I0818538

חומש קורן

THE KOREN ḤUMASH

TRANSLATION AND COMMENTARY BY
RABBI LORD JONATHAN SACKS

FIRST EDITION

THE MAGERMAN EDITION

חומש קורן
THE KOREN ḤUMASH

TRANSLATION AND COMMENTARY BY

Rabbi Lord Jonathan Sacks זצ״ל

KOREN PUBLISHERS JERUSALEM

The Koren Ḥumash
Translation and commentary by Rabbi Lord Jonathan Sacks
The Magerman Edition
First Hebrew-English Edition, 2025

Koren Publishers Jerusalem Ltd.
POB 4044, Jerusalem 91040, ISRAEL
POB 8531, New Milford, CT 06776-8531, USA

www.korenpub.com

The publication of this book was made possible
through the generous support of *The Jewish Book Trust.*

Hardcover, ISBN 978-965-7844-86-1

Printed in PRC

First printing

KH1

We have been blessed in our lives, by virtue of our philanthropic endeavors, to meet some of the most amazing and beautiful souls in the Jewish world. The pinnacle of those blessings was the time we shared with Rabbi Lord Jonathan Sacks and his wife, Lady Elaine Sacks.

As a part of the project to support the new translation of the Tanakh, along with Rabbi Sacks' new translation of and commentary on the Ḥumash, we were blessed with the opportunity to spend a few *Shabbatot* with Lord and Lady Sacks, to hear Rabbi Sacks speak in our community, and to have him spend time celebrating *ḥagim* with our community's children at school events. Learning from Rabbi Sacks is a privilege and a pleasure he has shared with the world through his publications and public speaking. Spending time with Rabbi Sacks – the man, the beautiful *neshama* – is more rare, and those experiences we had with him in our home and in our community, at Shabbat meals and on Shabbat afternoon walks, are priceless experiences we will never forget.

Rabbi Lord Jonathan Sacks was the authentic Torah voice for our generation, simultaneously steeped in Torah tradition and deeply engaged with people of all faiths. He succinctly understood and eloquently conveyed both the particular Jewish identity of our sacred writings as well as their universal relevance.

We pray that this unique, traditional, painstakingly researched and annotated translation of and commentary on the Ḥumash enlivens Torah for *klal Yisrael*, unites us in our traditions, inspires us with new, and old, ways of thinking, and ultimately brings us closer to the Redemption.

Debra and David Magerman
Philadelphia, Pennsylvania

CONTENTS

BERESHIT/GENESIS

Parasha · Haftara

SHEMOT/EXODUS

VAYIKRA/LEVITICUS

BEMIDBAR/NUMBERS

DEVARIM/DEUTERONOMY

SPECIAL HAFTAROT

PUBLISHER'S PREFACE
THE KOREN ḤUMASH

The publication of the new *Koren Ḥumash* with commentary by Rabbi Lord Jonathan Sacks is a time of celebration, but one that is bittersweet. Its publication close to his fifth yahrzeit is a reminder that his living presence is no longer with us, but also that his Torah lives on and continues to grow in influence. Rabbi Sacks' enthusiasm, joyful scholarship, erudition, and penetrating insight permeated all his writings, conveying to us and to future generations that our Torah is a limitless source of wisdom, faith, and moral clarity. We were well into this ambitious endeavor when he went into hospital, from which he fully expected to return.

I cannot write a preface for him; no one can. But his many books on Ḥumash – the *Covenant & Conversation* series, and those exploring leadership, ethics, spirituality, life-changing ideas, and belief – speak for themselves. These works, alongside his astonishing range of books, articles, and lectures – all of which have marshalled to complete Rabbi Sacks' commentary – reveal the depth, breadth, and relevance of the Torah's messages for the current age. The Torah is, as the Rabbis teach, "betrothed" to the Jewish people; yet it also contains the blueprint for a healthy and holy society that has universal relevance. Rabbi Sacks was our guide through the bewildering thickets of modernity, our guide to a fresh and refreshing engagement with Torah, and we gratefully follow the path he has charted for us.

His passing leaves a void which no one in this generation fills. We hope these writings will engage, provoke, and inspire the next generation of Torah scholars, teachers, laypeople, and indeed all God-seekers.

In the best of circumstances, the creation of this Ḥumash would be a collaboration of many. It is my privilege to thank them.

This project, the sister project of *The Koren Tanakh* which was published two years ago, has been sponsored by our friends Debra and David Magerman of Philadelphia and Jerusalem. With continual encouragement and no lack of patience, they shared the vision that animated both Rabbi Sacks and Koren, and enabled us to create this work you hold in your hands. For my colleagues at Koren, we thank you; for the many future generations who will read and use this Ḥumash weekly, we are forever in your debt.

We thank the family of Rabbi Sacks, Lady Elaine Sacks and her children Joshua, Dina, and Gila, for their encouragement and commitment, particularly after his passing. The leadership of The Rabbi Sacks Legacy, its chief executive, and my friends, Joanna Benarroch and Alan Sacks, provided encouragement during the awful days of 2020 and 2021, when we felt leaderless, and they continue to be valued and cherished partners.

Jessica Sacks' scholarship and erudition is not simply hereditary but unique to her, and she engaged with her uncle's writings with compassion and dedication. Rabbi Reuven Ziegler oversaw the entire project, and Dayan Ivan Binstock of the London Beth Din reviewed the Ḥumash.

Management of the editorial side was led by Gila Chitiz and Ashirah Firszt, and the production and design side was led by Rabbi Avishai Magence and Caryn Meltz; the typography was designed by Esther Be'er and Tomi Mager. I would also like to acknowledge Dr. Joel B. Wolowelsky for the initial commentary drafts; Rabbi Julian Sinclair, Yaffa Aranoff, Dr. Yoel Finkelman, and Tani Bednarsh for their review and comments; Debbie Ismailoff and Ita Olesker for copyediting; Rabbi Yedidya Naveh for authoring and translating the haftara commentary; Tali Simon, Doron Chitiz, and Avichai Gamdani for proofreading; Eliyahu Misgav for the cover design; and Gila Chitiz, Tani Bednarsh, and Elchanan Spitz for creating a database of books, essays, articles, and broadcasts of Rabbi Sacks.

Rabbi Sacks taught: "In Judaism we not only learn to live; we live to learn. In study, we make Torah real in the mind so that we can make it actual in the world." We pray that this masterful commentary on the Torah will allow countless people to ascend to ever greater heights in *living* and *learning*, to internalize the Torah's relevance to the individual and to society, and to help heal our fractured world.

Matthew Miller, Publisher
Jerusalem, Tishrei 5786 (October 2025)

EDITOR'S NOTE

Rabbi Sacks intended that this Ḥumash be his flagship project, one in which he could incorporate many of his timeless messages and ideas. "Traditional commentaries," he wrote of the Haggada, "are usually close readings of individual words and phrases rather than reflections on the meaning of the whole. That is a classic Jewish response, and I have not hesitated to do likewise.... But it is the great themes, the overarching principles, that are often neglected or taken for granted." These great themes – freedom and responsibility, love and justice, the meaning of the covenant between God and humanity and God and Israel – were for Rabbi Sacks the lifeblood of Judaism, and their text is the Torah as we read it week by week.

After translating the Ḥumash for *The Koren Tanakh*, Rabbi Sacks began writing his commentary, beginning with the book of Exodus. Regretfully, he was unable to see it to completion. The Ḥumash editorial team at Koren, led by Rabbi Sacks' niece Jessica Sacks, compiled the rest of the Ḥumash commentary from his vast array of books, articles, commentaries, and lectures. The work was always done with Rabbi Sacks' intention for the Ḥumash commentary as our guiding light, mission statement, and purpose. Great care was taken to present his invaluable ideas and messages in his own words, only adapting and reshaping them to preserve his style in the new format. We pray that we have managed to bring Rabbi Sacks' words alive through the Torah and his dream project to fruition. May this work allow his beautiful Torah to enlighten and inspire all of us for generations to come.

Haftarot

Following the Humash section are the haftarot according to the various customs of the Ashkenazim, Sepharadim, Yemenites, and Chabad. Chabad follows the Ashkenazi custom unless indicated otherwise. We included a short commentary for each haftara, originally written in Hebrew by Rabbi David Nativ (for Koren's Humash Yisrael) and translated by Rabbi Yedidya Naveh. The commentary for the special haftarot was composed especially for this volume by Rabbi Yedidya Naveh. We hope that these commentaries provide the reader with the context to appreciate the significance of the words of the prophets and their depth and timeless teachings.

TORAH READINGS FOR SPECIAL DAYS

Rosh Ḥodesh	Numbers 28:1–15, p. 1065
Fast Days	Exodus 32:11–14, p. 591 Continues with Exodus 34:1–10, p. 601
Ninth of Av	Shaḥarit: Deuteronomy 4:25–40, p. 1167 Minḥa: See Fast Days, above
Ḥanukka – Day 1	Ashkenazim: Numbers 7:1–17, p. 909 Sepharadim: Numbers 6:22–7:17, p. 907
Ḥanukka – Days 2–7	Read the offering for the respective day, Numbers 7:18–53, p. 913 On Rosh Ḥodesh, read the Rosh Ḥodesh reading from the first Torah scroll, and the Ḥanukka reading from the second Torah scroll.
Ḥanukka – Day 8	Numbers 7:54–8:4, p. 917
Purim	Exodus 17:8–16, p. 481
Purim on Shabbat (in Walled Cities)	Exodus 17:8–16, p. 481 *Haftara*: Same as Shabbat Zakhor

TORAH READINGS FOR FESTIVALS

Pesaḥ – Day 1	Exodus 12:21–51, p. 443 On Shabbat, Sepharadim read Exodus 12:14–51, p. 439 *Maftir*: Numbers 28:16–25, p. 1069
Day 2	Leviticus 22:26–23:44, p. 805 In Israel: *Revi'i* (second Torah scroll): Numbers 28:19–25, p. 1069 In the Diaspora: *Maftir*: Same as Day 1
Day 3	Exodus 13:1–16, p. 449 *Revi'i* (second Torah scroll): Numbers 28:19–25, p. 1069

Day 4	Exodus 22:24–23:19, p. 521 (If it falls on a Sunday, Sepharadim read the passage for Day 3.) *Revi'i* (second Torah scroll): Numbers 28:19–25, p. 1069
Day 5	Exodus 34:1–26, p. 601 (If it falls on a Monday, Sepharadim read the passage for Day 4.) *Revi'i* (second Torah scroll): Numbers 28:19–25, p. 1069
Day 6	Numbers 9:1–14, p. 927 *Revi'i* (second Torah scroll): Numbers 28:19–25, p. 1069
Shabbat Ḥol HaMoed Pesaḥ	Exodus 33:12–34:26, p. 599 *Maftir*: Numbers 28:19–25, p. 1069
Day 7	Exodus 13:17–15:26, p. 455 *Maftir*: Numbers 28:19–25, p. 1069
Day 8 (Diaspora)	Deuteronomy 15:19–16:17, p. 1253 On Shabbat: Deuteronomy 14:22–16:17, p. 1243 *Maftir*: Numbers 28:19–25, p. 1069
Shavuot – Day 1	Exodus 19:1–20:23, p. 491 *Maftir*: Numbers 28:26–31, p. 1069
Day 2 (Diaspora)	Deuteronomy 15:19–16:17, p. 1253 On Shabbat: Deuteronomy 14:22–16:17, p. 1243 *Maftir*: Same as Day 1
Rosh HaShana – Day 1	Genesis 21:1–34, p. 125 *Maftir*: Numbers 29:1–6, p. 1071
Day 2	Genesis 22:1–24, p. 131 *Maftir*: Same as Day 1
Yom Kippur – Shaharit	Leviticus 16:1–34, p. 759 *Maftir*: Numbers 29:7–11, p. 1073

Minḥa	Leviticus 18:1–30, p. 773
Sukkot – Day 1	Leviticus 22:26–23:44, p. 805 *Maftir*: Numbers 29:12–16, p. 1073
Day 2	Israel: Numbers 29:17–19, p. 1075 Diaspora: Same as Day 1
Day 3	Israel: Numbers 29:20–22, p. 1075 Diaspora: Numbers 29:17–25, p. 1075
Day 4	Israel: Numbers 29:23–25, p. 1075 Diaspora: Numbers 29:20–28, p. 1075
Day 5	Israel: Numbers 29:26–28, p. 1075 Diaspora: Numbers 29:23–31, p. 1075
Day 6	Israel: Numbers 29:29–31, p. 1075 Diaspora: Numbers 29:26–34, p. 1075
Hoshana Rabba	Israel: Numbers 29:32–34, p. 1077 Diaspora: Numbers 29:26–34, p. 1075
Shabbat Ḥol HaMoed Sukkot	Exodus 33:12–34:26, p. 599 *Maftir*: Read the offering for the respective day (in the Diaspora adding the offering for the previous day).
Shemini Atzeret (Diaspora)	Deuteronomy 15:19–16:17, p. 1253 On Shabbat: Deuteronomy 14:22–16:17, p. 1243 *Maftir*: Numbers 29:35–30:1, p. 1077
Simḥat Torah (Israel and Diaspora)	First Torah scroll: Deuteronomy 33:1–34:12, p. 1395 Second Torah scroll: Genesis 1:1–2:3, p. 5 Third Torah scroll (*Maftir*): Numbers 29:35–30:1, p. 1077

NUMBER OF VERSES PER PARASHA

BERESHIT/GENESIS

Bereshit	146 pesukim	Vayetze	148 pesukim
Noaḥ	153 pesukim	Vayishlaḥ	153 pesukim
Lekh Lekha	126 pesukim	Vayeshev	112 pesukim
Vayera	147 pesukim	Miketz	146 pesukim
Ḥayei Sara	105 pesukim	Vayigash	106 pesukim
Toledot	106 pesukim	Vayeḥi	85 pesukim

SHEMOT/EXODUS

Shemot	124 pesukim	Teruma	96 pesukim
Vaera	121 pesukim	Tetzaveh	101 pesukim
Bo	106 pesukim	Ki Tisa	139 pesukim
Beshalaḥ	116 pesukim	Vayak'hel	122 pesukim
Yitro	75 pesukim	Pekudei	92 pesukim
Mishpatim	118 pesukim		

VAYIKRA/LEVITICUS

Vayikra	111 pesukim	Aḥarei Mot	80 pesukim
Tzav	97 pesukim	Kedoshim	64 pesukim
Shemini	91 pesukim	Emor	124 pesukim
Tazria	67 pesukim	Behar	57 pesukim
Metzora	90 pesukim	Beḥukotai	78 pesukim

BEMIDBAR/NUMBERS

Bemidbar	159 pesukim	Ḥukat	87 pesukim
Naso	176 pesukim	Balak	104 pesukim
Behaalotekha	136 pesukim	Pinḥas	168 pesukim
Shelaḥ	119 pesukim	Matot	112 pesukim
Koraḥ	95 pesukim	Masei	132 pesukim

DEVARIM/DEUTERONOMY

Devarim	105 pesukim	Ki Tavo	122 pesukim
Vaetḥanan	122 pesukim	Nitzavim	40 pesukim
Ekev	111 pesukim	Vayelekh	30 pesukim
Re'eh	126 pesukim	Haazinu	52 pesukim
Shofetim	97 pesukim	Vezot Haberakha	41 pesukim
Ki Tetzeh	110 pesukim		

BLESSINGS BEFORE AND AFTER READING THE TORAH (ASHKENAZI CUSTOM)

Before reading the Torah, the Oleh says:

Oleh: בָּרְכוּ Bless the LORD, the blessed One.

Cong: בָּרוּךְ Bless the LORD, the blessed One, for ever and all time.

Oleh: בָּרוּךְ Bless the LORD, the blessed One, for ever and all time.

Blessed are You, LORD our God, King of the Universe,
who has chosen us from all peoples
and has given us His Torah.
Blessed are You, LORD, Giver of the Torah.

After the reading, the oleh recites:

Oleh: בָּרוּךְ Blessed are You, LORD our God, King of the Universe,
who has given us the Torah of truth,
and everlasting life He has planted in our midst.
Blessed are You, LORD, Giver of the Torah.

BLESSINGS BEFORE AND AFTER READING THE HAFTARA

Before reading the Haftara, the person called up for Maftir recites:

בָּרוּךְ Blessed are You, LORD our God, King of the Universe, who chose good prophets and was pleased with their words, spoken in truth. Blessed are You, LORD, who chooses the Torah, His servant Moses, His people Israel, and the prophets of truth and righteousness.

After the Haftara, the person called up for Maftir recites the following blessings:

בָּרוּךְ Blessed are You, LORD our God King of the Universe, Rock of all worlds, righteous for all generations, the faithful God who says and does, speaks and fulfills, all of whose words are truth and righteousness. You are faithful, LORD our God, and faithful are Your words, not one of which returns unfulfilled, for You, God, are a faithful (and compassionate) King. Blessed are You, LORD, faithful in all His words.

ברכות התורה (מנהג אשכנזים)

Before קריאת התורה*, the* עולה *says:*

עולה: בָּרְכוּ אֶת יהוה הַמְבֹרָךְ.

קהל: בָּרוּךְ יהוה הַמְבֹרָךְ לְעוֹלָם וָעֶד.

עולה: בָּרוּךְ יהוה הַמְבֹרָךְ לְעוֹלָם וָעֶד.

בָּרוּךְ אַתָּה יהוה, אֱלֹהֵינוּ מֶלֶךְ הָעוֹלָם
אֲשֶׁר בָּחַר בָּנוּ מִכָּל הָעַמִּים וְנָתַן לָנוּ אֶת תּוֹרָתוֹ.
בָּרוּךְ אַתָּה יהוה, נוֹתֵן הַתּוֹרָה.

After קריאת התורה*, the* עולה *says:*

עולה: בָּרוּךְ אַתָּה יהוה, אֱלֹהֵינוּ מֶלֶךְ הָעוֹלָם
אֲשֶׁר נָתַן לָנוּ תּוֹרַת אֱמֶת וְחַיֵּי עוֹלָם נָטַע בְּתוֹכֵנוּ.
בָּרוּךְ אַתָּה יהוה, נוֹתֵן הַתּוֹרָה.

ברכות ההפטרה

Before reading the הפטרה*, the person called up for* מפטיר *says:*

בָּרוּךְ אַתָּה יהוה אֱלֹהֵינוּ מֶלֶךְ הָעוֹלָם, אֲשֶׁר בָּחַר בִּנְבִיאִים טוֹבִים. וְרָצָה בְדִבְרֵיהֶם הַנֶּאֱמָרִים בֶּאֱמֶת. בָּרוּךְ אַתָּה יהוה, הַבּוֹחֵר בַּתּוֹרָה וּבְמֹשֶׁה עַבְדּוֹ, וּבְיִשְׂרָאֵל עַמּוֹ וּבִנְבִיאֵי הָאֱמֶת וָצֶדֶק.

After the הפטרה*, the person called up for* מפטיר *says the following blessings:*

בָּרוּךְ אַתָּה יהוה, אֱלֹהֵינוּ מֶלֶךְ הָעוֹלָם, צוּר כָּל הָעוֹלָמִים, צַדִּיק בְּכָל הַדּוֹרוֹת, הָאֵל הַנֶּאֱמָן, הָאוֹמֵר וְעוֹשֶׂה, הַמְדַבֵּר וּמְקַיֵּם, שֶׁכָּל דְּבָרָיו אֱמֶת וָצֶדֶק. נֶאֱמָן אַתָּה הוּא יהוה אֱלֹהֵינוּ וְנֶאֱמָנִים דְּבָרֶיךָ, וְדָבָר אֶחָד מִדְּבָרֶיךָ אָחוֹר לֹא יָשׁוּב רֵיקָם, כִּי אֵל מֶלֶךְ נֶאֱמָן (וְרַחֲמָן) אָתָּה. בָּרוּךְ אַתָּה יהוה, הָאֵל הַנֶּאֱמָן בְּכָל דְּבָרָיו.

רַחֵם Have compassion on Zion for it is the source of our life, and save the one grieved in spirit swiftly in our days. Blessed are You, Lord, who makes Zion rejoice in her children.

שַׂמְּחֵנוּ Grant us joy, Lord our God, through Elijah the prophet Your servant, and through the kingdom of the house of David Your anointed – may he soon come and gladden our hearts. May no stranger sit on his throne, and may others no longer inherit his glory, for You took an oath to him by Your holy name that his light would never be extinguished. Blessed are You, Lord, Shield of David.

On Shabbat, including Shabbat Ḥol HaMo'ed Pesaḥ, say:

עַל הַתּוֹרָה For the Torah, for divine worship, for the prophets, and for this Sabbath day which You, Lord our God, have given us for holiness and rest, honor and glory – for all these we thank and bless You, Lord our God, and may Your name be blessed by the mouth of all that lives, continually, for ever and all time. Blessed are You, Lord, who sanctifies the Sabbath.

On Yom Tov and on Shabbat Ḥol HaMo'ed Sukkot, say (adding on Shabbat the words in parentheses):

עַל הַתּוֹרָה For the Torah, for Divine worship, for the prophets, (for this Sabbath day) and for this day of

On Pesaḥ: the Festival of Matzot
On Shavuot: the Festival of Shavuot
On Sukkot: the Festival of Sukkot
On Shemini Atzeret and Simḥat Torah: the Festival of Shemini Atzeret

which You, Lord our God, have given us (for holiness and rest),
for joy and gladness, honor and glory –
for all these we thank and bless You, Lord our God,
and may Your name be blessed by the mouth of all that lives,
continually, for ever and all time.
Blessed are You, Lord, who sanctifies (the Sabbath), Israel and the festivals. (Amen.)

רַחֵם עַל צִיּוֹן כִּי הִיא בֵּית חַיֵּינוּ, וְלַעֲלוּבַת נֶפֶשׁ תּוֹשִׁיעַ בִּמְהֵרָה בְיָמֵינוּ. בָּרוּךְ אַתָּה יהוה, מְשַׂמֵּחַ צִיּוֹן בְּבָנֶיהָ.

שַׂמְּחֵנוּ יהוה אֱלֹהֵינוּ בְּאֵלִיָּהוּ הַנָּבִיא עַבְדֶּךָ, וּבְמַלְכוּת בֵּית דָּוִד מְשִׁיחֶךָ, בִּמְהֵרָה יָבוֹא וְיָגֵל לִבֵּנוּ. עַל כִּסְאוֹ לֹא יֵשֶׁב זָר, וְלֹא יִנְחֲלוּ עוֹד אֲחֵרִים אֶת כְּבוֹדוֹ, כִּי בְשֵׁם קָדְשְׁךָ נִשְׁבַּעְתָּ לּוֹ שֶׁלֹּא יִכְבֶּה נֵרוֹ לְעוֹלָם וָעֶד. בָּרוּךְ אַתָּה יהוה, מָגֵן דָּוִד.

On שבת, including שבת חול המועד פסח, say:

עַל הַתּוֹרָה וְעַל הָעֲבוֹדָה וְעַל הַנְּבִיאִים וְעַל יוֹם הַשַּׁבָּת הַזֶּה, שֶׁנָּתַתָּ לָּנוּ יהוה אֱלֹהֵינוּ לִקְדֻשָּׁה וְלִמְנוּחָה, לְכָבוֹד וּלְתִפְאָרֶת. עַל הַכֹּל יהוה אֱלֹהֵינוּ אֲנַחְנוּ מוֹדִים לָךְ וּמְבָרְכִים אוֹתָךְ, יִתְבָּרַךְ שִׁמְךָ בְּפִי כָּל חַי תָּמִיד לְעוֹלָם וָעֶד. בָּרוּךְ אַתָּה יהוה, מְקַדֵּשׁ הַשַּׁבָּת.

On יום טוב and on שבת חול המועד סוכות,
say (adding on שבת the words in parentheses):

עַל הַתּוֹרָה וְעַל הָעֲבוֹדָה וְעַל הַנְּבִיאִים (בשבת: וְעַל יוֹם הַשַּׁבָּת הַזֶּה), וְעַל יוֹם

בפסח: חַג הַמַּצּוֹת הַזֶּה

בשבועות: חַג הַשָּׁבוּעוֹת הַזֶּה

בסוכות: חַג הַסֻּכּוֹת הַזֶּה

בשמיני עצרת ובש״ת: (הַ)שְּׁמִינִי חַג (הָ)עֲצֶרֶת הַזֶּה

שֶׁנָּתַתָּ לָּנוּ, יהוה אֱלֹהֵינוּ (בשבת: לִקְדֻשָּׁה וְלִמְנוּחָה)
לְשָׂשׂוֹן וּלְשִׂמְחָה, לְכָבוֹד וּלְתִפְאָרֶת.
עַל הַכֹּל יהוה אֱלֹהֵינוּ אֲנַחְנוּ מוֹדִים לָךְ וּמְבָרְכִים אוֹתָךְ.
יִתְבָּרַךְ שִׁמְךָ בְּפִי כָּל חַי תָּמִיד לְעוֹלָם וָעֶד.
בָּרוּךְ אַתָּה יהוה, מְקַדֵּשׁ (בשבת: הַשַּׁבָּת וְ)יִשְׂרָאֵל וְהַזְּמַנִּים. (אָמֵן.)

BLESSINGS BEFORE AND AFTER READING THE TORAH (SEPHARDIC CUSTOM)

Before reading the Torah, the Oleh says:

Oleh: The Lord is with you *Cong:* May the Lord bless you

Oleh: בָּרוּךְ Bless the Lord, the blessed One.

Cong: בָּרוּךְ Bless the Lord, the blessed One, for ever and all time.

Oleh: בָּרוּךְ Bless the Lord, the blessed One, for ever and all time.

Blessed are You, Lord our God, King of the Universe,
who has chosen us from all peoples
and has given us His Torah.
Blessed are You, Lord, Giver of the Torah.

After the reading, the oleh recites:

Oleh: Blessed are You, Lord our God, King of the Universe,
who has given us His Torah, the Torah of truth, and everlasting life He has planted in our midst.
Blessed are You, Lord, Giver of the Torah.

BLESSINGS BEFORE AND AFTER READING THE HAFTARA

Before reading the Haftara, the person called up for Maftir recites:

בָּרוּךְ Blessed are You, Lord our God, King of the Universe, who chose good prophets and was pleased with their words, spoken in truth. Blessed are You, Lord, who chose the Torah, His servant Moses, His people Israel, and the prophets of truth and righteousness.

After reading the Haftara, he recites:

גֹּאֲלֵנוּ Our Redeemer, the Lord of hosts is His name, Holy One of Israel *Isaiah 47*

בָּרוּךְ Blessed are You, Lord our God, King of the Universe, Rock of all worlds, righteous for all generations, the faithful God who says and does, speaks and fulfills, all of whose words are truth and righteousness.

בְּרכות התורה (מנהג ספרדים)

Before קריאת התורה, the עולה says:

עולה: **יהוה עִמָּכֶם** קהל: **יְבָרֶכְךָ יהוה**

עולה: **(רַבָּנָן) בָּרְכוּ אֶת יהוה הַמְבֹרָךְ.**

קהל: **בָּרוּךְ יהוה הַמְבֹרָךְ לְעוֹלָם וָעֶד.**

עולה: **בָּרוּךְ יהוה הַמְבֹרָךְ לְעוֹלָם וָעֶד.**

בָּרוּךְ אַתָּה יהוה, אֱלֹהֵינוּ מֶלֶךְ הָעוֹלָם,
אֲשֶׁר בָּחַר בָּנוּ מִכָּל הָעַמִּים, וְנָתַן לָנוּ אֶת תּוֹרָתוֹ.
בָּרוּךְ אַתָּה יהוה, נוֹתֵן הַתּוֹרָה.

After the reading, the עולה recites:

עולה: **בָּרוּךְ אַתָּה יהוה, אֱלֹהֵינוּ מֶלֶךְ הָעוֹלָם**
אֲשֶׁר נָתַן לָנוּ (אֶת) תּוֹרָתוֹ תּוֹרַת אֱמֶת
וְחַיֵּי עוֹלָם נָטַע בְּתוֹכֵנוּ.
בָּרוּךְ אַתָּה יהוה, נוֹתֵן הַתּוֹרָה.

ברכות ההפטרה

Before reading the הפטרה, the person called up for מפטיר recites:

בָּרוּךְ אַתָּה יהוה אֱלֹהֵינוּ מֶלֶךְ הָעוֹלָם, אֲשֶׁר בָּחַר בִּנְבִיאִים טוֹבִים, וְרָצָה בְדִבְרֵיהֶם הַנֶּאֱמָרִים בֶּאֱמֶת. בָּרוּךְ אַתָּה יהוה, הַבּוֹחֵר בַּתּוֹרָה וּבְמֹשֶׁה עַבְדּוֹ, וּבְיִשְׂרָאֵל עַמּוֹ וּבִנְבִיאֵי הָאֱמֶת וְהַצֶּדֶק.

After reading the הפטרה, he recites:

גֹּאֲלֵנוּ יהוה צְבָאוֹת שְׁמוֹ, קְדוֹשׁ יִשְׂרָאֵל: ישעיה מז

בָּרוּךְ אַתָּה יהוה, אֱלֹהֵינוּ מֶלֶךְ הָעוֹלָם, צוּר כָּל הָעוֹלָמִים, צַדִּיק בְּכָל הַדּוֹרוֹת, הָאֵל הַנֶּאֱמָן, הָאוֹמֵר וְעוֹשֶׂה, מְדַבֵּר וּמְקַיֵּם, כִּי כָל דְּבָרָיו אֱמֶת וָצֶדֶק. נֶאֱמָן אַתָּה הוּא יהוה אֱלֹהֵינוּ וְנֶאֱמָנִים דְּבָרֶיךָ, וְדָבָר אֶחָד מִדְּבָרֶיךָ

You are faithful, Lord our God, and faithful are Your words, not one of which returns unfulfilled, for You, God, are a faithful (and compassionate) King. Blessed are You, Lord, faithful in all His words.

רַחֵם Have compassion on Zion for it is the source of our life, and save the one grieved in spirit swiftly in our days. Blessed are You, Lord, who makes Zion rejoice in her children.

שַׂמְּחֵנוּ Grant us joy, Lord our God, through Elijah the prophet Your servant, and through the kingdom of the house of David Your anointed – may he soon come and gladden our hearts. May no stranger sit on his throne, and may others no longer inherit his glory, for You took an oath to him by Your holy name that his light would never be extinguished. Blessed are You, Lord, Shield of David.

On Shabbat, including Shabbat Ḥol HaMo'ed Pesaḥ, say:

עַל הַתּוֹרָה For the Torah, for divine worship, for the prophets, and for this Sabbath day which You, Lord our God, have given us for holiness and rest, honor and glory – for all these we thank and bless You, Lord our God, and may Your name be blessed by the mouth of all that lives, continually, for ever and all time. Blessed are You, Lord, who sanctifies the Sabbath.

On Yom Tov and on Shabbat Ḥol HaMo'ed Sukkot, say (adding on Shabbat the words in parentheses):

עַל הַתּוֹרָה For the Torah, for Divine worship, for the prophets,
(for this Sabbath day) and for this day of

On Pesaḥ: the Festival of Matzot
On Shavuot: the Festival of Shavuot
On Sukkot: the Festival of Sukkot
On Shemini Atzeret and Simḥat Torah: the Festival of Shemini Atzeret

which You, Lord our God, have given us (for holiness and rest),
for joy and gladness, honor and glory –
for all these we thank and bless You, Lord our God,
and may Your name be blessed by the mouth of all that lives,
continually, for ever and all time.

אָחוֹר לֹא יָשׁוּב רֵיקָם, כִּי אֵל מֶלֶךְ נֶאֱמָן (וְרַחֲמָן) אָתָּה. בָּרוּךְ אַתָּה יהוה, הָאֵל הַנֶּאֱמָן בְּכָל דְּבָרָיו.

רַחֵם עַל צִיּוֹן כִּי הִיא בֵּית חַיֵּינוּ, וְלַעֲלוּבַת נֶפֶשׁ תּוֹשִׁיעַ בִּמְהֵרָה בְיָמֵינוּ. בָּרוּךְ אַתָּה יהוה, מְשַׂמֵּחַ צִיּוֹן בְּבָנֶיהָ.

שַׂמְּחֵנוּ יהוה אֱלֹהֵינוּ בְּאֵלִיָּהוּ הַנָּבִיא עַבְדֶּךָ, וּבְמַלְכוּת בֵּית דָּוִד מְשִׁיחֶךָ, בִּמְהֵרָה יָבוֹא וְיָגֵל לִבֵּנוּ. עַל כִּסְאוֹ לֹא יֵשֵׁב זָר, וְלֹא יִנְחֲלוּ עוֹד אֲחֵרִים אֶת כְּבוֹדוֹ, כִּי בְשֵׁם קָדְשְׁךָ נִשְׁבַּעְתָּ לּוֹ שֶׁלֹּא יִכְבֶּה נֵרוֹ לְעוֹלָם וָעֶד. בָּרוּךְ אַתָּה יהוה, מָגֵן דָּוִד.

On שבת*, including* שבת חול המועד פסח*, say:*

עַל הַתּוֹרָה וְעַל הָעֲבוֹדָה וְעַל הַנְּבִיאִים וְעַל יוֹם הַשַּׁבָּת הַזֶּה, שֶׁנָּתַתָּ לָּנוּ יהוה אֱלֹהֵינוּ לִקְדֻשָּׁה וְלִמְנוּחָה, לְכָבוֹד וּלְתִפְאָרֶת. עַל הַכֹּל יהוה אֱלֹהֵינוּ אֲנַחְנוּ מוֹדִים לָךְ וּמְבָרְכִים אוֹתָךְ, יִתְבָּרַךְ שִׁמְךָ בְּפִי כָּל חַי תָּמִיד לְעוֹלָם וָעֶד. בָּרוּךְ אַתָּה יהוה, מְקַדֵּשׁ הַשַּׁבָּת. אָמֵן.

On יום טוב *and on* שבת חול המועד סוכות*,*
say (adding on שבת *the words in parentheses):*

עַל הַתּוֹרָה וְעַל הָעֲבוֹדָה וְעַל הַנְּבִיאִים (בשבת: וְעַל יוֹם הַשַּׁבָּת הַזֶּה), וְעַל יוֹם

בפסח: חַג הַמַּצּוֹת הַזֶּה, וְעַל יוֹם טוֹב מִקְרָא קֹדֶשׁ הַזֶּה
בשבועות: חַג הַשָּׁבוּעוֹת הַזֶּה, וְעַל יוֹם טוֹב מִקְרָא קֹדֶשׁ הַזֶּה
בסוכות: חַג הַסֻּכּוֹת הַזֶּה, וְעַל יוֹם טוֹב מִקְרָא קֹדֶשׁ הַזֶּה
בשמיני עצרת ובש״ת: שְׁמִינִי חַג עֲצֶרֶת הַזֶּה, וְעַל יוֹם טוֹב מִקְרָא קֹדֶשׁ הַזֶּה

שֶׁנָּתַתָּ לָּנוּ, יהוה אֱלֹהֵינוּ (בשבת: לִקְדֻשָּׁה וְלִמְנוּחָה)
לְשָׂשׂוֹן וּלְשִׂמְחָה, לְכָבוֹד וּלְתִפְאָרֶת.
עַל הַכֹּל יהוה אֱלֹהֵינוּ אֲנַחְנוּ מוֹדִים לָךְ וּמְבָרְכִים אוֹתָךְ.
יִתְבָּרַךְ שִׁמְךָ בְּפִי כָּל חַי תָּמִיד לְעוֹלָם וָעֶד.
בָּרוּךְ אַתָּה יהוה, מְקַדֵּשׁ (בשבת: הַשַּׁבָּת וְ)יִשְׂרָאֵל וְהַזְּמַנִּים. (אָמֵן.)

בראשית
GENESIS

and how we should behave (ethics). But it does so in a way quite unlike the philosophical classics from Plato to Wittgenstein. To put it at its simplest: Philosophy is *truth as system*. Genesis is *truth as story*. It is a unique work, philosophy in the narrative mode.

So we learn about what exists by way of a story about creation. We learn about knowledge through a tangled tale of the first man, the first woman, a serpent, and a tree. We begin to understand human freedom and its abuse through the story of Kayin. We learn how to behave through the lives of Avraham and Sara and their children. It is this that has helped to make Tanakh the most widely read and influential book in the history of civilization. Only the gifted few can fully understand a philosophical classic, but everyone can relate to a story.

Everyone can understand Genesis, yet not understand at the same level; that is another feature of the book. Each of its stories has layer upon layer of meaning and significance, which we only grasp after repeated readings. Our understanding of the book grows as we grow. Each age adds insights, commentaries, and interpretations of its own. The book's literary style allows it to be read afresh in each generation. Only stories have this depth, this ambiguity, this principled multiplicity of meanings.

Torah is God's book of humanity, and each of us is a chapter in its unfinished story. Its words form our covenant with Heaven. And as we listen and respond, we add our voice to the unbroken conversation between the Jewish people and its destiny.

THE BOOK OF GENESIS

Genesis, the book of Bereshit, is as its name suggests, about beginnings: the birth of the universe, the origins of humanity, and the first chapters in the story of the people that would be known as Israel. It tells of how this people began, first as an individual, Avraham, who heard a call to leave his home and begin a journey, then as a family; it closes as the extended family stands on the threshold of becoming a nation. The journey turns out to be unexpectedly complicated and fraught with setbacks. In a sense, it continues till today. This is part of what makes Genesis so vivid. We can relate to its characters and their dilemmas. We are part of their world, as they are of ours. This is our story; this is where we came from; this is our journey.

But this is not all Genesis is. Rambam makes the fundamental point that *reshit* does not mean "beginning" in the sense of "first of a chronological sequence." For that, Biblical Hebrew has other words. *Reshit* implies the most significant element, the part that stands for the whole, the foundation, the principle. Genesis is Judaism's foundational work, a philosophy of the human condition under the sovereignty of God.

This is a difficult point to understand, because there is no other book quite like it. It is not myth. It is not history in the conventional sense, a mere recording of events. Nor is it theology: Genesis is less about God than about human beings and their relationship with God. The theology is almost always implicit rather than explicit. What Genesis is, in fact, is *philosophy written in a deliberately non-philosophical way*. It deals with all the central questions of philosophy: what exists (ontology), what can we know (epistemology), are we free (philosophical psychology),

Parashat Bereshit

1 1 2 When God began creating heaven and earth, the earth
was void and desolate, there was darkness on the face of
the deep, and the spirit of God moved over the waters.
3 4 God said, "Let there be light." And there was light. God

Parashat Lekh Lekha, does it narrow in on the particular. As far as Plato was concerned, knowledge starts with the particular – this tree, this person; looking at these you begin to realize that what is interesting is not this tree but tree-ness, not this person, but the universal things that make a person a person. Following Plato, Western thought has not been interested in the particular or parochial. It considers truth to be universal and eternal or not truth at all. Judaism is structurally unique – it is the only world religion ever to believe in a universal God, the God of all peoples, times, and places, and at the same time to believe in a particular way of life that not all people have to follow, because there is more than one way to find God. The structure we see in Genesis – first universal, then particular – recurs repeatedly in our prayers and our thought. It is a basic form of the Jewish mind.

LET THERE BE...

> Just as God is called gracious, so you be gracious. Just as He is called merciful, so you be merciful. The prophets described the Almighty by all the various attributes: long-suffering, abounding in kindness... powerful, and so on – to teach us that these qualities are good and righteous and that a human being should cultivate them, and thus imitate God as far as we can. (*Hilkhot Deot* 1:11)

Implicit in the first chapter of Genesis is a momentous challenge: Just as God is creative, so you be creative. What is more, it tells us how to be creative – namely, in three stages. The first is the stage of saying, "Let there be." What is truly creative is not science or technology per se, but the word. Because we can speak, we can think and therefore imagine a world different from the one that currently exists. Creation begins with the creative word, the idea, the vision, the dream. The first stage in creation is imagination.

The second stage is for us the most difficult. "And there was...." It is one thing to conceive an idea, another to execute it. Between the intention and the fact, the dream and the reality, lies struggle, opposition, and the fallibility of the human will. It is all too easy, having tried and failed, to conclude that nothing ultimately can be achieved, that the world

פרשת בראשית

א א ב בְּרֵאשִׁית בָּרָא אֱלֹהִים אֵת הַשָּׁמַיִם וְאֵת הָאָרֶץ: וְהָאָרֶץ א
הָיְתָה תֹהוּ וָבֹהוּ וְחֹשֶׁךְ עַל־פְּנֵי תְהוֹם וְרוּחַ אֱלֹהִים מְרַחֶפֶת
ג ד עַל־פְּנֵי הַמָּיִם: וַיֹּאמֶר אֱלֹהִים יְהִי־אוֹר וַיְהִי־אוֹר: וַיַּרְא

BERESHIT

The Book of Books starts with the beginning of beginnings: the creation of the universe and life. The story is told from two different perspectives, first as cosmology (the origins of matter), then as anthropology (the birth of humanity).

The first narrative (Gen. 1:1–2:3) emphasizes harmony and order. God creates the universe in six days and dedicates the seventh as a day of holiness and rest. The second (2:4–3:24) focuses on humanity, not as a biological species but as persons-in-relation. God fashions man, sees that "it is not good for man to be alone" (2:18), and then fashions the woman. The serpent tempts them; they sin and are banished from the garden.

From then on, the human drama unfolds as tragedy. Kayin murders his brother. By the end of the *parasha*, God sees "how great man's wickedness was upon the earth" (6:5) and "regretted that He had made man on earth" (6:6). God creates order; man creates chaos. The question that remains to challenge us is: which will prevail?

1:1 בְּרֵאשִׁית בָּרָא אֱלֹהִים *When God began creating* – Rashi begins his commentary: "Rabbi Yitzḥak said: The Torah should have begun with the verse 'This month shall be to you the beginning of months' (Ex. 12:2), which was the first mitzva given to Israel." To understand a book, one needs to know to which genre it belongs. What Rashi is succinctly saying in his enigmatic question is that the Torah is not a book of history, even though it includes history. It is not a book of science, even though the first chapter of Genesis is the necessary prelude to science, representing as it does the first time people saw the universe as the product of a single creative will, and therefore as intelligible rather than capricious and mysterious. The Torah is, first and last, a book about how to live.

Rashi gives one answer to his question. I would suggest an additional one. Jewish ethics is not confined to law. It includes virtues of character, general principles, and role models. It is conveyed not only by commandments but also by stories. And so the book of how to live opens with the most fundamental question of all. As the psalm (8:4) puts it: "What are mortals, that You should be mindful of them?"

1:1 אֵת הַשָּׁמַיִם וְאֵת הָאָרֶץ *Heaven and earth* – The Torah begins with the universal, and only later, in chapter 12,

saw the light: it was good; and God separated the light
5 from the darkness. And God called the light "day," and the
darkness He called "night." There was evening, and there
was morning – one day.
6 Then God said, "Let an expanse stretch through the

---

justice, compassion, faithfulness, loving-kindness, the dignity of the individual, and the sanctity of life.

1:4 וַיַּבְדֵּל אֱלֹהִים בֵּין הָאוֹר וּבֵין הַחֹשֶׁךְ *God separated the light from the darkness* – "I am the LORD; there is no other, forming light, creating darkness, making peace, creating evil" (Is. 45:7). The first act of creation inspired the single most emphatic rejection of dualism in the Bible. Dualism is the view that there is not one force operative in the universe but two: a force of good and a force of evil. Evil, in this worldview, comes not from God but from an independent force: Satan, the Devil, Lucifer, the Prince of Darkness, and the many other names given to the force that is not God but is opposed to Him and those who worship Him. This idea, which has surfaced in sectarian forms in each of the Abrahamic monotheisms, as well as in secular totalitarianisms, is one of the most dangerous in all of history. It divides humanity into the unshakably good and the irredeemably evil, giving rise to a long history of bloodshed and barbarism of the kind we see being enacted today in many parts of the world in the name of holy war against the greater and lesser Satan. Dualism is not monotheism, and the Sages, who called it *shetei reshuyot*, "two powers" or "two domains" (Berakhot 33b), were right to reject it utterly. In the words of historian Jeffrey Russel, dualism "denied the unity and omnipotence of God in order to preserve His perfect goodness." Further, it allows people to commit "altruistic evil": evil committed in a sacred cause, in the name of high ideals. Dualism resolves complexity. But monotheism requires the ability to handle complexity. God who creates light brings back the darkness also. "There was evening, and there was morning – one day."

1:6 וִיהִי מַבְדִּיל *Let it separate* – The narrative of creation is tightly structured. For three days, God creates domains – light and dark, sea and sky, sea and dry land. Order is a matter of distinction and separation; the verb *lehavdil*, to separate and divide, appears five times in Genesis 1. For the next three days, He populates those domains with their appropriate contents: the sun, moon, and stars; fish and birds; land animals and man. The seventh day, the Sabbath, is the apotheosis of creation: an enduring symbol of the world at peace with itself and its maker, the first thing in the Torah to be called holy.

אֱלֹהִים אֶת־הָאוֹר כִּי־טוֹב וַיַּבְדֵּל אֱלֹהִים בֵּין הָאוֹר וּבֵין
ה הַחֹשֶׁךְ: וַיִּקְרָא אֱלֹהִים ׀ לָאוֹר יוֹם וְלַחֹשֶׁךְ קָרָא לָיְלָה
וַיְהִי־עֶרֶב וַיְהִי־בֹקֶר יוֹם אֶחָד:
ו וַיֹּאמֶר אֱלֹהִים יְהִי רָקִיעַ בְּתוֹךְ הַמָּיִם וִיהִי מַבְדִּיל בֵּין

is as it is, and that all human endeavor is destined to end in failure. Yet Judaism holds the opposite, that though creation is difficult, laborious, and fraught with setbacks, we are summoned to it as our essential human vocation: "It is not for you to complete the work," said R. Tarfon, "but neither are you free to desist from it" (Avot 2:16). There is a lovely rabbinic phrase: *Maḥashava tova HaKadosh barukh Hu metzarefa lemaaseh* (Tosefta, Pe'ah 1:4). This is usually translated as "God considers a good intention as if it were the deed." I translate it differently: "When a human being has a good intention, God joins in helping it become a deed," meaning, He gives us the strength, if not now, then eventually, to turn it into achievement. If the first stage in creation is imagination, the second is will.

Finally: "God saw…it was good." This is the hardest of the three stages of creation to understand. But Genesis makes clear that to see that someone is good and to say so is a creative act. There may be some few individuals who are inescapably evil, but they are few. Within almost all of us is something positive and unique but which is all too easily injured, and which grows only when exposed to the sunlight of someone else's recognition and praise. To see the good in others and let them see themselves in the mirror of our regard is to help someone grow to become the best they can be. "Greater," says the Talmud, "is one who causes others to do good than one who does good himself" (Bava Batra 9a). To help others become what they can be is to give birth to creativity in someone else's soul. This is done not by criticism but by searching out the good in others, and helping them see it, own it, and live it.

"God saw… it was good" – this too is part of the work of creation, the subtlest and most beautiful of all. When we recognize the goodness in someone, we do more than create it; we help it become creative. This is what God does for us, and what He calls us to do for others.

1:4 כִּי־טוֹב *It was good – Tov,* "good," is a moral word. The Torah in Genesis 1 is telling us something radical. The reality to which Torah is a guide (the word "Torah" itself means "guide," "instruction," or "law") is *moral* and *ethical*. The question Genesis seeks to answer is not "How did the universe come into being?" but "How then shall we live?" This is the Torah's most significant paradigm shift. The universe that God made and that we inhabit is not about power or dominance but about *tov* and *ra*, good and evil. For the first time, here, religion is ethicized. God, we are told, cares about

7 water; let it separate water from water." So God made the
expanse, and it separated the water beneath the expanse
8 from the water above. And so it was. God called the
expanse "heavens." There was evening, and there was
morning – a second day.
9 Then God said, "Let the water beneath the heavens be
gathered to one place, and let dry ground appear." And
10 so it was. God called the dry ground "earth," and the
gathered waters He called "seas." And God saw: it was
11 good. Then God said, "Let the earth produce vegetation:
seed-bearing plants and trees of all the kinds on earth
12 that grow seed-bearing fruit." And so it was. The earth
produced vegetation: plants bearing seeds, each of its
kind, and trees bearing fruit containing seeds, each of its
13 kind. And God saw: it was good. There was evening, and
there was morning – a third day.
14 Then God said, "Let there be lights in the heavens'
expanse to separate day from night and to serve for signs
15 and seasons, days and years. They shall be lights in the
heavens' expanse, shining upon the earth." And so it was.
16 God made the two great lights – the greater light to rule
by day and the lesser light to rule by night – and the stars.

---

work of His hands' (Is. 5:12). How do we know that it is one's duty to calculate the cycles and planetary courses? Because it is written, 'For this will be your wisdom and understanding in the eyes of the peoples' (Deut. 4:6). What wisdom and understanding is in the sight of the peoples? Say, that is the science of cycles and planets" (Shabbat 75a).

The Sages attached religious dignity and integrity to science, both as human wisdom and as an insight into the divine wisdom evident in the cosmos. The Babylonian Talmud sees the study of astronomy, for those who are capable of it, as a religious duty. There is a blessing to be recited on seeing "one of the sages of the nations of the world." For the Sages to institute a blessing – a religious act of thanksgiving – over Greek and Roman scholars showed a remarkable open-mindedness to wisdom, whatever its source. The heavenly bodies are intended not just to exist, but also as "signs" to be studied, to help us navigate in time and space. Rambam sees science as a way to the love and awe of God.

ז מַיִם לָמָיִם: וַיַּעַשׂ אֱלֹהִים אֶת־הָרָקִיעַ וַיַּבְדֵּל בֵּין הַמַּיִם
אֲשֶׁר מִתַּחַת לָרָקִיעַ וּבֵין הַמַּיִם אֲשֶׁר מֵעַל לָרָקִיעַ וַיְהִי־
ח כֵן: וַיִּקְרָא אֱלֹהִים לָרָקִיעַ שָׁמָיִם וַיְהִי־עֶרֶב וַיְהִי־בֹקֶר יוֹם
שֵׁנִי:
ט וַיֹּאמֶר אֱלֹהִים יִקָּווּ הַמַּיִם מִתַּחַת הַשָּׁמַיִם אֶל־מָקוֹם אֶחָד
י וְתֵרָאֶה הַיַּבָּשָׁה וַיְהִי־כֵן: וַיִּקְרָא אֱלֹהִים ׀ לַיַּבָּשָׁה אֶרֶץ
יא וּלְמִקְוֵה הַמַּיִם קָרָא יַמִּים וַיַּרְא אֱלֹהִים כִּי־טוֹב: וַיֹּאמֶר
אֱלֹהִים תַּדְשֵׁא הָאָרֶץ דֶּשֶׁא עֵשֶׂב מַזְרִיעַ זֶרַע עֵץ פְּרִי
יב עֹשֶׂה פְּרִי לְמִינוֹ אֲשֶׁר זַרְעוֹ־בוֹ עַל־הָאָרֶץ וַיְהִי־כֵן: וַתּוֹצֵא
הָאָרֶץ דֶּשֶׁא עֵשֶׂב מַזְרִיעַ זֶרַע לְמִינֵהוּ וְעֵץ עֹשֶׂה־פְּרִי אֲשֶׁר
יג זַרְעוֹ־בוֹ לְמִינֵהוּ וַיַּרְא אֱלֹהִים כִּי־טוֹב: וַיְהִי־עֶרֶב וַיְהִי־בֹקֶר
יוֹם שְׁלִישִׁי:
יד וַיֹּאמֶר אֱלֹהִים יְהִי מְאֹרֹת בִּרְקִיעַ הַשָּׁמַיִם לְהַבְדִּיל בֵּין
הַיּוֹם וּבֵין הַלָּיְלָה וְהָיוּ לְאֹתֹת וּלְמוֹעֲדִים וּלְיָמִים וְשָׁנִים:
טו וְהָיוּ לִמְאוֹרֹת בִּרְקִיעַ הַשָּׁמַיִם לְהָאִיר עַל־הָאָרֶץ וַיְהִי־כֵן:
טז וַיַּעַשׂ אֱלֹהִים אֶת־שְׁנֵי הַמְּאֹרֹת הַגְּדֹלִים אֶת־הַמָּאוֹר הַגָּדֹל
לְמֶמְשֶׁלֶת הַיּוֹם וְאֶת־הַמָּאוֹר הַקָּטֹן לְמֶמְשֶׁלֶת הַלַּיְלָה

1:12 לְמִינֵהוּ *Each of its kind* – The key recurring word is *leminehem, lemino, lemina.* God creates plants, animals, birds, fish *leminehem,* according to their different kinds. The essence of Genesis 1 is ordered diversity. This is the priestly way of seeing the world, one which we will see expressed most clearly in the book of Leviticus. For the priest, the moral life is something we learn by honoring the distinctions God has taught us to see in the structure of reality. There is milk, a sign of life, and meat, a sign of death. There is plant life and there is animal life. There are brothers and others. Each has its boundaries that must be respected. That is sacred ontology and it creates an ethic of holiness. Its theoretical foundations lie here in Genesis 1.

1:14 וְהָיוּ לְאֹתֹת וּלְמוֹעֲדִים *To serve for signs and seasons* – Nature is something we can observe and learn from. "He who knows how to calculate the cycles and planetary courses, but does not, of him Scripture says, '[They] feast…never once turning to look at the LORD's workings, never once noticing the

17 God set them in the heavens' expanse to shine upon the
18 earth, to rule by day and by night and to separate light
19 from darkness. And God saw that it was good. There was
evening, and there was morning – a fourth day.
20 Then God said, "Let the water teem with swarms of
living creatures, and let birds fly over the earth across the
21 heavens' expanse." So God created the great sea serpents,
and all the kinds of crawling, living things that swarm in
the water, and all the kinds of winged, flying creatures.
22 And God saw that it was good. God blessed them, saying:
"Be fertile and multiply and fill the waters of the seas, and
23 let flying creatures multiply on earth." There was evening,
and there was morning – a fifth day.
24 Then God said, "Let the land produce every kind of living
thing: all the different species of cattle, crawling things,
25 and wild animals of the earth." And so it was. God made
the different kinds of wild animals of the earth, and cattle,
and all the species of creature that creep upon land. And
26 God saw that it was good. Then God said, "Let us make
humankind in our image, our likeness, that they may
rule over the fish of the sea and the flying creatures of

> and fleas and gnats, they too are part of the creation of the world. Through all does the Holy One, blessed be He, make manifest His mission, even through the serpent, even through the gnat, even through the frog. (Bereshit Rabba 10:8)

Biodiversity is a source of wonder to the psalmist: "How many are Your works, LORD. You made them all in wisdom; the earth is full of Your creations" (Ps. 104:24).

1:22 וַיְבָרֶךְ אֹתָם אֱלֹהִים *God blessed them* – God's first blessings are not addressed to Adam, but to animals. Rambam warns us against an anthropocentric view of reality. "The universe does not exist for man's sake, but each being exists for its own sake and not because of some other thing" (*Guide for the Perplexed* III:13). To be sure, humanity with its unique capacity for moral choice is the focus of the Torah's concerns, but Genesis sets forth a view of nature which is not man-centered – but God-centered.

MAN IN GOD'S IMAGE

Genesis 1:26–27 is not so much a metaphysical statement about the nature of

יז וְאֵת הַכּוֹכָבִים׃ וַיִּתֵּן אֹתָם אֱלֹהִים בִּרְקִיעַ הַשָּׁמָיִם לְהָאִיר
יח עַל־הָאָרֶץ׃ וְלִמְשֹׁל בַּיּוֹם וּבַלַּיְלָה וּלֲהַבְדִּיל בֵּין הָאוֹר וּבֵין
יט הַחֹשֶׁךְ וַיַּרְא אֱלֹהִים כִּי־טוֹב׃ וַיְהִי־עֶרֶב וַיְהִי־בֹקֶר יוֹם
רְבִיעִי׃
כ וַיֹּאמֶר אֱלֹהִים יִשְׁרְצוּ הַמַּיִם שֶׁרֶץ נֶפֶשׁ חַיָּה וְעוֹף יְעוֹפֵף
כא עַל־הָאָרֶץ עַל־פְּנֵי רְקִיעַ הַשָּׁמָיִם׃ וַיִּבְרָא אֱלֹהִים אֶת־
הַתַּנִּינִם הַגְּדֹלִים וְאֵת כָּל־נֶפֶשׁ הַחַיָּה ׀ הָרֹמֶשֶׂת אֲשֶׁר שָׁרְצוּ
הַמַּיִם לְמִינֵהֶם וְאֵת כָּל־עוֹף כָּנָף לְמִינֵהוּ וַיַּרְא אֱלֹהִים
כב כִּי־טוֹב׃ וַיְבָרֶךְ אֹתָם אֱלֹהִים לֵאמֹר פְּרוּ וּרְבוּ וּמִלְאוּ אֶת־
כג הַמַּיִם בַּיַּמִּים וְהָעוֹף יִרֶב בָּאָרֶץ׃ וַיְהִי־עֶרֶב וַיְהִי־בֹקֶר יוֹם
חֲמִישִׁי׃
כד וַיֹּאמֶר אֱלֹהִים תּוֹצֵא הָאָרֶץ נֶפֶשׁ חַיָּה לְמִינָהּ בְּהֵמָה וָרֶמֶשׂ
כה וְחַיְתוֹ־אֶרֶץ לְמִינָהּ וַיְהִי־כֵן׃ וַיַּעַשׂ אֱלֹהִים אֶת־חַיַּת הָאָרֶץ
לְמִינָהּ וְאֶת־הַבְּהֵמָה לְמִינָהּ וְאֵת כָּל־רֶמֶשׂ הָאֲדָמָה לְמִינֵהוּ
כו וַיַּרְא אֱלֹהִים כִּי־טוֹב׃ וַיֹּאמֶר אֱלֹהִים נַעֲשֶׂה אָדָם בְּצַלְמֵנוּ
כִּדְמוּתֵנוּ וְיִרְדּוּ בִדְגַת הַיָּם וּבְעוֹף הַשָּׁמַיִם וּבַבְּהֵמָה וּבְכָל־

1:21 אֶת הַתַּנִּינִם הַגְּדֹלִים *The great sea serpents* – In Ugaritic mythology, the god of the sky does battle with the god of the sea, a "great sea serpent," and out of his victory establishes dry land, usually over the dead body of his victim. But in Genesis there is no myth. God speaks and the universe comes into being. Genesis 1 is the beginning of the end of the mythic imagination. No longer is the universe seen as unpredictable. It is the work of a single, rational creative will. This is what will make science possible: science was born when people stopped telling stories about nature and instead observed it. Nor is the God of Genesis – as were the gods of myth – at best indifferent, at worst actively hostile to human beings. Genesis speaks of a God who endows humanity with His image. Thus, science and monotheism come hand in hand. We need science to understand the universe, and we need religion to guide our way within it, from the world as it is to the world as it ought to be.

1:21 כָּל־נֶפֶשׁ הַחַיָּה הָרֹמֶשֶׂת *All the kinds of crawling, living things* – God delights in diversity. The Rabbis sensed it when they said:

> Even those creatures you hold superfluous in the world, such as the flies

the heavens, the cattle and all the earth, and every living
27 creature that moves upon the earth." So God created
humankind in His image: in the image of God He created
28 him; male and female He created them. God blessed them,
saying, "Be fertile and multiply. Fill the earth and subdue it.
Rule over the fish of the sea, and the flying creatures of the
heavens, and every living thing that moves upon the earth."
29 Then God said, "I give you all these seed-bearing plants on
the face of the earth and every tree with seed-bearing fruit.
30 They shall be yours to eat. And to all the beasts of the earth
and birds of the heavens and everything that crawls over
the earth and has within it living spirit – I give every green
31 plant for food." And so it was. Then God saw all that He had
made: and it was very good. There was evening, and there
was morning – the sixth day.

---

use nature only in the service of God, its maker. To exploit nature rapaciously for our own ends is *ultra vires*. It breaks the condition on which man was made.

1:28 פְּרוּ וּרְבוּ *Be fertile and multiply* – All of nature shares with God the property of being creative, of bringing new life into being, but only humanity shares with God the moral choice of bringing new life into the world. Only for Adam and Ḥava is the phrase "Be fertile and multiply" experienced not just as a blessing but as a command. Bringing children into the world thus presupposes moral responsibility, for one might have chosen otherwise. That responsibility for those one has brought into existence extends to caring for them in their dependency, and to ensuring that they will have a world to inherit.

1:28 מִלְאוּ אֶת־הָאָרֶץ וְכִבְשֻׁהָ *Fill the earth and subdue it* – Rabbi Joseph Soloveitchik, in *The Lonely Man of Faith*, noted that in the phrase "and subdue it" we receive our mandate to be masters of our environment. As a result of developments over time – in knowledge, control, medical technology, education, and our range of resources and facilities – we are able to address problems in ways that previous generations were unable to do. Our attitudes to situations such as old age and disability evolve with our expanded possibilities. The more we are active and not passive, the more we can shape our circumstances rather than be shaped by them, the more dignified is our existence.

1:31 טוֹב מְאֹד *Very good* – Seven times in Genesis 1 the word "good" appears, the last with the addition of the word "very," meaning that the universe is not just good in its individual elements but also in their complex interaction. Natural (or

כז הָאָ֔רֶץ וּבְכָל־הָרֶ֖מֶשׂ הָֽרֹמֵ֥שׂ עַל־הָאָֽרֶץ׃ וַיִּבְרָ֨א אֱלֹהִ֤ים ׀
אֶת־הָֽאָדָם֙ בְּצַלְמ֔וֹ בְּצֶ֥לֶם אֱלֹהִ֖ים בָּרָ֣א אֹת֑וֹ זָכָ֥ר וּנְקֵבָ֖ה
כח בָּרָ֥א אֹתָֽם׃ וַיְבָ֣רֶךְ אֹתָם֮ אֱלֹהִים֒ וַיֹּ֨אמֶר לָהֶ֜ם אֱלֹהִ֗ים פְּר֥וּ
וּרְב֛וּ וּמִלְא֥וּ אֶת־הָאָ֖רֶץ וְכִבְשֻׁ֑הָ וּרְד֞וּ בִּדְגַ֤ת הַיָּם֙ וּבְע֣וֹף
כט הַשָּׁמַ֔יִם וּבְכָל־חַיָּ֖ה הָֽרֹמֶ֥שֶׂת עַל־הָאָֽרֶץ׃ וַיֹּ֣אמֶר אֱלֹהִ֗ים
הִנֵּה֩ נָתַ֨תִּי לָכֶ֜ם אֶת־כָּל־עֵ֣שֶׂב ׀ זֹרֵ֣עַ זֶ֗רַע אֲשֶׁר֙ עַל־פְּנֵ֣י כָל־
הָאָ֔רֶץ וְאֶת־כָּל־הָעֵ֛ץ אֲשֶׁר־בּ֥וֹ פְרִי־עֵ֖ץ זֹרֵ֣עַ זָ֑רַע לָכֶ֥ם יִֽהְיֶ֖ה
ל לְאָכְלָֽה׃ וּֽלְכָל־חַיַּ֣ת הָ֠אָרֶץ וּלְכָל־ע֨וֹף הַשָּׁמַ֜יִם וּלְכֹ֣ל ׀ רוֹמֵ֣שׂ
עַל־הָאָ֗רֶץ אֲשֶׁר־בּוֹ֙ נֶ֣פֶשׁ חַיָּ֔ה אֶת־כָּל־יֶ֥רֶק עֵ֖שֶׂב לְאָכְלָ֑ה
לא וַֽיְהִי־כֵֽן׃ וַיַּ֤רְא אֱלֹהִים֙ אֶת־כָּל־אֲשֶׁ֣ר עָשָׂ֔ה וְהִנֵּה־ט֖וֹב מְאֹ֑ד
וַֽיְהִי־עֶ֥רֶב וַֽיְהִי־בֹ֖קֶר י֥וֹם הַשִּׁשִּֽׁי׃

Momentous ideas made the West what it is, ideas like human rights, the abolition of slavery, the equal worth of all, and justice based on the principle that right is sovereign over might. All of these ultimately derived from the statement in the first chapter of the Torah that we are made in God's image and likeness. No other text has had a greater influence on moral thought, nor has any other civilization ever held a higher vision of what we are called on to be.

1:26 נַעֲשֶׂה אָדָם *Let us make humankind* – There are several understandings of this enigmatic first-person plural. The view put forth by Rabbi Samson Raphael Hirsch is striking. According to Rabbi Hirsch, "us" refers to the rest of creation. Before making mankind, with its potential for disrupting nature, God invites nature itself to give its assent. The implied condition is that man will

the human person as it is *a political protest against the very basis of hierarchical, class- or caste-based societies,* whether in ancient or modern times.

The phrase "in the image of God" would not have been unfamiliar to the first readers of the Torah; they knew it well. It was commonplace in the first civilizations, Mesopotamia and ancient Egypt, that certain people were said to be in the image of God. These were the kings of the Mesopotamian city-states and the pharaohs of Egypt. Nothing could have been more radical than to say that not just kings and rulers are God's image. We all are. In some fundamental sense we are all equal in dignity and ultimate worth, for we are all in God's image regardless of color, culture, or creed, physical form or mental ability. Today the idea is still daring; how much more so must it have been in an age of absolute rulers with absolute power.

2 1 So the heavens and the earth were finished, and all their
2 vast array. On the seventh day God finished the work that
He had done, and on the seventh day He rested from all
3 the work that He had done. God blessed the seventh day
and sanctified it, because on it He rested from all His
work, from all that God had created and done.
4 This is the story of the heavens and the earth when they SHENI
were created, on the day the LORD God made earth and
5 heaven. No shrub of the field yet grew on earth, and no
plant had yet sprouted, for the LORD God had not yet
brought rain upon the earth, and there was no one to
6 work the land. A mist would rise up from the earth and

---

rested from all His work, from all that God had created." The sentence should finish there. In fact, though, there is one extra word in the Hebrew, *laasot*, translated here "and done," but which literally means "to do," "to make," "to function."

Ibn Ezra and Abrabanel interpret it to mean "[He had created it] in such a way that it would continue to create itself." God as we see Him in Genesis 2 is a gardener, not a mechanic, one who plants systems that grow. It is a universe impossible to predict in detail, one that gives rise to agencies that are themselves creative. Without stretching the text too far, we might say that *laasot* means, quite simply, "to evolve."

THE SECOND STORY OF CREATION

To introduce us to a new perspective, the Bible uses a device more familiar to us from film than from ancient literature. The first two chapters of Genesis tell the story of creation twice, each time with a different focus. The first chapter uses a wide-angled lens to take in the whole panoply of the universe and man's place in it. In the second, the camera zooms in on man himself, the fissile combination of "dust of the land" and "breath of God," no longer part of nature but the lonely being only too aware of the gift of self-consciousness that now isolates him from the animals.

Genesis 1 tells us about creation and nature, the reality mapped by the natural sciences. It speaks about humanity as the biological species, *Homo sapiens*. What is distinctive about humans as a species is precisely our godlike powers of dominating nature and exercising control of the forces that shape the physical world. This is a matter of fact, not value, and it has increased exponentially throughout the relatively short period of human civilization. Power is morally neutral. It can be used to heal or wound, build or destroy.

Genesis 2, by contrast, is about morality and responsibility. It tells us

ב א ב וַיְכֻלּוּ הַשָּׁמַיִם וְהָאָרֶץ וְכָל־צְבָאָם׃ וַיְכַל אֱלֹהִים בַּיּוֹם
הַשְּׁבִיעִי מְלַאכְתּוֹ אֲשֶׁר עָשָׂה וַיִּשְׁבֹּת בַּיּוֹם הַשְּׁבִיעִי מִכָּל־
ג מְלַאכְתּוֹ אֲשֶׁר עָשָׂה׃ וַיְבָרֶךְ אֱלֹהִים אֶת־יוֹם הַשְּׁבִיעִי
וַיְקַדֵּשׁ אֹתוֹ כִּי בוֹ שָׁבַת מִכָּל־מְלַאכְתּוֹ אֲשֶׁר־בָּרָא אֱלֹהִים
לַעֲשׂוֹת׃
ד אֵלֶּה תוֹלְדוֹת הַשָּׁמַיִם וְהָאָרֶץ בְּהִבָּרְאָם בְּיוֹם עֲשׂוֹת יְהוָה ב שני
ה אֱלֹהִים אֶרֶץ וְשָׁמָיִם׃ וְכֹל ׀ שִׂיחַ הַשָּׂדֶה טֶרֶם יִהְיֶה בָאָרֶץ
וְכָל־עֵשֶׂב הַשָּׂדֶה טֶרֶם יִצְמָח כִּי לֹא הִמְטִיר יְהוָה אֱלֹהִים
ו עַל־הָאָרֶץ וְאָדָם אַיִן לַעֲבֹד אֶת־הָאֲדָמָה׃ וְאֵד יַעֲלֶה מִן־

---

scientific) law, moral law, and religious or ritual law are all part of the same phenomenon: the God-given, law-governed structure of reality. When this is honored by human beings, there is order. When it is violated, there is chaos and violence.

THE SEVENTH DAY

The Hebrew text until this point is precisely structured around the number seven, in ways not always apparent in translation. The word "good" appears seven times. The word "God" appears thirty-five times. The words "heavens" and "earth" each appear twenty-one times. The words "light" and "day" occur seven times in the first paragraph. The first verse contains seven words, the second fourteen words. This paragraph, describing the seventh day, contains thirty-five words, and so on. The passage as a whole contains 67 x 7 words. The entire passage is structured like a fractal, so that the sevenfold motif of the text as a whole is mirrored at lower levels of magnitude. The Sabbath, then, is woven into the pattern of creation.

The Sabbath was and remains a revolutionary idea. Many ancient religions had their holy days. But none had a day on which it was forbidden to work. Rabbinic tradition says that when the Torah was first translated into Greek, the translators changed this sentence to make it comprehensible. Instead of "On the seventh day God finished the work that He had done," the translators wrote, "On the sixth day...." It is as if they knew that the Greeks could understand that in six days God made the universe but not that on the seventh He made rest – that rest itself is a creation. Rest is the creation which allows us to enjoy all other creations. Just as clear space surrounds a page or frames a picture, so clear time is the frame in which we set our work, giving it the dignity of art.

2:3 אֲשֶׁר בָּרָא אֱלֹהִים לַעֲשׂוֹת *That God had created and done* – "Because on it He

7 water all the face of the land. Then the LORD God formed
man from the dust of the land and breathed the breath of
life into his nostrils, and the man became a living being.
8 The LORD God planted a garden in Eden, in the east, and
9 there he put the man He had formed. And from the land,
the LORD God caused all kinds of trees to grow, pleasant
to look at and good to eat from, and the Tree of Life stood
in the middle of the garden, and the Tree of Knowledge
10 of good and evil. A river flows from Eden to water this
garden, and from there divides into four headwaters.
11 The name of the first is Pishon. It surrounds the land of
12 Ḥavila, where there is gold. And the gold of that land is
13 good; bdellium and rock crystal are there also. The name
of the second river is Giḥon; it is the one that surrounds
14 the land of Kush. The name of the third river is the Tigris,
and it flows to the east of Assyria. The fourth river is the
15 Euphrates. The LORD God took the man and placed him
16 in the Garden of Eden to work it and safeguard it. And

The first – *le'ovda* – literally means "to serve it." The human being is thus both master and servant of nature. The second – *leshomra* – means "to guard it." This is the verb used in later biblical legislation to describe the responsibilities of a guardian of property that belongs to someone else. This guardian must exercise vigilance while protecting, and is personally liable for losses that occur through negligence. This is perhaps the best short definition of humanity's responsibility for nature as the Bible conceives it. We do not own nature – "The LORD owns the earth and all it contains" (Ps. 24:1). We are its stewards on behalf of God, who created and owns everything. As guardians of the earth, we are duty-bound to respect its integrity.

If we see our role as masters of the earth as a unique opportunity to truly serve and care for the planet, its creatures, and its resources, then we can reclaim our status as stewards of the world, and raise our new generations in an environment much closer to that of Eden.

THE TREE OF KNOWLEDGE OF GOOD AND EVIL

Why does God forbid the fruit that produces one of the highest forms of knowledge – the knowledge of good and evil? Indeed, do Adam and Ḥava not already have this knowledge *before* eating the fruit, in virtue of being in the image of God? Surely this is implied in the very fact that they are commanded

ז הָאָ֖רֶץ וְהִשְׁקָ֥ה אֶֽת־כָּל־פְּנֵֽי־הָאֲדָמָֽה׃ וַיִּיצֶר֩ יְהוָ֨ה אֱלֹהִ֜ים
אֶת־הָֽאָדָ֗ם עָפָר֙ מִן־הָ֣אֲדָמָ֔ה וַיִּפַּ֥ח בְּאַפָּ֖יו נִשְׁמַ֣ת חַיִּ֑ים
ח וַיְהִ֥י הָֽאָדָ֖ם לְנֶ֥פֶשׁ חַיָּֽה׃ וַיִּטַּ֞ע יְהוָ֧ה אֱלֹהִ֛ים גַּן־בְּעֵ֖דֶן מִקֶּ֑דֶם
ט וַיָּ֣שֶׂם שָׁ֔ם אֶת־הָֽאָדָ֖ם אֲשֶׁ֥ר יָצָֽר׃ וַיַּצְמַ֞ח יְהוָ֤ה אֱלֹהִים֙ מִן־
הָ֣אֲדָמָ֔ה כָּל־עֵ֛ץ נֶחְמָ֥ד לְמַרְאֶ֖ה וְט֣וֹב לְמַאֲכָ֑ל וְעֵ֤ץ הַֽחַיִּים֙
י בְּת֣וֹךְ הַגָּ֔ן וְעֵ֕ץ הַדַּ֖עַת ט֥וֹב וָרָֽע׃ וְנָהָר֙ יֹצֵ֣א מֵעֵ֔דֶן לְהַשְׁק֖וֹת
יא אֶת־הַגָּ֑ן וּמִשָּׁם֙ יִפָּרֵ֔ד וְהָיָ֖ה לְאַרְבָּעָ֥ה רָאשִֽׁים׃ שֵׁ֥ם הָֽאֶחָ֖ד
פִּישׁ֑וֹן ה֣וּא הַסֹּבֵ֗ב אֵ֚ת כָּל־אֶ֣רֶץ הַֽחֲוִילָ֔ה אֲשֶׁר־שָׁ֖ם הַזָּהָֽב׃
יב יג וּזֲהַ֛ב הָאָ֥רֶץ הַהִ֖וא ט֑וֹב שָׁ֥ם הַבְּדֹ֖לַח וְאֶ֥בֶן הַשֹּֽׁהַם׃ וְשֵֽׁם־
יד הַנָּהָ֥ר הַשֵּׁנִ֖י גִּיח֑וֹן ה֣וּא הַסּוֹבֵ֔ב אֵ֖ת כָּל־אֶ֥רֶץ כּֽוּשׁ׃ וְשֵׁ֨ם
הַנָּהָ֤ר הַשְּׁלִישִׁי֙ חִדֶּ֔קֶל ה֥וּא הַהֹלֵ֖ךְ קִדְמַ֣ת אַשּׁ֑וּר וְהַנָּהָ֥ר
טו הָֽרְבִיעִ֖י ה֥וּא פְרָֽת׃ וַיִּקַּ֛ח יְהוָ֥ה אֱלֹהִ֖ים אֶת־הָֽאָדָ֑ם וַיַּנִּחֵ֣הוּ
טז בְגַן־עֵ֔דֶן לְעָבְדָ֖הּ וּלְשָׁמְרָֽהּ׃ וַיְצַו֙ יְהוָ֣ה אֱלֹהִ֔ים עַל־הָֽאָדָ֖ם

---

about the moral limits of power. Not everything we *can* do *may* we do. The earth is not ours. It belongs to God who made it. Therefore we are not the owners of nature but its custodians. We are here to serve it and to safeguard it.

2:7 וַיְהִי הָאָדָם לְנֶפֶשׁ חַיָּה *The man became a living being* – Targum Onkelos translates this as "and man became *ruaḥ memalela*, a *speaking* spirit." Indeed, what singles out *Homo sapiens* among other animals is the ability to speak. Because we can speak, we can think, and therefore imagine a world different from the one that currently exists. Language – and with it the ability to remember a distant past and conceptualize a distant future – lies at the heart of our uniqueness as the image of God. Just as God makes the natural world by words ("God said… and so it was"), so we make the human world by words, which is why Judaism takes words so seriously: "Death and life are in the power of the tongue," says the book of Proverbs (18:21). Already at the opening of the Torah, at the very beginning of creation, is foreshadowed the Jewish doctrine of revelation: that God reveals Himself to humanity not in the sun, the stars, the wind, or the storm but in and through words – sacred words that make us co-partners with God in the work of redemption.

2:15 לְעָבְדָהּ וּלְשָׁמְרָהּ *To work it and safeguard it* – Immediately after reading of man's rights we are given a statement of man's responsibilities. The two Hebrew verbs used here are significant.

the Lord God commanded the man: "You are free to eat
17 from any tree in the garden. But the Tree of Knowledge of
good and evil – you may not eat from that, for on the day
18 you eat of it, you shall die." Then the Lord God said, "It is
not good for man to be alone. I will make a fitting partner

You cannot escape it by hiding. Your conscience accompanies you wherever you go, regardless of whether you are seen by others. As God tells Shmuel, "Man sees what the eyes see, but the Lord sees into the heart" (I Sam. 16:7). Judaism, with its belief in an invisible God who created the world with words, is an attempt to base the moral life on something other than appearance, honor, and shame. This is the innocence lost by Adam and Ḥava. With effort, it can be regained.

2:17 לֹא תֹאכַל *You may not eat* – On the sixth day, God makes His most fateful decision: to create a being who, like Himself, has the capacity to create. Yet the ability to create goes hand in hand with the ability to destroy. The danger immediately becomes clear. God tells the first man not to eat of the fruit of one tree. Let us set aside for the moment the nature of the tree; its presence in the garden represents the fact that *creation has boundaries* – the most important being the boundary between the permitted and forbidden. That is why there has to be, even in paradise, something that is forbidden. When the first two human beings eat of the forbidden fruit, the essential harmony between man and nature is broken. Humanity loses its innocence. For the first time, *nature* (the world we find) and *culture* (the world we make) come into conflict. The result is paradise lost.

2:18 לֹא־טוֹב *It is not good* – Throughout the first chapter of Genesis, the universe unfolds as a majestic set of verses in the song of creation: "And God said, 'Let there be….' And there was…. And God saw that it was good." Then, like an unexpected discord in a Mozart symphony, for the first time we hear the fateful words "*not* good." What, in the divinely ordered scheme of things, could possibly be not good? "It is not good for man to be alone." With the birth of the individual, something else makes its first appearance in the human story: solitude, and with it, the search for relationship.

This discovery flows directly from monotheism. In the world of myth, the gods were never alone. They conversed, argued, schemed, and fought. The stage of heaven was crowded. The Torah for the first time envisages a God who is radically alone, and thus allows man to see himself as radically alone, which is to say, conscious of his solitude. So, within the briefest possible span, the Torah sets out the twin poles of human existence – the dignity of man as the image of God, and the incompleteness of man, the relationship-seeking animal. From this point

יז לֵאמֹר מִכֹּל עֵץ־הַגָּן אָכֹל תֹּאכֵל׃ וּמֵעֵץ הַדַּעַת טוֹב וָרָע
יח לֹא תֹאכַל מִמֶּנּוּ כִּי בְּיוֹם אֲכָלְךָ מִמֶּנּוּ מוֹת תָּמוּת׃ וַיֹּאמֶר
יְהוָה אֱלֹהִים לֹא־טוֹב הֱיוֹת הָאָדָם לְבַדּוֹ אֶעֱשֶׂה־לּוֹ עֵזֶר

by God to be fertile and multiply, to fill the earth and subdue it, and not to eat of the Tree of Knowledge. For someone to understand a command, they must know it is good to obey and bad to disobey. What then changes when they eat the fruit? These questions go so deep that they threaten to make the entire narrative incomprehensible.

Rambam's answer is perplexing. Before eating the fruit, he says, the first humans knew the difference between truth and falsehood. What they acquired by eating the fruit was knowledge of "things generally accepted" (*Guide for the Perplexed* I:2). What does Rambam mean by "things generally accepted"? Is morality mere convention? Surely not. What Rambam means is that, after eating the fruit, the man and woman were embarrassed that they were naked, and *that* is a matter of social convention.

Adam and Ḥava begin life naked and "not ashamed" (Gen. 2:25). This is the first reference to shame in the Bible, albeit in its absence. The serpent tells the woman that if she eats from the fruit her "eyes will be opened" (3:5). Note the significance of this. They have not been blind until now. In what respect will their eyes be opened? This seems to be an explicit reference to a mode of moral judgment, "knowing good and evil," that has to do with sight rather than sound. The woman looks at the tree and sees that it is "enticing to the eyes." The text also adds that it is "desirable too for granting insight" – the Targum interprets the verb *lehaskil* as referring specifically to sight, in line with the serpent's assertion that eating the fruit will open her eyes. Accordingly, I have translated it as "granting insight."

The couple eat, their eyes are opened, they know that they are naked, and they seek to cover their nakedness. Every element of this is visual. The most interesting line is the one that reads: "They heard the sound ['the voice'] of the LORD God walking in the garden in the cool of the day, and the man and his wife hid from the LORD God among the trees of the garden" (3:8). Everything about this verse is strange. Voices don't walk. And you can't hide from God. Adam and Ḥava have become utterly sight-oriented. That is why they think you can hide. That is why they experience a voice walking as if it were itself something to be seen rather than to be heard.

Philosophers, among them Bernard Williams, have pointed out that shame cultures are usually visual. Shame has to do with how you appear (or imagine you appear) in other people's eyes. The instinctive reaction to shame is to wish you were invisible, or somewhere else. Guilt, by contrast, is much more internal.

19 for him." The LORD God formed all the wild animals, and
all the birds of the heavens, out of the land. He brought
them to the man to see what he would call them, and
whatever he called each living thing, that became its
20 name. So the man gave names to all the animals, the birds SHELISHI
of the heavens, and all the wild creatures. But he found
21 no fitting partner for himself. Then the LORD God made
the man fall into a deep sleep, and while he was sleeping
He took one of his ribs and closed the flesh in its place.
22 And the LORD God built the rib He had taken from the
23 man into a woman. He brought her to the man. And the
man said: "This, at last, is bone of my bones and flesh of
my flesh. This shall be called Woman, for from Man was
24 this one taken." That is why a man leaves his father and

---

estimated six thousand – and they have certain features in common, reflecting what has been called a depth grammar, which shapes and is shaped by the human brain. But languages are also different, and lead us to experience and understand the world in different ways.

Shown three objects, a chicken, a cow, and a clump of grass, and asked, "Which two go together?" American children choose the chicken and the cow – both members of the same class: animal. Chinese children choose the cow and the grass – where there are cows there is grass. American children learn nouns faster than verbs, but South Asian children learn verbs faster than nouns. Nouns are about classification; verbs are about relationships. The language you speak affects how you experience and understand the world and how you navigate through it. God partners with Adam, not only in creating the world, but in forming the language of which our inner landscape is formed.

If we are to find meaning, depth, and resonance in life, we must choose a language of deeds as we choose a language of words. Among the many moralities available, there is one that, as Jews, is ours. Here, Adam's work of classification shows him that relationship is missing. His moral world is just beginning to take shape.

2:23 כִּי מֵאִישׁ לֻקֳחָה זֹּאת *For from man was this one taken* – Waking to see the woman, man utters his first words, and in so doing creates the first poem. At the first reading, it sounds as if man is claiming ontological priority. First there was man; only afterward was there woman. Man comes from God and woman comes from man. That is how the classic Christian theologians read the text. But the Hebrew contains a nuance missed in

יט כְּנֶגְדּֽוֹ׃ וַיִּצֶר֩ יהוה אֱלֹהִ֜ים מִן־הָֽאֲדָמָ֗ה כׇּל־חַיַּ֤ת הַשָּׂדֶה֙
וְאֵת֙ כׇּל־ע֣וֹף הַשָּׁמַ֔יִם וַיָּבֵא֙ אֶל־הָ֣אָדָ֔ם לִרְא֖וֹת מַה־יִּקְרָא־
כ ל֑וֹ וְכֹל֩ אֲשֶׁ֨ר יִקְרָא־ל֧וֹ הָֽאָדָ֛ם נֶ֥פֶשׁ חַיָּ֖ה ה֥וּא שְׁמֽוֹ׃ וַיִּקְרָ֨א שלישי
הָֽאָדָ֜ם שֵׁמ֗וֹת לְכׇל־הַבְּהֵמָה֙ וּלְע֣וֹף הַשָּׁמַ֔יִם וּלְכֹ֖ל חַיַּ֣ת
כא הַשָּׂדֶ֑ה וּלְאָדָ֕ם לֹֽא־מָצָ֥א עֵ֖זֶר כְּנֶגְדּֽוֹ׃ וַיַּפֵּל֩ יהוה אֱלֹהִ֧ים ׀
תַּרְדֵּמָ֛ה עַל־הָאָדָ֖ם וַיִּישָׁ֑ן וַיִּקַּ֗ח אַחַת֙ מִצַּלְעֹתָ֔יו וַיִּסְגֹּ֥ר בָּשָׂ֖ר
כב תַּחְתֶּֽנָּה׃ וַיִּבֶן֩ יהוה אֱלֹהִ֧ים ׀ אֶת־הַצֵּלָ֛ע אֲשֶׁר־לָקַ֥ח מִן־
כג הָֽאָדָ֖ם לְאִשָּׁ֑ה וַיְבִאֶ֖הָ אֶל־הָֽאָדָֽם׃ וַיֹּאמֶר֮ הָֽאָדָם֒ זֹ֣את
הַפַּ֗עַם עֶ֚צֶם מֵֽעֲצָמַ֔י וּבָשָׂ֖ר מִבְּשָׂרִ֑י לְזֹאת֙ יִקָּרֵ֣א אִשָּׁ֔ה כִּ֥י
כד מֵאִ֖ישׁ לֻֽקֳחָה־זֹּֽאת׃ עַל־כֵּן֙ יַעֲזׇב־אִ֔ישׁ אֶת־אָבִ֖יו וְאֶת־אִמּ֑וֹ

onward the entire human story will be about the gradual unfolding of relationships into ever-widening spheres – the nuclear family, the extended family, the tribe, the federation of tribes, the nation, humanity.

2:18 הֱיוֹת הָאָדָם לְבַדּוֹ *For man to be alone* – God feels for the existential isolation of the first man. God empathizes. He enters into the human mind. He feels what we feel. There is no such moment in any other ancient religious literature. What is radical about biblical monotheism is not just that there is only one God, not just that He is the source of all that exists, but that God is closer to us than we are to ourselves. God knows the loneliness of the first man before the first man knows it of himself.

In Genesis 1, God creates the universe. Nothing vaster can be imagined. And yet, almost in the same breath as it speaks of the panoply of creation, the Torah tells us that God takes time to breathe the breath of life into the first human, give him dignified work, enter his loneliness, make him a wife, and robe them both with garments when the time comes for them to leave Eden and make their way in the world.

Creation of things is relatively easy; creation of relationships is hard. Never think of people as things. Never think of people as types: they are individuals. Never be content with creating systems: care also about relationships. It is by loving people that we learn to love God and feel the fullness of His love for us.

2:19 לִרְאוֹת מַה־יִּקְרָא־לוֹ *To see what he would call them* – The first thing God gives Adam is the gift of naming the animals, using words to categorize and thus begin to understand the world around us. Judaism is a religion of language, a sustained meditation on the power of words.

The world has many languages – an

mother and cleaves to his wife and they become one flesh.
25 The man and his wife were both naked, but they were
3 1 not ashamed. The serpent was the slyest of all the wild
animals the LORD God had made. "Did God say," it asked
the woman, "that you must not eat from any tree in the
2 garden?" The woman told the serpent, "We may eat the
3 fruit of the trees in the garden, but God did say, 'You must
not eat fruit from the tree in the middle of the garden, and
4 you must not touch it, or you will die.'" But the serpent
5 told the woman, "You will not die; God knows that on
the day you eat from it your eyes will be opened, and you
6 will be like God, knowing good and evil." The woman
saw that the tree was ripe for eating, enticing to the eyes,
and desirable too for granting insight. She took some
of its fruit and ate, and she gave some to her husband

---

love of one's neighbor, love of the stranger. That love is a flame lit in marriage and the family. Morality is the love between husband and wife, parent and child – uncommanded because it is assumed to be natural – extended outward to the world.

3:6 וְכִי תַאֲוָה הוּא לָעֵינַיִם...לְהַשְׂכִּיל *Enticing to the eyes... insight* – Heinrich Graetz, the nineteenth-century historian, summed up the difference between biblical Judaism and all other cultures of its time:

The pagan perceives the Divine in nature through the medium of the eye, and he becomes conscious of it as something to be looked at. On the other hand, to the Jew who conceives God as being outside of nature and prior to it, the Divine manifests itself through the will and through the medium of the ear. He becomes conscious of it as something to be heeded and listened to.

The word the Torah uses instead of "to obey" is the root *sh-m-a*, which means (1) to listen, (2) to hear, (3) to attend, (4) to understand, (5) to internalize, (6) to respond in action, and thus (7) to obey. This is a fact of the highest significance, because it tells us that the Torah is not a series of heteronomous (other-given) commands that call for mere obedience. The divine command is one that God issues in the expectation that we will understand, internalize, and act accordingly. It is at the heart of what Rabbi Dr. David Weiss Halivni calls Judaism's "predilection for justified law," law that speaks to the mind and to human understanding.

In his book *Kol HaNevua*, Rabbi David Cohen, the disciple of Rav Kook known as "the nazirite," pointed out that the visual nature of the pagan religious experience, and the aural nature

כה וְדָבַק בְּאִשְׁתּוֹ וְהָיוּ לְבָשָׂר אֶחָד׃ וַיִּהְיוּ שְׁנֵיהֶם עֲרוּמִּים
ג א הָאָדָם וְאִשְׁתּוֹ וְלֹא יִתְבֹּשָׁשׁוּ׃ וְהַנָּחָשׁ הָיָה עָרוּם מִכֹּל
חַיַּת הַשָּׂדֶה אֲשֶׁר עָשָׂה יהוה אֱלֹהִים וַיֹּאמֶר אֶל־הָאִשָּׁה
ב אַף כִּי־אָמַר אֱלֹהִים לֹא תֹאכְלוּ מִכֹּל עֵץ הַגָּן׃ וַתֹּאמֶר
ג הָאִשָּׁה אֶל־הַנָּחָשׁ מִפְּרִי עֵץ־הַגָּן נֹאכֵל׃ וּמִפְּרִי הָעֵץ אֲשֶׁר
בְּתוֹךְ־הַגָּן אָמַר אֱלֹהִים לֹא תֹאכְלוּ מִמֶּנּוּ וְלֹא תִגְּעוּ בּוֹ פֶּן
ד ה תְּמֻתוּן׃ וַיֹּאמֶר הַנָּחָשׁ אֶל־הָאִשָּׁה לֹא־מוֹת תְּמֻתוּן׃ כִּי
יֹדֵעַ אֱלֹהִים כִּי בְּיוֹם אֲכָלְכֶם מִמֶּנּוּ וְנִפְקְחוּ עֵינֵיכֶם וִהְיִיתֶם
ו כֵּאלֹהִים יֹדְעֵי טוֹב וָרָע׃ וַתֵּרֶא הָאִשָּׁה כִּי טוֹב הָעֵץ לְמַאֲכָל
וְכִי תַאֲוָה־הוּא לָעֵינַיִם וְנֶחְמָד הָעֵץ לְהַשְׂכִּיל וַתִּקַּח מִפִּרְיוֹ

---

translation. Biblical Hebrew contains two words for "man," *adam* and *ish*. *Adam* is the species. It means, roughly, *Homo sapiens*. *Ish* is the individual, the person. Until this point, the Bible has consistently used the word *adam*. This is the first occurrence of the word *ish*, and it comes after the word *isha*, "woman."

Here the Bible is signalling a momentous proposition. Adam has to pronounce his wife's name before he can pronounce his own. I have to say "you" before I can say "I." *I have to acknowledge the other before I can truly understand myself.* Not only can I not live alone, I cannot think, know, understand alone.

Sociologists from George Herbert Mead to Peter Berger, and philosophers from Wittgenstein to Charles Taylor, have pointed out that identity is born in conversation. That is because we exist as persons-in-relation. Without language there is no relationship, and without relationship there is no personhood.

▶

2:24 וְדָבַק בְּאִשְׁתּוֹ *And cleaves to his wife* – One woman, one man. We do not always remember how revolutionary this model is. The establishment of monogamy goes against the normal grain of social change. Normally the values of a society are those imposed on it by the ruling class. And the ruling class stands to gain from promiscuity and polygamy, which multiply the chances of their genes being handed on. From monogamy the rich and powerful lose and the poor and powerless gain. Monogamy did not immediately become the norm, even within the world of the Tanakh. But many of its most famous stories are critiques that point the way to monogamy. Its development was a triumph for the equal dignity of all.

All the great civilizations share the "golden rule" of reciprocity. What is new and remarkable in the Torah is the idea that *love*, not just reciprocity, is the driving principle of the moral life: love of God,

7 and he too ate. The eyes of both of them were opened,
and they realized that they were naked. So they sewed
fig leaves together and made coverings for themselves.
8 They heard the sound of the LORD God walking in the
garden in the cool of the day, and the man and his wife
hid from the LORD God among the trees of the garden.
9 10 The LORD God called to the man: "Where are you?" He
answered, "I heard Your voice in the garden, and I was
11 afraid, because I was naked. So I hid." "Who told you,"
God asked, "that you were naked? Have you eaten from
12 the tree from which I commanded you not to eat?" The
man said, "The woman You put here with me – she gave
13 me fruit from the tree and I ate." Then the LORD God
said to the woman, "What is this you have done?" The
14 woman said, "The serpent beguiled me and I ate." And
the LORD God said to the serpent, "Because you have
done this, you are accursed more than all the animals
and all wild beasts. You will creep on your belly and dust

---

listen to the voice of anger, as in the case of Kayin? Or will we follow the voice of God calling on us to make this a more just and gracious world?

3:12 הָאִשָּׁה אֲשֶׁר נָתַתָּה עִמָּדִי *The woman You put here* – Adam blames the woman. The woman blames the serpent. The result is that they are both punished and exiled from Eden. Genesis is a set of variations on the theme of family, and none runs smoothly. With Adam and Ḥava comes conflict. With each successive generation, new tensions arise. This is the great power of the Book of Books and the reason why it has never lost its hold on the human imagination: It is about us, people we can recognize and identify with. The real dramas are not the ones fought in court or in the battlefield. They are the ones fought and resolved in the home, between parents and children, between siblings, between husbands and wives. No literature more systematically expresses the dignity of the personal, the high moral drama of everyday life with its defensiveness, its petty betrayals, its self-deception.

Families are not ideal worlds. They are significant precisely because they are real worlds with people we know and trust. Working out our tensions with them, we learn how to resolve our tensions with society. And yes, they have their share of pain. It is the pain of life lived in relationship. Without it we could not learn to love.

ז וַתֹּאכַל וַתִּתֵּן גַּם־לְאִישָׁהּ עִמָּהּ וַיֹּאכַל׃ וַתִּפָּקַחְנָה עֵינֵי
שְׁנֵיהֶם וַיֵּדְעוּ כִּי עֵירֻמִּם הֵם וַיִּתְפְּרוּ עֲלֵה תְאֵנָה וַיַּעֲשׂוּ
ח לָהֶם חֲגֹרֹת׃ וַיִּשְׁמְעוּ אֶת־קוֹל יהוה אֱלֹהִים מִתְהַלֵּךְ בַּגָּן
לְרוּחַ הַיּוֹם וַיִּתְחַבֵּא הָאָדָם וְאִשְׁתּוֹ מִפְּנֵי יהוה אֱלֹהִים
ט בְּתוֹךְ עֵץ הַגָּן׃ וַיִּקְרָא יהוה אֱלֹהִים אֶל־הָאָדָם וַיֹּאמֶר לוֹ
י אַיֶּכָּה׃ וַיֹּאמֶר אֶת־קֹלְךָ שָׁמַעְתִּי בַּגָּן וָאִירָא כִּי־עֵירֹם אָנֹכִי
יא וָאֵחָבֵא׃ וַיֹּאמֶר מִי הִגִּיד לְךָ כִּי עֵירֹם אָתָּה הֲמִן־הָעֵץ אֲשֶׁר
יב צִוִּיתִיךָ לְבִלְתִּי אֲכָל־מִמֶּנּוּ אָכָלְתָּ׃ וַיֹּאמֶר הָאָדָם הָאִשָּׁה
יג אֲשֶׁר נָתַתָּה עִמָּדִי הִוא נָתְנָה־לִּי מִן־הָעֵץ וָאֹכֵל׃ וַיֹּאמֶר
יהוה אֱלֹהִים לָאִשָּׁה מַה־זֹּאת עָשִׂית וַתֹּאמֶר הָאִשָּׁה הַנָּחָשׁ
יד הִשִּׁיאַנִי וָאֹכֵל׃ וַיֹּאמֶר יהוה אֱלֹהִים ׀ אֶל־הַנָּחָשׁ כִּי עָשִׂיתָ
זֹּאת אָרוּר אַתָּה מִכָּל־הַבְּהֵמָה וּמִכֹּל חַיַּת הַשָּׂדֶה עַל־גְּחֹנְךָ

of the Jewish one, affects our most basic metaphors of knowing. To this day, in English, almost all our words for understanding or intellect are governed by the metaphor of sight. We speak of insight, hindsight, foresight, vision, and imagination. We say, "It appears that...." When we understand something we say, "I see."

The Babylonian Talmud, by contrast, consistently uses the metaphor of hearing. When a proof is about to be brought, it says, *Ta shma*, "Come and hear." When it speaks of inference it says, *Shema mina*, "Hear from this." When someone disagrees with a proposition, it says, *Lo shemiya lei*, "He could not hear it." In Judaism, knowledge is a form, not of seeing, but of listening. These conflicting forms of knowledge – not sexual desire or any of the other fanciful explanations that have been given of it – constitute the real drama of the sin of Adam and Ḥava in eating the forbidden fruit.

3:9 אַיֶּכָּה *Where are you?* – As Rabbi Shneur Zalman of Liadi pointed out, this call was not directed only to the first humans. It echoes in every generation. God teaches us what we ought to do, but He does not do it for us. With rare exceptions, God does not intervene in history. He acts *through* us, not *to* us. His is the voice that tells us that we can resist the evil within us as well as the evil that surrounds us. The great question, the question that the life we lead answers, is: Which voice will we listen to? Will we heed the voice of desire, as in the case of Adam and Ḥava? Will we

15 will you eat all the days of your life. I will plant hostility
between you and the woman, between your children and
hers. And man will strike your head, and you will strike
16 his heel." To the woman He said, "I will make
your pain in pregnancy searingly great; in sorrow will you
bear children. You will long for your husband, but he will
17 rule over you." To Adam He said, "Because you
listened to your wife and ate of the tree from which I
commanded you not to eat – cursed will be the land on
your account. By painful toil you will eat from it all the
18 days of your life. It will sprout thorns and thistles for
19 you, and you shall eat plants of the field. By the sweat
of your brow will you eat bread until you return to the
land, for from there you were taken. You are dust, and
20 you will return to dust." Then the man named his wife

---

emotions. Yet the Judaic answer is not that state beloved of the Greek philosophers, namely *ataraxia*, serenity, affectlessness, the "therapy of desire," nor is it the *nirvana* of the Eastern mystics. In Judaism, joy, exhilaration, strong emotion, and above all, love – "with all your heart, with all your soul, and with all your might" – are all part of the religious life. If we master our desires, they need not master us.

3:19 בְּזֵעַת אַפֶּיךָ *By the sweat of your brow* – The Jewish liturgy for Saturday night – the time that recalls the expulsion from Eden – culminates in a hymn to the values of work and the family (Ps. 128:2): "You shall eat the fruit of your labor; you shall be happy and thriving." Work has spiritual value. How so?

When the Holy One, blessed be He, told Adam, "Cursed will be the land on your account. It will sprout thorns and thistles," Adam wept. He said, "Master of the Universe, am I and my donkey to eat in the same manger?" But when he heard the words "By the sweat of your brow will you eat bread," he was consoled (Pesaḥim 118a).

Labor elevates man, for by it he *earns* his food. Animals find sustenance; only mankind creates it. As the thirteenth-century commentator Rabbeinu Baḥya put it, "The active participation of man in the creation of his own wealth is a sign of his spiritual greatness." The "thorns and thistles" are a curse; work itself is not a curse, but a blessing.

3:19 עָפָר אַתָּה וְאֶל עָפָר תָּשׁוּב *You are dust, and you will return to dust* – Until this point, death has not entered Adam's consciousness, but now he is brought face-to-face with it. It is now, too, that Adam remembers God's words to the woman. She will give birth to children – in pain,

טו תֵלֵ֔ךְ וְעָפָ֥ר תֹּאכַ֖ל כָּל־יְמֵ֥י חַיֶּֽיךָ׃ וְאֵיבָ֣ה ׀ אָשִׁ֗ית בֵּֽינְךָ֙ וּבֵ֣ין
הָֽאִשָּׁ֔ה וּבֵ֥ין זַרְעֲךָ֖ וּבֵ֣ין זַרְעָ֑הּ ה֚וּא יְשׁוּפְךָ֣ רֹ֔אשׁ וְאַתָּ֖ה
טז תְּשׁוּפֶ֥נּוּ עָקֵֽב׃ אֶל־הָאִשָּׁ֣ה אָמַ֗ר הַרְבָּ֤ה אַרְבֶּה֙
עִצְּבוֹנֵ֣ךְ וְהֵֽרֹנֵ֔ךְ בְּעֶ֖צֶב תֵּֽלְדִ֣י בָנִ֑ים וְאֶל־אִישֵׁךְ֙ תְּשׁ֣וּקָתֵ֔ךְ
יז וְה֖וּא יִמְשָׁל־בָּֽךְ׃ וּלְאָדָ֣ם אָמַ֗ר כִּ֣י שָׁמַ֘עְתָּ֮ לְק֣וֹל
אִשְׁתֶּ֗ךָ וַתֹּ֙אכַל֙ מִן־הָעֵ֔ץ אֲשֶׁ֤ר צִוִּיתִ֙יךָ֙ לֵאמֹ֔ר לֹ֥א תֹאכַ֖ל
מִמֶּ֑נּוּ אֲרוּרָ֤ה הָֽאֲדָמָה֙ בַּעֲבוּרֶ֔ךָ בְּעִצָּבוֹן֙ תֹּֽאכֲלֶ֔נָּה כֹּ֖ל יְמֵ֥י
יח חַיֶּֽיךָ׃ וְק֥וֹץ וְדַרְדַּ֖ר תַּצְמִ֣יחַֽ לָ֑ךְ וְאָכַלְתָּ֖ אֶת־עֵ֥שֶׂב הַשָּׂדֶֽה׃
יט בְּזֵעַ֤ת אַפֶּ֙יךָ֙ תֹּ֣אכַל לֶ֔חֶם עַ֤ד שֽׁוּבְךָ֙ אֶל־הָ֣אֲדָמָ֔ה כִּ֥י מִמֶּ֖נָּה
כ לֻקָּ֑חְתָּ כִּֽי־עָפָ֣ר אַ֔תָּה וְאֶל־עָפָ֖ר תָּשֽׁוּב׃ וַיִּקְרָ֧א הָֽאָדָ֛ם שֵׁ֥ם

3:15 בֵּין זַרְעֲךָ וּבֵין זַרְעָהּ *Between your children and hers* – And yet, in the prophet Yeshayahu's vision:

> A baby will play at the cobra's hole,
> and an infant's hand
> will explore the viper's nest.
> There will be no wrong or violence
> on all My holy mountain,
> for knowledge of the Lord will fill the earth
> as waters cover the ocean. (Is. 11:8–9)

By the eighth century BCE the prophets of Israel had become the first people in history to envisage a world at peace. Yeshayahu is the classic instance of this, foreseeing a time when "nation shall not raise sword against nation" (2:4), and, in a reversal of the conflicts that emerge from our story, the world will be in a state of *shalom*, the integrated diversity that constitutes peace.

3:16 אֶל־אִישֵׁךְ תְּשׁוּקָתֵךְ וְהוּא יִמְשָׁל־בָּךְ *You will long for your husband but he will rule over you* – The word "longing," *teshuka*, appears only twice elsewhere in Tanakh, in God's warning to Kayin about the danger of the violent anger he is feeling toward Hevel: "Sin is crouching at the door; it *longs to have you*, but you must rule over it" (Gen. 4:7), and much later, in Song of Songs: "I am my beloved's, and his longing is for me" (7:11). This is a fine instance of intertextuality. In both places in Genesis, longing is about the dangerous power of passion. It will cause Ḥava to be subservient to her husband and Kayin to be a slave to his emotions. In Song of Songs, *teshuka* is benign because it is mutual. In no other book in Tanakh do woman and man – and thus Israel and God – stand on such equal terms (the dominant voice in the Song is the woman). Longing, desire, passion – these are dangerously labile

21 Ḥava, for she would become the mother of all life. Then
the LORD God made garments of skins for Adam and
his wife and clothed them.
22 The LORD God then said, "Now that man has become REVI'I
like one of us, knowing good and evil, he must not be
allowed to reach out his hand and take also from the
23 Tree of Life, eat, and live forever." So the LORD God sent
him away from the Garden of Eden to work the land

---

worse, mankind has attained a new level of consciousness – but no possibility remains that we can overcome death.

There are two consolations for this. The first is that we are not just physical beings. God made the first human "from the dust of the land" (Gen. 2:7) but He breathed into him the breath of life. We may be mortal but there is within us something that is immortal. "The dust returns to the earth where it began, and the spirit returns to God who gave it" (Eccl. 12:7).

The second is that, even down here on earth, something of us lives on. For good or bad, our lives have an impact on other lives, and the ripples of our deeds spread ever outward across space and time.

So we may be mortal, but that does not reduce our life to insignificance, for we are part of something larger than ourselves, characters in a story that began early in the history of civilization and that will last as long as humankind.

We are dust of the earth but there is within us the breath of God. We fail, but we can still achieve greatness. We die, but the best part of us lives on. No man is a god. There is no life without error and shortcoming. Yet we have a higher intelligence than other species; we are self-conscious, but also self-reflective. We are in dialogue with our creator.

The hasidic master Rabbi Simcha Bunim of Peshisḥa said we should each have two pockets. In one should be a note saying: "I am but dust and ashes" (Gen. 18:27). In the other should be a note saying: "For my sake was the world created" (Mishna Sanhedrin 4:5). Life lives in the tension between our physical smallness and our spiritual greatness, the brevity of life and the eternity of the faith by which we live. Defeat, despair, and a sense of tragedy are always premature. Life is short, but when we lift our eyes to heaven, we walk tall.

3:23 לַעֲבֹד אֶת הָאֲדָמָה *To work the land* – The Sages were intrigued by the chronology of the narrative of Adam and Ḥava in the Garden of Eden. According to them, the entire drama of the creation and disobedience of Adam and Ḥava took place on the sixth day. On that day, they were made, they were commanded about the tree, they transgressed the command, and they were sentenced to exile. Not only were they condemned to leave the garden,

כא אִשְׁתּוֹ חַוָּה כִּי הִוא הָיְתָה אֵם כָּל־חָי: וַיַּעַשׂ יהוה אֱלֹהִים
לְאָדָם וּלְאִשְׁתּוֹ כָּתְנוֹת עוֹר וַיַּלְבִּשֵׁם:
כב וַיֹּאמֶר ׀ יהוה אֱלֹהִים הֵן הָאָדָם הָיָה כְּאַחַד מִמֶּנּוּ לָדַעַת ג רביעי
טוֹב וָרָע וְעַתָּה ׀ פֶּן־יִשְׁלַח יָדוֹ וְלָקַח גַּם מֵעֵץ הַחַיִּים וְאָכַל
כג וָחַי לְעֹלָם: וַיְשַׁלְּחֵהוּ יהוה אֱלֹהִים מִגַּן־עֵדֶן לַעֲבֹד אֶת־

---

to be sure, but she will bring new life into the world. Suddenly Adam knows that though we die, if we are privileged to have children, something of us will live on: our genes, our influence, our example, our ideals. That is our immortality. But this cannot be achieved alone.

Until he became aware of his mortality, Adam could think of his wife as a mere *ezer kenegdo* – as an assistant, not an equal. Now he knows otherwise. Without her, he cannot have children – and children are to be his share in eternity. With this awareness he ceases to think of her as an assistant. She is a person in her own right – more even than he, for it is she, not he, who will actually give birth. In this respect she is more like God than he can be, for God is He-who-brings-new-life-into-being. It is now that he turns to his wife and for the first time sees her as a person, giving her a personal name, Ḥava, meaning, "she who gives life."

3:21 וַיַּעַשׂ יהוה אֱלֹהִים לְאָדָם וּלְאִשְׁתּוֹ כָּתְנוֹת עוֹר וַיַּלְבִּשֵׁם *God made garments of skins for Adam and his wife and clothed them* – The first-century sage Rabbi Meir read the *ayin* of the word *or*, "skins," as an *alef* – and thus interprets the phrase "garments of skins" as "garments of light" (Bereshit Rabba 20:12). For Adam now saw that physical being, "nakedness," was not simply a source of shame. There is a spiritual dimension to the physical relationship between husband and wife. At one level it is the most animal of desires, but at another it is as close as we come to the principle of divine creativity itself, namely, that love creates life. It is only when we relate to one another as persons possessed of non-negotiable dignity that we respond to the "image of God" in the other.

In a sense, the whole of Judaism – or at least *mitzvot bein adam lehavero*, "the commands between us and our fellow human beings" – is an extended commentary on this idea. The rules of justice, mercy, charity, compassion, regard for the poor, love for the neighbor and the stranger, delicacy of speech, and sensitivity to the easily injured feelings of others are all variants on the theme of respect for the human other as an image and likeness of the Divine Other. It is when Ḥava receives her name that God robes the couple in garments of light.

3:22 פֶּן יִשְׁלַח יָדוֹ... וָחַי לְעֹלָם *He must not be allowed to… live forever* – For better or

▶

24 from which he had been taken. He drove out the man,
and east of the Garden of Eden He placed the cherubim
and the flaming, whirling sword to guard the way to the
4 1 Tree of Life. The man knew his wife Ḥava, and
she conceived and gave birth to Kayin. She said, "With
2 the LORD's help I have made a man." Later, she gave birth
to his brother Hevel. Hevel became a shepherd, while

God as power, God as justice. Thus far Adam has only used nouns, first for the animals, and then for his wife, whom he calls *isha*, "woman." He has moved from nature to culture – of which language is the first step – but he has not yet understood the concept of a person.

Judaism was much more than the discovery of monotheism, the discovery of a single unified God. That idea is contained in the word *Elokim*. It was also the discovery that God is a "person" – that the fact that we are persons, with loves, fears, hopes, and dreams, is not an accidental by-product of evolution, but rather an echo of the ultimate reality of the cosmos. That is the world-transforming concept of *Hashem* – and it is only when Adam responds to Ḥava as a person that he can see himself as a person, and they can both experience God too through His proper name. At this moment humanity ceases to be a mere biological species and becomes *Homo religiosus*, man-in-search-of-God who meets *Hashem*, God-in-search-of-man.

In other words, our relationship to God parallels our relationship to one another. Only when we respect and recognize the uniqueness of another person are we capable of respecting and recognizing the uniqueness of God Himself. *Hashem* is not a noun but a name. It refers to God not as a power, or even the totality of all powers, but as a person, a "Thou." *Hashem* is the One who speaks to us and to whom we speak, who loves us as a person loves, who hears our prayers, forgives our failures, gives us strength in times of crisis, and teaches us the path of life. A philosopher can come to the realization that the universe has an author, a creator, a first cause, a "prime mover." But only a prophet (or a child of Avraham and the nation of prophets) can relate to God as a person, as the consecration of the personal, the Divinity that underwrites our humanity.

4:2 הֶבֶל *Hevel* – Hevel's name is, among other things, the keyword of the Book of Ecclesiastes; as the King James Version translates: "Vanity of vanities; all is vanity." *Hevel* has also been translated as "meaningless," "pointless," "futile," "useless." These translations miss the point. *Hevel* is a word for "breath." Jews speak of the soul, or the spiritual dimension of humankind, in language drawn from the act of breathing. In Hebrew, words for soul – such as *nefesh*, *ruaḥ*, *neshama* – are all types of breath. *Hevel* means a shallow,

כד הָאֲדָמָה אֲשֶׁר לֻקַּח מִשָּׁם׃ וַיְגָרֶשׁ אֶת־הָאָדָם וַיַּשְׁכֵּן מִקֶּדֶם
לְגַן־עֵדֶן אֶת־הַכְּרֻבִים וְאֵת לַהַט הַחֶרֶב הַמִּתְהַפֶּכֶת לִשְׁמֹר
ד א אֶת־דֶּרֶךְ עֵץ הַחַיִּים׃ וְהָאָדָם יָדַע אֶת־חַוָּה
אִשְׁתּוֹ וַתַּהַר וַתֵּלֶד אֶת־קַיִן וַתֹּאמֶר קָנִיתִי אִישׁ אֶת־יְהוָה׃
ב וַתֹּסֶף לָלֶדֶת אֶת־אָחִיו אֶת־הָבֶל וַיְהִי־הֶבֶל רֹעֵה צֹאן

---

but as the day reached its close and night began to fall, they experienced darkness for the first time (Avot DeRabbi Natan 42; Devarim Rabba 13).

In compassion, God allowed them a stay of sentence. They were given an extra day in Eden – namely the Sabbath. For the whole of that day, the sun did not set. As it too came to a close, *God showed the first human beings how to make light* (Pesikta Rabbati 23; Pirkei DeRabbi Eliezer 20). This, according to the Sages, is the reason we light a *Havdala* candle at the end of the Sabbath to inaugurate the new week.

There is, in other words, a fundamental difference between the light of the first day ("God said, 'Let there be light'") and that of the eighth day. The light of the first day is the illumination God makes. The light of the eighth day is the illumination God teaches *us* to make. It symbolizes our "partnership with God in the work of creation" (Shabbat 10a, 119b). There is no more beautiful image than this of how God empowers us to join Him in bringing light to the world. On the Sabbath we remember God's creation. On the eighth day (Motza'ei Shabbat) we celebrate *our* creativity as the image and partner of God.

God seeks to confer dignity on the beings He made in His image as an act of love. He does not hide the secrets of the universe from us. He does not seek to keep mankind in a state of ignorance or dependence. The creative God empowers us to be creative and begins by teaching us how. He wants us to be guardians of the world He has entrusted to our care.

4:1 וְהָאָדָם יָדַע *The man knew* – The Hebrew word *daat*, usually translated as "knowledge," does not mean knowledge at all in the Greek sense, as a form of cognition. It means intimacy, relationship, the touch of soul and soul. In the Western Hellenistic tradition, knowledge involves detachment. In Judaism, knowledge is attachment; it is intimacy. Only that which you love can you really know.

4:1 קָנִיתִי אִישׁ אֶת יהוה *With the LORD's help I have made a man* – Only after the man has given his wife a proper name do we find the Torah referring to God Himself by His proper name alone. Until now He has been described as either *Elokim* or *Hashem Elokim* – *Elokim* being the impersonal aspect of God: God as law,

3 Kayin was a worker of the land. Time passed, and Kayin
4 brought fruit of the land as an offering to the LORD. Hevel
too brought an offering: fat portions from the firstborn
of his flock. The LORD looked favorably on Hevel and
5 his offering, but upon Kayin and his offering He did not
look with favor. Kayin became very angry, and his face
6 downcast. The LORD said to Kayin, "Why are you angry;
7 why is your face downcast? If you act well, will you not
be uplifted? If you fail to act well, sin is crouching at the
door; it longs to have you, but you must rule over it."
8 Then Kayin said to his brother Hevel – and when they

4:7 וְאַתָּה תִּמְשָׁל־בּוֹ *But you must rule over it* – We can rephrase this a little more technically nowadays. Kayin is experiencing a rush of emotion to the amygdala, the so-called reptile brain with its fight-or-flight reactions, including anger. God is urging him to use his prefrontal cortex, more rational and deliberative, capable of thinking beyond the immediacy of me, here, now. The choice – God is saying – is in your hands. You are free to do what you choose. But actions have consequences. You cannot overeat and take no exercise, and at the same time stay healthy. You cannot act selfishly and win the respect of other people. You cannot allow injustices to prevail and sustain a cohesive society. You cannot let rulers use power for their own ends without destroying the basis of a free and gracious social order. There is nothing mystical about these ideas. They are eminently intelligible. But they are also, and inescapably, moral. Neuroscience has shown us where in the brain the battle for freedom is fought, but it has not shown us freedom itself. This we can know only introspectively, from within. Sin is crouching at the door. But we can rule over our own minds.

4:8 וַיֹּאמֶר קַיִן אֶל הֶבֶל אָחִיו *Kayin said to his brother Hevel* – The verse contains fractured syntax. It says, "Then Kayin said," but it does not say *what* he says. To turn it into a coherent sentence, translations usually add words not in the original, or paraphrase the verb from "said" to "talked with" or "had words with." In so doing, however, they completely miss the point of the verse. Style mirrors substance. The fractured syntax represents the fractured relationship. The conversation breaks down. "Then Kayin said" – but his speech gets no further, and there is nothing but tension and silence. When words fail, violence begins.

Violence, Alan Brien once wrote, is the repartee of the inarticulate. If we can speak together, we will be able to live together. Speech heals hate; silence incubates it. Such is the verdict of Jewish narrative and law.

ג וְקַיִן הָיָה עֹבֵד אֲדָמָה׃ וַיְהִי מִקֵּץ יָמִים וַיָּבֵא קַיִן מִפְּרִי
ד הָאֲדָמָה מִנְחָה לַיהוה׃ וְהֶבֶל הֵבִיא גַם־הוּא מִבְּכֹרוֹת צֹאנוֹ
ה וּמֵחֶלְבֵהֶן וַיִּשַׁע יהוה אֶל־הֶבֶל וְאֶל־מִנְחָתוֹ׃ וְאֶל־קַיִן
ו וְאֶל־מִנְחָתוֹ לֹא שָׁעָה וַיִּחַר לְקַיִן מְאֹד וַיִּפְּלוּ פָּנָיו׃ וַיֹּאמֶר
ז יהוה אֶל־קָיִן לָמָּה חָרָה לָךְ וְלָמָּה נָפְלוּ פָנֶיךָ׃ הֲלוֹא אִם־
תֵּיטִיב שְׂאֵת וְאִם לֹא תֵיטִיב לַפֶּתַח חַטָּאת רֹבֵץ וְאֵלֶיךָ
ח תְּשׁוּקָתוֹ וְאַתָּה תִּמְשָׁל־בּוֹ׃ וַיֹּאמֶר קַיִן אֶל־הֶבֶל אָחִיו וַיְהִי

fleeting, ephemeral breath. Ecclesiastes is a sustained meditation on mortality. All the wealth and glory even the greatest accumulate means nothing, because all that separates us from non-existence is a mere breath. Kayin, in contrast, means not only "to make" but also "to acquire," "to possess," "to own." The Hebrew word *baal*, the name of the chief Canaanite god, has the same range of meanings: "to own," "to possess," "to exercise power over someone or something." That for the Bible is the ultimate idolatry. The earth belongs to God. God does not sanctify the will to power. This, as the Bible understands it, is the fundamental conflict within the human condition: the struggle between the *will to power* and the *will to life*.

Hevel represents mortal human life – a mortality that comes less from sin than from the fact that we are embodied souls in a physical world subject to deterioration and decay. All that separates us from the grave is the breath God breathed into us (Gen. 2:7). We are *hevel*, mere breath. But it is God's breath. Life is holy.

4:5 וַיִּחַר לְקַיִן מְאֹד *Kayin became very angry* – The reason God rejects Kayin's offering becomes clear in Kayin's reaction. Imagine the following: You offer someone a gift. Politely, they refuse it. How do you respond? There are two possibilities. You can ask yourself, "What did I do wrong?" or you can be angry with the intended recipient. If you respond in the first way, you were genuinely trying to please the other person. If the second, it becomes retrospectively clear that your concern was not with the other but with yourself. You were trying to assert your own dominance by putting the other in your debt. That is what sacrifices were in the pagan world: attempts to appease, placate, or bribe the gods, thereby coercing or manipulating them into doing one's will – whether sending rain, victory in battle, or restoring past imperial glories. This is the exact opposite of what the Torah views as true faith: humility in the face of God, respect for the integrity of creation, and reverence for human life – the only thing that bears the image of God.

were in the field, Kayin rose up against his brother Hevel
9 and killed him. The Lord asked Kayin, "Where is your
brother, Hevel?" "I do not know," he said. "Am I my
10 brother's keeper?" He said, "What is it you have done?
The voice of your brother's blood cries out to Me from the
11 land! Now you are cursed, more so than the land that has
opened its mouth to receive your brother's blood from
12 your hand. When you work the land, it will no longer
grant you its powers. You will be a fugitive wanderer over
13 the land." Kayin said to the Lord, "My sin is more than
14 I can bear. You have banished me today from the face of
the land, and from Your face too I will be hidden. I will
be a fugitive wanderer over the land, and whoever finds
15 me will kill me." The Lord said to him, "Whoever then
kills Kayin will suffer vengeance seven times over." Then
the Lord put a mark on Kayin so that none who found
16 him would kill him. So Kayin departed from the Lord's
presence and lived in the land of Nod, east of Eden.
17 Kayin knew his wife, and she conceived and gave birth to
Ḥanokh. He built a city, naming it Ḥanokh after his son.
18 Ḥanokh had a son Irad, and Irad had a son Meḥuyael.
Meḥiyael had a son Metushael, and Metushael had a son
19 Lemekh. Lemekh married two women, one named Ada ḤAMISHI

God of love, and practiced cruelty in the name of the God of compassion. When this happens, God speaks, sometimes in a still, small voice almost inaudible beneath the clamor of those claiming to speak on His behalf. What He says at such times is: *Not in My Name.*

4:19 לֶמֶךְ *Lemekh* – Among Lemekh's family's prodigious achievements, only his song, which tells us of the violence becoming endemic in human society, earns more than a few words. The Hebrew Bible is uninterested in *Homo sapiens* the biological species. It is even relatively uninterested in *Homo faber*, the tool-making, environment-changing life-form. And so it passes over, in short order, Yaval, "the ancestor of those who live in tents and raise livestock," Yuval, "the ancestor of all those who play the lyre and the pipe," and Tuval-Kayin, who "forged all kinds of bronze and iron tools." It is interested exclusively in *Homo religious,* the first humans to hear and respond to the divine voice.

ט בִּהְיוֹתָ֣ם בַּשָּׂדֶ֔ה וַיָּ֥קָם קַ֛יִן אֶל־הֶ֥בֶל אָחִ֖יו וַיַּהַרְגֵֽהוּ׃ וַיֹּ֤אמֶר
יהוה֙ אֶל־קַ֔יִן אֵ֖י הֶ֣בֶל אָחִ֑יךָ וַיֹּ֙אמֶר֙ לֹ֣א יָדַ֔עְתִּי הֲשֹׁמֵ֥ר אָחִ֖י
י אָנֹֽכִי׃ וַיֹּ֖אמֶר מֶ֣ה עָשִׂ֑יתָ ק֚וֹל דְּמֵ֣י אָחִ֔יךָ צֹעֲקִ֥ים אֵלַ֖י מִן־
יא הָאֲדָמָֽה׃ וְעַתָּ֖ה אָר֣וּר אָ֑תָּה מִן־הָֽאֲדָמָה֙ אֲשֶׁ֣ר פָּצְתָ֣ה אֶת־
יב פִּ֔יהָ לָקַ֛חַת אֶת־דְּמֵ֥י אָחִ֖יךָ מִיָּדֶֽךָ׃ כִּ֤י תַֽעֲבֹד֙ אֶת־הָ֣אֲדָמָ֔ה
יג לֹֽא־תֹסֵ֥ף תֵּת־כֹּחָ֖הּ לָ֑ךְ נָ֥ע וָנָ֖ד תִּֽהְיֶ֥ה בָאָֽרֶץ׃ וַיֹּ֥אמֶר קַ֖יִן
יד אֶל־יהוה גָּד֥וֹל עֲוֺנִ֖י מִנְּשֹֽׂא׃ הֵן֩ גֵּרַ֨שְׁתָּ אֹתִ֜י הַיּ֗וֹם מֵעַל֙ פְּנֵ֣י
הָאֲדָמָ֔ה וּמִפָּנֶ֖יךָ אֶסָּתֵ֑ר וְהָיִ֜יתִי נָ֤ע וָנָד֙ בָּאָ֔רֶץ וְהָיָ֥ה כָל־מֹצְאִ֖י
טו יַהַרְגֵֽנִי׃ וַיֹּ֧אמֶר ל֣וֹ יהוה לָכֵן֙ כָּל־הֹרֵ֣ג קַ֔יִן שִׁבְעָתַ֖יִם יֻקָּ֑ם
וַיָּ֨שֶׂם יהוה לְקַ֙יִן֙ א֔וֹת לְבִלְתִּ֥י הַכּוֹת־אֹת֖וֹ כָּל־מֹצְאֽוֹ׃
טז וַיֵּ֥צֵא קַ֖יִן מִלִּפְנֵ֣י יהוה וַיֵּ֥שֶׁב בְּאֶֽרֶץ־נ֖וֹד קִדְמַת־עֵֽדֶן׃
יז וַיֵּ֤דַע קַ֙יִן֙ אֶת־אִשְׁתּ֔וֹ וַתַּ֖הַר וַתֵּ֣לֶד אֶת־חֲנ֑וֹךְ וַֽיְהִי֙ בֹּ֣נֶה עִ֔יר
יח וַיִּקְרָא֙ שֵׁ֣ם הָעִ֔יר כְּשֵׁ֖ם בְּנ֥וֹ חֲנֽוֹךְ׃ וַיִּוָּלֵ֤ד לַֽחֲנוֹךְ֙ אֶת־עִירָ֔ד
וְעִירָ֕ד יָלַ֖ד אֶת־מְחוּיָאֵ֑ל וּמְחִיָּיאֵ֗ל יָלַד֙ אֶת־מְת֣וּשָׁאֵ֔ל
יט וּמְתוּשָׁאֵ֖ל יָלַ֥ד אֶת־לָֽמֶךְ׃ וַיִּֽקַּֽח־ל֥וֹ לֶ֖מֶךְ שְׁתֵּ֣י נָשִׁ֑ים שֵׁ֣ם חמישי

THE FIRST MURDER

That the Bible is preoccupied by violence is evident at the outset; it is a central theme in Genesis.

"If you act well, will you not be uplifted? If you fail to act well, sin is crouching at the door." This is God's warning to Kayin as soon as he feels the stirrings of anger. We have a disposition to do wrong, for we are driven by our desires. Other people also have desires. Sometimes both cannot be satisfied. The other stands in my way. So I am faced with a choice. Do I regard the other as an obstacle to be overridden or removed? Or do I recognize his or her integrity as another person with the same desires and rights as mine? Kayin chooses the first, and kills Hevel. Challenged by God, he replies, "Am I my brother's keeper?" meaning: "Am I responsible for his fate?" The road from denial of responsibility to violence and murder is slippery and short.

This, however, is not all. The first murder follows directly from the offerings brought by Kayin and Hevel, the first recorded act of worship. The connection between religion and violence is struck at the start.

Too often in the history of religion, people have killed in the name of the God of life, waged war in the name of the God of peace, hated in the name of the

20 and the other Tzila. Ada gave birth to Yaval. He was the
ancestor of those who live in tents and raise livestock.
21 His brother's name was Yuval. He was the ancestor of
22 all those who play the lyre and the pipe. Tzila, too, had
a son, Tuval-Kayin, who forged all kinds of bronze and
23 iron tools. Tuval-Kayin's sister was Naama. Lemekh
said to his wives: "Ada and Tzila, listen to my voice;
wives of Lemekh, heed my words. I killed a man for
24 wounding me, killed a boy for bruising me. If Kayin will
be avenged seven times, then Lemekh, seventy-seven."
25 Adam knew his wife again, and she gave birth to a son
and named him Shet, "because God has granted me
another child in place of Hevel," for Kayin had killed
26 him. And Shet too had a son, and named him Enosh.
That was when people began to pray in the name of the
5 1 LORD. This is the book of Adam's descendants: SHISHI
On the day God created humankind, He made them in the
2 likeness of God. Male and female He created them, and
on the day they were created, He blessed them and called
3 them Humankind. Adam lived one hundred and thirty
years and then had a son in his own likeness and image,
4 and named him Shet. After Shet was born, Adam lived
eight hundred years and had other sons and daughters.
5 Altogether Adam lived nine hundred and thirty years, and

Radical unconditioned freedom enters Western civilization in the first chapter of Genesis when the free God freely creates the universe, saying, "Let there be." Making humankind in His image, after His likeness, meant that He endowed us too with freedom. All life was created. Humans alone are creative. Every life-form has drives, inherent instincts of survival. Humans alone are capable of what philosophers call second-order evaluations, deciding which drives to pursue and which not. Other animals act. We alone bear responsibility for our acts because we could have chosen to act otherwise. Freedom is God's greatest gift to humankind but it is also the most fateful and terrifying. For it means that we alone have the power to destroy the work of God. This is the central drama of Tanakh and of Judaism as a whole. Will we use our freedom to respect order or misuse it to create chaos? Will we honor or dishonor the image of God that lives within the human heart and mind?

כ הָאַחַת עָדָה וְשֵׁם הַשֵּׁנִית צִלָּה: וַתֵּלֶד עָדָה אֶת־יָבָל הוּא
כא הָיָה אֲבִי יֹשֵׁב אֹהֶל וּמִקְנֶה: וְשֵׁם אָחִיו יוּבָל הוּא הָיָה
כב אֲבִי כָּל־תֹּפֵשׂ כִּנּוֹר וְעוּגָב: וְצִלָּה גַם־הִוא יָלְדָה אֶת־
תּוּבַל קַיִן לֹטֵשׁ כָּל־חֹרֵשׁ נְחֹשֶׁת וּבַרְזֶל וַאֲחוֹת תּוּבַל־
כג קַיִן נַעֲמָה: וַיֹּאמֶר לֶמֶךְ לְנָשָׁיו עָדָה וְצִלָּה שְׁמַעַן קוֹלִי
נְשֵׁי לֶמֶךְ הַאְזֵנָּה אִמְרָתִי כִּי אִישׁ הָרַגְתִּי לְפִצְעִי וְיֶלֶד
כד לְחַבֻּרָתִי: כִּי שִׁבְעָתַיִם יֻקַּם־קָיִן וְלֶמֶךְ שִׁבְעִים וְשִׁבְעָה:
כה וַיֵּדַע אָדָם עוֹד אֶת־אִשְׁתּוֹ וַתֵּלֶד בֵּן וַתִּקְרָא אֶת־שְׁמוֹ שֵׁת
כו כִּי שָׁת־לִי אֱלֹהִים זֶרַע אַחֵר תַּחַת הֶבֶל כִּי הֲרָגוֹ קָיִן: וּלְשֵׁת
גַּם־הוּא יֻלַּד־בֵּן וַיִּקְרָא אֶת־שְׁמוֹ אֱנוֹשׁ אָז הוּחַל לִקְרֹא
ה א בְּשֵׁם יהוה: זֶה סֵפֶר תּוֹלְדֹת אָדָם בְּיוֹם בְּרֹא ד ששי
ב אֱלֹהִים אָדָם בִּדְמוּת אֱלֹהִים עָשָׂה אֹתוֹ: זָכָר וּנְקֵבָה בְּרָאָם
ג וַיְבָרֶךְ אֹתָם וַיִּקְרָא אֶת־שְׁמָם אָדָם בְּיוֹם הִבָּרְאָם: וַיְחִי אָדָם
שְׁלֹשִׁים וּמְאַת שָׁנָה וַיּוֹלֶד בִּדְמוּתוֹ כְּצַלְמוֹ וַיִּקְרָא אֶת־שְׁמוֹ
ד שֵׁת: וַיִּהְיוּ יְמֵי־אָדָם אַחֲרֵי הוֹלִידוֹ אֶת־שֵׁת שְׁמֹנֶה מֵאֹת
ה שָׁנָה וַיּוֹלֶד בָּנִים וּבָנוֹת: וַיִּהְיוּ כָּל־יְמֵי אָדָם אֲשֶׁר־חַי תְּשַׁע

4:24 וְלֶמֶךְ שִׁבְעִים וְשִׁבְעָה *Lemekh, seventy-seven* – Early societies, René Girard has argued, did not yet have a legal system – laws, courts, prisons, and punishments – to enforce order. Instead they practiced reciprocity, the rule of tit for tat. They acted generously to others until they encountered a hostile response. They then did to the others what the others had done to them.

The trouble with this strategy is that it gives rise to potentially endless cycles of retaliation. It begins with a single act of murder. This sets in motion a blood feud, vendetta, or clan war. Short of mass assassination, there is no natural end to this cycle of retaliation.

5:3 בִּדְמוּתוֹ כְּצַלְמוֹ *In his own likeness and image* – As Adam's life reaches its end we are reminded of its beginning, and of the essence he passes on to his countless descendants, "the image of God."

The phrase raises a question. In Judaism *God has no image or likeness.* He has no image because He is not physical. He transcends the physical universe. Therefore He is free, unconstrained by the laws of matter. By making us in His image, He gave us also the power to be free.

6 then he died. Shet lived one hundred and five
7 years and then had a son, Enosh. After Enosh was born,
Shet lived eight hundred and seven years and had other
8 sons and daughters. Altogether, Shet lived nine hundred
9 and twelve years, and then he died. Enosh
10 lived ninety years and then had a son, Keinan. After
Keinan was born, Enosh lived eight hundred and fifteen
11 years and had other sons and daughters. Altogether,
Enosh lived nine hundred and five years, and then he
12 died. Keinan lived seventy years and had a son,
13 Mahalalel. After Mahalalel was born, Keinan lived eight
hundred and forty years and had other sons and daughters.
14 Altogether, Keinan lived nine hundred and ten years, and
15 then he died. Mahalalel lived sixty-five years and
16 had a son, Yered. After Yered was born, Mahalalel lived
eight hundred and thirty years and had other sons and
17 daughters. Altogether, Mahalalel lived eight hundred and
18 ninety-five years, and then he died. Yered lived
one hundred and sixty-two years and had a son, Ḥanokh.
19 After Ḥanokh was born, Yered lived eight hundred years
20 and had other sons and daughters. Altogether, Yered
lived nine hundred and sixty-two years, and then he
21 died. Ḥanokh lived sixty-five years and had
22 a son, Metushelaḥ. Ḥanokh walked faithfully with God
for three hundred years after Metushelaḥ was born, and
23 had other sons and daughters. Altogether, Ḥanokh lived
24 for three hundred and sixty-five years. Ḥanokh walked
faithfully with God and then he was no more, for God
25 took him. Metushelaḥ lived one hundred and SHEVI'I
26 eighty-seven years and had a son, Lemekh. After Lemekh
was born, Metushelaḥ lived seven hundred and eighty-
27 two years and had other sons and daughters. Altogether,
Metushelaḥ lived nine hundred and sixty-nine years, and
28 then he died. Lemekh lived one hundred and

ו מֵאוֹת שָׁנָה וּשְׁלֹשִׁים שָׁנָה וַיָּמֹת׃ וַיְחִי־שֵׁת
ז חָמֵשׁ שָׁנִים וּמְאַת שָׁנָה וַיּוֹלֶד אֶת־אֱנוֹשׁ׃ וַיְחִי־שֵׁת אַחֲרֵי
הוֹלִידוֹ אֶת־אֱנוֹשׁ שֶׁבַע שָׁנִים וּשְׁמֹנֶה מֵאוֹת שָׁנָה וַיּוֹלֶד בָּנִים
ח וּבָנוֹת׃ וַיִּהְיוּ כָּל־יְמֵי־שֵׁת שְׁתֵּים עֶשְׂרֵה שָׁנָה וּתְשַׁע מֵאוֹת
ט שָׁנָה וַיָּמֹת׃ וַיְחִי אֱנוֹשׁ תִּשְׁעִים שָׁנָה וַיּוֹלֶד אֶת־
י קֵינָן׃ וַיְחִי אֱנוֹשׁ אַחֲרֵי הוֹלִידוֹ אֶת־קֵינָן חֲמֵשׁ עֶשְׂרֵה שָׁנָה
יא וּשְׁמֹנֶה מֵאוֹת שָׁנָה וַיּוֹלֶד בָּנִים וּבָנוֹת׃ וַיִּהְיוּ כָּל־יְמֵי אֱנוֹשׁ
יב חָמֵשׁ שָׁנִים וּתְשַׁע מֵאוֹת שָׁנָה וַיָּמֹת׃ וַיְחִי קֵינָן
יג שִׁבְעִים שָׁנָה וַיּוֹלֶד אֶת־מַהֲלַלְאֵל׃ וַיְחִי קֵינָן אַחֲרֵי הוֹלִידוֹ
אֶת־מַהֲלַלְאֵל אַרְבָּעִים שָׁנָה וּשְׁמֹנֶה מֵאוֹת שָׁנָה וַיּוֹלֶד
יד בָּנִים וּבָנוֹת׃ וַיִּהְיוּ כָּל־יְמֵי קֵינָן עֶשֶׂר שָׁנִים וּתְשַׁע מֵאוֹת
טו שָׁנָה וַיָּמֹת׃ וַיְחִי מַהֲלַלְאֵל חָמֵשׁ שָׁנִים וְשִׁשִּׁים
טז שָׁנָה וַיּוֹלֶד אֶת־יָרֶד׃ וַיְחִי מַהֲלַלְאֵל אַחֲרֵי הוֹלִידוֹ אֶת־יֶרֶד
יז שְׁלֹשִׁים שָׁנָה וּשְׁמֹנֶה מֵאוֹת שָׁנָה וַיּוֹלֶד בָּנִים וּבָנוֹת׃ וַיִּהְיוּ
כָּל־יְמֵי מַהֲלַלְאֵל חָמֵשׁ וְתִשְׁעִים שָׁנָה וּשְׁמֹנֶה מֵאוֹת שָׁנָה
יח וַיָּמֹת׃ וַיְחִי־יֶרֶד שְׁתַּיִם וְשִׁשִּׁים שָׁנָה וּמְאַת שָׁנָה
יט וַיּוֹלֶד אֶת־חֲנוֹךְ׃ וַיְחִי־יֶרֶד אַחֲרֵי הוֹלִידוֹ אֶת־חֲנוֹךְ שְׁמֹנֶה
כ מֵאוֹת שָׁנָה וַיּוֹלֶד בָּנִים וּבָנוֹת׃ וַיִּהְיוּ כָּל־יְמֵי־יֶרֶד שְׁתַּיִם
כא וְשִׁשִּׁים שָׁנָה וּתְשַׁע מֵאוֹת שָׁנָה וַיָּמֹת׃ וַיְחִי חֲנוֹךְ
כב חָמֵשׁ וְשִׁשִּׁים שָׁנָה וַיּוֹלֶד אֶת־מְתוּשָׁלַח׃ וַיִּתְהַלֵּךְ חֲנוֹךְ אֶת־
הָאֱלֹהִים אַחֲרֵי הוֹלִידוֹ אֶת־מְתוּשֶׁלַח שְׁלֹשׁ מֵאוֹת שָׁנָה
כג וַיּוֹלֶד בָּנִים וּבָנוֹת׃ וַיְהִי כָּל־יְמֵי חֲנוֹךְ חָמֵשׁ וְשִׁשִּׁים שָׁנָה
כד וּשְׁלֹשׁ מֵאוֹת שָׁנָה׃ וַיִּתְהַלֵּךְ חֲנוֹךְ אֶת־הָאֱלֹהִים וְאֵינֶנּוּ כִּי־
כה לָקַח אֹתוֹ אֱלֹהִים׃ וַיְחִי מְתוּשֶׁלַח שֶׁבַע וּשְׁמֹנִים שביעי
כו שָׁנָה וּמְאַת שָׁנָה וַיּוֹלֶד אֶת־לָמֶךְ׃ וַיְחִי מְתוּשֶׁלַח אַחֲרֵי
הוֹלִידוֹ אֶת־לֶמֶךְ שְׁתַּיִם וּשְׁמוֹנִים שָׁנָה וּשְׁבַע מֵאוֹת שָׁנָה
כז וַיּוֹלֶד בָּנִים וּבָנוֹת׃ וַיִּהְיוּ כָּל־יְמֵי מְתוּשֶׁלַח תֵּשַׁע וְשִׁשִּׁים
כח שָׁנָה וּתְשַׁע מֵאוֹת שָׁנָה וַיָּמֹת׃ וַיְחִי־

29 eighty-two years and had a son. He named him Noaḥ,
saying, "This one will bring us comfort after all our labor
and the sorrow of our hands on the land the LORD has
30 cursed." After Noaḥ was born, Lemekh lived five hundred
and ninety-five years and had other sons and daughters.
31 Altogether, Lemekh lived seven hundred and seventy-
32 seven years, and then he died. After Noaḥ was
five hundred years old, Noaḥ had three sons: Shem,
6 1 Ḥam, and Yefet. Humans began to multiply on earth,
2 and daughters were born to them. When the sons of God
saw that the daughters of man were lovely, they began to
3 take whomever they chose to be wives to them. Then the
LORD said, "My spirit will not forever judge man; he is of
flesh. His life shall be but one hundred and twenty years."
4 In those days the Nefilim were on earth, and later also, for
the sons of God had gone to the daughters of man and
had children with them. These were the heroes of old,
men of legends.
5 The LORD saw how great man's wickedness was upon the
earth, and that his thoughts constantly inclined toward MAFTIR
6 evil. Then the LORD regretted that He had made man on

bring relief from man's work, but it is the release found in death. Not only does Noaḥ fail to lift God's curse upon the land, he lives through the worst curse of all. Noaḥ's greatness is also his weakness. Avraham is to begin his service of God by moving, leaving home, and traveling to a distant land. Noaḥ's gift is that, living through a time of widespread evil, he is not affected by it. He is unmoved. But he is also unable to grow. Noaḥ ("rest") stands still.

6:6 וַיִּנָּחֶם יהוה *The LORD regretted* – Having made human beings in His image, God sees the first man and woman disobey the first command, and the first human child commit the first murder. Within a short space of time "the earth had become... full of violence." God "saw how great man's wickedness was upon the earth." We then read one of the most searing sentences in religious literature. "The LORD regretted that He had made man on earth, and His heart was touched with sorrow" (Gen. 6:6). The *parasha* that started with the beginnings of creation ends with God's regret. It is now that the real story of the Torah – the faltering move toward the society we still seek to build – begins.

כט לֶמֶךְ שְׁתַּיִם וּשְׁמֹנִים שָׁנָה וּמְאַת שָׁנָה וַיּוֹלֶד בֵּן: וַיִּקְרָא
אֶת־שְׁמוֹ נֹחַ לֵאמֹר זֶה יְנַחֲמֵנוּ מִמַּעֲשֵׂנוּ וּמֵעִצְּבוֹן יָדֵינוּ
ל מִן־הָאֲדָמָה אֲשֶׁר אֵרְרָהּ יהוה: וַיְחִי־לֶמֶךְ אַחֲרֵי הוֹלִידוֹ
אֶת־נֹחַ חָמֵשׁ וְתִשְׁעִים שָׁנָה וַחֲמֵשׁ מֵאֹת שָׁנָה וַיּוֹלֶד בָּנִים
לא וּבָנוֹת: וַיְהִי כָּל־יְמֵי־לֶמֶךְ שֶׁבַע וְשִׁבְעִים שָׁנָה וּשְׁבַע מֵאוֹת
לב שָׁנָה וַיָּמֹת: וַיְהִי־נֹחַ בֶּן־חֲמֵשׁ מֵאוֹת שָׁנָה וַיּוֹלֶד
ו א נֹחַ אֶת־שֵׁם אֶת־חָם וְאֶת־יָפֶת: וַיְהִי כִּי־הֵחֵל הָאָדָם לָרֹב
ב עַל־פְּנֵי הָאֲדָמָה וּבָנוֹת יֻלְּדוּ לָהֶם: וַיִּרְאוּ בְנֵי־הָאֱלֹהִים
אֶת־בְּנוֹת הָאָדָם כִּי טֹבֹת הֵנָּה וַיִּקְחוּ לָהֶם נָשִׁים מִכֹּל אֲשֶׁר
ג בָּחָרוּ: וַיֹּאמֶר יהוה לֹא־יָדוֹן רוּחִי בָאָדָם לְעֹלָם בְּשַׁגָּם
ד הוּא בָשָׂר וְהָיוּ יָמָיו מֵאָה וְעֶשְׂרִים שָׁנָה: הַנְּפִלִים הָיוּ
בָאָרֶץ בַּיָּמִים הָהֵם וְגַם אַחֲרֵי־כֵן אֲשֶׁר יָבֹאוּ בְּנֵי הָאֱלֹהִים
אֶל־בְּנוֹת הָאָדָם וְיָלְדוּ לָהֶם הֵמָּה הַגִּבֹּרִים אֲשֶׁר מֵעוֹלָם
אַנְשֵׁי הַשֵּׁם:
ה וַיַּרְא יהוה כִּי רַבָּה רָעַת הָאָדָם בָּאָרֶץ וְכָל־יֵצֶר מַחְשְׁבֹת מפטיר
ו לִבּוֹ רַק רַע כָּל־הַיּוֹם: וַיִּנָּחֶם יהוה כִּי־עָשָׂה אֶת־הָאָדָם

5:29 זֶה יְנַחֲמֵנוּ *This one will bring us comfort* – There is something not quite right here. The root *n-ḥ-m* (for "comfort") does not yield the name Noaḥ but Menaḥem. The name Noaḥ comes from the word that means "to rest." Complex resonances are being set up. Noaḥ is the man who rests when he should act, for when disaster threatens the world he saves himself and his family, no one else. The text also contains a wordplay lost in translation. Noaḥ's Hebrew name, the two letters *nun-ḥet*, is an exact reversal of the word *ḥet-nun*, "grace," "favor," a key word in the story: "Noaḥ found *favor* in the LORD's sight" (Gen. 6:8). Noaḥ's grace is ambivalent, his life a reversal. Most significantly, the word used by Lemekh at Noaḥ's birth, *nun-ḥet-mem*, reappears later in the story with the opposite meaning to that which Lemekh intended: "The LORD saw how great man's wickedness was upon the earth, and that his thoughts constantly inclined toward evil. Then the LORD regretted [*vayinaḥem*] that He had made man on earth, and His heart was touched with sorrow" (6:5–6). *Nun-ḥet-mem* turns out to be a contronym. It means "relief" but also "regret," comfort but also discomfort. Noaḥ does

7 earth, and His heart was touched with sorrow. The LORD
said, "I will erase My creation, humankind, from the face
of the land – man, even animals and creeping things, even
8 birds of the heavens – for I regret having made them." But
Noaḥ found favor in the LORD's sight.

The haftara for Parashat Bereshit is on page 1408.
On Erev Rosh Ḥodesh Marḥeshvan read the haftara on page 1644.

ז בָּאָ֑רֶץ וַיִּתְעַצֵּ֖ב אֶל־לִבּֽוֹ׃ וַיֹּ֣אמֶר יהו֗ה אֶמְחֶ֨ה אֶת־הָאָדָ֤ם
אֲשֶׁר־בָּרָ֙אתִי֙ מֵעַל֙ פְּנֵ֣י הָֽאֲדָמָ֔ה מֵֽאָדָם֙ עַד־בְּהֵמָ֔ה עַד־
ח רֶ֖מֶשׂ וְעַד־ע֣וֹף הַשָּׁמָ֑יִם כִּ֥י נִחַ֖מְתִּי כִּ֥י עֲשִׂיתִֽם׃ וְנֹ֕חַ מָ֥צָא
חֵ֖ן בְּעֵינֵ֥י יהוֽה׃

The הפטרה *for* פרשת בראשית *is on page 1409.*
On ערב ראש חודש מרחשוון *read the haftara on page 1645.*

Parashat Noaḥ

6 9 This is the story of Noaḥ. Noaḥ was a righteous man, a
person of integrity in his generation; Noaḥ walked with
10 God. And Noaḥ had three sons: Shem, Ḥam, and Yefet.

Tigris-Euphrates valley (see the commentary of Rabbi David Tzvi Hoffman on Genesis 6 [Hebrew, 140]; he suggests that the flood may have been limited to centers of human habitation, rather than covering the whole earth). Excavations at Shurrupak, Kish, Uruk, and Ur – Avraham's birthplace – reveal evidence of clay flood deposits. Likewise, the Tower of Bavel reflects a historical reality, as we shall see.

However, the stories of the flood and Bavel are not merely historical, because the Torah is not history but means "teaching," "instruction." They are there because they represent a profound moral-social-political-spiritual truth about the human situation as the Torah sees it. The flood tells us what happens to civilization when individuals rule and there is no collective. Bavel tells us what happens when the collective rules and individuals are sacrificed to it.

After the two great failures of the flood and Bavel, Avraham will be called on to create a new form of social order that will give equal honor to the individual and the collective, personal responsibility and the common good. That remains the special gift of Jews and Judaism to the world.

6:9 צַדִּיק...בְּדֹרֹתָיו *Righteous... in his generation* – Noaḥ's gift is that, living through a time of widespread evil, he is not affected by it. He is unmoved. But he is also unable to grow. The Sages heard in the phrase "righteous... in his generation" a subtle criticism. Relative to his generation, he was righteous, but in absolute terms he was not.

What is Noaḥ's failure, according to the classic commentators? Told that there will be a flood and that he should build an ark, he busies himself in the labor. The text goes out of its way to emphasize his obedience, stating no less than three times that Noaḥ did "all that God commanded him." Throughout the whole of the narrative – the warning of the deluge, the building of the ark, the gathering of the animals, the beginning of the rain – Noaḥ says nothing. The silence, in contrast with the dialogues Avraham and Kayin have with God, is unmistakable. Noaḥ does not rebuke his contemporaries, nor does he pray for them, questioning the justice of the flood, as Avraham is to do for the people of the cities of the plain. Noaḥ, the righteous man, fails to exercise collective responsibility.

6:9 אֶת־הָאֱלֹהִים הִתְהַלֶּךְ־נֹחַ *Noaḥ walked with God* – The difference between Noaḥ and Avraham is eloquently summarized by the midrashic comment of Rabbi Yehuda (*Tanḥuma*, Lekh Lekha 26):

פרשת נח

ו ט אֵלֶּה תּוֹלְדֹת נֹחַ נֹחַ אִישׁ צַדִּיק תָּמִים הָיָה בְּדֹרֹתָיו אֶת־ ה
י הָאֱלֹהִים הִתְהַלֶּךְ־נֹחַ׃ וַיּוֹלֶד נֹחַ שְׁלֹשָׁה בָנִים אֶת־שֵׁם

NOAḤ

Parashat Noaḥ brings to a close the eleven chapters that precede the call to Avraham and the beginning of the special relationship between him and his descendants, and God. During these chapters, the Torah gives prominence to four stories: Adam and Ḥava, Kayin and Hevel, Noaḥ and the generation of the flood, and the Tower of Bavel. Each represents another step in the maturation of humanity.

The first thing we learn as children is that our acts are under our control (*personal* responsibility). This is what Adam and Ḥava tried to deny when, faced with primal failure, the man blamed the woman and the woman blamed the serpent. The next lesson is that not everything we *can* do, we *may* do (*moral* responsibility). We cannot say, like Kayin, "Am I my brother's keeper?" and justify the harm we cause. The next stage, which we arrive at here in our *parasha*, is the realization that we have a duty not just to ourselves but to those on whom we have an influence (*collective* responsibility). This is the test that Noaḥ fails. The story of Bavel, as we shall see, demonstrates the failure of *ontological* responsibility – the idea that something beyond us makes a call on us. There is an author of being; therefore there is an authority beyond mankind to whom, when acting morally, we respond. This will close the first cycle of the story of mankind, preparing us for God's call to Avraham, "Go" (Gen. 12:1).

THE FLOOD AND THE TOWER

The *parasha* begins and ends with two great events, the flood on the one hand, Bavel and its tower on the other. On the face of it they have nothing in common. The failings of the generation of the flood are explicit. "The earth had become corrupt in God's sight, full of violence" (Gen. 6:11). Wickedness, violence, corruption: this is the language of systemic moral failure.

Bavel, by contrast, seems almost idyllic. "The whole world spoke the same language, the same words" (11:1). The builders are bent on construction, not destruction. It is far from clear what their sin is. Yet from the Torah's point of view Bavel represents another serious wrong turn, because immediately thereafter God summons Avraham to begin an entirely new chapter in the religious story of humankind.

Both the flood and the Tower of Bavel are rooted in actual historical events, even if the narrative is not couched in the language of descriptive history. Mesopotamia had many flood myths, all of which testify to the memory of disastrous inundations, especially on the flat lands of the

11 The earth had become corrupt in God's sight, full of
12 violence. And when God saw how corrupt the earth had
become, all flesh corrupting its ways upon the
13 earth, God said to Noaḥ, "The end of all flesh
has come before Me, for the earth is full of violence
because of them. I am about to destroy them, along with
14 all the earth. So make yourself an ark of cypress wood.
Make it with compartments and coat it in pitch inside
15 and out. This is how you shall make it: the ark shall be
three hundred cubits long, fifty cubits wide, and thirty
16 cubits high. Make a window for the ark, and taper the
latter to within a cubit of the top. Put a door in the side of

---

the ark itself. But what exactly is it? Rashi quotes a midrash in which two Rabbis disagree as to its meaning: "Some say this was a window; others say that it was a precious stone that gave light to them" (Bereshit Rabba 31:11). The precious stone had the miraculous quality of being able to generate light within the darkness.

It remains fascinating to ask why the Rabbis of the Midrash would spend time on a question that has no practical relevance. There will be – God promised this in this *parasha* – no further flood. There will be no new Noaḥ. In any future threat to the existence of the planet, an ark floating on the water will not be sufficient to save humankind. So why should it matter what source of illumination Noaḥ had in the ark during those tempestuous days? What is the lesson for the generations?

I would like to offer a midrashic speculation. The answer, I suggest, lies in the history of the Hebrew language. Throughout the biblical era, the word *teva* meant an ark. More generally, it meant "box." However, by the time of the Midrash, *teva* had come also to mean "word."

It seems to me that the Rabbis of the Midrash were not so much commenting on Noaḥ and the ark as they were reflecting on a fundamental question of Torah. Where and what is the *tzohar*, the brightness, the source of illumination? Does it come solely from within, or also from without? Does the Torah come with a window or a precious stone?

There are certainly those who believed that Torah is self-sufficient, illuminated by a precious stone that generates its own light. There are, however, other views. Most famously, Rambam believed that a knowledge of science and philosophy – a window to the outside world – was essential to understanding God's word. He made the radical suggestion, in the *Mishneh Torah* (*Hilkhot Yesodei HaTorah* 2:2), that it was precisely these forms of study that were the way to the love and fear of God.

יא אֶת־חָם וְאֶת־יָפֶת׃ וַתִּשָּׁחֵת הָאָרֶץ לִפְנֵי הָאֱלֹהִים וַתִּמָּלֵא
יב הָאָרֶץ חָמָס׃ וַיַּרְא אֱלֹהִים אֶת־הָאָרֶץ וְהִנֵּה נִשְׁחָתָה כִּי־
יג הִשְׁחִית כָּל־בָּשָׂר אֶת־דַּרְכּוֹ עַל־הָאָרֶץ׃ וַיֹּאמֶר
אֱלֹהִים לְנֹחַ קֵץ כָּל־בָּשָׂר בָּא לְפָנַי כִּי־מָלְאָה הָאָרֶץ חָמָס
יד מִפְּנֵיהֶם וְהִנְנִי מַשְׁחִיתָם אֶת־הָאָרֶץ׃ עֲשֵׂה לְךָ תֵּבַת עֲצֵי־
גֹפֶר קִנִּים תַּעֲשֶׂה אֶת־הַתֵּבָה וְכָפַרְתָּ אֹתָהּ מִבַּיִת וּמִחוּץ
טו בַּכֹּפֶר׃ וְזֶה אֲשֶׁר תַּעֲשֶׂה אֹתָהּ שְׁלֹשׁ מֵאוֹת אַמָּה אֹרֶךְ
טז הַתֵּבָה חֲמִשִּׁים אַמָּה רָחְבָּהּ וּשְׁלֹשִׁים אַמָּה קוֹמָתָהּ׃ צֹהַר ׀
תַּעֲשֶׂה לַתֵּבָה וְאֶל־אַמָּה תְּכַלֶּנָּה מִלְמַעְלָה וּפֶתַח הַתֵּבָה

"Noaḥ walked with God" – The meaning of this phrase can be understood by means of a parable. A king had two sons, one grown up, the other a child. To the child, he said: "Walk with me." But to the adult son, he said: "Walk before me."

So it was that to Avraham, God said: "Walk before Me in integrity" (Gen. 17:1). But of Noaḥ, the Torah says that he "walked with God" (6:9).

Noaḥ is the paradigm of biblical obedience. But faith is more than obedience. It is the courage to take the risk and walk ahead, the courage to create.

6:11 וַתִּשָּׁחֵת הָאָרֶץ... וַתִּמָּלֵא הָאָרֶץ חָמָס *Corrupt…full of violence* – It was Thomas Hobbes (1588–1679) who, without referring to the flood, gave it its best explanation. Before there were political institutions – a stable ruler, an effective government, and enforceable laws – people would be in a state of permanent and violent chaos as they competed for scarce resources – "a war of every man against every man." There would be "continual fear, and danger of violent death; and the life of man, solitary, poor, nasty, brutish, and short." Such situations exist today in a whole series of failed or failing states. That is precisely the Torah's description of life before the flood. When there is no rule of law to constrain individuals, the world is filled with violence.

6:14 עֲשֵׂה לְךָ תֵּבַת עֲצֵי־גֹפֶר *Make yourself an ark of cypress wood* – Noaḥ's ark, his *teva*, contrasts with the *teva*, or "basket," in which Moshe is saved as a child. Moshe, who three times in his early years intervenes when he sees injustice, is the antitype of Noaḥ, the exemplum of obedience to authority.

6:16 צֹהַר תַּעֲשֶׂה לַתֵּבָה *Make a window* – There is a difficulty understanding what *tzohar* means, since the word does not appear anywhere else in Tanakh. Everyone agrees that it is referring to a source of illumination. It will give light within

17 the ark and make lower, middle, and upper decks. And
I – I am about to bring floodwaters over the earth to
destroy all flesh that has within it the breath of life under
18 the heavens. Everything on earth will die. But I will
establish My covenant with you, and you will enter the
ark – you, your sons, your wife, and your sons' wives with
19 you. And you shall take two of each living creature, male
20 and female, into the ark to keep alive with you. Of every
kind of bird, animal, and wild beast, bring two to keep
21 alive. As for you, take all the food to be eaten and store it:
22 it will be for food for you and for them." Noaḥ did so: all
7 1 that God commanded him, he fulfilled. Then the LORD SHENI
said to Noaḥ, "Enter the ark, you and all your household,
for I have seen you alone to be righteous before Me in this
2 generation. Take seven and seven of every pure animal,
seven pairs, and two of every animal that is not pure, of
3 each kind a pair. Also take seven pairs of each kind of bird,
male and female, to keep their kind alive across the earth.
4 For in seven days' time I will send rain on the earth for
forty days and forty nights, and I will wipe from the face
5 of the earth every living creature I have made." Noaḥ did
6 all that the LORD commanded him. Noaḥ was six hundred

(Gen. 6:9) is praise or criticism may well be related to this. Some say that perfect "in his generation" means that he was perfect only relative to the low standard then prevailing. Had he lived in the generation of Avraham, they claim, he would have been insignificant. Others say the opposite: if in a wicked generation Noaḥ was righteous, how much greater he would have been in a generation with role models like Avraham.

The argument, it seems to me, turns on whether Noaḥ's isolation is part of his character – he is a loner – or merely a necessary tactic in that time and place. If he is naturally a loner, he would not gain by the presence of heroes like Avraham. He would be impervious to influence, whether for good or bad. If he is not a loner by nature but merely by circumstance, then in another age he would seek out kindred spirits and become greater still.

7:5 וַיַּעַשׂ נֹחַ כְּכֹל אֲשֶׁר צִוָּהוּ יהוה *Noaḥ did all that the LORD commanded him* – Noaḥ is the only person in Tanakh called a *tzaddik*, "righteous." Yet Noaḥ's righteousness is turned inward. He has no influence on his contemporaries. Is he,

יז בְּצִדָּהּ תָּשִׂים תַּחְתִּיִּם שְׁנִיִּם וּשְׁלִשִׁים תַּעֲשֶׂהָ: וַאֲנִי הִנְנִי
מֵבִיא אֶת־הַמַּבּוּל מַיִם עַל־הָאָרֶץ לְשַׁחֵת כָּל־בָּשָׂר אֲשֶׁר־
יח בּוֹ רוּחַ חַיִּים מִתַּחַת הַשָּׁמָיִם כֹּל אֲשֶׁר־בָּאָרֶץ יִגְוָע: וַהֲקִמֹתִי
אֶת־בְּרִיתִי אִתָּךְ וּבָאתָ אֶל־הַתֵּבָה אַתָּה וּבָנֶיךָ וְאִשְׁתְּךָ
יט וּנְשֵׁי־בָנֶיךָ אִתָּךְ: וּמִכָּל־הָחַי מִכָּל־בָּשָׂר שְׁנַיִם מִכֹּל תָּבִיא
כ אֶל־הַתֵּבָה לְהַחֲיֹת אִתָּךְ זָכָר וּנְקֵבָה יִהְיוּ: מֵהָעוֹף לְמִינֵהוּ
וּמִן־הַבְּהֵמָה לְמִינָהּ מִכֹּל רֶמֶשׂ הָאֲדָמָה לְמִינֵהוּ שְׁנַיִם מִכֹּל
כא יָבֹאוּ אֵלֶיךָ לְהַחֲיוֹת: וְאַתָּה קַח־לְךָ מִכָּל־מַאֲכָל אֲשֶׁר
כב יֵאָכֵל וְאָסַפְתָּ אֵלֶיךָ וְהָיָה לְךָ וְלָהֶם לְאָכְלָה: וַיַּעַשׂ נֹחַ כְּכֹל
ז א אֲשֶׁר צִוָּה אֹתוֹ אֱלֹהִים כֵּן עָשָׂה: וַיֹּאמֶר יהוה לְנֹחַ בֹּא־ שני
אַתָּה וְכָל־בֵּיתְךָ אֶל־הַתֵּבָה כִּי־אֹתְךָ רָאִיתִי צַדִּיק לְפָנַי
ב בַּדּוֹר הַזֶּה: מִכֹּל ׀ הַבְּהֵמָה הַטְּהוֹרָה תִּקַּח־לְךָ שִׁבְעָה
שִׁבְעָה אִישׁ וְאִשְׁתּוֹ וּמִן־הַבְּהֵמָה אֲשֶׁר לֹא טְהֹרָה הִוא
ג שְׁנַיִם אִישׁ וְאִשְׁתּוֹ: גַּם מֵעוֹף הַשָּׁמַיִם שִׁבְעָה שִׁבְעָה זָכָר
ד וּנְקֵבָה לְחַיּוֹת זֶרַע עַל־פְּנֵי כָל־הָאָרֶץ: כִּי לְיָמִים עוֹד שִׁבְעָה
אָנֹכִי מַמְטִיר עַל־הָאָרֶץ אַרְבָּעִים יוֹם וְאַרְבָּעִים לָיְלָה
וּמָחִיתִי אֶת־כָּל־הַיְקוּם אֲשֶׁר עָשִׂיתִי מֵעַל פְּנֵי הָאֲדָמָה:
ה ו וַיַּעַשׂ נֹחַ כְּכֹל אֲשֶׁר־צִוָּהוּ יהוה: וְנֹחַ בֶּן־שֵׁשׁ מֵאוֹת שָׁנָה

Science, which allows us to understand the world as God's work, and humanities, which explore the human person as God's image, have an honorable place within the Jewish worldview. They have religious dignity; they are the gift of God. *We need to open a series of windows so that the world can illuminate our understanding of Torah, and so that the Torah, in turn, may guide us as we seek to make our way through the world.*

7:1 אֹתְךָ רָאִיתִי צַדִּיק *I have seen you alone to be righteous* – Noaḥ is a good man in a bad age. But his influence on the life of his contemporaries is, apparently, nonexistent. It is reasonable to assume that these two facts – Noaḥ's righteousness and his lack of influence on his contemporaries – are intimately related. Noaḥ preserves his virtue by separating himself from his environment. That is how, in a world gone mad, he stays sane.

The famous debate among the Sages as to whether the phrase "perfect" or "a person of integrity in his generation"

years old when the floodwaters came upon the earth.
7 Noaḥ, with his sons, his wife, and his sons' wives, came
8 into the ark to escape the waters of the flood. The pure
animals, the animals that were not pure, the birds, and all
9 that walked the earth came two by two to Noaḥ into the
ark, male and female, as God had commanded Noaḥ.
10 Thus, after seven days the floodwaters came upon the
11 earth. In the six hundredth year of Noaḥ's life, in the
second month, on the seventeenth of the month – on that
day, all the wellsprings of the great deep burst, and the
12 heavens' floodgates opened. The rain fell on the earth for
13 forty days and forty nights. On that very day, Noaḥ, his
sons, Shem, Ḥam, and Yefet, Noaḥ's wife, and his sons'
14 three wives entered the ark. With them came every kind
of wild beast, every kind of animal, every creeping,
crawling creature of the land, every kind of flying creature,
15 every bird, and each winged thing. They came to Noaḥ, to
the ark, two by two, of all flesh that had within it the
16 breath of life. They came, male and female of all flesh,
as God had commanded him. Then the LORD shut him
17 in. For forty days the flood came upon the earth. The SHELISHI
waters swelled, lifting the ark so that it rose above the
18 land. The waters surged, swelling enormously on the
earth, and the ark began to drift on the surface of the
19 water. The waters surged ever more, until all the high
20 mountains beneath all the heavens were covered. Fifteen
cubits above them the waters surged as the mountains
21 were covered. All flesh that moved upon the earth
perished – birds, animals, wild beasts, and all the creatures

---

probability of changing minds is small. That is because the moral life is a life we share with others. We are, in some sense, responsible for the society of which we are a part. There are times when each of us must lead.

Hasidim used to call Noaḥ a *tzaddik im peltz*, "a righteous man in a fur coat." There are two ways of keeping warm on a cold day. You can wear a fur coat or light a fire. Wear a fur coat and you warm only yourself. Light a fire and you warm others. Jews are supposed to light a fire.

ז וְהַמַּבּוּל הָיָה מַיִם עַל־הָאָרֶץ׃ וַיָּבֹא נֹחַ וּבָנָיו וְאִשְׁתּוֹ וּנְשֵׁי־
ח בָנָיו אִתּוֹ אֶל־הַתֵּבָה מִפְּנֵי מֵי הַמַּבּוּל׃ מִן־הַבְּהֵמָה
הַטְּהוֹרָה וּמִן־הַבְּהֵמָה אֲשֶׁר אֵינֶנָּה טְהֹרָה וּמִן־הָעוֹף וְכֹל
ט אֲשֶׁר־רֹמֵשׂ עַל־הָאֲדָמָה׃ שְׁנַיִם שְׁנַיִם בָּאוּ אֶל־נֹחַ אֶל־
י הַתֵּבָה זָכָר וּנְקֵבָה כַּאֲשֶׁר צִוָּה אֱלֹהִים אֶת־נֹחַ׃ וַיְהִי
יא לְשִׁבְעַת הַיָּמִים וּמֵי הַמַּבּוּל הָיוּ עַל־הָאָרֶץ׃ בִּשְׁנַת שֵׁשׁ־
מֵאוֹת שָׁנָה לְחַיֵּי־נֹחַ בַּחֹדֶשׁ הַשֵּׁנִי בְּשִׁבְעָה־עָשָׂר יוֹם
לַחֹדֶשׁ בַּיּוֹם הַזֶּה נִבְקְעוּ כָּל־מַעְיְנוֹת תְּהוֹם רַבָּה וַאֲרֻבֹּת
יב הַשָּׁמַיִם נִפְתָּחוּ׃ וַיְהִי הַגֶּשֶׁם עַל־הָאָרֶץ אַרְבָּעִים יוֹם
יג וְאַרְבָּעִים לָיְלָה׃ בְּעֶצֶם הַיּוֹם הַזֶּה בָּא נֹחַ וְשֵׁם־וְחָם וָיֶפֶת
בְּנֵי־נֹחַ וְאֵשֶׁת נֹחַ וּשְׁלֹשֶׁת נְשֵׁי־בָנָיו אִתָּם אֶל־הַתֵּבָה׃
יד הֵמָּה וְכָל־הַחַיָּה לְמִינָהּ וְכָל־הַבְּהֵמָה לְמִינָהּ וְכָל־
הָרֶמֶשׂ הָרֹמֵשׂ עַל־הָאָרֶץ לְמִינֵהוּ וְכָל־הָעוֹף לְמִינֵהוּ כֹּל
טו צִפּוֹר כָּל־כָּנָף׃ וַיָּבֹאוּ אֶל־נֹחַ אֶל־הַתֵּבָה שְׁנַיִם שְׁנַיִם מִכָּל־
טז הַבָּשָׂר אֲשֶׁר־בּוֹ רוּחַ חַיִּים׃ וְהַבָּאִים זָכָר וּנְקֵבָה מִכָּל־בָּשָׂר
יז בָּאוּ כַּאֲשֶׁר צִוָּה אֹתוֹ אֱלֹהִים וַיִּסְגֹּר יְהוָה בַּעֲדוֹ׃ וַיְהִי שלישי
הַמַּבּוּל אַרְבָּעִים יוֹם עַל־הָאָרֶץ וַיִּרְבּוּ הַמַּיִם וַיִּשְׂאוּ אֶת־
יח הַתֵּבָה וַתָּרָם מֵעַל הָאָרֶץ׃ וַיִּגְבְּרוּ הַמַּיִם וַיִּרְבּוּ מְאֹד עַל־
יט הָאָרֶץ וַתֵּלֶךְ הַתֵּבָה עַל־פְּנֵי הַמָּיִם׃ וְהַמַּיִם גָּבְרוּ מְאֹד מְאֹד
עַל־הָאָרֶץ וַיְכֻסּוּ כָּל־הֶהָרִים הַגְּבֹהִים אֲשֶׁר־תַּחַת כָּל־
כ הַשָּׁמָיִם׃ חֲמֵשׁ עֶשְׂרֵה אַמָּה מִלְמַעְלָה גָּבְרוּ הַמָּיִם וַיְכֻסּוּ
כא הֶהָרִים׃ וַיִּגְוַע כָּל־בָּשָׂר ׀ הָרֹמֵשׂ עַל־הָאָרֶץ בָּעוֹף וּבַבְּהֵמָה

after the flood, haunted by guilt? Does he think of the lives he might have saved if only he had spoken out, whether to his contemporaries or to God? We cannot be sure. The text is suggestive but not conclusive.

The Torah sets a high standard for the moral life. It is not enough to be righteous if that means turning our backs on a society that is guilty of wrongdoing. We must take a stand. We must protest. We must register dissent even if the

22 that swarm on the earth, and all humankind. Everything
on dry land that had breath of life in its nostrils died.
23 Every living thing on the face of the earth was wiped out:
from humans to animals, from creeping creatures to
winged birds of the heavens, all were wiped from the
earth. Only Noaḥ and those with him in the ark survived.
24 For one hundred fifty days, the waters surged over the
8 1 earth. Then God remembered Noaḥ and all the wild
beasts and animals with him in the ark. God sent a wind
2 over the earth, and the waters began to subside. The
wellsprings of the deep and heavens' floodgates closed,
3 and the heavens' rains were reined in. The water steadily
receded from the earth, and by the end of one hundred
4 fifty days, the water had abated. In the seventh month, on
the seventeenth day of the month, the ark came to rest on
5 the mountains of Ararat. The water continued to abate
until the tenth month, and on the first day of the tenth
6 month, the mountaintops became visible. After forty days
7 Noaḥ opened the window he had made in the ark and sent
a raven forth. It flew to and fro until the water on the earth
8 had dried. After that he sent forth a dove to see whether
9 the water had subsided from the face of the land. But the
dove found no resting place to plant its foot, and so it
returned to him, to the ark, for water still covered the face
of the earth completely. He reached out his hand and
10 brought the dove back to him, into the ark. Then he waited
another seven days, and again he sent the dove forth from
11 the ark. The dove came back to him in the evening – and
in its beak was a freshly picked olive leaf. Noaḥ knew then
12 that the water had subsided from the earth. He waited
another seven days and again sent forth the dove – and it
13 returned to him no more. So it was that, by the first day of
the first month of Noaḥ's six hundred and first year, the
water on the earth dried up. Noaḥ removed the covering
14 of the ark and saw that the face of the land was dry. By the
twenty-seventh day of the second month, the earth had
15 dried completely. Then God said to Noaḥ, REVI'I

וּבַחַיָּה וּבְכָל־הַשֶּׁרֶץ הַשֹּׁרֵץ עַל־הָאָרֶץ וְכֹל הָאָדָם׃
כב כֹּל אֲשֶׁר נִשְׁמַת־רוּחַ חַיִּים בְּאַפָּיו מִכֹּל אֲשֶׁר בֶּחָרָבָה
כג מֵתוּ׃ וַיִּמַח אֶת־כָּל־הַיְקוּם ׀ אֲשֶׁר ׀ עַל־פְּנֵי הָאֲדָמָה מֵאָדָם
עַד־בְּהֵמָה עַד־רֶמֶשׂ וְעַד־עוֹף הַשָּׁמַיִם וַיִּמָּחוּ מִן־הָאָרֶץ
כד וַיִּשָּׁאֶר אַךְ־נֹחַ וַאֲשֶׁר אִתּוֹ בַּתֵּבָה׃ וַיִּגְבְּרוּ הַמַּיִם עַל־הָאָרֶץ
ח א חֲמִשִּׁים וּמְאַת יוֹם׃ וַיִּזְכֹּר אֱלֹהִים אֶת־נֹחַ וְאֵת כָּל־הַחַיָּה ו
וְאֶת־כָּל־הַבְּהֵמָה אֲשֶׁר אִתּוֹ בַּתֵּבָה וַיַּעֲבֵר אֱלֹהִים רוּחַ
ב עַל־הָאָרֶץ וַיָּשֹׁכּוּ הַמָּיִם׃ וַיִּסָּכְרוּ מַעְיְנֹת תְּהוֹם וַאֲרֻבֹּת
ג הַשָּׁמָיִם וַיִּכָּלֵא הַגֶּשֶׁם מִן־הַשָּׁמָיִם׃ וַיָּשֻׁבוּ הַמַּיִם מֵעַל
הָאָרֶץ הָלוֹךְ וָשׁוֹב וַיַּחְסְרוּ הַמַּיִם מִקְצֵה חֲמִשִּׁים וּמְאַת
ד יוֹם׃ וַתָּנַח הַתֵּבָה בַּחֹדֶשׁ הַשְּׁבִיעִי בְּשִׁבְעָה־עָשָׂר יוֹם לַחֹדֶשׁ
ה עַל הָרֵי אֲרָרָט׃ וְהַמַּיִם הָיוּ הָלוֹךְ וְחָסוֹר עַד הַחֹדֶשׁ הָעֲשִׂירִי
ו בָּעֲשִׂירִי בְּאֶחָד לַחֹדֶשׁ נִרְאוּ רָאשֵׁי הֶהָרִים׃ וַיְהִי מִקֵּץ
אַרְבָּעִים יוֹם וַיִּפְתַּח נֹחַ אֶת־חַלּוֹן הַתֵּבָה אֲשֶׁר עָשָׂה׃
ז וַיְשַׁלַּח אֶת־הָעֹרֵב וַיֵּצֵא יָצוֹא וָשׁוֹב עַד־יְבֹשֶׁת הַמַּיִם מֵעַל
ח הָאָרֶץ׃ וַיְשַׁלַּח אֶת־הַיּוֹנָה מֵאִתּוֹ לִרְאוֹת הֲקַלּוּ הַמַּיִם מֵעַל
ט פְּנֵי הָאֲדָמָה׃ וְלֹא־מָצְאָה הַיּוֹנָה מָנוֹחַ לְכַף־רַגְלָהּ וַתָּשָׁב
אֵלָיו אֶל־הַתֵּבָה כִּי־מַיִם עַל־פְּנֵי כָל־הָאָרֶץ וַיִּשְׁלַח יָדוֹ
י וַיִּקָּחֶהָ וַיָּבֵא אֹתָהּ אֵלָיו אֶל־הַתֵּבָה׃ וַיָּחֶל עוֹד שִׁבְעַת יָמִים
יא אֲחֵרִים וַיֹּסֶף שַׁלַּח אֶת־הַיּוֹנָה מִן־הַתֵּבָה׃ וַתָּבֹא אֵלָיו הַיּוֹנָה
לְעֵת עֶרֶב וְהִנֵּה עֲלֵה־זַיִת טָרָף בְּפִיהָ וַיֵּדַע נֹחַ כִּי־קַלּוּ הַמַּיִם
יב מֵעַל הָאָרֶץ׃ וַיִּיָּחֶל עוֹד שִׁבְעַת יָמִים אֲחֵרִים וַיְשַׁלַּח אֶת־
יג הַיּוֹנָה וְלֹא־יָסְפָה שׁוּב־אֵלָיו עוֹד׃ וַיְהִי בְּאַחַת וְשֵׁשׁ־
מֵאוֹת שָׁנָה בָּרִאשׁוֹן בְּאֶחָד לַחֹדֶשׁ חָרְבוּ הַמַּיִם מֵעַל הָאָרֶץ
וַיָּסַר נֹחַ אֶת־מִכְסֵה הַתֵּבָה וַיַּרְא וְהִנֵּה חָרְבוּ פְּנֵי הָאֲדָמָה׃
יד וּבַחֹדֶשׁ הַשֵּׁנִי בְּשִׁבְעָה וְעֶשְׂרִים יוֹם לַחֹדֶשׁ יָבְשָׁה
טו הָאָרֶץ׃ וַיְדַבֵּר אֱלֹהִים אֶל־נֹחַ לֵאמֹר׃ ז רביעי

16 "Leave the ark – you, and your wife, your sons, and your
17 sons' wives with you. And every living thing with you –
birds, animals, and all wild beasts that walk the earth –
bring them out with you. Let them swarm again on the
18 earth and be fertile and multiply upon it." So Noaḥ came
19 out with his sons, his wife, and his sons' wives. Every
beast, creeping thing, winged creature, everything that
creeps across the earth, emerged from the ark by families.
20 Then Noaḥ built an altar to the LORD and, taking of each
of the kinds of pure animals and pure birds, sacrificed

---

its ways upon the earth" (Gen. 6:11–12). God brings a flood that wipes away all life, until – with the exception of Noaḥ, his family, and the animals in the ark – the earth has returned to the state it was in at the beginning of the Torah, when "the earth was void and desolate, there was darkness on the face of the deep, and the spirit of God moved over the waters" (1:2). Now, God begins again.

This is the point at which the Torah confronts what Christianity is later to call "original sin," but in a quite different way. God makes a covenant with all humanity, based on the prohibition of murder ("One who sheds the blood of man....") The Sages were eventually to identify seven "Noahide" laws, but the principle is essentially the same. God no longer makes maximal demands: He makes minimal ones. This is what contemporary philosophers call a "thin" morality, the basic requirements of human conduct as such.

God does not condemn humankind; He does not hold it guilty or incapable of good. Rather, He lowers His requirements to the level at which an acceptable degree of virtue is humanly achievable. Enough, He seems to say, that you honor the sanctity of life and the basic human decencies.

But that is not the end of the story. If it were, the Torah would merely be one work of moral philosophy among many others, articulating the "thin" principles universal to the human condition. Instead it makes a surprising move. God asks one individual – eventually a family, a tribe, a collection of tribes, a nation – to serve as an exemplary role model, to be as it were a living case study in what it is to live closely and continuously in the presence of God. In Lon Fuller's terms, in his book *The Morality of Law*, the covenant of Noaḥ is "the morality of duty" – the minimum standard, the kind of thing you enact as law. The covenant of Avraham is "the morality of aspiration," the ideals at which we aim: Avraham is a role model of life at its best.

God, we are reminded, also loves those He does not choose for that morality of aspiration. They are part of His covenant with humanity – part of the covenant of the morality of duty.

טז יז צֵא מִן־הַתֵּבָה אַתָּה וְאִשְׁתְּךָ וּבָנֶיךָ וּנְשֵׁי־בָנֶיךָ אִתָּךְ׃ כָּל־
הַחַיָּה אֲשֶׁר־אִתְּךָ מִכָּל־בָּשָׂר בָּעוֹף וּבַבְּהֵמָה וּבְכָל־הָרֶמֶשׂ
הָרֹמֵשׂ עַל־הָאָרֶץ הוצא אִתָּךְ וְשָׁרְצוּ בָאָרֶץ וּפָרוּ וְרָבוּ הַיְצֵא
יח יט עַל־הָאָרֶץ׃ וַיֵּצֵא־נֹחַ וּבָנָיו וְאִשְׁתּוֹ וּנְשֵׁי־בָנָיו אִתּוֹ׃ כָּל־
הַחַיָּה כָּל־הָרֶמֶשׂ וְכָל־הָעוֹף כֹּל רוֹמֵשׂ עַל־הָאָרֶץ
כ לְמִשְׁפְּחֹתֵיהֶם יָצְאוּ מִן־הַתֵּבָה׃ וַיִּבֶן נֹחַ מִזְבֵּחַ לַיהוָה וַיִּקַּח
מִכֹּל ׀ הַבְּהֵמָה הַטְּהֹרָה וּמִכֹּל הָעוֹף הַטָּהֹר וַיַּעַל עֹלֹת

8:16 צֵא מִן־הַתֵּבָה *Leave the ark* – There are many midrashic comments on Noaḥ and his place in the history of faith, but one is unrivaled in its sharpness:

> Once the waters had abated, Noaḥ should have left the ark. However, Noaḥ said to himself, "I entered with God's permission, as it says, 'Enter the ark' (Gen. 7:1). Shall I now leave without permission?" The Holy One, blessed be He, said to him, "Is it permission, then, that you are seeking? Very well, then, here is permission," as it is said, "[Then God said to Noaḥ,] 'Leave the ark'" (8:17).
>
> R. Yehuda b. Ilai said: If I had been there, I would have broken down the ark and taken myself out. (*Tanḥuma*, Noaḥ 13–14)

To understand this midrash, one must read the story of the flood carefully, with an ear to the pace of the narrative. The story begins rapidly. God announces the imminent destruction of life on earth. He orders Noaḥ to build an ark, specifying its precise measurements. Details follow as to what Noaḥ must take with him. The rain comes; the earth is flooded; Noaḥ and those with him are the sole survivors. The rain ceases and the water abates.

We expect to read next that Noaḥ emerges. Instead the narrative slows down, and for fourteen verses almost nothing happens. The water recedes. The ark comes to rest. Noaḥ opens a window and sends out a raven. Then he sends out a dove. He waits seven days and sends it out again. It returns with an olive leaf. Another seven days pass. He sends the dove a third time. This time it does not return, but Noaḥ still does not step out onto dry land. Eventually God Himself says, "Leave the ark," and only then does Noaḥ do so. The midrash is unmistakable in its note of exasperation. When it comes to rebuilding a shattered world, you do not wait for permission.

THE NOAHIDE COVENANT

The story of the first eight chapters of Genesis is tragic but simple: creation, followed by de-creation, followed by re-creation. God creates order. Humans then destroy that order to the point where "the earth had become…full of violence," with "all flesh corrupting

21 burnt offerings on the altar. The LORD smelled the fragrant
aroma and said in His heart, "Never again will I curse the
land because of man; the devisings of the human heart are
evil from its youth. And never again will I destroy all life as
22 I have done. As long as earth and time endure – sowing
time and harvest, cold and heat, summer, winter, day, and
9 1 night will not cease." Then God blessed Noaḥ and his
sons, saying to them, "Be fertile, multiply, fill the earth.

---

has given way to divine compassion. In making His covenant with Noaḥ, *God rejects rejection.*

8:22 עֹד כָּל־יְמֵי הָאָרֶץ *As long as earth and time endure* – The real subject of the Torah is not our faith in God, which is often faltering, but His unfailing faith in us. *The Torah is not man's book of God. It is God's book of man.* God never stops believing in us, loving us, and hoping for the best from us. There are moments when He almost despairs. Yet – God has patience. God has forgiveness. God has compassion. God has love. For centuries, theologians and philosophers have been looking at religion upside down. The real phenomenon at its heart, the mystery and the miracle, is not our faith in God, but God's faith in us.

There may be times in our lives – certainly there have been in mine – when the sun disappears and we enter the cloud of black despair. King David knew these feelings well. They are the theme of several psalms. People can be brutal to one another. There are some who, having suffered pain themselves, find relief in inflicting it on others. You can lose faith in humanity, or in yourself, or both. At such times, the knowledge that God has faith in us is transformative, redemptive. As David said in Psalms: *Were my father and my mother to forsake me, the LORD would take me in* (27:10).

We may lose heart; God never will. We may despair; God will give us hope. God believes in us even if we don't believe in ourselves. We may sin and disappoint and come short again and again, but God never ceases to forgive us when we fail and lift us when we fall.

As long as God's faith endures, dawn will continue to follow dark, spring follow winter. Have faith in God's faith in us and you will find the path from darkness to light.

THE NOAHIDE COVENANT: "OBJECTIVE" MORALITY

The two great principles of the Noahide covenant happen also to be the first two principles to have been established by computer simulation. The Prisoner's Dilemma imagines the following scenario: Police arrest two men on suspicion of a serious crime. They do not have enough evidence to convict them; at most they have evidence sufficient to prove them guilty of a lesser offense.

כא בַּמִּזְבֵּחַ: וַיָּרַח יְהוָה אֶת־רֵיחַ הַנִּיחֹחַ וַיֹּאמֶר יְהוָה אֶל־לִבּוֹ
לֹא אֹסִף לְקַלֵּל עוֹד אֶת־הָאֲדָמָה בַּעֲבוּר הָאָדָם כִּי יֵצֶר
לֵב הָאָדָם רַע מִנְּעֻרָיו וְלֹא־אֹסִף עוֹד לְהַכּוֹת אֶת־כָּל־חַי
כב כַּאֲשֶׁר עָשִׂיתִי: עֹד כָּל־יְמֵי הָאָרֶץ זֶרַע וְקָצִיר וְקֹר וָחֹם
ט א וְקַיִץ וָחֹרֶף וְיוֹם וָלַיְלָה לֹא יִשְׁבֹּתוּ: וַיְבָרֶךְ אֱלֹהִים אֶת־
נֹחַ וְאֶת־בָּנָיו וַיֹּאמֶר לָהֶם פְּרוּ וּרְבוּ וּמִלְאוּ אֶת־הָאָרֶץ:

It is inscribed into the terms of the covenant itself that God sets His image on everyone.

8:21 יֵצֶר לֵב הָאָדָם *The devisings of the human heart* – Reading the story closely, it seems that God created humans in the faith that they would *naturally* choose the right and the good. They would not need to eat the fruit of the Tree of Knowledge of good and evil; calculation, reflection, decision – all the things we associate with knowledge – would not be necessary. They would act as God wanted them to act, because they had been created in His own image.

It did not turn out that way. Adam and Ḥava sinned, Kayin committed murder, and within a few generations the world was reduced to chaos. Everything else in the universe was *tov*, "good." But "the devisings of the human heart" – the *yetzer* – are not.

We now know the neuroscience behind this. We have a prefrontal cortex that evolved to allow humans to think and act reflectively, considering the consequences of their deeds. But this is slower and weaker than the amygdala (what the Jewish mystics called the *nefesh habehemit*, the animal soul), which produces, even before we have had time to think, the fight-or-flight reactions without which humans before civilization would simply not have survived.

The problem is that these reactions can be deeply destructive. Often they lead to violence. It is not that we only do evil. Empathy and compassion are as natural to us as are fear and aggression. The problem is that fear lies just beneath the surface of human interaction, and it can overwhelm all our other instincts.

Daniel Goleman calls this an *amygdala hijack*: "Emotions make us pay attention right now – this is urgent – and give us an immediate action plan without having to think twice." Impulsive action is often destructive because it is undertaken without thought of consequences. Therefore, Rambam argued, many of the laws of the Torah constitute a training in virtue simply by making us think before we act.

8:21 רַע מִנְּעֻרָיו *Evil from its youth* – A new principle enters the relationship between God and humanity. Where earlier the wickedness of the human heart was a reason to destroy the earth, it now becomes a reason *not* to destroy it. Divine justice

2 Fear and dread of you shall fall upon all beasts of the
earth, upon all winged creatures of the heavens, upon all
that creeps upon the land and all fish of the sea. Into your
3 hand they are given. Every moving thing that lives shall
be food for you; I allow them all to you, like green plants.
4 5 But flesh with its lifeblood still in it you may not eat. And
for your own lifeblood I will demand account; I will
demand it from every wild beast. For human life I will

---

the blood of man – by man shall his blood be shed" (Gen. 9:6). This is measure for measure (in Hebrew, *midda keneged midda*), or retributive justice: as you do, so shall you be done to.

In 1989, however, Martin Nowak produced a program that beats Tit-for-Tat. He called it Generous. It overcame one weakness of Tit-for-Tat, namely that when you meet a particularly nasty opponent, you get drawn into a potentially endless and destructive cycle of retaliation, which is bad for both sides. Generous avoided this possibility by randomly but periodically forgetting the last move of its opponent, thus allowing the relationship to begin again. What Nowak had produced, in fact, was a computer simulation of *forgiveness.*

After the flood, God vows: "Never again will I curse the land because of man; the devisings of the human heart are evil from its youth. And never again will I destroy all life as I have done" (8:21). This is the principle of divine compassion.

There is, then, an objective basis for morality. It rests on two key ideas: justice and forgiveness, or what the Sages called *middat hadin* and *middat haraḥamim.* Without these, no group can survive.

9:3 נָתַתִּי לָכֶם אֶת־כֹּל *I allow them all to you* – Adam and Ḥava were vegetarian. God only permitted eating meat after the flood. Rabbi Yosef Albo's theory, in his *Sefer HaIkkarim,* is that killing animals for food is inherently wrong. It involves taking the life of a sentient being to satisfy our needs. After the world becomes "full of violence," and is destroyed by the flood, God has to lower His demands. *Let humans kill animals,* He said, *rather than kill human beings.*

According to Rabbi Albo, Noaḥ offers an animal sacrifice in thanksgiving for having survived the flood. God sees that human beings need this way of expressing themselves. They are genetically predisposed to violence ("the devisings of the human heart are evil from its youth"). If society is to survive, humans will need to be able to direct their violence toward nonhuman animals, whether as food or sacrificial offerings. The crucial line to be drawn is between human and nonhuman. The permission to kill animals is accompanied by an absolute prohibition against killing human beings, "for in the image of God has God made man" (Gen. 9:6).

ב וּמוֹרַאֲכֶם וְחִתְּכֶם יִהְיֶה עַל כָּל־חַיַּת הָאָרֶץ וְעַל כָּל־
עוֹף הַשָּׁמָיִם בְּכֹל אֲשֶׁר תִּרְמֹשׂ הָאֲדָמָה וּבְכָל־דְּגֵי הַיָּם
ג בְּיֶדְכֶם נִתָּנוּ׃ כָּל־רֶמֶשׂ אֲשֶׁר הוּא־חַי לָכֶם יִהְיֶה לְאָכְלָה
ד כְּיֶרֶק עֵשֶׂב נָתַתִּי לָכֶם אֶת־כֹּל׃ אַךְ־בָּשָׂר בְּנַפְשׁוֹ דָמוֹ לֹא
ה תֹאכֵלוּ׃ וְאַךְ אֶת־דִּמְכֶם לְנַפְשֹׁתֵיכֶם אֶדְרֹשׁ מִיַּד כָּל־חַיָּה

Their aim is to get them to inform on one another. They therefore put them in separate rooms, with no possible communication between them, and offer them a deal. If one informs and the other stays silent, the informant will go free, and the other will receive a jail sentence of ten years. If both inform, they will be sentenced to five years each. If both stay silent, they will be found guilty of the lesser offense and be sentenced to a year in prison.

It does not take long to work out that for each, the optimal decision is to inform. The result, however, is that they both receive a five-year sentence, whereas if they had both stayed silent, they would have received only one year. The Prisoner's Dilemma establishes the paradoxical, but deeply significant, fact that two people, each pursuing their own self-interest, generate an outcome which is bad for them, both individually and collectively.

What people suspected, and were eventually able to prove, is that the Prisoner's Dilemma yields its paradoxical result only if it is played once. If it is played over and over – the so-called "iterated Prisoner's Dilemma" – the parties eventually learn that they are doing themselves, as well as the other person, harm. Once they discover this, they learn to cooperate.

At this point, game theory provided sociobiologists with an answer to a question that had long puzzled Darwinians, including Charles Darwin himself. In the struggle for survival, the fittest wins. Despite this, all human societies value altruistic behavior, and some forms of it can be found in nonhuman species.

In the late 1970s, a competition was announced to find the computer program that did best at playing the iterated Prisoner's Dilemma against itself and other opponents. The winning program was devised by Anatol Rapoport, and was called Tit-for-Tat. It was dazzlingly simple: it began by cooperating, and then repeated the last move of its opponent, working on the rule of "What you did to me, I will do to you," or "measure for measure." This was the first time scientific proof had been given for any moral principle.

What is fascinating about this chain of discoveries is that it precisely mirrors the central principle of the covenant God made with Noaḥ: "One who sheds

demand account, of every man toward his fellow man:
6 One who sheds the blood of man – by man shall his
7 blood be shed, for in God's image man was made. As for
you, be fertile and multiply, abound on earth and become
8 many on it." Then God said to Noaḥ and to his ḤAMISHI
9 sons with him: "I – I am about to establish My covenant
10 with you and your descendants after you, and with every
living creature that is with you – the birds, the animals,
and all the wild beasts of earth that are with you,
everything that left the ark, every living creature on
11 earth. I will establish My covenant with you, that never
again may all life be destroyed by the waters of a flood;
never again will there be a flood to destroy the earth."
12 God said, "This is the sign of the covenant I am making
between Me and you – and every living creature with
13 you – for all generations to come. I have laid down My
bow in the clouds to be the sign of the covenant between

---

not in my image is nonetheless in God's image – that is the basis of God's covenant with Noaḥ, a universal requirement of all cultures if they are to honor God who gave us life.

9:10 לְכׇל חַיַּת הָאָרֶץ *Every living creature on earth* – The concept of the covenant with Noaḥ tells us that, prior to our particular commitments to this faith or that, this culture, nation, civilization or that, we are human beings, cast together in a fate which grows more interconnected with every passing century, each passing year. We have a duty, not just to ourselves, our families and friends, but also to the ever-widening concentric circles – community, society, humanity – of which we are a part. We are responsible for what we could do, but did not, to alleviate the human condition. To be sure, these responsibilities are not open-ended; we can't do it all. We have limited time, energy, and resources, and those with whom we are most closely bound in a web of obligations have a right to expect that we will give them priority. But what applies to a community applies to society, and ultimately to the world: We are worth what we are willing to share. Each of us has a contribution to make, and "whether we do much or we do little, what matters is that our heart is turned to Heaven" (Menaḥot 110a).

9:13 לְאוֹת בְּרִית *The sign of the covenant* – When we read Genesis and Exodus superficially, it seems as if the covenants of Noaḥ, Avraham, and Sinai are the same sort of thing. But they are not.

אֶדְרְשֶׁנּוּ וּמִיַּד הָאָדָם מִיַּד אִישׁ אָחִיו אֶדְרֹשׁ אֶת־נֶפֶשׁ
ו הָאָדָם: שֹׁפֵךְ דַּם הָאָדָם בָּאָדָם דָּמוֹ יִשָּׁפֵךְ כִּי בְּצֶלֶם אֱלֹהִים
ז עָשָׂה אֶת־הָאָדָם: וְאַתֶּם פְּרוּ וּרְבוּ שִׁרְצוּ בָאָרֶץ וּרְבוּ־
ח בָהּ: וַיֹּאמֶר אֱלֹהִים אֶל־נֹחַ וְאֶל־בָּנָיו אִתּוֹ לֵאמֹר: חמישי
ט וַאֲנִי הִנְנִי מֵקִים אֶת־בְּרִיתִי אִתְּכֶם וְאֶת־זַרְעֲכֶם אַחֲרֵיכֶם:
י וְאֵת כָּל־נֶפֶשׁ הַחַיָּה אֲשֶׁר אִתְּכֶם בָּעוֹף בַּבְּהֵמָה וּבְכָל־
חַיַּת הָאָרֶץ אִתְּכֶם מִכֹּל יֹצְאֵי הַתֵּבָה לְכֹל חַיַּת הָאָרֶץ:
יא וַהֲקִמֹתִי אֶת־בְּרִיתִי אִתְּכֶם וְלֹא־יִכָּרֵת כָּל־בָּשָׂר עוֹד מִמֵּי
יב הַמַּבּוּל וְלֹא־יִהְיֶה עוֹד מַבּוּל לְשַׁחֵת הָאָרֶץ: וַיֹּאמֶר אֱלֹהִים
זֹאת אוֹת־הַבְּרִית אֲשֶׁר־אֲנִי נֹתֵן בֵּינִי וּבֵינֵיכֶם וּבֵין כָּל־נֶפֶשׁ
יג חַיָּה אֲשֶׁר אִתְּכֶם לְדֹרֹת עוֹלָם: אֶת־קַשְׁתִּי נָתַתִּי בֶּעָנָן
יד וְהָיְתָה לְאוֹת בְּרִית בֵּינִי וּבֵין הָאָרֶץ: וְהָיָה בְּעַנְנִי עָנָן עַל־

9:6 בָּאָדָם דָּמוֹ יִשָּׁפֵךְ *By man shall his blood be shed* – Many Torah passages are constructed in the form of a mirror-image symmetry, technically known as chiasmus: a sequence with the form ABC-CBA, where the second half reverses the order of the first. A precise example is this six-word commandment, which forms the central element of the Noahide covenant:

[A] One who sheds [B] the blood [C] of man [C] by man [B] shall his blood [A] be shed.

This is more than a stylistic device. It is the expression of one of the Torah's most profound beliefs, namely, the reciprocal nature of justice. Those who do good are blessed with good. Those who do evil, suffer evil. What happens to us is a mirror image of what we do. Thus, form mirrors substance: mirror-image symmetry is the literary equivalent of a just world.

9:6 בְּצֶלֶם אֱלֹהִים *In God's image* – This sounds like a restatement of Genesis 1. In fact it is the opposite. Genesis 1 tells us that *we* are in God's image. Genesis 9 tells us that the *other person* is in God's image. Genesis 1 speaks of the preeminence of humankind ("Fill the earth and subdue it"). Genesis 9 declares the prohibition of murder. Between the two lies tragedy. Granted mastery over nature, human beings used that power to attempt mastery over other human beings, and the result – from Kayin to the flood – was violence and murder. It still is. That is why Genesis 9 is *not a repetition but a reversal* of Genesis 1.

Genesis 1 is about the self, Genesis 9 about the human Other. *One who is*

14 Me and the earth. Whenever I bring clouds over the earth
15 and the rainbow appears in the clouds, I will remember
My covenant that binds Me and you and every living
creature of all flesh so that never again will the waters
16 become a flood to destroy all life. The rainbow will be
there in the cloud, and I will see it, remembering the
eternal covenant between God and every living creature,
17 all flesh upon the earth." So said God to Noaḥ: "This is the
sign of the covenant that I have established between Me
and all flesh that is on earth."
18 Noaḥ's sons who came out from the ark were Shem, Ḥam, SHISHI
19 and Yefet. Ḥam was the father of Kenaan. These three
were Noaḥ's sons; and from them all the world branched
20 out. Noaḥ began to be a man of the land, and he planted
21 a vineyard. He drank some of the wine, became drunk,
22 and lay uncovered in his tent. Ḥam, father of Kenaan,
saw his father's nakedness and told his two brothers who

---

destroy all life – though not guaranteeing that humanity might not do so of its own accord – God has begun the world again, this time with Noaḥ in place of Adam, father of a new start to the human story. Genesis 9 is therefore parallel to Genesis 1. In both there is a keyword, repeated seven times, but it is a different word. In Genesis 1 the word is *tov*, "good." In Genesis 9, the word is *brit*, "covenant."

The terms of the human condition have changed. God acknowledges now that "the devisings of the human heart are evil from its youth" (Gen. 8:21), despite the fact that we were created in God's image. The difference is that there is only one God. If there were only one human being, he or she might live at peace with the world. But we know that this could not be the case because *lo tov* – "it is not good – for man to be alone" (2:18). We are social animals. And when one human being thinks he or she has godlike powers vis-à-vis another human being, the result is violence. Therefore, thinking yourself godlike, if you are human, all too human, is very dangerous indeed.

When we call something *good*, we are speaking about how it is in itself. But when we speak of *covenant*, we are talking about relationships. A covenant is a moral bond between persons. God teaches Noaḥ – and through him all humanity – that we should think, *not of ourselves but of the human other*, as being in the image of God. That is the only way to save ourselves from violence and self-destruction. The great religious challenge is: can I see a trace of God in the face of a stranger?

טו הָאָרֶץ וְנִרְאֲתָה הַקֶּשֶׁת בֶּעָנָן: וְזָכַרְתִּי אֶת־בְּרִיתִי אֲשֶׁר
בֵּינִי וּבֵינֵיכֶם וּבֵין כָּל־נֶפֶשׁ חַיָּה בְּכָל־בָּשָׂר וְלֹא־יִהְיֶה עוֹד
טז הַמַּיִם לְמַבּוּל לְשַׁחֵת כָּל־בָּשָׂר: וְהָיְתָה הַקֶּשֶׁת בֶּעָנָן
וּרְאִיתִיהָ לִזְכֹּר בְּרִית עוֹלָם בֵּין אֱלֹהִים וּבֵין כָּל־נֶפֶשׁ חַיָּה
יז בְּכָל־בָּשָׂר אֲשֶׁר עַל־הָאָרֶץ: וַיֹּאמֶר אֱלֹהִים אֶל־נֹחַ זֹאת
אוֹת־הַבְּרִית אֲשֶׁר הֲקִמֹתִי בֵּינִי וּבֵין כָּל־בָּשָׂר אֲשֶׁר עַל־
הָאָרֶץ:
יח וַיִּהְיוּ בְנֵי־נֹחַ הַיֹּצְאִים מִן־הַתֵּבָה שֵׁם וְחָם וָיָפֶת וְחָם ח ששי
יט הוּא אֲבִי כְנָעַן: שְׁלֹשָׁה אֵלֶּה בְּנֵי־נֹחַ וּמֵאֵלֶּה נָפְצָה כָל־
כ כא הָאָרֶץ: וַיָּחֶל נֹחַ אִישׁ הָאֲדָמָה וַיִּטַּע כָּרֶם: וַיֵּשְׁתְּ מִן־
כב הַיַּיִן וַיִּשְׁכָּר וַיִּתְגַּל בְּתוֹךְ אָהֳלֹה: וַיַּרְא חָם אֲבִי כְנַעַן

The covenants of Avraham and Sinai are covenants of faith. But the covenant of Noaḥ says nothing about faith. The world has been almost destroyed by a flood. All mankind, all life, with the exception of Noaḥ's ark, has shared the same fate. There is a famous prophecy in Isaiah 11 that one day, "wolf will lie down beside lamb." So far it has only happened once: in Noaḥ's ark. Why there? Not because they were friends, but because otherwise they would drown. That is a covenant of fate.

In the Noahide covenant God is saying: Never again will I destroy the world. But I cannot promise that *you* will never destroy it because I have given you free will. All I can do is teach you *how* not to destroy the world.

This code, the covenant of Noaḥ, has three dimensions. The first, as we have seen, is *the sanctity of human life*.

The second is *the integrity of the created world*. If we read the chapter carefully we see that *five times* God insists that the covenant of Noaḥ is not merely with humanity, but with all life on earth.

The third lies in the symbol of the covenant, the rainbow. Rabbi Samson Raphael Hirsch suggests that this sign represents the white light of God refracted into the infinite shadings of the spectrum (commentary on Gen. 9:14). This is what I have called the dignity of difference: unity in heaven creates diversity here on earth.

These three dimensions define the covenant of fate. Note that the covenant of fate *precedes* the covenant of faith, because faith is particular, but fate is universal. Without these foundations of human solidarity, we cannot survive.

9:17 הַבְּרִית אֲשֶׁר הֲקִמֹתִי *The covenant that I have established* – Vowing never again to

23 were outside. Shem and Yefet then took a cloak and put
it over both their shoulders. They walked backward and
covered their father's nakedness, averting their faces so as
24 not to see the nakedness of their father. Noaḥ woke from
his wine and realized what his youngest son had done to
25 him. He said, "Cursed be Kenaan! The lowest of slaves
26 shall he be to his brothers." Then he said, "Blessed be
27 the LORD, God of Shem; Kenaan shall be his slave. May
God enlarge Yefet, and let him dwell in the tents of Shem;
28 Kenaan shall be his slave." After the flood Noaḥ lived
29 three hundred and fifty years. Noaḥ lived a total of nine
hundred and fifty years, and he died.
10 1 These are the descendants of Noaḥ's sons, Shem, Ḥam,
and Yefet; after the flood, children were born to them.
2 Yefet's sons were Gomer, Magog, Madai, Yavan, Tuval,
3 Meshekh, and Tiras. Gomer's sons were Ashkenaz, Rifat,
4 and Togarma. Yavan's sons were Elisha, Tarshish, Kitim,
5 and Dodanim. From these the seagoing nations spread
out to their territories, each with its own language, by
6 their clans and their nations. Ḥam's sons were Kush,
7 Mitzrayim, Put, and Kenaan. Kush's sons were Seva,
Ḥavila, Savta, Raama, and Savtekha. Raama's sons were
8 Sheva and Dedan. Kush was the father of Nimrod, the
9 first mighty warrior on earth. He was a mighty hunter
before the LORD, which is why people still say, "Like
10 Nimrod, a mighty hunter before the LORD." His kingdom
began with Babylon, Erekh, Akad, and Kalneh in the
11 land of Shinar. From that land, Ashur went out and built
12 Nineveh, Reḥovot Ir, Kalaḥ, and Resen between Nineveh
13 and Kalaḥ; that is the great city. Mitzrayim fathered
14 the Ludim, Anamim, Lehavim and Naftuḥim, Patrusim,

that their father – the sole human being worthy of rescue during the flood – has become debased. Noaḥ's end – drunk, disheveled, an embarrassment to his children – eloquently tells us that if you save yourself while doing nothing to save the world, you do not even save yourself. Noaḥ, so the narrative seems to suggest, could not live with the guilt of survival.

כג אֵת עֶרְוַת אֲבִיו וַיַּגֵּד לִשְׁנֵי־אֶחָיו בַּחוּץ: וַיִּקַּח שֵׁם וָיֶפֶת
אֶת־הַשִּׂמְלָה וַיָּשִׂימוּ עַל־שְׁכֶם שְׁנֵיהֶם וַיֵּלְכוּ אֲחֹרַנִּית
וַיְכַסּוּ אֵת עֶרְוַת אֲבִיהֶם וּפְנֵיהֶם אֲחֹרַנִּית וְעֶרְוַת אֲבִיהֶם
כד לֹא רָאוּ: וַיִּיקֶץ נֹחַ מִיֵּינוֹ וַיֵּדַע אֵת אֲשֶׁר־עָשָׂה לוֹ בְּנוֹ
כה הַקָּטָן: וַיֹּאמֶר אָרוּר כְּנָעַן עֶבֶד עֲבָדִים יִהְיֶה לְאֶחָיו:
כו וַיֹּאמֶר בָּרוּךְ יְהוָה אֱלֹהֵי שֵׁם וִיהִי כְנַעַן עֶבֶד לָמוֹ:
כז יַפְתְּ אֱלֹהִים לְיֶפֶת וְיִשְׁכֹּן בְּאׇהֳלֵי־שֵׁם וִיהִי כְנַעַן עֶבֶד
כח לָמוֹ: וַיְחִי־נֹחַ אַחַר הַמַּבּוּל שְׁלֹשׁ מֵאוֹת שָׁנָה וַחֲמִשִּׁים
כט שָׁנָה: וַיְהִי כׇּל־יְמֵי־נֹחַ תְּשַׁע מֵאוֹת שָׁנָה וַחֲמִשִּׁים שָׁנָה
וַיָּמֹת:

י א וְאֵלֶּה תּוֹלְדֹת בְּנֵי־נֹחַ שֵׁם חָם וָיָפֶת וַיִּוָּלְדוּ לָהֶם בָּנִים
ב אַחַר הַמַּבּוּל: בְּנֵי יֶפֶת גֹּמֶר וּמָגוֹג וּמָדַי וְיָוָן וְתֻבָל וּמֶשֶׁךְ
ג ד וְתִירָס: וּבְנֵי גֹּמֶר אַשְׁכְּנַז וְרִיפַת וְתֹגַרְמָה: וּבְנֵי יָוָן אֱלִישָׁה
ה וְתַרְשִׁישׁ כִּתִּים וְדֹדָנִים: מֵאֵלֶּה נִפְרְדוּ אִיֵּי הַגּוֹיִם בְּאַרְצֹתָם
ו אִישׁ לִלְשֹׁנוֹ לְמִשְׁפְּחֹתָם בְּגוֹיֵהֶם: וּבְנֵי חָם כּוּשׁ וּמִצְרַיִם
ז וּפוּט וּכְנָעַן: וּבְנֵי כוּשׁ סְבָא וַחֲוִילָה וְסַבְתָּה וְרַעְמָה
ח וְסַבְתְּכָא וּבְנֵי רַעְמָה שְׁבָא וּדְדָן: וְכוּשׁ יָלַד אֶת־נִמְרֹד
ט הוּא הֵחֵל לִהְיוֹת גִּבֹּר בָּאָרֶץ: הוּא־הָיָה גִבֹּר־צַיִד לִפְנֵי
י יְהוָה עַל־כֵּן יֵאָמַר כְּנִמְרֹד גִּבּוֹר צַיִד לִפְנֵי יְהוָה: וַתְּהִי
רֵאשִׁית מַמְלַכְתּוֹ בָּבֶל וְאֶרֶךְ וְאַכַּד וְכַלְנֵה בְּאֶרֶץ שִׁנְעָר:
יא מִן־הָאָרֶץ הַהִוא יָצָא אַשּׁוּר וַיִּבֶן אֶת־נִינְוֵה וְאֶת־רְחֹבֹת
יב עִיר וְאֶת־כָּלַח: וְאֶת־רֶסֶן בֵּין נִינְוֵה וּבֵין כָּלַח הִוא הָעִיר
יג הַגְּדֹלָה: וּמִצְרַיִם יָלַד אֶת־לוּדִים וְאֶת־עֲנָמִים וְאֶת־לְהָבִים
יד וְאֶת־נַפְתֻּחִים: וְאֶת־פַּתְרֻסִים וְאֶת־כַּסְלֻחִים אֲשֶׁר יָצְאוּ

9:23 עֶרְוַת אֲבִיהֶם *The nakedness of their father* – The opening of the *parasha* was full of expectation; no one else in the Torah receives such accolades as Noaḥ. Yet the last scene of his life is full of pathos. The decorousness of Shem and Yefet's behavior cannot hide from us the embarrassment they feel at knowing

Kasluḥim – from whom the Philistines descended – and
15 the Kaftorim. Kenaan fathered Tzidon,
16 his firstborn, and Ḥet, and the Jebusites, Amorites, and
17 18 Girgashites, the Hivites, Arkites, and Sinites, the Arvadites,
Zemarites, and Hamatites. Later, the Canaanite families
19 were dispersed. The Canaanite borders were from Sidon
toward Gerar near Aza, and toward Sedom, Amora, Adma,
20 and Tzevoyim, near Lasha. These were the descendants of
Ḥam, by their clans and their languages, with their lands
21 and their nations. Sons were also born to Shem.
The older brother of Yefet, he was the ancestor of all the
22 sons of Ever. Shem's sons were Elam, Ashur, Arpakhshad,
23 Lud, and Aram. Aram's sons were Utz, Ḥul, Geter, and
24 Mash. Arpakhshad was the father of Shelaḥ, and Shelaḥ
25 was the father of Ever. To Ever, two sons were born. One
was named Peleg, for in his time the earth was divided.
26 His brother was named Yoktan. Yoktan was the father of
27 Almodad, Shelef, Ḥatzarmavet, Yeraḥ, Hadoram, Uzal,
28 29 Dikla, Oval, Avimael, Sheva, Ofir, Ḥavila, and Yovav; all
30 these were Yoktan's sons. Their settlements extended from
31 Mesha toward Sefar, in the eastern hill country. These
were the descendants of Shem, by their clans and their
32 languages, with their lands and their nations. These, then,
are the clans of the sons of Noaḥ, by their lines, in their
nations. And from these, the nations spread out across the
earth after the flood.
11 1 The whole world spoke the same language, the same SHEVI'I
2 words. And as the people migrated from the east they

and ecological. It depends on respect for boundaries – in a word, *order*.

The opposite of order is Bavel – "confusion." The builders of the tower defy the principle stated in the book of Psalms: "The heavens are the LORD's; but He has granted the earth to mankind" (Ps. 115:16). The Hebrew word *avera*, like its English equivalent, "transgression," means "straying across a boundary, entering forbidden territory." It is a failure to engage in *havdala*, knowing the difference between one thing and another and what belongs where. Aspiring to make their home in heaven, the builders of Bavel fail to honor the distinction between man and God.

Their punishment precisely fits the

טו מִשָּׁם פְּלִשְׁתִּים וְאֶת־כַּפְתֹּרִים׃ וּכְנַעַן יָלַד אֶת־
טז צִידֹן בְּכֹרוֹ וְאֶת־חֵת׃ וְאֶת־הַיְבוּסִי וְאֶת־הָאֱמֹרִי וְאֵת
יז יח הַגִּרְגָּשִׁי׃ וְאֶת־הַחִוִּי וְאֶת־הַעַרְקִי וְאֶת־הַסִּינִי׃ וְאֶת־
הָאַרְוָדִי וְאֶת־הַצְּמָרִי וְאֶת־הַחֲמָתִי וְאַחַר נָפֹצוּ מִשְׁפְּחוֹת
יט הַכְּנַעֲנִי׃ וַיְהִי גְּבוּל הַכְּנַעֲנִי מִצִּידֹן בֹּאֲכָה גְרָרָה
עַד־עַזָּה בֹּאֲכָה סְדֹמָה וַעֲמֹרָה וְאַדְמָה וּצְבֹיִם עַד־
כ לָשַׁע׃ אֵלֶּה בְנֵי־חָם לְמִשְׁפְּחֹתָם לִלְשֹׁנֹתָם בְּאַרְצֹתָם
כא בְּגוֹיֵהֶם׃ וּלְשֵׁם יֻלַּד גַּם־הוּא אֲבִי כָּל־בְּנֵי־
כב עֵבֶר אֲחִי יֶפֶת הַגָּדוֹל׃ בְּנֵי שֵׁם עֵילָם וְאַשּׁוּר וְאַרְפַּכְשַׁד וְלוּד
כג כד וַאֲרָם׃ וּבְנֵי אֲרָם עוּץ וְחוּל וְגֶתֶר וָמַשׁ׃ וְאַרְפַּכְשַׁד יָלַד אֶת־
כה שָׁלַח וְשֶׁלַח יָלַד אֶת־עֵבֶר׃ וּלְעֵבֶר יֻלַּד שְׁנֵי בָנִים שֵׁם הָאֶחָד
כו פֶּלֶג כִּי בְיָמָיו נִפְלְגָה הָאָרֶץ וְשֵׁם אָחִיו יָקְטָן׃ וְיָקְטָן יָלַד
כז אֶת־אַלְמוֹדָד וְאֶת־שָׁלֶף וְאֶת־חֲצַרְמָוֶת וְאֶת־יָרַח׃ וְאֶת־
כח הֲדוֹרָם וְאֶת־אוּזָל וְאֶת־דִּקְלָה׃ וְאֶת־עוֹבָל וְאֶת־אֲבִימָאֵל
כט וְאֶת־שְׁבָא׃ וְאֶת־אוֹפִר וְאֶת־חֲוִילָה וְאֶת־יוֹבָב כָּל־אֵלֶּה
ל בְּנֵי יָקְטָן׃ וַיְהִי מוֹשָׁבָם מִמֵּשָׁא בֹּאֲכָה סְפָרָה הַר הַקֶּדֶם׃
לא אֵלֶּה בְנֵי־שֵׁם לְמִשְׁפְּחֹתָם לִלְשֹׁנֹתָם בְּאַרְצֹתָם לְגוֹיֵהֶם׃
לב אֵלֶּה מִשְׁפְּחֹת בְּנֵי־נֹחַ לְתוֹלְדֹתָם בְּגוֹיֵהֶם וּמֵאֵלֶּה נִפְרְדוּ
הַגּוֹיִם בָּאָרֶץ אַחַר הַמַּבּוּל׃
יא א ב וַיְהִי כָל־הָאָרֶץ שָׂפָה אֶחָת וּדְבָרִים אֲחָדִים׃ וַיְהִי בְּנָסְעָם ט שביעי

THE TOWER OF BAVEL

Bavel is a story about the relationship between heaven and earth. Specifically, it echoes the first verse in the Torah: "When God began creating heaven and earth...." Bavel is what happens when human beings, in full exercise of their creative powers, attempt to build a cosmopolis, the city as man-made universe in which they, not God, rule.

One of the key words of the first chapter of Genesis, as we noted there, is the root *b-d-l*, "to distinguish, separate, impose, and respect order." At the end of creation, immediately prior to the Sabbath, God "saw all that He had made, and it was *very* good," meaning: Each thing was good in itself, and *very* good in relation to all else. The goodness of the world in Genesis 1 is ontological

found a valley in the land of Shinar and settled there.
3 They said to each other, "Come, let us make bricks, let us
bake them thoroughly." They used bricks for stone and tar
4 for mortar. And they said, "Come, let us build ourselves
a city and a tower that reaches the heavens, and make a

The whole land was of one speech and a shared vocabulary: an enforced shared speech by imperial conquest. This describes the practice of the world's first empires. We have historical evidence dating back to the neo-Assyrians who asserted their supremacy by insisting that their language was the only one to be used by the nations and populations they had defeated. In other words, this is an attempt to frustrate the natural process which has already been described in the previous chapter, which talked about the emergence of seventy languages and human diversity.

The great nineteenth-century commentator Rabbi Naftali Tzvi Yehuda Berlin questions the apparent repetition: "the same language, the same words." "The same words," Rabbi Berlin suggests, means "they all had the same opinions," they were of like mind. There is nothing dangerous in this initially. They all want to build a city and a tower. The danger lies in the future. Having built a cosmopolis, a total and totalizing man-made environment, the risk is that they will impose a man-made uniformity on all who live there. There will be no freedom of speech, no dignity of dissent. Any disagreement will be held to endanger the necessary unity of the *polis*, the city-state (*Haamek Davar* on Gen. 11:4). Rabbi Berlin, who taught in the yeshiva of Volozhin in Belarus, died in 1893, before the Russian Revolution, but in retrospect his words were prophetic. Bavel was, he implied, the first totalitarianism.

11:3 וְנִשְׂרְפָה לִשְׂרֵפָה *Let us bake them thoroughly* – The men on the plain at Shinar make a technological discovery. They learn how to make bricks by pouring clay into molds, drying it in the sun, and eventually firing it in kilns. This gives them the first processed (as opposed to entirely natural) building material in history, enabling the construction of buildings on a larger scale and reaching greater heights than hitherto. As after so many other technological advances, they immediately conclude that they now have the power of gods. They are no longer subject to nature. They have become its masters. They will storm the heavens. Their man-made environment – the city with its ziggurat or artificial mountain – will replicate the structure of the cosmos, but here they will rule, not God. It is a supreme act of hubris, but one committed time and again in history.

11:4 עִיר וּמִגְדָּל *A city and a tower* – These towers – of which the remains of at least thirty have been discovered – were man-made "holy mountains," the mountain being the place where heaven and earth

ג מִקֶּדֶם וַיִּמְצְאוּ בִקְעָה בְּאֶרֶץ שִׁנְעָר וַיֵּשְׁבוּ שָׁם׃ וַיֹּאמְרוּ
אִישׁ אֶל־רֵעֵהוּ הָבָה נִלְבְּנָה לְבֵנִים וְנִשְׂרְפָה לִשְׂרֵפָה וַתְּהִי
ד לָהֶם הַלְּבֵנָה לְאָבֶן וְהַחֵמָר הָיָה לָהֶם לַחֹמֶר׃ וַיֹּאמְרוּ הָבָה ׀
נִבְנֶה־לָּנוּ עִיר וּמִגְדָּל וְרֹאשׁוֹ בַשָּׁמַיִם וְנַעֲשֶׂה־לָּנוּ שֵׁם פֶּן־

---

crime. By creating disorder, they inherit disorder, an inability to communicate with one another and thus engage in the collaborative activity on which all human achievement depends. By dishonoring language – God creates the world with words, because words create order, classifying and labeling distinctions – their language is dishonored. By aspiring to reach heaven by technological prowess rather than moral conduct, the builders of Bavel discover that not only do we fail to reach heaven, we also lose our compact nature, our unity, on earth.

Bavel is a profound commentary on the human desire to take the place of God. The word "responsibility" comes from the word "response." It implies the existence of an Other who has legitimate claims on my conduct, for or to whom I am accountable. The Hebrew equivalent, *aḥrayut*, derives from the word *aḥer*, meaning "other." Responsibility is intrinsically relational. H. Richard Niebuhr defines the biblical ethic of responsibility as the principle "God is acting in all actions upon you. So respond to all actions upon you as to respond to His action." In other words, your life is a personal communication from God, who awaits your reply.

Bavel represents the failure of ontological responsibility, the idea that we are accountable to something or someone beyond ourselves. Fired by technological progress, the men on the plain of Shinar attempt to construct a self-sufficient universe in which man is accountable only to himself. "The possession of unlimited power," wrote Lord Acton of the later city-state of Athens, "corrodes the conscience, hardens the heart, and confounds the understanding of monarchs.... It is bad to be oppressed by a minority, but it is worse to be oppressed by a majority.... The philosophy that was then in the ascendent taught them that there is no law superior to that of the State – the lawgiver is above the law. It followed that the sovereign people had a right to do whatever was within its power, and was bound by no rule of right or wrong but its own judgment of expediency."

The result was that "the emancipated people... became a tyrant." Responsibility is *response*-ability: accountability to an authority beyond us, in the here and now. The alternative, from Bavel to Nazi Germany and Soviet Communism, is a story of human blood shed on the altar dedicated to the greater glory of humankind.

11:1 וַיְהִי כָל הָאָרֶץ שָׂפָה אֶחָת וּדְבָרִים אֲחָדִים *The whole world spoke... the same words* – Perhaps the whole land, not the whole world.

name for ourselves. Otherwise we will be scattered across
5 the face of the earth." But the LORD came down to see
the city and the tower being built by the children of men.
6 The LORD said, "If, as one people with one language, they
have begun to do this, nothing they plan to do will be
7 impossible for them. Let us go down and confuse their
language so that one will not understand the speech of
8 another." From there the LORD scattered them all over

11:4 עַל פְּנֵי כָל הָאָרֶץ *Across the face of the earth* – The essence of Genesis 1 is ordered diversity. By attempting to suppress the individuality of the nations they conquer and their distinct languages, the Mesopotamians, the builders of Bavel, transgress that set of harmonious boundaries created by God: biodiversity in Genesis 1, human diversity in Genesis 10.

11:5 וַיֵּרֶד יהוה *The LORD came down* – The world of myth, against which Judaism is a sustained protest, is one in which boundaries are not observed. To the Judaic mind this is paganism, and it is never morally neutral. God creates order; man creates chaos – and the result is inevitably destructive.

The most fundamental boundary is the one created first: the differentiation between "heaven" and "earth." Defying this boundary is the sin of the builders of the tower. Their aspiration to "reach the heavens" is laughable, and indeed the Torah makes a joke of it. They think that their construction – three hundred feet high – has reached the heavens, whereas God has to "come down" to look at it.

When human beings try to become more than human, they quickly become less than human. Only when God is God can man be man. That means keeping heaven and earth distinct, organizing the latter only under the conscious sovereignty of the former. Without this there is little to prevent human beings from sacrificing the many for the sake of the few, or the few for the sake of the many. Humility in the presence of divine order is our last, best safeguard against mankind arrogating to itself power without restraint, might without right. Bavel means chaos, confusion, and the loss of that order which is a precondition of both nature – the world God creates – and culture – the world we create.

11:7 וְנָבְלָה שָׁם שְׂפָתָם *Confuse their language* – The story is shot through with literary devices: inversions, wordplays, ironies, and puns. It is chiastic, beginning and ending with the same words, *kol haaretz* ("The whole world/the earth"). In the middle comes the word *shamayim*, "the heavens." There is a lot of assonance: *sham*, *shem*, *shamayim*. One of the most masterly effects is that the two keywords, *l-v-n*, "brick," and *n-v-l*, "confuse," are precise inversions of one

ה נָפוּץ עַל־פְּנֵי כָל־הָאָרֶץ׃ וַיֵּרֶד יהוֹה לִרְאֹת אֶת־הָעִיר
ו וְאֶת־הַמִּגְדָּל אֲשֶׁר בָּנוּ בְּנֵי הָאָדָם׃ וַיֹּאמֶר יהוֹה הֵן עַם
אֶחָד וְשָׂפָה אַחַת לְכֻלָּם וְזֶה הַחִלָּם לַעֲשׂוֹת וְעַתָּה לֹא־
ז יִבָּצֵר מֵהֶם כֹּל אֲשֶׁר יָזְמוּ לַעֲשׂוֹת׃ הָבָה נֵרְדָה וְנָבְלָה
ח שָׁם שְׂפָתָם אֲשֶׁר לֹא יִשְׁמְעוּ אִישׁ שְׂפַת רֵעֵהוּ׃ וַיָּפֶץ יהוֹה

---

most visibly meet. Inscriptions on several of these buildings, decoded by archaeologists, refer, as does the Torah, to the idea that their top "reaches heaven." The largest – the great ziggurat of Babylon to which the Torah refers – was a structure of seven stories, three hundred feet high, on a base of roughly the same dimensions.

The pride of the people of Bavel lies in their newfound technological ability to construct buildings of unprecedented grandeur. They do not realize that the greatest creative power is language – a message signaled in the opening verses of the Torah with the grand simplicity of the repeated formula "God said... and there was." What is holy for the Torah is not power, but the use to which we put it, and this is intrinsically linked to language – the medium in which we frame our ideals, construct imaginative possibilities, and call others to join us in realizing them. The word is prior to the work. With great poetic justice, it is not a technical problem that causes the builders to abandon the project, but rather the loss of the ability to communicate.

11:4 פֶּן־נָפוּץ *Otherwise we will be scattered* – The people are attempting to frustrate God's command in Genesis 1, "Be fruitful and multiply. Fill the earth." They attempt to concentrate in a city. Throughout the Torah we find a critique of urban civilization. The first city is founded by the first murderer, following the first fratricide. The city is born in blood. The people of Sedom do not like strangers. They do not see them as protected by law – nor even by the conventions of hospitality. There is a clear suggestion of sexual depravity and potential violence. There is also the idea of a crowd, a mob. People in a crowd can commit crimes they would not dream of doing on their own. Not by accident are the patriarchs and matriarchs not city dwellers.

In Bavel, human life is cheap. (When the tower was being built, said the Sages, if a person fell and died, no one noticed. If a brick fell, they wept.) In Egypt, entire populations – among them, eventually, the children of Israel – can be pressed into service as a labor force to build pyramids, temples, and monuments, many of which still stand today.

The Tanakh is not opposed to cities as such. In a sense, the Torah project is to sustain strong face-to-face communities even within cities. The antitype of the dehumanizing city is Jerusalem, home of the Divine Presence. But that, at this stage of history, lies long in the future.

the earth, and they abandoned the building of the city.
9 That is why it was called Bavel, because it was there that
the LORD confused the language of all the earth; and
from there the LORD scattered them all across the face
of the earth.
10 These are the descendants of Shem. When Shem was
one hundred years old, he had a son, Arpakhshad,
11 two years after the flood. After Arpakhshad was born,
Shem lived five hundred years and had other sons and
12 daughters. When Arpakhshad was thirty-five
13 years old, he had a son, Shelaḥ. After Shelaḥ was born,
Arpakhshad lived four hundred and three years and had
14 other sons and daughters. When Shelaḥ
15 was thirty years old, he had a son, Ever. After Ever was
born, Shelaḥ lived four hundred and three years and had
16 other sons and daughters. Ever lived thirty-
17 four years and then had a son, Peleg. After Peleg was
born, Ever lived four hundred and thirty years and had
18 other sons and daughters. Peleg lived thirty
19 years and then had a son, Reu. After Reu was born,

11:31 וַיִּקַּח תֶּרַח אֶת אַבְרָם בְּנוֹ *Teraḥ took his son Avram* – The story of Avraham can be read in two ways, depending on how we reconcile the end of chapter 11 with the beginning of chapter 12. One reading emphasizes discontinuity. Avraham breaks with all that went before. The other emphasizes continuity. Teraḥ, his father, has already begun to wrestle with idolatry. He has set out on the long walk to the land which will eventually become holy, but stops halfway. Avraham completes the journey his father began.

Perhaps childhood itself has the same ambiguity. There are times, especially in adolescence, when we tell ourselves that we are breaking with our parents, charting a path that is completely new. Only in retrospect, many years later, do we realize how much we owe our parents – how, even at those moments when we felt most strongly that we were setting out on a journey uniquely our own, we were, in fact, living out the ideals and aspirations that we learned from them.

We see, then, that the break between Parashat Noaḥ and Parashat Lekh Lekha is more than a technical one. It allows us two perspectives on the continuity or otherwise between the first, universal chapter of the human story, and the particular story of Avraham's journey, which is about to begin.

ט אֹתָם מִשָּׁם עַל־פְּנֵי כָל־הָאָרֶץ וַיַּחְדְּלוּ לִבְנֹת הָעִיר׃ עַל־כֵּן
קָרָא שְׁמָהּ בָּבֶל כִּי־שָׁם בָּלַל יְהוָה שְׂפַת כָּל־הָאָרֶץ וּמִשָּׁם
הֱפִיצָם יְהוָה עַל־פְּנֵי כָּל־הָאָרֶץ׃
י אֵלֶּה תּוֹלְדֹת שֵׁם שֵׁם בֶּן־מְאַת שָׁנָה וַיּוֹלֶד אֶת־אַרְפַּכְשָׁד
יא שְׁנָתַיִם אַחַר הַמַּבּוּל׃ וַיְחִי־שֵׁם אַחֲרֵי הוֹלִידוֹ אֶת־אַרְפַּכְשַׁד
יב חֲמֵשׁ מֵאוֹת שָׁנָה וַיּוֹלֶד בָּנִים וּבָנוֹת׃ וְאַרְפַּכְשַׁד
יג חַי חָמֵשׁ וּשְׁלֹשִׁים שָׁנָה וַיּוֹלֶד אֶת־שָׁלַח׃ וַיְחִי אַרְפַּכְשַׁד
אַחֲרֵי הוֹלִידוֹ אֶת־שֶׁלַח שָׁלֹשׁ שָׁנִים וְאַרְבַּע מֵאוֹת שָׁנָה
יד וַיּוֹלֶד בָּנִים וּבָנוֹת׃ וְשֶׁלַח חַי שְׁלֹשִׁים שָׁנָה וַיּוֹלֶד
טו אֶת־עֵבֶר׃ וַיְחִי־שֶׁלַח אַחֲרֵי הוֹלִידוֹ אֶת־עֵבֶר שָׁלֹשׁ שָׁנִים
טז וְאַרְבַּע מֵאוֹת שָׁנָה וַיּוֹלֶד בָּנִים וּבָנוֹת׃ וַיְחִי־
יז עֵבֶר אַרְבַּע וּשְׁלֹשִׁים שָׁנָה וַיּוֹלֶד אֶת־פָּלֶג׃ וַיְחִי־עֵבֶר
אַחֲרֵי הוֹלִידוֹ אֶת־פֶּלֶג שְׁלֹשִׁים שָׁנָה וְאַרְבַּע מֵאוֹת שָׁנָה
יח וַיּוֹלֶד בָּנִים וּבָנוֹת׃ וַיְחִי־פֶלֶג שְׁלֹשִׁים שָׁנָה
יט וַיּוֹלֶד אֶת־רְעוּ׃ וַיְחִי־פֶלֶג אַחֲרֵי הוֹלִידוֹ אֶת־רְעוּ תֵּשַׁע

---

another. As so often in the Torah, literary technique is closely related to the moral or spiritual message being conveyed. In this case the wordplay draws attention to the phenomenon of inversion itself. The results of human behavior are often the opposite of what was intended. The builders want to concentrate humanity in one place: "Let us build ourselves a city.... Otherwise we will be scattered across the face of the earth" (Gen. 11:4). The result is that they are dispersed: "From there the LORD scattered them all over the earth" (11:8). They want to "make a name" for themselves, and they do, but the name they make – Bavel – becomes an eternal symbol of confusion.

11:9 וּמִשָּׁם הֱפִיצָם יהוה *From there the LORD scattered them* – When, at the end of the Bavel story, God "confused the language" of the builders, He is not creating a new state of affairs but restoring the old. *When a single culture is imposed on all, suppressing the diversity of languages and traditions, this is an assault on our God-given differences,* and the result is tyranny and oppression. The Torah is showing us how – and why – the unity of God coexists with the diversity of humankind.

Peleg lived two hundred and nine years and had other
20 sons and daughters. Reu lived thirty-two
21 years and then had a son, Serug. After Serug was born,
Reu lived two hundred and seven years and had other
22 sons and daughters. Serug lived thirty years
23 and then had a son, Naḥor. After Naḥor was born,
Serug lived two hundred years and had other sons and
24 daughters. Naḥor lived twenty-nine years and
25 then had a son, Teraḥ. After Teraḥ was born, Naḥor
lived one hundred and nineteen years and had other
26 sons and daughters. Teraḥ lived seventy years
27 and fathered Avram, Naḥor, and Haran. These are the
descendants of Teraḥ. Teraḥ was the father of Avram,
28 Naḥor, and Haran, and Haran had a son, Lot. While his
father Teraḥ was still alive, Haran died in the land of his
29 birth, Ur Kasdim. Avram and Naḥor married; the name MAFTIR
of Avram's wife was Sarai, and the name of Naḥor's wife
was Milka. She was the daughter of Haran, father of Milka
30 31 and Yiska. And Sarai was barren – she had no child. Teraḥ
took his son Avram, and his grandson Lot, son of Haran,
and his daughter-in-law Sarai, his son Avram's wife, and
together they set out from Ur Kasdim to go to the land
of Canaan. But when they arrived at Ḥaran, they settled
32 there. Teraḥ lived two hundred and five years, and he died
in Ḥaran.

The haftara for Parashat Noaḥ is on page 1412.
On Rosh Ḥodesh Marḥeshvan some read the haftara on page 1640.

כ שְׁנֵים וּמָאתַיִם שָׁנָה וַיּוֹלֶד בָּנִים וּבָנוֹת׃ וַיְחִי
כא רְעוּ שְׁתַּיִם וּשְׁלֹשִׁים שָׁנָה וַיּוֹלֶד אֶת־שְׂרוּג׃ וַיְחִי רְעוּ אַחֲרֵי
הוֹלִידוֹ אֶת־שְׂרוּג שֶׁבַע שָׁנִים וּמָאתַיִם שָׁנָה וַיּוֹלֶד בָּנִים
כב וּבָנוֹת׃ וַיְחִי שְׂרוּג שְׁלֹשִׁים שָׁנָה וַיּוֹלֶד אֶת־נָחוֹר׃
כג וַיְחִי שְׂרוּג אַחֲרֵי הוֹלִידוֹ אֶת־נָחוֹר מָאתַיִם שָׁנָה וַיּוֹלֶד בָּנִים
כד וּבָנוֹת׃ וַיְחִי נָחוֹר תֵּשַׁע וְעֶשְׂרִים שָׁנָה וַיּוֹלֶד
כה אֶת־תָּרַח׃ וַיְחִי נָחוֹר אַחֲרֵי הוֹלִידוֹ אֶת־תֶּרַח תְּשַׁע־עֶשְׂרֵה
כו שָׁנָה וּמְאַת שָׁנָה וַיּוֹלֶד בָּנִים וּבָנוֹת׃ וַיְחִי־תֶרַח
כז שִׁבְעִים שָׁנָה וַיּוֹלֶד אֶת־אַבְרָם אֶת־נָחוֹר וְאֶת־הָרָן׃ וְאֵלֶּה
תּוֹלְדֹת תֶּרַח תֶּרַח הוֹלִיד אֶת־אַבְרָם אֶת־נָחוֹר וְאֶת־הָרָן
כח וְהָרָן הוֹלִיד אֶת־לוֹט׃ וַיָּמָת הָרָן עַל־פְּנֵי תֶּרַח אָבִיו בְּאֶרֶץ
כט מוֹלַדְתּוֹ בְּאוּר כַּשְׂדִּים׃ וַיִּקַּח אַבְרָם וְנָחוֹר לָהֶם נָשִׁים שֵׁם מפטיר
אֵשֶׁת־אַבְרָם שָׂרָי וְשֵׁם אֵשֶׁת־נָחוֹר מִלְכָּה בַּת־הָרָן אֲבִי־
ל לא מִלְכָּה וַאֲבִי יִסְכָּה׃ וַתְּהִי שָׂרַי עֲקָרָה אֵין לָהּ וָלָד׃ וַיִּקַּח
תֶּרַח אֶת־אַבְרָם בְּנוֹ וְאֶת־לוֹט בֶּן־הָרָן בֶּן־בְּנוֹ וְאֵת שָׂרַי
כַּלָּתוֹ אֵשֶׁת אַבְרָם בְּנוֹ וַיֵּצְאוּ אִתָּם מֵאוּר כַּשְׂדִּים לָלֶכֶת
לב אַרְצָה כְּנַעַן וַיָּבֹאוּ עַד־חָרָן וַיֵּשְׁבוּ שָׁם׃ וַיִּהְיוּ יְמֵי־תֶרַח
חָמֵשׁ שָׁנִים וּמָאתַיִם שָׁנָה וַיָּמָת תֶּרַח בְּחָרָן׃

The הפטרה *for* פרשת נח *is on page 1413.*
On ראש חודש מרחשוון *some read the* הפטרה *on page 1641.*

Parashat Lekh Lekha

12 1 The LORD said to Avram, "Go – from your land, your
birthplace, and your father's house – to the land that I

harmony but in dissonance. If God created the world, then why does He allow man to destroy the world? Can God have made the world only to abandon it?

From time immemorial to the present, there have always been two ways of seeing the world. The first view says there is no God. There are contending forces, chance and necessity – the chance that produces variation, and the necessity that gives the strong victory over the weak. From this perspective, the evolution of the universe is inexorable and blind, and therefore we never know *why*. There is no why. There is no palace. There are only flames.

The second view insists that there is a God. All that exists or transpires does so because He willed it. Therefore, all injustice is an illusion. Perhaps the world itself is an illusion. When the innocent suffer, it is to teach them to find faith through suffering, the soul's strength through the body's torments. Evil is the cloak that masks the good. There is a question, but there is always an answer, for if we could understand God we would know that the world is as it is because it would be less good were it otherwise. There is a palace. Therefore there are no flames.

The faith of Avraham begins in the refusal to accept either answer. Suppose both God and evil exist? Suppose there are both the palace and the flames?

It is in that cry, that sacred discontent, that Avraham's journey begins. At the heart of reality is a contradiction between order and chaos, and it has no resolution at the level of thought. It can be resolved only at the level of action, only by making the world other than it is. To be a Jew is to have the courage to refuse easy answers; to reject either consolation or despair. God exists; therefore life has a purpose. Evil exists; therefore we have not yet achieved that purpose. Until then we must travel, just as Avraham and Sara traveled, to begin the task of shaping a different kind of world.

What haunts us about the midrash is not just Avraham's question, but God's reply. He says, in effect, "I am here," without explaining the flames. He does not attempt to put out the fire. It is as if, instead, He were calling for help. God made the building. Man set it on fire. Only man can put out the flames. Avraham asks God, "Where are You?" God replies, "I am here; where are you?" Man asks God, "Why did You abandon me?" So begins a dialogue between earth and heaven, which has not ceased for four thousand years. In these questions, which only the other can answer, God and man find one another. Perhaps only together can they extinguish the flames.

פרשת לך לך

יב א וַיֹּאמֶר יהוה אֶל־אַבְרָם לֶךְ־לְךָ מֵאַרְצְךָ וּמִמּוֹלַדְתְּךָ וּמִבֵּית י

LEKH LEKHA

In response to the call of God, Avraham and Sara begin their journey to a new land and a new kind of faith, which will become the context of the entire Jewish drama thereafter.

Avraham's life is a culmination of all that has gone before. The first four dramas of Genesis dealt with the evasion and abdication of responsibility. Adam denies personal responsibility. Kayin denies moral responsibility. Noaḥ fails the test of collective responsibility. Bavel was a rejection of ontological responsibility (see ch. 11, "The Tower of Bavel"). Avraham represents the turning point, offering a counterpoint to the previous failures.

The first words of God to Avraham, as we shall see, are a call to personal responsibility. By entering into battle, in Genesis 14, to rescue (not his brother, but his brother's son) Lot, Avraham exercises *moral* responsibility. Unlike Kayin, he *is* his brother's keeper. As the drama builds in the next *parasha,* he will display collective and finally ontological responsibility in the greatest trial of all.

AVRAHAM'S CALL

Tradition offers several explanations of how Avraham and Sara's journey began. According to one, Avraham was the iconoclast who broke his father's idols. According to another, he was the philosopher who, seeing people worship the sun and the stars, asked, "But who created *them*?" But the Midrash contains a third and altogether more radical reading:

> "The Lord said to Avram: 'Go....'" To what may this be compared? To a man who was traveling from place to place when he saw a palace in flames. He wondered, "Is it possible that the palace lacks an owner?" The owner of the palace looked out and said, "I am the owner of the palace." So Avraham our father said, "Is it possible that the world lacks a ruler?" The Holy One, blessed be He, looked out and said to him, "I am the ruler, the sovereign of the universe." (*Midrash HaGadol*, Bereishit 12:1)

This is a deeply enigmatic passage. Avraham sees a palace. The world has order, and therefore it has a creator. But the palace is in flames. The world is full of *dis*order, of evil, violence, and injustice. Now, no one builds a building and then deserts it. If there is a fire, there must be someone to put it out. The building must have an owner. If so, where is he? That is the question, and it gives Avraham no peace. With this we arrive at the starting point of Jewish faith. Faith is born not in the answer but in the question, not in

2 will show you. I will make you a great nation, and I will
bless you and make your name great. You will become a
3 blessing. And I will bless those who bless you, and those

When power was worshipped, it meant constructing a society that cared for the powerless, the widow, orphan, and stranger. During centuries in which the mass of mankind was sunk in ignorance, it meant honoring education as the key to human dignity and creating schools to provide universal literacy. In ages of radical individualism like today, it means knowing that we are not what we own but what we share, not what we buy but what we give. To be a Jew is to be willing to hear the still, small voice of eternity urging us to travel, move, go on ahead, continuing Avraham's journey toward that unknown destination at the far horizon of hope.

12:1 מֵאַרְצְךָ וּמִמּוֹלַדְתְּךָ וּמִבֵּית אָבִיךָ *From your land, your birthplace, and your father's house* – The call to Avraham is a counter-commentary to the three great determinisms of the modern world. Karl Marx held that behavior is determined by structures of power in society, among them the ownership of land. Therefore God said, "Go from your land." Spinoza believed human conduct is given by the instincts we acquire at birth (what we now might call genetic determinism). Therefore God said, "Go from your birthplace." Freud held that we are shaped by early experiences in childhood. Therefore God said, "Go from your father's house." Avraham is the refutation of determinism. There are structures of power, but we can stand outside them. There are genetic influences on our behavior, but we can master them. We are shaped by our parents, but we can go beyond them. Avraham's journey is as much psychological as geographical. Like the Israelites in Moshe's day, he is traveling to freedom.

12:1 אֶל־הָאָרֶץ אֲשֶׁר אַרְאֶךָּ *To the land that I will show you* – Rashi, following an ancient exegetic tradition, translates God's opening words as "Journey for yourself" (Gen. 12:1). According to him, God is saying, "Travel for your own benefit and good. There I will make you into a great nation; here you will not have the merit of having children." In His first words to Avraham, God is already intimating that what seems like a sacrifice is, in the long run, not so. Sometimes we have to give up our past in order to acquire a future. "Go for yourself" – believe in what you can become.

12:2 וֶהְיֵה בְּרָכָה *You will become a blessing* – There has never been anyone like Avraham, yet the Torah is exceptionally understated in its account of him. Leaving aside midrashic interpretations, the Torah's presentation of Avraham does not fit any conventional image of the religious hero. To be sure, he is a man of exemplary virtue. But if we were asked to characterize him with adjectives, the words that spring to mind – gentle, kind, gracious – are not those usually associated

ב אָבִיךָ אֶל־הָאָרֶץ אֲשֶׁר אַרְאֶךָּ׃ וְאֶעֶשְׂךָ לְגוֹי גָּדוֹל וַאֲבָרֶכְךָ

ג וַאֲגַדְּלָה שְׁמֶךָ וֶהְיֵה בְּרָכָה׃ וַאֲבָרְכָה מְבָרְכֶיךָ וּמְקַלֶּלְךָ

12:1 לֶךְ־לְךָ *Go* – In Hebrew the suggestive phrase is *Lekh lekha* – literally, "Go for yourself," or possibly "Go to yourself." A more midrashic interpretation takes the phrase to mean "Go *with* yourself" – meaning, by traveling from place to place you will extend your influence not over one land but many:

> When the Holy One said to Avraham, "Go – from your land, your birthplace, and your father's house" what did Avraham resemble? A jar of scent with a tight-fitting lid put away in a corner so that its fragrance could not go forth. As soon as it was moved from that place and opened, its fragrance began to spread. So the Holy One said to Avraham, "Avraham, many good deeds are in you. Travel about from place to place, so that the greatness of your name will go forth in My world." (Bereshit Rabba 39:2)

Avraham is commanded to leave his place in order to testify to the existence of a God not bounded by place – creator and sovereign of the entire universe. Avraham and Sara are to be like perfume, leaving a trace of their presence wherever they go. Implicit in this midrash is the idea that the fate of the first Jews already prefigured that of their descendants, who would be scattered throughout the world in order to spread knowledge of God throughout the world. Unusually, exile is seen here not as punishment but as a necessary corollary of a faith that sees God everywhere. *Lekh lekha* means "Go with yourself" – your beliefs, your way of life, your faith.

12:1 לֶךְ־לְךָ מֵאַרְצְךָ *Go – from your land* – There is another interpretation of the phrase *Lekh lekha*: "Go by yourself." Only a person willing to stand alone, singular and unique, can worship the God who is alone, singular and unique. Only one able to leave behind the natural sources of identity – home, family, culture and society – can encounter God who stands above and beyond nature. Avraham's children are summoned to be the people that defy the laws of nature because they refuse to define themselves as the products of nature. That is not to say that economic or biological or psychological forces have no part to play in human behavior. They do. But with sufficient imagination, determination, discipline, and courage we can rise above them. Avraham does. So, at most times, will his children.

Lekh Lekha in this sense means being prepared to take an often lonely journey: "Go by yourself." To be a child of Avraham is to have the courage to be different, to challenge the idols of the age, whatever the idols and whichever the age. In an era of polytheism, that meant seeing the universe as the product of a single creative will – and therefore not meaningless but coherent, meaningful.

who curse you I will curse. And through you, all the
4 families of the earth will be blessed." So Avram went, as
the LORD had told him, and with him went Lot. Avram
5 was seventy-five years old when he left Ḥaran. Avram
took Sarai his wife, and Lot his nephew, and all the wealth
they had acquired and the people they had gathered in
Ḥaran. They set out to go to the land of Canaan, and they
6 entered the land of Canaan. Avram traveled through the
land to the region of Shekhem, to the Oak of Moreh.
7 The Canaanites were then in the land. Then the LORD
appeared to Avram and said, "To your descendants I will
give this land." There he built an altar to the LORD, who
8 had appeared to him. And from there he moved on to the
hills east of Beit El, and pitched his tent with Beit El to
the west and Ai to the east. There he built an altar to the
9 LORD and called on the name of the LORD. Then Avram
journeyed on, traveling toward the Negev.

---

hopefully for blessing, on many cultures. This has been a recurring theme of Jewish experience.

12:4 כַּאֲשֶׁר דִּבֶּר אֵלָיו יהוה *As the LORD had told him* – Avraham is a new human type: the person whose life is a response to the call of God. Until now, with the exception of Noaḥ, we have encountered human beings for whom God's command is a constraint from which they try to break free, by violence in the case of Kayin and the generation of the flood, by hubris in the case of the builders of Bavel. Avraham is different. For him, the command is life itself. God speaks; Avraham listens and acts, without resistance on the one hand, and with pride on the other. His life is an answer to God's question; his existence is lived in the conscious presence of the divine will.

With Avraham a new faith is born: the faith of responsibility, in which the divine command and the human act meet and give birth to a new and blessed order, built on the principles of righteousness and justice. Judaism is supremely a religion of freedom – not freedom in the modern sense, the ability to do what we *like*, but in the ethical sense of the ability to choose to do what we *should*, to become co-architects with God of a just and gracious social order. The former leads to a culture of rights, the latter to a culture of responsibilities: to *freedom as responsibility*.

ד אָאֹר וְנִבְרְכוּ בְךָ כֹּל מִשְׁפְּחֹת הָאֲדָמָה: וַיֵּלֶךְ אַבְרָם כַּאֲשֶׁר
דִּבֶּר אֵלָיו יְהוָה וַיֵּלֶךְ אִתּוֹ לוֹט וְאַבְרָם בֶּן־חָמֵשׁ שָׁנִים
ה וְשִׁבְעִים שָׁנָה בְּצֵאתוֹ מֵחָרָן: וַיִּקַּח אַבְרָם אֶת־שָׂרַי אִשְׁתּוֹ
וְאֶת־לוֹט בֶּן־אָחִיו וְאֶת־כָּל־רְכוּשָׁם אֲשֶׁר רָכָשׁוּ וְאֶת־הַנֶּפֶשׁ
אֲשֶׁר־עָשׂוּ בְחָרָן וַיֵּצְאוּ לָלֶכֶת אַרְצָה כְּנַעַן וַיָּבֹאוּ אַרְצָה
ו כְּנָעַן: וַיַּעֲבֹר אַבְרָם בָּאָרֶץ עַד מְקוֹם שְׁכֶם עַד אֵלוֹן מוֹרֶה
ז וְהַכְּנַעֲנִי אָז בָּאָרֶץ: וַיֵּרָא יְהוָה אֶל־אַבְרָם וַיֹּאמֶר לְזַרְעֲךָ
אֶתֵּן אֶת־הָאָרֶץ הַזֹּאת וַיִּבֶן שָׁם מִזְבֵּחַ לַיהוָה הַנִּרְאֶה אֵלָיו:
ח וַיַּעְתֵּק מִשָּׁם הָהָרָה מִקֶּדֶם לְבֵית־אֵל וַיֵּט אָהֳלֹה בֵּית־אֵל
מִיָּם וְהָעַי מִקֶּדֶם וַיִּבֶן־שָׁם מִזְבֵּחַ לַיהוָה וַיִּקְרָא בְּשֵׁם יְהוָה:
ט וַיִּסַּע אַבְרָם הָלוֹךְ וְנָסוֹעַ הַנֶּגְבָּה:

12:3 וְנִבְרְכוּ בְךָ כֹּל מִשְׁפְּחֹת הָאֲדָמָה *All the families of the earth will be blessed* – Half promise, half command. Avraham, unlike Adam and Noaḥ, is not a symbol of humanity as a whole. He is an individual singled out for a particular destiny. His children, too, become a people singled out for a particular destiny. Why Avraham is chosen, we never discover. That is one of the great enigmas of the Tanakh. But to what end he is chosen, we discover at the very beginning: to be a blessing. Not to his family or to God alone, but to all the peoples on earth. Somehow he will enrich the lives of others, of cultures and faiths very different from his own. Some will bless him for this, others will curse him. That much is known in advance. But the lives of his descendants will be peculiarly interwoven with the history of many nations, and they will leave their mark,

with the founder of a new faith. They are the kind of attributes to which any of us could aspire. None of us can be an Avraham, but all of us can take him as a role model.

Avraham is the paradigm of an unheroic hero, one who (in Rambam's lovely phrase) "does what is right because it is right" (*Hilkhot Teshuva* 10:2) and not for the sake of popularity or fame. As the founder of Judaism, Avraham gives us a vision of what it is to live directly and immediately in the presence of God, who knows our thoughts, our hopes, our fears, our dreams. This involves a radically new kind of heroism: the heroism of decency and goodness, integrity and faithfulness, the humble, unostentatious heroism of being willing to live by one's convictions though all the world thinks otherwise, being true to the call of eternity, not the noise of now.

10 There was a famine in the land. Avram went down to
Egypt to stay there for a while because the famine in the
11 land was severe. And as his arrival in Egypt drew close, he
said to Sarai his wife, "I know what a beautiful woman you
12 are. When the Egyptians see you, they will say, 'She is his
13 wife'; they will kill me and keep you alive. Please, say you
are my sister. Then I will be treated well for your sake, and
14 because of you my life will be spared." When Avram came SHENI
to Egypt, the Egyptians saw the woman, saw that she was
15 very beautiful indeed. And when Pharaoh's officials saw
her, they praised her to Pharaoh, and the woman was
16 taken into Pharaoh's palace. He treated Avram well for
her sake: he acquired flocks, herds, donkeys, male and
17 female servants, she-donkeys, and camels. But the LORD
struck Pharaoh and his household with terrible afflictions
18 because of Avram's wife Sarai. Pharaoh summoned Avram
and said, "What have you done to me? Why did you not
19 tell me she was your wife? Why did you say 'She is my
sister,' so that I took her as a wife? Now – here is your
20 wife. Take her. Go." Pharaoh gave orders to his men about
him, and they sent him on his way, together with his wife
13 1 and all that he had. Then Avram went up from Egypt to
the Negev with his wife and all he had, and with him went
2 Lot. And Avram had become very wealthy in cattle, silver,
3 and gold. From the Negev he continued on his journey to
Beit El, to the site between Beit El and Ai where his tent
4 had previously been, and where he had first made an altar.

---

this lack of faith that Avraham's children were sentenced to exile in Egypt centuries later.

No religion has held a higher view of humanity than the book that tells us we are each in the image and likeness of God. Yet none has been more honest about the failings of even the greatest. God does not ask us to be perfect. He asks us, instead, to take risks in pursuit of the right and the good, and to acknowledge the mistakes we will inevitably make. In Judaism, the moral life is about learning and growing, knowing that even the greatest have failings and even the worst have saving graces. It calls for humility about ourselves and generosity toward others. This unique blend of idealism and realism is morality at its most demanding and mature.

י וַיְהִי רָעָב בָּאָרֶץ וַיֵּרֶד אַבְרָם מִצְרַיְמָה לָגוּר שָׁם כִּי־כָבֵד
יא הָרָעָב בָּאָרֶץ: וַיְהִי כַּאֲשֶׁר הִקְרִיב לָבוֹא מִצְרָיְמָה וַיֹּאמֶר
אֶל־שָׂרַי אִשְׁתּוֹ הִנֵּה־נָא יָדַעְתִּי כִּי אִשָּׁה יְפַת־מַרְאֶה אָתְּ:
יב וְהָיָה כִּי־יִרְאוּ אֹתָךְ הַמִּצְרִים וְאָמְרוּ אִשְׁתּוֹ זֹאת וְהָרְגוּ אֹתִי
יג וְאֹתָךְ יְחַיּוּ: אִמְרִי־נָא אֲחֹתִי אָתְּ לְמַעַן יִיטַב־לִי בַעֲבוּרֵךְ
יד וְחָיְתָה נַפְשִׁי בִּגְלָלֵךְ: וַיְהִי כְּבוֹא אַבְרָם מִצְרָיְמָה וַיִּרְאוּ שני
טו הַמִּצְרִים אֶת־הָאִשָּׁה כִּי־יָפָה הִוא מְאֹד: וַיִּרְאוּ אֹתָהּ שָׂרֵי
פַרְעֹה וַיְהַלְלוּ אֹתָהּ אֶל־פַּרְעֹה וַתֻּקַּח הָאִשָּׁה בֵּית פַּרְעֹה:
טז וּלְאַבְרָם הֵיטִיב בַּעֲבוּרָהּ וַיְהִי־לוֹ צֹאן־וּבָקָר וַחֲמֹרִים
יז וַעֲבָדִים וּשְׁפָחֹת וַאֲתֹנֹת וּגְמַלִּים: וַיְנַגַּע יְהוָה ׀ אֶת־פַּרְעֹה
יח נְגָעִים גְּדֹלִים וְאֶת־בֵּיתוֹ עַל־דְּבַר שָׂרַי אֵשֶׁת אַבְרָם: וַיִּקְרָא
פַרְעֹה לְאַבְרָם וַיֹּאמֶר מַה־זֹּאת עָשִׂיתָ לִּי לָמָּה לֹא־הִגַּדְתָּ
יט לִּי כִּי אִשְׁתְּךָ הִוא: לָמָה אָמַרְתָּ אֲחֹתִי הִוא וָאֶקַּח אֹתָהּ לִי
כ לְאִשָּׁה וְעַתָּה הִנֵּה אִשְׁתְּךָ קַח וָלֵךְ: וַיְצַו עָלָיו פַּרְעֹה אֲנָשִׁים
יג א וַיְשַׁלְּחוּ אֹתוֹ וְאֶת־אִשְׁתּוֹ וְאֶת־כָּל־אֲשֶׁר־לוֹ: וַיַּעַל אַבְרָם
מִמִּצְרַיִם הוּא וְאִשְׁתּוֹ וְכָל־אֲשֶׁר־לוֹ וְלוֹט עִמּוֹ הַנֶּגְבָּה:
ב ג וְאַבְרָם כָּבֵד מְאֹד בַּמִּקְנֶה בַּכֶּסֶף וּבַזָּהָב: וַיֵּלֶךְ לְמַסָּעָיו
מִנֶּגֶב וְעַד־בֵּית־אֵל עַד־הַמָּקוֹם אֲשֶׁר־הָיָה שָׁם אָהֳלֹה
ד בַּתְּחִלָּה בֵּין בֵּית־אֵל וּבֵין הָעָי: אֶל־מְקוֹם הַמִּזְבֵּחַ אֲשֶׁר־

12:10 וַיֵּרֶד אַבְרָם מִצְרַיְמָה *Avram went down to Egypt* – In an extraordinary series of observations on Parashat Lekh Lekha, Ramban (Rabbi Moshe ben Naḥman Girondi, or Naḥmanides) delivers harsh criticisms of Avraham and Sara. The first has to do with Avraham's decision, after arriving at the land of Canaan, to leave and go to Egypt because "there was a famine in the land" (Gen. 12:10). According to Ramban (commentary on Gen. 12:10, based on Zohar, Tazria, 52a), Avraham should have stayed in Canaan; he should have had faith in God that He would sustain him despite the famine. Avraham's decision to leave was not his only error; he also put Sara in a position in which she was compelled to tell a lie. In saying that she was Avraham's sister and not his wife, she was taken into Pharaoh's harem where she might have been forced into adultery. This is a very harsh judgment, made more so by Ramban's further assertion that it was because of

▶

5 There Avram called on the name of the LORD. Lot, who SHELISHI
6 went with Avram, had flocks, herds, and tents as well, and
the land could not support them living together; so many
were their possessions that they were unable to live side
7 by side. A dispute broke out between Avram's herdsmen
and those of Lot; and the Canaanites and the Perizzites
8 were then too living in the land. Avram said to Lot,
"Please, let there be no friction between me and you, and
between my herdsmen and yours, for we are brothers.
9 The whole land lies before you; please separate yourself
from me. If you go to the left, I will go to the right; if you
10 go to the right, I will go to the left." Lot raised his eyes
and saw that the whole plain of the Jordan up to Tzoar
was well watered. It was like the garden of the LORD, like
the land of Egypt; this was before the LORD destroyed
11 Sedom and Amora. So Lot chose for himself the entire
plain of the Jordan. He traveled eastward, and the two
12 men separated. Avram settled in the land of Canaan while
Lot settled in the cities of the plain, pitching his tent near
13 Sedom. But the people of Sedom were evil, great sinners
14 against the LORD. After Lot had separated from him, the
LORD said to Avram, "Raise your eyes and look around
15 from where you are to the north, south, east, and west. All
the land you see I will give to you and your descendants
16 forever. I will make your descendants like the dust of the
earth: if anyone could count the dust of the earth, then
17 could your descendants be counted. Get up and walk
through the length and breadth of the land, for to you

None of this is apparent to Lot at the time. We imagine him standing on a hilltop surveying the panorama. He has no way of knowing the character of the people in the towns he sees, nor what will be their ultimate fate. Evidently Lot's character failure lies in the fact that he "raised his eyes and saw." Like Ḥava when she saw that the fruit of the Tree of Knowledge was "enticing to the eyes" (Gen. 3:6), Lot judges by appearances. The children of the covenant follow sound, not sight, the voice of God in the depths of the soul, not the seductive surfaces of the visible. So Avraham loses his first potential heir.

ה עָשָׂה שָׁם בָּרִאשֹׁנָה וַיִּקְרָא שָׁם אַבְרָם בְּשֵׁם יהוה׃ וְגַם־ שלישי
ו לְלוֹט הַהֹלֵךְ אֶת־אַבְרָם הָיָה צֹאן־וּבָקָר וְאֹהָלִים׃ וְלֹא־
נָשָׂא אֹתָם הָאָרֶץ לָשֶׁבֶת יַחְדָּו כִּי־הָיָה רְכוּשָׁם רָב וְלֹא
ז יָכְלוּ לָשֶׁבֶת יַחְדָּו׃ וַיְהִי־רִיב בֵּין רֹעֵי מִקְנֵה־אַבְרָם וּבֵין
ח רֹעֵי מִקְנֵה־לוֹט וְהַכְּנַעֲנִי וְהַפְּרִזִּי אָז יֹשֵׁב בָּאָרֶץ׃ וַיֹּאמֶר
אַבְרָם אֶל־לוֹט אַל־נָא תְהִי מְרִיבָה בֵּינִי וּבֵינֶךָ וּבֵין רֹעַי
ט וּבֵין רֹעֶיךָ כִּי־אֲנָשִׁים אַחִים אֲנָחְנוּ׃ הֲלֹא כָל־הָאָרֶץ
לְפָנֶיךָ הִפָּרֶד נָא מֵעָלָי אִם־הַשְּׂמֹאל וְאֵימִנָה וְאִם־הַיָּמִין
י וְאַשְׂמְאִילָה׃ וַיִּשָּׂא־לוֹט אֶת־עֵינָיו וַיַּרְא אֶת־כָּל־כִּכַּר הַיַּרְדֵּן
כִּי כֻלָּהּ מַשְׁקֶה לִפְנֵי ׀ שַׁחֵת יהוה אֶת־סְדֹם וְאֶת־עֲמֹרָה
יא כְּגַן־יהוה כְּאֶרֶץ מִצְרַיִם בֹּאֲכָה צֹעַר׃ וַיִּבְחַר־לוֹ לוֹט אֵת
כָּל־כִּכַּר הַיַּרְדֵּן וַיִּסַּע לוֹט מִקֶּדֶם וַיִּפָּרְדוּ אִישׁ מֵעַל אָחִיו׃
יב אַבְרָם יָשַׁב בְּאֶרֶץ־כְּנָעַן וְלוֹט יָשַׁב בְּעָרֵי הַכִּכָּר וַיֶּאֱהַל עַד־
יג יד סְדֹם׃ וְאַנְשֵׁי סְדֹם רָעִים וְחַטָּאִים לַיהוה מְאֹד׃ וַיהוה אָמַר
אֶל־אַבְרָם אַחֲרֵי הִפָּרֶד־לוֹט מֵעִמּוֹ שָׂא־נָא עֵינֶיךָ וּרְאֵה
מִן־הַמָּקוֹם אֲשֶׁר־אַתָּה שָׁם צָפֹנָה וָנֶגְבָּה וָקֵדְמָה וָיָמָּה׃
טו כִּי אֶת־כָּל־הָאָרֶץ אֲשֶׁר־אַתָּה רֹאֶה לְךָ אֶתְּנֶנָּה וּלְזַרְעֲךָ
טז עַד־עוֹלָם׃ וְשַׂמְתִּי אֶת־זַרְעֲךָ כַּעֲפַר הָאָרֶץ אֲשֶׁר ׀ אִם־
יז יוּכַל אִישׁ לִמְנוֹת אֶת־עֲפַר הָאָרֶץ גַּם־זַרְעֲךָ יִמָּנֶה׃ קוּם

13:10 וַיִּשָּׂא־לוֹט אֶת־עֵינָיו *Lot raised his eyes* – Lot chooses the good land with evil inhabitants. Evidently, he puts the material before the moral and spiritual. This alone is sufficient to tell us that, as far as the covenant is concerned, he is not a child of Avraham.

The text goes out of its way to emphasize this, using a prolepsis – telling us in advance things we would not otherwise discover until later. The verse links Sedom with Egypt, the full significance of which we will not realize until the book of Exodus. We are told that in the future, Sedom and Amora will be destroyed. Twice the text stresses the wickedness of their inhabitants. The people are "evil" and "great sinners."

18 shall I give it." So Avram took his tent and came to settle
by the Oaks of Mamre, in Ḥevron. There he built an altar
to the Lord.
14 1 In the days of Amrafel, king of Shinar, Aryokh, king of REVI'I
Elasar, Kedorlaomer, king of Eilam, and Tidal, king of
2 Goyim, they all waged war against Bera, king of Sedom,
Birsha, king of Amora, Shinav, king of Adma, and Shemever,
king of Tzevoyim, and the king of Bela – that is, Tzoar.
3 These had all come together in Siddim Valley – now the
4 Dead Sea; for twelve years they had served Kedorlaomer,
5 but in the thirteenth year they had rebelled. In the
fourteenth year Kedorlaomer and his allied kings came and
defeated the Refaim in Ashterot Karnayim, the Zuzim in
6 Ham, the Eimim in Shaveh Kiryatayim, and the Horites in
the hill country of Se'ir as far as Eil Paran by the wilderness.
7 Then they swung back and came to Ein Mishpat – that is,
Kadesh – conquering the whole territory of the Amalekites,
8 as well as the Amorites living in Ḥatzetzon Tamar. Then
the kings of Sedom, Amora, Adma, Tzevoyim, and Bela –
that is, Tzoar – marched out and drew up their battle lines
9 in Siddim Valley against Kedorlaomer, king of Eilam, Tidal,
king of Goyim, Amrafel, king of Shinar, and Aryokh, king
10 of Elasar: four kings battling five. The Siddim Valley was
riddled with tar pits, and when the kings of Sedom and
Amora tried to flee, they fell into them. The others fled to
11 the mountains. The victors seized all the possessions of
12 Sedom and Amora and all the food, and they left, taking
with them – since he had been living in Sedom – Avram's
13 nephew, Lot, and his possessions. A fugitive came and
reported this to Avram the Hebrew, who was then living
near the Oaks of Mamre the Amorite, a kinsman of Avram's
14 allies, Eshkol and Aner. When Avram heard that his own
kinsman had been taken captive, he marshaled the three

---

a call. They have a vision, not of what is, but of what might be. They think outside the box. They march to a different tune.

To be a Jew is to be willing to challenge the prevailing consensus when, as so often happens, nations slip into

יח הִתְהַלֵּךְ בָּאָרֶץ לְאָרְכָּהּ וּלְרָחְבָּהּ כִּי לְךָ אֶתְּנֶנָּה: וַיֶּאֱהַל
אַבְרָם וַיָּבֹא וַיֵּשֶׁב בְּאֵלֹנֵי מַמְרֵא אֲשֶׁר בְּחֶבְרוֹן וַיִּבֶן־שָׁם
מִזְבֵּחַ לַיהוָה:
יד א וַיְהִי בִּימֵי אַמְרָפֶל מֶלֶךְ־שִׁנְעָר אַרְיוֹךְ מֶלֶךְ אֶלָּסָר כְּדָרְלָעֹמֶר יא רביעי
ב מֶלֶךְ עֵילָם וְתִדְעָל מֶלֶךְ גּוֹיִם: עָשׂוּ מִלְחָמָה אֶת־בֶּרַע מֶלֶךְ
סְדֹם וְאֶת־בִּרְשַׁע מֶלֶךְ עֲמֹרָה שִׁנְאָב ׀ מֶלֶךְ אַדְמָה וְשֶׁמְאֵבֶר
ג מֶלֶךְ צביים וּמֶלֶךְ בֶּלַע הִיא־צֹעַר: כָּל־אֵלֶּה חָבְרוּ אֶל־עֵמֶק צְבוֹיִם
ד הַשִּׂדִּים הוּא יָם הַמֶּלַח: שְׁתֵּים עֶשְׂרֵה שָׁנָה עָבְדוּ אֶת־
ה כְּדָרְלָעֹמֶר וּשְׁלֹשׁ־עֶשְׂרֵה שָׁנָה מָרָדוּ: וּבְאַרְבַּע עֶשְׂרֵה
שָׁנָה בָּא כְדָרְלָעֹמֶר וְהַמְּלָכִים אֲשֶׁר אִתּוֹ וַיַּכּוּ אֶת־רְפָאִים
בְּעַשְׁתְּרֹת קַרְנַיִם וְאֶת־הַזּוּזִים בְּהָם וְאֵת הָאֵימִים בְּשָׁוֵה
ו קִרְיָתָיִם: וְאֶת־הַחֹרִי בְּהַרְרָם שֵׂעִיר עַד אֵיל פָּארָן אֲשֶׁר
ז עַל־הַמִּדְבָּר: וַיָּשֻׁבוּ וַיָּבֹאוּ אֶל־עֵין מִשְׁפָּט הִוא קָדֵשׁ וַיַּכּוּ
אֶת־כָּל־שְׂדֵה הָעֲמָלֵקִי וְגַם אֶת־הָאֱמֹרִי הַיֹּשֵׁב בְּחַצְצֹן
ח תָּמָר: וַיֵּצֵא מֶלֶךְ־סְדֹם וּמֶלֶךְ עֲמֹרָה וּמֶלֶךְ אַדְמָה וּמֶלֶךְ
צביים וּמֶלֶךְ בֶּלַע הִוא־צֹעַר וַיַּעַרְכוּ אִתָּם מִלְחָמָה בְּעֵמֶק צְבוֹיִם
ט הַשִּׂדִּים: אֵת כְּדָרְלָעֹמֶר מֶלֶךְ עֵילָם וְתִדְעָל מֶלֶךְ גּוֹיִם
וְאַמְרָפֶל מֶלֶךְ שִׁנְעָר וְאַרְיוֹךְ מֶלֶךְ אֶלָּסָר אַרְבָּעָה מְלָכִים
י אֶת־הַחֲמִשָּׁה: וְעֵמֶק הַשִּׂדִּים בֶּאֱרֹת בֶּאֱרֹת חֵמָר וַיָּנֻסוּ
יא מֶלֶךְ־סְדֹם וַעֲמֹרָה וַיִּפְּלוּ־שָׁמָּה וְהַנִּשְׁאָרִים הֶרָה נָּסוּ: וַיִּקְחוּ
יב אֶת־כָּל־רְכֻשׁ סְדֹם וַעֲמֹרָה וְאֶת־כָּל־אָכְלָם וַיֵּלֵכוּ: וַיִּקְחוּ
אֶת־לוֹט וְאֶת־רְכֻשׁוֹ בֶּן־אֲחִי אַבְרָם וַיֵּלֵכוּ וְהוּא יֹשֵׁב בִּסְדֹם:
יג וַיָּבֹא הַפָּלִיט וַיַּגֵּד לְאַבְרָם הָעִבְרִי וְהוּא שֹׁכֵן בְּאֵלֹנֵי מַמְרֵא
הָאֱמֹרִי אֲחִי אֶשְׁכֹּל וַאֲחִי עָנֵר וְהֵם בַּעֲלֵי בְרִית־אַבְרָם:
יד וַיִּשְׁמַע אַבְרָם כִּי נִשְׁבָּה אָחִיו וַיָּרֶק אֶת־חֲנִיכָיו יְלִידֵי בֵיתוֹ

14:14 וַיָּרֶק אֶת חֲנִיכָיו *He marshaled* – Leaders lead. That does not mean to say that they do not follow. But what they follow is different from what most people follow. They do not conform for the sake of conforming. They follow an inner voice,

hundred eighteen trained men born in his household,
15 and went in pursuit as far as Dan. He divided his forces
against the captors at night and defeated them, pursuing
16 them to Ḥova, north of Damascus. He recovered all the
plunder, as well as his kinsman Lot and his possessions, the
17 women, and the other survivors as well. When he returned
from defeating Kedorlaomer and the kings with him, the
king of Sedom came out to greet him at Shaveh Valley –
18 that is, the Valley of the King. And Malki Tzedek, king of
Shalem, offered bread and wine. He was a priest of God
19 Most High, and he blessed Avram, saying: "Blessed be

---

them to the standards of simple, human morality, not those of divine ethics or holiness.

When his nephew Lot chooses to live among the people of Sedom, about whom the Tanakh says that they "were evil, great sinners against the Lord" (13:13), Avraham does not criticize him. Nor does he condemn them. To the contrary, he now fights a battle on their behalf. When, in the next *parasha*, he hears that God is planning to punish them, he will plead for them, in one of the most audacious prayers in the Tanakh: "Shall the judge of all the earth not do justice?" (18:25).

Avraham does not seek to impose his views on others. Yet his contemporaries sense that there is something special, Godly, about him. Malki Tzedek, king of Shalem, salutes him with the words "Blessed be Avram by God Most High, Maker of heaven and earth" (14:19). The Hittites say to him, "You are a prince of God in our midst" (23:6). Avraham impresses his contemporaries by the way he lives, not the way he forces, or even urges, others to live.

14:18 מַלְכִּי צֶדֶק מֶלֶךְ שָׁלֵם *Malki Tzedek, king of Shalem* – The God who appears to Avraham also appears to Malki Tzedek, king of Shalem, described as "a priest of God Most High" though not party to the Abrahamic covenant. He appears to Avimelekh, king of the Philistines, and to Lavan, Yaakov's high-handed father-in-law. Even an Egyptian Pharaoh can relate to the Divine. After Yosef has interpreted his dream, Pharaoh says, "Could we find another like him, a man who has within him the spirit of God?"

The Torah seems to delight in this discovery of godliness outside the Abrahamic covenant. When, in the early centuries CE, the Sages said that the righteous of every nation have a share in the World to Come, they were doing no more than making explicit a view implicit in the Torah throughout, that Israel has no monopoly on virtue or wisdom or grace.

טו שְׁמֹנָה עָשָׂר וּשְׁלֹשׁ מֵאוֹת וַיִּרְדֹּף עַד־דָּן׃ וַיֵּחָלֵק עֲלֵיהֶם ׀
לַיְלָה הוּא וַעֲבָדָיו וַיַּכֵּם וַיִּרְדְּפֵם עַד־חוֹבָה אֲשֶׁר מִשְּׂמֹאל
טז לְדַמָּשֶׂק׃ וַיָּשֶׁב אֵת כָּל־הָרְכֻשׁ וְגַם אֶת־לוֹט אָחִיו וּרְכֻשׁוֹ
יז הֵשִׁיב וְגַם אֶת־הַנָּשִׁים וְאֶת־הָעָם׃ וַיֵּצֵא מֶלֶךְ־סְדֹם לִקְרָאתוֹ
אַחֲרֵי שׁוּבוֹ מֵהַכּוֹת אֶת־כְּדָרְלָעֹמֶר וְאֶת־הַמְּלָכִים אֲשֶׁר
יח אִתּוֹ אֶל־עֵמֶק שָׁוֵה הוּא עֵמֶק הַמֶּלֶךְ׃ וּמַלְכִּי־צֶדֶק מֶלֶךְ
יט שָׁלֵם הוֹצִיא לֶחֶם וָיָיִן וְהוּא כֹהֵן לְאֵל עֶלְיוֹן׃ וַיְבָרְכֵהוּ וַיֹּאמַר

---

worshipping the old gods. We make a mistake when we think of idols in terms of their physical appearance – statues, figurines, icons. In that sense they belong to ancient times we have long outgrown. Instead, the right way to think of idols is in terms of what they represent. They symbolize power. That is what Ra was for the Egyptians, what Baal was for the Canaanites, what Zeus was for the Greeks, and what missiles and bombs are for terrorists and rogue states today.

Power allows us to rule over others without their consent. Judaism is a sustained critique of power. It is about how a nation can be formed on the basis of shared commitment and collective responsibility. It is about how to construct a society that honors the human person as the image and likeness of God. It is about a vision, never fully realized but never abandoned, of a world based on justice and compassion. Here Avraham stands up to power in defense of his nephew. We notice that he himself is a force to be reckoned with, but his military prowess and leadership are only used here, once, in defense of others.

14:14 וַיִּרְדֹּף *He… went in pursuit* – The unique structure of biblical spirituality – its calibrated tension between the universality of justice and the particularity of love – is the most compelling way I know of giving religious expression to *both* our common humanity *and* our religious differences.

Consider the life of Avraham. Readers of the Tanakh are so familiar with his story that they often fail to notice how strange it is. Here is the father of monotheism, yet in the biblical text itself Abraham breaks no idol, challenges no polytheist, and establishes no new religious movement. Other than an ambiguous hint that Avraham took with him on his journey "the people (literally, 'souls') they had gathered" (Gen. 12:5), which may refer to converts they had made but may equally merely refer to their servants, they attract no disciples.

He lives among people whose beliefs and practices are alien to his own, yet he does not reprimand them, except when the servants of Avimelekh, a king with whom he had made a treaty, seize one of the wells he has dug (21:25). He holds

Avram by God Most High, Maker of heaven and earth,
20 and blessed be God Most High who delivered your foes
into your hand." Then Avram gave him a tenth of
21 everything. And the king of Sedom said to Avram, "Give ḤAMISHI
22 me the people, and keep the possessions for yourself." But
Avram said to the king of Sedom, "I raise my hand in oath
to the LORD, God Most High, Maker of heaven and earth,
23 that I will not accept anything of yours, not even a thread
or a shoe strap, so that you never shall say, 'I made Avram
24 rich.' I will accept nothing but what my young men have
eaten and the share that belongs to the men who went
with me – Aner, Eshkol, and Mamre; let them have their
15 1 share." After these events the word of the LORD
came to Avram in a vision, saying: "Do not be afraid,
Avram. I am your shield. Your reward shall be very great."
2 But Avram said, "My Lord GOD, what will You have given
me if I remain childless, and the one who will take charge

---

message is being woven into our being. To move from one generation to the next requires a series of miracles. At every stage in the transition from Avraham and Sara to Yitzḥak, continuity seems impossible. Nature is against it. Prediction rules otherwise. At times even Heaven itself seems to decree against it. We are Jews today by virtue of miracles. How then do we survive?

The story of Avraham and Sara and their longing for a child, the promises, the delay, the hope, the despair, the torments and trials, could have no other effect than to create, at the very beginning of Jewish time, a focus bordering on an obsession with Jewish children.

No people can have cared more for their children, invested more energy in them and shaped the whole of their religious life so decisively in order to hand on to them what they find precious. *Avraham and Sara have a child because they so nearly do not have a child.* Judaism has never taken its children for granted, because Jews have known what it is like to be an Avraham or Sara.

Let us not treat the future lightly. When God promises Avraham that his reward will be very great, he replies: "My Lord GOD, what will You have given me if I remain childless?" That is the question eternity asks of us. What meaning will our lives and the lives of our ancestors have if they are not lent immortality by our continuity, by our bringing it about that we have Jewish grandchildren? If we would only remember the many miracles it took to bring us to this hour, we would willingly do our duty to ensure that the next generation stays Jewish, and the

כ בָּרוּךְ אַבְרָם לְאֵל עֶלְיוֹן קֹנֵה שָׁמַיִם וָאָרֶץ: וּבָרוּךְ אֵל עֶלְיוֹן
כא אֲשֶׁר־מִגֵּן צָרֶיךָ בְּיָדֶךָ וַיִּתֶּן־לוֹ מַעֲשֵׂר מִכֹּל: וַיֹּאמֶר מֶלֶךְ־ חמישי
כב סְדֹם אֶל־אַבְרָם תֶּן־לִי הַנֶּפֶשׁ וְהָרְכֻשׁ קַח־לָךְ: וַיֹּאמֶר
אַבְרָם אֶל־מֶלֶךְ סְדֹם הֲרִמֹתִי יָדִי אֶל־יהוה אֵל עֶלְיוֹן קֹנֵה
כג שָׁמַיִם וָאָרֶץ: אִם־מִחוּט וְעַד שְׂרוֹךְ־נַעַל וְאִם־אֶקַּח מִכָּל־
כד אֲשֶׁר־לָךְ וְלֹא תֹאמַר אֲנִי הֶעֱשַׁרְתִּי אֶת־אַבְרָם: בִּלְעָדַי
רַק אֲשֶׁר אָכְלוּ הַנְּעָרִים וְחֵלֶק הָאֲנָשִׁים אֲשֶׁר הָלְכוּ אִתִּי
טו א עָנֵר אֶשְׁכֹּל וּמַמְרֵא הֵם יִקְחוּ חֶלְקָם: אַחַר | יב
הַדְּבָרִים הָאֵלֶּה הָיָה דְבַר־יהוה אֶל־אַבְרָם בַּמַּחֲזֶה לֵאמֹר
ב אַל־תִּירָא אַבְרָם אָנֹכִי מָגֵן לָךְ שְׂכָרְךָ הַרְבֵּה מְאֹד: וַיֹּאמֶר
אַבְרָם אֲדֹנָי יֱהוִה מַה־תִּתֶּן־לִי וְאָנֹכִי הוֹלֵךְ עֲרִירִי וּבֶן־מֶשֶׁק

15:1 אַל תִּירָא אַבְרָם *Do not be afraid, Avram* – It is after he faces the sword to save Lot that God tells Avram, "I am your shield." Each year we tell the story of Avraham's call from God to leave his home and travel to "the land that I will show you." I call that the journey into insecurity. Life has been highly insecure for Jews for four thousand years. We are still on that journey. A lot of people are struck by the history of Jewish suffering. I am always struck by the history of Jewish recovery from suffering. What gives a people the strength to keep going? It is that feeling that you can face the future without fear if you know you are not alone. It is that famous line in Psalm 23: "Though I walk through the valley of the shadow of death, I fear no evil, for You are with me." That, I think, is the positive reason for faith in the twenty-first century. We can handle anything so long as we have the humility to know that we are answerable to something much greater than ourselves.

THE PROMISE OF CHILDREN

The first recorded words of man to God in the history of the covenant are a plea for there to be future generations. The first Jew fears he will be the last.

According to the Torah, had nature taken its course, Sara would not have had a child and there would be no Jewish people. If Avraham had had his way and been content with Yishmael, there would have been no Jewish people. If – Yitzḥak having been born – the word from Heaven telling Avraham to stay his hand had been delayed, there would have been no Jewish people. On such slender avoidance of the probable does Jewish continuity rest.

It is as if, from the beginning, a

3 of my household is Eliezer of Damascus?" Avram said,
"You have given me no children. A man of my household
4 will be my heir." Then the word of the LORD came to him:
"That man will not be your heir; one who comes forth
5 from your own loins will be your heir." He took him
outside and said, "Look at the heavens and count the
stars – if indeed you can count them." He said to him,
6 "That is how your descendants will be." And because
Avram put his trust in the LORD, He reckoned it to him as
7 righteousness. And He told him, "I am the LORD who SHISHI
brought you out from Ur Kasdim to give you this land to
8 possess it." And he said, "My Lord GOD, how shall I know
9 that I will possess it?" And He said to him, "Take for Me a
three-year-old heifer, and a three-year-old goat, and a
three-year-old ram, and a turtledove, and a young pigeon."
10 And he took all these and cut them in two and put each
half opposite its other half, but the birds he did not cut.
11 Birds of prey descended on the carcasses, but Avram
12 drove them away. And so it was that, as the sun went

covenant between God and the children of Israel at Mount Sinai. *Emuna,* in this context, means that both parties remain loyal to its terms.

Only against this background can we understand how faith, in Judaism, can be a communal phenomenon. The key concepts of Judaism – creation, revelation, redemption – do not refer to the relationship between God and an individual soul. They refer to the relationship between God and humanity, or God and an entire people. God creates the world not for lonely Adam but for people who marry and have children and build societies. It is Israel the people which experiences slavery and liberation; Israel the people which accepts the covenant and its commands; Israel which is charged in its collective life with being "witnesses of God" and exemplars of righteousness. The prophet Yeḥezkel, in his vision of the valley of dry bones, sees the resurrection of the dead as something which happens to a nation, not simply to individuals. *Emuna,* as it resonates through the verses of the Tanakh, is the faithfulness of a people to its shared and public undertaking. Individuals may sin, whole groups may break away, but the people as a whole endures, and despite its many rebellions remains faithful to the terms of the covenant.

ג בֵּיתִי הוּא דַּמֶּשֶׂק אֱלִיעֶזֶר: וַיֹּאמֶר אַבְרָם הֵן לִי לֹא נָתַתָּה
ד זָרַע וְהִנֵּה בֶן־בֵּיתִי יוֹרֵשׁ אֹתִי: וְהִנֵּה דְבַר־יהוה אֵלָיו לֵאמֹר
ה לֹא יִירָשְׁךָ זֶה כִּי־אִם אֲשֶׁר יֵצֵא מִמֵּעֶיךָ הוּא יִירָשֶׁךָ: וַיּוֹצֵא
אֹתוֹ הַחוּצָה וַיֹּאמֶר הַבֶּט־נָא הַשָּׁמַיְמָה וּסְפֹר הַכּוֹכָבִים
ו אִם־תּוּכַל לִסְפֹּר אֹתָם וַיֹּאמֶר לוֹ כֹּה יִהְיֶה זַרְעֶךָ: וְהֶאֱמִן
ז בַּיהוה וַיַּחְשְׁבֶהָ לּוֹ צְדָקָה: וַיֹּאמֶר אֵלָיו אֲנִי יהוה אֲשֶׁר ששי
הוֹצֵאתִיךָ מֵאוּר כַּשְׂדִּים לָתֶת לְךָ אֶת־הָאָרֶץ הַזֹּאת
ח ט לְרִשְׁתָּהּ: וַיֹּאמַר אֲדֹנָי יֱהֹוִה בַּמָּה אֵדַע כִּי אִירָשֶׁנָּה: וַיֹּאמֶר
אֵלָיו קְחָה לִי עֶגְלָה מְשֻׁלֶּשֶׁת וְעֵז מְשֻׁלֶּשֶׁת וְאַיִל מְשֻׁלָּשׁ
י וְתֹר וְגוֹזָל: וַיִּקַּח־לוֹ אֶת־כָּל־אֵלֶּה וַיְבַתֵּר אֹתָם בַּתָּוֶךְ וַיִּתֵּן
יא אִישׁ־בִּתְרוֹ לִקְרַאת רֵעֵהוּ וְאֶת־הַצִּפֹּר לֹא בָתָר: וַיֵּרֶד
יב הָעַיִט עַל־הַפְּגָרִים וַיַּשֵּׁב אֹתָם אַבְרָם: וַיְהִי הַשֶּׁמֶשׁ לָבוֹא

generation after that. Jewish continuity is the greatest gift we can bring to the future and the past.

15:2 דַּמֶּשֶׂק אֱלִיעֶזֶר *Eliezer of Damascus* – The reference to Eliezer has taken on a new intelligibility in the light of ancient documents from the Nuzi archives, which show that it was a well-established practice in Avraham's day for childless individuals to adopt someone, even a slave, as a son. He would then have all the attendant duties and rights of a natural son and heir. Whether or not Avraham has adopted his slave Eliezer, it is clear that with the departure of Lot, there is no one else he can look to.

15:6 וְהֶאֱמִן בַּיהוה *Avram put his trust in the* Lord – The Hebrew word *emuna* is usually translated as "faith" or "belief." But like many words which lie at the center of a unique way of life, it defies exact translation. When Avraham, old and childless, is told that he will have as many descendants as the stars of the sky, he "put his trust in [*vehe'emin*] God," who "reckoned it to him as righteousness." This means less that Avraham believes he will have a child than that he trusts in God who has given His word. When Hoshea describes God's relationship with Israel he says, "I will betroth you to Me in faithfulness [*be'emuna*]." By this he means fidelity, loyalty, staying together in troubled times. *Emuna* conveys strength, firmness, and tenacity. It characterizes a moral relationship between persons, a mutuality of trust and dedication. As these two examples suggest, it is often a relationship created by words – a promise given, a betrothal spoken – and signals the power of language to express binding commitments. The key undertaking in Judaism is the

down, a deep sleep fell upon Avram and a deep, dark
13 dread came upon him. And God said to Avram, "Know
with certainty that your descendants will be migrants in a
land not their own, and there they will be enslaved and
14 oppressed for four hundred years. But I will bring judgment
on the nation they will serve, and afterward they will go
15 free with great wealth. As for you, you will join your
16 ancestors in peace; you will be buried in ripe old age. And
the fourth generation will return here, for the guilt of the
17 Amorites is not yet resolved." And when the sun set and it

---

to Egypt" (Gen. 12:10). He senses danger, fearing that the Egyptians will kill him and take Sara into the royal harem. Sara, saying that she is Avraham's sister, is indeed taken into Pharaoh's palace, which is then visited by a series of plagues. Pharaoh then sends the couple away.

The episode seems to disturb the narrative logic of the patriarchal story. Why, if God wants Avraham to go to the land of Canaan, does He force him to leave almost as soon as he has arrived? Midrash Rabba, an early rabbinic commentary, linking that episode with what is foretold here, gives what is undoubtedly the correct answer:

> The Holy One, blessed be He, said to our father Avraham, "Go forth and tread a path for your children." For you find that everything written in connection with Avraham is written in connection with his children. Of Avraham it is written, "*There was a famine in the land*" [Gen. 12:10], and of Israel it is written, "*For two years now there has been famine in the land*" [45:6]. Of Avraham: "*Avram went down to Egypt*" [12:10]. Of Israel: "*Our ancestors went down to Egypt*" [Num. 20:15]. Of Avraham: "*To stay there for a while*" [Gen. 12:10]. Of Israel: "*We have come to stay for a while in your land*" [47:4]. (Bereshit Rabba 40:6)

And so on through a long series of linguistic and substantive parallels between Avraham's fate and the later experience of the Israelites. The exiles of Avraham, Yitzḥak, and Yaakov are, in other words, prefigurations of what is now foretold explicitly in *brit bein habetarim*, the covenant between the pieces. It is as if the patriarchs and matriarchs of the Jewish people had *rehearsed in advance* the fate of their children, not necessarily knowing they were doing so, but nonetheless *laying the foundations of future hope*. The Israelites, exiled and enslaved, would be liberated and redeemed, not only because God said so, but because He had *done so* in the past. He had already shown, several times in different ways, that He was with the ancestors of the nation, protecting them and bringing them safely back.

וְתַרְדֵּמָה נָפְלָה עַל־אַבְרָם וְהִנֵּה אֵימָה חֲשֵׁכָה גְדֹלָה
יג נֹפֶלֶת עָלָיו׃ וַיֹּאמֶר לְאַבְרָם יָדֹעַ תֵּדַע כִּי־גֵר ׀ יִהְיֶה זַרְעֲךָ
בְּאֶרֶץ לֹא לָהֶם וַעֲבָדוּם וְעִנּוּ אֹתָם אַרְבַּע מֵאוֹת שָׁנָה׃
יד וְגַם אֶת־הַגּוֹי אֲשֶׁר יַעֲבֹדוּ דָּן אָנֹכִי וְאַחֲרֵי־כֵן יֵצְאוּ בִּרְכֻשׁ
טו גָּדוֹל׃ וְאַתָּה תָּבוֹא אֶל־אֲבֹתֶיךָ בְּשָׁלוֹם תִּקָּבֵר בְּשֵׂיבָה
טז טוֹבָה׃ וְדוֹר רְבִיעִי יָשׁוּבוּ הֵנָּה כִּי לֹא־שָׁלֵם עֲוֺן הָאֱמֹרִי
יז עַד־הֵנָּה׃ וַיְהִי הַשֶּׁמֶשׁ בָּאָה וַעֲלָטָה הָיָה וְהִנֵּה תַנּוּר עָשָׁן

15:14 וְאַחֲרֵי־כֵן יֵצְאוּ *Afterward they will go free* – This vision, with its "deep, dark dread," foretells, like the future prophets, enslavement and redemption, exile and return. Centuries after Avraham's time, the Talmud (Makkot 24a) will describe how the great Sages, Rabban Gamliel, R. Elazar b. Azarya, R. Yehoshua, and R. Akiva, looked out upon the ruins of the Temple. Three of them wept. But R. Akiva gave them a message of consolation. The prophets, he said, foresaw this day of destruction, and it has come to pass. But they also foresaw a later day when the city would be rebuilt. Since one vision has come true, so will the other. The day will come when Zekharya's prophecy will be fulfilled: "Old men and old women will sit in the squares of Jerusalem… and the city squares will be full and alive with young boys and girls playing" (Zech. 8:4–5). Nineteen hundred years later, one Sabbath afternoon in Jerusalem, I lived to see R. Akiva's hope come true. *If only he had known,* I thought. If only R. Akiva had known how long it would take, how many exiles, expulsions, persecutions, pogroms, blood libels, inquisitions, and Crusades Jews would first have to endure. If only he had known of the Holocaust and its millions of innocent victims gassed and turned to ashes. Would he not have wept? Would he still have kept his faith? In that moment of truth I knew the answer. Yes, *all the more would he have held to his faith,* knowing that God could not have led this people so long through the valley of the shadow of death without one day bringing them to the city of peace.

15:14 וְאַחֲרֵי־כֵן יֵצְאוּ בִּרְכֻשׁ גָּדוֹל *Afterward… with great wealth* – One of the most striking facts about the patriarchal families is that they all experience exile. Avraham and Yitzḥak are both forced, through famine, to travel to the land of the Philistines. Yaakov suffers exile twice, once to escape Esav, a second time to be rejoined with his son Yosef. In none of these is exile the result of sin, and it is the first instance that provides the interpretive clue to the rest. It occurs earlier in our *parasha,* almost immediately after God's call to Avraham to leave his land, birthplace, and father's house: "There was a famine in the land. Avram went down

was very dark, a smoking furnace appeared and a blazing
18 torch passed between these pieces. On that day the Lord
made a covenant with Avram: "To your descendants I will
give this land, from the River of Egypt to the great river
19 Euphrates, the land of the Kenites, the Kenizzites, the
20 21 Kadmonites, the Hittites, the Perizzites, the Refaim, the
Amorites, the Canaanites, the Girgashites, and the
16 1 Jebusites." Sarai, Avram's wife, had borne him no
children; but she had an Egyptian maidservant named
2 Hagar. Sarai said to Avram, "The Lord has kept me from
having children. Come now to my maid. Perhaps through
her I might build a family." And Avram listened to Sarai.
3 So it was that, after living in Canaan for ten years, Avram's
wife Sarai took Hagar, her Egyptian maidservant, and
4 gave her to her husband Avram to be his wife. He came to
Hagar and she conceived. And when she realized that she
was pregnant, she began to look upon her mistress with
5 contempt. Sarai said to Avram, "The abuse I suffer is your
fault. I laid my servant in your arms and now that she
knows she is pregnant, she looks upon me with contempt.

The message seems clear. Just as Avraham was chosen out of all humankind, so is Yitzḥak. But this is not a straightforward story. Yitzḥak is not the firstborn. Yishmael is. What we seem to have here is a *displacement narrative*. In almost all societies where birth order has a bearing on rank, the oldest (usually male) child succeeds to the role occupied by the father. Here the order is reversed. The result, happy for Sara and Yitzḥak, is tragic for Hagar and Yishmael.

Peeling away the layers of this complex and subtle text, we will discover another story altogether. The rabbis heard discordant notes in the narrative, and realized that it is conveying a different and surprising message. Only a superficial reading yields the conclusion: Yitzḥak chosen, Yishmael rejected. In fact, here, at the first generational succession in the Abrahamic covenant, the Torah contains not only a narrative but also a counter-narrative. *Yishmael is not vilified.* As we shall see, despite the fact that Avraham, Sara, and Yitzḥak are the heroes of the story as a whole, in the two crucial scenes in the desert our imaginative sympathies are with Hagar and her child. That is what gives the story its counter-intuitive depth.

יח וְלַפִּיד אֵשׁ אֲשֶׁר עָבַר בֵּין הַגְּזָרִים הָאֵלֶּה׃ בַּיּוֹם הַהוּא כָּרַת
יהוה אֶת־אַבְרָם בְּרִית לֵאמֹר לְזַרְעֲךָ נָתַתִּי אֶת־הָאָרֶץ
יט הַזֹּאת מִנְּהַר מִצְרַיִם עַד־הַנָּהָר הַגָּדֹל נְהַר־פְּרָת׃ אֶת־
כ הַקֵּינִי וְאֶת־הַקְּנִזִּי וְאֵת הַקַּדְמֹנִי׃ וְאֶת־הַחִתִּי וְאֶת־הַפְּרִזִּי
כא וְאֶת־הָרְפָאִים׃ וְאֶת־הָאֱמֹרִי וְאֶת־הַכְּנַעֲנִי וְאֶת־הַגִּרְגָּשִׁי
טז א וְאֶת־הַיְבוּסִי׃ וְשָׂרַי אֵשֶׁת אַבְרָם לֹא יָלְדָה לוֹ וְלָהּ יג
ב שִׁפְחָה מִצְרִית וּשְׁמָהּ הָגָר׃ וַתֹּאמֶר שָׂרַי אֶל־אַבְרָם הִנֵּה־
נָא עֲצָרַנִי יהוה מִלֶּדֶת בֹּא־נָא אֶל־שִׁפְחָתִי אוּלַי אִבָּנֶה
ג מִמֶּנָּה וַיִּשְׁמַע אַבְרָם לְקוֹל שָׂרָי׃ וַתִּקַּח שָׂרַי ׀ אֵשֶׁת אַבְרָם
אֶת־הָגָר הַמִּצְרִית שִׁפְחָתָהּ מִקֵּץ עֶשֶׂר שָׁנִים לְשֶׁבֶת אַבְרָם
ד בְּאֶרֶץ כְּנָעַן וַתִּתֵּן אֹתָהּ לְאַבְרָם אִישָׁהּ לוֹ לְאִשָּׁה׃ וַיָּבֹא
אֶל־הָגָר וַתַּהַר וַתֵּרֶא כִּי הָרָתָה וַתֵּקַל גְּבִרְתָּהּ בְּעֵינֶיהָ׃
ה וַתֹּאמֶר שָׂרַי אֶל־אַבְרָם חֲמָסִי עָלֶיךָ אָנֹכִי נָתַתִּי שִׁפְחָתִי
בְּחֵיקֶךָ וַתֵּרֶא כִּי הָרָתָה וָאֵקַל בְּעֵינֶיהָ יִשְׁפֹּט יהוה בֵּינִי

HAGAR

This is the first story of sibling rivalry in Avraham's family, and it begins with heartache. Avram has been promised countless children. Yet the years pass and still he and Sara have no child. In despair, Sara proposes an arrangement. Hagar is to become a surrogate mother. Then as now it is a procedure fraught with potential conflict.

Hagar does conceive, and this alters the relationship between the two women. Hagar "began to look upon her mistress with contempt." As the bearer of Avraham's child, she is no longer content to be treated as a servant. Sara notices the change and reacts angrily. Uncharacteristically, Avraham shrugs off the dilemma. "Your maid is in your own hands. Do with her whatever you think best." Sara ill-treats Hagar, who flees into the desert. There she is met by an angel who tells her to go back. She returns and Yishmael is born.

In the next chapter, God appears to Avraham and reaffirms His covenant with him, adding for the first time a command: circumcision. Avraham is to undergo this operation. So is Yishmael. It will become the sign of the covenantal family. The revelation, however, contains a twist. Despite the fact that Avraham now has a son, God tells him he will have another, born to him by Sara. A year later, Yitzḥak is born.

6 Let the LORD judge between me and you!" Avram said to
Sarai, "Your maid is in your own hands. Do with her
whatever you think best." Sarai treated her harshly – and
7 Hagar ran away from her. An angel of the LORD found her
near a spring of water in the desert, the spring by the road
8 to Shur. He said, "Hagar, maidservant of Sarai, where have
you come from and where are you going?" She said, "I am
9 running away from my mistress Sarai." The angel of the
LORD said to her, "Go back to your mistress; submit
10 yourself under her hand." And the angel of the LORD
added: "I will greatly multiply your descendants; they will
11 be too many to count." Said the angel of the LORD: "You
are pregnant and will give birth to a son. You shall name
12 him Yishmael, for the LORD has heard your affliction. He
will become a wild donkey of a man; his hand will be
against everyone, and everyone's hand against him. He
13 will live up against all his brothers." She gave a name to the
LORD who had spoken to her: "You are the God who sees
me," for she said: "Have I not here seen Him who sees
14 me?" That is why the well is called Be'er Laḥai Ro'i. It is

---

No one in the Torah is portrayed as perfect. No religious literature was ever further from hagiography, idealization, and hero worship. Rabbi Tzvi Hirsch Chajes explains that the tendency of Midrash to make the heroes seem perfect and the villains completely evil is entirely for educational reasons. It is difficult to teach ethics through stories whose characters are fraught with complexity and ambiguity. The moral life is not something we understand in depth all at once. As children we hear stories of heroes and villains. We learn basic distinctions: right and wrong, good and bad, permitted and forbidden. As we grow, though, we begin to realize how difficult some decisions are. Do I go to Egypt? Do I stay in Canaan? Do I show compassion to my servant's child despite the risk that he may be a bad influence on my child who has been chosen by God for a sacred mission? Anyone who thinks such decisions are easy is not yet morally mature. So the best way of teaching ethics is to do so by way of stories that can be read at different levels at different times in life. When we first read the story we may think that the wild Yishmael is something quite different from the righteous Avraham. As we return to the story again and again, however, we begin to realize that the complexities of the son are bound up with the complexities of the father.

ו וּבֵינֶֽיךָ׃ וַיֹּאמֶר אַבְרָם אֶל־שָׂרַי הִנֵּה שִׁפְחָתֵךְ בְּיָדֵךְ עֲשִׂי־לָהּ
ז הַטּוֹב בְּעֵינָיִךְ וַתְּעַנֶּהָ שָׂרַי וַתִּבְרַח מִפָּנֶיהָ׃ וַיִּמְצָאָהּ מַלְאַךְ
ח יהוה עַל־עֵין הַמַּיִם בַּמִּדְבָּר עַל־הָעַיִן בְּדֶרֶךְ שׁוּר׃ וַיֹּאמַר
הָגָר שִׁפְחַת שָׂרַי אֵי־מִזֶּה בָאת וְאָנָה תֵלֵכִי וַתֹּאמֶר מִפְּנֵי
ט שָׂרַי גְּבִרְתִּי אָנֹכִי בֹּרַחַת׃ וַיֹּאמֶר לָהּ מַלְאַךְ יהוה שׁוּבִי
י אֶל־גְּבִרְתֵּךְ וְהִתְעַנִּי תַּחַת יָדֶיהָ׃ וַיֹּאמֶר לָהּ מַלְאַךְ יהוה
יא הַרְבָּה אַרְבֶּה אֶת־זַרְעֵךְ וְלֹא יִסָּפֵר מֵרֹב׃ וַיֹּאמֶר לָהּ מַלְאַךְ
יהוה הִנָּךְ הָרָה וְיֹלַדְתְּ בֵּן וְקָרָאת שְׁמוֹ יִשְׁמָעֵאל כִּי־שָׁמַע
יב יהוה אֶל־עָנְיֵךְ׃ וְהוּא יִהְיֶה פֶּרֶא אָדָם יָדוֹ בַכֹּל וְיַד כֹּל בּוֹ
יג וְעַל־פְּנֵי כָל־אֶחָיו יִשְׁכֹּן׃ וַתִּקְרָא שֵׁם־יהוה הַדֹּבֵר אֵלֶיהָ
יד אַתָּה אֵל רֳאִי כִּי אָמְרָה הֲגַם הֲלֹם רָאִיתִי אַחֲרֵי רֹאִי׃ עַל־
כֵּן קָרָא לַבְּאֵר בְּאֵר לַחַי רֹאִי הִנֵּה בֵין־קָדֵשׁ וּבֵין בָּרֶד׃

16:6 וַתְּעַנֶּהָ שָׂרַי *Sarai treated her harshly* – Note the characterization of the key figures, especially Avraham and Sara. No reader can fail to sense the harsh light in which Sara is portrayed in her relationship with Hagar and Yishmael. Having proposed the idea of Hagar sleeping with Avraham, she later blames Avraham: "*The abuse I suffer is your fault*" (Gen. 16:5). Avraham, for his part, seems caught helplessly in the tension between the two women.

The Hebrew text uses a significant word to describe Sara's treatment of Hagar: *vate'ane'a*, literally, she "oppressed" her. The Hebrew verb is the same as will later be used to describe the Egyptians: they "oppressed" the Israelites (Ex. 1:11–12). It also appears in Deuteronomy in the text of remembrance to be recited by the Israelites on bringing first fruits to the Temple ("The Egyptians dealt cruelly with us and *oppressed* us … and the Lord … saw our *oppression*, our toil, and our enslavement," Deut. 26:6–7). Hagar is herself an Egyptian (Gen. 16:3). There is a subtle hint here that the experience of the Israelites at the hands of the Egyptians will mirror the Egyptian Hagar's experience at the hands of Sara. This unmistakably qualifies the simple stereotype: Israelites good, Egyptians bad.

16:12 פֶּרֶא אָדָם *A wild donkey of a man* – Ramban writes (on Gen. 16:6): "Our mother [Sara] transgressed in this affliction, as did Avraham by allowing her to do so. So God heard her [Hagar's] affliction and gave her a son who would be *a wild donkey of a man* to afflict the seed of Avraham and Sara with all kinds of affliction."

15 still there between Kadesh and Bered. So Hagar bore
Avram a son, and Avram gave the name Yishmael to the
16 son that she had borne. Avram was eighty-six years old
17 1 when Hagar bore him Yishmael. When Avram was
ninety-nine years old, the LORD appeared to him and
2 said, "I am El Shaddai. Walk before Me in integrity, and I
will establish My covenant between Me and you, and
3 make you exceedingly numerous." Avram fell facedown.
4 And God said to him, "As for Me – this is My covenant
5 with you: you shall be father to a multitude of nations. No
longer shall you be called Avram. Your name will be
Avraham, for I have made you father to a multitude of
6 nations. I will make you exceptionally fertile, I will turn
7 you into nations; kings will come from you. I will establish SHEVI'I
My covenant between Me and you and your descendants
after you throughout the generations: an eternal covenant.
8 I will be God to you and your descendants after you, and
I will give you and your descendants after you the land
where you now live as strangers, the whole land of
Canaan, an everlasting possession, and I will be their
9 God." Then God said to Avraham, "As for you, you shall
keep My covenant, you and your descendants after you
10 throughout their generations. This is My covenant, kept
between Me and you and your descendants after you:

---

words of Milton Himmelfarb, "caught up in things great and inexplicable."

17:10 הִמּוֹל לָכֶם כָּל־זָכָר *Every male among you shall be circumcised* – As the incident in Egypt exemplified (Gen. 12:10–17), sexual relationships are the test of a society's morals. Do I respect other people as persons in their own right, or do I see them as means to my ends, instruments of my pleasure? Do I relate to you in freedom and dignity, or do I simply use you? The nature of the sexual encounter will – not immediately, but eventually – affect all other social relationships. Marriage is the moralization of sex, and the breakdown of marriage is the beginning of the disintegration of society, a fact that virtually every civilization has learned too late. The sign of the covenant, therefore, will be circumcision, because man needs to be reminded in one place more than others of the binding force of moral obligation.

טו ותלד הגר לאברם בן ויקרא אברם שם־בנו אשר־ילדה
טז הגר ישמעאל: ואברם בן־שמנים שנה ושש שנים בלדת־
יז א הגר את־ישמעאל לאברם: ויהי אברם בן־ יד
תשעים שנה ותשע שנים וירא יהוה אל־אברם ויאמר
ב אליו אני־אל שדי התהלך לפני והיה תמים: ואתנה בריתי
ג ביני ובינך וארבה אותך במאד מאד: ויפל אברם על־פניו
ד וידבר אתו אלהים לאמר: אני הנה בריתי אתך והיית
ה לאב המון גוים: ולא־יקרא עוד את־שמך אברם והיה
ו שמך אברהם כי אב־המון גוים נתתיך: והפרתי אתך
ז במאד מאד ונתתיך לגוים ומלכים ממך יצאו: והקמתי שביעי
את־בריתי ביני ובינך ובין זרעך אחריך לדרתם לברית
ח עולם להיות לך לאלהים ולזרעך אחריך: ונתתי לך
ולזרעך אחריך את ׀ ארץ מגריך את כל־ארץ כנען
ט לאחזת עולם והייתי להם לאלהים: ויאמר אלהים אל־
אברהם ואתה את־בריתי תשמר אתה וזרעך אחריך
י לדרתם: זאת בריתי אשר תשמרו ביני וביניכם ובין זרעך

קודי **בְּרִית עוֹלָם** *An eternal covenant* – Through thirty-seven long and difficult centuries, Jews have remained faithful to the mandate given by God to Avraham in the first words of covenantal history: "And through you, all the families of the earth will be blessed." And we are their heirs. Was there ever a more challenging proposition than this?

As individuals, there is nothing remarkable about Jews. In our *parasha* we have seen even our heroes in a far from ideal light. There have been many theories, Jewish and non-Jewish, which attribute to us an innate genius, a racial gift, a genetic endowment, a mystic difference. None is convincing. Removed from our traditions, our past, our way of life, and our community, within three generations or less we merge into the wider landscape and become invisible. Individually we are ordinary. Collectively we become something else – we are charged with responsibility, and that call propels us forward. For that reason we always set as our first and highest goal the transmission of identity across the generations. A Jewish child knew that he or she was something special, that he or she was, in the

11 every male among you shall be circumcised. You must
circumcise the flesh of your foreskin – this shall be the sign
12 of the covenant between Me and you. Throughout the
generations, every male among you shall be circumcised at
the age of eight days, including the slave born in your
household, including one acquired from a stranger not
13 descended from you. All must be circumcised – those born
in your household, those acquired with your money – and
My covenant in your flesh will be a covenant everlasting.
14 Any uncircumcised male, whose foreskin has not been
circumcised, shall be severed from his people; he has
15 broken My covenant." God then said to Avraham,
"As for Sarai your wife, you shall no longer call her Sarai.
16 Her name will be Sara. I will bless her and give you a son
by her. I will bless her so that she shall birth nations; kings
17 of peoples shall descend from her." Avraham fell on his
face and laughed. "Can a hundred-year-old man become
a father?" he said to himself. "Can Sara, at ninety, bear a
18 child?" To God Avraham said, "If only Yishmael might
19 live before You!" God said, "Nonetheless, Sara your wife
will bear you a son, and you shall name him Yitzḥak. I will
establish My covenant with him as an everlasting
20 covenant for his descendants after him. As for Yishmael –
I have heard you. I will bless him and make him fertile
and multiply him exceedingly. He will become father of
21 twelve princes, and I will make of him a great nation. But
I will establish My covenant with Yitzḥak, whom Sara

---

establish My covenant with Yitzḥak – By the time the *parasha* ends, we have heard four promises of children and seen three prospective heirs, Lot, Eliezer, and Yishmael, fail to fit the specification. Lot makes his home among evildoers. Eliezer is not part of the patriarchal family. Yishmael will become "a wild donkey of a man: his hand will be against everyone, and everyone's hand against him" (Gen. 16:12).

What are we to make of all this? Undoubtedly, one theme is miraculous birth. Sara, like Rivka and Raḥel after her, is infertile, so the children born to them are marked as divine gifts – in a strong sense, God's children.

יא אַחֲרֶיךָ הִמּוֹל לָכֶם כָּל־זָכָר: וּנְמַלְתֶּם אֵת בְּשַׂר עָרְלַתְכֶם
יב וְהָיָה לְאוֹת בְּרִית בֵּינִי וּבֵינֵיכֶם: וּבֶן־שְׁמֹנַת יָמִים יִמּוֹל לָכֶם
כָּל־זָכָר לְדֹרֹתֵיכֶם יְלִיד בָּיִת וּמִקְנַת־כֶּסֶף מִכֹּל בֶּן־נֵכָר
יג אֲשֶׁר לֹא מִזַּרְעֲךָ הוּא: הִמּוֹל ׀ יִמּוֹל יְלִיד בֵּיתְךָ וּמִקְנַת
יד כַּסְפֶּךָ וְהָיְתָה בְרִיתִי בִּבְשַׂרְכֶם לִבְרִית עוֹלָם: וְעָרֵל ׀ זָכָר
אֲשֶׁר לֹא־יִמּוֹל אֶת־בְּשַׂר עָרְלָתוֹ וְנִכְרְתָה הַנֶּפֶשׁ הַהִוא
טו מֵעַמֶּיהָ אֶת־בְּרִיתִי הֵפַר: וַיֹּאמֶר אֱלֹהִים אֶל־
אַבְרָהָם שָׂרַי אִשְׁתְּךָ לֹא־תִקְרָא אֶת־שְׁמָהּ שָׂרָי כִּי שָׂרָה
טז שְׁמָהּ: וּבֵרַכְתִּי אֹתָהּ וְגַם נָתַתִּי מִמֶּנָּה לְךָ בֵּן וּבֵרַכְתִּיהָ
יז וְהָיְתָה לְגוֹיִם מַלְכֵי עַמִּים מִמֶּנָּה יִהְיוּ: וַיִּפֹּל אַבְרָהָם עַל־
פָּנָיו וַיִּצְחָק וַיֹּאמֶר בְּלִבּוֹ הַלְּבֶן מֵאָה־שָׁנָה יִוָּלֵד וְאִם־שָׂרָה
יח הֲבַת־תִּשְׁעִים שָׁנָה תֵּלֵד: וַיֹּאמֶר אַבְרָהָם אֶל־הָאֱלֹהִים לוּ
יט יִשְׁמָעֵאל יִחְיֶה לְפָנֶיךָ: וַיֹּאמֶר אֱלֹהִים אֲבָל שָׂרָה אִשְׁתְּךָ
יֹלֶדֶת לְךָ בֵּן וְקָרָאתָ אֶת־שְׁמוֹ יִצְחָק וַהֲקִמֹתִי אֶת־בְּרִיתִי
כ אִתּוֹ לִבְרִית עוֹלָם לְזַרְעוֹ אַחֲרָיו: וּלְיִשְׁמָעֵאל שְׁמַעְתִּיךָ
הִנֵּה ׀ בֵּרַכְתִּי אֹתוֹ וְהִפְרֵיתִי אֹתוֹ וְהִרְבֵּיתִי אֹתוֹ בִּמְאֹד
כא מְאֹד שְׁנֵים־עָשָׂר נְשִׂיאִם יוֹלִיד וּנְתַתִּיו לְגוֹי גָּדוֹל: וְאֶת־
בְּרִיתִי אָקִים אֶת־יִצְחָק אֲשֶׁר תֵּלֵד לְךָ שָׂרָה לַמּוֹעֵד הַזֶּה

17:20 שְׁנֵים־עָשָׂר נְשִׂיאִם *Twelve princes* – Note the extraordinary length to which the text goes to insist that *Yishmael will be blessed by God*. This is stated four times, the first and last times to Hagar, the second and third to Avraham himself (Gen. 16:9–12; 17:20; 21:13, 18). The first, above in 16:10, *repeats to Hagar the promise God made to Avraham*, that his children would be too numerous to count (15:5). The handmaid will be blessed just as Avraham, the "knight of faith," will be. Here, the promise of "twelve princes" reminds us of Yaakov's twelve sons, each of whom becomes a tribe. The phrase "a great nation" likewise echoes God's promise to Avraham (12:2). He is being promised by God that, although Yitzḥak will continue the covenant, Yishmael will, in worldly terms, be no less great, perhaps greater. Certainly he will have a share in Avraham's blessing.

17:21 וְאֶת־בְּרִיתִי אָקִים אֶת־יִצְחָק *I will*

▶

22 will bear to you this time next year." When He finished
23 speaking with him, God went up from Avraham. On that
very day, Avraham took his son Yishmael, along with all
those born in his house or acquired with money, every
male in Avraham's household, and circumcised the flesh
24 of their foreskins as God had instructed him. Avraham MAFTIR
25 was ninety-nine years old when he was circumcised, and
26 his son Yishmael was thirteen. That very day, Avraham
27 and his son Yishmael were circumcised; and all the men
of his household, whether home-born or acquired from
strangers, were circumcised together with him.

The haftara for Parashat Lekh Lekha is on page 1414.

change takes time. *Faith is the ability to live with delay without losing trust in the promise; to experience disappointment without losing hope, to know that the road between the real and the ideal is long and yet be willing to undertake the journey.*

Jews are often restless and impatient: in the Talmud they are described (by a Sadducee) as an *ama peziza*, a "rash people" (Shabbat 88a). Yet none has waited longer – for freedom and equality, for the return to the land, and for the Messiah. To wait without despair, to hope and keep on hoping: that is the faith of Avraham and Sara's children, the faith that they themselves lived. And though it was shot through with disappointments, and though they themselves sometimes gave expression to their doubts and fears, it did not prove in vain. Jews kept faith alive. Faith kept the Jewish people alive.

כב בִּשְׁנָה הָאַחֶרֶת: וַיְכַל לְדַבֵּר אִתּוֹ וַיַּעַל אֱלֹהִים מֵעַל
כג אַבְרָהָם: וַיִּקַּח אַבְרָהָם אֶת־יִשְׁמָעֵאל בְּנוֹ וְאֵת כׇּל־יְלִידֵי
בֵיתוֹ וְאֵת כׇּל־מִקְנַת כַּסְפּוֹ כׇּל־זָכָר בְּאַנְשֵׁי בֵּית אַבְרָהָם
וַיָּמׇל אֶת־בְּשַׂר עׇרְלָתָם בְּעֶצֶם הַיּוֹם הַזֶּה כַּאֲשֶׁר דִּבֶּר אִתּוֹ
כד אֱלֹהִים: וְאַבְרָהָם בֶּן־תִּשְׁעִים וָתֵשַׁע שָׁנָה בְּהִמֹּלוֹ בְּשַׂר מפטיר
כה עׇרְלָתוֹ: וְיִשְׁמָעֵאל בְּנוֹ בֶּן־שְׁלֹשׁ עֶשְׂרֵה שָׁנָה בְּהִמֹּלוֹ אֵת
כו בְּשַׂר עׇרְלָתוֹ: בְּעֶצֶם הַיּוֹם הַזֶּה נִמּוֹל אַבְרָהָם וְיִשְׁמָעֵאל
כז בְּנוֹ: וְכׇל־אַנְשֵׁי בֵיתוֹ יְלִיד בָּיִת וּמִקְנַת־כֶּסֶף מֵאֵת בֶּן־נֵכָר
נִמֹּלוּ אִתּוֹ:

The הפטרה *for* פרשת לך לך *is on page 1415.*

But there is also a counter-theme, moving in the opposite direction. The patriarchs and prophets move in the real world, not a world of magic and myth and larger-than-life legend. Avraham begins a journey, but it is beset by obstacles. He receives a promise, but its fulfillment is long delayed and fraught with diversions and false turns.

Avraham's journey, like that of Moshe and the Israelites in a later generation, takes longer than they or we expect. There is no sudden transition from here to the Promised Land, from starting point to destination. Taking Genesis literally, the universe might be made in seven days, but anything in the human world that involves profound

Parashat Vayera

18 1 The Lord appeared to him by the Oaks of Mamre as he was sitting at the entrance to his tent in the heat of the day.

---

lords" or "sirs," it has no special sanctity. Jewish law rules that in the later scene with Lot, *adonai* is read as "sirs," but in the case of Avraham it is read as "Lord."

This is an extraordinary fact, because it suggests that *Avraham actually interrupts God as He is about to speak, asking Him to wait while he attends to the visitors.* Faced with a choice between listening to God and offering hospitality to what seem to be human beings, Avraham chooses the latter. God accedes to his request, and waits while Avraham brings the visitors food and drink, before engaging him in dialogue about the fate of Sedom.

What the passage is telling us is something of immense profundity. The idolaters of Avraham's time worshipped the forces of nature as gods. They worshipped power and the powerful. Avraham knows, however, that God is not *in* nature but *beyond* nature. There is only one thing in the universe on which He has set His image: the human person, *every* person, powerful and powerless alike.

Avraham knows the paradoxical truth that to live the life of faith is to see the trace of God in the face of the stranger. It is easy to receive the Divine Presence when God appears as God. What is difficult is to sense the Divine Presence when it comes disguised as three anonymous passersby. Avraham knows that serving God and offering hospitality to strangers are not two things but one. That, we are to understand, is Avraham's greatness.

18:1 וַיֵּרָא אֵלָיו יהוה... כְּחֹם הַיּוֹם *The Lord appeared to him... in the heat of the day* – What was the content of this revelation? According to the reading explained above ("The Three Visitors"), God appears to tell Avraham of His plan to destroy Sedom; the intervening passage is an interruption. For Rambam, on the other hand, "the general statement that the Lord appeared to Avraham is followed by the description of the way in which that appearance of the Lord took place, namely, that Avraham first saw three men; he ran and spoke to them" (*Moreh Nevukhim* II:42). Our verse, in that case, is a chapter heading. First the Torah states, in general terms, that God appeared to Avraham, then it describes how: in a vision of three men. Verse 1 is a superscription to the chapter as a whole, not a separate incident.

Rashi's explanation is different. The previous chapter has told of Avraham's circumcision at the age of ninety-nine. Following the midrashic assumption that God's conduct is a model for ours, Rashi infers that God's appearance in the first verse is "to visit the sick"

פרשת וירא

יח א וַיֵּרָא אֵלָיו יְהוָֹה בְּאֵלֹנֵי מַמְרֵא וְהוּא יֹשֵׁב פֶּתַח־הָאֹהֶל כְּחֹם טו

VAYERA

God appears to Avraham. Three strangers pass by. Avraham engages in a momentous dialogue with God about justice. Lot, with his wife and two of his daughters, is rescued from the destruction of Sedom. Eventually, the promised child, Yitzḥak, is born to Sara. The *parasha* ends with the great test of *akedat Yitzḥak* (the binding of Yitzḥak).

In Lekh Lekha we saw Avraham accept *personal* and *moral* responsibility. Now we see him accept *collective* responsibility. He prays for the inhabitants of Sedom, even though he knows they are sinful, on the grounds that there may be innocent, righteous people among them. They are not his kin, not part of his specific covenant with God, but they are human beings, and Avraham feels the imperative of praying, even arguing with God, on their behalf.

In contrast to the builders of Bavel, he also demonstrates *ontological* responsibility, the duty of human beings to respond to the otherness, and the command, of God. This is the basis of the greatest of his trials, his willingness to sacrifice even his son if God so commands it. Avraham knows that we are but "dust and ashes" (Gen. 18:27) in the face of the Infinite. His task is to obey the will of Heaven on earth, encapsulated in the words "to keep the way of the Lord, by doing what is right and just" (18:19).

THE THREE VISITORS

The interpretation of this chapter hinges upon the way we translate the word *Adonai* in Avraham's appeal: "*Adonai,* if I have found favor in your sight, please do not pass your servant by." *Adonai* can be a reference to one of the names of God. It can also be read as "my lords" or "sirs." In the first case, Avraham would be addressing God: "Please God, do not leave. Stay while I serve the visitors." In the second, he would be speaking to the passersby, asking them not to pass by but to stay, rest, and eat. (The sentence shifts between singular and plural because, in this reading, Avraham is addressing the men collectively, but specifically directing his words to the one he takes to be their leader or senior.)

Normally, differences of interpretation of biblical narrative have no halakhic implications. They are matters of legitimate disagreement. This case of Avraham's addressee is unusual, however, because if we translate *Adonai* as "Lord" it is a holy name, and both the writing of the word by a scribe, and the way we treat a parchment or document containing it, have special stringencies in Jewish law. If, by contrast, we translate it as "my

2 Avraham looked up and saw three men standing nearby.
The moment he saw them, he ran from the opening of his
tent to greet them, and bowed down low to the ground.
3 He said, "My Lord, if I have found favor in your sight,
4 please do not pass your servant by. Let a little water be
brought so that you can wash your feet and rest under the
5 tree. Since you are passing by your servant, let me bring a
morsel of bread so that you can be refreshed before you
go on your way." They replied, "Do just as you say."
6 Avraham rushed to Sara in the tent and said, "Hurry – three
7 *se'a* of fine flour; knead it and bake bread." Avraham
himself ran to the herd and took a tender choice calf and
8 gave it to the young man, who hurried to prepare it. He
brought curds and milk and the calf that had been
prepared, and set them before them, standing by them as
9 they ate, under the tree. They asked him, "Where is your
10 wife Sara?" "There, in the tent," he replied. Then one of
them said, "I will return to you this time next year, and
your wife Sara will have a son." Sara was listening at the
11 opening of the tent behind him. Avraham and Sara were
already old, advanced in years; the way of women no
12 longer visited Sara. So Sara laughed to herself, saying,
"Now that I am worn out, can I have this pleasure? With
13 my lord an old man?" Then the LORD said to Avraham,
"Why did Sara laugh and say, 'Can I really have a child,
14 now that I am old?' Is anything beyond the LORD's
powers? At the due time next year I will return to you,
15 and Sara will have a son." Sara, because she was afraid, SHENI

haShekhina, "greater is hospitality than welcoming the Divine Presence" (Shabbat 127a; Shevuot 35b).

18:8 עֹמֵד עֲלֵיהֶם *Standing by them* – Using a very literal reading of the verses, Rabbi Shalom of Belz notes that in verse 2, the visitors are spoken of as standing *above* Avraham (*nitzavim alav*), while in verse 8, Avraham is described as standing *above them* (*omed aleihem*). At first, the visitors were higher than Avraham because they were angels and he a mere human being. But when he gave them food and drink and shelter, he stood even higher than the angels (cited in *Peninei Ḥasidut* on Gen. 18:2).

ב הַיּוֹם: וַיִּשָּׂא עֵינָיו וַיַּרְא וְהִנֵּה שְׁלֹשָׁה אֲנָשִׁים נִצָּבִים עָלָיו
ג וַיַּרְא וַיָּרָץ לִקְרָאתָם מִפֶּתַח הָאֹהֶל וַיִּשְׁתַּחוּ אָרְצָה: וַיֹּאמַר
אֲדֹנָי אִם־נָא מָצָאתִי חֵן בְּעֵינֶיךָ אַל־נָא תַעֲבֹר מֵעַל עַבְדֶּךָ:
ד יֻקַּח־נָא מְעַט־מַיִם וְרַחֲצוּ רַגְלֵיכֶם וְהִשָּׁעֲנוּ תַּחַת הָעֵץ:
ה וְאֶקְחָה פַת־לֶחֶם וְסַעֲדוּ לִבְּכֶם אַחַר תַּעֲבֹרוּ כִּי־עַל־כֵּן
עֲבַרְתֶּם עַל־עַבְדְּכֶם וַיֹּאמְרוּ כֵּן תַּעֲשֶׂה כַּאֲשֶׁר דִּבַּרְתָּ:
ו וַיְמַהֵר אַבְרָהָם הָאֹהֱלָה אֶל־שָׂרָה וַיֹּאמֶר מַהֲרִי שְׁלֹשׁ סְאִים
ז קֶמַח סֹלֶת לוּשִׁי וַעֲשִׂי עֻגוֹת: וְאֶל־הַבָּקָר רָץ אַבְרָהָם וַיִּקַּח
ח בֶּן־בָּקָר רַךְ וָטוֹב וַיִּתֵּן אֶל־הַנַּעַר וַיְמַהֵר לַעֲשׂוֹת אֹתוֹ: וַיִּקַּח
חֶמְאָה וְחָלָב וּבֶן־הַבָּקָר אֲשֶׁר עָשָׂה וַיִּתֵּן לִפְנֵיהֶם וְהוּא
ט עֹמֵד עֲלֵיהֶם תַּחַת הָעֵץ וַיֹּאכֵלוּ: וַיֹּאמְרוּ אֵלָיו אַיֵּה שָׂרָה
י אִשְׁתֶּךָ וַיֹּאמֶר הִנֵּה בָאֹהֶל: וַיֹּאמֶר שׁוֹב אָשׁוּב אֵלֶיךָ כָּעֵת
חַיָּה וְהִנֵּה־בֵן לְשָׂרָה אִשְׁתֶּךָ וְשָׂרָה שֹׁמַעַת פֶּתַח הָאֹהֶל
יא וְהוּא אַחֲרָיו: וְאַבְרָהָם וְשָׂרָה זְקֵנִים בָּאִים בַּיָּמִים חָדַל
יב לִהְיוֹת לְשָׂרָה אֹרַח כַּנָּשִׁים: וַתִּצְחַק שָׂרָה בְּקִרְבָּהּ לֵאמֹר
יג אַחֲרֵי בְלֹתִי הָיְתָה־לִּי עֶדְנָה וַאדֹנִי זָקֵן: וַיֹּאמֶר יְהוָה אֶל־
אַבְרָהָם לָמָּה זֶּה צָחֲקָה שָׂרָה לֵאמֹר הַאַף אֻמְנָם אֵלֵד וַאֲנִי
יד זָקַנְתִּי: הֲיִפָּלֵא מֵיְהוָה דָּבָר לַמּוֹעֵד אָשׁוּב אֵלֶיךָ כָּעֵת חַיָּה
טו וּלְשָׂרָה בֵן: וַתְּכַחֵשׁ שָׂרָה ׀ לֵאמֹר לֹא צָחַקְתִּי כִּי ׀ יָרֵאָה שני

(commentary on Gen. 18:1), teaching us the mitzva by divine example. Normally, a divine appearance is a prelude to an act of communication, but here, not so. God "appeared" without saying anything. There are times – visiting the sick – when mere presence is enough.

18:4 וְהִשָּׁעֲנוּ תַּחַת הָעֵץ *Rest under the tree* – Unbeknown to Avraham, these passersby are angels, bringing news that Sara will have a child, Yitzḥak, first child of the covenant. At the dawn of Jewish time, an association is being struck: God shows kindness to those who show kindness to strangers. The Hebrew letter *bet*, with which the Torah begins, also means "house." It is open at one side, signaling graphically that a Jewish home is one that is open to visitors and strangers. From the story of Avraham the Rabbis derive the rule – no mere figure of speech but meant categorically – that *gedola hakhnassat orḥim mikabbalat pnei*

denied it: "I did not laugh," she said. But He said, "Not so.
16 You laughed." The men got up to leave and looked down
toward Sedom. Avraham accompanied them to see them
17 on their way. The LORD said, "Shall I hide from Avraham
18 what I am about to do? Avraham is about to become a
great and mighty nation, and through him all the nations
19 on earth will be blessed. For I have chosen him so that he
may direct his children and his household after him to
keep the way of the LORD by doing what is right and just,
that the LORD may bring about for Avraham what He
20 spoke of for him." Then the LORD said, "The outcry
against Sedom and Amora is great, and their sin is very
21 grave. I shall go down now and see if they have really
done as much as the outcry that has reached Me. If not, I
22 will know." The men turned from there and went toward

---

is why Judaism – the religion for which justice is central – is a religion of argument and debate, for the sake of Heaven, even if it involves argument with Heaven itself. And it begins here with Avraham, the man empowered by God to argue with God so that justice might be seen to be done.

18:19 לַעֲשׂוֹת צְדָקָה וּמִשְׁפָּט *By doing what is right and just* – The Bible tells us very little about Avraham that might explain why he is chosen for the mission he undertakes. It does not call him righteous, as it does in the case of Noaḥ. It does not portray him as a miracle worker, as it does Moshe. The only place in the Bible to explain why Avraham is chosen is this verse. He is chosen because he will hand his way of life on to future generations.

The words of this explanation imply three things about what it is to be an heir of Avraham. On the most basic level, it means that we are the guardians of our children's future. We must ensure that they have a world to inherit. Today that means political, economic, and environmental sustainability.

Second, education – directing our children and our household after us – is a sacred task. Teach children to love, and they will have hope. Teach them to hate, and they will have only anger and the desire for revenge. Thinking about the past leads to war. Thinking about the future helps us to make peace.

Third, what is the end goal of this education? How are we to keep the way of the Lord? By doing what is right and just. That is the test. If religious people do what is right and just, they are keeping the way. If they do not, then somehow they have lost their way.

טז וַיֹּאמֶר ׀ לֹא כִּי צָחָקְתְּ׃ וַיָּקֻמוּ מִשָּׁם הָאֲנָשִׁים וַיַּשְׁקִפוּ
יז עַל־פְּנֵי סְדֹם וְאַבְרָהָם הֹלֵךְ עִמָּם לְשַׁלְּחָם׃ וַיהוה אָמָר
יח הַמְכַסֶּה אֲנִי מֵאַבְרָהָם אֲשֶׁר אֲנִי עֹשֶׂה׃ וְאַבְרָהָם הָיוֹ יִהְיֶה
יט לְגוֹי גָּדוֹל וְעָצוּם וְנִבְרְכוּ־בוֹ כֹּל גּוֹיֵי הָאָרֶץ׃ כִּי יְדַעְתִּיו
לְמַעַן אֲשֶׁר יְצַוֶּה אֶת־בָּנָיו וְאֶת־בֵּיתוֹ אַחֲרָיו וְשָׁמְרוּ דֶּרֶךְ
יהוה לַעֲשׂוֹת צְדָקָה וּמִשְׁפָּט לְמַעַן הָבִיא יהוה עַל־אַבְרָהָם
כ אֵת אֲשֶׁר־דִּבֶּר עָלָיו׃ וַיֹּאמֶר יהוה זַעֲקַת סְדֹם וַעֲמֹרָה כִּי־
כא רָבָּה וְחַטָּאתָם כִּי כָבְדָה מְאֹד׃ אֵרְדָה־נָּא וְאֶרְאֶה
כב הַכְּצַעֲקָתָהּ הַבָּאָה אֵלַי עָשׂוּ ׀ כָּלָה וְאִם־לֹא אֵדָעָה׃ וַיִּפְנוּ
מִשָּׁם הָאֲנָשִׁים וַיֵּלְכוּ סְדֹמָה וְאַבְרָהָם עוֹדֶנּוּ עֹמֵד לִפְנֵי

AVRAHAM INTERCEDES FOR SEDOM

This is a turning point in the history of the spirit. How can finite, fallible human beings challenge God Himself, and this, not in opposition to faith, but as part of the life of faith itself? How, in our *parasha*, can Avraham, who describes himself as mere "dust and ashes" (Gen. 18:27), confront "the judge of all the earth" (18:25), challenging God's verdict on the people of Sedom?

The answer is given by the Torah itself. It is clear that this speech of God's is an invitation to Avraham to speak. "Shall I hide from Avraham what I am about to do?" asks God. Not only does He invite Avraham to speak; He even signals in advance the words He wants Avraham to use – "right" (*tzedek/tzedaka*) and "just" (*mishpat*). These constitute "the way of the Lord" (18:19) that God wants Avraham to teach his children.

Avraham responds by using precisely these words in his challenge. He uses the root *tz-d-k* seven times. He uses the root *sh-p-t* twice, at the beginning and end of the key sentence: "Shall the judge [*hashofet*] of all the earth not do justice [*mishpat*]?" (18:25).

God wants Avraham and his descendants to be agents of justice. *For justice to be done and seen to be done, both sides must be heard.* There must be not only an advocate for the prosecution but also for the defense. That is what God wants of Avraham: to be the defense attorney for the people of Sedom; to argue their case; to be the voice of the other side. And that is precisely what Avraham does.

God needs humanity to become His partner in the administration of justice. He needs to hear a dissenting voice. No judge, however omniscient and infallible, can execute justice in the absence of counterargument. That

23 Sedom, while Avraham still stood before the LORD. Then
Avraham stepped forward and said: "Would You really
24 sweep away the righteous with the wicked? What if there
are fifty righteous people in the city? Would You really
sweep it away and not spare the place for the sake of the
25 fifty righteous people in it? Far be it from You to do such
a thing – to kill the righteous with the wicked, treating
the righteous like the wicked. Far be it from You! Shall
26 the judge of all the earth not do justice?" The LORD said,
"If I find fifty righteous people in the city of Sedom, I will
27 spare the whole place for their sake." Then Avraham
spoke up again and said, "Now that I have dared to speak
28 to the Lord, though I am mere dust and ashes, what if the
righteous are five less than fifty? Will You destroy the
whole city for the lack of five people?" He said, "If I find
29 forty-five there, I will not destroy it." He spoke to Him yet
again, saying, "What if only forty are found there?" He
30 said, "I will refrain for the sake of the forty." Then he said,
"Please, may the Lord not be angry, but let me speak.
What if only thirty are found there?" He answered, "I will
31 refrain if I find thirty there." "Now that I have dared to
speak to the Lord," he said, "what if only twenty are found
there?" He said, "I will not destroy, for the sake of the
32 twenty." Then he said, "Please, may the Lord not be angry,

---

justice and mercy which binds both creature and Creator, reaching a climax in this question of Avraham's.

What then, for Judaism, is the connection between religion, law, and morality? Is "justice" by definition what the "judge" decides, or is He bound by a code that exists outside Him? The answer is that law, as portrayed in the Torah, is *covenantal*. It is born in the mutual agreement of God and humanity to engage in constructing a society on the foundations of compassion, righteousness, and justice. God and man come together to form a covenant which binds both to a morality that each recognizes as righteous and just, much as two partners come together to form a marriage which both recognize as imposing obligations. Neither God nor man arbitrarily invent morality, just as neither husband nor wife invent marriage. By entering into a covenant, both agree to bind themselves to one another within its terms. Thus love is translated into a moral relationship whose terms are law.

כג יהוה: וַיִּגַּשׁ אַבְרָהָם וַיֹּאמַר הַאַף תִּסְפֶּה צַדִּיק עִם־רָשָׁע:
כד אוּלַי יֵשׁ חֲמִשִּׁים צַדִּיקִם בְּתוֹךְ הָעִיר הַאַף תִּסְפֶּה וְלֹא־תִשָּׂא
כה לַמָּקוֹם לְמַעַן חֲמִשִּׁים הַצַּדִּיקִם אֲשֶׁר בְּקִרְבָּהּ: חָלִלָה לְּךָ
מֵעֲשֹׂת ׀ כַּדָּבָר הַזֶּה לְהָמִית צַדִּיק עִם־רָשָׁע וְהָיָה כַצַּדִּיק
כָּרָשָׁע חָלִלָה לָּךְ הֲשֹׁפֵט כָּל־הָאָרֶץ לֹא יַעֲשֶׂה מִשְׁפָּט:
כו וַיֹּאמֶר יהוה אִם־אֶמְצָא בִסְדֹם חֲמִשִּׁים צַדִּיקִם בְּתוֹךְ הָעִיר
כז וְנָשָׂאתִי לְכָל־הַמָּקוֹם בַּעֲבוּרָם: וַיַּעַן אַבְרָהָם וַיֹּאמַר הִנֵּה־
כח נָא הוֹאַלְתִּי לְדַבֵּר אֶל־אֲדֹנָי וְאָנֹכִי עָפָר וָאֵפֶר: אוּלַי יַחְסְרוּן
חֲמִשִּׁים הַצַּדִּיקִם חֲמִשָּׁה הֲתַשְׁחִית בַּחֲמִשָּׁה אֶת־כָּל־הָעִיר
כט וַיֹּאמֶר לֹא אַשְׁחִית אִם־אֶמְצָא שָׁם אַרְבָּעִים וַחֲמִשָּׁה: וַיֹּסֶף
עוֹד לְדַבֵּר אֵלָיו וַיֹּאמַר אוּלַי יִמָּצְאוּן שָׁם אַרְבָּעִים וַיֹּאמֶר
ל לֹא אֶעֱשֶׂה בַּעֲבוּר הָאַרְבָּעִים: וַיֹּאמֶר אַל־נָא יִחַר לַאדֹנָי
וַאֲדַבֵּרָה אוּלַי יִמָּצְאוּן שָׁם שְׁלֹשִׁים וַיֹּאמֶר לֹא אֶעֱשֶׂה אִם־
לא אֶמְצָא שָׁם שְׁלֹשִׁים: וַיֹּאמֶר הִנֵּה־נָא הוֹאַלְתִּי לְדַבֵּר אֶל־
אֲדֹנָי אוּלַי יִמָּצְאוּן שָׁם עֶשְׂרִים וַיֹּאמֶר לֹא אַשְׁחִית בַּעֲבוּר
לב הָעֶשְׂרִים: וַיֹּאמֶר אַל־נָא יִחַר לַאדֹנָי וַאֲדַבְּרָה אַךְ־הַפַּעַם

18:24 צַדִּיקִם בְּתוֹךְ הָעִיר *Righteous people in the city* – Rabbi Samson Raphael Hirsch once asked whom Avraham might have had in mind when he asked God to spare Sedom if it contained ten righteous people. What would it have been like to be righteous in such a corrupt civilization? He answered that such a person would not be "one who keeps to his own four walls." He would instead be one who "is to be found 'in the midst of the city' – *betokh ha'ir* – and in lively connection with everything and everybody." Even in Sedom, to be righteous is not to be segregated. It is to be a participant in society, challenging it where it needs to be challenged, but not abandoning it.

18:25 הֲשֹׁפֵט כָּל־הָאָרֶץ לֹא יַעֲשֶׂה מִשְׁפָּט *Shall the judge of all the earth not do justice?* – Perhaps the single greatest contribution of Israel to the religious heritage of mankind is what is often called ethical monotheism: the idea that God is not merely the author of the moral law but is Himself bound by it. It is this that gives rise to some of the most awe-inspiring passages in the Tanakh in which Moshe, Yirmeyahu, Iyov, and others argue with God on the basis of the shared code of

but let me speak just once more. What if only ten are
found there?" He said, "I will not destroy, for the sake of
33 the ten." When the LORD had finished speaking with
Avraham, He left. And Avraham went back to his place.
19 1 The two angels arrived at Sedom in the evening, while Lot SHELISHI
was sitting in the city gate. Lot saw them, and rose to greet
2 them, bowing with his face to the ground. He said,
"Please, my lords, turn aside to your servant's house, stay
the night, wash your feet, and then go on your way early in
the morning." "No," they said, "we will spend the night in
3 the square." But he was so insistent that they followed him
to his house and came in. He made a feast for them and

---

covenant with God. Yet even as he calls himself a "migrant and a visitor" (23:4), the Hittites see him as "a prince of God in our midst" (23:6). That equation has not changed. Non-Jews respect Jews who respect Judaism. They are embarrassed by Jews who are embarrassed by Judaism. Never be ambivalent about who and what you are.

19:3 מַצּוֹת *Unleavened bread* – Lot makes matzot. On this, Rashi makes a strange comment: *Pesaḥ haya*, he writes. It was Passover. How could Lot have the foresight to know that the date of the angels' visit would one day become the festival of Passover? And why should he be observing its laws generations before it became a reality?

Rashi is hinting that Lot's experience in Sedom will be repeated in Egypt, this time on a national scale. Like Lot, the Israelites will settle in their new home and grow affluent. Rabbi Joseph Soloveitchik made an insightful comment about the opening of the book of Exodus (*Divrei Hashkafa*, 41–43). The first verse reads, "And these are the names of the sons of Yisrael who came (*haba'im*) to Egypt" (Ex. 1:1). The Hebrew verb appears in the present tense rather than the past. In fact, the Israelites had come generations before, but in the eyes of the Egyptians it was as if they had just arrived. The new Pharaoh, announcing his program of persecution, justifies it with the words "If war breaks out they may join our enemies and fight against us" (1:10). In the eyes of the Egyptians, they are not citizens but aliens, just as the people of Sedom see Lot. The Israelites, for their part, "acquired holdings" in Egypt (Gen. 47:27), implying that they intend to make it their home. It is not easy for Moshe to get them to leave. In the end they are "driven out" by the Egyptians (Ex. 12:39), just as Lot is physically dragged by the angels from Sedom (Gen. 19:16).

Sadly, this has often been the fate of Jews. Facing danger, they were slow to see it – in Spain in the fifteenth century,

אוּלַי יִמָּצְאוּן שָׁם עֲשָׂרָה וַיֹּאמֶר לֹא אַשְׁחִית בַּעֲבוּר
לג הָעֲשָׂרָה׃ וַיֵּלֶךְ יהוה כַּאֲשֶׁר כִּלָּה לְדַבֵּר אֶל־אַבְרָהָם
יט א וְאַבְרָהָם שָׁב לִמְקֹמוֹ׃ וַיָּבֹאוּ שְׁנֵי הַמַּלְאָכִים סְדֹמָה בָּעֶרֶב טז שלישי
וְלוֹט יֹשֵׁב בְּשַׁעַר־סְדֹם וַיַּרְא־לוֹט וַיָּקָם לִקְרָאתָם וַיִּשְׁתַּחוּ
ב אַפַּיִם אָרְצָה׃ וַיֹּאמֶר הִנֶּה נָּא־אֲדֹנַי סוּרוּ נָא אֶל־בֵּית
עַבְדְּכֶם וְלִינוּ וְרַחֲצוּ רַגְלֵיכֶם וְהִשְׁכַּמְתֶּם וַהֲלַכְתֶּם לְדַרְכְּכֶם
ג וַיֹּאמְרוּ לֹּא כִּי בָרְחוֹב נָלִין׃ וַיִּפְצַר־בָּם מְאֹד וַיָּסֻרוּ אֵלָיו
וַיָּבֹאוּ אֶל־בֵּיתוֹ וַיַּעַשׂ לָהֶם מִשְׁתֶּה וּמַצּוֹת אָפָה וַיֹּאכֵלוּ׃

LOT IN SEDOM

Having chosen to put down roots in the Jordan Valley and the cities of the plain, Lot and his family become profoundly assimilated. His daughters marry local men; Lot rises to public position. Sedom is where Lot sees himself as belonging – so much so that the visitors have to drag him away physically.

Lot's sense of belonging, however, is either naivete or self-deception. The text makes this clear at three points. The first is the attempted sexual assault on Lot's visitors (Gen. 19:4–5). Evidently the people of Sedom do not take kindly to strangers. This is the first hint that perhaps Lot is also, in their eyes, a stranger.

The second indication is brutally explicit: "'Get out of our way,' they replied [to Lot, when he begged them to respect his visitors]. Then they said, 'This fellow came here as a migrant and now he is setting himself up as a judge! We will treat you worse than them'" (19:9).

The third comes when, telling his daughters' husbands that they must escape because the city is about to be destroyed, "his sons-in-law thought him laughable" (19:14). Lot's elaborate new identity is about to come crashing down about him. He has not been accepted in this place. Sedom hates strangers, they still consider Lot a stranger, and his sons-in-law regard him as a fool.

Yet despite this, he hesitates. He has invested too much of himself into the project of making his home among the people of the plain. Now he faces the ultimate existential question: "Who am I?" Having tried so hard to become one of them, he finds it almost impossible to tear himself away.

The lives of Lot and Avraham exemplify for all time the contrast between ambivalence and the security that comes from knowing who one is and why. Lot, who has tried to become someone else, finds himself regarded by his neighbors as an alien, an arriviste, an interloper. To his own sons-in-law he is "laughable." Avraham lives a different kind of life. He fights a war on behalf of his neighbors. He prays for them. But he lives apart, true to his faith, his mission, and his

4 baked unleavened bread, and they ate. They had not yet
gone to bed when all the townsmen, the men of Sedom –
young and old, all the people from every
5 quarter – surrounded the house. They called to Lot,
"Where are the men who came to you tonight? Bring
6 them out to us so that we may know them." Lot went out
7 to speak to them, shutting the door behind him, and said,
8 "My brothers, please do not do this evil. I have two
daughters who have never known a man. Let me bring
them out to you; you may do what you like with them.
But do not do anything to these men, for they have come
9 under the protection of my roof." "Get out of our way,"
they replied. "This fellow came here as a migrant and now
he is setting himself up as a judge! We will treat you worse
than them." They pressed hard against Lot and moved
10 forward to break down the door. But the men inside
reached out and pulled Lot back into the house and shut
11 the door behind him. Then they struck the men at the
door, young and old, with blindness so that they wore
12 themselves out trying in vain to find the door. The visitors
said to Lot, "Who else do you have here – children-in-
law, sons, daughters, or anyone else in the city? Bring
13 them out of here, because we are about to destroy this
place. So great is the outcry against them before the Lord
14 that He has sent us to destroy it." Lot went out and spoke
to his sons-in-law, the men who were betrothed to his
daughters, and told them, "Get up and leave this place:
the Lord is about to destroy the city!" But his sons-in-
15 law thought him laughable. As dawn was breaking, the
angels hurried Lot. "Get up," they said. "Take your wife
and your two daughters here, or you will be swept away
16 amid the city's sin." Still he hesitated. So the men seized

The *shalshelet* is an unusual note, going up and down, up and down, as if unable to move forward to the next note. The sixteenth-century commentator Rabbi Yosef Ibn Kaspi (in his commentary on Gen. 19:16) best defined what it was meant to convey: namely, a psychological state of uncertainty and indecision. We

ד טֶרֶם יִשְׁכָּבוּ וְאַנְשֵׁי הָעִיר אַנְשֵׁי סְדֹם נָסַבּוּ עַל־הַבַּיִת מִנַּעַר
ה וְעַד־זָקֵן כָּל־הָעָם מִקָּצֶה: וַיִּקְרְאוּ אֶל־לוֹט וַיֹּאמְרוּ לוֹ אַיֵּה
הָאֲנָשִׁים אֲשֶׁר־בָּאוּ אֵלֶיךָ הַלָּיְלָה הוֹצִיאֵם אֵלֵינוּ וְנֵדְעָה
ו אֹתָם: וַיֵּצֵא אֲלֵהֶם לוֹט הַפֶּתְחָה וְהַדֶּלֶת סָגַר אַחֲרָיו:
ז ח וַיֹּאמַר אַל־נָא אַחַי תָּרֵעוּ: הִנֵּה־נָא לִי שְׁתֵּי בָנוֹת אֲשֶׁר
לֹא־יָדְעוּ אִישׁ אוֹצִיאָה־נָּא אֶתְהֶן אֲלֵיכֶם וַעֲשׂוּ לָהֶן כַּטּוֹב
בְּעֵינֵיכֶם רַק לָאֲנָשִׁים הָאֵל אַל־תַּעֲשׂוּ דָבָר כִּי־עַל־כֵּן בָּאוּ
ט בְּצֵל קֹרָתִי: וַיֹּאמְרוּ ׀ גֶּשׁ־הָלְאָה וַיֹּאמְרוּ הָאֶחָד בָּא־לָגוּר
וַיִּשְׁפֹּט שָׁפוֹט עַתָּה נָרַע לְךָ מֵהֶם וַיִּפְצְרוּ בָאִישׁ בְּלוֹט מְאֹד
י וַיִּגְּשׁוּ לִשְׁבֹּר הַדָּלֶת: וַיִּשְׁלְחוּ הָאֲנָשִׁים אֶת־יָדָם וַיָּבִיאוּ
יא אֶת־לוֹט אֲלֵיהֶם הַבָּיְתָה וְאֶת־הַדֶּלֶת סָגָרוּ: וְאֶת־הָאֲנָשִׁים
אֲשֶׁר־פֶּתַח הַבַּיִת הִכּוּ בַּסַּנְוֵרִים מִקָּטֹן וְעַד־גָּדוֹל וַיִּלְאוּ
יב לִמְצֹא הַפָּתַח: וַיֹּאמְרוּ הָאֲנָשִׁים אֶל־לוֹט עֹד מִי־לְךָ פֹה
חָתָן וּבָנֶיךָ וּבְנֹתֶיךָ וְכֹל אֲשֶׁר־לְךָ בָּעִיר הוֹצֵא מִן־הַמָּקוֹם:
יג כִּי־מַשְׁחִתִים אֲנַחְנוּ אֶת־הַמָּקוֹם הַזֶּה כִּי־גָדְלָה צַעֲקָתָם
יד אֶת־פְּנֵי יְהוָה וַיְשַׁלְּחֵנוּ יְהוָה לְשַׁחֲתָהּ: וַיֵּצֵא לוֹט וַיְדַבֵּר ׀
אֶל־חֲתָנָיו ׀ לֹקְחֵי בְנֹתָיו וַיֹּאמֶר קוּמוּ צְּאוּ מִן־הַמָּקוֹם הַזֶּה
כִּי־מַשְׁחִית יְהוָה אֶת־הָעִיר וַיְהִי כִמְצַחֵק בְּעֵינֵי חֲתָנָיו:
טו וּכְמוֹ הַשַּׁחַר עָלָה וַיָּאִיצוּ הַמַּלְאָכִים בְּלוֹט לֵאמֹר קוּם קַח
אֶת־אִשְׁתְּךָ וְאֶת־שְׁתֵּי בְנֹתֶיךָ הַנִּמְצָאֹת פֶּן־תִּסָּפֶה בַּעֲוֺן
טז הָעִיר: וַיִּתְמַהְמָהּ ׀ וַיַּחֲזִיקוּ הָאֲנָשִׁים בְּיָדוֹ וּבְיַד־אִשְׁתּוֹ וּבְיַד

in Europe in the twentieth. How could a country to which they had contributed so much turn against them? How could they, who had lived there for so long, not be accepted? This delay – the recurrence of Lot's ambivalence – was fraught with risk. The people of history was sometimes deaf to the warning signals of history. This too, tragically, is part of the Passover story, and it begins with Lot in Sedom. Rashi's comment is profound: without knowing it, Lot is living through the first Passover.

19:16 וַיִּתְמַהְמָהּ *He hesitated* – The Torah does not have a word for ambivalence. It does, however, have a tune for it. This is the rare note known as the *shalshelet*.

him, his wife, and his two daughters by the hand and led
them safely outside the city, for the LORD had mercy
17 upon him. As soon as they had brought them out, one
said, "Run for your life. Do not look back. Do not stop
anywhere in the plain. Flee to the mountains or you will
18 be swept away." But Lot said to them, "No, my lords,
19 please. Your servant has found favor in your eyes, and you
have done me great kindness in saving my life. But I
cannot flee to the mountains; the disaster would overtake
20 me, and I would die. There is a town here close enough
for refuge. It is small. Let me flee there – is it not small? – so
21 that I might survive." "Very well," he said, "I will grant this REVI'I
request also; I will not overthrow the town of which you
22 speak. But hurry. Flee there, because I cannot do anything
23 until you reach it." That is why the town is called Tzoar. By
the time Lot reached Tzoar, the sun had risen over the
24 land. Then the LORD rained down sulfur and fire on
Sedom and Amora. Out of the heavens it came from the
25 LORD. He overthrew those cities, and the whole plain,
and all the cities' inhabitants, and the vegetation on the
26 land. But Lot's wife looked back – and she was turned
27 into a pillar of salt. Avraham rose early the next morning
and returned to the place where he had stood before the
28 LORD. He looked down toward Sedom and Amora and
all the land of the plain, and he saw thick smoke rising

---

the more he or she will agonize over whether they have made the right choice. They have second thoughts; they need reassurance; they "look back."

19:26 וַתַּבֵּט אִשְׁתּוֹ מֵאַחֲרָיו *Lot's wife looked back – To mend the past, first you have to secure the future.* I learned this from Holocaust survivors. Many of them did not speak about those years, even to their spouses or their children, sometimes for as long as forty or fifty years. Only when they had secured the future did they allow themselves to look back at the past. Only when they had built a life did they permit themselves to remember death. I think the Holocaust survivors knew that if they turned and looked back, they, like Lot's wife who disobeyed the angels, would be reduced to the salt of tears.

שְׁתֵּ֣י בְנֹתָ֔יו בְּחֶמְלַ֥ת יְהוָ֖ה עָלָ֑יו וַיֹּצִאֻ֥הוּ וַיַּנִּחֻ֖הוּ מִח֥וּץ לָעִֽיר׃
יז וַיְהִי֩ כְהוֹצִיאָ֨ם אֹתָ֜ם הַח֗וּצָה וַיֹּ֙אמֶר֙ הִמָּלֵ֣ט עַל־נַפְשֶׁ֔ךָ אַל־
תַּבִּ֣יט אַחֲרֶ֔יךָ וְאַֽל־תַּעֲמֹ֖ד בְּכָל־הַכִּכָּ֑ר הָהָ֥רָה הִמָּלֵ֖ט פֶּן־
יח יט תִּסָּפֶֽה׃ וַיֹּ֥אמֶר ל֖וֹט אֲלֵהֶ֑ם אַל־נָ֖א אֲדֹנָֽי׃ הִנֵּה־נָ֠א מָצָ֨א
עַבְדְּךָ֣ חֵן֮ בְּעֵינֶ֒יךָ֒ וַתַּגְדֵּ֣ל חַסְדְּךָ֗ אֲשֶׁ֤ר עָשִׂ֙יתָ֙ עִמָּדִ֔י לְהַחֲי֖וֹת
אֶת־נַפְשִׁ֑י וְאָנֹכִ֗י לֹ֤א אוּכַל֙ לְהִמָּלֵ֣ט הָהָ֔רָה פֶּן־תִּדְבָּקַ֥נִי
כ הָרָעָ֖ה וָמַֽתִּי׃ הִנֵּה־נָ֠א הָעִ֨יר הַזֹּ֧את קְרֹבָ֛ה לָנ֥וּס שָׁ֖מָּה וְהִ֣וא
מִצְעָ֑ר אִמָּלְטָ֨ה נָּ֜א שָׁ֗מָּה הֲלֹ֥א מִצְעָ֛ר הִ֖וא וּתְחִ֥י נַפְשִֽׁי׃
כא וַיֹּ֣אמֶר אֵלָ֔יו הִנֵּה֙ נָשָׂ֣אתִי פָנֶ֔יךָ גַּ֖ם לַדָּבָ֣ר הַזֶּ֑ה לְבִלְתִּ֛י הָפְכִּ֥י רביעי
כב אֶת־הָעִ֖יר אֲשֶׁ֥ר דִּבַּֽרְתָּ׃ מַהֵר֙ הִמָּלֵ֣ט שָׁ֔מָּה כִּ֣י לֹ֤א אוּכַל֙
לַעֲשׂ֣וֹת דָּבָ֔ר עַד־בֹּאֲךָ֖ שָׁ֑מָּה עַל־כֵּ֛ן קָרָ֥א שֵׁם־הָעִ֖יר צֽוֹעַר׃
כג כד הַשֶּׁ֖מֶשׁ יָצָ֣א עַל־הָאָ֑רֶץ וְל֖וֹט בָּ֥א צֹֽעֲרָה׃ וַֽיהוָ֗ה הִמְטִ֧יר
עַל־סְדֹ֛ם וְעַל־עֲמֹרָ֖ה גָּפְרִ֣ית וָאֵ֑שׁ מֵאֵ֥ת יְהוָ֖ה מִן־הַשָּׁמָֽיִם׃
כה וַיַּהֲפֹךְ֙ אֶת־הֶֽעָרִ֣ים הָאֵ֔ל וְאֵ֖ת כָּל־הַכִּכָּ֑ר וְאֵת֙ כָּל־יֹשְׁבֵ֣י
כו הֶעָרִ֔ים וְצֶ֖מַח הָאֲדָמָֽה׃ וַתַּבֵּ֥ט אִשְׁתּ֖וֹ מֵאַחֲרָ֑יו וַתְּהִ֖י נְצִ֥יב
כז מֶֽלַח׃ וַיַּשְׁכֵּ֥ם אַבְרָהָ֖ם בַּבֹּ֑קֶר אֶל־הַ֨מָּק֔וֹם אֲשֶׁר־עָ֥מַד שָׁ֖ם
כח אֶת־פְּנֵ֥י יְהוָֽה׃ וַיַּשְׁקֵ֗ף עַל־פְּנֵ֤י סְדֹם֙ וַעֲמֹרָ֔ה וְעַ֥ל כָּל־פְּנֵ֖י
אֶ֣רֶץ הַכִּכָּ֑ר וַיַּ֗רְא וְהִנֵּ֤ה עָלָה֙ קִיטֹ֣ר הָאָ֔רֶץ כְּקִיטֹ֖ר הַכִּבְשָֽׁן׃

---

discussed the nature of Lot's indecision above (see "Lot in Sedom"). The graphic notation of the *shalshelet* itself looks like a streak of lightning, a "zigzag movement" (*tenua meuvetet*), a mark that goes repeatedly backward and forward. It conveys frozen motion. Lot is a prime example of what Leon Festinger called cognitive dissonance. According to Festinger, the need to avoid dissonance and the unbearable tension it creates is fundamental to human beings. It is this tension that Lot cannot resolve – and which is signaled by the *shalshelet* over "he hesitated."

Festinger's theory also explains the behavior of Lot's wife, who "looked back – and was turned into a pillar of salt" (Gen. 19:26). Festinger called this syndrome "post-decision dissonance." He predicted that the more important the issue, the longer the person delays a decision, and the harder it is to reverse,

▶

29 from the land like smoke from a kiln. So it was, that when
God destroyed the cities of the plain, He remembered
Avraham and brought Lot out of the overthrow that
30 overturned the cities where Lot had lived. Lot went up
from Tzoar and settled in the hills together with his two
daughters because he was afraid to stay in Tzoar. He and
31 his two daughters settled in a cave. The elder said to the
younger, "Our father is old, and there is no man left on
32 earth to come to us in the normal way of the world. Let us
get our father drunk with wine and then sleep with him,
so that we may raise a new generation through our father."
33 That night they gave their father wine to drink. Then the
elder daughter went in and slept with him. He was
34 unaware when she lay down and when she arose. The
next day, the elder said to the younger, "Last night I slept
with my father. Let us get him to drink wine again tonight,
then you go in and sleep with him. So may we preserve
35 our family line through our father." So that night they got
their father to drink wine again, and the younger went
and slept with him. And he was unaware when she lay
36 down and when she arose. And so both of Lot's daughters
37 became pregnant by their father. The elder had a son,
whom she named Moav. He is the ancestor of the
38 Moabites of today. The younger also had a son, whom she
named Ben Ami. And he is the ancestor of the Amonites
20 1 of today. Avraham then journeyed on to the
Negev region, settling between Kadesh and Shur. For a
2 while he lived as a stranger in Gerar. There Avraham said
of his wife Sara, "She is my sister." Avimelekh, king of

---

kindness, and compassion. A free society, implies the Bible, is a moral society, for if there is corruption and injustice, there will no longer be social cohesion. The powerful will oppress the powerless. The rich will be at best indifferent to, at worst exploitative of, the plight of the poor. Each will seek his or her own advantage rather than the common good. Society will become demoralized, people will not rally to its defense, and if it does not fall, like Sedom, to an enemy without, it will implode from within.

כט וַיְהִי בְּשַׁחֵת אֱלֹהִים אֶת־עָרֵי הַכִּכָּר וַיִּזְכֹּר אֱלֹהִים אֶת־
אַבְרָהָם וַיְשַׁלַּח אֶת־לוֹט מִתּוֹךְ הַהֲפֵכָה בַּהֲפֹךְ אֶת־הֶעָרִים
ל אֲשֶׁר־יָשַׁב בָּהֵן לוֹט: וַיַּעַל לוֹט מִצּוֹעַר וַיֵּשֶׁב בָּהָר וּשְׁתֵּי
בְנֹתָיו עִמּוֹ כִּי יָרֵא לָשֶׁבֶת בְּצוֹעַר וַיֵּשֶׁב בַּמְּעָרָה הוּא וּשְׁתֵּי
לא בְנֹתָיו: וַתֹּאמֶר הַבְּכִירָה אֶל־הַצְּעִירָה אָבִינוּ זָקֵן וְאִישׁ אֵין
לב בָּאָרֶץ לָבוֹא עָלֵינוּ כְּדֶרֶךְ כָּל־הָאָרֶץ: לְכָה נַשְׁקֶה אֶת־אָבִינוּ
לג יַיִן וְנִשְׁכְּבָה עִמּוֹ וּנְחַיֶּה מֵאָבִינוּ זָרַע: וַתַּשְׁקֶיןָ אֶת־אֲבִיהֶן
יַיִן בַּלַּיְלָה הוּא וַתָּבֹא הַבְּכִירָה וַתִּשְׁכַּב אֶת־אָבִיהָ וְלֹא־יָדַע
לד בְּשִׁכְבָהּ וּבְקוּמָהּ: וַיְהִי מִמָּחֳרָת וַתֹּאמֶר הַבְּכִירָה אֶל־
הַצְּעִירָה הֵן־שָׁכַבְתִּי אֶמֶשׁ אֶת־אָבִי נַשְׁקֶנּוּ יַיִן גַּם־הַלַּיְלָה
לה וּבֹאִי שִׁכְבִי עִמּוֹ וּנְחַיֶּה מֵאָבִינוּ זָרַע: וַתַּשְׁקֶיןָ גַּם בַּלַּיְלָה
הַהוּא אֶת־אֲבִיהֶן יָיִן וַתָּקָם הַצְּעִירָה וַתִּשְׁכַּב עִמּוֹ וְלֹא־יָדַע
לו לז בְּשִׁכְבָהּ וּבְקֻמָהּ: וַתַּהֲרֶיןָ שְׁתֵּי בְנוֹת־לוֹט מֵאֲבִיהֶן: וַתֵּלֶד
הַבְּכִירָה בֵּן וַתִּקְרָא שְׁמוֹ מוֹאָב הוּא אֲבִי־מוֹאָב עַד־הַיּוֹם:
לח וְהַצְּעִירָה גַם־הִוא יָלְדָה בֵּן וַתִּקְרָא שְׁמוֹ בֶּן־עַמִּי הוּא אֲבִי
כ א בְנֵי־עַמּוֹן עַד־הַיּוֹם: וַיִּסַּע מִשָּׁם אַבְרָהָם יז
ב אַרְצָה הַנֶּגֶב וַיֵּשֶׁב בֵּין־קָדֵשׁ וּבֵין שׁוּר וַיָּגָר בִּגְרָר: וַיֹּאמֶר
אַבְרָהָם אֶל־שָׂרָה אִשְׁתּוֹ אֲחֹתִי הִוא וַיִּשְׁלַח אֲבִימֶלֶךְ מֶלֶךְ

19:29 הַהֲפֵכָה בַּהֲפֹךְ אֶת הֶעָרִים *The overthrow that overturned the cities* – This language will be echoed in the opening chapter of Isaiah, describing the "overturning" of Judah, which, but for God's sparing of a few survivors "would have been like Sedom" (Is. 1:7, 9). What is the sin of Sedom that causes its utter destruction? The Mishna (Avot 5:14) summarizes the ethos of the city: "What is mine is mine, and what is yours is yours." The Talmud (Sanhedrin 109a ff.) describes a city where, though no individual breaks the rules, there is no compassion, and so no safety for the vulnerable.

In the book of Isaiah, the prophet's prescription for escaping the fate of Sedom is clearly stated: "Seek justice. Correct what is cruel. Rule justice for orphans. Fight the widows' cause" (Is. 1:17).

The point is that it is not the responsibility of any particular group within society, but of everyone. That is what citizenship in a covenantal society is: co-responsibility for justice, equity,

3 Gerar, sent for Sara and took her as his own. But God
came to Avimelekh in a dream one night and told him,
"You will die because of the woman you have taken. She
4 is already married." Avimelekh had not gone near her, so
he said, "Lord, would You destroy an innocent nation?
5 Did he not tell me, 'She is my sister'? Did she not say, 'He
is my brother'? I have acted from an innocent heart, with
6 clean hands." Then, in the dream, God said to him, "I too
knew that you acted from an innocent heart, and so I kept
you from sinning against Me. That is why I did not let you
7 touch her. But now, give back the man's wife. He is a
prophet. He will pray for you and you will live. But if you
do not give her back, know that you and all your people
8 are to die." Early the next morning, Avimelekh summoned
all his servants and told them all this – they were very
9 afraid. Then Avimelekh summoned Avraham and said,
"What have you done to us? What wrong have I done
you? Why have you brought such onerous guilt upon me
and my kingdom? You have done to me that which should
10 never be done. What were you thinking of," asked
11 Avimelekh, "that you did such a thing?" Avraham replied,
"I thought, 'There is no fear of God in this place. They will
12 kill me because of my wife.' Besides, she really is my sister.

---

visitors – angels – who smite the people with blindness saves Lot's family from violence.

In the fifth case (Gen. 34), Shekhem, a local prince, rapes and abducts Dina when she "went out to visit some of the local girls," leading Shimon and Levi to practice deception and bloodshed in the course of rescuing her.

Then comes a marginal case, the story of Yehuda and Tamar, more complex than the others and not part of the overall pattern (see ch. 38 and commentary there).

Finally there is the sixth episode, when Potifar's wife attempts to seduce Yosef. Failing, she accuses him of rape and has him imprisoned.

In other words, there is a continuing theme in Genesis 12–50, a contrast between the people of the Abrahamic covenant and their neighbors. It is not about idolatry, but rather about adultery, promiscuity, seduction, rape, and sexually motivated violence.

This gives us an entirely new way of thinking about Abrahamic faith. *Emuna*, the Hebrew word normally translated as "faith," does not mean a body of dogma,

ג גְּרָר וַיִּקַּח אֶת־שָׂרָה: וַיָּבֹא אֱלֹהִים אֶל־אֲבִימֶלֶךְ בַּחֲלוֹם
הַלָּיְלָה וַיֹּאמֶר לוֹ הִנְּךָ מֵת עַל־הָאִשָּׁה אֲשֶׁר־לָקַחְתָּ וְהִוא
ד בְּעֻלַת בָּעַל: וַאֲבִימֶלֶךְ לֹא קָרַב אֵלֶיהָ וַיֹּאמַר אֲדֹנָי הֲגוֹי
ה גַּם־צַדִּיק תַּהֲרֹג: הֲלֹא הוּא אָמַר־לִי אֲחֹתִי הִוא וְהִיא־גַם־
הוּא אָמְרָה אָחִי הוּא בְּתָם־לְבָבִי וּבְנִקְיֹן כַּפַּי עָשִׂיתִי זֹאת:
ו וַיֹּאמֶר אֵלָיו הָאֱלֹהִים בַּחֲלֹם גַּם אָנֹכִי יָדַעְתִּי כִּי בְתָם־לְבָבְךָ
עָשִׂיתָ זֹּאת וָאֶחְשֹׂךְ גַּם־אָנֹכִי אוֹתְךָ מֵחֲטוֹ־לִי עַל־כֵּן לֹא־
ז נְתַתִּיךָ לִנְגֹּעַ אֵלֶיהָ: וְעַתָּה הָשֵׁב אֵשֶׁת־הָאִישׁ כִּי־נָבִיא
הוּא וְיִתְפַּלֵּל בַּעַדְךָ וֶחְיֵה וְאִם־אֵינְךָ מֵשִׁיב דַּע כִּי־מוֹת
ח תָּמוּת אַתָּה וְכָל־אֲשֶׁר־לָךְ: וַיַּשְׁכֵּם אֲבִימֶלֶךְ בַּבֹּקֶר וַיִּקְרָא
לְכָל־עֲבָדָיו וַיְדַבֵּר אֶת־כָּל־הַדְּבָרִים הָאֵלֶּה בְּאָזְנֵיהֶם
ט וַיִּירְאוּ הָאֲנָשִׁים מְאֹד: וַיִּקְרָא אֲבִימֶלֶךְ לְאַבְרָהָם וַיֹּאמֶר
לוֹ מֶה־עָשִׂיתָ לָּנוּ וּמֶה־חָטָאתִי לָךְ כִּי־הֵבֵאתָ עָלַי וְעַל־
מַמְלַכְתִּי חֲטָאָה גְדֹלָה מַעֲשִׂים אֲשֶׁר לֹא־יֵעָשׂוּ עָשִׂיתָ
י עִמָּדִי: וַיֹּאמֶר אֲבִימֶלֶךְ אֶל־אַבְרָהָם מָה רָאִיתָ כִּי עָשִׂיתָ
יא אֶת־הַדָּבָר הַזֶּה: וַיֹּאמֶר אַבְרָהָם כִּי אָמַרְתִּי רַק אֵין־יִרְאַת
יב אֱלֹהִים בַּמָּקוֹם הַזֶּה וַהֲרָגוּנִי עַל־דְּבַר אִשְׁתִּי: וְגַם־אָמְנָה

20:11 וַהֲרָגוּנִי עַל־דְּבַר אִשְׁתִּי *They will kill me because of my wife* – This theme appears no less than six (possibly even seven) times in Genesis. Whenever a member of the covenantal family leaves his or her own space and enters the wider world of their contemporaries, they encounter a world of sexual depravity.

Three times, Avraham (Gen. 12 and 20) and Yitzḥak (Gen. 26) are forced to leave their homes because of famine. On all three occasions, the husband fears he will be killed so that the local ruler can take his wife into his harem. All three times they put forward the story that their wife is actually their sister. At worst this is a lie, at best a half-truth. In all three cases the local ruler (Pharaoh, Avimelekh), protests their behavior when the truth becomes known. Clearly, the fear of death is real or the patriarchs would not be party to deception.

In the fourth case, Lot in Sedom (Gen. 19), the people cluster round Lot's house demanding that he bring out his two visitors so that they can be raped. Lot offers them his virgin daughters instead. Only swift action by the

▶

She is the daughter of my father though not of my mother,
13 and she became my wife. When God made me wander
from my father's house, I said to her, 'Do me this kindness:
14 wherever we go, say of me, "He is my brother."'" Avimelekh
gave Avraham sheep, cattle, and male and female slaves,
15 and returned his wife Sara to him. Avimelekh said, "Here
16 is my land. Live wherever you wish." To Sara he said, "I am
giving your brother a thousand pieces of silver. This will
allay the suspicions of everyone who is with you. You are
17 fully vindicated." Then Avraham prayed to God, and God
healed Avimelekh, his wife, and his female slaves so they
18 could again have children, for the LORD had prevented all
the women in Avimelekh's household from bearing
21 1 children, because of Sara, Avraham's wife. The
LORD remembered Sara as He had said He would, and
2 acted for Sara as He had promised. Sara became pregnant
and bore a son to Avraham in his old age at the very time
3 God had promised. Avraham named his newborn son,
4 whom Sara had borne him, Yitzḥak. And when Yitzḥak his
son was eight days old, Avraham circumcised him as God
5 had commanded. Avraham was one hundred years old ḤAMISHI
6 when his son Yitzḥak was born to him. Sara said, "God has
brought me laughter; all those who hear will laugh with
7 me." Then she said, "Who would have told Avraham, 'Sara
will nurse children'? Yet I have borne a son in his old age."
8 The child grew and was weaned; on the day Yitzḥak was
9 weaned, Avraham held a great feast. But Sara saw the son
whom Hagar the Egyptian had borne Avraham mocking.
10 She said to Avraham, "Drive out that slave woman and

---

get to understanding God's love for us.

21:3 יִצְחָק *Yitzḥak* – The name Yitzḥak means "he will laugh." Yitzḥak, the first Jewish child, hints at the fact that though we may suffer many trials, we will eventually know the laughter of joy. Jewish history has often been written in tears, but that is neither its essence nor its destiny.

21:9 מְצַחֵק *Mocking* – Literally, "laughing." The verb *tz-ḥ-k* is a recurring motif in the story of Avraham and Sara. It

יג אֲחֹתִי בַת־אָבִי הִוא אַךְ לֹא בַת־אִמִּי וַתְּהִי־לִי לְאִשָּׁה׃ וַיְהִי
כַּאֲשֶׁר הִתְעוּ אֹתִי אֱלֹהִים מִבֵּית אָבִי וָאֹמַר לָהּ זֶה חַסְדֵּךְ
אֲשֶׁר תַּעֲשִׂי עִמָּדִי אֶל כָּל־הַמָּקוֹם אֲשֶׁר נָבוֹא שָׁמָּה אִמְרִי־
יד לִי אָחִי הוּא׃ וַיִּקַּח אֲבִימֶלֶךְ צֹאן וּבָקָר וַעֲבָדִים וּשְׁפָחֹת
טו וַיִּתֵּן לְאַבְרָהָם וַיָּשֶׁב לוֹ אֵת שָׂרָה אִשְׁתּוֹ׃ וַיֹּאמֶר אֲבִימֶלֶךְ
טז הִנֵּה אַרְצִי לְפָנֶיךָ בַּטּוֹב בְּעֵינֶיךָ שֵׁב׃ וּלְשָׂרָה אָמַר הִנֵּה
נָתַתִּי אֶלֶף כֶּסֶף לְאָחִיךְ הִנֵּה הוּא־לָךְ כְּסוּת עֵינַיִם לְכֹל
יז אֲשֶׁר אִתָּךְ וְאֵת כֹּל וְנֹכָחַת׃ וַיִּתְפַּלֵּל אַבְרָהָם אֶל־הָאֱלֹהִים
וַיִּרְפָּא אֱלֹהִים אֶת־אֲבִימֶלֶךְ וְאֶת־אִשְׁתּוֹ וְאַמְהֹתָיו וַיֵּלֵדוּ׃
יח כִּי־עָצֹר עָצַר יְהוָה בְּעַד כָּל־רֶחֶם לְבֵית אֲבִימֶלֶךְ עַל־דְּבַר
כא א שָׂרָה אֵשֶׁת אַבְרָהָם׃ וַיהוָה פָּקַד אֶת־שָׂרָה כַּאֲשֶׁר יח
ב אָמָר וַיַּעַשׂ יְהוָה לְשָׂרָה כַּאֲשֶׁר דִּבֵּר׃ וַתַּהַר וַתֵּלֶד שָׂרָה
ג לְאַבְרָהָם בֵּן לִזְקֻנָיו לַמּוֹעֵד אֲשֶׁר־דִּבֶּר אֹתוֹ אֱלֹהִים׃ וַיִּקְרָא
אַבְרָהָם אֶת־שֶׁם־בְּנוֹ הַנּוֹלַד־לוֹ אֲשֶׁר־יָלְדָה־לּוֹ שָׂרָה
ד יִצְחָק׃ וַיָּמָל אַבְרָהָם אֶת־יִצְחָק בְּנוֹ בֶּן־שְׁמֹנַת יָמִים כַּאֲשֶׁר
ה צִוָּה אֹתוֹ אֱלֹהִים׃ וְאַבְרָהָם בֶּן־מְאַת שָׁנָה בְּהִוָּלֶד לוֹ אֵת חמישי
ו יִצְחָק בְּנוֹ׃ וַתֹּאמֶר שָׂרָה צְחֹק עָשָׂה לִי אֱלֹהִים כָּל־הַשֹּׁמֵעַ
ז יִצְחַק־לִי׃ וַתֹּאמֶר מִי מִלֵּל לְאַבְרָהָם הֵינִיקָה בָנִים שָׂרָה
ח כִּי־יָלַדְתִּי בֵן לִזְקֻנָיו׃ וַיִּגְדַּל הַיֶּלֶד וַיִּגָּמַל וַיַּעַשׂ אַבְרָהָם
ט מִשְׁתֶּה גָדוֹל בְּיוֹם הִגָּמֵל אֶת־יִצְחָק׃ וַתֵּרֶא שָׂרָה אֶת־בֶּן־
י הָגָר הַמִּצְרִית אֲשֶׁר־יָלְדָה לְאַבְרָהָם מְצַחֵק׃ וַתֹּאמֶר

---

a set of principles, or a cluster of beliefs often held on non-rational grounds. *Emuna* means faithfulness, loyalty, fidelity, honoring your commitments, and acting in such a way as to inspire trust. It has to do with relationships, first and foremost with marriage.

When a society loses faith, eventually it loses the very idea of a sexual ethic, and the result in the long term is violence and the exploitation of the powerless by the powerful. Women suffer. Children suffer. There is a breakdown of trust where it matters most. So it was in the days of the patriarchs. Sadly, so it is today. Judaism, by contrast, is the sanctification of relationship, of the love between husband and wife which is as close as we will ever

her son, for the son of that slave woman must not share
11 the inheritance with my son, with Yitzḥak." This distressed
12 Avraham greatly because of his son. But God told
Avraham, "Do not be distressed about the boy or about
your slave. Listen to whatever Sara tells you, because it is
through Yitzḥak that your descendants will be reckoned.
13 But I will make the slave's son too into a nation, because
14 he is your child." Early the next morning Avraham took
bread and a skin of water and gave them to Hagar. He
placed them on her shoulder, and together with the child,
he sent her away. She went wandering in the Be'er Sheva
15 desert. When the water in the skin was all gone, she cast
16 the child away under one of the bushes and went and
sat down at a distance, about a bowshot away, saying, "I

---

emotional states. The scenes involving Hagar, however, are etched with emotional intensity.

To understand the significance of this, we have to realize that Genesis 21, the sending away of Yishmael, is parallel to Genesis 22, *akedat Yitzḥak*. In both, Avraham undergoes a trial involving the potential loss of a son. Yishmael and Yitzḥak, the two children, are both only dimly aware of what is happening. In both, they are about to die until Heaven intervenes, in the first case by providing a well of water, in the second, a ram to be offered as a sacrifice in Yitzḥak's place. The similarities serve to highlight the differences.

The story of *akedat Yitzḥak* is notable for its complete absence of emotion. God commands, Avraham obeys. Throughout the ordeal Avraham says nothing to God except for one word at the beginning and the end: *Hineni*, "Here I am" (22:1, 11).

By contrast, the episode involving Hagar and Yishmael is saturated with emotion. Hagar weeps: She "went and sat down at a distance, about a bowshot away, saying, 'I cannot watch the child die.' Sitting there, at a distance, she raised her voice and wept" (21:16). Yishmael weeps: "God heard the boy crying" (21:17). There is a pathos here that is rare in biblical prose. There can be no doubt that the narrative is written to enlist our sympathy in a way it does not in the case of Yitzḥak. We *identify* with Hagar and Yishmael; we are *awed* by Avraham and Yitzḥak. The latter is a religious drama, the former a human one, and its very humanity gives it power.

There is a moral reason for this complexity, and it is fundamental. Violence between groups begins in the in-group/out-group dichotomy. I identify with my side, and am suspicious of the other side. In situations of stress, sympathy for the other side can come to seem like a kind of betrayal. It is this that the Yishmael story

לְאַבְרָהָ֔ם גָּרֵ֛שׁ הָאָמָ֥ה הַזֹּ֖את וְאֶת־בְּנָ֑הּ כִּ֣י לֹ֤א יִירַשׁ֙ בֶּן־
יא הָאָמָ֣ה הַזֹּ֔את עִם־בְּנִ֖י עִם־יִצְחָֽק׃ וַיֵּ֧רַע הַדָּבָ֛ר מְאֹ֖ד בְּעֵינֵ֣י
יב אַבְרָהָ֑ם עַ֖ל אוֹדֹ֥ת בְּנֽוֹ׃ וַיֹּ֨אמֶר אֱלֹהִ֜ים אֶל־אַבְרָהָ֗ם אַל־יֵרַ֤ע
בְּעֵינֶ֙יךָ֙ עַל־הַנַּ֣עַר וְעַל־אֲמָתֶ֔ךָ כֹּל֩ אֲשֶׁ֨ר תֹּאמַ֥ר אֵלֶ֛יךָ שָׂרָ֖ה
יג שְׁמַ֣ע בְּקֹלָ֑הּ כִּ֣י בְיִצְחָ֔ק יִקָּרֵ֥א לְךָ֖ זָֽרַע׃ וְגַ֥ם אֶת־בֶּן־הָאָמָ֖ה
יד לְג֣וֹי אֲשִׂימֶ֑נּוּ כִּ֥י זַרְעֲךָ֖ הֽוּא׃ וַיַּשְׁכֵּ֣ם אַבְרָהָ֣ם ׀ בַּבֹּ֡קֶר וַיִּֽקַּח־
לֶחֶם֩ וְחֵ֨מַת מַ֜יִם וַיִּתֵּ֣ן אֶל־הָ֠גָ֠ר שָׂ֧ם עַל־שִׁכְמָ֛הּ וְאֶת־הַיֶּ֖לֶד
טו וַֽיְשַׁלְּחֶ֑הָ וַתֵּ֣לֶךְ וַתֵּ֔תַע בְּמִדְבַּ֖ר בְּאֵ֥ר שָֽׁבַע׃ וַיִּכְל֥וּ הַמַּ֖יִם
טז מִן־הַחֵ֑מֶת וַתַּשְׁלֵ֣ךְ אֶת־הַיֶּ֔לֶד תַּ֖חַת אַחַ֥ד הַשִּׂיחִֽם׃ וַתֵּ֨לֶךְ
וַתֵּ֩שֶׁב֩ לָ֨הּ מִנֶּ֜גֶד הַרְחֵ֗ק כִּמְטַחֲוֵ֣י קֶ֔שֶׁת כִּ֣י אָֽמְרָ֔ה אַל־אֶרְאֶ֖ה

appears seven times in the narrative (Gen. 17:17; 18:12, 13, 15; 21:6 – twice – and 21:9), and in the Pentateuch the sevenfold repetition of a word is always significant. It signals a keyword around which the text is thematized.

Avraham "laughs" when he hears the news that he and Sara will have a son (17:17). So does Sara (18:12), for which she is rebuked by God. The name Yitzḥak, as we have seen, means "he will laugh." When he is born, Sara says, "God has brought me laughter; all those who hear will laugh with me" (21:6). *Tzḥok* has a whole range of senses, from *joy* to *disbelief* to *disdain*. In a later chapter it even has sexual undertones: "enjoying himself (with his wife)" (26:8). At this point the text is deliberately ambiguous, leaving it to us, the readers, to decide whether Sara is right to take offense (Yishmael is mocking) or wrong (he is sharing in the general celebration).

Sara's judgment, however, is unambiguous, her tone dismissive: "Drive out that *slave woman* and her son, for the son of that slave woman must not share the inheritance with my son, with Yitzḥak" (21:10). Not only does she not dignify either mother or child by calling them by name; her language has changed since chapter 16. Then she called Hagar a "maid" (*shifḥa*). Now she has become a "slave" (*ama*).

21:13 כִּי זַרְעֲךָ הוּא *Because he is your child* – The text makes a fine distinction between biological and ascribed identity. Yishmael, says God to Avraham, "*is* your child" (Gen. 21:13), while "it is through Yitzḥak that *your descendants will be reckoned*" (21:12). The former promises worldly greatness, the latter covenantal *responsibility*. Yet God recognizes that Yishmael *remains Avraham's son and will be blessed accordingly*.

THE BANISHMENT OF YISHMAEL

In general, the Hebrew Bible is highly reticent in telling us about people's

cannot watch the child die." Sitting there, at a distance,
17 she raised her voice and wept. God heard the boy crying,
and an angel of God called to Hagar from the heavens and
said to her, "Hagar, what is wrong? Fear not. God has
18 heard the boy's cry there, where he is. Go, raise up the
boy and take him by the hand, for I will make of him a
19 great nation." Then God opened her eyes and she saw a
well of water. She went and filled the skin with water and
20 gave the boy to drink. God was with the boy as he grew.
He lived in the desert and became an expert with the
21 bow. In the Paran desert he lived, and his mother took
him a wife from Egypt.
22 At that time, Avimelekh and Pikhol, commander of his SHISHI
troops, said to Avraham, "God is with you in all you do.
23 Now swear to me here before God that you will not deal
falsely with me or with my children or grandchildren.
Show me and the land where you have lived as a stranger

The ministering angels rose to accuse [Yishmael]. They said, "Lord of the Universe, here is someone who will one day slay Your children with thirst. Will You now provide him with a well?"

He said to them, "What is he *now*, righteous or wicked?"

They said, "Righteous."

He said to them, "I judge man *only as he is at the moment*."

(Bereshit Rabba 53:14)

Yishmael was rescued *baasher hu sham*, "there, where he is." Meaning: for what he is *now*, an innocent child, not for what he might *predictably become*.

In this exchange, the angels argue that God must foresee his ultimate destiny and act accordingly. God rejects the argument. Man is judged only for what he is, not for what he might become. So Yishmael is saved. At the heart of *teshuva* is the faith in human free will, which makes *no destiny inevitable*. No future is inevitable, for where we will be is dependent on *baasher hu sham*: the direction we *now* choose to face.

Sometimes repentance is hampered by the burden of the past. Yishmael, in contrast, is haunted by his future, which seemed by all reasonable expectations to be nonexistent. This sense of futurelessness is a universal of certain moods of despair. The verse answers this persistent nightmare with the most radical assurance. The "now" of *teshuva* is stronger than any human rejection, any pre-scripted future.

יז בְּמוֹת הַיָּלֶד וַתֵּשֶׁב מִנֶּגֶד וַתִּשָּׂא אֶת־קֹלָהּ וַתֵּבְךְּ: וַיִּשְׁמַע
אֱלֹהִים אֶת־קוֹל הַנַּעַר וַיִּקְרָא מַלְאַךְ אֱלֹהִים ׀ אֶל־הָגָר
מִן־הַשָּׁמַיִם וַיֹּאמֶר לָהּ מַה־לָּךְ הָגָר אַל־תִּירְאִי כִּי־שָׁמַע
יח אֱלֹהִים אֶל־קוֹל הַנַּעַר בַּאֲשֶׁר הוּא־שָׁם: קוּמִי שְׂאִי אֶת־
יט הַנַּעַר וְהַחֲזִיקִי אֶת־יָדֵךְ בּוֹ כִּי־לְגוֹי גָּדוֹל אֲשִׂימֶנּוּ: וַיִּפְקַח
אֱלֹהִים אֶת־עֵינֶיהָ וַתֵּרֶא בְּאֵר מָיִם וַתֵּלֶךְ וַתְּמַלֵּא אֶת־
כ הַחֵמֶת מַיִם וַתַּשְׁקְ אֶת־הַנָּעַר: וַיְהִי אֱלֹהִים אֶת־הַנַּעַר וַיִּגְדָּל
כא וַיֵּשֶׁב בַּמִּדְבָּר וַיְהִי רֹבֶה קַשָּׁת: וַיֵּשֶׁב בְּמִדְבַּר פָּארָן וַתִּקַּח־
לוֹ אִמּוֹ אִשָּׁה מֵאֶרֶץ מִצְרָיִם:
כב וַיְהִי בָּעֵת הַהִוא וַיֹּאמֶר אֲבִימֶלֶךְ וּפִיכֹל שַׂר־צְבָאוֹ אֶל־ ששי
אַבְרָהָם לֵאמֹר אֱלֹהִים עִמְּךָ בְּכֹל אֲשֶׁר־אַתָּה עֹשֶׂה:
כג וְעַתָּה הִשָּׁבְעָה לִּי בֵאלֹהִים הֵנָּה אִם־תִּשְׁקֹר לִי וּלְנִינִי
וּלְנֶכְדִּי כַּחֶסֶד אֲשֶׁר־עָשִׂיתִי עִמְּךָ תַּעֲשֶׂה עִמָּדִי וְעִם־הָאָרֶץ

---

is challenging. At the first critical juncture for the covenantal family – the birth of its first children – we feel for Sara and Yitzḥak. She is the first Jewish mother, and he the first Jewish child. *But we also feel for Hagar and Yishmael.* We enter their world, see through their eyes, empathize with their emotions. That is how the narrative is written, to enlist our sympathy. We weep with them, feeling their outcast state. *As does God.* Yishmael means "he whom God has heard." For it is God who hears their tears, comforts them, saves them from death, and gives them His blessing.

21:17 שָׁמַע אֱלֹהִים אֶל־קוֹל הַנַּעַר *God has heard the boy's cry* – The voice breaks in on an almost unbearable moment. Yishmael has been cast away, in turn, by Sara, then Avraham, then Hagar. He was born, as it were, to the wrong parents. He has no share in the destiny mapped out for the seed of Avraham. His tears on the point of death, though they are tears of a child, belong almost to *objective despair*. There is no place for him in the story.

The angel represents, therefore, a mercy as radical as it is total. We recall it when, throughout the month of Elul and the days of *teshuva*, we read Psalm 27: "Were my father and my mother to forsake me, the LORD would take me in" (Ps. 27:10). There is no rejection which includes God's rejection.

21:17 בַּאֲשֶׁר הוּא־שָׁם *There, where he is* – A midrash records a conversation between God and the angels at this point:

24 the same kindness I have shown to you." Avraham said,
25 "I swear." Then Avraham rebuked Avimelekh for the
26 well of water that Avimelekh's servants had seized. But
Avimelekh said, "I do not know who has done this. You
did not tell me; I had not heard about it until today."
27 Avraham then brought sheep and cattle and gave them
to Avimelekh, and the two of them forged a covenant.
28 Avraham set apart seven ewe lambs from the flock.
29 Avimelekh asked him, "What is the meaning of these
30 seven ewe lambs you have set apart?" He replied, "Accept
these seven lambs from me as testimony that I dug this
31 well." That is why that place is called Be'er Sheva, because
32 there the two men swore an oath. Thus they made a
pact at Be'er Sheva. And then Avimelekh and Pikhol,
commander of his troops, returned to the land of the
33 Philistines. Avraham planted a tamarisk tree in Be'er
Sheva, and there he called on the name of the Lord, the
34 Everlasting God. Avraham stayed on in the land of the
Philistines for many days.
22 1 After these things, God tested Avraham. "Avraham!" SHEVI'I
2 He said. And Avraham replied, "Here I am." Then God

---

the whole of Jewish law. God created the universe. Therefore, God is the ultimate owner of the universe. The legal term for this is "eminent domain." God has the right to prescribe the conditions under which we may benefit from the universe. It is to establish this legal fact – not to tell us about the cosmology of the Big Bang – that the Torah begins with the story of creation.

In the ancient world, up to and including the time of the Roman Empire, children were considered the legal property of their parents. They had no rights. Under the Roman principle of *patria potestas*, a father could do whatever he wished with his child, including putting him to death. Infanticide was well known in antiquity.

It is this principle that underlies the entire practice of child sacrifice, which was widespread throughout the pagan world. The Torah is horrified by child sacrifice, which it sees as the worst of all sins. It therefore seeks to establish, in the case of children, what it establishes in the case of the universe as a whole, the land of Israel, and the people of Israel. We do not own our children. We are merely their guardians on God's behalf.

Only the most dramatic event could establish an idea so revolutionary and unprecedented in the ancient world.

כד כה אֲשֶׁר־גַּרְתָּה בָּהּ: וַיֹּאמֶר אַבְרָהָם אָנֹכִי אִשָּׁבֵעַ: וְהוֹכִחַ
אַבְרָהָם אֶת־אֲבִימֶלֶךְ עַל־אֹדוֹת בְּאֵר הַמַּיִם אֲשֶׁר גָּזְלוּ
כו עַבְדֵי אֲבִימֶלֶךְ: וַיֹּאמֶר אֲבִימֶלֶךְ לֹא יָדַעְתִּי מִי עָשָׂה אֶת־
הַדָּבָר הַזֶּה וְגַם־אַתָּה לֹא־הִגַּדְתָּ לִּי וְגַם אָנֹכִי לֹא שָׁמַעְתִּי
כז בִּלְתִּי הַיּוֹם: וַיִּקַּח אַבְרָהָם צֹאן וּבָקָר וַיִּתֵּן לַאֲבִימֶלֶךְ
כח וַיִּכְרְתוּ שְׁנֵיהֶם בְּרִית: וַיַּצֵּב אַבְרָהָם אֶת־שֶׁבַע כִּבְשֹׂת
כט הַצֹּאן לְבַדְּהֶן: וַיֹּאמֶר אֲבִימֶלֶךְ אֶל־אַבְרָהָם מָה הֵנָּה שֶׁבַע
ל כְּבָשֹׂת הָאֵלֶּה אֲשֶׁר הִצַּבְתָּ לְבַדָּנָה: וַיֹּאמֶר כִּי אֶת־שֶׁבַע
כְּבָשֹׂת תִּקַּח מִיָּדִי בַּעֲבוּר תִּהְיֶה־לִּי לְעֵדָה כִּי חָפַרְתִּי אֶת־
לא הַבְּאֵר הַזֹּאת: עַל־כֵּן קָרָא לַמָּקוֹם הַהוּא בְּאֵר שָׁבַע כִּי שָׁם
לב נִשְׁבְּעוּ שְׁנֵיהֶם: וַיִּכְרְתוּ בְרִית בִּבְאֵר שָׁבַע וַיָּקָם אֲבִימֶלֶךְ
לג וּפִיכֹל שַׂר־צְבָאוֹ וַיָּשֻׁבוּ אֶל־אֶרֶץ פְּלִשְׁתִּים: וַיִּטַּע אֶשֶׁל
לד בִּבְאֵר שָׁבַע וַיִּקְרָא־שָׁם בְּשֵׁם יהוה אֵל עוֹלָם: וַיָּגָר אַבְרָהָם
בְּאֶרֶץ פְּלִשְׁתִּים יָמִים רַבִּים:

כב א וַיְהִי אַחַר הַדְּבָרִים הָאֵלֶּה וְהָאֱלֹהִים נִסָּה אֶת־אַבְרָהָם יט שביעי
ב וַיֹּאמֶר אֵלָיו אַבְרָהָם וַיֹּאמֶר הִנֵּנִי: וַיֹּאמֶר קַח־נָא אֶת־

AKEDAT YITZHAK

Throughout Tanakh, the gravest sin is child sacrifice. The Torah and Prophets denounce it in the strongest terms. Mesha king of Moab uses it in his campaign against Israel (II Kings 3:26–27). How can the Torah regard as Avraham's supreme achievement that he was willing to do what the worst of idolaters do?

To answer this fully, we must consider an overriding theme of the Torah as a whole. First principle: God owns the land of Israel. That is why He can command the return of property to its original owners in the Jubilee year: "The land shall not be sold in perpetuity, for the land is Mine. You are merely migrants and visitors to Me" (Lev. 25:23).

Second principle: God owns the children of Israel since He redeemed them from slavery. Therefore they cannot be turned into permanent slaves: "For they are My servants whom I brought out from Egypt: they cannot be sold as slaves" (25:42).

Third principle: God is the ultimate owner of all that exists. That is why we must make a blessing over anything we enjoy (Berakhot 35a).

This is the jurisprudential basis of

said, "Take your son, your only one, the one whom you
love – Yitzḥak – and go to the land of Moria. There, offer
him up as a burnt offering on one of the mountains,
3 the one that I will show you." Early the next morning
Avraham rose and saddled his donkey. With him he took
two of his young men and Yitzḥak his son. He cut wood
for the offering and set out toward the place of which God
4 had told him. On the third day Avraham looked up and,
5 in the distance, he saw the place. He told his young men,
"Stay here with the donkey. I and the boy will go there
6 and worship. Then we will come back to you." Avraham
took the wood for the offering and placed it on Yitzḥak
his son. He himself took the fire and the knife. The two
7 of them walked together. Then Yitzḥak said to his father,
Avraham, "Father?" Avraham said, "Here I am, my son."
Yitzḥak said, "Here is the fire and the wood, but where is
8 the lamb for the burnt offering?" And Avraham replied,
"God will see to a lamb for an offering, my son." The two
9 of them walked on together. They came to the place of

---

relationship with Him, the individual was suddenly given significance – not just fathers but also mothers, and not just parents but also children. No longer were they fused into a single unit, with a single controlling will. They were each to become persons in their own right, with their own identity and integrity.

First separate, then connect. That seems to be the Jewish way. That is how God created the universe, by first separating domains – day and night, upper and lower waters, sea and dry land – then allowing them to be filled. And that is how we create real personal relationships. By separating and leaving space for the other. Parents should not seek to control children. Spouses should not seek to control one another. It is the carefully calibrated distance between us in which relationship allows each party to grow.

Changes like this do not happen overnight, and they do not happen without wrenching dislocations. That is what is happening at both ends of the Avraham story. At the beginning of his mission, Avraham is told to separate himself from his father, and toward the end he is told to separate himself, in different ways, from each of his two sons. God tells him to listen to Sara and send Yishmael away. God tells him to sacrifice Yitzḥak, "your son, your only one, the one whom you love." These painful episodes are extreme representations – the agonizing birth pangs – of a new way of thinking about humanity.

22:8 אֱלֹהִים יִרְאֶה לּוֹ הַשֶּׂה לְעֹלָה בְּנִי *God will*

בִּנְךָ אֶת־יְחִידְךָ אֲשֶׁר־אָהַבְתָּ אֶת־יִצְחָק וְלֶךְ־לְךָ אֶל־
אֶרֶץ הַמֹּרִיָּה וְהַעֲלֵהוּ שָׁם לְעֹלָה עַל אַחַד הֶהָרִים אֲשֶׁר
ג אֹמַר אֵלֶיךָ: וַיַּשְׁכֵּם אַבְרָהָם בַּבֹּקֶר וַיַּחֲבֹשׁ אֶת־חֲמֹרוֹ וַיִּקַּח
אֶת־שְׁנֵי נְעָרָיו אִתּוֹ וְאֵת יִצְחָק בְּנוֹ וַיְבַקַּע עֲצֵי עֹלָה וַיָּקָם
ד וַיֵּלֶךְ אֶל־הַמָּקוֹם אֲשֶׁר־אָמַר־לוֹ הָאֱלֹהִים: בַּיּוֹם הַשְּׁלִישִׁי
ה וַיִּשָּׂא אַבְרָהָם אֶת־עֵינָיו וַיַּרְא אֶת־הַמָּקוֹם מֵרָחֹק: וַיֹּאמֶר
אַבְרָהָם אֶל־נְעָרָיו שְׁבוּ־לָכֶם פֹּה עִם־הַחֲמוֹר וַאֲנִי וְהַנַּעַר
ו נֵלְכָה עַד־כֹּה וְנִשְׁתַּחֲוֶה וְנָשׁוּבָה אֲלֵיכֶם: וַיִּקַּח אַבְרָהָם
אֶת־עֲצֵי הָעֹלָה וַיָּשֶׂם עַל־יִצְחָק בְּנוֹ וַיִּקַּח בְּיָדוֹ אֶת־הָאֵשׁ
ז וְאֶת־הַמַּאֲכֶלֶת וַיֵּלְכוּ שְׁנֵיהֶם יַחְדָּו: וַיֹּאמֶר יִצְחָק אֶל־
אַבְרָהָם אָבִיו וַיֹּאמֶר אָבִי וַיֹּאמֶר הִנֶּנִּי בְנִי וַיֹּאמֶר הִנֵּה
ח הָאֵשׁ וְהָעֵצִים וְאַיֵּה הַשֶּׂה לְעֹלָה: וַיֹּאמֶר אַבְרָהָם אֱלֹהִים
ט יִרְאֶה־לּוֹ הַשֶּׂה לְעֹלָה בְּנִי וַיֵּלְכוּ שְׁנֵיהֶם יַחְדָּו: וַיָּבֹאוּ אֶל־

That is what the story of *akedat Yitzḥak* is about. When the angel calls to Avraham, "Do not lift your hand against the boy…for you have not withheld from Me your son" (Gen. 22:12), this is what it means. God does not want Avraham to sacrifice his child. God wants him to renounce ownership of his child – then to "do nothing to him." The story of the *akeda* is a polemic against the idea, universal to all pagan cultures, that children are the property of their parents.

22:2 לֶךְ־לְךָ *Go* – God's words "Go (*Lekh lekha*) to the land of Moria" inevitably remind us of God's first summons: "Go (*Lekh lekha*) from your land, your birthplace, and your father's house" (Gen. 12:1). These are the only two places in which this phrase occurs in the Torah. Avraham's last trial echoes his first. Note that the first trial meant that Avraham had to abandon his father, thereby looking as if he were neglecting his duties as a son. So, whether as a father to his sons or as a son to his father, Avraham is commanded to act in ways that seem the exact opposite of what we would expect and how we should behave. This is too strange to be accidental. Essentially, what we are seeing in these events is *the birth of the individual.*

In ancient times, and in antiquity in Greece and Rome, the basic social unit was not the individual but the family, under the absolute rule of its male head. The Torah was a radical break with this mindset. Monotheism was more than simply the belief in one God. Because each human was in His image, and because each could be in direct

which God had spoken. There Avraham built an altar and
arranged the wood. Then he bound Yitzḥak his son and
10 laid him on the altar on top of the wood. Avraham reached
11 out his hand and took hold of the knife to slay his son. But
an angel of the Lord called out to him from the heavens,
12 "Avraham! Avraham!" He said, "Here I am." "Do not lift
your hand against the boy; do nothing to him, for now I
know that you fear God: for you have not withheld from
13 Me your son, your only one." Avraham looked up and
saw a ram caught in a thicket by its horns. Avraham went,
took hold of the ram, and offered it up as a burnt offering
14 in place of his son. And Avraham named the place The
Lord Will See. To this day it is said, "On the mountain of
15 the Lord, He will be seen." Then the angel of the Lord
called to Avraham from the heavens a second time
16 and said, "By My own Self I swear, says the Lord, that
because you have done this and have not withheld your
17 son, your only one, I will bless you greatly and make
your descendants as many as the stars of the heavens, as
the sand on the seashore. Your descendants will possess
18 their enemies' gate, and through your descendants will
all nations of the earth be blessed, because you have
19 listened to My voice." Avraham returned to his young
men, and together they set out and went to Be'er Sheva,
and Avraham stayed on in Be'er Sheva.
20 Some time later, Avraham was told, "Milka too has had MAFTIR
21 children with your brother Naḥor: Utz, his firstborn,

---

whether Avraham has the strength to give up something he loves. He has shown this time and time again. *The trial is to see whether Avraham can live with what seemed to be a clear contradiction between God's word now, and God's word previously – God's promise.*

Faith is not certainty; it is the courage to live with uncertainty. Avraham has what the poet John Keates called "negative capability – that is, when a man is capable of being in uncertainties, mysteries, doubts, without any irritable reaching after fact and reason." He knows the promises will come true; he can live with the uncertainty of not knowing how or when.

הַמָּקוֹם אֲשֶׁר אָמַר־לוֹ הָאֱלֹהִים וַיִּבֶן שָׁם אַבְרָהָם אֶת־
הַמִּזְבֵּחַ וַיַּעֲרֹךְ אֶת־הָעֵצִים וַיַּעֲקֹד אֶת־יִצְחָק בְּנוֹ וַיָּשֶׂם
י אֹתוֹ עַל־הַמִּזְבֵּחַ מִמַּעַל לָעֵצִים: וַיִּשְׁלַח אַבְרָהָם אֶת־יָדוֹ
יא וַיִּקַּח אֶת־הַמַּאֲכֶלֶת לִשְׁחֹט אֶת־בְּנוֹ: וַיִּקְרָא אֵלָיו מַלְאַךְ
יהוה מִן־הַשָּׁמַיִם וַיֹּאמֶר אַבְרָהָם ׀ אַבְרָהָם וַיֹּאמֶר הִנֵּנִי:
יב וַיֹּאמֶר אַל־תִּשְׁלַח יָדְךָ אֶל־הַנַּעַר וְאַל־תַּעַשׂ לוֹ מְאוּמָה
כִּי ׀ עַתָּה יָדַעְתִּי כִּי־יְרֵא אֱלֹהִים אַתָּה וְלֹא חָשַׂכְתָּ אֶת־בִּנְךָ
יג אֶת־יְחִידְךָ מִמֶּנִּי: וַיִּשָּׂא אַבְרָהָם אֶת־עֵינָיו וַיַּרְא וְהִנֵּה־אַיִל
אַחַר נֶאֱחַז בַּסְּבַךְ בְּקַרְנָיו וַיֵּלֶךְ אַבְרָהָם וַיִּקַּח אֶת־הָאַיִל
יד וַיַּעֲלֵהוּ לְעֹלָה תַּחַת בְּנוֹ: וַיִּקְרָא אַבְרָהָם שֵׁם־הַמָּקוֹם
הַהוּא יהוה ׀ יִרְאֶה אֲשֶׁר יֵאָמֵר הַיּוֹם בְּהַר יהוה יֵרָאֶה:
טו טז וַיִּקְרָא מַלְאַךְ יהוה אֶל־אַבְרָהָם שֵׁנִית מִן־הַשָּׁמָיִם: וַיֹּאמֶר
בִּי נִשְׁבַּעְתִּי נְאֻם־יהוה כִּי יַעַן אֲשֶׁר עָשִׂיתָ אֶת־הַדָּבָר הַזֶּה
יז וְלֹא חָשַׂכְתָּ אֶת־בִּנְךָ אֶת־יְחִידֶךָ: כִּי־בָרֵךְ אֲבָרֶכְךָ וְהַרְבָּה
אַרְבֶּה אֶת־זַרְעֲךָ כְּכוֹכְבֵי הַשָּׁמַיִם וְכַחוֹל אֲשֶׁר עַל־שְׂפַת
יח הַיָּם וְיִרַשׁ זַרְעֲךָ אֵת שַׁעַר אֹיְבָיו: וְהִתְבָּרְכוּ בְזַרְעֲךָ כֹּל גּוֹיֵי
יט הָאָרֶץ עֵקֶב אֲשֶׁר שָׁמַעְתָּ בְּקֹלִי: וַיָּשָׁב אַבְרָהָם אֶל־נְעָרָיו
וַיָּקֻמוּ וַיֵּלְכוּ יַחְדָּו אֶל־בְּאֵר שָׁבַע וַיֵּשֶׁב אַבְרָהָם בִּבְאֵר
שָׁבַע:
כ וַיְהִי אַחֲרֵי הַדְּבָרִים הָאֵלֶּה וַיֻּגַּד לְאַבְרָהָם לֵאמֹר הִנֵּה יָלְדָה מפטיר
כא מִלְכָּה גַם־הִוא בָּנִים לְנָחוֹר אָחִיךָ: אֶת־עוּץ בְּכֹרוֹ וְאֶת־בּוּז

---

see to… my son – Avraham's elusive statements to the servants and to Yitzḥak are usually taken as diplomatic evasions. I believe, however, that Avraham means exactly what he says. He is living the contradiction. He believes that the God who has promised him a son will not allow him to sacrifice that son. But he does not know how the contradiction between God's promise and His command will resolve itself.

The trial is *not* to see whether Avraham has the courage to sacrifice his son. The practice was commonplace in the ancient world, and completely abhorrent to Judaism. The trial is *not* to see

22 his brother Buz, Kemuel, father of Aram, Kesed, Ḥazo,
23 Pildash, Yidlaf, and Betuel." Betuel had a daughter Rivka.
Milka bore these eight sons to Avraham's brother Naḥor.
24 His concubine, named Reuma, also had children: Tevaḥ,
Gaḥam, Taḥash, and Maakha.

The haftara for Parashat Vayera is on page 1418.

---

greeted by the two servants on his safe return from Mount Moria. He should be there to mourn his departed mother, Sara. Yet only Avraham is mentioned. Yitzḥak should be there to at least discuss, with his father and his father's servant, his future wife. Yet the arrangement is made between Avraham and his servant with no mention of Yitzḥak's wishes. Yitzḥak does not die on the mountain, but something in him does die – only to be revived when he marries. Then "he took Rivka as his wife, and he loved her; and Yitzḥak was comforted..." (Gen. 24:67). Here, as the *parasha* ends, Rivka quietly enters the narrative, hinting toward the first stage in Yitzḥak's healing.

כב אָחִיו וְאֶת־קְמוּאֵל אֲבִי אֲרָם: וְאֶת־כֶּשֶׂד וְאֶת־חֲזוֹ וְאֶת־
כג פִּלְדָּשׁ וְאֶת־יִדְלָף וְאֵת בְּתוּאֵל: וּבְתוּאֵל יָלַד אֶת־רִבְקָה
כד שְׁמֹנָה אֵלֶּה יָלְדָה מִלְכָּה לְנָחוֹר אֲחִי אַבְרָהָם: וּפִילַגְשׁוֹ
וּשְׁמָהּ רְאוּמָה וַתֵּלֶד גַּם־הִוא אֶת־טֶבַח וְאֶת־גַּחַם וְאֶת־
תַּחַשׁ וְאֶת־מַעֲכָה:

The הפטרה *for* פרשת וירא *is on page 1419.*

22:23 רִבְקָה *Rivka* – What happens to Yitzḥak after the *akeda*? As soon as the angel has stopped Avraham from sacrificing his son, Yitzḥak drops out of the picture. The text tells us that Avraham returns to the two servants who accompanied them on the way, but there is no mention of Yitzḥak.

What does this mean? We can only speculate. But if silences mean something, they suggest that *even an arrested sacrifice has a victim*. Yitzḥak may not have died physically, but the text seems to make him disappear, literarily, through three scenes in which his presence is central. He should be there to greet and be

Parashat Ḥayei Sara

23 1 Sara's lifetime – the years of Sara's life – were one hundred
2 and twenty-seven. Sara died in Kiryat Arba – that is,
Ḥevron – in the land of Canaan. And Avraham came to
3 mourn for Sara and to weep for her. Then Avraham rose

---

of the spirit. These things constituted a life of uncertainty and decades of unmet hopes.

Nietzsche was one of the most brilliant thinkers of the modern age, and also one of the most dangerous. Yet one of his most famous remarks is both profound and true: *He who has a why in life can bear almost any how*. Avraham and Sara are among the supreme examples in all history of what it is to have a "why" in life. The entire course of their lives came as a response to a call – a divine call to live in a land where they would be strangers, abandon every conventional form of security, and have the faith to believe that by living by the standards of righteousness and justice, they would be taking the first step to establishing a nation, a land, a faith and a way of life that would be a blessing to all humankind.

Surviving whatever fate threw at them, however much it seemed to derail their mission, Avraham and Sara knew that what makes a life satisfying is not external but internal, a sense of purpose, mission, of starting something that would be continued by those who came after them, of bringing something new into the world by the way they lived their lives. What mattered was the inside, not the outside; their faith, not their often-troubled circumstances.

Faith helps us to find the "why" that allows us to bear almost any "how." The serenity of Sara's (and later, Avraham's) death is eternal testimony to how they lived.

23:3 וַיָּקָם אַבְרָהָם *Then Avraham rose* – Avraham's grief is described in a mere five Hebrew words. Then immediately we read, "And Avraham rose from beside his dead." From here on, he engages in a flurry of activity with two aims in mind: first to buy a plot of land in which to bury Sara, second to find a wife for his son.

We have observed two people in the Torah who look back, one by implication, the other explicitly. Noaḥ ends his life drunk. The Torah does not say why but we can guess. He has lost an entire world. It is not hard to imagine this righteous man overwhelmed by grief as he replays in his mind all that has happened, wondering whether he might have done something to save more lives or avert the catastrophe.

Lot's wife, against the instruction of the angels, does look back as the cities of the plain disappear under fire and brimstone and the anger of God. Immediately

פרשת חיי שרה

כג א וַיִּהְיוּ חַיֵּי שָׂרָה מֵאָה שָׁנָה וְעֶשְׂרִים שָׁנָה וְשֶׁבַע שָׁנִים שְׁנֵי
ב חַיֵּי שָׂרָה: וַתָּמָת שָׂרָה בְּקִרְיַת אַרְבַּע הִוא חֶבְרוֹן בְּאֶרֶץ
ג כְּנָעַן וַיָּבֹא אַבְרָהָם לִסְפֹּד לְשָׂרָה וְלִבְכֹּתָהּ: וַיָּקָם אַבְרָהָם

ḤAYEI SARA

By the time the *parasha* begins, Avraham has received two promises – both stated five times. The first is of a land (12:7; 13:14–17; 15:7; 15:18–21; 17:7–8), the second of children (12:2; 13:16; 15:5; 17:4–5; 22:17). Both are remarkable promises. The land in its length and breadth will be Avraham's and his children's as "an everlasting possession." Avraham will have as many children as the dust of the earth, the stars of the sky, and the sand on the seashore. What, though, is the reality at the time Sara dies? Avraham owns no land and has only one son, unmarried, to be the bearer of the covenant.

Ḥayei Sara contains three narratives. First comes the death of Sara, and Avraham's purchase of a burial plot for her, the first part of the Holy Land to be owned by the people of the covenant. Next is the search for a wife for Yitzḥak, the first Jewish child. Finally, we hear of the last period of Avraham's life, and of his death. A land: Israel. And children: Jewish continuity. The astonishing fact is that today, four thousand years later, they remain the dominant concerns of Jews throughout the world – the safety and security of Israel as the Jewish home, and the future of the Jewish people. Avraham's hopes and fears are ours.

The *parasha*, then, tells a difficult story. Yes, Avraham will have a land. He will have countless children. But these things will not happen soon, or suddenly, or easily. Nor will they occur without human effort. The future will happen, but it is we – inspired, empowered, given strength by the promise – who must bring it about.

THE YEARS OF SARA'S LIFE

A well-known comment by Rashi on the apparently superfluous phrase "the years of Sara's life" states: "The word 'years' is repeated [in the Hebrew] and without a number to indicate that they were all equally good." How could anyone say that the years of Sara's life were equally good? Twice, first in Egypt, then in Gerar, she was taken against her wishes into a royal harem.

There were the years when, despite God's repeated promise of many children, she was infertile, unable to have even a single child. There was the time when she persuaded Avraham to take her handmaid, Hagar, and have a child by her, which caused her great strife

4 from beside his dead and spoke to the Hittites. He said, "I
am a migrant and a visitor among you. Sell me a burial
5 site here so that I can bury my dead." The Hittites
6 answered Avraham, "Hear us, my lord. You are a prince of
God in our midst. Bury your dead in the choicest of our
tombs. None of us will refuse you his tomb to bury your
7 dead." Avraham rose and bowed down to the Hittites, the
8 people of the land, and said to them, "If you are willing to
allow me to bury the dead that lies before me, then hear
me and intercede on my behalf with Efron son of Tzoḥar.
9 Let him sell me the cave of Makhpela that he owns, at the

---

a field with a cave in which to bury Sara. It is a tense, even humiliating, encounter. The Hittites say one thing and mean another. As a group they say, "Bury your dead in the choicest of our tombs" (Gen. 23:6). Efron, the owner of the field Avraham wants to buy, says: "Hear me. I give you the field and I give you the cave that is in it. In the presence of my people, I give it to you. Bury your dead" (23:11).

As the narrative makes clear, this elaborate generosity is a façade for some extremely hard bargaining. Avraham knows he is "a migrant and a visitor among you" (23:4), meaning, among other things, that he has no right to own land. That is the force of their reply which, stripped of its overlay of courtesy, means: "Use one of our burial sites. You may not acquire your own."

Avraham is not deterred. He insists that he wants to buy his own. Efron's reply – "It is yours. I give it to you" – is in fact the prelude to a demand for a highly inflated price. Finally, however, Avraham fulfills his wish. The transfer of ownership is recorded in precise legal prose (23:17–20) to signal that, at last, Avraham owns part of the land. It is a small part: one field and a cave. A burial place, bought at great expense. That is as much of the divine promise of the land as Avraham will see in his lifetime.

23:6 נְשִׂיא אֱלֹהִים אַתָּה בְּתוֹכֵנוּ *You are a prince of God in our midst* – This is the first instance, and the classic example, of *kiddush Hashem* in the Torah. Noaḥ's righteousness was turned inward. He had no influence on his contemporaries. Lot chose the way of assimilation. He tried to merge into the society, Sedom, in which he had chosen to live. Avraham is different. He fights for his neighbors and prays for them but he does not become like them. He lives out the principle that has been the Jewish imperative ever since: be true to your faith and a blessing to others regardless of their faith. What is the result? When Avraham comes before the Hittites, they say to him: "You are a prince of God in our midst."

ד מֵעַל פְּנֵי מֵתוֹ וַיְדַבֵּר אֶל־בְּנֵי־חֵת לֵאמֹר׃ גֵּר־וְתוֹשָׁב אָנֹכִי
עִמָּכֶם תְּנוּ לִי אֲחֻזַּת־קֶבֶר עִמָּכֶם וְאֶקְבְּרָה מֵתִי מִלְּפָנָי׃
ה ו וַיַּעֲנוּ בְנֵי־חֵת אֶת־אַבְרָהָם לֵאמֹר לוֹ׃ שְׁמָעֵנוּ ׀ אֲדֹנִי נְשִׂיא
אֱלֹהִים אַתָּה בְּתוֹכֵנוּ בְּמִבְחַר קְבָרֵינוּ קְבֹר אֶת־מֵתֶךָ אִישׁ
ז מִמֶּנּוּ אֶת־קִבְרוֹ לֹא־יִכְלֶה מִמְּךָ מִקְּבֹר מֵתֶךָ׃ וַיָּקָם אַבְרָהָם
ח וַיִּשְׁתַּחוּ לְעַם־הָאָרֶץ לִבְנֵי־חֵת׃ וַיְדַבֵּר אִתָּם לֵאמֹר אִם־
יֵשׁ אֶת־נַפְשְׁכֶם לִקְבֹּר אֶת־מֵתִי מִלְּפָנַי שְׁמָעוּנִי וּפִגְעוּ־לִי
ט בְּעֶפְרוֹן בֶּן־צֹחַר׃ וְיִתֶּן־לִי אֶת־מְעָרַת הַמַּכְפֵּלָה אֲשֶׁר־לוֹ

she is turned into a pillar of salt, unable to move on.

Against the background of these two stories, Avraham sets a different precedent. He marks his loss, and then he rises from it. Avraham hears the future calling to him.

23:4 גֵּר וְתוֹשָׁב *A migrant and a visitor* – This is the first time we encounter the phrase *ger vetoshav*. It is no mere formulaic utterance; Avraham is acknowledging his legal lack of standing. As a stranger and temporary resident, he has no entitlement to own land. He depends on the goodwill of the Hittites even to begin the conversation with the cave's owner, Efron.

Reading this for the first time, we assume that the text represents Israel's prehistory. Genesis is about the promise, not the fulfillment. One day, this will change. Israel will become a nation with its own land. Time passes. Israel goes into exile. It is redeemed from slavery. Moshe leads the people out of Egypt on their way to the land. There, we cannot but expect, the people will find a home. At last, they will own the land. They will no longer be as Avraham was. Then, in one of the great paradigm-shifting moments of the Bible, the twenty-fifth chapter of Leviticus turns this expectation on its head: "The land shall not be sold in perpetuity, for the land is Mine. You are merely migrants and visitors to Me" (Lev. 25:23).

The fate of Avraham's family, we now discover, will be not temporary but permanent – permanently temporary. They will know no certainty, have no fixed and unconditional home, even in the land of promise. Avraham has been told, in a dark vision of exile, that his offspring will be "migrants in a land not their own" (Gen. 15:13). That, we thought, meant Egypt. It turns out to mean Israel as well. This is the central, haunting irony of the Pentateuch. Even at their greatest moments, the people of the covenant will be strangers at home. This is how they will learn to make strangers feel at home.

23:4 תְּנוּ לִי אֲחֻזַּת קֶבֶר *Sell me a burial site* – Avraham undergoes a lengthy bargaining process with the Hittites to buy

edge of his field. Ask him to sell it to me at the full price as
10 a burial site in your midst." Efron was sitting among the
Hittites. Efron the Hittite answered Avraham in the
hearing of all the Hittites who had come to the city gate.
11 He said, "No, my lord, hear me. I give you the field and I
give you the cave that is in it. In the presence of my people,
12 I give it to you. Bury your dead." Avraham bowed down
13 again before the people of the land and said to Efron in
their hearing, "Please, would that you would hear me. I
give you the money for the field. Take it from me so that I
14 can bury my dead there." Efron answered Avraham and
15 said to him, "My lord, hear me. A piece of land worth four
hundred silver shekel – what is that between you and me?
16 Bury your dead." Avraham heard Efron. He weighed out
for him the price he had mentioned in the Hittites' hearing:
four hundred silver shekel at the merchants' standard rate.
17 So Efron's field in Makhpela near Mamre – the field, its SHENI
18 cave, and all the trees within the field's borders – passed to
Avraham as his possession, in the presence of all the
19 Hittites who had come to the city gate. Avraham then
buried Sara his wife in the cave in the field of Makhpela
near Mamre – that is, Ḥevron – in the land of Canaan.
20 Thus the field and its cave passed from the Hittites to
24 1 Avraham as a burial site. Avraham was old,
advanced in years, and the Lord had blessed him in all
2 things. And Avraham said to the senior servant of his
household, who was in charge of all he had, "Place your
3 hand under my thigh. I want you to swear by the Lord,
God of heaven and earth, that you will not take a wife for
my son from among the daughters of the Canaanites
4 among whom I live. Instead, go to my land and birthplace,
5 and there find a wife for Yitzḥak my son." The servant
asked, "What if the woman does not want to come back
with me to this land? Shall I bring your son back to the
6 land from which you came?" Avraham said to him, "Be
7 sure not to take my son back there. The Lord, God of the
heavens, took me from my father's house and from the

אֲשֶׁר בִּקְצֵה שָׂדֵהוּ בְּכֶסֶף מָלֵא יִתְּנֶנָּה לִּי בְּתוֹכְכֶם לַאֲחֻזַּת־
י קָבֶר׃ וְעֶפְרוֹן יֹשֵׁב בְּתוֹךְ בְּנֵי־חֵת וַיַּעַן עֶפְרוֹן הַחִתִּי אֶת־
יא אַבְרָהָם בְּאָזְנֵי בְנֵי־חֵת לְכֹל בָּאֵי שַׁעַר־עִירוֹ לֵאמֹר׃ לֹא־
אֲדֹנִי שְׁמָעֵנִי הַשָּׂדֶה נָתַתִּי לָךְ וְהַמְּעָרָה אֲשֶׁר־בּוֹ לְךָ נְתַתִּיהָ
יב לְעֵינֵי בְנֵי־עַמִּי נְתַתִּיהָ לָּךְ קְבֹר מֵתֶךָ׃ וַיִּשְׁתַּחוּ אַבְרָהָם
יג לִפְנֵי עַם־הָאָרֶץ׃ וַיְדַבֵּר אֶל־עֶפְרוֹן בְּאָזְנֵי עַם־הָאָרֶץ לֵאמֹר
אַךְ אִם־אַתָּה לוּ שְׁמָעֵנִי נָתַתִּי כֶּסֶף הַשָּׂדֶה קַח מִמֶּנִּי
יד וְאֶקְבְּרָה אֶת־מֵתִי שָׁמָּה׃ וַיַּעַן עֶפְרוֹן אֶת־אַבְרָהָם לֵאמֹר
טו לוֹ׃ אֲדֹנִי שְׁמָעֵנִי אֶרֶץ אַרְבַּע מֵאֹת שֶׁקֶל־כֶּסֶף בֵּינִי וּבֵינְךָ
טז מַה־הִוא וְאֶת־מֵתְךָ קְבֹר׃ וַיִּשְׁמַע אַבְרָהָם אֶל־עֶפְרוֹן
וַיִּשְׁקֹל אַבְרָהָם לְעֶפְרֹן אֶת־הַכֶּסֶף אֲשֶׁר דִּבֶּר בְּאָזְנֵי בְנֵי־
יז חֵת אַרְבַּע מֵאוֹת שֶׁקֶל כֶּסֶף עֹבֵר לַסֹּחֵר׃ וַיָּקָם ׀ שְׂדֵה שני
עֶפְרוֹן אֲשֶׁר בַּמַּכְפֵּלָה אֲשֶׁר לִפְנֵי מַמְרֵא הַשָּׂדֶה וְהַמְּעָרָה
אֲשֶׁר־בּוֹ וְכָל־הָעֵץ אֲשֶׁר בַּשָּׂדֶה אֲשֶׁר בְּכָל־גְּבֻלוֹ סָבִיב׃
יח לְאַבְרָהָם לְמִקְנָה לְעֵינֵי בְנֵי־חֵת בְּכֹל בָּאֵי שַׁעַר־עִירוֹ׃
יט וְאַחֲרֵי־כֵן קָבַר אַבְרָהָם אֶת־שָׂרָה אִשְׁתּוֹ אֶל־מְעָרַת שְׂדֵה
כ הַמַּכְפֵּלָה עַל־פְּנֵי מַמְרֵא הִוא חֶבְרוֹן בְּאֶרֶץ כְּנָעַן׃ וַיָּקָם
הַשָּׂדֶה וְהַמְּעָרָה אֲשֶׁר־בּוֹ לְאַבְרָהָם לַאֲחֻזַּת־קָבֶר מֵאֵת
כד א בְּנֵי־חֵת׃ וְאַבְרָהָם זָקֵן בָּא בַּיָּמִים וַיהוָה בֵּרַךְ כ
ב אֶת־אַבְרָהָם בַּכֹּל׃ וַיֹּאמֶר אַבְרָהָם אֶל־עַבְדּוֹ זְקַן בֵּיתוֹ
ג הַמֹּשֵׁל בְּכָל־אֲשֶׁר־לוֹ שִׂים־נָא יָדְךָ תַּחַת יְרֵכִי׃ וְאַשְׁבִּיעֲךָ
בַּיהוָה אֱלֹהֵי הַשָּׁמַיִם וֵאלֹהֵי הָאָרֶץ אֲשֶׁר לֹא־תִקַּח אִשָּׁה
ד לִבְנִי מִבְּנוֹת הַכְּנַעֲנִי אֲשֶׁר אָנֹכִי יוֹשֵׁב בְּקִרְבּוֹ׃ כִּי אֶל־אַרְצִי
ה וְאֶל־מוֹלַדְתִּי תֵּלֵךְ וְלָקַחְתָּ אִשָּׁה לִבְנִי לְיִצְחָק׃ וַיֹּאמֶר אֵלָיו
הָעֶבֶד אוּלַי לֹא־תֹאבֶה הָאִשָּׁה לָלֶכֶת אַחֲרַי אֶל־הָאָרֶץ
הַזֹּאת הֶהָשֵׁב אָשִׁיב אֶת־בִּנְךָ אֶל־הָאָרֶץ אֲשֶׁר־יָצָאתָ
ו מִשָּׁם׃ וַיֹּאמֶר אֵלָיו אַבְרָהָם הִשָּׁמֶר לְךָ פֶּן־תָּשִׁיב אֶת־בְּנִי
ז שָׁמָּה׃ יְהוָה ׀ אֱלֹהֵי הַשָּׁמַיִם אֲשֶׁר לְקָחַנִי מִבֵּית אָבִי וּמֵאֶרֶץ

land of my birth. He spoke to me and swore to me, 'To
your descendants I will give this land.' He will send His
angel before you, and there you will find a wife for my
8 son. But if the woman does not want to come back with
you, then you will be released from this oath to me. Just
9 do not take my son back there." So the servant placed his
hand under his master Avraham's thigh and swore this by
10 an oath to him. The servant then took ten of his master's SHELISHI
camels, laden with all his master's bounty, and set out to
11 Aram Naharayim, to the city of Naḥor. By the well outside
the city, he had the camels kneel. It was evening, the time
12 when the women came out to draw water. "LORD, God of
my master Avraham," he said, "please, grant me success

---

man's [and woman's] life" is their "little, nameless, unremembered acts / Of kindness and of love."

24:12 וַיֹּאמַ֓ר *He said* – The masoretic tradition has placed a *shalshelet* over this word, the musical note meant to convey a psychological state of uncertainty and indecision (see note on Gen. 19:16). The commentators identify multiple sources of ambivalence at this point. The Midrash, however, offers the most insightful explanation: Eliezer has mixed feelings about the mission itself. Until that point, says the Midrash (Bereshit Rabba 59:9), he had been "sitting and weighing whether his own daughter was suitable for Yitzḥak." He hoped, in other words, that one way or another, Avraham's estate would pass to him.

There are two cues that led the Midrash to this hypothesis. The first is that when Avraham first spoke to God about his childlessness, he said: "My Lord GOD, what will You have given me if I remain childless, and the one who will take charge of my household is Eliezer of Damascus?" (Gen. 15:2). Eliezer, at that time, was Avraham's putative heir. The second is that when Avraham charges his servant with the mission to find a wife for his son, Eliezer replies, "What if (*ulai*) the woman does not want to come back with me to this land?" (24:5). As Ibn Ezra notes, the word *ulai* is not neutral (commentary on Psalms 116:16). It signifies an emotional involvement in the outcome: one wishes for the eventuality to either come to pass or not come to pass. Eliezer's "what if" may be an unconscious expression of the fact that, with half his mind, he wants the mission to fail. This would once again place him or his daughter in a position to be Avraham's heir. It is therefore with profoundly mixed feelings that he prays for the woman who is to be God's choice of Yitzḥak's wife to appear.

מוֹלַדְתִּי וַאֲשֶׁר דִּבֶּר־לִי וַאֲשֶׁר נִשְׁבַּע־לִי לֵאמֹר לְזַרְעֲךָ אֶתֵּן
אֶת־הָאָרֶץ הַזֹּאת הוּא יִשְׁלַח מַלְאָכוֹ לְפָנֶיךָ וְלָקַחְתָּ אִשָּׁה
ח לִבְנִי מִשָּׁם׃ וְאִם־לֹא תֹאבֶה הָאִשָּׁה לָלֶכֶת אַחֲרֶיךָ וְנִקִּיתָ
ט מִשְּׁבֻעָתִי זֹאת רַק אֶת־בְּנִי לֹא תָשֵׁב שָׁמָּה׃ וַיָּשֶׂם הָעֶבֶד
אֶת־יָדוֹ תַּחַת יֶרֶךְ אַבְרָהָם אֲדֹנָיו וַיִּשָּׁבַע לוֹ עַל־הַדָּבָר הַזֶּה׃
י וַיִּקַּח הָעֶבֶד עֲשָׂרָה גְמַלִּים מִגְּמַלֵּי אֲדֹנָיו וַיֵּלֶךְ וְכָל־טוּב שלישי
אֲדֹנָיו בְּיָדוֹ וַיָּקָם וַיֵּלֶךְ אֶל־אֲרַם נַהֲרַיִם אֶל־עִיר נָחוֹר׃
יא וַיַּבְרֵךְ הַגְּמַלִּים מִחוּץ לָעִיר אֶל־בְּאֵר הַמָּיִם לְעֵת עֶרֶב
יב לְעֵת צֵאת הַשֹּׁאֲבֹת׃ וַיֹּאמַר ׀ יהוה אֱלֹהֵי אֲדֹנִי אַבְרָהָם

THE SERVANT'S TEST

Avraham does not tell his servant (unnamed in the text but traditionally identified as Eliezer) to look for any specific traits of character. He simply tells him to find someone from his own extended family. Eliezer, however, formulates a test: "By this I will know that You have shown kindness (*ḥesed*) to my master." His use of the word *ḥesed* here is no accident, for it is the very characteristic he is looking for in the future wife of the first Jewish child, Yitzḥak, and he finds it in Rivka. *Ḥesed,* what I define as "love as deed," is central to the Jewish value system.

Ḥesed – providing shelter for the homeless, food for the hungry, or assistance to the poor; visiting the sick; comforting mourners; and providing a dignified burial for all – became constitutive of Jewish life. During the many centuries of exile and dispersion, Jewish communities were built around these needs. There were *ḥevrot,* "friendly societies," for each of them.

Through *ḥesed,* Jews humanized fate as, they believed, God's *ḥesed* humanizes the world. As God acts toward us with love, so we are called on to act lovingly to one another. The world does not operate solely on the basis of impersonal principles like power or justice, but also on the deeply personal basis of vulnerability, attachment, care, and concern, recognizing us as individuals with unique needs and potentialities.

Ḥesed also added a word to the English language. In 1535, Myles Coverdale published the first-ever translation of the Hebrew Bible into English. It was when he came to this word that he realized that there was no word in English which captured its meaning. It was then that, to translate it, he coined the word "loving-kindness."

Ḥesed is what leads Eliezer to choose Rikva to become the first Jewish bride. It brings redemption to the world and it can change lives. Wordsworth was right when he wrote in his poem "Tintern Abbey" that the "best portion of a good

13 today and show kindness to my master Avraham. I am
standing here by the spring and the daughters of the
14 townspeople are coming out to draw water. If I say to a
young woman, 'Please lower your jar so that I can drink,'
and she replies, 'Drink, and I will water your camels also,'
let her be the one You have chosen for Your servant
Yitzḥak. By this I will know that You have shown kindness
15 to my master." Before he had even finished speaking,
Rivka, daughter of Betuel son of Milka, the wife of
Avraham's brother Naḥor, came out with her jar on her
16 shoulder. The young woman was very beautiful, a virgin
whom no man had known. She went down to the spring,
17 filled her jar, and came up. The servant ran to meet her
and said, "Please let me sip a little water from your jar."
18 She said, "Drink, my lord," and quickly lowered her jar to
19 her hand and let him drink. When she had let him drink
his fill, she said, "I will draw water for your camels, too,
20 until they have had enough to drink." Quickly she
emptied her jar into the trough and ran back to the well to
21 draw more water; she drew for all his camels. The man
stood gazing at her, silently wondering whether the Lord
22 had made his journey successful. When the camels had
finished drinking, the man took a gold ring weighing a
half shekel and two gold bracelets for her arms weighing
23 ten shekel, and he asked, "Whose daughter are you?
Please tell me, is there room in your father's house for us
24 to spend the night?" She answered him, "I am the
25 daughter of Betuel, the son Milka bore to Naḥor." She
added, "We have plenty of straw and fodder, as well as

---

the most passive of the patriarchs. Rivka is his opposite – initiating, full of energy. It is the people not like us who make us grow. When building a team, we need to recognize where we are weak and surround ourselves by people who are strong in those areas. Often this applies in family life as well. Marriage is the supreme embodiment of openness to otherness. It was and is the single greatest source of beauty in ordinary lives – moral beauty. It is a song scored for two different voices in complex harmony.

יג הַקְרֵה־נָא לְפָנַי הַיּוֹם וַעֲשֵׂה־חֶסֶד עִם אֲדֹנִי אַבְרָהָם: הִנֵּה
אָנֹכִי נִצָּב עַל־עֵין הַמָּיִם וּבְנוֹת אַנְשֵׁי הָעִיר יֹצְאֹת לִשְׁאֹב
יד מָיִם: וְהָיָה הַנַּעֲרָ אֲשֶׁר אֹמַר אֵלֶיהָ הַטִּי־נָא כַדֵּךְ וְאֶשְׁתֶּה
וְאָמְרָה שְׁתֵה וְגַם־גְּמַלֶּיךָ אַשְׁקֶה אֹתָהּ הֹכַחְתָּ לְעַבְדְּךָ
טו לְיִצְחָק וּבָהּ אֵדַע כִּי־עָשִׂיתָ חֶסֶד עִם־אֲדֹנִי: וַיְהִי־הוּא טֶרֶם
כִּלָּה לְדַבֵּר וְהִנֵּה רִבְקָה יֹצֵאת אֲשֶׁר יֻלְּדָה לִבְתוּאֵל בֶּן־
טז מִלְכָּה אֵשֶׁת נָחוֹר אֲחִי אַבְרָהָם וְכַדָּהּ עַל־שִׁכְמָהּ: וְהַנַּעֲרָ
טֹבַת מַרְאֶה מְאֹד בְּתוּלָה וְאִישׁ לֹא יְדָעָהּ וַתֵּרֶד הָעַיְנָה
יז וַתְּמַלֵּא כַדָּהּ וַתָּעַל: וַיָּרָץ הָעֶבֶד לִקְרָאתָהּ וַיֹּאמֶר הַגְמִיאִינִי
יח נָא מְעַט־מַיִם מִכַּדֵּךְ: וַתֹּאמֶר שְׁתֵה אֲדֹנִי וַתְּמַהֵר וַתֹּרֶד
יט כַּדָּהּ עַל־יָדָהּ וַתַּשְׁקֵהוּ: וַתְּכַל לְהַשְׁקֹתוֹ וַתֹּאמֶר גַּם לִגְמַלֶּיךָ
כ אֶשְׁאָב עַד אִם־כִּלּוּ לִשְׁתֹּת: וַתְּמַהֵר וַתְּעַר כַּדָּהּ אֶל־הַשֹּׁקֶת
כא וַתָּרָץ עוֹד אֶל־הַבְּאֵר לִשְׁאֹב וַתִּשְׁאַב לְכָל־גְּמַלָּיו: וְהָאִישׁ
מִשְׁתָּאֵה לָהּ מַחֲרִישׁ לָדַעַת הַהִצְלִיחַ יהוה דַּרְכּוֹ אִם־לֹא:
כב וַיְהִי כַּאֲשֶׁר כִּלּוּ הַגְּמַלִּים לִשְׁתּוֹת וַיִּקַּח הָאִישׁ נֶזֶם זָהָב
בֶּקַע מִשְׁקָלוֹ וּשְׁנֵי צְמִידִים עַל־יָדֶיהָ עֲשָׂרָה זָהָב מִשְׁקָלָם:
כג וַיֹּאמֶר בַּת־מִי אַתְּ הַגִּידִי נָא לִי הֲיֵשׁ בֵּית־אָבִיךְ מָקוֹם לָנוּ
כד לָלִין: וַתֹּאמֶר אֵלָיו בַּת־בְּתוּאֵל אָנֹכִי בֶּן־מִלְכָּה אֲשֶׁר יָלְדָה
כה לְנָחוֹר: וַתֹּאמֶר אֵלָיו גַּם־תֶּבֶן גַּם־מִסְפּוֹא רַב עִמָּנוּ גַּם־

24:19 גַּם לִגְמַלֶּיךָ אֶשְׁאָב *I will draw water for your camels, too* – While fulfilling the stranger's request for water, Rivka identifies a need he has not mentioned and meets that as well. "Someone else's physical needs are my spiritual obligation," a Jewish mystic taught. The truths of religion are exalted, but its duties are close at hand.

Jewish ethics is refreshingly down to earth. If someone is in need, give. If someone is lonely, invite them home. If someone you know has recently been bereaved, visit them and give them comfort. If you know of someone who has lost their job, do all you can to help them find another. The Sages called this "imitating God." It is the test by which the servant unerringly recognizes our second founding mother.

24:20 וַתָּרָץ עוֹד *And ran back* – Yitzḥak is

26 room for you to spend the night." The man bowed low, REVI'I
27 prostrating himself to the LORD. He said, "Blessed be
the LORD, God of my master Avraham, who has not
withheld His kindness and faithfulness from my master.
As for me – the LORD has guided me on the way to the
28 house of my master's close family." The young woman
29 ran and told all this to her mother's household. Rivka
had a brother named Lavan; he ran outside to the man
30 at the spring. He had seen the ring, and the bracelets on
his sister's arms, and had heard his sister Rivka tell what
the man had said to her. He came up to the man who
31 was still standing by the camels at the spring, and said,
"Come. The LORD bless you! Why are you standing
outside? I have made room in the house and prepared a
32 place for the camels." So the man entered the house, the
camels were unloaded, straw and fodder were brought
for the camels, and water was brought for him and his
33 men to wash their feet. Food was set before him to eat,
but he said, "I will not eat until I have said what I have to
34 say." "Speak, then," said Lavan. "I am Avraham's servant,"
35 he said. "The LORD has blessed my master greatly, and
he has prospered. He has given him sheep and cattle,

tradition, were far stronger than they are now. Normally it was expected that a child would act in accordance with the will of his or her parents in all things. Strikingly, the halakhists did not follow this line. Writing in the thirteenth century, Rabbi Shlomo Ibn Adret (Rashba, 1235–1310) argued that getting married is a positive commandment. As the wishes of God take precedence over those of human beings, parental wishes cannot override the desire of a child to marry and fulfill the mitzva. Since the child wants to do God's will, he is not bound to do his parents' will if it collides with his own in the choice of a marriage partner. As for Yitzḥak, Rashba argues that he was unique. Yitzḥak was a "perfect offering," a child of special sanctity; having been offered at the altar, he was not allowed to leave the land of Israel – in contrast to Avraham and Yaakov, both of whom traveled to Egypt. Had this not been so, says Rashba, he would certainly have undertaken the journey himself to choose a wife (*Teshuvot HaMeyuḥasot LeHaRamban*, 272). As it is, the text is explicit in assuring us that once Rivka has entered Yitzḥak's life, "he loved her."

כו כז מָקוֹם לָלִין: וַיִּקֹּד הָאִישׁ וַיִּשְׁתַּחוּ לַיהוָה: וַיֹּאמֶר בָּרוּךְ יהוה רביעי
אֱלֹהֵי אֲדֹנִי אַבְרָהָם אֲשֶׁר לֹא־עָזַב חַסְדּוֹ וַאֲמִתּוֹ מֵעִם אֲדֹנִי
כח אָנֹכִי בַּדֶּרֶךְ נָחַנִי יהוה בֵּית אֲחֵי אֲדֹנִי: וַתָּרָץ הַנַּעֲרָ וַתַּגֵּד
כט לְבֵית אִמָּהּ כַּדְּבָרִים הָאֵלֶּה: וּלְרִבְקָה אָח וּשְׁמוֹ לָבָן וַיָּרָץ
ל לָבָן אֶל־הָאִישׁ הַחוּצָה אֶל־הָעָיִן: וַיְהִי | כִּרְאֹת אֶת־הַנֶּזֶם
וְאֶת־הַצְּמִדִים עַל־יְדֵי אֲחֹתוֹ וּכְשָׁמְעוֹ אֶת־דִּבְרֵי רִבְקָה
אֲחֹתוֹ לֵאמֹר כֹּה־דִבֶּר אֵלַי הָאִישׁ וַיָּבֹא אֶל־הָאִישׁ וְהִנֵּה
לא עֹמֵד עַל־הַגְּמַלִּים עַל־הָעָיִן: וַיֹּאמֶר בּוֹא בְּרוּךְ יהוה לָמָּה
לב תַעֲמֹד בַּחוּץ וְאָנֹכִי פִּנִּיתִי הַבַּיִת וּמָקוֹם לַגְּמַלִּים: וַיָּבֹא
הָאִישׁ הַבַּיְתָה וַיְפַתַּח הַגְּמַלִּים וַיִּתֵּן תֶּבֶן וּמִסְפּוֹא לַגְּמַלִּים
לג וּמַיִם לִרְחֹץ רַגְלָיו וְרַגְלֵי הָאֲנָשִׁים אֲשֶׁר אִתּוֹ: ויישם לְפָנָיו וַיּוּשַׂם
לֶאֱכֹל וַיֹּאמֶר לֹא אֹכַל עַד אִם־דִּבַּרְתִּי דְּבָרָי וַיֹּאמֶר דַּבֵּר:
לד לה וַיֹּאמַר עֶבֶד אַבְרָהָם אָנֹכִי: וַיהוה בֵּרַךְ אֶת־אֲדֹנִי מְאֹד
וַיִּגְדָּל וַיִּתֶּן־לוֹ צֹאן וּבָקָר וְכֶסֶף וְזָהָב וַעֲבָדִם וּשְׁפָחֹת וּגְמַלִּים

24:34 עֶבֶד אַבְרָהָם אָנֹכִי *I am Avraham's servant* – Eliezer repeats the Torah's first detailed description of a marriage arrangement. The highly involved narrative is striking. Yitzḥak takes no part in the process. There is no indication that his father consults him, that he gives his consent to the arrangement, or that his views were taken into account in any way. Only after Rivka arrives do we hear of his reaction in a few brief words.

This is consistent with the general impression we have of Yitzḥak as a figure in the shadow of Avraham, who does what his father does rather than strike out in any new direction of his own.

The Torah's next presentation of marriage will be different. Esav and Yaakov each choose their own wives. Yet once again there is an emphasis on parental wishes. Esav chooses wives who become "a source of bitter sorrow to Yitzḥak and Rivka" (Gen. 26:35). Yaakov, by contrast, "obeyed his father and mother" by going to find a wife from his mother's family (28:7).

These episodes raise the question of the role of parental authority in marriage. To what extent is Avraham's initiative in choosing, or getting his servant to choose, a wife for his son normative? Does a parent have a right, in Judaism, to determine who their child will marry?

This issue was much debated in the Middle Ages, an era in which parental authority, as well as respect for age and

silver and gold, male and female servants, camels and
36 donkeys. My master's wife Sara bore my master a son in
37 her old age, and he committed to his son all that is his. My
master made me swear, saying, 'You must not take a wife
for my son from among the daughters of the Canaanites
38 in whose land I live. Instead you must go to my father's
39 house and family and there find a wife for my son.' I asked
my master, 'What if the woman does not want to come
40 back with me?' He answered, 'The LORD before whom I
have walked will send His angel with you to make your
journey a success, so that you may find a wife for my son
41 from my family and father's house. You are released from
this vow only if you come to my family and they refuse to
give her to you. Then you are released from my vow.'
42 Today, when I came to the spring, I said, 'LORD, God of
my master Avraham, if You will, please grant success to
43 this journey on which I have come. I am standing here by
a spring of water. The woman who comes out to draw
water, to whom I say, "Please let me sip a little water from
44 your jar," and who says to me, "Drink, and I will also draw
for your camels" – let her be the one the LORD has chosen
45 for my master's son.' Before I had even finished speaking
to myself, Rivka came out with her jar on her shoulder.
She went down to the spring and drew water, and I asked
46 her, 'Please, let me drink.' She immediately lowered her
jar and said, 'Drink, and I will also water your camels.' So
47 I drank, and she gave the camels water too. I asked her,
'Whose daughter are you?' She said, 'The daughter of
Betuel son of Naḥor, whom Milka bore to him.' So I
48 placed a ring on her nose and bracelets on her arms. I
bowed low and prostrated myself to the LORD, and
blessed the LORD, God of my master Avraham, who led
me on the right way to take the daughter of my master's
49 brother for his son. Now, if you are willing to show
kindness and faithfulness to my master, tell me; and if
not, tell me that, so that I may move on, right or left."
50 Lavan and Betuel answered, "This is surely from the

לו וַחֲמֹרִים: וַתֵּלֶד שָׂרָה אֵשֶׁת אֲדֹנִי בֵן לַאדֹנִי אַחֲרֵי זִקְנָתָהּ
לז וַיִּתֶּן־לוֹ אֶת־כָּל־אֲשֶׁר־לוֹ: וַיַּשְׁבִּעֵנִי אֲדֹנִי לֵאמֹר לֹא־תִקַּח
לח אִשָּׁה לִבְנִי מִבְּנוֹת הַכְּנַעֲנִי אֲשֶׁר אָנֹכִי יֹשֵׁב בְּאַרְצוֹ: אִם־לֹא
לט אֶל־בֵּית־אָבִי תֵּלֵךְ וְאֶל־מִשְׁפַּחְתִּי וְלָקַחְתָּ אִשָּׁה לִבְנִי: וָאֹמַר
מ אֶל־אֲדֹנִי אֻלַי לֹא־תֵלֵךְ הָאִשָּׁה אַחֲרָי: וַיֹּאמֶר אֵלָי יְהוָה
אֲשֶׁר־הִתְהַלַּכְתִּי לְפָנָיו יִשְׁלַח מַלְאָכוֹ אִתָּךְ וְהִצְלִיחַ דַּרְכֶּךָ
מא וְלָקַחְתָּ אִשָּׁה לִבְנִי מִמִּשְׁפַּחְתִּי וּמִבֵּית אָבִי: אָז תִּנָּקֶה
מֵאָלָתִי כִּי תָבוֹא אֶל־מִשְׁפַּחְתִּי וְאִם־לֹא יִתְּנוּ לָךְ וְהָיִיתָ
מב נָקִי מֵאָלָתִי: וָאָבֹא הַיּוֹם אֶל־הָעָיִן וָאֹמַר יְהוָה אֱלֹהֵי אֲדֹנִי כא
אַבְרָהָם אִם־יֶשְׁךָ־נָּא מַצְלִיחַ דַּרְכִּי אֲשֶׁר אָנֹכִי הֹלֵךְ עָלֶיהָ:
מג הִנֵּה אָנֹכִי נִצָּב עַל־עֵין הַמָּיִם וְהָיָה הָעַלְמָה הַיֹּצֵאת לִשְׁאֹב
מד וְאָמַרְתִּי אֵלֶיהָ הַשְׁקִינִי־נָא מְעַט־מַיִם מִכַּדֵּךְ: וְאָמְרָה אֵלַי
גַּם־אַתָּה שְׁתֵה וְגַם לִגְמַלֶּיךָ אֶשְׁאָב הִוא הָאִשָּׁה אֲשֶׁר־
מה הֹכִיחַ יְהוָה לְבֶן־אֲדֹנִי: אֲנִי טֶרֶם אֲכַלֶּה לְדַבֵּר אֶל־לִבִּי
וְהִנֵּה רִבְקָה יֹצֵאת וְכַדָּהּ עַל־שִׁכְמָהּ וַתֵּרֶד הָעַיְנָה וַתִּשְׁאָב
מו וָאֹמַר אֵלֶיהָ הַשְׁקִינִי נָא: וַתְּמַהֵר וַתּוֹרֶד כַּדָּהּ מֵעָלֶיהָ
וַתֹּאמֶר שְׁתֵה וְגַם־גְּמַלֶּיךָ אַשְׁקֶה וָאֵשְׁתְּ וְגַם הַגְּמַלִּים
מז הִשְׁקָתָה: וָאֶשְׁאַל אֹתָהּ וָאֹמַר בַּת־מִי אַתְּ וַתֹּאמֶר בַּת־
בְּתוּאֵל בֶּן־נָחוֹר אֲשֶׁר יָלְדָה־לּוֹ מִלְכָּה וָאָשִׂם הַנֶּזֶם עַל־
מח אַפָּהּ וְהַצְּמִידִים עַל־יָדֶיהָ: וָאֶקֹּד וָאֶשְׁתַּחֲוֶה לַיהוָה וָאֲבָרֵךְ
אֶת־יְהוָה אֱלֹהֵי אֲדֹנִי אַבְרָהָם אֲשֶׁר הִנְחַנִי בְּדֶרֶךְ אֱמֶת
מט לָקַחַת אֶת־בַּת־אֲחִי אֲדֹנִי לִבְנוֹ: וְעַתָּה אִם־יֶשְׁכֶם עֹשִׂים
חֶסֶד וֶאֱמֶת אֶת־אֲדֹנִי הַגִּידוּ לִי וְאִם־לֹא הַגִּידוּ לִי וְאֶפְנֶה
נ עַל־יָמִין אוֹ עַל־שְׂמֹאל: וַיַּעַן לָבָן וּבְתוּאֵל וַיֹּאמְרוּ מֵיְהוָה

LORD: there is nothing for us to say to you, bad or good.
51 Here is Rivka in front of you. Take her; go. Let her be the
52 wife of your master's son, as the LORD has spoken." When
Avraham's servant heard these words, he bowed down to
53 the ground before the LORD. The servant brought out ḤAMISHI
gold and silver jewelry and clothes and gave them to
Rivka. He also gave costly gifts to her brother and her
54 mother. Then he and his men ate and drank and spent the
night there. When they got up the next morning he said,
55 "Send me on my way to my master." But her brother and
her mother replied, "Let the young woman stay with us a
56 year or ten months. Then she may go." "Do not delay me,"
he said, "now that the LORD has made my journey a
success. Let me leave so that I may go back to my master."
57 They replied, "Let us call the young woman and ask her."
58 So they called Rivka and asked her, "Will you go with this
59 man?" She replied, "I will." So they sent their sister Rivka
on her way, together with her nurse and Avraham's
60 servant and his men. They blessed Rivka and said to her,
"Our sister, may you grow into thousands of myriads, and
61 may your descendants possess their enemies' gates." Then
Rivka set off with her maids, riding on camels and following
62 the man. The servant took Rivka and went. Yitzḥak was

---

itself a product of Hellenistic as well as Hebraic culture, it was assumed to suggest a form of knowledge. In Biblical Hebrew it has no such connotation. *Emuna* means many things – trust, loyalty, fidelity, strength, firmness, affirmation, caring. All these things have to do not with knowledge but with the relationship between persons. They are about willingness to make a binding commitment in the conscious presence of uncertainty. Faith is a marriage; marriage is an act of faith. It is the redemption of loneliness so that we can face the future without fear. Anyone who has had the privilege of a happy marriage knows that it is the most important and beautiful thing in life.

24:60 וַיְבָרְכוּ אֶת־רִבְקָה *They blessed Rivka* – There has long been a custom among Sephardim – increasingly adopted by Ashkenazim – to mark the birth of a daughter with a special ceremony known as *zeved habat* ("the gift of a daughter"), during which the baby is named and blessed. The blessing given to Rivka by her family is a traditional part of this service.

נא יָצָא הַדָּבָר לֹא נוּכַל דַּבֵּר אֵלֶיךָ רַע אוֹ־טוֹב׃ הִנֵּה־רִבְקָה
לְפָנֶיךָ קַח וָלֵךְ וּתְהִי אִשָּׁה לְבֶן־אֲדֹנֶיךָ כַּאֲשֶׁר דִּבֶּר יְהוָה׃
נב וַיְהִי כַּאֲשֶׁר שָׁמַע עֶבֶד אַבְרָהָם אֶת־דִּבְרֵיהֶם וַיִּשְׁתַּחוּ
נג אַרְצָה לַיהוָה׃ וַיּוֹצֵא הָעֶבֶד כְּלֵי־כֶסֶף וּכְלֵי זָהָב וּבְגָדִים חמישי
נד וַיִּתֵּן לְרִבְקָה וּמִגְדָּנֹת נָתַן לְאָחִיהָ וּלְאִמָּהּ׃ וַיֹּאכְלוּ וַיִּשְׁתּוּ
הוּא וְהָאֲנָשִׁים אֲשֶׁר־עִמּוֹ וַיָּלִינוּ וַיָּקוּמוּ בַבֹּקֶר וַיֹּאמֶר
נה שַׁלְּחֻנִי לַאדֹנִי׃ וַיֹּאמֶר אָחִיהָ וְאִמָּהּ תֵּשֵׁב הַנַּעֲרָ אִתָּנוּ יָמִים
נו אוֹ עָשׂוֹר אַחַר תֵּלֵךְ׃ וַיֹּאמֶר אֲלֵהֶם אַל־תְּאַחֲרוּ אֹתִי וַיהוָה
נז הִצְלִיחַ דַּרְכִּי שַׁלְּחוּנִי וְאֵלְכָה לַאדֹנִי׃ וַיֹּאמְרוּ נִקְרָא לַנַּעֲרָ
נח וְנִשְׁאֲלָה אֶת־פִּיהָ׃ וַיִּקְרְאוּ לְרִבְקָה וַיֹּאמְרוּ אֵלֶיהָ הֲתֵלְכִי
נט עִם־הָאִישׁ הַזֶּה וַתֹּאמֶר אֵלֵךְ׃ וַיְשַׁלְּחוּ אֶת־רִבְקָה אֲחֹתָם
ס וְאֶת־מֵנִקְתָּהּ וְאֶת־עֶבֶד אַבְרָהָם וְאֶת־אֲנָשָׁיו׃ וַיְבָרְכוּ אֶת־
רִבְקָה וַיֹּאמְרוּ לָהּ אֲחֹתֵנוּ אַתְּ הֲיִי לְאַלְפֵי רְבָבָה וְיִירַשׁ
סא זַרְעֵךְ אֵת שַׁעַר שֹׂנְאָיו׃ וַתָּקָם רִבְקָה וְנַעֲרֹתֶיהָ וַתִּרְכַּבְנָה
עַל־הַגְּמַלִּים וַתֵּלַכְנָה אַחֲרֵי הָאִישׁ וַיִּקַּח הָעֶבֶד אֶת־רִבְקָה

24:55 תֵּשֵׁב הַנַּעֲרָ אִתָּנוּ יָמִים אוֹ עָשׂוֹר *Let the young woman stay… or ten months* This is one of the longest chapters in the Torah. As with the purchase of the cave of Makhpela, so here: acquiring a daughter-in-law will take much money and hard negotiation. The servant, on arriving in the vicinity of Avraham's family, immediately finds the girl, Rivka, before he has even finished praying for God's help. Securing her family's agreement is another matter. He brings out gold, silver, and clothing for the girl. He gives her brother and mother costly gifts. The family has a celebratory meal. But when the servant wants to leave, brother and mother say, "Let the young woman stay with us." Lavan, Rivka's brother, plays a role not unlike that of Efron: the show of generosity and concern conceals a tough, even exploitative, determination to make a profitable deal.

24:58 אֵלֵךְ *I will* – Rivka's family hesitates to send her out into the unknown. She does not hesitate. It is fitting, for this is what a marriage is: a journey across an unknown land, with nothing to protect you from the elements except one another. It may not be much, but it is everything.

Marriage is a paradigm of faith. Because the word "faith" – *emuna* – entered Europe through Christianity,

just coming back from the direction of Be'er Laḥai Ro'i,
63 for he was then living in the Negev. He had gone out in
the field toward evening to meditate. Looking up, he
64 saw – there were camels approaching. Rivka too looked
up – and saw Yitzḥak. She jumped down from the camel
65 and asked the servant, "Who is that man walking in the
field toward us?" The servant replied, "That is my master."
66 And she took her veil and covered herself. The servant
67 told Yitzḥak all he had done. And Yitzḥak brought her
into the tent of his mother Sara. He took Rivka as his
wife, and he loved her. And Yitzḥak was comforted after
his mother's death.
25 1 2 Avraham took another wife, whose name was Ketura. She SHISHI
bore him Zimran, Yokshan, Medan, Midyan, Yishbak, and
3 Shuaḥ; Yokshan was the father of Sheva and Dedan. The

---

they pray. Yitzḥak is just about to meet the woman with whom he will share his life. For him, prayer is the prelude to a human relationship. Our openness to God shapes and is shaped by our openness to other people. Love of God is, or should be, interwoven with our love for human beings.

In prayer we do not simply speak; God, and the traditions of Jewish faith, speak through us. The very words we use are not our own, but those of thousands of years of our people's history, distilling the response to innumerable encounters with God. We become a channel through which flows the energy of Jewish history – the force of creation and the drive toward redemption. While the prayer lasts, we make those energies our own.

A genuine human conversation is a preparation for, and a microcosmic version of, the act of prayer. For in prayer I attend to the presence of God, listening as well as speaking, opening myself up to a reality other and infinitely vaster than my own, and I become a different person as a result. It is not monologue but dialogue. That is prayer as *siḥa*.

24:64 וַתִּשָּׂא רִבְקָה אֶת עֵינֶיהָ וַתֵּרֶא אֶת יִצְחָק *Rivka too looked up – and saw Yitzḥak* – The great transformative experiences – love, a sudden sense of beauty, an upsurge of happiness – happen unpredictably and leave us, in Wordsworth's famous phrase, "surprised by joy."

25:1 קְטוּרָה *Ketura* – The Sages identify Ketura with Hagar. It is not unusual for people in the Torah to have more than one name; Yitro, Moshe's father-in-law, has seven. Hagar is called Ketura, tradition has it, because "her acts gave forth fragrance like incense (*ketoret*)" (Bereshit Rabba 51:4).

סב וַיֵּלַךְ: וְיִצְחָק בָּא מִבּוֹא בְּאֵר לַחַי רֹאִי וְהוּא יוֹשֵׁב בְּאֶרֶץ
סג הַנֶּגֶב: וַיֵּצֵא יִצְחָק לָשׂוּחַ בַּשָּׂדֶה לִפְנוֹת עָרֶב וַיִּשָּׂא עֵינָיו
סד וַיַּרְא וְהִנֵּה גְמַלִּים בָּאִים: וַתִּשָּׂא רִבְקָה אֶת־עֵינֶיהָ וַתֵּרֶא
סה אֶת־יִצְחָק וַתִּפֹּל מֵעַל הַגָּמָל: וַתֹּאמֶר אֶל־הָעֶבֶד מִי־הָאִישׁ
הַלָּזֶה הַהֹלֵךְ בַּשָּׂדֶה לִקְרָאתֵנוּ וַיֹּאמֶר הָעֶבֶד הוּא אֲדֹנִי
סו וַתִּקַּח הַצָּעִיף וַתִּתְכָּס: וַיְסַפֵּר הָעֶבֶד לְיִצְחָק אֵת כָּל־
סז הַדְּבָרִים אֲשֶׁר עָשָׂה: וַיְבִאֶהָ יִצְחָק הָאֹהֱלָה שָׂרָה אִמּוֹ
וַיִּקַּח אֶת־רִבְקָה וַתְּהִי־לוֹ לְאִשָּׁה וַיֶּאֱהָבֶהָ וַיִּנָּחֵם יִצְחָק
אַחֲרֵי אִמּוֹ:

כה א ב וַיֹּסֶף אַבְרָהָם וַיִּקַּח אִשָּׁה וּשְׁמָהּ קְטוּרָה: וַתֵּלֶד לוֹ אֶת־ כב ששי
זִמְרָן וְאֶת־יָקְשָׁן וְאֶת־מְדָן וְאֶת־מִדְיָן וְאֶת־יִשְׁבָּק וְאֶת־
ג שׁוּחַ: וְיָקְשָׁן יָלַד אֶת־שְׁבָא וְאֶת־דְּדָן וּבְנֵי דְדָן הָיוּ אַשּׁוּרִם

24:63 לָשׂוּחַ בַּשָּׂדֶה *To meditate* – The word *siḥa* means not only meditation but also, and primarily, conversation. When the Talmud says, in the context of Yitzḥak, *ein siḥa ela tefilla*, we could translate this phrase as "conversation is a form of prayer" – and in a profound sense, it is so.

Prayer is a conversation between heaven and earth. But conversation is also a prayer – for in true conversation, I open myself up to the reality of another person. I enter his or her world. I begin to see things from a perspective not my own. In the touch of two selves, both are changed.

How appropriate, therefore, is the fact that Yitzḥak is seen praying immediately prior to his first encounter with the woman who was to become his wife. Avraham and Yaakov are alone when

24:63 לִפְנוֹת עָרֶב *Toward evening* – The three patriarchs are traditionally associated with the three daily prayer services respectively. My predecessor as chief rabbi, the late Lord Jakobovits of blessed memory, used to point out that the position of the sun at the times of the various services mirrors the stories of the patriarchs themselves. In the morning, the sun is in the east – and Avraham, who "rose early" (Gen. 19:27) to meet God, began his life in the east, in Ur Kasdim, namely Mesopotamia. In the early afternoon, the sun is overhead in the middle of the sky – reminding us of Yitzḥak, who spent his entire life within the land of Canaan, later to become the land of Israel. In the evening, when Yaakov "chanced upon" God (28:11), the sun is in the west, as was Yaakov, who ended his life in the west, in exile in Egypt.

4 sons of Dedan were Ashurim, Letushim, and Leumim. The
sons of Midyan were Eifa, Efer, Ḥanokh, Avida, and Eldaa;
5 all these were descendants of Ketura. Avraham left all that
6 was his to Yitzḥak – while he was still living he gave gifts to
the sons of his concubines and sent them eastward, away
7 from his son Yitzḥak, to the land of the East. These are the
days, the years of Avraham's life: he lived one hundred and
8 seventy-five years. Avraham breathed his last and died in
his ripe old age, aged and satisfied, and was gathered to his
9 people. His sons, Yitzḥak and Yishmael, buried him in the
cave of Makhpela, near Mamre, in the field of Efron son of
10 Tzoḥar the Hittite – the field Avraham had bought from
the Hittites. There Avraham was buried with Sara his wife.
11 After Avraham's death, God blessed Yitzḥak his son, who
was then living near Be'er Laḥai Ro'i.

---

simply, to have done what you were called on to do, to have made a beginning, and then to have passed on the baton to the next generation.

25:9 יִצְחָק וְיִשְׁמָעֵאל בָּנָיו *His sons, Yitzḥak and Yishmael* – Until now, we have assumed that the two half-brothers have lived in total isolation from one another. Yet the Torah places them together at the funeral without a word of explanation.

There is an extraordinary midrash, in Pirkei DeRabbi Eliezer (30), which tells of how Avraham twice visited his son Yishmael after his banishment. On the first occasion, Yishmael was not at home. His wife, not knowing Avraham's identity, refused the stranger bread and water. Yishmael, continues the midrash, divorced her and married a woman named Fatima. This time, when Avraham visited, again not disclosing his identity, the woman gave him food and drink. The midrash then says, "Avraham stood and prayed before the Holy One, blessed be He, and Yishmael's house became filled with all good things. When Yishmael returned, his wife told him about it, and Yishmael knew that his father still loved him." Father and son were reconciled.

This hidden story of Ḥayei Sara has immense consequence for our time. Jews and Muslims both trace their descent from Avraham – Jews through Yitzḥak, Muslims through Yishmael. The fact that both sons stand together at their father's funeral tells us that they too were reunited. Yes, there was conflict and separation, but that was the beginning, not the end. There is hope for the future in this story of the past. Avraham loved both his sons, and, in the end, is laid to rest by both.

ד וּלְטוּשִׁם וּלְאֻמִּים: וּבְנֵי מִדְיָן עֵיפָה וָעֵפֶר וַחֲנֹךְ וַאֲבִידָע
ה וְאֶלְדָּעָה כָּל־אֵלֶּה בְּנֵי קְטוּרָה: וַיִּתֵּן אַבְרָהָם אֶת־כָּל־
ו אֲשֶׁר־לוֹ לְיִצְחָק: וְלִבְנֵי הַפִּילַגְשִׁים אֲשֶׁר לְאַבְרָהָם נָתַן
אַבְרָהָם מַתָּנֹת וַיְשַׁלְּחֵם מֵעַל יִצְחָק בְּנוֹ בְּעוֹדֶנּוּ חַי קֵדְמָה
ז אֶל־אֶרֶץ קֶדֶם: וְאֵלֶּה יְמֵי שְׁנֵי־חַיֵּי אַבְרָהָם אֲשֶׁר־חָי מְאַת
ח שָׁנָה וְשִׁבְעִים שָׁנָה וְחָמֵשׁ שָׁנִים: וַיִּגְוַע וַיָּמָת אַבְרָהָם
ט בְּשֵׂיבָה טוֹבָה זָקֵן וְשָׂבֵעַ וַיֵּאָסֶף אֶל־עַמָּיו: וַיִּקְבְּרוּ אֹתוֹ
יִצְחָק וְיִשְׁמָעֵאל בָּנָיו אֶל־מְעָרַת הַמַּכְפֵּלָה אֶל־שְׂדֵה עֶפְרֹן
י בֶּן־צֹחַר הַחִתִּי אֲשֶׁר עַל־פְּנֵי מַמְרֵא: הַשָּׂדֶה אֲשֶׁר־קָנָה
אַבְרָהָם מֵאֵת בְּנֵי־חֵת שָׁמָּה קֻבַּר אַבְרָהָם וְשָׂרָה אִשְׁתּוֹ:
יא וַיְהִי אַחֲרֵי מוֹת אַבְרָהָם וַיְבָרֶךְ אֱלֹהִים אֶת־יִצְחָק בְּנוֹ וַיֵּשֶׁב
יִצְחָק עִם־בְּאֵר לַחַי רֹאִי:

AVRAHAM'S DEATH

This is a deeply serene description of old age and dying. There is also an earlier verse, no less moving: "Avraham was old, advanced in years, and the LORD had blessed him in all things" (Gen. 24:1).

Whether we think of children or the land – the two key divine promises to Avraham and Sara – the reality they saw fell far short of what they might have felt entitled to expect. Yet – in Ḥayei Sara, Avraham does two things: he buys the first plot in the land of Canaan, and he arranges for the marriage of Yitzḥak. One field and a cave; one child, Yitzḥak, married and with children, was enough for Avraham to die in peace.

Lao-Tzu, the Chinese sage, said that a journey of a thousand miles begins with a single step. To that Judaism adds, "It is not for you to complete the work but neither are you free to desist from it" (Avot 2:16). The meaning is clear. If you ensure that your children will continue to live for what you have lived for, then you can have faith that they will continue your journey until eventually they reach the destination. Avraham is able to die serenely because he has faith in God and faith that others would complete what he began. The same is surely true of Sara.

To place your life in God's hands, to have faith that whatever happens to you happens for a reason, to know that you are part of a larger narrative, and to believe that others will continue what you began, is to achieve a satisfaction in life that cannot be destroyed by circumstance. To be happy does not mean that you have everything you want or everything you were promised. It means,

12 These are the descendants of Avraham's son Yishmael, SHEVI'I
whom Sara's maidservant, Hagar the Egyptian, bore to
13 Avraham. The names of Yishmael's sons, in the order of
their birth, are: Nevayot – Yishmael's firstborn, Kedar,
14 15 Adbe'el, Mivsam, Mishma, Duma, Massa, Ḥadad, Teima,
16 Yetur, Nafish, and Kedma. These were Yishmael's sons, and MAFTIR
these are their names by their villages and encampments:
17 twelve princes and their tribes. These were the years of
Yishmael's life: he lived one hundred and thirty-seven
years. He breathed his last and died, and was gathered to
18 his people. The Ishmaelites dwelt from Ḥavila to Shur, up
against Egypt, all the way to Assyria, settling up against all
their brothers.

The haftara for Parashat Ḥayei Sara is on page 1422.

יב וְאֵ֛לֶּה תֹּלְדֹ֥ת יִשְׁמָעֵ֖אל בֶּן־אַבְרָהָ֑ם אֲשֶׁ֨ר יָֽלְדָ֜ה הָגָ֧ר שביעי
יג הַמִּצְרִ֛ית שִׁפְחַ֥ת שָׂרָ֖ה לְאַבְרָהָֽם׃ וְאֵ֗לֶּה שְׁמוֹת֙ בְּנֵ֣י יִשְׁמָעֵ֔אל
בִּשְׁמֹתָ֖ם לְתוֹלְדֹתָ֑ם בְּכֹ֤ר יִשְׁמָעֵאל֙ נְבָיֹ֔ת וְקֵדָ֥ר וְאַדְבְּאֵ֖ל
יד טו וּמִבְשָֽׂם׃ וּמִשְׁמָ֥ע וְדוּמָ֖ה וּמַשָּֽׂא׃ חֲדַ֣ד וְתֵימָ֔א יְט֥וּר נָפִ֖ישׁ
טז וָקֵֽדְמָה׃ אֵ֣לֶּה הֵ֞ם בְּנֵ֣י יִשְׁמָעֵאל֮ וְאֵ֣לֶּה שְׁמֹתָם֒ בְּחַצְרֵיהֶ֖ם מפטיר
יז וּבְטִֽירֹתָ֑ם שְׁנֵים־עָשָׂ֥ר נְשִׂיאִ֖ם לְאֻמֹּתָֽם׃ וְאֵ֗לֶּה שְׁנֵי֙ חַיֵּ֣י
יִשְׁמָעֵ֔אל מְאַ֥ת שָׁנָ֛ה וּשְׁלֹשִׁ֥ים שָׁנָ֖ה וְשֶׁ֣בַע שָׁנִ֑ים וַיִּגְוַ֣ע וַיָּ֔מָת
יח וַיֵּאָ֖סֶף אֶל־עַמָּֽיו׃ וַיִּשְׁכְּנ֨וּ מֵֽחֲוִילָ֜ה עַד־שׁ֗וּר אֲשֶׁר֙ עַל־פְּנֵ֣י
מִצְרַ֔יִם בֹּאֲכָ֖ה אַשּׁ֑וּרָה עַל־פְּנֵ֥י כָל־אֶחָ֖יו נָפָֽל׃

The הפטרה *for* פרשת חיי שרה *is on page 1423.*

Parashat Toledot

25 19 This is the story of Yitzḥak, son of Avraham: Avraham

Yet, reading this parasha, we cannot but identify with Esav, not Yaakov. We feel their father's shock – "Yitzḥak was seized with a violent fit of trembling" (Gen. 27:33) – as he realizes that his younger son has deceived him. We empathize with Esav, whose first thought is not anger against his brother but simple love for Yitzḥak: "Bless me, me too, my father" (27:34). Then comes Yitzḥak's helplessness – "What then can I do for you, my son?" (27:37) – and Esav's weeping, all the more poignant given what we know of him, that he is strong, a hunter, a man not given to tears. The scene of the two together, robbed of what should have been a moment of tenderness and intimacy – son feeding father, father blessing son – is deeply affecting. There is only one other scene like it in the Ḥumash: Hagar and Yishmael, alone in the heat of the desert, without water, about to die. The comparison is deliberate. Just as there, so here, our sympathies are being enlisted on behalf of the elder son.

The real doubt, however, lies in the way the text describes Yaakov's conduct. Whatever else the covenant is, we feel, it cannot be *this*: a blessing taken by deceit, a destiny acquired by disguise. Did God not say of Avraham, "For I have chosen him so that he may direct his children and his household after him to keep the way of the Lord by doing what is right and just" (Gen. 18:19)? Righteousness, justice, integrity, truth – these are key words of covenantal ethics, and we strain to see how they could be applied to Yaakov's conduct toward his blind father. Besides which, Yitzḥak may be deceived, but is God? The idea is absurd. Had God wanted the blessing to go to Yaakov, not Esav, He would have told that to Yitzḥak, as He told Avraham about Yitzḥak and Yishmael. There is just enough discord to make us wonder if we have read the story correctly. In the end we will discover that our unease was justified and that nothing in the story is as it seems – but only at the end. The suspense is maintained until the final scene, many years and two *parashot* later. Even then, only the most careful listening reveals the unexpected truth.

25:19 אַבְרָהָם הוֹלִיד אֶת יִצְחָק *Avraham was Yitzḥak's father* – The first half of the sentence tells us that Yitzḥak was Avraham's son. Why then does the text repeat, "Avraham was Yitzḥak's father"? The Sages offer a possible explanation (Bava Metzia 87a). Immediately prior to the story of Yitzḥak's birth, in Genesis 20, we are told that Sara was taken into the harem of Avimelekh, king of Gerar. Gossip may have suggested that Avraham was infertile, that Yitzḥak's true father was Avimelekh. Hence the

פרשת תולדת

כה יט וְאֵלֶּה תּוֹלְדֹת יִצְחָק בֶּן־אַבְרָהָם אַבְרָהָם הוֹלִיד אֶת־יִצְחָק׃ כג

TOLEDOT

Toledot tells the story of Yitzḥak and Rivka's twin sons, Yaakov and Esav, who struggle in the womb and seem destined to clash throughout their lives and those of their descendants. It contains two great passages: the birth and childhood of the boys, and the scene in which Yaakov, at Rivka's behest, dresses in Esav's clothes and takes his blessing from their father Yitzḥak. Between them is a narrative about Yitzḥak and Rivka traveling to Gerar because of famine, very similar to that told about Avraham and Sara in Genesis 20.

The *parasha* contains themes of similarity and difference – the almost seamless continuity between Avraham and Yitzḥak followed by the conflict and rivalry between Yitzḥak's two very different sons. On the surface, the stories of Yitzḥak and Yishmael and of Yaakov and Esav are about sibling rivalry and the displacement of the elder by the younger. Beneath the surface, however, the Sages heard a counter-narrative telling the opposite story: *the birth of the younger does not displace the older*. We are led to ask – what if the Torah understands, as did Freud and René Girard, and as did Greek and Roman myth, that sibling rivalry is the most primal form of violence? And what if, rather than endorsing it, it set out to undermine it, subvert it, challenge it, and eventually replace it with another, quite different way of understanding our relationship with God and with the human Other? What if, in this regard, Genesis is a more profound, multi-leveled, transformative text than we have taken it to be? These questions are central to our reading of Parashat Toledot.

YAAKOV AND ESAV

Nowhere are narrative and counter-narrative more subtly interwoven than in the story of Yaakov and Esav. It is a work of awesome brilliance and, once we have understood its hidden message, it is clear that it is intended as a forceful refutation of sibling rivalry, the major source of conflict in the stories of Genesis. Its significance, set at the very center of the book, is unmistakable. Once we have decoded the mystery of Yaakov, our understanding of covenant and identity will be changed forever.

The surface narrative is a paradigm, almost a caricature, of the trope of displacement – a story of the younger child displacing the older as heir to power. From Avraham to Menashe and Efrayim, this theme punctuates the book of Genesis. The first time we see the twins, at their birth, the younger Yaakov is already clinging to the heels of the firstborn Esav.

20 was Yitzḥak's father. When Yitzḥak was forty he married
Rivka, daughter of Betuel the Aramean of Padan Aram,
21 sister of Lavan the Aramean. And Yitzḥak pleaded with
the LORD on behalf of his wife, for she was childless. The
22 LORD granted his plea and Rivka became pregnant. But
the children clashed within her. She said, "If this is so,
23 why am I living?" So she went to inquire of the LORD. The
LORD said to her, "Two nations are inside your womb;
two peoples are to part from you. People will overpower
24 people, and the greater shall the younger serve." When

---

informs Yitzḥak of the oracle she hears before the twins, Esav and Yaakov, are born. The consequences of this silence will continue to unfold throughout the children's lives.

25:23 שְׁנֵי גוֹיִם בְּבִטְנֵךְ *Two nations are inside your womb* – This is a rare example in the Torah of an oracle as opposed to a prophecy. Oracles – a familiar form of supernatural communication in the ancient world – were normally obscure and cryptic, unlike the normal form of Israelite prophecy. This may well be the technical meaning of the phrase "she went to inquire of the LORD," which puzzled the medieval commentators.

The scene reminds us of the Delphic oracle in *Oedipus Rex* who tells Laius that he will be killed by his son. The story begins with the end, and the tension lies in waiting to see how it comes to pass. Nowhere else does the Tanakh come so close to Greek tragedy; fate and tragedy belong together, which is what makes this passage so unexpected, so *unbiblical*. The Torah rejects the idea of inescapable fate, a preordained future. Yet these verses set up an expectation, shaping the way we interpret all that follows. The story that begins with the words "The greater will the younger serve" seems destined to end with Yitzḥak's blessing to Yaakov, given against his intentions: "Be lord over your brothers, and may your mother's sons bow down to you" (Gen. 27:29). Not so. The oracle will continue to unfold in unexpected ways.

25:23 וְרַב יַעֲבֹד צָעִיר *The greater will the younger serve* – The word *et*, signaling the object of the verb, is missing here (as noted by Radak and Rabbi Yosef Ibn Kaspi). Normally in Biblical Hebrew, the subject precedes the verb, and the object follows – but not always. Thus, while the phrase told to Rivka might mean "the older shall serve the younger," it could also mean "the younger shall serve the older." This reading, though it leans on poetic rather than conventional use of grammar, is supported by the unusual musical notation (*tipḥa-merkha-sof pasuk* in place of the normal *merkha-tipḥa-sof pasuk*).

What is more, *rav* and *tza'ir* are

כ וַיְהִי יִצְחָק בֶּן־אַרְבָּעִים שָׁנָה בְּקַחְתּוֹ אֶת־רִבְקָה בַּת־בְּתוּאֵל
כא הָאֲרַמִּי מִפַּדַּן אֲרָם אֲחוֹת לָבָן הָאֲרַמִּי לוֹ לְאִשָּׁה: וַיֶּעְתַּר
יִצְחָק לַיהוה לְנֹכַח אִשְׁתּוֹ כִּי עֲקָרָה הִוא וַיֵּעָתֶר לוֹ יהוה
כב וַתַּהַר רִבְקָה אִשְׁתּוֹ: וַיִּתְרֹצְצוּ הַבָּנִים בְּקִרְבָּהּ וַתֹּאמֶר אִם־
כג כֵּן לָמָּה זֶּה אָנֹכִי וַתֵּלֶךְ לִדְרֹשׁ אֶת־יהוה: וַיֹּאמֶר יהוה לָהּ
שְׁנֵי גיים בְּבִטְנֵךְ וּשְׁנֵי לְאֻמִּים מִמֵּעַיִךְ יִפָּרֵדוּ וּלְאֹם מִלְאֹם גּוֹיִם
כד יֶאֱמָץ וְרַב יַעֲבֹד צָעִיר: וַיִּמְלְאוּ יָמֶיהָ לָלֶדֶת וְהִנֵּה תוֹמִם

double emphasis of our verse: not only was Avraham Yitzḥak's father, but also everyone could see this because father and son looked exactly alike.

The Sages link this idea to another detail in the text: Avraham and Sara are the first people in the Torah described as being old (Gen. 24:1), despite the fact that many previously mentioned biblical characters lived to a much greater age.

Until Avraham, people did not age. But people who saw Avraham would say, "That is Yitzḥak," and people who saw Yitzḥak would say, "That is Avraham," and so Avraham prayed to grow old, and this is the meaning of [the phrase] "Avraham was old" (Sanhedrin 103b).

Yitzḥak is the least individuated of the patriarchs; in some places his story directly echoes that of his father. Sensitive to this, the Rabbis told a profound psychological story. The close physical resemblance between Avraham and Yitzḥak refuted the charge of those who said Avraham was not the real father. At first, indeed, he looked like his clone. Eventually, however, Avraham has to pray for the deed to be undone. It is the space we make for otherness that makes love something other than narcissism and parenthood something greater than self-replication. We are each in God's image but no one else's.

25:22 וַתֵּלֶךְ לִדְרֹשׁ אֶת יהוה *So she went to inquire of the Lord* – The Netziv made the sharp observation that Rivka's "relationship with Yitzḥak was not the same as that between Sara and Avraham or Raḥel and Yaakov. When they had a problem, they were not afraid to speak about it. Not so with Rivka" (*Haamek Davar* on Gen. 24:65).

The Netziv senses a distance from the very first moment when Rivka sees Yitzḥak "had gone out in the field…to meditate" (Gen. 24:63), at which point she "took her veil and covered herself" (24:65). He comments, "She covered herself out of awe and a sense of inadequacy, as if she felt she was unworthy to be his wife, and from then on this trepidation was fixed in her mind."

Their relationship, suggests the Netziv, was never casual, candid, and communicative. The result is, at a series of critical moments, a failure of communication. It seems likely that Rivka never

the time came for her to give birth, there were twins in her
25 womb. The first came out red. His whole body was like a
26 hairy cloak, so they named him Esav. Then his brother
emerged, his hand grasping Esav's heel, so he named him
Yaakov. Yitzḥak was sixty years old when they were born.
27 The boys grew up. Esav became a skilled hunter, a man of
the field, while Yaakov was an innocent man who stayed
28 among the tents. Yitzḥak loved Esav because he ate of his
29 game, but Rivka loved Yaakov. Once when Yaakov was
30 cooking a stew, Esav came in exhausted from the field. He
said to Yaakov, "Let me gulp down some of that red stuff.
I am starved!" – that is how he came to be named Edom.
31 32 Yaakov said, "First sell me your birthright." And Esav said,
"Look, I am about to die. What use to me is a birthright?"
33 But Yaakov said, "Swear to me first." So he swore, and sold
34 Yaakov his birthright. Yaakov then gave Esav bread and
lentil stew. He ate, drank, got up, and left. Thus – Esav
disdained his birthright.

---

meaning that Esav trapped and deceived Yitzḥak. He pretended to be more religious than he was (*Tanḥuma,* Toledot 8, quoted by Rashi on Gen. 25:27). There is, though, a quite different explanation, closer to the plain sense of the text: Yitzḥak *loves Esav because Esav is his son, and that is what fathers do.* They love their children unconditionally. That does not mean that Yitzḥak cannot see the faults in Esav's character. But it does mean that Yitzḥak knows that *a father must love his son because he is his son.* Yitzḥak is teaching us a fundamental lesson in parenthood.

To take seriously the idea, central to Judaism, of *Avinu Malkeinu,* that our King is first and foremost our parent, is to invest our relationship with God with the most profound emotions. God wrestles with us, as does a parent with a child. We wrestle with Him as a child does with his or her parents. The relationship is sometimes tense, conflictual, even painful, yet what gives it its depth is the knowledge that it is unbreakable. Whatever happens, a parent is still a parent, and a child is still a child. The bond may be deeply damaged, but it is never broken beyond repair.

Unconditional love is not uncritical, but it is unbreakable. That is how we should love our children – for it is how God loves us.

25:34 וַיִּבֶז עֵשָׂו אֶת־הַבְּכֹרָה *Esav disdained his birthright* – Yaakov drives a hard bargain: my stew for your birthright. Esav agrees and in a staccato succession of five consecutive verbs – literally: "he ate, drank, got

כה בְּבִטְנָהּ׃ וַיֵּצֵא הָרִאשׁוֹן אַדְמוֹנִי כֻּלּוֹ כְּאַדֶּרֶת שֵׂעָר וַיִּקְרְאוּ
כו שְׁמוֹ עֵשָׂו׃ וְאַחֲרֵי־כֵן יָצָא אָחִיו וְיָדוֹ אֹחֶזֶת בַּעֲקֵב עֵשָׂו
וַיִּקְרָא שְׁמוֹ יַעֲקֹב וְיִצְחָק בֶּן־שִׁשִּׁים שָׁנָה בְּלֶדֶת אֹתָם׃
כז וַיִּגְדְּלוּ הַנְּעָרִים וַיְהִי עֵשָׂו אִישׁ יֹדֵעַ צַיִד אִישׁ שָׂדֶה וְיַעֲקֹב
כח אִישׁ תָּם יֹשֵׁב אֹהָלִים׃ וַיֶּאֱהַב יִצְחָק אֶת־עֵשָׂו כִּי־צַיִד בְּפִיו
כט וְרִבְקָה אֹהֶבֶת אֶת־יַעֲקֹב׃ וַיָּזֶד יַעֲקֹב נָזִיד וַיָּבֹא עֵשָׂו מִן־
ל הַשָּׂדֶה וְהוּא עָיֵף׃ וַיֹּאמֶר עֵשָׂו אֶל־יַעֲקֹב הַלְעִיטֵנִי נָא מִן־
הָאָדֹם הָאָדֹם הַזֶּה כִּי עָיֵף אָנֹכִי עַל־כֵּן קָרָא־שְׁמוֹ אֱדוֹם׃
לא לב וַיֹּאמֶר יַעֲקֹב מִכְרָה כַיּוֹם אֶת־בְּכֹרָתְךָ לִי׃ וַיֹּאמֶר עֵשָׂו
לג הִנֵּה אָנֹכִי הוֹלֵךְ לָמוּת וְלָמָּה־זֶּה לִי בְּכֹרָה׃ וַיֹּאמֶר יַעֲקֹב
הִשָּׁבְעָה לִּי כַּיּוֹם וַיִּשָּׁבַע לוֹ וַיִּמְכֹּר אֶת־בְּכֹרָתוֹ לְיַעֲקֹב׃
לד וְיַעֲקֹב נָתַן לְעֵשָׂו לֶחֶם וּנְזִיד עֲדָשִׁים וַיֹּאכַל וַיֵּשְׁתְּ וַיָּקָם
וַיֵּלַךְ וַיִּבֶז עֵשָׂו אֶת־הַבְּכֹרָה׃

25:28 וַיֶּאֱהַב יִצְחָק אֶת־עֵשָׂו *Yitzḥak loved Esav* – Is it conceivable that Yitzḥak loves Esav merely because he has a taste for wild game? He surely knows that his elder son is a man of mercurial temperament who lives in the emotions of the moment. Even if this does not trouble him, the next episode involving Esav clearly will: "When Esav was forty years old, he married Yehudit daughter of Be'eri the Hittite, and Basmat daughter of Eilon the Hittite. These were a source of bitter sorrow to Yitzḥak and Rivka" (Gen. 26:34–35). Esav has made himself at home among the Hittites and all they represented in terms of religion, culture, and morality.

Yet Yitzḥak clearly *does* love Esav. The Sages gave an explanation. They interpreted the phrase "skilled hunter" as

not opposites. The opposite of *tza'ir* ("younger") is *bekhir* ("older" or "firstborn"). *Rav* does not mean "older." It means "great" or possibly "chief." This linking of two terms as if they were polar opposites, when in fact they are not, further destabilizes the meaning. Who was the *rav*? The elder? The leader? The chief? The more numerous?

These ambiguities are not accidental, but integral to the text. The subtlety is such that we do not notice them at first, but later, when the narrative does not turn out as expected, we are forced to go back and notice what at first we missed: that the words Rivka heard may mean "the greater will serve the younger" or "the younger will serve the greater," and that the identities of the two are not at all obvious.

26 1 Another famine afflicted the land, apart from the earlier
famine in Avraham's days, and Yitzḥak went to Avimelekh,
2 king of the Philistines, in Gerar. The LORD had appeared to
him: "Do not go down to Egypt," He had said. "Stay in the
3 land I tell you of. Bide in this land and I will be with you
and bless you, for I am going to give all these lands to you
and your descendants, fulfilling the oath I swore to
4 Avraham your father. I will make your descendants as
many as the stars of the heavens, and I will give them all
these lands. All the nations of the earth will bless themselves
5 by your descendants, because Avraham listened to My
voice and kept My charge: My commandments, My
6 statutes, and My laws." So Yitzḥak now settled in Gerar. SHENI
7 The men of the place inquired after his wife; "She is my
sister," he said. He was terrified to say "She is my wife." "The
men of the place might kill me for Rivka," he thought, "she
8 is so beautiful." When he had already been there for some
time, Avimelekh, king of the Philistines, looked down from
a window and saw Yitzḥak enjoying himself with his wife
9 Rivka. Avimelekh summoned Yitzḥak. "She is your wife,"
he said. "Why did you say, 'She is my sister'?" Yitzḥak
10 replied, "I thought I might die because of her." "What is
this you have done to us?" said Avimelekh. "One of the
people might have slept with your wife, and you would
11 have brought guilt upon us." Avimelekh then issued an
order to all the people: "Whoever touches this man or his
12 wife shall be put to death." Yitzḥak planted crops in that
land, and that year he reaped a hundredfold because the
13 LORD had blessed him. The man became rich; he prospered SHELISHI
14 more and more until he became very wealthy. He had
flocks and herds and a large retinue of servants, and the
15 Philistines envied him. So the Philistines stopped up all the
wells that his father's servants had dug in the time of his

---

explanations are made, and the moment passes. In both cases Avimelekh promises the patriarchs security. Yet in both cases, there is a troubled aftermath, as we shall see.

כו א וַיְהִי רָעָב בָּאָרֶץ מִלְּבַד הָרָעָב הָרִאשׁוֹן אֲשֶׁר הָיָה בִּימֵי
אַבְרָהָם וַיֵּלֶךְ יִצְחָק אֶל־אֲבִימֶלֶךְ מֶלֶךְ־פְּלִשְׁתִּים גְּרָרָה:
ב וַיֵּרָא אֵלָיו יהוה וַיֹּאמֶר אַל־תֵּרֵד מִצְרָיְמָה שְׁכֹן בָּאָרֶץ
ג אֲשֶׁר אֹמַר אֵלֶיךָ: גּוּר בָּאָרֶץ הַזֹּאת וְאֶהְיֶה עִמְּךָ וַאֲבָרְכֶךָּ
כִּי־לְךָ וּלְזַרְעֲךָ אֶתֵּן אֶת־כָּל־הָאֲרָצֹת הָאֵל וַהֲקִמֹתִי אֶת־
ד הַשְּׁבֻעָה אֲשֶׁר נִשְׁבַּעְתִּי לְאַבְרָהָם אָבִיךָ: וְהִרְבֵּיתִי אֶת־
זַרְעֲךָ כְּכוֹכְבֵי הַשָּׁמַיִם וְנָתַתִּי לְזַרְעֲךָ אֵת כָּל־הָאֲרָצֹת הָאֵל
ה וְהִתְבָּרְכוּ בְזַרְעֲךָ כֹּל גּוֹיֵי הָאָרֶץ: עֵקֶב אֲשֶׁר־שָׁמַע אַבְרָהָם
ו בְּקֹלִי וַיִּשְׁמֹר מִשְׁמַרְתִּי מִצְוֹתַי חֻקּוֹתַי וְתוֹרֹתָי: וַיֵּשֶׁב יִצְחָק שני
ז בִּגְרָר: וַיִּשְׁאֲלוּ אַנְשֵׁי הַמָּקוֹם לְאִשְׁתּוֹ וַיֹּאמֶר אֲחֹתִי הִוא
כִּי יָרֵא לֵאמֹר אִשְׁתִּי פֶּן־יַהַרְגֻנִי אַנְשֵׁי הַמָּקוֹם עַל־רִבְקָה
ח כִּי־טוֹבַת מַרְאֶה הִוא: וַיְהִי כִּי־אָרְכוּ־לוֹ שָׁם הַיָּמִים וַיַּשְׁקֵף
אֲבִימֶלֶךְ מֶלֶךְ פְּלִשְׁתִּים בְּעַד הַחַלּוֹן וַיַּרְא וְהִנֵּה יִצְחָק
ט מְצַחֵק אֵת רִבְקָה אִשְׁתּוֹ: וַיִּקְרָא אֲבִימֶלֶךְ לְיִצְחָק וַיֹּאמֶר
אַךְ הִנֵּה אִשְׁתְּךָ הִוא וְאֵיךְ אָמַרְתָּ אֲחֹתִי הִוא וַיֹּאמֶר אֵלָיו
י יִצְחָק כִּי אָמַרְתִּי פֶּן־אָמוּת עָלֶיהָ: וַיֹּאמֶר אֲבִימֶלֶךְ מַה־זֹּאת
עָשִׂיתָ לָּנוּ כִּמְעַט שָׁכַב אַחַד הָעָם אֶת־אִשְׁתֶּךָ וְהֵבֵאתָ
יא עָלֵינוּ אָשָׁם: וַיְצַו אֲבִימֶלֶךְ אֶת־כָּל־הָעָם לֵאמֹר הַנֹּגֵעַ בָּאִישׁ
יב הַזֶּה וּבְאִשְׁתּוֹ מוֹת יוּמָת: וַיִּזְרַע יִצְחָק בָּאָרֶץ הַהִוא וַיִּמְצָא
יג בַּשָּׁנָה הַהִוא מֵאָה שְׁעָרִים וַיְבָרְכֵהוּ יהוה: וַיִּגְדַּל הָאִישׁ שלישי
יד וַיֵּלֶךְ הָלוֹךְ וְגָדֵל עַד כִּי־גָדַל מְאֹד: וַיְהִי־לוֹ מִקְנֵה־צֹאן
טו וּמִקְנֵה בָקָר וַעֲבֻדָּה רַבָּה וַיְקַנְאוּ אֹתוֹ פְּלִשְׁתִּים: וְכָל־
הַבְּאֵרֹת אֲשֶׁר חָפְרוּ עַבְדֵי אָבִיו בִּימֵי אַבְרָהָם אָבִיו סִתְּמוּם

---

up, left, despised his birthright" – reveals his character: mercurial, impetuous, no match for the subtle Yaakov.

26:6 וַיֵּשֶׁב יִצְחָק בִּגְרָר *So Yitzḥak now settled in Gerar* – This story reads almost like a replay of Genesis 20, a generation later. In both cases the couple pass themselves off as brother and sister. The deception is discovered. Avimelekh is indignant,

16 father Avraham, filling them with earth. Avimelekh said
to Yitzḥak, "Move away from us. You have become much
17 too powerful for us." So Yitzḥak left and camped in the
18 valley of Gerar and settled there. And he reopened the
wells that had been dug in the time of his father Avraham,
which the Philistines had stopped up after Avraham died,
and gave them the same names his father had given them.
19 Yitzḥak's servants dug in the valley and discovered a well
20 of fresh water, but the shepherds of Gerar quarreled with
Yitzḥak's shepherds, claiming that the water was theirs.
So he called the well Esek, because they contended with
21 him there. They dug another well, and there was a quarrel
22 about that too; so he called it Sitna. He moved on from
there and dug another well, and this time they did not
quarrel over it; so he named this one Reḥovot. "Now the

---

will, in any case, become theirs, once the famine ends and Yitzḥak returns home.

More than hate destroys the hated, it destroys the hater. In this too, Yitzḥak and the Philistines are a portent of what will eventually happen to the Israelites in Egypt. By the time of the plague of locusts, we read: "Pharaoh's officials then said to him, 'How long must we leave this man to ensnare us? Send the people forth to serve the LORD their God. Do you not yet know that Egypt is being destroyed?'" (Ex. 10:7).

In effect they said to Pharaoh: "You may think you are harming the Israelites. In fact you are harming us." This is the self-destructive nature of hate.

26:18 כַּשֵּׁמֹת אֲשֶׁר־קָרָא לָהֶן אָבִיו *The same names his father had given them* – Yitzḥak does not strive to be original. He "reopened the wells that had been dug in the time of his father Avraham, which the Philistines had stopped up after Avraham died, and *gave them the same names*." He is content to be a link in the chain of generations, faithful to what his father started.

Yitzḥak represents the faith of persistence, the courage of continuity. He is the first Jewish child, and he represents the single greatest challenge of being a Jewish child: to continue the journey our ancestors began, rather than drifting from it, thereby bringing the journey to an end before it has reached its destination. And Yitzḥak, because of that faith, is able to achieve the most elusive of goals, namely peace – because he never gives up. When one effort fails, he begins again. So it is with all great achievement: one part originality, nine parts persistence.

26:22 רְחֹבוֹת *Reḥovot* – How fitting it is that the town that today carries the

טז פְּלִשְׁתִּ֔ים וַיְמַלְא֖וּם עָפָֽר׃ וַיֹּ֥אמֶר אֲבִימֶ֖לֶךְ אֶל־יִצְחָ֑ק לֵ֚ךְ
יז מֵֽעִמָּ֔נוּ כִּֽי־עָצַֽמְתָּ מִמֶּ֖נּוּ מְאֹֽד׃ וַיֵּ֥לֶךְ מִשָּׁ֖ם יִצְחָ֑ק וַיִּ֥חַן בְּנַֽחַל־
יח גְּרָ֖ר וַיֵּ֥שֶׁב שָֽׁם׃ וַיָּ֨שָׁב יִצְחָ֜ק וַיַּחְפֹּ֣ר ׀ אֶת־בְּאֵרֹ֣ת הַמַּ֗יִם אֲשֶׁ֤ר
חָֽפְרוּ֙ בִּימֵי֙ אַבְרָהָ֣ם אָבִ֔יו וַיְסַתְּמ֣וּם פְּלִשְׁתִּ֔ים אַחֲרֵ֖י מ֣וֹת
אַבְרָהָ֑ם וַיִּקְרָ֤א לָהֶן֙ שֵׁמ֔וֹת כַּשֵּׁמֹ֕ת אֲשֶׁר־קָרָ֥א לָהֶ֖ן אָבִֽיו׃
יט וַיַּחְפְּר֥וּ עַבְדֵֽי־יִצְחָ֖ק בַּנָּ֑חַל וַיִּ֨מְצְאוּ־שָׁ֔ם בְּאֵ֖ר מַ֥יִם חַיִּֽים׃
כ וַיָּרִ֜יבוּ רֹעֵ֣י גְרָ֗ר עִם־רֹעֵ֥י יִצְחָ֛ק לֵאמֹ֖ר לָ֣נוּ הַמָּ֑יִם וַיִּקְרָ֤א
כא שֵֽׁם־הַבְּאֵר֙ עֵ֔שֶׂק כִּ֥י הִֽתְעַשְּׂק֖וּ עִמּֽוֹ׃ וַֽיַּחְפְּרוּ֙ בְּאֵ֣ר אַחֶ֔רֶת
כב וַיָּרִ֖יבוּ גַּם־עָלֶ֑יהָ וַיִּקְרָ֥א שְׁמָ֖הּ שִׂטְנָֽה׃ וַיַּעְתֵּ֣ק מִשָּׁ֗ם וַיַּחְפֹּר֙
בְּאֵ֣ר אַחֶ֔רֶת וְלֹ֥א רָב֖וּ עָלֶ֑יהָ וַיִּקְרָ֤א שְׁמָהּ֙ רְחֹב֔וֹת וַיֹּ֕אמֶר

STOPPING UP THE WELLS

Centuries later, Pharaoh will say, at the beginning of the book of Exodus, "You see that the Israelite people are many and *more powerful* than we. Come, let us deal wisely with them in case they increase, and if war breaks out they may join our enemies and fight against us and escape from the land" (Ex. 1:9–10). The same word, *atzum*, "power/powerful," is Avimelekh's stated reason for sending Yitzḥak away now: "You have become much too powerful for us." Our passage signals the birth of one of the deadliest of human phenomena, antisemitism.

Amy Chua's thesis, in her book *World on Fire*, is that any conspicuously successful minority will attract envy that may deepen into hate and provoke violence. All three conditions are essential. The hated group must be *conspicuous*, for otherwise it would not be singled out. It must be *successful*, for otherwise it would not be envied. And it must be a *minority*, for otherwise it would not be attacked.

More specifically, according to Hannah Arendt (in part 1 of *The Origins of Totalitarianism*), what gives rise to antisemitism is the phenomenon of "wealth without power." Antisemitism is a complex, protean phenomenon because antisemites must be able to hold together two beliefs that seem to contradict one another: Jews are so powerful that they should be feared, and at the same time so powerless that they can be attacked without fear. Emotions are not rational; there is a world of difference between *rationality* and *rationalization*. "Wealth without power" precisely describes the position of Yitzḥak among the Philistines.

The Philistines do not ask Yitzḥak to share his water with them. They do not ask him to teach them how he (and his father) discovered a source of water that they – residents of the place – did not. They do not even simply ask him to move on. The act of "stopping up" the wells harms them more than it harms Yitzḥak. It robs them of a resource that

LORD has given us space," he said, "and we will flourish in
23 24 the land." From there he went up to Be'er Sheva. That REVI'I
night the LORD appeared to him and said, "I am the God
of your father Avraham. Do not be afraid, for I am with
you. I will bless you and multiply your descendants for the
25 sake of Avraham My servant." Yitzḥak built an altar there
and called on the name of the LORD. There he pitched his
26 tent, and there his servants dug a well. Avimelekh came to
him from Gerar, with Aḥuzat his advisor and Pikhol the
27 commander of his troops. Yitzḥak said to them, "Why
have you come to me? You hate me; you sent me away
28 from you." They said, "We have seen clearly that the LORD
is with you, so we say: Let there be a pact between you and
29 us. Let us make a covenant with you that you will do us no
harm, just as we did not touch you, just as we have done
you nothing but good and we sent you on your way in
30 peace. And now – the LORD bless you." Yitzḥak made ḤAMISHI
31 them a feast, and they ate and drank. Early in the morning
they rose and exchanged oaths, and Yitzḥak sent them on
32 their way. They parted from him in peace. That day,
Yitzḥak's servants came and told him about the well that
33 they had dug; they said, "We have found water." He named
it Shiva, which is why the town is called Be'er Sheva to this
34 day. When Esav was forty years old, he married
Yehudit daughter of Be'eri the Hittite, and Basmat daughter
35 of Eilon the Hittite. These were a source of bitter sorrow to
27 1 Yitzḥak and Rivka. When Yitzḥak had grown
old, when his eyes had grown so dim that he could not see,
he summoned his elder son Esav. "My son," he said. Esav
2 replied, "Here I am." He said, "I am old, and I do not know

---

the name – given to him by God Himself before Yitzḥak was born – means what the psalm means when it says, "May those who sowed in tears reap in joy" (126:5). Faith means the courage to persist through all the setbacks, all the grief, never giving up, never accepting defeat. For at the end, despite the opposition, the envy, and the hate, lie the broad spaces, Reḥovot, and the laughter, Yitzḥak: the serenity of the destination after the storms along the way.

כג כִּי־עַתָּה הִרְחִיב יְהוָה לָנוּ וּפָרִינוּ בָאָרֶץ: וַיַּעַל מִשָּׁם בְּאֵר רביעי
כד שָׁבַע: וַיֵּרָא אֵלָיו יְהוָה בַּלַּיְלָה הַהוּא וַיֹּאמֶר אָנֹכִי אֱלֹהֵי
אַבְרָהָם אָבִיךָ אַל־תִּירָא כִּי־אִתְּךָ אָנֹכִי וּבֵרַכְתִּיךָ וְהִרְבֵּיתִי
כה אֶת־זַרְעֲךָ בַּעֲבוּר אַבְרָהָם עַבְדִּי: וַיִּבֶן שָׁם מִזְבֵּחַ וַיִּקְרָא
בְּשֵׁם יְהוָה וַיֶּט־שָׁם אָהֳלוֹ וַיִּכְרוּ־שָׁם עַבְדֵי־יִצְחָק בְּאֵר:
כו וַאֲבִימֶלֶךְ הָלַךְ אֵלָיו מִגְּרָר וַאֲחֻזַּת מֵרֵעֵהוּ וּפִיכֹל שַׂר־
כז צְבָאוֹ: וַיֹּאמֶר אֲלֵהֶם יִצְחָק מַדּוּעַ בָּאתֶם אֵלָי וְאַתֶּם
כח שְׂנֵאתֶם אֹתִי וַתְּשַׁלְּחוּנִי מֵאִתְּכֶם: וַיֹּאמְרוּ רָאוֹ רָאִינוּ כִּי־
הָיָה יְהוָה ׀ עִמָּךְ וַנֹּאמֶר תְּהִי נָא אָלָה בֵּינוֹתֵינוּ בֵּינֵינוּ וּבֵינֶךָ
כט וְנִכְרְתָה בְרִית עִמָּךְ: אִם־תַּעֲשֵׂה עִמָּנוּ רָעָה כַּאֲשֶׁר לֹא
נְגַעֲנוּךָ וְכַאֲשֶׁר עָשִׂינוּ עִמְּךָ רַק־טוֹב וַנְּשַׁלֵּחֲךָ בְּשָׁלוֹם אַתָּה
ל עַתָּה בְּרוּךְ יְהוָה: וַיַּעַשׂ לָהֶם מִשְׁתֶּה וַיֹּאכְלוּ וַיִּשְׁתּוּ: חמישי
לא וַיַּשְׁכִּימוּ בַבֹּקֶר וַיִּשָּׁבְעוּ אִישׁ לְאָחִיו וַיְשַׁלְּחֵם יִצְחָק וַיֵּלְכוּ
לב מֵאִתּוֹ בְּשָׁלוֹם: וַיְהִי ׀ בַּיּוֹם הַהוּא וַיָּבֹאוּ עַבְדֵי יִצְחָק וַיַּגִּדוּ
לוֹ עַל־אֹדוֹת הַבְּאֵר אֲשֶׁר חָפָרוּ וַיֹּאמְרוּ לוֹ מָצָאנוּ מָיִם:
לג וַיִּקְרָא אֹתָהּ שִׁבְעָה עַל־כֵּן שֵׁם־הָעִיר בְּאֵר שֶׁבַע עַד הַיּוֹם
לד הַזֶּה: וַיְהִי עֵשָׂו בֶּן־אַרְבָּעִים שָׁנָה וַיִּקַּח אִשָּׁה
אֶת־יְהוּדִית בַּת־בְּאֵרִי הַחִתִּי וְאֶת־בָּשְׂמַת בַּת־אֵילֹן הַחִתִּי:
כז לה א וַתִּהְיֶיןָ מֹרַת רוּחַ לְיִצְחָק וּלְרִבְקָה: וַיְהִי כִּי־זָקֵן כד
יִצְחָק וַתִּכְהֶיןָ עֵינָיו מֵרְאֹת וַיִּקְרָא אֶת־עֵשָׂו ׀ בְּנוֹ הַגָּדֹל
ב וַיֹּאמֶר אֵלָיו בְּנִי וַיֹּאמֶר אֵלָיו הִנֵּנִי: וַיֹּאמֶר הִנֵּה־נָא זָקַנְתִּי

---

name that Yitzḥak gave the site of this third well is the home of the Weizmann Institute of Science, the Faculty of Agriculture of the Hebrew University, and the Kaplan hospital, allied to the Medical School of the Hebrew University. Israel Belkind, one of the founders of the settlement in 1890, called it Reḥovot precisely because of this verse: "He named this one Reḥovot, [saying,] 'Now the Lord has given us space… and we will flourish in the land.'"

I find it moving that Yitzḥak, who undergoes so many trials, from the *akeda* (the binding of Yitzḥak) when he was young, to the rivalry between his sons when he is old and blind, carries a name that means "He will laugh." Perhaps

3 when I will die. So now, take your weapons, your quiver
and bow, and go out into the field and hunt me some
4 game. Then make me delicious food, prepared in the way
that I love, and bring it to me to eat so that my soul may
5 bless you before I die." When Yitzḥak was speaking to
Esav his son, Rivka was listening. Esav went out into the
6 field to hunt game to bring back. And Rivka said to her
son Yaakov, "I overheard your father say to your brother
7 Esav, 'Fetch me some game and make me delicious food
so that I may eat and give you my blessing before the
8 Lord before I die.' Now, my son, listen carefully to my
9 instructions. Go to the flock and bring me two choice
young goats. I will make them into delicious food, in the
10 way he loves. Then take it to your father to eat so that he
11 may give you his blessing before he dies." Yaakov said to
Rivka his mother, "My brother Esav is hairy, but I have
12 smooth skin. What if my father touches me? I will look to
him like a fraud and bring upon myself not a blessing but a
13 curse." But his mother replied, "Your curse will be on me,
14 my son. Do as I say. Go; fetch them for me." So he went,
took the goats, and brought them to his mother, and his
mother prepared delicious food in the way his father
15 loved. Then Rivka took her elder son Esav's best clothes,
which were with her in the house, and put them on Yaakov,
16 her younger son. She put the goatskins on his hands and
17 the smooth part of his neck. She then handed her son

It is about God and destiny and spiritual vocation. It is about the future of an entire people, since God has repeatedly told Avraham that he will be the ancestor of a great nation who will be a blessing to humanity as a whole.

Rivka is not Lady Macbeth. This is the woman whom Avraham's servant chose to be the wife of his master's son because she is kind, because at the well she gave water to a stranger and to his camels also. If she has no other way of ensuring that the blessing will go to one who will cherish it and live it, then in this case, she must reason, the end justifies the means. This is one way of reading the story, and it is taken by many of the commentators. As the narrative continues, however, a more complex picture is to emerge.

ג לֹא יָדַעְתִּי יוֹם מוֹתִי: וְעַתָּה שָׂא־נָא כֵלֶיךָ תֶּלְיְךָ וְקַשְׁתֶּךָ
ד וְצֵא הַשָּׂדֶה וְצוּדָה לִּי צידה: וַעֲשֵׂה־לִי מַטְעַמִּים כַּאֲשֶׁר צָיִד
אָהַבְתִּי וְהָבִיאָה לִּי וְאֹכֵלָה בַּעֲבוּר תְּבָרֶכְךָ נַפְשִׁי בְּטֶרֶם
ה אָמוּת: וְרִבְקָה שֹׁמַעַת בְּדַבֵּר יִצְחָק אֶל־עֵשָׂו בְּנוֹ וַיֵּלֶךְ עֵשָׂו
ו הַשָּׂדֶה לָצוּד צַיִד לְהָבִיא: וְרִבְקָה אָמְרָה אֶל־יַעֲקֹב בְּנָהּ
לֵאמֹר הִנֵּה שָׁמַעְתִּי אֶת־אָבִיךָ מְדַבֵּר אֶל־עֵשָׂו אָחִיךָ
ז לֵאמֹר: הָבִיאָה לִּי צַיִד וַעֲשֵׂה־לִי מַטְעַמִּים וְאֹכֵלָה
ח וַאֲבָרֶכְכָה לִפְנֵי יהוה לִפְנֵי מוֹתִי: וְעַתָּה בְנִי שְׁמַע בְּקֹלִי
ט לַאֲשֶׁר אֲנִי מְצַוָּה אֹתָךְ: לֶךְ־נָא אֶל־הַצֹּאן וְקַח־לִי מִשָּׁם
שְׁנֵי גְּדָיֵי עִזִּים טֹבִים וְאֶעֱשֶׂה אֹתָם מַטְעַמִּים לְאָבִיךָ כַּאֲשֶׁר
י אָהֵב: וְהֵבֵאתָ לְאָבִיךָ וְאָכָל בַּעֲבֻר אֲשֶׁר יְבָרֶכְךָ לִפְנֵי מוֹתוֹ:
יא וַיֹּאמֶר יַעֲקֹב אֶל־רִבְקָה אִמּוֹ הֵן עֵשָׂו אָחִי אִישׁ שָׂעִר וְאָנֹכִי
יב אִישׁ חָלָק: אוּלַי יְמֻשֵּׁנִי אָבִי וְהָיִיתִי בְעֵינָיו כִּמְתַעְתֵּעַ
יג וְהֵבֵאתִי עָלַי קְלָלָה וְלֹא בְרָכָה: וַתֹּאמֶר לוֹ אִמּוֹ עָלַי
יד קִלְלָתְךָ בְּנִי אַךְ שְׁמַע בְּקֹלִי וְלֵךְ קַח־לִי: וַיֵּלֶךְ וַיִּקַּח וַיָּבֵא
טו לְאִמּוֹ וַתַּעַשׂ אִמּוֹ מַטְעַמִּים כַּאֲשֶׁר אָהֵב אָבִיו: וַתִּקַּח רִבְקָה
אֶת־בִּגְדֵי עֵשָׂו בְּנָהּ הַגָּדֹל הַחֲמֻדֹת אֲשֶׁר אִתָּהּ בַּבָּיִת
טז וַתַּלְבֵּשׁ אֶת־יַעֲקֹב בְּנָהּ הַקָּטָן: וְאֵת עֹרֹת גְּדָיֵי הָעִזִּים
יז הִלְבִּישָׁה עַל־יָדָיו וְעַל חֶלְקַת צַוָּארָיו: וַתִּתֵּן אֶת־הַמַּטְעַמִּים

27:4 כַּאֲשֶׁר אָהַבְתִּי *Prepared in the way that I love* – This is not Yitzḥak's physical appetite speaking. It is his wish to be filled with the smell and taste he associates with his elder son, so that he can bless him in a mood of focused love. We will hear this in the wording of the blessing he gives, which is imbued with his son's particular scent, that of "a field the LORD has blessed" (Gen. 27:27).

27:10 בַּעֲבֻר אֲשֶׁר יְבָרֶכְךָ *So that he may give you his blessing* – Rivka has watched the twins grow up. She knows that Esav is a hunter, a man of violence. She has seen that he is impetuous, a man of impulse rather than calm reflection. She has seen him sell his birthright for a bowl of soup. No one who despises his birthright can be the trusted guardian of a covenant intended for eternity.

The blessing, she perceives, has to go to Yaakov. This is, after all, not just a matter of relationships within the family.

Yaakov the delicious food and bread that she had prepared.
18 He went in to his father; "My father," he said. His father
19 replied, "Here I am. Who are you, my son?" Yaakov said to
his father, "I am Esav your firstborn. I have done as you
asked. Please sit up and eat some of my game so that your
20 soul may bless me." Yitzḥak asked his son, "How did you
find it so quickly, my son?" He replied, "The LORD your
21 God brought it about for me." Then Yitzḥak said to Yaakov,
"Come close and let me feel you, my son, to know – are
22 you really my son Esav?" Yaakov came close to Yitzḥak his
father, who felt him and said, "The voice is the voice of
23 Yaakov, but the hands are the hands of Esav." He did not
recognize him, because his hands were hairy like those of
24 his brother Esav. And he blessed him. "Are you really my
25 son Esav?" he asked. He replied, "I am." "Then serve me
and let me eat some of my son's game so that my soul may
bless you." He served him food and he ate, he brought him
26 wine and he drank. Then Yaakov's father Yitzḥak said to
27 him, "Come close and kiss me, my son." So he came close
and kissed him, and Yitzḥak smelled the smell of his
clothes and blessed him, saying: "The smell of my son is
28 the smell of a field the LORD has blessed. God endow you SHISHI
with dew of heaven, the cream of the land, much grain and
wine. May peoples serve you; may nations bow down to
you. Be lord over your brothers, and may your mother's
sons bow down to you. A curse on those who curse you;
30 on those who bless you, blessing." Yitzḥak had finished
blessing Yaakov, and Yaakov had just left his father Yitzḥak,
31 when his brother Esav came back from the hunt. He too
had prepared delicious food and brought it to his father.
And he said to his father, "Let my father sit up and eat
some of his son's game so that your soul may bless me."
32 "Who are you?" asked his father Yitzḥak. "I am your son,

---

voice is the voice of Yaakov, but the hands are the hands of Esav"). Eventually, Yitzḥak trusts the evidence of taste, touch, and smell over sound, and gives Yaakov the blessing.

יח וְאֶת־הַלֶּחֶם אֲשֶׁר עָשָׂתָה בְּיַד יַעֲקֹב בְּנָהּ׃ וַיָּבֹא אֶל־אָבִיו
יט וַיֹּאמֶר אָבִי וַיֹּאמֶר הִנֶּנִּי מִי אַתָּה בְּנִי׃ וַיֹּאמֶר יַעֲקֹב אֶל־
אָבִיו אָנֹכִי עֵשָׂו בְּכֹרֶךָ עָשִׂיתִי כַּאֲשֶׁר דִּבַּרְתָּ אֵלָי קוּם־נָא
כ שְׁבָה וְאָכְלָה מִצֵּידִי בַּעֲבוּר תְּבָרְכַנִּי נַפְשֶׁךָ׃ וַיֹּאמֶר יִצְחָק
אֶל־בְּנוֹ מַה־זֶּה מִהַרְתָּ לִמְצֹא בְּנִי וַיֹּאמֶר כִּי הִקְרָה יהוה
כא אֱלֹהֶיךָ לְפָנָי׃ וַיֹּאמֶר יִצְחָק אֶל־יַעֲקֹב גְּשָׁה־נָּא וַאֲמֻשְׁךָ בְּנִי
כב הַאַתָּה זֶה בְּנִי עֵשָׂו אִם־לֹא׃ וַיִּגַּשׁ יַעֲקֹב אֶל־יִצְחָק אָבִיו
כג וַיְמֻשֵּׁהוּ וַיֹּאמֶר הַקֹּל קוֹל יַעֲקֹב וְהַיָּדַיִם יְדֵי עֵשָׂו׃ וְלֹא הִכִּירוֹ
כד כִּי־הָיוּ יָדָיו כִּידֵי עֵשָׂו אָחִיו שְׂעִרֹת וַיְבָרְכֵהוּ׃ וַיֹּאמֶר אַתָּה
כה זֶה בְּנִי עֵשָׂו וַיֹּאמֶר אָנִי׃ וַיֹּאמֶר הַגִּשָׁה לִּי וְאֹכְלָה מִצֵּיד בְּנִי
לְמַעַן תְּבָרֶכְךָ נַפְשִׁי וַיַּגֶּשׁ־לוֹ וַיֹּאכַל וַיָּבֵא לוֹ יַיִן וַיֵּשְׁתְּ׃
כו כז וַיֹּאמֶר אֵלָיו יִצְחָק אָבִיו גְּשָׁה־נָּא וּשְׁקָה־לִּי בְּנִי׃ וַיִּגַּשׁ וַיִּשַּׁק־
לוֹ וַיָּרַח אֶת־רֵיחַ בְּגָדָיו וַיְבָרְכֵהוּ וַיֹּאמֶר רְאֵה רֵיחַ בְּנִי כְּרֵיחַ
כח שָׂדֶה אֲשֶׁר בֵּרֲכוֹ יהוה׃ וְיִתֶּן־לְךָ הָאֱלֹהִים מִטַּל הַשָּׁמַיִם כה ששי
כט וּמִשְׁמַנֵּי הָאָרֶץ וְרֹב דָּגָן וְתִירֹשׁ׃ יַעַבְדוּךָ עַמִּים וְיִשְׁתַּחֲוֻ לְךָ
לְאֻמִּים הֱוֵה גְבִיר לְאַחֶיךָ וְיִשְׁתַּחֲווּ לְךָ בְּנֵי אִמֶּךָ אֹרְרֶיךָ
ל אָרוּר וּמְבָרְכֶיךָ בָּרוּךְ׃ וַיְהִי כַּאֲשֶׁר כִּלָּה יִצְחָק לְבָרֵךְ אֶת־
יַעֲקֹב וַיְהִי אַךְ יָצֹא יָצָא יַעֲקֹב מֵאֵת פְּנֵי יִצְחָק אָבִיו וְעֵשָׂו
לא אָחִיו בָּא מִצֵּידוֹ׃ וַיַּעַשׂ גַּם־הוּא מַטְעַמִּים וַיָּבֵא לְאָבִיו
וַיֹּאמֶר לְאָבִיו יָקֻם אָבִי וְיֹאכַל מִצֵּיד בְּנוֹ בַּעֲבֻר תְּבָרְכַנִּי
לב נַפְשֶׁךָ׃ וַיֹּאמֶר לוֹ יִצְחָק אָבִיו מִי־אָתָּה וַיֹּאמֶר אֲנִי בִּנְךָ

27:22 וְהַיָּדַיִם יְדֵי עֵשָׂו *But the hands are the hands of Esav* – Three times, Yitzḥak expresses doubts – giving Yaakov three opportunities to admit the truth. He does not. Far from glossing over the morally ambiguous nature of Yaakov's conduct, the text goes out of its way to emphasize it.

The deception is possible only because Yitzḥak cannot see. The text at this point is almost an essay on the senses. Deprived of one (sight), Yitzḥak uses the other four. He *tastes* the food, *touches* Yaakov's hands (which Rivka has covered with goatskins), and *smells* his clothes ("The smell of my son is the smell of a field the Lord has blessed," Gen. 27:27). He *hears* his voice ("The

33 your firstborn, Esav," he replied. Yitzhak was seized with a
violent fit of trembling. "Who then was it that hunted
game and brought it to me? I ate it all before you came,
34 and I blessed him – and he will be blessed." When Esav
heard his father's words, he burst into a loud and bitter cry.
35 He said to his father, "Bless me, me too, my father!" "Your
brother came in deceit and took your blessing," he replied.
36 Esav said, "Is he not rightly named Yaakov? Twice he has
supplanted me. He took my birthright and now he has
taken my blessing." And then, "Do you not have any
37 blessing left for me?" Yitzhak answered Esav, "I have made
him lord over you and given him all his brothers as
servants. I have endowed him with grain and wine. What
38 then can I do for you, my son?" Esav said to his father,
"Have you only one blessing, father? Bless me, me too, my
39 father!" And Esav wept aloud. His father Yitzhak answered

---

blessing could have been framed as a just consequence of Esav's sale of the birthright. Instead the text, at this moment, directs our feelings toward nothing but compassion.

"BLESS ME TOO"

Yitzhak knows the pain of the displacement narrative. We recall that when Yitzhak and Rivka first met, "Yitzhak was just coming back from the direction of Be'er Lahai Ro'i" (Gen. 24:62). We had encountered this place only once before. It is where the angel appeared to Hagar when, pregnant, she fled from Sara who was treating her harshly (16:14). An ingenious midrash says that when Yitzhak heard that Avraham sent his servant to find a wife for him, he said to himself, "Can I live with a wife while my father lives alone? I will go and return Hagar to him" (*Midrash HaGadol* on Gen. 24:62). A later verse tells us that "after Avraham's death, God blessed his son Yitzhak, who then lived near Be'er Lahai Roi" (25:11). On this, the Midrash says that even after his father's death, Yitzhak continued to live near Hagar and treated her with respect (Midrash Aggada and Bereshit Rabbati ad loc.).

It seems that Yitzhak, who himself was almost sacrificed, never forgets how Hagar and her son – his half-brother Yishmael – were sent away. The Midrash says that Yitzhak reunited Hagar with Avraham after Sara's death. The biblical text tells us that Yitzhak and Yishmael stood together at Avraham's grave (25:9). Somehow the divided family is reunited, seemingly at the instigation of Yitzhak.

If this is so, then Yitzhak's love for Esav is simply explained. It is as if

לג בְּכוֹרְךָ עֵשָׂו׃ וַיֶּחֱרַד יִצְחָק חֲרָדָה גְּדֹלָה עַד־מְאֹד וַיֹּאמֶר
מִי־אֵפוֹא הוּא הַצָּד־צַיִד וַיָּבֵא לִי וָאֹכַל מִכֹּל בְּטֶרֶם תָּבוֹא
לד וָאֲבָרְכֵהוּ גַּם־בָּרוּךְ יִהְיֶה׃ כִּשְׁמֹעַ עֵשָׂו אֶת־דִּבְרֵי אָבִיו
וַיִּצְעַק צְעָקָה גְּדֹלָה וּמָרָה עַד־מְאֹד וַיֹּאמֶר לְאָבִיו בָּרְכֵנִי
לה גַם־אָנִי אָבִי׃ וַיֹּאמֶר בָּא אָחִיךָ בְּמִרְמָה וַיִּקַּח בִּרְכָתֶךָ׃
לו וַיֹּאמֶר הֲכִי קָרָא שְׁמוֹ יַעֲקֹב וַיַּעְקְבֵנִי זֶה פַעֲמַיִם אֶת־בְּכֹרָתִי
לָקָח וְהִנֵּה עַתָּה לָקַח בִּרְכָתִי וַיֹּאמַר הֲלֹא־אָצַלְתָּ לִּי בְּרָכָה׃
לז וַיַּעַן יִצְחָק וַיֹּאמֶר לְעֵשָׂו הֵן גְּבִיר שַׂמְתִּיו לָךְ וְאֶת־כָּל־אֶחָיו
נָתַתִּי לוֹ לַעֲבָדִים וְדָגָן וְתִירֹשׁ סְמַכְתִּיו וּלְכָה אֵפוֹא מָה
לח אֶעֱשֶׂה בְּנִי׃ וַיֹּאמֶר עֵשָׂו אֶל־אָבִיו הַבְרָכָה אַחַת הִוא־לְךָ
לט אָבִי בָּרְכֵנִי גַם־אָנִי אָבִי וַיִּשָּׂא עֵשָׂו קֹלוֹ וַיֵּבְךְּ׃ וַיַּעַן יִצְחָק

27:38 הַבְרָכָה אַחַת הִוא לְךָ אָבִי *Have you only one blessing, father?* – There is a humanity here that defies all stereotypes and conventional categorizations. Esav is a child loved by his father and loving him in return. This is so striking that, despite the generally negative evaluation of Esav in the midrashic literature, this fact shines through: "R. Shimon b. Gamliel said: No man ever honored his father as I did mine, yet I found that Esav honored his father even more than I did" (Devarim Rabba 1:15).

There is at times a tendency on the part of the Midrash to separate biblical characters into the wholly good and wholly bad, and for this there are good pedagogic reasons, as Rabbi Tzvi Hirsch Chajes points out (*Mavo HaAggadot*). To serve effectively as role models, biblical heroes must be seen as consistently heroic, non-heroes as systematic villains.

Yet beneath this overlay of Midrash, the Torah teaches a different and equally important message: Even heroes have their faults and non-heroes their virtues, and these virtues are important to God. "The Holy One, blessed be He, does not withhold the reward of any creature," said the Sages (Pesaḥim 118a). The Esav who emerges from the Torah has none of Avraham's faith, Yitzḥak's steadfastness, or Yaakov's persistence. He is carved of an altogether coarser grain. But he is not without his humanity, his filial loyalty, and a decent if quick-tempered disposition.

This too is part of the Torah's message. Just as we cannot predict God's actions in advance ("I will be what I will be," Ex. 3:14; "I will be gracious to whom I choose to be gracious, and will show mercy to whom I decide to show mercy," 33:19), so we cannot predict in advance where God's image will shine in the affairs of mankind. The loss of Yitzḥak's

him and said: "Of the cream of the land your home shall
40 be, of the dew of heaven above. By your sword you will
live, and your brother you will serve; but when you break
41 loose, you will throw off his yoke from your neck." Esav
resented Yaakov because of the blessing his father had
given him. "The days of mourning for my father are
approaching," he said to himself, "and then I will kill my
42 brother Yaakov." When Rivka was told what her elder son
Esav had said, she summoned her younger son Yaakov and
said, "Your brother Esav is consoling himself with the
43 thought of killing you. Now, my son, listen to me. Flee at
44 once to my brother Lavan in Ḥaran. Stay with him a while,
45 until your brother's rage subsides. When your brother is

---

loose – Many years later, the brothers are to meet again after a long estrangement (Gen. 32–33). Yaakov will be terrified of the encounter. He will bow down to Esav seven times. He will call him "my lord." He will refer to himself as "your servant." The roles will have been reversed. The blessing Yitzḥak gives Esav here casts a new light on the ambiguity of the oracle to Rivka in verse 23. Does older serve younger, or does younger serve older? It is an example of one of the most remarkable of all the Torah's narrative devices – the power of the future to transform our understanding of the past. Sometimes it is only later that we understand now. New situations retrospectively disclose new meanings in the text. This is the essence of Midrash.

27:44 וְיָשַׁבְתָּ עִמּוֹ יָמִים אֲחָדִים *Stay with him a while* – *Yamim aḥadim*, literally, "a few days." To Yaakov, Rivka explains her need for this separation with a rhetorical question: "Why should I lose you both in one day?" (Gen. 27:45). To Yitzḥak she uses another, more heartrending still: "If Yaakov marries a Hittite woman like them ... why should I go on living?" (27:46).

I remember the first time I heard the idea of the family being intellectually abused. As a teenager I heard these words from a renowned anthropologist on the BBC: "Far from being the basis of the good society, the family, with its narrow privacy and tawdry secrets, is the source of all our discontents."

What kind of family did this lecturer grow up in? I wondered at the time. It did not sound like any I knew. I saw honest men and women building a life together, caring for their children and working to give them chances they never had. "Haven in a heartless world" is what Christopher Lasch called his book on the subject.

Families are not fairy tales whose

אָבִיו וַיֹּאמֶר אֵלָיו הִנֵּה מִשְׁמַנֵּי הָאָרֶץ יִהְיֶה מוֹשָׁבֶךָ וּמִטַּל
מ הַשָּׁמַיִם מֵעָל׃ וְעַל־חַרְבְּךָ תִחְיֶה וְאֶת־אָחִיךָ תַּעֲבֹד וְהָיָה
מא כַּאֲשֶׁר תָּרִיד וּפָרַקְתָּ עֻלּוֹ מֵעַל צַוָּארֶךָ׃ וַיִּשְׂטֹם עֵשָׂו אֶת־
יַעֲקֹב עַל־הַבְּרָכָה אֲשֶׁר בֵּרְכוֹ אָבִיו וַיֹּאמֶר עֵשָׂו בְּלִבּוֹ יִקְרְבוּ
מב יְמֵי אֵבֶל אָבִי וְאַהַרְגָה אֶת־יַעֲקֹב אָחִי׃ וַיֻּגַּד לְרִבְקָה אֶת־
דִּבְרֵי עֵשָׂו בְּנָהּ הַגָּדֹל וַתִּשְׁלַח וַתִּקְרָא לְיַעֲקֹב בְּנָהּ הַקָּטָן
מג וַתֹּאמֶר אֵלָיו הִנֵּה עֵשָׂו אָחִיךָ מִתְנַחֵם לְךָ לְהָרְגֶךָ׃ וְעַתָּה
מד בְנִי שְׁמַע בְּקֹלִי וְקוּם בְּרַח־לְךָ אֶל־לָבָן אָחִי חָרָנָה׃ וְיָשַׁבְתָּ
מה עִמּוֹ יָמִים אֲחָדִים עַד אֲשֶׁר־תָּשׁוּב חֲמַת אָחִיךָ׃ עַד־שׁוּב

Yitzḥak has said: I know what Esav is. He is strong, wild, unpredictable, possibly violent. It is impossible that he should be the person entrusted with the covenant and its spiritual demands. *But he, too, is my child.* I refuse to sacrifice him, as my father almost sacrificed me. I refuse to send him away, as my parents sent Hagar and Yishmael away. My love for my son is unconditional. I do not ignore who or what he is. But I will love him anyway, even if I do not love everything he does – because that is how God loves us, unconditionally, even if He does not love everything we do. I will bless him. I will hold him close. And I believe that one day that love may make him a better person than he might otherwise have been.

In this one act of loving Esav, Yitzḥak redeems the pain of two of the most difficult moments in his father Avraham's life: the sending away of Hagar and Yishmael and *akedat Yitzḥak*. A silence surrounds Yitzḥak in the text from the moment of the *akeda*. Esav here prompts him to voice an answer: "Have you only one blessing, father?" No. A parent has a blessing for every child. The past need not be repeated. Love can heal both the lover and the loved.

27:39 מִשְׁמַנֵּי הָאָרֶץ *Of the cream of the land* – The "cream of the land" and the "dew of heaven" are plentiful enough, Yitzḥak implies, for there to be enough for both sons. More significant is his qualification of Yaakov's supremacy. It will last, he says, only as long as he does not misuse it. If he acts harshly, Esav will "throw off his yoke" from his neck. For the first time, a doubt enters our understanding of the brothers' respective fates. Until now we have been led to believe that the narrative has reached closure. The elder (Esav) will serve the younger (Yaakov). Now, it is suddenly less clear. Perhaps Esav will not serve Yaakov after all. Perhaps Yaakov will misuse his power and Esav will rebel – a small incongruity, but a significant one.

27:40 וְהָיָה כַּאֲשֶׁר תָּרִיד *But when you break*

no longer angry with you and has forgotten what you did
to him, I will send word to you to come back. Why should
46 I lose you both in one day?" Rivka then said to Yitzḥak, "I
loathe my life because of these Hittite women. If Yaakov
marries a Hittite woman like them, one of the women of
28 1 the land, why should I go on living?" So Yitzḥak called
Yaakov to him. He blessed him and charged him: "You are
2 not to marry a Canaanite woman. Go at once to Padan
Aram, to the house of your mother's father Betuel, and
there marry a daughter of your mother's brother Lavan.
3 May El Shaddai bless you, make you fertile, and multiply
4 you so that you become a community of peoples. May He
grant Avraham's blessing to you and your descendants,
that you may possess the land where you live as a stranger,
5 which God gave to Avraham." Then Yitzḥak sent Yaakov SHEVI'I
on his way. He went toward Padan Aram, to Lavan son of
Betuel the Aramean, brother of Rivka, Yaakov and Esav's
6 mother. Esav learned that Yitzḥak had blessed Yaakov and
sent him to Padan Aram to find a wife, and that when he

---

different. They are about *children* and a *land*. It is this blessing that Yitzḥak gives Yaakov here. This is the blessing Yitzḥak intended for Yaakov all along.

Yaakov's blessing has nothing to do with wealth or power. It has to do with the children he will teach to be heirs of the covenant, and the land where his descendants will seek to create a society based on the covenant of law and love.

Each of us has a blessing that is our own. That is true not just of Yitzḥak but also of Yishmael, not just of Yaakov but also of Esav. The moral could not be more powerful. Never seek your brother's blessing. Be content with your own.

28:4 לְרִשְׁתְּךָ אֶת אֶרֶץ מְגֻרֶיךָ *The land where... you live as a stranger* – Avraham's blessing, now passed on to Yaakov, is the promise of a future sovereignty neither will live to see. No sooner does Avraham arrive in the land "that I will show you" (Gen. 13:1) than famine forces him to leave. Throughout the Tanakh the land of Israel is never a simple destination, a place at which you simply arrive. It is indeed a geographical location, a country on the map, but it is more than that. It is the place we travel toward, symbol of a not-yet-realized future. That future, mapped out in greater detail in the book of Deuteronomy and in the visionary images of the prophets, is the perfect society: what Judaism is to call the Messianic age.

אַף־אָחִיךָ מִמְּךָ וְשָׁכַח אֵת אֲשֶׁר־עָשִׂיתָ לּוֹ וְשָׁלַחְתִּי
מו וּלְקַחְתִּיךָ מִשָּׁם לָמָה אֶשְׁכַּל גַּם־שְׁנֵיכֶם יוֹם אֶחָד׃ וַתֹּאמֶר
רִבְקָה אֶל־יִצְחָק קַצְתִּי בְחַיַּי מִפְּנֵי בְּנוֹת חֵת אִם־לֹקֵחַ יַעֲקֹב
אִשָּׁה מִבְּנוֹת־חֵת כָּאֵלֶּה מִבְּנוֹת הָאָרֶץ לָמָּה לִּי חַיִּים׃
כח א וַיִּקְרָא יִצְחָק אֶל־יַעֲקֹב וַיְבָרֶךְ אֹתוֹ וַיְצַוֵּהוּ וַיֹּאמֶר לוֹ לֹא־
ב תִקַּח אִשָּׁה מִבְּנוֹת כְּנָעַן׃ קוּם לֵךְ פַּדֶּנָה אֲרָם בֵּיתָה בְתוּאֵל
ג אֲבִי אִמֶּךָ וְקַח־לְךָ מִשָּׁם אִשָּׁה מִבְּנוֹת לָבָן אֲחִי אִמֶּךָ׃ וְאֵל
ד שַׁדַּי יְבָרֵךְ אֹתְךָ וְיַפְרְךָ וְיַרְבֶּךָ וְהָיִיתָ לִקְהַל עַמִּים׃ וְיִתֶּן־לְךָ
אֶת־בִּרְכַּת אַבְרָהָם לְךָ וּלְזַרְעֲךָ אִתָּךְ לְרִשְׁתְּךָ אֶת־אֶרֶץ
ה מְגֻרֶיךָ אֲשֶׁר־נָתַן אֱלֹהִים לְאַבְרָהָם׃ וַיִּשְׁלַח יִצְחָק אֶת־ שביעי
יַעֲקֹב וַיֵּלֶךְ פַּדֶּנָה אֲרָם אֶל־לָבָן בֶּן־בְּתוּאֵל הָאֲרַמִּי אֲחִי
ו רִבְקָה אֵם יַעֲקֹב וְעֵשָׂו׃ וַיַּרְא עֵשָׂו כִּי־בֵרַךְ יִצְחָק אֶת־יַעֲקֹב
וְשִׁלַּח אֹתוֹ פַּדֶּנָה אֲרָם לָקַחַת־לוֹ מִשָּׁם אִשָּׁה בְּבָרְכוֹ אֹתוֹ

last line is "and they all lived happily ever after." They are places of conflict and stress. But they are also places where we learn to resolve those conflicts by honest communication, mutual understanding, and forgiveness. The family is where we learn the grammar of emotional intelligence by not giving up when the going gets tough. It is our ongoing seminar on the meaning of loyalty.

Families are where love is written not in poetry but in prose. There is a beauty, undemonstrative, unselfconscious, that lives in a thousand small gestures of listening, caring, helping, giving, for no ulterior motive other than the fact that here we are "we," not "I."

The discord in Rivka's sons' lives, from the womb and into adulthood, makes her question the value of her own. Her *yamim aḥadim* of separation from Yaakov will, as it turns out, be long. But Yaakov hopes to build his own family. For him, years will pass *keyamim aḥadim*, as but a few days, "so great was his love for [Raḥel]" (29:20). It is worth taking a risk for this. We can face the future without fear when we sense we will not face it alone.

28:4 בִּרְכַּת אַבְרָהָם *Avraham's blessing* – We now see that Yitzḥak fully understands the nature of his two sons. He loves Esav but this does not blind him to the fact that Yaakov will be the heir of the covenant. Therefore Yitzḥak has prepared two sets of blessings, one for Esav, the other for Yaakov. He blesses Esav (Gen. 27:28–29) with the gifts he feels he will appreciate: wealth and power. The covenantal blessings that God gave Avraham and Yitzḥak are completely

blessed him, he commanded him not to marry a Canaanite
7 woman, and that Yaakov had obeyed his father and mother MAFTIR
8 and had gone to Padan Aram. Esav realized then that the
9 Canaanite women displeased his father Yitzḥak. So Esav
went to Yishmael and took Maḥalat, daughter of Avraham's
son Yishmael, a sister of Nevayot, to be his wife, with his
other wives.

The haftara for Parashat Toledot is on page 1426.
On Erev Rosh Ḥodesh Kislev read the haftara on page 1644.

---

loves. As for Yaakov, the consequences last a lifetime, resulting in strife between his wives and between his children. "Few and hard have been the years of my life" (47:9), he says to Pharaoh as an old man. Four lives are scarred by one act which was not necessary in the first place.

Such is the human price we pay for a failure to communicate. The Torah is exceptionally candid about such matters, which is what makes it so powerful a guide to life: real life, among real people with real problems. Communication matters. For us, speech is life. Life is relationship. And human relationships only exist because we can speak. We can tell other people our hopes, our fears, our feelings and thoughts.

Parents and leaders must establish a culture in which honest, open, respectful communication takes place, one that involves not just speaking but also listening. Without it, tragedy is waiting in the wings.

ז וַיְצַו עָלָיו לֵאמֹר לֹא־תִקַּח אִשָּׁה מִבְּנוֹת כְּנָעַן: וַיִּשְׁמַע מפטיר
ח יַעֲקֹב אֶל־אָבִיו וְאֶל־אִמּוֹ וַיֵּלֶךְ פַּדֶּנָה אֲרָם: וַיַּרְא עֵשָׂו כִּי
ט רָעוֹת בְּנוֹת כְּנָעַן בְּעֵינֵי יִצְחָק אָבִיו: וַיֵּלֶךְ עֵשָׂו אֶל־יִשְׁמָעֵאל
וַיִּקַּח אֶת־מָחֲלַת ׀ בַּת־יִשְׁמָעֵאל בֶּן־אַבְרָהָם אֲחוֹת נְבָיוֹת
עַל־נָשָׁיו לוֹ לְאִשָּׁה:

The הפטרה *for* פרשת תולדת *is on page 1427.*
On ערב ראש חודש כסלו *some read the* הפטרה *on page 1645.*

28:8 וַיַּרְא עֵשָׂו *Esav realized* – We learned before this story began, in Gen. 26:34, of the distress Esav's marriages cause his parents. Esav only learns of it now, indirectly. The failures of communication in this family have cost them dearly. Yitzḥak never did intend to give the blessing of the covenant to Esav. He intended to give each child the blessing that suited him. Why did Rivka not understand this? Because she and her husband did not communicate.

Now let us count the consequences of the deceit. Yitzḥak, old and blind, feels betrayed by Yaakov. He "was seized with a violent fit of trembling" (Gen. 27:33) when he realized what had happened, saying to Esav, "Your brother came in deceit" (27:35). Esav likewise feels betrayed and feels such violent hatred toward Yaakov that he vows to kill him. Rivka is forced to send Yaakov into exile, thus depriving herself for more than two decades of the company of the son she

PARASHAT VAYETZE

28 10 Yaakov left Be'er Sheva and journeyed toward Ḥaran. In
11 time he chanced upon a certain place and decided to
spend the night there, because the sun had set. He took
some stones of the place and put them under his head,

(a) *shevaḥ*, praise, the first three blessings; (b) *bakasha*, request, the middle blessings, and (c) *hodaya*, thanks or acknowledgment, the last three blessings.

Shevaḥ is a preparation. On this ladder of words, thoughts, and emotions, we move from the world around us, perceived by the senses, to an awareness of that which lies beyond the world. *Bakasha*, the central section, is standing in the Presence itself. *Hodaya* is leave-taking. We slowly make our way back to our mundane concerns, the arena of actions and interactions within which we live. The spiritual form of the first and last actions – entry and leave-taking – are dramatized by taking three steps forward, and at the end, three steps back. There is a basic shape – a deep grammar – of prayer; the inspiration for this is Yaakov's vision.

Prayer is a ladder. The first stage is the climb, the second is standing in heaven, and the third is bringing a fragment of heaven down to earth. For Yaakov realizes when he wakes from his vision that God is in *this* place. Heaven is not somewhere else, but is here – even if we are alone and afraid – if only we realize it.

28:11 וַיִּפְגַּע בַּמָּקוֹם *He chanced upon a certain place* – Later, in Rabbinic Hebrew, the word *hamakom*, "the Place," came to mean "God." Hence in a poetic way the phrase *vayifga bamakom* could be read as "Yaakov chanced upon, had an unexpected encounter with, God." On the basis of this passage the Sages assert that "Yaakov instituted the evening prayer" (Berakhot 26b). Avraham, who instituted Shaḥarit, sought God before God sought him. Yitzḥak's prayer, Minḥa, is described as a *siḥa*, literally, a conversation or dialogue. There are two parties to a dialogue – Yitzḥak represents the religious experience as conversation between the word of God and the word of mankind. Yaakov's prayer is very different. He does not initiate it. His thoughts are elsewhere – on Esav from whom he is escaping, and on Lavan to whom he is journeying. Into this troubled mind comes a vision of God and the angels and a stairway connecting earth and heaven. He has done nothing to prepare for it. It is unexpected. Yaakov literally "chances upon" God as we can sometimes encounter a familiar face among a crowd of strangers. This is a meeting brought about by God, not man. That is one reason why Yaakov's prayer, Maariv, could not be made the basis of

פרשת ויצא

כח יא וַיֵּצֵא יַעֲקֹב מִבְּאֵר שָׁבַע וַיֵּלֶךְ חָרָנָה׃ וַיִּפְגַּע בַּמָּקוֹם וַיָּלֶן כו
שָׁם כִּי־בָא הַשֶּׁמֶשׁ וַיִּקַּח מֵאַבְנֵי הַמָּקוֹם וַיָּשֶׂם מְרַאֲשֹׁתָיו

VAYETZE

Yaakov leaves home in flight from Esav, only to find himself in a fraught relationship with Lavan, his uncle, with whom he takes refuge. He falls in love with Lavan's younger daughter Raḥel, and agrees to work the seven years to earn her hand in marriage. When the wedding eventually takes place, Yaakov wakes the next morning to discover that Lavan has substituted the elder, Leah, in place of Raḥel. Yaakov later marries Raḥel as well, but there is tension between the sisters. Leah, unloved, is blessed with children; Raḥel, loved, is not. Interwoven with this is another tension between Yaakov and Lavan – about flocks, wages, and ownership – which eventually leads Yaakov to flee again, this time homeward.

Parashat Vayetze is framed by these two journeys. Yaakov, we see, is the man whose deepest spiritual encounters happen when he is on a journey, fleeing from one danger to another, alone and afraid at the dead of night.

THE VISION OF THE LADDER

The two encounters in this *parasha* and the next – the ladder and the wrestling match (Gen. 32:24) – provide us with powerful metaphors for spiritual life. Here we see it represented as climbing a ladder, rung by rung. Each day, week, month, or year, when we study and understand more, we come a little closer to heaven, learning to stand above the fray, rise above our reactive emotions, and begin to sense the complexity of the human condition. That is faith as a ladder.

The Zohar (I, 201b) identifies the ladder in Yaakov's vision with prayer: we who pray stand on earth, yet our prayers reach heaven. I would like to suggest that this primal vision does not merely give us a paradigm of prayer. Its impact extends to influence the very *structure* of Jewish liturgy. A close study of the liturgy reveals a prevalent symmetrical three-part structure, A-B-A, which has the following form: (a) ascent, (b) standing in the Presence, (c) descent. For example, Shaḥarit, the morning service, begins with (a) *Pesukei DeZimra*, a series of psalms which constitute a preparation for prayer. It moves on to (b) prayer-proper: the *Shema* with its three blessings, and the *Amida*, standing prayer. It ends with (c) a series of concluding hymns including *Ashrei*, itself a key element of *Pesukei DeZimra*. The threefold pattern of Shaḥarit is repeated in microcosm in the structure of the *Amida*. It too follows a three-part pattern:

12 and in that place lay down to sleep. And he dreamed: He
saw a ladder set upon the ground, whose top reached the
heavens. On it, angels of God went up and came down.
13 The LORD stood over him there and said, "I am the LORD,
the God of Avraham your father, and the God of Yitzḥak.
The land on which you lie I will give to you and your
14 descendants. Your descendants shall be like the dust of the
earth, and you will spread out to the west, the east, the
north, and the south. Through you and your descendants,
15 all the families of the earth will be blessed. I am with you.
I will protect you wherever you go and I will bring you
back to this land, for I will not leave you until I have done
16 what I have spoken of to you." Then Yaakov awoke from
his sleep and said, "Truly, the LORD is in this place – and
17 I did not know it!" He was afraid and said, "How full of
awe is this place! This is none other than the House of
18 God, and this the gate of the heavens!" Yaakov rose early

---

used to say, "A person needs to cry to his Father in the heavens with a powerful voice from the depths of his heart. Then God will listen to his voice and turn to his cry. And it may be that from this act itself, all doubts and obstacles that are keeping him back from true service of God will fall from him and be completely nullified" (*Likkutei Maharan* 2:46).

That is our heritage from Yaakov: the knowledge that we may fall, but we fall into the arms of God. Though others may lose faith in us, and though we may even lose faith in ourselves, God never loses faith in us. God is there, beside us, within us, urging us to stand and move on, for there is a task to do that we have not yet done and that we were created to fulfill. As for Yaakov, so for us, it feels in such a moment as if we are waking from sleep and realizing, as if for the first time, that "truly, the LORD is in this place." The place has not changed, but we have. Suddenly, with a certainty that is unmistakable, we know that we are not alone, that God is there and has been all along.

28:17 זֶה שַׁעַר הַשָּׁמָיִם *This the gate of the heavens* – "The house of God" came to refer to the synagogue, for prayer is "the gate of the heavens."

Prayer has two dimensions, one mysterious, the other not. There are too many cases of prayers being answered for us to deny that it makes a difference to our fate. I once heard the following story. A man in a Nazi concentration camp lost the will to live – and in the death camps, if you lost the will to live, you died. That night he poured out his

יב וַיִּשְׁכַּב בַּמָּקוֹם הַהוּא׃ וַיַּחֲלֹם וְהִנֵּה סֻלָּם מֻצָּב אַרְצָה
וְרֹאשׁוֹ מַגִּיעַ הַשָּׁמָיְמָה וְהִנֵּה מַלְאֲכֵי אֱלֹהִים עֹלִים וְיֹרְדִים
יג בּוֹ׃ וְהִנֵּה יהוה נִצָּב עָלָיו וַיֹּאמַר אֲנִי יהוה אֱלֹהֵי אַבְרָהָם
אָבִיךָ וֵאלֹהֵי יִצְחָק הָאָרֶץ אֲשֶׁר אַתָּה שֹׁכֵב עָלֶיהָ לְךָ
יד אֶתְּנֶנָּה וּלְזַרְעֶךָ׃ וְהָיָה זַרְעֲךָ כַּעֲפַר הָאָרֶץ וּפָרַצְתָּ יָמָּה
וָקֵדְמָה וְצָפֹנָה וָנֶגְבָּה וְנִבְרֲכוּ בְךָ כָּל־מִשְׁפְּחֹת הָאֲדָמָה
טו וּבְזַרְעֶךָ׃ וְהִנֵּה אָנֹכִי עִמָּךְ וּשְׁמַרְתִּיךָ בְּכֹל אֲשֶׁר־תֵּלֵךְ
וַהֲשִׁבֹתִיךָ אֶל־הָאֲדָמָה הַזֹּאת כִּי לֹא אֶעֱזָבְךָ עַד אֲשֶׁר
טז אִם־עָשִׂיתִי אֵת אֲשֶׁר־דִּבַּרְתִּי לָךְ׃ וַיִּיקַץ יַעֲקֹב מִשְּׁנָתוֹ
יז וַיֹּאמֶר אָכֵן יֵשׁ יהוה בַּמָּקוֹם הַזֶּה וְאָנֹכִי לֹא יָדָעְתִּי׃ וַיִּירָא
וַיֹּאמַר מַה־נּוֹרָא הַמָּקוֹם הַזֶּה אֵין זֶה כִּי אִם־בֵּית אֱלֹהִים
יח וְזֶה שַׁעַר הַשָּׁמָיִם׃ וַיַּשְׁכֵּם יַעֲקֹב בַּבֹּקֶר וַיִּקַּח אֶת־הָאֶבֶן

---

a regular obligation. None of us knows when the presence of God will suddenly intrude into our lives.

28:12 וַיַּחֲלֹם *And he dreamed* – Not a nightmare but an epiphany. Yaakov signifies God's encounter with us – unplanned, unexpected – the vision, the voice, the call we can never know in advance but which leaves us transformed.

28:14 כַּעֲפַר הָאָרֶץ... וְנִבְרֲכוּ בְךָ כָּל מִשְׁפְּחֹת הָאֲדָמָה *Like the dust of the earth.... all the families of the earth will be blessed* – Avraham, who described himself as "dust and ashes" (Gen. 18:27), was an *Ivri*, a Hebrew, one who wanders from place to place, whose sole security is his faith. To be a Jew has often meant just that. But he also bequeathed through Yaakov that half promise, half command: "You will become a blessing" (12:2). Avraham and Yaakov, unlike Adam and Noaḥ, are not symbols of humanity as a whole. They are individuals singled out for a particular destiny. Their children become a people singled out for a particular destiny. Why Avraham was chosen, we never discover. That is one of the great enigmas of the Bible. But to what end he was chosen, we discover at the very beginning: to be a blessing. Not to his family or to God alone; somehow he will enrich the lives of others, of cultures and faiths very different from his own. The lives of his descendants will be peculiarly interwoven with the history of many nations, and they will leave their mark, hopefully for blessing, on many cultures.

28:16 וְאָנֹכִי לֹא יָדָעְתִּי *And I did not know it* – At times we may feel utterly alone. We are not. Rav Naḥman of Breslav, who knew what it was to be broken-hearted,

the next morning, took the stone he had placed under his
19 head, set it up as a pillar, and poured oil on top of it. He
named the place Beit El; the town was originally called
20 Luz. Yaakov then made a vow. "If God will be with me,"
he said, "protecting me on this journey I am taking, giving
21 me bread to eat and clothes to wear, and if I return in
peace to my father's house, then the LORD will be my
22 God. This stone I set up as a pillar will become a house of
God, and of all that You give me I will dedicate a tenth to
29 1 You." Yaakov began traveling again and came to the land SHENI
2 of the people of the East. There he saw a well in a field.
Three flocks of sheep were lying beside it because this

---

and the poor, and eventually in *maaser kesafim*, the practice of giving a tenth of one's income to charity. We worship God spiritually by helping His creations physically. That is why, when the Temple was destroyed and the sacrifices came to an end, *tzedaka* became a substitute:

> R. Dostai son of R. Yannai taught: Consider the difference between the Holy One and a king of flesh and blood. If a man brings a present to the king, it may or may not be accepted. Even if it is accepted, it remains doubtful whether the man will be admitted into the king's presence. Not so with the Holy One. A person who gives even a small coin to a beggar is deemed worthy of being admitted to behold the Divine Presence, as it is written, "I shall behold Your face through charity, and when I awake, shall be satisfied with Your likeness" (Ps. 17:15). (Bava Batra 10a)

Charity is a form of prayer, a preliminary to prayer. To know God is to act with justice and compassion, to recognize His image in other people, and to hear the silent cry of those in need. The mishnaic Sage R. Yehuda b. Ilai gave this poetic expression:

> There are ten strong things in the world: Rock is strong, but iron breaks it. Iron is strong, but fire melts it. Fire is strong, but water extinguishes it. Water is strong, but the clouds carry it. The clouds are strong, but the wind drives them. The wind is strong, but man withstands it. Man is strong, but fear weakens him. Fear is strong, but wine removes it. Wine is strong, but sleep overcomes it. Sleep is strong, but death stands over it. What is stronger even than death? Acts of charity. For it is written, "*Tzedaka* delivers from death" (Prov. 10:2). (Bava Batra 10a)

This is why, when Yaakov swears his allegiance to God, worship and charity are two inseparable sides of the same commitment.

אֲשֶׁר־שָׂם מְרַאֲשֹׁתָיו וַיָּשֶׂם אֹתָהּ מַצֵּבָה וַיִּצֹק שֶׁמֶן עַל־
יט רֹאשָׁהּ: וַיִּקְרָא אֶת־שֵׁם־הַמָּקוֹם הַהוּא בֵּית־אֵל וְאוּלָם לוּז
כ שֵׁם־הָעִיר לָרִאשֹׁנָה: וַיִּדַּר יַעֲקֹב נֶדֶר לֵאמֹר אִם־יִהְיֶה
אֱלֹהִים עִמָּדִי וּשְׁמָרַנִי בַּדֶּרֶךְ הַזֶּה אֲשֶׁר אָנֹכִי הוֹלֵךְ וְנָתַן־
כא לִי לֶחֶם לֶאֱכֹל וּבֶגֶד לִלְבֹּשׁ: וְשַׁבְתִּי בְשָׁלוֹם אֶל־בֵּית אָבִי
כב וְהָיָה יהוה לִי לֵאלֹהִים: וְהָאֶבֶן הַזֹּאת אֲשֶׁר־שַׂמְתִּי מַצֵּבָה
יִהְיֶה בֵּית אֱלֹהִים וְכֹל אֲשֶׁר תִּתֶּן־לִי עַשֵּׂר אֲעַשְּׂרֶנּוּ לָךְ:
כט א ב וַיִּשָּׂא יַעֲקֹב רַגְלָיו וַיֵּלֶךְ אַרְצָה בְנֵי־קֶדֶם: וַיַּרְא וְהִנֵּה בְאֵר שני
בַּשָּׂדֶה וְהִנֵּה־שָׁם שְׁלֹשָׁה עֶדְרֵי־צֹאן רֹבְצִים עָלֶיהָ כִּי מִן־

heart in prayer. The next morning, he was transferred to work in the camp kitchen. There he was able, when the guards were not looking, to steal some potato peelings. It was these peelings that kept him alive. I heard this story from his son.

There is, however, a second dimension which is non-mysterious. Less than prayer changes the world, it changes us. In prayer, we escape from the prison of the self and see the world, including ourselves, from the outside. Prayer is where the relentless first-person singular, the "I," falls silent for a moment.

When Yaakov wakes from his sleep he says, "Truly, the Lord is in this place *ve'anokhi lo yadati*." *Lo yadati* means "I did not know"; *anokhi* means, again, "I," which in this sentence is superfluous. To translate it literally we would have to say, "And I, I did not know it!" How, asks Rabbi Pinchas Horowitz (*Panim Yafot*), do we come to know that "the Lord is in this place"? By *ve'anokhi lo yadati* – not knowing the I.

Sometimes it takes a great crisis to make us realize how self-centered we have been. The only question strong enough to endow existence with meaning is not "What do I need from life?" but "What does life need from me?" That is the question we hear when we truly pray. More than an act of speaking, prayer is an act of listening – to what God wants from us, here, now. More than prayer changes God, it changes us. It lets us see, feel, know that "the Lord is in this place." How do we reach that awareness? By moving beyond the first-person singular, so that for a moment, like Yaakov, we can say, "I know not the I." In the silence of the "I," we meet the "Thou" of God.

28:22 עַשֵּׂר אֲעַשְּׂרֶנּוּ לָךְ *I will dedicate a tenth* – Yaakov itemizes his side of the agreement – the commitment that "the Lord will be my God" – into two resolutions: "This stone… will become a house of God" and "of all that You give me I will dedicate a tenth to You." This second promise is later to find expression in the *maasrot* dedicated to the Levites

was the well from which the flocks were watered. The top
3 of it was covered with a large stone. When all the flocks
were gathered there, the stone would be rolled from the
mouth of the well and the sheep watered. The stone
4 would then be put back in place on top of the well. Yaakov
asked the shepherds, "Brothers, where are you from?"
5 "We are from Ḥaran," they replied. He asked, "Do you
know Lavan son of Naḥor?" "We know him," they said.
6 He asked, "Is he well?" "He is well," they said, "and look,
here is his daughter Raḥel coming with the sheep."
7 "Look," he said, "it is still broad daylight. It is not yet time
to gather in the animals. Water the flocks and take them
8 back to pasture." But they said, "We cannot do that until
all the flocks are gathered and the stone is rolled from the
9 top of the well. Only then can we water the flocks." While
he was still talking with them, Raḥel came with her
10 father's sheep; she was a shepherdess. When Yaakov saw
Raḥel, daughter of his mother's brother Lavan, with
Lavan's sheep, he stepped forward, rolled the stone from
the top of the well, and watered his uncle Lavan's sheep.
11 12 And Yaakov kissed Raḥel – and wept aloud. And Yaakov
told Raḥel that he was related to her father: he was Rivka's
13 son. She ran to tell her father. When Lavan heard the
news about Yaakov, his sister's son, he ran to meet him.
He embraced and kissed him and brought him to his
14 house. Yaakov told Lavan all that had happened. Lavan
said to him, "You are truly of my own bones, my own
15 flesh." And Yaakov stayed with him for a month. Then
Lavan said to him, "If you are my brother, does that mean
you should work for me for nothing? Tell me what your
16 hire should be." Lavan had two daughters. The elder was

29:13 וַיְחַבֶּק־לוֹ וַיְנַשֶּׁק־לוֹ *Embraced and kissed him* – In age after age, Jews sought refuge from those who, like Esav, sought to kill them. The nations who gave them refuge seemed at first to be benefactors. But they demanded a price. As we shall see (ch. 30, "An Aramean Sought My Father's Death"), Lavan's behavior is the paradigm of antisemites through the ages.

הַבְּאֵר הַהִוא יַשְׁקוּ הָעֲדָרִים וְהָאֶבֶן גְּדֹלָה עַל־פִּי הַבְּאֵר׃
ג וְנֶאֶסְפוּ־שָׁמָּה כָל־הָעֲדָרִים וְגָלְלוּ אֶת־הָאֶבֶן מֵעַל פִּי הַבְּאֵר
וְהִשְׁקוּ אֶת־הַצֹּאן וְהֵשִׁיבוּ אֶת־הָאֶבֶן עַל־פִּי הַבְּאֵר
ד לִמְקֹמָהּ׃ וַיֹּאמֶר לָהֶם יַעֲקֹב אַחַי מֵאַיִן אַתֶּם וַיֹּאמְרוּ מֵחָרָן
ה אֲנָחְנוּ׃ וַיֹּאמֶר לָהֶם הַיְדַעְתֶּם אֶת־לָבָן בֶּן־נָחוֹר וַיֹּאמְרוּ
ו יָדָעְנוּ׃ וַיֹּאמֶר לָהֶם הֲשָׁלוֹם לוֹ וַיֹּאמְרוּ שָׁלוֹם וְהִנֵּה רָחֵל
ז בִּתּוֹ בָּאָה עִם־הַצֹּאן׃ וַיֹּאמֶר הֵן עוֹד הַיּוֹם גָּדוֹל לֹא־עֵת
ח הֵאָסֵף הַמִּקְנֶה הַשְׁקוּ הַצֹּאן וּלְכוּ רְעוּ׃ וַיֹּאמְרוּ לֹא נוּכַל
עַד אֲשֶׁר יֵאָסְפוּ כָּל־הָעֲדָרִים וְגָלְלוּ אֶת־הָאֶבֶן מֵעַל פִּי
ט הַבְּאֵר וְהִשְׁקִינוּ הַצֹּאן׃ עוֹדֶנּוּ מְדַבֵּר עִמָּם וְרָחֵל ׀ בָּאָה
י עִם־הַצֹּאן אֲשֶׁר לְאָבִיהָ כִּי רֹעָה הִוא׃ וַיְהִי כַּאֲשֶׁר רָאָה
יַעֲקֹב אֶת־רָחֵל בַּת־לָבָן אֲחִי אִמּוֹ וְאֶת־צֹאן לָבָן אֲחִי אִמּוֹ
וַיִּגַּשׁ יַעֲקֹב וַיָּגֶל אֶת־הָאֶבֶן מֵעַל פִּי הַבְּאֵר וַיַּשְׁקְ אֶת־צֹאן
יא לָבָן אֲחִי אִמּוֹ׃ וַיִּשַּׁק יַעֲקֹב לְרָחֵל וַיִּשָּׂא אֶת־קֹלוֹ וַיֵּבְךְּ׃
יב וַיַּגֵּד יַעֲקֹב לְרָחֵל כִּי אֲחִי אָבִיהָ הוּא וְכִי בֶן־רִבְקָה הוּא
יג וַתָּרָץ וַתַּגֵּד לְאָבִיהָ׃ וַיְהִי כִשְׁמֹעַ לָבָן אֶת־שֵׁמַע ׀ יַעֲקֹב
בֶּן־אֲחֹתוֹ וַיָּרָץ לִקְרָאתוֹ וַיְחַבֶּק־לוֹ וַיְנַשֶּׁק־לוֹ וַיְבִיאֵהוּ
יד אֶל־בֵּיתוֹ וַיְסַפֵּר לְלָבָן אֵת כָּל־הַדְּבָרִים הָאֵלֶּה׃ וַיֹּאמֶר לוֹ
טו לָבָן אַךְ עַצְמִי וּבְשָׂרִי אָתָּה וַיֵּשֶׁב עִמּוֹ חֹדֶשׁ יָמִים׃ וַיֹּאמֶר
לָבָן לְיַעֲקֹב הֲכִי־אָחִי אַתָּה וַעֲבַדְתַּנִי חִנָּם הַגִּידָה לִּי מַה־
טז מַשְׂכֻּרְתֶּךָ׃ וּלְלָבָן שְׁתֵּי בָנוֹת שֵׁם הַגְּדֹלָה לֵאָה וְשֵׁם הַקְּטַנָּה

29:10 כַּאֲשֶׁר רָאָה יַעֲקֹב אֶת־רָחֵל *When Yaakov saw Raḥel* – Notice the sharp contrast with the earlier scene at which Avraham's servant sought a wife for his master's son at a well. Here it is Yaakov, not the woman, who is active. Rolling the stone off the well is a feat of considerable strength, as well as a daring defiance of local custom, not attributes we have hitherto associated with the quiet son of Yitzḥak. Evidently, Yaakov is seized with strong emotion. He kisses Raḥel; he weeps. The text at least raises the possibility that he has performed his act of bravado to impress her with both his strength and his kindness. It may be love at first sight.

▶

17 called Leah and the younger Raḥel. Leah had sensitive
18 eyes; Raḥel was beautiful and lovely. And Yaakov was in SHELISHI
love with Raḥel, so he said, "I will work for you seven
19 years for your younger daughter Raḥel." Lavan replied,
"Better that I give her to you than to some other man.
20 Stay on with me." So Yaakov worked for Raḥel seven
years. But so great was his love for her that they seemed to
21 him but a few days. Then Yaakov said to Lavan, "Give me
22 my wife – my time is done, let me come to her." So Lavan
23 brought together all the local people and made a feast. In
the evening he took his daughter Leah and brought her in
24 to him, and he came to her. Lavan also gave his servant
25 Zilpa to his daughter Leah as her maid. Then came
morning – and it was Leah. Yaakov said to Lavan, "What
is this you have done to me? I served you for Raḥel, did I
26 not? Why did you deceive me?" Lavan said, "This is not
done in our country – to marry off the younger before the

---

both labor and time. Not before and not afterward do we find in the Torah such romantic passion.

29:25 וְהִנֵּה־הִוא לֵאָה *And it was Leah* – Lavan has made it impossible for Yaakov to backtrack. He has invited "all the local people" to be witnesses to the marriage celebration. They could not know that he had promised that the bride would be Raḥel. They will have assumed, Lavan implies, that it would be Leah, since the local custom is that the elder is married first. Besides which, has Lavan in fact promised Raḥel? His answer, seven years earlier, when Yaakov first asked for Raḥel, was curiously evasive and oblique: "Better that I give her to you than to some other man. Stay on with me" (Gen. 29:19). It may be that he had already then formed the intention to deceive.

29:25 וְלָמָּה רִמִּיתָנִי *Why did you deceive me?* – Listen carefully to the text. The word Yaakov uses with Lavan, "Why did you deceive me [*rimitani*]?" is the very word Yitzḥak used to describe Yaakov's behavior in taking Esav's blessing: "Your brother came in deceit [*mirma*]" (Gen. 27:35). The word Lavan uses to describe the younger sibling is *tze'ira*, the word that appears in Rikva's oracle about Yaakov and Esav: "The greater shall the younger [*tza'ir*] serve" (25:23).

Even the sentence Lavan uses to justify the deception – "This is not done in our country – to marry off the younger before the firstborn" – is deeply ironic. Does Lavan know that this, in effect, is what Yaakov once did in another place? The irony may be unintentional. Lavan may not know, but we, the readers, do. And so surely does Yaakov himself.

יז רָחֵל: וְעֵינֵי לֵאָה רַכּוֹת וְרָחֵל הָיְתָה יְפַת־תֹּאַר וִיפַת מַרְאֶה:
יח וַיֶּאֱהַב יַעֲקֹב אֶת־רָחֵל וַיֹּאמֶר אֶעֱבָדְךָ שֶׁבַע שָׁנִים בְּרָחֵל שלישי
יט בִּתְּךָ הַקְּטַנָּה: וַיֹּאמֶר לָבָן טוֹב תִּתִּי אֹתָהּ לָךְ מִתִּתִּי אֹתָהּ
כ לְאִישׁ אַחֵר שְׁבָה עִמָּדִי: וַיַּעֲבֹד יַעֲקֹב בְּרָחֵל שֶׁבַע שָׁנִים
כא וַיִּהְיוּ בְעֵינָיו כְּיָמִים אֲחָדִים בְּאַהֲבָתוֹ אֹתָהּ: וַיֹּאמֶר יַעֲקֹב
אֶל־לָבָן הָבָה אֶת־אִשְׁתִּי כִּי מָלְאוּ יָמָי וְאָבוֹאָה אֵלֶיהָ:
כב כג וַיֶּאֱסֹף לָבָן אֶת־כָּל־אַנְשֵׁי הַמָּקוֹם וַיַּעַשׂ מִשְׁתֶּה: וַיְהִי בָעֶרֶב
כד וַיִּקַּח אֶת־לֵאָה בִתּוֹ וַיָּבֵא אֹתָהּ אֵלָיו וַיָּבֹא אֵלֶיהָ: וַיִּתֵּן לָבָן
כה לָהּ אֶת־זִלְפָּה שִׁפְחָתוֹ לְלֵאָה בִתּוֹ שִׁפְחָה: וַיְהִי בַבֹּקֶר
וְהִנֵּה־הִוא לֵאָה וַיֹּאמֶר אֶל־לָבָן מַה־זֹּאת עָשִׂיתָ לִּי הֲלֹא
כו בְרָחֵל עָבַדְתִּי עִמָּךְ וְלָמָּה רִמִּיתָנִי: וַיֹּאמֶר לָבָן לֹא־יֵעָשֶׂה

29:17 וְעֵינֵי לֵאָה רַכּוֹת *Leah had sensitive eyes* – The word *rakot* could mean many things: beautiful (Onkelos and Rashbam), weak (Ramban and Radak), or sensitive. Rabbi Naftali Tzvi Yehuda Berlin suggests that Leah is unable to go out with the flocks because the bright sunlight hurts her eyes (*Haamek Davar*). But the word is more significant than that. It means – as Rashi, Radak, and midrashic tradition explain – "Leah is easily moved to tears." Sensitive, easily hurt, she will know that she is Yaakov's lesser love, and it will cause her pain. In a few deft strokes, which we only notice if we are listening carefully, the text has sketched Leah's situation and character.

29:20 וַיִּהְיוּ בְעֵינָיו כְּיָמִים אֲחָדִים *Seemed to him but a few days* – For several verses we have been kept in suspense. After a month, when Lavan asks Yaakov what he would like his wages to be in return for the work he expects from him, the text makes clear what we suspected at the outset. Yaakov has fallen in love with Raḥel. Yaakov is following his eyes, not generally considered a good thing in Tanakh. Ḥava followed her eyes in desiring the forbidden fruit (Gen. 3:6). Shmuel, seeing the sons of Yishai, among whom God has told him is Israel's future king, initially chooses Eliav, who looks the part. He is told by God that he has judged wrongly: "Do not consider his appearance or height, for I have rejected him. The Lord does not look at the things man looks at. Man looks at the outward appearance, but the Lord looks at the heart" (I Sam. 16:7). Yet Yaakov is deeply in love. The Torah tells us this in one of its most beautiful lines: "So Yaakov worked for Raḥel seven years. But so great was his love for her that they seemed to him but a few days" (Gen. 29:20). He is oblivious to

27 firstborn. Wait until the bridal week of this one is over
and then we will give you the other one also, in return for
28 your serving me another seven years." Yaakov did so. He
completed Leah's bridal week; then Lavan gave him his
29 daughter Raḥel as a wife. Lavan gave his servant Bilha to
30 his daughter Raḥel as her maid. And Yaakov came also to
Raḥel; and he loved Raḥel more than Leah. And he
31 served him for another seven years. When the LORD saw
that Leah was unloved, He opened her womb, but Raḥel
32 was barren. Leah became pregnant and had a son. She
named him Reuven, saying, "The LORD has seen my

Yet though the text is semantically strange, is it psychologically lucid. Leah knows that Yaakov's heart is elsewhere. She may be loved but she feels the lesser love as a rejection. The words "the LORD saw" mean that God feels her sense of humiliation. Lavan's deception has human consequences, and they are tragic. Leah weeps inwardly for the husband she has acquired as a result of her father's wiles, the husband whose love is for someone else.

Judaism is supremely a religion of love: three loves. "Love the LORD your God with all your heart, with all your soul, and with all your might" (Deut. 6:5); "Love your neighbor as your own self" (Lev. 19:18); and "Love the stranger, for you yourselves were strangers" (Deut. 10:19).

But without justice, love alone is insufficient to sustain the world, insufficient even to maintain peace within a family. Yaakov's love for Raḥel, and later Yosef, is the cause of conflict between his two wives and their sons, and Yaakov pays heavily for it. Love is not enough, for it leaves the less loved feeling unloved, and the result is conflict and sometimes tragedy.

Much of the moral life is generated by this tension between love and justice. It is no accident that this is the theme of many of the narratives of Genesis. Genesis is about people and their relationships while the rest of the Torah is predominantly about society.

At the heart of the moral life is a conflict with no simple resolution. Weaving together these two strands of love (Yaakov's intense feelings for Raḥel) and justice (the deceiver deceived), the story of Yaakov, Raḥel, and Leah turns out to be an essential prelude to the book of Exodus and the covenant between God and Israel, based on love and justice. For without justice, love is blind; and without love, justice is impersonal and cold. Yaakov's family needs both – and so do we.

29:32 וַתִּקְרָא שְׁמוֹ *She named him* – Read superficially, these verses are no more than a genealogy, a list of births, of the

כז כֵּן בִּמְקוֹמֵנוּ לָתֵת הַצְּעִירָה לִפְנֵי הַבְּכִירָה: מַלֵּא שְׁבֻעַ
זֹאת וְנִתְּנָה לְךָ גַּם־אֶת־זֹאת בַּעֲבֹדָה אֲשֶׁר תַּעֲבֹד עִמָּדִי
כח עוֹד שֶׁבַע־שָׁנִים אֲחֵרוֹת: וַיַּעַשׂ יַעֲקֹב כֵּן וַיְמַלֵּא שְׁבֻעַ
כט זֹאת וַיִּתֶּן־לוֹ אֶת־רָחֵל בִּתּוֹ לוֹ לְאִשָּׁה: וַיִּתֵּן לָבָן לְרָחֵל
ל בִּתּוֹ אֶת־בִּלְהָה שִׁפְחָתוֹ לָהּ לְשִׁפְחָה: וַיָּבֹא גַּם אֶל־רָחֵל
וַיֶּאֱהַב גַּם־אֶת־רָחֵל מִלֵּאָה וַיַּעֲבֹד עִמּוֹ עוֹד שֶׁבַע־שָׁנִים
לא אֲחֵרוֹת: וַיַּרְא יהוה כִּי־שְׂנוּאָה לֵאָה וַיִּפְתַּח אֶת־רַחְמָהּ כז
לב וְרָחֵל עֲקָרָה: וַתַּהַר לֵאָה וַתֵּלֶד בֵּן וַתִּקְרָא שְׁמוֹ רְאוּבֵן כִּי

If these hints are signaling how the passage should be read, then the narrative is an example, unparalleled in its drama, of the single most fundamental moral axiom of the Torah, *midda keneged midda*, measure for measure (Shabbat 105b). Those who deceive will be deceived.

THE RIVALRY OF LEAH AND RAḤEL

Torah is written to be read aloud, and several of its literary devices are based on the timed sequence of the audial. Time and again, the Torah makes use of the fact that a later word has the power to confound expectations that have been formed based on what has been heard thus far. In our story we know that Yaakov loves Raḥel, and has been married to Leah against his will. Then we read: "Yaakov came also [*gam*] to Raḥel; and he [also, *gam*] loved Raḥel…" (Gen. 29:30).

The implication at this point is clear. The repeated *gam*, "also," leads us to believe that the two sisters are equal in Yaakov's eyes. The story of the deception has – or so we must suppose on the basis of what we have so far heard – a happy ending after all. Yaakov has married both. He loves them both. The sibling rivalry that is so pronounced a theme of Genesis seems to finally be reaching a positive resolution.

The next word sends our expectation crashing to the ground: "…more than Leah" (29:30).

This is an ungrammatical construction. The words "also" and "more than" do not belong together in the same sentence. The effect – like a sudden discord in the middle of a Mozart symphony – is strident and shocking. Yaakov does not love the two sisters equally. He may love them both, but his passion is for Raḥel.

Immediately after, in verse 31, we read that Leah is *senua* – "hated." This is a phrase that cannot be understood literally. The previous verse has just said that Leah was not *senua*, but loved. The commentators and translators wrestled with this difficulty. Ramban (in his second interpretation) and Radak both read the word *senua* not as "hated" but as "[relatively] unloved" (commentaries on Gen. 29:31; we reflect this reading in our translation).

33 affliction. Now my husband will love me." She became
pregnant again and had a son. She said, "The LORD has
heard that I am unloved, so He has given me this son
34 also," and she named him Shimon. She became pregnant
again and had a son and said, "Now that I have borne him
three sons, my husband will walk with me." That is why he
35 was named Levi. She became pregnant again and had a
son. She said, "This time I will praise the LORD," so she
named him Yehuda. Then she ceased having children.
30 1 Aware that she had borne Yaakov no children, Raḥel
became envious of her sister. To Yaakov she said, "Give
2 me children! If not, let me die!" Yaakov grew angry with
Raḥel, and said, "Am I in place of God, who has kept you

"The LORD saw that Leah was unloved.") Reuven is to know this and to feel his mother's shame and his father's apparent indifference intensely. Later, we will see the contrast between the hesitant Reuven and the confident – even overconfident – Yosef, loved and favored by his father. If we want our children to have the confidence to act when action is needed, then we need, from the beginning, to empower, encourage, and praise them.

29:35 הַפַּעַם אוֹדֶה אֶת יהוה *This time I will praise the LORD* – After three children have been born and brought Leah no closer to gaining the love she longs for, she seems to let her expectation go. *Hodaya,* appreciation, the acknowledgment that what we have is a gift, is one of the most profound religious emotions. To thank God is to know that I am not less worthwhile because someone else is more successful. Through prayer I know that I am valued for what I am. I learn to cherish what I have, rather than be diminished by what I do not have. To be a Jew – *Yehudi,* the name we acquired from Yehuda – is to offer thanks and praise.

30:2 הֲתַחַת אֱלֹהִים אָנֹכִי... *Am I in place of God...* – We are not all destined to have children. The rabbis said that the good we do constitutes our *toledot,* our posterity (Rashi on Gen. 6:9). But the Torah recognizes the agony of infertility: to wait in hope and wait again.

Lacking a solution to Raḥel's problem, Yaakov reacts in anger to her pain. His harsh words prompt her to suggest her own solution. He cannot stand in for God. Let a concubine stand in for her. When Yaakov fell in love he followed his eyes. The world of appearances is a false world of masks, disguises, and concealments. Yaakov must learn to listen.

Listen deeply to those you love and who love you. Listening is not easy. I confess I find it formidably hard. But listening alone bridges the abyss between soul and soul, self and other, I and the

לג אמרה כי־ראה יהוה בעניי כי עתה יאהבני אישי: ותהר
עוד ותלד בן ותאמר כי־שמע יהוה כי־שנואה אנכי ויתן־
לד לי גם־את־זה ותקרא שמו שמעון: ותהר עוד ותלד בן
ותאמר עתה הפעם ילוה אישי אלי כי־ילדתי לו שלשה
לה בנים על־כן קרא־שמו לוי: ותהר עוד ותלד בן ותאמר
הפעם אודה את־יהוה על־כן קראה שמו יהודה ותעמד
ל א מלדת: ותרא רחל כי לא ילדה ליעקב ותקנא רחל
באחתה ותאמר אל־יעקב הבה־לי בנים ואם־אין מתה
ב אנכי: ויחר־אף יעקב ברחל ויאמר התחת אלהים אנכי

kind of which there are many in Genesis. Heard while attuned to Leah's plight, however, what we hear is heartbreaking. Leah is pleading for attention. Each of the names of her first three children is a cry to her husband Yaakov – to see, to listen, to be attached, to notice, to love her. Sadly, the lack of relationship between Yaakov and Leah at the birth of her children is carried through in the years to come. Yaakov's relationship with Reuven, Shimon, and Levi breaks down completely, with Reuven after the episode of Bilha's couch, with Shimon and Levi after the incident with Shekhem. On his deathbed he curses instead of blessing them (see ch. 49). Yet it is from Levi that Israel's spiritual leaders will come – Moshe, Aharon, Miriam, and eventually the *kohanim* and *levi'im* (priests and Levites); it is from Yehuda that will come its kings, David and his descendants.

Through painful experience, Yaakov must learn a truth about love: It not only unites, it also divides. It did so in his childhood, when Yitzḥak loved Esav and Rivka loved Yaakov. It does so again when he marries two sisters. It will do so a third time when he loves Raḥel's child Yosef more than his other sons. What Yaakov learns – and what we learn, hearing his story – is that love is not enough. We must also heed those who feel unloved. Without that, there will be conflict and tragedy. But to heed the unloved requires a specific capacity: the ability to listen – in Yaakov's case, to the unspoken tears of Leah and her feeling of rejection, made explicit in the names she gives her sons.

29:32 כי ראה יהוה *The Lord has seen* – Reuven is Yaakov's firstborn. Yaakov is to say of him on his deathbed, "Reuven, you are my firstborn, my strength, first fruit of my manhood, excelling in rank, excelling in power" (Gen. 49:3). This is an impressive tribute, suggesting physical presence and commanding demeanor. But at his birth, his father's attention is elsewhere; he does not care for either Leah or her sons. (The text itself says,

3 from having children?" "Here is Bilha my slave," she said.
"Come to her. Let her give birth on my knees so that I too
4 can build a family through her." So she gave him her maid
5 Bilha as a wife. Yaakov came to her, and she became
6 pregnant and bore Yaakov a son. Then Raḥel said, "God
has vindicated me. He has listened to my voice and given
7 me a son." So she named him Dan. Bilha, Raḥel's maid,
became pregnant again and bore Yaakov a second son.
8 And Raḥel said, "I have struggled hard with my sister and
9 I have won." So she named him Naftali. Leah realized that
she was no longer having children, so she took her maid
10 Zilpa and gave her to Yaakov as a wife. And Leah's maid
11 Zilpa bore Yaakov a son. Leah said, "Good fortune has
12 come!" So she named him Gad. Then Zilpa, Leah's maid,
13 bore Yaakov a second son. Leah said, "How blessed I am;
young girls will call me blessed." So she named him Asher.
14 During the wheat harvest, Reuven went for a walk and REVI'I
found mandrakes in the field. He brought them to his
mother Leah. Raḥel said to Leah, "Please give me some of
15 your son's mandrakes." She replied, "Is it not enough that
you have taken away my husband? Now you want to take
my son's mandrakes too!" "Very well," said Raḥel. "Let
him sleep with you tonight in exchange for your son's
16 mandrakes." When Yaakov came back from the field that
evening, Leah went out to meet him and said, "You are to
come to me, for I have hired you with my son's mandrakes."
17 So that night he slept with her. God listened to Leah, and

---

This is the only time that angry words are reported between the two sisters. Reuven, seeking to help Leah, ends up creating a scene in which her bitterness rises to the surface. Returning with the mandrakes, he might have bided his time until Leah was alone, but he does not. Reuven carries with him a lack of confidence, an uncertainty that at critical moments robs him of his capacity to carry through a course of action that he knows to be right. As we shall see later on with more consequence (see ch. 37, "Reuven's Good Intentions), he begins well but fails to drive the deed to closure.

ג אֲשֶׁר־מָנַע מִמֵּךְ פְּרִי־בָטֶן׃ וַתֹּאמֶר הִנֵּה אֲמָתִי בִלְהָה בֹּא
ד אֵלֶיהָ וְתֵלֵד עַל־בִּרְכַּי וְאִבָּנֶה גַם־אָנֹכִי מִמֶּנָּה׃ וַתִּתֶּן־לוֹ
ה אֶת־בִּלְהָה שִׁפְחָתָהּ לְאִשָּׁה וַיָּבֹא אֵלֶיהָ יַעֲקֹב׃ וַתַּהַר בִּלְהָה
ו וַתֵּלֶד לְיַעֲקֹב בֵּן׃ וַתֹּאמֶר רָחֵל דָּנַנִּי אֱלֹהִים וְגַם שָׁמַע בְּקֹלִי
ז וַיִּתֶּן־לִי בֵּן עַל־כֵּן קָרְאָה שְׁמוֹ דָּן׃ וַתַּהַר עוֹד וַתֵּלֶד בִּלְהָה
ח שִׁפְחַת רָחֵל בֵּן שֵׁנִי לְיַעֲקֹב׃ וַתֹּאמֶר רָחֵל נַפְתּוּלֵי אֱלֹהִים ׀
ט נִפְתַּלְתִּי עִם־אֲחֹתִי גַּם־יָכֹלְתִּי וַתִּקְרָא שְׁמוֹ נַפְתָּלִי׃ וַתֵּרֶא
לֵאָה כִּי עָמְדָה מִלֶּדֶת וַתִּקַּח אֶת־זִלְפָּה שִׁפְחָתָהּ וַתִּתֵּן
י אֹתָהּ לְיַעֲקֹב לְאִשָּׁה׃ וַתֵּלֶד זִלְפָּה שִׁפְחַת לֵאָה לְיַעֲקֹב בֵּן׃
יא יב וַתֹּאמֶר לֵאָה בגד וַתִּקְרָא אֶת־שְׁמוֹ גָּד׃ וַתֵּלֶד זִלְפָּה שִׁפְחַת בָּא גָד
יג לֵאָה בֵּן שֵׁנִי לְיַעֲקֹב׃ וַתֹּאמֶר לֵאָה בְּאָשְׁרִי כִּי אִשְּׁרוּנִי בָּנוֹת
יד וַתִּקְרָא אֶת־שְׁמוֹ אָשֵׁר׃ וַיֵּלֶךְ רְאוּבֵן בִּימֵי קְצִיר־חִטִּים רביעי
וַיִּמְצָא דוּדָאִים בַּשָּׂדֶה וַיָּבֵא אֹתָם אֶל־לֵאָה אִמּוֹ וַתֹּאמֶר
טו רָחֵל אֶל־לֵאָה תְּנִי־נָא לִי מִדּוּדָאֵי בְּנֵךְ׃ וַתֹּאמֶר לָהּ הַמְעַט
קַחְתֵּךְ אֶת־אִישִׁי וְלָקַחַת גַּם אֶת־דּוּדָאֵי בְּנִי וַתֹּאמֶר רָחֵל
טז לָכֵן יִשְׁכַּב עִמָּךְ הַלַּיְלָה תַּחַת דּוּדָאֵי בְנֵךְ׃ וַיָּבֹא יַעֲקֹב מִן־
הַשָּׂדֶה בָּעֶרֶב וַתֵּצֵא לֵאָה לִקְרָאתוֹ וַתֹּאמֶר אֵלַי תָּבוֹא כִּי
שָׂכֹר שְׂכַרְתִּיךָ בְּדוּדָאֵי בְּנִי וַיִּשְׁכַּב עִמָּהּ בַּלַּיְלָה הוּא׃
יז וַיִּשְׁמַע אֱלֹהִים אֶל־לֵאָה וַתַּהַר וַתֵּלֶד לְיַעֲקֹב בֵּן חֲמִישִׁי׃

Divine. Jewish spirituality is the art of listening.

30:14 וַיָּבֵא אֹתָם אֶל־לֵאָה אִמּוֹ *He brought them to his mother Leah* – From the context it appears that mandrakes were believed to be both an aphrodisiac and a fertility drug. Reuven's first thought is to give them to his mother Leah. This tells us something about Reuven. He is not thinking about himself, but about her. He knows she feels unloved and identifies with her anguish with all the sensitivity of an eldest child. He hopes that, with the aid of the mandrakes, Leah will be able to win Yaakov's attention, perhaps even his love.

It is a strikingly mature and thoughtful act. Yet it has negative consequences. It provokes a bitter row between the two sisters, Leah and Raḥel. Raḥel sees the mandrakes and wants them for herself.

▶

18 she became pregnant and bore Yaakov a fifth son. Leah
said, "God has rewarded me for giving my maid to my
19 husband," so she named him Yissakhar. Leah became
20 pregnant again and bore Yaakov a sixth son. "God has
given me a precious gift," said Leah. "This time my
husband will honor me, for I have borne him six sons," so
21 she named him Zevulun. Later she gave birth to a daughter
22 and named her Dina. Then God remembered Raḥel and
23 listened to her and enabled her to conceive. She became
pregnant and gave birth to a son. She said, "God has taken
24 away my shame," and she named him Yosef, saying, "May
25 the Lord grant me another son also." After Raḥel had
given birth to Yosef, Yaakov said to Lavan, "Release me to
26 go home to my own land. Give me my wives and my
children for whom I have worked for you, and let me go.
You know very well how much work I have done for you."
27 But Lavan said to him, "If you will allow me to say so, I
have learned by divination that it is because of you that
28 the Lord has blessed me." He added, "Name your hire ḤAMISHI
29 and I will pay it." Yaakov said, "You know well how I have
worked for you and how your livestock have fared under
30 my care. You had little before I came, but it has swelled
into much. The Lord has blessed you wherever I have

At some stage, however, the passage was placed in another context: the Mishna specifies that it be read and expounded on Seder night (Pesaḥim 4:10). What could be the connection between "My ancestor was a wandering Aramean" and the exodus?

Let me suggest an explanation. We have here a phrase with two quite different meanings, depending on the context in which we read it. The Sages formulated the principle that *maasei avot siman lebanim*, "the acts of the fathers are a sign for their children." The classic example, as we have seen, occurs in Genesis 12 when, almost immediately after arriving in the land of Canaan, Avraham and Sara are forced into exile in Egypt. Avraham's life is at risk. Sara is taken into Pharaoh's harem. God then strikes Pharaoh's household with plagues, and Pharaoh sends them away. The parallels between this and the story of the exodus are obvious. The event appears to recur both in Avraham's life and in Yitzḥak's.

Living with Lavan, however, Yaakov loses his freedom. He becomes, in effect, his father-in-law's slave. Eventually he

יח וַתֹּאמֶר לֵאָה נָתַן אֱלֹהִים שְׂכָרִי אֲשֶׁר־נָתַתִּי שִׁפְחָתִי לְאִישִׁי
יט וַתִּקְרָא שְׁמוֹ יִשָּׂשכָר׃ וַתַּהַר עוֹד לֵאָה וַתֵּלֶד בֵּן־שִׁשִּׁי
כ לְיַעֲקֹב׃ וַתֹּאמֶר לֵאָה זְבָדַנִי אֱלֹהִים ׀ אֹתִי זֵבֶד טוֹב הַפַּעַם
יִזְבְּלֵנִי אִישִׁי כִּי־יָלַדְתִּי לוֹ שִׁשָּׁה בָנִים וַתִּקְרָא אֶת־שְׁמוֹ
כא כב זְבֻלוּן׃ וְאַחַר יָלְדָה בַּת וַתִּקְרָא אֶת־שְׁמָהּ דִּינָה׃ וַיִּזְכֹּר כח
אֱלֹהִים אֶת־רָחֵל וַיִּשְׁמַע אֵלֶיהָ אֱלֹהִים וַיִּפְתַּח אֶת־רַחְמָהּ׃
כג כד וַתַּהַר וַתֵּלֶד בֵּן וַתֹּאמֶר אָסַף אֱלֹהִים אֶת־חֶרְפָּתִי׃ וַתִּקְרָא
כה אֶת־שְׁמוֹ יוֹסֵף לֵאמֹר יֹסֵף יְהוָה לִי בֵּן אַחֵר׃ וַיְהִי כַּאֲשֶׁר
יָלְדָה רָחֵל אֶת־יוֹסֵף וַיֹּאמֶר יַעֲקֹב אֶל־לָבָן שַׁלְּחֵנִי וְאֵלְכָה
כו אֶל־מְקוֹמִי וּלְאַרְצִי׃ תְּנָה אֶת־נָשַׁי וְאֶת־יְלָדַי אֲשֶׁר עָבַדְתִּי
אֹתְךָ בָּהֵן וְאֵלֵכָה כִּי אַתָּה יָדַעְתָּ אֶת־עֲבֹדָתִי אֲשֶׁר
כז עֲבַדְתִּיךָ׃ וַיֹּאמֶר אֵלָיו לָבָן אִם־נָא מָצָאתִי חֵן בְּעֵינֶיךָ
כח נִחַשְׁתִּי וַיְבָרְכֵנִי יְהוָה בִּגְלָלֶךָ׃ וַיֹּאמַר נָקְבָה שְׂכָרְךָ עָלַי חמישי
כט וְאֶתֵּנָה׃ וַיֹּאמֶר אֵלָיו אַתָּה יָדַעְתָּ אֵת אֲשֶׁר עֲבַדְתִּיךָ וְאֵת
ל אֲשֶׁר־הָיָה מִקְנְךָ אִתִּי׃ כִּי מְעַט אֲשֶׁר־הָיָה לְךָ לְפָנַי וַיִּפְרֹץ
לָרֹב וַיְבָרֶךְ יְהוָה אֹתְךָ לְרַגְלִי וְעַתָּה מָתַי אֶעֱשֶׂה גַם־אָנֹכִי

AN ARAMEAN SOUGHT MY FATHER'S DEATH

The narrative of Yaakov in Lavan's house gives rise to the strangest passage in the Haggada. Commenting on Deuteronomy 26:5, the passage we expound on Seder night, it says as follows: "*Arami oved avi* – Go [to the verse] and learn what Lavan the Aramean sought to do to our father Yaakov: Pharaoh condemned only the boys to death, but Lavan sought to uproot everything."

The plain sense of the verse from Deuteronomy cannot be "[Lavan] an Aramean [tried to] destroy my father," because, as Ibn Ezra points out, *oved* is an intransitive verb meaning "lost," "wandering," or "on the brink of perishing." The text of *arami oved avi,* originally, had nothing to do with Passover. It appears in the Torah as the text of the declaration to be said on bringing first fruits to the Temple on Shavuot. In that context, the literal translation, "My ancestor was a wandering Aramean," makes eminent sense. The text is contrasting the past, when the patriarchs were forced to wander from place to place, with the present, when, thanks to God, the Israelites have a land of their own.

▶

been. Now, when can I do likewise for my own household?"
31 Lavan asked, "What shall I give you?" Yaakov replied, "Do
not give me anything. If you do this one thing for me, I will
32 continue to shepherd and guard your flocks. Let me go
through all your flocks today and remove every speckled or
spotted sheep, every dark-colored lamb, and every spotted
33 or speckled goat. They shall be my hire. Let my honesty
testify for me in the future, whenever you come to check
the wages you have paid me. Any goat not speckled or
spotted or any lamb not dark colored in my possession
34 shall be considered stolen." Lavan said, "Agreed. Let it be as
35 you have said." That day Lavan removed the streaked or
spotted goats, all the speckled or spotted female
goats – every one that had a trace of white – and every dark-
36 colored lamb. These he placed in the care of his sons. Then
he put a three-day-journey's distance between him and
37 Yaakov. Yaakov tended the rest of Lavan's flock. Yaakov
took fresh shoots of poplar, almond, and plane trees and
peeled white strips in them, exposing the white of the

---

anger, his rage, is that Yaakov maintains his dignity and independence. Faced with a near-impossible existence as his father-in-law's slave, Yaakov always finds a way of carrying on. Yes, he has been cheated of his beloved Raḥel, but he works so that he can marry her too. Yes, he has been forced to work for nothing, but he uses his superior knowledge of animal husbandry to propose a deal which will allow him to build flocks of his own that will allow him to maintain what is now a large family. Hemmed in on all sides, he finds a way out. His methods are not those he would have chosen in other circumstances. He has to outwit an extremely cunning adversary. Yet in a seemingly impossible situation Yaakov retains his dignity, independence, and freedom. Yaakov is no man's slave.

30:37 וַיִּקַּח־לוֹ יַעֲקֹב מַקַּל לִבְנֶה *Yaakov took fresh shoots*– Yaakov embarks on an extraordinary course of action. In charge of the flocks, he goes through an elaborate procedure involving peeled branches of poplar, almond, and plane trees, which he places with their drinking water. The result is that, though Lavan has removed all the streaked animals from the flock, those that remain do in fact produce streaked and spotted offspring.

How this happens has intrigued not only the commentators (who mostly assume that it was a miracle, God's way

לא לְבֵיתִי: וַיֹּאמֶר מָה אֶתֶּן־לָךְ וַיֹּאמֶר יַעֲקֹב לֹא־תִתֶּן־לִי
מְאוּמָה אִם־תַּעֲשֶׂה־לִּי הַדָּבָר הַזֶּה אָשׁוּבָה אֶרְעֶה צֹאנְךָ
לב אֶשְׁמֹר: אֶעֱבֹר בְּכָל־צֹאנְךָ הַיּוֹם הָסֵר מִשָּׁם כָּל־שֶׂה ׀ נָקֹד
וְטָלוּא וְכָל־שֶׂה־חוּם בַּכְּשָׂבִים וְטָלוּא וְנָקֹד בָּעִזִּים וְהָיָה
לג שְׂכָרִי: וְעָנְתָה־בִּי צִדְקָתִי בְּיוֹם מָחָר כִּי־תָבוֹא עַל־שְׂכָרִי
לְפָנֶיךָ כֹּל אֲשֶׁר־אֵינֶנּוּ נָקֹד וְטָלוּא בָּעִזִּים וְחוּם בַּכְּשָׂבִים
לד לה גָּנוּב הוּא אִתִּי: וַיֹּאמֶר לָבָן הֵן לוּ יְהִי כִדְבָרֶךָ: וַיָּסַר בַּיּוֹם
הַהוּא אֶת־הַתְּיָשִׁים הָעֲקֻדִּים וְהַטְּלֻאִים וְאֵת כָּל־הָעִזִּים
הַנְּקֻדּוֹת וְהַטְּלֻאֹת כֹּל אֲשֶׁר־לָבָן בּוֹ וְכָל־חוּם בַּכְּשָׂבִים וַיִּתֵּן
לו בְּיַד־בָּנָיו: וַיָּשֶׂם דֶּרֶךְ שְׁלֹשֶׁת יָמִים בֵּינוֹ וּבֵין יַעֲקֹב וְיַעֲקֹב
לז רֹעֶה אֶת־צֹאן לָבָן הַנּוֹתָרֹת: וַיִּקַּח־לוֹ יַעֲקֹב מַקַּל לִבְנֶה
לַח וְלוּז וְעַרְמוֹן וַיְפַצֵּל בָּהֵן פְּצָלוֹת לְבָנוֹת מַחְשֹׂף הַלָּבָן

---

has to escape, without letting Lavan know he is going. In this respect, Yaakov's experience is closer to the exodus than that of Avraham or Yitzhak. No one stopped them from leaving. No one pursued them. It is Yaakov's experience in the house of Lavan that becomes the sharpest prefiguration of the exodus.

What then are we to make of the Haggada's comment "Pharaoh condemned only the boys to death, but Lavan sought to uproot everything"? The answer is not that Lavan sought to kill all the members of Yaakov's family. Quite the opposite. Yaakov works for some twenty years to earn his family and flocks. Yet Lavan still claims they are his. Were God not to intervene, he would keep Yaakov's entire family as prisoners. He seeks "to uproot everything" by denying them all the chance to go free.

It was the genius of the Sages to give a verse related to the bringing of the first fruits an interpretation that connects it with Passover. And though it gives a far-fetched reading of the phrase, it gives a compelling interpretation to the narrative of Yaakov in Lavan's house. It tells us that the third patriarch, whose descent to Egypt will actually begin the story of the exodus, himself undergoes an exodus experience in his youth. *Maasei avot siman lebanim*, "the acts of the fathers are a sign for their children." Our ancestors experienced exile and exodus as if to say to their descendants: This is not unknown territory. And God was with us then; He will be with you now.

30:31 לֹא תִתֶּן לִי מְאוּמָה *Do not give me anything* – The thing that arouses Lavan's

38 shoots. Then he set the peeled shoots in all the water
troughs so that they would be in front of the flocks when
they came to drink. They would mate when they came to
39 drink, and since they mated by the shoots, they bore
40 streaked, speckled, and spotted young. Yaakov set apart
the young of the flock, and he made the others belonging
to Lavan face the streaked and dark-colored animals.
Thus he bred separate flocks for himself, and he did not
41 let them breed with Lavan's flocks. Whenever the stronger
animals were mating, Yaakov would place the shoots in
the troughs facing them so that they mated facing the
42 shoots. But the weaker animals he did not put there, so
43 the weaker went to Lavan and the stronger to Yaakov. Thus
the man's wealth swelled into a fortune. He had large
flocks, female and male servants, camels and donkeys.
31 1 Yaakov heard that Lavan's sons were saying, "Yaakov has
taken everything our father owned; of what belonged to
2 our father, he has made all these riches." And Yaakov saw
that Lavan's manner toward him was not what it had
3 been. The Lord said to Yaakov, "Go back to the land of
4 your fathers where you were born; I will be with you." So
Yaakov sent word to Raḥel and Leah to come out to the
5 field where his flock was. He said to them, "I see that your
father's manner toward me is not what it used to be. But
6 the God of my father has been with me. You well know

---

here, as in the story of Yitzḥak in Gerar, Amy Chua's three conditions for the persecution of a minority (see ch. 26, "Stopping up the Wells"). Yaakov is a minority, outnumbered by Lavan's family. He is successful, and it is conspicuous. You can see it by looking at his flocks.

As with Lavan, so through the ages, the host society would eventually turn against the Jews. They claimed that Jews were exploiting them rather than what was in fact the case, that they were exploiting the Jews. And when Jews succeeded, they accused them of theft: "The flocks are my flocks! All that you see is mine!" (Gen. 31:43). They forgot that Jews had contributed massively to national prosperity. The fact that Jews had salvaged some self-respect, some independence, that they too had prospered, made antisemites not just envious but angry. That was when it became dangerous to be a Jew.

לח אֲשֶׁר עַל־הַמַּקְלוֹת׃ וַיַּצֵּג אֶת־הַמַּקְלוֹת אֲשֶׁר פִּצֵּל בָּרְהָטִים
בְּשִׁקְתוֹת הַמָּיִם אֲשֶׁר תָּבֹאןָ הַצֹּאן לִשְׁתּוֹת לְנֹכַח הַצֹּאן
לט וַיֵּחַמְנָה בְּבֹאָן לִשְׁתּוֹת׃ וַיֶּחֱמוּ הַצֹּאן אֶל־הַמַּקְלוֹת וַתֵּלַדְןָ
מ הַצֹּאן עֲקֻדִּים נְקֻדִּים וּטְלֻאִים׃ וְהַכְּשָׂבִים הִפְרִיד יַעֲקֹב וַיִּתֵּן
פְּנֵי הַצֹּאן אֶל־עָקֹד וְכָל־חוּם בְּצֹאן לָבָן וַיָּשֶׁת לוֹ עֲדָרִים
מא לְבַדּוֹ וְלֹא שָׁתָם עַל־צֹאן לָבָן׃ וְהָיָה בְּכָל־יַחֵם הַצֹּאן
הַמְקֻשָּׁרוֹת וְשָׂם יַעֲקֹב אֶת־הַמַּקְלוֹת לְעֵינֵי הַצֹּאן בָּרְהָטִים
מב לְיַחְמֵנָּה בַּמַּקְלוֹת׃ וּבְהַעֲטִיף הַצֹּאן לֹא יָשִׂים וְהָיָה הָעֲטֻפִים
מג לְלָבָן וְהַקְּשֻׁרִים לְיַעֲקֹב׃ וַיִּפְרֹץ הָאִישׁ מְאֹד מְאֹד וַיְהִי־לוֹ
לא א צֹאן רַבּוֹת וּשְׁפָחוֹת וַעֲבָדִים וּגְמַלִּים וַחֲמֹרִים׃ וַיִּשְׁמַע אֶת־
דִּבְרֵי בְנֵי־לָבָן לֵאמֹר לָקַח יַעֲקֹב אֵת כָּל־אֲשֶׁר לְאָבִינוּ
ב וּמֵאֲשֶׁר לְאָבִינוּ עָשָׂה אֵת כָּל־הַכָּבֹד הַזֶּה׃ וַיַּרְא יַעֲקֹב
ג אֶת־פְּנֵי לָבָן וְהִנֵּה אֵינֶנּוּ עִמּוֹ כִּתְמוֹל שִׁלְשׁוֹם׃ וַיֹּאמֶר יהוה כט
אֶל־יַעֲקֹב שׁוּב אֶל־אֶרֶץ אֲבוֹתֶיךָ וּלְמוֹלַדְתֶּךָ וְאֶהְיֶה עִמָּךְ׃
ד וַיִּשְׁלַח יַעֲקֹב וַיִּקְרָא לְרָחֵל וּלְלֵאָה הַשָּׂדֶה אֶל־צֹאנוֹ׃
ה וַיֹּאמֶר לָהֶן רֹאֶה אָנֹכִי אֶת־פְּנֵי אֲבִיכֶן כִּי־אֵינֶנּוּ אֵלַי כִּתְמֹל
ו שִׁלְשֹׁם וֵאלֹהֵי אָבִי הָיָה עִמָּדִי׃ וְאַתֵּנָה יְדַעְתֶּן כִּי בְּכָל־כֹּחִי

of assuring Yaakov's welfare) but also scientists. Some argue that Yaakov must have had an understanding of genetics. Two unspotted sheep can produce spotted offspring. Yaakov has doubtless noticed this in his many years of tending Lavan's flocks.

Others have suggested that prenatal nutrition can have an epigenetic effect – that is, it can cause a certain gene to be expressed which might not have been otherwise. If the peeled branches of poplar, almond, and plane trees are added to the water the sheep drank, they might affect the agouti gene that determines the color of fur in sheep and mice. However it happens, the result is evidently dramatic.

31:2 אֵינֶנּוּ עִמּוֹ כִּתְמוֹל שִׁלְשׁוֹם *Not what it had been* – Throughout the ages, antisemites saw in Jews people who would make them rich. Wherever Jews went they brought prosperity to their hosts. Yet they refused to be mere chattels. They refused to be owned. They had their own identity and way of life; they insisted on the basic human right to be free. We see

how I have worked for your father with all my strength.
7 Your father cheated me, changing my wages ten times,
8 but God has not let him harm me. If he said, 'The speckled
animals shall be your hire,' then all the flock would give
birth to speckled young. If he said, 'The streaked animals
shall be your hire,' then all the flock would give birth to
9 streaked young. God has taken your father's livestock and
10 given it to me. Once, during the breeding season, I had a
dream: I saw that the rams mounting the flock were
11 streaked, speckled, or spotted. And in the dream an angel
12 of God said to me, 'Yaakov.' I replied, 'Here I am.' He said,
'Look up and see that all the rams mounting the flock are
streaked, speckled, or spotted, for I have seen all that
13 Lavan is doing to you. I am the God of Beit El, where you
anointed a pillar and made a vow to Me. Now – leave this
land at once and return to the land where you were born.'"
14 Raḥel and Leah answered him, "Do we still have a share
15 in the inheritance of our father's estate? He treats us like
16 strangers. He has sold us and spent the money. All the
wealth that God has taken from our father belongs to us
17 and our children. So do whatever God has told you." So SHISHI
18 Yaakov put his children and wives on camels and drove
all the livestock and wealth he had accumulated – the
livestock he had acquired in Padan Aram – heading for
19 his father Yitzḥak in the land of Canaan. Meanwhile,
when Lavan had gone to shear his sheep, Raḥel had stolen
20 her father's household gods. Yaakov deceived Lavan the

---

stolen them. Yaakov indignantly denies this and says, "If you find your gods with anyone here, they shall not live" (31:32). Several chapters later, we will read that Raḥel dies prematurely, on the way. The possibility hinted at by the text, articulated by a midrash and by Rashi (Bereshit Rabba; Zohar ad loc.) is that, unwittingly, Yaakov has condemned her to death.

As with Rivka and Yitzḥak a generation earlier, misunderstanding flows from a failure of communication. Had Rivka told Yitzḥak about the oracle, and had Raḥel told Yaakov about the *terafim*, tragedy might have been averted. Judaism is a religion of holy words, and one of the themes of Genesis as a whole is the power of speech to create, mislead,

ז עָבַדְתִּי אֶת־אֲבִיכֶן: וַאֲבִיכֶן הֵתֶל בִּי וְהֶחֱלִף אֶת־מַשְׂכֻּרְתִּי
ח עֲשֶׂרֶת מֹנִים וְלֹא־נְתָנוֹ אֱלֹהִים לְהָרַע עִמָּדִי: אִם־כֹּה יֹאמַר
נְקֻדִּים יִהְיֶה שְׂכָרֶךָ וְיָלְדוּ כָל־הַצֹּאן נְקֻדִּים וְאִם־כֹּה יֹאמַר
ט עֲקֻדִּים יִהְיֶה שְׂכָרֶךָ וְיָלְדוּ כָל־הַצֹּאן עֲקֻדִּים: וַיַּצֵּל אֱלֹהִים
י אֶת־מִקְנֵה אֲבִיכֶם וַיִּתֶּן־לִי: וַיְהִי בְּעֵת יַחֵם הַצֹּאן וָאֶשָּׂא
עֵינַי וָאֵרֶא בַּחֲלוֹם וְהִנֵּה הָעַתֻּדִים הָעֹלִים עַל־הַצֹּאן עֲקֻדִּים
יא נְקֻדִּים וּבְרֻדִּים: וַיֹּאמֶר אֵלַי מַלְאַךְ הָאֱלֹהִים בַּחֲלוֹם יַעֲקֹב
יב וָאֹמַר הִנֵּנִי: וַיֹּאמֶר שָׂא־נָא עֵינֶיךָ וּרְאֵה כָּל־הָעַתֻּדִים
הָעֹלִים עַל־הַצֹּאן עֲקֻדִּים נְקֻדִּים וּבְרֻדִּים כִּי רָאִיתִי אֵת
יג כָּל־אֲשֶׁר לָבָן עֹשֶׂה לָּךְ: אָנֹכִי הָאֵל בֵּית־אֵל אֲשֶׁר מָשַׁחְתָּ
שָּׁם מַצֵּבָה אֲשֶׁר נָדַרְתָּ לִּי שָׁם נֶדֶר עַתָּה קוּם צֵא מִן־הָאָרֶץ
יד הַזֹּאת וְשׁוּב אֶל־אֶרֶץ מוֹלַדְתֶּךָ: וַתַּעַן רָחֵל וְלֵאָה וַתֹּאמַרְנָה
טו לוֹ הַעוֹד לָנוּ חֵלֶק וְנַחֲלָה בְּבֵית אָבִינוּ: הֲלוֹא נָכְרִיּוֹת
טז נֶחְשַׁבְנוּ לוֹ כִּי מְכָרָנוּ וַיֹּאכַל גַּם־אָכוֹל אֶת־כַּסְפֵּנוּ: כִּי כָל־
הָעֹשֶׁר אֲשֶׁר הִצִּיל אֱלֹהִים מֵאָבִינוּ לָנוּ הוּא וּלְבָנֵינוּ וְעַתָּה
יז כֹּל אֲשֶׁר אָמַר אֱלֹהִים אֵלֶיךָ עֲשֵׂה: וַיָּקָם יַעֲקֹב וַיִּשָּׂא אֶת־ ששי
יח בָּנָיו וְאֶת־נָשָׁיו עַל־הַגְּמַלִּים: וַיִּנְהַג אֶת־כָּל־מִקְנֵהוּ וְאֶת־
כָּל־רְכֻשׁוֹ אֲשֶׁר רָכָשׁ מִקְנֵה קִנְיָנוֹ אֲשֶׁר רָכַשׁ בְּפַדַּן אֲרָם
יט לָבוֹא אֶל־יִצְחָק אָבִיו אַרְצָה כְּנָעַן: וְלָבָן הָלַךְ לִגְזֹז אֶת־
כ צֹאנוֹ וַתִּגְנֹב רָחֵל אֶת־הַתְּרָפִים אֲשֶׁר לְאָבִיהָ: וַיִּגְנֹב יַעֲקֹב

31:19 וַתִּגְנֹב רָחֵל *Raḥel had stolen* – We are reminded of an earlier episode (see note on Gen. 25:22). Yitzḥak, we recall, loved Esav; Rivka loved Yaakov. At least one possible explanation, offered by Abrabanel (commentary on Gen. 25:28), is that Rivka had been told by God, before the twins were born, that "the greater shall the younger serve" (Gen. 25:23). Hence her attachment to Yaakov, the younger, and her determination that he, not Esav, should have Yitzḥak's blessing.

Here, Raḥel steals her father's *terafim,* "icons" or "household gods," when they leave Lavan to return to the land of Canaan. She does not tell Yaakov that she has done so. The text says explicitly, "Yaakov did not know" (31:32). When Lavan pursues and catches up with them, he accuses Yaakov's party of having

21 Aramean by not telling him that he was running away. He
fled with all he had, crossed the Euphrates, and headed
22 for the hill country of Gilad. On the third day, Lavan was
23 told that Yaakov had fled. Taking his kinsmen with him,
he pursued him for seven days, catching up with him in
24 the hill country of Gilad. That night God came to Lavan
the Aramean in a dream and said to him, "Take care not
25 to say anything to Yaakov for good or for bad." When
Lavan overtook him, Yaakov had pitched his tent in the
hill country, and Lavan and his kinsmen too encamped in
26 the hill country of Gilad. Lavan said to Yaakov, "What
have you done? You have deceived me, and carried off my
27 daughters like captives of the sword. Why did you leave
secretly? Why did you deceive me by not telling me? I
would have sent you off with celebration and song, with
28 tambourines and harps. You did not even let me kiss my
grandchildren and daughters goodbye. You have behaved
29 foolishly. I have the power to harm you, but last night
your father's God spoke to me and said, 'Take care not to
30 say anything to Yaakov for good or for bad.' I realize you
left because you longed so much for your father's house.
31 But why did you steal my gods?" Yaakov answered Lavan,
saying, "I was afraid; I thought you would take your
32 daughters away from me by force. But if you find your
gods with anyone here, they shall not live. In the presence
of our kinsmen, see if there is anything of yours here, and
take it." Yaakov did not know that Raḥel was the one who
33 had stolen them. So Lavan went into Yaakov's tent, Leah's
tent, and the tents of the two female slaves, but found
34 nothing. Leaving Leah's tent, he entered Raḥel's. But
Raḥel had taken the household gods and put them inside
a camel cushion, and was sitting on them; and Lavan
35 rummaged through the tent but found nothing. She said
to her father, "Do not be angry, my lord, but I cannot get
up for you, for the way of women is with me now." So he
36 searched but did not find his household gods. Yaakov
became indignant and confronted Lavan. "What is my

כא אֶת־לֵ֥ב לָבָ֖ן הָאֲרַמִּ֑י עַל־בְּלִי֙ הִגִּ֣יד ל֔וֹ כִּ֥י בֹרֵ֖חַ הֽוּא׃ וַיִּבְרַ֥ח
הוּא֙ וְכָל־אֲשֶׁר־ל֔וֹ וַיָּ֖קָם וַיַּעֲבֹ֣ר אֶת־הַנָּהָ֑ר וַיָּ֥שֶׂם אֶת־פָּנָ֖יו
כב כג הַ֥ר הַגִּלְעָֽד׃ וַיֻּגַּ֥ד לְלָבָ֖ן בַּיּ֣וֹם הַשְּׁלִישִׁ֑י כִּ֥י בָרַ֖ח יַעֲקֹֽב׃ וַיִּקַּ֤ח
אֶת־אֶחָיו֙ עִמּ֔וֹ וַיִּרְדֹּ֣ף אַחֲרָ֔יו דֶּ֖רֶךְ שִׁבְעַ֣ת יָמִ֑ים וַיַּדְבֵּ֥ק אֹת֖וֹ
כד בְּהַ֥ר הַגִּלְעָֽד׃ וַיָּבֹ֧א אֱלֹהִ֛ים אֶל־לָבָ֥ן הָאֲרַמִּ֖י בַּחֲלֹ֣ם הַלָּ֑יְלָה
וַיֹּ֣אמֶר ל֗וֹ הִשָּׁ֧מֶר לְךָ֛ פֶּן־תְּדַבֵּ֥ר עִֽם־יַעֲקֹ֖ב מִטּ֥וֹב עַד־רָֽע׃
כה וַיַּשֵּׂ֥ג לָבָ֖ן אֶֽת־יַעֲקֹ֑ב וְיַעֲקֹ֗ב תָּקַ֤ע אֶת־אָהֳלוֹ֙ בָּהָ֔ר וְלָבָ֛ן
כו תָּקַ֥ע אֶת־אֶחָ֖יו בְּהַ֥ר הַגִּלְעָֽד׃ וַיֹּ֤אמֶר לָבָן֙ לְיַעֲקֹ֔ב מֶ֣ה עָשִׂ֔יתָ
כז וַתִּגְנֹ֖ב אֶת־לְבָבִ֑י וַתְּנַהֵג֙ אֶת־בְּנֹתַ֔י כִּשְׁבֻי֖וֹת חָֽרֶב׃ לָ֤מָּה
נַחְבֵּ֙אתָ֙ לִבְרֹ֔חַ וַתִּגְנֹ֖ב אֹתִ֑י וְלֹא־הִגַּ֣דְתָּ לִּ֔י וָֽאֲשַׁלֵּחֲךָ֛ בְּשִׂמְחָ֥ה
כח וּבְשִׁרִ֖ים בְּתֹ֥ף וּבְכִנּֽוֹר׃ וְלֹ֣א נְטַשְׁתַּ֔נִי לְנַשֵּׁ֥ק לְבָנַ֖י וְלִבְנֹתָ֑י
כט עַתָּ֖ה הִסְכַּ֥לְתָּ עֲשֽׂוֹ׃ יֶשׁ־לְאֵ֣ל יָדִ֔י לַעֲשׂ֥וֹת עִמָּכֶ֖ם רָ֑ע וֵאלֹהֵ֨י
אֲבִיכֶ֜ם אֶ֣מֶשׁ ׀ אָמַ֧ר אֵלַ֣י לֵאמֹ֗ר הִשָּׁ֧מֶר לְךָ֛ מִדַּבֵּ֥ר עִֽם־יַעֲקֹ֖ב
ל מִטּ֥וֹב עַד־רָֽע׃ וְעַתָּה֙ הָלֹ֣ךְ הָלַ֔כְתָּ כִּֽי־נִכְסֹ֥ף נִכְסַ֖פְתָּה לְבֵ֣ית
לא אָבִ֑יךָ לָ֥מָּה גָנַ֖בְתָּ אֶת־אֱלֹהָֽי׃ וַיַּ֥עַן יַעֲקֹ֖ב וַיֹּ֣אמֶר לְלָבָ֑ן כִּ֣י
לב יָרֵ֔אתִי כִּ֣י אָמַ֔רְתִּי פֶּן־תִּגְזֹ֥ל אֶת־בְּנוֹתֶ֖יךָ מֵעִמִּֽי׃ עִ֠ם אֲשֶׁ֨ר
תִּמְצָ֜א אֶת־אֱלֹהֶ֘יךָ֮ לֹ֣א יִֽחְיֶה֒ נֶ֣גֶד אַחֵ֧ינוּ הַכֶּר־לְךָ֛ מָ֥ה עִמָּדִ֖י
לג וְקַֽח־לָ֑ךְ וְלֹֽא־יָדַ֣ע יַעֲקֹ֔ב כִּ֥י רָחֵ֖ל גְּנָבָֽתַם׃ וַיָּבֹ֨א לָבָ֜ן בְּאֹ֥הֶל־
יַעֲקֹ֣ב ׀ וּבְאֹ֣הֶל לֵאָ֗ה וּבְאֹ֛הֶל שְׁתֵּ֥י הָאֲמָהֹ֖ת וְלֹ֣א מָצָ֑א וַיֵּצֵא֙
לד מֵאֹ֣הֶל לֵאָ֔ה וַיָּבֹ֖א בְּאֹ֥הֶל רָחֵֽל׃ וְרָחֵ֞ל לָקְחָ֣ה אֶת־הַתְּרָפִ֗ים
וַתְּשִׂמֵ֛ם בְּכַ֥ר הַגָּמָ֖ל וַתֵּ֣שֶׁב עֲלֵיהֶ֑ם וַיְמַשֵּׁ֥שׁ לָבָ֛ן אֶת־כָּל־
לה הָאֹ֖הֶל וְלֹ֥א מָצָֽא׃ וַתֹּ֣אמֶר אֶל־אָבִ֗יהָ אַל־יִ֙חַר֙ בְּעֵינֵ֣י אֲדֹנִ֔י
כִּ֣י ל֤וֹא אוּכַל֙ לָק֣וּם מִפָּנֶ֔יךָ כִּי־דֶ֥רֶךְ נָשִׁ֖ים לִ֑י וַיְחַפֵּ֕שׂ וְלֹ֥א
לו מָצָ֖א אֶת־הַתְּרָפִֽים׃ וַיִּ֥חַר לְיַעֲקֹ֖ב וַיָּ֣רֶב בְּלָבָ֑ן וַיַּ֤עַן יַעֲקֹב֙

crime?" he asked Lavan. "What wrong did I do that you
37 come chasing after me? You have rummaged through all
my possessions. What have you found that belongs to
your house? Put it here in front of my kinsmen and yours
38 and let them decide between the two of us! For the
twenty years I was with you, your sheep and goats did not
miscarry. Not once did I take a ram from your flock as
39 food. I never brought you an animal torn by wild beasts. I
bore the loss myself. Whether it was stolen by day or by
40 night you demanded payment from me. By day I was
ravaged by the heat; at night by the freezing cold. Sleep
41 fled from my eyes. Twenty years I spent working in your
household – fourteen for your two daughters and six for
42 your flock – and ten times you changed my wages. Had
the God of my father – the God of Avraham, the Fear of
Yitzḥak – not been with me, you would have sent me
away empty-handed. But God saw my plight and the toil
43 of my hands, and He rebuked you last night." Then Lavan SHEVI'I
spoke up and said to Yaakov, "The daughters are my
daughters. The children are my children. The flocks are
my flocks. All that you see is mine. But what can I do now
about my daughters or the children they have borne?

---

gave them the capacity for self-sacrifice. Moshe taught them to be passionate fighters for justice. But Yaakov gives them this: the knowledge that precisely when you feel most alone, God is still with you, giving you the courage to hope and the strength to dream.

31:43 וְכֹל אֲשֶׁר־אַתָּה רֹאֶה לִי הוּא *All that you see is mine* – It turns out that everything Lavan has ostensibly given Yaakov, in his own mind he has not given at all. Lavan treats Yaakov as his property, his slave. He is a non-person. In his eyes Yaakov has no rights, no independent existence. He has given Yaakov his daughters in marriage but still claims that they and their children belong to him, not Yaakov. He has given Yaakov an agreement as to the animals that will be his as his wages, yet still he insists that "the flocks are my flocks." Put this way, we begin to see Yaakov in a new light. Yaakov stands for minorities and small nations everywhere. Yaakov is the refusal to let large powers crush the few, the weak, the refugee. Yaakov refuses to define himself as a slave, someone else's property. He maintains his inner dignity and freedom. He contributes to other people's

לז וַיֹּאמֶר לְלָבָן מַה־פִּשְׁעִי מַה חַטָּאתִי כִּי דָלַקְתָּ אַחֲרָי׃ כִּֽי־
מִשַּׁשְׁתָּ אֶת־כָּל־כֵּלַי מַה־מָּצָאתָ מִכֹּל כְּלֵי־בֵיתֶךָ שִׂים כֹּה
לח נֶגֶד אַחַי וְאַחֶיךָ וְיוֹכִיחוּ בֵּין שְׁנֵינוּ׃ זֶה עֶשְׂרִים שָׁנָה אָנֹכִי
עִמָּךְ רְחֵלֶיךָ וְעִזֶּיךָ לֹא שִׁכֵּלוּ וְאֵילֵי צֹאנְךָ לֹא אָכָלְתִּי׃
לט טְרֵפָה לֹא־הֵבֵאתִי אֵלֶיךָ אָנֹכִי אֲחַטֶּנָּה מִיָּדִי תְּבַקְשֶׁנָּה
מ גְּנֻבְתִי יוֹם וּגְנֻבְתִי לָיְלָה׃ הָיִיתִי בַיּוֹם אֲכָלַנִי חֹרֶב וְקֶרַח
מא בַּלָּיְלָה וַתִּדַּד שְׁנָתִי מֵעֵינָי׃ זֶה־לִּי עֶשְׂרִים שָׁנָה בְּבֵיתֶךָ
עֲבַדְתִּיךָ אַרְבַּע־עֶשְׂרֵה שָׁנָה בִּשְׁתֵּי בְנֹתֶיךָ וְשֵׁשׁ שָׁנִים
מב בְּצֹאנֶךָ וַתַּחֲלֵף אֶת־מַשְׂכֻּרְתִּי עֲשֶׂרֶת מֹנִים׃ לוּלֵי אֱלֹהֵי
אָבִי אֱלֹהֵי אַבְרָהָם וּפַחַד יִצְחָק הָיָה לִי כִּי עַתָּה רֵיקָם
שִׁלַּחְתָּנִי אֶת־עָנְיִי וְאֶת־יְגִיעַ כַּפַּי רָאָה אֱלֹהִים וַיּוֹכַח אָמֶשׁ׃
מג וַיַּעַן לָבָן וַיֹּאמֶר אֶל־יַעֲקֹב הַבָּנוֹת בְּנֹתַי וְהַבָּנִים בָּנַי וְהַצֹּאן שביעי
צֹאנִי וְכֹל אֲשֶׁר־אַתָּה רֹאֶה לִי־הוּא וְלִבְנֹתַי מָה־אֶעֱשֶׂה

---

harm, or heal. Lavan is charged "not to say anything to Yaakov for good or for bad" (31:24). Raḥel's own silence and Yaakov's careless speech may cost them everything.

31:42 לוּלֵי אֱלֹהֵי אָבִי...הָיָה לִי *Had the God of my father... not been with me* – Yaakov is not what Noaḥ was: "righteous... a person of integrity in his generation," one who "walked with God" (Gen. 6:9). He does not, like Avraham, leave his land, his birthplace, and his father's house in response to a divine call. He does not, like Yitzḥak, offer himself up as a sacrifice. Nor does he have the burning sense of justice and willingness to intervene that we see in the vignettes of Moshe's early life. Yet we are defined for all time as the descendants of Yaakov, the children of Israel. Faith and courage may falter at certain moments. But the legacy of Yaakov is always with us.

Yaakov becomes the father of the people who will have their closest encounter with God in what Moshe is later to describe as "a barren, howling waste" (Deut. 32:10). Uniquely, Jews have survived a whole series of exiles, and though at first they said, "How can we sing the LORD's song on foreign soil?" (Ps. 137:4) they discovered that the *Shekhina*, the Divine Presence, was still with them. Though they had lost everything else, they had not lost contact with God. They could still discover that "the LORD is in this place – and I did not know it!" (Gen. 28:16).

Avraham gave Jews the courage to challenge the idols of the age. Yitzḥak

44 Come now, let us make a covenant, you and I, and let it be
45 a witness between us." So Yaakov took a stone and set it
46 up as a pillar. Yaakov said to his kinsmen, "Gather stones."
They took stones and made a mound, and there by the
47 mound they ate. Lavan called it Yegar Sahaduta, while
48 Yaakov called it Galed. Lavan said, "This mound is a
witness between me and you this day." That is why it is
49 called Galed. It is also called Mitzpa because he said,
"May the Lord keep watch between me and you when
50 we are out of each other's sight. If you mistreat my
daughters or take other wives besides my daughters, even
though no one else is present, remember that God is the
51 witness between me and you." Lavan said to Yaakov,
"Here is the mound and here is the pillar I have set up
52 between us. This mound is a witness, and the pillar is a
witness, that I will not go past this mound on your side
and that you will not go past this mound and pillar on my
53 side with intent to do harm. May the God of Avraham,
the god of Naḥor, and the god of their father be our
54 judge." Yaakov swore by the Fear of his father Yitzḥak. He
offered a sacrifice on the hill and invited his kinsmen to
break bread. And they ate and spent the night upon that
55 hill. Lavan rose early the next morning. He kissed his MAFTIR
grandchildren and daughters goodbye and blessed them.
32 1 Lavan then left to return home. Yaakov continued on his

---

or guarantor of a particular relationship." Having cemented their peace agreement, Lavan invoking "the god of Naḥor," Yaakov "the Fear of Yitzḥak" (Gen. 31:53), Lavan is able to kiss his grandchildren, bless his daughters, before sending them on their way.

31:55 וַיְבָרֶךְ אֶתְהֶם *And blessed them* – The story ends, against all odds, with Lavan's blessing. If Lavan is the eternal paradigm of hatred of conspicuously successful minorities, then Yaakov is the eternal paradigm of the human capacity to survive the hatred of others. In this strange way Yaakov becomes the voice of hope in the conversation of humankind, the living proof that hate never wins the final victory; freedom does.

מד לָאֵלֶּה הַיּוֹם אוֹ לִבְנֵיהֶן אֲשֶׁר יָלָדוּ: וְעַתָּה לְכָה נִכְרְתָה
מה בְרִית אֲנִי וָאָתָּה וְהָיָה לְעֵד בֵּינִי וּבֵינֶךָ: וַיִּקַּח יַעֲקֹב אָבֶן
מו וַיְרִימֶהָ מַצֵּבָה: וַיֹּאמֶר יַעֲקֹב לְאֶחָיו לִקְטוּ אֲבָנִים וַיִּקְחוּ
מז אֲבָנִים וַיַּעֲשׂוּ־גָל וַיֹּאכְלוּ שָׁם עַל־הַגָּל: וַיִּקְרָא־לוֹ לָבָן יְגַר
מח שָׂהֲדוּתָא וְיַעֲקֹב קָרָא לוֹ גַּלְעֵד: וַיֹּאמֶר לָבָן הַגַּל הַזֶּה עֵד
מט בֵּינִי וּבֵינְךָ הַיּוֹם עַל־כֵּן קָרָא־שְׁמוֹ גַּלְעֵד: וְהַמִּצְפָּה אֲשֶׁר
נ אָמַר יִצֶף יְהוָה בֵּינִי וּבֵינֶךָ כִּי נִסָּתֵר אִישׁ מֵרֵעֵהוּ: אִם־תְּעַנֶּה
אֶת־בְּנֹתַי וְאִם־תִּקַּח נָשִׁים עַל־בְּנֹתַי אֵין אִישׁ עִמָּנוּ רְאֵה
נא אֱלֹהִים עֵד בֵּינִי וּבֵינֶךָ: וַיֹּאמֶר לָבָן לְיַעֲקֹב הִנֵּה ׀ הַגַּל הַזֶּה
נב וְהִנֵּה הַמַּצֵּבָה אֲשֶׁר יָרִיתִי בֵּינִי וּבֵינֶךָ: עֵד הַגַּל הַזֶּה וְעֵדָה
הַמַּצֵּבָה אִם־אָנִי לֹא־אֶעֱבֹר אֵלֶיךָ אֶת־הַגַּל הַזֶּה וְאִם־אַתָּה
לֹא־תַעֲבֹר אֵלַי אֶת־הַגַּל הַזֶּה וְאֶת־הַמַּצֵּבָה הַזֹּאת לְרָעָה:
נג אֱלֹהֵי אַבְרָהָם וֵאלֹהֵי נָחוֹר יִשְׁפְּטוּ בֵינֵינוּ אֱלֹהֵי אֲבִיהֶם
נד וַיִּשָּׁבַע יַעֲקֹב בְּפַחַד אָבִיו יִצְחָק: וַיִּזְבַּח יַעֲקֹב זֶבַח
בָּהָר וַיִּקְרָא לְאֶחָיו לֶאֱכָל־לָחֶם וַיֹּאכְלוּ לֶחֶם וַיָּלִינוּ בָּהָר:
נה וַיַּשְׁכֵּם לָבָן בַּבֹּקֶר וַיְנַשֵּׁק לְבָנָיו וְלִבְנוֹתָיו וַיְבָרֶךְ אֶתְהֶם וַיֵּלֶךְ מפטיר
לב א וַיָּשָׁב לָבָן לִמְקֹמוֹ: וְיַעֲקֹב הָלַךְ לְדַרְכּוֹ וַיִּפְגְּעוּ־בוֹ מַלְאֲכֵי

---

prosperity but he defeats every attempt to be exploited. Yaakov is the voice that says: I too am human. I too have rights. I too am free.

31:50 רְאֵה אֱלֹהִים עֵד *God is the witness* – The key word in biblical ethics is *brit*, or "covenant." In a covenant, parties come together to pledge themselves to a code of mutual loyalty and protection. Like a contract, a covenant is born in the recognition that no individual can achieve his or her ends in isolation. Because we are different, we each have strengths that others need, and weaknesses that others can remedy. Unlike a contract, however, a covenant is more than a narrow legal agreement bound by mutual interest. It involves a commitment to go beyond the letter of the law, and to sustain the relationship even at times when it seems to go against the interests of one of the parties. As Daniel Elazar puts it, "in its heart of hearts, a covenant is an agreement in which a higher moral force, traditionally God, is either a direct party to

2 way – and angels of God encountered him. When he
saw them, Yaakov said, "This is God's own camp," and he
named the place Maḥanayim.

The haftara for Parashat Vayetze is on page 1432.

---

appears: *vayifga* (28:11) – *vayifgeu* (32:2). Our verses here are recited, in some traditions, after *Tefillat HaDerekh*, the Traveler's Prayer.

From Yaakov we know we can find God not only in the holy or familiar places but also in the midst of a journey, alone at night. The most profound of all spiritual experiences, the base of all others, is the knowledge that, even when we are far from all that is familiar, we are never alone.

ב אֱלֹהִים: וַיֹּאמֶר יַעֲקֹב כַּאֲשֶׁר רָאָם מַחֲנֵה אֱלֹהִים זֶה וַיִּקְרָא
שֵׁם־הַמָּקוֹם הַהוּא מַחֲנָיִם:

The הפטרה *for* פרשת ויצא *is on page 1433.*

32:2 וַיִּקְרָא שֵׁם־הַמָּקוֹם הַהוּא מַחֲנָיִם *He named the place Maḥanayim* – Literally, "two camps," a phrase that will gain new resonances in the coming days (Gen. 32:7–8, 11). At the start of this *parasha,* we saw Yaakov fleeing from Esav and about to meet Lavan; now he is fleeing in the opposite direction, from Lavan to Esav, a meeting that fills him with dread (32:7). This journey, like Yaakov's first, contains an encounter with angels and a place of God; in both, the same verb

Parashat Vayishlaḥ

32 3 Yaakov sent messengers ahead of him to his brother Esav
4 in the land of Se'ir, the country of Edom. He instructed
them, "Say the following to my lord Esav: 'Your servant
Yaakov says, "I have been staying with Lavan; until now I
5 have remained there. And I have acquired cattle, donkeys,

---

was born holding on to Esav's heel. He bought Esav's birthright. He stole Esav's blessing. When his blind father asked him who he was, he replied, "I am Esav your firstborn" (Gen. 27:19). Yaakov was the child who wanted to be Esav.

Esav was the elder. Esav was strong, physically mature, a hunter. Above all, Esav was his father's favorite (25:28). Yaakov is the paradigm of what the French literary theorist and anthropologist René Girard called *mimetic desire*, meaning, we want what someone else wants, because we want to *be* that someone else. Most of us have such feelings from time to time. Girard argues that this has been the main source of conflict throughout history. The tension between Yaakov and Esav rises to an unbearable intensity when Esav discovers that Yaakov has taken the blessing Yitzḥak has reserved for him, and vows to kill Yaakov when Yitzḥak is no longer alive.

Yaakov flees to Lavan, where he encounters more conflict; he is on his way home when he hears that Esav is coming to meet him. In an unusually strong description of emotion the Torah tells us that Yaakov is "acutely afraid and distressed" (32:7) – frightened, no doubt, that Esav will try to kill him, and perhaps distressed that his brother's animosity is not without cause.

As long as Yaakov seeks to be Esav there is tension, conflict, rivalry. Esav feels cheated; Yaakov feels fear. On this night, about to meet Esav again after an absence of twenty-two years, Yaakov, "left alone," wrestles with himself. Finally, he throws off the image of Esav, the person he wants to be, which he has carried with him all these years. This is the critical moment in Yaakov's life.

After his wrestling match, Yaakov undergoes a change of personality. He gives back to Esav the blessing he has taken from him. The previous day he has given him back the material blessing by sending him a wealth of livestock. Now he gives him back the blessing that said, "Be lord over your brothers, and may your mother's sons bow down to you" (27:29). He even uses the words "Please accept *my blessing*." The result is that the two brothers meet and part in peace.

Yaakov, more than anyone else in Genesis, is surrounded by conflict. We have to resolve the tension in ourselves before we can do so for others. This may involve great struggle, but the outcome

פרשת וישלח

לב ג וַיִּשְׁלַח יַעֲקֹב מַלְאָכִים לְפָנָיו אֶל־עֵשָׂו אָחִיו אַרְצָה שֵׂעִיר ל
ד שְׂדֵה אֱדוֹם: וַיְצַו אֹתָם לֵאמֹר כֹּה תֹאמְרוּן לַאדֹנִי לְעֵשָׂו
כֹּה אָמַר עַבְדְּךָ יַעֲקֹב עִם־לָבָן גַּרְתִּי וָאֵחַר עַד־עָתָּה:
ה וַיְהִי־לִי שׁוֹר וַחֲמוֹר צֹאן וְעֶבֶד וְשִׁפְחָה וָאֶשְׁלְחָה לְהַגִּיד

VAYISHLAḤ

Vayishlaḥ tells the story of the meeting, after an estrangement that lasted twenty-two years, between Yaakov and Esav. Hearing that his brother is coming to meet him with a force of four hundred men, Yaakov is "acutely afraid and distressed" (Gen. 32:7). That night he wrestles with a mysterious stranger, in an episode that ends with his being given a new name, Yisrael. The next day the two brothers meet, not in violence but in peace. They embrace and then go their separate ways.

Yaakov's safe return to the land is not to be a happy ending, however. Dina, Yaakov's daughter – the only Jewish daughter mentioned in the entire patriarchal narrative – leaves the safety of home to go out to "see the daughters of the land" (34:1). She is raped and abducted by a local prince, Shekhem. The aftermath of this event brings untold suffering and bloodshed, and an apparent end to Yaakov's chance of living peacefully with his neighbors.

Following the death of Yitzḥak, the *parasha* that gives Israel its name ends with a proud genealogy of the descendants of Esav. Yaakov does not emerge as the triumphant, dominant brother. His heroism lies in the image of him wrestling with the angel of destiny and inner conflict and saying, "I will not let you go until you bless me" (32:26). That is how he rescues hope from catastrophe – as Jews have always done. Our darkest nights have always been preludes to our most creative dawns.

YAAKOV FACES ESAV

Yaakov is about to meet his brother Esav after an estrangement of twenty-two years. In a way unparalleled anywhere else in Genesis, the narrative builds up suspense. Yaakov is afraid. He divides his camp into two, that at least one may survive. He prays. He sends emissaries with gifts. He takes his family and possessions across the river. He makes every possible preparation, takes every possible precaution. Yet still we sense his disquiet. It is then that one of the most haunting scenes in the Torah takes place.

To understand the mysterious episode of Yaakov's nocturnal struggle with the stranger, we must step back and observe Yaakov's life trajectory. Yaakov

sheep, and male and female servants. I am sending this
6 message to my lord to find favor in your eyes.'"" And
when the messengers returned to Yaakov, they said, "We
came to your brother Esav. He is on his way to meet you,
7 and with him, four hundred men." Yaakov was acutely
afraid and distressed. He divided the people with him
into two camps, along with the flocks, the cattle, and the
8 camels. "If Esav comes and attacks one camp," he thought,
9 "the other camp may still survive." Then Yaakov prayed,
"God of my father Avraham and God of my father Yitzḥak,
LORD, You who said to me, 'Go back to the land where
10 you were born and I will deal well with you,' I am
unworthy of all the kindnesses and the faithfulness that
You have bestowed upon Your servant. When I crossed
the Jordan I had only my staff, and now I have become
11 two camps. Rescue me, I pray, from my brother's hand,
from the hand of Esav. I am afraid he will come and kill us
12 all, mothers and children alike. Yet You said, 'I will deal
well with you and make your descendants countless, like
13 the sand of the sea.'" He spent the night there. Then, from SHENI
what he had at hand, he selected a gift for his brother
14 Esav: two hundred female goats, twenty male goats, two
15 hundred ewes, twenty rams, thirty milk camels and their
young, forty cows, ten bulls, twenty female donkeys, and

---

overrides another (the prohibition against killing) does not mean that, faced with such a choice, Yaakov is without qualms. Sometimes being moral means that one experiences distress at having to make such a choice. Doing the right thing may mean that one does not feel remorse or guilt, but one still feels regret or grief about the action that needs to be taken.

A moral system which leaves room for the existence of dilemmas is one that does not attempt to eliminate the complexities of the moral life. In a conflict between two rights or two wrongs, there may be a proper way to act – the lesser of two evils, or the greater of two goods – but this does not cancel out all emotional pain. These mixed feelings were born thousands of years ago, when Yaakov, father of the Jewish people, experienced not only the physical fear of defeat but the moral distress of victory. Only those who are capable of feeling both can defend their bodies without endangering their souls.

ו לַאדֹנִי לִמְצֹא־חֵן בְּעֵינֶיךָ׃ וַיָּשֻׁבוּ הַמַּלְאָכִים אֶל־יַעֲקֹב
לֵאמֹר בָּאנוּ אֶל־אָחִיךָ אֶל־עֵשָׂו וְגַם הֹלֵךְ לִקְרָאתְךָ
ז וְאַרְבַּע־מֵאוֹת אִישׁ עִמּוֹ׃ וַיִּירָא יַעֲקֹב מְאֹד וַיֵּצֶר לוֹ וַיַּחַץ
אֶת־הָעָם אֲשֶׁר־אִתּוֹ וְאֶת־הַצֹּאן וְאֶת־הַבָּקָר וְהַגְּמַלִּים
ח לִשְׁנֵי מַחֲנוֹת׃ וַיֹּאמֶר אִם־יָבוֹא עֵשָׂו אֶל־הַמַּחֲנֶה הָאַחַת
ט וְהִכָּהוּ וְהָיָה הַמַּחֲנֶה הַנִּשְׁאָר לִפְלֵיטָה׃ וַיֹּאמֶר יַעֲקֹב אֱלֹהֵי
אָבִי אַבְרָהָם וֵאלֹהֵי אָבִי יִצְחָק יהוה הָאֹמֵר אֵלַי שׁוּב
י לְאַרְצְךָ וּלְמוֹלַדְתְּךָ וְאֵיטִיבָה עִמָּךְ׃ קָטֹנְתִּי מִכֹּל הַחֲסָדִים
וּמִכָּל־הָאֱמֶת אֲשֶׁר עָשִׂיתָ אֶת־עַבְדֶּךָ כִּי בְמַקְלִי עָבַרְתִּי
יא אֶת־הַיַּרְדֵּן הַזֶּה וְעַתָּה הָיִיתִי לִשְׁנֵי מַחֲנוֹת׃ הַצִּילֵנִי נָא מִיַּד
אָחִי מִיַּד עֵשָׂו כִּי־יָרֵא אָנֹכִי אֹתוֹ פֶּן־יָבוֹא וְהִכַּנִי אֵם עַל־
יב בָּנִים׃ וְאַתָּה אָמַרְתָּ הֵיטֵב אֵיטִיב עִמָּךְ וְשַׂמְתִּי אֶת־זַרְעֲךָ
יג כְּחוֹל הַיָּם אֲשֶׁר לֹא־יִסָּפֵר מֵרֹב׃ וַיָּלֶן שָׁם בַּלַּיְלָה הַהוּא שני
יד וַיִּקַּח מִן־הַבָּא בְיָדוֹ מִנְחָה לְעֵשָׂו אָחִיו׃ עִזִּים מָאתַיִם
טו וּתְיָשִׁים עֶשְׂרִים רְחֵלִים מָאתַיִם וְאֵילִים עֶשְׂרִים׃ גְּמַלִּים
מֵינִיקוֹת וּבְנֵיהֶם שְׁלֹשִׁים פָּרוֹת אַרְבָּעִים וּפָרִים עֲשָׂרָה

is an immense strength. No one is stronger than the person who knows who and what he is.

32:7 וַיִּירָא יַעֲקֹב מְאֹד וַיֵּצֶר לוֹ *Yaakov was acutely afraid and distressed* – Why the duplication? What is the difference between fear and distress? According to Rashi (quoting Bereshit Rabba 76:2), the first is a physical anxiety, the second a moral one. It is one thing to fear one's own death, quite another to contemplate being the cause of someone else's. If Esav were to try to kill Yaakov, he would be justified in fighting back, if necessary at the cost of Esav's life. Yet Yaakov is distressed at the possibility of being forced to kill *even if it is entirely justified.*

What we are encountering here is the concept of a moral dilemma. This phrase is often used imprecisely, to mean a moral problem, a difficult ethical decision. In numerous situations, two duties conflict and we have meta-halakhic principles to tell us which takes priority. There is always a decision-procedure and thus a determinate answer to the question "What should I do?"

But a dilemma is not simply a conflict. It arises in cases of conflict between right and right, or between wrong and wrong. The fact that one principle (self-defense)

16 ten male donkeys. He put them in the care of his servants,
each herd by itself, and he told the servants, "Go on ahead
17 of me. Keep a space between the herds." He instructed
the first, "When my brother Esav meets you and asks, 'To
whom do you belong? Where are you going? Who owns
18 all these animals ahead of you?' you must say, 'They
belong to your servant Yaakov; they are a gift sent to my
19 lord Esav – and he is coming behind us.'" He likewise
instructed the second and third and all the others who
followed the herds, "You shall say the same thing to Esav
20 when you meet him. Also say, 'Your servant Yaakov is
coming behind us.'" He thought, "I will pacify him with
these gifts I am sending on ahead. Then I will face him.
21 Perhaps he will accept me." So the gifts went on ahead of
22 him, while he remained in the camp that night. That night
Yaakov got up and took his two wives, two maidservants,
23 and eleven sons and crossed the ford of the Yabok. He
took them and crossed the stream with them and then
24 brought across all that he had. And Yaakov was left alone.

never be bought at the cost of others. That knowledge alone – that Yaakov and Esav can each have their own blessings without envying one another – is enough to remove many, even most, of the conflicts by which people cause one another pain.

32:24 וַיֵּאָבֵק אִישׁ עִמּוֹ *And a man wrestled with him* – Everything about this story is mysterious. It takes place at a liminal time between night and dawn, at an unspecified location, with no explanation, after the most elaborately conceived and executed preparations for any event in Genesis. Yaakov has prepared himself for three things: diplomacy, war, and prayer. He has sent huge gifts of cattle to appease Esav's anger. He has divided his camp in two so that even if one is destroyed the other might survive. He has prayed to God. He has covered every eventuality, adopted every strategy, anticipated, seemingly, every outcome – but not the one that actually happens, the appearance of an unnamed adversary who fights with him.

There is no way we can make ourselves immune to crises. That is the human condition and we cannot escape it. Faith is not certainty; it is the courage to live with uncertainty. Indeed, that is why we need faith: because life is uncertain. Even in the twenty-first century when we know so much about the universe, cosmology, the human genome,

טז אֲתֹנֹ֥ת עֶשְׂרִ֖ים וַעְיָרִ֥ם עֲשָׂרָֽה׃ וַיִּתֵּן֙ בְּיַד־עֲבָדָ֔יו עֵ֥דֶר עֵ֖דֶר
לְבַדּ֑וֹ וַיֹּ֤אמֶר אֶל־עֲבָדָיו֙ עִבְר֣וּ לְפָנַ֔י וְרֶ֣וַח תָּשִׂ֔ימוּ בֵּ֥ין עֵ֖דֶר
יז וּבֵ֥ין עֵֽדֶר׃ וַיְצַ֥ו אֶת־הָרִאשׁ֖וֹן לֵאמֹ֑ר כִּ֣י יִֽפְגָּשְׁךָ֞ עֵשָׂ֣ו אָחִ֗י
וּשְׁאֵֽלְךָ֙ לֵאמֹ֔ר לְמִי־אַ֙תָּה֙ וְאָ֣נָה תֵלֵ֔ךְ וּלְמִ֖י אֵ֥לֶּה לְפָנֶֽיךָ׃
יח וְאָֽמַרְתָּ֙ לְעַבְדְּךָ֣ לְיַעֲקֹ֔ב מִנְחָ֥ה הִוא֙ שְׁלוּחָ֔ה לַאדֹנִ֖י לְעֵשָׂ֑ו
יט וְהִנֵּ֥ה גַם־ה֖וּא אַחֲרֵֽינוּ׃ וַיְצַ֞ו גַּ֣ם אֶת־הַשֵּׁנִ֗י גַּ֚ם אֶת־הַשְּׁלִישִׁ֔י
גַּ֚ם אֶת־כׇּל־הַהֹ֣לְכִ֔ים אַחֲרֵ֥י הָעֲדָרִ֖ים לֵאמֹ֑ר כַּדָּבָ֤ר הַזֶּה֙
כ תְּדַבְּר֣וּן אֶל־עֵשָׂ֔ו בְּמֹצַאֲכֶ֖ם אֹתֽוֹ׃ וַאֲמַרְתֶּ֕ם גַּ֗ם הִנֵּ֛ה עַבְדְּךָ֥
יַעֲקֹ֖ב אַחֲרֵ֑ינוּ כִּֽי־אָמַ֞ר אֲכַפְּרָ֣ה פָנָ֗יו בַּמִּנְחָה֙ הַהֹלֶ֣כֶת לְפָנָ֔י
כא וְאַחֲרֵי־כֵן֙ אֶרְאֶ֣ה פָנָ֔יו אוּלַ֖י יִשָּׂ֥א פָנָֽי׃ וַתַּעֲבֹ֥ר הַמִּנְחָ֖ה עַל־
כב פָּנָ֑יו וְה֛וּא לָ֥ן בַּלַּֽיְלָה־הַה֖וּא בַּֽמַּחֲנֶֽה׃ וַיָּ֣קׇם ׀ בַּלַּ֣יְלָה ה֗וּא
וַיִּקַּ֞ח אֶת־שְׁתֵּ֤י נָשָׁיו֙ וְאֶת־שְׁתֵּ֣י שִׁפְחֹתָ֔יו וְאֶת־אַחַ֥ד עָשָׂ֖ר
כג יְלָדָ֑יו וַֽיַּעֲבֹ֔ר אֵ֖ת מַעֲבַ֥ר יַבֹּֽק׃ וַיִּקָּחֵ֔ם וַיַּעֲבִרֵ֖ם אֶת־הַנָּ֑חַל
כד וַיַּעֲבֵ֖ר אֶת־אֲשֶׁר־לֽוֹ׃ וַיִּוָּתֵ֥ר יַעֲקֹ֖ב לְבַדּ֑וֹ וַיֵּאָבֵ֥ק אִישׁ֙ עִמּ֔וֹ

32:24 וַיִּוָּתֵר יַעֲקֹב לְבַדּוֹ *And Yaakov was left alone* – Rashi's grandson, Rashbam, gives an extraordinary interpretation of Yaakov's wrestling match (commentary on Gen. 32). Fearing the confrontation with Esav, Yaakov wanted to run away. He was already apart from his family when God sent an angel to wrestle with him to prevent him from doing so. On this reading, God is teaching Yaakov how to wrestle with his fears and defeat them.

What actually happens the next day, when Yaakov finally comes face-to-face with Esav? Instead of attacking him, Esav runs to meet him and embraces him (Gen. 32:1). There is no anger, no violence, no lingering trace of resentment. Everything Yaakov fears fails to happen. Is this mere coincidence, happenstance? Were Yaakov's fears simply misplaced? I believe the Torah is teaching a deeper truth, that once Yaakov has resolved the conflict within himself, he removes the source of tension between himself and Esav. Even animals sense fear. Predators chase those who run away. The way of safety is to stay calm and still.

An inner sense of self-confidence and trust does not mean that one will never have to fight battles. Economics and politics are intrinsically conflictual. Much of life is a zero-sum competition for scarce goods in which some win, some lose. But spiritual goods – love, trust, friendship, the pursuit of knowledge – are not zero-sum. The more we share, the more we have. So our deepest psychological and spiritual goods need

25 And a man wrestled with him until dawn. When he saw
that he could not overpower him, the man wrenched
Yaakov's hip in its socket so that the socket of Yaakov's
26 hip was strained as he wrestled with the man. "Let me go,"
said the man, "for dawn is breaking." But he replied, "I
27 will not let you go unless you bless me." "What is your
28 name?" asked the man. "Yaakov," he replied. "No longer
will your name be Yaakov, but Yisrael," said the man, "for
you have struggled with God and with men and have
29 prevailed." Yaakov asked, "Please tell me your name." But
he said, "Why do you ask my name?" and he blessed him
30 there. Yaakov named the place Peniel, "for I have seen SHELISHI
31 God face-to-face and yet my life has been spared." The
sun was rising on him as he moved on from Penuel,
32 limping on his thigh. That is why, to this day, the Israelites
do not eat the sciatic nerve by the hip socket: because he
33 1 wrenched Yaakov's hip socket at the sciatic nerve. Yaakov

---

Esav and Lavan. Now, the text seems to suggest, he has struggled with God Himself.

32:31 צֹלֵעַ עַל־יְרֵכוֹ *Limping on his thigh* – Whatever Yaakov's struggle represents, it leaves a lasting mark. Crisis is real; the suffering to which it gives rise can cut deep. Even when you survive, you limp; long afterward, perhaps for a lifetime, you bear the scars. But they are honorable scars. They tell that you fought and won, and greater is one who fought and won than one who, fearing confrontation, takes the path of least resistance and submits.

The heroes of our faith do not live charmed lives. They suffer exiles, know danger, have their hopes disappointed and their expectations delayed. They fight, they struggle, but they neither give in nor give up. They are not serene. Sometimes they laugh in disbelief; there are times when they fear, tremble, weep, and even give way to anger. For they are human beings, not angels; they are people with whom we can identify, not saints to be worshipped. Yaakov teaches us that we cannot preempt crisis, nor should we minimize it, but we can survive it, thus becoming worthy of bearing the name of one who has struggled with God and with men and prevailed.

32:32 עַד הַיּוֹם הַזֶּה *To this day* – This passage above all others has seemed, at times of trauma, to epitomize Jewish destiny. For the Sages of the second century CE, it described the confrontation between Jews and Rome. For Ramban in thirteenth-century Spain, it foreshadowed

כה עַד עֲלוֹת הַשָּׁחַר: וַיַּרְא כִּי לֹא יָכֹל לוֹ וַיִּגַּע בְּכַף־יְרֵכוֹ וַתֵּקַע
כו כַּף־יֶרֶךְ יַעֲקֹב בְּהֵאָבְקוֹ עִמּוֹ: וַיֹּאמֶר שַׁלְּחֵנִי כִּי עָלָה הַשָּׁחַר
כז וַיֹּאמֶר לֹא אֲשַׁלֵּחֲךָ כִּי אִם־בֵּרַכְתָּנִי: וַיֹּאמֶר אֵלָיו מַה־שְּׁמֶךָ
כח וַיֹּאמֶר יַעֲקֹב: וַיֹּאמֶר לֹא יַעֲקֹב יֵאָמֵר עוֹד שִׁמְךָ כִּי אִם־
כט יִשְׂרָאֵל כִּי־שָׂרִיתָ עִם־אֱלֹהִים וְעִם־אֲנָשִׁים וַתּוּכָל: וַיִּשְׁאַל
יַעֲקֹב וַיֹּאמֶר הַגִּידָה־נָּא שְׁמֶךָ וַיֹּאמֶר לָמָּה זֶּה תִּשְׁאַל לִשְׁמִי
ל וַיְבָרֶךְ אֹתוֹ שָׁם: וַיִּקְרָא יַעֲקֹב שֵׁם הַמָּקוֹם פְּנִיאֵל כִּי־רָאִיתִי שלישי
לא אֱלֹהִים פָּנִים אֶל־פָּנִים וַתִּנָּצֵל נַפְשִׁי: וַיִּזְרַח־לוֹ הַשֶּׁמֶשׁ
לב כַּאֲשֶׁר עָבַר אֶת־פְּנוּאֵל וְהוּא צֹלֵעַ עַל־יְרֵכוֹ: עַל־כֵּן לֹא־
יֹאכְלוּ בְנֵי־יִשְׂרָאֵל אֶת־גִּיד הַנָּשֶׁה אֲשֶׁר עַל־כַּף הַיָּרֵךְ עַד
לג א הַיּוֹם הַזֶּה כִּי נָגַע בְּכַף־יֶרֶךְ יַעֲקֹב בְּגִיד הַנָּשֶׁה: וַיִּשָּׂא יַעֲקֹב

---

and the workings of the human brain, there is one thing we do not know and never will: what tomorrow will bring.

32:26 לֹא אֲשַׁלֵּחֲךָ כִּי אִם בֵּרַכְתָּנִי *I will not let you go unless you bless me* – These words of Yaakov to the angel lie at the very core of surviving crisis. Each of us knows from personal experience that events that seemed disappointing, painful, even humiliating at the time can be the most important in our lives. Through them we learned how to try harder next time; or they taught us a truth about ourselves; or they shifted our life into a new and more fruitful direction. We learn, not from our successes but from our failures. We mature and grow strong and become more understanding and forgiving through the mistakes we make. A protected life is a fragile and superficial life. Strength comes from knowing the worst and refusing to give in. Yaakov/Yisrael has bequeathed us many gifts, but few more valuable than the obstinacy and resilience that can face hard times and say of them: "I will not let you go until you bless me." I will not give up or move on until I have extracted something positive from this pain and turned it into blessing.

32:30 כִּי רָאִיתִי אֱלֹהִים *For I have seen God* – Throughout the episode we do not even know who the adversary is. The text itself calls him "a man"; according to the prophet Hoshea, it is an angel (Hos. 12:4); for the Sages, it is the guardian angel of Esav (Bereshit Rabba 77:3, cited in Rashi on Gen. 32:24). Yaakov himself has no doubt. It is God. The adversary himself implies as much when he gives Yaakov the name Yisrael: "for you have struggled with God and with men and have prevailed." Hitherto, we have seen Yaakov struggle with human beings, with

looked up – and saw Esav coming with his four hundred
men. So he divided the children among Leah, Raḥel, and
2 the two maidservants. He put the maidservants and their
children first, Leah and her children behind, and Raḥel
3 and Yosef at the rear. And he went ahead of them, bowing
down to the ground seven times until he came close to
4 his brother. Esav ran to meet him and embraced him. He
threw his arms around his neck and kissed him, and they
5 wept. Esav looked up and saw the women and children.
He asked, "Who are these with you?" Yaakov answered,
"They are the children God has graciously given your
6 servant." Then the maidservants and their children came
7 forward and bowed down. Leah and her children came REVI'I
forward and bowed down. And last, Yosef and Raḥel
8 approached and bowed down. Esav asked, "What did you
mean by all the procession that I met before?" He said,
9 "To find favor in your eyes, my lord." But Esav said, "I
have plenty, my brother. Let what is yours remain yours."
10 "No, please," said Yaakov. "If I have found favor in your
eyes, accept this gift from me, for seeing your face is like
seeing the face of God, and you have shown me favor.

---

of Yaakov's struggle and the mark it left on him. It is fundamental to who we are as Jews.

33:4 וַיָּרָץ עֵשָׂו לִקְרָאתוֹ וַיְחַבְּקֵהוּ *Esav ran… and embraced him* – When Esav finally appears, all Yaakov's fears of the previous day turn out to be unfounded. He "runs" to meet Yaakov, throws his arms around his neck, kisses him, and weeps. That is not to say that Yaakov's fears were irrational. They were not. After all, Esav had vowed revenge twenty-two years before ("The days of mourning for my father are approaching… and then I will kill my brother Yaakov" [Gen. 27:41]). Esav, however, turns out to be an impulsive man who lives in the mood of the moment. He has none of Cassius's "lean and hungry look" or Iago's cold calculation. He is quick to anger, quick to forget. The anticlimax when the brothers meet is consistent with Esav's character, if not with Yaakov's fears.

33:10 כִּרְאֹת פְּנֵי אֱלֹהִים *Like seeing the face of God* – These words of Yaakov's echo his remark after the wrestling match, "Yaakov named the place Peniel, 'for I have seen God *face*-to-*face* and yet my life has been spared'" (Gen. 32:30). Altogether, chapters 32 and 33 echo time and again

עֵינָיו וַיַּרְא וְהִנֵּה עֵשָׂו בָּא וְעִמּוֹ אַרְבַּע מֵאוֹת אִישׁ וַיַּחַץ
ב אֶת־הַיְלָדִים עַל־לֵאָה וְעַל־רָחֵל וְעַל שְׁתֵּי הַשְּׁפָחוֹת: וַיָּשֶׂם
אֶת־הַשְּׁפָחוֹת וְאֶת־יַלְדֵיהֶן רִאשֹׁנָה וְאֶת־לֵאָה וִילָדֶיהָ
ג אַחֲרֹנִים וְאֶת־רָחֵל וְאֶת־יוֹסֵף אַחֲרֹנִים: וְהוּא עָבַר לִפְנֵיהֶם
ד וַיִּשְׁתַּחוּ אַרְצָה שֶׁבַע פְּעָמִים עַד־גִּשְׁתּוֹ עַד־אָחִיו: וַיָּרָץ
עֵשָׂו לִקְרָאתוֹ וַיְחַבְּקֵהוּ וַיִּפֹּל עַל־צַוָּארָו וַיִּשָּׁקֵהוּ וַיִּבְכּוּ:
ה וַיִּשָּׂא אֶת־עֵינָיו וַיַּרְא אֶת־הַנָּשִׁים וְאֶת־הַיְלָדִים וַיֹּאמֶר
מִי־אֵלֶּה לָּךְ וַיֹּאמַר הַיְלָדִים אֲשֶׁר־חָנַן אֱלֹהִים אֶת־עַבְדֶּךָ:
ו ז וַתִּגַּשְׁןָ הַשְּׁפָחוֹת הֵנָּה וְיַלְדֵיהֶן וַתִּשְׁתַּחֲוֶיןָ: וַתִּגַּשׁ גַּם־לֵאָה רביעי
ח וִילָדֶיהָ וַיִּשְׁתַּחֲווּ וְאַחַר נִגַּשׁ יוֹסֵף וְרָחֵל וַיִּשְׁתַּחֲווּ: וַיֹּאמֶר
מִי לְךָ כָּל־הַמַּחֲנֶה הַזֶּה אֲשֶׁר פָּגָשְׁתִּי וַיֹּאמֶר לִמְצֹא־חֵן
ט בְּעֵינֵי אֲדֹנִי: וַיֹּאמֶר עֵשָׂו יֶשׁ־לִי רָב אָחִי יְהִי לְךָ אֲשֶׁר־לָךְ:
י וַיֹּאמֶר יַעֲקֹב אַל־נָא אִם־נָא מָצָאתִי חֵן בְּעֵינֶיךָ וְלָקַחְתָּ
מִנְחָתִי מִיָּדִי כִּי עַל־כֵּן רָאִיתִי פָנֶיךָ כִּרְאֹת פְּנֵי אֱלֹהִים

---

the persecution of Jews at the hands of medieval Christianity. It is no less evocative in the wake of the Jewish encounter with Enlightenment. It is a heavy burden to be singled out by God to be different.

Man tries to flee from chosenness. The Israelites in the wilderness try to return to Egypt. Yona seeks to escape his prophetic mission. Yeḥezkel predicts a time when Israel will want to "be like the nations, like the families of the lands" (Ezek. 20:32). In the nineteenth century, Jews sought in normalization a release from the destiny of differentness. But in the Holocaust, their way was blocked by the angel of death. We will never fully understand those dark biblical passages in which God turns His people toward life by the threat of death. Why must Jews endure suffering to continue to exist as a people? That remains a mystery no prophet has ever fathomed. Like Yaakov after his struggle, the Jewish people limps, still scarred by that encounter. But those who remain have, like Yaakov, taken up the journey again, no longer seeking flight from fate but instead determined to survive as Jews. The State of Israel, Diaspora Jewish activism, and a renascent Orthodoxy all express this fundamental affirmation. The Jewish people has returned to its perennial vocation: to be Israel, the people of the covenant, though this means struggling with God and with man. Thus the earliest law given to Israel alone is a reminder

11 Please accept my blessing that was brought to you, for
God has been gracious to me, and I have everything."

33:11 קַח נָא אֶת בִּרְכָתִי *Please accept my blessing* – First, Yaakov "went ahead of them, bowing down to the ground seven times" (Gen. 33:3). "Then the maidservants and their children came forward and bowed down. Leah and her children came forward and bowed down. And last, Yosef and Raḥel approached and bowed down" (33:6–7). The threefold repetition is significant, as is Yaakov's cautious way of presenting his family.

No less striking is Yaakov's use of language. Five times he calls Esav *adoni*, "my lord." Twice he calls himself Esav's *eved*, "servant." As with his physical gesture of sevenfold prostration, so with his sevenfold use of the words *adon* and *eved*, this is the choreography of self-abasement.

How are we to connect this with the wrestling match of the previous night? Surely Yaakov won a victory over his adversary. At the very least he refused to let him go until he received a blessing. The new name implied that henceforth Yaakov should have no doubts about his ability to survive any conflict. A man who has "struggled with God and with men and prevailed" is not one who needs to bow down to anyone. We would have expected Yaakov to show confidence rather than servility.

Esav initially refuses Yaakov's gifts, saying, "I have plenty [*yesh li rav*], my brother." Yaakov's reply is enigmatic:

> "No, please … if I have found favor in your eyes, accept this gift [*minḥa*] from me.… Please accept my blessing that was brought to you, for God has been gracious to me, and I have everything [*yesh li khol*]." (33:10–11)

We noted above that Yaakov is symbolically giving back the blessing he took all those years before. "Please accept [not just 'my gift' but also] '*my blessing*.'" The herds and flocks he sends to Esav represent wealth ("dew of heaven, the cream of the land," 27:28). The sevenfold bowing and calling himself "your servant" and Esav "my lord" represent power ("Be lord over your brothers, and may your mother's sons bow down to you," 27:29). Yaakov's blessing (28:3–4) has nothing to do with wealth or power. It has to do with children and a land – children he will instruct in the ways of the covenant and a land in which his descendants would strive to construct a covenantal society based on justice and compassion, law and love. Yaakov alters Esav's words, "I have plenty," into his own "I have everything" – meaning, "I no longer need either wealth or power to be complete."

He has, instead, to be himself, a person whose ears are attuned to the call of the Author of all. He has to be true to that which cannot be bought by wealth or controlled by power, namely, the human spirit as the breath of God, human dignity as the image of God.

יא וַתִּרְצֵנִי׃ קַח־נָא אֶת־בִּרְכָתִי֙ אֲשֶׁ֣ר הֻבָ֣את לָ֔ךְ כִּֽי־חַנַּ֥נִי

with variants on the word *panim*. This is missed in translation, because *panim* has many forms in Hebrew not evident in English. To take one example, 32:20 contains the Hebrew word *four times* – the second half of the verse, translated hyper-literally, reads: "He thought, 'I will wipe [the anger from] his *face* with these gifts I am sending on ahead of my *face*. Then I will see his *face*. Perhaps he will lift up my *face*.'" There is a drama here and it has to do with faces: the face of Esav, of Yaakov, and of God Himself. We are reminded that when Yaakov received Esav's blessing, Yitzḥak was blind. Yitzḥak gave the blessing to Yaakov only because *he could not see Yaakov's face*.

The lives of the patriarchs are significant not only for what they tell us about the past but also for what they tell us about the present – for their challenges are ours. Avraham is the man who has the strength of conviction to stand apart from the culture of his time. What carries him through is love (*ḥesed*) – love of God and, yes, the love of humanity that shines through all his deeds and words. Yitzḥak is the man who knows the reality of sacrifice. He lives, he survives, but not without seeing the knife lifted against him. He knows to the core of his being that to be a child of the covenant is neither easy nor safe. What carries him through is courage (*gevura*) – and for whatever reason, the historical record is clear: to remain Jewish takes courage.

In connection with Yaakov, though, the prophet Mikha speaks of *truth* ("You will show truth to Yaakov" [Mic. 7:20]). This does not imply truth in a cognitive sense (what are the facts?) but rather truth in an existential sense: Who am I? To which story do I belong and what part am I called on to play? The search for cognitive truth is not specific to the Abrahamic covenant. It is the heritage of all mankind. The truth with which Yaakov spends much of his life wrestling is quite different. It is a truth about identity. Central to it are the words *face* (in which mirror do I look to see who I am?), *name* (by which term do I know myself?), and *blessing* (to what destiny am I called?).

It is as if the man with whom he wrestled in the night says to him, "In the past you struggled to be Esav. In the future you will struggle to be yourself. In the past you held on to Esav's heel. In the future you will hold on to God. You will not let go of Him; He will not let go of you. Now let go of Esav so that you can be free to hold on to God." Ours is another face, an alternative destiny, an altogether different blessing from Esav's. The face that is truly ours is the one we see reflected back at us by God. That is the meaning of the priestly blessing "May the Lord *raise His face* toward you and grant you *peace*" (Num. 6:26). Peace comes when we let go of the desire to be someone else and see our reflection in the face of God.

12 Yaakov pressed him, and he accepted. Then Esav said,
13 "Let us be on our way. I will go beside you." But Yaakov
said, "My lord knows that the children are fragile, and I
must care for the nursing sheep and cattle. If they are
14 driven hard even for one day, all the flocks will die. Let
my lord go on ahead of his servant, and I will go slowly at
the pace of the livestock before me and the pace of the
15 children until I come to my lord in Se'ir." Esav said, "Let
me leave some of my people with you." "Why do that?"
16 he said. "Just let me find favor in the eyes of my lord." So
17 that day Esav started back on his way to Se'ir, and Yaakov
journeyed on to Sukkot. There he built himself a house
and made huts for his livestock; that is why he named the
18 place Sukkot. Thus Yaakov, having come from
Padan Aram, arrived safely at the town of Shekhem in
19 Canaan, and he set up camp within sight of the town. He
bought the plot of ground where he pitched his tent from
the sons of Ḥamor, father of Shekhem, for one hundred
20 *kesita* of silver. There he erected an altar and named it El
34 1 Elohei Yisrael. Dina, the daughter whom Leah ḤAMISHI
had borne to Yaakov, went out to see the daughters of the
2 land. When Shekhem son of Ḥamor the Hivite, prince of
the land, saw her, he took hold of her, lay with her, and

---

he does not call the place "House" (as in Beit El or Beit Leḥem). *He calls it Sukkot, "cattle sheds."* It is as if Yaakov, consciously or unconsciously, already knows that to live the life of the covenant means to be ready to move on, to travel, to journey, to grow.

We will learn from the laws of the Jubilee (Lev. 26:34–35) that if we live as if the land is permanently ours, our stay there will be temporary. If we live as if it is only temporarily so, we will live there permanently. In this world of time and change, growth and decay, only God and His word are permanent. One of the most poignant lines in the book of Psalms – a verse cherished by the French Jewish philosopher Emmanuel Levinas – says, "I am but a stranger on earth – do not hide Your commandments from me" (Ps. 119:19). To be a Jew is to stay light on your feet, ready to begin the next stage of the journey, literally or metaphorically. An Englishman's home is his castle, they used to say. But a Jew's home is a tent, a tabernacle, a sukka. We know that life on earth is a temporary dwelling. That is why we value each moment and its newness.

יב אֱלֹהִים וְכִי יֶשׁ־לִי־כֹל וַיִּפְצַר־בּוֹ וַיִּקָּח: וַיֹּאמֶר נִסְעָה וְנֵלֵכָה
יג וְאֵלְכָה לְנֶגְדֶּךָ: וַיֹּאמֶר אֵלָיו אֲדֹנִי יֹדֵעַ כִּי־הַיְלָדִים רַכִּים
וְהַצֹּאן וְהַבָּקָר עָלוֹת עָלָי וּדְפָקוּם יוֹם אֶחָד וָמֵתוּ כָּל־הַצֹּאן:
יד יַעֲבָר־נָא אֲדֹנִי לִפְנֵי עַבְדּוֹ וַאֲנִי אֶתְנָהֲלָה לְאִטִּי לְרֶגֶל
הַמְּלָאכָה אֲשֶׁר־לְפָנַי וּלְרֶגֶל הַיְלָדִים עַד אֲשֶׁר־אָבֹא אֶל־
טו אֲדֹנִי שֵׂעִירָה: וַיֹּאמֶר עֵשָׂו אַצִּיגָה־נָּא עִמְּךָ מִן־הָעָם
טז אֲשֶׁר אִתִּי וַיֹּאמֶר לָמָּה זֶּה אֶמְצָא־חֵן בְּעֵינֵי אֲדֹנִי: וַיָּשָׁב
יז בַּיּוֹם הַהוּא עֵשָׂו לְדַרְכּוֹ שֵׂעִירָה: וְיַעֲקֹב נָסַע סֻכֹּתָה וַיִּבֶן
לוֹ בָּיִת וּלְמִקְנֵהוּ עָשָׂה סֻכֹּת עַל־כֵּן קָרָא שֵׁם־הַמָּקוֹם
יח סֻכּוֹת: וַיָּבֹא יַעֲקֹב שָׁלֵם עִיר שְׁכֶם אֲשֶׁר בְּאֶרֶץ לא
יט כְּנַעַן בְּבֹאוֹ מִפַּדַּן אֲרָם וַיִּחַן אֶת־פְּנֵי הָעִיר: וַיִּקֶן אֶת־חֶלְקַת
הַשָּׂדֶה אֲשֶׁר נָטָה־שָׁם אָהֳלוֹ מִיַּד בְּנֵי־חֲמוֹר אֲבִי שְׁכֶם
כ בְּמֵאָה קְשִׂיטָה: וַיַּצֶּב־שָׁם מִזְבֵּחַ וַיִּקְרָא־לוֹ אֵל אֱלֹהֵי
לד א יִשְׂרָאֵל: וַתֵּצֵא דִינָה בַּת־לֵאָה אֲשֶׁר יָלְדָה לְיַעֲקֹב חמישי
ב לִרְאוֹת בִּבְנוֹת הָאָרֶץ: וַיַּרְא אֹתָהּ שְׁכֶם בֶּן־חֲמוֹר הַחִוִּי

33:17 וְיַעֲקֹב נָסַע *Yaakov journeyed on* – At almost every significant juncture in our history we have wrestled with civilizations who worshipped the gods of nature: wealth or power. Israel never knew the power of great empires, their invincible armies and weapons of destruction. When it longed for those things, as in the days of Shlomo, it lost its way.

Israel's strength never lay in itself, but in that which was other and greater than itself: the power that transcends all earthly powers, and the wealth that is not physical but spiritual, a matter of mind and heart. Despite this, Jews have often wished to be someone else, the Esavs of the age.

That is a feeling we must ultimately reject. The Torah does not ask us to think badly of Esav. To the contrary, it commands us: "Do not despise an Edomite [i.e., a descendant of Esav], for he is your kin" (Deut. 23:8). It does, however, ask us to wrestle alone, at night, in the depths of our soul, and discover the face, the name, and the blessing that are ours.

33:17 עַל־כֵּן קָרָא שֵׁם־הַמָּקוֹם סֻכּוֹת *He named the place Sukkot* – The point is linguistic, but the message is remarkable. *Yaakov has just become the first member of the covenantal family to build a house, yet*

3 violated her. He became deeply drawn to Dina, Yaakov's
daughter, and, in love with the young woman, he spoke to
4 her heart. Shekhem said to his father Ḥamor, "Take this
5 girl as a wife for me." When Yaakov heard that he had
defiled his daughter Dina, his sons were in the field with
his livestock, and so he stayed silent until they came
6 home. Shekhem's father Ḥamor came to Yaakov to speak
7 with him. Meanwhile, Yaakov's sons, having heard what
had happened, came back from the field. They were
shocked and furious, for Shekhem had committed an
outrage in Israel by sleeping with Yaakov's daughter. Such
8 a thing cannot be done! But Ḥamor spoke with them and
said, "My son Shekhem has his heart set upon your
9 daughter. Please give her to him as his wife. Intermarry
with us. Give us your daughters and take our daughters
10 for yourselves. Settle with us. The land is open to you. Live
11 here, trade here, acquire property here." Then Shekhem
said to Dina's father and brothers, "Let me but find favor

---

itself, it too will need to have recourse to violence. "The irony is that successful defense against a power-maximizing aggressor requires a society to become more like the society that threatens it. Power can be stopped only by power."

There are, in other words, four possible outcomes: (1) destruction, (2) subjugation, (3) withdrawal, and (4) imitation. "In every one of these outcomes," writes Schmookler, *"the ways of power are spread throughout the system."* If you introduce a single violent tribe into the region, violence will eventually prevail, however the other tribes choose to respond. That is the tragedy of the human condition.

Shekhem's single act of violence against Dina forces two of Yaakov's sons into violent reprisal. In the end everyone involved is either contaminated or dead. It is indicative of the moral depth of the Torah that it does not hide this terrible truth from us by depicting one side as guilty, the other as innocent.

Violence defiles us all. It did then. It does now.

34:3 וַתִּדְבַּק נַפְשׁוֹ בְּדִינָה *He became deeply drawn to Dina* – Compare this with the description of Amnon, son of King David, who rapes his half-sister Tamar. That story too is a tale of bloody revenge. But the text says about Amnon that after raping Tamar, he "hated her with a fierce hatred; his hatred for her was fiercer than the love he had felt toward her. And Amnon said to her, 'Get up! Be gone!'" (II Sam. 13:15). Shekhem is not like that at all. He falls in love with Dina and wants to marry her.

ג נְשִׂיא הָאָרֶץ וַיִּקַּח אֹתָהּ וַיִּשְׁכַּב אֹתָהּ וַיְעַנֶּהָ׃ וַתִּדְבַּק נַפְשׁוֹ
בְּדִינָה בַּת־יַעֲקֹב וַיֶּאֱהַב אֶת־הַנַּעֲרָ וַיְדַבֵּר עַל־לֵב הַנַּעֲרָ׃
ד וַיֹּאמֶר שְׁכֶם אֶל־חֲמוֹר אָבִיו לֵאמֹר קַח־לִי אֶת־הַיַּלְדָּה
ה הַזֹּאת לְאִשָּׁה׃ וְיַעֲקֹב שָׁמַע כִּי טִמֵּא אֶת־דִּינָה בִתּוֹ וּבָנָיו
ו הָיוּ אֶת־מִקְנֵהוּ בַּשָּׂדֶה וְהֶחֱרִשׁ יַעֲקֹב עַד־בֹּאָם׃ וַיֵּצֵא חֲמוֹר
ז אֲבִי־שְׁכֶם אֶל־יַעֲקֹב לְדַבֵּר אִתּוֹ׃ וּבְנֵי יַעֲקֹב בָּאוּ מִן־הַשָּׂדֶה
כְּשָׁמְעָם וַיִּתְעַצְּבוּ הָאֲנָשִׁים וַיִּחַר לָהֶם מְאֹד כִּי נְבָלָה עָשָׂה
ח בְיִשְׂרָאֵל לִשְׁכַּב אֶת־בַּת־יַעֲקֹב וְכֵן לֹא יֵעָשֶׂה׃ וַיְדַבֵּר חֲמוֹר
אִתָּם לֵאמֹר שְׁכֶם בְּנִי חָשְׁקָה נַפְשׁוֹ בְּבִתְּכֶם תְּנוּ נָא אֹתָהּ
ט לוֹ לְאִשָּׁה׃ וְהִתְחַתְּנוּ אֹתָנוּ בְּנֹתֵיכֶם תִּתְּנוּ־לָנוּ וְאֶת־בְּנֹתֵינוּ
י תִּקְחוּ לָכֶם׃ וְאִתָּנוּ תֵּשֵׁבוּ וְהָאָרֶץ תִּהְיֶה לִפְנֵיכֶם שְׁבוּ
יא וּסְחָרוּהָ וְהֵאָחֲזוּ בָּהּ׃ וַיֹּאמֶר שְׁכֶם אֶל־אָבִיהָ וְאֶל־אַחֶיהָ

DINA AND SHEKHEM

The story of Dina seems to lack any kind of moral message. No one comes out of it well. Shekhem, the prince, would seem to be the chief villain. It is he who abducts and rapes Dina in the first place. Ḥamor, his father, fails to reprimand him or order Dina's release. Shimon and Levi are guilty of a horrendous act of violence. The other brothers engage in looting the town. Yaakov seems passive throughout. He neither acts nor instructs his sons on how to act. Even Dina herself seems at best to have been guilty of carelessness in going out into what is clearly a dangerous neighborhood – recall that both Avraham and Yitzḥak, her great-grandfather and grandfather, feared for their own lives because of the lawlessness of the times, particularly with regard to the abduction of women.

Who is in the right and who in the wrong is left conspicuously undecided in the text. The overall effect is a story with no irredeemable villains and no stainless heroes. Why then is it told at all? Stories do not appear in the Torah merely because they happened. *Torah* means "teaching," "instruction," "guidance." What teaching does the Torah want us to draw from this narrative out of which no one emerges well?

There is an important thought experiment devised by Andrew Schmookler known as the parable of the tribes. Imagine a group of tribes living close to one another. All choose the way of peace except one that is willing to use violence to achieve its ends. What happens to the peace-seeking tribes? One is defeated and destroyed by the violent tribe. A second is conquered and subjugated. A third flees to some remote and inaccessible place. If the fourth seeks to defend

12 in your eyes and I will give whatever you ask. Set the
bridal price and gifts as high as you like. I will give
whatever you ask of me; only give me the young woman
13 as my wife." Yaakov's sons responded to Shekhem and his
father Ḥamor, and they spoke deceptively: he had, after
14 all, defiled their sister Dina. They told them, "We cannot
do this. To give our sister to an uncircumcised man would
15 be a disgrace to us. Only on one condition will we agree
with you: If you become like us, circumcising all your
16 males, then we will give you our daughters and take your
daughters for ourselves. We will live with you and become
17 one people. If you do not agree to be circumcised, we will
18 take our daughter and go." Their words gratified Ḥamor
19 and his son Shekhem. The young man, the most honored
of his father's family, lost no time in doing it, because he
20 longed for Yaakov's daughter. Ḥamor and his son
Shekhem came to the town gate and spoke to their fellow
21 townsmen. "These people are friendly toward us," they
said. "Let them live in the land and trade in it. We have
space enough for them. We can marry their daughters
22 and they can marry ours. But only on one condition will
they agree to dwell with us as one people. Every male
23 among us must be circumcised as they are. Will not their
livestock, property, and all their animals be ours? Let us,
then, agree to their terms and let them settle among us."
24 All the people who went out by the town gate listened to
Ḥamor and his son Shekhem, and all the males who went
25 out by the town gate were circumcised. On the third day,
when the people were weak from pain, two of Yaakov's

perception of their predicament. The text, however, does not demonize the people of Shekhem and does not paint any of Yaakov's family in a completely positive light. It uses the same word for "deceptively" that it has used previously about Yaakov taking Esav's blessing and Lavan substituting Leah for Raḥel. In its description of all the characters – from Dina herself to her excessively violent rescuers, to the plundering other brothers and the passive Yaakov – the text seems written deliberately to alienate our sympathies.

יב אֶמְצָא־חֵן בְּעֵינֵיכֶם וַאֲשֶׁר תֹּאמְרוּ אֵלַי אֶתֵּן: הַרְבּוּ עָלַי
מְאֹד מֹהַר וּמַתָּן וְאֶתְּנָה כַּאֲשֶׁר תֹּאמְרוּ אֵלָי וּתְנוּ־לִי אֶת־
יג הַנַּעֲרָ לְאִשָּׁה: וַיַּעֲנוּ בְנֵי־יַעֲקֹב אֶת־שְׁכֶם וְאֶת־חֲמוֹר אָבִיו
יד בְּמִרְמָה וַיְדַבֵּרוּ אֲשֶׁר טִמֵּא אֵת דִּינָה אֲחֹתָם: וַיֹּאמְרוּ
אֲלֵיהֶם לֹא נוּכַל לַעֲשׂוֹת הַדָּבָר הַזֶּה לָתֵת אֶת־אֲחֹתֵנוּ
טו לְאִישׁ אֲשֶׁר־לוֹ עָרְלָה כִּי־חֶרְפָּה הִוא לָנוּ: אַךְ־בְּזֹאת נֵאוֹת
טז לָכֶם אִם תִּהְיוּ כָמֹנוּ לְהִמֹּל לָכֶם כָּל־זָכָר: וְנָתַנּוּ אֶת־בְּנֹתֵינוּ
לָכֶם וְאֶת־בְּנֹתֵיכֶם נִקַּח־לָנוּ וְיָשַׁבְנוּ אִתְּכֶם וְהָיִינוּ לְעַם
יז אֶחָד: וְאִם־לֹא תִשְׁמְעוּ אֵלֵינוּ לְהִמּוֹל וְלָקַחְנוּ אֶת־בִּתֵּנוּ
יח וְהָלָכְנוּ: וַיִּיטְבוּ דִבְרֵיהֶם בְּעֵינֵי חֲמוֹר וּבְעֵינֵי שְׁכֶם בֶּן־חֲמוֹר:
יט וְלֹא־אֵחַר הַנַּעַר לַעֲשׂוֹת הַדָּבָר כִּי חָפֵץ בְּבַת־יַעֲקֹב וְהוּא
כ נִכְבָּד מִכֹּל בֵּית אָבִיו: וַיָּבֹא חֲמוֹר וּשְׁכֶם בְּנוֹ אֶל־שַׁעַר
כא עִירָם וַיְדַבְּרוּ אֶל־אַנְשֵׁי עִירָם לֵאמֹר: הָאֲנָשִׁים הָאֵלֶּה
שְׁלֵמִים הֵם אִתָּנוּ וְיֵשְׁבוּ בָאָרֶץ וְיִסְחֲרוּ אֹתָהּ וְהָאָרֶץ הִנֵּה
רַחֲבַת־יָדַיִם לִפְנֵיהֶם אֶת־בְּנֹתָם נִקַּח־לָנוּ לְנָשִׁים וְאֶת־
כב בְּנֹתֵינוּ נִתֵּן לָהֶם: אַךְ־בְּזֹאת יֵאֹתוּ לָנוּ הָאֲנָשִׁים לָשֶׁבֶת
אִתָּנוּ לִהְיוֹת לְעַם אֶחָד בְּהִמּוֹל לָנוּ כָּל־זָכָר כַּאֲשֶׁר הֵם
כג נִמֹּלִים: מִקְנֵהֶם וְקִנְיָנָם וְכָל־בְּהֶמְתָּם הֲלוֹא לָנוּ הֵם אַךְ
כד נֵאוֹתָה לָהֶם וְיֵשְׁבוּ אִתָּנוּ: וַיִּשְׁמְעוּ אֶל־חֲמוֹר וְאֶל־שְׁכֶם
בְּנוֹ כָּל־יֹצְאֵי שַׁעַר עִירוֹ וַיִּמֹּלוּ כָּל־זָכָר כָּל־יֹצְאֵי שַׁעַר עִירוֹ:
כה וַיְהִי בַיּוֹם הַשְּׁלִישִׁי בִּהְיוֹתָם כֹּאֲבִים וַיִּקְחוּ שְׁנֵי־בְנֵי־יַעֲקֹב

34:13 וַיַּעֲנוּ... אָבִיו בְּמִרְמָה *They spoke deceptively* – Shimon and Levi, Dina's brothers, realize that they must act to rescue her. It is an almost impossible assignment. The hostage-taker is no ordinary individual. As the son of the king, he cannot be confronted directly. The king is unlikely to order his son to release her. The other townspeople, if challenged, will come to the prince's defense. It is Shimon and Levi against the town, two against many. Even were all of Yaakov's sons to be enlisted, they would still be outnumbered. Shimon and Levi must resort to a ruse.

This appears to be the brothers'

sons, Shimon and Levi, Dina's brothers, took their swords,
entered the unsuspecting town, and killed every single
26 male. They killed Ḥamor and his son Shekhem by the
27 sword, took Dina from Shekhem's house and left. Yaakov's
sons came upon the dead and plundered the town that
28 had defiled their sister. They took their flocks, their cattle,
their donkeys, and everything else of theirs in the town
29 and out in the field. Their wealth, their children, and their
women they took captive and looted, and all that was in
30 the houses. Yaakov said to Shimon and Levi, "You have
brought trouble upon me – you have made me odious to
the inhabitants of the land, the Canaanites and Perizzites.
I am few in number, and if they join forces and attack me,
31 I and my household will be destroyed." But they said,
"Should our sister be treated like a whore?"
35 1 God said to Yaakov, "Arise, go up to Beit El. Stay there,
and there build an altar to God, who appeared to you as
2 you fled your brother Esav." Yaakov told his household
and everyone with him, "Be rid of the alien gods you
have with you. Purify yourselves and change your
3 clothes. Then come, let us go up to Beit El, and there
I will make an altar to God, who answered me in my
time of trouble and who has been with me wherever
4 I have gone." They gave Yaakov all the alien gods they
had, and even the rings in their ears, and Yaakov buried
5 them under a terebinth near Shekhem. As they set out,
the terror of God fell on the surrounding towns so that

39a) is not restricted to Israel. It applies to all societies. As Isaac Arama would write in the fifteenth century, any crime known about and allowed to continue ceases to be an offense of individuals only and becomes a sin of the community as a whole (*Akedat Yitzḥak*, Bereshit, Vayera 20, s.v. *UVeMidrash*).

Ramban disagrees (in his commentary on Gen. 34:13). The principle of collective responsibility does not, in his view, apply to non-Jewish societies. The Noahide covenant requires every society to set up courts of law, but it does not imply that a failure to prosecute a wrongdoer involves all members of the society in a capital crime.

שִׁמְעוֹן וְלֵוִי אֲחֵי דִינָה אִישׁ חַרְבּוֹ וַיָּבֹאוּ עַל־הָעִיר בֶּטַח
כו וַיַּהַרְגוּ כָּל־זָכָר׃ וְאֶת־חֲמוֹר וְאֶת־שְׁכֶם בְּנוֹ הָרְגוּ לְפִי־חָרֶב
כז וַיִּקְחוּ אֶת־דִּינָה מִבֵּית שְׁכֶם וַיֵּצֵאוּ׃ בְּנֵי יַעֲקֹב בָּאוּ עַל־
כח הַחֲלָלִים וַיָּבֹזּוּ הָעִיר אֲשֶׁר טִמְּאוּ אֲחוֹתָם׃ אֶת־צֹאנָם
וְאֶת־בְּקָרָם וְאֶת־חֲמֹרֵיהֶם וְאֵת אֲשֶׁר־בָּעִיר וְאֶת־אֲשֶׁר
כט בַּשָּׂדֶה לָקָחוּ׃ וְאֶת־כָּל־חֵילָם וְאֶת־כָּל־טַפָּם וְאֶת־נְשֵׁיהֶם
ל שָׁבוּ וַיָּבֹזּוּ וְאֵת כָּל־אֲשֶׁר בַּבָּיִת׃ וַיֹּאמֶר יַעֲקֹב אֶל־שִׁמְעוֹן
וְאֶל־לֵוִי עֲכַרְתֶּם אֹתִי לְהַבְאִישֵׁנִי בְּיֹשֵׁב הָאָרֶץ בַּכְּנַעֲנִי
וּבַפְּרִזִּי וַאֲנִי מְתֵי מִסְפָּר וְנֶאֶסְפוּ עָלַי וְהִכּוּנִי וְנִשְׁמַדְתִּי אֲנִי
לא וּבֵיתִי׃ וַיֹּאמְרוּ הַכְזוֹנָה יַעֲשֶׂה אֶת־אֲחוֹתֵנוּ׃

לה

א וַיֹּאמֶר אֱלֹהִים אֶל־יַעֲקֹב קוּם עֲלֵה בֵית־אֵל וְשֶׁב־שָׁם וַעֲשֵׂה־
שָׁם מִזְבֵּחַ לָאֵל הַנִּרְאֶה אֵלֶיךָ בְּבָרְחֲךָ מִפְּנֵי עֵשָׂו אָחִיךָ׃
ב וַיֹּאמֶר יַעֲקֹב אֶל־בֵּיתוֹ וְאֶל כָּל־אֲשֶׁר עִמּוֹ הָסִרוּ אֶת־אֱלֹהֵי
ג הַנֵּכָר אֲשֶׁר בְּתֹכְכֶם וְהִטַּהֲרוּ וְהַחֲלִיפוּ שִׂמְלֹתֵיכֶם׃ וְנָקוּמָה
וְנַעֲלֶה בֵּית־אֵל וְאֶעֱשֶׂה־שָּׁם מִזְבֵּחַ לָאֵל הָעֹנֶה אֹתִי בְּיוֹם
ד צָרָתִי וַיְהִי עִמָּדִי בַּדֶּרֶךְ אֲשֶׁר הָלָכְתִּי׃ וַיִּתְּנוּ אֶל־יַעֲקֹב אֵת
כָּל־אֱלֹהֵי הַנֵּכָר אֲשֶׁר בְּיָדָם וְאֶת־הַנְּזָמִים אֲשֶׁר בְּאָזְנֵיהֶם
ה וַיִּטְמֹן אֹתָם יַעֲקֹב תַּחַת הָאֵלָה אֲשֶׁר עִם־שְׁכֶם׃ וַיִּסָּעוּ וַיְהִי ו
חִתַּת אֱלֹהִים עַל־הֶעָרִים אֲשֶׁר סְבִיבוֹתֵיהֶם וְלֹא רָדְפוּ אַחֲרֵי

34:31 הַכְזוֹנָה יַעֲשֶׂה אֶת־אֲחוֹתֵנוּ *Should our sister be treated like a whore?* – Yaakov condemns his sons. His sons reject the criticism. Who is in the right and who in the wrong are left conspicuously undecided in the text. The debate continued and was taken up by two of the greatest rabbis in the Middle Ages. Rambam takes the side of Shimon and Levi. They were justified in what they did, he says. The other members of the town saw what Shekhem had done, knew that he was guilty of a crime, and yet neither brought him to court nor rescued the girl. They were therefore accomplices in his guilt. What Shekhem had done was a capital crime, and by sheltering him the townspeople were implicated (*Hilkhot Melakhim* 9:14). This is, incidentally, a fascinating ruling since it suggests that for Rambam the rule that "all Israel are responsible for one another" (Shevuot

6 no one pursued Yaakov's sons. Yaakov and all the people
with him came to Luz – that is, Beit El – in the land of
7 Canaan. There he built an altar and called the place El Beit
El, because it was there that God had revealed Himself to
8 him as he fled his brother. Devora, Rivka's nurse, died and
was buried under the oak outside Beit El. And so it was
named Oak of Weeping.
9 After Yaakov had returned from Padan Aram God
10 appeared to him again and blessed him. God said to
him, "Your name is Yaakov; no longer shall you be called
Yaakov; Yisrael shall be your name." Thus He named him
11 Yisrael. God said to him: "I am El Shaddai. Be fertile and
multiply. A nation, a community of nations will come to
12 be from you. Of your loins, kings shall come forth. The SHISHI
land I gave to Avraham and Yitzḥak I surely give to you;
13 to your descendants after you I will give the land." God
went up from him at the place where He had spoken
14 with him. Yaakov set up a stone pillar at the place where
God had talked with him, and on it he offered a libation

---

this is what people call you." *Be a prince. Be royalty. Be upright. Be yourself. Do not long to be someone else.* This will turn out to be a challenge not just now but many times in the Jewish future.

Centuries later, the prophet Hoshea says, "But also with Yehuda the LORD has a dispute: He will visit upon Yaakov as he deserves, as befits his deeds – He will repay him. In the womb he grasped his brother by the heel, and with all his strength he struggled with God" (Hos. 12:3–4). The name Yaakov seems to connote a lack of truth, of uprightness. Yirmeyahu uses it to mean someone who practices deception: "Let each man be on guard against his fellow, and let no one trust his own brother, for every brother acts deceitfully [*akov yaakov*], and every friend spreads slander" (Jer. 9:3). *And the fact that the Torah and tradition still use the word Yaakov, not just Israel, tells us that this impulse has not disappeared.* Yaakov seems to have wrestled with this throughout his life, and we still do today. It takes courage to be different, a minority, countercultural. It is easy to live for the moment, like Esav, or to "be like the peoples of the world," as Yeḥezkel says. It can be much harder to stand tall, and true to our principles.

I believe the challenge issued by the angel still echoes today. Are we Yaakov, evasive, embarrassed by who we are? Or are we Yisrael, with the courage to stand upright and walk tall in the path of faith?

ו בְּנֵי יַעֲקֹב׃ וַיָּבֹא יַעֲקֹב לוּזָה אֲשֶׁר בְּאֶרֶץ כְּנַעַן הִוא בֵּית־אֵל
ז הוּא וְכָל־הָעָם אֲשֶׁר־עִמּוֹ׃ וַיִּבֶן שָׁם מִזְבֵּחַ וַיִּקְרָא לַמָּקוֹם
אֵל בֵּית־אֵל כִּי שָׁם נִגְלוּ אֵלָיו הָאֱלֹהִים בְּבָרְחוֹ מִפְּנֵי אָחִיו׃
ח וַתָּמָת דְּבֹרָה מֵינֶקֶת רִבְקָה וַתִּקָּבֵר מִתַּחַת לְבֵית־אֵל תַּחַת
הָאַלּוֹן וַיִּקְרָא שְׁמוֹ אַלּוֹן בָּכוּת׃
ט וַיֵּרָא אֱלֹהִים אֶל־יַעֲקֹב עוֹד בְּבֹאוֹ מִפַּדַּן אֲרָם וַיְבָרֶךְ אֹתוֹ׃ לב
י וַיֹּאמֶר־לוֹ אֱלֹהִים שִׁמְךָ יַעֲקֹב לֹא־יִקָּרֵא שִׁמְךָ עוֹד יַעֲקֹב כִּי
יא אִם־יִשְׂרָאֵל יִהְיֶה שְׁמֶךָ וַיִּקְרָא אֶת־שְׁמוֹ יִשְׂרָאֵל׃ וַיֹּאמֶר לוֹ
אֱלֹהִים אֲנִי אֵל שַׁדַּי פְּרֵה וּרְבֵה גּוֹי וּקְהַל גּוֹיִם יִהְיֶה מִמֶּךָּ
יב וּמְלָכִים מֵחֲלָצֶיךָ יֵצֵאוּ׃ וְאֶת־הָאָרֶץ אֲשֶׁר נָתַתִּי לְאַבְרָהָם ששי
יג וּלְיִצְחָק לְךָ אֶתְּנֶנָּה וּלְזַרְעֲךָ אַחֲרֶיךָ אֶתֵּן אֶת־הָאָרֶץ׃ וַיַּעַל
יד מֵעָלָיו אֱלֹהִים בַּמָּקוֹם אֲשֶׁר־דִּבֶּר אִתּוֹ׃ וַיַּצֵּב יַעֲקֹב מַצֵּבָה
בַּמָּקוֹם אֲשֶׁר־דִּבֶּר אִתּוֹ מַצֶּבֶת אָבֶן וַיַּסֵּךְ עָלֶיהָ נֶסֶךְ וַיִּצֹק

35:8 אַלּוֹן בָּכוּת *Oak of Weeping* – This is our only reference to Rivka's nurse Devora, who presumably took this same path with her charge many years earlier. We are made conscious of the passage of time, and of the death and grief that are bound up with that. This is, as Rambam said, "the way of the world" (*Hilkhot Avel* 13:11). We are embodied souls. We are flesh and blood. We grow old. We lose those we love. Outwardly we struggle to maintain our composure but inwardly we weep. According to one tradition, cited by Rashi, our verse also hints at "another weeping": Rivka's own death.

35:10 וַיִּקְרָא אֶת שְׁמוֹ יִשְׂרָאֵל *Thus He named him Yisrael* – Note, first, that this is not an adjustment of an existing name by the change or addition of a letter, as when God changed Avram's name to Avraham, or Sarai's to Sara. It is an entirely new name, as if to signal that what it represents is a complete change of character. Second, the name change happens not once but twice. Third – and this is the puzzle of puzzles – *having said twice that his name will no longer be Yaakov, the Torah continues to call him Yaakov*. God Himself does so. So do we, every time we pray to the God of Avraham, Yitzḥak, and Yaakov.

How then are we to understand what, first the stranger, then God, said to Yaakov? *Not as a statement but as a request, a challenge, an invitation*. Read it not as "Your name *shall* no longer be Yaakov but Yisrael"; instead read it as "*Let* your name no longer be Yaakov but Yisrael," meaning, "Act in such a way that

15 and poured oil. And Yaakov named the place where God
16 had spoken to him Beit El. From Beit El they moved on.
While they were still some distance from Efrat, Raḥel
17 began to give birth; her labor pains were intense. When
her labor was at its worst, the midwife said to her, "Don't
18 be afraid. You have another son." But she was dying. With
her last breath, she named him Ben Oni; but his father
19 called him Binyamin. So Raḥel died and was buried on
20 the road to Efrat – that is, Beit Leḥem. Yaakov erected a
pillar at her grave. To this day, that pillar marks Raḥel's
21 grave. Yisrael traveled on, pitching his tent beyond
22 Migdal Eder. While Yisrael was staying in that region,
Reuven went and lay with his father's concubine Bilha.
And Yisrael heard –

---

when Avshalom does the same with his father David's concubine (II Sam. 16:21). Rashi, following midrashic tradition, prefers a gentler explanation. When Raḥel dies, Yaakov, who until now slept in her tent, moves his bed to the tent of Bilha, her handmaid. This, for Reuven, is an unbearable provocation. It is bad enough that Yaakov preferred Raḥel to her sister Leah, but intolerable to Reuven that he should prefer her handmaid to his mother. Reuven therefore moves Yaakov's bed from Bilha's tent to Leah's.

Even according to this interpretation, however, it is clear that Yaakov misunderstands the act and believes that his son has in fact usurped his place. He never forgets or forgives the incident and on his deathbed he reminds Reuven of it: "Unstable as water, you shall not excel, for you went up onto your father's bed and defiled it – went up onto my couch" (Gen. 49:4).

Describing the event, the Torah uses an unusual stylistic device. After the words "And Yisrael heard," the masoretic text indicates a paragraph break in the middle of a sentence. The effect is to signal a silence, a complete breakdown in communication. Hence the pathos of the rabbinic interpretation of the passage, which certainly fits all we know about Reuven. He is not seeking to displace Yaakov but rather to draw his father's attention to the hurt and distress of Leah. Yet Yaakov says nothing, giving Reuven no opportunity to clear his name or explain why he did what he did. This is not the first or last time we will meet Reuven as a tragic figure, "seen" but not heard.

טו עָלֶיהָ שָׁמֶן: וַיִּקְרָא יַעֲקֹב אֶת־שֵׁם הַמָּקוֹם אֲשֶׁר דִּבֶּר אִתּוֹ
טז שָׁם אֱלֹהִים בֵּית־אֵל: וַיִּסְעוּ מִבֵּית אֵל וַיְהִי־עוֹד כִּבְרַת־
יז הָאָרֶץ לָבוֹא אֶפְרָתָה וַתֵּלֶד רָחֵל וַתְּקַשׁ בְּלִדְתָּהּ: וַיְהִי
בְהַקְשֹׁתָהּ בְּלִדְתָּהּ וַתֹּאמֶר לָהּ הַמְיַלֶּדֶת אַל־תִּירְאִי כִּי־
יח גַם־זֶה לָךְ בֵּן: וַיְהִי בְּצֵאת נַפְשָׁהּ כִּי מֵתָה וַתִּקְרָא שְׁמוֹ
יט בֶּן־אוֹנִי וְאָבִיו קָרָא־לוֹ בִנְיָמִין: וַתָּמָת רָחֵל וַתִּקָּבֵר בְּדֶרֶךְ
כ אֶפְרָתָה הִוא בֵּית לָחֶם: וַיַּצֵּב יַעֲקֹב מַצֵּבָה עַל־קְבֻרָתָהּ
כא הִוא מַצֶּבֶת קְבֻרַת־רָחֵל עַד־הַיּוֹם: וַיִּסַּע יִשְׂרָאֵל וַיֵּט
כב אָהֳלֹה מֵהָלְאָה לְמִגְדַּל־עֵדֶר: וַיְהִי בִּשְׁכֹּן יִשְׂרָאֵל בָּאָרֶץ
הַהִוא וַיֵּלֶךְ רְאוּבֵן וַיִּשְׁכַּב אֶת־בִּלְהָה פִּילֶגֶשׁ אָבִיו וַיִּשְׁמַע
יִשְׂרָאֵל

35:18 **וְאָבִיו קָרָא־לוֹ בִנְיָמִין** *But his father called him Binyamin* – Yaakov's youngest son, like him, is named twice – Ben Oni, "the son of my suffering," by Raḥel, and Binyamin, "the son of my strength, my right hand," by Yaakov.

To be a Jew is to carry the name Yisrael, meaning "one who struggles with God and men and [yet] prevails." Yisrael, who would not let the stranger go until he blessed him. His is the wrestling match each of us has to undergo when evil threatens or tragedy strikes. Faith is the refusal to let go until you have turned suffering into a blessing. Rabbi Naḥman of Breslov taught a parable:

Sometimes when people are joyous and dancing, they grab a man from outside the dancing circle, one who is sad and melancholy, and force him to join them in their dance. Thus it is with joy: when a person is happy, his own sadness and suffering stand off on the side. But it is a higher achievement to struggle and pursue that sadness, bringing it too into the joy, until it is transformed… you grab hold of this suffering, and force it to join with you in the rejoicing, just as in the parable.

Yaakov's story in our *parasha* ends with a death and a birth. The loss of Raḥel is a wound that will remain with him always. And yet he is challenged again to transform suffering, making even the angel of death join, for a moment, the dance of life.

35:22 **וַיִּשְׁכַּב אֶת בִּלְהָה** *Lay with… Bilha* – Read literally, this suggests that Reuven took his father's place in Bilha's tent – an almost Oedipal act of displacement, as we discover later in the Bible

23 Yaakov had twelve sons. The sons of Leah were Reuven,
Yaakov's firstborn, Shimon, Levi, Yehuda, Yissakhar, and
24 Zevulun. The sons of Raḥel were Yosef and Binyamin.
25 The sons of Raḥel's maid Bilha were Dan and Naftali.
26 The sons of Leah's maid Zilpa were Gad and Asher. These
were the sons of Yaakov, born to him in Padan Aram.
27 Yaakov came home to his father Yitzḥak at Mamre, near
Kiryat Arba – that is, Ḥevron – where Avraham and
28 Yitzḥak had lived as strangers. Yitzḥak lived one hundred
29 and eighty years. Then he breathed his last, and died, and
was gathered to his people, aged, satisfied with his years.
His sons Esav and Yaakov buried him.

36 1 2 These are the descendants of Esav – that is, Edom. Esav

---

Yaakov's meetings with angels are described by the same verb *p-g-a* (28:11, 32:1), which means "a chance encounter," as if they took Yaakov by surprise, which clearly they did. Yaakov's most spiritual moments are ones he does not plan. He is thinking of other things, about what he is leaving behind and what lies ahead of him. He is, as it were, "surprised by God."

Not everyone can aspire to the loving faith and total trust of an Avraham, or to the seclusion of a Yitzḥak. But Yaakov is someone we understand. We can feel his fear, understand his pain at the tensions in his family, and sympathize with his deep longing for a life of quietude and peace (the Sages say about the opening words of the next *parasha* that "Yaakov longed to live in peace, but was immediately thrust into the troubles of Yosef" [Bereshit Rabba 84:3; Rashi on Gen. 37:2]).

The point is not just that Yaakov is the most human of the patriarchs, but rather that at the depths of his despair he is lifted to the greatest heights of spirituality. He is the man who encounters angels. He is the person surprised by God. He is the one who, at the very moments he feels most alone, discovers that he is not alone, that God is with him, that he is accompanied by angels.

The path chosen by Yaakov/Yisrael is not for the fainthearted. *S'iz shver tzu zayn a Yid*, they used to say: "It's hard to be a Jew." In some ways, it still is. It is not easy to face our fears and wrestle with them, refusing to let go until we have turned them into renewed strength and blessing. But speaking personally, I would have it no other way. Judaism is not faith as illusion, seeing the world through rose-tinted lenses as we would wish it to be. It is faith as relentless honesty, seeing evil as evil and fighting it to our human, all-too-human utmost. That struggle is our vocation and what makes us the children of Yaakov.

כג וַיִּהְיוּ בְנֵי־יַעֲקֹב שְׁנֵים עָשָׂר: בְּנֵי לֵאָה בְּכוֹר יַעֲקֹב רְאוּבֵן
כד וְשִׁמְעוֹן וְלֵוִי וִיהוּדָה וְיִשָּׂשכָר וּזְבֻלוּן: בְּנֵי רָחֵל יוֹסֵף וּבִנְיָמִן:
כה כו וּבְנֵי בִלְהָה שִׁפְחַת רָחֵל דָּן וְנַפְתָּלִי: וּבְנֵי זִלְפָּה שִׁפְחַת לֵאָה
כז גָּד וְאָשֵׁר אֵלֶּה בְּנֵי יַעֲקֹב אֲשֶׁר יֻלַּד־לוֹ בְּפַדַּן אֲרָם: וַיָּבֹא
יַעֲקֹב אֶל־יִצְחָק אָבִיו מַמְרֵא קִרְיַת הָאַרְבַּע הִוא חֶבְרוֹן
כח אֲשֶׁר־גָּר־שָׁם אַבְרָהָם וְיִצְחָק: וַיִּהְיוּ יְמֵי יִצְחָק מְאַת שָׁנָה
כט וּשְׁמֹנִים שָׁנָה: וַיִּגְוַע יִצְחָק וַיָּמָת וַיֵּאָסֶף אֶל־עַמָּיו זָקֵן וּשְׂבַע
יָמִים וַיִּקְבְּרוּ אֹתוֹ עֵשָׂו וְיַעֲקֹב בָּנָיו:
לו א ב וְאֵלֶּה תֹּלְדוֹת עֵשָׂו הוּא אֱדוֹם: עֵשָׂו לָקַח אֶת־נָשָׁיו מִבְּנוֹת

THE CHILDREN OF ISRAEL

As the narrative breaks off at a tense moment, we take stock again of a genealogy. On this occasion what we hear is a list of what will become the tribes of Israel. For we are "the children of Israel." Why is Yaakov named as the father of our people, the hero of our faith? We are "the congregation of Yaakov." Yet it is Avraham who began the Jewish journey, Yitzḥak who was willing to be sacrificed, Yosef who will save his family in the years of famine, Moshe who will lead the people out of Egypt and give it its laws. It is Yehoshua who will take the people into the Promised Land, David who will become its greatest king, Shlomo who will build the Temple, and the prophets through the ages who will become the voice of God.

Yaakov is different. What makes him unique is that he has his most intense encounters with God – they are the most dramatic in the whole book of Genesis – in the midst of the journey, alone, at night, far from home, fleeing from one danger to the next, from Esav to Lavan on the outward journey, from Lavan to Esav on his homecoming.

In the midst of the first journey he has the blazing epiphany of the ladder stretching from earth to heaven, with angels ascending and descending, moving him to say on waking, "Truly, the Lord is in this place – and I did not know it.... This is none other than the House of God, and this the gate of the heavens" (Gen. 28:16–17). None of the other patriarchs, not even Moshe, has a vision quite like this.

On the second, in our *parasha,* he has the haunting, enigmatic wrestling match with the man/angel/God, which leaves him limping but permanently transformed – the only person in the Torah to receive from God an entirely new name, Yisrael, which may mean "one who has struggled with God and with men" or "one who has become a prince [*sar*] before God."

took wives from among the daughters of Canaan: Ada
daughter of Eilon the Hittite, and Oholivama daughter
3 of Ana, granddaughter of Tzivon the Hivite – and also
4 Basmat, daughter of Yishmael and sister of Nevayot. Ada
5 bore Elifaz to Esav, and Basmat bore Reuel. Oholivama
bore Yeush, Yalam, and Koraḥ. These were the sons of
6 Esav, born in the land of Canaan. Esav took his wives, sons
and daughters, and all the members of his household,
together with his livestock, his other animals, and all the
possessions he had acquired in Canaan, and he moved to
7 another region, away from his brother Yaakov, for their
possessions were too great for them to remain together;
because of all their livestock, the land where they were
8 living could not support them both. So Esav settled in
9 the hill country of Se'ir. Esav is Edom. These, then, are
the descendants of Esav, ancestor of the Edomites, in the
10 hill country of Se'ir. These are the names of Esav's sons:
Elifaz, son of Esav's wife Ada, and Reuel, son of Esav's
11 wife Basmat. The sons of Elifaz were Teiman, Omar,
12 Tzefo, Gatam, and Kenaz. Timna, a concubine of Esav's
son Elifaz, bore him Amalek. These are the descendants
13 of Esav's wife Ada. The sons of Reuel were Naḥat, Zeraḥ,
Shama, and Miza. These were the descendants of Esav's
14 wife Basmat. The sons of Oholivama, daughter of Ana
and granddaughter of Tzivon, Esav's wife, whom she bore
15 to Esav, were Yeush, Yalam, and Koraḥ. These were the
tribal chiefs among Esav's descendants. The sons of Elifaz,
Esav's firstborn, were the chiefs Teiman, Omar, Tzefo,
16 Kenaz, Koraḥ, Gatam, and Amalek. These were the chiefs
descended from Elifaz in Edom; they were grandsons
17 of Ada. The sons of Esav's son Reuel were the chiefs
Naḥat, Zeraḥ, Shama, and Miza. These were the chiefs
descended from Reuel in Edom; they were grandsons of
18 Esav's wife Basmat. The sons of Esav's wife Oholivama
were the chiefs Yeush, Yalam, and Koraḥ. These were the
chiefs descended from Esav's wife Oholivama daughter
19 of Ana. These were the sons of Esav – that is, Edom – and

כְּנָעַן אֶת־עָדָה בַּת־אֵילוֹן הַחִתִּי וְאֶת־אָהֳלִיבָמָה בַּת־עֲנָה
ג בַּת־צִבְעוֹן הַחִוִּי׃ וְאֶת־בָּשְׂמַת בַּת־יִשְׁמָעֵאל אֲחוֹת נְבָיוֹת׃
ד וַתֵּלֶד עָדָה לְעֵשָׂו אֶת־אֱלִיפָז וּבָשְׂמַת יָלְדָה אֶת־רְעוּאֵל׃
ה וְאָהֳלִיבָמָה יָלְדָה אֶת־יְעִישׁ וְאֶת־יַעְלָם וְאֶת־קֹרַח אֵלֶּה יְעוּשׁ
ו בְּנֵי עֵשָׂו אֲשֶׁר יֻלְּדוּ־לוֹ בְּאֶרֶץ כְּנָעַן׃ וַיִּקַּח עֵשָׂו אֶת־נָשָׁיו
וְאֶת־בָּנָיו וְאֶת־בְּנֹתָיו וְאֶת־כָּל־נַפְשׁוֹת בֵּיתוֹ וְאֶת־מִקְנֵהוּ
וְאֶת־כָּל־בְּהֶמְתּוֹ וְאֵת כָּל־קִנְיָנוֹ אֲשֶׁר רָכַשׁ בְּאֶרֶץ כְּנָעַן
ז וַיֵּלֶךְ אֶל־אֶרֶץ מִפְּנֵי יַעֲקֹב אָחִיו׃ כִּי־הָיָה רְכוּשָׁם רָב מִשֶּׁבֶת
יַחְדָּו וְלֹא יָכְלָה אֶרֶץ מְגוּרֵיהֶם לָשֵׂאת אֹתָם מִפְּנֵי מִקְנֵיהֶם׃
ח ט וַיֵּשֶׁב עֵשָׂו בְּהַר שֵׂעִיר עֵשָׂו הוּא אֱדוֹם׃ וְאֵלֶּה תֹּלְדוֹת
י עֵשָׂו אֲבִי אֱדוֹם בְּהַר שֵׂעִיר׃ אֵלֶּה שְׁמוֹת בְּנֵי־עֵשָׂו אֱלִיפַז
יא בֶּן־עָדָה אֵשֶׁת עֵשָׂו רְעוּאֵל בֶּן־בָּשְׂמַת אֵשֶׁת עֵשָׂו׃ וַיִּהְיוּ
יב בְּנֵי אֱלִיפָז תֵּימָן אוֹמָר צְפוֹ וְגַעְתָּם וּקְנַז׃ וְתִמְנַע ׀ הָיְתָה
פִילֶגֶשׁ לֶאֱלִיפַז בֶּן־עֵשָׂו וַתֵּלֶד לֶאֱלִיפַז אֶת־עֲמָלֵק אֵלֶּה בְּנֵי
יג עָדָה אֵשֶׁת עֵשָׂו׃ וְאֵלֶּה בְּנֵי רְעוּאֵל נַחַת וָזֶרַח שַׁמָּה וּמִזָּה
יד אֵלֶּה הָיוּ בְּנֵי בָשְׂמַת אֵשֶׁת עֵשָׂו׃ וְאֵלֶּה הָיוּ בְּנֵי אָהֳלִיבָמָה
בַת־עֲנָה בַּת־צִבְעוֹן אֵשֶׁת עֵשָׂו וַתֵּלֶד לְעֵשָׂו אֶת־יְעִישׁ יְעוּשׁ
טו וְאֶת־יַעְלָם וְאֶת־קֹרַח׃ אֵלֶּה אַלּוּפֵי בְנֵי־עֵשָׂו בְּנֵי אֱלִיפַז
בְּכוֹר עֵשָׂו אַלּוּף תֵּימָן אַלּוּף אוֹמָר אַלּוּף צְפוֹ אַלּוּף קְנַז׃
טז אַלּוּף־קֹרַח אַלּוּף גַּעְתָּם אַלּוּף עֲמָלֵק אֵלֶּה אַלּוּפֵי אֱלִיפַז
יז בְּאֶרֶץ אֱדוֹם אֵלֶּה בְּנֵי עָדָה׃ וְאֵלֶּה בְּנֵי רְעוּאֵל בֶּן־עֵשָׂו
אַלּוּף נַחַת אַלּוּף זֶרַח אַלּוּף שַׁמָּה אַלּוּף מִזָּה אֵלֶּה אַלּוּפֵי
יח רְעוּאֵל בְּאֶרֶץ אֱדוֹם אֵלֶּה בְּנֵי בָשְׂמַת אֵשֶׁת עֵשָׂו׃ וְאֵלֶּה
בְּנֵי אָהֳלִיבָמָה אֵשֶׁת עֵשָׂו אַלּוּף יְעוּשׁ אַלּוּף יַעְלָם אַלּוּף
יט קֹרַח אֵלֶּה אַלּוּפֵי אָהֳלִיבָמָה בַּת־עֲנָה אֵשֶׁת עֵשָׂו׃ אֵלֶּה

20 these were their chiefs. These are the sons of Se'ir SHEVI'I
the Horite who were settled in the land: Lotan, Shoval,
21 Tzivon, Ana, Dishon, Etzer, and Dishan. These were the
chiefs of the Horites, descendants of Se'ir in the land of
22 Edom. Lotan's sons were Ḥori and Heimam. Timna was
23 Lotan's sister. Shoval's sons were Alvan, Manaḥat, Eival,
24 Shefo, and Onam. Tzivon's sons were Aya and Ana. This
is the Ana who discovered hot springs in the desert while
25 pasturing the donkeys of his father Tzivon. Ana's children
26 were Dishon and Oholivama daughter of Ana. Dishon's
27 sons were Ḥemdan, Eshban, Yitran, and Keran. Etzer's
28 sons were Bilhan, Zaavan, and Akan. Dishan's sons were
29 Utz and Aran. These were the tribal chiefs of the Horites:
30 chiefs Lotan, Shoval, Tzivon, Ana, Dishon, Etzer, and
Dishan. These were the Horite chiefs by their divisions in
the land of Se'ir.
31 These were the kings who reigned in Edom before any
32 king reigned over the Israelites. Bela son of Beor became
33 king in Edom. His city was named Dinhava. When Bela
died, Yovav son of Zeraḥ from Botzra succeeded him as
34 king. When Yovav died, Ḥusham from the land of the
35 Temanites succeeded him as king. When Ḥusham died,

relationship with Him. Yaakov was loved by his mother, Esav by his father – but what of God who is neither father nor mother, but both and more than both? Love rejects comparisons. Yaakov is Yaakov, heir to the covenant. Esav is Esav, doing what he does, being what he is, enjoying his own heritage and blessing. What a simple truth and how beautifully, subtly, it is conveyed. It is one of the Torah's most profound messages to humanity – and how deeply (in an age of "the clash of civilizations") the world needs to hear it today.

Something of the deepest possible consequence, therefore, is being intimated here. The choice of one does not mean the rejection of the other. Esav too will have his blessing, his heritage, his land. He too will have children who become kings, who will rule and not be ruled. He too will have his virtues recognized, above all his love and respect for his father. Not all are chosen for the rigors, spiritual and existential, of the Abrahamic covenant, but each has his or her place in the scheme of things, each has his or her virtues, talents, gifts. Each is precious in the eyes of God.

כ בְּנֵי־עֵשָׂו וְאֵלֶּה אַלּוּפֵיהֶם הוּא אֱדוֹם׃ אֵלֶּה שביעי
בְנֵי־שֵׂעִיר הַחֹרִי יֹשְׁבֵי הָאָרֶץ לוֹטָן וְשׁוֹבָל וְצִבְעוֹן וַעֲנָה׃
כא וְדִשׁוֹן וְאֵצֶר וְדִישָׁן אֵלֶּה אַלּוּפֵי הַחֹרִי בְּנֵי שֵׂעִיר בְּאֶרֶץ
כב אֱדוֹם׃ וַיִּהְיוּ בְנֵי־לוֹטָן חֹרִי וְהֵימָם וַאֲחוֹת לוֹטָן תִּמְנָע׃
כג כד וְאֵלֶּה בְּנֵי שׁוֹבָל עַלְוָן וּמָנַחַת וְעֵיבָל שְׁפוֹ וְאוֹנָם׃ וְאֵלֶּה בְנֵי־
צִבְעוֹן וְאַיָּה וַעֲנָה הוּא עֲנָה אֲשֶׁר מָצָא אֶת־הַיֵּמִם בַּמִּדְבָּר
כה בִּרְעֹתוֹ אֶת־הַחֲמֹרִים לְצִבְעוֹן אָבִיו׃ וְאֵלֶּה בְנֵי־עֲנָה דִּשֹׁן
כו וְאָהֳלִיבָמָה בַּת־עֲנָה׃ וְאֵלֶּה בְּנֵי דִישָׁן חֶמְדָּן וְאֶשְׁבָּן וְיִתְרָן
כז כח וּכְרָן׃ אֵלֶּה בְּנֵי־אֵצֶר בִּלְהָן וְזַעֲוָן וַעֲקָן׃ אֵלֶּה בְנֵי־דִישָׁן
כט עוּץ וַאֲרָן׃ אֵלֶּה אַלּוּפֵי הַחֹרִי אַלּוּף לוֹטָן אַלּוּף שׁוֹבָל אַלּוּף
ל צִבְעוֹן אַלּוּף עֲנָה׃ אַלּוּף דִּשֹׁן אַלּוּף אֵצֶר אַלּוּף דִּישָׁן אֵלֶּה
אַלּוּפֵי הַחֹרִי לְאַלֻּפֵיהֶם בְּאֶרֶץ שֵׂעִיר׃
לא וְאֵלֶּה הַמְּלָכִים אֲשֶׁר מָלְכוּ בְּאֶרֶץ אֱדוֹם לִפְנֵי מְלָךְ־מֶלֶךְ
לב לִבְנֵי יִשְׂרָאֵל׃ וַיִּמְלֹךְ בֶּאֱדוֹם בֶּלַע בֶּן־בְּעוֹר וְשֵׁם עִירוֹ
לג דִּנְהָבָה׃ וַיָּמָת בָּלַע וַיִּמְלֹךְ תַּחְתָּיו יוֹבָב בֶּן־זֶרַח מִבָּצְרָה׃
לד לה וַיָּמָת יוֹבָב וַיִּמְלֹךְ תַּחְתָּיו חֻשָׁם מֵאֶרֶץ הַתֵּימָנִי׃ וַיָּמָת חֻשָׁם

36:31 אֲשֶׁר מָלְכוּ...לִפְנֵי מְלָךְ־מֶלֶךְ לִבְנֵי יִשְׂרָאֵל *Who reigned… before any king reigned over the Israelites* – It is not surprising that Yaakov's first desire was to be like Esav. Esav is *Homo naturalis*, a man of nature. He knows that *homo homini lupus est*, "man is wolf to man." He has the strength and skill to fight and win in the Darwinian struggle to survive and the Hobbesian war of "all against all." These are his natural battlegrounds, and he relishes the contest. Long "before any king reigned over the Israelites," the descendants of Esav can boast legendary rulers.

Esav is the archetypal hero of a hundred myths and legends of the ancient world (and of action movies today). He is not without dignity, nor does he lack human feelings. The Midrash, for sound educational reasons, turned Esav into a bad man. The Torah itself is altogether more subtle and profound. Esav is not a bad man; he is a natural man, celebrating the Homeric virtues and the Nietzschean will to power.

To be chosen does not mean that others are unchosen. To be secure in one's relationship with God does not depend on negating the possibility that others too may have a (different)

Hadad son of Bedad, who defeated Midyan in the country
of Moav, succeeded him as king. His city was named Avit.
36 When Hadad died, Samla from Masreka succeeded him
37 as king. When Samla died, Sha'ul from Reḥovot HaNahar
38 succeeded him as king. When Sha'ul died, Baal Ḥanan
39 son of Akhbor succeeded him as king. When Baal Ḥanan
son of Akhbor died, Hadar succeeded him as king. His
city was named Pa'u, and his wife's name was Meheitavel,
40 daughter of Matred, daughter of Mei Zahav. These were MAFTIR
the chiefs descended from Esav, by their clans, localities,
41 and names: the chiefs Timna, Alva, Yetet, Oholivama,
42 Ela, Pinon, Kenaz, Teiman, Mivtzar, Magdiel, and Iram.
43 These were the chiefs of Edom – of Esav, ancestor of the
Edomites – each with their own settlements in the land
that they held.

The haftara for Parashat Vayishlaḥ is on page 1438.

וַיִּמְלֹךְ תַּחְתָּיו הֲדַד בֶּן־בְּדַד הַמַּכֶּה אֶת־מִדְיָן בִּשְׂדֵה מוֹאָב
לו וְשֵׁם עִירוֹ עֲוִית: וַיָּמָת הֲדָד וַיִּמְלֹךְ תַּחְתָּיו שַׂמְלָה מִמַּשְׂרֵקָה:
לז לח וַיָּמָת שַׂמְלָה וַיִּמְלֹךְ תַּחְתָּיו שָׁאוּל מֵרְחֹבוֹת הַנָּהָר: וַיָּמָת
לט שָׁאוּל וַיִּמְלֹךְ תַּחְתָּיו בַּעַל חָנָן בֶּן־עַכְבּוֹר: וַיָּמָת בַּעַל חָנָן
בֶּן־עַכְבּוֹר וַיִּמְלֹךְ תַּחְתָּיו הֲדַר וְשֵׁם עִירוֹ פָּעוּ וְשֵׁם אִשְׁתּוֹ
מ מְהֵיטַבְאֵל בַּת־מַטְרֵד בַּת מֵי זָהָב: וְאֵלֶּה שְׁמוֹת אַלּוּפֵי עֵשָׂו מפטיר
לְמִשְׁפְּחֹתָם לִמְקֹמֹתָם בִּשְׁמֹתָם אַלּוּף תִּמְנָע אַלּוּף עַלְוָה
מא מב אַלּוּף יְתֵת: אַלּוּף אָהֳלִיבָמָה אַלּוּף אֵלָה אַלּוּף פִּינֹן: אַלּוּף
מג קְנַז אַלּוּף תֵּימָן אַלּוּף מִבְצָר: אַלּוּף מַגְדִּיאֵל אַלּוּף עִירָם
אֵלֶּה ׀ אַלּוּפֵי אֱדוֹם לְמֹשְׁבֹתָם בְּאֶרֶץ אֲחֻזָּתָם הוּא עֵשָׂו אֲבִי
אֱדוֹם:

The הפטרה *for* פרשת וישלח *is on page 1439.*

Parashat Vayeshev

37 1 Yaakov settled where his father had lived as a stranger,
2 in the land of Canaan. This is the story of Yaakov. Yosef,
seventeen years old, was shepherding the flock with his
brothers, an assistant to the sons of his father's wives
Bilha and Zilpa. And Yosef brought his father bad reports
3 of them. Now, Yisrael loved Yosef more than all his other
sons, for he was a child of his old age; he made him an
4 ornately colored robe. But when his brothers saw that
their father loved him more than any of them, they hated
5 him and could not say a peaceful word to him. Then Yosef
had a dream, and when he told it to his brothers, they
6 hated him still more. "Listen to this dream I had," he said.
7 "We were binding sheaves in the field when my sheaf

---

there broke upon him the storm of Yosef" (Rashi, commentary on Gen. 37:2, based on Bereshit Rabba 84:3).

37:4 וַיִּשְׂנְאוּ אֹתוֹ *They hated him* – The text sets up a contrast between love and hate. Twice we read that Yaakov loves Yosef, twice that his brothers hate him. They hate him *because* their father loves him. The same pair of verbs, "to love" and "to hate," have already appeared in the story of Yaakov's wives, the sisters Raḥel and Leah (Gen. 29:30–31). This is a crucial point, the core of the problem Genesis is intent on exploring. To create a universe, Genesis implies, is easy. It takes up no more than a single chapter (1:1–2:3). To create a human relationship is difficult. Yaakov's love for Yosef – innocent, human, benign – generates envy and hate. It is this honest confrontation with complexity that makes Genesis so profound a religious text. It refuses to simplify the human condition.

37:4 וְלֹא יָכְלוּ דַּבְּרוֹ לְשָׁלֹם *Could not say a peaceful word to him* – What this means, says Rabbi Yonatan Eybeshutz, is that had the brothers spoken, they could have told Yosef of their resentments. Yosef would be aware of their feelings and might moderate his behavior in some way. Once real communication had taken place, the brothers might have spoken their way to peace. As it is, the brothers' inability to speak allows hatred to fester until they plot to kill him, eventually deciding to sell him as a slave, fracturing the family and causing their father inconsolable grief. As we have already seen several times in Genesis, a failure of words again begets tragedy.

פרשת וישב

לז א ב וַיֵּשֶׁב יַעֲקֹב בְּאֶרֶץ מְגוּרֵי אָבִיו בְּאֶרֶץ כְּנָעַן: אֵלֶּה ׀ תֹּלְדוֹת לג
יַעֲקֹב יוֹסֵף בֶּן־שְׁבַע־עֶשְׂרֵה שָׁנָה הָיָה רֹעֶה אֶת־אֶחָיו בַּצֹּאן
וְהוּא נַעַר אֶת־בְּנֵי בִלְהָה וְאֶת־בְּנֵי זִלְפָּה נְשֵׁי אָבִיו וַיָּבֵא
ג יוֹסֵף אֶת־דִּבָּתָם רָעָה אֶל־אֲבִיהֶם: וְיִשְׂרָאֵל אָהַב אֶת־יוֹסֵף
ד מִכָּל־בָּנָיו כִּי־בֶן־זְקֻנִים הוּא לוֹ וְעָשָׂה לוֹ כְּתֹנֶת פַּסִּים: וַיִּרְאוּ
אֶחָיו כִּי־אֹתוֹ אָהַב אֲבִיהֶם מִכָּל־אֶחָיו וַיִּשְׂנְאוּ אֹתוֹ וְלֹא
ה יָכְלוּ דַּבְּרוֹ לְשָׁלֹם: וַיַּחֲלֹם יוֹסֵף חֲלוֹם וַיַּגֵּד לְאֶחָיו וַיּוֹסִפוּ
ו עוֹד שְׂנֹא אֹתוֹ: וַיֹּאמֶר אֲלֵיהֶם שִׁמְעוּ־נָא הַחֲלוֹם הַזֶּה
ז אֲשֶׁר חָלָמְתִּי: וְהִנֵּה אֲנַחְנוּ מְאַלְּמִים אֲלֻמִּים בְּתוֹךְ הַשָּׂדֶה

VAYESHEV

With Vayeshev, the story shifts from Yaakov to his children. The tension we have already sensed between Leah and Raḥel is transferred to the next generation in the form of the rivalry between Yosef and his brothers, the story whose twists and turns take us to the end of Genesis.

Yosef is Yaakov's favorite son, firstborn of his beloved Raḥel. The envy and antagonism of his brothers leads them to sell Yosef into slavery in Egypt, an act that will many years later result in the entire family, by then a nation, being enslaved.

The story of Yosef is full of fascinating vignettes, homing in on the characters of Reuven, Yehuda, Tamar, Yaakov, and others. Common to them all is the power of the narrative to confound our expectations. Reuven, the firstborn, seems to suffer self-doubt that robs him of the courage to take decisive action. Tamar turns out to be a paradigm of moral sensibility and courage. Part of the continuing power of these stories lies in their defiance of narrative convention. You can never predict in advance, the Torah seems to suggest, where virtue is to be found.

37:1 וַיֵּשֶׁב יַעֲקֹב *Yaakov settled* – The story of Yosef begins on an ominous note which tends to be lost in translation: "Yaakov settled [*vayeshev*] where his father had lived as a stranger [*be'eretz megurei aviv*]." The contrast between the two verbs, "to settle, dwell" and "to sojourn, live as a stranger" – to live securely and insecurely – suggests that Yaakov wants what Avraham and Yitzḥak did not have: tranquility. Having fled twice, once from his brother Esav, a second time from his father-in-law Lavan, he longs for a quiet life. He will not achieve it. The Sages said: "Yaakov sought to dwell in peace; immediately

rose and stood upright and your sheaves gathered around
8 mine and bowed down to it." His brothers said to him,
"Do you mean to be king over us? Do you mean to rule
over us?" Then they hated him even more for his dreams
9 and for what he said. Then he had another dream and told
it to his brothers. "I had another dream," he said. "This
time, the sun, moon, and eleven stars were bowing down
10 to me." When he told his father as well as his brothers,
his father rebuked him and said, "What kind of dream is
this that you have had? Shall we really come, I and your
mother and your brothers, to bow to the ground before
11 you?" His brothers were jealous of him; but his father
12 kept the matter in mind. When his brothers had gone to SHENI
13 pasture their father's flock near Shekhem, Yisrael said to
Yosef, "Come, your brothers are pasturing the flocks near
Shekhem; I will send you to them." Yosef said, "Here I
14 am." He said to him, "Go and see how your brothers and
the flocks are doing, and bring me back word," and he
sent him from the Ḥevron Valley, from where he walked
15 to Shekhem. A man found him wandering lost among
16 the fields and asked him, "What are you looking for?" He
replied, "I'm looking for my brothers. Can you tell me
17 where they are pasturing the sheep?" "They have moved
on from here," said the man. "I heard them say, 'Let us
go to Dotan.'" So Yosef went after his brothers and found

---

no Yosef the viceroy, no storage of food during the years of plenty, no descent of Yosef's family to Egypt, no exile, no slavery, no exodus. The message could not be more significant. When Heaven intends something to happen, and it seems to be impossible, sometimes it sends an angel down to earth – an angel who does not know he or she is an angel – to move the story from here to there.

I believe that there are times when we feel lost, and then someone says or does something that lifts us or points the way to a new direction and destination. Years later, looking back, we see how important that intervention was, even though it seemed slight at the time. That is when we know that we too encountered an angel who didn't know he or she was an angel.

וְהִנֵּה קָמָה אֲלֻמָּתִי וְגַם־נִצָּבָה וְהִנֵּה תְסֻבֶּינָה אֲלֻמֹּתֵיכֶם
ח וַתִּשְׁתַּחֲוֶיןָ לַאֲלֻמָּתִי׃ וַיֹּאמְרוּ לוֹ אֶחָיו הֲמָלֹךְ תִּמְלֹךְ עָלֵינוּ
אִם־מָשׁוֹל תִּמְשֹׁל בָּנוּ וַיּוֹסִפוּ עוֹד שְׂנֹא אֹתוֹ עַל־חֲלֹמֹתָיו
ט וְעַל־דְּבָרָיו׃ וַיַּחֲלֹם עוֹד חֲלוֹם אַחֵר וַיְסַפֵּר אֹתוֹ לְאֶחָיו
וַיֹּאמֶר הִנֵּה חָלַמְתִּי חֲלוֹם עוֹד וְהִנֵּה הַשֶּׁמֶשׁ וְהַיָּרֵחַ וְאַחַד
י עָשָׂר כּוֹכָבִים מִשְׁתַּחֲוִים לִי׃ וַיְסַפֵּר אֶל־אָבִיו וְאֶל־אֶחָיו
וַיִּגְעַר־בּוֹ אָבִיו וַיֹּאמֶר לוֹ מָה הַחֲלוֹם הַזֶּה אֲשֶׁר חָלָמְתָּ
הֲבוֹא נָבוֹא אֲנִי וְאִמְּךָ וְאַחֶיךָ לְהִשְׁתַּחֲוֺת לְךָ אָרְצָה׃
יא יב וַיְקַנְאוּ־בוֹ אֶחָיו וְאָבִיו שָׁמַר אֶת־הַדָּבָר׃ וַיֵּלְכוּ אֶחָיו שני
יג לִרְעוֹת אֶת־צֹאן אֲבִיהֶם בִּשְׁכֶם׃ וַיֹּאמֶר יִשְׂרָאֵל אֶל־יוֹסֵף
הֲלוֹא אַחֶיךָ רֹעִים בִּשְׁכֶם לְכָה וְאֶשְׁלָחֲךָ אֲלֵיהֶם וַיֹּאמֶר לוֹ
יד הִנֵּנִי׃ וַיֹּאמֶר לוֹ לֶךְ־נָא רְאֵה אֶת־שְׁלוֹם אַחֶיךָ וְאֶת־שְׁלוֹם
הַצֹּאן וַהֲשִׁבֵנִי דָּבָר וַיִּשְׁלָחֵהוּ מֵעֵמֶק חֶבְרוֹן וַיָּבֹא שְׁכֶמָה׃
טו וַיִּמְצָאֵהוּ אִישׁ וְהִנֵּה תֹעֶה בַּשָּׂדֶה וַיִּשְׁאָלֵהוּ הָאִישׁ לֵאמֹר
טז מַה־תְּבַקֵּשׁ׃ וַיֹּאמֶר אֶת־אַחַי אָנֹכִי מְבַקֵּשׁ הַגִּידָה־נָּא לִי
יז אֵיפֹה הֵם רֹעִים׃ וַיֹּאמֶר הָאִישׁ נָסְעוּ מִזֶּה כִּי שָׁמַעְתִּי אֹמְרִים

37:15 וַיִּמְצָאֵהוּ אִישׁ וְהִנֵּה תֹעֶה *A man found him wandering* – I know of no comparable passage in the Torah: three verses dedicated to an apparently trivial, eminently forgettable detail of someone having to ask directions from a stranger. Who is this unnamed man? And what conceivable message does the episode hold for future generations, for us? Rashi says he is the angel Gavriel. Ibn Ezra says he is a passerby. Ramban, however, says that "the Holy One, blessed be He, sent him a guide without his knowledge."

I am not sure whether Ramban meant without Yosef's knowledge or without the guide's knowledge. I prefer to think both. The anonymous man – so the Torah is intimating – represents an intrusion of providence to make sure that Yosef goes to where he is supposed to be, so that the rest of the drama can unfold. He may not know he has such a role. Yosef surely does not know. To put it as simply as I can: *He is an angel who does not know he is an angel.* He has a vital role in the story. Without him, none of the events that take up the rest of the Torah will happen: no Yosef the slave,

18 them at Dotan. They saw him in the distance, and by the
19 time he reached them, they had plotted to kill him. "Here
20 comes the dreamer!" they said to one another. "Now let
us kill him and throw him into one of the pits – we can
say that a wild animal ate him – then we shall see what
21 will come of his dreams!" When Reuven heard this, he
tried to save him from them. "Let us not kill him," he said.
22 "Do not shed blood," said Reuven. "Throw him into this
pit in the desert, but do not lay hands on him." His plan
23 was to rescue him and bring him back to his father. So SHELISHI
when Yosef came to his brothers, they stripped him of his

---

however, Yosef is taken from the pit and sold to a passing caravan of merchants. Reuven, unaware of all this, returns to the pit to rescue Yosef but finds him gone. He is bereft. "He … went back to his brothers, and said, 'The boy is gone, and I – where can I turn?'" (Gen. 37:30).

Commenting on this episode, the Midrash (Vayikra Rabba 34:8) states that if Reuven had only known that the Holy One, blessed be He, would record his intentions to save Yosef, he would have picked Yosef up on his shoulders and carried him back to his father.

If Reuven had only known, says the Midrash. If only he had known that the Torah would write of him, "When Reuven heard this, he saved him from them" – known that his intention was recognized and valued by God as if it were the deed – he might have found the courage to carry it through into action. But Reuven cannot know. He has not read the story. None of us can read the story of our life – we can only live it. The result is that we live in and with uncertainty. Doubt can lead to delay until the moment is lost. In an instant of arrested intention, Reuven loses his chance of changing history.

Reuven cannot read his story, but we can. Observing Reuven, we can see that God loves each of us, and that this can be a source of formidable strength. God heeds those not heard. He loves those whom others do not love. Reuven, still a young man, does not yet know this. But we, reading his story and the rest of Tanakh, do.

We are here for a reason, conceived in love, brought into being by the One who brought the universe into being, who knows our innermost thoughts, values our good intentions, and has more faith in us than we have in ourselves. That, if only we meditate on it, gives us the strength to turn intention into deed, lifting us from the person we might have been into the person we become.

יח נֵלְכָ֖ה דֹּתָ֑יְנָה וַיֵּ֤לֶךְ יוֹסֵף֙ אַחַ֣ר אֶחָ֔יו וַיִּמְצָאֵ֖ם בְּדֹתָֽן׃ וַיִּרְא֥וּ
אֹת֖וֹ מֵרָחֹ֑ק וּבְטֶ֙רֶם֙ יִקְרַ֣ב אֲלֵיהֶ֔ם וַיִּֽתְנַכְּל֥וּ אֹת֖וֹ לַהֲמִיתֽוֹ׃
יט וַיֹּאמְר֖וּ אִ֣ישׁ אֶל־אָחִ֑יו הִנֵּ֗ה בַּ֛עַל הַחֲלֹמ֥וֹת הַלָּזֶ֖ה בָּֽא׃
כ וְעַתָּ֞ה ׀ לְכ֣וּ וְנַהַרְגֵ֗הוּ וְנַשְׁלִכֵ֙הוּ֙ בְּאַחַ֣ד הַבֹּר֔וֹת וְאָמַ֕רְנוּ
כא חַיָּ֥ה רָעָ֖ה אֲכָלָ֑תְהוּ וְנִרְאֶ֕ה מַה־יִּהְי֖וּ חֲלֹמֹתָֽיו׃ וַיִּשְׁמַ֣ע
כב רְאוּבֵ֔ן וַיַּצִּלֵ֖הוּ מִיָּדָ֑ם וַיֹּ֕אמֶר לֹ֥א נַכֶּ֖נּוּ נָֽפֶשׁ׃ וַיֹּאמֶר֩ אֲלֵהֶ֨ם ׀
רְאוּבֵ֜ן אַל־תִּשְׁפְּכוּ־דָ֗ם הַשְׁלִ֣יכוּ אֹת֗וֹ אֶל־הַבּ֤וֹר הַזֶּה֙ אֲשֶׁ֣ר
בַּמִּדְבָּ֔ר וְיָ֖ד אַל־תִּשְׁלְחוּ־ב֑וֹ לְמַ֗עַן הַצִּ֤יל אֹתוֹ֙ מִיָּדָ֔ם לַהֲשִׁיב֖וֹ
כג אֶל־אָבִֽיו׃ וַיְהִ֕י כַּאֲשֶׁר־בָּ֥א יוֹסֵ֖ף אֶל־אֶחָ֑יו וַיַּפְשִׁ֤טוּ אֶת־ שלישי

37:18 וַיִּרְאוּ אֹתוֹ מֵרָחֹק *In the distance* – Imagine the scene. They can't see his face. All they can see is the "ornately colored robe" that so upsets them because it constantly reminds them that it is he, not they, whom their father loves. From far away, we don't see people as human beings, and when we stop seeing people as human beings, and they become instead symbols, objects of envy or hate, people can do terrible things to one another.

37:20 וְנִרְאֶה מַה יִּהְיוּ חֲלֹמֹתָיו *What will come of his dreams* – Here, the irony could not be more explicit. The words mean one thing to the brothers, the opposite to us, the listeners. Once we have reached the end of the story and go back to read it a second time, we realize that the very act intended to frustrate the dreams by killing the dreamer is the beginning of a sequence of events that will make the dreams come true.

REUVEN'S GOOD INTENTIONS

The brothers realize that, alone with no one to see them, they can kill Yosef and concoct a tale that will be impossible to refute. Only Reuven protests. It is at this point the Torah does something it does nowhere else. It makes a statement that, construed literally, is obviously false. The text states, literally: "When Reuven heard this, he saved [Yosef] from them." He did not. The discrepancy is so obvious that most translations, ours included, simply do not translate the phrase literally. What Reuven actually does is to attempt to save him. The Hebrew phrase tells us what might have been, not what actually is.

Reuven's plan is simple. He tells the brothers, in verse 22, not to kill Yosef but to let him die. The text – unusually, for it is rare for the Torah to describe a person's thoughts – explains Reuven's intent: his plan is to persuade the brothers to leave Yosef in the pit so that, when their attention is elsewhere, he can come back to it, lift him out, and take him home.

While Reuven is somewhere else,

24 robe, the ornately colored robe he was wearing, and they
took him and threw him into the pit. The pit was empty;
25 there was no water in it. And they sat down and ate their
meal. Looking up, they saw a caravan of Ishmaelites
coming from Gilad, their camels laden with spices, balm,
26 and myrrh, to be taken to Egypt. Yehuda said to his
brothers, "What do we gain by killing our brother and
27 covering his blood? Let's sell him to the Ishmaelites and
not harm him with our own hands. After all, he is our
brother, our own flesh and blood." His brothers agreed.
28 Some Midianite traders passed by and they pulled Yosef
up out of the pit, and they sold him to the Ishmaelites
for twenty pieces of silver. They then brought Yosef to

---

another perspective, it is the working out of a providential pattern whose end was announced (in Yosef's dreams) at the beginning.

37:26 מַה בֶּצַע כִּי נַהֲרֹג אֶת אָחִינוּ *What do we gain by killing our brother?* – Note that he does not say, "It is wrong to kill our brother." He says, "What do we gain?" This is the language not of principle but of pragmatism. Note too that he proposes selling Yosef as a slave at the very moment he recognizes that "he is our brother, our own flesh and blood." It is as if Yehuda were echoing Kayin when he said, "Am I my brother's keeper?" (Gen. 4:9).

37:28 וַיִּמְכְּרוּ אֶת יוֹסֵף *And they sold him* – It is a confusing episode. *Who* sells Yosef to the Ishmaelites? Is it the brothers or the Midianites? The subject "they" is ambiguous.

The commentators offered many interpretations. Of these, the simplest is given by Rashbam, who reads it as follows: The brothers, having thrown Yosef into the pit, sit down some distance away to eat. Reuven sneaks back to rescue Yosef, but finds the pit empty and cries, "The boy is gone, and I – where can I turn?" Rashbam points out that the brothers do not calm him by telling him they have sold Yosef. They seem as surprised as he is. It follows that the brothers, having seen the Ishmaelites in the distance, decide to sell Yosef to them, but before they have the chance to do so, a second group of travelers, the Midianites, hear Yosef's cries, see the possibility of selling him to the Ishmaelites, and do so.

In other words, the brothers intend to sell Yosef, and Yosef is sold, but *not by the brothers*. They seek to do the deed, and the deed is done, but not by them.

Unusually, but of immense significance, the Torah is telling us something about divine providence. Between intention and outcome there was an intervention – the appearance of the Midianites. We are being given a rare glimpse of

כג יוֹסֵף אֶת־כֻּתָּנְתּוֹ אֶת־כְּתֹנֶת הַפַּסִּים אֲשֶׁר עָלָיו׃ וַיִּקָּחֻהוּ
כד וַיַּשְׁלִכוּ אֹתוֹ הַבֹּרָה וְהַבּוֹר רֵק אֵין בּוֹ מָיִם׃ וַיֵּשְׁבוּ לֶאֱכָל־
לֶחֶם וַיִּשְׂאוּ עֵינֵיהֶם וַיִּרְאוּ וְהִנֵּה אֹרְחַת יִשְׁמְעֵאלִים בָּאָה
מִגִּלְעָד וּגְמַלֵּיהֶם נֹשְׂאִים נְכֹאת וּצְרִי וָלֹט הוֹלְכִים לְהוֹרִיד
כו מִצְרָיְמָה׃ וַיֹּאמֶר יְהוּדָה אֶל־אֶחָיו מַה־בֶּצַע כִּי נַהֲרֹג אֶת־
כז אָחִינוּ וְכִסִּינוּ אֶת־דָּמוֹ׃ לְכוּ וְנִמְכְּרֶנּוּ לַיִּשְׁמְעֵאלִים וְיָדֵנוּ
כח אַל־תְּהִי־בוֹ כִּי־אָחִינוּ בְשָׂרֵנוּ הוּא וַיִּשְׁמְעוּ אֶחָיו׃ וַיַּעַבְרוּ
אֲנָשִׁים מִדְיָנִים סֹחֲרִים וַיִּמְשְׁכוּ וַיַּעֲלוּ אֶת־יוֹסֵף מִן־הַבּוֹר
וַיִּמְכְּרוּ אֶת־יוֹסֵף לַיִּשְׁמְעֵאלִים בְּעֶשְׂרִים כָּסֶף וַיָּבִיאוּ אֶת־

37:25 וְהִנֵּה אֹרְחַת יִשְׁמְעֵאלִים *They saw a caravan of Ishmaelites* – Here is another apparently random encounter. The story of Yosef is carefully constructed to be read on at least two levels. On the one hand, it is a story of chance human interactions. It is a tale of parental favoritism and sibling rivalry. People speak, have emotions, and make decisions that have consequences. It might have been otherwise.

Read at another level, it is a story of divine providence in which the end is foretold at the beginning – one of the very few such stories in the Bible. The outcome is announced through the dreams. Yosef will become a leader. His brothers will bow down to him. As in a Greek tragedy, every act, whatever its intention, has the effect of leading toward the predestined end.

On the one hand, the story of Yosef can be read as pure chance. At the key moment, he might not have found his brothers. He might have wandered around looking for them and then returned home. The traders may not have passed by at the decisive moment, unknowingly averting his death. The entire drama of Yosef's fall and rise might never have happened.

On the other hand, divine providence is active at every stage.

In case we miss the point, the Torah is to put it explicitly in Yosef's mouth. "Do not be distressed or angry with yourselves that you sold me here, for God sent me ahead of you to save lives.... So then, it was not you who sent me here, but God" (Gen. 45:5–8).

The Bible is making, here and elsewhere, a philosophical point of some delicacy and power. It is rejecting the law of contradiction: either *p* or not-*p*. It is rejecting what William Blake called "single vision." It is telling us that there may be no unequivocal answer to the question "Was event X a chance event, or was it intended by divine design?" It may be both. From one perspective, the story of Yosef is a series of random events, mingled with a series of human decisions that might have been otherwise. From

29 Egypt. Reuven returned to the pit – and Yosef was not
30 there. He tore his clothes, went back to his brothers, and
31 said, "The boy is gone, and I – where can I turn?" They
took Yosef's robe, slaughtered a goat, and dipped the
32 robe in the blood. They had the ornately colored robe
brought to their father, and they said, "We found this. Try
33 to identify it. Is it your son's robe or not?" He recognized
it and said, "It is my son's robe! A wild animal must have
34 eaten him! Yosef has been torn limb from limb!" Yaakov
tore his clothes, put sackcloth on his loins, and mourned
35 for his son for many days. All his sons and daughters tried
to comfort him, but he refused to be comforted and said,
"I will go down to Sheol mourning for my son." His father
36 wept for him. Meanwhile, the Medanites had sold him in
Egypt to Potifar, one of Pharaoh's officials, captain of the
guard.

38 1 Around that time, Yehuda left his brothers and camped REVI'I
2 near an Adulamite named Ḥira. There, Yehuda met
the daughter of Shua, a Canaanite, and he married her
3 and came to her. She became pregnant and had a son,
4 whom he named Er. She became pregnant again and
5 had another son, and she named him Onan. She had
yet another son and named him Shela; Yehuda was in
6 Keziv when she gave birth to him. Yehuda took a wife for
7 his firstborn, Er; her name was Tamar. But Er, Yehuda's
firstborn, was wicked in the LORD's sight, and the LORD
8 took his life. Yehuda then said to Onan, "Go in to your

---

optimism is. It carries with it a considerable price. When the prophets saw evil in the world, they refused to be comforted; those who hope refuse to be comforted while the hoped-for outcome is not yet reached. Theodicy is a comfort bought too cheaply. Given their history of suffering, Jews were rarely optimists. But they never gave up hope.

TAMAR

Spliced within the story of Yosef is the story of Yehuda and the death of his children. Into this dark scenario enters one of the more unexpected heroines of the Torah, Tamar. The text gives us no inclination as to who she is, but from her entry into the narrative, this fascinating and mysterious figure begins

כט יוֹסֵף מִצְרָיְמָה: וַיָּשָׁב רְאוּבֵן אֶל־הַבּוֹר וְהִנֵּה אֵין־יוֹסֵף
ל בַּבּוֹר וַיִּקְרַע אֶת־בְּגָדָיו: וַיָּשָׁב אֶל־אֶחָיו וַיֹּאמַר הַיֶּלֶד
לא אֵינֶנּוּ וַאֲנִי אָנָה אֲנִי־בָא: וַיִּקְחוּ אֶת־כְּתֹנֶת יוֹסֵף וַיִּשְׁחֲטוּ
לב שְׂעִיר עִזִּים וַיִּטְבְּלוּ אֶת־הַכֻּתֹּנֶת בַּדָּם: וַיְשַׁלְּחוּ אֶת־כְּתֹנֶת
הַפַּסִּים וַיָּבִיאוּ אֶל־אֲבִיהֶם וַיֹּאמְרוּ זֹאת מָצָאנוּ הַכֶּר־נָא
לג הַכְּתֹנֶת בִּנְךָ הִוא אִם־לֹא: וַיַּכִּירָהּ וַיֹּאמֶר כְּתֹנֶת בְּנִי חַיָּה
לד רָעָה אֲכָלָתְהוּ טָרֹף טֹרַף יוֹסֵף: וַיִּקְרַע יַעֲקֹב שִׂמְלֹתָיו וַיָּשֶׂם
לה שַׂק בְּמָתְנָיו וַיִּתְאַבֵּל עַל־בְּנוֹ יָמִים רַבִּים: וַיָּקֻמוּ כָל־בָּנָיו
וְכָל־בְּנֹתָיו לְנַחֲמוֹ וַיְמָאֵן לְהִתְנַחֵם וַיֹּאמֶר כִּי־אֵרֵד אֶל־בְּנִי
לו אָבֵל שְׁאֹלָה וַיֵּבְךְּ אֹתוֹ אָבִיו: וְהַמְּדָנִים מָכְרוּ אֹתוֹ אֶל־
מִצְרָיִם לְפוֹטִיפַר סְרִיס פַּרְעֹה שַׂר הַטַּבָּחִים:
לח א וַיְהִי בָּעֵת הַהִוא וַיֵּרֶד יְהוּדָה מֵאֵת אֶחָיו וַיֵּט עַד־אִישׁ לד רביעי
ב עֲדֻלָּמִי וּשְׁמוֹ חִירָה: וַיַּרְא־שָׁם יְהוּדָה בַּת־אִישׁ כְּנַעֲנִי וּשְׁמוֹ
ג שׁוּעַ וַיִּקָּחֶהָ וַיָּבֹא אֵלֶיהָ: וַתַּהַר וַתֵּלֶד בֵּן וַיִּקְרָא אֶת־שְׁמוֹ
ד ה עֵר: וַתַּהַר עוֹד וַתֵּלֶד בֵּן וַתִּקְרָא אֶת־שְׁמוֹ אוֹנָן: וַתֹּסֶף עוֹד
וַתֵּלֶד בֵּן וַתִּקְרָא אֶת־שְׁמוֹ שֵׁלָה וְהָיָה בִכְזִיב בְּלִדְתָּהּ אֹתוֹ:
ו ז וַיִּקַּח יְהוּדָה אִשָּׁה לְעֵר בְּכוֹרוֹ וּשְׁמָהּ תָּמָר: וַיְהִי עֵר בְּכוֹר
ח יְהוּדָה רַע בְּעֵינֵי יְהוָה וַיְמִתֵהוּ יְהוָה: וַיֹּאמֶר יְהוּדָה לְאוֹנָן

---

the workings of providence in history. Nothing in the Yosef story happens by chance – and where an event most looks like chance, that is where divine intervention is most evident in retrospect.

37:35 וַיְמָאֵן לְהִתְנַחֵם *He refused to be comforted* – The Sages asked: Why did Yaakov refuse to be comforted? There are laws of mourning in Judaism, and they go back to its earliest days. There is the week of mourning; there is the first month; in some cases it takes a year. But there is a limit. Excessive mourning is seen in Judaism as a rebellion against reality. We are mortal. No one and nothing lives forever. Why then does Yaakov refuse to be comforted?

The traditional answer is surely the right one. Yaakov refuses to be comforted because he refuses to give up hope that Yosef is still alive – as, indeed, he is (Bereshit Rabba 84:21).

Hope is not costless in the way that

brother's wife and fulfill your duty as her brother-in-law.
9 Provide children for your brother." But Onan knew that
the children would not be considered his. Whenever he
came to his brother's wife, he let his seed go to waste on
the ground so as not to have children in his brother's
10 name. What he did was wicked in the LORD's sight, and
11 so He took his life also. Then Yehuda said to his daughter-
in-law Tamar, "Live as a widow in your father's house
until my son Shela grows up" – for he thought he too
might die like his brothers. So Tamar went to live in her
12 father's house. A long time passed, and Yehuda's wife,
Shua's daughter, died. When he had completed his time
of mourning, he and his neighbor Ḥira the Adulamite
13 went to join his sheepshearers in Timna. Tamar was told,
"Your father-in-law is going to Timna to shear his sheep."
14 And she took off her widow's clothes and covered herself
with a veil. Disguised, she sat at the entrance to Einayim
on the road to Timna, for she had seen that Shela was now
grown up and yet she had not been given to him as a wife.
15 Yehuda saw her and thought she was a prostitute, because
16 she had covered her face. Not realizing that she was his

---

tribute to the exemplary virtues of the women. Yehuda says of Tamar, "She is more righteous than I" (Gen. 38:26). Boaz says of Ruth, "This last kindness is yet greater than your first, for you have not gone after the young men, poor or rich" (Ruth 3:10).

These similarities are surely too pronounced to be accidental, and it is the Book of Ruth itself, in its closing lines, that provides the connection. The beginning of David's family tree is the son, Peretz, born to Yehuda and Tamar. The seventh generation is the son, Oved, born to Ruth and Boaz. The family tree of Israel's great and future king includes both Tamar and Ruth, two women whose virtue and loyalty, kindness and discretion, surely contributed to David's greatness.

I find it exceptionally moving that the Bible should cast in these heroic roles two figures at the extreme margins of Israelite society: women, childless widows, outsiders. Tamar and Ruth, powerless except for their moral courage, write their names into Jewish history as role models who gave birth to royalty – to remind us, in case we ever forget, that true royalty lies in love and faithfulness, and that greatness often exists where we expect it least.

ט בֹּ֛א אֶל־אֵ֥שֶׁת אָחִ֖יךָ וְיַבֵּ֣ם אֹתָ֑הּ וְהָקֵ֥ם זֶ֖רַע לְאָחִֽיךָ׃ וַיֵּ֣דַע
אוֹנָ֔ן כִּ֛י לֹּ֥א ל֖וֹ יִהְיֶ֣ה הַזָּ֑רַע וְהָיָ֞ה אִם־בָּ֨א אֶל־אֵ֤שֶׁת אָחִיו֙
י וְשִׁחֵ֣ת אַ֔רְצָה לְבִלְתִּ֥י נְתָן־זֶ֖רַע לְאָחִֽיו׃ וַיֵּ֛רַע בְּעֵינֵ֥י יְהוָ֖ה
יא אֲשֶׁ֣ר עָשָׂ֑ה וַיָּ֖מֶת גַּם־אֹתֽוֹ׃ וַיֹּ֣אמֶר יְהוּדָ֡ה לְתָמָר֩ כַּלָּת֨וֹ
שְׁבִ֣י אַלְמָנָ֣ה בֵֽית־אָבִ֗יךְ עַד־יִגְדַּל֙ שֵׁלָ֣ה בְנִ֔י כִּ֣י אָמַ֔ר פֶּן־
יב יָמ֥וּת גַּם־ה֖וּא כְּאֶחָ֑יו וַתֵּ֣לֶךְ תָּמָ֔ר וַתֵּ֖שֶׁב בֵּ֥ית אָבִֽיהָ׃ וַיִּרְבּוּ֙
הַיָּמִ֔ים וַתָּ֖מָת בַּת־שׁ֣וּעַ אֵֽשֶׁת־יְהוּדָ֑ה וַיִּנָּ֣חֶם יְהוּדָ֗ה וַיַּ֜עַל
יג עַל־גֹּֽזְזֵ֤י צֹאנוֹ֙ ה֗וּא וְחִירָ֛ה רֵעֵ֥הוּ הָעֲדֻלָּמִ֖י תִּמְנָֽתָה׃ וַיֻּגַּ֥ד
יד לְתָמָ֖ר לֵאמֹ֑ר הִנֵּ֥ה חָמִ֛יךְ עֹלֶ֥ה תִמְנָ֖תָה לָגֹ֥ז צֹאנֽוֹ׃ וַתָּסַר֩
בִּגְדֵ֨י אַלְמְנוּתָ֜הּ מֵעָלֶ֗יהָ וַתְּכַ֤ס בַּצָּעִיף֙ וַתִּתְעַלָּ֔ף וַתֵּ֙שֶׁב֙
בְּפֶ֣תַח עֵינַ֔יִם אֲשֶׁ֖ר עַל־דֶּ֣רֶךְ תִּמְנָ֑תָה כִּ֤י רָאֲתָה֙ כִּֽי־גָדַ֣ל
טו שֵׁלָ֔ה וְהִ֕וא לֹא־נִתְּנָ֥ה ל֖וֹ לְאִשָּֽׁה׃ וַיִּרְאֶ֣הָ יְהוּדָ֔ה וַֽיַּחְשְׁבֶ֖הָ
טז לְזוֹנָ֑ה כִּ֥י כִסְּתָ֖ה פָּנֶֽיהָ׃ וַיֵּ֨ט אֵלֶ֜יהָ אֶל־הַדֶּ֗רֶךְ וַיֹּ֙אמֶר֙ הָֽבָה־נָּ֔א

---

to dominate the story. Tamar bears an uncanny resemblance to one other figure in Tanakh: Ruth, daughter-in-law of Naomi, eponymous heroine of one of the gentlest and loveliest books of the Hebrew Bible. The resemblances between their respective stories are many and striking.

Both women are driven by a specific kind of loyalty: the loyalty that motivates the biblical law of *yibbum*, levirate marriage. The Torah says about the childless widow who marries her brother-in-law and then has a child, "The firstborn son whom she bears will perpetuate the name of the dead brother, so that his name is not erased from Israel" (Deut. 25:6). Likewise the Book of Ruth explains, in the context of her marriage to Boaz, that "the dead man's name will not be cut off from among his brothers" (Ruth 4:10). Both, in other words, keep faith with their dead husbands in seeking to have a child who will bear his name. Each, too, exhibits loyalty to their in-laws, Ruth in refusing to be parted from Naomi, and Tamar, I will argue, in ensuring that she will not put her father-in-law Yehuda to shame (see note on v. 25).

In both stories, an extended form of levirate marriage is involved, and in both cases, the man who becomes the father of the child or children – Yehuda and Boaz – is not the closest in line. For Tamar, this was Shela, Yehuda's third son; for Ruth it was the anonymous Peloni Almoni (this phrase has come, in Hebrew, to mean "Mr. So-and-so" or "Mr. What's-his-name").

Finally, in both cases, the men pay

daughter-in-law, he turned aside to her on the road and
said, "Come, let me sleep with you." She said, "What will
17 you give me to sleep with you?" He said, "I will send you a
young goat from my flock." "Only if you give me something
18 as a pledge until you send it," she said. "What pledge should
I give you?" he asked. She answered, "Your seal and cord,
and the staff in your hand." He gave them to her and went
19 in to her – and she became pregnant by him. She got up
and left, removed her veil, and put on her widow's clothes
20 again. And Yehuda sent the young goat by his neighbor
the Adulamite, to recover the pledge from the woman, but
21 he could not find her. He asked the local men, "Where is
the cult prostitute, the one by the roadside at Einayim?"
22 They said, "No cult prostitute has been here." So he went
back to Yehuda and said, "I could not find her. Besides,
the local men said that there was no cult prostitute there."
23 Yehuda said, "Let her keep what she has or we will become
a laughingstock. I tried to send her this young goat, but you
24 could not find her." About three months later, Yehuda was
told, "Your daughter-in-law Tamar has behaved as a loose
woman; in fact she has become pregnant by her harlotry."
25 "Take her out and let her be burned," Yehuda said. As she
was being brought out, she sent her father-in-law a message:
"I am pregnant by the man to whom these belong." She
added, "Please identify to whom this seal and cord and

---

concern to protect human dignity. Psychological injury may be no less harmful – is often even more so – than physical injury. Hence the rule: never humiliate, never put to shame, never take refuge in the excuse that they were only words, that no physical harm was done.

Tamar, a childless widow, unable to remarry, is a person without position or power. Is it this that gives her unusual insight into the fact that psychological pain can be as serious as physical pain, that loss of dignity is a kind of loss of life? It says something about the nature of Jewish spirituality that the Torah attributes this moral greatness to her and not to a direct member of the covenantal family – to one of Yaakov's sons – and that the Rabbis took her deed as a binding precedent for all of us.

Tamar takes her sense of shame and uses it to sensitize herself to avoiding shaming others. Can we, dare we, do less?

אָבוֹא אֵלַיִךְ כִּי לֹא יָדַע כִּי כַלָּתוֹ הִוא וַתֹּאמֶר מַה־תִּתֶּן־לִּי
יז כִּי תָבוֹא אֵלָי: וַיֹּאמֶר אָנֹכִי אֲשַׁלַּח גְּדִי־עִזִּים מִן־הַצֹּאן
יח וַתֹּאמֶר אִם־תִּתֵּן עֵרָבוֹן עַד שָׁלְחֶךָ: וַיֹּאמֶר מָה הָעֵרָבוֹן
אֲשֶׁר אֶתֶּן־לָּךְ וַתֹּאמֶר חֹתָמְךָ וּפְתִילֶךָ וּמַטְּךָ אֲשֶׁר בְּיָדֶךָ
יט וַיִּתֶּן־לָהּ וַיָּבֹא אֵלֶיהָ וַתַּהַר לוֹ: וַתָּקָם וַתֵּלֶךְ וַתָּסַר צְעִיפָהּ
כ מֵעָלֶיהָ וַתִּלְבַּשׁ בִּגְדֵי אַלְמְנוּתָהּ: וַיִּשְׁלַח יְהוּדָה אֶת־גְּדִי
הָעִזִּים בְּיַד רֵעֵהוּ הָעֲדֻלָּמִי לָקַחַת הָעֵרָבוֹן מִיַּד הָאִשָּׁה וְלֹא
כא מְצָאָהּ: וַיִּשְׁאַל אֶת־אַנְשֵׁי מְקֹמָהּ לֵאמֹר אַיֵּה הַקְּדֵשָׁה הִוא
כב בָעֵינַיִם עַל־הַדָּרֶךְ וַיֹּאמְרוּ לֹא־הָיְתָה בָזֶה קְדֵשָׁה: וַיָּשָׁב
אֶל־יְהוּדָה וַיֹּאמֶר לֹא מְצָאתִיהָ וְגַם אַנְשֵׁי הַמָּקוֹם אָמְרוּ
כג לֹא־הָיְתָה בָזֶה קְדֵשָׁה: וַיֹּאמֶר יְהוּדָה תִּקַּח־לָהּ פֶּן נִהְיֶה
כד לָבוּז הִנֵּה שָׁלַחְתִּי הַגְּדִי הַזֶּה וְאַתָּה לֹא מְצָאתָהּ: וַיְהִי ׀
כְּמִשְׁלֹשׁ חֳדָשִׁים וַיֻּגַּד לִיהוּדָה לֵאמֹר זָנְתָה תָּמָר כַּלָּתֶךָ
כה וְגַם הִנֵּה הָרָה לִזְנוּנִים וַיֹּאמֶר יְהוּדָה הוֹצִיאוּהָ וְתִשָּׂרֵף: הִוא
מוּצֵאת וְהִיא שָׁלְחָה אֶל־חָמִיהָ לֵאמֹר לְאִישׁ אֲשֶׁר־אֵלֶּה
לּוֹ אָנֹכִי הָרָה וַתֹּאמֶר הַכֶּר־נָא לְמִי הַחֹתֶמֶת וְהַפְּתִילִים

38:25 לְמִי הַחֹתֶמֶת וְהַפְּתִילִים וְהַמַּטֶּה הָאֵלֶּה *To whom this seal and cord and staff belong* – With great ingenuity and boldness, Tamar has broken through the bind in which Yehuda placed her. She has fulfilled her duty to the dead. But no less significantly, at least in one classic interpretation, she has spared Yehuda shame. By sending him a coded message – the pledge – she has ensured that he will know that he himself is the father of the child, but that no one else will. To do this, she takes the enormous risk of being put to death for adultery.

Her behavior is to become a model; the Rabbis inferred from her conduct a strong moral rule: "It is better that a person throw himself into a fiery furnace rather than shame his neighbor in public" (Bava Metzia 59a). This acute sensitivity to humiliation displayed by Tamar permeates much of rabbinic thought. The Talmud even includes in the definition of *onaat devarim*, "verbal oppression," the act of reminding a person of a past they may find shameful.

Judaism is a religion of words. God created the natural world with words. We create – and sometimes destroy – the social world with words. That is one reason why Judaism has so strong an ethic of speech. The other reason, surely, is its

▶

26 staff belong." Yehuda recognized them and said, "She is
more righteous than I. It was because I did not give her
to Shela my son." He did not know her intimately again.
27 When the time came for her to give birth, there were
28 twins in her womb. As she was in labor one child put out a
hand, so the midwife took a crimson thread and tied it to
29 his wrist, saying, "This one came out first." But he pulled
his hand back and then his brother came out. She said,
"How you have burst through!" So he was named Peretz.
30 Then his brother came out with the crimson thread on his
39 1 wrist. He was named Zeraḥ. Meanwhile, Yosef ḤAMISHI
had been brought down to Egypt. Potifar, an Egyptian, one
of Pharaoh's officials and captain of the guard, had bought
him from the Ishmaelites who had brought him there.
2 The LORD was with Yosef, and he became a successful
3 man. He lived in the house of his Egyptian master. And
his master saw that the LORD was with him and that the
4 LORD granted him success in all he did; Yosef found favor
in his eyes and became his personal attendant. Potifar put
him in charge of his household, giving him responsibility
5 for all he owned. From the moment he put him in charge
of his household and all he owned, the LORD blessed
the Egyptian's household because of Yosef. The LORD's
6 blessing was in all he owned, in house and field. And so he
left all he had in Yosef's hands and, with him there, he had
no concern for anything but the food he ate. Now, Yosef
7 was well built and handsome, and after a while, his master's SHISHI
8 wife cast her eyes on Yosef. "Lie with me," she said. But
he refused. "With me here," he told her, "my master does

---

the musical note meant to convey a psychological state of uncertainty and indecision.

We can imagine the conflict in Yosef's mind at this moment. On the one hand, his entire moral sense says: "No." It would be a betrayal of everything his family stands for: their ethic of sexual propriety and their strong sense of identity as children of the covenant. It would also be, as Yosef himself says, a betrayal of Potifar.

And yet, the temptation must be intense. He is in an urban civilization of a kind he has not seen before. It is his first experience of "bright lights, big city." He is far from home. No one can see him. After

כו וְהַמַּטֶּה הָאֵלֶּה׃ וַיַּכֵּר יְהוּדָה וַיֹּאמֶר צָדְקָה מִמֶּנִּי כִּי־עַל־כֵּן
כז לֹא־נְתַתִּיהָ לְשֵׁלָה בְנִי וְלֹא־יָסַף עוֹד לְדַעְתָּהּ׃ וַיְהִי בְּעֵת
כח לִדְתָּהּ וְהִנֵּה תְאוֹמִים בְּבִטְנָהּ׃ וַיְהִי בְלִדְתָּהּ וַיִּתֶּן־יָד וַתִּקַּח
הַמְיַלֶּדֶת וַתִּקְשֹׁר עַל־יָדוֹ שָׁנִי לֵאמֹר זֶה יָצָא רִאשֹׁנָה׃
כט וַיְהִי ׀ כְּמֵשִׁיב יָדוֹ וְהִנֵּה יָצָא אָחִיו וַתֹּאמֶר מַה־פָּרַצְתָּ עָלֶיךָ
ל פָּרֶץ וַיִּקְרָא שְׁמוֹ פָּרֶץ׃ וְאַחַר יָצָא אָחִיו אֲשֶׁר עַל־יָדוֹ
לט א הַשָּׁנִי וַיִּקְרָא שְׁמוֹ זָרַח׃ וְיוֹסֵף הוּרַד מִצְרָיְמָה לה חמישי
וַיִּקְנֵהוּ פּוֹטִיפַר סְרִיס פַּרְעֹה שַׂר הַטַּבָּחִים אִישׁ מִצְרִי מִיַּד
ב הַיִּשְׁמְעֵאלִים אֲשֶׁר הוֹרִדֻהוּ שָׁמָּה׃ וַיְהִי יְהוָה אֶת־יוֹסֵף וַיְהִי
ג אִישׁ מַצְלִיחַ וַיְהִי בְּבֵית אֲדֹנָיו הַמִּצְרִי׃ וַיַּרְא אֲדֹנָיו כִּי יְהוָה
ד אִתּוֹ וְכֹל אֲשֶׁר־הוּא עֹשֶׂה יְהוָה מַצְלִיחַ בְּיָדוֹ׃ וַיִּמְצָא יוֹסֵף
חֵן בְּעֵינָיו וַיְשָׁרֶת אֹתוֹ וַיַּפְקִדֵהוּ עַל־בֵּיתוֹ וְכָל־יֶשׁ־לוֹ נָתַן
ה בְּיָדוֹ׃ וַיְהִי מֵאָז הִפְקִיד אֹתוֹ בְּבֵיתוֹ וְעַל כָּל־אֲשֶׁר יֶשׁ־לוֹ
וַיְבָרֶךְ יְהוָה אֶת־בֵּית הַמִּצְרִי בִּגְלַל יוֹסֵף וַיְהִי בִּרְכַּת יְהוָה
ו בְּכָל־אֲשֶׁר יֶשׁ־לוֹ בַּבַּיִת וּבַשָּׂדֶה׃ וַיַּעֲזֹב כָּל־אֲשֶׁר־לוֹ
בְּיַד־יוֹסֵף וְלֹא־יָדַע אִתּוֹ מְאוּמָה כִּי אִם־הַלֶּחֶם אֲשֶׁר־
ז הוּא אוֹכֵל וַיְהִי יוֹסֵף יְפֵה־תֹאַר וִיפֵה מַרְאֶה׃ וַיְהִי אַחַר ששי
הַדְּבָרִים הָאֵלֶּה וַתִּשָּׂא אֵשֶׁת־אֲדֹנָיו אֶת־עֵינֶיהָ אֶל־יוֹסֵף
ח וַתֹּאמֶר שִׁכְבָה עִמִּי׃ וַיְמָאֵן ׀ וַיֹּאמֶר אֶל־אֵשֶׁת אֲדֹנָיו הֵן

38:26 צָדְקָה מִמֶּנִּי *She is more righteous than I* – This moment is a turning point in history. Yehuda is the first person in the Torah to explicitly admit he is wrong. We do not realize it yet, but this seems to be the moment at which he acquires the depth of character necessary for him to become the first real *baal teshuva,* the first penitent. We see this years later, when he – the man who proposed selling Yosef as a slave – becomes the man who is willing to spend the rest of his life in slavery so that his brother Binyamin can go free (Gen. 44:33). I have argued elsewhere that it is from here that we learn the principle that a penitent stands higher than even a perfectly righteous individual (Berakhot 34b). While Yehuda the penitent becomes the ancestor of Israel's kings, Yosef the righteous is only a viceroy, *mishneh lemelekh,* second to the king.

39:8 וַיְמָאֵן *But he refused* – Over "he refused" tradition has placed a *shalshelet,*

not concern himself with the running of the house; he has
9 entrusted me with all that he owns. No one in this house
has greater authority than I. He has withheld nothing from
me except you, because you are his wife. How could I do so
10 great a wrong? It would be a sin against God!" And though
she spoke to Yosef day after day, he would not consent to
11 lie with her or be with her. One day he came into the house
to do his work and none of the other servants were there.
12 She caught him by his cloak and said, "Lie with me!" He
13 ran away from her and fled outside. When she saw that he
had left his cloak in her hand and had run out of the house,
14 she called out to her servants and said to them, "Look! He
brought us a Hebrew to mock us! He came to me to lie
15 with me, but I screamed. And when he heard me scream
and cry for help, he left his cloak with me and ran outside."
16 She kept his cloak beside her until his master came home.
17 Then she told him the same story: "The Hebrew slave you
18 brought us came to me to mock me. I screamed and called
for help, and he left his cloak with me and ran outside."
19 When his master heard the story his wife told him – "This
20 is what your servant did to me!" – he was incensed. Yosef's
master had him put in prison, where the king's prisoners
21 were confined. He remained there in prison. But the Lord
was with Yosef and showed him kindness, granting him
22 favor in the eyes of the prison warden. The warden put
Yosef in charge of all the prisoners in the jail. Everything
23 done there was under his direction. The warden did not
need to pay attention to anything he had entrusted to him,
because the Lord was with him, giving him success in all
he did.

The Talmud (Sota 36b) gives a graphic description of his inner torment: "The image of his father appeared to him in the window and said, 'Yosef, your brothers' names are destined to be inscribed on the stones of the [High Priest's] breastplate, and you will be among them. Do you want your name to be erased? Do you want to be called an adulterer?'"

We have seen above how Reuven was thwarted by not knowing what was "destined to be written" (see ch. 37, "Reuven's Good Intentions"). The Talmud here proposes the complementary story. Yosef,

אֲדֹנִי לֹא־יָדַע אִתִּי מַה־בַּבָּיִת וְכֹל אֲשֶׁר־יֶשׁ־לוֹ נָתַן בְּיָדִי׃
ט אֵינֶנּוּ גָדוֹל בַּבַּיִת הַזֶּה מִמֶּנִּי וְלֹא־חָשַׂךְ מִמֶּנִּי מְאוּמָה כִּי
אִם־אוֹתָךְ בַּאֲשֶׁר אַתְּ־אִשְׁתּוֹ וְאֵיךְ אֶעֱשֶׂה הָרָעָה הַגְּדֹלָה
י הַזֹּאת וְחָטָאתִי לֵאלֹהִים׃ וַיְהִי כְּדַבְּרָהּ אֶל־יוֹסֵף יוֹם ׀ יוֹם
יא וְלֹא־שָׁמַע אֵלֶיהָ לִשְׁכַּב אֶצְלָהּ לִהְיוֹת עִמָּהּ׃ וַיְהִי כְּהַיּוֹם
הַזֶּה וַיָּבֹא הַבַּיְתָה לַעֲשׂוֹת מְלַאכְתּוֹ וְאֵין אִישׁ מֵאַנְשֵׁי הַבַּיִת
יב שָׁם בַּבָּיִת׃ וַתִּתְפְּשֵׂהוּ בְּבִגְדוֹ לֵאמֹר שִׁכְבָה עִמִּי וַיַּעֲזֹב בִּגְדוֹ
יג בְּיָדָהּ וַיָּנָס וַיֵּצֵא הַחוּצָה׃ וַיְהִי כִּרְאוֹתָהּ כִּי־עָזַב בִּגְדוֹ בְּיָדָהּ
יד וַיָּנָס הַחוּצָה׃ וַתִּקְרָא לְאַנְשֵׁי בֵיתָהּ וַתֹּאמֶר לָהֶם לֵאמֹר
רְאוּ הֵבִיא לָנוּ אִישׁ עִבְרִי לְצַחֶק בָּנוּ בָּא אֵלַי לִשְׁכַּב עִמִּי
טו וָאֶקְרָא בְּקוֹל גָּדוֹל׃ וַיְהִי כְשָׁמְעוֹ כִּי־הֲרִימֹתִי קוֹלִי וָאֶקְרָא
טז וַיַּעֲזֹב בִּגְדוֹ אֶצְלִי וַיָּנָס וַיֵּצֵא הַחוּצָה׃ וַתַּנַּח בִּגְדוֹ אֶצְלָהּ עַד־
יז בּוֹא אֲדֹנָיו אֶל־בֵּיתוֹ׃ וַתְּדַבֵּר אֵלָיו כַּדְּבָרִים הָאֵלֶּה לֵאמֹר
יח בָּא אֵלַי הָעֶבֶד הָעִבְרִי אֲשֶׁר־הֵבֵאתָ לָּנוּ לְצַחֶק בִּי׃ וַיְהִי
יט כַּהֲרִימִי קוֹלִי וָאֶקְרָא וַיַּעֲזֹב בִּגְדוֹ אֶצְלִי וַיָּנָס הַחוּצָה׃ וַיְהִי
כִשְׁמֹעַ אֲדֹנָיו אֶת־דִּבְרֵי אִשְׁתּוֹ אֲשֶׁר דִּבְּרָה אֵלָיו לֵאמֹר
כ כַּדְּבָרִים הָאֵלֶּה עָשָׂה לִי עַבְדֶּךָ וַיִּחַר אַפּוֹ׃ וַיִּקַּח אֲדֹנֵי יוֹסֵף
אֹתוֹ וַיִּתְּנֵהוּ אֶל־בֵּית הַסֹּהַר מְקוֹם אֲשֶׁר־אסורי הַמֶּלֶךְ אֲסִירֵי
כא אֲסוּרִים וַיְהִי־שָׁם בְּבֵית הַסֹּהַר׃ וַיְהִי יְהוָה אֶת־יוֹסֵף וַיֵּט
כב אֵלָיו חָסֶד וַיִּתֵּן חִנּוֹ בְּעֵינֵי שַׂר בֵּית־הַסֹּהַר׃ וַיִּתֵּן שַׂר בֵּית־
הַסֹּהַר בְּיַד־יוֹסֵף אֵת כָּל־הָאֲסִירִם אֲשֶׁר בְּבֵית הַסֹּהַר וְאֵת
כג כָּל־אֲשֶׁר עֹשִׂים שָׁם הוּא הָיָה עֹשֶׂה׃ אֵין ׀ שַׂר בֵּית־הַסֹּהַר
רֹאֶה אֶת־כָּל־מְאוּמָה בְּיָדוֹ בַּאֲשֶׁר יְהוָה אִתּוֹ וַאֲשֶׁר־הוּא
עֹשֶׂה יְהוָה מַצְלִיחַ׃

all the hostility he has suffered in his childhood, being propositioned by Potifar's wife must be flattering as well as seductive. It is a decisive moment. A slave, with no realistic hope of rescue – is he to become an Egyptian, with all the sexual laissez-faire that implies? Or will he remain faithful to his past, his conscience, his identity? The *shalshelet* is an elegant commentary on Yosef's *crise de conscience*.

40 1 Some time later, the Egyptian king's cupbearer and baker SHEVI'I
2 gave offense to their master, the king of Egypt. Pharaoh was
angry with the two officials, his chief cupbearer, and his
3 chief baker, and he placed them in custody in the house of
the captain of the guard, in the very place where Yosef was
4 confined. The captain of the guard assigned them to Yosef
and it was he who attended them. When they had been in
5 custody for some time, the two of them – the imprisoned
cupbearer and baker of the king of Egypt – each had a
dream on the same night, each dream seeming to carry
6 its own meaning. When Yosef came to them the next
7 morning, he saw that they were both distressed. He asked
Pharaoh's officials who were in custody with him in his
master's house, "Why are you looking so troubled today?"
8 "We both had dreams," they told him, "but there is no one
to interpret them." Yosef replied, "Interpretation belongs
9 to God. Tell me your dreams." So the chief cupbearer told
his dream to Yosef and said to him, "In my dream I saw a
10 vine in front of me. The vine had three branches. As soon
as it budded, it blossomed, and its clusters ripened into
11 grapes. Pharaoh's cup was in my hand; I took the grapes
and squeezed them into Pharaoh's cup, and I placed the
12 cup in his hand." "This is what it means," Yosef said. "The
13 three branches are three days. In three days Pharaoh will
lift your head and restore you to your position. You will
place Pharaoh's cup in his hand again, as you did when you

---

than a wave in the ocean, a grain of sand on the seashore, dust on the surface of infinity. Is it conceivable that with one act we could change the trajectory of our life, let alone that of humanity as a whole? Our *parasha* tells us that yes, it is. A stranger's directions, a brother's hesitation, a chance encounter in the wilderness, all have so far changed the course of Yosef's story and, by extension, Jewish history. Now in prison, home to the most powerless, Yosef's attentiveness to his fellow inmates will ultimately – though indirectly – change the course of world events. If the opportunity to help a vulnerable other presents itself, advises Rambam, do not hesitate. Our next act might tilt the balance of someone else's life and our own. We are not inconsequential. We can make a difference to our world. When we do so, we become God's partners in the work of redemption.

מ א וַיְהִ֗י אַחַר֙ הַדְּבָרִ֣ים הָאֵ֔לֶּה חָֽטְא֛וּ מַשְׁקֵ֥ה מֶֽלֶךְ־מִצְרַ֖יִם שביעי
ב וְהָאֹפֶ֑ה לַאֲדֹנֵיהֶ֖ם לְמֶ֥לֶךְ מִצְרָֽיִם׃ וַיִּקְצֹ֣ף פַּרְעֹ֔ה עַ֖ל שְׁנֵ֣י
ג סָרִיסָ֑יו עַ֚ל שַׂ֣ר הַמַּשְׁקִ֔ים וְעַ֖ל שַׂ֥ר הָאוֹפִֽים׃ וַיִּתֵּ֨ן אֹתָ֜ם
בְּמִשְׁמַ֗ר בֵּ֛ית שַׂ֥ר הַטַּבָּחִ֖ים אֶל־בֵּ֣ית הַסֹּ֑הַר מְק֕וֹם אֲשֶׁ֥ר
ד יוֹסֵ֖ף אָס֥וּר שָֽׁם׃ וַ֠יִּפְקֹד שַׂ֣ר הַטַּבָּחִ֧ים אֶת־יוֹסֵ֛ף אִתָּ֖ם וַיְשָׁ֣רֶת
ה אֹתָ֑ם וַיִּהְי֥וּ יָמִ֖ים בְּמִשְׁמָֽר׃ וַיַּֽחַלְמוּ֩ חֲל֨וֹם שְׁנֵיהֶ֜ם אִ֤ישׁ חֲלֹמוֹ֙
בְּלַ֣יְלָה אֶחָ֔ד אִ֖ישׁ כְּפִתְר֣וֹן חֲלֹמ֑וֹ הַמַּשְׁקֶ֣ה וְהָאֹפֶ֗ה אֲשֶׁר֙
ו לְמֶ֣לֶךְ מִצְרַ֔יִם אֲשֶׁ֥ר אֲסוּרִ֖ים בְּבֵ֥ית הַסֹּֽהַר׃ וַיָּבֹ֧א אֲלֵיהֶ֛ם
ז יוֹסֵ֖ף בַּבֹּ֑קֶר וַיַּ֣רְא אֹתָ֔ם וְהִנָּ֖ם זֹעֲפִֽים׃ וַיִּשְׁאַ֞ל אֶת־סְרִיסֵ֣י
פַרְעֹ֗ה אֲשֶׁ֨ר אִתּ֧וֹ בְמִשְׁמַ֛ר בֵּ֥ית אֲדֹנָ֖יו לֵאמֹ֑ר מַדּ֛וּעַ פְּנֵיכֶ֥ם
ח רָעִ֖ים הַיּֽוֹם׃ וַיֹּאמְר֣וּ אֵלָ֔יו חֲל֣וֹם חָלַ֔מְנוּ וּפֹתֵ֖ר אֵ֣ין אֹת֑וֹ
וַיֹּ֨אמֶר אֲלֵהֶ֜ם יוֹסֵ֗ף הֲל֤וֹא לֵֽאלֹהִים֙ פִּתְרֹנִ֔ים סַפְּרוּ־נָ֖א לִֽי׃
ט וַיְסַפֵּ֧ר שַׂר־הַמַּשְׁקִ֛ים אֶת־חֲלֹמ֖וֹ לְיוֹסֵ֑ף וַיֹּ֣אמֶר ל֔וֹ בַּחֲלוֹמִ֕י
י וְהִנֵּה־גֶ֖פֶן לְפָנָֽי׃ וּבַגֶּ֖פֶן שְׁלֹשָׁ֣ה שָׂרִיגִ֑ם וְהִ֤וא כְפֹרַ֙חַת֙ עָלְתָ֣ה
יא נִצָּ֔הּ הִבְשִׁ֥ילוּ אַשְׁכְּלֹתֶ֖יהָ עֲנָבִֽים׃ וְכ֥וֹס פַּרְעֹ֖ה בְּיָדִ֑י וָאֶקַּ֣ח
אֶת־הָֽעֲנָבִ֗ים וָאֶשְׂחַ֤ט אֹתָם֙ אֶל־כּ֣וֹס פַּרְעֹ֔ה וָאֶתֵּ֥ן אֶת־
יב הַכּ֖וֹס עַל־כַּ֥ף פַּרְעֹֽה׃ וַיֹּ֤אמֶר לוֹ֙ יוֹסֵ֔ף זֶ֖ה פִּתְרֹנ֑וֹ שְׁלֹ֙שֶׁת֙
יג הַשָּׂ֣רִגִ֔ים שְׁלֹ֥שֶׁת יָמִ֖ים הֵֽם׃ בְּע֣וֹד ׀ שְׁלֹ֣שֶׁת יָמִ֗ים יִשָּׂ֤א
פַרְעֹה֙ אֶת־רֹאשֶׁ֔ךָ וַהֲשִֽׁיבְךָ֖ עַל־כַּנֶּ֑ךָ וְנָתַתָּ֤ כוֹס־פַּרְעֹה֙ בְּיָד֔וֹ

with his father's love at the front of his mind, knows that his better self will one day be recognized.

40:8 סַפְּרוּ־נָא לִי *Tell me your dreams* – In his *Hilkhot Teshuva*, Rambam makes one of the most empowering statements in religious literature. Having explained that we and the world are judged by the majority of our deeds, he continues: "Therefore we should see ourselves throughout the year as if our deeds and those of the world are evenly poised between good and bad, so that our next act may change both the balance of our lives and that of the world" (*Hilkhot Teshuva* 3:4). We can make a difference, and it is potentially immense. That should be our mindset, always.

Few statements are more at odds with the way the world seems to us most of the time. Each of us knows that there is only one of us, and that there are billions of others in the world. What conceivable difference can we make? We are no more

14 were his cupbearer. When it goes well with you, remember
me and do me this kindness: mention me to Pharaoh so as
15 to free me from this place. The truth is that I was kidnapped
from the land of the Hebrews. Here too, I have done
16 nothing to deserve being placed in this pit." The chief baker
saw that he had given a favorable interpretation, so he said
to Yosef, "I too had a dream. There were three baskets of
17 white bread on my head. In the top basket were all sorts of
baked food that Pharaoh eats, but birds were eating them
18 out of the basket above my head." "This is what it means,"
19 Yosef said. "The three baskets are three days. In three days
Pharaoh will lift your head from your body; he will hang
20 you from a stake, and birds will eat your flesh." The third MAFTIR
day was Pharaoh's birthday. He made a feast for all his
servants, and from among them he singled out his chief
21 cupbearer and chief baker. He restored the chief cupbearer
to his position so that, as before, he placed the cup in
22 Pharaoh's hand. But he hung up the chief baker, as Yosef
23 had predicted. Still, the chief cupbearer did not remember
Yosef; he forgot him.

The haftara for Parashat Vayeshev is on page 1442.
On Ḥanukka read the haftara on page 1648.

the man who saves an entire region from famine and starvation, the one Jewish tradition calls "the *tzaddik*" (Yoma 35b). The human condition is not inherently tragic. Heroes are not fated to fall.

Yosef's story is a precise reversal of the narrative structure of Sophocles's *Oedipus*. Everything Laius and his son Oedipus do to *avert* the tragic fate announced by the oracle in fact brings it closer to fulfillment, whereas in the story of Yosef, every episode that seems to be leading to tragedy turns out in retrospect to be a necessary step to saving lives and fulfilling Yosef's dreams.

Do not think you understand the story of your life at halftime. That is the lesson of Yosef. There is no way of predicting how the story will end on the basis of the events narrated in Parashat Vayeshev. The turning point in his life is a highly improbable event that could not be predicted but which changes all else, not just for him but for large numbers of people and for the eventual course of Jewish history. God's hand is at work, even when Yosef feels abandoned by every human being he has encountered.

Judaism is the opposite of tragedy. Every bad thing that has happened to you thus far may be the necessary prelude to the good things that are about to happen because you have been strengthened and given courage by your ability to survive. Seen through the eye of faith, today's curse may be the beginning of tomorrow's blessing.

יד כַּמִּשְׁפָּט הָרִאשׁוֹן אֲשֶׁר הָיִיתָ מַשְׁקֵהוּ: כִּי אִם־זְכַרְתַּנִי
אִתְּךָ כַּאֲשֶׁר יִיטַב לָךְ וְעָשִׂיתָ־נָּא עִמָּדִי חָסֶד וְהִזְכַּרְתַּנִי
טו אֶל־פַּרְעֹה וְהוֹצֵאתַנִי מִן־הַבַּיִת הַזֶּה: כִּי־גֻנֹּב גֻּנַּבְתִּי מֵאֶרֶץ
הָעִבְרִים וְגַם־פֹּה לֹא־עָשִׂיתִי מְאוּמָה כִּי־שָׂמוּ אֹתִי בַּבּוֹר:
טז וַיַּרְא שַׂר־הָאֹפִים כִּי טוֹב פָּתָר וַיֹּאמֶר אֶל־יוֹסֵף אַף־אֲנִי
יז בַּחֲלוֹמִי וְהִנֵּה שְׁלֹשָׁה סַלֵּי חֹרִי עַל־רֹאשִׁי: וּבַסַּל הָעֶלְיוֹן
מִכֹּל מַאֲכַל פַּרְעֹה מַעֲשֵׂה אֹפֶה וְהָעוֹף אֹכֵל אֹתָם מִן־הַסַּל
יח מֵעַל רֹאשִׁי: וַיַּעַן יוֹסֵף וַיֹּאמֶר זֶה פִּתְרֹנוֹ שְׁלֹשֶׁת הַסַּלִּים
יט שְׁלֹשֶׁת יָמִים הֵם: בְּעוֹד ׀ שְׁלֹשֶׁת יָמִים יִשָּׂא פַרְעֹה אֶת־
רֹאשְׁךָ מֵעָלֶיךָ וְתָלָה אוֹתְךָ עַל־עֵץ וְאָכַל הָעוֹף אֶת־בְּשָׂרְךָ
כ מֵעָלֶיךָ: וַיְהִי ׀ בַּיּוֹם הַשְּׁלִישִׁי יוֹם הֻלֶּדֶת אֶת־פַּרְעֹה וַיַּעַשׂ מפטיר
מִשְׁתֶּה לְכָל־עֲבָדָיו וַיִּשָּׂא אֶת־רֹאשׁ ׀ שַׂר הַמַּשְׁקִים וְאֶת־
כא רֹאשׁ שַׂר הָאֹפִים בְּתוֹךְ עֲבָדָיו: וַיָּשֶׁב אֶת־שַׂר הַמַּשְׁקִים
כב עַל־מַשְׁקֵהוּ וַיִּתֵּן הַכּוֹס עַל־כַּף פַּרְעֹה: וְאֵת שַׂר הָאֹפִים
כג תָּלָה כַּאֲשֶׁר פָּתַר לָהֶם יוֹסֵף: וְלֹא־זָכַר שַׂר־הַמַּשְׁקִים אֶת־
יוֹסֵף וַיִּשְׁכָּחֵהוּ:

The הפטרה *for* פרשת וישב *is on page 1443.*
On חנוכה *read the* הפטרה *on page 1649.*

40:23 וישכחהו *He forgot him* – The last line of the *parasha* delivers one of the cruelest blows of fate in the Torah. Seemingly his one chance of escape to freedom is now lost. Yosef the beloved son in his magnificent robe has become Yosef the prisoner, bereft of hope. This is as near the Torah gets to Greek tragedy. It is a tale of Yosef's hubris leading, step after step, to his nemesis. Every good thing that happens to him turns out to be only the prelude to some new and unforeseen misfortune.

Two years later, at the beginning of the next *parasha*, we discover that all this has been leading to Yosef's supreme elevation. From the lowest pit he has risen to dizzying heights.

What is stunning about the way this story is told in the Torah is that it is constructed to lead us, as readers, in precisely the wrong direction. Parashat Vayeshev has the form of a Greek tragedy. Yosef has flaws in his character. He is vain about his appearance; he brings his father evil reports about his brothers (Gen. 37:2; Rashi; and see Bereshit Rabba 84:7); his narcissism leads directly to the advances of Potifar's wife (*Tanḥuma*, Vayeshev 8).

But the story of which he is a part is not a Greek tragedy. By its end – the death of Yosef in the final chapter of Genesis – he has become a different human being entirely, one who forgives his brothers the crime they committed against him,

Parashat Miketz

41 1 Two years passed. Then Pharaoh had a dream: he was
2 standing by the Nile when seven handsome, healthy cows
came up out of the river and grazed among the reeds.
3 Then seven other cows came up from the river after them,

remember Yosef, he *forgot* him" (40:23). The anticlimax is intense, emphasized by the double verb, "did not remember" and "forgot." We sense Yosef waiting day after day for news. None comes. His last, best hope has gone. He will never go free. Or so it seems.

To understand the power of this anticlimax, we must remember that only since the invention of printing and the free availability of books have we been accustomed to tell what happens next merely by turning a page. For many centuries, there were no printed books. People knew the biblical story primarily by *listening* to it week by week. Someone hearing the story for the first time would have to wait a week to discover what Yosef's fate would be.

The *parasha* break is thus a kind of real-life equivalent to the delay Yosef experienced in jail, which, as we now read, took "two years." It is then that Pharaoh has two dreams that no one in the court can interpret, prompting the chief butler to remember the man he had met in prison. Yosef is now transformed within hours from a prisoner-without-hope to viceroy of the greatest empire of the ancient world.

God answers our prayers – but often not when we thought or how we thought. Yosef seeks to get out of prison, and he does get out of prison. But not immediately, and not because the butler keeps his promise. The story is telling us something fundamental about the relationship between our dreams and our achievements. Yosef is the great dreamer of the Torah, and he becomes a leader, as he dreamed he would. But first he has to hone his practical and administrative skills, first in Potifar's house, then in prison. Even when God assures us that something will happen, it will not happen without our effort. A divine promise is not a *substitute for* human responsibility. To the contrary, it is a *call to* responsibility.

But effort alone is not enough. We need *siyyata diShmaya*, "the help of Heaven." We need the humility to acknowledge that we are dependent on forces not under our control. No one in Genesis invokes God more often than Yosef. He credits God for each of his successes. He recognizes that without God he could not have done what he does. And out of that humility comes patience.

פרשת מקץ

מא א וַיְהִ֕י מִקֵּ֖ץ שְׁנָתַ֣יִם יָמִ֑ים וּפַרְעֹ֣ה חֹלֵ֔ם וְהִנֵּ֖ה עֹמֵ֥ד עַל־הַיְאֹֽר׃ לו
ב וְהִנֵּ֣ה מִן־הַיְאֹ֗ר עֹלֹת֙ שֶׁ֣בַע פָּר֔וֹת יְפ֥וֹת מַרְאֶ֖ה וּבְרִיאֹ֣ת בָּשָׂ֑ר
ג וַתִּרְעֶ֖ינָה בָּאָֽחוּ׃ וְהִנֵּ֞ה שֶׁ֧בַע פָּר֣וֹת אֲחֵר֗וֹת עֹל֤וֹת אַחֲרֵיהֶן֙

MIKETZ

Miketz is dominated by two of the great encounters in the Torah. The first brings about the reversal in Yosef's fortunes. Forgotten and abandoned in prison, he is brought out to interpret Pharaoh's dreams, which he does with ease. Having told Pharaoh that the dreams portend eventual drought and famine, he then articulates a solution to the problem. Pharaoh, impressed, appoints Yosef to high office in Egypt, second only to himself.

The second occurs when Yosef's brothers, driven by famine in Canaan, come to Egypt to buy food. They come before Yosef, but fail to recognize him as their brother, though he recognizes them. Yosef, without disclosing his identity, sets in motion a complex scenario, designed to test his brothers, that reaches a climax in the next *parasha*.

Three tensions come to the fore in this *parasha*. First, the subtle interplay between human choice and divine intervention is traced more delicately here than anywhere else in Tanakh. Next, the conversation between Pharaoh and Yosef exemplifies the interplay of particularity and universality in Judaism. Third, the meeting between Yosef and his brothers takes place in the context of three other narratives of recognition and nonrecognition in Genesis. This turns out to be one of the book's major themes: appearance and reality in human interaction, the difference between who we seem to be and who we are. These three tensions lie at the heart of Judaism, and they reach their fullest exposition here, in the story of Yosef.

"TWO YEARS PASSED"

For the first time in the whole story, Yosef decided, at the end of last week's *parasha*, to take fate into his own hands. Knowing that the chief butler was about to be restored to his position, he asked him to bring his case to the attention of Pharaoh: "When it goes well with you, remember me and do me this kindness: mention me to Pharaoh so as to free me from this place. The truth is that I was kidnapped from the land of the Hebrews. Here too, I have done nothing to deserve being placed in this pit" (Gen. 40:14–15).

A double injustice has been done, and Yosef sees this as his one chance of regaining his freedom. But the end of the *parasha* delivers a devastating blow: "Still, the chief cupbearer *did not*

ugly and gaunt, and stood beside them by the riverbank.
4 The ugly, gaunt cows ate up the seven handsome, healthy
5 cows. Pharaoh awoke. Falling back to sleep, he had a
second dream: he saw seven ears of grain, ripe and robust,
6 growing on a single stalk. Suddenly, seven other ears
sprouted after them, thin and scorched by the east wind.
7 The thin ears swallowed up the seven ripe, full ears.
8 Pharaoh awoke – and realized it had been a dream. In the
morning his mind was troubled, so he sent for all the
magicians and sages of Egypt. Pharaoh told them his
dream, but no one could offer an interpretation that
9 satisfied him. Then the chief cupbearer said to Pharaoh, "I
10 must recall my sins today. Once, Pharaoh was angry with
his servants and placed me and the chief baker in custody
11 in the house of the captain of the guard. One night he and
I each had a dream, and each dream seemed to have its
12 own meaning. With us was a young Hebrew, a slave of the
captain of the guard. We told him our dreams and he
interpreted them for us, telling each of us the meaning of
13 his dream. Things turned out exactly as he interpreted
them to us. I was restored to my position, and the baker
14 was hung up." So Pharaoh sent for Yosef. He was rushed
from the dungeon, had his hair cut, changed his clothes,
15 and came before Pharaoh. Pharaoh said to Yosef, "I had a SHENI
dream and no one can interpret it; I have heard that when
16 you hear a dream you can interpret it." "Not I," replied
Yosef to Pharaoh. "God will give Pharaoh the answer that
17 he needs." Pharaoh told Yosef: "In my dream, I was standing
18 by the bank of the Nile when seven handsome, healthy
cows came up out of the river and grazed among the reeds.
19 Then after them came seven other cows, scrawny, very
sickly, and thin – I never saw such sickly cows in all Egypt.

human story. Judaism found a simple way of resolving the paradox. For the bad we do, we take responsibility. For the good we achieve, we thank God. In this, Yosef is our mentor.

מִן־הַיְאֹר רָעוֹת מַרְאֶה וְדַקּוֹת בָּשָׂר וַתַּעֲמֹדְנָה אֵצֶל הַפָּרוֹת
ד עַל־שְׂפַת הַיְאֹר: וַתֹּאכַלְנָה הַפָּרוֹת רָעוֹת הַמַּרְאֶה וְדַקֹּת
הַבָּשָׂר אֵת שֶׁבַע הַפָּרוֹת יְפֹת הַמַּרְאֶה וְהַבְּרִיאֹת וַיִּיקַץ
ה פַּרְעֹה: וַיִּישָׁן וַיַּחֲלֹם שֵׁנִית וְהִנֵּה ׀ שֶׁבַע שִׁבֳּלִים עֹלוֹת בְּקָנֶה
ו אֶחָד בְּרִיאוֹת וְטֹבוֹת: וְהִנֵּה שֶׁבַע שִׁבֳּלִים דַּקּוֹת וּשְׁדוּפֹת
ז קָדִים צֹמְחוֹת אַחֲרֵיהֶן: וַתִּבְלַעְנָה הַשִּׁבֳּלִים הַדַּקּוֹת אֵת
שֶׁבַע הַשִּׁבֳּלִים הַבְּרִיאוֹת וְהַמְּלֵאוֹת וַיִּיקַץ פַּרְעֹה וְהִנֵּה
ח חֲלוֹם: וַיְהִי בַבֹּקֶר וַתִּפָּעֶם רוּחוֹ וַיִּשְׁלַח וַיִּקְרָא אֶת־כָּל־
חַרְטֻמֵּי מִצְרַיִם וְאֶת־כָּל־חֲכָמֶיהָ וַיְסַפֵּר פַּרְעֹה לָהֶם אֶת־
ט חֲלֹמוֹ וְאֵין־פּוֹתֵר אוֹתָם לְפַרְעֹה: וַיְדַבֵּר שַׂר הַמַּשְׁקִים
י אֶת־פַּרְעֹה לֵאמֹר אֶת־חֲטָאַי אֲנִי מַזְכִּיר הַיּוֹם: פַּרְעֹה קָצַף
עַל־עֲבָדָיו וַיִּתֵּן אֹתִי בְּמִשְׁמַר בֵּית שַׂר הַטַּבָּחִים אֹתִי וְאֵת
יא שַׂר הָאֹפִים: וַנַּחַלְמָה חֲלוֹם בְּלַיְלָה אֶחָד אֲנִי וָהוּא אִישׁ
יב כְּפִתְרוֹן חֲלֹמוֹ חָלָמְנוּ: וְשָׁם אִתָּנוּ נַעַר עִבְרִי עֶבֶד לְשַׂר
הַטַּבָּחִים וַנְּסַפֶּר־לוֹ וַיִּפְתָּר־לָנוּ אֶת־חֲלֹמֹתֵינוּ אִישׁ כַּחֲלֹמוֹ
יג פָּתָר: וַיְהִי כַּאֲשֶׁר פָּתַר־לָנוּ כֵּן הָיָה אֹתִי הֵשִׁיב עַל־כַּנִּי
יד וְאֹתוֹ תָלָה: וַיִּשְׁלַח פַּרְעֹה וַיִּקְרָא אֶת־יוֹסֵף וַיְרִיצֻהוּ מִן־
טו הַבּוֹר וַיְגַלַּח וַיְחַלֵּף שִׂמְלֹתָיו וַיָּבֹא אֶל־פַּרְעֹה: וַיֹּאמֶר פַּרְעֹה שני
אֶל־יוֹסֵף חֲלוֹם חָלַמְתִּי וּפֹתֵר אֵין אֹתוֹ וַאֲנִי שָׁמַעְתִּי עָלֶיךָ
טז לֵאמֹר תִּשְׁמַע חֲלוֹם לִפְתֹּר אֹתוֹ: וַיַּעַן יוֹסֵף אֶת־פַּרְעֹה
יז לֵאמֹר בִּלְעָדָי אֱלֹהִים יַעֲנֶה אֶת־שְׁלוֹם פַּרְעֹה: וַיְדַבֵּר פַּרְעֹה
יח אֶל־יוֹסֵף בַּחֲלֹמִי הִנְנִי עֹמֵד עַל־שְׂפַת הַיְאֹר: וְהִנֵּה מִן־
הַיְאֹר עֹלֹת שֶׁבַע פָּרוֹת בְּרִיאוֹת בָּשָׂר וִיפֹת תֹּאַר וַתִּרְעֶינָה
יט בָּאָחוּ: וְהִנֵּה שֶׁבַע פָּרוֹת אֲחֵרוֹת עֹלוֹת אַחֲרֵיהֶן דַּלּוֹת
וְרָעוֹת תֹּאַר מְאֹד וְרַקּוֹת בָּשָׂר לֹא־רָאִיתִי כָהֵנָּה בְּכָל־אֶרֶץ

41:16 בִּלְעָדָי *Not I* – When Yosef is forced to act harshly, he weeps. But when he speaks of his successes, he attributes them to God. As R. Akiva said: "All is foreseen yet freedom of choice is given" (Avot 3:15). We and God are co-authors of the

20 Then the thin, sickly cows ate up the first seven healthy
21 cows. But when they had eaten them you could not tell
that they had eaten them, for they still looked as bad as
22 before. Then I awoke. In my dream I then saw seven ears
23 of grain, ripe and full, growing on a single stalk. Suddenly,
seven other ears sprouted after them, shriveled, thin, and
24 scorched by the east wind, and the thin ears swallowed
the seven good ears. I told this to the magicians, but none
25 could explain it to me." Yosef said to Pharaoh, "The two
dreams of Pharaoh are one and the same. God has told
26 Pharaoh what He is about to do. The seven good cows are
seven years, and so too the seven good ears are seven
27 years. It is one and the same dream. The seven thin, sickly
cows that came up after them are seven years, as are the
seven empty ears scorched by the east wind. They are
28 seven years of famine. It is as I have told Pharaoh: God has
29 shown Pharaoh what He is about to do. Seven years are
coming when there will be great abundance throughout
30 the land of Egypt. But after them will come seven years of
famine, when all the abundance in Egypt will be forgotten.
31 Famine will ravage the land. So devastating will the famine
be that no one in the land will know anything of abundance
32 anymore. As for Pharaoh having the same dream twice,
this means that the matter has already been decided by
33 God, and He is soon to bring it about. So now let Pharaoh

---

reign of King Djoser (c. twenty-eighth century BCE):

> I was in distress on the Great Throne, and those who are in the palace were in heart's affliction from a very great evil, since the Nile had not come in my time for a space of seven years. Grain was scant, fruits were dried up, and everything which they eat was short. (*Understanding Genesis*)

What Pharaoh terms "the spirit of God" (41:38) in Yosef might in this case be something that we would call "insight."

41:32 וּמְמַהֵר הָאֱלֹהִים לַעֲשֹׂתוֹ *He is soon to bring it about* – Pharaoh has not one dream, but two: one about cows, the other about ears of grain. Yosef explains that they are, substantively, the same dream, conveying the same message through different images. In the immediate context, this is just another piece of information about Egypt and its future.

כ מִצְרַיִם לָרֹעַ: וַתֹּאכַלְנָה הַפָּרוֹת הָרַקּוֹת וְהָרָעוֹת אֵת שֶׁבַע
כא הַפָּרוֹת הָרִאשֹׁנוֹת הַבְּרִיאֹת: וַתָּבֹאנָה אֶל־קִרְבֶּנָה וְלֹא
נוֹדַע כִּי־בָאוּ אֶל־קִרְבֶּנָה וּמַרְאֵיהֶן רַע כַּאֲשֶׁר בַּתְּחִלָּה
כב וָאִיקָץ: וָאֵרֶא בַּחֲלֹמִי וְהִנֵּה ׀ שֶׁבַע שִׁבֳּלִים עֹלֹת בְּקָנֶה
כג אֶחָד מְלֵאֹת וְטֹבוֹת: וְהִנֵּה שֶׁבַע שִׁבֳּלִים צְנֻמוֹת דַּקּוֹת
כד שְׁדֻפוֹת קָדִים צֹמְחוֹת אַחֲרֵיהֶם: וַתִּבְלַעְןָ הַשִּׁבֳּלִים הַדַּקֹּת
אֵת שֶׁבַע הַשִּׁבֳּלִים הַטֹּבוֹת וָאֹמַר אֶל־הַחַרְטֻמִּים וְאֵין
כה מַגִּיד לִי: וַיֹּאמֶר יוֹסֵף אֶל־פַּרְעֹה חֲלוֹם פַּרְעֹה אֶחָד הוּא
כו אֵת אֲשֶׁר הָאֱלֹהִים עֹשֶׂה הִגִּיד לְפַרְעֹה: שֶׁבַע פָּרֹת הַטֹּבֹת
שֶׁבַע שָׁנִים הֵנָּה וְשֶׁבַע הַשִּׁבֳּלִים הַטֹּבֹת שֶׁבַע שָׁנִים הֵנָּה
כז חֲלוֹם אֶחָד הוּא: וְשֶׁבַע הַפָּרוֹת הָרַקּוֹת וְהָרָעֹת הָעֹלֹת
אַחֲרֵיהֶן שֶׁבַע שָׁנִים הֵנָּה וְשֶׁבַע הַשִּׁבֳּלִים הָרֵקוֹת שְׁדֻפוֹת
כח הַקָּדִים יִהְיוּ שֶׁבַע שְׁנֵי רָעָב: הוּא הַדָּבָר אֲשֶׁר דִּבַּרְתִּי אֶל־
כט פַּרְעֹה אֲשֶׁר הָאֱלֹהִים עֹשֶׂה הֶרְאָה אֶת־פַּרְעֹה: הִנֵּה שֶׁבַע
ל שָׁנִים בָּאוֹת שָׂבָע גָּדוֹל בְּכָל־אֶרֶץ מִצְרָיִם: וְקָמוּ שֶׁבַע שְׁנֵי
רָעָב אַחֲרֵיהֶן וְנִשְׁכַּח כָּל־הַשָּׂבָע בְּאֶרֶץ מִצְרָיִם וְכִלָּה הָרָעָב
לא אֶת־הָאָרֶץ: וְלֹא־יִוָּדַע הַשָּׂבָע בָּאָרֶץ מִפְּנֵי הָרָעָב הַהוּא
לב אַחֲרֵי־כֵן כִּי־כָבֵד הוּא מְאֹד: וְעַל הִשָּׁנוֹת הַחֲלוֹם אֶל־
פַּרְעֹה פַּעֲמָיִם כִּי־נָכוֹן הַדָּבָר מֵעִם הָאֱלֹהִים וּמְמַהֵר
לג הָאֱלֹהִים לַעֲשֹׂתוֹ: וְעַתָּה יֵרֶא פַרְעֹה אִישׁ נָבוֹן וְחָכָם

41:27 שֶׁבַע שְׁנֵי רָעָב *Seven years of famine* – Yosef's interpretations are neither magical nor miraculous. In the case of the butler and baker, he remembers that in three days' time it will be Pharaoh's birthday (Gen. 40:20). It was the custom of rulers to make a feast on their birthday and decide the fate of certain individuals (in Britain, the monarch's birthday honors continue this tradition). It is reasonable therefore to assume that the butler's and baker's dreams relate to this event and their unconscious hopes and fears (Ibn Ezra on 40:12 and Bekhor Shor on 40:12 both make this suggestion).

In the case of Pharaoh's dreams, Yosef may know ancient Egyptian traditions about seven-year famines. Nahum Sarna quotes an Egyptian text from the

seek out an astute, wise man and set him over the land of
34 Egypt. Let Pharaoh appoint overseers across the land and
take a fifth of Egypt's harvest during the seven years of
35 abundance. Let them gather all that food in these coming
good years, storing the grain under Pharaoh's aegis so that
36 there is food under guard in all the cities. The food should
be held in reserve for the land when the seven years of
famine come to Egypt, so that the country is not ruined
37 by the famine." The plan seemed good to Pharaoh and all
38 his officials. Pharaoh said to them, "Could we find another
39 like him, a man who has within him the spirit of God?" So SHELISHI
Pharaoh said to Yosef, "Since God has made all this
known to you, there can be no one else as astute or as

---

divinity that shapes our ends, rough-hew them how we will." It is only in retrospect that we understand the story of our life.

41:37 וַיִּיטַב הַדָּבָר *The plan seemed good* – Yosef has three gifts that many people have in isolation but few have in combination. The first is that he dreams dreams. Dreaming is often thought to be impractical. Not so; it is one of the most practical things we can do. There are people who spend months planning a holiday but not even a day planning a life. They let themselves be carried by the winds of chance and circumstance. That is a mistake. It is our dreams that give us direction.

Second, Yosef can interpret the dreams of others. Leaders interpret other people's dreams. They articulate the inchoate. They find a way of expressing the hopes and fears of a generation. Martin Luther King Jr.'s "I have a dream" speech was about taking the hopes of African Americans and giving them wings. Similarly, it is not Yosef's dreams that made him a leader; it is Pharaoh's. Our own dreams give us direction; it is other people's dreams that give us opportunity.

Yosef's most impressive achievement, though, is his third gift, the ability to implement dreams, solving the problem for which they are an early warning. No sooner has he told of a seven-year famine than he continues, without pause, to provide a solution.

Good leaders either are, or surround themselves with, problem solvers. It is easy to see what is going wrong. What makes someone a leader is the ability to find a way of putting it right.

Dream dreams, understand and articulate the dreams of others, and find ways of turning a dream into a reality – these three gifts are Yosef's lessons in leadership.

PHARAOH, YOSEF, AND *ELOKIM*

Pharaonic Egypt was not a monotheistic culture. To be sure, there was a brief

לד וִישִׁיתֵהוּ עַל־אֶרֶץ מִצְרָיִם׃ יַעֲשֶׂה פַרְעֹה וְיַפְקֵד פְּקִדִים
עַל־הָאָרֶץ וְחִמֵּשׁ אֶת־אֶרֶץ מִצְרַיִם בְּשֶׁבַע שְׁנֵי הַשָּׂבָע׃
לה וְיִקְבְּצוּ אֶת־כָּל־אֹכֶל הַשָּׁנִים הַטֹּבוֹת הַבָּאֹת הָאֵלֶּה
לו וְיִצְבְּרוּ־בָר תַּחַת יַד־פַּרְעֹה אֹכֶל בֶּעָרִים וְשָׁמָרוּ׃ וְהָיָה
הָאֹכֶל לְפִקָּדוֹן לָאָרֶץ לְשֶׁבַע שְׁנֵי הָרָעָב אֲשֶׁר תִּהְיֶיןָ בְּאֶרֶץ
לז מִצְרָיִם וְלֹא־תִכָּרֵת הָאָרֶץ בָּרָעָב׃ וַיִּיטַב הַדָּבָר בְּעֵינֵי פַרְעֹה
לח וּבְעֵינֵי כָּל־עֲבָדָיו׃ וַיֹּאמֶר פַּרְעֹה אֶל־עֲבָדָיו הֲנִמְצָא כָזֶה לז
לט אִישׁ אֲשֶׁר רוּחַ אֱלֹהִים בּוֹ׃ וַיֹּאמֶר פַּרְעֹה אֶל־יוֹסֵף אַחֲרֵי שלישי
הוֹדִיעַ אֱלֹהִים אוֹתְךָ אֶת־כָּל־זֹאת אֵין־נָבוֹן וְחָכָם כָּמוֹךָ׃

Viewed within the full context of Yosef's life story, however, it changes our entire understanding of events. For it is not Pharaoh alone who has two dreams with a similar structure. Yosef does as well. At the very beginning of the story, he dreams, once of sheaves of wheat bowing down to his sheaf, and then about the sun, moon, and stars bowing down to him.

At that stage we had no idea what the dreams signified. Were they a prophecy, or the fruit of the fevered imagination of an overindulged, overambitious boy? The tension in Yosef's narrative depends on this ambiguity. Only now, chapters and years later, are we given the vital information: a dream, repeated in different images, is not just a dream. It is a message sent by God about a future that will soon come to pass. Only in retrospect do we realize that Yosef's double dream was a sign that this too was no mere imagining. Yosef really is destined to be a leader to whom his family will bow.

There are several possible reasons why we were not given this information earlier. It may be that Yosef has only now come to understand it. Or it may simply be a literary device to create and maintain tension in the unfolding plot. It is also possible, though, that it signals something altogether deeper about the human condition seen through the eyes of faith. On the surface, the story of Yosef is about human beings and their relationships. It is not a happy story. People betray people. Dreams are mere dreams. Hopes are destined to be dashed on the rocks of reality.

But as events unfold in Miketz, we realize that at a deeper level some other force has been at work all along. God has been monitoring the entire sequence of events, arranging the necessary strategic interventions to ensure that the outcome will be as planned. This is not obvious, as it is, for example, in the story of the exodus. Here it is concealed. It takes reflection and the ability to read beneath the surface to sense it at all. This is more than a story about Yosef. It is a story about each of us. In Shakespeare's words, "There's a

40 wise as you. You shall be in charge of my court, and by
your command shall all my people be directed. Only the
41 throne itself will make me greater than you." Then
Pharaoh said to Yosef, "I hereby place you in charge of all
42 the land of Egypt." Pharaoh removed his signet ring from
his hand and placed it on Yosef's. He had him robed in
garments of the finest linen, and placed a gold chain around
43 his neck. He had him ride in the chariot of his second-in-
command, and ahead of him people proclaimed, "*Avrekh*."
44 Thus was he given authority over all Egypt. Pharaoh told
Yosef, "I am Pharaoh, but without your consent no one will
45 lift hand or foot in all Egypt." And Pharaoh gave Yosef the
name Tzafenat Paneaḥ and gave him Asnat, daughter of
Potifera, priest of On, as his wife. Thus Yosef went out to
46 oversee Egypt. When he entered the service of Pharaoh,
king of Egypt, Yosef was thirty years old. Leaving Pharaoh's

the totality of all powers." Moving from the ancient to the contemporary world, we might say that *Elokim* is God as He is disclosed by science: the Big Bang, the various forces that give the universe its configuration, and the genetic code that shapes life from the simplest bacterium to *Homo sapiens*.

Hashem is a word of different logical form. It is, according to HaLevi, God's proper name. Just as "the first patriarch" (a generic description) was called Avraham (a name), so "the Author of being" (*Elokim*) has a proper name, *Hashem*.

The story of Yosef is one of those relatively rare narratives in Tanakh in which a Jew (Israelite/Hebrew) comes to play a prominent part in a gentile society. As we search in the twenty-first century for a way to avoid a "clash of civilizations," it seems to me that humanity can learn much from the ancient and still compelling way of understanding the human condition that arises from his story. We are all "the image and likeness" of God – the One God we call *Elokim*. But there are many ways, each distinct and unique, in which different cultures and civilizations define their relationship with the Author of all being. We do not presume to judge them, except insofar as they succeed or fail in honoring the basic, universal principles of human dignity. We as Jews are (or should be) secure in our relationship with *Hashem*, the God who has revealed Himself in the intimacy of love, whose expression is Torah. Today, as then, the challenge of faith is to be true to our particular heritage while being a blessing to others, whatever their heritage. That is a formula for peace and graciousness in an era badly in need of both.

מ אַתָּה תִּהְיֶה עַל־בֵּיתִי וְעַל־פִּיךָ יִשַּׁק כָּל־עַמִּי רַק הַכִּסֵּא
מא אֶגְדַּל מִמֶּךָּ׃ וַיֹּאמֶר פַּרְעֹה אֶל־יוֹסֵף רְאֵה נָתַתִּי אֹתְךָ עַל
מב כָּל־אֶרֶץ מִצְרָיִם׃ וַיָּסַר פַּרְעֹה אֶת־טַבַּעְתּוֹ מֵעַל יָדוֹ וַיִּתֵּן
אֹתָהּ עַל־יַד יוֹסֵף וַיַּלְבֵּשׁ אֹתוֹ בִּגְדֵי־שֵׁשׁ וַיָּשֶׂם רְבִד הַזָּהָב
מג עַל־צַוָּארוֹ׃ וַיַּרְכֵּב אֹתוֹ בְּמִרְכֶּבֶת הַמִּשְׁנֶה אֲשֶׁר־לוֹ וַיִּקְרְאוּ
מד לְפָנָיו אַבְרֵךְ וְנָתוֹן אֹתוֹ עַל כָּל־אֶרֶץ מִצְרָיִם׃ וַיֹּאמֶר פַּרְעֹה
אֶל־יוֹסֵף אֲנִי פַרְעֹה וּבִלְעָדֶיךָ לֹא־יָרִים אִישׁ אֶת־יָדוֹ וְאֶת־
מה רַגְלוֹ בְּכָל־אֶרֶץ מִצְרָיִם׃ וַיִּקְרָא פַרְעֹה שֵׁם־יוֹסֵף צָפְנַת
פַּעְנֵחַ וַיִּתֶּן־לוֹ אֶת־אָסְנַת בַּת־פּוֹטִי פֶרַע כֹּהֵן אֹן לְאִשָּׁה
מו וַיֵּצֵא יוֹסֵף עַל־אֶרֶץ מִצְרָיִם׃ וְיוֹסֵף בֶּן־שְׁלֹשִׁים שָׁנָה בְּעָמְדוֹ
לִפְנֵי פַּרְעֹה מֶלֶךְ־מִצְרָיִם וַיֵּצֵא יוֹסֵף מִלִּפְנֵי פַרְעֹה וַיַּעֲבֹר

period under Ikhnaton (Amenhotep IV), when the official religion was reformed in the direction of monolatry (worship of one god without disputing the existence of others). But this was short-lived, and certainly not at the time of Yosef. The entire biblical portrayal of Egypt is predicated on the people's belief in many gods, against whom God will "execute judgments" (Ex. 12:12) in the days of Moshe. Why then does Yosef take it for granted that Pharaoh will understand his reference to God – an assumption proved correct when Pharaoh twice uses the word himself? What is the significance of the word *Elokim*?

Tanakh generally and the Torah specifically have two primary ways of referring to God, the four-letter name we allude to as *Hashem* ("the name" par excellence, translated here as LORD) and the word *Elokim*.

The Sages understood the difference in terms of the distinction between God-as-justice (*Elokim*) and God-as-mercy (*Hashem*). However, the philosopher-poet of the eleventh century, Yehuda HaLevi, proposed a quite different distinction, based not on ethical attributes but on modes of relationship (*Kuzari* IV:1). HaLevi's view was this: The ancients worshipped forces of nature, which they personified as gods. Each was known as *El* or *Eloah*. The word *El* therefore generically means "a force, a power, an element of nature." The fundamental difference between those belief systems and Judaism was that Judaism believed that the forces of nature were not independent and autonomous. They represented a single totality, one creative will, the Author of being. The Torah therefore speaks of *Elokim* in the plural, meaning, "the sum of all forces,

presence, Yosef traveled throughout the land of Egypt.
47 During the seven years of plenty the land produced in
48 profusion. He gathered all the grain produced during the
seven years of plenty in Egypt and stored it in the cities.
In each city he stored the grain grown in the surrounding
49 fields. Yosef stored so much grain that it was like the sand
of the sea. They had to stop keeping records because it
50 was beyond measure. Before the years of famine came,
two sons were born to Yosef by Asnat daughter of Potifera,
51 priest of On. Yosef named his firstborn Menashe, saying,
"God has made me forget all my troubles and all my
52 father's family." The second son he named Efrayim, saying,
"God has made me fruitful in the land of my affliction."
53 The seven years of abundance in Egypt came to an end, REVI'I

In a later age, a man not otherwise known for his positive psychology will sit down to write a letter to his coreligionists in a foreign land. The man is Yirmeyahu. The people to whom he is writing are the Jews who have been taken captive to Babylon after their defeat at its hands, a defeat that included the destruction of the Temple, the central symbol of their nation and the sign that God was in their midst.

We know exactly what the feeling of those exiles was. A psalm has recorded it in the most powerful way: "By the rivers of Babylon, there we sat and wept as we remembered Zion.... How can we sing the Lord's song on foreign soil?" (Ps. 137:1, 4).

This is, of course, what Yirmeyahu predicted. But there is no air of triumphalism in his letter, no "I told you so." What he writes is massively counterintuitive. Yet it would be no exaggeration to say that it will change the course of Jewish history, perhaps even, in an indirect way, that of Western civilization as a whole. This is what he writes:

> Build houses and dwell in them; plant gardens and eat their fruit. Take wives, and beget sons and daughters. Take wives for your sons and give your daughters to husbands so that they may give birth to sons and daughters. Multiply there; do not be diminished. Seek the welfare of the city to which I have exiled you, and pray on its behalf to the Lord, for in its peace there shall be peace for you. (Jer. 29:5–7)

What Yirmeyahu is saying is that it is possible to survive in exile with your identity intact, your appetite for life undiminished, while contributing to the wider society and praying to God on its behalf. Yirmeyahu is introducing into history a highly consequential idea: the idea of a creative minority.

מז בכל־ארץ מצרים: ותעש הארץ בשבע שני השבע
מח לקמצים: ויקבץ את־כל־אכל | שבע שנים אשר היו בארץ
מצרים ויתן־אכל בערים אכל שדה־העיר אשר סביבתיה
מט נתן בתוכה: ויצבר יוסף בר כחול הים הרבה מאד עד
נ כי־חדל לספר כי־אין מספר: וליוסף ילד שני בנים בטרם
תבוא שנת הרעב אשר ילדה־לו אסנת בת־פוטי פרע
נא כהן און: ויקרא יוסף את־שם הבכור מנשה כי־נשני
נב אלהים את־כל־עמלי ואת כל־בית אבי: ואת שם השני
נג קרא אפרים כי־הפרני אלהים בארץ עניי: ותכלינה שבע רביעי

41:49 כִּי אֵין מִסְפָּר *It was beyond measure* – The great break of Judaism from the ancient world of magic, mystery, and myth was the deconsecration of nature that followed from the fact that God created nature by an act of will, and by making us in His image, gave us too the creative power of will. That meant that for Jews, holiness lies not in the way the world is, but in the way it ought to be. Poverty, disease, famine, injustice, and the exploitation of the powerless by the powerful are not the will of God. They may be part of human nature, but we have the power to rise above nature. God wants us not to accept but to heal, to cure, to prevent. So Jews have tended to become, out of all proportion to their numbers, lawyers fighting injustice, doctors fighting disease, teachers fighting ignorance, economists fighting poverty, and (especially in modern Israel) agricultural technologists finding new ways to grow food in environments where it has never grown before.

Thus, in our *parasha*, Yosef interprets the dream as asked, diagnosing the problem. There will be a famine lasting seven years. But it is what he does next that is world-changing. He sees this not as a fate to be endured but as a problem to be solved. Then, without fuss, he solves it, saving a whole region from death by starvation.

What can be changed need not be endured. Human suffering is not a fate to be borne, but a challenge to be overcome. This is Yosef's life-changing idea. What can be healed is not holy. God does not want us to accept poverty and pain, but to cure them.

41:52 כִּי־הִפְרַנִי אֱלֹהִים בְּאֶרֶץ עָנְיִי *Fruitful in the land of my affliction* – Yosef names his firstborn child Menashe, thanking God who "has *made me forget* (*nashani*) all my troubles and all my father's family" (Gen. 41:51). The pain of exile is numbed by forgetting his past and identity. By the time Efrayim is born, Yosef's feelings have changed.

54 and the seven years of famine began, just as Yosef had said
they would. There was famine in all the other lands, but
55 throughout Egypt there was food. When all Egypt began
to feel the famine, the people cried to Pharaoh for food.
Pharaoh told all the Egyptians, "Go to Yosef. Whatever
56 he tells you – do." The famine spread over the entire
country. Yosef then opened all the storehouses and sold
grain to the Egyptians, for the famine was worsening
57 throughout Egypt. People from all over the region came
to Egypt to buy grain from Yosef, because all across the
42 1 land the famine was devastating. Knowing that there was
grain in Egypt, Yaakov said to his sons, "Why do you keep
2 looking at one another?" He said, "I have heard that there
is grain in Egypt. Go down there and buy some for us so
3 that we may live and not die." So ten of Yosef's brothers
4 went down to buy grain in Egypt. But Yaakov did not
send Yosef's brother Binyamin with them, for he was
5 afraid that harm might come to him. So Yisrael's sons
were among those who came to buy grain, the famine
6 having reached as far as the land of Canaan. Yosef was the
governor of the land; it was he who dispensed food to all
its people. When Yosef's brothers arrived, they bowed

---

to mind is revenge. The text, however, explicitly rules this out. At every stage of the stratagem, Yosef weeps. He weeps at their first meeting (Gen. 42:24), again at the second (43:30), and a third time at the end of Yehuda's speech (45:2). People taking revenge do not weep. Yosef is doing something he finds personally painful yet morally necessary. He bears them – as he says when he reveals his identity – no malice. He has forgiven them. Why then does he put them through such fear and subject them to such a trial?

I have argued elsewhere (*Not in God's Name*, ch. 1) that the source of violence lies in our need to exist in groups, which leads to in-group altruism and out-group hostility. The pathological form of this is the dualism that divides humanity into children of light and children of darkness, the one all good, the other all evil. *It follows that the most profound moralizing experience, the only one capable of defeating dualism, is to undergo role reversal.* Imagine a Crusader in the Middle Ages, or a German in 1939, discovering that he is a Jew. There can be no more life-changing trial than finding yourself *on the other side.*

That, in essence, is what Yosef is

נד שְׁנֵי הַשָּׂבָע אֲשֶׁר הָיָה בְּאֶרֶץ מִצְרָיִם: וַתְּחִלֶּינָה שֶׁבַע שְׁנֵי
הָרָעָב לָבוֹא כַּאֲשֶׁר אָמַר יוֹסֵף וַיְהִי רָעָב בְּכָל־הָאֲרָצוֹת
נה וּבְכָל־אֶרֶץ מִצְרַיִם הָיָה לָחֶם: וַתִּרְעַב כָּל־אֶרֶץ מִצְרַיִם
וַיִּצְעַק הָעָם אֶל־פַּרְעֹה לַלָּחֶם וַיֹּאמֶר פַּרְעֹה לְכָל־מִצְרַיִם
נו לְכוּ אֶל־יוֹסֵף אֲשֶׁר־יֹאמַר לָכֶם תַּעֲשׂוּ: וְהָרָעָב הָיָה עַל
כָּל־פְּנֵי הָאָרֶץ וַיִּפְתַּח יוֹסֵף אֶת־כָּל־אֲשֶׁר בָּהֶם וַיִּשְׁבֹּר
נז לְמִצְרַיִם וַיֶּחֱזַק הָרָעָב בְּאֶרֶץ מִצְרָיִם: וְכָל־הָאָרֶץ בָּאוּ
מב א מִצְרַיְמָה לִשְׁבֹּר אֶל־יוֹסֵף כִּי־חָזַק הָרָעָב בְּכָל־הָאָרֶץ: וַיַּרְא
יַעֲקֹב כִּי יֶשׁ־שֶׁבֶר בְּמִצְרָיִם וַיֹּאמֶר יַעֲקֹב לְבָנָיו לָמָּה
ב תִּתְרָאוּ: וַיֹּאמֶר הִנֵּה שָׁמַעְתִּי כִּי יֶשׁ־שֶׁבֶר בְּמִצְרָיִם רְדוּ־
ג שָׁמָּה וְשִׁבְרוּ־לָנוּ מִשָּׁם וְנִחְיֶה וְלֹא נָמוּת: וַיֵּרְדוּ אֲחֵי־יוֹסֵף
ד עֲשָׂרָה לִשְׁבֹּר בָּר מִמִּצְרָיִם: וְאֶת־בִּנְיָמִין אֲחִי יוֹסֵף לֹא־
ה שָׁלַח יַעֲקֹב אֶת־אֶחָיו כִּי אָמַר פֶּן־יִקְרָאֶנּוּ אָסוֹן: וַיָּבֹאוּ בְּנֵי
יִשְׂרָאֵל לִשְׁבֹּר בְּתוֹךְ הַבָּאִים כִּי־הָיָה הָרָעָב בְּאֶרֶץ כְּנָעַן:
ו וְיוֹסֵף הוּא הַשַּׁלִּיט עַל־הָאָרֶץ הוּא הַמַּשְׁבִּיר לְכָל־עַם

This maps a new path for the Jewish people, but the wisdom Yirmeyahu applies is born here. In the past Yosef may have found relief in forgetting his heritage. When Efrayim is born, however, he stands fully in the presence of the God of his fathers, even in "the land of his affliction," bringing life to himself and those around him.

YOSEF AND HIS BROTHERS MEET AGAIN

What happens when the brothers arrive in Egypt is wholly counterintuitive. The story is nearing closure. Yosef has become a ruler. His brothers have bowed down to him. All that remains is for Yaakov and Yosef's younger brother Binyamin to be brought to Egypt. There they will make their obeisance, and the end foretold at the beginning, in Yosef's childhood dreams, will be complete. We cannot but expect this to happen, given the story thus far.

What is going on in this strange and apparently pointless diversion? Why Yosef's false accusation? Why the deception and intrigue? Why force the brothers to bring Binyamin? How does it advance the narrative or tell us something we need to know? In terms of the dreams, it delays their fulfillment rather than hastens it.

The first explanation that comes

7 down to him, their faces to the ground. Yosef recognized
his brothers as soon as he saw them, but he acted like a
stranger and spoke harshly to them. "Where have you
come from?" he asked. They replied, "From the land of
8 Canaan – to buy food." Yosef recognized his brothers, but
9 they did not recognize him. Then Yosef remembered the

Tzafenat Pane'aḥ, who wears Egyptian robes of office and whom they assume cannot even speak their language. Eventually Yosef forces them to recognize that just as a brother can be a stranger (when kept "at a distance"), so a stranger can turn out to be a brother.

The dual meaning of the verb *n-k-r* gathers into itself the whole force and dramatic conflict of Genesis as a sustained exploration of recognition and estrangement, closeness and distance. It tells us that if only we listen closely to the voice of the other, we will find that beneath the skin we *are* brothers and sisters, members of the human family under the parenthood of God. When others become brothers and conflict is transformed into conciliation, we have begun the journey to society-as-a-family, and the redemptive drama can begin.

42:8 וְהֵם לֹא הִכִּרֻהוּ *They did not recognize him* – The encounter between Yosef and his brothers is the fifth in a series of stories in which clothes play a key role. The first is Yaakov who dresses in Esav's clothes while bringing his father a meal so that he can take his brother's blessing. The second is Yosef's "ornately colored robe" which the brothers bring back to their father stained in blood, saying that a wild animal must have seized him. The third is the story of Tamar taking off her widow's dress, covering herself with a veil, and making herself look as if she were a prostitute. The fourth is the robe Yosef leaves in the hands of Potifar's wife while escaping her attempt to seduce him. The fifth is the one in our *parasha*, in which Pharaoh dresses Yosef as a high-ranking Egyptian, with clothes of linen, a gold chain, and the royal signet ring.

What all five cases have in common is that they facilitate deception. In each case, they bring about a situation in which things are not as they seem. Appearances deceive. It is therefore with a frisson of discovery that we realize that the Hebrew word for garment, *b-g-d*, is also the Hebrew word for "betrayal," as in the confession formula, *Ashamnu, bagadnu*, "We have been guilty, we have acted treacherously."

Is this a mere literary conceit, a way of linking a series of otherwise unconnected stories? Or is there something more fundamental at stake?

"Yosef recognized his brothers, but they did not recognize him." The reason they did not recognize him is that, from the start, they allowed their feelings to be guided by what they saw, the "ornately colored robe" that inflamed their envy of

ז הָאָרֶץ וַיָּבֹאוּ אֲחֵי יוֹסֵף וַיִּשְׁתַּחֲווּ־לוֹ אַפַּיִם אָרְצָה: וַיַּרְא
יוֹסֵף אֶת־אֶחָיו וַיַּכִּרֵם וַיִּתְנַכֵּר אֲלֵיהֶם וַיְדַבֵּר אִתָּם קָשׁוֹת
וַיֹּאמֶר אֲלֵהֶם מֵאַיִן בָּאתֶם וַיֹּאמְרוּ מֵאֶרֶץ כְּנַעַן לִשְׁבָּר־
ח ט אֹכֶל: וַיַּכֵּר יוֹסֵף אֶת־אֶחָיו וְהֵם לֹא הִכִּרֻהוּ: וַיִּזְכֹּר יוֹסֵף אֵת

---

forcing his brothers to do. He is putting them through the intensely painful yet morally transformative ordeal of role reversal. They suspected him of ambition. Now they learn what it is to be under suspicion. They planned to sell him as a slave. Now they know what it feels like to face enslavement. They made Yaakov go through the grief of losing a son. Now they must witness that grief again, this time through no fault of their own. Above all, they treated their brother as a stranger. *Now they must learn that the stranger,* Tzafenat Pane'aḥ, ruler of Egypt, *is actually their brother.*

42:7 וַיַּכִּרֵם *Yosef recognized* – In Hebrew the root *n-k-r* is a contranym – one word with two contradictory meanings. It can mean "to recognize" or the opposite, "to be a stranger," someone who is *not* recognized. The root appears four times in these two verses, three in the sense of recognition, one in the sense of estrangement. "Yosef *recognized* his brothers, but they did *not recognize* him," and Yosef "*recognized* his brothers... but he *acted like a stranger.*"

The power of this contranym is intense. The central question of Genesis is: Are human beings friends or strangers, brothers or others? That has been hammering at our consciousness since Kayin and Hevel, the first human children. All those years before, Yosef's brothers "*saw him in the distance,* and by the time he reached them, they had plotted to kill him" (Gen. 37:18). This sentence, like so many others in the story of Yosef, has two meanings. On the surface, it means what it says: they saw him approach, and they planned murder. At another level, however, it is a philosophical statement about love and hate. They were able to contemplate fratricide because "they saw him at a distance" (Rabbi Ḥayyim of Kossov, *Torat Ḥayyim* on Gen. 37:18). They refused to allow him to come close. They could see his cloak, but in Emmanuel Levinas's terminology, they could not yet see his "face," his reality as a person. Distant physically, they would not let him come close emotionally.

Soon after, Yehuda uttered the devastatingly ironic words "Let's sell him to the Ishmaelites and not harm him with our own hands. *After all, he is our brother,* our own flesh and blood" (37:27). Genesis is about recognition and nonrecognition in the deepest sense, about the willingness to accord dignity to the other rather than see the other as a threat.

The irony of Yosef is that his siblings do not recognize him, in Egypt, as their brother. *They recognize him only as a stranger,* an Egyptian ruler called

dreams he had dreamed about them. "You are spies!" he
said. "You have come to see where our land is exposed."
10 "No, my lord," they said. "Your servants have come to buy
11 food. We all are sons of the same man. We are honest men.
12 Your servants are not spies." "Lies," he said. "You have
13 come to see where our land is exposed." "We were once
twelve brothers," they replied, "sons of one man in Canaan.
14 The youngest is now with our father, and one is gone." But
15 Yosef said, "It is as I said to you – you are spies. This is how
you will be tested. By Pharaoh's life, you will not leave this
16 place unless your youngest brother comes here. Let one of
you go and fetch your brother. The rest of you will remain
confined here. This will test whether or not you are telling
17 the truth. If not, by Pharaoh's life, you are spies." He had
18 them placed in custody for three days. On the third day,
Yosef said to them, "If you do this you will live, for I am a
19 God-fearing man. If you are honest, let one of your ḤAMISHI
brothers stay here in prison while the rest of you go and
20 take back grain for your starving households. Then bring
your youngest brother to me so that your words can be
21 verified and you will not die." They agreed. And they said
to one another, "We are guilty, guilty because of what we
did to our brother. We saw his suffering when he pleaded

in their sacks, they tremble: "What is this that God has done to us?" (Gen. 41:28).

42:21 אֲבָל אֲשֵׁמִים אֲנַחְנוּ *We are guilty* – The Talmud says that "when sufferings come upon a person, he should examine his deeds" (Berakhot 5a). This seems to suggest that suffering is a sign of our having done something wrong and that we are being punished. But that is not what the Talmud means.

Rabbi Joseph Soleveitchik, in his essay "*Kol Dodi Dofek*," writes that when the Talmud sets out the halakhic approach to suffering, it is not seeking to answer the question "Why did this happen?" but rather "*Given* that this has happened, what then shall I do?" When it instructs us to examine our lives and undergo repentance, it does not mean that suffering is punishment. It means that suffering is a source of personal challenge and spiritual growth which we would never have experienced otherwise. The pain is not diminished by this realization. But through it we find a way of living through pain without endless, fruitless thoughts of what might have been.

הַחֲלֹמוֹת אֲשֶׁר חָלַם לָהֶם וַיֹּאמֶר אֲלֵהֶם מְרַגְּלִים אַתֶּם
י לִרְאוֹת אֶת־עֶרְוַת הָאָרֶץ בָּאתֶם׃ וַיֹּאמְרוּ אֵלָיו לֹא אֲדֹנִי
יא וַעֲבָדֶיךָ בָּאוּ לִשְׁבָּר־אֹכֶל׃ כֻּלָּנוּ בְּנֵי אִישׁ־אֶחָד נָחְנוּ כֵּנִים
יב אֲנַחְנוּ לֹא־הָיוּ עֲבָדֶיךָ מְרַגְּלִים׃ וַיֹּאמֶר אֲלֵהֶם לֹא כִּי־עֶרְוַת
יג הָאָרֶץ בָּאתֶם לִרְאוֹת׃ וַיֹּאמְרוּ שְׁנֵים עָשָׂר עֲבָדֶיךָ אַחִים ׀
אֲנַחְנוּ בְּנֵי אִישׁ־אֶחָד בְּאֶרֶץ כְּנָעַן וְהִנֵּה הַקָּטֹן אֶת־אָבִינוּ
יד הַיּוֹם וְהָאֶחָד אֵינֶנּוּ׃ וַיֹּאמֶר אֲלֵהֶם יוֹסֵף הוּא אֲשֶׁר דִּבַּרְתִּי
טו אֲלֵכֶם לֵאמֹר מְרַגְּלִים אַתֶּם׃ בְּזֹאת תִּבָּחֵנוּ חֵי פַרְעֹה אִם־
טז תֵּצְאוּ מִזֶּה כִּי אִם־בְּבוֹא אֲחִיכֶם הַקָּטֹן הֵנָּה׃ שִׁלְחוּ מִכֶּם
אֶחָד וְיִקַּח אֶת־אֲחִיכֶם וְאַתֶּם הֵאָסְרוּ וְיִבָּחֲנוּ דִּבְרֵיכֶם
יז הַאֱמֶת אִתְּכֶם וְאִם־לֹא חֵי פַרְעֹה כִּי מְרַגְּלִים אַתֶּם׃ וַיֶּאֱסֹף
יח אֹתָם אֶל־מִשְׁמָר שְׁלֹשֶׁת יָמִים׃ וַיֹּאמֶר אֲלֵהֶם יוֹסֵף בַּיּוֹם לח
יט הַשְּׁלִישִׁי זֹאת עֲשׂוּ וִחְיוּ אֶת־הָאֱלֹהִים אֲנִי יָרֵא׃ אִם־כֵּנִים חמישי
אַתֶּם אֲחִיכֶם אֶחָד יֵאָסֵר בְּבֵית מִשְׁמַרְכֶם וְאַתֶּם לְכוּ הָבִיאוּ
כ שֶׁבֶר רַעֲבוֹן בָּתֵּיכֶם׃ וְאֶת־אֲחִיכֶם הַקָּטֹן תָּבִיאוּ אֵלַי וְיֵאָמְנוּ
כא דִבְרֵיכֶם וְלֹא תָמוּתוּ וַיַּעֲשׂוּ־כֵן׃ וַיֹּאמְרוּ אִישׁ אֶל־אָחִיו
אֲבָל אֲשֵׁמִים ׀ אֲנַחְנוּ עַל־אָחִינוּ אֲשֶׁר רָאִינוּ צָרַת נַפְשׁוֹ

---

their younger brother. Judge by appearances and you will miss the deeper truth about situations and people. You will even miss God Himself, for God cannot be seen, only heard. That is why the primary imperative in Judaism is *Shema Yisrael*, "Listen, Israel" (Deut. 6:4), and it is why, when we say the first line of the *Shema*, we place our hand over our eyes so that we cannot see.

Appearances deceive. Clothes betray. Deep understanding, whether of God or of human beings, needs the ability to listen.

42:20 וְיֵאָמְנוּ דִבְרֵיכֶם *So that your words can be verified* – This is illogical. The existence of another brother has nothing to do with whether or not they are spies. Indeed, were they to bring a child, there would be no way an Egyptian ruler would be able to tell whether he was their brother or not. The strangeness of the request does not, however, raise doubts in the minds of the brothers. They know they are in trouble; that is all. When, on the journey back, they discover that the silver they have paid for the grain has been returned to them

▶

with us but we did not listen. That is why this trouble has
22 come upon us." Then Reuven spoke up: "Did I not tell
you not to sin against the boy? But you would not listen.
23 Now comes the reckoning for his blood." They did not
realize that Yosef could understand them, for a translator
24 stood between them. And Yosef turned away from them
and wept. Then he turned back to them and spoke again.
He had Shimon taken from them and placed in chains
25 before their eyes. Yosef gave orders to fill their bags with
grain and put each man's money back in his sack. They
were to be given provisions for the journey. After this was
26 done for them, they loaded their grain on their donkeys
27 and left. As one of them was opening his sack to feed his
donkey at the place where they stopped for the night, he
28 saw his money right there at the top of his pack. "My
money has been returned!" he told his brothers. "There it
is in my pack!" Their hearts sank. Trembling, they turned
to one another, saying, "What is this that God has done
29 to us?" When they came to their father Yaakov in the land
of Canaan, they told him all that had happened to them.
30 They said, "The man who is the lord of the land spoke to
31 us harshly. He accused us of spying on the land. We said
32 to him, 'We are honest men; we are not spies. We were
twelve brothers, sons of the same father. One is gone, and
33 the youngest is now with our father in Canaan.' Then the
man who is lord of the land said to us, 'This is how I will
know that you are honest men. Leave one of your brothers
with me, take something for your starving households,
34 and go. Then bring your youngest brother to me. Then I
will know that you are not spies but honest men. And
then I will give you back your brother, and you can trade
35 in the land.'" They began emptying their sacks, and there
in each one's sack was his money bag. When they and
36 their father saw the money bags, they were afraid. Their
father Yaakov said to them, "You have taken my children
away from me. Yosef is gone. Shimon is gone. Now you
37 want to take Binyamin? All this I must suffer!" Reuven

בְּהִתְחַנְנוֹ אֵלֵינוּ וְלֹא שָׁמָעְנוּ עַל־כֵּן בָּאָה אֵלֵינוּ הַצָּרָה
כב הַזֹּאת: וַיַּעַן רְאוּבֵן אֹתָם לֵאמֹר הֲלוֹא אָמַרְתִּי אֲלֵיכֶם ׀
לֵאמֹר אַל־תֶּחֶטְאוּ בַיֶּלֶד וְלֹא שְׁמַעְתֶּם וְגַם־דָּמוֹ הִנֵּה
כג כד נִדְרָשׁ: וְהֵם לֹא יָדְעוּ כִּי שֹׁמֵעַ יוֹסֵף כִּי הַמֵּלִיץ בֵּינֹתָם: וַיִּסֹּב
מֵעֲלֵיהֶם וַיֵּבְךְּ וַיָּשָׁב אֲלֵהֶם וַיְדַבֵּר אֲלֵהֶם וַיִּקַּח מֵאִתָּם
כה אֶת־שִׁמְעוֹן וַיֶּאֱסֹר אֹתוֹ לְעֵינֵיהֶם: וַיְצַו יוֹסֵף וַיְמַלְאוּ אֶת־
כְּלֵיהֶם בָּר וּלְהָשִׁיב כַּסְפֵּיהֶם אִישׁ אֶל־שַׂקּוֹ וְלָתֵת לָהֶם
כו צֵדָה לַדָּרֶךְ וַיַּעַשׂ לָהֶם כֵּן: וַיִּשְׂאוּ אֶת־שִׁבְרָם עַל־חֲמֹרֵיהֶם
כז וַיֵּלְכוּ מִשָּׁם: וַיִּפְתַּח הָאֶחָד אֶת־שַׂקּוֹ לָתֵת מִסְפּוֹא לַחֲמֹרוֹ
כח בַּמָּלוֹן וַיַּרְא אֶת־כַּסְפּוֹ וְהִנֵּה־הוּא בְּפִי אַמְתַּחְתּוֹ: וַיֹּאמֶר
אֶל־אֶחָיו הוּשַׁב כַּסְפִּי וְגַם הִנֵּה בְאַמְתַּחְתִּי וַיֵּצֵא לִבָּם
וַיֶּחֶרְדוּ אִישׁ אֶל־אָחִיו לֵאמֹר מַה־זֹּאת עָשָׂה אֱלֹהִים לָנוּ:
כט וַיָּבֹאוּ אֶל־יַעֲקֹב אֲבִיהֶם אַרְצָה כְּנָעַן וַיַּגִּידוּ לוֹ אֵת כָּל־
ל הַקֹּרֹת אֹתָם לֵאמֹר: דִּבֶּר הָאִישׁ אֲדֹנֵי הָאָרֶץ אִתָּנוּ קָשׁוֹת
לא וַיִּתֵּן אֹתָנוּ כִּמְרַגְּלִים אֶת־הָאָרֶץ: וַנֹּאמֶר אֵלָיו כֵּנִים אֲנָחְנוּ
לב לֹא הָיִינוּ מְרַגְּלִים: שְׁנֵים־עָשָׂר אֲנַחְנוּ אַחִים בְּנֵי אָבִינוּ
לג הָאֶחָד אֵינֶנּוּ וְהַקָּטֹן הַיּוֹם אֶת־אָבִינוּ בְּאֶרֶץ כְּנָעַן: וַיֹּאמֶר
אֵלֵינוּ הָאִישׁ אֲדֹנֵי הָאָרֶץ בְּזֹאת אֵדַע כִּי כֵנִים אַתֶּם אֲחִיכֶם
לד הָאֶחָד הַנִּיחוּ אִתִּי וְאֶת־רַעֲבוֹן בָּתֵּיכֶם קְחוּ וָלֵכוּ: וְהָבִיאוּ
אֶת־אֲחִיכֶם הַקָּטֹן אֵלַי וְאֵדְעָה כִּי לֹא מְרַגְּלִים אַתֶּם כִּי
לה כֵנִים אַתֶּם אֶת־אֲחִיכֶם אֶתֵּן לָכֶם וְאֶת־הָאָרֶץ תִּסְחָרוּ: וַיְהִי
הֵם מְרִיקִים שַׂקֵּיהֶם וְהִנֵּה־אִישׁ צְרוֹר־כַּסְפּוֹ בְּשַׂקּוֹ וַיִּרְאוּ
לו אֶת־צְרֹרוֹת כַּסְפֵּיהֶם הֵמָּה וַאֲבִיהֶם וַיִּירָאוּ: וַיֹּאמֶר אֲלֵהֶם
יַעֲקֹב אֲבִיהֶם אֹתִי שִׁכַּלְתֶּם יוֹסֵף אֵינֶנּוּ וְשִׁמְעוֹן אֵינֶנּוּ וְאֶת־
לז בִּנְיָמִן תִּקָּחוּ עָלַי הָיוּ כֻלָּנָה: וַיֹּאמֶר רְאוּבֵן אֶל־אָבִיו לֵאמֹר

said to his father, "You may kill my two sons if I do not
bring him back to you; entrust him to my care and I will
38 bring him back to you." "My son will not go down with
you," said Yaakov. "His brother is dead, and he is all I have
left. If any harm comes to him on the way, you will bring
43 1 down my gray head in grief to Sheol." The famine in the
2 land continued to be severe. When they had eaten all the
grain they had brought from Egypt, their father said to
3 them, "Go back and buy us some more food." But Yehuda
said to him, "The man warned us, 'Do not appear before
4 me unless your brother is with you.' If you agree to send
5 our brother with us, we will go and buy you food. But if
you will not send him, we cannot go. The man told us,
'Do not appear before me unless your brother is with
6 you.'" Yisrael said, "Why did you bring this trouble on me
7 by telling the man you had another brother?" They
replied, "The man kept asking about us and our family: 'Is
your father still alive?' he asked. 'Do you have a brother?'
We simply answered his questions. How could we know
8 that he would say, 'Bring your brother here'?" And Yehuda
said to his father Yisrael, "Send the boy with me. Let us be
on our way so that we, you, and our children may live and
9 not die. I myself am the guarantee for his safety: you may
hold me personally responsible. If I do not bring him

mortality: If the Other I love is eternal, then I am made eternal by our love.

Yaakov has survived the loss of Raḥel, compounded by the loss of her beloved first son. To survive the loss of her second, Binyamin, would be inconceivable. It would be, in every meaningful sense, the end of Yaakov's life.

43:9 אָנֹכִי אֶעֶרְבֶנּוּ *I myself am the guarantee* – Yehuda pledges himself and his freedom against Yaakov's "loan" of Binyamin. Just as Yaakov's life is bound up in his son's, so are Yehuda's freedom and well-being now conditional on Binyamin's. The language will be echoed in the Sages' maxim *Kol Yisrael arevin zeh bazeh*, literally, "All Israel are guarantors for one another." The people of Israel are "a single body and a single soul," moved by one another's pain, sharing responsibility for their collective fate. More than any other factor, that attitude preserved the Jewish nation through the deepest crises of its history, and sustains us today.

אֶת־שְׁנֵי בָנַי תָּמִית אִם־לֹא אֲבִיאֶנּוּ אֵלֶיךָ תְּנָה אֹתוֹ עַל־יָדִי
לח וַאֲנִי אֲשִׁיבֶנּוּ אֵלֶיךָ: וַיֹּאמֶר לֹא־יֵרֵד בְּנִי עִמָּכֶם כִּי־אָחִיו
מֵת וְהוּא לְבַדּוֹ נִשְׁאָר וּקְרָאָהוּ אָסוֹן בַּדֶּרֶךְ אֲשֶׁר תֵּלְכוּ־בָהּ
מג א וְהוֹרַדְתֶּם אֶת־שֵׂיבָתִי בְּיָגוֹן שְׁאוֹלָה: וְהָרָעָב כָּבֵד בָּאָרֶץ:
ב וַיְהִי כַּאֲשֶׁר כִּלּוּ לֶאֱכֹל אֶת־הַשֶּׁבֶר אֲשֶׁר הֵבִיאוּ מִמִּצְרָיִם
ג וַיֹּאמֶר אֲלֵיהֶם אֲבִיהֶם שֻׁבוּ שִׁבְרוּ־לָנוּ מְעַט־אֹכֶל: וַיֹּאמֶר
אֵלָיו יְהוּדָה לֵאמֹר הָעֵד הֵעִד בָּנוּ הָאִישׁ לֵאמֹר לֹא־תִרְאוּ
ד פָנַי בִּלְתִּי אֲחִיכֶם אִתְּכֶם: אִם־יֶשְׁךָ מְשַׁלֵּחַ אֶת־אָחִינוּ
ה אִתָּנוּ נֵרְדָה וְנִשְׁבְּרָה לְךָ אֹכֶל: וְאִם־אֵינְךָ מְשַׁלֵּחַ לֹא נֵרֵד
כִּי־הָאִישׁ אָמַר אֵלֵינוּ לֹא־תִרְאוּ פָנַי בִּלְתִּי אֲחִיכֶם אִתְּכֶם:
ו וַיֹּאמֶר יִשְׂרָאֵל לָמָה הֲרֵעֹתֶם לִי לְהַגִּיד לָאִישׁ הַעוֹד לָכֶם
ז אָח: וַיֹּאמְרוּ שָׁאוֹל שָׁאַל־הָאִישׁ לָנוּ וּלְמוֹלַדְתֵּנוּ לֵאמֹר
הַעוֹד אֲבִיכֶם חַי הֲיֵשׁ לָכֶם אָח וַנַּגֶּד־לוֹ עַל־פִּי הַדְּבָרִים
ח הָאֵלֶּה הֲיָדוֹעַ נֵדַע כִּי יֹאמַר הוֹרִידוּ אֶת־אֲחִיכֶם: וַיֹּאמֶר
יְהוּדָה אֶל־יִשְׂרָאֵל אָבִיו שִׁלְחָה הַנַּעַר אִתִּי וְנָקוּמָה וְנֵלֵכָה
ט וְנִחְיֶה וְלֹא נָמוּת גַּם־אֲנַחְנוּ גַם־אַתָּה גַּם־טַפֵּנוּ: אָנֹכִי
אֶעֶרְבֶנּוּ מִיָּדִי תְּבַקְשֶׁנּוּ אִם־לֹא הֲבִיאֹתִיו אֵלֶיךָ וְהִצַּגְתִּיו

Yosef's brothers do not know that in this case it is he who is designing a situation of unfolding horror that will feel like a cruel repayment of their earlier crimes. Their test will be to see whether they bow to this apparent punishment and allow history to repeat, or whether they translate guilt into responsibility, and turn their past around.

42:38 בְּיָגוֹן שְׁאוֹלָה *In grief to Sheol* – The Hebrew word *Sheol* means the underworld, the realm of the dead. In Song of Songs we will read, "For love is as powerful as death itself, and jealousy unyielding as Sheol" (8:6). Why the same forceful use of language here and there?

Song of Songs signals that lovers belong to one another at the deepest level of their being. Any kind of betrayal of such a relationship is an ultimate wound and causes existential pain. Love and death are both inexorable, irresistible forces. Death is the extinction of self into nothingness. Love is the extinction of self into the other. Giving myself to the other, I live in the other's life. Thus the love of God is the force that defeats

back and set him before you, I will have sinned against
10 you for all time. We could have been there and back twice
11 if we had not hesitated so long." And then their father
Yisrael said to them, "If that is how it must be, then do
this. Take some of the best produce of the land in your
bags, and bring them to the man as a gift – a little balm
and a little honey, some spices and myrrh, pistachio nuts
12 and almonds. Take with you double the money. Return
the money that was put back into your sacks. Perhaps it
13 was a mistake. And take your brother. Go back to the man
14 at once. May El Shaddai grant you mercy before the man,
that he may send your other brother forth to you, and
Binyamin. And as for me, if I am to be bereaved, I will be
15 bereaved." So the men took the gift and double the money
and set out with Binyamin. They went to Egypt and
16 presented themselves to Yosef. When Yosef saw Binyamin SHISHI
with them, he said to his house steward, "Take these men
to my house. Slaughter an animal and prepare a meal, for
17 they will dine with me at noon." The man did as Yosef said
18 and brought them to Yosef's house. The men were
frightened that they were being brought to Yosef's house.
They said, "We have been brought here because of the
money that was put back in our sacks the first time. He
wants to attack us, seize us as slaves, and take our donkeys."
19 So they went up to Yosef's steward and spoke to him at the
20 entrance to the house. "If you please, my lord," they said,
21 "we came here once before to buy food. But at the place
where we stopped for the night, we opened our bags and
each of us found his money, in its exact weight, in the
22 mouth of his bag. So we have brought it back with us. We
have also brought additional money to buy food. We do
23 not know who put our money in our bags." He replied,
"All is well. Do not be afraid. Your God, the God of your
father, must have placed a hidden gift in your bags. I
received the money you paid." Then he brought Shimon
24 out to them. He brought the brothers into Yosef's house,
gave them water to bathe their feet, and had fodder brought

י לְפָנֶיךָ וְחָטָאתִי לְךָ כָּל־הַיָּמִים׃ כִּי לוּלֵא הִתְמַהְמָהְנוּ כִּי־
יא עַתָּה שַׁבְנוּ זֶה פַעֲמָיִם׃ וַיֹּאמֶר אֲלֵהֶם יִשְׂרָאֵל אֲבִיהֶם
אִם־כֵּן ׀ אֵפוֹא זֹאת עֲשׂוּ קְחוּ מִזִּמְרַת הָאָרֶץ בִּכְלֵיכֶם
וְהוֹרִידוּ לָאִישׁ מִנְחָה מְעַט צֳרִי וּמְעַט דְּבַשׁ נְכֹאת וָלֹט
יב בָּטְנִים וּשְׁקֵדִים׃ וְכֶסֶף מִשְׁנֶה קְחוּ בְיֶדְכֶם וְאֶת־הַכֶּסֶף
הַמּוּשָׁב בְּפִי אַמְתְּחֹתֵיכֶם תָּשִׁיבוּ בְיֶדְכֶם אוּלַי מִשְׁגֶּה הוּא׃
יג יד וְאֶת־אֲחִיכֶם קָחוּ וְקוּמוּ שׁוּבוּ אֶל־הָאִישׁ׃ וְאֵל שַׁדַּי יִתֵּן לט
לָכֶם רַחֲמִים לִפְנֵי הָאִישׁ וְשִׁלַּח לָכֶם אֶת־אֲחִיכֶם אַחֵר
טו וְאֶת־בִּנְיָמִין וַאֲנִי כַּאֲשֶׁר שָׁכֹלְתִּי שָׁכָלְתִּי׃ וַיִּקְחוּ הָאֲנָשִׁים
אֶת־הַמִּנְחָה הַזֹּאת וּמִשְׁנֶה־כֶּסֶף לָקְחוּ בְיָדָם וְאֶת־בִּנְיָמִן
טז וַיָּקֻמוּ וַיֵּרְדוּ מִצְרַיִם וַיַּעַמְדוּ לִפְנֵי יוֹסֵף׃ וַיַּרְא יוֹסֵף אִתָּם ששי
אֶת־בִּנְיָמִין וַיֹּאמֶר לַאֲשֶׁר עַל־בֵּיתוֹ הָבֵא אֶת־הָאֲנָשִׁים
הַבָּיְתָה וּטְבֹחַ טֶבַח וְהָכֵן כִּי אִתִּי יֹאכְלוּ הָאֲנָשִׁים בַּצָּהֳרָיִם׃
יז וַיַּעַשׂ הָאִישׁ כַּאֲשֶׁר אָמַר יוֹסֵף וַיָּבֵא הָאִישׁ אֶת־הָאֲנָשִׁים
יח בֵּיתָה יוֹסֵף׃ וַיִּירְאוּ הָאֲנָשִׁים כִּי הוּבְאוּ בֵּית יוֹסֵף וַיֹּאמְרוּ
עַל־דְּבַר הַכֶּסֶף הַשָּׁב בְּאַמְתְּחֹתֵינוּ בַּתְּחִלָּה אֲנַחְנוּ מוּבָאִים
לְהִתְגֹּלֵל עָלֵינוּ וּלְהִתְנַפֵּל עָלֵינוּ וְלָקַחַת אֹתָנוּ לַעֲבָדִים
יט וְאֶת־חֲמֹרֵינוּ׃ וַיִּגְּשׁוּ אֶל־הָאִישׁ אֲשֶׁר עַל־בֵּית יוֹסֵף וַיְדַבְּרוּ
כ אֵלָיו פֶּתַח הַבָּיִת׃ וַיֹּאמְרוּ בִּי אֲדֹנִי יָרֹד יָרַדְנוּ בַּתְּחִלָּה
כא לִשְׁבָּר־אֹכֶל׃ וַיְהִי כִּי־בָאנוּ אֶל־הַמָּלוֹן וַנִּפְתְּחָה אֶת־
אַמְתְּחֹתֵינוּ וְהִנֵּה כֶסֶף־אִישׁ בְּפִי אַמְתַּחְתּוֹ כַּסְפֵּנוּ בְּמִשְׁקָלוֹ
כב וַנָּשֶׁב אֹתוֹ בְּיָדֵנוּ׃ וְכֶסֶף אַחֵר הוֹרַדְנוּ בְיָדֵנוּ לִשְׁבָּר־אֹכֶל
כג לֹא יָדַעְנוּ מִי־שָׂם כַּסְפֵּנוּ בְּאַמְתְּחֹתֵינוּ׃ וַיֹּאמֶר שָׁלוֹם לָכֶם
אַל־תִּירָאוּ אֱלֹהֵיכֶם וֵאלֹהֵי אֲבִיכֶם נָתַן לָכֶם מַטְמוֹן
בְּאַמְתְּחֹתֵיכֶם כַּסְפְּכֶם בָּא אֵלָי וַיּוֹצֵא אֲלֵהֶם אֶת־שִׁמְעוֹן׃
כד וַיָּבֵא הָאִישׁ אֶת־הָאֲנָשִׁים בֵּיתָה יוֹסֵף וַיִּתֶּן־מַיִם וַיִּרְחֲצוּ

25 for their donkeys. They set out their gifts in preparation
for Yosef's arrival at noon, because they had heard that
26 they were going to eat there. When Yosef entered the
house, they presented him with the gifts they had brought
27 and bowed low to the ground before him. He asked them
how they were. Then he asked, "How is the elderly father
28 about whom you spoke? Is he still alive?" They said, "Your
servant our father is alive and well." They bowed down
29 and prostrated themselves. Then he looked up and saw his
brother Binyamin, his mother's son, and asked, "Is this
your youngest brother, the one you mentioned to me?"
30 And he said, "God be gracious to you, my son." At that, he SHEVI'I
hurried out, for he was overcome with feeling toward his
brother and was on the verge of tears. He went into a
31 private room and there he wept. He washed his face and
came out, controlling himself. "Serve the food," he said.
32 They served him apart, them apart, and the Egyptians
who ate with him apart, for the Egyptians could not eat
with Hebrews, since to Egyptians that was considered
33 abhorrent. Seated by his direction in order of age, oldest to
34 youngest, they looked at one another in amazement. He
sent them portions from his table, giving Binyamin five
times as much as anyone else. And they drank and grew
44 1 merry with him. Then Yosef instructed his steward, "Fill
the men's bags with as much food as they can carry, and

---

life, for the realization of his dreams and his elevation to a position of power. Yosef does everything he can for his brothers and makes it as clear as he possibly can that he does not harbor a grudge against them for what they did to him all those many years before. Still, all those years later, his brothers will not trust him and will fear that he may still seek their harm. Rav Lichtenstein comments: "[Yosef] weeps over the weakness inherent in power, over the terrible price that he has paid for it. His dreams have indeed been realized, on some level, but the tragedy remains just as real. The torn shreds of the family have not been made completely whole."

The gap between public grandeur and private vulnerability is nowhere better illustrated than here. Yosef is surrounded by Egyptian admirers and supporters, and now his brothers are with him. None of these imagine that, in his private room, he weeps.

כה רַגְלֵיהֶם וַיִּתֵּן מִסְפּוֹא לַחֲמֹרֵיהֶם: וַיָּכִינוּ אֶת־הַמִּנְחָה עַד־
כו בּוֹא יוֹסֵף בַּצָּהֳרָיִם כִּי שָׁמְעוּ כִּי־שָׁם יֹאכְלוּ לָחֶם: וַיָּבֹא יוֹסֵף
הַבַּיְתָה וַיָּבִיאוּ לוֹ אֶת־הַמִּנְחָה אֲשֶׁר־בְּיָדָם הַבָּיְתָה
כז וַיִּשְׁתַּחֲווּ־לוֹ אָרְצָה: וַיִּשְׁאַל לָהֶם לְשָׁלוֹם וַיֹּאמֶר הֲשָׁלוֹם
כח אֲבִיכֶם הַזָּקֵן אֲשֶׁר אֲמַרְתֶּם הַעוֹדֶנּוּ חָי: וַיֹּאמְרוּ שָׁלוֹם
כט לְעַבְדְּךָ לְאָבִינוּ עוֹדֶנּוּ חָי וַיִּקְּדוּ וַיִּשְׁתַּחֲוּ: וַיִּשָּׂא עֵינָיו וַיַּרְא
אֶת־בִּנְיָמִין אָחִיו בֶּן־אִמּוֹ וַיֹּאמֶר הֲזֶה אֲחִיכֶם הַקָּטֹן אֲשֶׁר
ל אֲמַרְתֶּם אֵלָי וַיֹּאמַר אֱלֹהִים יָחְנְךָ בְּנִי: וַיְמַהֵר יוֹסֵף כִּי־ שביעי
נִכְמְרוּ רַחֲמָיו אֶל־אָחִיו וַיְבַקֵּשׁ לִבְכּוֹת וַיָּבֹא הַחַדְרָה וַיֵּבְךְּ
לא לב שָׁמָּה: וַיִּרְחַץ פָּנָיו וַיֵּצֵא וַיִּתְאַפַּק וַיֹּאמֶר שִׂימוּ לָחֶם: וַיָּשִׂימוּ
לוֹ לְבַדּוֹ וְלָהֶם לְבַדָּם וְלַמִּצְרִים הָאֹכְלִים אִתּוֹ לְבַדָּם כִּי לֹא
יוּכְלוּן הַמִּצְרִים לֶאֱכֹל אֶת־הָעִבְרִים לֶחֶם כִּי־תוֹעֵבָה הִוא
לג לְמִצְרָיִם: וַיֵּשְׁבוּ לְפָנָיו הַבְּכֹר כִּבְכֹרָתוֹ וְהַצָּעִיר כִּצְעִרָתוֹ
לד וַיִּתְמְהוּ הָאֲנָשִׁים אִישׁ אֶל־רֵעֵהוּ: וַיִּשָּׂא מַשְׂאֹת מֵאֵת פָּנָיו
אֲלֵהֶם וַתֵּרֶב מַשְׂאַת בִּנְיָמִן מִמַּשְׂאֹת כֻּלָּם חָמֵשׁ יָדוֹת
א וַיִּשְׁתּוּ וַיִּשְׁכְּרוּ עִמּוֹ: וַיְצַו אֶת־אֲשֶׁר עַל־בֵּיתוֹ לֵאמֹר מַלֵּא מד
אֶת־אַמְתְּחֹת הָאֲנָשִׁים אֹכֶל כַּאֲשֶׁר יוּכְלוּן שְׂאֵת וְשִׂים

43:30 וַיֵּבְךְּ שָׁמָּה *And there he wept* – No one in the Tanakh weeps as much as Yosef. Esav wept when he discovered that Yaakov had taken his blessing (Gen. 27:38). Yaakov wept when he saw the love of his life, Raḥel, for the first time (29:11). Both brothers, Yaakov and Esav, wept when they met again after their long estrangement (33:4). Yaakov wept when told that his beloved son Yosef was dead (37:35).

But Yosef's seven acts of weeping have no parallel. They span the full spectrum of emotion, from painful memory to the complicated joy of being reunited, first here, with his brother Binyamin, then with his father Yaakov. There are the complex tears immediately before and after he discloses his identity to his brothers, and there are the tears of bereavement at Yaakov's deathbed. The most intriguing are the last, the tears he sheds when he hears that his brothers fear that he will take revenge on them now that their father is no longer alive.

In his essay "Yosef's Tears," Rav Aharon Lichtenstein suggests that that last act of weeping is an expression of the price Yosef pays, over the course of his

2 put each one's money in the mouth of his bag. Then put
my chalice – the silver chalice – in the mouth of the
youngest one's bag, along with the money for his grain."
3 He did as Yosef told him. As morning showed its first
light, the men were sent on their way with their donkeys.
4 They had not gone far from the city when Yosef said to his
steward, "Go after the men at once. When you catch up
with them, say to them, 'Why have you repaid good with
5 evil? Is it not from this that my master drinks and that he
uses for divination? It is a wicked thing you have done.'"
6 He caught up with them and repeated those words to
7 them. But they said to him, "How can my lord say such
things? Heaven forbid that we should do such a thing!
8 Look, we brought back to you from Canaan the money
we found in the mouths of our bags. Why would we steal
9 silver or gold from your master's house? If any of your
servants is found with it, he shall die, and the rest of us
10 will become my lord's slaves." "Let it be as you say," he
replied, "but only the one with whom it is found shall be
11 my slave. The rest of you can go free." Each of them
quickly lowered his bag to the ground, and each opened
12 his bag. He searched, beginning with the oldest and
ending with the youngest. The chalice was found in
13 Binyamin's bag. The brothers tore their clothes. Each
loaded his donkey again, and they returned to the city.
14 Yehuda and his brothers came to Yosef's house – he was MAFTIR
still there – and they threw themselves on the ground
15 before him. Yosef said to them, "What is this thing you
have done? Do you not know that a man like me can find

In effect, Yosef has constructed a controlled experiment in "perfect repentance." When the cup is found in Binyamin's sack and the brothers say, "We are now my lord's slaves" (44:16), Yosef replies, "Heaven forbid that I should do such a thing.…The man in whose possession the chalice was found will become my slave. As for the rest of you, go back to your father in peace" (44:17). He gives them the chance to walk away in freedom if they are willing to leave Binyamin as a slave. This is the moment of trial.

ב כֶּסֶף־אִישׁ בְּפִי אַמְתַּחְתּוֹ: וְאֶת־גְּבִיעִי גְּבִיעַ הַכֶּסֶף תָּשִׂים
בְּפִי אַמְתַּחַת הַקָּטֹן וְאֵת כֶּסֶף שִׁבְרוֹ וַיַּעַשׂ כִּדְבַר יוֹסֵף אֲשֶׁר
ג ד דִּבֵּר: הַבֹּקֶר אוֹר וְהָאֲנָשִׁים שֻׁלְּחוּ הֵמָּה וַחֲמֹרֵיהֶם: הֵם
יָצְאוּ אֶת־הָעִיר לֹא הִרְחִיקוּ וְיוֹסֵף אָמַר לַאֲשֶׁר עַל־בֵּיתוֹ
קוּם רְדֹף אַחֲרֵי הָאֲנָשִׁים וְהִשַּׂגְתָּם וְאָמַרְתָּ אֲלֵהֶם לָמָּה
ה שִׁלַּמְתֶּם רָעָה תַּחַת טוֹבָה: הֲלוֹא זֶה אֲשֶׁר יִשְׁתֶּה אֲדֹנִי בּוֹ
ו וְהוּא נַחֵשׁ יְנַחֵשׁ בּוֹ הֲרֵעֹתֶם אֲשֶׁר עֲשִׂיתֶם: וַיַּשִּׂגֵם וַיְדַבֵּר
ז אֲלֵהֶם אֶת־הַדְּבָרִים הָאֵלֶּה: וַיֹּאמְרוּ אֵלָיו לָמָּה יְדַבֵּר אֲדֹנִי
ח כַּדְּבָרִים הָאֵלֶּה חָלִילָה לַעֲבָדֶיךָ מֵעֲשׂוֹת כַּדָּבָר הַזֶּה: הֵן
כֶּסֶף אֲשֶׁר מָצָאנוּ בְּפִי אַמְתְּחֹתֵינוּ הֱשִׁיבֹנוּ אֵלֶיךָ מֵאֶרֶץ
ט כְּנָעַן וְאֵיךְ נִגְנֹב מִבֵּית אֲדֹנֶיךָ כֶּסֶף אוֹ זָהָב: אֲשֶׁר יִמָּצֵא
אִתּוֹ מֵעֲבָדֶיךָ וָמֵת וְגַם־אֲנַחְנוּ נִהְיֶה לַאדֹנִי לַעֲבָדִים:
י וַיֹּאמֶר גַּם־עַתָּה כְדִבְרֵיכֶם כֶּן־הוּא אֲשֶׁר יִמָּצֵא אִתּוֹ יִהְיֶה־
יא לִּי עָבֶד וְאַתֶּם תִּהְיוּ נְקִיִּם: וַיְמַהֲרוּ וַיּוֹרִדוּ אִישׁ אֶת־
יב אַמְתַּחְתּוֹ אָרְצָה וַיִּפְתְּחוּ אִישׁ אַמְתַּחְתּוֹ: וַיְחַפֵּשׂ בַּגָּדוֹל
יג הֵחֵל וּבַקָּטֹן כִּלָּה וַיִּמָּצֵא הַגָּבִיעַ בְּאַמְתַּחַת בִּנְיָמִן: וַיִּקְרְעוּ
יד שִׂמְלֹתָם וַיַּעֲמֹס אִישׁ עַל־חֲמֹרוֹ וַיָּשֻׁבוּ הָעִירָה: וַיָּבֹא יְהוּדָה מפטיר
וְאֶחָיו בֵּיתָה יוֹסֵף וְהוּא עוֹדֶנּוּ שָׁם וַיִּפְּלוּ לְפָנָיו אָרְצָה:
טו וַיֹּאמֶר לָהֶם יוֹסֵף מָה־הַמַּעֲשֶׂה הַזֶּה אֲשֶׁר עֲשִׂיתֶם הֲלוֹא

44:10 אֲשֶׁר יִמָּצֵא אִתּוֹ הוּא יִהְיֶה־לִּי עָבֶד *The one… shall be my slave* – They had sold their brother into slavery. How would they act if placed in the same situation again? Yosef plans the scene with meticulous care. He must create a situation in which they can purchase their freedom by leaving one of their number as a slave. It cannot be one of the brothers chosen at random. It must be one of whom they are jealous, as they were of Yosef. That is why he chooses Binyamin, the other son of Raḥel, his father's favorite wife. He has to add one further element. What provoked them to rage many years earlier was the physical emblem of favoritism, the richly embroidered cloak. That is why, in an otherwise inexplicable detail, when the brothers return with Binyamin and sit to eat their meal, "he sent them portions from his table, giving Binyamin *five times as much* as anyone else" (Gen. 43:34).

16 out the truth by divination?" Yehuda replied, "What can
we say to my lord? What can we speak? How can we
prove our innocence? God has uncovered your servants'
guilt! We are now my lord's slaves – we and the one in
17 whose possession the chalice was found." "Heaven forbid
that I should do such a thing," he said. "The man in
whose possession the chalice was found will become my
slave. As for the rest of you, go back to your father in
peace."

The haftara for Parashat Miketz is on page 1446.
On Ḥanukka read the haftara on page 1648 (even on Rosh Ḥodesh or Erev Rosh Ḥodesh Tevet). On the second Shabbat of Ḥanukka read the haftara on page 1652.

---

a slave to a strange land far from home. This is not revenge, for which Yosef has neither desire nor need. It is, rather, the only way they will understand what evil feels like from the other side, not as perpetrator but as victim. That is the necessary prelude to repentance, itself the most compelling proof that we are free. Kayin is able to commit murder because, as he says, "Am I my brother's keeper?" (Gen. 4:9). He does not feel Hevel's pain. He feels only his own at having his offering rejected. *The way we learn not to commit evil is to experience an event from the perspective of the victim.* Yehuda's repentance – showing that he *is* his brother Binyamin's keeper – redeems not only his own earlier sin, but also Kayin's.

In learning what this ordeal teaches them, the brothers enact the greatest of biblical themes: the defeat of tragedy in the name of hope.

טז יְדַעְתֶּם כִּי־נַחֵשׁ יְנַחֵשׁ אִישׁ אֲשֶׁר כָּמֹנִי׃ וַיֹּאמֶר יְהוּדָה
מַה־נֹּאמַר לַאדֹנִי מַה־נְּדַבֵּר וּמַה־נִּצְטַדָּק הָאֱלֹהִים מָצָא
אֶת־עֲוֺן עֲבָדֶיךָ הִנֶּנּוּ עֲבָדִים לַאדֹנִי גַּם־אֲנַחְנוּ גַּם אֲשֶׁר־
יז נִמְצָא הַגָּבִיעַ בְּיָדוֹ׃ וַיֹּאמֶר חָלִילָה לִּי מֵעֲשׂוֹת זֹאת הָאִישׁ
אֲשֶׁר נִמְצָא הַגָּבִיעַ בְּיָדוֹ הוּא יִהְיֶה־לִּי עָבֶד וְאַתֶּם עֲלוּ
לְשָׁלוֹם אֶל־אֲבִיכֶם׃

The הפטרה *for* פרשת מקץ *is on page 1447.*
On חנוכה *read the* הפטרה *on page 1649 (even on* ראש חודש *or* ערב ראש חודש טבת*). On the second* שבת *of* חנוכה *read the* הפטרה *on page 1653.*

44:16 הִנֶּנּוּ עֲבָדִים לַאדֹנִי *We are now my lord's slaves* – The length and weight of Yosef's story testifies that, within the highly structured book of Genesis, it is resolving the tension not of that generation alone, but of all that went before. Genesis is about failure and learning from failure, discovering that we can change. Yaakov discovers this after a long night of wrestling with the angel. His sons discover it after a long period of suspense and fear.

Here, as we have seen, it happens through role reversal. The most fundamental fact about consciousness is that I cannot feel someone else's pain. I can only feel my own. This is the source of the human tendency to divide the world into brothers and others, kin and non-kin, friends and strangers, the "Us" to whom I belong, and the "Them," the Other, to whom I do not belong. That is why the covenantal family, the children of Israel, begin their collective life as a nation in Egypt, as slaves, so that they will know from the inside what it feels like to be on the other side.

That is what Yosef is forcing his brothers to do. They must undergo what he went through when he was sold as

Parashat Vayigash

44 18 But Yehuda stepped forward to him. "If you please, my
lord," he said, "let your servant speak a word in my lord's
hearing. Do not be angry with me, you who are the equal
19 of Pharaoh. My lord asked his servants, 'Do you have a

---

every way. Which is why it was only when Yehuda came close to Yosef – *Vayigash* – that the coldness between them thawed, and they became brothers, not strangers to one another. Distance damaged the relationship. *Vayigash* – Yehuda's act of drawing close – restored it.

YEHUDA'S TEST

Yehuda's final confrontation can only be fully understood in the context of his initial behavior toward Yosef. It is Yehuda, in his first recorded words, who suggested selling Yosef into slavery:

> Yehuda said to his brothers, "What do we gain by killing our brother and covering his blood? Let's sell him to the Ishmaelites and not harm him with our own hands. After all, he is our brother, our own flesh and blood." His brothers agreed. (Gen. 37:26–27)

This is a speech of monstrous callousness. There is no mention of the evil of murder, merely a pragmatic calculation ("What do we gain?"). At the very moment he calls Yosef "our own flesh and blood," Yehuda is proposing to sell him as a slave. At this point, Yehuda is the last person from whom we expect great things.

However, Yehuda – more than anyone else in the Torah – changes. The man we see confronting Yosef all these years later is not the same personality as the one who spoke when Yosef was trapped in the pit. Then he was prepared to see his brother sold into slavery. Now he is prepared to suffer that fate himself rather than see Binyamin held as a slave.

It is a precise reversal of character. Callousness has been replaced with concern. Indifference to his brother's fate has been transformed into courage on his behalf. Yehuda is willing to suffer what he once inflicted on Yosef so that the same fate should not befall Binyamin. At this point Yosef reveals his identity. We know why. Yehuda has passed the test that Yosef has carefully constructed for him. Yosef wants to know if Yehuda has changed. He has.

This is a highly significant moment in the history of the human spirit. Yehuda is the first penitent – the first *baal teshuva* – in the Torah.

Yosef is consistently known to tradition as *hatzaddik*, "the righteous." He also becomes *mishneh lamelekh*, "second to the king." Yehuda, however, becomes

פרשת ויגש

מד יח וַיִּגַּ֨שׁ אֵלָ֜יו יְהוּדָ֗ה וַיֹּאמֶר֮ בִּ֣י אֲדֹנִי֒ יְדַבֶּר־נָ֨א עַבְדְּךָ֤ דָבָר֙ מ
יט בְּאָזְנֵ֣י אֲדֹנִ֔י וְאַל־יִ֥חַר אַפְּךָ֖ בְּעַבְדֶּ֑ךָ כִּ֥י כָמ֖וֹךָ כְּפַרְעֹֽה׃ אֲדֹנִ֣י

VAYIGASH

Vayigash begins with the climactic scene in which Yosef finally reveals himself to his brothers. Moved by Yehuda's impassioned plea for Binyamin's freedom, in return for which he declares himself ready to take Binyamin's place as a slave, Yosef discloses his identity and the estrangement of the brothers comes to an end. On Yosef's instructions, they return to Yaakov with the news that his beloved son is still alive, and the family is reunited. Egypt, meanwhile, is spared from mass starvation under Yosef's direction, at the cost of major upheavals, the significance of which will only be fully apparent in Exodus.

Yosef's forgiveness is the bridge between Genesis and Exodus. The first is about the children of Israel as a family, the second is about them as a nation. Central to both is the experience of slavery, first Yosef's and finally the entire people's.

44:18 וַיִּגַּשׁ אֵלָיו יְהוּדָה *Yehuda stepped forward to him* – What do porcupines do in winter? asked Schopenhauer. If they come too close to one another, they injure each other. If they stay too far apart, they freeze. Life, for porcupines, is a delicate balance between closeness and distance. It is hard to get it right and dangerous to get it wrong. And so it is for us.

That is the force of the word that gives our *parasha* its name: *Vayigash*, literally, "And he came close." For perhaps the first time in his life, Yehuda comes close to his brother Yosef. The irony is, of course, that he does not know it is Yosef. But that one act of coming close melts all of Yosef's reserve, all his defenses, and as if unable to stop himself, he finally discloses his identity.

This moment contrasts with another, many chapters, and many years, earlier: "They saw him in the distance, and by the time he reached them, they had plotted to kill him" (Gen. 37:18).

At the beginning of the story, when Yosef was sent by his father to see how the brothers were doing, tending the sheep, they saw him from far away, from a distance. They couldn't see his face. All they could see was the "ornately colored robe" (37:3) that so upsets them because it reminded them that it was he and not they whom their father loved. From far away, we don't see people as human beings, and when we stop seeing people as human beings, they become instead objects of envy or hate. Yosef and his brothers were too far apart in

20 father or a brother?' And we told my lord, 'We have an
elderly father and there is a young son, a child of his old
age. When his brother died, he was the only one of his
21 mother's sons left, and his father loves him.' Then you said
to your servants, 'Bring him to me that I may set eyes on
22 him.' But we said to my lord, 'The boy cannot leave his
23 father. If he left him, his father would die.' Then you told
your servants, 'Unless your youngest brother comes with
24 you, you shall not see my face again.' When we went back
to your servant my father, we told him what my lord had
25 said. Then our father said, 'Go back and buy a little more
26 food.' We said, 'We cannot go. We can go only if our
youngest brother is with us. If he is not with us, we cannot
27 see the man's face.' Then your servant, my father, said to
28 us, 'You know that my wife bore me two sons. One is
gone from me, and I said, "He must have been torn to
29 pieces." I have not seen him since. If you take this one
from me and harm befalls him, you will bring down my
30 gray head in grief to Sheol.' So now, if the boy is not with
us when I go back to your servant my father, so bound

---

moon – his father and mother – would bow down to him.

This angered Yaakov, and Yosef knew it. His father had rebuked him. It was outrageous to suggest that his parents would prostrate themselves before him. It was wrong to imagine it, all the more so to say it.

Yosef did not communicate with his father because he believed his father no longer wanted to see him or hear from him. His father had terminated the relationship. That was a reasonable inference from the facts as Yosef knew them. He could not have known that Yaakov still loved him, that his brothers had deceived their father by showing him Yosef's bloodstained cloak, and that his father mourned for him and "refused to be comforted." We know these facts because the Torah tells us. But Yosef, far away, in another land, serving as a slave, could not know. This places the story in a completely new and tragic light.

Yosef's first thought when the truth is revealed is not about Yehuda or Binyamin, but about Yaakov. A doubt he has harbored for twenty-two years has been shown to be unfounded. Hence his first question: "Is my father really still alive?" (Gen. 45:3).

כ שָׁאַל אֶת־עֲבָדָיו לֵאמֹר הֲיֵשׁ־לָכֶם אָב אוֹ־אָח: וַנֹּאמֶר
אֶל־אֲדֹנִי יֶשׁ־לָנוּ אָב זָקֵן וְיֶלֶד זְקֻנִים קָטָן וְאָחִיו מֵת וַיִּוָּתֵר
כא הוּא לְבַדּוֹ לְאִמּוֹ וְאָבִיו אֲהֵבוֹ: וַתֹּאמֶר אֶל־עֲבָדֶיךָ הוֹרִדֻהוּ
כב אֵלָי וְאָשִׂימָה עֵינִי עָלָיו: וַנֹּאמֶר אֶל־אֲדֹנִי לֹא־יוּכַל הַנַּעַר
כג לַעֲזֹב אֶת־אָבִיו וְעָזַב אֶת־אָבִיו וָמֵת: וַתֹּאמֶר אֶל־עֲבָדֶיךָ
אִם־לֹא יֵרֵד אֲחִיכֶם הַקָּטֹן אִתְּכֶם לֹא תֹסִפוּן לִרְאוֹת פָּנָי:
כד וַיְהִי כִּי עָלִינוּ אֶל־עַבְדְּךָ אָבִי וַנַּגֶּד־לוֹ אֵת דִּבְרֵי אֲדֹנִי:
כה כו וַיֹּאמֶר אָבִינוּ שֻׁבוּ שִׁבְרוּ־לָנוּ מְעַט־אֹכֶל: וַנֹּאמֶר לֹא נוּכַל
לָרֶדֶת אִם־יֵשׁ אָחִינוּ הַקָּטֹן אִתָּנוּ וְיָרַדְנוּ כִּי־לֹא נוּכַל
כז לִרְאוֹת פְּנֵי הָאִישׁ וְאָחִינוּ הַקָּטֹן אֵינֶנּוּ אִתָּנוּ: וַיֹּאמֶר עַבְדְּךָ
כח אָבִי אֵלֵינוּ אַתֶּם יְדַעְתֶּם כִּי שְׁנַיִם יָלְדָה־לִּי אִשְׁתִּי: וַיֵּצֵא
הָאֶחָד מֵאִתִּי וָאֹמַר אַךְ טָרֹף טֹרָף וְלֹא רְאִיתִיו עַד־הֵנָּה:
כט וּלְקַחְתֶּם גַּם־אֶת־זֶה מֵעִם פָּנַי וְקָרָהוּ אָסוֹן וְהוֹרַדְתֶּם אֶת־
ל שֵׂיבָתִי בְּרָעָה שְׁאֹלָה: וְעַתָּה כְּבֹאִי אֶל־עַבְדְּךָ אָבִי וְהַנַּעַר

the father of Israel's kings. Where the penitent Yehuda stands, even the perfectly righteous Yosef cannot stand. However great an individual may be in virtue of his or her natural character, greater still is one who is capable of growth and change. That is the power of penitence, and it begins with Yehuda.

44:28 אַךְ טָרֹף טֹרָף *"He must have been torn to pieces"* – It is one of the great questions we naturally ask each time we read the story of Yosef. Why does he not, at some time during their twenty-two-year separation, send word to his father that he is alive? Yosef knows how much his father loves him. He must know how much their separation grieves him. He does not know what Yaakov thinks has happened to him, but he knows that it is his duty to communicate with him when the opportunity arises, to tell his father that he is alive and well. Why then does he not?

The story of Yosef's descent into slavery and exile began when his father sent him, alone, to see how the brothers were faring. It was there, at that meeting far from home, that they plotted to kill him, lowered him into a pit, and eventually sold him as a slave. What else could he conclude, as he reflected on the events that led up to his sale as a slave, other than that Yaakov had deliberately placed him in this danger? Why? Because of the immediately prior event, when Yosef had told his father that the sun and

31 together are their lives that when he sees that the boy is SHENI
not with us, he will die. Your servants will have brought
down the gray head of your servant, our father, in grief to
32 Sheol. Your servant offered himself to my father as a
guarantee for the boy. I said, 'If I do not bring him back to
33 you, I will have sinned against my father for all time.' So,
please, let your servant stay as my lord's slave in place of
34 the boy, and let the boy go back with his brothers. For
how can I go back to my father if the boy is not with me?
I could not bear to see the misery that would overwhelm
45 1 my father!" Yosef could no longer control himself in the
company of all his attendants. He cried out, "Have
everyone leave my presence!" So no one else was with
2 Yosef when he revealed himself to his brothers. He wept
so loudly that the Egyptians could hear him, and the
3 news reached Pharaoh's palace. Yosef said to his brothers,
"I am Yosef. Is my father really still alive?" His brothers
were so bewildered at his presence that they could not

---

repentance-and-forgiveness culture, the first of its kind in the world.

Humanity changes the day Yosef forgives his brothers. When we forgive and are worthy of being forgiven, we are no longer prisoners of our past.

45:3 אֲנִי יוֹסֵף *I am Yosef* – One of the key concepts of Judaism is *teshuva*, a complex concept involving remorse, repentance, and return. If we understand the three necessary components of *teshuva*, the logic of Yosef's course of action becomes clear. The drama to which he subjects his brothers is leading them – for the first time in recorded history – through the three stages of *teshuva*: (1) admission of guilt, (2) confession, and (3) behavioral change.

Yehuda, the very brother who was responsible for selling Yosef into slavery (Gen. 37:27), now offers to sacrifice his own freedom rather than let Binyamin be held as a slave. The circumstances are similar to what they were years earlier, but Yehuda's behavior is now diametrically opposite to what it was then. He has the opportunity and ability to repeat the offense, but he does not do so. Yehuda has fulfilled the conditions set out by the Sages and Rambam for "perfect *teshuva*" (*Hilkhot Teshuva* 2:1). As soon as he does so, Yosef reveals his identity and the drama is at an end. Not dreams, not revenge, but *teshuva* is what has driven Yosef all along.

God does not demand perfection; by giving us free will He empowers us

לא אֵינֶנּוּ אִתָּנוּ וְנַפְשׁוֹ קְשׁוּרָה בְנַפְשׁוֹ: וְהָיָה כִּרְאוֹתוֹ כִּי־אֵין שני
הַנַּעַר וָמֵת וְהוֹרִידוּ עֲבָדֶיךָ אֶת־שֵׂיבַת עַבְדְּךָ אָבִינוּ בְּיָגוֹן
לב שְׁאֹלָה: כִּי עַבְדְּךָ עָרַב אֶת־הַנַּעַר מֵעִם אָבִי לֵאמֹר אִם־לֹא
לג אֲבִיאֶנּוּ אֵלֶיךָ וְחָטָאתִי לְאָבִי כָּל־הַיָּמִים: וְעַתָּה יֵשֶׁב־נָא
לד עַבְדְּךָ תַּחַת הַנַּעַר עֶבֶד לַאדֹנִי וְהַנַּעַר יַעַל עִם־אֶחָיו: כִּי־
אֵיךְ אֶעֱלֶה אֶל־אָבִי וְהַנַּעַר אֵינֶנּוּ אִתִּי פֶּן אֶרְאֶה בָרָע אֲשֶׁר
מה א יִמְצָא אֶת־אָבִי: וְלֹא־יָכֹל יוֹסֵף לְהִתְאַפֵּק לְכֹל הַנִּצָּבִים
עָלָיו וַיִּקְרָא הוֹצִיאוּ כָל־אִישׁ מֵעָלָי וְלֹא־עָמַד אִישׁ אִתּוֹ
ב בְּהִתְוַדַּע יוֹסֵף אֶל־אֶחָיו: וַיִּתֵּן אֶת־קֹלוֹ בִּבְכִי וַיִּשְׁמְעוּ
ג מִצְרַיִם וַיִּשְׁמַע בֵּית פַּרְעֹה: וַיֹּאמֶר יוֹסֵף אֶל־אֶחָיו אֲנִי יוֹסֵף
הַעוֹד אָבִי חָי וְלֹא־יָכְלוּ אֶחָיו לַעֲנוֹת אֹתוֹ כִּי נִבְהֲלוּ מִפָּנָיו:

YOSEF FORGIVES HIS BROTHERS

This is the first recorded moment in history in which one human being forgives another. The first time God forgives is after the sin of the golden calf. God does not forgive Adam and Ḥava or Kayin. He mitigates their punishment, but mitigation is not forgiveness. God does not forgive the generation of the flood, or the builders of Bavel, or the sinners of Sedom.

God, in short, does not forgive human beings until human beings learn to forgive. It takes Yosef to bring forgiveness into the world. Had God forgiven first, He would have made the human situation worse, not better. People would have said, "Why shouldn't I harm others? After all, God forgives." This is what God has been waiting for.

Forgiveness transformed the human situation. For the first time it established the possibility that we are not condemned endlessly to repeat the past. Genuine forgiveness only exists in a culture in which repentance exists. Repentance presupposes that we are free and morally responsible agents who are capable of change, specifically the change that comes about when we recognize that something we have done is wrong and we are responsible and must never do it again. When I repent, I show I can change. The future is not predestined. I can make it different from what it might have been. And when I forgive, I show that my action is not mere reaction, as revenge would be. Forgiveness breaks the irreversibility of the past. The possibility of that kind of moral transformation simply did not exist in ancient Greece or any other pagan culture. To put it technically, Greece was a shame-and-honor culture. Judaism was a guilt-

4 answer him. "Come close to me, please," said Yosef to his
brothers. They came close, and he said, "I am your brother
5 Yosef, whom you sold into Egypt. And now, do not be
distressed or angry with yourselves that you sold me here,
6 for God sent me ahead of you to save lives. For two years
now there has been famine in the land, and for another
7 five years there will be no plowing or reaping. So God
sent me ahead of you to ensure your survival in the land,
8 and to save your lives by a great deliverance. So then, it SHELISHI
was not you who sent me here, but God. He has made me
a father to Pharaoh, lord of his whole household and ruler
9 of all Egypt. Hurry back to my father and tell him, 'This is
what your son Yosef says: God has made me lord of all
10 Egypt. Come down to me without delay. You may live in
the region of Goshen where you will be close to me, you,
your children, and your grandchildren, your flocks and
11 herds and all that is yours. I will provide for you there, for
there are still five years of famine to come. Otherwise
you, your household, and all who belong to you will be
12 destitute.' You and my brother Binyamin can see with
13 your own eyes that it is I who am speaking to you. Tell my
father about all the honor accorded to me in Egypt and
about everything you have seen. Hurry now – bring my
14 father here." Then he threw his arms around his brother
Binyamin's neck and wept, and Binyamin wept on his
15 neck; he kissed all his brothers and wept over them. Only

---

that he could act as their protector in the years to come. It is a moment of supreme generosity of spirit.

To achieve this, Yosef has had to rethink the entire sequence of events. He no longer sees it in terms of a wrong done against him by his brothers. He sees it as part of a providential plan to bring him to where God needs him to be ("So then, it was not you who sent me here, but God"). He thinks not only of the moment twenty-two years earlier when he was sold as a slave, but of its long-term consequences. Before he can come to terms with his brothers, Yosef has to come to terms with himself and his experiences. Forgiveness lifts the forgiver even more than the one who is forgiven.

45:15 וְאַחֲרֵי כֵן *Only after that* – Yosef has reframed his entire past. He no longer sees himself as a man wronged by his

ד וַיֹּאמֶר יוֹסֵף אֶל־אֶחָיו גְּשׁוּ־נָא אֵלַי וַיִּגָּשׁוּ וַיֹּאמֶר אֲנִי יוֹסֵף
ה אֲחִיכֶם אֲשֶׁר־מְכַרְתֶּם אֹתִי מִצְרָיְמָה: וְעַתָּה | אַל־תֵּעָצְבוּ
וְאַל־יִחַר בְּעֵינֵיכֶם כִּי־מְכַרְתֶּם אֹתִי הֵנָּה כִּי לְמִחְיָה שְׁלָחַנִי
ו אֱלֹהִים לִפְנֵיכֶם: כִּי־זֶה שְׁנָתַיִם הָרָעָב בְּקֶרֶב הָאָרֶץ וְעוֹד
ז חָמֵשׁ שָׁנִים אֲשֶׁר אֵין־חָרִישׁ וְקָצִיר: וַיִּשְׁלָחֵנִי אֱלֹהִים
לִפְנֵיכֶם לָשׂוּם לָכֶם שְׁאֵרִית בָּאָרֶץ וּלְהַחֲיוֹת לָכֶם לִפְלֵיטָה
ח גְּדֹלָה: וְעַתָּה לֹא־אַתֶּם שְׁלַחְתֶּם אֹתִי הֵנָּה כִּי הָאֱלֹהִים שלישי
וַיְשִׂימֵנִי לְאָב לְפַרְעֹה וּלְאָדוֹן לְכָל־בֵּיתוֹ וּמֹשֵׁל בְּכָל־אֶרֶץ
ט מִצְרָיִם: מַהֲרוּ וַעֲלוּ אֶל־אָבִי וַאֲמַרְתֶּם אֵלָיו כֹּה אָמַר בִּנְךָ
יוֹסֵף שָׂמַנִי אֱלֹהִים לְאָדוֹן לְכָל־מִצְרָיִם רְדָה אֵלַי אַל־
י תַּעֲמֹד: וְיָשַׁבְתָּ בְאֶרֶץ־גֹּשֶׁן וְהָיִיתָ קָרוֹב אֵלַי אַתָּה וּבָנֶיךָ
יא וּבְנֵי בָנֶיךָ וְצֹאנְךָ וּבְקָרְךָ וְכָל־אֲשֶׁר־לָךְ: וְכִלְכַּלְתִּי אֹתְךָ
שָׁם כִּי־עוֹד חָמֵשׁ שָׁנִים רָעָב פֶּן־תִּוָּרֵשׁ אַתָּה וּבֵיתְךָ וְכָל־
יב אֲשֶׁר־לָךְ: וְהִנֵּה עֵינֵיכֶם רֹאוֹת וְעֵינֵי אָחִי בִנְיָמִין כִּי־פִי
יג הַמְדַבֵּר אֲלֵיכֶם: וְהִגַּדְתֶּם לְאָבִי אֶת־כָּל־כְּבוֹדִי בְּמִצְרַיִם
וְאֵת כָּל־אֲשֶׁר רְאִיתֶם וּמִהַרְתֶּם וְהוֹרַדְתֶּם אֶת־אָבִי הֵנָּה:
יד וַיִּפֹּל עַל־צַוְּארֵי בִנְיָמִן־אָחִיו וַיֵּבְךְּ וּבִנְיָמִן בָּכָה עַל־צַוָּארָיו:
טו וַיְנַשֵּׁק לְכָל־אֶחָיו וַיֵּבְךְּ עֲלֵהֶם וְאַחֲרֵי כֵן דִּבְּרוּ אֶחָיו אִתּוֹ:

---

to make mistakes. All He asks is that we acknowledge our mistakes and commit ourselves not to make them again – in a word, that we be capable of *teshuva*. Yehuda, by undergoing Yosef's test, demonstrates that the children of Israel have become *baalei teshuva*, masters of repentance, capable of learning from, and growing through, their mistakes. Jewish history, starting with exile and exodus in Egypt, can now begin.

45:8 וְעַתָּה לֹא־אַתֶּם שְׁלַחְתֶּם אֹתִי הֵנָּה כִּי הָאֱלֹהִים

▶

It was not you who sent me here, but God – Yosef makes no reference to the brothers' plot to kill him or to the fact that they sold him into slavery. He makes no mention of the lost years he spent, first as Potifar's slave, then as a prisoner in jail. Not only does he forgive them, he does everything possible to relieve them from a sense of guilt. He tells them that they were not really responsible; that it had been God's plan all along; that it had been for the best, so that he could save lives during the years of famine, and so

16 after that could his brothers speak to him. When the news
reached Pharaoh's palace that Yosef's brothers had come,
17 Pharaoh and his officials were gratified. Pharaoh said to
Yosef, "Tell your brothers, 'Do this: Load your animals
18 and go back to Canaan. Bring your father and your families
and come to me. I will give you the best of the land of
19 Egypt; you shall live off the cream of the land. You are also REVI'I
instructed to do this: Take wagons from Egypt for your
20 children and wives. Bring your father and come. Do not
trouble yourselves about your belongings, for the best of
21 all Egypt will be yours.'" Yisrael's sons did so. Yosef gave
them wagons as Pharaoh had ordered, and gave them
22 provisions for the journey. To each he gave new clothes,
but to Binyamin he gave three hundred pieces of silver and
23 five sets of clothes. To his father he sent the following: ten
donkeys loaded with the best things of Egypt and ten
female donkeys loaded with grain, bread, and food for his
24 father's journey. He sent his brothers on their way; and as
they were leaving, he said to them, "Do not quarrel on the
25 way." So they went up out of Egypt and came to their
26 father Yaakov in Canaan. They told him, "Yosef is still
alive; in fact, he is ruler over all Egypt." His heart stood
27 still; he did not believe them. But when they told him
everything Yosef had said to them, and when he saw the
wagons that Yosef had sent to carry him back, Yaakov's
28 spirit was filled with new life. Yisrael said, "It is enough: ḤAMISHI
Yosef my son is still alive. I must go and see him before I
46 1 die." So Yisrael set out with all he had. When he reached
Be'er Sheva, he offered up sacrifices to the God of his
2 father Yitzḥak. And God spoke to Yisrael in a night

---

movements in psychotherapy in the modern world. He has shown the power of reframing. We cannot change the past. But by changing the way we think about the past, we can change the future.

Whatever situation we are in, by reframing it we can change our entire response, giving us the strength to survive, the courage to persist, and the resilience to emerge, on the far side of darkness, into the light of a new and better day.

טז וְהַקֹּל֩ נִשְׁמַ֨ע בֵּ֤ית פַּרְעֹה֙ לֵאמֹ֔ר בָּ֖אוּ אֲחֵ֣י יוֹסֵ֑ף וַיִּיטַב֙ בְּעֵינֵ֣י
יז פַרְעֹ֔ה וּבְעֵינֵ֖י עֲבָדָֽיו׃ וַיֹּ֤אמֶר פַּרְעֹה֙ אֶל־יוֹסֵ֔ף אֱמֹ֥ר אֶל־
אַחֶ֖יךָ זֹ֣את עֲשׂ֑וּ טַֽעֲנוּ֙ אֶת־בְּעִ֣ירְכֶ֔ם וּלְכוּ־בֹ֖אוּ אַ֥רְצָה כְּנָֽעַן׃
יח וּקְח֧וּ אֶת־אֲבִיכֶ֛ם וְאֶת־בָּתֵּיכֶ֖ם וּבֹ֣אוּ אֵלָ֑י וְאֶתְּנָ֣ה לָכֶ֗ם
יט אֶת־טוּב֙ אֶ֣רֶץ מִצְרַ֔יִם וְאִכְל֖וּ אֶת־חֵ֥לֶב הָאָֽרֶץ׃ וְאַתָּ֥ה רביעי
צֻוֵּ֖יתָה זֹ֣את עֲשׂ֑וּ קְחוּ־לָכֶם֩ מֵאֶ֨רֶץ מִצְרַ֜יִם עֲגָל֗וֹת לְטַפְּכֶם֙
כ וְלִנְשֵׁיכֶ֔ם וּנְשָׂאתֶ֥ם אֶת־אֲבִיכֶ֖ם וּבָאתֶֽם׃ וְעֵ֣ינְכֶ֔ם אַל־תָּחֹ֖ס
כא עַל־כְּלֵיכֶ֑ם כִּי־ט֛וּב כָּל־אֶ֥רֶץ מִצְרַ֖יִם לָכֶ֥ם הֽוּא׃ וַיַּֽעֲשׂוּ־כֵן֙
בְּנֵ֣י יִשְׂרָאֵ֔ל וַיִּתֵּ֨ן לָהֶ֥ם יוֹסֵ֛ף עֲגָל֖וֹת עַל־פִּ֣י פַרְעֹ֑ה וַיִּתֵּ֥ן לָהֶ֛ם
כב צֵדָ֖ה לַדָּֽרֶךְ׃ לְכֻלָּ֥ם נָתַ֛ן לָאִ֖ישׁ חֲלִפ֣וֹת שְׂמָלֹ֑ת וּלְבִנְיָמִ֤ן
כג נָתַן֙ שְׁלֹ֣שׁ מֵא֣וֹת כֶּ֔סֶף וְחָמֵ֖שׁ חֲלִפֹ֥ת שְׂמָלֹֽת׃ וּלְאָבִ֞יו שָׁלַ֤ח
כְּזֹאת֙ עֲשָׂרָ֣ה חֲמֹרִ֔ים נֹשְׂאִ֖ים מִטּ֣וּב מִצְרָ֑יִם וְעֶ֣שֶׂר אֲתֹנֹ֡ת
כד נֹ֠שְׂאֹת בָּ֣ר וָלֶ֧חֶם וּמָז֛וֹן לְאָבִ֖יו לַדָּֽרֶךְ׃ וַיְשַׁלַּ֥ח אֶת־אֶחָ֖יו
כה וַיֵּלֵ֑כוּ וַיֹּ֣אמֶר אֲלֵהֶ֔ם אַֽל־תִּרְגְּז֖וּ בַּדָּֽרֶךְ׃ וַֽיַּעֲל֖וּ מִמִּצְרָ֑יִם וַיָּבֹ֙אוּ֙
כו אֶ֣רֶץ כְּנַ֔עַן אֶל־יַעֲקֹ֖ב אֲבִיהֶֽם׃ וַיַּגִּ֨דוּ ל֜וֹ לֵאמֹ֗ר ע֚וֹד יוֹסֵ֣ף חַ֔י
וְכִֽי־ה֥וּא מֹשֵׁ֖ל בְּכָל־אֶ֣רֶץ מִצְרָ֑יִם וַיָּ֣פָג לִבּ֔וֹ כִּ֥י לֹא־הֶאֱמִ֖ין
כז לָהֶֽם׃ וַיְדַבְּר֣וּ אֵלָ֗יו אֵ֣ת כָּל־דִּבְרֵ֤י יוֹסֵף֙ אֲשֶׁ֣ר דִּבֶּ֣ר אֲלֵהֶ֔ם
וַיַּרְא֙ אֶת־הָעֲגָל֔וֹת אֲשֶׁר־שָׁלַ֥ח יוֹסֵ֖ף לָשֵׂ֣את אֹת֑וֹ וַתְּחִ֕י ר֖וּחַ
כח יַעֲקֹ֥ב אֲבִיהֶֽם׃ וַיֹּ֙אמֶר֙ יִשְׂרָאֵ֔ל רַ֖ב עוֹד־יוֹסֵ֣ף בְּנִ֣י חָ֑י אֵלְכָ֥ה חמישי
מו א וְאֶרְאֶ֖נּוּ בְּטֶ֥רֶם אָמֽוּת׃ וַיִּסַּ֤ע יִשְׂרָאֵל֙ וְכָל־אֲשֶׁר־ל֔וֹ וַיָּבֹ֖א
ב בְּאֵ֣רָה שָּׁ֑בַע וַיִּזְבַּ֣ח זְבָחִ֔ים לֵאלֹהֵ֖י אָבִ֥יו יִצְחָֽק׃ וַיֹּ֨אמֶר
אֱלֹהִ֤ים ׀ לְיִשְׂרָאֵל֙ בְּמַרְאֹ֣ת הַלַּ֔יְלָה וַיֹּ֖אמֶר יַעֲקֹ֣ב ׀ יַעֲקֹ֑ב

This single act of reframing allows Yosef to live without a burning sense of anger and injustice. It transforms the negative energies of feelings about the past into focused attention on the future. It enables him to be reconciled with his brothers. Yosef, without knowing it, has become the precursor of one of the great

brothers. He has come to see himself as a man charged with a life-saving mission by God. Everything that has happened to him was necessary so that he could achieve his purpose in life: to save an entire region from starvation during a famine, and to provide a safe haven for his family.

3 vision: "Yaakov, Yaakov." He replied, "Here I am." "I am
God, the God of your father," He said. "Do not be afraid
to go down to Egypt, for there I will make of you a great
4 nation. I Myself will go down to Egypt with you, and I
Myself will also bring you back; and Yosef's hand will
5 close your eyes." Then Yaakov left Be'er Sheva. Yisrael's
sons took their father Yaakov and their children and wives
6 in the wagons that Pharaoh had sent to carry him. They
took their livestock and all the possessions they had
acquired in Canaan. So Yaakov and all his descendants
7 came to Egypt. He brought with him to Egypt his sons
and grandsons, daughters and granddaughters, and all his
8 descendants. These are the names of the children
of Israel – Yaakov and his descendants – who came to
9 Egypt: Reuven, Yaakov's firstborn, and Reuven's sons,
10 Ḥanokh, Palu, Ḥetzron, and Karmi. Shimon's sons were
Yemuel, Yamin, Ohad, Yakhin, Tzoḥar, and Sha'ul, son of
11 the Canaanite woman. Levi's sons were Gershon, Kehat,
12 and Merari. Yehuda's sons were Er, Onan, Shela, Peretz,
and Zeraḥ – but Er and Onan had died in Canaan. Peretz's
13 sons were Ḥetzron and Ḥamul. Yissakhar's sons were
14 Tola, Puva, Yov, and Shimron. Zevulun's sons were Sered,
15 Elon, and Yaḥliel. These were the sons whom Leah bore
to Yaakov in Padan Aram, besides his daughter Dina. In
16 all, male and female, they numbered thirty-three. Gad's
sons were Tzifyon, Ḥagi, Shuni, Etzbon, Eri, Arodi, and
17 Areli. Asher's sons were Yimna, Yishva, Yishvi, and Beria.
Their sister was Seraḥ. Beria's sons were Ḥever and Malkiel.

---

forever, for you have filled my spirit with new life."

"It is our task," said Itzhak Perlman, "to make music with what remains." In his book, *Musicophilia*, the late Oliver Sacks (no relation, alas) told the poignant story of Clive Wearing, an eminent musicologist who was struck by acute amnesia. He was unable to remember anything for more than a few seconds. Unable to thread experiences together, he was caught in an endless present that had no connection with anything that had gone before. He had no past at all.

Two things broke through his isolation. One was his love for his wife. The

ג וַיֹּאמֶר הִנֵּנִי׃ וַיֹּאמֶר אָנֹכִי הָאֵל אֱלֹהֵי אָבִיךָ אַל־תִּירָא
ד מֵרְדָה מִצְרַיְמָה כִּי־לְגוֹי גָּדוֹל אֲשִׂימְךָ שָׁם׃ אָנֹכִי אֵרֵד עִמְּךָ
מִצְרַיְמָה וְאָנֹכִי אַעַלְךָ גַם־עָלֹה וְיוֹסֵף יָשִׁית יָדוֹ עַל־עֵינֶיךָ׃
ה וַיָּקָם יַעֲקֹב מִבְּאֵר שָׁבַע וַיִּשְׂאוּ בְנֵי־יִשְׂרָאֵל אֶת־יַעֲקֹב
אֲבִיהֶם וְאֶת־טַפָּם וְאֶת־נְשֵׁיהֶם בָּעֲגָלוֹת אֲשֶׁר־שָׁלַח פַּרְעֹה
ו לָשֵׂאת אֹתוֹ׃ וַיִּקְחוּ אֶת־מִקְנֵיהֶם וְאֶת־רְכוּשָׁם אֲשֶׁר רָכְשׁוּ
ז בְּאֶרֶץ כְּנַעַן וַיָּבֹאוּ מִצְרָיְמָה יַעֲקֹב וְכָל־זַרְעוֹ אִתּוֹ׃ בָּנָיו
וּבְנֵי בָנָיו אִתּוֹ בְּנֹתָיו וּבְנוֹת בָּנָיו וְכָל־זַרְעוֹ הֵבִיא אִתּוֹ
ח מִצְרָיְמָה׃ וְאֵלֶּה שְׁמוֹת בְּנֵי־יִשְׂרָאֵל הַבָּאִים
ט מִצְרַיְמָה יַעֲקֹב וּבָנָיו בְּכֹר יַעֲקֹב רְאוּבֵן׃ וּבְנֵי רְאוּבֵן חֲנוֹךְ
י וּפַלּוּא וְחֶצְרֹן וְכַרְמִי׃ וּבְנֵי שִׁמְעוֹן יְמוּאֵל וְיָמִין וְאֹהַד וְיָכִין
יא וְצֹחַר וְשָׁאוּל בֶּן־הַכְּנַעֲנִית׃ וּבְנֵי לֵוִי גֵּרְשׁוֹן קְהָת וּמְרָרִי׃
יב וּבְנֵי יְהוּדָה עֵר וְאוֹנָן וְשֵׁלָה וָפֶרֶץ וָזָרַח וַיָּמָת עֵר וְאוֹנָן
יג בְּאֶרֶץ כְּנַעַן וַיִּהְיוּ בְנֵי־פֶרֶץ חֶצְרֹן וְחָמוּל׃ וּבְנֵי יִשָּׂשכָר תּוֹלָע
יד טו וּפֻוָּה וְיוֹב וְשִׁמְרֹן׃ וּבְנֵי זְבֻלוּן סֶרֶד וְאֵלוֹן וְיַחְלְאֵל׃ אֵלֶּה ׀
בְּנֵי לֵאָה אֲשֶׁר יָלְדָה לְיַעֲקֹב בְּפַדַּן אֲרָם וְאֵת דִּינָה בִתּוֹ
טז כָּל־נֶפֶשׁ בָּנָיו וּבְנוֹתָיו שְׁלֹשִׁים וְשָׁלֹשׁ׃ וּבְנֵי גָד צִפְיוֹן וְחַגִּי
יז שׁוּנִי וְאֶצְבֹּן עֵרִי וַאֲרוֹדִי וְאַרְאֵלִי׃ וּבְנֵי אָשֵׁר יִמְנָה וְיִשְׁוָה
וְיִשְׁוִי וּבְרִיעָה וְשֶׂרַח אֲחֹתָם וּבְנֵי בְרִיעָה חֶבֶר וּמַלְכִּיאֵל׃

46:17 וְשֶׂרַח אֲחֹתָם *Their sister was Seraḥ* – Seraḥ will be mentioned again in a list of the Israelites who left Egypt (Num. 26:46). This inspires midrashic traditions about her longevity and her role in carrying knowledge of the past through the time of slavery to younger generations. A medieval midrash in *Sefer HaYashar* tells that the brothers are afraid, when they come back from Egypt, that the sudden revelation that Yosef is still alive will come as too great a shock to Yaakov, and that he will not believe them. They ask Seraḥ, who is "good and wise and could play the harp" to bear the news for them. Seraḥ weaves their message into a beautiful song, which she sings to Yaakov, accompanying herself on the harp. After hearing the words sung several times, Yaakov understands that they are true, and blesses his granddaughter, "Daughter, let death have no hold on you

18 These were the children of Zilpa, whom Lavan had
given to his daughter Leah; these she bore to Yaakov –
19 sixteen in all. The sons of Yaakov's wife Raḥel were Yosef
20 and Binyamin. In Egypt Menashe and Efrayim were born
to Yosef; Asnat, daughter of Potifera priest of On, bore
21 them to him. Binyamin's sons were Bela, Bekher, Ashbel,
Gera, Naaman, Eḥi, Rosh, Mupim, Ḥupim, and Ard.
22 These are the children Raḥel bore to Yaakov – fourteen in
23 24 all. Dan's son was Ḥushim. Naftali's sons were Yaḥtze'el,
25 Guni, Yetzer, and Shilem. These were the sons born to
Yaakov by Bilha, whom Lavan had given to his daughter
26 Raḥel – seven in all. So the number of people who came
to Egypt with Yaakov – his direct descendants, not
27 including his sons' wives – were sixty-six in all. Yosef's
sons, born to him in Egypt, were two in number. Thus the
total number of Yaakov's family who came to Egypt was
28 seventy. He sent Yehuda ahead of him to SHISHI
Yosef to show him the way to Goshen. When they came to
29 the region of Goshen, Yosef harnessed his chariot and
rode to Goshen to greet his father Yisrael. He presented
himself to him, threw his arms around his neck, and wept
30 on his shoulder for a long time. "Now I can die," said
Yisrael to Yosef. "I have seen your face! You are still alive!"
31 Yosef said to his brothers and his father's household, "I

---

breaks into time. Faith is the ability to hear the music beneath the noise.

46:30 כִּי עוֹדְךָ חָי *You are still alive* – After years of grief without resolution, Yaakov is now satisfied.

Yaakov has "refused to be comforted" (Gen. 37:35) until he sees Yosef again. The Jewish people took after him. Yirmeyahu heard it in a later age: "A sound is heard in Rama: wailing, bitter weeping. It is Raḥel, weeping for her children. *She refuses to be consoled* for her children, for they are gone. This is what the Lord said…'There is a reward for your labor,' declares the Lord, 'and they will return from the land of the enemy. There is hope for your future,' declares the Lord" (Jer. 31:14–15).

And Raḥel's children did return to the land. Jerusalem is once again the Jewish home. All the evidence may suggest otherwise: it may seem to signify irretrievable loss, a decree of history that cannot be overturned, a fate that

יח אֵ֣לֶּה בְּנֵ֣י זִלְפָּ֔ה אֲשֶׁר־נָתַ֥ן לָבָ֖ן לְלֵאָ֣ה בִתּ֑וֹ וַתֵּ֤לֶד אֶת־אֵ֙לֶּה֙
יט לְיַעֲקֹ֔ב שֵׁ֥שׁ עֶשְׂרֵ֖ה נָֽפֶשׁ׃ בְּנֵי֙ רָחֵ֣ל אֵ֣שֶׁת יַעֲקֹ֔ב יוֹסֵ֖ף וּבִנְיָמִֽן׃
כ וַיִּוָּלֵ֣ד לְיוֹסֵף֮ בְּאֶ֣רֶץ מִצְרַיִם֒ אֲשֶׁ֤ר יָֽלְדָה־לּוֹ֙ אָֽסְנַ֔ת בַּת־פּ֥וֹטִי
כא פֶ֖רַע כֹּהֵ֣ן אֹ֑ן אֶת־מְנַשֶּׁ֖ה וְאֶת־אֶפְרָֽיִם׃ וּבְנֵ֣י בִנְיָמִ֗ן בֶּ֤לַע וָבֶ֙כֶר֙
כב וְאַשְׁבֵּ֔ל גֵּרָ֥א וְנַעֲמָ֖ן אֵחִ֣י וָרֹ֑אשׁ מֻפִּ֥ים וְחֻפִּ֖ים וָאָֽרְדְּ׃ אֵ֚לֶּה
כג בְּנֵ֣י רָחֵ֔ל אֲשֶׁ֥ר יֻלַּ֖ד לְיַעֲקֹ֑ב כָּל־נֶ֖פֶשׁ אַרְבָּעָ֥ה עָשָֽׂר׃ וּבְנֵי־דָ֖ן
כד כה חֻשִֽׁים׃ וּבְנֵ֖י נַפְתָּלִ֑י יַחְצְאֵ֥ל וְגוּנִ֖י וְיֵ֥צֶר וְשִׁלֵּֽם׃ אֵ֚לֶּה בְּנֵ֣י
בִלְהָ֔ה אֲשֶׁר־נָתַ֥ן לָבָ֖ן לְרָחֵ֣ל בִּתּ֑וֹ וַתֵּ֧לֶד אֶת־אֵ֛לֶּה לְיַעֲקֹ֖ב
כו כָּל־נֶ֥פֶשׁ שִׁבְעָֽה׃ כָּל־הַנֶּ֨פֶשׁ הַבָּאָ֤ה לְיַעֲקֹב֙ מִצְרַ֙יְמָה֙ יֹצְאֵ֣י
כז יְרֵכ֔וֹ מִלְּבַ֖ד נְשֵׁ֣י בְנֵֽי־יַעֲקֹ֑ב כָּל־נֶ֖פֶשׁ שִׁשִּׁ֥ים וָשֵֽׁשׁ׃ וּבְנֵ֥י יוֹסֵ֛ף
אֲשֶׁר־יֻלַּד־ל֥וֹ בְמִצְרַ֖יִם נֶ֣פֶשׁ שְׁנָ֑יִם כָּל־הַנֶּ֧פֶשׁ לְבֵית־יַעֲקֹ֛ב
כח הַבָּ֥אָה מִצְרַ֖יְמָה שִׁבְעִֽים׃ וְאֶת־יְהוּדָ֞ה שָׁלַ֤ח מא ששי
לְפָנָיו֙ אֶל־יוֹסֵ֔ף לְהוֹרֹ֥ת לְפָנָ֖יו גֹּ֑שְׁנָה וַיָּבֹ֖אוּ אַ֥רְצָה גֹּֽשֶׁן׃
כט וַיֶּאְסֹ֤ר יוֹסֵף֙ מֶרְכַּבְתּ֔וֹ וַיַּ֛עַל לִקְרַֽאת־יִשְׂרָאֵ֥ל אָבִ֖יו גֹּ֑שְׁנָה
ל וַיֵּרָ֣א אֵלָ֗יו וַיִּפֹּל֙ עַל־צַוָּארָ֔יו וַיֵּ֥בְךְּ עַל־צַוָּארָ֖יו עֽוֹד׃ וַיֹּ֥אמֶר
יִשְׂרָאֵ֛ל אֶל־יוֹסֵ֖ף אָמ֣וּתָה הַפָּ֑עַם אַחֲרֵי֙ רְאוֹתִ֣י אֶת־פָּנֶ֔יךָ כִּ֥י
לא עוֹדְךָ֖ חָֽי׃ וַיֹּ֨אמֶר יוֹסֵ֤ף אֶל־אֶחָיו֙ וְאֶל־בֵּ֣ית אָבִ֔יו אֶֽעֱלֶ֖ה

other was music. He could still sing, play the organ, and conduct a choir with all his old skill and verve.

What was it about music that enabled him, while playing or conducting, to overcome amnesia? Sacks quotes the philosopher of music, Victor Zuckerkandl, who wrote, "Hearing a melody is hearing, having heard, and being about to hear, all at once…. Every melody declares to us that the past can be there without being remembered, the future without being foreknown." Music is a form of sensed continuity that can sometimes break through the most overpowering disconnections in our experience of time. Seraḥ's song allows Yaakov to integrate new knowledge that completely disrupts his experience of his past and future. She is blessed in return to become a symbol and bearer of a people's continuity through the horrific alienation of slavery.

Faith is more like music than science. Science analyzes; music integrates. And as music connects note to note, so faith connects episode to episode, life to life, age to age in a timeless melody that

will go and speak to Pharaoh. I will tell him, 'My brothers
and my father's household have come to me from Canaan.
32 The men are shepherds. They tend livestock. They have
33 brought their sheep and cattle and all they have.' When
Pharaoh summons you and asks, 'What is your occupation?'
34 you should say, 'We and our fathers have tended livestock
all our lives.' Then you will be allowed to settle in the region
of Goshen, because the Egyptians abominate all who keep
47 1 sheep." So Yosef went and told Pharaoh. He said, "My
father and brothers, together with their flocks, herds, and
all they have, have come from Canaan and are now in the
2 region of Goshen." He chose five of his brothers and
3 presented them to Pharaoh. Pharaoh asked the brothers,
"What is your occupation?" They replied, "Your servants
4 are shepherds, as our fathers were before." And they said
to Pharaoh, "We have come to stay for a while in your
land because the famine is severe in Canaan and there is
no pasture for your servants' flocks. Please, then, let your
5 servants settle in the region of Goshen." Pharaoh said to

The city is a dehumanizing environment and potentially a place where people worship symbolic representations of themselves. To this day, the temples, colossi, and pyramids of Egypt are awe-inspiring. They were meant to be. But there is a question to be asked about monumental architecture through the ages, much of it religious: At whose cost was it built? Virtually none was produced without exploitation on a massive scale. In Genesis and Exodus we hear little about the idolatry and pagan rituals that were later to earn the scorn of the prophets. We hear much, however, about something else, namely the hierarchical society by which some presume to rule over others. This, to the Torah, is unforgivable.

The Israelites will be commanded to create *a society that is not Egypt*, that is different, opposite, counter-cultural. It will be a society in which even slaves rest every seventh day and breathe the wide air of freedom. And those at the margins of society – as the Israelites with their alien lifestyle were in Egypt – are to be treated with dignity and included in national celebrations. This is the drama of Exodus, but the seeds of it are already to be found here. In Genesis, the lives of shepherds, from Hevel to Yisrael's children, are set in contrast with four cities: Ḥanokh, Bavel, Sedom, and finally, the urban capital of Egypt. What the Torah is telling us, implicitly, is how and why Abrahamic monotheism was born.

וְאַגִּידָה לְפַרְעֹה וְאֹמְרָה אֵלָיו אַחַי וּבֵית־אָבִי אֲשֶׁר בְּאֶרֶץ־
לב כְּנַעַן בָּאוּ אֵלָי׃ וְהָאֲנָשִׁים רֹעֵי צֹאן כִּי־אַנְשֵׁי מִקְנֶה הָיוּ
לג וְצֹאנָם וּבְקָרָם וְכָל־אֲשֶׁר לָהֶם הֵבִיאוּ׃ וְהָיָה כִּי־יִקְרָא לָכֶם
לד פַּרְעֹה וְאָמַר מַה־מַּעֲשֵׂיכֶם׃ וַאֲמַרְתֶּם אַנְשֵׁי מִקְנֶה הָיוּ
עֲבָדֶיךָ מִנְּעוּרֵינוּ וְעַד־עַתָּה גַּם־אֲנַחְנוּ גַּם־אֲבֹתֵינוּ בַּעֲבוּר
מז א תֵּשְׁבוּ בְּאֶרֶץ גֹּשֶׁן כִּי־תוֹעֲבַת מִצְרַיִם כָּל־רֹעֵה צֹאן׃ וַיָּבֹא
יוֹסֵף וַיַּגֵּד לְפַרְעֹה וַיֹּאמֶר אָבִי וְאַחַי וְצֹאנָם וּבְקָרָם וְכָל־
ב אֲשֶׁר לָהֶם בָּאוּ מֵאֶרֶץ כְּנָעַן וְהִנָּם בְּאֶרֶץ גֹּשֶׁן׃ וּמִקְצֵה אֶחָיו
ג לָקַח חֲמִשָּׁה אֲנָשִׁים וַיַּצִּגֵם לִפְנֵי פַרְעֹה׃ וַיֹּאמֶר פַּרְעֹה
אֶל־אֶחָיו מַה־מַּעֲשֵׂיכֶם וַיֹּאמְרוּ אֶל־פַּרְעֹה רֹעֵה צֹאן עֲבָדֶיךָ
ד גַּם־אֲנַחְנוּ גַּם־אֲבוֹתֵינוּ׃ וַיֹּאמְרוּ אֶל־פַּרְעֹה לָגוּר בָּאָרֶץ
בָּאנוּ כִּי־אֵין מִרְעֶה לַצֹּאן אֲשֶׁר לַעֲבָדֶיךָ כִּי־כָבֵד הָרָעָב
ה בְּאֶרֶץ כְּנָעַן וְעַתָּה יֵשְׁבוּ־נָא עֲבָדֶיךָ בְּאֶרֶץ גֹּשֶׁן׃ וַיֹּאמֶר

must be accepted. Jews never believed the evidence because they had something else to set against it – a faith, a trust, an unbreakable hope that proved stronger than historical inevitability. It is not too much to say that Jewish survival was sustained in that hope. And that hope came from a simple – or perhaps not so simple – phrase in the life of Yaakov. He refused to be comforted. And so – while we live in a world still scarred by violence, poverty, and injustice – must we.

46:34 תּוֹעֲבַת מִצְרַיִם כָּל רֹעֵה צֹאן *The Egyptians abominate all who keep sheep* – Their objection, historically, was a religious one. But in our narrative we are receiving our first intimation that Israel, with its humble shepherd origins, is to form a counterculture in relation to the urban superpower of Egypt.

All the patriarchs were shepherds. They moved from place to place. They lived in tents. They spent much of their time alone, far from the noise of the city, where they could be in communion with God.

Their lifestyle reflected some of the values of an earlier time. Hunter-gatherer societies were relatively egalitarian. It was only with the birth of agriculture and the division of labor, of trade and trading centers and economic surplus and marked inequalities of wealth, concentrated in cities with their distinctive hierarchies of power, that a whole cluster of phenomena began to appear – not just the benefits of civilization but the downside also.

6 Yosef, "Your father and brothers have come to you. The
land of Egypt is open before you. Settle your father and
brothers in the best part of the land. Let them live in
the region of Goshen, and if there are able men among
them, you may give them charge of my own livestock."
7 Then Yosef brought his father Yaakov and presented him
8 before Pharaoh. Yaakov blessed Pharaoh, and Pharaoh
9 asked Yaakov, "How old are you?" Yaakov said to Pharaoh,
"The years of my wandering are one hundred and thirty.
Few and hard have been the years of my life, and I have
not reached the age my fathers reached in their own
10 wanderings." Yaakov blessed Pharaoh and left his presence.
11 Yosef settled his father and brothers, giving them holdings SHEVI'I
in the best part of Egypt, in the region of Ramesses, as
12 Pharaoh had instructed. And Yosef provided his father, his
brothers, and all his father's household with food, befitting
13 the numbers of their dependents. And there was no food
across the land, because the famine was so severe. Egypt
14 and Canaan languished because of the famine. Yosef
collected all the money that was to be found in Egypt and
Canaan in payment for the grain the people were buying,
15 and he brought it into Pharaoh's palace. When the money
in Egypt and Canaan was gone, all the Egyptians came to
Yosef, saying, "Give us food. Why should we die before
your eyes just because there is no more money left?"
16 "Bring your livestock," said Yosef, "and I will sell you food
in exchange for your livestock since there is no more
17 money left." So they brought their livestock to Yosef, and
he gave them food in exchange for horses, sheep, cattle,
and donkeys. He supplied them with food that year in
18 exchange for all their livestock. That year passed, and they
came to him the following year and said, "We cannot hide
from my lord that the money is gone and the livestock
belongs to you. There is nothing left for my lord except
19 our bodies and our land. Why should we and our land die
before your eyes? Acquire us and our land in exchange for
food, and we with our land will be slaves to Pharaoh. Give

ו פַּרְעֹה אֶל־יוֹסֵף לֵאמֹר אָבִיךָ וְאַחֶיךָ בָּאוּ אֵלֶיךָ: אֶרֶץ
מִצְרַיִם לְפָנֶיךָ הִוא בְּמֵיטַב הָאָרֶץ הוֹשֵׁב אֶת־אָבִיךָ וְאֶת־
אַחֶיךָ יֵשְׁבוּ בְּאֶרֶץ גֹּשֶׁן וְאִם־יָדַעְתָּ וְיֶשׁ־בָּם אַנְשֵׁי־חַיִל
ז וְשַׂמְתָּם שָׂרֵי מִקְנֶה עַל־אֲשֶׁר־לִי: וַיָּבֵא יוֹסֵף אֶת־יַעֲקֹב
ח אָבִיו וַיַּעֲמִדֵהוּ לִפְנֵי פַרְעֹה וַיְבָרֶךְ יַעֲקֹב אֶת־פַּרְעֹה: וַיֹּאמֶר
ט פַּרְעֹה אֶל־יַעֲקֹב כַּמָּה יְמֵי שְׁנֵי חַיֶּיךָ: וַיֹּאמֶר יַעֲקֹב אֶל־
פַּרְעֹה יְמֵי שְׁנֵי מְגוּרַי שְׁלֹשִׁים וּמְאַת שָׁנָה מְעַט וְרָעִים הָיוּ
יְמֵי שְׁנֵי חַיַּי וְלֹא הִשִּׂיגוּ אֶת־יְמֵי שְׁנֵי חַיֵּי אֲבֹתַי בִּימֵי
י מְגוּרֵיהֶם: וַיְבָרֶךְ יַעֲקֹב אֶת־פַּרְעֹה וַיֵּצֵא מִלִּפְנֵי פַרְעֹה:
יא וַיּוֹשֵׁב יוֹסֵף אֶת־אָבִיו וְאֶת־אֶחָיו וַיִּתֵּן לָהֶם אֲחֻזָּה בְּאֶרֶץ שביעי
מִצְרַיִם בְּמֵיטַב הָאָרֶץ בְּאֶרֶץ רַעְמְסֵס כַּאֲשֶׁר צִוָּה פַרְעֹה:
יב וַיְכַלְכֵּל יוֹסֵף אֶת־אָבִיו וְאֶת־אֶחָיו וְאֵת כָּל־בֵּית אָבִיו לֶחֶם
יג לְפִי הַטָּף: וְלֶחֶם אֵין בְּכָל־הָאָרֶץ כִּי־כָבֵד הָרָעָב מְאֹד
יד וַתֵּלַהּ אֶרֶץ מִצְרַיִם וְאֶרֶץ כְּנַעַן מִפְּנֵי הָרָעָב: וַיְלַקֵּט יוֹסֵף
אֶת־כָּל־הַכֶּסֶף הַנִּמְצָא בְאֶרֶץ־מִצְרַיִם וּבְאֶרֶץ כְּנַעַן בַּשֶּׁבֶר
טו אֲשֶׁר־הֵם שֹׁבְרִים וַיָּבֵא יוֹסֵף אֶת־הַכֶּסֶף בֵּיתָה פַרְעֹה: וַיִּתֹּם
הַכֶּסֶף מֵאֶרֶץ מִצְרַיִם וּמֵאֶרֶץ כְּנַעַן וַיָּבֹאוּ כָל־מִצְרַיִם אֶל־
יוֹסֵף לֵאמֹר הָבָה־לָּנוּ לֶחֶם וְלָמָּה נָמוּת נֶגְדֶּךָ כִּי אָפֵס כָּסֶף:
טז וַיֹּאמֶר יוֹסֵף הָבוּ מִקְנֵיכֶם וְאֶתְּנָה לָכֶם בְּמִקְנֵיכֶם אִם־
יז אָפֵס כָּסֶף: וַיָּבִיאוּ אֶת־מִקְנֵיהֶם אֶל־יוֹסֵף וַיִּתֵּן לָהֶם יוֹסֵף
לֶחֶם בַּסּוּסִים וּבְמִקְנֵה הַצֹּאן וּבְמִקְנֵה הַבָּקָר וּבַחֲמֹרִים
יח וַיְנַהֲלֵם בַּלֶּחֶם בְּכָל־מִקְנֵהֶם בַּשָּׁנָה הַהִוא: וַתִּתֹּם הַשָּׁנָה
הַהִוא וַיָּבֹאוּ אֵלָיו בַּשָּׁנָה הַשֵּׁנִית וַיֹּאמְרוּ לוֹ לֹא־נְכַחֵד
מֵאֲדֹנִי כִּי אִם־תַּם הַכֶּסֶף וּמִקְנֵה הַבְּהֵמָה אֶל־אֲדֹנִי לֹא
יט נִשְׁאַר לִפְנֵי אֲדֹנִי בִּלְתִּי אִם־גְּוִיָּתֵנוּ וְאַדְמָתֵנוּ: לָמָּה נָמוּת
לְעֵינֶיךָ גַּם־אֲנַחְנוּ גַּם־אַדְמָתֵנוּ קְנֵה־אֹתָנוּ וְאֶת־אַדְמָתֵנוּ
בַּלָּחֶם וְנִהְיֶה אֲנַחְנוּ וְאַדְמָתֵנוּ עֲבָדִים לְפַרְעֹה וְתֶן־זֶרַע

us seed so that we can live and not die and so that the land
20 does not become desolate." Thus Yosef acquired all the land
of Egypt for Pharaoh. Each Egyptian sold his field, because
the famine had become too much for them. So the land
21 became Pharaoh's. As for the people, he transferred them
22 town by town from one end of Egypt to the other. The only
land he did not acquire was that of the priests, because they
received an allotment of food from Pharaoh; they were able
to live on the allotment that Pharaoh gave them, and so they
23 did not sell their land. Yosef said to the people, "Today I
have acquired you and your land for Pharaoh. Here is seed
24 for you to sow the land. When the harvest comes, give one-
fifth to Pharaoh. Four-fifths shall be yours as seed for your
fields and as food for you, your households, and your
25 children." "You have saved our lives," they said. "May we MAFTIR
find favor in the eyes of my lord – we shall be slaves to
26 Pharaoh." So Yosef made it a law, as it is to this day, governing

---

question. We tend to assume that the enslavement of the Israelites in Egypt was a consequence of, and punishment for, the brothers selling Yosef as a slave. But Yosef himself turns the Egyptians into a nation of slaves. What is more, he creates the highly centralized power that will eventually be used against his people.

It may be that the Torah intends no criticism of Yosef. He is acting loyally to Pharaoh and judiciously to Egypt as a whole. Or it may be that there is an implied criticism of his character. As a child, he dreamt of power; as an adult he exercises it – but Judaism is critical of power and those who seek it.

Certainly, this entire passage represents the first intrusion of politics into the life of the family of the covenant. From the beginning of Exodus to the end of Deuteronomy, politics will dominate the narrative. But Yosef's appointment to a key position in the Egyptian court is our first introduction to it. And what it is telling us about is the sheer ambiguity of power. On the one hand, you cannot create or sustain a society without it. On the other hand, it almost cries out to be abused. Power is dangerous, even when used with the best of intentions by the best of people.

Tradition called Yosef *hatzaddik*, "the righteous." At the same time, the Talmud says that he died before his brothers "because he assumed airs of authority" (Berakhot 55a). Even a *tzaddik* with the best of intentions, when he or she enters politics and assumes airs of authority, can make mistakes. The great challenge of politics – ongoing and

כ וְנִחְיֶה וְלֹא נָמוּת וְהָאֲדָמָה לֹא תֵשָׁם: וַיִּקֶן יוֹסֵף אֶת־כׇּל־
אַדְמַת מִצְרַיִם לְפַרְעֹה כִּי־מָכְרוּ מִצְרַיִם אִישׁ שָׂדֵהוּ כִּי־חָזַק
כא עֲלֵהֶם הָרָעָב וַתְּהִי הָאָרֶץ לְפַרְעֹה: וְאֶת־הָעָם הֶעֱבִיר אֹתוֹ
כב לֶעָרִים מִקְצֵה גְבוּל־מִצְרַיִם וְעַד־קָצֵהוּ: רַק אַדְמַת הַכֹּהֲנִים
לֹא קָנָה כִּי חֹק לַכֹּהֲנִים מֵאֵת פַּרְעֹה וְאָכְלוּ אֶת־חֻקָּם אֲשֶׁר
כג נָתַן לָהֶם פַּרְעֹה עַל־כֵּן לֹא מָכְרוּ אֶת־אַדְמָתָם: וַיֹּאמֶר
יוֹסֵף אֶל־הָעָם הֵן קָנִיתִי אֶתְכֶם הַיּוֹם וְאֶת־אַדְמַתְכֶם
כד לְפַרְעֹה הֵא־לָכֶם זֶרַע וּזְרַעְתֶּם אֶת־הָאֲדָמָה: וְהָיָה
בַּתְּבוּאֹת וּנְתַתֶּם חֲמִישִׁית לְפַרְעֹה וְאַרְבַּע הַיָּדֹת יִהְיֶה
לָכֶם לְזֶרַע הַשָּׂדֶה וּלְאׇכְלְכֶם וְלַאֲשֶׁר בְּבָתֵּיכֶם וְלֶאֱכֹל
כה לְטַפְּכֶם: וַיֹּאמְרוּ הֶחֱיִתָנוּ נִמְצָא־חֵן בְּעֵינֵי אֲדֹנִי וְהָיִינוּ מפטיר
כו עֲבָדִים לְפַרְעֹה: וַיָּשֶׂם אֹתָהּ יוֹסֵף לְחֹק עַד־הַיּוֹם הַזֶּה עַל־

THE EGYPTIANS BECOME SLAVES

By this stage in the famine, the Egyptians have used up all their money buying grain. They come to Yosef asking for food, telling him they will die without it, and he replies by telling them that he will sell it to them in exchange for ownership of their livestock. They willingly do so: they bring their horses, donkeys, sheep, and cattle. The next year he sells them grain in exchange for their land. The result of these transactions is that within a short period of time – seemingly a mere three years – he has transferred to Pharaoh's ownership all the money, livestock, and private land, with the exception of the land of the priests, which he allowed them to retain.

Not only this, but the Torah tells us that Yosef "transferred [the people] town by town from one end of Egypt to the other" (Gen. 47:21) – a policy of enforced resettlement that would eventually be used against Israel by the Assyrians.

The question is: Is Yosef right to do this? Seemingly, he does it of his own accord. He is not asked to do so by Pharaoh. The result, however, of all these policies is that unprecedented wealth and power are now concentrated in Pharaoh's hand – power that will eventually be used against the Israelites. More seriously, twice we encounter the phrase *avadim lePharo*, "slaves to Pharaoh" (47:19, 25) – one of the key phrases in the exodus account and in the answer to the questions of the child in the Seder service (Deut. 6:21). With this difference: *that it was said, not by the Israelites, but by the Egyptians.*

This passage raises a most serious

land in Egypt, that one-fifth of all produce belongs to
Pharaoh. Only the land of the priests did not become
27 Pharaoh's. Thus Yisrael settled in the land of Egypt, in the
region of Goshen. They acquired holdings in it and were
fertile and greatly increased in number.

The haftara for Parashat Vayigash is on page 1448

live together in peace, then they cannot form a stable society or a cohesive nation. Rambam explains that forgiveness and the associated command not to bear a grudge (Lev. 19:18) are essential to the survival of society: "For as long as one nurses a grievance and keeps it in mind, one may come to take vengeance. The Torah emphatically warns us not to bear a grudge, so that the impression of the wrong shall be quite obliterated and be no longer remembered. This is the right principle. It alone makes civilization and human relationships possible (*Hilkhot Deot* 7:8). Forgiveness is not merely personal; it is also political. It is essential to the life of any nation that seeks to maintain its independence for long. There is no greater proof of this than Jewish history itself. Twice Israel suffered defeat and exile. The first – the conquest of the Northern Kingdom, followed a century and a half later by the destruction of the First Temple and the Babylonian exile – was a direct consequence of the division of the kingdom into two after the death of Shlomo. The second – defeat at the hands of the Romans and the destruction of the Second Temple – was the result of intense factionalism and internal strife, *sinat ḥinam*.

When people lack the ability to forgive, they are unable to resolve conflict. The result is division, factionalism, and the fragmentation of a nation into competing groups and sects. What individuals practice in the family can determine the course of nations. Those who seek freedom must learn to forgive.

אַדְמַת מִצְרַיִם לְפַרְעֹה לַחֹמֶשׁ רַק אַדְמַת הַכֹּהֲנִים לְבַדָּם
כז לֹא הָיְתָה לְפַרְעֹה׃ וַיֵּשֶׁב יִשְׂרָאֵל בְּאֶרֶץ מִצְרַיִם בְּאֶרֶץ גֹּשֶׁן
וַיֵּאָחֲזוּ בָהּ וַיִּפְרוּ וַיִּרְבּוּ מְאֹד׃

The הפטרה *for* פרשת ויגש *is on page 1449.*

---

ever-present – is to keep policies humane and ensure that politicians remain humble, so that power, always so dangerous, is not used for harm.

47:27 וַיֵּשֶׁב יִשְׂרָאֵל בְּאֶרֶץ מִצְרַיִם *Settled in the land of Egypt* – The real significance of this passage goes far beyond the story of Yosef and his brothers. It is the essential prelude to the book of Exodus and the birth of Israel as a nation. The book of Genesis is, among other things, a set of variations on the theme of sibling rivalry: Kayin and Hevel, Yitzḥak and Yishmael, Yaakov and Esav, Yosef and his brothers. The book begins with fratricide and ends with reconciliation. There is a clear pattern to the final scene of each of the four narratives:

1. Kayin/Hevel	Murder
2. Yitzḥak/Yishmael	The two stand together at Avraham's funeral
3. Yaakov/Esav	Meet, embrace, go their separate ways
4. Yosef/brothers	Forgiveness, reconciliation, coexistence

In the development of these four narratives, the Torah is making a fundamental statement. If brothers cannot

Parashat Vayeḥi

47 28 Yaakov lived in Egypt for seventeen years; the years of his
29 life were one hundred and forty-seven. As the time of his
death drew near, he summoned his son Yosef and said to
him, "If I have found favor in your eyes, place your hand
under my thigh and promise to deal kindly and truly
30 with me: do not bury me in Egypt. Let me lie with my
fathers. Carry me from Egypt and bury me where they
31 are buried." "I will do as you say," he replied. Yaakov said,
"Swear to me," and Yosef swore. Then, at the head of the
bed, Yisrael bowed.
48 1 Some time later, Yosef was told, "Your father is ill." He
brought with him his two sons, Menashe and Efrayim.
2 And when Yaakov was told, "Your son Yosef has come to
see you," Yisrael summoned his strength and sat up in the
3 bed. Yaakov said to Yosef, "El Shaddai appeared to me in
4 Luz in the land of Canaan. He blessed me and said to me,
'I will make you fruitful and increase your numbers. I will
make you a community of peoples, and I will give this
land to your descendants as an everlasting possession.'
5 Now, the two sons who were born to you in Egypt before
I came here shall be considered mine: Efrayim and
6 Menashe will be like Reuven and Shimon to me. Any
child born to you after shall be yours; in any inheritance
they will be reckoned under the names of their brothers.

48:2 וַיִּתְחַזֵּק יִשְׂרָאֵל וַיֵּשֶׁב עַל־הַמִּטָּה *Yisrael summoned his strength and sat up* – The Sages said, "A prisoner cannot release himself from prison" (Berakhot 5b). It takes someone else to lift you from depression. That is why Judaism is so insistent on not leaving people alone at times of maximum vulnerability. Hence the principles of visiting the sick, comforting mourners, including the lonely ("the migrants, orphans, and widows") in festive celebrations, and offering hospitality. Yaakov is at the end of his strength, but when he hears his loved ones have come to visit him, he finds the strength to lift himself.

פרשת ויחי

מז כח וַיְחִי יַעֲקֹב בְּאֶרֶץ מִצְרַיִם שְׁבַע עֶשְׂרֵה שָׁנָה וַיְהִי יְמֵי־
כט יַעֲקֹב שְׁנֵי חַיָּיו שֶׁבַע שָׁנִים וְאַרְבָּעִים וּמְאַת שָׁנָה: וַיִּקְרְבוּ
יְמֵי־יִשְׂרָאֵל לָמוּת וַיִּקְרָא ׀ לִבְנוֹ לְיוֹסֵף וַיֹּאמֶר לוֹ אִם־נָא
מָצָאתִי חֵן בְּעֵינֶיךָ שִׂים־נָא יָדְךָ תַּחַת יְרֵכִי וְעָשִׂיתָ עִמָּדִי
ל חֶסֶד וֶאֱמֶת אַל־נָא תִקְבְּרֵנִי בְּמִצְרָיִם: וְשָׁכַבְתִּי עִם־אֲבֹתַי
וּנְשָׂאתַנִי מִמִּצְרַיִם וּקְבַרְתַּנִי בִּקְבֻרָתָם וַיֹּאמַר אָנֹכִי אֶעֱשֶׂה
לא כִדְבָרֶךָ: וַיֹּאמֶר הִשָּׁבְעָה לִי וַיִּשָּׁבַע לוֹ וַיִּשְׁתַּחוּ יִשְׂרָאֵל
עַל־רֹאשׁ הַמִּטָּה:
מח א וַיְהִי אַחֲרֵי הַדְּבָרִים הָאֵלֶּה וַיֹּאמֶר לְיוֹסֵף הִנֵּה אָבִיךָ חֹלֶה מב
ב וַיִּקַּח אֶת־שְׁנֵי בָנָיו עִמּוֹ אֶת־מְנַשֶּׁה וְאֶת־אֶפְרָיִם: וַיַּגֵּד
לְיַעֲקֹב וַיֹּאמֶר הִנֵּה בִּנְךָ יוֹסֵף בָּא אֵלֶיךָ וַיִּתְחַזֵּק יִשְׂרָאֵל
ג וַיֵּשֶׁב עַל־הַמִּטָּה: וַיֹּאמֶר יַעֲקֹב אֶל־יוֹסֵף אֵל שַׁדַּי נִרְאָה־
ד אֵלַי בְּלוּז בְּאֶרֶץ כְּנָעַן וַיְבָרֶךְ אֹתִי: וַיֹּאמֶר אֵלַי הִנְנִי מַפְרְךָ
וְהִרְבִּיתִךָ וּנְתַתִּיךָ לִקְהַל עַמִּים וְנָתַתִּי אֶת־הָאָרֶץ הַזֹּאת
ה לְזַרְעֲךָ אַחֲרֶיךָ אֲחֻזַּת עוֹלָם: וְעַתָּה שְׁנֵי־בָנֶיךָ הַנּוֹלָדִים
לְךָ בְּאֶרֶץ מִצְרַיִם עַד־בֹּאִי אֵלֶיךָ מִצְרַיְמָה לִי־הֵם אֶפְרַיִם
ו וּמְנַשֶּׁה כִּרְאוּבֵן וְשִׁמְעוֹן יִהְיוּ־לִי: וּמוֹלַדְתְּךָ אֲשֶׁר־הוֹלַדְתָּ
ז אַחֲרֵיהֶם לְךָ יִהְיוּ עַל שֵׁם אֲחֵיהֶם יִקָּרְאוּ בְּנַחֲלָתָם: וַאֲנִי ׀

VAYEḤI

With Parashat Vayeḥi, the book of Genesis, full of conflicts within the family, comes to a serene end. Yaakov, reunited with his beloved Yosef, sees his grandsons, the only such scene in the Torah. He blesses them; then, on his deathbed, he blesses his twelve sons. He dies and is buried in the cave of Makhpela with his parents and grandparents. Yosef forgives his brothers a second time, and he himself dies, having assured his brothers that God will eventually bring the family back to the Promised Land. The long patriarchal narrative is at an end, and a new period – the birth of Israel as a nation – is about to begin.

7 For I – as I was returning from Padan, Raḥel died beside
me in Canaan while we were still on the way, a short
distance from Efrat. And I buried her there beside the
8 road to Efrat – that is, Beit Leḥem." Then Yisrael looked
9 at Yosef's sons and said, "Who are these?" Yosef told his
father, "They are my sons God has given me here." "Please
bring them to me," Yaakov said, "so that I can bless them."
10 Yisrael's eyes were heavy with age and he could not see. SHENI
So Yosef brought them close to him, and he kissed and
11 embraced them. Yisrael said to Yosef, "I never expected to
see you again, and now God has shown me your children
12 as well." Yosef then took them from between his knees
13 and bowed low, his face to the ground. Yosef took both of
them, Efrayim on his right to Yisrael's left, and Menashe

---

the stay of his family in Egypt will not be a short one, for God has told him so (Gen. 46:3–4). And he knows his grandsons' names.

> Yosef named his firstborn Menashe, saying, "God has made me forget (*nashani*) all my troubles and all my father's family." The second son he named Efrayim, saying, "God has made me fruitful (*fara*) in the land of my affliction." (41:51–52)

With the utmost brevity, the Torah has intimated an experience of exile that is to be repeated many times across the centuries. At first, Yosef felt relief. The years as a slave, then a prisoner, were over. In Canaan, he had been the youngest of eleven brothers in a family of shepherds. Now, in Egypt, he was at the center of the greatest civilization of the ancient world, second only to Pharaoh in rank and power. No one reminded him of his background. With his royal robes and ring and chariot, he was an Egyptian prince (as Moshe was later to be). The past was a bitter memory he sought to remove from his mind. Menashe means "forgetting."

But as time passed, Yosef began to feel quite different emotions. Yes, he had arrived; he had achieved the power and greatness of which he had dreamed in his youth. But the Egyptian nation was not his, nor was its culture. To be sure, his family was, by any worldly terms, undistinguished, unsophisticated. Yet they remained his family. Though they were no more than shepherds (a class the Egyptians despised), they had been spoken to by God – not the gods of the sun, the river, and death, the Egyptian pantheon – but God, the creator of heaven and earth, who did not make His home in temples and pyramids and panoplies of power, but who spoke in the human

בְּבֹאִי מִפַּדָּן מֵתָה עָלַי רָחֵל בְּאֶרֶץ כְּנַעַן בַּדֶּרֶךְ בְּעוֹד כִּבְרַת־
אֶרֶץ לָבֹא אֶפְרָתָה וָאֶקְבְּרֶהָ שָּׁם בְּדֶרֶךְ אֶפְרָת הִוא בֵּית
ח ט לָחֶם: וַיַּרְא יִשְׂרָאֵל אֶת־בְּנֵי יוֹסֵף וַיֹּאמֶר מִי־אֵלֶּה: וַיֹּאמֶר
יוֹסֵף אֶל־אָבִיו בָּנַי הֵם אֲשֶׁר־נָתַן־לִי אֱלֹהִים בָּזֶה וַיֹּאמַר
י קָחֶם־נָא אֵלַי וַאֲבָרְכֵם: וְעֵינֵי יִשְׂרָאֵל כָּבְדוּ מִזֹּקֶן לֹא יוּכַל שני
יא לִרְאוֹת וַיַּגֵּשׁ אֹתָם אֵלָיו וַיִּשַּׁק לָהֶם וַיְחַבֵּק לָהֶם: וַיֹּאמֶר
יִשְׂרָאֵל אֶל־יוֹסֵף רְאֹה פָנֶיךָ לֹא פִלָּלְתִּי וְהִנֵּה הֶרְאָה אֹתִי
יב אֱלֹהִים גַּם אֶת־זַרְעֶךָ: וַיּוֹצֵא יוֹסֵף אֹתָם מֵעִם בִּרְכָּיו וַיִּשְׁתַּחוּ
יג לְאַפָּיו אָרְצָה: וַיִּקַּח יוֹסֵף אֶת־שְׁנֵיהֶם אֶת־אֶפְרַיִם בִּימִינוֹ
מִשְּׂמֹאל יִשְׂרָאֵל וְאֶת־מְנַשֶּׁה בִשְׂמֹאלוֹ מִימִין יִשְׂרָאֵל וַיַּגֵּשׁ

48:11 וְהִנֵּה הֶרְאָה אֹתִי אֱלֹהִים גַּם אֶת־זַרְעֶךָ *And now God has shown me your children as well* – We begin the Sabbath, as Yaakov will tell us in verse 20, blessing our children as he did his grandchildren. With an exquisite sense of symmetry, just as we begin the Sabbath with a grandparent's blessing so we end it with the words "May you live to see your children's children. Peace be on Israel" (Ps. 128:6, part of the Maariv service at the conclusion of the Sabbath).

What is the connection between grandchildren and peace? Surely this: that those who think about grandchildren care about the future, and those who think about the future make peace. It is those who constantly think of the past, of slights and humiliations and revenge, who make war.

To bless grandchildren and be blessed by them, to teach them and to be taught by them – these are the highest Jewish privileges and the serene end of Yaakov's troubled life. He, who has known so much suffering, can now talk of "the angel who has delivered me from all harm" (Gen. 48:16).

EFRAYIM AND MENASHE – THE FIRST CHILDREN OF EXILE

The drama of younger and older brothers, which haunts the book of Genesis from Kayin and Hevel onward, reaches a strange climax in the story of Yosef's children. In light of all the conflict in his life and in his family's past, it is not difficult to understand the care Yosef takes to ensure that Yaakov blesses the firstborn first. Why, then, has his father seemingly not learned? Besides which, what possible reason could he have for favoring the younger of his grandchildren over the elder? He has not seen them before. He knows nothing about them. Why does Yaakov favor Efrayim over Menashe?

The explanation lies in the two things Yaakov does know. He knows that

14 on his left to Yisrael's right, and brought them close. Yisrael
reached out his right hand and put it on Efrayim's head,
even though he was the younger. And, crossing his hands,
he put his left hand on Menashe's head even though he
15 was the firstborn. He blessed Yosef and said, "God before
whom my fathers walked – Avraham and Yitzḥak – God
16 who has been my shepherd all my life to now, the angel
who has delivered me from all harm, may He bless the
boys. Through them may my name be recalled, and the
names of my fathers, Avraham and Yitzḥak. May they
17 grow to a multitude upon the land." When Yosef saw that SHELISHI
his father had placed his right hand on Efrayim's head, he
was displeased. He took hold of his father's hand to move
18 it from Efrayim's head to Menashe's head. Yosef said to
his father, "Not so, father. This is the firstborn. Put your
19 right hand on his head." But his father refused: "I know,
my son, I know. He too will be a people, and he too will
become great, but his younger brother will become even
greater, and his descendants will become an abundance
20 of nations." On that day, he blessed them: "By you shall
Israel bless, saying: May God make you like Efrayim and
21 Menashe." He put Efrayim before Menashe. Then Yisrael
said to Yosef, "I am about to die, but God will be with

---

remembers the past and future of which he is a part.

48:20 כְּאֶפְרַיִם וְכִמְנַשֶּׁה *Like Efrayim and Menashe* – This is the blessing that Jewish parents use on Friday night to bless their sons. Why this blessing of all the blessings in the Torah? My predecessor Lord Jakobovits gave a most lovely explanation. He said that though there are many instances in the Torah and Tanakh in which parents bless their children, this is the only example of a grandparent blessing grandchildren.

Between parents and children, he said, there are often tensions. Parents worry about their children. Children sometimes rebel against their parents. The relationship is not always smooth.

Not so with grandchildren. There the relationship is one of love untroubled by tension or anxiety. When a grandparent blesses a grandchild he or she does so with a full heart. That is why this blessing by Yaakov of his grandchildren is to become the model of blessing across the generations.

יד אֵלָיו: וַיִּשְׁלַח יִשְׂרָאֵל אֶת־יְמִינוֹ וַיָּשֶׁת עַל־רֹאשׁ אֶפְרַיִם
וְהוּא הַצָּעִיר וְאֶת־שְׂמֹאלוֹ עַל־רֹאשׁ מְנַשֶּׁה שִׂכֵּל אֶת־יָדָיו
טו כִּי מְנַשֶּׁה הַבְּכוֹר: וַיְבָרֶךְ אֶת־יוֹסֵף וַיֹּאמַר הָאֱלֹהִים אֲשֶׁר
הִתְהַלְּכוּ אֲבֹתַי לְפָנָיו אַבְרָהָם וְיִצְחָק הָאֱלֹהִים הָרֹעֶה אֹתִי
טז מֵעוֹדִי עַד־הַיּוֹם הַזֶּה: הַמַּלְאָךְ הַגֹּאֵל אֹתִי מִכָּל־רָע יְבָרֵךְ
אֶת־הַנְּעָרִים וְיִקָּרֵא בָהֶם שְׁמִי וְשֵׁם אֲבֹתַי אַבְרָהָם וְיִצְחָק
יז וְיִדְגּוּ לָרֹב בְּקֶרֶב הָאָרֶץ: וַיַּרְא יוֹסֵף כִּי־יָשִׁית אָבִיו יַד־ שלישי
יְמִינוֹ עַל־רֹאשׁ אֶפְרַיִם וַיֵּרַע בְּעֵינָיו וַיִּתְמֹךְ יַד־אָבִיו לְהָסִיר
יח אֹתָהּ מֵעַל רֹאשׁ־אֶפְרַיִם עַל־רֹאשׁ מְנַשֶּׁה: וַיֹּאמֶר יוֹסֵף
אֶל־אָבִיו לֹא־כֵן אָבִי כִּי־זֶה הַבְּכֹר שִׂים יְמִינְךָ עַל־רֹאשׁוֹ:
יט וַיְמָאֵן אָבִיו וַיֹּאמֶר יָדַעְתִּי בְנִי יָדַעְתִּי גַּם־הוּא יִהְיֶה־לְּעָם
וְגַם־הוּא יִגְדָּל וְאוּלָם אָחִיו הַקָּטֹן יִגְדַּל מִמֶּנּוּ וְזַרְעוֹ יִהְיֶה
כ מְלֹא־הַגּוֹיִם: וַיְבָרְכֵם בַּיּוֹם הַהוּא לֵאמוֹר בְּךָ יְבָרֵךְ יִשְׂרָאֵל
לֵאמֹר יְשִׂמְךָ אֱלֹהִים כְּאֶפְרַיִם וְכִמְנַשֶּׁה וַיָּשֶׂם אֶת־אֶפְרַיִם
כא לִפְנֵי מְנַשֶּׁה: וַיֹּאמֶר יִשְׂרָאֵל אֶל־יוֹסֵף הִנֵּה אָנֹכִי מֵת וְהָיָה

---

heart as a voice, lifting a simple family to moral greatness.

By the time his second son was born, Yosef had undergone a profound change of heart. To be sure, he had all the trappings of earthly success – "God has made me fruitful" – but Egypt had become "the land of my affliction." Why? Because it was exile. By calling this child Efrayim, he was remembering what, when Menashe was born, he was trying to forget: who he was, where he came from, where he belonged.

On this reading, Yaakov's blessing of Efrayim over Menashe has nothing to do with their ages and everything to do with their names.

Knowing that these were the first two children of his family to be born in exile, knowing too that the exile will be prolonged and at times difficult and dark, Yaakov seeks to signal to all future generations that there will be a constant tension between the desire to forget (to assimilate, acculturate, anaesthetize the hope of a return) and the promptings of memory (the knowledge that this is exile, that we are part of another story, that our ultimate home is somewhere else).

The child of forgetting (Menashe) may have blessings. But greater are the blessings of a child (Efrayim) who

▶

you and will bring you back to the land of your fathers.
22 And to you I give one portion more than your brothers,
which I took from the Amorites by my sword and my
bow."
49 1 Then Yaakov called for his sons and said, "Gather together REVI'I
so that I can tell you what will happen to you in the days to
2 come. Assemble and listen, Yaakov's sons. Listen to your
3 father Yisrael. Reuven, you are my firstborn, my strength,
first fruit of my manhood, excelling in rank, excelling in

---

blessings to the eldest three sons, Reuven, Shimon, and Levi, read more like curses than blessings. There is discernible tension here. Yet the fact is that he is blessing all twelve together in the same room at the same time. We have not seen this before. There is no record of Avraham blessing either Yishmael or Yitzḥak. Yitzḥak blesses Esav and Yaakov separately. The mere fact that Yaakov is able to gather his sons together is unprecedented, and important. In the next chapter – the first of Exodus – the Israelites are, for the first time, described as a people. It is hard to see how they could live together as a people if they could not live together as a family.

The Torah is giving us an unexpected message here: The family is prior to all else, to the land, the nation, politics, economics, the pursuit of power, and the accumulation of wealth. From an external point of view, the impressive story is that Yosef reaches the heights of power in Egypt. The Egyptians themselves mourn the death of his father Yaakov and accompany the family on their way to bury him, so that the Canaanites, seeing the entourage, say, "Egypt is in deep mourning here" (Gen. 50:11). But that is externality. When we turn the page and begin the book of Exodus, we discover that the position of the Israelites in Egypt is very vulnerable indeed, and all the power Yosef has centralized in the hands of Pharaoh will eventually be used against them. Genesis is not about power. It is about families. Because that is where life together begins.

The book, then, ends on these three important resolutions: First, that grandparents are part of the family, and their blessing is important. Second, Yaakov shows that it is possible to bless all your children, even if you have a fractured relationship with some of them. Third, Yosef shows that it is possible to forgive your siblings even if they have done you great harm.

That, surprisingly, is what Genesis is about. Not about the creation of the world, which can be described in a single chapter, but about how to handle family conflict. As soon as Avraham's descendants can create strong families, they can move from Genesis to Exodus and their birth as a nation.

כב אֱלֹהִים עִמָּכֶם וְהֵשִׁיב אֶתְכֶם אֶל־אֶרֶץ אֲבֹתֵיכֶם: וַאֲנִי
נָתַתִּי לְךָ שְׁכֶם אַחַד עַל־אַחֶיךָ אֲשֶׁר לָקַחְתִּי מִיַּד הָאֱמֹרִי
בְּחַרְבִּי וּבְקַשְׁתִּי:
מט א וַיִּקְרָא יַעֲקֹב אֶל־בָּנָיו וַיֹּאמֶר הֵאָסְפוּ וְאַגִּידָה לָכֶם אֵת מג רביעי
ב אֲשֶׁר־יִקְרָא אֶתְכֶם בְּאַחֲרִית הַיָּמִים: הִקָּבְצוּ וְשִׁמְעוּ
ג בְּנֵי יַעֲקֹב וְשִׁמְעוּ אֶל־יִשְׂרָאֵל אֲבִיכֶם: רְאוּבֵן בְּכֹרִי

YAAKOV'S DEATHBED SPEECH

Yaakov summons his children, wishing to bless them before he dies. The text begins with a strange semi-repetition: "Gather together so that I can tell you what will happen to you in the days to come. Assemble and listen.... Listen to your father Yisrael" (Gen. 49:1–2). The two verses seem to be saying the same thing twice, with one difference. In the first, there is a reference to "what will happen to you in the days to come" (literally, "at the end of days"). This is missing from the second.

Rashi, following the Talmud, says that "Yaakov wished to reveal what would happen in the end, but the Divine Presence was removed from him" (Rashi on Gen. 49:1; Pesaḥim 56a; Bereshit Rabba 99:5). He tried to foresee the future but found he could not.

This is no minor detail. It is a fundamental feature of Jewish spirituality. We believe that we cannot predict the future when it comes to human beings. We *make* the future by our choices. We cannot obtain the script. The future is radically open.

Do not believe that the future is written. There is no fate we cannot change, no prediction we cannot defy. We are not predestined to fail; neither are we preordained to succeed. We do not predict the future, because we make the future: by our choices, our willpower, our persistence, and our determination to survive.

The proof is the Jewish people itself. The first reference to Israel outside the Tanakh is engraved on the Merneptah Stele, inscribed around 1225 BCE by Pharaoh Merneptah IV, Ramesses II's successor. It reads: "Israel is laid waste, her seed is no more." It is, in short, an obituary. The Jewish people have been written off many times by their enemies, but they remain, after almost four millennia, still young and strong.

That is why, when Yaakov wants to tell his children what will happen to them in the future, the Divine Spirit is taken away from him. Our children continue to surprise us, as we continue to surprise others. Made in the image of God, we are free. Sustained by the blessings of God, we can become greater than anyone, even ourselves, could foresee.

49:2 הִקָּבְצוּ וְשִׁמְעוּ *Assemble and listen* – Yaakov blesses his twelve sons. His

4 power. Unstable as water, you shall not excel, for you went
up onto your father's bed and defiled it – went up onto
my couch.
5 Shimon and Levi are brothers; weapons of violence their
6 wares. Let me never join their council, nor my honor be
of their assembly. For in their anger they killed men; at
7 their whim they hamstrung oxen. Cursed be their anger,
for it is most fierce, and their fury, for it is most cruel. I
will divide them up in Yaakov, and scatter them in Israel.
8 Yehuda, your brothers shall praise you. Your hand will
be on the neck of your foes. To you will your father's
9 sons bow. Yehuda is a lion's cub. From the prey, my son,
you have risen. Like a lion he crouches, lies down, like
10 a lioness; who dares to rouse him? The scepter shall not
pass from Yehuda, nor the staff from between his feet, so
that tribute will come to him and the homage of nations
11 be his. He tethers his donkey to vines, to the vine bough
his donkey's colt; he washes his clothes in wine, his robe

Reuven, then, is the greatest "might-have-been" in the Torah. His story is of potential unfulfilled, virtue not quite realized, greatness so close yet unachieved. It is impossible not to recognize in Reuven a person of the highest ethical sensibilities. He is a person of good intentions. He cares. He thinks. He is not led by the crowd or by his darker instincts. He penetrates to the moral core of a situation. That is the first thing we notice about him. The second, however, is that somehow his interventions backfire. They fail to achieve their effect. Attempting to make things better, Reuven makes them worse. Though he has conscience, he lacks courage. He knows what is right, but lacks the resolve to do it boldly and decisively. The Torah clearly wants us to reflect on Reuven's character. Between the lines it tells us what stands between what might have been and what was.

49:5 כְּלֵי חָמָס מְכֵרֹתֵיהֶם *Weapons of violence their wares* – Yaakov's horror at the action of his sons in chapter 34 does not end there. He returns to it now, on his deathbed, and in effect curses them. We are reminded of Andrew Schmookler's point, that "power is like a contaminant, a disease, which once introduced will gradually but inexorably become universal" (see ch. 34, "Dina and Shekhem"). Because Shimon and Levi misused force in their youth, Yaakov feels he must "scatter them in Israel" and deny them further power. The two brothers' tribes are separated on the map of Israel, and never allowed territorial strength.

ד אַתָּה כֹּחִי וְרֵאשִׁית אוֹנִי יֶתֶר שְׂאֵת וְיֶתֶר עָז: פַּחַז כַּמַּיִם
אַל־תּוֹתַר כִּי עָלִיתָ מִשְׁכְּבֵי אָבִיךָ אָז חִלַּלְתָּ יְצוּעִי
עָלָה:
ה ו שִׁמְעוֹן וְלֵוִי אַחִים כְּלֵי חָמָס מְכֵרֹתֵיהֶם: בְּסֹדָם
אַל־תָּבֹא נַפְשִׁי בִּקְהָלָם אַל־תֵּחַד כְּבֹדִי כִּי בְאַפָּם
ז הָרְגוּ אִישׁ וּבִרְצֹנָם עִקְּרוּ־שׁוֹר: אָרוּר אַפָּם כִּי
עָז וְעֶבְרָתָם כִּי קָשָׁתָה אֲחַלְּקֵם בְּיַעֲקֹב וַאֲפִיצֵם
בְּיִשְׂרָאֵל:
ח יְהוּדָה אַתָּה יוֹדוּךָ אַחֶיךָ יָדְךָ בְּעֹרֶף אֹיְבֶיךָ יִשְׁתַּחֲווּ לְךָ
ט בְּנֵי אָבִיךָ: גּוּר אַרְיֵה יְהוּדָה מִטֶּרֶף בְּנִי עָלִיתָ כָּרַע רָבַץ
י כְּאַרְיֵה וּכְלָבִיא מִי יְקִימֶנּוּ: לֹא־יָסוּר שֵׁבֶט מִיהוּדָה
וּמְחֹקֵק מִבֵּין רַגְלָיו עַד כִּי־יָבֹא שִׁילֹה וְלוֹ יִקְּהַת עַמִּים:
יא אֹסְרִי לַגֶּפֶן עִירֹה וְלַשֹּׂרֵקָה בְּנִי אֲתֹנוֹ כִּבֵּס בַּיַּיִן לְבֻשׁוֹ

49:3–4 יֶתֶר שְׂאֵת וְיֶתֶר עָז: פַּחַז כַּמַּיִם *Excelling in power. Unstable as water* – By now we have a rich, composite, and penetrating portrait of Reuven – and we now know that the psychological key to his character is already given at his birth (see comments on 29:32 and 30:14 and ch. 37, "Reuven's Good Intentions"). Yaakov is a hero of faith, the man who gave Israel its name. Yet the complexity of Yaakov's character is light-years away from the idealized heroes of other religious traditions. In Yaakov we discover that the life of faith is not simple. We also discover something else. Every virtue carries with it a corresponding danger. The person who is overgenerous may condemn his own family to poverty. The individual (like Aharon – see Mishna Avot 1:12) who chooses peace at any price can sometimes allow those around him to make a golden calf. There is no single authoritative role model in Judaism. Instead there are many: Avraham, Yitzḥak, and Yaakov; Moshe, Aharon, and Miriam; kings, prophets, and priests; masters of halakha and Aggada; Sages and saints, poets and philosophers. The reason is that no one can embody all the virtues all the time. A strength here is a weakness there.

Yaakov loved, passionately and deeply. That was his strength, but also his weakness. His love for Raḥel meant that he could not bestow equal favor on Leah. His longing for a child by Raḥel meant that there was something lacking in his relationship with Leah's firstborn, Reuven. Had he loved less, there might have been no problem. He might have divided his attention more equally. But had he loved less, he would not have been Yaakov.

12 in the blood of grapes. His eyes are darker than wine, and
his teeth whiter than milk.
13 Zevulun will live by the seashore; he will be a haven for
ships. To Sidon his border will reach.
14 Yissakhar is a strong-boned donkey, lying down among
15 the sheep pens. Seeing how good is his resting place, and
how pleasant is the land, he will bend his shoulder to the
16 load, and work like a slave in harness. Dan will
17 seek justice for his people as one of Israel's tribes. Dan:
a snake by the roadside, a viper upon the path that bites
18 the horse's heel, so that its rider falls backward. I wait for
19 Your salvation, LORD. Gad will be raided by ḤAMISHI
20 raiders, but he then will raid at their heels. From
Asher will come rich food, he will proffer the king's
21 delights. Naftali is a deer set free, bearing
22 loveliest fawns. Yosef is a fruitful vine, a
fruitful vine by a spring, whose branches spread over a
23 wall. Archers attacked him with bitterness, shot at him,
24 harassed him. But his bow stopped steady, and his arms
held firm because of the hand of the Mighty One of
25 Yaakov, the Shepherd, Yisrael's Rock, because of the God
of your father who will help you, because of Shaddai who
will bless you with blessings of heaven above, blessings of
the deep that lies under, blessings of breast and of womb.

---

and temptation. Does the misconduct of leaders affect our judgment of them as leaders or not? Judaism suggests it should. The prophet Natan was unsparing in his criticism of King David for consorting with another man's wife. But Judaism also takes note of what happens next.

What matters, suggests the Torah, is that you repent – you recognize and admit your wrongdoings, and you change as a result. As Rabbi Joseph B. Soloveitchik pointed out, both Sha'ul and David, Israel's first two kings, sinned. Both were reprimanded by a prophet. Both said *ḥatati*, "I have sinned" (I Sam. 15:24; II Sam. 12:13). But their fates were radically different. Sha'ul lost the throne; David did not. The reason, said Rabbi Soloveitchik, was that David confessed immediately. Sha'ul prevaricated and made excuses before admitting his sin (*Kol Dodi Dofek*, 26). Yehuda takes ownership of his darker side. Ultimately this is what makes him "like a lion," full of strength that he can choose to harness for the good.

יב וּבְדַם־עֲנָבִים סוּתֹה: חַכְלִילִי עֵינַיִם מִיָּיִן וּלְבֶן־שִׁנַּיִם
מֵחָלָב:
יג זְבוּלֻן לְחוֹף יַמִּים יִשְׁכֹּן וְהוּא לְחוֹף אֳנִיֹּת וְיַרְכָתוֹ עַל־
צִידֹן:
יד טו יִשָּׂשכָר חֲמֹר גָּרֶם רֹבֵץ בֵּין הַמִּשְׁפְּתָיִם: וַיַּרְא מְנֻחָה כִּי
טוֹב וְאֶת־הָאָרֶץ כִּי נָעֵמָה וַיֵּט שִׁכְמוֹ לִסְבֹּל וַיְהִי לְמַס־
טז עֹבֵד: דָּן יָדִין עַמּוֹ כְּאַחַד שִׁבְטֵי יִשְׂרָאֵל:
יז יְהִי־דָן נָחָשׁ עֲלֵי־דֶרֶךְ שְׁפִיפֹן עֲלֵי־אֹרַח הַנֹּשֵׁךְ עִקְּבֵי־סוּס
יח יט וַיִּפֹּל רֹכְבוֹ אָחוֹר: לִישׁוּעָתְךָ קִוִּיתִי יהוה: גָּד חמישי
כ גְּדוּד יְגוּדֶנּוּ וְהוּא יָגֻד עָקֵב: מֵאָשֵׁר שְׁמֵנָה לַחְמוֹ
כא וְהוּא יִתֵּן מַעֲדַנֵּי־מֶלֶךְ: נַפְתָּלִי אַיָּלָה שְׁלֻחָה
כב הַנֹּתֵן אִמְרֵי־שָׁפֶר: בֵּן פֹּרָת יוֹסֵף בֵּן פֹּרָת
כג עֲלֵי־עָיִן בָּנוֹת צָעֲדָה עֲלֵי־שׁוּר: וַיְמָרְרֻהוּ וָרֹבּוּ וַיִּשְׂטְמֻהוּ
כד בַּעֲלֵי חִצִּים: וַתֵּשֶׁב בְּאֵיתָן קַשְׁתּוֹ וַיָּפֹזּוּ זְרֹעֵי יָדָיו מִידֵי
כה אֲבִיר יַעֲקֹב מִשָּׁם רֹעֶה אֶבֶן יִשְׂרָאֵל: מֵאֵל אָבִיךָ וְיַעְזְרֶךָּ
וְאֵת שַׁדַּי וִיבָרְכֶךָּ בִּרְכֹת שָׁמַיִם מֵעָל בִּרְכֹת תְּהוֹם רֹבֶצֶת

49:12 חַכְלִילִי עֵינַיִם מִיָּיִן וּלְבֶן־שִׁנַּיִם מֵחָלָב *His eyes are darker than wine, and his teeth whiter than milk* – As we have noted before with regard to Yehuda, "Where penitents stand even the perfectly righteous cannot stand" (Berakhot 34b; see note on 38:26). The Talmud brings a prooftext from Isaiah for this principle: "Peace, peace, to those far away and near" (Is. 57:19), placing the far (the penitent sinner) before the near (the perfectly righteous). However, almost certainly the real source is here in the story of Yosef and Yehuda.

Perhaps Yehuda's future was already implicit in his name, for though the verb *lehodot* from which it is derived means "to thank," it is also related to the verb *lehitvadot,* which means "to admit" or "to confess" – and confession is, according to Rambam, the core of the command to repent.

Leaders make mistakes. That is an occupational hazard of the role. Managers follow the rules, but leaders find themselves in situations for which there are no rules. What is more, leaders are also human, and their mistakes often have nothing to do with leadership and everything to do with human weakness

26 May your father's blessing surpass even the blessings of
my forebears – to the bounds of the everlasting hills. May
they rest on the head of Yosef, on the brow of the elect of
his brothers.
27 Binyamin is a ravening wolf, devouring prey in the SHISHI
28 morning, and by evening dividing the plunder." All
these are the twelve tribes of Israel, and this is what their
father said to them when he blessed them, giving each
29 his particular blessing. Then he gave them instruction,
saying, "I am about to be gathered to my people. Bury
me with my fathers in the cave in the field of Efron the
30 Hittite, the cave in the field of Makhpela near Mamre in
Canaan, which Avraham bought, together with the field,
31 from Efron the Hittite as a burial place. There Avraham
and his wife Sara are buried, there Yitzḥak and his wife
32 Rivka are buried, and there I buried Leah. The field
33 and the cave in it were bought from the Hittites." There
Yaakov finished instructing his sons. And he drew his feet
back onto the bed, breathed his last, and was gathered to
50 1 his people. Yosef fell on his father's face and wept over

---

tend to develop an equilibrium. If a child stammers, everyone in the family adjusts to it. Therefore, if the child is to lose their stammer, all the relationships within the family will have to be renegotiated. Not only must the child change. So must everyone else.

By and large, we tend to resist change. We settle into patterns of behavior as they become more and more comfortable, like a well-used armchair. How do you create an atmosphere within a family that encourages change and makes it unthreatening? The answer Lena discovered was praise. She told the families with whom she was working that every day they must notice each member of the family doing something right, and say so – specifically, positively, and thankfully. She was creating, within each home, an atmosphere of mutual regard and continuous positive reinforcement. She wanted the atmosphere of the home to be one in which people felt safe to change and help others to do so.

Yaakov's deathbed blessings are not without criticism. Nonetheless, he gives each child an emblem for his own particular strength, which even today suffuses Jewish iconography and art and inspires us with the potential he saw in his sons.

כו תַּחַת בִּרְכֹת שָׁדַיִם וָרָחַם׃ בִּרְכֹת אָבִיךָ גָּבְרוּ עַל־בִּרְכֹת
הוֹרַי עַד־תַּאֲוַת גִּבְעֹת עוֹלָם תִּהְיֶיןָ לְרֹאשׁ יוֹסֵף וּלְקָדְקֹד
נְזִיר אֶחָיו׃
כז בִּנְיָמִין זְאֵב יִטְרָף בַּבֹּקֶר יֹאכַל עַד וְלָעֶרֶב יְחַלֵּק שָׁלָל׃ ששי
כח כָּל־אֵלֶּה שִׁבְטֵי יִשְׂרָאֵל שְׁנֵים עָשָׂר וְזֹאת אֲשֶׁר־דִּבֶּר לָהֶם
כט אֲבִיהֶם וַיְבָרֶךְ אוֹתָם אִישׁ אֲשֶׁר כְּבִרְכָתוֹ בֵּרַךְ אֹתָם׃ וַיְצַו
אוֹתָם וַיֹּאמֶר אֲלֵהֶם אֲנִי נֶאֱסָף אֶל־עַמִּי קִבְרוּ אֹתִי אֶל־
ל אֲבֹתָי אֶל־הַמְּעָרָה אֲשֶׁר בִּשְׂדֵה עֶפְרוֹן הַחִתִּי׃ בַּמְּעָרָה
אֲשֶׁר בִּשְׂדֵה הַמַּכְפֵּלָה אֲשֶׁר־עַל־פְּנֵי מַמְרֵא בְּאֶרֶץ כְּנָעַן
אֲשֶׁר קָנָה אַבְרָהָם אֶת־הַשָּׂדֶה מֵאֵת עֶפְרֹן הַחִתִּי לַאֲחֻזַּת־
לא קָבֶר׃ שָׁמָּה קָבְרוּ אֶת־אַבְרָהָם וְאֵת שָׂרָה אִשְׁתּוֹ שָׁמָּה
קָבְרוּ אֶת־יִצְחָק וְאֵת רִבְקָה אִשְׁתּוֹ וְשָׁמָּה קָבַרְתִּי אֶת־
לב לֵאָה׃ מִקְנֵה הַשָּׂדֶה וְהַמְּעָרָה אֲשֶׁר־בּוֹ מֵאֵת בְּנֵי־חֵת׃
לג וַיְכַל יַעֲקֹב לְצַוֺּת אֶת־בָּנָיו וַיֶּאֱסֹף רַגְלָיו אֶל־הַמִּטָּה וַיִּגְוַע
נ א וַיֵּאָסֶף אֶל־עַמָּיו׃ וַיִּפֹּל יוֹסֵף עַל־פְּנֵי אָבִיו וַיֵּבְךְּ עָלָיו וַיִּשַּׁק־

49:28 וַיְבָרֶךְ אוֹתָם אִישׁ אֲשֶׁר כְּבִרְכָתוֹ *Giving each his particular blessing* – One of the most important tasks of a leader, a parent, or a friend is focused praise. We see this illustrated in Pirkei Avot (2:8), in which Rabban Yoḥanan b. Zakkai enumerates the praises of his five beloved students: Eliezer b. Hyrcanus: a plastered well that never loses a drop; Yehoshua b. Ḥananya: happy is the one who gave him birth; Yosei the Priest: a pious man; Shimon b. Netanel: a man who fears sin; and Elazar b. Arakh: an ever-flowing spring.

It is not difficult to create followers. But how does a teacher encourage these followers to become creative intellects in their own right? It is far harder to create leaders than to create followers. Rabban Yoḥanan b. Zakkai was a great teacher because five of his students became giants in their own right. The Mishna is telling us how he did it: with focused praise. He showed each of his pupils where their particular strength lay.

I discovered the transformative power of focused praise from one of the more remarkable people I ever met, the late Lena Rustin. Lena was a speech therapist, specializing in helping children who struggled with stammers. Lena believed that the young children she was treating – they were, on average, around five years old – had to be understood in the context of their families. Families

2 him and kissed him. Then Yosef instructed his servants
the physicians to embalm his father. So the physicians
3 embalmed Yisrael. It took them forty days; that was the
time required for embalming. The Egyptians mourned him
4 for seventy days. When the period of mourning was over,
Yosef spoke to Pharaoh's court: "If I have found favor in
your eyes, please speak to Pharaoh on my behalf. Tell him,
5 'My father made me swear an oath, saying, "I am about to
die. Bury me in the grave I prepared for myself in the land
of Canaan." Now let me go up and bury my father; then I
6 will return.'" Pharaoh said, "Go and bury your father as he
7 had you swear." So Yosef went up to bury his father. With
him went all Pharaoh's officials, the elders of his palace,
8 and all the other elders of Egypt, together with all Yosef's
household, his brothers, and his father's household. They
left only their children and flocks and herds in Goshen.
9 With them too went a chariot brigade and horsemen; it was
10 a very large retinue. When they reached the threshing floor
of Atad, beyond the Jordan, they held a great and solemn
lamentation, and Yosef observed a seven-day period of
11 mourning for his father. When the Canaanites who lived
there saw the mourning at the threshing floor of Atad they
said, "Egypt is in deep mourning here"; that is why the place
12 beyond the Jordan was called Avel Mitzrayim. So his sons
13 did as he had instructed them. They carried him to Canaan
and buried him in the cave of the field of Makhpela, near
Mamre, which Avraham had bought as a burial site from
14 Efron the Hittite. After burying his father, Yosef returned
to Egypt together with his brothers and all those who
15 had accompanied him to his father's burial. When Yosef's
brothers knew that their father was dead, they said, "What
if Yosef really hates us and decides to pay us back for all the
16 wrong we did to him?" So they sent word to Yosef saying,
"Your father gave these instructions before his death:
17 'This is what you are to say to Yosef: "Please forgive the
crime and sin of your brothers who inflicted such harm
upon you."' That being so, please forgive the crime of these

ב לוֹ: וַיְצַו יוֹסֵף אֶת־עֲבָדָיו אֶת־הָרֹפְאִים לַחֲנֹט אֶת־אָבִיו
ג וַיַּחַנְטוּ הָרֹפְאִים אֶת־יִשְׂרָאֵל: וַיִּמְלְאוּ־לוֹ אַרְבָּעִים יוֹם
כִּי כֵּן יִמְלְאוּ יְמֵי הַחֲנֻטִים וַיִּבְכּוּ אֹתוֹ מִצְרַיִם שִׁבְעִים יוֹם:
ד וַיַּעַבְרוּ יְמֵי בְכִיתוֹ וַיְדַבֵּר יוֹסֵף אֶל־בֵּית פַּרְעֹה לֵאמֹר אִם־
נָא מָצָאתִי חֵן בְּעֵינֵיכֶם דַּבְּרוּ־נָא בְּאָזְנֵי פַרְעֹה לֵאמֹר:
ה אָבִי הִשְׁבִּיעַנִי לֵאמֹר הִנֵּה אָנֹכִי מֵת בְּקִבְרִי אֲשֶׁר כָּרִיתִי
לִי בְּאֶרֶץ כְּנַעַן שָׁמָּה תִּקְבְּרֵנִי וְעַתָּה אֶעֱלֶה־נָּא וְאֶקְבְּרָה
ו אֶת־אָבִי וְאָשׁוּבָה: וַיֹּאמֶר פַּרְעֹה עֲלֵה וּקְבֹר אֶת־אָבִיךָ
ז כַּאֲשֶׁר הִשְׁבִּיעֶךָ: וַיַּעַל יוֹסֵף לִקְבֹּר אֶת־אָבִיו וַיַּעֲלוּ אִתּוֹ
ח כָּל־עַבְדֵי פַרְעֹה זִקְנֵי בֵיתוֹ וְכֹל זִקְנֵי אֶרֶץ־מִצְרָיִם: וְכֹל בֵּית
יוֹסֵף וְאֶחָיו וּבֵית אָבִיו רַק טַפָּם וְצֹאנָם וּבְקָרָם עָזְבוּ בְּאֶרֶץ
ט גֹּשֶׁן: וַיַּעַל עִמּוֹ גַּם־רֶכֶב גַּם־פָּרָשִׁים וַיְהִי הַמַּחֲנֶה כָּבֵד מְאֹד:
י וַיָּבֹאוּ עַד־גֹּרֶן הָאָטָד אֲשֶׁר בְּעֵבֶר הַיַּרְדֵּן וַיִּסְפְּדוּ־שָׁם מִסְפֵּד
יא גָּדוֹל וְכָבֵד מְאֹד וַיַּעַשׂ לְאָבִיו אֵבֶל שִׁבְעַת יָמִים: וַיַּרְא יוֹשֵׁב
הָאָרֶץ הַכְּנַעֲנִי אֶת־הָאֵבֶל בְּגֹרֶן הָאָטָד וַיֹּאמְרוּ אֵבֶל־כָּבֵד
זֶה לְמִצְרָיִם עַל־כֵּן קָרָא שְׁמָהּ אָבֵל מִצְרַיִם אֲשֶׁר בְּעֵבֶר
יב יג הַיַּרְדֵּן: וַיַּעֲשׂוּ בָנָיו לוֹ כֵּן כַּאֲשֶׁר צִוָּם: וַיִּשְׂאוּ אֹתוֹ בָנָיו
אַרְצָה כְּנַעַן וַיִּקְבְּרוּ אֹתוֹ בִּמְעָרַת שְׂדֵה הַמַּכְפֵּלָה אֲשֶׁר
קָנָה אַבְרָהָם אֶת־הַשָּׂדֶה לַאֲחֻזַּת־קֶבֶר מֵאֵת עֶפְרֹן הַחִתִּי
יד עַל־פְּנֵי מַמְרֵא: וַיָּשָׁב יוֹסֵף מִצְרַיְמָה הוּא וְאֶחָיו וְכָל־הָעֹלִים
טו אִתּוֹ לִקְבֹּר אֶת־אָבִיו אַחֲרֵי קָבְרוֹ אֶת־אָבִיו: וַיִּרְאוּ אֲחֵי־
יוֹסֵף כִּי־מֵת אֲבִיהֶם וַיֹּאמְרוּ לוּ יִשְׂטְמֵנוּ יוֹסֵף וְהָשֵׁב יָשִׁיב
טז לָנוּ אֵת כָּל־הָרָעָה אֲשֶׁר גָּמַלְנוּ אֹתוֹ: וַיְצַוּוּ אֶל־יוֹסֵף לֵאמֹר
יז אָבִיךָ צִוָּה לִפְנֵי מוֹתוֹ לֵאמֹר: כֹּה־תֹאמְרוּ לְיוֹסֵף אָנָּא שָׂא

50:16 אָבִיךָ צִוָּה לִפְנֵי מוֹתוֹ לֵאמֹר *Your father gave these instructions* – Years earlier, when Yosef revealed his true identity to them, he appeared to have forgiven them for selling him as a slave. Yet the brothers are not wholly reassured. Maybe he did not mean what he said. Perhaps he still harbors resentment. Perhaps the

servants of your father's God." Yosef wept as they spoke to
18 him. Then his brothers came and threw themselves down
19 before him and said, "We are your slaves." But Yosef said
20 to them, "Do not be afraid. Am I in place of God? You
intended to harm me, but God intended it for good, to

---

multitudes of" but "most" of his brothers. Most but not all. Rashi (quoting Megilla 16b) says that some members of the Sanhedrin were critical of him because his political involvement (his "closeness to the king") distracted from the time he spent studying Torah. Ibn Ezra says, simply, "It is impossible to satisfy everyone, because people are envious [of other people's success]."

At a deeper level, we can recall Hegel's famous master-slave dialectic, an idea that had huge influence on nineteenth-century, especially Marxist, thought. Hegel argued that the early history of humanity was marked by a struggle for power in which some became masters, others slaves. On the face of it, masters rule while slaves obey. But in fact, the master is dependent on his slaves – he has leisure only because they do the work, and he is the master only because he is recognized as such by his slaves.

Meanwhile, the slave, through his or her work, acquires his own dignity as a producer. Thus the slave has "inner freedom" while the master has "inner bondage." This tension creates a dialectic – a conflict worked out through history – reaching equilibrium only when there are neither masters nor slaves, but merely human beings who treat one another not as means to an end but as ends in themselves. Thus understood, Yosef's tears are a prelude to the master-slave drama about to be enacted in the book of Exodus between Pharaoh and the Israelites.

We are reminded that Torah, Tanakh, and Judaism as a whole are a sustained critique of power. Prior to the Messianic age we cannot do without it – consider the tragedies Jews suffered in the centuries in which they lacked it. But power alienates. It breeds suspicion and distrust. It diminishes those it is used against, and thus diminishes those who use it.

Power may be a necessary evil, but it is an evil, and the less we have need of it, the better. Even Yosef the righteous weeps when he sees the extent to which power has set him apart from his brothers. Judaism is about an alternative social order which depends not on power but on love, loyalty, and the mutual responsibility created by covenant.

50:19 הֲתַחַת אֱלֹהִים אָנִי *Am I in place of God?* – A book replete with tensions, hatred, and competition ends with forgiveness. This closing is essential to the biblical drama of redemption, for if brothers cannot live together, how can nations? And if nations cannot live together, how can the human world

נָא פֶּשַׁע אַחֶיךָ וְחַטָּאתָם כִּי־רָעָה גְמָלוּךָ וְעַתָּה שָׂא נָא
יח לְפֶשַׁע עַבְדֵי אֱלֹהֵי אָבִיךָ וַיֵּבְךְּ יוֹסֵף בְּדַבְּרָם אֵלָיו׃ וַיֵּלְכוּ גַּם־
יט אֶחָיו וַיִּפְּלוּ לְפָנָיו וַיֹּאמְרוּ הִנֶּנּוּ לְךָ לַעֲבָדִים׃ וַיֹּאמֶר אֲלֵהֶם
כ יוֹסֵף אַל־תִּירָאוּ כִּי הֲתַחַת אֱלֹהִים אָנִי׃ וְאַתֶּם חֲשַׁבְתֶּם

---

only reason he has not yet taken revenge is respect for Yaakov. There was a convention that there is to be no settling of scores between siblings in the lifetime of the father. We know this from an earlier episode. After Yaakov took his brother's blessing, Esav said, "The days of mourning for my father are approaching... and then I will kill my brother Yaakov" (Gen. 27:41). Now the brothers are afraid.

The text makes it as plain as possible that the story they tell Yosef is a lie. If Yaakov had really said those words, he would have said them to Yosef himself. The time to have done so was on his deathbed in the previous chapter. The brothers' tale is what we may call a "white lie." Its primary aim was not to deceive but to ease a potentially explosive situation. Perhaps that is why Yosef weeps, understanding that his brothers still think him capable of revenge.

The Sages derived a principle from this text. *Mutar leshanot mipnei hashalom*: "It is permitted to tell an untruth (literally, 'to change' the facts) for the sake of peace" (Yevamot 65b). A white lie can be permitted in Jewish law.

Our grasp of truth is partial, fragmentary, incomplete. That is the human condition. The way to peace is to realize this. Truth matters, but peace matters more. That is Judaism's considered judgment. Many of the greatest crimes in history were committed by those who believed they were in possession of the truth while their opponents were sunk in error. To make peace between brothers, the Torah sanctions a statement that is less than the whole truth. Dishonesty? No. Tact, sensitivity, discretion? Yes. That is an idea both eminently sensible and humane.

50:17 וַיֵּבְךְּ יוֹסֵף *Yosef wept* – On the surface, Yosef holds all the power. His family are entirely dependent on him. But at a deeper level it is the other way round. He still yearns for their acceptance, their recognition, their closeness. He weeps at almost every stage of the fraught encounter with his family in Egypt.

Yosef and Mordekhai/Esther are supreme examples of Jews who reached positions of influence and power in non-Jewish circles. In early modern times in Europe they were called *Hofjuden*, "Court Jews," and other Jews often held deeply ambivalent feelings about them. The last verse in the Book of Esther says that "Mordekhai the Jew was second in command to King Aḥashverosh and revered too among the Jews – beloved of all the multitudes of his brothers (*lerov eḥav*)" (Esther 10:3). Rabbinic Hebrew reads that last phrase differently – not "all the

bring about what is now being done: the saving of many
21 lives. So, do not be afraid. I myself will provide for you SHEVI'I
and your children." And he comforted them and spoke
22 to their hearts. Yosef remained in Egypt together with his
father's family, and he lived one hundred and ten years.
23 Yosef saw the third generation of Efrayim's children, and MAFTIR
the children of Menashe's son Makhir were also born on
24 Yosef's knees. Yosef said to his brothers, "I am about to
die. But God will surely take note of you and bring you
out of this land to the land He promised to Avraham,
25 Yitzḥak, and Yaakov." Then Yosef bound the children of
Israel by an oath: "When God takes note of you, carry

---

to closure by showing that sibling rivalry is not written indelibly into the human script. We can change, repent, and grow. The brothers show that they have changed when they demonstrate that they are no longer willing to let Binyamin – the Yosef-substitute – be enslaved (Gen. 44:33). Yosef, by his act of reconciliation, shows that he is not captive to the past and its resentments. His statement to his brothers shows the power of a religious vision to reframe history, liberating ourselves from the otherwise violent dynamic of revenge and retaliation. In a real sense, then, freedom extends to more than our ability to choose between alternative futures. It includes the freedom to reshape our understanding of the past, healing some of its legacy of pain. The point could not be more significant in the context of the sibling rivalries among cultures today. The past does not dictate the future. To the contrary, a future of reconciliation can, in some measure at least, retroactively redeem the past.

50:25 וְהַעֲלִתֶם אֶת־עַצְמֹתַי מִזֶּה *Carry my bones up from this place* – Wherever Jews were scattered, they saw their condition as *galut*, "exile," rather than mere dispersions, *tefutzot*. There were places like Germany, where they had lived for a thousand years. There were others, like Babylonia, in which there was continuous Jewish settlement for two and a half thousand years. Yet Jews saw themselves, and were seen by others, as being *here* but belonging *elsewhere*. This did not mean, as their critics claimed, that they had dual loyalties. Few groups were as loyal to their societies and non-Jewish rulers as were the Jews. They made significant contributions to the nations in which they lived, and whenever possible, added vastly to the arts, sciences, medicine, and the economy.

Since the days of Yirmeyahu they remembered his instruction to "seek the welfare of the city to which I have exiled you; and pray on its behalf to the Lord, for in its peace there shall be peace for

עָלַי רָעָה אֱלֹהִים חֲשָׁבָהּ לְטֹבָה לְמַעַן עֲשֹׂה כַּיּוֹם הַזֶּה
כא לְהַחֲיֹת עַם־רָב׃ וְעַתָּה אַל־תִּירָאוּ אָנֹכִי אֲכַלְכֵּל אֶתְכֶם שביעי
כב וְאֶת־טַפְּכֶם וַיְנַחֵם אוֹתָם וַיְדַבֵּר עַל־לִבָּם׃ וַיֵּשֶׁב יוֹסֵף
בְּמִצְרַיִם הוּא וּבֵית אָבִיו וַיְחִי יוֹסֵף מֵאָה וָעֶשֶׂר שָׁנִים׃
כג וַיַּרְא יוֹסֵף לְאֶפְרַיִם בְּנֵי שִׁלֵּשִׁים גַּם בְּנֵי מָכִיר בֶּן־מְנַשֶּׁה יֻלְּדוּ מפטיר
כד עַל־בִּרְכֵּי יוֹסֵף׃ וַיֹּאמֶר יוֹסֵף אֶל־אֶחָיו אָנֹכִי מֵת וֵאלֹהִים
פָּקֹד יִפְקֹד אֶתְכֶם וְהֶעֱלָה אֶתְכֶם מִן־הָאָרֶץ הַזֹּאת אֶל־
כה הָאָרֶץ אֲשֶׁר נִשְׁבַּע לְאַבְרָהָם לְיִצְחָק וּלְיַעֲקֹב׃ וַיַּשְׁבַּע
יוֹסֵף אֶת־בְּנֵי יִשְׂרָאֵל לֵאמֹר פָּקֹד יִפְקֹד אֱלֹהִים אֶתְכֶם

survive? Only now, with the reconciliation of Yosef and his brothers, can the story move on to the birth of Israel as a nation, passing from the crucible of slavery to the constitution of freedom as a people under the sovereignty of God.

We now see the profound overarching structure of the book of Genesis. It begins with God creating the universe in freedom. It ends with Yaakov's family on the brink of creating a new social universe of freedom which begins in slavery, but ends in the giving and receiving of the Torah, Israel's "constitution of liberty." Israel is charged with the task of changing the moral vision of mankind, but it can only do so if individual Jews, of whom the forerunners were Yaakov's children, are capable of changing themselves – that ultimate assertion of freedom we call *teshuva*. Time then becomes an arena of change in which the future redeems the past and a new concept is born – the idea of hope.

and Ḥava sin, but deny responsibility. Both instead define themselves as victims: "The woman You put here with me – she gave me fruit"; "the serpent beguiled me" (Gen. 3:12, 13). By the end of Genesis, however, Yosef, who really was a victim, refuses to define himself as such. He says to his brothers, "You intended to harm me, but God intended … to bring about what is now being done: the saving of many lives. So, do not be afraid. I myself will provide for you and your children." This is an immensely significant transformation. Instead of asking, "Who did this to me?" Yosef asks about his suffering, "What redemptive deed has this put me in a position to perform?" He looks forward, not back. Instead of blaming others, he exercises responsibility. Yosef represents the first great biblical rejection of the culture of victimhood, the reaction that caused the first humans to lose paradise.

50:20 אֱלֹהִים חֲשָׁבָהּ לְטֹבָה *God intended it for good* – At the start of the book, Adam ▶

50:21 וַיְנַחֵם אוֹתָם *And he comforted them* – The Yosef story brings Genesis

26 my bones up from this place." Yosef died at the age of
one hundred and ten. He was embalmed and placed in a
coffin there, in Egypt.

The haftara for Parashat Vayeḥi is on page 1450.

---

reason enough to turn away with despair from the realm of human affairs and to hold in contempt the human capacity for freedom.

What transforms the human situation from tragedy to hope, she argues, is the possibility of forgiveness. Forgiving is "the only reaction which does not merely re-act but acts anew and unexpectedly, unconditioned by the act which provoked it and therefore freeing from its consequences both the one who forgives and the one who is forgiven."

Atonement and forgiveness are the supreme expressions of human freedom – the freedom to act differently in the future than one did in the past, the freedom not to be trapped in a cycle of vengeance and retaliation. Only those who can forgive can be free. Only a civilization based on forgiveness can construct a future that is not an endless repetition of the past. That, surely, is why the golden age of Judaism is perpetually in the future.

It was this revolutionary concept of time – based on human freedom – that Judaism contributed to the world. Many ancient cultures believed in cyclical time, in which all things return to their beginning. The Greeks developed a sense of tragic time, in which the ship of dreams is destined to founder on the hard rocks of reality. Europe of the Enlightenment introduced the idea of linear time, with its close cousin, progress. Judaism believes in covenantal time, well described by Harold Fisch: "The covenant is a condition of our existence in time.... We cooperate with its purposes never quite knowing where it will take us, for 'the readiness is all.'" In a lovely phrase, he speaks of the Jewish imagination as shaped by "the unappeased memory of a future still to be fulfilled."

Tragedy gives rise to pessimism. Cyclical time leads to acceptance. Linear time begets optimism. Covenantal time gives birth to hope. These are radically different ways of relating to life and the universe. They are expressed in the different kinds of stories people tell. Jewish time always faces an open future. The last chapter is not yet written. The Messiah has not yet come. Until then, the story continues – and we, together with God, are the co-authors of the next chapter.

כו וְהַעֲלִתֶם אֶת־עַצְמֹתַי מִזֶּה: וַיָּמָת יוֹסֵף בֶּן־מֵאָה וָעֶשֶׂר
שָׁנִים וַיַּחַנְטוּ אֹתוֹ וַיִּישֶׂם בָּאָרוֹן בְּמִצְרָיִם:

The הפטרה *for* פרשת ויחי *is on page 1451.*

you" (Jer. 29:7; see note on Gen. 41:52). But they knew that, at some date in the future, the Jewish people would return home. They never mistook the immediate for the ultimate. It was this more than anything that preserved their identity as a distinctive people, and sustained hope during the long centuries of exile and expulsion. It preserved Jews against the internal decay that has beset every other civilization. Forgetfulness of the past, heedlessness of the long-term future, and a loss of moral purpose in the pursuit of the here and now has been the beginning of the decline of other cultures. The sense of *galut* was the Jewish immune system. It meant that the past and future were as real as the present. This consciousness, inherited perhaps from Yosef, has saved Jews from the ravages of time.

THE ENDING THAT IS NOT AN ENDING

The story of the people of the covenant begins with God's call to Avraham to leave his land and travel "to the land that I will show you" (Gen. 12:1). Yet no sooner does he arrive than he is forced by famine to go to Egypt. That is the fate repeated by Yaakov and his children. Genesis ends not with life in Israel but with a death in Egypt, and Yosef's last request: "I am about to die. But God will surely take note of you and bring you out of this land to the land He promised to Avraham, Yitzḥak, and Yaakov.... When God takes note of you, carry my bones up from this place" (50:24–25). A hope not yet realized, a journey not yet ended, a destination just beyond the horizon.

Normally we expect a story to create a tension that is resolved on the final page. The Tanakh defies narrative convention. Time and again, never more so than here, it introduces us to the story without an ending which looks forward to an open future rather than reaching closure. Is there some connection between this narrative form and the theme with which Yosef's story ends, namely forgiveness?

Hannah Arendt in *The Human Condition* offers us a profound insight into the connection between forgiveness and time. Human action, she argues, is potentially tragic. We can never foresee the consequences of our acts, but once done, they cannot be undone. This is

שמות
EXODUS

It said that people could escape, could survive, and could defy the mightiest of empires. It said that faith is more powerful than power. Hope lies just beyond the visible horizon of hopelessness.

The story, however, does not end at the exodus. A free society is a moral achievement. The Ten Commandments, with their emphasis on the sanctity of life, the integrity of the family, respect for truth and for the property of others, summarize the essentials of a decent society in so short and simple a way as to be memorized by – engraved on the hearts of – an entire people. They remain the world's most famous moral code. This is the culmination of what the Torah has been about all along. To have a free society, there must be rule of law. In Exodus, then, we find the inseparable interweaving of narrative and law that will become the hallmark of Judaism.

It is an extraordinary drama – theological, political, but also human. That is why it has never lost its hold on those who know it, and why it continues to inspire us with the belief that when we open ourselves to the force of the Divine, extraordinary things can happen.

THE BOOK OF EXODUS

The book of Exodus, second of the Mosaic books, is not only a key text in Jewish history. It is also one of the most influential in the history of the West, its metanarrative of hope. In 1776, in Philadelphia, preparing for the American Declaration of Independence, Benjamin Franklin and Thomas Jefferson offered their designs for a seal for the new United States. Franklin proposed that it should bear a picture of Moshe lifting his staff to divide the Sea of Reeds, with the motto "Rebellion to tyrants is obedience to God." Jefferson preferred a picture of the Israelites in the wilderness being "led by a cloud by day and a pillar of fire at night." The American story – its "civil religion"– is supremely the story of the exodus.

That story told of how a small group, fleeing persecution, escaped, undertook a journey through a wilderness, crossed a sea in search of the Promised Land, and there sought to create a "new birth of freedom." The way would be long and hard. There would be diversions and digressions, resistances and rebellions. Yet that is what the founders of America sought, and their inspiration was the story of the Israelites as set out in the book of Exodus.

▶

Parashat Shemot

1 1 And these are the names of the sons of Yisrael who
came to Egypt with Yaakov, each with his household:
2 3 Reuven, Shimon, Levi and Yehuda; Yissakhar, Zevulun
4 5 and Binyamin; Dan and Naftali; Gad and Asher. The

numbers. The Egyptians were obsessed with numbers. It was the number of Israelites that gave them fear. They forced the Israelites to produce a precise number of bricks each day. Nations that quantify human life, reducing populations to numbers, eventually lose their humanity.

THE PEOPLE OF ISRAEL

As we move from Genesis to Exodus, the entire biblical landscape changes. The Jewish project is about to take on substance and form. For the first time, politics enters the narrative, center stage. God is to intervene in history in a series of miracles and wonders that have no precedent and no real sequels. For the first time we will encounter law in all its nuances – Torah, mitzva, *ḥok,* and *mishpat* – as the substance of the divine will. And for the first time we will encounter a transformative leader, Moshe, who emerges from the shadows of a strange, improbable childhood to become, despite his many hesitations, the man who is to leave his mark on the Jewish people to this day.

The reason for all these changes is the appearance, early in the first chapter of Exodus, of one word we have not heard before in connection with the covenantal family: the word *am,* "people" (Ex. 1:9). Not accidentally, it is an outsider, Pharaoh, who uses it first, for it is he who first realizes the change that has come about. What had been a family has become a nation. With that, the very terms of Israel's existence are transformed.

Genesis was about individuals and their relationships. One of its recurring themes was the difficulty the matriarchs – Sara, Rivka, and Raḥel – had in conceiving children. Despite grandiose promises – that they would have as many children as the stars of the sky, the sands of the seashore, and the dust of the earth – having even a single child turned out to be difficult, even miraculous. Yet as we turn the pages and begin the new book, all of that vanishes, and a family of seventy members becomes a nation with six hundred thousand adult males. The Israelites, we are told in a cascade of verbs, "were fruitful and burgeoned; they multiplied and became exceptionally strong, until the land was filled with them" (1:7). Even the attempt by Pharaoh to limit childbirth by subjecting the Israelites to hard labor fails completely: "The more they were oppressed, the more they increased" (1:12).

Exodus is about the birth of a nation,

פרשת שמות

א א וְאֵלֶּה שְׁמוֹת בְּנֵי יִשְׂרָאֵל הַבָּאִים מִצְרָיְמָה אֵת יַעֲקֹב אִישׁ א
ב ג וּבֵיתוֹ בָּאוּ׃ רְאוּבֵן שִׁמְעוֹן לֵוִי וִיהוּדָה׃ יִשָּׂשכָר זְבוּלֻן
ה ד וּבִנְיָמִן׃ דָּן וְנַפְתָּלִי גָּד וְאָשֵׁר׃ וַיְהִי כָּל־נֶפֶשׁ יֹצְאֵי יֶרֶךְ־יַעֲקֹב

SHEMOT

Here, the drama of Exodus begins. In exile, the Jewish people multiply, until they are no longer a family but a nation. Pharaoh, fearing that they pose a threat to Egypt, enslaves them and orders their male children killed. Moshe, an Israelite child adopted by Pharaoh's daughter, is chosen by God to confront Pharaoh and lead the people to freedom. Reluctantly, Moshe agrees, but his initial intervention only makes things worse, and on this tense note the *parasha* ends. On the surface, Exodus is about freedom, slavery, and the fate of nations, but it is also about the power of individuals, driven by justice or compassion, to defy tyrants and change the course of history.

1:1 וְאֵלֶּה *And these* – The word "and" signals an unbroken continuity between Genesis and Exodus, as does the opening genealogy, a more detailed version of which has already appeared in Genesis 46:8–27 (Ramban). Genesis is about the birth of Israel as a family. Exodus is about the birth of Israel as a nation. The two are inseparable. Even as a nation, Israel will still feel a sense of shared fate and mutual responsibility as if it were a single extended family.

What was promised or distantly foreseen in Genesis becomes real at the beginning of Exodus: the promise of many children, of becoming "a great nation" (Gen. 12:1), and the nocturnal vision, with its "deep, dark dread" in which Avraham was told that his descendants would become strangers in a land not their own, where they would be enslaved and mistreated (ch. 15).

Narrative continuity is not merely a literary feature of the Torah. It is also part of its theology. For the Torah, history is meaningful. It tells a story. This was a unique conception of time. For Jews, as historian J. H. Plumb put it, "The past was no longer static, a mere store of information, example and event, but dynamic, an unfolding story." Exodus is the unfolding of the themes set out in Genesis.

1:1 שְׁמוֹת *The names* – Proper names are a marker of individuality, difference, distinctiveness. This follows from Judaism's insistence on the sanctity of human life and the dignity of the individual as the image and likeness of God (Gen. 9:6). When the Nazis sought to dehumanize Jews in the concentration camps, they took away their names and gave them

descendants of Yaakov were seventy in all, and Yosef was
6 already in Egypt. Then Yosef died, and all his brothers,
7 and all that generation. But the Israelites were fruitful and
burgeoned; they multiplied and became exceptionally
strong, until the land was filled with them.
8 Then a new king arose over Egypt, who had not known
9 Yosef. And he said to his people, "You see that the
Israelite people are many and more powerful than we.

Period (c. 1650–c. 1550 BCE). The Hyksos were a Semitic people who were traders and were at first welcomed, settling at Avaris. They prospered, attracted other non-Egyptian groups to join them, and eventually built up economic, political, and military power. It seems that this period remained a vivid part of national memory. The fear was that now another non-native population would take over the rule of this proud and ancient empire. Not all evil is irrational, but neither does the rationality of fear justify evil.

1:8 אֲשֶׁר לֹא־יָדַע אֶת־יוֹסֵף *Who had not known Yosef* – Genesis ends on an almost serene note. Yaakov has found his long-lost son. The family has been reunited. Yosef has forgiven his brothers. Under his protection and influence the family has settled in Goshen, one of the most prosperous regions of Egypt. They now have homes, property, food, the protection of Yosef, and the favor of Pharaoh. It must have seemed one of the golden moments of Avraham's family's history.

Then, as has happened so often since, "a new king arose over Egypt, who had not known Yosef" (Ex. 1:8). There is a political climate change. The family falls out of favor. Pharaoh tells his advisors: "You see that the Israelite people are many and more powerful than we. Come, let us deal wisely with them in case they increase" (vv. 9–10). And so the whole mechanism of oppression moves into operation: forced labor that turns into slavery that becomes attempted genocide.

The story is engraved in our memory. We tell it every year, and in summary form in our prayers every day. It is part of what it is to be a Jew. Yet there is one phrase that shines out from the narrative: "But the more they were oppressed, the more they increased and spread" (v. 12). This, no less than oppression itself, is part of what it means to be a Jew. The worse things get, the stronger we become. Jews are the people who not only survive but thrive in adversity.

Jewish history is not merely a story of Jews enduring catastrophes that might have spelled the end to less tenacious groups. It is the fact that after every disaster, Jews renewed themselves. They discovered some hitherto hidden reservoir of spirit that fueled new forms of collective self-expression as the carriers of God's message to the world.

1:9 עַם בְּנֵי יִשְׂרָאֵל *The Israelite people* – Though we are a fractious people, crisis

ו שִׁבְעִים נָפֶשׁ וְיוֹסֵף הָיָה בְמִצְרָיִם׃ וַיָּמָת יוֹסֵף וְכָל־אֶחָיו
ז וְכֹל הַדּוֹר הַהוּא׃ וּבְנֵי יִשְׂרָאֵל פָּרוּ וַיִּשְׁרְצוּ וַיִּרְבּוּ וַיַּעַצְמוּ
בִּמְאֹד מְאֹד וַתִּמָּלֵא הָאָרֶץ אֹתָם׃
ח וַיָּקָם מֶלֶךְ־חָדָשׁ עַל־מִצְרָיִם אֲשֶׁר לֹא־יָדַע אֶת־יוֹסֵף׃
ט וַיֹּאמֶר אֶל־עַמּוֹ הִנֵּה עַם בְּנֵי יִשְׂרָאֵל רַב וְעָצוּם מִמֶּנּוּ׃

described variously as an *am*, "people," *goy*, "nation," *kahal*, "congregation," and *eda*, "community." No sooner do we see this than we understand what the Jewish project was intended from the outset to be. It is about politics, society, and the principles on which a people can come together to form associations. It is about justice, freedom, and the rule of law. It is about the sanctity of life and human dignity. Ultimately it is about the use and misuse of power. Exodus places frankly before us the risks inherent in power. It can be used to oppress, enslave, and, in extremis, to kill. That is what Pharaoh proposes at the beginning of Exodus.

It is important to understand precisely what is being argued in these opening pages. Pharaoh is not portrayed as the embodiment of evil. He is not a Haman. His people are not the Amalekites. Pharaoh is driven by political motives, not hate: "Come, let us deal wisely with them in case they increase, and if war breaks out they may join our enemies and fight against us" (1:10).

This is not a simple story of good versus evil. It is a critique of the politics of power, empires, hierarchical societies, and the division of populations into free human beings and slaves. Lord Acton summed it up in his famous dictum that "all power tends to corrupt and absolute power corrupts absolutely." In its place, the Torah proposes a different kind of politics, based not on power but on covenant, the free agreement of a free people who accord absolute sovereignty to God alone. The idea could hardly be more radical, and it has shaped the history of the West.

1:8 מֶלֶךְ־חָדָשׁ *A new king* – The Torah nowhere identifies which particular Pharaoh this was. There may be a suggestion here that the person matters less than the role, that the conduct of Pharaoh as described here and later has less to do with his personality and more to do with the system he leads and embodies. Its entire structure – a highly hierarchical society, with absolute power held by rulers, while much of the rest of the population is used as a conscripted labor force to construct monumental buildings – has an inherent tendency to cruelty.

The "new king," however, may refer to one of the rulers of the "new kingdom" which wrested back power from the foreign Hyksos (*heqau-khasut* in ancient Egyptian, "rulers from foreign lands"), who ruled the northern part of the country during the Second Intermediate

10 Come, let us deal wisely with them in case they increase,
and if war breaks out they may join our enemies and fight
11 against us and escape from the land." So they placed slave
masters over the Israelites to oppress them with forced

so the Israelites became accustomed to it rather than trying to flee. First Pharaoh issued a proclamation calling on all Egyptians and Israelites to work on his construction projects for pay. Pharaoh himself joined them (Sota 11a). After a month, the Egyptians gradually withdrew, leaving the Israelites working alone. Then they stopped being paid. By then the Israelites had become slaves and the Egyptians their taskmasters. Gradualism later became part of the Nazi program of genocide.

1:10 וְנוֹסַף גַּם־הוּא עַל־שֹׂנְאֵינוּ *They may join our enemies* – We do not have other ancient descriptions of the events of the exodus. But we have enough background information to understand the context in which a pharaoh would say this. It makes eminent sense, given the conditions of the time. A great drama was to begin that would leave its mark ever afterward on the life of the group whose descendants are the Jews of today.

The contrast between the two peoples could not have been greater. Egypt at that time was an indomitable power. It held sway over the whole ancient Near East. Ramesses II conducted successful campaigns against the Hittites and the Libyans and launched punitive raids against Edom and Moav. He used the technical prowess and prosperity of Egypt to undertake a series of monumental building projects that have few rivals in the ancient world. He had colossal statues of himself erected throughout the country. The prefix "Ra" in his name tells us that he was seen as the sun god, a divine being whose rule was written in the heavens and whose word carried absolute command.

The Israelites, for their part, were a landless people, entirely at the mercy of the Egyptians. They had no power and, at first, no effective leadership. They were easily conscripted into forced labor. No group seemed less likely to become the people of eternity.

Had anyone suggested at the time that it would not be the Egypt of the pharaohs that would survive and change the moral landscape of the world, but instead a group of Hebrew slaves, it would have seemed an ultimate absurdity. The Egyptians believed that the Israelites were already on the verge of extinction. The earliest known reference to Israel outside the Bible is an inscription produced by Ramesses's successor, Merneptah, in the thirteenth century BCE. The Merneptah Stele, a giant slab of black granite that stands today in the Cairo Museum, contains these words: "Israel is laid waste. His seed is no more."

י הָבָה נִּתְחַכְּמָה לוֹ פֶּן־יִרְבֶּה וְהָיָה כִּי־תִקְרֶאנָה מִלְחָמָה
וְנוֹסַף גַּם־הוּא עַל־שֹׂנְאֵינוּ וְנִלְחַם־בָּנוּ וְעָלָה מִן־הָאָרֶץ׃
יא וַיָּשִׂימוּ עָלָיו שָׂרֵי מִסִּים לְמַעַן עַנֹּתוֹ בְּסִבְלֹתָם וַיִּבֶן עָרֵי

unites us. As the Rabbis said: when it comes to the history of Jewish suffering, "the latter troubles make us forget the earlier ones" (Berakhot 13a). The entire book of Genesis is taken up with arguments within the family, between husbands and wives, parents and children, and between siblings. But as soon as the book of Exodus begins, the Israelites are faced with exile and slavery, and for the first time we hear the phrase *am Benei Yisrael*, "the Israelite people." Earlier rivalries have been forgotten, and a divided family has become a united people.

1:9 רַב וְעָצוּם מִמֶּנּוּ *More powerful than we* – Thus Pharaoh says to his people, but he cannot have believed this, or he would not risk provoking the Israelites by ordering the murder of every male child. In the case of antisemitism there is always a discrepancy between what Israel's enemies say and what they believe. They say that Hebrews/Israelites/Jews are powerful in order to arouse fear that mutates into hate, but they know that in fact they are, in earthly terms, powerless. They would not seek a confrontation that they believed they would lose.

At the same time, Pharaoh is speaking to real anxieties on the part of the people. We mentioned above that before our narrative began, northern Egypt had come under the rule of the Hyksos, a Semitic-speaking group from the coastal Levant. Their culture was Asiatic, they worshipped Baal Tzefon, the Canaanite storm god, and they preserved their non-Egyptian names. They built a huge citadel on the Nile. This period was preserved as a trauma in Egyptian memories as a time when the created order itself was overturned. The Israelites, with their distinctive identity and faith, could easily be portrayed as a new danger akin to the Hyksos. This would have readily been believed by the population as a whole.

Note that in the history of antisemitism, hate usually emerges in the wake of an event, unrelated to Jews, that was perceived by the host culture as a humiliation. The French defeat in the Franco-Prussian War of 1870 led to the antisemitism that reached a climax in the Dreyfus affair. German defeat in the First World War and the punitive terms of the Treaty of Versailles led to Nazism. The deep humiliation felt by the Egyptians as they remembered the Hyksos may well be the background to the events of this and the following chapters.

1:10 נִתְחַכְּמָה לוֹ *Deal wisely with them* – According to the Midrash, the "wise dealing" of Pharaoh consisted of inflicting slavery slowly and by degrees,

labor; they built supply cities for Pharaoh: Pitom and
12 Ramesses. But the more they were oppressed, the more
they increased and spread; and the Egyptians came to
13 dread the Israelites. The Egyptians imposed backbreaking
14 labor on the Israelites, embittering their lives with harsh
work in mortar and brick and all field labors; all the
work they forced upon them was intended to break
15 them. Then the king of Egypt said to the midwives of the
16 Hebrews – one named Shifra, the other Puah – "When
you help a Hebrew woman give birth, look on the birth
stool. If it is a boy, kill him, and if it is a girl, let her live."

MIDWIVES TO THE HEBREWS

Who were Shifra and Puah? The truth is, we do not know. One midrash identifies them with Moshe's mother Yokheved and sister Miriam, using a midrashic technique of identifying unknown characters with characters who are more elaborated upon (Sota 11b, Rashi there). However, in describing them the Torah uses an ambiguous phrase. It calls them *hameyaldot haIvriot*, which could mean either "the Hebrew midwives" or "the midwives to the Hebrews." On the second interpretation, they may not have been Hebrews at all, but Egyptians. This is the view taken, among others, by the scholar and statesman Abrabanel and the Italian commentator Shmuel David Luzzatto. Luzzatto's reasoning is simple: could Pharaoh realistically have expected Hebrew women to murder their own people's children? Rather than decide one way or the other, it seems clear that the Torah's ambiguity on this point is deliberate. We do not know who they are or which people they belong to because their particular form of moral courage transcends nationality and race. In essence, they are being asked to commit a "crime against humanity," and the fact that they refuse to do so tells us something about the ethical parameters of humanity as such. Though Shifra and Puah are seemingly minor figures in the narrative, they are giants in the story of humanity. All we know about them is that they "feared God and did not do as the king of Egypt ordered them" (Ex. 1:17). In those words, a precedent is set that will eventually become the basis of the United Nations Universal Declaration of Human Rights. Shifra and Puah, by refusing to obey an immoral order, redefine the moral imagination of the world.

Shifra and Puah are the first of six courageous women who will play a vital part in the story of Israel's redemption in this *parasha*. The others are Yokheved and Miriam, Pharaoh's daughter, and Moshe's wife Tzipora. Moshe may be the central character in the unfolding drama of Israel's redemption, but without these women, there would be no Moshe. Their moral courage is a vital element in the story.

יב מִסְכְּנוֹת לְפַרְעֹה אֶת־פִּתֹם וְאֶת־רַעַמְסֵס׃ וְכַאֲשֶׁר יְעַנּוּ
יג אֹתוֹ כֵּן יִרְבֶּה וְכֵן יִפְרֹץ וַיָּקֻצוּ מִפְּנֵי בְּנֵי יִשְׂרָאֵל׃ וַיַּעֲבִדוּ
יד מִצְרַיִם אֶת־בְּנֵי יִשְׂרָאֵל בְּפָרֶךְ׃ וַיְמָרְרוּ אֶת־חַיֵּיהֶם בַּעֲבֹדָה
קָשָׁה בְּחֹמֶר וּבִלְבֵנִים וּבְכָל־עֲבֹדָה בַּשָּׂדֶה אֵת כָּל־עֲבֹדָתָם
טו אֲשֶׁר־עָבְדוּ בָהֶם בְּפָרֶךְ׃ וַיֹּאמֶר מֶלֶךְ מִצְרַיִם לַמְיַלְּדֹת
הָעִבְרִיֹּת אֲשֶׁר שֵׁם הָאַחַת שִׁפְרָה וְשֵׁם הַשֵּׁנִית פּוּעָה׃
טז וַיֹּאמֶר בְּיַלֶּדְכֶן אֶת־הָעִבְרִיּוֹת וּרְאִיתֶן עַל־הָאָבְנָיִם אִם־בֵּן

1:11 אֶת־פִּתֹם וְאֶת־רַעַמְסֵס *Pitom and Ramesses* – Pitom or Per-Atum is the modern Tell el-Mashkuta in the eastern delta, a day's journey from Ramesses. Ramesses or Per-Ramses, "the house of Ramesses," was constructed near the old Hyksos capital of Avaris, where Ramesses's father, Seti I, had built a summer palace. Construction continued for twenty years, and a series of mansions, administrative buildings, and barracks grew up around the palace until it became a city. Documents from the time attest to the rich abundance of food that grew in the area, and there were granaries well stocked with wheat, the "supplies" referred to in the verse. As Toby Wilkinson describes it: "The royal quarter, covering four square miles, was located in a natural stronghold on the banks of the Nile, protected by canals and sand promontories. Court poets penned eulogies on the splendor of Ramesses's palaces.... The steps leading to the throne dais were adorned with prostrate images of the king's enemies, so that he might tread them underfoot each time he ascended or descended." This was very close to the Israelites' region in the land of Goshen and explains why Moshe is able to visit the Pharaoh often during the events preceding the exodus.

1:14 וַיְמָרְרוּ אֶת־חַיֵּיהֶם *Embittering their lives* – Jewish tradition would relate this term to the bitter herbs at the Seder service (Ex. 12:8). Note the fourfold repetition in this verse of the Hebrew root *a-v-d*, "slave, forced labor," as if to emphasize the intensity and relentlessness of the oppression. Both the previous verse and this one end with the word *befarekh*, meaning backbreaking labor, inhuman and dehumanizing work, of a kind that would later be forbidden to be demanded by one Israelite of another (Lev. 25:43, 46). According to Egyptian documents of the period, recently discovered, brickmaking quotas issued by slave masters were only rarely reached. It seems, therefore, to have been a deliberate policy toward slaves and prisoners of war to set them work targets that were virtually impossible to achieve, a form of physical and mental torture that may be what the Torah is referring to here as cruel or "backbreaking."

17 But the midwives feared God, and did not do as the king
18 of Egypt ordered them. They let the babies live. Then the SHENI
king of Egypt summoned the midwives and demanded,
"Why have you done this; why have you let the children
19 live?" But "Hebrew women," the midwives replied, "are
not like Egyptians. They are full of vigor, and have already
20 given birth by the time the midwife arrives." God was
good to the midwives; and the people multiplied and
21 grew very strong. And because the midwives feared God,
22 He granted them households. Then Pharaoh commanded
his entire people, saying, "Throw every boy that is born
into the Nile, and let all the girls live."
2 1 A man of the house of Levi went and married a daughter
2 of Levi. And she became pregnant and gave birth to a son.

---

the death of the firstborn. A fundamental theme here, as it was after the flood, is the sanctity of life, every life, even that of the young child. The reference to the entire people is a further emphasis on the fact that what was happening was public: all the people were complicit in the slow genocide of the male Israelite newborns. One of the fundamental unanswered questions about the Holocaust is: how was it that so many knew but did not protest? Evil, when initiated at the top of the social-political structure, is often contagious. That is why the Torah emphasizes the counter-examples, the midwives here, and Pharaoh's daughter in the next chapter. It is possible to take a stand against evil.

2:1 וַיֵּלֶךְ אִישׁ מִבֵּית לֵוִי וַיִּקַּח אֶת־בַּת־לֵוִי *A man of the house of Levi went and married a daughter of Levi* – The Talmud records the existential dilemma faced by Jews in the second century CE, having experienced the destruction of the Temple, the brutal suppression of the Bar Kokhba rebellion, and the Hadrianic persecutions. A statement in the name of R. Yishmael reads: "From the day that a government has come to power which issues cruel decrees against us and forbids us to observe the Torah and its commands… we ought by rights to bind ourselves not to marry and beget children, with the result that the seed of Avraham our father would come to an end of its own accord" (Bava Batra 60b). This haunting passage tells us that there were profoundly religious Jews like R. Yishmael who believed that on rational grounds one should not bring Jewish children into a world which had experienced nightmare. But R. Yishmael added that were this to be issued as a ruling it would not be obeyed, for the faith of ordinary Jews transcends logic.

Does this mean an irrational faith? The Rabbis implicitly posed the question

יז הוּא וַהֲמִתֶּן אֹתוֹ וְאִם־בַּת הִוא וָחָיָה׃ וַתִּירֶאןָ הַמְיַלְּדֹת
אֶת־הָאֱלֹהִים וְלֹא עָשׂוּ כַּאֲשֶׁר דִּבֶּר אֲלֵיהֶן מֶלֶךְ מִצְרָיִם
יח וַתְּחַיֶּיןָ אֶת־הַיְלָדִים׃ וַיִּקְרָא מֶלֶךְ־מִצְרַיִם לַמְיַלְּדֹת וַיֹּאמֶר שני
יט לָהֶן מַדּוּעַ עֲשִׂיתֶן הַדָּבָר הַזֶּה וַתְּחַיֶּיןָ אֶת־הַיְלָדִים׃ וַתֹּאמַרְןָ
הַמְיַלְּדֹת אֶל־פַּרְעֹה כִּי לֹא כַנָּשִׁים הַמִּצְרִיֹּת הָעִבְרִיֹּת כִּי־
כ חָיוֹת הֵנָּה בְּטֶרֶם תָּבוֹא אֲלֵהֶן הַמְיַלֶּדֶת וְיָלָדוּ׃ וַיֵּיטֶב
כא אֱלֹהִים לַמְיַלְּדֹת וַיִּרֶב הָעָם וַיַּעַצְמוּ מְאֹד׃ וַיְהִי כִּי־יָרְאוּ
כב הַמְיַלְּדֹת אֶת־הָאֱלֹהִים וַיַּעַשׂ לָהֶם בָּתִּים׃ וַיְצַו פַּרְעֹה לְכָל־
עַמּוֹ לֵאמֹר כָּל־הַבֵּן הַיִּלּוֹד הַיְאֹרָה תַּשְׁלִיכֻהוּ וְכָל־הַבַּת
תְּחַיּוּן׃
ב א ב וַיֵּלֶךְ אִישׁ מִבֵּית לֵוִי וַיִּקַּח אֶת־בַּת־לֵוִי׃ וַתַּהַר הָאִשָּׁה וַתֵּלֶד

It is notable that only two, Yokheved and Miriam, are clearly Israelite. Pharaoh's daughter and Tzipora are clearly not, and the identity of Shifra and Puah is uncertain. The entire Exodus narrative is a delicate counterpoint between the particularity of Israel – "My son, My firstborn" (4:22) – and the universality of the moral law. We will see this several times in the following chapters.

Not every nation is expected to be holy. But every nation is expected to be moral. Thus we are presented with role models, such as these non-Israelite women, whose principled stand against tyranny and persecution transcends all ethnic and cultural boundaries.

1:21 וַיַּעַשׂ לָהֶם בָּתִּים *He granted them households* – The story of Shifra and Puah is not a tragedy. It ends with a curious phrase: God "granted them households." What does this mean? Luzzatto (see above, "Midwives to the Hebrews") offers an insightful interpretation. Sometimes women become midwives when they are unable to have children of their own. That, he suggests, was the case with Shifra and Puah. Because they saved children's lives, God rewarded them – measure for measure – with children of their own ("households," meaning families). "In reward for the righteous women of that generation, our ancestors were redeemed from Egypt" (Sota 11b). Shifra and Puah were two of those women, heroines of the spirit, giants in the story of humankind.

1:22 וַיְצַו פַּרְעֹה לְכָל־עַמּוֹ *Then Pharaoh commanded his entire people* – This is the beginning of a terrible crime against humanity – the mass murder of children – that will eventually return to haunt Pharaoh and his people. This is the message of the first plague, the river that turned into blood, and the last plague,

She saw what a fine child he was, and for three months she
3 kept him hidden. And when she could no longer hide him,
she took a papyrus basket and coated it with tar and pitch.
She laid the child in it and placed it among the reeds by
4 the bank of the Nile, and his sister stood by at a distance to
5 see what would happen to him. Pharaoh's daughter came
down to bathe in the Nile, while her attendants walked
by the riverbank. She saw the basket among the reeds and

2:3 וַתָּשֶׂם בַּסּוּף עַל־שְׂפַת הַיְאֹר *Placed it among the reeds by the bank of the Nile* – I try to imagine the courage of a woman willing to have a child once the decree has been issued to "throw every boy that is born into the Nile" (Ex. 1:22). The scene is Germany, 1939. Anti-Jewish edicts are in force. There is a sense of impending tragedy. To have a child at that time is a supreme act of hope in the midst of despair. That is the bravery of Yokheved.

What do we know about her? Surprisingly little. We see Yokheved's resourcefulness. For three months she hides the child. When she can do so no longer, she makes a papyrus basket and sets him afloat on the Nile, hoping he will be noticed and saved. Like many biblical women, she is a person of action, determination, and courage.

She gives birth to three children destined for greatness: Miriam, the prophetess; Aharon, Israel's first High Priest; and Moshe, its greatest leader. She endows her children, genetically or by example, with the gift of leadership. She and her husband are both from the tribe of Levi. A few chapters earlier, the Torah has told us that on his deathbed Yaakov delivers both a prediction and a curse: "Shimon and Levi are brothers; weapons of violence their wares. Let me never join their council, nor my honor be of their assembly. For in their anger they killed men, at their whim they hamstrung oxen. Cursed be their anger, for it is most fierce, and their fury, for it is most cruel" (Gen. 49:5–7).

We hear little subsequently about Shimon. But the children of Levi defy Yaakov's low opinion. From their ranks will eventually come not only the three leaders of the exodus, but Israel's priests and Levites, its spiritual ministers, for all time. There is more than a hint that something in Yokheved – her capacity for hope or her faith in life – transforms, in her children, violence into courage, and aggression into an unshakable determination to rescue people and set them on the path to liberty. She has the subtle gift of transforming vice into virtue. She becomes the mother of Israel's leaders.

PHARAOH'S DAUGHTER

Pharaoh afflicts the children of Israel, but it is another member of his own family who saves the decisive vestige of hope. Pharaoh's daughter is one of the most unexpected heroes of the Hebrew Bible. Without her, Moshe might not

ג בֵּן וַתֵּרֶא אֹתוֹ כִּי־טוֹב הוּא וַתִּצְפְּנֵהוּ שְׁלֹשָׁה יְרָחִים: וְלֹא־
יָכְלָה עוֹד הַצְּפִינוֹ וַתִּקַּח־לוֹ תֵּבַת גֹּמֶא וַתַּחְמְרָה בַחֵמָר
וּבַזָּפֶת וַתָּשֶׂם בָּהּ אֶת־הַיֶּלֶד וַתָּשֶׂם בַּסּוּף עַל־שְׂפַת הַיְאֹר:
ד ה וַתֵּתַצַּב אֲחֹתוֹ מֵרָחֹק לְדֵעָה מַה־יֵּעָשֶׂה לוֹ: וַתֵּרֶד בַּת־
פַּרְעֹה לִרְחֹץ עַל־הַיְאֹר וְנַעֲרֹתֶיהָ הֹלְכֹת עַל־יַד הַיְאֹר
וַתֵּרֶא אֶת־הַתֵּבָה בְּתוֹךְ הַסּוּף וַתִּשְׁלַח אֶת־אֲמָתָהּ וַתִּקָּחֶהָ:

elsewhere in the form of a projected dialogue between Amram, "a man of the house of Levi," and his daughter Miriam, at the time of Pharaoh's decree (Sota 12a). In this interpretation, Amram and the other Israelite men, seeing that every male Israelite child was to be cast into the river and drowned, thereupon divorced their wives and refused to have children. Amram's daughter protested. The decision, she said, was worse than Pharaoh's decree. It condemned both boys and girls. It deprived them of both this world and the next. Amram relented and he and his wife had a son: Moshe. The implication is clear. From faith comes redemption. Trust in the future is not always rational, but neither is it irrational. Rather it is, in crisis, the critical test of religious courage.

2:2 וַתֵּרֶא אֹתוֹ כִּי־טוֹב *She saw what a fine child he was* – Literally, "She saw him that he was good." This language is an echo of the creation narrative: "And God saw… it was good" (Gen. 1:4, 10, 12, 18, 21, 25, 31). This is one of a series of evocations of the early chapters of Genesis (compare, for instance, the language of Ex. 1:7 with that of Gen. 1:28), suggesting that what we are reading is the story of a new creation: a covenanted nation that will emerge from the crucible of suffering to carry the Divine Presence in its midst.

2:2 וַתִּצְפְּנֵהוּ *She kept him hidden* – In standard versions of mythology, a ruler receives a warning about a child about to be born to him. The ruler takes steps to kill the child or let him die. The child is saved, often by being placed in a basket and floated down a river, and raised by people of humble birth. Only later does he learn that he has royal blood.

The story of Moshe is the precise opposite. He is found and raised by royalty – an Egyptian princess, Pharaoh's daughter – and learns that he is in fact not royalty but a member of what has become, in Egyptian eyes, a pariah people. The Moshe story is a subtle and brilliant assault on the concept, central (though not exclusive) to polytheistic religions, of a human hierarchy, in which rulers are marked from the outset by royal blood. Moshe is the representative of a people every member of whom has been adopted by God, a point made in the first words Moshe is commanded to say to Pharaoh: "Israel is My son, My firstborn" (Ex. 4:22).

6 sent her maid to fetch it. When she opened it she saw him
there, the child; the boy was crying, and she was moved
to pity for him: "This must be one of the Hebrew boys."
7 Then his sister asked Pharaoh's daughter, "Shall I go and
fetch one of the Hebrew women to nurse the child for
8 you?" "Go," said Pharaoh's daughter. So the girl went away
9 and called the child's mother. "Take this child," Pharaoh's
daughter told her. "Nurse him for me, and I will pay you
your wage." So the woman took the child and nursed him.
10 The child grew, and she brought him to Pharaoh's daughter
and he became her son. She named him Moshe, "because,"

---

who were so righteous that they entered paradise in their lifetime (Derekh Eretz Zuta 1).

Moral courage can sometimes be found in the heart of darkness. That the Torah itself tells the story the way it does has enormous implications. It means that when it comes to people, we must never generalize, never stereotype. The Egyptians were not all evil: even from Pharaoh himself a heroine was born. Nothing could signal more powerfully that the Torah is not an ethnocentric text; that we must recognize virtue wherever we find it, even among our enemies; and that the basic core of human values – humanity, compassion, courage – is truly universal. Faith may not be; goodness is.

2:6 וְהִנֵּה־נַעַר בֹּכֶה *The boy was crying* – The verse begins by calling Moshe a baby (*yeled*) and ends by calling him a boy or youth (*naar*). Rashi explains that "he cried in an adult way." On this, Rabbi Meir Shapiro of Lublin commented: "There are two ways of crying. A child cries when it is in pain. An adult cries when it sees someone else in pain." Already the princess felt in Moshe a sensitivity to the suffering of others.

2:7 וַתֹּאמֶר אֲחֹתוֹ אֶל־בַּת־פַּרְעֹה *Then his sister asked Pharaoh's daughter* – This encounter on the banks of the Nile, between an Egyptian princess and a young Israelite child, Moshe's sister Miriam, is profoundly moving. The contrast between them – in terms of age, culture, status, and power – could not be greater. Yet their deep humanity bridges all the differences, all the distance. Two heroines. May they inspire us.

2:10 וַתִּקְרָא שְׁמוֹ מֹשֶׁה *She named him Moshe* – It takes a while before we realize that there is something strange about this sentence. It presupposes that Pharaoh's daughter spoke Hebrew. It also makes the impossible assumption that not only would she adopt a Hebrew child in direct contravention to her father's decree that every male child be killed, but would advertise the fact by giving him a Hebrew name. In short, the

ו וַתִּפְתַּח וַתִּרְאֵהוּ אֶת־הַיֶּלֶד וְהִנֵּה־נַעַר בֹּכֶה וַתַּחְמֹל עָלָיו
ז וַתֹּאמֶר מִיַּלְדֵי הָעִבְרִים זֶה׃ וַתֹּאמֶר אֲחֹתוֹ אֶל־בַּת־פַּרְעֹה
הַאֵלֵךְ וְקָרָאתִי לָךְ אִשָּׁה מֵינֶקֶת מִן הָעִבְרִיֹּת וְתֵינִק לָךְ
ח אֶת־הַיָּלֶד׃ וַתֹּאמֶר־לָהּ בַּת־פַּרְעֹה לֵכִי וַתֵּלֶךְ הָעַלְמָה
ט וַתִּקְרָא אֶת־אֵם הַיָּלֶד׃ וַתֹּאמֶר לָהּ בַּת־פַּרְעֹה הֵילִיכִי
אֶת־הַיֶּלֶד הַזֶּה וְהֵינִקִהוּ לִי וַאֲנִי אֶתֵּן אֶת־שְׂכָרֵךְ וַתִּקַּח
י הָאִשָּׁה הַיֶּלֶד וַתְּנִיקֵהוּ׃ וַיִּגְדַּל הַיֶּלֶד וַתְּבִאֵהוּ לְבַת־פַּרְעֹה
וַיְהִי־לָהּ לְבֵן וַתִּקְרָא שְׁמוֹ מֹשֶׁה וַתֹּאמֶר כִּי מִן־הַמַּיִם

have lived. The whole story of the exodus would have been different. Yet she is not an Israelite. She has nothing to gain, and everything to lose, by her courage. Yet she seems to have no doubt, experiences no misgivings, makes no hesitation.

Pharaoh's daughter goes to bathe in the Nile, while her maids walk along the Nile's edge. She sees the basket in the reeds and sends her slave girl to fetch it. First she sees that it is a child and has pity on it. This is a natural, human, compassionate reaction. Only then does it dawn on her who the child must be. Who else would abandon a child? She remembers her father's decree against the Hebrews. Instantly the situation has changed. To save the baby would mean disobeying the royal command. That would be serious enough for an ordinary Egyptian, doubly so for a member of the royal family.

Nor is she alone when the event happens. Her maids are with her; her slave girl is standing beside her. She must face the risk that one of them, in a fit of pique, or even mere gossip, will tell someone about it. Rumors flourish in royal courts. Yet she does not shift her ground. She does not tell one of her servants to take the baby and hide it with a family far away. She has the courage of her compassion. She does not flinch.

Nor is this simply a moment's pity. She remains committed to the child's welfare, taking the riskiest of strategies. She will adopt him and bring him up as her own son. This is courage of a high order.

Who then is Pharaoh's daughter? Nowhere is she explicitly named. However, the first book of Chronicles (4:18) mentions a daughter of Pharaoh, named Bitya, and it was she the Sages identified as the woman who saved Moshe. The name Bitya (sometimes rendered as Batya) means "the daughter of God." From this, the Sages drew one of their most striking lessons: "The Holy One, blessed be He, said to her: 'Moshe was not your son, yet you called him your son. You are not My daughter, but I shall call you My daughter'" (Vayikra Rabba 1:3). They added that she was one of the few people (tradition enumerates nine)

11 she said, "I drew him out of the water." One day, when SHELISHI
Moshe had grown up, he went out to his people and saw
their forced labor. And he noticed an Egyptian striking a
12 Hebrew: one of his brothers. Looking this way and that
and seeing no one, he struck down the Egyptian and hid
13 his body in the sand. The next day he went out and saw
two Hebrews fighting. He asked the guilty one, "Why are
14 you striking your own neighbor?" The man said, "Who
made you a ruler and judge over us? Do you intend to kill
me as you killed the Egyptian?" Then Moshe was afraid.
15 "Surely," he thought, "the thing has become known." Word
reached Pharaoh and he sought to kill Moshe. But Moshe
fled his presence and went to live in the land of Midyan.
16 There he sat down beside a well. The priest of Midyan had
seven daughters; they came to draw water and filled the
17 troughs to water their father's flock. Then the shepherds
arrived and started to drive the young women away. But
Moshe stood up to defend them, and then watered their
18 flock. When the sisters returned to Reuel their father,

Although Moshe had many names, the only one by which he is known in the whole Torah is the one given to him by the daughter of Pharaoh. Even the Holy One, blessed be He, did not call him by any other name."

2:11 וַיֵּצֵא אֶל־אֶחָיו *He went out to his people* – Miriam's strategy has worked: having been nursed by his own mother during his early years, he knows that the slaves he sees are "his people," "his brothers." To be a Jew is to know that one cannot be indifferent when one's people are suffering. "Israel," said R. Shimon b. Yoḥai, "is like a single body with one soul. When one is injured, all feel the pain." Moshe identifies with the Israelites at considerable cost to himself.

The passage is a brief tutorial in leadership. First Moshe goes out to the people. Though he did not grow up with them, he identifies with them. Second, he sees their suffering. He sees what they need to be liberated from and cannot do by themselves. Third, "looking this way and that" and seeing no one else prepared to act, he acts. There will be many years before he will be summoned to lead the people, but he is already acting like a leader.

2:17 וַיָּקָם מֹשֶׁה וַיּוֹשִׁעָן *Moshe stood up to defend them* – Leadership begins with taking responsibility. Contrast the opening of Genesis with the opening of Exodus. The opening chapters of Genesis

יא מְשִׁיתִֽהוּ׃ וַיְהִ֣י ׀ בַּיָּמִ֣ים הָהֵ֗ם וַיִּגְדַּ֤ל מֹשֶׁה֙ וַיֵּצֵ֣א אֶל־אֶחָ֔יו שלישי
וַיַּ֖רְא בְּסִבְלֹתָ֑ם וַיַּרְא֙ אִ֣ישׁ מִצְרִ֔י מַכֶּ֥ה אִישׁ־עִבְרִ֖י מֵאֶחָֽיו׃
יב וַיִּ֤פֶן כֹּה֙ וָכֹ֔ה וַיַּ֖רְא כִּ֣י אֵ֣ין אִ֑ישׁ וַיַּךְ֙ אֶת־הַמִּצְרִ֔י וַֽיִּטְמְנֵ֖הוּ
יג בַּחֽוֹל׃ וַיֵּצֵא֙ בַּיּ֣וֹם הַשֵּׁנִ֔י וְהִנֵּ֛ה שְׁנֵֽי־אֲנָשִׁ֥ים עִבְרִ֖ים נִצִּ֑ים
יד וַיֹּ֙אמֶר֙ לָֽרָשָׁ֔ע לָ֥מָּה תַכֶּ֖ה רֵעֶֽךָ׃ וַ֠יֹּאמֶר מִ֣י שָֽׂמְךָ֞ לְאִ֨ישׁ
שַׂ֤ר וְשֹׁפֵט֙ עָלֵ֔ינוּ הַלְהָרְגֵ֙נִי֙ אַתָּ֣ה אֹמֵ֔ר כַּאֲשֶׁ֥ר הָרַ֖גְתָּ אֶת־
טו הַמִּצְרִ֑י וַיִּירָ֤א מֹשֶׁה֙ וַיֹּאמַ֔ר אָכֵ֖ן נוֹדַ֥ע הַדָּבָֽר׃ וַיִּשְׁמַ֤ע פַּרְעֹה֙
אֶת־הַדָּבָ֣ר הַזֶּ֔ה וַיְבַקֵּ֖שׁ לַהֲרֹ֣ג אֶת־מֹשֶׁ֑ה וַיִּבְרַ֤ח מֹשֶׁה֙ מִפְּנֵ֣י
טז פַרְעֹ֔ה וַיֵּ֥שֶׁב בְּאֶֽרֶץ־מִדְיָ֖ן וַיֵּ֥שֶׁב עַל־הַבְּאֵֽר׃ וּלְכֹהֵ֥ן מִדְיָ֖ן
שֶׁ֣בַע בָּנ֑וֹת וַתָּבֹ֣אנָה וַתִּדְלֶ֗נָה וַתְּמַלֶּ֙אנָה֙ אֶת־הָ֣רְהָטִ֔ים
יז לְהַשְׁק֖וֹת צֹ֥אן אֲבִיהֶֽן׃ וַיָּבֹ֥אוּ הָרֹעִ֖ים וַֽיְגָרְשׁ֑וּם וַיָּ֤קָם מֹשֶׁה֙
יח וַיּ֣וֹשִׁעָ֔ן וַיַּ֖שְׁקְ אֶת־צֹאנָֽם׃ וַתָּבֹ֔אנָה אֶל־רְעוּאֵ֖ל אֲבִיהֶ֑ן

Hebrew etymology of the name is only half of the story.

Moshe – in the form Mose, Mses or Messes – is in fact an Egyptian word. It figures in the names of several Pharaohs, including Thutmose, and most significantly Ramesses himself. The word means "child." Understanding this, we stand before one of the Torah's boldest and most revolutionary strokes. Years later, two men are to be involved in a monumental confrontation: Ramesses and Moshe. Their names tell us what is at stake. Ramesses means "child of the sun god Ra." Ramesses, as we have seen, saw himself as a god and erected a temple at Abu Simbel to that proposition. Moshe is simply, anonymously, "a child" – with no more identification than that, exactly as there is no name given to his parents when we first encounter them in the biblical text, other than the bare description, "A man of the house of Levi went and married a daughter of Levi" (Ex. 2:1).

In the Torah, it is parents who give a child its name, and in the case of a special individual, God Himself. It is God who gives the name Yitzḥak to the first Jewish child; God's angel who gives Yaakov the name Yisrael; God who changes the names of Avram and Sarai to Avraham and Sara. We have already encountered one adoptive name – Tzafenat Pane'aḥ – the name by which Yosef was known in Egypt; yet in the Torah, Yosef remains Yosef. How surpassingly strange that the hero of the exodus, greatest of all the prophets, should bear not the name Amram and Yokheved have undoubtedly used thus far, but the one given to him by his adoptive mother, an Egyptian princess. A midrash (Shemot Rabba 1:26) draws our attention to the fact: "This is the reward for those who do kindness.

he asked them, "How is it that you have come back so
19 quickly today?" They said, "An Egyptian rescued us from
the shepherds. He even drew water for us and watered the
20 flock." "Where is he?" he asked his daughters. "Why did
you leave him there? Invite him in to have something to
21 eat." Moshe accepted an invitation to stay with the man,
22 and he gave Moshe his daughter Tzipora in marriage. She
gave birth to a son, and Moshe named him Gershom,
saying, "I have been a stranger in an alien land."
23 Years passed, and the king of Egypt died. The Israelites
sighed in their enslavement and cried out, and from their
24 servitude their plea for help rose up to God. And God
heard their groaning, and remembered His covenant
25 with Avraham, with Yitzḥak, and with Yaakov. God saw
3 1 the Israelites, and God knew. One day Moshe REVI'I
was tending the flock of his father-in-law Yitro, priest of
Midyan. He led the flock to the far side of the wilderness
2 and came to Ḥorev, the mountain of God. Then an angel

2:24 וַיִּשְׁמַע אֱלֹהִים *And God heard* – In the Torah the word *shema* means more than "hear." It means "listen, pay attention, and act accordingly." This explains an unusual feature of Biblical Hebrew, namely that it has no word that means "obey." Judaism does not demand blind obedience. To the contrary, it asks us, as far as possible, to understand the reasons for the commandments, though their full wisdom will always be beyond our understanding. Obedience in Judaism is a form of active listening. Premodern English used the word "hearken" to convey this, but there is now no word in common usage that has this precise sense. By "God heard," our verse means "He attended to the cries of the Israelites and set it in the context of the promise He had given the patriarchs that He would bring their children safely out of slavery and back to the land of Israel."

2:25 וַיֵּדַע אֱלֹהִים *And God knew* – As we see throughout the Torah, the verb "know" in Hebrew means something quite different from its meaning in Greek and subsequent Western thought. Knowledge, for the Greeks, was a form of cognition, a detached appraisal of facts. In the Torah, knowledge is not simply an intellectual attribute. It also has consequences for emotion and action. In this case, "and God knew" means that He not only saw the suffering of the Israelites. He was pained by it, and determined to act to redeem them.

יט וַיֹּאמֶר מַדּוּעַ מִהַרְתֶּן בֹּא הַיּוֹם: וַתֹּאמַרְןָ אִישׁ מִצְרִי הִצִּילָנוּ
כ מִיַּד הָרֹעִים וְגַם־דָּלֹה דָלָה לָנוּ וַיַּשְׁקְ אֶת־הַצֹּאן: וַיֹּאמֶר אֶל־
בְּנֹתָיו וְאַיּוֹ לָמָּה זֶּה עֲזַבְתֶּן אֶת־הָאִישׁ קִרְאֶן לוֹ וְיֹאכַל לָחֶם:
כא וַיּוֹאֶל מֹשֶׁה לָשֶׁבֶת אֶת־הָאִישׁ וַיִּתֵּן אֶת־צִפֹּרָה בִתּוֹ לְמֹשֶׁה:
כב וַתֵּלֶד בֵּן וַיִּקְרָא אֶת־שְׁמוֹ גֵּרְשֹׁם כִּי אָמַר גֵּר הָיִיתִי בְּאֶרֶץ
נָכְרִיָּה:
כג וַיְהִי בַיָּמִים הָרַבִּים הָהֵם וַיָּמָת מֶלֶךְ מִצְרַיִם וַיֵּאָנְחוּ בְנֵי־
יִשְׂרָאֵל מִן־הָעֲבֹדָה וַיִּזְעָקוּ וַתַּעַל שַׁוְעָתָם אֶל־הָאֱלֹהִים
כד מִן־הָעֲבֹדָה: וַיִּשְׁמַע אֱלֹהִים אֶת־נַאֲקָתָם וַיִּזְכֹּר אֱלֹהִים
כה אֶת־בְּרִיתוֹ אֶת־אַבְרָהָם אֶת־יִצְחָק וְאֶת־יַעֲקֹב: וַיַּרְא
ג א אֱלֹהִים אֶת־בְּנֵי יִשְׂרָאֵל וַיֵּדַע אֱלֹהִים: וּמֹשֶׁה ב רביעי
הָיָה רֹעֶה אֶת־צֹאן יִתְרוֹ חֹתְנוֹ כֹּהֵן מִדְיָן וַיִּנְהַג אֶת־הַצֹּאן
ב אַחַר הַמִּדְבָּר וַיָּבֹא אֶל־הַר הָאֱלֹהִים חֹרֵבָה: וַיֵּרָא מַלְאַךְ

are about failures of responsibility. Confronted by God with their sin, Adam blames Ḥava; Ḥava blames the serpent. Kayin says, "Am I my brother's keeper?" (Gen. 4:9). Even Noaḥ, "righteous… in his generation" (6:9), has no effect on his contemporaries.

By contrast, at the beginning of Exodus, Moshe takes responsibility. When he sees an Egyptian beating an Israelite, he intervenes. When he sees two Israelites fighting, he intervenes. In Midyan, when he sees shepherds abusing the daughters of Yitro, he intervenes. Moshe, an Israelite brought up as an Egyptian, could have avoided each of these confrontations, yet he does not. He is the supreme case of one who says: when I see wrong, if no one else is prepared to act, I will.

At the heart of Judaism are three beliefs about leadership: We are free. We are responsible. And together we can change the world.

2:22 גֵּר הָיִיתִי בְּאֶרֶץ נָכְרִיָּה *I have been a stranger in an alien land* – A double estrangement: he is "a stranger" from Israel the people; strange too in Egypt the "alien" land. Charles Péguy said that "being elsewhere" was "the great and secret virtue, the great vocation of this people." Even in Israel, says the Torah, "you are merely migrants and visitors to Me" (Lev. 25:23). To be a Jew is to fully know the contingency of life, the lack of ultimate, this-worldly security and yet still to fight for justice and believe that the battle can be won because with us is a force greater than we are, greater than we can know.

of the LORD appeared to him in flames of fire from the
midst of a bush – and he saw – the bush was ablaze with
3 fire but was not consumed. Moshe said, "I must turn aside
4 to see this wonder. Why does the bush not burn up?" The
LORD saw that he had turned aside to look, and God
called to him from within the bush: "Moshe, Moshe." He
5 answered, "Here I am." Then God said, "Do not come
close. Remove the shoes from your feet, for the place

3:4 הִנֵּנִי *Here I am* – This single word is the ultimate human response to the call of God. When God summons us, He calls our name, and the most profound reply is simply *Hineni*, "Here I am." So said Avraham at the beginning of the binding of Yitzḥak (Gen. 22:1). So said Yaakov when God told him not to be afraid to go to Egypt (46:2). So Moshe says now, as God appears to him at the burning bush (Ex. 3:4). So the young Shmuel will say when God appears to him at night (I Sam. 3:4), and Yeshayahu in the mystical vision that will mark the beginning of his mission (Is. 6:8). At the beginning of the human story, God called to Adam and Ḥava in Eden, "Where are you?" (Gen. 3:9). So He has done ever since: He calls to each one of us, here where we are, this person, in this situation, at this time, saying: there is an act only you can do, a situation only you can address, a moment that, if not seized, may never come again. God commands in generalities but calls in particulars. He knows our gifts, and He knows the needs of the world. That is why we are here. There is an act only we can do, and only at this time, and that is our task. The sum of these tasks is the meaning of our life, the purpose of our existence, the story we are called on to write.

There is no life without a task, no person without a talent, no situation without its possibility of sanctification. When God calls, He whispers our name – and the greatest reply is simply *Hineni*, "Here I am," ready to heed Your call, to mend a fragment of Your all-too-broken world. Rabbi Ḥayyim of Volozhin enjoins us: "Let nobody in Israel, God forbid, ask himself: What am I, and what can my humble acts achieve in the world? Let him rather understand this, that he may know it and fix it in his thoughts: Not one detail of his acts, his words, and his thoughts, is ever lost. Each one leads back to its origin, where it takes effect in the height of heights."

3:5 שַׁל־נְעָלֶיךָ מֵעַל רַגְלֶיךָ *Remove the shoes from your feet* – Shoes were not worn by the priests in their service at the Temple. Yehoshua was told by "the commander of the LORD's hosts" to "remove the shoes from your feet, for the place where you stand is holy" (Josh. 5:15). Since shoes were worn as protection from dirt, wearing them in a holy place or in the presence of royalty was considered disrespectful.

יְהוָ֥ה אֵלָ֛יו בְּלַבַּת־אֵ֖שׁ מִתּ֣וֹךְ הַסְּנֶ֑ה וַיַּ֗רְא וְהִנֵּ֤ה הַסְּנֶה֙ בֹּעֵ֣ר
ג בָּאֵ֔שׁ וְהַסְּנֶ֖ה אֵינֶ֥נּוּ אֻכָּֽל׃ וַיֹּ֣אמֶר מֹשֶׁ֔ה אָסֻֽרָה־נָּ֣א וְאֶרְאֶ֔ה
ד אֶת־הַמַּרְאֶ֥ה הַגָּדֹ֖ל הַזֶּ֑ה מַדּ֖וּעַ לֹא־יִבְעַ֥ר הַסְּנֶֽה׃ וַיַּ֥רְא
יְהוָ֖ה כִּ֣י סָ֣ר לִרְא֑וֹת וַיִּקְרָא֩ אֵלָ֨יו אֱלֹהִ֜ים מִתּ֣וֹךְ הַסְּנֶ֗ה
ה וַיֹּ֛אמֶר מֹשֶׁ֥ה מֹשֶׁ֖ה וַיֹּ֥אמֶר הִנֵּֽנִי׃ וַיֹּ֖אמֶר אַל־תִּקְרַ֣ב הֲלֹ֑ם
שַׁל־נְעָלֶ֙יךָ֙ מֵעַ֣ל רַגְלֶ֔יךָ כִּ֣י הַמָּק֗וֹם אֲשֶׁ֤ר אַתָּה֙ עוֹמֵ֣ד עָלָ֔יו

THE BURNING BUSH

In this singularly powerful event, which marks the beginning of the exodus from Egypt, God reveals three characteristics that have molded Jewish spirituality ever since.

First, He is a God of history, not the abstract God of philosophy, nor even the intimate God of personal salvation. He is concerned with the behavior of mankind, with society, freedom, and the politics of suffering. The consolation He offers lies in historical and political change: the exodus of a people and the building of a new social order.

Secondly, He is a God who cherishes freedom. Often the Mosaic books return to the theme, and always with reference to the exodus. Free your slaves in the year of release. Do not let them work for you on the seventh day. Remember that you were once a slave in the land of Egypt. It is as if any loss of freedom is an assault on the image of God that is man.

Thirdly, He is a God who wants His people never to forget the experience of being a minority without power. Do not oppress a stranger, commands the Bible, because you understand the heart of a stranger – you were once strangers yourselves. Plead the cause of the widow and the orphan, the underprivileged. Power corrupts, the Bible seems to argue, unless we carry in our memories the thought of what it is to be without power. Social justice is born not so much of political theory as it is of the sharp pain of injustice and the decision, having felt it, never to inflict it. "I know their anguish" (Ex. 3:7), says God – and we too are commanded to keep it in mind.

3:2 מִתּוֹךְ הַסְּנֶה *From the midst of a bush* – In Hebrew, the word *sneh*, "bush," appears three times in this one verse for emphasis. This is not a grand epiphany. The flickering flames made their home in the lowliest of vegetation. The highest of the high can be present in the lowest of the low. Already there is a hint of the anti-hierarchical thrust of monotheism, even if it takes many centuries fully to emerge. That God would make His first appearance in the exodus story in so humble a setting stands in the strongest possible contrast to ancient Egypt, where an appearance of a god was supposed to take place at an auspicious and predictable time in a magnificent building permanently consecrated as sacred space.

▶

6 where you stand is holy ground. I," He said, "am the God
of your father, the God of Avraham, the God of Yitzḥak,
and the God of Yaakov." Then Moshe hid his face, for he
7 was afraid to look at God. The LORD continued, "I have
seen My people's suffering in Egypt; I have heard them
8 cry out amid their oppressors; I know their anguish. So I
have come to rescue them from the hand of the Egyptians
and bring them up from that land to one that is good, spacious, a land flowing with milk and honey, the place of the
Canaanites, Hittites, Amorites, Perizzites, Hivites, and Je-
9 busites. Now the cry of the Israelites has reached Me; I
have seen the oppression the Egyptians subject them to.
10 So go: I am sending you to Pharaoh to bring My people,
11 the Israelites, out of Egypt." But "who am I," said Moshe
to God, "to go to Pharaoh, to bring the Israelites out of
12 Egypt?" God replied, "I will be with you. Proof that I have
sent you will come when, having brought the people out
of Egypt, you come to serve God upon this mountain."
13 Moshe said to God, "When I go to the Israelites and tell
them, 'Your fathers' God has sent me to you,' they will
14 ask me, 'What is His name?' What shall I say?" God replied
to Moshe, "I will be what I will be." He said, "This is what

---

to let the Israelites go, and an Israelite people he knows from his youth to be not easily led. This deeply human portrayal of Moshe leads into a remarkable conversation with God, sometimes fraught, but also caring, supportive, and full of hope. The exchange signals what will come to be one of Israel's most distinctive features: the extended conversation between heaven and earth out of which are born world-transforming energies that will eventually triumph over seemingly insuperable obstacles. On one level the story of the exodus is about divine miracles in the face of which human beings are powerless. At another level, the present chapter tells us that God needs Moshe. Divine energy needs human vehicles to bring it down to earth.

The most moving moment in this encounter comes when Moshe utters his first words to God: "Who am I?" The greatest leader who ever lived said, "Who am I?" We may be small in our own eyes but there is greatness within us when we hear and heed the divine call.

I WILL BE WHAT I WILL BE

God's enigmatic reply to Moshe was translated into Greek as *ego eimi ho on,*

ו אַדְמַת־קֹ֖דֶשׁ הֽוּא׃ וַיֹּ֗אמֶר אָנֹכִי֙ אֱלֹהֵ֣י אָבִ֔יךָ אֱלֹהֵ֧י אַבְרָהָ֛ם
אֱלֹהֵ֥י יִצְחָ֖ק וֵאלֹהֵ֣י יַעֲקֹ֑ב וַיַּסְתֵּ֤ר מֹשֶׁה֙ פָּנָ֔יו כִּ֣י יָרֵ֔א מֵהַבִּ֖יט
ז אֶל־הָאֱלֹהִֽים׃ וַיֹּ֣אמֶר יהוה רָאֹ֥ה רָאִ֛יתִי אֶת־עֳנִ֥י עַמִּ֖י אֲשֶׁ֣ר
בְּמִצְרָ֑יִם וְאֶת־צַעֲקָתָ֤ם שָׁמַ֙עְתִּי֙ מִפְּנֵ֣י נֹגְשָׂ֔יו כִּ֥י יָדַ֖עְתִּי אֶת־
ח מַכְאֹבָֽיו׃ וָאֵרֵ֞ד לְהַצִּיל֣וֹ ׀ מִיַּ֣ד מִצְרַ֗יִם וּֽלְהַעֲלֹתוֹ֮ מִן־הָאָ֣רֶץ
הַהִוא֒ אֶל־אֶ֤רֶץ טוֹבָה֙ וּרְחָבָ֔ה אֶל־אֶ֛רֶץ זָבַ֥ת חָלָ֖ב וּדְבָ֑שׁ
אֶל־מְק֤וֹם הַֽכְּנַעֲנִי֙ וְהַֽחִתִּ֔י וְהָֽאֱמֹרִי֙ וְהַפְּרִזִּ֔י וְהַחִוִּ֖י וְהַיְבוּסִֽי׃
ט וְעַתָּ֕ה הִנֵּ֛ה צַעֲקַ֥ת בְּנֵֽי־יִשְׂרָאֵ֖ל בָּ֣אָה אֵלָ֑י וְגַם־רָאִ֙יתִי֙ אֶת־
י הַלַּ֔חַץ אֲשֶׁ֥ר מִצְרַ֖יִם לֹחֲצִ֥ים אֹתָֽם׃ וְעַתָּ֣ה לְכָ֔ה וְאֶֽשְׁלָחֲךָ֖
יא אֶל־פַּרְעֹ֑ה וְהוֹצֵ֛א אֶת־עַמִּ֥י בְנֵֽי־יִשְׂרָאֵ֖ל מִמִּצְרָֽיִם׃ וַיֹּ֤אמֶר
מֹשֶׁה֙ אֶל־הָ֣אֱלֹהִ֔ים מִ֣י אָנֹ֔כִי כִּ֥י אֵלֵ֖ךְ אֶל־פַּרְעֹ֑ה וְכִ֥י אוֹצִ֛יא
יב אֶת־בְּנֵ֥י יִשְׂרָאֵ֖ל מִמִּצְרָֽיִם׃ וַיֹּ֙אמֶר֙ כִּֽי־אֶהְיֶ֣ה עִמָּ֔ךְ וְזֶה־לְּךָ֣
הָא֔וֹת כִּ֥י אָנֹכִ֖י שְׁלַחְתִּ֑יךָ בְּהוֹצִיאֲךָ֤ אֶת־הָעָם֙ מִמִּצְרַ֔יִם
יג תַּֽעַבְדוּן֙ אֶת־הָ֣אֱלֹהִ֔ים עַ֖ל הָהָ֥ר הַזֶּֽה׃ וַיֹּ֨אמֶר מֹשֶׁ֜ה אֶל־
הָאֱלֹהִ֗ים הִנֵּ֨ה אָנֹכִ֣י בָא֮ אֶל־בְּנֵ֣י יִשְׂרָאֵל֒ וְאָמַרְתִּ֣י לָהֶ֔ם אֱלֹהֵ֥י
אֲבוֹתֵיכֶ֖ם שְׁלָחַ֣נִי אֲלֵיכֶ֑ם וְאָֽמְרוּ־לִ֣י מַה־שְּׁמ֔וֹ מָ֥ה אֹמַ֖ר
יד אֲלֵהֶֽם׃ וַיֹּ֤אמֶר אֱלֹהִים֙ אֶל־מֹשֶׁ֔ה אֶֽהְיֶ֖ה אֲשֶׁ֣ר אֶֽהְיֶ֑ה וַיֹּ֗אמֶר

Shoes are a human artifact, symbolizing our powers of rational creativity, raising us protectively above the rough terrain of nature. But this cannot bring us to the holy. For that we must make ourselves vulnerable to a dimension outside and beyond ourselves. That vulnerability is what was symbolized when Moshe, and later the priests, removed their shoes when entering holy ground.

3:11 מִי אָנֹכִי *Who am I* – Moshe's second question at the burning bush is "Who are you?" His first question, though, is *mi anokhi* – "Who am I?"

Israel was to be summoned to create a new kind of society, one that would be the opposite of Egypt. In the dramatic scene that unfolds in this chapter, we encounter a new kind of leader, the opposite of the kind of leadership associated with the pharaohs of Egypt. Moshe has none of the splendor and pride associated with rule in the ancient Near East. He has doubts, trepidations, and a profound sense of his own inadequacy. He is not driven by ambition or a sense of destiny. To the contrary, he feels overwhelmed by the double challenge of an all-powerful Egypt unlikely to agree

15 you shall tell the Israelites: I will be sent me to you." Then
God said to Moshe, "You shall say this to the Israelites: The
Lord God of your fathers, the God of Avraham, the God
of Yitzḥak, and the God of Yaakov, has sent me to you. This
is My name forever, and this is how I will be remembered
16 through the ages. Go, gather the elders of Israel and tell ḤAMISHI

---

in constant dialogue with His people, urging, warning, challenging, forgiving. When Malakhi says in the name of God, "I am the Lord. I have not changed" (Mal. 3:6), He is not speaking about His essence as pure being, the unmoved mover, but about His moral commitments. God keeps His promises even when His children break theirs. Time, however, becomes something understood as a narrative, a journey or a quest. Throughout the Torah, the Promised Land lies in the future. Avraham, Yitzḥak, and Yaakov do not acquire it. Even Moshe, who spends forty years leading the people there, does not get to enter it. It is always just beyond. Soon but not yet. All this is hinted at in those three Hebrew words that mean "I will be what I will be." I am the God of the future tense.

3:15 יהוה אֱלֹהֵי אֲבֹתֵיכֶם *The Lord God of your fathers* – This phrase suggests some fundamental propositions. First, identity runs through genealogy. It is a matter of who my parents were, who their parents were, and so on. This is not always true. There are adopted children. There are children who make a conscious break from their parents. But for most of us, identity lies in uncovering the story of our ancestors, which, in the case of Jews, given the unparalleled dislocations of Jewish life, is almost always a tale of journeys, courage, suffering or escapes from suffering, and sheer endurance.

Second, it is not simply that God was the God of their ancestors. He is also the God who makes certain promises: that He will bring them from slavery to freedom, from exile to the Promised Land. The Israelites are part of a narrative extended over time. They are part of an unfinished story, and God is about to write the next chapter.

What is more, when God tells Moshe that He is the God of the Israelites' ancestors, He adds, "This is My name forever, and this is how I will be remembered [*zikhri*] through the ages." God is saying here that He is beyond time – "This is My name forever" – but when it comes to human understanding, He lives within time, "through the ages." The way He does this is through the handing on of memory: "This is how I will be remembered." Identity is not just a matter of who my parents were. It is also a matter of what they remembered and handed on to me. Personal identity is shaped by individual memory. Group identity is formed by collective memory.

טו כֹּה תֹאמַר לִבְנֵי יִשְׂרָאֵל אֶהְיֶה שְׁלָחַנִי אֲלֵיכֶם׃ וַיֹּאמֶר עוֹד
אֱלֹהִים אֶל־מֹשֶׁה כֹּה תֹאמַר אֶל־בְּנֵי יִשְׂרָאֵל יהוה אֱלֹהֵי
אֲבֹתֵיכֶם אֱלֹהֵי אַבְרָהָם אֱלֹהֵי יִצְחָק וֵאלֹהֵי יַעֲקֹב שְׁלָחַנִי
טז אֲלֵיכֶם זֶה־שְּׁמִי לְעֹלָם וְזֶה זִכְרִי לְדֹר דֹּר׃ לֵךְ וְאָסַפְתָּ אֶת־ חמישי

He will be a God of surprises. He will do things never seen before, create signs and wonders that will be spoken about for thousands of years. They will set in motion wave after wave of repercussions. People will learn that slavery is not an inevitable condition, that might is not right, that empires are not impregnable, and that a tiny people like the Israelites can do great things if they attach their destiny to Heaven. None of this could be predicted in advance. God is saying to Moshe and to the people: You will have to trust Me. The destination to which I am calling you is just beyond the visible horizon.

It is very hard to understand how revolutionary this was. Ancient religions were deeply conservative, designed to show that the existing social hierarchy was inevitable, part of the deep structure of reality, timeless and unchangeable. Just as there was a hierarchy in the heavens, and another within the animal kingdom, so there was a hierarchy in human society. That was order. Anything that challenged it represented chaos. Until Israel appeared on the scene, religion was a way of consecrating the status quo. That is what the story of Israel would overturn.

Far from being timeless and immutable, God in the Torah is active, engaged,

and into Latin as *ego sum qui sum*, meaning "I am who I am," or "I am He who is." The early and medieval Christian theologians all understood the phrase to be speaking about ontology, the metaphysical nature of God's existence. It meant that He was "Being-itself, timeless, immutable, incorporeal, understood as the subsisting act of all existing." Augustine defines God as that which does not change and cannot change. Aquinas, continuing the same tradition, reads the Exodus formula as saying that God is "true being, that is being that is eternal, immutable, simple, self-sufficient, and the cause and principle of every creature."

But this is the God of the philosophers, not the God of the prophets. *Ehyeh asher ehyeh* means none of these things. It means "I will be what, where, or how I will be." The essential element of the phrase is the dimension omitted by all the early Christian translations, namely the future tense. There is no way, God is telling Moshe, that he or anyone else can know in advance what God is about to do. He tells him in general terms that He is about to rescue the Israelites from the hands of the Egyptians – but as for specifics, Moshe and the people will know God not through His essence but through His acts. The future tense is key here. They cannot know Him until He acts.

them: The LORD God of your fathers appeared to me – the
God of Avraham, Yitzḥak, and Yaakov – saying: I have tak-
en note of you and I have seen what is being inflicted upon
17 you in Egypt. And I promise to bring you out of the misery of Egypt to the land of the Canaanites and Hittites, the
Amorites and Perizzites, the Hivites and Jebusites, to a land
18 flowing with milk and honey. They will listen to you. Then
you and the elders of Israel shall go to the king of Egypt
and tell him, 'The LORD God of the Hebrews has revealed
Himself to us. Send us forth now for a three-day journey
19 into the wilderness to sacrifice to the LORD our God.' But I
know that even by a mighty hand the king of Egypt would
20 not send you forth. So I will stretch out My hand and strike
Egypt with all the wonders I will do there. After that, he
21 will send you forth. And I will grant this people favor in
the eyes of the Egyptians, so that when you leave, you
22 will not leave empty-handed. Every woman shall ask her
neighbor, ask any woman lodging with her, for objects of
silver and gold, and clothing, and you shall put these on
4 1 your sons and daughters, and despoil the Egyptians." But
Moshe replied, "They will not believe me. They will not

amply justified. The people are fractious. Moshe calls them a "stiff-necked people" (Deut. 9:6). Time and again during the wilderness years they complain, sin, and want to return to Egypt. Moshe is not wrong in his estimate of their character. Yet God reprimands him, indeed punishes him, by whitening his hand with "an impure blight" (see note on v. 6). A fundamental principle of Jewish leadership is intimated here for the first time: a leader does not need faith in himself, but he must have faith in the people he is to lead.

That, according to the Sages, is what God is teaching Moshe: What matters is not whether they believe in you, but whether you believe in them. Unless you believe in them, you cannot lead in the way a prophet must lead. You must identify with them and have faith in them, seeing not only their surface faults but also their underlying virtues. Otherwise, you will be no better than a detached intellectual – and that is the beginning of the end. You will think yourself superior to others, and that is a corruption of the soul. If you do not believe in the people, eventually you will not even believe in God.

Who is a leader? To this, the Jewish answer is one who identifies with his or her people, mindful of their faults, to be

זִקְנֵי יִשְׂרָאֵל וְאָמַרְתָּ אֲלֵהֶם יהוה אֱלֹהֵי אֲבֹתֵיכֶם נִרְאָה
אֵלַי אֱלֹהֵי אַבְרָהָם יִצְחָק וְיַעֲקֹב לֵאמֹר פָּקֹד פָּקַדְתִּי אֶתְכֶם
יז וְאֶת־הֶעָשׂוּי לָכֶם בְּמִצְרָיִם: וָאֹמַר אַעֲלֶה אֶתְכֶם מֵעֳנִי
מִצְרַיִם אֶל־אֶרֶץ הַכְּנַעֲנִי וְהַחִתִּי וְהָאֱמֹרִי וְהַפְּרִזִּי וְהַחִוִּי
יח וְהַיְבוּסִי אֶל־אֶרֶץ זָבַת חָלָב וּדְבָשׁ: וְשָׁמְעוּ לְקֹלֶךָ וּבָאתָ
אַתָּה וְזִקְנֵי יִשְׂרָאֵל אֶל־מֶלֶךְ מִצְרַיִם וַאֲמַרְתֶּם אֵלָיו יהוה
אֱלֹהֵי הָעִבְרִיִּים נִקְרָה עָלֵינוּ וְעַתָּה נֵלְכָה־נָּא דֶּרֶךְ שְׁלֹשֶׁת
יט יָמִים בַּמִּדְבָּר וְנִזְבְּחָה לַיהוה אֱלֹהֵינוּ: וַאֲנִי יָדַעְתִּי כִּי לֹא־
כ יִתֵּן אֶתְכֶם מֶלֶךְ מִצְרַיִם לַהֲלֹךְ וְלֹא בְּיָד חֲזָקָה: וְשָׁלַחְתִּי
אֶת־יָדִי וְהִכֵּיתִי אֶת־מִצְרַיִם בְּכֹל נִפְלְאֹתַי אֲשֶׁר אֶעֱשֶׂה
כא בְּקִרְבּוֹ וְאַחֲרֵי־כֵן יְשַׁלַּח אֶתְכֶם: וְנָתַתִּי אֶת־חֵן הָעָם־הַזֶּה
כב בְּעֵינֵי מִצְרָיִם וְהָיָה כִּי תֵלֵכוּן לֹא תֵלְכוּ רֵיקָם: וְשָׁאֲלָה
אִשָּׁה מִשְּׁכֶנְתָּהּ וּמִגָּרַת בֵּיתָהּ כְּלֵי־כֶסֶף וּכְלֵי זָהָב וּשְׂמָלֹת
וְשַׂמְתֶּם עַל־בְּנֵיכֶם וְעַל־בְּנֹתֵיכֶם וְנִצַּלְתֶּם אֶת־מִצְרָיִם:
ד א וַיַּעַן מֹשֶׁה וַיֹּאמֶר וְהֵן לֹא־יַאֲמִינוּ לִי וְלֹא יִשְׁמְעוּ בְּקֹלִי כִּי

4:1 וְהֵן לֹא־יַאֲמִינוּ לִי *They will not believe me* – The sages, ultrasensitive to nuances in the text, noticed two important features of this response. The first is that God has already told Moshe, "They will listen to you" (Ex. 3:18). Moshe's reply seems to contradict God's prior assurance. To be sure, the commentators offered various harmonizing interpretations. Ibn Ezra suggests that God had told Moshe that the elders would listen to him, whereas Moshe expressed doubts about the mass of the people. Ramban says that Moshe did not doubt that they would believe initially, but he thought that they would lose faith as soon as they saw that Pharaoh would not let them go. There are other explanations, but the fact remains that according to this verse, Moshe is not satisfied by God's assurance. His own experience of the fickleness of the people (one of them, years earlier, has already said, "Who made you a ruler and judge over us?" [2:14]) makes him doubt that they will be easy to lead. Whereas Moshe's other refusals focus on his own sense of inadequacy, here he speaks not about himself but about the people. They will not believe him.

The text implies that Moshe is entitled to have doubts about his own worthiness for the task. What he is not entitled to do is to have doubts about the people. His doubts, it will transpire, are

listen to me. They will say, 'The LORD has not appeared
2 to you.'" "What is that in your hand?" asked the LORD.
3 "A staff," he replied. "Throw it to the ground." He threw
it, and it turned into a snake; and Moshe fled back from
4 it. The LORD told Moshe, "Reach out your hand and take
hold of its tail." He reached out his hand and grasped it,
5 and in his hand it turned back into a staff. "This is so that
they will believe that the LORD God of their fathers, the
God of Avraham, Yitzḥak, and Yaakov, appeared to you."
6 The LORD spoke to him again: "Put your hand inside
your cloak." He put his hand inside his cloak; when he
7 took it out it was as white as snow. "Put it back inside your
cloak," He said. Moshe put his hand back inside his cloak,
8 and when he took it out the skin color had returned. "If
they do not believe you and are not persuaded by the first
sign, they will believe the evidence of the second sign.
9 And if they do not believe either of these signs, and will
not listen to you, then take some water from the Nile and
spill it on the ground. The water you take from the Nile
10 will become blood on the ground." Then Moshe said to
the LORD, "Please, my LORD, I am not a man of words;
I was not yesterday, nor the day before, and still I am not
since You spoke to Your servant. I am slow of speech

The Sages arrived at the following comment (Shabbat 97a):

> Reish Lakish said: He who entertains a suspicion against the innocent will be bodily afflicted, as it is written, "Moshe replied: 'They will not believe me.'" However, it was known to the Holy One, blessed be He, that Israel would believe. He said to Moshe: "They are believers, the children of believers, but you will ultimately disbelieve… as it is said, '[But the LORD said to Moshe…] "Because you did not put your trust in Me"'" (Num. 20:12).

4:10 לֹא אִישׁ דְּבָרִים אָנֹכִי *I am not a man of words* – Some suggest that Moshe had a speech defect, perhaps a stammer. It may be simply that, having spent much of his adult life as a solitary shepherd, he is unused to speaking, especially in public. It may be, however, that far from being a disqualification, this is an important qualification (see Malbim). God chose an infertile, aged couple to be the progenitors of a nation that would

ב יֹאמְרוּ לֹא־נִרְאָה אֵלֶיךָ יהוה: וַיֹּאמֶר אֵלָיו יהוה מזה בְיָדֶךָ מַה־זֶּה
ג וַיֹּאמֶר מַטֶּה: וַיֹּאמֶר הַשְׁלִיכֵהוּ אַרְצָה וַיַּשְׁלִכֵהוּ אַרְצָה וַיְהִי
ד לְנָחָשׁ וַיָּנָס מֹשֶׁה מִפָּנָיו: וַיֹּאמֶר יהוה אֶל־מֹשֶׁה שְׁלַח יָדְךָ
ה וֶאֱחֹז בִּזְנָבוֹ וַיִּשְׁלַח יָדוֹ וַיַּחֲזֶק־בּוֹ וַיְהִי לְמַטֶּה בְּכַפּוֹ: לְמַעַן
יַאֲמִינוּ כִּי־נִרְאָה אֵלֶיךָ יהוה אֱלֹהֵי אֲבֹתָם אֱלֹהֵי אַבְרָהָם
ו אֱלֹהֵי יִצְחָק וֵאלֹהֵי יַעֲקֹב: וַיֹּאמֶר יהוה לוֹ עוֹד הָבֵא־נָא
יָדְךָ בְּחֵיקֶךָ וַיָּבֵא יָדוֹ בְּחֵיקוֹ וַיּוֹצִאָהּ וְהִנֵּה יָדוֹ מְצֹרַעַת
ז כַּשָּׁלֶג: וַיֹּאמֶר הָשֵׁב יָדְךָ אֶל־חֵיקֶךָ וַיָּשֶׁב יָדוֹ אֶל־חֵיקוֹ
ח וַיּוֹצִאָהּ מֵחֵיקוֹ וְהִנֵּה־שָׁבָה כִּבְשָׂרוֹ: וְהָיָה אִם־לֹא יַאֲמִינוּ
לָךְ וְלֹא יִשְׁמְעוּ לְקֹל הָאֹת הָרִאשׁוֹן וְהֶאֱמִינוּ לְקֹל הָאֹת
ט הָאַחֲרוֹן: וְהָיָה אִם־לֹא יַאֲמִינוּ גַּם לִשְׁנֵי הָאֹתוֹת הָאֵלֶּה
וְלֹא יִשְׁמְעוּן לְקֹלֶךָ וְלָקַחְתָּ מִמֵּימֵי הַיְאֹר וְשָׁפַכְתָּ הַיַּבָּשָׁה
י וְהָיוּ הַמַּיִם אֲשֶׁר תִּקַּח מִן־הַיְאֹר וְהָיוּ לְדָם בַּיַּבָּשֶׁת: וַיֹּאמֶר
מֹשֶׁה אֶל־יהוה בִּי אֲדֹנָי לֹא אִישׁ דְּבָרִים אָנֹכִי גַּם מִתְּמוֹל
גַּם מִשִּׁלְשֹׁם גַּם מֵאָז דַּבֶּרְךָ אֶל־עַבְדֶּךָ כִּי כְבַד־פֶּה וּכְבַד

sure, but convinced also of their potential greatness and their preciousness in the sight of God. In effect, God is saying to Moshe: Those people of whom you have doubts are believers. They are My people, and they are your people. Just as you believe in Me, so you must believe in them.

4:6 מְצֹרַעַת כַּשָּׁלֶג *White as snow* – In Hebrew, *metzoraat*. The biblical disease *tzaraat* was mistakenly translated in the Septuagint as leprosy, the bacterial infection, untreatable until the twentieth century, now known as Hansen's disease. The two illnesses have vastly different symptoms, and the mistranslation has historically compounded the stigma attached to Hansen's disease, causing unnecessary shame to sufferers who were already ostracized. We have therefore avoided the traditional translation. *Tzaraat* is always presented as a set of visible symptoms inflicted by God, so we have chosen to translate it "an impure blight," or here, simply "whiteness."

What, then, is the significance of this particular sign? The Sages recalled that later, Miriam was punished with *tzaraat* for speaking negatively about Moshe (Num. 12:10). In general, this "blight" was understood as a punishment for *lashon hara*, derogatory speech. Moshe, perhaps, had been guilty of the same sin.

11 and tongue." "Who gives man speech?" said the LORD
to him. "Who makes people dumb or deaf? Who gives
12 them sight or blindness? Is it not I, the LORD? Now go. I
13 will help you speak and I will teach you what to say." But
14 "Please, my LORD," he said, "send someone else." Then
the LORD's anger blazed against Moshe. "Have you not a
brother, Aharon the Levite? He, I know, is able to speak.
Even now he is setting out to meet you, and when he sees
15 you his heart will rejoice. You shall speak to him and place

---

and why. Often His faith in us is greater than our faith in ourselves.

4:14 וְשָׂמַח בְּלִבּוֹ *His heart will rejoice* – Aharon, we may have thought, might have many reasons not to rejoice on seeing Moshe return. The brothers did not grow up together. Moshe was adopted by Pharaoh's daughter and raised in an Egyptian palace, while Aharon remained with the Israelites. Nor have they been together during the Israelites' sufferings. Moshe, fearing for his life, fled to Midyan.

Besides this, Moshe is Aharon's younger brother, and yet it is Moshe who is about to become the leader of the people. Always in the past, when the younger has taken something the elder might have believed belonged naturally to him, there was jealousy, animosity; this story played out at every stage of the book of Genesis. Each generation there, however, improved upon the last. Kayin killed Hevel, but Yosef and his brothers were reconciled. All of this has prepared the way for the fifth story of siblings in the Torah, one that will gloriously transcend all the others. Among Yokheved's children there is no rivalry. It is Miriam who watches over the young Moshe and ensures he knows who his parents and his people are. It is Aharon who acts as Moshe's spokesman in Egypt, and who becomes the first priest to stand beside the greatest of the prophets. The implication is that *only when a people has overcome its internal rivalries is it ready for the journey from slavery to freedom.*

And so, against all expectations, God assures Moshe: "When Aharon sees you, his heart will rejoice." And so it does: "The LORD said to Aharon, 'Go and meet Moshe in the wilderness.' And he went and met him at God's mountain, and kissed him" (Ex. 4:27).

Moshe and Aharon are quite different in temperament and role. Moshe is the man of truth, Aharon of peace. Without truth, there can be no vision to inspire a nation. But without internal peace, there is no nation to inspire. Their roles are in creative tension. Yet they work side by side, each respecting the distinctive gift of the other. As the Midrash says, "And kissed him" [the brothers kissed when they met] – This means: each rejoiced at the other's greatness (Shemot Rabba 5:10).

יא לְשׁוֹן אָנֹכִי׃ וַיֹּאמֶר יְהֹוָה אֵלָיו מִי שָׂם פֶּה לָאָדָם אוֹ מִי־
יָשׂוּם אִלֵּם אוֹ חֵרֵשׁ אוֹ פִקֵּחַ אוֹ עִוֵּר הֲלֹא אָנֹכִי יְהֹוָה׃
יב וְעַתָּה לֵךְ וְאָנֹכִי אֶהְיֶה עִם־פִּיךָ וְהוֹרֵיתִיךָ אֲשֶׁר תְּדַבֵּר׃
יג יד וַיֹּאמֶר בִּי אֲדֹנָי שְׁלַח־נָא בְּיַד־תִּשְׁלָח׃ וַיִּחַר־אַף יְהֹוָה
בְּמֹשֶׁה וַיֹּאמֶר הֲלֹא אַהֲרֹן אָחִיךָ הַלֵּוִי יָדַעְתִּי כִּי־דַבֵּר יְדַבֵּר
הוּא וְגַם הִנֵּה־הוּא יֹצֵא לִקְרָאתֶךָ וְרָאֲךָ וְשָׂמַח בְּלִבּוֹ׃

eventually become numerous. Three of the matriarchs ("mothers"), Sara, Rivka, and Raḥel, were unable to have children. God chooses a fractious, often rebellious people to be the bearers of His covenant. He chooses one who is not a man of words to be the bearer of His word. Those whom God chooses testify in themselves to something beyond themselves. *The man God chooses to deliver His word to the world is a man who cannot naturally deliver words.* What Moshe reasonably sees as a disqualification is in fact part of his qualification.

Those who hear Moshe know that his words come from a source beyond himself. Moshe does not yet understand this, partly because his mission has not yet begun, partly because there has never before in Israel been a prophet like him who addresses an entire nation and gives them instruction from Heaven, and whose words, written down, will become holy and canonical. Other prophets also expressed a sense of inadequacy in giving voice to the divine word. Yeshayahu said, "My mouth has been defiled" (Is. 6:5). Yirmeyahu said, "I am not capable of speaking, for I am still only a boy" (Jer. 1:6). Only the true prophet understands how difficult it is to translate the voice of heaven into the language of earth. The prophets spoke not because they could but because they must. "The LORD God speaks; who would not prophesy?" (Amos 3:8).

4:13 שְׁלַח־נָא בְּיַד־תִּשְׁלָח *Send someone else* – This response provokes divine anger because God has answered all of Moshe's hesitations and doubts. All that is left is an overwhelming sense of inadequacy, as if Moshe believes that he cannot do this, he is not a leader, he is not known to the Israelites, he has not grown up with them or suffered with them. Note how profoundly human is the Torah's portrayal of Moshe: the greatest of men, yet fraught with doubts and hesitations. What Moshe does not understand, however, was that each of his weaknesses is a strength: his youth in Egypt, his long stay in Midyan, his speech defect, his anger at injustice will all prove to be invaluable to his role. Ultimately, though, what provokes divine anger is his lack of faith in God's faith in him. That is one doubt too far. When God calls, He knows whom He is calling

words in his mouth. I will help you both to speak, and I
16 will teach you what to do. He will speak on your behalf
to the people – he will be your voice; and you will be his
17 access to God. Take this staff in your hand. With it, you
shall perform the signs."
18 Moshe left and returned to Yeter his father-in-law. He SHISHI
said to him, "Let me go back to my brothers in Egypt, to
see if they are still alive." Yitro said to him, "Go in peace."
19 While Moshe was still in Midyan, the LORD said to him,
"Go, return to Egypt. All those who sought your life have
20 died." So Moshe took his wife and sons and put them on

It is a unique interpretation, sobering in its implications. Here are three great men, Yaakov, Moshe, and Yona, yet all three, according to Rashbam, are afraid. Of what? None is a coward.

They are afraid, essentially, of their mission. This is not physical fear. It is the fear that comes from a feeling of personal inadequacy. "Who am I…to bring the Israelites out of Egypt?" (Ex. 3:11) asks Moshe at the burning bush. Sometimes the greatest have the least self-confidence, because they know how immense is the responsibility and how small they feel in relation to it.

I sometimes feel that, consciously or subconsciously, some take flight from Judaism for this very reason. Who are we to be God's witnesses to the world, a light to the nations, role models for others? If even spiritual giants like Moshe sought to flee, how much more so you and me? This fear of unworthiness is one that surely most of us have had at some time or other.

The reason it is wrong is not that it is untrue, but that it is irrelevant. Writers grow by writing. Teachers grow by teaching. It is only by overcoming our sense of inadequacy that we throw ourselves into the task and find ourselves lifted and enlarged by so doing.

In Shakespeare's words: "Be not afraid of greatness: some are born great, some achieve greatness, and some have greatness thrust upon 'em." That is why God wrestled with Yaakov, Moshe, and Yona and would not let them escape. We may not be born great, but we have greatness thrust upon us. For we are all children of the man who was given the name Yisrael: one who struggled with God and with men and prevailed.

4:20 וַיִּקַּח מֹשֶׁה אֶת־אִשְׁתּוֹ וְאֶת־בָּנָיו *Moshe took his wife and sons* – Thus far we have only heard of one son, Gershom. The reference to "sons" in the plural may be an indication that the second son has only recently been born. If so, this might explain Moshe's reluctance to give him a circumcision. Circumcision was considered dangerous in the course of a journey.

טו וְדִבַּרְתָּ אֵלָיו וְשַׂמְתָּ אֶת־הַדְּבָרִים בְּפִיו וְאָנֹכִי אֶהְיֶה עִם־פִּיךָ
טז וְעִם־פִּיהוּ וְהוֹרֵיתִי אֶתְכֶם אֵת אֲשֶׁר תַּעֲשׂוּן: וְדִבֶּר־הוּא
לְךָ אֶל־הָעָם וְהָיָה הוּא יִהְיֶה־לְּךָ לְפֶה וְאַתָּה תִּהְיֶה־לּוֹ
יז לֵאלֹהִים: וְאֶת־הַמַּטֶּה הַזֶּה תִּקַּח בְּיָדֶךָ אֲשֶׁר תַּעֲשֶׂה־בּוֹ
אֶת־הָאֹתֹת:
יח וַיֵּלֶךְ מֹשֶׁה וַיָּשָׁב ׀ אֶל־יֶתֶר חֹתְנוֹ וַיֹּאמֶר לוֹ אֵלְכָה־נָּא ג ששי
וְאָשׁוּבָה אֶל־אַחַי אֲשֶׁר־בְּמִצְרַיִם וְאֶרְאֶה הַעוֹדָם חַיִּים
יט וַיֹּאמֶר יִתְרוֹ לְמֹשֶׁה לֵךְ לְשָׁלוֹם: וַיֹּאמֶר יהוה אֶל־מֹשֶׁה
בְּמִדְיָן לֵךְ שֻׁב מִצְרָיִם כִּי־מֵתוּ כָּל־הָאֲנָשִׁים הַמְבַקְשִׁים
כ אֶת־נַפְשֶׁךָ: וַיִּקַּח מֹשֶׁה אֶת־אִשְׁתּוֹ וְאֶת־בָּנָיו וַיַּרְכִּבֵם עַל־

THE ENCOUNTER ON THE WAY TO EGYPT

What follows is an obscure episode in the life of Moshe, as shocking as it is enigmatic. On his way back to Egypt, "The Lord confronted Moshe and was about to kill him" (Ex. 4:24). Tzipora then saves Moshe's life by giving their son a *brit mila*. How are we to understand this?

Rashbam (on Gen. 32:29) takes this as an instance of what Robert Alter has classed as a type-scene, that is, a stylized episode that happens more than once in Tanakh. One obvious example is young-man-meets-future-wife-at-well, a scene enacted with variations three times in the Torah: in the case of Avraham's servant and Rivka, Yaakov and Raḥel, and of course Moshe and Tzipora. There are differences between them, but sufficient similarities to make us realize that we are dealing with a convention. Rashbam compares the encounter here to Yaakov's nocturnal struggle with an unknown man and to the story of the prophet Yona. It is the latter that provides the key to understanding both the earlier narratives. Yona seeks to escape from his mission to go to Nineveh to warn the people that the city is about to be destroyed if they do not repent. He flees in a boat to Tarshish, but God brings a storm that threatens to sink the ship. The prophet is then thrown into the sea and swallowed by a giant fish that later vomits him out alive. Yona thus realizes that flight is impossible.

The same, says Rashbam, applies to Moshe, who has repeatedly expressed his reluctance to undertake the task God has set him. Evidently, Moshe is still prevaricating even after beginning the journey. Some commentators suggest that he has agreed with his father-in-law that at least one of his children will be brought up not as an Israelite but as a Midianite. Tzipora's prompt and decisive action saves a life.

a donkey, and he set out to return to Egypt, taking in his
21 hand the staff of God. The LORD said to Moshe, "When
you return to Egypt, see that you perform for Pharaoh
all the wonders I have placed in your power. But still I
will strengthen his heart and he will not send the people
22 forth. Tell Pharaoh: This is what the LORD says, 'Israel
23 is My son, My firstborn. I have told you: Send forth My
son, so that he may serve Me. If you refuse to let him go,
24 I will kill your son, your firstborn.'" At a lodging place
on the way, the LORD confronted Moshe and was about
25 to kill him. But Tzipora took a flint knife and cut off her
son's foreskin, throwing it down at his feet, and said,
26 "You are a bridegroom of blood to me." So He let him
go. Then "A bridegroom of blood," she said, "because of
circumcision."
27 The LORD said to Aharon, "Go and meet Moshe in the

---

an extraordinary humanization of the relationship between earth and heaven, implying as it does that every human is the child, or the image, of God, and that He is about to take Israel, a small and currently enslaved people, as His firstborn.

4:25 וַתִּקַּח צִפֹּרָה צֹר *Tzipora took a flint knife* – Though Moshe is the central figure in the drama of the exodus, there is a striking emphasis on the roles of six women, without whom there would not have been a Moshe. There is Yokheved, his mother, who had the courage to have a child at a time when all male Israelite children faced death. There is Miriam, his sister, who followed his fate and ensured that he knew who his people were. There are Shifra and Puah, the two midwives, who defy Pharaoh's decree of genocide. There is Pharaoh's daughter, who rescues Moshe and adopts him, knowing that in doing so she is acting in contravention of her father's will. And there is Tzipora, Moshe's Midianite wife, who accompanies him on his mission and here saves his life.

These are six stories of outstanding moral courage and they are all about women, at least two of whom, Tzipora and Pharaoh's daughter, are not Israelites (the identity of the midwives is left uncertain, perhaps deliberately so, see ch. 1, "Midwives to the Hebrews"). It is the women who recognize the sanctity of life and refuse to obey orders that desecrate life. It is the women who, fearing God, are fearless in the face of danger and of human evil. It is the women who embody compassion as well as courage – and justice without compassion is not justice.

הַחֲמֹר וַיָּשָׁב אַרְצָה מִצְרָיִם וַיִּקַּח מֹשֶׁה אֶת־מַטֵּה הָאֱלֹהִים
כא בְּיָדוֹ׃ וַיֹּאמֶר יהוה אֶל־מֹשֶׁה בְּלֶכְתְּךָ לָשׁוּב מִצְרַיְמָה רְאֵה
כׇּל־הַמֹּפְתִים אֲשֶׁר־שַׂמְתִּי בְיָדֶךָ וַעֲשִׂיתָם לִפְנֵי פַרְעֹה וַאֲנִי
כב אֲחַזֵּק אֶת־לִבּוֹ וְלֹא יְשַׁלַּח אֶת־הָעָם׃ וְאָמַרְתָּ אֶל־פַּרְעֹה
כג כֹּה אָמַר יהוה בְּנִי בְכֹרִי יִשְׂרָאֵל׃ וָאֹמַר אֵלֶיךָ שַׁלַּח אֶת־בְּנִי
וְיַעַבְדֵנִי וַתְּמָאֵן לְשַׁלְּחוֹ הִנֵּה אָנֹכִי הֹרֵג אֶת־בִּנְךָ בְּכֹרֶךָ׃
כד כה וַיְהִי בַדֶּרֶךְ בַּמָּלוֹן וַיִּפְגְּשֵׁהוּ יהוה וַיְבַקֵּשׁ הֲמִיתוֹ׃ וַתִּקַּח
צִפֹּרָה צֹר וַתִּכְרֹת אֶת־עׇרְלַת בְּנָהּ וַתַּגַּע לְרַגְלָיו וַתֹּאמֶר
כו כִּי חֲתַן־דָּמִים אַתָּה לִי׃ וַיִּרֶף מִמֶּנּוּ אָז אָמְרָה חֲתַן דָּמִים
לַמּוּלֹת׃
כז וַיֹּאמֶר יהוה אֶל־אַהֲרֹן לֵךְ לִקְרַאת מֹשֶׁה הַמִּדְבָּרָה וַיֵּלֶךְ

4:22 בְּנִי בְּכֹרִי יִשְׂרָאֵל *Israel is My son, My firstborn* – Biblical monotheism was a revolution thousands of years in advance of the culture of the West. The exodus was more than the liberation of slaves. It was a redrawing of the moral and political landscape. If the image of God is to be found not only in kings but in the human person as such, then all power that dehumanizes is *ipso facto* an abuse of power. Slavery, seen by all ancient thinkers as part of the natural order, becomes morally wrong, an offense not only against man but against God. When God tells Moshe to talk to Pharaoh of "Israel [...] My son, My firstborn" (Ex. 4:22), He is announcing to the most powerful ruler of the ancient world that though these people may be your slaves, they are My children. The story of the plagues in Egypt is as much political as theological. Theologically it affirms that the creator of nature is supreme over the forces of nature. Politically it declares that over every human power stands the sovereignty of God, defender and guarantor of the rights of mankind.

This formulation, "My son, My firstborn," is one of the most revolutionary in the entire history of religion. Throughout history, individuals were singled out for reverence or obedience as the child of (or chief intermediary with) God or the gods. One individual was seen as divine or semidivine. That was true of ancient Egypt but also of virtually every other religion since. In this one phrase, however, a new order altogether is announced, one in which every single individual can see him- or herself as the child of God, and correspondingly see God not only as the supreme deity, creator of the universe, but also, and essentially, as a parent. There is between Him and the Israelites a relationship of kinship, responsibility, and love. This is

wilderness." And he went and met him at God's mountain,
28 and kissed him. And Moshe told Aharon all that the
LORD had said about his mission, and all the miraculous
29 signs He had commanded him to perform. So Moshe and
30 Aharon went and gathered all the elders of Israel. Aharon
told them everything the LORD had said to Moshe, and
31 he performed the signs before the people. And the people
believed. When they heard that the LORD was watching
over the Israelites, and that He had seen their misery, they
5 1 bowed their heads and prostrated themselves. After this, SHEVI'I
Moshe and Aharon came to Pharaoh; they said, "Thus
says the LORD, God of Israel: Send My people forth so
that they may hold a festival for Me in the wilderness."
2 But Pharaoh said, "Who is this LORD that I should obey
Him and send Israel forth? I do not know the LORD, and
3 I will not send Israel forth." "The God of the Hebrews has
revealed Himself to us," they said. "Let us take a three-
day journey into the wilderness and sacrifice to the LORD
our God, or He may strike us with the plague or with the
4 sword." The king of Egypt said to them, "Why, Moshe and
Aharon, would you take the people from their work? Get
5 back to your labor! Look," said Pharaoh, "how numerous
the people of the land have become; and yet you would

---

people to do so in Egypt. A minor religious request is met by blunt refusal.

5:2 לֹא יָדַעְתִּי אֶת־יהוה *I do not know the LORD* – The meaning is: Regardless of whether there is such a God, in this territory I am the sole authority. I recognize no other. Where I and the gods I represent have sovereignty, no other has legitimacy. Other peoples may have their gods, but at best their power is territorially limited. Already hinted at here is the radical implication of monotheism: that the God of Israel is the God of everywhere, and the God of the Hebrews is the God of everyone. This challenges the entire structure of territorially constituted national or local deities. Egypt may have known a brief period of proto-monotheism under Akhenaten, but it was decisively rejected after his death. Pharaoh's long battle against accepting the reality of the God of Israel is no accident, nor is it mere stubbornness of character. The religion of Israel challenges the very essence of the social structure and hierarchical worldview of Egypt and the pharaohs.

כח וַיִּפְגְּשֵׁהוּ בְּהַר הָאֱלֹהִים וַיִּשַּׁק־לוֹ׃ וַיַּגֵּד מֹשֶׁה לְאַהֲרֹן אֵת
כָּל־דִּבְרֵי יהוה אֲשֶׁר שְׁלָחוֹ וְאֵת כָּל־הָאֹתֹת אֲשֶׁר צִוָּהוּ׃
כט ל וַיֵּלֶךְ מֹשֶׁה וְאַהֲרֹן וַיַּאַסְפוּ אֶת־כָּל־זִקְנֵי בְּנֵי יִשְׂרָאֵל׃ וַיְדַבֵּר
אַהֲרֹן אֵת כָּל־הַדְּבָרִים אֲשֶׁר־דִּבֶּר יהוה אֶל־מֹשֶׁה וַיַּעַשׂ
לא הָאֹתֹת לְעֵינֵי הָעָם׃ וַיַּאֲמֵן הָעָם וַיִּשְׁמְעוּ כִּי־פָקַד יהוה
ה א אֶת־בְּנֵי יִשְׂרָאֵל וְכִי רָאָה אֶת־עָנְיָם וַיִּקְּדוּ וַיִּשְׁתַּחֲווּ׃ וְאַחַר שביעי
בָּאוּ מֹשֶׁה וְאַהֲרֹן וַיֹּאמְרוּ אֶל־פַּרְעֹה כֹּה־אָמַר יהוה אֱלֹהֵי
ב יִשְׂרָאֵל שַׁלַּח אֶת־עַמִּי וְיָחֹגּוּ לִי בַּמִּדְבָּר׃ וַיֹּאמֶר פַּרְעֹה מִי
יהוה אֲשֶׁר אֶשְׁמַע בְּקֹלוֹ לְשַׁלַּח אֶת־יִשְׂרָאֵל לֹא יָדַעְתִּי
ג אֶת־יהוה וְגַם אֶת־יִשְׂרָאֵל לֹא אֲשַׁלֵּחַ׃ וַיֹּאמְרוּ אֱלֹהֵי
הָעִבְרִים נִקְרָא עָלֵינוּ נֵלֲכָה־נָּא דֶּרֶךְ שְׁלֹשֶׁת יָמִים בַּמִּדְבָּר
ד וְנִזְבְּחָה לַיהוה אֱלֹהֵינוּ פֶּן־יִפְגָּעֵנוּ בַּדֶּבֶר אוֹ בֶחָרֶב׃ וַיֹּאמֶר
אֲלֵהֶם מֶלֶךְ מִצְרַיִם לָמָּה מֹשֶׁה וְאַהֲרֹן תַּפְרִיעוּ אֶת־הָעָם
ה מִמַּעֲשָׂיו לְכוּ לְסִבְלֹתֵיכֶם׃ וַיֹּאמֶר פַּרְעֹה הֵן־רַבִּים עַתָּה

5:1 שַׁלַּח אֶת־עַמִּי *Send My people forth* – As instructed by God (Ex. 3:18) they make a relatively minor demand, a mere three days' journey into the wilderness, and for a specifically religious reason. The point is to reveal the character of Pharaoh and the regime over which he presides. They have not asked for freedom or for the right permanently to leave. Their simple request, and the punitive response from Pharaoh, illustrate the kind of society Egypt has become. The Egyptians themselves had many religious festivals. A text from the time of Ramesses II itemizes forty-six of them, many of them involving large public ceremonies. Egyptian records also show that workmen were given time off to perform religious duties, so what Moshe and Aharon were asking for was no more than standard practice at the time. The Egyptians would certainly have understood the importance of allowing people to fulfill their religious obligations, and the danger of divine anger if they do not. The point being made by the Torah here is that not only would Pharaoh not contemplate giving the Israelites the freedom to leave permanently. He would not even accede to the minimal request Moshe and Aharon make. Many episodes in Genesis showed that it was impossible for the covenantal family to live by their ideals in a Canaanite society ruled by peoples of a very different culture. We now see that it is impossible for the Israelite

6 have them rest from their labors." That day, Pharaoh gave
7 orders to the people's taskmasters and foremen: "Do not
give the people straw for bricks as before. Let them go
8 and gather their own straw. But require them to make the
same quota of bricks as before. Do not reduce it. They
are lazy. That is why they are crying out, 'Send us forth
9 to sacrifice to our God.' Make the work harder for the
people; and make sure they do it instead of listening to
10 lies." So the taskmasters and foremen went out and told
the people, "This is what Pharaoh says: I will no longer
11 give you straw. You must go and get your own straw
wherever you can find it. Your production must not fall
12 short of what it was." So the people spread out all over
13 Egypt to collect stubble for straw. The taskmasters kept
pressuring them, saying, "Complete your daily work
14 quota just as when there was straw." And the Israelite
foremen whom Pharaoh's slave drivers had appointed
were flogged. "Why have you not fulfilled your quota of
bricks," they were asked, "either yesterday or today as you
15 did before?" The Israelite foremen came and protested to
Pharaoh, "Why are you treating your servants like this?
16 Your servants are given no straw, yet they tell us, 'Make
bricks!' We are being flogged for your people's failing."
17 But he said, "Lazy, that is what you are – lazy! That is why
you keep saying, 'Send us forth to sacrifice to the Lord.'
18 Now go. Get to work. Straw will not be given you, and you
19 must complete your count of bricks." When the Israelite
foremen saw that they were not to reduce each day's
20 quota, they knew that harm was coming to them. Leaving
Pharaoh, they met Moshe and Aharon, who stood
21 awaiting them. They said to them, "May the Lord look
on you and judge, because you have made us repellent
in the eyes of Pharaoh and his officials; you have put a

of Moshe. He has been charged by God with a message and mission of deliverance. Instead, conditions have become worse. That is a point that tests the faith of both the people and the leader. Hence Moshe's anguished cry to God.

ו עַם־הָאָ֖רֶץ וְהִשְׁבַּתֶּ֥ם אֹתָ֖ם מִסִּבְלֹתָֽם׃ וַיְצַ֥ו פַּרְעֹ֖ה בַּיּ֣וֹם
ז הַה֑וּא אֶת־הַנֹּגְשִׂ֣ים בָּעָ֔ם וְאֶת־שֹׁטְרָ֖יו לֵאמֹֽר׃ לֹ֣א תֹאסִפ֞וּן
לָתֵ֨ת תֶּ֥בֶן לָעָ֛ם לִלְבֹּ֥ן הַלְּבֵנִ֖ים כִּתְמ֣וֹל שִׁלְשֹׁ֑ם הֵ֚ם יֵֽלְכ֔וּ
ח וְקֹשְׁשׁ֥וּ לָהֶ֖ם תֶּֽבֶן׃ וְאֶת־מַתְכֹּ֨נֶת הַלְּבֵנִ֜ים אֲשֶׁ֨ר הֵ֤ם עֹשִׂים֙
תְּמ֣וֹל שִׁלְשֹׁ֔ם תָּשִׂ֣ימוּ עֲלֵיהֶ֔ם לֹ֥א תִגְרְע֖וּ מִמֶּ֑נּוּ כִּֽי־נִרְפִּ֣ים
ט הֵ֔ם עַל־כֵּ֗ן הֵ֤ם צֹעֲקִים֙ לֵאמֹ֔ר נֵלְכָ֖ה נִזְבְּחָ֥ה לֵאלֹהֵֽינוּ׃ תִּכְבַּ֧ד
הָעֲבֹדָ֛ה עַל־הָאֲנָשִׁ֖ים וְיַֽעֲשׂוּ־בָ֑הּ וְאַל־יִשְׁע֖וּ בְּדִבְרֵי־שָֽׁקֶר׃
י וַ֠יֵּצְאוּ נֹגְשֵׂ֤י הָעָם֙ וְשֹׁ֣טְרָ֔יו וַיֹּאמְר֥וּ אֶל־הָעָ֖ם לֵאמֹ֑ר כֹּ֚ה אָמַ֣ר
יא פַּרְעֹ֔ה אֵינֶ֛נִּי נֹתֵ֥ן לָכֶ֖ם תֶּֽבֶן׃ אַתֶּ֗ם לְכ֤וּ קְחוּ֙ לָכֶ֣ם תֶּ֔בֶן מֵאֲשֶׁ֖ר
יב תִּמְצָ֑אוּ כִּ֛י אֵ֥ין נִגְרָ֛ע מֵעֲבֹדַתְכֶ֖ם דָּבָֽר׃ וַיָּ֥פֶץ הָעָ֖ם בְּכָל־
יג אֶ֣רֶץ מִצְרָ֑יִם לְקֹשֵׁ֥שׁ קַ֖שׁ לַתֶּֽבֶן׃ וְהַנֹּגְשִׂ֖ים אָצִ֣ים לֵאמֹ֑ר כַּלּ֤וּ
יד מַעֲשֵׂיכֶם֙ דְּבַר־י֣וֹם בְּיוֹמ֔וֹ כַּאֲשֶׁ֖ר בִּהְי֥וֹת הַתֶּֽבֶן׃ וַיֻּכּ֗וּ שֹׁטְרֵי֙
בְּנֵ֣י יִשְׂרָאֵ֔ל אֲשֶׁר־שָׂ֣מוּ עֲלֵהֶ֔ם נֹגְשֵׂ֥י פַרְעֹ֖ה לֵאמֹ֑ר מַדּוּעַ֩ לֹ֨א
כִלִּיתֶ֜ם חָקְכֶ֤ם לִלְבֹּן֙ כִּתְמ֣וֹל שִׁלְשֹׁ֔ם גַּם־תְּמ֖וֹל גַּם־הַיּֽוֹם׃
טו וַיָּבֹ֗אוּ שֹֽׁטְרֵי֙ בְּנֵ֣י יִשְׂרָאֵ֔ל וַיִּצְעֲק֥וּ אֶל־פַּרְעֹ֖ה לֵאמֹ֑ר לָ֧מָּה
טז תַעֲשֶׂ֛ה כֹ֖ה לַעֲבָדֶֽיךָ׃ תֶּ֗בֶן אֵ֤ין נִתָּן֙ לַעֲבָדֶ֔יךָ וּלְבֵנִ֛ים אֹמְרִ֥ים
יז לָ֖נוּ עֲשׂ֑וּ וְהִנֵּ֧ה עֲבָדֶ֛יךָ מֻכִּ֖ים וְחָטָ֥את עַמֶּֽךָ׃ וַיֹּ֛אמֶר נִרְפִּ֥ים
אַתֶּ֖ם נִרְפִּ֑ים עַל־כֵּן֙ אַתֶּ֣ם אֹֽמְרִ֔ים נֵלְכָ֖ה נִזְבְּחָ֥ה לַיהוָֽה׃
יח וְעַתָּה֙ לְכ֣וּ עִבְד֔וּ וְתֶ֖בֶן לֹא־יִנָּתֵ֣ן לָכֶ֑ם וְתֹ֥כֶן לְבֵנִ֖ים תִּתֵּֽנוּ׃
יט וַיִּרְא֞וּ שֹׁטְרֵ֧י בְנֵי־יִשְׂרָאֵ֛ל אֹתָ֖ם בְּרָ֣ע לֵאמֹ֑ר לֹא־תִגְרְע֥וּ
כ מִלִּבְנֵיכֶ֖ם דְּבַר־י֥וֹם בְּיוֹמֽוֹ׃ וַֽיִּפְגְּעוּ֙ אֶת־מֹשֶׁ֣ה וְאֶֽת־אַהֲרֹ֔ן
כא נִצָּבִ֖ים לִקְרָאתָ֑ם בְּצֵאתָ֖ם מֵאֵ֥ת פַּרְעֹֽה׃ וַיֹּאמְר֣וּ אֲלֵהֶ֔ם
יֵ֧רֶא יהוָ֛ה עֲלֵיכֶ֖ם וְיִשְׁפֹּ֑ט אֲשֶׁ֧ר הִבְאַשְׁתֶּ֣ם אֶת־רֵיחֵ֗נוּ בְּעֵינֵי֙

5:21 יֵרֶא יהוה עֲלֵיכֶם וְיִשְׁפֹּט *May the* LORD *look on you and judge* – This is an extremely sharp response to Moshe and Aharon, calling down divine judgment on them for making the situation of the Israelites, already bad, even more unbearable. This is a critical moment in the story of the exodus and in the life

▶

22 sword in their hands to kill us." Then Moshe returned to MAFTIR
the LORD and said, "Why, LORD, have You brought harm
23 to this people? Is this why You sent me? Ever since I came
to Pharaoh to speak in Your name, he has dealt worse
with this people; and You have done nothing to deliver
6 1 Your people." But the LORD said to Moshe, "Now you are
about to see what I will do to Pharaoh. By a mighty hand
he will send them forth, and by a mighty hand he will
drive them from his land."

The haftara for Parashat Shemot is on page 1452.

---

a screen of mystery, but they are there. For without them, life is "a tale told by an idiot, full of sound and fury, signifying nothing" (*Macbeth*). The faith of the Bible is neither optimistic nor naive. It contains no theodicies, no systematic answers, no easy consolations. At times, in the books of Job and Ecclesiastes and Lamentations, it comes close to the abyss of pain and despair. "I turned again and saw," says Ecclesiastes, "...the victims' tears and none to console them" (4:1). "It was," says Lamentations, "as if [God] were the enemy" (2:5). But the people of the book refused to stop wrestling with the question. To believe was painful, but to disbelieve was too easy, too superficial, untrue. The rabbi of Klausenburg, Rabbi Yekutiel Yehuda Halberstam, who survived Auschwitz and lost his wife and eleven children in the Holocaust, once said:

> The biggest miracle of all is that we, the survivors of the Holocaust, after all that we witnessed and lived through, still believe and have faith in the Almighty God, may His name be blessed. This, my friends, is the miracle of miracles, the greatest miracle ever to have taken place.

As he said these words, he wept. But still he believed.

What we see in Exodus is that it is those who argue who may become the agents of change. It is as if God intervenes in history only in response to a human call. God calls to us, but we too must call to Him. When those two calls meet, transformation takes place.

כב פַּרְעֹה֙ וּבְעֵינֵ֣י עֲבָדָ֔יו לָֽתֶת־חֶ֥רֶב בְּיָדָ֖ם לְהָרְגֵֽנוּ׃ וַיָּ֧שָׁב מֹשֶׁ֛ה מפטיר
אֶל־יְהֹוָ֖ה וַיֹּאמַ֑ר אֲדֹנָ֗י לָמָ֤ה הֲרֵעֹ֙תָה֙ לָעָ֣ם הַזֶּ֔ה לָ֥מָּה זֶּ֖ה
כג שְׁלַחְתָּֽנִי׃ וּמֵאָ֞ז בָּ֤אתִי אֶל־פַּרְעֹה֙ לְדַבֵּ֣ר בִּשְׁמֶ֔ךָ הֵרַ֖ע לָעָ֣ם
ו א הַזֶּ֑ה וְהַצֵּ֖ל לֹא־הִצַּ֥לְתָּ אֶת־עַמֶּֽךָ׃ וַיֹּ֤אמֶר יהוה֙ אֶל־מֹשֶׁ֔ה
עַתָּ֣ה תִרְאֶ֔ה אֲשֶׁ֥ר אֶֽעֱשֶׂ֖ה לְפַרְעֹ֑ה כִּ֣י בְיָ֤ד חֲזָקָה֙ יְשַׁלְּחֵ֔ם
וּבְיָד֙ חֲזָקָ֔ה יְגָרְשֵׁ֖ם מֵאַרְצֽוֹ׃

The הפטרה *for* פרשת שמות *is on page 1453.*

5:22 לָמָה הֲרֵעֹתָה לָעָם הַזֶּה *Why, Lord, have You brought harm to this people?* – Moshe, like Avraham, feels empowered by Heaven to challenge God Himself in the name of ideals God espouses. This is his first great act of pleading with Heaven on behalf of the people, something he will do at other supreme moments of crisis.

Those who ask in the Tanakh about the apparent injustices of the world are not doubters or sceptics. They are Judaism's supreme prophets. They do not ask because they lack belief; they ask because they believe. If there were no Judge, there would be no justice and no question. There *is* a Judge. When then will justice be done? Above all else, Jewish thought through the centuries has been a sustained meditation on this question, never finding a final answer, realizing that here was a sacred mystery no human mind could penetrate. All other requests Moshe made on behalf of the Jewish people, says the Talmud (Berakhot 7a), were granted except this: to understand why the righteous suffer.

As tenaciously as those questioners ask, so they hold firm to the faith without which there is no question: that there is a moral rule governing the universe and that what happens to us is in some way related to what we do. Good is rewarded and evil has no ultimate dominion. No Jewish belief is more central than this. It forms the core of the Hebrew Bible, the writings of the rabbis, and the speculation of the Jewish mystics. Reward and punishment may be individual or collective, immediate or deferred, in this world or the next, apparent or veiled behind

Parashat Vaera

6 2 Then God spoke to Moshe. "I am the Lord," He said
3 to him. "As El Shaddai I appeared to Avraham, Yitzḥak,

---

the beginning, end, and middle of the speech.

What is meant by the opening proposition? "As El Shaddai I appeared to Avraham, Yitzḥak, and Yaakov –" but not "by My name the Lord." The verse distinguishes between El Shaddai (often rendered "Almighty God") and the four-letter name which, because of its sanctity, Jewish tradition referred to simply as *Hashem* – "the name" par excellence. As the classic Jewish commentators point out, the verse must be read with great care. It does not say that God did not "make this name known" to the patriarchs. God uses the phrase "I am the Lord" to both Avraham (Gen. 15:7) and Yaakov (28:13). Yet a fundamental distinction is being made between the experience the patriarchs had of God, and the experience the Israelites are about to have. What is it? Rashi's explanation (on Ex. 6:3) is the simplest and most elegant:

> It is not written here "[My name 'the Lord'] I did not make known to them" but rather "[By the name 'the Lord'] I did not make Myself known to them" – meaning, I was not recognized by them in My attribute of "keeping faith," by reason of which My name is "the Lord," namely that I am faithful to fulfill My word. For I made promises to them but I did not fulfill them [during their lifetime].

The patriarchs received the covenantal promise. They would become a nation. They would inherit a land. Yet as the book of Genesis reaches its close, the family numbers a mere seventy souls in exile in Egypt. Now, the fulfillment of those promises is about to begin. Already in the first chapter of Exodus, we hear, for the first time, the phrase "the Israelite *people*" (Ex. 1:9). Israel has at last become a nation. Moshe has been told, by God, that He will bring them to a good and spacious land, "a land flowing with milk and honey" (3:8). "The Lord" therefore means the God who acts in history to fulfill His promises. The significance of this act, we shall see, goes far beyond the Israelite story.

6:2 אֲנִי יהוה *I am the Lord* – This brief sentence contains two transitions, from "spoke" to "said," and from "God" to "the Lord." Although these nuances are untranslatable in English, they both represent a move from justice to compassion, from harsh to gentle, from detached to intimate and confiding. God responded sharply to Moshe's question at the end of last week's *parasha*, "Why, Lord, have You brought harm to this

פרשת וארא

ו ב ג וַיְדַבֵּ֥ר אֱלֹהִ֖ים אֶל־מֹשֶׁ֑ה וַיֹּ֥אמֶר אֵלָ֖יו אֲנִ֥י יְהוָֽה׃ וָאֵרָ֗א ד

VAERA

In Vaera, the story of the exodus begins in earnest, with an unprecedented series of divine interventions into history. Time and again plagues hit the Egyptians. Moshe repeatedly asks Pharaoh to release the people. Repeatedly, Pharaoh refuses. All the power of imperial Egypt is powerless against the God of creation and redemption. The plagues are a lesson, to Pharaoh and to the world, that there is something higher than power. There is justice, liberty, human dignity, the sanctity of life.

I AM THE LORD

Having given Moshe a brief and forceful answer to his anxieties at the end of last week's *parasha*, God now, in a separate address, explains to him in detail the world-changing significance of what is about to transpire. Nehama Leibowitz and others point out that the speech is a chiasmus:

Then God spoke to Moshe:

A. I am the LORD.

B. As El Shaddai I appeared to Avraham, Yitzḥak, and Yaakov – but by My name the LORD I did not make Myself known to them.

C. And I made a covenant with them to give them the land of Canaan…

D. And now, I have heard the groaning of the Israelites, whom the Egyptians are holding as slaves, and I remember My covenant.

E. Therefore, say to the Israelites: I am the LORD,

D1. and I will free you from the forced labor of the Egyptians.…Then you will know that I am the LORD your God…

C1. And I will bring you to the land that I promised to give

B1. to Avraham, Yitzḥak, and Yaakov; to you I will give it as a possession.

A1. I am the LORD.

The first and second halves of the speech each contain exactly fifty words in the Hebrew text. B and B1 are about the patriarchs; C and C1 about the land; D and D1 about Egypt and slavery. The first half is about the past, the second about the future. The first half refers to the Israelites in the third person ("them"), the second in the second person ("you"). The entire speech turns on the threefold repetition of "I am the LORD" – at

and Yaakov – but by My name the LORD I did not make
4 Myself known to them. And I made a covenant with them
to give them the land of Canaan, the land where they lived
5 as strangers. And now, I have heard the groaning of the
Israelites whom the Egyptians are holding as slaves, and
6 I remember My covenant. Therefore, say to the Israelites:
I am the LORD, and I will free you from the forced labor
of the Egyptians, I will rescue you from slavery. I will
liberate you with an arm stretched forth and with great
7 acts of judgment. I will take you as My people and I will
be your God. Then you will know that I am the LORD your
8 God, freeing you from Egyptian forced labor. And I will
bring you to the land that I promised to give to Avraham,

---

into being, nor is He reached only in the private recesses of the soul. At a certain point He intervenes in history, to rescue His people from slavery and set them on the path to freedom. This is the revolution, at once political and intellectual.

Judaism is the escape into history, the unique attempt to endow events with meaning, and to see in the chronicles of mankind something more than a mere succession of happenings – to see history as nothing less than a drama of redemption in which the fate of a nation reflects its loyalty or otherwise to a covenant with God.

Some 3,300 years ago, God tells Moshe that He will intervene in the arena of time, not only (though primarily) to rescue the Israelites but also "to have My name known throughout the land" (Ex. 9:16). The script of history will bear the mark of a hand – not human, but divine. And it begins with these words: "Therefore, say to the Israelites: I am the LORD, and I will free you from the forced labor of the Egyptians."

6:8 וְהֵבֵאתִי אֶתְכֶם *I will bring you* – The Mishna in Pesaḥim (10:1) speaks of four cups of wine at the Passover Seder. Traditionally, the first cup corresponds to "I will free you," the second to "I will rescue you," the third to "I will liberate you," and the fourth to "I will take you." Geographically, God will take the Israelites out of Egypt, physically He will save them from oppression, legally He will liberate them from Pharaoh's rule, and spiritually He will take them under His own protection and tutelage. Each of the four cups is a stage on the way to freedom, a way of pausing and giving thanks. The rabbis of the Middle Ages debated whether a fifth cup, corresponding to this fifth promise: "I will bring you to the land that I promised," should be drunk during the time of exile. Out of respect for Rambam

אֶל־אַבְרָהָם אֶל־יִצְחָק וְאֶל־יַעֲקֹב בְּאֵל שַׁדָּי וּשְׁמִי יהוה
ד לֹא נוֹדַעְתִּי לָהֶם׃ וְגַם הֲקִמֹתִי אֶת־בְּרִיתִי אִתָּם לָתֵת לָהֶם
ה אֶת־אֶרֶץ כְּנָעַן אֵת אֶרֶץ מְגֻרֵיהֶם אֲשֶׁר־גָּרוּ בָהּ׃ וְגַם ׀ אֲנִי
שָׁמַעְתִּי אֶת־נַאֲקַת בְּנֵי יִשְׂרָאֵל אֲשֶׁר מִצְרַיִם מַעֲבִדִים
ו אֹתָם וָאֶזְכֹּר אֶת־בְּרִיתִי׃ לָכֵן אֱמֹר לִבְנֵי־יִשְׂרָאֵל אֲנִי יהוה
וְהוֹצֵאתִי אֶתְכֶם מִתַּחַת סִבְלֹת מִצְרַיִם וְהִצַּלְתִּי אֶתְכֶם
מֵעֲבֹדָתָם וְגָאַלְתִּי אֶתְכֶם בִּזְרוֹעַ נְטוּיָה וּבִשְׁפָטִים גְּדֹלִים׃
ז וְלָקַחְתִּי אֶתְכֶם לִי לְעָם וְהָיִיתִי לָכֶם לֵאלֹהִים וִידַעְתֶּם כִּי
אֲנִי יהוה אֱלֹהֵיכֶם הַמּוֹצִיא אֶתְכֶם מִתַּחַת סִבְלוֹת מִצְרָיִם׃
ח וְהֵבֵאתִי אֶתְכֶם אֶל־הָאָרֶץ אֲשֶׁר נָשָׂאתִי אֶת־יָדִי לָתֵת

people?" (Ex. 5:22). Now He speaks again as the loving God who is about to redeem His people.

6:3 וּשְׁמִי יהוה לֹא נוֹדַעְתִּי לָהֶם *But by My name the Lord I did not make Myself known* – The patriarchs knew God by the four-letter name "the Lord." It occurs 165 times in Genesis. In an earlier comment ("I am the Lord") we discussed Rashi's decoding of the verse: The patriarchs knew the God of promise. The Israelites were now about to see the God who delivers on a national scale. Note that the root *y-d-a* in Hebrew does not mean "to know" in a purely cognitive sense. It means "to have direct and immediate experience" of something. The patriarchs knew that God would fulfill His promises, but they did not live to see the full realization of the covenant.

In the ancient world, the idea of a God who promises would not have made sense outside Israel. "The Lord" is not a natural force, as in polytheism, or even the totality of natural forces. For this we have the word "God." "The Lord" is the concept of a God who places Himself under moral obligations for the future, hence a God who acts in history, who says "I will be who I will be." God told Avraham, "I am the Lord" (Gen. 15:7) in the vision in which He revealed to him that his descendants would be strangers in the land not their own, where they would be enslaved and mistreated. The repetition of these words to Moshe here creates a vast temporal arch between Avraham and Moshe, the first and last scenes of exile.

6:6 וְהוֹצֵאתִי אֶתְכֶם מִתַּחַת סִבְלֹת מִצְרַיִם *I will free you from the forced labor of the Egyptians* – What is revolutionary in Judaism is not simply the concept of monotheism – that the universe is not a blind clash of conflicting powers but the result of a single creative will. It is that God is *involved* in His creation. God is not simply the force that brought the universe

Yitzḥak, and Yaakov; to you I will give it as a possession. I
9 am the Lord." Moshe told this to the Israelites, but in the
brokenness of their spirit and the brutal labor they did
not listen to him.
10 11 Then the Lord said to Moshe, "Go, tell Pharaoh, king
12 of Egypt, to send the Israelites forth from his land." But
Moshe said to the Lord, "The Israelites, You see, have
not listened to me. How then will Pharaoh listen? And I
am a man of uncircumcised lips."

---

disease on earth because that is the way the world is; that is how God made it and wants it. That isn't Judaism at all. When it comes to the poverty and pain of the world, ours is a religion of protest, not acceptance. God is to be found in this world, not just the next. But for us to climb to spiritual heights we must first have satisfied our material needs.

Alleviating poverty, curing disease, ensuring the rule of law, and respecting human rights: these are spiritual tasks no less than prayer and Torah study. To be sure, the latter are higher, but the former are prior. People cannot hear God's message if their spirit is broken and their labor harsh.

6:12 וְאֵיךְ יִשְׁמָעֵנִי פַרְעֹה *How then will Pharaoh listen?* – This is a mode of reasoning known as *kal vaḥomer*, or *a fortiori*. If the Israelites, who are the beneficiaries of my message, do not listen, how much less so is Pharaoh likely to listen. Moshe seems aware that the argument he mounts is not a strong one. The text has already told us that the Israelites do not listen because of "the brokenness of their spirit and the brutal labor," which does not apply to Pharaoh. So Moshe adds, "I am a man of uncircumcised lips." God tacitly acknowledges this by including Aharon, the more fluent speaker, in the instructions.

6:12 עֲרַל שְׂפָתָיִם *Uncircumcised lips* – This is another reference to his speech defect, or perhaps to a sense on the part of Moshe that, being all too human, he lacks the inspirational quality that might be expected in a person who claims to be the voice of God. His broken speech makes it difficult for people to be in awe of him as a holy man. He is more likely to evoke laughter or contempt than fear and trembling.

Moshe has not yet internalized the fact that he is never destined to succeed by words alone. God has already told him at the burning bush, "But I know that even by a mighty hand the king of Egypt would not send you forth" (Ex. 3:19). He is part of a drama larger than even he, greatest of the prophets, can understand at the time. Pharaoh cannot accede to the request, however eloquently it is made, without demeaning his stature as an emperor and demigod.

אֹתָהּ לְאַבְרָהָם לְיִצְחָק וּלְיַעֲקֹב וְנָתַתִּי אֹתָהּ לָכֶם מוֹרָשָׁה
ט אֲנִי יהוה׃ וַיְדַבֵּר מֹשֶׁה כֵּן אֶל־בְּנֵי יִשְׂרָאֵל וְלֹא שָׁמְעוּ אֶל־
מֹשֶׁה מִקֹּצֶר רוּחַ וּמֵעֲבֹדָה קָשָׁה׃
יא וַיְדַבֵּר יהוה אֶל־מֹשֶׁה לֵּאמֹר׃ בֹּא דַבֵּר אֶל־פַּרְעֹה מֶלֶךְ
יב מִצְרָיִם וִישַׁלַּח אֶת־בְּנֵי־יִשְׂרָאֵל מֵאַרְצוֹ׃ וַיְדַבֵּר מֹשֶׁה לִפְנֵי
יהוה לֵאמֹר הֵן בְּנֵי־יִשְׂרָאֵל לֹא־שָׁמְעוּ אֵלַי וְאֵיךְ יִשְׁמָעֵנִי
פַרְעֹה וַאֲנִי עֲרַל שְׂפָתָיִם׃

Now we find that Moshe was both right and wrong, right that they do not listen to him, but wrong about why. It has nothing to do with his failures as a leader or a public speaker. In fact, it has nothing to do with Moshe at all. They do not listen "in the brokenness of their spirit and the brutal labor." In other words: *if you want to improve people's spiritual situation, you must first improve their physical situation.* That is one of the most humanizing insights of Judaism.

Rambam emphasizes this in his *Guide for the Perplexed* (III:27). The Torah, he says, has two aims: the well-being of the soul and the well-being of the body. The well-being of the soul is something inward and spiritual, but the well-being of the body requires a strong society and economy, where there is the rule of law, division of labor, and the promotion of trade. We have bodily well-being when all our physical needs are supplied, but none of us can do this on our own. We specialize and exchange. That is why we need a good, strong, just society.

Most religions are cultures of acceptance. There is poverty, hunger, and

(*Hilkhot Ḥametz UMatza* 8:10), we pour this extra cup, because of the promise. Out of respect for Rashi (Pesaḥim 118a), we do not drink it, because the promise is not yet fulfilled.

In our times, the Jewish people have returned to the land. According to one sage (the late Rabbi Menahem Kasher), we should now drink the fifth cup. Be that as it may, according to the sages, unresolved halakhic disputes will one day be resolved by Eliyahu. (According to one popular understanding, the word *teiku*, "Let it stand [undecided]," refers to Eliyahu: "[Eliyahu] the Tishbite will come and answer questions and problems"). It is thus the untouched fifth cup that became known as the cup of Eliyahu. It represents the hope that kept the Jewish people alive through the darkest night of exile.

6:9 וְלֹא שָׁמְעוּ אֶל־מֹשֶׁה *They did not listen to him* – When Moshe first met God at the burning bush, God told him to lead, and Moshe demurred on the grounds that the people would not listen to him. He was not a man of words. He lacked eloquence. He could not sway crowds. He was not an inspirational leader.

13 The LORD spoke to Moshe and Aharon; and He charged
them with regard to the Israelites and to Pharaoh,
king of Egypt, to bring the Israelites out of the land of
14 Egypt. These were the heads of their ancestral SHENI
houses. The sons of Reuven, Yisrael's firstborn, were
Ḥanokh, Palu, Ḥetzron, and Karmi; these were the families
15 of Reuven. Shimon's sons were Yemuel, Yamin, Ohad,
Yakhin, Tzoḥar, and Sha'ul, son of a Canaanite woman;
16 these are the families of Shimon. These are the names of
Levi's sons by their lineage: Gershon, Kehat, and Merari.
17 Levi lived one hundred thirty-seven years. The sons of
18 Gershon were Livni and Shimi, by their families. The
sons of Kehat were Amram, Yitzhar, Ḥevron, and Uziel.
19 Kehat lived one hundred thirty-three years. The sons of
Merari were Maḥli and Mushi. These are the families of
20 the Levites by their lineage. Amram married Yokheved,
his father's sister, who bore him Aharon and Moshe.
21 Amram lived one hundred thirty-seven years. The sons
22 of Yitzhar were Koraḥ, Nefeg, and Zikhri. The sons of
23 Uziel were Mishael, Eltzafan, and Sitri. Aharon married
Elisheva, daughter of Aminadav and sister of Naḥshon,
and she bore him Nadav and Avihu, Elazar and Itamar.
24 The sons of Koraḥ were Asir, Elkana, and Aviasaf; these

We are given surprisingly detailed information about Koraḥ, and about Aharon's son Elazar and his grandson Pinḥas. The two sons of Moshe, Gershom and Eliezer, are not mentioned. This is not the usual genealogy of the kind the Torah inserts at various occasions, but rather an advance identification of leading figures, not only from earlier generations but also in the future. Moshe's sons will not inherit his office, unlike Aharon's who will. It will be Elazar who becomes Aharon's successor, because Nadav and Avihu die prematurely. Elazar's son Pinḥas will play a leading role in a key episode in Israel's history. Koraḥ will eventually challenge Moshe's leadership, as will two figures from the tribe of Reuven. All these future events are hinted at in this genealogy.

6:20 וַיִּקַּח עַמְרָם אֶת־יוֹכֶבֶד דֹּדָתוֹ לוֹ לְאִשָּׁה *Amram married Yokheved, his father's sister* – Marriages of this kind were forbidden in later Torah law (Lev. 18:12), but not at the time. It is striking that the Torah does not suppress this fact about the marriage that yielded Israel three great leaders, Moshe, Aharon, and Miriam.

יג וַיְדַבֵּר יְהוָה אֶל־מֹשֶׁה וְאֶל־אַהֲרֹן וַיְצַוֵּם אֶל־בְּנֵי יִשְׂרָאֵל
וְאֶל־פַּרְעֹה מֶלֶךְ מִצְרָיִם לְהוֹצִיא אֶת־בְּנֵי־יִשְׂרָאֵל מֵאֶרֶץ
יד מִצְרָיִם: אֵלֶּה רָאשֵׁי בֵית־אֲבֹתָם בְּנֵי רְאוּבֵן בְּכֹר שני
יִשְׂרָאֵל חֲנוֹךְ וּפַלּוּא חֶצְרֹן וְכַרְמִי אֵלֶּה מִשְׁפְּחֹת רְאוּבֵן:
טו וּבְנֵי שִׁמְעוֹן יְמוּאֵל וְיָמִין וְאֹהַד וְיָכִין וְצֹחַר וְשָׁאוּל בֶּן־
טז הַכְּנַעֲנִית אֵלֶּה מִשְׁפְּחֹת שִׁמְעוֹן: וְאֵלֶּה שְׁמוֹת בְּנֵי־לֵוִי
לְתֹלְדֹתָם גֵּרְשׁוֹן וּקְהָת וּמְרָרִי וּשְׁנֵי חַיֵּי לֵוִי שֶׁבַע וּשְׁלֹשִׁים
יז יח וּמְאַת שָׁנָה: בְּנֵי גֵרְשׁוֹן לִבְנִי וְשִׁמְעִי לְמִשְׁפְּחֹתָם: וּבְנֵי
קְהָת עַמְרָם וְיִצְהָר וְחֶבְרוֹן וְעֻזִּיאֵל וּשְׁנֵי חַיֵּי קְהָת שָׁלֹשׁ
יט וּשְׁלֹשִׁים וּמְאַת שָׁנָה: וּבְנֵי מְרָרִי מַחְלִי וּמוּשִׁי אֵלֶּה
כ מִשְׁפְּחֹת הַלֵּוִי לְתֹלְדֹתָם: וַיִּקַּח עַמְרָם אֶת־יוֹכֶבֶד דֹּדָתוֹ
לוֹ לְאִשָּׁה וַתֵּלֶד לוֹ אֶת־אַהֲרֹן וְאֶת־מֹשֶׁה וּשְׁנֵי חַיֵּי עַמְרָם
כא שֶׁבַע וּשְׁלֹשִׁים וּמְאַת שָׁנָה: וּבְנֵי יִצְהָר קֹרַח וָנֶפֶג וְזִכְרִי:
כב כג וּבְנֵי עֻזִּיאֵל מִישָׁאֵל וְאֶלְצָפָן וְסִתְרִי: וַיִּקַּח אַהֲרֹן אֶת־
אֱלִישֶׁבַע בַּת־עַמִּינָדָב אֲחוֹת נַחְשׁוֹן לוֹ לְאִשָּׁה וַתֵּלֶד לוֹ
כד אֶת־נָדָב וְאֶת־אֲבִיהוּא אֶת־אֶלְעָזָר וְאֶת־אִיתָמָר: וּבְנֵי
קֹרַח אַסִּיר וְאֶלְקָנָה וַאֲבִיאָסָף אֵלֶּה מִשְׁפְּחֹת הַקָּרְחִי:

6:14 אֵלֶּה רָאשֵׁי *These were the heads* – The genealogy at this point marks a pause in the narrative. We have reached the end of the first phase: Moshe's intercession, the reliance on human efforts, and Pharaoh's initial obduracy. The narrative is now about to move from natural to supernatural, from request to sign to plague. To root these wondrous events in human history the text gives us a genealogy, with special emphasis on the tribe of Levi and the leadership of Moshe, Aharon, Aharon's sons, and in one case, Pinḥas, Aharon's grandson. This foreshadows the family's future role as priests. Levi was Yaakov's third son. Out of respect to the two older sons, a brief genealogy is given also for Reuven and Shimon. The genealogy supplies the information conspicuously withheld in chapter 2, where with the exception of his sister Miriam, Moshe's family appears anonymously. Until now, the emphasis has been on Moshe the individual. Now we see him as fully part of his people. He and Aharon may have been chosen by God to perform signs and wonders but they remain resolutely part of the family of the covenant.

25 are the families of the Korahites. Elazar, Aharon's son,
married one of the daughters of Putiel, and she bore him
Pinḥas. These were the heads of the Levite clans by their
26 families. These were the Aharon and Moshe to whom the
Lord said, "Bring the Israelites out of Egypt, by their
27 battalions." It was they who spoke up to Pharaoh, king
of Egypt, to bring the Israelites out of Egypt – this same
28 Moshe and Aharon. So it came to pass on the day the
29 Lord spoke to Moshe in Egypt. The Lord said SHELISHI
to Moshe, "I am the Lord. Tell Pharaoh, king of Egypt,
30 all that I am telling you." But Moshe replied to the Lord,
"You know that I have uncircumcised lips. How then will
Pharaoh listen to me?"
7 1 Then the Lord said to Moshe, "I am making you now
like a god to Pharaoh, and your brother Aharon will be
2 your prophet. All that I command you, you are to speak,
and your brother Aharon to convey to Pharaoh, that he
3 send the Israelites forth from his land. But I will harden
Pharaoh's heart and multiply My signs and wonders in

gods, destined to join them after death. Ramesses II went further, having himself portrayed as a god at the temple at Abu Simbel. Just as there was a confrontation between Moshe (a mere "child") and Ramesses ("child of the sun god Ra"), so there is between the pharaoh who considers himself a god and Moshe, who knows he is all too human. Yet, says God, you will be a "god" to Pharaoh because, in your humility, My presence will shine through you, and Pharaoh will see that there is a force in the universe that transcends all the powers of nature and of empire. Pharaoh, arrogant, will be humbled. You, humble, will be uplifted. The lowliest of all peoples will be set free while the greatest of all empires will meet its nemesis.

THE HARDENING OF PHARAOH'S HEART

The Egyptians – pharaohs especially – were preoccupied by death. Their funerary practices were elaborate in the extreme and were meant to prepare the person for life after death. According to Egyptian myth, the deceased underwent a trial to establish their worthiness to enjoy life after death in Aaru, the Field of Reeds, where souls live on in pleasure for eternity. They believed that the soul resides in the heart, and the trial consisted of the ceremony of the Weighing

כה וְאֶלְעָזָר בֶּן־אַהֲרֹן לָקַח־לוֹ מִבְּנוֹת פּוּטִיאֵל לוֹ לְאִשָּׁה
וַתֵּלֶד לוֹ אֶת־פִּינְחָס אֵלֶּה רָאשֵׁי אֲבוֹת הַלְוִיִּם לְמִשְׁפְּחֹתָם:
כו הוּא אַהֲרֹן וּמֹשֶׁה אֲשֶׁר אָמַר יהוה לָהֶם הוֹצִיאוּ אֶת־בְּנֵי
כז יִשְׂרָאֵל מֵאֶרֶץ מִצְרַיִם עַל־צִבְאֹתָם: הֵם הַמְדַבְּרִים אֶל־
פַּרְעֹה מֶלֶךְ־מִצְרַיִם לְהוֹצִיא אֶת־בְּנֵי־יִשְׂרָאֵל מִמִּצְרָיִם
כח הוּא מֹשֶׁה וְאַהֲרֹן: וַיְהִי בְּיוֹם דִּבֶּר יהוה אֶל־מֹשֶׁה בְּאֶרֶץ
כט מִצְרָיִם: וַיְדַבֵּר יהוה אֶל־מֹשֶׁה לֵּאמֹר אֲנִי יהוה שלישי
דַּבֵּר אֶל־פַּרְעֹה מֶלֶךְ מִצְרַיִם אֵת כָּל־אֲשֶׁר אֲנִי דֹּבֵר אֵלֶיךָ:
ל וַיֹּאמֶר מֹשֶׁה לִפְנֵי יהוה הֵן אֲנִי עֲרַל שְׂפָתַיִם וְאֵיךְ יִשְׁמַע
אֵלַי פַּרְעֹה:
ז א וַיֹּאמֶר יהוה אֶל־מֹשֶׁה רְאֵה נְתַתִּיךָ אֱלֹהִים לְפַרְעֹה וְאַהֲרֹן
ב אָחִיךָ יִהְיֶה נְבִיאֶךָ: אַתָּה תְדַבֵּר אֵת כָּל־אֲשֶׁר אֲצַוֶּךָּ וְאַהֲרֹן
ג אָחִיךָ יְדַבֵּר אֶל־פַּרְעֹה וְשִׁלַּח אֶת־בְּנֵי־יִשְׂרָאֵל מֵאַרְצוֹ: וַאֲנִי
אַקְשֶׁה אֶת־לֵב פַּרְעֹה וְהִרְבֵּיתִי אֶת־אֹתֹתַי וְאֶת־מוֹפְתַי

6:26 אַהֲרֹן וּמֹשֶׁה *Aharon and Moshe* – The names are given here in their chronological order, as opposed to their leadership positions. The Netziv suggests that in this verse, which speaks about the Israelites, Aharon takes priority since he is well known to and beloved by the people. Moshe, who has spent much of his life in an Egyptian palace and in Midyan, is relatively unknown to them. The next verse, however, speaks of their address to Pharaoh. Here Moshe takes precedence, since he is well known to the court and respected for his Egyptian ways (*Haamek Davar*).

The Sages, cited by Rashi, comment that the Torah is emphasizing that both brothers were equal in their worthiness, in their stature, in their rank. This again signals the end of the sibling rivalry that preoccupied much of the book of Genesis.

7:1 אֱלֹהִים לְפַרְעֹה *Like a god to Pharaoh* – Until now, Moshe has been described as a god to Aharon, in the sense of instructing him what to say. Here, however, the phrase has a sharper import. Central to the biblical vision is the absolute distinction between God and human beings. Humans are in the image of God, but they are not God. Hence the astonishingly realistic portrayal of the heroes of the Bible, each of whom is finite, frail, and fallible. Moshe argues, doubts, loses heart, yet he is the greatest leader we have known. The pharaohs, on the other hand, saw themselves as children of the

4 the land of Egypt. Still Pharaoh will not listen to you.
Then I will set My hand against Egypt and, with great
acts of judgment, bring My battalions, My people the
5 Israelites, forth out of the land of Egypt. When I stretch
out My hand against Egypt and bring the Israelites out
from among them, the Egyptians will know that I am
6 the Lord." Moshe and Aharon did so; they did exactly
7 as the Lord commanded them. Moshe was eighty
years old, and Aharon eighty-three, when they spoke to
Pharaoh.

8 9 Then the Lord said to Moshe, and to Aharon, "When REVI'I
Pharaoh says to you, 'Perform a miracle,' tell Aharon:
Take your staff and throw it down before Pharaoh and
10 it will become a serpent." So Moshe and Aharon went to

---

the story in a new way. It is less about free will than about the universality of morality. Pharaoh's conduct toward the Israelites was not only an offense against them but also against his own people's values. The narrative is telling us that *certain things are wrong, whoever does them and whoever they are done against.* They are wrong by Egyptian standards too. That is true of Pharaoh's decision to kill all male Israelite children. It is an unforgivable sin; that is the beginning of the eventually unstoppable hardening and heavying of the heart.

Pharaoh, in his repeated refusal to let the people go, may justify his decision on the grounds that he is securing *Ma'at*, order, against the threat of a growing minority in the midst of Egypt. However, with each plague the country is reduced to ever greater chaos. Tyrannies often justify themselves on the grounds that they are securing order. God is showing Egypt and ultimately the world that right is sovereign over might, that political order may not be secured at the cost of murder and oppression. The order Pharaoh seeks to protect is built on a foundation of injustice: the enslavement of the many for the benefit of the few. The more he tries to defend it, the heavier his heart grows.

7:9 לְתַנִּין *A serpent* – Evidently this is not the same sign as the one given to Moshe at the burning bush. There the text uses the word *naḥash*. Here it uses the word *tanin*. This word appears in Genesis 1:21 meaning a sea monster. Here the reference is to a crocodile, the deadly animal of which there were many in the Nile. An ancient Egyptian story tells of a magician, Ubaaner, who made a model of a crocodile out of wax, which then came alive and ate its intended victim. Sobek, one of the gods of the Nile, was often portrayed as a crocodile. The sign produced by Moshe and Aharon would thus be meaningful to

ד בְּאֶרֶץ מִצְרָיִם: וְלֹא־יִשְׁמַע אֲלֵכֶם פַּרְעֹה וְנָתַתִּי אֶת־יָדִי
בְּמִצְרָיִם וְהוֹצֵאתִי אֶת־צִבְאֹתַי אֶת־עַמִּי בְנֵי־יִשְׂרָאֵל מֵאֶרֶץ
ה מִצְרַיִם בִּשְׁפָטִים גְּדֹלִים: וְיָדְעוּ מִצְרַיִם כִּי־אֲנִי יהוה בִּנְטֹתִי
אֶת־יָדִי עַל־מִצְרָיִם וְהוֹצֵאתִי אֶת־בְּנֵי־יִשְׂרָאֵל מִתּוֹכָם:
ו ז וַיַּעַשׂ מֹשֶׁה וְאַהֲרֹן כַּאֲשֶׁר צִוָּה יהוה אֹתָם כֵּן עָשׂוּ: וּמֹשֶׁה
בֶּן־שְׁמֹנִים שָׁנָה וְאַהֲרֹן בֶּן־שָׁלֹשׁ וּשְׁמֹנִים שָׁנָה בְּדַבְּרָם
אֶל־פַּרְעֹה:
ח ט וַיֹּאמֶר יהוה אֶל־מֹשֶׁה וְאֶל־אַהֲרֹן לֵאמֹר: כִּי יְדַבֵּר אֲלֵכֶם ה רביעי
פַּרְעֹה לֵאמֹר תְּנוּ לָכֶם מוֹפֵת וְאָמַרְתָּ אֶל־אַהֲרֹן קַח אֶת־
י מַטְּךָ וְהַשְׁלֵךְ לִפְנֵי־פַרְעֹה יְהִי לְתַנִּין: וַיָּבֹא מֹשֶׁה וְאַהֲרֹן

of the Heart. Other organs were removed after death, but the heart was left because it was needed for the trial.

On one side of the scales was a feather. On the other was placed the heart. If the heart was as light as the feather, the dead could continue to Aaru. If it was heavier, it was devoured by the goddess Ammit, and its owner was condemned to live in Duat, the underworld. An illustration, on papyrus in *The Book of the Dead,* shows the ceremony, undertaken in the Hall of Two Truths, overseen by Anubis, the Egyptian god of the dead.

The root *k-v-d,* "to make heavy," would thus have had a highly specific meaning for the Egyptians of that time. It would imply that Pharaoh's heart had become heavier than a feather. He would fail the heart-weighing ceremony and be denied what was most important to him – the prospect of joining the gods in the afterlife.

No one would have been in doubt as to why this was so. The feather represented *Ma'at,* the central Egyptian value that included the concepts of truth, balance, order, harmony, justice, morality, and law. This was fundamental to Egyptian culture, and it was the task of the Pharaoh to ensure that it prevailed. *Ma'at* means cosmic order. Its absence invites chaos. A Pharaoh whose heart had become heavier than the *Ma'at* feather was not only endangering his own afterlife, but threatening the entire people over whom he ruled with turmoil and disarray.

One of the things the deceased was supposed to do as part of the trial was to make a series of forty-two negative confessions, declaring himself innocent of the kind of sin that would exclude him from Paradise. They included: "I have not done injury to men. I have not oppressed those beneath me. I have not murdered. I have not commanded murder. I have not caused suffering to men." Pharaoh had done these things. If the "heavying" of his heart is an allusion to the Weighing of the Heart ceremony, it allows us to read

Pharaoh and did just as the Lord had commanded. Aharon
threw down his staff before Pharaoh and his officials, and it
11 became a serpent. Pharaoh then summoned his sages and
sorcerers, and the Egyptian magicians did the same thing by
12 their sorcery. Each threw down his staff, and they became
13 serpents – but Aharon's staff swallowed up theirs. Pharaoh,
nonetheless, was obstinate, and he would not listen to
14 them, just as the Lord had predicted. Then the
Lord said to Moshe, "Pharaoh's heart is unyielding. He
15 refuses to send the people forth. So go to Pharaoh in the
morning as he goes out to the water. Place yourself by the
bank of the Nile where you will encounter him, taking in
16 your hand the staff that turned into a snake. Say to him:
The Lord, God of the Hebrews, has sent me to tell you:
Send My people forth, so that they may serve Me in the
17 wilderness. So far, you have not listened. This is what the
Lord says: This will make it known to you that I am the
Lord. With the staff in my hand I will strike the water in
18 the Nile and it will become blood. The fish in the Nile

The plagues themselves have an underlying structure. The first nine are divided into three groups of three. For the first plague in each triad, Moshe is commanded to confront Pharaoh in the morning in the open, usually by the Nile. For the second, he is commanded to go to Pharaoh in the palace. The third in each group occurs without warning (Rashbam). Another way of categorizing them is to see them as five groups of two. The first two, blood and frogs, both emerge from the Nile. The second pair, lice and swarms of insects, are irritants. The third, the deadly epidemic and boils, are bodily conditions, affecting animals then humans. The fourth, hail and locusts, destroy the produce of the field. The fifth pair, darkness and the death of the firstborn, blot out, first light, then life.

The plagues are intended to show Pharaoh and his people the powerlessness of the gods in which they believe. What is at stake in this confrontation is the difference between myth – in which the gods are mere powers, to be tamed, propitiated, or manipulated – and biblical monotheism, in which ethics (justice, compassion, human dignity) constitute the meeting point of God and mankind. The symbolism of these plagues, often lost on us, would have been immediately apparent to the Egyptians.

7:17 וְנֶהֶפְכוּ לְדָם *It will become blood* – Again, this may be a reference to Egyptian

אֶל־פַּרְעֹה וַיַּעֲשׂוּ־כֵן כַּאֲשֶׁר צִוָּה יהוה וַיַּשְׁלֵךְ אַהֲרֹן אֶת־
יא מַטֵּהוּ לִפְנֵי פַרְעֹה וְלִפְנֵי עֲבָדָיו וַיְהִי לְתַנִּין׃ וַיִּקְרָא גַּם־
פַּרְעֹה לַחֲכָמִים וְלַמְכַשְּׁפִים וַיַּעֲשׂוּ גַם־הֵם חַרְטֻמֵּי מִצְרַיִם
יב בְּלַהֲטֵיהֶם כֵּן׃ וַיַּשְׁלִיכוּ אִישׁ מַטֵּהוּ וַיִּהְיוּ לְתַנִּינִם וַיִּבְלַע
יג מַטֵּה־אַהֲרֹן אֶת־מַטֹּתָם׃ וַיֶּחֱזַק לֵב פַּרְעֹה וְלֹא שָׁמַע אֲלֵהֶם
יד כַּאֲשֶׁר דִּבֶּר יהוה׃ וַיֹּאמֶר יהוה אֶל־מֹשֶׁה כָּבֵד
טו לֵב פַּרְעֹה מֵאֵן לְשַׁלַּח הָעָם׃ לֵךְ אֶל־פַּרְעֹה בַּבֹּקֶר הִנֵּה יֹצֵא
הַמַּיְמָה וְנִצַּבְתָּ לִקְרָאתוֹ עַל־שְׂפַת הַיְאֹר וְהַמַּטֶּה אֲשֶׁר־
טז נֶהְפַּךְ לְנָחָשׁ תִּקַּח בְּיָדֶךָ׃ וְאָמַרְתָּ אֵלָיו יהוה אֱלֹהֵי הָעִבְרִים
שְׁלָחַנִי אֵלֶיךָ לֵאמֹר שַׁלַּח אֶת־עַמִּי וְיַעַבְדֻנִי בַּמִּדְבָּר וְהִנֵּה
יז לֹא־שָׁמַעְתָּ עַד־כֹּה׃ כֹּה אָמַר יהוה בְּזֹאת תֵּדַע כִּי אֲנִי יהוה
הִנֵּה אָנֹכִי מַכֶּה ׀ בַּמַּטֶּה אֲשֶׁר־בְּיָדִי עַל־הַמַּיִם אֲשֶׁר בַּיְאֹר
יח וְנֶהֶפְכוּ לְדָם׃ וְהַדָּגָה אֲשֶׁר־בַּיְאֹר תָּמוּת וּבָאַשׁ הַיְאֹר וְנִלְאוּ

---

the Egyptians. Yeḥezkel (29:3) calls Pharaoh a great crocodile. Thus, the sign is intended to convey that Pharaoh is being confronted by a power greater than any he could summon.

THE PLAGUES

The plagues have three aims: to persuade Pharaoh to let the Israelites go, to punish him and his people for their wrongs, and to communicate to Pharaoh and Egypt that there is a supreme power above and beyond all the forces operative in the universe, a power dedicated to justice and human dignity. The demonstration of God's power that is about to follow is as much for the Egyptians as for the Israelites. The Egyptians worship nature, personified as a series of gods. During the plagues, they will see a power higher than nature, capable of overriding their own most powerful gods. This is important for moral and political reasons. Only if there is a power greater than that of the greatest empire can universal human values like the sanctity of life override the will of the ruler. The gods of the ancient world were deifications of power. Since you worship power, God is saying tacitly to the Egyptians, I will show you a greater power. In the plagues, I will be speaking a language you understand.

The basic requirements of morality are universal. They derive from the covenant with Noaḥ, they are written into human nature, and they apply to all nations. An unjust empire may achieve military and architectural greatness, but in the absence of goodness, it will not survive.

will die; the Nile will stink and the Egyptians will be
19 unable to drink its water." Then the LORD said
to Moshe, "Tell Aharon: Take your staff and stretch out
your hand over the waters of Egypt, their rivers, canals,
ponds, and reservoirs, and they will turn into blood.
There will be blood throughout Egypt, even inside vessels
20 of wood and of stone." Moshe and Aharon did just as the
LORD commanded. Aharon raised his staff, in full view
of Pharaoh and his officials, and struck the water of the
21 Nile, and all the Nile's water turned into blood. The Nile
fish died, and the river stank so that the Egyptians could
not drink its water. Throughout the land of Egypt, blood
22 appeared. But the Egyptian magicians did the same thing
by their sorcery. So Pharaoh's heart remained adamant,
and he would not listen to them, just as the LORD had
23 predicted. Pharaoh turned and went back into his palace
24 and did not take even this to heart. The Egyptians all dug
along the Nile to get drinking water, unable to drink of
25 the waters of the Nile. And seven days went by after the
LORD's striking of the Nile.
26 Then the LORD said to Moshe, "Go to Pharaoh and say to
him: This is what the LORD says: Send My people forth,
27 so that they may serve Me. And if you should refuse to
send them forth – I will scourge your land with frogs
28 from end to end. The Nile will teem with frogs. They

7:22 וַיַּעֲשׂוּ־כֵן חַרְטֻמֵּי מִצְרַיִם בְּלָטֵיהֶם *But the Egyptian magicians did the same thing by their sorcery* – Magic was integral to the culture of ancient Egypt, and magicians were an important class within its society, thought to be able to cure illness, remove bad luck, and curse enemies and opponents. A bitterly ironic note is being struck here. The magicians, intent on demonstrating their skills, are oblivious to the fact that they are making the situation worse, not better. Constructive magic would have been to turn the blood back into water.

This is a classic example of the human tendency to demonstrate power without asking whether its use improves or harms the human condition. "I can" prevails over "I should."

7:27 הִנֵּה אָנֹכִי נֹגֵף אֶת־כָּל־גְּבוּלְךָ בַּצְפַרְדְּעִים *I will scourge your land with frogs* – The reference is probably to the frog goddess

יט מִצְרַיִם לִשְׁתּוֹת מַיִם מִן־הַיְאֹר׃ וַיֹּאמֶר
יהוה אֶל־מֹשֶׁה אֱמֹר אֶל־אַהֲרֹן קַח מַטְּךָ וּנְטֵה־יָדְךָ עַל־
מֵימֵי מִצְרַיִם עַל־נַהֲרֹתָם ׀ עַל־יְאֹרֵיהֶם וְעַל־אַגְמֵיהֶם וְעַל
כָּל־מִקְוֵה מֵימֵיהֶם וְיִהְיוּ־דָם וְהָיָה דָם בְּכָל־אֶרֶץ מִצְרַיִם
כ וּבָעֵצִים וּבָאֲבָנִים׃ וַיַּעֲשׂוּ־כֵן מֹשֶׁה וְאַהֲרֹן כַּאֲשֶׁר ׀ צִוָּה יהוה
וַיָּרֶם בַּמַּטֶּה וַיַּךְ אֶת־הַמַּיִם אֲשֶׁר בַּיְאֹר לְעֵינֵי פַרְעֹה וּלְעֵינֵי
כא עֲבָדָיו וַיֵּהָפְכוּ כָּל־הַמַּיִם אֲשֶׁר־בַּיְאֹר לְדָם׃ וְהַדָּגָה אֲשֶׁר־
בַּיְאֹר מֵתָה וַיִּבְאַשׁ הַיְאֹר וְלֹא־יָכְלוּ מִצְרַיִם לִשְׁתּוֹת מַיִם
כב מִן־הַיְאֹר וַיְהִי הַדָּם בְּכָל־אֶרֶץ מִצְרָיִם׃ וַיַּעֲשׂוּ־כֵן חַרְטֻמֵּי
מִצְרַיִם בְּלָטֵיהֶם וַיֶּחֱזַק לֵב־פַּרְעֹה וְלֹא־שָׁמַע אֲלֵהֶם כַּאֲשֶׁר
כג דִּבֶּר יהוה׃ וַיִּפֶן פַּרְעֹה וַיָּבֹא אֶל־בֵּיתוֹ וְלֹא־שָׁת לִבּוֹ גַּם־
כד לָזֹאת׃ וַיַּחְפְּרוּ כָל־מִצְרַיִם סְבִיבֹת הַיְאֹר מַיִם לִשְׁתּוֹת כִּי
כה לֹא יָכְלוּ לִשְׁתֹּת מִמֵּימֵי הַיְאֹר׃ וַיִּמָּלֵא שִׁבְעַת יָמִים אַחֲרֵי
הַכּוֹת־יהוה אֶת־הַיְאֹר׃
כו וַיֹּאמֶר יהוה אֶל־מֹשֶׁה בֹּא אֶל־פַּרְעֹה וְאָמַרְתָּ אֵלָיו כֹּה
כז אָמַר יהוה שַׁלַּח אֶת־עַמִּי וְיַעַבְדֻנִי׃ וְאִם־מָאֵן אַתָּה לְשַׁלֵּחַ
כח הִנֵּה אָנֹכִי נֹגֵף אֶת־כָּל־גְּבוּלְךָ בַּצְפַרְדְּעִים׃ וְשָׁרַץ הַיְאֹר

---

tradition. A text known as the Admonitions of Ipuwer contains the statement that "the river is blood," one of the symptoms of its vivid description of the collapse of order and the reign of chaos. The Nile was the supreme source of life for ancient Egypt. Its water turning to blood transforms it into a symbol of death. Hence this is not just a wonder but a sign, a symbol. The river that turns to blood is a dramatic enactment of the fact that the Nile, source of life, had become a source of death when male Israelite children were thrown into it to be drowned. That crime, intended to be hidden, is now proclaimed to all in the most graphic way.

The cosmic order is being overturned. Pharaoh, seen as sustainer of that order, is being challenged in his own terms and in his own domain. Pharaohs were known to be capable of rewriting their own history, obliterating the more shameful episodes and aggrandizing their achievements. The plagues are saying, in effect, that there are crimes that cannot be concealed. Nature itself bears witness to the guilt of those who commit crimes against humanity.

will come up into your palace, into your bedroom and
up onto your bed, into the houses of your officials and
of all your people, into your ovens and your kneading
29 pans. The frogs shall climb up onto you and your people
8 1 and all your officials." The LORD said to Moshe, "Speak
to Aharon: Stretch out your hand that holds your staff
over the rivers, the canals, and the pools, and cause frogs
2 to climb up and out onto the land of Egypt." So Aharon
stretched out his hand over the waters of Egypt, and
3 frogs climbed up and covered the Egyptian land. But the
magicians used their sorcery and did the same, making
4 frogs climb up over the land of Egypt. Then Pharaoh
called for Moshe and Aharon and said, "Pray to the LORD
to take the frogs away from me and from my people, and
I will send your people forth to sacrifice to the LORD."
5 Moshe said to Pharaoh, "Gloat over me: you name the
time when I should pray that the frogs be removed, for
you and your officials, and your people, from you and
6 your homes, remaining only in the Nile." "Tomorrow,"
he replied. Moshe said, "It will be as you say. Then you

---

the case of Egypt of the nineteenth dynasty, it resulted in a society in which the most important single institution was the army. This is not freedom but oppression.

8:5 הִתְפָּאֵר עָלַי *Gloat over me* – Alternatively, "I give you the honor." Moshe is offering Pharaoh a face-saving formula. He recognizes that one of the difficulties Pharaoh would confront in conceding the Israelites' request is a loss of face before his councilors, court, and people. A mighty emperor finds it difficult to capitulate to slaves. Moshe therefore offers Pharaoh the chance to say: "I ended the plague, specifying exactly when it would end." Sometimes a face-saving formula is part of conflict resolution.

In a slightly different reading, Moshe, apparently on his own initiative, "gives Pharaoh the honor" of naming a specific time when the plague will stop, precisely because the river turning red, and an attack of frogs, were not unknown in Egypt, albeit on a far lower scale. It is thus more than possible that Pharaoh, his court, and the Egyptians as a whole might regard these things as freak natural occurrences. Moshe wants to show Pharaoh a clear sign that they are nothing of the kind, that they have been sent by God, who is supremely powerful even in Egypt, where other gods are believed to rule.

8:6 לְמַעַן תֵּדַע *Then you will know* – Note again, as throughout the story, the

צְפַרְדְּעִים וְעָלוּ וּבָאוּ בְּבֵיתֶךָ וּבַחֲדַר מִשְׁכָּבְךָ וְעַל־מִטָּתֶךָ
כט וּבְבֵית עֲבָדֶיךָ וּבְעַמֶּךָ וּבְתַנּוּרֶיךָ וּבְמִשְׁאֲרוֹתֶיךָ׃ וּבְכָה
ח א וּבְעַמְּךָ וּבְכָל־עֲבָדֶיךָ יַעֲלוּ הַצְפַרְדְּעִים׃ וַיֹּאמֶר יהוה אֶל־
מֹשֶׁה אֱמֹר אֶל־אַהֲרֹן נְטֵה אֶת־יָדְךָ בְּמַטֶּךָ עַל־הַנְּהָרֹת
עַל־הַיְאֹרִים וְעַל־הָאֲגַמִּים וְהַעַל אֶת־הַצְפַרְדְּעִים עַל־אֶרֶץ
ב מִצְרָיִם׃ וַיֵּט אַהֲרֹן אֶת־יָדוֹ עַל מֵימֵי מִצְרָיִם וַתַּעַל הַצְּפַרְדֵּעַ
ג וַתְּכַס אֶת־אֶרֶץ מִצְרָיִם׃ וַיַּעֲשׂוּ־כֵן הַחַרְטֻמִּים בְּלָטֵיהֶם
ד וַיַּעֲלוּ אֶת־הַצְפַרְדְּעִים עַל־אֶרֶץ מִצְרָיִם׃ וַיִּקְרָא פַרְעֹה
לְמֹשֶׁה וּלְאַהֲרֹן וַיֹּאמֶר הַעְתִּירוּ אֶל־יהוה וְיָסֵר הַצְפַרְדְּעִים
ה מִמֶּנִּי וּמֵעַמִּי וַאֲשַׁלְּחָה אֶת־הָעָם וְיִזְבְּחוּ לַיהוה׃ וַיֹּאמֶר מֹשֶׁה
לְפַרְעֹה הִתְפָּאֵר עָלַי לְמָתַי ׀ אַעְתִּיר לְךָ וְלַעֲבָדֶיךָ וּלְעַמְּךָ
לְהַכְרִית הַצְפַרְדְּעִים מִמְּךָ וּמִבָּתֶּיךָ רַק בַּיְאֹר תִּשָּׁאַרְנָה׃
ו וַיֹּאמֶר לְמָחָר וַיֹּאמֶר כִּדְבָרְךָ לְמַעַן תֵּדַע כִּי־אֵין כַּיהוה

Heqet, Egyptian goddess of life, birth, and fertility, also associated with midwives. There may be a suggestion here of Pharaoh's first instructions to the midwives, to kill the male Israelite children at birth. The frogs would not only have been a source of irritation; they would have been an extension of the guilt of the river turning into blood, the sign now moving inland and coming close to the people. Again, the Egyptian magicians, obsessed with demonstrating their own power, are portrayed ironically. Far from making the frogs go away, they deepen the curse and produce even more.

8:4 הַעְתִּירוּ אֶל־יהוה *Pray to the Lord* – This is the first time Pharaoh asks Moshe and Aharon to intervene on his behalf with God. Note that Pharaoh now uses the four-letter name of God, when earlier he said, "Who is this Lord…? I do not know the Lord." He uses the name twice, as if to emphasize the point: he now knows the Lord. This seems to be a momentary act of contrition on his part; it does not last for long.

8:4 וַאֲשַׁלְּחָה אֶת־הָעָם *And I will send your people forth* – This is the first of what will be many instances of Pharaoh making a promise and then failing to keep it. Recall that this entire episode began with God saying that He was going to reveal Himself in His attribute of fulfilling covenantal promises (see ch. 6, "I am the Lord"). God keeps His word and we must keep ours. That is the essence of covenant. In politics, power is secondary. Fidelity, honoring one's word, keeping one's commitments, is primary. Without fidelity, there is no trust. A society without trust can only be maintained by the use of force. In

7 will know that there is none like the Lord our God. The HAMISHI
frogs will depart from you and from your homes, your
officials, all your people. They will only remain in the
8 Nile." Moshe and Aharon departed Pharaoh's presence,
and Moshe cried out to the Lord about the frogs He
9 had brought upon Pharaoh. The Lord did as Moshe
said, and the frogs in the houses, courtyards, and fields
10 died; they gathered them up into heaping piles, and the
11 stench filled the whole land. But when Pharaoh saw that
respite had come, he hardened his heart and would not
12 listen, just as the Lord had predicted. Then
the Lord said to Moshe, "Tell Aharon: Extend your staff
and strike the dust of the earth; all over Egypt it will be
13 transformed into lice." They did so. Aharon extended
the hand that held his staff and struck the dust of the
earth, and suddenly there were lice on the people, on
the animals. The dust of the earth was turned to lice all
14 across Egypt. The magicians tried to produce lice with
their sorcery, but they could not. Meanwhile the lice still
15 infested people and animals alike. "This," the magicians
told Pharaoh, "is the finger of God." But Pharaoh's heart
was toughened, and – as the Lord had predicted – he

---

not necessarily true of all moral principles, but it is certainly true of justice.

8:10 וַיִּצְבְּרוּ אֹתָם *They gathered them up* – The same root is used in Genesis (*tz-b-r*) to describe how the Egyptians, under Yosef's tutelage, gathered up grain to store for use during the years of famine (Gen. 41:35). This fine use of intertextuality highlights the fact that Egypt availed itself of Yosef's wisdom to avoid catastrophe, but then forgot Yosef and persecuted his people, thus creating catastrophe.

8:10 וַתִּבְאַשׁ הָאָרֶץ *The stench filled the whole land* – This graphic description is intended to give us a sense of what Egypt looks and feels like at this moment. You can smell decay and death everywhere. The fish have died. Now the frogs have died. At least some of the people may be wondering: are we next?

THE FINGER OF GOD

In a sense, this is the first appearance in the Torah of an idea, surprisingly persistent in religious thinking even today, called "the god of the gaps." This holds that a miracle is something for which we cannot yet find a scientific explanation.

ז אֱלֹהֵינוּ׃ וְסָרוּ הַֽצְפַרְדְּעִים מִמְּךָ וּמִבָּתֶּיךָ וּמֵעֲבָדֶיךָ וּמֵעַמֶּךָ חמישי
ח רַק בַּיְאֹר תִּשָּׁאַרְנָה׃ וַיֵּצֵא מֹשֶׁה וְאַהֲרֹן מֵעִם פַּרְעֹה וַיִּצְעַק
מֹשֶׁה אֶל־יהוה עַל־דְּבַר הַצְפַרְדְּעִים אֲשֶׁר־שָׂם לְפַרְעֹה׃
ט וַיַּעַשׂ יהוה כִּדְבַר מֹשֶׁה וַיָּמֻתוּ הַֽצְפַרְדְּעִים מִן־הַבָּתִּים מִן־
י הַחֲצֵרֹת וּמִן־הַשָּׂדֹת׃ וַיִּצְבְּרוּ אֹתָם חֳמָרִם חֳמָרִם וַתִּבְאַשׁ
יא הָאָרֶץ׃ וַיַּרְא פַּרְעֹה כִּי הָיְתָה הָֽרְוָחָה וְהַכְבֵּד אֶת־לִבּוֹ וְלֹא
יב שָׁמַע אֲלֵהֶם כַּאֲשֶׁר דִּבֶּר יהוה׃ וַיֹּאמֶר יהוה
אֶל־מֹשֶׁה אֱמֹר אֶל־אַהֲרֹן נְטֵה אֶת־מַטְּךָ וְהַךְ אֶת־עֲפַר
יג הָאָרֶץ וְהָיָה לְכִנִּם בְּכָל־אֶרֶץ מִצְרָיִם׃ וַיַּעֲשׂוּ־כֵן וַיֵּט אַהֲרֹן
אֶת־יָדוֹ בְמַטֵּהוּ וַיַּךְ אֶת־עֲפַר הָאָרֶץ וַתְּהִי הַכִּנָּם בָּאָדָם
וּבַבְּהֵמָה כָּל־עֲפַר הָאָרֶץ הָיָה כִנִּים בְּכָל־אֶרֶץ מִצְרָיִם׃
יד וַיַּעֲשׂוּ־כֵן הַחַרְטֻמִּים בְּלָטֵיהֶם לְהוֹצִיא אֶת־הַכִּנִּים וְלֹא יָכֹלוּ
טו וַתְּהִי הַכִּנָּם בָּאָדָם וּבַבְּהֵמָה׃ וַיֹּאמְרוּ הַחַרְטֻמִּם אֶל־פַּרְעֹה
אֶצְבַּע אֱלֹהִים הִוא וַיֶּחֱזַק לֵב־פַּרְעֹה וְלֹא־שָׁמַע אֲלֵהֶם

emphasis is on the impression the plagues make on the Egyptians, not the Israelites. As far as the Israelites are concerned, the only significant plague is the last one, the death of the firstborn. That is how matters are framed at the very beginning of Moshe's mission, when God tells him to tell Pharaoh, "Israel is My son, My firstborn. I have told you: Send forth My son, so that he may serve Me. If you refuse to let him go, I will kill your son, your firstborn" (Ex. 4:22). That plague happens so that Pharaoh and the Egyptians will set the Israelites free. The other plagues happen so that the Egyptians should know that "there is none like the Lord our God."

Israel does not need miracles to learn that slavery is wrong or that power corrupts. They have learned it by being a powerless minority in a land not theirs. Egypt, however, does. And indeed the story of the exodus is to become a source of inspiration to many powerless minorities in the course of the centuries, and to lead them to fight and often to win their freedom. It is important for the Egyptians to understand that their system of moral order is showing fatal signs of self-contradiction, and that what they have thought of as strength is in fact weakness. One of the consequences of monotheism is that if there is a single God who is sovereign everywhere, then there is a single moral domain whose fundamental principles hold everywhere. That is

16 would not listen to them. Then the LORD said
to Moshe, "Rise up early in the morning and confront
Pharaoh as he goes out to the water; tell him: This is what
the LORD says: Send My people forth, so that they may
17 serve Me. If you refuse to send them forth, I will send
swarms of insects onto you, your officials, your people,
and your houses. The Egyptians' houses will be filled
with swarms of insects; the ground they stand upon will
18 be covered by them. On that day, I will set the land of
Goshen, where My people live, apart – there, there will
be no swarms – and then you will know that I am the

---

of devastation, and the civilizations they built declined and died, to be remembered only in relics and ruins. Humility is the only antidote to hubris. However great we are, we are small in the scheme of things. That is what God showed the Egyptians in the plague of lice.

8:16 שַׁלַּח עַמִּי וְיַעַבְדֻנִי *Send My people forth, so that they may serve Me* – The Torah does not frame the move from slavery to freedom in terms of the ability to do what you like. Rather, it promotes the freedom to do what you ought. That, for the intellectual architects of freedom in the modern world, such as John Locke, was the difference between liberty and license. Letting the people go – escaping tyranny – was not in and of itself a prelude to freedom. The key distinction throughout the exodus narrative is not between slavery and freedom but between servitude to a human ruler and service to God, creator of all. It is the second way that honors humanity, because it involves acknowledging as our sovereign the One who created each of us in His image.

Thus ends the first cycle of three plagues. The effect has been to move from Egypt's central symbol, the Nile, to homes throughout the land in the form of frogs, to something as tiny and almost invisible as lice. The sense of some large assault on the people and the land has become more and more pervasive as if they were harbingers of some terrible judgment.

8:17 הֶעָרֹב *Swarms of insects* – Others read "wild animals." However, the reading of the plague as insects accords better with the parallelism of the plague of lice, and makes more sense in terms of the Torah's description of "houses being filled" with them.

8:18 כִּי אֲנִי יהוה בְּקֶרֶב הָאָרֶץ *That I am the LORD, here on earth* – Among the most serious enablers of evil is the idea that no one sees what we are doing, that there is no ultimate justice in the world, that

טז כַּאֲשֶׁר דִּבֶּר יְהוָה: וַיֹּאמֶר יְהוָה אֶל־מֹשֶׁה הַשְׁכֵּם ו
בַּבֹּקֶר וְהִתְיַצֵּב לִפְנֵי פַרְעֹה הִנֵּה יוֹצֵא הַמָּיְמָה וְאָמַרְתָּ אֵלָיו
יז כֹּה אָמַר יְהוָה שַׁלַּח עַמִּי וְיַעַבְדֻנִי: כִּי אִם־אֵינְךָ מְשַׁלֵּחַ
אֶת־עַמִּי הִנְנִי מַשְׁלִיחַ בְּךָ וּבַעֲבָדֶיךָ וּבְעַמְּךָ וּבְבָתֶּיךָ אֶת־
הֶעָרֹב וּמָלְאוּ בָּתֵּי מִצְרַיִם אֶת־הֶעָרֹב וְגַם הָאֲדָמָה אֲשֶׁר־הֵם
יח עָלֶיהָ: וְהִפְלֵיתִי בַיּוֹם הַהוּא אֶת־אֶרֶץ גֹּשֶׁן אֲשֶׁר עַמִּי עֹמֵד
עָלֶיהָ לְבִלְתִּי הֱיוֹת־שָׁם עָרֹב לְמַעַן תֵּדַע כִּי אֲנִי יְהוָה בְּקֶרֶב

Science is natural; religion is supernatural. In the magicians' terms – what magicians (or technocrats) cannot reproduce must be the result of divine intervention. This approach leads inevitably to the conclusion that religion and science are opposed. The more we can explain scientifically or control technologically, the less need we have for faith. As the scope of science expands, the place of God progressively diminishes to a vanishing point.

What the Torah is intimating here is that this is a pagan mode of thought, not a Jewish one. The Egyptians admit that Moshe and Aharon are genuine prophets when they perform wonders beyond the scope of their own magic. But this is not why we believe in Moshe and Aharon. On this, Rambam (*Hilkhot Yesodei HaTorah* 8:1) is unequivocal. The primary way in which we encounter God is not through miracles but through His word – the revelation – Torah – which is the Jewish people's constitution as a nation under the sovereignty of God.

To be sure, God is in the events which, seeming to defy nature, we call miracles. But He is also in nature itself. Far from diminishing our religious sense, science (rightly understood) should enlarge it, teaching us to see "how many are Your works, LORD; You made them all in wisdom" (Ps. 104:24). Above all, God is to be found in the voice heard at Sinai, teaching us how to construct a society that will be the opposite of Egypt: in which the few do not enslave the many, nor are strangers mistreated.

The best argument against the world of ancient Egypt was divine irony. The cultic priests and magicians who think they can control the sun and the Nile discover that they cannot even produce a louse. What the Egyptian magicians (and their latter-day successors) do not understand is that power over nature is not an end in itself, but solely the means to *ethical* ends. The lice are God's joke at the expense of the magicians who believe that because they control the forces of nature, they are masters of human destiny. They are wrong.

Technological prowess has led human beings, time and again, to believe that they were like gods. They could scale the heavens, bend nature to their purposes, and construct vast edifices to their glory. Yet in their wake they left a trail

19 LORD, here on earth. Between My people and yours I will SHISHI
mark out a separation; tomorrow, this sign will come to
20 be." The LORD did so. Great swarms of insects infested
Pharaoh's palace and the houses of his officials. All across
21 Egypt, swarms of insects devastated the land. Pharaoh
called for Moshe and Aharon. "Go," he said, "and sacrifice
22 to your God here in the land." But Moshe replied, "That
would not be right for us to do; our sacrifice to the LORD
our God is an abomination to the Egyptians. If, before
the Egyptians' eyes, we offer the sacrifice they consider
23 an abomination, will they not stone us to death? Send
us forth, three days' journey into the wilderness, to
sacrifice there to the LORD our God, as He will instruct

---

differences between two of these groups led to a war, which required the Roman army to suppress it. Moshe is therefore being realistic, as well as understanding Pharaoh's mindset, when he suspects that, in Pharaoh's concession, he and his people are being invited into a trap.

MOSHE'S REQUEST

At no stage does Moshe say explicitly that he is proposing that the people should be allowed to leave permanently, never to return. He talks of a three-day journey. There is an argument between him and Pharaoh as to who is to go. Moshe consistently asks for permission to worship God at some place that is not Egypt. But he does not speak about freedom. Why not? Why does he create, and not correct, a false impression?

The terms of this encounter between Moshe and Pharaoh are part of a wider pattern that we have already observed in the Torah. When Yaakov leaves Lavan we read: "Yaakov deceived Lavan the Aramean by not telling him that he was running away" (Gen. 31:20). He has to tell at best a half-truth when Esav suggests that they travel together (33:13–14). When Yaakov's sons are trying to rescue their sister Dina, who has been raped and abducted by Shekhem the Hivite, they "spoke deceptively" (34:13) when Shekhem and his father propose that the entire family should come and settle with them.

Earlier still we find that three times Avraham and Yitzḥak, forced to leave home because of famine, have to pretend that they are their wives' brothers, not their husbands, because they fear that otherwise they will be killed so that Sara or Rivka can be taken into the king's harem (chs. 12, 20, 26).

These echoes cannot be entirely accidental or coincidental to the biblical narrative as a whole. The implication seems to be this: Without their own land, Jews in the biblical age are in danger if they tell the truth. They are at constant

יט הָאָֽרֶץ׃ וְשַׂמְתִּ֣י פְדֻ֔ת בֵּ֥ין עַמִּ֖י וּבֵ֣ין עַמֶּ֑ךָ לְמָחָ֥ר יִהְיֶ֖ה הָאֹ֥ת ששי
כ הַזֶּֽה׃ וַיַּ֤עַשׂ יהוה֙ כֵּ֔ן וַיָּבֹא֙ עָרֹ֣ב כָּבֵ֔ד בֵּ֥יתָה פַרְעֹ֖ה וּבֵ֣ית
עֲבָדָ֑יו וּבְכָל־אֶ֧רֶץ מִצְרַ֛יִם תִּשָּׁחֵ֥ת הָאָ֖רֶץ מִפְּנֵ֥י הֶעָרֹֽב׃
כא וַיִּקְרָ֣א פַרְעֹ֔ה אֶל־מֹשֶׁ֖ה וּֽלְאַהֲרֹ֑ן וַיֹּ֗אמֶר לְכ֛וּ זִבְח֥וּ לֵאלֹהֵיכֶ֖ם
כב בָּאָֽרֶץ׃ וַיֹּ֣אמֶר מֹשֶׁ֗ה לֹ֤א נָכוֹן֙ לַעֲשׂ֣וֹת כֵּ֔ן כִּ֚י תּוֹעֲבַ֣ת מִצְרַ֔יִם
נִזְבַּ֖ח לַיהוָ֣ה אֱלֹהֵ֑ינוּ הֵ֣ן נִזְבַּ֞ח אֶת־תּוֹעֲבַ֥ת מִצְרַ֛יִם לְעֵינֵיהֶ֖ם
כג וְלֹ֥א יִסְקְלֻֽנוּ׃ דֶּ֚רֶךְ שְׁלֹ֣שֶׁת יָמִ֔ים נֵלֵ֖ךְ בַּמִּדְבָּ֑ר וְזָבַ֙חְנוּ֙ לַיהוָ֣ה

God is distant. This plague is meant to bring home to the Egyptians that God is everywhere, sees everything, and calls us all into judgment.

8:19 וְשַׂמְתִּי פְדֻת *I will mark out a separation* – The phrase "I will mark out a separation" – *Vehifleti* – comes from the same root as "wonder." The wonder is that a blind phenomenon of nature could make such a distinction between different religious and ethnic groups. God must be directing events. Geographically the distinction is facilitated by the positioning of the Israelites at the northern end of the Nile Delta, in Lower Egypt. It is as if God were saying through Moshe to Pharaoh: You have singled out this people for oppression; I will single them out for protection.

8:21 וַיִּקְרָא פַרְעֹה אֶל־מֹשֶׁה וּלְאַהֲרֹן *Pharaoh called for Moshe and Aharon* – Note that he no longer turns to his magicians. He knows the plagues are intensifying, that the force driving them is beyond their replication or control. He must therefore turn directly to Moshe. He proposes a compromise response to the request of the Israelites. Yes, they may worship their God. At this point it seems as if he has acceded to their request. With one word, however, the last in his utterance, he takes it back. They may worship but only "in the land." They may not leave Egypt. Pharaoh's deteriorating character is manifest in the fact that the offer he makes here is less than he made in the previous plague, where he promised to let the people go. He must know that it will be unacceptable to Moshe.

Moshe's reply is calm and intentionally uses language that Pharaoh will understand. Rather than insisting on nothing less than their complete freedom, he appeals to Pharaoh's understanding that for the Israelites to worship their God in a public manner in Egypt would be an invitation to violence.

8:22 תּוֹעֲבַת מִצְרַיִם *An abomination to the Egyptians* – Shadal (on this verse) quotes the Greek historian Plutarch on how an Egyptian king fostered different religions among his diverse population, to prevent them coming together to unite against his rule and possibly dethrone him. On one occasion, religious

24 us.” Pharaoh said, “I will send you forth; you shall
sacrifice to the LORD your God in the wilderness. Just do
25 not go far away. Pray for me.” Moshe said, “I am going to
leave you and pray to the LORD. Tomorrow, the swarms
of insects will move on from Pharaoh, his officials, and
his people. But let Pharaoh no more deceive us, refusing
to send the people forth to make their sacrifice to the
26 27 LORD.” Moshe left Pharaoh and prayed to the LORD. And
the LORD did what Moshe asked. He diverted the swarms
of insects from Pharaoh, his officials, his people – not one
28 was left behind. But this time too, Pharaoh hardened his
heart and did not send the people forth.
9 1 Then the LORD said to Moshe, “Go to Pharaoh. Tell him:
This is what the LORD, God of the Hebrews, says: Send My
2 people forth to serve Me. If you refuse to send them forth,
3 if you continue to hold them back, the LORD’s hand will
turn against your livestock in the field. A deadly epidemic
will strike horses, donkeys, and camels, cattle and flocks.
4 But the LORD will set Israel’s livestock apart from Egypt’s;

---

truth. Where there is freedom there can be truth. Without it, there cannot. A society in which people are forced to be less than fully honest merely to survive and not provoke further oppression is anathema to God, whose seal is truth.

9:3 יַד־יהוה *The LORD’s hand* – The lice were “the finger of God.” This plague is the hand of the LORD. The expression “the hand of the LORD” was familiar in the ancient Near East. It signified power, sometimes punitive, sometimes coercive. The change in terminology signals an intensification of the plagues from temporary discomfort to permanent and serious loss. God through Moshe is showing Pharaoh how self-destructive his behavior is. Pharaoh intends to harm the Israelites, but they will not be harmed. They will not lose any of their cattle to the disease. It will be his own people who suffer. Those who seek to harm others end by harming themselves.

9:3 דֶּבֶר *A deadly epidemic* – A cattle disease, this constitutes a devastating assault on the Egyptian economy. Naturalistically, this may be a disease conveyed by the rotting frogs. As a sign, it may be intended to show the vulnerability of the various animal gods in Egyptian culture. More simply, by harming the Egyptian economy and people’s livelihoods, it shows again that the country is suffering by prolonging the suffering of the

כד אֱלֹהֵינוּ כַּאֲשֶׁר יֹאמַר אֵלֵינוּ: וַיֹּאמֶר פַּרְעֹה אָנֹכִי אֲשַׁלַּח
אֶתְכֶם וּזְבַחְתֶּם לַיהוה אֱלֹהֵיכֶם בַּמִּדְבָּר רַק הַרְחֵק לֹא־
כה תַרְחִיקוּ לָלֶכֶת הַעְתִּירוּ בַּעֲדִי: וַיֹּאמֶר מֹשֶׁה הִנֵּה אָנֹכִי יוֹצֵא
מֵעִמָּךְ וְהַעְתַּרְתִּי אֶל־יהוה וְסָר הֶעָרֹב מִפַּרְעֹה מֵעֲבָדָיו
וּמֵעַמּוֹ מָחָר רַק אַל־יֹסֵף פַּרְעֹה הָתֵל לְבִלְתִּי שַׁלַּח אֶת־הָעָם
כו לִזְבֹּחַ לַיהוה: וַיֵּצֵא מֹשֶׁה מֵעִם פַּרְעֹה וַיֶּעְתַּר אֶל־יהוה:
כז וַיַּעַשׂ יהוה כִּדְבַר מֹשֶׁה וַיָּסַר הֶעָרֹב מִפַּרְעֹה מֵעֲבָדָיו וּמֵעַמּוֹ
כח לֹא נִשְׁאַר אֶחָד: וַיַּכְבֵּד פַּרְעֹה אֶת־לִבּוֹ גַּם בַּפַּעַם הַזֹּאת
וְלֹא שִׁלַּח אֶת־הָעָם:

ט
א וַיֹּאמֶר יהוה אֶל־מֹשֶׁה בֹּא אֶל־פַּרְעֹה וְדִבַּרְתָּ אֵלָיו כֹּה־
ב אָמַר יהוה אֱלֹהֵי הָעִבְרִים שַׁלַּח אֶת־עַמִּי וְיַעַבְדֻנִי: כִּי
ג אִם־מָאֵן אַתָּה לְשַׁלֵּחַ וְעוֹדְךָ מַחֲזִיק בָּם: הִנֵּה יַד־יהוה
הוֹיָה בְּמִקְנְךָ אֲשֶׁר בַּשָּׂדֶה בַּסּוּסִים בַּחֲמֹרִים בַּגְּמַלִּים בַּבָּקָר
ד וּבַצֹּאן דֶּבֶר כָּבֵד מְאֹד: וְהִפְלָה יהוה בֵּין מִקְנֵה יִשְׂרָאֵל

risk of being killed or at best enslaved.

Why must they deceive? Because they are powerless in an age of power. They are a small family, at best a small nation, in an age of empires. They have to use their wits to survive. By and large they do not tell lies, but they can create a false impression. This is not how things should be. But it is how they were before Jews had their own land, their one and only defensible space. It is how people in impossible situations are forced to be if they are to exist at all.

No one should be forced to live a lie. When your nation is being enslaved, however, and its male children murdered, you have to liberate them by whatever means are possible. Moshe, who has already seen that his first encounter with Pharaoh made things worse for his people – they still have to make the same quota of bricks but now also have to gather their own straw (Ex. 5:6–8) – does not want to risk making them worse still.

The Torah here is not condoning deceit. To the contrary, it is condemning a system in which telling the truth may put your life at risk, as it still does in many tyrannical or totalitarian societies today. Judaism – a religion of dissent, questioning, and "arguments for the sake of Heaven" – is a faith that values intellectual honesty and moral truthfulness above all things. Every *Amida* ends with the prayer "My God, guard my tongue from evil and my lips from deceitful speech." The Torah is showing us here the connection between freedom and

5 none belonging to the Israelites will die. The LORD has set
His appointed time; tomorrow the LORD will bring this
6 about in the land." And the next day, the LORD brought
it to be. All the livestock of the Egyptians perished, but
7 of the Israelites' livestock, not one creature died. Pharaoh
investigated the matter and discovered that not one
among Israel's livestock had died. But still Pharaoh's heart
remained hard, and he would not send the people forth.
8 Then the LORD said to Moshe and Aharon, "Take a
handful of soot from a furnace and throw it up in the air
9 before Pharaoh's eyes. It will become a cloud of dust over
all the land of Egypt, and on people and animals it will
become a rash, breaking out into boils on people and
10 animals throughout the land of Egypt." So they took soot
from the furnace and stood before Pharaoh. Moshe threw
it up in the air, and it became a rash that broke into boils on
11 people and animals. The magicians could not stand before

---

used by the Israelites. This sixth plague suggests that the resource that they use for building is now about to be used for destructive purposes. There may be a distant reminder here of the backbreaking labor of brick making that the Egyptians imposed on the Israelites.

Boils in the Bible seem to be a peculiarly difficult trial. In the book that bears his name, Iyov withstands many terrible tragedies and does not lose faith until his body is covered with boils, at which point he breaks down and curses his fate. Here, the Torah adds that not only can the magicians not replicate this plague – since their failure to replicate the third plague, their inability has been taken for granted – but they are so badly afflicted by it that they can no longer stand. Moshe and Aharon are standing before Pharaoh, but the magicians are no longer able to stand before them. Having tried to humiliate Moshe and Aharon, now the magicians themselves are humiliated. Magicians in the ancient world also had a role as physicians. Now they cannot heal themselves. Their magic has failed them.

The description of the effects of the plague – a rash breaking out into boils – answers to symptoms of anthrax, a known disease in ancient Egypt (see Deut. 28:27). If this is indeed the nature of the plague, it again suggests an intertwined presence of both supernatural and natural. Moshe and Aharon's act in throwing the soot into the air signals that what is about to happen next should not be treated as a mere natural occurrence.

ה וּבֵין מִקְנֵה מִצְרָיִם וְלֹא יָמוּת מִכׇּל־לִבְנֵי יִשְׂרָאֵל דָּבָר׃ וַיָּשֶׂם
יְהוָה מוֹעֵד לֵאמֹר מָחָר יַעֲשֶׂה יְהוָה הַדָּבָר הַזֶּה בָּאָרֶץ׃
ו וַיַּעַשׂ יְהוָה אֶת־הַדָּבָר הַזֶּה מִמָּחֳרָת וַיָּמׇת כֹּל מִקְנֵה מִצְרָיִם
ז וּמִמִּקְנֵה בְנֵי־יִשְׂרָאֵל לֹא־מֵת אֶחָד׃ וַיִּשְׁלַח פַּרְעֹה וְהִנֵּה
לֹא־מֵת מִמִּקְנֵה יִשְׂרָאֵל עַד־אֶחָד וַיִּכְבַּד לֵב פַּרְעֹה וְלֹא
שִׁלַּח אֶת־הָעָם׃
ח וַיֹּאמֶר יְהוָה אֶל־מֹשֶׁה וְאֶל־אַהֲרֹן קְחוּ לָכֶם מְלֹא חׇפְנֵיכֶם
ט פִּיחַ כִּבְשָׁן וּזְרָקוֹ מֹשֶׁה הַשָּׁמַיְמָה לְעֵינֵי פַרְעֹה׃ וְהָיָה לְאָבָק
עַל כׇּל־אֶרֶץ מִצְרָיִם וְהָיָה עַל־הָאָדָם וְעַל־הַבְּהֵמָה לִשְׁחִין
י פֹּרֵחַ אֲבַעְבֻּעֹת בְּכׇל־אֶרֶץ מִצְרָיִם׃ וַיִּקְחוּ אֶת־פִּיחַ הַכִּבְשָׁן
וַיַּעַמְדוּ לִפְנֵי פַרְעֹה וַיִּזְרֹק אֹתוֹ מֹשֶׁה הַשָּׁמָיְמָה וַיְהִי שְׁחִין
יא אֲבַעְבֻּעֹת פֹּרֵחַ בָּאָדָם וּבַבְּהֵמָה׃ וְלֹא־יָכְלוּ הַחַרְטֻמִּים

Israelites. The Egyptians, not the Israelites, repeatedly become the losers. The plagues are intensifying in seriousness. No longer about temporary discomfort, they are now about laying waste to the country and its natural resources.

There is a wordplay between *dever*, "epidemic," in this verse, and the threefold appearance of *davar*, "word" or "thing," in the subsequent three verses. Unheeded, the word can turn into a plague.

9:7 וַיִּשְׁלַח פַּרְעֹה *Pharaoh investigated the matter* – Unlike other natural disasters, plagues spread. There are no effective boundaries. Pharaoh is thus genuinely perplexed as to how the Israelites' cattle are unaffected. He sends officials to the Israelite territory in Goshen to see whether it is true that none of their cattle have died. They confirm that it is. By now, Pharaoh has unmistakable evidence that a vast power is arrayed against him, and that he can disarm it by the simple act of letting the Israelites leave his country. Yet he does not do so. This act of sending people to check whether the Israelites have been protected, and then ignoring the evidence that they bring back, represents, perhaps, an extreme case of the confirmation bias in which we take note of the evidence that supports our view, and ignore that which negates it. This is a high point in Pharaoh's obstinacy: from this point onward, for the last five plagues, the text will tell us that God hardens, strengthens, or makes heavy his heart.

9:8 מְלֹא חׇפְנֵיכֶם פִּיחַ *A handful of soot* – The Egyptians used furnaces to fire bricks, in addition to the sun-dried method

Moshe because of their boils; for the boils had affected
12 them as they had the rest of the Egyptians. But the LORD
strengthened Pharaoh's heart, and he would not listen to
13 them, just as the LORD had told Moshe. Then
the LORD said to Moshe, "Rise up early in the morning
and confront Pharaoh. Tell him: This is what the LORD,
God of the Hebrews, says: Send My people forth to serve
14 Me, or this time I will set the full force of My plagues
upon you, your officials, and your people so that you will
15 know that there is none like Me in all the world. By now
I could have stretched out My hand and struck you and
your people with an epidemic that would have wiped
16 you off the face of the earth. But I have let you survive for
this purpose – to show you My power, and to have My
17 name known throughout the land. You are still abusing SHEVI'I

---

them. Their acts appear to the outside as ever more irrational. And they are indeed self-destructive. But Pharaoh is now a prisoner within the cage he has made for himself. Having steadfastly refused, in the name of *Ma'at,* order, to grant the Israelites their freedom to leave, he cannot back down now without making himself a laughingstock. Hence the irony and pathos of these last plagues. Pharaoh, having turned free men into slaves, is now himself a slave of the system he has created.

9:14 אֲנִי שֹׁלֵחַ אֶת־כָּל־מַגֵּפֹתַי אֶל־לִבְּךָ *I will set the full force of My plagues upon you* – The Hebrew emphasizes that they will be sent (literally) "into your heart." The point of the plagues is not just the physical phenomena they constitute, but rather the effect they have on Pharaoh and his people. They are not just wonders; they are signs. A sign is an encoded message. It communicates. A wonder, by contrast, conveys no message. It produces awe. A sign exists within culture, a wonder within nature. To the Israelites, the plagues are wonders. To the Egyptians, they are signs. They embody a truth, that there is a God of all the earth and all humanity, who stands above all other powers and represents a universal ethic of respect for persons. Rarely does God intervene in history as intensely as He does in the course of the exodus. But this story is meant to be handed on across the generations, giving hope to the hopeless and dignity to those ground down. There is a moral shape to events. As Dr. Martin Luther King, Jr. said: "The arc of a moral universe is long, but it bends toward justice."

9:16 סַפֵּר שְׁמִי בְּכָל־הָאָרֶץ *My name known throughout the land* – In the ancient

לַעֲמֹד לִפְנֵי מֹשֶׁה מִפְּנֵי הַשְּׁחִין כִּי־הָיָה הַשְּׁחִין בַּחֲרְטֻמִּם
יב וּבְכָל־מִצְרָיִם׃ וַיְחַזֵּק יהוה אֶת־לֵב פַּרְעֹה וְלֹא שָׁמַע אֲלֵהֶם
יג כַּאֲשֶׁר דִּבֶּר יהוה אֶל־מֹשֶׁה׃ וַיֹּאמֶר יהוה אֶל־
מֹשֶׁה הַשְׁכֵּם בַּבֹּקֶר וְהִתְיַצֵּב לִפְנֵי פַרְעֹה וְאָמַרְתָּ אֵלָיו
יד כֹּה־אָמַר יהוה אֱלֹהֵי הָעִבְרִים שַׁלַּח אֶת־עַמִּי וְיַעַבְדֻנִי׃ כִּי ׀
בַּפַּעַם הַזֹּאת אֲנִי שֹׁלֵחַ אֶת־כָּל־מַגֵּפֹתַי אֶל־לִבְּךָ וּבַעֲבָדֶיךָ
טו וּבְעַמֶּךָ בַּעֲבוּר תֵּדַע כִּי אֵין כָּמֹנִי בְּכָל־הָאָרֶץ׃ כִּי עַתָּה
שָׁלַחְתִּי אֶת־יָדִי וָאַךְ אוֹתְךָ וְאֶת־עַמְּךָ בַּדָּבֶר וַתִּכָּחֵד מִן־
טז הָאָרֶץ׃ וְאוּלָם בַּעֲבוּר זֹאת הֶעֱמַדְתִּיךָ בַּעֲבוּר הַרְאֹתְךָ
יז אֶת־כֹּחִי וּלְמַעַן סַפֵּר שְׁמִי בְּכָל־הָאָרֶץ׃ עוֹדְךָ מִסְתּוֹלֵל שביעי

9:12 וַיְחַזֵּק יהוה אֶת־לֵב פַּרְעֹה *But the LORD strengthened Pharaoh's heart* – This is the first time that God is described as hardening or strengthening Pharaoh's heart. Significantly, it happens in the sixth plague. During the first five, Pharaoh's refusal to let the Israelites go was his own choice. Rashi (on Ex. 7:3) understands God's hardening of Pharaoh's heart in the last five plagues as a form of punishment for the first five. Rambam interprets it as meaning that "repentance was withheld from him, and the liberty to turn from his wickedness was not accorded to him" (*Hilkhot Teshuva* 6:3). Rabbi Yosef Albo and Sforno suggest the opposite. God hardens Pharaoh's heart precisely to restore his free will. After the succession of plagues that have devastated the land, Pharaoh is under overwhelming pressure to let the Israelites go. Were he to do so, it would not be out of free choice, but rather under force majeure. God therefore toughens – strengthens – Pharaoh's heart so that even after the first five plagues he is genuinely free to say yes or no (*Sefer HaIkkarim* 4:25; Sforno on Ex. 7:3). Simplest and most profound are the words of the talmudic Sages about the *yetzer hara*, the evil impulse: "R. Assi said: At first the evil impulse is as thin as a spider's gossamer, but in the end it is as thick as a cart rope. Rava said: At first the evil impulse is called a 'wayfarer,' then a 'guest,' then finally a 'master'" (Sukka 52a–b). Evil traps the evildoer in its mesh. Slowly but surely he or she loses freedom and becomes not evil's master but its slave.

Meanwhile, the plagues are deepening. Animal disease has affected the cattle. Boils have had such an impact that Pharaoh's own court magicians are unable to stand. Shortly, his court will beg him to let the Israelites go. Pharaoh is becoming more and more isolated, as often happens to absolute rulers when they lose the support of those around

18 your power over My people, refusing to let them go. And
so this time tomorrow I will bring a hailstorm on Egypt
heavier than any it has suffered, from the day Egypt was
19 established until now. Give an order now to bring in
your livestock and all else you have in the field. Anyone
or any animal in the open, any not brought under shelter,
20 will die when the hail beats down." Those of Pharaoh's
officials who feared the LORD's word hurried to bring in
21 their slaves and livestock. And those who set no stock in
the LORD's word kept their slaves and livestock where they
were in the fields.
22 The LORD said to Moshe, "Reach your hand out to
the sky, that hail may fall on all the land of Egypt, on
the people and the animals and everything growing in
23 Egypt's fields." Moshe raised his staff toward the sky; the
LORD sent thunderclaps and hail. Fire struck the ground,
and the LORD rained down hail on the land of Egypt.
24 The hail, with fire blazing inside it, battered so hard that
there had been nothing like it anywhere in Egypt since it

---

the speech is unprecedentedly long and emphatic. "I could," He says, "have destroyed you completely. But I have let you survive so that you will know who and what I am. You are still 'abusing your power' (Ex. 9:17) over My people. What you have been doing to them will now be done to you."

There is a sense of progression in the plagues. The first six were set in motion by the inundation of the Nile. First came the plague of blood. The change in the water would have sent the frogs to land. Their decomposing bodies may have been fertile breeding grounds for the lice, the swarms of flies and the infections they carried with them affecting first cattle, then humans. Various accounts of the plagues analyzed on naturalistic lines of epidemiology link these first six plagues together as a closely related group in the months following the inundation of the Nile in September-October. The last cycle of three plagues are set later, however, nearer harvest time, culminating in the tenth plague in the month of Nisan, that is, spring.

9:24 וְאֵשׁ מִתְלַקַּחַת בְּתוֹךְ הַבָּרָד *The hail, with fire blazing inside it* – A miracle within a miracle: Fire and ice coexist as they would not naturally do (Rashi, Ibn Ezra). The same phrase appears in the mystical vision of Yeḥezkel, when he sees "a cloud with flashing lightning" (Ezek. 1:4). The hail might have borne

יח בְּעַמִּי לְבִלְתִּי שַׁלְּחָם: הִנְנִי מַמְטִיר כָּעֵת מָחָר בָּרָד כָּבֵד
מְאֹד אֲשֶׁר לֹא־הָיָה כָמֹהוּ בְּמִצְרַיִם לְמִן־הַיּוֹם הִוָּסְדָה וְעַד־
יט עָתָּה: וְעַתָּה שְׁלַח הָעֵז אֶת־מִקְנְךָ וְאֵת כָּל־אֲשֶׁר לְךָ בַּשָּׂדֶה
כָּל־הָאָדָם וְהַבְּהֵמָה אֲשֶׁר־יִמָּצֵא בַשָּׂדֶה וְלֹא יֵאָסֵף הַבַּיְתָה
כ וְיָרַד עֲלֵהֶם הַבָּרָד וָמֵתוּ: הַיָּרֵא אֶת־דְּבַר יהוה מֵעַבְדֵי
כא פַּרְעֹה הֵנִיס אֶת־עֲבָדָיו וְאֶת־מִקְנֵהוּ אֶל־הַבָּתִּים: וַאֲשֶׁר
לֹא־שָׂם לִבּוֹ אֶל־דְּבַר יהוה וַיַּעֲזֹב אֶת־עֲבָדָיו וְאֶת־מִקְנֵהוּ
בַּשָּׂדֶה:
כב וַיֹּאמֶר יהוה אֶל־מֹשֶׁה נְטֵה אֶת־יָדְךָ עַל־הַשָּׁמַיִם וִיהִי בָרָד
בְּכָל־אֶרֶץ מִצְרָיִם עַל־הָאָדָם וְעַל־הַבְּהֵמָה וְעַל כָּל־עֵשֶׂב
כג הַשָּׂדֶה בְּאֶרֶץ מִצְרָיִם: וַיֵּט מֹשֶׁה אֶת־מַטֵּהוּ עַל־הַשָּׁמַיִם
וַיהוה נָתַן קֹלֹת וּבָרָד וַתִּהֲלַךְ־אֵשׁ אָרְצָה וַיַּמְטֵר יהוה בָּרָד
כד עַל־אֶרֶץ מִצְרָיִם: וַיְהִי בָרָד וְאֵשׁ מִתְלַקַּחַת בְּתוֹךְ הַבָּרָד
כָּבֵד מְאֹד אֲשֶׁר לֹא־הָיָה כָמֹהוּ בְּכָל־אֶרֶץ מִצְרַיִם מֵאָז

---

world, each nation had its gods, and they were territorially limited. They were gods of this place, not that. This is the essential meaning of Pharaoh's remark to Moshe when he demands the Israelites' release in the name of God. Pharaoh replies: "Who is this Lord that I should obey Him and send Israel forth? I do not know the Lord, and I will not send Israel forth" (Ex. 5:2). This does not mean that he does not know who the God of the Israelites is. It means that within Egypt, the gods of Egypt rule. The book of Exodus presents the idea of a God not territorially bound, a God of anywhere and everywhere.

9:22 נְטֵה אֶת־יָדְךָ *Reach your hand out* – Now begins the third cycle of plagues (see ch. 7, "The Plagues") and an intensification of the drama they represent. Not only will they be devastating. They will be an unmistakable sign to Egypt that "the time is out of joint," that order has been turned into chaos, that the very forces of nature are fighting against them, that there is a supreme power beyond all the powers that they have traditionally worshipped, and that their resistance to God is destined to fail. At this point, Aharon disappears from the scene and Moshe alone stands before Pharaoh.

As happens with the first of each of the three plague cycles, God sends a message to Pharaoh, telling him why these devastating events are about to befall him and his people. In this case,

25 first became a nation. The hail struck everything in the
open field throughout all Egypt: people, animals, and
everything growing in the fields, and it smashed asunder
26 every tree. Only in Goshen, where the Israelites lived,
27 no hail fell. Then Pharaoh sent for Moshe and Aharon
and said to them, "This time I have sinned. The Lord is
28 in the right, and I and my people are guilty. Pray to the
Lord. Enough of God's thunder and hail – I will send
29 you forth. You need not wait any longer." Moshe said to
him, "As I leave the city, I will spread out my hands to the
Lord. The thunder will stop and there will be no more
hail. You will then know that the world belongs to the
30 Lord. But I know that you and your officials still do not
31 hold the Lord God in awe." By then the flax and barley
had been destroyed, because the barley was ripe and

---

outside the city. Why would He not speak to him within the city? Because it was full of abominations and idols" (*Mekhilta DeRabbi Yishmael, Massekhta Defisha* 1).

The seat of politics is not where we meet God. The secularization of politics is driven by a religious vision. It says that power is not to be sacralized. Rulers, kings, and emperors are not holy. They are there to serve, not to be served. All power is subject to the overarching imperatives of the right and the just. The moment it oversteps those limits, it is *ultra vires* and may rightly be opposed.

Furthermore, for the first time, God and religion are deterritorialized. God created everything. He is God of everywhere. There is no longer a god of this city and a god of that, of these people as opposed to those. God is intervening to deliver one nation out of another, what we would call today an international intervention in defense of human rights.

Note that it is not the hail, but the stopping of the hail, that will teach Pharaoh that "the world belongs to the Lord." God's greatness lies not only in power, but in the limitation of power, not only in His ability to create but also in His ability to cease. All natural forces continue until their energy is no more. God alone can say "stop." That is why the Sabbath, when God stopped creating, is holy. God's ability to stop the hail is greater than His ability to bring it in the first place (Rabbi Samson Raphael Hirsch). At the end of the *parasha* we are left in suspense; as the story continues to unfold we will witness God conclusively saying to Pharaoh, as to the sea (Job 38:11), "Just this far and no more."

כה הָיְתָה לְגוֹי: וַיַּךְ הַבָּרָד בְּכָל־אֶרֶץ מִצְרַיִם אֵת כָּל־אֲשֶׁר
בַּשָּׂדֶה מֵאָדָם וְעַד־בְּהֵמָה וְאֵת כָּל־עֵשֶׂב הַשָּׂדֶה הִכָּה
כו הַבָּרָד וְאֶת־כָּל־עֵץ הַשָּׂדֶה שִׁבֵּר: רַק בְּאֶרֶץ גֹּשֶׁן אֲשֶׁר־שָׁם
כז בְּנֵי יִשְׂרָאֵל לֹא הָיָה בָּרָד: וַיִּשְׁלַח פַּרְעֹה וַיִּקְרָא לְמֹשֶׁה
וּלְאַהֲרֹן וַיֹּאמֶר אֲלֵהֶם חָטָאתִי הַפָּעַם יהוה הַצַּדִּיק וַאֲנִי
כח וְעַמִּי הָרְשָׁעִים: הַעְתִּירוּ אֶל־יְהוָה וְרַב מִהְיֹת קֹלֹת אֱלֹהִים
כט וּבָרָד וַאֲשַׁלְּחָה אֶתְכֶם וְלֹא תֹסִפוּן לַעֲמֹד: וַיֹּאמֶר אֵלָיו
מֹשֶׁה כְּצֵאתִי אֶת־הָעִיר אֶפְרֹשׂ אֶת־כַּפַּי אֶל־יְהוָה הַקֹּלוֹת
יֶחְדָּלוּן וְהַבָּרָד לֹא יִהְיֶה־עוֹד לְמַעַן תֵּדַע כִּי לַיהוָה הָאָרֶץ:
ל וְאַתָּה וַעֲבָדֶיךָ יָדַעְתִּי כִּי טֶרֶם תִּירְאוּן מִפְּנֵי יְהוָה אֱלֹהִים:
לא וְהַפִּשְׁתָּה וְהַשְּׂעֹרָה נֻכָּתָה כִּי הַשְּׂעֹרָה אָבִיב וְהַפִּשְׁתָּה

---

traces of a volcanic eruption, the ash from such an eruption, borne by the wind, precipitating the hailstorm. The hailstorm is unlikely to have had a specific religious connotation for the Egyptians. There were various sky gods, but none that seems to correlate with this kind of weather. The general impression, though, would have been powerful. The heavens are communicating their anger.

Hailstorms were rare in Egypt but could happen with devastating force. The language here is emphatic and unusual, emphasizing that such a storm has never happened since "Egypt … first became a nation" – a phrase frequently found in ancient Egyptian literature, but not in Hebrew literature. God is thus speaking to Pharaoh in his own language and idiom. Now He gives advance warning to Pharaoh and his court that they should take shelter, and protect the animals that survived the fifth plague. This has the effect that those who believe are saved the effects of the plague and those who do not are not.

9:27 חָטָאתִי הַפָּעַם *This time I have sinned* – This is the first expression of remorse on the part of Pharaoh. But it seems too brief and pro forma. Pharaoh divides the guilt between himself and his people. He peremptorily orders Moshe to pray to the Lord. Moshe takes him at his word and assures him the hailstorm will end, but makes it clear that he does not believe that Pharaoh is sincere.

9:29 כְּצֵאתִי אֶת־הָעִיר *As I leave the city* – Moshe cannot pray within the city lest people think he is praying to its gods. No one in Egypt now doubts God's power, but they may well doubt His identity. The Mekhilta goes further: "If Moshe would only pray outside the city, how much more so would God only speak to him

32 the flax in bud. But the wheat and emmer had not been
33 destroyed, because they ripen later. Moshe left Pharaoh MAFTIR
and the city and spread out his hands to the LORD. The
thunder and hail stopped; the rain did not pound the
34 earth anymore. But when Pharaoh saw that the rain,
hail, and thunder had stopped, he once more turned to
sinfulness. He hardened his heart; his officials likewise.
35 Pharaoh's heart was strengthened and he refused to send
the Israelites forth, just as the LORD had predicted at
Moshe's hand.

The haftara for Parashat Vaera is on page 1460.
On Rosh Ḥodesh Shevat read the haftara on page 1640.

לב לג גִּבְעֹֽל׃ וְהַחִטָּ֥ה וְהַכֻּסֶּ֖מֶת לֹ֣א נֻכּ֑וּ כִּ֥י אֲפִילֹ֖ת הֵֽנָּה׃ וַיֵּצֵ֨א מֹשֶׁ֜ה מפטיר
מֵעִ֤ם פַּרְעֹה֙ אֶת־הָעִ֔יר וַיִּפְרֹ֥שׂ כַּפָּ֖יו אֶל־יְהוָ֑ה וַיַּחְדְּל֤וּ הַקֹּלוֹת֙
לד וְהַבָּרָ֔ד וּמָטָ֖ר לֹא־נִתַּ֥ךְ אָֽרְצָה׃ וַיַּ֣רְא פַּרְעֹ֗ה כִּֽי־חָדַ֨ל הַמָּטָ֧ר
לה וְהַבָּרָ֛ד וְהַקֹּלֹ֖ת וַיֹּ֣סֶף לַחֲטֹ֑א וַיַּכְבֵּ֥ד לִבּ֖וֹ ה֥וּא וַעֲבָדָֽיו׃ וַיֶּחֱזַק֙
לֵ֣ב פַּרְעֹ֔ה וְלֹ֥א שִׁלַּ֖ח אֶת־בְּנֵ֣י יִשְׂרָאֵ֑ל כַּאֲשֶׁ֛ר דִּבֶּ֥ר יְהוָ֖ה בְּיַד־
מֹשֶֽׁה׃

The הפטרה *for* פרשת וארא *is on page 1461.*
On ראש חודש שבט *read the* הפטרה *on page 1641.*

Parashat Bo

10 1 Then the Lord said to Moshe, "Go to Pharaoh. I have
hardened his heart and his officials', that I may display
2 these My signs before him, and so that you may tell your
children and grandchildren how I made the Egyptians a
laughingstock by the signs I revealed among them; and
3 know that I am the Lord." Moshe and Aharon came to
Pharaoh and said to him, "Thus says the Lord, God of
the Hebrews: How much longer will you refuse to submit
4 to Me? Send My people forth to serve Me. For if you
refuse to send My people forth, tomorrow I bring locusts

God hardens someone's heart, this does not mean that they forfeit their free will.

10:2 וּלְמַעַן תְּסַפֵּר בְּאָזְנֵי בִנְךָ וּבֶן־בִּנְךָ *And so that you may tell your children and grandchildren* – For the first time, the full significance of the plagues is made clear. It is not limited to Egypt or to that time. That there exists a power greater than the mightiest empire in the ancient world is a proposition to have resonance far beyond the boundaries of Egypt. And in our verse, we learn that it will provide a lesson beyond its time. It would be a story to be handed on across the generations, as it has been from the days of Moshe until today. Those who forget how freedom was won eventually lose it. Those who lived through these events died long ago, but their story never will. That was part of the divine plan from the outset: to tell a story about the liberation of slaves that would lead eventually to a civilization based on freedom, justice, and human rights.

10:3 עַד־מָתַי מֵאַנְתָּ לֵעָנֹת מִפָּנָי *How much longer will you refuse to submit to Me?* – There is a new tone of assertiveness here. Patience has worn thin. The Israelites are suffering. The Egyptians are suffering. Only Pharaoh's obstinacy stands in the way of the relief of both nations. Moshe and Aharon are no longer the importuning representatives of the powerless nation of slaves. They occupy the higher moral ground and can speak with authority.

10:4 אַרְבֶּה *Locusts* – The desert locust is a devastating visitor to the Middle East, Africa, and Asia even today. A swarm can be 460 square miles in size and contain between forty and eighty million locusts in less than half a square mile. Each locust can eat its weight in plants each day, so a swarm of this size would eat 423 million pounds of plants every day.

Egypt was ravaged by them from time to time and whenever there was an attack of locusts, people would be

פרשת בא

י א וַיֹּאמֶר יהוה אֶל־מֹשֶׁה בֹּא אֶל־פַּרְעֹה כִּי־אֲנִי הִכְבַּדְתִּי אֶת־ ז
ב לִבּוֹ וְאֶת־לֵב עֲבָדָיו לְמַעַן שִׁתִי אֹתֹתַי אֵלֶּה בְּקִרְבּוֹ: וּלְמַעַן
תְּסַפֵּר בְּאָזְנֵי בִנְךָ וּבֶן־בִּנְךָ אֵת אֲשֶׁר הִתְעַלַּלְתִּי בְּמִצְרַיִם
ג וְאֶת־אֹתֹתַי אֲשֶׁר־שַׂמְתִּי בָם וִידַעְתֶּם כִּי־אֲנִי יהוה: וַיָּבֹא
מֹשֶׁה וְאַהֲרֹן אֶל־פַּרְעֹה וַיֹּאמְרוּ אֵלָיו כֹּה־אָמַר יהוה אֱלֹהֵי
הָעִבְרִים עַד־מָתַי מֵאַנְתָּ לֵעָנֹת מִפָּנָי שַׁלַּח עַמִּי וְיַעַבְדֻנִי:
ד כִּי אִם־מָאֵן אַתָּה לְשַׁלֵּחַ אֶת־עַמִּי הִנְנִי מֵבִיא מָחָר אַרְבֶּה

BO

Parashat Bo introduces the institution of storytelling as a fundamental religious duty, recalling and re-enacting the events of the exodus every year, and in particular, making children central to the story. If we are the story we tell about ourselves, then as long as we never lose the story, we will never lose our identity.

Cultures are shaped by the range of stories to which they give rise. Some of these have a special role in shaping the self-understanding of those who tell them. We call them master-narratives. They are about large, ongoing groups of people: the tribe, the nation, the civilization. They hold the group together horizontally across space and vertically across time, giving it a shared identity handed on across the generations.

None has been more powerful than the exodus story, whose frame and context is set out in our *parasha*. It gave Jews the most tenacious identity ever held by a nation. In the eras of oppression, it gave hope of freedom. At times of exile, it promised return. It told two hundred generations of Jewish children who they were and of what story they were a part. It became the world's master-narrative of liberty, adopted by an astonishing variety of groups, from Puritans in the seventeenth century to African-Americans in the nineteenth and to Tibetan Buddhists today.

I believe that I am a character in our people's story, with my own chapter to write, and so are we all. To be a Jew is to see yourself as part of that story, to make it live in our time, and to do your best to hand it on to those who will come after us. All of this begins in Parashat Bo.

10:1 אֶת־לִבּוֹ וְאֶת־לֵב עֲבָדָיו *His heart and his officials'* – In fact, though, as we read in verse 7, the officials do experience a change of heart, warning Pharaoh that he is making a mistake that will cost him and his country dearly. This is strong evidence that even when the Torah says that

5 to your land. They will cover the landscape so that you
will not be able to see the ground. They will eat what little
remains after the hail, including all the trees that grow up
6 from your soil. They will fill your palaces, your officials'
houses, and all the houses of Egypt. Your parents and
grandparents never saw anything like this, from the day
they arrived upon this earth until today." Then Moshe
7 turned and left Pharaoh. Pharaoh's officials then said to
him, "How long must we leave this man to ensnare us?
Send the people forth to serve the Lord their God.
Do you not yet know that Egypt is being destroyed?"
8 Moshe and Aharon were summoned back to Pharaoh,
and he said to them, "Go and serve the Lord your God.
9 Who exactly will be going?" "With our youths and our
elderly folk we will go," said Moshe, "with our sons and
our daughters, our sheep and our cattle, we all must go,
10 for it will be our festival of the Lord." He replied, "The
Lord be with you if I let you and your children go!
11 Look – evil is staring you in the face. No! Let the men

---

in order to accelerate the transportation of Jews to Auschwitz. He endangered his own war efforts for the sake of continuing his genocidal program against the Jews. This was evil for evil's sake. The law of history articulated in this chapter continues to hold true: hate destroys the hater. Evil has two faces. The first – turned to the outside world – is what it does to its victim. The second – turned within – is what it does to its perpetrator. Evil traps the evildoer in its mesh. Slowly but surely, he or she loses freedom and becomes not evil's master but its slave.

10:9 בִּנְעָרֵינוּ וּבִזְקֵנֵינוּ *With our youths and our elderly folk* – It was the very young and the old who were sent straight to the gas chambers during the Holocaust. They were deemed of no use. Likewise, to a civilization like ancient Egypt, able-bodied men represented the wealth of the nation. Moshe is signaling a different set of values. We care about our young and our old. Our young are our future, our old are our past, and both are precious to us and to God. We owe respect to those who brought us into being and care for those we have brought into being. The phrase "with our youths and our elderly folk" has become familiar as an expression of Jewish collective responsibility, as if to say: We will not abandon anyone. "All Jews are responsible for one another" (Shevuot 39a).

10:10 רָעָה נֶגֶד פְּנֵיכֶם *Evil is staring you in the face* – The Hebrew *raa* may be an

ה בִּגְבֻלֶךָ׃ וְכִסָּה אֶת־עֵין הָאָרֶץ וְלֹא יוּכַל לִרְאֹת אֶת־הָאָרֶץ
וְאָכַל ׀ אֶת־יֶתֶר הַפְּלֵטָה הַנִּשְׁאֶרֶת לָכֶם מִן־הַבָּרָד וְאָכַל
ו אֶת־כָּל־הָעֵץ הַצֹּמֵחַ לָכֶם מִן־הַשָּׂדֶה׃ וּמָלְאוּ בָתֶּיךָ וּבָתֵּי
כָל־עֲבָדֶיךָ וּבָתֵּי כָל־מִצְרַיִם אֲשֶׁר לֹא־רָאוּ אֲבֹתֶיךָ וַאֲבוֹת
אֲבֹתֶיךָ מִיּוֹם הֱיוֹתָם עַל־הָאֲדָמָה עַד הַיּוֹם הַזֶּה וַיִּפֶן וַיֵּצֵא
ז מֵעִם פַּרְעֹה׃ וַיֹּאמְרוּ עַבְדֵי פַרְעֹה אֵלָיו עַד־מָתַי יִהְיֶה זֶה
לָנוּ לְמוֹקֵשׁ שַׁלַּח אֶת־הָאֲנָשִׁים וְיַעַבְדוּ אֶת־יהוה אֱלֹהֵיהֶם
ח הֲטֶרֶם תֵּדַע כִּי אָבְדָה מִצְרָיִם׃ וַיּוּשַׁב אֶת־מֹשֶׁה וְאֶת־אַהֲרֹן
אֶל־פַּרְעֹה וַיֹּאמֶר אֲלֵהֶם לְכוּ עִבְדוּ אֶת־יהוה אֱלֹהֵיכֶם מִי
ט וָמִי הַהֹלְכִים׃ וַיֹּאמֶר מֹשֶׁה בִּנְעָרֵינוּ וּבִזְקֵנֵינוּ נֵלֵךְ בְּבָנֵינוּ
י וּבִבְנוֹתֵנוּ בְּצֹאנֵנוּ וּבִבְקָרֵנוּ נֵלֵךְ כִּי חַג־יהוה לָנוּ׃ וַיֹּאמֶר
אֲלֵהֶם יְהִי כֵן יהוה עִמָּכֶם כַּאֲשֶׁר אֲשַׁלַּח אֶתְכֶם וְאֶת־טַפְּכֶם
יא רְאוּ כִּי רָעָה נֶגֶד פְּנֵיכֶם׃ לֹא כֵן לְכוּ־נָא הַגְּבָרִים וְעִבְדוּ

reminded of the most massive attack of all (Bekhor Shor, and see Joel 1). The locusts completed the work of the hail by destroying the wheat and the spelt that had remained after the hailstorm. Once, Yosef provided the country with grain during the seven years of famine. Now, nature is doing the reverse: destroying all the crops in the field. There is an echo here of the first words of God to Avraham: "And I will bless those who bless you, and those who curse you I will curse" (Gen. 12:33).

10:6 אֲבֹתֶיךָ וַאֲבוֹת אֲבֹתֶיךָ *Your parents and grandparents* – A contrast with the earlier phrase, "your children and grandchildren." The Israelites look, in hope, to future generations. The Egyptians, in fear, turn toward the past.

10:6 וַיִּפֶן *Then Moshe turned* – It is one of the customs of absolute rulers that one does not turn their back on them. You leave, still facing them, bowing, and walking backward. The fact that Moshe turned and exited meant that he was not obeying this protocol, and by implication showing that he believed that Pharaoh's authority no longer commanded in one respect. For the first time, in the next verse, Pharaoh's own officials will tell him his policy has failed. Egypt is being destroyed. Much better to let the people leave than to allow this succession of disasters to continue.

Tragically, tyrants are held captive by their hate, and they lead their own people to destruction. In the closing stages of the Second World War, Hitler diverted trains from the Russian front

go and serve the LORD. That is what you are asking for."
Then Pharaoh had Moshe and Aharon expelled from his
12 presence. The LORD said to Moshe, "Reach out SHENI
your hand over Egypt so that locusts swarm over the land
and eat everything growing there, all that is left after the
13 hail." So Moshe stretched out his staff over Egypt, and the
LORD caused an east wind to blow across the land all that
day and night. By morning, the east wind had brought the
14 locusts. They invaded all of Egypt and settled throughout
its land in a dense swarm. Never before had there been
15 such a plague of locusts, nor will there ever be again. They
covered all the landscape until the ground was black.
They ate all that was left after the hail: all the plants and
all the fruit. Nothing green remained on trees or plants
16 throughout all Egypt. In haste, Pharaoh summoned
Moshe and Aharon and said, "I have sinned against the
17 LORD your God and you. Forgive my sin now, one more
time. Pray to the LORD your God to take this death away
18 from me." Moshe left Pharaoh's presence and prayed to
19 the LORD. And the LORD turned the wind, westerly and
very strong, and lifted the locusts and swept them into
the Sea of Reeds. Not one locust remained anywhere in
20 Egypt. But the LORD strengthened Pharaoh's heart and
he would not send the Israelites forth.
21 Then the LORD said to Moshe, "Reach out your hand

The naturalistic explanation again focuses our attention on the moral dimension of the plague. In Egyptian mythology, Pharaoh and the entire structure of its society represented order against the ever-threatening forces of chaos. Sheer chaos has now been unleashed against the land and its inhabitants. It is as if creation itself were protesting the injustice being perpetrated against an afflicted people who only sought the opportunity to leave the land and worship their own God.

10:17 שָׂא נָא חַטָּאתִי *Forgive my sin* – This is Pharaoh's first request for forgiveness, a measure of how far, finally, the reality of the plagues is beginning to close in on the ruler of Egypt. His prayer "to take this death away from me" is his darkest utterance thus far.

את־יהוה כי אתה אתם מבקשים ויגרש אתם מאת פני
יב פרעה: ויאמר יהוה אל־משה נטה ידך על־ שני
ארץ מצרים בארבה ויעל על־ארץ מצרים ויאכל את־
יג כל־עשב הארץ את כל־אשר השאיר הברד: ויט משה
את־מטהו על־ארץ מצרים ויהוה נהג רוח־קדים בארץ
כל־היום ההוא וכל־הלילה הבקר היה ורוח הקדים נשא
יד את־הארבה: ויעל הארבה על כל־ארץ מצרים וינח בכל
גבול מצרים כבד מאד לפניו לא־היה כן ארבה כמהו
טו ואחריו לא יהיה־כן: ויכס את־עין כל־הארץ ותחשך
הארץ ויאכל את־כל־עשב הארץ ואת כל־פרי העץ אשר
הותיר הברד ולא־נותר כל־ירק בעץ ובעשב השדה בכל־
טז ארץ מצרים: וימהר פרעה לקרא למשה ולאהרן ויאמר
יז חטאתי ליהוה אלהיכם ולכם: ועתה שא נא חטאתי אך
הפעם והעתירו ליהוה אלהיכם ויסר מעלי רק את־המות
יח יט הזה: ויצא מעם פרעה ויעתר אל־יהוה: ויהפך יהוה רוח־
ים חזק מאד וישא את־הארבה ויתקעהו ימה סוף לא
כ נשאר ארבה אחד בכל גבול מצרים: ויחזק יהוה את־לב
פרעה ולא שלח את־בני ישראל:
כא ויאמר יהוה אל־משה נטה ידך על־השמים ויהי חשך על־

allusion to the Egyptian sun god Ra, as if Pharaoh were saying, "Your God may have done wonders for you, but our god has evil in store" (cf. Rashi). This would make sense in terms of the next plague, darkness, which was an eclipse of the sun god of Egypt.

10:13 ויהוה נהג רוח־קדים *The Lord caused an east wind* – The text does not say that God created the locusts out of nothing or brought them in defiance of the laws of nature. A sirocco from the southeast like the wind that blasted the ears of corn in an earlier pharaoh's dream (Gen. 41:21) is precisely what would have brought a dense swarm of locusts, given the damp earth left by the plague of hail, which is particularly conducive to the hatching of large numbers of locusts.

toward the sky to bring darkness down over Egypt –
22 darkness so deep it can be felt." Moshe reached out his
hand toward the sky, and all across Egypt it was pitch dark
23 for three days. For three days, no one could see anyone
else or even move. But in the Israelites' homes, they had
24 light. Then Pharaoh summoned Moshe and said, "Go, SHELISHI
serve the LORD. Just leave your flocks and herds. Your
25 children may go with you." "Then give us sacrifices and
burnt offerings to present to the LORD our God," said
26 Moshe. "Our livestock must go with us. Not a hoof can
be left behind. We must take them to serve the LORD our
God, for until we arrive, we will not know what we must use

We can now understand the significance of the ninth plague. The greatest god in the Egyptian pantheon was Ra or Re, the sun god. The name of the Pharaoh often associated with the exodus, Ramesses II, means, as we have seen, *messes*, "son of" Ra. Egypt – so its people believed – was ruled by the sun. Its human ruler was semidivine, the child of the sun god. In the beginning of time, according to Egyptian myth, the sun god ruled together with Nun, the primeval waters. Eventually there were many deities. Ra then created human beings from his tears. Seeing, however, that they were deceitful, he sent the goddess Hathor to destroy them; only a few survived.

The obliteration of the sun in the ninth plague signals that there is a power greater than Ra. Yet this signified less the power of God over the sun than the rejection by God of a civilization that turned one man into an absolute ruler – and that could tolerate the murder of children because that is what Ra himself did.

When God tells Moshe to say to Pharaoh, "Israel is My son, My firstborn," He is saying: I am the God who cares for His children, not one who kills His children. The ninth plague is a divine act of communication that says: there is not only physical darkness but also moral darkness. The best test of a civilization is to see how it treats children, its own and others'.

10:21 וְיָמֵשׁ חֹשֶׁךְ *Darkness so deep it can be felt* – The phrase suggests what happened: a *ḥamsin*, a sandstorm of a kind not unfamiliar in Egypt, which can last for several days, producing sand- and dust-filled air that obliterates the light of the sun: "darkness so deep it can be felt." A *ḥamsin* is usually produced by a southern wind that blows into Egypt from the Sahara Desert. The worst sandstorm is usually the first of the season, in March. This fits the dating of the plague, which happened shortly before the death of the firstborn, on Passover.

כב אֶרֶץ מִצְרָיִם וְיָמֵשׁ חֹשֶׁךְ: וַיֵּט מֹשֶׁה אֶת־יָדוֹ עַל־הַשָּׁמָיִם
כג וַיְהִי חֹשֶׁךְ־אֲפֵלָה בְּכָל־אֶרֶץ מִצְרַיִם שְׁלֹשֶׁת יָמִים: לֹא־
רָאוּ אִישׁ אֶת־אָחִיו וְלֹא־קָמוּ אִישׁ מִתַּחְתָּיו שְׁלֹשֶׁת יָמִים
כד וּלְכָל־בְּנֵי יִשְׂרָאֵל הָיָה אוֹר בְּמוֹשְׁבֹתָם: וַיִּקְרָא פַרְעֹה אֶל־ שלישי
מֹשֶׁה וַיֹּאמֶר לְכוּ עִבְדוּ אֶת־יהוה רַק צֹאנְכֶם וּבְקַרְכֶם יֻצָּג
כה גַּם־טַפְּכֶם יֵלֵךְ עִמָּכֶם: וַיֹּאמֶר מֹשֶׁה גַּם־אַתָּה תִּתֵּן בְּיָדֵנוּ
כו זְבָחִים וְעֹלֹת וְעָשִׂינוּ לַיהוה אֱלֹהֵינוּ: וְגַם־מִקְנֵנוּ יֵלֵךְ עִמָּנוּ
לֹא תִשָּׁאֵר פַּרְסָה כִּי מִמֶּנּוּ נִקַּח לַעֲבֹד אֶת־יהוה אֱלֹהֵינוּ
וַאֲנַחְנוּ לֹא־נֵדַע מַה־נַּעֲבֹד אֶת־יהוה עַד־בֹּאֵנוּ שָׁמָּה:

THE PLAGUE OF DARKNESS

The ninth plague seems out of sequence. Thus far there have been eight plagues, and they have become steadily more serious. The first two seemed more like omens than anything else. The third and fourth caused worry, not crisis. The fifth affected animals, not human beings.

The sixth, boils, was again a discomfort, but a serious one, no longer an external issue but a bodily affliction. The seventh and eighth destroyed the Egyptian grain. Now there is no food. Still to come is the tenth plague, the death of the firstborn, in retribution for Pharaoh's murder of Israelite children. It is this that will break Pharaoh's resolve.

So we would expect the ninth plague to be very serious indeed, something that threatens, even if it does not take, human life. Instead it seems like an anticlimax: Darkness is a nuisance, but no more. Why then does it happen now?

The answer lies in a line from *Dayeinu*, the song we sing as part of the Haggada: "If God had executed judgment against them [the Egyptians] but had not done so against their gods, it would have been sufficient."

Not all the plagues are directed, in the first instance, against the Egyptians. Some are intended to show them the powerlessness of the gods in which they believed – we saw this most clearly in the first two plagues, which were symbolic representations of the Egyptian murder of Israelite children. These had a quite different symbolism for the Israelites, and for us. To the Egyptians' victims, their meaning was moral. They represented the rule of retributive justice: As you do, so shall you be done to.

Unlike all the other plagues, the significance of the tenth is disclosed to Moshe even before he sets out on his mission: "Tell Pharaoh: This is what the Lord says, 'Israel is My son, My firstborn. I have told you: Send forth My son.... If you refuse to let him go, I will kill your son, your firstborn'" (Ex. 4:22–23). The tenth plague is to be the enactment of retributive justice; the first nine are a prelude.

27 to serve the LORD." But the LORD strengthened Pharaoh's
heart, and he would not agree to send the people forth.
28 "Leave my presence," said Pharaoh. "Take care never to
see my face again, because on the day you do, that day
29 you will die!" Moshe replied, "As you say: I will not see
your face again."
11 1 Then the LORD said to Moshe, "One last plague will I
send against Pharaoh, against Egypt. After that, he will
send you forth from here, and when he does, he will
2 drive you out completely. Now tell the people, men and
women, to ask of their neighbors articles of silver and
3 of gold." The LORD granted the people favor in the eyes
of the Egyptians. And the man Moshe, too, was held in
high regard in the land of Egypt, among both Pharaoh's
4 officials and the people. Moshe said, REVI'I
"This is what the LORD says: Around midnight I will move
5 throughout Egypt, and every firstborn son in Egypt will
die, from Pharaoh's firstborn presiding on his throne to
the firstborn of the slave girl at her hand mill; the firstborn
6 of the cattle as well. A scream will ring out across Egypt,
unlike any that has been before, or any that will be again.
7 But among the Israelites not a dog will bare its tongue at
man or beast. Then you will know that the LORD is setting
8 Israel apart from Egypt. And all these officials of yours
will come and bow down to me, saying, 'Leave, you and
all the people behind you.' After that, I will leave." He
9 turned and left Pharaoh, blazing with anger. The

---

though it is from that of Egypt, has undeniable force. There is something remarkable that they did not fully understand but for which they have increasing awe. Thus their attitude to the Israelites shifts from contempt to respect.

11:3 הָאִישׁ מֹשֶׁה *The man Moshe* – The Egyptians recognized that Moshe had given Pharaoh every opportunity to avoid the plagues, and that he had ended them when requested to do so. He had been consistent in his words and legitimate in his request, unlike Pharaoh who showed obstinacy, made promises and failed to keep them, and held his own people hostage to his failure to let the Israelites leave.

11:8 בָּחֳרִי־אָף *Blazing with anger* – Moshe displays anger here for the first time in

כז כח וַיְחַזֵּק יְהוָה אֶת־לֵב פַּרְעֹה וְלֹא אָבָה לְשַׁלְּחָם: וַיֹּאמֶר־לוֹ
פַרְעֹה לֵךְ מֵעָלָי הִשָּׁמֶר לְךָ אַל־תֹּסֶף רְאוֹת פָּנַי כִּי בְּיוֹם
כט רְאֹתְךָ פָנַי תָּמוּת: וַיֹּאמֶר מֹשֶׁה כֵּן דִּבַּרְתָּ לֹא־אֹסִף עוֹד
רְאוֹת פָּנֶיךָ:
יא א וַיֹּאמֶר יְהוָה אֶל־מֹשֶׁה עוֹד נֶגַע אֶחָד אָבִיא עַל־פַּרְעֹה ח
וְעַל־מִצְרַיִם אַחֲרֵי־כֵן יְשַׁלַּח אֶתְכֶם מִזֶּה כְּשַׁלְּחוֹ כָּלָה
ב גָּרֵשׁ יְגָרֵשׁ אֶתְכֶם מִזֶּה: דַּבֶּר־נָא בְּאָזְנֵי הָעָם וְיִשְׁאֲלוּ
אִישׁ ׀ מֵאֵת רֵעֵהוּ וְאִשָּׁה מֵאֵת רְעוּתָהּ כְּלֵי־כֶסֶף וּכְלֵי
ג זָהָב: וַיִּתֵּן יְהוָה אֶת־חֵן הָעָם בְּעֵינֵי מִצְרָיִם גַּם ׀ הָאִישׁ
מֹשֶׁה גָּדוֹל מְאֹד בְּאֶרֶץ מִצְרַיִם בְּעֵינֵי עַבְדֵי־פַרְעֹה וּבְעֵינֵי
ד הָעָם: וַיֹּאמֶר מֹשֶׁה כֹּה אָמַר יְהוָה כַּחֲצֹת רביעי
ה הַלַּיְלָה אֲנִי יוֹצֵא בְּתוֹךְ מִצְרָיִם: וּמֵת כָּל־בְּכוֹר בְּאֶרֶץ
מִצְרַיִם מִבְּכוֹר פַּרְעֹה הַיֹּשֵׁב עַל־כִּסְאוֹ עַד בְּכוֹר הַשִּׁפְחָה
ו אֲשֶׁר אַחַר הָרֵחָיִם וְכֹל בְּכוֹר בְּהֵמָה: וְהָיְתָה צְעָקָה גְדֹלָה
בְּכָל־אֶרֶץ מִצְרָיִם אֲשֶׁר כָּמֹהוּ לֹא נִהְיָתָה וְכָמֹהוּ לֹא תֹסִף:
ז וּלְכֹל ׀ בְּנֵי יִשְׂרָאֵל לֹא יֶחֱרַץ־כֶּלֶב לְשֹׁנוֹ לְמֵאִישׁ וְעַד־בְּהֵמָה
לְמַעַן תֵּדְעוּן אֲשֶׁר יַפְלֶה יְהוָה בֵּין מִצְרַיִם וּבֵין יִשְׂרָאֵל:
ח וְיָרְדוּ כָל־עֲבָדֶיךָ אֵלֶּה אֵלַי וְהִשְׁתַּחֲווּ־לִי לֵאמֹר צֵא אַתָּה
וְכָל־הָעָם אֲשֶׁר־בְּרַגְלֶיךָ וְאַחֲרֵי־כֵן אֵצֵא וַיֵּצֵא מֵעִם־פַּרְעֹה
ט בָּחֳרִי־אָף: וַיֹּאמֶר יְהוָה אֶל־מֹשֶׁה לֹא־

11:3 וַיִּתֵּן יהוה אֶת־חֵן הָעָם בְּעֵינֵי מִצְרָיִם *The Lord granted the people favor in the eyes of the Egyptians* – In fulfillment of his promise to Moshe at the burning bush (Ex. 3:21). The Egyptians are generous in their release of the Israelites, as the Israelites will later be commanded to be on the release of any of their own slaves (see Deut. 15:14). They do not blame the Israelites for the plagues. They recognize the justice of their cause.

Once the Egyptians have seen the power that was working on behalf of the Israelites, greater than anything they know within their own pantheon, they began to realize that the Israelites are not mere slaves. They are people in their own right. Their own religion, different

LORD said to Moshe, "Pharaoh will not listen to you, that
10 My wonders may be multiplied in Egypt." Moshe and
Aharon had produced all these wonders before Pharaoh,
but the LORD strengthened Pharaoh's heart, and he did
12 1 not let the Israelites leave his land. Then the
LORD spoke to Moshe and Aharon in the land of Egypt.
2 He said, "This month shall be to you the beginning of
months; the opening of the year, this month will be for

If you are to be free, then time is the first thing you must learn to master. Part of the beauty of Judaism, and surely this is so for other faiths also, is that it gently restores control over time. Three times a day we stop what we are doing and turn to God in prayer. We recover perspective. We inhale a deep breath of eternity. Nor do we rush our meals. Before eating, and afterward, we say a blessing. That too allows us to focus attention on simple pleasures, turning our daily bread into momentary epiphany.

Under pressure of time we tend to ignore the things that are important but not urgent. The Sabbath, unusual amid the stresses of modern life, is a time dedicated to the things that are important but not urgent, like eating together as a family, or celebrating together as a community, or simply giving thanks. These are the things that flood a life with unexpected happiness. Religious ritual is a way of structuring time so that we, not employers, the market, or the media, are in control. Life needs its pauses, its chapter breaks, if the soul is to have space to breathe. Otherwise, we may not be in Egypt but we can still be slaves.

12:2 לָכֶם *To you* – The determination of the calendar, and with it the date of the festivals, was handed over to the human court, unlike the seventh day that was made holy by God at the beginning of creation.

The Jewish calendar is both lunar and solar. Months are determined by the moon, and last either twenty-nine or thirty days. In ancient times, the length depended on eye-witnesses coming to the *beit din* and saying, "We saw the new moon." The seasons, however, are determined by the sun. To ensure an alignment between the lunar and solar calendars, there is a system of seven leap years in every cycle of nineteen years – a leap year involving an extra month, Adar 2. This additional Adar would also be established by the court. Hence on the Sabbath we speak of God who "sanctifies the Sabbath" but on festivals we speak of God who "sanctifies Israel who sanctify the festive seasons."

12:2 רֹאשׁ חֳדָשִׁים *The beginning of months* – Hebrew months tended to be numbered rather than named, as were the days of the week. This may have been to avoid using

יִשְׁמַע אֲלֵיכֶם פַּרְעֹה לְמַעַן רְבוֹת מוֹפְתַי בְּאֶרֶץ מִצְרָיִם׃
י וּמֹשֶׁה וְאַהֲרֹן עָשׂוּ אֶת־כָּל־הַמֹּפְתִים הָאֵלֶּה לִפְנֵי פַרְעֹה
וַיְחַזֵּק יהוה אֶת־לֵב פַּרְעֹה וְלֹא־שִׁלַּח אֶת־בְּנֵי־יִשְׂרָאֵל
יב א מֵאַרְצוֹ׃ וַיֹּאמֶר יהוה אֶל־מֹשֶׁה וְאֶל־אַהֲרֹן בְּאֶרֶץ
ב מִצְרַיִם לֵאמֹר׃ הַחֹדֶשׁ הַזֶּה לָכֶם רֹאשׁ חֳדָשִׁים רִאשׁוֹן הוּא

these confrontations, yet it was the capacity for righteous indignation that marked Moshe as a leader many years before. The Egyptians had lacked this capacity. The "scream" (Ex. 11:6) echoes the verb that was used of the Israelites when their cry was heard in heaven (3:7, 9). The Egyptians were silent while the Israelites were persecuted for many years. Now that what they did to others is being done to them, they are no longer silent. Their anguished cries fill the night (Rabbi Samson Raphael Hirsch). Meanwhile, Pharaoh's personal authority has been eroded by his capricious behavior. "Your own officials," says Moshe to Pharaoh, "will bow down to me rather than you."

"THIS MONTH SHALL BE TO YOU..."
The texture of the narrative changes here. At the very height of the drama, as the final plague has been announced but not yet happened, we move from Egypt to the Israelites. Before talking about preparations for the exodus, God commands Moshe and Aharon to instruct the people on what will become a new foundation of their faith: the calendar. Events in Egypt will not remain simply as a historical past. They will shape the way that the Israelites experience time. The month of the exodus will become, each year, a month of new beginnings. It will be a time of memory and reenactment, of reexperiencing the story and handing it on to future generations. It will become the basis of their identity.

According to Jewish tradition, this is the first command the Jewish people ever received: the command to establish a calendar. Why? The Israelites are still slaves in Egypt. They are longing for freedom. They are about to begin the long journey across the desert. Why do they need a command about calendars and holy days? What has a diary to do with liberty?

Rabbi Avraham Pam explained it in the following way: The difference between a slave and a free human being does not lie in how long or hard each works. Free people often work long hours doing arduous tasks. The difference lies in who controls time. A slave works until he or she is allowed to stop. A free person decides when to begin and end. Control over time is the essential difference between slavery and freedom. Control over the calendar gave the Israelites authority over time. The first command to the Israelites was thus an essential prelude to freedom. It is said: Learn how to value time and make it holy. "Teach us to count our days rightly, that our hearts may grow wise" (Ps. 90:12).

3 you. Speak to the entire community of Israel and say: On
the tenth of this month each man must take a lamb for
4 his family; one for every household. If the household is
too small for a lamb, let him and a close neighbor take
a lamb together, to suit the number of people involved;
they shall be counted for the lamb in proportion to their
5 eating. A one-year-old male shall you take, flawless, from
6 among the sheep or goats. You shall guard it until the
fourteenth day of this month. And then, in the afternoon,
7 all the community of Israel shall slaughter it. They shall
then take some of the blood and put it on the two sides
and top of the doorframes of the houses where they are
8 to eat the lamb. They shall eat the meat that night, roasted
over a fire; with unleavened bread and bitter herbs they

---

contrasts with the ninth plague of darkness in which "no one could see anyone else" (Ex. 10:23).

The Seder service, in which we yearly reenact this meal, opens with a strange invitation: "This is the bread of oppression our fathers ate in the land of Egypt. Let all who are hungry come in and eat." What hospitality is it to offer the hungry this taste of suffering? In fact, this is a profound insight into the nature of slavery and freedom. Matza represents two things: the food of slaves, and the bread eaten by the Israelites as they leave Egypt in liberty. What transforms the bread of oppression into the bread of freedom is *the willingness to share it.* One who fears tomorrow does not offer his bread to others. One who is willing to divide his food with a stranger has already shown himself capable of fellowship and faith, the two things from which hope is born. The Seder returns us to the solidarity of that original moment on the cusp of freedom.

12:7 עַל־שְׁתֵּי הַמְּזוּזֹת וְעַל־הַמַּשְׁקוֹף *Two sides and top of the doorframes* – The door is a symbol of a threshold, in this case between the interior – the inner lives of the Israelites – and the Egyptian exterior. The blood of the sacrifice is the sign that the Israelites are willing to practice their faith despite knowing that it constitutes an abomination to the Egyptians. Moshe has told Pharaoh that it would be dangerous for the Israelites to worship God in Egypt, implying that they would sacrifice animals held holy by the Egyptians. The offering is thus a mark of religious courage. It is this willingness to keep faith with God despite the risks that serves as a protection at a time of divine anger.

12:8 מַצּוֹת *Unleavened bread* – This was mentioned during the story of the two visitors to Lot in Sedom (Gen. 19:3), as bread that could be prepared speedily. Already in advance of the exodus, there is a hint that it would be undertaken in

ג לָכֶם לְחׇדְשֵׁי הַשָּׁנָה׃ דַּבְּרוּ אֶל־כׇּל־עֲדַת יִשְׂרָאֵל לֵאמֹר
בֶּעָשֹׂר לַחֹדֶשׁ הַזֶּה וְיִקְחוּ לָהֶם אִישׁ שֶׂה לְבֵית־אָבֹת שֶׂה
ד לַבָּיִת׃ וְאִם־יִמְעַט הַבַּיִת מִהְיוֹת מִשֶּׂה וְלָקַח הוּא וּשְׁכֵנוֹ
הַקָּרֹב אֶל־בֵּיתוֹ בְּמִכְסַת נְפָשֹׁת אִישׁ לְפִי אׇכְלוֹ תָּכֹסּוּ
ה עַל־הַשֶּׂה׃ שֶׂה תָמִים זָכָר בֶּן־שָׁנָה יִהְיֶה לָכֶם מִן־הַכְּבָשִׂים
ו וּמִן־הָעִזִּים תִּקָּחוּ׃ וְהָיָה לָכֶם לְמִשְׁמֶרֶת עַד אַרְבָּעָה עָשָׂר
יוֹם לַחֹדֶשׁ הַזֶּה וְשָׁחֲטוּ אֹתוֹ כֹּל קְהַל עֲדַת־יִשְׂרָאֵל בֵּין
ז הָעַרְבָּיִם׃ וְלָקְחוּ מִן־הַדָּם וְנָתְנוּ עַל־שְׁתֵּי הַמְּזוּזֹת וְעַל־
ח הַמַּשְׁקוֹף עַל הַבָּתִּים אֲשֶׁר־יֹאכְלוּ אֹתוֹ בָּהֶם׃ וְאָכְלוּ אֶת־
הַבָּשָׂר בַּלַּיְלָה הַזֶּה צְלִי־אֵשׁ וּמַצּוֹת עַל־מְרֹרִים יֹאכְלֻהוּ׃

---

names that could have had idolatrous associations. This first month was sometimes called Aviv, meaning the ripening of ears of barley. Later, after the Babylonian exile, it became known as Nisan.

The fixing of the calendar on the basis of the exodus for the first time brought into the calendar the concept of historical time, time as an arena of change, from slavery to freedom, from Egypt to the Promised Land.

12:3 עֲדַת יִשְׂרָאֵל *Community of Israel* – This is the first time the term has been applied to the Israelites. It refers specifically to the people as a religious entity, a congregation bearing witness together (*eda* from the word *ed*, "a witness") to the sovereignty of God. At the beginning of Exodus, the Israelites were called an *am*, a "people," for the first time (Ex. 1:9). The difference between *am* and *eda* is best expressed in Rabbi Joseph B. Soloveitchik's terminology as the difference between *brit goral*, a covenant of fate, and *brit yeud*, a covenant of faith or destiny. A community of fate is defined by what happens to it. The *brit goral* was born in the experience of slavery in Egypt. A community of faith is defined by what it seeks to do and build. The *brit yeud* was formed in the revelation at Sinai. The reason that *eda* appears here for the first time is that it is here that Israel receives its first commands, turning it into a religious community directed to the service of God. This is an essential part of their journey to freedom. Serving God, they have begun their liberation from servitude to human principalities and powers.

12:4 וְלָקַח הוּא וּשְׁכֵנוֹ הַקָּרֹב אֶל־בֵּיתוֹ *Let him and a close neighbor take a lamb together* – The shared meal bonds people together. The sense of kinship, of family bonds, of eating together and caring for one another, will prove essential to the people in their journey to freedom. It

9 shall eat it. Do not eat it raw or boiled in water; it must be
roasted over fire with its head, its legs, and its inner parts.
10 Do not leave any of it until morning; any left over until
11 morning you shall burn with fire. This is how you shall eat
it: your belt secured, the sandals on your feet, your staff
12 in your hand. Eat it in haste. It is the LORD's Passover. I
will pass through the land of Egypt that night, and will
kill every firstborn in Egypt, man and beast. Against all
the gods of Egypt I will execute judgments. I am the
13 LORD. The blood will be your sign on the houses where
you are. I will see the blood and I will pass over you. No
deadly plague will touch you when I strike the land of
14 Egypt. This day will become a memorial for you; you will
celebrate it as a festival to the LORD for all generations, a

---

told us, "For seven days, eat matza and bitter herbs."

In fact, Rashi's interpretation is profound. Why were our ancestors slaves? Why did God allow it to happen? God wanted us at the beginning of history, of our history, to lose our freedom so that we would never let it be lost again. He wanted us to know what it feels like to be a slave, so that we would become the world's most consistent fighters for freedom. Why have we walked as a people through the "valley of the shadow of death" so many times? So that we never forget the sanctity of life. What you once lose, you never take for granted. This is why, even as they celebrate their freedom, the people taste their bitterness, as we do to this day.

12:11 פֶּסַח *Passover* – The word means to "skip over." It is understood to refer to the LORD passing over the houses of the Israelites during the night of the last plague.

Throughout the biblical period, there were two quite different holy times. Passover referred specifically to the fourteenth of Nisan, while the festival that we nowadays call by that name began on the fifteenth and was known as *Ḥag HaMatzot*, the Festival of Unleavened Bread. Only in the postbiblical era did the two come to be known by the same name.

12:14 הַיּוֹם הַזֶּה לָכֶם לְזִכָּרוֹן *This day... a memorial for you* – In ancient Israel, a new concept of time was born. This did more than change the history of the West; in a sense, it created it. Until Tanakh, time was generally conceived as a series of eternal recurrences, endlessly repeating a pattern that belonged to the immutable structure of the universe. The seasons – spring, summer, autumn, winter – and the lifecycle – birth, growth, decline, and death – were a reiterated sequence in which nothing fundamentally changed.

ט אַל־תֹּאכְלוּ מִמֶּנּוּ נָא וּבָשֵׁל מְבֻשָּׁל בַּמָּיִם כִּי אִם־צְלִי־אֵשׁ
י רֹאשׁוֹ עַל־כְּרָעָיו וְעַל־קִרְבּוֹ׃ וְלֹא־תוֹתִירוּ מִמֶּנּוּ עַד־בֹּקֶר
יא וְהַנֹּתָר מִמֶּנּוּ עַד־בֹּקֶר בָּאֵשׁ תִּשְׂרֹפוּ׃ וְכָכָה תֹּאכְלוּ אֹתוֹ
מָתְנֵיכֶם חֲגֻרִים נַעֲלֵיכֶם בְּרַגְלֵיכֶם וּמַקֶּלְכֶם בְּיֶדְכֶם וַאֲכַלְתֶּם
יב אֹתוֹ בְּחִפָּזוֹן פֶּסַח הוּא לַיהוָה׃ וְעָבַרְתִּי בְאֶרֶץ־מִצְרַיִם
בַּלַּיְלָה הַזֶּה וְהִכֵּיתִי כָל־בְּכוֹר בְּאֶרֶץ מִצְרַיִם מֵאָדָם וְעַד־
יג בְּהֵמָה וּבְכָל־אֱלֹהֵי מִצְרַיִם אֶעֱשֶׂה שְׁפָטִים אֲנִי יְהוָה׃ וְהָיָה
הַדָּם לָכֶם לְאֹת עַל הַבָּתִּים אֲשֶׁר אַתֶּם שָׁם וְרָאִיתִי אֶת־
הַדָּם וּפָסַחְתִּי עֲלֵכֶם וְלֹא־יִהְיֶה בָכֶם נֶגֶף לְמַשְׁחִית בְּהַכֹּתִי
יד בְּאֶרֶץ מִצְרָיִם׃ וְהָיָה הַיּוֹם הַזֶּה לָכֶם לְזִכָּרוֹן וְחַגֹּתֶם אֹתוֹ חַג

---

haste. The fact that the Israelites were to eat it with their loins girded and their sandals on their feet, ready to leave, suggests that urgency was associated with this particular kind of bread. The Torah does not directly associate it with slavery, but Ibn Ezra suggests that slaves were given unleavened bread because, being hard, it takes longer to digest. It removes hunger for longer than ordinary bread. In the Seder, therefore, it has two symbolisms. It is the bread of oppression which becomes the bread of freedom. The difference between freedom and slavery lies not in the quality of the bread we eat, but in the state of mind in which we eat it.

12:8 מְרֹרִים *Bitter herbs* – In the first chapter of Exodus we read that the Egyptians "embittered" the lives of the Israelites through hard labor (Ex. 1:14), so the verbal connection makes it likely that the bitterness of the herbs was symbolic of the Israelites' experience that they were about to leave.

This is the interpretation preserved in the Haggada. On Seder night, each of us must see ourselves as if we had personally left Egypt. "As it says, on that day you must tell your child, *baavur zeh asa Hashem li betzeiti miMitzrayim* – 'This is because of what the Lord did for *me* [not "my ancestors"], when I left Egypt'" (13:8). As we shall see there, Rashi reads this verse counterintuitively: "Why did God take me out of Egypt? *Baavur 'zeh'*: In order that I should fulfill *these mitzvot* of eating matza and bitter herbs." In other words, I am not doing this because of the past. The past happened so that I would do this, all these centuries later. This seems incomprehensible. Can we have gone through all that suffering in Egypt just so that we would eat matza and bitter herbs? If so, God could have left out the whole episode of Egypt. We need not have endured slavery. He could just have

15 celebration that will be an everlasting law. For seven days
you shall eat unleavened bread. By the first day you shall
have removed leaven from your houses, for the soul of
anyone who eats leavened bread from the first day to the
16 seventh will be severed from Israel. The first day shall be
a sacred assembly and the seventh day shall be a sacred
assembly. On them no work may be done but preparing
the food for everyone to eat. That alone may you do.
17 Safeguard the unleavened bread, because on this very day
I will have brought your battalions out of Egypt. You shall
observe this day for all generations; it is an everlasting law.
18 From the fourteenth day of the first month in the evening
until the twenty-first day of the month in the evening,
19 you may eat only unleavened bread. During these seven
days, leaven must not be found in your houses. Anyone,
whether newcomer or native born, who eats leavened
food will have his soul severed from the community of
20 Israel. Eat nothing leavened. Wherever you may live, you
shall eat unleavened bread."

---

houses" (Ex. 12:15). This involves the physical removal of all leaven and is the source of the command of *biur ḥametz*, the burning or destruction of leavened products. (2) "No bread or leavening shall be seen in all your land" (13:7). (3) "During these seven days, leaven must not be found in your houses" (12:19). Whereas the first source enjoins a positive act to remove all *ḥametz*, the second and third are the negative corollaries, forbidding us to leave any leaven or leavened products in our possession.

These are unique commands. Not only must we (at least on Seder night) eat matza, not only must we refrain, throughout the festival, from eating leavened bread or any product that has even the slightest admixture of *ḥametz*, we must also ensure that no leaven or leaven-containing food is in our possession and we must take active steps to remove it, destroy it, and disown it. We do not find such extreme measures in the case of any other forbidden food. The halakhic logic is the temporary nature of the ban on leaven. During the rest of the year it is permitted. Therefore, were there any in the house or in our ownership during the festival we might come to eat it inadvertently; hence we must remove it completely (*Sefer Mitzvot Katan*, 222). The psychological logic is that Passover is a time of departure, the beginning of a journey, the transformation of a nation from slavery to freedom. Clearing the house of *ḥametz* is a symbolic jettisoning of the past, the preparation for a leave-taking.

טו לַיהוָה לְדֹרֹתֵיכֶם חֻקַּת עוֹלָם תְּחָגֻּהוּ: שִׁבְעַת יָמִים מַצּוֹת
תֹּאכֵלוּ אַךְ בַּיּוֹם הָרִאשׁוֹן תַּשְׁבִּיתוּ שְּׂאֹר מִבָּתֵּיכֶם כִּי ׀ כָּל־
אֹכֵל חָמֵץ וְנִכְרְתָה הַנֶּפֶשׁ הַהִוא מִיִּשְׂרָאֵל מִיּוֹם הָרִאשֹׁן
טז עַד־יוֹם הַשְּׁבִעִי: וּבַיּוֹם הָרִאשׁוֹן מִקְרָא־קֹדֶשׁ וּבַיּוֹם הַשְּׁבִיעִי
מִקְרָא־קֹדֶשׁ יִהְיֶה לָכֶם כָּל־מְלָאכָה לֹא־יֵעָשֶׂה בָהֶם אַךְ
יז אֲשֶׁר יֵאָכֵל לְכָל־נֶפֶשׁ הוּא לְבַדּוֹ יֵעָשֶׂה לָכֶם: וּשְׁמַרְתֶּם אֶת־
הַמַּצּוֹת כִּי בְּעֶצֶם הַיּוֹם הַזֶּה הוֹצֵאתִי אֶת־צִבְאוֹתֵיכֶם מֵאֶרֶץ
מִצְרָיִם וּשְׁמַרְתֶּם אֶת־הַיּוֹם הַזֶּה לְדֹרֹתֵיכֶם חֻקַּת עוֹלָם:
יח בָּרִאשֹׁן בְּאַרְבָּעָה עָשָׂר יוֹם לַחֹדֶשׁ בָּעֶרֶב תֹּאכְלוּ מַצֹּת
יט עַד יוֹם הָאֶחָד וְעֶשְׂרִים לַחֹדֶשׁ בָּעָרֶב: שִׁבְעַת יָמִים שְׂאֹר
לֹא יִמָּצֵא בְּבָתֵּיכֶם כִּי ׀ כָּל־אֹכֵל מַחְמֶצֶת וְנִכְרְתָה הַנֶּפֶשׁ
כ הַהִוא מֵעֲדַת יִשְׂרָאֵל בַּגֵּר וּבְאֶזְרַח הָאָרֶץ: כָּל־מַחְמֶצֶת
לֹא תֹאכֵלוּ בְּכֹל מוֹשְׁבֹתֵיכֶם תֹּאכְלוּ מַצּוֹת:

This is variously called cyclical, or cosmological, or mythic time.

A world of cyclical time is one in which nothing ultimately changes. All that lives, dies, but life itself lives on. Winds, storms, floods, and drought wreak devastation, but nature recovers, homes are rebuilt, fields are replanted, and the cycle begins again. Myth justifies the status quo. Inequalities are seen as written into the structure of the universe. All attempts to change society are destined to fail. People are what they are, and the world is what it has always been. At best this view leads to resignation, at worst to despair. There is no ultimate meaning in history.

The Jewish understanding of time that emerges from Tanakh, by contrast, was utterly revolutionary. For the first time people began to conceive that God had created the universe in freedom, and that by making man in His image, He endowed him too with freedom. That being so, he might be different tomorrow from what he was today, and if he could change himself, he could begin to change the world. Time became an arena of change. With this, the concept of history (as opposed to myth) was born.

12:15 תַּשְׁבִּיתוּ שְּׂאֹר מִבָּתֵּיכֶם *You shall have removed leaven from your houses* – The Torah not only commands us to eat matza on Passover and to avoid eating leaven or leavened products. It also contains three distinct commands about removing all leaven from our property and possession: (1) "By the first day you shall have removed leaven from your

21 Then Moshe called together all the elders of Israel and HAMISHI
instructed them, "Each select or acquire one of the
flock for yourselves, for your families and slaughter the
22 Passover sacrifice. Take a bunch of hyssop, dip it in the
blood in the bowl, and put some of the blood on the top
and two sides of the doorframe. None of you shall leave
23 by the doors of your houses until morning. When the
LORD passes through to strike Egypt and sees the blood
on the top and sides of a doorframe, He will pass over
that doorway and will not let the destroyer enter your
24 houses to strike you down. Keep this as a law for you
25 and for your children forever. When you enter the land
the LORD will give you as He has promised, you shall
26 keep this ceremony. And when your children say to you,
27 'What does this ceremony mean to you?' you shall say,
'It is the Passover sacrifice to the LORD who passed over
the houses of the Israelites in Egypt, for He struck the
Egyptians; but our homes, He spared.'" Then the people

---

ages for putting education first. Where others built castles and palaces, Jews built schools and houses of study. From this flowed all the familiar achievements in which we take collective pride: the fact that Jews knew their texts even in ages of mass illiteracy; the record of Jewish scholarship and intellect; the astonishing overrepresentation of Jews among the shapers of the modern mind; the Jewish reputation, sometimes admired, sometimes feared, sometimes caricatured for mental agility, argument, debate, and the ability to see all sides of a disagreement.

Moshe wanted us to teach our children a story. He wanted us to help our children understand who they are, where they came from, what happened to their ancestors to make them the distinctive people they became, and what moments in their history shaped their lives and dreams. He wanted us to give our children an identity by turning history into memory, and memory itself into a sense of responsibility. Jews were not summoned to be a nation of intellectuals. They were called on to be actors in a drama of redemption, a people invited by God to bring blessings into the world by the way they lived and sanctified life.

The long walk to freedom is not just a matter of history and politics, let alone miracles. It has to do with the relationship between parents and children. It is about telling the story and passing it on across the generations. It is about a sense of God's presence in our lives. It is about making space for transcendence, wonder,

כא וַיִּקְרָא מֹשֶׁה לְכָל־זִקְנֵי יִשְׂרָאֵל וַיֹּאמֶר אֲלֵהֶם מִשְׁכוּ וּקְחוּ חמישי
כב לָכֶם צֹאן לְמִשְׁפְּחֹתֵיכֶם וְשַׁחֲטוּ הַפָּסַח׃ וּלְקַחְתֶּם אֲגֻדַּת
אֵזוֹב וּטְבַלְתֶּם בַּדָּם אֲשֶׁר־בַּסַּף וְהִגַּעְתֶּם אֶל־הַמַּשְׁקוֹף
וְאֶל־שְׁתֵּי הַמְּזוּזֹת מִן־הַדָּם אֲשֶׁר בַּסָּף וְאַתֶּם לֹא תֵצְאוּ אִישׁ
כג מִפֶּתַח־בֵּיתוֹ עַד־בֹּקֶר׃ וְעָבַר יהוה לִנְגֹּף אֶת־מִצְרַיִם וְרָאָה
אֶת־הַדָּם עַל־הַמַּשְׁקוֹף וְעַל שְׁתֵּי הַמְּזוּזֹת וּפָסַח יהוה עַל־
כד הַפֶּתַח וְלֹא יִתֵּן הַמַּשְׁחִית לָבֹא אֶל־בָּתֵּיכֶם לִנְגֹּף׃ וּשְׁמַרְתֶּם
כה אֶת־הַדָּבָר הַזֶּה לְחָק־לְךָ וּלְבָנֶיךָ עַד־עוֹלָם׃ וְהָיָה כִּי־תָבֹאוּ
אֶל־הָאָרֶץ אֲשֶׁר יִתֵּן יהוה לָכֶם כַּאֲשֶׁר דִּבֵּר וּשְׁמַרְתֶּם אֶת־
כו הָעֲבֹדָה הַזֹּאת׃ וְהָיָה כִּי־יֹאמְרוּ אֲלֵיכֶם בְּנֵיכֶם מָה הָעֲבֹדָה
כז הַזֹּאת לָכֶם׃ וַאֲמַרְתֶּם זֶבַח־פֶּסַח הוּא לַיהוה אֲשֶׁר פָּסַח
עַל־בָּתֵּי בְנֵי־יִשְׂרָאֵל בְּמִצְרַיִם בְּנָגְפּוֹ אֶת־מִצְרַיִם וְאֶת־בָּתֵּינוּ

EDUCATION

This is the first of four references to children and their instruction in connection with the exodus – three of them in Exodus 12 and 13. They became the "four children" of the Haggada. Already at the outset, one of the most distinctive features of Judaism is enshrined in Jewish law: the centrality of education as the conversation between the generations.

A study from Emory University shows that having a family narrative connects children to something larger than themselves. It helps them make sense of how they fit into the world that existed before they were born. It gives them the starting point of an identity. That in turn becomes the basis of confidence. It enables children to say: This is who I am. This is the story of which I am a part. These are the people who came before me and whose descendant I am. These are the roots of which I am the stem reaching upward toward the sun.

Three times in the course of the *parasha* (Ex. 12:26–27; 13:8, 14), Moshe turns to the theme of responding to one's children's questions. He speaks not about tomorrow but about the distant future. He does not celebrate the moment of liberation. Instead he wants to ensure that it will form part of the people's memory until the end of time. He wants each generation to pass on the story to the next. He wants Jewish parents to become educators, and Jewish children to be guardians of the past for the sake of the future. Inspired by God, Moshe teaches the Israelites the lesson arrived at via a different route by the Chinese: *If you plan for a year, plant rice. If you plan for a decade, plant a tree. If you plan for a century, educate a child.*

Jews became famous throughout the

28 bowed down and prostrated themselves. The Israelites
proceeded to do exactly as the LORD had commanded
29 Moshe and Aharon. It happened at midnight: SHISHI
the LORD struck down all the firstborn in Egypt, from
the firstborn of Pharaoh, presiding on his throne, to the
firstborn of the prison captives, and all the firstborn
30 cattle. Pharaoh arose that night, he and all his officials and
all Egypt – for a great scream rang out across Egypt, for
31 there was no house without its dead. That night, Pharaoh
summoned Moshe and Aharon and said, "Get up, get out
from among my people, you and the Israelites. Go. Serve
32 the LORD exactly as you requested; take your sheep and
cattle also, just as you said. Just go. But bless me too."
33 The Egyptians too urged the people to make haste and
34 leave the land. "All of us will die," they said. The people
took their dough before it could rise, carrying it on their
35 shoulders in kneading pans wrapped in their clothing. As
Moshe had told them, the Israelites had requested items
36 of silver and gold, and clothing, of the Egyptians, and
the LORD had given the people favor in the eyes of the
Egyptians and they had granted their request. Thus they
despoiled Egypt.

---

they should not do so. They should bear the Egyptians no ill will. Why? In this brief command we have one of the most profound insights into the nature of a free society.

A people driven by hate cannot be free. Had the people carried with them a burden of hatred and a desire for revenge, Moshe would have taken the Israelites out of Egypt, but he would not have taken Egypt out of the Israelites. They would still be there, bound by chains of anger as restricting as any metal. To be free you have to let go of hate.

There is a fundamental difference between living *with* the past and living *in* the past. Judaism is a religion of memory. We remember the exodus annually, even daily. But we do so for the sake of the future, not the past. "Do not oppress a stranger," says the Torah, because "you know what it is to be a stranger" (Ex. 23:9). In other words: what you suffered, do not inflict. Memory is a moral tutorial. In Santayana's famous words: "Those who cannot remember the past are destined to repeat it." Israel remembers its past precisely in order *not* to repeat it.

כח הַצִּיל וַיִּקֹּד הָעָם וַיִּשְׁתַּחֲווּ: וַיֵּלְכוּ וַיַּעֲשׂוּ בְּנֵי יִשְׂרָאֵל כַּאֲשֶׁר
כט צִוָּה יהוה אֶת־מֹשֶׁה וְאַהֲרֹן כֵּן עָשׂוּ: וַיְהִי | בַּחֲצִי ט ששי
הַלַּיְלָה וַיהוה הִכָּה כָל־בְּכוֹר בְּאֶרֶץ מִצְרַיִם מִבְּכֹר פַּרְעֹה
הַיֹּשֵׁב עַל־כִּסְאוֹ עַד בְּכוֹר הַשְּׁבִי אֲשֶׁר בְּבֵית הַבּוֹר וְכֹל
ל בְּכוֹר בְּהֵמָה: וַיָּקָם פַּרְעֹה לַיְלָה הוּא וְכָל־עֲבָדָיו וְכָל־
מִצְרַיִם וַתְּהִי צְעָקָה גְדֹלָה בְּמִצְרָיִם כִּי־אֵין בַּיִת אֲשֶׁר
לא אֵין־שָׁם מֵת: וַיִּקְרָא לְמֹשֶׁה וּלְאַהֲרֹן לַיְלָה וַיֹּאמֶר קוּמוּ
צְּאוּ מִתּוֹךְ עַמִּי גַּם־אַתֶּם גַּם־בְּנֵי יִשְׂרָאֵל וּלְכוּ עִבְדוּ אֶת־
לב יהוה כְּדַבֶּרְכֶם: גַּם־צֹאנְכֶם גַּם־בְּקַרְכֶם קְחוּ כַּאֲשֶׁר דִּבַּרְתֶּם
לג וָלֵכוּ וּבֵרַכְתֶּם גַּם־אֹתִי: וַתֶּחֱזַק מִצְרַיִם עַל־הָעָם לְמַהֵר
לד לְשַׁלְּחָם מִן־הָאָרֶץ כִּי אָמְרוּ כֻּלָּנוּ מֵתִים: וַיִּשָּׂא הָעָם אֶת־
בְּצֵקוֹ טֶרֶם יֶחְמָץ מִשְׁאֲרֹתָם צְרֻרֹת בְּשִׂמְלֹתָם עַל־שִׁכְמָם:
לה וּבְנֵי־יִשְׂרָאֵל עָשׂוּ כִּדְבַר מֹשֶׁה וַיִּשְׁאֲלוּ מִמִּצְרַיִם כְּלֵי־כֶסֶף
לו וּכְלֵי זָהָב וּשְׂמָלֹת: וַיהוה נָתַן אֶת־חֵן הָעָם בְּעֵינֵי מִצְרַיִם
וַיַּשְׁאִלוּם וַיְנַצְּלוּ אֶת־מִצְרָיִם:

gratitude, humility, empathy, love, forgiveness, and compassion, ornamented by ritual, song, and prayer. These help to give a child confidence, trust, and hope, along with a sense of identity, belonging, and at-home-ness in the universe.

12:32 וּבֵרַכְתֶּם גַּם־אֹתִי *But bless me too* – Finally, too late, in the midst of grief, Pharaoh poignantly acknowledges that there is a power in the universe greater than Egypt and its gods.

12:35 כְּלֵי־כֶסֶף וּכְלֵי זָהָב *Items of silver and gold* – Why the silver and gold? The Israelites are in such a hurry to leave, and the Egyptians so hasty in urging their departure, that they do not even have time for the dough to rise. Why then is God so insistent that they take the time to ask for these parting gifts? What conceivable use do they have for them in the long journey across the wilderness?

It is not until we reach the end of the Mosaic books that we can begin to understand it. Moshe insists: "Do not despise an Edomite, for he is your kin. Do not despise an Egyptian, for you lived as a stranger in his land" (Deut. 23:8).

This is remarkable. The Israelites were enslaved by the Egyptians. They owe them no debt of gratitude. On the contrary, they are entitled to feel a lingering resentment. Yet Moshe insists that

37 The Israelites traveled from Ramesses to Sukkot. There
were about six hundred thousand men on foot, quite apart
38 from the children. And a great variety of other people
went up with them, as well as large droves of livestock,
39 flocks and cattle. With the dough they had brought from
Egypt, they baked cakes of unleavened bread, not risen.
They had been driven out of Egypt and could not delay,
40 and had prepared no other provisions. The Israelites had
41 lived in Egypt for four hundred thirty years. At the end of
four hundred thirty years, to the very day, all the LORD's
42 battalions left Egypt. All that night, the LORD watched
over them to bring them out of Egypt; and still this night
is kept as one of watchfulness for the LORD throughout
the generations of Israel.
43 The LORD said to Moshe and Aharon, "This is the law of
44 the Passover sacrifice. No foreigner may eat of it. But any

---

is a critique of empires and imperialism. I can define imperialism in the same words that I define religious fundamentalism today. Imperialism, like fundamentalism, is the attempt to impose a single truth on a plural world.

The Tanakh does not gloss over the fact that biblical Israel was an ethnic mix; it seems to go out of its way to emphasize it. There are two ways of reading the story of the exodus. One is as a tale of divine intervention in history; this is how we have read the text so far. The other is about how Moshe turned a ragtag crowd of escaping slaves, fractious, fearful, and disputatious, into a cohesive nation with an identity so strong that it was able to survive devastating defeats, as well as a two-thousand-year exile. That nation continued to see itself as a nation even when scattered and dispersed across the world. How do you create that kind of identity out of diversity? How do you build this sort of loyalty, this sense of identity, without coercion? The answer will unfold through the rest of the Torah.

12:39 וְלֹא יָכְלוּ לְהִתְמַהְמֵהַּ *They... could not delay* – The Egyptians were pressing them to leave. The same verb appears in Genesis 19:16 when the angels urged Lot and his family to leave Sedom because the city was about to be destroyed. Lot delayed, and it was almost fatal. Here, God brings about a sequence of events that makes it impossible for the Israelites to delay in the event that they have second thoughts. Their frequently expressed longing to return to Egypt during their years in the desert shows how necessary this was. Had they delayed, they might never have left.

לז וַיִּסְעוּ בְנֵי־יִשְׂרָאֵל מֵרַעְמְסֵס סֻכֹּתָה כְּשֵׁשׁ־מֵאוֹת אֶלֶף
לח רַגְלִי הַגְּבָרִים לְבַד מִטָּף׃ וְגַם־עֵרֶב רַב עָלָה אִתָּם וְצֹאן
לט וּבָקָר מִקְנֶה כָּבֵד מְאֹד׃ וַיֹּאפוּ אֶת־הַבָּצֵק אֲשֶׁר הוֹצִיאוּ
מִמִּצְרַיִם עֻגֹת מַצּוֹת כִּי לֹא חָמֵץ כִּי־גֹרְשׁוּ מִמִּצְרַיִם וְלֹא יָכְלוּ
מ לְהִתְמַהְמֵהַּ וְגַם־צֵדָה לֹא־עָשׂוּ לָהֶם׃ וּמוֹשַׁב בְּנֵי יִשְׂרָאֵל
מא אֲשֶׁר יָשְׁבוּ בְּמִצְרָיִם שְׁלֹשִׁים שָׁנָה וְאַרְבַּע מֵאוֹת שָׁנָה׃ וַיְהִי
מִקֵּץ שְׁלֹשִׁים שָׁנָה וְאַרְבַּע מֵאוֹת שָׁנָה וַיְהִי בְּעֶצֶם הַיּוֹם
מב הַזֶּה יָצְאוּ כָּל־צִבְאוֹת יהוה מֵאֶרֶץ מִצְרָיִם׃ לֵיל שִׁמֻּרִים
הוּא לַיהוה לְהוֹצִיאָם מֵאֶרֶץ מִצְרָיִם הוּא־הַלַּיְלָה הַזֶּה
לַיהוה שִׁמֻּרִים לְכָל־בְּנֵי יִשְׂרָאֵל לְדֹרֹתָם׃
מג וַיֹּאמֶר יהוה אֶל־מֹשֶׁה וְאַהֲרֹן זֹאת חֻקַּת הַפָּסַח כָּל־בֶּן־
מד נֵכָר לֹא־יֹאכַל בּוֹ׃ וְכָל־עֶבֶד אִישׁ מִקְנַת־כָּסֶף וּמַלְתָּה

Moshe's message is: remember, but not in order to hate.

That means drawing a line over the resentments of the past. That is why, when a slave went free, his master had to give him gifts. This was not to compensate for the fact of slavery. There is no way of giving back the years spent in servitude. But there is a way of ensuring that the parting is done with goodwill, with some symbolic compensation. The gifts allow the former slave to reach emotional closure, to feel that a new chapter is beginning, to leave without anger and a sense of humiliation. One who has received gifts finds it hard to hate. That is the significance of the silver and gold taken from the Egyptians by the Israelites at the express command of God.

12:38 עֵרֶב רַב *A great variety of other people* – The Bible has a strange but unmistakable fascination with diversity. One of the oddest elements of the biblical narrative is the way it describes the Israelites, not as a unified nation but as a group of twelve tribes. As early as this verse, we hear of the *erev rav*, an unidentified "variety of others" or "mixed multitude" who leave Egypt as part of Israel. Biblical Israel is a nation whose unity is not ethnic but civic. That is why, for example, the twenty-fifth chapter of Leviticus will be about minority rights. The *ger* – a migrant or "resident alien" is one who does not share the religion of the majority, but does share its political culture.

We sometimes forget, because Judaism is quite old, that the Bible presents Judaism or Abrahamic faith as a latecomer, not as the original faith of humanity. By the time Moshe appears, Egypt is already old. The Judaic project

slave who has been acquired for money and circumcised
45 may eat it. No gentile resident or hired laborer may eat of
46 it. It should be eaten in a single house; bring none of the
47 meat outside the house. Do not break any of its bones. All
48 the community of Israel shall observe this. If a stranger lives
among you and wishes to offer a Passover sacrifice to the
Lord, every male in his household must be circumcised.
Then he may join in observing it and be like a native born.
49 But no uncircumcised man may eat of it. There shall be
one and the same law for the native born and the stranger
50 who lives among you." All the Israelites did exactly as the
51 Lord had commanded Moshe and Aharon. And
on that very day the Lord brought the Israelites out of
Egypt in their battalions.
13 1 2 The Lord said to Moshe, "Consecrate every firstborn to SHEVI'I
Me. Man and beast, the first to emerge from every womb
3 among the Israelites is Mine." Moshe said to the people,
"Remember this day, the day you left Egypt, the house of
slaves, when with a mighty hand the Lord rescued you
4 from here. No leaven may be eaten. Today, in the month
5 of Aviv, you are leaving. And when the Lord brings
you into the land of the Canaanites, Hittites, Amorites,
Hivites, and Jebusites, the land that He promised your
ancestors He would give you – one flowing with milk and
with honey – you shall keep this ceremony in this month.
6 For seven days you shall eat unleavened bread; the
7 seventh day shall be a festival to the Lord. Unleavened
bread shall be eaten for those seven days; no bread or

---

service, since it was their lives that had been protected by God during the last plague. When this service was later transferred to the tribe of Levi and to the priests, the father of a firstborn was to redeem his son for the sum of five shekels (Num. 18:16) in a ceremony known as *pidyon haben*. The substance of this ceremony has not changed since biblical times, though the wording we now use is more recent. Thus the exodus is to be recalled in perpetuity not only by the celebration of Passover but also by the dedication of firstborn animals to God, and by the redemption of firstborn males.

מה מו אִתּוֹ אָז יֹאכַל בּוֹ׃ תּוֹשָׁב וְשָׂכִיר לֹא־יֹאכַל בּוֹ׃ בְּבַיִת אֶחָד
יֵאָכֵל לֹא־תוֹצִיא מִן־הַבַּיִת מִן־הַבָּשָׂר חוּצָה וְעֶצֶם לֹא
מז מח תִשְׁבְּרוּ־בוֹ׃ כָּל־עֲדַת יִשְׂרָאֵל יַעֲשׂוּ אֹתוֹ׃ וְכִי־יָגוּר אִתְּךָ גֵּר
וְעָשָׂה פֶסַח לַיהוה הִמּוֹל לוֹ כָל־זָכָר וְאָז יִקְרַב לַעֲשֹׂתוֹ וְהָיָה
מט כְּאֶזְרַח הָאָרֶץ וְכָל־עָרֵל לֹא־יֹאכַל בּוֹ׃ תּוֹרָה אַחַת יִהְיֶה
נ לָאֶזְרָח וְלַגֵּר הַגָּר בְּתוֹכְכֶם׃ וַיַּעֲשׂוּ כָּל־בְּנֵי יִשְׂרָאֵל כַּאֲשֶׁר
נא צִוָּה יהוה אֶת־מֹשֶׁה וְאֶת־אַהֲרֹן כֵּן עָשׂוּ׃ וַיְהִי
בְּעֶצֶם הַיּוֹם הַזֶּה הוֹצִיא יהוה אֶת־בְּנֵי יִשְׂרָאֵל מֵאֶרֶץ מִצְרַיִם
עַל־צִבְאֹתָם׃

יג א ב וַיְדַבֵּר יהוה אֶל־מֹשֶׁה לֵּאמֹר׃ קַדֶּשׁ־לִי כָל־בְּכוֹר פֶּטֶר כָּל־ שביעי
ג רֶחֶם בִּבְנֵי יִשְׂרָאֵל בָּאָדָם וּבַבְּהֵמָה לִי הוּא׃ וַיֹּאמֶר מֹשֶׁה י
אֶל־הָעָם זָכוֹר אֶת־הַיּוֹם הַזֶּה אֲשֶׁר יְצָאתֶם מִמִּצְרַיִם מִבֵּית
עֲבָדִים כִּי בְּחֹזֶק יָד הוֹצִיא יהוה אֶתְכֶם מִזֶּה וְלֹא יֵאָכֵל
ד ה חָמֵץ׃ הַיּוֹם אַתֶּם יֹצְאִים בְּחֹדֶשׁ הָאָבִיב׃ וְהָיָה כִי־יְבִיאֲךָ
יהוה אֶל־אֶרֶץ הַכְּנַעֲנִי וְהַחִתִּי וְהָאֱמֹרִי וְהַחִוִּי וְהַיְבוּסִי אֲשֶׁר
נִשְׁבַּע לַאֲבֹתֶיךָ לָתֶת לָךְ אֶרֶץ זָבַת חָלָב וּדְבָשׁ וְעָבַדְתָּ
ו אֶת־הָעֲבֹדָה הַזֹּאת בַּחֹדֶשׁ הַזֶּה׃ שִׁבְעַת יָמִים תֹּאכַל מַצֹּת
ז וּבַיּוֹם הַשְּׁבִיעִי חַג לַיהוה׃ מַצּוֹת יֵאָכֵל אֵת שִׁבְעַת הַיָּמִים
וְלֹא־יֵרָאֶה לְךָ חָמֵץ וְלֹא־יֵרָאֶה לְךָ שְׂאֹר בְּכָל־גְּבֻלֶךָ׃

12:49 לַגֵּר הַגָּר בְּתוֹכְכֶם *The stranger who lives among you* – This is a *ger tzedek*, a convert to Judaism. This principle of "one and the same law" for the born Jew and the convert establishes the people of the covenant as a community of faith, not just an ethnic group defined by biological descent from Avraham and Sara. The covenant with Avraham was based on kinship. The covenant to be initiated between God and Israel is to be based on consent. Those who choose to become Jews are not to be discriminated against in any way. Racism is forbidden in Judaism, unlike fifteenth-century Spain where, by the law of *limpieza de sangre*, "purity of blood," prejudice against Jews continued even after they had converted – an anticipation of the Nuremberg Laws in Nazi Germany.

13:2 קַדֶּשׁ־לִי כָל־בְּכוֹר *Consecrate every firstborn* – Originally, until the sin of the golden calf, the firstborn of all tribes were consecrated to perform God's

▶

8 leavening shall be seen in all your land. On that day you
must tell your child, 'This is because of what the LORD
9 did for me when I left Egypt.' It shall be a sign on your
arm, a reminder between your eyes, so that the LORD's
teaching be on your tongue, for with a mighty hand the
10 LORD brought you out of Egypt. Celebrate this law each
year at its set time.
11 When the LORD brings you to the land of the Canaanites,
as He promised you and your ancestors, and He gives it
12 to you, you shall give over to the LORD the first to emerge
from every womb. Every male firstborn of your animals
13 shall be His. You shall redeem every firstborn donkey
with a lamb; otherwise, you must break the donkey's
neck. You must redeem every firstborn among your sons.
14 And in the future, when your children ask, 'What is this?' MAFTIR
you shall answer, 'With a mighty hand the LORD brought

---

fundamentals of faith, worn as gestures of love and dedication.

13:14 מַה־זֹּאת *What is this?* – In context, the child is asking about the law of the firstborn. In the Haggada, however, this is the question attributed to the simple child, and it is asked in the context of the Passover ritual. Note how concerned the Torah is that a parent should take the questions of a child seriously. In fact, according to the Haggada, parents should encourage their children to ask questions. It is part of the logic of the Torah that we understand its commands and practices, that we question what we do not understand, and that we internalize what we do understand.

Children are naturally spiritual. They are fascinated by the vastness of the universe and our place in it. They have the same sense of wonder that we find in some of the greatest of the psalms. They love stories, songs, and rituals. They like the shape and structure they give to time, and relationships, and the moral life. To be sure, skeptics and atheists have often derided religion as a child's view of reality, but that only serves to strengthen the corollary, that a child's view of reality is instinctively, intuitively religious. Deprive a child of that by ridiculing faith, abandoning ritual, and focusing instead on academic achievement and other forms of success, and you starve him or her of some of the most important elements of emotional and psychological well-being.

Spirituality plays a part in a child's resilience, physical and mental health, and healing. It is a key dimension of adolescence and its intense search for

ח וְהִגַּדְתָּ לְבִנְךָ בַּיּוֹם הַהוּא לֵאמֹר בַּעֲבוּר זֶה עָשָׂה יהוה
ט לִי בְּצֵאתִי מִמִּצְרָיִם: וְהָיָה לְךָ לְאוֹת עַל־יָדְךָ וּלְזִכָּרוֹן בֵּין
עֵינֶיךָ לְמַעַן תִּהְיֶה תּוֹרַת יהוה בְּפִיךָ כִּי בְּיָד חֲזָקָה הוֹצִאֲךָ
י יהוה מִמִּצְרָיִם: וְשָׁמַרְתָּ אֶת־הַחֻקָּה הַזֹּאת לְמוֹעֲדָהּ מִיָּמִים
יָמִימָה:
יא וְהָיָה כִּי־יְבִאֲךָ יהוה אֶל־אֶרֶץ הַכְּנַעֲנִי כַּאֲשֶׁר נִשְׁבַּע לְךָ
יב וְלַאֲבֹתֶיךָ וּנְתָנָהּ לָךְ: וְהַעֲבַרְתָּ כָל־פֶּטֶר־רֶחֶם לַיהוה וְכָל־
יג פֶּטֶר ׀ שֶׁגֶר בְּהֵמָה אֲשֶׁר יִהְיֶה לְךָ הַזְּכָרִים לַיהוה: וְכָל־
פֶּטֶר חֲמֹר תִּפְדֶּה בְשֶׂה וְאִם־לֹא תִפְדֶּה וַעֲרַפְתּוֹ וְכֹל בְּכוֹר
יד אָדָם בְּבָנֶיךָ תִּפְדֶּה: וְהָיָה כִּי־יִשְׁאָלְךָ בִנְךָ מָחָר לֵאמֹר מפטיר
מַה־זֹּאת וְאָמַרְתָּ אֵלָיו בְּחֹזֶק יָד הוֹצִיאָנוּ יהוה מִמִּצְרָיִם

13:8 וְהִגַּדְתָּ לְבִנְךָ *You must tell your child* – This is taken in the Haggada as a commandment to instruct a child even if he or she does not ask a question. The task of education, of inducting a child into the history of its people, begins very young, even before the child has questions. The verb used in this verse is the source of the name of the Haggada, for the recounting of the story of the exodus on the night of Passover. This response has traditionally had two radically different interpretations. According to Rashbam it means: I am doing what I am doing now because of what God did for me (and my ancestors) in Egypt. I am expressing gratitude for what happened then. However, according to Rashi and Ibn Ezra, as we saw earlier, it means: God acted in Egypt so that I would do what I am doing now, *so that* I would serve Him and strive to do His will. On the first interpretation, the present is a commemoration of the past. On the second, the past was a preparation for the present and future.

13:9 וְהָיָה לְךָ לְאוֹת *It shall be a sign* – The texts, contained in leather boxes, known as tefillin – related to *tefilla*, meaning "prayer" – are worn as a sign on the arm, symbolic of action, and a reminder between the eyes, signifying thought. The tefillin contain four sections from the Torah (Ex. 13:1–10, 11–16; Deut. 6:4–9, 11:13–21). They thus combine passages declaring the unity and sovereignty of God, commitment to the commandments, and – as in these two passages – the engagement of God in history and the deliverance of His people from slavery.

The texts contained in the tefillin embody what could have been abstract ideas. It is the genius of Judaism to turn such ideas into concrete actions and physical symbols. Tefillin, in particular, represent a daily engagement with the

15 us out of Egypt, the house of slaves. And when Pharaoh
was obstinate and refused to set us free, the LORD killed
all the firstborn sons in Egypt, man and beast alike. That
is why I sacrifice every male firstborn animal to the LORD,
16 and redeem all my firstborn sons.' It shall be a sign on your
arm and an emblem between your eyes – with a mighty
hand the LORD rescued us from Egypt."

The haftara for Parashat Bo is on page 1464.

army. But to defend a free society you need schools. You need families and an educational system in which ideals are passed on from one generation to the next, and never lost, or despaired of, or obscured. There has never been a more profound understanding of freedom. It is not difficult, Moshe was saying, to gain liberty, but to sustain it is the work of a hundred generations. Forget it and you lose it.

Freedom needs three institutions: parenthood, education, and memory. You must tell your children about slavery and the long journey to liberation. They must annually taste the bread of affliction and the bitter herbs of slave labor. They must know what oppression feels like if they are to fight against it in every age. So Jews became the people whose passion was education, whose citadels were schools, and whose heroes were teachers. The result was that by the time the Second Temple was destroyed, Jews had constructed the world's first system of universal compulsory education, paid for by public funds. None has given education a higher position in the scale of communal priorities. From the very outset, Israel knew that freedom cannot be created by legislation, nor can it be sustained by political structures alone. This basic principle is so crucial to Judaism that it is established here in Parashat Bo – before the Torah has even been given.

טו מִבֵּית עֲבָדִים: וַיְהִי כִּי־הִקְשָׁה פַרְעֹה לְשַׁלְּחֵנוּ וַיַּהֲרֹג יְהוָה
כָּל־בְּכוֹר בְּאֶרֶץ מִצְרַיִם מִבְּכֹר אָדָם וְעַד־בְּכוֹר בְּהֵמָה
עַל־כֵּן אֲנִי זֹבֵחַ לַיהוָה כָּל־פֶּטֶר רֶחֶם הַזְּכָרִים וְכָל־בְּכוֹר
טז בָּנַי אֶפְדֶּה: וְהָיָה לְאוֹת עַל־יָדְכָה וּלְטוֹטָפֹת בֵּין עֵינֶיךָ כִּי
בְּחֹזֶק יָד הוֹצִיאָנוּ יְהוָה מִמִּצְרָיִם:

The הפטרה *for* פרשת בא *is on page 1465.*

identity and purpose. The teenage years often take the form of a spiritual quest. And when there is a cross generational bond through which children and parents come to share a sense of connection to something larger, an enormous inner strength is born. Indeed, the parent-child relationship, especially in Judaism, mirrors the relationship between God and us.

That is why Moshe so often emphasizes the role of the *question* in the process of education: "When your child asks you…" (Deut. 6:20) – a feature ritualized at the Seder table in the form of the *Ma Nishtana*. Judaism is a questioning and argumentative faith, in which even the greatest ask questions of God, and in which the Rabbis of the Mishna and Midrash constantly disagree.

You cannot build a healthy society out of emotionally unhealthy families and angry and conflicted children. Faith begins in families. Hope is born in the home.

13:14 וְאָמַרְתָּ אֵלָיו *You shall answer* – About to gain their freedom, the Israelites are told that they have to become a nation of educators. That is what makes Moshe a great leader. What the Torah is teaching is that freedom is won, not on the battlefield, nor in the political arena, nor in the courts, national or international, but in the human imagination and will. To defend a country you need an

Parashat Beshalaḥ

13 17 When Pharaoh let the people go, God did not lead them
through the land of the Philistines, though it was the
shorter way. "If the people face war," thought God, "they
18 will change their minds and go back to Egypt." So He led
them on a roundabout course, by way of the wilderness,
to the Sea of Reeds. The Israelites left Egypt armed for
19 battle. And Moshe took with him the remains of Yosef,
who had bound the Israelites by oath: "When God comes
20 to your aid, bring my remains with you out of here." They
set out from Sukkot and camped at Etam, at the edge of
21 the desert. The Lord went ahead of them by day in a
column of cloud to guide them, and at night in a column

Egypt.'" For Rambam, this minor detail in the larger story is a key text. Why did God not simply put courage into their hearts? Because God does not intervene in human nature. It is no accident that the generation that left Egypt was not the generation to cross the Jordan and enter the Promised Land. That privilege will belong to their children:

> It was the result of God's wisdom that the Israelites were led about in the wilderness until they acquired courage. For it is a well-known fact that traveling in the wilderness, deprived of bodily enjoyments like bathing, produces courage.... Besides, another generation arose during the wanderings, which had not been accustomed to degradation and slavery. (*Guide for the Perplexed* III:32)

In other words: it takes a generation born in freedom to build a society of freedom. It is hard to overemphasize the importance of this insight. Change takes time. Even God Himself does not force the pace. He led the Israelites on a circuitous route, knowing that they could not face the full challenge of liberty immediately. There are no shortcuts on the long walk to freedom. The rest of the Torah is the story of this extended detour.

13:19 אֶת־עַצְמוֹת יוֹסֵף *The remains of Yosef* – A moving fulfillment of Yosef's last request, shortly before he died (Gen. 50:25). It was a mark of honor that the remains were carried by Moshe himself. There are cultures that forget the past and there are cultures that are held captive by the past. Jews do neither. We carry the past with us.

13:21 בְּעַמּוּד עָנָן לַנְחֹתָם הַדֶּרֶךְ *A column of cloud to guide them* – One of the most beautiful sentences in the whole of

פרשת בשלח

יג יז וַיְהִ֗י בְּשַׁלַּ֣ח פַּרְעֹה֮ אֶת־הָעָם֒ וְלֹא־נָחָ֣ם אֱלֹהִ֗ים דֶּ֚רֶךְ אֶ֣רֶץ
פְּלִשְׁתִּ֔ים כִּ֥י קָר֖וֹב ה֑וּא כִּ֣י ׀ אָמַ֣ר אֱלֹהִ֗ים פֶּֽן־יִנָּחֵ֥ם הָעָ֛ם
יח בִּרְאֹתָ֥ם מִלְחָמָ֖ה וְשָׁ֥בוּ מִצְרָֽיְמָה׃ וַיַּסֵּ֨ב אֱלֹהִ֧ים ׀ אֶת־הָעָ֛ם
דֶּ֥רֶךְ הַמִּדְבָּ֖ר יַם־ס֑וּף וַחֲמֻשִׁ֛ים עָל֥וּ בְנֵֽי־יִשְׂרָאֵ֖ל מֵאֶ֥רֶץ
יט מִצְרָֽיִם׃ וַיִּקַּ֥ח מֹשֶׁ֛ה אֶת־עַצְמ֥וֹת יוֹסֵ֖ף עִמּ֑וֹ כִּי֩ הַשְׁבֵּ֨עַ
הִשְׁבִּ֜יעַ אֶת־בְּנֵ֤י יִשְׂרָאֵל֙ לֵאמֹ֔ר פָּקֹ֨ד יִפְקֹ֤ד אֱלֹהִים֙ אֶתְכֶ֔ם
כ וְהַעֲלִיתֶ֧ם אֶת־עַצְמֹתַ֛י מִזֶּ֖ה אִתְּכֶֽם׃ וַיִּסְע֖וּ מִסֻּכֹּ֑ת וַֽיַּחֲנ֣וּ
כא בְאֵתָ֔ם בִּקְצֵ֖ה הַמִּדְבָּֽר׃ וַֽיהוָ֡ה הֹלֵךְ֩ לִפְנֵיהֶ֨ם יוֹמָ֜ם בְּעַמּ֤וּד
עָנָן֙ לַנְחֹתָ֣ם הַדֶּ֔רֶךְ וְלַ֛יְלָה בְּעַמּ֥וּד אֵ֖שׁ לְהָאִ֣יר לָהֶ֑ם לָלֶ֖כֶת

BESHALAḤ

Parashat Beshalaḥ begins with a battle, it ends with a battle, and in the middle is the great miracle, the turning point – the crossing of the Reed Sea. As so often in the Mosaic books, we are presented with a chiasmus, a literary structure of the form ABCBA, in which the end is a mirror image of the beginning, and the climax is at the center.

Occupying the central role in Parashat Beshalaḥ is the episode of the Reed Sea, which turns out to be a division in more than one sense. Literally, the waters are divided. But metaphorically, the fate of the Israelites is also divided: into a before and after. Before, they are still in Egyptian territory, still – that is to say – under the sway of Pharaoh. It is no accident that Pharaoh and his chariots pursue the Israelites to the very edge of their territory. Anywhere within Egypt, Pharaoh rules – or at least, he believes he does.

Once across the sea, however, the Israelites have traversed a boundary. They are now in no-man's-land, the desert. Again it is no accident that here, where no king rules, they can experience with pristine clarity the sovereignty of God. Israel becomes the first – historically, the only – people to be ruled directly by God. The Reed Sea was a boundary between two domains – in this case the boundary between human and divine rule. Once crossed, there is no going back.

THE JOURNEY BEGINS

The journey from Egypt begins with a detour: "God did not lead them through the land of the Philistines. ...'If the people face war,' thought God, 'they will change their minds and go back to

▶

of fire to give them light, so that they might travel day and
22 night. Neither the column of cloud by day nor that of fire
by night once departed from the people.
14 1 2 Then the LORD said to Moshe, "Speak to the Israelites and
tell them to turn back and camp in front of Pi HaḤirot,
between Migdol and the sea, before Baal Tzefon. Encamp
3 facing it, by the sea. Pharaoh will think that the Israelites
are lost across the land, that they are trapped in the desert.
4 I will toughen Pharaoh's heart, and he will pursue them.
I will be glorified over Pharaoh and all his force, and the
Egyptians will know that I am the LORD." And so they did.
5 When the king of Egypt was told that the Israelites had
escaped, he and his officials changed their minds about
the people: "What have we done, releasing the Israelites
6 from serving us?" So the king harnessed his chariot and
7 brought out his army. He took six hundred elite chariots
and all the other chariots of Egypt, with officers over
8 them all. The LORD strengthened the heart of Pharaoh,
king of Egypt, and he pursued the Israelites, who were
9 leaving in defiance of them. The Egyptians, with all the SHENI
king's horses and chariots, cavalry and infantry, chased
and caught up with them as they were encamped by the
10 sea near Pi HaḤirot, before Baal Tzefon. Pharaoh drew
near – the Israelites looked up: there were the Egyptians
thundering after them. They were terrified and cried to
11 the LORD for help. "Were there no graves in Egypt?" they
asked Moshe. "Is that why you brought us here to die in
the desert? What have you done to us, bringing us out of
12 Egypt? Did we not tell you in Egypt: Leave us alone – let

it, and still take the risk of commitment.

Judaism is not described as a state of being. It is about walking, about the way, about following the call of God. The road is long, the work is hard, and there will be many setbacks and false turnings. We need grit, resilience, stamina, and persistence. In place of a column of cloud leading the way, we need the advice of mentors and the encouragement of friends. But the journey is exhilarating, and there is no other way.

כב יוֹמָם וָלָיְלָה: לֹא־יָמִישׁ עַמּוּד הֶעָנָן יוֹמָם וְעַמּוּד הָאֵשׁ
לָיְלָה לִפְנֵי הָעָם:
יד א וַיְדַבֵּר יהוה אֶל־מֹשֶׁה לֵּאמֹר: ב דַּבֵּר אֶל־בְּנֵי יִשְׂרָאֵל וְיָשֻׁבוּ
וְיַחֲנוּ לִפְנֵי פִּי הַחִירֹת בֵּין מִגְדֹּל וּבֵין הַיָּם לִפְנֵי בַּעַל צְפֹן
ג נִכְחוֹ תַחֲנוּ עַל־הַיָּם: וְאָמַר פַּרְעֹה לִבְנֵי יִשְׂרָאֵל נְבֻכִים
ד הֵם בָּאָרֶץ סָגַר עֲלֵיהֶם הַמִּדְבָּר: וְחִזַּקְתִּי אֶת־לֵב־פַּרְעֹה
וְרָדַף אַחֲרֵיהֶם וְאִכָּבְדָה בְּפַרְעֹה וּבְכָל־חֵילוֹ וְיָדְעוּ מִצְרַיִם
ה כִּי־אֲנִי יהוה וַיַּעֲשׂוּ־כֵן: וַיֻּגַּד לְמֶלֶךְ מִצְרַיִם כִּי בָרַח הָעָם
וַיֵּהָפֵךְ לְבַב פַּרְעֹה וַעֲבָדָיו אֶל־הָעָם וַיֹּאמְרוּ מַה־זֹּאת
ו עָשִׂינוּ כִּי־שִׁלַּחְנוּ אֶת־יִשְׂרָאֵל מֵעָבְדֵנוּ: וַיֶּאְסֹר אֶת־רִכְבּוֹ
ז וְאֶת־עַמּוֹ לָקַח עִמּוֹ: וַיִּקַּח שֵׁשׁ־מֵאוֹת רֶכֶב בָּחוּר וְכֹל רֶכֶב
ח מִצְרָיִם וְשָׁלִשִׁם עַל־כֻּלּוֹ: וַיְחַזֵּק יהוה אֶת־לֵב פַּרְעֹה מֶלֶךְ
מִצְרַיִם וַיִּרְדֹּף אַחֲרֵי בְּנֵי יִשְׂרָאֵל וּבְנֵי יִשְׂרָאֵל יֹצְאִים בְּיָד
ט רָמָה: וַיִּרְדְּפוּ מִצְרַיִם אַחֲרֵיהֶם וַיַּשִּׂיגוּ אוֹתָם חֹנִים עַל־הַיָּם שני
כָּל־סוּס רֶכֶב פַּרְעֹה וּפָרָשָׁיו וְחֵילוֹ עַל־פִּי הַחִירֹת לִפְנֵי בַּעַל
י צְפֹן: וּפַרְעֹה הִקְרִיב וַיִּשְׂאוּ בְנֵי־יִשְׂרָאֵל אֶת־עֵינֵיהֶם וְהִנֵּה
מִצְרַיִם ׀ נֹסֵעַ אַחֲרֵיהֶם וַיִּירְאוּ מְאֹד וַיִּצְעֲקוּ בְנֵי־יִשְׂרָאֵל
יא אֶל־יהוה: וַיֹּאמְרוּ אֶל־מֹשֶׁה הֲמִבְּלִי אֵין־קְבָרִים בְּמִצְרַיִם
לְקַחְתָּנוּ לָמוּת בַּמִּדְבָּר מַה־זֹּאת עָשִׂיתָ לָּנוּ לְהוֹצִיאָנוּ
יב מִמִּצְרָיִם: הֲלֹא־זֶה הַדָּבָר אֲשֶׁר דִּבַּרְנוּ אֵלֶיךָ בְמִצְרַיִם

Judaism occurs early in the book of Yirmeya (2:2). Speaking to the Israelites, who have hitherto been seen as a fractious and rebellious people, God says, "I recall on your behalf the devotion of your youth, your bridal love, when you followed Me into the wilderness, a land unseeded," an unknown land. Yirmeyahu is telling us that God loves the Jewish people because they had the courage to take a risk, to go into a place they had never seen before, with no map and no roads, just the column of cloud and the column of fire.

We all face an unknown and unknowable future. Every single course of action we take, every commitment, has its underside of doubt. That is what faith is. Not the absence of doubt, but the ability to recognize doubt, live with

us serve the Egyptians. Better a life in servitude to Egypt
13 than death in the desert." But Moshe told the people,
"Fear not. Stand firm and see the deliverance the Lord
will bring you today. The Egyptians you see today, you
14 shall never see again. The Lord will fight for you. You
stay silent."
15 The Lord said to Moshe, "Why are you crying out to Me? SHELISHI
16 Speak to the Israelites; have them move forward. Raise
your staff, stretch out your hand over the sea and divide
it, and the Israelites will walk through the sea on dry land.
17 I will strengthen the Egyptians' hearts and they will go
after them. Then will My glory bear down hard upon
18 Pharaoh and his entire army, his chariots and cavalry. And
when My glory bears down upon Pharaoh, his chariots
and cavalry, the Egyptians will know that I am the Lord."
19 Then the angel of God who had been traveling ahead of
the Israelite camp moved and went behind them, and the
column of cloud moved from in front of them to their
20 rear. It came between the Egyptian and Israelite camps,
as cloud and darkness for one, but lighting the night for
21 the other, keeping the two apart all night. Then Moshe

---

through the parted sea while the Egyptians were forced to encamp in the darkness. It is also symbolic of good and evil, characterized throughout Tanakh as forms, respectively, of light and darkness. When God then "looked down at the Egyptian army" (Ex. 14:24), a metaphorical expression of intense divine involvement, the verb "looked down" (*sh-k-f*) recalls the narrative of the destruction of Sedom (Gen. 19:28). Here as there, it is intended to convey the idea that God is high above those who hold themselves to be above God. The people are passive at this point; they are witnesses to a drama playing out between God and Egypt.

14:20 וְלֹא־קָרַב זֶה אֶל־זֶה כָּל־הַלָּיְלָה *Keeping the two apart all night* – Literally, "They did not draw near one to another all night." The only other appearance of the phrase *zeh el zeh*, "one to another," in Tanakh is the basis for the *Kedusha* section of each *Amida* prayer: "And they [the angels] called out *one to another*, 'Holy, holy, holy – the Lord of Hosts'" (Is. 6:3). This verbal echo inspired a midrash with halakhic implications. According to the Talmud (Megilla 10b; Sanhedrin 39b), when the angels wished to sing the Song of the Sea, God silenced them: "Shall you sing a song while My creatures are drowning?" God does not rejoice in the

לֵאמֹר חֲדַל מִמֶּנּוּ וְנַעַבְדָה אֶת־מִצְרָיִם כִּי טוֹב לָנוּ עֲבֹד אֶת־
יג מִצְרַיִם מִמֻּתֵנוּ בַּמִּדְבָּר: וַיֹּאמֶר מֹשֶׁה אֶל־הָעָם אַל־תִּירָאוּ
הִתְיַצְּבוּ וּרְאוּ אֶת־יְשׁוּעַת יהוה אֲשֶׁר־יַעֲשֶׂה לָכֶם הַיּוֹם
כִּי אֲשֶׁר רְאִיתֶם אֶת־מִצְרַיִם הַיּוֹם לֹא תֹסִפוּ לִרְאֹתָם עוֹד
יד עַד־עוֹלָם: יהוה יִלָּחֵם לָכֶם וְאַתֶּם תַּחֲרִשׁוּן:
טו וַיֹּאמֶר יהוה אֶל־מֹשֶׁה מַה־תִּצְעַק אֵלָי דַּבֵּר אֶל־בְּנֵי־יִשְׂרָאֵל יא שלישי
טז וְיִסָּעוּ: וְאַתָּה הָרֵם אֶת־מַטְּךָ וּנְטֵה אֶת־יָדְךָ עַל־הַיָּם
יז וּבְקָעֵהוּ וְיָבֹאוּ בְנֵי־יִשְׂרָאֵל בְּתוֹךְ הַיָּם בַּיַּבָּשָׁה: וַאֲנִי הִנְנִי
מְחַזֵּק אֶת־לֵב מִצְרַיִם וְיָבֹאוּ אַחֲרֵיהֶם וְאִכָּבְדָה בְּפַרְעֹה
יח וּבְכָל־חֵילוֹ בְּרִכְבּוֹ וּבְפָרָשָׁיו: וְיָדְעוּ מִצְרַיִם כִּי־אֲנִי יהוה
יט בְּהִכָּבְדִי בְּפַרְעֹה בְּרִכְבּוֹ וּבְפָרָשָׁיו: וַיִּסַּע מַלְאַךְ הָאֱלֹהִים
הַהֹלֵךְ לִפְנֵי מַחֲנֵה יִשְׂרָאֵל וַיֵּלֶךְ מֵאַחֲרֵיהֶם וַיִּסַּע עַמּוּד הֶעָנָן
כ מִפְּנֵיהֶם וַיַּעֲמֹד מֵאַחֲרֵיהֶם: וַיָּבֹא בֵּין ׀ מַחֲנֵה מִצְרַיִם וּבֵין
מַחֲנֵה יִשְׂרָאֵל וַיְהִי הֶעָנָן וְהַחֹשֶׁךְ וַיָּאֶר אֶת־הַלָּיְלָה וְלֹא־
כא קָרַב זֶה אֶל־זֶה כָּל־הַלָּיְלָה: וַיֵּט מֹשֶׁה אֶת־יָדוֹ עַל־הַיָּם

14:13 אַל־תִּירָאוּ *Fear not* – The Sages, their ears ever attuned to nuance, detected four responses in Moshe's words:

> Our ancestors were divided into four groups at the sea. One group said, "Let us throw ourselves into the sea." Another said, "Let us go back to Egypt." A third said, "Let us wage war against them." A fourth said, "Let us cry out against them." To the first, who said, "Let us throw ourselves into the sea," Moshe said, "Stand firm and see the deliverance the LORD will bring." To the second, who said, "Let us go back to Egypt," he said, "The Egyptians you see today, you shall never see again." To the third, who said, "Let us wage war against them," he said, "The LORD will fight for you." To the fourth, who said, "Let us cry out against them," he said, "You stay silent." (Yerushalmi, Taanit 2:5.)

The battle against the Egyptians, we are assured, was a divine act, not a human one. The point is stressed by the enigmatic scene that unfolds in the night. The cloud between the camps appears "as cloud and darkness for one, but lighting the night for the other." This may mean that, as in the ninth plague, there was light for the Israelites, darkness for the Egyptians (Rashi on Ex. 20:14) – a suspension of the laws of nature. This allowed the Israelites to journey onward

stretched out his hand over the sea, and the LORD drove
the sea back by a strong east wind all night, turning it to
22 dry land and dividing the waters. So the Israelites walked
through the sea on dry land. To their right and left, the
23 water was like a wall. The Egyptians chased after them.
All Pharaoh's horses, chariots, and cavalry followed them
24 into the sea. During the last watch of the night, the LORD
looked down at the Egyptian army from a column of fire

There are, then, two possible perspectives on the crossing of the Reed Sea, two ways of reading the biblical narrative. To some, the miracle was the suspension of the laws of nature. To others, the fact that there was a naturalistic explanation did not make the event any less miraculous. That the Israelites should arrive at the sea precisely where the waters were unexpectedly shallow, that a strong east wind should blow when and how it did, and that the Egyptians' greatest military asset should have proved their undoing – all these things were wonders, and we have never forgotten them.

14:22 מִימִינָם וּמִשְּׂמֹאלָם *To their right and left* – The symbolism of the sea reminds us of the ancient ceremony of covenant making. The key verb of covenant is "to cut." An animal, or several animals, were divided, and the parties to the covenant stood or sat between them. The division of things normally united or whole stood as a symbol of the unification of entities (persons, tribes, nations) previously divided. In this context, a key passage is the covenant "cut" between God and Avraham in Genesis 15. God tells Avraham to cut various animals in half and arrange the halves opposite each other. "On that day the LORD made [literally, 'cut'] a covenant with Avram" (Gen. 15:18).

So at the Reed Sea, the Israelites passed "between the pieces" (the waters, rather than the halves of animals) in a ratification of the covenant with Avraham. They passed from one domain to another, from being slaves – *avadim* – to Pharaoh to becoming servants – *avadim* – to God. This surely is the meaning of the phrase in the Song of the Sea: "until Your people crossed, LORD, until the people You acquired crossed over" (Ex. 15:16).

The crossing of the sea is both an act of covenant making and a transfer of possession. The Israelites are now God's possession rather than Pharaoh's. They have entered new territory, not just geographically but also existentially.

Geula, redemption, is a legal as well as religious term. It means "to buy back." Thus God, redeeming the Israelites, became in legal terms their owner. "For it is to Me that *the Israelites are servants*. They are My servants, whom I brought out of the land of Egypt. I am the LORD your God" (Lev. 25:55).

וַיּוֹלֶךְ יהוה | אֶת־הַיָּם בְּרוּחַ קָדִים עַזָּה כָּל־הַלַּיְלָה וַיָּשֶׂם
כב אֶת־הַיָּם לֶחָרָבָה וַיִּבָּקְעוּ הַמָּיִם: וַיָּבֹאוּ בְנֵי־יִשְׂרָאֵל בְּתוֹךְ
כג הַיָּם בַּיַּבָּשָׁה וְהַמַּיִם לָהֶם חוֹמָה מִימִינָם וּמִשְּׂמֹאלָם: וַיִּרְדְּפוּ
מִצְרַיִם וַיָּבֹאוּ אַחֲרֵיהֶם כֹּל סוּס פַּרְעֹה רִכְבּוֹ וּפָרָשָׁיו אֶל־
כד תּוֹךְ הַיָּם: וַיְהִי בְּאַשְׁמֹרֶת הַבֹּקֶר וַיַּשְׁקֵף יהוה אֶל־מַחֲנֵה

downfall of the wicked. Sympathy should know no religious or national borders. The division of the Sea of Reeds, at which the Egyptians died, took place on the seventh day of Passover, and this, according to the *Beit Yosef* (*siman* 490), is the reason why full Hallel is not said on that day as it is on other festivals.

THE SPLITTING OF THE SEA

The splitting of the Reed Sea is engraved in Jewish memory. We recite it daily during the morning service, at the transition from the *Pesukei DeZimra* to the beginning of communal prayer. We speak of it again after the *Shema*, just before the *Amida*. It was the supreme miracle of the exodus. But in what sense?

The passage can be read in two ways. The first is that what happened was a suspension of the laws of nature. It was a supernatural event. The waters stood, literally, like a wall.

The second is that what happened was miraculous not because the laws of nature were suspended. To the contrary, as computer simulation has shown, the exposure of dry land at a particular point in the Reed Sea can be a natural outcome of the strong east wind. What made it miraculous is that it happened just there, just then, when the Israelites seemed trapped, unable to go forward because of the sea, unable to turn back because of the Egyptian army pursuing them.

There is a significant difference between these two interpretations. The first appeals to our sense of wonder. How extraordinary that the laws of nature should be suspended to allow an escaping people to go free. It is a story to appeal to the imagination.

But the naturalistic explanation is wondrous at another level entirely. Here the Torah is using the device of irony. What made the Egyptians of the time of Ramesses so formidable was the fact that they possessed the latest and most powerful form of military technology, the horse-drawn chariot. It made them unbeatable in battle, and fearsome.

What happens at the sea is poetic justice of the most exquisite kind. There is only one circumstance in which a group of people traveling by foot can escape a highly trained army of charioteers, namely, when the route passes through a muddy seabed. The people can walk across, but the chariot wheels get stuck in the mud. The Egyptian army can neither advance nor retreat. The wind drops. The water returns. The powerful are now powerless, while the powerless have made their way to freedom.

25 and cloud and threw them into a panic, clogging their
chariot wheels so that it was hard for them to move. The
Egyptians said, "Let us flee from the Israelites. The Lord
is fighting for them against Egypt."
26 Then the Lord said to Moshe, "Stretch out your hand REVI'I
over the sea. The waters will flow back over the Egyptians
27 and their chariots and cavalry." Moshe stretched out his
hand over the sea, and at daybreak the water came back in
full force. The Egyptians fled at its approach but the Lord
28 swept them into the sea. The waters returned, covering
the chariots, the cavalry, and the whole Egyptian army
that had followed the Israelites into the sea. Not one of
29 them remained. But the Israelites had walked through
the sea on dry land, with a wall of water to their right
30 and left. That day, the Lord saved the Israelites from the
Egyptians. And when the Israelites saw the Egyptians
31 dead on the seashore, and witnessed the wondrous
power the Lord had unleashed against the Egyptians,
the people were in awe of the Lord, and they believed in
Him and in Moshe His servant.

---

not go. Strength has turned to weakness, and what gave the Egyptian army its speed now mires them in immobility.

14:28 לֹא־נִשְׁאַר בָּהֶם עַד־אֶחָד *Not one of them remained* – This is the moral climax of the episode. Pharaoh had decreed that every male Israelite child be drowned. The first plague, in which the river turned into blood, was intended to remind the Egyptians that they were being punished for this crime, but the plague made no impression on Pharaoh. He merely instructed his magicians to show that they could do likewise. Now the punishment comes, measure for measure: those who drowned innocent children were themselves drowned. According to Targum Onkelos this is the meaning of Yitro's later statement, "He brought upon them what they schemed against others" (Ex. 18:11). The miracle at the sea was intended to demonstrate the moral truth that evil eventually turns against its perpetrator.

14:31 וַיַּאֲמִינוּ בַּיהוה וּבְמֹשֶׁה עַבְדּוֹ *They believed in Him and in Moshe His servant* – This is the first time the people are described as believing in Moshe's leadership. The phrase "His servant" is pointed in this context. The rulers of the ancient world saw themselves as demigods who commanded obedience. The Torah insists that the truth is the opposite:

מִצְרַיִם בְּעַמּוּד אֵשׁ וְעָנָן וַיָּהָם אֵת מַחֲנֵה מִצְרָיִם׃ וַיָּסַר כה
אֵת אֹפַן מַרְכְּבֹתָיו וַיְנַהֲגֵהוּ בִּכְבֵדֻת וַיֹּאמֶר מִצְרַיִם אָנוּסָה
מִפְּנֵי יִשְׂרָאֵל כִּי יהוה נִלְחָם לָהֶם בְּמִצְרָיִם׃
וַיֹּאמֶר יהוה אֶל־מֹשֶׁה נְטֵה אֶת־יָדְךָ עַל־הַיָּם וְיָשֻׁבוּ הַמַּיִם כו רביעי
עַל־מִצְרַיִם עַל־רִכְבּוֹ וְעַל־פָּרָשָׁיו׃ וַיֵּט מֹשֶׁה אֶת־יָדוֹ עַל־ כז
הַיָּם וַיָּשָׁב הַיָּם לִפְנוֹת בֹּקֶר לְאֵיתָנוֹ וּמִצְרַיִם נָסִים לִקְרָאתוֹ
וַיְנַעֵר יהוה אֶת־מִצְרַיִם בְּתוֹךְ הַיָּם׃ וַיָּשֻׁבוּ הַמַּיִם וַיְכַסּוּ כח
אֶת־הָרֶכֶב וְאֶת־הַפָּרָשִׁים לְכֹל חֵיל פַּרְעֹה הַבָּאִים אַחֲרֵיהֶם
בַּיָּם לֹא־נִשְׁאַר בָּהֶם עַד־אֶחָד׃ וּבְנֵי יִשְׂרָאֵל הָלְכוּ בַיַּבָּשָׁה כט
בְּתוֹךְ הַיָּם וְהַמַּיִם לָהֶם חֹמָה מִימִינָם וּמִשְּׂמֹאלָם׃ וַיּוֹשַׁע ל
יהוה בַּיּוֹם הַהוּא אֶת־יִשְׂרָאֵל מִיַּד מִצְרָיִם וַיַּרְא יִשְׂרָאֵל
אֶת־מִצְרַיִם מֵת עַל־שְׂפַת הַיָּם׃ וַיַּרְא יִשְׂרָאֵל אֶת־הַיָּד לא
הַגְּדֹלָה אֲשֶׁר עָשָׂה יהוה בְּמִצְרַיִם וַיִּירְאוּ הָעָם אֶת־יהוה
וַיַּאֲמִינוּ בַּיהוה וּבְמֹשֶׁה עַבְדּוֹ׃

14:25 וַיָּסַר אֵת אֹפַן מַרְכְּבֹתָיו וַיְנַהֲגֵהוּ בִּכְבֵדֻת *Clogging their chariot wheels* – As we saw earlier, in the time of the Torah, Egypt was famous for its horses. They still were, in the time of Shlomo, five centuries later (1 Kings 10:26–29). No other nation could rival them. This meant that they could out-maneuver any rival military force. Horses gave them speed, and chariots gave them protection. They were impregnable, and the sight of six hundred of them approaching would have been terrifying to a well-drilled army, let alone an unruly, disorganized group of slaves.

When the Israelites lost heart and blamed Moshe for bringing them out of Egypt, Moshe's reply was short and sharp: "The LORD will fight for you. You stay silent" (Ex. 14:14). The scene resonates with the message of the book of Psalms:

> He does not take delight in the strength of horses, or pleasure in the fleetness of man. The LORD takes pleasure in those who fear Him, who put their hope in His loyalty. (Ps. 147:10–11)

While the Israelites watch, the chariots become bogged down in the mud. By the time the Egyptians realize what is happening, they are trapped. The mightiest army of the ancient world is defeated, and its warriors drowned, not by a superior army, not by human opposition at all, but by their own folly in being so focused on capturing the Israelites that they ignored the fact that they were driving into mud where their chariots could

15 1 And then, Moshe and the Israelites sang this song to the
LORD: I will sing to the LORD, for He has triumphed in
glory; / horse and horseman He hurled into the sea. /
2 The LORD is my strength and song – / and now my
salvation. / This is my God, I will glorify Him, / my
3 father's God, I will exalt Him. / The LORD is a Master of

---

was divinely inspired to sing it in unison. It was a moment of collective epiphany, and it expressed itself as song.

When language aspires to the transcendent and the soul longs to break free of the gravitational pull of the earth, it modulates into song. Goethe said, "Religious worship cannot do without music. It is one of the foremost means to work upon man with an effect of marvel." Mystics go further and speak of the song of the universe, what Pythagoras called "the music of the spheres." This is what Psalm 19 means when it says, "The heavens tell of God's glory; the skies proclaim His handiwork. . . . There is no speech, there are no words, their voice is not heard, yet their music carries across the land, their words to the end of the earth." Beneath the silence, audible only to the inner ear, creation sings to its Creator. Words are the language of the mind. Music is the language of the soul.

15:2 עָזִּי וְזִמְרָת יָהּ *The LORD is my strength and song* – This verse is echoed in Isaiah 12:2, which is part of the *Havdala* service, encouraging us as we begin the new week. It could also be translated "my strength and might." The root *z-m-r* means both "to sing" and "to prune," and thus by extension "to cut off" an enemy.

Our faith is expressed in our music. When we pray, we do not read; we sing. When we engage with sacred texts, we do not recite; we chant. Every text and every time has, in Judaism, its own specific melody. There are different tunes for Shaḥarit, Minḥa, and Maariv, the morning, afternoon, and evening prayers. There are different melodies and moods for the prayers for a weekday, the Sabbath, the three pilgrimage festivals, Passover, Shavuot, and Sukkot (which have much musically in common but also tunes distinctive to each), and for the *Yamim Nora'im*, Rosh HaShana and Yom Kippur.

There are different tunes for different texts. There is one kind of cantillation for Torah, another for the *haftara* from the prophetic books, and yet another for *Ketuvim*, the Writings, especially the five Megillot. There is a particular chant for studying the texts of the written Torah, for studying Mishna and Gemara. So by music alone we can tell what kind of day it is and what kind of text is being used. There is a map of holy words and it is written in melodies and songs. Perhaps that's what prayer, faith, spirituality really are: more like poetry than prose, more like music than speech.

15:2 אֱלֹהֵי אָבִי וַאֲרֹמְמֶנְהוּ *My father's God, I will exalt Him* – What you love, your

טו א אָז יָשִׁיר־מֹשֶׁה וּבְנֵי יִשְׂרָאֵל אֶת־הַשִּׁירָה הַזֹּאת לַיהוָה
וַיֹּאמְרוּ לֵאמֹר אָשִׁירָה לַיהוָה כִּי־גָאֹה גָּאָה סוּס
ב וְרֹכְבוֹ רָמָה בַיָּם׃ עָזִּי וְזִמְרָת יָהּ וַיְהִי־לִי
לִישׁוּעָה זֶה אֵלִי וְאַנְוֵהוּ אֱלֹהֵי
ג אָבִי וַאֲרֹמְמֶנְהוּ׃ יְהוָה אִישׁ מִלְחָמָה יְהוָה

greatness is humility, and to be a leader is to be a servant. On this, the Sages asked: What is it to be a leader of the Jewish people? Is it to hold official authority, of which the supreme example is a king? Is it to have the kind of personal relationship with one's followers that rests not on honor and deference but on encouraging people to grow, accept responsibility, and continue the journey you have begun? Or is it something in between?

There is no single answer. At times, Moshe asserted his authority (for example, during the Koraḥ rebellion). At another, he said, "Would that all the Lord's people were prophets" (Num. 11:29). There are times when it is important to show that "there is only one leader for the generation, not two" (Sanhedrin 8a), and others when the highest mark of leadership is inviting others to share in it (Sanhedrin ad loc.).

We are each called on to fill a number of leadership roles: as parents, teachers, friends, team members, and team leaders. And there is no one Torah model of leadership. There is no doubt, however, that Judaism favors as an ideal the role of parent, encouraging those we lead to continue the journey we have begun, and go further than we did. A good leader creates followers. A great leader creates leaders. That was Moshe's greatest achievement – that he left behind him a people willing, in each generation, to accept responsibility for taking further the great task he had begun.

THE SONG OF THE SEA

For the first time since their departure from Egypt, the Israelites do something together. They sing. In recollection of that moment, tradition has named the week when we read this passage *Shabbat Shira*, the Sabbath of Song. The first of the great celebratory songs in Israel's history, it subsequently became known as "the song" par excellence. The song has three strophes: the first (vv. 1–6) celebrating the victory at the sea, the second (7–11) restating it in more vivid imagery, and the third (12–18) looking toward the future. The concluding verse of each strophe (vv. 6, 11, and 18) is a majestic statement of God's sovereignty and might. There are several views in the Mishna, Tosefta, and Talmud (Sota 30b) as to how it was sung. Some say that the Israelites repeated "I will sing to the Lord" after each verse; others that they sang it line by line after Moshe; others that Moshe began each line and the Israelites completed it; yet others (a view adopted by Rashi) that the entire people

4 war; / the LORD is His name. / Pharaoh's chariots and
army / He hurled into the sea; / the best of his officers /
5 drowned in the Sea of Reeds. / The deep waters covered
6 them; / they sank to the depths like a stone. / Your right
hand, LORD, majestic in power, / Your right hand, LORD,
7 shatters the enemy. / In the greatness of Your majesty, You
overthrew those who rose against You. / You sent forth
8 Your rage; it consumed them like stubble. / By the blast of
Your nostrils the waters heaped; / the surge stood upright
as a wall; / the deeps congealed at the heart of the sea. /
9 The enemy said, "I will give chase, will overtake, / I will
divide the spoils. / My desire shall gorge its fill of them. /
I will draw my sword, / and my hand destroy them." /
10 You blew with Your wind; the sea covered over them. /
11 They sank like lead in mighty waters. / Who is like You,
LORD, among the mighty? / Who is like You – majestic
12 in holiness, / awesome in glory, working wonders? / You
reached out Your right hand – / the earth swallowed
13 them up. / In Your love, You guided out the people You

---

is full of light, said the Jewish mystics, if we only know how to open our eyes. The Psalms are a symphony of praise. They say: See the glory of creation. Look at all the beauty that surrounds you. Listen to the song of a bird. Look carefully at the beauty of a tree, its leaves shimmering in the breeze. Pause and inhale the sheer miracle of being. Remind yourself, slowly, gently: I am here. The universe is here. I am alive. I am free. I am capable of love and I am loved. And I will praise the force that made all this and allowed me to be here and see it.

Then feel the restlessness subside, the striving cease, the pulse slow, and know for a moment the sheer blessedness of being. It is there, waiting to be uncovered, in the secret places of the soul. Praise is where the journey into happiness begins.

Among my favorite lines of poetry are the words of W. H. Auden about the power of the imagination to liberate us from negative emotion:

> In the desert of the heart
> Let the healing fountain start.
> In the prison of his days
> Teach the free man how to praise.

15:13 נָחִיתָ בְחַסְדְּךָ... נֵהַלְתָּ בְעָזְּךָ *In Your love, You guided.... In Your strength, You led* – Both phrases are suggestive of a shepherd leading his sheep, and indeed, both are echoed in Psalm 23, "The LORD

ד שְׁמוֹ׃ מַרְכְּבֹת פַּרְעֹה וְחֵילוֹ יָרָה בַיָּם וּמִבְחַר
ה שָׁלִשָׁיו טֻבְּעוּ בְיַם־סוּף׃ תְּהֹמֹת יְכַסְיֻמוּ יָרְדוּ בִמְצוֹלֹת
ו כְּמוֹ־אָבֶן׃ יְמִינְךָ יהוה נֶאְדָּרִי בַּכֹּחַ יְמִינְךָ
ז יהוה תִּרְעַץ אוֹיֵב׃ וּבְרֹב גְּאוֹנְךָ תַּהֲרֹס
ח קָמֶיךָ תְּשַׁלַּח חֲרֹנְךָ יֹאכְלֵמוֹ כַּקַּשׁ׃ וּבְרוּחַ
אַפֶּיךָ נֶעֶרְמוּ מַיִם נִצְּבוּ כְמוֹ־נֵד
ט נֹזְלִים קָפְאוּ תְהֹמֹת בְּלֶב־יָם׃ אָמַר
אוֹיֵב אֶרְדֹּף אַשִּׂיג אֲחַלֵּק שָׁלָל תִּמְלָאֵמוֹ
י נַפְשִׁי אָרִיק חַרְבִּי תּוֹרִישֵׁמוֹ יָדִי׃ נָשַׁפְתָּ
בְרוּחֲךָ כִּסָּמוֹ יָם צָלְלוּ כַּעוֹפֶרֶת בְּמַיִם
יא אַדִּירִים׃ מִי־כָמֹכָה בָּאֵלִם יהוה מִי
כָּמֹכָה נֶאְדָּר בַּקֹּדֶשׁ נוֹרָא תְהִלֹּת עֹשֵׂה
יב יג פֶלֶא׃ נָטִיתָ יְמִינְךָ תִּבְלָעֵמוֹ אָרֶץ׃ נָחִיתָ
בְחַסְדְּךָ עַם־זוּ גָּאָלְתָּ נֵהַלְתָּ בְעָזְּךָ אֶל־נְוֵה

---

children will learn to love. And there is no other way to teach your children. It is not only what you say to them. It is not even what you do to them. It is the way your life reflects your loves. Those are the things our children absorb and, hopefully, make their own. Or, as the English poet William Wordsworth wrote in his great poem, "The Prelude": "What we love others will love, and we will show them how."

15:11 נוֹרָא תְהִלֹּת *Awesome in glory* – One of the many, many Hebrew words for praise. In one sentence alone, the Siddur mentions *lehodot, lehallel, leshabe'aḥ, lefa'er, leromem, lehader, levarekh, le'aleh, ulekales.* To be a Jew is to live amidst the praise of God. It is the air our spirit breathes, the music the Jewish soul sings. We gave the English language the word *halleluya,* "praise be to God," and the book of Psalms remains the most beautiful poetry of praise ever written.

Jewish prayer always starts with praise. It takes different forms in different services, but it is always there before anything else. Why? Because on the bad days we can be distracted by worry, depressed by anxiety, clouded by fear. We turn in on ourselves, as if we were shut in a small, airless room, unable to see the sunlight or breathe the free air.

Which is why prayer as praise is so important. It says: Don't look in; look out. Don't look down; look up. The world

▶

redeemed. / In Your strength, You led them to Your holy
14 abode. / Nations heard and they trembled; / terror seized
15 the Philistines. / The chiefs of Edom were dismayed,
then, / Moav's leaders were seized with trembling, / the
16 people of Canaan melted away. / Dread, terror fell upon
them; / by Your arm's power they were stilled as stone – /
until Your people crossed, LORD, / until the people You
17 acquired crossed over. / You will bring them, You will
plant them on the mountain, Your heritage – / the place,
LORD, that You made for Your dwelling, / the Sanctuary,
18 LORD, that Your hands established. / The LORD will reign
19 for ever and all time. // This they sang when Pharaoh's
horses, chariots, and cavalry had gone into the sea /
and the LORD had brought the waters of the sea back
over them / while the Israelites had walked on dry land
through the sea.

20 Then Miriam, the prophetess, sister of Aharon, took a
tambourine in her hand, and all the women followed her
21 with tambourines and dance. And Miriam led them in

---

a miraculous experience, nor merely an escape from defeat and death, but also a fundamental rite of passage: Israel has become the nation whose sovereign is God Himself.

15:19 וּבְנֵי יִשְׂרָאֵל הָלְכוּ בַיַּבָּשָׁה בְּתוֹךְ הַיָּם *The Israelites had walked on dry land through the sea* – Emil Fackenheim has spoken of "epoch-making events" that transform the course of history. The French philosopher Alain Badiou has similarly proposed the concept of an "event" as a "rupture in ontology" through which individuals are brought face-to-face with a truth that changes them and their world. It is as if all normal perception fades away and we know that we are in the presence of something momentous, to which we sense we must remain faithful for the rest of our lives. It is through transformative events that we feel ourselves addressed, summoned, by something beyond history, breaking through into history. In this sense, the division of the Reed Sea was something other and deeper than a suspension of the laws of nature. It was the transformative moment at which the people "were in awe of the LORD, and they believed in Him and in Moshe His servant" (Ex. 14:31) and called themselves "the people You acquired" (15:16).

יד קָדְשֶׁךָ׃ שָׁמְעוּ עַמִּים יִרְגָּזוּן חִיל
טו אָחַז יֹשְׁבֵי פְּלָשֶׁת׃ אָז נִבְהֲלוּ אַלּוּפֵי
אֱדוֹם אֵילֵי מוֹאָב יֹאחֲזֵמוֹ רָעַד נָמֹגוּ
טז כֹּל יֹשְׁבֵי כְנָעַן׃ תִּפֹּל עֲלֵיהֶם אֵימָתָה
וָפַחַד בִּגְדֹל זְרוֹעֲךָ יִדְּמוּ כָּאָבֶן עַד־
יַעֲבֹר עַמְּךָ יְהוָה עַד־יַעֲבֹר עַם־זוּ
יז קָנִיתָ׃ תְּבִאֵמוֹ וְתִטָּעֵמוֹ בְּהַר נַחֲלָתְךָ מָכוֹן
לְשִׁבְתְּךָ פָּעַלְתָּ יְהוָה מִקְּדָשׁ אֲדֹנָי כּוֹנְנוּ
יח יט יָדֶיךָ׃ יְהוָה ׀ יִמְלֹךְ לְעֹלָם וָעֶד׃ כִּי
בָא סוּס פַּרְעֹה בְּרִכְבּוֹ וּבְפָרָשָׁיו בַּיָּם וַיָּשֶׁב יְהוָה עֲלֵהֶם אֶת־מֵי
הַיָּם וּבְנֵי יִשְׂרָאֵל הָלְכוּ בַיַּבָּשָׁה בְּתוֹךְ הַיָּם׃

כ וַתִּקַּח מִרְיָם הַנְּבִיאָה אֲחוֹת אַהֲרֹן אֶת־הַתֹּף בְּיָדָהּ וַתֵּצֶאןָ
כא כָל־הַנָּשִׁים אַחֲרֶיהָ בְּתֻפִּים וּבִמְחֹלֹת׃ וַתַּעַן לָהֶם מִרְיָם שִׁירוּ
כב לַיהוָה כִּי־גָאֹה גָּאָה סוּס וְרֹכְבוֹ רָמָה בַיָּם׃ וַיַּסַּע

is my Shepherd." The contrast is striking between the military images of God acting against the enemies of His people, and the pastoral imagery here of God's tender concern for His people, His flock. The assertion that immediately follows, that the people of the land would be terrified when they heard of the miracle at the Reed Sea, was confirmed by later reports in the days of Yehoshua (Josh. 2:9–11).

15:17 מִקְּדָשׁ אֲדֹנָי כּוֹנְנוּ יָדֶיךָ *The Sanctuary… that Your hands established* – The building of the Temple by Shlomo, begun "in the four hundred and eightieth year after the Israelites left Egypt" (I Kings 6:1), is the only event in the history of Israel to be dated by reference to the exodus. And here, as the Israelites cross the Reed Sea, they end their song by looking forward to the building of the Temple.

The Temple was the symbol of the presence of God among a people that had established itself as a sovereign power in its own land. The building of the Temple was thus the final act in the drama begun by the exodus, and brought it to closure.

15:18 יְהוָה יִמְלֹךְ לְעֹלָם וָעֶד *The Lord will reign for ever* – A key verse, marking the first time in the Torah that God has been described as a king. Crossing the sea has been for the Israelites not just

song: Sing to the LORD, for He has triumphed in glory; /
22 horse and horseman He hurled into the sea. Moshe
then led the Israelites from the Sea of Reeds out into the
desert of Shur. For three days, they journeyed across the
23 desert without finding water. Eventually they came to
Mara, but they could not drink the water there because it
24 was bitter; because of this it was named Mara. The people
25 railed against Moshe – "What are we to drink?" Moshe
cried out to the LORD. And the LORD showed him a piece
of wood, which he threw into the water – and the water
became sweet. It was there that the LORD gave His people
decree and law; it was there that He put them to the test.
26 He said, "If you listen faithfully to the voice of the LORD
your God, doing what is right in His eyes, heeding His
commands and keeping His decrees, I will not bring on
you any of the sicknesses I brought on the Egyptians, for

15:25 וַיּוֹרֵהוּ יהוה עֵץ וַיַּשְׁלֵךְ אֶל־הַמַּיִם *The LORD showed him a piece of wood, which he threw into the water* – One would not expect that further "polluting" the water would make it fit for drinking. A beautiful midrash explores the symbolism of this event: "See how different are the ways of God from the ways of flesh and blood. Flesh and blood seek to use sweetness to heal bitterness. But the One at whose word the world became – He is not so. Rather, He uses bitterness to heal bitterness. How so? He places the thing that harms into the thing that is harmed – and uses it to perform a miracle" (Mekhilta). We often seek to "cure" suffering through distraction and denial. That is not God's way. Pain and loneliness are forms of energy that can be transformed if we turn them outward, using them to recognize and redeem someone else's pain and loneliness. To heal where others harm, mend where others destroy, to redeem evil by turning its negative energies to good: these are the mark of the ethics of responsibility, born in the radical faith that God calls on us to exercise our freedom by becoming His partners in the work of creation. "Good represents the reality of which God is the dream," wrote Iris Murdoch. And in the words of W. B. Yeats, "In dreams begin responsibilities." Among many survivors of unspeakable tragedy I sense an extraordinary gesture of *tikkun*, mending. When we face up to evil courageously, as free people, we find that though it can never be justified as the will of God, it can in some ways be redeemed. Perhaps this is the message the Sages heard in this brief story, just days after the end of the people's centuries-long slavery.

מֹשֶׁה אֶת־יִשְׂרָאֵל מִיַּם־סוּף וַיֵּצְאוּ אֶל־מִדְבַּר־שׁוּר וַיֵּלְכוּ
כג שְׁלֹשֶׁת־יָמִים בַּמִּדְבָּר וְלֹא־מָצְאוּ מָיִם: וַיָּבֹאוּ מָרָתָה וְלֹא
יָכְלוּ לִשְׁתֹּת מַיִם מִמָּרָה כִּי מָרִים הֵם עַל־כֵּן קָרָא־שְׁמָהּ
כד כה מָרָה: וַיִּלֹּנוּ הָעָם עַל־מֹשֶׁה לֵּאמֹר מַה־נִּשְׁתֶּה: וַיִּצְעַק אֶל־
יהוה וַיּוֹרֵהוּ יהוה עֵץ וַיַּשְׁלֵךְ אֶל־הַמַּיִם וַיִּמְתְּקוּ הַמָּיִם שָׁם
כו שָׂם לוֹ חֹק וּמִשְׁפָּט וְשָׁם נִסָּהוּ: וַיֹּאמֶר אִם־שָׁמוֹעַ תִּשְׁמַע
לְקוֹל ׀ יהוה אֱלֹהֶיךָ וְהַיָּשָׁר בְּעֵינָיו תַּעֲשֶׂה וְהַאֲזַנְתָּ לְמִצְוֹתָיו
וְשָׁמַרְתָּ כָּל־חֻקָּיו כָּל־הַמַּחֲלָה אֲשֶׁר־שַׂמְתִּי בְמִצְרַיִם לֹא־

15:22 שְׁלֹשֶׁת־יָמִים *Three days* – This is how long it takes, from the euphoric moment when the people "witnessed the wondrous power the LORD had unleashed against the Egyptians... and they believed in Him and in Moshe His servant" (Ex. 14:31) for their doubts to spill out into protest.

Two of the most powerful parodies of the "scientific" approach to faith (what is believable is only that which is empirically confirmed) are contained in the book of Exodus. God "empirically" confirms His existence to Pharaoh through the plagues, but at the same time gives him the "strength" or "hardness" of heart to disbelieve. And in our *parasha*, God demonstrates His presence to the Israelites at the division of the Reed Sea: they "see" and therefore "believe," yet here in the very next passage they are rebellious again. The faith that requires this kind of confirmation is not faith.

A fundamental axiom of Torah is that God is not seen but heard. He is not to be found in "objective" history (events as they are grasped by the senses) but in covenantal history (events as they are perceived through the "word" of faith). Genesis is a set of variations on the dissonance between the divine word (the promise of children and a land) and empirical reality (the childlessness of the matriarchs and the landlessness of the patriarchs).

The only empirical claim the Torah makes about itself is that the people who live by its covenant will, obscurely but unmistakably, testify to the presence of God in history. This I believe to be true.

One of the great Enlightenment ideas is that texts (religious texts especially) are a veil covering a pristine core of historical truth, which must be removed if objectivity is to be arrived at. This is a way not of reading the Bible but of misreading it, to which the most eloquent commentary is the Bible itself. God is not seen with the senses but heard with the ear of faith. He is, to use Buber's terms, not in the "It" of empiricism but the "Thou" of relationship: the relationship of loyalty, fidelity, and trust whose formal expression is covenant.

27 I am the LORD – your Healer." And then they ḤAMISHI
arrived at Eilim, where there were twelve springs and
seventy date palms. They encamped there by the water.
16 1 They set out from Eilim, and on the fifteenth day of the
second month after leaving Egypt, the congregation of
Israel all arrived at the desert of Sin, between Eilim and
2 Sinai. In the desert, all the community started railing
3 against Moshe and Aharon. The Israelites said to them, "If
only we had died by the LORD's hand in Egypt, when we sat
by the fleshpots and ate our fill of bread. Instead, you have
brought us out into this desert to kill the entire assembly
4 by starvation." Then the LORD said to Moshe,
"I am going to rain down bread from heaven. Let the
people go out and gather enough for each day; I will test
5 them to see whether they will follow My law or not. On
the sixth day, they will have to prepare what they bring in.
It will be twice as much as they gather on all other days."
6 So Moshe and Aharon told all the Israelites, "At evening
you will know that it was the LORD who brought you out
7 of Egypt, and by morning you shall see the LORD's glory,
for He has heard you railing against Him. As for us, what
8 are we that you rail against us?" Then Moshe said, "In the
evening, the LORD will give you meat to eat, and in the
morning bread to fill you, for He has heard you railing
against Him. We – what are we? It is not us you rail against,
9 but the LORD." Then Moshe said to Aharon, "Tell all the
community of Israel to come before the LORD, because

---

yield of the land…. The manna stopped falling the day after they had eaten from the yield of the land"). To them, freedom means building a society, creating farms, plowing the land, producing our own food. The Zohar, indeed, calls manna *nahama dekisufa*, the bread of shame. Why? Because we did not work for it.

We should not need miracles, nor should we rely on them. Judaism is a religion that celebrates law: the natural law that governs the physical universe, and the moral law that governs the human universe. God is found in order, not in the miraculous suspension of that order. Faith is about seeing the miraculous in the everyday, not about waiting every day for the miraculous.

כז אֲשֶׁים עָלֶיךָ כִּי אֲנִי יהוה רֹפְאֶךָ׃ וַיָּבֹאוּ אֵילִמָה חמישי
וְשָׁם שְׁתֵּים עֶשְׂרֵה עֵינֹת מַיִם וְשִׁבְעִים תְּמָרִים וַיַּחֲנוּ־שָׁם
טז א עַל־הַמָּיִם׃ וַיִּסְעוּ מֵאֵילִם וַיָּבֹאוּ כָּל־עֲדַת בְּנֵי־יִשְׂרָאֵל
אֶל־מִדְבַּר־סִין אֲשֶׁר בֵּין־אֵילִם וּבֵין סִינָי בַּחֲמִשָּׁה עָשָׂר
ב יוֹם לַחֹדֶשׁ הַשֵּׁנִי לְצֵאתָם מֵאֶרֶץ מִצְרָיִם׃ וילינו כָּל־ וַיִּלּוֹנוּ
ג עֲדַת בְּנֵי־יִשְׂרָאֵל עַל־מֹשֶׁה וְעַל־אַהֲרֹן בַּמִּדְבָּר׃ וַיֹּאמְרוּ
אֲלֵהֶם בְּנֵי יִשְׂרָאֵל מִי־יִתֵּן מוּתֵנוּ בְיַד־יהוה בְּאֶרֶץ מִצְרַיִם
בְּשִׁבְתֵּנוּ עַל־סִיר הַבָּשָׂר בְּאָכְלֵנוּ לֶחֶם לָשֹׂבַע כִּי־הוֹצֵאתֶם
אֹתָנוּ אֶל־הַמִּדְבָּר הַזֶּה לְהָמִית אֶת־כָּל־הַקָּהָל הַזֶּה
ד בָּרָעָב׃ וַיֹּאמֶר יהוה אֶל־מֹשֶׁה הִנְנִי מַמְטִיר יב
לָכֶם לֶחֶם מִן־הַשָּׁמָיִם וְיָצָא הָעָם וְלָקְטוּ דְּבַר־יוֹם בְּיוֹמוֹ
ה לְמַעַן אֲנַסֶּנּוּ הֲיֵלֵךְ בְּתוֹרָתִי אִם־לֹא׃ וְהָיָה בַּיּוֹם הַשִּׁשִּׁי
וְהֵכִינוּ אֵת אֲשֶׁר־יָבִיאוּ וְהָיָה מִשְׁנֶה עַל אֲשֶׁר־יִלְקְטוּ יוֹם ׀
ו יוֹם׃ וַיֹּאמֶר מֹשֶׁה וְאַהֲרֹן אֶל־כָּל־בְּנֵי יִשְׂרָאֵל עֶרֶב וִידַעְתֶּם
ז כִּי יהוה הוֹצִיא אֶתְכֶם מֵאֶרֶץ מִצְרָיִם׃ וּבֹקֶר וּרְאִיתֶם אֶת־
כְּבוֹד יהוה בְּשָׁמְעוֹ אֶת־תְּלֻנֹּתֵיכֶם עַל־יהוה וְנַחְנוּ מָה כִּי
ח תלונו עָלֵינוּ׃ וַיֹּאמֶר מֹשֶׁה בְּתֵת יהוה לָכֶם בָּעֶרֶב בָּשָׂר תַלִּינוּ
לֶאֱכֹל וְלֶחֶם בַּבֹּקֶר לִשְׂבֹּעַ בִּשְׁמֹעַ יהוה אֶת־תְּלֻנֹּתֵיכֶם
אֲשֶׁר־אַתֶּם מַלִּינִם עָלָיו וְנַחְנוּ מָה לֹא־עָלֵינוּ תְלֻנֹּתֵיכֶם
ט כִּי עַל־יהוה׃ וַיֹּאמֶר מֹשֶׁה אֶל־אַהֲרֹן אֱמֹר אֶל־כָּל־עֲדַת

16:1 בַּחֲמִשָּׁה עָשָׂר יוֹם לַחֹדֶשׁ הַשֵּׁנִי *The fifteenth day of the second month* – This was one month after leaving Egypt. Rashi explains: "Because that was the day the supply of matza ran out and they needed food…and the manna fell on the sixteenth [of Iyar], and that was Sunday."

The timing mentioned here, as we shall later see, appears to be the reason behind the Sadducee ruling that we begin the counting of the Omer "the day after the Sabbath" (Lev. 23:15), meaning Sunday. To them, it celebrated the freedom of being in the wilderness and receiving sustenance from heaven by a miracle.

The Pharisees, however, link the counting of the Omer not to the beginning, but to the end of the period of the manna (Josh. 5:11–12, "On the day after the Passover sacrifice, they ate of the

10 He has heard your railing." As soon as Aharon had spoken
to the whole community of Israel, they looked toward the
desert – and the glory of the LORD appeared in the midst of
cloud.
11 12 The LORD spoke to Moshe and said, "I have heard the SHISHI
Israelites' railing. Tell them: At twilight you shall eat meat,
and in the morning your fill of bread. Then you will know
13 that I am the LORD your God." That evening a flock of
quail flew in and covered the camp; next morning a layer
14 of dew surrounded the camp. When the dew covering
lifted, fine flakes covered the floor of the desert like fine
15 frost on the ground. When the Israelites saw it, they asked
one another, "What is it?" for they did not recognize it.
Moshe said to them, "This is the bread the LORD has
16 given you to eat. This is what the LORD has instructed:
Each of you gather as much as you need, an omer for
every person; each take enough for all the people in your
17 tent." The people of Israel did so. Some gathered more,
18 others less. But when they measured it with an omer
measure, those who had gathered much had none left
over, and those who gathered but little did not fall short.
19 All had gathered as much as they could eat. "Let no one
20 leave any over for the morning," said Moshe; but they
did not listen to Moshe. Some of them left part of it till
morning, and it became worm infested and stank. Moshe
21 was enraged with them. Every morning they gathered it,
all as much as they could eat, and when the sun grew hot,
22 it melted away. When the sixth day came, they gathered
a double portion, two omer each. All the leaders of the
23 community came and reported this to Moshe. "This," he
told them, "is what the LORD has said: Tomorrow is a day
of rest, a holy Sabbath to the LORD. Bake now what you
need to bake and cook what you need to cook. Whatever
24 is left, keep carefully aside for the morning." So they
put it aside until the morning, as Moshe had instructed
25 them, and it did not stink, nor did worms infest it. And
Moshe said, "Today, eat this, for today is a Sabbath to the

י בְּנֵי יִשְׂרָאֵל קִרְבוּ לִפְנֵי יהוה כִּי שָׁמַע אֵת תְּלֻנֹּתֵיכֶם: וַיְהִי
כְּדַבֵּר אַהֲרֹן אֶל־כָּל־עֲדַת בְּנֵי־יִשְׂרָאֵל וַיִּפְנוּ אֶל־הַמִּדְבָּר
וְהִנֵּה כְּבוֹד יהוה נִרְאָה בֶּעָנָן:
יא יב וַיְדַבֵּר יהוה אֶל־מֹשֶׁה לֵּאמֹר: שָׁמַעְתִּי אֶת־תְּלוּנֹּת בְּנֵי ששי
יִשְׂרָאֵל דַּבֵּר אֲלֵהֶם לֵאמֹר בֵּין הָעַרְבַּיִם תֹּאכְלוּ בָשָׂר
יג וּבַבֹּקֶר תִּשְׂבְּעוּ־לָחֶם וִידַעְתֶּם כִּי אֲנִי יהוה אֱלֹהֵיכֶם: וַיְהִי
בָעֶרֶב וַתַּעַל הַשְּׂלָו וַתְּכַס אֶת־הַמַּחֲנֶה וּבַבֹּקֶר הָיְתָה שִׁכְבַת
יד הַטַּל סָבִיב לַמַּחֲנֶה: וַתַּעַל שִׁכְבַת הַטָּל וְהִנֵּה עַל־פְּנֵי
טו הַמִּדְבָּר דַּק מְחֻסְפָּס דַּק כַּכְּפֹר עַל־הָאָרֶץ: וַיִּרְאוּ בְנֵי־
יִשְׂרָאֵל וַיֹּאמְרוּ אִישׁ אֶל־אָחִיו מָן הוּא כִּי לֹא יָדְעוּ מַה־
הוּא וַיֹּאמֶר מֹשֶׁה אֲלֵהֶם הוּא הַלֶּחֶם אֲשֶׁר נָתַן יהוה לָכֶם
טז לְאָכְלָה: זֶה הַדָּבָר אֲשֶׁר צִוָּה יהוה לִקְטוּ מִמֶּנּוּ אִישׁ לְפִי
אָכְלוֹ עֹמֶר לַגֻּלְגֹּלֶת מִסְפַּר נַפְשֹׁתֵיכֶם אִישׁ לַאֲשֶׁר בְּאָהֳלוֹ
יז תִּקָּחוּ: וַיַּעֲשׂוּ־כֵן בְּנֵי יִשְׂרָאֵל וַיִּלְקְטוּ הַמַּרְבֶּה וְהַמַּמְעִיט:
יח וַיָּמֹדּוּ בָעֹמֶר וְלֹא הֶעְדִּיף הַמַּרְבֶּה וְהַמַּמְעִיט לֹא הֶחְסִיר
יט אִישׁ לְפִי־אָכְלוֹ לָקָטוּ: וַיֹּאמֶר מֹשֶׁה אֲלֵהֶם אִישׁ אַל־יוֹתֵר
כ מִמֶּנּוּ עַד־בֹּקֶר: וְלֹא־שָׁמְעוּ אֶל־מֹשֶׁה וַיּוֹתִרוּ אֲנָשִׁים מִמֶּנּוּ
כא עַד־בֹּקֶר וַיָּרֻם תּוֹלָעִים וַיִּבְאַשׁ וַיִּקְצֹף עֲלֵהֶם מֹשֶׁה: וַיִּלְקְטוּ
כב אֹתוֹ בַּבֹּקֶר בַּבֹּקֶר אִישׁ כְּפִי אָכְלוֹ וְחַם הַשֶּׁמֶשׁ וְנָמָס: וַיְהִי ׀
בַּיּוֹם הַשִּׁשִּׁי לָקְטוּ לֶחֶם מִשְׁנֶה שְׁנֵי הָעֹמֶר לָאֶחָד וַיָּבֹאוּ
כג כָּל־נְשִׂיאֵי הָעֵדָה וַיַּגִּידוּ לְמֹשֶׁה: וַיֹּאמֶר אֲלֵהֶם הוּא אֲשֶׁר
דִּבֶּר יהוה שַׁבָּתוֹן שַׁבַּת־קֹדֶשׁ לַיהוה מָחָר אֵת אֲשֶׁר־
תֹּאפוּ אֵפוּ וְאֵת אֲשֶׁר־תְּבַשְּׁלוּ בַּשֵּׁלוּ וְאֵת כָּל־הָעֹדֵף הַנִּיחוּ
כד לָכֶם לְמִשְׁמֶרֶת עַד־הַבֹּקֶר: וַיַּנִּיחוּ אֹתוֹ עַד־הַבֹּקֶר כַּאֲשֶׁר
כה צִוָּה מֹשֶׁה וְלֹא הִבְאִישׁ וְרִמָּה לֹא־הָיְתָה־בּוֹ: וַיֹּאמֶר מֹשֶׁה
אִכְלֻהוּ הַיּוֹם כִּי־שַׁבָּת הַיּוֹם לַיהוה הַיּוֹם לֹא תִמְצָאֻהוּ

26 Lord; today you will not find it on the ground. Six days
shall you gather it, but on the seventh day, the Sabbath,
27 it will not be there." Some people did go out to gather it
28 on the seventh day; but they found none. Then
the Lord said to Moshe, "How long will you refuse to
29 keep My commandments and laws? Understand that
the Lord has given you a Sabbath – that is why He gave
you two days' bread on the sixth day. You shall each rest
where you are: let no man depart from where he is on
30 the seventh day." So the people rested on the seventh day.
31 The House of Israel named it manna. It looked like white
coriander seeds, and tasted like wafers made with honey.
32 Moshe said, "This is what the Lord commands: Let an
omer of it be kept carefully aside for your descendants,
that they may see the bread I fed you in the desert when
33 I brought you out of Egypt." Moshe said to Aharon,
"Take an urn, put an omer of manna in it, and place it
34 before the Lord to be kept for future generations." As the

---

smartphones, and the demands of 24/7 availability.

God wants the Israelites to begin their one-day-in-seven rehearsal of freedom almost as soon as they leave Egypt, because real freedom, of the seven-days-in-seven kind, takes time, centuries, millennia. The Torah regards slavery as wrong, but it does not abolish it immediately because people are not yet ready. Neither Britain nor America abolished it until the nineteenth century, and even then not without a struggle. Yet the outcome is inevitable once the Sabbath has been set in motion. Slaves who know freedom one day in seven will eventually rise against their chains.

16:33 לְדֹרֹתֵיכֶם *For future generations* – Religions are guardians of memory. Much of Judaism is timeless – our beliefs, our values, our way of life. The days, the years, the centuries pass, but Judaism and the Jewish people remain. But there is something else in Jewish existence that renders us acutely sensitive to time. In one of the classics of modern Jewish scholarship, *Zakhor*, Professor Yosef Hayim Yerushalmi writes: "It was ancient Israel that first assigned a decisive significance to history and thus forged a new world-view….'The heavens,' in the words of the psalmist, might still 'tell of God's glory' (Ps. 19:2), but it was human history that revealed His will and purpose…. Far from attempting a flight from history, biblical religion allows itself to be saturated by it and is

כו בַּשָּׂדֶה: שֵׁשֶׁת יָמִים תִּלְקְטֻהוּ וּבַיּוֹם הַשְּׁבִיעִי שַׁבָּת לֹא
כז יִהְיֶה־בּוֹ: וַיְהִי בַּיּוֹם הַשְּׁבִיעִי יָצְאוּ מִן־הָעָם לִלְקֹט וְלֹא
כח מָצָאוּ: וַיֹּאמֶר יהוה אֶל־מֹשֶׁה עַד־אָנָה יג
כט מֵאַנְתֶּם לִשְׁמֹר מִצְוֹתַי וְתוֹרֹתָי: רְאוּ כִּי־יהוה נָתַן לָכֶם
הַשַּׁבָּת עַל־כֵּן הוּא נֹתֵן לָכֶם בַּיּוֹם הַשִּׁשִּׁי לֶחֶם יוֹמָיִם שְׁבוּ ׀
ל אִישׁ תַּחְתָּיו אַל־יֵצֵא אִישׁ מִמְּקֹמוֹ בַּיּוֹם הַשְּׁבִיעִי: וַיִּשְׁבְּתוּ
לא הָעָם בַּיּוֹם הַשְּׁבִעִי: וַיִּקְרְאוּ בֵית־יִשְׂרָאֵל אֶת־שְׁמוֹ מָן
לב וְהוּא כְּזֶרַע גַּד לָבָן וְטַעְמוֹ כְּצַפִּיחִת בִּדְבָשׁ: וַיֹּאמֶר מֹשֶׁה
זֶה הַדָּבָר אֲשֶׁר צִוָּה יהוה מְלֹא הָעֹמֶר מִמֶּנּוּ לְמִשְׁמֶרֶת
לְדֹרֹתֵיכֶם לְמַעַן ׀ יִרְאוּ אֶת־הַלֶּחֶם אֲשֶׁר הֶאֱכַלְתִּי אֶתְכֶם
לג בַּמִּדְבָּר בְּהוֹצִיאִי אֶתְכֶם מֵאֶרֶץ מִצְרָיִם: וַיֹּאמֶר מֹשֶׁה
אֶל־אַהֲרֹן קַח צִנְצֶנֶת אַחַת וְתֶן־שָׁמָּה מְלֹא־הָעֹמֶר מָן
לד וְהַנַּח אֹתוֹ לִפְנֵי יהוה לְמִשְׁמֶרֶת לְדֹרֹתֵיכֶם: כַּאֲשֶׁר צִוָּה

THE SABBATH

The Sabbath is among the first commands the Israelites receive on leaving Egypt. They are not to gather manna on the seventh day. Instead, a double portion will fall on the sixth. To this day we have two challot on the Sabbath, in memory of that time. On this day, we do not live from hand to mouth.

The Sabbath changed the way the world thought about time. Prior to Judaism, people measured time either by the sun – the solar calendar of 365 days aligning us with the seasons – or by the moon, that is, by months of roughly thirty days. The idea of the seven-day week – which has no counterpart in nature – was born in the Torah and spread throughout the world via Christianity and Islam. We have years because of the sun, months because of the moon, and weeks because of the Jews.

What the Sabbath did and still does is to create space within our lives and within society as a whole in which we are truly free. Free from the pressures of work, free from the demands of ruthless employers, free from the siren calls of a consumer society urging us to spend our way to happiness, free to be ourselves in the company of those we love. Somehow this one day has renewed its meaning in generation after generation, despite the most profound economic and industrial change. In Moshe's day it meant freedom from slavery to Pharaoh. In the nineteenth and early twentieth century it meant freedom from sweatshop working conditions of long hours for little pay. In ours, it means freedom from emails,

LORD commanded Moshe, so Aharon placed it before
35 the Ark of Testimony to be kept with care. The Israelites
ate manna for forty years, until they came to the land
where they could settle down. They ate the manna until
36 they came to the border of Canaan. An omer is a tenth of
an ephah.
17 1 All the community of Israel moved on after that from the SHEVI'I
desert of Sin, traveling from place to place as the LORD
guided them, and they camped at Refidim, but there was
2 no water there for the people to drink. The people started
to wrangle with Moshe. "Give us water to drink," they
raged. "Why do you wrangle with me?" asked Moshe.
3 "Why are you testing the LORD?" But the people were
thirsty for water. They railed against Moshe, "Why did
you bring us out of Egypt? Was it to kill me, my children,
4 and all my livestock by thirst?" "What shall I do with this
people?" Moshe cried to the LORD. "Another moment
5 and they will stone me." The LORD answered Moshe,
"Walk out to face the people taking some of the elders of
Israel with you. Take the staff with which you struck the
6 Nile in your hand, and go. I will be there before you by
the rock at Ḥorev. Strike the rock; water will come out of
it and the people will drink." And that is what Moshe did,

But then the climate changes. Eventually, it always does. That is when many businesses and politicians and marriages fail. There are times when even the greatest people stumble. At such moments, character is tested. The great human beings are not those who never fail. They are those who survive failure, who never give up or give in. They keep trying. They treat failure as a learning experience. And from every refusal to be defeated, they become stronger, wiser, and more determined.

That is the story of Moshe's life. Eventually he will become the man of whom it was said that he was "a hundred and twenty years old when he died," a man whose "eyes had not grown dim, nor his vitality fled" (Deut. 34:7). If there are times when we too feel discouraged and demoralized, it is important to remember that even the greatest people failed; what made them great is that they kept going.

לה יְהוָה אֶל־מֹשֶׁה וַיַּנִּיחֵהוּ אַהֲרֹן לִפְנֵי הָעֵדֻת לְמִשְׁמָרֶת: וּבְנֵי
יִשְׂרָאֵל אָכְלוּ אֶת־הַמָּן אַרְבָּעִים שָׁנָה עַד־בֹּאָם אֶל־אֶרֶץ
נוֹשָׁבֶת אֶת־הַמָּן אָכְלוּ עַד־בֹּאָם אֶל־קְצֵה אֶרֶץ כְּנָעַן:
לו וְהָעֹמֶר עֲשִׂרִית הָאֵיפָה הוּא:
יז א וַיִּסְעוּ כָּל־עֲדַת בְּנֵי־יִשְׂרָאֵל מִמִּדְבַּר־סִין לְמַסְעֵיהֶם עַל־ שביעי
ב פִּי יְהוָה וַיַּחֲנוּ בִּרְפִידִים וְאֵין מַיִם לִשְׁתֹּת הָעָם: וַיָּרֶב
הָעָם עִם־מֹשֶׁה וַיֹּאמְרוּ תְּנוּ־לָנוּ מַיִם וְנִשְׁתֶּה וַיֹּאמֶר לָהֶם
ג מֹשֶׁה מַה־תְּרִיבוּן עִמָּדִי מַה־תְּנַסּוּן אֶת־יְהוָה: וַיִּצְמָא שָׁם
הָעָם לַמַּיִם וַיָּלֶן הָעָם עַל־מֹשֶׁה וַיֹּאמֶר לָמָּה זֶּה הֶעֱלִיתָנוּ
מִמִּצְרַיִם לְהָמִית אֹתִי וְאֶת־בָּנַי וְאֶת־מִקְנַי בַּצָּמָא:
ד וַיִּצְעַק מֹשֶׁה אֶל־יְהוָה לֵאמֹר מָה אֶעֱשֶׂה לָעָם הַזֶּה עוֹד מְעַט
ה וּסְקָלֻנִי: וַיֹּאמֶר יְהוָה אֶל־מֹשֶׁה עֲבֹר לִפְנֵי הָעָם וְקַח אִתְּךָ
מִזִּקְנֵי יִשְׂרָאֵל וּמַטְּךָ אֲשֶׁר הִכִּיתָ בּוֹ אֶת־הַיְאֹר קַח בְּיָדְךָ
ו וְהָלָכְתָּ: הִנְנִי עֹמֵד לְפָנֶיךָ שָּׁם ׀ עַל־הַצּוּר בְּחֹרֵב וְהִכִּיתָ
בַצּוּר וְיָצְאוּ מִמֶּנּוּ מַיִם וְשָׁתָה הָעָם וַיַּעַשׂ כֵּן מֹשֶׁה לְעֵינֵי

inconceivable apart from it." Jews are a people of memory.

As the Israelites left Egypt, they were taught to reenact the story for their children. In but a few verses, they will be told to remember the battle with Amalek. In between, the everyday miracle of the manna is archived too for future memory. Even as they live it, the national story is being inscribed.

17:3 וַיָּלֶן הָעָם עַל־מֹשֶׁה *They railed against Moshe* – Note that as early as their first complaint (Ex. 14:11), the people have blamed Moshe, as if the decision were his, not God's – an ominous precursor of many complaints that were to follow during their time in the wilderness. His successes have been celebrated, but in times of difficulty the people turn against him.

In every field, leaders are tested not by their successes but by their response to failure. It can sometimes be easy to succeed. The conditions may be favorable. The economic, political, or personal climate is good. When there is an economic boom, most businesses flourish. In the first months after a general election, the successful leader carries the charisma of victory. In the first year, most marriages are happy. It takes no special skill to succeed in good times.

7 before the eyes of the elders of Israel. He named the place
Masa and Meriva, because the people had quarreled and
had tested the LORD, demanding, "Is the LORD among
us or not?"
8 9 Then, at Refidim, Amalek came and attacked Israel. Moshe
said to Yehoshua, "Choose men for us, and go out and do
battle against Amalek. Tomorrow I will stand on top of the

A leader, we learn, must empower the team. He cannot do the work for them; they must do it for themselves. But he must, at the same time, give them the absolute confidence that they can succeed. During the battle, he must betray no sign of weakness or doubt.

Yet all leaders have their moments of exhaustion. Moshe's hands "grew heavy." At such times the leader needs support – even Moshe needs the help of Aharon and Ḥur. In the end, though, his upraised hands were the sign the Israelites needed that God was giving them the strength to prevail, and they did.

"Not with valor and not with strength, but with My spirit," said the prophet (Zech. 4:6). Jewish history is a sustained set of variations on this theme. A small people that, in the face of difficulty, continues to look up will win great victories and achieve great things.

17:9 וְצֵא הִלָּחֵם בַּעֲמָלֵק *Do battle against Amalek* – Our *parasha* began with God's concern that "if the people face war… they will change their minds and go back to Egypt" (Ex. 13:17). Yet it ends with another battle, against the Amalekites. And here, *there is no complaint on the part of the people*, no fear, no trauma, no despair. Faced by the Amalekites, the Israelites do not say they want to return to Egypt. Their sheer silence stands in the strongest possible contrast to their earlier complaints about water and food. The Israelites turn out to be good warriors. Having crossed the sea, the people have no way back. They have crossed the Rubicon. Their boats and bridges are burned. They look only forward, for there is no return.

Rashbam connects Yaakov's wrestling match with the angel to the episode in which Moshe, returning to Egypt, is attacked by God (4:24), and also links this to Yona on the stormy ship (commentary on Gen. 32:21–29). All three, he says, were overcome by fear at the danger or difficulty that confronted them, and each wanted to escape. Yaakov's angel, Moshe's encounter, and the tempest that threatened to sink Yona's ship were all ways in which Heaven cut off the line of retreat.

Any great undertaking comes with fear. Often we fear failure. Sometimes we even fear success. We long for the security of the familiar, the life we have known. We are afraid of uncharted territory, and the journey itself exposes our vulnerability. Rashbam is telling us that

ז זִקְנֵי יִשְׂרָאֵל: וַיִּקְרָא שֵׁם הַמָּקוֹם מַסָּה וּמְרִיבָה עַל־רִיב ׀
בְּנֵי יִשְׂרָאֵל וְעַל נַסֹּתָם אֶת־יהוה לֵאמֹר הֲיֵשׁ יהוה בְּקִרְבֵּנוּ
אִם־אָיִן:
ח ט וַיָּבֹא עֲמָלֵק וַיִּלָּחֶם עִם־יִשְׂרָאֵל בִּרְפִידִם: וַיֹּאמֶר מֹשֶׁה אֶל־
יְהוֹשֻׁעַ בְּחַר־לָנוּ אֲנָשִׁים וְצֵא הִלָּחֵם בַּעֲמָלֵק מָחָר אָנֹכִי

AMALEK

The contrast between God's expectations from Israel before and after the crossing of the Reed Sea could not be more complete. Before, facing the approaching Egyptians, Moshe said to the people: "Stand firm and see the deliverance the LORD will bring you today.... The LORD will fight for you; you stay silent" (Ex. 14:13). In other words: Do nothing. God will do it for you. And He did.

In the case of the Amalekites, however, Moshe says to Yehoshua, "Choose men for us, and go out and do battle against Amalek" (17:9). Yehoshua does so and the people wage war. This is the great transition: the Israelites are moving from a situation in which the leader (with the help of God) does everything for the people, to one in which the leader empowers the people to do it for themselves.

The Torah focuses our attention on one detail as the battle with Amalek begins: Moshe climbs to the top of a hill overlooking the battlefield, with a staff in his hand:

> Whenever Moshe held his hand high, the Israelites prevailed, but whenever he let his hand drop, the Amalekites prevailed. But Moshe's hands grew heavy. So they took a stone and placed it under him and he sat, while Aharon and Ḥur held up his hands, one on each side, so that his hands held true until sunset. (17:11–12)

What is going on here? The passage could be read in two ways. The staff in Moshe's hand – with which he performed miracles in Egypt and at the sea – might be a sign that the Israelites' victory was a miraculous one. Alternatively, it might simply be a reminder to the Israelites that God was with them, giving them strength.

A mishna resolves the question, which is very unusual, since the Mishna in general is a book of law rather than biblical commentary.

> Did the hands of Moshe make or break [the course of the] war? Rather, the text implies that whenever the Israelites looked up and dedicated their hearts to their Father in heaven, they prevailed, but otherwise they fell. (Mishna Rosh HaShana 3:8)

Neither the staff nor Moshe's upraised hands were performing a miracle. They were simply reminding the Israelites to look up to heaven and remember that God was with them. This gave them the confidence and courage to win.

10 hill with the staff of God in my hand." Yehoshua fought
the Amalekites as Moshe had directed him, while Moshe,
11 Aharon, and Ḥur climbed to the top of the hill. Whenever
Moshe held his hand high, the Israelites prevailed, but
whenever he let his hand drop, the Amalekites prevailed.
12 But Moshe's hands grew heavy. So they took a stone and
placed it under him and he sat, while Aharon and Ḥur
held up his hands, one on each side, so that his hands held
13 true until sunset. And Yehoshua overcame Amalek and his
people by the sword.
14 Then the LORD said to Moshe, "Write this as a memorial MAFTIR
on a scroll, and commit it to Yehoshua's ears: I will erase
the memory of Amalek, utterly, from under the heavens."
15 Moshe built an altar and named it "The LORD Is My
16 Banner," saying, "There is a hand on the LORD's throne.
The LORD will be at war with Amalek throughout the
ages."

The haftara for Parashat Beshalaḥ is on page 1470.

Egypt'" (Ex. 13:17). The closing verse says: "The LORD will be at war with Amalek throughout the ages" (17:16).

The difference between them is between the war God fights for us, and the war we fight for God. The first is miraculous, the second only metaphorically so. The war God fights changes nature, even to the point of dividing a sea. But the war we fight changes us – and that is something God cannot do for us. We can only do it for ourselves. As long as the Israelites were totally dependent on God, they remained querulous and quarrelsome, in a state of arrested development. Only when they fought their own battles did they eventually – and painfully slowly – begin to acknowledge God. This battle – the one that requires our courage, our eyes turned to heaven – is the one that continues as the journey starts in earnest, and onward to this day.

י נִצָּב עַל־רֹאשׁ הַגִּבְעָה וּמַטֵּה הָאֱלֹהִים בְּיָדִי׃ וַיַּעַשׂ יְהוֹשֻׁעַ
כַּאֲשֶׁר אָמַר־לוֹ מֹשֶׁה לְהִלָּחֵם בַּעֲמָלֵק וּמֹשֶׁה אַהֲרֹן וְחוּר
יא עָלוּ רֹאשׁ הַגִּבְעָה׃ וְהָיָה כַּאֲשֶׁר יָרִים מֹשֶׁה יָדוֹ וְגָבַר יִשְׂרָאֵל
יב וְכַאֲשֶׁר יָנִיחַ יָדוֹ וְגָבַר עֲמָלֵק׃ וִידֵי מֹשֶׁה כְּבֵדִים וַיִּקְחוּ־אֶבֶן
וַיָּשִׂימוּ תַחְתָּיו וַיֵּשֶׁב עָלֶיהָ וְאַהֲרֹן וְחוּר תָּמְכוּ בְיָדָיו מִזֶּה
יג אֶחָד וּמִזֶּה אֶחָד וַיְהִי יָדָיו אֱמוּנָה עַד־בֹּא הַשָּׁמֶשׁ׃ וַיַּחֲלֹשׁ
יְהוֹשֻׁעַ אֶת־עֲמָלֵק וְאֶת־עַמּוֹ לְפִי־חָרֶב׃
יד וַיֹּאמֶר יהוה אֶל־מֹשֶׁה כְּתֹב זֹאת זִכָּרוֹן בַּסֵּפֶר וְשִׂים בְּאָזְנֵי מפטיר
יְהוֹשֻׁעַ כִּי־מָחֹה אֶמְחֶה אֶת־זֵכֶר עֲמָלֵק מִתַּחַת הַשָּׁמָיִם׃
טו טז וַיִּבֶן מֹשֶׁה מִזְבֵּחַ וַיִּקְרָא שְׁמוֹ יהוה ׀ נִסִּי׃ וַיֹּאמֶר כִּי־יָד
עַל־כֵּס יָהּ מִלְחָמָה לַיהוה בַּעֲמָלֵק מִדֹּר דֹּר׃

The הפטרה *for* פרשת בשלח *is on page 1471.*

if we have these feelings we should not feel ashamed. Even the greatest people have felt fear. Courage is not fearlessness. It is, in the words of a well-known book title, feeling the fear but doing it anyway.

Sometimes the only way to do this is to know that there is no way back. That is what crossing the Reed Sea meant for the Israelites, and why it was essential that they experienced it at an early stage in their journey. It marked the point of no return, the line of no retreat, the critical point at which they could only move forward.

17:16 מִדֹּר דֹּר *Throughout the ages* – The opening and closing verses of Beshalaḥ both contain as their key word *milḥama*, "war." The opening verse states: "When Pharaoh let the people go, God did not lead them through the land of the Philistines, though it was the shorter way. 'If the people face war,' thought God, 'they will change their minds and go back to

Parashat Yitro

18 1 Moshe's father-in-law Yitro, priest of Midyan, heard about
all that God had done for Moshe and for His people Israel
2 when the Lord brought Israel out of Egypt. Yitro had
received Moshe's wife Tzipora after he had sent her home,
3 together with her two sons. One was named Gershom, for
Moshe had said, "I have been a stranger in a foreign land,"
4 and the other, Eliezer, for he had said, "My father's God
5 has helped me, saving me from Pharaoh's sword." And now
Moshe's father-in-law Yitro came to Moshe in the desert,
bringing his sons and his wife, to where he was encamped
6 by the mountain of God. Yitro sent word to Moshe, "I am
coming to you – your father-in-law Yitro – together with
7 your wife and both of your sons." Moshe went out to greet
his father-in-law and bowed down and kissed him. Each
asked after the other's welfare, and they went inside the
8 tent. And Moshe told his father-in-law all that the Lord
had done to Pharaoh and the Egyptians, for Israel's sake,
all the hardship they had encountered along the way,
9 and how the Lord had rescued them. Yitro delighted in
all the good that the Lord had done for Israel, in His
10 liberating them from the Egyptians, and said, "Blessed be
the Lord who has rescued you from Egypt and Pharaoh

Hasidim say of the Baal Shem Tov that he would travel around the little towns and villages of Eastern Europe, asking Jews how they were. However poor or troubled they were, invariably they would reply, "*Barukh Hashem*." It was an instinctive expression of faith, and every Jew knew it. They might have lacked the learning of the great talmudic scholar, or the wealth of the successful, but they believed they had much to thank God for, and they did so. When asked what he was doing and why, the Baal Shem Tov would reply by quoting the verse "But You are the Holy One, enthroned on Israel's praises" (Ps. 22:4). Every time a Jew says *Barukh Hashem*, he or she is helping to make a throne for the *Shekhina*, the Divine Presence.

Three people in the Torah use this expression – but all of them are non-Jews, people outside the Abrahamic covenant.

פרשת יתרו

יח א וַיִּשְׁמַע יִתְרוֹ כֹהֵן מִדְיָן חֹתֵן מֹשֶׁה אֵת כָּל־אֲשֶׁר עָשָׂה יד
אֱלֹהִים לְמֹשֶׁה וּלְיִשְׂרָאֵל עַמּוֹ כִּֽי־הוֹצִיא יְהוָה אֶת־יִשְׂרָאֵל
ב מִמִּצְרָיִם: וַיִּקַּח יִתְרוֹ חֹתֵן מֹשֶׁה אֶת־צִפֹּרָה אֵשֶׁת מֹשֶׁה
ג אַחַר שִׁלּוּחֶיהָ: וְאֵת שְׁנֵי בָנֶיהָ אֲשֶׁר שֵׁם הָאֶחָד גֵּרְשֹׁם כִּי
ד אָמַר גֵּר הָיִיתִי בְּאֶרֶץ נָכְרִיָּה: וְשֵׁם הָאֶחָד אֱלִיעֶזֶר כִּֽי־אֱלֹהֵי
ה אָבִי בְּעֶזְרִי וַיַּצִּלֵנִי מֵחֶרֶב פַּרְעֹה: וַיָּבֹא יִתְרוֹ חֹתֵן מֹשֶׁה
וּבָנָיו וְאִשְׁתּוֹ אֶל־מֹשֶׁה אֶל־הַמִּדְבָּר אֲשֶׁר־הוּא חֹנֶה שָׁם
ו הַר הָאֱלֹהִים: וַיֹּאמֶר אֶל־מֹשֶׁה אֲנִי חֹתֶנְךָ יִתְרוֹ בָּא אֵלֶיךָ
ז וְאִשְׁתְּךָ וּשְׁנֵי בָנֶיהָ עִמָּהּ: וַיֵּצֵא מֹשֶׁה לִקְרַאת חֹתְנוֹ וַיִּשְׁתַּחוּ
וַיִּשַּׁק־לוֹ וַיִּשְׁאֲלוּ אִישׁ־לְרֵעֵהוּ לְשָׁלוֹם וַיָּבֹאוּ הָאֹהֱלָה:
ח וַיְסַפֵּר מֹשֶׁה לְחֹתְנוֹ אֵת כָּל־אֲשֶׁר עָשָׂה יְהוָה לְפַרְעֹה
וּלְמִצְרַיִם עַל אוֹדֹת יִשְׂרָאֵל אֵת כָּל־הַתְּלָאָה אֲשֶׁר מְצָאָתַם
ט בַּדֶּרֶךְ וַיַּצִּלֵם יְהוָה: וַיִּחַדְּ יִתְרוֹ עַל כָּל־הַטּוֹבָה אֲשֶׁר־עָשָׂה
י יְהוָה לְיִשְׂרָאֵל אֲשֶׁר הִצִּילוֹ מִיַּד מִצְרָיִם: וַיֹּאמֶר יִתְרוֹ בָּרוּךְ
יְהוָה אֲשֶׁר הִצִּיל אֶתְכֶם מִיַּד מִצְרַיִם וּמִיַּד פַּרְעֹה אֲשֶׁר

YITRO

Parashat Yitro is divided into two episodes. In the first (ch. 18), Israel receives its first system of governance – devolved to leaders of thousands, hundreds, fifties, and tens – at the advice of Yitro, Moshe's father-in-law, whose name the *parasha* bears. In the second (chs. 19–20), it receives its eternal constitution by way of a covenant with God, making the entire nation into "a kingdom of priests." A brief summation of its key elements is given by the voice of God Himself in the form of the Ten Commandments (or Utterances). The twin tablets with their ten commands are the enduring symbol of eternal law under the sovereignty of God.

Both episodes, Yitro and the revelation at Sinai, have one theme in common, namely the *delegation, distribution, and democratization* of human leadership. Only God can rule alone.

18:10 בָּרוּךְ יהוה *Blessed be the Lord* – The quintessential Jewish expression of thanks, gratitude, and acknowledgment is *barukh Hashem*, meaning "thank God" or "praise be to the Lord."

11 and liberated the people from the Egyptians' hands. Now
I know that the LORD is greater than all gods – for He
brought upon them what they schemed against others."
12 Then Yitro brought a burnt offering and sacrifices to
God. And Aharon and all the elders of Israel came to
13 break bread with Moshe's father-in-law before God. The SHENI
next day Moshe sat to serve the people as judge. From
14 morning to evening the people stood before him. When
Moshe's father-in-law saw everything Moshe did for
the people, he asked, "What is this that you do for the
people? Why do you sit alone while all the people stand
15 over you from morning to evening?" "The people come
16 to me to inquire of God," Moshe replied. "When they
have a dispute, they come to me and I judge between
one neighbor and another, and I make God's laws and

---

society. For there are indeed among the nations people who recognize well-authenticated propositions (*devarim me'usharim*).

The forms and structures of governance are not specifically Jewish. They are part of *ḥokhma*, the wisdom of humankind. Jews have known many forms of leadership. In fact, the Torah says about monarchy that a time will come when the people say, "I will set a king over me, like all the surrounding nations" (Deut. 17:14) – the only case in the entire Torah in which the people of Israel are commanded – or permitted – to imitate other nations. There is nothing uniquely Jewish about political structures.

Religion does not specify an ideal form of government, but it does provide us with a set of values or principles against which a system can be judged. What are they? The first is the epic statement of the opening chapter of the Tanakh, that the human individual is created "in the image of God" (Gen. 1:27). This is a religious and ethical proposition. But it is also a political one. The person is prior to the collective. The starting point of political theory must lie in the rights, freedom, and dignity of the individual, not in those of the state. It is this that forms the biblical basis of modern political theory, and an eternal protest against totalitarianism.

The idea that humanity is created in the image of God is a subtle one, because central to the Tanakh is the idea that God has no image. His very name, God tells Moshe, is *Ehyeh asher Ehyeh*, "I will be what I will be" (Ex. 3:14). God is Being in its infinite, open-ended unpredictability. What is divine about humanity is its diversity, not its uniformity.

But the individual is not self-sufficient. Each of us lacks some gift that

יא הִצִּיל אֶת־הָעָם מִתַּחַת יַד־מִצְרָיִם׃ עַתָּה יָדַעְתִּי כִּי־גָדוֹל
יב יְהוָה מִכָּל־הָאֱלֹהִים כִּי בַדָּבָר אֲשֶׁר זָדוּ עֲלֵיהֶם׃ וַיִּקַּח
יִתְרוֹ חֹתֵן מֹשֶׁה עֹלָה וּזְבָחִים לֵאלֹהִים וַיָּבֹא אַהֲרֹן וְכֹל ׀
זִקְנֵי יִשְׂרָאֵל לֶאֱכָל־לֶחֶם עִם־חֹתֵן מֹשֶׁה לִפְנֵי הָאֱלֹהִים׃
יג וַיְהִי מִמָּחֳרָת וַיֵּשֶׁב מֹשֶׁה לִשְׁפֹּט אֶת־הָעָם וַיַּעֲמֹד הָעָם שני
יד עַל־מֹשֶׁה מִן־הַבֹּקֶר עַד־הָעָרֶב׃ וַיַּרְא חֹתֵן מֹשֶׁה אֵת כָּל־
אֲשֶׁר־הוּא עֹשֶׂה לָעָם וַיֹּאמֶר מָה־הַדָּבָר הַזֶּה אֲשֶׁר אַתָּה
עֹשֶׂה לָעָם מַדּוּעַ אַתָּה יוֹשֵׁב לְבַדֶּךָ וְכָל־הָעָם נִצָּב עָלֶיךָ
טו מִן־בֹּקֶר עַד־עָרֶב׃ וַיֹּאמֶר מֹשֶׁה לְחֹתְנוֹ כִּי־יָבֹא אֵלַי הָעָם
טז לִדְרֹשׁ אֱלֹהִים׃ כִּי־יִהְיֶה לָהֶם דָּבָר בָּא אֵלַי וְשָׁפַטְתִּי בֵּין
אִישׁ וּבֵין רֵעֵהוּ וְהוֹדַעְתִּי אֶת־חֻקֵּי הָאֱלֹהִים וְאֶת־תּוֹרֹתָיו׃

The first is Noaḥ: "Blessed be the Lord, God of Shem" (Gen. 9:26). The second is Avraham's servant, presumed to be Eliezer, whom Avraham sends to find a wife for Yitzḥak: "Blessed be the Lord, God of my master Avraham, who has not withheld His kindness and faithfulness from my master" (24:27). The third is Yitro here. You do not need to be Jewish to have a sense of reverence for the Creator or to recognize, as Yitro did, His hand in miraculous events.

God is universal. Therefore humanity, created in His image, is universal. This is an essential reminder. The great problems humanity faces are global, while our most effective political agencies are at most national. We need to find a way of combining our universal humanity with our cultural and religious particularity.

No one demonstrates this better than Yitro. His wise advice, coming, as it were, from the outside, gives Israel its first system of governance. The religion of Israel is not the religion of everyone, but the God of Israel is the God of everyone. You do not have to be Jewish to be good, wise, or beloved of God.

YITRO ADVISES MOSHE

One of the classic commentaries, *Ohr HaḤayyim* (authored by Rabbi Ḥayyim Ibn Attar of Morocco, later of Israel, 1696–1743) made a striking observation on Yitro's lesson to Moshe:

> It seems to me that the reason [that this teaching came from Yitro] is that God wanted to show the Israelites of that generation – and of all generations – that there are among the nations of the world great masters of understanding and intellect (*gedolim behavana u'vehaskala*). The example of this was Yitro: his advice and the way he chose to organize a

17 teachings known." Moshe's father-in-law said to him,
18 "What you are doing is not good. You will be worn away,
and this people along with you. It is too heavy a burden
19 for you. You cannot carry it alone. Now listen to me, let
me advise you; and may God be with you. You speak for
the people before God, and bring their concerns to Him.
20 And you must acquaint them with His precepts and laws,
and make known to them the path they are to walk and
21 the way they must act. You, as well, must seek out among
the people capable men – God-fearing, trustworthy
men, who despise corruption; and appoint them over
the people as leaders of thousands, hundreds, fifties, and

because "he added a passage to the Torah beginning [here with the words] 'You, as well, must seek out'" (18:21).

The Kotzker pointed out that the passage that Yitro added to the Torah does not begin, "Seek out." It begins several verses earlier when he says, "What you are doing is not good" (18:17). The answer the Kotzker gives is simple. Saying "What you are doing is not good" is not an addition to the Torah – it is merely stating a problem. The addition consists of the solution: delegate. It is easy to see what is going wrong. What makes someone a leader is the ability to find a way of putting it right.

18:21 שָׂרֵי אֲלָפִים שָׂרֵי מֵאוֹת שָׂרֵי חֲמִשִּׁים וְשָׂרֵי עֲשָׂרֹת *Leaders of thousands, hundreds, fifties, and tens* – The great nineteenth-century scholar the Netziv (Rabbi Naftali Tzvi Yehuda Berlin) made an unexpected, counterintuitive observation on this point (*Harḥev Davar* on Ex. 18:23). The Talmud (Sanhedrin 6b) teaches that Moshe preferred strict justice to peace. He was not a man to compromise or mediate. In addition, as the greatest of the prophets, he knew almost instantly which of the parties before him was innocent and which guilty, who had right on his side and who did not. It was therefore impossible for him to mediate, since this is only permitted before the judge has reached a verdict, which in Moshe's case was almost immediately.

By delegating the judicial function downward, Moshe would bring ordinary people – with no special prophetic or legal gifts – into the seats of judgment. Precisely because they *lacked* Moshe's intuitive knowledge of law and justice, they were able to propose equitable solutions, and an equitable solution is one in which both sides feel they have been heard. Both gain; both believe the result is fair.

Moshe was the *ish haElokim* (Ps. 90:1), the supreme "man of God." Yet there was, the Netziv implies, one thing he could not do, which others – less great in every other respect – could

יז וַיֹּאמֶר חֹתֵן מֹשֶׁה אֵלָיו לֹא־טוֹב הַדָּבָר אֲשֶׁר אַתָּה עֹשֶׂה׃
יח נָבֹל תִּבֹּל גַּם־אַתָּה גַּם־הָעָם הַזֶּה אֲשֶׁר עִמָּךְ כִּי־כָבֵד מִמְּךָ
יט הַדָּבָר לֹא־תוּכַל עֲשֹׂהוּ לְבַדֶּךָ׃ עַתָּה שְׁמַע בְּקֹלִי אִיעָצְךָ
וִיהִי אֱלֹהִים עִמָּךְ הֱיֵה אַתָּה לָעָם מוּל הָאֱלֹהִים וְהֵבֵאתָ
כ אַתָּה אֶת־הַדְּבָרִים אֶל־הָאֱלֹהִים׃ וְהִזְהַרְתָּה אֶתְהֶם
אֶת־הַחֻקִּים וְאֶת־הַתּוֹרֹת וְהוֹדַעְתָּ לָהֶם אֶת־הַדֶּרֶךְ יֵלְכוּ
כא בָהּ וְאֶת־הַמַּעֲשֶׂה אֲשֶׁר יַעֲשׂוּן׃ וְאַתָּה תֶחֱזֶה מִכָּל־הָעָם
אַנְשֵׁי־חַיִל יִרְאֵי אֱלֹהִים אַנְשֵׁי אֱמֶת שֹׂנְאֵי בָצַע וְשַׂמְתָּ
עֲלֵהֶם שָׂרֵי אֲלָפִים שָׂרֵי מֵאוֹת שָׂרֵי חֲמִשִּׁים וְשָׂרֵי עֲשָׂרֹת׃

---

someone else has. To achieve anything we must form associations, and this gives rise to the political process. Rambam puts it thus:

> This great variety [among humans] and the necessity of social life are essential elements in man's nature. But the well-being of society demands that there should be a leader able to regulate the actions of man; he must complete every shortcoming, remove every excess, and prescribe for the conduct of all, so that the natural variety should be counterbalanced by the uniformity of legislation, and the order of society be well established. I therefore maintain that the Law, though not a product of nature, is nonetheless not entirely foreign to nature. (*Guide for the Perplexed* II:40)

People are different, but they must be able to form societies. This requires laws, a legislator, and a source of legislative authority. Humanity needs political structures. In the narrative of our *parasha,* a legal system exists and must be honed before the laws are even given. We need *ḥokhma* to support Torah, and in this case it comes from Yitro.

18:17 לֹא־טוֹב *Not good* – Moshe must learn to delegate and share the burden of leadership. Interestingly, the sentence "What you are doing is not good (*lo tov*)" is one of only two places in the Torah where the phrase "not good" occurs. The other (Gen. 2:18) is "It is not good for man to be alone." We cannot live alone; we cannot lead alone. That is one of the axioms of biblical anthropology. The Hebrew word for life, *ḥayyim*, is in the plural, as if to signify that life is essentially shared.

18:21 וְאַתָּה תֶחֱזֶה... אַנְשֵׁי־חַיִל *Seek out… capable men* – The Kotzker Rebbe once drew attention to a difficulty in Rashi's writing. In the opening verse of our *parasha* (Ex. 18:1), Rashi says that Yitro was given the name Yeter ("he added")

22 tens. Have them serve as daily judges for the people; let
them bring the major cases to you, but judge the minor
ones themselves. In this way they will lighten your load,
23 and bear it together with you. If you do this, and God so
commands, then you will endure, and all these people
24 will be able to go home in peace." Moshe listened to
25 his father-in-law and did all that he said. Moshe chose SHELISHI
capable men from all Israel and made them chiefs over the
people, leaders of thousands, hundreds, fifties, and tens.
26 They judged the people every day. Any major case they
brought to Moshe, but they decided every minor matter
27 themselves. Then Moshe parted from his father-in-law,
and the latter went forth, back to his own land.
19 1 On the first day of the third month after the Israelites REVI'I
2 had left Egypt they came to the Sinai Desert. Setting
out from Refidim they had arrived at the Sinai Desert,
encamping in the wilderness, and there Israel camped,
3 facing the mountain, while Moshe went up to God.
And the LORD called to him from the mountain: "This
is what you shall say to the House of Yaakov, what you
4 shall tell the people of Israel: You yourselves have seen

"There Israel [singular] camped." Rashi, always sensitive to the nuances of the biblical text, spells out the implication. At this moment, he writes, the people of Israel are "like one person with one heart." They have been transformed from the plural to the singular. Within sight of Mount Sinai, within reach of revelation, about to receive their call and consummation as a people, they are united.

19:3 בֵּית יַעֲקֹב *The House of Yaakov* – According to the Sages, when God was about to give the Torah at Sinai, He told Moshe to consult first with the women and only then with the men. This is the meaning of the verse "This is what you shall say to the House of Yaakov, what you shall tell the people of Israel." The House of Yaakov, our Sages tell us, refers to the women (Mekhilta DeRabbi Yishmael 19:3:1). Shemot Rabba gives various explanations for this idea, never questioning the fact that women received the Torah first.

In 1917, Sarah Schenirer founded the first Bais Yaakov school for women, naming it after our verse. Since then, women have risen in the ranks of Torah scholars. The Belzer Rebbe, a great hasidic leader, and the Chofetz Chaim, the major Torah scholar of his

כב וְשָׁפְטוּ אֶת־הָעָם בְּכָל־עֵת וְהָיָה כָּל־הַדָּבָר הַגָּדֹל יָבִיאוּ
אֵלֶיךָ וְכָל־הַדָּבָר הַקָּטֹן יִשְׁפְּטוּ־הֵם וְהָקֵל מֵעָלֶיךָ וְנָשְׂאוּ
כג אִתָּךְ: אִם אֶת־הַדָּבָר הַזֶּה תַּעֲשֶׂה וְצִוְּךָ אֱלֹהִים וְיָכָלְתָּ עֲמֹד
כד וְגַם כָּל־הָעָם הַזֶּה עַל־מְקֹמוֹ יָבֹא בְשָׁלוֹם: וַיִּשְׁמַע מֹשֶׁה
כה לְקוֹל חֹתְנוֹ וַיַּעַשׂ כֹּל אֲשֶׁר אָמָר: וַיִּבְחַר מֹשֶׁה אַנְשֵׁי־חַיִל שלישי
מִכָּל־יִשְׂרָאֵל וַיִּתֵּן אֹתָם רָאשִׁים עַל־הָעָם שָׂרֵי אֲלָפִים
כו שָׂרֵי מֵאוֹת שָׂרֵי חֲמִשִּׁים וְשָׂרֵי עֲשָׂרֹת: וְשָׁפְטוּ אֶת־הָעָם
בְּכָל־עֵת אֶת־הַדָּבָר הַקָּשֶׁה יְבִיאוּן אֶל־מֹשֶׁה וְכָל־הַדָּבָר
כז הַקָּטֹן יִשְׁפּוּטוּ הֵם: וַיְשַׁלַּח מֹשֶׁה אֶת־חֹתְנוֹ וַיֵּלֶךְ לוֹ אֶל־
אַרְצוֹ:
יט א בַּחֹדֶשׁ הַשְּׁלִישִׁי לְצֵאת בְּנֵי־יִשְׂרָאֵל מֵאֶרֶץ מִצְרָיִם בַּיּוֹם רביעי
ב הַזֶּה בָּאוּ מִדְבַּר סִינָי: וַיִּסְעוּ מֵרְפִידִים וַיָּבֹאוּ מִדְבַּר סִינַי
ג וַיַּחֲנוּ בַּמִּדְבָּר וַיִּחַן־שָׁם יִשְׂרָאֵל נֶגֶד הָהָר: וּמֹשֶׁה עָלָה
אֶל־הָאֱלֹהִים וַיִּקְרָא אֵלָיו יהוה מִן־הָהָר לֵאמֹר כֹּה תֹאמַר
ד לְבֵית יַעֲקֹב וְתַגֵּיד לִבְנֵי יִשְׂרָאֵל: אַתֶּם רְאִיתֶם אֲשֶׁר עָשִׂיתִי

---

achieve. They could bring peace between contending parties. They could create nonviolent, noncoercive forms of conflict resolution. Not knowing the law with the depth that Moshe did, not having his intuitive sense of truth, they had instead to exercise patience. They had to listen to both sides. They had to arrive at an equitable verdict that both parties could see as fair. A mediator has different gifts from a prophet, a liberator, a lawgiver – more modest perhaps, but sometimes no less necessary. That is why the delegation of judgment would not only help Moshe avoid total exhaustion; it would also help "all these people" to "go home in peace."

Judaism is a social faith. It is about networks of relationship. It is about families, communities, and ultimately a nation, in which each of us, great or small, has a role to play. There is something ordinary individuals (heads of thousands, hundreds, tens) can achieve that even Moshe in all his glory cannot achieve. That is why a nation is greater than any individual, and why each of us has something to give.

19:2 וַיִּחַן־שָׁם יִשְׂרָאֵל *There Israel camped* – Rashi notes that when the Israelites arrive in the wilderness of Sinai prior to receiving the Ten Commandments, the Torah's description shifts from the plural to the singular: *Vayiḥan sham Yisrael,*

what I did to the Egyptians: how I lifted you up on eagles'
5 wings and brought you to Me. Now, if you faithfully
heed My voice and keep My covenant, you will be My
treasure among all the peoples, although the whole earth
6 is Mine. A kingdom of priests and a holy nation you
shall be to Me. These are the words you must speak to

---

the universe as God's work and the Bible as God's will. God wants us to be the people who are true to our faith, while being a blessing to others regardless of their faith. Jews are the voice of hope in the conversation of humankind. That is what we were chosen for, and I can think of no higher vocation.

A KINGDOM OF PRIESTS AND A HOLY NATION

This phrase was to become the mission statement of the Jewish people. Indeed, with the possible exception of the United States, the Jewish people is the only nation ever to have had a mission statement. Most are defined in terms of language, geography, political structure, long association, and the like. Jews became a nation by adopting a task, by covenanting with God. Absent that, it is hard to say what it is to be a Jew.

What is a kingdom of priests? Jews never were literally a kingdom of priests. Priesthood fell to Aharon and his sons. What is more, priesthood is not seen by the Torah as a distinctively Jewish phenomenon. Yitro, for instance, is described as a Midianite priest.

Ibn Ezra and Ramban interpret the word to mean "servants." A priest is one consecrated to the service of God. This is now to be the task of all Israelites. Others – Saadia Gaon, Rashi, Rashbam – understand it to mean princes, based on II Samuel 18:1. There, David's sons are described as *kohanim,* which cannot mean priests and must mean royalty, princes. The Israelites are called on to be *a nation of servant leaders.*

I want to suggest a different interpretation, by looking at the wider context against which the biblical narrative is set. The earliest writing systems involved a huge number of hieroglyphic or pictographic symbols. The result was that in each society where there was writing, there was a literate elite, a knowledge class, often involved in administration. Only the few had access to knowledge, and so to power. The invention of the alphabet reduced the number of symbols needed to be learned to less than thirty. We cannot give a precise date for the first alphabet – sometime between 1800 and 2000 BCE seems likely. But unlike the pre-alphabetical scripts, the alphabet seems to have been invented only once. All the hundreds of scripts that exist are direct or indirect descendants of the proto-Semitic writing from the Sinai Desert.

Was it divine providence that led to this invention becoming available at exactly the right time and place to be used by the Israelites for the holiest of

לְמִצְרָיִם וָאֶשָּׂא אֶתְכֶם עַל־כַּנְפֵי נְשָׁרִים וָאָבִא אֶתְכֶם אֵלָי׃
ה וְעַתָּה אִם־שָׁמוֹעַ תִּשְׁמְעוּ בְּקֹלִי וּשְׁמַרְתֶּם אֶת־בְּרִיתִי
ו וִהְיִיתֶם לִי סְגֻלָּה מִכָּל־הָעַמִּים כִּי־לִי כָּל־הָאָרֶץ׃ וְאַתֶּם טו
תִּהְיוּ־לִי מַמְלֶכֶת כֹּהֲנִים וְגוֹי קָדוֹשׁ אֵלֶּה הַדְּבָרִים אֲשֶׁר

generation, both blessed this endeavor. After World War II, in America, Rabbi Joseph B. Soloveitchik and the Lubavitcher Rebbe promoted the role of women as students of Torah and teachers of Torah. From this revolution came thousands of new Torah teachers and hundreds of thousands of new Torah learners, drawing support in part from this midrashic tradition.

The call to "the House of Yaakov" and "the people of Israel" – the Torah's "constitution of liberty" – includes everyone: men, women, and children. It is the first moment, by thousands of years, that citizenship is conceived as being universal. With this, something unprecedented enters the human horizon, though it will take centuries, millennia, before its full implications will be understood. At Sinai, the politics of freedom are born.

19:4 אַתֶּם רְאִיתֶם *You yourselves have seen* – The emphasis is on the immediacy of the experience. The people have witnessed a divine intervention into history. They have been redeemed from slavery under Pharaoh. God is now proposing that they become a nation under His own direct sovereignty in fulfillment of what He had earlier told Moshe: "I will take you as My people and I will be your God" (Ex. 6:7). This will mark the culmination of their seven-week journey from servitude to law-governed liberty.

19:5 וִהְיִיתֶם לִי סְגֻלָּה מִכָּל־הָעַמִּים *My treasure among all the peoples* – God is the creator of the universe and the God of all humanity, but through the covenant, Israel is to have a special closeness to Him. In "heeding My voice and keeping My covenant," they undertake to be His emissaries and exemplars, His ambassadors to humanity, probably the most challenging vocation anyone has ever been given. It does not mean that we are better than anyone else. It does not mean that we are worse. It means that the task to which we have been summoned is different. A chosen people is not a master race but its opposite: a servant community. Some nations in the history of humanity have given the world the idea of beauty, or of science, or of philosophy, or of music. It has been our task always to be God's witnesses in the world. In Jewish history we see time and time again, in multiple and variegated ways, that Jews have always been a people who testify in themselves to something greater than themselves. Jews have always done extraordinary things because they were challenged by God to perform this daunting task – the task of acting to bring humanity to see

7 the Israelites." So Moshe came and summoned the elders HAMISHI
of the people, and set before them all that the LORD had
8 commanded him. And the people answered as one – "All
that the LORD has spoken we will do." Moshe brought

holy nation." At Sinai, the Jewish people, until then mainly an aggregate of individuals linked by family, memory, and the experience of exodus, fully became a body politic, with the Torah as its written constitution. The Vilna Gaon notes the connection between the words *goy*, "nation," and *geviya*, "body." A nation is a group of individuals whose relationship to one another is as of limbs to a body. Sinai creates the terms of collective existence. Henceforth the Israelites are implicated in one another's fate.

What does it mean to be a holy nation? Holiness is the space we make for God. Holiness is that bounded emptiness filled by the Divine Presence. In addition to the holiness of empty time (the Sabbath) and the holiness of empty space (the Tabernacle), the phrase "holy nation" designates a third emptiness: the empty throne (cathedra, seat of authority). The place occupied in other nations by the monarch, ruler, or pharaoh is in the case of Israel to be left empty for God. Israel is to become a republic of faith under His direct sovereignty. He is the author of its constitution, the framer of its rules, the one who guides it through its long journeys, sustains it in hours of need, and gives it hope in times of crisis. The essence of the Sinai revelation is that the Israelites become the first – indeed the only – nation formed on the basis of a covenant with God.

19:8 וַיַּעֲנוּ כָל־הָעָם יַחְדָּו *And the people answered as one* – Only when the people have signaled their consent does God proceed with the covenant and the accompanying revelation. The fact of choice is fundamental, for the Tanakh portrays God not as an overwhelming force, but as a constitutional sovereign. The supreme power, God, grants His people the freedom to decide whether or not to enter into the covenant. Thus is born the first principle of a free society: there is no justified government without the consent of the governed, even if the governor is Creator of heaven and earth.

No less essential is the participation of the whole people, for each must give his or her consent. It is a point the Tanakh emphasizes twice: "And *all the people* answered as one" (Ex. 19:8, literally translated); "*The people all* responded with one voice" (24:3). This is not democracy in the modern or even the Greek sense, but it is a corollary of the idea that the human person as such is in the image of God. In covenant as the Tanakh understands it, each individual has significance, dignity, moral worth, the right to be heard, a voice.

Despite the abyss between the infinite power of God and the finitude of humankind, at the heart of the Sinai covenant is the idea of reciprocity and mutuality. It is God's call to human responsibility.

ז תְּדַבֵּר אֶל־בְּנֵי יִשְׂרָאֵל: וַיָּבֹא מֹשֶׁה וַיִּקְרָא לְזִקְנֵי הָעָם וַיָּשֶׂם חמישי
ח לִפְנֵיהֶם אֵת כָּל־הַדְּבָרִים הָאֵלֶּה אֲשֶׁר צִוָּהוּ יהוה: וַיַּעֲנוּ כָל־
הָעָם יַחְדָּו וַיֹּאמְרוּ כֹּל אֲשֶׁר־דִּבֶּר יהוה נַעֲשֶׂה וַיָּשֶׁב מֹשֶׁה

---

purposes, namely, recording the divine word? Or was it this new development that allowed the Israelites to develop the consciousness – the high levels of abstraction, essential to monotheism, made possible by literacy – that allowed them to decipher the word of the One God? One way or another, the alphabet created a possibility that never existed before, namely of a society of mass, even universal, literacy.

Functionally, a priest in the ancient world was one who could read and write. A kingdom of priests is therefore *a nation of universal literacy*. The law God was about to reveal at Mount Sinai would become the possession of every member of the nation. He or she could know it, read it, study it, internalize it, and make it their own.

Torah was not a code written by a distant king, imposed by force. Nor was it an esoteric mystery understood by only a scholarly elite. It was to be available to, and intelligible by, everyone. God was to become a teacher, Israel His pupils, and the Torah the text that bound them to one another. Every Jew was expected to be both a prince and a servant, a student and a teacher; that is to say, every one of them was called on to be a leader.

Never was leadership more profoundly democratized.

19:6 גּוֹי קָדוֹשׁ *A holy nation* – The concept of a nation is fundamental to Judaism, because the nation is a basic unit of culture. As a sociopolitical entity, it constructs its own form of order through law, ritual, and custom. It is where many smaller groupings, families and communities, come together to create the basic terms of their common life. And God wants His presence to inform public life – otherwise He would have limited His concerns to the individual and the soul.

Judaism knows the faith of individuals: that is what Genesis is about, and the book of Psalms, the lexicon of the soul in dialogue with God. Judaism also knows the faith of humanity as a whole: that is the meaning of the first eleven chapters of Genesis and their culmination in the Noahide covenant, the covenant God makes with all mankind. But Judaism's great concerns are with the life we construct together and the terms on which we do so: justice, compassion, human dignity, peace, the limited and proper conduct of war, care for the dependent, welfare for the poor, concern for the long-term viability of the environment, and above all, the rule of law, in which strong and weak, powerful and powerless, are subject to the same code of conduct applied equally to all. These institutions and ideals are essentially political; hence they require the constitution of a nation as a political entity. That is the meaning of the phrase *goy kadosh*, "a

9 their answer back to the Lord. Then the Lord said to
Moshe, "I will come to you in a dense cloud, that the
people may hear Me speaking to you. They will then
believe you forever." When Moshe reported the words of
10 the people to the Lord, the Lord said to Moshe, "Go to
the people and consecrate them today and tomorrow; let
11 them wash their clothes and be ready for the third day, for
on that third day the Lord will descend on Mount Sinai
12 before all the peoples' eyes. Set a boundary for the people
around the mountain; tell them to take care not to ascend
to it, nor even touch its edge. Anyone who touches the
13 mountain must be put to death. No hand shall touch
him: he shall be stoned or shot with arrows; beast or
man, he shall not live. When the ram's horn sounds a long
14 blast – only then may they go up on the mountain." So
Moshe came down from the mountain to the people;
he consecrated them and they cleansed their clothes.
15 "Be ready for the third day," he told them, "and do not
16 draw close to your wives." The third day came; and that
morning there was thunder and lightning and a dense
cloud on the mountain and the sound of a ram's horn,
17 intensely loud, and all the people in the camp shook. Then
Moshe led the people out of the camp to meet God, and
18 they stood at the foot of the mountain. Mount Sinai was
enveloped in smoke because the Lord had descended on
it in fire. Smoke billowed up from it as if from a furnace,
19 and the mountain shook violently as one. As the sound
of the ram's horn grew louder and louder, Moshe spoke
20 and God answered him aloud. And the Lord descended SHISHI
on Mount Sinai, to the top of the mountain, and called
21 Moshe to the mountaintop, and Moshe ascended. The
Lord told Moshe, "Go back down – warn the people not
to force their way through to look at the Lord, or many
22 will die. Even priests who come near to the Lord must
first consecrate themselves, or the Lord will break out
23 against them." Moshe replied to the Lord, "The people
cannot climb Mount Sinai. You Yourself warned us to set

ט אֶת־דִּבְרֵי הָעָם אֶל־יְהוָה: וַיֹּאמֶר יְהוָה אֶל־מֹשֶׁה הִנֵּה
אָנֹכִי בָּא אֵלֶיךָ בְּעַב הֶעָנָן בַּעֲבוּר יִשְׁמַע הָעָם בְּדַבְּרִי עִמָּךְ
וְגַם־בְּךָ יַאֲמִינוּ לְעוֹלָם וַיַּגֵּד מֹשֶׁה אֶת־דִּבְרֵי הָעָם אֶל־
י יְהוָה: וַיֹּאמֶר יְהוָה אֶל־מֹשֶׁה לֵךְ אֶל־הָעָם וְקִדַּשְׁתָּם הַיּוֹם
יא וּמָחָר וְכִבְּסוּ שִׂמְלֹתָם: וְהָיוּ נְכֹנִים לַיּוֹם הַשְּׁלִישִׁי כִּי ׀ בַּיּוֹם
יב הַשְּׁלִשִׁי יֵרֵד יְהוָה לְעֵינֵי כָל־הָעָם עַל־הַר סִינָי: וְהִגְבַּלְתָּ
אֶת־הָעָם סָבִיב לֵאמֹר הִשָּׁמְרוּ לָכֶם עֲלוֹת בָּהָר וּנְגֹעַ בְּקָצֵהוּ
יג כָּל־הַנֹּגֵעַ בָּהָר מוֹת יוּמָת: לֹא־תִגַּע בּוֹ יָד כִּי־סָקוֹל יִסָּקֵל
אוֹ־יָרֹה יִיָּרֶה אִם־בְּהֵמָה אִם־אִישׁ לֹא יִחְיֶה בִּמְשֹׁךְ הַיֹּבֵל
יד הֵמָּה יַעֲלוּ בָהָר: וַיֵּרֶד מֹשֶׁה מִן־הָהָר אֶל־הָעָם וַיְקַדֵּשׁ
טו אֶת־הָעָם וַיְכַבְּסוּ שִׂמְלֹתָם: וַיֹּאמֶר אֶל־הָעָם הֱיוּ נְכֹנִים
טז לִשְׁלֹשֶׁת יָמִים אַל־תִּגְּשׁוּ אֶל־אִשָּׁה: וַיְהִי בַיּוֹם הַשְּׁלִישִׁי
בִּהְיֹת הַבֹּקֶר וַיְהִי קֹלֹת וּבְרָקִים וְעָנָן כָּבֵד עַל־הָהָר וְקֹל
יז שֹׁפָר חָזָק מְאֹד וַיֶּחֱרַד כָּל־הָעָם אֲשֶׁר בַּמַּחֲנֶה: וַיּוֹצֵא מֹשֶׁה
אֶת־הָעָם לִקְרַאת הָאֱלֹהִים מִן־הַמַּחֲנֶה וַיִּתְיַצְּבוּ בְּתַחְתִּית
יח הָהָר: וְהַר סִינַי עָשַׁן כֻּלּוֹ מִפְּנֵי אֲשֶׁר יָרַד עָלָיו יְהוָה בָּאֵשׁ
יט וַיַּעַל עֲשָׁנוֹ כְּעֶשֶׁן הַכִּבְשָׁן וַיֶּחֱרַד כָּל־הָהָר מְאֹד: וַיְהִי קוֹל
הַשֹּׁפָר הוֹלֵךְ וְחָזֵק מְאֹד מֹשֶׁה יְדַבֵּר וְהָאֱלֹהִים יַעֲנֶנּוּ בְקוֹל:
כ וַיֵּרֶד יְהוָה עַל־הַר סִינַי אֶל־רֹאשׁ הָהָר וַיִּקְרָא יְהוָה לְמֹשֶׁה ששי
כא אֶל־רֹאשׁ הָהָר וַיַּעַל מֹשֶׁה: וַיֹּאמֶר יְהוָה אֶל־מֹשֶׁה רֵד
כב הָעֵד בָּעָם פֶּן־יֶהֶרְסוּ אֶל־יְהוָה לִרְאוֹת וְנָפַל מִמֶּנּוּ רָב: וְגַם
הַכֹּהֲנִים הַנִּגָּשִׁים אֶל־יְהוָה יִתְקַדָּשׁוּ פֶּן־יִפְרֹץ בָּהֶם יְהוָה:
כג וַיֹּאמֶר מֹשֶׁה אֶל־יְהוָה לֹא־יוּכַל הָעָם לַעֲלֹת אֶל־הַר סִינָי

19:20 וַיֵּרֶד יהוה *And the Lord descended* – Rambam explains that this is a figurative expression. God, beyond space, does not literally ascend or descend. The word "descend" in this context refers to revelation (*Guide for the Perplexed* I:10). There was thunder, lightning, smoke, and fire, and the mountain itself trembled. The Israelites felt a terrifying, palpable sense of the closeness of God. It was a unique moment: heaven and earth seemed almost to touch.

24 a boundary around the mountain and consecrate it." The
LORD said to him, "Go down, and come back together
with Aharon. But do not let the priests or people force
their way through to come up to the LORD, or He will
25 break out against them." So Moshe went down to the
20 1 people and told them. Then God spoke all these
2 words: "I am the LORD your God who brought
you out of the land of Egypt, out of the house of slaves.

---

theft, and bearing false witness – establish the basic institutions on which society depends. Marriage is sacred because it is the human bond closest in approximation to the covenant between us and God. It is the human institution par excellence that depends on loyalty and fidelity, and it is the matrix of a free society. The prohibition against theft establishes the integrity of property. The prohibition of false testimony is the precondition of justice.

Finally comes the stand-alone prohibition against envying your neighbor's house, wife, slave, maid, ox, donkey, or anything else belonging to him or her. This seems odd if we think of the Ten Commandments as statutes, but not if we think of them as the basic principles of a free society. Envy is the failure to understand the principle of creation as set out in Genesis 1, that everything has its place in the scheme of things. Each of us has our own task and our own blessings, and we are each loved and cherished by God. Live by these truths and there is order. Abandon them and there is chaos. Nothing is more pointless and destructive than to let someone else's happiness diminish your own.

So the prohibition of envy counters the most basic force undermining the social harmony and order that are the aim of the Ten Commandments as a whole. Not only do they forbid it; they also help us rise above it. Thirty-three centuries after they were first given, the Ten Commandments remain the simplest, shortest guide to the creation and maintenance of a good society.

20:2 אָנֹכִי יהוה אֱלֹהֶיךָ *I am the LORD your God* – As the Midrash narrates this moment:

> When the Holy One, blessed be He, gave the Torah, no bird called, no fowl took flight, no ox lowed, the *ofanim* did not fly, the *seraphim* did not utter "Holy, holy," the ocean did not stir, created man did not speak: the whole world was silent and still – and the voice emerged: "I am the LORD your God." (Shemot Rabba 29)

"Judaism is full of silences," said Elie Wiesel, "but we don't talk about them." Undergirding all human speech is that sense of "something far more deeply interfused," as Wordsworth called it. Beneath the noise there is the music, the hymn of creation to its Creator, but

כִּי־אַתָּה הַעֵדֹתָה בָּנוּ לֵאמֹר הַגְבֵּל אֶת־הָהָר וְקִדַּשְׁתּוֹ:

כד וַיֹּאמֶר אֵלָיו יהוה לֶךְ־רֵד וְעָלִיתָ אַתָּה וְאַהֲרֹן עִמָּךְ וְהַכֹּהֲנִים

כה וְהָעָם אַל־יֶהֶרְסוּ לַעֲלֹת אֶל־יהוה פֶּן־יִפְרָץ־בָּם: וַיֵּרֶד

כ א מֹשֶׁה אֶל־הָעָם וַיֹּאמֶר אֲלֵהֶם: וַיְדַבֵּר אֱלֹהִים

ב אֵת כָּל־הַדְּבָרִים הָאֵלֶּה לֵאמֹר: אָנֹכִי יהוה

אֱלֹהֶיךָ אֲשֶׁר הוֹצֵאתִיךָ מֵאֶרֶץ מִצְרַיִם מִבֵּית עֲבָדִים:

THE TEN COMMANDMENTS

The Ten Commandments that appear in Parashat Yitro have long held a special place not only in Judaism but also within the broader configuration of values we call the Judeo-Christian ethic. They remain the supreme expression of the higher law to which all human law is bound. Most depictions of the Ten Commandments divide them into two, because of the "two tablets of stone" (Deut. 4:13) on which they were engraved. The first five, roughly speaking, are about the relationship between humans and God, the second five about the relationship between humans and other humans. However, it seems to me that the commandments are also structured, like the ten plagues, in three groups of three, with a tenth that is set apart from the rest.

The first three – no other gods besides Me, no graven images, and no taking of God's name in vain – define the Jewish people as "one nation under God." God is our ultimate sovereign. Therefore all other earthly rule is subject to the overarching imperatives linking Israel to God. God is a living force: make no graven images. And sovereignty presupposes reverence: do not take My name in vain. These first three commands, through which the people declare their obedience and loyalty to God above all else, establish the single most important principle of a free society, namely the *moral limits of power.*

The second three commands – the Sabbath, honoring parents, and the prohibition of murder – are all about the principle of *the createdness of life*. They establish limits to the idea of autonomy, namely, that we are free to do whatever we like so long as it does not harm others. The Sabbath is the day dedicated to seeing God as Creator and the universe as His creation. Hence, one day in seven, human hierarchies are suspended and everyone is free. Honoring parents acknowledges our human createdness. It tells us that not everything that matters is the result of our choice, chief of which is the fact that we exist at all. "Do not murder" restates the central principle of the universal Noahide covenant that murder is not just a crime against man but a sin against God in whose image we are created. Thus, commands four to six tell us to remember where we came from if we are to be mindful of how to live.

The third three – against adultery,

3 4 Have no other gods than Me. Do not make for yourself
any carved image or likeness of any creature in the
heavens above or the earth beneath or the water beneath
5 the earth. Do not bow down to them or worship them,
for I the LORD your God demand absolute loyalty. For
those who hate Me, I hold the descendants to account for
the sins of the fathers to the third and fourth generation,
6 but to those who love Me and keep My commands – I
7 shall act with faithful love for thousands. Do
not speak the name of the LORD your God in vain, for the
LORD will not hold guiltless those who speak His name
in vain.
8 9 Remember the Sabbath to keep it holy. Six days you
10 shall work, and carry out all your labors, but the seventh
is a Sabbath to the LORD your God. On it, do no work –
neither you, nor your son or daughter, your male or female

---

of vicarious guilt or punishment. "To the third and fourth generation" – if they also reject Me.

The other side of this equation follows in the next verse. Jewish identity, historically, has constantly been learned and relearned, enacted and reinforced, and passed on as a precious gift to the next generation. The secret of Jewish continuity is that Jews cared about it. They created continuity by making the transmission of tradition their first duty and greatest joy.

20:7 לֹא תִשָּׂא אֶת־שֵׁם־יהוה אֱלֹהֶיךָ לַשָּׁוְא *Do not speak the name… in vain* – T. S. Eliot believed that blasphemy was no longer possible. He thought that you could blaspheme only if you profoundly believed in the reality of that which you profaned. No one, according to Eliot, believed that strongly anymore. Yet in our day, other religions have made blasphemy front-page news throughout the world, and it has led to the shedding of blood. Are we fated to live between these two extremes?

A free society is a moral achievement, and it is made by us and our habits of thought, speech, and deed. Even as we revere God's name, it is not our task to conquer or convert the world or enforce uniformity of belief. It is our task to be a blessing to the world. To invoke God to justify violence is not an act of sanctity but of sacrilege. It is in itself a kind of blasphemy. It is to take God's name in vain.

20:10 אַתָּה וּבִנְךָ וּבִתֶּךָ עַבְדְּךָ וַאֲמָתְךָ וּבְהֶמְתֶּךָ וְגֵרְךָ *You, nor your son or daughter… servant… livestock… migrant* – The difference between a holiday and a holy day is that a holiday is private; a holy day is public. We take a vacation as individuals

ג ד לֹא־יִהְיֶה לְךָ אֱלֹהִים אֲחֵרִים עַל־פָּנָי: לֹא־תַעֲשֶׂה לְךָ פֶסֶל
וְכָל־תְּמוּנָה אֲשֶׁר בַּשָּׁמַיִם מִמַּעַל וַאֲשֶׁר בָּאָרֶץ מִתָּחַת
ה וַאֲשֶׁר בַּמַּיִם מִתַּחַת לָאָרֶץ: לֹא־תִשְׁתַּחֲוֶה לָהֶם וְלֹא
תָעָבְדֵם כִּי אָנֹכִי יהוה אֱלֹהֶיךָ אֵל קַנָּא פֹּקֵד עֲוֹן אָבֹת
ו עַל־בָּנִים עַל־שִׁלֵּשִׁים וְעַל־רִבֵּעִים לְשֹׂנְאָי: וְעֹשֶׂה חֶסֶד
ז לַאֲלָפִים לְאֹהֲבַי וּלְשֹׁמְרֵי מִצְוֺתָי: לֹא תִשָּׂא אֶת־
שֵׁם־יהוה אֱלֹהֶיךָ לַשָּׁוְא כִּי לֹא יְנַקֶּה יהוה אֵת אֲשֶׁר־יִשָּׂא
אֶת־שְׁמוֹ לַשָּׁוְא:
ח ט זָכוֹר אֶת־יוֹם הַשַּׁבָּת לְקַדְּשׁוֹ: שֵׁשֶׁת יָמִים תַּעֲבֹד וְעָשִׂיתָ
י כָּל־מְלַאכְתֶּךָ: וְיוֹם הַשְּׁבִיעִי שַׁבָּת לַיהוה אֱלֹהֶיךָ לֹא־
תַעֲשֶׂה כָל־מְלָאכָה אַתָּה ׀ וּבִנְךָ וּבִתֶּךָ עַבְדְּךָ וַאֲמָתְךָ

---

to hear it we need to create a kind of silence of the soul. We need to learn to listen – and listening is an art, one of the greatest there is.

There is a listening beyond words, a silence that gives meaning to speech. In that silence, we know and are known by God. God is the personal dimension of existence, the "Thou" beneath the "It," the "Ought" beyond the "Is," the Self that speaks to self in moments of total disclosure. Opening ourselves to the universe, we find God reaching out to us. At that moment we make the life-changing discovery that though we seem utterly insignificant, we are utterly significant, a fragment of God's presence in the world. Eternity preceded us; infinity will come after us. Yet we know that this day, this moment, this place, this circumstance, is full of the light of infinite radiance, whose proof is the mere fact that we are here to experience it. Faith is where God and human beings touch across the abyss of infinity. Feeling, we are felt. Acting, we are acted upon. Living, we are lived. And if we make ourselves transparent to existence, then our lives too radiate that Divine Presence which, celebrating life, gives life to those whose lives we touch.

20:5 עַל־שִׁלֵּשִׁים וְעַל־רִבֵּעִים *To the third and fourth generation* – Deuteronomy 24:16 tells us, "A person shall be put to death only for his own sin." Yirmeya 31:28–29 and Yehezkel 18:2–4 both reinforce the point that there is no intergenerational transfer of guilt. So what then is the meaning of "I hold the descendants to account for the sins of the fathers"? According to Sanhedrin 27b, children are only punished for the sins of their parents if they themselves commit those sins. The phrase is therefore a warning to parents not to have a negative influence on their children, not a statement

servant, your livestock, or the migrant within your gates.
11 For in six days the LORD made heaven and earth, the sea,
and all that they contain, and He rested on the seventh
day. And so the LORD blessed the Sabbath day and made
12 it holy. Honor your father and mother. Then
you will live long in the land that the LORD your God is
13 giving you. Do not murder. Do not
commit adultery. Do not steal. Do not

---

market economy are counterbalanced by a world in which money does not count, in which we are all equal citizens. The Jewish writer Ahad Ha'am was surely correct when he said that more than the Jews have kept the Sabbath, the Sabbath has kept the Jews. It was and is the one day in seven in which we live out all those values which are in danger of being obscured in the daily rush of events, the day in which we stop making a living and learn instead simply how to live.

20:12 כַּבֵּד אֶת־אָבִיךָ וְאֶת־אִמֶּךָ *Honor your father and mother* – As we have seen, the first five commands are generally considered to be about our relationship with God, the second five about our relationships with our fellow humans. The command to honor parents, the fifth command, belongs to the first group because it is about the duties we owe to those who brought us into being. Collectively, they represent ontological gratitude, an attitude of thankfulness and respect to those to whom we owe the gift of life itself.

20:13 לֹא תִנְאָף *Do not commit adultery* – In marriage we ask for and offer a commitment to share not this or that aspect of life but life itself. Marriage is the supreme example of a moral bond. Like all things seriously worthwhile, it involves the realization of a possibility at the price of excluding others. Every relationship has its rows, its tensions, its disappointments, its languid passages, but marriage is where we live through these things in the knowledge – given by commitment, renewed by love's rituals – that they will not drive us apart. Marriage is surrounded by a wall (the Rabbis called it a "hedge of roses") that we may not cross. On the other side is adultery.

Adultery involves putting short-term pleasure ahead of lifelong happiness. It sets my desires above my feeling for, and obligation to, others. It devalues the currency of commitment: the word spoken, the pledge given, the promise undertaken. And like so many ostensibly unpublic acts, it affects the world around us. What we do today others may do in the future, affected, consciously or unconsciously, by our example. We tacitly teach our partners, friends, and above all our children, that despite our most serious undertakings, the word of another person cannot be trusted. When that happens, we are all diminished.

יא וּבְהֶמְתֶּךָ וְגֵרְךָ אֲשֶׁר בִּשְׁעָרֶיךָ׃ כִּי שֵׁשֶׁת־יָמִים עָשָׂה יְהוָה
אֶת־הַשָּׁמַיִם וְאֶת־הָאָרֶץ אֶת־הַיָּם וְאֶת־כָּל־אֲשֶׁר־בָּם
וַיָּנַח בַּיּוֹם הַשְּׁבִיעִי עַל־כֵּן בֵּרַךְ יְהוָה אֶת־יוֹם הַשַּׁבָּת
יב וַיְקַדְּשֵׁהוּ׃ כַּבֵּד אֶת־אָבִיךָ וְאֶת־
אִמֶּךָ לְמַעַן יַאֲרִכוּן יָמֶיךָ עַל הָאֲדָמָה אֲשֶׁר־יְהוָה אֱלֹהֶיךָ
יג נֹתֵן לָךְ׃ לֹא תִרְצָח לֹא
תִנְאָף לֹא תִגְנֹב לֹא־

---

choosing to do so for our own enjoyment. The biblical Sabbath, by contrast, is a collective good. Michael Walzer writes that it is "enjoined for everyone, enjoyed by everyone." He also notes the paradox of holy days. They are an abridgment of liberty – a holy day is not one on which we are free to do what we like. Nonetheless, "the historical experience of the Sabbath is not an experience of unfreedom. The overwhelming sense conveyed in Jewish literature, secular as well as religious, is that the day was eagerly looked forward to and joyfully welcomed – precisely as a day of release, a day of expansiveness and leisure." It is expansive the way a public park is expansive: by not being private property. The Sabbath is time we, not I, own. It is essential that on the Sabbath no one – not slaves, servants, employees, even farm animals – can be made to work against their will.

20:11 וַיְקַדְּשֵׁהוּ *Made it holy* – The universe was created in six days, yet creation itself involved seven days. The seventh day is declared by God Himself to be holy. The holy is where human beings renounce their independence and self-sufficiency, the very things that are the mark of their humanity, and for a moment acknowledge their utter dependence on He who spoke and brought the universe into being. The essence of the Sabbath is that it is a day of not doing, a cessation, a stopping point, a pause, an absence of activity.

The Sabbath is the time when humans cease, for a day, to be creators and become conscious of themselves as creations. Just as God had to make space for the finite, so human beings have to make space for the infinite. One way to understand the holy, then, is that it is a time or space that in itself testifies to the existence of something beyond itself. The Sabbath points to a time beyond time; to creation.

The Sabbath is one of those phenomena which you have to live in order to understand. For countless generations of Jews, it was the moment at which we renew our attachment to family and community, during which we live the truth that the world is not wholly ours to bend to our will but something given to us in trust to conserve for future generations, and in which the inequalities of a

14 bear false witness against your neighbor. Do not
crave your neighbor's house. Do not
crave your neighbor's wife, his male or female servant,
his ox, his donkey, or anything else that is your
neighbor's."
15 Every one of the people witnessed the thunder and SHEVI'I
lightning and the sound of the ram's horn and the smoke-
covered mountain; they saw and they shook – and they
16 stood at a distance, and said to Moshe, "Speak to us yourself
and we will listen, but let not God say any more to us, or
17 we will die." "Do not be afraid," said Moshe to the people,
"God has come to lift you up, so that the awe of Him will
18 be with you always, keeping you from sin." But the people
remained at a distance while Moshe approached the thick
19 darkness where God was. Then the LORD said MAFTIR
to Moshe, "This is what you shall tell the Israelites: You
yourselves have seen that I, from the heavens, have spoken

---

freedom without justice, but there is no justice without each of us accepting individual and collective responsibility for "telling the truth, the whole truth, and nothing but the truth."

20:14 לֹא תַחְמֹד *Do not crave* – Envy, desiring what someone else has, is an emotion, not a thought, a word, or a deed. Surely, one would think, we cannot help our emotions. They used to be called the "passions," precisely because we are passive in relation to them. So how can envy be forbidden at all? Surely it only makes sense to command or forbid matters that are within our control. In any case, why should the occasional spasm of envy matter if it does not lead to anything harmful to other people?

It matters because envy is one of the prime drivers of violence in society. It is what led Kayin to murder Hevel. Most poignantly, envy lay at the heart of the hatred of the brothers for Yosef. They resented his special treatment at the hands of their father, the richly embroidered cloak he wore, and his dreams of becoming the ruler of them all. That is what led them to contemplate killing him and eventually to sell him as a slave.

The antidote to envy is gratitude. "Who is rich?" asked Ben Zoma, and replied, "One who rejoices in what he has" (Mishna Avot 4:1). Through gratitude we learn to celebrate what we have instead of thinking about what other people have, and to be what we are instead of wanting to be what we are not.

יד תַעֲנֶה בְרֵעֲךָ עֵד שָׁקֶר: לֹא
תַחְמֹד בֵּית רֵעֶךָ לֹא־
תַחְמֹד אֵשֶׁת רֵעֶךָ וְעַבְדּוֹ וַאֲמָתוֹ וְשׁוֹרוֹ וַחֲמֹרוֹ וְכֹל אֲשֶׁר
לְרֵעֶךָ:
טו וְכָל־הָעָם רֹאִים אֶת־הַקּוֹלֹת וְאֶת־הַלַּפִּידִם וְאֵת קוֹל הַשֹּׁפָר שביעי
טז וְאֶת־הָהָר עָשֵׁן וַיַּרְא הָעָם וַיָּנֻעוּ וַיַּעַמְדוּ מֵרָחֹק: וַיֹּאמְרוּ
אֶל־מֹשֶׁה דַּבֵּר־אַתָּה עִמָּנוּ וְנִשְׁמָעָה וְאַל־יְדַבֵּר עִמָּנוּ
יז אֱלֹהִים פֶּן־נָמוּת: וַיֹּאמֶר מֹשֶׁה אֶל־הָעָם אַל־תִּירָאוּ כִּי
לְבַעֲבוּר נַסּוֹת אֶתְכֶם בָּא הָאֱלֹהִים וּבַעֲבוּר תִּהְיֶה יִרְאָתוֹ
יח עַל־פְּנֵיכֶם לְבִלְתִּי תֶחֱטָאוּ: וַיַּעֲמֹד הָעָם מֵרָחֹק וּמֹשֶׁה נִגַּשׁ
יט אֶל־הָעֲרָפֶל אֲשֶׁר־שָׁם הָאֱלֹהִים: וַיֹּאמֶר מפטיר
יהוה אֶל־מֹשֶׁה כֹּה תֹאמַר אֶל־בְּנֵי יִשְׂרָאֵל אַתֶּם רְאִיתֶם

When marriage is betrayed, something of our world has been lost – and it is not something small. Love freely given and freely received, the sharing of a life, is the most profound redemption ever experienced from loneliness, the point at which the political and moral enterprise begin. A world of safe distances, of reservations and precautions, can never hope to recapture that state. We, individually and collectively, are the guardians of the world of trust, and the family is its birthplace.

20:13 לֹא תִגְנֹב *Do not steal* – Whereas Jefferson defined as inalienable rights those of "life, liberty, and the pursuit of happiness," John Locke, closer in spirit to the Tanakh, saw them as "life, liberty, or possession." The biblical respect for property rights is a revolution against the ancient world and the power it gave rulers to regard the property of the tribe or the people as their own. By contrast, when Moshe finds his leadership challenged by the Israelites during the Koraḥ rebellion, he says about his relation to the people, "I have not taken a single donkey from them, nor have I wronged any one of them" (Num. 16:15). For a ruler to abuse property rights is, for the Tanakh, one of the great corruptions of power. Judaism is the religion of a people born in slavery and longing for redemption. The great assault of slavery against human dignity is that it deprives me of the ownership of the wealth I create.

20:13 לֹא תַעֲנֶה בְרֵעֲךָ עֵד שָׁקֶר *Do not bear false witness* – A just society needs more than a structure of laws, courts, and enforcement agencies. There is no

20 to you. Have no others alongside Me; make yourselves
21 no silver gods, no golden gods. Make for Me an altar of
earth and on that sacrifice your burnt offerings and peace
offerings, your sheep and your cattle. Wherever I cause My
name to be invoked, I will come to you and I will bless you.
22 If you make Me an altar of stones, do not build it of hewn
23 stone, for in wielding a sword upon it, you profane it. Do
not ascend to My altar with steps, for your nakedness must
not be exposed on it.

The haftara for Parashat Yitro is on page 1478.

---

their spears into pruning hooks. Nation shall not raise sword against nation; no more will they learn to make war" (Is. 2:4). His vision of a world in which "there will be no wrong or violence on all My holy mountain, for the knowledge of the LORD will fill the earth as waters cover the ocean" (11:9) is part of the Tanakh's decisive break with the ethic of militarism that dominated the ancient world. The vision of peace would not be revived, outside the Judeo-Christian tradition, until Kant's secular essay on "perpetual peace" in 1795. No soul was ever saved by hate. No truth was ever proved by violence. No redemption was ever brought by holy war. The sword, though sometimes necessary, cannot build the altar, only profane it. It is with this hint that we conclude the *parasha*, and the narrative of our founding and greatest revelation.

כִּי מִן־הַשָּׁמַיִם דִּבַּרְתִּי עִמָּכֶם׃ לֹא תַעֲשׂוּן אִתִּי אֱלֹהֵי כֶסֶף כ
וֵאלֹהֵי זָהָב לֹא תַעֲשׂוּ לָכֶם׃ מִזְבַּח אֲדָמָה תַּעֲשֶׂה־לִּי וְזָבַחְתָּ כא
עָלָיו אֶת־עֹלֹתֶיךָ וְאֶת־שְׁלָמֶיךָ אֶת־צֹאנְךָ וְאֶת־בְּקָרֶךָ
בְּכָל־הַמָּקוֹם אֲשֶׁר אַזְכִּיר אֶת־שְׁמִי אָבוֹא אֵלֶיךָ וּבֵרַכְתִּיךָ׃
וְאִם־מִזְבַּח אֲבָנִים תַּעֲשֶׂה־לִּי לֹא־תִבְנֶה אֶתְהֶן גָּזִית כִּי כב
חַרְבְּךָ הֵנַפְתָּ עָלֶיהָ וַתְּחַלְלֶהָ׃ וְלֹא־תַעֲלֶה בְמַעֲלֹת עַל־ כג
מִזְבְּחִי אֲשֶׁר לֹא־תִגָּלֶה עֶרְוָתְךָ עָלָיו׃

The הפטרה *for* פרשת יתרו *is on page 1479.*

20:22 כִּי חַרְבְּךָ הֵנַפְתָּ עָלֶיהָ וַתְּחַלְלֶהָ *In wielding a sword upon it, you profane it* – Despite the apparent militarism of the early texts of Judaism, their underlying value was always peace. In the book of Samuel, when David wishes to build the Ark a permanent home, God tells him not to build the Temple, assuring him that the work would be done by his son, Shlomo. David explains this in his own words in Chronicles: "The word of the Lord came to me, saying, 'You have shed much blood and waged mighty wars – you will not build a House for My name, for you have shed too much blood upon the earth before Me'" (I Chr. 22:8).

By the eighth century BCE the prophets of Israel became the first people in history to envisage a world at peace. The classic instance is Yeshayahu, who foresaw a time when the nations "shall beat their swords into plowshares,

Parashat Mishpatim

21 1 And these are the laws that you shall set before them. If you
buy a Hebrew slave, he shall serve for six years, but in the
3 seventh he shall go forth free, without paying anything. If
he came alone, he shall leave alone. But if he was a married

Three remarkable propositions are being set out here. The first is that just as the general principles of Judaism (*Aseret HaDibrot* means not "Ten Commandments" but "Ten Utterances" or overarching principles) are divine, so are the details. There are those who believe that what is holy in Judaism is its broad vision, never so compellingly expressed as in the Decalogue at Sinai. The truth, however, is that "just as the former were given at Sinai, so these were given at Sinai." The greatness of Judaism is not simply in its noble vision, but in the way it brings this vision down to earth in detailed legislation.

The second principle, no less fundamental, is that civil law is not secular law. We do not believe in the idea "render to Caesar what is Caesar's and to God what belongs to God." We believe in the separation of powers but not in the secularization of law or the spiritualization of faith. The Sanhedrin or Supreme Court must be placed near the Temple to teach that law itself must be driven by a religious vision.

The third principle is the idea that law does not belong to lawyers. It is the heritage of every Jew. Legal knowledge is not the closely guarded property of an elite. It is – in the famous phrase – the "heritage of Yaakov's assembly" (Deut. 33:4). Judaism expected everyone to know and understand the law.

SLAVERY

We have read in the first part of Exodus about the Israelites' historic experience of slavery. So, understandably, the social legislation of Mishpatim begins with slavery. What is fascinating is not only what it says but what it doesn't say.

It doesn't say: abolish slavery. Surely it should have done that. Is that not the whole point of the story thus far? Yosef's brothers sell him into slavery. Generations later, when a pharaoh arises who "had not known Yosef" (Ex. 1:8), the entire Israelite people become Egypt's slaves. Slavery, like vengeance, is a vicious circle that has no natural end. Why not, then, give it a supernatural end? Why did God not say, "There shall be no more slavery"?

The Torah has already given us an implicit answer. Change is possible in human nature but it takes time: time on a vast scale, centuries, even millennia. There is little doubt that in terms of the Torah's value system, the exercise of power by one person over another,

פרשת משפטים

כא א ב וְאֵ֙לֶּה֙ הַמִּשְׁפָּטִ֔ים אֲשֶׁ֥ר תָּשִׂ֖ים לִפְנֵיהֶֽם׃ כִּ֤י תִקְנֶה֙ עֶ֣בֶד טז
ג עִבְרִ֔י שֵׁ֥שׁ שָׁנִ֖ים יַעֲבֹ֑ד וּבַּ֨שְּׁבִעִ֔ת יֵצֵ֥א לַֽחָפְשִׁ֖י חִנָּֽם׃ אִם־
בְּגַפּ֥וֹ יָבֹ֖א בְּגַפּ֣וֹ יֵצֵ֑א אִם־בַּ֤עַל אִשָּׁה֙ ה֔וּא וְיָצְאָ֥ה אִשְׁתּ֖וֹ

MISHPATIM

Following the revelation at Mount Sinai, Parashat Mishpatim fleshes out the details of the law that was to govern the Israelites: laws relating to slaves and their release; personal injuries and property laws; laws of social responsibility, justice, and compassion; and laws relating to the Sabbath and the festivals. It ends with a ratification of the covenant, and Moshe ascending the mountain for forty days.

The contrast between the *parasha* of Yitro and that of Mishpatim is immense. In the former, the Torah takes us to the greatest encounter ever between human beings and God, the revelation at Mount Sinai, with its broad statement of principles, the Ten Commandments. In the latter, we are plunged into a plethora of detail. We seem to move from the sublime to the prosaic, from an all-encompassing moral and spiritual vision to the small print of a legal code.

Mishpatim, with its detailed rules and regulations, can sometimes seem an anticlimax after the breathtaking grandeur of the revelation at Sinai. It should not be. Parashat Yitro contains the vision, but God is in the details. God is in heaven, but we honor Him here on earth: that is what Torah – the word that means "law, teaching, ethical instruction" – is about. It is precisely through law that we enact spiritual truths in physical circumstances, creating fragments of heaven in our interactions on earth.

21:1 וְאֵלֶּה הַמִּשְׁפָּטִים *And these are the laws* – Rashi comments on this verse:

> *And these are the laws* – Wherever [the Torah] uses the word "these" it signals a discontinuity with what has been stated previously. Wherever it uses the term "and these" it signals a continuity. Just as the former commands were given at Sinai, so these were given at Sinai. Why then are the civil laws placed in juxtaposition with the laws concerning the altar? To tell you to place the Sanhedrin near the Temple.
>
> *That you shall set before them* – You should not think, "I will teach them a section of law two or three times until they know the words verbatim but I will not take the trouble to make them understand the reason and its significance." Therefore the Torah states, "That you shall set before them," like a fully laid table with everything ready for eating.

4 man, his wife shall leave with him. If his master gave him a
wife and she bore him sons or daughters, the woman and
her children shall remain her master's, while he shall leave
5 alone. But if the slave declares, 'I love my master, my wife,
6 and my children; I do not want to go free,' then his master
shall bring him before the judges. He shall take him to the
door or to the doorpost and pierce his ear with an awl;
7 after that he shall then remain his slave forever. If
a man sells his daughter as a maidservant, she does not
8 go free in the usual way of slaves. If her master, who
intended to wed her, finds that he dislikes her, he must let
her be redeemed. He has no right to sell her to foreigners,
9 because he has broken faith with her. If he intends her

> The ear that heard on Mount Sinai: "For it is to Me that the Israelites are servants," and he nevertheless went ahead and acquired a master for himself, should [have his ear] pierced.

A Hebrew slave is to go free after six years. If the slave has grown so used to his condition that he wishes not to go free, then he undergoes a stigmatizing ceremony, having his ear pierced, which thereafter remains as a visible sign of shame. These stipulations have the effect of turning slavery from a lifelong fate into a temporary condition, and one that is perceived to be a humiliation rather than something written indelibly into the human script.

21:7 וְכִי־יִמְכֹּר אִישׁ אֶת־בִּתּוֹ לְאָמָה *If a man sells his daughter as a maidservant* – The Rabbis refused to rationalize poverty. It is not a blessed condition. It is, they said, "a kind of death" and "worse than fifty plagues." They said:

> Nothing is harder to bear than poverty, for he who is crushed by poverty is like one to whom all the troubles of the world cling and upon whom all the curses of Deuteronomy have descended. If all other troubles were placed on one side and poverty on the other, poverty would outweigh them all.

Poverty in the ancient world, as in too many places today, can lead directly to slavery. The Torah does not gloss this fact over, but it does demand that we recognize the humanity of the person caught in this net. The Rabbis had the sanest view of poverty I know, and they did so because most of them were poor. They neither valued poverty, nor did they see in the distribution of wealth a divinely ordained social order. I know of nothing in the literature of Judaism that speaks of submissively accepting one's "station in life"; neither may the needy be exploited without restraint. We are a community, sharing a collective fate and responsibility.

ד עִמּוֹ: אִם־אֲדֹנָיו יִתֶּן־לוֹ אִשָּׁה וְיָלְדָה־לוֹ בָנִים אוֹ בָנוֹת
ה הָאִשָּׁה וִילָדֶיהָ תִּהְיֶה לַאדֹנֶיהָ וְהוּא יֵצֵא בְגַפּוֹ: וְאִם־
אָמֹר יֹאמַר הָעֶבֶד אָהַבְתִּי אֶת־אֲדֹנִי אֶת־אִשְׁתִּי וְאֶת־בָּנָי
ו לֹא אֵצֵא חָפְשִׁי: וְהִגִּישׁוֹ אֲדֹנָיו אֶל־הָאֱלֹהִים וְהִגִּישׁוֹ אֶל־
הַדֶּלֶת אוֹ אֶל־הַמְּזוּזָה וְרָצַע אֲדֹנָיו אֶת־אָזְנוֹ בַּמַּרְצֵעַ וַעֲבָדוֹ
ז לְעֹלָם: וְכִי־יִמְכֹּר אִישׁ אֶת־בִּתּוֹ לְאָמָה לֹא תֵצֵא
ח כְּצֵאת הָעֲבָדִים: אִם־רָעָה בְּעֵינֵי אֲדֹנֶיהָ אֲשֶׁר־לֹא יְעָדָהּ לוֹ
ט וְהֶפְדָּהּ לְעַם נָכְרִי לֹא־יִמְשֹׁל לְמָכְרָהּ בְּבִגְדוֹ־בָהּ: וְאִם־לִבְנוֹ
י יִיעָדֶנָּה כְּמִשְׁפַּט הַבָּנוֹת יַעֲשֶׂה־לָּהּ: אִם־אַחֶרֶת יִקַּח־לוֹ

without their consent, is a fundamental assault against human dignity. This is not just true of the relationship between master and slave. It is even true, according to many classic Jewish commentators, of the relationship between king and subjects, rulers and ruled.

So slavery is to be abolished, but it is a fundamental principle of God's relationship with us that He does not force us to change faster than we are able to do of our own free will. Mishpatim does not abolish slavery, but it sets in motion a series of fundamental laws that will lead people, albeit at their own pace, to abolish it of their own accord.

In these laws, a fundamental change is taking place in the nature of slavery. No longer is it a permanent status; it is a temporary condition. A Hebrew slave goes free after seven years. He or she knows this. Liberty awaits the slave not at the whim of the master but by divine command. When you know that within a fixed time you are going to be free, you may be a slave in body, but in your own mind you are a free human being who has temporarily lost his or her liberty.

A slave may stay a slave, but not without being reminded that this is not what God wants for His people. The result of these laws was to create a dynamic that would in the end lead to an abolition of slavery, at a time of free human choosing.

God has patience, though it is often sorely tried. He wants slavery abolished but He wants it to be done by free human beings coming to see of their own accord the evil it is and the evil it does. The God of history, who taught us to study history, has faith that eventually we will learn the lesson of history: that freedom is indivisible. We must grant freedom to others if we truly seek it for ourselves.

21:6 וְרָצַע אֲדֹנָיו אֶת־אָזְנוֹ בַּמַּרְצֵעַ *Pierce his ear with an awl* – Rashi explains:

> Why was the ear chosen to be pierced rather than all the other limbs of the body? Said R. Yoḥanan b. Zakkai:

for his son, he shall grant her all the rights of a daughter.
10 If he marries another woman alongside her, he shall not
11 reduce her food, her clothing, or marital rights. If he
fails her in any of these three things, she shall go forth
12 free without paying anything. One person who
13 strikes another so that he dies shall be put to death. If he
did not lie in wait to harm him, but it came about by an
act of God – I am setting apart a place where he may find
14 refuge. But if someone schemes against another
and kills him by stealth, you shall take him even from My
15 altar and he shall die. One who wounds his father
16 or mother shall be put to death. One who
kidnaps a person shall be put to death, whether the victim
17 has been sold or found in his possession. One
who curses his father or mother shall be put to
18 death. If two people fight and one strikes
another with a stone or with his fist – if the victim does
19 not die but is confined to bed, and afterward he gets up
and walks outdoors even leaning on a cane, the assailant is
absolved, but he must pay for the victim's loss of time and
20 provide for his cure. If a man strikes his slave, SHENI
male or female, with a rod and the slave dies there and
21 then, the death shall be avenged. But if the slave survives
a day, two days – since the money lost is the master's, the
22 death shall not be avenged. If two men fight and
one of them hits a pregnant woman, and she miscarries
but suffers no irreparable injury herself, the offender
must be fined, as the woman's husband demands and as
23 the judges rule. But if she suffers an irreparable injury, he

---

philosopher Philo, turns to this passage.

Philo follows the Septuagint, the Greek translation of the Tanakh made in the third century BCE during the reign of Ptolemy II. There are numerous divergences between the Septuagint and the Hebrew text, and this is one of them.

The Greek version translates *ason* not as "calamity," but rather as "form." Now, according to Philo, the verses are talking about damage to the fetus. In the first case, "there is no *ason*" means the fetus was "unformed" – i.e., the woman miscarries, but the fetus was at an early

יא שְׁאֵרָהּ כְּסוּתָהּ וְעֹנָתָהּ לֹא יִגְרָע: וְאִם־שְׁלָשׁ־אֵלֶּה לֹא
יב יַעֲשֶׂה לָהּ וְיָצְאָה חִנָּם אֵין כָּסֶף: מַכֵּה אִישׁ וָמֵת
יג מוֹת יוּמָת: וַאֲשֶׁר לֹא צָדָה וְהָאֱלֹהִים אִנָּה לְיָדוֹ וְשַׂמְתִּי לְךָ
יד מָקוֹם אֲשֶׁר יָנוּס שָׁמָּה: וְכִי־יָזִד אִישׁ עַל־רֵעֵהוּ
טו לְהָרְגוֹ בְעָרְמָה מֵעִם מִזְבְּחִי תִּקָּחֶנּוּ לָמוּת: וּמַכֵּה
טז אָבִיו וְאִמּוֹ מוֹת יוּמָת: וְגֹנֵב אִישׁ וּמְכָרוֹ וְנִמְצָא
יז בְיָדוֹ מוֹת יוּמָת: וּמְקַלֵּל אָבִיו וְאִמּוֹ מוֹת
יח יוּמָת: וְכִי־יְרִיבֻן אֲנָשִׁים וְהִכָּה־אִישׁ אֶת־
יט רֵעֵהוּ בְּאֶבֶן אוֹ בְאֶגְרֹף וְלֹא יָמוּת וְנָפַל לְמִשְׁכָּב: אִם־יָקוּם
וְהִתְהַלֵּךְ בַּחוּץ עַל־מִשְׁעַנְתּוֹ וְנִקָּה הַמַּכֶּה רַק שִׁבְתּוֹ יִתֵּן
כ וְרַפֹּא יְרַפֵּא: וְכִי־יַכֶּה אִישׁ אֶת־עַבְדּוֹ אוֹ אֶת־ שני
כא אֲמָתוֹ בַּשֵּׁבֶט וּמֵת תַּחַת יָדוֹ נָקֹם יִנָּקֵם: אַךְ אִם־יוֹם אוֹ יוֹמַיִם
כב יַעֲמֹד לֹא יֻקַּם כִּי כַסְפּוֹ הוּא: וְכִי־יִנָּצוּ אֲנָשִׁים
וְנָגְפוּ אִשָּׁה הָרָה וְיָצְאוּ יְלָדֶיהָ וְלֹא יִהְיֶה אָסוֹן עָנוֹשׁ יֵעָנֵשׁ
כג כַּאֲשֶׁר יָשִׁית עָלָיו בַּעַל הָאִשָּׁה וְנָתַן בִּפְלִלִים: וְאִם־אָסוֹן

TEXT AND INTERPRETATION: THE CASE OF ACCIDENTAL MISCARRIAGE

The word *ason*, irreparable injury, apparently means a fatal accident. The law under consideration is about harm to an innocent third party when people are engaged in a public and potentially murderous fight. If the third party is a pregnant woman, and as a result of being hit she miscarries but suffers no other injury, the person responsible must pay compensation for the loss of the unborn child, but suffers no other penalty. If, however, the woman dies, he is guilty of a much more serious offence (the Sages disagreed as to whether this means that he is liable to capital punishment or not [Sanhedrin 79a]).

On this interpretation, causing a woman to miscarry – being responsible for the death of a fetus – is not a capital offense. Until birth, the fetus does not have the legal status of a person. Such was the view of the Sages in the land of Israel.

However, the Alexandrian Jewish community during the late Second Temple period developed its own traditions, at times quite different from those of the rabbinic mainstream. In one of his works, its most famous member, the

24 must compensate life for life, eye for eye, tooth for tooth,
25 hand for hand, foot for foot, burn for burn, wound for
26 wound, bruise for bruise. If a man should strike
the eye of his slave, male or female, and maim it, he must
27 send the slave out free on account of his eye. If he knocks
out the tooth of his slave, male or female, he must send
the slave out free on account of his tooth.
28 If an ox gores a man or a woman to death, the ox shall be
stoned, and its flesh not eaten, but the owner of the ox
29 shall not be liable. But if the ox has already gored in the
past, and its owner was warned but failed to guard it, and
it kills a man or a woman, the ox shall be stoned, and its

---

meaning retributive justice or the rule of law, and specifically with cases delineating a person's responsibility to compensate for harm he or she causes others. A free society must be governed by law, impartially administered, through which the guilty are punished, the innocent acquitted, the injured compensated, and human rights secured. *Tzedaka*, by contrast, refers to distributive justice, a less procedural and more substantive idea, which becomes the focus from 22:21. God, for the Israelites, is actively concerned with the economic and political order, especially with those who, because they lack power, or even a voice, became the victims of injustice and inequity.

The society the Israelites are to construct, we are told, will stand as a living contrast to what they have experienced in Egypt: poverty, persecution, and enslavement. Their release from bondage was only the first stage on their journey to freedom. The second – their covenant with God – involves collective responsibility to ensure that no one will be excluded from the shared graciousness of the community and its life. This requires both *mishpat*, the rule of law, and *tzedaka*, a just distribution of resources, a fair chance at a dignified livelihood. This view has close affinities with Amartya Sen's concept of "development as freedom":

> The adult who lacks the means of having medical treatment for an ailment from which she suffers is not only prey to preventable morbidity and possibly escapable mortality, but may also be denied the freedom to do various things – for herself and for others – that she may wish to do as a responsible human being. The bonded laborer born into semi-slavery, the subjugated girl child stifled by a repressive society, the helpless landless laborer without substantial means of earning an income are all deprived not only in terms of well-being, but also in terms of the ability to lead responsible lives, which are

כד יִהְיֶה וְנָתַתָּה נֶפֶשׁ תַּחַת נָפֶשׁ: עַיִן תַּחַת עַיִן שֵׁן תַּחַת שֵׁן יָד
כה תַּחַת יָד רֶגֶל תַּחַת רָגֶל: כְּוִיָּה תַּחַת כְּוִיָּה פֶּצַע תַּחַת פָּצַע
כו חַבּוּרָה תַּחַת חַבּוּרָה: וְכִי־יַכֶּה אִישׁ אֶת־עֵין עַבְדּוֹ
אוֹ־אֶת־עֵין אֲמָתוֹ וְשִׁחֲתָהּ לַחָפְשִׁי יְשַׁלְּחֶנּוּ תַּחַת עֵינוֹ:
כז וְאִם־שֵׁן עַבְדּוֹ אוֹ־שֵׁן אֲמָתוֹ יַפִּיל לַחָפְשִׁי יְשַׁלְּחֶנּוּ תַּחַת
שִׁנּוֹ:
כח וְכִי־יִגַּח שׁוֹר אֶת־אִישׁ אוֹ אֶת־אִשָּׁה וָמֵת סָקוֹל יִסָּקֵל
כט הַשּׁוֹר וְלֹא יֵאָכֵל אֶת־בְּשָׂרוֹ וּבַעַל הַשּׁוֹר נָקִי: וְאִם שׁוֹר
נַגָּח הוּא מִתְּמֹל שִׁלְשֹׁם וְהוּעַד בִּבְעָלָיו וְלֹא יִשְׁמְרֶנּוּ
וְהֵמִית אִישׁ אוֹ אִשָּׁה הַשּׁוֹר יִסָּקֵל וְגַם־בְּעָלָיו יוּמָת:

---

stage of development. The next verse speaks of a fetus "that has form," i.e., the woman was at a later stage of pregnancy. In this view, feticide – and hence abortion – can be a capital crime, an act of murder.

Judaism followed the opinion of the Sages of the land of Israel. In Judaism, abortion is not murder. Still, while a fetus may not be a person in Jewish law, it is a potential person, and must therefore be protected. We permit abortion to save the life of the mother or to protect her from life-threatening illness.

However, Philo's reading had an impact on the development of Christian teaching. The first Christian texts were written in Greek rather than Hebrew. The early Christian teachings on abortion thus followed Philo rather than the Sages. If the fetus was formed, then causing its death was murder. So taught Tertullian in the second century.

It is fascinating to see how this difference arose – over a difference in understanding of a single word, *ason*. This is the fundamental truth behind the Jewish belief in *Torah Shebe'al Peh*, the "Oral Law": The meaning of a text is not given by the text itself. Between a text and its meaning stands the act of interpretation. Rules of interpretation handed down across the generations guide our reading. There have been sectarian groups within Judaism – Sadducees, Karaites, and others – who accepted the Written Torah but not the Oral Law, but in reality such a doctrine is untenable. We need an authoritative tradition of interpretation – in Judaism, the Oral Law – to give us a basis not only to understand the text, but also to apply it to new circumstances without departing from its fundamental truths.

21:29 וְהוּעַד בִּבְעָלָיו *Its owner was warned* – The *parasha* entitled Mishpatim begins, as we might expect, with *mishpat*,

30 owner also shall be put to death. If a ransom is imposed
on his life, then he shall pay whatever is imposed on him
31 and redeem his life. This rule also applies if the ox gores
32 a minor son or daughter, but if the ox gores a slave, male
or female, the owner shall give thirty shekels of silver to
33 the master, and the ox must be stoned. If a man
uncovers a hole or digs one and fails to cover it, and an
34 ox or a donkey falls into it, the one responsible for the
pit shall make restitution. He shall give its owner its full
35 value, and the dead animal shall be his. If one
man's ox injures another's so that it dies, they shall sell
the live ox and share the money. The dead animal they
36 shall also share. If, however, it is known that the ox had
gored in the past, and still the owner failed to guard it,
he shall pay an ox for an ox, and the dead animal shall be
37 his. If a man steals an ox or a sheep and kills it or
sells it, he shall pay five oxen for an ox, four sheep for a
22 1 sheep. If a burglar is caught tunneling in, and is struck and
2 killed, there is no bloodguilt on his account. But if the sun
has risen on him, there is bloodguilt on his account. A
thief must make restitution; if he lacks the means, he shall
3 be sold as a slave to repay his debt. If what he stole – an
ox, ass, or sheep – is found alive in his possession, he shall
4 pay double. If a person lets a field or vineyard be SHELISHI
damaged, either by letting his livestock loose or by letting

---

possibility of a fight with his brother Esav in Parashat Vayishlaḥ (Gen. 32:7): In the words of the Midrash, "He was 'acutely afraid' that he might be killed; he was 'distressed' that he might kill" (Rashi on Bereshit Rabba 76:2).

If Esav were to try to kill Yaakov, Yaakov would be justified in fighting back, if necessary at the cost of Esav's life. Why then should this possibility raise moral qualms? The principle at stake, according to the *Siftei Ḥakhamim*, is the minimum use of force. Yaakov was distressed at the possibility that in the heat of conflict he might kill some of the combatants when injury alone might have been all that was necessary to defend the lives of those – including himself – who were under attack. Even the heroes of the Tanakh struggle with situations of moral uncertainty. But halakha is here beginning to give us a framework through which to examine and refine our moral choices.

ל אִם־כֹּפֶר יוּשַׁת עָלָיו וְנָתַן פִּדְיֹן נַפְשׁוֹ כְּכֹל אֲשֶׁר־יוּשַׁת
לא עָלָיו׃ אוֹ־בֵן יִגָּח אוֹ־בַת יִגָּח כַּמִּשְׁפָּט הַזֶּה יֵעָשֶׂה לּוֹ׃
לב אִם־עֶבֶד יִגַּח הַשּׁוֹר אוֹ אָמָה כֶּסֶף ׀ שְׁלֹשִׁים שְׁקָלִים יִתֵּן
לג לַאדֹנָיו וְהַשּׁוֹר יִסָּקֵל׃ וְכִי־יִפְתַּח אִישׁ
בּוֹר אוֹ כִּי־יִכְרֶה אִישׁ בֹּר וְלֹא יְכַסֶּנּוּ וְנָפַל־שָׁמָּה שּׁוֹר אוֹ
לד חֲמוֹר׃ בַּעַל הַבּוֹר יְשַׁלֵּם כֶּסֶף יָשִׁיב לִבְעָלָיו וְהַמֵּת יִהְיֶה־
לה לּוֹ׃ וְכִי־יִגֹּף שׁוֹר־אִישׁ אֶת־שׁוֹר רֵעֵהוּ
וָמֵת וּמָכְרוּ אֶת־הַשּׁוֹר הַחַי וְחָצוּ אֶת־כַּסְפּוֹ וְגַם אֶת־הַמֵּת
לו יֶחֱצוּן׃ אוֹ נוֹדַע כִּי שׁוֹר נַגָּח הוּא מִתְּמוֹל שִׁלְשֹׁם וְלֹא
יִשְׁמְרֶנּוּ בְּעָלָיו שַׁלֵּם יְשַׁלֵּם שׁוֹר תַּחַת הַשּׁוֹר וְהַמֵּת יִהְיֶה־
לז לּוֹ׃ כִּי יִגְנֹב־אִישׁ שׁוֹר אוֹ־שֶׂה וּטְבָחוֹ
אוֹ מְכָרוֹ חֲמִשָּׁה בָקָר יְשַׁלֵּם תַּחַת הַשּׁוֹר וְאַרְבַּע־צֹאן
כב א תַּחַת הַשֶּׂה׃ אִם־בַּמַּחְתֶּרֶת יִמָּצֵא הַגַּנָּב וְהֻכָּה וָמֵת
ב אֵין לוֹ דָּמִים׃ אִם־זָרְחָה הַשֶּׁמֶשׁ עָלָיו דָּמִים לוֹ שַׁלֵּם יְשַׁלֵּם
ג אִם־אֵין לוֹ וְנִמְכַּר בִּגְנֵבָתוֹ׃ אִם־הִמָּצֵא תִמָּצֵא בְיָדוֹ הַגְּנֵבָה
ד מִשּׁוֹר עַד־חֲמוֹר עַד־שֶׂה חַיִּים שְׁנַיִם יְשַׁלֵּם׃ כִּי שלישי
יַבְעֶר־אִישׁ שָׂדֶה אוֹ־כֶרֶם וְשִׁלַּח אֶת־בְּעִירֹה וּבִעֵר בִּשְׂדֵה

contingent on having certain basic freedoms. Responsibility requires freedom.

Individual freedom may be best described, as Isaiah Berlin argued, in terms of "negative liberty," namely the absence of constraints (*ḥofesh*). But *collective* freedom (*ḥerut*) is something else. It means, among other things, that my freedom is not bought at the price of yours. The theology and the legal details of *tzedaka* will be expanded upon in Leviticus and Deuteronomy, but the basic principles are laid out in our *parasha*. Freedom means

responsibility as *mishpat*, delineated in the cases here, and also responsibility as *tzedaka*.

22:1 אִם־בַּמַּחְתֶּרֶת יִמָּצֵא הַגַּנָּב *If a burglar is caught tunneling in* – Where the Ten Commandments presented us with moral absolutes: "Do not murder," we now begin to deal with situations of moral complexity. Self-defense, we see here, is permitted in Jewish law (Sanhedrin 72a). Yet the rules of defense and self-defense are not an open-ended permission to kill. We recall Yaakov's emotional state as he prepared for the

them graze in someone else's field, he must repay the best
5 of his field or vineyard. If a fire is started and
spreads to thorns, so that grain is destroyed, stacked or
standing or growing in the field, the person who started
6 the fire must redress the damage. If one person
entrusts another with money or goods, and they are
stolen from his house, then if the thief is found he must
7 pay double. If the thief is not found, then the owner of
the house must swear before the court that he has not laid
8 hands on his neighbor's goods himself. In every case of
betrayal of trust, whether concerning an ox, donkey or
sheep, clothing, or any loss that one can point to and say,
'This is it,' – both parties' claims shall be brought to the
court. The one the court finds guilty shall pay the other
9 double. If one person entrusts another with a
donkey, ox, sheep, or any animal, for safekeeping, and
10 it dies or is injured or is carried away unseen, an oath
before the Lord shall settle between them; if the second
man swears that he did not lay his hands on his charge,
then the owner must accept this, and no restitution
11 need be made. But if the charge was stolen from him, he
12 must make restitution to the owner. If it was torn by a
wild animal and the second man brings the remains as
evidence, he need not make good the loss.
13 If one person borrows a creature from his neighbor, and
it is injured or dies while the owner is not there, he must
14 make restitution. But if the owner was present, he need not
make restitution; if the animal was hired, only the hiring
15 fee is due. If a man seduces a virgin who is not
betrothed, and lies with her, he must pay her bride price
16 and marry her. If her father refuses to let him marry her, he
17 must still pay out the full bride price for virgins. Do
18 not allow a witch to live. And any person who lies with an
19 animal shall be put to death. Whoever sacrifices
20 to any other deity shall be utterly destroyed. Do not
oppress a stranger or exploit him, for you yourselves were
21 strangers in the land of Egypt. Do not abuse a widow or

ה אַחֵר מֵיטַב שָׂדֵהוּ וּמֵיטַב כַּרְמוֹ יְשַׁלֵּם׃ כִּי־תֵצֵא
אֵשׁ וּמָצְאָה קֹצִים וְנֶאֱכַל גָּדִישׁ אוֹ הַקָּמָה אוֹ הַשָּׂדֶה
ו שַׁלֵּם יְשַׁלֵּם הַמַּבְעִר אֶת־הַבְּעֵרָה׃ כִּי־יִתֵּן
אִישׁ אֶל־רֵעֵהוּ כֶּסֶף אוֹ־כֵלִים לִשְׁמֹר וְגֻנַּב מִבֵּית הָאִישׁ
ז אִם־יִמָּצֵא הַגַּנָּב יְשַׁלֵּם שְׁנָיִם׃ אִם־לֹא יִמָּצֵא הַגַּנָּב וְנִקְרַב
בַּעַל־הַבַּיִת אֶל־הָאֱלֹהִים אִם־לֹא שָׁלַח יָדוֹ בִּמְלֶאכֶת
ח רֵעֵהוּ׃ עַל־כָּל־דְּבַר־פֶּשַׁע עַל־שׁוֹר עַל־חֲמוֹר עַל־שֶׂה
עַל־שַׂלְמָה עַל־כָּל־אֲבֵדָה אֲשֶׁר יֹאמַר כִּי־הוּא זֶה עַד
הָאֱלֹהִים יָבֹא דְּבַר־שְׁנֵיהֶם אֲשֶׁר יַרְשִׁיעֻן אֱלֹהִים יְשַׁלֵּם
ט שְׁנַיִם לְרֵעֵהוּ׃ כִּי־יִתֵּן אִישׁ אֶל־רֵעֵהוּ חֲמוֹר
אוֹ־שׁוֹר אוֹ־שֶׂה וְכָל־בְּהֵמָה לִשְׁמֹר וּמֵת אוֹ־נִשְׁבַּר אוֹ־
י נִשְׁבָּה אֵין רֹאֶה׃ שְׁבֻעַת יהוה תִּהְיֶה בֵּין שְׁנֵיהֶם אִם־לֹא
יא שָׁלַח יָדוֹ בִּמְלֶאכֶת רֵעֵהוּ וְלָקַח בְּעָלָיו וְלֹא יְשַׁלֵּם׃ וְאִם־
יב גָּנֹב יִגָּנֵב מֵעִמּוֹ יְשַׁלֵּם לִבְעָלָיו׃ אִם־טָרֹף יִטָּרֵף יְבִאֵהוּ עֵד
הַטְּרֵפָה לֹא יְשַׁלֵּם׃
יג וְכִי־יִשְׁאַל אִישׁ מֵעִם רֵעֵהוּ וְנִשְׁבַּר אוֹ־מֵת בְּעָלָיו אֵין־עִמּוֹ
יד שַׁלֵּם יְשַׁלֵּם׃ אִם־בְּעָלָיו עִמּוֹ לֹא יְשַׁלֵּם אִם־שָׂכִיר הוּא בָּא
טו בִּשְׂכָרוֹ׃ וְכִי־יְפַתֶּה אִישׁ בְּתוּלָה אֲשֶׁר לֹא־אֹרָשָׂה
טז וְשָׁכַב עִמָּהּ מָהֹר יִמְהָרֶנָּה לּוֹ לְאִשָּׁה׃ אִם־מָאֵן יְמָאֵן אָבִיהָ
יז לְתִתָּהּ לוֹ כֶּסֶף יִשְׁקֹל כְּמֹהַר הַבְּתוּלֹת׃ מְכַשֵּׁפָה
יח יט לֹא תְחַיֶּה׃ כָּל־שֹׁכֵב עִם־בְּהֵמָה מוֹת יוּמָת׃ זֹבֵחַ
כ לָאֱלֹהִים יָחֳרָם בִּלְתִּי לַיהוה לְבַדּוֹ׃ וְגֵר לֹא־תוֹנֶה וְלֹא
כא תִלְחָצֶנּוּ כִּי־גֵרִים הֱיִיתֶם בְּאֶרֶץ מִצְרָיִם׃ כָּל־אַלְמָנָה וְיָתוֹם

22:20 כִּי־גֵרִים הֱיִיתֶם בְּאֶרֶץ מִצְרָיִם *For you yourselves were strangers in the land of Egypt* – Mishpatim contains many laws of social justice – against taking advantage of a widow or orphan, for example, or taking interest on a loan to a fellow member of the covenantal community. The first and last of these laws, however, is the much-repeated command against harming a *ger*, a "stranger" or "migrant."

22 an orphan. For if you do abuse them, if they cry out to
23 Me, I will unquestionably heed their cry. My anger will
flare and I will kill you by the sword – and then your wives
will be widows and your children orphans.
24 If you lend money to one of My people who is poor, do
not act with him as a harsh creditor, and do not charge him
25 interest. If you take your neighbor's garment as collateral,
26 return it to him before the sun sets, because it is his only
clothing, the sole covering for his skin. What else does
he have in which to sleep? And if he cries out to Me, I will
27 be listening: I am gracious. Do not curse a judge, REVI'I

---

terms of speech, there is. God's greatness is that He hears the unheard. Hearing is presented as the basis of both justice and compassion in the great social legislation of these verses.

In Judaism, we believe we connect to God in three different ways: creation, revelation, redemption. To see the beauty of creation is one way God speaks to us. When we sit and learn Torah, especially when we sit and learn Torah together, we are hearing God's word. When we look at how Rashi refracted that word – and Ramban, and Rashbam, and Ibn Ezra – we are hearing that several-thousand-year-old conversation between heaven and earth that we call the Written Torah and the Oral Torah. And when we become part of that conversation we see God in revelation.

But there is a third way: redemption. When we hear the cry of a child or the cry of a person dying of hunger, we are hearing God calling to us to be His partner in the work of redemption. This is encountering God in a different way, one that is much more active than in creation and revelation, but one where we feel we are partners with God in making the world a little better. This is what is being modeled in our verse. God hears and holds us to account for the suffering of others; God hears and demonstrates the attention we must pay in order to bring that suffering to an end.

22:26 כִּי־חַנּוּן אָנִי *I am gracious* – This is law with a human face. Superficially, we are dealing with a simple economic transaction. Someone borrows money and gives the lender an item of clothing as security for the repayment of the loan, an everyday occurrence in ancient times. Yet the Torah insists that we must not forget the existential human situation. The borrower may be poor. The cloak may be the only one he has. The lender must not forget this fact. In strict, legal terms, he may be within his rights simply to hold on to the pledge, but a decent society depends on more than legal rights.

God Himself says about the poor borrower's cries, "I will be listening: I

כב לֹא תְעַנּוּן׃ אִם־עַנֵּה תְעַנֶּה אֹתוֹ כִּי אִם־צָעֹק יִצְעַק אֵלַי
כג שָׁמֹעַ אֶשְׁמַע צַעֲקָתוֹ׃ וְחָרָה אַפִּי וְהָרַגְתִּי אֶתְכֶם בֶּחָרֶב
וְהָיוּ נְשֵׁיכֶם אַלְמָנוֹת וּבְנֵיכֶם יְתֹמִים׃
כד אִם־כֶּסֶף ׀ תַּלְוֶה אֶת־עַמִּי אֶת־הֶעָנִי עִמָּךְ לֹא־תִהְיֶה לוֹ כְּנֹשֶׁה יז
כה לֹא־תְשִׂימוּן עָלָיו נֶשֶׁךְ׃ אִם־חָבֹל תַּחְבֹּל שַׂלְמַת רֵעֶךָ עַד־
כו בֹּא הַשֶּׁמֶשׁ תְּשִׁיבֶנּוּ לוֹ׃ כִּי הִוא כְסוּתֹה לְבַדָּהּ הִוא שִׂמְלָתוֹ
לְעֹרוֹ בַּמֶּה יִשְׁכָּב וְהָיָה כִּי־יִצְעַק אֵלַי וְשָׁמַעְתִּי כִּי־חַנּוּן
כז אָנִי׃ אֱלֹהִים לֹא תְקַלֵּל וְנָשִׂיא בְעַמְּךָ לֹא תָאֹר׃ רביעי

Clearly something fundamental is at stake here.

According to R. Eliezer, the Torah "warns against the wronging of a *ger* in thirty-six places; others say, in forty-six places" (Bava Metzia 59b). Whatever the precise number, the repetition throughout the Mosaic books is remarkable. Sometimes the stranger is mentioned along with the poor; other times, with the widow and orphan. On several occasions the Torah specifies: "There shall be one law for you, for migrant and for native born alike" (Lev. 24:22; see also Ex. 12:49; Num. 15:16, 29). Not only must the stranger not be wronged; he or she must be included in the positive welfare provisions of Jewish society.

The Torah asks: why should you not hate the stranger? Because you once stood where he stands now. You know the heart of the stranger because you were once a stranger in the land of Egypt. If you are human, so is he. If he is less than human, so are you. You must fight the hatred in your heart, says God, as I once fought the greatest ruler and the strongest empire in the ancient world on your behalf. I made you into the world's archetypal strangers so that you would fight for the rights of strangers.

There is only one reply strong enough to answer the question "Why should I not hate the stranger?": because the stranger is me.

22:24 אִם־כֶּסֶף תַּלְוֶה אֶת־עַמִּי אֶת־הֶעָנִי *If you lend money to one of My people who is poor* – According to Rashi, the Hebrew word *im*, which often means "if," should here be understood as "when." Helping the poor is not an option but an obligation. Society needs morality, a concern for the welfare of others, an active commitment to justice and compassion, a willingness to ask not just what is good for me, but what is good for all of us together.

22:26 וְשָׁמַעְתִּי *I will be listening* – The emphasis on listening lies at the heart of the unique intimacy Jews feel with God. In terms of power, there is no possible relationship between an infinite Creator and His finite creations. In

28 and do not deride a leader of your people. Do not delay
offerings from your harvest of grain or wine. The firstborn
29 of your sons you must give to Me. Likewise with your
oxen and sheep; let them stay with their mothers for seven
30 days, and on the eighth, give them over to Me. You are to
be My holy people. Do not eat flesh torn by beasts in the
23 1 wild. Throw it to the dogs. Do not accept a false
report. Do not join with an unscrupulous person to bear
2 corrupt witness. Do not follow the crowd to do evil. When
you give testimony in a lawsuit, do not pervert justice by
3 siding with the crowd. Do not show favoritism even to a
4 poor man in a dispute. If you come across your
enemy's ox or donkey going astray – bring it back to
5 him. If you see the donkey of someone who

---

ignore the fact that the donkey is laboring under its load. It is innocent. Why should it suffer?

The second principle is stronger still. It says, in effect: Your enemy is also a human being. Hostility may divide you, but there is something deeper that connects you: the covenant of human solidarity. Distress, difficulty – these things transcend the language of difference. A decent society will be one in which enemies do not allow their rancor or animosity to prevent them from coming to one another's assistance when they need help. If someone is in trouble, help. Don't stop to ask if they are friend or foe. Get involved.

There is more at stake than merely helping someone in distress. There is also the challenge of overcoming estrangement, distance, and ill feeling. The phrase "resist the impulse to leave it there" (Ex. 23:5) seems superfluous, but it is not. What it highlights is that when we see our enemy suffering, our first instinct is to pass by. Hence part of the logic of the command is to suppress the evil inclination.

There is something distinctive about the Torah's approach to hatred and enemies. It is realistic rather than utopian. It does not say, "Love your enemy." It says to help him. Saints apart, we cannot love our enemies, and if we try to, we may pay a high psychological price. Instead the Torah says: When your enemy is in trouble, come to his assistance. That way, part of the hatred will be dissipated. The fault lines between people can be redrawn so that erstwhile enemies are on the same side, not opposite sides, of the table. Sometimes, all it takes is a shared task that both can achieve together but neither can do alone. Who knows whether help given may not turn hostility to gratitude and from there to friendship? That is a practical way of moving beyond hate. At the heart of the law of

כח כט מְלֵאָתְךָ וְדִמְעֲךָ לֹא תְאַחֵר בְּכוֹר בָּנֶיךָ תִּתֶּן־לִי׃ כֵּן־תַּעֲשֶׂה
לְשֹׁרְךָ לְצֹאנֶךָ שִׁבְעַת יָמִים יִהְיֶה עִם־אִמּוֹ בַּיּוֹם הַשְּׁמִינִי
ל תִּתְּנוֹ־לִי׃ וְאַנְשֵׁי־קֹדֶשׁ תִּהְיוּן לִי וּבָשָׂר בַּשָּׂדֶה טְרֵפָה לֹא
כג א תֹאכֵלוּ לַכֶּלֶב תַּשְׁלִכוּן אֹתוֹ׃ לֹא תִשָּׂא שֵׁמַע
ב שָׁוְא אַל־תָּשֶׁת יָדְךָ עִם־רָשָׁע לִהְיֹת עֵד חָמָס׃ לֹא־תִהְיֶה
אַחֲרֵי־רַבִּים לְרָעֹת וְלֹא־תַעֲנֶה עַל־רִב לִנְטֹת אַחֲרֵי רַבִּים
ג ד לְהַטֹּת׃ וְדָל לֹא תֶהְדַּר בְּרִיבוֹ׃ כִּי תִפְגַּע שׁוֹר
ה אֹיִבְךָ אוֹ חֲמֹרוֹ תֹּעֶה הָשֵׁב תְּשִׁיבֶנּוּ לוֹ׃ כִּי־

am gracious." God, the lawgiver, is not a remote abstraction. He is a direct personal presence in the lives of those who keep His law. And just as God tempers justice with compassion, so must His people do likewise.

23:2 וְלֹא־תַעֲנֶה עַל־רִב לִנְטֹת *Do not pervert justice* – God may be found in the innermost depths of the human soul, but God is equally to be found in the public square and in the structures of society: the marketplace, the corridors of power, and the courts of law. There must be no gap, no dissociation of sensibilities, between the court of justice (the meeting place of man and man) and the Temple (the meeting place of man and God).

23:2 אַחֲרֵי רַבִּים לְהַטֹּת *Siding with the crowd* – Do not assume that a majority is always right. The herd instinct is to be avoided. Popular sentiment often conflicts with truth and justice. We must not sacrifice individual judgment to conform to the crowd when we suspect they may be wrong.

23:3 וְדָל לֹא תֶהְדַּר בְּרִיבוֹ *Do not show favoritism even to a poor man* – In Judaism, God is our lawgiver. This is foreshadowed in the first chapter of the Torah, with its statement of the equal and absolute dignity of the human person as the image of God (Gen. 1:27). Law and justice are primary vehicles of equality. That is why society must be based on the rule of law, impartially administered, treating all alike. Charity is one thing, justice another. We must never pervert the latter for the sake of the former. Each has its specific place in the moral life and they must not be confused.

23:4 שׁוֹר אֹיִבְךָ *Your enemy's ox* – There are two principles at stake in these laws. One is concern for the animal. Jewish law forbids *tzaar baalei ḥayim*, the needless infliction of pain on animals. (Other examples in the Torah include sending the mother bird away [Deut. 22:6] and not muzzling an ox when it is treading grain [25:4].) It is as if the Torah is saying: A conflict between two human beings should not lead either of them to

hates you, fallen under its load, resist the impulse to leave
6 it there. Help him to release it. Do not subvert ḤAMISHI
7 the rights of the needy when they come to court. Keep far
from a false charge. Do not bring death on the innocent
8 and righteous, for I will not acquit the wrongdoer. Take no
bribe, for bribes blind the sighted and subvert the cause
9 of the just. Do not oppress a stranger. You know what it is
to be a stranger, for you yourselves were strangers in the
10 land of Egypt. For six years, sow your land and gather its
11 crops, but in the seventh let it rest and lie fallow. Let the
needy of your people eat from it, and what they leave, let

---

stranger – together with the historical reminder that "you yourselves were slaves in the land of Egypt." It is as if, in this series of laws, we are nearing the core of the mystery of Jewish existence itself. What is the Torah implying?

To be a Jew is to be a stranger. It seems that this was why Avraham was commanded to leave his land, home, and father's house; why, long before Yosef was born, Avraham was already told that his descendants would be strangers in a land not their own; why Moshe had to suffer personal exile before assuming leadership of the people; why the Israelites underwent persecution before inheriting their own land; and why the Torah is so insistent that this experience should become a permanent part of their collective memory. The Israelites in Egypt knew what it was to be marginal and isolated, to suffer and be treated like pariahs. You will not succeed in caring for the stranger, implies God, until you yourselves know in your very bones and sinews what it feels like to be a stranger.

SHEMITTA AND THE SABBATH

The Torah here juxtaposes two commands enjoining periodic rest. On the Sabbath all agricultural work is forbidden "so that your ox and donkey may rest" (Ex. 23:12). The Sabbath sets a limit to our intervention in nature and the pursuit of economic growth. We become conscious that we are creations, not just creators. The earth is not ours, but God's. For six days it is handed over to us, but on the seventh we symbolically abdicate that power. We may perform no "work," which is to say, an act that alters the state of something for human purposes. The Sabbath is a weekly reminder of the integrity of nature and the boundaries of human striving.

The seventh year, like the seventh day, must also be a time of rest – in this case for the land. The law, with its stipulation that the produce of the field should be available to all, appears here because of its association with other commands to have care for the poor. We see here a convergence of the interests

תִרְאֶה חֲמוֹר שֹׂנַאֲךָ רֹבֵץ תַּחַת מַשָּׂאוֹ וְחָדַלְתָּ מֵעֲזֹב לוֹ עָזֹב
ו תַּעֲזֹב עִמּוֹ: לֹא תַטֶּה מִשְׁפַּט אֶבְיֹנְךָ בְּרִיבוֹ: חמישי
ז מִדְּבַר־שֶׁקֶר תִּרְחָק וְנָקִי וְצַדִּיק אַל־תַּהֲרֹג כִּי לֹא־אַצְדִּיק
ח רָשָׁע: וְשֹׁחַד לֹא תִקָּח כִּי הַשֹּׁחַד יְעַוֵּר פִּקְחִים וִיסַלֵּף דִּבְרֵי
ט צַדִּיקִים: וְגֵר לֹא תִלְחָץ וְאַתֶּם יְדַעְתֶּם אֶת־נֶפֶשׁ הַגֵּר כִּי־
י גֵרִים הֱיִיתֶם בְּאֶרֶץ מִצְרָיִם: וְשֵׁשׁ שָׁנִים תִּזְרַע אֶת־אַרְצֶךָ
יא וְאָסַפְתָּ אֶת־תְּבוּאָתָהּ: וְהַשְּׁבִיעִת תִּשְׁמְטֶנָּה וּנְטַשְׁתָּהּ
וְאָכְלוּ אֶבְיֹנֵי עַמֶּךָ וְיִתְרָם תֹּאכַל חַיַּת הַשָּׂדֶה כֵּן־תַּעֲשֶׂה

the overladen donkey is one of Judaism's most beautiful axioms: "Who is a hero? One who turns an enemy into a friend" (Avot DeRabbi Natan 23).

23:7 נָקִי וְצַדִּיק *The innocent and righteous* – This is the basis of the ruling that if fresh evidence comes to light after an individual has been deemed guilty, the case may be reopened. The reverse is not the case. If the accused has been acquitted, no retrial is ordered.

23:9 כִּי־גֵרִים הֱיִיתֶם בְּאֶרֶץ מִצְרָיִם *For you yourselves were strangers in the land of Egypt* – According to Ramban (on Ex. 22:22), this command has two dimensions. The first is the relative powerlessness of the stranger. He or she is not surrounded by family, friends, neighbors, a community of those ready to come to their defense. Therefore, the Torah warns against wronging them because God has made Himself protector of those who have no one else to defend them. This is the political dimension of the command.

The second reason is the psychological vulnerability of the stranger. Moshe himself, while living among the Midianites, said: "I have been a stranger in an alien land" (2:22). The stranger is one who lives outside the normal securities of home and belonging. He or she is, or feels, alone – and throughout the Torah, God is especially sensitive to the sigh of the oppressed, the feelings of the rejected, the cry of the unheard. That is the emotional dimension of the command.

Rabbi Ḥayyim Ibn Attar (*Ohr HaḤayyim* on 22:20) adds a further fascinating insight. It may be, he says, that the very sanctity that Israelites feel as children of the covenant may lead them to look down on those who lack a similar lineage. Therefore they are commanded not to feel superior to the *ger*, but instead to remember the degradation their ancestors experienced in Egypt. This becomes a command of humility in the face of strangers.

Whichever way we look at it, there is something striking about this almost endlessly iterated concern for the

the wild animals eat. Do the same with your vineyards
12 and olive groves. For six days carry out your work, but
on the seventh you must cease, so that your ox and
donkey may rest, and even the children of maidservants
13 and strangers be revived. Take care in all that I have said
to you. Never invoke the names of other gods; let them
14 never pass your lips. Three times a year, celebrate a festival
15 for Me. Keep the Festival of Unleavened Bread. For seven
days, eat unleavened bread as I commanded you, at the
time appointed, in the month of Aviv, for at that time
you left Egypt. Do not appear before Me empty-handed.
16 Likewise, keep the Festival of the Harvest, of the first
fruits of the produce that you sowed in the field. Keep the
Festival of Ingathering at the end of the year, when you
17 gather in the fruit of your labor from the field. Three times
a year, all the males among you shall appear before the
18 Master, the LORD. Do not offer the blood of My sacrifice
together with anything leavened. Do not let the fat of My
19 festive offering remain until morning. Bring the best first
fruits of your land to the House of the LORD your God.
Do not boil a kid in the milk of its mother.
20 I am sending a messenger ahead of you to guard you on SHISHI
the way and to bring you to the place that I have prepared.

---

and soul. Hence the Judaic imperative is neither hedonistic nor ascetic, but rather transformative. We are commanded not to indulge in the act of eating nor to abhor it, but rather to *sanctify* it. From this flow the dietary laws, a key element of *kedusha*, the life of holiness.

23:20 הִנֵּה אָנֹכִי שֹׁלֵחַ מַלְאָךְ *I am sending a messenger* – The Haggada, with its insistence that God brought us out of Egypt "not through an angel, not through a seraph, not through any emissary," is striking for its almost complete omission of any reference to Moshe and his part in the redemption. The emphasis throughout is on the saving acts of God. The pharaohs, by contrast, were regarded as incarnate gods, usually of the sun. The Torah was the first document in history to insist that God cannot be identified either with a phenomenon of nature or with a human being, however exalted.

This separation nonetheless allows a possibility of communication. God speaks to mankind. Mankind speaks to God. Between them lies the bond of language.

יב לְכַרְמְךָ לְזֵיתֶךָ: שֵׁשֶׁת יָמִים תַּעֲשֶׂה מַעֲשֶׂיךָ וּבַיּוֹם הַשְּׁבִיעִי
תִּשְׁבֹּת לְמַעַן יָנוּחַ שׁוֹרְךָ וַחֲמֹרֶךָ וְיִנָּפֵשׁ בֶּן־אֲמָתְךָ וְהַגֵּר:
יג וּבְכֹל אֲשֶׁר־אָמַרְתִּי אֲלֵיכֶם תִּשָּׁמֵרוּ וְשֵׁם אֱלֹהִים אֲחֵרִים
יד לֹא תַזְכִּירוּ לֹא יִשָּׁמַע עַל־פִּיךָ: שָׁלֹשׁ רְגָלִים תָּחֹג לִי בַּשָּׁנָה:
טו אֶת־חַג הַמַּצּוֹת תִּשְׁמֹר שִׁבְעַת יָמִים תֹּאכַל מַצּוֹת כַּאֲשֶׁר
צִוִּיתִךָ לְמוֹעֵד חֹדֶשׁ הָאָבִיב כִּי־בוֹ יָצָאתָ מִמִּצְרָיִם וְלֹא־
טז יֵרָאוּ פָנַי רֵיקָם: וְחַג הַקָּצִיר בִּכּוּרֵי מַעֲשֶׂיךָ אֲשֶׁר תִּזְרַע
בַּשָּׂדֶה וְחַג הָאָסִף בְּצֵאת הַשָּׁנָה בְּאָסְפְּךָ אֶת־מַעֲשֶׂיךָ
יז מִן־הַשָּׂדֶה: שָׁלֹשׁ פְּעָמִים בַּשָּׁנָה יֵרָאֶה כָּל־זְכוּרְךָ אֶל־פְּנֵי
יח הָאָדֹן ׀ יהוה: לֹא־תִזְבַּח עַל־חָמֵץ דַּם־זִבְחִי וְלֹא־יָלִין
יט חֵלֶב־חַגִּי עַד־בֹּקֶר: רֵאשִׁית בִּכּוּרֵי אַדְמָתְךָ תָּבִיא בֵּית
יהוה אֱלֹהֶיךָ לֹא־תְבַשֵּׁל גְּדִי בַּחֲלֵב אִמּוֹ:
כ הִנֵּה אָנֹכִי שֹׁלֵחַ מַלְאָךְ לְפָנֶיךָ לִשְׁמָרְךָ בַּדָּרֶךְ וְלַהֲבִיאֲךָ אֶל־ ששי

of people and land, what we call today an ethic of sustainability. What the Sabbath does for humans and animals, the Sabbatical Year does for the people as a whole and for the land. The earth, too, is entitled to its periodic rest. The Torah warns that if the Israelites do not respect this, they will suffer exile: "Then shall the land make appeasement for its Sabbaths, for as long as it lies desolate and you are in your enemies' lands. Then the land will rest and make appeasement for its Sabbaths" (Lev. 26:34).

Behind this are two concerns. One is environmental. As Rambam points out (*Guide for the Perplexed* III:39), land which is overexploited eventually erodes and loses its fertility. The Israelites were therefore commanded to conserve the soil by giving it periodic fallow years, not pursuing short-term gain at the cost of long-term desolation. The second, no less significant, is theological. "The land," says God, "is Mine; you are merely migrants and visitors to Me" (Lev. 25:23). We are guests on earth. What we possess, we do not own, we merely hold in trust. There are conditions to that trust, the most fundamental of which is that we must show concern for the good of all

23:19 לֹא־תְבַשֵּׁל גְּדִי בַּחֲלֵב אִמּוֹ *Do not boil a kid in the milk of its mother* – This is an instance of the general prohibition of mixing meat and milk, which is stated three times in the Torah to forbid (1) the cooking itself, (2) eating, and (3) deriving benefit from the mixture. Judaism sees the human situation in terms of integration and balance. We are body

21 Heed his presence and listen to his voice. Do not rebel
against him, for he will not let your transgression pass,
22 because My name is with him. But if you listen carefully
to him and do all that I tell you, then I will be an enemy
23 to your enemies, a foe to your foes. When My messenger
goes ahead of you and brings you to the Amorites,
Hittites, Perizzites, Canaanites, Hivites, and Jebusites,
24 and I wipe them out, do not bow down to their gods or
worship them, and do not do as they do. Demolish their
25 gods and shatter their worship pillars. Serve the Lord
your God, and He will bless your bread, your water. I will
26 banish all sickness from your midst. No woman SHEVI'I
in your land will suffer miscarriage or barrenness. I will
27 fill out the full measure of your years. I will send My
terror before you, throwing into panic all the people you
come upon. All you will see of your enemies will be their
28 fleeing backs. I will send hornets ahead of you, and they
will drive the Hivites, Canaanites, and Hittites out before
29 you. I will not drive them out in a single year, lest the land
become desolate and the wild animals too numerous for
30 you. No – little by little I will drive them out before you,
as you burgeon and come to take possession of the land.
31 I will set your borders from the Sea of Reeds to the Sea of
the Philistines, and from the wilderness to the Euphrates,
for I will deliver the inhabitants of the land into your
32 hands: you will drive them out before you. Make no
33 covenant with them and their gods. They must not stay in
your land, for they would make you sin against Me. If you
worship their gods, it will be a trap for you."
24 1 Then He said to Moshe, "Ascend to the Lord, you and
Aharon, Nadav and Avihu, and seventy of Israel's elders

---

mighty deeds with the forces of nature at his command. Rather, he and his successors are "messengers." The prophets (as Ralbag understands the work *malakh* here), or the angels who inspire them (as others interpret), are God's messengers, able to ensure our safe passage only if we "listen carefully to him and do all that I" – God – "tell you."

כא הַמָּקוֹם אֲשֶׁר הֲכִנֹתִי: הִשָּׁמֶר מִפָּנָיו וּשְׁמַע בְּקֹלוֹ אַל־תַּמֵּר
כב בּוֹ כִּי לֹא יִשָּׂא לְפִשְׁעֲכֶם כִּי שְׁמִי בְּקִרְבּוֹ: כִּי אִם־שָׁמוֹעַ
תִּשְׁמַע בְּקֹלוֹ וְעָשִׂיתָ כֹּל אֲשֶׁר אֲדַבֵּר וְאָיַבְתִּי אֶת־אֹיְבֶיךָ
כג וְצַרְתִּי אֶת־צֹרְרֶיךָ: כִּי־יֵלֵךְ מַלְאָכִי לְפָנֶיךָ וֶהֱבִיאֲךָ אֶל־
הָאֱמֹרִי וְהַחִתִּי וְהַפְּרִזִּי וְהַכְּנַעֲנִי הַחִוִּי וְהַיְבוּסִי וְהִכְחַדְתִּיו:
כד לֹא־תִשְׁתַּחֲוֶה לֵאלֹהֵיהֶם וְלֹא תָעָבְדֵם וְלֹא תַעֲשֶׂה
כְּמַעֲשֵׂיהֶם כִּי הָרֵס תְּהָרְסֵם וְשַׁבֵּר תְּשַׁבֵּר מַצֵּבֹתֵיהֶם:
כה וַעֲבַדְתֶּם אֵת יהוה אֱלֹהֵיכֶם וּבֵרַךְ אֶת־לַחְמְךָ וְאֶת־מֵימֶיךָ
כו וַהֲסִרֹתִי מַחֲלָה מִקִּרְבֶּךָ: לֹא תִהְיֶה מְשַׁכֵּלָה שביעי
כז וַעֲקָרָה בְּאַרְצֶךָ אֶת־מִסְפַּר יָמֶיךָ אֲמַלֵּא: אֶת־אֵימָתִי אֲשַׁלַּח
לְפָנֶיךָ וְהַמֹּתִי אֶת־כָּל־הָעָם אֲשֶׁר תָּבֹא בָּהֶם וְנָתַתִּי אֶת־
כח כָּל־אֹיְבֶיךָ אֵלֶיךָ עֹרֶף: וְשָׁלַחְתִּי אֶת־הַצִּרְעָה לְפָנֶיךָ וְגֵרְשָׁה
כט אֶת־הַחִוִּי אֶת־הַכְּנַעֲנִי וְאֶת־הַחִתִּי מִלְּפָנֶיךָ: לֹא אֲגָרְשֶׁנּוּ
מִפָּנֶיךָ בְּשָׁנָה אֶחָת פֶּן־תִּהְיֶה הָאָרֶץ שְׁמָמָה וְרַבָּה עָלֶיךָ
ל חַיַּת הַשָּׂדֶה: מְעַט מְעַט אֲגָרְשֶׁנּוּ מִפָּנֶיךָ עַד אֲשֶׁר תִּפְרֶה
לא וְנָחַלְתָּ אֶת־הָאָרֶץ: וְשַׁתִּי אֶת־גְּבֻלְךָ מִיַּם־סוּף וְעַד־יָם
פְּלִשְׁתִּים וּמִמִּדְבָּר עַד־הַנָּהָר כִּי ׀ אֶתֵּן בְּיֶדְכֶם אֵת יֹשְׁבֵי
לב הָאָרֶץ וְגֵרַשְׁתָּמוֹ מִפָּנֶיךָ: לֹא־תִכְרֹת לָהֶם וְלֵאלֹהֵיהֶם
לג בְּרִית: לֹא יֵשְׁבוּ בְּאַרְצְךָ פֶּן־יַחֲטִיאוּ אֹתְךָ לִי כִּי תַעֲבֹד
אֶת־אֱלֹהֵיהֶם כִּי־יִהְיֶה לְךָ לְמוֹקֵשׁ:
כד א וְאֶל־מֹשֶׁה אָמַר עֲלֵה אֶל־יהוה אַתָּה וְאַהֲרֹן נָדָב וַאֲבִיהוּא

In the world of myth there was no need for revelation. The gods constantly revealed themselves, in the rising and setting sun, the rain that fell, the wind that blew. In Judaism, revelation is both necessary and possible, and takes place not through a show of power but through the communication of meaning, namely words, promises, commands, and prayers. Language becomes invested with holiness. In the Torah, God speaks to us. In prayer, we speak to God. Because God is God, man can become man. This was an utterly new form of religious consciousness, and remains only incompletely understood today.

Moshe was not a Jewish equivalent of Pharaoh, a man-god, a doer of

2 and bow down from afar. Moshe alone shall approach
the Lord. The others must not come close, nor shall the
3 people come up with him." Moshe came and told the
people all the Lord's words and laws, and the people all
responded with one voice, "All that the Lord has spoken
4 we shall do." Then Moshe wrote down all the Lord's
words. Early the next morning he rose and built an altar
at the base of the mountain, and also twelve pillars for the
5 twelve tribes of Israel. Then he sent young men of Israel,
and they sacrificed bulls as burnt offerings and peace
6 offerings to the Lord. Moshe took half the blood and put
7 it in bowls. The other half he sprinkled on the altar. Then
he took the book of the covenant and read it aloud to the
people. They replied, "All that the Lord has spoken we
8 shall do and we shall heed." Then Moshe took the blood,

(*yishme'u*) the speech of another" (Gen. 11:7).

According to this last explanation, when the Israelites put "doing" before "understanding," they were giving expression to a profound philosophical truth. There are certain things we only understand by doing. We only understand leadership by leading. We only understand authorship by writing. We only understand music by listening. Reading books about these things is not enough. So it is with faith. We only truly understand Judaism by living in accordance with its commands. You cannot comprehend a faith from the outside. Doing leads to understanding.

The modern Western mind tends to put things in the opposite order. We seek to understand what we are committing ourselves to before making the commitment. That is fine when what is at stake is signing a contract, buying a new mobile phone, or purchasing a subscription, but not when making a deep existential commitment. The only way to understand marriage is to get married. The only way to understand whether a certain career path is right for you is to actually try it for an extended period. Those who hover on the edge of a commitment, reluctant to make a decision until all the facts are in, will eventually find that life has passed them by. The only way to understand a way of life is to take the risk of living it. So, *naaseh venishma* – we shall do, and eventually, through extended practice and long exposure, we shall understand.

24:7 נַעֲשֶׂה *We shall do* – The Israelites are described by the Torah as ratifying the covenant three times: once before they heard the commandments and twice afterward. There is a fascinating difference between the way the Torah

ב וְשִׁבְעִים מִזִּקְנֵי יִשְׂרָאֵל וְהִשְׁתַּחֲוִיתֶם מֵרָחֹק׃ וְנִגַּשׁ מֹשֶׁה
ג לְבַדּוֹ אֶל־יְהוָה וְהֵם לֹא יִגָּשׁוּ וְהָעָם לֹא יַעֲלוּ עִמּוֹ׃ וַיָּבֹא
מֹשֶׁה וַיְסַפֵּר לָעָם אֵת כָּל־דִּבְרֵי יְהוָה וְאֵת כָּל־הַמִּשְׁפָּטִים
וַיַּעַן כָּל־הָעָם קוֹל אֶחָד וַיֹּאמְרוּ כָּל־הַדְּבָרִים אֲשֶׁר־דִּבֶּר
ד יְהוָה נַעֲשֶׂה׃ וַיִּכְתֹּב מֹשֶׁה אֵת כָּל־דִּבְרֵי יְהוָה וַיַּשְׁכֵּם בַּבֹּקֶר
וַיִּבֶן מִזְבֵּחַ תַּחַת הָהָר וּשְׁתֵּים עֶשְׂרֵה מַצֵּבָה לִשְׁנֵים עָשָׂר
ה שִׁבְטֵי יִשְׂרָאֵל׃ וַיִּשְׁלַח אֶת־נַעֲרֵי בְּנֵי יִשְׂרָאֵל וַיַּעֲלוּ עֹלֹת
ו וַיִּזְבְּחוּ זְבָחִים שְׁלָמִים לַיהוָה פָּרִים׃ וַיִּקַּח מֹשֶׁה חֲצִי הַדָּם
ז וַיָּשֶׂם בָּאַגָּנֹת וַחֲצִי הַדָּם זָרַק עַל־הַמִּזְבֵּחַ׃ וַיִּקַּח סֵפֶר הַבְּרִית
וַיִּקְרָא בְּאָזְנֵי הָעָם וַיֹּאמְרוּ כֹּל אֲשֶׁר־דִּבֶּר יְהוָה נַעֲשֶׂה
ח וְנִשְׁמָע׃ וַיִּקַּח מֹשֶׁה אֶת־הַדָּם וַיִּזְרֹק עַל־הָעָם וַיֹּאמֶר הִנֵּה

WE SHALL DO AND WE SHALL HEED

Two words that we read toward the end of our *parasha* – *naaseh venishma*, "we shall do and we shall heed" – are among the most famous in Judaism. They are what our ancestors said when they accepted the covenant at Sinai.

What, though, do the words actually mean? *Naaseh* is straightforward. It means "we shall do." It is about action, behavior, deed. But *nishma* is unclear. It could mean "we shall hear." But it could also mean "we shall obey" or "we shall heed." Or it could mean "we shall understand." Here are some of the classic ways of interpreting *naaseh venishma*:

1. "We shall do and then we shall hear." This is the view of the Talmud (Shabbat 88a) and Rashi. The people expressed their total faith in God. They accepted the covenant even before they heard its terms. They said "we shall do" before they knew what it was that God wanted them to do.
2. "We shall do [what we have already been commanded until now] and we shall obey [all future commands]." This is the view of Rashbam. The Israelites' statement thus looked both back and forward. The people understood that they were on a spiritual as well as a physical journey and they might not know all the details of the law at once. *Nishma* here means not "to hear" but "to heed, hearken, obey; to respond faithfully in deed."
3. "We shall do and we shall understand" (Rabbi Yitzḥak Arama in *Akedat Yitzḥak*). The word *shema* can have the sense of understanding, as in God's statement about the Tower of Bavel: "Let us go down and confuse their language so that one will not understand

sprinkled it on the people, and said, "This is the blood of
the covenant that the LORD is making with you regarding
9 all these words." Then Moshe went up with Aharon, Nadav,
10 Avihu, and seventy of Israel's elders. They saw a vision of
the God of Israel, and beneath His feet what looked like a
11 lapis lazuli pavement as clear as the sky itself. And He did

---

distinct literary genres that have very little overlap. Most books of law do not contain narratives, and most narratives do not contain law. Even if people in Britain or America today know the history behind a given law, there is no canonical text that brings the two together. In any case, in most societies there are many different ways of telling the story. Moreover, most laws are enacted without a statement of why they came to be, what they were intended to achieve, and what historical experience led to their enactment.

So the Torah is a unique combination of *nomos* and narrative, history and law, the formative experiences of a nation and the way that nation sought to live its collective life so as never to forget the lessons it learned along the way. It brings together vision and detail in a way that has never been surpassed.

That is how we must lead if we want people to come with us, giving of their best. There must be a vision to inspire us, telling us why we should do what we are asked to do. There must be a narrative: this is what happened, this is who we are, and this is why the vision is so important to us. Then there must be the law, the code, the fastidious attention to detail, that allow us to translate vision into reality and turn the pain of the past into the blessings of the future. That extraordinary combination, to be found in almost no other law code, is what gives Torah its enduring power – hence "the covenant that the LORD is making with you regarding *all* these words."

24:10 וַיִּרְאוּ *They saw a vision* – This mystical, visual experience of God is striking – perhaps shocking – in the context of the earthbound legal passages that surround it. Why is it here?

As we have discussed, law and narrative are intimately bound up in the Torah. Ideas do not appear from nowhere, nor are all thoughts possible within every configuration of culture. The world of myth was profoundly conservative. Indeed, throughout most of history, religions and civilizations have tended to reinforce, rather than challenge, the status quo. They have taught acceptance, not protest; continuity, not revolution. Their governing assumption has been that the world is as it is because that is the nature of things. In the struggle for survival, the strong win, the weak die, power rules, and fate is blind. From where, then, do the thoughts arise that we can change the world and humanize it, making it less random and cruel and

דַּם־הַבְּרִית֙ אֲשֶׁ֨ר כָּרַ֤ת יְהוָה֙ עִמָּכֶ֔ם עַ֥ל כָּל־הַדְּבָרִ֖ים הָאֵֽלֶּה׃
ט וַיַּ֥עַל מֹשֶׁ֖ה וְאַהֲרֹ֑ן נָדָב֙ וַאֲבִיה֔וּא וְשִׁבְעִ֖ים מִזִּקְנֵ֥י יִשְׂרָאֵֽל׃
י וַיִּרְא֕וּ אֵ֖ת אֱלֹהֵ֣י יִשְׂרָאֵ֑ל וְתַ֣חַת רַגְלָ֗יו כְּמַעֲשֵׂה֙ לִבְנַ֣ת הַסַּפִּ֔יר
יא וּכְעֶ֥צֶם הַשָּׁמַ֖יִם לָטֹֽהַר׃ וְאֶל־אֲצִילֵי֙ בְּנֵ֣י יִשְׂרָאֵ֔ל לֹ֥א שָׁלַ֖ח

it comes to halakha, the way of Jewish doing, we seek consensus.

By contrast, though there are undoubtedly principles of Jewish faith, *when it comes to spirituality there is no single normative Jewish approach.* Judaism has had its priests and prophets, its rationalists and mystics, its philosophers and poets. Tanakh speaks in a multiplicity of voices. The Torah contains law and narrative, history and mystic vision, ritual and prayer. There are norms about how to act as Jews. But there are few about how to think and feel as Jews. We do the godly deed "together." We respond to His commands "with one voice." But we hear God's presence in many ways, for though God is one, we are all different, and we encounter Him each in our own way.

24:8 עַל כָּל־הַדְּבָרִים הָאֵלֶּה *Regarding all these words* – The word "Torah" is untranslatable because it means several different things that appear together only in the book that bears that name. Torah means "law." But it also means "teaching," "instruction," "guidance," or more generally, "direction." It is also the generic name for the five books, from Genesis to Deuteronomy, that comprise both narrative and law.

In general, law and narrative are two

describes the first two of these responses and the third:

> And the people *answered as one* – "All that the Lord has spoken we will do (*naaseh*)." (Ex. 19:8)
>
> Moshe came and told the people all the Lord's words and laws, and the people *all responded with one voice,* "All that the Lord has spoken we shall do (*naaseh*)." (24:3)
>
> Then he took the book of the covenant and read it aloud to the people. They *replied,* "All that the Lord has spoken we shall do and we shall heed (*naaseh venishma*)." (24:7)

The first two responses, which refer only to action (*naaseh*), are given unanimously. The people respond "as one." They do so "with one voice." The third, which refers not only to doing but also to listening or understanding (*nishma*), involves no unanimity. *Nishma* here means many things, as we have seen: listening, paying attention, understanding, absorbing, internalizing, and obeying. It refers, in other words, *to the spiritual, inward dimension of Judaism.*

From this, an important consequence follows. Judaism is a *community of doing* rather than of "hearing." There is an authoritative code of Jewish law. When

the leaders of Israel no harm – and they looked upon God
12 and they ate and they drank. The LORD said to
Moshe, "Ascend to Me on the mountain, and as you stand
there I will give you the stone tablets with the teaching
and commandments that I have written to instruct the
13 people." So Moshe set out with Yehoshua, his disciple,
14 and ascended the mountain of God. He told the elders,
"Wait for us here until we return to you. Aharon and Ḥur
will stay here with you; whoever has a dispute shall go to
15 them." As Moshe climbed the mountain, it was covered in MAFTIR
16 a cloud. The glory of the LORD rested on Mount Sinai, and
the cloud covered it for six days. On the seventh, He called
17 to Moshe from within the cloud. To the Israelites the
appearance of the LORD's glory on the mountaintop was
18 like consuming fire. Moshe entered the cloud and climbed
the mountain, and he stayed there for forty days and forty
nights.

The haftara for Parashat Mishpatim is on page 1482.
On Rosh Ḥodesh Adar I read the haftara on page 1640.
On Erev Rosh Ḥodesh Adar I read the haftara on page 1644.
However, on the Shabbat of Parashat Shekalim, even if it also Rosh Ḥodesh or Erev Rosh Ḥodesh Adar I, read the haftara on page 1654.

---

the past, and because we can imagine it, we can decide to act in such a way as to begin to bring it about. When God is conceived of as both beyond the natural universe *and* endowing humanity with His most distinctive attribute, creativity, a momentous human freedom is born. For the first time, religion becomes a world-transforming rather than world-accepting force. When the elders experience God enthroned above a paving "as clear as the sky itself," when the people of Israel sense His presence over the mountaintop "like consuming fire" (Ex. 24:17), they know that they are accountable to something and someone beyond their own realm. The moral and the mystical are intertwined. It is with this knowledge that we enter the *parashot* of the *Mishkan* (Tabernacle).

יב יָדוֹ וַיֶּחֱזוּ אֶת־הָאֱלֹהִים וַיֹּאכְלוּ וַיִּשְׁתּוּ׃ וַיֹּאמֶר
יהוה אֶל־מֹשֶׁה עֲלֵה אֵלַי הָהָרָה וֶהְיֵה־שָׁם וְאֶתְּנָה לְךָ
אֶת־לֻחֹת הָאֶבֶן וְהַתּוֹרָה וְהַמִּצְוָה אֲשֶׁר כָּתַבְתִּי לְהוֹרֹתָם׃
יג וַיָּקָם מֹשֶׁה וִיהוֹשֻׁעַ מְשָׁרְתוֹ וַיַּעַל מֹשֶׁה אֶל־הַר הָאֱלֹהִים׃
יד וְאֶל־הַזְּקֵנִים אָמַר שְׁבוּ־לָנוּ בָזֶה עַד אֲשֶׁר־נָשׁוּב אֲלֵיכֶם
טו וְהִנֵּה אַהֲרֹן וְחוּר עִמָּכֶם מִי־בַעַל דְּבָרִים יִגַּשׁ אֲלֵהֶם׃ וַיַּעַל מפטיר
טז מֹשֶׁה אֶל־הָהָר וַיְכַס הֶעָנָן אֶת־הָהָר׃ וַיִּשְׁכֹּן כְּבוֹד־יהוה
עַל־הַר סִינַי וַיְכַסֵּהוּ הֶעָנָן שֵׁשֶׁת יָמִים וַיִּקְרָא אֶל־מֹשֶׁה
יז בַּיּוֹם הַשְּׁבִיעִי מִתּוֹךְ הֶעָנָן׃ וּמַרְאֵה כְּבוֹד יהוה כְּאֵשׁ אֹכֶלֶת
יח בְּרֹאשׁ הָהָר לְעֵינֵי בְּנֵי יִשְׂרָאֵל׃ וַיָּבֹא מֹשֶׁה בְּתוֹךְ הֶעָנָן
וַיַּעַל אֶל־הָהָר וַיְהִי מֹשֶׁה בָּהָר אַרְבָּעִים יוֹם וְאַרְבָּעִים
לָיְלָה׃

The הפטרה for פרשת משפטים is on page 1483.
On ראש חודש אדר א׳ read the הפטרה on page 1641.
On ערב ראש חודש אדר א׳ read the haftara on page 1645.
However, on the שבת of פרשת שקלים, even if it also ראש חודש or ערב ראש חודש אדר א׳, read the הפטרה on page 1655.

creating within its deserts oases of justice and gardens of grace?

The key idea is *transcendence*, that God is to be found not within nature but beyond it. "The heavens are My throne; the world, My footstool" (Is. 66:1). At a stroke, this idea relativized all human institutions. Nothing in society is as it is because it could not be otherwise. God is free: therefore the human person, created in His image, is also free. Hierarchy, inequality, the corruptions of power, the exploitation of the weak, imperial conquest, and the enslavement of peoples are not justified merely because they exist. For the first time a gap is opened up between "is" and "ought." Not everything that is, is good. Not all that is done is right. We can imagine a world different from the way it is now and has been in

Parashat Teruma

25 1 2 The Lord spoke to Moshe, saying, "Tell the Israelites to
take an offering for Me; take My offering from all whose

---

almost ungovernable group. Moshe, their deliverer, comes to them with the news that they are about to go free. His first intervention, however, only makes things worse, and the people complain. Eventually the people leave, but Pharaoh and his army pursue them. Trapped between the approaching Egyptian chariots and the Sea of Reeds, again the Israelites complain. Moshe performs a miracle. The sea divides. But three days later, they are complaining again, this time about the lack of water.

Some six weeks later, at Mount Sinai, they receive the great revelation. God speaks directly to the people and they forge a covenant. Moshe ascends the mountain to receive the tablets on which the covenant provisions are engraved. While he is away, the Israelites commit their greatest sin: the worshipping of the golden calf. The episode will be told in Exodus 32–34, in the middle of the account of the making of the Tabernacle, so clearly there is some connection between them.

Putting all this together we arrive at the boldest of all Exodus's political statements. A nation – at least, the kind of nation the Israelites are called on to become – is *created through the act of creation itself*. Not all the miracles of Exodus combined, not even the revelation at Sinai itself, turn the Israelites into a nation. In commanding Moshe to get the people to make the Tabernacle, God is in effect saying: *To turn a group of individuals into a covenantal nation, they must build something together.*

Freedom cannot be conferred by an outside force, not even by God Himself. It can be achieved only by collective, collaborative effort on the part of the people. Hence the construction of the Tabernacle. A people is made by making. A nation is built by building. What they built was a "home" for the Divine Presence. The Tabernacle, placed at the center of the camp with the tribes arrayed around it, symbolized the public square, the common good, the voice that had summoned them to collective freedom. It was a visible emblem of community. Within the Tabernacle was the Ark, within the Ark were the tablets of stone, and on the tablets of stone were written the details of the covenant. It was the home of their constitution of liberty. What was true for the Israelites holds true in each generation. Society, like the Tabernacle, is the home we must build together.

25:2 כָּל־אִישׁ אֲשֶׁר יִדְּבֶנּוּ לִבּוֹ *All whose heart moves them to give* – The emphasis is on the voluntary nature of the gifts. Yet

פרשת תרומה

כה א ב וַיְדַבֵּר יְהוָה אֶל־מֹשֶׁה לֵּאמֹר׃ דַּבֵּר אֶל־בְּנֵי יִשְׂרָאֵל וְיִקְחוּ־ יח
לִי תְּרוּמָה מֵאֵת כָּל־אִישׁ אֲשֶׁר יִדְּבֶנּוּ לִבּוֹ תִּקְחוּ אֶת־

TERUMA

Parashat Teruma begins the longest single passage in the book of Exodus, continuing to the end of the book and interrupted only by the episode of the golden calf. Its subject is the *Mishkan*, the Tabernacle or Sanctuary that the Israelites were commanded to make as a center of worship and as a visible sign of the presence of God in their midst. The length and painstaking detail of the narrative indicate that the Divine Presence is not brought fully to earth in sudden moments of inspiration but through the long and collaborative process through which the people Israel fashions its life in accordance with the divine command. Israel is a people at whose center is the space we make for God. In the desert it was in the Tabernacle in the middle of the camp, in Israel it was in the Temple in Jerusalem, elsewhere it was in the synagogue at the core of the community. Jews wrestled with the paradox of the encounter between the infinity of God and the finitude of man. When Solomon dedicated the Temple he said, "For will God truly dwell on earth? If the heavens – the highest heavens – cannot contain You, how will this House that I have built?" (I Kings 8:27). The answer the Torah gave is that God exists in the space we make for Him, and the purpose of the Sanctuary is to open such a space at the heart of our collective life.

CALLING FOR CONTRIBUTIONS

The early chapters of Exodus are all about the politics of freedom. But the last section, beginning here and covering roughly a third of the book, is taken up with an apparently minor and irrelevant episode told and retold in exhaustive detail: the construction of the Tabernacle.

This was the first house of worship built by the Israelites. It was a modest affair, made of poles, beams, skins, and drapes, all of which could be taken apart, carried on their journeys, and reassembled at their next encampment. It had, or so it seems, no lasting significance. Once the Israelites had entered the land, the Tabernacle was left in Shilo for several centuries until King David established Jerusalem as the capital of the newly united kingdom, and his son Shlomo built the Temple. So why is the story of the Tabernacle told at such length?

The Torah is a political as well as a spiritual text, and it tells a political story. Despite the miracles, the essential narrative is remarkably human. The Israelites are portrayed as a querulous,

3 heart moves them to give. These are the offerings you
4 shall receive from them: gold, silver and bronze; sky-blue,
5 purple, and scarlet wool; linen and goats' hair; rams' hides
6 dyed red and fine leather; acacia wood; oil for the lamps;
7 spices for the anointing oil and the fragrant incense; and
rock crystal together with other precious stones for the
8 ephod and breast piece. They shall make Me a Sanctuary
9 and I will dwell in their midst. Form the Tabernacle
and form all of its furnishings following the patterns

---

because of a random fluctuation in the quantum field, if our moral convictions are self-serving means of self-preservation, and our spiritual aspirations mere delusions, then it is difficult to feel gratitude for the gift of life. There is no gift if there is no giver. There is only a series of meaningless accidents, and it is difficult to feel gratitude for an accident.

The Torah therefore tells us something simple and practical. Give, and you will come to see life as a gift. *You don't need to be able to prove God exists. All you need is to be thankful that you exist – and the rest will follow.* That is how God came to be close to the Israelites through the building of the Sanctuary. *Where people give voluntarily to one another and to holy causes, that is where the Divine Presence rests.*

Hence the resonant word that gives its name to this *parasha*: Teruma. I've translated it as "an offering," but it actually has a subtly different meaning for which there is no simple English equivalent. It means "something you lift up" by dedicating it to a sacred cause. You lift it up, and then it lifts you up.

25:8 בְּתוֹכָם *In their midst* – The Jewish mystics pointed out the linguistic strangeness of this verse. It should have said, "They shall make Me a Sanctuary and I will dwell in it," the Sanctuary, not "and I will dwell in their midst." The reason for this wording is that the Divine Presence lives not in a building, but in its builders, not in a physical place but in the human heart. The Sanctuary was not a place in which the objective existence of God was somehow more concentrated than elsewhere. Rather, it was a place whose holiness had the effect of opening hearts to the One worshipped there. God exists everywhere, but not everywhere do we feel the presence of God in the same way. The essence of "the holy" is that it is a place where we set aside all human devices and desires and enter a domain wholly set aside for God.

If the concept of the *Mishkan*, the Tabernacle, is that God lives in the human heart whenever it opens itself unreservedly to Heaven, then the way is open to the synagogue: the supreme statement of the idea that if God is everywhere, He can be reached anywhere. After the destruction of the Temple, the synagogue became Jerusalem in exile,

ג תְּרוּמָתִי׃ וְזֹאת הַתְּרוּמָה אֲשֶׁר תִּקְחוּ מֵאִתָּם זָהָב וָכֶסֶף
ד ה וּנְחֹשֶׁת׃ וּתְכֵלֶת וְאַרְגָּמָן וְתוֹלַעַת שָׁנִי וְשֵׁשׁ וְעִזִּים׃ וְעֹרֹת
ו אֵילִם מְאָדָּמִים וְעֹרֹת תְּחָשִׁים וַעֲצֵי שִׁטִּים׃ שֶׁמֶן לַמָּאֹר
ז בְּשָׂמִים לְשֶׁמֶן הַמִּשְׁחָה וְלִקְטֹרֶת הַסַּמִּים׃ אַבְנֵי־שֹׁהַם
ח וְאַבְנֵי מִלֻּאִים לָאֵפֹד וְלַחֹשֶׁן׃ וְעָשׂוּ לִי מִקְדָּשׁ וְשָׁכַנְתִּי
ט בְּתוֹכָם׃ כְּכֹל אֲשֶׁר אֲנִי מַרְאֶה אוֹתְךָ אֵת תַּבְנִית הַמִּשְׁכָּן

25:3 וְזֹאת הַתְּרוּמָה אֲשֶׁר תִּקְחוּ מֵאִתָּם *The offerings you shall receive from them* – How do you feel the presence of God in the midst of everyday life? The answer, I believe, is in the name of this *parasha*, Teruma. It means "an offering." God said to Moshe: "Tell the Israelites to take an offering for Me; take My offering from all whose heart moves them to give" (Ex. 25:2). In other words, the best way of encountering God is to give.

The very act of giving flows from, or leads to, the understanding that what we give is part of what we were given. It is a way of giving thanks, an act of gratitude. That is the difference in the human mind between the presence of God and the absence of God.

If God is present, it means that what we have is His. He created the universe. He made us. He gave us life. He breathed into us the very air we breathe. All around us is the majesty, the plenitude, of God's generosity: the light of the sun, the green of the leaves, the song of the birds.

When life is something given, you acknowledge this by giving back. But *if life is not a given because there is no giver*, if the universe came into existence only

the Sanctuary and its service were overwhelmingly compulsory, not voluntary. The regular offerings were minutely prescribed. So too were the contributions. During the initial construction of the Sanctuary, everyone had to give a half shekel for the silver sockets. In addition, there was an annual mandatory half shekel for the sacrifices. Why then was the Sanctuary specifically to be built through voluntary donations?

The Sanctuary was intended to stand at the heart, geographical and spiritual, of a nation that had been taken by God from slavery to freedom. The faith of Israel therefore had to be an expression of liberty. Faith, coerced, is not faith. Worship, forced, is not true worship. A Sanctuary built by conscripted labor conflicts with the very nature of God to whom it is dedicated.

It was thus not accidental, but of the essence, that the first House of God – small and portable – was built through free, uncoerced, voluntary contributions. For God lives not in houses of wood and stone, but in the minds and souls of free human beings. He is to be found not in monumental architecture, but in the willing heart.

10 that I show you. Make an Ark of acacia wood,
two and a half cubits long, a cubit and a half wide, and
11 a cubit and a half high. Overlay it with pure gold, inside
12 and out, and around it make a gold rim. Cast four gold
rings for it and place them on its four corners, two rings

---

universe. We are charged with creating order in the human universe. That means painstaking care in what we say, what we do, and what we must restrain ourselves from doing. There is a precise choreography to the moral and spiritual life as there is a precise architecture to the Tabernacle. Being good, specifically being holy, is not a matter of acting as the spirit moves us. It is a matter of aligning ourselves to the Will that made the world. Law, structure, precision: of these things the cosmos is made and without them it would cease to be. The fact that the Torah records the precise dimensions of the Tabernacle signals that the same applies to human behavior.

25:10 וְעָשׂוּ אֲרוֹן עֲצֵי שִׁטִּים *Make an Ark of acacia wood – Ve'asu* – literally, "they shall make." God instructs Moshe in the making of the Sanctuary and its appurtenances, detail by detail. In each case the verb is in the second-person singular: *vetzipita, ve'asita, veyatzakta, venatata, veheveta,* "you shall cover…you shall make…you shall pour…you shall place… you shall bring." However, there is one exception to this rule: the Ark. There the verb is in the third-person plural. Why "they shall make," not "you"? Why the shift from the singular to the plural?

The Ark was made to hold the tablets of stone given to Moshe by God at Mount Sinai. The Torah calls the tablets "the testimony" since they were the physical symbol of the Sinai covenant. According to the Sages, "both the [complete second set of] tablets and the fragments of the [first] tablets [which Moshe broke after the golden calf] were in the Ark" (Berakhot 8b; Bava Batra 14b; Menaḥot 99a). The Ark, in short, symbolized and represented Torah.

The reason, therefore, that the construction of the Ark is commanded in the plural is that everyone is to have a share in it (see Ramban on this verse). Unlike other aspects of service in the Sanctuary or Temple, Torah is the heritage of everyone. All Israel were parties to the covenant. All were expected to know and study its terms. Judaism might know other hierarchies, but when it came to knowledge, study, and the dignity conferred by scholarship, everyone stood on equal footing. That is why, here alone in its list of the component parts of the Sanctuary, the Torah shifts from the second-person singular to the third-person plural. When it comes to the Ark, home and symbol of the most significant form of knowledge, everyone must have an equal share.

י וְאֵ֗ת תַּבְנִ֛ית כָּל־כֵּלָ֖יו וְכֵ֥ן תַּעֲשֽׂוּ׃ וְעָשׂ֥וּ אֲר֖וֹן
עֲצֵ֣י שִׁטִּ֑ים אַמָּתַ֨יִם וָחֵ֜צִי אָרְכּ֗וֹ וְאַמָּ֤ה וָחֵ֙צִי֙ רָחְבּ֔וֹ וְאַמָּ֥ה
יא וָחֵ֖צִי קֹמָתֽוֹ׃ וְצִפִּיתָ֤ אֹתוֹ֙ זָהָ֣ב טָה֔וֹר מִבַּ֥יִת וּמִח֖וּץ תְּצַפֶּ֑נּוּ
יב וְעָשִׂ֧יתָ עָלָ֛יו זֵ֥ר זָהָ֖ב סָבִֽיב׃ וְיָצַ֣קְתָּ לּ֗וֹ אַרְבַּע֙ טַבְּעֹ֣ת זָהָ֔ב
וְנָתַתָּ֕ה עַ֖ל אַרְבַּ֣ע פַּעֲמֹתָ֑יו וּשְׁתֵּ֣י טַבָּעֹ֗ת עַל־צַלְעוֹ֙ הָאֶחָ֔ת

the home of the Jewish heart. It is the ultimate expression of monotheism – that wherever we gather to turn our hearts toward Heaven, there the Divine Presence can be found.

THE DETAILS OF THE TABERNACLE
Moshe is shown a pattern image of what the Tabernacle is to look like: "the patterns that I show you" (see Ibn Ezra). What is the eternal significance of the dimensions of this modest, portable, temporary construction? To put the question more sharply still: Is not the very idea of a specific size for the home of the *Shekhina*, the Divine Presence, liable to mislead? A transcendent God cannot be contained in space. What difference could it make whether the Tabernacle was large or small? Either way, it was a symbol, a focus, of the Divine Presence that is everywhere, wherever human beings open their heart to God. Its exact dimensions should not matter.

Torah commentators, especially Nehama Leibowitz, have drawn attention to the way the terminology of the construction of the Tabernacle is the same as that used to describe God's creation of the universe. The key Hebrew words – for *make, see, complete, bless, sanctify, work, behold* – appear in both texts. The latter creation mirrors the former. As God made the universe, so He instructed the Israelites to make the *Mishkan*. The Tabernacle was, in other words, a microcosmos, a symbolic reminder of the world God made. The fact that the Divine Presence rested within it was not meant to suggest that God is here not there, in this place not that. It was meant to signal, powerfully and palpably, that just as God exists within its walls, so too does He exist throughout the macrocosmos. It was a man-made structure to focus attention on the divinely created universe. It was in space what the Sabbath is in time: a reminder of creation.

The dimensions of the universe are precise, mathematically exact. Had they differed in even the slightest degree, the universe, or life, would not exist. The misplacement of even a few of the 3.1 billion letters in the human genome can lead to devastating genetic conditions. The famous "butterfly effect" – the beating of a butterfly's wing somewhere may cause a tsunami elsewhere, thousands of miles away – tells us that small actions can have large consequences. Precision matters. Order matters. That is the message the Tabernacle was intended to convey.

God creates order in the natural

13 on one side and two on the other. Make staves of acacia
14 wood and overlay them with gold; place these staves in
the rings on the sides of the Ark so that the Ark may be
15 carried. The staves must stay in the rings of the Ark; they
16 must not be removed. Inside the Ark, place the tablets of
17 the Covenant that I will give you. Make an Ark cover of SHENI
pure gold, two and a half cubits long and a cubit and a
18 half wide. Make two cherubim of beaten gold and place
19 them at the two ends of the cover: one cherub at one end
and one at the other; the cherubim shall be made of one
20 piece with the cover. These cherubim should have wings
spread upward, sheltering the cover. They should face
21 one another, and look toward the cover. Place the cover
on top of the Ark, and inside the Ark place the tablets of
22 the Covenant that I will give you. There, from above the
cover, between the two cherubim, above the Ark of the
Testimony, I will meet with you and speak with you, and
give you all My commands to the Israelites.
23 Make a table of acacia wood, two cubits long, a cubit wide,
24 and a cubit and a half high. Overlay it with pure gold and

---

by discerning it in another. God lives in *the between* that joins self to self through acts of covenantal kindness, *ḥesed*.

Emmanuel Levinas was right to see the concept of "face" as fundamental to our humanity. Society is faceless; *ḥesed* is a relationship of face-to-face. The Torah repeatedly emphasizes that we cannot see God face-to-face. It follows that we can only see God in the face of another.

25:22 מֵעַל הַכַּפֹּרֶת *There, from above the cover* – At the heart of the Tabernacle, framed between the two cherubim, where in a different shrine one might expect to find the graven image of a god, God will reveal Himself from an empty space.

The holy, in the Tanakh, simply means *God's domain* – those points in time and space at which His presence is peculiarly visible. That is what Yeshayahu means when he says of Israel: "'You are My witnesses,' so says the Lord…'that I am He'" (Is. 43:10). Holiness is the space vacated by us so that God's presence can be felt in our midst. Every time we set aside our desires in order to act on the basis of God's will, not our own, we engage in self-limitation – we take up a little less space ourselves, creating the space in which God can be felt. The everyday world is the space God makes for us. *Kedusha*, holiness, is the space we make for God.

יג וּשְׁתֵּי טַבָּעֹת עַל־צַלְעוֹ הַשֵּׁנִית: וְעָשִׂיתָ בַדֵּי עֲצֵי שִׁטִּים
יד וְצִפִּיתָ אֹתָם זָהָב: וְהֵבֵאתָ אֶת־הַבַּדִּים בַּטַּבָּעֹת עַל צַלְעֹת
טו הָאָרֹן לָשֵׂאת אֶת־הָאָרֹן בָּהֶם: בְּטַבְּעֹת הָאָרֹן יִהְיוּ הַבַּדִּים
טז לֹא יָסֻרוּ מִמֶּנּוּ: וְנָתַתָּ אֶל־הָאָרֹן אֵת הָעֵדֻת אֲשֶׁר אֶתֵּן
יז אֵלֶיךָ: וְעָשִׂיתָ כַפֹּרֶת זָהָב טָהוֹר אַמָּתַיִם וָחֵצִי אָרְכָּהּ וְאַמָּה שני
יח וָחֵצִי רָחְבָּהּ: וְעָשִׂיתָ שְׁנַיִם כְּרֻבִים זָהָב מִקְשָׁה תַּעֲשֶׂה
יט אֹתָם מִשְּׁנֵי קְצוֹת הַכַּפֹּרֶת: וַעֲשֵׂה כְּרוּב אֶחָד מִקָּצָה מִזֶּה
וּכְרוּב־אֶחָד מִקָּצָה מִזֶּה מִן־הַכַּפֹּרֶת תַּעֲשׂוּ אֶת־הַכְּרֻבִים
כ עַל־שְׁנֵי קְצוֹתָיו: וְהָיוּ הַכְּרֻבִים פֹּרְשֵׂי כְנָפַיִם לְמַעְלָה סֹכְכִים
בְּכַנְפֵיהֶם עַל־הַכַּפֹּרֶת וּפְנֵיהֶם אִישׁ אֶל־אָחִיו אֶל־הַכַּפֹּרֶת
כא יִהְיוּ פְּנֵי הַכְּרֻבִים: וְנָתַתָּ אֶת־הַכַּפֹּרֶת עַל־הָאָרֹן מִלְמָעְלָה
כב וְאֶל־הָאָרֹן תִּתֵּן אֶת־הָעֵדֻת אֲשֶׁר אֶתֵּן אֵלֶיךָ: וְנוֹעַדְתִּי
לְךָ שָׁם וְדִבַּרְתִּי אִתְּךָ מֵעַל הַכַּפֹּרֶת מִבֵּין שְׁנֵי הַכְּרֻבִים
אֲשֶׁר עַל־אֲרוֹן הָעֵדֻת אֵת כָּל־אֲשֶׁר אֲצַוֶּה אוֹתְךָ אֶל־בְּנֵי
יִשְׂרָאֵל:
כג וְעָשִׂיתָ שֻׁלְחָן עֲצֵי שִׁטִּים אַמָּתַיִם אָרְכּוֹ וְאַמָּה רָחְבּוֹ וְאַמָּה
כד וָחֵצִי קֹמָתוֹ: וְצִפִּיתָ אֹתוֹ זָהָב טָהוֹר וְעָשִׂיתָ לּוֹ זֵר זָהָב סָבִיב:

25:20 וּפְנֵיהֶם אִישׁ אֶל־אָחִיו *They should face one another* – This strange and lovely detail begs for explanation. Above the Ark are to be two figures, cherubim, their faces turned to one another. Ostensibly this was a great risk. The Israelites had been told not to make any likeness that might be worshipped as a god, an idol. Why then were the figures introduced into the Holy of Holies?

The Sages say the cherubim were like children (Rashi, based on Sukka 5b), or, in another interpretation, that they were intertwined like lovers (Yoma 54a). It was *between the two cherubim* that God spoke to Moshe. The message of this symbol is so significant that it is deemed by God Himself to be sufficient to outweigh the risk of misunderstanding. *God speaks where two persons turn their faces to one another* in love, embrace, generosity, and care. God's presence is everywhere. But not everywhere are we ready to receive it. When we open our "I" to another's "Thou" – that is where God lives. We discover God's image in ourself

25 around it make a gold rim. Make a frame a handbreadth
wide all around, and around the frame also make a gold
26 rim. Make for it four gold rings, and place the rings on the
27 four corners where the four legs are. The rings should be
attached next to the frame as holders for staves to carry the
28 table. Make the staves of acacia wood and overlay them
29 with gold; by these the table shall be carried. You must
also make, out of pure gold, its bowls, spoons, pitchers,
30 and jars for pouring libations. On this table the showbread
must be placed before Me at all times.
31 Make a candelabrum of pure gold. Its base and shaft, cups,
knobs, and flowers shall be hammered from a single piece.
32 Six branches shall extend from its sides, three on one side,
33 three on the other. On each branch there shall be three
finely crafted cups, each with a knob and a flower. All six
branches extending from the candelabrum shall be like
34 this. The shaft of the candelabrum shall have four finely
35 crafted cups, each with a knob and a flower. For the six
branches that extend from the candelabrum, there must
36 be a knob at the base of each pair of branches. The knobs
and their branches shall be of one piece with it, the whole

---

sun on the fourth day], it was so strong and pellucid that one could see from one end of the world to the other, but God was afraid that the wicked might abuse it. What did He do? He reserved that light for the righteous in the World to Come. But now and then there are great men who are blessed and privileged to see it. I think that Rembrandt was one of them, and the light in his pictures is the very light that God created on Genesis day."

I suspect that what Rabbi Kook saw in those paintings was Rembrandt's ability to convey the beauty of ordinary people. He makes no attempt to beautify or idealize his subjects. The light that shines from them is, simply, their humanity.

How fitting that one of the most iconic symbols in Jewish art was to be the Menora, the seven-branched candelabrum. In Rome, the Arch of Titus was erected by Titus's brother Domitian to commemorate the victorious Roman siege of Jerusalem in the year 70. It shows Roman soldiers carrying away the spoils of war, most famously the Menora. Rome won that military conflict. Yet its civilization declined and fell, while Jews and Judaism survived. We survive "not with valor and not with strength" but by the quality of our light.

כה וְעָשִׂיתָ לּוֹ מִסְגֶּרֶת טֹפַח סָבִיב וְעָשִׂיתָ זֵר־זָהָב לְמִסְגַּרְתּוֹ
כו סָבִיב: וְעָשִׂיתָ לּוֹ אַרְבַּע טַבְּעֹת זָהָב וְנָתַתָּ אֶת־הַטַּבָּעֹת עַל
כז אַרְבַּע הַפֵּאֹת אֲשֶׁר לְאַרְבַּע רַגְלָיו: לְעֻמַּת הַמִּסְגֶּרֶת תִּהְיֶיןָ
כח הַטַּבָּעֹת לְבָתִּים לְבַדִּים לָשֵׂאת אֶת־הַשֻּׁלְחָן: וְעָשִׂיתָ אֶת־
הַבַּדִּים עֲצֵי שִׁטִּים וְצִפִּיתָ אֹתָם זָהָב וְנִשָּׂא־בָם אֶת־הַשֻּׁלְחָן:
כט וְעָשִׂיתָ קְּעָרֹתָיו וְכַפֹּתָיו וּקְשׂוֹתָיו וּמְנַקִּיֹּתָיו אֲשֶׁר יֻסַּךְ בָּהֵן
ל זָהָב טָהוֹר תַּעֲשֶׂה אֹתָם: וְנָתַתָּ עַל־הַשֻּׁלְחָן לֶחֶם פָּנִים לְפָנַי
תָּמִיד:
לא וְעָשִׂיתָ מְנֹרַת זָהָב טָהוֹר מִקְשָׁה תֵּיעָשֶׂה הַמְּנוֹרָה יְרֵכָהּ
לב וְקָנָהּ גְּבִיעֶיהָ כַּפְתֹּרֶיהָ וּפְרָחֶיהָ מִמֶּנָּה יִהְיוּ: וְשִׁשָּׁה קָנִים
יֹצְאִים מִצִּדֶּיהָ שְׁלֹשָׁה ׀ קְנֵי מְנֹרָה מִצִּדָּהּ הָאֶחָד וּשְׁלֹשָׁה
לג קְנֵי מְנֹרָה מִצִּדָּהּ הַשֵּׁנִי: שְׁלֹשָׁה גְבִעִים מְשֻׁקָּדִים בַּקָּנֶה
הָאֶחָד כַּפְתֹּר וָפֶרַח וּשְׁלֹשָׁה גְבִעִים מְשֻׁקָּדִים בַּקָּנֶה
הָאֶחָד כַּפְתֹּר וָפָרַח כֵּן לְשֵׁשֶׁת הַקָּנִים הַיֹּצְאִים מִן־הַמְּנֹרָה:
לד לה וּבַמְּנֹרָה אַרְבָּעָה גְבִעִים מְשֻׁקָּדִים כַּפְתֹּרֶיהָ וּפְרָחֶיהָ: וְכַפְתֹּר
תַּחַת שְׁנֵי הַקָּנִים מִמֶּנָּה וְכַפְתֹּר תַּחַת שְׁנֵי הַקָּנִים מִמֶּנָּה
וְכַפְתֹּר תַּחַת־שְׁנֵי הַקָּנִים מִמֶּנָּה לְשֵׁשֶׁת הַקָּנִים הַיֹּצְאִים
לו מִן־הַמְּנֹרָה: כַּפְתֹּרֵיהֶם וּקְנֹתָם מִמֶּנָּה יִהְיוּ כֻּלָּהּ מִקְשָׁה

25:31 מְנֹרַת זָהָב טָהוֹר *A candelabrum of pure gold* – In the Tabernacle we meet the aesthetic side of Judaism – art that points to something beyond itself. The Tabernacle itself was a kind of microcosm of the universe, with one overriding particularity: that in it you felt the presence of something beyond – what the Torah calls "the glory of the LORD," which "filled the Tabernacle" (Ex. 40:35).

The strongest positive Jewish statement on art of which I am aware was made by Rabbi Avraham HaKohen Kook, the first Ashkenazic chief rabbi of (pre-state) Israel, describing his time in London during the First World War:

"I used to visit the National Gallery, and my favorite pictures were those of Rembrandt. I really think that Rembrandt was a *tzaddik*. Do you know that when I first saw Rembrandt's works, they reminded me of the rabbinic statement about the creation of light?

"We are told that when God created light [on the first day of creation, as opposed to the natural light of the

▶

37 of it a single, hammered piece of pure gold. Make its
seven lamps and mount them so that they light the space
38 39 in front of it. Make its tongs and pans of pure gold. All
40 these items shall be made from a talent of pure gold. Take
care to make them according to that design that is shown
26 1 to you on the mountain. As for the Tabernacle SHELISHI
itself, make it with ten sheets of finely spun linen and sky-
blue, purple, and scarlet wool, with a design of cherubim
2 worked into them. Each sheet shall be twenty-eight cubits
long and four cubits wide; all the sheets should be the
3 same size. Five of the sheets should be sewn together; the
4 other five likewise. Make loops of sky-blue wool on the
upper edge of the end sheet in the first set, and likewise on
the upper edge of the outermost sheet in the second set.
5 Make fifty loops on each sheet on one side and fifty on the
upper edge of the corresponding sheets in the other set,
6 with the loops opposite one another. And make fifty gold
clasps. With the clasps, join the sheets together so that
7 the Tabernacle becomes one whole. Make sheets of goats'
hair as a tent over the Tabernacle; make eleven of these
8 sheets. Each sheet shall be thirty cubits long and four
9 cubits wide, all eleven sheets the same size. Join five of

---

quarried enormous blocks of prime stone so that the foundations of the House would be laid with hewn stone" (I Kings 5:27–31).

Is this not precisely what the Israelites left Egypt to avoid, becoming a mere labor force for a ruler engaged in a grand project, even if it is the holiest of holies? Is this not, albeit temporarily and for a sacred cause, a new form of slavery?

No less fascinating is the explanation given in the second book of Samuel for why God, when David first mooted the idea of a Temple, said no:

> Shall you be the one to build a house for Me, for My abode? For I have not dwelt in a house from the day I brought the Israelites out of Egypt to this day; I have roamed in tent and tabernacle. But wherever I roamed, among all the Israelites, have I ever spoken a word to any of the tribes of Israel whom I charged to shepherd my people Israel, saying, "Why have you not built Me a cedarwood palace?" (II Sam. 7:5–7)

This reply contains a tantalizing suggestion: that God does not seek the glory of

לז אַחַת זָהָב טָהוֹר: וְעָשִׂיתָ אֶת־נֵרֹתֶיהָ שִׁבְעָה וְהֶעֱלָה
לח אֶת־נֵרֹתֶיהָ וְהֵאִיר עַל־עֵבֶר פָּנֶיהָ: וּמַלְקָחֶיהָ וּמַחְתֹּתֶיהָ
לט זָהָב טָהוֹר: כִּכַּר זָהָב טָהוֹר יַעֲשֶׂה אֹתָהּ אֵת כָּל־הַכֵּלִים
מ הָאֵלֶּה: וּרְאֵה וַעֲשֵׂה בְּתַבְנִיתָם אֲשֶׁר־אַתָּה מָרְאֶה
כו א בָּהָר: וְאֶת־הַמִּשְׁכָּן תַּעֲשֶׂה עֶשֶׂר יְרִיעֹת שֵׁשׁ יט שלישי
מָשְׁזָר וּתְכֵלֶת וְאַרְגָּמָן וְתֹלַעַת שָׁנִי כְּרֻבִים מַעֲשֵׂה חֹשֵׁב
ב תַּעֲשֶׂה אֹתָם: אֹרֶךְ ׀ הַיְרִיעָה הָאַחַת שְׁמֹנֶה וְעֶשְׂרִים בָּאַמָּה
וְרֹחַב אַרְבַּע בָּאַמָּה הַיְרִיעָה הָאֶחָת מִדָּה אַחַת לְכָל־
ג הַיְרִיעֹת: חֲמֵשׁ הַיְרִיעֹת תִּהְיֶיןָ חֹבְרֹת אִשָּׁה אֶל־אֲחֹתָהּ
ד וְחָמֵשׁ יְרִיעֹת חֹבְרֹת אִשָּׁה אֶל־אֲחֹתָהּ: וְעָשִׂיתָ לֻלְאֹת
תְּכֵלֶת עַל שְׂפַת הַיְרִיעָה הָאֶחָת מִקָּצָה בַּחֹבָרֶת וְכֵן תַּעֲשֶׂה
ה בִּשְׂפַת הַיְרִיעָה הַקִּיצוֹנָה בַּמַּחְבֶּרֶת הַשֵּׁנִית: חֲמִשִּׁים לֻלָאֹת
תַּעֲשֶׂה בַּיְרִיעָה הָאֶחָת וַחֲמִשִּׁים לֻלָאֹת תַּעֲשֶׂה בִּקְצֵה
הַיְרִיעָה אֲשֶׁר בַּמַּחְבֶּרֶת הַשֵּׁנִית מַקְבִּילֹת הַלֻּלָאֹת אִשָּׁה
ו אֶל־אֲחֹתָהּ: וְעָשִׂיתָ חֲמִשִּׁים קַרְסֵי זָהָב וְחִבַּרְתָּ אֶת־הַיְרִיעֹת
ז אִשָּׁה אֶל־אֲחֹתָהּ בַּקְּרָסִים וְהָיָה הַמִּשְׁכָּן אֶחָד: וְעָשִׂיתָ
יְרִיעֹת עִזִּים לְאֹהֶל עַל־הַמִּשְׁכָּן עַשְׁתֵּי־עֶשְׂרֵה יְרִיעֹת
ח תַּעֲשֶׂה אֹתָם: אֹרֶךְ ׀ הַיְרִיעָה הָאַחַת שְׁלֹשִׁים בָּאַמָּה וְרֹחַב
אַרְבַּע בָּאַמָּה הַיְרִיעָה הָאֶחָת מִדָּה אַחַת לְעַשְׁתֵּי עֶשְׂרֵה
ט יְרִיעֹת: וְחִבַּרְתָּ אֶת־חֲמֵשׁ הַיְרִיעֹת לְבָד וְאֶת־שֵׁשׁ הַיְרִיעֹת

A TENT

In one sense the Temple and the Tabernacle were similar things. They were both places of worship, at the symbolic center of society. Both involved the contributions of many kinds of people. Both were projects of society as a whole.

There was, however, a difference. The Tabernacle, a simple tent, was made out of voluntary contributions. The Temple, a palatial stone building, was not. To build it, Shlomo had to turn the Israelites into a vast labor force: "King Shlomo began to levy forced labor upon all of Israel; the levy was thirty thousand men. He had ten thousand men sent to Lebanon every month, in shifts; they would spend a month in Lebanon and two months at home.... At the king's command, they

▶

the sheets by themselves, and the other six by themselves.
10 Fold the sixth sheet over the front of the Tent. Make fifty
loops on the edge of the end sheet of one set, and fifty on
11 the edge of the end sheet of the other. Make, also, fifty
bronze clasps. Put the clasps through the loops, joining
12 the tent together so that it becomes one whole. As for the
additional length of the tent sheets, the extra half sheet
13 is to hang down at the rear of the Tabernacle. The extra
cubit at either end of each of the tent sheets should hang
over the sides of the Tabernacle to cover it on both sides.
14 Make a covering for the tent from rams' hides dyed red.
Above it make a covering of fine leather.
15 Make the upright boards for the Tabernacle of acacia REVI'I
16 wood. Each board shall be ten cubits long and one and
17 a half cubits wide. Each board should have two matching
tenons; all the Tabernacle's boards should be made in
18 this way. Make twenty boards for the southern side of
19 the Tabernacle, and forty silver sockets under the twenty
boards, two sockets under the first board for its two
20 tenons, and two under the next. For the second side of
the Tabernacle, the northern side, there should be twenty
21 boards, along with their forty silver sockets, two under
22 the first board and two under each of the others. Make
23 six boards for the west side of the Tabernacle, and two

subsequent ruler was able to reunite the tribes.

The Tabernacle and Temple, in contemporary language, mark the difference between society and state. Civil society, where the covenantal virtues are exercised, is made up of voluntary associations. When the state takes over the work of civil institutions, it is not the same thing under a different name: it is a different thing entirely. That is the difference between contract and covenant, between what people do because the government decides, and what they do out of a sense of shared commitment. Society is what we make together, all of us, without delegating away responsibility to others. Governments administer states. We, the people, build societies.

What can be done voluntarily cannot necessarily be done coercively. The Tabernacle, a fragile tent built of voluntary contributions, united the nation. The Temple, built by conscripted labor, divided it.

לְבָ֑ד וְכָפַלְתָּ֙ אֶת־הַיְרִיעָ֣ה הַשִּׁשִּׁ֔ית אֶל־מ֖וּל פְּנֵ֥י הָאֹֽהֶל׃
י וְעָשִׂ֜יתָ חֲמִשִּׁ֣ים לֻֽלָאֹ֗ת עַ֣ל שְׂפַ֤ת הַיְרִיעָה֙ הָֽאֶחָ֔ת הַקִּיצֹנָ֖ה
בַּחֹבָ֑רֶת וַחֲמִשִּׁ֣ים לֻֽלָאֹ֔ת עַ֚ל שְׂפַ֣ת הַיְרִיעָ֔ה הַחֹבֶ֖רֶת הַשֵּׁנִֽית׃
יא וְעָשִׂ֛יתָ קַרְסֵ֥י נְחֹ֖שֶׁת חֲמִשִּׁ֑ים וְהֵבֵאתָ֤ אֶת־הַקְּרָסִים֙ בַּלֻּ֣לָאֹ֔ת
יב וְחִבַּרְתָּ֥ אֶת־הָאֹ֖הֶל וְהָיָ֥ה אֶחָֽד׃ וְסֶ֙רַח֙ הָעֹדֵ֔ף בִּירִיעֹ֖ת
הָאֹ֑הֶל חֲצִ֤י הַיְרִיעָה֙ הָעֹדֶ֔פֶת תִּסְרַ֕ח עַ֖ל אֲחֹרֵ֥י הַמִּשְׁכָּֽן׃
יג וְהָאַמָּ֨ה מִזֶּ֜ה וְהָאַמָּ֣ה מִזֶּ֗ה בָּעֹדֵ֕ף בְּאֹ֖רֶךְ יְרִיעֹ֣ת הָאֹ֑הֶל
יד יִהְיֶ֨ה סָר֜וּחַ עַל־צִדֵּ֧י הַמִּשְׁכָּ֛ן מִזֶּ֥ה וּמִזֶּ֖ה לְכַסֹּתֽוֹ׃ וְעָשִׂ֤יתָ
מִכְסֶה֙ לָאֹ֔הֶל עֹרֹ֥ת אֵילִ֖ם מְאָדָּמִ֑ים וּמִכְסֵ֛ה עֹרֹ֥ת תְּחָשִׁ֖ים
מִלְמָֽעְלָה׃
טו טז וְעָשִׂ֥יתָ אֶת־הַקְּרָשִׁ֖ים לַמִּשְׁכָּ֑ן עֲצֵ֥י שִׁטִּ֖ים עֹמְדִֽים׃ עֶ֥שֶׂר רביעי
אַמּ֖וֹת אֹ֣רֶךְ הַקָּ֑רֶשׁ וְאַמָּה֙ וַחֲצִ֣י הָֽאַמָּ֔ה רֹ֖חַב הַקֶּ֥רֶשׁ הָאֶחָֽד׃
יז שְׁתֵּ֣י יָד֗וֹת לַקֶּ֙רֶשׁ֙ הָאֶחָ֔ד מְשֻׁלָּבֹ֔ת אִשָּׁ֖ה אֶל־אֲחֹתָ֑הּ כֵּ֣ן
יח תַּעֲשֶׂ֔ה לְכֹ֖ל קַרְשֵׁ֥י הַמִּשְׁכָּֽן׃ וְעָשִׂ֥יתָ אֶת־הַקְּרָשִׁ֖ים לַמִּשְׁכָּ֑ן
יט עֶשְׂרִ֣ים קֶ֔רֶשׁ לִפְאַ֖ת נֶ֥גְבָּה תֵימָֽנָה׃ וְאַרְבָּעִים֙ אַדְנֵי־כֶ֔סֶף
תַּעֲשֶׂ֕ה תַּ֖חַת עֶשְׂרִ֣ים הַקָּ֑רֶשׁ שְׁנֵ֨י אֲדָנִ֜ים תַּֽחַת־הַקֶּ֤רֶשׁ
הָאֶחָד֙ לִשְׁתֵּ֣י יְדֹתָ֔יו וּשְׁנֵ֧י אֲדָנִ֛ים תַּֽחַת־הַקֶּ֥רֶשׁ הָאֶחָ֖ד לִשְׁתֵּ֥י
כ יְדֹתָֽיו׃ וּלְצֶ֧לַע הַמִּשְׁכָּ֛ן הַשֵּׁנִ֖ית לִפְאַ֣ת צָפ֑וֹן עֶשְׂרִ֖ים קָֽרֶשׁ׃
כא וְאַרְבָּעִ֥ים אַדְנֵיהֶ֖ם כָּ֑סֶף שְׁנֵ֣י אֲדָנִ֗ים תַּ֚חַת הַקֶּ֣רֶשׁ הָאֶחָ֔ד
כב וּשְׁנֵ֣י אֲדָנִ֔ים תַּ֖חַת הַקֶּ֥רֶשׁ הָאֶחָֽד׃ וּֽלְיַרְכְּתֵ֥י הַמִּשְׁכָּ֖ן יָ֑מָּה
כג תַּעֲשֶׂ֖ה שִׁשָּׁ֥ה קְרָשִֽׁים׃ וּשְׁנֵ֤י קְרָשִׁים֙ תַּעֲשֶׂ֔ה לִמְקֻצְעֹ֖ת

great buildings. It is only the barest hint, but it lingers in the mind.

What was the result of this monumental building project? After Shlomo's death, the people came to his son and successor, Reḥavam, and staged a protest. "Your father made our yoke heavy – now, relieve the heavy workload and the harsh yoke your father placed upon us, and we will serve you" (I Kings 12:4). The elders who had counseled Shlomo told Reḥavam to grant their request. Reḥavam's young friends, however, told him to refuse. Reḥavam did refuse. The nation split in two, the ten northerly tribes declaring an independent kingdom under Yorovam. It was the end of the united kingdom. No

24 additional boards for the Tabernacle's rear corners. These
should adjoin each other at the bottom, and be joined
together at the top by a ring. So it should be for both
25 sides; they shall form the two corners. So there should be
eight boards and sixteen silver sockets, two sockets under
26 each board. Make crossbars, too, of acacia wood, five for
27 the boards of the first side of the Tabernacle, five for the
boards of the second side of the Tabernacle, and five for
the boards of the western side of the Tabernacle at the
28 rear. The central crossbar should go through the middle
29 of the boards from one end to the other. Overlay the
boards with gold, and make gold rings for the crossbars.
30 The crossbars too should be overlaid with gold. So shall
you set up the Tabernacle, according to the plan you were
31 shown on the mountain. Make a curtain of sky- ḤAMISHI
blue, purple, and scarlet wool, and finely spun linen with
32 a design of cherubim worked into it. Hang it on four gold-
covered posts of acacia wood with gold hooks, set on four
33 sockets of silver. Hang the curtain under the clasps and
bring the Ark of the Testimony behind it, so that the
curtain separates the holy place from the Holy of Holies.
34 Put the cover on the Ark of the Testimony in the Holy
35 of Holies. The table shall be placed on the north side of
the Tabernacle outside the curtain, and the candelabrum
36 on the south side, opposite the table. Make a screen for
the entrance to the Tent, embroidered with sky-blue,
37 purple, and scarlet wool and finely spun linen. Make five
posts of acacia wood for the screen and overlay them
with gold; their hooks, also, shall be of gold. Cast for
27 1 them, too, five sockets of bronze. Make the altar SHISHI
from acacia wood. It should be square, five cubits long,

Hobbes's account of the social contract was that it is in the interests of each of us to hand over some of our rights to a central power charged with ensuring the rule of law and the defense of the realm. Adam Smith's insight into the market economy was that if we each act to maximize our own advantage, the result is the growth of the commonwealth. Modern politics and economics were built on

כד הַמִּשְׁכָּן בַּיַּרְכָתָיִם: וְיִהְיוּ תֹאֲמִם מִלְּמַטָּה וְיַחְדָּו יִהְיוּ
תַמִּים עַל־רֹאשׁוֹ אֶל־הַטַּבַּעַת הָאֶחָת כֵּן יִהְיֶה לִשְׁנֵיהֶם
כה לִשְׁנֵי הַמִּקְצֹעֹת יִהְיוּ: וְהָיוּ שְׁמֹנָה קְרָשִׁים וְאַדְנֵיהֶם כֶּסֶף
שִׁשָּׁה עָשָׂר אֲדָנִים שְׁנֵי אֲדָנִים תַּחַת הַקֶּרֶשׁ הָאֶחָד וּשְׁנֵי
כו אֲדָנִים תַּחַת הַקֶּרֶשׁ הָאֶחָד: וְעָשִׂיתָ בְרִיחִם עֲצֵי שִׁטִּים
כז חֲמִשָּׁה לְקַרְשֵׁי צֶלַע־הַמִּשְׁכָּן הָאֶחָד: וַחֲמִשָּׁה בְרִיחִם
לְקַרְשֵׁי צֶלַע־הַמִּשְׁכָּן הַשֵּׁנִית וַחֲמִשָּׁה בְרִיחִם לְקַרְשֵׁי צֶלַע
כח הַמִּשְׁכָּן לַיַּרְכָתַיִם יָמָּה: וְהַבְּרִיחַ הַתִּיכֹן בְּתוֹךְ הַקְּרָשִׁים
כט מַבְרִחַ מִן־הַקָּצֶה אֶל־הַקָּצֶה: וְאֶת־הַקְּרָשִׁים תְּצַפֶּה
זָהָב וְאֶת־טַבְּעֹתֵיהֶם תַּעֲשֶׂה זָהָב בָּתִּים לַבְּרִיחִם וְצִפִּיתָ
ל אֶת־הַבְּרִיחִם זָהָב: וַהֲקֵמֹתָ אֶת־הַמִּשְׁכָּן כְּמִשְׁפָּטוֹ אֲשֶׁר
לא הָרְאֵיתָ בָּהָר: וְעָשִׂיתָ פָרֹכֶת תְּכֵלֶת וְאַרְגָּמָן כ חמישי
וְתוֹלַעַת שָׁנִי וְשֵׁשׁ מָשְׁזָר מַעֲשֵׂה חֹשֵׁב יַעֲשֶׂה אֹתָהּ כְּרֻבִים:
לב וְנָתַתָּה אֹתָהּ עַל־אַרְבָּעָה עַמּוּדֵי שִׁטִּים מְצֻפִּים זָהָב וָוֵיהֶם
לג זָהָב עַל־אַרְבָּעָה אַדְנֵי־כָסֶף: וְנָתַתָּה אֶת־הַפָּרֹכֶת תַּחַת
הַקְּרָסִים וְהֵבֵאתָ שָׁמָּה מִבֵּית לַפָּרֹכֶת אֵת אֲרוֹן הָעֵדוּת
וְהִבְדִּילָה הַפָּרֹכֶת לָכֶם בֵּין הַקֹּדֶשׁ וּבֵין קֹדֶשׁ הַקֳּדָשִׁים:
לד וְנָתַתָּ אֶת־הַכַּפֹּרֶת עַל אֲרוֹן הָעֵדֻת בְּקֹדֶשׁ הַקֳּדָשִׁים:
לה וְשַׂמְתָּ אֶת־הַשֻּׁלְחָן מִחוּץ לַפָּרֹכֶת וְאֶת־הַמְּנֹרָה נֹכַח
הַשֻּׁלְחָן עַל צֶלַע הַמִּשְׁכָּן תֵּימָנָה וְהַשֻּׁלְחָן תִּתֵּן עַל־צֶלַע
לו צָפוֹן: וְעָשִׂיתָ מָסָךְ לְפֶתַח הָאֹהֶל תְּכֵלֶת וְאַרְגָּמָן וְתוֹלַעַת
לז שָׁנִי וְשֵׁשׁ מָשְׁזָר מַעֲשֵׂה רֹקֵם: וְעָשִׂיתָ לַמָּסָךְ חֲמִשָּׁה עַמּוּדֵי
שִׁטִּים וְצִפִּיתָ אֹתָם זָהָב וָוֵיהֶם זָהָב וְיָצַקְתָּ לָהֶם חֲמִשָּׁה
כז א אַדְנֵי נְחֹשֶׁת: וְעָשִׂיתָ אֶת־הַמִּזְבֵּחַ עֲצֵי שִׁטִּים ששי

27:1 וְעָשִׂיתָ אֶת־הַמִּזְבֵּחַ *Make the altar* – The building of the Tabernacle is a preparation for an activity central to the Torah, yet in many ways foreign to us: sacrifice. The major institutions of the modern world were predicated on the model of the *rational actor*, that is, one who acts to maximize the benefits to him- or herself.

▶

2 five cubits wide, and three cubits high. Make horns for
it on its four corners, the horns being of one piece with
3 it, and overlay it with bronze. Make pots for removing
its ashes, together with shovels, basins, forks, and pans.
4 Make all of these of bronze. Make a grate of bronze mesh
for it, and on the mesh make four bronze rings at its four
5 corners. The grate should be set below, under the ledge
of the altar, so that the mesh reaches the middle of the
6 altar. And make staves of acacia wood for the altar, and
7 overlay them with bronze. Place the poles in the rings,
so that the poles will be on the two sides of the altar
8 when it is carried. Make it hollow, with planks; make it
9 as it was shown to you on the mountain. Make SHEVI'I
the courtyard of the Tabernacle thus: on the south side
there should be hangings a hundred cubits long of finely
spun linen, all the length of the courtyard on that side,
10 with twenty posts and their twenty bronze sockets. The
11 hooks and bands of the posts shall be of silver. Likewise
on the north side; the hangings shall be a hundred cubits
long, with twenty posts and their twenty corresponding
12 bronze sockets, with hooks and bands of silver. The width
of the hangings at the western end of the courtyard shall
be fifty cubits, and it should have ten posts and their ten
13 corresponding sockets. The width of the courtyard at the
14 front, facing east, shall be fifty cubits: fifteen cubits of

---

Talmud says that when a man divorces his first wife, "the altar sheds tears" (Gittin 90b). What is the connection between the altar and a marriage? Both, he said, are about sacrifices. Marriages fail when the partners are unwilling to make sacrifices for one another.

In the eleventh century, Rabbi Yehuda HaLevi expressed something close to awe at the fact that Jews stayed Jewish despite the fact that "with a word lightly spoken" they could have converted to the majority faith and lived a life of relative ease (*Kuzari* IV:23). Jews and Judaism survived despite the many sacrifices people had to make for it. Equally possible, though, is that Judaism survived *because* of those sacrifices. Where people make sacrifices for their ideals, the ideals stay strong. Not all sacrifice is holy. But the principle of sacrifice remains. It is the gift we bring to what and whom we love.

חָמֵשׁ אַמּוֹת אֹרֶךְ וְחָמֵשׁ אַמּוֹת רֹחַב רָבוּעַ יִהְיֶה הַמִּזְבֵּחַ
ב וְשָׁלֹשׁ אַמּוֹת קֹמָתוֹ׃ וְעָשִׂיתָ קַרְנֹתָיו עַל אַרְבַּע פִּנֹּתָיו מִמֶּנּוּ
ג תִּהְיֶיןָ קַרְנֹתָיו וְצִפִּיתָ אֹתוֹ נְחֹשֶׁת׃ וְעָשִׂיתָ סִּירֹתָיו לְדַשְּׁנוֹ
וְיָעָיו וּמִזְרְקֹתָיו וּמִזְלְגֹתָיו וּמַחְתֹּתָיו לְכָל־כֵּלָיו תַּעֲשֶׂה
ד נְחֹשֶׁת׃ וְעָשִׂיתָ לּוֹ מִכְבָּר מַעֲשֵׂה רֶשֶׁת נְחֹשֶׁת וְעָשִׂיתָ
ה עַל־הָרֶשֶׁת אַרְבַּע טַבְּעֹת נְחֹשֶׁת עַל אַרְבַּע קְצוֹתָיו׃ וְנָתַתָּה
אֹתָהּ תַּחַת כַּרְכֹּב הַמִּזְבֵּחַ מִלְּמָטָּה וְהָיְתָה הָרֶשֶׁת עַד
ו חֲצִי הַמִּזְבֵּחַ׃ וְעָשִׂיתָ בַדִּים לַמִּזְבֵּחַ בַּדֵּי עֲצֵי שִׁטִּים וְצִפִּיתָ
ז אֹתָם נְחֹשֶׁת׃ וְהוּבָא אֶת־בַּדָּיו בַּטַּבָּעֹת וְהָיוּ הַבַּדִּים עַל־
ח שְׁתֵּי צַלְעֹת הַמִּזְבֵּחַ בִּשְׂאֵת אֹתוֹ׃ נְבוּב לֻחֹת תַּעֲשֶׂה אֹתוֹ
ט כַּאֲשֶׁר הֶרְאָה אֹתְךָ בָּהָר כֵּן יַעֲשׂוּ׃ וְעָשִׂיתָ שביעי
אֵת חֲצַר הַמִּשְׁכָּן לִפְאַת נֶגֶב־תֵּימָנָה קְלָעִים לֶחָצֵר שֵׁשׁ
י מָשְׁזָר מֵאָה בָאַמָּה אֹרֶךְ לַפֵּאָה הָאֶחָת׃ וְעַמֻּדָיו עֶשְׂרִים
וְאַדְנֵיהֶם עֶשְׂרִים נְחֹשֶׁת וָוֵי הָעַמֻּדִים וַחֲשֻׁקֵיהֶם כָּסֶף׃
יא וְכֵן לִפְאַת צָפוֹן בָּאֹרֶךְ קְלָעִים מֵאָה אֹרֶךְ וְעַמֻּדָו עֶשְׂרִים
וְאַדְנֵיהֶם עֶשְׂרִים נְחֹשֶׁת וָוֵי הָעַמֻּדִים וַחֲשֻׁקֵיהֶם כָּסֶף׃
יב וְרֹחַב הֶחָצֵר לִפְאַת־יָם קְלָעִים חֲמִשִּׁים אַמָּה עַמֻּדֵיהֶם
יג עֲשָׂרָה וְאַדְנֵיהֶם עֲשָׂרָה׃ וְרֹחַב הֶחָצֵר לִפְאַת קֵדְמָה מִזְרָחָה
יד חֲמִשִּׁים אַמָּה׃ וַחֲמֵשׁ עֶשְׂרֵה אַמָּה קְלָעִים לַכָּתֵף עַמֻּדֵיהֶם

the foundation of the rational pursuit of self-interest.

There was nothing wrong with this. It was an attempt to create peace in a Europe that had for centuries been ravaged by war. The democratic state and the market economy were serious attempts to harness the power of self-interest to combat the destructive passions that led to violence. The fact that politics and economics were based on self-interest did not negate the possibility that families and communities were sustained by altruism. It was a good system, not a bad one.

Now, however, after several centuries, the idea of love-as-sacrifice has grown thin in many areas of life. We see this specifically in relationships. *Lose the concept of sacrifice within a society, and sooner or later marriage falters, parenthood declines, and the society slowly ages and dies.* My predecessor, Lord Jakobovits, had a lovely way of putting this. The

hangings with three posts and three sockets on one side,
15 and fifteen cubits of hangings with three posts and three
16 sockets on the other, and for the gate of the courtyard
there shall be an embroidered screen of twenty cubits of
sky-blue, purple, and scarlet wool and finely spun linen,
17 with four posts and four sockets. All the posts around the MAFTIR
courtyard should be banded with silver. Their hooks shall
18 be of silver, and their sockets of bronze. The courtyard
shall be a hundred cubits long, fifty cubits wide, and
five cubits high, with hangings of finely spun linen and
19 sockets of bronze. All the Tabernacle utensils, for every
use, as well as all its tent pegs and the tent pegs of the
courtyard, shall be of bronze.

The haftara for Parashat Teruma is on page 1488.
On Rosh Ḥodesh Adar I read the haftara on page 1640.
However, on the Shabbat of Parashat Shekalim, even if it also Rosh Ḥodesh or Erev Rosh Ḥodesh Adar, read the haftara on page 1654.

טו שְׁלֹשָׁ֔ה וְאַדְנֵיהֶ֖ם שְׁלֹשָֽׁה׃ וְלַכָּתֵף֙ הַשֵּׁנִ֔ית חֲמֵ֥שׁ עֶשְׂרֵ֖ה
טז קְלָעִ֑ים עַמֻּדֵיהֶ֣ם שְׁלֹשָׁ֔ה וְאַדְנֵיהֶ֖ם שְׁלֹשָֽׁה׃ וּלְשַׁ֨עַר הֶחָצֵ֜ר
מָסָ֣ךְ ׀ עֶשְׂרִ֣ים אַמָּ֗ה תְּכֵ֨לֶת וְאַרְגָּמָ֜ן וְתוֹלַ֧עַת שָׁנִ֛י וְשֵׁ֥שׁ
מָשְׁזָ֖ר מַעֲשֵׂ֣ה רֹקֵ֑ם עַמֻּדֵיהֶם֙ אַרְבָּעָ֔ה וְאַדְנֵיהֶ֖ם אַרְבָּעָֽה׃
יז כׇּל־עַמּוּדֵ֨י הֶחָצֵ֤ר סָבִיב֙ מְחֻשָּׁקִ֣ים כֶּ֔סֶף וָוֵיהֶ֖ם כָּ֑סֶף וְאַדְנֵיהֶ֖ם מפטיר
יח נְחֹֽשֶׁת׃ אֹ֣רֶךְ הֶחָצֵר֩ מֵאָ֨ה בָֽאַמָּ֜ה וְרֹ֣חַב ׀ חֲמִשִּׁ֣ים בַּחֲמִשִּׁ֗ים
יט וְקֹמָ֛ה חָמֵ֥שׁ אַמּ֖וֹת שֵׁ֣שׁ מָשְׁזָ֑ר וְאַדְנֵיהֶ֖ם נְחֹֽשֶׁת׃ לְכֹל֙ כְּלֵ֣י
הַמִּשְׁכָּ֔ן בְּכֹ֖ל עֲבֹדָת֑וֹ וְכׇל־יְתֵדֹתָ֛יו וְכׇל־יִתְדֹ֥ת הֶחָצֵ֖ר
נְחֹֽשֶׁת׃

The הפטרה *for* פרשת תרומה *is on page 1489.*
On ראש חודש אדר א׳ *read the* הפטרה *on page 1641.*
However, on the שבת *of* פרשת שקלים*, even if it also* ראש חודש
or ערב ראש חודש אדר א׳*, read the* הפטרה *on page 1655.*

Parashat Tetzaveh

27 20 Command the Israelites to bring you pure oil from
crushed olives for light, to kindle the lamp, every night.
21 From evening to morning, before the LORD, Aharon and
his sons shall set it up to burn in the Tent of Meeting,
outside the curtain that veils the Ark of the Testimony.
This shall be a rule for all time for the Israelites, throughout
28 1 their generations. From among the Israelites,
draw your brother Aharon and his sons close to you to

---

various Sages who fell ill. When asked, "Are your sufferings precious to you?" they replied, "Neither they nor their reward" (Berakhot 5b). There is no glorification of hardships here. When they befall us or someone close to us, they can lead us to despair. Alternatively, we can respond stoically. We can practice the attribute of *gevura*, strength in adversity. But there is a third possibility. We can respond with compassion, kindness, and love. We can become like the olive which, when crushed, produces the pure oil that fuels the light of holiness.

27:21 אַהֲרֹן וּבָנָיו *Aharon and his sons* – Moshe the prophet dominates four of the five books of the Torah. Tetzaveh, as commentators have noted, is the only *parasha* from the birth of Moshe at the beginning of the book of Exodus to the end of Deuteronomy that does not contain his name. For most of the narrative he is front and center. Here, he is in the background. Several interpretations have been offered.

The Vilna Gaon suggests that it is related to the fact that in most years Parashat Tetzaveh is read during the week in which the seventh of Adar falls: the day of Moshe's death. During this week we sense the loss of the greatest leader in Jewish history – and his absence from Tetzaveh expresses that loss.

The Baal HaTurim (on Ex. 27:20) relates it to Moshe's plea, in next week's *parasha*, for God to forgive Israel. "If not," says Moshe, "please blot me out of the book You have written" (32:32). There is a principle that "the curse of a Sage comes true, even if it was conditional" (Makkot 11a). Thus for one week his name was "blotted out" from the Torah.

Whatever the reason, in Parashat Tetzaveh, for once, it is Aharon, the first of the priests, who holds center stage, undiminished by the rival presence of his brother. For whereas Moshe lit the fire in the souls of the Jewish people, it was Aharon who tended the flame and turned it into a *ner tamid*, literally, "an eternal light."

פרשת תצוה

כז כ וְאַתָּה תְּצַוֶּה ׀ אֶת־בְּנֵי יִשְׂרָאֵל וְיִקְחוּ אֵלֶיךָ שֶׁמֶן זַיִת זָךְ כא
כא כָּתִית לַמָּאוֹר לְהַעֲלֹת נֵר תָּמִיד: בְּאֹהֶל מוֹעֵד מִחוּץ
לַפָּרֹכֶת אֲשֶׁר עַל־הָעֵדֻת יַעֲרֹךְ אֹתוֹ אַהֲרֹן וּבָנָיו מֵעֶרֶב
עַד־בֹּקֶר לִפְנֵי יְהוָה חֻקַּת עוֹלָם לְדֹרֹתָם מֵאֵת בְּנֵי
כח א יִשְׂרָאֵל: וְאַתָּה הַקְרֵב אֵלֶיךָ אֶת־אַהֲרֹן אָחִיךָ

TETZAVEH

In Parashat Tetzaveh, the role of the priests in the service of the Tabernacle takes center stage. For once the limelight is no longer on Moshe, but on his brother Aharon, the High Priest. We read about the task of the priesthood, their robes of office and their consecration, as well as further details about the Tabernacle itself.

For the first time we find the Torah speaking about *sacred vestments,* those of the priests and the High Priest worn while officiating in the sacred place. For the first time too we encounter this phrase, used about the vestments: *lekhavod ulet-iferet,* "for glory and for splendor" (Ex. 28:2). Until this point, *kavod* in the sense of glory or honor was attributed only to God. As for *tiferet,* this is the first time it appears in the Torah.

With Parashat Tetzaveh, something new enters Judaism: *Torat Kohanim,* the world and mindset of the priest. Rapidly it became a central dimension of Judaism. It dominates the next book of the Torah, Leviticus.

27:20 לְהַעֲלֹת נֵר תָּמִיד *To kindle the lamp, every night* – Our *parasha* begins with the words "Command the Israelites to bring you pure oil from crushed olives for light, to kindle the lamp, every night" (Ex. 27:20). The Sages drew a comparison between the olive and the Jewish people:

> R. Yehoshua b. Levi asked: Why is Israel compared to an olive? Just as an olive is first bitter, then sweet, so Israel suffers in the present but great good is stored up for them in the time to come. And just as the olive only yields its oil by being crushed – as it is written, "pure oil from crushed olives for light" – so Israel fulfills [its full potential in] the Torah only when it is pressed by suffering. (*Midrash Pitron Torah* on Num. 13:2)

The oil was, of course, for the candelabrum, whose perpetual light symbolizes the divine light that floods the universe for those who see it through the eyes of faith. To produce this light, the olives must be crushed.

The Talmud gives an account of

serve Me as priests – Aharon and his sons Nadav and
2 Avihu, Elazar and Itamar. Make sacred vestments for your
3 brother Aharon, for glory and for splendor. Speak to all

---

for splendor"? The answer, I suggest, lies in the analysis given by the nineteenth-century sociologist Max Weber. Weber was fascinated by the question of leadership. What is it that gives some individuals authority over others? His most famous insight – it has become part of the language of everyday speech – is that certain rare figures have what he called charisma. Charismatic leaders, by the force of their personality, are able to exercise influence over others.

Yet charisma begins to die almost as soon as it is born. Charismatic authority is personal. It is unique to the individual who wields it, and it cannot be replicated over time. But a group, in order to survive, needs a form of leadership that is resistant to change. That is why, after the appearance in its midst of a charismatic leader, the group must undergo what Weber called the routinization of charisma. This is the process whereby a certain form of authority is vested, not in an individual-as-individual but in an individual (or group) as bearers-of-an-office. Thus charisma is handed down from generation to generation in an orderly and predictable way.

Parashat Tetzaveh describes exactly this in the process through which Moshe invests priestly authority in Aharon and his sons. The *bigdei kehuna*, the "priestly vestments," are its visible symbol. The priests are – by virtue of birth and descent, not personal qualities – the carriers of sacred office. Their work is holy. Their domain is the Tabernacle, the physical embodiment of sacred space. They are charged with mediating between the people and God. Their clothes mark their office and role.

In a famous phrase, the book of Psalms proclaims, "Your priests are robed in righteousness" (Ps. 132:9). It is clear then that the phrase in Tetzaveh, "for glory and for splendor," does not mean "for the glory and splendor of the priest." It means "for the glory of God and the splendor of His presence" (Sforno on Ex. 28:2). The task of the priest – and the message of his clothes – was to be a "signal of transcendence," to point *in* himself to something *beyond* himself, to be a living symbol of the Divine Presence in the midst of the nation.

28:3 וְאַתָּה תְּדַבֵּר *Speak* – Three times the word *ve'ata*, "And you," appears in the Hebrew: "[*And you*] command the Israelites" (about the oil for the candelabrum that Aharon and his sons would keep alight) (Ex. 27:20); "[*And you*] draw your brother Aharon and his sons close to you..." (28:1); "[*And you*] speak to all the skilled craftsmen" (and command them to make the vestments Aharon and the other priests would wear) (28:3). The Torah emphasizes God's

וְאֶת־בָּנָיו אִתּוֹ מִתּוֹךְ בְּנֵי יִשְׂרָאֵל לְכַהֲנוֹ־לִי אַהֲרֹן נָדָב
ב וַאֲבִיהוּא אֶלְעָזָר וְאִיתָמָר בְּנֵי אַהֲרֹן: וְעָשִׂיתָ בִגְדֵי־קֹדֶשׁ
ג לְאַהֲרֹן אָחִיךָ לְכָבוֹד וּלְתִפְאָרֶת: וְאַתָּה תְּדַבֵּר אֶל־כָּל־

28:1 לְכַהֲנוֹ־לִי *To serve Me as priests* – At its heart, Judaism is a priestly religion. We can see this through the very organization of the Mosaic books. They are organized as a chiastic or mirror-image structure, of the form ABCBA. Here is the simplest way of describing it:

- A. Genesis: prehistory of Israel
  - B. Exodus: the journey to Sinai
    - C. Leviticus: priesthood, sacrifice, and holiness
  - B1. Numbers: the journey from Sinai
- A1. Deuteronomy: the future of Israel

In a chiasmus, the key term is the middle one. The middle book of the Pentateuch, Leviticus, is about priests and the service of the Sanctuary. So too is the last third of Exodus (25–40) and the first third of Numbers (1–10). We tend to forget this, because the narrative drama lies elsewhere, and besides, we have not had a Temple and sacrifices for almost two thousand years.

Judaism is a religion of ritual, of repeated daily deeds. It is a religion of holiness whose focus is both on the home and on the house of worship, the successor institution to the Tabernacle. It is a religion of education, and the priests were the first educators (Deut. 30:10; Mal. 2:4–7). All the great achievements of Israel's kings and the incandescent moral passion of Israel's prophets would not have been possible without the continuity and devotion of the priests. This constancy and dedication of the priesthood is beautifully summed up by the opening verses of Tetzaveh. *Kindle the lamp every night… throughout their generations* (Ex. 27:20–21).

PRIESTLY VESTMENTS

With the words "for glory and for splendor," something new enters Jewish life. Never before have we encountered clothes marking off their wearers as holy people charged with a particular function in religious life.

This whole section of the biblical narrative strikes us as strange, given all we know of what has come before. Avraham, Yitzḥak, and Yaakov did not wear special clothes. Nor did Moshe. They were shepherds. They dressed simply. In any event, what they wore is utterly irrelevant to the biblical message. As Erich Auerbach noted in his classic study, "Odysseus' Scar," the great difference between Homer and the Torah is that Homer constantly describes appearances; the Torah rarely does. Throughout Genesis, whenever a garment is a key element in the story, it involves some deception or betrayal.

Why then did God command Moshe to set in motion the making of special garments for the priests, "for glory and

the skilled craftsmen whom I have endowed with a spirit
of wisdom, and have them make Aharon's vestments;
4 these will consecrate him to serve Me as priest. These are
the garments they shall make: a breast piece, an ephod, a
robe, a quilted tunic, a miter, and a sash; sacred vestments
shall they make, for your brother Aharon and his sons to
5 serve Me in. They should use gold, and sky-blue, purple,
and scarlet wool, and fine linen.
6 They are to make the ephod of finely spun linen
embroidered with gold, and sky-blue, purple, and scarlet
7 wool. It should have two shoulder pieces attached to its
8 two edges so that it can be joined together. The decorated
waistband on it shall be like it and of one piece with it,
made of gold, of sky-blue, purple, and scarlet wool, and
9 finely spun linen. Take two rock crystal stones and
10 engrave on them the names of Yisrael's sons: six names on
one stone and the remaining six names on the other, in
11 the order of their birth. Engrave the two stones with the

---

a difference. Why? Rambam gives this explanation:

> In order to exalt the Temple, those who ministered there received great honor, and the priests and Levites were therefore distinguished from the rest. It was commanded that the priest should be clothed properly with the most splendid and fine clothes, "sacred vestments for glory and for splendor"... for the multitude does not estimate man by his true form but by... the beauty of his garments, and the Temple was to be held in great reverence by all. (*Guide for the Perplexed* III:45)

Rambam suggests that to those who really understand the religious life, appearances should not matter, but "the multitude," the masses, are not like that. They are impressed by spectacle, the glitter of gold, the jewels of the breast piece, and the pristine purity of white linen robes.

Taking Rambam a step further, we may note that this chimes with an immense body of recent research into neuroscience, evolutionary psychology, and behavioral economics which has established beyond doubt that we are not, for the most part, rational animals. It is not that we are incapable of reason, but that reason alone does not move us to action. For that, we need emotion – and emotion goes deeper than the prefrontal cortex, the brain's center of conscious reflection. Art speaks

חַכְמֵי־לֵב אֲשֶׁר מִלֵּאתִיו רוּחַ חָכְמָה וְעָשׂוּ אֶת־בִּגְדֵי אַהֲרֹן
ד לְקַדְּשׁוֹ לְכַהֲנוֹ־לִי׃ וְאֵלֶּה הַבְּגָדִים אֲשֶׁר יַעֲשׂוּ חֹשֶׁן וְאֵפוֹד
וּמְעִיל וּכְתֹנֶת תַּשְׁבֵּץ מִצְנֶפֶת וְאַבְנֵט וְעָשׂוּ בִגְדֵי־קֹדֶשׁ
ה לְאַהֲרֹן אָחִיךָ וּלְבָנָיו לְכַהֲנוֹ־לִי׃ וְהֵם יִקְחוּ אֶת־הַזָּהָב
וְאֶת־הַתְּכֵלֶת וְאֶת־הָאַרְגָּמָן וְאֶת־תּוֹלַעַת הַשָּׁנִי וְאֶת־
הַשֵּׁשׁ׃
ו וְעָשׂוּ אֶת־הָאֵפֹד זָהָב תְּכֵלֶת וְאַרְגָּמָן תּוֹלַעַת שָׁנִי וְשֵׁשׁ
ז מָשְׁזָר מַעֲשֵׂה חֹשֵׁב׃ שְׁתֵּי כְתֵפֹת חֹבְרֹת יִהְיֶה־לּוֹ אֶל־שְׁנֵי
ח קְצוֹתָיו וְחֻבָּר׃ וְחֵשֶׁב אֲפֻדָּתוֹ אֲשֶׁר עָלָיו כְּמַעֲשֵׂהוּ מִמֶּנּוּ
ט יִהְיֶה זָהָב תְּכֵלֶת וְאַרְגָּמָן וְתוֹלַעַת שָׁנִי וְשֵׁשׁ מָשְׁזָר׃ וְלָקַחְתָּ
אֶת־שְׁתֵּי אַבְנֵי־שֹׁהַם וּפִתַּחְתָּ עֲלֵיהֶם שְׁמוֹת בְּנֵי יִשְׂרָאֵל׃
י שִׁשָּׁה מִשְּׁמֹתָם עַל הָאֶבֶן הָאֶחָת וְאֶת־שְׁמוֹת הַשִּׁשָּׁה
יא הַנּוֹתָרִים עַל־הָאֶבֶן הַשֵּׁנִית כְּתוֹלְדֹתָם׃ מַעֲשֵׂה חָרַשׁ אֶבֶן

insistence that it be Moshe who bestows this honor on Aharon.

Moshe must show the people – and Aharon himself – that he has the humility, the power of self-effacement, needed to make space for someone else to share in the leadership of the people, someone whose strengths are not his, whose role is different, someone who may be more popular, closer to the people, than Moshe – as in fact Aharon turns out to be.

It takes a special kind of character to make space for those whom one is entitled to see as rivals. Early on, when they met after the revelation at the burning bush, Aharon showed that character in relation to Moshe, and now Moshe is called on to show it in relation to Aharon. True leadership involves humility and magnanimity. The smaller the ego, the greater the leader.

THE AESTHETIC IN JUDAISM

The aesthetic dimension does not always figure prominently in Judaism. The great empires – Mesopotamia, Egypt, Assyria, Babylon, Greece, and Rome – built monumental palaces and temples. Their royal courts were marked by magnificent robes, cloaks, crowns, and regalia. Judaism, by contrast, often seems almost puritanical in its avoidance of pomp and display. Worshipping the invisible God, Judaism tended to devalue the visual in favor of the oral and aural: words heard, rather than appearances seen.

Yet the service of the Tabernacle and Temple were different. Here appearances – dignity, beauty – made

names of Yisrael's sons as a gem cutter engraves a seal, then
12 mount them in gold filigree settings. Place the two stones
on the shoulder pieces of the ephod as remembrance
stones for the sons of Yisrael. Thus will Aharon carry their
names on his shoulders as a remembrance before the
13 14 Lord. Make gold filigree settings and two sets of SHENI
pure gold chains braided into cords, and attach the cords
15 of chains to the settings. Make a breast piece for
judgment. Make it with the same skilled craftsmanship as
the ephod: of gold, of sky-blue, purple, and scarlet wool,
16 and of finely spun linen. It shall be square and folded
17 double, a span long and a span wide. Mount four rows of
precious stones onto it: the first row a carnelian, an
18 olivine, and a garnet; the second row an emerald, a lapis
19 lazuli, and a green quartz; the third row an amber, a jet,
20 and a sardonyx; and the fourth an aquamarine, a rock
crystal, and an opal. Mount them in gold filigree settings.
21 The stones shall correspond to the names of Yisrael's
sons. Each stone should be engraved like a seal, with one
22 of the names of the twelve tribes. Make chains of pure

---

piece were then woven (Yoma 72a). The *ḥoshen* – the breast piece – is a piece of fabric woven of this yarn and then folded over with the Urim and Tumim placed inside. On its front, twelve precious stones bearing the names of the twelve tribes are attached in a golden setting.

The detailed descriptions of these beautiful objects confirm what we noted above: that there is a place for the aesthetic in *avoda*, divine service. In the words of the Song of the Sea: *Zeh Keli ve'anvehu*, "This is my God, I will glorify Him" (Ex. 15:3). For beauty inspires love, and from love flows the service of the heart.

28:21 בְּנֵי־יִשְׂרָאֵל... לִשְׁנֵי עָשָׂר שָׁבֶט *Yisrael's sons.... the twelve tribes* – The families descended from Yaakov were clans when the book began. Now they are tribes. For the next several centuries, Israel will remain an amphictyony: a federation of tribes.

The central insight of monotheism is that if God is the parent of humanity, then we are all members of a single family. The Enlightenment gave us the concept of universal rights, but this remains a thin morality, stronger in abstract ideas than in its grip on the moral imagination. Far more powerful is the biblical idea that those in need are our brothers and sisters. Early Israelite religion was the attempt to create

פִּתּוּחֵי חֹתָם תְּפַתַּח אֶת־שְׁתֵּי הָאֲבָנִים עַל־שְׁמֹת בְּנֵי
יב יִשְׂרָאֵל מֻסַבֹּת מִשְׁבְּצוֹת זָהָב תַּעֲשֶׂה אֹתָם: וְשַׂמְתָּ אֶת־
שְׁתֵּי הָאֲבָנִים עַל כִּתְפֹת הָאֵפֹד אַבְנֵי זִכָּרֹן לִבְנֵי יִשְׂרָאֵל
וְנָשָׂא אַהֲרֹן אֶת־שְׁמוֹתָם לִפְנֵי יְהוָה עַל־שְׁתֵּי כְתֵפָיו
יג יד לְזִכָּרֹן: וְעָשִׂיתָ מִשְׁבְּצֹת זָהָב: וּשְׁתֵּי שַׁרְשְׁרֹת שני
זָהָב טָהוֹר מִגְבָּלֹת תַּעֲשֶׂה אֹתָם מַעֲשֵׂה עֲבֹת וְנָתַתָּה אֶת־
טו שַׁרְשְׁרֹת הָעֲבֹתֹת עַל־הַמִּשְׁבְּצֹת: וְעָשִׂיתָ חֹשֶׁן
מִשְׁפָּט מַעֲשֵׂה חֹשֵׁב כְּמַעֲשֵׂה אֵפֹד תַּעֲשֶׂנּוּ זָהָב תְּכֵלֶת
טז וְאַרְגָּמָן וְתוֹלַעַת שָׁנִי וְשֵׁשׁ מָשְׁזָר תַּעֲשֶׂה אֹתוֹ: רָבוּעַ יִהְיֶה
יז כָּפוּל זֶרֶת אָרְכּוֹ וְזֶרֶת רָחְבּוֹ: וּמִלֵּאתָ בוֹ מִלֻּאַת אֶבֶן
אַרְבָּעָה טוּרִים אָבֶן טוּר אֹדֶם פִּטְדָה וּבָרֶקֶת הַטּוּר הָאֶחָד:
יח יט וְהַטּוּר הַשֵּׁנִי נֹפֶךְ סַפִּיר וְיַהֲלֹם: וְהַטּוּר הַשְּׁלִישִׁי לֶשֶׁם שְׁבוֹ
כ וְאַחְלָמָה: וְהַטּוּר הָרְבִיעִי תַּרְשִׁישׁ וְשֹׁהַם וְיָשְׁפֵה מְשֻׁבָּצִים
כא זָהָב יִהְיוּ בְּמִלּוּאֹתָם: וְהָאֲבָנִים תִּהְיֶיןָ עַל־שְׁמֹת בְּנֵי־
יִשְׂרָאֵל שְׁתֵּים עֶשְׂרֵה עַל־שְׁמֹתָם פִּתּוּחֵי חוֹתָם אִישׁ עַל־
כב שְׁמוֹ תִּהְיֶיןָ לִשְׁנֵי עָשָׂר שָׁבֶט: וְעָשִׂיתָ עַל־הַחֹשֶׁן שַׁרְשֹׁת

to emotion. It moves us in ways that go deeper than words.

That is why great art has a spirituality that applies to the visual beauty and pageantry of the service of Tabernacle and Temple. We can define now the nature of the aesthetic in Judaism. It is art devoted to the greater glory of God. That is the implication of the fact that the word *kavod*, "glory," is attributed in the Torah only to God – and to the priest officiating in the House of God.

Judaism does not believe in art for art's sake, but in art in the service of God. Art gives back as a votive offering to God a little of the beauty He has made in this created world.

28:15 וְעָשִׂיתָ חֹשֶׁן *Make a breast piece* – The Torah instructs Moshe to use five different fibers for the priestly vestments (Ex. 28:5): gold thread; finely twisted linen (see Rashi on Ex. 25:4); and wool dyed in three different colors – sky-blue, purple, and scarlet. Six threads of each of the four fibers were spun together with a single gold thread to create one yarn. This composite yarn was then further spun to produce a yarn of twenty-eight threads from which the ephod and breast

23 gold, braided into cords, for the breast piece. Make the
breast piece two gold rings and attach them to its two
24 corners. Then fasten the two gold chains to the two gold
25 rings at the corners of the breast piece. Attach the other
ends of the chains to the two settings. They will thus be
26 joined to the ephod's shoulder pieces at the front. Make
two gold rings and place them at the two other corners of
the breast piece on the edge, inside, next to the ephod.
27 Make two more gold rings and attach them to the bottom
of the ephod's two shoulder pieces facing its front, close
28 to its seam and above the ephod's woven waistband. The
breast piece shall be held in place by a cord of sky blue
from its rings to the rings of the ephod, so that the breast
piece remains secured above the ephod's waistband, and
29 does not come loose from the ephod. Thus will Aharon
carry the names of Yisrael's sons on the breast piece of
judgment at his heart whenever he enters the Sanctuary,

had gone out in the field toward evening to meditate" (24:63). Yaakov instituted the evening prayer when he received his vision, at night, of a ladder stretching from earth to heaven (28:12–15). The Sages cited prooftexts to show that each of these was an occasion of prayer.

According to R. Yehoshua b. Levi, however, the prayers correspond to the daily sacrifices: The morning and afternoon prayers represent the morning and afternoon offerings. The evening prayer mirrors the completion of the sacrificial process (the burning of the limbs), which was done at night.

When prophets prayed, they used words. They addressed God directly in speech. Prophetic prayer in the Bible is spontaneous. We think of Avraham's prayer on behalf of Sedom and Amora, Yaakov's prayer before his encounter with Esav, Moshe's prayer to God to forgive the Israelites after the golden calf. No two such prayers are alike.

Quite different was the service of the priests. Here, what was primary was the sacrifice, not the words – in fact, for the most part the priestly worship took place in silence. The actions of the priests were precisely regulated; moreover, any deviation, such as the spontaneous offering of Aharon's two sons, Nadav and Avihu, was fraught with danger. The priests did the same thing, in the same place, at the same time, following a daily, weekly, monthly, and yearly cycle.

The patriarchs spoke to God because they felt moved to do so, not because there was an obligation to pray. Throughout the biblical era, the primary form

כג גַּבְלֻת מַעֲשֵׂה עֲבֹת זָהָב טָהוֹר: וְעָשִׂיתָ עַל־הַחֹשֶׁן שְׁתֵּי
טַבְּעוֹת זָהָב וְנָתַתָּ אֶת־שְׁתֵּי הַטַּבָּעוֹת עַל־שְׁנֵי קְצוֹת
כד הַחֹשֶׁן: וְנָתַתָּה אֶת־שְׁתֵּי עֲבֹתֹת הַזָּהָב עַל־שְׁתֵּי הַטַּבָּעֹת
כה אֶל־קְצוֹת הַחֹשֶׁן: וְאֵת שְׁתֵּי קְצוֹת שְׁתֵּי הָעֲבֹתֹת תִּתֵּן
עַל־שְׁתֵּי הַמִּשְׁבְּצוֹת וְנָתַתָּה עַל־כִּתְפוֹת הָאֵפֹד אֶל־מוּל
כו פָּנָיו: וְעָשִׂיתָ שְׁתֵּי טַבְּעוֹת זָהָב וְשַׂמְתָּ אֹתָם עַל־שְׁנֵי קְצוֹת
כז הַחֹשֶׁן עַל־שְׂפָתוֹ אֲשֶׁר אֶל־עֵבֶר הָאֵפוֹד בָּיְתָה: וְעָשִׂיתָ
שְׁתֵּי טַבְּעוֹת זָהָב וְנָתַתָּה אֹתָם עַל־שְׁתֵּי כִתְפוֹת הָאֵפוֹד
מִלְּמַטָּה מִמּוּל פָּנָיו לְעֻמַּת מֶחְבַּרְתּוֹ מִמַּעַל לְחֵשֶׁב הָאֵפוֹד:
כח וְיִרְכְּסוּ אֶת־הַחֹשֶׁן מִטַּבְּעֹתָו אֶל־טַבְּעֹת הָאֵפוֹד בִּפְתִיל
תְּכֵלֶת לִהְיוֹת עַל־חֵשֶׁב הָאֵפוֹד וְלֹא־יִזַּח הַחֹשֶׁן מֵעַל
כט הָאֵפוֹד: וְנָשָׂא אַהֲרֹן אֶת־שְׁמוֹת בְּנֵי־יִשְׂרָאֵל בְּחֹשֶׁן
הַמִּשְׁפָּט עַל־לִבּוֹ בְּבֹאוֹ אֶל־הַקֹּדֶשׁ לְזִכָּרֹן לִפְנֵי־יְהוָה

a heterogenous, classless, decentralized association of tribes conceived as a brotherhood – and at least in larger measure than in Canaanite society, as a sisterhood – of social, economic, and political equals. When the High Priest carries the people's "remembrance before the Lord" (Ex. 28:29), then it is not in the form of one name, one symbol, but of twelve: twelve brothers, twelve stones, all different, all precious.

PROPHETIC AND PRIESTLY PRAYER

The breast piece with its Urim and Tumim will perform the function of an oracle, something through which the High Priest can discern God's instructions. The prophets, too, convey God's will. What then is the difference between them? Priests and prophets represent not just two different roles, but two different ways of being, two distinct modes of consciousness. This is reflected in a talmudic debate on the nature of prayer:

> It has been stated: R. Yosei son of R. Ḥanina said: The [morning, afternoon, and evening] prayers were instituted by the patriarchs. R. Yehoshua b. Levi said: The prayers were instituted to replace the daily sacrifices. (Berakhot 26b)

According to R. Yosei son of R. Ḥanina, the patriarchs set the precedent for prayer. Avraham established the morning prayer, as it is said, "Avraham rose early the next morning and returned to the place where he had stood before the Lord" (Gen. 19:27). Yitzḥak instituted the afternoon prayer, as it is said, "He

30 as a remembrance before the LORD at all times. Place the
Urim and Tumim in the breast piece of judgment so that
they too will be at Aharon's heart when he comes before
the LORD. Aharon will then always be carrying at his heart
31 Israel's means of judgment, before the LORD. Make SHELISHI
32 the robe of the ephod entirely of sky-blue wool. It should
have an opening for the head in the middle with a woven
border around it like the neck of a coat of mail, so that it
33 does not tear. Around the hem of the robe make
pomegranates of sky-blue, purple, and scarlet wool, and
34 between them put gold bells, so that gold bells and
pomegranates alternate around the hem of the robe.
35 Aharon shall wear this robe whenever he ministers, and
its sound will be heard when he enters the Sanctuary
before the LORD and when he leaves, so that he will not
36 die. Make a headplate of pure gold and
37 engrave on it, as on a seal: Holy to the LORD. Attach a
cord of sky blue to it, so that it can be fixed to the miter,

---

the presence of the aesthetic dimension of the service of the Sanctuary. It had beauty, gravitas, and majesty. In the time of the Temple it had music. There were choirs of Levites singing psalms. Beauty speaks to emotion and emotion to the soul, lifting us in ways reason cannot do to heights of love and awe, taking us above the narrow confines of the self into the circle at whose center is God.

The Sanctuary and priesthood introduced into Jewish life the ethic of *kedusha*, holiness, which strengthened the values of loyalty, respect, and the sacred by creating an environment of reverence, the humility felt by the people once they had these symbols of the Divine Presence in their midst. As Rambam wrote in a famous passage in *Guide for the Perplexed* (III:51), we do not act when in the presence of a king as we do when we are merely in the company of friends or family. In the Sanctuary people sensed they were in the presence of the King.

Reverence gives power to ritual, ceremony, social conventions, and civilities. It helps transform autonomous individuals into a collectively responsible group. You cannot sustain a national identity or even a marriage without loyalty. You cannot socialize successive generations without respect for figures of authority. You cannot defend the nonnegotiable value of human dignity without a sense of the sacred. That is why the prophetic ethic of justice and compassion had to be supplemented with the priestly ethic of holiness.

ל תָּמִיד: וְנָתַתָּ אֶל־חֹשֶׁן הַמִּשְׁפָּט אֶת־הָאוּרִים וְאֶת־הַתֻּמִּים
וְהָיוּ עַל־לֵב אַהֲרֹן בְּבֹאוֹ לִפְנֵי יְהוָה וְנָשָׂא אַהֲרֹן אֶת־מִשְׁפַּט
לא בְּנֵי־יִשְׂרָאֵל עַל־לִבּוֹ לִפְנֵי יְהוָה תָּמִיד: וְעָשִׂיתָ שלישי
לב אֶת־מְעִיל הָאֵפוֹד כְּלִיל תְּכֵלֶת: וְהָיָה פִי־רֹאשׁוֹ בְּתוֹכוֹ
שָׂפָה יִהְיֶה לְפִיו סָבִיב מַעֲשֵׂה אֹרֵג כְּפִי תַחְרָא יִהְיֶה־לּוֹ לֹא
לג יִקָּרֵעַ: וְעָשִׂיתָ עַל־שׁוּלָיו רִמֹּנֵי תְּכֵלֶת וְאַרְגָּמָן וְתוֹלַעַת שָׁנִי
לד עַל־שׁוּלָיו סָבִיב וּפַעֲמֹנֵי זָהָב בְּתוֹכָם סָבִיב: פַּעֲמֹן זָהָב
לה וְרִמּוֹן פַּעֲמֹן זָהָב וְרִמּוֹן עַל־שׁוּלֵי הַמְּעִיל סָבִיב: וְהָיָה עַל־
אַהֲרֹן לְשָׁרֵת וְנִשְׁמַע קוֹלוֹ בְּבֹאוֹ אֶל־הַקֹּדֶשׁ לִפְנֵי יְהוָה
לו וּבְצֵאתוֹ וְלֹא יָמוּת: וְעָשִׂיתָ צִּיץ זָהָב טָהוֹר
לז וּפִתַּחְתָּ עָלָיו פִּתּוּחֵי חֹתָם קֹדֶשׁ לַיהוָה: וְשַׂמְתָּ אֹתוֹ עַל־
פְּתִיל תְּכֵלֶת וְהָיָה עַל־הַמִּצְנָפֶת אֶל־מוּל פְּנֵי־הַמִּצְנֶפֶת

of organized worship was the sacrifices offered by the priests, first in the Tabernacle, later in the Temple, on behalf of the whole people. Only when the Temple was destroyed did prayer replace sacrifice. For Rambam, at the heart of prayer is the prophetic experience of the individual in conversation with God. For Ramban, by contrast, prayer is the collective worship of the Jewish people, a continuation of the pattern set by the Temple service.

Jewish prayer as it has existed for almost two thousand years is a synthesis of two modes of biblical spirituality, supremely exemplified by two brothers: Moshe the prophet and Aharon the High Priest. Without the prophetic tradition, we would have no spontaneity. Without the priestly tradition, we would have no continuity. The Rabbis brought together what, for more than a thousand years, had existed apart: the prophetic and priestly traditions, one with its emphasis on the heart, the other with its fixed forms.

Moshe was the lonely man of faith, wrestling with God. Aharon was closer to the community, ministering to God on their behalf. Our heritage derives from both. The priestly dimension of worship – collective, structured, never changing – is the other hemisphere of the Jewish mind, the voice of eternity in the midst of time.

28:35 וְלֹא יָמוּת *So that he will not die* – Transgression of this dress code would condemn the priest to death. A deep solemnity surrounds the beauty. The service of the Sanctuary performed by the priests in their vestments worn *lekhavod*, "for glory," established the principle of respect. That explains, as we have noted,

38 affixed to the miter's front. It shall remain on Aharon's
forehead, that Aharon may bear away all guilt that arises
from the holy offerings the Israelites consecrate, from
all their sacred gifts; it shall be on his forehead always,
39 that they may find favor in the LORD's sight. Quilt the
tunic of fine linen. Make a miter out of fine linen, and
40 an embroidered sash. Make tunics, sashes, and caps for
41 Aharon's sons, for glory and for splendor. Put these on
your brother Aharon and his sons; then anoint, ordain,
42 and consecrate them to serve Me as priests. Make them
linen trousers to cover their nakedness, reaching from
43 waist to thigh. They must be worn by Aharon and his sons
whenever they enter the Tent of Meeting or approach the
altar to minister in the Sanctuary so that they do not incur
guilt and die. This shall be a law for Aharon and his
29 1 descendants for all time. This is what you must REVI'I
do to consecrate them to serve Me as priests. Take a young
2 bull, two unblemished rams, and unleavened bread,
unleavened loaves mixed with oil, and unleavened wafers
3 brushed with oil – all made of fine wheat flour. Place these
in a basket and bring them in the basket together with the

---

between Moshe and Aharon. Here, for the first time, there is no hint of sibling rivalry (some develops later in Numbers 12, but is resolved by Moshe's humility). The brothers work together from the very outset of the mission to lead the Israelites to freedom. They address the people together. They stand together when confronting Pharaoh. They perform signs and wonders together. They share leadership in the wilderness together. For the first time, brothers function as a team, with different gifts, different talents, different roles, but without hostility, each complementing the other.

The story of Aharon and Moshe, the fifth chapter in the biblical story of brotherhood, is where, finally, fraternity reaches the heights. And that surely is the meaning of Psalm 133, with its explicit reference to Aharon and his sacred garments: "How good and pleasant it is when brothers dwell together – like fragrant oil on the head flowing down onto the beard, Aharon's beard that flows down over the collar of his robes" (Ps. 133:1–2). It was thanks to Aharon, and the honor he showed Moshe, that at last brothers learned to live together in unity.

לח יִהְיֶה: וְהָיָה עַל־מֵצַח אַהֲרֹן וְנָשָׂא אַהֲרֹן אֶת־עֲוֺן הַקֳּדָשִׁים
אֲשֶׁר יַקְדִּישׁוּ בְּנֵי יִשְׂרָאֵל לְכָל־מַתְּנֹת קָדְשֵׁיהֶם וְהָיָה
לט עַל־מִצְחוֹ תָּמִיד לְרָצוֹן לָהֶם לִפְנֵי יהוה: וְשִׁבַּצְתָּ הַכְּתֹנֶת
שֵׁשׁ וְעָשִׂיתָ מִצְנֶפֶת שֵׁשׁ וְאַבְנֵט תַּעֲשֶׂה מַעֲשֵׂה רֹקֵם:
מ וְלִבְנֵי אַהֲרֹן תַּעֲשֶׂה כֻתֳּנֹת וְעָשִׂיתָ לָהֶם אַבְנֵטִים וּמִגְבָּעוֹת
מא תַּעֲשֶׂה לָהֶם לְכָבוֹד וּלְתִפְאָרֶת: וְהִלְבַּשְׁתָּ אֹתָם אֶת־אַהֲרֹן
אָחִיךָ וְאֶת־בָּנָיו אִתּוֹ וּמָשַׁחְתָּ אֹתָם וּמִלֵּאתָ אֶת־יָדָם
מב וְקִדַּשְׁתָּ אֹתָם וְכִהֲנוּ־לִי: וַעֲשֵׂה לָהֶם מִכְנְסֵי־בָד לְכַסּוֹת
מג בְּשַׂר עֶרְוָה מִמָּתְנַיִם וְעַד־יְרֵכַיִם יִהְיוּ: וְהָיוּ עַל־אַהֲרֹן וְעַל־
בָּנָיו בְּבֹאָם ׀ אֶל־אֹהֶל מוֹעֵד אוֹ בְגִשְׁתָּם אֶל־הַמִּזְבֵּחַ לְשָׁרֵת
בַּקֹּדֶשׁ וְלֹא־יִשְׂאוּ עָוֺן וָמֵתוּ חֻקַּת עוֹלָם לוֹ וּלְזַרְעוֹ
כט א אַחֲרָיו: וְזֶה הַדָּבָר אֲשֶׁר תַּעֲשֶׂה לָהֶם לְקַדֵּשׁ כב רביעי
אֹתָם לְכַהֵן לִי לְקַח פַּר אֶחָד בֶּן־בָּקָר וְאֵילִם שְׁנַיִם תְּמִימִם:
ב וְלֶחֶם מַצּוֹת וְחַלֹּת מַצֹּת בְּלוּלֹת בַּשֶּׁמֶן וּרְקִיקֵי מַצּוֹת
ג מְשֻׁחִים בַּשָּׁמֶן סֹלֶת חִטִּים תַּעֲשֶׂה אֹתָם: וְנָתַתָּ אוֹתָם
עַל־סַל אֶחָד וְהִקְרַבְתָּ אֹתָם בַּסָּל וְאֶת־הַפָּר וְאֵת שְׁנֵי

28:43 חֻקַּת עוֹלָם לוֹ וּלְזַרְעוֹ אַחֲרָיו *A law for Aharon and his descendants for all time* – One of the recurring themes of Genesis is sibling rivalry. This story is told, at ever-increasing length, four times: between Kayin and Hevel, Yitzḥak and Yishmael, Yaakov and Esav, and Yosef and his brothers.

There is an identifiable pattern to this set of narratives, best seen in the way each ends. The story of Kayin and Hevel ends with murder, fratricide. Yitzḥak and Yishmael – though they grow up apart – are seen together at Avraham's funeral. Evidently there had been a reconciliation, though this is told between the lines (and spelled out in Midrash), not directly in the text. Yaakov and Esav meet, embrace, and go their separate ways. Yosef and his brothers are reconciled and live together in peace, Yosef providing them with food, land, and protection. Genesis is telling us a story of great consequence. Fraternity – one of the key words of the French Revolution – is not simple or straightforward. It is often fraught with conflict and contention. Yet slowly, brothers can learn that there is another way.

But it is not the end of the story. There is a fifth chapter, the relationship

4 young bull and two rams. Bring Aharon and his sons to
the entrance of the Tent of Meeting, and you shall wash
5 them with water. Then take the vestments and dress
Aharon in the tunic, the robe of the ephod, the ephod
itself, and the breast piece. Fasten the ephod on him by its
6 woven waistband. Put the miter on his head and on the
7 miter place the sacred diadem. Take the anointing oil,
8 pour it on his head, and anoint him. Then bring his sons
9 forward and dress them with the tunics. Gird Aharon and
his sons with the sashes and fasten their headdresses. The
priesthood shall be theirs as a law for all time. Thus you
10 shall ordain Aharon and his sons. Then bring the young
bull in front of the Tent of Meeting, and have Aharon and
11 his sons lay their hands on its head. Slaughter the bull
before the Lord at the entrance of the Tent of Meeting.
12 Take some of the bull's blood and put it on the horns of
the altar with your finger. Pour out the rest of the blood at
13 the base of the altar. Take all the fat that covers the
entrails, the diaphragm of the liver, and the two kidneys
with the fat around them, and burn them on the altar.
14 Burn the bull's flesh, its hide, and its waste outside the
15 camp; it is a purification offering. Then take one of the
rams and have Aharon and his sons lay their hands upon
16 its head, then slaughter it; let them take its blood and
17 sprinkle it on all the sides of the altar. Cut the ram into
pieces, wash its entrails and legs, and put them with its
18 pieces and its head. Burn the entire ram on the altar. It is
a burnt offering to the Lord, a pleasing aroma, a fire
19 offering to the Lord. Then take the second ram, and have HAMISHI
20 Aharon and his sons lay their hands on its head. Slaughter
the ram, take some of its blood and put it on the ridges of
the right ears of Aharon and his sons, and on the thumbs
of their right hands and on the big toes of their right feet.
Sprinkle the rest of the blood on the sides of the altar.
21 Collect some of the blood on the altar and some of the
anointing oil and sprinkle it on Aharon and his vestments,
and on his sons and his sons' vestments. Then he, and his

ד הָאֵילִם׃ וְאֶת־אַהֲרֹן וְאֶת־בָּנָיו תַּקְרִיב אֶל־פֶּתַח אֹהֶל מוֹעֵד
ה וְרָחַצְתָּ אֹתָם בַּמָּיִם׃ וְלָקַחְתָּ אֶת־הַבְּגָדִים וְהִלְבַּשְׁתָּ אֶת־
אַהֲרֹן אֶת־הַכֻּתֹּנֶת וְאֵת מְעִיל הָאֵפֹד וְאֶת־הָאֵפֹד וְאֶת־
ו הַחֹשֶׁן וְאָפַדְתָּ לוֹ בְּחֵשֶׁב הָאֵפֹד׃ וְשַׂמְתָּ הַמִּצְנֶפֶת עַל־רֹאשׁוֹ
ז וְנָתַתָּ אֶת־נֵזֶר הַקֹּדֶשׁ עַל־הַמִּצְנָפֶת׃ וְלָקַחְתָּ אֶת־שֶׁמֶן
ח הַמִּשְׁחָה וְיָצַקְתָּ עַל־רֹאשׁוֹ וּמָשַׁחְתָּ אֹתוֹ׃ וְאֶת־בָּנָיו תַּקְרִיב
ט וְהִלְבַּשְׁתָּם כֻּתֳּנֹת׃ וְחָגַרְתָּ אֹתָם אַבְנֵט אַהֲרֹן וּבָנָיו וְחָבַשְׁתָּ
לָהֶם מִגְבָּעֹת וְהָיְתָה לָהֶם כְּהֻנָּה לְחֻקַּת עוֹלָם וּמִלֵּאתָ יַד־
י אַהֲרֹן וְיַד־בָּנָיו׃ וְהִקְרַבְתָּ אֶת־הַפָּר לִפְנֵי אֹהֶל מוֹעֵד וְסָמַךְ
יא אַהֲרֹן וּבָנָיו אֶת־יְדֵיהֶם עַל־רֹאשׁ הַפָּר׃ וְשָׁחַטְתָּ אֶת־הַפָּר
יב לִפְנֵי יְהוָה פֶּתַח אֹהֶל מוֹעֵד׃ וְלָקַחְתָּ מִדַּם הַפָּר וְנָתַתָּה
עַל־קַרְנֹת הַמִּזְבֵּחַ בְּאֶצְבָּעֶךָ וְאֶת־כָּל־הַדָּם תִּשְׁפֹּךְ אֶל־
יג יְסוֹד הַמִּזְבֵּחַ׃ וְלָקַחְתָּ אֶת־כָּל־הַחֵלֶב הַמְכַסֶּה אֶת־הַקֶּרֶב
וְאֵת הַיֹּתֶרֶת עַל־הַכָּבֵד וְאֵת שְׁתֵּי הַכְּלָיֹת וְאֶת־הַחֵלֶב אֲשֶׁר
יד עֲלֵיהֶן וְהִקְטַרְתָּ הַמִּזְבֵּחָה׃ וְאֶת־בְּשַׂר הַפָּר וְאֶת־עֹרוֹ וְאֶת־
טו פִּרְשׁוֹ תִּשְׂרֹף בָּאֵשׁ מִחוּץ לַמַּחֲנֶה חַטָּאת הוּא׃ וְאֶת־הָאַיִל
הָאֶחָד תִּקָּח וְסָמְכוּ אַהֲרֹן וּבָנָיו אֶת־יְדֵיהֶם עַל־רֹאשׁ הָאָיִל׃
טז וְשָׁחַטְתָּ אֶת־הָאָיִל וְלָקַחְתָּ אֶת־דָּמוֹ וְזָרַקְתָּ עַל־הַמִּזְבֵּחַ
יז סָבִיב׃ וְאֶת־הָאַיִל תְּנַתֵּחַ לִנְתָחָיו וְרָחַצְתָּ קִרְבּוֹ וּכְרָעָיו
יח וְנָתַתָּ עַל־נְתָחָיו וְעַל־רֹאשׁוֹ׃ וְהִקְטַרְתָּ אֶת־כָּל־הָאַיִל
הַמִּזְבֵּחָה עֹלָה הוּא לַיהוָה רֵיחַ נִיחוֹחַ אִשֶּׁה לַיהוָה הוּא׃
יט וְלָקַחְתָּ אֵת הָאָיִל הַשֵּׁנִי וְסָמַךְ אַהֲרֹן וּבָנָיו אֶת־יְדֵיהֶם עַל־ חמישי
כ רֹאשׁ הָאָיִל׃ וְשָׁחַטְתָּ אֶת־הָאַיִל וְלָקַחְתָּ מִדָּמוֹ וְנָתַתָּה
עַל־תְּנוּךְ אֹזֶן אַהֲרֹן וְעַל־תְּנוּךְ אֹזֶן בָּנָיו הַיְמָנִית וְעַל־בֹּהֶן
יָדָם הַיְמָנִית וְעַל־בֹּהֶן רַגְלָם הַיְמָנִית וְזָרַקְתָּ אֶת־הַדָּם עַל־
כא הַמִּזְבֵּחַ סָבִיב׃ וְלָקַחְתָּ מִן־הַדָּם אֲשֶׁר עַל־הַמִּזְבֵּחַ וּמִשֶּׁמֶן
הַמִּשְׁחָה וְהִזֵּיתָ עַל־אַהֲרֹן וְעַל־בְּגָדָיו וְעַל־בָּנָיו וְעַל־בִּגְדֵי

sons with him, and their vestments, will be consecrated.
22 From the ram take its fat parts – the broad tail, the fat that
covers the entrails, the diaphragm of the liver, and the
two kidneys with the fat on them – and the right thigh,
23 for this is the ram of ordination. From the basket of
unleavened bread before the Lord, take one loaf of bread,
24 one loaf of oil bread, and one wafer. Place all of these on
the palms of Aharon and his sons, and have them wave
25 them as a wave offering before the Lord. Then take them
from their hands and burn them on the altar with the
burnt offering, for a pleasing aroma before the Lord. It is
26 a fire offering to the Lord. Take the breast of Aharon's
ram of ordination and wave it as a wave offering before
27 the Lord; it shall be your portion. From Aharon and his
sons' ram of ordination, consecrate the breast, the wave
28 offering and the thigh, the upraised gift. These parts shall
be the Israelites' due to Aharon and his sons for all time.
They are the Israelites' gift from their peace offerings,
29 their gift to the Lord. Aharon's sacred vestments shall
pass on to his sons after him. In them they shall be
30 anointed and ordained. The son who succeeds him as
priest, entering the Tent of Meeting to minister in the
31 Sanctuary, shall wear them for seven days. Take the ram
of ordination and, in the sacred precinct, cook its flesh.

Religious ritual and spirituality are two quite different things. Spirituality is the direct encounter with God. Religion is the behavior we adopt when we express our sense of belonging to a group who, at key points in its history, encountered the Divine. You can be spiritual without being religious. You can be religious without being spiritual. It is almost like the distinction between love and marriage. Love is an emotion. Marriage is an institution. They are linked, but they are not the same.

In this respect, religion is like being married to the Divine Presence. A person may experience long stretches of loyalty between the moments of high passion. Spirituality is the poetry of the soul. Religion is the prose. If they come together, however, as they did in the choreography of the wave offering, we may touch upon something of the priests' experience of a life "upraised" and consecrated to God.

כב בָּנָיו אִתּוֹ וְקָדַשׁ הוּא וּבְגָדָיו וּבָנָיו וּבִגְדֵי בָנָיו אִתּוֹ׃ וְלָקַחְתָּ
מִן־הָאַיִל הַחֵלֶב וְהָאַלְיָה וְאֶת־הַחֵלֶב ׀ הַמְכַסֶּה אֶת־הַקֶּרֶב
וְאֵת יֹתֶרֶת הַכָּבֵד וְאֵת ׀ שְׁתֵּי הַכְּלָיֹת וְאֶת־הַחֵלֶב אֲשֶׁר
כג עֲלֵיהֶן וְאֵת שׁוֹק הַיָּמִין כִּי אֵיל מִלֻּאִים הוּא׃ וְכִכַּר לֶחֶם
אַחַת וְחַלַּת לֶחֶם שֶׁמֶן אַחַת וְרָקִיק אֶחָד מִסַּל הַמַּצּוֹת
כד אֲשֶׁר לִפְנֵי יְהוָה׃ וְשַׂמְתָּ הַכֹּל עַל כַּפֵּי אַהֲרֹן וְעַל כַּפֵּי בָנָיו
כה וְהֵנַפְתָּ אֹתָם תְּנוּפָה לִפְנֵי יְהוָה׃ וְלָקַחְתָּ אֹתָם מִיָּדָם
וְהִקְטַרְתָּ הַמִּזְבֵּחָה עַל־הָעֹלָה לְרֵיחַ נִיחוֹחַ לִפְנֵי יְהוָה אִשֶּׁה
כו הוּא לַיהוָה׃ וְלָקַחְתָּ אֶת־הֶחָזֶה מֵאֵיל הַמִּלֻּאִים אֲשֶׁר
לְאַהֲרֹן וְהֵנַפְתָּ אֹתוֹ תְּנוּפָה לִפְנֵי יְהוָה וְהָיָה לְךָ לְמָנָה׃
כז וְקִדַּשְׁתָּ אֵת ׀ חֲזֵה הַתְּנוּפָה וְאֵת שׁוֹק הַתְּרוּמָה אֲשֶׁר הוּנַף
וַאֲשֶׁר הוּרָם מֵאֵיל הַמִּלֻּאִים מֵאֲשֶׁר לְאַהֲרֹן וּמֵאֲשֶׁר לְבָנָיו׃
כח וְהָיָה לְאַהֲרֹן וּלְבָנָיו לְחָק־עוֹלָם מֵאֵת בְּנֵי יִשְׂרָאֵל כִּי תְרוּמָה
הוּא וּתְרוּמָה יִהְיֶה מֵאֵת בְּנֵי־יִשְׂרָאֵל מִזִּבְחֵי שַׁלְמֵיהֶם
כט תְּרוּמָתָם לַיהוָה׃ וּבִגְדֵי הַקֹּדֶשׁ אֲשֶׁר לְאַהֲרֹן יִהְיוּ לְבָנָיו
ל אַחֲרָיו לְמָשְׁחָה בָהֶם וּלְמַלֵּא־בָם אֶת־יָדָם׃ שִׁבְעַת יָמִים
יִלְבָּשָׁם הַכֹּהֵן תַּחְתָּיו מִבָּנָיו אֲשֶׁר יָבֹא אֶל־אֹהֶל מוֹעֵד
לא לְשָׁרֵת בַּקֹּדֶשׁ׃ וְאֵת אֵיל הַמִּלֻּאִים תִּקָּח וּבִשַּׁלְתָּ אֶת־בְּשָׂרוֹ

29:24 תְּנוּפָה לִפְנֵי יהוה *A wave offering before the Lord* – The ritual is described in more detail in the Talmud: "He extends [the offering to each of the four directions] and brings them back, then raises and lowers them. R. Ḥiyya b. Abba says in the name of R. Yoḥanan: He extends it and brings it back in order to dedicate it to Him to whom the four directions belong. He raises and lowers it in order to dedicate it to Him to whom the heavens and earth belong" (Menaḥot 62a). We recognize these gestures from the Sukkot ritual of the four species. The priests enact the ritual side of religion, the side that is perhaps hardest to relate to looking in from the outside.

The Baal Shem Tov, champion of the worship of the heart, compared those atheists who mock religion to a deaf man who for the first time comes upon a violinist playing in the town square while the townspeople, moved by the lilt and rhythm of his playing, dance in joy. Unable to hear the music, he concludes that they are all mad.

32 Aharon and his sons shall eat the meat of the ram, and
the bread in the basket, near the entrance of the Tent of
33 Meeting. They shall eat these things, through which
atonement will be made, to be ordained and consecrated.
Because they are consecrated no layman may eat of them.
34 If any of the meat of the ordination ram or any of the bread
is left over until morning, you shall burn what remains
35 with fire. It must not be eaten, for it is consecrated. This
is what you must do for Aharon and his sons, just as I
have commanded you. Their ordination shall take seven
36 days. Each day, offer a bull as a purification offering for
atonement. Purify the altar by making atonement for it,
37 and consecrate it by anointing it. For seven days, make
atonement for the altar and consecrate it, so that the altar
becomes holy of holies – and anything that touches it will
38 become holy. This is what you shall offer on the SHISHI
39 altar: two yearling lambs each day, with constancy. Offer
one lamb in the morning, and the other in the afternoon.

---

in which various Sages put forward their idea of *klal gadol baTorah*, "the great principle of the Torah." Ben Azzai says it is the verse "This is the book of Adam's descendants: On the day God created humankind, He made them in the likeness of God" (Gen. 5:1). Ben Zoma says that there is a more embracing principle: "Listen, Israel: the LORD our God – the LORD is one" (Deut. 6:4). Ben Nannas says there is a yet more embracing principle: "Love your neighbor as your own self" (Lev. 19:18). Ben Pazi says we find a more embracing principle still. He quotes a verse from this *parasha*: "Offer one lamb in the morning, and the other in the afternoon" (Ex. 29:39). In a word: "routine." The passage concludes: "The law follows Ben Pazi."

The meaning of Ben Pazi's statement is clear: all the high ideals in the world count for little until they are turned into habits of action that become habits of the heart. We can all recall moments of insight when we had a great idea, a transformative thought, the glimpse of a project that could change our lives. A day, a week, or a year later the thought has been forgotten or become a distant memory, at best a might-have-been.

The people who change the world, whether in small or epic ways, are those who turn peak experiences into daily routines, who know that the details matter, and who have developed the discipline of hard work, sustained over time.

Judaism's greatness is that it takes high ideals and exalted visions – the

לב בְּמָקֹם קָדֹשׁ: וְאָכַל אַהֲרֹן וּבָנָיו אֶת־בְּשַׂר הָאַיִל וְאֶת־הַלֶּחֶם
לג אֲשֶׁר בַּסָּל פֶּתַח אֹהֶל מוֹעֵד: וְאָכְלוּ אֹתָם אֲשֶׁר כֻּפַּר בָּהֶם
לְמַלֵּא אֶת־יָדָם לְקַדֵּשׁ אֹתָם וְזָר לֹא־יֹאכַל כִּי־קֹדֶשׁ הֵם:
לד וְאִם־יִוָּתֵר מִבְּשַׂר הַמִּלֻּאִים וּמִן־הַלֶּחֶם עַד־הַבֹּקֶר וְשָׂרַפְתָּ
לה אֶת־הַנּוֹתָר בָּאֵשׁ לֹא יֵאָכֵל כִּי־קֹדֶשׁ הוּא: וְעָשִׂיתָ לְאַהֲרֹן
וּלְבָנָיו כָּכָה כְּכֹל אֲשֶׁר־צִוִּיתִי אֹתָכָה שִׁבְעַת יָמִים תְּמַלֵּא
לו יָדָם: וּפַר חַטָּאת תַּעֲשֶׂה לַיּוֹם עַל־הַכִּפֻּרִים וְחִטֵּאתָ עַל־
לז הַמִּזְבֵּחַ בְּכַפֶּרְךָ עָלָיו וּמָשַׁחְתָּ אֹתוֹ לְקַדְּשׁוֹ: שִׁבְעַת יָמִים
תְּכַפֵּר עַל־הַמִּזְבֵּחַ וְקִדַּשְׁתָּ אֹתוֹ וְהָיָה הַמִּזְבֵּחַ קֹדֶשׁ קָדָשִׁים
לח כָּל־הַנֹּגֵעַ בַּמִּזְבֵּחַ יִקְדָּשׁ: וְזֶה אֲשֶׁר תַּעֲשֶׂה עַל־ ששי
לט הַמִּזְבֵּחַ כְּבָשִׂים בְּנֵי־שָׁנָה שְׁנַיִם לַיּוֹם תָּמִיד: אֶת־הַכֶּבֶשׂ
הָאֶחָד תַּעֲשֶׂה בַבֹּקֶר וְאֵת הַכֶּבֶשׂ הַשֵּׁנִי תַּעֲשֶׂה בֵּין

29:33 אֲשֶׁר כֻּפַּר בָּהֶם *Through which atonement will be made* – Rituals of atonement are to form a large part of the Tabernacle's, later the Temple's, function. Interestingly, R. Akiva's response to the end of the Temple and its atonement rites is not to be one of mourning, but a paradoxical sense of uplift. Tragedy will not defeat hope. Indeed, it will bring about a spiritual advance. Far from being separated from God, the sinner will now be able to become closer to the Divine Presence. His words are these: "Happy are you, O Israel. Before whom are you being purified and who purifies you? Your Father who is in heaven" (Yoma 85b).

He meant this: Now that there is no Temple and no High Priest, atonement need no longer be vicarious. The sinner can obtain forgiveness directly. All he or she needs to do is confess the sin, express remorse, and resolve not to repeat it in the future. Atonement is no longer mediated by a third party. It needs no priest, no sacrifice, and no Temple ritual. It is a direct relationship between the individual and God. This is one of rabbinic Judaism's most magnificent ideas – the concept, long prefigured in the Torah but never explicitly set out as such, of *teshuva*, the "return" of the sinner to God. This, then, is where our rituals of *teshuva* begin. For now, atonement is enacted publicly. The priests enter their new office in a state of moral and spiritual cleanliness, unburdened by the past.

THE REGULAR BURNT OFFERING

Any form of sustained spiritual growth requires daily effort and regular rituals. Hence the remarkable aggadic passage (brought in the preface of *Ein Yaakov*)

40 With the first lamb offer a tenth measure of fine flour
mixed with a quarter of a hin of beaten oil, and a quarter
41 of a hin of wine as a libation. Offer the other lamb in the
afternoon together with a grain offering and libation as in
the morning, as a pleasing aroma, a fire offering to the
42 LORD. This shall be the regular burnt offering throughout
your generations at the entrance of the Tent of Meeting
before the LORD. There I will meet with you, there I will
43 speak to you, and there I will meet with the Israelites. It
44 will be sanctified by My glory. I will consecrate the Tent
of Meeting and the altar. I will also consecrate Aharon
45 and his sons to serve Me as priests. I will have My presence
46 dwell among the Israelites and I shall be their God. Then
they will know that I am the LORD their God, who
brought them out of Egypt to dwell among them. I am
the LORD their God.
30 1 Make an altar on which to burn incense; make it of acacia SHEVI'I
2 wood. It shall be square, a cubit long, a cubit wide, and
3 two cubits high, its horns of one piece with it. Overlay it
with pure gold on its top, all around its sides, and on its
4 horns, and around it make a gold molding. Make two gold
rings for it under its molding on both sides to hold the
5 staves used to carry it. Make the staves of acacia wood and
6 overlay them with gold. Put it in front of the screen that
veils the Ark of the Testimony, in front of the cover above
7 the Ark, where I will meet with you. Aharon should burn
incense on it every morning when he tends the lamps,
8 and before evening when he lights the lamps. It shall be MAFTIR
a perpetual incense offering before the LORD throughout

---

priestly dimension of Judaism, set out in this *parasha* and throughout the book of Leviticus. These rituals have an effect. We now know through PET and fMRI scans that repeated spiritual exercise reconfigures the brain. It gives us inner resilience. It makes us more grateful. It gives us a sense of basic trust in the source of our being. It shapes our identity, the way we act and talk and think.

The more you seek spiritual heights, the more you need the ritual and routine of halakha, the Jewish "way" to God.

מ הָֽעַרְבָּֽיִם׃ וְעִשָּׂרֹן סֹלֶת בָּלוּל בְּשֶׁמֶן כָּתִית רֶבַע הַהִין וְנֵסֶךְ
מא רְבִיעִת הַהִין יָיִן לַכֶּבֶשׂ הָאֶחָֽד׃ וְאֵת הַכֶּבֶשׂ הַשֵּׁנִי תַּעֲשֶׂה
בֵּין הָֽעַרְבָּיִם כְּמִנְחַת הַבֹּקֶר וּכְנִסְכָּהּ תַּעֲשֶׂה־לָּהּ לְרֵיחַ נִיחֹחַ
מב אִשֶּׁה לַיהוָֽה׃ עֹלַת תָּמִיד לְדֹרֹתֵיכֶם פֶּתַח אֹֽהֶל־מוֹעֵד לִפְנֵי
מג יְהוָה אֲשֶׁר אִוָּעֵד לָכֶם שָׁמָּה לְדַבֵּר אֵלֶיךָ שָֽׁם׃ וְנֹעַדְתִּי שָׁמָּה
מד לִבְנֵי יִשְׂרָאֵל וְנִקְדַּשׁ בִּכְבֹדִֽי׃ וְקִדַּשְׁתִּי אֶת־אֹהֶל מוֹעֵד
וְאֶת־הַמִּזְבֵּחַ וְאֶת־אַהֲרֹן וְאֶת־בָּנָיו אֲקַדֵּשׁ לְכַהֵן לִֽי׃
מה מו וְשָׁכַנְתִּי בְּתוֹךְ בְּנֵי יִשְׂרָאֵל וְהָיִיתִי לָהֶם לֵאלֹהִֽים׃ וְיָדְעוּ כִּי
אֲנִי יְהוָה אֱלֹהֵיהֶם אֲשֶׁר הוֹצֵאתִי אֹתָם מֵאֶרֶץ מִצְרַיִם
לְשָׁכְנִי בְתוֹכָם אֲנִי יְהוָה אֱלֹהֵיהֶֽם׃

ל א וְעָשִׂיתָ מִזְבֵּחַ מִקְטַר קְטֹרֶת עֲצֵי שִׁטִּים תַּעֲשֶׂה אֹתֽוֹ׃ כג שביעי
ב אַמָּה אָרְכּוֹ וְאַמָּה רָחְבּוֹ רָבוּעַ יִהְיֶה וְאַמָּתַיִם קֹמָתוֹ מִמֶּנּוּ
ג קַרְנֹתָֽיו׃ וְצִפִּיתָ אֹתוֹ זָהָב טָהוֹר אֶת־גַּגּוֹ וְאֶת־קִירֹתָיו סָבִיב
ד וְאֶת־קַרְנֹתָיו וְעָשִׂיתָ לּוֹ זֵר זָהָב סָבִֽיב׃ וּשְׁתֵּי טַבְּעֹת זָהָב
תַּעֲשֶׂה־לּוֹ ׀ מִתַּחַת לְזֵרוֹ עַל שְׁתֵּי צַלְעֹתָיו תַּעֲשֶׂה עַל־שְׁנֵי
ה צִדָּיו וְהָיָה לְבָתִּים לְבַדִּים לָשֵׂאת אֹתוֹ בָּהֵֽמָּה׃ וְעָשִׂיתָ
ו אֶת־הַבַּדִּים עֲצֵי שִׁטִּים וְצִפִּיתָ אֹתָם זָהָֽב׃ וְנָתַתָּה אֹתוֹ
לִפְנֵי הַפָּרֹכֶת אֲשֶׁר עַל־אֲרֹן הָעֵדֻת לִפְנֵי הַכַּפֹּרֶת אֲשֶׁר
ז עַל־הָעֵדֻת אֲשֶׁר אִוָּעֵד לְךָ שָֽׁמָּה׃ וְהִקְטִיר עָלָיו אַהֲרֹן
קְטֹרֶת סַמִּים בַּבֹּקֶר בַּבֹּקֶר בְּהֵיטִיבוֹ אֶת־הַנֵּרֹת יַקְטִירֶֽנָּה׃
ח וּבְהַעֲלֹת אַהֲרֹן אֶת־הַנֵּרֹת בֵּין הָעַרְבַּיִם יַקְטִירֶנָּה קְטֹרֶת מפטיר

Judaism is about changing us so that we become creative artists whose greatest creation is our own life. And that needs daily rituals: the Shaḥarit, Minḥa, and Maariv prayers, the food we eat, the way we behave at work or in the home, the choreography of holiness which is the special contribution of the human person as God's image, belief in God's unity, and the love of neighbor – and turns them into patterns of behavior. Halakha, Jewish law, involves a set of routines that, like those of the great creative minds, give discipline to our lives and change the way we feel, think, and act.

9 your generations. Offer no unauthorized incense on it, or
10 any burnt offering, grain offering, or libation. Once a year
Aharon shall make atonement on its horns; once a year,
with the blood of the purification offering of atonement, he
shall make atonement on it, throughout your generations.
It is holy of holies to the LORD."

The haftara for Parashat Tetzaveh is on page 1492.
On the Shabbat of Parashat Zakhor or on Purim Meshulash in Jerusalem read the haftara on page 1658.

ט תָּמִ֛יד לִפְנֵ֥י יְהוָ֖ה לְדֹרֹתֵיכֶֽם׃ לֹֽא־תַעֲל֥וּ עָלָ֛יו קְטֹ֥רֶת זָרָ֖ה
י וְעֹלָ֣ה וּמִנְחָ֑ה וְנֵ֕סֶךְ לֹ֥א תִסְּכ֖וּ עָלָֽיו׃ וְכִפֶּ֤ר אַהֲרֹן֙ עַל־קַרְנֹתָ֔יו
אַחַ֖ת בַּשָּׁנָ֑ה מִדַּ֞ם חַטַּ֣את הַכִּפֻּרִ֗ים אַחַ֤ת בַּשָּׁנָה֙ יְכַפֵּ֣ר עָלָ֔יו
לְדֹרֹ֣תֵיכֶ֔ם קֹֽדֶשׁ־קָֽדָשִׁ֥ים ה֖וּא לַיהוָֽה׃

The הפטרה *for* פרשת תצוה *is on page 1493.*
On the שבת *of* פרשת זכור *or on* פורים משולש *in Jerusalem*
read the הפטרה *on page 1659*

Parashat Ki Tisa

30 11 12 The Lord said to Moshe, "When you take the census of
the Israelites, as you count, each must give ransom for his
life to the Lord, so that no plague strikes them when you
13 count them. Everyone numbered in the census shall give
half a shekel according to the Sanctuary weight, where the

---

assumption that there is strength in numbers. The larger the people, the stronger it is. That is why it is dangerous to count Jews. If we ever came to believe that there is strength in numbers we would, God forbid, give way to despair. For four thousand years the strength of the Jewish people has never lain in numbers.

Where then did it lie? To this the Torah gives an answer of great beauty. In effect, God tells Moshe, "Do not count Jews. *Ask them to give, and then count the contributions.* That is how you measure the strength of the Jewish people." In terms of numbers we are small. But in terms of our contributions, we are vast. In almost every age, Jews have given something special to the world. In one era it was the Tanakh, the most influential document in the history of the world. In later centuries Jews produced a never-ending stream of scholars, saints, poets, and philosophers.

It is not that Jews are brighter, cleverer, more energetic or talented than others. That is a racist doctrine and I reject it. Nor is it that Jews, more than others, are driven to succeed. That is at the heart of much antisemitic propaganda, and it is false. The simple answer, given in the Torah and engraved in Jewish sensibility, is that *to be a Jew is to be asked to give,* to contribute, to make a difference, to help in the monumental task that has engaged Jews since the dawn of our history, to make the world a home for the Divine Presence, a place of justice, compassion, human dignity, and the sanctity of life. Though our ancestors cherished their relationship with God, they never saw it as a privilege. Instead they saw it as a responsibility. God challenged them to give. In that familiar yet astonishing phrase, he invited them to be His "partners in the work of creation" (Shabbat 119b).

30:13 מַחֲצִית הַשֶּׁקֶל *Half a shekel* – Why should each person give specifically *half* a shekel? Moshe is saying: Never think that you need to do it all. Each of us must be conscious that we can't complete the task; we need someone else to make the shekel whole. But neither is our contribution insignificant. We contribute our half, confident that others will join us, perhaps inspired by what we do. We can change the world, but we need partners, and the best way of finding them is to lead by personal example. Virtue is contagious. One good deed begets another. What is important is that we begin.

פרשת כי תשא

ל יא יב וַיְדַבֵּר יְהוָה אֶל־מֹשֶׁה לֵּאמֹר: כִּי תִשָּׂא אֶת־רֹאשׁ בְּנֵי־
יִשְׂרָאֵל לִפְקֻדֵיהֶם וְנָתְנוּ אִישׁ כֹּפֶר נַפְשׁוֹ לַיהוָה בִּפְקֹד
יג אֹתָם וְלֹא־יִהְיֶה בָהֶם נֶגֶף בִּפְקֹד אֹתָם: זֶה ׀ יִתְּנוּ כָּל־הָעֹבֵר
עַל־הַפְּקֻדִים מַחֲצִית הַשֶּׁקֶל בְּשֶׁקֶל הַקֹּדֶשׁ עֶשְׂרִים גֵּרָה

KI TISA

Ki Tisa begins with the final details about the Tabernacle, including a collection of money from the people that is to serve as a census. The *parasha* then moves into high drama with one of the most gripping narratives in Jewish history. The people, panicking in the absence of Moshe (who is up the mountain, receiving the tablets from God), make a golden calf and dance before it. God tells Moshe to go down. Coming down the mountain, and facing Israel, he smashes the tablets, symbol of the covenant. He censures the people, then reascends the mountain in a prolonged attempt to reestablish the shattered relationship. God forgives and proclaims His attributes of mercy, which are part of our liturgy today. Moshe returns, with a second set of tablets, unaware that his face is now radiant.

THE CENSUS

The *parasha* begins with God's command to Moshe to take a census of the people. But it is phrased in a curious manner. Moshe is told not to count the people directly, but obliquely. Each is to give half a shekel and only thus was their number to be calculated.

The verse warns Moshe to do it this way, "so that no plague strikes them when you count them." Evidently, it is dangerous to count Jews. Many centuries later, ignoring this warning, King David took a census of the people, and disaster struck the nation (II Sam. 24). To this day, we do not needlessly count Jews, even to calculate whether there is a minyan (a quorum of ten men) in the synagogue. Our custom is to take a verse with ten words and use that instead. But why is it dangerous to count Jews?

The classic commentators on Exodus 30:12 give several answers. Rashi says that counting is fraught with the danger of the "evil eye." Rabbeinu Baḥya suggests that when people are counted, they are numbered as individuals, separated from the community. There is a danger that an individual's merit may be insufficient to save him from adverse judgment.

I want to suggest another explanation. Why do nations count their numbers? To estimate their strength – military, political, or economic. Behind the ancient practice of counting populations is the

shekel is twenty gerah. This half shekel is an offering to
14 the LORD. Every male over twenty is to be included in the
15 census and must give the LORD's offering. The rich shall
not give more, and the poor shall not give less, than this
half shekel. It is an offering to the LORD to redeem your
16 lives. Take this redemption money from the Israelites
and assign it for the service of the Tent of Meeting. It shall
be a remembrance for the Israelites before the LORD, to
redeem your lives."
17 18 The LORD said to Moshe, "Make a bronze laver with a
bronze base for washing. Place it between the Tent of
19 Meeting and the altar, and put water in it, for Aharon and
20 his sons to wash their hands and feet. When they enter
the Tent of Meeting or approach the altar to minister by
presenting a food offering to the LORD, they must wash
21 with water, so that they do not die. They must wash their
hands and feet so that they do not die; it shall be an eternal
law for them, for Aharon and his offspring, throughout
the generations."
22 23 Then the LORD said to Moshe, "Take the finest spices:
five hundred shekel of liquid myrrh, and half as much,
two hundred fifty, of fragrant cinnamon, as well as two
24 hundred fifty of aromatic cane, and five hundred shekel of
cassia – all according to the Sanctuary weight – and a hin of
25 olive oil. Make from these a sacred anointing oil, blended
26 as by a perfumer; it shall be a sacred anointing oil. With it,
anoint the Tent of Meeting and the Ark of the Testimony,
27 the table and all its utensils, the candelabrum and its
28 utensils, the incense altar, the sacrificial altar with all its
29 utensils, and the laver and its base. You shall consecrate
them and they will become holy of holies, and whatever
30 touches them will become holy. You shall anoint Aharon
and his sons and consecrate them to serve Me as priests.
31 And you shall tell the Israelites: This shall be My sacred
32 anointing oil throughout the generations. Do not pour it
on anyone else's body, and do not make any other oil with
the same formula. It is sacred, and shall remain sacred to

יד הַשֶּׁקֶל מַחֲצִית הַשֶּׁקֶל תְּרוּמָה לַיהוָה: כֹּל הָעֹבֵר עַל־
הַפְּקֻדִים מִבֶּן עֶשְׂרִים שָׁנָה וָמָעְלָה יִתֵּן תְּרוּמַת יהוה:
טו הֶעָשִׁיר לֹא־יַרְבֶּה וְהַדַּל לֹא יַמְעִיט מִמַּחֲצִית הַשָּׁקֶל לָתֵת
טז אֶת־תְּרוּמַת יהוה לְכַפֵּר עַל־נַפְשֹׁתֵיכֶם: וְלָקַחְתָּ אֶת־כֶּסֶף
הַכִּפֻּרִים מֵאֵת בְּנֵי יִשְׂרָאֵל וְנָתַתָּ אֹתוֹ עַל־עֲבֹדַת אֹהֶל
מוֹעֵד וְהָיָה לִבְנֵי יִשְׂרָאֵל לְזִכָּרוֹן לִפְנֵי יהוה לְכַפֵּר עַל־
נַפְשֹׁתֵיכֶם:
יז יח וַיְדַבֵּר יהוה אֶל־מֹשֶׁה לֵּאמֹר: וְעָשִׂיתָ כִּיּוֹר נְחֹשֶׁת וְכַנּוֹ
נְחֹשֶׁת לְרָחְצָה וְנָתַתָּ אֹתוֹ בֵּין־אֹהֶל מוֹעֵד וּבֵין הַמִּזְבֵּחַ
יט וְנָתַתָּ שָׁמָּה מָיִם: וְרָחֲצוּ אַהֲרֹן וּבָנָיו מִמֶּנּוּ אֶת־יְדֵיהֶם
כ וְאֶת־רַגְלֵיהֶם: בְּבֹאָם אֶל־אֹהֶל מוֹעֵד יִרְחֲצוּ־מַיִם וְלֹא יָמֻתוּ
אוֹ בְגִשְׁתָּם אֶל־הַמִּזְבֵּחַ לְשָׁרֵת לְהַקְטִיר אִשֶּׁה לַיהוָה:
כא וְרָחֲצוּ יְדֵיהֶם וְרַגְלֵיהֶם וְלֹא יָמֻתוּ וְהָיְתָה לָהֶם חָק־עוֹלָם
לוֹ וּלְזַרְעוֹ לְדֹרֹתָם:
כב כג וַיְדַבֵּר יהוה אֶל־מֹשֶׁה לֵּאמֹר: וְאַתָּה קַח־לְךָ בְּשָׂמִים
רֹאשׁ מָר־דְּרוֹר חֲמֵשׁ מֵאוֹת וְקִנְּמָן־בֶּשֶׂם מַחֲצִיתוֹ חֲמִשִּׁים
כד וּמָאתָיִם וּקְנֵה־בֹשֶׂם חֲמִשִּׁים וּמָאתָיִם: וְקִדָּה חֲמֵשׁ מֵאוֹת
כה בְּשֶׁקֶל הַקֹּדֶשׁ וְשֶׁמֶן זַיִת הִין: וְעָשִׂיתָ אֹתוֹ שֶׁמֶן מִשְׁחַת־
קֹדֶשׁ רֹקַח מִרְקַחַת מַעֲשֵׂה רֹקֵחַ שֶׁמֶן מִשְׁחַת־קֹדֶשׁ
כו יִהְיֶה: וּמָשַׁחְתָּ בוֹ אֶת־אֹהֶל מוֹעֵד וְאֵת אֲרוֹן הָעֵדֻת:
כז וְאֶת־הַשֻּׁלְחָן וְאֶת־כָּל־כֵּלָיו וְאֶת־הַמְּנֹרָה וְאֶת־כֵּלֶיהָ וְאֵת
כח מִזְבַּח הַקְּטֹרֶת: וְאֶת־מִזְבַּח הָעֹלָה וְאֶת־כָּל־כֵּלָיו וְאֶת־
כט הַכִּיֹּר וְאֶת־כַּנּוֹ: וְקִדַּשְׁתָּ אֹתָם וְהָיוּ קֹדֶשׁ קָדָשִׁים כָּל־הַנֹּגֵעַ
ל בָּהֶם יִקְדָּשׁ: וְאֶת־אַהֲרֹן וְאֶת־בָּנָיו תִּמְשָׁח וְקִדַּשְׁתָּ אֹתָם
לא לְכַהֵן לִי: וְאֶל־בְּנֵי יִשְׂרָאֵל תְּדַבֵּר לֵאמֹר שֶׁמֶן מִשְׁחַת־
לב קֹדֶשׁ יִהְיֶה זֶה לִי לְדֹרֹתֵיכֶם: עַל־בְּשַׂר אָדָם לֹא יִיסָךְ
וּבְמַתְכֻּנְתּוֹ לֹא תַעֲשׂוּ כָּמֹהוּ קֹדֶשׁ הוּא קֹדֶשׁ יִהְיֶה לָכֶם:

33 you. Whoever makes perfume like it or applies it to a
34 layperson shall be severed from his people." The
LORD said to Moshe, "Take sweet spices, equal parts of
35 stacte, onycha, galbanum, and pure frankincense and
make them into incense, blended as by a perfumer, salted,
36 pure and sacred. Beat some of it into powder and put part
of it before the covenant in the Tent of Meeting where I
37 will meet with you. It shall be holy of holies to you. Do
not make any incense with this formula for yourselves.
38 It must, for you, remain sacred to the LORD. The person
who makes any incense like it to use as perfume shall be
31 1 severed from his people." The LORD said to
2 Moshe, "See, I have called by name Betzalel, son of Uri,
3 son of Ḥur from the tribe of Yehuda, and I have filled him
with a divine spirit, with wisdom, understanding, and
4 knowledge in every craft. He will fashion works of art
5 in gold, silver, and bronze. He will cut stones for setting,
6 carve wood, and work in every craft. I have assigned to him
Oholiav, son of Aḥisamakh from the tribe of Dan. I have
also put wisdom into the heart of all the wise-hearted,
so that they will be able to make all I have commanded
7 you: the Tent of Meeting, the Ark of the Testimony and
8 its cover, and all other furnishings of the Tent; the table
and its utensils, the pure candelabrum and all its utensils,
9 the incense altar, the sacrificial altar with all its utensils,
10 the laver and its base, the service vestments, the sacred
vestments for Aharon the priest and the vestments for his

---

aesthetically. Shem has enlightened it spiritually and morally.

Yet as we see from the case of Betzalel, Judaism is not indifferent to aesthetics. The key to Betzalel lies in his name. It means "in the shadow of God." Betzalel's gift lay in his ability to communicate, through his work, that art is the shadow cast by God. Religious art is never "art for art's sake." It points to something beyond itself. The Tabernacle is to be a kind of microcosm of the universe, with one overriding particularity: that in it you felt the presence of something beyond – what the Torah calls "the glory of the LORD" which "filled the Tabernacle" (Ex. 40:35).

לג אִ֚ישׁ אֲשֶׁ֣ר יִרְקַ֣ח כָּמֹ֔הוּ וַאֲשֶׁ֥ר יִתֵּ֛ן מִמֶּ֖נּוּ עַל־זָ֑ר וְנִכְרַ֖ת
לד מֵעַמָּֽיו׃ וַיֹּאמֶר֩ יְהֹוָ֨ה אֶל־מֹשֶׁ֜ה קַח־לְךָ֣ סַמִּ֗ים
נָטָ֤ף ׀ וּשְׁחֵ֙לֶת֙ וְחֶלְבְּנָ֔ה סַמִּ֖ים וּלְבֹנָ֣ה זַכָּ֑ה בַּ֥ד בְּבַ֖ד יִהְיֶֽה׃
לה וְעָשִׂ֤יתָ אֹתָהּ֙ קְטֹ֔רֶת רֹ֖קַח מַעֲשֵׂ֣ה רוֹקֵ֑חַ מְמֻלָּ֖ח טָה֥וֹר
לו קֹֽדֶשׁ׃ וְשָׁחַקְתָּ֣ מִמֶּ֘נָּה֮ הָדֵק֒ וְנָתַתָּ֨ה מִמֶּ֜נָּה לִפְנֵ֤י הָעֵדֻת֙
בְּאֹ֣הֶל מוֹעֵ֔ד אֲשֶׁ֛ר אִוָּעֵ֥ד לְךָ֖ שָׁ֑מָּה קֹ֥דֶשׁ קָֽדָשִׁ֖ים תִּהְיֶ֥ה
לז לָכֶֽם׃ וְהַקְּטֹ֙רֶת֙ אֲשֶׁ֣ר תַּעֲשֶׂ֔ה בְּמַ֙תְכֻּנְתָּ֔הּ לֹ֥א תַעֲשׂ֖וּ לָכֶ֑ם
לח קֹ֛דֶשׁ תִּהְיֶ֥ה לְךָ֖ לַיהֹוָֽה׃ אִ֛ישׁ אֲשֶׁר־יַעֲשֶׂ֥ה כָמ֖וֹהָ לְהָרִ֣יחַ
לא א בָּ֑הּ וְנִכְרַ֖ת מֵעַמָּֽיו׃ וַיְדַבֵּ֥ר יְהֹוָ֖ה אֶל־מֹשֶׁ֥ה לֵּאמֹֽר׃ כד
ב רְאֵ֖ה קָרָ֣אתִֽי בְשֵׁ֑ם בְּצַלְאֵ֛ל בֶּן־אוּרִ֥י בֶן־ח֖וּר לְמַטֵּ֥ה יְהוּדָֽה׃
ג וָאֲמַלֵּ֥א אֹת֖וֹ ר֣וּחַ אֱלֹהִ֑ים בְּחָכְמָ֛ה וּבִתְבוּנָ֥ה וּבְדַ֖עַת וּבְכָל־
ד מְלָאכָֽה׃ לַחְשֹׁ֖ב מַחֲשָׁבֹ֑ת לַעֲשׂ֛וֹת בַּזָּהָ֥ב וּבַכֶּ֖סֶף וּבַנְּחֹֽשֶׁת׃
ה וּבַחֲרֹ֥שֶׁת אֶ֛בֶן לְמַלֹּ֖את וּבַחֲרֹ֣שֶׁת עֵ֑ץ לַעֲשׂ֖וֹת בְּכָל־מְלָאכָֽה׃
ו וַאֲנִ֞י הִנֵּ֧ה נָתַ֣תִּי אִתּ֗וֹ אֵ֣ת אָהֳלִיאָ֞ב בֶּן־אֲחִיסָמָךְ֙ לְמַטֵּה־
דָ֔ן וּבְלֵ֥ב כָּל־חֲכַם־לֵ֖ב נָתַ֣תִּי חָכְמָ֑ה וְעָשׂ֕וּ אֵ֖ת כָּל־אֲשֶׁ֥ר
ז צִוִּיתִֽךָ׃ אֵ֣ת ׀ אֹ֣הֶל מוֹעֵ֗ד וְאֶת־הָֽאָרֹן֙ לָֽעֵדֻ֔ת וְאֶת־הַכַּפֹּ֖רֶת
ח אֲשֶׁ֣ר עָלָ֑יו וְאֵ֖ת כָּל־כְּלֵ֥י הָאֹֽהֶל׃ וְאֶת־הַשֻּׁלְחָן֙ וְאֶת־כֵּלָ֔יו
וְאֶת־הַמְּנֹרָ֥ה הַטְּהֹרָ֖ה וְאֶת־כָּל־כֵּלֶ֑יהָ וְאֵ֖ת מִזְבַּ֥ח הַקְּטֹֽרֶת׃
ט וְאֶת־מִזְבַּ֥ח הָעֹלָ֖ה וְאֶת־כָּל־כֵּלָ֑יו וְאֶת־הַכִּיּ֖וֹר וְאֶת־כַּנּֽוֹ׃
י וְאֵ֖ת בִּגְדֵ֣י הַשְּׂרָ֑ד וְאֶת־בִּגְדֵ֤י הַקֹּ֙דֶשׁ֙ לְאַהֲרֹ֣ן הַכֹּהֵ֔ן וְאֶת־

31:2 בְּצַלְאֵל *Betzalel* – Betzalel is a rare type in the Tanakh – the artist, the craftsman, the shaper of beauty in the service of God, the man who, together with Oholiav, fashioned the articles associated with the Tabernacle. Judaism – in contrast to ancient Greece – did not cherish the visual arts. It was Rabbi Samson Raphael Hirsch who distinguished ancient Greece from ancient Israel in terms of the contrast between aesthetics and ethics. In his comment on the verse "May God enlarge Yefet, and let him dwell in the tents of Shem" (Gen. 9:27), he observes:

> The stem of Yefet reached its fullest blossoming in the Greeks; that of Shem in the Hebrews, Israel, who bore and bear the name (Shem) of God through the world of nations.... Yefet has ennobled the world

11 sons for when they serve as priests, the anointing oil, and
the fragrant incense for the Sanctuary; they shall make
them exactly as I have commanded you."
12 13 Then the LORD said to Moshe, "Speak to the Israelites
and say: Nevertheless, you shall keep My Sabbaths. It is
a sign between Me and you throughout the generations,
14 that you may know that I, the LORD, make you holy. Keep
the Sabbath, for it is holy to you. Whoever profanes it
shall be put to death. Whoever does work on it shall be
15 severed from his people. Six days shall work be done, but
the seventh day is a Sabbath of complete rest, sacred to
the LORD. Whoever does any work on the Sabbath shall
16 be put to death. The Israelites shall keep the Sabbath,
making it a day of rest throughout their generations as
17 a covenant forever. It is an eternal sign between Me and
the Israelites that in six days the LORD made heaven
and earth, and on the seventh day He ceased and was
18 revived." When He had finished speaking SHENI
to Moshe on Mount Sinai, He gave him the two tablets
of the Covenant, stone tablets, inscribed by the finger of
32 1 God. When the people saw that Moshe was long delayed
in coming down the mountain, they gathered around

---

it appears to. It will resume in Leviticus 25: "The LORD spoke to Moshe on Mount Sinai." That chapter is about principles of social justice: the Jubilee year, the release of debts, and the liberation of slaves, precisely the subjects we associate with Exodus. The obvious place for these laws is in Parashat Mishpatim.

What we have, then, between Exodus 24 and Leviticus 25 is a massive parenthesis, some forty chapters long. What caused it?

There is only one plausible candidate: the episode of the golden calf. Moshe ascends Mount Sinai after the great revelation. Eventually the people panic. Without Moshe how can they receive the will and word of God? They become a mob. Unused to such pressure, Aharon makes what turns out to be a disastrous decision and builds the calf.

Moshe is told by God, "Quick – go down. Your people… are acting ruinously" (Ex. 32:7). He prays to God to forgive them. He then goes down, smashes the tablets, burns the calf, has everyone drink its ashes, and has the Levites execute punishment against the main wrongdoers. Then he returns to God, asking again for forgiveness. God agrees,

יא בִּגְדֵי בָנָיו לְכַהֵן: וְאֵת שֶׁמֶן הַמִּשְׁחָה וְאֶת־קְטֹרֶת הַסַּמִּים
לַקֹּדֶשׁ כְּכֹל אֲשֶׁר־צִוִּיתִךָ יַעֲשׂוּ:
יב יג וַיֹּאמֶר יהוה אֶל־מֹשֶׁה לֵּאמֹר: וְאַתָּה דַּבֵּר אֶל־בְּנֵי יִשְׂרָאֵל
לֵאמֹר אַךְ אֶת־שַׁבְּתֹתַי תִּשְׁמֹרוּ כִּי אוֹת הִוא בֵּינִי וּבֵינֵיכֶם
יד לְדֹרֹתֵיכֶם לָדַעַת כִּי אֲנִי יהוה מְקַדִּשְׁכֶם: וּשְׁמַרְתֶּם אֶת־
הַשַּׁבָּת כִּי קֹדֶשׁ הִוא לָכֶם מְחַלְלֶיהָ מוֹת יוּמָת כִּי כָּל־הָעֹשֶׂה
טו בָהּ מְלָאכָה וְנִכְרְתָה הַנֶּפֶשׁ הַהִוא מִקֶּרֶב עַמֶּיהָ: שֵׁשֶׁת יָמִים
יֵעָשֶׂה מְלָאכָה וּבַיּוֹם הַשְּׁבִיעִי שַׁבַּת שַׁבָּתוֹן קֹדֶשׁ לַיהוה
טז כָּל־הָעֹשֶׂה מְלָאכָה בְּיוֹם הַשַּׁבָּת מוֹת יוּמָת: וְשָׁמְרוּ בְנֵי־
יִשְׂרָאֵל אֶת־הַשַּׁבָּת לַעֲשׂוֹת אֶת־הַשַּׁבָּת לְדֹרֹתָם בְּרִית
יז עוֹלָם: בֵּינִי וּבֵין בְּנֵי יִשְׂרָאֵל אוֹת הִוא לְעֹלָם כִּי־שֵׁשֶׁת יָמִים
עָשָׂה יהוה אֶת־הַשָּׁמַיִם וְאֶת־הָאָרֶץ וּבַיּוֹם הַשְּׁבִיעִי שָׁבַת
יח וַיִּנָּפַשׁ: וַיִּתֵּן אֶל־מֹשֶׁה כְּכַלֹּתוֹ לְדַבֵּר אִתּוֹ בְּהַר שני
סִינַי שְׁנֵי לֻחֹת הָעֵדֻת לֻחֹת אֶבֶן כְּתֻבִים בְּאֶצְבַּע אֱלֹהִים:
לב א וַיַּרְא הָעָם כִּי־בֹשֵׁשׁ מֹשֶׁה לָרֶדֶת מִן־הָהָר וַיִּקָּהֵל הָעָם
עַל־אַהֲרֹן וַיֹּאמְרוּ אֵלָיו קוּם ׀ עֲשֵׂה־לָנוּ אֱלֹהִים אֲשֶׁר יֵלְכוּ

31:17 וּבַיּוֹם הַשְּׁבִיעִי שָׁבַת וַיִּנָּפַשׁ *And on the seventh day He ceased and was revived* – The creation of the Tabernacle, we have seen, reflects the creation of the world. For six days God created the world and on the seventh day He rested (see Gen. 2:2). So we are instructed that for six days we too should labor to create, and on the seventh day we should rest. Why? Does an all-powerful God *need* to rest? And if we sometimes need to relax, can we be said to be imitating God?

Perhaps the simplest answer is this. All of nature is creative, but only God and humanity create consciously for a purpose. For us, unlike the plant or animal kingdoms, creation is not a process of ceaseless activity. It involves moments of contemplation when we reflect on *why* we act. We need time for thinking as well as for doing. So the Sabbath is a holy time, meaning time set apart, time out from the relentless pressures of activity: a day dedicated to thinking about the purpose of what we do.

THE GOLDEN CALF

The classical commentators, notably Ibn Ezra and Ramban, observed that the Sinai revelation does not end where

Aharon and said to him, "Get up, make us gods to go before
us. This man Moshe who brought us out of Egypt – we
2 have no idea what has become of him." So Aharon said to
them, "Remove the gold rings from the ears of your wives,
your sons, and your daughters and bring them to me."
3 So all the people took the gold rings from their ears and

32:2 וְהָבִיאוּ אֵלָי *Bring them to me* – Aharon is the de facto leader of the people in the absence of Moshe. Surely, Aharon should have seen the danger unfolding, and told them to wait, have patience and trust. What is going on in his mind?

Essentially there are three lines of defense among the commentators. According to the first, Aharon is playing for time. He tells the people to take the gold rings from the ears of their wives, sons, and daughters, reasoning to himself, "While they are quarreling with their children and wives about the gold, there will be a delay and Moshe will come" (Zohar).

The second defense is in the Talmud and is based on the fact that when Moshe departed to ascend the mountain, he left not just Aharon but also Ḥur in charge of the people (Ex. 24:14). Yet Ḥur does not figure in the narrative of the golden calf. According to the Talmud, Ḥur opposed the people, and was then killed by them. Aharon saw this and decided that proceeding with the making of the calf was the lesser of two evils: "'Can priest [Aharon] and prophet [Ḥur] be murdered in the Temple of the Lord?' (Lam. 2:20). If that happens, the people will never be forgiven. Better let them worship the golden calf, for which they may yet find forgiveness through repentance" (Sanhedrin 7a).

The third, argued by Ibn Ezra, is that the calf is not an idol at all, and what the Israelites are doing is, in Aharon's view, permissible. After all, their initial complaint is: "This man Moshe… we have no idea what has become of him" (Ex. 32:1). They do not want a god-substitute but a Moshe-substitute, an oracle, something through which they can discern God's instructions.

So there is a systematic attempt in the history of interpretation to mitigate or minimize Aharon's culpability, even to reveal heroic aspects of his actions. Recall the famous words of Hillel: "Be like the disciples of Aharon, loving peace, pursuing peace, loving people, and drawing them close to the Torah" (Avot 1:12). There are well-known aggadic traditions about how Aharon was able to turn enemies into friends and sinners into observers of the law. Sifra says that Aharon never said to anyone, "You have sinned" – all the more remarkable since one of the tasks of the High Priest was, once a year on Yom Kippur, to atone for the sins of the nation.

Peacemaking is not the only task of leadership. When Aharon is left to lead, the people make a golden calf. But neither is a passion for truth and justice sufficient. Moshe needs an Aharon to hold the people together. Every leadership

לְפָנֵינוּ כִּי־זֶה ׀ מֹשֶׁה הָאִישׁ אֲשֶׁר הֶעֱלָנוּ מֵאֶרֶץ מִצְרַיִם לֹא
ב יָדַעְנוּ מֶה־הָיָה לוֹ׃ וַיֹּאמֶר אֲלֵהֶם אַהֲרֹן פָּרְקוּ נִזְמֵי הַזָּהָב
ג אֲשֶׁר בְּאָזְנֵי נְשֵׁיכֶם בְּנֵיכֶם וּבְנֹתֵיכֶם וְהָבִיאוּ אֵלָי׃ וַיִּתְפָּרְקוּ

---

but only partially. The guilty will suffer but the people as a whole will survive.

Thus far, the story is clear. What happens next is not. First God says that the people must move on and continue their journey to the Promised Land. They do so only fifty chapters later, in Numbers 10. God then says that He will not be "among you" (Ex. 33:3). It would be too dangerous for God to be close to the people, given their tendency to provoke Him to anger. Moshe urges God to reconsider His decision. Then the subject changes to what seem to be metaphysical inquiries about the nature of God. In chapter 34 comes the famous scene in which God places Moshe in a crevice in a rock and passes before him, reciting the words that became known as God's Thirteen Attributes of Mercy.

Moshe, in this bewildering series of conversations, is exploring the fundamental parameters of the relationship between God and humanity. Can an infinite God be close to finite human beings? If not, what hope is there for humanity? So far the people have experienced God only as a terrifying, overwhelming force. In His apparent absence, however, they are lost. When they made the calf, wrongheaded though they were, they were seeking a way of encountering God without terror.

Predictability too has become problematic. It is as if Moshe says to God, "Sometimes You are angry, and sometimes You are moved by compassion. Precisely because You are free, we cannot predict which will prevail: punishment or forgiveness. But we have staked our entire existence on You. How can we live, not knowing when You will next be angry, and whether our prayers for forgiveness will succeed? What will happen in the future if the people sin and there is no Moshe to pray for them? There must be some sustainable order in the life of the spirit. There must be a structure of leadership that does not depend on chance."

This is one of the decisive moments in Judaism. The long digression between Exodus 23 and Leviticus 25 is, as Ramban saw (commentary on Lev. 25:1), entirely taken up with the consequences of the golden calf and the new relationship it inaugurated between God and the people. All of it – the appointment of the priests and Levites, the construction of the Sanctuary, the offerings to be made there, the special demands of purity for all who entered its precincts, the holiness demanded of a people with God in its midst – is about *bringing God close*, living safely in the constant presence of the Divine. This is God's answer to Moshe: "They shall make Me a Sanctuary and I will dwell (*veshakhanti*) in their midst" (Ex. 25:8).

4 brought them to Aharon. He took the gold from them
and, fashioning it with a chisel, made a molten calf. And
they said, "These, Israel, are your gods who brought you
5 out of Egypt!" Seeing this, Aharon built an altar in front
of it and announced, "Tomorrow will be a festival to the
6 LORD." The next day, they rose early and sacrificed burnt
offerings and brought peace offerings. The people sat
down to eat and drink and then stood up to engage in
revelry.
7 The LORD said to Moshe, "Quick – go down. Your people,
whom you brought out of Egypt, are acting ruinously.
8 They have deviated swiftly from the way I commanded
them; they have made themselves a molten calf and are
bowing down and sacrificing to it, saying, 'These, Israel,
9 are your gods who brought you out of Egypt!'" Then the
LORD said to Moshe, "I have seen this people; it is a stiff-
10 necked people. So do not try to stop Me when My anger
burns against them. I will put an end to them and make
11 of you a great nation." Moshe implored the LORD his
God, "Why, O LORD, unleash Your anger against Your
people, whom You brought out of Egypt with such vast

Israelites made the golden calf, Moshe sought to persuade God to forgive them, but God said, "I have already taken an oath that '*whoever sacrifices to any other deity shall be utterly destroyed*' (Ex. 22:19). I cannot retract what I have said." Moshe replied, "LORD of the universe, You have given me the power to annul oaths, for You taught me that one who takes an oath cannot break their word but a scholar can absolve them. I hereby absolve You of Your vow." (Abridged from Shemot Rabba 43:4)

According to the Sages this original act of divine forgiveness, the one on which Yom Kippur is based, came about through the annulment of a vow, when Moshe annulled the vow of God. The Sages understood the verse "Then the LORD *relented* from the evil He had spoken of doing to His people" (Ex. 32:14) to mean that God expressed regret for the vow He had taken – a precondition for a vow to be annulled.

This is why *Kol Nidrei*, the prayer with which we begin Yom Kippur, is a formula for the annulment of vows. We must always strive to fulfill our promises. But given the choice between justice and

כָּל־הָעָם אֶת־נִזְמֵי הַזָּהָב אֲשֶׁר בְּאָזְנֵיהֶם וַיָּבִיאוּ אֶל־אַהֲרֹן׃
ד וַיִּקַּח מִיָּדָם וַיָּצַר אֹתוֹ בַּחֶרֶט וַיַּעֲשֵׂהוּ עֵגֶל מַסֵּכָה וַיֹּאמְרוּ
ה אֵלֶּה אֱלֹהֶיךָ יִשְׂרָאֵל אֲשֶׁר הֶעֱלוּךָ מֵאֶרֶץ מִצְרָיִם׃ וַיַּרְא
אַהֲרֹן וַיִּבֶן מִזְבֵּחַ לְפָנָיו וַיִּקְרָא אַהֲרֹן וַיֹּאמַר חַג לַיהוה
ו מָחָר׃ וַיַּשְׁכִּימוּ מִמָּחֳרָת וַיַּעֲלוּ עֹלֹת וַיַּגִּשׁוּ שְׁלָמִים וַיֵּשֶׁב
הָעָם לֶאֱכֹל וְשָׁתוֹ וַיָּקֻמוּ לְצַחֵק׃
ז וַיְדַבֵּר יהוה אֶל־מֹשֶׁה לֶךְ־רֵד כִּי שִׁחֵת עַמְּךָ אֲשֶׁר הֶעֱלֵיתָ
ח מֵאֶרֶץ מִצְרָיִם׃ סָרוּ מַהֵר מִן־הַדֶּרֶךְ אֲשֶׁר צִוִּיתִם עָשׂוּ לָהֶם
עֵגֶל מַסֵּכָה וַיִּשְׁתַּחֲווּ־לוֹ וַיִּזְבְּחוּ־לוֹ וַיֹּאמְרוּ אֵלֶּה אֱלֹהֶיךָ
ט יִשְׂרָאֵל אֲשֶׁר הֶעֱלוּךָ מֵאֶרֶץ מִצְרָיִם׃ וַיֹּאמֶר יהוה אֶל־מֹשֶׁה
י רָאִיתִי אֶת־הָעָם הַזֶּה וְהִנֵּה עַם־קְשֵׁה־עֹרֶף הוּא׃ וְעַתָּה
הַנִּיחָה לִּי וְיִחַר־אַפִּי בָהֶם וַאֲכַלֵּם וְאֶעֱשֶׂה אוֹתְךָ לְגוֹי גָּדוֹל׃
יא וַיְחַל מֹשֶׁה אֶת־פְּנֵי יהוה אֱלֹהָיו וַיֹּאמֶר לָמָה יהוה יֶחֱרֶה

---

team needs both a voice of truth and a force for peace – both a Moshe and an Aharon.

32:3 וַיָּבִיאוּ אֶל־אַהֲרֹן *Brought them to Aharon* – One of the most striking characteristics of the children of Israel is that, whenever they are asked, they give. When asked to make a donation to the building of the Sanctuary, they give without demur. When asked to contribute to the golden calf, they do likewise. The golden calf is an idol. The Sanctuary is the home of the Divine Presence. There is nothing in common between them except this, that they both come into being through voluntary donations. The Talmud Yerushalmi (Shekalim 1:1) expresses amazement: "One cannot understand the nature of this people: if appealed to for the calf they give; if appealed to for the Sanctuary they give." Jewishly, to live is to give.

32:11 וַיְחַל מֹשֶׁה *Moshe implored* – Moshe's prayers, as recorded in the Torah, are daring. But the Midrash makes them more audacious still. The text introducing Moshe's prayer begins with the Hebrew words "*Vayeḥal Moshe*" (Ex. 32:11). Normally these are translated as "Moshe besought, implored, entreated, pleaded, or attempted to pacify" God. However, *the same verb is used in the context of annulling or breaking a vow* (Num. 30:3). On this basis the Sages advanced a remarkable interpretation:

> [*Vayeḥal Moshe* means] "Moshe *absolved God of His vow*." When the

12 power and mighty force? Why should the Egyptians be
able to say that You brought them out with evil intent, to
kill them in the mountains and purge them from the face
of the earth? Turn from Your fierce anger and relent from
13 doing evil to Your people. Remember Avraham, Yitzḥak,
and Yisrael, Your servants, to whom You swore by Your
very Self, telling them, 'I will make your descendants as
many as the stars of the heavens, and give them this land
14 of which I spoke, to inherit forever.'" Then the LORD
relented from the evil He had spoken of doing to His
people.
15 Then Moshe turned and came down the mountain with
the two tablets of testimony in his hand, inscribed on
16 both sides, front and back. The tablets were the work of
God, and the writing was God's writing, engraved on the
17 tablets. When Yehoshua heard the noise of the people
shouting, he said to Moshe, "The sound of war is coming
18 from the camp." But Moshe said, "It is neither the sound
of triumph nor the wailing of defeat. What I hear is the
19 sound of revelry." As he approached the camp and saw
the calf and the dancing, Moshe's anger blazed, and he
flung the tablets from his hands and smashed them at
20 the foot of the mountain. Then he took the calf that they
had made, burned it with fire, ground it to fine powder,
scattered it on the water, and made the Israelites drink it.

---

its success, not on power, but on moral obligation. It places a greater burden on the educated conscience, requires unique institutions, and needs constant education. The people must know the law; they must hand it on to their children; they must speak of it constantly until it becomes part of their innermost being. But the gain is immense. It means that Israel, if it is loyal to the covenant, will keep the law, not because of fear of arrest, trial, and punishment, but because of their love of God, their concern for their neighbors, and their shared sense of past and future. With this, we can appreciate the strangest fact of all in Jewish history – that without sovereignty and a land, without police or an army, without any of the normal accoutrements of nationhood, the Jewish people kept Jewish law voluntarily in exile for two thousand years.

אַפְּךָ בְּעַמֶּךָ אֲשֶׁר הוֹצֵאתָ מֵאֶרֶץ מִצְרַיִם בְּכֹחַ גָּדוֹל וּבְיָד
יב חֲזָקָה׃ לָמָּה יֹאמְרוּ מִצְרַיִם לֵאמֹר בְּרָעָה הוֹצִיאָם לַהֲרֹג
אֹתָם בֶּהָרִים וּלְכַלֹּתָם מֵעַל פְּנֵי הָאֲדָמָה שׁוּב מֵחֲרוֹן אַפֶּךָ
יג וְהִנָּחֵם עַל־הָרָעָה לְעַמֶּךָ׃ זְכֹר לְאַבְרָהָם לְיִצְחָק וּלְיִשְׂרָאֵל
עֲבָדֶיךָ אֲשֶׁר נִשְׁבַּעְתָּ לָהֶם בָּךְ וַתְּדַבֵּר אֲלֵהֶם אַרְבֶּה אֶת־
זַרְעֲכֶם כְּכוֹכְבֵי הַשָּׁמָיִם וְכָל־הָאָרֶץ הַזֹּאת אֲשֶׁר אָמַרְתִּי
יד אֶתֵּן לְזַרְעֲכֶם וְנָחֲלוּ לְעֹלָם׃ וַיִּנָּחֶם יהוה עַל־הָרָעָה אֲשֶׁר
דִּבֶּר לַעֲשׂוֹת לְעַמּוֹ׃
טו וַיִּפֶן וַיֵּרֶד מֹשֶׁה מִן־הָהָר וּשְׁנֵי לֻחֹת הָעֵדֻת בְּיָדוֹ לֻחֹת כה
טז כְּתֻבִים מִשְּׁנֵי עֶבְרֵיהֶם מִזֶּה וּמִזֶּה הֵם כְּתֻבִים׃ וְהַלֻּחֹת
מַעֲשֵׂה אֱלֹהִים הֵמָּה וְהַמִּכְתָּב מִכְתַּב אֱלֹהִים הוּא חָרוּת
יז עַל־הַלֻּחֹת׃ וַיִּשְׁמַע יְהוֹשֻׁעַ אֶת־קוֹל הָעָם בְּרֵעֹה וַיֹּאמֶר
יח אֶל־מֹשֶׁה קוֹל מִלְחָמָה בַּמַּחֲנֶה׃ וַיֹּאמֶר אֵין קוֹל עֲנוֹת
יט גְּבוּרָה וְאֵין קוֹל עֲנוֹת חֲלוּשָׁה קוֹל עַנּוֹת אָנֹכִי שֹׁמֵעַ׃ וַיְהִי
כַּאֲשֶׁר קָרַב אֶל־הַמַּחֲנֶה וַיַּרְא אֶת־הָעֵגֶל וּמְחֹלֹת וַיִּחַר־אַף
מֹשֶׁה וַיַּשְׁלֵךְ מִיָּדָו אֶת־הַלֻּחֹת וַיְשַׁבֵּר אֹתָם תַּחַת הָהָר׃
כ וַיִּקַּח אֶת־הָעֵגֶל אֲשֶׁר עָשׂוּ וַיִּשְׂרֹף בָּאֵשׁ וַיִּטְחַן עַד אֲשֶׁר־

---

forgiveness, forgiveness is generally to be preferred. Invoking this principle, *Kol Nidrei* recalls the first Yom Kippur, when the Almighty let His compassion override His justice, the basis of all divine forgiveness.

32:16 חָרוּת עַל־הַלֻּחֹת *Engraved on the tablets* – In Pirkei Avot (6:2), the Sages saw in this verse a brilliant play on words. Noting the similarity between *ḥerut,* "freedom," and *ḥarut,* "engraved," they reread "engraved on the tablets" as "freedom on the tablets." The Rabbis said, "Read not *ḥarut* but *ḥerut* [not 'engraved' but 'freedom'], for the only person who is truly free is one who occupies himself with Torah study." What they meant was that if the law is engraved on the hearts of its citizens, it does not need to be enforced by police. True freedom – *ḥerut* – is the ability to control oneself without having to be controlled by others, accepting voluntarily the moral restraints without which liberty becomes license and society itself a battleground of warring instincts and desires.

This idea of freedom depends, for

21 "What did this people do to you," said Moshe to Aharon,
"that you should have brought so great a sin upon it?"
22 Aharon replied, "Do not be angry with me. You know that
23 the people are set on evil. They said to me, 'Make us gods
to go before us. This man Moshe who brought us out of
24 Egypt – we have no idea what has become of him.' So I
told them, 'Who has gold? Take it off.' They gave it to me,
25 I threw it into the fire – and out came this calf." Moshe
saw that the people were running wild, for Aharon had
let them run beyond control and become a laughingstock
26 to their enemies. So Moshe stood at the gate of the camp
and said, "Who is for the LORD? Come to me." All the
27 Levites rallied round him. He said to them, "This is what
the LORD God of Israel says: Let each of you put sword on
thigh and go back and forth from gate to gate throughout
28 the camp – slaying brother, neighbor, kinsman." The
Levites did as Moshe had ordered. Some three thousand
29 people fell that day. Moshe said, "Dedicate yourselves
to the LORD today. You have been willing to act even
against your son or brother. May He bestow a blessing
30 on you this day." On the following day, Moshe said to the
people, "You have committed a grievous sin. Now I must
go back up to the LORD. Perhaps I can secure atonement
31 for your sin." So Moshe went back to the LORD and said,
"I beg of You. This people has committed a grievous
32 sin. They made gods of gold for themselves. But now, if
only You would forgive their sin – but if not, please blot
33 me out of the book You have written." The LORD said
to Moshe, "I will blot out of My book those who have

Moshe to restore order now. He does so only by the most dramatic action: smashing the tablets and grinding the calf to dust. The Israelites at the foot of the mountain know nothing of how close they had come to being utterly destroyed.

32:32 מִסִּפְרְךָ אֲשֶׁר כָּתָבְתָּ *The book You have written* – On Rosh HaShana and Yom Kippur, we ask God to inscribe us in the book of life. The idea that our lives are written in a book by God goes back to the daring ultimatum that Moshe presents to God here: forgive their sin

כא דק ויזר על־פני המים וישק את־בני ישראל׃ ויאמר משה
אל־אהרן מה־עשה לך העם הזה כי־הבאת עליו חטאה
כב גדלה׃ ויאמר אהרן אל־יחר אף אדני אתה ידעת את־
כג העם כי ברע הוא׃ ויאמרו לי עשה־לנו אלהים אשר ילכו
לפנינו כי־זה ׀ משה האיש אשר העלנו מארץ מצרים לא
כד ידענו מה־היה לו׃ ואמר להם למי זהב התפרקו ויתנו־לי
כה ואשלכהו באש ויצא העגל הזה׃ וירא משה את־העם כי
כו פרע הוא כי־פרעה אהרן לשמצה בקמיהם׃ ויעמד משה
בשער המחנה ויאמר מי ליהוה אלי ויאספו אליו כל־בני
כז לוי׃ ויאמר להם כה־אמר יהוה אלהי ישראל שימו איש־
חרבו על־ירכו עברו ושובו משער לשער במחנה והרגו
כח איש־את־אחיו ואיש את־רעהו ואיש את־קרבו׃ ויעשו
בני־לוי כדבר משה ויפל מן־העם ביום ההוא כשלשת
כט אלפי איש׃ ויאמר משה מלאו ידכם היום ליהוה כי איש
ל בבנו ובאחיו ולתת עליכם היום ברכה׃ ויהי ממחרת
ויאמר משה אל־העם אתם חטאתם חטאה גדלה ועתה
לא אעלה אל־יהוה אולי אכפרה בעד חטאתכם׃ וישב משה
אל־יהוה ויאמר אנא חטא העם הזה חטאה גדלה ויעשו
לב להם אלהי זהב׃ ועתה אם־תשא חטאתם ואם־אין מחני
לג נא מספרך אשר כתבת׃ ויאמר יהוה אל־משה מי אשר

32:24 ויתנו־לי *They gave it to me* – Aharon blames the people. He denies responsibility for making the calf. "I threw it into the fire, and out came this calf!" This is the same kind of denial of responsibility we recall from the story of Adam and Ḥava (Gen. 3). The man says, "It was the woman." The woman says, "It was the serpent." It wasn't me. I was the victim, not the perpetrator. In anyone, such evasion is a moral failure; in a leader, all the more so.

It is easy to be critical of people who fail the leadership test when it involves defying the crowd, but it is hard to oppose a mob. They can ignore you, remove you, even assassinate you. Even Moshe was helpless in the face of the people during the later episode of the spies (Num. 14:5). Nor is it easy for

34 sinned against Me. Now go and lead the people to the
place about which I have spoken to you. My messenger
shall go before you. But when the time comes for Me to
35 punish, I will punish them for their sin." Thus the LORD
struck the people with a plague for what they had done
33 1 with the calf Aharon had made. The LORD said
to Moshe, "Go. Set out from here – you and the people
you brought out of Egypt – to the land I promised to
Avraham, Yitzḥak, and Yaakov, saying, 'I will give this to
2 your descendants.' I will send a messenger ahead of you
and drive out the Canaanites and Amorites, the Hittites
3 and the Perizzites, the Hivites, and the Jebusites. You will
come to a land flowing with milk and honey, but I will
not go among you, because you are a stiff-necked people;
4 I might destroy you on the way." When the people heard
this distressing news, they were grief-stricken. None put
5 on their finery; for the LORD had said to Moshe, "Tell
the Israelites: You are a stiff-necked people. If for one
moment I were to go among you, I might destroy you. So
now take off your finery; and I will consider what to do
6 with you." So the Israelites stripped themselves of their
7 finery from Mount Ḥorev onward. Moshe took the tent
and pitched it at a distance outside the camp, calling it the
Tent of Meeting. Whoever sought the LORD would go to
8 the Tent of Meeting, outside the camp. And when Moshe

---

point. He does go down. He does punish the guilty. He does pray for God to forgive the people. Having restored order to the people, Moshe now introduces an entirely new approach. He is, in effect, saying to God: What the people need is not for *me* to be close to them. I am just a human, here today, gone tomorrow. But You are eternal. You are their God. They need *You* to be close to them.

It is as if Moshe is saying: Until now, they have experienced You delivering plague after plague to the Egyptians, bringing the world's greatest empire to its knees, dividing the sea, overturning the very order of nature itself. At Mount Sinai, merely hearing Your voice, they were so overwhelmed that they said: If we continue to hear the voice, "we will die" (Ex. 20:16). The people need, says Moshe, to experience not only the *greatness* of God but the *closeness* of God, not just God heard in thunder and lightning at the top of the mountain, not just

לד חֲטָא־לִי אֶמְחֶנּוּ מִסִּפְרִי: וְעַתָּה לֵךְ ׀ נְחֵה אֶת־הָעָם אֶל
אֲשֶׁר־דִּבַּרְתִּי לָךְ הִנֵּה מַלְאָכִי יֵלֵךְ לְפָנֶיךָ וּבְיוֹם פָּקְדִי
לה וּפָקַדְתִּי עֲלֵהֶם חַטָּאתָם: וַיִּגֹּף יהוה אֶת־הָעָם עַל אֲשֶׁר עָשׂוּ
לג א אֶת־הָעֵגֶל אֲשֶׁר עָשָׂה אַהֲרֹן: וַיְדַבֵּר יהוה אֶל־
מֹשֶׁה לֵךְ עֲלֵה מִזֶּה אַתָּה וְהָעָם אֲשֶׁר הֶעֱלִיתָ מֵאֶרֶץ מִצְרָיִם
אֶל־הָאָרֶץ אֲשֶׁר נִשְׁבַּעְתִּי לְאַבְרָהָם לְיִצְחָק וּלְיַעֲקֹב לֵאמֹר
ב לְזַרְעֲךָ אֶתְּנֶנָּה: וְשָׁלַחְתִּי לְפָנֶיךָ מַלְאָךְ וְגֵרַשְׁתִּי אֶת־הַכְּנַעֲנִי
ג הָאֱמֹרִי וְהַחִתִּי וְהַפְּרִזִּי הַחִוִּי וְהַיְבוּסִי: אֶל־אֶרֶץ זָבַת חָלָב
וּדְבָשׁ כִּי לֹא אֶעֱלֶה בְּקִרְבְּךָ כִּי עַם־קְשֵׁה־עֹרֶף אַתָּה פֶּן־
ד אֲכֶלְךָ בַּדָּרֶךְ: וַיִּשְׁמַע הָעָם אֶת־הַדָּבָר הָרָע הַזֶּה וַיִּתְאַבָּלוּ
ה וְלֹא־שָׁתוּ אִישׁ עֶדְיוֹ עָלָיו: וַיֹּאמֶר יהוה אֶל־מֹשֶׁה אֱמֹר אֶל־
בְּנֵי־יִשְׂרָאֵל אַתֶּם עַם־קְשֵׁה־עֹרֶף רֶגַע אֶחָד אֶעֱלֶה בְקִרְבְּךָ
וְכִלִּיתִיךָ וְעַתָּה הוֹרֵד עֶדְיְךָ מֵעָלֶיךָ וְאֵדְעָה מָה אֶעֱשֶׂה־לָּךְ:
ו ז וַיִּתְנַצְּלוּ בְנֵי־יִשְׂרָאֵל אֶת־עֶדְיָם מֵהַר חוֹרֵב: וּמֹשֶׁה יִקַּח
אֶת־הָאֹהֶל וְנָטָה־לוֹ ׀ מִחוּץ לַמַּחֲנֶה הַרְחֵק מִן־הַמַּחֲנֶה
וְקָרָא לוֹ אֹהֶל מוֹעֵד וְהָיָה כָּל־מְבַקֵּשׁ יהוה יֵצֵא אֶל־אֹהֶל
ח מוֹעֵד אֲשֶׁר מִחוּץ לַמַּחֲנֶה: וְהָיָה כְּצֵאת מֹשֶׁה אֶל־הָאֹהֶל

---

or blot me out of the book you have written. When Jews – the people of the book – think of life, they think of a book. Our lives are each a chapter in the book of Jewish life, of which we, with God, are the co-authors.

33:8 וְהָיָה כְּצֵאת מֹשֶׁה *When Moshe went out* – At times of distress, a leader has to be close to the people, not distant. For Moshe, then, to leave the camp must be demoralizing. This is a cryptic text, but it seems to me that the most powerful interpretation is this: Moshe is making an audacious prayer, so audacious that the Torah does not state it directly and explicitly. We have to reconstruct it from clues within the text.

The previous chapter implies that the people panic because of the absence of Moshe, their leader. God Himself implies as much when He says to Moshe, "Go down. *Your* people, whom *you* brought up out of Egypt, are acting ruinously" (Ex. 32:7). The suggestion is that Moshe's absence or distance was the cause of the sin. He should have stayed closer to the people. Moshe takes the

went out to the Tent, all the people would rise, standing
at the openings of their tents, and watch Moshe until he
9 had entered the Tent. When Moshe entered the Tent,
the pillar of cloud would descend and stand at the Tent's
10 opening while He spoke with Moshe. When the people
saw the pillar of cloud standing at the Tent's opening, all
the people would rise and bow down, each at the opening
11 of his own tent. The LORD would speak to Moshe face-
to-face, as one person speaks to his friend. And then
Moshe would return to the camp, but his young disciple,
Yehoshua son of Nun, did not leave the Tent.

12 Moshe said to the LORD, "You told me to lead this people SHELISHI
forth, but You have not let me know whom You will send
with me. And You said, 'I have known you by name,
13 and you have found favor in My sight.' So now, if I have
found favor in Your sight, please show me Your ways, so
that I may know You and continue to find favor in Your
14 sight. And look upon this nation: it is Your people." "My
presence," He replied, "will go with you, and I will grant
15 you rest." Then Moshe said to Him, "If Your presence
16 does not go with us, do not make us leave this place. For
unless You go with us, how shall it be known that I and
Your people have found favor in Your sight? That is how
I and Your people are distinguished from every other
people on the face of the earth."

17 Then the LORD said to Moshe, "In this too I will do what REVI'I
you ask, for you have found favor in My sight; for I know
18 you by name." Then Moshe said, "Show me, please, Your

could not now enter the Tent of Meeting, because the cloud had settled on it, and *the glory of the LORD* filled the Tabernacle" (Ex. 40:34–35). If, like Rabbi Yehuda HaLevi (Kuzari 1:97) we understand the institution of the Tabernacle as a divine response to the sin of the golden calf, and an acceptance by God of Moshe's plea that He come close to the people, then we become conscious of God's glory in the Tent of Meeting as the very closeness that the Israelites need. We cannot see God's *face*, we cannot understand God's *ways*, but we can encounter God's *glory* whenever we build a home for His presence here on earth.

יָקוּמוּ כָּל־הָעָם וְנִצְּבוּ אִישׁ פֶּתַח אָהֳלוֹ וְהִבִּיטוּ אַחֲרֵי מֹשֶׁה
ט עַד־בֹּאוֹ הָאֹהֱלָה: וְהָיָה כְּבֹא מֹשֶׁה הָאֹהֱלָה יֵרֵד עַמּוּד
י הֶעָנָן וְעָמַד פֶּתַח הָאֹהֶל וְדִבֶּר עִם־מֹשֶׁה: וְרָאָה כָל־הָעָם
אֶת־עַמּוּד הֶעָנָן עֹמֵד פֶּתַח הָאֹהֶל וְקָם כָּל־הָעָם וְהִשְׁתַּחֲווּ
יא אִישׁ פֶּתַח אָהֳלוֹ: וְדִבֶּר יהוה אֶל־מֹשֶׁה פָּנִים אֶל־פָּנִים
כַּאֲשֶׁר יְדַבֵּר אִישׁ אֶל־רֵעֵהוּ וְשָׁב אֶל־הַמַּחֲנֶה וּמְשָׁרְתוֹ
יְהוֹשֻׁעַ בִּן־נוּן נַעַר לֹא יָמִישׁ מִתּוֹךְ הָאֹהֶל:
יב וַיֹּאמֶר מֹשֶׁה אֶל־יהוה רְאֵה אַתָּה אֹמֵר אֵלַי הַעַל אֶת־הָעָם שלישי
הַזֶּה וְאַתָּה לֹא הוֹדַעְתַּנִי אֵת אֲשֶׁר־תִּשְׁלַח עִמִּי וְאַתָּה
יג אָמַרְתָּ יְדַעְתִּיךָ בְשֵׁם וְגַם־מָצָאתָ חֵן בְּעֵינָי: וְעַתָּה אִם־נָא
מָצָאתִי חֵן בְּעֵינֶיךָ הוֹדִעֵנִי נָא אֶת־דְּרָכֶךָ וְאֵדָעֲךָ לְמַעַן
יד אֶמְצָא־חֵן בְּעֵינֶיךָ וּרְאֵה כִּי עַמְּךָ הַגּוֹי הַזֶּה: וַיֹּאמַר פָּנַי יֵלֵכוּ
טו וַהֲנִחֹתִי לָךְ: וַיֹּאמֶר אֵלָיו אִם־אֵין פָּנֶיךָ הֹלְכִים אַל־תַּעֲלֵנוּ
טז מִזֶּה: וּבַמֶּה ׀ יִוָּדַע אֵפוֹא כִּי־מָצָאתִי חֵן בְּעֵינֶיךָ אֲנִי וְעַמֶּךָ
הֲלוֹא בְּלֶכְתְּךָ עִמָּנוּ וְנִפְלֵינוּ אֲנִי וְעַמְּךָ מִכָּל־הָעָם אֲשֶׁר
עַל־פְּנֵי הָאֲדָמָה:
יז וַיֹּאמֶר יהוה אֶל־מֹשֶׁה גַּם אֶת־הַדָּבָר הַזֶּה אֲשֶׁר דִּבַּרְתָּ רביעי
יח אֶעֱשֶׂה כִּי־מָצָאתָ חֵן בְּעֵינַי וָאֵדָעֲךָ בְּשֵׁם: וַיֹּאמַר הַרְאֵנִי נָא

---

prophetic revelation such as mine, but as a perpetual presence in the valley below. That is why Moshe removes the tent and pitches it outside the camp, as if to say to God: It is not my presence the people need in their midst, but Yours.

33:13 הוֹדִעֵנִי נָא אֶת־דְּרָכֶךָ *Please show me Your ways* – As noted earlier, Moshe seeks here to understand the very nature of God Himself. Is it possible for God to be close to where people are? Can transcendence become immanence? Can the God who is vaster than the universe live within the universe in a predictable, comprehensible way, not just in the form of miraculous intervention?

33:18 הַרְאֵנִי נָא אֶת־כְּבֹדֶךָ *Show me, please, Your glory* – We do not know exactly what is meant by God's glory, but we find a clue at the very end of the book of Exodus. When the Tabernacle is finished and assembled we read this: "Then the cloud covered the Tent of Meeting, and *the glory of the Lord* filled the Tabernacle. Moshe

19 glory." And He said, "I will cause all My goodness to
pass before you and in your presence I will proclaim My
name: The LORD. But I will be gracious to whom I choose
to be gracious, and will show mercy to whom I decide to
20 show mercy. Nor," He said, "can you see My face. For no
21 one can see Me and live." Then the LORD said, "Look,
there is a place by Me where you may stand on the rock,
22 and while My glory passes by I will put you in a cleft of
the rock, and I will shield you with My hand until I have
23 passed. Then I will take My hand away, and you will see
My back, but My face may not be seen."
34 1 The LORD said to Moshe, "Carve two tablets of stone HAMISHI
like the first, and I will inscribe on them the words that
2 were on the first tablets that you broke. Be ready in the
morning. Climb Mount Sinai in the morning and present
3 yourself to Me there on the mountaintop. Let no one
come up with you. No one else should be seen anywhere
on the mountain, nor may flocks or herds graze near the
4 mountain." So Moshe carved two stone tablets like the
first. He rose early in the morning and climbed Mount
Sinai, as the LORD had commanded him. In his hand
5 he took the two tablets of stone. The LORD descended
in a cloud and stood with him there, and proclaimed the

An "awakening from above" may change nature, but it does not necessarily change human nature. Those to whom it happens are passive. While it lasts, it is overwhelming – but only while it lasts. Thereafter, people revert to what they were. An "awakening from below," by contrast, leaves a permanent mark. Because human beings have taken the initiative, something in them changes. They now know they are capable of great things, and because they did so once, they are aware that they can do so again. An awakening from above temporarily transforms the external world; an awakening from below permanently transforms our internal world.

In Judaism, the natural is greater than the supernatural in the sense that an "awakening from below" is more powerful in transforming us, and longer lasting in its effects, than is an "awakening from above." That was why the second tablets survived intact while the first did not. Divine intervention changes nature, but it is human initiative – our approach to God – that changes us.

יט אֶת־כְּבֹדֶךָ׃ וַיֹּאמֶר אֲנִי אַעֲבִיר כָּל־טוּבִי עַל־פָּנֶיךָ וְקָרָאתִי
בְשֵׁם יהוה לְפָנֶיךָ וְחַנֹּתִי אֶת־אֲשֶׁר אָחֹן וְרִחַמְתִּי אֶת־אֲשֶׁר
כ אֲרַחֵם׃ וַיֹּאמֶר לֹא תוּכַל לִרְאֹת אֶת־פָּנָי כִּי לֹא־יִרְאַנִי
כא הָאָדָם וָחָי׃ וַיֹּאמֶר יהוה הִנֵּה מָקוֹם אִתִּי וְנִצַּבְתָּ עַל־הַצּוּר׃
כב וְהָיָה בַּעֲבֹר כְּבֹדִי וְשַׂמְתִּיךָ בְּנִקְרַת הַצּוּר וְשַׂכֹּתִי כַפִּי עָלֶיךָ
כג עַד־עָבְרִי׃ וַהֲסִרֹתִי אֶת־כַּפִּי וְרָאִיתָ אֶת־אֲחֹרָי וּפָנַי לֹא
יֵרָאוּ׃

לד א וַיֹּאמֶר יהוה אֶל־מֹשֶׁה פְּסָל־לְךָ שְׁנֵי־לֻחֹת אֲבָנִים כָּרִאשֹׁנִים חמישי
וְכָתַבְתִּי עַל־הַלֻּחֹת אֶת־הַדְּבָרִים אֲשֶׁר הָיוּ עַל־הַלֻּחֹת
ב הָרִאשֹׁנִים אֲשֶׁר שִׁבַּרְתָּ׃ וֶהְיֵה נָכוֹן לַבֹּקֶר וְעָלִיתָ בַבֹּקֶר
ג אֶל־הַר סִינַי וְנִצַּבְתָּ לִי שָׁם עַל־רֹאשׁ הָהָר׃ וְאִישׁ לֹא־
יַעֲלֶה עִמָּךְ וְגַם־אִישׁ אַל־יֵרָא בְּכָל־הָהָר גַּם־הַצֹּאן וְהַבָּקָר
ד אַל־יִרְעוּ אֶל־מוּל הָהָר הַהוּא׃ וַיִּפְסֹל שְׁנֵי־לֻחֹת אֲבָנִים
כָּרִאשֹׁנִים וַיַּשְׁכֵּם מֹשֶׁה בַבֹּקֶר וַיַּעַל אֶל־הַר סִינַי כַּאֲשֶׁר
ה צִוָּה יהוה אֹתוֹ וַיִּקַּח בְּיָדוֹ שְׁנֵי לֻחֹת אֲבָנִים׃ וַיֵּרֶד יהוה בֶּעָנָן

33:19 וְרִחַמְתִּי אֶת־אֲשֶׁר אֲרַחֵם *Will show mercy to whom I decide to show mercy* – Even as God consents to show aspects of His glory, Moshe is reminded that there is an element of divine justice that must always elude human comprehension. We cannot fully enter into the mind of another human being, how much less so the mind of the Creator.

34:1 פְּסָל־לְךָ שְׁנֵי־לֻחֹת אֲבָנִים כָּרִאשֹׁנִים *Carve two tablets of stone like the first* – The first tablets made by God are smashed. The second tablets, the joint work of God and Moshe, remain intact. Surely the opposite should be true: the greater the holiness, the more eternal the object. Why was the more holy object broken while the less holy stayed whole?

This question leads us to a fundamental principle in Jewish spirituality. The Zohar distinguishes between two types of Divine-human encounter, calling them *itaruta dele'eyla* and *itaruta deletata*, respectively "an awakening from above" and "an awakening from below." The first is initiated by God, the second by mankind. An "awakening from above" is a supernatural event that bursts through the chains of causality that at other times bind the natural world. An "awakening from below" originates in human beings.

6 name: The LORD. And the LORD passed before him, and
proclaimed, "The LORD, the LORD, God compassionate
and gracious, slow to anger, abounding in kindness and
7 truth, extending kindness for thousands of generations,
forgiving sin, rebellion, and error, but who does not
acquit the guilty, holding descendants to account for
the sins of the fathers, children and grandchildren to
8 the third and fourth generation." Moshe quickly bowed

---

13. *And acquitting*: Literally, "cleansing" those who repent.

Note that this last attribute was derived by deliberately cutting the verse off before the end – the emphatic negative in the Hebrew is *venakeh lo yenakeh*, literally, "and acquitting He will not acquit." (This very different conclusion is discussed in the next comment.)

34:7 לֹא יְנַקֶּה *Who does not acquit the guilty* – God is compassionate and lives in love and forgiveness. This is an essential element of Jewish faith. But the Torah includes a caveat. There is compassion but there is also justice.

Why so? Why must there be punishment as well as forgiveness? The Sages said that "when God created the universe He did so under the attribute of justice, but then saw it could not survive. What did He do? He added compassion to justice and created the world" (Rashi on Gen. 1:1). This statement prompts the same question: Why did God not abandon justice altogether? Why is forgiveness alone not enough?

Some fascinating recent research provides us with an extraordinary and unexpected answer. Studies show that those who believe in a punitive God cheat and steal less than those who believe in a forgiving God. What is more, however, people who believe in a punitive God also punish people less than others who believe in a forgiving God. Subjects who believe that, as the Torah says, God "does not acquit the guilty" are more willing to leave punishment to God. Those who focus on divine forgiveness are more likely to practice human retribution or revenge.

A world without divine justice would be one where there is more resentment, punishment, and crime – and less public-spiritedness and forgiveness, even among religious believers. The more we believe that God punishes the guilty, the more forgiving we can become. The less we believe that God punishes the guilty, the more resentful and punitive we become. This is a counterintuitive truth, yet one that allows us to see the profound wisdom of the Torah in helping us create a humane and compassionate society. This is why, at the very moment He is declaring His compassion, grace, and forgiveness, God insists that He does not leave the guilty unpunished.

ו וַיִּתְיַצֵּב עִמּוֹ שָׁם וַיִּקְרָא בְשֵׁם יהוה: וַיַּעֲבֹר יהוה ׀ עַל־פָּנָיו
וַיִּקְרָא יהוה ׀ יהוה אֵל רַחוּם וְחַנּוּן אֶרֶךְ אַפַּיִם וְרַב־חֶסֶד
ז וֶאֱמֶת: נֹצֵר חֶסֶד לָאֲלָפִים נֹשֵׂא עָוֺן וָפֶשַׁע וְחַטָּאָה וְנַקֵּה
לֹא יְנַקֶּה פֹּקֵד ׀ עֲוֺן אָבוֹת עַל־בָּנִים וְעַל־בְּנֵי בָנִים עַל־
ח שִׁלֵּשִׁים וְעַל־רִבֵּעִים: וַיְמַהֵר מֹשֶׁה וַיִּקֹּד אַרְצָה וַיִּשְׁתָּחוּ:

THE THIRTEEN ATTRIBUTES OF MERCY

The Thirteen Attributes of Mercy, the name given by the Sages to God's declaration here, are the basis of all *Seliḥot*, prayers for forgiveness, for they are God's self-definition as the source of compassion and pardon that frames the moral life. They tell us that God "do[es] not desire the death of the wicked one, but that he should turn from his course and live" (Ezek. 33:11). When we repent and make good the harm we have done, God forgives. It is as if God is binding Himself to forgive the penitent in each generation by this description of Himself. The Thirteen Attributes derived by the Sages are as follows:

1. *The Lord:* The name that signifies God's attribute of compassion as opposed to strict justice.
2. *The Lord:* God retains the same compassion even after we have sinned, thus making repentance possible.
3. *God*: The power and force through which God sustains the universe and all that lives.
4. *Compassionate*: The root *r-ḥ-m* (from the Hebrew word *raḥum*, meaning "compassionate") is the same as "womb." Hence, it means the kind of compassion a mother has for a child.
5. *Gracious*: The root *ḥ-n-n* (from the Hebrew word *ḥanun*, meaning "gracious") refers to behavior that comes from the generosity of the one who does it, not the merits of the one to whom, or for whom, it is done.
6. *Slow to anger*: Thus giving time for wrongdoers to repent.
7. *Abounding in kindness*: According to a person's needs, not their deserts.
8. *And truth*: Giving a just reward to those who do His will.
9. *Extending kindness for thousands of generations*: God remembers through the ages the kindness of the patriarchs and the merits of our ancestors.
10. *Forgiving sin*: Sins committed knowingly.
11. *Rebellion*: Sins committed in a spirit of defiance.
12. *And error*: Sins committed unwittingly, either because we did not know what we were doing or did not know that it was forbidden.

9 and prostrated himself, and he said, "If now I have found
favor in Your sight, O Lord, please, let my Lord go among
us. Though this is a stiff-necked people, pardon our sins
10 and errors, and keep us as Your own." The LORD said, SHISHI
"Now am I hereby making a covenant. Before your entire
people I will perform such wonders as never have been
performed anywhere on earth, for any nation. All the
peoples you live among shall see: how awe-inspiring are
11 the deeds that I the LORD will do for you. Be vigilant
in what I am commanding you this day. I am going to
drive out before you the Amorites, Canaanites, Hittites,
12 Perizzites, Hivites, and Jebusites. Take care not to make
a treaty with the inhabitants of the land you are going
13 to; for they would become a dangerous trap to you. Tear
down their altars, smash their worship pillars, and cut
14 down their sacred trees, for you must worship no other
god. The LORD, known to demand absolute loyalty, is
15 your God who demands it indeed. You must not make a
treaty with the inhabitants of the land, for they will lust
after their gods and sacrifice to them; they will invite you
16 to join them and you will eat of their sacrifice, and you
will take their daughters as wives for your sons, and their
daughters will lust after their gods and cause your sons

Almighty God, look upon this people with favor, because what is now their greatest vice will one day be their most heroic virtue. They are indeed an obstinate people. When they have everything to thank You for, they complain. Mere weeks after hearing Your voice they make a golden calf. But just as now they are stiff-necked in their disobedience, so one day they will be equally stiff-necked in their loyalty. Nations will call on them to assimilate, but they will refuse. Mightier religions will urge them to convert, but they will resist. They will suffer humiliation, persecution, even torture and death because of the name they bear and the faith they profess, but they will stay true to the covenant their ancestors made with You. They will go to their deaths saying *Ani maamin*, "I believe." This is a people awesome in its obstinacy – and though now it is their failing, there will be times far into the future when it will be their noblest strength. (Cited in Aaron Yaakov Greenberg, ed., *Itturei Torah*)

ט וַיֹּאמֶר אִם־נָא מָצָאתִי חֵן בְּעֵינֶיךָ אֲדֹנָי יֵלֶךְ־נָא אֲדֹנָי
בְּקִרְבֵּנוּ כִּי עַם־קְשֵׁה־עֹרֶף הוּא וְסָלַחְתָּ לַעֲוֺנֵנוּ וּלְחַטָּאתֵנוּ
י וּנְחַלְתָּנוּ: וַיֹּאמֶר הִנֵּה אָנֹכִי כֹּרֵת בְּרִית נֶגֶד כָּל־עַמְּךָ ששי
אֶעֱשֶׂה נִפְלָאֹת אֲשֶׁר לֹא־נִבְרְאוּ בְכָל־הָאָרֶץ וּבְכָל־הַגּוֹיִם
וְרָאָה כָל־הָעָם אֲשֶׁר־אַתָּה בְקִרְבּוֹ אֶת־מַעֲשֵׂה יהוה כִּי־
יא נוֹרָא הוּא אֲשֶׁר אֲנִי עֹשֶׂה עִמָּךְ: שְׁמָר־לְךָ אֵת אֲשֶׁר אָנֹכִי
מְצַוְּךָ הַיּוֹם הִנְנִי גֹרֵשׁ מִפָּנֶיךָ אֶת־הָאֱמֹרִי וְהַכְּנַעֲנִי וְהַחִתִּי
יב וְהַפְּרִזִּי וְהַחִוִּי וְהַיְבוּסִי: הִשָּׁמֶר לְךָ פֶּן־תִּכְרֹת בְּרִית לְיוֹשֵׁב
הָאָרֶץ אֲשֶׁר אַתָּה בָּא עָלֶיהָ פֶּן־יִהְיֶה לְמוֹקֵשׁ בְּקִרְבֶּךָ:
יג כִּי אֶת־מִזְבְּחֹתָם תִּתֹּצוּן וְאֶת־מַצֵּבֹתָם תְּשַׁבֵּרוּן וְאֶת־
יד אֲשֵׁרָיו תִּכְרֹתוּן: כִּי לֹא תִשְׁתַּחֲוֶה לְאֵל אַחֵר כִּי יהוה
טו קַנָּא שְׁמוֹ אֵל קַנָּא הוּא: פֶּן־תִּכְרֹת בְּרִית לְיוֹשֵׁב הָאָרֶץ
וְזָנוּ | אַחֲרֵי אֱלֹהֵיהֶם וְזָבְחוּ לֵאלֹהֵיהֶם וְקָרָא לְךָ וְאָכַלְתָּ
טז מִזִּבְחוֹ: וְלָקַחְתָּ מִבְּנֹתָיו לְבָנֶיךָ וְזָנוּ בְנֹתָיו אַחֲרֵי אֱלֹהֵיהֶן

34:9 כִּי עַם־קְשֵׁה־עֹרֶף הוּא *Though this is a stiff-necked people* – The Hebrew word *ki*, most often meaning "because," reads as though Moshe is in fact citing a reason for God remaining with the Israelites. Yet this is the very attribute that God had previously given for wishing to abandon them: "Then the LORD said to Moshe, 'I have seen this people; it is a stiff-necked people. So do not try to stop Me when My anger burns against them. I will put an end to them'" (Ex. 32:9–10).

How can Moshe invoke the people's obstinacy as the very reason for God to maintain His presence among them? The commentators offer a variety of interpretations. Rashi reads the word *ki* as "if": "If they are stiff-necked, then forgive them." Ibn Ezra and *Ḥizkuni,* reflected in our translation, read it as "although" or "despite the fact that" (*af al pi*). Alternatively, suggests Ibn Ezra, the verse might be read as "[I admit that] it is a stiff-necked people – therefore forgive our wickedness and our sin, and take us as Your inheritance."

There is a striking line of interpretation that can be traced across the centuries. In the twentieth century it was given expression by Rabbi Yitzchak Nissenbaum. The fact that Rabbi Nissenbaum lived and died in the Warsaw Ghetto gives added poignancy to his words. The argument he attributed to Moshe is this:

17 to do as they do. Make for yourselves no molten gods.
18 Keep the Festival of Unleavened Bread. For seven days,
eat unleavened bread as I commanded you, at the time
appointed, in the month of Aviv, because in that month
19 you left Egypt. The first to emerge from every womb
is Mine; among all your livestock, firstborn cattle, and
20 sheep. Redeem each firstborn donkey with a sheep; if you
do not redeem it, you must break its neck. Also redeem
all your firstborn sons. Do not appear before Me empty-
21 handed. Six days you shall work, but on the seventh day
you shall rest, ceasing from labor even at plowing time
22 and harvest time. Observe the Festival of Weeks, of the
first fruits of the wheat harvest, as well as the Festival of
23 Ingathering at the close of the year. Three times a year all
the males among you shall appear before the Master, the
24 LORD, God of Israel. For I will banish nations before you
and enlarge your territory. No one will covet your land
when you go up, three times a year, to appear before the
25 LORD your God. Do not offer the blood of My sacrifice
with anything leavened. Do not let any of the Passover
26 festival sacrifice remain until morning. Bring the best first
fruits of your land to the House of the LORD your God.
Do not cook a kid in the milk of its mother."

The Sabbath tells us that happiness lies not in what we buy, but in what we are; that true contentment is to be found not by seeking what we lack but by giving thanks for what we have; and that we should never allow ourselves to be so busy making a living that we have all too little time to live. Above all, we should never be led by the crowd when it stampedes in pursuit of gain, for that is how gold becomes a golden calf.

34:26 לֹא־תְבַשֵּׁל גְּדִי בַּחֲלֵב אִמּוֹ *Do not cook a kid in the milk of its mother* – This is the origin of the prohibition against mixing meat and milk. Rambam infers from its association with the festivals that this was an idolatrous practice associated with pagan festivities (*Guide for the Perplexed* III:48). The pagan imagination often celebrated the blurring of boundaries: man-god, man-beast, androgyny, and other hybrids. The biblical imagination, on the other hand, is predicated on clear boundaries.

יז וְהִזְנוּ֙ אֶת־בָּנֶ֔יךָ אַחֲרֵ֖י אֱלֹהֵיהֶֽן׃ אֱלֹהֵ֥י מַסֵּכָ֖ה לֹ֥א תַעֲשֶׂה־
יח לָּֽךְ׃ אֶת־חַ֣ג הַמַּצּוֹת֮ תִּשְׁמֹר֒ שִׁבְעַ֨ת יָמִ֜ים תֹּאכַ֤ל מַצּוֹת֙
אֲשֶׁ֣ר צִוִּיתִ֔ךָ לְמוֹעֵ֖ד חֹ֣דֶשׁ הָאָבִ֑יב כִּ֚י בְּחֹ֣דֶשׁ הָֽאָבִ֔יב יָצָ֖אתָ
יט מִמִּצְרָֽיִם׃ כָּל־פֶּ֥טֶר רֶ֖חֶם לִ֑י וְכָֽל־מִקְנְךָ֙ תִּזָּכָ֔ר פֶּ֖טֶר שׁ֥וֹר
כ וָשֶֽׂה׃ וּפֶ֤טֶר חֲמוֹר֙ תִּפְדֶּ֣ה בְשֶׂ֔ה וְאִם־לֹ֥א תִפְדֶּ֖ה וַעֲרַפְתּ֑וֹ
כא כֹּ֣ל בְּכ֤וֹר בָּנֶ֙יךָ֙ תִּפְדֶּ֔ה וְלֹא־יֵרָא֥וּ פָנַ֖י רֵיקָֽם׃ שֵׁ֤שֶׁת יָמִים֙
כב תַּעֲבֹ֔ד וּבַיּ֥וֹם הַשְּׁבִיעִ֖י תִּשְׁבֹּ֑ת בֶּחָרִ֥ישׁ וּבַקָּצִ֖יר תִּשְׁבֹּֽת׃ וְחַ֤ג
שָׁבֻעֹת֙ תַּעֲשֶׂ֣ה לְךָ֔ בִּכּוּרֵ֖י קְצִ֣יר חִטִּ֑ים וְחַג֙ הָֽאָסִ֔יף תְּקוּפַ֖ת
כג הַשָּׁנָֽה׃ שָׁלֹ֥שׁ פְּעָמִ֖ים בַּשָּׁנָ֑ה יֵרָאֶה֙ כָּל־זְכ֣וּרְךָ֔ אֶת־פְּנֵ֛י הָֽאָדֹ֥ן ׀
כד יְהוָ֖ה אֱלֹהֵ֥י יִשְׂרָאֵֽל׃ כִּֽי־אוֹרִ֤ישׁ גּוֹיִם֙ מִפָּנֶ֔יךָ וְהִרְחַבְתִּ֖י אֶת־
גְּבֻלֶ֑ךָ וְלֹא־יַחְמֹ֥ד אִישׁ֙ אֶת־אַרְצְךָ֔ בַּעֲלֹֽתְךָ֗ לֵרָאוֹת֙ אֶת־פְּנֵי֙
כה יְהוָ֣ה אֱלֹהֶ֔יךָ שָׁלֹ֥שׁ פְּעָמִ֖ים בַּשָּׁנָֽה׃ לֹֽא־תִשְׁחַ֥ט עַל־חָמֵ֖ץ
כו דַּם־זִבְחִ֑י וְלֹא־יָלִ֣ין לַבֹּ֔קֶר זֶ֖בַח חַ֥ג הַפָּֽסַח׃ רֵאשִׁ֗ית בִּכּוּרֵי֙
אַדְמָ֣תְךָ֔ תָּבִ֕יא בֵּ֖ית יְהוָ֣ה אֱלֹהֶ֑יךָ לֹֽא־תְבַשֵּׁ֥ל גְּדִ֖י בַּחֲלֵ֥ב
אִמּֽוֹ׃

34:21 **וּבַיּוֹם הַשְּׁבִיעִי תִּשְׁבֹּת** *On the seventh day you shall rest* – Immediately before and after the golden calf event, Moshe gives the Israelites the same command, namely the Sabbath. The Sabbath is the antidote to the golden calf.

The golden calf is a symbol of what can happen when people turn gold, a medium of exchange, into an object of worship. The Sabbath, on the other hand, is the day when we stop thinking of the *price* of things and focus instead on the *value* of things. On the Sabbath we can't sell or buy. We can't work or pay others to work for us. It is the day dedicated to the celebration of the things that have value but no price. Husbands sing a song of praise to their wives. Parents bless their children. We take time to have a meal together with family and friends. In the synagogue we renew our sense of community. People share their joys with others and find comfort for their grief. We listen to Torah together, reminding ourselves of the story of which we are a part. We pray together, thanking God for our blessings.

The Sabbath is our refuge from what has become, by now, a consumer culture. There are limits to our striving, our labors, our consumption of the earth's finite resources. Any culture that loses its sense of limits eventually self-destructs.

▶

27 Then the LORD said to Moshe, "Write down these words, SHEVI'I
for in accordance with these words I have made a covenant
28 with you and with Israel." He stayed there with the LORD
for forty days and forty nights, eating no bread and
drinking no water. And on the tablets, He wrote the words
29 of the covenant, the Ten Commandments. When Moshe
came down from Mount Sinai with the two tablets of
testimony in his hand, he was unaware that the skin of
his face shone with light, because he had been speaking
30 with God. When Aharon and all the Israelites saw the
light that shone from the skin of Moshe's face, they were
31 afraid to come close to him. But Moshe called them, and
Aharon and all the community leaders came back to him,
32 and Moshe spoke. After that, all the Israelites approached, MAFTIR
and he instructed them in all that the LORD had spoken
33 to him on Mount Sinai. And when Moshe had finished
34 speaking to them, he veiled his face. Whenever Moshe
came before the LORD to speak with Him, he would
remove the veil until he came out. When he came out
35 and told the Israelites what he had been commanded, the
Israelites would see how the skin of Moshe's face shone
with light, and he would veil his face again until he went
back in to speak with Him.

The haftara for Parashat Ki Tisa is on page 1494.
On Purim Meshulash in Jerusalem read the haftara on page 1658.
On the Shabbat of Parashat Para read the haftara on page 1662.

---

are given of this phrase. One reads it as "a loud voice that was never heard again," the other as "a loud voice that did not cease," i.e., a voice that was always heard again. Both are true. The first refers to the Written Torah, given once and never to be repeated. The second applies to the Oral Torah, whose study has never ceased.

It also helps us understand why it is only after the second tablets, not the first, that "when Moshe came down from Mount Sinai with the two tablets of testimony in his hand, he was unaware that the skin of his face shone with light, because he had been speaking with God" (Ex. 34:29). Receiving the first tablets, Moshe is passive. Therefore, nothing in him changes. For the second, he is active. He has a share in the making. He carves the stone on which the words are to be engraved. That is why he becomes a different person. His face shines.

כז וַיֹּאמֶר יהוה אֶל־מֹשֶׁה כְּתׇב־לְךָ אֶת־הַדְּבָרִים הָאֵלֶּה כִּי כו שביעי
עַל־פִּי ׀ הַדְּבָרִים הָאֵלֶּה כָּרַתִּי אִתְּךָ בְּרִית וְאֶת־יִשְׂרָאֵל׃
כח וַיְהִי־שָׁם עִם־יהוה אַרְבָּעִים יוֹם וְאַרְבָּעִים לַיְלָה לֶחֶם לֹא
אָכַל וּמַיִם לֹא שָׁתָה וַיִּכְתֹּב עַל־הַלֻּחֹת אֵת דִּבְרֵי הַבְּרִית
כט עֲשֶׂרֶת הַדְּבָרִים׃ וַיְהִי בְּרֶדֶת מֹשֶׁה מֵהַר סִינַי וּשְׁנֵי לֻחֹת
הָעֵדֻת בְּיַד־מֹשֶׁה בְּרִדְתּוֹ מִן־הָהָר וּמֹשֶׁה לֹא־יָדַע כִּי קָרַן
ל עוֹר פָּנָיו בְּדַבְּרוֹ אִתּוֹ׃ וַיַּרְא אַהֲרֹן וְכׇל־בְּנֵי יִשְׂרָאֵל אֶת־
לא מֹשֶׁה וְהִנֵּה קָרַן עוֹר פָּנָיו וַיִּירְאוּ מִגֶּשֶׁת אֵלָיו׃ וַיִּקְרָא אֲלֵהֶם
מֹשֶׁה וַיָּשֻׁבוּ אֵלָיו אַהֲרֹן וְכׇל־הַנְּשִׂאִים בָּעֵדָה וַיְדַבֵּר מֹשֶׁה
לב אֲלֵהֶם׃ וְאַחֲרֵי־כֵן נִגְּשׁוּ כׇּל־בְּנֵי יִשְׂרָאֵל וַיְצַוֵּם אֵת כׇּל־
לג אֲשֶׁר דִּבֶּר יהוה אִתּוֹ בְּהַר סִינָי׃ וַיְכַל מֹשֶׁה מִדַּבֵּר אִתָּם מפטיר
לד וַיִּתֵּן עַל־פָּנָיו מַסְוֶה׃ וּבְבֹא מֹשֶׁה לִפְנֵי יהוה לְדַבֵּר אִתּוֹ
יָסִיר אֶת־הַמַּסְוֶה עַד־צֵאתוֹ וְיָצָא וְדִבֶּר אֶל־בְּנֵי יִשְׂרָאֵל
לה אֵת אֲשֶׁר יְצֻוֶּה׃ וְרָאוּ בְנֵי־יִשְׂרָאֵל אֶת־פְּנֵי מֹשֶׁה כִּי קָרַן
עוֹר פְּנֵי מֹשֶׁה וְהֵשִׁיב מֹשֶׁה אֶת־הַמַּסְוֶה עַל־פָּנָיו עַד־בֹּאוֹ
לְדַבֵּר אִתּוֹ׃

The הפטרה *for* פרשת כי תשא *is on page 1495.*
On פורים משולש *in Jerusalem read the* הפטרה *on page 1659.*
On the שבת *of* פרשת פרה *read the* הפטרה *on page 1663.*

34:29 קָרַן עוֹר פָּנָיו *The skin of his face shone with light* – According to tradition, when Moshe was given the first tablets, he was given only *Torah Shebikhtav*, the Written Torah. At the time of the second tablets, he was given *Torah Shebe'al Peh*, the Oral Torah as well. The difference between the Written and Oral Torah is profound. The first is the word of God, with no human contribution. The second is a partnership – the word of God as interpreted by the mind of man. Any attempt to reduce the Oral Torah to the Written – by relying on prophecy or divine communication – mistakes its essential nature as the collaborative partnership between God and man, where revelation meets interpretation. Thus, the difference between the two precisely mirrors that between the first and second tablets. The first were divine, the second the result of Divine-human collaboration. This helps us understand a glorious ambiguity. The Torah says that at Sinai the Israelites heard a "loud voice *velo yasaf*" (Deut. 5:19). Two contradictory interpretations

PARASHAT VAYAK'HEL

35 1 Moshe assembled all the community of Israel and said to
them, "These are the things the LORD has commanded
2 you to do. For six days, let work be done, but the seventh
must be sacred to you. It is a Sabbath of complete rest
dedicated to the LORD. Whoever does work on it shall be
3 put to death. Do not light a fire in any of your dwellings
on the Sabbath day."

---

that they said the same prayers, at the same time, all facing the same spot, Jerusalem. They observed the same festivals, honored the same days. They were a community in time, not in space.

This idea has halachic implications:

> R. Yitzḥak said to R. Naḥman: Why did the master not come to the synagogue to pray? R. Naḥman said to him: I was [weak and] unable to come.... R. Yitzḥak said: The master should tell the congregation to send a messenger when the congregation is praying to come and inform the master [so that you may pray at the same time]. As R. Yoḥanan said in the name of R. Shimon b. Yoḥai: ... "But as for me, may my prayer come to You, LORD, in a moment of favor" (Ps. 69:14). When is a time of favor? The time when the congregation is praying. (Berakhot 7b–8a)

In other words, even if one is unable to go to the synagogue, one should try to pray at the same time as the community. Rabbi Joseph B. Soloveitchik explains that if one does so, one's prayer is joined to that of the community.

Rabbi Shneur Zalman of Liadi once said to his disciples, "One must live with the times." The disciples were puzzled; surely Judaism is timeless. Eventually the Rebbe's brother, Rabbi Yehuda Leib, explained, "He meant one must live with the weekly *parasha*." Somehow or other, that must be the time zone in which Jews live.

We live in the intersection between the timely and the timeless, between what is happening now and what God said to us over three thousand years ago. By praying at the same time as the rest of the community, we become "like one person with one heart" (Rashi on Ex. 19:2). There is such a thing as a community in time. This is why the narrative of the Tabernacle is inseparable from the law of the Sabbath.

35:3 בְּיוֹם הַשַּׁבָּת *On the Sabbath day* – The Talmud raises the following question: What happens if you are far away from human habitation and you forget which

פרשת ויקהל

לה א וַיַּקְהֵל מֹשֶׁה אֶת־כׇּל־עֲדַת בְּנֵי יִשְׂרָאֵל וַיֹּאמֶר אֲלֵהֶם אֵלֶּה
ב הַדְּבָרִים אֲשֶׁר־צִוָּה יהוה לַעֲשֹׂת אֹתָם: שֵׁשֶׁת יָמִים תֵּעָשֶׂה
מְלָאכָה וּבַיּוֹם הַשְּׁבִיעִי יִהְיֶה לָכֶם קֹדֶשׁ שַׁבַּת שַׁבָּתוֹן
ג לַיהוה כׇּל־הָעֹשֶׂה בוֹ מְלָאכָה יוּמָת: לֹא־תְבַעֲרוּ אֵשׁ בְּכֹל
מֹשְׁבֹתֵיכֶם בְּיוֹם הַשַּׁבָּת:

VAYAK'HEL

Immediately after his return from the mountaintop, having secured forgiveness for the people for the sin of the golden calf, Moshe assembles them and commands them first about the Sabbath and then about the making of the Tabernacle. The *parasha* repeats much of what was said earlier in Parashat Teruma, with this difference: there, we read the instructions; here, the Torah reports on their execution. The people give willingly, and Betzalel and Oholiav, the craftsmen, fashion the various structures. Our *parasha* raises questions about why the long account of the Tabernacle appears in Exodus, a book concerned with nation-building, the Torah's understanding of community, and the place of aesthetics in Judaism.

THE SABBATH AND THE SANCTUARY

Why here does Moshe repeat the commandment of keeping the Sabbath? The conventional and authoritative explanation is that this passage shows us that the Sabbath takes priority over the building of the Tabernacle. But the passage also has another meaning. God is saying, "I am going to give the Jewish people two sanctuaries, not one. The first is the Tabernacle, a sanctuary in space, in place. The second is the Sabbath, a sanctuary in time."

Why do we need both? Because we have a principle in Judaism: "Before God brings a sickness to the world, He brings the cure" (Megilla 13b). God knew that the day would come when Jews would suffer exile and dispersion. They would no longer have a Temple in Jerusalem; they would no longer have a land; they would no longer have a home. "Even so," says God, "however dispersed you are, you will still have a sanctuary. It will exist not in space, but in time. That sanctuary is called the Sabbath. It will happen not because you are together physically in one place, but because spiritually you will be together at the same time."

And so it happened. Jews lost all the attributes of a people. They weren't living in the same place, under the same conditions, or within the same culture. What forged them as one people was

4 Then Moshe said to all the community of Israel, "This is
5 what the LORD has commanded. Bring of what is yours
an offering to the LORD. Let everyone whose heart
moves him bring an offering to the LORD: gold, silver,
6 and bronze; sky-blue, purple, and scarlet wool; linen and
7 goats' hair; rams' hides dyed red and fine leather; acacia
8 wood; oil for the lamp; spices for the anointing oil and
9 the fragrant incense; and rock crystal together with other
10 precious stones for the ephod and breast piece. And let
all among you who are skilled come and make the things
11 that the LORD has commanded: the Tabernacle, its tent
and covering, its hooks and frames, its bars, posts, and
12 sockets; the Ark and its staves, the cover and the curtain
13 for the screen; the table, its staves and all its utensils, and
14 the showbread; the candelabrum for light, together with
15 its utensils, lamps, and the oil for lighting; the incense
altar with its staves, the anointing oil and the fragrant
incense, and the entrance screen for the entrance of the
16 Tabernacle; the sacrificial altar, its bronze grate, its staves

---

poor may have the opposite effect. Even a novelist may not know how the story will turn out until he has written it.

One possible response to this is simply to let things happen as they will. This kind of resignation, however, is wholly out of keeping with the Judaic view of history. The other solution, then, is to reveal the end at the beginning. That is the meaning of the Sabbath. It is not simply a day of rest. It is an anticipation of "the end of history," the Messianic age. On it, we recover the lost harmonies of the Garden of Eden. We do not strive to do; we are content to be. We are not allowed to exercise power or dominance over other human beings, nor even domestic animals. Rich and poor inhabit the Sabbath alike, with equal dignity and freedom. The Sabbath is a dress rehearsal for an ideal society that has not yet come to pass.

God wanted us to know what we were aiming for, so that we would not lose our way in the wilderness of time. That is why, when it came to the human execution of the building, the Sabbath came first, even though the Messianic age, the "Sabbath of history," will come last. God is "telling of the end from the beginning" (Is. 46:10) – the fulfilled rest that follows creative labor, the peace that will one day take the place of strife – so that, before beginning the journey, we catch a glimpse of the destination.

ד וַיֹּאמֶר מֹשֶׁה אֶל־כָּל־עֲדַת בְּנֵי־יִשְׂרָאֵל לֵאמֹר זֶה הַדָּבָר
ה אֲשֶׁר־צִוָּה יהוה לֵאמֹר: קְחוּ מֵאִתְּכֶם תְּרוּמָה לַיהוה כֹּל
נְדִיב לִבּוֹ יְבִיאֶהָ אֵת תְּרוּמַת יהוה זָהָב וָכֶסֶף וּנְחֹשֶׁת:
ו ז וּתְכֵלֶת וְאַרְגָּמָן וְתוֹלַעַת שָׁנִי וְשֵׁשׁ וְעִזִּים: וְעֹרֹת אֵילִם
ח מְאָדָּמִים וְעֹרֹת תְּחָשִׁים וַעֲצֵי שִׁטִּים: וְשֶׁמֶן לַמָּאוֹר וּבְשָׂמִים
ט לְשֶׁמֶן הַמִּשְׁחָה וְלִקְטֹרֶת הַסַּמִּים: וְאַבְנֵי־שֹׁהַם וְאַבְנֵי
י מִלֻּאִים לָאֵפוֹד וְלַחֹשֶׁן: וְכָל־חֲכַם־לֵב בָּכֶם יָבֹאוּ וְיַעֲשׂוּ
יא אֵת כָּל־אֲשֶׁר צִוָּה יהוה: אֶת־הַמִּשְׁכָּן אֶת־אָהֳלוֹ וְאֶת־
מִכְסֵהוּ אֶת־קְרָסָיו וְאֶת־קְרָשָׁיו אֶת־בְּרִיחָו אֶת־עַמֻּדָיו
יב וְאֶת־אֲדָנָיו: אֶת־הָאָרֹן וְאֶת־בַּדָּיו אֶת־הַכַּפֹּרֶת וְאֵת פָּרֹכֶת
יג הַמָּסָךְ: אֶת־הַשֻּׁלְחָן וְאֶת־בַּדָּיו וְאֶת־כָּל־כֵּלָיו וְאֵת לֶחֶם
יד הַפָּנִים: וְאֶת־מְנֹרַת הַמָּאוֹר וְאֶת־כֵּלֶיהָ וְאֶת־נֵרֹתֶיהָ וְאֵת
טו שֶׁמֶן הַמָּאוֹר: וְאֶת־מִזְבַּח הַקְּטֹרֶת וְאֶת־בַּדָּיו וְאֵת שֶׁמֶן
הַמִּשְׁחָה וְאֵת קְטֹרֶת הַסַּמִּים וְאֶת־מָסַךְ הַפֶּתַח לְפֶתַח
טז הַמִּשְׁכָּן: אֵת ׀ מִזְבַּח הָעֹלָה וְאֶת־מִכְבַּר הַנְּחֹשֶׁת אֲשֶׁר־לוֹ

---

day it is? How do you observe the Sabbath? Two answers are offered:

> R. Huna said: "If one is traveling on a road or in the wilderness and does not know when the Sabbath falls, he must count six days [from the day he realizes he has forgotten] and observe one." R. Ḥiyya b. Rav said: "He must observe one, and then count six [week]days." On what do they differ? One master holds that it is like the world's creation. The other holds that it is like [the case of] Adam. (Shabbat 69b)

From God's point of view, the Sabbath was the seventh day. From the point of view of the first human beings – created on the sixth day – the Sabbath was the first. We now have an insight into why, in God's instruction to Moshe in Parashat Ki Tisa, the command of the Sabbath appears after the details of the construction of the Tabernacle, while here, in Moshe's instruction to the people, it appears before. For God, the Sabbath was the last day of creation; for human beings it was the first.

In divine creation, there is no gap between intention and execution. God spoke, and the world came into existence. With human beings, it is otherwise. Creativity is fraught with risk. The law of unintended consequences tells us that revolutions rarely turn out as planned. Policies designed to help the

17 and all its utensils, the laver and its base; the hangings of
the courtyard, its posts and its sockets, and the screen
18 for the gate of the court; the tent pegs of the Tabernacle
19 and of the courtyard and their ropes; the vestments for
ministering in the Sanctuary, and the sacred vestments
for Aharon the priest and for his sons for their priestly
20 service." So all the community of Israel left Moshe's
21 presence. And they came, everyone whose heart inspired SHENI
him and whose spirit moved him, and brought an
offering for the LORD, to be used for the Tent of Meeting
22 and all its service, and for the sacred vestments. All whose
hearts moved them – the men with the women – brought
brooches, earrings, signet rings and pendants, all kinds
of gold ornaments, together with all those who gave gold
23 as a wave offering to the LORD. Everyone who had sky-
blue, purple, or scarlet wool, linen or goats' hair, rams'
24 hides dyed red or fine leather brought them. Whoever
could make an offering of silver or bronze brought it as
an offering to the LORD, as did everyone who had acacia
25 wood that could be used for the work. Every skilled
woman spun with her own hands, and brought what
she had spun: sky-blue, purple, and scarlet wool and fine
26 linen. All the women whose hearts inspired them used
27 their skill to spin the goats' hair. The leaders brought rock
crystal stones and other precious stones for setting in the
28 ephod and the breast piece, together with spices and oil
for the light, the anointing oil and the fragrant incense.
29 So the Israelites – all the men and women whose hearts
moved them to bring anything for the work that the
LORD, through Moshe, had commanded – brought it as a
freewill offering to the LORD.

individuals. Moses turned the *kehilla* with its diversity into a community with a singleness of purpose, while preserving the range of the gifts they each brought to God.

Society is what we build together. A nation is made by contributions, not claims; active citizenship, not rights; what we give, not what we demand. Every member of the group must be

יז אֶת־בַּדָּיו וְאֶת־כָּל־כֵּלָיו אֶת־הַכִּיֹּר וְאֶת־כַּנּוֹ: אֵת קַלְעֵי
הֶחָצֵר אֶת־עַמֻּדָיו וְאֶת־אֲדָנֶיהָ וְאֵת מָסַךְ שַׁעַר הֶחָצֵר:
יח אֶת־יִתְדֹת הַמִּשְׁכָּן וְאֶת־יִתְדֹת הֶחָצֵר וְאֶת־מֵיתְרֵיהֶם:
יט אֶת־בִּגְדֵי הַשְּׂרָד לְשָׁרֵת בַּקֹּדֶשׁ אֶת־בִּגְדֵי הַקֹּדֶשׁ לְאַהֲרֹן
כ הַכֹּהֵן וְאֶת־בִּגְדֵי בָנָיו לְכַהֵן: וַיֵּצְאוּ כָּל־עֲדַת בְּנֵי־יִשְׂרָאֵל
כא מִלִּפְנֵי מֹשֶׁה: וַיָּבֹאוּ כָּל־אִישׁ אֲשֶׁר־נְשָׂאוֹ לִבּוֹ וְכֹל אֲשֶׁר שני
נָדְבָה רוּחוֹ אֹתוֹ הֵבִיאוּ אֶת־תְּרוּמַת יהוה לִמְלֶאכֶת אֹהֶל
כב מוֹעֵד וּלְכָל־עֲבֹדָתוֹ וּלְבִגְדֵי הַקֹּדֶשׁ: וַיָּבֹאוּ הָאֲנָשִׁים עַל־
הַנָּשִׁים כֹּל ׀ נְדִיב לֵב הֵבִיאוּ חָח וָנֶזֶם וְטַבַּעַת וְכוּמָז כָּל־כְּלִי
כג זָהָב וְכָל־אִישׁ אֲשֶׁר הֵנִיף תְּנוּפַת זָהָב לַיהוה: וְכָל־אִישׁ
אֲשֶׁר־נִמְצָא אִתּוֹ תְּכֵלֶת וְאַרְגָּמָן וְתוֹלַעַת שָׁנִי וְשֵׁשׁ וְעִזִּים
כד וְעֹרֹת אֵילִם מְאָדָּמִים וְעֹרֹת תְּחָשִׁים הֵבִיאוּ: כָּל־מֵרִים
תְּרוּמַת כֶּסֶף וּנְחֹשֶׁת הֵבִיאוּ אֵת תְּרוּמַת יהוה וְכֹל אֲשֶׁר
כה נִמְצָא אִתּוֹ עֲצֵי שִׁטִּים לְכָל־מְלֶאכֶת הָעֲבֹדָה הֵבִיאוּ: וְכָל־
אִשָּׁה חַכְמַת־לֵב בְּיָדֶיהָ טָווּ וַיָּבִיאוּ מַטְוֶה אֶת־הַתְּכֵלֶת
כו וְאֶת־הָאַרְגָּמָן אֶת־תּוֹלַעַת הַשָּׁנִי וְאֶת־הַשֵּׁשׁ: וְכָל־הַנָּשִׁים
כז אֲשֶׁר נָשָׂא לִבָּן אֹתָנָה בְּחָכְמָה טָווּ אֶת־הָעִזִּים: וְהַנְּשִׂאִם
הֵבִיאוּ אֵת אַבְנֵי הַשֹּׁהַם וְאֵת אַבְנֵי הַמִּלֻּאִים לָאֵפוֹד וְלַחֹשֶׁן:
כח וְאֶת־הַבֹּשֶׂם וְאֶת־הַשָּׁמֶן לְמָאוֹר וּלְשֶׁמֶן הַמִּשְׁחָה וְלִקְטֹרֶת
כט הַסַּמִּים: כָּל־אִישׁ וְאִשָּׁה אֲשֶׁר נָדַב לִבָּם אֹתָם לְהָבִיא
לְכָל־הַמְּלָאכָה אֲשֶׁר צִוָּה יהוה לַעֲשׂוֹת בְּיַד־מֹשֶׁה הֵבִיאוּ
בְנֵי־יִשְׂרָאֵל נְדָבָה לַיהוה:

35:29 כָּל־אִישׁ וְאִשָּׁה אֲשֶׁר נָדַב לִבָּם אֹתָם לְהָבִיא... נְדָבָה לַיהוה *All the men and women whose hearts moved them to bring anything... as a freewill offering to the* LORD – Moshe emphasizes that each has something different to give: "Bring of what is yours an offering to the LORD. Let everyone whose heart moves him bring an offering to the LORD: gold, silver and bronze.... And let all among you who are skilled come and make the things that the LORD has commanded..." (Ex. 35:5, 10). The beauty of a *kehilla* – a community – is that when it is driven by a constructive purpose, it gathers together the distinct and separate contributions of many

30 Then Moshe said to the Israelites, "Know that the LORD SHELISHI /SHENI/
has summoned by name Betzalel, son of Uri, son of Ḥur,
31 of the tribe of Yehuda, and has filled him with a divine
spirit of wisdom, understanding, and knowledge in
32 every craft, to devise designs, working in gold, silver, and
33 bronze, as well as cutting stones for setting, carving wood,
34 and working in every other craft. He has also given him
the ability to teach others, together with Oholiav, son of
35 Aḥisamakh of the tribe of Dan. He has filled them with
the skill to do all kinds of work, as engravers, designers,
embroiderers in sky-blue, purple, or scarlet wool or fine
linen, and as weavers. They will be able to carry out all the
36 1 necessary work and design. And so Betzalel and Oholiav
shall carry out everything the LORD has commanded,
together with all the skilled people to whom the LORD
has granted expertise and acumen to do all the work
2 necessary for the service of the Sanctuary." Then Moshe
summoned Betzalel and Oholiav and all the skilled
craftsmen to whom God had given expertise and who
were inspired to dedicate themselves and come to carry

(28:2). The very terms applied to Betzalel – wisdom, understanding, and knowledge – are applied by the book of Proverbs to God Himself as creator of the universe:

> The LORD founded the earth with wisdom;
> He established the heavens with discernment;
> With His knowledge were the depths carved out,
> And the sky dropped dew. (Prov. 3:19–20)

The Greeks, and many in the Western world who inherited their tradition, believed in the holiness of beauty. Keats gave succinct expression to this creed in the last lines of his "Ode to a Grecian Urn": "Beauty is Truth, truth is beauty, that is all/Ye know on earth and all ye need to know." Jews believe in the opposite: *hadrat kodesh*, the beauty of holiness: "Render to the LORD the glory due His name; bow to the LORD in the splendor of holiness" (Ps. 29:2). Art in Judaism always has a spiritual purpose: to make us aware of the universe as a work of art, testifying to the supreme Artist, God Himself.

ל ויאמר משה אל-בני ישראל ראו קרא יהוה בשם בצלאל שלישי
לא בן-אורי בן-חור למטה יהודה: וימלא אתו רוח אלהים /שני/
לב בחכמה בתבונה ובדעת ובכל-מלאכה: ולחשב מחשבת
לג לעשת בזהב ובכסף ובנחשת: ובחרשת אבן למלאת
לד ובחרשת עץ לעשות בכל-מלאכת מחשבת: ולהורת
לה נתן בלבו הוא ואהליאב בן-אחיסמך למטה-דן: מלא
אתם חכמת-לב לעשות כל-מלאכת חרש | וחשב ורקם
בתכלת ובארגמן בתולעת השני ובשש וארג עשי כל-
לו א מלאכה וחשבי מחשבת: ועשה בצלאל ואהליאב וכל |
איש חכם-לב אשר נתן יהוה חכמה ותבונה בהמה לדעת
לעשת את-כל-מלאכת עבדת הקדש לכל אשר-צוה
ב יהוה: ויקרא משה אל-בצלאל ואל-אהליאב ואל כל-
איש חכם-לב אשר נתן יהוה חכמה בלבו כל אשר

able to make a unique contribution and then feel that it has been valued. What matters is that together we build something none of us could make alone. Each must be able to say with pride: I helped make this.

35:33 לעשות בכל-מלאכת מחשבת *Working in every other craft* – The Israelites worshipped the invisible God who transcended the universe. Other than the human person, God has no image. Even when He revealed Himself to the people at Sinai, "you heard the sound of words but saw no image; there was only a voice" (Deut. 4:12). Given the intense connection – until around the eighteenth century – between art and religion, image-making was seen as potentially idolatrous. Hence the second of the Ten Commandments: "Do not make for yourself any carved image or likeness of any creature in the heavens above or the earth beneath or the waters beneath the earth" (Ex. 20:4). This concern continued long after the biblical era. The Greeks, who achieved unrivaled excellence in the visual arts, were, in the religious sphere, still a pagan people of myth and mystery, while the Romans had a disturbing tendency to turn caesars into gods and erect statues to them.

Yet as we see from the case of Betzalel, Judaism is not indifferent to aesthetics. The concept of *hiddur mitzva*, "beautifying the commandment," meant, for the Sages, that we should strive to fulfill the commands in the most aesthetically pleasing way. The priestly garments were meant to be "for glory and for splendor"

3 out the work. From Moshe they received all the offerings
the Israelites had brought for the work of the Sanctuary.
And the people kept bringing him additional gifts every
4 morning. So all the craftsmen engaged in the work of the
5 Sanctuary left what they were doing, and said to Moshe,
"The people are bringing more than is necessary for the
6 work the LORD has commanded us to do." Moshe ordered
an announcement to be made throughout the camp: "Let
no man or woman make anything more as an offering for
7 the Sanctuary." So the people brought no more; for what
they already had was more than enough for all the work
8 that was to be done. All the skilled craftsmen REVI'I
among those engaged in the work made the Tabernacle
with ten sheets of fine linen and sky-blue, purple, and
9 scarlet wool, with a woven design of cherubim. All the
sheets were of the same size: twenty-eight cubits long
10 and four cubits wide. Five sheets were sewn together, and
11 likewise the second five. He made loops of sky-blue wool
on the edge of the outermost sheet of the first set and
12 likewise on the outermost sheet of the second set: fifty
loops on the first sheet and fifty on the edge of the end
sheet of the other set, so that the loops were opposite one
13 another. He made fifty gold clasps and used them to fasten
the two sets of sheets together so that the Tabernacle
was all of one piece.

14 He made sheets of goats' hair for a tent over the
15 Tabernacle. There were eleven such sheets. All eleven
were the same size: thirty cubits long and four cubits
16 wide. He joined five of the sheets into one set and six
17 into another. He made fifty loops on the edge of the
outermost sheet of the first set, and fifty loops on the edge

ג נְשָׂא֣וֹ לִבּ֔וֹ לְקָרְבָ֥ה אֶל־הַמְּלָאכָ֖ה לַעֲשֹׂ֥ת אֹתָֽהּ׃ וַיִּקְח֞וּ
מִלִּפְנֵ֣י מֹשֶׁ֗ה אֵ֤ת כָּל־הַתְּרוּמָה֙ אֲשֶׁ֨ר הֵבִ֜יאוּ בְּנֵ֣י יִשְׂרָאֵ֗ל
לִמְלֶ֛אכֶת עֲבֹדַ֥ת הַקֹּ֖דֶשׁ לַעֲשֹׂ֣ת אֹתָ֑הּ וְ֠הֵם הֵבִ֨יאוּ אֵלָ֥יו ע֛וֹד
ד נְדָבָ֖ה בַּבֹּ֥קֶר בַּבֹּֽקֶר׃ וַיָּבֹ֙אוּ֙ כָּל־הַ֣חֲכָמִ֔ים הָעֹשִׂ֕ים אֵ֖ת כָּל־
מְלֶ֣אכֶת הַקֹּ֑דֶשׁ אִ֥ישׁ אִֽישׁ מִמְּלַאכְתּ֖וֹ אֲשֶׁר־הֵ֥מָּה עֹשִֽׂים׃
ה וַיֹּאמְרוּ֙ אֶל־מֹשֶׁ֣ה לֵּאמֹ֔ר מַרְבִּ֥ים הָעָ֖ם לְהָבִ֑יא מִדֵּ֤י הָעֲבֹדָה֙
ו לַמְּלָאכָ֔ה אֲשֶׁר־צִוָּ֥ה יְהוָ֖ה לַעֲשֹׂ֥ת אֹתָֽהּ׃ וַיְצַ֣ו מֹשֶׁ֗ה וַיַּעֲבִ֨ירוּ
ק֥וֹל בַּֽמַּחֲנֶה֮ לֵאמֹר֒ אִ֣ישׁ וְאִשָּׁ֗ה אַל־יַעֲשׂוּ־ע֛וֹד מְלָאכָ֖ה
ז לִתְרוּמַ֣ת הַקֹּ֑דֶשׁ וַיִּכָּלֵ֥א הָעָ֖ם מֵהָבִֽיא׃ וְהַמְּלָאכָ֗ה הָיְתָ֥ה דַיָּ֛ם
ח לְכָל־הַמְּלָאכָ֖ה לַעֲשׂ֣וֹת אֹתָ֑הּ וְהוֹתֵֽר׃ וַיַּעֲשׂ֨וּ רביעי
כָל־חֲכַם־לֵ֜ב בְּעֹשֵׂ֧י הַמְּלָאכָ֛ה אֶת־הַמִּשְׁכָּ֖ן עֶ֣שֶׂר יְרִיעֹ֑ת
שֵׁ֣שׁ מָשְׁזָ֗ר וּתְכֵ֤לֶת וְאַרְגָּמָן֙ וְתוֹלַ֣עַת שָׁנִ֔י כְּרֻבִ֛ים מַעֲשֵׂ֥ה
ט חֹשֵׁ֖ב עָשָׂ֥ה אֹתָֽם׃ אֹ֜רֶךְ הַיְרִיעָ֣ה הָאַחַ֗ת שְׁמֹנֶ֤ה וְעֶשְׂרִים֙
בָּֽאַמָּ֔ה וְרֹ֙חַב֙ אַרְבַּ֣ע בָּֽאַמָּ֔ה הַיְרִיעָ֖ה הָאֶחָ֑ת מִדָּ֥ה אַחַ֖ת
י לְכָל־הַיְרִיעֹֽת׃ וַיְחַבֵּר֙ אֶת־חֲמֵ֣שׁ הַיְרִיעֹ֔ת אַחַ֖ת אֶל־אֶחָ֑ת
יא וְחָמֵ֤שׁ יְרִיעֹת֙ חִבַּ֔ר אַחַ֖ת אֶל־אֶחָֽת׃ וַיַּ֜עַשׂ לֻלְאֹ֣ת תְּכֵ֗לֶת
עַ֣ל שְׂפַ֤ת הַיְרִיעָה֙ הָאֶחָ֔ת מִקָּצָ֖ה בַּמַּחְבָּ֑רֶת כֵּ֤ן עָשָׂה֙ בִּשְׂפַ֣ת
יב הַיְרִיעָ֔ה הַקִּ֣יצוֹנָ֔ה בַּמַּחְבֶּ֖רֶת הַשֵּׁנִֽית׃ חֲמִשִּׁ֣ים לֻלָאֹ֗ת עָשָׂה֮
בַּיְרִיעָ֣ה הָאֶחָת֒ וַחֲמִשִּׁ֣ים לֻלָאֹ֗ת עָשָׂה֙ בִּקְצֵ֣ה הַיְרִיעָ֔ה אֲשֶׁ֖ר
יג בַּמַּחְבֶּ֣רֶת הַשֵּׁנִ֑ית מַקְבִּילֹת֙ הַלֻּ֣לָאֹ֔ת אַחַ֖ת אֶל־אֶחָֽת׃ וַ֗יַּעַשׂ
חֲמִשִּׁ֖ים קַרְסֵ֣י זָהָ֑ב וַיְחַבֵּ֨ר אֶת־הַיְרִיעֹ֜ת אַחַ֤ת אֶל־אַחַת֙
בַּקְּרָסִ֔ים וַיְהִ֥י הַמִּשְׁכָּ֖ן אֶחָֽד׃
יד וַ֙יַּעַשׂ֙ יְרִיעֹ֣ת עִזִּ֔ים לְאֹ֖הֶל עַל־הַמִּשְׁכָּ֑ן עַשְׁתֵּי־עֶשְׂרֵ֥ה יְרִיעֹ֖ת
טו עָשָׂ֥ה אֹתָֽם׃ אֹ֗רֶךְ הַיְרִיעָ֤ה הָֽאַחַת֙ שְׁלֹשִׁ֣ים בָּֽאַמָּ֔ה וְאַרְבַּ֣ע
אַמּ֔וֹת רֹ֖חַב הַיְרִיעָ֣ה הָאֶחָ֑ת מִדָּ֣ה אַחַ֔ת לְעַשְׁתֵּ֥י עֶשְׂרֵ֖ה
טז יְרִיעֹֽת׃ וַיְחַבֵּ֛ר אֶת־חֲמֵ֥שׁ הַיְרִיעֹ֖ת לְבָ֑ד וְאֶת־שֵׁ֥שׁ הַיְרִיעֹ֖ת
יז לְבָֽד׃ וַיַּ֜עַשׂ לֻלָאֹ֣ת חֲמִשִּׁ֗ים עַ֚ל שְׂפַ֣ת הַיְרִיעָ֔ה הַקִּיצֹנָ֖ה
בַּמַּחְבָּ֑רֶת וַחֲמִשִּׁ֣ים לֻלָאֹ֗ת עָשָׂה֙ עַל־שְׂפַ֣ת הַיְרִיעָ֔ה הַחֹבֶ֖רֶת

18 of the second set. He made fifty bronze clasps to join the
19 tent together into a single piece. And for the tent he made
a covering of rams' skins dyed red, with a covering of fine
20 leather above. Then he made the upright boards ḤAMISHI
21 for the Tabernacle from acacia wood. Each was ten cubits
22 long and a cubit and a half wide. Each board had two
matching tenons; all the Tabernacle's boards were made
23 24 in this way. He made twenty boards for the south side, and
forty silver sockets to go under them, two sockets under
25 each board, one under each tenon. For the second side
of the Tabernacle, the north side, he made twenty boards
26 27 and their forty silver sockets, two under each board. For
the rear of the Tabernacle on the west side he made six
28 boards, along with two boards for each of the rear corners
29 of the Tabernacle. They were even at the bottom, and
joined at the top by a ring. This was so for the other corner
30 also. So there were eight boards and sixteen silver sockets,
31 two under each board. He made crossbars of acacia wood,
32 five for the boards of the first side of the Tabernacle, five
for the boards of the second, and five for those of the rear
33 of the Tabernacle on the west side. He made the central
crossbar to go across the middles of the boards from one
34 end to the other. He overlaid the boards with gold, and
made gold rings to hold the crossbars; he overlaid the
35 crossbars themselves with gold. He made the curtain of
sky-blue, purple, and scarlet wool and finely spun linen,
36 with a design of cherubim worked into it. He also made

Eight Chapters (*Shemona Perakim*) – the introduction to Rambam's commentary on Mishna Avot – he speaks about the therapeutic power of beauty and its importance:

> Someone afflicted with melancholy may dispel it by listening to music and various kinds of song, by strolling in gardens, by experiencing beautiful buildings, by associating with beautiful pictures, and similar sorts of things that broaden the soul. (Ch. 5)

Art, in short, is balm to the soul.

This is true of the products of human artistry, but also of the process. God, taught R. Akiva, deliberately left the world unfinished so that it could be completed by the work of human beings

יח הַשֵּׁנִית: וַיַּעַשׂ קַרְסֵי נְחֹשֶׁת חֲמִשִּׁים לְחַבֵּר אֶת־הָאֹהֶל לִהְיֹת
יט אֶחָד: וַיַּעַשׂ מִכְסֶה לָאֹהֶל עֹרֹת אֵילִם מְאָדָּמִים וּמִכְסֵה
כ עֹרֹת תְּחָשִׁים מִלְמָעְלָה: וַיַּעַשׂ אֶת־הַקְּרָשִׁים חמישי
כא לַמִּשְׁכָּן עֲצֵי שִׁטִּים עֹמְדִים: עֶשֶׂר אַמֹּת אֹרֶךְ הַקָּרֶשׁ וְאַמָּה
כב וַחֲצִי הָאַמָּה רֹחַב הַקֶּרֶשׁ הָאֶחָד: שְׁתֵּי יָדֹת לַקֶּרֶשׁ הָאֶחָד
מְשֻׁלָּבֹת אַחַת אֶל־אֶחָת כֵּן עָשָׂה לְכֹל קַרְשֵׁי הַמִּשְׁכָּן:
כג וַיַּעַשׂ אֶת־הַקְּרָשִׁים לַמִּשְׁכָּן עֶשְׂרִים קְרָשִׁים לִפְאַת נֶגֶב
כד תֵּימָנָה: וְאַרְבָּעִים אַדְנֵי־כֶסֶף עָשָׂה תַּחַת עֶשְׂרִים הַקְּרָשִׁים
שְׁנֵי אֲדָנִים תַּחַת־הַקֶּרֶשׁ הָאֶחָד לִשְׁתֵּי יְדֹתָיו וּשְׁנֵי אֲדָנִים
כה תַּחַת־הַקֶּרֶשׁ הָאֶחָד לִשְׁתֵּי יְדֹתָיו: וּלְצֶלַע הַמִּשְׁכָּן הַשֵּׁנִית
כו לִפְאַת צָפוֹן עָשָׂה עֶשְׂרִים קְרָשִׁים: וְאַרְבָּעִים אַדְנֵיהֶם
כֶּסֶף שְׁנֵי אֲדָנִים תַּחַת הַקֶּרֶשׁ הָאֶחָד וּשְׁנֵי אֲדָנִים תַּחַת
כז הַקֶּרֶשׁ הָאֶחָד: וּלְיַרְכְּתֵי הַמִּשְׁכָּן יָמָּה עָשָׂה שִׁשָּׁה קְרָשִׁים:
כח כט וּשְׁנֵי קְרָשִׁים עָשָׂה לִמְקֻצְעֹת הַמִּשְׁכָּן בַּיַּרְכָתָיִם: וְהָיוּ
תוֹאֲמִם מִלְּמַטָּה וְיַחְדָּו יִהְיוּ תַמִּים אֶל־רֹאשׁוֹ אֶל־הַטַּבַּעַת
ל הָאֶחָת כֵּן עָשָׂה לִשְׁנֵיהֶם לִשְׁנֵי הַמִּקְצֹעֹת: וְהָיוּ שְׁמֹנָה
קְרָשִׁים וְאַדְנֵיהֶם כֶּסֶף שִׁשָּׁה עָשָׂר אֲדָנִים שְׁנֵי אֲדָנִים שְׁנֵי
לא אֲדָנִים תַּחַת הַקֶּרֶשׁ הָאֶחָד: וַיַּעַשׂ בְּרִיחֵי עֲצֵי שִׁטִּים חֲמִשָּׁה
לב לְקַרְשֵׁי צֶלַע־הַמִּשְׁכָּן הָאֶחָת: וַחֲמִשָּׁה בְרִיחִם לְקַרְשֵׁי צֶלַע־
הַמִּשְׁכָּן הַשֵּׁנִית וַחֲמִשָּׁה בְרִיחִם לְקַרְשֵׁי הַמִּשְׁכָּן לַיַּרְכָתַיִם
לג יָמָּה: וַיַּעַשׂ אֶת־הַבְּרִיחַ הַתִּיכֹן לִבְרֹחַ בְּתוֹךְ הַקְּרָשִׁים מִן־
לד הַקָּצֶה אֶל־הַקָּצֶה: וְאֶת־הַקְּרָשִׁים צִפָּה זָהָב וְאֶת־טַבְּעֹתָם
לה עָשָׂה זָהָב בָּתִּים לַבְּרִיחִם וַיְצַף אֶת־הַבְּרִיחִם זָהָב: וַיַּעַשׂ
אֶת־הַפָּרֹכֶת תְּכֵלֶת וְאַרְגָּמָן וְתוֹלַעַת שָׁנִי וְשֵׁשׁ מָשְׁזָר
לו מַעֲשֵׂה חֹשֵׁב עָשָׂה אֹתָהּ כְּרֻבִים: וַיַּעַשׂ לָהּ אַרְבָּעָה עַמּוּדֵי

36:35 עָשָׂה אֹתָהּ כְּרֻבִים *With a design of cherubim worked into it* – The makers of the Tabernacle are not only craftsmen following the measurements and materials prescribed. Artistic creativity is required too. In the work known as the ▶

four posts of acacia wood for it and overlaid them with
gold. Their hooks were of gold, and he cast for them four
37 sockets of silver. He made an embroidered screen for
the entrance of the Tent, of sky-blue, purple, and scarlet
38 wool and finely spun linen, as well as five posts with their
hooks. He overlaid their tops and bands with gold, but
their five sockets were of bronze.
37 1 Betzalel made the Ark of acacia wood, two and a half
cubits long, a cubit and a half wide, and a cubit and a half
2 high. He overlaid it with pure gold inside and out, and
3 encircled it around with a gold rim. He cast four gold
rings for its four corners, two rings on one side and two
4 on the other. He made staves of acacia wood and overlaid
5 them with gold. He then placed the staves in the rings
6 on the Ark's sides so that it could be carried. He made
a cover of pure gold, two and a half cubits long and a
7 cubit and a half wide. He made two cherubim of beaten
8 gold for the two ends of the cover, one cherub at one end
and one at the other. He made them of one piece with
9 the cover, and the wings of the cherubim were spread
upward, sheltering the cover. They faced each other, their
faces toward the cover.
10 He made a table of acacia wood, two cubits long, a cubit
11 wide, and a cubit and a half high. He overlaid it with pure
12 gold and around it made a gold rim. He also made a frame
a handbreadth wide around it and made a gold rim for
13 the frame. He cast four gold rings and placed the rings
14 on the corners of its four legs. The rings were close to the
15 frame to hold the staves used to carry the table. He made
the staves for carrying the table of acacia wood overlaid
16 with gold. The articles for the table – the bowls, spoons,

essentials of a free society. The second, no less significant, however, is creativity. Work is more than mere labor. Biblical Hebrew has two words to express the difference: *melakha* is work as creation; *avoda* is work as service or servitude. Both are central to the Tabernacle, a labor of love.

שִׁטִּים וַיְצַפֵּם זָהָב וָוֵיהֶם זָהָב וַיִּצֹק לָהֶם אַרְבָּעָה אַדְנֵי־
לז כָסֶף: וַיַּעַשׂ מָסָךְ לְפֶתַח הָאֹהֶל תְּכֵלֶת וְאַרְגָּמָן וְתוֹלַעַת
לח שָׁנִי וְשֵׁשׁ מָשְׁזָר מַעֲשֵׂה רֹקֵם: וְאֶת־עַמּוּדָיו חֲמִשָּׁה וְאֶת־
וָוֵיהֶם וְצִפָּה רָאשֵׁיהֶם וַחֲשֻׁקֵיהֶם זָהָב וְאַדְנֵיהֶם חֲמִשָּׁה
נְחֹשֶׁת:

לז א וַיַּעַשׂ בְּצַלְאֵל אֶת־הָאָרֹן עֲצֵי שִׁטִּים אַמָּתַיִם וָחֵצִי אָרְכּוֹ כז
ב וְאַמָּה וָחֵצִי רָחְבּוֹ וְאַמָּה וָחֵצִי קֹמָתוֹ: וַיְצַפֵּהוּ זָהָב טָהוֹר
ג מִבַּיִת וּמִחוּץ וַיַּעַשׂ לוֹ זֵר זָהָב סָבִיב: וַיִּצֹק לוֹ אַרְבַּע טַבְּעֹת
זָהָב עַל אַרְבַּע פַּעֲמֹתָיו וּשְׁתֵּי טַבָּעֹת עַל־צַלְעוֹ הָאֶחָת
ד וּשְׁתֵּי טַבָּעֹת עַל־צַלְעוֹ הַשֵּׁנִית: וַיַּעַשׂ בַּדֵּי עֲצֵי שִׁטִּים וַיְצַף
ה אֹתָם זָהָב: וַיָּבֵא אֶת־הַבַּדִּים בַּטַּבָּעֹת עַל צַלְעֹת הָאָרֹן
ו לָשֵׂאת אֶת־הָאָרֹן: וַיַּעַשׂ כַּפֹּרֶת זָהָב טָהוֹר אַמָּתַיִם וָחֵצִי
ז אָרְכָּהּ וְאַמָּה וָחֵצִי רָחְבָּהּ: וַיַּעַשׂ שְׁנֵי כְרֻבִים זָהָב מִקְשָׁה
ח עָשָׂה אֹתָם מִשְּׁנֵי קְצוֹת הַכַּפֹּרֶת: כְּרוּב־אֶחָד מִקָּצָה מִזֶּה
וּכְרוּב־אֶחָד מִקָּצָה מִזֶּה מִן־הַכַּפֹּרֶת עָשָׂה אֶת־הַכְּרֻבִים
ט מִשְּׁנֵי קצוותו: וַיִּהְיוּ הַכְּרֻבִים פֹּרְשֵׂי כְנָפַיִם לְמַעְלָה סֹכְכִים קְצוֹתָיו
בְּכַנְפֵיהֶם עַל־הַכַּפֹּרֶת וּפְנֵיהֶם אִישׁ אֶל־אָחִיו אֶל־הַכַּפֹּרֶת
הָיוּ פְּנֵי הַכְּרֻבִים:
י וַיַּעַשׂ אֶת־הַשֻּׁלְחָן עֲצֵי שִׁטִּים אַמָּתַיִם אָרְכּוֹ וְאַמָּה רָחְבּוֹ
יא וְאַמָּה וָחֵצִי קֹמָתוֹ: וַיְצַף אֹתוֹ זָהָב טָהוֹר וַיַּעַשׂ לוֹ זֵר זָהָב
יב סָבִיב: וַיַּעַשׂ לוֹ מִסְגֶּרֶת טֹפַח סָבִיב וַיַּעַשׂ זֵר־זָהָב לְמִסְגַּרְתּוֹ
יג סָבִיב: וַיִּצֹק לוֹ אַרְבַּע טַבְּעֹת זָהָב וַיִּתֵּן אֶת־הַטַּבָּעֹת עַל
יד אַרְבַּע הַפֵּאֹת אֲשֶׁר לְאַרְבַּע רַגְלָיו: לְעֻמַּת הַמִּסְגֶּרֶת הָיוּ
טו הַטַּבָּעֹת בָּתִּים לַבַּדִּים לָשֵׂאת אֶת־הַשֻּׁלְחָן: וַיַּעַשׂ אֶת־
הַבַּדִּים עֲצֵי שִׁטִּים וַיְצַף אֹתָם זָהָב לָשֵׂאת אֶת־הַשֻּׁלְחָן:
טז וַיַּעַשׂ אֶת־הַכֵּלִים ׀ אֲשֶׁר עַל־הַשֻּׁלְחָן אֶת־קְעָרֹתָיו וְאֶת־

(*Tanḥuma,* Tazria 5). The creative God seeks creativity from mankind. Work gives human beings two things. First it gives a person independence, one of the ▶

jars, and pitchers for pouring libations – he made of pure
gold.
17 He made the candelabrum of pure beaten gold. Its base SHISHI /SHELISHI/
and shaft, cups, knobs, and flowers were hammered
18 from a single piece. Six branches extended from its sides,
19 three on one side, three on the other. On each of the six
branches extending from the candelabrum were three
20 finely crafted cups, each with a knob and a flower. On the
candelabrum itself there were four finely crafted cups,
21 each with a knob and a flower. At the base of each of the
three pairs of branches extending from the candelabrum
22 there was a knob of one piece with it; their knobs and
branches were of one piece with it, so that the whole of it
23 was a single piece of pure beaten gold. Its seven lamps and
24 its tongs and pans were of pure gold; it and all its utensils
were made from a talent of pure gold.
25 He made the incense altar of acacia wood, square, a cubit
long, a cubit wide, and two cubits high, with horns of one
26 piece with it. He overlaid its top, its sides all around, and
its horns with pure gold and around it he made a gold
27 molding. Under the molding he made two gold rings on
the two sides, to hold the staves by which it was carried.
28 The staves themselves were made of acacia wood, overlaid
29 with gold. As well as this, with the skill of a perfumer,

Does faith make a difference? And is it possible to have faith, even in the twenty-first century, after all we have learned from science? The answer to both questions is yes. Jewish faith isn't irrational or naive or prescientific. Faith is what I call a framing belief.

Compare trust. Is it right or wrong to go through life trusting people? Some do. Some don't. If you trust people, some of them will take advantage of you, and it will hurt. If you go through life cynical and suspicious, you will protect yourself against betrayal, but never know love or friendship, the deep communion of souls. There are some things you cannot achieve without trust. So which is the rational option: trust or suspicion? There is no rational option. These are framing beliefs.

So it is with faith. When all the science is in – when we know exactly when and how the universe came into being – the question will still be open. Does life have a meaning, a higher purpose? Are all our prayers in vain? Is

כַּפֹּתָיו וְאֵת מְנַקִּיֹּתָיו וְאֶת־הַקְּשָׂוֺת אֲשֶׁר יֻסַּךְ בָּהֵן זָהָב
טָהוֹר׃
יז וַיַּעַשׂ אֶת־הַמְּנֹרָה זָהָב טָהוֹר מִקְשָׁה עָשָׂה אֶת־הַמְּנֹרָה ששי /שלישי/
יח יְרֵכָהּ וְקָנָהּ גְּבִיעֶיהָ כַּפְתֹּרֶיהָ וּפְרָחֶיהָ מִמֶּנָּה הָיוּ׃ וְשִׁשָּׁה
קָנִים יֹצְאִים מִצִּדֶּיהָ שְׁלֹשָׁה ׀ קְנֵי מְנֹרָה מִצִּדָּהּ הָאֶחָד
יט וּשְׁלֹשָׁה קְנֵי מְנֹרָה מִצִּדָּהּ הַשֵּׁנִי׃ שְׁלֹשָׁה גְבִעִים מְשֻׁקָּדִים
בַּקָּנֶה הָאֶחָד כַּפְתֹּר וָפֶרַח וּשְׁלֹשָׁה גְבִעִים מְשֻׁקָּדִים בְּקָנֶה
אֶחָד כַּפְתֹּר וָפָרַח כֵּן לְשֵׁשֶׁת הַקָּנִים הַיֹּצְאִים מִן־הַמְּנֹרָה׃
כ וּבַמְּנֹרָה אַרְבָּעָה גְבִעִים מְשֻׁקָּדִים כַּפְתֹּרֶיהָ וּפְרָחֶיהָ׃
כא וְכַפְתֹּר תַּחַת שְׁנֵי הַקָּנִים מִמֶּנָּה וְכַפְתֹּר תַּחַת שְׁנֵי הַקָּנִים
מִמֶּנָּה וְכַפְתֹּר תַּחַת־שְׁנֵי הַקָּנִים מִמֶּנָּה לְשֵׁשֶׁת הַקָּנִים
כב הַיֹּצְאִים מִמֶּנָּה׃ כַּפְתֹּרֵיהֶם וּקְנֹתָם מִמֶּנָּה הָיוּ כֻּלָּהּ מִקְשָׁה
כג אַחַת זָהָב טָהוֹר׃ וַיַּעַשׂ אֶת־נֵרֹתֶיהָ שִׁבְעָה וּמַלְקָחֶיהָ
כד וּמַחְתֹּתֶיהָ זָהָב טָהוֹר׃ כִּכָּר זָהָב טָהוֹר עָשָׂה אֹתָהּ וְאֵת
כָּל־כֵּלֶיהָ׃
כה וַיַּעַשׂ אֶת־מִזְבַּח הַקְּטֹרֶת עֲצֵי שִׁטִּים אַמָּה אָרְכּוֹ וְאַמָּה
כו רָחְבּוֹ רָבוּעַ וְאַמָּתַיִם קֹמָתוֹ מִמֶּנּוּ הָיוּ קַרְנֹתָיו׃ וַיְצַף אֹתוֹ
זָהָב טָהוֹר אֶת־גַּגּוֹ וְאֶת־קִירֹתָיו סָבִיב וְאֶת־קַרְנֹתָיו וַיַּעַשׂ
כז לוֹ זֵר זָהָב סָבִיב׃ וּשְׁתֵּי טַבְּעֹת זָהָב עָשָׂה־לוֹ ׀ מִתַּחַת לְזֵרוֹ
עַל שְׁתֵּי צַלְעֹתָיו עַל שְׁנֵי צִדָּיו לְבָתִּים לְבַדִּים לָשֵׂאת אֹתוֹ
כח כט בָּהֶם׃ וַיַּעַשׂ אֶת־הַבַּדִּים עֲצֵי שִׁטִּים וַיְצַף אֹתָם זָהָב׃ וַיַּעַשׂ
אֶת־שֶׁמֶן הַמִּשְׁחָה קֹדֶשׁ וְאֶת־קְטֹרֶת הַסַּמִּים טָהוֹר מַעֲשֵׂה

37:29 וְאֶת־קְטֹרֶת הַסַּמִּים טָהוֹר מַעֲשֵׂה רֹקֵחַ *With the skill of a perfumer… the fragrant incense* – While sacrifices were offered only in the Tabernacle and later the Temple, the Mishna tells us that the scent of the incense spread out so far from Jerusalem that "goats… on Mount Mikhvar [beyond the River Jordan] would sneeze" (Tamid 3:8). As with worship, so with knowledge; there are things that are limited and measurable, and things, equally real, that cannot be pinned down and yet color everything else. What we call "faith" falls in the latter category.

▶

he prepared the sacred anointing oil and the fragrant
38 1 incense. He made the sacrificial altar of acacia SHEVI'I /REVI'I/
wood, square, five cubits long, five cubits wide, and three
2 cubits high. He made horns on its four corners, of one
3 piece with it, and then overlaid it with bronze. He made all
the altar's utensils: pots, shovels, basins, forks, and pans,
4 out of bronze. He made a grate of bronze mesh beneath
the ledge, extending downward to the middle of the altar.
5 Four rings were cast for the four corners of the bronze
6 mesh, to hold the staves, which were made of acacia wood
7 and overlaid with bronze. He placed the staves in the rings
on the sides of the altar so that it could be carried. The
8 altar itself was hollow, made of planks. He made
the bronze laver and its bronze base from the mirrors
of the women who served at the entrance of the Tent
9 of Meeting. He made the courtyard thus: on
the south side, the hangings were of finely spun linen, a

---

did not hesitate to donate them to the Tabernacle project. Now at first Moshe considered the mirrors distasteful and inappropriate, because these objects indulged the evil inclination. But the Holy One, blessed be He, said: You should accept these mirrors, for they are dearer to Me than any of the other donations the people have brought. For it was these mirrors that assisted Israel to burgeon to huge numbers in Egypt. While the women's husbands were exhausting themselves with oppressive labor in the fields, their wives would bring them food and drink to sustain them.

The Egyptians sought not merely to enslave but also to put an end to the people of Israel. One way of doing so was to kill all male children. Another was to interrupt normal family life. The people, both men and women, were laboring all day. At night, says the Midrash, they were forbidden to return home. The intention was to destroy both privacy and sexual desire, so that the Israelites would have no more children.

The women realized this, and decided to frustrate Pharaoh's plan. As Rashi writes,

> As they visited with their men, the women would invite them to gaze at their reflections in the mirrors. Flirting with her husband, a wife would say: "You know I'm more beautiful than you are!" This sort of talk had the effect of arousing the men who would sleep with their wives, who would then conceive and give birth there as the verse states: "Beneath

לח א רֹקֵחַ׃ וַיַּעַשׂ אֶת־מִזְבַּח הָעֹלָה עֲצֵי שִׁטִּים שביעי /רביעי/
חָמֵשׁ אַמּוֹת אָרְכּוֹ וְחָמֵשׁ־אַמּוֹת רָחְבּוֹ רָבוּעַ וְשָׁלֹשׁ אַמּוֹת
ב קֹמָתוֹ׃ וַיַּעַשׂ קַרְנֹתָיו עַל אַרְבַּע פִּנֹּתָיו מִמֶּנּוּ הָיוּ קַרְנֹתָיו
ג וַיְצַף אֹתוֹ נְחֹשֶׁת׃ וַיַּעַשׂ אֶת־כָּל־כְּלֵי הַמִּזְבֵּחַ אֶת־הַסִּירֹת
וְאֶת־הַיָּעִים וְאֶת־הַמִּזְרָקֹת אֶת־הַמִּזְלָגֹת וְאֶת־הַמַּחְתֹּת
ד כָּל־כֵּלָיו עָשָׂה נְחֹשֶׁת׃ וַיַּעַשׂ לַמִּזְבֵּחַ מִכְבָּר מַעֲשֵׂה רֶשֶׁת
ה נְחֹשֶׁת תַּחַת כַּרְכֻּבּוֹ מִלְּמַטָּה עַד־חֶצְיוֹ׃ וַיִּצֹק אַרְבַּע טַבָּעֹת
ו בְּאַרְבַּע הַקְּצָוֹת לְמִכְבַּר הַנְּחֹשֶׁת בָּתִּים לַבַּדִּים׃ וַיַּעַשׂ
ז אֶת־הַבַּדִּים עֲצֵי שִׁטִּים וַיְצַף אֹתָם נְחֹשֶׁת׃ וַיָּבֵא אֶת־
הַבַּדִּים בַּטַּבָּעֹת עַל צַלְעֹת הַמִּזְבֵּחַ לָשֵׂאת אֹתוֹ בָּהֶם
ח נְבוּב לֻחֹת עָשָׂה אֹתוֹ׃ וַיַּעַשׂ אֵת הַכִּיּוֹר נְחֹשֶׁת
וְאֵת כַּנּוֹ נְחֹשֶׁת בְּמַרְאֹת הַצֹּבְאֹת אֲשֶׁר צָבְאוּ פֶּתַח אֹהֶל
ט מוֹעֵד׃ וַיַּעַשׂ אֶת־הֶחָצֵר לִפְאַת ׀ נֶגֶב תֵּימָנָה

there nothing beyond the physical universe? Are all our hopes illusions and our aspirations no more than self-deluding dreams?

Faith and faithlessness are framing beliefs. But which we choose makes all the difference. You can live without optimism and trust, just as you can live without music or a sense of humor. But it is a limited life. And in the same way, you can live without faith. But you will miss out on all that comes from the belief that life has a meaning, that God created the universe in love and forgiveness and asks us to love and forgive others. Like the smell of the incense enveloping Jerusalem, the mystery that is faith can pervade our lives and fill them, unmistakably, with a scent of holiness.

WOMEN AND THE MAKING OF THE TABERNACLE

The Torah goes out of its way to emphasize the role women played in making the Tabernacle. Indeed, an unusual locution in Ex. 35:22, *haanashim al hanashim*, "the men with the women," implies that the women came to make their donations first, and the men merely followed their lead (Ibn Ezra, Ramban, Rabbeinu Baḥya).

This cryptic verse hints at a further perspective. The Sages (*Tanḥuma*, Pekudei 9) told a story about it, retold here by Rashi:

> The Israelite women were in possession of mirrors that they used when adorning themselves. And yet, they

10 hundred cubits long, with twenty posts and their twenty
bronze sockets. The posts' hooks and bands were of
11 silver. Likewise on the north side: the hangings were a
hundred cubits long, with twenty pillars and their bronze
12 sockets, and hooks and bands of silver. On the west side
the hangings were fifty cubits long, with ten posts and ten
13 sockets, and hooks and bands of silver. The east side was
14 also fifty cubits long: fifteen cubits of hangings with three
15 posts and three sockets on one side, and fifteen cubits of
hangings with three posts and three sockets on the other.
16 All the hangings of the courtyard were of finely spun linen.
17 The sockets for the posts were of bronze, the posts' hooks
and bands were of silver, and their tops were overlaid with
18 silver; all the posts had silver bands. At the entrance of the MAFTIR
courtyard there was an embroidered screen of sky-blue,
purple, and scarlet wool and finely spun linen, twenty

---

most precious love of all. The women, who offered to God the mirrors through which they aroused their husbands' love in the dark days of Egypt, understand what it means to love God "with all your heart, with all your soul, and with all your might" (Deut. 6:5).

THE COMPLETION OF THE BUILDING WORK

From the Ark of the Covenant to the bronze pegs, the Tabernacle and its furnishings are now complete. But this is not enough: After the making of the golden calf in Parashat Ki Tisa, life needed to begin again. A shattered people had to be rebuilt. This is the other story of our *parasha*. The verb *vayak'hel*, "[Moshe] assembled," is crucial to an understanding of his task. For the use of this word at the start of the *parasha* reminds us of an earlier occasion on which it appeared:

> When the people saw that Moshe was long delayed in coming down the mountain, they gathered (*vayikahel*) around Aharon and said to him, "Get up, make us gods to go before us." (Ex. 32:1)

Vayak'hel is the redemption of a past misdemeanor. Just as the sin of the calf was committed by the people acting as a community (a *kahal* or *kehilla*), so atonement is to be achieved by their again acting as a *kehilla*, this time by making a home for the Divine Presence as they earlier sought to make a substitute for it. Just as the people were assembled for bad, so they have now been gathered for good.

י קַלְעֵי הֶחָצֵר שֵׁשׁ מָשְׁזָר מֵאָה בָּאַמָּה: עַמּוּדֵיהֶם עֶשְׂרִים
וְאַדְנֵיהֶם עֶשְׂרִים נְחֹשֶׁת וָוֵי הָעַמּוּדִים וַחֲשֻׁקֵיהֶם כָּסֶף:
יא וְלִפְאַת צָפוֹן מֵאָה בָאַמָּה עַמּוּדֵיהֶם עֶשְׂרִים וְאַדְנֵיהֶם
יב עֶשְׂרִים נְחֹשֶׁת וָוֵי הָעַמּוּדִים וַחֲשֻׁקֵיהֶם כָּסֶף: וְלִפְאַת־יָם
קְלָעִים חֲמִשִּׁים בָּאַמָּה עַמּוּדֵיהֶם עֲשָׂרָה וְאַדְנֵיהֶם עֲשָׂרָה
יג וָוֵי הָעַמֻּדִים וַחֲשׁוּקֵיהֶם כָּסֶף: וְלִפְאַת קֵדְמָה מִזְרָחָה
יד חֲמִשִּׁים אַמָּה: קְלָעִים חֲמֵשׁ־עֶשְׂרֵה אַמָּה אֶל־הַכָּתֵף
טו עַמּוּדֵיהֶם שְׁלֹשָׁה וְאַדְנֵיהֶם שְׁלֹשָׁה: וְלַכָּתֵף הַשֵּׁנִית מִזֶּה
וּמִזֶּה לְשַׁעַר הֶחָצֵר קְלָעִים חֲמֵשׁ עֶשְׂרֵה אַמָּה עַמֻּדֵיהֶם
טז שְׁלֹשָׁה וְאַדְנֵיהֶם שְׁלֹשָׁה: כָּל־קַלְעֵי הֶחָצֵר סָבִיב שֵׁשׁ מָשְׁזָר:
יז וְהָאֲדָנִים לָעַמֻּדִים נְחֹשֶׁת וָוֵי הָעַמּוּדִים וַחֲשׁוּקֵיהֶם כֶּסֶף
וְצִפּוּי רָאשֵׁיהֶם כָּסֶף וְהֵם מְחֻשָּׁקִים כֶּסֶף כֹּל עַמֻּדֵי הֶחָצֵר:
יח וּמָסַךְ שַׁעַר הֶחָצֵר מַעֲשֵׂה רֹקֵם תְּכֵלֶת וְאַרְגָּמָן וְתוֹלַעַת מפטיר

the apple tree I roused you where your mother bore you" (Song. 8:5). This is why the mirrors are referred to as *mar'ot hatzove'ot* ["mirrors of the women who served," but also: "mirrors of the hosts," that is, the mirrors of the multitudes of Israelite children who were born thanks to their use]. And this is why the mirrors were repurposed to make the laver.

Intimate relations resumed. The women conceived. Because of this was there a new generation of Jewish children. The women, by their faith, courage, and ingenuity, secured Jewish survival.

The story tells us that without the faith of women, Jews and Judaism would never have survived. But it also tells us something fundamental to the Jewish understanding of love in the religious life. Where classical Greece drew a distinction between *eros* (love as intense physical desire) and *agape* (a calm, detached love of humanity in general and things in general), Judaism sees love as supremely both physical *and* spiritual. This is the love we find in passages like Psalms 63:2: "My soul thirsts for You, my flesh longs for You in a parched and weary land that has no water." This is not the language of meditation or contemplation, philosophical or mystical. It is the language of passion.

Moshe, in Rashi's account of our verse, believes that closeness to God is about celibacy and purity. God teaches him otherwise, that passionate love, when offered as a gift to God, is the

cubits long and five cubits wide, like the hangings of the
19 courtyard. It had four posts with four bronze sockets and
with hooks and bands of silver; their tops were overlaid
20 with silver. All the tent pegs for the Tabernacle and the
surrounding courtyard were of bronze.

The haftara for Parashat Vayak'hel is on page 1502.
When Vayak'hel and Pekudei are read together read the haftara on 1506.

On the Shabbat of Parashat Shekalim read the haftara on page 1654.
On the Shabbat of Parashat Para read the haftara on page 1662.
On the Shabbat of Parashat HaḤodesh read the haftara on page 1666.

---

dignity of labor and creative endeavor. It brought to closure their birth as a nation and it symbolized the challenge of the future. The society they were summoned to create in the land of Israel would be one in which everyone would play their part. As John Ruskin wrote, "The highest reward for a man's toil is not what he gets from it, but what he becomes by it." Or as the early Zionist settlers said, they came to the land "*livnot u'lehibanot,* to build and to be built."

Hence the principle of Judaism that we are called on to become co-creators with God. And hence, too, the corollary: that leaders do not do the work on behalf of the people. They teach people how to do the work. It is not what God does for us but what we do for God that allows us to reach dignity and responsibility. A community is a group of people who build something together. "All your children will be students of the Lord, and great will be your children's peace": How do you lay the groundwork for peace? asked the Rabbis. By turning children into builders.

שְׁנִי וְשֵׁשׁ מָשְׁזָר וְעֶשְׂרִים אַמָּה אֹרֶךְ וְקוֹמָה בְרֹחַב חָמֵשׁ
יט אַמּוֹת לְעֻמַּת קַלְעֵי הֶחָצֵר׃ וְעַמֻּדֵיהֶם אַרְבָּעָה וְאַדְנֵיהֶם
אַרְבָּעָה נְחֹשֶׁת וָוֵיהֶם כֶּסֶף וְצִפּוּי רָאשֵׁיהֶם וַחֲשֻׁקֵיהֶם כָּסֶף׃
כ וְכָל־הַיְתֵדֹת לַמִּשְׁכָּן וְלֶחָצֵר סָבִיב נְחֹשֶׁת׃

The הפטרה *for* פרשת ויקהל *is on page 1503.*
When ויקהל *and* פקודי *are read together read the* הפטרה *on page 1507.*

On the שבת *of* פרשת שקלים *read the* הפטרה *on page 1655.*
On the שבת *of* פרשת פרה *read the* הפטרה *on page 1663.*
On the שבת *of* פרשת החודש *read the* הפטרה *on page 1667.*

This simple action has transformed the Israelites. During the whole time the Tabernacle was being constructed, there were no complaints, no rebellions, no dissension. The people contributed – some gold or silver or bronze, some brought skins and drapes, others gave their time and skill. They gave so much that Moshe had to order them to stop.

The people had to become God's "partners in the work of creation" (Shabbat 10a). That, I believe, is what the Sages meant when they reinterpreted a verse in the book of Isaiah: "All your children will be students of the Lord, and great will be your children's peace" (54:13). To this the Rabbis added a comment, based on a Hebrew wordplay: "Call them not 'your children' (*banayikh*) but 'your builders' (*bonayikh*)" (Berakhot 64a). People have to become builders if they are to grow from childhood to adulthood.

The building of the Tabernacle was the first great project the Israelites undertook together. It involved their generosity and skill. It gave them the chance to give back to God a little of what He had given them. It conferred on them the

Parashat Pekudei

38 21 These are the accounts of the Tabernacle, the Tabernacle
of testimony, recorded at Moshe's command by the
22 Levites under Itamar, son of Aharon the priest. Betzalel,
son of Uri, son of Ḥur, from the tribe of Yehuda, made
23 everything that the Lord had commanded Moshe. He
was assisted by Oholiav, son of Aḥisamakh, from the tribe
of Dan, an engraver, designer, and embroiderer in sky-blue,
24 purple, and scarlet wool and fine linen. All the
gold used in all the sacred work, donated as wave offerings,

Moshe issued a detailed reckoning to avoid coming under suspicion that he had personally appropriated some of the donated money. Note the emphasis that the accounting was undertaken not by Moshe himself but "by the Levites under Itamar," in other words, by independent auditors.

Accusations of corruption and personal enrichment have often been leveled against leaders, both with and without justification. We might think that since God sees all we do, this is enough to safeguard against wrongdoing. Yet Judaism never says this. When humans commit a sin they worry that other people might see them. They forget that God certainly sees them. Temptation befuddles the brain, and no one should believe they are immune to it.

Interestingly, a later passage in Tanakh seems to indicate that Moshe's accounting was not strictly necessary. The book of Kings relates an episode in which, during the reign of King Yehoash, money was raised for the restoration of the Temple: "They did not need to keep track of the men who received the money to pay out to the workers, for they dealt honestly" (II Kings 12:16).

Moshe, a man of complete honesty, may thus have acted "beyond the strict requirement of the law" (Berakhot 45b). It is precisely the fact that Moshe did not need to do what he did that gives the passage its force. Trust is of the essence in public life. There must be transparency and accountability when it comes to public funds even if the people involved have impeccable reputations. A nation that suspects its leaders of corruption cannot function effectively as a free, just, and open society.

It is the mark of a good society that public leadership is seen as a form of service rather than a means to power, which is all too easily abused. A free society is built on moral foundations, and those must be unshakable. Moshe's personal example, in giving an accounting of the funds that had been collected for the first collective project of the Jewish people, sets a vital precedent for all time.

פרשת פקודי

לח כא אֵלֶּה פְקוּדֵי הַמִּשְׁכָּן מִשְׁכַּן הָעֵדֻת אֲשֶׁר פֻּקַּד עַל־פִּי מֹשֶׁה כח
כב עֲבֹדַת הַלְוִיִּם בְּיַד אִיתָמָר בֶּן־אַהֲרֹן הַכֹּהֵן: וּבְצַלְאֵל בֶּן־
אוּרִי בֶן־חוּר לְמַטֵּה יְהוּדָה עָשָׂה אֵת כָּל־אֲשֶׁר־צִוָּה
כג יְהוָה אֶת־מֹשֶׁה: וְאִתּוֹ אָהֳלִיאָב בֶּן־אֲחִיסָמָךְ לְמַטֵּה־
דָן חָרָשׁ וְחֹשֵׁב וְרֹקֵם בַּתְּכֵלֶת וּבָאַרְגָּמָן וּבְתוֹלַעַת הַשָּׁנִי
כד וּבַשֵּׁשׁ: כָּל־הַזָּהָב הֶעָשׂוּי לַמְּלָאכָה בְּכֹל
מְלֶאכֶת הַקֹּדֶשׁ וַיְהִי | זְהַב הַתְּנוּפָה תֵּשַׁע וְעֶשְׂרִים כִּכָּר

PEKUDEI

With Pekudei, the book of Exodus reaches its end, if not its closure. Moshe orders an account to be made of all the donations given for the construction of the Tabernacle and how they were used. The priestly garments are sewn. No sooner has Moshe finally erected the Tabernacle than there is an epiphany, a majestic disclosure of the Divine Presence. After a tale full of setbacks, the Israelites have made a home for God, and His presence is now constantly in their midst.

Concluding the book of Exodus will enable us to look back at its remarkable narrative structure, the pattern beneath the surface, showing how tightly it, together with Genesis, forms a literary unity of immense coherence and power, in which, through a series of dramas both personal and political, the meaning of the universe and our place within it are explored.

THE ACCOUNTS OF THE TABERNACLE

Parashat Pekudei derives its name from the detailed account, or reckoning, of the contributions made toward the construction of the Tabernacle. Its opening passage lists the exact amounts of gold, silver, and bronze collected, and the purposes to which they were put. Why did Moshe give this precise accounting? A midrash suggests an answer:

> "And watch Moshe" (Ex. 33:8) – People criticized Moshe. They used to say to one another, "…Moshe is eating and drinking what belongs to us. All that he has belongs to us." The other would reply: "A man who is in charge of the work of the Sanctuary – what do you expect? That he should not get rich?" As soon as he heard this, Moshe replied, "By your life, as soon as the Sanctuary is complete, I will make a full reckoning with you." (*Tanḥuma*, Buber, Pekudei 4)

came to twenty-nine talents and 730 shekels according
25 to the Sanctuary weight. The silver of those recorded in
the census came to a hundred talents and 1,775 shekels,
26 according to the Sanctuary weight. One beka – half a
shekel according to the Sanctuary weight – was given by
each of the 603,550 men aged twenty or over included
27 in the census. A hundred talents of silver were used for
casting the sockets of the Sanctuary and the curtain, one
talent for each socket: a hundred talents for the hundred
28 sockets. Of 1,775 shekels he made the hooks and bands of
29 the posts and their silver-plated tops. The bronze given
as an offering came to seventy talents and 2,400 shekels.
30 With this were made the sockets for the entrance of the
Tent of Meeting, the bronze altar with its bronze mesh,
31 and all the utensils of the altar, the sockets around the
courtyard, the sockets at the courtyard gate, and all
the tent pegs for the Tabernacle and the surrounding
39 1 courtyard. From the sky-blue, purple, and scarlet wool
they made woven garments for ministering in the
Sanctuary. They also made sacred vestments for Aharon,
as the LORD commanded Moshe.

Do these two passages, taken together, tell us something larger about the biblical vision? The first eleven chapters of Genesis and the book of Exodus as a whole tell a story of human failure – a failure to observe the moral order by which life, liberty, and human dignity are sacred. The result in both cases was catastrophe: in the first, a world ruined by the flood, in the second, an Egypt devastated by the plagues. Both stories involve a physical construction, an ark and a Tabernacle, and in both, the Torah's emphasis is on precise dimensions ordained by God and faithfully carried out by human beings.

There is, to be sure, a great difference between these two structures. Noaḥ needed the ark only until the floodwaters subsided. The Israelites need the Tabernacle, or some equivalent of it (the Temple, later the synagogue), forever. Yet both were symbols of order in a disordered world. The Tabernacle will be the symbolic focus of Israel's collective life. It tells them that they are a nation at whose center is the Divine Presence. It bears witness to the sovereignty of right over might, the rule of justice over the rule of power. It is their ark in the wilderness. Without sacred order, there is no social order.

There is deep symbolism here: God creates order. Human beings create chaos.

כה וּשְׁבַ֧ע מֵא֛וֹת וּשְׁלֹשִׁ֖ים שֶׁ֑קֶל בְּשֶׁ֖קֶל הַקֹּֽדֶשׁ׃ וְכֶ֛סֶף פְּקוּדֵ֥י
הָעֵדָ֖ה מְאַ֣ת כִּכָּ֑ר וְאֶ֨לֶף וּשְׁבַ֜ע מֵא֗וֹת וַחֲמִשָּׁ֧ה וְשִׁבְעִ֛ים
כו שֶׁ֖קֶל בְּשֶׁ֥קֶל הַקֹּֽדֶשׁ׃ בֶּ֚קַע לַגֻּלְגֹּ֔לֶת מַחֲצִ֥ית הַשֶּׁ֖קֶל
בְּשֶׁ֣קֶל הַקֹּ֑דֶשׁ לְכֹ֨ל הָעֹבֵ֜ר עַל־הַפְּקֻדִ֗ים מִבֶּ֨ן עֶשְׂרִ֤ים
שָׁנָה֙ וָמַ֔עְלָה לְשֵׁשׁ־מֵא֥וֹת אֶ֙לֶף֙ וּשְׁלֹ֣שֶׁת אֲלָפִ֔ים וַחֲמֵ֥שׁ
כז מֵא֖וֹת וַחֲמִשִּֽׁים׃ וַֽיְהִ֗י מְאַת֙ כִּכַּ֣ר הַכֶּ֔סֶף לָצֶ֕קֶת אֵ֚ת אַדְנֵ֣י
הַקֹּ֔דֶשׁ וְאֵ֖ת אַדְנֵ֣י הַפָּרֹ֑כֶת מְאַ֧ת אֲדָנִ֛ים לִמְאַ֥ת הַכִּכָּ֖ר
כח כִּכָּ֥ר לָאָֽדֶן׃ וְאֶת־הָאֶ֜לֶף וּשְׁבַ֤ע הַמֵּאוֹת֙ וַחֲמִשָּׁ֣ה וְשִׁבְעִ֔ים
כט עָשָׂ֥ה וָוִ֖ים לָעַמּוּדִ֑ים וְצִפָּ֥ה רָאשֵׁיהֶ֖ם וְחִשַּׁ֥ק אֹתָֽם׃ וּנְחֹ֥שֶׁת
ל הַתְּנוּפָ֖ה שִׁבְעִ֣ים כִּכָּ֑ר וְאַלְפַּ֥יִם וְאַרְבַּע־מֵא֖וֹת שָֽׁקֶל׃ וַיַּ֣עַשׂ
בָּ֗הּ אֶת־אַדְנֵי֙ פֶּ֚תַח אֹ֣הֶל מוֹעֵ֔ד וְאֵת֙ מִזְבַּ֣ח הַנְּחֹ֔שֶׁת וְאֶת־
לא מִכְבַּ֥ר הַנְּחֹ֖שֶׁת אֲשֶׁר־ל֑וֹ וְאֵ֖ת כׇּל־כְּלֵ֥י הַמִּזְבֵּֽחַ׃ וְאֶת־
אַדְנֵ֤י הֶֽחָצֵר֙ סָבִ֔יב וְאֶת־אַדְנֵ֖י שַׁ֣עַר הֶחָצֵ֑ר וְאֵ֨ת כׇּל־יִתְדֹ֧ת
לט א הַמִּשְׁכָּ֛ן וְאֶת־כׇּל־יִתְדֹ֥ת הֶחָצֵ֖ר סָבִֽיב׃ וּמִן־הַתְּכֵ֤לֶת
וְהָֽאַרְגָּמָן֙ וְתוֹלַ֣עַת הַשָּׁנִ֔י עָשׂ֥וּ בִגְדֵי־שְׂרָ֖ד לְשָׁרֵ֣ת בַּקֹּ֑דֶשׁ
וַֽיַּעֲשׂ֞וּ אֶת־בִּגְדֵ֤י הַקֹּ֙דֶשׁ֙ אֲשֶׁ֣ר לְאַהֲרֹ֔ן כַּאֲשֶׁ֛ר צִוָּ֥ה יְהֹוָ֖ה
אֶת־מֹשֶֽׁה׃

39:1 כַּאֲשֶׁר צִוָּה יהוה אֶת־מֹשֶׁה *As the Lord commanded Moshe* – Parashat Pekudei, and with it the book of Exodus as a whole, draws to a conclusion with an extraordinary emphasis on obedience. This phrase, "as the Lord commanded Moshe," appears seven times in the passage describing how the Israelites constructed the Tabernacle, and the formula "as the Lord commanded" appears three additional times in the summarizing verses, 39:32–43. In the next chapter, narrating how Moshe set up the Tabernacle, seven times we hear the phrase "as the Lord commanded him." Where have we heard this language before?

The answer takes us back to another construction project, the first in the Torah: Noaḥ's ark. Three times we hear virtually the same phrase:

> Noaḥ did so: all that *God commanded him, he fulfilled.* (Gen. 6:22)
>
> Noaḥ did *all that the Lord commanded him.* (7:5)
>
> They came, male and female of all flesh, *as God had commanded him.* (7:16)

2 He made the ephod of gold, with sky-blue, purple, and SHENI
3 scarlet wool and finely spun linen. They hammered out /ḤAMISHI/
thin sheets of gold and cut strands to be worked into the
sky-blue, purple, and scarlet wool and fine linen – highly
4 skilled work. They made fixed shoulder pieces for the
5 ephod; these were affixed to its two ends. Its decorated
waistband was like it and of one piece with the ephod,
made with gold, with sky-blue, purple, and scarlet
wool and finely spun linen, as the LORD commanded
6 Moshe. They mounted the rock crystal stones in
gold filigree settings and engraved them as a seal with the
7 names of Yisrael's sons. He fastened them on the shoulder
pieces of the ephod as remembrance stones for Yisrael's
sons, as the LORD commanded Moshe.
8 He made the breast piece with the same skilled craftsmanship as the ephod: of gold, of sky-blue, purple, and
9 scarlet wool, and of finely spun linen. It was square and
10 folded double, a span long and a span wide. Then they
mounted four rows of precious stones on it. The first
11 row was a carnelian, an olivine, and a garnet; the second
row was an emerald, a lapis lazuli, and a green quartz;
12 13 the third row was an amber, a jet, and a sardonyx; and
the fourth was an aquamarine, a rock crystal, and an
14 opal. They were mounted in gold filigree settings. There
were twelve stones, one for each of the names of Yisrael's
sons. Each was engraved like a seal with the name of one
15 of the twelve tribes. For the breast piece they made chains
16 of pure gold, braided like cords. They made two gold
filigree settings and two gold rings, and attached the rings
17 to two of the corners of the breast piece. They fastened
the two gold chains to the rings at the corners of the
18 breast piece, and the other ends of the chains to the two
settings, attaching them to the ephod's shoulder pieces
19 at the front. They made two gold rings and placed them
at the two other corners of the breast piece on the edge,

ב וַיַּ֙עַשׂ֙ אֶת־הָאֵפֹ֔ד זָהָ֕ב תְּכֵ֥לֶת וְאַרְגָּמָ֖ן וְתוֹלַ֣עַת שָׁנִ֑י וְשֵׁ֖שׁ שני /חמישי/
ג מָשְׁזָֽר׃ וַֽיְרַקְּע֞וּ אֶת־פַּחֵ֣י הַזָּהָב֮ וְקִצֵּ֣ץ פְּתִילִם֒ לַעֲשׂ֗וֹת בְּת֤וֹךְ
הַתְּכֵ֙לֶת֙ וּבְת֣וֹךְ הָֽאַרְגָּמָ֔ן וּבְת֖וֹךְ תּוֹלַ֣עַת הַשָּׁנִ֑י וּבְת֥וֹךְ הַשֵּׁ֖שׁ
ד מַעֲשֵׂ֥ה חֹשֵֽׁב׃ כְּתֵפֹ֥ת עָֽשׂוּ־ל֖וֹ חֹבְרֹ֑ת עַל־שְׁנֵ֥י קצוותו חֻבָּֽר׃ קְצוֹתָ֖יו
ה וְחֵ֨שֶׁב אֲפֻדָּת֜וֹ אֲשֶׁ֣ר עָלָ֗יו מִמֶּ֣נּוּ הוּא֮ כְּמַעֲשֵׂהוּ֒ זָהָ֗ב תְּכֵ֧לֶת
וְאַרְגָּמָ֛ן וְתוֹלַ֥עַת שָׁנִ֖י וְשֵׁ֣שׁ מָשְׁזָ֑ר כַּאֲשֶׁ֛ר צִוָּ֥ה יְהוָ֖ה אֶת־
ו מֹשֶֽׁה׃ וַֽיַּעֲשׂוּ֙ אֶת־אַבְנֵ֣י הַשֹּׁ֔הַם מֻֽסַבֹּ֖ת מִשְׁבְּצֹ֣ת
ז זָהָ֑ב מְפֻתָּחֹת֙ פִּתּוּחֵ֣י חוֹתָ֔ם עַל־שְׁמ֖וֹת בְּנֵ֥י יִשְׂרָאֵֽל׃ וַיָּ֣שֶׂם
אֹתָ֗ם עַ֚ל כִּתְפֹ֣ת הָֽאֵפֹ֔ד אַבְנֵ֥י זִכָּר֖וֹן לִבְנֵ֣י יִשְׂרָאֵ֑ל כַּאֲשֶׁ֛ר
צִוָּ֥ה יְהוָ֖ה אֶת־מֹשֶֽׁה׃
ח וַיַּ֧עַשׂ אֶת־הַחֹ֛שֶׁן מַעֲשֵׂ֥ה חֹשֵׁ֖ב כְּמַעֲשֵׂ֣ה אֵפֹ֑ד זָהָ֗ב תְּכֵ֧לֶת
ט וְאַרְגָּמָ֛ן וְתוֹלַ֥עַת שָׁנִ֖י וְשֵׁ֥שׁ מָשְׁזָֽר׃ רָב֧וּעַ הָיָ֛ה כָּפ֖וּל עָשׂ֣וּ
י אֶת־הַחֹ֑שֶׁן זֶ֧רֶת אָרְכּ֛וֹ וְזֶ֥רֶת רָחְבּ֖וֹ כָּפֽוּל׃ וַיְמַ֨לְאוּ־ב֔וֹ
אַ֖רְבָּעָה ט֣וּרֵי אָ֑בֶן ט֗וּר אֹ֤דֶם פִּטְדָה֙ וּבָרֶ֔קֶת הַטּ֖וּר הָאֶחָֽד׃
יא יב וְהַטּ֖וּר הַשֵּׁנִ֑י נֹ֥פֶךְ סַפִּ֖יר וְיָהֲלֹֽם׃ וְהַטּ֖וּר הַשְּׁלִישִׁ֑י לֶ֥שֶׁם
יג שְׁב֖וֹ וְאַחְלָֽמָה׃ וְהַטּוּר֙ הָרְבִיעִ֔י תַּרְשִׁ֥ישׁ שֹׁ֖הַם וְיָשְׁפֵ֑ה
יד מֽוּסַבֹּ֛ת מִשְׁבְּצ֥וֹת זָהָ֖ב בְּמִלֻּאֹתָֽם׃ וְ֠הָאֲבָנִים עַל־שְׁמֹ֨ת בְּנֵֽי־
יִשְׂרָאֵ֥ל הֵ֛נָּה שְׁתֵּ֥ים עֶשְׂרֵ֖ה עַל־שְׁמֹתָ֑ם פִּתּוּחֵ֨י חֹתָ֜ם אִ֣ישׁ
טו עַל־שְׁמ֔וֹ לִשְׁנֵ֥ים עָשָׂ֖ר שָֽׁבֶט׃ וַיַּעֲשׂ֥וּ עַל־הַחֹ֛שֶׁן שַׁרְשְׁרֹ֥ת
טז גַּבְלֻ֖ת מַעֲשֵׂ֣ה עֲבֹ֑ת זָהָ֖ב טָהֽוֹר׃ וַֽיַּעֲשׂ֗וּ שְׁתֵּי֙ מִשְׁבְּצֹ֣ת זָהָ֔ב
וּשְׁתֵּ֖י טַבְּעֹ֣ת זָהָ֑ב וַֽיִּתְּנ֗וּ אֶת־שְׁתֵּי֙ הַטַּבָּעֹ֔ת עַל־שְׁנֵ֖י קְצ֥וֹת
יז הַחֹֽשֶׁן׃ וַֽיִּתְּנ֗וּ שְׁתֵּי֙ הָעֲבֹתֹ֣ת הַזָּהָ֔ב עַל־שְׁתֵּ֖י הַטַּבָּעֹ֑ת עַל־
יח קְצ֖וֹת הַחֹֽשֶׁן׃ וְאֵ֨ת שְׁתֵּ֤י קְצוֹת֙ שְׁתֵּ֣י הָעֲבֹתֹ֔ת נָתְנ֖וּ עַל־
שְׁתֵּ֣י הַֽמִּשְׁבְּצֹ֑ת וַֽיִּתְּנֻ֛ם עַל־כִּתְפֹ֥ת הָאֵפֹ֖ד אֶל־מ֥וּל פָּנָֽיו׃
יט וַֽיַּעֲשׂ֗וּ שְׁתֵּי֙ טַבְּעֹ֣ת זָהָ֔ב וַיָּשִׂ֖ימוּ עַל־שְׁנֵ֣י קְצ֣וֹת הַחֹ֑שֶׁן עַל־

Yet when human beings create their own symbolic order – the ark, the Tabernacle – by precise and exacting obedience to God's command, there is a chance for humanity to survive.

20 inside, next to the ephod. Then they made two more gold
rings and attached them to the bottom of the ephod's two
shoulder pieces facing the priest's front, close to the seam
21 and above the ephod's woven waistband. They tied the
rings of the breast piece to the rings of the ephod with a
sky-blue cord, connecting it to the waistband so that the
breast piece would remain secured to the ephod, as the
LORD had commanded Moshe.
22 They made the robe of the ephod woven entirely of sky- SHELISHI /SHISHI/
23 blue wool, with an opening in the center like the neck of
a coat of mail, with a woven border around it so that it
24 would not tear. They made pomegranates of finely spun
sky-blue, purple, and scarlet wool around the hem of
25 the robe. And they made bells of pure gold and attached
26 them around the hem between the pomegranates. The
bells and pomegranates alternated around the hem of
the robe worn for ministering, as the LORD commanded
27 Moshe. For Aharon and his sons, they made
28 tunics woven from fine linen, together with a linen miter,
29 linen headdresses, and trousers of finely spun linen. The
sash was embroidered out of finely spun linen and sky-
blue, purple, and scarlet wool, as the LORD commanded
30 Moshe. They made the headplate, the holy
diadem, of pure gold and engraved on it, as on a seal:
31 Holy to the LORD. Then they attached a sky-blue cord to
it to affix it to the miter, as the LORD had commanded
32 Moshe. Thus all the work on the Tabernacle,
the Tent of Meeting, was completed. The Israelites

20:11). Rav Nissim Gaon (990–1062) in his introduction to the Talmud says that humans have been bound by the commands of morality since man first walked on earth. Individually, we can and should be moral, regardless of our specific religious commitments.

But man is a social animal. We form societies. And societies beat to a different pulse than do individuals. Reinhold Niebuhr made this distinction famous in the title of his book, *Moral Man and Immoral Society*. We do not act en masse the way we do alone. That is why societies of people not themselves wicked can perform collective acts of great evil.

כ שְׂפָתוֹ אֲשֶׁר אֶל־עֵבֶר הָאֵפֹד בָּיְתָה׃ וַיַּעֲשׂוּ שְׁתֵּי טַבְּעֹת
זָהָב וַיִּתְּנֻם עַל־שְׁתֵּי כִתְפֹת הָאֵפֹד מִלְּמַטָּה מִמּוּל פָּנָיו
כא לְעֻמַּת מַחְבַּרְתּוֹ מִמַּעַל לְחֵשֶׁב הָאֵפֹד׃ וַיִּרְכְּסוּ אֶת־הַחֹשֶׁן
מִטַּבְּעֹתָיו אֶל־טַבְּעֹת הָאֵפֹד בִּפְתִיל תְּכֵלֶת לִהְיֹת עַל־
חֵשֶׁב הָאֵפֹד וְלֹא־יִזַּח הַחֹשֶׁן מֵעַל הָאֵפֹד כַּאֲשֶׁר צִוָּה יהוה
אֶת־מֹשֶׁה׃
כב כג וַיַּעַשׂ אֶת־מְעִיל הָאֵפֹד מַעֲשֵׂה אֹרֵג כְּלִיל תְּכֵלֶת׃ וּפִי־ שלישי /ששי/
כד הַמְּעִיל בְּתוֹכוֹ כְּפִי תַחְרָא שָׂפָה לְפִיו סָבִיב לֹא יִקָּרֵעַ׃ וַיַּעֲשׂוּ
עַל־שׁוּלֵי הַמְּעִיל רִמּוֹנֵי תְּכֵלֶת וְאַרְגָּמָן וְתוֹלַעַת שָׁנִי מָשְׁזָר׃
כה וַיַּעֲשׂוּ פַעֲמֹנֵי זָהָב טָהוֹר וַיִּתְּנוּ אֶת־הַפַּעֲמֹנִים בְּתוֹךְ הָרִמֹּנִים
כו עַל־שׁוּלֵי הַמְּעִיל סָבִיב בְּתוֹךְ הָרִמֹּנִים׃ פַּעֲמֹן וְרִמֹּן פַּעֲמֹן
וְרִמֹּן עַל־שׁוּלֵי הַמְּעִיל סָבִיב לְשָׁרֵת כַּאֲשֶׁר צִוָּה יהוה אֶת־
כז מֹשֶׁה׃ וַיַּעֲשׂוּ אֶת־הַכָּתְנֹת שֵׁשׁ מַעֲשֵׂה אֹרֵג
כח לְאַהֲרֹן וּלְבָנָיו׃ וְאֵת הַמִּצְנֶפֶת שֵׁשׁ וְאֶת־פַּאֲרֵי הַמִּגְבָּעֹת
כט שֵׁשׁ וְאֶת־מִכְנְסֵי הַבָּד שֵׁשׁ מָשְׁזָר׃ וְאֶת־הָאַבְנֵט שֵׁשׁ מָשְׁזָר
וּתְכֵלֶת וְאַרְגָּמָן וְתוֹלַעַת שָׁנִי מַעֲשֵׂה רֹקֵם כַּאֲשֶׁר צִוָּה יהוה
ל אֶת־מֹשֶׁה׃ וַיַּעֲשׂוּ אֶת־צִיץ נֵזֶר־הַקֹּדֶשׁ זָהָב טָהוֹר
לא וַיִּכְתְּבוּ עָלָיו מִכְתַּב פִּתּוּחֵי חוֹתָם קֹדֶשׁ לַיהוה׃ וַיִּתְּנוּ עָלָיו
פְּתִיל תְּכֵלֶת לָתֵת עַל־הַמִּצְנֶפֶת מִלְמָעְלָה כַּאֲשֶׁר צִוָּה יהוה
לב אֶת־מֹשֶׁה׃ וַתֵּכֶל כָּל־עֲבֹדַת מִשְׁכַּן אֹהֶל

39:32 וַתֵּכֶל כָּל־עֲבֹדַת מִשְׁכַּן אֹהֶל מוֹעֵד *Thus all the work on the Tabernacle, the Tent of Meeting, was completed* – The placement of the Tabernacle at the heart of the camp suggests that societies need, in the public domain, a constant reminder of the presence of God. That, after all, is why the Tabernacle appears in Exodus, not Genesis. Genesis is about individuals, Exodus about societies. Individuals can be moral without being conventionally religious. You do not need to believe in God to rescue a drowning child, give food to the hungry or shelter to the homeless. The Torah describes the courage, for example, of Pharaoh's daughter without implying that she was in receipt of a divine revelation. The Torah seems to use the phrase "fear of God" in roughly the same way as we speak about the moral sense (see Gen.

did everything exactly as the LORD had commanded
Moshe.
33 They brought the Tabernacle to Moshe: the Tent and REVI'I
all its furnishings, its clasps, frames, crossbars, posts,
34 and sockets; the covering of reddened rams' hides and
the covering of fine leather and the curtain that covered
35 the screen; the Ark of the Testimony and its carrying
36 staves; the Ark cover; the table with all its utensils; the
37 showbread; the pure gold candelabrum with its row of
lamps and all its accessories, together with the oil for
38 lighting; the gold altar, the anointing oil, the fragrant
incense, and the curtain for the entrance to the Tent;
39 the bronze altar with its bronze mesh, its staves, and all
40 its utensils; the laver with its base; the hangings for the
courtyard, its posts and sockets, and the screen for the
courtyard gate; the ropes and tent pegs for the courtyard;
all the furnishings for the service of the Tabernacle, the
41 Tent of Meeting; and the woven garments for ministering
in the Sanctuary, both the sacred vestments for Aharon
the priest and the vestments for his sons to wear when
42 serving as priests. The Israelites had completed all the
43 work exactly as the LORD commanded Moshe. Moshe

---

and dispersed among the nations, never knowing when they would be forced to leave and find a new home. In the fifteenth century alone, Jews were expelled from Vienna and Linz in 1421, from Cologne in 1424, Augsburg in 1439, Bavaria in 1442, Moravia in 1454, Perugia in 1485, Vicenza in 1486, Parma in 1488, Milan and Lucca in 1489, Spain in 1492, and Portugal in 1497.

How did they survive, their identity intact, their faith, though sorely challenged, still strong? Because they believed that God was with them, even in exile. Because they were sustained by the line from Psalms (23:4), "Though I walk through the valley of the shadow of death, I fear no evil, for You are with me." Because they still had the Torah, God's unbreakable covenant, with its promise that "yet even then, when they are in the land of their enemies, I will not reject them nor despise them and annihilate them, will not break My covenant with them, for I am the LORD their God" (Lev. 26:44). The Torah became, in the famous phrase of Heinrich Heine, "the portable homeland of the Jew."

מוֹעֵד וַיַּעֲשׂוּ בְּנֵי יִשְׂרָאֵל כְּכֹל אֲשֶׁר צִוָּה יְהוָה אֶת־מֹשֶׁה כֵּן
עָשׂוּ׃
לג וַיָּבִיאוּ אֶת־הַמִּשְׁכָּן אֶל־מֹשֶׁה אֶת־הָאֹהֶל וְאֶת־כָּל־כֵּלָיו כט רביעי
לד קְרָסָיו קְרָשָׁיו בְּרִיחָו וְעַמֻּדָיו וַאֲדָנָיו׃ וְאֶת־מִכְסֵה עוֹרֹת
הָאֵילִם הַמְאָדָּמִים וְאֶת־מִכְסֵה עֹרֹת הַתְּחָשִׁים וְאֵת
לה פָּרֹכֶת הַמָּסָךְ׃ אֶת־אֲרוֹן הָעֵדֻת וְאֶת־בַּדָּיו וְאֵת הַכַּפֹּרֶת׃
לו לז אֶת־הַשֻּׁלְחָן אֶת־כָּל־כֵּלָיו וְאֵת לֶחֶם הַפָּנִים׃ אֶת־הַמְּנֹרָה
הַטְּהֹרָה אֶת־נֵרֹתֶיהָ נֵרֹת הַמַּעֲרָכָה וְאֶת־כָּל־כֵּלֶיהָ וְאֵת
לח שֶׁמֶן הַמָּאוֹר׃ וְאֵת מִזְבַּח הַזָּהָב וְאֵת שֶׁמֶן הַמִּשְׁחָה וְאֵת
לט קְטֹרֶת הַסַּמִּים וְאֵת מָסַךְ פֶּתַח הָאֹהֶל׃ אֵת ׀ מִזְבַּח הַנְּחֹשֶׁת
וְאֶת־מִכְבַּר הַנְּחֹשֶׁת אֲשֶׁר־לוֹ אֶת־בַּדָּיו וְאֶת־כָּל־כֵּלָיו
מ אֶת־הַכִּיֹּר וְאֶת־כַּנּוֹ׃ אֵת קַלְעֵי הֶחָצֵר אֶת־עַמֻּדֶיהָ וְאֶת־
אֲדָנֶיהָ וְאֶת־הַמָּסָךְ לְשַׁעַר הֶחָצֵר אֶת־מֵיתָרָיו וִיתֵדֹתֶיהָ
מא וְאֵת כָּל־כְּלֵי עֲבֹדַת הַמִּשְׁכָּן לְאֹהֶל מוֹעֵד׃ אֶת־בִּגְדֵי הַשְּׂרָד
לְשָׁרֵת בַּקֹּדֶשׁ אֶת־בִּגְדֵי הַקֹּדֶשׁ לְאַהֲרֹן הַכֹּהֵן וְאֶת־בִּגְדֵי
מב בָנָיו לְכַהֵן׃ כְּכֹל אֲשֶׁר־צִוָּה יְהוָה אֶת־מֹשֶׁה כֵּן עָשׂוּ בְּנֵי
מג יִשְׂרָאֵל אֵת כָּל־הָעֲבֹדָה׃ וַיַּרְא מֹשֶׁה אֶת־כָּל־הַמְּלָאכָה

Without the Divine Presence symbolized at the heart of the camp, human beings will do what they have always done: oppress one another, fight with one another, and exploit one another. There can be no just society without some collective form of *yirat Shamayim*, some "reverence for Heaven." This moment, then – the completion and placement of the Tabernacle, in full view of all, at the center of the camp – is the culmination of Exodus.

39:35 אֶת־אֲרוֹן הָעֵדֻת וְאֶת־בַּדָּיו *The Ark… its carrying staves* – The Torah has already stipulated that "the staves must stay in the rings of the Ark; they must not be removed" (Ex. 25:15). Rabbi Samson Raphael Hirsch explained that the ark is to be permanently ready when the need arises for the Israelites to travel. Why is the same not true about the other objects in the Tabernacle, such as the altar and the candelabrum? To show supremely, said Rabbi Hirsch, that the Torah is not limited to any one place.

And so it came to be. Throughout history Jews found themselves scattered

▶

saw that all the work had been done just as the LORD had
commanded – and Moshe blessed them.
40 1 2 Then the LORD spoke to Moshe, saying, "On the first day HAMISHI /SHEVI'I/
of the first month you shall set up the Tabernacle of the
3 Tent of Meeting. Put in it the Ark of the Testimony, and
4 screen the Ark with the curtain. Bring in the table and set
5 it. Bring in the candelabrum and light its lamps. Put the
golden incense altar in front of the Ark of the Testimony,
6 and hang the screen for the Tabernacle's entrance. Put the
sacrificial altar in front of the entrance of the Tabernacle
7 of the Tent of Meeting. Place the laver between the Tent
8 of Meeting and the altar, and put water in it. Arrange
the courtyard all around, and put in place the screen for
9 the courtyard gate. Take the anointing oil and anoint
the Tabernacle and everything in it. Consecrate it and
10 all its furnishings so that it becomes holy. Anoint the
sacrificial altar and all its utensils, consecrating it so
11 that it becomes holy of holies. Anoint the laver with its
12 base, making it holy. Then bring Aharon and his sons to
the entrance of the Tent of Meeting, and cleanse them
13 with water. Robe Aharon with the sacred vestments
and anoint him and consecrate him, that he may serve
14 Me as priest. Then bring his sons forward, robe them
15 with tunics, and anoint them as you anointed their
father, that they may serve Me as priests. Through this
anointing, theirs will become an everlasting priesthood
16 throughout the generations." Moshe did exactly as the
17 LORD had commanded him. On the first day SHISHI

have gifts, capacities that can lie dormant throughout life until someone awakens them. We can achieve heights of which we never thought ourselves capable. All it takes is for us to meet someone who believes in us, challenges us, and then, when we have responded to the challenge, blesses and celebrates our achievements.

That is what Moshe does for the Israelites after the sin of the golden calf. First he gets them to create, and then he blesses them and their creation with one of the simplest and most moving of all blessings, that the *Shekhina* should dwell in the work of their hands.

וְהִנֵּה עָשׂוּ אֹתָהּ כַּאֲשֶׁר צִוָּה יְהוָה כֵּן עָשׂוּ וַיְבָרֶךְ אֹתָם
מֹשֶׁה׃

מ א ב וַיְדַבֵּר יְהוָה אֶל־מֹשֶׁה לֵּאמֹר׃ בְּיוֹם־הַחֹדֶשׁ הָרִאשׁוֹן בְּאֶחָד חמישי
ג לַחֹדֶשׁ תָּקִים אֶת־מִשְׁכַּן אֹהֶל מוֹעֵד׃ וְשַׂמְתָּ שָׁם אֵת אֲרוֹן /שביעי/
ד הָעֵדוּת וְסַכֹּתָ עַל־הָאָרֹן אֶת־הַפָּרֹכֶת׃ וְהֵבֵאתָ אֶת־הַשֻּׁלְחָן
וְעָרַכְתָּ אֶת־עֶרְכּוֹ וְהֵבֵאתָ אֶת־הַמְּנֹרָה וְהַעֲלֵיתָ אֶת־נֵרֹתֶיהָ׃
ה וְנָתַתָּה אֶת־מִזְבַּח הַזָּהָב לִקְטֹרֶת לִפְנֵי אֲרוֹן הָעֵדֻת וְשַׂמְתָּ
ו אֶת־מָסַךְ הַפֶּתַח לַמִּשְׁכָּן׃ וְנָתַתָּה אֵת מִזְבַּח הָעֹלָה לִפְנֵי
ז פֶּתַח מִשְׁכַּן אֹהֶל־מוֹעֵד׃ וְנָתַתָּ אֶת־הַכִּיֹּר בֵּין־אֹהֶל מוֹעֵד
ח וּבֵין הַמִּזְבֵּחַ וְנָתַתָּ שָׁם מָיִם׃ וְשַׂמְתָּ אֶת־הֶחָצֵר סָבִיב וְנָתַתָּ
ט אֶת־מָסַךְ שַׁעַר הֶחָצֵר׃ וְלָקַחְתָּ אֶת־שֶׁמֶן הַמִּשְׁחָה וּמָשַׁחְתָּ
אֶת־הַמִּשְׁכָּן וְאֶת־כָּל־אֲשֶׁר־בּוֹ וְקִדַּשְׁתָּ אֹתוֹ וְאֶת־כָּל־
י כֵּלָיו וְהָיָה קֹדֶשׁ׃ וּמָשַׁחְתָּ אֶת־מִזְבַּח הָעֹלָה וְאֶת־כָּל־כֵּלָיו
יא וְקִדַּשְׁתָּ אֶת־הַמִּזְבֵּחַ וְהָיָה הַמִּזְבֵּחַ קֹדֶשׁ קָדָשִׁים׃ וּמָשַׁחְתָּ
יב אֶת־הַכִּיֹּר וְאֶת־כַּנּוֹ וְקִדַּשְׁתָּ אֹתוֹ׃ וְהִקְרַבְתָּ אֶת־אַהֲרֹן וְאֶת־
יג בָּנָיו אֶל־פֶּתַח אֹהֶל מוֹעֵד וְרָחַצְתָּ אֹתָם בַּמָּיִם׃ וְהִלְבַּשְׁתָּ
אֶת־אַהֲרֹן אֵת בִּגְדֵי הַקֹּדֶשׁ וּמָשַׁחְתָּ אֹתוֹ וְקִדַּשְׁתָּ אֹתוֹ
יד טו וְכִהֵן לִי׃ וְאֶת־בָּנָיו תַּקְרִיב וְהִלְבַּשְׁתָּ אֹתָם כֻּתֳּנֹת׃ וּמָשַׁחְתָּ
אֹתָם כַּאֲשֶׁר מָשַׁחְתָּ אֶת־אֲבִיהֶם וְכִהֲנוּ לִי וְהָיְתָה לִהְיֹת
טז לָהֶם מָשְׁחָתָם לִכְהֻנַּת עוֹלָם לְדֹרֹתָם׃ וַיַּעַשׂ מֹשֶׁה כְּכֹל
יז אֲשֶׁר צִוָּה יְהוָה אֹתוֹ כֵּן עָשָׂה׃ וַיְהִי בַּחֹדֶשׁ ששי

39:43 וַיְבָרֶךְ אֹתָם מֹשֶׁה *And Moshe blessed them* – As Israel's first creative achievement reaches its culmination, Moshe blesses them, saying, according to the Sages (Sifrei Bemidbar, Pinḥas 143), "May it be God's will that His presence rests in the work of your hands." Our potential greatness is that we can create structures, relationships, and lives that become homes for the Divine Presence. Blessing them and celebrating their achievement, Moshe shows them what they could be. That is potentially a life-changing experience.

Not all of us can paint like Monet or compose like Mozart. But we each

of the first month of the second year the Tabernacle was
18 set up. Moshe set up the Tabernacle, placed its sockets,
erected its frames, inserted its bars, and put up its posts.
19 He spread the tent over the Tabernacle and placed the
covering over the tent, as the Lord had commanded
20 him. He took the covenant and put it in the
Ark. He inserted the carrying staves into the Ark and
21 placed the cover on top of it. He brought the Ark into
the Tabernacle and hung the cloth curtain, screening off
the Ark of the Testimony, as the Lord had commanded
22 him. He put the table in the Tent of Meeting,
outside the curtain on the north side of the Tabernacle,
23 and arranged the bread on it before the Lord, as the

---

refined. "Where there is much desire to learn, there of necessity will be much arguing, much writing, many opinions; for *opinion in men is but knowledge in the making.*" The path to truth passes through the city of many voices. The strength and vigor of argument within a culture is a measure of its spiritual health.

His refutation of those who believed that society requires us all to hold the same faith is based on the building of the Temple. It is absurd to insist on uniformity, as if:

> While the temple of the Lord was building, some cutting, some squaring the marble, others hewing the cedars, there should be a sort of irrational men who could not consider there must be many schisms and many dissections made in the quarry and in the timber, ere the house of God can be built. And when every stone is laid artfully together, it cannot be united into a continuity, it can but be contiguous in this world; neither can every piece of the building be of one form; nay rather the perfection consists in this, that, out of many moderate varieties and brotherly dissimilitudes that are not vastly disproportional, arises the goodly and the graceful symmetry that commends the whole pile and structure. (*Areopagitica*, 1644)

Society, for Milton, is the arena in which all sorts of groups, different yet linked in a collective task, each have a contribution to make to "the whole pile and structure." It is precisely this integrated diversity that gives society its complex beauty, its "goodly and gracious symmetry." Just as God creates the natural universe, so we are called on to create the social universe – a universe, like that of the planets and stars, that is ordered, rule-governed, a space of integrated diversity, a world we can see and say, as God saw and said, that it is good.

הָרִאשׁוֹן בַּשָּׁנָה הַשֵּׁנִית בְּאֶחָד לַחֹדֶשׁ הוּקַם הַמִּשְׁכָּן׃
יח וַיָּקֶם מֹשֶׁה אֶת־הַמִּשְׁכָּן וַיִּתֵּן אֶת־אֲדָנָיו וַיָּשֶׂם אֶת־קְרָשָׁיו
יט וַיִּתֵּן אֶת־בְּרִיחָיו וַיָּקֶם אֶת־עַמּוּדָיו׃ וַיִּפְרֹשׂ אֶת־הָאֹהֶל
עַל־הַמִּשְׁכָּן וַיָּשֶׂם אֶת־מִכְסֵה הָאֹהֶל עָלָיו מִלְמָעְלָה
כ כַּאֲשֶׁר צִוָּה יְהוָה אֶת־מֹשֶׁה׃ וַיִּקַּח וַיִּתֵּן
אֶת־הָעֵדֻת אֶל־הָאָרֹן וַיָּשֶׂם אֶת־הַבַּדִּים עַל־הָאָרֹן וַיִּתֵּן
כא אֶת־הַכַּפֹּרֶת עַל־הָאָרֹן מִלְמָעְלָה׃ וַיָּבֵא אֶת־הָאָרֹן אֶל־
הַמִּשְׁכָּן וַיָּשֶׂם אֵת פָּרֹכֶת הַמָּסָךְ וַיָּסֶךְ עַל אֲרוֹן הָעֵדוּת
כב כַּאֲשֶׁר צִוָּה יְהוָה אֶת־מֹשֶׁה׃ וַיִּתֵּן אֶת־הַשֻּׁלְחָן
בְּאֹהֶל מוֹעֵד עַל יֶרֶךְ הַמִּשְׁכָּן צָפֹנָה מִחוּץ לַפָּרֹכֶת׃
כג וַיַּעֲרֹךְ עָלָיו עֵרֶךְ לֶחֶם לִפְנֵי יְהוָה כַּאֲשֶׁר צִוָּה יְהוָה אֶת־

THE COMPLETION AND CONSTRUCTION OF THE TABERNACLE

The date of the completion of the Tabernacle – the first day of the first month (Ex. 40:17) – is the anniversary of creation, as well as the day on which dry land appeared after the flood (Gen. 8:13), the start of the recreated universe after the great destruction. A set of linguistic parallels between the Israelites' construction of the Tabernacle and God's creation of the universe culminates at its end: "Moshe saw that all the work had been done… and Moshe blessed them"; "And so Moshe completed the work" (Ex. 39:43, 40:33; compare Gen. 1:31–2:3). The effect is to suggest that the Tabernacle was the human counterpart of the divine creation of the universe. Though the creation of the universe takes a mere thirty-four verses (Gen. 1:1–2:3), the making of the Tabernacle takes several hundred. Although the Torah is interested in the natural universe, the home God makes for man, it is even more interested in the social universe, the home man makes for God.

The world had but a single Creator, but the Tabernacle constructed by man was built out of difference and diversity. Each of the Israelites brought his or her own distinctive contribution. Each was valued equally. The Tabernacle was built out of the differential contributions of the various groups and tribes. It represented *orchestrated diversity*, or in social terms, integration without assimilation. Because we are not the same, we each have something unique to contribute, something only we can give.

In an age of religious conformity, John Milton argued that God wants difference, for it is only through the clash of opinions that truth is honed and

24 Lord had commanded him. He placed the
candelabrum in the Tent of Meeting, opposite the table,
25 on the Tabernacle's south side, and lit the lamps before the
26 Lord, as the Lord had commanded him. He
placed the golden altar in the Tent of Meeting, in front
27 of the curtain, and on it he burned fragrant incense, as
28 the Lord had commanded him. He hung the SHEVI'I
29 curtain at the entrance of the Tabernacle. He put the
sacrificial altar at the entrance of the Tabernacle of the
Tent of Meeting, and on it sacrificed a burnt offering
and a grain offering, as the Lord had commanded
30 him. He placed the laver between the Tent of
Meeting and the altar, and in it he put water for washing.
31 Moshe, Aharon, and his sons would wash their hands and
32 feet there, for they washed themselves whenever they
went into the Tent of Meeting or approached the altar,
33 as the Lord had commanded Moshe. Then
he set up the courtyard around the Tabernacle and the
altar, and hung the curtain for the courtyard gate. And so
Moshe completed the work.
34 Then the cloud covered the Tent of Meeting, and the glory MAFTIR
35 of the Lord filled the Tabernacle. Moshe could not now
enter the Tent of Meeting, because the cloud had settled
on it, and the glory of the Lord filled the Tabernacle.
36 In all the journeys of the Israelites, when the cloud rose
37 from the Tabernacle, they would set out. But if the cloud
did not lift, they did not move on; they waited until it had

---

made it; they prepared the structured space the Divine Presence would fill. Forty days after the revelation at Sinai, the Israelites made a golden calf. But after constructing the Sanctuary, that generation will make no more idols. That is the difference between the things that are done for us and the things we have a share in doing ourselves. The former change us for a moment, the latter for a lifetime.

EXODUS: THE NARRATIVE STRUCTURE

Human creation mirrors divine creation. Thus, the end of Exodus brings us back to the beginning of Genesis. On close examination, we see that Genesis and

כד מֹשֶׁה׃ וַיָּשֶׂם אֶת־הַמְּנֹרָה בְּאֹהֶל מוֹעֵד
כה נֹכַח הַשֻּׁלְחָן עַל יֶרֶךְ הַמִּשְׁכָּן נֶגְבָּה׃ וַיַּעַל הַנֵּרֹת לִפְנֵי יְהוָה
כו כַּאֲשֶׁר צִוָּה יְהוָה אֶת־מֹשֶׁה׃ וַיָּשֶׂם אֶת־מִזְבַּח
כז הַזָּהָב בְּאֹהֶל מוֹעֵד לִפְנֵי הַפָּרֹכֶת׃ וַיַּקְטֵר עָלָיו קְטֹרֶת
כח סַמִּים כַּאֲשֶׁר צִוָּה יְהוָה אֶת־מֹשֶׁה׃ וַיָּשֶׂם שביעי
כט אֶת־מָסַךְ הַפֶּתַח לַמִּשְׁכָּן׃ וְאֵת מִזְבַּח הָעֹלָה שָׂם פֶּתַח
מִשְׁכַּן אֹהֶל־מוֹעֵד וַיַּעַל עָלָיו אֶת־הָעֹלָה וְאֶת־הַמִּנְחָה
ל כַּאֲשֶׁר צִוָּה יְהוָה אֶת־מֹשֶׁה׃ וַיָּשֶׂם אֶת־
הַכִּיֹּר בֵּין־אֹהֶל מוֹעֵד וּבֵין הַמִּזְבֵּחַ וַיִּתֵּן שָׁמָּה מַיִם לְרָחְצָה׃
לא וְרָחֲצוּ מִמֶּנּוּ מֹשֶׁה וְאַהֲרֹן וּבָנָיו אֶת־יְדֵיהֶם וְאֶת־רַגְלֵיהֶם׃
לב בְּבֹאָם אֶל־אֹהֶל מוֹעֵד וּבְקָרְבָתָם אֶל־הַמִּזְבֵּחַ יִרְחָצוּ כַּאֲשֶׁר
לג צִוָּה יְהוָה אֶת־מֹשֶׁה׃ וַיָּקֶם אֶת־הֶחָצֵר סָבִיב
לַמִּשְׁכָּן וְלַמִּזְבֵּחַ וַיִּתֵּן אֶת־מָסַךְ שַׁעַר הֶחָצֵר וַיְכַל מֹשֶׁה
אֶת־הַמְּלָאכָה׃
לד וַיְכַס הֶעָנָן אֶת־אֹהֶל מוֹעֵד וּכְבוֹד יְהוָה מָלֵא אֶת־הַמִּשְׁכָּן׃ מפטיר
לה וְלֹא־יָכֹל מֹשֶׁה לָבוֹא אֶל־אֹהֶל מוֹעֵד כִּי־שָׁכַן עָלָיו הֶעָנָן
לו וּכְבוֹד יְהוָה מָלֵא אֶת־הַמִּשְׁכָּן׃ וּבְהֵעָלוֹת הֶעָנָן מֵעַל
לז הַמִּשְׁכָּן יִסְעוּ בְּנֵי יִשְׂרָאֵל בְּכֹל מַסְעֵיהֶם׃ וְאִם־לֹא יֵעָלֶה

40:34 וּכְבוֹד יהוה מָלֵא אֶת־הַמִּשְׁכָּן *The glory of the Lord filled the Tabernacle* – The Torah speaks about the revelations of "the Lord's glory" at Mount Sinai and the Tabernacle in almost identical terms:

> Mount Sinai: "The glory of the Lord rested on Mount Sinai, and the cloud covered it for six days. On the seventh, He called to Moshe from within the cloud." (Ex. 24:16)

> The Tabernacle: "Then the cloud covered the Tent of Meeting, and the glory of the Lord filled the Tabernacle." (40:34)

The difference between them is that the sanctity of Mount Sinai was momentary, while that of the Tabernacle (later transferred to the Temple) is permanent. The revelation at Sinai was conducted by God. So overwhelming was it that the people say to Moshe, "Let not God say any more to us or we will die" (20:16). By contrast, the Tabernacle involves human labor. The Israelites

38 lifted. The LORD's cloud was over the Tabernacle by day,
and fire was in it at night, in view of all the House of Israel
through all their journeys.

The haftara for Parashat Pekudei is on page 1506.
On the Shabbat of Parashat Shekalim read the haftara on page 1654. On the Shabbat of Parashat Para read the haftara on page 1662. On the Shabbat of Parashat HaḤodesh read the haftara on page 1666.

---

just as God created order in the universe, so we are called on to create order in our personal lives and in society as a whole. We are God's image; we are God's children; we are God's partners.

40:38 בְּכָל־מַסְעֵיהֶם *Through all their journeys* – The Tabernacle is constructed in such a way as to be portable. It will be dismantled and its parts carried as the Israelites make their way to the next stage of their journey. When the time comes for the Israelites to move on, the cloud moves from its resting place above the Tent of Meeting to a position outside the camp, signaling the direction they must now take.

However, there is a small but significant difference between the two instances of the phrase "in all their journeys," one in verse 36 and one in verse 38. In the first instance the words are to be taken literally. When the cloud lifted and moved on ahead, the Israelites knew they were about to travel. In the second instance, the words cannot be taken literally, as the cloud was not "over the Tabernacle" in all their journeys. On the contrary: It was there only when they stopped traveling and instead pitched camp. During the journeys the cloud went on ahead.

Noting this, Rashi (on Ex. 40:38) makes the following comment: "The word *masa* can denote a destination.... The desert locations are referred to as such because they served as resting places prior to the nation setting out again." The point is linguistic, yet Rashi has encapsulated in a few brief words the existential truth at the heart of Judaism. In Jewish history, even an encampment is called a journey. So long as we have not yet reached our destination, even a place of rest is merely temporary.

To be a Jew is to travel, and to know that here where we are is a mere resting place, not yet a home. It is defined not by the fact that we are here, but by the knowledge that eventually – after a day, a week, a year, a century, sometimes even a millennium – we will have to move on. Thus, the portable Tabernacle, even more than the Temple in Jerusalem, became the symbol of Jewish life.

How and why it happened is contained in those simple words of Rashi at the end of Exodus. Even when at rest, Jews knew that they would one day have to uproot their tents, dismantle the Tabernacle, and move on. Even an encampment is called a journey. A people that never stops traveling is one that never grows old or stale or complacent. It may live in the here and now, but it is always conscious of the distant past and the still-beckoning future. It is with this word, with its two entwined meanings, that the book of Exodus comes to a close. The journey through the wilderness has begun.

לח הֶעָנָן וְלֹא יִסְעוּ עַד־יוֹם הֵעָלֹתוֹ׃ כִּי עֲנַן יְהוָה עַל־הַמִּשְׁכָּן
יוֹמָם וְאֵשׁ תִּהְיֶה לַיְלָה בּוֹ לְעֵינֵי כָל־בֵּית־יִשְׂרָאֵל בְּכָל־
מַסְעֵיהֶם׃

The הפטרה *for* פרשת פקודי *is on page 1507.*
On the שבת *of* פרשת שקלים *read the* הפטרה *on page 1655. On the* שבת *of* פרשת פרה *read the* הפטרה *on page 1663. On the* שבת *of* פרשת החודש *read the* הפטרה *on page 1667.*

Exodus are joined as a single mirror-image symmetry, whose structure is this:

- Creation of the universe (Gen. 1–3)
  - Humanity and its failings (3–6)
    - Flood (7–10)
      - Hubris: The Tower of Bavel (11)
        - The family of the covenant (12–50)
        - The people of the covenant (Ex. 1–4)
      - Hubris: Pharaoh (5–6)
    - Plagues (7–11)
  - The people and their failings (12–18; 32–33)
- Creation of the Sanctuary (25–31; 34–40)

The difference between Genesis and Exodus is that the *family* of the covenant has become the *people* of the covenant. Framing the narrative as a whole are the creation of the universe and the creation of the Tabernacle.

At the heart of Genesis and Exodus are journeys: Avraham's from the east in Genesis, Moshe's from the west in Exodus. There is, the narrative implies, a way back from sin to harmony, exile to return. Seen from this perspective, the Sanctuary is more than an atonement for the sin of the golden calf. It is also a kind of atonement for the sin of Adam and Ḥava in Eden. After the flood, God accepts the fact of human sinfulness. After the golden calf, He accepts the fact of Israel's collective sinfulness. When people sacrifice – when they offer something of themselves to God – God will grant atonement. The second tablets that rested in the Ark as a permanent sign of divine forgiveness are thus, for Israel, the counterpart of the rainbow in the days of Noaḥ, with its promise that God would never again destroy all life. God is just, but God forgives. Human beings are sinful, but humans can be forgiven.

The ideal society, according to the Torah, is one of *ordered liberty*, brought about by the rule of law. So the presence of the Sanctuary with its precisely ordered spaces at the heart of the camp is not just a symbol of God's presence, but also of God's order, which characterizes both creation (natural order, science) and redemption (social order, justice). The ordered society the Israelites are commanded to create brings to a kind of closure the story with which the Torah began, God's creation of an ordered universe.

Genesis-Exodus, then, is a single literary unit, in which the meaning of the universe and our place within it is explored through a series of dramas, some personal, others political, yet adding up to a momentous proposition: that

ויקרא
LEVITICUS

psychopathology of hatred and violence. It contains one of the most remarkable of religious ideas, that we are summoned to be holy because God is holy. Not only are we created in God's image, we are called on to act in God's ways.

At a more practical but no less profound level, Vayikra sets out an entire infrastructure for justice and equity in political and economic life. It humanizes slavery and sets in motion a process that must end in its abolition. It speaks about debt relief and the return of ancestral land in the Jubilee year.

Vayikra is a precisely structured book, divided into three parts. The first (chs. 1–10) is about the holy. Specifically, it is about sacrifices and how to come close to God in the House of God. The second part (chs. 11–16) is set at the boundary between the holy and the world. It is about the things that prevent us from entering sacred space. The third (chs. 17–27) is about taking the holy into the world. The book begins with an elite, the priests, sons of Aharon, a minority within a minority, one specific family within the tribe of Levi. It culminates in a call from God to the entire nation. It begins in the Sanctuary, but ends in society. It democratizes *kedusha*, holiness, the sign of God's presence, so that it becomes part of the life of the whole people.

THE BOOK OF VAYIKRA

The third book of the Torah is markedly different from the others. It contains no journey. It is set entirely at Sinai. It occupies only a brief section of time: a single month. There is almost no narrative. Yet set at the center of the Mosaic books, it is the key to understanding Israel's vocation as "a kingdom of priests and a holy nation" (Ex. 19:6), the first collective mission statement in history. Vayikra was not the first name the Sages gave the book. They called it *Torat Kohanim*, "The Law of the Priests," because much of it is about the Sanctuary and its service, the world of the priests. Hence its English name, Leviticus, from the Greek and Latin meaning "matters concerning the Levites," the tribe from which the priests came.

Much of the book is indeed about the work of the priests and the Sanctuary. But the book is larger than that. It opens out into broad vistas of personal morality and social justice. The great code in Leviticus 19 tells us that every Jew, not just a priestly elite, is called on to be holy. So tradition eventually settled on the name Vayikra, "He called."

Vayikra is a – perhaps even *the* – key text of Judaism. It is here that we read for the first time the command to "love your neighbor as your own self" (Lev. 19:18). It is the source of the even greater moral principle "The stranger... love him as your own self, for you yourselves were strangers in the land of Egypt" (19:34). It is Leviticus that forbids us to exact vengeance or bear a grudge, taking a stand against the

Parashat Vayikra

1 1 The Lord called to Moshe. From the Tent of Meeting He

---

expression signifying a casual encounter and uncleanness, as it says, 'The Lord met Bilam' (Num. 23:16)." For Rashi, the verb "to call" denotes something more than mere speech. It implies affection, intimacy, a relationship of love.

In the final *parasha* of the book of Leviticus, Parashat Beḥukotai, we encounter an echo of *vayikar*, the meeting of happenstance. There, the passage known as the *tokheḥa*, the "warning" or "rebuke," tells of the curses that will befall the Israelites if they fail to keep their covenant with God. These curses contain a recurring motif: the word *keri*, an unusual word which by the mishnaic period will denote "uncleanness," as hinted by Rashi above. It appears seven times in the *tokheḥa* – always a sign of significance – and nowhere else in the whole Torah.

The commentators disagree as to what the word *keri* means there. Saadia Gaon understands it as "if you are rebellious," and Ibn Ezra as "if you are overconfident." Rambam, however, understands *keri*, like *vayikar*, to be related to *mikreh*, "chance," the way of the world. To regard something as *mikreh* means to see it as if it had no larger significance. That, he says, is not how we as Jews should view our fate (*Hilkhot Taanit* 1:1–3).

The difference between *vayikra* and *vayikar* lies in the small *alef*. An *alef* is almost inaudible. The small *alef* in the Torah scroll at the beginning of the word *Vayikra* is almost invisible. It is as if the Torah were intimating that the presence of God in history will not always be as clear as it was during the exodus or the division of the Sea of Reeds. Often, it will depend on our own sensitivity. For those who look, it will be visible. For those who listen, it will be audible. But we will need to look and listen. God does not force His presence on us against our will. We have to search Him out.

If we choose *not* to see or hear, then *Vayikra* will become *Vayikar*. God's call will be inaudible. History will seem no more than "a tale / Told by an idiot, full of sound and fury, / Signifying nothing" (*Macbeth*). It is a self-fulfilling expectation. *If you believe that history is chance, then it will become so.*

But if you believe otherwise, it will be otherwise. The word *vayikra* at the beginning and the sevenfold *keri* at the end enfold the priestly book in prophetic time. Israel's timeless encounters with God allow it to negotiate safely the currents and rapids of history. We must all choose: will we live the life of *vayikra*, calling, or *keri* – vocation or accident, destiny or chance?

פרשת ויקרא

א א וַיִּקְרָא אֶל־מֹשֶׁה וַיְדַבֵּר יהוה אֵלָיו מֵאֹהֶל מוֹעֵד לֵאמֹר׃ א

VAYIKRA

This *parasha*, with which the book opens, details the various kinds of sacrifices the Israelites brought to the Tabernacle. There were five: the burnt offering (*ola*), the grain offering (*minḥa*), the peace offering (*shelamim*), the purification offering (*ḥatat*), and the guilt offering (*asham*).

Sacrifice, in the broadest sense, is the fundamental activity in relation to the holy. God sacrifices something of Himself to make space for us. We sacrifice something of ourselves to make space for Him. Sacrifice is what God allows us to give Him, to show our love and gratitude for what He has given us.

The discussion of sacrifices in Parashat Vayikra raises many fascinating questions. Among them, as we shall see, are the issue of how the sacrificial service relates to prophetic ethics, the symbolic meaning of sacrifice, how sacrifices can teach us about the nature of sin itself, and what the description of the sacrifice brought by an elder or judge can tell us about the nature and challenges of leadership.

THE LORD CALLED

The phrase "The Lord called to Moshe" is clearly a prelude. Once we get to "He spoke to him and said," we know we are about to hear substantive details. The redundancy of using three verbs for God's speech ("called," "spoke," and "said") cries out for attention. What is more, there is something strangely conspicuous about the way the first of these three verbs is written in a Torah scroll. Its last letter, an *alef*, is written small – almost to the point of invisibility. The standard-size letters spell out the word *vayikar*, meaning "he encountered" or "he chanced upon." Unlike *vayikra*, which refers to a call, a meeting by request, *vayikar* suggests the opposite: an accidental meeting, a mere happenstance.

The Sages, always alert to the way a word in one place chimes with one in another, recall that *vayikar* is the verb the Torah uses for God's encounter with the pagan prophet Bilam (Num. 23:16). Rashi comments: "All [God's] communications [to Moshe], whether they use the words 'speak' or 'say' or 'command,' were preceded by a call [*keria*], which is a term of endearment, used by the angels when they address one another, as it is said, 'And they called out one to another' [*vekara zeh el zeh*, Is. 6:3]. However, to the prophets of the nations of the world, His appearance is described by an

2 spoke to him and said, "Speak to the Israelites. Say: When
one of you brings an animal offering to the LORD, you
3 may bring it either from the herd or from the flock. If the
offering is a burnt offering from the herd, one must offer a
male animal without blemish. The one making the offering
shall bring it to the entrance to the Tent of Meeting to be
4 accepted on his behalf before the LORD; and, that it be
accepted on his behalf, to make his atonement, he shall lay
5 his hand on the head of the burnt offering and shall have
the bull slaughtered before the LORD. And Aharon's sons
the priests shall present the blood, dashing it against each
side of the altar at the entrance to the Tent of Meeting.

---

interpretation of Rabbi Shneur Zalman of Liadi (see previous comment), each of the three types of animal mentioned in the verse – *behema*, "animal," *bakar*, "cattle," and *tzon*, "flock" – represents a separate animal-like feature of the human personality.

Behema represents the animal instinct itself. The word refers to domesticated animals. It does not imply the savage instincts of the predator. It means something more tame. Animals spend their time searching for food. Their lives are bounded by the struggle to survive. To sacrifice the animal within us is to be moved by something more than mere survival. The godly soul within us is the force that makes us look up, beyond the physical world, beyond mere survival, in search of meaning, purpose, goal.

The Hebrew word *bakar*, "cattle," reminds us of the word *boker*, "dawn," literally, "to break through," as the first rays of sunlight break through the darkness of night. Cattle, stampeding, break through barriers. Unless constrained by fences, cattle are no respecters of boundaries. To sacrifice the *bakar* is to learn to recognize and respect boundaries – between holy and profane, pure and impure, permitted and forbidden. Barriers of the mind can sometimes be stronger than walls.

Finally, the word *tzon*, "flock," represents the herd instinct – the powerful drive to move in a given direction because others are doing likewise. The great figures of Judaism – Avraham, Moshe, the prophets – were distinguished precisely by their ability to stand apart from the herd, to be different, to challenge the idols of the age, to refuse to capitulate to the intellectual fashions of the moment. That, ultimately, is the meaning of holiness in Judaism.

We can transcend the *behema*, the *bakar*, and the *tzon*. By bringing that which is animal within us close to God, we allow the material to be suffused with the spiritual. We become no longer slaves of nature but servants of the living God.

ב דַּבֵּר אֶל־בְּנֵי יִשְׂרָאֵל וְאָמַרְתָּ אֲלֵהֶם אָדָם כִּי־יַקְרִיב מִכֶּם
קָרְבָּן לַיהוָה מִן־הַבְּהֵמָה מִן־הַבָּקָר וּמִן־הַצֹּאן תַּקְרִיבוּ אֶת־
ג קָרְבַּנְכֶם: אִם־עֹלָה קָרְבָּנוֹ מִן־הַבָּקָר זָכָר תָּמִים יַקְרִיבֶנּוּ
ד אֶל־פֶּתַח אֹהֶל מוֹעֵד יַקְרִיב אֹתוֹ לִרְצֹנוֹ לִפְנֵי יְהוָה: וְסָמַךְ
ה יָדוֹ עַל רֹאשׁ הָעֹלָה וְנִרְצָה לוֹ לְכַפֵּר עָלָיו: וְשָׁחַט אֶת־בֶּן
הַבָּקָר לִפְנֵי יְהוָה וְהִקְרִיבוּ בְּנֵי אַהֲרֹן הַכֹּהֲנִים אֶת־הַדָּם
וְזָרְקוּ אֶת־הַדָּם עַל־הַמִּזְבֵּחַ סָבִיב אֲשֶׁר־פֶּתַח אֹהֶל מוֹעֵד:

1:2 קָרְבָּן לַיהוה מִן־הַבְּהֵמָה *An animal offering* – Rabbi Shneur Zalman of Liadi, the first Rebbe of Lubavitch, noticed a grammatical oddity in our verse. In Hebrew, the word order of the sentence is unexpected. We would expect to read: *Adam mikem ki yakriv*, "When one of you offers a sacrifice." Instead, it says *Adam ki yakriv mikem*, literally, "When one offers a sacrifice *of you*." The essence of sacrifice, said Rabbi Shneur Zalman (*Likkutei Torah*, Vayikra 2a ff.), is that we offer ourselves. We bring to God our faculties, our energies, our thoughts and emotions. The physical form of sacrifice – an animal offered on the altar – is an external manifestation of an inner act. The real sacrifice is *mikem*, "of you." We give God something of ourselves.

What exactly is it that we give God when we offer a sacrifice? The Jewish mystics, among them Rabbi Shneur Zalman, spoke about two souls that each of us has – the animal soul (*nefesh habahamit*) and the godly soul. On the one hand we are physical beings. We are part of nature. We have physical needs: food, drink, shelter. We are born, we live, we die.

Yet we are not simply animals. We have immortal longings. We can think, speak, and communicate. We can reach out to others. We are the one life-form known to us in the universe that can ask the question "why?" We can formulate ideas and be moved by high ideals. Physically, we are almost nothing; spiritually, we are brushed by the wings of eternity. We have a godly soul. What we offer God is not just an animal, but also the *nefesh habahamit*, the animal soul within us.

The noun *korban*, "sacrifice," and the verb *lehakriv*, "to offer something as a sacrifice," actually mean "that which is brought close" and "the act of bringing close." The key element is not only giving something up (the usual meaning of sacrifice), but rather bringing something close to God. *Lehakriv* is to bring the animal element within us to be transformed through the divine fire that once burned on the altar, and still burns at the heart of prayer if we truly seek closeness to God.

1:2 מִן־הַבָּקָר וּמִן־הַצֹּאן *From the herd or from the flock* – In the allegorical

6 The burnt offering shall then be skinned and cut into
7 pieces. The sons of Aharon the priest shall arrange wood
8 on the fire they will have placed upon the altar. Then
Aharon's sons the priests shall arrange the pieces of the
sacrifice, with the head and the fat, upon the wood on the
9 altar fire; the inner organs and legs shall first be washed
with water. The priest shall then burn it all on the altar as
a burnt offering, an offering of fire, a pleasing aroma to
10 the LORD. If the offering is a burnt offering from
the flock, whether a sheep or a goat, one must offer a male
11 without blemish. The one making the sacrifice shall have
it slaughtered on the north side of the altar before the
LORD, and Aharon's sons the priests shall dash its blood
12 against each side of the altar. The sacrifice shall be cut into
pieces, including the head and the fat, and the priest shall
13 arrange these upon the wood on the altar fire, the inner
organs and legs having been washed with water. The
priest shall then offer it all, sending it up in smoke upon
the altar as a burnt offering, an offering of fire, a pleasing
aroma to the LORD.
14 If the offering for the LORD is to be a burnt offering of fowl, SHENI
15 one may offer doves or pigeons. The priest shall bring the
offering to the altar, sever its neck, and burn it on the altar;
16 its blood shall be drained against the altar wall: the priest
shall remove the crop with its feathers and throw that to
the east side of the altar, to the place where the ashes are
17 gathered. Then he shall tear the bird open by its wings,

---

approximates what a parent gives a child, namely, life itself? Yet it is so, and the reverse is also true. The cruelest thing a child can do is *not* to acknowledge his or her parents. The Talmud attributes to R. Akiva the phrase *Avinu Malkenu*, "Our Father, our King" (Taanit 25b). Those two words encapsulate the essence of Jewish worship. God is king – maker and sovereign of the vast universe. Yet even before God is our king, He is our father, our parent, the one who brought us into being in love, who nurtured and sustained us, who taught us His ways, and who tenderly watches over our destiny. Sacrifice – the gift we bring to God – is the gift of the made to its Maker, the owned to its Owner, the child to its Parent. If creation is an act of love, sacrifice is an acknowledgment of that love.

ו ז וְהִפְשִׁיט אֶת־הָעֹלָה וְנִתַּח אֹתָהּ לִנְתָחֶיהָ׃ וְנָתְנוּ בְּנֵי אַהֲרֹן
ח הַכֹּהֵן אֵשׁ עַל־הַמִּזְבֵּחַ וְעָרְכוּ עֵצִים עַל־הָאֵשׁ׃ וְעָרְכוּ בְּנֵי
אַהֲרֹן הַכֹּהֲנִים אֵת הַנְּתָחִים אֶת־הָרֹאשׁ וְאֶת־הַפָּדֶר עַל־
ט הָעֵצִים אֲשֶׁר עַל־הָאֵשׁ אֲשֶׁר עַל־הַמִּזְבֵּחַ׃ וְקִרְבּוֹ וּכְרָעָיו
יִרְחַץ בַּמָּיִם וְהִקְטִיר הַכֹּהֵן אֶת־הַכֹּל הַמִּזְבֵּחָה עֹלָה אִשֵּׁה
י רֵיחַ־נִיחוֹחַ לַיהוָה׃ וְאִם־מִן־הַצֹּאן קָרְבָּנוֹ מִן־
יא הַכְּשָׂבִים אוֹ מִן־הָעִזִּים לְעֹלָה זָכָר תָּמִים יַקְרִיבֶנּוּ׃ וְשָׁחַט
אֹתוֹ עַל יֶרֶךְ הַמִּזְבֵּחַ צָפֹנָה לִפְנֵי יְהוָה וְזָרְקוּ בְּנֵי אַהֲרֹן
יב הַכֹּהֲנִים אֶת־דָּמוֹ עַל־הַמִּזְבֵּחַ סָבִיב׃ וְנִתַּח אֹתוֹ לִנְתָחָיו
וְאֶת־רֹאשׁוֹ וְאֶת־פִּדְרוֹ וְעָרַךְ הַכֹּהֵן אֹתָם עַל־הָעֵצִים אֲשֶׁר
יג עַל־הָאֵשׁ אֲשֶׁר עַל־הַמִּזְבֵּחַ׃ וְהַקֶּרֶב וְהַכְּרָעַיִם יִרְחַץ בַּמָּיִם
וְהִקְרִיב הַכֹּהֵן אֶת־הַכֹּל וְהִקְטִיר הַמִּזְבֵּחָה עֹלָה הוּא אִשֵּׁה
רֵיחַ נִיחֹחַ לַיהוָה׃
יד וְאִם מִן־הָעוֹף עֹלָה קָרְבָּנוֹ לַיהוָה וְהִקְרִיב מִן־הַתֹּרִים אוֹ שני
טו מִן־בְּנֵי הַיּוֹנָה אֶת־קָרְבָּנוֹ׃ וְהִקְרִיבוֹ הַכֹּהֵן אֶל־הַמִּזְבֵּחַ
וּמָלַק אֶת־רֹאשׁוֹ וְהִקְטִיר הַמִּזְבֵּחָה וְנִמְצָה דָמוֹ עַל קִיר
טז הַמִּזְבֵּחַ׃ וְהֵסִיר אֶת־מֻרְאָתוֹ בְּנֹצָתָהּ וְהִשְׁלִיךְ אֹתָהּ אֵצֶל
יז הַמִּזְבֵּחַ קֵדְמָה אֶל־מְקוֹם הַדָּשֶׁן׃ וְשִׁסַּע אֹתוֹ בִכְנָפָיו לֹא

1:9 רֵיחַ־נִיחוֹחַ לַיהוָה *A pleasing aroma to the* LORD – The sacrifices of the biblical age were ways in which the individual or the nation said, in effect: What we have, God, is really Yours. The world exists because of You. *We* exist because of You. Nothing we have is ultimately ours. The gesture of sacrifice is, on the face of it, absurd. What we give to God is something that already belongs to Him. As King David said: "Who am I and who are my people that we should have the power to offer so freely? For all is from You, and we have given You only what is Yours" (1 Chr. 29:14). Yet to *give back* to God is a profound instinct of the soul. Doing so, we acknowledge our dependency. We cast off the carapace of self-absorption. That is why, in one of its most striking phrases, the Torah speaks of sacrifice as being *rei'aḥ niḥo'aḥ*, "a pleasing aroma," to God.

One of the sweetest savors of parenthood is when a child, grown to maturity, brings a parent a gift to express his or her thanks. This too may seem absurd. What can a child give a parent that remotely

without dividing it completely. The priest shall then send
it up in smoke upon the altar, on the wood of the altar fire.
It is a burnt offering, an offering of fire, a pleasing aroma
2 1 to the LORD. When one brings a grain offering
to the LORD, it shall be of fine flour. The one who brings
the sacrifice shall pour oil over it, then place incense upon
2 it, and bring it to Aharon's sons, the priests. From this, the
priest shall scoop out a handful of its fine flour and oil,
together with all its incense, and send this remembrance
up in smoke upon the altar as an offering of fire, a pleasing
3 aroma to the LORD. What remains of the grain offering
shall belong to Aharon and his sons; it is holy of holies
4 among the fire offerings to the LORD. When you
bring a grain offering baked in an oven, it shall be of fine
flour: unleavened loaves mixed with oil or unleavened
5 wafers spread with oil. If your offering is grain
prepared on a griddle, it shall be of fine flour mixed with
6 oil, and unleavened. Crumble it into pieces and pour oil
7 over it; this is a grain offering. If your offering is SHELISHI
8 grain prepared in a pan, it shall be of fine flour in oil. You
shall bring the grain offering made in one of these ways
to the LORD, presenting it to the priest, who will bring it
9 to the altar. The priest shall lift a remembrance from the
grain offering and send it up in smoke upon the altar as an
10 offering of fire, a pleasing aroma to the LORD. What is left
of this grain offering shall belong to Aharon and his sons;
11 it is holy of holies among the fire offerings to the LORD. No
grain offering that you bring to the LORD shall be made
with leaven, for no leaven or honey may be used in a fire
12 offering to the LORD, sent up in smoke. You may bring
them as offerings of first produce to the LORD, but they
13 may not be offered on the altar as a pleasing aroma. You
shall season all your grain offerings with salt; do not omit

Judaism continues to be a religion of rituals, and it is this that sustains its continuity through time, etching its days with the charisma of grace, more like a marriage than a romance but no less moving for the quietness of its beauty.

יַבְדִּיל וְהִקְטִיר אֹתוֹ הַכֹּהֵן הַמִּזְבֵּחָה עַל־הָעֵצִים אֲשֶׁר עַל־
ב א הָאֵשׁ עֹלָה הוּא אִשֵּׁה רֵיחַ נִיחֹחַ לַיהוָה׃ וְנֶפֶשׁ
כִּי־תַקְרִיב קָרְבַּן מִנְחָה לַיהוָה סֹלֶת יִהְיֶה קָרְבָּנוֹ וְיָצַק
ב עָלֶיהָ שֶׁמֶן וְנָתַן עָלֶיהָ לְבֹנָה׃ וֶהֱבִיאָהּ אֶל־בְּנֵי אַהֲרֹן
הַכֹּהֲנִים וְקָמַץ מִשָּׁם מְלֹא קֻמְצוֹ מִסָּלְתָּהּ וּמִשַּׁמְנָהּ עַל כָּל־
לְבֹנָתָהּ וְהִקְטִיר הַכֹּהֵן אֶת־אַזְכָּרָתָהּ הַמִּזְבֵּחָה אִשֵּׁה רֵיחַ
ג נִיחֹחַ לַיהוָה׃ וְהַנּוֹתֶרֶת מִן־הַמִּנְחָה לְאַהֲרֹן וּלְבָנָיו קֹדֶשׁ
ד קָדָשִׁים מֵאִשֵּׁי יְהוָה׃ וְכִי תַקְרִב קָרְבַּן מִנְחָה
מַאֲפֵה תַנּוּר סֹלֶת חַלּוֹת מַצֹּת בְּלוּלֹת בַּשֶּׁמֶן וּרְקִיקֵי מַצּוֹת
ה מְשֻׁחִים בַּשָּׁמֶן׃ וְאִם־מִנְחָה עַל־הַמַּחֲבַת
ו קָרְבָּנֶךָ סֹלֶת בְּלוּלָה בַשֶּׁמֶן מַצָּה תִהְיֶה׃ פָּתוֹת אֹתָהּ פִּתִּים
ז וְיָצַקְתָּ עָלֶיהָ שָׁמֶן מִנְחָה הִוא׃ וְאִם־ שלישי
ח מִנְחַת מַרְחֶשֶׁת קָרְבָּנֶךָ סֹלֶת בַּשֶּׁמֶן תֵּעָשֶׂה׃ וְהֵבֵאתָ
אֶת־הַמִּנְחָה אֲשֶׁר יֵעָשֶׂה מֵאֵלֶּה לַיהוָה וְהִקְרִיבָהּ אֶל־
ט הַכֹּהֵן וְהִגִּישָׁהּ אֶל־הַמִּזְבֵּחַ׃ וְהֵרִים הַכֹּהֵן מִן־הַמִּנְחָה
אֶת־אַזְכָּרָתָהּ וְהִקְטִיר הַמִּזְבֵּחָה אִשֵּׁה רֵיחַ נִיחֹחַ לַיהוָה׃
י וְהַנּוֹתֶרֶת מִן־הַמִּנְחָה לְאַהֲרֹן וּלְבָנָיו קֹדֶשׁ קָדָשִׁים מֵאִשֵּׁי
יא יְהוָה׃ כָּל־הַמִּנְחָה אֲשֶׁר תַּקְרִיבוּ לַיהוָה לֹא תֵעָשֶׂה חָמֵץ
כִּי כָל־שְׂאֹר וְכָל־דְּבַשׁ לֹא־תַקְטִירוּ מִמֶּנּוּ אִשֶּׁה לַיהוָה׃
יב קָרְבַּן רֵאשִׁית תַּקְרִיבוּ אֹתָם לַיהוָה וְאֶל־הַמִּזְבֵּחַ לֹא־יַעֲלוּ
יג לְרֵיחַ נִיחֹחַ׃ וְכָל־קָרְבַּן מִנְחָתְךָ בַּמֶּלַח תִּמְלָח וְלֹא תַשְׁבִּית
מֶלַח בְּרִית אֱלֹהֶיךָ מֵעַל מִנְחָתֶךָ עַל כָּל־קָרְבָּנְךָ תַּקְרִיב

2:1 סלת *Fine flour* – Flour was milled painstakingly with hand mills, and fine white wheat flour was the most labor intensive and desirable kind. Its preparation evoked the devotion of the priest, the endlessly repeated, precisely prescribed rites, the humble, unspectacular acts of devotion that translate faith into the lives of its followers.

Torat Kohanim sees the religious life as built on the foundations of its rituals that, barring catastrophe, never change. Even though we no longer have a Temple or sacrifices or a functioning priesthood,

▶

from your grain offering the salt of your covenant with
14 God. You shall offer salt with all your offerings. If
you bring a grain offering of first produce to the LORD, it
shall be brought as soon as it ripens on the stalk. Roasted
in fire, crushed from fresh kernels; thus shall you bring
15 the grain offering of first produce. You shall put oil and
16 incense on it; it is a grain offering. The priest shall send
its remembrance up in smoke – some of the crushed new
grain and oil together with all of the incense – as a fire
offering to the LORD.

3 1 If one's sacrifice is a peace offering, and brought from REVI'I
the herd, whether male or female, the animal one offers
2 before the LORD must be without blemish. The one
bringing the offering shall lay his hand on its head and
have it slaughtered at the entrance to the Tent of Meeting.
Aharon's sons the priests shall dash the blood against
3 each side of the altar. A priest shall present of the peace
offering a fire offering to the LORD: the fat that covers the
4 entrails and all the fat surrounding them; the two kidneys
and the fat that is on them at the loins; and the diaphragm
of the liver, which should be removed with the kidneys.

God and caring for one's fellow humans, and they are disconnected. Judaism rejects the concept of two disconnected domains. Psychologically, ethically, and spiritually, they are part of a single indivisible system. To serve God is to serve humanity.

That was the point made memorably by Mikha: "Man, God has told you what is good and what the LORD seeks from you: only to do justice, love goodness, and walk modestly with your God" (Mic. 6:8). Yirmeyahu said of King Yoshiyahu: "He took up the cause of the poor and the destitute with good results. 'That is the way to know Me,' declares the LORD" (Jer. 22:16). Knowing God, said Yirmeyahu, means caring for those in need.

Rambam said essentially the same at the end of *Guide for the Perplexed* (III:54). He quotes Yirmeyahu: "'Someone may boast only of his conscious devotion to Me, for I the LORD act with loving-kindness, justice, and righteousness in the world. For it is these things that I desire,' declares the LORD" (Jer. 9:23). To know God is to know what it is to act with kindness, justice, and righteousness.

יד מֶלַח׃ וְאִם־תַּקְרִיב מִנְחַת בִּכּוּרִים לַיהוָה
אָבִיב קָלוּי בָּאֵשׁ גֶּרֶשׂ כַּרְמֶל תַּקְרִיב אֵת מִנְחַת בִּכּוּרֶיךָ׃
טו טז וְנָתַתָּ עָלֶיהָ שֶׁמֶן וְשַׂמְתָּ עָלֶיהָ לְבֹנָה מִנְחָה הִוא׃ וְהִקְטִיר
הַכֹּהֵן אֶת־אַזְכָּרָתָהּ מִגִּרְשָׂהּ וּמִשַּׁמְנָהּ עַל כָּל־לְבֹנָתָהּ אִשֶּׁה
לַיהוָה׃

ג א וְאִם־זֶבַח שְׁלָמִים קָרְבָּנוֹ אִם מִן־הַבָּקָר הוּא מַקְרִיב אִם־זָכָר רביעי
ב אִם־נְקֵבָה תָּמִים יַקְרִיבֶנּוּ לִפְנֵי יהוָה׃ וְסָמַךְ יָדוֹ עַל־רֹאשׁ
קָרְבָּנוֹ וּשְׁחָטוֹ פֶּתַח אֹהֶל מוֹעֵד וְזָרְקוּ בְּנֵי אַהֲרֹן הַכֹּהֲנִים
ג אֶת־הַדָּם עַל־הַמִּזְבֵּחַ סָבִיב׃ וְהִקְרִיב מִזֶּבַח הַשְּׁלָמִים
אִשֶּׁה לַיהוָה אֶת־הַחֵלֶב הַמְכַסֶּה אֶת־הַקֶּרֶב וְאֵת כָּל־
ד הַחֵלֶב אֲשֶׁר עַל־הַקֶּרֶב׃ וְאֵת שְׁתֵּי הַכְּלָיֹת וְאֶת־הַחֵלֶב
אֲשֶׁר עֲלֵהֶן אֲשֶׁר עַל־הַכְּסָלִים וְאֶת־הַיֹּתֶרֶת עַל־הַכָּבֵד

PEACE OFFERING

The act of bringing a sacrifice was fraught with ambiguity. Jews were not the only people in ancient times to have temples, priests, and sacrifices. Almost everyone did. It was precisely here that the religion of ancient Israel came closest, outwardly, to the practices of their pagan neighbors. But the sacrificial systems of other cultures were based on totally different beliefs. In many religions sacrifices were seen as a way of placating or appeasing the gods. The Aztecs believed that sacrificial offerings fed the gods who sustained the universe. Walter Burkert speculated that the ancient Greeks experienced guilt when they killed animals for food, so they offered sacrifices as a way of appeasing their consciences.

All these ideas are alien to Judaism. God cannot be bribed or appeased. Nor can we bring Him anything that is not His. God sustains the universe; the universe does not sustain Him. And wrongs righted by sacrifice do not excuse other wrongs. So intention and mindset were essential in the sacrificial system. The thought that "if I bring a sacrifice to God, He will overlook my other faults" – in effect, the idea that I can bribe the Judge of all the earth – turns a sacred act into a pagan one, and produces precisely the opposite result than the one intended by the Torah. It turns religious worship from a way to the right and the good into a way of easing the conscience of those who practice the wrong and the bad.

The danger of the sacrificial system, said the prophets, is that it can lead people to think that there are two domains, the Temple and the world, serving

5 Aharon's sons shall send all these up in smoke upon the
altar, along with the burnt offering on the wood on the
altar fire – a fire offering, a pleasing aroma to the Lord.
6 If one's offering is a peace offering from the flock, whether
7 male or female, it must be without blemish. If one brings
a sheep as his offering, he shall present it before the
8 Lord. He shall lay his hand on the head of the offering
and have it slaughtered at the entrance to the Tent of
Meeting. Aharon's sons the priests shall dash the blood
9 against each side of the altar. The priest shall present the
fat from the peace offering as a fire offering to the Lord:
the whole broad tail, removed close to the backbone;
the fat that covers the entrails and all the fat surrounding
10 them; the two kidneys and the fat that is on them at the
loins; and the diaphragm of the liver, which should be
11 removed with the kidneys. The priest shall send these up
in smoke upon the altar: foodstuffs – a fire offering to the
Lord.
12 If the sacrifice is a goat, the one bringing it shall present
13 it before the Lord. He shall lay his hand on the head of
the offering and have it slaughtered at the entrance to
the Tent of Meeting. Aharon's sons the priests shall dash
14 the blood against each side of the altar. The priest shall
present of the offering a fire offering to the Lord: the fat
that covers the entrails and all the fat surrounding them;
15 the two kidneys and the fat that is on them at the loins;
and the diaphragm of the liver, which should be removed
16 with the kidneys. The priest shall send these up in smoke
upon the altar: foodstuffs – a fire offering to the Lord. All
17 the fatty parts belong to the Lord: this is an everlasting
statute throughout your generations in all your dwellings:
you shall not eat either that fat or blood."
4 1 2 The Lord spoke to Moshe: "Tell the Israelites: If a HAMISHI
person sins unintentionally with regard to any of the

forgotten either the law or some relevant fact. To give a contemporary example: Suppose the phone rings on the Sabbath and you answer it. Assuming this

ה עַל־הַכְּלָיוֹת יְסִירֶנָּה׃ וְהִקְטִירוּ אֹתוֹ בְנֵֽי־אַהֲרֹן֮ הַמִּזְבֵּ֒חָה
עַל־הָעֹלָ֔ה אֲשֶׁ֥ר עַל־הָעֵצִ֖ים אֲשֶׁ֣ר עַל־הָאֵ֑שׁ אִשֵּׁ֛ה רֵ֥יחַ
נִיחֹ֖חַ לַיהוָֽה׃
ו וְאִם־מִן־הַצֹּ֧אן קָרְבָּנ֛וֹ לְזֶ֥בַח שְׁלָמִ֖ים לַיהוָ֑ה זָכָר֙ א֣וֹ נְקֵבָ֔ה
ז תָּמִ֖ים יַקְרִיבֶֽנּוּ׃ אִם־כֶּ֥שֶׂב הֽוּא־מַקְרִ֖יב אֶת־קָרְבָּנ֑וֹ וְהִקְרִ֥יב
ח אֹת֖וֹ לִפְנֵ֥י יְהוָֽה׃ וְסָמַ֤ךְ אֶת־יָדוֹ֙ עַל־רֹ֣אשׁ קָרְבָּנ֔וֹ וְשָׁחַ֣ט
אֹת֔וֹ לִפְנֵ֖י אֹ֣הֶל מוֹעֵ֑ד וְ֠זָֽרְקוּ בְּנֵ֨י אַהֲרֹ֧ן אֶת־דָּמ֛וֹ עַל־הַמִּזְבֵּ֖חַ
ט סָבִֽיב׃ וְהִקְרִ֨יב מִזֶּ֣בַח הַשְּׁלָמִים֮ אִשֶּׁ֣ה לַיהוָה֒ חֶלְבּוֹ֙ הָֽאַלְיָ֣ה
תְמִימָ֔ה לְעֻמַּ֥ת הֶעָצֶ֖ה יְסִירֶ֑נָּה וְאֶת־הַחֵ֙לֶב֙ הַמְכַסֶּ֣ה אֶת־
י הַקֶּ֔רֶב וְאֵת֙ כָּל־הַחֵ֔לֶב אֲשֶׁ֖ר עַל־הַקֶּֽרֶב׃ וְאֵת֙ שְׁתֵּ֣י הַכְּלָיֹ֔ת
וְאֶת־הַחֵ֙לֶב֙ אֲשֶׁ֣ר עֲלֵהֶ֔ן אֲשֶׁ֖ר עַל־הַכְּסָלִ֑ים וְאֶת־הַיֹּתֶ֙רֶת֙
יא עַל־הַכָּבֵ֔ד עַל־הַכְּלָיֹ֖ת יְסִירֶֽנָּה׃ וְהִקְטִיר֥וֹ הַכֹּהֵ֖ן הַמִּזְבֵּ֑חָה
לֶ֥חֶם אִשֶּׁ֖ה לַיהוָֽה׃
יב יג וְאִ֖ם עֵ֣ז קָרְבָּנ֑וֹ וְהִקְרִיב֖וֹ לִפְנֵ֥י יְהוָֽה׃ וְסָמַ֤ךְ אֶת־יָדוֹ֙ עַל־
רֹאשׁ֔וֹ וְשָׁחַ֣ט אֹת֔וֹ לִפְנֵ֖י אֹ֣הֶל מוֹעֵ֑ד וְ֠זָֽרְקוּ בְּנֵ֨י אַהֲרֹ֧ן אֶת־דָּמ֛וֹ
יד עַל־הַמִּזְבֵּ֖חַ סָבִֽיב׃ וְהִקְרִ֤יב מִמֶּ֙נּוּ֙ קָרְבָּנ֔וֹ אִשֶּׁ֖ה לַיהוָ֑ה אֶת־
הַחֵ֙לֶב֙ הַֽמְכַסֶּ֣ה אֶת־הַקֶּ֔רֶב וְאֵת֙ כָּל־הַחֵ֔לֶב אֲשֶׁ֖ר עַל־הַקֶּֽרֶב׃
טו וְאֵת֙ שְׁתֵּ֣י הַכְּלָיֹ֔ת וְאֶת־הַחֵ֙לֶב֙ אֲשֶׁ֣ר עֲלֵהֶ֔ן אֲשֶׁ֖ר עַל־הַכְּסָלִ֑ים
טז וְאֶת־הַיֹּתֶ֙רֶת֙ עַל־הַכָּבֵ֔ד עַל־הַכְּלָיֹ֖ת יְסִירֶֽנָּה׃ וְהִקְטִירָ֥ם
הַכֹּהֵ֖ן הַמִּזְבֵּ֑חָה לֶ֤חֶם אִשֶּׁה֙ לְרֵ֣יחַ נִיחֹ֔חַ כָּל־חֵ֖לֶב לַיהוָֽה׃
יז חֻקַּ֤ת עוֹלָם֙ לְדֹרֹ֣תֵיכֶ֔ם בְּכֹ֖ל מוֹשְׁבֹתֵיכֶ֑ם כָּל־חֵ֥לֶב וְכָל־דָּ֖ם לֹ֥א
תֹאכֵֽלוּ׃

ד א ב וַיְדַבֵּ֥ר יְהוָ֖ה אֶל־מֹשֶׁ֥ה לֵּאמֹֽר׃ דַּבֵּ֞ר אֶל־בְּנֵ֤י יִשְׂרָאֵל֙ לֵאמֹ֔ר ב חמישי
נֶ֗פֶשׁ כִּֽי־תֶחֱטָ֤א בִשְׁגָגָה֙ מִכֹּל֙ מִצְוֺ֣ת יְהוָ֔ה אֲשֶׁ֖ר לֹ֣א תֵעָשֶׂ֑ינָה

4:2 נֶפֶשׁ כִּי־תֶחֱטָא בִשְׁגָגָה *If a person sins unintentionally* – The *ḥatat* is often translated as "sin offering"; from the same Hebrew root are derived the words both for "sin" and "purification." The sins for which a purification offering had to be brought were those committed inadvertently, *beshogeg*. The sinner had

Lord's commands, doing what should not be done; any
3 transgression – if it is the anointed priest who sins, bringing
guilt upon his people, he shall bring an unblemished
young bull to the Lord as a purification offering for the
4 sin he has committed. He shall bring the bull before the
Lord at the entrance to the Tent of Meeting, lay his hand
upon the bull's head, and slaughter the bull before the
5 Lord. The anointed priest shall take some of the bull's
6 blood and bring it into the Tent of Meeting. The priest
shall dip his finger into the blood and sprinkle of it seven
times before the Lord in front of the Sanctuary's inner
7 curtain. Then the priest shall apply some of the blood to
the horns of the altar of fragrant incense, which is in the
Tent of Meeting before the Lord. The rest of the bull's
blood he shall pour out at the base of the altar of burnt
8 offerings, at the entrance to the Tent of Meeting. He
shall remove all the fat from the bull of the purification
offering: the fat that covers the entrails and all the fat
9 surrounding them; the two kidneys and the fat that is on
them at the loins; and the diaphragm of the liver, which
10 should be removed with the kidneys, just as it is removed
from the ox of the peace offering. The priest shall send

The law of the sin offering reminds us that we can do harm unintentionally, and this can have consequences, both physical and psychological. The best way of putting things right, of achieving purification, is to make a sacrifice: to do something that costs us something. In ancient times, that took the form of a sacrifice offered on the altar at the Temple. Nowadays, the best way of doing so is to give money to charity (*tzedaka*) or perform an act of kindness to others (*ḥesed*). The prophet said so long ago: "For it is goodness I yearn for, not sacrifice" (Hos. 6:6). Charity and kindness are our substitutes for sacrifice, and like the sin offering of old, they help mend what is broken in the world and in our soul.

The sin offering tells us that the wrong we do, or let happen, even if we did not intend it, still requires atonement. Unfashionable though this is, a morality that speaks about action, not just intention – about what happens through us even if we did not mean to do it – is more compelling, more true to the human situation, than one that speaks of intention alone.

ג וְעָשָׂה מֵאַחַת מֵהֵנָּה: אִם הַכֹּהֵן הַמָּשִׁיחַ יֶחֱטָא לְאַשְׁמַת
הָעָם וְהִקְרִיב עַל חַטָּאתוֹ אֲשֶׁר חָטָא פַּר בֶּן־בָּקָר תָּמִים
ד לַיהוָה לְחַטָּאת: וְהֵבִיא אֶת־הַפָּר אֶל־פֶּתַח אֹהֶל מוֹעֵד
לִפְנֵי יְהוָה וְסָמַךְ אֶת־יָדוֹ עַל־רֹאשׁ הַפָּר וְשָׁחַט אֶת־הַפָּר
ה לִפְנֵי יְהוָה: וְלָקַח הַכֹּהֵן הַמָּשִׁיחַ מִדַּם הַפָּר וְהֵבִיא אֹתוֹ
ו אֶל־אֹהֶל מוֹעֵד: וְטָבַל הַכֹּהֵן אֶת־אֶצְבָּעוֹ בַּדָּם וְהִזָּה מִן־
ז הַדָּם שֶׁבַע פְּעָמִים לִפְנֵי יְהוָה אֶת־פְּנֵי פָּרֹכֶת הַקֹּדֶשׁ: וְנָתַן
הַכֹּהֵן מִן־הַדָּם עַל־קַרְנוֹת מִזְבַּח קְטֹרֶת הַסַּמִּים לִפְנֵי יְהוָה
אֲשֶׁר בְּאֹהֶל מוֹעֵד וְאֵת ׀ כָּל־דַּם הַפָּר יִשְׁפֹּךְ אֶל־יְסוֹד מִזְבַּח
ח הָעֹלָה אֲשֶׁר־פֶּתַח אֹהֶל מוֹעֵד: וְאֶת־כָּל־חֵלֶב פַּר הַחַטָּאת
יָרִים מִמֶּנּוּ אֶת־הַחֵלֶב הַמְכַסֶּה עַל־הַקֶּרֶב וְאֵת כָּל־הַחֵלֶב
ט אֲשֶׁר עַל־הַקֶּרֶב: וְאֵת שְׁתֵּי הַכְּלָיֹת וְאֶת־הַחֵלֶב אֲשֶׁר עֲלֵיהֶן
אֲשֶׁר עַל־הַכְּסָלִים וְאֶת־הַיֹּתֶרֶת עַל־הַכָּבֵד עַל־הַכְּלָיוֹת
י יְסִירֶנָּה: כַּאֲשֶׁר יוּרַם מִשּׁוֹר זֶבַח הַשְּׁלָמִים וְהִקְטִירָם הַכֹּהֵן

is a biblical-level prohibition, you would only be liable for a purification offering if either you forgot the law that you may not answer a phone on the Sabbath, or you forgot the fact that that day was the Sabbath. For a moment you thought it was Friday or Sunday.

It is just this kind of act that we do not tend to see as a sin at all. It was a mistake. You forgot. You did not mean to do anything wrong. And when you realize that inadvertently you have broken the Sabbath, you are more likely to feel regret than remorse. You feel sorry but not guilty.

We think of a sin as something we did intentionally, yielding to temptation perhaps, or in a moment of rebellion. That is what Jewish law calls *bezadon* in Biblical Hebrew or *bemezid* in Rabbinic Hebrew. That is the kind of act we would have thought calls for a sin offering. In Jewish law, though, such an act cannot be atoned for by an offering at all. So how are we to make sense of the sin offering?

The answer is that our acts leave traces in the world. The very fact that unintentional sins require atonement tells us that we cannot dissociate ourselves from our actions by saying, "I didn't mean to do it." Wrong was done – and it was done by us. Therefore we must perform an act that signals our contrition. We cannot just walk away as if the act had nothing to do with us.

11 these up in smoke upon the altar of burnt offerings. But
the bull's skin and all its flesh, together with its head, legs,
12 entrails, and dung – all the rest of the bull – he shall take
to a ritually pure place outside the camp, to the ash heap,
and burn upon a wood fire; at the ash heap it shall be
burned.
13 If it is the entire community of Israel that commits an
unintentional sin, the congregation unwittingly violating
one of the LORD's commands, doing what must not be
14 done, when the sin that they committed becomes known,
the community shall bring a young bull as a purification
15 offering, presenting it before the Tent of Meeting. The
community elders shall lay their hands on the bull's head
before the LORD and, before the LORD, the bull shall be
16 slaughtered. The anointed priest shall take some of the
17 bull's blood into the Tent of Meeting. The priest shall dip
his finger into the blood and sprinkle it seven times before
18 the LORD in front of the curtain. Then he shall apply some
of the blood to the horns of the altar before the LORD in
the Tent of Meeting, and pour out all the rest at the base
of the altar of burnt offerings, at the entrance to the Tent
19 of Meeting. Then he shall remove all its fat and send it up
20 in smoke upon the altar. He shall do the same with this
bull as he does with the bull of his purification offering;
he shall do the same with this. So shall the priest make
21 atonement for the people, and they shall be forgiven. The
priest shall then take the bull outside the camp and burn
it just as he burns the first bull. This is the community's
purification offering.
22 When a leader sins unintentionally with regard to any of
the LORD's commands, doing what must not be done and
23 thus incurring guilt, when the sin that he has committed
is made known to him, he shall bring an unblemished

---

a ruler, king, judge, elder, or prince. Usually it refers to the holder of political power. Why does the Torah consider this type of leadership particularly prone to error? Sforno (on Lev. 4:21–22) cites the phrase "Yeshurun grew fat, and kicked"

יא עַל מִזְבַּח הָעֹלָה׃ וְאֶת־עוֹר הַפָּר וְאֶת־כָּל־בְּשָׂרוֹ עַל־רֹאשׁוֹ
יב וְעַל־כְּרָעָיו וְקִרְבּוֹ וּפִרְשׁוֹ׃ וְהוֹצִיא אֶת־כָּל־הַפָּר אֶל־מִחוּץ
לַמַּחֲנֶה אֶל־מָקוֹם טָהוֹר אֶל־שֶׁפֶךְ הַדֶּשֶׁן וְשָׂרַף אֹתוֹ עַל־
עֵצִים בָּאֵשׁ עַל־שֶׁפֶךְ הַדֶּשֶׁן יִשָּׂרֵף׃
יג וְאִם כָּל־עֲדַת יִשְׂרָאֵל יִשְׁגּוּ וְנֶעְלַם דָּבָר מֵעֵינֵי הַקָּהָל וְעָשׂוּ
יד אַחַת מִכָּל־מִצְוֺת יהוה אֲשֶׁר לֹא־תֵעָשֶׂינָה וְאָשֵׁמוּ׃ וְנוֹדְעָה
הַחַטָּאת אֲשֶׁר חָטְאוּ עָלֶיהָ וְהִקְרִיבוּ הַקָּהָל פַּר בֶּן־בָּקָר
טו לְחַטָּאת וְהֵבִיאוּ אֹתוֹ לִפְנֵי אֹהֶל מוֹעֵד׃ וְסָמְכוּ זִקְנֵי הָעֵדָה
אֶת־יְדֵיהֶם עַל־רֹאשׁ הַפָּר לִפְנֵי יהוה וְשָׁחַט אֶת־הַפָּר לִפְנֵי
טז יהוה׃ וְהֵבִיא הַכֹּהֵן הַמָּשִׁיחַ מִדַּם הַפָּר אֶל־אֹהֶל מוֹעֵד׃
יז וְטָבַל הַכֹּהֵן אֶצְבָּעוֹ מִן־הַדָּם וְהִזָּה שֶׁבַע פְּעָמִים לִפְנֵי יהוה
יח אֵת פְּנֵי הַפָּרֹכֶת׃ וּמִן־הַדָּם יִתֵּן ׀ עַל־קַרְנֹת הַמִּזְבֵּחַ אֲשֶׁר
לִפְנֵי יהוה אֲשֶׁר בְּאֹהֶל מוֹעֵד וְאֵת כָּל־הַדָּם יִשְׁפֹּךְ אֶל־יְסוֹד
יט מִזְבַּח הָעֹלָה אֲשֶׁר־פֶּתַח אֹהֶל מוֹעֵד׃ וְאֵת כָּל־חֶלְבּוֹ יָרִים
כ מִמֶּנּוּ וְהִקְטִיר הַמִּזְבֵּחָה׃ וְעָשָׂה לַפָּר כַּאֲשֶׁר עָשָׂה לְפַר
הַחַטָּאת כֵּן יַעֲשֶׂה־לּוֹ וְכִפֶּר עֲלֵהֶם הַכֹּהֵן וְנִסְלַח לָהֶם׃
כא וְהוֹצִיא אֶת־הַפָּר אֶל־מִחוּץ לַמַּחֲנֶה וְשָׂרַף אֹתוֹ כַּאֲשֶׁר שָׂרַף
אֵת הַפָּר הָרִאשׁוֹן חַטַּאת הַקָּהָל הוּא׃
כב אֲשֶׁר נָשִׂיא יֶחֱטָא וְעָשָׂה אַחַת מִכָּל־מִצְוֺת יהוה אֱלֹהָיו
כג אֲשֶׁר לֹא־תֵעָשֶׂינָה בִּשְׁגָגָה וְאָשֵׁם׃ אוֹ־הוֹדַע אֵלָיו חַטָּאתוֹ
אֲשֶׁר חָטָא בָּהּ וְהֵבִיא אֶת־קָרְבָּנוֹ שְׂעִיר עִזִּים זָכָר תָּמִים׃

THE SINS OF LEADERS

The Torah prescribes four different kinds of offerings, depending on the offender. One is the High Priest, a second is "the entire community" (understood by the Sages to mean the great Sanhedrin, the Supreme Court), a third is "a leader" (*nasi*), and the fourth is an ordinary individual. In three of the four cases, the law is introduced by the word *im*, "if" – if such a person commits a sin. In the case of the leader, however, the law is prefaced by the word *asher*, "when." It is *possible* that a High Priest, the Supreme Court, or an individual may err. But in the case of a leader, the *nasi*, it is probable or even certain.

Nasi is the generic word for a leader:

24 male goat as his offering. He shall lay his hand upon the
goat's head, and it shall be slaughtered in the place where
burnt offerings are slaughtered before the LORD. It is a
25 purification offering. The priest shall take some of the
blood from the purification offering with his finger, and
apply it to the horns of the altar of burnt offerings. The
rest of the blood he shall pour out at the base of the altar
26 of burnt offerings. He shall send up all its fat in smoke
upon the altar, like the fat of the peace offerings. So shall
the priest make atonement for that leader for his sin, and
he will be forgiven.
27 If an individual among the people sins unintentionally SHISHI
with regard to any of the LORD's commands, doing what
28 should not be done and thus incurring guilt, when the sin
he has committed is made known to him, he shall bring an
unblemished female goat as his offering to atone for the
29 sin that he committed. He shall lay his hand on the head
of the purification offering, and it shall be slaughtered in
30 the same place as the burnt offerings. The priest shall take
some of its blood with his finger, and apply it to the horns
of the altar of burnt offerings. The rest of the blood he shall
31 pour out at the base of the altar. The priest shall remove

---

science. A ruler sometimes has to make decisions that a conscientious individual would shrink from in private life. He may have to wage a war, knowing that some will die. In many cases, only after the event will the leader know whether the decision was justified. Leaders make mistakes. As the Torah signals, it is only a matter of "when," not "if."

The Jewish approach to leadership is thus an unusual combination of realism and idealism – realistic in its acknowledgment that leaders inevitably make mistakes, idealistic in its constant subjection of politics to ethics, power to responsibility, pragmatism to conscience. What matters is not that leaders never get it wrong, but that they are always exposed to prophetic critique and that they constantly engage in Torah study to remind themselves of transcendent standards and ultimate aims. The most important thing from a Torah perspective is that a leader is sufficiently honest to admit his mistakes. Hence the significance of the purification offering.

Leadership, then, demands two kinds of courage: the strength to take a risk, and the humility to admit when a risk fails.

כד וְסָמַךְ יָדוֹ עַל־רֹאשׁ הַשָּׂעִיר וְשָׁחַט אֹתוֹ בִּמְקוֹם אֲשֶׁר־
כה יִשְׁחַט אֶת־הָעֹלָה לִפְנֵי יהוה חַטָּאת הוּא׃ וְלָקַח הַכֹּהֵן
מִדַּם הַחַטָּאת בְּאֶצְבָּעוֹ וְנָתַן עַל־קַרְנֹת מִזְבַּח הָעֹלָה וְאֶת־
כו דָּמוֹ יִשְׁפֹּךְ אֶל־יְסוֹד מִזְבַּח הָעֹלָה׃ וְאֶת־כָּל־חֶלְבּוֹ יַקְטִיר
הַמִּזְבֵּחָה כְּחֵלֶב זֶבַח הַשְּׁלָמִים וְכִפֶּר עָלָיו הַכֹּהֵן מֵחַטָּאתוֹ
וְנִסְלַח לוֹ׃
כז וְאִם־נֶפֶשׁ אַחַת תֶּחֱטָא בִשְׁגָגָה מֵעַם הָאָרֶץ בַּעֲשֹׂתָהּ אַחַת ששי
כח מִמִּצְוֺת יהוה אֲשֶׁר לֹא־תֵעָשֶׂינָה וְאָשֵׁם׃ אוֹ הוֹדַע אֵלָיו
חַטָּאתוֹ אֲשֶׁר חָטָא וְהֵבִיא קָרְבָּנוֹ שְׂעִירַת עִזִּים תְּמִימָה
כט נְקֵבָה עַל־חַטָּאתוֹ אֲשֶׁר חָטָא׃ וְסָמַךְ אֶת־יָדוֹ עַל רֹאשׁ
ל הַחַטָּאת וְשָׁחַט אֶת־הַחַטָּאת בִּמְקוֹם הָעֹלָה׃ וְלָקַח הַכֹּהֵן
מִדָּמָהּ בְּאֶצְבָּעוֹ וְנָתַן עַל־קַרְנֹת מִזְבַּח הָעֹלָה וְאֶת־כָּל־דָּמָהּ
לא יִשְׁפֹּךְ אֶל־יְסוֹד הַמִּזְבֵּחַ׃ וְאֶת־כָּל־חֶלְבָּהּ יָסִיר כַּאֲשֶׁר הוּסַר

(Deut. 32:15). Those who have advantages over others, whether of wealth or power, can lose their moral sense.

Rabbi Elie Munk, citing the Zohar, explains that the High Priest and the Sanhedrin were in constant contact with that which was holy. They lived in a world of ideals. The king or political ruler, by contrast, was involved in secular affairs: war and peace, the administration of government, and international relations. They were more likely to sin because their day-to-day concerns were not religious but pragmatic.

Rabbi Meir Simḥa of Dvinsk (*Meshekh Ḥokhma* on Lev. 4:21–22) points out that a king was especially vulnerable to being led astray by popular sentiment. Neither a priest nor a judge in the Sanhedrin was answerable to the people. The king, however, relied on popular support. Thus, for a whole series of reasons, a political leader is more exposed to temptation and error than a priest or judge.

I would also add that politics is an arena of conflict. It deals in matters – specifically the pursuit of wealth or power – that are, in the short term, zero-sum games. The more I have, the less you have. Politics is the mediation of conflict by justice backed with power. Whatever course a politician takes, it will please some and anger others. From this, there is no escape.

Politics also involves difficult judgments. A leader must balance competing claims and will sometimes get it wrong.

There are no universal rules when it comes to leadership. It is an art, not a

all its fat, just as the fat is removed from a peace offering,
and send it up in smoke upon the altar as a pleasing aroma
to the Lord. So shall the priest make atonement for that
person, and he will be forgiven.
32 If one brings a sheep as a purification offering, it shall be
33 an unblemished female. One shall lay one's hand upon the
head of the purification offering, and it shall be slaughtered
34 in the place where burnt offerings are slaughtered. The
priest shall take some of its blood with his finger, and
apply it to the horns of the altar of burnt offerings. The
rest of the blood he shall pour out at the base of the altar.
35 He shall remove all its fat, as the fat of a sheep is removed
from a peace offering. The priest shall send it up in smoke
upon the altar with the other fire offerings to the Lord.
So shall the priest make atonement for that person for the
sin that he committed, and he will be forgiven.
5 1 If a person sins by failing to testify after hearing a public
adjuration to do so: if he knows or has seen something,
2 yet does not speak up, and thus bears his guilt; or sins
through touching an impure thing – the carcass of an
impure beast, or a carcass of impure livestock, or the
carcass of an impure creeping creature – and it escapes
3 his notice, and while impure, he incurs guilt; or sins by
touching human impurity of any kind that makes him
impure, and it escapes his notice, but later he realizes his
4 guilt; or sins by making a verbal oath to do something,
bad or good – whatever one might carelessly swear – and
it escapes his attention, but later he realizes his guilt; in
5 any one of these ways – when he realizes the guilt he has
incurred in any of these ways, he shall confess the sin he
6 has committed, and bring the amends of his guilt to the
Lord for the sin he has committed: a female sheep or
goat as a purification offering. So shall the priest make

failure, and that He has faith in us even when we lose faith in ourselves, can be a life-changing experience. That is when we discover that, even in a secular age, God is still there, open to us whenever we are willing to open ourselves to Him.

חֵ֣לֶב מֵעַל־זֶ֣בַח הַשְּׁלָמִ֗ים וְהִקְטִ֤יר הַכֹּהֵן֙ הַמִּזְבֵּ֔חָה לְרֵ֥יחַ
נִיחֹ֖חַ לַֽיהוָ֑ה וְכִפֶּ֥ר עָלָ֛יו הַכֹּהֵ֖ן וְנִסְלַ֥ח לֽוֹ׃
לב וְאִם־כֶּ֥בֶשׂ יָבִ֛יא קָרְבָּנ֖וֹ לְחַטָּ֑את נְקֵבָ֥ה תְמִימָ֖ה יְבִיאֶֽנָּה׃
לג וְסָמַךְ֙ אֶת־יָד֔וֹ עַ֖ל רֹ֣אשׁ הַֽחַטָּ֑את וְשָׁחַ֤ט אֹתָהּ֙ לְחַטָּ֔את
לד בִּמְק֕וֹם אֲשֶׁ֥ר יִשְׁחַ֖ט אֶת־הָעֹלָֽה׃ וְלָקַ֨ח הַכֹּהֵ֜ן מִדַּ֤ם הַֽחַטָּאת֙
בְּאֶצְבָּע֔וֹ וְנָתַ֕ן עַל־קַרְנֹ֖ת מִזְבַּ֣ח הָעֹלָ֑ה וְאֶת־כָּל־דָּמָ֣הּ יִשְׁפֹּ֔ךְ
לה אֶל־יְס֖וֹד הַמִּזְבֵּֽחַ׃ וְאֶת־כָּל־חֶלְבָּ֣הּ יָסִ֗יר כַּאֲשֶׁ֨ר יוּסַ֥ר חֵֽלֶב־
הַכֶּשֶׂב֮ מִזֶּ֣בַח הַשְּׁלָמִים֒ וְהִקְטִ֨יר הַכֹּהֵ֤ן אֹתָם֙ הַמִּזְבֵּ֔חָה
עַ֖ל אִשֵּׁ֣י יְהוָ֑ה וְכִפֶּ֨ר עָלָ֧יו הַכֹּהֵ֛ן עַל־חַטָּאת֥וֹ אֲשֶׁר־חָטָ֖א
וְנִסְלַ֥ח לֽוֹ׃

ה א וְנֶ֣פֶשׁ כִּֽי־תֶחֱטָ֗א וְשָֽׁמְעָה֙ ק֣וֹל אָלָ֔ה וְה֣וּא עֵ֔ד א֥וֹ רָאָ֖ה א֣וֹ
ב יָדָ֑ע אִם־ל֥וֹא יַגִּ֖יד וְנָשָׂ֥א עֲוֺנֽוֹ׃ א֣וֹ נֶ֗פֶשׁ אֲשֶׁ֣ר תִּגַּע֮ בְּכָל־דָּבָ֣ר
טָמֵא֒ אוֹ֩ בְנִבְלַ֨ת חַיָּ֜ה טְמֵאָ֗ה א֚וֹ בְּנִבְלַת֙ בְּהֵמָ֣ה טְמֵאָ֔ה
א֕וֹ בְּנִבְלַ֖ת שֶׁ֣רֶץ טָמֵ֑א וְנֶעְלַ֣ם מִמֶּ֔נּוּ וְה֥וּא טָמֵ֖א וְאָשֵֽׁם׃
ג א֣וֹ כִ֤י יִגַּע֙ בְּטֻמְאַ֣ת אָדָ֔ם לְכֹל֙ טֻמְאָת֔וֹ אֲשֶׁ֥ר יִטְמָ֖א בָּ֑הּ
ד וְנֶעְלַ֣ם מִמֶּ֔נּוּ וְה֥וּא יָדַ֖ע וְאָשֵֽׁם׃ א֣וֹ נֶ֡פֶשׁ כִּ֣י תִשָּׁבַע֩ לְבַטֵּ֨א
בִשְׂפָתַ֜יִם לְהָרַ֣ע ׀ א֣וֹ לְהֵיטִ֗יב לְ֠כֹל אֲשֶׁ֨ר יְבַטֵּ֧א הָאָדָ֛ם
בִּשְׁבֻעָ֖ה וְנֶעְלַ֣ם מִמֶּ֑נּוּ וְהוּא־יָדַ֥ע וְאָשֵׁ֖ם לְאַחַ֥ת מֵאֵֽלֶּה׃
ה וְהָיָ֥ה כִֽי־יֶאְשַׁ֖ם לְאַחַ֣ת מֵאֵ֑לֶּה וְהִ֨תְוַדָּ֔ה אֲשֶׁ֥ר חָטָ֖א עָלֶֽיהָ׃
ו וְהֵבִ֣יא אֶת־אֲשָׁמ֣וֹ לַֽיהוָ֡ה עַ֣ל חַטָּאתוֹ֩ אֲשֶׁ֨ר חָטָ֜א נְקֵבָ֨ה
מִן־הַצֹּ֛אן כִּשְׂבָּ֥ה אֽוֹ־שְׂעִירַ֥ת עִזִּ֖ים לְחַטָּ֑את וְכִפֶּ֥ר עָלָ֛יו

5:5 וְהִתְוַדָּה *He shall confess* – Leviticus establishes Judaism's culture of repentance. In our daily and annual prayers for forgiveness, God asks us: What have you done with your life thus far? Have you thought about others or only about yourself? Have you brought healing to a place of human pain or hope where you found despair? You may have avoided malicious actions, but have you sinned by inattention? You may have been a success, but have you also been a blessing?

To ask these questions in the company of others publicly willing to confess their faults, knowing that God forgives every failure we acknowledge as a

7 atonement for that person for his sin. If he cannot afford a
sheep, he shall bring two doves or two pigeons as his guilt
offering to the LORD, one as a purification offering and the
8 other as a burnt offering. He shall bring them to the priest,
who will offer the first as a purification offering, severing
9 its neck at the back without detaching the head. Then he
shall sprinkle some of the blood of the purification offering
against the side of the altar; the rest of the blood shall be
10 drained out at its base. This is the purification offering. He
shall then offer the second bird as a burnt offering in the
prescribed way. So shall the priest make atonement for
that person for the sin he has committed, and he will be
11 forgiven. If he cannot afford two doves or two SHEVI'I
pigeons, he shall bring the purification offering of a tenth
of an ephah of fine flour as the sacrifice for his sin. He shall
not put any oil on it, nor place on it any incense, for it is a
12 purification offering. He shall bring it to the priest, and the
priest shall lift a handful from it – its remembrance – and
send it up in smoke upon the altar with the LORD's fire
13 offerings. It is a purification offering. Thus shall the priest
make atonement for that person for whichever one of
these sins he has committed, and he will be forgiven.
The rest of the offering, as in the case of a grain offering,
14 shall belong to the priest." And the LORD spoke
15 to Moshe: "If a person commits a trespass, sinning
unintentionally with respect to any of the LORD's sacred
objects, he shall bring an unblemished ram from the flock,
valued in silver shekel by the Sanctuary weight, as his
16 guilt offering to the LORD; it is a guilt offering. He shall
make restitution for his trespass against the sacred object,
adding one-fifth to its value and giving it to the priest. The

---

more than the outer form of the essential act, which is *coming close in love through giving up something of ourselves to the Beloved*. Those who cannot sacrifice cannot love. Love, loyalty, sacrifice: these are what bind us to the other, defeating the solipsism and narcissism that leave us small and alone.

ז הַכֹּהֵן מֵחַטָּאתוֹ: וְאִם־לֹא תַגִּיעַ יָדוֹ דֵּי שֶׂה וְהֵבִיא אֶת־
אֲשָׁמוֹ אֲשֶׁר חָטָא שְׁתֵּי תֹרִים אוֹ־שְׁנֵי בְנֵי־יוֹנָה לַיהוָה אֶחָד
ח לְחַטָּאת וְאֶחָד לְעֹלָה: וְהֵבִיא אֹתָם אֶל־הַכֹּהֵן וְהִקְרִיב
אֶת־אֲשֶׁר לַחַטָּאת רִאשׁוֹנָה וּמָלַק אֶת־רֹאשׁוֹ מִמּוּל
ט עָרְפּוֹ וְלֹא יַבְדִּיל: וְהִזָּה מִדַּם הַחַטָּאת עַל־קִיר הַמִּזְבֵּחַ
י וְהַנִּשְׁאָר בַּדָּם יִמָּצֵה אֶל־יְסוֹד הַמִּזְבֵּחַ חַטָּאת הוּא: וְאֶת־
הַשֵּׁנִי יַעֲשֶׂה עֹלָה כַּמִּשְׁפָּט וְכִפֶּר עָלָיו הַכֹּהֵן מֵחַטָּאתוֹ
יא אֲשֶׁר־חָטָא וְנִסְלַח לוֹ: וְאִם־לֹא תַשִּׂיג יָדוֹ שביעי
לִשְׁתֵּי תֹרִים אוֹ לִשְׁנֵי בְנֵי־יוֹנָה וְהֵבִיא אֶת־קָרְבָּנוֹ אֲשֶׁר
חָטָא עֲשִׂירִת הָאֵפָה סֹלֶת לְחַטָּאת לֹא־יָשִׂים עָלֶיהָ שֶׁמֶן
יב וְלֹא־יִתֵּן עָלֶיהָ לְבֹנָה כִּי חַטָּאת הִוא: וֶהֱבִיאָהּ אֶל־הַכֹּהֵן
וְקָמַץ הַכֹּהֵן ׀ מִמֶּנָּה מְלוֹא קֻמְצוֹ אֶת־אַזְכָּרָתָהּ וְהִקְטִיר
יג הַמִּזְבֵּחָה עַל אִשֵּׁי יְהוָה חַטָּאת הִוא: וְכִפֶּר עָלָיו הַכֹּהֵן
עַל־חַטָּאתוֹ אֲשֶׁר־חָטָא מֵאַחַת מֵאֵלֶּה וְנִסְלַח לוֹ וְהָיְתָה
יד לַכֹּהֵן כַּמִּנְחָה: וַיְדַבֵּר יְהוָה אֶל־מֹשֶׁה לֵּאמֹר:
טו נֶפֶשׁ כִּי־תִמְעֹל מַעַל וְחָטְאָה בִּשְׁגָגָה מִקָּדְשֵׁי יְהוָה וְהֵבִיא
אֶת־אֲשָׁמוֹ לַיהוָה אַיִל תָּמִים מִן־הַצֹּאן בְּעֶרְכְּךָ כֶּסֶף־
טז שְׁקָלִים בְּשֶׁקֶל־הַקֹּדֶשׁ לְאָשָׁם: וְאֵת אֲשֶׁר חָטָא מִן־הַקֹּדֶשׁ

5:7 אֲשָׁמוֹ *Offering* – As we have seen, the Hebrew word for sacrifice, *korban*, comes from the root *k-r-v*, which means to bring or come close to God. Yet the very ideas of *closeness* and *distance* seem inappropriate when speaking of God, who does not occupy physical space.

The barrier between us and God is not physical; it is metaphysical, psychological. It comes from our sense that we are self-sufficient. We overcome this tragic loneliness by giving something of ourselves away – and here the two senses of the word *korban*, sacrificing and coming close, come together. This is one reason why, under the wedding canopy, the groom gives the bride a ring. A gift bespeaks love, and love – the space we make for the other – is the redemption of our solitude. In ancient times, when flocks and herds were the measure of a person's wealth, our ancestors brought sacrificial animals as their gift of love.

Even then, though, they were no

priest shall make his atonement with the ram of the guilt
offering, and he will be forgiven.
17 If a person sins without realizing it, doing any of the things
that the Lord commanded not to be done, he incurs
18 guilt and is subject to punishment. He shall bring an
unblemished ram from the flock, of the appropriate value,
as a guilt offering to the priest. The priest shall atone for
him for that unintentional sin, committed unknowingly,
19 and he will be forgiven. This is a guilt offering, for he had
incurred guilt before the Lord."
20 21 The Lord spoke to Moshe: "If a person sins, committing
a trespass against the Lord by lying to his neighbor
about a deposit or pledge, or by robbery, or by defrauding
22 his neighbor, or by finding lost property and lying about
it; if he swears falsely about anything he does in any of
23 the ways a person sins, afterward acknowledging guilt for
the sin, he shall return what he took by robbery or fraud,
or the deposit left with him for safekeeping, or the lost
24 property that he found, or anything else about which he MAFTIR
swore falsely. He shall repay its value and add to that a
fifth; he shall pay this to its owner on the day he presents
25 his guilt offering. And as his guilt offering to the Lord
he shall bring the priest an unblemished ram from the
26 flock of the appropriate value. The priest shall make his

---

of the world, the individual driven by a glimpse of perfection can come to find it in an alternative reality, the world within the soul in whose quietude can be heard the mystic reverberations of infinity.

Judaism's most revolutionary gesture is to have declined this consolation. With unusual courage, often in dire circumstances, Jews have felt called on to bring the presence of God into the public places of our shared life. We must resist the flight into solitude, for we are called on neither to forsake nor to accept the world but to change it, creating in its midst a society of justice and compassion, equity and moral integrity, never yielding to despair even after a succession of failures. God is not in another world but in this, the world of deceit and desire, collision and collusion. He is here, less as a presence than as a challenge, a call, a summons, a command. And so, when we betray the trust on which society is built, it is God we trespass against.

יְשַׁלֵּם וְאֶת־חֲמִישִׁתוֹ יוֹסֵף עָלָיו וְנָתַן אֹתוֹ לַכֹּהֵן וְהַכֹּהֵן יְכַפֵּר
עָלָיו בְּאֵיל הָאָשָׁם וְנִסְלַח לוֹ׃
יז וְאִם־נֶפֶשׁ כִּי תֶחֱטָא וְעָשְׂתָה אַחַת מִכׇּל־מִצְוֺת יהוה אֲשֶׁר
יח לֹא תֵעָשֶׂינָה וְלֹא־יָדַע וְאָשֵׁם וְנָשָׂא עֲוֺנוֹ׃ וְהֵבִיא אַיִל תָּמִים
מִן־הַצֹּאן בְּעֶרְכְּךָ לְאָשָׁם אֶל־הַכֹּהֵן וְכִפֶּר עָלָיו הַכֹּהֵן עַל
יט שִׁגְגָתוֹ אֲשֶׁר־שָׁגָג וְהוּא לֹא־יָדַע וְנִסְלַח לוֹ׃ אָשָׁם הוּא
אָשֹׁם אָשַׁם לַיהוה׃
כ כא וַיְדַבֵּר יהוה אֶל־מֹשֶׁה לֵּאמֹר׃ נֶפֶשׁ כִּי תֶחֱטָא וּמָעֲלָה מַעַל
בַּיהוה וְכִחֵשׁ בַּעֲמִיתוֹ בְּפִקָּדוֹן אוֹ־בִתְשׂוּמֶת יָד אוֹ בְגָזֵל
כב אוֹ עָשַׁק אֶת־עֲמִיתוֹ׃ אוֹ־מָצָא אֲבֵדָה וְכִחֶשׁ בָּהּ וְנִשְׁבַּע
עַל־שָׁקֶר עַל־אַחַת מִכֹּל אֲשֶׁר־יַעֲשֶׂה הָאָדָם לַחֲטֹא בָהֵנָּה׃
כג וְהָיָה כִּי־יֶחֱטָא וְאָשֵׁם וְהֵשִׁיב אֶת־הַגְּזֵלָה אֲשֶׁר גָּזָל אוֹ
אֶת־הָעֹשֶׁק אֲשֶׁר עָשָׁק אוֹ אֶת־הַפִּקָּדוֹן אֲשֶׁר הׇפְקַד אִתּוֹ
כד אוֹ אֶת־הָאֲבֵדָה אֲשֶׁר מָצָא׃ אוֹ מִכֹּל אֲשֶׁר־יִשָּׁבַע עָלָיו מפטיר
לַשֶּׁקֶר וְשִׁלַּם אֹתוֹ בְּרֹאשׁוֹ וַחֲמִשִׁתָיו יֹסֵף עָלָיו לַאֲשֶׁר
כה הוּא לוֹ יִתְּנֶנּוּ בְּיוֹם אַשְׁמָתוֹ׃ וְאֶת־אֲשָׁמוֹ יָבִיא לַיהוה אַיִל
כו תָּמִים מִן־הַצֹּאן בְּעֶרְכְּךָ לְאָשָׁם אֶל־הַכֹּהֵן׃ וְכִפֶּר עָלָיו

5:21 וּמָעֲלָה מַעַל בַּיהוה *A trespass against the Lord* – Faith, for many Western thinkers, was something encountered in the privacy of the soul. There are religious traditions built around the private experiences of the individual. But they are not Judaism. Solitude, for the Torah, is not humanity's highest state, nor is it the condition in which we come most fully into the presence of God. The individual must share his life with others.

The Torah's narratives about persons-in-relation are often painful. They tell a story of conflicts, rivalries, jealousies, antagonisms, rifts, murmurings, and rebellions. In our collective life we seldom if ever reach the serenity that sometimes comes upon an individual when, alone, he or she contemplates the universe. Nonetheless it is here that we must struggle to make a space for God.

Religion has often been humanity's most profound source of consolation. It is hard to live long in the company of society without deep disillusionment. Faced with the apparent arbitrariness

atonement before the LORD, and he will be forgiven for whatever he did to incur this guilt."

The haftara for Parashat Vayikra is on page 1510.
On the Shabbat of Parashat HaḤodesh read the haftara on page 1666.

something similar but different, namely appeasement, usually accompanied by an act of self-abasement. In a guilt culture it makes sense to confess your sins. In a shame culture it makes no sense at all – instead it becomes all-important to cover up your wrongdoing by any means possible.

Ultimately, guilt cultures produce strong individuals precisely because they force us to accept responsibility. When things go wrong we don't waste time blaming others. We don't luxuriate in that most addictive, destructive drug, victimhood. We say, honestly and seriously, "I'm sorry. Forgive me. Now let me do what I can to put it right." That way, we and the people we offend can move on. Through our mistakes we discover the strength to heal, learn, and grow. Shame cultures produce people who conform. Guilt cultures produce people with the courage to be free.

הַכֹּהֵן לִפְנֵי יְהוָה וְנִסְלַח לוֹ עַל־אַחַת מִכֹּל אֲשֶׁר־יַעֲשֶׂה
לְאַשְׁמָה בָהּ׃

The הפטרה *for* פרשת ויקרא *is on page 1511.*
On the שבת *of* פרשת החודש *read the* הפטרה *on page 1667.*

5:26 לְאַשְׁמָה בָהּ *This guilt* – After repaying and compensating the victim of a crime, the criminal brings a guilt offering. There is a key distinction between guilt cultures and shame cultures. Guilt cultures conceive of morality as a voice within – the voice of conscience that tells us whether or not we have done wrong. Shame cultures think of morality as an external demand – what other people expect of us. To feel shame is to experience or imagine what one looks like in the sight of others who pass judgment on us. Shame cultures are other-directed. Guilt cultures are inner directed. Guilt cultures make a sharp distinction between the sinner and the sin. The act may be wrong, but the agent's integrity as a person remains intact. That is why guilt can be relieved by remorse, confession, restitution, and the resolve never to behave that way again. In guilt cultures there is repentance and forgiveness. Shame is not like that. It is a stain on the sinner that cannot be fully removed. A shame culture does not provide forgiveness; it offers

Parashat Tzav

6 1 2 The Lord spoke to Moshe: "Instruct Aharon and his
sons: This is the law of the burnt offering. The burnt
offering shall remain on the altar hearth all night until the
morning, and the altar fire shall be kept alight upon it.

---

have wanted in an ideal world. What He wanted was *avoda*: He wanted the Israelites to worship Him. But they, accustomed to religious practices in the ancient world, could not yet conceive of *avoda shebalev*, the "service of the heart," namely prayer. They were accustomed to the way things were done in Egypt (and virtually everywhere else at that time), where worship meant sacrifice. On this reading, Yirmeyahu in the *haftara* meant that from a divine perspective sacrifices were *bediavad*, not *lekhatḥila*, an after-the-fact concession, not something desired at the outset.

A third interpretation is that the entire sequence of events from Exodus 25 to Leviticus 25 was a response to the episode of the golden calf. This, I argued in Parashat Ki Tisa, represented a passionate need on the part of the people to have God close, not distant; in the camp, not at the top of the mountain; accessible to everyone, not just Moshe; and on a daily basis, not just at rare moments of miracle. Though central to the Judaism we know now, this was not part of God's original intention for the Israelites.

This debate aside, Yirmeyahu's message in the *haftara* is clear: his insistence on the moral dimension of Judaism: "I the Lord act with loving-kindness, justice, and righteousness in the world, for it is these things that I desire" (Jer. 9:23). What is genuinely unexpected is that the Sages joined sections of the Torah and passages from the prophetic literature so different from one another that they sound as if they are coming from different universes with different laws of gravity.

Judaism is a choral symphony scored for many voices. It is an ongoing argument between different points of view. Without detailed laws, no sacrifices. Without sacrifices in the biblical age, no coming close to God. But if there are only sacrifices with no prophetic voice, then people may serve God while abusing their fellow humans. They may think themselves righteous while they are, in fact, merely self-righteous.

I believe that this fugue between Torah and haftara, priestly and prophetic voices, is one of Judaism's great glories. We hear in both voices how to act and why. Without the how, action is lame; without the why, behavior is blind. Combine priestly detail and prophetic vision and you have spiritual greatness.

פרשת צו

ו א ב וַיְדַבֵּ֥ר יְהוָ֖ה אֶל־מֹשֶׁ֥ה לֵּאמֹֽר׃ צַ֤ו אֶֽת־אַהֲרֹן֙ וְאֶת־בָּנָ֣יו
לֵאמֹ֔ר זֹ֥את תּוֹרַ֖ת הָעֹלָ֑ה הִ֣וא הָעֹלָ֡ה עַל֩ מוֹקְדָ֨ה עַל־

TZAV

Parashat Tzav continues the laws of sacrifices begun in the previous *parasha,* this time from the perspective of the priests performing the ritual. Rules are set out for burnt and grain offerings, sin and guilt offerings, and peace offerings, each with its own specific procedures. Details are then set out for the induction of Aharon and his sons into office, prior to the inauguration of the service of the Sanctuary.

A rigorous set of laws is now established for those who enter the Sanctuary's sacred space. They are differential: some for the High Priest, others for ordinary priests, yet others for the people as a whole. The result is to be a form of Divine Presence, known in Rabbinic Hebrew as the *Shekhina,* very different from the God of creation who makes universes and the God of redemption who overthrows empires. This is the God who is close, who can be met in fixed places at predictable times, who travels with the people in the desert and will later be with them even in exile. This is God as *shakhen,* as "neighbor," and also as *kavod,* "glory." This is God as He gives a specific kind of dignity to man.

6:2 צַו אֶת־אַהֲרֹן וְאֶת־בָּנָיו לֵאמֹר זֹאת תּוֹרַת הָעֹלָה *Instruct Aharon and his sons: This is the law of the burnt offering* – Fascinatingly, while the *parasha* presents the sacrificial service as a key element of Jewish worship, the *haftara,* the reading from the Prophets, that the Sages selected for Parashat Tzav appears immediately to negate the very substance of the *parasha*:

> For when I brought your forefathers out of Egypt, I did not speak to them, nor did I command them about matters of burnt offerings and sacrifices. Rather, this is what I commanded them: Heed My voice so that I will be your God and you will be My people. Walk in all the ways as I will command you so that it will be good for you. (Jer. 7:22–23)

What does this mean? The simplest interpretation is that it means "I did not *only* give them commands about burnt offerings and sacrifices." I commanded them but they were not the whole of the law, nor were they even its primary purpose.

A second interpretation is the famously controversial view of Rambam (*Guide for the Perplexed* III:32) that the sacrifices were not what God would

3 The priest shall dress in his linen vestments, with linen
undergarments against his skin. He shall lift the ashes of
the burnt offering that the fire consumed on the altar, and
4 place them by the altar's side. Then he shall take off his
vestments, put on other garments, and take the ashes to a
5 ritually pure place outside the camp. The altar fire shall be
kept alight; it shall not go out. Every morning the priest
shall add wood to it, lay out the burnt offering upon it,
and send the fat parts of the peace offering up in smoke
6 upon it. A daily fire shall be kept alight on the altar; it shall
7 not go out. This is the law of the grain offering.
Aharon's sons shall bring these before the LORD in front
8 of the altar. The priest shall lift a handful of the fine flour
and oil from the grain offering, and all the incense on it,
and send this remembrance up in smoke upon the altar as
9 a pleasing aroma to the LORD. Aharon and his sons shall
eat what is left of it. It shall be eaten as unleavened bread in
a holy place; in the courtyard of the Tent of Meeting shall
10 they eat it. It shall not be baked with any leaven. I have
given it as their portion of My fire offerings; it is holy of
holies, like the purification offering and the guilt offering.

---

sacrifice possibly mean in a religion in which God is the creator and owner of all?

The simplest answer is this: *We love what we are willing to make sacrifices for.* The verb "to love," *a-h-v*, is related to the verbs *h-v-h*, *h-v-v*, and *y-h-v*, all of which have the sense of giving, bringing, or offering.

That is why, when they were a nation of farmers and shepherds, the Israelites demonstrated their love of God by bringing Him a symbolic gift of their flocks and herds, their grain and fruit, that is, their livelihood. To love is to want to bring an offering to the Beloved. To love is to give. This is true in many aspects of life. A happily married couple is constantly making sacrifices for one another. Parents make huge sacrifices for their children. People drawn to a calling often sacrifice remunerative careers for the sake of their ideals. In ages of patriotism, people make sacrifices for their country. In strong communities people make sacrifices for one another when someone is in distress or needs help. Sacrifice is the superglue of relationship. It bonds us to one another. Sacrifice is the choreography of love.

הַמִּזְבֵּחַ כָּל־הַלַּיְלָה עַד־הַבֹּקֶר וְאֵשׁ הַמִּזְבֵּחַ תּוּקַד בּוֹ׃ וְלָבַשׁ ג
הַכֹּהֵן מִדּוֹ בַד וּמִכְנְסֵי־בַד יִלְבַּשׁ עַל־בְּשָׂרוֹ וְהֵרִים אֶת־
הַדֶּשֶׁן אֲשֶׁר תֹּאכַל הָאֵשׁ אֶת־הָעֹלָה עַל־הַמִּזְבֵּחַ וְשָׂמוֹ אֵצֶל
ד הַמִּזְבֵּחַ׃ וּפָשַׁט אֶת־בְּגָדָיו וְלָבַשׁ בְּגָדִים אֲחֵרִים וְהוֹצִיא
ה אֶת־הַדֶּשֶׁן אֶל־מִחוּץ לַמַּחֲנֶה אֶל־מָקוֹם טָהוֹר׃ וְהָאֵשׁ עַל־
הַמִּזְבֵּחַ תּוּקַד־בּוֹ לֹא תִכְבֶּה וּבִעֵר עָלֶיהָ הַכֹּהֵן עֵצִים בַּבֹּקֶר
בַּבֹּקֶר וְעָרַךְ עָלֶיהָ הָעֹלָה וְהִקְטִיר עָלֶיהָ חֶלְבֵי הַשְּׁלָמִים׃
ו ז אֵשׁ תָּמִיד תּוּקַד עַל־הַמִּזְבֵּחַ לֹא תִכְבֶּה׃ וְזֹאת
תּוֹרַת הַמִּנְחָה הַקְרֵב אֹתָהּ בְּנֵי־אַהֲרֹן לִפְנֵי יְהוָה אֶל־פְּנֵי
ח הַמִּזְבֵּחַ׃ וְהֵרִים מִמֶּנּוּ בְּקֻמְצוֹ מִסֹּלֶת הַמִּנְחָה וּמִשַּׁמְנָהּ וְאֵת
כָּל־הַלְּבֹנָה אֲשֶׁר עַל־הַמִּנְחָה וְהִקְטִיר הַמִּזְבֵּחַ רֵיחַ נִיחֹחַ
ט אַזְכָּרָתָהּ לַיהוָה׃ וְהַנּוֹתֶרֶת מִמֶּנָּה יֹאכְלוּ אַהֲרֹן וּבָנָיו מַצּוֹת
י תֵּאָכֵל בְּמָקוֹם קָדֹשׁ בַּחֲצַר אֹהֶל־מוֹעֵד יֹאכְלוּהָ׃ לֹא תֵאָפֶה
חָמֵץ חֶלְקָם נָתַתִּי אֹתָהּ מֵאִשָּׁי קֹדֶשׁ קָדָשִׁים הִוא כַּחַטָּאת

6:6 אֵשׁ תָּמִיד תּוּקַד עַל־הַמִּזְבֵּחַ *A daily fire shall be kept alight on the altar* – One of our most potent symbols is the *ner tamid,* the everlasting light that, like the bush Moshe saw in the desert, "was ablaze with fire but was not consumed." We are an eternal people bound to the eternal God. The days, the years, the centuries pass, but Judaism and the Jewish people remain. This fire must be tended from morning to morning. The Jewish people have always translated identity into action. "No people," wrote Matthew Arnold, "ever felt so strongly as the people of the Old Testament, the Hebrew people, that conduct is three-fourths of our life and its largest concern." In the thirteenth century the *Sefer HaḤinukh* expressed the same truth in slightly different words: "The heart is drawn after the deed" (mitzva 16). That is one of the central truths of Torah and halakha. To be a Jew requires an ongoing program of Jewish learning and Jewish doing. We are what we do; our everyday rituals tend the flame.

6:7 תּוֹרַת הַמִּנְחָה *The law of the grain offering – Minḥa,* the grain offering brought alongside all other sacrifices, literally means "gift" or "tribute." Sacrifice is not the same act across cultures. One must seek to understand a practice in terms of the distinctive beliefs of the culture in which it takes place. What then could

11 Any male among Aharon's descendants may eat it as their
eternal share of the LORD's fire offerings throughout their
generations; anything that touches it is sanctified."
12 13 The LORD spoke to Moshe: "This is the offering of SHENI
Aharon and his sons that each shall present to the LORD
on the day when he is anointed: one-tenth of an ephah of
fine flour as a continual grain offering, half in the morning
14 and half in the evening. It shall be made on a griddle with
oil. You shall bring it well mixed, and offer it in pieces
like a crumbled grain offering, as a pleasing aroma to the
15 LORD. The priest among Aharon's sons who is anointed
to succeed him shall prepare it; it is the LORD's perpetual
16 share, to be sent up in smoke in its entirety. Any grain
offering from a priest shall be wholly burned; it shall not
be eaten."
17 18 The LORD spoke to Moshe: "Tell Aharon and his sons:
This is the law of the purification offering. The purification
offering shall be slaughtered before the LORD at the place
where burnt offerings are slaughtered; it is holy of holies.
19 The priest who offers it as a purification offering shall eat
of it. It shall be eaten in a holy place, in the courtyard of
20 the Tent of Meeting. Anything that touches its flesh is
sanctified; if any of its blood splashes on a garment, you
21 shall wash that part in a holy place. An earthen vessel in
which it was cooked shall be broken, but if it was cooked
in a bronze vessel, that shall be scoured and rinsed with

Ritual turns us from lonely individuals into members of the covenant.

The American anthropologist Roy A. Rappaport argues that ritual is the enactment of meaning. Human beings are meaning-seeking animals, and one way of achieving meaning is through language. But language also allows us to tell lies. Ritual does not speak, it enacts. Ritual inducts us into a world of shared values. We may sometimes betray those values, but by taking part in the ritual we enter the world they define. Without ritual, there is no community, no continuity, and no shared structure of meanings. The priest is inducted then, with a sacrifice that is "wholly burned; it shall not be eaten" (Lev. 6:16). He is leaving the everyday world of functionality and entering one of ritual, meaning, and holiness.

יא וְכָאָשָׁם: כָּל־זָכָר בִּבְנֵי אַהֲרֹן יֹאכְלֶנָּה חָק־עוֹלָם לְדֹרֹתֵיכֶם
מֵאִשֵּׁי יהוה כֹּל אֲשֶׁר־יִגַּע בָּהֶם יִקְדָּשׁ:
יב יג וַיְדַבֵּר יהוה אֶל־מֹשֶׁה לֵּאמֹר: זֶה קָרְבַּן אַהֲרֹן וּבָנָיו אֲשֶׁר־ ג שני
יַקְרִיבוּ לַיהוה בְּיוֹם הִמָּשַׁח אֹתוֹ עֲשִׂירִת הָאֵפָה סֹלֶת מִנְחָה
יד תָּמִיד מַחֲצִיתָהּ בַּבֹּקֶר וּמַחֲצִיתָהּ בָּעָרֶב: עַל־מַחֲבַת בַּשֶּׁמֶן
תֵּעָשֶׂה מֻרְבֶּכֶת תְּבִיאֶנָּה תֻּפִינֵי מִנְחַת פִּתִּים תַּקְרִיב רֵיחַ־
טו נִיחֹחַ לַיהוה: וְהַכֹּהֵן הַמָּשִׁיחַ תַּחְתָּיו מִבָּנָיו יַעֲשֶׂה אֹתָהּ
טז חָק־עוֹלָם לַיהוה כָּלִיל תָּקְטָר: וְכָל־מִנְחַת כֹּהֵן כָּלִיל תִּהְיֶה
לֹא תֵאָכֵל:
יז יח וַיְדַבֵּר יהוה אֶל־מֹשֶׁה לֵּאמֹר: דַּבֵּר אֶל־אַהֲרֹן וְאֶל־בָּנָיו
לֵאמֹר זֹאת תּוֹרַת הַחַטָּאת בִּמְקוֹם אֲשֶׁר תִּשָּׁחֵט הָעֹלָה
יט תִּשָּׁחֵט הַחַטָּאת לִפְנֵי יהוה קֹדֶשׁ קָדָשִׁים הִוא: הַכֹּהֵן
הַמְחַטֵּא אֹתָהּ יֹאכְלֶנָּה בְּמָקוֹם קָדֹשׁ תֵּאָכֵל בַּחֲצַר אֹהֶל
כ מוֹעֵד: כֹּל אֲשֶׁר־יִגַּע בִּבְשָׂרָהּ יִקְדָּשׁ וַאֲשֶׁר יִזֶּה מִדָּמָהּ עַל־
כא הַבֶּגֶד אֲשֶׁר יִזֶּה עָלֶיהָ תְּכַבֵּס בְּמָקוֹם קָדֹשׁ: וּכְלִי־חֶרֶשׂ אֲשֶׁר
תְּבֻשַּׁל־בּוֹ יִשָּׁבֵר וְאִם־בִּכְלִי נְחֹשֶׁת בֻּשָּׁלָה וּמֹרַק וְשֻׁטַּף

6:13 בְּיוֹם הִמָּשַׁח אֹתוֹ *On the day when he is anointed* – Moshe took up his mantle with no great ceremony; not so Aharon, who assumes office in a carefully ordered ceremony. This feature of Aharon's initiation befits his distinctive role. Unlike prophets and kings, the priest does not live in the world of everyday. He is the guardian of sacred space and time, the points at which we withdraw from the world to remind ourselves how small we are and how brief are our lives, yet how great they can be when we allow ourselves to be brushed by the wings of eternity. In a word, the priest inhabits the world of *ritual,* where each human act coincides with divine will, and order is safeguarded against the threat of chaos.

Ritual has fared badly in the West. Many see ritual as part of the mindset of myth and magic. But ritual in Leviticus is not magic or primitive technology. We serve God not to bring success, but to be close to Him because He is clarity in a world of confusion, life in a world too often obsessed with death, the enduring presence in the midst of change.

As such, ritual binds us to Jews in other times and places. More than anything else, the shared life of ritual sustained Jews as a nation through two thousand years of exile and dispersion.

▶

22 water. Any male among the priests may eat of it; it is
23 holy of holies. But no purification offering shall be eaten
from which blood is brought inside the Tent of Meeting
to make atonement within the Sanctuary; that shall be
burned with fire.
7 1 And this is the law of the guilt offering; it is holy of holies.
2 The guilt offering shall be slaughtered at the place where
burnt offerings are slaughtered, and its blood dashed
3 against each side of the altar. All its fat shall be offered: the
4 broad tail, the fat covering the entrails, the two kidneys
and the fat around them at the loins, and the diaphragm
5 of the liver, which shall be removed with the kidneys. The
priest shall turn these into smoke on the altar as a fire
6 offering for the Lord; it is a guilt offering. Any male priest
may eat of it and it shall be eaten in a holy place; it is holy
7 of holies. The guilt offering follows the same law as the
purification offering: it belongs to the priest who makes
8 atonement with it. The priest who offers any person's
burnt offering shall keep the skin of the burnt offering
9 that he has offered. Any grain offering baked in an oven or
prepared in a pan or griddle also belongs to the priest who
10 offers it, while every other grain offering, whether mixed
with oil or dry, shall belong equally to all of Aharon's
sons.
11 This is the law of the peace sacrifice that one may offer SHELISHI
12 to the Lord: If it is offered for thanksgiving, one offers

from catastrophe. That instinct – to offer thanks to a force, a presence, over and above natural circumstances and human intervention – is itself a signal of transcendence. Though not a proof of the existence of God, it is nonetheless an intimation of something deeply spiritual in the human heart. It tells us that we are not random concatenations of selfish genes, blindly reproducing themselves. Our bodies may be products of nature ("You are dust, and you will return to dust" [Gen. 3:19]), but there is something within us that reaches out to Someone beyond us: the soul of the universe, the divine "You" to whom we offer our thanks. That is what was once expressed in the thanksgiving offering, and still is, in the *HaGomel* prayer and many others.

כב בַּמָּיִם׃ כָּל־זָכָר בַּכֹּהֲנִים יֹאכַל אֹתָהּ קֹדֶשׁ קָדָשִׁים הִוא׃
כג וְכָל־חַטָּאת אֲשֶׁר יוּבָא מִדָּמָהּ אֶל־אֹהֶל מוֹעֵד לְכַפֵּר בַּקֹּדֶשׁ
לֹא תֵאָכֵל בָּאֵשׁ תִּשָּׂרֵף׃
ז א ב וְזֹאת תּוֹרַת הָאָשָׁם קֹדֶשׁ קָדָשִׁים הוּא׃ בִּמְקוֹם אֲשֶׁר יִשְׁחֲטוּ
אֶת־הָעֹלָה יִשְׁחֲטוּ אֶת־הָאָשָׁם וְאֶת־דָּמוֹ יִזְרֹק עַל־הַמִּזְבֵּחַ
ג סָבִיב׃ וְאֵת כָּל־חֶלְבּוֹ יַקְרִיב מִמֶּנּוּ אֵת הָאַלְיָה וְאֶת־הַחֵלֶב
ד הַמְכַסֶּה אֶת־הַקֶּרֶב׃ וְאֵת שְׁתֵּי הַכְּלָיֹת וְאֶת־הַחֵלֶב אֲשֶׁר
עֲלֵיהֶן אֲשֶׁר עַל־הַכְּסָלִים וְאֶת־הַיֹּתֶרֶת עַל־הַכָּבֵד עַל־
ה הַכְּלָיֹת יְסִירֶנָּה׃ וְהִקְטִיר אֹתָם הַכֹּהֵן הַמִּזְבֵּחָה אִשֶּׁה לַיהוָה
ו אָשָׁם הוּא׃ כָּל־זָכָר בַּכֹּהֲנִים יֹאכְלֶנּוּ בְּמָקוֹם קָדוֹשׁ יֵאָכֵל
ז קֹדֶשׁ קָדָשִׁים הוּא׃ כַּחַטָּאת כָּאָשָׁם תּוֹרָה אַחַת לָהֶם הַכֹּהֵן
ח אֲשֶׁר יְכַפֶּר־בּוֹ לוֹ יִהְיֶה׃ וְהַכֹּהֵן הַמַּקְרִיב אֶת־עֹלַת אִישׁ עוֹר
ט הָעֹלָה אֲשֶׁר הִקְרִיב לַכֹּהֵן לוֹ יִהְיֶה׃ וְכָל־מִנְחָה אֲשֶׁר תֵּאָפֶה
בַּתַּנּוּר וְכָל־נַעֲשָׂה בַמַּרְחֶשֶׁת וְעַל־מַחֲבַת לַכֹּהֵן הַמַּקְרִיב
י אֹתָהּ לוֹ תִהְיֶה׃ וְכָל־מִנְחָה בְלוּלָה־בַשֶּׁמֶן וַחֲרֵבָה לְכָל־בְּנֵי
אַהֲרֹן תִּהְיֶה אִישׁ כְּאָחִיו׃
יא יב וְזֹאת תּוֹרַת זֶבַח הַשְּׁלָמִים אֲשֶׁר יַקְרִיב לַיהוָה׃ אִם עַל־ שלישי
תּוֹדָה יַקְרִיבֶנּוּ וְהִקְרִיב ׀ עַל־זֶבַח הַתּוֹדָה חַלּוֹת מַצּוֹת

THANKSGIVING

The first words we are taught to say each morning, immediately on waking, are *Modeh/Moda ani*, "I give thanks." We thank before we think. The source of the command to give thanks is the *korban toda*, the thanksgiving offering.

Though we have been without sacrifices for almost two thousand years, a trace of this command survives in the form of the *HaGomel* blessing, "Who bestows good things on the unworthy," said in the synagogue, at the time of the reading of the Torah, by one who has survived a hazardous situation. This is defined by the Sages (on the basis of Psalm 107) as one who has survived a sea crossing, traveled across a desert, recovered from serious illness, or been released from captivity (Berakhot 54b).

Insurance companies sometimes describe natural catastrophes as "acts of God." Human emotion tends to do the opposite. God is in the good news, the miraculous deliverance, the escape

unleavened loaves mixed with oil with the thanksgiving
sacrifice, and unleavened wafers spread with oil, and
13 loaves of fine flour mixed with oil. This offering, together
with loaves of leavened bread, he shall present with the
14 peace sacrifice of thanksgiving. Of these he shall offer one
of each kind as a gift raised up to the Lord. This shall
belong to the priest who dashed the blood of the peace
15 offering. The flesh of the peace sacrifice of thanksgiving
shall be eaten on the day it is offered; you may not leave
16 any of it to the morning. If the sacrifice is to fulfill a vow,
however, or is a freewill offering, it shall be eaten on the
day when one offers the sacrifice, while what is left over
17 may be eaten the next day. Whatever of the flesh of the
sacrifice is left over on the third day shall be burned with
18 fire. If any of the flesh of the peace sacrifice is eaten on the
third day, it shall not be accepted, nor shall it be credited
to the one who offered it. It is offensive, and anyone who
19 eats of it is liable to punishment. Flesh that touches any
impure thing shall not be eaten; it shall be burned with

---

bring *shalom* – well-being, peace – into the world.

7:19 וְהַבָּשָׂר אֲשֶׁר־יִגַּע בְּכָל־טָמֵא *Flesh that touches any impure thing* – There is a famous midrash in which a Roman challenges Rabban Yoḥanan b. Zakkai on the ritual of the red heifer. The Roman finds the law incomprehensible, irrational, and superstitious. Yoḥanan b. Zakkai asks the Roman whether he believes in exorcism. The Roman says he does. Well then, says Yoḥanan, that is what the rite of the red heifer is, a kind of exorcism. It expels unclean spirits. The Roman, satisfied, leaves.

There then follows a remarkable scene. The students turn to Rabban Yoḥanan and say, "You gave him an answer to satisfy a Roman, but what will you answer us?" Yoḥanan then says, "Know that it is not death that defiles or the ritual that purifies. Rather, God is saying: 'I have established a statute and instituted a decree, and you have no permission to transgress them'" (Bemidbar Rabba, Ḥukat 19).

The passage is telling us that not only do we find the laws of purity hard to understand. So do the Sages, or at least the disciples of the Sages. However, we should not misunderstand Rabban Yoḥanan's reply to his students. It has often been taken to mean that the laws we call *ḥukim*, "statutes," have no reason, or at least none we can understand.

בְּלוּלֹ֣ת בַּשֶּׁ֔מֶן וּרְקִיקֵ֥י מַצּ֖וֹת מְשֻׁחִ֣ים בַּשָּׁ֑מֶן וְסֹ֣לֶת
יג מֻרְבֶּ֔כֶת חַלֹּ֖ת בְּלוּלֹ֥ת בַּשָּֽׁמֶן׃ עַל־חַלֹּת֙ לֶ֣חֶם חָמֵ֔ץ יַקְרִ֖יב
יד קָרְבָּנ֑וֹ עַל־זֶ֖בַח תּוֹדַ֥ת שְׁלָמָֽיו׃ וְהִקְרִ֨יב מִמֶּ֤נּוּ אֶחָד֙ מִכָּל־
קָרְבָּ֔ן תְּרוּמָ֖ה לַֽיהוָ֑ה לַכֹּהֵ֗ן הַזֹּרֵ֛ק אֶת־דַּ֥ם הַשְּׁלָמִ֖ים ל֥וֹ
טו יִהְיֶֽה׃ וּבְשַׂ֗ר זֶ֚בַח תּוֹדַ֣ת שְׁלָמָ֔יו בְּי֥וֹם קָרְבָּנ֖וֹ יֵאָכֵ֑ל לֹֽא־
טז יַנִּ֥יחַ מִמֶּ֖נּוּ עַד־בֹּֽקֶר׃ וְאִם־נֶ֣דֶר ׀ א֣וֹ נְדָבָ֗ה זֶ֚בַח קָרְבָּנ֔וֹ
בְּי֛וֹם הַקְרִיב֥וֹ אֶת־זִבְח֖וֹ יֵאָכֵ֑ל וּמִֽמָּחֳרָ֔ת וְהַנּוֹתָ֥ר מִמֶּ֖נּוּ
יז יֵאָכֵֽל׃ וְהַנּוֹתָ֖ר מִבְּשַׂ֣ר הַזָּ֑בַח בַּיּוֹם֙ הַשְּׁלִישִׁ֔י בָּאֵ֖שׁ יִשָּׂרֵֽף׃
יח וְאִ֣ם הֵאָכֹ֣ל יֵ֠אָכֵל מִבְּשַׂר־זֶ֨בַח שְׁלָמָ֜יו בַּיּ֣וֹם הַשְּׁלִישִׁי֮ לֹ֣א
יֵרָצֶה֒ הַמַּקְרִ֣יב אֹת֔וֹ לֹ֥א יֵחָשֵׁ֛ב ל֖וֹ פִּגּ֣וּל יִהְיֶ֑ה וְהַנֶּ֛פֶשׁ הָאֹכֶ֥לֶת
יט מִמֶּ֖נּוּ עֲוֺנָ֥הּ תִּשָּֽׂא׃ וְהַבָּשָׂ֞ר אֲשֶׁר־יִגַּ֤ע בְּכָל־טָמֵא֙ לֹ֣א יֵאָכֵ֔ל

7:13 זֶבַח תּוֹדַת שְׁלָמָיו *Peace sacrifice of thanksgiving* – The thanksgiving offering is one of several kinds of "peace sacrifices," so named, according to one interpretation in the Sifra, because "one who brings one brings peace (*shalom*) to the world." We now know of the multiple effects of developing gratitude. It improves physical health and immunity against disease. Thankfulness reduces toxic emotions such as resentment, frustration, and regret, and makes depression less likely. It helps people avoid overreacting to negative experiences by seeking revenge. It enhances self-respect, making it less likely that you will envy others for their achievements or success. Saying "thank you" enhances friendships and elicits better performance from employees. Grateful people tend to have better relationships.

Jewish prayer is an ongoing seminar in gratitude. Our morning prayers open with the *Birkot HaShaḥar*, the morning blessings, in which we give thanks to God for giving us back our consciousness after sleep, for the human body and our restored soul, the earth we stand on and the freedom with which we rise, and so on through a repeated refrain of thanks. What this does is to *foreground the background*, focusing our attention on the things we normally take for granted. It is a cognitive shift designed to make us attentive to the myriad blessings with which we are surrounded.

This is neither easy nor natural. For sound biological reasons, we are hyperalert to potential threats and dangers. It takes focused attention to become aware, day to day, of how much we have to be grateful for. That, in different ways, is the logic of prayer, of making blessings, of the Sabbath, and many other elements of Jewish life. And learning to offer up thanks is a way to

fire. As for other flesh, any ritually pure person may eat
20 it, but one who eats the flesh of a peace sacrifice to the
LORD in a state of impurity shall be severed from his
21 people. When anyone touches any impure thing – human
impurity, or an impure animal, or any impure, detested
creature – and then eats flesh from the LORD's peace
sacrifice, that person shall be severed from his people."
22 23 The LORD spoke to Moshe: "Tell the Israelites: Do not
24 eat the fat of an ox, sheep, or goat. The fat of one of these
that died naturally or was killed by another animal may be
25 put to other use, but you may not eat it. For anyone who
eats the fat of an animal of which a fire offering could be
26 offered to the LORD – he is severed from his people. Do
not eat any blood, whether that of a bird or of an animal,

For Rambam (*Guide for the Perplexed* III:46), it is part of the Torah's extended battle against idolatry. Idolators believed that blood was the food of the spirits, and that by eating it they would have "something in common with the spirits." Eating blood is forbidden because of its association with idolatry.

Ramban (on Lev. 17:13) says, contrariwise, that the ban has to do with human nature. We are affected by what we eat. Eating blood, implies Ramban, makes us cruel, bestial, animal-like.

Barbara Ehrenreich, in her book *Blood Rites: Origins and History of the Passions of War*, argues that one of the most formative experiences of the first human beings must have been the terror of being attacked by an animal predator. They knew that the likely outcome was that one of the group, usually an outsider, an invalid, a child, or perhaps an animal, would fall as prey, giving the others a chance to escape. It was this embedded memory that became the basis of subsequent sacrificial rites. As she puts it, "The sacrificial ritual in many ways mimics the crisis of a predator's attack. An animal or perhaps a human member of the group is singled out for slaughter, often in a spectacularly bloody manner." The eating of the victim and his or its blood temporarily occupies the predator, allowing the rest of the group to escape in safety. That is why blood is offered to the gods.

Ehrenreich's view is that the sacrificial response – fear and guilt – survives to the present as part of our genetic endowment from earlier times. It leaves two legacies: one, the human tendency to band together in the face of an external threat; the other, the willingness to risk self-sacrifice for the sake of the group. These emotions appear at times of war. They are not the *cause* of war,

כ בָּאֵשׁ יִשָּׂרֵף וְהַבָּשָׂר כָּל־טָהוֹר יֹאכַל בָּשָׂר׃ וְהַנֶּפֶשׁ אֲשֶׁר־
תֹּאכַל בָּשָׂר מִזֶּבַח הַשְּׁלָמִים אֲשֶׁר לַיהוָה וְטֻמְאָתוֹ עָלָיו
כא וְנִכְרְתָה הַנֶּפֶשׁ הַהִוא מֵעַמֶּיהָ׃ וְנֶפֶשׁ כִּי־תִגַּע בְּכָל־טָמֵא
בְּטֻמְאַת אָדָם אוֹ ׀ בִּבְהֵמָה טְמֵאָה אוֹ בְּכָל־שֶׁקֶץ טָמֵא
וְאָכַל מִבְּשַׂר־זֶבַח הַשְּׁלָמִים אֲשֶׁר לַיהוָה וְנִכְרְתָה הַנֶּפֶשׁ
כב כג הַהִוא מֵעַמֶּיהָ׃ וַיְדַבֵּר יְהוָה אֶל־מֹשֶׁה לֵּאמֹר׃ דַּבֵּר אֶל־
בְּנֵי יִשְׂרָאֵל לֵאמֹר כָּל־חֵלֶב שׁוֹר וְכֶשֶׂב וָעֵז לֹא תֹאכֵלוּ׃
כד וְחֵלֶב נְבֵלָה וְחֵלֶב טְרֵפָה יֵעָשֶׂה לְכָל־מְלָאכָה וְאָכֹל לֹא
כה תֹאכְלֻהוּ׃ כִּי כָּל־אֹכֵל חֵלֶב מִן־הַבְּהֵמָה אֲשֶׁר יַקְרִיב מִמֶּנָּה
כו אִשֶּׁה לַיהוָה וְנִכְרְתָה הַנֶּפֶשׁ הָאֹכֶלֶת מֵעַמֶּיהָ׃ וְכָל־דָּם לֹא

What I believe Rabban Yoḥanan was doing was making a sharp distinction – made in our time by philosopher John Rawls – between two kinds of rules: *regulatory* and *constitutive*. Regulatory rules, as their name implies, regulate something that exists independently of the rules. There were employers and employees before there was employment law. A practice exists and then come the laws to ensure fairness, justice, and so on. In Judaism, *mishpatim*, social legislation, are of this kind.

Constitutive laws *create* a practice. The laws of chess create the game called chess. Without the laws, there is no game. Rabban Yoḥanan was saying that the laws of purity are like this. They are not like medicine, because impurity is not like a disease. Before there were laws of purity, death did not defile and the waters did not purify. The laws created a new reality, but that does not mean that they are irrational or incomprehensible. Chapters 11–16 will give us a broad mapping of the Torah's rules of purity and impurity. Here we see them introduced in their natural context – the Tabernacle with its sacrifices.

THE PROHIBITION AGAINST EATING BLOOD

The ban on eating blood is not just one prohibition among others; it is fundamental to the Torah. It occupies a central place in the covenant God makes with Noaḥ – and through him, all humanity – after the flood: "But flesh with its lifeblood still in it you may not eat" (Gen. 9:4). So too, Moshe returns to the subject in his great closing addresses in the book of Deuteronomy: "But make sure that you do not eat the blood, for blood is life, and you must not eat the life with the meat" (Deut. 12:23).

What is so wrong about eating blood? Rambam and Ramban offer apparently conflicting interpretations.

27 in any of your dwellings. Anyone who eats any blood shall
be cut off from his people."
28 29 And the LORD spoke to Moshe: "Tell the Israelites: One
who brings a peace sacrifice to the LORD is to bring the
offering of his peace sacrifice before the LORD himself;
30 with his own hands he shall present the LORD's fire
offerings. He shall bring the animal's fat and breast so that
the breast can be displayed, this way and that, as a wave
31 offering before the LORD. The priest shall send the fat up
in smoke upon the altar, but the breast shall go to Aharon
32 and his sons. The right thigh of your peace offering you
33 shall give as an upraised gift to the priest. The one among
the sons of Aharon who offers the blood and fat of the
peace offering shall receive the right thigh as his portion.
34 For I have taken from the peace sacrifices of the Israelites
the breast of the wave offering and the thigh of the
upraised gift, and given them to Aharon the priest and
to his sons as their perpetual share from the Israelites.
35 This is the anointed right of Aharon and his sons from
the LORD's fire offerings from the day they are presented
36 to serve the LORD as priests; when the LORD anointed
them as priests He commanded that these be given them
by the Israelites as their perpetual share throughout the
37 generations." This, then, is the law for the burnt offering,
the grain offering, the purification offering, the guilt
offering, the ordination offering, and the peace offering,

---

for the burnt offering – The major part of Leviticus is a series of God's direct speeches to Moshe. The formulation in this verse, part of the book's frame, concludes the series of speeches concerning the sacrifices, and will continue on to different areas of ritual law.

Judaism's fundamental solution to the distance between God and man is *language*. Words alone have the power to cross the abyss between finite humans and the infinite God. God spoke to Adam, Kayin, Noaḥ, the patriarchs and matriarchs, and, of course, "the LORD spoke to Moshe."

Direct divine communication is a solution that worked for individuals. What happens when the Israelites become a nation? The answer comes in the form of this forty-chapter digression in the story of the Israelites' journey from Egypt to the Promised Land: a

כז תֹּאכְלוּ בְּכֹל מוֹשְׁבֹתֵיכֶם לָעוֹף וְלַבְּהֵמָה׃ כָּל־נֶפֶשׁ אֲשֶׁר־
תֹּאכַל כָּל־דָּם וְנִכְרְתָה הַנֶּפֶשׁ הַהִוא מֵעַמֶּיהָ׃
כח כט וַיְדַבֵּר יְהוָה אֶל־מֹשֶׁה לֵּאמֹר׃ דַּבֵּר אֶל־בְּנֵי יִשְׂרָאֵל לֵאמֹר
הַמַּקְרִיב אֶת־זֶבַח שְׁלָמָיו לַיהוָה יָבִיא אֶת־קָרְבָּנוֹ לַיהוָה
ל מִזֶּבַח שְׁלָמָיו׃ יָדָיו תְּבִיאֶינָה אֵת אִשֵּׁי יְהוָה אֶת־הַחֵלֶב
עַל־הֶחָזֶה יְבִיאֶנּוּ אֵת הֶחָזֶה לְהָנִיף אֹתוֹ תְּנוּפָה לִפְנֵי
לא יְהוָה׃ וְהִקְטִיר הַכֹּהֵן אֶת־הַחֵלֶב הַמִּזְבֵּחָה וְהָיָה הֶחָזֶה
לב לְאַהֲרֹן וּלְבָנָיו׃ וְאֵת שׁוֹק הַיָּמִין תִּתְּנוּ תְרוּמָה לַכֹּהֵן מִזִּבְחֵי
לג שַׁלְמֵיכֶם׃ הַמַּקְרִיב אֶת־דַּם הַשְּׁלָמִים וְאֶת־הַחֵלֶב מִבְּנֵי
לד אַהֲרֹן לוֹ תִהְיֶה שׁוֹק הַיָּמִין לְמָנָה׃ כִּי אֶת־חֲזֵה הַתְּנוּפָה
וְאֵת ׀ שׁוֹק הַתְּרוּמָה לָקַחְתִּי מֵאֵת בְּנֵי־יִשְׂרָאֵל מִזִּבְחֵי
שַׁלְמֵיהֶם וָאֶתֵּן אֹתָם לְאַהֲרֹן הַכֹּהֵן וּלְבָנָיו לְחָק־עוֹלָם מֵאֵת
לה בְּנֵי יִשְׂרָאֵל׃ זֹאת מִשְׁחַת אַהֲרֹן וּמִשְׁחַת בָּנָיו מֵאִשֵּׁי יְהוָה
לו בְּיוֹם הִקְרִיב אֹתָם לְכַהֵן לַיהוָה׃ אֲשֶׁר צִוָּה יְהוָה לָתֵת לָהֶם
בְּיוֹם מָשְׁחוֹ אֹתָם מֵאֵת בְּנֵי יִשְׂרָאֵל חֻקַּת עוֹלָם לְדֹרֹתָם׃
לז זֹאת הַתּוֹרָה לָעֹלָה לַמִּנְחָה וְלַחַטָּאת וְלָאָשָׁם וְלַמִּלּוּאִים

---

but they invest it with "the profound feelings – dread, awe, and the willingness to sacrifice – that make it 'sacred' to us." They help explain why it is so easy to mobilize people by conjuring up the specter of an external enemy.

Evolutionary psychology has taught us about these genetic residues from earlier times which – because they are not rational – cannot be cured by reason alone, but only by ritual, strict prohibition, and habituation. The contemporary world continues to be scarred by violence and terror. Sadly, the ban against blood sacrifice is still relevant.

In this perspective, we can see that Rambam and Ramban were both correct. Rambam was right to see in blood sacrifice a central idolatrous practice. Ramban was equally correct to see it as a symptom of human cruelty. The instinct against which it is a protest – sacrificing life to exorcise fear – still lives on.

We now sense the profound wisdom of the law forbidding the eating of blood. Only thus could human beings be gradually cured of a deeply ingrained instinct, deriving from a world of predators and prey, in which the key choice is to kill or be killed.

7:37 זֹאת הַתּוֹרָה לָעֹלָה *This, then, is the law*

38 which the LORD commanded Moshe at Mount Sinai
when he commanded the Israelites to bring their offerings
to the LORD, in the Wilderness of Sinai.
8 1 2 The LORD said to Moshe: "Take Aharon, and his sons REVI'I
with him, the vestments, the anointing oil, a bull for
the purification offering, two rams, and a basket of
3 unleavened bread, and assemble the whole community
4 at the entrance to the Tent of Meeting." Moshe did as
the LORD commanded him; and the community was
5 assembled at the entrance to the Tent of Meeting. And
Moshe told the community, "This is what the LORD has
6 commanded us to do." Then Moshe brought Aharon and
7 his sons close, and he washed them with water. He put the
tunic on Aharon, tied the sash around him, clothed him
in the robe, and placed the ephod on him. He bound the
ephod's decorated belt about him, securing the ephod to
8 him. Then he put the breast piece on him, and inside the
9 breast piece he placed the Urim and Tumim. On his head
he placed the miter, and on the miter in front, he placed
the golden head plate, the holy diadem, as the LORD had
10 commanded him. Then Moshe took the anointing oil
and anointed the Tabernacle and everything in it; thus
11 he consecrated them. He sprinkled some of the oil on the
altar seven times. He anointed the altar and all its vessels,
and the laver and its base, thus consecrating them.
12 Some of the anointing oil he poured on Aharon's head,
13 anointing him, consecrating him. Then Moshe brought
close Aharon's sons, dressed them in their tunics, bound

---

expression. Without prophecy, a society can become corrupt at the top. But without priesthood, it can erode from below. It can lose its structures of family and community life, within which the civic virtues are learned and enacted. Prophecy is dramatic; priesthood is not. Prophecy makes headlines; priesthood rarely does. But both are necessary to the civil order. Without the matrix of institutions within which individual responsibility and the moral sentiments are nurtured, no freedoms are secure for long. Here, the entire nation is called to witness the inauguration of the first priests. While their work will be contained in the Tabernacle, it will be of the utmost significance to the community as a whole.

לח וּלְזֶבַח הַשְּׁלָמִים: אֲשֶׁר צִוָּה יְהוָה אֶת־מֹשֶׁה בְּהַר סִינָי
בְּיוֹם צַוֺּתוֹ אֶת־בְּנֵי יִשְׂרָאֵל לְהַקְרִיב אֶת־קָרְבְּנֵיהֶם לַיהוָה
בְּמִדְבַּר סִינָי:

ח א ב וַיְדַבֵּר יְהוָה אֶל־מֹשֶׁה לֵּאמֹר: קַח אֶת־אַהֲרֹן וְאֶת־בָּנָיו אִתּוֹ ד רביעי
וְאֵת הַבְּגָדִים וְאֵת שֶׁמֶן הַמִּשְׁחָה וְאֵת ׀ פַּר הַחַטָּאת וְאֵת
ג שְׁנֵי הָאֵילִים וְאֵת סַל הַמַּצּוֹת: וְאֵת כָּל־הָעֵדָה הַקְהֵל אֶל־
ד פֶּתַח אֹהֶל מוֹעֵד: וַיַּעַשׂ מֹשֶׁה כַּאֲשֶׁר צִוָּה יְהוָה אֹתוֹ וַתִּקָּהֵל
ה הָעֵדָה אֶל־פֶּתַח אֹהֶל מוֹעֵד: וַיֹּאמֶר מֹשֶׁה אֶל־הָעֵדָה זֶה
ו הַדָּבָר אֲשֶׁר־צִוָּה יְהוָה לַעֲשׂוֹת: וַיַּקְרֵב מֹשֶׁה אֶת־אַהֲרֹן
ז וְאֶת־בָּנָיו וַיִּרְחַץ אֹתָם בַּמָּיִם: וַיִּתֵּן עָלָיו אֶת־הַכֻּתֹּנֶת וַיַּחְגֹּר
אֹתוֹ בָּאַבְנֵט וַיַּלְבֵּשׁ אֹתוֹ אֶת־הַמְּעִיל וַיִּתֵּן עָלָיו אֶת־הָאֵפֹד
ח וַיַּחְגֹּר אֹתוֹ בְּחֵשֶׁב הָאֵפֹד וַיֶּאְפֹּד לוֹ בּוֹ: וַיָּשֶׂם עָלָיו אֶת־
ט הַחֹשֶׁן וַיִּתֵּן אֶל־הַחֹשֶׁן אֶת־הָאוּרִים וְאֶת־הַתֻּמִּים: וַיָּשֶׂם
אֶת־הַמִּצְנֶפֶת עַל־רֹאשׁוֹ וַיָּשֶׂם עַל־הַמִּצְנֶפֶת אֶל־מוּל פָּנָיו
אֵת צִיץ הַזָּהָב נֵזֶר הַקֹּדֶשׁ כַּאֲשֶׁר צִוָּה יְהוָה אֶת־מֹשֶׁה:
י וַיִּקַּח מֹשֶׁה אֶת־שֶׁמֶן הַמִּשְׁחָה וַיִּמְשַׁח אֶת־הַמִּשְׁכָּן וְאֶת־
יא כָּל־אֲשֶׁר־בּוֹ וַיְקַדֵּשׁ אֹתָם: וַיַּז מִמֶּנּוּ עַל־הַמִּזְבֵּחַ שֶׁבַע
פְּעָמִים וַיִּמְשַׁח אֶת־הַמִּזְבֵּחַ וְאֶת־כָּל־כֵּלָיו וְאֶת־הַכִּיֹּר
יב וְאֶת־כַּנּוֹ לְקַדְּשָׁם: וַיִּצֹק מִשֶּׁמֶן הַמִּשְׁחָה עַל רֹאשׁ אַהֲרֹן
יג וַיִּמְשַׁח אֹתוֹ לְקַדְּשׁוֹ: וַיַּקְרֵב מֹשֶׁה אֶת־בְּנֵי אַהֲרֹן וַיַּלְבִּשֵׁם

---

series of revelations spoken to Moshe and then recorded, structured, and ordered as the priestly code, *Torat Kohanim*.

8:3 וְאֵת כָּל־הָעֵדָה הַקְהֵל *Assemble the whole community* – Why must the whole people come to the initiation of the priesthood? I suggest that it is because the priesthood plays an essential part in protecting a society's integrity. Religions help safeguard governments against corruption. They can do this in two distinct ways corresponding to the biblical realms of prophecy and priesthood. Prophecy has a critical function. Yeḥezkel defined his role as "watchman" to the House of Israel, giving warnings of impending catastrophe (Ezek. 3:17, 33:7). But priesthood is about constructing communities where the life of faith is given tangible

sashes about them, and placed their headdresses on them,
14 just as the LORD had commanded him. Moshe drew close ḤAMISHI
the bull for the purification offering, and Aharon and his
15 sons laid their hands on its head. It was slaughtered, and
Moshe took the blood and applied it with his finger to all
the altar's horns, purifying the altar. The rest of the blood
he poured out at the altar's base. Thus he consecrated it so
16 that, upon it, atonement could be made. Moshe removed
all the fat around the entrails, the diaphragm of the liver,
the two kidneys and their fat, and sent them up in smoke
17 upon the altar. But the rest of the bull, its skin, its flesh,
and its dung, he burned with fire outside the camp as
18 the LORD had commanded him. Then Moshe drew close
the ram for the burnt offering, and Aharon and his sons
19 laid their hands on its head. Moshe slaughtered it and
20 dashed the blood against each side of the altar. He cut
the ram into pieces and sent the head, pieces, and suet up
21 in smoke. After washing the entrails and legs with water,
Moshe sent the entire ram up in smoke upon the altar. It
was a burnt offering for a pleasing aroma: a fire offering to
22 the LORD, as the LORD had commanded Moshe. Moshe SHISHI
then drew close the second ram, the ram of ordination.
23 Aharon and his sons laid their hands upon its head. It
was slaughtered; and Moshe took some of its blood and

At the burning bush, Moshe had repeatedly resisted God's call to lead the people. Eventually God told him that Aharon would go with him, helping him speak (Ex. 4:14–16). The Talmud says that at that moment Moshe lost the chance to be a priest. "Originally [said God], I had intended that you would be the priest and Aharon your brother would be a Levite. Now he will be the priest and you will be a Levite" (Zevaḥim 102a).

That is Moshe's inner struggle, conveyed by the *shalshelet*. He is about to induct his brother into an office he himself will never hold. He surely feels joy for his brother, but he cannot altogether avoid a sense of loss. Perhaps he already senses that though he is the prophet and liberator, Aharon will have a privilege Moshe is denied, namely, seeing his children and their descendants inherit his role. The son of a priest is a priest. The son of a prophet is rarely a prophet. To say yes to who we are, we have to have the

כֻּתֳּנֹת וַיַּחְגֹּר אֹתָם אַבְנֵט וַיַּחֲבֹשׁ לָהֶם מִגְבָּעוֹת כַּאֲשֶׁר
יד צִוָּה יְהוָה אֶת־מֹשֶׁה: וַיַּגֵּשׁ אֵת פַּר הַחַטָּאת וַיִּסְמֹךְ אַהֲרֹן חמישי
טו וּבָנָיו אֶת־יְדֵיהֶם עַל־רֹאשׁ פַּר הַחַטָּאת: וַיִּשְׁחָט וַיִּקַּח מֹשֶׁה
אֶת־הַדָּם וַיִּתֵּן עַל־קַרְנוֹת הַמִּזְבֵּחַ סָבִיב בְּאֶצְבָּעוֹ וַיְחַטֵּא
אֶת־הַמִּזְבֵּחַ וְאֶת־הַדָּם יָצַק אֶל־יְסוֹד הַמִּזְבֵּחַ וַיְקַדְּשֵׁהוּ
טז לְכַפֵּר עָלָיו: וַיִּקַּח אֶת־כָּל־הַחֵלֶב אֲשֶׁר עַל־הַקֶּרֶב וְאֵת
יֹתֶרֶת הַכָּבֵד וְאֶת־שְׁתֵּי הַכְּלָיֹת וְאֶת־חֶלְבְּהֶן וַיַּקְטֵר מֹשֶׁה
יז הַמִּזְבֵּחָה: וְאֶת־הַפָּר וְאֶת־עֹרוֹ וְאֶת־בְּשָׂרוֹ וְאֶת־פִּרְשׁוֹ שָׂרַף
יח בָּאֵשׁ מִחוּץ לַמַּחֲנֶה כַּאֲשֶׁר צִוָּה יְהוָה אֶת־מֹשֶׁה: וַיַּקְרֵב
אֵת אֵיל הָעֹלָה וַיִּסְמְכוּ אַהֲרֹן וּבָנָיו אֶת־יְדֵיהֶם עַל־רֹאשׁ
יט הָאָיִל: וַיִּשְׁחָט וַיִּזְרֹק מֹשֶׁה אֶת־הַדָּם עַל־הַמִּזְבֵּחַ סָבִיב:
כ וְאֶת־הָאַיִל נִתַּח לִנְתָחָיו וַיַּקְטֵר מֹשֶׁה אֶת־הָרֹאשׁ וְאֶת־
כא הַנְּתָחִים וְאֶת־הַפָּדֶר: וְאֶת־הַקֶּרֶב וְאֶת־הַכְּרָעַיִם רָחַץ בַּמָּיִם
וַיַּקְטֵר מֹשֶׁה אֶת־כָּל־הָאַיִל הַמִּזְבֵּחָה עֹלָה הוּא לְרֵיחַ־נִיחֹחַ
כב אִשֶּׁה הוּא לַיהוָה כַּאֲשֶׁר צִוָּה יְהוָה אֶת־מֹשֶׁה: וַיַּקְרֵב אֶת־ ששי
הָאַיִל הַשֵּׁנִי אֵיל הַמִּלֻּאִים וַיִּסְמְכוּ אַהֲרֹן וּבָנָיו אֶת־יְדֵיהֶם
כג עַל־רֹאשׁ הָאָיִל: וַיִּשְׁחָט ׀ וַיִּקַּח מֹשֶׁה מִדָּמוֹ וַיִּתֵּן עַל־תְּנוּךְ

8:23 וַיִּשְׁחָט *It was slaughtered* – Over the word *vayishḥat,* "slaughtered," there is a *shalshelet* (chain). This rare note appears in the Torah four times only. Each time it is a sign of an inner crisis. There is not the slightest sign in the text that suggests that Moshe is undergoing a crisis here, yet we may intuit what Moshe's inner turmoil is about. Until now he has led the Jewish people. Aharon, his older brother, assisted him, accompanying him on his missions to Pharaoh, acting as his spokesman, aide, and second-in-command. Now, however, Aharon is about to undertake a new leadership role in his own right. No longer will he be a shadow of Moshe. He will do what Moshe himself cannot. He will preside over the daily offerings in the Tabernacle. He will mediate the *avoda,* the Israelites' sacred service to God. Once a year on Yom Kippur he will perform the service that will secure atonement for the people from its sins. Aharon is about to become the one kind of leader Moshe is not destined to be: a High Priest.

The Talmud adds a further dimension to the poignancy of the moment.

applied it to the ridge of Aharon's right ear, to his right
24 thumb, and to his right big toe. He drew Aharon's sons
close and put some of the blood on the ridges of their
right ears, on their right thumbs, and on their right big
toes. Moshe dashed the rest of the blood against each of
25 the altar's sides. Then he took the fat, the broad tail, all the
fat around the entrails, the diaphragm of the liver, and the
26 two kidneys with their fat, as well as the right thigh. He
took a loaf of unleavened bread from the basket, before
the Lord, and also one loaf of oil bread, and one wafer,
27 and placed them on the fat and on the right thigh. All of
this he placed on the palms of Aharon and of his sons, and
displayed them this way and that as a wave offering before
28 the Lord. Then Moshe took them from their hands and
burnt them upon the altar with the burnt offering. This
was the ordination offering, a pleasing aroma, a fire
29 offering to the Lord. Moshe then took the breast and
waved it as a wave offering before the Lord. This was
Moshe's portion of the ordination ram, as the Lord had
30 commanded him. Moshe took some of the anointing oil SHEVI'I
and some of the blood from the altar and sprinkled it on
Aharon and on his vestments, and on his sons and theirs.
Thus Moshe consecrated Aharon and his vestments,
31 and his sons and their vestments. Then Moshe said to
Aharon and his sons: "Cook the meat at the entrance to
the Tent of Meeting and eat it there together with the
bread in the basket of the ordination offering, as I have
32 charged you: Aharon and his sons shall eat it. Whatever
33 is left over of the meat and the bread, burn with fire. Do MAFTIR
not leave the entrance to the Tent of Meeting for seven
days, until the days of your ordination are complete, for
34 your ordination will take seven days, each like today. This
is what the Lord has commanded to be done to make

---

both facts if he is to be honest with himself. And great leaders, if they are to be honest with those they lead, must be honest with themselves.

אזן־אהרן הימנית ועל־בהן ידו הימנית ועל־בהן רגלו
כד הימנית: ויקרב את־בני אהרן ויתן משה מן־הדם על־
תנוך אזנם הימנית ועל־בהן ידם הימנית ועל־בהן רגלם
כה הימנית ויזרק משה את־הדם על־המזבח סביב: ויקח
את־החלב ואת־האליה ואת־כל־החלב אשר על־הקרב
ואת יתרת הכבד ואת־שתי הכלית ואת־חלבהן ואת שוק
כו הימין: ומסל המצות אשר | לפני יהוה לקח חלת מצה
אחת וחלת לחם שמן אחת ורקיק אחד וישם על־החלבים
כז ועל שוק הימין: ויתן את־הכל על כפי אהרן ועל כפי בניו
כח וינף אתם תנופה לפני יהוה: ויקח משה אתם מעל כפיהם
ויקטר המזבחה על־העלה מלאים הם לריח ניחח אשה
כט הוא ליהוה: ויקח משה את־החזה ויניפהו תנופה לפני
יהוה מאיל המלאים למשה היה למנה כאשר צוה יהוה
ל את־משה: ויקח משה משמן המשחה ומן־הדם אשר שביעי
על־המזבח ויז על־אהרן על־בגדיו ועל־בניו ועל־בגדי בניו
אתו ויקדש את־אהרן את־בגדיו ואת־בניו ואת־בגדי בניו
לא אתו: ויאמר משה אל־אהרן ואל־בניו בשלו את־הבשר
פתח אהל מועד ושם תאכלו אתו ואת־הלחם אשר בסל
לב המלאים כאשר צויתי לאמר אהרן ובניו יאכלהו: והנותר
לג בבשר ובלחם באש תשרפו: ומפתח אהל מועד לא תצאו מפטיר
שבעת ימים עד יום מלאת ימי מלאיכם כי שבעת ימים
לד ימלא את־ידכם: כאשר עשה ביום הזה צוה יהוה לעשת

---

courage to say no to who we are not. Pain and internal conflict are involved. But we emerge less conflicted than we were before. That is the meaning of the *shalshelet*.

This applies especially to leaders. There are things Moshe is not destined to do. He will not become a priest. That task falls to Aharon. He will not lead the people across the Jordan. That will be Yehoshua's role. Moshe has to accept

35 your atonement. Stay, then, at the entrance to the Tent of
Meeting for seven days, day and night, keeping the Lord's
charge – and you will not die. This is what I have been
36 commanded." And Aharon and his sons did everything
that the Lord had commanded through Moshe.

The haftara for Parashat Tzav is on page 1514.
On the Shabbat of Parashat Para read the haftara on page 1662.
On Shabbat HaGadol read the haftara on page 1672

---

universe on which God has set His image. A sin against any person is a sin against God.

It is specifically in the book of sacrifices, Leviticus, that we find the twin commands to love your neighbor as yourself, and love the stranger (Lev. 19:18, 33–34). The sacrifices that express our love and awe of God should lead to love of the neighbor and the stranger. There should be a seamless transition from commands between us and God to commands between us and our fellow humans.

Amos, Hoshea, Yeshayahu, Mikha, and Yirmeyahu all witnessed societies in which people were punctilious in bringing their offerings to the Temple, but in which there was bribery, corruption, perversion of justice, abuse of power, and the exploitation of the powerless by the powerful. The prophets saw in this a profound and dangerous contradiction.

To love God is to love our fellow humans. To honor God is to honor our fellow humans. We may not ask God to listen to us if we are unwilling to listen to others. We may not ask God to forgive us if we are unwilling to forgive others. To know God is to seek to imitate Him, which means, said Yirmeyahu (Jer. 9:23) and Rambam (*Guide for the Perplexed* III:54), to exercise kindness, justice, and righteousness. This requires true obedience paired with an inner moral compass; in the prophet Mikha's summary, "only to do justice, love goodness, and walk modestly with your God" (Mic. 6:8).

לה לְכַפֵּר עֲלֵיכֶם׃ וּפֶתַח אֹהֶל מוֹעֵד תֵּשְׁבוּ יוֹמָם וָלַיְלָה שִׁבְעַת
יָמִים וּשְׁמַרְתֶּם אֶת־מִשְׁמֶרֶת יהוה וְלֹא תָמוּתוּ כִּי־כֵן צֻוֵּיתִי׃
לו וַיַּעַשׂ אַהֲרֹן וּבָנָיו אֵת כָּל־הַדְּבָרִים אֲשֶׁר־צִוָּה יהוה בְּיַד־
מֹשֶׁה׃

The הפטרה *for* פרשת צו *is on page 1515.*
On the שבת *of* פרשת פרה *read the* הפטרה *on page 1663.*
On שבת הגדול *read the* הפטרה *on page 1673.*

JUSTICE AND OBEDIENCE

We have not had the sacrificial service since the destruction of the Second Temple almost two thousand years ago. What is deeply relevant today, however, is the *critique* of sacrifices we find among the prophets of the First Temple. That critique was sharp and deep and formed many of their most powerful addresses including the *haftara* for Parashat Tzav.

Strongest of all is the beginning of the book of Isaiah, read on *Shabbat Ḥazon* (before the Ninth of Av):

> "Why," says the Lord, "would I want all these offerings? I am sated with burnt offerings, with rams and fleshy creatures' fat, the blood of bulls and sheep and goats – I do not want them. You come, appear before Me. Who asked all this of you, who asked you for all this: trampling My courtyards? Bring no more your empty gifts – they are foul incense to Me." (Is. 1:11–13)

This entire line of thought, sustained across centuries, is extraordinary. The people were being criticized not for disobeying God's law but for obeying it. What distressed the prophets to the core of their being was the idea that you could serve God and at the same time act disdainfully, cruelly, unjustly, insensitively, or callously toward other people. "So long as I am in God's good graces, that is all that matters." If you think that, they seem to say, then you haven't understood either God or Torah.

The first thing the Torah tells us about humanity is that we are each in the image and likeness of God Himself. Therefore, if you wrong a human being, you are abusing the only creation in the

Parashat Shemini

9 1 On the eighth day, Moshe called to Aharon and his sons,
2 and to the elders of Israel. "Take a bull calf for yourself as
a purification offering," he told Aharon, "and a ram for a
burnt offering, both without blemish, and offer them up
3 before the Lord. Then tell the Israelites: Take a goat for a
purification offering, and a calf and a lamb, both yearlings
4 without blemish, for a burnt offering, a bull and a ram
for a peace offering to offer up before the Lord, and a
grain offering mixed with oil – for on this day the Lord
5 will be revealed to you." They brought what Moshe had

---

eighth day. The light of the first day was created by God. The light of the eighth day is what God taught us to create. It symbolizes our "partnership with God in the work of creation" (Shabbat 10a, 119b). On the Sabbath we remember God's creation. On the eighth day (Motza'ei Shabbat) we celebrate our creativity as the image and partner of God. (This, according to the Sages, is the reason we light a *Havdala* candle at the end of the Sabbath to inaugurate the new week (Pesikta Rabbati 23).

We believe that God wants human beings to exercise power responsibly, creatively, and within limits set by the integrity of nature. The rabbinic account of how God taught Adam and Ḥava the secret of making fire is the precise opposite of the Greek myth of Prometheus, who stole the spark of fire that Zeus wanted to keep as a divine secret. God seeks to confer dignity on the beings He made in His image as an act of love. He does not hide the secrets of the universe from us. The creative God empowers us to be creative and begins by teaching us how. That is the symbolism of the eighth day.

We now understand the symbolic significance of the eighth day in relation to the Tabernacle. As we have noted elsewhere, the linguistic parallels in the Torah show that the construction of the Tabernacle in the wilderness mirrors the divine creation of the world. The Tabernacle was intended to be a miniature universe, constructed by human beings. Just as God made the earth as a home for mankind, so the Israelites in the wilderness built the Tabernacle as a symbolic home for God.

Thus the day it begins is, figuratively as well as literally, the eighth day. If the first day represents divine creation, the eighth day signifies human creation under the tutelage and sovereignty of God.

פרשת שמיני

ט א וַיְהִי֙ בַּיּ֣וֹם הַשְּׁמִינִ֔י קָרָ֣א מֹשֶׁ֔ה לְאַהֲרֹ֖ן וּלְבָנָ֑יו וּלְזִקְנֵ֖י יִשְׂרָאֵֽל׃
ב וַיֹּ֣אמֶר אֶֽל־אַהֲרֹ֗ן קַח־לְךָ֞ עֵ֣גֶל בֶּן־בָּקָ֧ר לְחַטָּ֛את וְאַ֥יִל
ג לְעֹלָ֖ה תְּמִימִ֑ם וְהַקְרֵ֖ב לִפְנֵ֥י יהוֽה׃ וְאֶל־בְּנֵ֥י יִשְׂרָאֵ֖ל תְּדַבֵּ֣ר
לֵאמֹ֑ר קְח֤וּ שְׂעִיר־עִזִּים֙ לְחַטָּ֔את וְעֵ֨גֶל וָכֶ֧בֶשׂ בְּנֵי־שָׁנָ֛ה
ד תְּמִימִ֖ם לְעֹלָֽה׃ וְשׁ֨וֹר וָאַ֜יִל לִשְׁלָמִ֗ים לִזְבֹּ֙חַ֙ לִפְנֵ֣י יהו֔ה
ה וּמִנְחָ֖ה בְּלוּלָ֣ה בַשָּׁ֑מֶן כִּ֣י הַיּ֔וֹם יהו֖ה נִרְאָ֥ה אֲלֵיכֶֽם׃ וַיִּקְח֗וּ

SHEMINI

Parashat Shemini tells the story of the inauguration of the Tabernacle. For many chapters we have read of the preparations for the moment at which God would bring His presence to rest in the midst of the people. Five *parashot* (Teruma, Tetzaveh, Ki Tisa, Vayak'hel, and Pekudei) describe the instructions for building the Sanctuary. Two (Vayikra, Tzav) detail the sacrificial offerings to be brought there. All is now ready. For seven days, beginning on the twenty-third of Adar, Moshe consecrated Aharon and the priests. Now, on Rosh Ḥodesh Nisan, the eighth day, the time has come for Aharon to begin his service, ministering to the people on behalf of God. This is the day about which the Sages say that God rejoiced as much as He had at the creation of the universe (Megilla 10b). Yet the celebration is overshadowed by the shocking deaths of two of Aharon's sons, Nadav and Avihu, who offered an "unauthorized fire" (Lev. 10:1) at the inauguration ceremony.

The second half of the *parasha* details the dietary laws, a list of permitted and forbidden species, animals, fish, and birds. Why are these laws placed here? We shall see that in fact they have a deep connection to the Sanctuary.

THE EIGHTH DAY

To understand the symbolism of the "eighth day," the phrase that gives this *parasha* its name, let us go back to creation itself, more specifically to the conclusion of the first Sabbath. The Midrash tells us:

> With the going out of the Sabbath, the celestial light began to fade. Adam was afraid that the serpent would attack him in the dark. Therefore, God illuminated his understanding, and he learned to rub two stones against each other and produce light for his needs. (Bereshit Rabba 12:6)

There is a fundamental difference between the light of the first day ("God said, 'Let there be light'" [Gen. 1:3]) and that of the

commanded to the space before the Tent of Meeting, and
all the community drew near and stood before the Lord.
6 Moshe said, "This is what the Lord has commanded you to
7 do so that the Lord's glory be revealed to you." Moshe said
to Aharon, "Approach the altar, prepare your purification
offering and burnt offering, and make atonement for you
and for the people. Then prepare the people's offering to
make atonement for them, as the Lord has commanded."
8 Aharon drew close to the altar and slaughtered the calf
9 of his purification offering. Aharon's sons presented
him with the blood, and he dipped his finger into it and
applied the blood to the horns of the altar; the rest of the
10 blood he poured out at the altar's base. Then he sent the
fat, the kidneys, and the diaphragm of the liver from the
purification offering up in smoke upon the altar as the
11 Lord had commanded Moshe, and he burned the flesh
12 and skin with fire outside the camp. Then he slaughtered
the burnt offering. Aharon's sons presented him with the
13 blood, and he dashed it on each side of the altar. Then
they presented him with the burnt offering in its pieces,
with its head, and he sent them up in smoke upon the
14 altar. Having washed the entrails and legs, he sent them
up in smoke upon the altar with the burnt offering.
15 Then he brought close the people's offering. He took the
goat of the people's purification offering, slaughtered it,
and prepared it as a purification offering like the first.
16 He presented the burnt offering and sacrificed it in the
17 prescribed way. He then presented the grain offering, SHENI
took a handful from it, and sent this portion up in smoke

Until now Aharon has been in all respects second to Moshe. Yes, he had been at his side throughout, helping him speak and lead. But there is a vast psychological difference between being second-in-command and being a leader in your own right. We probably all know of examples of people who quite readily serve in an assisting capacity but who are terrified at the prospect of leading on their own.

Whichever explanation is true – and perhaps they all are – Aharon is reticent at taking on his new role, and Moshe has to give him the confidence to step forward. "This," he therefore tells him, "is what you have been chosen to do."

אֵת אֲשֶׁר צִוָּה מֹשֶׁה אֶל־פְּנֵי אֹהֶל מוֹעֵד וַיִּקְרְבוּ כׇּל־הָעֵדָה
ו וַיַּעַמְדוּ לִפְנֵי יהוה׃ וַיֹּאמֶר מֹשֶׁה זֶה הַדָּבָר אֲשֶׁר־צִוָּה
ז יהוה תַּעֲשׂוּ וְיֵרָא אֲלֵיכֶם כְּבוֹד יהוה׃ וַיֹּאמֶר מֹשֶׁה אֶל־
אַהֲרֹן קְרַב אֶל־הַמִּזְבֵּחַ וַעֲשֵׂה אֶת־חַטָּאתְךָ וְאֶת־עֹלָתֶךָ
וְכַפֵּר בַּעַדְךָ וּבְעַד הָעָם וַעֲשֵׂה אֶת־קׇרְבַּן הָעָם וְכַפֵּר בַּעֲדָם
ח כַּאֲשֶׁר צִוָּה יהוה׃ וַיִּקְרַב אַהֲרֹן אֶל־הַמִּזְבֵּחַ וַיִּשְׁחַט אֶת־
ט עֵגֶל הַחַטָּאת אֲשֶׁר־לוֹ׃ וַיַּקְרִבוּ בְּנֵי אַהֲרֹן אֶת־הַדָּם אֵלָיו
וַיִּטְבֹּל אֶצְבָּעוֹ בַּדָּם וַיִּתֵּן עַל־קַרְנוֹת הַמִּזְבֵּחַ וְאֶת־הַדָּם
י יָצַק אֶל־יְסוֹד הַמִּזְבֵּחַ׃ וְאֶת־הַחֵלֶב וְאֶת־הַכְּלָיֹת וְאֶת־
הַיֹּתֶרֶת מִן־הַכָּבֵד מִן־הַחַטָּאת הִקְטִיר הַמִּזְבֵּחָה כַּאֲשֶׁר
יא צִוָּה יהוה אֶת־מֹשֶׁה׃ וְאֶת־הַבָּשָׂר וְאֶת־הָעוֹר שָׂרַף בָּאֵשׁ
יב מִחוּץ לַמַּחֲנֶה׃ וַיִּשְׁחַט אֶת־הָעֹלָה וַיַּמְצִאוּ בְּנֵי אַהֲרֹן אֵלָיו
יג אֶת־הַדָּם וַיִּזְרְקֵהוּ עַל־הַמִּזְבֵּחַ סָבִיב׃ וְאֶת־הָעֹלָה הִמְצִיאוּ
יד אֵלָיו לִנְתָחֶיהָ וְאֶת־הָרֹאשׁ וַיַּקְטֵר עַל־הַמִּזְבֵּחַ׃ וַיִּרְחַץ
אֶת־הַקֶּרֶב וְאֶת־הַכְּרָעָיִם וַיַּקְטֵר עַל־הָעֹלָה הַמִּזְבֵּחָה׃
טו וַיַּקְרֵב אֵת קׇרְבַּן הָעָם וַיִּקַּח אֶת־שְׂעִיר הַחַטָּאת אֲשֶׁר לָעָם
טז וַיִּשְׁחָטֵהוּ וַיְחַטְּאֵהוּ כָּרִאשׁוֹן׃ וַיַּקְרֵב אֶת־הָעֹלָה וַיַּעֲשֶׂהָ
יז כַּמִּשְׁפָּט׃ וַיַּקְרֵב אֶת־הַמִּנְחָה וַיְמַלֵּא כַפּוֹ מִמֶּנָּה וַיַּקְטֵר שני

9:7 קְרַב אֶל־הַמִּזְבֵּחַ *Approach the altar* – The Sages sense a nuance in the words "Approach the altar," as if Aharon were standing at a distance from it, reluctant to come near. They said: "Initially Aharon was ashamed to come close. Moshe said to him, 'Do not be ashamed. This is what you have been chosen to do'" (Rashi on Lev. 9:7, quoting Sifra, Shemini 9:8).

Why is Aharon ashamed? Tradition gives two explanations, both brought by Ramban (on Lev. 9:7). The first is that Aharon is overwhelmed by trepidation at coming so close to the Divine Presence. The second is that Aharon, seeing the "horns" of the altar, is reminded of the golden calf, his great sin. How could he, who played a key role in that terrible event, now take on the role of atoning for the people's sins? Moshe has to remind him that it is precisely to atone for sins that the altar was made; the fact that he had been chosen by God to be High Priest is an unequivocal sign that he has been forgiven.

There is perhaps a third explanation.

18 upon the altar, with the morning's burnt offering. He
slaughtered the ox and the ram: the people's peace
sacrifice. Aharon's sons presented him with the blood,
19 and he dashed it against each side of the altar, and the fat
parts of the ox and ram: the broad tail, the covering fat,
20 the kidneys, and the diaphragm of the liver. They laid the
fat parts over the breasts, and he sent them up in smoke
21 upon the altar. But the breasts and right thigh Aharon
displayed, this way and that, as a wave offering before the
22 LORD, as Moshe had commanded. Then Aharon raised
his hands to the people and blessed them. And, having
presented the purification offering, the burnt offering,
23 and the peace sacrifice, he stepped down. Moshe and
Aharon entered the Tent of Meeting; when they came
out, they blessed the people, and the glory of the LORD
24 was revealed to all the people. And from before the LORD, SHELISHI
fire came forth. It consumed the burnt offering and the
fat pieces on the altar; and all the people saw it, and cried
out for joy, and threw themselves facedown upon the
10 1 ground. Aharon's sons Nadav and Avihu took their fire
pans, put fire in them, and placed incense upon it, and
they offered unauthorized fire before the LORD: fire He

(what the kabbalists called *tzimtzum*) to create space for human action. No other act more profoundly indicates the love and generosity implicit in creation. God as we encounter Him in the Torah is like a parent who knows He must hold back, let go, refrain from intervening, if His children are to become responsible and mature.

However, to be true to God's purposes, there must be times and places at which humanity experiences the reality of the Divine. The holy is that segment of time and space God has reserved for His presence. Those times and places require absolute obedience. The most fundamental mistake – the mistake of Nadav and Avihu – is to take the powers that belong to man's encounter with the world, and apply them to man's encounter with the Divine. Had Nadav and Avihu used their own initiative to fight evil and injustice, the human domain, they would have been heroes. Because they used their own initiative in the arena of the holy, they erred. They asserted their own presence in the absolute presence of God.

That is the function of the holy – it is the point at which "I am" is silent in the

יח עַל־הַמִּזְבֵּחַ מִלְּבַד עֹלַת הַבֹּקֶר: וַיִּשְׁחַט אֶת־הַשּׁוֹר וְאֶת־
הָאַיִל זֶבַח הַשְּׁלָמִים אֲשֶׁר לָעָם וַיַּמְצִאוּ בְּנֵי אַהֲרֹן אֶת־הַדָּם
יט אֵלָיו וַיִּזְרְקֵהוּ עַל־הַמִּזְבֵּחַ סָבִיב: וְאֶת־הַחֲלָבִים מִן־הַשּׁוֹר
כ וּמִן־הָאַיִל הָאַלְיָה וְהַמְכַסֶּה וְהַכְּלָיֹת וְיֹתֶרֶת הַכָּבֵד: וַיָּשִׂימוּ
כא אֶת־הַחֲלָבִים עַל־הֶחָזוֹת וַיַּקְטֵר הַחֲלָבִים הַמִּזְבֵּחָה: וְאֵת
הֶחָזוֹת וְאֵת שׁוֹק הַיָּמִין הֵנִיף אַהֲרֹן תְּנוּפָה לִפְנֵי יְהוָה
כב כַּאֲשֶׁר צִוָּה מֹשֶׁה: וַיִּשָּׂא אַהֲרֹן אֶת־יָדָו אֶל־הָעָם וַיְבָרְכֵם
כג וַיֵּרֶד מֵעֲשֹׂת הַחַטָּאת וְהָעֹלָה וְהַשְּׁלָמִים: וַיָּבֹא מֹשֶׁה וְאַהֲרֹן
אֶל־אֹהֶל מוֹעֵד וַיֵּצְאוּ וַיְבָרְכוּ אֶת־הָעָם וַיֵּרָא כְבוֹד־יְהוָה
כד אֶל־כָּל־הָעָם: וַתֵּצֵא אֵשׁ מִלִּפְנֵי יְהוָה וַתֹּאכַל עַל־הַמִּזְבֵּחַ שלישי
אֶת־הָעֹלָה וְאֶת־הַחֲלָבִים וַיַּרְא כָּל־הָעָם וַיָּרֹנּוּ וַיִּפְּלוּ עַל־
י א פְּנֵיהֶם: וַיִּקְחוּ בְנֵי־אַהֲרֹן נָדָב וַאֲבִיהוּא אִישׁ מַחְתָּתוֹ וַיִּתְּנוּ
בָהֵן אֵשׁ וַיָּשִׂימוּ עָלֶיהָ קְטֹרֶת וַיַּקְרִיבוּ לִפְנֵי יְהוָה אֵשׁ זָרָה

NADAV AND AVIHU

Celebration turns to tragedy when the two eldest sons of Aharon die. The shock is immense. The Sages and commentators offer many explanations. Nadav and Avihu die because: they enter the Holy of Holies (*Tanḥuma*, Buber, Aḥarei Mot 7); they are not wearing the requisite clothes (Vayikra Rabba 20:9); they take fire from the kitchen, not the altar (*Tanḥuma* ad loc.); they do not consult Moshe and Aharon (*Yalkut Shimoni* 1:524); nor do they consult one another (*Tanḥuma* ad loc.). According to some they are guilty of hubris. They are impatient to assume leadership roles themselves (Aggada, Buber, Vayikra 10); and they have not married, considering themselves above such things (Vayikra Rabba 20:10). Yet others see their deaths as delayed punishment for an earlier sin, when at Mount Sinai "they ate and they drank" in the presence of God (Ex. 24:9–11).

The explanation explicit in the Torah itself is that Nadav and Avihu died because they offered unauthorized – literally, "strange" – fire, meaning "fire He had not commanded" (Lev. 10:1). To understand the significance of this, we must remind ourselves of the meaning of *kadosh*, "holy," and thus of *mikdash* as the home of the holy, and of its place in the world.

The word *olam*, "universe," is semantically linked to the word *ne'elam*, "hidden." *Creation involves concealment*. To give mankind some of his own creative powers – the use of language to think, communicate, understand, imagine alternative futures, and choose between them – God must do more than create *Homo sapiens*. He must efface Himself

2 had not commanded. And fire came forth from before the
LORD and consumed them. They died before the LORD.
3 Moshe said to Aharon, "Of this the LORD spoke when
He said: I will be sanctified through those close to Me,
and before all the people I will be honored." And Aharon
4 was silent. Moshe called to Mishael and Eltzafan, sons of
Uziel, Aharon's uncle; "Draw near," he said, "carry your
kinsmen from the Sanctuary and take them outside the
5 camp." They approached and, as Moshe had instructed
them, they carried Nadav and Avihu out by their tunics
6 to a place outside the camp. Moshe said to Aharon and
to Elazar and Itamar his sons, "Do not dishevel your hair

Prophecy and priesthood involve different tasks, different sensibilities. The priest serves God in a way that never changes over time (except of course when the Temple was destroyed and its service, presided over by the priests, came to an end). The prophet serves God in a way that is constantly changing. When people are at ease, the prophet warns of forthcoming catastrophe. When they suffer and are in the depths of despair, the prophets bring consolation and hope.

The words said by the priest are always the same. The priestly blessing uses the same words today as it did in the days of Moshe and Aharon. But the words used by the prophet are never the same. "No two prophets use the same style" (Sanhedrin 89a). For a prophet, spontaneity is of the essence. But for the priest engaged in divine service, it is out of place.

10:3 וַיִּדֹּם אַהֲרֹן *Aharon was silent* – Moshe tries to comfort his brother, who has lost two of his sons. He tells him that God has said, "I will be sanctified through those close to Me" (Lev. 10:3). According to Rashi, he is saying, "Now I see that they [Nadav and Avihu] were greater than you and me." The holier the person, the more demanding is God with them.

It is as if Moshe were saying to Aharon: "My brother, do not give up now. We have come so far. I know your heart is broken. So is mine. Did we not think – you and I – that our troubles were behind us, that after all we suffered in Egypt, and at the Sea of Reeds, and in the battle against Amalek, and in the sin of the golden calf, we were finally safe and free? And now this has happened. Aharon, don't give up, don't lose faith, don't despair. Your children died not because they were evil but because they were holy. Though their act was wrong, their intentions were good. They merely tried too hard." But despite Moshe's words of consolation, "Aharon was silent," lost in a grief too deep for words.

ב אֲשֶׁר לֹא צִוָּה אֹתָם׃ וַתֵּצֵא אֵשׁ מִלִּפְנֵי יהוה וַתֹּאכַל אוֹתָם
ג וַיָּמֻתוּ לִפְנֵי יהוה׃ וַיֹּאמֶר מֹשֶׁה אֶל־אַהֲרֹן הוּא אֲשֶׁר־דִּבֶּר
יהוה ׀ לֵאמֹר בִּקְרֹבַי אֶקָּדֵשׁ וְעַל־פְּנֵי כָל־הָעָם אֶכָּבֵד וַיִּדֹּם
ד אַהֲרֹן׃ וַיִּקְרָא מֹשֶׁה אֶל־מִישָׁאֵל וְאֶל אֶלְצָפָן בְּנֵי עֻזִּיאֵל
דֹּד אַהֲרֹן וַיֹּאמֶר אֲלֵהֶם קִרְבוּ שְׂאוּ אֶת־אֲחֵיכֶם מֵאֵת פְּנֵי־
ה הַקֹּדֶשׁ אֶל־מִחוּץ לַמַּחֲנֶה׃ וַיִּקְרְבוּ וַיִּשָּׂאֻם בְּכֻתֳּנֹתָם אֶל־
ו מִחוּץ לַמַּחֲנֶה כַּאֲשֶׁר דִּבֶּר מֹשֶׁה׃ וַיֹּאמֶר מֹשֶׁה אֶל־אַהֲרֹן

> Aharon's sons Nadav and Avihu took their fire pans, put fire in them, and placed incense upon it; and they offered unauthorized fire before the LORD, fire He had not commanded. (10:1)

Then there was the counterfire from heaven:

> And fire came forth from before the LORD and consumed them. They died before the LORD. (10:2)

The message is simple and intensely serious: Religion is not what the European Enlightenment thought it would become: mute, marginal, and mild. It is fire – and like fire, it warms but it also burns.

10:2 וַיָּמֻתוּ לִפְנֵי יהוה *They died before the LORD* – The highest virtue for the priest is obedience: doing as God told us to do. Prophets, by contrast, often acted on the spur of the moment. That is what Moshe does when he smashes the tablets on seeing the golden calf.

Why then is spontaneity wrong for Nadav and Avihu, but right for Moshe? overwhelming presence of "there is." That is what Nadav and Avihu forget – that to enter holy space or time requires ontological humility, the total renunciation of human initiative and desire. When we confuse God's will with our will, we turn the holy – the source of life – into something unholy and a source of death.

10:2 וַתֵּצֵא אֵשׁ *And fire came forth* – The story of Nadav and Avihu reminds us yet again of the warning first spelled out in the days of Kayin and Hevel. *The first act of worship led to the first murder* (Gen. 4). Worship generates power, which can be benign but can also be profoundly dangerous.

The episode of Nadav and Avihu is written in three kinds of fire. First there is the fire from heaven:

> And from before the LORD, fire came forth. It consumed the burnt offering. (Lev. 9:24)

This was the fire of favor, consummating the service of the Sanctuary. Then came the "unauthorized fire" offered by the two sons.

or tear your clothes or you will die and bring fury down
upon the whole community. Your brothers, the whole
House of Israel, may mourn the burning that the LORD
7 has brought about. But you must not leave the entrance
to the Tent of Meeting or you will die, for the LORD's
anointing oil is upon you." They did as Moshe had told
them.
8 9 And the LORD spoke to Aharon: "You and your sons must
not drink wine or strong drink when you enter the Tent
of Meeting, so that you do not die. This is an everlasting
10 statute throughout your generations, to enable you to
distinguish between sacred and profane, and between
11 impure and pure, and to teach the Israelites all the statutes
that the LORD has spoken to them through Moshe."

Otherwise it can eventually become a raging inferno, spreading destruction and claiming lives. Intoxication in the arena of the sacred is dangerous. That is why Judaism contains so many laws and so much attention to detail – and the closer we come to God, the more details we need.

10:10 וּבֵין הַטָּמֵא וּבֵין הַטָּהוֹר *Between impure and pure* – The sequence of passages beginning with chapter 11 of Leviticus (toward the end of Parashat Shemini), occupying the whole of Parashot Tazria and Metzora and culminating in chapter 16 (the opening of Parashat Aḥarei Mot), is a tightly organized sequence of laws revolving around the keywords *tameh* and *tahor*, "impure" and "pure." The purity sequence is preceded by a general statement about the role of the priests: "to distinguish between sacred (*kodesh*) and profane (*ḥol*), and between impure (*tameh*) and pure (*tahor*)." That was one of the fundamental priestly duties, to "distinguish," differentiate, and maintain the boundaries between different states and conditions, especially those that had to do with the strict demands of holy space, the Tabernacle, and later, the Temple.

The story of creation tells us that nature is not a blind struggle between contending forces in which the strongest wins and power is the most important gift. To the contrary: The universe is fundamentally good. It is a place of ordered harmony, the intelligible design of a single Creator. That harmony is constantly threatened by mankind. In the covenant with Noaḥ, God establishes a minimum threshold of order for human civilization. In the covenant with Israel, He establishes a higher code of holiness. The principle of holiness, as of creation itself, is the maintenance of boundaries, within which every form of life receives its due.

וּלְאֶלְעָזָ֣ר וּלְאִֽיתָמָ֣ר ׀ בָּנָ֡יו רָאשֵׁיכֶ֣ם אַל־תִּפְרָ֣עוּ ׀ וּבִגְדֵיכֶ֤ם
לֹֽא־תִפְרֹ֙מוּ֙ וְלֹ֣א תָמֻ֔תוּ וְעַ֥ל כָּל־הָעֵדָ֖ה יִקְצֹ֑ף וַאֲחֵיכֶם֙ כָּל־
ז בֵּ֣ית יִשְׂרָאֵ֔ל יִבְכּוּ֙ אֶת־הַשְּׂרֵפָ֔ה אֲשֶׁ֖ר שָׂרַ֥ף יְהוָֽה׃ וּמִפֶּ֩תַח֩
אֹ֨הֶל מוֹעֵ֜ד לֹ֤א תֵֽצְאוּ֙ פֶּן־תָּמֻ֔תוּ כִּי־שֶׁ֛מֶן מִשְׁחַ֥ת יְהוָ֖ה
עֲלֵיכֶ֑ם וַֽיַּעֲשׂ֖וּ כִּדְבַ֥ר מֹשֶֽׁה׃
ח ט וַיְדַבֵּ֣ר יְהוָ֔ה אֶֽל־אַהֲרֹ֖ן לֵאמֹֽר׃ יַ֣יִן וְשֵׁכָ֞ר אַל־תֵּ֣שְׁתְּ ׀ אַתָּ֣ה ׀ ה
וּבָנֶ֣יךָ אִתָּ֔ךְ בְּבֹאֲכֶ֖ם אֶל־אֹ֣הֶל מוֹעֵ֑ד וְלֹ֣א תָמֻ֑תוּ חֻקַּ֥ת עוֹלָ֖ם
י לְדֹרֹתֵיכֶֽם׃ וּֽלְהַבְדִּ֔יל בֵּ֥ין הַקֹּ֖דֶשׁ וּבֵ֣ין הַחֹ֑ל וּבֵ֥ין הַטָּמֵ֖א וּבֵ֥ין
יא הַטָּהֽוֹר׃ וּלְהוֹרֹ֖ת אֶת־בְּנֵ֣י יִשְׂרָאֵ֑ל אֵ֚ת כָּל־הַ֣חֻקִּ֔ים אֲשֶׁ֨ר
דִּבֶּ֧ר יְהוָ֛ה אֲלֵיהֶ֖ם בְּיַד־מֹשֶֽׁה׃

10:9 יַיִן וְשֵׁכָר *Wine or strong drink* – One of the rabbinic explanations of Nadav and Avihu's sin is that they had been drinking alcohol (Vayikra Rabba 12:1). The service of the priests touches upon the highest intensity of relationship with God – yet it requires control, decorum, sobriety.

Nadav and Avihu were "enthusiasts," not in the contemporary sense but in the sense in which the word was used in the seventeenth and eighteenth centuries. Enthusiasts then were people who, full of religious passion, believed that God was inspiring them to do deeds in defiance of law and convention. They were very spiritual but they were also potentially very dangerous. David Hume in particular saw that enthusiasm in this sense is diametrically opposed to the mindset of priesthood. In his words, "All enthusiasts have been free from the yoke of ecclesiastics, and have expressed great independence of devotion; with a contempt of forms, ceremonies, and traditions."

Priests understand the power, and thus the potential danger, of the sacred. That is why holy places, times, and rituals must be guarded with precise rules. To bring unauthorized fire to the Tabernacle might seem a small offense, but a single unauthorized act in the realm of the holy causes a breach in the laws around the sacred that can grow in time to a gaping hole. Enthusiasm, harmless though it might be in some of its manifestations, can quickly become extremism, fanaticism, and religiously motivated violence. As Hume observed, "Human reason and even morality are rejected [by enthusiasts] as fallacious guides, and the fanatic madman delivers himself over blindly" to what he believes to be divine inspiration, but what may in fact be overheated self-importance or frenzied rage.

Precisely because it gives rise to such intense passions, religious life in particular needs the constraints of law and ritual, the entire intricate minuet of worship, so that the fire of faith is contained, giving light and a glimpse of the glory of God.

12 Moshe told Aharon, and Elazar and Itamar, the two sons REVI'I
left to him, "Take the grain offering left over after the fire
offerings to the LORD and eat it unleavened beside the
13 altar, for it is holy of holies. You must eat it in a holy place
because it is your share, and that of your sons, from the
14 LORD's fire offerings, for so I have been commanded. But
you and your sons and daughters may eat the breast of
the wave offering and the thigh of the upraised gift in
any ritually pure place, for these have been given to you
from the peace sacrifices of Israel as your portion and the
15 portion of your children. The thigh for the upraised gift
and the breast for the wave offering are to be brought, with
the fat of the fire offering, to be waved as a wave offering
before the LORD. These are to be your share and that of
your children forever, as the LORD has commanded."
16 Moshe inquired about the goat for the purification ḤAMISHI
offering, and discovered that it had been burned. He
was furious with Elazar and Itamar, the two sons left to
17 Aharon. "Why did you not eat the purification offering
in the holy area?" he asked. "It is holy of holies, and it has
been given to you to remove the guilt of the community
18 and atone for them before the LORD. Because its blood
was not to be brought into the inner Sanctuary, you
should have eaten it in the Sanctuary, as I commanded."
19 It was Aharon who replied to Moshe, "They offered their
purification offering and their burnt offerings before the
LORD today – but such things have happened to me.
Would it really have been right in the LORD's eyes if I had
20 eaten a purification offering today?" Moshe listened; and
it was right in his eyes.

In this exchange between two brothers, a momentous courage is born: the courage of an Aharon who has the strength to grieve and not accept easy consolation, and the courage of a Moshe who has the strength to keep going despite grief. It is almost as if we are present at the birth of an emotional configuration that will characterize the Jewish people in centuries to come. Jews are a people who have had more than their share of suffering. Like Aharon, they did

יב וַיְדַבֵּר מֹשֶׁה אֶל־אַהֲרֹן וְאֶל אֶלְעָזָר וְאֶל־אִיתָמָר ׀ בָּנָיו רביעי
הַנּוֹתָרִים קְחוּ אֶת־הַמִּנְחָה הַנּוֹתֶרֶת מֵאִשֵּׁי יהוה וְאִכְלוּהָ
יג מַצּוֹת אֵצֶל הַמִּזְבֵּחַ כִּי קֹדֶשׁ קָדָשִׁים הִוא: וַאֲכַלְתֶּם אֹתָהּ
בְּמָקוֹם קָדוֹשׁ כִּי חָקְךָ וְחָק־בָּנֶיךָ הִוא מֵאִשֵּׁי יהוה כִּי־כֵן
יד צֻוֵּיתִי: וְאֵת חֲזֵה הַתְּנוּפָה וְאֵת ׀ שׁוֹק הַתְּרוּמָה תֹּאכְלוּ
בְּמָקוֹם טָהוֹר אַתָּה וּבָנֶיךָ וּבְנֹתֶיךָ אִתָּךְ כִּי־חָקְךָ וְחָק־
טו בָּנֶיךָ נִתְּנוּ מִזִּבְחֵי שַׁלְמֵי בְּנֵי יִשְׂרָאֵל: שׁוֹק הַתְּרוּמָה
וַחֲזֵה הַתְּנוּפָה עַל אִשֵּׁי הַחֲלָבִים יָבִיאוּ לְהָנִיף תְּנוּפָה
לִפְנֵי יהוה וְהָיָה לְךָ וּלְבָנֶיךָ אִתְּךָ לְחָק־עוֹלָם כַּאֲשֶׁר צִוָּה
טז יהוה: וְאֵת ׀ שְׂעִיר הַחַטָּאת דָּרֹשׁ דָּרַשׁ מֹשֶׁה וְהִנֵּה שֹׂרָף חמישי
וַיִּקְצֹף עַל־אֶלְעָזָר וְעַל־אִיתָמָר בְּנֵי אַהֲרֹן הַנּוֹתָרִם לֵאמֹר:
יז מַדּוּעַ לֹא־אֲכַלְתֶּם אֶת־הַחַטָּאת בִּמְקוֹם הַקֹּדֶשׁ כִּי קֹדֶשׁ
קָדָשִׁים הִוא וְאֹתָהּ ׀ נָתַן לָכֶם לָשֵׂאת אֶת־עֲוֺן הָעֵדָה
יח לְכַפֵּר עֲלֵיהֶם לִפְנֵי יהוה: הֵן לֹא־הוּבָא אֶת־דָּמָהּ אֶל־
הַקֹּדֶשׁ פְּנִימָה אָכוֹל תֹּאכְלוּ אֹתָהּ בַּקֹּדֶשׁ כַּאֲשֶׁר צִוֵּיתִי:
יט וַיְדַבֵּר אַהֲרֹן אֶל־מֹשֶׁה הֵן הַיּוֹם הִקְרִיבוּ אֶת־חַטָּאתָם
וְאֶת־עֹלָתָם לִפְנֵי יהוה וַתִּקְרֶאנָה אֹתִי כָּאֵלֶּה וְאָכַלְתִּי
כ חַטָּאת הַיּוֹם הַיִּיטַב בְּעֵינֵי יהוה: וַיִּשְׁמַע מֹשֶׁה וַיִּיטַב
בְּעֵינָיו:

10:20 וַיִּשְׁמַע מֹשֶׁה וַיִּיטַב בְּעֵינָיו *Moshe listened; and it was right in his eyes* – Aharon is in a state of grief. But, Moshe implies, Aharon is not simply a private person. He is the High Priest. The people need him to perform his duties, whatever his inner feelings. To this Aharon replies: "Would it really have been right in the Lord's eyes if I had eaten a purification offering today?" (Lev. 10:19). The words are opaque and we can only guess at their precise import. Perhaps they mean this: "I know that in general, a High Priest is forbidden to mourn as if he were an ordinary individual. That is the law, and I accept it. But had I acted on this inaugural day as if nothing had happened, as if my sons had not died, would this not seem to the people as if I were heartless, as if the service of God meant a renunciation of my humanity?" This time, Moshe is silent. Aharon is right, and Moshe knows it.

11 1 The LORD spoke to Moshe and Aharon, saying to them: SHISHI
2 "Tell the Israelites: These are the creatures that you may
3 eat among the land mammals: You may eat any animal
that has divided hoofs, fully split, and chews the cud.
4 Among those that chew the cud or have divided hoofs you
must not eat the following: the camel, because though it
chews the cud, it does not have divided hoofs, and so it
5 is impure for you; the hyrax, though it chews the cud,
does not have divided hoofs and so it is impure for you;
6 the hare, though it chews the cud, does not have divided

> bird or anything that creeps upon the ground that I have set apart (*hivdalti*) from you to regard as impure. Be holy to Me, for I the LORD am holy, and I have set you apart (*vaavdil*) from all other peoples to be My own.

The keywords here are "holy" and *lehavdil*, "to distinguish/set apart." Here we encounter an additional dimension of holiness. *To be holy is to make distinctions, to recognize and honor the divine order of creation.* Originally, according to the Torah, human beings (and animals) were to be vegetarians ("I give you all these seed-bearing plants on the face of the earth and every tree with seed-bearing fruit. They shall be yours to eat" [Gen. 1:29]). After the flood, humanity was permitted to eat meat, with the exception of blood (ch. 9). A concession was made to the human tendency to violence. It is as if God had said: If you must kill, then kill animals, not human beings.

However, the people of Israel were to serve as role models of a higher ideal. They are permitted to kill animals for food, but only those that best exemplify divine order. Amphibians were forbidden because they lack a definite place. Others are forbidden because they lack a clear form – sea creatures that lack a shape defined by fins and scales, and land animals that are not ruminants with clearly defined cloven hoofs. Creatures that prey on others are also forbidden.

The Sanctuary, with its partitions, represents *boundary-making in space*. The dietary laws, with their divisions of permitted and forbidden, represent *boundary-making in life*, in the act of eating, the most natural of human activities. This vision epitomizes the priestly voice within Judaism. It is a vision of great beauty. It sees the world as a place of order in which everything has its place and dignity within the richly differentiated tapestry of creation. To be holy is to be a guardian of that order, a task delegated to us by God. That is both an intellectual and ethical challenge: intellectually, to be able to recognize the boundaries and limits of nature; ethically, to have the humility to preserve and conserve the world for the sake of generations yet to come.

יא א ב וַיְדַבֵּר יְהוָה אֶל־מֹשֶׁה וְאֶל־אַהֲרֹן לֵאמֹר אֲלֵהֶם: דַּבְּרוּ ו ששי
אֶל־בְּנֵי יִשְׂרָאֵל לֵאמֹר זֹאת הַחַיָּה אֲשֶׁר תֹּאכְלוּ מִכׇּל־
ג הַבְּהֵמָה אֲשֶׁר עַל־הָאָרֶץ: כֹּל ׀ מַפְרֶסֶת פַּרְסָה וְשֹׁסַעַת
ד שֶׁסַע פְּרָסֹת מַעֲלַת גֵּרָה בַּבְּהֵמָה אֹתָהּ תֹּאכֵלוּ: אַךְ אֶת־זֶה
לֹא תֹאכְלוּ מִמַּעֲלֵי הַגֵּרָה וּמִמַּפְרִסֵי הַפַּרְסָה אֶת־הַגָּמָל
כִּי־מַעֲלֵה גֵרָה הוּא וּפַרְסָה אֵינֶנּוּ מַפְרִיס טָמֵא הוּא לָכֶם:
ה וְאֶת־הַשָּׁפָן כִּי־מַעֲלֵה גֵרָה הוּא וּפַרְסָה לֹא יַפְרִיס טָמֵא
ו הוּא לָכֶם: וְאֶת־הָאַרְנֶבֶת כִּי־מַעֲלַת גֵּרָה הִוא וּפַרְסָה לֹא

not lose their humanity. But neither did they lose their capacity to continue, to carry on, to hope. Like Moshe, they never lost faith in God. But like Aharon, they never allowed that faith to anaesthetize their feelings, their human vulnerability.

That, it seems to me, is what happened to the Jewish people after the Holocaust. There were, and are, no words to silence the grief or end the tears. Yet, like Moshe, the Jewish people found the strength to continue, to reaffirm hope in the face of despair. A mere three years after coming eye to eye with the angel of death, the Jewish people, by establishing the State of Israel, made the single most powerful affirmation in two thousand years that *am Yisrael ḥai,* the Jewish people lives.

Faith does not render us invulnerable to tragedy, but it gives us the strength to mourn and then, despite everything, to carry on.

THE DIETARY LAWS

Many explanations have been given of the Torah's dietary laws. Some see them as rules of hygiene. Others see them as a discipline of self-restraint. In the words of the talmudic sage Rav: "The commandments were given to refine human beings" (Bereshit Rabba 44:1). Yet others see in them a set of laws that have no logic other than the fact that they were given by God. However, the simplest explanation is the one given here by the Torah itself:

> I am the Lord your God. Consecrate yourselves and be holy, for I am holy.... I am the Lord, who brought you up out of Egypt to be your God. Be holy, for I am holy...to distinguish (*lehavdil*) between the impure and the pure and between creatures that may be eaten and those that may not. (Lev. 11:44–47)

A similar statement appears later in Leviticus (20:24–26):

> I am the Lord your God, who has set you apart (*hivdalti*) from all other peoples. You, then, shall set pure apart (*vehivdaltem*) from impure animals, pure from impure birds. Do not make yourselves detestable by an animal or

7 hoofs and so it is impure for you; the pig, though it has
fully divided hoofs, does not chew the cud and so it is
8 impure for you. You may not eat the flesh of these animals
9 or touch their carcasses; they are impure for you. These
you may eat among the creatures of the water: anything
in the water, whether in sea or in stream, that has fins and
10 scales may be eaten, whereas anything in the sea or the
stream that does not have fins and scales, whether one
of the swarming creatures of the water or any other of
11 living creature there, is detestable to you and will remain
so. You may not eat their flesh, and you shall detest their
12 carcasses. Anything in the water that does not have fins or
13 scales is detestable to you. Among the birds, the following
you shall regard as detestable – being detested they shall
not be eaten: the griffon vulture, the bearded vulture,
14 the lappet-faced vulture, the kite, any kind of buzzard,
15 16 any kind of raven, the ostrich, the swallow, the gull, any
17 kind of sparrow hawk, the little owl, the cormorant, the
18 short-eared owl, the barn owl, the pelican, the Egyptian
19 vulture, the stork, any kind of heron, the hoopoe, and
20 the bat. All swarming, flying creatures that crawl on
21 fours are detestable to you, but you may eat those
swarming, flying creatures that crawl on four legs, with
legs jointed above their feet with which they hop on the
22 ground. Of these you may eat the following: any kind of
23 locust, bald locust, cricket, or grasshopper. Every other
swarming, flying, crawling creature on fours is detestable
24 to you. You become impure through these: whoever
touches their carcasses shall be impure until evening,
25 and whoever moves their carcasses shall immerse his
26 clothes and be impure until evening. All livestock with
divided hoofs that are not completely split, or that do
not chew the cud, are impure for you; whoever touches

means "the compassionate one." How can a bird called "compassion" possibly be unclean? They answered: The *ḥasida* has compassion only for its own kind. Compassion only for your own is not compassion.

ז הִפְרִ֑יסָה טְמֵאָ֥ה הִ֖וא לָכֶֽם׃ וְֽאֶת־הַֽחֲזִ֡יר כִּֽי־מַפְרִ֨יס פַּרְסָ֜ה
ה֗וּא וְשֹׁסַ֥ע שֶׁ֙סַע֙ פַּרְסָ֔ה וְה֖וּא גֵּרָ֣ה לֹֽא־יִגָּ֑ר טָמֵ֥א ה֖וּא
ח לָכֶֽם׃ מִבְּשָׂרָם֙ לֹ֣א תֹאכֵ֔לוּ וּבְנִבְלָתָ֖ם לֹ֣א תִגָּ֑עוּ טְמֵאִ֥ים הֵ֖ם
ט לָכֶֽם׃ אֶת־זֶה֙ תֹּֽאכְל֔וּ מִכֹּ֖ל אֲשֶׁ֣ר בַּמָּ֑יִם כֹּ֣ל אֲשֶׁר־לוֹ֩ סְנַפִּ֨יר
י וְקַשְׂקֶ֜שֶׂת בַּמַּ֗יִם בַּיַּמִּ֛ים וּבַנְּחָלִ֖ים אֹתָ֥ם תֹּאכֵֽלוּ׃ וְכֹל֩ אֲשֶׁ֨ר
אֵֽין־ל֜וֹ סְנַפִּ֣יר וְקַשְׂקֶ֗שֶׂת בַּיַּמִּים֙ וּבַנְּחָלִ֔ים מִכֹּל֙ שֶׁ֣רֶץ הַמַּ֔יִם
יא וּמִכֹּ֛ל נֶ֥פֶשׁ הַֽחַיָּ֖ה אֲשֶׁ֣ר בַּמָּ֑יִם שֶׁ֥קֶץ הֵ֖ם לָכֶֽם׃ וְשֶׁ֖קֶץ יִהְי֣וּ
יב לָכֶ֑ם מִבְּשָׂרָם֙ לֹ֣א תֹאכֵ֔לוּ וְאֶת־נִבְלָתָ֖ם תְּשַׁקֵּֽצוּ׃ כֹּ֣ל אֲשֶׁ֥ר
יג אֵֽין־ל֛וֹ סְנַפִּ֥יר וְקַשְׂקֶ֖שֶׂת בַּמָּ֑יִם שֶׁ֥קֶץ ה֖וּא לָכֶֽם׃ וְאֶת־אֵ֙לֶּה֙
תְּשַׁקְּצ֣וּ מִן־הָע֔וֹף לֹ֥א יֵאָכְל֖וּ שֶׁ֣קֶץ הֵ֑ם אֶת־הַנֶּ֙שֶׁר֙ וְאֶת־
יד טו הַפֶּ֔רֶס וְאֵ֖ת הָעָזְנִיָּֽה׃ וְאֶת־הַדָּאָ֔ה וְאֶת־הָאַיָּ֖ה לְמִינָֽהּ׃ אֵ֥ת
טז כָּל־עֹרֵ֖ב לְמִינֽוֹ׃ וְאֵת֙ בַּ֣ת הַֽיַּעֲנָ֔ה וְאֶת־הַתַּחְמָ֖ס וְאֶת־הַשָּׁ֑חַף
יז וְאֶת־הַנֵּ֖ץ לְמִינֵֽהוּ׃ וְאֶת־הַכּ֥וֹס וְאֶת־הַשָּׁלָ֖ךְ וְאֶת־הַיַּנְשֽׁוּף׃
יח יט וְאֶת־הַתִּנְשֶׁ֥מֶת וְאֶת־הַקָּאָ֖ת וְאֶת־הָרָחָֽם׃ וְאֵת֙ הַחֲסִידָ֔ה
כ הָאֲנָפָ֖ה לְמִינָ֑הּ וְאֶת־הַדּֽוּכִיפַ֖ת וְאֶת־הָעֲטַלֵּֽף׃ כֹּ֚ל שֶׁ֣רֶץ
כא הָע֔וֹף הַהֹלֵ֖ךְ עַל־אַרְבַּ֑ע שֶׁ֥קֶץ ה֖וּא לָכֶֽם׃ אַ֣ךְ אֶת־זֶה֙ תֹּֽאכְל֔וּ
מִכֹּל֙ שֶׁ֣רֶץ הָע֔וֹף הַהֹלֵ֖ךְ עַל־אַרְבַּ֑ע אֲשֶׁר־לֹ֤א כְרָעַ֙יִם֙ מִמַּ֣עַל לוֹ
כב לְרַגְלָ֔יו לְנַתֵּ֥ר בָּהֵ֖ן עַל־הָאָֽרֶץ׃ אֶת־אֵ֤לֶּה מֵהֶם֙ תֹּאכֵ֔לוּ אֶת־
הָֽאַרְבֶּ֣ה לְמִינ֔וֹ וְאֶת־הַסָּלְעָ֖ם לְמִינֵ֑הוּ וְאֶת־הַחַרְגֹּ֣ל לְמִינֵ֔הוּ
כג וְאֶת־הֶחָגָ֖ב לְמִינֵֽהוּ׃ וְכֹל֙ שֶׁ֣רֶץ הָע֔וֹף אֲשֶׁר־ל֖וֹ אַרְבַּ֣ע רַגְלָ֑יִם
כד שֶׁ֥קֶץ ה֖וּא לָכֶֽם׃ וּלְאֵ֖לֶּה תִּטַּמָּ֑אוּ כָּל־הַנֹּגֵ֥עַ בְּנִבְלָתָ֖ם יִטְמָ֥א
כה עַד־הָעָֽרֶב׃ וְכָל־הַנֹּשֵׂ֖א מִנִּבְלָתָ֑ם יְכַבֵּ֥ס בְּגָדָ֖יו וְטָמֵ֥א עַד־
כו הָעָֽרֶב׃ לְכָֽל־הַבְּהֵמָ֡ה אֲשֶׁ֣ר הִוא֩ מַפְרֶ֨סֶת פַּרְסָ֜ה וְשֶׁ֣סַע ׀
אֵינֶ֣נָּה שֹׁסַ֗עַת וְגֵרָה֙ אֵינֶ֣נָּה מַעֲלָ֔ה טְמֵאִ֥ים הֵ֖ם לָכֶ֑ם כָּל־

11:19 הַחֲסִידָה *The stork* – Ramban links the laws of *kashrut* to the characteristics of different groups of animals. We eat tame herbivores but not predators, because we are affected by what we eat. The Jewish mystics once asked: Why, then, is the *ḥasida*, the stork, an unclean animal? Its name in Hebrew literally

27 them becomes impure. Among four-footed animals, all
those that walk on their paws are impure for you; anyone
touching their carcasses shall be impure until evening.
28 One who moves their carcasses shall immerse his clothes
and be impure until evening; these animals are impure
29 for you. Among the creatures that creep along
the ground, the following are impure for you: the ferret,
30 the mouse, every kind of spiny-tailed lizard, the legless
lizard, the chameleon, the lizard, the skink, and the mole
31 rat. Of all the creatures that creep along the ground, these
are impure for you; whoever touches them when they are
32 dead shall be impure until evening. And if any of these SHEVI'I
dies and falls on something – a wooden vessel, clothing,
leather goods or sackcloth, any utensil with which work is
done – it renders it impure. The article must be immersed
in water and then remains impure until evening, when it
33 will become pure again. If any of these falls into a pottery
jar, everything inside it becomes impure; you must
34 smash the pot. Edible food becomes impure in such a jar
if water has been poured over; any drinkable beverage in
35 such a jar becomes impure. Anything on which a part of
one of their dead bodies falls becomes impure. If it is an
oven or stove, it must be broken into pieces; it is impure
36 for you and will remain so. A spring or cistern holding
water remains pure, but anyone who touches one of their
37 dead bodies in it becomes impure. If any part of their
dead bodies falls on seed that has been planted, the seed
38 remains pure. But if water has been poured over the seed
and afterward any part of their dead bodies falls upon it,
39 it is rendered impure for you. If an animal of a
kind that you are allowed to eat dies naturally, one who
40 touches its carcass shall be impure until evening. Anyone
who eats of its carcass must immerse his clothes, and he
remains impure until evening. Anyone who moves the
carcass must immerse his clothes, and he remains impure
41 until evening. All creatures that swarm on the earth are
42 detested; they shall not be eaten. Of these swarming

כז הַנֹּגֵעַ בָּהֶם יִטְמָא׃ וְכֹל ׀ הוֹלֵךְ עַל־כַּפָּיו בְּכָל־הַחַיָּה הַהֹלֶכֶת
עַל־אַרְבַּע טְמֵאִים הֵם לָכֶם כָּל־הַנֹּגֵעַ בְּנִבְלָתָם יִטְמָא עַד־
כח הָעָרֶב׃ וְהַנֹּשֵׂא אֶת־נִבְלָתָם יְכַבֵּס בְּגָדָיו וְטָמֵא עַד־הָעָרֶב
כט טְמֵאִים הֵמָּה לָכֶם׃ וְזֶה לָכֶם הַטָּמֵא בַּשֶּׁרֶץ
ל הַשֹּׁרֵץ עַל־הָאָרֶץ הַחֹלֶד וְהָעַכְבָּר וְהַצָּב לְמִינֵהוּ׃ וְהָאֲנָקָה
לא וְהַכֹּחַ וְהַלְּטָאָה וְהַחֹמֶט וְהַתִּנְשָׁמֶת׃ אֵלֶּה הַטְּמֵאִים לָכֶם
לב בְּכָל־הַשָּׁרֶץ כָּל־הַנֹּגֵעַ בָּהֶם בְּמֹתָם יִטְמָא עַד־הָעָרֶב׃ וְכֹל
אֲשֶׁר־יִפֹּל עָלָיו מֵהֶם ׀ בְּמֹתָם יִטְמָא מִכָּל־כְּלִי־עֵץ אוֹ בֶגֶד
אוֹ־עוֹר אוֹ שָׂק כָּל־כְּלִי אֲשֶׁר־יֵעָשֶׂה מְלָאכָה בָּהֶם בַּמַּיִם
לג יוּבָא וְטָמֵא עַד־הָעֶרֶב וְטָהֵר׃ וְכָל־כְּלִי־חֶרֶשׂ אֲשֶׁר־יִפֹּל שביעי
לד מֵהֶם אֶל־תּוֹכוֹ כֹּל אֲשֶׁר בְּתוֹכוֹ יִטְמָא וְאֹתוֹ תִשְׁבֹּרוּ׃ מִכָּל־
הָאֹכֶל אֲשֶׁר יֵאָכֵל אֲשֶׁר יָבוֹא עָלָיו מַיִם יִטְמָא וְכָל־מַשְׁקֶה
לה אֲשֶׁר יִשָּׁתֶה בְּכָל־כְּלִי יִטְמָא׃ וְכֹל אֲשֶׁר־יִפֹּל מִנִּבְלָתָם ׀
עָלָיו יִטְמָא תַּנּוּר וְכִירַיִם יֻתָּץ טְמֵאִים הֵם וּטְמֵאִים יִהְיוּ
לו לָכֶם׃ אַךְ מַעְיָן וּבוֹר מִקְוֵה־מַיִם יִהְיֶה טָהוֹר וְנֹגֵעַ בְּנִבְלָתָם
לז יִטְמָא׃ וְכִי יִפֹּל מִנִּבְלָתָם עַל־כָּל־זֶרַע זֵרוּעַ אֲשֶׁר יִזָּרֵעַ טָהוֹר
לח הוּא׃ וְכִי יֻתַּן־מַיִם עַל־זֶרַע וְנָפַל מִנִּבְלָתָם עָלָיו טָמֵא הוּא
לט לָכֶם׃ וְכִי יָמוּת מִן־הַבְּהֵמָה אֲשֶׁר־הִיא לָכֶם
מ לְאָכְלָה הַנֹּגֵעַ בְּנִבְלָתָהּ יִטְמָא עַד־הָעָרֶב׃ וְהָאֹכֵל מִנִּבְלָתָהּ
יְכַבֵּס בְּגָדָיו וְטָמֵא עַד־הָעָרֶב וְהַנֹּשֵׂא אֶת־נִבְלָתָהּ יְכַבֵּס
מא בְּגָדָיו וְטָמֵא עַד־הָעָרֶב׃ וְכָל־הַשֶּׁרֶץ הַשֹּׁרֵץ עַל־הָאָרֶץ
מב שֶׁקֶץ הוּא לֹא יֵאָכֵל׃ כֹּל הוֹלֵךְ עַל־גָּחוֹן וְכֹל ׀ הוֹלֵךְ עַל־

things you shall not eat any, those that move on their
bellies or crawl on all fours or on many feet – for they
43 are all detestable. Do not make yourselves detestable by
contact with any of these swarming creatures. Do not
44 defile yourselves with them or be defiled by them. I am
the Lord your God. Consecrate yourselves and be holy,
for I am holy. Do not defile yourselves with any swarming
45 creature that crawls on the ground. I am the Lord, who MAFTIR
brought you up out of Egypt to be your God. Be holy,
46 for I am holy." This is the law concerning animals, birds,
all creatures that live in water and all that swarm on the
47 earth, to distinguish between the impure and the pure
and between creatures that may be eaten and those that
may not.

The haftara for Parashat Shemini is on page 1518.
On the Shabbat of Parashat HaḤodesh read the haftara on page 1666.

most overt example of a much broader principle: we cannot apply Torah to the world unless we understand the world.

To fully apply the Torah's dietary laws, we need an understanding of zoology. To apply Torah to the human mind, one must understand psychology and psychiatry. To apply it to society, we must understand sociology and anthropology. To cure poverty, we must understand economics. To avoid environmental catastrophe, we need to understand botany, biology, climatology, and much else besides. All these things come under the general heading of *ḥokhma,* "wisdom," which I define as the knowledge that helps us see the universe as God's work and the human person as God's image – in other words, the sciences and humanities broadly conceived.

There was a time when a purely instrumental reason was given for Jews pursuing secular studies. You needed it to get a job and earn a living. The Sages gave another reason. It gave Jews, and by implication Judaism, respect in the eyes of the world. There was a deeper reason still. It allowed us to see the wisdom of God's creation. It led, said Rambam, to the love and fear of God. I have argued that within the logic of Judaism as a whole, there is another reason. To realize the Torah's vision we need *ḥokhma.* To repair the world, you have to understand it.

אַרְבַּע עַד כָּל־מַרְבֵּה רַגְלַיִם לְכָל־הַשֶּׁרֶץ הַשֹּׁרֵץ עַל־הָאָרֶץ
מג לֹא תֹאכְלוּם כִּי־שֶׁקֶץ הֵם׃ אַל־תְּשַׁקְּצוּ אֶת־נַפְשֹׁתֵיכֶם
מד בְּכָל־הַשֶּׁרֶץ הַשֹּׁרֵץ וְלֹא תִטַּמְּאוּ בָּהֶם וְנִטְמֵתֶם בָּם׃ כִּי
אֲנִי יהוה אֱלֹהֵיכֶם וְהִתְקַדִּשְׁתֶּם וִהְיִיתֶם קְדֹשִׁים כִּי קָדוֹשׁ
אָנִי וְלֹא תְטַמְּאוּ אֶת־נַפְשֹׁתֵיכֶם בְּכָל־הַשֶּׁרֶץ הָרֹמֵשׂ עַל־
מה הָאָרֶץ׃ כִּי ׀ אֲנִי יהוה הַמַּעֲלֶה אֶתְכֶם מֵאֶרֶץ מִצְרַיִם לִהְיֹת מפטיר
מו לָכֶם לֵאלֹהִים וִהְיִיתֶם קְדֹשִׁים כִּי קָדוֹשׁ אָנִי׃ זֹאת תּוֹרַת
הַבְּהֵמָה וְהָעוֹף וְכֹל נֶפֶשׁ הַחַיָּה הָרֹמֶשֶׂת בַּמָּיִם וּלְכָל־נֶפֶשׁ
מז הַשֹּׁרֶצֶת עַל־הָאָרֶץ׃ לְהַבְדִּיל בֵּין הַטָּמֵא וּבֵין הַטָּהֹר וּבֵין
הַחַיָּה הַנֶּאֱכֶלֶת וּבֵין הַחַיָּה אֲשֶׁר לֹא תֵאָכֵל׃

The הפטרה *for* פרשת שמיני *is on page 1519.*
On the שבת *of* פרשת החודש *read the* הפטרה *on page 1667.*

11:44 וִהְיִיתֶם קְדֹשִׁים כִּי קָדוֹשׁ אָנִי *Be holy, for I am holy* – Eating and procreation are the most primal activities, shared with most other forms of life. Without sexual relations there is no continuation of the species. Without food, even the individual cannot survive. These have been approached in radically different ways by human cultures.

On the one hand, there are hedonistic cultures in which food and sexuality are seen as pleasures and pursued as such. On the other are ascetic cultures – marked by monastic seclusion – in which sexual relations are avoided and eating kept to a minimum. The former emphasize the body, the latter the soul.

Judaism, by contrast, sees the human situation in terms of integration and balance. We are body *and* soul. Hence the Judaic imperative, neither hedonistic nor ascetic, but transformative: we are commanded to *sanctify* both eating and sexual relations. From this flow the dietary laws and the laws of family purity (*nidda* and *mikveh*), two key elements of *kedusha*, the life of holiness. Here we have discussed eating; we will turn to family purity in the coming *parashot.*

11:46 זֹאת תּוֹרַת הַבְּהֵמָה וְהָעוֹף וְכֹל נֶפֶשׁ הַחַיָּה *This is the law concerning… all creatures* – We owe our translations of the species listed here to the scholarship of natural historians such as Yehuda Feliks and Zohar Amar. This passage is perhaps the

Parashat Tazria

12 1 2 The Lord spoke to Moshe: "Tell the Israelites: If a woman
conceives and gives birth to a son, she shall be impure for
3 seven days, as she is during her menstrual period. On the
4 eighth day, the child's foreskin shall be circumcised. For
thirty-three days she shall wait, bleeding pure blood, but

---

of the answer, but there may be a way of understanding the command in the wider context of the Torah as a whole.

To see why this might be, we must look back to the first book of the Torah, Genesis. What makes the patriarchs different? How do Avraham and his family mark a new beginning? The book, as we noted there, gives us an inescapable clue. Whenever a member of the covenantal family finds him- or herself entering another society, there is always a moment of danger – and the danger is always rooted in an absence of sexual ethics. There are six such episodes: Sara and then Rivka (twice) are threatened with being abducted into a royal harem because of their beauty; two visitors come to Lot's house in Sedom and the local populace threatens to rape them; Dina is raped by the local prince, Shekhem. Finally, Potifar's wife attempts to seduce Yosef and falsely accuses him of rape.

Hence the conclusion that a key difference between the matriarchs and patriarchs of Genesis and their neighbors was their sexual ethics. Note that the problem is violence around sexuality, and the abuse of power, rather than sexuality itself. When some humans became richer and more powerful than others, kings, rulers, and pharaohs – human alpha males – could command almost open-ended gratification of sexual desire, hence Avraham and Yitzḥak's fears that they would be killed so that their wives could be taken into a harem.

The Torah views this cluster of behaviors with abhorrence. Such behavior privileges some people against others. It turns women into instruments of male desire. It places power, not love, at the heart of human relationships. It treats women as objects rather than as subjects with equal dignity and integrity. It divorces sex from compassion and dishonors the most intimate human bond.

Now we understand why the sign of the covenant is circumcision. *Brit mila* is the consecration of sexual desire. Our instincts are not evil in themselves. The religious life is not a matter of self-denial and renunciation. But neither is it hedonism, the unrestrained pursuit of pleasure. Instinct has its darker side, which culminates in violence. For faith to be more than the worship of power, it must affect the most intimate relationship between men and women. In a society founded on covenant, male-female relationships

פרשת תזריע

יב א ב וַיְדַבֵּר יְהוָה אֶל־מֹשֶׁה לֵּאמֹר: דַּבֵּר אֶל־בְּנֵי יִשְׂרָאֵל לֵאמֹר ז
אִשָּׁה כִּי תַזְרִיעַ וְיָלְדָה זָכָר וְטָמְאָה שִׁבְעַת יָמִים כִּימֵי נִדַּת
ג ד דְּוֺתָהּ תִּטְמָא: וּבַיּוֹם הַשְּׁמִינִי יִמּוֹל בְּשַׂר עָרְלָתוֹ: וּשְׁלֹשִׁים

TAZRIA

Parashat Tazria continues the laws of purity and impurity begun in Parashat Shemini. One of the key roles of the priest was to distinguish *tahor* from *tameh*, pure from impure, the latter debarring an individual from entering the sacred space of the Sanctuary.

These categories flow from the contrast between God and human beings. God is immortal; humans are mortal. God is spiritual; humans are also physical. And whatever is physical is subject to disease and decay. Conditions that render a person *tameh* are those that testify to our mortality and physicality. People who had a reminder of mortality in ways specified by the Torah may not enter holy space until they are healed and purified.

The *parasha* begins with laws relating to childbirth – the impurity it brings, and also the command to circumcise a male child on the eighth day. It continues with laws relating to a still-unidentified disease, *tzaraat*, often translated as leprosy, but referring to something other and larger than the disease because it affects not only people but also clothes and houses. The *parasha* describes some of the symptoms, which may appear following a skin inflammation. It is the task of the priest to examine such symptoms, declaring the person clean or unclean or to be quarantined until a clearer diagnosis can be made. The Sages see *tzaraat* as a punishment for the sin of evil speech.

CIRCUMCISION

Parashat Tazria opens with the command that, for males, is the distinguishing mark of Jewish identity: circumcision. The question arises: Why this sign above all others? Why a physical mark on the flesh, and why this part of the flesh? What does it tell us about the nature of Jewish identity?

There is no explicit answer to these questions in the Torah, and the commentators offer several explanations. According to Midrash Sekhel Tov (on Gen. 17:11) and *Sefer HaḤinukh* (positive command 2), it serves as an outward sign to differentiate Jews from gentiles. It is like the other signs such as tzitzit, tefillin, and mezuza, different in that it is actually a part of one's body. Rambam (*Guide for the Perplexed* III:49) explains that it is a unifying mark that identifies Jews as part of a nation. Ramban (on Gen. 17:11) sees it as a way of conferring *kedusha*, sanctity, on the act of procreation.

Each of these is an important part

until her time of purification is completed, she must not
5 touch anything holy or enter the Sanctuary. If she gives
birth to a daughter, she shall be impure – as she is during
her menstrual period – for two weeks, and bleeds in purity
6 for sixty-six days. When the days of her purification are
complete, whether for a son or a daughter, she shall bring
a yearling sheep to the priest at the entrance to the Tent
of Meeting as a burnt offering and a pigeon or dove as a

As we have noted, the Tabernacle, and later the Temple, were symbols of the presence of God within the human domain. God is eternal and spiritual. We and the universe are physical, and whatever is physical is subject to birth, growth, decline, decay, and death. It is these things that must be excluded from the Sanctuary if we are to have the experience of standing in the presence of eternity.

What bars us, therefore, from entering the holy is anything that reminds us or others of our mortality. Hence the supreme source of impurity is death: contact with or proximity to a dead body. Paradoxically, childbirth defiles, even though it represents new life. The reason may be that until recently, it was a hazard fraught with the risk of death. Many babies were stillborn, many died young, and many mothers died giving birth. The very loss of blood was dangerous. So childbirth may render one impure because it is an encounter with the risk of death. Alternatively, it may simply be that it defiles because it is a reminder of the passing of the generations. Birth, like death, is a signal of mortality. The Tabernacle, and later the Temple, is the space set aside for consciousness of eternity.

12:6 וּבִמְלֹאת יְמֵי טָהֳרָהּ *When the days of her purification are complete* – There is a halakhic principle: "One who is engaged in a mitzva is exempt from other *mitzvot*" (Sukka 25a). It is as if God were saying to the mother: "For forty days in the case of a boy, and doubly so in the case of a girl (for the daughter herself contains the potential to beget and nurture future life), I exempt you from coming before Me in the place of holiness because you are fully engaged in one of the holiest acts of all, nurturing and caring for your child. Unlike others, you do not need to visit the Temple to be attached to life in all its sacred splendor. You are experiencing it yourself, directly and with every fiber of your being. Days, weeks, from now you will come and give thanks before Me (together with offerings for having come through a moment of danger). But for now, look upon your child with wonder." Childbirth exempts the new mother from attendance at the Temple because her bedside replicates the experience of the Temple. She knows what it is for love to beget life and in the midst of mortality to be touched by an intimation of immortality.

יוֹם וּשְׁלֹשֶׁת יָמִים תֵּשֵׁב בִּדְמֵי טָהֳרָה בְּכָל־קֹדֶשׁ לֹא־תִגָּע
ה וְאֶל־הַמִּקְדָּשׁ לֹא תָבֹא עַד־מְלֹאת יְמֵי טָהֳרָהּ: וְאִם־נְקֵבָה
תֵלֵד וְטָמְאָה שְׁבֻעַיִם כְּנִדָּתָהּ וְשִׁשִּׁים יוֹם וְשֵׁשֶׁת יָמִים
ו תֵּשֵׁב עַל־דְּמֵי טָהֳרָה: וּבִמְלֹאת ׀ יְמֵי טָהֳרָהּ לְבֵן אוֹ לְבַת
תָּבִיא כֶּבֶשׂ בֶּן־שְׁנָתוֹ לְעֹלָה וּבֶן־יוֹנָה אוֹ־תֹר לְחַטָּאת

must be built on something other and gentler than male dominance, masculine power, sexual desire, and the drive to own, control, possess. The alpha male must become the caring husband. Sex must be sanctified and tempered by mutual respect. The sexual drive must be circumcised and circumscribed so that it no longer seeks to possess and is instead content to love.

12:3 יִמּוֹל בְּשַׂר עָרְלָתוֹ *The child's foreskin shall be circumcised* – Why is the commandment of *brit mila*, already given to Avraham, repeated here? Rambam gives an explanation in his commentary on the Mishna (Ḥullin 7:6). Although Avraham was given the command of circumcision as the sign of God's covenant with him, the covenant God made with the Israelites at Mount Sinai superseded all previous commands. Therefore, our performing circumcision today is not because of the command to Avraham, but because it was repeated as part of the covenant at Sinai. The command is historically linked with Avraham but legislatively with the revelation to Moshe.

OFFERINGS AFTER CHILDBIRTH

The laws at the start of this *parasha*, about the sacrifices brought by a woman who has given birth, have challenged and puzzled the commentators. We could easily understand if she had to bring a thanksgiving offering. But instead she must bring a burnt offering, together with a purification offering. Why does she need atonement? Here are some of the suggestions of the commentators:

Ibn Ezra (on Lev. 21:6) says that during the anguish of labor, the woman may have thought or expressed ideas that were sinful or that she now regrets (such as vowing not to have future relations with her husband). Ramban (on Lev. 12:7) explains that the sacrifices are a kind of "ransom" for having survived the dangers of childbirth, as well as a form of prayer for a full recovery. Rabbi Meir Simḥa of Dvinsk suggests that the burnt offering is like an *olat re'iya*, an offering brought when appearing at the Temple on festivals. The woman thus celebrates her ability to appear before God at the Temple (*Meshekh Ḥokhma* on Lev. 12:6).

Without displacing any of these ideas, we might suggest another perspective. This is related to the words *tameh* and *tahor*, impure and pure. *Tameh* does not mean "defiled." It is a technical term referring to people being in a condition that prevents them from entering the Tabernacle or Temple. *Tahor* means the opposite, that they may enter.

7 purification offering. The priest shall present it before the
LORD and make atonement for her; so shall she be purified
of her source of blood." This is the law for a woman who
8 bears a child, male or female. "But if she cannot afford
a sheep, she may bring two doves or two pigeons – one
for the burnt offering and the other for the purification
offering. The priest will then make atonement for her, and
she shall be pure."

---

would offer a sacrifice after the birth of a child (Lev. 12:6–8). No record exists of a formal prayer offered on such occasions; there may have been no fixed text. Ḥana's prayer after the birth of Shmuel (I Sam. 2:1–10) is, however, a powerful example of such a song of thanksgiving. Ritual is what we use to declare the sanctity of life and its milestones. It gives public, collective expression to one of the essential underpinnings of morality.

12:8 אֶחָד לְעֹלָה *One for the burnt offering* – This offering is a reminder of *akedat Yitzḥak* (the binding of Yitzḥak), and of the animal sacrificed in his place (Gen. 22:13). I argued there that *akedat Yitzḥak* was intended as a protest against the absolute power parents had over children in the ancient world – *patria potestas*, as it was called in Roman law. The child was regarded as the property of his parents. A father had total legal power over a child, even to the extent of life and death.

The Torah makes an implicit comment on this in its account of the name given to the first human child. Ḥava called him Kayin – from the Hebrew meaning "ownership" – saying, "With the LORD's help I have made [literally, 'acquired'] a man" (4:1). Treat your child as a possession and you may inadvertently turn him into a murderer, the text implies.

The narrative of the binding of Yitzḥak is a statement that parents do not own their children. The story of Yitzḥak's birth also points in that direction. He was born when Sara was already post-menopausal (18:11), incapable of having a child naturally. Yitzḥak was clearly a special gift of God. As the first Jewish child, he became the precedent for subsequent generations. The binding was intended to establish that children belong to God. Parents are merely their guardians. The same idea lies behind the ritual of the redemption of the firstborn.

In similar fashion, Ḥana dedicated her child, Shmuel, to God (I Sam. 1), as did the wife of Manoaḥ, mother of Shimshon (Judges 13). In each case, the mother brought a burnt offering, as did Avraham, in lieu of the child. By so doing she acknowledged that she was not the owner of the child, merely its guardian. In bringing the offering it was as if she had said: "God, I know I should dedicate this child entirely to Your service. Please accept this offering in his place."

ז אֶל־פֶּ֥תַח אֹֽהֶל־מוֹעֵ֖ד אֶל־הַכֹּהֵֽן׃ וְהִקְרִיב֞וֹ לִפְנֵ֤י יהוה֙ וְכִפֶּ֣ר
עָלֶ֔יהָ וְטָהֲרָ֖ה מִמְּקֹ֣ר דָּמֶ֑יהָ זֹ֤את תּוֹרַת֙ הַיֹּלֶ֔דֶת לַזָּכָ֖ר א֥וֹ
ח לַנְּקֵבָֽה׃ וְאִם־לֹ֨א תִמְצָ֣א יָדָהּ֮ דֵּ֣י שֶׂה֒ וְלָקְחָ֣ה שְׁתֵּֽי־תֹרִ֗ים
א֤וֹ שְׁנֵי֙ בְּנֵ֣י יוֹנָ֔ה אֶחָ֥ד לְעֹלָ֖ה וְאֶחָ֣ד לְחַטָּ֑את וְכִפֶּ֥ר עָלֶ֛יהָ
הַכֹּהֵ֖ן וְטָהֵֽרָה׃

12:7 זֹאת תּוֹרַת הַיֹּלֶדֶת *The law for a woman who bears a child* – It is common to divide the religious life in Judaism into two dimensions. On the one side, the priesthood and the Sanctuary, and on the other, the prophets and the people. The priests focused on the relationship between the people and God, *mitzvot bein adam laMakom*. Prophets focused on the relationship between the people and one another, *mitzvot bein adam leḥavero*. The priests supervised ritual and the prophets spoke about ethics. One group was concerned with holiness, the other with virtue. You don't need to be holy to be good. You need to be good to be holy, but that is an entrance requirement, not what being holy is about. Pharaoh's daughter, who rescued Moshe when he was a baby, was good but not holy. These are two separate ideas.

I would like to challenge that conception. The prophetic virtues of *ḥesed* and *mishpat* are close to those that prevail today in the liberal democracies of the West – kindness, or protection from harm, and fairness. That is a measure of the impact of the Hebrew Bible on the West, but that is another story for another time. The point is that kindness and fairness are about relationships between individuals. The priesthood and the Sanctuary, however, also made a moral difference. The priestly values of loyalty, respect, and sanctity, though frequently neglected in secularized societies, have been shown to be important, even essential, in sustaining community over time.

Sanctity involves the need to ring-fence certain values we regard as non-negotiable. They are not mine to do with as I wish. These are the things we call *sacred*, sacrosanct, not to be treated lightly or defiled. Reverence is what gives power to social conventions, civilities, ceremony, and ritual.

Not all societies see a need for rituals after birth. Nothing is more "natural" than procreation. Every living thing engages in it. Sociobiologists go so far as to argue that a human being is a gene's way of creating another gene. In the Torah, childbirth is wondrous. To be a parent is the closest any of us come to God Himself. Women, unlike men, know what it is to bring new life out of themselves, as God brings life out of Himself. The idea is beautifully captured in the verse in which, leaving Eden, Adam turns to his wife and calls her Ḥava "for she would become the mother of all life" (Gen. 3:20).

And so, in Temple times, mothers

13 1 2 The Lord spoke to Moshe and Aharon: "When a person
has a swelling, a rash, or a bright patch on his skin, and
it develops on his skin into what seems to be an impure
blight, he shall be brought to the priests, to Aharon or
3 one of his sons. The priest shall examine the disease on
his skin. If hair in the diseased part has turned white and
the disease appears to be deeper than the skin, then it is
the disease of an impure blight. When the priest sees this,
4 he shall declare the person impure. But if the bright patch
on the skin is white but does not appear to be deeper than
the skin and the hair in it has not turned white, the priest
5 shall quarantine the patient for seven days. On the seventh
day the priest shall examine him again. If the disease has
remained the same in appearance and not spread on the
patient's skin, the priest shall quarantine him for another
6 seven days. On the seventh day the priest shall examine SHENI
it again. If the diseased area has receded and not spread
over the skin, the priest shall declare the patient pure; it
was only a rash. He shall immerse his clothes, and he shall

---

sickness and health, being ill and being cured. The category of *tuma* relates to mortality, and skin disease is the most publicly visible reminder of our physicality. "A *metzora* [an individual with *tzaraat*] is like one who is dead," say the Sages (Nedarim 64b).

What are we to make of a phenomenon that does not correspond to anything in our experience? How could there be a condition that makes sense to Moshe and the Israelites, but not to us?

The Sages were guided here by the principle that "the word of Torah may be poor in one place but rich in another" (Yerushalmi, Rosh HaShana 3:5), meaning that an obscure text can sometimes be understood by considering other passages elsewhere. The most obvious clue is Moshe's warning in Deuteronomy:

> Take great care in cases of impure blight. Carefully do whatever the Levitical priests instruct you.... Remember what the Lord your God did to Miriam on your way when you left Egypt. (Deut. 24:8–9)

The connection between *tzaraat* and "what the Lord your God did to Miriam" lies in an episode in the book of Numbers (12:1–2) when Miriam and Aharon spoke disparagingly about Moshe. This juxtaposition provides grounding for the link between *tzaraat* and evil speech, a theme that we will continue to explore below.

יג א ב וַיְדַבֵּר יהוה אֶל־מֹשֶׁה וְאֶל־אַהֲרֹן לֵאמֹר: אָדָם כִּי־יִהְיֶה
בְעוֹר־בְּשָׂרוֹ שְׂאֵת אוֹ־סַפַּחַת אוֹ בַהֶרֶת וְהָיָה בְעוֹר־בְּשָׂרוֹ
לְנֶגַע צָרָעַת וְהוּבָא אֶל־אַהֲרֹן הַכֹּהֵן אוֹ אֶל־אַחַד מִבָּנָיו
ג הַכֹּהֲנִים: וְרָאָה הַכֹּהֵן אֶת־הַנֶּגַע בְּעוֹר־הַבָּשָׂר וְשֵׂעָר בַּנֶּגַע
הָפַךְ | לָבָן וּמַרְאֵה הַנֶּגַע עָמֹק מֵעוֹר בְּשָׂרוֹ נֶגַע צָרַעַת
ד הוּא וְרָאָהוּ הַכֹּהֵן וְטִמֵּא אֹתוֹ: וְאִם־בַּהֶרֶת לְבָנָה הִוא
בְּעוֹר בְּשָׂרוֹ וְעָמֹק אֵין־מַרְאֶהָ מִן־הָעוֹר וּשְׂעָרָה לֹא־הָפַךְ
ה לָבָן וְהִסְגִּיר הַכֹּהֵן אֶת־הַנֶּגַע שִׁבְעַת יָמִים: וְרָאָהוּ הַכֹּהֵן
בַּיּוֹם הַשְּׁבִיעִי וְהִנֵּה הַנֶּגַע עָמַד בְּעֵינָיו לֹא־פָשָׂה הַנֶּגַע
ו בָּעוֹר וְהִסְגִּירוֹ הַכֹּהֵן שִׁבְעַת יָמִים שֵׁנִית: וְרָאָה הַכֹּהֵן אֹתוֹ שני
בַּיּוֹם הַשְּׁבִיעִי שֵׁנִית וְהִנֵּה כֵּהָה הַנֶּגַע וְלֹא־פָשָׂה הַנֶּגַע

TZARAAT: THE IMPURE BLIGHT

Much of Parashat Tazria and the following *parasha*, Metzora, are about the condition known as *tzaraat*. The Septuagint, the early Greek translation of the Hebrew Bible, translated the word as *lepra*, giving rise to a long tradition identifying it with leprosy, now known as Hansen's disease.

Some such disease, involving skin discoloration and sores, is implied in the stories of Miriam and Naaman, both of whom were smitten by *tzaraat*. However, this cannot be the meaning of the term, at least in the present context. As Rambam (*Hilkhot Tumat Tzaraat* 16:10) and Sforno (on Lev. 13:2) – both of whom were doctors – point out, the symptoms described in the Torah correspond neither to leprosy nor to any other known disease.

Tzaraat as described in Parashot Tazria and Metzora refers not only to various skin conditions but also to discolorations on clothes and the walls of houses. Rambam (ibid.) emphasizes this when he writes:

> *Tzaraat* is a comprehensive term covering a number of dissimilar conditions. So, whiteness in a person's skin is called *tzaraat*. The falling off of some of his hair on the head or the chin is called *tzaraat*. A change of color in garments or in houses is called *tzaraat*.

There is no disease that affects not only people but also clothes and walls.

Moreover, the Torah is not a book of medicine. It was priests, not doctors, who supervised cases of *tzaraat*. The language of *tuma* and *tahara*, impurity and purity, in which the whole section is couched, is quite different from the concepts of

7 be pure. But if the rash does spread over the skin after he
has appeared before the priest for purification, he must
8 appear before the priest again. If the priest sees that the
rash has indeed spread over the skin, he shall declare the
person impure; it is a blight.
9 When a person has a blight-like disease, he shall be
10 brought to the priest, and the priest shall look. If there
is a white swelling in the skin that has turned the hair
11 white, and within the swelling there is healthy flesh, it is a
chronic blight on the skin of his body, and the priest shall
pronounce the patient impure; he need not quarantine
12 him, for he is definitely impure. If, however, the blight has
spread over the skin, so that it covers all of the patient's
13 skin from head to foot, wherever the priest can see, the
priest shall make an examination, and if the blight has
covered all his body, he shall pronounce him pure of the
14 disease; if he has turned completely white, he is pure. But
as soon as healthy flesh appears, the patient is impure.
15 The priest shall examine the healthy flesh and pronounce
him impure; the healthy flesh is impure, for it indicates
16 a blight. But if the healthy flesh turns white again, the
17 patient shall come back to the priest. The priest shall
examine him, and if the disease has indeed whitened, the
priest shall pronounce the patient pure, and he shall be
pure.
18
19 When one has a boil on his skin and it heals, and in the SHELISHI
place of the boil there comes a white swelling or a bright
patch of white and reddish color, this shall be shown to
20 the priest. The priest shall then make an examination,
and if the area appears lower than the rest of the skin
and its hair has turned white, the priest shall declare the

of Psalms always inspires in me a certain awe. It says of God that "He counts the number of the stars, calling each by name" (Ps. 147:4). To call someone or something by a name is to endow it with significance for what it uniquely is. Even a blighted person is not subjected to exclusion before he receives the priest's individual close attention and care.

ז בָּעוֹר וְטִהֲרוֹ הַכֹּהֵן מִסְפַּחַת הִוא וְכִבֶּס בְּגָדָיו וְטָהֵר׃ וְאִם־
פָּשֹׂה תִפְשֶׂה הַמִּסְפַּחַת בָּעוֹר אַחֲרֵי הֵרָאֹתוֹ אֶל־הַכֹּהֵן
ח לְטָהֳרָתוֹ וְנִרְאָה שֵׁנִית אֶל־הַכֹּהֵן׃ וְרָאָה הַכֹּהֵן וְהִנֵּה פָּשְׂתָה
הַמִּסְפַּחַת בָּעוֹר וְטִמְּאוֹ הַכֹּהֵן צָרַעַת הִוא׃
ט י נֶגַע צָרַעַת כִּי תִהְיֶה בְּאָדָם וְהוּבָא אֶל־הַכֹּהֵן׃ וְרָאָה הַכֹּהֵן
וְהִנֵּה שְׂאֵת־לְבָנָה בָּעוֹר וְהִיא הָפְכָה שֵׂעָר לָבָן וּמִחְיַת בָּשָׂר
יא חַי בַּשְׂאֵת׃ צָרַעַת נוֹשֶׁנֶת הִוא בְּעוֹר בְּשָׂרוֹ וְטִמְּאוֹ הַכֹּהֵן
יב לֹא יַסְגִּרֶנּוּ כִּי טָמֵא הוּא׃ וְאִם־פָּרוֹחַ תִּפְרַח הַצָּרַעַת בָּעוֹר
וְכִסְּתָה הַצָּרַעַת אֵת כָּל־עוֹר הַנֶּגַע מֵרֹאשׁוֹ וְעַד־רַגְלָיו
יג לְכָל־מַרְאֵה עֵינֵי הַכֹּהֵן׃ וְרָאָה הַכֹּהֵן וְהִנֵּה כִסְּתָה הַצָּרַעַת
אֶת־כָּל־בְּשָׂרוֹ וְטִהַר אֶת־הַנָּגַע כֻּלּוֹ הָפַךְ לָבָן טָהוֹר הוּא׃
יד טו וּבְיוֹם הֵרָאוֹת בּוֹ בָּשָׂר חַי יִטְמָא׃ וְרָאָה הַכֹּהֵן אֶת־הַבָּשָׂר
טז הַחַי וְטִמְּאוֹ הַבָּשָׂר הַחַי טָמֵא הוּא צָרַעַת הוּא׃ אוֹ כִי
יז יָשׁוּב הַבָּשָׂר הַחַי וְנֶהְפַּךְ לְלָבָן וּבָא אֶל־הַכֹּהֵן׃ וְרָאָהוּ
הַכֹּהֵן וְהִנֵּה נֶהְפַּךְ הַנֶּגַע לְלָבָן וְטִהַר הַכֹּהֵן אֶת־הַנֶּגַע טָהוֹר
הוּא׃
יח יט וּבָשָׂר כִּי־יִהְיֶה בוֹ־בְעֹרוֹ שְׁחִין וְנִרְפָּא׃ וְהָיָה בִּמְקוֹם שלישי
הַשְּׁחִין שְׂאֵת לְבָנָה אוֹ בַהֶרֶת לְבָנָה אֲדַמְדָּמֶת וְנִרְאָה
כ אֶל־הַכֹּהֵן׃ וְרָאָה הַכֹּהֵן וְהִנֵּה מַרְאֶהָ שָׁפָל מִן־הָעוֹר
וּשְׂעָרָהּ הָפַךְ לָבָן וְטִמְּאוֹ הַכֹּהֵן נֶגַע־צָרַעַת הִוא בַּשְּׁחִין

13:10 וְרָאָה הַכֹּהֵן *The priest shall look* – A priest is not a doctor, and an impure blight is not a natural disease. Yet from this lengthy passage we see that diagnosing it requires repeated careful examinations. Expertise is needed – and so is care. The priest must make minute observations and remember the patient so that he can note changes in his or her symptoms. We may imagine the elements of a doctor-patient relationship.

The dazzling assertion at the heart of the Hebrew Bible is that God "raise[s] His face toward us" (Num. 6:26), knowing, loving, and challenging each of us in our singularity. If the religious voice has one thing to say above all others, it is that each of us counts. One line in the book

▶

patient impure: it is a case of blight that has broken out
21 in the boil. But if the priest examines it and there is no
white hair in it and it does not appear lower than the skin,
but it has not receded, then the priest shall quarantine the
22 patient for seven days. If it spreads in the skin, the priest
23 shall declare him impure; it is a blight. But if the bright
patch remains in one place and does not spread, it is scar
tissue from the boil, and the priest shall declare the patient
24 pure. When one has a burn on his skin and the REVI'I /SHENI/
raw flesh of the burn becomes a bright patch, either white
25 and reddish or only white, the priest shall examine it, and if
the hair in the bright patch has turned white and it appears
to be deeper than the skin, then it is a blight. It has broken
out in the burn, and the priest shall pronounce the patient
26 impure: it is a blight. But if the priest examines it and there
is no white hair in the spot and it appears no deeper than
the skin, but it has not receded, the priest shall quarantine
27 him for seven days. The priest shall examine him on the
seventh day. If the disease is spreading on the skin, then
28 the priest shall declare him impure; it is a blight. But if the
spot remains in its place and has not spread on the skin,
but has receded, then it was a swelling from the burn,
and the priest shall pronounce him pure; it is merely scar
tissue from the burn.

---

committing all three cardinal sins: idolatry, incest, and murder. They said that it kills three people: the one who says it, the one he says it about, and the one who listens to it (Arakhin 15b). We do not say, "Sticks and stones may break my bones but words will never harm me." To the contrary, words can cause emotional injuries that are as painful as physical ones, perhaps more so.

The negative force of *lashon hara*, however, has grown exponentially in the age of social media. It is far easier to be critical, offensive, scathing, and destructive when communicating electronically because of the so-called "disinhibition effect" which occurs when people are not speaking face-to-face. Imagine a world in which those who posted negative, hurtful, or malicious remarks about others carried a visible mark of shame, and for a period were excluded from public places and the company of others – in short, suffered the fate of the *metzora*. This would be a world in which people would think twice before using speech to harm others.

כא פָּרָחָה: וְאִם ׀ יִרְאֶנָּה הַכֹּהֵן וְהִנֵּה אֵין־בָּהּ שֵׂעָר לָבָן וּשְׁפָלָה
אֵינֶנָּה מִן־הָעוֹר וְהִיא כֵהָה וְהִסְגִּירוֹ הַכֹּהֵן שִׁבְעַת יָמִים:
כב כג וְאִם־פָּשֹׂה תִפְשֶׂה בָּעוֹר וְטִמֵּא הַכֹּהֵן אֹתוֹ נֶגַע הִוא: וְאִם־
תַּחְתֶּיהָ תַּעֲמֹד הַבַּהֶרֶת לֹא פָשָׂתָה צָרֶבֶת הַשְּׁחִין הִוא
כד וְטִהֲרוֹ הַכֹּהֵן: אוֹ בָשָׂר כִּי־יִהְיֶה בְעֹרוֹ מִכְוַת־ רביעי /שני/
אֵשׁ וְהָיְתָה מִחְיַת הַמִּכְוָה בַּהֶרֶת לְבָנָה אֲדַמְדֶּמֶת אוֹ
כה לְבָנָה: וְרָאָה אֹתָהּ הַכֹּהֵן וְהִנֵּה נֶהְפַּךְ שֵׂעָר לָבָן בַּבַּהֶרֶת
וּמַרְאֶהָ עָמֹק מִן־הָעוֹר צָרַעַת הִוא בַּמִּכְוָה פָּרָחָה וְטִמֵּא
כו אֹתוֹ הַכֹּהֵן נֶגַע צָרַעַת הִוא: וְאִם ׀ יִרְאֶנָּה הַכֹּהֵן וְהִנֵּה אֵין־
בַּבַּהֶרֶת שֵׂעָר לָבָן וּשְׁפָלָה אֵינֶנָּה מִן־הָעוֹר וְהִוא כֵהָה
כז וְהִסְגִּירוֹ הַכֹּהֵן שִׁבְעַת יָמִים: וְרָאָהוּ הַכֹּהֵן בַּיּוֹם הַשְּׁבִיעִי
אִם־פָּשֹׂה תִפְשֶׂה בָּעוֹר וְטִמֵּא הַכֹּהֵן אֹתוֹ נֶגַע צָרַעַת הִוא:
כח וְאִם־תַּחְתֶּיהָ תַעֲמֹד הַבַּהֶרֶת לֹא־פָשְׂתָה בָעוֹר וְהִוא
כֵהָה שְׂאֵת הַמִּכְוָה הִוא וְטִהֲרוֹ הַכֹּהֵן כִּי־צָרֶבֶת הַמִּכְוָה
הִוא:

13:21 וְהִסְגִּירוֹ הַכֹּהֵן שִׁבְעַת יָמִים *Shall quarantine the patient for seven days* – Why was the *metzora* required to quarantine outside the camp? Again, the episode in which Miriam will be struck with *tzaraat* for seven days for speaking ill of Moshe informs the Sages' astonishing insight of seeing the disfiguring blight as a symbol and symptom of evil speech. The Talmud takes the word *metzora* to be an abbreviated form of the phrase *motzi shem ra,* meaning slander (Arakhin 15b).

Identifying a connection between *tzaraat* and evil speech helps us understand certain other features of the phenomenon. The most obvious sign of *tzaraat* was a whitening of the skin. The phrase the Sages used to describe shaming someone was *malbin penei ḥavero,* someone who "causes his fellow's face to turn white" (Bava Metzia 59a). Thus, the punishment was measure for measure. Negative words that could turn someone else's face white are punished by the skin of the speaker turning white. Moreover, malicious speech is usually spoken in private, the fiction being that words conveyed confidentially will stay confidential. The punishment is the most public possible. The nature of *tzaraat* testified to the kind of sin that provoked it.

The Sages spoke more dramatically about *lashon hara* than any other offense. They said that it was as bad as

29 When a man or woman has a disease on the scalp or ḤAMISHI
30 beard, and the priest examines the disease and finds that
it appears to be deeper than the skin, and has fine blond
hairs in it, the priest shall declare the person impure. It
31 is a scaling eruption, a blight of the head or beard. If the
priest examines the scaling and it appears no deeper than
the skin but there is no black hair in it, then the priest
shall quarantine the person with the scaling eruption
32 for seven days, and on the seventh day the priest shall
examine the disease. If the scaling has not spread, and
there is no blond hair among it, and the scaling appears
33 to be no deeper than the skin, then the patient shall shave
himself, but shall not shave the scaled part; and the priest
shall quarantine the person with the scaling eruption for
34 a further seven days. On the seventh day the priest shall
examine the scaling, and if it has not spread in the skin and
it appears to be no deeper than the skin, then the priest
shall pronounce the patient pure; he shall immerse his
35 clothes and be pure. But if the scaling spreads in the skin
36 after he is declared pure, and when the priest examines
him, if the scaling has spread in the skin, the priest need
37 not seek the blond hair; he is impure. But if it appears to
him that the scaling is unchanged and if black hair has
grown in among it, the eruption is healed and is pure, and
38 the priest shall declare the person pure. When a
man or a woman has white patches on the skin of his or
39 her body, the priest shall examine them, and if the patches
on the skin are dull white, it is merely a rash breaking out
40 on the skin; the person is pure. If a man loses the SHISHI /SHELISHI/
41 hair on his head, it is merely baldness; he is pure. If he
loses the hair from his forehead, it is merely a receding
42 hairline; he is pure. But if there is a white and reddish
diseased area on his bald spot or receding hairline, it is a
blight erupting in his bald spot or at his receding hairline.
43 The priest shall examine him, and if the diseased swelling
is a white and reddish area on his bald spot or receding
44 hairline, resembling a blight in the skin of the body, he is

כט ל וְאִישׁ֙ א֣וֹ אִשָּׁ֔ה כִּֽי־יִהְיֶ֥ה ב֖וֹ נָ֑גַע בְּרֹ֖אשׁ א֥וֹ בְזָקָֽן׃ וְרָאָ֨ה הַכֹּהֵ֜ן ח חמישי
אֶת־הַנֶּ֗גַע וְהִנֵּ֤ה מַרְאֵ֙הוּ֙ עָמֹ֣ק מִן־הָע֔וֹר וּב֛וֹ שֵׂעָ֥ר צָהֹ֖ב דָּ֑ק
וְטִמֵּ֨א אֹת֤וֹ הַכֹּהֵן֙ נֶ֣תֶק ה֔וּא צָרַ֧עַת הָרֹ֛אשׁ א֥וֹ הַזָּקָ֖ן הֽוּא׃
לא וְכִֽי־יִרְאֶ֨ה הַכֹּהֵ֜ן אֶת־נֶ֣גַע הַנֶּ֗תֶק וְהִנֵּ֤ה אֵין־מַרְאֵ֙הוּ֙ עָמֹ֣ק
מִן־הָע֔וֹר וְשֵׂעָ֥ר שָׁחֹ֖ר אֵ֣ין בּ֑וֹ וְהִסְגִּ֧יר הַכֹּהֵ֛ן אֶת־נֶ֥גַע הַנֶּ֖תֶק
לב שִׁבְעַ֥ת יָמִֽים׃ וְרָאָ֨ה הַכֹּהֵ֥ן אֶת־הַנֶּגַע֮ בַּיּ֣וֹם הַשְּׁבִיעִי֒ וְהִנֵּה֙
לֹא־פָשָׂ֣ה הַנֶּ֔תֶק וְלֹא־הָ֥יָה ב֖וֹ שֵׂעָ֣ר צָהֹ֑ב וּמַרְאֵ֣ה הַנֶּ֔תֶק
לג אֵ֥ין עָמֹ֖ק מִן־הָעֽוֹר׃ וְהִ֨תְגַּלָּ֔ח וְאֶת־הַנֶּ֖תֶק לֹ֣א יְגַלֵּ֑חַ וְהִסְגִּ֨יר
לד הַכֹּהֵ֧ן אֶת־הַנֶּ֛תֶק שִׁבְעַ֥ת יָמִ֖ים שֵׁנִֽית׃ וְרָאָה֩ הַכֹּהֵ֨ן אֶת־
הַנֶּ֜תֶק בַּיּ֣וֹם הַשְּׁבִיעִ֗י וְ֠הִנֵּה לֹא־פָשָׂ֤ה הַנֶּ֙תֶק֙ בָּע֔וֹר וּמַרְאֵ֕הוּ
אֵינֶ֥נּוּ עָמֹ֖ק מִן־הָע֑וֹר וְטִהַ֤ר אֹתוֹ֙ הַכֹּהֵ֔ן וְכִבֶּ֥ס בְּגָדָ֖יו וְטָהֵֽר׃
לה לו וְאִם־פָּשֹׂ֥ה יִפְשֶׂ֛ה הַנֶּ֖תֶק בָּע֑וֹר אַחֲרֵ֖י טָהֳרָתֽוֹ׃ וְרָאָ֙הוּ֙ הַכֹּהֵ֔ן
וְהִנֵּ֛ה פָּשָׂ֥ה הַנֶּ֖תֶק בָּע֑וֹר לֹֽא־יְבַקֵּ֥ר הַכֹּהֵ֛ן לַשֵּׂעָ֥ר הַצָּהֹ֖ב טָמֵ֥א
לז הֽוּא׃ וְאִם־בְּעֵינָ֞יו עָמַ֤ד הַנֶּ֙תֶק֙ וְשֵׂעָ֨ר שָׁחֹ֤ר צָֽמַח־בּוֹ֙ נִרְפָּ֣א
לח הַנֶּ֖תֶק טָה֣וֹר ה֑וּא וְטִהֲר֖וֹ הַכֹּהֵֽן׃ וְאִישׁ֙ אֽוֹ־אִשָּׁ֔ה
לט כִּֽי־יִהְיֶ֥ה בְעוֹר־בְּשָׂרָ֖ם בֶּהָרֹ֑ת בֶּהָרֹ֖ת לְבָנֹֽת׃ וְרָאָ֣ה הַכֹּהֵ֗ן
וְהִנֵּ֛ה בְעוֹר־בְּשָׂרָ֥ם בֶּהָרֹ֖ת כֵּה֣וֹת לְבָנֹ֑ת בֹּ֥הַק ה֛וּא פָּרַ֥ח
מ בָּע֖וֹר טָה֥וֹר הֽוּא׃ וְאִ֕ישׁ כִּ֥י יִמָּרֵ֖ט רֹאשׁ֑וֹ קֵרֵ֥חַ ששי /שלישי/
מא ה֖וּא טָה֥וֹר הֽוּא׃ וְאִם֙ מִפְּאַ֣ת פָּנָ֔יו יִמָּרֵ֖ט רֹאשׁ֑וֹ גִּבֵּ֥חַ ה֖וּא
מב טָה֥וֹר הֽוּא׃ וְכִֽי־יִהְיֶ֤ה בַקָּרַ֙חַת֙ א֣וֹ בַגַּבַּ֔חַת נֶ֖גַע לָבָ֣ן אֲדַמְדָּ֑ם
מג צָרַ֤עַת פֹּרַ֙חַת֙ ה֔וּא בְּקָרַחְתּ֖וֹ א֥וֹ בְגַבַּחְתּֽוֹ׃ וְרָאָ֨ה אֹת֜וֹ הַכֹּהֵ֗ן
וְהִנֵּ֤ה שְׂאֵת־הַנֶּ֙גַע֙ לְבָנָ֣ה אֲדַמְדֶּ֔מֶת בְּקָרַחְתּ֖וֹ א֣וֹ בְגַבַּחְתּ֑וֹ
מד כְּמַרְאֵ֥ה צָרַ֖עַת ע֥וֹר בָּשָֽׂר׃ אִישׁ־צָר֥וּעַ ה֖וּא טָמֵ֣א ה֑וּא טַמֵּ֧א

a blighted person; he is impure. The priest shall declare
45 him impure; he has a blight on his scalp. And a blighted
person, one bearing the disease – his clothes shall be torn
and the hair of his head disarrayed. And he shall cover his
46 upper lip as he cries out, 'Impure, impure.' He shall be in
a state of impurity for as long as he has the disease; he is
impure. He shall live apart; outside the camp shall be his
47 dwelling. When a blight appears in a garment,
48 whether the garment is of wool or of linen, or in the warp
or in the weft of the linen or wool cloth, in leather or
49 anything made of leather, if the infection shows as green
or red in the garment, the leather, the warp or the weft, or
the article of leather, it is a case of the impure blight and
50 shall be shown to the priest. And the priest shall examine
the disease and quarantine the diseased article for seven
51 days. He shall examine the disease on the seventh day.
If the disease has spread in the garment, the warp or the

Elazar's town, his disciples came to greet him. The man who had been insulted said to them, "Is this the person you call a great man? May there not be many more like him in Israel." When the disciples discovered what their rabbi had said, they agreed that he had done wrong, but added, "Forgive him because he is a great scholar." The man did so on the condition that R. Shimon would agree not to speak likewise in the future (Taanit 20b). The fact that the Talmud records such episodes, critical of the Sages, is eloquent of the need to wrestle with prejudice and the difficulty we have in coming to terms with disability, illness, and physical difference.

Against this, Judaism directs us to integrate people with disabilities into the community. We must reach out to those who have a family member affected by illness and make them feel that they are full participants in the community. The behavioral model here is *avelut*, mourning. When faced with grief, the natural reaction is what halakha defines as *aninut* (the period of mourning before the burial). This is a time of trauma, in which we are emotionally isolated by distress. In the Torah, the appearance of a person with an impure blight, with torn clothes and covered face, is like that of a mourner (Moed Katan 15a), and this is not accidental. The whole thrust of the Jewish laws of mourning and of comforting the bereaved is to lead the mourner back from isolation to reintegration into the community. If this applies to the bereaved, all the more so does it apply to those who are concerned with life.

מה יְטַמְּאֶנּוּ הַכֹּהֵן בְּרֹאשׁוֹ נִגְעוֹ׃ וְהַצָּרוּעַ אֲשֶׁר־בּוֹ הַנֶּגַע בְּגָדָיו
יִהְיוּ פְרֻמִים וְרֹאשׁוֹ יִהְיֶה פָרוּעַ וְעַל־שָׂפָם יַעְטֶה וְטָמֵא ׀
מו טָמֵא יִקְרָא׃ כָּל־יְמֵי אֲשֶׁר הַנֶּגַע בּוֹ יִטְמָא טָמֵא הוּא בָּדָד
מז יֵשֵׁב מִחוּץ לַמַּחֲנֶה מוֹשָׁבוֹ׃ וְהַבֶּגֶד כִּי־יִהְיֶה בוֹ
מח נֶגַע צָרָעַת בְּבֶגֶד צֶמֶר אוֹ בְּבֶגֶד פִּשְׁתִּים׃ אוֹ בִשְׁתִי אוֹ בְעֵרֶב
מט לַפִּשְׁתִּים וְלַצָּמֶר אוֹ בְעוֹר אוֹ בְּכָל־מְלֶאכֶת עוֹר׃ וְהָיָה הַנֶּגַע
יְרַקְרַק ׀ אוֹ אֲדַמְדָּם בַּבֶּגֶד אוֹ בָעוֹר אוֹ־בַשְּׁתִי אוֹ־בָעֵרֶב אוֹ
נ בְּכָל־כְּלִי־עוֹר נֶגַע צָרַעַת הוּא וְהָרְאָה אֶת־הַכֹּהֵן׃ וְרָאָה
נא הַכֹּהֵן אֶת־הַנֶּגַע וְהִסְגִּיר אֶת־הַנֶּגַע שִׁבְעַת יָמִים׃ וְרָאָה
אֶת־הַנֶּגַע בַּיּוֹם הַשְּׁבִיעִי כִּי־פָשָׂה הַנֶּגַע בַּבֶּגֶד אוֹ־בַשְּׁתִי

ILLNESS AND OSTRACIZATION

This passage details quintessential expressions of shame to which the blighted individual is subjected. First is the *stigma*: the public marks of disgrace or dishonor (the torn clothes, unkempt hair). Then comes the *ostracism:* temporary exclusion from the normal affairs of society. These have nothing to do with illness and everything to do with social disapproval. This is what makes the law of *tzaraat* so hard to understand at first: it is one of the rare appearances of public shaming in a non-shame, guilt-based culture. It happened, though, not because society had expressed its disapproval but because God was signaling that it should do so. Malicious gossip, *lashon hara*, undermines relationships, erodes the social bond, and damages trust. It, uniquely in Jewish culture, deserves to be exposed and shamed.

For centuries, Hansen's disease sufferers enacted, with variations, the scene described here. The mistranslation of *tzaraat* as leprosy amplified the stigma they anyway suffered. The stigmatization of disease and disability, however, is something all societies must grapple with. Often we do not know what to do when faced by someone with a severe disability or illness. To avoid our own awkwardness we may shun the affected family, or on the other hand try too hard. Through our own embarrassment, we may create embarrassment in others.

The Talmud, with great candor, tells us of the difficulty some of the Sages had in overcoming their instinctive stigmatizing feelings. It relates, for example, that R. Shimon b. Elazar was once on a journey when he saw an individual who was disfigured. He asked the man, "Are all the people in your town as deformed as you are?" The man replied, "If you do not like the pot, go and complain to the potter [i.e., to God who made me this way]." When they arrived at R. Shimon b.

weft, or the leather, whatever the leather is used for, the
52 infection is a malignant disease blight; it is impure. The
garment shall be burned – or the warp or weft, wool or
linen, or any article of leather that is infected – for it is
53 a malignant disease blight; it must be burned in fire. If,
however, the priest examines it and the disease has not
spread in the garment, the warp or the weft, or the article
54 of leather, then the priest shall command the article in
which the disease appears to be washed, and he shall
55 quarantine it for another seven days. After this washing SHEVI'I /REVI'I/
the priest shall once more examine the diseased article.
If the diseased area has not changed color, though the
disease has not spread, it is impure. You shall burn it in
fire, whether the mark of decay is on the inside or on the
56 outside. But if the priest examines it and the diseased area MAFTIR
has faded after washing, he shall tear it out of the garment
57 or the leather or the warp or the weft. If it appears again in
the garment, in the warp or weft, or in the leather article,
it is erupting. Whatever has the disease, you shall burn
58 with fire. But the garment, or the warp or weft, or the
leather article from which the disease departs after you
have washed it shall be washed a second time and then
59 be pure." This is the law concerning the disease blight in a
garment of wool or of linen, in warp or in weft, or in any
article made of leather, to determine whether it is pure
or impure.

The haftara for Parashat Tazria is on page 1524.
When Tazria and Metzora are read together, read the haftara on page 1528.
On the Shabbat of Parashat HaḤodesh read the haftara on page 1666.

אוֹ־בָעֵ֗רֶב א֚וֹ בָע֔וֹר לְכֹ֛ל אֲשֶׁר־יֵעָשֶׂ֥ה הָע֖וֹר לִמְלָאכָ֑ה צָרַ֧עַת
נב מַמְאֶ֛רֶת הַנֶּ֖גַע טָמֵ֥א הֽוּא׃ וְשָׂרַ֨ף אֶת־הַבֶּ֜גֶד א֥וֹ אֶת־הַשְּׁתִ֣י ׀
א֣וֹ אֶת־הָעֵ֗רֶב בַּצֶּ֙מֶר֙ א֣וֹ בַפִּשְׁתִּ֔ים א֚וֹ אֶת־כָּל־כְּלִ֣י הָע֔וֹר
אֲשֶׁר־יִהְיֶ֥ה ב֖וֹ הַנָּ֑גַע כִּֽי־צָרַ֤עַת מַמְאֶ֙רֶת֙ הִ֔וא בָּאֵ֖שׁ תִּשָּׂרֵֽף׃
נג וְאִם֮ יִרְאֶ֣ה הַכֹּהֵן֒ וְהִנֵּה֙ לֹֽא־פָשָׂ֣ה הַנֶּ֔גַע בַּבֶּ֕גֶד א֥וֹ בַשְּׁתִ֖י א֣וֹ
נד בָעֵ֑רֶב א֖וֹ בְּכָל־כְּלִי־עֽוֹר׃ וְצִוָּה֙ הַכֹּהֵ֔ן וְכִ֨בְּס֔וּ אֵ֥ת אֲשֶׁר־בּ֖וֹ
נה הַנָּ֑גַע וְהִסְגִּיר֥וֹ שִׁבְעַת־יָמִ֖ים שֵׁנִֽית׃ וְרָאָ֨ה הַכֹּהֵ֜ן אַחֲרֵ֣י ׀ שביעי
הֻכַּבֵּ֣ס אֶת־הַנֶּ֗גַע וְ֠הִנֵּה לֹֽא־הָפַ֨ךְ הַנֶּ֤גַע אֶת־עֵינוֹ֙ וְהַנֶּ֣גַע לֹֽא־ /רביעי/
פָשָׂ֔ה טָמֵ֣א ה֔וּא בָּאֵ֖שׁ תִּשְׂרְפֶ֑נּוּ פְּחֶ֣תֶת הִ֔וא בְּקָרַחְתּ֖וֹ א֥וֹ
נו בְגַבַּחְתּֽוֹ׃ וְאִם֮ רָאָ֣ה הַכֹּהֵן֒ וְהִנֵּה֙ כֵּהָ֣ה הַנֶּ֔גַע אַחֲרֵ֖י הֻכַּבֵּ֣ס
אֹת֑וֹ וְקָרַ֣ע אֹת֗וֹ מִן־הַבֶּ֙גֶד֙ א֣וֹ מִן־הָע֔וֹר א֥וֹ מִן־הַשְּׁתִ֖י א֥וֹ
נז מִן־הָעֵֽרֶב׃ וְאִם־תֵּרָאֶ֨ה ע֜וֹד בַּ֠בֶּגֶד אֽוֹ־בַשְּׁתִ֤י אֽוֹ־בָעֵ֙רֶב֙ מפטיר
אֽוֹ־בְכָל־כְּלִי־ע֔וֹר פֹּרַ֖חַת הִ֑וא בָּאֵ֣שׁ תִּשְׂרְפֶ֔נּוּ אֵ֥ת אֲשֶׁר־בּ֖וֹ
נח הַנָּֽגַע׃ וְהַבֶּ֡גֶד אֽוֹ־הַשְּׁ֠תִי אֽוֹ־הָעֵ֜רֶב אֽוֹ־כָל־כְּלִ֤י הָעוֹר֙ אֲשֶׁ֣ר
נט תְּכַבֵּ֔ס וְסָ֥ר מֵהֶ֖ם הַנָּ֑גַע וְכֻבַּ֥ס שֵׁנִ֖ית וְטָהֵֽר׃ זֹ֡את תּוֹרַ֣ת נֶֽגַע־
צָרַ֩עַת֩ בֶּ֨גֶד הַצֶּ֜מֶר ׀ א֣וֹ הַפִּשְׁתִּ֗ים א֤וֹ הַשְּׁתִי֙ א֣וֹ הָעֵ֔רֶב א֖וֹ
כָּל־כְּלִי־ע֑וֹר לְטַהֲר֖וֹ א֥וֹ לְטַמְּאֽוֹ׃

The הפטרה *for* פרשת תזריע *is on page 1525.*
When תזריע *and* מצרע *are read together, read the* הפטרה *on page 1529.*
On the שבת *of* פרשת החודש *read the* הפטרה *on page 1667.*

Parashat Metzora

14 1 2 The Lord spoke to Moshe: "This shall be the law of
the person with an impure blight on the day he is to be
3 purified. He shall be brought to see the priest, and the
priest shall go out of the camp to examine him. If the
4 disease is healed in the blighted person, the priest shall
command two living ritually pure birds, and cedarwood,
scarlet wool, and hyssop to be brought for the one who
5 is to be purified. The priest shall command one of the
birds to be slaughtered into an earthen vessel, over living

---

of speech. It is why humans developed language in the first place.

If this is so, it explains why the prohibitions against gossip and *lashon hara* are so often honored in the breach, not the observance. So common is *lashon hara* that one of the giants of modern Jewry, Rabbi Yisrael Meir HaKohen (the Chofetz Chaim) devoted much of his life to combatting it. Yet it persists, as anyone who has ever been part of a human group knows from personal experience. You can know it is wrong, yet you and others do it anyway.

In our *parasha* the bearer of *lashon hara* is temporarily separated from the rest of society, condemned to live outside the camp as long as the condition lasts. The primary way to avoid *lashon hara* is to practice silence, and indeed the Sages were eloquent on the importance of silence (Mishna Avot 1:17, 3:13). Silence saves us from evil speech but in and of itself it achieves nothing positive. The challenge is to step back and see whether another form of "grooming speech" can create a more healthy community bond. Alongside the grave sin of *lashon hara*, there must in principle be a concept of *lashon hatov*, good speech, and it must be more than a mere negation of its opposite.

One of the most important tasks of a leader, a parent, or a friend is focused praise. In any relationship that matters to you, deliver praise daily. Seeing and praising the good in people makes them better people, makes you a better person, and strengthens the bond between you. Praise an act, a word, a gesture that was kind or sensitive or generous or thoughtful. The praise must be focused on that one act, not generalized. It must be genuine: it must come from the heart. And as a recipient, learn also to accept the praise.

Language is the air we breathe as social beings. Hence the statement in Proverbs (18:21), "Death and life" – both – "are in the power of the tongue." Evil speech destroys relationships. Good speech mends them.

פרשת מצרע

יד א ב וידבר יהוה אל־משה לאמר: זאת תהיה תורת המצרע ט
ג ביום טהרתו והובא אל־הכהן: ויצא הכהן אל־מחוץ
למחנה וראה הכהן והנה נרפא נגע־הצרעת מן־הצרוע:
ד וצוה הכהן ולקח למטהר שתי־צפרים חיות טהרות ועץ
ה ארז ושני תולעת ואזב: וצוה הכהן ושחט את־הצפור

METZORA

Parashat Metzora opens by continuing the description of the process of purification for the phenomenon known as *tzaraat,* the decay that causes skin disease in humans and discoloration in garments and the walls of houses.

In the previous *parasha,* Tazria, we noted the connection, already hinted at in the Torah, between *tzaraat* and *lashon hara,* evil speech. We shall continue to delve into this connection in Parashat Metzora. The second part of the *parasha* discusses the rules of impurity from bodily discharges, which help us grasp the concepts of *tuma* and *tahara,* impurity and purity, in general.

REINTEGRATION

If *tzaraat* were a disease, then the sufferer's temporary removal from the camp (Lev. 13:46) would clearly be a form of quarantine. But if it is a punishment for malicious speech, then we understand it differently. High morale was essential to the Israelites' survival in the desert. Evil speech creates division between one person and another, undermining trust, weakening community bonds, and destroying morale. The entire community suffers.

Yet there is a reason why it is hard to cure people of *lashon hara.* Robin Dunbar, in his famous book *Grooming, Gossip, and the Evolution of Language* argues that, in nature, groups are held together by devoting a considerable amount of time to building relationships and alliances. Nonhuman primates do this by "grooming," stroking and cleaning one another's skin. But this is very time-consuming and puts a limit on the size of the group.

Humans developed language as a more effective form of grooming. You can only stroke one animal or person at a time, but you can talk to several at a time. The specific form of language that bonds a group together, says Dunbar, is gossip – because this is the way members of the group can learn who to trust and who not to. So gossip is not one form of speech among others. According to Dunbar, it is the most primal of all uses

6 water. Then he shall take the living bird, together with
the cedarwood, the scarlet wool, and the hyssop, and dip
them and the living bird in the blood of the bird that was
7 killed over living water. With these he shall sprinkle seven
times over the one who is to be purified of the blight to
purify him; and he shall set the living bird free into the
8 open field. The one who is to be purified shall then wash
his clothes, shave off all his hair, and immerse himself
in water; then he shall be purified. After that he may
come into the camp, but he shall dwell outside his tent
9 for seven days. On the seventh day he shall shave all the
hair from his head, his beard, and his eyebrows. When he
has shaved off all his hair, he shall wash his clothes and
10 immerse his body in water, and he shall be pure. On the
eighth day he shall take two unblemished male lambs and
one unblemished ewe lamb in its first year, with three-
tenths of an ephah of fine flour mixed with oil as a grain
11 offering, and one *log* of oil. The priest who purifies shall
present the one to be purified, together with these, to the
12 LORD at the entrance to the Tent of Meeting. The priest
shall take one of the male lambs and offer it as a guilt
offering, along with the *log* of oil; he shall display these,
13 this way and that, as a wave offering before the LORD. He SHENI
shall slaughter the lamb in the place where purification
offerings and burnt offerings are slaughtered within the
holy place. For the guilt offering, like the purification
14 offering, belongs to the priest and is holy of holies. The
priest shall take some of the blood of the guilt offering
and apply it to the ridge of the right ear, to the right
thumb, and to the right big toe of the one who is to be
15 purified. The priest shall pour some of the *log* of oil into
16 his own left palm, dip his right finger into the oil in his
left hand, and sprinkle of the oil with his finger seven
17 times before the LORD. The priest shall apply some of
the remaining oil in his hand to the ridge of the right ear,
to the right thumb, and to the right big toe of the one
18 who is to be purified, over the guilt offering blood. What

ו הָאֶחָת אֶל־כְּלִי־חֶרֶשׂ עַל־מַיִם חַיִּים׃ אֶת־הַצִּפֹּר הַחַיָּה
יִקַּח אֹתָהּ וְאֶת־עֵץ הָאֶרֶז וְאֶת־שְׁנִי הַתּוֹלַעַת וְאֶת־הָאֵזֹב
וְטָבַל אוֹתָם וְאֵת ׀ הַצִּפֹּר הַחַיָּה בְּדַם הַצִּפֹּר הַשְּׁחֻטָה
ז עַל הַמַּיִם הַחַיִּים׃ וְהִזָּה עַל הַמִּטַּהֵר מִן־הַצָּרַעַת שֶׁבַע
פְּעָמִים וְטִהֲרוֹ וְשִׁלַּח אֶת־הַצִּפֹּר הַחַיָּה עַל־פְּנֵי הַשָּׂדֶה׃
ח וְכִבֶּס הַמִּטַּהֵר אֶת־בְּגָדָיו וְגִלַּח אֶת־כָּל־שְׂעָרוֹ וְרָחַץ בַּמַּיִם
וְטָהֵר וְאַחַר יָבוֹא אֶל־הַמַּחֲנֶה וְיָשַׁב מִחוּץ לְאָהֳלוֹ שִׁבְעַת
ט יָמִים׃ וְהָיָה בַיּוֹם הַשְּׁבִיעִי יְגַלַּח אֶת־כָּל־שְׂעָרוֹ אֶת־רֹאשׁוֹ
וְאֶת־זְקָנוֹ וְאֵת גַּבֹּת עֵינָיו וְאֶת־כָּל־שְׂעָרוֹ יְגַלֵּחַ וְכִבֶּס אֶת־
י בְּגָדָיו וְרָחַץ אֶת־בְּשָׂרוֹ בַּמַּיִם וְטָהֵר׃ וּבַיּוֹם הַשְּׁמִינִי יִקַּח
שְׁנֵי־כְבָשִׂים תְּמִימִם וְכַבְשָׂה אַחַת בַּת־שְׁנָתָהּ תְּמִימָה
וּשְׁלֹשָׁה עֶשְׂרֹנִים סֹלֶת מִנְחָה בְּלוּלָה בַשֶּׁמֶן וְלֹג אֶחָד
יא שָׁמֶן׃ וְהֶעֱמִיד הַכֹּהֵן הַמְטַהֵר אֵת הָאִישׁ הַמִּטַּהֵר וְאֹתָם
יב לִפְנֵי יְהוָה פֶּתַח אֹהֶל מוֹעֵד׃ וְלָקַח הַכֹּהֵן אֶת־הַכֶּבֶשׂ
הָאֶחָד וְהִקְרִיב אֹתוֹ לְאָשָׁם וְאֶת־לֹג הַשָּׁמֶן וְהֵנִיף אֹתָם
יג תְּנוּפָה לִפְנֵי יְהוָה׃ וְשָׁחַט אֶת־הַכֶּבֶשׂ בִּמְקוֹם אֲשֶׁר יִשְׁחַט שני
אֶת־הַחַטָּאת וְאֶת־הָעֹלָה בִּמְקוֹם הַקֹּדֶשׁ כִּי כַּחַטָּאת
יד הָאָשָׁם הוּא לַכֹּהֵן קֹדֶשׁ קָדָשִׁים הוּא׃ וְלָקַח הַכֹּהֵן מִדַּם
הָאָשָׁם וְנָתַן הַכֹּהֵן עַל־תְּנוּךְ אֹזֶן הַמִּטַּהֵר הַיְמָנִית וְעַל־
טו בֹּהֶן יָדוֹ הַיְמָנִית וְעַל־בֹּהֶן רַגְלוֹ הַיְמָנִית׃ וְלָקַח הַכֹּהֵן
טז מִלֹּג הַשָּׁמֶן וְיָצַק עַל־כַּף הַכֹּהֵן הַשְּׂמָאלִית׃ וְטָבַל הַכֹּהֵן
אֶת־אֶצְבָּעוֹ הַיְמָנִית מִן־הַשֶּׁמֶן אֲשֶׁר עַל־כַּפּוֹ הַשְּׂמָאלִית
וְהִזָּה מִן־הַשֶּׁמֶן בְּאֶצְבָּעוֹ שֶׁבַע פְּעָמִים לִפְנֵי יְהוָה׃
יז וּמִיֶּתֶר הַשֶּׁמֶן אֲשֶׁר עַל־כַּפּוֹ יִתֵּן הַכֹּהֵן עַל־תְּנוּךְ אֹזֶן הַמִּטַּהֵר
הַיְמָנִית וְעַל־בֹּהֶן יָדוֹ הַיְמָנִית וְעַל־בֹּהֶן רַגְלוֹ הַיְמָנִית עַל דַּם
יח הָאָשָׁם׃ וְהַנּוֹתָר בַּשֶּׁמֶן אֲשֶׁר עַל־כַּף הַכֹּהֵן יִתֵּן עַל־רֹאשׁ

remains of the oil in his hand the priest shall pour on the
head of the one to be purified. Thus shall the priest make
19 his atonement before the LORD. Then the priest shall offer
the purification offering to make atonement for the one
to be purified of his defilement. Then he shall slaughter
20 the burnt offering. The priest shall offer the burnt offering
and the grain offering on the altar. Thus shall the priest
21 make his atonement, and he shall be purified. If, SHELISHI /ḤAMISHI/
however, the person is poor and cannot afford so much,
he shall take one male lamb as a guilt offering to be made a
wave offering to make his atonement, and one-tenth of an
ephah of fine flour mixed with oil as a grain offering, and
22 a *log* of oil, and two doves or two pigeons, such as he can
afford; one shall be a purification offering and the other

Jerusalem danced before the boys and wives were chosen, they would wear borrowed clothes "so as not to put to shame those who did not have" (Mishna Taanit 4:8).

Another example: The festival of Passover involves a major upheaval in the running of a household. No leavened ingredient may be eaten or even kept in the home. If one uses earthenware vessels, different utensils must be used for cooking and eating (metal utensils, by contrast, can be made kosher for Passover). The third-century Babylonian community followed the rulings of their great leader, Rav. But one of his rulings had severe implications. Any earthenware pot that had been used for cooking during the year, and so had absorbed some leaven, must not merely be put away during Passover, but actually broken and disposed of. In effect this meant that families had to buy complete new sets of cooking equipment each year. This created a concentrated seasonal demand for earthenware pots, and in the free market, traders were quick to take advantage and raise their prices. It was the kind of situation of exploitation familiar to us from the prophetic literature.

Rav's contemporary and friend, Shmuel, responded immediately. He gathered the merchants together and informed them that unless they held their prices steady, he would pronounce in accordance with the more lenient tradition, which held that old pots need not be broken, simply stored away. It worked (Pesaḥim 30a).

Many, perhaps most, of the innovations of the Rabbis had a similar motive. They were guardians of the tradition, but they were also guardians of the unity of the people, and they were aware that nothing could be more destructive of that unity than a Judaism that was identified with a particular economic class.

יט הַמִּטַּהֵר וְכִפֶּר עָלָיו הַכֹּהֵן לִפְנֵי יהוה׃ וְעָשָׂה הַכֹּהֵן אֶת־
הַחַטָּאת וְכִפֶּר עַל־הַמִּטַּהֵר מִטֻּמְאָתוֹ וְאַחַר יִשְׁחַט אֶת־
כ הָעֹלָה׃ וְהֶעֱלָה הַכֹּהֵן אֶת־הָעֹלָה וְאֶת־הַמִּנְחָה הַמִּזְבֵּחָה
כא וְכִפֶּר עָלָיו הַכֹּהֵן וְטָהֵר׃ וְאִם־דַּל הוּא שלישי
וְאֵין יָדוֹ מַשֶּׂגֶת וְלָקַח כֶּבֶשׂ אֶחָד אָשָׁם לִתְנוּפָה לְכַפֵּר עָלָיו /חמישי/
כב וְעִשָּׂרוֹן סֹלֶת אֶחָד בָּלוּל בַּשֶּׁמֶן לְמִנְחָה וְלֹג שָׁמֶן׃ וּשְׁתֵּי
תֹרִים אוֹ שְׁנֵי בְּנֵי יוֹנָה אֲשֶׁר תַּשִּׂיג יָדוֹ וְהָיָה אֶחָד חַטָּאת

14:20 וְכִפֶּר עָלָיו הַכֹּהֵן וְטָהֵר *Thus shall the priest make his atonement, and he shall be purified* – *Lehakriv,* as we have noted, means "to bring close." The key element of a sacrifice is bringing something close to God. The animal, or *behema,* sacrificed represents the animal, instinctual element within us to be brought close to God and transformed through the divine fire that burned on the altar.

By an irony of history, this idea has become suddenly contemporary. Darwinism, the decoding of the human genome, and scientific materialism (the idea that the material is all there is) have led to the widespread conclusion that we are all animals, nothing more, nothing less. We share 98 percent of our genes with the primates. On this view, *Homo sapiens* exists by mere accident. We are the result of a random series of genetic mutations and just happened to be more adapted to survival than other species. The *nefesh habahamit,* the animal soul, is all there is.

The refutation of this idea lies in the very act of sacrifice itself. We can redirect our animal instincts and rise above mere survival. We can transcend the *behema* in us. No animal is capable of self-transformation, but we are. By bringing that which is animal within us close to God, we allow the material to be suffused with the spiritual and we become something else: no longer slaves of nature but servants of the living God.

14:22 אֲשֶׁר תַּשִּׂיג יָדוֹ *Such as he can afford* – Tabernacle requirements should not put the person recovering from a blight in the position of a beggar. If we were to ask what a religious tradition can contribute to the problem of poverty, one would have to recognize that charity is only part of the answer. In the Talmud we find that fundamental to the Rabbis' conception of Judaism was the idea that its practice should never impoverish or be beyond the reach of the poor. This was not a theoretical issue. Judaism did make economic demands, and it is important that these should not be divisive. Hence, for instance, the institutions that burials should be as simple as possible (Moed Katan 27b), and that on the special festive days when the girls of

23 a burnt offering. On the eighth day of his purification, he
shall bring them to the priest at the entrance to the Tent
24 of Meeting before the LORD. The priest shall take the
lamb of the guilt offering, together with the *log* of oil, and
move them this way and that as a wave offering before the
25 LORD. Then he shall slaughter the guilt offering lamb. The
priest shall take some of the blood of the guilt offering and
apply it to the ridge of the right ear, to the right thumb,
and to the right big toe of the one who is to be purified.
26 The priest shall then pour some of the oil into his own left
27 palm, and, using his right finger, shall sprinkle of the oil
28 that is in his left hand seven times before the LORD. He
shall apply some of the oil remaining in his hand to the
ridge of the right ear, to the right thumb, and to the right
big toe of the person to be purified, over the guilt offering
29 blood. What remains of the oil in his hand the priest shall
pour on the head of the one to be purified, to make his
30 atonement before the LORD. He shall then offer up one
31 of the doves or pigeons the person could afford; whatever
he can afford, one as a purification offering, and the other
as a burnt offering, together with the grain offering; and
thus shall the priest make atonement for the person who
32 is to be purified before the LORD." This is the law for a
person who has an impure blight and cannot afford the
regular offerings for his purification.
33 34 The LORD spoke to Moshe and to Aharon: "When REVI'I /SHISHI/
you enter the land of Canaan that I am giving you as a
possession, and I afflict a house in the land you possess
35 with an impure blight, the owner of the house shall come

he continued in his wickedness until they were burned, the garments that he wore would suffer a change. If he repented they would again become clean. But if he continued in his wickedness until they were burned, his skin would suffer a change and he would become infected by *tzaraat* and be set apart and alone until he no longer engaged in the conversation of the wicked which is scoffing and slander. (*Hilkhot Tumat Tzaraat* 16:10)

Evil speech is subversive: it is a sin

כג וְהָאֶחָד עֹלָה׃ וְהֵבִיא אֹתָם בַּיּוֹם הַשְּׁמִינִי לְטָהֳרָתוֹ אֶל־
כד הַכֹּהֵן אֶל־פֶּתַח אֹהֶל־מוֹעֵד לִפְנֵי יהוה׃ וְלָקַח הַכֹּהֵן אֶת־
כֶּבֶשׂ הָאָשָׁם וְאֶת־לֹג הַשָּׁמֶן וְהֵנִיף אֹתָם הַכֹּהֵן תְּנוּפָה לִפְנֵי
כה יהוה׃ וְשָׁחַט אֶת־כֶּבֶשׂ הָאָשָׁם וְלָקַח הַכֹּהֵן מִדַּם הָאָשָׁם
וְנָתַן עַל־תְּנוּךְ אֹזֶן־הַמִּטַּהֵר הַיְמָנִית וְעַל־בֹּהֶן יָדוֹ הַיְמָנִית
כו וְעַל־בֹּהֶן רַגְלוֹ הַיְמָנִית׃ וּמִן־הַשֶּׁמֶן יִצֹק הַכֹּהֵן עַל־כַּף הַכֹּהֵן
כז הַשְּׂמָאלִית׃ וְהִזָּה הַכֹּהֵן בְּאֶצְבָּעוֹ הַיְמָנִית מִן־הַשֶּׁמֶן אֲשֶׁר
כח עַל־כַּפּוֹ הַשְּׂמָאלִית שֶׁבַע פְּעָמִים לִפְנֵי יהוה׃ וְנָתַן הַכֹּהֵן
מִן־הַשֶּׁמֶן ׀ אֲשֶׁר עַל־כַּפּוֹ עַל־תְּנוּךְ אֹזֶן הַמִּטַּהֵר הַיְמָנִית
וְעַל־בֹּהֶן יָדוֹ הַיְמָנִית וְעַל־בֹּהֶן רַגְלוֹ הַיְמָנִית עַל־מְקוֹם
כט דַּם הָאָשָׁם׃ וְהַנּוֹתָר מִן־הַשֶּׁמֶן אֲשֶׁר עַל־כַּף הַכֹּהֵן יִתֵּן
ל עַל־רֹאשׁ הַמִּטַּהֵר לְכַפֵּר עָלָיו לִפְנֵי יהוה׃ וְעָשָׂה אֶת־
הָאֶחָד מִן־הַתֹּרִים אוֹ מִן־בְּנֵי הַיּוֹנָה מֵאֲשֶׁר תַּשִּׂיג יָדוֹ׃
לא אֵת אֲשֶׁר־תַּשִּׂיג יָדוֹ אֶת־הָאֶחָד חַטָּאת וְאֶת־הָאֶחָד
עֹלָה עַל־הַמִּנְחָה וְכִפֶּר הַכֹּהֵן עַל הַמִּטַּהֵר לִפְנֵי יהוה׃
לב זֹאת תּוֹרַת אֲשֶׁר־בּוֹ נֶגַע צָרָעַת אֲשֶׁר לֹא־תַשִּׂיג יָדוֹ
בְּטָהֳרָתוֹ׃
לג לד וַיְדַבֵּר יהוה אֶל־מֹשֶׁה וְאֶל־אַהֲרֹן לֵאמֹר׃ כִּי תָבֹאוּ אֶל־ י רביעי /ששי/
אֶרֶץ כְּנַעַן אֲשֶׁר אֲנִי נֹתֵן לָכֶם לַאֲחֻזָּה וְנָתַתִּי נֶגַע צָרַעַת
לה בְּבֵית אֶרֶץ אֲחֻזַּתְכֶם׃ וּבָא אֲשֶׁר־לוֹ הַבַּיִת וְהִגִּיד לַכֹּהֵן

14:34 וְנָתַתִּי נֶגַע צָרַעַת בְּבֵית אֶרֶץ אֲחֻזַּתְכֶם *And I afflict a house in the land you possess* – Rambam, on the basis of rabbinic traditions, gives a remarkable account of why *tzaraat* afflicts both inanimate objects like walls and clothes, and human beings:

> It [*tzaraat*] was a sign and wonder among the Israelites to warn them against slanderous speaking. For if a man uttered slander, the walls of his house would suffer a change. If he repented, the house would again become clean. But if he continued in his wickedness until the house was torn down, leather objects in his house on which he sat or lay would suffer a change. If he repented they would again become clean. But if

and tell the priest, 'It looks to me as if there were some
36 disease in the house.' The priest shall instruct them to
empty the house before he goes to examine the disease, to
prevent everything in the house from becoming impure.
37 After that, the priest shall go to examine the house. He
shall look at the disease. If the disease is in the walls of
the house with greenish or reddish spots that appear to
38 go deep into the wall, the priest shall go out to the door
39 of the house and shut the house up for seven days. On the
seventh day, the priest shall return; he shall examine the
40 disease and, if it has spread in the walls of the house, the
priest shall order the stones in which the disease appears
to be removed and thrown into a ritually impure place
41 outside the town. He shall have the inside of the house
scraped all around, and the plaster that they scrape off
shall be poured out in an impure place outside the city.
42 They shall take other stones and put them in the place of
those stones, and take new plaster and replaster the house.
43 If the disease breaks out again in the house after the stones
have been removed and the house has been scraped and
44 plastered, the priest shall come back and examine it. If the
disease has spread, then there is malignant blight in the
45 house; it is impure. He shall have the house torn down,
its stones, timber, and all the plaster from the house, and
have them all taken outside the town to an impure place.
46 Anyone who entered the house while it was shut up shall
47 be impure until the evening. Anyone who slept in the
house shall wash his clothes; anyone who ate in the house
48 shall wash his clothes. If, however, the priest comes and
examines it and the disease has not spread in the house
after its plastering, then the priest shall pronounce the
49 house pure; the disease is healed. He shall take two birds,
and cedarwood, scarlet wool, and hyssop to purify the

---

public shaming. Never say or do in private what you would be ashamed to read about on the front page of tomorrow's newspapers. That is the basic theme of the law of *tzaraat*.

לו לֵאמֹר כְּנֶגַע נִרְאָה לִי בַּבָּיִת: וְצִוָּה הַכֹּהֵן וּפִנּוּ אֶת־הַבַּיִת
בְּטֶרֶם יָבֹא הַכֹּהֵן לִרְאוֹת אֶת־הַנֶּגַע וְלֹא יִטְמָא כָּל־אֲשֶׁר
לז בַּבָּיִת וְאַחַר כֵּן יָבֹא הַכֹּהֵן לִרְאוֹת אֶת־הַבָּיִת: וְרָאָה
אֶת־הַנֶּגַע וְהִנֵּה הַנֶּגַע בְּקִירֹת הַבַּיִת שְׁקַעֲרוּרֹת יְרַקְרַקֹּת
לח אוֹ אֲדַמְדַּמֹּת וּמַרְאֵיהֶן שָׁפָל מִן־הַקִּיר: וְיָצָא הַכֹּהֵן מִן־
הַבַּיִת אֶל־פֶּתַח הַבָּיִת וְהִסְגִּיר אֶת־הַבַּיִת שִׁבְעַת יָמִים:
לט וְשָׁב הַכֹּהֵן בַּיּוֹם הַשְּׁבִיעִי וְרָאָה וְהִנֵּה פָּשָׂה הַנֶּגַע בְּקִירֹת
מ הַבָּיִת: וְצִוָּה הַכֹּהֵן וְחִלְּצוּ אֶת־הָאֲבָנִים אֲשֶׁר בָּהֵן הַנָּגַע
מא וְהִשְׁלִיכוּ אֶתְהֶן אֶל־מִחוּץ לָעִיר אֶל־מָקוֹם טָמֵא: וְאֶת־
הַבַּיִת יַקְצִעַ מִבַּיִת סָבִיב וְשָׁפְכוּ אֶת־הֶעָפָר אֲשֶׁר הִקְצוּ
מב אֶל־מִחוּץ לָעִיר אֶל־מָקוֹם טָמֵא: וְלָקְחוּ אֲבָנִים אֲחֵרוֹת
וְהֵבִיאוּ אֶל־תַּחַת הָאֲבָנִים וְעָפָר אַחֵר יִקַּח וְטָח אֶת־הַבָּיִת:
מג וְאִם־יָשׁוּב הַנֶּגַע וּפָרַח בַּבַּיִת אַחַר חִלֵּץ אֶת־הָאֲבָנִים וְאַחֲרֵי
מד הִקְצוֹת אֶת־הַבַּיִת וְאַחֲרֵי הִטּוֹחַ: וּבָא הַכֹּהֵן וְרָאָה וְהִנֵּה
פָּשָׂה הַנֶּגַע בַּבָּיִת צָרַעַת מַמְאֶרֶת הִוא בַּבַּיִת טָמֵא הוּא:
מה וְנָתַץ אֶת־הַבַּיִת אֶת־אֲבָנָיו וְאֶת־עֵצָיו וְאֵת כָּל־עֲפַר הַבָּיִת
מו וְהוֹצִיא אֶל־מִחוּץ לָעִיר אֶל־מָקוֹם טָמֵא: וְהַבָּא אֶל־הַבַּיִת
מז כָּל־יְמֵי הִסְגִּיר אֹתוֹ יִטְמָא עַד־הָעָרֶב: וְהַשֹּׁכֵב בַּבַּיִת יְכַבֵּס
מח אֶת־בְּגָדָיו וְהָאֹכֵל בַּבַּיִת יְכַבֵּס אֶת־בְּגָדָיו: וְאִם־בֹּא יָבֹא
הַכֹּהֵן וְרָאָה וְהִנֵּה לֹא־פָשָׂה הַנֶּגַע בַּבַּיִת אַחֲרֵי הִטֹּחַ אֶת־
מט הַבָּיִת וְטִהַר הַכֹּהֵן אֶת־הַבַּיִת כִּי נִרְפָּא הַנָּגַע: וְלָקַח לְחַטֵּא

that seeks to conceal itself. People who speak badly about others do so in private, in hushed, conspiratorial tones, and often deny that they have done so. What connects the different types of *tzaraat* – garments, the walls of houses, and skin – is that they themselves are boundaries between inside and outside, and holiness depends on the health and strength of boundaries.

That is why, as long as the condition of *tzaraat* existed, what had been done in private was broadcast in public, first by the walls of the offender's house, then by his clothes, and finally by his skin. It was not just a punishment. It was a

50 house. He shall slaughter one of the birds in an earthen
51 vessel over living water. He shall take the cedarwood, the
hyssop, the scarlet wool, and the living bird and dip them
in the blood of the slaughtered bird, in the living water,
52 and sprinkle the house seven times. He shall purify the
house with the blood of the bird and the living water,
with the living bird, the cedarwood, the hyssop, and the
53 scarlet wool. And he shall send the living bird forth free
outside the city, into the open field. Thus shall he make
54 atonement for the house, and it shall be purified." This HAMISHI
is the law for every impure blight of disease, for a scaling
55 56 eruption, for blight of a garment or a house, and for
57 swellings, eruptions, and bright patches on the skin, to
determine when they are impure and when they are pure.
This is the law of the blight.
15 1 2 The Lord spoke to Moshe and Aharon: "Speak to the
Israelites. Say: When any man has a genital discharge, he
3 is rendered impure. This is the impurity brought about by
his discharge: whether his member allows the discharge
to flow or whether it blocks it, the discharge renders him
4 impure, so that any bed he lies upon and any object he sits
5 upon becomes impure. Anyone who touches his bed shall
wash his clothes, immerse in water, and remain impure
6 until evening. Anyone who sits on something he has sat
upon shall wash his clothes, immerse in water, and remain
7 impure until evening. Anyone who touches his body shall
wash his clothes, immerse in water, and remain impure
8 until evening. If the man with the discharge spits on a
person who is pure, that person shall wash his clothes,
immerse in water, and remain impure until evening.
9 Any saddle on which the man with the discharge rides
10 becomes impure. Anyone who touches anything that was
underneath him shall be impure until evening. Anyone

represented a kind of death, the death of the unfertilized egg and of the possibility that month of new life. Seminal and other discharges likewise defiled because they too were signs of the body functioning in non-normal ways.

נ אֶת־הַבַּיִת שְׁתֵּי צִפֳּרִים וְעֵץ אֶרֶז וּשְׁנִי תוֹלַעַת וְאֵזֹב׃ וְשָׁחַט
נא אֶת־הַצִּפֹּר הָאֶחָת אֶל־כְּלִי־חֶרֶשׂ עַל־מַיִם חַיִּים׃ וְלָקַח
אֶת־עֵץ־הָאֶרֶז וְאֶת־הָאֵזֹב וְאֵת ׀ שְׁנִי הַתּוֹלַעַת וְאֵת הַצִּפֹּר
הַחַיָּה וְטָבַל אֹתָם בְּדַם הַצִּפֹּר הַשְּׁחוּטָה וּבַמַּיִם הַחַיִּים וְהִזָּה
נב אֶל־הַבַּיִת שֶׁבַע פְּעָמִים׃ וְחִטֵּא אֶת־הַבַּיִת בְּדַם הַצִּפּוֹר
וּבַמַּיִם הַחַיִּים וּבַצִּפֹּר הַחַיָּה וּבְעֵץ הָאֶרֶז וּבָאֵזֹב וּבִשְׁנִי
נג הַתּוֹלָעַת׃ וְשִׁלַּח אֶת־הַצִּפֹּר הַחַיָּה אֶל־מִחוּץ לָעִיר אֶל־
נד פְּנֵי הַשָּׂדֶה וְכִפֶּר עַל־הַבַּיִת וְטָהֵר׃ זֹאת הַתּוֹרָה לְכָל־נֶגַע חמישי
נה נו הַצָּרַעַת וְלַנָּתֶק׃ וּלְצָרַעַת הַבֶּגֶד וְלַבָּיִת׃ וְלַשְׂאֵת וְלַסַּפַּחַת
נז וְלַבֶּהָרֶת׃ לְהוֹרֹת בְּיוֹם הַטָּמֵא וּבְיוֹם הַטָּהֹר זֹאת תּוֹרַת
הַצָּרָעַת׃

טו א ב וַיְדַבֵּר יְהוָה אֶל־מֹשֶׁה וְאֶל־אַהֲרֹן לֵאמֹר׃ דַּבְּרוּ אֶל־בְּנֵי יא
יִשְׂרָאֵל וַאֲמַרְתֶּם אֲלֵהֶם אִישׁ אִישׁ כִּי יִהְיֶה זָב מִבְּשָׂרוֹ
ג זוֹבוֹ טָמֵא הוּא׃ וְזֹאת תִּהְיֶה טֻמְאָתוֹ בְּזוֹבוֹ רָר בְּשָׂרוֹ אֶת־
ד זוֹבוֹ אוֹ־הֶחְתִּים בְּשָׂרוֹ מִזּוֹבוֹ טֻמְאָתוֹ הִוא׃ כָּל־הַמִּשְׁכָּב
אֲשֶׁר יִשְׁכַּב עָלָיו הַזָּב יִטְמָא וְכָל־הַכְּלִי אֲשֶׁר־יֵשֵׁב עָלָיו
ה יִטְמָא׃ וְאִישׁ אֲשֶׁר יִגַּע בְּמִשְׁכָּבוֹ יְכַבֵּס בְּגָדָיו וְרָחַץ בַּמַּיִם
ו וְטָמֵא עַד־הָעָרֶב׃ וְהַיֹּשֵׁב עַל־הַכְּלִי אֲשֶׁר־יֵשֵׁב עָלָיו הַזָּב
ז יְכַבֵּס בְּגָדָיו וְרָחַץ בַּמַּיִם וְטָמֵא עַד־הָעָרֶב׃ וְהַנֹּגֵעַ בִּבְשַׂר
ח הַזָּב יְכַבֵּס בְּגָדָיו וְרָחַץ בַּמַּיִם וְטָמֵא עַד־הָעָרֶב׃ וְכִי־יָרֹק
הַזָּב בַּטָּהוֹר וְכִבֶּס בְּגָדָיו וְרָחַץ בַּמַּיִם וְטָמֵא עַד־הָעָרֶב׃
ט י וְכָל־הַמֶּרְכָּב אֲשֶׁר יִרְכַּב עָלָיו הַזָּב יִטְמָא׃ וְכָל־הַנֹּגֵעַ בְּכֹל
אֲשֶׁר יִהְיֶה תַחְתָּיו יִטְמָא עַד־הָעָרֶב וְהַנּוֹשֵׂא אוֹתָם יְכַבֵּס
יא בְּגָדָיו וְרָחַץ בַּמַּיִם וְטָמֵא עַד־הָעָרֶב׃ וְכֹל אֲשֶׁר יִגַּע־בּוֹ

15:2 זָב מִבְּשָׂרוֹ *A genital discharge* – The supreme source of impurity is death: contact with or proximity to a dead body. Likewise, the flow of menstrual blood and the reproductive cycle is a sign of human mortality. The appearance of menstrual blood was a sign that the woman was not pregnant, so it may have

▶

who moves such an item shall wash his clothes, immerse
11 in water, and be impure until evening. If the man with
the discharge touches someone without first washing
his hands with water, that person shall wash his clothes,
12 immerse in water, and remain impure until evening. Any
earthen vessel that the man with the discharge touches
shall be broken, any wooden vessel immersed in water.
13 When the man with the discharge is purified of it, he shall
count seven days for his purification. Then he shall wash
his clothes and immerse his body in flowing water; then he
14 is pure. On the eighth day he shall take two doves or two
pigeons before the LORD to the entrance of the Tent of
15 Meeting and give them to the priest. The priest shall offer
them, one as a purification offering, the other as a burnt
offering. Thus shall the priest make the man's atonement
16 before the LORD after his discharge. If a man has SHISHI /SHEVI'I/
an emission of semen, he shall immerse his entire body in
17 water, and he remains impure until evening. Any clothing
or leather on which there is an emission of semen shall
be washed in water and shall be impure until evening.
18 And any woman with whom a man lies carnally – both
partners shall immerse in water and remain impure until
evening.
19 When a woman has a discharge of blood that is her usual
bodily discharge, she retains her menstrual status for
seven days. Any person who touches her then shall be
20 impure until evening. Anything on which she lies or sits
21 during her menstrual time becomes impure. Whoever
touches her bed shall wash his clothes, immerse in water,

This is the Torah's form of chaos theory: as the beating of a butterfly's wing can cause a typhoon on the other side of the earth, so small breaches in boundaries can lead, in time, to anarchy and tyranny. Knowing how rapid the descent can be from civilization to barbarism, the priestly sensibility is vigilant in maintaining what Wallace Stevens called the "blessed rage for order." That "a man…cleaves to his wife and they become one flesh" (2:24) is part of the order of Eden. Yet that bond too requires the clear drawing of boundaries, its space set apart.

הַזָּב וְיָדָיו לֹא־שָׁטַף בַּמָּיִם וְכִבֶּס בְּגָדָיו וְרָחַץ בַּמַּיִם וְטָמֵא
יב עַד־הָעָרֶב׃ וּכְלִי־חֶרֶשׂ אֲשֶׁר־יִגַּע־בּוֹ הַזָּב יִשָּׁבֵר וְכָל־כְּלִי־
יג עֵץ יִשָּׁטֵף בַּמָּיִם׃ וְכִי־יִטְהַר הַזָּב מִזּוֹבוֹ וְסָפַר לוֹ שִׁבְעַת
יָמִים לְטָהֳרָתוֹ וְכִבֶּס בְּגָדָיו וְרָחַץ בְּשָׂרוֹ בְּמַיִם חַיִּים וְטָהֵר׃
יד וּבַיּוֹם הַשְּׁמִינִי יִקַּח־לוֹ שְׁתֵּי תֹרִים אוֹ שְׁנֵי בְּנֵי יוֹנָה וּבָא ׀
טו לִפְנֵי יהוה אֶל־פֶּתַח אֹהֶל מוֹעֵד וּנְתָנָם אֶל־הַכֹּהֵן׃ וְעָשָׂה
אֹתָם הַכֹּהֵן אֶחָד חַטָּאת וְהָאֶחָד עֹלָה וְכִפֶּר עָלָיו הַכֹּהֵן
טז לִפְנֵי יהוה מִזּוֹבוֹ׃ וְאִישׁ כִּי־תֵצֵא מִמֶּנּוּ שִׁכְבַת־זָרַע ששי
יז וְרָחַץ בַּמַּיִם אֶת־כָּל־בְּשָׂרוֹ וְטָמֵא עַד־הָעָרֶב׃ וְכָל־בֶּגֶד /שביעי/
וְכָל־עוֹר אֲשֶׁר־יִהְיֶה עָלָיו שִׁכְבַת־זָרַע וְכֻבַּס בַּמַּיִם וְטָמֵא
יח עַד־הָעָרֶב׃ וְאִשָּׁה אֲשֶׁר יִשְׁכַּב אִישׁ אֹתָהּ שִׁכְבַת־זָרַע
וְרָחֲצוּ בַמַּיִם וְטָמְאוּ עַד־הָעָרֶב׃
יט וְאִשָּׁה כִּי־תִהְיֶה זָבָה דָּם יִהְיֶה זֹבָהּ בִּבְשָׂרָהּ שִׁבְעַת יָמִים
כ תִּהְיֶה בְנִדָּתָהּ וְכָל־הַנֹּגֵעַ בָּהּ יִטְמָא עַד־הָעָרֶב׃ וְכֹל אֲשֶׁר
תִּשְׁכַּב עָלָיו בְּנִדָּתָהּ יִטְמָא וְכֹל אֲשֶׁר־תֵּשֵׁב עָלָיו יִטְמָא׃
כא וְכָל־הַנֹּגֵעַ בְּמִשְׁכָּבָהּ יְכַבֵּס בְּגָדָיו וְרָחַץ בַּמַּיִם וְטָמֵא עַד־

15:18 וְטָמְאוּ עַד־הָעָרֶב *Remain impure until evening* – God does not ask of us to sacrifice or devalue our physicality. To the contrary, we are part of the physical world He created, and this is where He wants us to serve Him. Nonetheless, lines have to be drawn and boundaries maintained between God's domain and ours. This is the function of the purity laws.

The word *tameh* in one or other of its forms appears no less than 106 times in Leviticus, while the root *tahor* appears 62 times. The root *tameh* appears only 285 times in Tanakh as a whole, and *tahor* 207 times, so that Leviticus accounts for around one-third of the occurrences of these words in the Hebrew Bible's thirty-nine books. The only rival in this respect is the book of Ezekiel. Yeḥezkel was both a prophet and a priest, and his is the most identifiably priestly voice in the non-Mosaic books. How does the priestly domain of regulatory order touch upon the prophetic domain of love and justice?

It was failure to observe the boundary between permitted and forbidden that caused Adam and Ḥava to be exiled from Eden. Within a generation, the first murder had taken place, and before long "the earth had become… full with violence" (Gen. 6:11).

22 and remain impure until evening. Whoever touches any
object she has sat upon shall wash his clothes, immerse in
23 water, and remain impure until evening. Whether it be a
bed or any object she sits upon, when one touches it he
24 shall be impure until evening. If a man has sexual relations
with her, her menstrual status is extended to him; he too
shall be impure for seven days, and any bed he lies upon
25 is rendered impure. Whenever a woman has a
discharge of blood for many days at a time other than her
menstrual period, or if she has a discharge beyond her
menstrual period, she shall be impure as long as she has
26 the discharge, as she is in her menstrual time. Any bed she
lies upon while she has this discharge shall be treated like
the bed she uses during her menstruation, and any object
she sits upon becomes impure, as during her menstrual
27 time. Whoever touches these things is rendered impure;
he shall wash his clothes, immerse in water, and remain
28 impure until evening. When the woman's discharge ends,
she shall count seven days; after that, she will be purified.
29 On the eighth day she shall take two doves or two pigeons SHEVI'I
and bring them to the priest at the entrance to the Tent
30 of Meeting. The priest shall prepare one as a purification
offering and the other as a burnt offering. Thus shall the
priest make her atonement before the LORD following
31 her impure discharge. You must separate the Israelites MAFTIR
from their own impurity so that they do not die in their

---

the two organizing principles of the priestly mind, are about the intense and vigilant preparation we must make before entering God's space. God is that which is not mortal, finite, and physical. Therefore, whatever inescapably reminds us of our physicality and mortality – whether it be birth or death, or a skin disease, or the flow of menstrual blood, or the unusual discharge of some bodily fluid, or contact with the carcass of a repulsive animal – conveys *tuma*, that is, a state from which we must be cleansed before entering the domain of the holy.

There is nothing intrinsically defiling about our physicality. To the contrary, the Torah asks us to seek God within the physical world, to sanctify rather than forswear physical pleasures such as eating and drinking and the marital bond.

כב הָעָרֶב: וְכָל־הַנֹּגֵעַ בְּכָל־כְּלִי אֲשֶׁר־תֵּשֵׁב עָלָיו יְכַבֵּס בְּגָדָיו
כג וְרָחַץ בַּמַּיִם וְטָמֵא עַד־הָעָרֶב: וְאִם עַל־הַמִּשְׁכָּב הוּא
אוֹ עַל־הַכְּלִי אֲשֶׁר־הִוא יֹשֶׁבֶת־עָלָיו בְּנָגְעוֹ־בוֹ יִטְמָא
כד עַד־הָעָרֶב: וְאִם שָׁכֹב יִשְׁכַּב אִישׁ אֹתָהּ וּתְהִי נִדָּתָהּ
עָלָיו וְטָמֵא שִׁבְעַת יָמִים וְכָל־הַמִּשְׁכָּב אֲשֶׁר־יִשְׁכַּב עָלָיו
כה יִטְמָא: וְאִשָּׁה כִּי־יָזוּב זוֹב דָּמָהּ יָמִים רַבִּים בְּלֹא יב
עֶת־נִדָּתָהּ אוֹ כִי־תָזוּב עַל־נִדָּתָהּ כָּל־יְמֵי זוֹב טֻמְאָתָהּ כִּימֵי
כו נִדָּתָהּ תִּהְיֶה טְמֵאָה הִוא: כָּל־הַמִּשְׁכָּב אֲשֶׁר תִּשְׁכַּב עָלָיו
כָּל־יְמֵי זוֹבָהּ כְּמִשְׁכַּב נִדָּתָהּ יִהְיֶה־לָּהּ וְכָל־הַכְּלִי אֲשֶׁר
כז תֵּשֵׁב עָלָיו טָמֵא יִהְיֶה כְּטֻמְאַת נִדָּתָהּ: וְכָל־הַנּוֹגֵעַ בָּם
כח יִטְמָא וְכִבֶּס בְּגָדָיו וְרָחַץ בַּמַּיִם וְטָמֵא עַד־הָעָרֶב: וְאִם־
כט טָהֲרָה מִזּוֹבָהּ וְסָפְרָה־לָּהּ שִׁבְעַת יָמִים וְאַחַר תִּטְהָר: וּבַיּוֹם שביעי
הַשְּׁמִינִי תִּקַּח־לָהּ שְׁתֵּי תֹרִים אוֹ שְׁנֵי בְּנֵי יוֹנָה וְהֵבִיאָה
ל אוֹתָם אֶל־הַכֹּהֵן אֶל־פֶּתַח אֹהֶל מוֹעֵד: וְעָשָׂה הַכֹּהֵן אֶת־
הָאֶחָד חַטָּאת וְאֶת־הָאֶחָד עֹלָה וְכִפֶּר עָלֶיהָ הַכֹּהֵן לִפְנֵי
לא יְהוָה מִזּוֹב טֻמְאָתָהּ: וְהִזַּרְתֶּם אֶת־בְּנֵי־יִשְׂרָאֵל מִטֻּמְאָתָם מפטיר
וְלֹא יָמֻתוּ בְּטֻמְאָתָם בְּטַמְּאָם אֶת־מִשְׁכָּנִי אֲשֶׁר בְּתוֹכָם:

15:31 בְּטַמְּאָם אֶת־מִשְׁכָּנִי *Making My Tabernacle impure* – The concepts of purity and impurity, as we know, have their main application in relation to the holy space of the Sanctuary. To enter its precincts one has to be pure, or purified. The chief exception is a woman's issue of menstrual blood, from which she had to be purified not only to enter the Temple, but also to resume physical relations with her husband. In general, "pure" and "impure" are not categories applying to life as a whole. They are not ethical terms like good and bad, right and wrong, which apply to secular as well as sacred space and time. They only exist because God has stipulated that they exist, just as, for example, the Sabbath only exists because God so ordered it. You cannot tell that a certain day was the Sabbath because, say, of the quality of the light or the air or the temperature. So the concept of impurity is not like the idea of uncleanliness, which could have physical manifestations. *Tuma* and *tahara* are spiritual categories brought into being by God's command.

The concepts of holiness and purity,

impurity by making My Tabernacle impure in their
32 midst." This is the law concerning the man who is impure
33 because of a discharge or seminal emission, the woman
during her menstrual period, the man or woman who has
a discharge, and the man who has sexual relations with a
woman who is impure.

The haftara for Parashat Metzora is on page 1528
(even when Tazria and Metzora are read together).
On Shabbat HaGadol read the haftara on page 1672.
On Rosh Ḥodesh Iyar read the haftara on page 1640.
On Erev Rosh Ḥodesh Iyar read the haftara on page 1644.

---

we should deny them, but simply to remind ourselves that God utterly transcends all such accidents and attributes of materiality. In the Temple we are in the presence of radical transcendence.

לב זֹ֥את תּוֹרַ֖ת הַזָּ֑ב וַאֲשֶׁ֨ר תֵּצֵ֥א מִמֶּ֛נּוּ שִׁכְבַת־זֶ֖רַע לְטָמְאָה־
לג בָֽהּ׃ וְהַדָּוָה֙ בְּנִדָּתָ֔הּ וְהַזָּב֙ אֶת־זוֹב֔וֹ לַזָּכָ֖ר וְלַנְּקֵבָ֑ה וּלְאִ֕ישׁ
אֲשֶׁ֥ר יִשְׁכַּ֖ב עִם־טְמֵאָֽה׃

The הפטרה *for* פרשת מצרע *is on page 1529*
(even when תוריע *and* מצרע *are read together).*
On שבת הגדול *read the* הפטרה *on page 1673.*
On ראש חודש אייר *read the* הפטרה *on page 1641.*
On ערב ראש חודש אייר *read the* הפטרה *on page 1645.*

There is nothing ascetic or otherworldly about the Torah's ethic.

Rather, we have to ensure that we have divested ourselves of all lingering traces of that which reminds us of our mortality and physicality, our vulnerability to disease, decay, and death, not because we can escape them, nor that

▶

Parashat Aḥarei Mot

16 1 After the deaths of Aharon's two sons – when they
came close to the Lord and died – the Lord spoke to
2 Moshe. "Tell your brother Aharon," said the Lord to
Moshe, "that he may not come at any time into the holy
place inside the inner curtain in front of the cover on
the Ark, or he will die – for in a cloud above the cover

---

the High Priest confess and atone for the sins of all Israel, sins he did not commit? The answer, surely, is that while Judaism has a strong sense of individual dignity and responsibility, it has an equally strong sense of collective responsibility. "All of Israel," says the Talmud, "are sureties for one another." Ours is not a religion of hermits, living apart from society and communing solely with God. The heroes and heroines of the Torah are fathers and mothers, people set in the context of their families and societies. On Yom Kippur we confess together, publicly and aloud. We say not "I have sinned" but "We have sinned."

Yom Kippur is a day of awe. Yet the Talmud calls it one of the most joyous days of the year. Rightly so, for its message is that as long as we breathe, there is no final verdict on our lives. "Prayer, penitence and charity have the power to turn aside the evil decree."

Throughout our history, on Yom Kippur, Jews who have grown distant, Jews who were forced to disavow their faith in public, even those who had been excommunicated, joined the congregation in prayer. It is the moment when the doors of belonging are opened, and those who have been estranged return.

The Hebrew word *teshuva,* usually translated as "penitence," in fact means returning, retracing our steps, coming home. *Teshuva* as a "return" belongs to the biblical vision in which sin means dislocation, and punishment is exile: Adam and Ḥava's exile from Eden, Israel's exile from its land (see Lev. 24:28). A sin is an act that does not belong, one that transgresses the moral boundaries of the world. Those who act in ways that do not belong find eventually that they do not belong. Increasingly, they place themselves outside the relationships – of family, of community, and of being at one with history – that make them who they are. The most characteristic sense of sin is less one of guilt than of being lost. *Teshuva* means finding your way back home again. On this day of days we hear His voice, gently calling us to come home.

פרשת אחרי מות

טז א וַיְדַבֵּר יְהוָה אֶל־מֹשֶׁה אַחֲרֵי מוֹת שְׁנֵי בְּנֵי אַהֲרֹן בְּקָרְבָתָם
ב לִפְנֵי־יְהוָה וַיָּמֻתוּ׃ וַיֹּאמֶר יְהוָה אֶל־מֹשֶׁה דַּבֵּר אֶל־אַהֲרֹן
אָחִיךָ וְאַל־יָבֹא בְכָל־עֵת אֶל־הַקֹּדֶשׁ מִבֵּית לַפָּרֹכֶת אֶל־
פְּנֵי הַכַּפֹּרֶת אֲשֶׁר עַל־הָאָרֹן וְלֹא יָמוּת כִּי בֶּעָנָן אֵרָאֶה

AḤAREI MOT

Parashat Aḥarei Mot describes the service of the High Priest on the Day of Atonement. This is a dramatic and highly charged ritual during which he casts lots on two identical goats, one of which is offered as a sacrifice, while the other is sent into the wilderness to die, the so-called "scapegoat." The entry of the High Priest into the Holy of Holies marks the spiritual high point of the Jewish year.

The *parasha* also outlines the prohibition against eating blood, and the laws of forbidden sexual relations, both of them aspects of the life of purity God asks of the Jewish people. Beginning, then, "after the deaths of Aharon's two sons [Nadav and Avihu] – when they came close to the LORD and died," the *parasha* closes a cycle that deals with the boundaries that protect lives lived in the presence of God.

YOM KIPPUR

Yom Kippur, the Day of Atonement, is the supreme moment of Jewish time, a day of fasting and prayer, introspection and self-judgment. At no other time are we so sharply conscious of standing before God, of *being known*.

The Torah speaks of holy places. The land of Israel is holy. Holier still is Jerusalem, and in Jerusalem the holiest site will be the Temple. Within the Temple – then within the Tabernacle – is the supremely sacred place known as the Holy of Holies.

There is holy time. There are the festivals. Above them is the Sabbath. Above even that is the one day in the year known as *Shabbat Shabbaton*, the most holy day of all, Yom Kippur.

There are holy people. Israel is called a "holy people" (Deut. 7:6). Among them is a tribe of special sanctity, the Levites, and within it are individuals who are holier still, the *kohanim* or priests. Among them is a person who is supremely holy, the High Priest.

In the Tabernacle, the holiest man is to enter the holiest place on the holiest day of the year and seek atonement for his people. Since the destruction of the Temple, we no longer have the holiest place and person. But we still have the day itself: holy time, along with the possibility of repentance and purification.

At the core of the day's service is *vidui*, confession (Lev. 16:21). How can

3 I appear. This is how Aharon is to enter the holy place:
with a young bull as a purification offering and a ram as
4 a burnt offering; he shall put on the sacred linen tunic
with linen undergarments covering his body. He shall
bind the linen sash around himself and wrap a linen
turban about his head. These are sacred vestments; he
shall immerse himself in water and only then put them
5 on. From the community of Israel he shall take two male
goats for a purification offering and a ram for a burnt
6 offering. And Aharon shall bring close the bull for his

(see Gen. 25:34 and the note there; see also the note on Gen. 36:31). Yaakov is the opposite. He acts and thinks long-term. That is what he does when he seizes the opportunity to buy Esav's birthright, when he works for seven years for Raḥel, a period that "seemed to him but a few days" (29:20), and when he fixes terms with Lavan for payment for his labor. Rebuking his son Yosef for the seeming presumptuousness of his dreams, the Torah tells us that the brothers were jealous of Yosef "but his father kept the matter in mind" (37:11). Yaakov never acts impulsively. He thinks long and hard.

The two goats of the High Priest's service symbolize a duality within each of us: "The voice is the voice of Yaakov, but the hands are the hands of Esav" (27:22). The power of ritual is that it does not speak in abstractions. It is gripping, visceral. We each have an inner Esav and Yaakov, the impulsive, emotional brain and the reflective, deliberative one. Our fate, our life script, will be determined by which we choose. Will our life be lived "for the Lord," or rather "for Azazel," left to the random vicissitudes of chance?

Who are you? That is the question Yom Kippur forces us to ask ourselves, as Yitzḥak asked Yaakov (27:18). To be Yaakov, we have to release and relinquish the Esav within us, the impulsiveness that can lead us to sell our birthright for a bowl of soup, to lose eternity in the pursuit of desire.

16:6 פַּר הַחַטָּאת אֲשֶׁר־לוֹ *His purification* – The bull is designated as a purification offering for the High Priest himself. Rashi learns from the words "his purification" that the bull must be purchased with his own money. This is in contrast to the two goats, which atone for the whole Jewish people and are bought with public funds. The High Priest is required to confess his sins and those of his family. This is the first of three acts of atonement by the High Priest on this day: first for himself and his family, then for the priesthood as a whole (v. 11), and only then for the whole nation (v. 21). The message is clear: we must purify ourselves before we can purify others.

ג עַל־הַכַּפֹּרֶת׃ בְּזֹאת יָבֹא אַהֲרֹן אֶל־הַקֹּדֶשׁ בְּפַר בֶּן־בָּקָר
ד לְחַטָּאת וְאַיִל לְעֹלָה׃ כְּתֹנֶת־בַּד קֹדֶשׁ יִלְבָּשׁ וּמִכְנְסֵי־בַד
יִהְיוּ עַל־בְּשָׂרוֹ וּבְאַבְנֵט בַּד יַחְגֹּר וּבְמִצְנֶפֶת בַּד יִצְנֹף בִּגְדֵי־
ה קֹדֶשׁ הֵם וְרָחַץ בַּמַּיִם אֶת־בְּשָׂרוֹ וּלְבֵשָׁם׃ וּמֵאֵת עֲדַת בְּנֵי
יִשְׂרָאֵל יִקַּח שְׁנֵי־שְׂעִירֵי עִזִּים לְחַטָּאת וְאַיִל אֶחָד לְעֹלָה׃
ו וְהִקְרִיב אַהֲרֹן אֶת־פַּר הַחַטָּאת אֲשֶׁר־לוֹ וְכִפֶּר בַּעֲדוֹ וּבְעַד

16:4 כְּתֹנֶת־בַּד קֹדֶשׁ יִלְבָּשׁ *Sacred linen tunic* – In public, the High Priest appears in garments of gold, "for glory and for splendor" (Ex. 28:2). Alone with God, however, he is to dress in the simplest linen garments. In the encounter with God, honesty, simplicity, and humility are needed. Some say that it is in memory of this that many men wear a kittel, a plain white robe, on Yom Kippur.

THE RITUAL OF THE TWO GOATS

Central to the Yom Kippur ritual, prescribed in the Torah and expounded in the Mishna, are two goats. They are, for all intents and purposes, indistinguishable from one another; they are chosen to be as similar as possible in size and appearance. They are brought before the High Priest and lots are drawn, one bearing the words "For the LORD," the other, "For Azazel." The first is offered as a sacrifice. Over the second, the High Priest confesses the sins of the nation, and it is then taken away into the desert hills where it plunges to its death. Tradition tells us that a red thread would be attached to its horns, half of which was removed before the animal was sent away. If the rite had been effective, the red thread would turn to white.

Two animals, alike in appearance but different in fate, suggest the idea of twins. This and other clues led classic commentators such as Ramban and Abrabanel to the conclusion that the goats symbolized the most famous of the Torah's twins, Yaakov and Esav. The word *se'ir*, "goat," is associated in the Torah with Esav. He and his descendants lived in the land of Se'ir, while he himself was *sa'ir*, "hairy" (Gen. 27:11). The red thread that is tied to the scapegoat in the Mishna's account recalls Edom – from *adom*, "red" – Esav's other name. The "two male goats" of the High Priest's rites remind us of the "two choice young goats" (27:9) served to Yitzḥak in the scene of Yaakov's deception.

The two goats of the High Priest's service, then, evoke the figures of Yaakov and Esav. What do those brothers represent in the context of Yom Kippur? Midrashic tradition tends to portray Esav as an evildoer. The Torah itself is more nuanced. Esav is not a figure of evil. His father loved him and sought to bless him. Rather, he is the man of impulse

purification offering, to make atonement for him and
7 for his family. He shall take the two goats and set them
before the LORD at the entrance to the Tent of Meeting.
8 Aharon shall cast lots over the two goats, one lot marked
9 'For the LORD,' the other 'For Azazel.' The goat on which
the lot for the LORD fell, Aharon should bring close and
10 offer up as a purification offering. But the goat on which
the lot fell for Azazel shall be presented alive before the
LORD; atonement shall be made over it; it shall be sent
11 forth, away into the wilderness to Azazel. Aharon shall
bring close the bull for his purification offering to make
atonement for him and for his family; he shall slaughter
12 the bull as his purification offering. He shall then take
a pan full of burning coals from the altar, from before
the LORD, and two handfuls of finely ground fragrant
13 incense, and bring them inside the inner curtain. He shall
place the incense on the fire before the LORD so that the
cloud of incense conceals the cover on top of the Ark of
14 the Testimony, so that he does not die. He shall take some
of the bull's blood and sprinkle it with his finger on the
cover on the east side. Then, in front of the cover, he shall

---

held to be responsible for the plight of the community. As the French scholar René Girard described the phenomenon:

> The persecutors convince themselves that a small number of people, or even a single individual, despite his relative weakness is extremely harmful to the whole of society.... He will be responsible for the cure, since he was responsible for the sickness.

Hence the demonization that has time and again led to pogroms, massacres, and genocides. Societies find it easier to blame a scapegoat than to face their own problems honestly and openly.

Projecting violence within the group onto an innocent outsider who is held guilty and killed to preserve the group is a vicious idea. The biblical scapegoat is precisely not a scapegoat in Girard's sense. Two features of the High Priest's ritual were crucial in this respect: (1) that the sacrifice was an animal, not a person; and (2) that the goat is dedicated by confession (v. 21). This is not an occasion for denying responsibility by blaming the victim, but to the contrary, an acceptance of responsibility in the context of repentance and atonement.

ז בֵּיתוֹ׃ וְלָקַח אֶת־שְׁנֵי הַשְּׂעִירִם וְהֶעֱמִיד אֹתָם לִפְנֵי יְהוָה
ח פֶּתַח אֹהֶל מוֹעֵד׃ וְנָתַן אַהֲרֹן עַל־שְׁנֵי הַשְּׂעִירִם גֹּרָלוֹת
ט גּוֹרָל אֶחָד לַיהוָה וְגוֹרָל אֶחָד לַעֲזָאזֵל׃ וְהִקְרִיב אַהֲרֹן
אֶת־הַשָּׂעִיר אֲשֶׁר עָלָה עָלָיו הַגּוֹרָל לַיהוָה וְעָשָׂהוּ חַטָּאת׃
י וְהַשָּׂעִיר אֲשֶׁר עָלָה עָלָיו הַגּוֹרָל לַעֲזָאזֵל יָעֳמַד־חַי לִפְנֵי
יא יְהוָה לְכַפֵּר עָלָיו לְשַׁלַּח אֹתוֹ לַעֲזָאזֵל הַמִּדְבָּרָה׃ וְהִקְרִיב
אַהֲרֹן אֶת־פַּר הַחַטָּאת אֲשֶׁר־לוֹ וְכִפֶּר בַּעֲדוֹ וּבְעַד בֵּיתוֹ
יב וְשָׁחַט אֶת־פַּר הַחַטָּאת אֲשֶׁר־לוֹ׃ וְלָקַח מְלֹא־הַמַּחְתָּה
גַּחֲלֵי־אֵשׁ מֵעַל הַמִּזְבֵּחַ מִלִּפְנֵי יְהוָה וּמְלֹא חָפְנָיו קְטֹרֶת
יג סַמִּים דַּקָּה וְהֵבִיא מִבֵּית לַפָּרֹכֶת׃ וְנָתַן אֶת־הַקְּטֹרֶת עַל־
הָאֵשׁ לִפְנֵי יְהוָה וְכִסָּה ׀ עֲנַן הַקְּטֹרֶת אֶת־הַכַּפֹּרֶת אֲשֶׁר
יד עַל־הָעֵדוּת וְלֹא יָמוּת׃ וְלָקַח מִדַּם הַפָּר וְהִזָּה בְאֶצְבָּעוֹ
עַל־פְּנֵי הַכַּפֹּרֶת קֵדְמָה וְלִפְנֵי הַכַּפֹּרֶת יַזֶּה שֶׁבַע־פְּעָמִים

16:8 לַעֲזָאזֵל *For Azazel* – What is the meaning of "Azazel," to which the second goat was sent? It appears nowhere else in Scripture. Three major theories emerged as to its meaning. According to the Sages and Rashi, it means "a steep, rocky, or hard place." In other words, the word is a description of its destination.

The second, suggested by Ibn Ezra and Ramban (see note on 17:7), is that Azazel represented a realm of spirits, demons, or fallen angels. In this sense it is like the word "Gehinnom," often understood as "hell," though in fact it was merely a valley outside of Jerusalem. The craggy, angular desert, hostile to human habitation, was a symbol of chaos and danger.

The third interpretation is that the word simply means "the goat [*ez*] that was sent away [*azal*]." This led to the addition of a new word to the English language. In 1530, William Tyndale produced the first printed English translation of the Hebrew Bible, an act then illegal and for which he paid with his life. Seeking to translate "Azazel" into English, he called it "the escapegoat," i.e., the goat that was sent away and released. In the course of time, the first letter was dropped, and the word "scapegoat" was born.

"Scapegoating," as we use the word today, means blaming someone else for our troubles. Faced with problems that it cannot solve, all too often a group ensures its psychic survival by projecting its inner conflicts onto an external cause,

15 sprinkle some of the blood with his finger seven times. He
shall then slaughter the goat for the people's purification
offering, bring its blood inside the inner curtain, and do
with it as he did with the blood of the bull, sprinkling it on
16 the cover and before the cover. In this way, he shall make
atonement for the Sanctuary – from the impurity of the
Israelites, from their rebellions and all their sins. And he
shall do the same for the Tent of Meeting, which is with
17 them in the midst of their impurity. No one shall be in
the Tent of Meeting from the time Aharon enters to make
atonement in the Sanctuary until he comes out. Thus he
shall make atonement for himself, for his house, and for
18 the whole assembly of Israel. He shall then go out to the SHENI
altar that is before the LORD and make its atonement. He
shall take some of the bull's blood and some of the goat's
19 blood and apply it to each of the altar's horns. He shall
sprinkle some of the blood upon it with his finger seven
times, to purify it and sanctify it from the impurity of
20 the Israelites. When he has finished making atonement
for the Sanctuary, the Tent of Meeting, and the altar, he
21 shall bring close the live goat. Aharon shall lay both his
hands on the head of the live goat and confess over it all
the Israelites' iniquities and rebellions, all of their sins,

---

Second, there is *tahara*, purification, something normally done in a different context altogether, namely the removal of *tuma*, ritual defilement, which could arise from a number of different causes, among them contact with a dead body, skin disease, or nocturnal discharge. Atonement has to do with guilt. Purification has to do with contamination or pollution. These are usually two separate worlds. The difference between guilt cultures and shame cultures is something we have discussed elsewhere (see note on Lev. 5:26). Guilt attaches to the act, not the person. Guilt can be "atoned for" by remorse and restitution, by achieving forgiveness. Shame cannot be removed by forgiveness. We still feel the stigma, the degradation. We feel defiled by the knowledge of our disgrace.

On Yom Kippur, the one day in the year when everyone shares in the process of confession, repentance, atonement, and purification, they are brought together. Yom Kippur confronts our sins as a community bound by mutual responsibility. It deals, in other words, with the social as well as the personal

טו מִן־הַדָּם בְּאֶצְבָּעוֹ: וְשָׁחַט אֶת־שְׂעִיר הַחַטָּאת אֲשֶׁר לָעָם
וְהֵבִיא אֶת־דָּמוֹ אֶל־מִבֵּית לַפָּרֹכֶת וְעָשָׂה אֶת־דָּמוֹ כַּאֲשֶׁר
עָשָׂה לְדַם הַפָּר וְהִזָּה אֹתוֹ עַל־הַכַּפֹּרֶת וְלִפְנֵי הַכַּפֹּרֶת:
טז וְכִפֶּר עַל־הַקֹּדֶשׁ מִטֻּמְאֹת בְּנֵי יִשְׂרָאֵל וּמִפִּשְׁעֵיהֶם לְכָל־
חַטֹּאתָם וְכֵן יַעֲשֶׂה לְאֹהֶל מוֹעֵד הַשֹּׁכֵן אִתָּם בְּתוֹךְ טֻמְאֹתָם:
יז וְכָל־אָדָם לֹא־יִהְיֶה ׀ בְּאֹהֶל מוֹעֵד בְּבֹאוֹ לְכַפֵּר בַּקֹּדֶשׁ עַד־
יח צֵאתוֹ וְכִפֶּר בַּעֲדוֹ וּבְעַד בֵּיתוֹ וּבְעַד כָּל־קְהַל יִשְׂרָאֵל: וְיָצָא שני
אֶל־הַמִּזְבֵּחַ אֲשֶׁר לִפְנֵי־יְהוָה וְכִפֶּר עָלָיו וְלָקַח מִדַּם הַפָּר
יט וּמִדַּם הַשָּׂעִיר וְנָתַן עַל־קַרְנוֹת הַמִּזְבֵּחַ סָבִיב: וְהִזָּה עָלָיו
מִן־הַדָּם בְּאֶצְבָּעוֹ שֶׁבַע פְּעָמִים וְטִהֲרוֹ וְקִדְּשׁוֹ מִטֻּמְאֹת
כ בְּנֵי יִשְׂרָאֵל: וְכִלָּה מִכַּפֵּר אֶת־הַקֹּדֶשׁ וְאֶת־אֹהֶל מוֹעֵד
כא וְאֶת־הַמִּזְבֵּחַ וְהִקְרִיב אֶת־הַשָּׂעִיר הֶחָי: וְסָמַךְ אַהֲרֹן אֶת־
שְׁתֵּי יָדָו עַל רֹאשׁ הַשָּׂעִיר הַחַי וְהִתְוַדָּה עָלָיו אֶת־כָּל־
עֲוֺנֹת בְּנֵי יִשְׂרָאֵל וְאֶת־כָּל־פִּשְׁעֵיהֶם לְכָל־חַטֹּאתָם וְנָתַן

16:21 אֶת־כָּל־עֲוֺנֹת בְּנֵי יִשְׂרָאֵל *All of their sins* – Purification and guilt offerings are familiar features of the Torah and a normal part of the service of the Tabernacle. The service of Yom Kippur is different, however, in one salient respect. In every other case, the sin is confessed over the animal that is sacrificed. On Yom Kippur, the High Priest confesses the sins of the people over the animal that is not sacrificed, the scapegoat that is sent away, "carry[ing] all their iniquities upon itself" (v. 22). Rambam explains as follows:

> There is no doubt that sins cannot be carried like a burden and taken off the shoulder of one being to be laid on that of another being. But these ceremonies are of a symbolic character, and serve to impress people with a certain idea, and to induce them to repent – as if to say: we have freed ourselves of our previous deeds, cast them behind our backs, and removed them from us as far as possible. (*Guide for the Perplexed* III:46)

Expiation demands a ritual, some dramatic representation of the removal of sin and the wiping clean of the past. Why the unique ritual here? The answer is that two distinct processes are involved in Yom Kippur: "On this day, atonement shall be made for you [*yekhaper*] to purify you [*letaher*]; of all your sins you shall be purified before the LORD" (v. 30).

First there is *kappara*, atonement.

putting them on the head of the goat and then sending it
away into the wilderness with the person designated for
22 the task. The goat shall carry all their iniquities upon itself
to a desolate place, and then the goat shall be sent forth
23 into the wilderness. Then Aharon shall enter the Tent
of Meeting, take off the linen vestments he was wearing
when he entered the Sanctuary, and leave them there.
24 He shall immerse his body in water in a holy place and
put on his vestments. Then he shall come out and offer
his burnt offering and the burnt offering of the people,
25 to make atonement for himself and for the people. And SHELISHI
he shall send the fat of the purification offering up in /SHENI/
26 smoke upon the altar. The man who sent forth the goat
for Azazel shall wash his clothes and immerse his body
27 in water; after that he may return to the camp. The
purification offering bull and the purification offering
goat, whose blood was brought in to make atonement
in the inner Sanctuary, shall be removed from the camp.
Their skin, flesh, and dung shall be burned with fire.
28 The one who burns them shall wash his clothes and
immerse his body in water. After that, he too may return
29 to the camp. This shall be an everlasting statute for you:

---

never changed throughout the generations, so long as the Temple stood.

Moshe's prayers on behalf of the people were full of audacity, what the Sages called *ḥutzpa kelapei Shemaya*, "audacity toward Heaven," reaching a climax in the astonishing words "But now, if only You would forgive their sin – but if not, please blot me out of the book You have written" (Ex. 32:32). Aharon's behavior, by contrast, is marked by obedience, humility, and confession. There are purification rituals, sin offerings, and atonements, for his own sins and those of his "house" as well as those of the people.

Few moments in the Torah rival in intensity the dialogue between Moshe and God after the golden calf. But the question thereafter is: how will we achieve forgiveness in the future, without a Moshe, or prophets, or direct access to God? Great moments change history. But what changes us is the unspectacular habit of doing certain acts again and again until they reconfigure the brain and change our habits of the heart.

אֹתָם עַל־רֹאשׁ הַשָּׂעִיר וְשִׁלַּח בְּיַד־אִישׁ עִתִּי הַמִּדְבָּרָה׃
כב וְנָשָׂא הַשָּׂעִיר עָלָיו אֶת־כָּל־עֲוֺנֹתָם אֶל־אֶרֶץ גְּזֵרָה וְשִׁלַּח
כג אֶת־הַשָּׂעִיר בַּמִּדְבָּר׃ וּבָא אַהֲרֹן אֶל־אֹהֶל מוֹעֵד וּפָשַׁט
אֶת־בִּגְדֵי הַבָּד אֲשֶׁר לָבַשׁ בְּבֹאוֹ אֶל־הַקֹּדֶשׁ וְהִנִּיחָם שָׁם׃
כד וְרָחַץ אֶת־בְּשָׂרוֹ בַמַּיִם בְּמָקוֹם קָדוֹשׁ וְלָבַשׁ אֶת־בְּגָדָיו וְיָצָא
וְעָשָׂה אֶת־עֹלָתוֹ וְאֶת־עֹלַת הָעָם וְכִפֶּר בַּעֲדוֹ וּבְעַד הָעָם׃
כה כו וְאֵת חֵלֶב הַחַטָּאת יַקְטִיר הַמִּזְבֵּחָה׃ וְהַמְשַׁלֵּחַ אֶת־הַשָּׂעִיר שלישי
לַעֲזָאזֵל יְכַבֵּס בְּגָדָיו וְרָחַץ אֶת־בְּשָׂרוֹ בַּמָּיִם וְאַחֲרֵי־כֵן יָבוֹא /שני/
כז אֶל־הַמַּחֲנֶה׃ וְאֶת פַּר הַחַטָּאת וְאֵת ׀ שְׂעִיר הַחַטָּאת אֲשֶׁר
הוּבָא אֶת־דָּמָם לְכַפֵּר בַּקֹּדֶשׁ יוֹצִיא אֶל־מִחוּץ לַמַּחֲנֶה
כח וְשָׂרְפוּ בָאֵשׁ אֶת־עֹרֹתָם וְאֶת־בְּשָׂרָם וְאֶת־פִּרְשָׁם׃ וְהַשֹּׂרֵף
אֹתָם יְכַבֵּס בְּגָדָיו וְרָחַץ אֶת־בְּשָׂרוֹ בַּמָּיִם וְאַחֲרֵי־כֵן יָבוֹא
כט אֶל־הַמַּחֲנֶה׃ וְהָיְתָה לָכֶם לְחֻקַּת עוֹלָם בַּחֹדֶשׁ הַשְּׁבִיעִי

---

dimension of wrongdoing. Yom Kippur is about shame as well as guilt.

That is why an immensely powerful and dramatic ceremony has to take place during which people can feel and symbolically see their sins carried away to the desert, to no-man's-land. Judaism is a guilt culture, a culture of hope. Nonetheless, it acknowledges the existence of shame. When a whole society confesses its guilt together, individuals can be redeemed from shame.

16:29 לְחֻקַּת עוֹלָם *An everlasting statute* – The move from the first Yom Kippur in the desert to the second was a great transition in Jewish spirituality. The first Yom Kippur was the culmination of Moshe's efforts to secure forgiveness for the people after the sin of the golden calf (Ex. 32–34). The process, which began on the seventeenth of Tammuz, ended on the tenth of Tishrei – the day that later became Yom Kippur. That was the day when Moshe descended the mountain with the second set of tablets, the visible sign that God had reaffirmed His covenant with the people. The second Yom Kippur, one year later, initiates the series of rites set out in this *parasha* (Lev. 16), conducted in the Tabernacle (*Mishkan*) by Aharon in his role as High Priest.

The differences between the two are immense. Moshe acted as a prophet. Aharon functions as a priest. Moshe's encounter was ad hoc, a unique, unrepeatable drama between heaven and earth. Aharon's is the opposite. The rules he follows

on the tenth day of the seventh month, you must afflict
yourselves. You shall perform no work at all – neither the
30 native born nor the migrant living among you. On this
day, atonement shall be made for you to purify you; of all
31 your sins you shall be purified before the LORD. It shall
be a Sabbath of complete rest for you, and on it you shall
32 afflict yourselves. This is an everlasting statute. The priest
who is anointed and ordained to succeed his father and
serve as priest shall perform the atonement, wearing the
33 sacred linen vestments. He shall make atonement for the
innermost Sanctuary, for the Tent of Meeting, and for the
altar. He shall make atonement for the priests and for all
34 the people of the community. This shall be an everlasting
statute for you, making atonement for the Israelites once
a year for all their sins." And as the LORD commanded
Moshe, so it was done.
17 1 2 The LORD spoke to Moshe: "Speak to Aharon, his sons, REVI'I
and all the Israelites. Say: This is what the LORD has
3 commanded: Any Israelite who slaughters an ox, sheep,

---

roots of life in the conscious presence of God.

It is from the period of the destruction of the Temple that a remarkable statement appears in the Mishna:

> R. Akiva said: Happy are you, Israel. Who is it before whom you are purified and who purifies you? Your Father in heaven. As it is said: "I will sprinkle over you purifying waters, and you will be cleansed." And it further says: "The hope of Israel is the LORD." Just as a fountain purifies the impure, so does the Holy One, blessed be He, purify Israel. (Yoma 8:9)

This statement embodies a transformative insight. First, note the radical midrashic reading of the text. The words *mikveh Yisrael Adonai* mean "The hope of Israel is the LORD" (Jer. 17:13). However, the root *k-v-h* has two meanings. One is "hope." The other is "a collection or gathering," hence "a gathering of water" and thus *mikveh*, a ritual bath, a place you go to be purified. R. Akiva uses this ambiguity to read the phrase as "God is the ritual bath of Israel," a daringly mystical vision. In his reading, God is the ritual bath into which we plunge ourselves in order to be cleansed. According to R. Akiva, even with no Temple, we may immerse ourselves in God and emerge pure, our sins dissolved.

בֶּעָשׂוֹר לַחֹדֶשׁ תְּעַנּוּ אֶת־נַפְשֹׁתֵיכֶם וְכָל־מְלָאכָה לֹא תַעֲשׂוּ
ל הָאֶזְרָח וְהַגֵּר הַגָּר בְּתוֹכְכֶם׃ כִּי־בַיּוֹם הַזֶּה יְכַפֵּר עֲלֵיכֶם
לא לְטַהֵר אֶתְכֶם מִכֹּל חַטֹּאתֵיכֶם לִפְנֵי יְהוָה תִּטְהָרוּ׃ שַׁבַּת
לב שַׁבָּתוֹן הִיא לָכֶם וְעִנִּיתֶם אֶת־נַפְשֹׁתֵיכֶם חֻקַּת עוֹלָם׃ וְכִפֶּר
הַכֹּהֵן אֲשֶׁר־יִמְשַׁח אֹתוֹ וַאֲשֶׁר יְמַלֵּא אֶת־יָדוֹ לְכַהֵן תַּחַת
לג אָבִיו וְלָבַשׁ אֶת־בִּגְדֵי הַבָּד בִּגְדֵי הַקֹּדֶשׁ׃ וְכִפֶּר אֶת־מִקְדַּשׁ
הַקֹּדֶשׁ וְאֶת־אֹהֶל מוֹעֵד וְאֶת־הַמִּזְבֵּחַ יְכַפֵּר וְעַל הַכֹּהֲנִים
לד וְעַל־כָּל־עַם הַקָּהָל יְכַפֵּר׃ וְהָיְתָה־זֹּאת לָכֶם לְחֻקַּת עוֹלָם
לְכַפֵּר עַל־בְּנֵי יִשְׂרָאֵל מִכָּל־חַטֹּאתָם אַחַת בַּשָּׁנָה וַיַּעַשׂ
כַּאֲשֶׁר צִוָּה יְהוָה אֶת־מֹשֶׁה׃
יז א ב וַיְדַבֵּר יְהוָה אֶל־מֹשֶׁה לֵּאמֹר׃ דַּבֵּר אֶל־אַהֲרֹן וְאֶל־בָּנָיו יג רביעי
וְאֶל כָּל־בְּנֵי יִשְׂרָאֵל וְאָמַרְתָּ אֲלֵיהֶם זֶה הַדָּבָר אֲשֶׁר־צִוָּה
ג יְהוָה לֵאמֹר׃ אִישׁ אִישׁ מִבֵּית יִשְׂרָאֵל אֲשֶׁר יִשְׁחַט שׁוֹר
אוֹ־כֶשֶׂב אוֹ־עֵז בַּמַּחֲנֶה אוֹ אֲשֶׁר יִשְׁחַט מִחוּץ לַמַּחֲנֶה׃

16:29 תְּעַנּוּ אֶת־נַפְשֹׁתֵיכֶם *You must afflict yourselves* – Although on Yom Kippur the High Priest atones for the sins of the nation, this does not mean that others are able to leave him to act vicariously on their behalf. They have to enter into the penitential spirit of the day through fasting and other afflictions. The ceremony as a whole is intended to create a national mood of repentance.

16:30 לִפְנֵי יהוה תִּטְהָרוּ *You shall be purified before the Lord* – There is a difference between *kappara*, atonement, and *tahara*, purification (see note on v. 21). Atonement – literally, "erasing" or "covering over" – refers to the sinful act. It is not merely forgiven. It is, as it were, deleted from the record. Purification refers to the person. Sin defiles the sinner. We feel soiled, stained. Yom Kippur, if we have internalized its message, removes the stain, and we are made pure again.

16:31 וְהָיְתָה־זֹּאת לָכֶם לְחֻקַּת עוֹלָם *An everlasting statute for you* – With the loss of the Temple, priesthood, and sacrifices, the institutional base of atonement ceased to exist. The service of Yom Kippur as prescribed in this *parasha* became impossible. How then could the people, individually and collectively, renew and restore their relationship with God? How could they live without an overwhelming sense of guilt? It was a crisis without parallel and went to the very

4 or goat inside or outside the camp without then bringing
it to the entrance of the Tent of Meeting to bring close an
offering to the LORD before the LORD's Tabernacle will
be considered guilty of bloodshed. He has shed blood;
5 he shall be severed from his people. For the Israelites
must bring the sacrifices they have been offering in the
open fields – to the LORD, to the priest at the entrance
of the Tent of Meeting, and offer them as peace sacrifices
6 to the LORD. The priest shall dash the blood against the
LORD's altar at the entrance to the Tent of Meeting and
send the fat up in smoke as a pleasing aroma to the LORD;
7 and no more may they offer sacrifices to the goat demons
to whom they prostitute themselves. This shall be an
everlasting statute for them throughout their generations.
8 And you shall tell them: Anyone of the House of Israel ḤAMISHI /SHELISHI/
or any migrant living among you who offers up a burnt
9 offering or other sacrifice and does not bring it to the
entrance of the Tent of Meeting to offer it to the LORD
10 shall be severed from his people. Anyone of the House of
Israel, or any migrant living among you, who eats blood – I
will set My face against that person who eats blood and
11 will sever him from his people, for the life of a creature is
in its blood. I have given it to you to make atonement for
your lives on the altar, for blood, which is bound up with
12 life, atones. That is why I have told the Israelites: None of
you may eat blood, nor may any migrant living among you
13 eat blood. Any Israelite or migrant living among you who
hunts an animal or bird that may be eaten shall pour out
14 its blood and cover it with earth, for the life of all flesh – its
blood is its life. That is why I have said to the Israelites:
You must not eat any creature's blood, because the life

Correspondingly, every transgression in Judaism is a way of putting the "I" before the "we." Whenever we put personal advantage over collective interest, or private inclination before the laws of the community, sooner or later, we sin. That is why the severest punishment in Judaism is one that is not inflicted by people: *karet*, literally being "severed" from the community.

ד וְאֶל־פֶּתַח אֹהֶל מוֹעֵד לֹא הֱבִיאוֹ לְהַקְרִיב קָרְבָּן לַיהוָה
לִפְנֵי מִשְׁכַּן יְהוָה דָּם יֵחָשֵׁב לָאִישׁ הַהוּא דָּם שָׁפָךְ וְנִכְרַת
ה הָאִישׁ הַהוּא מִקֶּרֶב עַמּוֹ: לְמַעַן אֲשֶׁר יָבִיאוּ בְּנֵי יִשְׂרָאֵל
אֶת־זִבְחֵיהֶם אֲשֶׁר הֵם זֹבְחִים עַל־פְּנֵי הַשָּׂדֶה וֶהֱבִיאֻם
לַיהוָה אֶל־פֶּתַח אֹהֶל מוֹעֵד אֶל־הַכֹּהֵן וְזָבְחוּ זִבְחֵי שְׁלָמִים
ו לַיהוָה אוֹתָם: וְזָרַק הַכֹּהֵן אֶת־הַדָּם עַל־מִזְבַּח יְהוָה פֶּתַח
ז אֹהֶל מוֹעֵד וְהִקְטִיר הַחֵלֶב לְרֵיחַ נִיחֹחַ לַיהוָה: וְלֹא־יִזְבְּחוּ
עוֹד אֶת־זִבְחֵיהֶם לַשְּׂעִירִם אֲשֶׁר הֵם זֹנִים אַחֲרֵיהֶם חֻקַּת
ח עוֹלָם תִּהְיֶה־זֹּאת לָהֶם לְדֹרֹתָם: וַאֲלֵהֶם תֹּאמַר אִישׁ אִישׁ חמישי /שלישי/
מִבֵּית יִשְׂרָאֵל וּמִן־הַגֵּר אֲשֶׁר־יָגוּר בְּתוֹכָם אֲשֶׁר־יַעֲלֶה
ט עֹלָה אוֹ־זָבַח: וְאֶל־פֶּתַח אֹהֶל מוֹעֵד לֹא יְבִיאֶנּוּ לַעֲשׂוֹת
י אֹתוֹ לַיהוָה וְנִכְרַת הָאִישׁ הַהוּא מֵעַמָּיו: וְאִישׁ אִישׁ מִבֵּית
יִשְׂרָאֵל וּמִן־הַגֵּר הַגָּר בְּתוֹכָם אֲשֶׁר יֹאכַל כָּל־דָּם וְנָתַתִּי
פָנַי בַּנֶּפֶשׁ הָאֹכֶלֶת אֶת־הַדָּם וְהִכְרַתִּי אֹתָהּ מִקֶּרֶב עַמָּהּ:
יא כִּי־נֶפֶשׁ הַבָּשָׂר בַּדָּם הִוא וַאֲנִי נְתַתִּיו לָכֶם עַל־הַמִּזְבֵּחַ
יב לְכַפֵּר עַל־נַפְשֹׁתֵיכֶם כִּי־הַדָּם הוּא בַּנֶּפֶשׁ יְכַפֵּר: עַל־כֵּן
אָמַרְתִּי לִבְנֵי יִשְׂרָאֵל כָּל־נֶפֶשׁ מִכֶּם לֹא־תֹאכַל דָּם וְהַגֵּר
יג הַגָּר בְּתוֹכְכֶם לֹא־יֹאכַל דָּם: וְאִישׁ אִישׁ מִבְּנֵי יִשְׂרָאֵל
וּמִן־הַגֵּר הַגָּר בְּתוֹכָם אֲשֶׁר יָצוּד צֵיד חַיָּה אוֹ־עוֹף אֲשֶׁר
יד יֵאָכֵל וְשָׁפַךְ אֶת־דָּמוֹ וְכִסָּהוּ בֶּעָפָר: כִּי־נֶפֶשׁ כָּל־בָּשָׂר דָּמוֹ
בְנַפְשׁוֹ הוּא וָאֹמַר לִבְנֵי יִשְׂרָאֵל דַּם כָּל־בָּשָׂר לֹא תֹאכֵלוּ כִּי

17:4 וְנִכְרַת הָאִישׁ הַהוּא מִקֶּרֶב עַמּוֹ *Severed from his people* – Every commandment in Judaism, every "Thou shalt" and "Thou shalt not," is a way of putting the "we" before the "I." When we rest on the Sabbath, for example, we do not engage in private relaxation. If we did, we would spend the seventh day pursuing individual hobbies or whatever else we chose. The Sabbath is instead a day of public rest. It is a day of "we," not "I." Similarly, here, sacrificial slaughter is centralized. One cannot, as in the days of the patriarchs, set up a private altar for private worship. Judaism is a faith less of individual salvation than of collective redemption.

▶

of every creature is bound up with its blood. All who
15 eat it will be severed. Anyone, native born or migrant,
who eats an animal that has died of itself or been torn
by beasts shall wash his clothes, immerse in water, and
remain impure until evening; then he shall be purified.
16 If he does not wash or immerse his body, he shall bear
his guilt."
18 1/2 The LORD spoke to Moshe: "Speak to the Israelites. Say:
3 I am the LORD your God. You shall not do as they do in
the land of Egypt where you lived. Nor shall you do as
they do in the land of Canaan where I am bringing you;
4 do not follow their practices. Observe My laws, keep My
5 statutes and follow them; I am the LORD your God. Keep
My statutes and laws, for by them a person shall live; I am
6 the LORD. No one among you shall draw close SHISHI
to any near relative to expose their nakedness; I am the
7 LORD. You shall not expose your father's and
mother's nakedness. She is your mother; you shall not

---

the safety of marriage and the family is a strict set of taboos defining who is *not* a potential partner.

A sexual ethic is therefore not just one among many features of Judaism. It is of its essence, for there is the closest possible connection between how we relate to God and how we relate to those to whom we are closest: our husband or wife, and our children. That is why Genesis, the story of our beginnings, deals only cursorily with the creation of the universe, and briefly with politics. Instead, it is a series of narratives about families, marriage partners, parents, children, and siblings.

One of the signs of ancient polytheistic cultures was the absence, subjectivity, or relativity of sexual ethics. Adultery, infidelity, promiscuity, and sexual and child abuse were commonplace. That is the world Genesis contrasts with the life of the covenant. Sexuality is often the primary force behind violence, and sexual decadence the first sign of civilizational decline.

So this passage, despite its seeming remoteness from the themes of Yom Kippur, is telling us a fundamental truth about Judaism as a whole. Holiness is expressed in our most intimate relationships within the family: in the love that is loyal and generous, self-sacrificing and kind, in the sensitivity of marriage partners to one another and their needs, and in our ability to recognize the integrity-of-otherness that lies at the heart of love.

טו נֶפֶשׁ כָּל־בָּשָׂר דָּמוֹ הִוא כָּל־אֹכְלָיו יִכָּרֵת׃ וְכָל־נֶפֶשׁ אֲשֶׁר
תֹּאכַל נְבֵלָה וּטְרֵפָה בָּאֶזְרָח וּבַגֵּר וְכִבֶּס בְּגָדָיו וְרָחַץ בַּמַּיִם
טז וְטָמֵא עַד־הָעֶרֶב וְטָהֵר׃ וְאִם לֹא יְכַבֵּס וּבְשָׂרוֹ לֹא יִרְחָץ
וְנָשָׂא עֲוֺנוֹ׃
יח א ב וַיְדַבֵּר יְהוָה אֶל־מֹשֶׁה לֵּאמֹר׃ דַּבֵּר אֶל־בְּנֵי יִשְׂרָאֵל וְאָמַרְתָּ יד
ג אֲלֵהֶם אֲנִי יְהוָה אֱלֹהֵיכֶם׃ כְּמַעֲשֵׂה אֶרֶץ־מִצְרַיִם אֲשֶׁר
יְשַׁבְתֶּם־בָּהּ לֹא תַעֲשׂוּ וּכְמַעֲשֵׂה אֶרֶץ־כְּנַעַן אֲשֶׁר אֲנִי
מֵבִיא אֶתְכֶם שָׁמָּה לֹא תַעֲשׂוּ וּבְחֻקֹּתֵיהֶם לֹא תֵלֵכוּ׃
ד אֶת־מִשְׁפָּטַי תַּעֲשׂוּ וְאֶת־חֻקֹּתַי תִּשְׁמְרוּ לָלֶכֶת בָּהֶם אֲנִי
ה יְהוָה אֱלֹהֵיכֶם׃ וּשְׁמַרְתֶּם אֶת־חֻקֹּתַי וְאֶת־מִשְׁפָּטַי אֲשֶׁר
ו יַעֲשֶׂה אֹתָם הָאָדָם וָחַי בָּהֶם אֲנִי יְהוָה׃ אִישׁ ששי
אִישׁ אֶל־כָּל־שְׁאֵר בְּשָׂרוֹ לֹא תִקְרְבוּ לְגַלּוֹת עֶרְוָה אֲנִי
ז יְהוָה׃ עֶרְוַת אָבִיךָ וְעֶרְוַת אִמְּךָ לֹא תְגַלֵּה אִמְּךָ

FORBIDDEN RELATIONSHIPS

This passage on forbidden sexual relationships is the Torah reading for the afternoon of Yom Kippur. Despite the passage directly following the text from the description of the Yom Kippur rituals, the choice of synagogue reading seems arbitrary. Why specifically these prohibitions on a day when we atone for sins of all kinds? Among the classic explanations, Rashi (on Megilla 31a) says that sexual sins are common and the desire to commit them is part of the human condition. Rambam states that sexual desire is, for most people and in all eras, the strongest of all inclinations to sin (*Hilkhot Issurei Bia* 22:18–19).

The passage itself raises questions. Why does it begin with the statement "I am the LORD your God" (Lev. 18:2)? Why the contrast with the behavior of the Egyptians and the Canaanites? Why are sexual sins so serious as to warrant the exile of Israel from its land?

Judaism was and is opposed to a worldview – whether in its ancient forms of myth, or its modern pseudo-scientific counterpart, the neo-Darwinian myth of the "selfish gene" – that the fundamental human drive is to perpetuate one's genes. Against this, Judaism sets an ethic of love and loyalty, whereby two parties, each respecting the integrity of the other, come together in a bond of mutual commitment and fidelity. The human counterpart of the covenant between God and humanity is marriage as a covenant between husband and wife. Essential to

8 expose her nakedness. You shall not expose
the nakedness of your father's wife; it is your father's
9 nakedness. You shall not expose the nakedness of
your sister – whether she is your father's daughter or your
mother's, whether born into the household or outside,
10 you shall not expose her nakedness. You
shall not expose the nakedness of your son's
daughter or your daughter's daughter; it is your own
11 nakedness. The nakedness of your father's wife's
daughter, born to your father – she is your sister; do not
12 expose her nakedness. You shall not expose the
nakedness of your father's sister; she is of your father's
13 flesh. You shall not expose the nakedness
of your mother's sister, for she is of your mother's
14 flesh. You shall not expose the nakedness of
your father's brother – do not draw close to his wife; she
15 is your aunt. You shall not expose the nakedness
of your daughter-in-law: she is your son's wife; do not
16 expose her nakedness. You shall not expose
the nakedness of your brother's wife; it is your brother's
17 nakedness. You shall not expose the
nakedness of a woman and her daughter, nor shall you
marry her son's daughter or her daughter's daughter,
exposing her nakedness; they are of the same flesh; it
18 would be depravity. Do not marry a woman to be a rival to
her sister, exposing her nakedness while her sister is alive.
19 Do not draw close to a woman to expose her nakedness
20 while she bears the impurity of her menstruation. Do not
have carnal relations with your neighbor's wife, becoming
21 impure through her. Do not give any of your children
over to be sacrificed to Molekh, profaning the name of
22 your God; I am the LORD. Do not lie with a male as with SHEVI'I /REVI'I/
23 a woman; this is an abhorrent act. Do not have carnal
relations with any animal, through it making yourself
impure; nor may a woman give herself to an animal to
24 mate with it – this is perversion. Do not make yourselves
impure in any of these ways, for it is by all these that the

ח הִ֔וא לֹ֥א תְגַלֶּ֖ה עֶרְוָתָֽהּ׃ עֶרְוַ֥ת אֵֽשֶׁת־אָבִ֖יךָ
ט לֹ֣א תְגַלֵּ֑ה עֶרְוַ֥ת אָבִ֖יךָ הִֽוא׃ עֶרְוַ֨ת אֲחֽוֹתְךָ֤
בַת־אָבִ֙יךָ֙ א֣וֹ בַת־אִמֶּ֔ךָ מוֹלֶ֣דֶת בַּ֔יִת א֖וֹ מוֹלֶ֣דֶת ח֑וּץ לֹ֥א
י תְגַלֶּ֖ה עֶרְוָתָֽן׃ עֶרְוַ֤ת בַּת־בִּנְךָ֙ א֣וֹ בַת־בִּתְּךָ֔
יא לֹ֥א תְגַלֶּ֖ה עֶרְוָתָ֑ן כִּ֥י עֶרְוָתְךָ֖ הֵֽנָּה׃ עֶרְוַ֨ת
בַּת־אֵ֤שֶׁת אָבִ֙יךָ֙ מוֹלֶ֣דֶת אָבִ֔יךָ אֲחוֹתְךָ֖ הִ֑וא לֹ֥א תְגַלֶּ֖ה
יב עֶרְוָתָֽהּ׃ עֶרְוַ֥ת אֲחוֹת־אָבִ֖יךָ לֹ֣א תְגַלֵּ֑ה שְׁאֵ֥ר
יג אָבִ֖יךָ הִֽוא׃ עֶרְוַ֥ת אֲחוֹת־אִמְּךָ֖ לֹ֣א תְגַלֵּ֑ה כִּֽי־
יד שְׁאֵ֥ר אִמְּךָ֖ הִֽוא׃ עֶרְוַ֥ת אֲחִֽי־אָבִ֖יךָ לֹ֣א תְגַלֵּ֑ה אֶל־
טו אִשְׁתּוֹ֙ לֹ֣א תִקְרָ֔ב דֹּדָֽתְךָ֖ הִֽוא׃ עֶרְוַ֥ת כַּלָּתְךָ֖ לֹ֣א
טז תְגַלֵּ֑ה אֵ֤שֶׁת בִּנְךָ֙ הִ֔וא לֹ֥א תְגַלֶּ֖ה עֶרְוָתָֽהּ׃ עֶרְוַ֥ת
יז אֵֽשֶׁת־אָחִ֖יךָ לֹ֣א תְגַלֵּ֑ה עֶרְוַ֥ת אָחִ֖יךָ הִֽוא׃ עֶרְוַ֥ת
אִשָּׁ֥ה וּבִתָּ֖הּ לֹ֣א תְגַלֵּ֑ה אֶת־בַּת־בְּנָ֞הּ וְאֶת־בַּת־בִּתָּ֗הּ לֹ֤א
יח תִקַּח֙ לְגַלּ֣וֹת עֶרְוָתָ֔הּ שַׁאֲרָ֥ה הֵ֖נָּה זִמָּ֥ה הִֽוא׃ וְאִשָּׁ֥ה אֶל־
יט אֲחֹתָ֖הּ לֹ֣א תִקָּ֑ח לִצְרֹ֗ר לְגַלּ֧וֹת עֶרְוָתָ֛הּ עָלֶ֖יהָ בְּחַיֶּֽיהָ׃ וְאֶל־
כ אִשָּׁ֖ה בְּנִדַּ֣ת טֻמְאָתָ֑הּ לֹ֣א תִקְרַ֔ב לְגַלּ֖וֹת עֶרְוָתָֽהּ׃ וְאֶל־אֵ֙שֶׁת֙
כא עֲמִֽיתְךָ֔ לֹא־תִתֵּ֥ן שְׁכָבְתְּךָ֖ לְזָ֑רַע לְטָמְאָה־בָֽהּ׃ וּמִֽזַּרְעֲךָ֥
לֹא־תִתֵּ֖ן לְהַעֲבִ֣יר לַמֹּ֑לֶךְ וְלֹ֧א תְחַלֵּ֛ל אֶת־שֵׁ֥ם אֱלֹהֶ֖יךָ
כב אֲנִ֥י יְהוָֽה׃ וְאֶ֨ת־זָכָ֔ר לֹ֥א תִשְׁכַּ֖ב מִשְׁכְּבֵ֣י אִשָּׁ֑ה תּוֹעֵבָ֖ה שביעי /רביעי/
כג הִֽוא׃ וּבְכָל־בְּהֵמָ֛ה לֹא־תִתֵּ֥ן שְׁכָבְתְּךָ֖ לְטָמְאָה־בָ֑הּ וְאִשָּׁ֗ה
כד לֹֽא־תַעֲמֹ֞ד לִפְנֵ֧י בְהֵמָ֛ה לְרִבְעָ֖הּ תֶּ֥בֶל הֽוּא׃ אַל־תִּֽטַּמְּא֖וּ
בְּכָל־אֵ֑לֶּה כִּ֤י בְכָל־אֵ֙לֶּה֙ נִטְמְא֣וּ הַגּוֹיִ֔ם אֲשֶׁר־אֲנִ֥י מְשַׁלֵּ֖חַ

nations I am casting out before you made themselves
25 impure. And so the land itself became impure, and I held
it to account for its sins, and the land vomited out its
26 inhabitants. But you shall keep My statutes and My laws
and do none of these abhorrent acts, neither the native
27 born nor the migrant living among you. The people who
lived in the land before you committed all these abhorrent
28 acts and the land became impure. Let the land not vomit MAFTIR
you out for making it impure, as it vomited out the nation
29 there before you, for anyone who performs any of these
30 abhorrent acts shall be severed from his people. Keep My
charge and do not follow any of these abhorrent practices
that were followed before you; do not by them make
yourselves impure; I am the Lord your God."

The haftara for Parashat Aḥarei Mot is on page 1532.
When Aḥarei Mot and Kedoshim are read together, read the hafara on page 1534.
On Shabbat HaGadol read the haftara on page 1672.

consciousness of God at its center. God asks the Jewish people to become a role model for humanity by the society they build on the principles of justice and the rule of law, and concern for the welfare of the poor and vulnerable – a society in which all have equal dignity under the sovereignty of God.

A society needs a land, a home, a location in space where a nation can shape its own destiny in accord with its deepest aspirations and ideals. *Only in Israel is the fulfillment of the commands a society-building exercise,* shaping the contours of a culture as a whole. Only in Israel can we fulfill the commands in a land, a landscape, and a language saturated with Jewish memories and hopes. Only in Israel does the calendar track the rhythms of the Jewish year. In Israel, Judaism is part of the public square, not just the private, sequestered space of synagogue, school, and home. That is the significance of the return to Zion in modern times. It is the Jewish return to the full terms of the covenant. Jews are the people of the covenant charged with bringing the Divine Presence down to earth in the shared spaces of our collective life, not by force, not by power, but by influence, "'with My spirit,' says the Lord" (Zech. 4:6).

The right to inherit the land, our *parasha* tells us, comes hand in hand with a duty to live individually and collectively by the standards of fidelity, of justice and compassion, of love of family, neighbor, and stranger, which alone constitute our mission and destiny: a holy people in the holy land.

כה מִפְּנֵיכֶם: וַתִּטְמָא הָאָרֶץ וָאֶפְקֹד עֲוֺנָהּ עָלֶיהָ וַתָּקִא הָאָרֶץ
כו אֶת־יֹשְׁבֶיהָ: וּשְׁמַרְתֶּם אַתֶּם אֶת־חֻקֹּתַי וְאֶת־מִשְׁפָּטַי וְלֹא
תַעֲשׂוּ מִכֹּל הַתּוֹעֵבֹת הָאֵלֶּה הָאֶזְרָח וְהַגֵּר הַגָּר בְּתוֹכְכֶם:
כז כִּי אֶת־כָּל־הַתּוֹעֵבֹת הָאֵל עָשׂוּ אַנְשֵׁי־הָאָרֶץ אֲשֶׁר לִפְנֵיכֶם
כח וַתִּטְמָא הָאָרֶץ: וְלֹא־תָקִיא הָאָרֶץ אֶתְכֶם בְּטַמַּאֲכֶם אֹתָהּ מפטיר
כט כַּאֲשֶׁר קָאָה אֶת־הַגּוֹי אֲשֶׁר לִפְנֵיכֶם: כִּי כָּל־אֲשֶׁר יַעֲשֶׂה
מִכֹּל הַתּוֹעֵבֹת הָאֵלֶּה וְנִכְרְתוּ הַנְּפָשׁוֹת הָעֹשֹׂת מִקֶּרֶב
ל עַמָּם: וּשְׁמַרְתֶּם אֶת־מִשְׁמַרְתִּי לְבִלְתִּי עֲשׂוֹת מֵחֻקּוֹת
הַתּוֹעֵבֹת אֲשֶׁר נַעֲשׂוּ לִפְנֵיכֶם וְלֹא תִטַּמְּאוּ בָּהֶם אֲנִי יְהֹוָה
אֱלֹהֵיכֶם:

The הפטרה *for* פרשת אחרי מות *is on page 1533*
When אחרי מות *and* קדשים *are read together, read the* הפטרה *on page 1535.*
On שבת הגדול *read the* הפטרה *on page 1673.*

THE LAW AND THE LAND

This verse raises a question. Reward and punishment in the Torah are often based on the principle of *midda keneged midda*, measure for measure. The punishment fits the crime. So, for example, *Shemitta*, the Sabbatical year, is a commandment relating to the land. The punishment for its non-observance is exile from the land (Lev. 26:35). But sexual offenses have nothing to do with the land. They are commands relating to person, not place. Why should their punishment be exile?

Ramban's answer is that not only some, but *all* the commands, are fundamentally directed to the land of Israel. To be sure, not all of them are conditional on it. But it is there that they receive their main fulfillment. Outside Israel, he says, it is impossible to encounter God directly. Over all other lands, God has set intermediaries (angels, stars, celestial powers). Only in Israel is His providence direct and unmediated. That is what gives the land its primary sanctity. Hence the land does not, in his words, "tolerate the worshippers of idols or those who practice immorality" (commentary on Lev. 18:25).

We may understand Ramban's account non-mystically. Outside Israel, Jews are subject to other powers. They are not under the direct, unmediated rule of God. The commands continue in force, but they are no longer the laws of an independent people. They are like an ongoing rehearsal for a state of affairs no longer experienced, but remembered, and awaited in the future, when Israel would once again come home and live as God's people in His land.

Taken collectively, the commands of the Torah are a prescription for the construction of a society with the

Parashat Kedoshim

19 1 2 The LORD spoke to Moshe: "Speak to all the community
of Israel. Say: Be holy, for I am holy; I, the LORD your
3 God. Each one of you, revere your mother and father and

---

precisely from the priestly voice – from which we would least expect it.

Holiness, we learn here, belongs to all of us when we turn our lives into the service of God, and society into a home for the Divine Presence. That is the moral life as lived by the kingdom of priests: a world where we aspire to come close to God by coming close, in justice and love, to our fellow humans.

BE HOLY

We are commanded to be holy *because God is holy*. Yet surely holiness is precisely what separates God from human beings. "For I am God, I am not a man; within you, My holiness dwells" says the prophet Hoshea (11:9). *Kadosh*, "holy," means "distinct, set apart," above, beyond. Holiness is what makes God, God: transcendent, eternal, beyond imagination. How can we, mere mortals – "this quintessence of dust," as Hamlet put it – be godlike?

The Sages (Sifra, Kedoshim 1:1) understand the command to be holy to mean "be *perushim*" that is, "be separate, practice abstinence, exercise self-restraint." Rashi in his commentary on the Torah understands this narrowly, applying it specifically to sexual conduct. Ramban reads it more broadly, and holds that it applies more generally to moderation and self-restraint in all matters. The Torah forbids certain activities and permits others. When it says "be holy" it means, according to Ramban, to practice self-restraint even in the domain of the permitted. Don't be a glutton, even if what you are eating is kosher. Don't be an alcoholic even if what you are drinking is kosher wine. Don't be, in his famous phrase, a *naval birshut haTorah*, "a scoundrel with Torah license" (commentary on Lev. 19:2).

Rambam arrives at a similar idea, from a different source:

> The LORD will establish you as His holy people, just as He has sworn to you, if you keep the LORD your God's commandments *and walk in His ways*. (Deut. 28:9)

From this, Rambam infers (*Hilkhot Deot* 1:6) that we are commanded to develop certain traits of character – to be gracious, merciful, and righteous, as God is gracious, merciful, and righteous. To be holy is, as far as we can, to imitate God.

Taking the *parasha* as a whole, however, we may discern an additional aspect of holiness. To be holy, we are

פרשת קדשים

יט א ב וַיְדַבֵּר יְהוָה אֶל־מֹשֶׁה לֵּאמֹר: דַּבֵּר אֶל־כָּל־עֲדַת בְּנֵי־ טו
יִשְׂרָאֵל וְאָמַרְתָּ אֲלֵהֶם קְדֹשִׁים תִּהְיוּ כִּי קָדוֹשׁ אֲנִי יְהוָה
ג אֱלֹהֵיכֶם: אִישׁ אִמּוֹ וְאָבִיו תִּירָאוּ וְאֶת־שַׁבְּתֹתַי תִּשְׁמֹרוּ

KEDOSHIM

Until now Vayikra has been largely about sacrifices, purity, the Sanctuary, and the priesthood. It has been, in short, about a holy place, holy offerings, and the elite of holy people – Aharon and his descendants – who minister there.

With Parashat Kedoshim, the laws of holiness are broadened and democratized from the world of the Sanctuary and priests to that of the Israelites as a whole, commanding them to be holy because "I am holy; I, the Lord your God" (Lev. 19:2). The opening chapter contains the famous commands to love the neighbor and the stranger, the prohibition against taking revenge, as well as other laws more ritual in character. The second half of the *parasha* deals with forbidden sexual relations and other prohibited pagan practices. The apparently unrelated laws in the *parasha* represent a unique moral vision, that of the priestly consciousness.

19:2 דַּבֵּר אֶל־כָּל *Speak to all* – This is the first and only time in Leviticus that so inclusive an address is commanded. The Sages (Sifra, Kedoshim 1:1) say that it means that the contents of the chapter were proclaimed by Moshe to a formal gathering of the entire nation (*hak'hel*). It is the people as a whole who are commanded to "be holy," not just the priests. This is a radical democratization of holiness. It is life itself that is to be sanctified, as the chapter goes on to make clear. Holiness is to be made manifest in the way the nation makes its clothes and plants its fields, in the way justice is administered, workers are paid, and business conducted. The vulnerable – the deaf, the blind, the elderly, and the stranger – are to be afforded special protection. The whole society is to be governed by love, without resentments or revenge.

The idea, if not the details, had already been hinted at (see Ex. 19:6 and comments there). The first intimation is the monumental assertion in the first chapter of Genesis: "God created humankind in His image; in the image of God He created him; male and female He created them" (Gen. 1:27).

It is striking that these radically egalitarian statements are spoken in the priestly voice that Judaism calls *Torat Kohanim*. On the face of it, priests are not egalitarian. They all come from a single tribe, the Levites, and from a single family within the tribe – that of Aharon. So deep is the concept of equality written into monotheism that it emerges

4 keep My Sabbaths; I am the LORD your God. Do not
turn to idols or cast yourselves gods; I am the LORD your
5 God. When you offer a peace sacrifice to the LORD, offer
6 it in such a way that it may be accepted for you. It shall be
eaten on the day you sacrifice it or on the following day;
7 what is left on the third day shall be burned with fire. If
any of it is eaten on the third day, it is repugnant; it will
8 not be accepted. Anyone who eats it shall bear his guilt,
for he has desecrated what is holy to the LORD; he shall
9 be severed from his people. When you reap the harvest of
your land, do not reap all the way to the edge of your field
10 or gather the gleanings of your harvest. Do not harvest
your vineyard bare or gather the grapes that have fallen
there. Leave them for the poor and for the migrant; I am
11 the LORD your God. Do not steal; do not deceive; do
12 not lie to one another. Do not swear falsely by My name,
13 desecrating the name of your God; I am the LORD. Do
not defraud or rob your neighbor. Do not hold back
14 the wages of a hired worker until the morning. Do not
curse the deaf or put a stumbling-block before the blind.

---

is semantically linked to the word *ne'elam*, "hidden." "Holy" is the name we give to those special times, places, people, and deeds that are signals of transcendence, points at which the infinity of God becomes manifest within the finite world. The holiness of Israel, then, refers to the points within our life where we efface ourselves in order to become a vehicle through which God's light flows into the world. "Be holy, for I am holy; I, the LORD your God."

19:14 לֹא־תְקַלֵּל חֵרֵשׁ וְלִפְנֵי עִוֵּר לֹא תִתֵּן מִכְשֹׁל *Do not curse the deaf or put a stumbling-block before the blind* – These are two very different commands. The prohibition against putting a stumbling-block before the blind is readily understandable. It warns us against taking advantage of the disabled to cause them harm. The moral offense here is self-evident. But the first command, "Do not curse the deaf," is more far-reaching. On the face of it, cursing the deaf harms no one because the person you are insulting cannot hear what you are saying. Nonetheless, it is morally wrong. If we treat disrespectfully those who are deaf or disabled, even if they are unaware of it, we diminish their humanity and thereby our humanity. Even what may be thought of as a "victimless crime" affects who we are.

ד אֲנִ֖י יְהוָ֥ה אֱלֹהֵיכֶֽם׃ אַל־תִּפְנוּ֙ אֶל־הָ֣אֱלִילִ֔ם וֵֽאלֹהֵי֙
ה מַסֵּכָ֔ה לֹ֥א תַעֲשׂ֖וּ לָכֶ֑ם אֲנִ֖י יְהוָ֥ה אֱלֹהֵיכֶֽם׃ וְכִ֧י תִזְבְּח֛וּ
ו זֶ֥בַח שְׁלָמִ֖ים לַֽיהוָ֑ה לִֽרְצֹנְכֶ֖ם תִּזְבָּחֻֽהוּ׃ בְּי֧וֹם זִבְחֲכֶ֛ם
יֵאָכֵ֖ל וּמִֽמָּחֳרָ֑ת וְהַנּוֹתָר֙ עַד־י֣וֹם הַשְּׁלִישִׁ֔י בָּאֵ֖שׁ יִשָּׂרֵֽף׃
ז וְאִ֛ם הֵאָכֹ֥ל יֵאָכֵ֖ל בַּיּ֣וֹם הַשְּׁלִישִׁ֑י פִּגּ֥וּל ה֖וּא לֹ֥א יֵרָצֶֽה׃
ח וְאֹֽכְלָיו֙ עֲוֺנ֣וֹ יִשָּׂ֔א כִּֽי־אֶת־קֹ֥דֶשׁ יְהוָ֖ה חִלֵּ֑ל וְנִכְרְתָ֛ה הַנֶּ֥פֶשׁ
ט הַהִ֖וא מֵעַמֶּֽיהָ׃ וּֽבְקֻצְרְכֶם֙ אֶת־קְצִ֣יר אַרְצְכֶ֔ם לֹ֧א תְכַלֶּ֛ה
י פְּאַ֥ת שָׂדְךָ֖ לִקְצֹ֑ר וְלֶ֥קֶט קְצִֽירְךָ֖ לֹ֥א תְלַקֵּֽט׃ וְכַרְמְךָ֙ לֹ֣א
תְעוֹלֵ֔ל וּפֶ֥רֶט כַּרְמְךָ֖ לֹ֣א תְלַקֵּ֑ט לֶֽעָנִ֤י וְלַגֵּר֙ תַּעֲזֹ֣ב אֹתָ֔ם
יא אֲנִ֖י יְהוָ֥ה אֱלֹהֵיכֶֽם׃ לֹ֖א תִּגְנֹ֑בוּ וְלֹא־תְכַחֲשׁ֥וּ וְלֹֽא־תְשַׁקְּר֖וּ
יב אִ֥ישׁ בַּעֲמִיתֽוֹ׃ וְלֹֽא־תִשָּׁבְע֥וּ בִשְׁמִ֖י לַשָּׁ֑קֶר וְחִלַּלְתָּ֛ אֶת־
יג שֵׁ֥ם אֱלֹהֶ֖יךָ אֲנִ֥י יְהוָֽה׃ לֹא־תַעֲשֹׁ֥ק אֶת־רֵעֲךָ֖ וְלֹ֣א תִגְזֹ֑ל
יד לֹֽא־תָלִ֞ין פְּעֻלַּ֥ת שָׂכִ֛יר אִתְּךָ֖ עַד־בֹּֽקֶר׃ לֹא־תְקַלֵּ֣ל חֵרֵ֔שׁ
וְלִפְנֵ֣י עִוֵּ֔ר לֹ֥א תִתֵּ֖ן מִכְשֹׁ֑ל וְיָרֵ֥אתָ מֵּאֱלֹהֶ֖יךָ אֲנִ֥י יְהוָֽה׃

taught, is to love your neighbor and to love the stranger. It means not stealing, lying, or deceiving others. It means not standing idly by when someone else's life is in danger. It means not cursing the deaf or putting a stumbling block before the blind, that is, insulting or taking advantage of others even when they are completely unaware of it – because God is not unaware of it.

It means not planting your field with different kinds of seed, not crossbreeding your livestock, or wearing clothes made of a forbidden mixture of wool and linen – or as we would put it nowadays, respecting the integrity of the environment. It means not conforming with whatever happens to be the idolatry of the time – and every age has its idols. It means being honest in business, doing justice, treating your employees well, and sharing your blessings (in those days, parts of the harvest) with others.

Above all, "be holy" means: have the courage to be different. That is the root meaning of *kadosh* in Hebrew. It means, as we saw above, something distinctive and set apart.

To be holy means to bear witness to the presence of God in our, and our people's, lives. Israel – the Jewish people – is the people who in themselves give testimony to One beyond themselves. That is what Judaism's rituals are about: reminding us of the presence of the Divine.

The infinite light of God is hidden in the finite spaces of the physical universe. Indeed, the word *olam*, "universe,"

15 Fear your God; I am the Lord. Do not pervert justice: SHENI /ḤAMISHI/
do not show partiality to the poor or deference to the
16 great; judge your fellow man fairly. Do not go around as a
gossipmonger among your people. Do not stand by while
17 your neighbor's life is in danger; I am the Lord. Do not
hate your brother in your heart. Admonish your fellow

---

satisfied. But that has not made us indifferent to the needs of others.

Especially when interpreted broadly, then, this command is a high moral requirement, and a challenging element of the holiness code.

LAWS OF SOCIAL RELATIONS

Verses 17 and 18, taken as a pair, speak volumes of the biblical concept of love. The Torah does not begin these verses with the command to love. Instead it starts with the hard case: What to do with a neighbor, or brother, whom you dislike, even hate? He may have harmed you, offended you, insulted you. He may have acted in a way that you deeply believe is wrong. Your hatred, let us say, is not irrational. What to do? To command blandly that you must stifle your feelings is naive and unlikely to be effective. Freud coined the phrase "the return of the repressed" to signal that feelings we consciously deny have a way of returning in full and destructive force.

Hence, "Do not hate your brother in your heart" is followed by phrase 2: "Admonish your fellow." Instead of silencing your feelings, verbalize them. You may not hate your brother in your heart; instead, you have to confront the person openly and honestly. As Ramban explains:

> The verse is saying, "Do not hate your brother in your heart when he does something to you against your will, but instead remonstrate with him, saying, 'Why did you do this to me?' And you will not bear sin because of him by covering up your hatred in your heart, for when you remonstrate with him, he will justify himself before you, or he will regret his action and admit his sin, and you will forgive him." (commentary on Lev. 19:17)

A key example of where this did not happen is the story of Yosef and his brothers:

> Now, Yisrael loved Yosef more than all his other sons, for he was a child of his old age; he made him an ornately colored robe. But when his brothers saw that their father loved him more than any of them, they hated him and could not say a peaceful word to him. (Gen. 37:3–4)

On this, Rabbi Yonatan Eybeshutz (c. 1690–1764) comments: "Had they been able to sit together as a group, they would have spoken to one another and remonstrated with each other, and would eventually have made their peace with one another" (*Tiferet Yehonatan* on Gen. 37:4). The tragedy of conflict is that

טו לֹא־תַעֲשׂוּ עָוֶל בַּמִּשְׁפָּט לֹא־תִשָּׂא פְנֵי־דָל וְלֹא תֶהְדַּר שני /חמישי/
טז פְּנֵי גָדוֹל בְּצֶדֶק תִּשְׁפֹּט עֲמִיתֶךָ: לֹא־תֵלֵךְ רָכִיל בְּעַמֶּיךָ
יז לֹא תַעֲמֹד עַל־דַּם רֵעֶךָ אֲנִי יְהוָה: לֹא־תִשְׂנָא אֶת־אָחִיךָ
בִּלְבָבֶךָ הוֹכֵחַ תּוֹכִיחַ אֶת־עֲמִיתֶךָ וְלֹא־תִשָּׂא עָלָיו חֵטְא:

19:15 לֹא־תִשָּׂא פְנֵי־דָל *Do not show partiality to the poor* – Precisely because its whole moral code is oriented toward compassion, the Tanakh commands that compassion, the substrate of judgment, must not distort judgment. The preservation of impartiality, the balance of claims, the reciprocity of rights and obligations, and the interdependence of apparently opposed interests are values essential to Jewish legal procedure. These are the characteristics that are often summed up by saying that Judaism is a religion of law. I prefer to describe it as the rule that moral passion must yield to moral rationality if it is to achieve its ends.

19:16 לֹא תַעֲמֹד *Do not stand by* – Alongside the prohibition against murder (Ex. 20:13) we also have an obligation to intervene when we see a person's life endangered. The law has complex implications in the area of charitable giving. Consider this interpretation of a controversial verse in Grace after Meals: "I was once young, now I am old, yet I have not seen the righteous forsaken, with their children begging for bread" (Ps. 37:25).

Surely throughout history there were times when the righteous were forsaken. Indeed this is one of the questions that, according to the Talmud, Moshe asked God: "Why do the righteous suffer?" (Berakhot 7a). The English writer Edmond Blunden wrote a poem, "Report on Experience," on this theme:

> I have been young, and now am not too old;
> And I have seen the righteous forsaken,
> His health, his honor, and his quality taken.
> This is not what we were formerly told.

I once heard a beautiful explanation from Rabbi Moses Feuerstein of Boston. The key phrase of the verse is *lo ra'iti*, standardly translated as "I have not seen." The verb *ra'iti*, though, occurs twice in the Book of Esther with a quite different meaning. "For how can I live to see (*ra'iti*) the evil that will come upon my people; how can I live to see (*ra'iti*) the loss of those I am born of?" (Esther 8:6). The verb here does not mean literally "to see." It means to stand by and watch, to be a passive witness, a disengaged spectator. *Ra'iti* in this sense means seeing and doing nothing to help. That, for Esther as for the psalmist, is a moral impossibility. You may not, in other words, "stand by while your neighbor's life is in danger." You *are* your brother's keeper. The verse ends the Grace after Meals with a moral commitment. Yes, we have eaten and are

18 and do not bear guilt on his account. Do not take revenge
or bear a grudge against any one among your people, but

> makes possible the settlement of the earth and social relations among human beings. (*Hilkhot Deot* 7:8)

For Rambam, as for other interpreters of Jewish law, forgiveness is an essential precondition of social existence.

19:17 הוֹכֵחַ תּוֹכִיחַ *Admonish* – One of the Rabbis said to Rabba:

> [The Torah says] *hokhe'aḥ tokhiaḥ,* meaning "you shall admonish your fellow repeatedly" [because the verb is doubled, it implies you should admonish him more than once]. Might this mean *hokhe'aḥ,* admonish him once, and *tokhiaḥ,* a second time? No, he replied, the word *hokhe'aḥ* means: even a hundred times. Why then does it add the word *tokhiaḥ*? Had there been only a single verb, I would have known that the law applies to a master admonishing his disciple. How do we know that it applies even to a disciple admonishing his master? From the phrase *hokhe'aḥ tokhiaḥ,* implying: under all circumstances (Bava Metzia 31a).

This is significant because it establishes a principle of *critical followership*. Judaism commands almost unlimited respect for teachers. "Let reverence for your teacher be as great as your reverence for Heaven," said the Sages (Avot 4:12). Despite this, the Talmud understands the Torah to be commanding us to remonstrate even with our teacher or leader, should we see him or her doing something wrong. Uncritical followership and habits of silent obedience give rise to the corruptions of power, and sometimes to avoidable catastrophes.

The very act of learning in rabbinic Judaism is conceived as active debate, a kind of gladiatorial contest of the mind: "Even a teacher and disciple, even a father and son, when they sit to study Torah together become enemies to one another. But they do not move from there until they have become beloved to one another" (Kiddushin 30b).

Hence the talmudic saying, "Much wisdom I have learned from my teacher, more from my colleagues, but most from my students" (Taanit 7a). Despite the reverence we owe our teachers, we owe them also our best efforts at questioning and challenging their ideas. This is essential to the rabbinical ideal of learning as a collaborative pursuit of truth.

19:18 לֹא־תִקֹּם *Do not take revenge* – There is a fundamental difference between justice and revenge. Revenge is personal, justice impersonal. Revenge involves taking the law into your own hands. Justice is the opposite. It means handing over your cause to an impartial tribunal to examine the evidence and apply the law. The move from revenge to justice is fundamental. When courts and the legal process take the place of retaliation, it is no longer the Montagues against the

יח לֹא־תִקֹּם וְלֹא־תִטֹּר אֶת־בְּנֵי עַמֶּךָ וְאָהַבְתָּ לְרֵעֲךָ כָּמוֹךָ

a high value on reconciliation and knows the dangers if it is not forthcoming. One of the examples given by Rambam is the biblical story of Avshalom and Amnon. Amnon had raped Avshalom's sister Tamar. At the time, Avshalom said nothing. He appeared to have either forgiven or forgotten the offense. Two years later, however, Avshalom took his revenge and had Amnon killed. Silence is no evidence of forgiveness. Better, concludes Rambam, to confront the wrongdoer directly and "if he repents and requests forgiveness, then one must forgive and not be harsh" (*Hilkhot Deot* 6:6).

This is not always necessary. To forgive without the dialectic of accusation and apology, as an unconditional act of grace, is equally mandated, and a sign of moral greatness:

> If someone is sinned against by another and the offended party does not wish to rebuke him or say anything to him – perhaps because the sinner is simpleminded or distraught – then if one forgives him in his heart and bears no animosity against him and does not rebuke him, this is indeed the way of saintliness [*middat ḥasidut*]. (*Hilkhot Deot* 6:9)

One way or another,

> the wrong done should be completely blotted out from a person's heart and not remembered. This is the appropriate character trait and

it prevents people from talking together and listening to one another. Thus the bitterest conflicts are self-perpetuating.

The inner logic of the two verses is this: Love your neighbor as yourself. But not all neighbors are lovable. There are those who, out of envy or malice, have done you harm. God does not command you to be angels, without any of the emotions natural to human beings. He does, however, forbid you to hate. That is why, when someone does you wrong, you must confront him. You must tell him of your feelings of hurt and distress. It may be that you misunderstood. Or it may be that he meant to do you harm, but now, faced with the reality of the injury he has done you, he may repent of what he did. If, however, you fail to talk it through, you might bear a grudge and in time, come to take revenge.

The Torah both articulates the highest of ideals, and at the same time speaks to us as human beings. If we were angels it would be easy to love one another. But we are not. An ethic that commands us to love our enemies, without teaching how, is unliveable. Instead, the Torah sets out a realistic program. By being honest with one another, talking things through, we may be able to achieve reconciliation – not always, but often. How much distress and bloodshed might be spared if humanity heeded this command.

19:17 לֹא־תִשְׂנָא אֶת־אָחִיךָ בִּלְבָבֶךָ *Do not hate your brother in your heart* – Jewish law sets

love your neighbor as your own self; I am the Lord.
19 Keep My decrees. Do not crossbreed different kinds of
animal, do not plant your field with two kinds of seed

"LOVE YOUR NEIGHBOR AS YOUR OWN SELF"

This iconic command is surely easier said than performed. But there are cases where love flows easily and naturally for most people: for instance, the love of parents for their child. The parents love their child because they stand in a special relationship to the child; the parents have brought the child into being.

In several dazzling passages in the Tanya, the classic statement of Chabad thought, Rabbi Schneur Zalman of Liadi spells out a mystical theology of love. In the Tanya, it is not simply that the soul in its relation to the body is like God in His relation to the world, but that every godly soul is literally a part of God. Man, at his most spiritual level, does more than relate to God: he contains part of the reality of God.

But God, as Rambam lays down as one of the principles of the Jewish faith, is One and indivisible. How then can many souls each be a part of something that cannot be split or analyzed into parts? The truth is, at the deepest level, the entire community of Jewish souls is a single unity, standing in relation to one another as do the limbs of the body – many parts but a single entity. (See Tanya, especially chapter 2.)

The radical conclusion of Rabbi Schneur Zalman's mysticism is that, at the level of soul, every Jew is related to every other with complete identity. Between each Jew is a bond closer even than the closest we can speak of in non-mystical terminology, the bond between parent and child. "Love your neighbor as your own self" – because he is yourself. If we could attain this level of perception, then that love would flow unforced and without limits.

But how do we get there? When we think of human beings as bodies, then certainly each is separate and distinct. It is only when we relate to ourselves and others at the level of the soul that we can begin to sense the unity. And hence the task of the mystic – and, in truth, the task of Judaism as a whole – is to move from body to soul, from reactions prompted by ordinary physical stimuli to those wholly spiritual in character and motivation (Tanya, chapter 32).

The result of this approach is a profound emphasis on the love of every Jew – an emphasis that flows not simply from an emotion of benevolence but from a new way of viewing our identity and that of our fellow. It places a simultaneous stress on two things that might, in any other context, seem incompatible: the infinite worth of the individual and the literal unity of the whole Jewish people. The individual, because he is a part of God and every fragment of infinity is infinite. The community, because, at the level of soul, there are no divisions that set person against person.

יט אֲנִ֖י יהוֽה׃ אֶת־חֻקֹּתַי֮ תִּשְׁמֹרוּ֒ בְּהֶמְתְּךָ֙ לֹא־תַרְבִּ֣יעַ כִּלְאַ֔יִם
שָׂדְךָ֖ לֹא־תִזְרַ֣ע כִּלְאָ֑יִם וּבֶ֤גֶד כִּלְאַ֙יִם֙ שַֽׁעַטְנֵ֔ז לֹ֥א יַעֲלֶ֖ה

Capulets but both under the impartial rule of law. Justice is not revenge. It is the only sane alternative to it.

What the prophets mean when they say in the name of God that "vengeance is Mine" is that there are forms of justice that only God can execute. Only for the God of justice are revenge and retribution the same thing. When the psalmist prays, "O God of retribution, LORD – O God of retribution, shine forth" (Ps. 94:1)," he means: God, let there be justice in this world. But You must do it, not us. We can judge individuals in courts of law, but we cannot judge nations. We can wage war to defend ourselves, but we cannot wage war to execute justice: You alone are the Judge of all the earth. *The call for divine vengeance is a renunciation of human vengeance while keeping faith in the ultimate rule of justice in the affairs of humankind.*

Vengeance is a profoundly dangerous human instinct. Wrongs must be righted through the due process of law, and larger questions of ultimate justice belong to God. To commit violence in the name of God is to forget the difference between God and humankind. There are some things, and vengeance is one, that belong to Heaven, not to fallible creatures of earth.

19:18 וְלֹא־תִטֹּר *Or bear a grudge* – What is the difference between taking revenge and bearing a grudge? The Sages give the following homely example:

> What is taking vengeance? If X says to Y, "Lend me your sickle," and Y refuses to lend it. The next day, Y says to X, "Lend me your axe," and X replies, "I will not lend you an axe, because you refused to lend me a sickle." That is forbidden by "You shall not take vengeance." (Sifra, Kedoshim 2:4 [10])

The prohibition against bearing a grudge is even more demanding:

> Y says to X, "Lend me your sickle," and X replies, "Take it. I am not like you who would not lend me an axe." That is what is forbidden by the law "You shall not bear a grudge." (Sifra, Kedoshim 2:4 [11])

Why is this a sin? On the face of it, the second person has acted correctly. He has *not* taken revenge. Rambam provides an explanation: "One should wipe the offense from his heart and not continue to bear a grudge, for as long as he continues to bear a grudge and remembers [the wrong done to him] he may come to take revenge" (*Hilkhot Deot* 7:8). Animosity is not a safe emotion. It can explode into action at any time. The prohibition against bearing a grudge, implies Rambam, is a kind of "fence," a protective barrier around the command not to take revenge. Not only is revenge forbidden but so is anything that might lead to it.

▶

intermixed, and do not wear clothing made from two
20 materials combined. If a man has carnal relations with
a woman who is a slave designated for another man, and
who has not been redeemed or given her freedom, there
shall be punishment but they shall not be put to death
21 since she has not been freed. The man shall bring his
guilt offering to the LORD at the entrance of the Tent of
22 Meeting: a ram for a guilt offering. The priest shall make
his atonement before the LORD with the ram of the guilt
offering for the sin that he committed, and the sin he
committed shall be forgiven.
23 When you enter the land and plant any tree for food, you SHELISHI
shall regard its fruit as forbidden. For three years it shall
24 be forbidden to you; it must not be eaten. In the fourth
year, all its fruit shall be holy, to give praise to the LORD.
25 In the fifth year you may eat its fruit – and so shall its yield
26 proliferate for you; I am the LORD your God. Do not eat
any creature with its blood. Do not practice divination or
27 seek omens. Do not cut off the hair on the sides of your
28 head or destroy the edges of your beard. Do not gash
your body for the dead or put tattoo marks on yourself; I
29 am the LORD. Do not profane your daughter by making
her a prostitute, that the land shall not be prostituted,
30 the land filled with depravity. Keep My Sabbaths, revere
31 My Sanctuary; I am the LORD. Do not turn to ghosts or
inquire of spirits, rendering yourself impure; I am the
32 LORD your God. Stand up in the presence of the white-
haired and show respect to the elderly; revere your God;
33 I am the LORD. When a stranger lives with you REVI'I /SHISHI/
34 in your land, do not wrong him. The stranger living with
you shall be like one of your native born to you: love him
as your own self, for you yourselves were strangers in the

---

none of these. It was simply that their society honored the elderly. So should we. It may or may not add years to their life, but it will add life to their years.

19:34 וְאָהַבְתָּ לוֹ כָּמוֹךָ *Love him as your own self* – Leviticus 19 teaches us a third love, in addition to that of God and our neighbor: love for "the stranger living

כ עָלֶיךָ׃ וְאִישׁ כִּי־יִשְׁכַּב אֶת־אִשָּׁה שִׁכְבַת־זֶרַע וְהִוא שִׁפְחָה
נֶחֱרֶפֶת לְאִישׁ וְהָפְדֵּה לֹא נִפְדָּתָה אוֹ חֻפְשָׁה לֹא נִתַּן־לָהּ
כא בִּקֹּרֶת תִּהְיֶה לֹא יוּמְתוּ כִּי־לֹא חֻפָּשָׁה׃ וְהֵבִיא אֶת־אֲשָׁמוֹ
כב לַיהוָה אֶל־פֶּתַח אֹהֶל מוֹעֵד אֵיל אָשָׁם׃ וְכִפֶּר עָלָיו הַכֹּהֵן
בְּאֵיל הָאָשָׁם לִפְנֵי יְהוָה עַל־חַטָּאתוֹ אֲשֶׁר חָטָא וְנִסְלַח
לוֹ מֵחַטָּאתוֹ אֲשֶׁר חָטָא׃
כג וְכִי־תָבֹאוּ אֶל־הָאָרֶץ וּנְטַעְתֶּם כָּל־עֵץ מַאֲכָל וַעֲרַלְתֶּם טז שלישי
עָרְלָתוֹ אֶת־פִּרְיוֹ שָׁלֹשׁ שָׁנִים יִהְיֶה לָכֶם עֲרֵלִים לֹא יֵאָכֵל׃
כד כה וּבַשָּׁנָה הָרְבִיעִת יִהְיֶה כָּל־פִּרְיוֹ קֹדֶשׁ הִלּוּלִים לַיהוָה׃ וּבַשָּׁנָה
הַחֲמִישִׁת תֹּאכְלוּ אֶת־פִּרְיוֹ לְהוֹסִיף לָכֶם תְּבוּאָתוֹ אֲנִי יְהוָה
כו כז אֱלֹהֵיכֶם׃ לֹא תֹאכְלוּ עַל־הַדָּם לֹא תְנַחֲשׁוּ וְלֹא תְעוֹנֵנוּ׃ לֹא
כח תַקִּפוּ פְּאַת רֹאשְׁכֶם וְלֹא תַשְׁחִית אֵת פְּאַת זְקָנֶךָ׃ וְשֶׂרֶט
לָנֶפֶשׁ לֹא תִתְּנוּ בִּבְשַׂרְכֶם וּכְתֹבֶת קַעֲקַע לֹא תִתְּנוּ בָּכֶם
כט אֲנִי יְהוָה׃ אַל־תְּחַלֵּל אֶת־בִּתְּךָ לְהַזְנוֹתָהּ וְלֹא־תִזְנֶה הָאָרֶץ
ל וּמָלְאָה הָאָרֶץ זִמָּה׃ אֶת־שַׁבְּתֹתַי תִּשְׁמֹרוּ וּמִקְדָּשִׁי תִּירָאוּ
לא אֲנִי יְהוָה׃ אַל־תִּפְנוּ אֶל־הָאֹבֹת וְאֶל־הַיִּדְּעֹנִים אַל־תְּבַקְשׁוּ
לב לְטָמְאָה בָהֶם אֲנִי יְהוָה אֱלֹהֵיכֶם׃ מִפְּנֵי שֵׂיבָה תָּקוּם וְהָדַרְתָּ
לג פְּנֵי זָקֵן וְיָרֵאתָ מֵּאֱלֹהֶיךָ אֲנִי יְהוָה׃ וְכִי־יָגוּר אִתְּךָ רביעי /ששי/
לד גֵּר בְּאַרְצְכֶם לֹא תוֹנוּ אֹתוֹ׃ כְּאֶזְרָח מִכֶּם יִהְיֶה לָכֶם הַגֵּר ׀
הַגָּר אִתְּכֶם וְאָהַבְתָּ לוֹ כָּמוֹךָ כִּי־גֵרִים הֱיִיתֶם בְּאֶרֶץ מִצְרָיִם

19:32 וְהָדַרְתָּ פְּנֵי זָקֵן *Show respect to the elderly* – The Tanakh takes it as axiomatic that a society is judged by the way it treats the most vulnerable: the very young and the very old. One of the beautiful aspects of Jewish life, in our synagogues, old-age homes, and extended families, is the conversation and friendship between the young and the old, between grandparents and grandchildren, sometimes even into the fourth generation; the young sharing their dreams with the old; the old sharing their memories with the young.

Years ago, the late Alastair Cooke in one of his *Letters from America* radio programs spoke about a remote region whose inhabitants lived to a great old age. A team of researchers went to discover their secret. Was it the climate, or the diet, or their genes? The answer was

35 land of Egypt; I am the LORD your God. Do not falsify
measures – not of length, nor of weight, nor of volume.
36 You shall have honest scales, honest weights, an honest
ephah, and an honest hin. I am the LORD your God, who
37 brought you out of the land of Egypt. Keep all My decrees
and laws and fulfill them; I am the LORD."
20 1 2 The LORD spoke to Moshe: "Tell the Israelites: Any HAMISHI
person – any Israelite or any migrant residing among
Israel – who sacrifices any of his children to Molekh shall
3 be put to death. The people of the land shall stone him, and
I Myself will set My face against that person; I will sever
him from his people because, in sacrificing his children
to Molekh, he defiles My Sanctuary; he desecrates My
4 holy name. If the people of the land close their eyes to a
man as he sacrifices his children to Molekh – if they do
5 not put him to death – I Myself will set My face against
him and his family; I will sever him from his people, and
with him all who follow him in going astray after Molekh.
6 And anyone who turns to ghosts or spirits, going astray
after them – I will set My face against him and sever him
7 from his people. Consecrate yourselves and be holy, for

As we survey the Torah and rabbinic literature, however, we find less concern with the question "What kind of economy should we have?" than with the question "How can we ensure the economy we have is an ethical enterprise?" Economic systems, like political ones, change over time, yet the Torah's concerns are timeless: Within a given system, how can we mitigate its hazards and injustices? How can we protect human dignity? How can we preserve fair dealing and integrity? How can we recognize the exigencies of economic endeavor and at the same time keep alive other and more spacious values? Jewish law and ethics devote great attention, sometimes at the level of broad principle, often in minute detail, to what John Gray calls "the moral foundations of market institutions."

According to Rava, when a person comes to the next world for judgment, the first question he is asked is "Did you deal honestly in business?" (Shabbat 31a). Honest scales and accurate weights and measures are to be a symbol for the hugely important halakhic field of business ethics. The Rabbis established supervisors to check on these measures, just as we now have supervisors of *kashrut*.

לה אני יהוה אלהיכם: לא־תעשו עול במשפט במדה במשקל
לו ובמשורה: מאזני צדק אבני־צדק איפת צדק והין צדק יהיה
לכם אני יהוה אלהיכם אשר־הוצאתי אתכם מארץ מצרים:
לז ושמרתם את־כל־חקתי ואת־כל־משפטי ועשיתם אתם אני
יהוה:

כ א ב וידבר יהוה אל־משה לאמר: ואל־בני ישראל תאמר חמישי
איש איש מבני ישראל ומן־הגר | הגר בישראל אשר
יתן מזרעו למלך מות יומת עם הארץ ירגמהו באבן:
ג ואני אתן את־פני באיש ההוא והכרתי אתו מקרב עמו
כי מזרעו נתן למלך למען טמא את־מקדשי ולחלל את־
ד שם קדשי: ואם העלם יעלימו עם הארץ את־עיניהם
מן־האיש ההוא בתתו מזרעו למלך לבלתי המית אתו:
ה ושמתי אני את־פני באיש ההוא ובמשפחתו והכרתי
אתו ואת | כל־הזנים אחריו לזנות אחרי המלך מקרב
ו עמם: והנפש אשר תפנה אל־האבת ואל־הידענים לזנת
אחריהם ונתתי את־פני בנפש ההוא והכרתי אתו מקרב
ז עמו: והתקדשתם והייתם קדשים כי אני יהוה אלהיכם:

---

poor; at others, with the widow and orphan. On several occasions, the Torah specifies: "You shall have the same law for the stranger as for the native born" (Ex. 12:49; Lev. 24:22; Num. 15:16, 29). Not only must the stranger not be wronged, he or she must be included in the positive welfare provisions of Israelite/Jewish society. But here the law goes beyond this; the stranger must be loved.

19:36 מאזני צדק *Honest scales* – There have been many hypotheses as to the religious origins of the market economy.

with you." It is easier to love your neighbor as yourself because throughout most of history, your neighbors were often like yourself, in culture, class, nationality, and ethnicity. The challenge is to love the stranger, the one who is not like you.

The Sages noted the repeated emphasis on the stranger in biblical law. According to R. Eliezer, the Torah "warns against the wronging of a *ger* in thirty-six places; others say: in forty-six places" (Bava Metzia 59b). Whatever the precise number, the repetition throughout the Mosaic books is remarkable. Sometimes the stranger is mentioned along with the

SHISHI /SHEVI'I/

8 I am the Lord your God. Keep My decrees and fulfill
9 them; I am the Lord, who makes you holy. One who
curses his father or mother shall be put to death. Since
he has cursed his father or mother, his bloodguilt is upon
10 him. If a man commits adultery with a married woman,
another man's wife, both the adulterer and the adulteress
11 shall be put to death. If a man lies with his father's wife,
he has exposed his father's nakedness; both of them
12 shall be put to death; their bloodguilt is upon them. If
a man lies with his daughter-in-law, both of them shall
be put to death. They have committed perversion; their
13 bloodguilt is upon them. If a man lies with a male as he
would with a woman, both have performed an abhorrent
act; they shall be put to death; their bloodguilt is upon
14 them. If a man marries a woman and also her mother, it
is depravity. He and they shall be burned by fire; there
15 must be no depravity among you. If a man lies with an
animal, he shall be put to death and you shall kill the
16 animal. If a woman approaches an animal to mate with
it, you shall kill the woman and the animal; they shall
17 both be put to death; their bloodguilt is upon them. If a
man takes his sister – his father's daughter or his mother's
daughter – and they see one another's nakedness, it is a
deep disgrace; they shall be severed in the sight of their
people. He has exposed his sister's nakedness; he shall
18 bear his guilt. If a man lies with a menstruating woman
and exposes her nakedness, he has laid her hidden source
bare; she has exposed the source of her blood; both of
19 them shall be severed from their people. Do not expose
the nakedness of your mother's sister or your father's
sister, because that is to lay bare your own near relative;

---

it with the sense of the transcendent? More than any other institution, the family turns the everyday into unself-conscious beauty. Halakha is the genius of taking an ordinary life in ordinary circumstances and making it a home for the Divine Presence.

ח וּשְׁמַרְתֶּם אֶת־חֻקֹּתַי וַעֲשִׂיתֶם אֹתָם אֲנִי יְהוָה מְקַדִּשְׁכֶם׃ ששי /שביעי/
ט כִּי־אִישׁ אִישׁ אֲשֶׁר יְקַלֵּל אֶת־אָבִיו וְאֶת־אִמּוֹ מוֹת יוּמָת
י אָבִיו וְאִמּוֹ קִלֵּל דָּמָיו בּוֹ׃ וְאִישׁ אֲשֶׁר יִנְאַף אֶת־אֵשֶׁת אִישׁ
אֲשֶׁר יִנְאַף אֶת־אֵשֶׁת רֵעֵהוּ מוֹת־יוּמַת הַנֹּאֵף וְהַנֹּאָפֶת׃
יא וְאִישׁ אֲשֶׁר יִשְׁכַּב אֶת־אֵשֶׁת אָבִיו עֶרְוַת אָבִיו גִּלָּה מוֹת־
יב יוּמְתוּ שְׁנֵיהֶם דְּמֵיהֶם בָּם׃ וְאִישׁ אֲשֶׁר יִשְׁכַּב אֶת־כַּלָּתוֹ
יג מוֹת יוּמְתוּ שְׁנֵיהֶם תֶּבֶל עָשׂוּ דְּמֵיהֶם בָּם׃ וְאִישׁ אֲשֶׁר יִשְׁכַּב
אֶת־זָכָר מִשְׁכְּבֵי אִשָּׁה תּוֹעֵבָה עָשׂוּ שְׁנֵיהֶם מוֹת יוּמָתוּ
יד דְּמֵיהֶם בָּם׃ וְאִישׁ אֲשֶׁר יִקַּח אֶת־אִשָּׁה וְאֶת־אִמָּהּ זִמָּה
הִוא בָּאֵשׁ יִשְׂרְפוּ אֹתוֹ וְאֶתְהֶן וְלֹא־תִהְיֶה זִמָּה בְּתוֹכְכֶם׃
טו וְאִישׁ אֲשֶׁר יִתֵּן שְׁכָבְתּוֹ בִּבְהֵמָה מוֹת יוּמָת וְאֶת־הַבְּהֵמָה
טז תַּהֲרֹגוּ׃ וְאִשָּׁה אֲשֶׁר תִּקְרַב אֶל־כָּל־בְּהֵמָה לְרִבְעָה אֹתָהּ
וְהָרַגְתָּ אֶת־הָאִשָּׁה וְאֶת־הַבְּהֵמָה מוֹת יוּמָתוּ דְּמֵיהֶם בָּם׃
יז וְאִישׁ אֲשֶׁר־יִקַּח אֶת־אֲחֹתוֹ בַּת־אָבִיו אוֹ בַת־אִמּוֹ וְרָאָה
אֶת־עֶרְוָתָהּ וְהִיא תִרְאֶה אֶת־עֶרְוָתוֹ חֶסֶד הוּא וְנִכְרְתוּ
יח לְעֵינֵי בְּנֵי עַמָּם עֶרְוַת אֲחֹתוֹ גִּלָּה עֲוֺנוֹ יִשָּׂא׃ וְאִישׁ אֲשֶׁר־
יִשְׁכַּב אֶת־אִשָּׁה דָּוָה וְגִלָּה אֶת־עֶרְוָתָהּ אֶת־מְקֹרָהּ הֶעֱרָה
וְהִוא גִּלְּתָה אֶת־מְקוֹר דָּמֶיהָ וְנִכְרְתוּ שְׁנֵיהֶם מִקֶּרֶב עַמָּם׃
יט וְעֶרְוַת אֲחוֹת אִמְּךָ וַאֲחוֹת אָבִיךָ לֹא תְגַלֵּה כִּי אֶת־שְׁאֵרוֹ

20:18 אֶת־מְקֹרָהּ הֶעֱרָה *He has laid her hidden source bare* – The devaluing of the family and the legitimation of sexual license, whether it takes place in ancient Greece or the contemporary West, is the beginning of the end of a social system. The human person needs to learn a "Thou" before it can coherently pronounce the "I." We need to be cared for before we can learn to care for others. We need the formative experience of personal stability if as adults we are to make the sacrifices necessary to sustain a stable social order. And so, moral agents need to grow within families – families which themselves contain boundaries between free individuals.

Our passage lays the foundation of an intricate code of investing the love between husband and wife with a discipline, a structure, a rhythm, turning prose into religious poetry. How do you take an ordinary life and imbue

20 both shall bear their guilt. If a man lies with his aunt, he
has exposed his uncle's nakedness. Both parties shall bear
21 their guilt; they shall die childless. For a man to marry his
brother's wife – that is taboo. He has exposed his brother's
22 nakedness; both parties shall be childless. Keep all My
decrees and all My laws and fulfill them, so that the land
to which I am bringing you to settle will not vomit you out.
23 Do not follow the practices of the nation I am driving out SHEVI'I
before you, for they did all these things and I was disgusted
24 with them. I have told you: You shall possess their land; I
am giving it to you to possess. It is a land that flows with
milk and with honey. I am the LORD your God, who has
25 set you apart from all other peoples. You, then, shall set MAFTIR
pure apart from impure animals, pure from impure birds.
Do not make yourselves detestable by an animal or bird
or anything that creeps upon the ground that I have set
26 apart from you to regard as impure. Be holy to Me, for I
the LORD am holy, and I have set you apart from all other
27 peoples to be My own. A man or woman who seeks ghosts
or spirits shall be put to death. They shall be stoned; their
bloodguilt is on them."

The haftara for Parashat Kedoshim is on page 1534
(even when Aḥarei Mot and Kedoshim are read together).
On Rosh Ḥodesh Iyar read the haftara on page 1640.

---

his task to make these distinctions and teach them to others. He knows that different life-forms have their own niche in the environment. That is why the ethic of holiness includes rules like: Don't mate with different kinds of animals, don't plant a field with different kinds of seeds, and don't wear clothing woven from two kinds of material.

The ethic of holiness tells us that God made each of us in love. Therefore, if we seek to imitate God – "Be holy for I am holy, I, the LORD your God" (Lev. 19:2) – we too must love humanity, and not in the abstract but in the concrete form of the neighbor and the stranger.

There is something unique and contemporary about the ethic of holiness. It tells us that morality and ecology are closely related. They both honor creation: the world as God's work and humanity as God's image. The integrity of humanity and the natural environment go together. The natural universe and humanity were both created by God, and we are charged to protect the first and love the second. The *parasha* has expanded this double imperative into numerous detailed guidelines, all under the heading "Be holy."

כ הֶעֱרָה עֲוֺנָם יִשָּׂאוּ׃ וְאִישׁ אֲשֶׁר יִשְׁכַּב אֶת־דֹּדָתוֹ עֶרְוַת
כא דֹּדוֹ גִּלָּה חֶטְאָם יִשָּׂאוּ עֲרִירִים יָמֻתוּ׃ וְאִישׁ אֲשֶׁר יִקַּח
אֶת־אֵשֶׁת אָחִיו נִדָּה הִוא עֶרְוַת אָחִיו גִּלָּה עֲרִירִים יִהְיוּ׃
כב וּשְׁמַרְתֶּם אֶת־כָּל־חֻקֹּתַי וְאֶת־כָּל־מִשְׁפָּטַי וַעֲשִׂיתֶם אֹתָם
וְלֹא־תָקִיא אֶתְכֶם הָאָרֶץ אֲשֶׁר אֲנִי מֵבִיא אֶתְכֶם שָׁמָּה
כג לָשֶׁבֶת בָּהּ׃ וְלֹא תֵלְכוּ בְּחֻקֹּת הַגּוֹי אֲשֶׁר־אֲנִי מְשַׁלֵּחַ שביעי
כד מִפְּנֵיכֶם כִּי אֶת־כָּל־אֵלֶּה עָשׂוּ וָאָקֻץ בָּם׃ וָאֹמַר לָכֶם אַתֶּם
תִּירְשׁוּ אֶת־אַדְמָתָם וַאֲנִי אֶתְּנֶנָּה לָכֶם לָרֶשֶׁת אֹתָהּ אֶרֶץ
זָבַת חָלָב וּדְבָשׁ אֲנִי יְהוָה אֱלֹהֵיכֶם אֲשֶׁר־הִבְדַּלְתִּי אֶתְכֶם
כה מִן־הָעַמִּים׃ וְהִבְדַּלְתֶּם בֵּין־הַבְּהֵמָה הַטְּהֹרָה לַטְּמֵאָה מפטיר
וּבֵין־הָעוֹף הַטָּמֵא לַטָּהֹר וְלֹא־תְשַׁקְּצוּ אֶת־נַפְשֹׁתֵיכֶם
בַּבְּהֵמָה וּבָעוֹף וּבְכֹל אֲשֶׁר תִּרְמֹשׂ הָאֲדָמָה אֲשֶׁר־הִבְדַּלְתִּי
כו לָכֶם לְטַמֵּא׃ וִהְיִיתֶם לִי קְדֹשִׁים כִּי קָדוֹשׁ אֲנִי יְהוָה וָאַבְדִּל
כז אֶתְכֶם מִן־הָעַמִּים לִהְיוֹת לִי׃ וְאִישׁ אוֹ־אִשָּׁה כִּי־יִהְיֶה
בָהֶם אוֹב אוֹ יִדְּעֹנִי מוֹת יוּמָתוּ בָּאֶבֶן יִרְגְּמוּ אֹתָם דְּמֵיהֶם
בָּם׃

The הפטרה *for* פרשת קדשים *is on page 1535*
(even when אחרי מות *and* קדשים *are read together).*
On ראש חודש אייר *read the* הפטרה *on page 1641.*

20:26 וָאַבְדִּל אֶתְכֶם *I have set you apart* – The verb *b-d-l*, to divide, set apart, separate, distinguish, is a keyword used throughout Tanakh in relation to the priest. That is what a priest does. His task is "to distinguish between sacred and profane" (Lev. 10:10; see comment there) and "to distinguish between the impure and the pure" (Lev. 11:47; see ch. 11, "The Dietary Laws"). This is what God does for His people: "I have set you apart [*vaavdil*] from all other peoples to be My own."

There is one other place in which *b-d-l* is a keyword, namely, the story of creation in Genesis 1, where it occurs five times. God separates light and dark, day and night, upper and lower waters. For three days God demarcates different domains, then for the next three days, He places in each its appropriate objects or life-forms. As His last act of creation, He makes man after His "image and likeness" (see Gen. 1:26). This was clearly an act of love. "Beloved is man," said R. Akiva, "because he was created in [God's] image" (Avot 3:14). Genesis 1 defines the priestly moral imagination, which looks at creation as the work of God. The priest knows that everything has its place: sacred and profane, permitted and forbidden. It is

Parashat Emor

21 1 The LORD said to Moshe, "Speak to the priests, Aharon's
sons. Say: No one of you shall render himself impure for
2 any dead person among his people except for his nearest
3 relatives: his mother, father, son, daughter, or brother; or
his virgin sister who has remained close to him because she
has not married – for her, he may render himself impure.
4 But he shall not become impure for those he is related
5 to by marriage, and so become profane. Priests shall not
make bald patches on their heads, or shave off the edges
6 of their beards, or gash wounds into their flesh. They shall
be holy to their God and not profane God's name, for they
bring close the LORD's fire offerings, foodstuff offerings
7 to their God; therefore they shall be holy. They may not
marry a woman made profane by immorality, nor may
they marry a woman divorced from her husband, for they

---

were completely and permanently hidden from the world, it would be as if He were absent. From a human perspective there would be no difference between an unknowable God and a nonexistent God. Therefore God established the holy as the point at which the Eternal enters time and the Infinite enters space.

God's eternity stands in the sharpest possible contrast to our mortality. All that lives will one day die. All that is physical will one day erode and cease to be. Hence the extreme delicacy and danger of the Tabernacle or Temple, the point at which That-which-is-beyond-time-and-space enters time and space. Just as a highly sensitive experiment has to be conducted without the slightest contamination, so the holy space has to be kept free of conditions that bespeak human mortality.

Tuma should therefore not be thought of as "defilement," as if there were something wrong or sinful about it. *Tuma* is about mortality. Death bespeaks mortality, but so too does birth. A skin disease like *tzaraat* makes us vividly aware of the body. There is nothing wrong about any of these things, but they focus our attention on the physical, the mortal, the fragility of life.

It is notable, however, that a priest, even a High Priest, may perform the rites of a *met mitzva*, that is, one who has no one else to attend to his funeral. Here the basic requirement of human dignity overrides the priestly imperative of purity.

פרשת אמר

כא א וַיֹּאמֶר יהוה אֶל־מֹשֶׁה אֱמֹר אֶל־הַכֹּהֲנִים בְּנֵי אַהֲרֹן וְאָמַרְתָּ יז
ב אֲלֵהֶם לְנֶפֶשׁ לֹא־יִטַּמָּא בְּעַמָּיו: כִּי אִם־לִשְׁאֵרוֹ הַקָּרֹב אֵלָיו
ג לְאִמּוֹ וּלְאָבִיו וְלִבְנוֹ וּלְבִתּוֹ וּלְאָחִיו: וְלַאֲחֹתוֹ הַבְּתוּלָה
ד הַקְּרוֹבָה אֵלָיו אֲשֶׁר לֹא־הָיְתָה לְאִישׁ לָהּ יִטַּמָּא: לֹא יִטַּמָּא
ה בַּעַל בְּעַמָּיו לְהֵחַלּוֹ: לֹא־יקרחה קָרְחָה בְּרֹאשָׁם וּפְאַת יִקְרְחוּ
ו זְקָנָם לֹא יְגַלֵּחוּ וּבִבְשָׂרָם לֹא יִשְׂרְטוּ שָׂרָטֶת: קְדֹשִׁים יִהְיוּ
לֵאלֹהֵיהֶם וְלֹא יְחַלְּלוּ שֵׁם אֱלֹהֵיהֶם כִּי אֶת־אִשֵּׁי יהוה לֶחֶם
ז אֱלֹהֵיהֶם הֵם מַקְרִיבִם וְהָיוּ קֹדֶשׁ: אִשָּׁה זֹנָה וַחֲלָלָה לֹא יִקָּחוּ
וְאִשָּׁה גְּרוּשָׁה מֵאִישָׁהּ לֹא יִקָּחוּ כִּי־קָדֹשׁ הוּא לֵאלֹהָיו:

EMOR

Parashat Emor deals with two kinds of holiness: of people and of time. Chapter 21 relates to holy people: priests, and above them, the High Priest. Their close contact with the Sanctuary means that they must live with certain restrictions, namely, on contact with the dead and whom they may marry. Chapter 22 recaps similar laws relating to ordinary Israelites when they seek to enter the Sanctuary, as well as defects in animals that bar them from being offered as sacrifices. Chapter 23 is about holy time, the festivals of the year. Chapter 24 speaks about the candelabrum (menora), lit daily, and the showbread renewed weekly, and ends with a story – one of only two narratives in Leviticus – about the fate of a man who blasphemes in the course of a fight. It is this narrative that draws to a close the long Tabernacle cycle, before we take up the narrative where we left off in Exodus 24, "on Mount Sinai" (Lev. 25:1).

21:1 לְנֶפֶשׁ לֹא־יִטַּמָּא *No one of you shall render himself impure* – A priest may not touch or be under the same roof as a dead body. He must remain aloof from close contact with the dead, with the exception of a close relative. The law for the High Priest is stricter still. He may not allow himself to become ceremonially unclean even for a close relative.

To understand these laws and other purity regulations, we first have to return to the concept of the holy. God is beyond space and time, yet God created space and time as well as the physical entities that occupy space and time. God is therefore "concealed" (*ne'elam*) in our physical world (*olam*). Yet if God

8 are holy to their God. You shall treat a priest as holy, for
he brings close the offerings of foodstuffs to your God.
And he shall be holy to you, because I, the LORD, am holy
9 and make you holy. If the daughter of a priest profanes
herself by immorality, she profanes her father also; she
10 shall be burned with fire. The priest, the highest
among his brothers, on whose head the anointing oil
has been poured and who has been ordained to wear the
vestments, shall not dishevel his hair or tear his clothes.
11 He shall not go near the dead; even for his father or
12 mother he shall not render himself impure. He shall not
leave the Sanctuary, profaning his God's Sanctuary, for
the crown of his God's anointing oil rests upon him; I am
13 the LORD. He may marry a woman only in her virginity.
14 He may not marry a widow, a divorcée, or one profaned
by immorality. He may marry only a virgin from his own
15 people, so that he will not profane his children among
16 his people, for I, the LORD, sanctify him." The SHENI
17 LORD spoke to Moshe: "Tell Aharon: Any of your future
descendants who has a physical blemish may not draw

(Job 1–2). The logic of this seems absurd. How can a skin disease be a greater trial of faith than losing your children? It isn't. But what the book is saying is that when your body is afflicted, it can be hard, even impossible, to focus on spirituality. This has nothing to do with ultimate truth and everything to do with the human mind. You cannot give your mind to meditating on truth when you are hungry or thirsty, homeless or sick (*Guide for the Perplexed* III:27). And a skin disease or a bodily abnormality in one person tends to prompt in others the thought, "This could happen to me." They remind us of the "thousand natural shocks that flesh is heir to."

This is the logic – if logic is the right word – of *tuma*. It has nothing to do with rationality and everything to do with emotion. That which distracts from eternity and infinity by making us forcibly aware of our own mortality, of the fact that we are physical beings in a physical world – that is what we distance from the operation of holy precincts. Something similar may be said of the appearance of bodily abnormalities in the Tabernacle.

Needless to say, however, our attitudes to disability have changed significantly. The principle of integration, for instance, played a part in a sixteenth-century responsum of Rabbi Aharon Slonik. He had been asked whether a

ח וְקִדַּשְׁתּוֹ כִּי־אֶת־לֶחֶם אֱלֹהֶיךָ הוּא מַקְרִיב קָדֹשׁ יִהְיֶה־לָּךְ
ט כִּי קָדוֹשׁ אֲנִי יהוה מְקַדִּשְׁכֶם: וּבַת אִישׁ כֹּהֵן כִּי תֵחֵל לִזְנוֹת
י אֶת־אָבִיהָ הִיא מְחַלֶּלֶת בָּאֵשׁ תִּשָּׂרֵף: וְהַכֹּהֵן
הַגָּדוֹל מֵאֶחָיו אֲשֶׁר־יוּצַק עַל־רֹאשׁוֹ ׀ שֶׁמֶן הַמִּשְׁחָה וּמִלֵּא
אֶת־יָדוֹ לִלְבֹּשׁ אֶת־הַבְּגָדִים אֶת־רֹאשׁוֹ לֹא יִפְרָע וּבְגָדָיו לֹא
יא יִפְרֹם: וְעַל כָּל־נַפְשֹׁת מֵת לֹא יָבֹא לְאָבִיו וּלְאִמּוֹ לֹא יִטַּמָּא:
יב וּמִן־הַמִּקְדָּשׁ לֹא יֵצֵא וְלֹא יְחַלֵּל אֵת מִקְדַּשׁ אֱלֹהָיו כִּי נֵזֶר
יג שֶׁמֶן מִשְׁחַת אֱלֹהָיו עָלָיו אֲנִי יהוה: וְהוּא אִשָּׁה בִבְתוּלֶיהָ
יד יִקָּח: אַלְמָנָה וּגְרוּשָׁה וַחֲלָלָה זֹנָה אֶת־אֵלֶּה לֹא יִקָּח כִּי
טו אִם־בְּתוּלָה מֵעַמָּיו יִקַּח אִשָּׁה: וְלֹא־יְחַלֵּל זַרְעוֹ בְּעַמָּיו כִּי
טז אֲנִי יהוה מְקַדְּשׁוֹ: וַיְדַבֵּר יהוה אֶל־מֹשֶׁה לֵּאמֹר: שני
יז דַּבֵּר אֶל־אַהֲרֹן לֵאמֹר אִישׁ מִזַּרְעֲךָ לְדֹרֹתָם אֲשֶׁר יִהְיֶה בוֹ

A PRIEST WITH A PHYSICAL BLEMISH

Some forms of physical difference render a priest unfit for service in the Tabernacle. We might assume that this implies that someone who had such a disability is considered less than perfect, and thus debarred from high religious office. But Rambam, in *Guide for the Perplexed* (III:44), gives a quite different explanation. It was, he says, a concession to ill-informed sentiment. People wrongly judge an individual by his physical appearance rather than by his true form. God looks to the heart, but people judge by external appearances. Thus the Torah excludes priests with certain disabilities and physical differences from Temple service to avoid public disrespect. Rambam himself makes it clear that the priest with a physical disability is pleasing before God. The legislation surrounding the Temple, however, involves concessions to human prejudice.

Rambam's understanding of this set of laws emphasizes what human beings lack in empathy. Yet his idea may be taken in a slightly different direction by applying to it what we learned about *tuma* above (v.1). We saw that what unites the various types of ritual impurity is that they focus our attention on the physical. Therefore they are incompatible with the holy space of the Tabernacle, which is dedicated to the presence of the nonphysical, the Eternal Infinite that never dies or decays.

This is well illustrated at the beginning of the book of Job. Iyov loses everything: his flocks, his herds, his children. Yet his faith remains intact. Satan then proposes subjecting Iyov to an even greater trial, covering his body with sores

18 close to present foodstuff offerings to his God. No one
with a blemish shall approach: this includes one who is
19 blind, lame, disfigured, or deformed; or who has a broken
20 foot or hand; or who is a hunchback or a dwarf, or who
has a growth in his eye, a severe rash, scabs, or crushed
21 testicles. No descendant of Aharon the priest who has a
physical blemish shall draw near to present the Lord's fire
offerings; because of his blemish, he shall not approach to
22 present an offering of foodstuffs to his God. He may eat
the foodstuff offerings of his God, the holy of holies as
23 well as the holy. But he may not come close to the inner
curtain or approach the altar, because of his blemish;
he shall not profane My Sanctuary; I am the Lord who
24 makes them holy." Moshe told this to Aharon, his sons,
and all the Israelites.

22 1 2 The Lord spoke to Moshe: "Tell Aharon and his sons to
take great care with the sacred offerings that the Israelites
consecrate to Me, so that they do not profane My holy
3 name: I am the Lord. Tell them: If any descendant of
yours throughout the generations comes near the sacred
offerings that the Israelites have consecrated to the Lord
while in an impure state, he shall be severed from My
4 presence; I am the Lord. Any descendant of Aharon
who has a defiling blight of the skin or a discharge may
not eat of the sacred offerings until he becomes pure.
One who touches anything made impure by contact
5 with the dead, or who has had a seminal emission, or
who has touched any swarming thing or any person
6 who renders him impure – whatever his impurity – the
one who touches these things shall be impure until the
evening, and shall not eat of the sacred offerings until he
7 has washed his body in water. When the sun sets, he shall
become pure again and may eat of the sacred offerings,
8 for they are his food. He may not eat an animal found

disrespectfully, we diminish their humanity and thereby ours (see Lev. 19:14 and comment there). This too is part of our halakhic heritage.

יח מום לא יקרב להקריב לחם אלהיו: כי כל־איש אשר־בו
יט מום לא יקרב איש עור או פסח או חרם או שרוע: או
כ איש אשר־יהיה בו שבר רגל או שבר יד: או־גבן או־דק
כא או תבלל בעינו או גרב או ילפת או מרוח אשך: כל־איש
אשר־בו מום מזרע אהרן הכהן לא יגש להקריב את־אשי
כב יהוה מום בו את לחם אלהיו לא יגש להקריב: לחם אלהיו
כג מקדשי הקדשים ומן־הקדשים יאכל: אך אל־הפרכת לא
יבא ואל־המזבח לא יגש כי־מום בו ולא יחלל את־מקדשי
כד כי אני יהוה מקדשם: וידבר משה אל־אהרן ואל־בניו
ואל־כל־בני ישראל:

כב א ב וידבר יהוה אל־משה לאמר: דבר אל־אהרן ואל־בניו
וינזרו מקדשי בני־ישראל ולא יחללו את־שם קדשי
ג אשר הם מקדשים לי אני יהוה: אמר אלהם לדרתיכם
כל־איש ׀ אשר־יקרב מכל־זרעכם אל־הקדשים אשר
יקדישו בני־ישראל ליהוה וטמאתו עליו ונכרתה הנפש
ד ההוא מלפני אני יהוה: איש איש מזרע אהרן והוא צרוע
או זב בקדשים לא יאכל עד אשר יטהר והנגע בכל־טמא־
ה נפש או איש אשר־תצא ממנו שכבת־זרע: או־איש אשר
יגע בכל־שרץ אשר יטמא־לו או באדם אשר יטמא־
ו לו לכל טמאתו: נפש אשר תגע־בו וטמאה עד־הערב
ז ולא יאכל מן־הקדשים כי אם רחץ בשרו במים: ובא
השמש וטהר ואחר יאכל מן־הקדשים כי לחמו הוא:
ח ט נבלה וטרפה לא יאכל לטמאה־בה אני יהוה: ושמרו

blind man may be called to the reading of the Torah. After citing the authorities who rule affirmatively on the question, he adds the following consideration: "We must allow the blind … to be called to the Torah and to utter blessings, in order to include them in the acceptance of God's dominion and to give them spiritual satisfaction" (*Mas'at Binyamin* 62). Inclusion of those with disabilities within the faith community was, for him, a significant halakhic factor. If we treat others

▶

dead or one that was torn by wild animals, becoming
9 impure by doing so; I am the LORD. They shall keep
My charge and not bear guilt and die through it, having
10 profaned it. I am the LORD, who makes them holy. No
layman may eat of the sacred offerings, nor may a priest's
11 visitor or hired laborer eat of them. But if a priest acquires
a slave for money, the slave may eat of them, and those
12 born into his household also may eat his food. If a priest's
daughter marries a layman, she may no longer eat of the
13 sacred gifts. If a priest's daughter is a widow or a divorcée,
has no children, and returns to live in her father's house
as when she was young, she may eat her father's food
14 again; but no layperson may do so. If someone eats of the
sacred gift unintentionally, he shall make restitution to
15 the priest, adding an extra fifth to its value. The people
must not profane the sacred meats that Israelites bring as
16 offerings to the LORD or incur the penalty of iniquity by
eating their sacred offerings; for I, the LORD, make them
holy."
17 18 The LORD spoke to Moshe: "Speak to Aharon, his sons, SHELISHI
and all the Israelites. Say: When anyone of the House of
Israel or of the migrants living in Israel presents an offering
to the LORD as a burnt offering – whether in fulfillment
19 of a vow or as a freewill offering – to be acceptable on
your behalf, it must be an unblemished male from the
20 herd, or of the sheep or goats. Do not offer anything that
has a blemish, for it will not be accepted on your behalf.
21 When someone presents a peace sacrifice to the LORD
from the herd or flock – whether because of a spoken
vow or as a freewill offering – it must be unblemished
22 to be acceptable; there shall be no blemish on it. Do not
present to the LORD anything blind, injured, or maimed,
or with warts, a severe rash, or scabs. Do not place any
23 of these on the altar as a fire offering to the LORD. You
may offer as a freewill offering an ox or sheep with a limb
deformed or uncloven, but they will not be accepted in
24 fulfillment of a vow. Do not offer to the LORD an animal

אֶת־מִשְׁמַרְתִּי וְלֹא־יִשְׂאוּ עָלָיו חֵטְא וּמֵתוּ בוֹ כִּי יְחַלְּלֻהוּ
י אֲנִי יהוה מְקַדְּשָׁם: וְכָל־זָר לֹא־יֹאכַל קֹדֶשׁ תּוֹשַׁב כֹּהֵן
יא וְשָׂכִיר לֹא־יֹאכַל קֹדֶשׁ: וְכֹהֵן כִּי־יִקְנֶה נֶפֶשׁ קִנְיַן כַּסְפּוֹ הוּא
יב יֹאכַל בּוֹ וִילִיד בֵּיתוֹ הֵם יֹאכְלוּ בְלַחְמוֹ: וּבַת־כֹּהֵן כִּי תִהְיֶה
יג לְאִישׁ זָר הִוא בִּתְרוּמַת הַקֳּדָשִׁים לֹא תֹאכֵל: וּבַת־כֹּהֵן כִּי
תִהְיֶה אַלְמָנָה וּגְרוּשָׁה וְזֶרַע אֵין לָהּ וְשָׁבָה אֶל־בֵּית אָבִיהָ
יד כִּנְעוּרֶיהָ מִלֶּחֶם אָבִיהָ תֹּאכֵל וְכָל־זָר לֹא־יֹאכַל בּוֹ: וְאִישׁ
כִּי־יֹאכַל קֹדֶשׁ בִּשְׁגָגָה וְיָסַף חֲמִשִׁיתוֹ עָלָיו וְנָתַן לַכֹּהֵן אֶת־
טו הַקֹּדֶשׁ: וְלֹא יְחַלְּלוּ אֶת־קָדְשֵׁי בְּנֵי יִשְׂרָאֵל אֵת אֲשֶׁר־יָרִימוּ
טז לַיהוה: וְהִשִּׂיאוּ אוֹתָם עֲוֹן אַשְׁמָה בְּאָכְלָם אֶת־קָדְשֵׁיהֶם
כִּי אֲנִי יהוה מְקַדְּשָׁם:
יז יח וַיְדַבֵּר יהוה אֶל־מֹשֶׁה לֵּאמֹר: דַּבֵּר אֶל־אַהֲרֹן וְאֶל־בָּנָיו וְאֶל יח שלישי
כָּל־בְּנֵי יִשְׂרָאֵל וְאָמַרְתָּ אֲלֵהֶם אִישׁ אִישׁ מִבֵּית יִשְׂרָאֵל
וּמִן־הַגֵּר בְּיִשְׂרָאֵל אֲשֶׁר יַקְרִיב קָרְבָּנוֹ לְכָל־נִדְרֵיהֶם וּלְכָל־
יט נִדְבוֹתָם אֲשֶׁר־יַקְרִיבוּ לַיהוה לְעֹלָה: לִרְצֹנְכֶם תָּמִים זָכָר
כ בַּבָּקָר בַּכְּשָׂבִים וּבָעִזִּים: כֹּל אֲשֶׁר־בּוֹ מוּם לֹא תַקְרִיבוּ כִּי־
כא לֹא לְרָצוֹן יִהְיֶה לָכֶם: וְאִישׁ כִּי־יַקְרִיב זֶבַח־שְׁלָמִים לַיהוה
לְפַלֵּא־נֶדֶר אוֹ לִנְדָבָה בַּבָּקָר אוֹ בַצֹּאן תָּמִים יִהְיֶה לְרָצוֹן
כב כָּל־מוּם לֹא יִהְיֶה־בּוֹ: עַוֶּרֶת אוֹ שָׁבוּר אוֹ־חָרוּץ אוֹ־יַבֶּלֶת
אוֹ גָרָב אוֹ יַלֶּפֶת לֹא־תַקְרִיבוּ אֵלֶּה לַיהוה וְאִשֶּׁה לֹא־תִתְּנוּ
כג מֵהֶם עַל־הַמִּזְבֵּחַ לַיהוה: וְשׁוֹר וָשֶׂה שָׂרוּעַ וְקָלוּט נְדָבָה
כד תַּעֲשֶׂה אֹתוֹ וּלְנֵדֶר לֹא יֵרָצֶה: וּמָעוּךְ וְכָתוּת וְנָתוּק וְכָרוּת

22:11 וְכֹהֵן כִּי־יִקְנֶה נֶפֶשׁ *But if a priest acquires a slave* – All members of the priestly household – including slaves – are eligible to eat the sacrificial meats. Visitors, and family members who leave the household, are not. Covenant democratizes society. It is a politics of empowerment. The Torah places a striking emphasis on personal responsibility for the structures of grace within society – above all, the home. Everything dehumanizing about slavery is forbidden. Home is something we build together; though it may have its hierarchies, it still generates a sense of belonging.

whose testicles are bruised, crushed, torn, or cut off;
25 and do not do such things in your land. Do not accept
such animals from a migrant as an offering of foodstuffs
to your God. Because they are mutilated and blemished,
26 they will not be accepted on your behalf." The
27 LORD spoke to Moshe: "When an ox or sheep or goat
is born, it shall remain with its mother for seven days.
From the eighth day it is acceptable as a sacrifice, a fire
28 offering to the LORD, but do not slaughter an ox or sheep
29 and its young on the same day. When you sacrifice a
thanksgiving offering for the LORD, sacrifice it so that it
30 will be acceptable on your behalf. It shall be eaten on the
same day – leave none of it to the morning; I am the LORD.
31 32 Keep My commands and fulfill them; I am the LORD. Do
not profane My holy name – that I may be sanctified in
the midst of the Israelites. I am the LORD, who makes you

God trusts us enough to make us His ambassadors to an often faithless, brutal world. The choice is ours. Will our lives be a *kiddush Hashem*, or God forbid, the opposite? To do something that makes someone grateful that there is a God in heaven who inspires people to do good on earth is perhaps the greatest achievement to which anyone can aspire.

22:32 בְּתוֹךְ בְּנֵי יִשְׂרָאֵל *In the midst of the Israelites* – In context, the phrase suggests that God will be sanctified through the service of an entire people living in, or journeying to, its land. We encounter here, once again, the inclusive nature of the covenant. The Oral Tradition, however, understood "in the midst of" to mean ten men, a minyan, any public gathering of Jews for prayer.

Rabbi Joseph B. Soloveitchik explains this quorum for public prayer using the concept of *sheliḥut*, agency. Just as an agent acts on behalf of and represents the person who has empowered him, so whenever ten Jews assemble for holy purposes they represent not merely a congregation of worshippers but the Jewish people in its totality. They become "the embodiment of the entire *knesset Yisrael*":

> *Knesset Yisrael* is not just a collectivity, a crowd, a herd, or a multitude. It is a separate entity, a living individuality. It embraces not only contemporary Jews but also the entire history of those people who have lived and died with *Shema Yisrael* on their lips. It includes the heroes and the cowards, the great and the small, the well-known historical figures as well as the anonymous people who are buried in unmarked graves. All are part of *knesset Yisrael*. All are personified by ten

כה לֹא תַקְרִיבוּ לַיהוָה וּבְאַרְצְכֶם לֹא תַעֲשׂוּ: וּמִיַּד בֶּן־נֵכָר
לֹא תַקְרִיבוּ אֶת־לֶחֶם אֱלֹהֵיכֶם מִכׇּל־אֵלֶּה כִּי מׇשְׁחָתָם
כו בָּהֶם מוּם בָּם לֹא יֵרָצוּ לָכֶם: וַיְדַבֵּר יְהוָה אֶל־
כז מֹשֶׁה לֵּאמֹר: שׁוֹר אוֹ־כֶשֶׂב אוֹ־עֵז כִּי יִוָּלֵד וְהָיָה שִׁבְעַת
יָמִים תַּחַת אִמּוֹ וּמִיּוֹם הַשְּׁמִינִי וָהָלְאָה יֵרָצֶה לְקׇרְבַּן אִשֶּׁה
כח לַיהוָה: וְשׁוֹר אוֹ־שֶׂה אֹתוֹ וְאֶת־בְּנוֹ לֹא תִשְׁחֲטוּ בְּיוֹם אֶחָד:
כט ל וְכִי־תִזְבְּחוּ זֶבַח־תּוֹדָה לַיהוָה לִרְצֹנְכֶם תִּזְבָּחוּ: בַּיּוֹם הַהוּא
לא יֵאָכֵל לֹא־תוֹתִירוּ מִמֶּנּוּ עַד־בֹּקֶר אֲנִי יְהוָה: וּשְׁמַרְתֶּם
לב מִצְוֺתַי וַעֲשִׂיתֶם אֹתָם אֲנִי יְהוָה: וְלֹא תְחַלְּלוּ אֶת־שֵׁם
קׇדְשִׁי וְנִקְדַּשְׁתִּי בְּתוֹךְ בְּנֵי יִשְׂרָאֵל אֲנִי יְהוָה מְקַדִּשְׁכֶם:

22:32 וְלֹא תְחַלְּלוּ אֶת־שֵׁם קׇדְשִׁי *Do not profane My holy name* – The two commands, the prohibition against desecrating God's name, *ḥillul Hashem*, and the positive corollary, *kiddush Hashem*, touch on the very nature of Jewish identity. But in what sense can we sanctify or desecrate God's name?

A name is how we are known to others. God's "name" is therefore His standing in the world. Do people acknowledge Him, respect Him, honor Him? The commands of *kiddush Hashem* and *ḥillul Hashem* locate that responsibility in the conduct and fate of the Jewish people. This is what Yeshayahu meant when he said: "'You are My witnesses,' so says the Lord…'that I am He'" (Is. 43:10). Therefore, when we behave in such a way as to evoke admiration for Judaism as a faith and a way of life, that is a *kiddush Hashem*, a sanctification of God's name. When we do the opposite – when we betray that faith and way of life, causing people to have contempt for the God of Israel, and to say: I cannot respect a religion, or a God, that inspires people to behave in such a way – that is a *ḥillul Hashem*, a desecration of God's name.

No nation has ever been given a greater or more fateful responsibility. And we each have a share in this task. As Rambam elaborates in one of the passages from his law code, the *Mishneh Torah*, speaking of *kiddush Hashem*:

> If a person is scrupulous in his conduct, gentle in his conversation, pleasant toward his fellow creatures, affable in manner when receiving, not retorting even when affronted, but showing courtesy to all, even to those who treat him with disdain, conducting his business affairs with integrity… and doing more than his duty in all things, while avoiding extremes and exaggerations – such a person has sanctified God. (*Hilkhot Yesodei HaTorah* 5:11)

33 holy, who brought you out of Egypt to be your God: I am
the LORD."
23 1 2 The LORD spoke to Moshe: "Speak to the Israelites. Say: REVI'I
These are the LORD's appointed times that you shall
proclaim as sacred assemblies; these are My appointed

---

passages, it includes Rosh HaShana and Yom Kippur. It also tells us about the specific mitzvot of the festivals, most notably Sukkot: it is the only place where the Torah mentions the *arbaa minim*, the four species, and the command to live in a sukka. More puzzling is the fact that the Torah here seems to be calling the Sabbath a *moed*, an appointed time, and a *mikra kodesh*, a sacred assembly, which it does nowhere else. Leviticus 23 is telling its own story – a deeply spiritual one. Recall our argument (made by Yehuda HaLevi and Ibn Ezra) that almost the entire forty chapters between Exodus 24 and Leviticus 25 are a digression (see Ex. 32, "The Golden Calf"). These chapters came about because Moshe argued that the people needed God to be close. They wanted to encounter Him not only at the top of the mountain but also in the midst of the camp – as a constant presence in their lives. That is why God gave the Israelites the Sanctuary (Ex. 25–40) and its service (the book of Leviticus as a whole).

Thus, the list of the festivals in Leviticus emphasizes the dimension of encounter, closeness, the meeting of the human and the Divine. This explains why we find in this chapter, more than in any other, two key expressions. One is *moed*; the other is *mikra kodesh*.

The word *moed* does not just mean "appointed time." We find the same word in the phrase *ohel moed*, meaning "tent of meeting." If the *ohel moed* is the place where man and God meet, then the *moadim* in our chapter are the times when we and God meet. This idea is given beautiful expression in the last line of the mystical song we sing on the Sabbath, *Yedid Nefesh*: "Hurry, beloved, for the appointed time (*moed*) has come." *Moed* here means a tryst – an appointment made between lovers to meet at a certain time and place.

As for the phrase *mikra kodesh*, it comes from the same root as the word that gives the entire book its name: *Vayikra*, meaning "to be summoned in love." A *mikra kodesh* is not just a holy day. It is a meeting to which we have been called in affection by One who holds us close.

Much of the book of Leviticus is about the holiness of place, the Sanctuary. Some of it is about the holiness of people, the priests, and Israel as a whole. In chapter 23, the Torah turns to the holiness of time and the times of holiness.

We are spiritual beings but we are also physical beings. We cannot be spiritual all the time. But one day in seven, we stop working and enter the presence of the God of creation. On certain days of the year, the festivals, we celebrate the

לג הַמּוֹצִיא אֶתְכֶם מֵאֶרֶץ מִצְרַיִם לִהְיוֹת לָכֶם לֵאלֹהִים אֲנִי
יהוה:

כג א ב וַיְדַבֵּר יהוה אֶל־מֹשֶׁה לֵּאמֹר: דַּבֵּר אֶל־בְּנֵי יִשְׂרָאֵל וְאָמַרְתָּ רביעי
אֲלֵהֶם מוֹעֲדֵי יהוה אֲשֶׁר־תִּקְרְאוּ אֹתָם מִקְרָאֵי קֹדֶשׁ אֵלֶּה

> ordinary Jews who gather together to pray as a *tzibbur* (congregation).... There is only one *knesset Yisrael* and it prays with every minyan of ten.

The synagogue, in this understanding, is the recreation of the Jewish people. Those who gather there are more than a congregation. In a halakhic and mystical sense they are the congregation, the reembodiment here and now of the Jewish people as it stood at Sinai and pledged itself to God. In the synagogue, Jews anticipate not only the rebuilding of Jerusalem but also the physical and spiritual reunification of the Jewish nation. This is a deep and metaphysical idea, but it has been Judaism's genius to translate such ideas into living institutions, never more so than in the case of the synagogue. *Knesset Yisrael*, God's covenantal partner, is the community of all Jews past, present, and future, united as they stand before God in their houses of study and prayer as they once before stood at the foot of Mount Sinai.

22:32 אֲנִי יהוה מְקַדִּשְׁכֶם *I am the Lord, who makes you holy.* It is precisely in our day-to-day relationships, at work or among friends, in our dealings with people and the integrity, sensitivity, and generosity we bring to bear on them, that we most add or subtract to the respect those around us have for the values by which we live. Here, the greatest of biblical commands – to sanctify and not desecrate God's name – have their arena, their impact and influence. "Sanctifying the name" is no mere marginal addendum to the script of Jewish life but its very point: to bring God's presence into the world by making others aware that God's word sanctifies life.

THE JEWISH CALENDAR

There are three lengthy accounts of the festivals in the Torah: one here, a second one in Numbers 28–29, and the third in Deuteronomy 16. What is striking is how different they are. The long section on the festivals in Numbers is wholly dedicated to the special additional sacrifices (the *musafim*) brought on holy days. One of Deuteronomy's most important themes is its insistence that worship be centralized "in the place that the Lord will choose" (for example, Deut. 12:14), which will turn out to be Jerusalem. That is why, when it comes to the festivals, Deuteronomy speaks only of Passover, Shavuot, and Sukkot, and not Rosh HaShana or Yom Kippur, because only on those three was there a duty of *aliya laregel*, pilgrimage to the Temple.

Our passage too is distinctive. Unlike the Exodus and Deuteronomy

3 times. Work shall be done through six days, but the
seventh day shall be a Sabbath of complete rest, a sacred
assembly. You shall perform no work at all; it shall be a
Sabbath for the LORD in all your dwellings.
4 These are the LORD's appointed times, sacred assemblies,
5 which you shall proclaim at their appointed times. In the
first month, the fourteenth of the month in the afternoon is

Torah contains three distinct accounts of the Sabbath. The account in the first version of the Ten Commandments, "For in six days the LORD made heaven and earth" (Ex. 20:11), is the Sabbath of creation. The account in the second version, "Remember that you were slaves in Egypt and the LORD, your God, brought you out" (Deut. 5:15), is the Sabbath of redemption. The account here in Emor is the Sabbath of revelation. In revelation, God calls to humankind. That is why the middle book of the Torah begins with the word *vayikra*, "and He called." It is also why the Sabbath is, uniquely here, included in the days "that you shall proclaim (*tikre'u*) as sacred assemblies (*mikra'ei kodesh*)" (Lev. 23:4), with the double emphasis on the verb *k-r-a*, "call," "proclaim," "convoke." The Sabbath is the day on which, in the stasis of rest and the silence of the soul, we are invited to hear the call of God.

23:5 פֶּסַח *Passover* – There is a profound difference between the mentalities of ancient Greece and Judaism. Greek thought is *logical* while Jewish thought is *chronological*. Logical systems are ideally timeless. Chronological systems are embedded in time. Logical systems are contemplated. Chronological systems are lived. Thus for Jews the creation of the universe is not a metaphysical truth to be accepted. It is an experience to be lived one day in seven. The exodus from Egypt, likewise, is not a historical truth to be recorded. It is a dramatic episode to be reenacted every year. The calendar – the musical score of the symphony of time – is how we take truths from the abstract heavens or the distant past and make them real in our shared lives.

In the Torah, the festival we call Pesaḥ is consistently described as *Ḥag HaMatzot*, the Festival of Unleavened Bread (*Ḥag HaPesaḥ*, in the Torah, is confined to the fourteenth of Nisan, the day prior to the Seder, when the Paschal sacrifice was brought). Rabbi Levi Yitzḥak of Berdichev gave a beautiful explanation for this dual terminology. The name Pesaḥ signifies the greatness of God, who "passed over" (*pasaḥ*) the houses of the Israelites. The name *Ḥag HaMatzot* suggests the greatness of the Israelites, who followed God into the desert without any provisions. In the Torah God calls the festival *Ḥag HaMatzot* in praise of Israel. The Jewish people, though, calls the festival Pesaḥ in praise of God.

ג הֵם מוֹעֲדָי: שֵׁשֶׁת יָמִים תֵּעָשֶׂה מְלָאכָה וּבַיּוֹם הַשְּׁבִיעִי
שַׁבַּת שַׁבָּתוֹן מִקְרָא־קֹדֶשׁ כָּל־מְלָאכָה לֹא תַעֲשׂוּ שַׁבָּת
הִוא לַיהוָה בְּכֹל מוֹשְׁבֹתֵיכֶם:
ד אֵלֶּה מוֹעֲדֵי יהוה מִקְרָאֵי קֹדֶשׁ אֲשֶׁר־תִּקְרְאוּ אֹתָם
ה בְּמוֹעֲדָם: בַּחֹדֶשׁ הָרִאשׁוֹן בְּאַרְבָּעָה עָשָׂר לַחֹדֶשׁ בֵּין

God of history. The holiness of the Sabbath is determined by God alone because He alone created the universe. The holiness of the festivals is partially determined by us, by the fixing of the calendar, because history is a partnership between us and God. But in two respects they are the same. They are both times of meeting (*moed*), and they are both times when we feel ourselves called, summoned, invited as God's guests (*mikra kodesh*).

23:3 שַׁבַּת שַׁבָּתוֹן *Sabbath of complete rest* – This is one of several accounts of the Sabbath in the Torah. What do we learn here that we do not learn elsewhere? Famously, two versions of the Ten Commandments, as they appear in Exodus and Deuteronomy, contain two different versions of the Sabbath command. The Exodus account begins with the word *zakhor*, "remember." The Deuteronomy account begins with *shamor*, "keep," "guard," "protect." But they differ more profoundly in their very understanding of the nature and significance of the day. In the Exodus text the Sabbath is a reminder of creation. However, in the Deuteronomy text the Torah speaks about a historical event: the exodus. Deuteronomy teaches us to keep the Sabbath because He took our ancestors out of Egypt, from slavery to freedom. Even greater emphasis is placed on the fact that, one day in seven, no one is a slave.

We integrate both accounts into the text of the *Kiddush* we make on Friday night. The Sabbath is "a remembrance of creation" (*zikaron lemaaseh bereshit*) as well as a "reminder of the exodus" (*zekher leyetziat Mitzrayim*). However, once we set the Leviticus account in the context of these other two, a richer pattern emerges.

If we play close attention, we can hear three primary voices in the Torah. There are three voices because axiomatic to Jewish faith is the belief that God is encountered in three ways: in creation, revelation, and redemption. Rabbi Shimon ben Tzemaḥ Duran (1366–1441) argued that all of Rambam's Thirteen Principles of Faith could be reduced to these three. They represent the three basic relationships within which Judaism and human life are set. Creation is God's relationship to the world. Revelation is God's relationship with us. When we apply revelation to creation, the result is redemption: the world in which God's will and ours coincide.

We can now understand why the

6 the time for the Passover sacrifice to the LORD. The fifteenth
day of this month is the LORD's Festival of Unleavened
Bread; for seven days you shall eat unleavened bread.
7 The first day shall be a sacred assembly for you; you shall
8 perform no laborious work. And you shall present a fire
offering for the LORD for seven days; on the seventh day
there shall be a sacred assembly; you shall perform no
laborious work."
9 10 The LORD spoke to Moshe: "Speak to the Israelites. Say:
When you come to the land that I am giving you and
reap its harvest, bring the first sheaf of your harvest to
11 the priest. He shall display the sheaf this way and that
before the LORD for your acceptance; on the day after
12 the day of rest the priest shall display it. On the day
you display the sheaf this way and that, you shall offer a
yearling sheep without blemish as a burnt offering to the
13 LORD. Its grain offering shall be two-tenths of an ephah
of fine flour mixed with oil, a fire offering for the LORD,
a pleasing aroma; and its libation shall be a quarter of a
14 hin of wine. Until that day, until you bring this sacrifice
to your God, you shall eat no bread or roasted grain or
ripe grain. This is an everlasting statute throughout your
15 generations, in all your dwellings. And from
the day you bring the sheaf of the wave offering, the day
after the day of rest, you shall count for yourselves seven

---

the festivals of the Tanakh – Passover, Shavuot, and Sukkot – we see that each has a dual logic. On the one hand, they belong to cyclical time. They celebrate seasons of the year – Passover is the festival of spring, Shavuot of first fruits, and Sukkot of the autumn harvest.

However, they also belong to covenantal, historical time. They commemorate historic events. Passover celebrates the exodus from Egypt, Shavuot the giving of the Torah, and Sukkot the forty years of wandering in the wilderness. Thus, the counting of the Omer also has two temporal dimensions.

On the one hand, it belongs to cyclical time. The forty-nine days represent the period of the grain harvest, the time during which farmers had most to thank God for – for "bringing forth bread from the ground." Each day brought forth its own blessing in the form of new grain, and therefore called for its own act of thanksgiving. This is time as

ו הָעַרְבָּיִם פֶּסַח לַיהוָה: וּבַחֲמִשָּׁה עָשָׂר יוֹם לַחֹדֶשׁ הַזֶּה חַג
ז הַמַּצּוֹת לַיהוָה שִׁבְעַת יָמִים מַצּוֹת תֹּאכֵלוּ: בַּיּוֹם הָרִאשׁוֹן
מִקְרָא־קֹדֶשׁ יִהְיֶה לָכֶם כָּל־מְלֶאכֶת עֲבֹדָה לֹא תַעֲשׂוּ:
ח וְהִקְרַבְתֶּם אִשֶּׁה לַיהוָה שִׁבְעַת יָמִים בַּיּוֹם הַשְּׁבִיעִי מִקְרָא־
קֹדֶשׁ כָּל־מְלֶאכֶת עֲבֹדָה לֹא תַעֲשׂוּ:
ט וַיְדַבֵּר יְהוָה אֶל־מֹשֶׁה לֵּאמֹר: דַּבֵּר אֶל־בְּנֵי יִשְׂרָאֵל וְאָמַרְתָּ
אֲלֵהֶם כִּי־תָבֹאוּ אֶל־הָאָרֶץ אֲשֶׁר אֲנִי נֹתֵן לָכֶם וּקְצַרְתֶּם
אֶת־קְצִירָהּ וַהֲבֵאתֶם אֶת־עֹמֶר רֵאשִׁית קְצִירְכֶם אֶל־
יא הַכֹּהֵן: וְהֵנִיף אֶת־הָעֹמֶר לִפְנֵי יְהוָה לִרְצֹנְכֶם מִמָּחֳרַת
יב הַשַּׁבָּת יְנִיפֶנּוּ הַכֹּהֵן: וַעֲשִׂיתֶם בְּיוֹם הֲנִיפְכֶם אֶת־הָעֹמֶר
יג כֶּבֶשׂ תָּמִים בֶּן־שְׁנָתוֹ לְעֹלָה לַיהוָה: וּמִנְחָתוֹ שְׁנֵי עֶשְׂרֹנִים
סֹלֶת בְּלוּלָה בַשֶּׁמֶן אִשֶּׁה לַיהוָה רֵיחַ נִיחֹחַ וְנִסְכֹּה יַיִן
יד רְבִיעִת הַהִין: וְלֶחֶם וְקָלִי וְכַרְמֶל לֹא תֹאכְלוּ עַד־עֶצֶם
הַיּוֹם הַזֶּה עַד הֲבִיאֲכֶם אֶת־קָרְבַּן אֱלֹהֵיכֶם חֻקַּת עוֹלָם
טו לְדֹרֹתֵיכֶם בְּכֹל מֹשְׁבֹתֵיכֶם: וּסְפַרְתֶּם לָכֶם יט
מִמָּחֳרַת הַשַּׁבָּת מִיּוֹם הֲבִיאֲכֶם אֶת־עֹמֶר הַתְּנוּפָה שֶׁבַע

COUNTING THE OMER

This passage was the focus of a halachic disagreement during the period of the *geonim* (eighth to eleventh centuries). What is the law for someone who forgets to count one of the forty-nine days? May he continue to count the rest, or has he forfeited the entire command for that year? There were two views. According to Halakhot Gedolot (a work attributed to Rabbi Shimon Kayyara), the person has indeed forfeited the chance to fulfill the command. According to R. Ḥai Gaon he has not. He continues to count the remaining days, unaffected by his failure to count one of the forty-nine.

How are we to understand this argument? According to Halakhot Gedolot, the key phrase is "seven *complete* (*temimot*) weeks." One who forgets a day cannot satisfy the requirement of completeness. In this view, the forty-nine days constitute a single religious act, and if one of the parts is missing, the whole is defective. According to R. Ḥai Gaon, however, each day of the forty-nine is a separate command – "To the day after the seventh week, you shall count fifty days." If one fails to keep one of the commands, that is no impediment to keeping the others.

What is at stake here? If we look at

16 complete weeks. To the day after the seventh week, you
shall count fifty days; and then you shall present a new
17 grain offering to the LORD. You shall bring two loaves of
bread from your dwellings made with two-tenths of an
ephah of fine flour baked with leaven, as a wave offering:
18 first produce to the LORD. Together with the bread, you
shall present seven unblemished yearling male lambs, one
young bull, and two rams – these shall be a burnt offering
for the LORD with their grain offering and their libations,
19 a fire offering, a pleasing aroma to the LORD. And you
shall offer one he-goat as a purification offering and two
20 yearling male sheep as peace sacrifices. The priest shall
display them this way and that with the bread of the first
produce as a wave offering before the LORD together with
the two sheep; they shall be holy to the LORD and belong
21 to the priest. On that day you shall make a proclamation;
it shall be a sacred assembly for you; you shall perform no
laborious work. This is an everlasting statute throughout
22 your generations in all your dwellings. And when you
reap the harvest of your land, do not reap to the edge of
your field or gather the gleanings of your harvest. Leave
them for the poor and for the migrant; I am the LORD
your God."
23 24 Then the LORD spoke to Moshe: "Tell the Israelites: On ḤAMISHI
the first day of the seventh month, you shall observe
a day of rest, a commemoration with the sounding of
25 the ram's horn, a sacred assembly. You shall perform no
laborious work, and you shall bring close a fire offering
26 to the LORD." The LORD spoke to Moshe:

---

between these two opinions. Out of respect for R. Ḥai, we continue to count after missing a day, but out of respect for Halakhot Gedolot, we do so without a blessing.

Cyclical time is deeply conservative; covenantal time is revolutionary. It was the greatness of the biblical prophets to hear the music of covenant beneath the noise of events, giving history its shape and meaning as the long, slow journey to redemption. Both, however, find their expression in the counting of the Omer.

טז שַׁבָּתוֹת תְּמִימֹת תִּהְיֶינָה: עַד מִמָּחֳרַת הַשַּׁבָּת הַשְּׁבִיעִת
תִּסְפְּרוּ חֲמִשִּׁים יוֹם וְהִקְרַבְתֶּם מִנְחָה חֲדָשָׁה לַיהוָה:
יז מִמּוֹשְׁבֹתֵיכֶם תָּבִיאוּ | לֶחֶם תְּנוּפָה שְׁתַּיִם שְׁנֵי עֶשְׂרֹנִים
יח סֹלֶת תִּהְיֶינָה חָמֵץ תֵּאָפֶינָה בִּכּוּרִים לַיהוָה: וְהִקְרַבְתֶּם
עַל־הַלֶּחֶם שִׁבְעַת כְּבָשִׂים תְּמִימִם בְּנֵי שָׁנָה וּפַר בֶּן־בָּקָר
אֶחָד וְאֵילִם שְׁנָיִם יִהְיוּ עֹלָה לַיהוָה וּמִנְחָתָם וְנִסְכֵּיהֶם אִשֵּׁה
יט רֵיחַ־נִיחֹחַ לַיהוָה: וַעֲשִׂיתֶם שְׂעִיר־עִזִּים אֶחָד לְחַטָּאת
כ וּשְׁנֵי כְבָשִׂים בְּנֵי שָׁנָה לְזֶבַח שְׁלָמִים: וְהֵנִיף הַכֹּהֵן | אֹתָם
עַל לֶחֶם הַבִּכֻּרִים תְּנוּפָה לִפְנֵי יהוה עַל־שְׁנֵי כְּבָשִׂים קֹדֶשׁ
כא יִהְיוּ לַיהוָה לַכֹּהֵן: וּקְרָאתֶם בְּעֶצֶם | הַיּוֹם הַזֶּה מִקְרָא־
קֹדֶשׁ יִהְיֶה לָכֶם כָּל־מְלֶאכֶת עֲבֹדָה לֹא תַעֲשׂוּ חֻקַּת עוֹלָם
כב בְּכָל־מוֹשְׁבֹתֵיכֶם לְדֹרֹתֵיכֶם: וּבְקֻצְרְכֶם אֶת־קְצִיר אַרְצְכֶם
לֹא־תְכַלֶּה פְּאַת שָׂדְךָ בְּקֻצְרֶךָ וְלֶקֶט קְצִירְךָ לֹא תְלַקֵּט
לֶעָנִי וְלַגֵּר תַּעֲזֹב אֹתָם אֲנִי יהוה אֱלֹהֵיכֶם:
כג כד וַיְדַבֵּר יהוה אֶל־מֹשֶׁה לֵּאמֹר: דַּבֵּר אֶל־בְּנֵי יִשְׂרָאֵל חמישי
לֵאמֹר בַּחֹדֶשׁ הַשְּׁבִיעִי בְּאֶחָד לַחֹדֶשׁ יִהְיֶה לָכֶם שַׁבָּתוֹן
כה זִכְרוֹן תְּרוּעָה מִקְרָא־קֹדֶשׁ: כָּל־מְלֶאכֶת עֲבֹדָה לֹא תַעֲשׂוּ
כו וְהִקְרַבְתֶּם אִשֶּׁה לַיהוָה: וַיְדַבֵּר יהוה אֶל־מֹשֶׁה

R. Ḥai Gaon understood it. "Count fifty days" – each of which is a command in itself, unaffected by the days that came before or after.

But the Omer is also part of historical time. It represents the journey from Egypt to Sinai, from exodus to revelation. This is, in the biblical worldview, a crucial transition. In the exodus the people gained negative liberty: they ceased to be slaves. At Mount Sinai they gained a covenant: the rule of law, a constitution of liberty that made them free.

In this sense, the forty-nine days represent an unbroken historical sequence. There is no way of going directly from escape-from-tyranny to a free society – as we have discovered time and again. Here, time is an ordered sequence of events, a journey, a narrative. Miss one stage, and one may lose everything. This is time as Halakhot Gedolot understood it: "Count … seven complete weeks," with the emphasis on "full, complete, unbroken."

Halakha as we practice it mediates

27 "Hear: the tenth day of this seventh month is the Day of
Atonement. It shall be a sacred assembly for you, and
you shall afflict yourselves and bring a fire offering to
28 the Lord. You shall perform no work at all during this
entire day, for it is the Day of Atonement, there to make
29 atonement for you before the Lord your God. Anyone
who does not afflict himself for this whole day shall be
30 severed from his people, and if anyone performs any
work during this whole day, I will annihilate that person
31 from among his people. No work at all may you perform;
this is an everlasting statute throughout your generations
32 in all your dwellings. It is a Sabbath of complete rest for
you, and you shall afflict yourselves from the evening of
the ninth day of the month: from evening to evening shall
you observe your Sabbath."
33 34 The Lord spoke to Moshe: "Tell the Israelites: From the SHISHI
fifteenth day of this seventh month, for seven days shall be
35 the Festival of Tabernacles to the Lord. The first day shall
be a sacred assembly; on it, you shall perform no laborious
36 work. For seven days you must bring close a fire offering

Israel, reminders of the fertility of the land. Symbolizing nature and the cycle of the seasons – things common to all humanity – the four species represent the universality of the festival. By contrast, the command to live for seven days in huts (v. 42) represents the singular character of Jewish history, with its repeated experiences of exile and homecoming and its long journey across the wilderness of time.

Sukkot celebrates the dual nature of Jewish faith: the *universality of God* and the *particularity of Jewish existence*. We all need rain. We are all part of nature. We are all dependent on the complex ecology of the created world. Hence the four species. But each nation, civilization, religion is different. Whatever God's relationship to other nations (and He *has* a relationship with other nations – so Amos and Yeshayahu insist), Jews know Him through His saving acts in Israel's history. And as Jews, we are heirs to a history unlike that of any other people: small, vulnerable, suffering exile after exile, yet surviving. Hence the sukka.

Humanity is formed out of our commonalities and differences. Our differences give us our identity. Our commonalities give us our humanity. Sukkot brings both together: our uniqueness as a people and our participation in the universal fate of humankind.

כז לֵאמֹֽר׃ אַ֡ךְ בֶּעָשׂ֣וֹר לַחֹדֶשׁ֩ הַשְּׁבִיעִ֨י הַזֶּ֜ה י֣וֹם הַכִּפֻּרִ֥ים ה֛וּא
מִקְרָא־קֹ֙דֶשׁ֙ יִהְיֶ֣ה לָכֶ֔ם וְעִנִּיתֶ֖ם אֶת־נַפְשֹׁתֵיכֶ֑ם וְהִקְרַבְתֶּ֥ם
כח אִשֶּׁ֖ה לַֽיהוָֽה׃ וְכָל־מְלָאכָה֙ לֹ֣א תַעֲשׂ֔וּ בְּעֶ֖צֶם הַיּ֣וֹם הַזֶּ֑ה כִּ֣י
כט י֤וֹם כִּפֻּרִים֙ ה֔וּא לְכַפֵּ֣ר עֲלֵיכֶ֔ם לִפְנֵ֖י יהוה אֱלֹהֵיכֶֽם׃ כִּ֤י כָל־
הַנֶּ֙פֶשׁ֙ אֲשֶׁ֣ר לֹֽא־תְעֻנֶּ֔ה בְּעֶ֖צֶם הַיּ֣וֹם הַזֶּ֑ה וְנִכְרְתָ֖ה מֵֽעַמֶּֽיהָ׃
ל וְכָל־הַנֶּ֗פֶשׁ אֲשֶׁ֤ר תַּעֲשֶׂה֙ כָּל־מְלָאכָ֔ה בְּעֶ֖צֶם הַיּ֣וֹם הַזֶּ֑ה
לא וְהַֽאֲבַדְתִּ֛י אֶת־הַנֶּ֥פֶשׁ הַהִ֖וא מִקֶּ֥רֶב עַמָּֽהּ׃ כָּל־מְלָאכָ֖ה לֹ֣א
לב תַעֲשׂ֑וּ חֻקַּ֤ת עוֹלָם֙ לְדֹרֹ֣תֵיכֶ֔ם בְּכֹ֖ל מֹשְׁבֹתֵיכֶֽם׃ שַׁבַּ֨ת שַׁבָּת֥וֹן
ה֙וּא֙ לָכֶ֔ם וְעִנִּיתֶ֖ם אֶת־נַפְשֹׁתֵיכֶ֑ם בְּתִשְׁעָ֤ה לַחֹ֙דֶשׁ֙ בָּעֶ֔רֶב
מֵעֶ֣רֶב עַד־עֶ֔רֶב תִּשְׁבְּת֖וּ שַׁבַּתְּכֶֽם׃
לג לד וַיְדַבֵּ֥ר יהוה אֶל־מֹשֶׁ֥ה לֵּאמֹֽר׃ דַּבֵּ֛ר אֶל־בְּנֵ֥י יִשְׂרָאֵ֖ל לֵאמֹ֑ר ששי
בַּחֲמִשָּׁה֩ עָשָׂ֨ר י֜וֹם לַחֹ֣דֶשׁ הַשְּׁבִיעִ֗י הַזֶּ֔ה חַ֧ג הַסֻּכּ֛וֹת שִׁבְעַ֥ת
לה יָמִ֖ים לַֽיהוָֽה׃ בַּיּ֥וֹם הָרִאשׁ֖וֹן מִקְרָא־קֹ֑דֶשׁ כָּל־מְלֶ֥אכֶת עֲבֹדָ֖ה
לו לֹ֥א תַעֲשֽׂוּ׃ שִׁבְעַ֣ת יָמִ֔ים תַּקְרִ֥יבוּ אִשֶּׁ֖ה לַֽיהוָ֑ה בַּיּ֣וֹם הַשְּׁמִינִ֡י

23:34 חַג הַסֻּכּוֹת *Festival of Tabernacles* – Although all the festivals are listed together, they in fact represent two different cycles. The first is the cycle of Passover, Shavuot, and Sukkot. These tell the particularistic story of Jewish identity and history: the exodus (Passover), the revelation at Mount Sinai (Shavuot), and the journey through the wilderness (Sukkot). Celebrating them, we reenact the key moments of Jewish memory. We celebrate what it is to be a Jew.

There is, however, a second cycle: the festivals of the seventh month: Rosh HaShana, Yom Kippur, and Sukkot. Rosh HaShana and Yom Kippur are not only about Jews and Judaism. They are about God and humanity as a whole. The language of the prayers is different. We say: "Instill Your awe upon *all* Your works, and fear of You on *all* that You have created." The liturgy is strikingly universalistic. The Days of Awe are about the sovereignty of God over all humankind. On them, we reflect on the *human*, not just the Jewish, condition. On the festival of Sukkot the whole world is judged in the matter of rain (Mishna Rosh HaShana 1:2).

The two cycles to which Sukkot belongs are reflected in the day's mitzvot. The four species and the rituals associated with them (v. 40) are about rain. They were, says Rambam (*Guide for the Perplexed* III:43), the most readily available products of the land of

to the LORD. The eighth day shall be a sacred assembly
for you, and you shall present a fire offering to the LORD.
It is an assembly; you shall perform no laborious work.
37 These are the LORD's festivals, which you shall proclaim,
sacred assemblies to present a fire offering to the LORD:
burnt offering, grain offering, sacrifice, and libations, each
38 on its appointed day; in addition to the LORD's Sabbaths,
and in addition to your gifts and all your offerings in the
fulfillment of vows and all the freewill offerings that you
39 give to the LORD. Hear: on the fifteenth day of the seventh
month, when you have harvested the land's produce, you
shall celebrate a festival to the LORD for seven days. The
first day shall be a day of rest; the eighth day shall be a day
40 of rest. On the first day you shall take for yourselves fruit
of the majestic tree, branches of palm trees, boughs of the
leafy tree, and willows of the brook, and rejoice before the
41 LORD your God for seven days. You shall celebrate it as a
festival to the LORD for seven days in the year. It shall be an
everlasting statute throughout your generations; celebrate
42 this in the seventh month. For seven days you shall live in
43 huts. All those native born in Israel must live in huts, so that
future generations may know that I had the Israelites live in
huts when I brought them out of the land of Egypt; I am

faith. According to R. Akiva, while Passover and Shavuot represent God's love for the Jewish people, Sukkot represents the Jewish people's love for God. We find this idea in the words of Yirmeyahu that we say on Rosh HaShana. In the Torah, the story of the years in the wilderness is told in terms of the people's rebelliousness and obstinacy. Yirmeyahu, however, describes it quite differently: "I recall on your behalf the devotion of your youth, your bridal love – when you followed Me into the wilderness, a land unseeded" (Jer. 2:2).

It is easy to worship God when you have safety and security. But Israel came of age as a nation long before it knew such things. It was born in the desert, vulnerable, exposed, yet willing to follow the call of God. That was the miracle – faith in the midst of uncertainty. What R. Akiva was saying was: look at the sukka and you will see where our people was born. The sukka was the matrix of Jewish courage, the birthplace of a people obstinate in their loyalty to God.

מִקְרָא־קֹדֶשׁ יִהְיֶה לָכֶם וְהִקְרַבְתֶּם אִשֶּׁה לַיהוָה עֲצֶרֶת הִוא
לז כָּל־מְלֶאכֶת עֲבֹדָה לֹא תַעֲשׂוּ׃ אֵלֶּה מוֹעֲדֵי יְהוָה אֲשֶׁר־
תִּקְרְאוּ אֹתָם מִקְרָאֵי קֹדֶשׁ לְהַקְרִיב אִשֶּׁה לַיהוָה עֹלָה
לח וּמִנְחָה זֶבַח וּנְסָכִים דְּבַר־יוֹם בְּיוֹמוֹ׃ מִלְּבַד שַׁבְּתֹת יְהוָה
וּמִלְּבַד מַתְּנוֹתֵיכֶם וּמִלְּבַד כָּל־נִדְרֵיכֶם וּמִלְּבַד כָּל־נִדְבֹתֵיכֶם
לט אֲשֶׁר תִּתְּנוּ לַיהוָה׃ אַךְ בַּחֲמִשָּׁה עָשָׂר יוֹם לַחֹדֶשׁ הַשְּׁבִיעִי
בְּאָסְפְּכֶם אֶת־תְּבוּאַת הָאָרֶץ תָּחֹגּוּ אֶת־חַג־יְהוָה שִׁבְעַת
מ יָמִים בַּיּוֹם הָרִאשׁוֹן שַׁבָּתוֹן וּבַיּוֹם הַשְּׁמִינִי שַׁבָּתוֹן׃ וּלְקַחְתֶּם
לָכֶם בַּיּוֹם הָרִאשׁוֹן פְּרִי עֵץ הָדָר כַּפֹּת תְּמָרִים וַעֲנַף עֵץ־
עָבֹת וְעַרְבֵי־נָחַל וּשְׂמַחְתֶּם לִפְנֵי יְהוָה אֱלֹהֵיכֶם שִׁבְעַת
מא יָמִים׃ וְחַגֹּתֶם אֹתוֹ חַג לַיהוָה שִׁבְעַת יָמִים בַּשָּׁנָה חֻקַּת
מב עוֹלָם לְדֹרֹתֵיכֶם בַּחֹדֶשׁ הַשְּׁבִיעִי תָּחֹגּוּ אֹתוֹ׃ בַּסֻּכֹּת תֵּשְׁבוּ
מג שִׁבְעַת יָמִים כָּל־הָאֶזְרָח בְּיִשְׂרָאֵל יֵשְׁבוּ בַּסֻּכֹּת׃ לְמַעַן יֵדְעוּ
דֹרֹתֵיכֶם כִּי בַסֻּכּוֹת הוֹשַׁבְתִּי אֶת־בְּנֵי יִשְׂרָאֵל בְּהוֹצִיאִי

23:43 בְּהוֹצִיאִי אוֹתָם מֵאֶרֶץ מִצְרָיִם *I brought them out of the land of Egypt* – We observe Sukkot, says the Torah, "so that your descendants will know that I made the Israelites live in booths when I brought them out of Egypt." What, though, is special or miraculous about this fact? On this, the Talmud records two views (Sukka 11b). According to R. Eliezer, *sukkot* represent the clouds of glory that accompanied the Israelites on their journey. According to R. Akiva, however, *sukkot* represent exactly what they are: temporary dwellings, shacks with a canopy of leaves for a roof.

Regarding R. Eliezer's view, the miracle is self-evident. For forty years, God's sheltering presence protected the Israelites from heat by day, cold by night, and the wild animals and enemies they encountered on the way.

Regarding R. Akiva's view, though, the sukka seems to represent no miracle whatsoever. That the Israelites lived in temporary dwellings for forty years was only to be expected. That is how nomads live.

Perhaps, however, R. Eliezer and R. Akiva differed less on whether there was a miracle than on to whom it belonged. According to R. Eliezer, the miracle was God's. It was He who protected the people on their long walk to freedom. According to R. Akiva, the miracle was that of the Jewish people. Though the journey to the Promised Land took forty years, and the Israelites faced setbacks, they did not give up or lose

44 the LORD your God." Thus Moshe announced the LORD's
appointed times to the Israelites.
24 1 2 The LORD spoke to Moshe: "Command the Israelites to SHEVI'I
bring you pure oil from crushed olives for the light, to
3 kindle the lamp, every night. From evening to morning,
before the LORD, Aharon shall set it up outside the
curtain of the testimony in the Tent of Meeting to burn
each night. This shall be a rule for all time, throughout
4 your generations. Aharon shall set out the lamps on the
pure candelabrum each day before the LORD.
5 And you shall take fine flour and bake twelve loaves, two-
6 tenths of an ephah for each loaf. You shall place them
in two columns, six to each column, on the pure table
7 before the LORD. Lay pure incense on each stack, as a
remembrance for the bread, as a fire offering to the LORD.
8 Every Sabbath he shall set it out, always, before the LORD
9 on behalf of the Israelites: an everlasting covenant. It shall
belong to Aharon and his sons. They shall eat it in a holy
place because it is holy of holies among the LORD's fire
10 offerings, their perpetual share." A man went
out among the Israelites, the son of an Israelite woman
and an Egyptian man. And a fight broke out in the camp
between this son of an Israelite woman, and an Israelite

We need a regular reminder of the brevity of life itself, and hence the need to use time wisely. That is what we do on Rosh HaShana as we stand before God in judgment and pray to be written in the book of life.

We need a time when we confront our faults, apologize for the wrong we have done, make amends, resolve to change, and ask for forgiveness. That is the work of Yom Kippur.

We need to remind ourselves that we are on a journey, that we are "migrants and visitors" (Lev. 25:24) on earth, and that where we live is only a temporary dwelling. That is what we experience on Sukkot.

And we need, from time to time, to step back from the ceaseless pressures of work and find the rest in which we can celebrate our blessings, renew our relationships, and recover the full vigor of body and mind. That is the Sabbath.

Doubtless, most people know that these things are important. But knowing is not enough. These are elements of life that become real not just when we know them, but when we live them.

מד אֹתָם מֵאֶרֶץ מִצְרָיִם אֲנִי יְהוָה אֱלֹהֵיכֶם: וַיְדַבֵּר מֹשֶׁה אֶת־
מֹעֲדֵי יְהוָה אֶל־בְּנֵי יִשְׂרָאֵל:

כד א ב וַיְדַבֵּר יְהוָה אֶל־מֹשֶׁה לֵּאמֹר: צַו אֶת־בְּנֵי יִשְׂרָאֵל וְיִקְחוּ שביעי
אֵלֶיךָ שֶׁמֶן זַיִת זָךְ כָּתִית לַמָּאוֹר לְהַעֲלֹת נֵר תָּמִיד:
ג מִחוּץ לְפָרֹכֶת הָעֵדֻת בְּאֹהֶל מוֹעֵד יַעֲרֹךְ אֹתוֹ אַהֲרֹן
מֵעֶרֶב עַד־בֹּקֶר לִפְנֵי יְהוָה תָּמִיד חֻקַּת עוֹלָם לְדֹרֹתֵיכֶם:
ד עַל הַמְּנֹרָה הַטְּהֹרָה יַעֲרֹךְ אֶת־הַנֵּרוֹת לִפְנֵי יְהוָה
תָּמִיד:
ה וְלָקַחְתָּ סֹלֶת וְאָפִיתָ אֹתָהּ שְׁתֵּים עֶשְׂרֵה חַלּוֹת שְׁנֵי עֶשְׂרֹנִים
ו יִהְיֶה הַחַלָּה הָאֶחָת: וְשַׂמְתָּ אוֹתָם שְׁתַּיִם מַעֲרָכוֹת שֵׁשׁ
ז הַמַּעֲרָכֶת עַל הַשֻּׁלְחָן הַטָּהֹר לִפְנֵי יְהוָה: וְנָתַתָּ עַל־
הַמַּעֲרֶכֶת לְבֹנָה זַכָּה וְהָיְתָה לַלֶּחֶם לְאַזְכָּרָה אִשֶּׁה לַיהוָה:
ח בְּיוֹם הַשַּׁבָּת בְּיוֹם הַשַּׁבָּת יַעַרְכֶנּוּ לִפְנֵי יְהוָה תָּמִיד מֵאֵת
ט בְּנֵי־יִשְׂרָאֵל בְּרִית עוֹלָם: וְהָיְתָה לְאַהֲרֹן וּלְבָנָיו וַאֲכָלֻהוּ
בְּמָקוֹם קָדֹשׁ כִּי קֹדֶשׁ קָדָשִׁים הוּא לוֹ מֵאִשֵּׁי יְהוָה חָק־
י עוֹלָם: וַיֵּצֵא בֶּן־אִשָּׁה יִשְׂרְאֵלִית וְהוּא בֶּן־אִישׁ
מִצְרִי בְּתוֹךְ בְּנֵי יִשְׂרָאֵל וַיִּנָּצוּ בַּמַּחֲנֶה בֶּן הַיִּשְׂרְאֵלִית

23:44 מֹעֲדֵי יהוה אֶל־בְּנֵי יִשְׂרָאֵל *The LORD's appointed times to the Israelites* – Chapter 23 of Parashat Emor sets out a weekly, monthly, and yearly schedule of sacred times. This is continued and extended in Parashat Behar to seven- and fifty-year schedules. The Torah forces us to remember what contemporary culture regularly forgets: our lives must have dedicated times when we focus on the things that give life meaning. And because we are social animals, the most important times are the ones we share. The Jewish calendar is precisely that: a structure of shared time.

We all need an identity, and every identity comes with a story. So we need a time when we remind ourselves of the story of where we came from and why we are who we are. That happens on Passover, when we reenact the founding moment of our people as they began their long walk to freedom.

We need a moral code, an internalized satellite navigation system to guide us through the wilderness of time. That is what we celebrate on Shavuot when we relive the moment when our ancestors stood at Sinai, made their covenant with God, and heard Heaven declare the Ten Commandments.

11 man. The Israelite woman's son blasphemed the Name
and cursed – his mother's name was Shlomit, daughter of
Divri, of the tribe of Dan – and they brought him before
12 Moshe. They placed the man in custody until the LORD's
verdict would be pronounced to them.
13 14 And the LORD spoke to Moshe: "Take the one who
cursed outside the camp. All the people who heard him
shall lay their hands on his head – and then the whole
15 community shall stone him. Tell the Israelites: Anyone
16 who curses his God shall bear the sin, and anyone who
blasphemes the LORD's name shall be put to death: the
whole community shall stone him. Migrant and native
born alike: one who blasphemes the LORD's name shall

---

humans creating order, symbolized in the holy place they have made for God. We can summarize *Torat Kohanim* in a single sentence: *sacred order leads to social order*. The two are inextricably intertwined. When people lose their fear of God, eventually they lose their other inhibitions. They become creatures of impulse and desire, and the end of this long road is violence. It is an unpopular truth. The serpent is always waiting in the wings, saying to us as he said to Ḥava: "What harm is there in eating one forbidden fruit?" A world God created and pronounced good can all too easily be destroyed if we forget the concept of boundaries and the habits of self-restraint.

The fundamental issue addressed by the Torah is violence and the misuse of power. There is more than one way of thinking about violence. There is the way of wisdom: Judaism's insights into philosophy and the social sciences. There is the way of prophecy, focusing on emotion and the moral sense. And there is the way of priesthood, whose central insight is the connection between sacred order and social order. When human beings lose respect for God, they eventually lose respect for humanity.

The message of Leviticus throughout is that life itself is holy: people, not just priests; the whole of life, not just edited parts of it. So we have to be holy in the way we eat, the way we conduct our most intimate sexual relationships, and the way we use language. We must not curse even the deaf, let alone our parents, let alone God, because verbal abuse leads to physical abuse. Blasphemy injures society by desecrating the sacred. That is why, uniquely in this case, the witnesses are to lay their hands on the sinner, to indicate that this affects everyone. It is a sobering narrative, the negative side of the broader picture of the book: the priestly sanctification of life.

יא וְאִישׁ הַיִּשְׂרְאֵלִי: וַיִּקֹּב בֶּן־הָאִשָּׁה הַיִּשְׂרְאֵלִית אֶת־הַשֵּׁם
וַיְקַלֵּל וַיָּבִיאוּ אֹתוֹ אֶל־מֹשֶׁה וְשֵׁם אִמּוֹ שְׁלֹמִית בַּת־
יב דִּבְרִי לְמַטֵּה־דָן: וַיַּנִּיחֻהוּ בַּמִּשְׁמָר לִפְרֹשׁ לָהֶם עַל־פִּי
יְהוָה:
יג יד וַיְדַבֵּר יְהוָה אֶל־מֹשֶׁה לֵּאמֹר: הוֹצֵא אֶת־הַמְקַלֵּל אֶל־
מִחוּץ לַמַּחֲנֶה וְסָמְכוּ כָל־הַשֹּׁמְעִים אֶת־יְדֵיהֶם עַל־רֹאשׁוֹ
טו וְרָגְמוּ אֹתוֹ כָּל־הָעֵדָה: וְאֶל־בְּנֵי יִשְׂרָאֵל תְּדַבֵּר לֵאמֹר
טז אִישׁ אִישׁ כִּי־יְקַלֵּל אֱלֹהָיו וְנָשָׂא חֶטְאוֹ: וְנֹקֵב שֵׁם־יְהוָה
מוֹת יוּמָת רָגוֹם יִרְגְּמוּ־בוֹ כָּל־הָעֵדָה כַּגֵּר כָּאֶזְרָח בְּנָקְבוֹ־

THE EXECUTION OF THE BLASPHEMER

Leviticus, a book of law rather than narrative, is suddenly interrupted by a tragic and disturbing story: Two men start fighting. The details of their quarrel appear to be irrelevant. One of the men, however, in the course of the struggle, curses God, or possibly, uses the sacred Name to curse his opponent. Everyone present knows that something serious has happened. Taking God's name in vain is forbidden (Ex. 20:6). Just a few chapters earlier, we read that cursing your parents is a capital sin (Ex. 21:17; Lev. 20:9). Cursing God must surely be more serious still.

What the people are unsure of is whether the law applies to someone of mixed parentage. Hence God's answer: "Migrant and native born alike" (Lev. 24:16). In the course of the revelation, the people learn something else: "All the people who heard him shall lay their hands on his head" (24:14) prior to carrying out the punishment. In no other case of the death sentence, Rambam notes, do the witnesses lay their hands on the condemned man.

This stark episode represents the end of the long sequence of laws which began forty chapters earlier (in Ex. 25:1 – see Lev. 23, "The Jewish Calendar" and Ex. 32, "The Golden Calf"), about the Sanctuary and the code of holiness. Why end this literary unit, which stands at the very center of the Torah, with so negative a note?

The end of the book of Exodus gives us a clue. As we have noted (Ex. 40, "Exodus: The Narrative Structure"), Exodus ends the way Genesis begins: with an act of creation. In Genesis it was God's creation of the universe. In Exodus it was the Israelites' creation of the Sanctuary. The connection is deliberate. In the beginning, God created order. Then He gave humans free will and they proceeded to create chaos. Only with the completion of the Sanctuary do we find

17 be put to death. One who takes the life of any human
18 being shall be put to death. One who takes the life of an
19 animal shall make restitution for it: life for life. One who
injures his fellow man shall be penalized in proportion
20 to the injury inflicted: the cost of a broken bone for a
broken bone, of an eye for an eye, of a tooth for a tooth.
Just as he inflicted injury on another human being, so
21 shall he suffer the loss. One who kills an animal shall MAFTIR
make restitution for it; but one who kills a human being
22 shall be put to death. There shall be one law for you, for
migrant and for native born alike, for I am the LORD your
23 God." Moshe told this to the Israelites, and so they took
the blasphemer outside the camp and stoned him. Thus
the Israelites did as the LORD had commanded Moshe.

The haftara for Parashat Emor is on page 1540.

was consecrated. The story itself seems out of place.

Something is being conveyed here beyond the detailed points of law. The implication seems to be that what begins as an offense in one area, a crossing of boundaries, never ends there. An offense against God eventually leads to assaults against humans. Spiritual sins lead to physical crimes. Leviticus has been about the sanctity of time, person, and place. The Torah now turns to sanctity of speech. The priests have already been warned: "Do not profane My holy name, that I may be sanctified in the midst of the Israelites. I am the LORD who makes you holy" (Lev. 22:32). The story of the blasphemer tells us that the same applies to ordinary Israelites, "migrant and native born alike."

Judaism has been skeptical of the value of capital punishment certainly since the days of the Mishna, eighteen centuries ago, and has rarely practiced it since. But the drama of this incident, paired with the earlier drama of Nadav and Avihu, underscores the point. Once boundaries are disrespected, a process has begun that leads, not immediately but ultimately, to civilizational breakdown.

Sacred and secular, spiritual and physical, offenses against God and crimes against human beings are indissolubly connected. Sacred order and social order go together. Lose one – either one – and you will eventually lose the other. A sense of the sacred is what lifts us above instinct and protects us from our dysfunctional drives. That is the message with which the book of Leviticus draws toward its close.

שֵׁם יוּמָת: וְאִישׁ כִּי יַכֶּה כָּל־נֶפֶשׁ אָדָם מוֹת יוּמָת: וּמַכֵּה יז יח
נֶפֶשׁ־בְּהֵמָה יְשַׁלְּמֶנָּה נֶפֶשׁ תַּחַת נָפֶשׁ: וְאִישׁ כִּי־יִתֵּן מוּם יט
בַּעֲמִיתוֹ כַּאֲשֶׁר עָשָׂה כֵּן יֵעָשֶׂה לּוֹ: שֶׁבֶר תַּחַת שֶׁבֶר עַיִן כ
תַּחַת עַיִן שֵׁן תַּחַת שֵׁן כַּאֲשֶׁר יִתֵּן מוּם בָּאָדָם כֵּן יִנָּתֶן בּוֹ:
מפטיר וּמַכֵּה בְהֵמָה יְשַׁלְּמֶנָּה וּמַכֵּה אָדָם יוּמָת: מִשְׁפַּט אֶחָד כא כב
יִהְיֶה לָכֶם כַּגֵּר כָּאֶזְרָח יִהְיֶה כִּי אֲנִי יְהוָה אֱלֹהֵיכֶם: וַיְדַבֵּר כג
מֹשֶׁה אֶל־בְּנֵי יִשְׂרָאֵל וַיּוֹצִיאוּ אֶת־הַמְקַלֵּל אֶל־מִחוּץ
לַמַּחֲנֶה וַיִּרְגְּמוּ אֹתוֹ אָבֶן וּבְנֵי־יִשְׂרָאֵל עָשׂוּ כַּאֲשֶׁר צִוָּה
יְהוָה אֶת־מֹשֶׁה:

The הפטרה *for* פרשת אמר *is on page 1541.*

24:20 עַיִן תַּחַת עַיִן *An eye for an eye* – This is the famous and much misunderstood *lex talionis*, the law of retribution. As the Sages make clear, the principle of "an eye for an eye" was never meant literally (Bava Kamma 84a). A world based on a literal practice of an eye for an eye would eventually go blind. Other than in the case of murder, it meant monetary compensation. The principle is simply that the punishment must fit the crime. It was meant restrictively, to forbid either excessive leniency or excessive harshness. Philosopher Simon May writes:

> The widespread belief that the Hebrew Bible is all about vengeance and "an eye for an eye," while the Gospels supposedly invent love as an unconditional and universal value, must…count as one of the most extraordinary misunderstandings in all of Western history.

Because this misconception, focused on our verse, has fueled so much antisemitism over the centuries, we have translated the verse explicitly in line with the rabbinic understanding.

24:22 מִשְׁפַּט אֶחָד יִהְיֶה לָכֶם *There shall be one law* – What are these laws doing here, in the middle of the story of the blasphemer? Seemingly, they have nothing to do with it. The blasphemer has committed a sin against God. The laws that follow his story are about crimes against people or property. Moshe does not ask about injury. He asks about blasphemy. Besides which, he and the people already know the laws about injury and murder (Ex. 21:24–25). Yet they are presented seamlessly as part of a single narrative, as God's answer to Moshe's question. Leviticus, we recall, is not generally a book of narrative. It contains only one other story, about the deaths of two of Aharon's sons, Nadav and Avihu, on the day the Sanctuary

Parashat Behar

25 1 2 On Mount Sinai the Lord spoke to Moshe: "Speak to
the Israelites. Say: When you enter the land that I am
giving you, the land shall keep a Sabbath to the Lord.
3 For six years you may plant your fields, prune your
4 vineyards, and harvest their crops. But the seventh year
shall be to the land a Sabbath of complete rest, a Sabbath
to the Lord. You shall not sow your fields or prune your

Jubilee year, the release of debts, and the liberation of slaves. The obvious place for these laws is immediately after the civil legislation contained in Exodus 21–23, which deals with justice in the relationships between humans. The last forty chapters have forged a new identity for Israel as a people with God in its midst, bringing God close, living in the constant presence of the Divine. With this established, we now return to the basic terms of our covenant: the commitment to establish a just, compassionate, and equitable society.

25:4 שַׁבַּת שַׁבָּתוֹן יִהְיֶה לָאָרֶץ *To the land a Sabbath* – We owe to the mathematician Benoit Mandelbrot the concept of fractals, the discovery that phenomena in nature often display the same pattern at different levels of magnitude. A single rock looks like a mountain. Crystals, snowflakes, and ferns are made up of elements that have the same shape as the whole. Fractal geometry is the scientific equivalent of the mystical ability to sense the great in the small: "To see a World in a Grain of Sand / And a Heaven in a Wild Flower / Hold Infinity in the palm of your hand / and Eternity in an hour" (William Blake).

The Vilna Gaon saw this pattern in holy time. Parashat Emor showed, for him, that the structure of the week – six days of work followed by a seventh that is holy – is mirrored in the structure of the year – six festive days of lesser holiness plus a seventh, Yom Kippur, of supreme holiness. The same pattern now appears on an even larger scale: six ordinary years followed by the Sabbatical year of *Shemitta*, "release"; seven cycles of seven years, followed by the Jubilee year, *Yovel*, when the shofar was sounded proclaiming "liberty throughout the land to all its inhabitants" (Lev. 25:10).

At the core of this fractal structure is the original divine act of creation. God made the world in six days, culminating in the creation of man in His image; on the seventh day, He rested. Wherever the Torah wishes to emphasize the dimension of holiness it makes systematic use of the number and concept of seven. The Sabbath was an unprecedented innovation. It meant that one

פרשת בהר

כה א ב וַיְדַבֵּר יְהוָה אֶל־מֹשֶׁה בְּהַר סִינַי לֵאמֹר: דַּבֵּר אֶל־בְּנֵי
יִשְׂרָאֵל וְאָמַרְתָּ אֲלֵהֶם כִּי תָבֹאוּ אֶל־הָאָרֶץ אֲשֶׁר אֲנִי נֹתֵן
ג לָכֶם וְשָׁבְתָה הָאָרֶץ שַׁבָּת לַיהוָה: שֵׁשׁ שָׁנִים תִּזְרַע שָׂדֶךָ
ד וְשֵׁשׁ שָׁנִים תִּזְמֹר כַּרְמֶךָ וְאָסַפְתָּ אֶת־תְּבוּאָתָהּ: וּבַשָּׁנָה
הַשְּׁבִיעִת שַׁבַּת שַׁבָּתוֹן יִהְיֶה לָאָרֶץ שַׁבָּת לַיהוָה שָׂדְךָ לֹא

BEHAR

Our *parasha* consists of a single chapter that, despite its brevity, had a transformative impact on the social structure of ancient Israel and provided a unique solution to the otherwise intractable conflict between two fundamental ideals: freedom and equality. Much of human history has illustrated the fact that you can have freedom without equality (laissez-faire economics), or equality without freedom (Communism, socialism), but not both. The powerful insight of the Torah is that you can have both, but not at the same time. Therefore time itself has to become part of the solution, in the form of the seventh year and, after seven Sabbatical cycles, the Jubilee. These become periodic corrections to the distortions of the free market that allow some to become rich while others suffer the loss of land, home, and even freedom. There is the command to help the needy (Lev. 25:35). And there is the obligation to treat slaves not slavishly but as "a hired worker or a resident worker" (25:40). Through the periodic liberation of slaves, release of debts, and restoration of ancestral lands, the Torah provides a still-inspiring alternative to individualism on the one hand and collectivism on the other.

25:1 בְּהַר סִינַי *On Mount Sinai* – This is not a phrase that shouts for attention, until we recall that the book of Leviticus does not take place on Mount Sinai. It takes place in the wilderness of Sinai, at the foot of the mountain, not the top. The last time Mount Sinai figured in the narrative was when Moshe came down carrying the second set of tablets, the sign that God had reestablished His covenant with the people after the sin of the golden calf (Ex. 34). This verse, then, marks the end of the long digression that comes to repair the rupture caused by that sin (see Ex. 32, "The Golden Calf").

If we look at the substance of the chapter, we discover the same thing. It is not about a subject we immediately associate with Leviticus, which mostly speaks of the relationship between human beings and God. It is, though, precisely the subject we associate with the book of Exodus: social justice – specifically, the

5 vineyards; you shall not harvest what grows of itself or
gather the grapes of your unpruned vine; it is a year of rest
6 for the land. You may eat the land's Sabbath yield: you,
your male and female servants, and the hired worker and
7 resident worker who live with you, your livestock and the

---

and not homelessness but home. Anticipating by two millennia the theory of the fourteenth-century Islamic historian Ibn Khaldun, he predicts that over the course of time, precisely as they succeed, the Israelites will be at risk of losing their social cohesion and solidarity as a group. To prevent this, he sets forth a way of life built on covenant, memory, collective responsibility, justice, welfare, and social inclusion – still, to this day, the most powerful formula ever devised for a strong civil society.

"Who is wise?" Alexander asked the Elders of the Negev. "One who foresees the consequences," they responded (Tamid 32a). Leaders, if they are wise, think about the impact of their decisions many years from now.

THE JUBILEE YEAR

The words "proclaim liberty throughout the land" that appear in this *parasha* (v. 10) are inscribed on the Liberty Bell in Philadelphia. It was the chiming of this bell from the tower of Independence Hall on July 8, 1776, that summoned citizens to hear the first public reading of the American Declaration of Independence. Biblical freedom inspired American freedom, and many other freedoms. Seldom has an ancient idea more effectively proved its relevance to the contemporary world. The social program of Parashat Behar with its concern for economic justice, debt relief, welfare, and humane working conditions speaks with undiminished power to the problems of a global economy.

The Torah – this chapter especially – sets out the parameters of a society based on equality and liberty. These are eternal values. But they conflict. It is hard to pursue both fully at the same time. Communism, for instance, favors equality at the cost of liberty. Free market capitalism favors liberty at the cost of equality. How we construct the balance varies from age to age and place to place. In general the Rabbis favored markets and competition because they generated wealth, lowered prices, increased choice, reduced absolute levels of poverty, and in the course of time extended humanity's control over the environment, narrowing the extent to which we are the passive victims of circumstance and fate. They accepted the proposition that the greatest advances are often brought about through quite unspiritual drives. "I saw," says the author of Ecclesiastes, "that all the striving and all the skill: it is all but

ה תִזְרָ֔ע וְכַרְמְךָ֖ לֹ֥א תִזְמֹֽר׃ אֵ֣ת סְפִ֤יחַ קְצִֽירְךָ֙ לֹ֣א תִקְצ֔וֹר
וְאֶת־עִנְּבֵ֥י נְזִירֶ֖ךָ לֹ֣א תִבְצֹ֑ר שְׁנַ֥ת שַׁבָּת֖וֹן יִהְיֶ֥ה לָאָֽרֶץ׃
ו וְֽהָ֨יְתָ֜ה שַׁבַּ֨ת הָאָ֤רֶץ לָכֶם֙ לְאָכְלָ֔ה לְךָ֖ וּלְעַבְדְּךָ֣ וְלַאֲמָתֶ֑ךָ
ז וְלִשְׂכִֽירְךָ֙ וּלְתוֹשָׁ֣בְךָ֔ הַגָּרִ֖ים עִמָּֽךְ׃ וְלִ֨בְהֶמְתְּךָ֔ וְלַֽחַיָּ֖ה אֲשֶׁ֣ר

day in seven, all hierarchies of wealth and power were suspended. No one could be forced to work: not employees, or slaves, or even domestic animals. In the seventh year, debts were remitted and slaves sent free. In the Jubilee all ancestral land was returned to its original owners. These laws share a common logic: "For it is to Me that the Israelites are servants; they are My servants whom I brought out of the land of Egypt" (25:55). Those who are servants to God may not be slaves to man (Bava Metzia 10a). This is the idea woven into Jewish time from its very inception.

25:8 וְסָפַרְתָּ לְךָ *And you shall count* – In Parashat Emor and Parashat Behar there are two similar commands, both of which have to do with counting time. In Parashat Emor we read about the counting of the Omer, the forty-nine days between the second day of Passover and Shavuot. In Parashat Behar we read about the counting of the years to the Jubilee. There is, though, one significant difference between the two acts of counting. The counting of the Omer is in the plural: *usfartem lakhem*. The counting of the years is in the singular: *vesafarta lekha*. Oral Tradition interpreted the difference as referring to who is to do the counting. In the case of the Omer, the counting is the duty of each individual (Menaḥot 65b); hence the use of the plural. In the case of the Jubilee, the counting is the responsibility of the *beit din*, specifically the Supreme Court, the Sanhedrin (Sifra, Behar 2:2; *Hilkhot Shemitta VeYovel* 10:1). It is the duty of the Jewish people as a whole, performed centrally on their behalf by the court; hence the singular.

Implicit here is an important principle of leadership. As individuals we may count the days, but leaders must count the years. As private persons we can think about tomorrow, but in our role as leaders we must think long-term, focusing our eyes on the far horizon. Jewish history is replete with just such long-term thinking. When Moshe, on the eve of the exodus, focused the attention of the Israelites on how they would tell the story to their children in the years to come, he was taking the first step to making Judaism a religion built on education, study, and the life of the mind.

Throughout the book of Deuteronomy he exhibits stunning insight when he says that the Israelites will find that their real challenge will be not slavery but freedom, not poverty but affluence,

wild animals in your land – whatever the land produces is
8 there to be eaten. And you shall count off seven
Sabbaths of years – seven times seven years – so that the
9 seven Sabbath cycles total forty-nine years. Then you shall
sound the ram's horn. On the tenth day of the seventh
month, on the Day of Atonement, you shall sound the
10 horn all across your land. You shall consecrate the fiftieth
year and proclaim liberty throughout the land to all its
inhabitants. This shall be your Jubilee; each person shall
11 return to his hereditary home, each to his family. The
fiftieth year shall be a Jubilee for you. Do not sow, or reap
12 what grows of itself, or harvest the unpruned vines, for
it is a Jubilee; it shall be holy to you. You shall eat only
13 directly from the field. And in this Jubilee year, each
14 person shall return to his hereditary home. But when you SHENI
sell land to your fellow or buy it from him, brother must

---

responsibilities, and we are summoned to become God's partners in building a world less random and capricious, more equitable and humane.

25:14 אָחִיו *[His] brother* – Ten times the laws in Parashat Behar use the word *aḥ*, "brother" (here and vv. 14, 25, 35, 36, 39, 46, 47, and 48).

"Your brother" in these verses is not meant literally. At times it means "your relative," but mostly it means "your fellow Jew." This is a distinctive way of thinking about society and our obligations to others. Jews are not just citizens of the same nation or adherents of the same faith. We are members of the same extended family. On the festivals we relive the same memories. We were forged in the same crucible of suffering. We are more than friends. We are *mishpaḥa*, family.

It is the sense of family that has kept Jews linked in a web of mutual obligation despite the fact that they are scattered across the world. The Jewish people remains a family, often divided, always argumentative, but bound in a common bond of fate nonetheless. As our *parasha* reminds us, that person who has fallen is our brother or sister, and ours must be the hand that helps them rise again.

25:14 אַל־תּוֹנוּ אִישׁ אֶת־אָחִיו *Brother must not cheat brother* – On the basis of this command, the Rabbis, expounding and developing halakhot of business, established a threshold for fair profit. An overcharge of more than a sixth above the market price was in most cases sufficient to invalidate the sale. It was forbidden to mislead customers by making old goods look new, or covering bad produce with

ח בְּאַרְצֶךָ תִּהְיֶה כָל־תְּבוּאָתָהּ לֶאֱכֹל׃ וְסָפַרְתָּ
לְךָ שֶׁבַע שַׁבְּתֹת שָׁנִים שֶׁבַע שָׁנִים שֶׁבַע פְּעָמִים וְהָיוּ לְךָ
ט יְמֵי שֶׁבַע שַׁבְּתֹת הַשָּׁנִים תֵּשַׁע וְאַרְבָּעִים שָׁנָה׃ וְהַעֲבַרְתָּ
שׁוֹפַר תְּרוּעָה בַּחֹדֶשׁ הַשְּׁבִעִי בֶּעָשׂוֹר לַחֹדֶשׁ בְּיוֹם הַכִּפֻּרִים
י תַּעֲבִירוּ שׁוֹפָר בְּכָל־אַרְצְכֶם׃ וְקִדַּשְׁתֶּם אֵת שְׁנַת הַחֲמִשִּׁים
שָׁנָה וּקְרָאתֶם דְּרוֹר בָּאָרֶץ לְכָל־יֹשְׁבֶיהָ יוֹבֵל הִוא תִּהְיֶה
לָכֶם וְשַׁבְתֶּם אִישׁ אֶל־אֲחֻזָּתוֹ וְאִישׁ אֶל־מִשְׁפַּחְתּוֹ תָּשֻׁבוּ׃
יא יוֹבֵל הִוא שְׁנַת הַחֲמִשִּׁים שָׁנָה תִּהְיֶה לָכֶם לֹא תִזְרָעוּ וְלֹא
יב תִקְצְרוּ אֶת־סְפִיחֶיהָ וְלֹא תִבְצְרוּ אֶת־נְזִרֶיהָ׃ כִּי יוֹבֵל הִוא
יג קֹדֶשׁ תִּהְיֶה לָכֶם מִן־הַשָּׂדֶה תֹּאכְלוּ אֶת־תְּבוּאָתָהּ׃ בִּשְׁנַת
יד הַיּוֹבֵל הַזֹּאת תָּשֻׁבוּ אִישׁ אֶל־אֲחֻזָּתוֹ׃ וְכִי־תִמְכְּרוּ מִמְכָּר כ שני
לַעֲמִיתֶךָ אוֹ קָנֹה מִיַּד עֲמִיתֶךָ אַל־תּוֹנוּ אִישׁ אֶת־אָחִיו׃

one man's jealousy of another" (Eccl. 4:4). Or as the talmudic Sages put it, "Were it not for the evil inclination, no one would build a house, marry a wife, have children, or engage in business" (Kohelet Rabba 3:11). To a point, then, free trade and limited government (albeit with due provision for publicly funded education and welfare) are consistent with a biblical vision whose key concerns are freedom, justice, and personal independence. In Judaism, the state exists to serve the individual, not the individual the state.

But the market itself has unintended consequences, among them growing inequality. Poverty creates the need for loans, and the burden of debt can become cumulative and crippling. It can lead people to sell their land and even their freedom; in ancient times this meant selling oneself into slavery. Today it can mean debt bondage, "sweatshop" labor at less-than-subsistence wages, and other inescapable cycles of poverty. Hence the need for periodic redistribution: the cancellation of debts, the liberation of slaves, and the return of ancestral property (other than that within walled cities). That is the logic of the Sabbatical and Jubilee years.

In an age of vast inequalities of income within and between societies – in which, at the time of writing, a billion people lack adequate food and shelter, clean water, and medical facilities, and thirty thousand children die each day from preventable diseases – the vision of Parashat Behar still challenges us with its ideals. To be sure, the Torah is not an economic theory or a political party's program. It is about eternity, whereas politics is about the here and now. But it establishes guiding principles. Wealth and power are not privileges but

15 not cheat brother: you shall buy from your neighbor by
the number of years since the Jubilee; he shall sell to you by
16 the number of years left for harvesting. You shall increase
the price if the remaining years are many, and lower it if
they are few; what is being sold to you is the number of
17 harvests. You shall not cheat one another; you shall hold
18 your God in awe; I am the LORD your God. You shall
fulfill My statutes, and keep and act in accordance with
19 My laws – then you will live securely on the land. The land SHELISHI /SHENI/
will yield its fruit and you will eat your fill and live securely
20 there. If you should ask, 'What shall we eat in the seventh
year? We may not sow and may not harvest our crops' –
21 I will send My blessing over you in the sixth year and it
22 will yield three years' harvest. As you sow in the eighth
year, you will eat of the old harvest; you will still be eating
23 of the old when the crop of the ninth year comes. And the
land shall not be sold in perpetuity, for the land is Mine.
24 You are merely migrants and visitors to Me. Throughout

If the Jewish experience of economic enterprise teaches one thing it is that ethics and business are not adversaries. In the long run they need one another. It is one of the tasks of religious teaching to show that the long run must always inform the short term, so that economic profit does not lead to moral loss.

25:23 כִּי־לִי הָאָרֶץ *The land is Mine* – Because the land of Israel belongs to God, there can be no permanent freehold. God grants the Israelites possession of it on certain conditions, one of which is that the original owner can buy it back for a fair price at any time he has the money and wishes to do so (see vv. 25–28). The other is that in any case, it returns to the original owner in the Jubilee year.

Underlying these laws is something more fundamental than economics and politics. It is a still-revolutionary concept of property and ownership. Ultimately all things belong to God. This is a theological equivalent of the legal concept of eminent domain: the superior dominion of the sovereign power over all lands within its jurisdiction. In the case of Israel, eminent domain – both in relation to persons and to land – is vested in God.

Since God is the ultimate owner of the universe, what we possess, we do not own; we only hold in trust. There are conditions to that trust. The most fundamental, as is demonstrated throughout our *parasha*, is that we must show concern for the good of all, and may not use wealth or power in ways incompatible with human dignity.

טו בְּמִסְפַּר שָׁנִים אַחַר הַיּוֹבֵל תִּקְנֶה מֵאֵת עֲמִיתֶךָ בְּמִסְפַּר
טז שְׁנֵי־תְבוּאֹת יִמְכָּר־לָךְ׃ לְפִי ׀ רֹב הַשָּׁנִים תַּרְבֶּה מִקְנָתוֹ
וּלְפִי מְעֹט הַשָּׁנִים תַּמְעִיט מִקְנָתוֹ כִּי מִסְפַּר תְּבוּאֹת הוּא
יז מֹכֵר לָךְ׃ וְלֹא תוֹנוּ אִישׁ אֶת־עֲמִיתוֹ וְיָרֵאתָ מֵאֱלֹהֶיךָ כִּי אֲנִי
יח יהוה אֱלֹהֵיכֶם׃ וַעֲשִׂיתֶם אֶת־חֻקֹּתַי וְאֶת־מִשְׁפָּטַי תִּשְׁמְרוּ
יט וַעֲשִׂיתֶם אֹתָם וִישַׁבְתֶּם עַל־הָאָרֶץ לָבֶטַח׃ וְנָתְנָה הָאָרֶץ שלישי /שני/
כ פִּרְיָהּ וַאֲכַלְתֶּם לָשֹׂבַע וִישַׁבְתֶּם לָבֶטַח עָלֶיהָ׃ וְכִי תֹאמְרוּ
מַה־נֹּאכַל בַּשָּׁנָה הַשְּׁבִיעִת הֵן לֹא נִזְרָע וְלֹא נֶאֱסֹף אֶת־
כא תְּבוּאָתֵנוּ׃ וְצִוִּיתִי אֶת־בִּרְכָתִי לָכֶם בַּשָּׁנָה הַשִּׁשִּׁית וְעָשָׂת
כב אֶת־הַתְּבוּאָה לִשְׁלֹשׁ הַשָּׁנִים׃ וּזְרַעְתֶּם אֵת הַשָּׁנָה הַשְּׁמִינִת
וַאֲכַלְתֶּם מִן־הַתְּבוּאָה יָשָׁן עַד ׀ הַשָּׁנָה הַתְּשִׁיעִת עַד־בּוֹא
כג תְּבוּאָתָהּ תֹּאכְלוּ יָשָׁן׃ וְהָאָרֶץ לֹא תִמָּכֵר לִצְמִתֻת כִּי־לִי
כד הָאָרֶץ כִּי־גֵרִים וְתוֹשָׁבִים אַתֶּם עִמָּדִי׃ וּבְכֹל אֶרֶץ אֲחֻזַּתְכֶם

---

a layer of good. Jewish law recognizes no concept of *caveat emptor*. The onus of fair representation lies with the vendor, not the purchaser. Giving misleading advice was forbidden under the biblical rubric of not "putting a stumbling-block before the blind" (Lev. 19:14). These and a host of similar provisions legislated for fair dealing and integrity. The Rabbis recognized that a perfect market would not emerge of its own accord. Not everyone had access to full information, and this gave scope for unscrupulous practices and unfair profits, against which they took a strong stand.

The subject of Jewish economic ethics is vast – perhaps a quarter of Jewish law is devoted to it – and much of the literature is highly detailed and case specific. Throughout the centuries, Jewish businesspeople sought rabbinic guidance in difficult cases, as did communal leaders in framing public policies. The glory of Jewish law lies in its concreteness: the Rabbis would have appreciated Mies van der Rohe's dictum that "God is in the details."

What the Tanakh and its rabbinic interpreters understood so well is that the market cannot be sustained by market values alone. It depends on a surrounding matrix of virtue and on the institutions that sustain it: families, communities, beliefs, and traditions. It needs rules of integrity and fair dealing, and a mindset that sees the market as a place not of exploitation, but of mutual gain. Without these, its workings are too arbitrary and abrasive. With them, it is the best way we know of matching one person's talents to another's desires, of encouraging freedom, creativity, and dignity, and of enhancing the conditions of life for all.

the land that you possess, you must allow land to be
25 redeemed. If your brother grows poor and REVI'I
sells part of his hereditary land, his closest redeeming
relative shall come and redeem what his kinsman has
26 sold. If the person lacks a relative to redeem it, but later
27 prospers and can afford to buy it back, he shall calculate
the years since its sale and refund the balance to the one
to whom he sold it, and return to his hereditary home.
28 If he cannot afford to recover it, what was sold shall
remain in the possession of the buyer until the Jubilee
year; but at the Jubilee it shall be released, and he shall
29 return to his possession. One who sells a house ḤAMISHI /SHELISHI/
in a walled city retains the right to redeem it until a year
30 after its sale. This is the period of redemption. If it is not
redeemed before a full year has passed, the house in the

---

slavery. I will liberate (*vegaalti*) you with an arm stretched forth and with great acts of judgment. I will take you as My people, and I will be your God" (Ex. 6:6–7). At the Sea of Reeds the Israelites sang, "In Your love, You guided out the people You redeemed" (15:13). Only now, given the laws of Parashat Behar, do we understand the significance of the first words God commands Moshe to say to Pharaoh: "This is what the LORD says: 'Israel is My son, My firstborn'" (4:22). God is doing more than rescuing people from oppression or liberating slaves. He is engaged in an act of redemption, that is to say, exercising the right and responsibility of a close relative, in this case a father. The fusion here between law, ethics, and narrative, and between God's interventions in history and our duties within society, is complete. In the exodus, God was engaged in more than miracles. He was teaching us how we too ought to behave when people close to us fall into destitution.

This becomes an essential element of a world of hope, not in the trivial sense of wishing or wanting things to be better, but in the grounded confidence that things will become better. We are part of a society in which people know they have a duty to help out family members in distress. Our founding memory is of just such an act performed by God Himself.

25:29 יָמִים תִּהְיֶה גְאֻלָּתוֹ *The period of redemption* – Ramban explains that losing one's home through poverty is deeply painful and may be a source of shame. Because of this, a city home may be redeemed in the first year of being forced to sell it. If, however, the seller recovers his fortunes later, when he has already lived for a time in a new home, his emotional connection to the original

כה גְּאֻלָּה תִּתְּנוּ לָאָרֶץ׃ כִּי־יָמוּךְ אָחִיךָ וּמָכַר מֵאֲחֻזָּתוֹ רביעי
כו וּבָא גֹאֲלוֹ הַקָּרֹב אֵלָיו וְגָאַל אֵת מִמְכַּר אָחִיו׃ וְאִישׁ כִּי
כז לֹא יִהְיֶה־לּוֹ גֹּאֵל וְהִשִּׂיגָה יָדוֹ וּמָצָא כְּדֵי גְאֻלָּתוֹ׃ וְחִשַּׁב
אֶת־שְׁנֵי מִמְכָּרוֹ וְהֵשִׁיב אֶת־הָעֹדֵף לָאִישׁ אֲשֶׁר מָכַר־
כח לוֹ וְשָׁב לַאֲחֻזָּתוֹ׃ וְאִם לֹא־מָצְאָה יָדוֹ דֵּי הָשִׁיב לוֹ וְהָיָה
מִמְכָּרוֹ בְּיַד הַקֹּנֶה אֹתוֹ עַד שְׁנַת הַיּוֹבֵל וְיָצָא בַּיֹּבֵל וְשָׁב
כט לַאֲחֻזָּתוֹ׃ וְאִישׁ כִּי־יִמְכֹּר בֵּית־מוֹשַׁב עִיר חוֹמָה חמישי /שלישי/
וְהָיְתָה גְּאֻלָּתוֹ עַד־תֹּם שְׁנַת מִמְכָּרוֹ יָמִים תִּהְיֶה גְאֻלָּתוֹ׃
ל וְאִם לֹא־יִגָּאֵל עַד־מְלֹאת לוֹ שָׁנָה תְמִימָה וְקָם הַבַּיִת אֲשֶׁר־

REDEMPTION

The root *g-a-l,* which features in Parashat Behar nineteen times and in the next *parasha,* Beḥukotai, twelve times, means "to redeem." The basic idea of redemption is that the law provides for the possibility of reclaiming land, property, or even liberty itself if one has the means to do so. Our chapter discusses three cases in which an individual finds himself forced, through poverty, to sell something valuable. It may be land, or a house, or himself, sold as a slave. In each case, provision is made for a relative of the seller, or the seller himself should he suddenly find himself with the means to do so, to buy it back by providing the buyer with appropriate compensation. If neither of these is possible then redemption will automatically take place in the Jubilee year (with the exception of a house in a walled city).

In general, the market economy functions on the basis of binding exchange. If I sell something to a purchaser at a price both of us accept as fair, I cannot change my mind tomorrow and say, "I have decided not to sell it after all. Give it back and I will return your money." If the purchaser does not want to do so, I cannot force him. But there are certain things, says the Torah, that should not be left entirely to the vagaries of the market because they are too fundamental to self-respect and human flourishing. When it comes to land, a home, and freedom of employment, a distinction must be made between temporary poverty and permanent deprivation. In such cases, while respecting the integrity of the market – the redeemer must pay the proper market value of what he redeems – a basic law of justice takes priority. No one should be permanently disadvantaged because of temporary misfortune.

Redemption, however, is more than a legal idea. It is the way the Torah describes God's intervention in history to liberate the Israelites from slavery in Egypt. God tells Moshe, "I am the LORD, and I will free you from the forced labor of the Egyptians. I will rescue you from

walled city shall belong permanently to the buyer and
his descendants forever; it is not released at the Jubilee.
31 Houses in villages without surrounding walls, however,
are considered as if they were open country. They may
32 be redeemed, and they are released at the Jubilee. In
the Levitical towns – Levites always retain the right to
33 redeem houses in their ancestral towns. Levite property
that can be redeemed – houses sold in towns belonging
to them – shall be released at the Jubilee, because the
houses in Levitical towns are their ancestral possession
34 among the Israelites. But the pastureland around their
towns can never be sold, because that is their permanent
35 possession. If your brother becomes poor and
is struggling, extend him support – a migrant or visitor
36 also – that he may live among you. Do not take advance

---

who commits himself to keep the seven Noahide commands. A third view, more stringent, holds that it is someone who undertakes to keep all the commands of the Torah except one, the prohibition of meat not ritually slaughtered. The law follows the Sages. A *ger toshav* is thus a non-Jew living in Israel who accepts the Noahide laws binding on everyone.

Ger toshav legislation is one of the earliest extant forms of minority rights. According to Rambam, there is an obligation on Jews in Israel to establish courts of law for resident aliens to allow them to settle their own disputes – or disputes they have with Jews – according to the provisions of Noahide law. Rambam adds: "One should act toward resident aliens with the same respect and loving-kindness as one would to a fellow Jew" (*Hilkhot Melakhim* 10:12).

The difference between this and later "ways of peace" legislation (Gittin 61a), which also mandated equal treatment, is that the "ways of peace" apply to non-Jews without regard to their beliefs or religious practice. They date from a time when Jews were a minority in a predominantly non-Jewish, non-monotheistic environment. "Ways of peace" are essentially pragmatic rules of what today we would call good community relations and active citizenship in a diverse society. *Ger toshav* legislation cuts deeper. It is based not on pragmatism but religious principle. According to the Torah, you do not have to be Jewish in a Jewish society and land to have many of the rights of citizenship. You simply have to be moral.

Since the days of Moshe, minority rights have been central to the vision of the kind of society God wants us to create in the land of Israel. A strong sense of group identity can coexist with love of, and care for, the people who belong

בָּעִיר אֲשֶׁר־לֹא חֹמָה לַצְּמִיתֻת לַקֹּנֶה אֹתוֹ לְדֹרֹתָיו לֹא יֵצֵא לוֹ
לא בַּיֹּבֵל: וּבָתֵּי הַחֲצֵרִים אֲשֶׁר אֵין־לָהֶם חֹמָה סָבִיב עַל־שְׂדֵה
לב הָאָרֶץ יֵחָשֵׁב גְּאֻלָּה תִּהְיֶה־לּוֹ וּבַיֹּבֵל יֵצֵא: וְעָרֵי הַלְוִיִּם
לג בָּתֵּי עָרֵי אֲחֻזָּתָם גְּאֻלַּת עוֹלָם תִּהְיֶה לַלְוִיִּם: וַאֲשֶׁר יִגְאַל
מִן־הַלְוִיִּם וְיָצָא מִמְכַּר־בַּיִת וְעִיר אֲחֻזָּתוֹ בַּיֹּבֵל כִּי בָתֵּי עָרֵי
לד הַלְוִיִּם הִוא אֲחֻזָּתָם בְּתוֹךְ בְּנֵי יִשְׂרָאֵל: וּשְׂדֵה מִגְרַשׁ עָרֵיהֶם
לה לֹא יִמָּכֵר כִּי־אֲחֻזַּת עוֹלָם הוּא לָהֶם: וְכִי־יָמוּךְ כא
לו אָחִיךָ וּמָטָה יָדוֹ עִמָּךְ וְהֶחֱזַקְתָּ בּוֹ גֵּר וְתוֹשָׁב וָחַי עִמָּךְ: אַל־
תִּקַּח מֵאִתּוֹ נֶשֶׁךְ וְתַרְבִּית וְיָרֵאתָ מֵאֱלֹהֶיךָ וְחֵי אָחִיךָ עִמָּךְ:

home is no longer so strong. The reason why fields and rural homes return to their original owners in the Jubilee year is that they are not only homes, but a source of livelihood.

This relates to the Torah's strong sense of the dignity of labor. God Himself plants a garden and fashions the first human from the earth. The first man is himself charged with serving and protecting the garden. "The sleep of a worker is sweet," says Ecclesiastes (5:11). "You shall eat the fruit of your labor; you shall be happy and thriving," says Psalms (128:2). Flay carcasses rather than be dependent on others, says the third-century Rav (Yerushalmi, Berakhot 9:2). Someone who does not engage in *yishuv haolam*, constructive work, is invalid as a witness in Jewish law (Sanhedrin 24b). Work is an important source of dignity and self-respect. It has spiritual value, because earning our food is part of the stature, the creativity of the human condition. Judaism is opposed to the idea of a leisured class, and while a city dweller's attachment to their home is something that must be honored, it does not run as far or as deep as the importance of land to the one who works it.

THE RIGHTS OF STRANGERS

These verses spell out the rights of and obligations toward a *ger*. The Sages hold that the word *ger* (migrant) might mean one of two things. One was a *ger tzedek*, a convert to Judaism who had accepted all its commands and obligations. The other was the *ger toshav*, the "migrant" or "resident alien," who had not adopted the religion of Israel but who lived in the land of Israel. This passage relates to the latter group. There is an obligation to support and sustain a non-Jewish migrant. Not only does he have the right to live in the Holy Land, but he has the right to share in its welfare provisions.

Who then is a *ger toshav*? There are three views in the Talmud (Avoda Zara 64a). According to R. Meir, it is anyone who takes it upon himself not to worship idols. According to the Sages, it is one

or accrued interest from him; fear your God so that your
37 brother can live with you. Do not lend him your money at
38 interest or provide him with food at a profit. I am the LORD
your God, who brought you out of the land of Egypt to
39 give the land of Canaan to you, to be your God. If SHISHI /REVI'I/
your brother becomes poor and sells himself to you, do
40 not work him as a slave. He shall abide with you like a
hired worker or a resident worker and work for you until
41 the Jubilee year. Then he and his children shall be free to
leave you and return to their family and their ancestral
42 land. For they are My servants whom I brought out from
43 Egypt: they cannot be sold as slaves. Do not rule them
44 harshly with backbreaking labor; fear your God. As for
male or female slaves that you may have: from the nations
45 around you, you may acquire a male or female slave. You

---

creation of a culture of study and education, which dominated their lives and to which access was free, universal, and lifelong.

The Talmud tells the story of Rabban Gamliel's visit to the house of his deputy, R. Yehoshua, to apologize for mistreating him. Evidently stuck for a way of opening the conversation, Rabban Gamliel looked around R. Yehoshua's house, noticed that the walls were black, and said: "Judging by the walls, I can see that you must be a blacksmith." R. Yehoshua replied: "Alas for the generation of which you are the leader, seeing that you know nothing of the troubles of the scholars and how they have to make a living" (*Berakhot* 28a).

The story fascinates me, because it is apparent that Rabban Gamliel and R. Yehoshua were able to work and debate together day by day in the academy, one as its head, the other as his deputy, without the wealthy Rabban Gamliel being aware that R. Yehoshua was a poor man. To this day, this rings true as a description of the spirit of the learning community. (Its second implication, no less important, is that ignorance of the real economic difficulties of a people disqualifies a sage from being a leader.) In a covenantal society, anyone who is struggling financially, whether brother or stranger, is to be supported to the extent and in such a manner that they can "live among you": fully as one of you.

25:44 מֵהֶם תִּקְנוּ עֶבֶד וְאָמָה *Acquire a male or female slave* – Slavery is an assault on the human condition. To be "in the image of God" (Gen. 1:27) means to be summoned to a life of freedom (see note on Gen. 5:3). Yet the Torah does not abolish slavery. That is the paradox at the heart of Parashat Behar. Instead, the Torah sets in motion a process that will lead people to come of their own

לז/לח אֶת־כַּסְפְּךָ לֹא־תִתֵּן לוֹ בְּנֶשֶׁךְ וּבְמַרְבִּית לֹא־תִתֵּן אָכְלֶךָ׃ אֲנִי
יהוה אֱלֹהֵיכֶם אֲשֶׁר־הוֹצֵאתִי אֶתְכֶם מֵאֶרֶץ מִצְרָיִם לָתֵת
לט לָכֶם אֶת־אֶרֶץ כְּנַעַן לִהְיוֹת לָכֶם לֵאלֹהִים׃ וְכִי־ ששי /רביעי/
יָמוּךְ אָחִיךָ עִמָּךְ וְנִמְכַּר־לָךְ לֹא־תַעֲבֹד בּוֹ עֲבֹדַת עָבֶד׃
מ כְּשָׂכִיר כְּתוֹשָׁב יִהְיֶה עִמָּךְ עַד־שְׁנַת הַיֹּבֵל יַעֲבֹד עִמָּךְ׃
מא וְיָצָא מֵעִמָּךְ הוּא וּבָנָיו עִמּוֹ וְשָׁב אֶל־מִשְׁפַּחְתּוֹ וְאֶל־
מב אֲחֻזַּת אֲבֹתָיו יָשׁוּב׃ כִּי־עֲבָדַי הֵם אֲשֶׁר־הוֹצֵאתִי אֹתָם
מג מֵאֶרֶץ מִצְרָיִם לֹא יִמָּכְרוּ מִמְכֶּרֶת עָבֶד׃ לֹא־תִרְדֶּה בוֹ
מד בְּפָרֶךְ וְיָרֵאתָ מֵאֱלֹהֶיךָ׃ וְעַבְדְּךָ וַאֲמָתְךָ אֲשֶׁר יִהְיוּ־לָךְ
מה מֵאֵת הַגּוֹיִם אֲשֶׁר סְבִיבֹתֵיכֶם מֵהֶם תִּקְנוּ עֶבֶד וְאָמָה׃ וְגַם
מִבְּנֵי הַתּוֹשָׁבִים הַגָּרִים עִמָּכֶם מֵהֶם תִּקְנוּ וּמִמִּשְׁפַּחְתָּם

---

to other groups or to none. That is part of *Torat Kohanim,* ethics in the priestly mode: our common humanity precedes our religious differences. Minority rights are the best test of a free and just society.

25:35 וְחַי עִמָּךְ *That he may live among you* – "The highest degree of charity, exceeded by none," writes Rambam in his famous summary of the eight levels of *tzedaka,* "is that of a person who assists a poor Jew by providing him with a gift or loan or by accepting him into business partnership or by helping him find employment – in a word, by putting him where he can dispense with other people's aid. With reference to such help it is said, 'Extend him support – a migrant or visitor also – that he may live among you' (Lev. 25:35), which means to strengthen him in such a manner that his falling into want is prevented" (*Hilkhot Mattenot Aniyyim* 10:7).

Rambam's exquisitely calibrated ethic is shot through with psychological insight. What matters, he explains in the continuation of the above passage, is not how *much* you give, but *how* you do so. The poor must not be embarrassed. The rich must not be allowed to feel superior. We give, not to take pride in our generosity, still less to emphasize the dependency of others, but because we belong to a covenant of human solidarity.

Especially noteworthy is Rambam's insistence that giving somebody a job, or the means to start a business, is the highest charity of all. What is humiliating about poverty is dependence itself: the feeling of being beholden to others. One of the rules of *tzedaka* is that even the person who subsists through charity must give charity, and be given enough to give it. This concern for dignity, this democratizing tendency, was expressed by the Rabbis most potently in their

may also acquire them from among the migrants residing
with you and from their families among you who were
born in your land; they may be yours, in your possession.
46 They become hereditary property that you can bequeath
to your children; they may be your slaves, but over your
47 brother Israelites you may not rule so harshly. If SHEVI'I
a migrant or temporary resident prospers among you,
and your fellow Israelite becomes poor and is sold to a
migrant residing among you or to a branch of a foreign
48 family, the Israelite has the right, subsequent to the sale,
49 to be redeemed; one of his relatives may redeem him. His
uncle or cousin or any other blood relative may redeem
him, or if he can afford to do so, he may redeem himself.
50 Together with his owner, he shall calculate the time from
the year he was sold until the Jubilee year. The price of
his release shall be based on that number of years, as if he
51 had been there as a hired laborer. If many years remain,
he shall pay that proportion of his purchase price for his
52 redemption. If only a few years remain until the Jubilee
year, he shall calculate that and pay for the redemption
53 accordingly. He shall be with him like a worker hired year
by year; and never shall he be oppressed in his labors
54 while you look on. And if he is not redeemed in any of
these ways, he and his children shall be released in the
55 Jubilee year. For it is to Me that the Israelites are servants. MAFTIR
They are My servants whom I brought out of the land of

10a). We may not willingly forgo our own freedom. The Midrash (Sifra, Behar 9:6) links the final verses of the *parasha* (Lev. 26:2) to the case of the Jew enslaved to a non-Jew: "He should not say, 'Since my master breaks the Sabbath, I too shall break the Sabbath' – so it says, 'Keep My Sabbaths, revere My Sanctuary; I am the LORD': I am faithful to pay your reward." It may be wishful thinking to imagine a slave able to assert his right to rest on the Sabbath – but it is also a statement of principle.

The idea was perhaps given its most powerful expression by the late Viktor Frankl, a survivor of Auschwitz who, on the basis of his experiences there, founded a new school of psychotherapy. He said that in the camps, they took away everything that made us human except the one thing that can never be taken away – the freedom to decide how

אֲשֶׁר עִמָּכֶם אֲשֶׁר הוֹלִידוּ בְּאַרְצְכֶם וְהָיוּ לָכֶם לַאֲחֻזָּה׃
מו וְהִתְנַחַלְתֶּם אֹתָם לִבְנֵיכֶם אַחֲרֵיכֶם לָרֶשֶׁת אֲחֻזָּה לְעֹלָם
בָּהֶם תַּעֲבֹדוּ וּבְאַחֵיכֶם בְּנֵי־יִשְׂרָאֵל אִישׁ בְּאָחִיו לֹא־תִרְדֶּה
מז בוֹ בְּפָרֶךְ׃ וְכִי תַשִּׂיג יַד גֵּר וְתוֹשָׁב עִמָּךְ וּמָךְ שביעי
אָחִיךָ עִמּוֹ וְנִמְכַּר לְגֵר תּוֹשָׁב עִמָּךְ אוֹ לְעֵקֶר מִשְׁפַּחַת גֵּר׃
מח מט אַחֲרֵי נִמְכַּר גְּאֻלָּה תִּהְיֶה־לּוֹ אֶחָד מֵאֶחָיו יִגְאָלֶנּוּ׃ אוֹ־דֹדוֹ
אוֹ בֶן־דֹּדוֹ יִגְאָלֶנּוּ אוֹ־מִשְּׁאֵר בְּשָׂרוֹ מִמִּשְׁפַּחְתּוֹ יִגְאָלֶנּוּ אוֹ־
נ הִשִּׂיגָה יָדוֹ וְנִגְאָל׃ וְחִשַּׁב עִם־קֹנֵהוּ מִשְּׁנַת הִמָּכְרוֹ לוֹ עַד
שְׁנַת הַיֹּבֵל וְהָיָה כֶּסֶף מִמְכָּרוֹ בְּמִסְפַּר שָׁנִים כִּימֵי שָׂכִיר
נא יִהְיֶה עִמּוֹ׃ אִם־עוֹד רַבּוֹת בַּשָּׁנִים לְפִיהֶן יָשִׁיב גְּאֻלָּתוֹ
נב מִכֶּסֶף מִקְנָתוֹ׃ וְאִם־מְעַט נִשְׁאַר בַּשָּׁנִים עַד־שְׁנַת הַיֹּבֵל
נג וְחִשַּׁב־לוֹ כְּפִי שָׁנָיו יָשִׁיב אֶת־גְּאֻלָּתוֹ׃ כִּשְׂכִיר שָׁנָה בְּשָׁנָה
נד יִהְיֶה עִמּוֹ לֹא־יִרְדֶּנּוּ בְּפֶרֶךְ לְעֵינֶיךָ׃ וְאִם־לֹא יִגָּאֵל בְּאֵלֶּה
נה וְיָצָא בִּשְׁנַת הַיֹּבֵל הוּא וּבָנָיו עִמּוֹ׃ כִּי־לִי בְנֵי־יִשְׂרָאֵל עֲבָדִים מפטיר
עֲבָדַי הֵם אֲשֶׁר־הוֹצֵאתִי אוֹתָם מֵאֶרֶץ מִצְרָיִם אֲנִי יְהוָה

---

accord to the conclusion that it is wrong. It limits slavery and humanizes it. Every seventh day, slaves are to be granted rest and a taste of freedom. In the seventh year, Israelite slaves are to be set free. If they choose otherwise they are released in the Jubilee year. During their years of service they are to be treated like employees. They are not to be subjected to backbreaking or spirit-crushing labor (v. 43; cf. Ex. 1:13–14 and note on 1:14).

The challenge to which Torah legislation is an answer is: How can one create a social structure in which, of their own accord, people will eventually come to see slavery as wrong and freely choose to abandon it?

The answer lay in changing slavery from an ontological condition to a temporary circumstance: from what I am to a situation in which I find myself, now but not forever. No Israelite was allowed to be treated or to see himself as a slave. He might be reduced to slavery for a period of time, but this was a passing plight, not a permanent identity.

25:55 כִּי־לִי בְנֵי־יִשְׂרָאֵל עֲבָדִים *For it is to Me that the Israelites are servants* – The Talmud completes the phrase: "For it is to Me that the Israelites are servants; they may not be slaves to slaves" (Bava Metzia

26 1 Egypt; I am the Lord your God. You shall make no idols,
nor may you erect any divine image or worship pillar. Do
not set up any carved stone in your land and bow down to
2 it, for I am the Lord your God. Keep My Sabbaths, revere
My Sanctuary; I am the Lord.

The haftara for Parashat Behar is on page 1542.
When Behar and Beḥukotai are read together, read the haftara on page 1548.

out. The more it tires, the more it fails, until it dies in exhaustion. The one thing it forgets to do is to look up.

The main task of our *parasha* has been to safeguard the functional freedom of those most vulnerable to losing it. Here, however, it reminds us of the deeper significance and responsibility inherent in our own ontological freedom.

כו א אֱלֹהֵיכֶם: לֹא־תַעֲשׂוּ לָכֶם אֱלִילִם וּפֶסֶל וּמַצֵּבָה לֹא־תָקִימוּ
לָכֶם וְאֶבֶן מַשְׂכִּית לֹא תִתְּנוּ בְּאַרְצְכֶם לְהִשְׁתַּחֲוֺת עָלֶיהָ כִּי
ב אֲנִי יְהוָה אֱלֹהֵיכֶם: אֶת־שַׁבְּתֹתַי תִּשְׁמֹרוּ וּמִקְדָּשִׁי תִּירָאוּ
אֲנִי יְהוָה:

The haftara for פרשת בהר *is on page 1543.*
When בהר *and* בחקתי *are read together, read the* הפטרה *on page 1549.*

to respond. He stayed sane by conducting himself as a free man even when all his external freedoms had been taken away.

To be free is to refuse to be defined by circumstance. It is about the action that is not reaction. Our ability to see and do the unexpected is the link between human creativity and freedom. Wittgenstein once said that his aim as a philosopher was "to show the fly the way out of the fly bottle." The fly keeps banging its head against the glass in a vain attempt to get

Parashat Beḥukotai

26 3 If you follow My decrees, keep My commands, and fulfill
4 them, then I shall give you rain in its due time. The land
shall yield its crops and the trees of the field shall yield
5 their fruit. Your threshing season shall last until the grape
harvest; the grape harvest shall last until sowing time.
You shall eat your bread to the full and live securely in

(27:34) – are in fact the closing words of the covenantal revelation at Sinai.

COVENANTAL POLITICS

This chapter sets out, with great clarity, the terms of Jewish life under the covenant. It opens with an idyllic picture of the blessing of divine favor: If Israel follows God's decrees and keeps His commands, there will be rain, the earth will yield its fruit, there will be peace, the people will flourish, they will have children, and the Divine Presence will be in their midst. God will make them free.

Covenantal politics is moral politics, driving an elemental connection between the fate of a nation and its vocation. It sees nothing inevitable or even natural about the fate of a people. Israel will not follow the usual laws of the rise and fall of civilizations. Instead, it will be utterly dependent on moral considerations. If Israel stays true to its mission, it will flourish. If it drifts from its vocation, it will suffer.

In this model, statehood is a matter not of power but of ethical responsibility. One might have thought that this kind of politics robbed a nation of its freedom. Spinoza argued just this. "This, then, was the object of the ceremonial law," he wrote, "that men should do nothing of their own free will, but should always act under external authority, and should continually confess by their actions and thoughts that they were not their own masters" (*Tractatus Theologico-Politicus*). However, in this respect, Spinoza was wrong.

Covenant theology is emphatically a politics of liberty. I brought you from slavery to freedom, says God, and I empower you to be free. I will not intervene in your choices, but will instruct you on what choices you ought to make and teach you the constitution of liberty.

The first and most important principle is this: A nation cannot worship itself and survive. Sooner or later, power will corrupt those who wield it. If fortune favors it and it grows rich, it will become self-indulgent and eventually decadent. Its citizens will no longer have the courage to fight for their liberty, and it will fall to another, more Spartan power.

To stay free, a nation must worship something greater than itself, nothing

פרשת בחקתי

כו ג אִם־בְּחֻקֹּתַ֖י תֵּלֵ֑כוּ וְאֶת־מִצְוֺתַ֣י תִּשְׁמְר֔וּ וַעֲשִׂיתֶ֖ם אֹתָֽם׃ כב
ד וְנָתַתִּ֥י גִשְׁמֵיכֶ֖ם בְּעִתָּ֑ם וְנָתְנָ֤ה הָאָ֨רֶץ֙ יְבוּלָ֔הּ וְעֵ֣ץ הַשָּׂדֶ֔ה
ה יִתֵּ֖ן פִּרְיֽוֹ׃ וְהִשִּׂ֨יג לָכֶ֥ם דַּ֨יִשׁ֙ אֶת־בָּצִ֔יר וּבָצִ֖יר יַשִּׂ֣יג אֶת־
זָ֑רַע וַאֲכַלְתֶּ֤ם לַחְמְכֶם֙ לָשֹׂ֔בַע וִישַׁבְתֶּ֥ם לָבֶ֖טַח בְּאַרְצְכֶֽם׃

BEḤUKOTAI

This *parasha* is dominated by the passage in which God speaks of the blessings that will be experienced by the Israelites if they are faithful to the covenant and of the curses they will encounter if they are not. The blessings in Parashat Beḥukotai are brief and serene. The curses, by contrast, are long and terrifying. If Israel loses its way spiritually, say the curses, it will lose it physically, economically, and politically also. The nation will experience defeat and disaster. It will forfeit its freedom and its land. The perennial choice between blessing and curse that lies at the heart of Judaism creates a profound ethic of responsibility. So, in a strange way, belief in curses creates blessings.

At the end of the curses, there is a sudden change of key. God promises that even if Israel sins, it may suffer, but it will never die. Israel may betray the covenant but God never will.

26:3 אִם־בְּחֻקֹּתַי תֵּלֵכוּ *If you follow My decrees* – This *parasha*, like Parashat Behar, was stated "on Mount Sinai" (Lev. 27:34), continuing the Sinai revelation after the long insertion of the priestly code (see note on Lev. 25:1). This section is about the blessings and curses that come with the covenant: blessings if the people obey, curses if they do not. We know now, thanks to intensive study by scholars of the ancient Near East, that the covenant the Israelites made with God at Sinai was similar in form if not in substance to the suzerainty treaties of the time – peace agreements between two states, one strong, the other weak. These covenants had a highly formalized structure: preamble, historical prologue, then the terms and conditions, first in general terms and then in specific details. Witnesses are named. Provision is made for the deposition of the treaty and for regular public readings.

An essential element of these treaties was the reward for compliance and the punishment that would follow any breach. Even if we did not know this from the historical record we would know it from the book of Deuteronomy, which is structured as a covenant on a massive scale and which, near the end, details the rewards and punishments in a passage parallel to this one. The closing words of Leviticus – "These are the commands that the LORD gave Moshe"

6 your land. And I will grant peace in the land; when you lie SHENI
down, no one will make you afraid. I will cause dangerous
animals to cease in the land, and through that land no
7 sword shall pass. You shall chase your enemies, and
8 they shall fall before you by the sword. Five of you shall
chase away a hundred, and a hundred of you shall put ten
thousand to flight; your enemies shall fall before you by
9 the sword. I will turn to you and make you fruitful, make
you numerous, and I will uphold My covenant with you.
10 You shall eat the grain of long ago and take the old grain SHELISHI /ḤAMISHI/
11 out to make space for all the new. I shall set My dwelling
12 among you, and I shall not despise you; I shall walk among
13 you. I shall be your God, and you shall be My people. I am
the LORD your God, who brought you out of Egypt, to be
their slaves no more. I broke the bars of your yoke and led
you to walk with your heads held high.
14 But if you do not listen to Me and do not carry out all
15 these commands – if you spurn My decrees and despise

The repeated phrases – "If in spite of all this…" "If you still…" "If despite all this…" – come like hammerblows of fate.

Why are the curses almost three times as long as the blessings that precede them? The answer is not because God seeks to punish. The Talmud tells us that God weeps when He allows disaster to strike His people: "Woe to Me, that due to their sins I destroyed My House, burned My Temple and exiled them [My children] among the nations of the world" (Berakhot 3a). The curses are meant as a warning. They are intended to deter, scare, discourage.

Social scientists argue that bad has far more impact on us than good. We pay more attention to bad news than good news. Bad health makes more difference to us than good health. Criticism affects us more than praise. Humans are designed to take notice of and rapidly react to threat. Failing to notice a lion is more dangerous than failing to notice a ripened fruit on a tree. Recognizing the kindness of a friend is good and virtuous, but not as significant as ignoring the animosity of an enemy. One traitor can betray an entire nation.

It follows that the stick is a more powerful motivator than the carrot. Fear of the curse is more likely to affect behavior than desire for the blessing.

The central question to which the Torah is the answer is: can there be a society of law-governed liberty, in which the rule of law prevails without the use of human force, in which the rich honor their responsibilities to the poor, justice

ו וְנָתַתִּי שָׁלוֹם בָּאָרֶץ וּשְׁכַבְתֶּם וְאֵין מַחֲרִיד וְהִשְׁבַּתִּי שני
ז חַיָּה רָעָה מִן־הָאָרֶץ וְחֶרֶב לֹא־תַעֲבֹר בְּאַרְצְכֶם: וּרְדַפְתֶּם
ח אֶת־אֹיְבֵיכֶם וְנָפְלוּ לִפְנֵיכֶם לֶחָרֶב: וְרָדְפוּ מִכֶּם חֲמִשָּׁה מֵאָה
וּמֵאָה מִכֶּם רְבָבָה יִרְדֹּפוּ וְנָפְלוּ אֹיְבֵיכֶם לִפְנֵיכֶם לֶחָרֶב:
ט וּפָנִיתִי אֲלֵיכֶם וְהִפְרֵיתִי אֶתְכֶם וְהִרְבֵּיתִי אֶתְכֶם וַהֲקִימֹתִי
י אֶת־בְּרִיתִי אִתְּכֶם: וַאֲכַלְתֶּם יָשָׁן נוֹשָׁן וְיָשָׁן מִפְּנֵי חָדָשׁ שלישי /חמישי/
יא תּוֹצִיאוּ: וְנָתַתִּי מִשְׁכָּנִי בְּתוֹכְכֶם וְלֹא־תִגְעַל נַפְשִׁי אֶתְכֶם:
יב וְהִתְהַלַּכְתִּי בְּתוֹכְכֶם וְהָיִיתִי לָכֶם לֵאלֹהִים וְאַתֶּם תִּהְיוּ־
יג לִי לְעָם: אֲנִי יהוה אֱלֹהֵיכֶם אֲשֶׁר הוֹצֵאתִי אֶתְכֶם מֵאֶרֶץ
מִצְרַיִם מִהְיֹת לָהֶם עֲבָדִים וָאֶשְׁבֹּר מֹטֹת עֻלְּכֶם וָאוֹלֵךְ
אֶתְכֶם קוֹמְמִיּוּת:
יד וְאִם־לֹא תִשְׁמְעוּ לִי וְלֹא תַעֲשׂוּ אֵת כָּל־הַמִּצְוֺת הָאֵלֶּה:
טו וְאִם־בְּחֻקֹּתַי תִּמְאָסוּ וְאִם אֶת־מִשְׁפָּטַי תִּגְעַל נַפְשְׁכֶם

less than God, and must believe that all human beings are created in His image. It rests on the choice Moshe is later to define in these words: "I call heaven and earth as witnesses against you today: I have set before you life and death, the blessing and the curse. Choose life – so that you and your children may live" (Deut. 30:19).

26:6 וְנָתַתִּי שָׁלוֹם *I will grant peace* – Against the backdrop of the economic legislation in Parashat Behar, we are reminded that human interaction is not inescapably tragic. It is not destined to be agonistic, conflictual, a matter of victory for some and defeat for others. Market exchange turns difference into a form of blessing from which not only I, but others also, benefit. It follows organically that when the people of Israel obey the laws of fair exchange, and are blessed with abundant harvest, "I will grant peace in the land."

This is in large part what differentiated biblical sensibility from that of ancient Greece. The fact that – individually, collectively, culturally – we are different can have two outcomes. It can lead to war, or it can lead to trade. Greece, with its military virtues, valued the manly arts of war. Jews, with their deep experience of suffering and exile, learned early to prefer peace.

THE CURSES

This passage – traditionally known as the *tokheḥa*, "the admonition" – is one of the most terrifying passages in literature. To this day we read it sotto voce, so fearful is it and so difficult to internalize and imagine. It is all the more fearful given what we know of later Jewish history.

My laws, not keeping all My commands; violating My
16 covenant – then I will do this to you: I will appoint over
you terror, consumption, and fever, which make your
eyes fail and your spirit languish. In vain shall you sow
17 your seed, for your enemies will eat its yield. I shall set
My face against you. You will be struck down before your
enemies. Those who hate you will rule over you; you will
18 flee, though no one chases you. And if, in spite of all this,
you still will not listen to Me, I shall punish you seven
19 times over for your sins. I will break down the majesty
of your power. I will make your sky like iron, your land
20 like brass. Your strength will be spent in vain. Your land
will not yield its produce, nor the trees of the land their
21 fruit. If you still walk contrary to Me and refuse to listen

---

is today known as a victim culture. It locates the source of evil outside oneself. Someone else is to blame. The attraction of this logic can be overpowering. It calls for, and often evokes, compassion. It is, however, deeply destructive. It leads people to see themselves as objects, not subjects. The results are anger, resentment, rage, and a burning sense of injustice. None of these ever leads to freedom, since by its very logic this mindset abdicates responsibility for the current circumstances in which one finds oneself. Blaming others is the suicide of liberty.

Blaming oneself, by contrast, is difficult. It means living with constant self-criticism. It is not a route to peace of mind. Yet it is profoundly empowering. It implies that, precisely because we accept responsibility for the bad things that have happened, we also have the ability to chart a different course in the future. Within the terms set by covenant, the outcome depends on us.

The politics of responsibility is not easy. The curses of this chapter are the very reverse of comforting. Yet the consolations with which they end are not accidental, nor are they wishful thinking. They are testimony to the power of the human spirit when summoned to the highest vocation. A nation that sees itself as responsible for the evils that befall it is also a nation that has an inextinguishable power of recovery and return.

26:21 וְאִם־תֵּלְכוּ עִמִּי קֶרִי *Walk contrary* – The keyword of the curses is *keri*. The word appears here seven times – and nowhere else in the entire Tanakh. The basic principle is clear. "If you act toward Me with *keri* – says God – I will act toward you with *keri*," However, what the word means is not clear. The various translations include rebelliousness, obstinacy, indifference, hard-heartedness and reluctance. Rambam (*Hilkhot Taaniyot* 1:1–3), however, understands

טז לְבִלְתִּי עֲשׂוֹת אֶת־כׇּל־מִצְוֺתַי לְהַפְרְכֶם אֶת־בְּרִיתִי׃ אַף־אֲנִי
אֶעֱשֶׂה־זֹּאת לָכֶם וְהִפְקַדְתִּי עֲלֵיכֶם בֶּהָלָה אֶת־הַשַּׁחֶפֶת
וְאֶת־הַקַּדַּחַת מְכַלּוֹת עֵינַיִם וּמְדִיבֹת נָפֶשׁ וּזְרַעְתֶּם לָרִיק
יז זַרְעֲכֶם וַאֲכָלֻהוּ אֹיְבֵיכֶם׃ וְנָתַתִּי פָנַי בָּכֶם וְנִגַּפְתֶּם לִפְנֵי
יח אֹיְבֵיכֶם וְרָדוּ בָכֶם שֹׂנְאֵיכֶם וְנַסְתֶּם וְאֵין־רֹדֵף אֶתְכֶם׃ וְאִם־
עַד־אֵלֶּה לֹא תִשְׁמְעוּ לִי וְיָסַפְתִּי לְיַסְּרָה אֶתְכֶם שֶׁבַע עַל־
יט חַטֹּאתֵיכֶם׃ וְשָׁבַרְתִּי אֶת־גְּאוֹן עֻזְּכֶם וְנָתַתִּי אֶת־שְׁמֵיכֶם
כ כַּבַּרְזֶל וְאֶת־אַרְצְכֶם כַּנְּחֻשָׁה׃ וְתַם לָרִיק כֹּחֲכֶם וְלֹא־תִתֵּן
כא אַרְצְכֶם אֶת־יְבוּלָהּ וְעֵץ הָאָרֶץ לֹא יִתֵּן פִּרְיוֹ׃ וְאִם־תֵּלְכוּ
עִמִּי קֶרִי וְלֹא תֹאבוּ לִשְׁמֹעַ לִי וְיָסַפְתִּי עֲלֵיכֶם מַכָּה שֶׁבַע

---

is impartial, and the principles of welfare are such that extremes of poverty are eliminated? Such is the vision behind the covenant society inaugurated at Mount Sinai. It was essential, therefore, that the promise of reward and the threat of punishment be sufficiently powerful to have an impact on the people as a whole, for it was they who bore responsibility for the fate of the nation. They had to secure the rule of law without relying on a liberty-restricting government to do it for them.

The more people believe that God punishes wrongdoers, the less likely they are to cheat their fellow human beings when no one else is looking. When given the opportunity to punish someone violating a social norm, empirical research finds that believers in a punitive God are less likely to do so than others. In other words, belief that God will punish offenders makes people more forgiving.

The more we internalize the idea that we are accountable to Heaven for what we do, the less likely we are to give way to temptation by cheating or bending the rules. The more social institutions can rely on trust, the less they have to rely on laws, police, regulations, surveillance, and punishment as deterrence. So, in a strange way, belief in curses creates blessings. It gives people the strongest possible motive for self-restraint, promotes trust in society, and secures order while minimizing external constraints on freedom.

26:18 וְאִם־עַד־אֵלֶּה לֹא תִשְׁמְעוּ לִי *And if, in spite of all this, you still will not listen to Me* – In the face of suffering and loss, there are two fundamentally different questions an individual or nation can ask, and they lead to quite different outcomes. The first is "What did I, or we, do wrong?" The second is "Who did this to us?" It is not an exaggeration to say that this is the fundamental choice governing the destinies of people.

The latter leads inescapably to what

22 to Me, I will strike you seven times over for your sins: I
will send wild animals against you. They will bereave
you of your children and annihilate your cattle. They
will make you few in number and your roads will be
23 deserted. If, despite all this, you still do not accept My
24 discipline and still you walk contrary to Me, then I too
will walk contrary to you and strike you seven times over
25 for your sins. I will bring a sword against you to avenge
the broken covenant. If you retreat into your cities, I shall
send pestilence against you, and you will be delivered up
26 into your enemy's hand. When I cut off your supply of
bread, ten women shall bake bread in a single oven. They
will ration it out by weight, and you will eat but not be
27 full. If, despite all this, you still do not listen to
28 Me – if still you walk contrary to Me – then I, in My fury,
will walk contrary to you. I will punish you seven times
29 more for your sins: you shall eat the flesh of your own
30 sons; the flesh of your own daughters you shall eat. I will
destroy your high shrines, cut down your incense altars,
and heap your corpses on the corpses of your idols. I shall
31 despise you. I will turn your cities into ruins and make
your sanctuaries desolate. I will not savor your pleasing
32 aromas. I Myself will devastate the land, so that your
33 enemies who settle there will be appalled. I shall scatter
you among the nations; I will draw My sword against you.
34 Your land will be desolate; your cities, ruins. Then shall
the land make appeasement for its Sabbaths for as long as
it lies desolate and you are in your enemies' lands. Then
the land will rest and make appeasement for its Sabbaths.
35 In its desolation, the land will have the rest it did not have
36 during the Sabbaths when you were dwelling there. As for
the survivors, I will bring such insecurity into their hearts

midda keneged midda (Shabbat 105b). If Israel believes in divine providence, it will be blessed by divine providence. If it sees history as mere chance, then indeed they will be left to chance. And since Israel is a small nation surrounded by large empires, chance will not be kind to them.

כב כְּחַטֹּאתֵיכֶם: וְהִשְׁלַחְתִּי בָכֶם אֶת־חַיַּת הַשָּׂדֶה וְשִׁכְּלָה
אֶתְכֶם וְהִכְרִיתָה אֶת־בְּהֶמְתְּכֶם וְהִמְעִיטָה אֶתְכֶם וְנָשַׁמּוּ
כג דַּרְכֵיכֶם: וְאִם־בְּאֵלֶּה לֹא תִוָּסְרוּ לִי וַהֲלַכְתֶּם עִמִּי קֶרִי:
כד וְהָלַכְתִּי אַף־אֲנִי עִמָּכֶם בְּקֶרִי וְהִכֵּיתִי אֶתְכֶם גַּם־אָנִי שֶׁבַע
כה עַל־חַטֹּאתֵיכֶם: וְהֵבֵאתִי עֲלֵיכֶם חֶרֶב נֹקֶמֶת נְקַם־בְּרִית
וְנֶאֱסַפְתֶּם אֶל־עָרֵיכֶם וְשִׁלַּחְתִּי דֶבֶר בְּתוֹכְכֶם וְנִתַּתֶּם בְּיַד־
כו אוֹיֵב: בְּשִׁבְרִי לָכֶם מַטֵּה־לֶחֶם וְאָפוּ עֶשֶׂר נָשִׁים לַחְמְכֶם
בְּתַנּוּר אֶחָד וְהֵשִׁיבוּ לַחְמְכֶם בַּמִּשְׁקָל וַאֲכַלְתֶּם וְלֹא
כז תִשְׂבָּעוּ: וְאִם־בְּזֹאת לֹא תִשְׁמְעוּ לִי וַהֲלַכְתֶּם
כח עִמִּי בְּקֶרִי: וְהָלַכְתִּי עִמָּכֶם בַּחֲמַת־קֶרִי וְיִסַּרְתִּי אֶתְכֶם
כט אַף־אָנִי שֶׁבַע עַל־חַטֹּאתֵיכֶם: וַאֲכַלְתֶּם בְּשַׂר בְּנֵיכֶם וּבְשַׂר
ל בְּנֹתֵיכֶם תֹּאכֵלוּ: וְהִשְׁמַדְתִּי אֶת־בָּמֹתֵיכֶם וְהִכְרַתִּי אֶת־
חַמָּנֵיכֶם וְנָתַתִּי אֶת־פִּגְרֵיכֶם עַל־פִּגְרֵי גִּלּוּלֵיכֶם וְגָעֲלָה נַפְשִׁי
לא אֶתְכֶם: וְנָתַתִּי אֶת־עָרֵיכֶם חָרְבָּה וַהֲשִׁמּוֹתִי אֶת־מִקְדְּשֵׁיכֶם
לב וְלֹא אָרִיחַ בְּרֵיחַ נִיחֹחֲכֶם: וַהֲשִׁמֹּתִי אֲנִי אֶת־הָאָרֶץ וְשָׁמְמוּ
לג עָלֶיהָ אֹיְבֵיכֶם הַיֹּשְׁבִים בָּהּ: וְאֶתְכֶם אֱזָרֶה בַגּוֹיִם וַהֲרִיקֹתִי
אַחֲרֵיכֶם חָרֶב וְהָיְתָה אַרְצְכֶם שְׁמָמָה וְעָרֵיכֶם יִהְיוּ חָרְבָּה:
לד אָז תִּרְצֶה הָאָרֶץ אֶת־שַׁבְּתֹתֶיהָ כֹּל יְמֵי הָשַּׁמָּה וְאַתֶּם
בְּאֶרֶץ אֹיְבֵיכֶם אָז תִּשְׁבַּת הָאָרֶץ וְהִרְצָת אֶת־שַׁבְּתֹתֶיהָ:
לה כָּל־יְמֵי הָשַּׁמָּה תִּשְׁבֹּת אֵת אֲשֶׁר לֹא־שָׁבְתָה בְּשַׁבְּתֹתֵיכֶם
לו בְּשִׁבְתְּכֶם עָלֶיהָ: וְהַנִּשְׁאָרִים בָּכֶם וְהֵבֵאתִי מֹרֶךְ בִּלְבָבָם

keri to be related to *mikreh,* meaning "chance," the way of the world. To regard something as *mikreh* means to see it as if it had no larger significance. It just happened. That, says Rambam, is not how we as Jews should see our fate. It is not mere chance. This means that for Rambam, the curses at the end of Leviticus are not divine retribution as such. It will not be God who makes Israel suffer; it will be other human beings. What will happen is that God will withdraw His protection. Israel will have to face the world without the sheltering presence of God.

This, for Rambam, is an application of the principle of measure for measure,

in their enemies' lands that the sound of a windblown leaf
will make them run as if they fled the sword; and they
37 will fall, though no one is chasing them. They will stumble
over one another as if fleeing the sword, when no one
chases them. You will have no power to stand before your
38 enemies. You will perish among the nations; your enemies'
39 lands will devour you. Those of you who survive will
waste away in their enemies' lands because of their sins –
40 for their ancestors' sins also, they will waste away. But if
they confess their sins and those of their ancestors – their
trespass against Me and their walking contrary to Me,
41 which made Me walk contrary to them, bringing them
into their enemies' lands – if their obstinate hearts are
42 humbled and they atone for their sin, then I will remember
My covenant with Yaakov; and My covenant with Yitzḥak
and My covenant with Avraham I will also remember,
43 and I will remember the land. The land will be deserted,

---

political system and sovereign power. Our horizons of possibility are shaped by the society and culture within which we live. What is unusual about Judaism is that the principle applies to a people scattered throughout the world. Jews are linked to one another by the same ties of mutual responsibility that they had in the land – for it was the covenant that formed them as a nation and bound them to one another even as it bound them to God. Therefore, even when falling over one another in flight from their enemies, they will still be bound by mutual responsibility. They will still be a nation with a shared fate and destiny.

We can see now why the Sages chose their proof text from the curses of Parashat Beḥukotai. Most other Mosaic texts refer to Israel's fate as a nation in, and journeying toward, its land. But this passage spoke of exile and "the hiding of the face" of God. All Israel are responsible for one another, even in dispersion and defeat, even when they are no longer a nation in any conventional sense. Though they may be scattered across the world, divided by space, language, culture, and outward fortune, Jews remain a people, bound to one another in and through their covenant with God. Though they are parted physically, they remain united spiritually, and that unity will one day give them the strength to return to God and to the land He gave their ancestors.

And so it happened. Thus was a curse turned into a blessing, and a description of weakness turned into a source of indomitable strength.

בארצת איביהם ורדף אתם קול עלה נדף ונסו מנסת־
לז חרב ונפלו ואין רדף: וכשלו איש־באחיו כמפני־חרב
לח ורדף אין ולא־תהיה לכם תקומה לפני איביכם: ואבדתם
לט בגוים ואכלה אתכם ארץ איביכם: והנשארים בכם ימקו
בעונם בארצת איביכם ואף בעונת אבתם אתם ימקו:
מ והתודו את־עונם ואת־עון אבתם במעלם אשר מעלו־
מא בי ואף אשר־הלכו עמי בקרי: אף־אני אלך עמם בקרי
והבאתי אתם בארץ איביהם או־אז יכנע לבבם הערל ואז
מב ירצו את־עונם: וזכרתי את־בריתי יעקוב ואף את־בריתי
מג יצחק ואף את־בריתי אברהם אזכר והארץ אזכר: והארץ

COLLECTIVE RESPONSIBILITY

There is, on the face of it, nothing positive in this nightmare scenario. But the Sages learned from it a fundamental idea: "'They will stumble over one another' – read this as 'stumble because of one another's sins': this teaches that all Israelites are responsible for one another" (Sifra ad loc.; Shevuot 39a).

The rule of *kol Yisrael arevin zeh bazeh,* all Israel are responsible for one another, not just individually, but before God – is one of the great principles of rabbinic Judaism. We are all in the same boat. My actions do not affect me alone. They have consequences for the whole of society. The idea of collective destiny and responsibility is more than just a metaphor. It is constitutive of Jewish identity.

But why locate this principle here? "Stumbling over one another" is not a description of a nation bound by mutual suretyship. It is an account of panic. In their hurry to escape, people fall over one another. Each is concerned with his own safety, not the common good. Whatever prompted the rabbinic interpretation, it was not the plain sense of the verse. Conversely, the notion that Jews have collective responsibility, that their fate and destiny are interlinked, could have been found in many places throughout the Torah. The Torah, from Exodus onward, is dedicated to this principle. It is basic to Moshe's vision and to the people's experience. They suffered slavery together. They experienced liberation together. The second paragraph of the *Shema* (Deut. 11:13–17) teaches that the people will prosper together or suffer together. Why locate the principle of mutual responsibility among the Torah's curses?

To understand this, note first that there is nothing unique to Judaism in the idea that we are all implicated in one another's fate. That is true of the citizens of any nation under the same

making appeasement for its Sabbaths, lying desolate of
them, while they will be making appeasement for their
sins, because they rejected My laws, because they despised
44 My statutes. Yet even then, when they are in the land of
their enemies, I will not reject them nor despise them and
annihilate them, will not break My covenant with them,
45 for I am the Lord their God. I will remember for them

---

the people He chose to be a living example of faith. The covenant transforms our understanding of history. God has given His word and will not break it. Without these beliefs we would have no reason to hope.

History as conceived in this *parasha* is not utopian. No one reading this chapter can be an optimist. Yet no one sensitive to its message can abandon hope. Without belief in the covenant and its insistence of "Yet even then…" there might have been no Jewish people today.

26:44 כִּי אֲנִי יהוה אֱלֹהֵיהֶם *For I am the Lord their God* – This is a fundamental statement upon which Judaism rests. It says that though the people may be faithless to God, God will never be faithless to the people. He may judge them harshly but He will not forget their ancestors who followed Him. God does not break His promises even if we break ours.

This verse testifies against the traditional Christian doctrine known as supersessionism or replacement theology, which maintains that Christianity represents God's rejection of the Jewish people, the "old Israel." It says that God once had a covenant with the Jewish people, but no longer. His new chosen people are not Jews but Christians. That doctrine is incompatible with this passage in Parashat Beḥukotai. God may send His people into exile but they remain His people.

It is not an isolated verse. Examination of the Torah as a whole reveals an underlying principle, namely the *rejection of rejection*. At first, God rejects humanity, saving only Noaḥ, when He sees the world full of violence. Yet after the flood He vows: "Never again will I curse the land because of man; the devisings of the human heart are evil from its youth. And never again will I destroy all life as I have done" (Gen. 8:21). That is the first *rejection of rejection.*

Then come a series of sibling rivalries. The covenant passes through Yitzḥak not Yishmael, Yaakov not Esav. But God sees Hagar's and Yishmael's tears. Evidently, He sees Esav's also, for He later commands, "Do not despise an Edomite [i.e., a descendant of Esav], for he is your kin" (Deut. 23:8). Finally God brings it about that Levi, one of the children Yaakov curses on his deathbed – "Cursed be their anger, for it is most fierce, and their fury, for it is most cruel" (Gen. 49:7) – becomes the father

תֵּעָזֵב מֵהֶם וְתִרֶץ אֶת־שַׁבְּתֹתֶיהָ בָּהְשַׁמָּה מֵהֶם וְהֵם יִרְצוּ
אֶת־עֲוֺנָם יַעַן וּבְיַעַן בְּמִשְׁפָּטַי מָאָסוּ וְאֶת־חֻקֹּתַי גָּעֲלָה
מד נַפְשָׁם: וְאַף גַּם־זֹאת בִּהְיוֹתָם בְּאֶרֶץ אֹיְבֵיהֶם לֹא־מְאַסְתִּים
וְלֹא־גְעַלְתִּים לְכַלֹּתָם לְהָפֵר בְּרִיתִי אִתָּם כִּי אֲנִי יהוה
מה אֱלֹהֵיהֶם: וְזָכַרְתִּי לָהֶם בְּרִית רִאשֹׁנִים אֲשֶׁר הוֹצֵאתִי־אֹתָם

THE BIRTH OF HOPE

After the terrifying curses warning that if Israel betrays its divine mission, it will forfeit its freedom and land, there is a sudden change of key. The end of the chapter holds a turning point. It is the birth of hope: not hope as a dream, a wish, a desire, but as the very shape of history. God is just. He may punish. He may hide His face. But He will not break His word. He will fulfill His promise and redeem His children.

Hope is one of the great Jewish contributions to Western civilization. In the ancient world, there were tragic cultures in which people believed that the gods were at best indifferent to our existence, at worst actively malevolent. Then there is the secular culture of the contemporary West in which the universe is seen as a series of meaningless accidents with no redeeming purpose. Hope is not unknown in these cultures, but it is what Aristotle called "a waking dream," a private wish that things may be otherwise. Seen through the eyes of ancient Greece or contemporary science, there is nothing in the texture of reality to justify belief that the human condition could be other or better than it is.

There is nothing inevitable or even rational about hope. It cannot be inferred from any facts about the past or present. Those with a tragic sense of life hold that hope is an illusion and that a mature response to our place in the universe is to accept its meaninglessness and cultivate stoic acceptance. Judaism insists otherwise: that the reality that underlies the universe is not deaf to our prayers, blind to our aspirations, indifferent to our existence.

We hear this note at several points in the Torah. It occurs twice, for instance, at the end of Genesis when first Yaakov and then Yosef assure the other members of the covenantal family that their stay in Egypt will not be endless. God will honor His promise and bring them back to the Promised Land.

But the key text is here at the end of the curses of Leviticus. This is where God promises that even if Israel sins, it may suffer, but it will never have reason to utterly despair. It may experience exile, but eventually it will return.

Hope emerged as part of the spiritual landscape of Western civilization through this quite specific set of beliefs: that God exists, that He cares about us, that He has made a covenant with humanity and a further covenant with

the covenant with their ancestors whom I brought out of
Egypt in the sight of the nations, to be their God; I am the
46 Lord." These are the statutes, laws, and instructions that
the Lord established between Himself and the Israelites,
through Moshe, on Mount Sinai.
27 1 2 The Lord spoke to Moshe: "Speak to the Israelites. Say: REVI'I /SHISHI/
When a person makes a spoken vow to the Lord to give
3 the equivalent of the value of a person – if it is a male
from twenty to sixty years old, his equivalent is fifty
4 silver shekel by the Sanctuary weight. If it is a female, the
5 equivalent is thirty shekel. If the person's age is between
five and twenty years, the equivalent for a male is twenty
6 shekel, and for a female, ten shekel. If the age is between
one month and five years, the equivalent for a male is five
7 silver shekel; for a female, three silver shekel. If the age
is sixty years or more, the equivalent for a male is fifteen
8 shekel, and for a female, ten shekel. But if the person is
too poor to pay the full amount, he shall be presented to
the priest, who will assess him. The priest shall assess him
with reference to the means of the person making the
9 vow. If the vow concerns an animal of a type that
may be offered to the Lord, any such animal given to the

> have perished so long ago, these still exist, despite the efforts of so many powerful kings who have tried a hundred times to wipe them out, as their historians testify, and as can easily be judged by the natural order of things over such a long spell of years. They have always been preserved, however, and their preservation was foretold.... My encounter with this people amazes me.

There is pain in this history. Yet it remains astonishing. The curses of the *tokheḥa* came true – but so did the consolation. No nation was attacked so often. Empire after empire pronounced their destruction. Yet the empires vanished into oblivion while the people Israel still lives, small, vulnerable, yet still there, defying all the natural laws that govern the history of nations. There is a mystery here, as Pascal so clearly saw. Yet its basic formulation is clear, and despite all the odds it came true: the people of the eternal God became the people of eternity.

מֵאֶרֶץ מִצְרַיִם לְעֵינֵי הַגּוֹיִם לִהְיוֹת לָהֶם לֵאלֹהִים אֲנִי יְהוָה׃
מו אֵלֶּה הַחֻקִּים וְהַמִּשְׁפָּטִים וְהַתּוֹרֹת אֲשֶׁר נָתַן יְהוָה בֵּינוֹ וּבֵין
בְּנֵי יִשְׂרָאֵל בְּהַר סִינַי בְּיַד־מֹשֶׁה׃
כז א ב וַיְדַבֵּר יְהוָה אֶל־מֹשֶׁה לֵּאמֹר׃ דַּבֵּר אֶל־בְּנֵי יִשְׂרָאֵל וְאָמַרְתָּ כג רביעי /ששי/
ג אֲלֵהֶם אִישׁ כִּי יַפְלִא נֶדֶר בְּעֶרְכְּךָ נְפָשֹׁת לַיהוָה׃ וְהָיָה עֶרְכְּךָ
הַזָּכָר מִבֶּן עֶשְׂרִים שָׁנָה וְעַד בֶּן־שִׁשִּׁים שָׁנָה וְהָיָה עֶרְכְּךָ
ד חֲמִשִּׁים שֶׁקֶל כֶּסֶף בְּשֶׁקֶל הַקֹּדֶשׁ׃ וְאִם־נְקֵבָה הִוא וְהָיָה
ה עֶרְכְּךָ שְׁלֹשִׁים שָׁקֶל׃ וְאִם מִבֶּן־חָמֵשׁ שָׁנִים וְעַד בֶּן־עֶשְׂרִים
שָׁנָה וְהָיָה עֶרְכְּךָ הַזָּכָר עֶשְׂרִים שְׁקָלִים וְלַנְּקֵבָה עֲשֶׂרֶת
ו שְׁקָלִים׃ וְאִם מִבֶּן־חֹדֶשׁ וְעַד בֶּן־חָמֵשׁ שָׁנִים וְהָיָה עֶרְכְּךָ
הַזָּכָר חֲמִשָּׁה שְׁקָלִים כָּסֶף וְלַנְּקֵבָה עֶרְכְּךָ שְׁלֹשֶׁת שְׁקָלִים
ז כָּסֶף׃ וְאִם מִבֶּן־שִׁשִּׁים שָׁנָה וָמַעְלָה אִם־זָכָר וְהָיָה עֶרְכְּךָ
ח חֲמִשָּׁה עָשָׂר שָׁקֶל וְלַנְּקֵבָה עֲשָׂרָה שְׁקָלִים׃ וְאִם־מָךְ הוּא
מֵעֶרְכֶּךָ וְהֶעֱמִידוֹ לִפְנֵי הַכֹּהֵן וְהֶעֱרִיךְ אֹתוֹ הַכֹּהֵן עַל־פִּי
ט אֲשֶׁר תַּשִּׂיג יַד הַנֹּדֵר יַעֲרִיכֶנּוּ הַכֹּהֵן׃ וְאִם־
בְּהֵמָה אֲשֶׁר יַקְרִיבוּ מִמֶּנָּה קָרְבָּן לַיהוָה כֹּל אֲשֶׁר יִתֵּן מִמֶּנּוּ

of Israel's spiritual leaders, Moshe, Aharon, and Miriam. From now on, all Israel are chosen. That is the second rejection of rejection.

Even when Israel suffer exile and find themselves "in the land of their enemies," they will remain the children of God's covenant, which He will not break, because God does not abandon His people. They may be faithless to Him. He will not be faithless to them. That is the third rejection of rejection, stated in this *parasha*. The God of Avraham keeps His promises.

26:45 אֲנִי יהוה *I am the Lord* – Many attempts have been made to prove the existence of God. Theologians have argued on the basis of philosophy, and in some cases the natural sciences (the "argument from design"). Yet the Torah speaks of a different kind of proof altogether: the history of Israel.

The great mathematician and theologian Blaise Pascal wrote this:

> The Jewish people ... is not only of remarkable antiquity but has also lasted for a singularly long time.... For whereas the peoples of Greece and Italy, of Sparta, Athens, and Rome, and others who came so much later

10 Lord becomes sacred. One may not exchange it or offer a
substitute for it, either better for worse or worse for better;
and if one animal is substituted for another, both it and
11 the substitute become holy. If the vow involves any type
of impure animal, which cannot be offered to the Lord,
12 the animal shall be brought to stand before the priest. The
priest shall assess it, whether good or bad, and its value
13 shall accord to the priest's assessment. If the donor wishes
14 to redeem it, a fifth shall be added to its valuation. When
someone consecrates his house to be sacred to the Lord,
the priest shall assess it, whether good or bad, and its
15 value shall accord to the priest's assessment. If the donor
wishes to redeem it, he shall add a fifth to its valuation,
16 and it shall be his again. If someone consecrates part of ḤAMISHI /SHEVI'I/
his hereditary land to the Lord, its value shall be set in
relation to the seed needed to sow it: fifty silver shekel
17 for each homer of barley seed. If the person consecrates
his field from the Jubilee year, the value that has been set
18 stands. But if the person consecrates the field after the
Jubilee, the priest shall calculate its value in relation to
the number of years left until the next Jubilee year, and
19 the valuation shall be reduced accordingly. If the person
who consecrated the field wishes to redeem it, he shall
20 add a fifth to its valuation, and it shall be his again. But
if he does not redeem the field, or if it has been sold to
21 someone else, it can no longer be redeemed. When the
field is released in the Jubilee, it shall be holy to the Lord
like devoted land; it comes into the priest's possession.
22 If the person consecrates to the Lord a field he has SHISHI
23 purchased – not part of his hereditary land – the priest

---

it was Eli. He ran to see what he wanted but Eli told him he had not called. This happened a second time and then a third, and by then Eli realized that it was God calling the child. He told Shmuel that the next time the voice called his name, he should reply, "Speak, O Lord, for Your servant is listening" (I Sam. 3:9). It did not occur to the child that it might be God summoning him to a mission, but it was. In his case, consecration was linked to an audible calling.

י לַיהוָה יִהְיֶה־קֹּדֶשׁ: לֹא יַחֲלִיפֶנּוּ וְלֹא־יָמִיר אֹתוֹ טוֹב בְּרָע
אוֹ־רַע בְּטוֹב וְאִם־הָמֵר יָמִיר בְּהֵמָה בִּבְהֵמָה וְהָיָה־הוּא
יא וּתְמוּרָתוֹ יִהְיֶה־קֹּדֶשׁ: וְאִם כָּל־בְּהֵמָה טְמֵאָה אֲשֶׁר לֹא־
יַקְרִיבוּ מִמֶּנָּה קָרְבָּן לַיהוָה וְהֶעֱמִיד אֶת־הַבְּהֵמָה לִפְנֵי
יב הַכֹּהֵן: וְהֶעֱרִיךְ הַכֹּהֵן אֹתָהּ בֵּין טוֹב וּבֵין רָע כְּעֶרְכְּךָ הַכֹּהֵן
יג יד כֵּן יִהְיֶה: וְאִם־גָּאֹל יִגְאָלֶנָּה וְיָסַף חֲמִישִׁתוֹ עַל־עֶרְכֶּךָ: וְאִישׁ
כִּי־יַקְדִּשׁ אֶת־בֵּיתוֹ קֹדֶשׁ לַיהוָה וְהֶעֱרִיכוֹ הַכֹּהֵן בֵּין טוֹב
טו וּבֵין רָע כַּאֲשֶׁר יַעֲרִיךְ אֹתוֹ הַכֹּהֵן כֵּן יָקוּם: וְאִם־הַמַּקְדִּישׁ
יִגְאַל אֶת־בֵּיתוֹ וְיָסַף חֲמִישִׁית כֶּסֶף־עֶרְכְּךָ עָלָיו וְהָיָה לוֹ:
טז וְאִם ׀ מִשְּׂדֵה אֲחֻזָּתוֹ יַקְדִּישׁ אִישׁ לַיהוָה וְהָיָה עֶרְכְּךָ לְפִי חמישי /שביעי/
יז זַרְעוֹ זֶרַע חֹמֶר שְׂעֹרִים בַּחֲמִשִּׁים שֶׁקֶל כָּסֶף: אִם־מִשְּׁנַת
יח הַיֹּבֵל יַקְדִּישׁ שָׂדֵהוּ כְּעֶרְכְּךָ יָקוּם: וְאִם־אַחַר הַיֹּבֵל יַקְדִּישׁ
שָׂדֵהוּ וְחִשַּׁב־לוֹ הַכֹּהֵן אֶת־הַכֶּסֶף עַל־פִּי הַשָּׁנִים הַנּוֹתָרֹת
יט עַד שְׁנַת הַיֹּבֵל וְנִגְרַע מֵעֶרְכֶּךָ: וְאִם־גָּאֹל יִגְאַל אֶת־הַשָּׂדֶה
כ הַמַּקְדִּישׁ אֹתוֹ וְיָסַף חֲמִשִׁית כֶּסֶף־עֶרְכְּךָ עָלָיו וְקָם לוֹ: וְאִם־
לֹא יִגְאַל אֶת־הַשָּׂדֶה וְאִם־מָכַר אֶת־הַשָּׂדֶה לְאִישׁ אַחֵר
כא לֹא־יִגָּאֵל עוֹד: וְהָיָה הַשָּׂדֶה בְּצֵאתוֹ בַיֹּבֵל קֹדֶשׁ לַיהוָה
כב כִּשְׂדֵה הַחֵרֶם לַכֹּהֵן תִּהְיֶה אֲחֻזָּתוֹ: וְאִם אֶת־שְׂדֵה מִקְנָתוֹ ששי
כג אֲשֶׁר לֹא מִשְּׂדֵה אֲחֻזָּתוֹ יַקְדִּישׁ לַיהוָה: וְחִשַּׁב־לוֹ הַכֹּהֵן
אֵת מִכְסַת הָעֶרְכְּךָ עַד שְׁנַת הַיֹּבֵל וְנָתַן אֶת־הָעֶרְכְּךָ בַּיּוֹם

LAWS OF CONSECRATION

The closing passage of Leviticus delineates some of the rules of *hekdesh*, "consecrating" – the process of setting a house, a field, an animal, or even oneself aside to be "sacred to the Lord." Our passage presupposes that in many cases the consecration will be symbolic, and a monetary donation to the Tabernacle will substitute for the person, animal, or place set aside. But sometimes the consecration was quite literal.

One example is the story of the young Shmuel, dedicated by his mother Ḥana to serve in the Sanctuary at Shilo where he acted as an assistant to Eli the priest. In bed one night Shmuel heard a voice calling his name. He assumed

shall calculate its proportionate value until the Jubilee
year, and the donor shall pay its valuation on that day,
24 as a sacred donation to the Lord. In the Jubilee year the
field shall return to the person from whom it was bought,
25 whose hereditary land it was. All assessments shall follow
the Sanctuary standard, by which a shekel is twenty gerah.
26 A person cannot consecrate a firstborn animal, whether
ox or sheep, because, being a firstling, it already belongs
27 to the Lord. If it is an impure animal, it may be redeemed
for its valuation with a fifth added. If it is not redeemed,
28 it shall be sold at its assessed value. Nothing that a person
owns that has been devoted to the Lord – be it a person,
an animal, or inherited land – may be sold or redeemed.
29 Every devoted thing is holy of holies to the Lord. And no SHEVI'I
person condemned to utter destruction may be ransomed;
30 he must be put to death. All tithes from the land, whether
seed from the ground or fruit of the tree, belong to the
31 Lord; they are sacred to the Lord. If a person wishes to
redeem part of his tithe, he shall add a fifth to its value.
32 All tithes from the herd or flock – every tenth animal that MAFTIR
passes under the shepherd's staff – shall be sacred to the
33 Lord. One should not pick out the good from the bad or
make any substitution. But if a substitution is made, both
the item and its substitute shall be sacred; they cannot be
34 redeemed." These are the commands that the Lord gave
Moshe, on Mount Sinai, for the people of Israel.

The haftara for Parashat Beḥukotai is on page 1548 (even when Behar and Beḥukotai are read together).

holiness, summoning the people with whom He covenanted to a life driven by its energy, transformed by its alignment with the will and word of the Creator.

The end of the book, like its beginning, invites us to consider what it would mean for us to live a consecrated, dedicated life. We can suggest this as a guide: where what we want to do meets what needs to be done, that is where God wants us to be. For each of us God has a task: work to perform, a kindness to show, a gift to give, love to share, loneliness to ease, pain to heal, or broken lives to help mend. One of the great spiritual challenges for each of us is discerning that task, hearing *Vayikra*, God's call.

כד הַהוּא קֹדֶשׁ לַיהוָה: בִּשְׁנַת הַיּוֹבֵל יָשׁוּב הַשָּׂדֶה לַאֲשֶׁר קָנָהוּ
כה מֵאִתּוֹ לַאֲשֶׁר־לוֹ אֲחֻזַּת הָאָרֶץ: וְכָל־עֶרְכְּךָ יִהְיֶה בְּשֶׁקֶל
כו הַקֹּדֶשׁ עֶשְׂרִים גֵּרָה יִהְיֶה הַשָּׁקֶל: אַךְ־בְּכוֹר אֲשֶׁר יְבֻכַּר
לַיהוָה בִּבְהֵמָה לֹא־יַקְדִּישׁ אִישׁ אֹתוֹ אִם־שׁוֹר אִם־שֶׂה
כז לַיהוָה הוּא: וְאִם בַּבְּהֵמָה הַטְּמֵאָה וּפָדָה בְעֶרְכֶּךָ וְיָסַף
כח חֲמִשִׁתוֹ עָלָיו וְאִם־לֹא יִגָּאֵל וְנִמְכַּר בְּעֶרְכֶּךָ: אַךְ כָּל־חֵרֶם
אֲשֶׁר יַחֲרִם אִישׁ לַיהוָה מִכָּל־אֲשֶׁר־לוֹ מֵאָדָם וּבְהֵמָה
וּמִשְּׂדֵה אֲחֻזָּתוֹ לֹא יִמָּכֵר וְלֹא יִגָּאֵל כָּל־חֵרֶם קֹדֶשׁ־קָדָשִׁים
כט הוּא לַיהוָה: כָּל־חֵרֶם אֲשֶׁר יָחֳרַם מִן־הָאָדָם לֹא יִפָּדֶה שביעי
ל מוֹת יוּמָת: וְכָל־מַעְשַׂר הָאָרֶץ מִזֶּרַע הָאָרֶץ מִפְּרִי הָעֵץ
לא לַיהוָה הוּא קֹדֶשׁ לַיהוָה: וְאִם־גָּאֹל יִגְאַל אִישׁ מִמַּעַשְׂרוֹ
לב חֲמִשִׁיתוֹ יֹסֵף עָלָיו: וְכָל־מַעְשַׂר בָּקָר וָצֹאן כֹּל אֲשֶׁר־ מפטיר
לג יַעֲבֹר תַּחַת הַשָּׁבֶט הָעֲשִׂירִי יִהְיֶה־קֹּדֶשׁ לַיהוָה: לֹא יְבַקֵּר
בֵּין־טוֹב לָרַע וְלֹא יְמִירֶנּוּ וְאִם־הָמֵר יְמִירֶנּוּ וְהָיָה־הוּא
לד וּתְמוּרָתוֹ יִהְיֶה־קֹּדֶשׁ לֹא יִגָּאֵל: אֵלֶּה הַמִּצְוֹת אֲשֶׁר צִוָּה
יְהוָה אֶת־מֹשֶׁה אֶל־בְּנֵי יִשְׂרָאֵל בְּהַר סִינָי:

The הפטרה *for* פרשת בחקתי *is on page 1549*
(even when בהר *and* בחקתי *are read together).*

In a subtle way, then, the ending of the book recalls the beginning. *Vayikra*, Rashi told us then, means *to be called to a task in love*. This is the source of one of the key ideas of Western thought, namely, the concept of a *vocation* or a *calling*, that is, the choice of a career or way of life not just because you want to do it, or because it offers certain benefits, but because you feel *summoned* to it. You feel this is your meaning and mission in life. This is what you were placed on earth to do.

And why does the word appear at the beginning of the central book of the Torah? Because the book of Leviticus is about sacrifices, and a vocation is about sacrifice. *We are willing to make sacrifices when we feel they are part of the task we are called on to do.*

Not everyone who finds meaning in life does so in moral terms. But they almost always do so in terms of some project involving challenge, dedication, commitment, and effort that takes them beyond themselves. A world dominated by the self leads ultimately to meaninglessness. In Leviticus, God sets out an alternative: the mystery and majesty of

במדבר
NUMBERS

and battles fought. Both tell of a series of breakdowns of morale. In both books the people romanticize the past, thinking of Egypt not as a land of oppression but as a place of safety where they had food and security. In both, there is a major sin that threatens the entire future of the people: in Exodus, the golden calf, in Numbers, the episode of the spies.

A key difference is in the nature of the journey itself. In Exodus, it is a journey from; it is the story of an escape. In Numbers, it is a journey to, a story of approach and preparation. These are not just two halves of a single story. Exodus and Numbers represent two different kinds of liberty. Exodus is about negative freedom, *ḥofesh* in Hebrew. Numbers is about positive freedom, for which the Sages coined the word *ḥerut*. Negative freedom is what a slave acquires when he or she is liberated. There is no one to give you orders. But a society in which everyone is free to do what they choose is not a free society. It is anarchy. A free society requires codes and disciplines of self-restraint so that my freedom is not bought at the cost of yours. It is a society of law-governed liberty, or positive freedom. What matters in Exodus is how the people escape from Pharaoh. What matters in Numbers is how they rise to the challenge of self-rule and responsibility.

THE BOOK OF NUMBERS

Numbers is not an easy book to read. It is among the most self-critical books about what Nelson Mandela called "the long walk to freedom." Its message is that there is no shortcut to liberty. Numbers is a sober warning set in the midst of a text – the Torah – that remains the master narrative of hope.

The Mosaic books, especially Exodus and Numbers, are about the journey from slavery to freedom and from oppression to law-governed liberty. On the map, the distance traveled from Egypt to the Promised Land is not far. But the message of Numbers is that it always takes longer than you think. For the journey is not just physical, a walk across the desert. It is psychological, moral, and spiritual. It takes as long as the time needed for human beings to change.

Political change cannot be brought about by politics alone. It needs human transformation, brought about by rituals, habits of the heart, and a strenuous process of education. It comes along with knowledge born out of painful experience, preserved for future generations by acts of remembering. You cannot arrive at freedom merely by escaping from slavery. It is won only when a nation takes upon itself the responsibilities of self-restraint, courage, and patience.

Exodus and Numbers have much in common. Both tell of distances traversed

Parashat Bemidbar

1 1 The Lord spoke to Moshe in the Sinai Desert, in the
Tent of Meeting, on the first of the second month, in
the second year since their coming out from the land of
2 Egypt. He said: "Take a census of the entire community
of Israel by their clans and their ancestral houses, listing

Note also what is unique about the Jewish story. It is not unknown in the history of religion for founders to spend time alone – their "wilderness years" – during which their understanding of their mission takes shape. There are such stories told of the heroes of Buddhism, Christianity, and Islam. What is unique to the Jewish experience is that *this happened to an entire people*. It was not Moshe alone but the Israelites as a whole who experienced the wilderness years. This too is essential to the distributed and democratized nature of Jewish spirituality.

The way to the Holy Land lies through the wilderness. The desert was the place where the people could be alone with God. There, undistracted by the sight of natural or man-made beauty, they could hear God's voice directly. What they heard was a counterintuitive challenge: to take the pain of suffering in Egypt forward with them and redirect it into creating a society that would be the opposite of Egypt, not an empire built on power but a society of individuals of equal dignity under the sovereignty of God.

1:2 שְׂאוּ אֶת־רֹאשׁ כָּל־עֲדַת בְּנֵי־יִשְׂרָאֵל *Take a census* – The book of Numbers begins with a census of the Israelites. That is why this book is known in English as Numbers, rather than "In the Desert" or similar, as in Hebrew. This raises a number of questions: What is the significance of this act of counting? And why here at the beginning of the book? Rashi notes that this is not the first time the people have been counted. Their number was already given as they prepared to leave Egypt (Ex. 12:37). A more precise calculation was made when the adult males each gave a half shekel toward the building of the Sanctuary (ch. 30, 38:26). In Numbers, a third and fourth count took place. Why so often?

Rashi's answer is simple and moving:

> Because they [the children of Israel] are dear to Him, God counts them often. He counted them when they were about to leave Egypt. He counted them after the golden calf to establish how many were left. When He was about to cause His presence to rest on them [with the inauguration of the Sanctuary], He counted them again. (Rashi on Num. 1:1)

פרשת במדבר

א א וַיְדַבֵּר יְהוָה אֶל־מֹשֶׁה בְּמִדְבַּר סִינַי בְּאֹהֶל מוֹעֵד בְּאֶחָד א
לַחֹדֶשׁ הַשֵּׁנִי בַּשָּׁנָה הַשֵּׁנִית לְצֵאתָם מֵאֶרֶץ מִצְרַיִם לֵאמֹר׃
ב שְׂאוּ אֶת־רֹאשׁ כָּל־עֲדַת בְּנֵי־יִשְׂרָאֵל לְמִשְׁפְּחֹתָם לְבֵית

BEMIDBAR

The central theme of the book of Numbers is the second stage of the Israelites' journey, physically from Egypt to the Promised Land, mentally from slavery to freedom. This *parasha* and the following one are about the preparations for that journey, the first of which is to take a census. To inherit the land, the Israelites will have to fight battles. Hence the census, specifically of men between the ages of twenty and sixty – that is, those eligible to serve in war. The Levites are counted separately because it is not their role to fight but to minister in the Sanctuary.

Instructions are given as to the layout of the camp, which is to be arranged in a square with the Sanctuary in the middle. Three tribes are to set up their tents and banners on each side, while the Levites form an inner square. The order in which they encamp is also the order in which they will journey.

The duties of the family of Kehat – which also includes Moshe, Aharon, and Miriam, who have other roles – are spelled out. It is their task to carry the sacred objects, the Ark, table, candelabrum (menora), altars, curtains, and holy vessels used in the sacrificial service, when the Israelites journey. This task demands special care.

The name of our *parasha* underscores the fact that the founding drama of the Israelites as a nation under the sovereignty of God is enacted, not in the Promised Land, but in the wilderness on the way.

1:1 בְּמִדְבַּר סִינַי *The Sinai Desert* – The Egyptian-French poet Edmond Jabès (1912–91) noted the connection between *d-b-r*, "word," and *m-d-b-r*, "desert." For him, the wilderness experience is an essential and continuing feature of what it is to be a Jew: "With exemplary regularity the Jew chooses to set out for the desert, to go toward a renewed world that has become his origin." For Jabès, the desert – with its unearthly silence and emptiness – is the condition in which the Word can be heard. There, between sand and sky, the unmediated encounter takes place between God and His people. There is something stark and austere about the wilderness, as there is about Judaism. In no other religion do God and humanity stand in such direct closeness, engaging in such frank and direct dialogue. Judaism is faith stripped of all accretions of myth.

3 every male by name individually, twenty years of age
and upward: everyone in Israel who is capable of active
service. You and Aharon shall number them by their
4 divisions. And one man from each tribe shall join you in
5 the task, each the head of his ancestral house. These are
the names of the men who will assist you: from Reuven,
6 Elitzur son of Shedeiur; from Shimon, Shelumiel son of
7 Tzurishadai; from Yehuda, Naḥshon son of Aminadav;
8 9 from Yissakhar, Netanel son of Tzuar; from Zevulun,
10 Eliav son of Ḥelon. For the sons of Yosef: from Efrayim,
Elishama son of Amihud; from Menashe, Gamliel son of
11 12 Pedatzur. From Binyamin, Avidan son of Gidoni; from
13 Dan, Aḥiezer son of Amishadai; from Asher, Pagiel son
14 15 of Okhran; from Gad, Elyasaf son of Deuel; and from
16 Naftali, Aḥira son of Einan." These were the ones chosen
from the community, princes of their ancestral tribes;

One of the key divisions – anticipating by millennia the "separation of church and state" – was between the king, the head of state, on the one hand, and the High Priest, the most senior religious office, on the other.

This was revolutionary. The kings of Mesopotamian city-states and the pharaohs of Egypt were considered demigods or chief intermediaries with the gods. They officiated at supreme religious festivals. They were regarded as the representatives of heaven on earth.

In Judaism, by stark contrast, political leadership had little or no ritual function (other than the king's recital of the book of the covenant every seven years in the ritual known as *hak'hel*). Indeed, the chief objection to the Hasmonean kings on the part of the Sages was that they broke this ancient rule, some of them declaring themselves High Priests also. The Talmud records the objection: "Let the crown of kingship be sufficient for you. Leave the crown of priesthood to the sons of Aharon" (Kiddushin 66a). The effect of this principle was to *secularize power*.

No less fundamental was the division of religious leadership itself into two distinct functions: that of the prophet and the priest. Priests constituted a religious establishment. The prophets, at least those whose messages have been eternalized in Tanakh, were not an establishment but an anti-establishment, critical of the powers that be. It is the fate of establishments, especially those whose membership is a matter of birth, to become corrupt. That is why the prophets were essential. They were the world's first social critics, mandated by God to speak truth

ג אֲבֹתָם בְּמִסְפַּר שֵׁמוֹת כָּל־זָכָר לְגֻלְגְּלֹתָם: מִבֶּן עֶשְׂרִים שָׁנָה
וָמַעְלָה כָּל־יֹצֵא צָבָא בְּיִשְׂרָאֵל תִּפְקְדוּ אֹתָם לְצִבְאֹתָם
ד אַתָּה וְאַהֲרֹן: וְאִתְּכֶם יִהְיוּ אִישׁ אִישׁ לַמַּטֶּה אִישׁ רֹאשׁ
ה לְבֵית־אֲבֹתָיו הוּא: וְאֵלֶּה שְׁמוֹת הָאֲנָשִׁים אֲשֶׁר יַעַמְדוּ
ו אִתְּכֶם לִרְאוּבֵן אֱלִיצוּר בֶּן־שְׁדֵיאוּר: לְשִׁמְעוֹן שְׁלֻמִיאֵל
ז ח בֶּן־צוּרִישַׁדָּי: לִיהוּדָה נַחְשׁוֹן בֶּן־עַמִּינָדָב: לְיִשָּׂשכָר נְתַנְאֵל
ט י בֶּן־צוּעָר: לִזְבוּלֻן אֱלִיאָב בֶּן־חֵלֹן: לִבְנֵי יוֹסֵף לְאֶפְרַיִם
אֱלִישָׁמָע בֶּן־עַמִּיהוּד לִמְנַשֶּׁה גַּמְלִיאֵל בֶּן־פְּדָהצוּר:
יא יב יג לְבִנְיָמִן אֲבִידָן בֶּן־גִּדְעֹנִי: לְדָן אֲחִיעֶזֶר בֶּן־עַמִּישַׁדָּי: לְאָשֵׁר
יד טו פַּגְעִיאֵל בֶּן־עָכְרָן: לְגָד אֶלְיָסָף בֶּן־דְּעוּאֵל: לְנַפְתָּלִי אֲחִירַע
טז בֶּן־עֵינָן: אֵלֶּה קריאי הָעֵדָה נְשִׂיאֵי מַטּוֹת אֲבוֹתָם רָאשֵׁי קְרוּאֵי

For Rashi, the counting of the people was an act of divine love.

The phrase the Torah uses to describe the act of counting: *se'u et rosh*, literally, to "lift the head," is a strange, indirect expression. Biblical Hebrew contains many verbs meaning "to count": *limnot, lifkod, lispor, laḥshov*. Why does the Torah not use one of these words, choosing instead the roundabout expression "lift the heads" of the people?

In any census, head count, or roll call there is a tendency to focus on the total: the crowd, the multitude, the mass. Counting a group devalues the individual and tends to make him or her replaceable. If one soldier dies in battle, another will take his place. If one person leaves the organization, someone else can be hired to do his or her job. There is therefore a danger, when counting a nation, that each individual will feel insignificant. "What am I? What difference can I make? I am only one of millions, a mere wave in the ocean, a grain of sand on the seashore, dust on the surface of infinity." So God tells Moshe to "lift people's heads" and to show them that they each count; they all matter as individuals. To lift someone's head means to show them favor, to recognize them. If a census is taken in this way, it is a gesture of love.

PRINCES OF THE TRIBES

For the first time here, we meet those "chosen from the community" as representatives, "princes" of the tribes. One of the most important Jewish contributions to our understanding of leadership is its early insistence of what, in the eighteenth century, Montesquieu called "the separation of powers." Neither authority nor power was to be located in a single individual or office. Instead, leadership was divided between different kinds of roles.

17 they are the heads of Israel's clans. Moshe and Aharon
took these men, those who had been marked out by name,
18 and they convened the entire community on the first day
of the second month. And the people declared themselves
by their clans and their ancestral houses. All those over
twenty years old were counted individually by name,
19 as the LORD had commanded Moshe; so it was that he
20 counted them in the Sinai Desert. The children SHENI
of Reuven, Yisrael's firstborn – his descendants by their
clans and their ancestral families – the tally of their names,
each male aged twenty years and above: everyone capable
21 of active service, all counted individually – those counted
from the tribe of Reuven numbered 46,500.
22 Of the children of Shimon – his descendants by their clans
and their ancestral families – the tally of their names, each
male aged twenty years and above: everyone capable of
23 active service, all counted individually – those counted
from the tribe of Shimon numbered 59,300.

---

that this book has been written by your ancestors. Every single one of them has written a chapter in this book telling their story and handing it on to their children. And as you get to the end of the book, with a shock you see that that empty page has your name on it. And you realize that is the chapter that you have to write.

Can you just put that book back on the shelf and walk away and forget it? If you did, all those two hundred generations of your ancestors would have kept that book going in vain, because it would have stopped with you. You have to write your chapter in that book, and when the time comes, hand that book on to your children and grandchildren.

The Baal Shem Tov used a similar image. He said that the Jewish people are a living *sefer Torah*, and every Jew is one of its letters. It is an image that invites a question – *the* question: will we, in our lifetime, be letters in the scroll of the Jewish people?

At some stage, each of us must decide how to live our lives. We have many options, and no generation in history has had a wider choice. We can live for work or success or wealth or fame or power. We can have a whole series of lifestyles and relationships. We can explore any of a myriad of faiths, mysticisms, or therapies. There is only one constraint – namely, that however much of anything else we have, we have only one life, and it is short. How we live and what we live for are the most fateful decisions we ever make.

יז אַלְפֵי יִשְׂרָאֵל הֵם: וַיִּקַּח מֹשֶׁה וְאַהֲרֹן אֵת הָאֲנָשִׁים הָאֵלֶּה
יח אֲשֶׁר נִקְּבוּ בְּשֵׁמוֹת: וְאֵת כָּל־הָעֵדָה הִקְהִילוּ בְּאֶחָד לַחֹדֶשׁ
הַשֵּׁנִי וַיִּתְיַלְדוּ עַל־מִשְׁפְּחֹתָם לְבֵית אֲבֹתָם בְּמִסְפַּר שֵׁמוֹת
יט מִבֶּן עֶשְׂרִים שָׁנָה וָמַעְלָה לְגֻלְגְּלֹתָם: כַּאֲשֶׁר צִוָּה יהוה אֶת־
כ מֹשֶׁה וַיִּפְקְדֵם בְּמִדְבַּר סִינָי: וַיִּהְיוּ בְנֵי־רְאוּבֵן שני
בְּכֹר יִשְׂרָאֵל תּוֹלְדֹתָם לְמִשְׁפְּחֹתָם לְבֵית אֲבֹתָם בְּמִסְפַּר
שֵׁמוֹת לְגֻלְגְּלֹתָם כָּל־זָכָר מִבֶּן עֶשְׂרִים שָׁנָה וָמַעְלָה כֹּל
כא יֹצֵא צָבָא: פְּקֻדֵיהֶם לְמַטֵּה רְאוּבֵן שִׁשָּׁה וְאַרְבָּעִים אֶלֶף
וַחֲמֵשׁ מֵאוֹת:
כב לִבְנֵי שִׁמְעוֹן תּוֹלְדֹתָם לְמִשְׁפְּחֹתָם לְבֵית אֲבֹתָם פְּקֻדָיו
בְּמִסְפַּר שֵׁמוֹת לְגֻלְגְּלֹתָם כָּל־זָכָר מִבֶּן עֶשְׂרִים שָׁנָה וָמַעְלָה
כג כֹּל יֹצֵא צָבָא: פְּקֻדֵיהֶם לְמַטֵּה שִׁמְעוֹן תִּשְׁעָה וַחֲמִשִּׁים
אֶלֶף וּשְׁלֹשׁ מֵאוֹת:

to power. The essential lesson of the Torah is that leadership can never be confined to one class or role. It must always be distributed and divided. In ancient Israel, kings dealt with power, priests with holiness, and prophets with the integrity and faithfulness of society as a whole. In Judaism, leadership is less a *function* than a *field of tensions* between different roles, each with its own perspective and voice.

Leadership in Judaism is *counterpoint*, a musical form defined as "the technique of combining two or more melodic lines in such a way that they establish a harmonic relationship while retaining their linear individuality." In Leviticus, Moshe and Aharon lead the people side by side; in Numbers, the people's own representatives step forward, bringing an added layer of complexity to the dynamics of the people. It is this internal complexity that is ultimately to give Jewish leadership its vigor, saving it from entropy, the loss of energy over time.

TO BE COUNTED

Each man in the census is "counted individually by name" (Num. 1:18), a person in his own right within the tally. We can picture an allegory for this passage. Imagine that you are in an enormous library. You are wandering through, looking at all the titles of the books, and then suddenly you stop dead. There is a book and the cover has your name on it. You take it out, you open it up, and you see that there are several hundred pages of that book written by many different hands in different languages. And you try to work out what this book is. And with a shock, you realize

24 Of the children of Gad – his descendants by their clans
and their ancestral families – the tally of their names, each
male aged twenty years and above: everyone capable of
25 active service, all counted individually – those counted
from the tribe of Gad numbered 45,650.
26 Of the children of Yehuda – his descendants by their clans
and their ancestral families – the tally of their names, each
male aged twenty years and above: everyone capable of
27 active service, all counted individually – those counted
from the tribe of Yehuda numbered 74,600.
28 Of the children of Yissakhar – his descendants by their
clans and their ancestral families – the tally of their names,
each male aged twenty years and above: everyone capable
29 of active service, all counted individually – those counted
from the tribe of Yissakhar numbered 54,400.
30 Of the children of Zevulun – his descendants by their
clans and their ancestral families – the tally of their names,
each male aged twenty years and above: everyone capable
31 of active service, all counted individually – those counted
from the tribe of Zevulun numbered 57,400.
32 Of the children of Yosef: of the children of Efrayim – his
descendants by their clans and their ancestral families – the
tally of their names, each male aged twenty years and
above: everyone capable of active service, all counted
33 individually – those counted from the tribe of Efrayim
numbered 40,500.
34 Of the children of Menashe – his descendants by their
clans and their ancestral families – the tally of their names,
each male aged twenty years and above: everyone capable
35 of active service, all counted individually – those counted
from the tribe of Menashe numbered 32,200.

---

most moving story in the annals of mankind. Every one of us has our part to write in that story before handing the book on. The men of Moshe's census, reporting as fit for service if required, are shrouded in the past, together with their sisters, elders, and children. Yet we carry them all in our DNA, our names, and our story. We too are counted – individually, yet as part of the whole.

כד לִבְנֵי גָד תּוֹלְדֹתָם לְמִשְׁפְּחֹתָם לְבֵית אֲבֹתָם בְּמִסְפַּר שֵׁמוֹת
כה מִבֶּן עֶשְׂרִים שָׁנָה וָמַעְלָה כֹּל יֹצֵא צָבָא: פְּקֻדֵיהֶם לְמַטֵּה גָד
חֲמִשָּׁה וְאַרְבָּעִים אֶלֶף וְשֵׁשׁ מֵאוֹת וַחֲמִשִּׁים:
כו לִבְנֵי יְהוּדָה תּוֹלְדֹתָם לְמִשְׁפְּחֹתָם לְבֵית אֲבֹתָם
בְּמִסְפַּר שֵׁמֹת מִבֶּן עֶשְׂרִים שָׁנָה וָמַעְלָה כֹּל יֹצֵא צָבָא:
כז פְּקֻדֵיהֶם לְמַטֵּה יְהוּדָה אַרְבָּעָה וְשִׁבְעִים אֶלֶף וְשֵׁשׁ
מֵאוֹת:
כח לִבְנֵי יִשָּׂשכָר תּוֹלְדֹתָם לְמִשְׁפְּחֹתָם לְבֵית אֲבֹתָם
בְּמִסְפַּר שֵׁמֹת מִבֶּן עֶשְׂרִים שָׁנָה וָמַעְלָה כֹּל יֹצֵא צָבָא:
כט פְּקֻדֵיהֶם לְמַטֵּה יִשָּׂשכָר אַרְבָּעָה וַחֲמִשִּׁים אֶלֶף וְאַרְבַּע
מֵאוֹת:
ל לִבְנֵי זְבוּלֻן תּוֹלְדֹתָם לְמִשְׁפְּחֹתָם לְבֵית אֲבֹתָם בְּמִסְפַּר שֵׁמֹת
לא מִבֶּן עֶשְׂרִים שָׁנָה וָמַעְלָה כֹּל יֹצֵא צָבָא: פְּקֻדֵיהֶם לְמַטֵּה
זְבוּלֻן שִׁבְעָה וַחֲמִשִּׁים אֶלֶף וְאַרְבַּע מֵאוֹת:
לב לִבְנֵי יוֹסֵף לִבְנֵי אֶפְרַיִם תּוֹלְדֹתָם לְמִשְׁפְּחֹתָם לְבֵית
אֲבֹתָם בְּמִסְפַּר שֵׁמֹת מִבֶּן עֶשְׂרִים שָׁנָה וָמַעְלָה כֹּל יֹצֵא
לג צָבָא: פְּקֻדֵיהֶם לְמַטֵּה אֶפְרָיִם אַרְבָּעִים אֶלֶף וַחֲמֵשׁ
מֵאוֹת:
לד לִבְנֵי מְנַשֶּׁה תּוֹלְדֹתָם לְמִשְׁפְּחֹתָם לְבֵית אֲבֹתָם בְּמִסְפַּר
לה שֵׁמוֹת מִבֶּן עֶשְׂרִים שָׁנָה וָמַעְלָה כֹּל יֹצֵא צָבָא: פְּקֻדֵיהֶם
לְמַטֵּה מְנַשֶּׁה שְׁנַיִם וּשְׁלֹשִׁים אֶלֶף וּמָאתָיִם:

We can live life as a succession of moments spent, like coins, in return for pleasures of various kinds. Or we can see our life as though it were a letter of the alphabet. A letter on its own has no meaning, yet when letters are joined to others they make a word, words combine with others to make a sentence, sentences connect to make a paragraph, and paragraphs join to make a story. That is how the Baal Shem Tov understood life. Every Jew is a letter. Each Jewish family is a word, every community a sentence, and the Jewish people at any one time are a paragraph. The Jewish people through time constitute a story, the strangest and

36 Of the children of Binyamin – his descendants by their
clans and their ancestral families – the tally of their names,
each male aged twenty years and above: everyone capable
37 of active service, all counted individually – those counted
from the tribe of Binyamin numbered 35,400.
38 Of the children of Dan – his descendants by their clans
and their ancestral families – the tally of their names, each
male aged twenty years and above: everyone capable of
39 active service, all counted individually – those counted
from the tribe of Dan numbered 62,700.
40 Of the children of Asher – his descendants by their clans
and their ancestral families – the tally of their names, each
male aged twenty years and above: everyone capable of
41 active service, all counted individually – those counted
from the tribe of Asher numbered 41,500.
42 The children of Naftali – his descendants by their clans
and their ancestral families – the tally of their names, each
male aged twenty years and above: everyone capable of
43 active service, all counted individually – those counted
from the tribe of Naftali numbered 53,400.
44 These were the ones counted by Moshe, Aharon, and the
twelve princes of Israel, one from each ancestral house.
45 Thus the total number of the Israelites counted, by their
ancestral houses, aged twenty years and above – everyone
46 47 in Israel capable of active service – was 603,550. The
ancestral house of the Levites, however, was not counted
among them.
48 49 For the LORD had spoken to Moshe and said, "You shall not
count the tribe of Levi, nor take a census of them among
50 the Israelites. Instead, you shall appoint the Levites over
the Tabernacle of the Testimony, over all its utensils and
all that belongs to it. For they are to carry the Tabernacle
and all its utensils; they are to tend to it, and around the

---

of each of us and know what we are thinking, and this is what the blessing refers to. In other words, even in a massive crowd where, to human eyes, faces blur into a mass, God still relates to us as individuals, not as members of a crowd.

לו לִבְנֵי בִנְיָמִן תּוֹלְדֹתָם לְמִשְׁפְּחֹתָם לְבֵית אֲבֹתָם בְּמִסְפַּר שֵׁמֹת
לז מִבֶּן עֶשְׂרִים שָׁנָה וָמַעְלָה כֹּל יֹצֵא צָבָא׃ פְּקֻדֵיהֶם לְמַטֵּה
בִנְיָמִן חֲמִשָּׁה וּשְׁלֹשִׁים אֶלֶף וְאַרְבַּע מֵאוֹת׃
לח לִבְנֵי דָן תּוֹלְדֹתָם לְמִשְׁפְּחֹתָם לְבֵית אֲבֹתָם בְּמִסְפַּר שֵׁמֹת
לט מִבֶּן עֶשְׂרִים שָׁנָה וָמַעְלָה כֹּל יֹצֵא צָבָא׃ פְּקֻדֵיהֶם לְמַטֵּה
דָן שְׁנַיִם וְשִׁשִּׁים אֶלֶף וּשְׁבַע מֵאוֹת׃
מ לִבְנֵי אָשֵׁר תּוֹלְדֹתָם לְמִשְׁפְּחֹתָם לְבֵית אֲבֹתָם בְּמִסְפַּר שֵׁמֹת
מא מִבֶּן עֶשְׂרִים שָׁנָה וָמַעְלָה כֹּל יֹצֵא צָבָא׃ פְּקֻדֵיהֶם לְמַטֵּה
אָשֵׁר אֶחָד וְאַרְבָּעִים אֶלֶף וַחֲמֵשׁ מֵאוֹת׃
מב בְּנֵי נַפְתָּלִי תּוֹלְדֹתָם לְמִשְׁפְּחֹתָם לְבֵית אֲבֹתָם בְּמִסְפַּר שֵׁמֹת
מג מִבֶּן עֶשְׂרִים שָׁנָה וָמַעְלָה כֹּל יֹצֵא צָבָא׃ פְּקֻדֵיהֶם לְמַטֵּה
נַפְתָּלִי שְׁלֹשָׁה וַחֲמִשִּׁים אֶלֶף וְאַרְבַּע מֵאוֹת׃
מד אֵלֶּה הַפְּקֻדִים אֲשֶׁר פָּקַד מֹשֶׁה וְאַהֲרֹן וּנְשִׂיאֵי יִשְׂרָאֵל שְׁנֵים
מה עָשָׂר אִישׁ אִישׁ־אֶחָד לְבֵית־אֲבֹתָיו הָיוּ׃ וַיִּהְיוּ כָּל־פְּקוּדֵי
בְנֵי־יִשְׂרָאֵל לְבֵית אֲבֹתָם מִבֶּן עֶשְׂרִים שָׁנָה וָמַעְלָה כָּל־
מו יֹצֵא צָבָא בְּיִשְׂרָאֵל׃ וַיִּהְיוּ כָּל־הַפְּקֻדִים שֵׁשׁ־מֵאוֹת אֶלֶף
מז וּשְׁלֹשֶׁת אֲלָפִים וַחֲמֵשׁ מֵאוֹת וַחֲמִשִּׁים׃ וְהַלְוִיִּם לְמַטֵּה
אֲבֹתָם לֹא הָתְפָּקְדוּ בְּתוֹכָם׃
מח מט וַיְדַבֵּר יְהוָה אֶל־מֹשֶׁה לֵּאמֹר׃ אַךְ אֶת־מַטֵּה לֵוִי לֹא תִפְקֹד
נ וְאֶת־רֹאשָׁם לֹא תִשָּׂא בְּתוֹךְ בְּנֵי יִשְׂרָאֵל׃ וְאַתָּה הַפְקֵד
אֶת־הַלְוִיִּם עַל־מִשְׁכַּן הָעֵדֻת וְעַל כָּל־כֵּלָיו וְעַל כָּל־אֲשֶׁר־
לוֹ הֵמָּה יִשְׂאוּ אֶת־הַמִּשְׁכָּן וְאֶת־כָּל־כֵּלָיו וְהֵם יְשָׁרְתֻהוּ

1:46 שֵׁשׁ־מֵאוֹת אֶלֶף וּשְׁלֹשֶׁת אֲלָפִים וַחֲמֵשׁ מֵאוֹת וַחֲמִשִּׁים *603,550* – The number six hundred thousand, an approximation of the Torah's total here, became a proverbial quantity for a great number of Jews. For example, there is a wonderful blessing mentioned in the Talmud to be said on seeing six hundred thousand Israelites together in one place. It is: "Blessed are You, Lord… who discerns secrets" (Berakhot 58a; Rashi ad loc.). The Talmud explains that every person is different. We each have different attributes. We all think our own thoughts. Only God can enter the minds

51 Tabernacle they shall encamp. When the Tabernacle is to
move onward, the Levites shall take it down, and when
the Tabernacle is to encamp, the Levites shall erect it. Any
52 outsider who draws close to it shall be put to death. The
Israelites shall encamp in their respective camps, each
53 by his own banner, in his division. But the Levites shall
encamp around the Tabernacle of the Testimony, so that
fury does not engulf the community of the Israelites; the
Levites shall keep watch faithfully over the Tabernacle of
54 the Testimony." The Israelites did so; all that the LORD
had commanded Moshe, they fulfilled.
2 1 2 The LORD spoke to Moshe and Aharon: "The Israelites SHELISHI
shall camp, each by his banner, the ensign of his ancestral
house, positioned around the Tent of Meeting at a
3 distance. Camping to the east, toward the sunrise, shall
be the divisions under the banner of Yehuda. The leader
of Yehuda's descendants is Naḥshon son of Aminadav.
4 5 And his division numbers 74,600. Camping next to them
shall be the tribe of Yissakhar. The leader of Yissakhar's
6 descendants is Netanel son of Tzuar. And his division
7 numbers 54,400. Then the tribe of Zevulun. The leader
8 of Zevulun's descendants is Eliav son of Ḥelon. His
9 division numbers 57,400. The total number in Yehuda's

That is one of the striking differences between the synagogues and the cathedrals of the Middle Ages. In a cathedral you sense the vastness of God and the smallness of humankind. But in the Altneushul in Prague or the synagogues of the Ari and Rabbi Yosef Karo in Tzefat, you sense the closeness of God and the potential greatness of humankind.

2:2 מִנֶּגֶד סָבִיב לְאֹהֶל־מוֹעֵד *Positioned around the Tent of Meeting at a distance* – Immediately after the census we read of how the twelve tribes are to encamp, each equidistant from the Sanctuary. Each tribe is different, but (with the exception of the Levites) all are equal. They eat the same food; they drink the same water. None yet has lands of their own, for the desert has no owners. There is no economic or territorial conflict between them.

They have not yet begun building a society with all the inequalities to which society gives rise. For the moment, they are together, their tents forming a perfect square with the Sanctuary at its center.

נא וְסָבִיב לַמִּשְׁכָּן יַחֲנוּ: וּבִנְסֹעַ הַמִּשְׁכָּן יוֹרִידוּ אֹתוֹ הַלְוִיִּם
נב וּבַחֲנֹת הַמִּשְׁכָּן יָקִימוּ אֹתוֹ הַלְוִיִּם וְהַזָּר הַקָּרֵב יוּמָת: וְחָנוּ
בְּנֵי יִשְׂרָאֵל אִישׁ עַל־מַחֲנֵהוּ וְאִישׁ עַל־דִּגְלוֹ לְצִבְאֹתָם:
נג וְהַלְוִיִּם יַחֲנוּ סָבִיב לְמִשְׁכַּן הָעֵדֻת וְלֹא־יִהְיֶה קֶצֶף עַל־עֲדַת
בְּנֵי יִשְׂרָאֵל וְשָׁמְרוּ הַלְוִיִּם אֶת־מִשְׁמֶרֶת מִשְׁכַּן הָעֵדוּת:
נד וַיַּעֲשׂוּ בְּנֵי יִשְׂרָאֵל כְּכֹל אֲשֶׁר צִוָּה יהוה אֶת־מֹשֶׁה כֵּן
עָשׂוּ:

ב א ב וַיְדַבֵּר יהוה אֶל־מֹשֶׁה וְאֶל־אַהֲרֹן לֵאמֹר: אִישׁ עַל־דִּגְלוֹ ב שלישי
בְאֹתֹת לְבֵית אֲבֹתָם יַחֲנוּ בְּנֵי יִשְׂרָאֵל מִנֶּגֶד סָבִיב לְאֹהֶל־
ג מוֹעֵד יַחֲנוּ: וְהַחֹנִים קֵדְמָה מִזְרָחָה דֶּגֶל מַחֲנֵה יְהוּדָה
ד לְצִבְאֹתָם וְנָשִׂיא לִבְנֵי יְהוּדָה נַחְשׁוֹן בֶּן־עַמִּינָדָב: וּצְבָאוֹ
ה וּפְקֻדֵיהֶם אַרְבָּעָה וְשִׁבְעִים אֶלֶף וְשֵׁשׁ מֵאוֹת: וְהַחֹנִים
עָלָיו מַטֵּה יִשָּׂשכָר וְנָשִׂיא לִבְנֵי יִשָּׂשכָר נְתַנְאֵל בֶּן־צוּעָר:
ו ז וּצְבָאוֹ וּפְקֻדָיו אַרְבָּעָה וַחֲמִשִּׁים אֶלֶף וְאַרְבַּע מֵאוֹת: מַטֵּה
ח זְבוּלֻן וְנָשִׂיא לִבְנֵי זְבוּלֻן אֱלִיאָב בֶּן־חֵלֹן: וּצְבָאוֹ וּפְקֻדָיו
ט שִׁבְעָה וַחֲמִשִּׁים אֶלֶף וְאַרְבַּע מֵאוֹת: כָּל־הַפְּקֻדִים לְמַחֲנֵה

1:53 יַחֲנוּ סָבִיב לְמִשְׁכַּן הָעֵדֻת *Encamp around the Tabernacle of the Testimony* – The book of Numbers is about a people with the Divine Presence in its midst. God is no longer simply the distant, majestic creator of the universe and intervener in history. He is also close, the *Shekhina,* God as immanent as well as transcendent: God-as-neighbor. Jewish spirituality conceives of God in abstract and awe-inspiring ways: God is more distant than the furthest star and more eternal than time itself. Yet no religion has ever felt God to be closer. In Tanakh, the prophets argue with God. In the book of Psalms, King David speaks to Him in terms of utmost intimacy. In the Talmud, God listens to the debates between the Sages and accepts their rulings even when they go against a heavenly voice. God's relationship with Israel, said the prophets, is like that between a parent and a child, or between a husband and a wife. In Song of Songs, it is like that between two infatuated lovers. The Zohar, key text of Jewish mysticism, uses the most daring language of passion, as does *Yedid Nefesh,* the poem attributed to the sixteenth-century Tzefat kabbalist Rabbi Elazar Azikri.

▶

camp, in their divisions, is 186,400. They shall be the
10 first to set out. The divisions under the banner
of Reuven's camp shall be to the south. The leader of
11 Reuven's descendants is Elitzur son of Shedeiur. And
12 his division numbers 46,500. Camping next to them
shall be the tribe of Shimon. The leader of Shimon's
13 descendants is Shelumiel son of Tzurishadai. His
14 division numbers 59,300. Then the tribe of Gad: the
leader of Gad's descendants is Elyasaf son of Reuel.
15 16 And his division numbers 45,650. The total number in
Reuven's camp, in their divisions, is 151,450. They shall
17 set out second. And the Tent of Meeting
and the Levite camp shall set out in the midst of the
camps. All shall set out as they encamp, each in his own
18 place under his banner. The divisions under
the banner of Efrayim shall be to the west. The leader of
19 Efrayim's descendants is Elishama son of Amihud. And
20 his division numbers 40,500. Next to them shall be the
tribe of Menashe. The leader of Menashe's descendants
21 is Gamliel son of Pedatzur. His division numbers 32,200.
22 Then the tribe of Binyamin: the leader of Binyamin's
23 descendants is Avidan son of Gidoni. His division
24 numbers 35,400. The total number of men in Efrayim's
camp, in their divisions, is 108,100. They shall set out
25 third. The divisions under the banner of Dan
shall be to the north. The leader of Dan's descendants is
26 Aḥiezer son of Amishadai. His division numbers 62,700.
27 Camping next to them shall be the tribe of Asher. The
28 leader of Asher's descendants is Pagiel son of Okhran. His

is what the Israelites did in the days of Moshe when they journeyed forth into the wilderness, guided only by a pillar of cloud by day and fire by night. It took faith to challenge the religions of the ancient world, especially when they were embodied in the greatest empires of their time. Faith is the courage to take a risk for the sake of God or the Jewish people; to begin a journey to a distant destination knowing that there will be hazards along the way, but knowing also that God is with us, giving us strength if we align our will with His.

יְהוּדָה מְאַת אֶלֶף וּשְׁמֹנִים אֶלֶף וְשֵׁשֶׁת־אֲלָפִים וְאַרְבַּע־
י מֵאוֹת לְצִבְאֹתָם רִאשֹׁנָה יִסָּעוּ: דֶּגֶל מַחֲנֵה
רְאוּבֵן תֵּימָנָה לְצִבְאֹתָם וְנָשִׂיא לִבְנֵי רְאוּבֵן אֱלִיצוּר בֶּן־
יא שְׁדֵיאוּר: וּצְבָאוֹ וּפְקֻדָיו שִׁשָּׁה וְאַרְבָּעִים אֶלֶף וַחֲמֵשׁ
יב מֵאוֹת: וְהַחוֹנִם עָלָיו מַטֵּה שִׁמְעוֹן וְנָשִׂיא לִבְנֵי שִׁמְעוֹן
יג שְׁלֻמִיאֵל בֶּן־צוּרִישַׁדָּי: וּצְבָאוֹ וּפְקֻדֵיהֶם תִּשְׁעָה וַחֲמִשִּׁים
יד אֶלֶף וּשְׁלֹשׁ מֵאוֹת: וּמַטֵּה גָּד וְנָשִׂיא לִבְנֵי גָד אֶלְיָסָף בֶּן־
טו רְעוּאֵל: וּצְבָאוֹ וּפְקֻדֵיהֶם חֲמִשָּׁה וְאַרְבָּעִים אֶלֶף וְשֵׁשׁ
טז מֵאוֹת וַחֲמִשִּׁים: כָּל־הַפְּקֻדִים לְמַחֲנֵה רְאוּבֵן מְאַת אֶלֶף
וְאֶחָד וַחֲמִשִּׁים אֶלֶף וְאַרְבַּע־מֵאוֹת וַחֲמִשִּׁים לְצִבְאֹתָם
יז וּשְׁנִיִּם יִסָּעוּ: וְנָסַע אֹהֶל־מוֹעֵד מַחֲנֵה
הַלְוִיִּם בְּתוֹךְ הַמַּחֲנֹת כַּאֲשֶׁר יַחֲנוּ כֵּן יִסָּעוּ אִישׁ עַל־יָדוֹ
יח לְדִגְלֵיהֶם: דֶּגֶל מַחֲנֵה אֶפְרַיִם לְצִבְאֹתָם
יט יָמָּה וְנָשִׂיא לִבְנֵי אֶפְרַיִם אֱלִישָׁמָע בֶּן־עַמִּיהוּד: וּצְבָאוֹ
כ וּפְקֻדֵיהֶם אַרְבָּעִים אֶלֶף וַחֲמֵשׁ מֵאוֹת: וְעָלָיו מַטֵּה
כא מְנַשֶּׁה וְנָשִׂיא לִבְנֵי מְנַשֶּׁה גַּמְלִיאֵל בֶּן־פְּדָהצוּר: וּצְבָאוֹ
כב וּפְקֻדֵיהֶם שְׁנַיִם וּשְׁלֹשִׁים אֶלֶף וּמָאתָיִם: וּמַטֵּה בִּנְיָמִן וְנָשִׂיא
כג לִבְנֵי בִנְיָמִן אֲבִידָן בֶּן־גִּדְעֹנִי: וּצְבָאוֹ וּפְקֻדֵיהֶם חֲמִשָּׁה
כד וּשְׁלֹשִׁים אֶלֶף וְאַרְבַּע מֵאוֹת: כָּל־הַפְּקֻדִים לְמַחֲנֵה אֶפְרַיִם
מְאַת אֶלֶף וּשְׁמֹנַת־אֲלָפִים וּמֵאָה לְצִבְאֹתָם וּשְׁלִשִׁים
כה יִסָּעוּ: דֶּגֶל מַחֲנֵה דָן צָפֹנָה לְצִבְאֹתָם וְנָשִׂיא
כו לִבְנֵי דָן אֲחִיעֶזֶר בֶּן־עַמִּישַׁדָּי: וּצְבָאוֹ וּפְקֻדֵיהֶם שְׁנַיִם
כז וְשִׁשִּׁים אֶלֶף וּשְׁבַע מֵאוֹת: וְהַחֹנִם עָלָיו מַטֵּה אָשֵׁר
כח וְנָשִׂיא לִבְנֵי אָשֵׁר פַּגְעִיאֵל בֶּן־עָכְרָן: וּצְבָאוֹ וּפְקֻדֵיהֶם

2:9 רִאשֹׁנָה יִסָּעוּ *They shall be the first to set out* – A significant part of what faith is in Judaism is to have the courage to "be the first to set out," to pioneer, to do something new, to venture out into the unknown. That is what Avraham and Sara did when they left their land, their home, and their father's house. It

29 division numbers 41,500. Then the tribe of Naftali: the
leader of Naftali's descendants is Aḥira son of Einan.
30 31 His division numbers 53,400. The total number in Dan's
camp, in their divisions, is 157,600. They shall set out last,
by their banners."
32 These were the numbers of the Israelites by their
ancestral houses. The total number in the camps by their
33 divisions was 603,550. As the LORD had commanded
Moshe, the Levites were not counted among the other
34 Israelites. And so the Israelites did all that the LORD had
commanded Moshe. Thus they camped by their banners,
and thus they set out, each amid his clan and his ancestral
house.
3 1 These were the descendants of Aharon and Moshe at the REVI'I
2 time when the LORD spoke to Moshe at Mount Sinai. The
names of Aharon's sons were Nadav, the firstborn, Avihu,
3 Elazar, and Itamar. These were the names of Aharon's
sons, the anointed priests, ordained for priestly service.
4 But Nadav and Avihu died before the LORD when,
before the LORD, they offered unauthorized fire in the
Wilderness of Sinai; they had had no sons. And Elazar
and Itamar served as priests while their father Aharon
lived.
5 6 The LORD said to Moshe, "Bring close the tribe of Levi
7 and set them before Aharon the priest to assist him. They

---

this order, for without it you cannot enter the land, fight its battles, and create a society that is both just and free.

3:1 תּוֹלְדֹת אַהֲרֹן וּמֹשֶׁה *Descendants of Aharon and Moshe* – The genealogy begins with the words "These were the descendants of Aharon and Moshe" but goes on to list only Aharon's children. On this, the Rabbis say that because Moshe taught Aharon's children they were regarded as his own. In general, disciples are called children (see Rashi on Num. 3:1). Teachers open our eyes to the world. They give us curiosity and confidence. They connect us to our past and future. They are the guardians of our social heritage. We have many heroes today, and they are often celebrities. They come, they have their fifteen minutes of fame, and they go. But the influence of good teachers stays with us. They are the people who really shape our lives.

כט אֶחָד וְאַרְבָּעִים אֶלֶף וְחָמֵשׁ מֵאוֹת: וּמַטֵּה נַפְתָּלִי וְנָשִׂיא
ל לִבְנֵי נַפְתָּלִי אֲחִירַע בֶּן־עֵינָן: וּצְבָאוֹ וּפְקֻדֵיהֶם שְׁלֹשָׁה
לא וַחֲמִשִּׁים אֶלֶף וְאַרְבַּע מֵאוֹת: כָּל־הַפְּקֻדִים לְמַחֲנֵה דָן
מְאַת אֶלֶף וְשִׁבְעָה וַחֲמִשִּׁים אֶלֶף וְשֵׁשׁ מֵאוֹת לָאַחֲרֹנָה
יִסְעוּ לְדִגְלֵיהֶם:
לב אֵלֶּה פְּקוּדֵי בְנֵי־יִשְׂרָאֵל לְבֵית אֲבֹתָם כָּל־פְּקוּדֵי הַמַּחֲנֹת
לְצִבְאֹתָם שֵׁשׁ־מֵאוֹת אֶלֶף וּשְׁלֹשֶׁת אֲלָפִים וַחֲמֵשׁ מֵאוֹת
לג וַחֲמִשִּׁים: וְהַלְוִיִּם לֹא הָתְפָּקְדוּ בְּתוֹךְ בְּנֵי יִשְׂרָאֵל כַּאֲשֶׁר
לד צִוָּה יהוה אֶת־מֹשֶׁה: וַיַּעֲשׂוּ בְּנֵי יִשְׂרָאֵל כְּכֹל אֲשֶׁר־צִוָּה
יהוה אֶת־מֹשֶׁה כֵּן־חָנוּ לְדִגְלֵיהֶם וְכֵן נָסָעוּ אִישׁ לְמִשְׁפְּחֹתָיו
עַל־בֵּית אֲבֹתָיו:

ג א וְאֵלֶּה תּוֹלְדֹת אַהֲרֹן וּמֹשֶׁה בְּיוֹם דִּבֶּר יהוה אֶת־מֹשֶׁה בְּהַר ג רביעי
ב סִינָי: וְאֵלֶּה שְׁמוֹת בְּנֵי־אַהֲרֹן הַבְּכֹר | נָדָב וַאֲבִיהוּא אֶלְעָזָר
ג וְאִיתָמָר: אֵלֶּה שְׁמוֹת בְּנֵי אַהֲרֹן הַכֹּהֲנִים הַמְּשֻׁחִים אֲשֶׁר־
ד מִלֵּא יָדָם לְכַהֵן: וַיָּמָת נָדָב וַאֲבִיהוּא לִפְנֵי יהוה בְּהַקְרִבָם
אֵשׁ זָרָה לִפְנֵי יהוה בְּמִדְבַּר סִינַי וּבָנִים לֹא־הָיוּ לָהֶם וַיְכַהֵן
אֶלְעָזָר וְאִיתָמָר עַל־פְּנֵי אַהֲרֹן אֲבִיהֶם:
ה וַיְדַבֵּר יהוה אֶל־מֹשֶׁה לֵּאמֹר: הַקְרֵב אֶת־מַטֵּה לֵוִי
ו וְהַעֲמַדְתָּ אֹתוֹ לִפְנֵי אַהֲרֹן הַכֹּהֵן וְשֵׁרְתוּ אֹתוֹ: וְשָׁמְרוּ

2:34 כֵּן־חָנוּ לְדִגְלֵיהֶם *They camped by their banners* – The drama to which the whole Torah is a commentary is: *how can freedom co-exist with order*? This drama is set on the stage of history, and it plays itself out through multiple scenes. The basic shape of the narrative is roughly: First God creates order. Then people create chaos. Terrible consequences follow. God begins again, sometimes deeply grieved, but never losing His faith in the one life-form on which He set His image. As the book of Numbers opens, then, we see that there is to be an order to the way the tribes are encamped around the Tabernacle, and to the way they proceed when traveling. Each person has his or her place within the family, the tribe, and the nation. Everyone has been counted and each person counts. It is as if God is saying to the Israelites: This is what order looks like. Preserve and protect

shall keep his charge and that of the whole community
at the Tent of Meeting, carrying out the service of the
8 Tabernacle. Theirs shall be the charge of all the utensils of
the Tent of Meeting, and they shall keep, too, the charge of
the Israelites by performing the service of the Tabernacle.
9 Give the Levites over to Aharon and his sons; they among
10 the Israelites are to be dedicated wholly to him. Appoint
Aharon and his sons to attend to the priestly duties; any
outsider who draws close will die."
11 12 And the LORD spoke to Moshe: "In place of the firstborn,
the first to emerge from every womb among the Israelites,
I have taken the Levites from among the Israelites; the
13 Levites shall be Mine, for all the firstborn are Mine.
On the day I struck down all the firstborn in Egypt, I
consecrated every firstborn in Israel to Myself, man and
animal. They are to be Mine; I am the LORD."
14 Then the LORD spoke to Moshe in the Sinai Desert: ḤAMISHI
15 "Count the Levites by their ancestral houses and their
clans. Count every male a month old or more."
16 So Moshe counted them at the LORD's word as he was
17 commanded. These were the names of Levi's sons:
18 Gershon, Kehat, and Merari. These were the names of
19 Gershon's sons with their clans: Livni and Shimi. Kehat's
sons with their clans: Amram, Yitzhar, Ḥevron, and Uziel.

---

is free – it costs nothing to enter – so the Torah is free. It is God's gift to us (*Midrash Lekaḥ Tov*, Yitro 20:2).

But there is another, more spiritual reason. The desert is a place of silence. There is nothing visual to distract you, and there is no ambient noise to muffle sound. To be sure, when the Israelites received the Torah, there was thunder and lightning and the sound of a shofar. The earth felt as if it were shaking at its foundations. But in a later age, when the prophet Eliyahu stood at the same mountain after his confrontation with the prophets of Baal, he encountered God not in the whirlwind, or the fire, or the earthquake, but in the *kol demama daka*, the still, small voice, literally "the sound of a slender silence" (I Kings 19:9–12). I define this as the sound you can hear only if you are listening.

In the silence of the *midbar*, the desert, you can hear the *Medaber*, the Speaker, and the *medubar*, that which is spoken. To hear the voice of God you need a listening silence in the soul.

אֶת־מִשְׁמַרְתּוֹ וְאֶת־מִשְׁמֶרֶת כָּל־הָעֵדָה לִפְנֵי אֹהֶל מוֹעֵד
ח לַעֲבֹד אֶת־עֲבֹדַת הַמִּשְׁכָּן׃ וְשָׁמְרוּ אֶת־כָּל־כְּלֵי אֹהֶל מוֹעֵד
וְאֶת־מִשְׁמֶרֶת בְּנֵי יִשְׂרָאֵל לַעֲבֹד אֶת־עֲבֹדַת הַמִּשְׁכָּן׃
ט וְנָתַתָּה אֶת־הַלְוִיִּם לְאַהֲרֹן וּלְבָנָיו נְתוּנִם נְתוּנִם הֵמָּה לוֹ
י מֵאֵת בְּנֵי יִשְׂרָאֵל׃ וְאֶת־אַהֲרֹן וְאֶת־בָּנָיו תִּפְקֹד וְשָׁמְרוּ
אֶת־כְּהֻנָּתָם וְהַזָּר הַקָּרֵב יוּמָת׃
יא יב וַיְדַבֵּר יְהוָה אֶל־מֹשֶׁה לֵּאמֹר׃ וַאֲנִי הִנֵּה לָקַחְתִּי אֶת־הַלְוִיִּם
מִתּוֹךְ בְּנֵי יִשְׂרָאֵל תַּחַת כָּל־בְּכוֹר פֶּטֶר רֶחֶם מִבְּנֵי יִשְׂרָאֵל
יג וְהָיוּ לִי הַלְוִיִּם׃ כִּי לִי כָּל־בְּכוֹר בְּיוֹם הַכֹּתִי כָל־בְּכוֹר בְּאֶרֶץ
מִצְרַיִם הִקְדַּשְׁתִּי לִי כָל־בְּכוֹר בְּיִשְׂרָאֵל מֵאָדָם עַד־בְּהֵמָה
לִי יִהְיוּ אֲנִי יְהוָה׃
יד טו וַיְדַבֵּר יְהוָה אֶל־מֹשֶׁה בְּמִדְבַּר סִינַי לֵאמֹר׃ פְּקֹד אֶת־בְּנֵי חמישי
לֵוִי לְבֵית אֲבֹתָם לְמִשְׁפְּחֹתָם כָּל־זָכָר מִבֶּן־חֹדֶשׁ וָמַעְלָה
תִּפְקְדֵם׃
טז יז וַיִּפְקֹד אֹתָם מֹשֶׁה עַל־פִּי יְהוָה כַּאֲשֶׁר צֻוָּה׃ וַיִּהְיוּ־אֵלֶּה
יח בְנֵי־לֵוִי בִּשְׁמֹתָם גֵּרְשׁוֹן וּקְהָת וּמְרָרִי׃ וְאֵלֶּה שְׁמוֹת בְּנֵי־
יט גֵרְשׁוֹן לְמִשְׁפְּחֹתָם לִבְנִי וְשִׁמְעִי׃ וּבְנֵי קְהָת לְמִשְׁפְּחֹתָם

3:14 וַיְדַבֵּר יהוה אֶל־מֹשֶׁה בְּמִדְבַּר סִינַי לֵאמֹר *Then the Lord spoke to Moshe in the Sinai Desert* – Parashat Bemidbar is usually read on the Sabbath before Shavuot. Shavuot is the time of the giving of the Torah. *Bemidbar* means "in the desert." Why, in the fixing of the Torah reading cycle, was a link forged between the giving of the Torah and the particular fact of its emergence from the wilderness?

The Sages gave several interpretations. According to the Mekhilta, the Torah was given publicly, openly, and in a place no one owns because had it been given in the land of Israel, Jews would have said to the nations of the world, "You have no share in it." Instead, God seems to say, whoever wants to come and accept it, let them come and accept it (*Mekhilta*, Yitro, *BaḤodesh* 1).

Another explanation: Had the Torah been given in Israel, the national homeland of the Israelites, the nations of the world would have had an excuse for not accepting it. This follows the rabbinic tradition that before God gave the Torah to the Israelites, He offered it to all the other nations and each found a reason to decline (ibid., *BaḤodesh* 5).

Yet another: Just as the wilderness

20 Merari's sons with their clans: Maḥli and Mushi. These
21 were the Levite clans by their ancestral houses. Gershon
encompassed the clans of Livni and Shimi; these were the
22 Gershonite clans. Their total number of males a month
23 old and upward was 7,500. The Gershonite families were
24 to camp behind the Tabernacle to the west. And the
leader of the Gershonite families was Elyasaf son of Lael.
25 The charge of the sons of Gershon at the Tent of Meeting
was the Tabernacle and the tent, its covering, the screen
26 at the entrance to the Tent of Meeting, the curtains of
the courtyard, the screen at the entrance to the courtyard
surrounding the Tabernacle and altar, and its ropes – and all
27 the service related to these. Kehat encompassed
the clans of Amram, Yitzhar, Ḥevron, and Uziel; these
28 were the Kohatite clans. Their total number of males a
month old and upward was 8,600; these kept the charge of
29 the Sanctuary. The Kohatite families were to camp on the
30 south side of the Tabernacle. The leader of the ancestral
house of the Kohatite families was Elitzafan son of Uziel.
31 Their charge was the Ark, the table, the candelabrum, the
altars, and the sacred utensils used in their service, and the
32 screen and everything pertaining to it. Chief of the leaders
of the Levites was Elazar son of Aharon the priest; he was
appointed over those responsible for keeping charge of
33 the Sanctuary. Merari encompassed the clans of Maḥli
34 and Mushi; these were the Merarite families. The total
number of their males a month old and upward was 6,200.
35 The leader of the ancestral house of the Merarite families
was Tzuriel son of Aviḥayil; and they were to camp on
36 the north side of the Tabernacle. The Merarites were
appointed to take care of the frames, bars, posts, and bases
37 of the Tabernacle, all its utensils and accessories, as well as
the posts of the surrounding courtyard with their bases,
38 pegs, and ropes. Those who were to camp to the east of
the Tabernacle in front of the Tent of Meeting toward
the sunrise were Moshe, Aharon, and his sons. They were
charged, on the Israelites' behalf, to keep faithful watch

כ עַמְרָם וְיִצְהָר חֶבְרוֹן וְעֻזִּיאֵל׃ וּבְנֵי מְרָרִי לְמִשְׁפְּחֹתָם מַחְלִי
כא וּמוּשִׁי אֵלֶּה הֵם מִשְׁפְּחֹת הַלֵּוִי לְבֵית אֲבֹתָם׃ לְגֵרְשׁוֹן
מִשְׁפַּחַת הַלִּבְנִי וּמִשְׁפַּחַת הַשִּׁמְעִי אֵלֶּה הֵם מִשְׁפְּחֹת
כב הַגֵּרְשֻׁנִּי׃ פְּקֻדֵיהֶם בְּמִסְפַּר כָּל־זָכָר מִבֶּן־חֹדֶשׁ וָמָעְלָה
כג פְּקֻדֵיהֶם שִׁבְעַת אֲלָפִים וַחֲמֵשׁ מֵאוֹת׃ מִשְׁפְּחֹת הַגֵּרְשֻׁנִּי
כד אַחֲרֵי הַמִּשְׁכָּן יַחֲנוּ יָמָּה׃ וּנְשִׂיא בֵית־אָב לַגֵּרְשֻׁנִּי אֶלְיָסָף
כה בֶּן־לָאֵל׃ וּמִשְׁמֶרֶת בְּנֵי־גֵרְשׁוֹן בְּאֹהֶל מוֹעֵד הַמִּשְׁכָּן
כו וְהָאֹהֶל מִכְסֵהוּ וּמָסַךְ פֶּתַח אֹהֶל מוֹעֵד׃ וְקַלְעֵי הֶחָצֵר
וְאֶת־מָסַךְ פֶּתַח הֶחָצֵר אֲשֶׁר עַל־הַמִּשְׁכָּן וְעַל־הַמִּזְבֵּחַ
כז סָבִיב וְאֵת מֵיתָרָיו לְכֹל עֲבֹדָתוֹ׃ וְלִקְהָת
מִשְׁפַּחַת הָעַמְרָמִי וּמִשְׁפַּחַת הַיִּצְהָרִי וּמִשְׁפַּחַת הַחֶבְרֹנִי
כח וּמִשְׁפַּחַת הָעָזִּיאֵלִי אֵלֶּה הֵם מִשְׁפְּחֹת הַקְּהָתִי׃ בְּמִסְפַּר
כָּל־זָכָר מִבֶּן־חֹדֶשׁ וָמָעְלָה שְׁמֹנַת אֲלָפִים וְשֵׁשׁ מֵאוֹת
כט שֹׁמְרֵי מִשְׁמֶרֶת הַקֹּדֶשׁ׃ מִשְׁפְּחֹת בְּנֵי־קְהָת יַחֲנוּ עַל
ל יֶרֶךְ הַמִּשְׁכָּן תֵּימָנָה׃ וּנְשִׂיא בֵית־אָב לְמִשְׁפְּחֹת הַקְּהָתִי
לא אֱלִיצָפָן בֶּן־עֻזִּיאֵל׃ וּמִשְׁמַרְתָּם הָאָרֹן וְהַשֻּׁלְחָן וְהַמְּנֹרָה
וְהַמִּזְבְּחֹת וּכְלֵי הַקֹּדֶשׁ אֲשֶׁר יְשָׁרְתוּ בָּהֶם וְהַמָּסָךְ וְכֹל
לב עֲבֹדָתוֹ׃ וּנְשִׂיא נְשִׂיאֵי הַלֵּוִי אֶלְעָזָר בֶּן־אַהֲרֹן הַכֹּהֵן פְּקֻדַּת
לג שֹׁמְרֵי מִשְׁמֶרֶת הַקֹּדֶשׁ׃ לִמְרָרִי מִשְׁפַּחַת הַמַּחְלִי וּמִשְׁפַּחַת
לד הַמּוּשִׁי אֵלֶּה הֵם מִשְׁפְּחֹת מְרָרִי׃ וּפְקֻדֵיהֶם בְּמִסְפַּר כָּל־זָכָר
לה מִבֶּן־חֹדֶשׁ וָמָעְלָה שֵׁשֶׁת אֲלָפִים וּמָאתָיִם׃ וּנְשִׂיא בֵית־אָב
לְמִשְׁפְּחֹת מְרָרִי צוּרִיאֵל בֶּן־אֲבִיחָיִל עַל יֶרֶךְ הַמִּשְׁכָּן יַחֲנוּ
לו צָפֹנָה׃ וּפְקֻדַּת מִשְׁמֶרֶת בְּנֵי מְרָרִי קַרְשֵׁי הַמִּשְׁכָּן וּבְרִיחָיו
לז וְעַמֻּדָיו וַאֲדָנָיו וְכָל־כֵּלָיו וְכֹל עֲבֹדָתוֹ׃ וְעַמֻּדֵי הֶחָצֵר סָבִיב
לח וְאַדְנֵיהֶם וִיתֵדֹתָם וּמֵיתְרֵיהֶם׃ וְהַחֹנִים לִפְנֵי הַמִּשְׁכָּן קֵדְמָה
לִפְנֵי אֹהֶל־מוֹעֵד ׀ מִזְרָחָה מֹשֶׁה ׀ וְאַהֲרֹן וּבָנָיו שֹׁמְרִים
מִשְׁמֶרֶת הַמִּקְדָּשׁ לְמִשְׁמֶרֶת בְּנֵי יִשְׂרָאֵל וְהַזָּר הַקָּרֵב

over the Sanctuary. Any outsider who drew close would
39 die. The total number of Levites counted by Moshe and
Aharon at the LORD's command, by their clans, all the
40 males a month old and upward, was 22,000. Then SHISHI
the LORD said to Moshe, "Count all the firstborn Israelite
males a month of age and upward, taking a census of their
41 names. Take the Levites for Me – I am the LORD – in
place of all the firstborn of the Israelites, and the livestock
of the Levites in place of all the firstborn of the Israelites'
42 livestock." So Moshe counted all the firstborn of the
43 Israelites, as the LORD had commanded him. The total
number of firstborn males a month of age and upward, the
full tally of their names, was 22,273.
44 45 Then the LORD spoke to Moshe: "Take the Levites in
place of all the firstborn of Israel, and the livestock of
the Levites in place of their livestock. The Levites shall
46 be Mine; I am the LORD. As for the redemption of the
273 firstborn Israelites who exceed the number of the
47 Levites, collect five shekel for each, according to the
48 Sanctuary weight – a shekel being twenty gerah. Give the
money to Aharon and his sons as a redemption for the
49 additional Israelites." Moshe took the redemption money
from those who were over and above those redeemed by
50 the Levites; from the firstborn of the Israelites he took
silver weighing 1,365 shekel by the Sanctuary weight.

---

for firstborn males, the priesthood would have been an elite. However, it is not the priests alone who are to be holy; the people as a whole are commanded to "be holy" (Lev. 19:1–2). Life itself is to be sanctified. Holiness is to be made manifest in the way the nation makes its clothes and plants its fields, in the way justice is administered, workers are paid, and business conducted. The vulnerable – the deaf, the blind, the elderly, and the stranger – are to be afforded special protection. The whole society is to be governed by love, without resentments or revenge.

This is a radical democratization of holiness. When we turn our lives into the service of God, and society into a home for the Divine Presence, holiness belongs to all of us.

לט יוּמָת: כׇּל־פְּקוּדֵי הַלְוִיִּם אֲשֶׁר פָּקַד מֹשֶׁה וְאַהֲרֹן עַל־
פִּי יהוה לְמִשְׁפְּחֹתָם כׇּל־זָכָר מִבֶּן־חֹדֶשׁ וָמַעְלָה שְׁנַיִם
מ וְעֶשְׂרִים אָלֶף: וַיֹּאמֶר יהוה אֶל־מֹשֶׁה פְּקֹד ששי
כׇּל־בְּכֹר זָכָר לִבְנֵי יִשְׂרָאֵל מִבֶּן־חֹדֶשׁ וָמָעְלָה וְשָׂא אֵת
מא מִסְפַּר שְׁמֹתָם: וְלָקַחְתָּ אֶת־הַלְוִיִּם לִי אֲנִי יהוה תַּחַת
כׇּל־בְּכֹר בִּבְנֵי יִשְׂרָאֵל וְאֵת בֶּהֱמַת הַלְוִיִּם תַּחַת כׇּל־בְּכוֹר
מב בְּבֶהֱמַת בְּנֵי יִשְׂרָאֵל: וַיִּפְקֹד מֹשֶׁה כַּאֲשֶׁר צִוָּה יהוה אֹתוֹ
מג אֶת־כׇּל־בְּכוֹר בִּבְנֵי יִשְׂרָאֵל: וַיְהִי כׇל־בְּכוֹר זָכָר בְּמִסְפַּר
שֵׁמֹת מִבֶּן־חֹדֶשׁ וָמַעְלָה לִפְקֻדֵיהֶם שְׁנַיִם וְעֶשְׂרִים אֶלֶף
שְׁלֹשָׁה וְשִׁבְעִים וּמָאתָיִם:
מד מה וַיְדַבֵּר יהוה אֶל־מֹשֶׁה לֵּאמֹר: קַח אֶת־הַלְוִיִּם תַּחַת כׇּל־
בְּכוֹר בִּבְנֵי יִשְׂרָאֵל וְאֶת־בֶּהֱמַת הַלְוִיִּם תַּחַת בְּהֶמְתָּם
מו וְהָיוּ־לִי הַלְוִיִּם אֲנִי יהוה: וְאֵת פְּדוּיֵי הַשְּׁלֹשָׁה וְהַשִּׁבְעִים
מז וְהַמָּאתַיִם הָעֹדְפִים עַל־הַלְוִיִּם מִבְּכוֹר בְּנֵי יִשְׂרָאֵל: וְלָקַחְתָּ
חֲמֵשֶׁת חֲמֵשֶׁת שְׁקָלִים לַגֻּלְגֹּלֶת בְּשֶׁקֶל הַקֹּדֶשׁ תִּקָּח
מח עֶשְׂרִים גֵּרָה הַשָּׁקֶל: וְנָתַתָּה הַכֶּסֶף לְאַהֲרֹן וּלְבָנָיו פְּדוּיֵי
מט הָעֹדְפִים בָּהֶם: וַיִּקַּח מֹשֶׁה אֵת כֶּסֶף הַפִּדְיוֹם מֵאֵת הָעֹדְפִים
נ עַל פְּדוּיֵי הַלְוִיִּם: מֵאֵת בְּכוֹר בְּנֵי יִשְׂרָאֵל לָקַח אֶת־הַכֶּסֶף

3:41 תַּחַת כׇּל־בְּכֹר בִּבְנֵי יִשְׂרָאֵל *In place of all the firstborn of the Israelites* – On the face of it, the priesthood was not egalitarian. We have encountered four instances in the Torah thus far of non-Israelite priests: Malkitzedek, Avraham's contemporary, described as a priest of God Most High; Potifera, Yosef's father-in-law; the Egyptian priests as a whole, whose land Yosef did not nationalize; and Yitro, Moshe's father-in-law, a Midianite priest. The priesthood was not unique to Israel, and everywhere it was an elite. In Israel too, priests all came from a single tribe, the Levites, and from a single family within the tribe – that of Aharon. The Torah tells us that this was not God's original intention. Initially it was to have been the firstborns – those who were saved from the last of the Ten Plagues – who were charged with special holiness as the ministers of God. It was after the sin of the golden calf, in which only the tribe of Levi did not participate, that the change was made.

Even as a role reserved specifically

51 Moshe gave the redemption money to Aharon and his
sons, at the LORD's word, as the LORD had commanded
Moshe.
4 1 2 The LORD spoke to Moshe and Aharon: "Take a census SHEVI'I
of the Kohatites among the Levites, by their families and
3 their ancestral houses, from thirty to fifty years old: all
those able to go into service to perform the work of the
4 Tent of Meeting. This will be the service of the Kohatites
5 in the Tent of Meeting: the most sacred objects; when
the camp is about to set out, Aharon and his sons shall
come and take down the screening curtain and cover the
6 Ark of the Testimony with it. Then they shall put over it
a covering of fine leather, and over that a cloth of pure
7 blue, and then they shall insert its poles. On the table of
the showbread they shall spread a blue cloth, and on it
place the bowls, spoons, jars, and the libation pitchers;
and the bread of the Presence shall be on it constantly.
8 They shall spread over them a scarlet cloth, and then
cover it with a covering of fine leather; and then they shall
9 insert its poles. They shall take a blue cloth and cover the
candelabrum and its lamps, tongs, pans, and all the oil
10 vessels used in its service. Then they must put it and all
its utensils into a covering of fine leather, and place them
11 on a carrying frame. They shall spread a blue cloth on the
golden altar, and cover it with a covering of fine leather;
12 and then they shall insert its poles. Then they shall take
all the service utensils, with which they serve in the
Sanctuary, put them into a blue cloth, cover them with
a covering of fine leather, and place them on a carrying
13 frame. They shall remove the ashes from the altar and
14 spread a purple cloth over it. Then they shall place upon
it all the special implements with which they serve
there – the pans, the forks, the shovels, the basins, and
all the altar's utensils – and spread over it all a covering
15 of fine leather, and then insert its poles. When Aharon
and his sons have finished covering the Sanctuary and all
the furnishings of the Sanctuary, when the camp is ready

נא חֲמִשָּׁה וְשִׁשִּׁים וּשְׁלֹשׁ מֵאוֹת וָאֶלֶף בְּשֶׁקֶל הַקֹּדֶשׁ׃ וַיִּתֵּן
מֹשֶׁה אֶת־כֶּסֶף הַפְּדֻיִם לְאַהֲרֹן וּלְבָנָיו עַל־פִּי יהוה כַּאֲשֶׁר
צִוָּה יהוה אֶת־מֹשֶׁה׃
ד א ב וַיְדַבֵּר יהוה אֶל־מֹשֶׁה וְאֶל־אַהֲרֹן לֵאמֹר׃ נָשֹׂא אֶת־רֹאשׁ שביעי
ג בְּנֵי קְהָת מִתּוֹךְ בְּנֵי לֵוִי לְמִשְׁפְּחֹתָם לְבֵית אֲבֹתָם׃ מִבֶּן
שְׁלֹשִׁים שָׁנָה וָמַעְלָה וְעַד בֶּן־חֲמִשִּׁים שָׁנָה כָּל־בָּא לַצָּבָא
ד לַעֲשׂוֹת מְלָאכָה בְּאֹהֶל מוֹעֵד׃ זֹאת עֲבֹדַת בְּנֵי־קְהָת בְּאֹהֶל
ה מוֹעֵד קֹדֶשׁ הַקֳּדָשִׁים׃ וּבָא אַהֲרֹן וּבָנָיו בִּנְסֹעַ הַמַּחֲנֶה
ו וְהוֹרִדוּ אֵת פָּרֹכֶת הַמָּסָךְ וְכִסּוּ־בָהּ אֵת אֲרֹן הָעֵדֻת׃ וְנָתְנוּ
עָלָיו כְּסוּי עוֹר תַּחַשׁ וּפָרְשׂוּ בֶגֶד־כְּלִיל תְּכֵלֶת מִלְמָעְלָה
ז וְשָׂמוּ בַּדָּיו׃ וְעַל ׀ שֻׁלְחַן הַפָּנִים יִפְרְשׂוּ בֶּגֶד תְּכֵלֶת וְנָתְנוּ
עָלָיו אֶת־הַקְּעָרֹת וְאֶת־הַכַּפֹּת וְאֶת־הַמְּנַקִּיֹּת וְאֵת קְשׂוֹת
ח הַנָּסֶךְ וְלֶחֶם הַתָּמִיד עָלָיו יִהְיֶה׃ וּפָרְשׂוּ עֲלֵיהֶם בֶּגֶד תּוֹלַעַת
ט שָׁנִי וְכִסּוּ אֹתוֹ בְּמִכְסֵה עוֹר תָּחַשׁ וְשָׂמוּ אֶת־בַּדָּיו׃ וְלָקְחוּ ׀
בֶּגֶד תְּכֵלֶת וְכִסּוּ אֶת־מְנֹרַת הַמָּאוֹר וְאֶת־נֵרֹתֶיהָ וְאֶת־
מַלְקָחֶיהָ וְאֶת־מַחְתֹּתֶיהָ וְאֵת כָּל־כְּלֵי שַׁמְנָהּ אֲשֶׁר יְשָׁרְתוּ־
י לָהּ בָּהֶם׃ וְנָתְנוּ אֹתָהּ וְאֶת־כָּל־כֵּלֶיהָ אֶל־מִכְסֵה עוֹר תָּחַשׁ
יא וְנָתְנוּ עַל־הַמּוֹט׃ וְעַל ׀ מִזְבַּח הַזָּהָב יִפְרְשׂוּ בֶּגֶד תְּכֵלֶת
יב וְכִסּוּ אֹתוֹ בְּמִכְסֵה עוֹר תָּחַשׁ וְשָׂמוּ אֶת־בַּדָּיו׃ וְלָקְחוּ אֶת־
כָּל־כְּלֵי הַשָּׁרֵת אֲשֶׁר יְשָׁרְתוּ־בָם בַּקֹּדֶשׁ וְנָתְנוּ אֶל־בֶּגֶד
תְּכֵלֶת וְכִסּוּ אוֹתָם בְּמִכְסֵה עוֹר תָּחַשׁ וְנָתְנוּ עַל־הַמּוֹט׃
יג יד וְדִשְּׁנוּ אֶת־הַמִּזְבֵּחַ וּפָרְשׂוּ עָלָיו בֶּגֶד אַרְגָּמָן׃ וְנָתְנוּ עָלָיו
אֶת־כָּל־כֵּלָיו אֲשֶׁר יְשָׁרְתוּ עָלָיו בָּהֶם אֶת־הַמַּחְתֹּת אֶת־
הַמִּזְלָגֹת וְאֶת־הַיָּעִים וְאֶת־הַמִּזְרָקֹת כֹּל כְּלֵי הַמִּזְבֵּחַ וּפָרְשׂוּ
טו עָלָיו כְּסוּי עוֹר תַּחַשׁ וְשָׂמוּ בַדָּיו׃ וְכִלָּה אַהֲרֹן־וּבָנָיו לְכַסֹּת
אֶת־הַקֹּדֶשׁ וְאֶת־כָּל־כְּלֵי הַקֹּדֶשׁ בִּנְסֹעַ הַמַּחֲנֶה וְאַחֲרֵי־
כֵן יָבֹאוּ בְנֵי־קְהָת לָשֵׂאת וְלֹא־יִגְּעוּ אֶל־הַקֹּדֶשׁ וָמֵתוּ

to set out, then the Kohatites shall come to carry them;
but they must not touch the sacred objects lest they die.
These are what the Kohatites must carry for the Tent
16 of Meeting. The responsibility of Elazar son of Aharon
the priest is for the lighting oil, the fragrant incense, the
daily grain offering, and the anointing oil. He is also
responsible for the whole Tabernacle and all that is in it,
for the Sanctuary and all its utensils."
17 18 Again the LORD spoke to Moshe and Aharon: "Do not MAFTIR
let the tribe of the clans of Kehat be cut off from among
19 the Levites. So that they may live and not die when they
come close to the most sacred things, they must do
this: let Aharon and his sons go in and assign each man
20 his duties and what he must carry; but they themselves
must not go in and watch while the holy things are being
covered, for they would die."

The haftara for Parashat Bemidbar is on page 1554.
On Erev Rosh Ḥodesh Sivan read the haftara on page 1644.

---

know of bad habits we have to cure. But the real challenge is to know where God wants us to travel to. What task were we put in the world, in this time and place, with these gifts, to do?

There is a biological reason why this is so. We are genetically predisposed to react strongly to danger. Our deepest instincts are aroused. We move into the fight-or-flight mode, with our senses alert, our attention focused, and our adrenalin levels high. When it comes to *fleeing from*, we often find ourselves accessing strengths we did not know we had.

But *fleeing to* is something else entirely. It means making a home in a place where, literally or metaphorically, we have not been before. We become "strangers in a strange land." We need to learn new skills, shoulder new responsibilities, acquire new strengths. That calls for imagination and willpower. It involves the most unique of all human abilities: envisaging a future that has not yet been and acting to bring it about. Fleeing to is a journey into the unknown.

To be a Jew is to know that, in some sense, life is a journey. Hence the importance of knowing at the outset where we are traveling to, and never forgetting, never giving up.

The Israelites, in their journey, make a series of mistakes. They focus too much on the present (the food, the water) and too little on the future. When they face difficulties, they have too much fear and too little faith. They keep looking back to how things were instead of looking forward to how they might be. The result will be that almost an entire generation will experience exodus but not entry. Leaving is easy. Arriving is formidably hard.

טז אֵלֶּה מַשָּׂא בְנֵי־קְהָת בְּאֹהֶל מוֹעֵד: וּפְקֻדַּת אֶלְעָזָר ׀ בֶּן־
אַהֲרֹן הַכֹּהֵן שֶׁמֶן הַמָּאוֹר וּקְטֹרֶת הַסַּמִּים וּמִנְחַת הַתָּמִיד
וְשֶׁמֶן הַמִּשְׁחָה פְּקֻדַּת כָּל־הַמִּשְׁכָּן וְכָל־אֲשֶׁר־בּוֹ בְּקֹדֶשׁ
וּבְכֵלָיו:
יז יח וַיְדַבֵּר יהוה אֶל־מֹשֶׁה וְאֶל־אַהֲרֹן לֵאמֹר: אַל־תַּכְרִיתוּ אֶת־ ד מפטיר
יט שֵׁבֶט מִשְׁפְּחֹת הַקְּהָתִי מִתּוֹךְ הַלְוִיִּם: וְזֹאת ׀ עֲשׂוּ לָהֶם וְחָיוּ
וְלֹא יָמֻתוּ בְּגִשְׁתָּם אֶת־קֹדֶשׁ הַקֳּדָשִׁים אַהֲרֹן וּבָנָיו יָבֹאוּ
כ וְשָׂמוּ אוֹתָם אִישׁ אִישׁ עַל־עֲבֹדָתוֹ וְאֶל־מַשָּׂאוֹ: וְלֹא־יָבֹאוּ
לִרְאוֹת כְּבַלַּע אֶת־הַקֹּדֶשׁ וָמֵתוּ:

The הפטרה *for* פרשת במדבר *is on page 1555.*
On ערב ראש חודש סיון *read the* הפטרה *on page 1645.*

THE JOURNEY ONWARD

The books of Exodus and Numbers have some striking similarities. They are both about journeys. They both portray the Israelites as quarrelsome and ungrateful. Both contain stories about the people complaining about food and water. In both, the Israelites commit a major sin: in Exodus, the golden calf, in Numbers, the episode of the spies. In both, God threatens to destroy them and begin again with Moshe. Both times, Moshe's passionate appeal persuades God to forgive the people.

But, as we noted at the beginning of Numbers, there is a difference. Exodus is about a journey *from*. Numbers is about a journey *to*. By now, the people have already left Egypt far behind. They have received the Torah and built the Sanctuary. Now they are ready to move on. This time they are looking forward, not back. They are thinking not of the danger they are fleeing from but of the destination they are traveling toward, the Promised Land.

If we had never read the Torah before, we might have assumed that the second half of the journey would be more relaxed, the mood more hopeful. After all, the great dangers have passed. Pharaoh has let the people go. They have been saved at the Sea of Reeds. They have fought and defeated the Amalekites. What else do they have to worry about? They know that when God is with them, no force can prevail against them.

In fact, though, the opposite is the case. The mood of Numbers is palpably darker than it is in Exodus. The rebellions are more serious. Moshe's leadership is more hesitant. We see him giving way, at times, to anger and despair. The Torah, with great realism, is telling us something counterintuitive and of great significance. *The journey from is always easier than the journey to.*

It may take a revolution to depose a tyrant, but it is easier to do that than to create a genuinely free society with the rule of law and respect for human rights. Likewise in the life of individuals. We all

Parashat Naso

4 21 22 Then the Lord spoke to Moshe: "Take a census too of
the Gershonites, by their clans and their ancestral houses,
23 from thirty years old to fifty: all who go into service to
24 carry out the work of the Tent of Meeting. This will be the
25 service of the clans of Gershon, serving and carrying: they
shall carry the curtains of the Tabernacle and the Tent of

transformative potential of a single radical idea – that the human person as such, man or woman, rich or poor, powerful or powerless, is the image of God and therefore of non-negotiable, unquantifiable value. We stand equal in the presence of God. This idea is fundamental to Judaism. In Greek thought and throughout the European Enlightenment, what mattered were universals. In Judaism, what matters to God are individuals. There is a verse in Psalms (147:4) which says that God "counts the number of the stars, calling each by name." A name is a marker of uniqueness. Collective nouns group things together; proper names distinguish them as individuals. Only what we value do we name. (One of the most chilling acts of dehumanization in the extermination camps of Nazi Germany was that those who entered were never addressed by their names. Instead they were given a number, inscribed on their skin.)

God gives even the stars their names. All the more so does this apply to human beings. When God calls, He calls our name, to which the reply is simply *Hineni*, "Here I am." God – one and alone – meets us, one and alone, endowing us with a significance that cannot be quantified or measured by a census.

That is the nature of the censuses in the book of Numbers. There is a difference between a census commanded by God, who cherishes and holds special each individual, and a census undertaken by a human being, who merely assumes that there is strength in numbers. The phrase *naso et rosh*, translated idiomatically as "take a census," literally means that those being counted have "their heads raised" – the same verb as that used later in the priestly blessing: "May the Lord raise His face toward you" (Num. 6:26). God "raises our head" in the most profound way known to humankind, by assuring each of us of His special, enduring, unquantifiable love. As the Israelites prepare to become a society with the Divine Presence at its center, they have to be reminded that they are to become the pioneers of a new social order, whose most famous definition was given by the prophet Zekharya (4:6): "Not with valor and not with strength, but with My spirit, says the Lord of Hosts."

פרשת נשא

ד כא כב וַיְדַבֵּר יְהוָה אֶל־מֹשֶׁה לֵּאמֹר: נָשֹׂא אֶת־רֹאשׁ בְּנֵי גֵרְשׁוֹן
כג גַּם־הֵם לְבֵית אֲבֹתָם לְמִשְׁפְּחֹתָם: מִבֶּן שְׁלֹשִׁים שָׁנָה
וָמַעְלָה עַד בֶּן־חֲמִשִּׁים שָׁנָה תִּפְקֹד אוֹתָם כָּל־הַבָּא לִצְבֹא
כד צָבָא לַעֲבֹד עֲבֹדָה בְּאֹהֶל מוֹעֵד: זֹאת עֲבֹדַת מִשְׁפְּחֹת
כה הַגֵּרְשֻׁנִּי לַעֲבֹד וּלְמַשָּׂא: וְנָשְׂאוּ אֶת־יְרִיעֹת הַמִּשְׁכָּן וְאֶת־

NASO

Continuing the preparations for the Israelites' journey from Sinai to the Holy Land, Parashat Naso contains a mélange of subjects whose inner connection is not immediately obvious: the roles of two of the Levitical clans, Gershon and Merari; the census of the Levites as a group; rules about the purity of the camp; the law of the *sota* (the woman suspected of adultery); the nazirite; and the priestly blessing. The *parasha* concludes with a lengthy and repetitive account of the offerings brought by the tribes at the dedication of the Tabernacle. There is a logic holding together this apparently disconnected series. It lies in the last word of the priestly blessing (Num. 6:26): *shalom,* "peace." Much of the rest of the book of Numbers is a set of variations on the theme of internal dissension and strife. The theme that binds the laws and narrative of this *parasha,* we shall see, is that of making special efforts to preserve or restore peace between people.

THE CENSUS

Parashat Naso begins with a continuation of the census that gives the entire book its English name, "Numbers," itself based on the old rabbinic name, *Ḥumash HaPekudim,* the book of "counting" or "numbering."

In the ancient world, and to some extent still today, a census represented the principle that there is power in numbers. Specifically, counting the people was a way of knowing the size of the army a nation could muster. Numbers also determined a people's capacity to build monumental buildings like the Tower of Bavel spoken about in Genesis, or the giant pyramid of Giza, undertaken by Pharaoh Khufu around 2500 BCE, before even the birth of Avraham. In such a world, with the exception of the ruler and the elite, life was cheap. The Sages said about the Tower of Bavel that if a person fell and died, no one noticed. If a brick fell, they wept (Pirkei DeRabbi Eliezer 24). Size meant strength, military or economic. Life was measured in the mass.

The religion of Israel is a principled protest against this view. At this distance in time, it is hard to fully appreciate the

Meeting, its covering, the covering of fine leather that is
over it, the screen at the entrance to the Tent of Meeting,
26 the hangings for the courtyard, the curtain for the entrance
of the gate to the courtyard around the Tabernacle and
the altar, and their ropes, together with all the utensils
for their service and everything made for them; and they
27 will serve. All the carrying and service of the Gershonites
shall be performed at Aharon and his sons' command;
you shall assign to their charge all that they are to carry.
28 This is the service of the families of the Gershonites
for the Tent of Meeting. Their charge will be under the
29 authority of Itamar son of Aharon the priest. As
for the sons of Merari, you shall number them by their
30 clans and ancestral houses, from thirty years old to fifty,
all who go into service to carry out the work of the Tent
31 of Meeting. This is what they are charged to carry as the
whole of their service in the Tent of Meeting: the boards
32 of the Tabernacle, its crossbars, its posts, its sockets; and
the posts of the surrounding courtyard with their sockets,
pegs, and ropes, together with all their furnishings and
everything for their service. You shall assign each object
33 by name to the man charged with carrying it. This is the
service of the families of the Merarites, the whole of their
service for the Tent of Meeting, under the authority of
34 Itamar son of Aharon the priest." So Moshe and Aharon
and the leaders of the community counted the Kohatites
35 by their clans and their ancestral houses, from thirty years
old to fifty, all who went into the service of the Tent of
36 Meeting; and those numbered by their clans were 2,750.
37 These were the ones numbered from the clans of Kehat,
all who served in the Tent of Meeting, whom Moshe
and Aharon numbered at the LORD's command through
38 Moshe. Those numbered of the Gershonites, SHENI
39 by their families and ancestral houses, from thirty years
old to fifty: all who went into the service of the Tent of
40 Meeting – those numbered by their clans and ancestral
41 houses were 2,630. These were the ones numbered from

אֹהֶל מוֹעֵד מִכְסֵהוּ וּמִכְסֵה הַתַּחַשׁ אֲשֶׁר־עָלָיו מִלְמָעְלָה
כו וְאֶת־מָסַךְ פֶּתַח אֹהֶל מוֹעֵד: וְאֵת קַלְעֵי הֶחָצֵר וְאֶת־
מָסַךְ | פֶּתַח | שַׁעַר הֶחָצֵר אֲשֶׁר עַל־הַמִּשְׁכָּן וְעַל־הַמִּזְבֵּחַ
סָבִיב וְאֵת מֵיתְרֵיהֶם וְאֶת־כָּל־כְּלֵי עֲבֹדָתָם וְאֵת כָּל־אֲשֶׁר
כז יֵעָשֶׂה לָהֶם וְעָבָדוּ: עַל־פִּי אַהֲרֹן וּבָנָיו תִּהְיֶה כָּל־עֲבֹדַת
בְּנֵי הַגֵּרְשֻׁנִּי לְכָל־מַשָּׂאָם וּלְכֹל עֲבֹדָתָם וּפְקַדְתֶּם עֲלֵהֶם
כח בְּמִשְׁמֶרֶת אֵת כָּל־מַשָּׂאָם: זֹאת עֲבֹדַת מִשְׁפְּחֹת בְּנֵי
הַגֵּרְשֻׁנִּי בְּאֹהֶל מוֹעֵד וּמִשְׁמַרְתָּם בְּיַד אִיתָמָר בֶּן־אַהֲרֹן
כט הַכֹּהֵן: בְּנֵי מְרָרִי לְמִשְׁפְּחֹתָם לְבֵית־אֲבֹתָם
ל תִּפְקֹד אֹתָם: מִבֶּן שְׁלֹשִׁים שָׁנָה וָמַעְלָה וְעַד בֶּן־חֲמִשִּׁים
שָׁנָה תִּפְקְדֵם כָּל־הַבָּא לַצָּבָא לַעֲבֹד אֶת־עֲבֹדַת אֹהֶל
לא מוֹעֵד: וְזֹאת מִשְׁמֶרֶת מַשָּׂאָם לְכָל־עֲבֹדָתָם בְּאֹהֶל מוֹעֵד
לב קַרְשֵׁי הַמִּשְׁכָּן וּבְרִיחָיו וְעַמּוּדָיו וַאֲדָנָיו: וְעַמּוּדֵי הֶחָצֵר
סָבִיב וְאַדְנֵיהֶם וִיתֵדֹתָם וּמֵיתְרֵיהֶם לְכָל־כְּלֵיהֶם וּלְכֹל
לג עֲבֹדָתָם וּבְשֵׁמֹת תִּפְקְדוּ אֶת־כְּלֵי מִשְׁמֶרֶת מַשָּׂאָם: זֹאת
עֲבֹדַת מִשְׁפְּחֹת בְּנֵי מְרָרִי לְכָל־עֲבֹדָתָם בְּאֹהֶל מוֹעֵד
לד בְּיַד אִיתָמָר בֶּן־אַהֲרֹן הַכֹּהֵן: וַיִּפְקֹד מֹשֶׁה וְאַהֲרֹן וּנְשִׂיאֵי
לה הָעֵדָה אֶת־בְּנֵי הַקְּהָתִי לְמִשְׁפְּחֹתָם וּלְבֵית אֲבֹתָם: מִבֶּן
שְׁלֹשִׁים שָׁנָה וָמַעְלָה וְעַד בֶּן־חֲמִשִּׁים שָׁנָה כָּל־הַבָּא לַצָּבָא
לו לַעֲבֹדָה בְּאֹהֶל מוֹעֵד: וַיִּהְיוּ פְקֻדֵיהֶם לְמִשְׁפְּחֹתָם אַלְפַּיִם
לז שְׁבַע מֵאוֹת וַחֲמִשִּׁים: אֵלֶּה פְקוּדֵי מִשְׁפְּחֹת הַקְּהָתִי כָּל־
הָעֹבֵד בְּאֹהֶל מוֹעֵד אֲשֶׁר פָּקַד מֹשֶׁה וְאַהֲרֹן עַל־פִּי יְהוָה
לח בְּיַד־מֹשֶׁה: וּפְקוּדֵי בְּנֵי גֵרְשׁוֹן לְמִשְׁפְּחוֹתָם שני
לט וּלְבֵית אֲבֹתָם: מִבֶּן שְׁלֹשִׁים שָׁנָה וָמַעְלָה וְעַד בֶּן־חֲמִשִּׁים
מ שָׁנָה כָּל־הַבָּא לַצָּבָא לַעֲבֹדָה בְּאֹהֶל מוֹעֵד: וַיִּהְיוּ פְּקֻדֵיהֶם
לְמִשְׁפְּחֹתָם לְבֵית אֲבֹתָם אַלְפַּיִם וְשֵׁשׁ מֵאוֹת וּשְׁלֹשִׁים:
מא אֵלֶּה פְקוּדֵי מִשְׁפְּחֹת בְּנֵי גֵרְשׁוֹן כָּל־הָעֹבֵד בְּאֹהֶל מוֹעֵד

the families of the Gershonites, all who served in the
Tent of Meeting, whom Moshe and Aharon numbered
42 at the command of the LORD. Those numbered from
the clans of the Merarites, by their clans and ancestral
43 houses, from thirty years old to fifty, all who went into the
44 service of the Tent of Meeting – those numbered by their
45 clans were 3,200. These were the ones numbered from
the clans of the Merarites, whom Moshe and Aharon
46 numbered at the LORD's command through Moshe. All
the Levites, whom Moshe, Aharon, and the leaders of
47 Israel numbered by their clans and ancestral houses, from
thirty years old to fifty: all who entered to do the work of
service and the work of carrying relating to the Tent of
48 49 Meeting – those numbered were 8,580. At the command
of the LORD they were listed, and by the authority of
Moshe, each according to his service and to what he was
to carry; thus was each one numbered as the LORD had
commanded Moshe.
5 1 2 Then the LORD spoke to Moshe: "Command the Israelites SHELISHI
to send away from the camp anyone who has an impure
blight, or has had a discharge, or anyone made impure
3 by contact with the dead. Male or female, you must send
them away – send them away outside the camp, so that
they do not defile their camps, in the midst of which I
4 dwell." The Israelites did so: outside the camp they sent

---

priesthood has gone to just one man and his descendants: Aharon, Moshe's brother. Later in the *parasha* Moshe will turn to the toxic effects of jealousy in a marriage; to individuals who aspire to a higher level of holiness without having been born into the priesthood; to the leadership of the tribes, which could so easily fall into a trap of rivalry.

There is no way of eliminating entirely the danger of jealousy and envy, but Moshe gives us some pointers. Honor everyone equally. Pay special attention to potentially disaffected groups. Make each feel valued. Give everyone a moment in the limelight. Find ways in which those with a particular passion can express it, and ensure that everyone has a chance to contribute. Though there is no fail-safe way to avoid the politics of envy, leaders can and must strive to minimize it.

מב אֲשֶׁר פָּקַד מֹשֶׁה וְאַהֲרֹן עַל־פִּי יְהוָה׃ וּפְקוּדֵי מִשְׁפְּחֹת
מג בְּנֵי מְרָרִי לְמִשְׁפְּחֹתָם לְבֵית אֲבֹתָם׃ מִבֶּן שְׁלֹשִׁים שָׁנָה
וָמַעְלָה וְעַד בֶּן־חֲמִשִּׁים שָׁנָה כָּל־הַבָּא לַצָּבָא לַעֲבֹדָה
מד בְּאֹהֶל מוֹעֵד׃ וַיִּהְיוּ פְקֻדֵיהֶם לְמִשְׁפְּחֹתָם שְׁלֹשֶׁת אֲלָפִים
מה וּמָאתָיִם׃ אֵלֶּה פְקוּדֵי מִשְׁפְּחֹת בְּנֵי מְרָרִי אֲשֶׁר פָּקַד מֹשֶׁה
מו וְאַהֲרֹן עַל־פִּי יְהוָה בְּיַד־מֹשֶׁה׃ כָּל־הַפְּקֻדִים אֲשֶׁר פָּקַד
מֹשֶׁה וְאַהֲרֹן וּנְשִׂיאֵי יִשְׂרָאֵל אֶת־הַלְוִיִּם לְמִשְׁפְּחֹתָם וּלְבֵית
מז אֲבֹתָם׃ מִבֶּן שְׁלֹשִׁים שָׁנָה וָמַעְלָה וְעַד בֶּן־חֲמִשִּׁים שָׁנָה
כָּל־הַבָּא לַעֲבֹד עֲבֹדַת עֲבֹדָה וַעֲבֹדַת מַשָּׂא בְּאֹהֶל מוֹעֵד׃
מח מט וַיִּהְיוּ פְּקֻדֵיהֶם שְׁמֹנַת אֲלָפִים וַחֲמֵשׁ מֵאוֹת וּשְׁמֹנִים׃ עַל־פִּי
יְהוָה פָּקַד אוֹתָם בְּיַד־מֹשֶׁה אִישׁ אִישׁ עַל־עֲבֹדָתוֹ וְעַל־
מַשָּׂאוֹ וּפְקֻדָיו אֲשֶׁר־צִוָּה יְהוָה אֶת־מֹשֶׁה׃
ה א ב וַיְדַבֵּר יְהוָה אֶל־מֹשֶׁה לֵּאמֹר׃ צַו אֶת־בְּנֵי יִשְׂרָאֵל וִישַׁלְּחוּ שלישי
ג מִן־הַמַּחֲנֶה כָּל־צָרוּעַ וְכָל־זָב וְכֹל טָמֵא לָנָפֶשׁ׃ מִזָּכָר עַד־
נְקֵבָה תְּשַׁלֵּחוּ אֶל־מִחוּץ לַמַּחֲנֶה תְּשַׁלְּחוּם וְלֹא יְטַמְּאוּ
ד אֶת־מַחֲנֵיהֶם אֲשֶׁר אֲנִי שֹׁכֵן בְּתוֹכָם׃ וַיַּעֲשׂוּ־כֵן בְּנֵי יִשְׂרָאֵל

4:46 כָּל־הַפְּקֻדִים *All the Levites* – Moshe has now given each Levitical clan a special role in carrying the vessels, furnishings, and framework of the Tabernacle whenever the people journeyed from place to place. The most sacred objects are to be carried by the clan of Kehat. The Gershonites are to carry the cloths, coverings, and curtains. The Merarites are to carry the boards, crossbars, posts, and sockets that make up the Tabernacle's framework. Each clan is, in other words, to have a special role and place in the solemn procession as the House of God is carried through the desert.

What is the importance, here in the midst of the census, of defining the separate roles of the Levite families? Envy is a constant throughout history. Aeschylus said, "It is in the character of very few men to honor without envy a friend who has prospered." Even when people accept, in theory, the equal dignity of all, and even when they see leadership as service, the old dysfunctional passions die hard. People still resent the success of others. R. Elazar HaKappar said: "Envy, lust, and the pursuit of honor drive a person out of the world" (Avot 4:21). The Levites have reason to resent the fact that the

them. As the LORD spoke to Moshe, so the Israelites
did.
5 6 And the LORD spoke to Moshe: "Tell the Israelites: When
one man or woman commits any sin against another,
7 breaking faith with the LORD and incurring guilt, then
he or she shall confess the sin committed and make
restitution, adding a fifth to its value, and giving it all to
8 the one whom he has wronged. But if there is no relative
to whom restitution can be made for the wrong, the
restitution for that wrong shall go to the LORD, to the
priest, in addition to the ram of atonement by which
9 atonement is made on his behalf. All gifts the Israelites
10 present to the priest as sacred offerings shall be his. Each
priest's sacred offerings will be his; whatever anyone gives
him shall be his."
11 12 The LORD spoke to Moshe: "Speak to the Israelites and REVI'I
tell them: If any man's wife goes astray and is unfaithful
13 to him; if another man has sexual relations with her, and

"Mercy and truth collided; righteousness and peace clashed" (Ps. 85:11).

Mercy said, "Let him be created, because he will do merciful deeds."

Truth said, "Let him not be created, for he will be full of falsehood."

Righteousness said, "Let him be created, for he will do righteous deeds."

Peace said, "Let him not be created, for he will never cease quarreling."

What did the Holy One, blessed be He, do? He took truth and threw it to the ground. The angels said, "Sovereign of the Universe, why do You do thus to Your own seal, truth? Let truth arise from the ground." (Bereshit Rabba 8:5)

This midrash clothes in a story an audacious theological interpretation. God, it suggests, was in two minds before creating mankind. Yes, humanity is capable of great acts of altruism and self-sacrifice, but it is also constantly at war. Human beings tell lies and are full of strife. God takes truth and throws it to the ground, meaning: for life to be livable, truth on earth cannot be what it is in heaven. Truth in heaven may be platonic – eternal, harmonious, radiant. But man cannot aspire to such truth, and if he does, he will create conflict, not peace. In that case, says God, throwing truth to the ground, let human beings live by a different standard of truth, one that is human and thus conscious of its limitations. Truth on the ground is multiple, partial. Fragments of it lie everywhere.

וישלחו אותם אל-מחוץ למחנה כאשר דבר יהוה אל-
משה כן עשו בני ישראל:
ה וידבר יהוה אל-משה לאמר: דבר אל-בני ישראל איש
ו או-אשה כי יעשו מכל-חטאת האדם למעל מעל ביהוה
ז ואשמה הנפש ההוא: והתודו את-חטאתם אשר עשו
והשיב את-אשמו בראשו וחמישתו יסף עליו ונתן לאשר
ח אשם לו: ואם-אין לאיש גאל להשיב האשם אליו האשם
המושב ליהוה לכהן מלבד איל הכפרים אשר יכפר-בו
ט עליו: וכל-תרומה לכל-קדשי בני-ישראל אשר-יקריבו
י לכהן לו יהיה: ואיש את-קדשיו לו יהיו איש אשר-יתן
לכהן לו יהיה:
יא יב וידבר יהוה אל-משה לאמר: דבר אל-בני ישראל ואמרת ה רביעי
יג אלהם איש איש כי-תשטה אשתו ומעלה בו מעל: ושכב

THE RITUAL OF THE ACCUSED WIFE

The case of the *sota* concerns the woman suspected by her husband of adultery – a situation fraught with danger of violence and abuse. The Mishna (Sota 1:5) clarifies that the woman in this predicament has the choice either to divorce her husband, or to prove her innocence beyond equivocation. What struck the Sages most forcibly about the ritual of the *sota* is the fact that it involved obliterating the name of God, something strictly forbidden under other circumstances. The officiating priest recites a curse including God's name, writes it on a parchment scroll, and then dissolves the writing into specially prepared water. The results of the woman drinking this water will publicly indicate her guilt or innocence of her husband's charge. The Sages inferred from this that God was willing to renounce His own honor, allowing His name to be effaced, "in order to make peace between husband and wife" by clearing an innocent woman from suspicion (Sifrei, Naso 42). Though the ordeal was eventually abolished by Rabban Yoḥanan b. Zakkai after the destruction of the Second Temple, the law served as a reminder as to how important domestic peace is in the Jewish scale of values. Peace and truth, the two objectives of the ritual, are often elusive in relationships between people:

> R. Shimon said: When God was about to create Adam, the ministering angels split into contending groups. Some said, "Let him be created." Others said, "Let him not be created." That is why it is written:

this happens without the husband's knowledge because
she defiled herself in secret, there was no witness against
14 her, and she was not caught in the act – if a fit of jealousy
overcomes him, making him jealous over his wife who
has defiled herself, or a fit of jealousy overcomes him,
making him jealous over his wife who has not defiled
15 herself – then the man shall bring his wife to the priest
together with the prescribed offering for her, one-tenth
of an ephah of barley flour. He shall not pour oil on it
or place frankincense upon it, for it is a grain offering
of jealousy, a grain offering of remembrance, calling
16 attention to a wrong. The priest shall bring the woman
17 close and have her stand before the Lord. He shall then
take sacred water in an earthenware vessel, and pick up
some earth from the floor of the Tabernacle and place it
18 in the water. He shall have the woman stand before the
Lord, and loosen the hair of the woman's head, placing
on her palms the grain offering of remembrance, the grain
offering of jealousy. His hand shall hold the bitter water
19 that gives rise to a curse. And the priest shall administer
an oath to her, saying to the woman, 'If no man has had
sexual relations with you, and if you have not gone astray,
letting yourself be defiled while married to your husband,
may your innocence be established by this bitter, cursing
20 water. But if you have gone astray while married to your
husband, and if you have let yourself be defiled and a man
other than your husband has had relations with you' – the
priest shall here put the woman under the oath of the
curse, and say to her – 'the Lord make you a curse and
an oath among your people, when the Lord makes your
22 thigh sag and your belly swell; may this curse-causing
water enter your intestines and make your belly swell and
your thigh sag.' And the woman shall say, 'Amen, Amen.'

---

wife. If she has not, the husband's withdrawal and anger would be unacceptably harsh. The doubt must be resolved, and we have to go the extra mile to achieve that end.

אִישׁ אֹתָהּ שִׁכְבַת־זֶרַע וְנֶעְלַם מֵעֵינֵי אִישָׁהּ וְנִסְתְּרָה וְהִיא
יד נִטְמָאָה וְעֵד אֵין בָּהּ וְהִוא לֹא נִתְפָּשָׂה: וְעָבַר עָלָיו רוּחַ־
קִנְאָה וְקִנֵּא אֶת־אִשְׁתּוֹ וְהִוא נִטְמָאָה אוֹ־עָבַר עָלָיו רוּחַ־
טו קִנְאָה וְקִנֵּא אֶת־אִשְׁתּוֹ וְהִיא לֹא נִטְמָאָה: וְהֵבִיא הָאִישׁ
אֶת־אִשְׁתּוֹ אֶל־הַכֹּהֵן וְהֵבִיא אֶת־קָרְבָּנָהּ עָלֶיהָ עֲשִׂירִת
הָאֵיפָה קֶמַח שְׂעֹרִים לֹא־יִצֹק עָלָיו שֶׁמֶן וְלֹא־יִתֵּן עָלָיו
לְבֹנָה כִּי־מִנְחַת קְנָאֹת הוּא מִנְחַת זִכָּרוֹן מַזְכֶּרֶת עָוֹן:
טז יז וְהִקְרִיב אֹתָהּ הַכֹּהֵן וְהֶעֱמִדָהּ לִפְנֵי יהוה: וְלָקַח הַכֹּהֵן
מַיִם קְדֹשִׁים בִּכְלִי־חָרֶשׂ וּמִן־הֶעָפָר אֲשֶׁר יִהְיֶה בְּקַרְקַע
יח הַמִּשְׁכָּן יִקַּח הַכֹּהֵן וְנָתַן אֶל־הַמָּיִם: וְהֶעֱמִיד הַכֹּהֵן אֶת־
הָאִשָּׁה לִפְנֵי יהוה וּפָרַע אֶת־רֹאשׁ הָאִשָּׁה וְנָתַן עַל־כַּפֶּיהָ
אֵת מִנְחַת הַזִּכָּרוֹן מִנְחַת קְנָאֹת הִוא וּבְיַד הַכֹּהֵן יִהְיוּ מֵי
יט הַמָּרִים הַמְאָרְרִים: וְהִשְׁבִּיעַ אֹתָהּ הַכֹּהֵן וְאָמַר אֶל־הָאִשָּׁה
אִם־לֹא שָׁכַב אִישׁ אֹתָךְ וְאִם־לֹא שָׂטִית טֻמְאָה תַּחַת
כ אִישֵׁךְ הִנָּקִי מִמֵּי הַמָּרִים הַמְאָרְרִים הָאֵלֶּה: וְאַתְּ כִּי שָׂטִית
תַּחַת אִישֵׁךְ וְכִי נִטְמֵאת וַיִּתֵּן אִישׁ בָּךְ אֶת־שְׁכָבְתּוֹ מִבַּלְעֲדֵי
כא אִישֵׁךְ: וְהִשְׁבִּיעַ הַכֹּהֵן אֶת־הָאִשָּׁה בִּשְׁבֻעַת הָאָלָה וְאָמַר
הַכֹּהֵן לָאִשָּׁה יִתֵּן יהוה אוֹתָךְ לְאָלָה וְלִשְׁבֻעָה בְּתוֹךְ עַמֵּךְ
כב בְּתֵת יהוה אֶת־יְרֵכֵךְ נֹפֶלֶת וְאֶת־בִּטְנֵךְ צָבָה: וּבָאוּ הַמַּיִם
הַמְאָרְרִים הָאֵלֶּה בְּמֵעַיִךְ לַצְבּוֹת בֶּטֶן וְלַנְפִּל יָרֵךְ וְאָמְרָה

Each person, culture, and language has part of it; none has it all.

In many cases, truth and peace are conflicting values. Holding on to my conception of truth makes it hard for me to concede space to yours. A tradition is what it is, not only in virtue of the ideals it espouses, but also how it resolves conflicts between those values, and the Rabbis articulated an ethic heavily weighted toward peace. Heroism, they said, meant conquering oneself, not others. Lights of peace (the Sabbath candles) took precedence over lights of victory (the Ḥanukka candles) (Shabbat 23b; *Hilkhot Ḥanukka* 4:14). In the case of the husband possessed by jealousy, establishing truth is a prerequisite for peace. If the wife has been unfaithful, they are forbidden to continue to live as husband and

23 Then the priest shall write these curses on a scroll and
24 wash them off into the bitter water. He shall make the
woman drink the bitter water that causes a curse, and the
curse-causing water will enter into her and turn bitter.
25 The priest shall take the grain offering of jealousy from
the woman's hand, wave the grain offering before the
26 LORD, and bring it close to the altar. Then the priest shall
take a handful of the grain offering as a token, and burn it
on the altar, after which he shall make the woman drink
27 the water. He having given her the water to drink, then,
if she has let herself be defiled and behaved unfaithfully
toward her husband, the curse-causing water will turn
bitter, her belly will swell, her thigh will sag, and the
28 woman will become a curse among her people. But if the
woman has not let herself be defiled and is pure, then she
29 shall be cleared and will conceive children." This is the
law for cases of jealousy, when a woman goes astray with
someone in place of her husband and becomes defiled,
30 or when a fit of jealousy overcomes a man and he grows
jealous over his wife. He shall have the woman stand
before the LORD, and the priest will deal with her as all
31 this law prescribes. No guilt will attach to the husband,
but the woman in question will bear the punishment of
her offense.
6 1 2 Then the LORD spoke to Moshe: "Speak to the Israelites.
Say: When a man or a woman takes a special vow, the vow

God brings order out of *tohu vavohu*, chaos, creating a world in which each object and life-form has its place. Peace exists where each element in the system is valued as a vital part of the system as a whole and where there is no discord between them.

Peace is easily damaged and hard to repair. The doubt cast within this couple's marriage renders their coexistence impossible. To resolve this, the Sages noted, and to rehabilitate the couple's mutual trust, God is willing to let His own name be blotted out.

THE NAZIRITE

The nazirite is an individual who undertakes the special rules of holiness and abstinence: not to drink alcohol (or anything made from grapes), not to have his hair cut, and to avoid contact with the dead. Living as a nazirite was

כג הָאִשָּׁה אָמֵן ׀ אָמֵן׃ וְכָתַב אֶת־הָאָלֹת הָאֵלֶּה הַכֹּהֵן בַּסֵּפֶר
כד וּמָחָה אֶל־מֵי הַמָּרִים׃ וְהִשְׁקָה אֶת־הָאִשָּׁה אֶת־מֵי הַמָּרִים
כה הַמְאָרְרִים וּבָאוּ בָהּ הַמַּיִם הַמְאָרְרִים לְמָרִים׃ וְלָקַח הַכֹּהֵן
מִיַּד הָאִשָּׁה אֵת מִנְחַת הַקְּנָאֹת וְהֵנִיף אֶת־הַמִּנְחָה לִפְנֵי
כו יהוה וְהִקְרִיב אֹתָהּ אֶל־הַמִּזְבֵּחַ׃ וְקָמַץ הַכֹּהֵן מִן־הַמִּנְחָה
אֶת־אַזְכָּרָתָהּ וְהִקְטִיר הַמִּזְבֵּחָה וְאַחַר יַשְׁקֶה אֶת־הָאִשָּׁה
כז אֶת־הַמָּיִם׃ וְהִשְׁקָהּ אֶת־הַמַּיִם וְהָיְתָה אִם־נִטְמְאָה וַתִּמְעֹל
מַעַל בְּאִישָׁהּ וּבָאוּ בָהּ הַמַּיִם הַמְאָרְרִים לְמָרִים וְצָבְתָה
כח בִטְנָהּ וְנָפְלָה יְרֵכָהּ וְהָיְתָה הָאִשָּׁה לְאָלָה בְּקֶרֶב עַמָּהּ׃ וְאִם־
כט לֹא נִטְמְאָה הָאִשָּׁה וּטְהֹרָה הִוא וְנִקְּתָה וְנִזְרְעָה זָרַע׃ זֹאת
תּוֹרַת הַקְּנָאֹת אֲשֶׁר תִּשְׂטֶה אִשָּׁה תַּחַת אִישָׁהּ וְנִטְמָאָה׃
ל אוֹ אִישׁ אֲשֶׁר תַּעֲבֹר עָלָיו רוּחַ קִנְאָה וְקִנֵּא אֶת־אִשְׁתּוֹ
וְהֶעֱמִיד אֶת־הָאִשָּׁה לִפְנֵי יהוה וְעָשָׂה לָהּ הַכֹּהֵן אֵת כָּל־
לא הַתּוֹרָה הַזֹּאת׃ וְנִקָּה הָאִישׁ מֵעָוֹן וְהָאִשָּׁה הַהִוא תִּשָּׂא
אֶת־עֲוֺנָהּ׃

ו א ב וַיְדַבֵּר יהוה אֶל־מֹשֶׁה לֵּאמֹר׃ דַּבֵּר אֶל־בְּנֵי יִשְׂרָאֵל וְאָמַרְתָּ
אֲלֵהֶם אִישׁ אוֹ־אִשָּׁה כִּי יַפְלִא לִנְדֹּר נֶדֶר נָזִיר לְהַזִּיר לַיהוה׃

5:23 וּמָחָה אֶל־מֵי הַמָּרִים *Wash them off into the bitter water* – In a long analysis, the fifteenth-century Spanish commentator Rabbi Yitzḥak Arama explains that *shalom* does not mean merely the absence of strife. It means completeness, the harmonious working of a complex system, a state in which everything is in its proper place and all is at one with the physical and ethical laws governing the universe: "Peace is the thread of grace issuing from Him, may He be exalted, stringing together all beings.... It underlies and sustains the reality and unique existence of each" (*Akedat Yitzḥak*, ch. 74).

Similarly, Rabbi Yitzḥak Abrabanel writes (commentary on Avot 2:12):

> That is why God is called "Peace," because it is He who binds the world together and orders all things according to their particular character and posture. For when things are in their proper order, peace will reign.

This is a concept of peace heavily dependent on the vision of Genesis 1, in which

3 of a nazirite, to separate him or herself to the LORD, he
must separate himself from wine and strong drink. He
must drink neither vinegar made from wine nor vinegar
made from any other strong drink, nor may he drink any
4 juice made with grapes, nor eat fresh grapes or raisins. All
the days of his separation he must not eat anything that

altogether. He or she follows the "golden mean," the "middle way," the way of moderation and balance. He or she avoids the extremes of cowardice on the one hand, recklessness on the other, and thus acquires the virtue of courage. He or she avoids miserliness in one direction, prodigality in the other, and instead chooses the middle way of generosity. The sage weighs the conflicting pressures and avoids the extremes.

Is the aim of the moral life to achieve personal perfection? Or is it to create gracious relationships and a decent, just, compassionate society? The intuitive answer of most people would be to say: both. Rambam realized that they are in fact different enterprises.

It was this insight that led Rambam to his seemingly contradictory evaluations of the nazirite. The nazirite has chosen, at least for a period, to adopt a life of extreme self-denial. He has adopted the path of personal perfection. That is noble, commendable, and exemplary. That is why Rambam calls him "praiseworthy" and "the equal of a prophet."

But it is not the way of the sage – and if you seek to perfect society, you need sages. The sage is not an extremist – because he or she realizes that there are other people at stake. There are one's family, colleagues, and community. There is a country to defend and a society to help build. The sage knows he or she cannot leave all these commitments behind to pursue a life of solitary virtue. We are called on by God to live in the world and to strive toward a balance among the conflicting pressures on us – in society, not in seclusion.

6:4 מִכֹּל אֲשֶׁר יֵעָשֶׂה מִגֶּפֶן הַיַּיִן *Anything that comes from the grapevine* – "He makes... wine to cheer people's hearts," says the psalmist (Ps. 104:14–15), celebrating one of the sources of enjoyment God created for our benefit. Nonetheless, almost every religion knows the phenomenon of people who, in pursuit of spiritual purity, withdraw from the pleasures and temptations of the world. The ambivalence of Jews toward the life of self-denial may lie in the suspicion that it entered Judaism from the outside. There were ascetic movements in the first centuries of the Common Era in both the West (Greece) and the East (Iran) that saw the physical world as a place of corruption and strife. They were, in fact, dualists, holding that the true God was not the creator of the universe. The physical world was the work of a lesser, and evil, deity.

ג מִיַּיִן וְשֵׁכָר יַזִּיר חֹמֶץ יַיִן וְחֹמֶץ שֵׁכָר לֹא יִשְׁתֶּה וְכָל־מִשְׁרַת
ד עֲנָבִים לֹא יִשְׁתֶּה וַעֲנָבִים לַחִים וִיבֵשִׁים לֹא יֹאכֵל׃ כֹּל
יְמֵי נִזְרוֹ מִכֹּל אֲשֶׁר יֵעָשֶׂה מִגֶּפֶן הַיַּיִן מֵחַרְצַנִּים וְעַד־זָג

usually undertaken for a limited time period; the standard length was thirty days. The Torah calls the nazirite "holy to the LORD" (Num. 6:8). Intriguingly, however, it requires him, at the end of the period of his vow, to bring a purification offering, as if he had sinned (6:13–14).

This led to an ongoing disagreement between the Rabbis. According to R. Elazar, and later Ramban, the nazirite is praiseworthy. He has voluntarily undertaken a higher level of holiness. The reason he had to bring a sin offering was that he was now returning to ordinary life. His sin lay in *ceasing* to be a nazirite. R. Eliezer HaKappar and Shmuel held the opposite opinion. For them the sin lay in becoming a nazirite in the first place and thereby denying himself some of the pleasures God created and declared good. R. Eliezer added: "From this we may infer that if one who denies himself the enjoyment of wine is called a sinner, all the more so one who denies himself other pleasures of life" (Taanit 11a; Nedarim 10a).

Rambam, surprisingly, holds *both* views regarding the nazirite, positive and negative, in the same book – his law code the *Mishneh Torah*. In the section *Hilkhot Deot,* he adopts the negative position of R. Eliezer:

> A person may say: "Desire, honor, and the like are bad paths to follow and remove a person from the world; therefore I will completely separate myself from them and go to the other extreme." As a result, he does not eat meat or drink wine or take a wife or live in a decent house or wear decent clothing.... This too is bad, and it is forbidden to choose this way. (*Hilkhot Deot* 3:1)

Yet in *Hilkhot Nezirut* he rules in accordance with the positive evaluation of R. Elazar: "Whoever vows to God [to become a nazirite] by way of holiness, he does well and is praiseworthy.... Indeed Scripture considers him the equal of a prophet" (*Hilkhot Nezirut* 10:14).

The resolution of these two contradictory opinions lies in a remarkable insight into the nature of the moral life. What Rambam saw is that there is not a single model of the virtuous life. He identifies two, calling them the way of the saint (*ḥasid*) and the way of the sage (*ḥakham*).

The saint is a person of extremes. Rambam defines *ḥesed* as extreme behavior – good behavior, to be sure, but conduct in excess of what strict justice requires (*Guide for the Perplexed* III:52). So, for example, "if one avoids haughtiness to the utmost extent and becomes exceedingly humble, he is termed a saint (*ḥasid*)" (*Hilkhot Deot* 1:5).

The sage is a different kind of person

5 comes from the grapevine, from seed to skin. All the days
of his separation vow, no razor shall touch his head. Until
the completion of the time for which he separated himself
to the LORD, he shall be holy, and must let the locks of his
6 hair grow long. All the days of his separation to the LORD,
7 he must not come near a dead body. Even for his father
or mother or brother or sister, if they die, he must not
defile himself, for his vow of separation to his God is on
8 his head. All the days of his separation he is holy to the
9 LORD. If someone dies suddenly beside him, defiling his
consecrated head, he shall shave his head on the day of his
10 purification; on the seventh day he shall shave it. Then,
on the eighth day, he shall bring two turtledoves or two
young pigeons to the priest, to the entrance of the Tent of
11 Meeting. The priest will offer one as a purification offering
and the other as a burnt offering, and make atonement
for him for the guilt he incurred through contact with the
dead body. He shall consecrate his head anew on that day.
12 He must rededicate himself to the LORD for the full term
of his vow, and bring a yearling lamb as a guilt offering.
The former days are discounted because his separation
13 was defiled. This is the law of the nazirite: On the day
that the term of his nazirite vow is completed, he shall
14 be brought to the entrance to the Tent of Meeting. He
shall present his offering to the LORD: one male yearling
lamb without blemish for a burnt offering, one yearling
ewe lamb without blemish for a purification offering, one
15 ram without blemish for a peace offering, and a basket of
unleavened bread, loaves of fine flour mixed with olive oil,
and unleavened wafers smeared with olive oil, along with
16 their grain offering and libations. The priest shall present
these before the LORD and offer up his purification
17 offering and his burnt offering. He shall then offer the
ram as a sacrifice, a peace offering to the LORD, together
with the basket of unleavened bread. The priest shall also
18 offer his grain offering and his libation. The nazirite shall
shave his consecrated hair at the entrance to the Tent of

ה לֹא יֹאכֵל: כָּל־יְמֵי נֶדֶר נִזְרוֹ תַּעַר לֹא־יַעֲבֹר עַל־רֹאשׁוֹ
עַד־מְלֹאת הַיָּמִם אֲשֶׁר־יַזִּיר לַיהוה קָדֹשׁ יִהְיֶה גַּדֵּל פֶּרַע
ו שְׂעַר רֹאשׁוֹ: כָּל־יְמֵי הַזִּירוֹ לַיהוה עַל־נֶפֶשׁ מֵת לֹא יָבֹא:
ז לְאָבִיו וּלְאִמּוֹ לְאָחִיו וּלְאַחֹתוֹ לֹא־יִטַּמָּא לָהֶם בְּמֹתָם
ח כִּי נֵזֶר אֱלֹהָיו עַל־רֹאשׁוֹ: כֹּל יְמֵי נִזְרוֹ קָדֹשׁ הוּא לַיהוה:
ט וְכִי־יָמוּת מֵת עָלָיו בְּפֶתַע פִּתְאֹם וְטִמֵּא רֹאשׁ נִזְרוֹ וְגִלַּח
י רֹאשׁוֹ בְּיוֹם טָהֳרָתוֹ בַּיּוֹם הַשְּׁבִיעִי יְגַלְּחֶנּוּ: וּבַיּוֹם הַשְּׁמִינִי
יָבִא שְׁתֵּי תֹרִים אוֹ שְׁנֵי בְּנֵי יוֹנָה אֶל־הַכֹּהֵן אֶל־פֶּתַח אֹהֶל
יא מוֹעֵד: וְעָשָׂה הַכֹּהֵן אֶחָד לְחַטָּאת וְאֶחָד לְעֹלָה וְכִפֶּר עָלָיו
מֵאֲשֶׁר חָטָא עַל־הַנָּפֶשׁ וְקִדַּשׁ אֶת־רֹאשׁוֹ בַּיּוֹם הַהוּא:
יב וְהִזִּיר לַיהוה אֶת־יְמֵי נִזְרוֹ וְהֵבִיא כֶּבֶשׂ בֶּן־שְׁנָתוֹ לְאָשָׁם
יג וְהַיָּמִים הָרִאשֹׁנִים יִפְּלוּ כִּי טָמֵא נִזְרוֹ: וְזֹאת תּוֹרַת הַנָּזִיר
בְּיוֹם מְלֹאת יְמֵי נִזְרוֹ יָבִיא אֹתוֹ אֶל־פֶּתַח אֹהֶל מוֹעֵד:
יד וְהִקְרִיב אֶת־קָרְבָּנוֹ לַיהוה כֶּבֶשׂ בֶּן־שְׁנָתוֹ תָמִים אֶחָד
לְעֹלָה וְכַבְשָׂה אַחַת בַּת־שְׁנָתָהּ תְּמִימָה לְחַטָּאת וְאַיִל־
טו אֶחָד תָּמִים לִשְׁלָמִים: וְסַל מַצּוֹת סֹלֶת חַלֹּת בְּלוּלֹת בַּשֶּׁמֶן
טז וּרְקִיקֵי מַצּוֹת מְשֻׁחִים בַּשָּׁמֶן וּמִנְחָתָם וְנִסְכֵּיהֶם: וְהִקְרִיב
יז הַכֹּהֵן לִפְנֵי יהוה וְעָשָׂה אֶת־חַטָּאתוֹ וְאֶת־עֹלָתוֹ: וְאֶת־
הָאַיִל יַעֲשֶׂה זֶבַח שְׁלָמִים לַיהוה עַל סַל הַמַּצּוֹת וְעָשָׂה
יח הַכֹּהֵן אֶת־מִנְחָתוֹ וְאֶת־נִסְכּוֹ: וְגִלַּח הַנָּזִיר פֶּתַח אֹהֶל מוֹעֵד
אֶת־רֹאשׁ נִזְרוֹ וְלָקַח אֶת־שְׂעַר רֹאשׁ נִזְרוֹ וְנָתַן עַל־הָאֵשׁ

Therefore God – the true God – is not to be found in the physical world and its enjoyments but rather in disengagement from them.

We have seen that Judaism is in two minds about the nazirite. At least some of the negative evaluation of the nazirite among the Rabbis may have been driven by a desire to discourage Jews from imitating non-Jewish practices. Judaism strongly believes that God is to be found in the midst of the physical world that He created that is, in the first chapter of Genesis, seven times pronounced "good." According to many, it believes not in renouncing pleasure but in sanctifying it.

Meeting and take the hair of his consecrated head and
19 place it on the fire beneath the peace offering. The priest
shall take the boiled foreleg of the ram, one unleavened
loaf from the basket, and one unleavened wafer, and place
them on the hands of the nazirite after he has shaved his
20 consecrated head. The priest shall wave them as a wave
offering before the LORD. It is a sacred gift for the priest,
together with the breast of the wave offering and the
thigh of the upraised gift. After this the nazirite may drink
21 wine." This is the law of the nazirite who vows offerings
to the LORD as a nazirite. Whatever he can afford further
and vows to give, beyond what the law of the nazirite
obliges him to, that too shall he fulfill.
22 23 The LORD spoke to Moshe: "Tell Aharon and his
sons: This is how you are to bless the Israelites. Say to

---

holiness of Aharon and has commanded us to bless His people Israel with love." The last word, *be'ahava*, is unusual. It appears in no other blessing over the performance of a command. Ideally we should fulfill all the commands with love. But an absence of love does not invalidate any other command. Surely what matters is that the priests recite the blessing; God will do the rest. What difference does it make whether they do so in love or not?

The commentators wrestle with this. Some say that the fact that the priests are facing the people when they bless means that they are like the cherubim in the Tabernacle, who faced each other as a sign of love. Others change the word order. They say that the blessing really means: "who has made us holy with the holiness of Aharon and with love has commanded us to bless His people Israel." "Love" here refers to God's love for Israel, not the love of the priests.

However, it seems to me that the explanation is this: The Torah explicitly says that, though the priests say the words, it is God who sends the blessing. "They shall set My name upon the Israelites, and I will bless them." Normally when we fulfill a mitzva, we are doing something. But when the *kohanim* bless the people, they are not doing anything in and of themselves. Instead they are acting as channels through which God's blessing flows into the world and into our lives. An ancient midrash says: "The House of Israel said to the Holy One, blessed be He, 'LORD of the Universe, You order the priests to bless us? We need only Your blessing. Look down from Your holy habitation and bless Your people.' The Holy One, blessed be He, replied to them, 'Though I ordered the priests to bless you, I will stand together with them and bless you'" (*Tanḥuma*, Naso 15). Love enables this to happen.

יט אֲשֶׁר־תַּחַת זֶבַח הַשְּׁלָמִים: וְלָקַח הַכֹּהֵן אֶת־הַזְּרֹעַ בְּשֵׁלָה
מִן־הָאַיִל וְחַלַּת מַצָּה אַחַת מִן־הַסַּל וּרְקִיק מַצָּה אֶחָד וְנָתַן
כ עַל־כַּפֵּי הַנָּזִיר אַחַר הִתְגַּלְּחוֹ אֶת־נִזְרוֹ: וְהֵנִיף אוֹתָם הַכֹּהֵן ׀
תְּנוּפָה לִפְנֵי יהוה קֹדֶשׁ הוּא לַכֹּהֵן עַל חֲזֵה הַתְּנוּפָה וְעַל
כא שׁוֹק הַתְּרוּמָה וְאַחַר יִשְׁתֶּה הַנָּזִיר יָיִן: זֹאת תּוֹרַת הַנָּזִיר
אֲשֶׁר יִדֹּר קָרְבָּנוֹ לַיהוה עַל־נִזְרוֹ מִלְּבַד אֲשֶׁר־תַּשִּׂיג יָדוֹ
כְּפִי נִדְרוֹ אֲשֶׁר יִדֹּר כֵּן יַעֲשֶׂה עַל תּוֹרַת נִזְרוֹ:
כב כג וַיְדַבֵּר יהוה אֶל־מֹשֶׁה לֵּאמֹר: דַּבֵּר אֶל־אַהֲרֹן ׀
וְאֶל־בָּנָיו לֵאמֹר כֹּה תְבָרְכוּ אֶת־בְּנֵי יִשְׂרָאֵל אָמוֹר

THE PRIESTLY BLESSING

The priestly blessing is one of the oldest prayers in the world still in continuous use. It has been found in amulets from the early sixth century BCE, the time of the prophet Yirmeyahu. So ancient are these, that they are written not in the Hebrew alphabet as we recognize it today, which dates from the Babylonian exile, but rather in the ancient Paleo-Hebrew script, a direct descendant of the first alphabet known to humankind. The blessing was spoken by the priests in the Temple. It is said today by the priests in the *ḥazan*'s repetition of the *Amida*, in Israel every day, in most of the Diaspora only on festivals. It is used by parents when they bless their children on Friday night. It is often said to the bride and groom under the *ḥuppa*. It is among the shortest of blessings, a mere fifteen words long, but marked by beauty and simplicity.

It has a strong rhythmic structure. The lines contain three, five, and seven words respectively. In each, the second word is "the LORD." In all three verses, the first part refers to an activity on the part of God – "bless," "make His face shine," and "raise His face toward." The second part describes the effect of the blessing on us, giving us protection, grace, and peace.

The verses also travel inward, as it were. The first verse, "May the LORD bless you and watch over you," refers, as the commentators note, to material blessings: sustenance, physical health, and so on. The second, "May the LORD make His face shine on you and be gracious to you," refers to moral blessing. *Ḥen*, grace, is what we show to other people and they to us. The third is the most inward of all. The knowledge that God raises His face toward us – that we are not just an indiscernible face in a crowd but that God relates to us in our uniqueness and singularity – is the most profound and ultimate source of peace.

Before blessing the congregation in the synagogue, *kohanim* utter a benediction, instituted by the Sages, which is unique in its wording: "Blessed are you…who has made us holy with the

24 them: 'May the LORD bless you
25 and watch over you. May the LORD make His
26 face shine upon you and be gracious to you. May
the LORD raise His face toward you and grant you
27 peace.' They shall set My name upon the
7 1 Israelites, and I will bless them." On the day when HAMISHI
Moshe finished establishing the Tabernacle, he anointed
it and consecrated it. He anointed and consecrated the
2 altar, too, and all its utensils. And the princes of Israel,
leaders of their ancestral houses, drew close. They were
the princes of the tribes, the ones who had directed the

God "Make His face shine upon you," meaning, may His presence be evident in you. May He leave a visible trace of His Being on the face you show to others. How is that presence to be recognized? Not in severity, remoteness, or austerity but in the gentle smile that speaks to what Lincoln called "the better angels of our nature." That is grace.

6:26 יִשָּׂא יהוה פָּנָיו אֵלֶיךָ וְיָשֵׂם לְךָ שָׁלוֹם *May the LORD raise His face toward you and grant you peace* – To make peace in the world we must be at peace with ourselves. To be at peace with ourselves we must know that we are unconditionally valued. That does not often happen. People value us for what we can give them. That is conditional value, what the Sages called "love that is dependent on a cause" (Avot 5:16). God values us unconditionally. We are here because He wanted us to be. Our very existence testifies to His love. Unlike others, God never gives up on us. He rejects no one. He never loses faith, however many times we fail. When we fall, He lifts us. He believes in us more than we believe in ourselves. That, in human terms, is the meaning of "May the LORD raise His face toward you and give you peace."

6:27 וַאֲנִי אֲבָרְכֵם *I will bless them* – The most profound element of the blessing lies in the concluding sentence: "They shall set My name upon the Israelites, and I will bless them." In the ancient world, magi, oracles, and religious virtuosi were held to have the power of blessing. It was thought that blessing or curse lay within the power of the holy person. Holiness is not, though it is often confused with, self-importance. This is the meaning of "They shall set My name upon the Israelites, and I will bless them." It is not the priests who bless the people, but God. In themselves, they have no power. They are intermediaries, channels through which God's blessing flows. True holiness is transparency to the Divine.

THE OFFERINGS OF THE PRINCES

One of the most visible features of Numbers as a book – conspicuously so

כד כה לָהֶם׃ יְבָרֶכְךָ יהוה וְיִשְׁמְרֶךָ׃ יָאֵר
כו יהוה ׀ פָּנָיו אֵלֶיךָ וִיחֻנֶּךָּ׃ יִשָּׂא יהוה ׀ פָּנָיו אֵלֶיךָ
כז וְיָשֵׂם לְךָ שָׁלוֹם׃ וְשָׂמוּ אֶת־שְׁמִי עַל־בְּנֵי
ז א יִשְׂרָאֵל וַאֲנִי אֲבָרְכֵם׃ וַיְהִי בְּיוֹם כַּלּוֹת מֹשֶׁה חמישי
לְהָקִים אֶת־הַמִּשְׁכָּן וַיִּמְשַׁח אֹתוֹ וַיְקַדֵּשׁ אֹתוֹ וְאֶת־כָּל־
כֵּלָיו וְאֶת־הַמִּזְבֵּחַ וְאֶת־כָּל־כֵּלָיו וַיִּמְשָׁחֵם וַיְקַדֵּשׁ אֹתָם׃
ב וַיַּקְרִיבוּ נְשִׂיאֵי יִשְׂרָאֵל רָאשֵׁי בֵּית אֲבֹתָם הֵם נְשִׂיאֵי הַמַּטֹּת

Love means that we are focused not on ourselves but on another. Love is selflessness. And selflessness allows us to be a channel through which flows a force greater than ourselves.

6:24 יְבָרֶכְךָ יהוה וְיִשְׁמְרֶךָ *May the Lord bless you and watch over you* – Blessing in the Mosaic books always means material blessing. Against the idea basic to many other faith systems – which embrace poverty, asceticism, or other forms of self-denial – in Judaism, the world as God's creation is fundamentally good. Religion is neither otherworldly nor anti-worldly. It is precisely in the physical world that God's blessings are to be found.

But material blessings can sometimes dull our sensitivities toward God. The irony is that when we have the most to thank God for, often we thank Him least. We tend to remember God in times of crisis rather than in times of prosperity and peace.

This, more than any other factor, has led to the decline and fall of civilizations. In the early, pioneering years they are lifted by a collective vision and energy. Then as people become affluent they begin to lose the very qualities that made earlier generations great. They become less motivated by ideals than by the pursuit of pleasure. They think less of others, more of themselves. They begin to be deaf and blind to those in need. They become decadent. What happens to nations happens also to individuals and families. Hence the first blessing. "May the Lord… watch over you" means: may He protect you from the blessing turning into a curse.

6:25 יָאֵר יהוה פָּנָיו אֵלֶיךָ וִיחֻנֶּךָּ *May the Lord make His face shine upon you and be gracious to you* – Judaism highly values the intellect: study, questioning, ideas, argument, and the life of the mind. Yet in *Kaddish DeRabbanan*, the prayer we say after studying a rabbinic text, we pray for spiritual leaders who have "grace, loving-kindness, and compassion." The power of intellect is secondary to the personal qualities of sensitivity and graciousness. Grace is that quality which sees the best in others and seeks the best for others. It is a combination of gentleness and generosity.

The second priestly blessing is: May

3 census. And they brought their offerings before the LORD:
six covered wagons and twelve oxen – a wagon for every
two leaders, and for each one an ox. They presented them
4 5 before the Tabernacle. The LORD said to Moshe, "Accept
these from them and use them for service in the Tent of
Meeting. Give them to the Levites, to each according to
6 his service." Moshe took the wagons and the oxen, and
7 he gave them to the Levites. He gave two wagons and
four oxen to the Gershonites as their service required.
8 He gave four wagons and eight oxen to the Merarites
for their service under the supervision of Itamar son of
9 Aharon the priest. But to the Kohatites he gave none, for
their responsibility was for the sacred articles that had
10 to be carried on their shoulders. The princes presented
their dedication offering for the altar at the time when it
was anointed. The princes brought their offerings before
11 the altar. The LORD said to Moshe, "Each day one prince
is to bring close his offering for the dedication of the
12 altar." The one who presented his offering on the
first day was Naḥshon son of Aminadav, from the tribe of
13 Yehuda. His offering was one silver bowl weighing one
hundred and thirty shekel and one silver basin weighing

or king who represents authority and imposes it on the population. To the contrary, the Torah takes us through the slow growth of Israel as an entity – beginning with one couple, Avraham and Sara, who become a family, then an extended family, then a tribe, then a series of tribes. They are forged into a nation negatively by the experience of oppression in Egypt, positively by redemption and by the covenant they made with God at Mount Sinai. But those early structures – family, clan, tribe – remain important in the body politic, not just at the beginning but throughout.

We are not one thing. We have multiple identities, as members of this family, that neighborhood, this congregation, that religious faith, this ethnicity, that nation, and ultimately the human family itself, brothers and sisters under the parenthood of God. The insistence on one identity to the exclusion of all others is the mark of a potentially totalitarian regime. Hence the insistence of the book of Numbers on the continuing significance of the twelve tribes even when Israel is one nation under the One God.

ג הֵם הָעֹמְדִים עַל־הַפְּקֻדִים: וַיָּבִיאוּ אֶת־קָרְבָּנָם לִפְנֵי יְהוָה
שֵׁשׁ־עֶגְלֹת צָב וּשְׁנֵי־עָשָׂר בָּקָר עֲגָלָה עַל־שְׁנֵי הַנְּשִׂאִים
ד וְשׁוֹר לְאֶחָד וַיַּקְרִיבוּ אוֹתָם לִפְנֵי הַמִּשְׁכָּן: וַיֹּאמֶר יְהוָה
ה אֶל־מֹשֶׁה לֵּאמֹר: קַח מֵאִתָּם וְהָיוּ לַעֲבֹד אֶת־עֲבֹדַת אֹהֶל
ו מוֹעֵד וְנָתַתָּה אוֹתָם אֶל־הַלְוִיִּם אִישׁ כְּפִי עֲבֹדָתוֹ: וַיִּקַּח
מֹשֶׁה אֶת־הָעֲגָלֹת וְאֶת־הַבָּקָר וַיִּתֵּן אוֹתָם אֶל־הַלְוִיִּם:
ז אֵת ׀ שְׁתֵּי הָעֲגָלוֹת וְאֵת אַרְבַּעַת הַבָּקָר נָתַן לִבְנֵי גֵרְשׁוֹן
ח כְּפִי עֲבֹדָתָם: וְאֵת ׀ אַרְבַּע הָעֲגָלֹת וְאֵת שְׁמֹנַת הַבָּקָר
נָתַן לִבְנֵי מְרָרִי כְּפִי עֲבֹדָתָם בְּיַד אִיתָמָר בֶּן־אַהֲרֹן הַכֹּהֵן:
ט וְלִבְנֵי קְהָת לֹא נָתָן כִּי־עֲבֹדַת הַקֹּדֶשׁ עֲלֵהֶם בַּכָּתֵף יִשָּׂאוּ:
י וַיַּקְרִיבוּ הַנְּשִׂאִים אֵת חֲנֻכַּת הַמִּזְבֵּחַ בְּיוֹם הִמָּשַׁח אֹתוֹ
יא וַיַּקְרִיבוּ הַנְּשִׂיאִם אֶת־קָרְבָּנָם לִפְנֵי הַמִּזְבֵּחַ: וַיֹּאמֶר יְהוָה
אֶל־מֹשֶׁה נָשִׂיא אֶחָד לַיּוֹם נָשִׂיא אֶחָד לַיּוֹם יַקְרִיבוּ אֶת־
יב קָרְבָּנָם לַחֲנֻכַּת הַמִּזְבֵּחַ: וַיְהִי הַמַּקְרִיב בַּיּוֹם
הָרִאשׁוֹן אֶת־קָרְבָּנוֹ נַחְשׁוֹן בֶּן־עַמִּינָדָב לְמַטֵּה יְהוּדָה:
יג וְקָרְבָּנוֹ קַעֲרַת־כֶּסֶף אַחַת שְׁלֹשִׁים וּמֵאָה מִשְׁקָלָהּ מִזְרָק

in Parashat Naso – is the great attention it pays to tribes. The book begins with the people being counted according to tribe. Then we read about their positioning in the camp around the Tabernacle by tribe. The order in which they traveled in their journeys through the wilderness was also by tribe. In this *parasha,* at inordinate length we are told of the offerings of each tribe at the dedication of the Tabernacle, despite the fact that each brought exactly the same offering (Num. 7:1–89). Later in the book there is an account of how the land was to be allocated tribe by tribe. The book ends with the second half of the story of the daughters of Tzelofḥad, in which the leaders of their tribe bring a case to Moshe to ensure that their rights as a tribe are respected. In light of all this, the question remains insistent. Why tell the story this way? Why place the emphasis on tribes? Why was Israel not conceived as a united nation to begin with? Why orient the entire book of Numbers along the axis of tribal divisions and distinctions?

It seems that the Torah is telling us something compelling and fundamental, relevant not just then but still today. The Torah conceives of politics and identity from the ground up, not from the top down. It is not the ruler, emperor,

seventy shekel according to the Sanctuary weight, both
filled with fine flour mixed with oil for a grain offering;
14 one golden spoon weighing ten shekel, full of incense;
15 one young bull, one ram, and one yearling sheep for a
16 17 burnt offering; one goat for a purification offering; and
for the peace sacrifice two oxen, five rams, five male goats,
and five yearling sheep. This was the offering of Naḥshon
son of Aminadav.
18 On the second day Netanel son of Tzuar, prince of
19 Yissakhar, presented his offering. He presented as his
offering one silver bowl weighing one hundred and thirty
shekel and one silver basin weighing seventy shekel
according to the Sanctuary weight, both filled with fine
20 flour mixed with oil for a grain offering; one golden spoon
21 weighing ten shekel, full of incense; one young bull, one
22 ram, and one yearling sheep for a burnt offering; one goat
23 for a purification offering; and for the peace sacrifice two
oxen, five rams, five male goats, and five yearling sheep. This
was the offering of Netanel son of Tzuar.
24 On the third day came Eliav son of Ḥelon, prince of the
25 Zebulunites: His offering was one silver bowl weighing one
hundred and thirty shekel and one silver basin weighing
seventy shekel according to the Sanctuary weight, both
filled with fine flour mixed with oil for a grain offering;
26 27 one golden spoon weighing ten shekel, full of incense; one
young bull, one ram, and one yearling sheep for a burnt
28 29 offering; one goat for a purification offering; and for the
peace sacrifice two oxen, five rams, five male goats, and

repetitiousness of this particular passage cries out for explanation.

The long account of the offerings of the princes of the twelve tribes is a dramatic way of indicating that each was considered important enough to merit its own passage in the Torah. People will do destructive things if they feel slighted and not given their due role and recognition. The case of Koraḥ and his allies will be proof of this. By giving the princes of the tribes their share of honor and attention, the Torah is telling us how important it is to preserve the harmony of the nation by honoring all.

אֶחָד כֶּסֶף שִׁבְעִים שֶׁקֶל בְּשֶׁקֶל הַקֹּדֶשׁ שְׁנֵיהֶם ׀ מְלֵאִים
יד סֹלֶת בְּלוּלָה בַשֶּׁמֶן לְמִנְחָה: כַּף אַחַת עֲשָׂרָה זָהָב מְלֵאָה
טו קְטֹרֶת: פַּר אֶחָד בֶּן־בָּקָר אַיִל אֶחָד כֶּבֶשׂ־אֶחָד בֶּן־שְׁנָתוֹ
טז יז לְעֹלָה: שְׂעִיר־עִזִּים אֶחָד לְחַטָּאת: וּלְזֶבַח הַשְּׁלָמִים בָּקָר
שְׁנַיִם אֵילִם חֲמִשָּׁה עַתּוּדִים חֲמִשָּׁה כְּבָשִׂים בְּנֵי־שָׁנָה
חֲמִשָּׁה זֶה קָרְבַּן נַחְשׁוֹן בֶּן־עַמִּינָדָב:
יח יט בַּיּוֹם הַשֵּׁנִי הִקְרִיב נְתַנְאֵל בֶּן־צוּעָר נְשִׂיא יִשָּׂשכָר: הִקְרִב
אֶת־קָרְבָּנוֹ קַעֲרַת־כֶּסֶף אַחַת שְׁלֹשִׁים וּמֵאָה מִשְׁקָלָהּ
מִזְרָק אֶחָד כֶּסֶף שִׁבְעִים שֶׁקֶל בְּשֶׁקֶל הַקֹּדֶשׁ שְׁנֵיהֶם ׀
כ מְלֵאִים סֹלֶת בְּלוּלָה בַשֶּׁמֶן לְמִנְחָה: כַּף אַחַת עֲשָׂרָה זָהָב
כא מְלֵאָה קְטֹרֶת: פַּר אֶחָד בֶּן־בָּקָר אַיִל אֶחָד כֶּבֶשׂ־אֶחָד בֶּן־
כב כג שְׁנָתוֹ לְעֹלָה: שְׂעִיר־עִזִּים אֶחָד לְחַטָּאת: וּלְזֶבַח הַשְּׁלָמִים
בָּקָר שְׁנַיִם אֵילִם חֲמִשָּׁה עַתֻּדִים חֲמִשָּׁה כְּבָשִׂים בְּנֵי־שָׁנָה
חֲמִשָּׁה זֶה קָרְבַּן נְתַנְאֵל בֶּן־צוּעָר:
כד כה בַּיּוֹם הַשְּׁלִישִׁי נָשִׂיא לִבְנֵי זְבוּלֻן אֱלִיאָב בֶּן־חֵלֹן: קָרְבָּנוֹ
קַעֲרַת־כֶּסֶף אַחַת שְׁלֹשִׁים וּמֵאָה מִשְׁקָלָהּ מִזְרָק אֶחָד כֶּסֶף
שִׁבְעִים שֶׁקֶל בְּשֶׁקֶל הַקֹּדֶשׁ שְׁנֵיהֶם ׀ מְלֵאִים סֹלֶת בְּלוּלָה
כו כז בַשֶּׁמֶן לְמִנְחָה: כַּף אַחַת עֲשָׂרָה זָהָב מְלֵאָה קְטֹרֶת: פַּר
אֶחָד בֶּן־בָּקָר אַיִל אֶחָד כֶּבֶשׂ־אֶחָד בֶּן־שְׁנָתוֹ לְעֹלָה:
כח כט שְׂעִיר־עִזִּים אֶחָד לְחַטָּאת: וּלְזֶבַח הַשְּׁלָמִים בָּקָר שְׁנַיִם

7:18 בַּיּוֹם הַשֵּׁנִי *On the second day* – The gifts brought by the princes of each tribe are described in a series of long paragraphs repeated no less than twelve times, despite the fact that each prince brought an identical offering.

Why does the Torah spend so much time describing an event that could have been stated far more briefly by naming the princes and then simply telling us generically that each brought a silver bowl, a silver basin, and so on? The Rabbis made the assumption that every word of the Torah is meaningful. It tells us something we need to know, and does so in the fewest possible words. So the

five yearling sheep. This was the offering of Eliav son of
Ḥelon.
30 On the fourth day came Elitzur son of Shedeiur, prince
31 of the Reubenites: His offering was one silver bowl
weighing one hundred and thirty shekel and one silver
basin weighing seventy shekel according to the Sanctuary
weight, both filled with fine flour mixed with oil for a grain
32 offering; one golden spoon weighing ten shekel, full of
33 incense; one young bull, one ram, and one yearling sheep
34 for a burnt offering; one goat for a purification offering;
35 and for the peace sacrifice two oxen, five rams, five male
goats, and five yearling sheep. This was the offering of
Elitzur son of Shedeiur.
36 On the fifth day came Shelumiel son of Tzurishadai,
37 prince of the Simeonites: His offering was one silver bowl
weighing one hundred and thirty shekel and one silver
basin weighing seventy shekel according to the Sanctuary
weight, both filled with fine flour mixed with oil for a grain
38 offering; one golden spoon weighing ten shekel, full of
39 incense; one young bull, one ram, and one yearling sheep
40 for a burnt offering; one goat for a purification offering;
41 and for the peace sacrifice two oxen, five rams, five male
goats, and five yearling sheep. This was the offering of
Shelumiel son of Tzurishadai.
42 On the sixth day came Elyasaf son of Deuel, prince of the SHISHI
43 Gadites: His offering was one silver bowl weighing one
hundred and thirty shekel and one silver basin weighing

Victorian Anglo-Jew, Sir Moses Montefiore, "Sir Moses, how much are you worth?" Moses thought for a while and named a figure. The other replied, "That can't be right. It's a large sum but not large enough. By my calculation you must be worth ten times that amount."

The reply Sir Moses gave was moving and wise. "You didn't ask me how much I own. You asked me how much I'm worth. So I calculated the amount I have given to charity this year, and that is the figure I gave you. You see," he said, "we are worth what we are willing to share with others."

The Greeks knew about love as an emotion. In Judaism we propose that the love that changes lives is the love we do, the blessings we share, the offerings we bring.

אֵילִם חֲמִשָּׁה עַתֻּדִים חֲמִשָּׁה כְּבָשִׂים בְּנֵי־שָׁנָה חֲמִשָּׁה זֶה
קׇרְבַּן אֱלִיאָב בֶּן־חֵלֹן׃
ל לא בַּיּוֹם הָרְבִיעִי נָשִׂיא לִבְנֵי רְאוּבֵן אֱלִיצוּר בֶּן־שְׁדֵיאוּר׃ קׇרְבָּנוֹ
קַעֲרַת־כֶּסֶף אַחַת שְׁלֹשִׁים וּמֵאָה מִשְׁקָלָהּ מִזְרָק אֶחָד כֶּסֶף
שִׁבְעִים שֶׁקֶל בְּשֶׁקֶל הַקֹּדֶשׁ שְׁנֵיהֶם ׀ מְלֵאִים סֹלֶת בְּלוּלָה
לב לג בַשֶּׁמֶן לְמִנְחָה׃ כַּף אַחַת עֲשָׂרָה זָהָב מְלֵאָה קְטֹרֶת׃ פַּר
אֶחָד בֶּן־בָּקָר אַיִל אֶחָד כֶּבֶשׂ־אֶחָד בֶּן־שְׁנָתוֹ לְעֹלָה׃
לד לה שְׂעִיר־עִזִּים אֶחָד לְחַטָּאת׃ וּלְזֶבַח הַשְּׁלָמִים בָּקָר שְׁנַיִם
אֵילִם חֲמִשָּׁה עַתֻּדִים חֲמִשָּׁה כְּבָשִׂים בְּנֵי־שָׁנָה חֲמִשָּׁה זֶה
קׇרְבַּן אֱלִיצוּר בֶּן־שְׁדֵיאוּר׃
לו בַּיּוֹם הַחֲמִישִׁי נָשִׂיא לִבְנֵי שִׁמְעוֹן שְׁלֻמִיאֵל בֶּן־צוּרִישַׁדָּי׃
לז קׇרְבָּנוֹ קַעֲרַת־כֶּסֶף אַחַת שְׁלֹשִׁים וּמֵאָה מִשְׁקָלָהּ מִזְרָק
אֶחָד כֶּסֶף שִׁבְעִים שֶׁקֶל בְּשֶׁקֶל הַקֹּדֶשׁ שְׁנֵיהֶם ׀ מְלֵאִים
לח סֹלֶת בְּלוּלָה בַשֶּׁמֶן לְמִנְחָה׃ כַּף אַחַת עֲשָׂרָה זָהָב מְלֵאָה
לט קְטֹרֶת׃ פַּר אֶחָד בֶּן־בָּקָר אַיִל אֶחָד כֶּבֶשׂ־אֶחָד בֶּן־שְׁנָתוֹ
מ מא לְעֹלָה׃ שְׂעִיר־עִזִּים אֶחָד לְחַטָּאת׃ וּלְזֶבַח הַשְּׁלָמִים בָּקָר
שְׁנַיִם אֵילִם חֲמִשָּׁה עַתֻּדִים חֲמִשָּׁה כְּבָשִׂים בְּנֵי־שָׁנָה חֲמִשָּׁה
זֶה קׇרְבַּן שְׁלֻמִיאֵל בֶּן־צוּרִישַׁדָּי׃
מב מג בַּיּוֹם הַשִּׁשִּׁי נָשִׂיא לִבְנֵי גָד אֶלְיָסָף בֶּן־דְּעוּאֵל׃ קׇרְבָּנוֹ ששי
קַעֲרַת־כֶּסֶף אַחַת שְׁלֹשִׁים וּמֵאָה מִשְׁקָלָהּ מִזְרָק אֶחָד כֶּסֶף

A LITANY OF GIFTS

The lengthy, twelvefold repetition of the gifts of the tribes serves as a meditation on giving. Contributing to the common good is a constant calling upon each of us. To live a responsible life – a responsive life – is always to ask of yourself, "What is God calling me to do, here, where I am?" There is almost not a day that goes by when you cannot transform someone's life for the better, in some way. The word *ḥesed* means love, but it is the love we do as opposed to the love we feel; it is love-as-deed. That is the kind of love that changes lives. It's when we see the lonely and we reach out to welcome them. It's when we see the hungry and say: Come and eat with me, share my food. Let us eat together.

Someone once asked the great

seventy shekel according to the Sanctuary weight, both
filled with fine flour mixed with oil for a grain offering;
44 one golden spoon weighing ten shekel, full of incense;
45 one young bull, one ram, and one yearling sheep for a
46 47 burnt offering; one goat for a purification offering; and
for the peace sacrifice two oxen, five rams, five male goats,
and five yearling sheep. This was the offering of Elyasaf
son of Deuel.
48 On the seventh day came Elishama son of Amihud,
49 prince of the Efraimites: His offering was one silver bowl
weighing one hundred and thirty shekel and one silver
basin weighing seventy shekel according to the Sanctuary
weight, both filled with fine flour mixed with oil for a grain
50 offering; one golden spoon weighing ten shekel, full of
51 incense; one young bull, one ram, and one yearling sheep
52 for a burnt offering; one goat for a purification offering;
53 and for the peace sacrifice two oxen, five rams, five male
goats, and five yearling sheep. This was the offering of
Elishama son of Amihud.
54 On the eighth day came Gamliel son of Pedatzur, prince
55 of the Manassites: His offering was one silver bowl
weighing one hundred and thirty shekel and one silver
basin weighing seventy shekel according to the Sanctuary
weight, both filled with fine flour mixed with oil for a grain
56 offering; one golden spoon weighing ten shekel, full of
57 incense; one young bull, one ram, and one yearling sheep
58 for a burnt offering; one goat for a purification offering;
59 and for the peace sacrifice two oxen, five rams, five male
goats, and five yearling sheep. This was the offering of
Gamliel son of Pedatzur.
60 On the ninth day came Avidan son of Gidoni, prince
61 of the Benjaminites: His offering was one silver bowl
weighing one hundred and thirty shekel and one silver
basin weighing seventy shekel according to the Sanctuary
weight, both filled with fine flour mixed with oil for a grain
62 offering; one golden spoon weighing ten shekel, full of
63 incense; one young bull, one ram, and one yearling sheep

שִׁבְעִים שֶׁקֶל בְּשֶׁקֶל הַקֹּדֶשׁ שְׁנֵיהֶם ׀ מְלֵאִים סֹלֶת בְּלוּלָה
מד מה בַשֶּׁמֶן לְמִנְחָה׃ כַּף אַחַת עֲשָׂרָה זָהָב מְלֵאָה קְטֹרֶת׃ פַּר
אֶחָד בֶּן־בָּקָר אַיִל אֶחָד כֶּבֶשׂ־אֶחָד בֶּן־שְׁנָתוֹ לְעֹלָה׃
מו מז שְׂעִיר־עִזִּים אֶחָד לְחַטָּאת׃ וּלְזֶבַח הַשְּׁלָמִים בָּקָר שְׁנַיִם
אֵילִם חֲמִשָּׁה עַתֻּדִים חֲמִשָּׁה כְּבָשִׂים בְּנֵי־שָׁנָה חֲמִשָּׁה זֶה
קָרְבַּן אֶלְיָסָף בֶּן־דְּעוּאֵל׃
מח בַּיּוֹם הַשְּׁבִיעִי נָשִׂיא לִבְנֵי אֶפְרָיִם אֱלִישָׁמָע בֶּן־עַמִּיהוּד׃ ז
מט קָרְבָּנוֹ קַעֲרַת־כֶּסֶף אַחַת שְׁלֹשִׁים וּמֵאָה מִשְׁקָלָהּ מִזְרָק
אֶחָד כֶּסֶף שִׁבְעִים שֶׁקֶל בְּשֶׁקֶל הַקֹּדֶשׁ שְׁנֵיהֶם ׀ מְלֵאִים
נ סֹלֶת בְּלוּלָה בַשֶּׁמֶן לְמִנְחָה׃ כַּף אַחַת עֲשָׂרָה זָהָב מְלֵאָה
נא קְטֹרֶת׃ פַּר אֶחָד בֶּן־בָּקָר אַיִל אֶחָד כֶּבֶשׂ־אֶחָד בֶּן־שְׁנָתוֹ
נב נג לְעֹלָה׃ שְׂעִיר־עִזִּים אֶחָד לְחַטָּאת׃ וּלְזֶבַח הַשְּׁלָמִים בָּקָר
שְׁנַיִם אֵילִם חֲמִשָּׁה עַתֻּדִים חֲמִשָּׁה כְּבָשִׂים בְּנֵי־שָׁנָה חֲמִשָּׁה
זֶה קָרְבַּן אֱלִישָׁמָע בֶּן־עַמִּיהוּד׃
נד בַּיּוֹם הַשְּׁמִינִי נָשִׂיא לִבְנֵי מְנַשֶּׁה גַּמְלִיאֵל בֶּן־פְּדָהצוּר׃
נה קָרְבָּנוֹ קַעֲרַת־כֶּסֶף אַחַת שְׁלֹשִׁים וּמֵאָה מִשְׁקָלָהּ מִזְרָק
אֶחָד כֶּסֶף שִׁבְעִים שֶׁקֶל בְּשֶׁקֶל הַקֹּדֶשׁ שְׁנֵיהֶם ׀ מְלֵאִים
נו סֹלֶת בְּלוּלָה בַשֶּׁמֶן לְמִנְחָה׃ כַּף אַחַת עֲשָׂרָה זָהָב מְלֵאָה
נז קְטֹרֶת׃ פַּר אֶחָד בֶּן־בָּקָר אַיִל אֶחָד כֶּבֶשׂ־אֶחָד בֶּן־שְׁנָתוֹ
נח נט לְעֹלָה׃ שְׂעִיר־עִזִּים אֶחָד לְחַטָּאת׃ וּלְזֶבַח הַשְּׁלָמִים בָּקָר
שְׁנַיִם אֵילִם חֲמִשָּׁה עַתֻּדִים חֲמִשָּׁה כְּבָשִׂים בְּנֵי־שָׁנָה חֲמִשָּׁה
זֶה קָרְבַּן גַּמְלִיאֵל בֶּן־פְּדָהצוּר׃
ס סא בַּיּוֹם הַתְּשִׁיעִי נָשִׂיא לִבְנֵי בִנְיָמִן אֲבִידָן בֶּן־גִּדְעֹנִי׃ קָרְבָּנוֹ
קַעֲרַת־כֶּסֶף אַחַת שְׁלֹשִׁים וּמֵאָה מִשְׁקָלָהּ מִזְרָק אֶחָד כֶּסֶף
שִׁבְעִים שֶׁקֶל בְּשֶׁקֶל הַקֹּדֶשׁ שְׁנֵיהֶם ׀ מְלֵאִים סֹלֶת בְּלוּלָה
סב סג בַשֶּׁמֶן לְמִנְחָה׃ כַּף אַחַת עֲשָׂרָה זָהָב מְלֵאָה קְטֹרֶת׃ פַּר
אֶחָד בֶּן־בָּקָר אַיִל אֶחָד כֶּבֶשׂ־אֶחָד בֶּן־שְׁנָתוֹ לְעֹלָה׃

64 for a burnt offering; one goat for a purification offering;
65 and for the peace sacrifice two oxen, five rams, five male
goats, and five yearling sheep. This was the offering of
Avidan son of Gidoni.
66 On the tenth day came Aḥiezer son of Amishadai,
67 prince of the Danites: His offering was one silver bowl
weighing one hundred and thirty shekel and one silver
basin weighing seventy shekel according to the Sanctuary
weight, both filled with fine flour mixed with oil for a grain
68 offering; one golden spoon weighing ten shekel, full of
69 incense; one young bull, one ram, and one yearling sheep
70 for a burnt offering; one goat for a purification offering;
71 and for the peace sacrifice two oxen, five rams, five male
goats, and five yearling sheep. This was the offering of
Aḥiezer son of Amishadai.
72 On the eleventh day came Pagiel son of Okhran, prince of SHEVI'I
73 the Asherites: His offering was one silver bowl weighing
one hundred and thirty shekel and one silver basin
weighing seventy shekel according to the Sanctuary
weight, both filled with fine flour mixed with oil for a grain
74 offering; one golden spoon weighing ten shekel, full of
75 incense; one young bull, one ram, and one yearling sheep
76 for a burnt offering; one goat for a purification offering;
77 and for the peace sacrifice two oxen, five rams, five male
goats, and five yearling sheep. This was the offering of
Pagiel son of Okhran.
78 On the twelfth day came Aḥira son of Einan, prince of the
79 Naftalites: His offering was one silver bowl weighing one
hundred and thirty shekel and one silver basin weighing
seventy shekel according to the Sanctuary weight, both
filled with fine flour mixed with oil for a grain offering;
80 one golden spoon weighing ten shekel, full of incense;
81 one young bull, one ram, and one yearling sheep for a
82 83 burnt offering; one goat for a purification offering; and
for the peace sacrifice two oxen, five rams, five male goats,
and five yearling sheep. This was the offering of Aḥira son
of Einan.

סד סה שְׂעִיר־עִזִּ֥ים אֶחָ֖ד לְחַטָּֽאת׃ וּלְזֶ֣בַח הַשְּׁלָמִים֮ בָּקָ֣ר שְׁנַ֒יִם֒
אֵילִ֤ם חֲמִשָּׁה֙ עַתֻּדִ֣ים חֲמִשָּׁ֔ה כְּבָשִׂ֥ים בְּנֵֽי־שָׁנָ֖ה חֲמִשָּׁ֑ה זֶ֛ה
קָרְבַּ֥ן אֲבִידָ֖ן בֶּן־גִּדְעֹנִֽי׃
סו סז בַּיּוֹם֙ הָֽעֲשִׂירִ֔י נָשִׂ֖יא לִבְנֵ֣י דָ֑ן אֲחִיעֶ֖זֶר בֶּן־עַמִּֽישַׁדָּֽי׃ קָרְבָּנ֞וֹ
קַֽעֲרַת־כֶּ֣סֶף אַחַ֗ת שְׁלֹשִׁ֣ים וּמֵאָה֮ מִשְׁקָלָהּ֒ מִזְרָ֤ק אֶחָד֙ כֶּ֔סֶף
שִׁבְעִ֥ים שֶׁ֖קֶל בְּשֶׁ֣קֶל הַקֹּ֑דֶשׁ שְׁנֵיהֶ֣ם ׀ מְלֵאִ֗ים סֹ֛לֶת בְּלוּלָ֥ה
סח סט בַשֶּׁ֖מֶן לְמִנְחָֽה׃ כַּ֥ף אַחַ֛ת עֲשָׂרָ֥ה זָהָ֖ב מְלֵאָ֥ה קְטֹֽרֶת׃ פַּ֣ר
אֶחָ֞ד בֶּן־בָּקָ֗ר אַ֧יִל אֶחָ֛ד כֶּֽבֶשׂ־אֶחָ֥ד בֶּן־שְׁנָת֖וֹ לְעֹלָֽה׃
ע עא שְׂעִיר־עִזִּ֥ים אֶחָ֖ד לְחַטָּֽאת׃ וּלְזֶ֣בַח הַשְּׁלָמִים֮ בָּקָ֣ר שְׁנַ֒יִם֒
אֵילִ֤ם חֲמִשָּׁה֙ עַתֻּדִ֣ים חֲמִשָּׁ֔ה כְּבָשִׂ֥ים בְּנֵֽי־שָׁנָ֖ה חֲמִשָּׁ֑ה זֶ֛ה
קָרְבַּ֥ן אֲחִיעֶ֖זֶר בֶּן־עַמִּֽישַׁדָּֽי׃
עב בְּיוֹם֙ עַשְׁתֵּ֣י עָשָׂ֣ר י֔וֹם נָשִׂ֖יא לִבְנֵ֣י אָשֵׁ֑ר פַּגְעִיאֵ֖ל בֶּן־עָכְרָֽן׃ שביעי
עג קָרְבָּנ֞וֹ קַֽעֲרַת־כֶּ֣סֶף אַחַ֗ת שְׁלֹשִׁ֣ים וּמֵאָה֮ מִשְׁקָלָהּ֒ מִזְרָ֤ק
אֶחָד֙ כֶּ֔סֶף שִׁבְעִ֥ים שֶׁ֖קֶל בְּשֶׁ֣קֶל הַקֹּ֑דֶשׁ שְׁנֵיהֶ֣ם ׀ מְלֵאִ֗ים
עד סֹ֛לֶת בְּלוּלָ֥ה בַשֶּׁ֖מֶן לְמִנְחָֽה׃ כַּ֥ף אַחַ֛ת עֲשָׂרָ֥ה זָהָ֖ב מְלֵאָ֥ה
עה קְטֹֽרֶת׃ פַּ֣ר אֶחָ֞ד בֶּן־בָּקָ֗ר אַ֧יִל אֶחָ֛ד כֶּֽבֶשׂ־אֶחָ֥ד בֶּן־שְׁנָת֖וֹ
עו עז לְעֹלָֽה׃ שְׂעִיר־עִזִּ֥ים אֶחָ֖ד לְחַטָּֽאת׃ וּלְזֶ֣בַח הַשְּׁלָמִים֮ בָּקָ֣ר
שְׁנַ֒יִם֒ אֵילִ֤ם חֲמִשָּׁה֙ עַתֻּדִ֣ים חֲמִשָּׁ֔ה כְּבָשִׂ֥ים בְּנֵֽי־שָׁנָ֖ה חֲמִשָּׁ֑ה
זֶ֛ה קָרְבַּ֥ן פַּגְעִיאֵ֖ל בֶּן־עָכְרָֽן׃
עח בְּיוֹם֙ שְׁנֵ֣ים עָשָׂ֣ר י֔וֹם נָשִׂ֖יא לִבְנֵ֣י נַפְתָּלִ֑י אֲחִירַ֖ע בֶּן־עֵינָֽן׃
עט קָרְבָּנ֞וֹ קַֽעֲרַת־כֶּ֣סֶף אַחַ֗ת שְׁלֹשִׁ֣ים וּמֵאָה֮ מִשְׁקָלָהּ֒ מִזְרָ֤ק
אֶחָד֙ כֶּ֔סֶף שִׁבְעִ֥ים שֶׁ֖קֶל בְּשֶׁ֣קֶל הַקֹּ֑דֶשׁ שְׁנֵיהֶ֣ם ׀ מְלֵאִ֗ים
פ סֹ֛לֶת בְּלוּלָ֥ה בַשֶּׁ֖מֶן לְמִנְחָֽה׃ כַּ֥ף אַחַ֛ת עֲשָׂרָ֥ה זָהָ֖ב מְלֵאָ֥ה
פא קְטֹֽרֶת׃ פַּ֣ר אֶחָ֞ד בֶּן־בָּקָ֗ר אַ֧יִל אֶחָ֛ד כֶּֽבֶשׂ־אֶחָ֥ד בֶּן־שְׁנָת֖וֹ
פב פג לְעֹלָֽה׃ שְׂעִיר־עִזִּ֥ים אֶחָ֖ד לְחַטָּֽאת׃ וּלְזֶ֣בַח הַשְּׁלָמִים֮ בָּקָ֣ר
שְׁנַ֒יִם֒ אֵילִ֤ם חֲמִשָּׁה֙ עַתֻּדִ֣ים חֲמִשָּׁ֔ה כְּבָשִׂ֥ים בְּנֵֽי־שָׁנָ֖ה
חֲמִשָּׁ֑ה זֶ֛ה קָרְבַּ֥ן אֲחִירַ֖ע בֶּן־עֵינָֽן׃

84 All this was the dedication offering from the princes
of Israel for the altar at the time it was anointed: There
were twelve silver bowls, twelve silver basins, and twelve
85 golden spoons, each silver bowl weighing one hundred
and thirty shekel and each basin seventy shekel – so all the
silver in the utensils weighed two thousand four hundred
86 shekel according to the Sanctuary weight. There were
twelve gold spoons full of incense weighing ten shekel
each according to the Sanctuary weight – so all the gold
of the spoons weighed one hundred and twenty shekel.
87 The total number of the animals for the burnt offerings MAFTIR
was twelve bulls, twelve rams, and twelve yearling sheep,
along with their grain offerings. There were also twelve
88 goats for the purification offerings. The total number of
all the animals for the peace sacrifices was twenty-four
bulls, sixty rams, sixty goats, and sixty yearling sheep.
This was the dedication offering for the altar after it was
89 anointed. When Moshe entered the Tent of Meeting to
speak with the LORD, he would hear the Voice speaking to
him from above the cover over the Ark of the Covenant,
from between the two cherubim. Thus did He speak to
him.

The haftara for Parashat Naso is on page 1558.

Moshe leads, like many of us today, are still prone to ambition, aspiration, vanity. They still have the human desire for honor, status, and respect. This is to be one of the primary themes of the book of Numbers.

Throughout Parashat Naso, we have seen Moshe dealing sequentially with several of these potential dangers, implicit in the "second-best" status of the Levites, in the longing that a layman may have for special sanctity, and in the parallel primacy of the tribal leaders. The fact that corrective measures are laid out *before* the narratives of conflict that dominate many of the later chapters of Numbers is an instance of the principle that "God creates the cure before the disease" (*Midrash Lekaḥ Tov,* Shemot 3:1). Rambam writes that the whole Torah was given to make peace in the world (*Hilkhot Ḥanukka* 4:14). Parashat Naso is a series of practical lessons in how to ensure, as far as possible, that everyone feels recognized and respected, and that suspicion is defused and dissolved. It is not enough to pray for peace; we have to work for it.

פד זֹאת ׀ חֲנֻכַּת הַמִּזְבֵּחַ בְּיוֹם הִמָּשַׁח אֹתוֹ מֵאֵת נְשִׂיאֵי יִשְׂרָאֵל
קַעֲרֹת כֶּסֶף שְׁתֵּים עֶשְׂרֵה מִזְרְקֵי־כֶסֶף שְׁנֵים עָשָׂר כַּפּוֹת
פה זָהָב שְׁתֵּים עֶשְׂרֵה׃ שְׁלֹשִׁים וּמֵאָה הַקְּעָרָה הָאַחַת כֶּסֶף
וְשִׁבְעִים הַמִּזְרָק הָאֶחָד כֹּל כֶּסֶף הַכֵּלִים אַלְפַּיִם וְאַרְבַּע־
פו מֵאוֹת בְּשֶׁקֶל הַקֹּדֶשׁ׃ כַּפּוֹת זָהָב שְׁתֵּים־עֶשְׂרֵה מְלֵאֹת
קְטֹרֶת עֲשָׂרָה עֲשָׂרָה הַכַּף בְּשֶׁקֶל הַקֹּדֶשׁ כָּל־זְהַב הַכַּפּוֹת
פז עֶשְׂרִים וּמֵאָה׃ כָּל־הַבָּקָר לָעֹלָה שְׁנֵים עָשָׂר פָּרִים אֵילִם מפטיר
שְׁנֵים־עָשָׂר כְּבָשִׂים בְּנֵי־שָׁנָה שְׁנֵים עָשָׂר וּמִנְחָתָם וּשְׂעִירֵי
פח עִזִּים שְׁנֵים עָשָׂר לְחַטָּאת׃ וְכֹל בְּקַר ׀ זֶבַח הַשְּׁלָמִים עֶשְׂרִים
וְאַרְבָּעָה פָּרִים אֵילִם שִׁשִּׁים עַתֻּדִים שִׁשִּׁים כְּבָשִׂים בְּנֵי־
פט שָׁנָה שִׁשִּׁים זֹאת חֲנֻכַּת הַמִּזְבֵּחַ אַחֲרֵי הִמָּשַׁח אֹתוֹ׃ וּבְבֹא
מֹשֶׁה אֶל־אֹהֶל מוֹעֵד לְדַבֵּר אִתּוֹ וַיִּשְׁמַע אֶת־הַקּוֹל מִדַּבֵּר
אֵלָיו מֵעַל הַכַּפֹּרֶת אֲשֶׁר עַל־אֲרֹן הָעֵדֻת מִבֵּין שְׁנֵי הַכְּרֻבִים
וַיְדַבֵּר אֵלָיו׃

The הפטרה *for* פרשת נשא *is on page 1559.*

7:89 **וּבְבֹא מֹשֶׁה** *When Moshe entered* – In the Torah, which lays as its conceptual foundation the idea that all of us, regardless of color, culture, creed, or class, are in the image and likeness of God, God summons His people, Israel, to take the first steps to create what might eventually become a truly egalitarian society – or to put it more precisely, a society in which dignity, *kavod*, does not depend on power or wealth or an accident of birth.

Hence the concept, which we will explore more fully in Parashat Koraḥ, of *leadership as service*. The highest title accorded to Moshe in the Torah is that of *eved Hashem*, "the LORD's own servant" (Deut. 34:5). His highest praise is that he was "very humble, more so than any other man on earth" (Num. 12:3). To lead is to serve. Greatness is humility. As the book of Proverbs puts it, "A man's pride will bring him down; he who is lowly in spirit will grasp honor" (29:23).

The Torah points us in the direction of an ideal world, but it does not assume that we have reached it yet or are within striking distance. The people

Parashat Behaalotekha

8 1 2 And the Lord spoke to Moshe: "Speak to Aharon; say
to him: When you raise up the lamps, the seven lamps
3 shall light the space in front of the candelabrum." Aharon
did so; he mounted the lamps toward the front of the

---

that the two books of Maccabees, and others under the same title, should be called *sefarim ḥitzoni'im*, apocryphal works, while the festival we celebrate focuses on one symbolic detail of the original chain of events, not mentioned in the books of the Maccabees at all: that one cruse of pure, undefiled oil was found by the Maccabees among the wreckage and defilements of the Temple, just enough to light the candelabrum until more oil could be sourced.

To defend a country physically, as the Maccabees did, you need an army, but to defend a civilization you need education, educators, and schools. Those are the things that kept the Jewish spirit alive and the menora of Jewish values burning in an everlasting light throughout the centuries. In the hindsight of history, military victory is often secondary to the cultural victory of handing your values on to the next generation, and making sure that your children, and theirs, light up the world. The service of God first requires light. This is reflected in the ritual of the candelabrum here, remembered in the synagogue in the *ner tamid*, the everlasting light, and celebrated on Ḥanukka in the growing light of the *ḥanukiya*.

8:3 וַיַּעַשׂ כֵּן אַהֲרֹן *Aharon did so* – The simplicity of this daily ritual epitomizes the role of the priest. A priest engages in rites that in essence never change. One symbol of this was the candelabrum, tended each day so that a *ner tamid*, an everlasting light, burned in the Sanctuary as a sign of the presence of the eternal God. Priestly rituals followed a daily, weekly, monthly, and yearly cycle that never changed. Barring tragedies such as the destruction of the Temple, they could be calculated in advance until the end of time.

On the phrase "Aharon did so… *as the Lord had commanded Moshe*," Rashi comments, "This is stated *in order to praise Aharon*, that he did so [i.e., followed Moshe's instructions] without making any change." On the face of it, this is a very odd comment. Do we need to be told every occasion on which a priest – or anyone else, for that matter – did what God commanded? Is that an occasion for praise? It ought to be the norm. Only the exceptions are newsworthy.

I would suggest that Rashi is alluding to an earlier drama: the inauguration of the Tabernacle at which two of Aharon's sons, Nadav and Avihu, offered up "unauthorized fire before the Lord: fire He had not commanded," and they died (Lev.

פרשת בהעלתך

ח א ב וַיְדַבֵּ֥ר יְהוָ֖ה אֶל־מֹשֶׁ֥ה לֵּאמֹֽר׃ דַּבֵּר֙ אֶֽל־אַהֲרֹ֔ן וְאָמַרְתָּ֖ אֵלָ֑יו ח
בְּהַעֲלֹֽתְךָ֙ אֶת־הַנֵּרֹ֔ת אֶל־מוּל֙ פְּנֵ֣י הַמְּנוֹרָ֔ה יָאִ֖ירוּ שִׁבְעַ֥ת
ג הַנֵּרֽוֹת׃ וַיַּ֤עַשׂ כֵּן֙ אַהֲרֹ֔ן אֶל־מוּל֙ פְּנֵ֣י הַמְּנוֹרָ֔ה הֶעֱלָ֖ה נֵרֹתֶ֑יהָ

BEHAALOTEKHA

Parashat Behaalotekha begins with the final preparations for the Israelites' journey from the Sinai Desert to the Promised Land. There are instructions for Aharon, the High Priest, to tend to the lighting of the candelabrum (menora), and for consecrating the Levites into their special role as guardians of the sacred. Before setting out, the Israelites celebrate Passover, one year after the exodus itself, and provisions are made so that those who are unable to celebrate it at its proper time may do so a month later. Details are given about the cloud that signals when to encamp and when to move on. Moshe is commanded to make two silver trumpets to summon the people. The narrative then changes tone. The Israelites set out after their long stay in the Sinai Desert, but almost immediately there are problems, protests, and complaints. Moshe suffers his deepest emotional crisis. He prays to God to die. God tells him to gather seventy elders who will help him with the burdens of leadership. In the last scene of the *parasha*, Moshe's own sister and brother speak against him. Miriam is punished. Moshe, here described as the humblest of men, prays on her behalf. After a week's wait for Miriam to be healed, the people move on. Rare markings found in the Torah scroll in the middle of the *parasha* can be viewed as hints to a distinct division within the *parasha*. The two halves focus respectively on Aharon the priest and Moshe the prophet, and the uniqueness and challenges that accompany each role.

LIGHTING THE CANDELABRUM

The first instruction Aharon receives at the dedication of the Tabernacle is on the lighting of the candelabrum. Similarly, Ḥanukka, the festival named for the rededication of the Temple after its desecration by the Greeks, celebrates the moment when the Maccabees relit the candelabrum. Over time, Ḥanukka became associated with *ḥinukh*, a word meaning "education." What we rededicated after the battle with the Hellenizers was not a physical building – the Temple – but living embodiments of Judaism, namely, our children, our students, the people to whom we teach and hand on our heritage and values. History itself has a history, and what began as the festival of a military victory, recorded in the first and second books of Maccabees, became predominantly the festival of a spiritual and civilizational victory. Tradition ruled

4 candelabrum as the LORD had commanded Moshe. This
is how the candelabrum was made: of hammered gold,
hammered from its base to its flowers. According to
the vision that the LORD had shown Moshe, so was the
lampstand made.
5
6 The LORD spoke to Moshe: "Take the Levites from
7 among the Israelites and purify them. This is what you
shall do to them to purify them: Sprinkle upon them the
water of purification, and have them shave their whole
bodies and wash their clothes; then they will be purified.
8 They shall take a young bull with its grain offering of fine
flour mixed with oil. You, meanwhile, shall take a second
9 young bull for a purification offering. You shall bring the
Levites before the Tent of Meeting and assemble all the
10 community of Israel. Then you shall bring the Levites
forward before the LORD, and the Israelites shall lay their
11 hands upon the Levites. Aharon shall then present the
Levites before the LORD like a wave offering from the
Israelites, so that they may perform the LORD's service.
12 The Levites shall then lay their hands upon the heads
of the bulls, and Aharon shall offer one as a purification
offering and the other as a burnt offering to the LORD,
13 to make atonement for the Levites. You shall have the
Levites stand before Aharon and his sons, and then
14 present them like a wave offering to the LORD. Thus
you shall separate the Levites from among the other
15 Israelites; the Levites shall become Mine. After that, the SHENI
Levites shall enter to perform the service of the Tent of
Meeting, once you have purified them and presented
16 them as a wave offering. They are wholly given over to
Me from among the Israelites. I have taken them for
Myself in place of the first to emerge from every womb,
17 the firstborn of all the Israelites. For all the firstborn
among the Israelites, man and beast alike, are Mine;
on the day that I struck down the firstborn in Egypt, I
18 consecrated them to Myself. But I have now taken the
Levites in place of all the firstborn among the Israelites,

ד כַּאֲשֶׁר צִוָּה יהוה אֶת־מֹשֶׁה: וְזֶה מַעֲשֵׂה הַמְּנֹרָה מִקְשָׁה
זָהָב עַד־יְרֵכָהּ עַד־פִּרְחָהּ מִקְשָׁה הִוא כַּמַּרְאֶה אֲשֶׁר הֶרְאָה
יהוה אֶת־מֹשֶׁה כֵּן עָשָׂה אֶת־הַמְּנֹרָה:
ה ו וַיְדַבֵּר יהוה אֶל־מֹשֶׁה לֵּאמֹר: קַח אֶת־הַלְוִיִּם מִתּוֹךְ בְּנֵי
ז יִשְׂרָאֵל וְטִהַרְתָּ אֹתָם: וְכֹה־תַעֲשֶׂה לָהֶם לְטַהֲרָם הַזֵּה
עֲלֵיהֶם מֵי חַטָּאת וְהֶעֱבִירוּ תַעַר עַל־כָּל־בְּשָׂרָם וְכִבְּסוּ
ח בִגְדֵיהֶם וְהִטֶּהָרוּ: וְלָקְחוּ פַּר בֶּן־בָּקָר וּמִנְחָתוֹ סֹלֶת
ט בְּלוּלָה בַשָּׁמֶן וּפַר־שֵׁנִי בֶן־בָּקָר תִּקַּח לְחַטָּאת: וְהִקְרַבְתָּ
אֶת־הַלְוִיִּם לִפְנֵי אֹהֶל מוֹעֵד וְהִקְהַלְתָּ אֶת־כָּל־עֲדַת בְּנֵי
י יִשְׂרָאֵל: וְהִקְרַבְתָּ אֶת־הַלְוִיִּם לִפְנֵי יהוה וְסָמְכוּ בְנֵי־יִשְׂרָאֵל
יא אֶת־יְדֵיהֶם עַל־הַלְוִיִּם: וְהֵנִיף אַהֲרֹן אֶת־הַלְוִיִּם תְּנוּפָה לִפְנֵי
יב יהוה מֵאֵת בְּנֵי יִשְׂרָאֵל וְהָיוּ לַעֲבֹד אֶת־עֲבֹדַת יהוה: וְהַלְוִיִּם
יִסְמְכוּ אֶת־יְדֵיהֶם עַל רֹאשׁ הַפָּרִים וַעֲשֵׂה אֶת־הָאֶחָד חַטָּאת
יג וְאֶת־הָאֶחָד עֹלָה לַיהוה לְכַפֵּר עַל־הַלְוִיִּם: וְהַעֲמַדְתָּ אֶת־
הַלְוִיִּם לִפְנֵי אַהֲרֹן וְלִפְנֵי בָנָיו וְהֵנַפְתָּ אֹתָם תְּנוּפָה לַיהוה:
יד וְהִבְדַּלְתָּ אֶת־הַלְוִיִּם מִתּוֹךְ בְּנֵי יִשְׂרָאֵל וְהָיוּ לִי הַלְוִיִּם:
טו וְאַחֲרֵי־כֵן יָבֹאוּ הַלְוִיִּם לַעֲבֹד אֶת־אֹהֶל מוֹעֵד וְטִהַרְתָּ אֹתָם שני
טז וְהֵנַפְתָּ אֹתָם תְּנוּפָה: כִּי נְתֻנִים נְתֻנִים הֵמָּה לִי מִתּוֹךְ בְּנֵי
יִשְׂרָאֵל תַּחַת פִּטְרַת כָּל־רֶחֶם בְּכוֹר כֹּל מִבְּנֵי יִשְׂרָאֵל
יז לָקַחְתִּי אֹתָם לִי: כִּי לִי כָל־בְּכוֹר בִּבְנֵי יִשְׂרָאֵל בָּאָדָם
וּבַבְּהֵמָה בְּיוֹם הַכֹּתִי כָל־בְּכוֹר בְּאֶרֶץ מִצְרַיִם הִקְדַּשְׁתִּי
יח אֹתָם לִי: וָאֶקַּח אֶת־הַלְוִיִּם תַּחַת כָּל־בְּכוֹר בִּבְנֵי יִשְׂרָאֵל:

10:1–2). Nadav and Avihu were doing what they had seen Moshe do at moments of great spiritual intensity, namely, act on his own initiative. What they failed to understand was that he was a prophet; they were priests. A prophet responds to the unique circumstances of the here and now. The essence of priestly service is to do what you are commanded "without making any change" (Deut. 28:14). What the Torah is saying about Aharon at this point is that he understands his role. He is Aharon, not Moshe – a priest, not a prophet. He epitomizes *that which does not change.*

19 and I have given the Levites to Aharon and his sons
from among the Israelites, to perform the service of the
Israelites in the Tent of Meeting and to make atonement
for the Israelites, so that no plague will come among the
20 Israelites for drawing too close to the Sanctuary." Moshe,
Aharon, and all the community of Israel did this for the
Levites; all that the Lord commanded Moshe with
21 regard to the Levites, so the Israelites did. The Levites
purified themselves and washed their clothes. Aharon
presented them as a wave offering before the Lord, and
22 made atonement for them in order to purify them. And
after that, the Levites went in to perform their service
in the Tent of Meeting before Aharon and his sons. As
the Lord had commanded Moshe regarding the Levites,
23 so they did for them. And the Lord spoke to
24 Moshe: "The Levites: From twenty-five years upward
25 they shall go into the service of the Tent of Meeting. At
fifty years old they shall retire from the service and serve
26 no longer. They may assist their fellow Levites in carrying
out their duties in the Tent of Meeting, but shall not
perform the service itself. This is how you shall conduct
the Levites with regard to their duties."

9 1 The Lord spoke to Moshe in the Sinai Desert in the first SHELISHI
2 month of the second year after they had left Egypt: "Let the
Israelites offer the Passover sacrifice at its appointed time.
3 On the fourteenth day of this month in the afternoon you
shall offer it at its appointed time. Bring it in accordance
4 with all its decrees and laws." And so Moshe instructed the
5 Israelites to offer the Passover sacrifice. On the afternoon
of the fourteenth day of the first month they offered the

Torah acknowledges this, we know that in the inner reaches of our soul we can be honest with ourselves, we can acknowledge the ways in which we've fallen short. Those who cannot offer the Passover sacrifice, whether due to lack of planning or to circumstances beyond their control, are eager for another chance. They know that, in His forgiveness, God gives us the strength to heal what we have harmed, to try again, and to become the person He wants us to be.

יט וָאֶתְּנָה אֶת־הַלְוִיִּם נְתֻנִים ׀ לְאַהֲרֹן וּלְבָנָיו מִתּוֹךְ בְּנֵי יִשְׂרָאֵל
לַעֲבֹד אֶת־עֲבֹדַת בְּנֵי־יִשְׂרָאֵל בְּאֹהֶל מוֹעֵד וּלְכַפֵּר עַל־בְּנֵי
יִשְׂרָאֵל וְלֹא יִהְיֶה בִּבְנֵי יִשְׂרָאֵל נֶגֶף בְּגֶשֶׁת בְּנֵי־יִשְׂרָאֵל אֶל־
כ הַקֹּדֶשׁ: וַיַּעַשׂ מֹשֶׁה וְאַהֲרֹן וְכָל־עֲדַת בְּנֵי־יִשְׂרָאֵל לַלְוִיִּם
כְּכֹל אֲשֶׁר־צִוָּה יהוה אֶת־מֹשֶׁה לַלְוִיִּם כֵּן־עָשׂוּ לָהֶם בְּנֵי
כא יִשְׂרָאֵל: וַיִּתְחַטְּאוּ הַלְוִיִּם וַיְכַבְּסוּ בִּגְדֵיהֶם וַיָּנֶף אַהֲרֹן אֹתָם
כב תְּנוּפָה לִפְנֵי יהוה וַיְכַפֵּר עֲלֵיהֶם אַהֲרֹן לְטַהֲרָם: וְאַחֲרֵי־כֵן
בָּאוּ הַלְוִיִּם לַעֲבֹד אֶת־עֲבֹדָתָם בְּאֹהֶל מוֹעֵד לִפְנֵי אַהֲרֹן
וְלִפְנֵי בָנָיו כַּאֲשֶׁר צִוָּה יהוה אֶת־מֹשֶׁה עַל־הַלְוִיִּם כֵּן עָשׂוּ
כג כד לָהֶם: וַיְדַבֵּר יהוה אֶל־מֹשֶׁה לֵּאמֹר: זֹאת אֲשֶׁר
לַלְוִיִּם מִבֶּן חָמֵשׁ וְעֶשְׂרִים שָׁנָה וָמַעְלָה יָבוֹא לִצְבֹא צָבָא
כה בַּעֲבֹדַת אֹהֶל מוֹעֵד: וּמִבֶּן חֲמִשִּׁים שָׁנָה יָשׁוּב מִצְּבָא
כו הָעֲבֹדָה וְלֹא יַעֲבֹד עוֹד: וְשֵׁרֵת אֶת־אֶחָיו בְּאֹהֶל מוֹעֵד
לִשְׁמֹר מִשְׁמֶרֶת וַעֲבֹדָה לֹא יַעֲבֹד כָּכָה תַּעֲשֶׂה לַלְוִיִּם
בְּמִשְׁמְרֹתָם:

ט א וַיְדַבֵּר יהוה אֶל־מֹשֶׁה בְמִדְבַּר־סִינַי בַּשָּׁנָה הַשֵּׁנִית לְצֵאתָם שלישי
ב מֵאֶרֶץ מִצְרַיִם בַּחֹדֶשׁ הָרִאשׁוֹן לֵאמֹר: וְיַעֲשׂוּ בְנֵי־יִשְׂרָאֵל
ג אֶת־הַפָּסַח בְּמוֹעֲדוֹ: בְּאַרְבָּעָה עָשָׂר־יוֹם בַּחֹדֶשׁ הַזֶּה בֵּין
הָעַרְבַּיִם תַּעֲשׂוּ אֹתוֹ בְּמֹעֲדוֹ כְּכָל־חֻקֹּתָיו וּכְכָל־מִשְׁפָּטָיו
ד תַּעֲשׂוּ אֹתוֹ: וַיְדַבֵּר מֹשֶׁה אֶל־בְּנֵי יִשְׂרָאֵל לַעֲשֹׂת הַפָּסַח:
ה וַיַּעֲשׂוּ אֶת־הַפֶּסַח בָּרִאשׁוֹן בְּאַרְבָּעָה עָשָׂר יוֹם לַחֹדֶשׁ בֵּין

9:1 בַּשָּׁנָה הַשֵּׁנִית לְצֵאתָם מֵאֶרֶץ מִצְרַיִם בַּחֹדֶשׁ הָרִאשׁוֹן *The first month of the second year* – The first commemorative Passover, as opposed to the original Passover in Egypt, already presents the issue of people unable to fulfill the command as given.

My favorite sentence in the English language is Winston Churchill's definition of success: "going from failure to failure without loss of enthusiasm." The real difference is not between failure and success. The real difference is between failing and giving up and failing and keeping on going, missing the mark and recalculating the route. Because even the

Passover sacrifice in the Sinai Desert. Just as the LORD
6 commanded Moshe, so the Israelites did. But there were
people who were impure because of contact with the
dead, and they were unable to offer the Passover sacrifice
on that day. That very day they approached Moshe and
7 Aharon: "We have become impure because of contact
with the dead," these people said to him, "but must we
be debarred from presenting the LORD's offering at its
8 appointed time among all the Israelites?" "Wait," Moshe
replied, "and let me hear what the LORD commands
concerning you."
9 10 And the LORD spoke to Moshe: "Tell the Israelites:
When any of you or your future descendants are impure
because of contact with the dead, or away on a journey,
11 they may still offer a Passover sacrifice to the LORD. They
shall offer it in the afternoon of the fourteenth day of the
second month; then shall they eat it with unleavened bread
12 and bitter herbs. They shall not leave any of it over until
morning, nor shall they break any of its bones. They shall
offer it in compliance with all the rules of the Passover
13 sacrifice. But anyone who is ritually pure and not on a
journey, but still fails to offer the Passover sacrifice, that
person shall be severed from his people, because he did
not offer the LORD's sacrifice at its appointed time; he will
14 bear his guilt. If there is a migrant living among you and
he offers a Passover sacrifice to the LORD, he shall do so
in compliance with all its rules and laws. You shall have
15 one law for migrant and native born alike." On REVI'I
the day when the Tabernacle was erected, the cloud
covered the Tabernacle, the Tent of the Testimony, and
from evening until morning it hung over the Tabernacle
16 with the appearance of fire. It was always there; the cloud
17 covered the Tent, appearing at night as fire. Whenever the
cloud rose above the Tent, the Israelites would set out, and
wherever the cloud settled, the Israelites would encamp.
18 At the LORD's command, the Israelites set out, and at the
LORD's command they would encamp; for as long as the

הָעַרְבַּיִם בְּמִדְבַּר סִינָי כְּכֹל אֲשֶׁר צִוָּה יהוה אֶת־מֹשֶׁה כֵּן
ו עָשׂוּ בְּנֵי יִשְׂרָאֵל: וַיְהִי אֲנָשִׁים אֲשֶׁר הָיוּ טְמֵאִים לְנֶפֶשׁ
אָדָם וְלֹא־יָכְלוּ לַעֲשֹׂת־הַפֶּסַח בַּיּוֹם הַהוּא וַיִּקְרְבוּ לִפְנֵי
ז מֹשֶׁה וְלִפְנֵי אַהֲרֹן בַּיּוֹם הַהוּא: וַיֹּאמְרוּ הָאֲנָשִׁים הָהֵמָּה
אֵלָיו אֲנַחְנוּ טְמֵאִים לְנֶפֶשׁ אָדָם לָמָּה נִגָּרַע לְבִלְתִּי הַקְרִיב
ח אֶת־קָרְבַּן יהוה בְּמֹעֲדוֹ בְּתוֹךְ בְּנֵי יִשְׂרָאֵל: וַיֹּאמֶר אֲלֵהֶם
מֹשֶׁה עִמְדוּ וְאֶשְׁמְעָה מַה־יְצַוֶּה יהוה לָכֶם:
ט י וַיְדַבֵּר יהוה אֶל־מֹשֶׁה לֵּאמֹר: דַּבֵּר אֶל־בְּנֵי יִשְׂרָאֵל לֵאמֹר
אִישׁ אִישׁ כִּי־יִהְיֶה טָמֵא ׀ לָנֶפֶשׁ אוֹ בְדֶרֶךְ רְחֹקָה לָכֶם אוֹ
יא לְדֹרֹתֵיכֶם וְעָשָׂה פֶסַח לַיהוה: בַּחֹדֶשׁ הַשֵּׁנִי בְּאַרְבָּעָה עָשָׂר
יוֹם בֵּין הָעַרְבַּיִם יַעֲשׂוּ אֹתוֹ עַל־מַצּוֹת וּמְרֹרִים יֹאכְלֻהוּ:
יב לֹא־יַשְׁאִירוּ מִמֶּנּוּ עַד־בֹּקֶר וְעֶצֶם לֹא יִשְׁבְּרוּ־בוֹ כְּכָל־חֻקַּת
יג הַפֶּסַח יַעֲשׂוּ אֹתוֹ: וְהָאִישׁ אֲשֶׁר־הוּא טָהוֹר וּבְדֶרֶךְ לֹא־
הָיָה וְחָדַל לַעֲשׂוֹת הַפֶּסַח וְנִכְרְתָה הַנֶּפֶשׁ הַהִוא מֵעַמֶּיהָ
כִּי ׀ קָרְבַּן יהוה לֹא הִקְרִיב בְּמֹעֲדוֹ חֶטְאוֹ יִשָּׂא הָאִישׁ
יד הַהוּא: וְכִי־יָגוּר אִתְּכֶם גֵּר וְעָשָׂה פֶסַח לַיהוה כְּחֻקַּת
הַפֶּסַח וּכְמִשְׁפָּטוֹ כֵּן יַעֲשֶׂה חֻקָּה אַחַת יִהְיֶה לָכֶם וְלַגֵּר
טו וּלְאֶזְרַח הָאָרֶץ: וּבְיוֹם הָקִים אֶת־הַמִּשְׁכָּן רביעי
כִּסָּה הֶעָנָן אֶת־הַמִּשְׁכָּן לְאֹהֶל הָעֵדֻת וּבָעֶרֶב יִהְיֶה עַל־
טז הַמִּשְׁכָּן כְּמַרְאֵה־אֵשׁ עַד־בֹּקֶר: כֵּן יִהְיֶה תָמִיד הֶעָנָן יְכַסֶּנּוּ
יז וּמַרְאֵה־אֵשׁ לָיְלָה: וּלְפִי הֵעָלֹת הֶעָנָן מֵעַל הָאֹהֶל וְאַחֲרֵי
כֵן יִסְעוּ בְּנֵי יִשְׂרָאֵל וּבִמְקוֹם אֲשֶׁר יִשְׁכָּן־שָׁם הֶעָנָן שָׁם
יח יַחֲנוּ בְּנֵי יִשְׂרָאֵל: עַל־פִּי יהוה יִסְעוּ בְּנֵי יִשְׂרָאֵל וְעַל־פִּי
יהוה יַחֲנוּ כָּל־יְמֵי אֲשֶׁר יִשְׁכֹּן הֶעָנָן עַל־הַמִּשְׁכָּן יַחֲנוּ:

cloud rested on the Tabernacle, they continued to camp
19 there. Even when the cloud lingered over the Tabernacle
for many days, the Israelites kept the Lord's charge and
20 did not journey on. Sometimes the cloud would be over
the Tabernacle for just a few days; at the Lord's command
they would camp, and at the Lord's command they would
21 set out. Sometimes the cloud stayed only from evening to
morning, and in the morning it rose, and they set out. Day
22 or night, they would set out when the cloud rose. Whether
it was two days, or a month, or for many days together,
the Israelites would camp as long as the cloud rested over
the Tabernacle, and would not move on. They journeyed
23 only when the cloud rose. At the Lord's command they
camped, and at the Lord's command they set out. And
they kept the Lord's charge, the Lord's word through
Moshe.
10 1 2 The Lord spoke to Moshe: "Make two silver trumpets;
make them of hammered metal. Use them for summoning
3 the community and for having the camps set out. When
both are blown with a long note, the entire community

Rabbi Soloveitchik calls this the covenant of fate (*brit goral*). This is not a purely negative phenomenon. It gives rise to a powerful sense that we are part of a single story – that what we have in common is stronger than the things that separate us. The covenant of fate was born in the experience of slavery in Egypt.

But there is an additional element of Jewish identity. Rabbi Soloveitchik calls this the covenant of destiny (*brit yeud*), entered into at Mount Sinai. This defines the people of Israel not as the object of persecution but the subject of a unique vocation, to become "a kingdom of priests and a holy nation" (Ex. 19:6). Our task as a people of destiny is to bear witness to the presence of God through the way we lead our lives (Torah) and the path we chart as a people across the centuries (history) – a camp and a congregation. Sometimes the clarion call speaks to our sense of faith. We are God's people, His emissaries and ambassadors, charged with making His presence real in the world through healing deeds and leading holy lives. At other times the trumpet that sounds and summons us is the call of fate: Jewish lives endangered in Israel or the Diaspora. Whichever sound the silver instruments make, they call on that duality that makes Jews and Judaism inseparable. However deep the divisions between us, we remain one family in fate and faith.

יט וּבְהַאֲרִיךְ הֶעָנָן עַל־הַמִּשְׁכָּן יָמִים רַבִּים וְשָׁמְרוּ בְנֵי־יִשְׂרָאֵל
כ אֶת־מִשְׁמֶרֶת יהוה וְלֹא יִסָּעוּ׃ וְיֵשׁ אֲשֶׁר יִהְיֶה הֶעָנָן יָמִים
מִסְפָּר עַל־הַמִּשְׁכָּן עַל־פִּי יהוה יַחֲנוּ וְעַל־פִּי יהוה יִסָּעוּ׃
כא וְיֵשׁ אֲשֶׁר יִהְיֶה הֶעָנָן מֵעֶרֶב עַד־בֹּקֶר וְנַעֲלָה הֶעָנָן בַּבֹּקֶר
כב וְנָסָעוּ אוֹ יוֹמָם וָלַיְלָה וְנַעֲלָה הֶעָנָן וְנָסָעוּ׃ אוֹ־יֹמַיִם אוֹ־
חֹדֶשׁ אוֹ־יָמִים בְּהַאֲרִיךְ הֶעָנָן עַל־הַמִּשְׁכָּן לִשְׁכֹּן עָלָיו יַחֲנוּ
כג בְנֵי־יִשְׂרָאֵל וְלֹא יִסָּעוּ וּבְהֵעָלֹתוֹ יִסָּעוּ׃ עַל־פִּי יהוה יַחֲנוּ
וְעַל־פִּי יהוה יִסָּעוּ אֶת־מִשְׁמֶרֶת יהוה שָׁמָרוּ עַל־פִּי יהוה
בְּיַד־מֹשֶׁה׃
י א ב וַיְדַבֵּר יהוה אֶל־מֹשֶׁה לֵּאמֹר׃ עֲשֵׂה לְךָ שְׁתֵּי חֲצוֹצְרֹת כֶּסֶף ט
מִקְשָׁה תַּעֲשֶׂה אֹתָם וְהָיוּ לְךָ לְמִקְרָא הָעֵדָה וּלְמַסַּע אֶת־
ג הַמַּחֲנוֹת׃ וְתָקְעוּ בָּהֵן וְנוֹעֲדוּ אֵלֶיךָ כָּל־הָעֵדָה אֶל־פֶּתַח

CONGREGATION AND CAMP

This passage, with its juxtaposition of the words "congregation," *eda,* and "camp," *maḥaneh,* became a springboard for one of the most profound meditations of Rabbi Joseph B. Soloveitchik (1903–93). We have seen (see note on Ex. 12:3) that for Rabbi Soloveitchik (*Kol Dodi Dofek*), there are two ways in which people become a group – a community, society, or nation. The first is when they face a common enemy. They band together for mutual protection, knowing that only by so doing can they survive. Such a group is a *maḥaneh* – a camp, a defensive formation. Alternatively, people can come together because they share a vision, a set of ideals. This is what it means to be an *eda,* congregation. (*Eda* is related to the word *ed,* "witness.") A society built around a shared project is not a *maḥaneh* but an *eda* – not a camp but a congregation. A camp is brought into being by what happens to it from the outside. A congregation comes into existence by internal decision. The first is a response to what has happened to the group in the past. The second represents what the group seeks to achieve in the future. This duality was given its first expression with this command: "Make two silver trumpets; make them of hammered metal. Use them for summoning the community (*eda*), and for having the camps (*maḥanot*) set out."

The two types of groups represent, in the most profound sense, two different ways of existing and relating to the world. Our ancestors became a *maḥaneh* in Egypt, forged together by a crucible of slavery and suffering. Ever since, Jews have known that we are thrown together by circumstance. We share a history all too often written in tears.

shall assemble before you at the entrance to the Tent
4 of Meeting. If only one is blown, the princes, leaders of
5 Israel's divisions, shall assemble before you. When you
blow a series of short blasts, the camps on the east side
6 shall march, and when you blow a second series of short
blasts, the camps on the south side will march; thus shall a
7 series of short blasts signal them to move on. To assemble
the community, blow a long blast, not a series of short
8 blasts. Aharon's sons the priests shall blow the trumpets.
This shall be for you an everlasting decree throughout
9 your generations. When you go to war against an enemy
who is attacking you in your land, you shall blow short
blasts on the trumpets to be remembered before the
10 LORD your God, to be delivered from your enemies. And
on your days of rejoicing, your festivals and New Moons,
you shall blow the trumpets over your burnt offerings
and your peace offerings. They will be a reminder of you
before your God. I am the LORD your God."
11 On the twentieth day of the second month in the second ḤAMISHI
year, the cloud rose above the Tabernacle of the Covenant.
12 The Israelites set out on their journey from the Sinai
Desert, and the cloud came to rest in the Wilderness of
13 Paran. For the first time, at the LORD's command through
14 Moshe, they set out. The divisions of Yehuda's camp set
out first, under their banner. Leading that division was
15 Naḥshon son of Aminadav. Netanel son of Tzuar was
16 in charge of the division of the tribe of Yissakhar. Eliav
son of Ḥelon was in charge of the division of the tribe
17 of Zevulun. The Tabernacle was taken down, and the
18 Gershonites and the Merarites, who carried it, set out. The
divisions of the camp of Reuven set out next, under their
banner. Leading that division was Elitzur son of Shedeiur.
19 Shelumiel son of Tzurishadai was in charge of the division
20 of the tribe of Shimon. Elyasaf son of Deuel was in charge
21 of the division of the tribe of Gad. Then the Kohatites,
who carried the sacred objects, set out. By the time they
22 arrived, the Tabernacle would have been erected. The

ד אֹהֶל מוֹעֵד: וְאִם־בְּאַחַת יִתְקָעוּ וְנוֹעֲדוּ אֵלֶיךָ הַנְּשִׂיאִים
ה רָאשֵׁי אַלְפֵי יִשְׂרָאֵל: וּתְקַעְתֶּם תְּרוּעָה וְנָסְעוּ הַמַּחֲנוֹת
ו הַחֹנִים קֵדְמָה: וּתְקַעְתֶּם תְּרוּעָה שֵׁנִית וְנָסְעוּ הַמַּחֲנוֹת
ז הַחֹנִים תֵּימָנָה תְּרוּעָה יִתְקְעוּ לְמַסְעֵיהֶם: וּבְהַקְהִיל אֶת־
ח הַקָּהָל תִּתְקְעוּ וְלֹא תָרִיעוּ: וּבְנֵי אַהֲרֹן הַכֹּהֲנִים יִתְקְעוּ
ט בַּחֲצֹצְרוֹת וְהָיוּ לָכֶם לְחֻקַּת עוֹלָם לְדֹרֹתֵיכֶם: וְכִי־תָבֹאוּ
מִלְחָמָה בְּאַרְצְכֶם עַל־הַצַּר הַצֹּרֵר אֶתְכֶם וַהֲרֵעֹתֶם
בַּחֲצֹצְרֹת וְנִזְכַּרְתֶּם לִפְנֵי יְהוָה אֱלֹהֵיכֶם וְנוֹשַׁעְתֶּם מֵאֹיְבֵיכֶם:
י וּבְיוֹם שִׂמְחַתְכֶם וּבְמוֹעֲדֵיכֶם וּבְרָאשֵׁי חָדְשֵׁכֶם וּתְקַעְתֶּם
בַּחֲצֹצְרֹת עַל עֹלֹתֵיכֶם וְעַל זִבְחֵי שַׁלְמֵיכֶם וְהָיוּ לָכֶם לְזִכָּרוֹן
לִפְנֵי אֱלֹהֵיכֶם אֲנִי יְהוָה אֱלֹהֵיכֶם:
יא וַיְהִי בַּשָּׁנָה הַשֵּׁנִית בַּחֹדֶשׁ הַשֵּׁנִי בְּעֶשְׂרִים בַּחֹדֶשׁ נַעֲלָה חמישי
יב הֶעָנָן מֵעַל מִשְׁכַּן הָעֵדֻת: וַיִּסְעוּ בְנֵי־יִשְׂרָאֵל לְמַסְעֵיהֶם
יג מִמִּדְבַּר סִינָי וַיִּשְׁכֹּן הֶעָנָן בְּמִדְבַּר פָּארָן: וַיִּסְעוּ בָּרִאשֹׁנָה
יד עַל־פִּי יְהוָה בְּיַד־מֹשֶׁה: וַיִּסַּע דֶּגֶל מַחֲנֵה בְנֵי־יְהוּדָה
טו בָּרִאשֹׁנָה לְצִבְאֹתָם וְעַל־צְבָאוֹ נַחְשׁוֹן בֶּן־עַמִּינָדָב: וְעַל־
טז צְבָא מַטֵּה בְּנֵי יִשָּׂשכָר נְתַנְאֵל בֶּן־צוּעָר: וְעַל־צְבָא מַטֵּה
יז בְּנֵי זְבוּלֻן אֱלִיאָב בֶּן־חֵלֹן: וְהוּרַד הַמִּשְׁכָּן וְנָסְעוּ בְנֵי־גֵרְשׁוֹן
יח וּבְנֵי מְרָרִי נֹשְׂאֵי הַמִּשְׁכָּן: וְנָסַע דֶּגֶל מַחֲנֵה רְאוּבֵן לְצִבְאֹתָם
יט וְעַל־צְבָאוֹ אֱלִיצוּר בֶּן־שְׁדֵיאוּר: וְעַל־צְבָא מַטֵּה בְּנֵי שִׁמְעוֹן
כ שְׁלֻמִיאֵל בֶּן־צוּרִישַׁדָּי: וְעַל־צְבָא מַטֵּה בְנֵי־גָד אֶלְיָסָף
כא בֶּן־דְּעוּאֵל: וְנָסְעוּ הַקְּהָתִים נֹשְׂאֵי הַמִּקְדָּשׁ וְהֵקִימוּ אֶת־
כב הַמִּשְׁכָּן עַד־בֹּאָם: וְנָסַע דֶּגֶל מַחֲנֵה בְנֵי־אֶפְרַיִם לְצִבְאֹתָם

divisions of the camp of Efrayim set out next, under
their banner. Leading that division was Elishama son of
23 Amihud. Gamliel son of Pedatzur was in charge of the
24 division of the tribe of Menashe. Avidan son of Gidoni was
25 in charge of the division of the tribe of Binyamin. Then,
at the rear of the whole camp, the divisions of the camp
of Dan set out under their banner. Leading that division
26 was Aḥiezer son of Amishadai. Pagiel son of Okhran was
27 in charge of the division of the tribe of Asher. Aḥira son of
Einan was in charge of the division of the tribe of Naftali.
28 This was the order in which the Israelites set out in their
29 divisions. Moshe said to Ḥovav son of Reuel the
Midianite, Moshe's father-in-law, "We are setting out to
the place that the LORD said He would give us. Come with
us and we will be good to you, for the LORD has promised
30 good things to Israel." But he replied, "I will not come; I
31 must go back to my own land and my own people." "Please
do not leave us," said Moshe, "for you know where we
should camp in the wilderness; you would be our eyes.
32 If you come with us, whatever good the LORD does for
33 us, we will do for you." They journeyed from the LORD's
mountain for three days; and the Ark of the LORD's
Covenant went ahead of them for those three days to find
34 a resting place for them. The LORD's cloud was over them
35 by day as they journeyed from the camp. When SHISHI
the Ark set out, Moshe would say, "Arise, LORD; let Your

separating this one paragraph from the words that precede and follow it. Some rabbis went so far as to say that this shows that *these two sentences are a book in their own right*. In other words, Numbers is not one book but three (Soferim 6:1; Bereshit Rabba 64:8).

To consider the significance of this we must take it in the context of the structure of the three central books of the Torah: Exodus, Leviticus, and Numbers. The outer sections – the first nineteen chapters of Exodus and the last twenty-five of Numbers – are full of incidents. The Israelites leave Egypt and travel through the desert. There are dangers, battles, and miracles. We are in the presence of history. This is the world of the prophet. Here the dominant figure is Moshe.

כג וְעַל־צְבָאוֹ אֱלִישָׁמָע בֶּן־עַמִּיהוּד׃ וְעַל־צְבָא מַטֵּה בְּנֵי
כד מְנַשֶּׁה גַּמְלִיאֵל בֶּן־פְּדָהצוּר׃ וְעַל־צְבָא מַטֵּה בְּנֵי בִנְיָמִן
כה אֲבִידָן בֶּן־גִּדְעוֹנִי׃ וְנָסַע דֶּגֶל מַחֲנֵה בְנֵי־דָן מְאַסֵּף לְכָל־
כו הַמַּחֲנֹת לְצִבְאֹתָם וְעַל־צְבָאוֹ אֲחִיעֶזֶר בֶּן־עַמִּישַׁדָּי׃ וְעַל־
כז צְבָא מַטֵּה בְּנֵי אָשֵׁר פַּגְעִיאֵל בֶּן־עָכְרָן׃ וְעַל־צְבָא מַטֵּה בְּנֵי
כח נַפְתָּלִי אֲחִירַע בֶּן־עֵינָן׃ אֵלֶּה מַסְעֵי בְנֵי־יִשְׂרָאֵל לְצִבְאֹתָם
כט וַיִּסָּעוּ׃ וַיֹּאמֶר מֹשֶׁה לְחֹבָב בֶּן־רְעוּאֵל הַמִּדְיָנִי
חֹתֵן מֹשֶׁה נֹסְעִים ׀ אֲנַחְנוּ אֶל־הַמָּקוֹם אֲשֶׁר אָמַר יהוה
אֹתוֹ אֶתֵּן לָכֶם לְכָה אִתָּנוּ וְהֵטַבְנוּ לָךְ כִּי־יהוה דִּבֶּר־טוֹב
ל עַל־יִשְׂרָאֵל׃ וַיֹּאמֶר אֵלָיו לֹא אֵלֵךְ כִּי אִם־אֶל־אַרְצִי וְאֶל־
לא מוֹלַדְתִּי אֵלֵךְ׃ וַיֹּאמֶר אַל־נָא תַּעֲזֹב אֹתָנוּ כִּי ׀ עַל־כֵּן יָדַעְתָּ
לב חֲנֹתֵנוּ בַּמִּדְבָּר וְהָיִיתָ לָּנוּ לְעֵינָיִם׃ וְהָיָה כִּי־תֵלֵךְ עִמָּנוּ
וְהָיָה ׀ הַטּוֹב הַהוּא אֲשֶׁר יֵיטִיב יהוה עִמָּנוּ וְהֵטַבְנוּ לָךְ׃
לג וַיִּסְעוּ מֵהַר יהוה דֶּרֶךְ שְׁלֹשֶׁת יָמִים וַאֲרוֹן בְּרִית־יהוה
לד נֹסֵעַ לִפְנֵיהֶם דֶּרֶךְ שְׁלֹשֶׁת יָמִים לָתוּר לָהֶם מְנוּחָה׃ וַעֲנַן
לה יְהוָה עֲלֵיהֶם יוֹמָם בְּנָסְעָם מִן־הַמַּחֲנֶה׃ ׆ וַיְהִי ששי
בִּנְסֹעַ הָאָרֹן וַיֹּאמֶר מֹשֶׁה קוּמָה ׀ יהוה וְיָפֻצוּ אֹיְבֶיךָ וְיָנֻסוּ

10:30 לֹא אֵלֵךְ *I will not come* – It is perhaps not by coincidence that immediately after we read of Yitro's departure (Reuel is another name for Yitro), Moshe experiences burnout and despair (Num. 11:10–15). Something very similar will happen later in Parashat Ḥukat (ch. 20), where first we read of the death of Miriam, followed immediately by the scene in which the people ask for water and Moshe loses his temper and strikes the rock. This act costs him the chance to lead the people across the Jordan into the Promised Land.

It seems that in their different ways, Yitro and Miriam are essential emotional supports for Moshe. When they are there, he copes. When they are not, he loses his poise. Leaders need soulmates, people who lift their spirits and give them the strength to carry on. No one can lead alone.

A BOOK BETWEEN THE BOOKS

This passage is separated from the rest of the text by two inverted Hebrew letters, each a *nun*. The Rabbis proposed that they form a set of brackets, parentheses,

enemies be scattered, and Your foes flee before You."
36 When it came to rest, he would say, "Bring back, O LORD,
the myriad thousands of Israel."
11 1 The people began to rail bitterly in the LORD's presence.
And the LORD heard and was incensed; fire from the
LORD blazed against them, consuming at the edge of the

verses, flanked by an inverted *nun*, are the interlude between two movements of the symphony, the *adagio* of the stay and the *allegro* of the journey. What it tells us is simply this: that whether setting out or halting, the Ark must always be there at the heart of Jewish life, reminding us that God is to be found both in eternity and history, stasis and change, beyond time and within time, joining His fate to ours, the God of both priest and prophet, who gives us the patience to rest and the courage to move on.

10:35 וַיְהִי בִּנְסֹעַ הָאָרֹן *When the Ark set out* – The Israelites are about to begin the second half of their journey through the wilderness. They travel, tribe by tribe, in the order specified earlier in the book, with the Ark, symbolizing the Divine Presence, in their midst. So at the beginning and end of each stage on the way, Moshe will remind the people that they are not alone, nor are they defenseless. God is with them, giving them strength in battle and security in their resting places. We still say these verses in the synagogue when we take the *sefer Torah* out of the ark, and when we replace it.

11:1 וַיְהִי הָעָם כְּמִתְאֹנְנִים רַע *The people began to rail bitterly* – The Torah gives us no indication of what the people are complaining about. Usually we are told exactly what the issue is – but not here. The Torah seems to be implying that they are complaining because that is what they have become accustomed to doing, even when they have nothing specific to complain about. When that happens, the whole mood of the group is badly affected.

We are social animals. We are affected by those around us. Consciously or unconsciously, we conform to the norms of the group. Social phenomena are contagious. Already in the twelfth century, Rambam had codified social contagion as an axiom of Jewish law, writing that "it is in the nature of human beings to be influenced in their deeds and characters by their friends and companions and to act like the people of their country" (*Hilkhot Deot* 6:1).

The Torah – as understood by the Sages in the light of Jewish history from the days of Moshe to their own – attaches huge significance to the tone of conversation within a society as a whole, within communities, and even within families. Freedom depends on civility, on people speaking courteously of and to one another. Free people do not blame others for their misfortune. They accept and practice responsibility. They assume that if something bad has happened, they

לו מְשַׂנְאֶיךָ מִפָּנֶיךָ: וּבְנֻחֹה יֹאמַר שׁוּבָה יהוה רִבְבוֹת אַלְפֵי
יִשְׂרָאֵל: ׆
יא א וַיְהִי הָעָם כְּמִתְאֹנְנִים רַע בְּאָזְנֵי יהוה וַיִּשְׁמַע יהוה וַיִּחַר

However, within this outer wrapping are fifty-nine chapters – the last part of Exodus, the whole of Leviticus, and the first ten chapters of Numbers – in which the Israelites stay in the Sinai Desert. Time slows to a standstill. This is the world of the Tabernacle and the Temple, the universe of *kedusha,* holiness, in which the dominant figures are Aharon the High Priest and his descendants. Now, in our *parasha,* we have read, "The Lord spoke to Moshe in the Sinai Desert in the first month of the second year after they had left Egypt" (Num. 9:1). The historical narrative resumes.

There are aspects of Judaism – the laws of purity and impurity, permitted and forbidden, sacred and secular – that have barely changed through the centuries. This is where we encounter the holiness, the otherness, the eternity of God. But there are other aspects that are deeply enmeshed in time. Most of the books in Tanakh are about this dimension. They tell a story about the faithfulness or faithlessness of the people to their covenant with God. It is about politics and economics, battles won or lost, about Israel as a nation in a world of nations, and about its ability to stay true to its founding principles through the rapids of history.

If Israel were only a people of eternity, it would never have had an impact on history. Jews would have been a priestly sect like the one known to us from the Dead Sea Scrolls, holy and harmless, secluded and serene, in touch with the ethereal music of the spheres but not the substance of everyday life. If, on the other hand, Jews had been only a people of history, they would have disappeared in exile. They would have been like the Jebusites and Perizzites, a brief footnote in the history of a long-vanished past. Judaism lives in the creative tension between these two essential elements of its being.

Our passage, then, is set at a dividing line between two kinds of books. In two verses, it encapsulates Jewish history. There are times when Jews halt and encamp, when time itself seems to stop and the people feel close to eternity as they did in their prolonged stay in the desert of Sinai. And there are moments when the cloud shifts, the trumpet sounds, and it is time to move on. History beckons. Destiny calls. For God exists within, not just beyond, time and space and we have to engage in the world as it is, even as we aspire to the world as it ought to be.

These are the two books of Jewish life: the Judaism-of-eternity and the Judaism-of-history. Nowhere is the line between them clearer than it is here, as the long stay at Sinai comes to an end and the people have to gather their belongings and travel on. These two

2 camp. The people cried out to Moshe – Moshe prayed to
3 the LORD – and the fire subsided. And so that place was
named Tavera, because the LORD's fire had blazed against
4 them. The rabble in their midst began to have strong
cravings, and once again the Israelites began to weep,
5 saying, "Who will give us meat to eat? We remember
the fish we ate in Egypt at no cost, the cucumbers, and
the melons, and the leeks, and the onions, and the garlic.
6 But now our throats are dry. There is nothing at all but
7 this manna to look at." The manna was like coriander
8 seed, and like bdellium in color. The people went around
gathering it. Then they would grind it in a mill or crush
it in a mortar. They cooked it in a pot and they made
9 cakes from it; it tasted like cakes made with oil. When
the dew fell over the camp at night, the manna would
10 fall upon that. Moshe heard the people weeping clan by
clan, each one at his tent's opening. The LORD's anger
11 blazed intensely, and Moshe was distressed. "Why have
You treated Your servant so badly?" asked Moshe of the
LORD. "Why have I found so little favor in Your sight that
12 You lay all the burden of this people upon me? Was it I
who conceived all this people? Was it I who gave birth to

---

done before. Nor are they starving. Their complaint is not that they have no food. They have the manna. Their complaint is that it is boring. They have lost their appetite. They have reached the spiritual heights but they remain the same recalcitrant, ungrateful, small-minded people they were before.

The song *Dayeinu*, which we sing at the Passover Seder, is structured as a *tikkun*, a making right, for the ingratitude of the Israelites in the wilderness. A series of fifteen praises punctuated by the refrain *dayeinu*, "that would have been enough," it enumerates the kindnesses of God on the long journey from slavery to freedom. It is as if the poet were saying: Where they complained, let us give thanks. Each stage was a miracle. Each would have been enough to convince us that there is a Providence at work in our fate.

As the philosopher Hegel points out, slavery gives rise to a culture of ressentiment, a generalized discontent; and the Israelites were newly released slaves. One sign of freedom is the capacity for gratitude. Only a free person can give thanks with a full heart.

ב אַפּוֹ וַתִּבְעַר־בָּם אֵשׁ יהוה וַתֹּאכַל בִּקְצֵה הַמַּחֲנֶה: וַיִּצְעַק
הָעָם אֶל־מֹשֶׁה וַיִּתְפַּלֵּל מֹשֶׁה אֶל־יהוה וַתִּשְׁקַע הָאֵשׁ:
ג וַיִּקְרָא שֵׁם־הַמָּקוֹם הַהוּא תַּבְעֵרָה כִּי־בָעֲרָה בָם אֵשׁ יהוה:
ד וְהָאסַפְסֻף אֲשֶׁר בְּקִרְבּוֹ הִתְאַוּוּ תַּאֲוָה וַיָּשֻׁבוּ וַיִּבְכּוּ גַּם
ה בְּנֵי יִשְׂרָאֵל וַיֹּאמְרוּ מִי יַאֲכִלֵנוּ בָּשָׂר: זָכַרְנוּ אֶת־הַדָּגָה
אֲשֶׁר־נֹאכַל בְּמִצְרַיִם חִנָּם אֵת הַקִּשֻּׁאִים וְאֵת הָאֲבַטִּחִים
ו וְאֶת־הֶחָצִיר וְאֶת־הַבְּצָלִים וְאֶת־הַשּׁוּמִים: וְעַתָּה נַפְשֵׁנוּ
ז יְבֵשָׁה אֵין כֹּל בִּלְתִּי אֶל־הַמָּן עֵינֵינוּ: וְהַמָּן כִּזְרַע־גַּד הוּא
ח וְעֵינוֹ כְּעֵין הַבְּדֹלַח: שָׁטוּ הָעָם וְלָקְטוּ וְטָחֲנוּ בָרֵחַיִם אוֹ
דָכוּ בַּמְּדֹכָה וּבִשְּׁלוּ בַּפָּרוּר וְעָשׂוּ אֹתוֹ עֻגוֹת וְהָיָה טַעְמוֹ
ט כְּטַעַם לְשַׁד הַשָּׁמֶן: וּבְרֶדֶת הַטַּל עַל־הַמַּחֲנֶה לָיְלָה יֵרֵד
י הַמָּן עָלָיו: וַיִּשְׁמַע מֹשֶׁה אֶת־הָעָם בֹּכֶה לְמִשְׁפְּחֹתָיו אִישׁ
יא לְפֶתַח אָהֳלוֹ וַיִּחַר־אַף יהוה מְאֹד וּבְעֵינֵי מֹשֶׁה רָע: וַיֹּאמֶר
מֹשֶׁה אֶל־יהוה לָמָה הֲרֵעֹתָ לְעַבְדֶּךָ וְלָמָּה לֹא־מָצָתִי חֵן
יב בְּעֵינֶיךָ לָשׂוּם אֶת־מַשָּׂא כָּל־הָעָם הַזֶּה עָלָי: הֶאָנֹכִי הָרִיתִי
אֵת כָּל־הָעָם הַזֶּה אִם־אָנֹכִי יְלִדְתִּיהוּ כִּי־תֹאמַר אֵלַי שָׂאֵהוּ

---

must work together to put it right. When criticism is necessary, and it often is, they do so constructively. In any group, where the predominant tone is one of complaint, criticism, envy, backbiting, cynicism, and mutual suspicion, not only is the group itself weakened; a profound disempowerment also takes place. The ability to challenge leaders is essential, but generalized, unconstructive complaint is potentially disastrous.

11:6 אֵין כֹּל בִּלְתִּי אֶל־הַמָּן *Nothing at all but this manna* – Moshe has faced a similar challenge before. Back in the book of Exodus the people made the same complaint: "If only we had died by the Lord's hand in Egypt, when we sat by the fleshpots and ate our fill of bread. Instead, you have brought us out into this desert to kill the entire assembly by starvation" (Ex. 16:3).

Moshe, on that occasion, experienced no crisis. The people were hungry and needed food. That was a legitimate request. Since then, though, they have experienced the twin peaks of the revelation at Mount Sinai and the construction of the Tabernacle. They have come closer to God than any nation has ever

them all, that You should say to me, 'Carry them in your
bosom, as a nursemaid carries a baby,' to the land that You
13 swore to their fathers? Where am I to get meat to give all
this people when they come wailing to me, 'Give us meat
14 to eat'? I cannot bear all this people alone; the burden is
15 too heavy for me. If this is how You treat me, kill me now,
if I find any favor in Your sight, and let me not see my own
misery."
16 Then the LORD said to Moshe, "Gather for Me seventy of
Israel's elders, whom you know to be the people's elders
and officers, and bring them to the Tent of Meeting. Let

---

need a father-mother-nursemaid, but as adults who need to be educated to take individual and collective responsibility for their own future.

People become what their leader gives them the space to become. When that space is large, they grow into greatness.

THE SEVENTY ELDERS

The people's complaint about food has been the worst crisis in Moshe's life. Why? It was an appalling show of ingratitude, but not the first time the Israelites had behaved this way. He had faced and overcome such difficulties before. Each time, God had answered the people's requests. Moshe knew this. Why did this outburst of the people induce in him a complete breakdown?

Equally strange is God's reaction here. To be sure, it is a response to Moshe's complaint: "I cannot bear all this people alone" (Num. 11:14). Nevertheless, how will the appointment of elders address the crisis? He does not need deputies to help him find meat. Either it will appear by a miracle, or it will not appear at all. Nor does he need help in sharing the burdens of leadership. Already, on Yitro's advice, he has created a leadership infrastructure: heads of thousands, hundreds, fifties, and tens. How would a new appointment of seventy elders make a difference?

And why the emphasis on spirit in God's reply: "I will take some of the spirit that is on you and place it upon them" (11:17)? The elders do not need to become prophets to help Moshe in carrying out the burdens of leadership. Prophets help only in knowing what guidance to give the people – and for this, one prophet, Moshe, is sufficient. To put it bluntly: Either the seventy elders will deliver the same message as Moshe or they will not. If they do, they will be superfluous. If they do not, they will undermine his authority.

Yet it works. From this moment onward, Moshe's despair disappears. When Eldad and Meidad prophesy not in the Tent of Meeting but in the camp, Yehoshua senses a threat to Moshe's

בְחֵיקֶךָ כַּאֲשֶׁר יִשָּׂא הָאֹמֵן אֶת־הַיֹּנֵק עַל הָאֲדָמָה אֲשֶׁר
יג נִשְׁבַּעְתָּ לַאֲבֹתָיו: מֵאַיִן לִי בָּשָׂר לָתֵת לְכָל־הָעָם הַזֶּה כִּי־
יד יִבְכּוּ עָלַי לֵאמֹר תְּנָה־לָּנוּ בָשָׂר וְנֹאכֵלָה: לֹא־אוּכַל אָנֹכִי
טו לְבַדִּי לָשֵׂאת אֶת־כָּל־הָעָם הַזֶּה כִּי כָבֵד מִמֶּנִּי: וְאִם־כָּכָה ׀
אַתְּ־עֹשֶׂה לִּי הָרְגֵנִי נָא הָרֹג אִם־מָצָאתִי חֵן בְּעֵינֶיךָ וְאַל־
אֶרְאֶה בְּרָעָתִי:
טז וַיֹּאמֶר יְהֹוָה אֶל־מֹשֶׁה אֶסְפָה־לִּי שִׁבְעִים אִישׁ מִזִּקְנֵי י
יִשְׂרָאֵל אֲשֶׁר יָדַעְתָּ כִּי־הֵם זִקְנֵי הָעָם וְשֹׁטְרָיו וְלָקַחְתָּ

11:12 כַּאֲשֶׁר יִשָּׂא הָאֹמֵן אֶת־הַיֹּנֵק *As a nursemaid carries a baby* – Inevitably, when we read Moshe's anguished plea, our attention focuses on his wish to die. But this is not the most interesting part of his speech. Moshe is not the only Jewish leader to pray to die. So does Eliyahu. So does Yirmeyahu. So does Yona.

What is singular here is his statement that God told him to carry the people in his arms "as a nursemaid carries a baby." God never used those words or even remotely implied such a thing. He asked Moshe to lead but did not tell him how to lead. He told Moshe what to do, but never discussed with him his leadership style.

It seems that the Torah is here hinting that *the way Moshe conceives the role of leader is itself part of the problem*. His is the language of the leader-as-parent. Moshe is not a typical charismatic leader. He says of himself, "I am not a man of words" (Ex. 4:10). He is not particularly close to the people. Aharon is. Perhaps Miriam is also. Kalev has the power to calm the people, at least temporarily. Moshe has neither the gift nor the desire to sway crowds, attract a mass following, or win popularity. But Moshe, especially here, seems to feel that *the leader must do it all*. He must be the people's father, mother, and nursemaid. He must be the doer, the problem solver, omniscient and omnipotent. The trouble is that if the leader is a parent, then the followers remain children. They are totally dependent on him. They do not develop skills of their own. They do not acquire a sense of responsibility or the self-confidence that comes from exercising it.

Perhaps this is what God is hinting to Moshe when He tells him to take seventy elders to stand with him in the Tent of Meeting. He is telling Moshe that his task is not to solve the crisis of the people's demand for meat. His task is to inspire others with his spirit – delegating, empowering, guiding, and encouraging. God is telling Moshe that great leaders do not create followers; they create leaders. They share their inspiration. They give of their spirit to others. They do not see the people they lead as children who

17 them stand there with you. I will come down and speak
with you there, and I will take some of the spirit that is on
you and place it upon them; they will share the burden
of the people with you, and you will not have to bear it
18 alone. And say to the people: Consecrate yourselves for
tomorrow; you will then have meat to eat, for you have
been wailing in the presence of the LORD, 'Who will give
us meat to eat? It was better for us in Egypt.' The LORD
19 will give you meat, and you will eat. You will eat it not just
for one day, or two days, or five, or ten, or twenty days,
20 but for a whole month, until it comes out at your nostrils
and becomes nauseating to you; for you have rejected the
LORD who is among you and have come wailing in His
21 presence, 'Why ever did we leave Egypt?'" But Moshe
said, "Here I am among six hundred thousand men on
foot, and You say, 'I will give them meat to eat for a whole
22 month'! If whole flocks and herds were slaughtered for
them, would there be enough? If all the fish of the sea were
caught for them, would there be enough?!"
23 The LORD said to Moshe, "Does the LORD's hand fall

His vision is not his alone. He has planted it in others. Others, too, will continue his work after his lifetime. That was enough for him, as it must be for us. Once Moshe knows this, he can face the future with equanimity.

11:17 וְלֹא־תִשָּׂא אַתָּה לְבַדֶּךָ *You will not have to bear it alone* – It is as if God were saying to Moshe, "Remember what your father-in-law Yitro told you. Do not try to lead alone. Even you, the greatest of the prophets, are still human, and humans are social animals. Enlist others."

What is moving about this episode is that, at the moment of Moshe's maximum emotional vulnerability, God Himself speaks to Moshe as a friend. God is not (merely) the creator of the universe, Lord of history, sovereign, lawgiver, and redeemer. He is also close, tender, loving: "He heals the brokenhearted and binds up their wounds" (Ps. 147:3). He is always there: "The LORD is close to all who call on Him – to all who truly call on Him" (145:18). *Faith is the redemption of solitude.* It is about relationships – between us and God, us and our family, us and our neighbors, us and our people, us and humankind. Judaism is not about the lonely soul. It is about the bonds that bind us to one another and to the Author of all. It is, in the highest sense, about friendship.

יז אֹתָם אֶל־אֹהֶל מוֹעֵד וְהִתְיַצְּבוּ שָׁם עִמָּךְ: וְיָרַדְתִּי וְדִבַּרְתִּי
עִמְּךָ שָׁם וְאָצַלְתִּי מִן־הָרוּחַ אֲשֶׁר עָלֶיךָ וְשַׂמְתִּי עֲלֵיהֶם
יח וְנָשְׂאוּ אִתְּךָ בְּמַשָּׂא הָעָם וְלֹא־תִשָּׂא אַתָּה לְבַדֶּךָ: וְאֶל־
הָעָם תֹּאמַר הִתְקַדְּשׁוּ לְמָחָר וַאֲכַלְתֶּם בָּשָׂר כִּי בְּכִיתֶם
בְּאׇזְנֵי יְהוָה לֵאמֹר מִי יַאֲכִלֵנוּ בָּשָׂר כִּי־טוֹב לָנוּ בְּמִצְרָיִם
יט וְנָתַן יְהוָה לָכֶם בָּשָׂר וַאֲכַלְתֶּם: לֹא יוֹם אֶחָד תֹּאכְלוּן וְלֹא
יוֹמָיִם וְלֹא ׀ חֲמִשָּׁה יָמִים וְלֹא עֲשָׂרָה יָמִים וְלֹא עֶשְׂרִים יוֹם:
כ עַד ׀ חֹדֶשׁ יָמִים עַד אֲשֶׁר־יֵצֵא מֵאַפְּכֶם וְהָיָה לָכֶם לְזָרָא
יַעַן כִּי־מְאַסְתֶּם אֶת־יְהוָה אֲשֶׁר בְּקִרְבְּכֶם וַתִּבְכּוּ לְפָנָיו
כא לֵאמֹר לָמָּה זֶּה יָצָאנוּ מִמִּצְרָיִם: וַיֹּאמֶר מֹשֶׁה שֵׁשׁ־מֵאוֹת
אֶלֶף רַגְלִי הָעָם אֲשֶׁר אָנֹכִי בְּקִרְבּוֹ וְאַתָּה אָמַרְתָּ בָּשָׂר אֶתֵּן
כב לָהֶם וְאָכְלוּ חֹדֶשׁ יָמִים: הֲצֹאן וּבָקָר יִשָּׁחֵט לָהֶם וּמָצָא לָהֶם
אִם אֶת־כׇּל־דְּגֵי הַיָּם יֵאָסֵף לָהֶם וּמָצָא לָהֶם:
כג וַיֹּאמֶר יְהוָה אֶל־מֹשֶׁה הֲיַד יְהוָה תִּקְצָר עַתָּה תִרְאֶה יא

authority – yet Moshe responds with surpassing generosity of spirit, "Would that all the Lord's people were prophets" (11:29). In the next chapter, when his own brother and sister start complaining about him, he does nothing. The despair is gone. The crisis has passed. How?

God let Moshe see the influence he had on others. All the evidence seemed to suggest that he had none. When he heard the people complain of boredom after all they had received, Moshe was staring at his own defeat. There was no point in carrying on. If the people have not changed by now, it is a reasonable assumption that they never will. And so, for a brief moment, God would take "some of the spirit that is on you and place it upon them" so that Moshe can see the difference he has made to this one group. He needs a glimpse of how his spirit has communicated itself to them. Then he knows he has made a difference.

Little can he know that he – who encounters little in his lifetime but complaints and rebellions – will have so decisive an influence that the people of Israel thirty-three centuries later would still be studying and living by the words he transmitted. He is helping forge an identity that would prove more tenacious than any other in the history of mankind. He cannot know these things; he does not *need* to know these things. All he needs is to see that seventy elders have internalized his spirit and made his message their own. Then he knows that his life is not in vain. He has disciples.

short? Soon you shall see whether what I say comes true
24 or not." Moshe went out and told the people what the
LORD had said. He gathered seventy of the people's
25 elders and had them stand surrounding the Tent. Then
the LORD came down in the cloud and spoke to him, and
took some of the spirit that was upon him and placed it
on the seventy elders. When the spirit rested upon them,
26 they prophesied – but they did not do so again. Two men,
one named Eldad and the other Meidad, had remained in
the camp, yet the spirit rested upon them. Though they
were among those listed, they had not gone out to the
27 Tent – and they spoke prophecy in the camp. A young
man ran and told Moshe, "Eldad and Meidad are speaking
28 prophecy in the camp!" Yehoshua son of Nun, who had
been Moshe's disciple since his youth, said, "My lord
29 Moshe, stop them!" But Moshe replied, "Are you jealous
for me? Would that all the LORD's people were prophets,
30 that the LORD would put His spirit upon them all!" And SHEVI'I
Moshe returned to the camp together with the elders of
31 Israel. Then a wind from the LORD sprang up, sweeping

---

be a leader. The most important forms of leadership come not with position, title, or robes of office, not with prestige and power, but with the willingness to work with others to achieve what we cannot do alone; to speak, to listen, to teach, to learn, to treat other people's views with respect even if they disagree with us; to explain patiently and cogently why we believe what we believe and do what we do; to encourage others, praise their best endeavors, and challenge them to do better still. One should always choose influence rather than power. It helps change people into people who can change the world.

11:30 הוּא וְזִקְנֵי יִשְׂרָאֵל *Together with the elders of Israel* – God has spoken directly to Moshe's concerns. He tells him he will not have to lead alone in the future. There will be others to help him.

The Sages said, "A prisoner cannot release himself from prison" (Berakhot 5b). It takes someone else to lift you from depression. That is why Judaism is so insistent on not leaving people alone at times of maximum vulnerability. Hence the principles of visiting the sick, comforting mourners, including the lonely ("the migrant, the orphan, and the widow") in festive celebrations, and offering hospitality – an act said to

כד הֲיִקְרְךָ דְבָרִי אִם־לֹא: וַיֵּצֵא מֹשֶׁה וַיְדַבֵּר אֶל־הָעָם אֵת
דִּבְרֵי יהוה וַיֶּאֱסֹף שִׁבְעִים אִישׁ מִזִּקְנֵי הָעָם וַיַּעֲמֵד אֹתָם
כה סְבִיבֹת הָאֹהֶל: וַיֵּרֶד יהוה ׀ בֶּעָנָן וַיְדַבֵּר אֵלָיו וַיָּאצֶל מִן־
הָרוּחַ אֲשֶׁר עָלָיו וַיִּתֵּן עַל־שִׁבְעִים אִישׁ הַזְּקֵנִים וַיְהִי כְּנוֹחַ
כו עֲלֵיהֶם הָרוּחַ וַיִּתְנַבְּאוּ וְלֹא יָסָפוּ: וַיִּשָּׁאֲרוּ שְׁנֵי־אֲנָשִׁים ׀
בַּמַּחֲנֶה שֵׁם הָאֶחָד ׀ אֶלְדָּד וְשֵׁם הַשֵּׁנִי מֵידָד וַתָּנַח עֲלֵהֶם
הָרוּחַ וְהֵמָּה בַּכְּתֻבִים וְלֹא יָצְאוּ הָאֹהֱלָה וַיִּתְנַבְּאוּ בַּמַּחֲנֶה:
כז וַיָּרָץ הַנַּעַר וַיַּגֵּד לְמֹשֶׁה וַיֹּאמַר אֶלְדָּד וּמֵידָד מִתְנַבְּאִים
כח בַּמַּחֲנֶה: וַיַּעַן יְהוֹשֻׁעַ בִּן־נוּן מְשָׁרֵת מֹשֶׁה מִבְּחֻרָיו וַיֹּאמַר
כט אֲדֹנִי מֹשֶׁה כְּלָאֵם: וַיֹּאמֶר לוֹ מֹשֶׁה הַמְקַנֵּא אַתָּה לִי וּמִי
יִתֵּן כָּל־עַם יהוה נְבִיאִים כִּי־יִתֵּן יהוה אֶת־רוּחוֹ עֲלֵיהֶם:
ל לא וַיֵּאָסֵף מֹשֶׁה אֶל־הַמַּחֲנֶה הוּא וְזִקְנֵי יִשְׂרָאֵל: וְרוּחַ נָסַע ׀ שביעי

11:29 כִּי־יִתֵּן יהוה אֶת־רוּחוֹ עֲלֵיהֶם *The LORD would put His spirit upon them all* – Compare this magnanimous response to Moshe's conduct later when his leadership is challenged by Koraḥ and his followers. On that occasion, in effect, he prays that the ground swallow them up, that "they go down alive to Sheol [the netherworld]" (Num. 16:28–30). He is sharp, decisive, and unforgiving.

To understand the difference between Koraḥ on the one hand, and Eldad and Meidad on the other, it is essential to grasp the difference between two concepts often confused, namely power and influence. Power works by division ("divide and conquer"), influence by multiplication. Eldad and Meidad seek and receive no power. They merely receive the same influence – the divine spirit that has emanated from Moshe. They become prophets. That is why Moshe says, "Would that all the LORD's people were prophets, that the LORD would put His spirit upon them all!" (11:29). Prophecy is not a zero-sum game. When it comes to leadership as influence, the more we share, the more we have. Koraḥ, or at least some of his followers, sought power, and power is a zero-sum game. Moshe could not let the challenge of Koraḥ go unopposed without fatefully compromising his own authority.

Judaism is a sustained protest against what Hobbes in *The Leviathan* called the "general inclination of all mankind," namely "a perpetual and restless desire of power after power, that ceaseth only in death." That may be the reason why Jews have seldom exercised power for prolonged periods but have had an influence on the world out of all proportion to their numbers.

Not all of us have power, but we all have influence. That is why we can each

quail in from the sea and letting them fall near the camp,
about a day's journey on one side and a day's journey
on the other, around the camp and piled up two cubits
32 above the ground. All that day, all night, and all the next
day, the people went out and gathered quail. Even those
who gathered least gathered ten omer, and they spread
33 them out all around the camp. While the meat was still
between their teeth, before it was eaten, the LORD's anger
blazed against the people, and the LORD struck the people
34 with a very great plague. The place was named Kivrot
HaTaava, because there they buried the people who had
35 craved. And from Kivrot HaTaava the people journeyed
to Ḥatzerot, and at Ḥatzerot they stayed.
12 1 Once, Miriam and Aharon spoke against Moshe because
of his Kushite wife; he had married a Kushite woman.

Miriam is expressing her concern for the wives of Moshe's newly inspired leadership group. Her motives are honorable. Miriam is never less than a heroic and compassionate human being.

Yet because others less noble might derive the wrong lesson from her behavior, because – as we have seen – complaint is a social contagion, she is stigmatized for seven days by an unsightly skin condition. Many years later, Moshe is to recall this incident to remind the people how dangerous it is to "judge the judges" and heap unjustified criticism on leaders. Speech does not always have to be positive. The prophets of Israel were deeply critical of the failings of the generation. But speech does have to be constructive, creative, in intent.

Never give way to sibling rivalry. Never speak badly of others. Never underestimate the damaging effect of words. And the lead has to be given by the leaders. That is why God is angry with Miriam and Aharon. If leaders speak like this, how can one blame the people for doing likewise?

12:1 עַל־אֹדוֹת הָאִשָּׁה הַכֻּשִׁית *Because of his Kushite wife* – There are midrashic interpretations that read this passage differently, but it may be that Miriam and Aharon look down on Moshe's wife because, like Kushite women generally, she has dark skin (see Jer. 13:23). If so, this is one of the first recorded instances of color prejudice, and for this sin too Miriam is struck with leprosy.

Jews have been subjected to racism more and longer than any other nation on earth. Therefore we should be doubly careful never to be guilty of it ourselves. We believe that God created each of us, regardless of color, class, culture, or

מֵאֵת יהוה וַיָּגׇז שַׂלְוִים מִן־הַיָּם וַיִּטֹּשׁ עַל־הַמַּחֲנֶה כְּדֶרֶךְ
יוֹם כֹּה וּכְדֶרֶךְ יוֹם כֹּה סְבִיבוֹת הַמַּחֲנֶה וּכְאַמָּתַיִם עַל־פְּנֵי
לב הָאָרֶץ: וַיָּקׇם הָעָם כׇּל־הַיּוֹם הַהוּא וְכׇל־הַלַּיְלָה וְכֹל ׀ יוֹם
הַמׇּחֳרָת וַיַּאַסְפוּ אֶת־הַשְּׂלָו הַמַּמְעִיט אָסַף עֲשָׂרָה חֳמָרִים
לג וַיִּשְׁטְחוּ לָהֶם שָׁטוֹחַ סְבִיבוֹת הַמַּחֲנֶה: הַבָּשָׂר עוֹדֶנּוּ בֵּין
שִׁנֵּיהֶם טֶרֶם יִכָּרֵת וְאַף יהוה חָרָה בָעָם וַיַּךְ יהוה בָּעָם מַכָּה
לד רַבָּה מְאֹד: וַיִּקְרָא אֶת־שֵׁם־הַמָּקוֹם הַהוּא קִבְרוֹת הַתַּאֲוָה
לה כִּי־שָׁם קָבְרוּ אֶת־הָעָם הַמִּתְאַוִּים: מִקִּבְרוֹת הַתַּאֲוָה נָסְעוּ
הָעָם חֲצֵרוֹת וַיִּהְיוּ בַּחֲצֵרוֹת:
יב א וַתְּדַבֵּר מִרְיָם וְאַהֲרֹן בְּמֹשֶׁה עַל־אֹדוֹת הָאִשָּׁה הַכֻּשִׁית

be "greater than receiving the *Shekhina*" (Shabbat 127a). Precisely because depression isolates you from others, remaining alone intensifies the despair. What the seventy elders will subsequently do to help Moshe is unclear. But simply *being there with him* is part of the cure.

MIRIAM AND AHARON SPEAK ABOUT MOSHE

One of the fundamental themes of Genesis is sibling rivalry. It appears, with variations, five times: in the stories of Kayin and Hevel, Yitzḥak and Yishmael, Yaakov and Esav, Yosef and his brothers, and the two sisters Leah and Raḥel. Until now we have had no reason to associate this theme with life after the exodus. Miriam and Aharon, Moshe's siblings, have been until now admirably free of rivalry. Miriam watched over her brother's fate as a baby. Aharon has shared with Moshe the burden of leadership from the outset of his mission. Neither has uttered a word of criticism, still less of envy, until now.

What, then, is their complaint? A midrash tells us that Miriam said, in effect: "I am sorry for the wives of the elders, for if they have been filled with Moshe's spirit, they are likely to do what Moshe has done, namely discontinue marital relations." Miriam is critical of this, saying that God has spoken not just to Moshe, but to her and Aharon also, yet they have not discontinued marital relations with their spouses. Evidently she is making the complaint, not out of malice, but out of sympathy for the wives of the elders. Miriam and Aharon do not know what it means to be the unique individual that Moshe is. One can sympathize with Miriam's concern if she believes, as the midrash suggests, that Moshe's wife (and perhaps his children also) suffer from a lack of attention. That is one of the burdens of leadership in general (see note on Num. 27:13) – all the more so in the case of one who felt the need to be perpetually ready for a communication from God Himself.

▶

2 "Has the LORD spoken only through Moshe?" they said.
"Has He not spoken through us also?" The LORD heard
3 this. Now the man Moshe was very humble, more so than
4 any other man on earth. And suddenly the
LORD said to Moshe and Aharon and Miriam: "All three
of you, come out to the Tent of Meeting." So the three of
5 them went. The LORD came down in a column of cloud,
and, standing at the entrance to the Tent, called, "Aharon
6 and Miriam." The two of them came forward. The LORD
said: "Now listen to My words: When there is a prophet
among you, I make Myself known to him in a vision, I
7 speak to him in a dream. Not so with Moshe My servant:

An *anav* (the biblical word used in this chapter) is one who never thinks about himself because he has more important things to think about. I once heard someone say about a religious leader: "He took God so seriously that he didn't need to take himself seriously at all." That is biblical humility.

Humility is not self-abasement. It is not "self" anything. It is the ability to stand in silent awe in the presence of otherness – the Thou of God, the otherness of other people, the majesty of creation, the beauty of the world, the power of great ideas, the call of great ideals. Humility is the silence of the self in the presence of that which is greater than the self.

Humility – true humility – is one of the most expansive and life-enhancing of all virtues. It does not mean undervaluing yourself. It means valuing other people. It signals an openness to life's grandeur and the willingness to be surprised, uplifted, by goodness wherever one finds it.

Humility, then, is more than just a virtue; it is a form of perception, a language in which the "I" is silent so that I can hear the "Thou," the unspoken call beneath human speech, the divine whisper within all that moves, the voice of otherness that calls me to redeem its loneliness with the touch of love. Humility is what opens us to the world.

12:7 לֹא־כֵן עַבְדִּי מֹשֶׁה *Not so with Moshe My servant* – This description of Moshe's unique experience, coupled with Miriam's concern, if we accept that interpretation, for his neglected wife (see above, "Miriam and Aharon Speak About Moshe"), paint a poignantly ambivalent picture of the prophetic experience. It struck a chord with Rabbi Joseph B. Soloveitchik. "When the hour of estrangement strikes, the ordeal of the man of faith begins and he starts his withdrawal from society," he writes in his classic *The Lonely Man of Faith*. "He returns, like Moses of old, to his solitary hiding and to the abode of loneliness."

ב אֲשֶׁר לָקָח כִּי־אִשָּׁה כֻשִׁית לָקָח: וַיֹּאמְרוּ הֲרַק אַךְ־בְּמֹשֶׁה
ג דִּבֶּר יְהוָה הֲלֹא גַּם־בָּנוּ דִבֵּר וַיִּשְׁמַע יְהוָה: וְהָאִישׁ מֹשֶׁה עָנָו
ד מְאֹד מִכֹּל הָאָדָם אֲשֶׁר עַל־פְּנֵי הָאֲדָמָה: וַיֹּאמֶר
יְהוָה פִּתְאֹם אֶל־מֹשֶׁה וְאֶל־אַהֲרֹן וְאֶל־מִרְיָם צְאוּ
ה שְׁלָשְׁתְּכֶם אֶל־אֹהֶל מוֹעֵד וַיֵּצְאוּ שְׁלָשְׁתָּם: וַיֵּרֶד יְהוָה
בְּעַמּוּד עָנָן וַיַּעֲמֹד פֶּתַח הָאֹהֶל וַיִּקְרָא אַהֲרֹן וּמִרְיָם וַיֵּצְאוּ
ו שְׁנֵיהֶם: וַיֹּאמֶר שִׁמְעוּ־נָא דְבָרָי אִם־יִהְיֶה נְבִיאֲכֶם יְהוָה
ז בַּמַּרְאָה אֵלָיו אֶתְוַדָּע בַּחֲלוֹם אֲדַבֶּר־בּוֹ: לֹא־כֵן עַבְדִּי מֹשֶׁה

creed, in His image. If we look down on other people because of their race, then we are demeaning God's image and failing to treat others with *kevod habriyot,* human dignity.

According to this understanding of the verse, if we think less of a person because of the color of his or her skin, we are repeating the sin of Aharon and Miriam. "First correct yourself; then [seek to] correct others," says the Talmud (Bava Metzia 107b). The Tanakh contains negative evaluations of some other nations, but always and only because of their moral failures, never because of ethnicity or skin color.

12:3 וְהָאִישׁ מֹשֶׁה עָנָו מְאֹד *Now the man Moshe was very humble* – This is a novum in history. The idea that a leader's highest virtue is humility must have seemed absurd, almost self-contradictory, in the ancient world. Leaders were proud, magnificent, distinguished by their dress, appearance, and regal manner. They built temples in their own honor. They had triumphant inscriptions engraved for posterity. Their role was not to serve but to be served. Everyone else was expected to be humble, not they. Humility and majesty could not coexist.

In Judaism, this entire configuration was overturned. Leaders were to serve, not to be served. Moshe's highest accolade was to be called *eved Hashem,* God's servant. The architectural symbolism of the two great empires of the ancient world, the Mesopotamian ziggurat (Tower of Bavel) and the pyramids of Egypt, visually represented a hierarchical society, broad at the base, narrow at the top. The Jewish symbol, the candelabrum (menora), was the opposite, broad at the top, narrow at the base, as if to say that in Judaism the leader serves the people, not vice versa. Moshe's first response to God's call at the burning bush was one of humility: "Who am I… to bring the Israelites out of Egypt?" (Ex. 3:11). It was precisely this humility that qualified him to lead.

Humility is not what it is sometimes taken to be – a low estimate of oneself. True humility is mindlessness of self.

8 he is trusted in all My House: With him I speak mouth
to mouth, clearly, never in riddles. He sees the LORD's
form. Why, then, are you not afraid to speak against My
9 servant Moshe?" The LORD's anger flared against them;
10 and He departed. When the cloud withdrew from the
Tent, Miriam had been struck with an impure blight,
white as snow. Aharon turned toward Miriam and saw
11 that she was blighted. Aharon said to Moshe, "Please, my
lord, do not hold against us the sin that we have foolishly
12 committed! Let her not be like a stillborn child emerging
from its mother's womb with half its flesh eaten away!"
13 And Moshe cried out to the LORD, "Please, God, heal her
now!"

14 But the LORD said to Moshe: "If her father had spat in her MAFTIR
face, would she not be shamed for seven days? Let her be
shut out of the camp for seven days; after that, she may be
15 brought back." So Miriam was shut out of the camp for
seven days, and the people did not move on until Miriam
16 was brought back. After that, the people set out from
Ḥatzerot and encamped in the Wilderness of Paran.

The haftara for Parashat Behaalotekha is on page 1562.

Communal funds – they came to be known as *hekdesh*, the same term used in an earlier age for donations to the Temple – were put aside for the maintenance of hospices. In late medieval times the Jewish communities of Turkey, Italy, Germany, Poland, and the Netherlands supported hospitals, communal physicians, nurses, midwives, and visitation societies. The latter were by no means an afterthought. Particular concern was always taken to visit the sick, an activity invested with immense sensitivity and religious depth. The detailed guidelines in the *Shulkhan Arukh*, Rabbi Yosef Karo's authoritative code of law, give some sense of the reverence in which the command was held – for instance, "One should not visit the sick during the first three hours of the day, for every patient's illness is alleviated in the morning, and consequently he [the visitor] will not trouble himself to pray for him; and not during the last three hours of the day, for then his illness grows worse and one will give up hope of praying for him" (*Yoreh De'ah* 335). There is an understanding here that sincere prayer, like Moshe's prayer for Miriam, emerges from a deep identification with the patient's fate, despite the gulf in experience that illness creates. *Ḥesed* is the redemption of solitude, the bridge we build across the ontological abyss between I and Thou.

ח בְּכׇל־בֵּיתִי נֶאֱמָן הוּא׃ פֶּה אֶל־פֶּה אֲדַבֶּר־בּוֹ וּמַרְאֶה וְלֹא
בְחִידֹת וּתְמֻנַת יהוה יַבִּיט וּמַדּוּעַ לֹא יְרֵאתֶם לְדַבֵּר בְּעַבְדִּי
ט בְמֹשֶׁה׃ וַיִּחַר־אַף יהוה בָּם וַיֵּלַךְ׃ וְהֶעָנָן סָר מֵעַל הָאֹהֶל
וְהִנֵּה מִרְיָם מְצֹרַעַת כַּשָּׁלֶג וַיִּפֶן אַהֲרֹן אֶל־מִרְיָם וְהִנֵּה
יא מְצֹרָעַת׃ וַיֹּאמֶר אַהֲרֹן אֶל־מֹשֶׁה בִּי אֲדֹנִי אַל־נָא תָשֵׁת
יב עָלֵינוּ חַטָּאת אֲשֶׁר נוֹאַלְנוּ וַאֲשֶׁר חָטָאנוּ׃ אַל־נָא תְהִי
יג כַּמֵּת אֲשֶׁר בְּצֵאתוֹ מֵרֶחֶם אִמּוֹ וַיֵּאָכֵל חֲצִי בְשָׂרוֹ׃ וַיִּצְעַק
מֹשֶׁה אֶל־יהוה לֵאמֹר אֵל נָא רְפָא נָא לָהּ׃
יד וַיֹּאמֶר יהוה אֶל־מֹשֶׁה וְאָבִיהָ יָרֹק יָרַק בְּפָנֶיהָ הֲלֹא תִכָּלֵם מפטיר
שִׁבְעַת יָמִים תִּסָּגֵר שִׁבְעַת יָמִים מִחוּץ לַמַּחֲנֶה וְאַחַר
טו תֵּאָסֵף׃ וַתִּסָּגֵר מִרְיָם מִחוּץ לַמַּחֲנֶה שִׁבְעַת יָמִים וְהָעָם
טז לֹא נָסַע עַד הֵאָסֵף מִרְיָם׃ וְאַחַר נָסְעוּ הָעָם מֵחֲצֵרוֹת וַיַּחֲנוּ
בְּמִדְבַּר פָּארָן׃

The הפטרה *for* פרשת בהעלתך *is on page 1563.*

A sense of loneliness permeates Rabbi Soloveitchik's work, whether or not he is talking explicitly about it. His modern "halakhic man" has friends: but they are people of the mind. He "embraces the entire company of the sages of the *mesora*.... He walks alongside Rambam, listens to R. Akiva, senses the presence of Abaye and Rava." But his peers are of the past; the present offers him little. The people around him are impatient, secular. There is little in *Halakhic Man*, where there could have been so much, about the delights of intellectual companionship, *ḥevruta*. This is in strange contrast to talmudic Judaism itself, which has nothing positive to say about isolation. "There is either companionship or death" (Taanit 23a), said the Rabbis; "A sword is upon those who sit alone and study Torah" (Berakhot 63b). Nothing in the classic literature of rabbinic Judaism dwells in this land of anguish, conflict, isolation. When Rabbi Soloveitchik seeks a precedent he finds it in the Tanakh – in the prophets, or the voice of the lover in Song of Songs, or in the image of Adam and Ḥava alone in the universe.

12:13 **רְפָא נָא לָהּ** *Heal her now* – Moshe prays on Miriam's behalf one of the shortest prayers in Tanakh, a mere five words: "Please God, heal her now"– literally, "God, please, heal, please, her." God refuses to remove the punishment, but He does mitigate it, limiting the disfigurement to a week. When Miriam is ready to return to the camp, the Israelites move on.

Historically, Jews have always regarded the treatment of the sick as a fundamental priority. Doctors would treat the poor without charge.

Parashat Shelaḥ

13 1 2 Then the Lord spoke to Moshe: "Send out men to scout
the land of Canaan, which I am going to give to the
Israelites, one man from each of their ancestral tribes,

The divine hand surrounded them like a protective wall.

Canaan meant practical responsibility, the work of building up a nation. They would have to plow the land, and create and sustain an army, an economy, and a welfare system. They would have to do what every other nation does: live in the real world. What then would happen to their relationship with God? Yes, He would still be present in the rain that made crops grow, in the blessings of field and town, and in the Temple in Jerusalem that they would visit three times a year, but not intimately and miraculously, as He was in the desert. This is what the spies feared: not failure but success.

This, said the Rebbe, was a noble sin but still a sin. God wants us to live in the real world of nations, economies, and armies. God wants us, as He put it, to create "a dwelling place in the lower world." This is what Kalev saw. He knew that the Sanctuary was mere preparation and that redemption is its fulfillment: God wants us to bring the *Shekhina*, the Divine Presence, into everyday life. It is easy to find God in total seclusion and escape from responsibility. It is hard to find God in the office, in business, in farms and fields and factories and finance. But it is that challenge to which we are summoned: to create a space for God in the midst of this physical world that He created and seven times pronounced good. That is what ten of the spies failed to understand, and it was a spiritual failure that condemned an entire generation to forty years of futile wandering.

13:2 אֲנָשִׁים *Men* – Ten of these men are to come back with a negative report. The people will be demoralized, and as a result will lose their chance to enjoy their inheritance in the land promised to their ancestors. The daughters of Tzelofḥad, by contrast, love the land and do inherit it, as we will read in Parashat Pinḥas. What we love, we inherit. Comparing these two stories, Rabbi Ephrayim Luntschitz of Prague argued that God was not *commanding* Moshe to send men, but permitting him. God was saying, "From My perspective, seeing the future, it would have been better to send women, because they love and cherish the land and would never come to speak negatively about it. However, since you are convinced that these men are worthy and do indeed value the land, I give you permission to go ahead and send them" (*Keli Yakar* on Num. 13:2). Clearly, Moshe's calculation was wrong. And what we fail to love, we lose.

פרשת שלח

יג א ב וַיְדַבֵּר יְהוָה אֶל־מֹשֶׁה לֵּאמֹר: שְׁלַח־לְךָ אֲנָשִׁים וְיָתֻרוּ יב
אֶת־אֶרֶץ כְּנַעַן אֲשֶׁר־אֲנִי נֹתֵן לִבְנֵי יִשְׂרָאֵל אִישׁ אֶחָד

SHELAḤ

Parashat Shelaḥ tells the story of the spies sent by Moshe to survey the land. Ten return with an ambivalent report: the land is good but the people are giants and their cities are impregnable. Two, Yehoshua and Kalev, argue to the contrary but their confidence is ignored and the people, fearful and demoralized, say, "Let us appoint a leader and go back to Egypt" (Num. 14:4).

God is angry and threatens to destroy the people and start again with Moshe. Moshe intercedes and succeeds in averting this fate, but God insists that the people will be punished by having to spend forty years in the desert. Their children, not they, will enter the land. There then follows a series of laws about sacrifices, challah, and forgiveness for sins committed inadvertently. The legal section is interrupted by a brief section about a Sabbath desecrator. The *parasha* ends with the law about tzitzit, fringes on the corners of garments, a text recited daily as the third paragraph of the *Shema*. This constant reminder to control our responses to temptation emphasizes the difficulty of freedom – something that the desert generation will take forty years to overcome.

THE SENDING OF THE SPIES

Who sends the spies and to what end is not entirely clear. In our *parasha*, the text says that it is God who tells Moshe to do so (Num. 13:1–2). In Deuteronomy (1:22), Moshe says that it was the people who made the request. Either way, the result will be that an entire generation, demoralized by the spies' negative report, is deprived of the chance to enter the Promised Land.

In *Torah Studies*, Rabbi Menachem Mendel Schneerson offered a remarkable commentary on the episode of the spies. He raised the obvious question: The Torah emphasizes that the spies are all leaders, princes, heads of tribes. They know that God is with them, that with His help there is nothing they cannot do and that God would not promise them a land they could not conquer. Why then do they come back with a negative report?

His answer turns the conventional understanding of the spies upside down. They were, he said, not afraid of defeat. *They were afraid of victory.* What they said to the people was one thing, but what led them to say it was another thing entirely.

In the desert, they lived closely and continuously with God. He sent them manna from heaven, water from a rock, and surrounded them with clouds of glory. He guided them; His presence dwelt amongst them in the Tabernacle.

3 each a leader among them." So Moshe sent them at the
LORD's command from the Wilderness of Paran. They
4 were all leading men among the Israelites. These were
their names: from the tribe of Reuven, Shamua son of
5 6 Zakur; from the tribe of Shimon, Shafat son of Ḥori; from
7 the tribe of Yehuda, Kalev son of Yefuneh; from the tribe
8 of Yissakhar, Yigal son of Yosef; from the tribe of Efrayim,
9 Hoshea son of Nun; from the tribe of Binyamin, Palti son
10 of Rafu; from the tribe of Zevulun, Gadiel son of Sodi;
11 from the tribe of Yosef, from the tribe of Menashe, Gadi
12 son of Susi; from the tribe of Dan, Amiel son of Gemali;
13 14 from the tribe of Asher, Setur son of Mikhael; from the
15 tribe of Naftali, Naḥbi son of Vofsi; from the tribe of Gad,
16 Geuel son of Makhi. These were the names of the men
Moshe sent to scout the land. And Moshe named Hoshea
17 son of Nun Yehoshua. When Moshe sent them to scout
the land of Canaan, he told them, "Ascend there into the
18 Negev; then go up into the hill country. See what the land
is like. Are the people who live there strong or weak, few
19 or many? Is the land in which they live a good place or
bad? Are the cities in which they live open or fortified?
20 Is the soil rich or poor? Are there trees in it or not? Take

---

qualities are not predetermined; they can change and grow. People with a growth mindset do not fear failure. They relish challenges. They know that if they fail, they will try again until they succeed. I do not think it is coincidence that the two spies with a growth mindset are also the two who are unafraid of the risks and trials of conquering the land.

God does not ask us never to fail. He asks of us that we give of our best, and He forgives us when we fail. All He asks is that *we acknowledge our failures*. This gives us the courage to take risks. That is what Yehoshua and Kalev know, one through his name change, the other through the experience of his ancestor Yehuda.

Alone among the twelve spies, Yehoshua and Kalev show leadership. They tell the people that the conquest of the land is eminently achievable, not because they are all-powerful, but because God is with them. It is a paradoxical but deeply liberating truth: Fear of failure causes us to fail. It is the willingness to fail that allows us to succeed.

ג אִ֣ישׁ אֶחָ֨ד לְמַטֵּ֤ה אֲבֹתָיו֙ תִּשְׁלָ֔חוּ כֹּ֖ל נָשִׂ֥יא בָהֶֽם׃ וַיִּשְׁלַ֨ח
אֹתָ֥ם מֹשֶׁ֛ה מִמִּדְבַּ֥ר פָּארָ֖ן עַל־פִּ֣י יְהוָ֑ה כֻּלָּ֣ם אֲנָשִׁ֔ים רָאשֵׁ֥י
ד בְנֵֽי־יִשְׂרָאֵ֖ל הֵֽמָּה׃ וְאֵ֖לֶּה שְׁמוֹתָ֑ם לְמַטֵּ֣ה רְאוּבֵ֔ן שַׁמּ֖וּעַ
ה ו בֶּן־זַכּֽוּר׃ לְמַטֵּ֣ה שִׁמְע֔וֹן שָׁפָ֖ט בֶּן־חוֹרִֽי׃ לְמַטֵּ֣ה יְהוּדָ֔ה כָּלֵ֖ב
ז ח בֶּן־יְפֻנֶּֽה׃ לְמַטֵּ֣ה יִשָּׂשכָ֔ר יִגְאָ֖ל בֶּן־יוֹסֵֽף׃ לְמַטֵּ֥ה אֶפְרָ֖יִם
ט י הוֹשֵׁ֥עַ בִּן־נֽוּן׃ לְמַטֵּ֥ה בִנְיָמִ֖ן פַּלְטִ֥י בֶּן־רָפֽוּא׃ לְמַטֵּ֣ה
יא זְבוּלֻ֔ן גַּדִּיאֵ֖ל בֶּן־סוֹדִֽי׃ לְמַטֵּ֥ה יוֹסֵ֖ף לְמַטֵּ֣ה מְנַשֶּׁ֑ה גַּדִּ֖י בֶּן־
יב יג סוּסִֽי׃ לְמַטֵּ֣ה דָ֔ן עַמִּיאֵ֖ל בֶּן־גְּמַלִּֽי׃ לְמַטֵּ֣ה אָשֵׁ֔ר סְת֖וּר בֶּן־
יד טו מִיכָאֵֽל׃ לְמַטֵּ֣ה נַפְתָּלִ֔י נַחְבִּ֖י בֶּן־וָפְסִֽי׃ לְמַטֵּ֣ה גָ֔ד גְּאוּאֵ֖ל
טז בֶּן־מָכִֽי׃ אֵ֚לֶּה שְׁמ֣וֹת הָֽאֲנָשִׁ֔ים אֲשֶׁר־שָׁלַ֥ח מֹשֶׁ֖ה לָת֣וּר
יז אֶת־הָאָ֑רֶץ וַיִּקְרָ֥א מֹשֶׁ֛ה לְהוֹשֵׁ֥עַ בִּן־נ֖וּן יְהוֹשֻֽׁעַ׃ וַיִּשְׁלַ֤ח
אֹתָם֙ מֹשֶׁ֔ה לָת֖וּר אֶת־אֶ֣רֶץ כְּנָ֑עַן וַיֹּ֣אמֶר אֲלֵהֶ֗ם עֲל֥וּ זֶה֙
יח בַּנֶּ֔גֶב וַעֲלִיתֶ֖ם אֶת־הָהָֽר׃ וּרְאִיתֶ֥ם אֶת־הָאָ֖רֶץ מַה־הִ֑וא
וְאֶת־הָעָם֙ הַיֹּשֵׁ֣ב עָלֶ֔יהָ הֶחָזָ֥ק הוּא֙ הֲרָפֶ֔ה הַמְעַ֥ט ה֖וּא
יט אִם־רָֽב׃ וּמָ֣ה הָאָ֗רֶץ אֲשֶׁר־הוּא֙ יֹשֵׁ֣ב בָּ֔הּ הֲטוֹבָ֥ה הִ֖וא אִם־
רָעָ֑ה וּמָ֣ה הֶֽעָרִ֗ים אֲשֶׁר־הוּא֙ יוֹשֵׁ֣ב בָּהֵ֔נָּה הַבְּמַחֲנִ֖ים אִ֥ם
כ בְּמִבְצָרִֽים׃ וּמָ֣ה הָ֠אָרֶץ הַשְּׁמֵנָ֨ה הִ֜וא אִם־רָזָ֗ה הֲיֵֽשׁ־בָּ֥הּ

13:16 וַיִּקְרָא מֹשֶׁה לְהוֹשֵׁעַ... יְהוֹשֻׁעַ *And Moshe named Hoshea... Yehoshua* – A change of name in the Torah always implies a change of character or calling. Avram became Avraham. Yaakov became Yisrael. When our name changes, says Rambam in his discussion of repentance (*Hilkhot Teshuva* 2:4), it is as if we or someone else were saying, "You are not the same person as you were before."

Could this hint at what gift, what strength of character, Yehoshua and Kalev possess that the other ten spies do not? Kalev comes from the tribe of Yehuda, and Yehuda, we learn in the book of Genesis, was the first *baal teshuva*, the first penitent (see Gen. 38:26 and the note there, and Gen. 34, "Yehuda's Test"). He matured. He was taught a lesson by his daughter-in-law, Tamar. Yehuda is the clearest example in Genesis of someone who takes adversity as a learning experience rather than as failure.

Anyone who, like Yehoshua, has experienced a name change has likewise been inducted into what Carol Dweck calls a growth mindset. They know their

courage and bring back some of the fruit of the land" – it
21 was the season of the first ripe grapes. So they went up and SHENI
scouted the land from the Wilderness of Tzin to Reḥov,
22 near Levo Ḥamat. They went up through the Negev and
came to Ḥevron, where Aḥiman, Sheshai, and Talmai,
descendants of Anak, were dwelling. Ḥevron had been
23 built seven years before the Egyptian city of Tzoan. Then
they came to the Eshkol Ravine and there they cut down
a vine branch, and on it one cluster of grapes, which they
carried on a pole between two men. They also took some
24 pomegranates and figs. That place was named the Eshkol
Ravine, because of the cluster that the Israelites cut there.
25 They returned from scouting the land when forty days
26 had passed. As soon as they arrived they came to Moshe
and Aharon and to all the community of Israel at Kadesh
in the Wilderness of Paran, and brought their report to
them and to all the community, and showed them the
27 fruit of the land. They told Moshe, "We came to the land
you sent us to, and it is indeed flowing with milk and with
28 honey, and this is its fruit. But the people who live in the
land are fierce, and the cities are fortified and very large
29 indeed. We even saw the descendants of Anak there. In
the Negev region, Amalek lives; the Hittites, Jebusites,

There is a commentary here on the experience of Jews in the modern age. Two centuries ago, Jews in Europe were not ready for the challenge of an integrated society and some chose instead segregation and the voluntary ghetto. Ours, by contrast, is not the age of the spies but of their descendants, born in freedom. We have had time enough to realize that we can be at home in Western culture without it calling into question Jewish faith or Jewish life. Those who are strong do not need to live behind defensive walls. The model is Rambam. He showed that one could be a supreme exponent of Jewish law while at the same time contributing to philosophy, medicine, and many other disciplines of his time. Of course, there was only one Rambam, and not everyone has the strength to live in a world without walls. But the story of the spies tells us that our fears are sometimes exaggerated. Judaism is strong enough to withstand any challenge if we have the confidence of our faith. People who are strong do not have to live behind defensive walls.

עֵץ אִם־אַיִן וְהִתְחַזַּקְתֶּם וּלְקַחְתֶּם מִפְּרִי הָאָרֶץ וְהַיָּמִים
כא יְמֵי בִּכּוּרֵי עֲנָבִים: וַיַּעֲלוּ וַיָּתֻרוּ אֶת־הָאָרֶץ מִמִּדְבַּר־צִן עַד־ שני
כב רְחֹב לְבֹא חֲמָת: וַיַּעֲלוּ בַנֶּגֶב וַיָּבֹא עַד־חֶבְרוֹן וְשָׁם אֲחִימַן
שֵׁשַׁי וְתַלְמַי יְלִידֵי הָעֲנָק וְחֶבְרוֹן שֶׁבַע שָׁנִים נִבְנְתָה לִפְנֵי
כג צֹעַן מִצְרָיִם: וַיָּבֹאוּ עַד־נַחַל אֶשְׁכֹּל וַיִּכְרְתוּ מִשָּׁם זְמוֹרָה
וְאֶשְׁכּוֹל עֲנָבִים אֶחָד וַיִּשָּׂאֻהוּ בַמּוֹט בִּשְׁנָיִם וּמִן־הָרִמֹּנִים
כד וּמִן־הַתְּאֵנִים: לַמָּקוֹם הַהוּא קָרָא נַחַל אֶשְׁכּוֹל עַל אֹדוֹת
כה הָאֶשְׁכּוֹל אֲשֶׁר־כָּרְתוּ מִשָּׁם בְּנֵי יִשְׂרָאֵל: וַיָּשֻׁבוּ מִתּוּר
כו הָאָרֶץ מִקֵּץ אַרְבָּעִים יוֹם: וַיֵּלְכוּ וַיָּבֹאוּ אֶל־מֹשֶׁה וְאֶל־
אַהֲרֹן וְאֶל־כָּל־עֲדַת בְּנֵי־יִשְׂרָאֵל אֶל־מִדְבַּר פָּארָן קָדֵשָׁה
וַיָּשִׁיבוּ אֹתָם דָּבָר וְאֶת־כָּל־הָעֵדָה וַיַּרְאוּם אֶת־פְּרִי הָאָרֶץ:
כז וַיְסַפְּרוּ־לוֹ וַיֹּאמְרוּ בָּאנוּ אֶל־הָאָרֶץ אֲשֶׁר שְׁלַחְתָּנוּ וְגַם זָבַת
כח חָלָב וּדְבַשׁ הִוא וְזֶה־פִּרְיָהּ: אֶפֶס כִּי־עַז הָעָם הַיֹּשֵׁב בָּאָרֶץ
וְהֶעָרִים בְּצֻרוֹת גְּדֹלֹת מְאֹד וְגַם־יְלִדֵי הָעֲנָק רָאִינוּ שָׁם:
כט עֲמָלֵק יוֹשֵׁב בְּאֶרֶץ הַנֶּגֶב וְהַחִתִּי וְהַיְבוּסִי וְהָאֱמֹרִי יוֹשֵׁב

13:28 וְהֶעָרִים בְּצֻרוֹת *The cities are fortified* – There is a fascinating passage from *Midrash Tanḥuma* – cited by Rashi in his commentary – with far-reaching implications.

> How were they [the spies] to know [the people's] strength? [By looking at their cities:] Are they unwalled or fortified? If they live in unwalled cities, they are strong and trust in their own strength. If, however, they live in fortified cities, they are weak and insecure.

The spies report back, "But the people who live in the land are fierce, and the cities are fortified and very large indeed" (Num. 13:28). They said: the people are strong and so are the cities. Hence their conclusion: We cannot win. We should not even try.

Clearly, the sight of the cities made a deep impression on the spies. This makes psychological sense, and it accords with historical fact. The cities in ancient Canaan were indeed surrounded by high, thick walls, which made them seem impregnable. However, according to the Midrash, the spies drew precisely the wrong conclusion: the cities are strong; therefore the people are strong. In fact the opposite was the case: the cities are strong; therefore the people are weak.

and Amorites live in the hill country, and the Canaanites
30 live by the sea and by the Jordan." But Kalev silenced the
people around Moshe and said, "Let us go up at once and
31 take possession of it, for certainly we are able." The men
who had gone up with him said, "We cannot go up against
32 those people, for they are stronger than us." So they gave
the Israelites an adverse report of the land that they had
scouted: "The land which we have journeyed through
and scouted is a land that consumes its inhabitants; the
33 people we saw in it were tall and broad to a man. There we
saw the Nefilim – the descendants of Anak are from the
Nefilim. We looked to our own eyes like grasshoppers,
14 1 and so we were in theirs." All the community lifted their
2 heads and cried out – that night the people wept. And
all the Israelites railed against Moshe and Aharon; all the

---

get the word *meraglim*, "spies"). Neither of these words appear in our *parasha*. Instead, no less than twelve times, we encounter the rare verb *latur*. This word was revived in Modern Hebrew, where it means (and sounds like) "to tour." *Tayar* is a tourist. There is all the difference between a tourist and a spy.

Malbim (1809–79) explains the difference simply. *Latur* means to seek out the good. That is what tourists do. They go to the beautiful, the majestic, the inspiring (compare, for instance, Eccl. 1:13). They don't spend their time trying to find out what is bad. *Laḥpor* and *leragel* are the opposite. They are about searching out a place's weaknesses and vulnerabilities. That is spying. In Genesis 42, when the brothers come before Yosef in Egypt to buy food, he accuses them of being *meraglim*, "spies," a word that appears seven times in that one chapter. He also defines what it is to be a spy: "You have come to see where our land is exposed" (i.e., where it is undefended). The exclusive use of the verb *latur* in our *parasha* – repeated twelve times – is there to tell us that the twelve men are not being sent to spy. But only two of them understand this.

The reason ten of the twelve men come back with a negative report, then, is because they have misunderstood their mission. They believe it is their role to find out where the "land is exposed," where it is vulnerable, where its defenses could be overcome. They look and cannot find. The people are strong, and the cities impregnable.

In fact, they are meant to see what is good about the land, not what is bad. So, if they are not meant to be spies, what is the purpose of this mission? I suggest that the answer is to be found in a

ל בָּהָר וְהַכְּנַעֲנִי יֹשֵׁב עַל־הַיָּם וְעַל יַד הַיַּרְדֵּן׃ וַיַּהַס כָּלֵב אֶת־
הָעָם אֶל־מֹשֶׁה וַיֹּאמֶר עָלֹה נַעֲלֶה וְיָרַשְׁנוּ אֹתָהּ כִּי־יָכוֹל
לא נוּכַל לָהּ׃ וְהָאֲנָשִׁים אֲשֶׁר עָלוּ עִמּוֹ אָמְרוּ לֹא נוּכַל לַעֲלוֹת
לב אֶל־הָעָם כִּי־חָזָק הוּא מִמֶּנּוּ׃ וַיֹּצִיאוּ דִּבַּת הָאָרֶץ אֲשֶׁר
תָּרוּ אֹתָהּ אֶל־בְּנֵי יִשְׂרָאֵל לֵאמֹר הָאָרֶץ אֲשֶׁר עָבַרְנוּ בָהּ
לָתוּר אֹתָהּ אֶרֶץ אֹכֶלֶת יוֹשְׁבֶיהָ הִוא וְכָל־הָעָם אֲשֶׁר־רָאִינוּ
לג בְתוֹכָהּ אַנְשֵׁי מִדּוֹת׃ וְשָׁם רָאִינוּ אֶת־הַנְּפִילִים בְּנֵי עֲנָק מִן־
יד א הַנְּפִלִים וַנְּהִי בְעֵינֵינוּ כַּחֲגָבִים וְכֵן הָיִינוּ בְּעֵינֵיהֶם׃ וַתִּשָּׂא
כָּל־הָעֵדָה וַיִּתְּנוּ אֶת־קוֹלָם וַיִּבְכּוּ הָעָם בַּלַּיְלָה הַהוּא׃
ב וַיִּלֹּנוּ עַל־מֹשֶׁה וְעַל־אַהֲרֹן כֹּל בְּנֵי יִשְׂרָאֵל וַיֹּאמְרוּ אֲלֵהֶם

13:33 וְכֵן הָיִינוּ בְּעֵינֵיהֶם *And so we were in theirs* – Rabbi Menachem Mendel of Kotzk pointed out that the spies make one statement that is completely unwarranted. They are entitled to say, "We looked to our own eyes like grasshoppers." It accurately describes how they felt. But they are not entitled to say the second half of the sentence. They have no idea how they appeared in the eyes of the inhabitants of the land; they merely inferred it and were wrong.

They should have known this. They had even sung, along their fellow Israelites, a song at the sea that contained the words "Nations heard and they trembled.... the people of Canaan melted away" (Ex. 15:14–15). They should have known that the people of the land were afraid of them. And so it was, as Raḥav is to tell the spies sent by Yehoshua forty years later: "I know that the Lord has given you the land, and that dread of you has fallen upon us, for all the inhabitants of the land quake before you. For we have heard that the Lord dried up the waters of the Sea of Reeds before you" (Josh. 2:9–11).

Yet they assumed that others saw them as they saw themselves, projecting their sense of inadequacy onto the external world, with the result that they misinterpreted what they saw. Instead of ordinary people, they saw giants. Instead of towns, they saw impregnable fortresses, and they were afraid. The spies' confirmation bias meant that they paid selective attention to phenomena that gave them reasons to be afraid. Their perception was not in the world but in the mind.

THE SPIES' REPORT

The disastrous outcome of the twelve men's report invites us to re-examine the purpose of their mission. Biblical Hebrew has two verbs that mean "to spy": *laḥpor* and *leragel* (from which we

community said to them, "If only we had died in Egypt,
3 if only we had died in this wilderness! Why is the LORD
bringing us as far as this land only to fall by the sword?
Our wives and children will be made plunder. Would it
4 not be better for us to go back to Egypt?" So they said
to one another, "Let us appoint a leader and go back to
5 Egypt." Moshe and Aharon fell facedown before all the
6 assembled community of Israel. Yehoshua son of Nun
and Kalev son of Yefuneh, who were among those who
7 scouted the land, tore their clothes and said before the
entire community of Israel: "The land we journeyed
8 through and scouted is a very, very good land. If the SHELISHI
LORD favors us, He will bring us into this land, a land
flowing with milk and with honey, and He will give it to
9 us. Do not rebel against the LORD, and do not be afraid
of the people of the land, for they are no more than bread
for us. They have been stripped of their protection and
10 the LORD is with us. Do not be afraid of them!" The
community, all, threatened to stone them to death – but
then the LORD's glory was revealed to all the Israelites at
the Tent of Meeting.
11 The LORD said to Moshe, "How long will these people
provoke Me? How long will they fail to have faith in Me in
12 spite of all the signs I have performed among them? I will
strike them with a plague now and disinherit them, and
make you into a nation greater and mightier than they."
13 But Moshe said to the LORD, "The Egyptians will hear
about it, for by Your power You brought this people up
14 from among them, and they will tell the inhabitants of this

But Moshe has never seen the land. They need the independent testimony of eyewitnesses. And in fact, all twelve fulfill that mission. When they return, the first thing they say is: "We came to the land you sent us to, and it is indeed flowing with milk and with honey, and this is its fruit" (Num. 13:27). But because ten of them think their task is to be spies, they go on to say that the conquest is impossible – and disaster ensues. Only Yehoshua and Kalev have in fact understood the mission.

כָּל־הָעֵדָה לוּ־מַתְנוּ בְּאֶרֶץ מִצְרַיִם אוֹ בַּמִּדְבָּר הַזֶּה לוּ־
ג מָתְנוּ: וְלָמָה יְהוָה מֵבִיא אֹתָנוּ אֶל־הָאָרֶץ הַזֹּאת לִנְפֹּל
בַּחֶרֶב נָשֵׁינוּ וְטַפֵּנוּ יִהְיוּ לָבַז הֲלוֹא טוֹב לָנוּ שׁוּב מִצְרָיְמָה:
ד ה וַיֹּאמְרוּ אִישׁ אֶל־אָחִיו נִתְּנָה רֹאשׁ וְנָשׁוּבָה מִצְרָיְמָה: וַיִּפֹּל
מֹשֶׁה וְאַהֲרֹן עַל־פְּנֵיהֶם לִפְנֵי כָּל־קְהַל עֲדַת בְּנֵי יִשְׂרָאֵל:
ו וִיהוֹשֻׁעַ בִּן־נוּן וְכָלֵב בֶּן־יְפֻנֶּה מִן־הַתָּרִים אֶת־הָאָרֶץ קָרְעוּ
ז בִּגְדֵיהֶם: וַיֹּאמְרוּ אֶל־כָּל־עֲדַת בְּנֵי־יִשְׂרָאֵל לֵאמֹר הָאָרֶץ
ח אֲשֶׁר עָבַרְנוּ בָהּ לָתוּר אֹתָהּ טוֹבָה הָאָרֶץ מְאֹד מְאֹד: אִם־ שלישי
חָפֵץ בָּנוּ יְהוָה וְהֵבִיא אֹתָנוּ אֶל־הָאָרֶץ הַזֹּאת וּנְתָנָהּ לָנוּ
ט אֶרֶץ אֲשֶׁר־הִוא זָבַת חָלָב וּדְבָשׁ: אַךְ בַּיהוָה אַל־תִּמְרֹדוּ
וְאַתֶּם אַל־תִּירְאוּ אֶת־עַם הָאָרֶץ כִּי לַחְמֵנוּ הֵם סָר צִלָּם
י מֵעֲלֵיהֶם וַיהוָה אִתָּנוּ אַל־תִּירָאֻם: וַיֹּאמְרוּ כָּל־הָעֵדָה
לִרְגּוֹם אֹתָם בָּאֲבָנִים וּכְבוֹד יְהוָה נִרְאָה בְּאֹהֶל מוֹעֵד
אֶל־כָּל־בְּנֵי יִשְׂרָאֵל:

יא וַיֹּאמֶר יְהוָה אֶל־מֹשֶׁה עַד־אָנָה יְנַאֲצֻנִי הָעָם הַזֶּה וְעַד־ יג
אָנָה לֹא־יַאֲמִינוּ בִי בְּכֹל הָאֹתוֹת אֲשֶׁר עָשִׂיתִי בְּקִרְבּוֹ:
יב אַכֶּנּוּ בַדֶּבֶר וְאוֹרִשֶׁנּוּ וְאֶעֱשֶׂה אֹתְךָ לְגוֹי־גָּדוֹל וְעָצוּם מִמֶּנּוּ:
יג וַיֹּאמֶר מֹשֶׁה אֶל־יְהוָה וְשָׁמְעוּ מִצְרַיִם כִּי־הֶעֱלִיתָ בְכֹחֲךָ
יד אֶת־הָעָם הַזֶּה מִקִּרְבּוֹ: וְאָמְרוּ אֶל־יוֹשֵׁב הָאָרֶץ הַזֹּאת

passage in the Talmud (Kiddushin 41a) that states that it is forbidden for a man to marry a woman without seeing her first. The reason? Were he to marry without having seen her first, he might, when he does see her, find he is not attracted to her. Tensions will inevitably arise. Hence the idea: first see, then love.

The same applies to a marriage between a people and its land. The Israelites are traveling to the country promised to their ancestors. But none of them have ever seen it. How then can they be expected to muster the energies necessary to fight the coming battles? They are about to marry a land they have not seen.

The twelve are sent *latur*: their mission is to be the eyes of the congregation, letting them know the beauty and goodness of what lies ahead, the land that has been their destiny since the days of their ancestor Avraham.

Moshe has told them that the land is good. It is "flowing with milk and honey."

land. They have heard that You, LORD, are among these
people, that You, LORD, are seen face-to-face, that Your
cloud stands over them, that You go before them in a pillar
15 of cloud by day and in a pillar of fire by night. If You kill
this people like a single man, the nations that have heard
16 of Your fame will say, 'It was because the LORD was unable
to bring this people into the land He swore to them; that
17 is why He slaughtered them in the wilderness.' So now, let
my LORD's power be great, as You declared when You said:
18 'The LORD is slow to anger and abounding in kindness,
forgiving sin and rebellion, though He does not acquit
the guilty, but holds the descendants to account for the
sins of the fathers; children and grandchildren to the third
19 and fourth generation.' Please – pardon the sin of this
people in Your great kindness, as You have forgiven this
20 people from the time of Egypt until now." And the LORD
21 said, "I have forgiven them at your word. Yet as surely as I
22 live and as the LORD's glory fills the whole earth, none of
those who have seen My glory and the signs I performed
in Egypt and in the wilderness, and have tested Me these
23 ten times and not obeyed Me, shall see the land I swore to
their fathers. None of those who have provoked Me will
24 see it. But My servant Kalev, because he was filled with a
different spirit and has followed Me wholeheartedly – him
I will bring into the land he came to, and his descendants
25 will inherit it. The Amalekites and Canaanites are living in
the valleys; so turn tomorrow and head for the wilderness
by way of the Sea of Reeds."

---

done evil and rebelled, straying from Your commandments and Your laws" (Dan. 9:4–5). Others were said by Ezra (Ezra 9:10–11:15) and Neḥemya (Neh. 1:6–7). All three of these were composed in the aftermath of the Babylonian exile and the later return of Jews to a devastated land of Israel, and they represent the authentic Jewish response to calamity: "When sufferings come, search your deeds and return in repentance" (Berakhot 5a). All renewal, whether in the life of an individual or a nation, begins with spiritual and moral renewal, and this in turn begins with *seliḥa*, the act of saying sorry to God. These, and in particular the Thirteen Attributes, became the model for the *Seliḥot* we say today.

שָׁמְעוּ כִּי־אַתָּה יהוה בְּקֶרֶב הָעָם הַזֶּה אֲשֶׁר־עַיִן בְּעַיִן
נִרְאָה ׀ אַתָּה יהוה וַעֲנָנְךָ עֹמֵד עֲלֵהֶם וּבְעַמֻּד עָנָן אַתָּה
טו הֹלֵךְ לִפְנֵיהֶם יוֹמָם וּבְעַמּוּד אֵשׁ לָיְלָה: וְהֵמַתָּה אֶת־הָעָם
הַזֶּה כְּאִישׁ אֶחָד וְאָמְרוּ הַגּוֹיִם אֲשֶׁר־שָׁמְעוּ אֶת־שִׁמְעֲךָ
טז לֵאמֹר: מִבִּלְתִּי יְכֹלֶת יהוה לְהָבִיא אֶת־הָעָם הַזֶּה אֶל־
יז הָאָרֶץ אֲשֶׁר־נִשְׁבַּע לָהֶם וַיִּשְׁחָטֵם בַּמִּדְבָּר: וְעַתָּה יִגְדַּל־נָא
יח כֹּחַ אֲדֹנָי כַּאֲשֶׁר דִּבַּרְתָּ לֵאמֹר: יהוה אֶרֶךְ אַפַּיִם וְרַב־חֶסֶד
נֹשֵׂא עָוֺן וָפָשַׁע וְנַקֵּה לֹא יְנַקֶּה פֹּקֵד עֲוֺן אָבוֹת עַל־בָּנִים עַל־
יט שִׁלֵּשִׁים וְעַל־רִבֵּעִים: סְלַח־נָא לַעֲוֺן הָעָם הַזֶּה כְּגֹדֶל חַסְדֶּךָ
כ וְכַאֲשֶׁר נָשָׂאתָה לָעָם הַזֶּה מִמִּצְרַיִם וְעַד־הֵנָּה: וַיֹּאמֶר יהוה
כא סָלַחְתִּי כִּדְבָרֶךָ: וְאוּלָם חַי־אָנִי וְיִמָּלֵא כְבוֹד־יהוה אֶת־
כב כָּל־הָאָרֶץ: כִּי כָל־הָאֲנָשִׁים הָרֹאִים אֶת־כְּבֹדִי וְאֶת־אֹתֹתַי
אֲשֶׁר־עָשִׂיתִי בְמִצְרַיִם וּבַמִּדְבָּר וַיְנַסּוּ אֹתִי זֶה עֶשֶׂר פְּעָמִים
כג וְלֹא שָׁמְעוּ בְּקוֹלִי: אִם־יִרְאוּ אֶת־הָאָרֶץ אֲשֶׁר נִשְׁבַּעְתִּי
כד לַאֲבֹתָם וְכָל־מְנַאֲצַי לֹא יִרְאוּהָ: וְעַבְדִּי כָלֵב עֵקֶב הָיְתָה
רוּחַ אַחֶרֶת עִמּוֹ וַיְמַלֵּא אַחֲרָי וַהֲבִיאֹתִיו אֶל־הָאָרֶץ אֲשֶׁר־
כה בָּא שָׁמָּה וְזַרְעוֹ יוֹרִשֶׁנָּה: וְהָעֲמָלֵקִי וְהַכְּנַעֲנִי יוֹשֵׁב בָּעֵמֶק
מָחָר פְּנוּ וּסְעוּ לָכֶם הַמִּדְבָּר דֶּרֶךְ יַם־סוּף:

14:18 אֶרֶךְ אַפַּיִם *The Lord is slow to anger* – In this verse, Moshe is paraphrasing back to God the words (known as the Thirteen Attributes of Mercy) that God said to him on Mount Sinai (see Ex. 34:5–7 and the notes there). From this the Rabbis inferred:

> This teaches us that God, as it were, robed Himself as if He were a leader of prayer, and said to Moshe: "Whenever Israel sins, let them perform this rite before Me and I shall forgive them."… R. Yehuda said: There is a covenant that the Thirteen Attributes do not return unanswered. (Rosh HaShana 17b)

In Exodus, God taught Moshe how to pray.

We have records of a number of penitential pleas long before Jewish prayer was formalized. One, moving and eloquent, was said by Daniel in exile: "O Lord, the great and awesome God, who keeps the covenant and the love with those who love Him and keep His commandments: we have sinned, offended,

26 27 Then the LORD spoke to Moshe and Aharon: "How long REVI'I
shall this wicked community keep railing against Me? I
have heard the Israelites' complaints with which they rail
28 against Me. Tell them: 'As surely as I live,' says the LORD,
29 'I will do to you the very thing I heard you say. In this
wilderness your corpses will fall, all of your number, all
those listed in the census, from twenty years old and
30 upward: all those who have railed against Me. None of
you will enter the land that I promised to settle you in,
except for Kalev son of Yefuneh and Yehoshua son of
31 Nun. I will bring in your children, whom you said would
be taken captive, and they will know the land you rejected.
32 But as for you, your corpses will fall in this wilderness.
33 Your children will shepherd in the wilderness for forty
years, suffering for your faithlessness until the last of your
34 corpses lies here in the wilderness. For the number of
the days in which you scouted the land, forty days, you
shall bear your sins – for every day a year: forty years.
35 You will know what it is to oppose Me. I, the LORD, have
spoken.' This will I do to this entire wicked community
that has gathered together against Me. In this wilderness
36 they shall come to their end, and there they shall die." So
the men Moshe sent to scout the land, and who came
back and caused all the community to rail against him
37 by giving an adverse report of the land – those men who
gave the adverse report of the land died by a plague before

precipitating factor, not the underlying cause. Nor is the divine verdict, that the people are condemned to spend forty years in the wilderness, a punishment as such. It is a consequence of human nature. People long deprived of their freedom grow used to their chains.

It takes more than a few days or weeks to turn a population of slaves into a nation capable of handling the responsibilities of freedom. In the case of the Israelites it needs a generation born in liberty, hardened by the experience of the desert, untrammeled by habits of servitude. *Liberty is the work of more than one generation.* The forty years of wandering in the wilderness prefigure a much larger, longer journey that will eventuate in a society that sanctifies human life as the gift of God and the human person as the image of God.

כו כז וַיְדַבֵּר יהוה אֶל־מֹשֶׁה וְאֶל־אַהֲרֹן לֵאמֹר: עַד־מָתַי לָעֵדָה רביעי
הָרָעָה הַזֹּאת אֲשֶׁר הֵמָּה מַלִּינִים עָלָי אֶת־תְּלֻנּוֹת בְּנֵי
כח יִשְׂרָאֵל אֲשֶׁר הֵמָּה מַלִּינִים עָלַי שָׁמָעְתִּי: אֱמֹר אֲלֵהֶם חַי־אָנִי
נְאֻם־יהוה אִם־לֹא כַּאֲשֶׁר דִּבַּרְתֶּם בְּאָזְנָי כֵּן אֶעֱשֶׂה לָכֶם:
כט בַּמִּדְבָּר הַזֶּה יִפְּלוּ פִגְרֵיכֶם וְכָל־פְּקֻדֵיכֶם לְכָל־מִסְפַּרְכֶם
ל מִבֶּן עֶשְׂרִים שָׁנָה וָמָעְלָה אֲשֶׁר הֲלִינֹתֶם עָלָי: אִם־אַתֶּם
תָּבֹאוּ אֶל־הָאָרֶץ אֲשֶׁר נָשָׂאתִי אֶת־יָדִי לְשַׁכֵּן אֶתְכֶם בָּהּ
לא כִּי אִם־כָּלֵב בֶּן־יְפֻנֶּה וִיהוֹשֻׁעַ בִּן־נוּן: וְטַפְּכֶם אֲשֶׁר אֲמַרְתֶּם
לָבַז יִהְיֶה וְהֵבֵיאתִי אֹתָם וְיָדְעוּ אֶת־הָאָרֶץ אֲשֶׁר מְאַסְתֶּם
לב לג בָּהּ: וּפִגְרֵיכֶם אַתֶּם יִפְּלוּ בַּמִּדְבָּר הַזֶּה: וּבְנֵיכֶם יִהְיוּ רֹעִים
בַּמִּדְבָּר אַרְבָּעִים שָׁנָה וְנָשְׂאוּ אֶת־זְנוּתֵיכֶם עַד־תֹּם פִּגְרֵיכֶם
לד בַּמִּדְבָּר: בְּמִסְפַּר הַיָּמִים אֲשֶׁר־תַּרְתֶּם אֶת־הָאָרֶץ אַרְבָּעִים
יוֹם יוֹם לַשָּׁנָה יוֹם לַשָּׁנָה תִּשְׂאוּ אֶת־עֲוֺנֹתֵיכֶם אַרְבָּעִים
לה שָׁנָה וִידַעְתֶּם אֶת־תְּנוּאָתִי: אֲנִי יהוה דִּבַּרְתִּי אִם־לֹא ׀ זֹאת
אֶעֱשֶׂה לְכָל־הָעֵדָה הָרָעָה הַזֹּאת הַנּוֹעָדִים עָלָי בַּמִּדְבָּר
לו הַזֶּה יִתַּמּוּ וְשָׁם יָמֻתוּ: וְהָאֲנָשִׁים אֲשֶׁר־שָׁלַח מֹשֶׁה לָתוּר
אֶת־הָאָרֶץ וַיָּשֻׁבוּ וילונו עָלָיו אֶת־כָּל־הָעֵדָה לְהוֹצִיא וַיַּלִּינוּ
לז דִבָּה עַל־הָאָרֶץ: וַיָּמֻתוּ הָאֲנָשִׁים מוֹצִאֵי דִבַּת־הָאָרֶץ רָעָה

14:35 בַּמִּדְבָּר הַזֶּה יִתַּמּוּ *In this wilderness they shall come to their end* – We have already seen (Ex. 13, "The Journey Begins") that for Rambam the entry into the land was delayed for a generation so that it could be undertaken by those who had been born in the desert, since "it is a well-known fact that traveling in the wilderness deprived of bodily enjoyments like bathing produces courage, while the opposite produces faintheartedness. Besides, another generation arose during the wanderings that had not been accustomed to degradation and slavery" (*Guide for the Perplexed* III.32).

This is an unusual position, because *Rambam does not mention the spies at all.* It was, he implies, a given of the state of the people at the time and of the constraints of human nature. People cannot change overnight. It takes time to move from slavery to the responsibilities of freedom. It can take an entire generation, sometimes longer still. This is a radical suggestion because it implies that the negative report of the spies is only the

38 the LORD. And only Yehoshua son of Nun and Kalev son
of Yefuneh remained alive of all those men who went to
39 scout the land. When Moshe reported these words to
all the Israelites, the people were overcome with grief.
40 They rose early the next morning and climbed up to the
heights of the hill country, saying, "We are ready to go
up to the place that the LORD spoke of; we were wrong."
41 But Moshe said, "Why are you transgressing the LORD's
42 command? It will not work. Do not go up; the LORD is
not with you. Do not be struck down by your enemies.
43 Ahead of you are the Amalekites and Canaanites, and
you will fall by the sword. Because you have turned away
from following the LORD, the LORD will not be with you."
44 Defiantly, they went up to the heights of the hill country.
Neither the Ark of the LORD's Covenant nor Moshe left
45 the camp. And the Amalekites and Canaanites who lived
in that hill country came down, and fought them, and
crushed them, all the way to Ḥorma.
15 1 2 The LORD spoke to Moshe: "Speak to the Israelites. Say:
When you come to the land that I am giving you to live

That is the lesson of the spies. Despite the divine anger, the people are not condemned to permanent exile. But they have to face the fact that their children will achieve what they themselves are not ready for.

People still forget this. Wars have been undertaken, at least in part, in the name of democracy and freedom. Yet that is the work not of a war, but of education, society-building, and the slow acceptance of responsibility. It takes generations. Sometimes it never happens at all. The people – like the Israelites immediately after the spies' report – lose heart and want to go back to the predictable past ("Let us appoint a leader and go back to Egypt" – Num. 14:4), not the unseen, hazardous, demanding future. That is why, historically, there have been more tyrannies than democracies.

The politics of liberty demands patience. It needs years of struggle without giving up hope. The late Emmanuel Levinas spoke about "difficult freedom" – and freedom always is difficult. The story of the spies tells us that the generation who left Egypt was not yet ready for it. That is their tragedy.

But their children will be. That is their consolation.

לח בַּמַּגֵּפָה לִפְנֵי יְהוָה: וִיהוֹשֻׁעַ בִּן־נוּן וְכָלֵב בֶּן־יְפֻנֶּה חָיוּ מִן־
לט הָאֲנָשִׁים הָהֵם הַהֹלְכִים לָתוּר אֶת־הָאָרֶץ: וַיְדַבֵּר מֹשֶׁה
אֶת־הַדְּבָרִים הָאֵלֶּה אֶל־כָּל־בְּנֵי יִשְׂרָאֵל וַיִּתְאַבְּלוּ הָעָם
מ מְאֹד: וַיַּשְׁכִּמוּ בַבֹּקֶר וַיַּעֲלוּ אֶל־רֹאשׁ־הָהָר לֵאמֹר הִנֶּנּוּ
מא וְעָלִינוּ אֶל־הַמָּקוֹם אֲשֶׁר־אָמַר יְהוָה כִּי חָטָאנוּ: וַיֹּאמֶר
מֹשֶׁה לָמָּה זֶּה אַתֶּם עֹבְרִים אֶת־פִּי יְהוָה וְהִוא לֹא תִצְלָח:
מב אַל־תַּעֲלוּ כִּי אֵין יְהוָה בְּקִרְבְּכֶם וְלֹא תִּנָּגְפוּ לִפְנֵי אֹיְבֵיכֶם:
מג כִּי הָעֲמָלֵקִי וְהַכְּנַעֲנִי שָׁם לִפְנֵיכֶם וּנְפַלְתֶּם בֶּחָרֶב כִּי־עַל־כֵּן
מד שַׁבְתֶּם מֵאַחֲרֵי יְהוָה וְלֹא־יִהְיֶה יְהוָה עִמָּכֶם: וַיַּעְפִּלוּ לַעֲלוֹת
אֶל־רֹאשׁ הָהָר וַאֲרוֹן בְּרִית־יְהוָה וּמֹשֶׁה לֹא־מָשׁוּ מִקֶּרֶב
מה הַמַּחֲנֶה: וַיֵּרֶד הָעֲמָלֵקִי וְהַכְּנַעֲנִי הַיֹּשֵׁב בָּהָר הַהוּא וַיַּכּוּם
וַיַּכְּתוּם עַד־הַחָרְמָה:

טו א ב וַיְדַבֵּר יְהוָה אֶל־מֹשֶׁה לֵּאמֹר: דַּבֵּר אֶל־בְּנֵי יִשְׂרָאֵל וְאָמַרְתָּ יד
אֲלֵהֶם כִּי תָבֹאוּ אֶל־אֶרֶץ מוֹשְׁבֹתֵיכֶם אֲשֶׁר אֲנִי נֹתֵן לָכֶם:

14:41 וְהִוא לֹא תִצְלָח *It will not work* – Many philosophers tend to cluster at the extremes: either rigidly conservative or profoundly revolutionary. The current social order is either right or wrong. If it is right, we should not change it. If it is wrong, we should overthrow it. The fact that change takes time, even many generations, is not an idea easy to square with philosophy (even those philosophers, like Hegel and Marx, who factored in time, did so mechanically, speaking about "historical inevitability" rather than the unpredictable exercise of freedom). What we see playing out in this incident, however, is what I call the chronological imagination, as opposed to the Greek logical imagination. Logic lacks the dimension of time. Narrative holds a different kind of wisdom.

One of the odd facts about Western civilization in recent centuries is that the people who have been most eloquent about tradition have been deeply conservative, defenders of the status quo. Yet there is no reason why a tradition should be conservative. We can hand on to our children not only our past but also our unrealized ideals. We can want them to go beyond us, to travel further on the road to freedom than we were able to do. That, for example, is how the Seder service on Passover begins: "This year, slaves, next year free; this year here, next year in Israel." A tradition can be evolutionary without being revolutionary.

3 in, and you present a fire offering from the herd or from
the flock for a pleasing aroma to the LORD – whether it
be a burnt offering or a sacrifice to fulfill a spoken vow, or
4 brought as a freewill offering, or a festival offering – the
one who brings this offering to the LORD shall bring
with it a grain offering of a tenth of a measure of fine
5 flour mixed with a quarter of a hin of oil, and with the
burnt offering or the sacrifice, a quarter of a hin of wine
6 as a libation for every lamb. In the case of a ram, you shall
bring a grain offering of two-tenths of a measure of fine
7 flour mixed with a third of a hin of oil. You shall also offer
a third of a hin of wine as a libation, for a pleasing aroma
8 to the LORD. If, however, you offer an animal from the HAMISHI
herd as a burnt offering or as a sacrifice to fulfill a spoken
9 vow, or as a peace offering to the LORD, then you shall
bring with each animal a grain offering of three-tenths of
10 a measure of fine flour mixed with half a hin of oil. You
shall also offer half a hin of wine as a libation; it is a fire
11 offering, a pleasing aroma to the LORD. So shall it be with
12 each ox, each ram, and with any sheep or goat. However
13 many you offer, you shall do the same for each. Every
native-born person, presenting a fire offering as a pleasing
14 aroma to the LORD, shall perform them in this way. And
whensoever, through the generations, a migrant joins you
or lives among you, and he too prepares a fire offering for
a pleasing aroma to the LORD, he shall do just as you do.
15 There shall be one law for the congregation: as for you, so
for any migrant. It shall be an eternal decree throughout
the generations: you and the migrant shall be the same
16 before the LORD. One law and one rule for you and for
the migrant who lives among you."
17 18 The LORD spoke to Moshe: "Speak to the Israelites. Say: SHISHI
When you come to the land to which I am bringing you,

---

are all strangers to someone else. This is something Israel is expected not merely to know abstractly but to feel in the deepest recesses of its collective memory. "You yourselves were strangers in the land of Egypt" (Lev. 19:34).

ג וַעֲשִׂיתֶם אִשֶּׁה לַיהוה עֹלָה אוֹ־זֶבַח לְפַלֵּא־נֶדֶר אוֹ בִנְדָבָה
אוֹ בְּמֹעֲדֵיכֶם לַעֲשׂוֹת רֵיחַ נִיחֹחַ לַיהוה מִן־הַבָּקָר אוֹ מִן־
ד הַצֹּאן: וְהִקְרִיב הַמַּקְרִיב קָרְבָּנוֹ לַיהוה מִנְחָה סֹלֶת עִשָּׂרוֹן
ה בָּלוּל בִּרְבִעִית הַהִין שָׁמֶן: וְיַיִן לַנֶּסֶךְ רְבִיעִית הַהִין תַּעֲשֶׂה
ו עַל־הָעֹלָה אוֹ לַזָּבַח לַכֶּבֶשׂ הָאֶחָד: אוֹ לָאַיִל תַּעֲשֶׂה מִנְחָה
ז סֹלֶת שְׁנֵי עֶשְׂרֹנִים בְּלוּלָה בַשֶּׁמֶן שְׁלִשִׁית הַהִין: וְיַיִן לַנֶּסֶךְ
ח שְׁלִשִׁית הַהִין תַּקְרִיב רֵיחַ־נִיחֹחַ לַיהוה: וְכִי־תַעֲשֶׂה בֶן־ חמישי
ט בָּקָר עֹלָה אוֹ־זָבַח לְפַלֵּא־נֶדֶר אוֹ־שְׁלָמִים לַיהוה: וְהִקְרִיב
עַל־בֶּן־הַבָּקָר מִנְחָה סֹלֶת שְׁלֹשָׁה עֶשְׂרֹנִים בָּלוּל בַּשֶּׁמֶן
י חֲצִי הַהִין: וְיַיִן תַּקְרִיב לַנֶּסֶךְ חֲצִי הַהִין אִשֵּׁה רֵיחַ־נִיחֹחַ
יא לַיהוה: כָּכָה יֵעָשֶׂה לַשּׁוֹר הָאֶחָד אוֹ לָאַיִל הָאֶחָד אוֹ־לַשֶּׂה
יב בַכְּבָשִׂים אוֹ בָעִזִּים: כַּמִּסְפָּר אֲשֶׁר תַּעֲשׂוּ כָּכָה תַּעֲשׂוּ לָאֶחָד
יג כְּמִסְפָּרָם: כָּל־הָאֶזְרָח יַעֲשֶׂה־כָּכָה אֶת־אֵלֶּה לְהַקְרִיב אִשֵּׁה
יד רֵיחַ־נִיחֹחַ לַיהוה: וְכִי־יָגוּר אִתְּכֶם גֵּר אוֹ אֲשֶׁר־בְּתוֹכְכֶם
לְדֹרֹתֵיכֶם וְעָשָׂה אִשֵּׁה רֵיחַ־נִיחֹחַ לַיהוה כַּאֲשֶׁר תַּעֲשׂוּ
טו כֵּן יַעֲשֶׂה: הַקָּהָל חֻקָּה אַחַת לָכֶם וְלַגֵּר הַגָּר חֻקַּת עוֹלָם
טז לְדֹרֹתֵיכֶם כָּכֶם כַּגֵּר יִהְיֶה לִפְנֵי יהוה: תּוֹרָה אַחַת וּמִשְׁפָּט
אֶחָד יִהְיֶה לָכֶם וְלַגֵּר הַגָּר אִתְּכֶם:
יז יח וַיְדַבֵּר יהוה אֶל־מֹשֶׁה לֵּאמֹר: דַּבֵּר אֶל־בְּנֵי יִשְׂרָאֵל וְאָמַרְתָּ ששי
אֲלֵהֶם בְּבֹאֲכֶם אֶל־הָאָרֶץ אֲשֶׁר אֲנִי מֵבִיא אֶתְכֶם שָׁמָּה:

15:15 כָּכֶם כַּגֵּר יִהְיֶה לִפְנֵי יהוה *You and the migrant shall be the same before the* LORD – The Mosaic books never tire of this theme (see, for instance, Ex. 22:20 and the note there). For the ancient world generally, even for Plato and Aristotle, strangers were aliens, beyond the radius of concern, unentitled to civil rights or citizenship. Few things would have been less intelligible to them than the principle that "there shall be one law for the congregation: as for you, so for any migrant.… You and the migrant shall be the same before the LORD." This is part of Israel's moral struggle against tribalism and its modern successor, xenophobic nationalism. Strangers, too, have rights and make a legitimate claim on our humanity, for we

19 and eat the bread of the land, you shall set some aside
20 as an offering to the LORD. As the first portion of your
kneading, you shall set aside a loaf as an offering, like
21 the offering you present from the threshing floor. You
shall present to the LORD an offering from the first of
22 your kneading throughout your generations. If,
without intention, you fail to perform any of these
23 commandments that the LORD gave to Moshe, anything
that the LORD has commanded you through Moshe from
the day the LORD commanded it and onward – in all
24 generations to come – if it is done unintentionally by the
community, the entire community must offer one bull
from the herd as a burnt offering, a pleasing aroma to the
LORD, with its prescribed grain offering and libation, and
25 one goat as a purification offering. The priest shall then
make atonement for all the community of Israel and they
will be forgiven, because it was an accidental failing, and
because they brought their sacrifice, a fire offering to the
LORD and the purification offering for their error before
26 the LORD. The community of Israel and the migrants
living among them will all be forgiven, because all the
27 people acted in error. If it is an individual who SHEVI'I
sins inadvertently, he shall offer a year-old female goat as
28 a purification offering. The priest shall make atonement
before the LORD for the person who sinned inadvertently,
29 to atone for his sin, and he will be forgiven. There shall
be one law for one who inadvertently commits a sin,
whether he is a native-born Israelite or a migrant living
30 among them. However, if a person commits a sin high-
handedly, whether he is native born or a migrant, he
reviles the LORD and shall be severed from the people.
31 Because he despises the LORD's word and violates His
commandments, he will be severed utterly and must bear
his guilt."

The second reminds us that by expressing remorse for the past, we may not cancel the wrong we have done but we revoke the intention with which we did it.

יט וְהָיָה בַּאֲכָלְכֶם מִלֶּחֶם הָאָרֶץ תָּרִימוּ תְרוּמָה לַיהוָה׃
כ רֵאשִׁית עֲרִסֹתֵכֶם חַלָּה תָּרִימוּ תְרוּמָה כִּתְרוּמַת גֹּרֶן כֵּן
כא תָּרִימוּ אֹתָהּ׃ מֵרֵאשִׁית עֲרִסֹתֵיכֶם תִּתְּנוּ לַיהוָה תְּרוּמָה
כב לְדֹרֹתֵיכֶם׃ וְכִי תִשְׁגּוּ וְלֹא תַעֲשׂוּ אֵת כָּל־
כג הַמִּצְוֹת הָאֵלֶּה אֲשֶׁר־דִּבֶּר יְהוָה אֶל־מֹשֶׁה׃ אֵת כָּל־אֲשֶׁר
צִוָּה יְהוָה אֲלֵיכֶם בְּיַד־מֹשֶׁה מִן־הַיּוֹם אֲשֶׁר צִוָּה יְהוָה
כד וָהָלְאָה לְדֹרֹתֵיכֶם׃ וְהָיָה אִם מֵעֵינֵי הָעֵדָה נֶעֶשְׂתָה לִשְׁגָגָה
וְעָשׂוּ כָל־הָעֵדָה פַּר בֶּן־בָּקָר אֶחָד לְעֹלָה לְרֵיחַ נִיחֹחַ לַיהוָה
כה וּמִנְחָתוֹ וְנִסְכּוֹ כַּמִּשְׁפָּט וּשְׂעִיר־עִזִּים אֶחָד לְחַטָּת׃ וְכִפֶּר
הַכֹּהֵן עַל־כָּל־עֲדַת בְּנֵי יִשְׂרָאֵל וְנִסְלַח לָהֶם כִּי־שְׁגָגָה
הִוא וְהֵם הֵבִיאוּ אֶת־קָרְבָּנָם אִשֶּׁה לַיהוָה וְחַטָּאתָם לִפְנֵי
כו יְהוָה עַל־שִׁגְגָתָם׃ וְנִסְלַח לְכָל־עֲדַת בְּנֵי יִשְׂרָאֵל וְלַגֵּר
כז הַגָּר בְּתוֹכָם כִּי לְכָל־הָעָם בִּשְׁגָגָה׃ וְאִם־נֶפֶשׁ שביעי
אַחַת תֶּחֱטָא בִשְׁגָגָה וְהִקְרִיבָה עֵז בַּת־שְׁנָתָהּ לְחַטָּאת׃
כח וְכִפֶּר הַכֹּהֵן עַל־הַנֶּפֶשׁ הַשֹּׁגֶגֶת בְּחֶטְאָה בִשְׁגָגָה לִפְנֵי יְהוָה
כט לְכַפֵּר עָלָיו וְנִסְלַח לוֹ׃ הָאֶזְרָח בִּבְנֵי יִשְׂרָאֵל וְלַגֵּר הַגָּר
ל בְּתוֹכָם תּוֹרָה אַחַת יִהְיֶה לָכֶם לָעֹשֶׂה בִּשְׁגָגָה׃ וְהַנֶּפֶשׁ
אֲשֶׁר־תַּעֲשֶׂה ׀ בְּיָד רָמָה מִן־הָאֶזְרָח וּמִן־הַגֵּר אֶת־יְהוָה
לא הוּא מְגַדֵּף וְנִכְרְתָה הַנֶּפֶשׁ הַהִוא מִקֶּרֶב עַמָּהּ׃ כִּי דְבַר־
יְהוָה בָּזָה וְאֶת־מִצְוָתוֹ הֵפַר הִכָּרֵת ׀ תִּכָּרֵת הַנֶּפֶשׁ הַהִוא
עֲוֺנָה בָהּ׃

15:26 כִּי לְכָל־הָעָם בִּשְׁגָגָה *Because all the people acted in error* – This verse, which today is part of the *Kol Nidrei* liturgy, is interpreted by the Sages to signal two things for the generations: (1) that we can come together as a community to seek forgiveness, and (2) that through repentance, even deliberate sins come to be regarded as unintentional ones (Yoma 86b) and can thus be forgiven. The importance of the first is that we should never rely on our own personal merits. Judaism is the faith of a people and its communities, not just of individuals in their private lives.

32 When the Israelites were in the wilderness, they encoun-
33 tered a man gathering wood on the Sabbath. Those who
found him gathering wood brought him before Moshe
34 and Aharon, and before the whole community, and he
was placed in custody, because it had not been specified
35 what should be done to him. And the LORD said
to Moshe, "The man shall be put to death. The whole
36 community must stone him outside the camp." And so,
as the LORD had commanded Moshe, the whole community took him outside the camp and stoned him to
death.
37 The LORD said to Moshe: "Speak to the Israelites; tell MAFTIR
38 them to make fringes on the corners of their garments
throughout the generations. To the fringe on each

this story we turn to the laws of tzitzit. Part of what makes religion a force for honest and altruistic behavior is the daily remembrance that God sees what we do. Studies in social science posit that "watched people are nice people"; even a picture of eyes on the wall makes people act with more integrity and generosity. It is no coincidence that, as belief in a personal God has waned in the West, surveillance by CCTV and other means has increased. The gentle reminder of the tzitzit stands in contrast to the harsh enforcement of criminal law.

TZITZIT

Parashat Shelaḥ begins with the story of the spies. It ends with the laws of tzitzit, the fringes with their cord of blue to be placed on the corners of garments so the people will "remember all the LORD's commands and keep them" (Num. 15:39). This passage became the third paragraph of the *Shema*.

On the face of it, there is no connection between these bookends of the *parasha*. One is a historical incident, the other a timeless law. One concerns the fate of the nation, the other has to do with individual dress. However, a close reading reveals that the two are very much related. They are an instance of intertextuality – the interrelationship between two texts that shed light on one another. Their juxtaposition tells us something about both the narrative and the law.

Intertextuality is often signaled in the Torah by use of the same word or words in two passages. Our *parasha* never, as we noted above (ch. 14, "The Spies' Report"), uses the standard Hebrew word, based on the root *r-g-l*, that means "spy." Instead the word used is *latur*, which means not "to spy" but rather "to see," "to explore." It is this verb, in verse 39, that explains what the fringes are intended to prevent: "You shall

לב וַיִּהְיוּ בְנֵי־יִשְׂרָאֵל בַּמִּדְבָּר וַיִּמְצְאוּ אִישׁ מְקֹשֵׁשׁ עֵצִים
לג בְּיוֹם הַשַּׁבָּת׃ וַיַּקְרִיבוּ אֹתוֹ הַמֹּצְאִים אֹתוֹ מְקֹשֵׁשׁ
לד עֵצִים אֶל־מֹשֶׁה וְאֶל־אַהֲרֹן וְאֶל כָּל־הָעֵדָה׃ וַיַּנִּיחוּ אֹתוֹ
לה בַּמִּשְׁמָר כִּי לֹא פֹרַשׁ מַה־יֵּעָשֶׂה לוֹ׃ וַיֹּאמֶר
יהוה אֶל־מֹשֶׁה מוֹת יוּמַת הָאִישׁ רָגוֹם אֹתוֹ בָאֲבָנִים כָּל־
לו הָעֵדָה מִחוּץ לַמַּחֲנֶה׃ וַיֹּצִיאוּ אֹתוֹ כָּל־הָעֵדָה אֶל־מִחוּץ
לַמַּחֲנֶה וַיִּרְגְּמוּ אֹתוֹ בָּאֲבָנִים וַיָּמֹת כַּאֲשֶׁר צִוָּה יהוה אֶת־
מֹשֶׁה׃
לז לח וַיֹּאמֶר יהוה אֶל־מֹשֶׁה לֵּאמֹר׃ דַּבֵּר אֶל־בְּנֵי יִשְׂרָאֵל וְאָמַרְתָּ מפטיר
אֲלֵהֶם וְעָשׂוּ לָהֶם צִיצִת עַל־כַּנְפֵי בִגְדֵיהֶם לְדֹרֹתָם וְנָתְנוּ

15:32 אִישׁ מְקֹשֵׁשׁ עֵצִים בְּיוֹם הַשַּׁבָּת *A man gathering wood on the Sabbath* – This incident recalls the case of the blasphemer, which arose in Leviticus 24. We noted there ("The Execution of the Blasphemer") that the erosion of reverence for God in a society has implications in the social arena; hence the need for a decisive public response. What, then, is the critical social importance of the Sabbath?

The Sabbath is one of the most potent of all religious institutions. Few will disagree with Ahad Ha'am's famous judgment that "more than the Jews kept the Sabbath, the Sabbath kept the Jews." It created an alternative world in which differentiations based on work, income, or expenditure had no room in which to operate. At all times, even in those many Jewish communities that lived in grinding poverty, one saved in order to dress and eat well on the seventh day. It was impossible, on the Sabbath, to internalize the pariah image that antisemitism seemed to impose. The Sabbath created the coherence of the religious community. It also, perhaps, was decisive in preserving the attitudes which made the Jews so adaptable and socially mobile. It was, if you like, the insertion into the world of an alternative identity, in which the white tablecloth, the silver candlesticks, the leisurely meals, the assembled family, enacted rather than symbolized a freedom from the existing economic and social order.

The Sabbath still has enormous importance as a "public good," central to the shared culture of Judaism. Perhaps this is why this narrative comes to complement that of the blasphemer in Leviticus: reverence for the Sabbath, like reverence for God, protects the social fabric that unites us.

The scene of "religious coercion" and capital punishment feels foreign to Judaism at least since the time of the Mishna. Perhaps the Torah itself hints at a certain discomfort, for immediately after

39 corner they should attach a blue cord. And this shall be
your fringe: seeing it, you shall remember all the Lord's

My teacher Rabbi Nachum Rabinovitch gave this explanation: There are two kinds of clothing. There are the clothes we wear to project an image. A king, a judge, a soldier all wear clothing that conceals the individual and instead proclaims a role, an office, a rank. Such are the clothes we wear in public when we want to create a certain impression. But there are other clothes we wear when we are alone that may convey more powerfully than anything else the kind of person we really are: the artist in his studio, the writer at his desk, the gardener tending the roses. They are not dressed to create an impression. To the contrary, these people dress as they do because of what they are, not because of what they wish to seem.

In this striking way, tzitzit represents the dual nature of Judaism. On the one hand it is a way of life that is public, communal, shared with others across the world and through the ages. We keep the Sabbath, celebrate the festivals, and observe the dietary laws in a way that has hardly varied for many centuries. That is the public face of Judaism – the tallit we wear, the cloak woven out of the 613 threads, each a command.

But there is also our inner life as people of faith. There are things we can say to God that we can say to no one else. He knows our thoughts, hopes, fears, better than we know them ourselves. We speak to Him in the privacy of the soul, and He listens. That internal conversation – the opening of our heart to the One who brought us into existence in love – is not for public show. Like the fringed undergarment, it stays hidden. But it is no less real an aspect of Jewish spirituality. The two types of fringed garments represent the two dimensions of the life of faith – the outer persona and the inner person, the image we present to the world and the face we show only to God.

15:39 וּזְכַרְתֶּם *You shall remember* – Wittgenstein once said that "the work of the philosopher consists in assembling reminders for a particular purpose" (*Philosophical Investigations*). In the case of Judaism the purpose of the outward signs – tzitzit, mezuza, and tefillin – is precisely that: to assemble reminders, on our clothes, our homes, our arms and head, that certain things are wrong, and that even if no other human being sees us, God sees us and will call us to account.

"More devious is the heart than all else, and it is hopelessly sick. Who can know it?" said Yirmeyahu (Jer. 17:9). One of the blessings and curses of human nature is that we use our power of reason not always and only to act rationally, but also to rationalize and make excuses for the things we do, even when we know we should not have done them. The moral sense, wrote the social

לט עַל־צִיצִת הַכָּנָף פְּתִיל תְּכֵלֶת׃ וְהָיָה לָכֶם לְצִיצִת וּרְאִיתֶם
אֹתוֹ וּזְכַרְתֶּם אֶת־כָּל־מִצְוֹת יהוה וַעֲשִׂיתֶם אֹתָם וְלֹא

remember all the Lord's commands and keep them. You will not then go astray (*velo taturu*), following the lusts of your heart or of your eyes."

The verbal connection is usually missed in translation. In Hebrew, however, the echo is unmistakable – *veyaturu* in the case of the spies, *velo taturu* in the case of tzitzit.

Similarly, the word *u're'item*, "and you shall see," appears only three times in the Torah, two of them in this *parasha*. The first occurs in Moshe's briefing of the spies, translated as: "See what the land is like" (13:18). The second is in the command of the tzitzit, translated as: "Seeing it, you shall remember all the Lord's commands" (15:39).

What these connections have in common is that *t-u-r* and *u're'item* are both verbs of seeing. At stake is the testimony of our eyes. The spies saw, but misunderstood what they saw, because they doubted their ability to overcome their opponents. They attributed to objective reality what was in fact subjective self-doubt. Had that been rare, the Torah would not have legislated against it. It is, however, a common and fateful error.

Rabbi Joseph B. Soloveitchik taught that *tekhelet* and *lavan*, blue and white, the two colors of the tzitzit, represent two ways of viewing and understanding the world. In Hebrew, *lavan* signifies not only the color white but also clarity, rationality, and openness. The Torah wants us to understand the world, exploring natural phenomena with the methods of science, not to live in ignorance and obscurity. *Tekhelet*, the Sages said, resembles the sea, which is like the sky, which represents the celestial throne (Sota 17a). Blue represents distance, inapproachability, the ineffable – those elements of reality that are beyond our rational understanding and control, numinous, awe-inspiring. We seek to understand what can be understood, while what lies beyond the horizon of human understanding we interpret through an act of faith.

Tzitzit is, as the Torah says, a way of remembering the commandments. But it is significantly more than this. It is a call from God to see the world through Jewish eyes. Faith does not mean seeing the world as we would like it to be. Nor is it a matter of blaming the world for not being as we would wish. Faith is the courage to see the world precisely as it is while refusing to be intimidated by it.

15:38 לְדֹרֹתָם *Throughout the generations* – In the course of time, the custom has evolved to fulfill the command of tzitzit in two quite different ways: the first, in the form of a tallit (robe, shawl) which is worn *over* our other clothes, specifically while we pray; the second, in the form of an undergarment, worn *beneath* our outer clothing throughout the day.

commands and keep them. You will not then go astray,
40 following the lusts of your heart or of your eyes. This is
to remind you to keep all My commands, to remain holy
41 to your God. I am the LORD your God, who brought
you out of Egypt to be your God. I am the LORD your
God."

The haftara for Parashat Shelaḥ is on page 1564.

of conquest: it couldn't be done. They could have said, "It will be difficult, we will need courage and skill, but with God's help we will prevail." But they did not. Their thinking was a polarized either-or.

Another negative thought pattern is *mind-reading*. We assume we know what other people are thinking, when usually we are completely wrong because we are jumping to conclusions about them based on our own feelings, not theirs. That is what the spies did when they said, "We looked to our own eyes like grasshoppers, and *so we were in theirs*" (Num. 13:33).

A third is *blame*. In the wake of the spies' report, the people "railed against Moshe and Aharon" (14:1), as if to say, "It is all your fault. If only you had let us stay in Egypt!" People who blame others have already begun down the road to learned helplessness. They see themselves as powerless to change. They are the passive victims of forces beyond their control.

Applying cognitive behavioral therapy to the story of the spies reminds us how easy it is to fall into these and other forms of cognitive distortion. The result can be depression and despair – dangerous states of mind that need immediate medical or therapeutic attention.

What I find profoundly moving is the therapy the Torah itself prescribes. We have already noted the linguistic links between the story of the spies and our passage on tzitzit (see above, "Tzitzit"). The blue thread in the tzitzit, says the Talmud (Sota 17a), is there to remind us of the sea, the sky, and God's throne of glory. *Tekhelet*, the blue itself, was in the ancient world the mark of royalty. Thus the tzitzit is itself a form of cognitive behavioral therapy, saying: "Do not be afraid. God is with you. And do not give way to your emotions, because you are royalty: you are children of the King."

Never let negative emotions distort your perceptions. You are not a grasshopper. Those who oppose you are not giants. To see the world as it is, not as you are afraid it might be, let faith banish fear.

תָתוּרוּ אַחֲרֵי לְבַבְכֶם וְאַחֲרֵי עֵינֵיכֶם אֲשֶׁר־אַתֶּם זֹנִים
מ אַחֲרֵיהֶם: לְמַעַן תִּזְכְּרוּ וַעֲשִׂיתֶם אֶת־כׇּל־מִצְוֺתָי וִהְיִיתֶם
מא קְדֹשִׁים לֵאלֹהֵיכֶם: אֲנִי יְהֹוָה אֱלֹהֵיכֶם אֲשֶׁר הוֹצֵאתִי
אֶתְכֶם מֵאֶרֶץ מִצְרַיִם לִהְיוֹת לָכֶם לֵאלֹהִים אֲנִי יְהֹוָה
אֱלֹהֵיכֶם:

The הפטרה *for* פרשת שלח *is on page 1565.*

psychologist James Q. Wilson, "is not a strong beacon light radiating outward to illuminate in sharp outline all that it touches." It is, rather, "a small candle flame, casting vague and multiple shadows, flickering and sputtering in the strong winds of power and passion, greed and ideology." He added: "But brought close to the heart" it "dispels the darkness and warms the soul."

That, perhaps, is one of the lessons the Torah wishes us to draw from the story of the spies. Had they recalled what God had done to Egypt, the mightiest empire of the ancient world, they would not have said, "We cannot attack those people; they are stronger than we are" (Num. 13:31). But they were in the grip of fear. Strong emotion – fear especially – distorts our perception. It activates the amygdala, the source of our most primal reactions, causing it to override the prefrontal cortex that allows us to think rationally about the consequences of our decisions and to follow the right path.

Tzitzit, with their thread of blue, remind us of Heaven, and that is what we most need if we are consistently to act in accordance with the better angels of our nature.

15:39 אַחֲרֵי לְבַבְכֶם וְאַחֲרֵי עֵינֵיכֶם *Your heart or of your eyes* – Note the strange order of the parts of the body. Normally we would expect it to be the other way around, as Rashi says in his commentary on the verse "The eye sees and the heart desires." First we see, then we feel. But in fact the Torah reverses the order, thus anticipating the point Adam T. Beck later made in developing cognitive behavioral therapy, which is that often our feelings distort our perception. The heart determines what the eye sees. We interpret events in accordance with our feelings – often in negative ways that can be fatalistic and damaging to our self-respect. We can think ourselves into "learned helplessness."

The spies have clearly demonstrated this effect. One negative thought pattern identified by Beck is *all-or-nothing thinking*. Everything is either black or white, good or bad, easy or impossible. That was the spies' verdict on the possibility

Parashat Koraḥ

16 1 Koraḥ, son of Yitzhar son of Kehat son of Levi, together
with Datan and Aviram sons of Eliav and On son of

---

lose. It was easy to tap into their disappointment, resentment, and fear.

Moshe wins the argument against Koraḥ, but only at the cost of invoking a miracle in which the earth opens up and swallows his opponents. Yet this does not end the argument. The next day the people gather against Moshe, saying: "You have killed the Lord's people!" (Num. 17:6). In this kind of confrontation, there is no benign outcome. You can only aim at minimizing the tragedy.

There is a warning here to stay far from people, movements, and parties that demonize their opponents. A healthy culture welcomes argument and respects dissenting views. Resist with all your heart and soul any attempt to substitute power for truth.

16:1 וַיִּקַּח *Took* – The verb does not have an object in the Hebrew. What did Koraḥ take? Rashi begins his commentary (on Num. 16:1) by stating what he believes to be the plain sense: "Koraḥ took himself to one side." He separated himself from the community and prepared to start a revolt.

Rashi cites *Midrash Tanḥuma*, which seeks to fill gaps in the narrative and elucidate its subtler levels. In this vein, *Tanḥuma* (Koraḥ, 2) answers the question "What did Koraḥ take?" by saying that he took a blue cloak and asked, "Does a cloak made entirely of blue wool require tzitzit, or is it exempt?"

Koraḥ knows that even a blue cloak requires tzitzit, a set of fringes that contain a cord of blue; he knows that it would be difficult to explain this convincingly to a large and skeptical public. Koraḥ's aim is to make Moshe seem absurd, whatever he answers.

Clearly this is not the plain sense of the text. Neither Koraḥ nor any of his fellow rebels mention tzitzit. Their complaints are that Moshe acted high-handedly, appointed his brother as High Priest, and failed in his central mission of bringing the people to the Promised Land. Yet the Midrash is teaching something deep about leadership. Recall Koraḥ's opening words to Moshe and Aharon: "You have gone too far! All the community is holy, every one of them, and the Lord is in their midst. Why then do you set yourselves above the Lord's people?" (Num. 16:3). Was Koraḥ right? Is all the community holy? Our midrash does not answer this directly, but does so implicitly.

Commanding all men to wear tzitzit with their thread of blue, the color associated with royalty and Aharon's priestly robe, meant that they were all holy, noble, and worthy to be priests. Had

פרשת קרח

טז א וַיִּקַּח קֹרַח בֶּן־יִצְהָר בֶּן־קְהָת בֶּן־לֵוִי וְדָתָן וַאֲבִירָם בְּנֵי טו

KORAḤ

The rebellion of Koraḥ, which dominates this *parasha,* is the most devastating challenge to Moshe's leadership in the Torah. Building on the unrest and shattered hopes of the people following the incident of the spies, Koraḥ assembles a heterogeneous group of malcontents – some from his own tribe, some from that of Reuven, yet others who have leadership positions elsewhere – and renounces the leadership of Moshe and Aharon.

The rebellion fails – ended by the ground opening and swallowing the chief rebels – yet the complaints of the people continue. These end only when Aharon's staff, alone among the staffs for each tribe, buds, blossoms, and brings forth almonds, a paradigm of peaceful conflict resolution. The *parasha* ends with a legal section detailing the duties of the priests and Levites and the offerings to be given to them by the rest of the people.

THE KORAḤ REBELLION

The Koraḥ rebellion is not just the worst of many in the wilderness years. It is also different in kind. It is not about a problem the Israelites have encountered – a lack of food or water or a way through the sea or the prospect of having to fight a battle against giants. It is an ad hominem attack on Moshe and Aharon. Koraḥ and his fellow rebels accuse Moshe of nepotism, of failure, and above all of being a fraud – of attributing to God decisions and laws that Moshe has devised himself for his own ends.

In contemporary terms, the Koraḥ rebellion is a populist movement. Populism is the politics of anger. It appears when there is widespread discontent with political leaders, when people feel that heads of institutions are working in their own interest rather than that of the general public. People come to feel that the distribution of rewards is unfair: a few gain disproportionately and the many stay static or lose. Discontent takes the form of the rejection of current political and cultural elites. Populist politicians claim that they, and they alone, are the true voice of the people. Populists stir up resentment against the establishment. They are deliberately divisive and confrontational. They promise strong leadership that will give the people back what has been taken from them. Ramban is undoubtedly correct when he says (commentary on Num. 16:1) that such a challenge to Moshe's leadership would have been impossible at any earlier point. Only in the aftermath of the episode of the spies, when the people realized that they would not see the Promised Land in their lifetime, could discontent be stirred by Koraḥ and his assorted fellow travelers. They felt they had nothing to

2 Pelet – descendants of Reuven – took two hundred fifty
Israelite men, leaders of the community, chosen from
3 the assembly, men of repute, and confronted Moshe and
Aharon together. They said to them, "You have gone too
far. All the community is holy, every one of them, and the
LORD is in their midst. Why then do you set yourselves

---

a sense of grievance. Ibn Ezra adds that the final straw may have been Moshe's appointment of Yehoshua as his successor. Yehoshua came from the tribe of Efrayim, the son of Yosef. This may have revived memories of the old conflict between the children of Leah (of whom Reuven was the firstborn) and those of Raḥel, whose first child was Yosef.

The 250 other rebels, Ibn Ezra conjectures, were firstborns, still unreconciled to the fact that after the sin of the golden calf, the role of special service to God passed from the firstborn to the tribe of Levi.

The rebels share the mistake of seeing leadership in terms of status: the one before whom others prostrate themselves and to whom others defer. That is what leaders are in hierarchical societies. That is not what leadership is in the Torah. Of Moshe it says that he was "very humble, more so than any other man on earth" (Num. 12:3). A true leader is a servant, not a master. Seeking to set oneself above others is a moral failing, not a mark of stature. A leader is one who coordinates, giving structure and shape to the enterprise, making sure that everyone is following the same script, traveling in the same direction, acting as an ensemble rather than a collection of prima donnas.

We are *all* God's servants. As the Torah says, "For it is to Me that the Israelites are servants; they are My servants whom I brought out of the land of Egypt" (Lev. 25:55). It is not that Moshe is a different kind of being than we are all called on to be. It is that he epitomized true service of God to the utmost degree. *The less there is of self in one who serves God, the more there is of God.* Moshe was the supreme exemplar of R. Yoḥanan's principle that "where you find humility, there you find greatness" (*Midrash Lekaḥ Tov*, Ekev 15a). The greatest achievement of a leader is to have served God and helped others to do so. That is what Moshe understood, and what Koraḥ and his fellow rebels did not.

16:3 כָל־הָעֵדָה כֻּלָּם קְדֹשִׁים *All the community is holy, every one of them* – How should we understand Koraḥ's fundamental claim here? Ramban (on Num. 16:1) suggests that Koraḥ was protesting the transfer of priestly and Levitical duties to the tribe of Levi after the sin of the golden calf. Until then, that role had gone to the firstborn males in every family and tribe (see Ex. 34:20; Num. 3:12). Koraḥ was saying not that everyone was equally holy, but that the original plan, in which the firstborns were consecrated

ב אֱלִיאָב׃ וְאוֹן בֶּן־פֶּלֶת בְּנֵי רְאוּבֵן׃ וַיָּקֻמוּ לִפְנֵי מֹשֶׁה וַאֲנָשִׁים
מִבְּנֵי־יִשְׂרָאֵל חֲמִשִּׁים וּמָאתָיִם נְשִׂיאֵי עֵדָה קְרִאֵי מוֹעֵד
ג אַנְשֵׁי־שֵׁם׃ וַיִּקָּהֲלוּ עַל־מֹשֶׁה וְעַל־אַהֲרֹן וַיֹּאמְרוּ אֲלֵהֶם
רַב־לָכֶם כִּי כָל־הָעֵדָה כֻּלָּם קְדֹשִׁים וּבְתוֹכָם יהוה וּמַדּוּעַ

---

not God Himself summoned Israel to be a "kingdom of priests and a holy nation" (Ex. 19:6)? Koraḥ's mistake is saying that a robe that is entirely blue does not need tzitzit and, by analogy, saying that a congregation of leaders does not need a leader. The truth is otherwise. A holy people still needs a leader, just as a garment, every thread of which is blue, still needs a fringe. A garment that is entirely blue but which lacks tzitzit has no special sanctity. A blue cloak is still only a cloak. The function of the tzitzit is not to diminish the significance of the garment but to endow it with a special and recognizable character.

Koraḥ does, though, have one virtue. He sees that the Jewish people should aspire to be a "cloak that is entirely blue." He dies for his sins, but his sons survive, and many centuries later their descendants are to sing psalms in the Temple – a whole series of psalms bear their name (see Psalms 42, 44–49, 84–88). If ambition had not corrupted him, Koraḥ might have been a genuine leader. For though his claim is self-serving, he sees a real and moving truth, that if a people dedicates itself to God it can become a robe every strand of which is royal blue.

16:1 בֶּן־קְהָת בֶּן־לֵוִי *Son of Kehat son of Levi* – The genealogy given in the opening verse of the *parasha*: "Koraḥ son of Yitzhar son of Kehat son of Levi" – suggested to the Sages (Bemidbar Rabba 18:2) the nature of his discontent. Koraḥ was aggrieved that he had been passed over when leaders were appointed for the various clans. In Numbers 3:30 we read that "the leader of the ancestral house of the Kohatite families was Elitzafan son of Uziel." Uziel was the youngest of the four sons of Kehat. Koraḥ is the son of Yitzhar, the second eldest of the brothers. Having already felt slighted that his father's elder brother, Amram, provided the Israelites with their two supreme leaders, Moshe and Aharon, this further rejection is the final insult. He feels humiliated and is determined to bring Moshe and Aharon down.

16:1 בְּנֵי רְאוּבֵן *Descendants of Reuven* – Koraḥ's allies include two disaffected groups: the Reubenites, among them Datan and Aviram, and "two hundred fifty Israelite men, leaders of the community, chosen from the assembly, men of repute" (v. 2).

The Reubenites, suggests Ibn Ezra, felt that as descendants of Yaakov's firstborn, they were entitled to leadership positions, yet the tribe was systematically passed over when it came to leadership roles, leaving its members with

4 above the Lord's people?" When Moshe heard this, he
5 fell upon his face. Then he spoke to Koraḥ and all his
company. "In the morning," he said, "the Lord will make
known who is His and who is holy, and will bring that one
close to Him. The one He chooses will be the one He will
6 allow to come close. Do this: Let Koraḥ and his company
7 take censers. Tomorrow light fire in them and place
incense upon them before the Lord. The man whom the
Lord chooses – he is holy. It is you, sons of Levi, who
8 have gone too far!" Moshe said to Koraḥ, "Listen now,
9 you sons of Levi. Is it not enough for you that the God
of Israel has separated you from the Israelite community,
enabling you to come close to Him, to serve in the Lord's
Tabernacle, and stand in the presence of the community
10 to minister to them? He has brought you, and with you all
your fellow Levites, to be close to Him, and yet you seek
11 the priesthood also? And so you and all your company

---

power – they are not good men – but in one basic thing they are correct: all the congregation is holy, every one of them, and the Lord is in their midst.

16:4 וַיִּפֹּל עַל־פָּנָיו *He fell upon his face* – Moshe's first response is to fall facedown. Rashi says this was in near despair. Moshe had already prayed to God to forgive the people three times. He did not know how he could succeed a fourth time. Rashbam says he fell in prayer. Saadia Gaon and Ibn Ezra say he did so to receive prophetic guidance from God. Immediately after, in any case, he stands, composed.

16:5 בֹּקֶר *In the morning* – By deferring the test to the next day, Moshe is giving Koraḥ and his followers a chance to think again and back down. By choosing the test he does, he is warning the rebels of the risk they are taking. The people still vividly recall what had happened to Aharon's two sons, Nadav and Avihu, when they offered up incense and fire that "He had not commanded" (Lev. 10:1–2): they died. Once Moshe has proposed this test, Koraḥ and his fellows know that they are risking their lives.

16:10 וּבִקַּשְׁתֶּם גַּם־כְּהֻנָּה *Yet you seek the priesthood also* – Moshe speaks to Koraḥ directly. He knows that not all the rebels share the same discontent. He knows also that their apparent egalitarianism – "all the community is holy" (Num. 16:3) – is a veneer for personal ambition: Koraḥ wants Aharon's position as High Priest. Koraḥ is Moshe and Aharon's cousin and feels that the second leadership role, the high priesthood, should have gone to him. Moshe now reasons

ד תִּתְנַשְּׂאוּ עַל־קְהַל יְהוָה: וַיִּשְׁמַע מֹשֶׁה וַיִּפֹּל עַל־פָּנָיו:
ה וַיְדַבֵּר אֶל־קֹרַח וְאֶל־כָּל־עֲדָתוֹ לֵאמֹר בֹּקֶר וְיֹדַע יְהוָה
אֶת־אֲשֶׁר־לוֹ וְאֶת־הַקָּדוֹשׁ וְהִקְרִיב אֵלָיו וְאֵת אֲשֶׁר יִבְחַר־בּוֹ
ו יַקְרִיב אֵלָיו: זֹאת עֲשׂוּ קְחוּ־לָכֶם מַחְתּוֹת קֹרַח וְכָל־עֲדָתוֹ:
ז וּתְנוּ־בָהֵן ׀ אֵשׁ וְשִׂימוּ עֲלֵיהֶן ׀ קְטֹרֶת לִפְנֵי יְהוָה מָחָר
וְהָיָה הָאִישׁ אֲשֶׁר־יִבְחַר יְהוָה הוּא הַקָּדוֹשׁ רַב־לָכֶם בְּנֵי
ח ט לֵוִי: וַיֹּאמֶר מֹשֶׁה אֶל־קֹרַח שִׁמְעוּ־נָא בְּנֵי לֵוִי: הַמְעַט מִכֶּם
כִּי־הִבְדִּיל אֱלֹהֵי יִשְׂרָאֵל אֶתְכֶם מֵעֲדַת יִשְׂרָאֵל לְהַקְרִיב
אֶתְכֶם אֵלָיו לַעֲבֹד אֶת־עֲבֹדַת מִשְׁכַּן יְהוָה וְלַעֲמֹד לִפְנֵי
י הָעֵדָה לְשָׁרְתָם: וַיַּקְרֵב אֹתְךָ וְאֶת־כָּל־אַחֶיךָ בְנֵי־לֵוִי אִתָּךְ
יא וּבִקַּשְׁתֶּם גַּם־כְּהֻנָּה: לָכֵן אַתָּה וְכָל־עֲדָתְךָ הַנֹּעָדִים עַל־

---

as holy, was fairer than the system that replaced it. In transferring priestly functions to a single tribe, Moshe was in danger of creating a dynastic elite set apart from the rest of the population.

Yeshayahu Leibowitz argued for a different interpretation. Koraḥ said, "All the community *is* holy." He was basing himself on Moshe's own words in the command of tzitzit, "This is to remind you to keep all My commands, to *remain* holy to your God" (Num. 15:40). One is a statement of fact, the other is a command. Koraḥ was confusing the two.

A third possibility is that Koraḥ made the mistake of thinking that what applies to a community as a whole applies to each of its members. In Judaism, holiness is primarily collective, not individual. The community is holy, but that does not mean that everyone within it has the same level of holiness.

On each of these three interpretations, Koraḥ's core claim is wrong. I would argue, however, that Koraḥ's mistake lies not in saying that all members of the congregation are holy. Rather, it lies in his assertions – first that a group of people of equal dignity do not need a leader; second, that leaders "set themselves above" those they lead; and third, that there was no need to change the structures of holiness after the sin of the golden calf.

A profound egalitarian impulse exists at the heart of Judaism. It is grounded in the first chapter of the Torah, where God created human beings in His image and likeness. The Sages (Sanhedrin 4:5) derive from this first that we are each of infinite value: "an entire world." We each have the same ancestry; we are all children of Adam and Ḥava. No one is entitled to say, "My ancestors were greater than yours." Koraḥ and his fellow rebels, then, are wrong in their attempt to seize

have assembled to defy the Lord. Aharon – who is he
12 that you should have grievances against him?" After this,
Moshe sent for Datan and Aviram, sons of Eliav. But they
13 said, "We will not come up. Is it not enough that you
have brought us out of a land flowing with milk and with
honey to kill us in the desert, that you insist on lording
14 it over us? And more: you have not brought us to a land SHENI
flowing with milk and with honey, nor have you given
us an inheritance of cropland and vineyard. Would you
pull out these people's eyes?! We will not come up!"
15 Moshe became very angry and said to the Lord, "Pay
no attention to their offering. I have not taken a single
donkey from them, nor have I wronged any one of them."

---

she was struck with leprosy for speaking badly about him. It is an extraordinary thing to pray to God *not* to accept someone's offering. Sforno (on Num. 16:15) explains his behavior by saying that there is a rule that offenses against other people are atoned for only when they have forgiven you. "I," Moshe is saying to God, "refuse to forgive them."

16:15 לֹא חֲמוֹר אֶחָד מֵהֶם נָשָׂאתִי *I have not taken a single donkey from them* – Jewish tradition focuses on this specific moment in the Koraḥ story, by pairing this *parasha* with a *haftara* taken from the book of Samuel, in which the prophet, having anointed Sha'ul as king, says to the people: "Here I am. Testify against me in front of the Lord and in front of His anointed. Whose ox have I seized, and whose donkey have I seized? Whom have I cheated, and whom have I oppressed, and from whose hand have I taken a bribe and averted my eyes from him? Let me repay you" (I Sam. 12:3). Shmuel is experiencing the same emotion as Moshe: the shame and humiliation of feeling accused of something he did not do, after a lifetime of self-sacrificing service to others.

Koraḥ's rebellion is bound up in issues that are real and substantive. There are the repercussions of the sin of the golden calf. There was the crushing sense of loss after the episode of the spies. At such moments, a leader will be attacked and blamed personally. He will bear the brunt of people's anger. Moshe surely takes the right course of action in proposing the test of the incense offering. That will resolve the question of the priesthood. As for the resentments of the rebels, however, there is nothing Moshe can do.

Of all the challenges of leadership, not taking criticism personally and staying calm when the people you lead are angry with you may be the hardest of all. Depersonalizing attacks is the best way to deal with them. People get angry

יב יְהוָה וְאַהֲרֹן מַה־הוּא כִּי תלונו עָלָיו׃ וַיִּשְׁלַח מֹשֶׁה לִקְרֹא תַּלִּינוּ
יג לְדָתָן וְלַאֲבִירָם בְּנֵי אֱלִיאָב וַיֹּאמְרוּ לֹא נַעֲלֶה׃ הַמְעַט
כִּי הֶעֱלִיתָנוּ מֵאֶרֶץ זָבַת חָלָב וּדְבַשׁ לַהֲמִיתֵנוּ בַּמִּדְבָּר
יד כִּי־תִשְׂתָּרֵר עָלֵינוּ גַּם־הִשְׂתָּרֵר׃ אַף לֹא אֶל־אֶרֶץ זָבַת שני
חָלָב וּדְבַשׁ הֲבִיאֹתָנוּ וַתִּתֶּן־לָנוּ נַחֲלַת שָׂדֶה וָכָרֶם הַעֵינֵי
טו הָאֲנָשִׁים הָהֵם תְּנַקֵּר לֹא נַעֲלֶה׃ וַיִּחַר לְמֹשֶׁה מְאֹד וַיֹּאמֶר
אֶל־יְהוָה אַל־תֵּפֶן אֶל־מִנְחָתָם לֹא חֲמוֹר אֶחָד מֵהֶם

---

with him firmly: "Is it not enough for you that the God of Israel has separated you from the Israelite community?... He has brought you, and with you all your fellow Levites, to be close to Him, and yet you seek the priesthood also?" (Num. 16:9–10).

16:13 מֵאֶרֶץ זָבַת חָלָב וּדְבַשׁ *Out of a land flowing with milk and with honey* – Koraḥ has made classic populist claims. The establishment, represented by Moshe and Aharon, is corrupt. Moshe has kept the leadership roles within his immediate family instead of sharing them out more widely. Koraḥ has presented himself as the people's champion. The whole community, he says, is holy. There is nothing special about you, Moshe and Aharon. We have all seen God's miracles and heard His voice. We all helped build His Sanctuary. Koraḥ poses as the democrat – so that he can become the autocrat.

Next, he and his fellow rebels have mounted an impressive campaign of fake news. We have to infer this indirectly. When Moshe says to God, "I have not taken a single donkey from them, nor have I wronged any one of them" (Num. 16:15), it is clear that he has been accused of just that: exploiting his office for personal gain. When he says, "By this you will know that the Lord sent me to do these deeds; it was not my idea" (Num. 16:28), it is equally clear that he has been accused of presenting his own decisions as the will and word of God.

Most blatant, however, is the manipulative claim of Datan and Aviram: "Is it not enough that you have brought us out of a land flowing with milk and with honey to kill us in the desert, that you insist on lording it over us?" (Num. 16:13). This is the most tendentious speech in the Torah. It combines false nostalgia for Egypt as a "land flowing with milk and with honey," replacing their slavery there with the image of God's promised plenty for them in the Holy Land, blaming Moshe for the report of the spies, and accusing him of holding on to leadership for his own personal prestige. All three are outrageous lies.

16:15 אַל־תֵּפֶן אֶל־מִנְחָתָם *Pay no attention to their offering* – Moshe, as Israel's leader, had always prayed on behalf of the people, even for his sister Miriam when

16 Moshe said to Koraḥ, "You and your entire company
shall appear before the LORD tomorrow: you, they, and
17 Aharon. Each one shall take his censer, place incense
upon it, and present it before the LORD, each holding
his censer, two hundred fifty censers in all, and you and
18 Aharon likewise with yours." Each took his censer, placed
fire in it, put incense upon it, and stood at the entrance
19 to the Tent of Meeting, as did Moshe and Aharon. Koraḥ
gathered all his company against them to the entrance
to the Tent of Meeting. Then the glory of the LORD was
20 revealed to the entire community. The LORD SHELISHI
21 spoke to Moshe and Aharon: "Separate yourselves from
this community and let Me consume them in a moment."
22 They fell on their faces and said, "God, the God of the
spirit of all flesh, if one man sins, will You rage against the
23 entire community?" The LORD spoke to Moshe:
24 "Tell the community to move away from the dwellings

---

a conversation, scored for a multiplicity of voices. Koraḥ, who challenged Moshe and Aharon for leadership, was arguing for the sake not of truth, but of victory; he wanted to be a leader too.

In an argument for the sake of truth, if you win, you win, but if you lose, you also win, because being defeated by the truth is the only defeat that is also a victory. We are enlarged thereby. As R. Shimon HaAmsoni said: "Just as I received reward for the exposition, so I will receive reward for the retraction" (Kiddushin 57a). In an argument for the sake of victory, if you lose, you lose, but if you win, you also lose, for by diminishing your opponents, you diminish yourself.

The concept of "argument for the sake of Heaven" allowed the Sages to reframe disagreement as a unifying, not just a divisive, force. That is implicit in the radical idea that each of two opposing opinions can represent "the words of the living God" (Eiruvin 13b).

A free society depends on the dignity of dissent. We see it in rabbinic dialogues between Hillel and Shammai and their descendants. Dismiss a contrary view and you impoverish the entire culture. Knowing this does not stop politics from being abrasive, sometimes brutal. But it does mean that people recognize the humanity of their opponents, listen to them, and realize that other viewpoints have integrity. Great leaders seek not power but truth, not victory but healing. Koraḥ, as the antithesis of this approach, forever represents for Judaism the danger of "arguments not for the sake of Heaven."

טז נָשָׂאתִי וְלֹא הֲרֵעֹתִי אֶת־אַחַד מֵהֶם: וַיֹּאמֶר מֹשֶׁה אֶל־קֹרַח
אַתָּה וְכָל־עֲדָתְךָ הֱיוּ לִפְנֵי יהוה אַתָּה וָהֵם וְאַהֲרֹן מָחָר:
יז וּקְחוּ ׀ אִישׁ מַחְתָּתוֹ וּנְתַתֶּם עֲלֵיהֶם קְטֹרֶת וְהִקְרַבְתֶּם
לִפְנֵי יהוה אִישׁ מַחְתָּתוֹ חֲמִשִּׁים וּמָאתַיִם מַחְתֹּת וְאַתָּה
יח וְאַהֲרֹן אִישׁ מַחְתָּתוֹ: וַיִּקְחוּ אִישׁ מַחְתָּתוֹ וַיִּתְּנוּ עֲלֵיהֶם
אֵשׁ וַיָּשִׂימוּ עֲלֵיהֶם קְטֹרֶת וַיַּעַמְדוּ פֶּתַח אֹהֶל מוֹעֵד וּמֹשֶׁה
יט וְאַהֲרֹן: וַיַּקְהֵל עֲלֵיהֶם קֹרַח אֶת־כָּל־הָעֵדָה אֶל־פֶּתַח אֹהֶל
כ מוֹעֵד וַיֵּרָא כְבוֹד־יהוה אֶל־כָּל־הָעֵדָה: וַיְדַבֵּר שלישי
כא יהוה אֶל־מֹשֶׁה וְאֶל־אַהֲרֹן לֵאמֹר: הִבָּדְלוּ מִתּוֹךְ הָעֵדָה
כב הַזֹּאת וַאֲכַלֶּה אֹתָם כְּרָגַע: וַיִּפְּלוּ עַל־פְּנֵיהֶם וַיֹּאמְרוּ אֵל
אֱלֹהֵי הָרוּחֹת לְכָל־בָּשָׂר הָאִישׁ אֶחָד יֶחֱטָא וְעַל כָּל־הָעֵדָה
כג כד תִּקְצֹף: וַיְדַבֵּר יהוה אֶל־מֹשֶׁה לֵּאמֹר: דַּבֵּר
אֶל־הָעֵדָה לֵאמֹר הֵעָלוּ מִסָּבִיב לְמִשְׁכַּן־קֹרַח דָּתָן וַאֲבִירָם:

when leaders cannot magically make harsh realities disappear. Leaders in such circumstances are called on to accept that anger with grace.

THE NATURE OF THE ARGUMENT

It is striking how the Sages framed the conflict with Koraḥ. They insisted on the validity of argument in the public domain. They said that what was wrong with Koraḥ and his fellows was not the fact that they argued with Moshe and Aharon, or even the content of their claims, but rather the nature of their dispute:

> Every argument for the sake of Heaven will in the end be of permanent value, but every argument not for the sake of Heaven will not endure. Which is an argument for the sake of Heaven? The argument between Hillel and Shammai. Which is an argument not for the sake of Heaven? The argument of Koraḥ and his company. (Avot 5:17)

Meiri (*Beit HaBeḥira* ad loc.) and other medieval commentators understood the Sages to be distinguishing here between an argument for the sake of *truth* and one for the sake of *victory*. The Sages Hillel and Shammai argued for the sake of truth, the determination of God's will. The school of Hillel knew that more than one interpretation can be given. They studied the views of their opponents alongside, and even before, their own. They were "kindly and modest" (Eiruvin 13b) because they realized that truth is not an all-or-nothing affair. It is

25 of Koraḥ, Datan, and Aviram." Moshe rose and went to
26 Datan and Aviram. Israel's elders followed him. He spoke
to the community, saying: "Turn away now from the tents
of these wicked men. Do not touch anything of theirs, lest
27 you be swept away for all their sins." So they moved away
from around the dwellings of Koraḥ, Datan, and Aviram.
Datan and Aviram came out and stood at the openings of
28 their tents with their wives, children, and infants. Moshe
said, "By this you will know that the LORD sent me to do
29 these deeds; it was not my idea. If all these men die as
others do, and share the common fate of all humanity,
30 then the LORD has not sent me. But if the LORD creates
something entirely new, so that the ground opens its
mouth and swallows them and all they have, and they go
down alive to Sheol, then you will know that these men
31 have provoked the LORD." As soon as he had finished
speaking these words, the ground beneath them split
32 open. The earth opened its mouth and swallowed them
and their households, with all the people who pertained
33 to Koraḥ and all their possessions – they and all that was
theirs descended alive to Sheol – the earth closed over
them – and they perished from the midst of the assembly.
34 At their cry, all the Israelites around them fled, for they
35 said, "The earth could swallow us." And fire came forth
from the LORD and consumed the two hundred fifty men
17 1 who were offering incense. Then the LORD spoke
2 to Moshe: "Tell Elazar son of Aharon the priest to remove
the censers from the fire, for they have become holy. Scatter
3 the burning coals far and wide. And the censers of those
who committed a mortal sin – make them into hammered
plates as a covering for the altar. Having been offered
before the LORD, they have become holy. And they will be

all miraculous events which involve temporary suspension of natural or scientific law. The Mishna teaches that these events were programmed into nature at the outset. In general, Judaism emphasizes the law-like structure of the physical universe, as it says in Ecclesiastes, "There is nothing new beneath the sun" (1:9).

כה וַיָּ֣קָם מֹשֶׁ֔ה וַיֵּ֖לֶךְ אֶל־דָּתָ֣ן וַאֲבִירָ֑ם וַיֵּלְכ֥וּ אַחֲרָ֖יו זִקְנֵ֥י יִשְׂרָאֵֽל׃
כו וַיְדַבֵּ֨ר אֶל־הָעֵדָ֜ה לֵאמֹ֗ר ס֣וּרוּ נָ֡א מֵעַל֩ אָהֳלֵ֨י הָאֲנָשִׁ֤ים
הָֽרְשָׁעִים֙ הָאֵ֔לֶּה וְאַֽל־תִּגְּע֖וּ בְּכָל־אֲשֶׁ֣ר לָהֶ֑ם פֶּן־תִּסָּפ֖וּ בְּכָל־
כז חַטֹּאתָֽם׃ וַיֵּעָל֗וּ מֵעַ֧ל מִשְׁכַּן־קֹ֛רַח דָּתָ֥ן וַאֲבִירָ֖ם מִסָּבִ֑יב וְדָתָ֨ן
וַאֲבִירָ֜ם יָצְא֣וּ נִצָּבִ֗ים פֶּ֚תַח אָהֳלֵיהֶ֔ם וּנְשֵׁיהֶ֥ם וּבְנֵיהֶ֖ם וְטַפָּֽם׃
כח וַיֹּאמֶר֮ מֹשֶׁה֒ בְּזֹאת֙ תֵּֽדְע֔וּן כִּֽי־יְהוָ֣ה שְׁלָחַ֔נִי לַעֲשׂ֕וֹת אֵ֥ת כָּל־
כט הַֽמַּעֲשִׂ֖ים הָאֵ֑לֶּה כִּי־לֹ֖א מִלִּבִּֽי׃ אִם־כְּמ֤וֹת כָּל־הָֽאָדָם֙ יְמֻת֣וּן
אֵ֔לֶּה וּפְקֻדַּת֙ כָּל־הָ֣אָדָ֔ם יִפָּקֵ֖ד עֲלֵיהֶ֑ם לֹ֥א יְהוָ֖ה שְׁלָחָֽנִי׃
ל וְאִם־בְּרִיאָ֞ה יִבְרָ֣א יְהוָ֗ה וּפָצְתָ֨ה הָאֲדָמָ֤ה אֶת־פִּ֙יהָ֙ וּבָלְעָ֤ה
אֹתָם֙ וְאֶת־כָּל־אֲשֶׁ֣ר לָהֶ֔ם וְיָרְד֥וּ חַיִּ֖ים שְׁאֹ֑לָה וִידַעְתֶּ֕ם
לא כִּ֧י נִֽאֲצ֛וּ הָאֲנָשִׁ֥ים הָאֵ֖לֶּה אֶת־יְהוָֽה׃ וַיְהִי֙ כְּכַלֹּת֔וֹ לְדַבֵּ֕ר
אֵ֥ת כָּל־הַדְּבָרִ֖ים הָאֵ֑לֶּה וַתִּבָּקַ֥ע הָאֲדָמָ֖ה אֲשֶׁ֥ר תַּחְתֵּיהֶֽם׃
לב וַתִּפְתַּ֤ח הָאָ֙רֶץ֙ אֶת־פִּ֔יהָ וַתִּבְלַ֥ע אֹתָ֖ם וְאֶת־בָּתֵּיהֶ֑ם וְאֵ֤ת
לג כָּל־הָֽאָדָם֙ אֲשֶׁ֣ר לְקֹ֔רַח וְאֵ֖ת כָּל־הָרְכֽוּשׁ׃ וַיֵּ֨רְד֜וּ הֵ֣ם וְכָל־
אֲשֶׁ֥ר לָהֶ֛ם חַיִּ֖ים שְׁאֹ֑לָה וַתְּכַ֤ס עֲלֵיהֶם֙ הָאָ֔רֶץ וַיֹּאבְד֖וּ מִתּ֥וֹךְ
לד הַקָּהָֽל׃ וְכָל־יִשְׂרָאֵ֗ל אֲשֶׁ֛ר סְבִיבֹתֵיהֶ֖ם נָ֣סוּ לְקֹלָ֑ם כִּ֣י אָֽמְר֔וּ
לה פֶּן־תִּבְלָעֵ֖נוּ הָאָֽרֶץ׃ וְאֵ֥שׁ יָצְאָ֖ה מֵאֵ֣ת יְהוָ֑ה וַתֹּ֗אכַל אֵ֣ת
יז א הַחֲמִשִּׁ֤ים וּמָאתַ֙יִם֙ אִ֔ישׁ מַקְרִיבֵ֖י הַקְּטֹֽרֶת׃ וַיְדַבֵּ֥ר
ב יְהוָ֖ה אֶל־מֹשֶׁ֥ה לֵּאמֹֽר׃ אֱמֹ֨ר אֶל־אֶלְעָזָ֜ר בֶּן־אַהֲרֹ֣ן הַכֹּהֵ֗ן
וְיָרֵ֤ם אֶת־הַמַּחְתֹּת֙ מִבֵּ֣ין הַשְּׂרֵפָ֔ה וְאֶת־הָאֵ֖שׁ זְרֵה־הָ֑לְאָה
ג כִּ֖י קָדֵֽשׁוּ׃ אֵ֡ת מַחְתּוֹת֩ הַֽחַטָּאִ֨ים הָאֵ֜לֶּה בְּנַפְשֹׁתָ֗ם וְעָשׂ֨וּ
אֹתָ֜ם רִקֻּעֵ֤י פַחִים֙ צִפּ֣וּי לַמִּזְבֵּ֔חַ כִּֽי־הִקְרִיבֻ֥ם לִפְנֵֽי־יְהוָ֖ה

16:32 וַתִּפְתַּח הָאָרֶץ אֶת־פִּיהָ *The earth opened its mouth* – "The mouth of the earth," which opens to swallow Koraḥ, is listed in the Mishna as one of the "ten things created on the eve of the Sabbath at sunset" (Avot 5:6). In the coming *parashot* we will encounter more of these, including "the mouth of [Miriam's] well," which accompanied the Israelites on their journey (a midrashic tradition – Taanit 9a – arising from the juxtaposition of Miriam's death and the people's thirst; Num. 20:1–4), and "the mouth of [Bilam's] donkey," which spoke (Num. 22:28). These are

4 a sign for the Israelites." Elazar the priest took the bronze
censers that the men consumed by fire had presented,
5 and hammered them into a covering for the altar, as the
Lord had said to him through Moshe – a reminder for
the Israelites that no outsider, no one not descended
from Aharon, should offer incense before the Lord, and
become like Koraḥ and his company.
6 The next day the entire Israelite community complained
to Moshe and Aharon, "You have killed the Lord's
7 people!" As the community assembled against Moshe
and Aharon, they turned toward the Tent of Meeting. A
cloud was covering it, and the glory of the Lord appeared.
8 Moshe and Aharon came to the front of the Tent of
9 10 Meeting. And the Lord spoke to Moshe: "Get REVI'I
away from this community; let Me consume them in
11 an instant." They fell on their faces, and Moshe said to
Aharon, "Take the censer, put fire from the altar into it,
place incense upon it, and go quickly to the community
and make atonement for them. Fury has come forth
12 from the Lord; the plague has begun." Aharon took it as
Moshe said and ran into the midst of the assembly, for the
plague had already begun among the people. He offered
13 incense and made atonement for the people; he stood
between the dead and the living, and the plague was
14 halted; 14,700 died from that plague, in addition to those

---

against Moshe and Aharon, yet the leaders' response is to rush to the people's defense. The voice of Heaven often speaks in the language of justice. The people have sinned and must be punished. But at the same time, God sends His prophets to speak in the people's defense. If the prophet adopts the perspective of justice and he too condemns the people, then he has betrayed his mission.

This will not be the last time that punishment takes the form of a plague. We remember this poignantly in the *Taḥanun* prayer as we quote words spoken by David during a moment of crisis (II Sam. 24:14). The king had sinned by taking a census of the people. God, through the prophet Gad, offered him a choice: famine, war, or punishment directly from Heaven. David replied: "I am in grave torment.... Let us fall into the hand of the Lord, for His mercy is great." God's punishment, even a deadly epidemic, is better than suffering the cruelty of man.

ד וַיִּקְדָּשׁוּ וְיִהְיוּ לְאוֹת לִבְנֵי יִשְׂרָאֵל: וַיִּקַּח אֶלְעָזָר הַכֹּהֵן
אֵת מַחְתּוֹת הַנְּחֹשֶׁת אֲשֶׁר הִקְרִיבוּ הַשְּׂרֻפִים וַיְרַקְּעוּם
ה צִפּוּי לַמִּזְבֵּחַ: זִכָּרוֹן לִבְנֵי יִשְׂרָאֵל לְמַעַן אֲשֶׁר לֹא־יִקְרַב
אִישׁ זָר אֲשֶׁר לֹא מִזֶּרַע אַהֲרֹן הוּא לְהַקְטִיר קְטֹרֶת לִפְנֵי
יהוה וְלֹא־יִהְיֶה כְקֹרַח וְכַעֲדָתוֹ כַּאֲשֶׁר דִּבֶּר יהוה בְּיַד־
מֹשֶׁה לוֹ:
ו וַיִּלֹּנוּ כָּל־עֲדַת בְּנֵי־יִשְׂרָאֵל מִמָּחֳרָת עַל־מֹשֶׁה וְעַל־אַהֲרֹן
ז לֵאמֹר אַתֶּם הֲמִתֶּם אֶת־עַם יהוה: וַיְהִי בְּהִקָּהֵל הָעֵדָה
עַל־מֹשֶׁה וְעַל־אַהֲרֹן וַיִּפְנוּ אֶל־אֹהֶל מוֹעֵד וְהִנֵּה כִסָּהוּ
ח הֶעָנָן וַיֵּרָא כְּבוֹד יהוה: וַיָּבֹא מֹשֶׁה וְאַהֲרֹן אֶל־פְּנֵי אֹהֶל
ט י מוֹעֵד: וַיְדַבֵּר יהוה אֶל־מֹשֶׁה לֵּאמֹר: הֵרֹמּוּ רביעי
מִתּוֹךְ הָעֵדָה הַזֹּאת וַאֲכַלֶּה אֹתָם כְּרָגַע וַיִּפְּלוּ עַל־פְּנֵיהֶם:
יא וַיֹּאמֶר מֹשֶׁה אֶל־אַהֲרֹן קַח אֶת־הַמַּחְתָּה וְתֶן־עָלֶיהָ אֵשׁ
מֵעַל הַמִּזְבֵּחַ וְשִׂים קְטֹרֶת וְהוֹלֵךְ מְהֵרָה אֶל־הָעֵדָה וְכַפֵּר
יב עֲלֵיהֶם כִּי־יָצָא הַקֶּצֶף מִלִּפְנֵי יהוה הֵחֵל הַנָּגֶף: וַיִּקַּח אַהֲרֹן
כַּאֲשֶׁר ׀ דִּבֶּר מֹשֶׁה וַיָּרָץ אֶל־תּוֹךְ הַקָּהָל וְהִנֵּה הֵחֵל הַנֶּגֶף
יג בָּעָם וַיִּתֵּן אֶת־הַקְּטֹרֶת וַיְכַפֵּר עַל־הָעָם: וַיַּעֲמֹד בֵּין־הַמֵּתִים
יד וּבֵין הַחַיִּים וַתֵּעָצַר הַמַּגֵּפָה: וַיִּהְיוּ הַמֵּתִים בַּמַּגֵּפָה אַרְבָּעָה
עָשָׂר אֶלֶף וּשְׁבַע מֵאוֹת מִלְּבַד הַמֵּתִים עַל־דְּבַר־קֹרַח:

17:6 אַתֶּם הֲמִתֶּם אֶת־עַם יהוה *You have killed the LORD's people* – No sooner has Moshe finished than "the ground beneath them split open. The earth opened its mouth and swallowed them" (Num. 16:31–32). One cannot imagine a more dramatic vindication. God has shown, beyond possibility of doubt, that Moshe is right and the rebels wrong. Yet far from being apologetic and repentant, the people return the next morning still complaining – this time, not about who should lead whom but about the way Moshe has chosen to end the dispute: "The next day the entire Israelite community complained to Moshe and Aharon, 'You have killed the LORD's people'" (17:6). You may be right, they imply, and Koraḥ may have been wrong. But is this a way to win an argument?

17:11 וְהוֹלֵךְ מְהֵרָה... הֵחֵל הַנָּגֶף *Go quickly.... The plague has begun* – The plague is a punishment for the people's rebellion

15 who died on account of Koraḥ. And Aharon returned to
Moshe at the entrance to the Tent of Meeting – for the
plague had stopped.
16 17 Then the LORD spoke to Moshe: "Speak to the Israelites HAMISHI
and take from them twelve staffs, one for each ancestral
house, from all the leaders of their ancestral houses. Write
18 each man's name on his staff, and on Levi's staff write
Aharon's name, for there shall be one staff for the head of
19 each ancestral house. Place them in the Tent of Meeting
in front of the Ark of the Covenant, where I meet with
20 you. The staff of the man I choose – that will give flower.
Thus I will rid Myself of the incessant railings of the
21 Israelites against you." Moshe spoke to the Israelites,
and each of their leaders gave him a staff, one for each
leader, according to their ancestral houses, twelve staffs
22 with Aharon's staff among them. Moshe placed the staffs
23 before the LORD in the Tent of the Testimony. And the
following day Moshe entered the Tent of the Testimony,
and Aharon's staff, representing the House of Levi, had
given flower. It had budded, produced blossoms, and was
24 now bearing almonds. Moshe brought out all the staffs

---

miracle that swallowed up Koraḥ and his fellow rebels. Yet it does not end the conflict. It deepens it.

What ends it is the quiet, gentle miracle that shows that Aharon is the true emissary of the God of life. Not by accident is the verse that calls Torah a "tree of life" preceded by these words: "Its ways are the ways of pleasantness, and all of its paths are peaceful" (Prov. 3:17). This is the preferred form of conflict resolution in Judaism – not by force, but by pleasantness and peace.

17:23 וַיִּגְמֹל שְׁקֵדִים *Bearing almonds* – In the Near East, the almond is the first tree to blossom, its white flowers signaling the end of winter and the emergence of new life. The almond flowers also recall the gold flowers on the candelabrum (menora), lit daily by Aharon in the Sanctuary (Ex. 25:31, 37:17). The Hebrew word *tzitz*, used here to mean "blossom," recalls the *tzitz*, the headplate of pure gold worn as part of Aharon's headdress, on which were inscribed the words "Holy to the LORD" (28:36). The sprouting almond branch is therefore more than a sign. It is a multifaceted symbol of life, light, holiness, and the watchful presence of God.

After the episode of the spies, Moshe

טו וַיָּשָׁב אַהֲרֹן אֶל־מֹשֶׁה אֶל־פֶּתַח אֹהֶל מוֹעֵד וְהַמַּגֵּפָה
נֶעֱצָרָה׃
טז יז וַיְדַבֵּר יְהוָה אֶל־מֹשֶׁה לֵּאמֹר׃ דַּבֵּר ׀ אֶל־בְּנֵי יִשְׂרָאֵל וְקַח טז חמישי
מֵאִתָּם מַטֶּה מַטֶּה לְבֵית אָב מֵאֵת כָּל־נְשִׂיאֵהֶם לְבֵית
אֲבֹתָם שְׁנֵים עָשָׂר מַטּוֹת אִישׁ אֶת־שְׁמוֹ תִּכְתֹּב עַל־מַטֵּהוּ׃
יח וְאֵת שֵׁם אַהֲרֹן תִּכְתֹּב עַל־מַטֵּה לֵוִי כִּי מַטֶּה אֶחָד לְרֹאשׁ
יט בֵּית אֲבוֹתָם׃ וְהִנַּחְתָּם בְּאֹהֶל מוֹעֵד לִפְנֵי הָעֵדוּת אֲשֶׁר
כ אִוָּעֵד לָכֶם שָׁמָּה׃ וְהָיָה הָאִישׁ אֲשֶׁר אֶבְחַר־בּוֹ מַטֵּהוּ
יִפְרָח וַהֲשִׁכֹּתִי מֵעָלַי אֶת־תְּלֻנּוֹת בְּנֵי יִשְׂרָאֵל אֲשֶׁר הֵם
כא מַלִּינִם עֲלֵיכֶם׃ וַיְדַבֵּר מֹשֶׁה אֶל־בְּנֵי יִשְׂרָאֵל וַיִּתְּנוּ אֵלָיו ׀
כָּל־נְשִׂיאֵיהֶם מַטֶּה לְנָשִׂיא אֶחָד מַטֶּה לְנָשִׂיא אֶחָד לְבֵית
כב אֲבֹתָם שְׁנֵים עָשָׂר מַטּוֹת וּמַטֵּה אַהֲרֹן בְּתוֹךְ מַטּוֹתָם׃ וַיַּנַּח
כג מֹשֶׁה אֶת־הַמַּטֹּת לִפְנֵי יְהוָה בְּאֹהֶל הָעֵדֻת׃ וַיְהִי מִמָּחֳרָת
וַיָּבֹא מֹשֶׁה אֶל־אֹהֶל הָעֵדוּת וְהִנֵּה פָּרַח מַטֵּה־אַהֲרֹן לְבֵית
כד לֵוִי וַיֹּצֵא פֶרַח וַיָּצֵץ צִיץ וַיִּגְמֹל שְׁקֵדִים׃ וַיֹּצֵא מֹשֶׁה אֶת־כָּל־

THE SIGN OF THE STAFFS

The use of force never ends a conflict. It merely adds grievance to injury. What ends this conflict is not the miracle of the ground opening up and swallowing Moshe's opponents, but something else altogether: the visible symbol that Aharon is the chosen vehicle of the God of life. The gentle miracle of the dead wood that comes to life again, flowering and bearing fruit, anticipates the famous words of the book of Proverbs about the Torah: "It is a tree of life for those who grasp it; those who hold fast to it are fortunate" (3:18). Moshe and Aharon stand accused of failing in their mission. They have brought the people out of Egypt to bring them to the land of Israel. After the debacle of the spies, that hope has died. The stick that comes to life again (like Yeḥezkel's vision of the valley of dry bones, Ezek. 37) symbolizes that hope is not dead, merely deferred. The next generation will live and reach the destination. God is a God of life. What He touches does not die.

The episode of Koraḥ teaches us that there are two ways of resolving conflict: by force and by persuasion. The first negates your opponent. The second enlists your opponent, taking his or her challenge seriously and addressing it. Force never ends conflict – not even in the case of Moshe, not even when the force is miraculous. There never was a more decisive intervention than the

from before the LORD to all the Israelites. They saw. And
each man took back his staff.
25 Then the LORD said to Moshe, "Put back Aharon's staff SHISHI
in front of the Ark of the Covenant to serve as a sign to
rebels so that their railings against Me end, and they will
26 not die." Moshe did so. As the LORD commanded him,
so he did.
27 The Israelites said to Moshe, "We are going to die. We are
28 lost; all of us are lost. Whoever approaches the LORD's
18 1 Tabernacle is to die. Will we die out completely?" The
LORD said to Aharon: "You, your sons, and your ancestral
house shall bear any guilt connected with the Sanctuary,
and you and your sons will bear any guilt connected with
2 your priesthood. Bring with you also your brothers from
the tribe of Levi, your father's tribe. Let them join you
and minister to you and your sons before the Tent of the
3 Testimony. They shall discharge their duties to you and to
the Tent as a whole, but they must not draw close to the
utensils of the Sanctuary or the altar, or both they and you
4 will die. They will join you in discharging the duties of
the Tent of Meeting for all the service of the Tent; no
5 outsider shall draw near you. You shall discharge the
duties of the Sanctuary and the altar, so that fury may
6 never again fall upon the Israelites. I have singled out
your brothers, the Levites, from among the Israelites as a

---

the Levitical status became "a gift" for the tribe who were not involved in the sin. Monarchy was introduced only after the breakdown of law and order in the last days of the judges (I Sam. 8). Despite the fact that the Torah contains a command to appoint a king, still God said that in seeking a king the people had "rejected" Him (v. 7). It can be argued that neither monarchy nor the special status of the tribe of Levi and the family of Aharon were part of the original plan. They were responses to human weakness and failure.

Only thus can we understand the direction taken by Judaism after the destruction of the Second Temple. What emerged from this period was, by historical standards, an extraordinarily egalitarian structure, based not on kings and priests but on Torah study and the dignity of *knesset Yisrael*, the congregation of Israel as a whole. In place of sacrifices offered by priests came prayer

הַמַּטֹּת מִלִּפְנֵי יְהוָה אֶל־כָּל־בְּנֵי יִשְׂרָאֵל וַיִּרְאוּ וַיִּקְחוּ אִישׁ
מַטֵּהוּ׃
כה וַיֹּאמֶר יְהוָה אֶל־מֹשֶׁה הָשֵׁב אֶת־מַטֵּה אַהֲרֹן לִפְנֵי הָעֵדוּת ששי
לְמִשְׁמֶרֶת לְאוֹת לִבְנֵי־מֶרִי וּתְכַל תְּלוּנֹּתָם מֵעָלַי וְלֹא יָמֻתוּ׃
כו וַיַּעַשׂ מֹשֶׁה כַּאֲשֶׁר צִוָּה יְהוָה אֹתוֹ כֵּן עָשָׂה׃
כז וַיֹּאמְרוּ בְּנֵי יִשְׂרָאֵל אֶל־מֹשֶׁה לֵאמֹר הֵן גָּוַעְנוּ אָבַדְנוּ כֻּלָּנוּ
כח אָבָדְנוּ׃ כֹּל הַקָּרֵב ׀ הַקָּרֵב אֶל־מִשְׁכַּן יְהוָה יָמוּת הַאִם
יח א תַּמְנוּ לִגְוֺעַ׃ וַיֹּאמֶר יְהוָה אֶל־אַהֲרֹן אַתָּה וּבָנֶיךָ
וּבֵית־אָבִיךָ אִתָּךְ תִּשְׂאוּ אֶת־עֲוֺן הַמִּקְדָּשׁ וְאַתָּה וּבָנֶיךָ אִתָּךְ
ב תִּשְׂאוּ אֶת־עֲוֺן כְּהֻנַּתְכֶם׃ וְגַם אֶת־אַחֶיךָ מַטֵּה לֵוִי שֵׁבֶט
אָבִיךָ הַקְרֵב אִתָּךְ וְיִלָּווּ עָלֶיךָ וִישָׁרְתוּךָ וְאַתָּה וּבָנֶיךָ אִתָּךְ
ג לִפְנֵי אֹהֶל הָעֵדֻת׃ וְשָׁמְרוּ מִשְׁמַרְתְּךָ וּמִשְׁמֶרֶת כָּל־הָאֹהֶל
אַךְ אֶל־כְּלֵי הַקֹּדֶשׁ וְאֶל־הַמִּזְבֵּחַ לֹא יִקְרָבוּ וְלֹא־יָמֻתוּ
ד גַם־הֵם גַּם־אַתֶּם׃ וְנִלְווּ עָלֶיךָ וְשָׁמְרוּ אֶת־מִשְׁמֶרֶת אֹהֶל
ה מוֹעֵד לְכֹל עֲבֹדַת הָאֹהֶל וְזָר לֹא־יִקְרַב אֲלֵיכֶם׃ וּשְׁמַרְתֶּם
אֵת מִשְׁמֶרֶת הַקֹּדֶשׁ וְאֵת מִשְׁמֶרֶת הַמִּזְבֵּחַ וְלֹא־יִהְיֶה עוֹד
ו קֶצֶף עַל־בְּנֵי יִשְׂרָאֵל׃ וַאֲנִי הִנֵּה לָקַחְתִּי אֶת־אֲחֵיכֶם הַלְוִיִּם

---

faces an almost impossible task. How do you lead a people when they know they will not reach their destination in their lifetime? In the end, what stills the rebellion is the sight of Aharon's staff, a piece of dry wood coming to life again, bearing flowers and fruit. Having thought of themselves as condemned to die in the desert, they now realize that they too have borne fruit – their children – and that those children will complete the journey their parents began.

18:6 הִנֵּה לָקַחְתִּי אֶת־אֲחֵיכֶם הַלְוִיִּם *I have singled out your brothers* – Stepping back from the Koraḥ revolt and looking at Tanakh and Jewish history as a whole, we see that hierarchy was introduced into Judaism only in response to crisis. The restriction of priesthood to the sons of Aharon, and of secondary holiness to the Levites, only happened according to the Torah because of the sin of the golden calf. Had that not happened, sacred duties would have stayed the prerogative of the firstborn of all the tribes. The event highlighted the need for a new arrangement of sacred and profane, and

▶

gift to you, dedicated to the LORD to perform the service
7 of the Tent of Meeting. You and your sons shall take care
to perform the duties of your priesthood in all matters
pertaining to the altar and inside the curtain. I give you
your priestly service as a gift, but any outsider who draws
close will die."
8 The LORD spoke to Aharon: "I place in your charge the
offerings made to Me, all the sacred gifts of the Israelites. I
give them to you and your sons as an anointed right; this is
9 an everlasting decree. This is what belongs to you among
the holiest offerings, from the fire: all their offerings, their
grain offerings, their purification offerings, and their guilt
offerings. The holiest offerings that they bring to Me will
10 be yours and your sons'. You shall eat them in the way of
the holiest things. All your males may eat it; it is holy to
11 you. This too will be yours: as an everlasting statute I give
the upraised gifts of all the Israelites' wave offerings to
you, together with your sons and daughters. Anyone who
12 is ritually pure in your household may eat of them. All
the best of the oil, wine, and grain, the choice produce
13 that they give to the LORD, I give to you. The first fruits
of all that is in their land that they bring to the LORD will
be yours. Anyone who is pure in your household may eat
14 15 it. Everything that is set aside in Israel shall be yours. All
the first to emerge from the womb of any creature, human
or animal, that is offered to the LORD shall be yours. You
must, however, redeem firstborn boys and the firstborn of

> Moshe received the Torah from Sinai and handed it on to Yehoshua, who handed it on to the elders, the elders to the prophets, and the prophets to the Men of the Great Assembly. (Avot 1:1)

Prophecy was not a dynasty. It was available to anyone of the right character, dedication, and spirituality. The Rabbis also understood that since knowledge is power, and the distribution of power is the central concern of politics, the distribution of knowledge is the single greatest issue affecting the structure of society. It was not on the streets or behind the barricades but in the house of study that the Rabbis achieved the revolutionary ideal of a society of equal dignity under the sovereignty of God.

מתוך בני ישראל לכם מתנה נתנים ליהוה לעבד את־
ז עבדת אהל מועד: ואתה ובניך אתך תשמרו את־כהנתכם
לכל־דבר המזבח ולמבית לפרכת ועבדתם עבדת מתנה
אתן את־כהנתכם והזר הקרב יומת:
ח וידבר יהוה אל־אהרן ואני הנה נתתי לך את־משמרת
תרומתי לכל־קדשי בני־ישראל לך נתתים למשחה
ט ולבניך לחק־עולם: זה יהיה לך מקדש הקדשים מן־האש
כל־קרבנם לכל־מנחתם ולכל־חטאתם ולכל־אשמם
י אשר ישיבו לי קדש קדשים לך הוא ולבניך: בקדש
הקדשים תאכלנו כל־זכר יאכל אתו קדש יהיה־לך:
יא וזה־לך תרומת מתנם לכל־תנופת בני ישראל לך נתתים
ולבניך ולבנתיך אתך לחק־עולם כל־טהור בביתך יאכל
יב אתו: כל חלב יצהר וכל־חלב תירוש ודגן ראשיתם אשר־
יג יתנו ליהוה לך נתתים: בכורי כל־אשר בארצם אשר־
יד יביאו ליהוה לך יהיה כל־טהור בביתך יאכלנו: כל־חרם
טו בישראל לך יהיה: כל־פטר רחם לכל־בשר אשר־יקריבו
ליהוה באדם ובבהמה יהיה־לך אך ׀ פדה תפדה את

offered by everyone. In place of rule by kings came governance by "the townsfolk" or "the notables (*tovei ha'ir*) – not quite representative democracy but a move in that direction nonetheless.

Above all, though, came the belief that status was conferred by scholarship, Torah study. On this, the rabbis' remarks were forceful and unambiguous:

> With three crowns was Israel crowned.... The crown of priesthood was bestowed on Aharon and his descendants. The crown of kingship was conferred on David and his successors. But the crown of Torah is for all Israel. Whoever wishes, let him come and take it.... A Torah scholar of illegitimate birth takes precedence over an ignorant High Priest. (*Hilkhot Talmud Torah* 3:1–2)

Alongside statements like these went the creation of the world's first system of community-funded, universal education (Bava Batra 21a).

Significantly, the Rabbis traced their descent not from kings or priests – the two dynastic roles in Judaism – but to the prophets:

16 impure animals. Their redemption price from the age of
one month shall be set at five shekel of silver according to
17 the Sanctuary weight: twenty gerah per shekel. You must
not redeem the firstborn of an ox, sheep, or goat; they are
sacred. You must dash their blood on the altar and send
their fat up in smoke for a pleasing aroma to the LORD.
18 But their meat is yours. It shall be yours like the breast
19 of the wave offering and the right thigh. All the sacred
gifts that the Israelites raise up to the LORD I give to you,
your sons, and your daughters as an everlasting statute.
It is an everlasting covenant of salt before the LORD, for
20 you and for your descendants." The LORD said to Aharon:
"You will have no inheritance in their land, nor shall
you have any share among them. I am your share, your
21 inheritance, among the Israelites. And I give to SHEVI'I
the Levites all tithes in Israel as an inheritance in return
for the service they perform, the service in the Tent of
22 Meeting. From now the Israelites shall no longer come
close to the Tent of Meeting, or they will incur guilt and
23 die. Instead, the Levites will perform the service of the
Tent of Meeting, and they will bear responsibility for
their own sins; this is an everlasting decree through all
your generations. But among the Israelites they will not
24 inherit land, because I have given as an inheritance to the
Levites the tithe of the Israelites which they have lifted up
to the LORD as an upraised gift. That is why I have said of

---

us work to do, saying in His still, small voice: "Bring a fragment of My presence into other lives." Not only Levites, not only kings, but every person. What made Moshe and Yirmeyahu and David special was not that they had a high opinion of themselves – the opposite was the case – but that they heard and heeded the cry of human suffering. For them, injustice was not a fact but a call. They believed, not in themselves, but in the cause. They knew that when someone is drowning, you don't stop to ask who is the best swimmer. You jump in. Leadership is response-ability, the ability to respond. How different is this conception of greatness to Koraḥ's – and yet how much more profound a recognition of the dignity of every human life.

טז בְּכ֣וֹר הָֽאָדָ֗ם וְאֵ֛ת בְּכֽוֹר־הַבְּהֵמָ֥ה הַטְּמֵאָ֖ה תִּפְדֶּֽה׃ וּפְדוּיָו֙
מִבֶּן־חֹ֣דֶשׁ תִּפְדֶּ֔ה בְּעֶ֨רְכְּךָ֔ כֶּ֕סֶף חֲמֵ֥שֶׁת שְׁקָלִ֖ים בְּשֶׁ֣קֶל
יז הַקֹּ֑דֶשׁ עֶשְׂרִ֥ים גֵּרָ֖ה הֽוּא׃ אַ֣ךְ בְּכוֹר־שׁ֡וֹר אֽוֹ־בְכ֨וֹר כֶּ֜שֶׂב
אֽוֹ־בְכ֥וֹר עֵ֛ז לֹ֥א תִפְדֶּ֖ה קֹ֣דֶשׁ הֵ֑ם אֶת־דָּמָ֞ם תִּזְרֹ֤ק עַל־
הַמִּזְבֵּ֙חַ֙ וְאֶת־חֶלְבָּ֣ם תַּקְטִ֔יר אִשֶּׁ֛ה לְרֵ֥יחַ נִיחֹ֖חַ לַֽיהוה׃
יח וּבְשָׂרָ֖ם יִֽהְיֶה־לָּ֑ךְ כַּחֲזֵ֧ה הַתְּנוּפָ֛ה וּכְשׁ֥וֹק הַיָּמִ֖ין לְךָ֥ יִהְיֶֽה׃
יט כֹּ֣ל ׀ תְּרוּמֹ֣ת הַקֳּדָשִׁ֗ים אֲשֶׁ֨ר יָרִ֥ימוּ בְנֵֽי־יִשְׂרָאֵל֮ לַיהוה֒
נָתַ֣תִּֽי לְךָ֗ וּלְבָנֶ֧יךָ וְלִבְנֹתֶ֛יךָ אִתְּךָ֖ לְחָק־עוֹלָ֑ם בְּרִית֩ מֶ֨לַח
כ עוֹלָ֥ם הִוא֙ לִפְנֵ֣י יהוה֔ לְךָ֖ וּלְזַרְעֲךָ֥ אִתָּֽךְ׃ וַיֹּ֨אמֶר יהוה֜ אֶֽל־
אַהֲרֹ֗ן בְּאַרְצָם֙ לֹ֣א תִנְחָ֔ל וְחֵ֕לֶק לֹא־יִהְיֶ֥ה לְךָ֖ בְּתוֹכָ֑ם אֲנִ֤י
כא חֶלְקְךָ֙ וְנַחֲלָ֣תְךָ֔ בְּת֖וֹךְ בְּנֵ֥י יִשְׂרָאֵֽל׃ וְלִבְנֵ֣י לֵוִ֔י שביעי
הִנֵּ֛ה נָתַ֥תִּי כָּל־מַעֲשֵׂ֛ר בְּיִשְׂרָאֵ֖ל לְנַחֲלָ֑ה חֵ֤לֶף עֲבֹֽדָתָם֙
כב אֲשֶׁר־הֵ֣ם עֹֽבְדִ֔ים אֶת־עֲבֹדַ֖ת אֹ֥הֶל מוֹעֵֽד׃ וְלֹא־יִקְרְב֥וּ ע֛וֹד
כג בְּנֵ֥י יִשְׂרָאֵ֖ל אֶל־אֹ֣הֶל מוֹעֵ֑ד לָשֵׂ֥את חֵ֖טְא לָמֽוּת׃ וְעָבַ֨ד
הַלֵּוִ֜י ה֗וּא אֶת־עֲבֹדַת֙ אֹ֣הֶל מוֹעֵ֔ד וְהֵ֖ם יִשְׂא֣וּ עֲוֺנָ֑ם חֻקַּ֤ת
כד עוֹלָם֙ לְדֹרֹ֣תֵיכֶ֔ם וּבְתוֹךְ֙ בְּנֵ֣י יִשְׂרָאֵ֔ל לֹ֥א יִנְחֲל֖וּ נַחֲלָֽה׃ כִּ֞י
אֶת־מַעְשַׂ֣ר בְּנֵֽי־יִשְׂרָאֵ֗ל אֲשֶׁ֨ר יָרִ֤ימוּ לַיהוה֙ תְּרוּמָ֔ה נָתַ֥תִּי

18:20 אֲנִי חֶלְקְךָ וְנַחֲלָתְךָ *I am your share, your inheritance* – As the *parasha* ends we return to the special status of the Levites, against which Koraḥ rebelled. Interestingly, however, when Rambam comes to codify this idea, he brings us back to the universal element in Judaism's vision of spiritual aristocracy. Having established that the tribe of Levi was chosen to serve, to know God, and "to teach His upright ways and righteous laws," Rambam adds this:

> And not only the tribe of Levi, but any person in the world whose spirit stirs him, and he reaches an understanding from his own mind that he should set himself apart to serve and to know God… he is sanctified as holy of holies, and God is his portion and inheritance forever. (*Hilkhot Shemitta VeYovel* 13:12–13)

The hasidic master Rabbi Shlomo of Karlin (1738–92) said something beautiful and unexpected: "The greatest *yetzer hara* [inhibition against doing good] is that *we forget that we are children of the King*." All of us are here because God brought us into being in love and gave

them that they shall have no land inheritance among the
Israelites."
25 26 The Lord spoke to Moshe: "Speak to the Levites and say
to them: When you receive from the Israelites the tithe
that I have given you from them as your inheritance,
you shall lift up a tenth of it as an offering to the Lord, a
27 tithe of the tithe. It will be considered your own upraised
gift, like the grain of the threshing floor or the flow from
28 the winepress. So shall you set aside an offering to the
Lord from all the tithes that you take from the Israelites,
and you shall give it as an upraised gift to the Lord
29 for Aharon the priest. From all your gifts, you shall set
aside an offering to the Lord; of each the finest portion
30 shall be consecrated. Say to the Levites: When you have MAFTIR
presented the best portion of it, it will be reckoned to you
31 as the yield of the threshing floor and the winepress. You
and your household may eat of it anywhere, because this is
32 your payment for your service in the Tent of Meeting. You
will not bear guilt for it once you have separated out the
finest portion; then you will not be profaning the sacred
offerings of the Israelites, and will not die."

The haftara for Parashat Koraḥ is on page 1568.
On Rosh Ḥodesh Tamuz read the haftara on page 1640.

לַלְוִיִּם לְנַחֲלָה עַל־כֵּן אָמַרְתִּי לָהֶם בְּתוֹךְ בְּנֵי יִשְׂרָאֵל לֹא
יִנְחֲלוּ נַחֲלָה׃
כה כו וַיְדַבֵּר יְהוָה אֶל־מֹשֶׁה לֵּאמֹר׃ וְאֶל־הַלְוִיִּם תְּדַבֵּר וְאָמַרְתָּ יז
אֲלֵהֶם כִּי־תִקְחוּ מֵאֵת בְּנֵי־יִשְׂרָאֵל אֶת־הַמַּעֲשֵׂר אֲשֶׁר
נָתַתִּי לָכֶם מֵאִתָּם בְּנַחֲלַתְכֶם וַהֲרֵמֹתֶם מִמֶּנּוּ תְּרוּמַת יְהוָה
כז מַעֲשֵׂר מִן־הַמַּעֲשֵׂר׃ וְנֶחְשַׁב לָכֶם תְּרוּמַתְכֶם כַּדָּגָן מִן־הַגֹּרֶן
כח וְכַמְלֵאָה מִן־הַיָּקֶב׃ כֵּן תָּרִימוּ גַם־אַתֶּם תְּרוּמַת יְהוָה מִכֹּל
מַעְשְׂרֹתֵיכֶם אֲשֶׁר תִּקְחוּ מֵאֵת בְּנֵי יִשְׂרָאֵל וּנְתַתֶּם מִמֶּנּוּ
כט אֶת־תְּרוּמַת יְהוָה לְאַהֲרֹן הַכֹּהֵן׃ מִכֹּל מַתְּנֹתֵיכֶם תָּרִימוּ אֵת
ל כָּל־תְּרוּמַת יְהוָה מִכָּל־חֶלְבּוֹ אֶת־מִקְדְּשׁוֹ מִמֶּנּוּ׃ וְאָמַרְתָּ מפטיר
אֲלֵהֶם בַּהֲרִימְכֶם אֶת־חֶלְבּוֹ מִמֶּנּוּ וְנֶחְשַׁב לַלְוִיִּם כִּתְבוּאַת
לא גֹּרֶן וְכִתְבוּאַת יָקֶב׃ וַאֲכַלְתֶּם אֹתוֹ בְּכָל־מָקוֹם אַתֶּם וּבֵיתְכֶם
לב כִּי־שָׂכָר הוּא לָכֶם חֵלֶף עֲבֹדַתְכֶם בְּאֹהֶל מוֹעֵד׃ וְלֹא־תִשְׂאוּ
עָלָיו חֵטְא בַּהֲרִימְכֶם אֶת־חֶלְבּוֹ מִמֶּנּוּ וְאֶת־קָדְשֵׁי בְנֵי־
יִשְׂרָאֵל לֹא תְחַלְּלוּ וְלֹא תָמוּתוּ׃

The הפטרה *for* פרשת קרח *is on page 1569.*
On ראש חודש תמוז *read the* הפטרה *on page 1641.*

Parashat Ḥukat

19 1 2 The Lord spoke to Moshe and Aharon: "This is the
decree of the Law that the Lord commands. Tell the

Or perhaps, as Saadia Gaon put it, it is a command issued for no other reason than to reward us for obeying it (Emunot VeDeot, book III).

Rambam had a quite different view. He believed that no divine command was irrational. The *ḥukim* only appear to be inexplicable because we have forgotten the original context in which they were ordained. Each of them was a rejection of, and education against, some idolatrous practice, since forgotten, which is why we now find the commands hard to understand (*Guide for the Perplexed* III:31).

A third view, adopted by Ramban (commentary on Lev. 19:19) and further articulated by Rabbi Samson Raphael Hirsch, is that the *ḥukim* are laws designed to teach the integrity of nature. Nature has its own domains and boundaries; to cross them is to dishonor the divinely created order and to threaten nature itself. So we do not combine animal (wool) and vegetable (linen) textiles, or mix animal life (milk) and animal death (meat). As for the red heifer, Rabbi Hirsch says that the ritual is to cleanse humans from depression brought about by proximity to death.

My own view is that *ḥukim* are *commands deliberately intended to bypass the rational brain,* the prefrontal cortex. The root from which the word *ḥok* comes is *ḥ-k-k,* meaning "to engrave." Rituals cut deep below the surface of the mind, and for an important reason. We are not fully rational animals, and we can make momentous mistakes if we think we are. We have a limbic system, an emotional brain. We also have an extremely powerful set of reactions to potential danger, located in the amygdala, that lead us to flee, freeze, or fight. A moral system, to be adequate to the human condition, must recognize the nature of the human condition. It must speak to our fears.

The most profound fear most of us have is of death. Death defiles in the simplest, starkest sense. It makes mockery of virtue: the hero may die young while the coward lives to old age. And bereavement is tragic in a different way. To lose those we love is to have the fabric of our life torn, perhaps irreparably. Mortality opens an abyss between us and God's eternity.

It is this fear, existential and elemental, to which the rite of the heifer is addressed. Faith can rescue life from meaninglessness. "Rational knowledge," Tolstoy noted, "negates the meaning of life." Something, then, other than rational knowledge is needed. "Faith is the force of life. If a man lives, then he must believe in something.... Without faith it is impossible to live."

פרשת חקת

יט א ב וַיְדַבֵּר יְהוָה אֶל־מֹשֶׁה וְאֶל־אַהֲרֹן לֵאמֹר: זֹאת חֻקַּת
הַתּוֹרָה אֲשֶׁר־צִוָּה יְהוָה לֵאמֹר דַּבֵּר ׀ אֶל־בְּנֵי יִשְׂרָאֵל

ḤUKAT

Parashat Ḥukat begins with the law of the red heifer, judged by the Sages to be the most incomprehensible in the Torah. It became a classic example of a *ḥok*, a "statute," often understood as a law that has no reason, or at least none we can understand. The text then shifts from law to narrative. After the death of Miriam, the people find themselves without water. They complain to Moshe and Aharon, who turn to God. They then respond to the people in a way that seems to suggest anger. They are judged to have acted wrongly, and both are told they will not enter the land. Aharon dies. The people complain again and are attacked by venomous snakes. Moshe, at God's command, places a brass serpent on a pole, so that all who look up to it will be healed. The people sing a song about a miraculous well that gave them water. Moshe then leads the people into successful battles against Siḥon, king of the Emorites, and Og, king of Bashan.

The *parasha* demonstrates, as we shall see, one of the recurring themes in Numbers, the close connection between law and narrative, in this case between the law of the red heifer and the story that follows. The ideas of purification from death embodied in the law of the heifer preempt the deaths of Miriam and Aharon and the foreshadowing of Moshe's death in the wilderness. After this study in mortality, the Israelites meet hostile nations in battle, and despite their earlier fears, emerge triumphant.

THE DECREE OF THE LAW

Though the ritual of the red heifer has not been practiced since the days of the Temple, it nonetheless remains significant, in itself and for an understanding of what a *ḥok*, "statute," actually is. Other instances include the prohibitions against eating meat and milk together, wearing clothes of mixed wool and linen (*shaatnez*), and sowing a field with two kinds of grain (*kilayim*). The Sages recognized that whereas non-Jews might understand Jewish laws based on social justice (*mishpatim*) or historical memory (*edot*), commands such as the prohibition of eating meat and milk together seemed irrational and superstitious. The *ḥukim* were laws of which "Satan and the nations of the world made fun" (Yoma 67b).

There have been several very different explanations of *ḥukim*. The most famous is that a *ḥok* is a law whose logic we cannot understand. It makes sense to God, but it makes no sense to us.

Israelites to bring you a cow, completely red, without
3 blemish, on which no yoke has been laid. Give this to
Elazar the priest; it shall be taken outside the camp and
4 slaughtered in his presence. Elazar the priest shall take
some of its blood with his finger and sprinkle it seven
5 times toward the front of the Tent of Meeting. The cow
shall then be burned in front of him; its skin, flesh, and
6 blood shall be burned, together with its dung. The priest
shall take cedarwood, hyssop, and scarlet cloth and throw
7 them into the fire where the cow is burning. Then the
priest shall wash his clothes and bathe his body in water.
Afterward he may enter the camp, but he will remain
8 impure until that evening. The one who burned it shall
wash his clothes in water and bathe his body in water,
9 but he too will remain impure until evening. Meanwhile,
one who is pure shall gather up the ashes of the cow and
place them outside the camp in a pure place. And they
shall be kept by the Israelite community for the water of
10 lustration, as a purification offering. The one who gathers
the ashes of the cow shall likewise wash his clothes but

---

body dies but the spirit flows on. A generation dies but another is born. Lives may end but life does not. Those who live after us continue what we began, and we live on in them. Life is a never-ending stream, and a trace of us is carried onward to the future.

As physical beings, we all one day "return to dust" (Gen. 3:19), but we are reminded of two consolations. The first is that we are not just physical beings. God made the first human "from the dust of the land" (2:7), but He breathed into him the breath of life. "The dust returns to the earth where it began, and the spirit returns to God who gave it" (Eccl. 12:7).

The second is that, even down here on earth, something of us lives on, as it did for Aharon in the form of his sons who carry the name of the priesthood, as it did for Moshe in the form of his disciples who studied and lived by his words, and as it did for Miriam in the lives of all those she led and taught. For good or bad, our lives have an impact on other lives, and the ripples of our deeds spread ever outward across space and time. We are part of the undying river of life. So we may be mortal, but that does not reduce our life to insignificance, for we are part of something larger than ourselves, characters in a story that began early in the history of civilization and that will last as long as humankind.

וְיִקְחוּ אֵלֶיךָ פָרָה אֲדֻמָּה תְּמִימָה אֲשֶׁר אֵין־בָּהּ מוּם אֲשֶׁר
ג לֹא־עָלָה עָלֶיהָ עֹל׃ וּנְתַתֶּם אֹתָהּ אֶל־אֶלְעָזָר הַכֹּהֵן וְהוֹצִיא
ד אֹתָהּ אֶל־מִחוּץ לַמַּחֲנֶה וְשָׁחַט אֹתָהּ לְפָנָיו׃ וְלָקַח אֶלְעָזָר
הַכֹּהֵן מִדָּמָהּ בְּאֶצְבָּעוֹ וְהִזָּה אֶל־נֹכַח פְּנֵי אֹהֶל־מוֹעֵד
ה מִדָּמָהּ שֶׁבַע פְּעָמִים׃ וְשָׂרַף אֶת־הַפָּרָה לְעֵינָיו אֶת־עֹרָהּ
ו וְאֶת־בְּשָׂרָהּ וְאֶת־דָּמָהּ עַל־פִּרְשָׁהּ יִשְׂרֹף׃ וְלָקַח הַכֹּהֵן עֵץ
אֶרֶז וְאֵזוֹב וּשְׁנִי תוֹלָעַת וְהִשְׁלִיךְ אֶל־תּוֹךְ שְׂרֵפַת הַפָּרָה׃
ז וְכִבֶּס בְּגָדָיו הַכֹּהֵן וְרָחַץ בְּשָׂרוֹ בַּמַּיִם וְאַחַר יָבֹא אֶל־
ח הַמַּחֲנֶה וְטָמֵא הַכֹּהֵן עַד־הָעָרֶב׃ וְהַשֹּׂרֵף אֹתָהּ יְכַבֵּס בְּגָדָיו
ט בַּמַּיִם וְרָחַץ בְּשָׂרוֹ בַּמָּיִם וְטָמֵא עַד־הָעָרֶב׃ וְאָסַף ׀ אִישׁ
טָהוֹר אֵת אֵפֶר הַפָּרָה וְהִנִּיחַ מִחוּץ לַמַּחֲנֶה בְּמָקוֹם טָהוֹר
וְהָיְתָה לַעֲדַת בְּנֵי־יִשְׂרָאֵל לְמִשְׁמֶרֶת לְמֵי נִדָּה חַטָּאת הִוא׃
י וְכִבֶּס הָאֹסֵף אֶת־אֵפֶר הַפָּרָה אֶת־בְּגָדָיו וְטָמֵא עַד־הָעָרֶב

To defeat the defilement of contact with death, there must be a ritual that bypasses rational knowledge. Hence the rite of the red heifer, in which death is dissolved in the waters of life, and those on whom they are sprinkled are made pure again so that they can, after a time, enter the precincts of the *Shekhina* and reestablish contact with eternity.

THE RED HEIFER

In Parashat Ḥukat we read of the death of two of Israel's three great leaders in the wilderness, Miriam and Aharon, and the sentence of death decreed against Moshe, the greatest of them all. To counter that sense of loss and bereavement, the Torah employs one of Judaism's great principles: the Holy One, blessed be He, creates the remedy before the disease (Megilla 13b). Before any of the deaths are mentioned, we read about the strange ritual of the red heifer, which purifies people who have been in contact with death – the archetypal source of impurity.

Why this ritual? Even though the red heifer is a *ḥok,* as we saw above, it can also have a dimension of symbolic import. The red heifer itself is the starkest symbol of pure, animal life, untamed, undomesticated. The red, like the scarlet of the wool, is the color of blood, the essence of life. The cedar, tallest of trees, represents vegetative life. The hyssop symbolizes purity. All these are reduced to ash in the fire, a powerful drama of mortality. The ash itself is then dissolved in "living" – flowing – water (Num. 19:17), symbolizing continuity, the flow of life, and the potential of rebirth. The

remains impure until evening. This shall be an everlasting
decree for the Israelites and for any migrant living among
11 them. Whoever touches the dead body of any person shall
12 be impure for seven days. He must purify himself with
the water on the third and seventh days to become pure.
If he does not purify himself on the third and seventh
13 days, he will not be pure. Whoever touches a corpse of
a person who has died, and fails to purify himself, defiles
the LORD's Tabernacle. He shall be severed from Israel
because, since the water of lustration was not sprinkled
on him, he remains impure; his impurity is still with him.
14 This is the law: when a person dies in a tent, whoever
enters that tent and whoever is in it shall remain impure
15 for seven days. Any open vessel not sealed with a cover
16 shall be impure. Anyone in the open field who touches
a person killed by the sword, or who died naturally, or a
human bone or a grave, shall be impure for seven days.
17 For this impure person they shall take some of the ashes
of the burnt purification offering, and place living water
18 along with it into a vessel. A person who is pure shall then SHENI
take hyssop, dip it into the water, and sprinkle it on the
tent, on all the vessels, on the people who were there, and
on anyone who touched the bone, the slain person, or

As long as she was alive, there was water, i.e., life. Her death marked the beginning of the end of Moshe's generation, and the sign of this was the drying up of the well that had served the people until then.

We die, but life goes on – that is the symbolic statement of the red heifer rite. So long as there is a covenant between the dead, the living, and those not yet born, mortality is redeemed from tragedy. We will live on in our children or in those whose lives we touch. As dust dissolves in living water, so death dissolves in the stream of life itself.

The law of the red heifer is thus intimately related to the narrative that follows. Before we are exposed to the death of Miriam and Aharon and the decree of death against Moshe, the Torah provides us with metaphysical comfort. They died, but what they lived for did not die. The water ceased, but after an interval, it returned. We are destined to mourn the death of those close to us, but eventually we reconnect with (the water of) life. Law informs the narrative, and narrative explains the law.

יא וְהָיְתָה לִבְנֵי יִשְׂרָאֵל וְלַגֵּר הַגָּר בְּתוֹכָם לְחֻקַּת עוֹלָם: הַנֹּגֵעַ
יב בְּמֵת לְכָל־נֶפֶשׁ אָדָם וְטָמֵא שִׁבְעַת יָמִים: הוּא יִתְחַטָּא־
בוֹ בַּיּוֹם הַשְּׁלִישִׁי וּבַיּוֹם הַשְּׁבִיעִי יִטְהָר וְאִם־לֹא יִתְחַטָּא
יג בַּיּוֹם הַשְּׁלִישִׁי וּבַיּוֹם הַשְּׁבִיעִי לֹא יִטְהָר: כָּל־הַנֹּגֵעַ בְּמֵת
בְּנֶפֶשׁ הָאָדָם אֲשֶׁר־יָמוּת וְלֹא יִתְחַטָּא אֶת־מִשְׁכַּן יהוה
טִמֵּא וְנִכְרְתָה הַנֶּפֶשׁ הַהִוא מִיִּשְׂרָאֵל כִּי מֵי נִדָּה לֹא־זֹרַק
יד עָלָיו טָמֵא יִהְיֶה עוֹד טֻמְאָתוֹ בוֹ: זֹאת הַתּוֹרָה אָדָם כִּי־
יָמוּת בְּאֹהֶל כָּל־הַבָּא אֶל־הָאֹהֶל וְכָל־אֲשֶׁר בָּאֹהֶל יִטְמָא
טו שִׁבְעַת יָמִים: וְכֹל כְּלִי פָתוּחַ אֲשֶׁר אֵין־צָמִיד פָּתִיל עָלָיו
טז טָמֵא הוּא: וְכֹל אֲשֶׁר־יִגַּע עַל־פְּנֵי הַשָּׂדֶה בַּחֲלַל־חֶרֶב אוֹ
יז בְמֵת אוֹ־בְעֶצֶם אָדָם אוֹ בְקָבֶר יִטְמָא שִׁבְעַת יָמִים: וְלָקְחוּ
לַטָּמֵא מֵעֲפַר שְׂרֵפַת הַחַטָּאת וְנָתַן עָלָיו מַיִם חַיִּים אֶל־כֶּלִי:
יח וְלָקַח אֵזוֹב וְטָבַל בַּמַּיִם אִישׁ טָהוֹר וְהִזָּה עַל־הָאֹהֶל וְעַל־ שני
כָּל־הַכֵּלִים וְעַל־הַנְּפָשׁוֹת אֲשֶׁר הָיוּ־שָׁם וְעַל־הַנֹּגֵעַ בַּעֶצֶם

19:11 שִׁבְעַת יָמִים *Seven days* – We no longer have the red heifer and the seven-day purification ritual to help us confront death, but we do have the shiva, the seven days of mourning during which we are comforted by others and thereby reconnected with life. Our grief is gradually dissolved by the contact with friends and family who come to console us, as the ashes of the heifer were dissolved in the "living water" (Num. 19:17), and we emerge, still bereaved, but in some measure cleansed, purified, able again to face life.

We can emerge from the shadow of death if we allow ourselves to be healed by the God of life. Faith leads us back into life. To allow this to happen, however, we often need the help of others. It took a priest to sprinkle the waters of cleansing. In a different sense, it takes comforters to lift our grief during our period of mourning.

19:17 מַיִם חַיִּים *Living water* – The phrase "living water" is an explicit metaphor. Water is the source of all life – plant, animal, and human. In the desert, or more generally in the Middle East, you feel this with a peculiar vividness. Hence it became the symbol of God-who-is-life. Speaking in God's name, Yirmeyahu says of his generation, "Those who stray from Me will be written in the earth, for they have forsaken the source of living waters" (Jer. 17:13). We may understand the symbolic significance of the fact that when Miriam died, the flow of water to the Israelites ceased (see Num. 20:1–2).

19 any other corpse, or a grave. On the third day and seventh
day the person who is pure shall sprinkle it on the one
who is impure, thus purifying him on the seventh day. He
shall then wash his clothes and immerse in water, and at
20 evening he will be pure. Anyone who becomes impure and
fails to purify himself shall be severed from the assembly,
for he has defiled the LORD's Sanctuary. Since water of
21 lustration was not sprinkled on him, he is impure. This is
an everlasting decree for them. The one who sprinkles the
water of lustration shall wash his own clothes. Anyone
who had contact with the water of lustration shall remain
22 impure until evening. Anything the impure person
touches is rendered impure, and one who touches him
remains impure until evening."
20 1 The Israelites, all the community, arrived at the Wilderness
of Tzin in the first month, and the people stayed at Kadesh.
2 There Miriam died and was buried. And there was no

of friendship. He calls it the "friendship of trust" [*ḥaver habitaḥon*] and describes it as having someone in whom "you have absolute trust and with whom you are completely open and unguarded," knowing that the other person will neither take advantage of the confidences shared, nor share them with others. A careful reading of this episode within the broader context of Moshe's early life suggests that Miriam was Moshe's "trusted friend," the source of his emotional stability.

Yet only in this week's *parasha* do we begin to get a full sense of her influence, and this only by implication. For the first time, when the people complain of thirst, Moshe faces a challenge without Miriam, and for the first time he loses emotional control in the presence of the people. This is one of the effects of bereavement. Bereaved, you lose control of your emotions. You find yourself angry when the situation calls for calm. You hit when you should speak, and speak when you should be silent. Rambam, in another context, mentions that the *Shekhina* does not rest upon us when we are in a state of grief (*Shemona Perakim*, ch. 7). The loss of a sibling can be less expected and more profoundly disorienting than even the loss of a parent. And Miriam was no ordinary sibling. Moshe owes her his life and his identity.

Without Miriam, Moshe could never have become the human face of God to the Israelites, lawgiver, liberator, and prophet. Losing her, he not only lost his sister. He lost the human foundation of his life. This is why, despite facing the rock and the thirst twice before, Moshe for the first time loses emotional control.

יט אוֹ בֶחָלָל אוֹ בַמֵּת אוֹ בַקָּבֶר: וְהִזָּה הַטָּהֹר עַל־הַטָּמֵא
בַּיּוֹם הַשְּׁלִישִׁי וּבַיּוֹם הַשְּׁבִיעִי וְחִטְּאוֹ בַּיּוֹם הַשְּׁבִיעִי וְכִבֶּס
כ בְּגָדָיו וְרָחַץ בַּמַּיִם וְטָהֵר בָּעָרֶב: וְאִישׁ אֲשֶׁר־יִטְמָא וְלֹא
יִתְחַטָּא וְנִכְרְתָה הַנֶּפֶשׁ הַהִוא מִתּוֹךְ הַקָּהָל כִּי אֶת־מִקְדַּשׁ
כא יְהוָה טִמֵּא מֵי נִדָּה לֹא־זֹרַק עָלָיו טָמֵא הוּא: וְהָיְתָה לָהֶם
לְחֻקַּת עוֹלָם וּמַזֵּה מֵי־הַנִּדָּה יְכַבֵּס בְּגָדָיו וְהַנֹּגֵעַ בְּמֵי הַנִּדָּה
כב יִטְמָא עַד־הָעָרֶב: וְכֹל אֲשֶׁר־יִגַּע־בּוֹ הַטָּמֵא יִטְמָא וְהַנֶּפֶשׁ
הַנֹּגַעַת תִּטְמָא עַד־הָעָרֶב:
כ א וַיָּבֹאוּ בְנֵי־יִשְׂרָאֵל כָּל־הָעֵדָה מִדְבַּר־צִן בַּחֹדֶשׁ הָרִאשׁוֹן
ב וַיֵּשֶׁב הָעָם בְּקָדֵשׁ וַתָּמָת שָׁם מִרְיָם וַתִּקָּבֵר שָׁם: וְלֹא־

MOSHE AND MIRIAM

Immediately after the account of Miriam's death we read: "And there was no water for the community, and together they confronted Moshe and Aharon" (Num. 20:2). A famous talmudic passage (Taanit 9a) explains that it was in Miriam's merit that the Israelites had a well of water that miraculously accompanied them through their desert journeys. When Miriam died, the water ceased. This interpretation reads the sequence of events supernaturally. Miriam died. Then there was no water. From this, you can infer that until then there was water because Miriam was alive. It was a miracle in her merit (see note on v. 1).

However, there is another way of reading the passage. The connection between Miriam's death and the events that follow it may have less to do with a miraculous well and more to do with Moshe's response to the complaints of the Israelites.

Let us recall who Miriam was, for Moshe. She was his elder sister, who watched over his fate as he floated down the Nile in a pitched basket. She had the presence of mind, and the audacity, to speak to Pharaoh's daughter and arrange for the child to be nursed by an Israelite woman, Moshe's own mother Yokheved. Without Miriam, Moshe would have grown up not knowing who he was.

Miriam is a background presence throughout much of the narrative. We see her leading the women in song at the Sea of Reeds, so it is clear that she, like Aharon, has a leadership role. We gain a sense of how much she means to Moshe when she is punished after she and Aharon "spoke against Moshe because of his Kushite wife; he had married a Kushite woman" (Num. 12:1). Aharon turns helplessly to Moshe and asks him to intervene on her behalf, which he does. Moshe still cares deeply for her.

Leaders need confidants. Rambam, in his Commentary on the Mishna (Avot 1:6), counts this as one of the four kinds

water for the community, and together they confronted
3 Moshe and Aharon. The people contended with Moshe:
"If only we had died when our brothers died before the
4 LORD! Why have you brought the LORD's assembly
into this wilderness only for us and our livestock to die
5 here? Why did you take us up out of Egypt to bring us
to this dreadful place with no grain, no figs, no vines or
6 pomegranates – there is no water to drink!" Moshe and
Aharon went away from the assembly to the entrance
of the Tent of Meeting. They fell on their faces, and the
LORD's glory was revealed to them.
7 8 And the LORD spoke to Moshe: "Take the staff, you and SHELISHI /SHENI/
your brother Aharon, and assemble the community.
Speak to the rock before their eyes and it will give forth
water. You shall bring forth water for them from the
rock, giving the community and their animals to drink."
9 Moshe took the staff from before the LORD, as He had
10 commanded him. And Moshe and Aharon gathered
the assembly together before the rock. He said to them,
"Listen now, rebels! Shall we produce water for you
11 from this rock?" Then Moshe raised his hand and struck
the rock twice with his staff. Water gushed out, and the

---

even a little anger is wrong. Moshe is not only a leader but the supreme role model of the Israelites. Seeing his behavior, the people may have concluded that anger is permissible.

In addition, says Rambam, by losing his temper Moshe failed to respect the people and might have demoralized them. Knowing that Moshe was God's emissary, the people might have concluded that if Moshe was angry with them, so too was God. Yet they had done no more than ask for water. Giving the people the impression that God was angry with them was a failure to sanctify God's name. In anyone else, it would have been considered a minor offense. However, the greater the person, the more exacting are the standards God sets.

Thus, one moment's anger was sufficient to deprive Moshe of the reward surely most precious to him, of seeing the culmination of his work by leading the people across the Jordan and into the Promised Land.

ג הָיָה מַיִם לָעֵדָה וַיִּקָּהֲלוּ עַל־מֹשֶׁה וְעַל־אַהֲרֹן: וַיָּרֶב הָעָם
עִם־מֹשֶׁה וַיֹּאמְרוּ לֵאמֹר וְלוּ גָוַעְנוּ בִּגְוַע אַחֵינוּ לִפְנֵי יְהוָה:
ד וְלָמָה הֲבֵאתֶם אֶת־קְהַל יְהוָה אֶל־הַמִּדְבָּר הַזֶּה לָמוּת שָׁם
ה אֲנַחְנוּ וּבְעִירֵנוּ: וְלָמָה הֶעֱלִיתֻנוּ מִמִּצְרַיִם לְהָבִיא אֹתָנוּ
אֶל־הַמָּקוֹם הָרָע הַזֶּה לֹא ׀ מְקוֹם זֶרַע וּתְאֵנָה וְגֶפֶן וְרִמּוֹן
ו וּמַיִם אַיִן לִשְׁתּוֹת: וַיָּבֹא מֹשֶׁה וְאַהֲרֹן מִפְּנֵי הַקָּהָל אֶל־
פֶּתַח אֹהֶל מוֹעֵד וַיִּפְּלוּ עַל־פְּנֵיהֶם וַיֵּרָא כְבוֹד־יְהוָה
אֲלֵיהֶם:
ז ח וַיְדַבֵּר יְהוָה אֶל־מֹשֶׁה לֵּאמֹר: קַח אֶת־הַמַּטֶּה וְהַקְהֵל אֶת־ שלישי /שני/
הָעֵדָה אַתָּה וְאַהֲרֹן אָחִיךָ וְדִבַּרְתֶּם אֶל־הַסֶּלַע לְעֵינֵיהֶם
וְנָתַן מֵימָיו וְהוֹצֵאתָ לָהֶם מַיִם מִן־הַסֶּלַע וְהִשְׁקִיתָ אֶת־
ט הָעֵדָה וְאֶת־בְּעִירָם: וַיִּקַּח מֹשֶׁה אֶת־הַמַּטֶּה מִלִּפְנֵי
י יְהוָה כַּאֲשֶׁר צִוָּהוּ: וַיַּקְהִלוּ מֹשֶׁה וְאַהֲרֹן אֶת־הַקָּהָל אֶל־
פְּנֵי הַסָּלַע וַיֹּאמֶר לָהֶם שִׁמְעוּ־נָא הַמֹּרִים הֲמִן־הַסֶּלַע
יא הַזֶּה נוֹצִיא לָכֶם מָיִם: וַיָּרֶם מֹשֶׁה אֶת־יָדוֹ וַיַּךְ אֶת־
הַסֶּלַע בְּמַטֵּהוּ פַּעֲמָיִם וַיֵּצְאוּ מַיִם רַבִּים וַתֵּשְׁתְּ הָעֵדָה

20:10 שִׁמְעוּ־נָא הַמֹּרִים *Listen now, rebels* – Rambam writes in his work *Shemona Perakim* (ch. 4) that Moshe's sin lay in his anger – his intemperate words to the people, "Listen now, rebels!" To be sure, there were other occasions on which he lost his temper – or at least appeared to lose it. His reaction to the sin of the golden calf, for instance, was hardly relaxed. But that case was different. The Israelites had committed a sin. God Himself was threatening to destroy the people. Moshe had to act decisively and with sufficient force to restore order to a people wildly out of control.

Here, though, the people had not sinned. They were thirsty. God was not angry with them. Moshe's intemperate reaction was therefore wrong, says Rambam. In general, Rambam advocated moderation. Like Aristotle, he believed that emotional intelligence exists in striking a balance between excess and deficiency, too much and too little. Too much fear makes me a coward; too little makes me rash and foolhardy, taking unnecessary risks. The middle way is courage. There are, however, two exceptions, says Rambam: pride and anger. Even a little pride is too much. Likewise,

▶

12 community and their animals drank. But the
LORD said to Moshe and Aharon, "Because you did not
put your trust in Me to demonstrate My holiness in the
Israelites' eyes, you shall not bring this assembly into
13 the land that I am giving them." These were the waters of
Meriva, where the Israelites quarreled with the LORD and
14 where He showed them His holiness. Moshe REVI'I
sent messengers from Kadesh to the king of Edom:
"This is what your brother Israel says: 'You know all the
15 hardship we have encountered, how our ancestors went
down to Egypt and lived in Egypt for a long time. And the
16 Egyptians oppressed us and our forebears, and we cried
out to the LORD. He heard our voice, sent a messenger, and
He brought us out of Egypt. Now here we are in Kadesh,
17 a town adjoining your border. Please, let us pass through

and the rock is the way he observes precedent. Almost forty years earlier, in similar circumstances, God told him to take his staff and strike the rock. Now too, God tells him to take his staff. Evidently Moshe now infers that he is being told to act this time as he did before, which is what he does. He strikes the rock. But time has changed one essential detail. He is facing a new generation. The people he confronted the first time were those who had spent much of their lives as slaves in Egypt. Those he now faces were born in freedom in the wilderness.

There is a critical difference between slaves and free human beings. Slaves respond to orders. Free people do not. They must be educated, informed, instructed, taught – for if not, they will not learn to take responsibility. Slaves understand that a stick is used for striking. That is how slave masters compel obedience. But free human beings must not be struck. They respond not to power but persuasion. They need to be spoken to. What Moshe fails to hear is that the difference between God's command then and now ("strike the rock" and "speak to the rock") is of the essence. The symbolism in each case is precisely calibrated to the mentalities of two different generations.

A figure capable of leading slaves to freedom is not the same as one able to lead free human beings from a nomadic existence in the wilderness to the conquest and settlement of a land. Each age produces its leaders, and each leader is a function of an age. At the dawn of time, said the Rabbis, God showed Adam each generation and its searchers, each generation and its leaders (Avoda Zara 5a) – meaning, no two generations are alike. The world changes and leaders need to help us to adapt to the new without breaking faith with the old.

יב וּבְעִירָֽם׃ וַיֹּ֣אמֶר יְהוָה֮ אֶל־מֹשֶׁ֣ה וְאֶל־אַהֲרֹן֒
יַ֚עַן לֹא־הֶאֱמַנְתֶּ֣ם בִּ֔י לְהַ֨קְדִּישֵׁ֔נִי לְעֵינֵ֖י בְּנֵ֣י יִשְׂרָאֵ֑ל לָכֵ֗ן
לֹ֤א תָבִ֙יאוּ֙ אֶת־הַקָּהָ֣ל הַזֶּ֔ה אֶל־הָאָ֖רֶץ אֲשֶׁר־נָתַ֥תִּי לָהֶֽם׃
יג הֵ֚מָּה מֵ֣י מְרִיבָ֔ה אֲשֶׁר־רָב֥וּ בְנֵֽי־יִשְׂרָאֵ֖ל אֶת־יְהוָ֑ה וַיִּקָּדֵ֖שׁ
יד בָּֽם׃ וַיִּשְׁלַ֨ח מֹשֶׁ֧ה מַלְאָכִ֛ים מִקָּדֵ֖שׁ אֶל־מֶ֣לֶךְ יח רביעי
אֱד֑וֹם כֹּ֤ה אָמַר֙ אָחִ֣יךָ יִשְׂרָאֵ֔ל אַתָּ֣ה יָדַ֔עְתָּ אֵ֥ת כָּל־הַתְּלָאָ֖ה
טו אֲשֶׁ֥ר מְצָאָֽתְנוּ׃ וַיֵּרְד֤וּ אֲבֹתֵ֙ינוּ֙ מִצְרַ֔יְמָה וַנֵּ֥שֶׁב בְּמִצְרַ֖יִם
טז יָמִ֣ים רַבִּ֑ים וַיָּרֵ֥עוּ לָ֛נוּ מִצְרַ֖יִם וְלַאֲבֹתֵֽינוּ׃ וַנִּצְעַ֤ק אֶל־יְהוָה֙
וַיִּשְׁמַ֣ע קֹלֵ֔נוּ וַיִּשְׁלַ֣ח מַלְאָ֔ךְ וַיֹּצִאֵ֖נוּ מִמִּצְרָ֑יִם וְהִנֵּה֙ אֲנַ֣חְנוּ
יז בְקָדֵ֔שׁ עִ֖יר קְצֵ֥ה גְבוּלֶֽךָ׃ נַעְבְּרָה־נָּ֣א בְאַרְצֶ֗ךָ לֹ֤א נַעֲבֹר֙

MOSHE'S PUNISHMENT

It is one of the most perplexing passages in the Torah. Moshe the faithful shepherd, who has led the Israelites for forty years, is told that he will not enter the Promised Land.

What offense could warrant so great a punishment? Because the text does not make it clear, the commentators offer numerous theories, among them that of Rambam (see note on v. 10 above). Rashi (in his commentary here) says that Moshe's sin lay in striking the rock rather than speaking to it. Had Moshe done as he was commanded, the people would have learned an unforgettable lesson: "If a rock, which neither speaks nor hears nor is in need of sustenance, obeys the word of God, how much more so should we." Ramban (on Num. 20:8) says that the sin lay in saying, "Shall we bring forth water for you from this rock?" implying that what was at issue was human ability rather than divine miracle. Rabbi Yosef Albo (*Sefer HaIkkarim* IV:22) suggests that the sin lay in the fact that Moshe and Aharon fled from the congregation and fell on their faces rather than standing their ground, confident that God would answer their prayers. The nineteenth-century Italian exegete Rabbi Shmuel David Luzzatto was moved to remark, "Moshe committed one sin, yet the commentators have accused him of thirteen or more – each inventing some new iniquity."

However we identify Moshe's sin, there is a disproportion between it and its punishment. Could God not forgive Moshe? To deprive him of seeing the culmination of a lifetime's efforts appears unduly harsh.

It is difficult to hazard a different explanation of so debated a text, but there may be a way of seeing the entire episode that makes sense of what otherwise seems like a mystery.

The remarkable fact about Moshe

your land. We will not pass through any field or vineyard,
nor will we drink water from any well. We will go along
the King's Highway and not turn from it to the right or
18 the left until we have passed through your territory.'" But
Edom said to him, "You shall not pass through, or I will
19 come out against you with the sword." The Israelites said,
"We will keep to the beaten track. If we or our livestock
drink any of your water, we will pay for it. It is such a small
20 matter; we only want to pass through on foot." But they
said, "You will not pass through." And Edom came out
against them with a large fighting force, heavily armed.
21 Edom refused to let Israel pass through their territory,
and Israel turned away.

22 They set out from Kadesh, and all the Israelite community ḤAMISHI
23 arrived at Mount Hor. There at Mount Hor, by the border /SHELISHI/
of the land of Edom, the LORD said to Moshe and Aharon,
24 "Aharon is to be gathered to his people. He shall not enter
the land that I have given to the Israelites, because you
25 disobeyed My command at the waters of Meriva. Take
Aharon and his son Elazar, and bring them up onto
26 Mount Hor. Strip Aharon of his vestments and put them
on his son Elazar. There will Aharon be gathered in and
27 he will die." Moshe did as the LORD commanded. They
ascended Mount Hor in the sight of all the community.
28 Moshe stripped Aharon of his vestments and put them
on his son Elazar. And there, Aharon died, at the top of
the mountain; and Moshe and Elazar came down from
29 the mountain. When all the community saw that Aharon
had perished, the whole House of Israel wept for Aharon
21 1 for thirty days. When the Canaanite king of
Arad, dwelling in the Negev, heard that the Israelites were
coming by the way of Atarim, he attacked the Israelites
2 and took captives. And the Israelites vowed to the LORD:

in the Mishna: It is not for you to complete the task, but neither are you free to desist from it (Avot 2:16). The great challenges of humanity are too large to be completed in a single generation.

בַּשָּׂדֶה וּבְכֶרֶם וְלֹא נִשְׁתֶּה מֵי בְאֵר דֶּרֶךְ הַמֶּלֶךְ נֵלֵךְ לֹא
יח נִטֶּה יָמִין וּשְׂמֹאול עַד אֲשֶׁר־נַעֲבֹר גְּבֻלֶךָ: וַיֹּאמֶר אֵלָיו
יט אֱדוֹם לֹא תַעֲבֹר בִּי פֶּן־בַּחֶרֶב אֵצֵא לִקְרָאתֶךָ: וַיֹּאמְרוּ
אֵלָיו בְּנֵי־יִשְׂרָאֵל בַּמְסִלָּה נַעֲלֶה וְאִם־מֵימֶיךָ נִשְׁתֶּה אֲנִי
כ וּמִקְנַי וְנָתַתִּי מִכְרָם רַק אֵין־דָּבָר בְּרַגְלַי אֶעֱבֹרָה: וַיֹּאמֶר
לֹא תַעֲבֹר וַיֵּצֵא אֱדוֹם לִקְרָאתוֹ בְּעַם כָּבֵד וּבְיָד חֲזָקָה:
כא וַיְמָאֵן ׀ אֱדוֹם נְתֹן אֶת־יִשְׂרָאֵל עֲבֹר בִּגְבֻלוֹ וַיֵּט יִשְׂרָאֵל
מֵעָלָיו:
כב וַיִּסְעוּ מִקָּדֵשׁ וַיָּבֹאוּ בְנֵי־יִשְׂרָאֵל כָּל־הָעֵדָה הֹר הָהָר: חמישי /שלישי/
כג וַיֹּאמֶר יְהוָה אֶל־מֹשֶׁה וְאֶל־אַהֲרֹן בְּהֹר הָהָר עַל־גְּבוּל
כד אֶרֶץ־אֱדוֹם לֵאמֹר: יֵאָסֵף אַהֲרֹן אֶל־עַמָּיו כִּי לֹא יָבֹא אֶל־
הָאָרֶץ אֲשֶׁר נָתַתִּי לִבְנֵי יִשְׂרָאֵל עַל אֲשֶׁר־מְרִיתֶם אֶת־פִּי
כה לְמֵי מְרִיבָה: קַח אֶת־אַהֲרֹן וְאֶת־אֶלְעָזָר בְּנוֹ וְהַעַל אֹתָם
כו הֹר הָהָר: וְהַפְשֵׁט אֶת־אַהֲרֹן אֶת־בְּגָדָיו וְהִלְבַּשְׁתָּם אֶת־
כז אֶלְעָזָר בְּנוֹ וְאַהֲרֹן יֵאָסֵף וּמֵת שָׁם: וַיַּעַשׂ מֹשֶׁה כַּאֲשֶׁר צִוָּה
כח יְהוָה וַיַּעֲלוּ אֶל־הֹר הָהָר לְעֵינֵי כָּל־הָעֵדָה: וַיַּפְשֵׁט מֹשֶׁה
אֶת־אַהֲרֹן אֶת־בְּגָדָיו וַיַּלְבֵּשׁ אֹתָם אֶת־אֶלְעָזָר בְּנוֹ וַיָּמָת
כט אַהֲרֹן שָׁם בְּרֹאשׁ הָהָר וַיֵּרֶד מֹשֶׁה וְאֶלְעָזָר מִן־הָהָר: וַיִּרְאוּ
כָּל־הָעֵדָה כִּי גָוַע אַהֲרֹן וַיִּבְכּוּ אֶת־אַהֲרֹן שְׁלֹשִׁים יוֹם כֹּל
כא א בֵּית יִשְׂרָאֵל: וַיִּשְׁמַע הַכְּנַעֲנִי מֶלֶךְ־עֲרָד
יֹשֵׁב הַנֶּגֶב כִּי בָּא יִשְׂרָאֵל דֶּרֶךְ הָאֲתָרִים וַיִּלָּחֶם בְּיִשְׂרָאֵל
ב וַיִּשְׁבְּ ׀ מִמֶּנּוּ שֶׁבִי: וַיִּדַּר יִשְׂרָאֵל נֶדֶר לַיהוָה וַיֹּאמַר אִם־נָתֹן

20:29 וַיִּבְכּוּ אֶת־אַהֲרֹן שְׁלֹשִׁים יוֹם כֹּל בֵּית יִשְׂרָאֵל *The whole House of Israel wept for Aharon for thirty days* – Aharon dies, and the people mourn profoundly. Moshe too knows that his days are numbered. He will not live to cross the Jordan. He will die in sight of the land but without setting foot on it. Parashat Ḥukat is thus about mortality. It is about the death of an entire generation, symbolized in the fate of its three leaders (and in the ritual of the red heifer, as we saw above). It is about the discovery of a painful truth, most famously expressed by R. Tarfon

"If You give this people over into our hands, we will
3 utterly destroy their towns." The LORD listened to Israel's
plea and gave over the Canaanites. They completely
destroyed them and their cities; and so the place was
named Ḥorma.
4 They set out from Mount Hor by the way to the Reed Sea,
going around the land of Edom. But the people became
5 restive along the way. The people spoke out against God
and Moshe: "Why did you bring us up from Egypt to die
in the desert? There is no bread, there is no water; we
6 detest this miserable food!" The LORD sent venomous
snakes among the people; they bit the people, and many
7 Israelites died. The people came to Moshe and said, "We
sinned when we spoke against the LORD and you. Pray to
the LORD to take the snakes away from us." Moshe prayed
8 for the people. The LORD then said to Moshe, "Fashion
a snake and place it on a pole. Anyone who is bitten
9 shall look at that and live." Moshe fashioned a bronze
snake and placed it on a pole. When anyone was bitten
by a snake, he would look at the bronze snake and live.
10 11 The Israelites moved on and camped at Ovot. Then they SHISHI
moved on from Ovot, and camped at Iyei HaAvarim in the
12 wilderness bordering Moav to the east. From there they
13 moved on and camped at the Zered Stream. From there
they moved on and camped beyond the Arnon, in the
wilderness that extends from the border of the Amorites,
for the Arnon marks the border of Moav, between Moav
14 and the Amorites. That is why the Book of the Wars of the
15 LORD records: "Vahev in Sufa and the wadis, Arnon and

---

says it was a record of the Israelites' history begun in the time of Avraham. Some modern scholars suggest that it was a collection of epic poems telling of Israel's battles. The Torah is not the only ancient account of Israel's history; others were composed and later lost (see also I Kings 14:19, among other places).

The brief quotation from this work is cryptic, its meaning almost unintelligible. The Sages gave a midrashic interpretation that laid no claim to being the plain meaning of the verse but is nevertheless fascinating:

ג תִּתֵּן אֶת־הָעָם הַזֶּה בְּיָדִי וְהַחֲרַמְתִּי אֶת־עָרֵיהֶם: וַיִּשְׁמַע
יהוה בְּקוֹל יִשְׂרָאֵל וַיִּתֵּן אֶת־הַכְּנַעֲנִי וַיַּחֲרֵם אֶתְהֶם וְאֶת־
עָרֵיהֶם וַיִּקְרָא שֵׁם־הַמָּקוֹם חָרְמָה:
ד וַיִּסְעוּ מֵהֹר הָהָר דֶּרֶךְ יַם־סוּף לִסְבֹב אֶת־אֶרֶץ אֱדוֹם
ה וַתִּקְצַר נֶפֶשׁ־הָעָם בַּדָּרֶךְ: וַיְדַבֵּר הָעָם בֵּאלֹהִים וּבְמֹשֶׁה
לָמָה הֶעֱלִיתֻנוּ מִמִּצְרַיִם לָמוּת בַּמִּדְבָּר כִּי אֵין לֶחֶם וְאֵין
ו מַיִם וְנַפְשֵׁנוּ קָצָה בַּלֶּחֶם הַקְּלֹקֵל: וַיְשַׁלַּח יהוה בָּעָם
אֵת הַנְּחָשִׁים הַשְּׂרָפִים וַיְנַשְּׁכוּ אֶת־הָעָם וַיָּמָת עַם־רָב
ז מִיִּשְׂרָאֵל: וַיָּבֹא הָעָם אֶל־מֹשֶׁה וַיֹּאמְרוּ חָטָאנוּ כִּי־דִבַּרְנוּ
בַיהוה וָבָךְ הִתְפַּלֵּל אֶל־יהוה וְיָסֵר מֵעָלֵינוּ אֶת־הַנָּחָשׁ
ח וַיִּתְפַּלֵּל מֹשֶׁה בְּעַד הָעָם: וַיֹּאמֶר יהוה אֶל־מֹשֶׁה עֲשֵׂה לְךָ
שָׂרָף וְשִׂים אֹתוֹ עַל־נֵס וְהָיָה כָּל־הַנָּשׁוּךְ וְרָאָה אֹתוֹ וָחָי:
ט וַיַּעַשׂ מֹשֶׁה נְחַשׁ נְחֹשֶׁת וַיְשִׂמֵהוּ עַל־הַנֵּס וְהָיָה אִם־נָשַׁךְ
י הַנָּחָשׁ אֶת־אִישׁ וְהִבִּיט אֶל־נְחַשׁ הַנְּחֹשֶׁת וָחָי: וַיִּסְעוּ בְּנֵי ששי
יא יִשְׂרָאֵל וַיַּחֲנוּ בְּאֹבֹת: וַיִּסְעוּ מֵאֹבֹת וַיַּחֲנוּ בְּעִיֵּי הָעֲבָרִים
יב בַּמִּדְבָּר אֲשֶׁר עַל־פְּנֵי מוֹאָב מִמִּזְרַח הַשָּׁמֶשׁ: מִשָּׁם נָסָעוּ
יג וַיַּחֲנוּ בְּנַחַל זָרֶד: מִשָּׁם נָסָעוּ וַיַּחֲנוּ מֵעֵבֶר אַרְנוֹן אֲשֶׁר
בַּמִּדְבָּר הַיֹּצֵא מִגְּבֻל הָאֱמֹרִי כִּי אַרְנוֹן גְּבוּל מוֹאָב בֵּין
יד מוֹאָב וּבֵין הָאֱמֹרִי: עַל־כֵּן יֵאָמַר בְּסֵפֶר מִלְחֲמֹת יהוה
טו אֶת־וָהֵב בְּסוּפָה וְאֶת־הַנְּחָלִים אַרְנוֹן: וְאֶשֶׁד הַנְּחָלִים

THE BOOK OF THE WARS OF THE LORD

The *parasha* tells three stories of hostile encounters with other nations. In the first, Edom meets Israel's peaceful overtures with aggression, and Israel retreats. In this, the second, Arad also aggressively denies Israel passage through their land, but Israel appeals to God for support, and they destroy or "dedicate" the kingdom to God. The third and fourth times the situation arises, Israel conquers the lands of Amor and Bashan and settles there.

It is clear that we are moving into a new phase in the history of Israel's relations with other powers. What is meant here by "the Book of the Wars of the Lord"? Ḥizkuni holds that it was a book that existed in ancient times and was lost. For Rashi it was a list of miracles performed by God for Israel. Ibn Ezra

the wadi slopes that lead to the settlement of Ar and lie
16 along the border of Moav." And from there to Be'er, the
well where the LORD said to Moshe, "Gather the people,
17 and I will give them water." Then the Israelites
18 sang this song: "Spring up, well – sing to her – that the
nobles of the people carved out with their scepter and
19 their staffs." They went from the desert to Matana, from
20 Matana to Naḥaliel, from Naḥaliel to Bamot, and from
Bamot to the valley in the fields of Moav, to the top of
Pisga, overlooking the wasteland.
21 Then the Israelites sent messengers to Siḥon, king of the SHEVI'I /REVI'I/
22 Amorites: "Let us pass through your land. We will not
turn aside into any field or vineyard, nor will we drink
water from any well. We will walk on the King's Highway
23 until we have passed through your territory." But Siḥon
would not allow the Israelites to pass through his territory.
He gathered all his people and went out to confront the
Israelites in the wilderness. When he arrived at Yahatz, he

When two sides fight, not with weapons but with ideas, they recognize that their very disagreement presupposes an agreement – about the value of the argument itself. Two sages who dispute the interpretation of a text nonetheless agree on fundamentals: that the text is holy and binding, and we, who interpret it, revere both God and His word. Thus, in the "wars of the LORD," they attested, "there is love in the end."

21:17 אָז יָשִׁיר יִשְׂרָאֵל אֶת־הַשִּׁירָה הַזֹּאת *Then the Israelites sang this song* – The song Israel sings at the well is one of ten songs the Rabbis enumerated that were sung at key moments in the life of the nation. There is something profoundly spiritual about music. When language aspires to the transcendent, and the soul longs to break free of the gravitational pull of the earth, it modulates into song. Poetry, music, love, wonder – the things that have no survival value but which speak to our deepest sense of being – all tell us that we are not mere animals, assemblages of selfish genes. A song – even a spontaneous one – can capture the fleeting moment, so that even if the narrative is lost, the wonder of the event remains.

THE FIRST CONQUEST OF LAND

The third time the Israelites are attacked, they fight back fearlessly and make their first territorial conquest. To understand the transformation this demonstrates in the people, it is illustrative to see the further cultural metamorphosis that took place in Judaism between the biblical era and the age of the Rabbis. We

טו אֲשֶׁר נָטָה לְשֶׁבֶת עָר וְנִשְׁעַן לִגְבוּל מוֹאָב: וּמִשָּׁם בְּאֵרָה
הִוא הַבְּאֵר אֲשֶׁר אָמַר יהוה לְמֹשֶׁה אֱסֹף אֶת־הָעָם וְאֶתְּנָה
יז לָהֶם מָיִם: אָז יָשִׁיר יִשְׂרָאֵל אֶת־הַשִּׁירָה הַזֹּאת
יח עֲלִי בְאֵר עֱנוּ־לָהּ: בְּאֵר חֲפָרוּהָ שָׂרִים כָּרוּהָ נְדִיבֵי הָעָם
יט בִּמְחֹקֵק בְּמִשְׁעֲנֹתָם וּמִמִּדְבָּר מַתָּנָה: וּמִמַּתָּנָה נַחֲלִיאֵל
כ וּמִנַּחֲלִיאֵל בָּמוֹת: וּמִבָּמוֹת הַגַּיְא אֲשֶׁר בִּשְׂדֵה מוֹאָב רֹאשׁ
הַפִּסְגָּה וְנִשְׁקָפָה עַל־פְּנֵי הַיְשִׁימֹן:
כא וַיִּשְׁלַח יִשְׂרָאֵל מַלְאָכִים אֶל־סִיחֹן מֶלֶךְ־הָאֱמֹרִי לֵאמֹר: שביעי
כב אֶעְבְּרָה בְאַרְצֶךָ לֹא נִטֶּה בְּשָׂדֶה וּבְכֶרֶם לֹא נִשְׁתֶּה מֵי בְאֵר /רביעי/
כג בְּדֶרֶךְ הַמֶּלֶךְ נֵלֵךְ עַד אֲשֶׁר־נַעֲבֹר גְּבֻלֶךָ: וְלֹא־נָתַן סִיחֹן
אֶת־יִשְׂרָאֵל עֲבֹר בִּגְבֻלוֹ וַיֶּאֱסֹף סִיחֹן אֶת־כָּל־עַמּוֹ וַיֵּצֵא
לִקְרַאת יִשְׂרָאֵל הַמִּדְבָּרָה וַיָּבֹא יָהְצָה וַיִּלָּחֶם בְּיִשְׂרָאֵל:

> Even a teacher and disciple, even a father and son, when they sit to study Torah together become enemies to one another. But they do not move from there until they have become beloved to one another. Therefore it says, "*Vahev in sufa*," meaning "There is love in the end." (Kiddushin 30b)

The Rabbis read *vahev* as a derivative of the root *a-h-b*, meaning "to love," and *sufa* as related to the word *sof*, "an end." "*Vahev in sufa*" then means: there is love at the end. It is intriguing that the Sages interpret the phrase "the Wars of the Lord" as a reference to the debates within the house of study, the dialogue and disputation about Jewish law and the meaning of sacred texts. By the time this interpretation was offered, Jews no longer fought wars on the battlefield. The wars they were familiar with were intellectual, spiritual; they took place in the mind, their weapons were reason and tradition, their arena was the study hall, and their aim was to establish the meaning of God's word.

Yet there is more to the statement than this. There is an awareness of human conflict. The Sages do not speak of the house of study as an environment of peace and harmony. In Parashat Korah, we saw the name – argument for the sake of Heaven – that the Sages gave this conflict, thus attaching to it a spiritual dignity of its own. They went so far as to portray God as saying about the protagonists and their divergent views, "These and those are the words of the living God" (Eiruvin 13b; Gittin 6b). God *lives* in the cut and thrust of the house of study. He does not deliver the verdict in the debate; He empowers His sages to do that.

▶

24 launched an attack on the Israelites. The Israelites struck
him down with their swords and took possession of his
land from the Arnon to the Yabok, as far as the Amonites,
25 for the border of the Amonites was strong. The Israelites
took all these cities, and they settled in all the cities of the
Amorites, in Ḥeshbon and all its surrounding settlements.
26 Ḥeshbon was the city of Siḥon, king of the Amorites,
who had fought against the former king of Moav and had
27 taken all his land from him as far as the Arnon. That is
why the ballad singers sing: "Come to Ḥeshbon, build
28 and refound the town of Siḥon. For fire went forth from
Ḥeshbon, a flame from the town of Siḥon. It consumed
29 Ar of Moav the masters of Arnon's high shrines. Woe
for you, Moav! You are destroyed, men of Kemosh! He

---

will be no more weapons; therefore they are not a badge of honor but a burden and may not be worn on the Sabbath.

The Sages in the Mishna text cite a biblical verse in support of their view. R. Eliezer does not. Clearly, though, he must have had another biblical verse in mind. The Talmud (Shabbat 63a) fills in the gap:

> Abaye asked R. Dimi: "What is R. Eliezer's reason for maintaining that [weapons] are ornaments?"
>
> [He replied]: "Because it is written, 'Fasten your sword on your thigh, mighty one, in your majesty and splendor' (Ps. 45:4)."
>
> R. Kahana raised an objection to Mar, son of R. Huna: "But this refers to the words of the Torah!"
>
> He replied: "A verse cannot depart from its plain meaning."
>
> R. Kahana said: "When I was eighteen I knew the whole six orders [of the Mishna] yet I did not know until today that a verse cannot depart from its plain meaning."

Some two centuries after the original Mishna teaching, R. Kahana can *no longer understand* that when a psalm refers to a sword it actually means a sword. For him it is self-evident that it means "words," teachings, texts. With what else does the Jewish people defend itself, if not its sacred merits achieved by devotion to religious learning? To understand R. Eliezer's view a mere two or three centuries earlier, R. Kahana has to be exposed to a principle he had never considered before, namely, that one cannot ignore the literal meaning of a biblical text. Whatever else a verse means, it also means what it says. Reading Ḥukat today, we hear two voices intertwined: that of biblical Israel rising to independence and singing its own song. And that of the Sages and their heirs, searching the text for its fundamental truths, renewed in every generation, as of old.

כד וַיַּכֵּהוּ יִשְׂרָאֵל לְפִי־חָרֶב וַיִּירַשׁ אֶת־אַרְצוֹ מֵאַרְנֹן עַד־יַבֹּק
כה עַד־בְּנֵי עַמּוֹן כִּי עַז גְּבוּל בְּנֵי עַמּוֹן׃ וַיִּקַּח יִשְׂרָאֵל אֵת כָּל־
הֶעָרִים הָאֵלֶּה וַיֵּשֶׁב יִשְׂרָאֵל בְּכָל־עָרֵי הָאֱמֹרִי בְּחֶשְׁבּוֹן
כו וּבְכָל־בְּנֹתֶיהָ׃ כִּי חֶשְׁבּוֹן עִיר סִיחֹן מֶלֶךְ הָאֱמֹרִי הִוא וְהוּא
נִלְחַם בְּמֶלֶךְ מוֹאָב הָרִאשׁוֹן וַיִּקַּח אֶת־כָּל־אַרְצוֹ מִיָּדוֹ עַד־
כז אַרְנֹן׃ עַל־כֵּן יֹאמְרוּ הַמֹּשְׁלִים בֹּאוּ חֶשְׁבּוֹן תִּבָּנֶה וְתִכּוֹנֵן
כח עִיר סִיחוֹן׃ כִּי־אֵשׁ יָצְאָה מֵחֶשְׁבּוֹן לֶהָבָה מִקִּרְיַת סִיחֹן
כט אָכְלָה עָר מוֹאָב בַּעֲלֵי בָּמוֹת אַרְנֹן׃ אוֹי־לְךָ מוֹאָב אָבַדְתָּ
עַם־כְּמוֹשׁ נָתַן בָּנָיו פְּלֵיטִם וּבְנֹתָיו בַּשְּׁבִית לְמֶלֶךְ אֱמֹרִי

---

see it, for instance, in an extraordinary conversation, reported in the Talmud, between the Jewish Sages in the late first century CE. The subject under discussion is a detail in the laws of the Sabbath. In Jewish law one may not carry objects on the seventh day, whether from a private domain into the street or in the street itself. Wearing clothes, however, is clearly not carrying. Here, the Sages debate a borderline case: wearing a sword. Is this *wearing*, in which case it is permitted, or is it *carrying*, in which case it is forbidden?

What is at stake in fact goes to the heart of the value system of Jews between the two great rebellions against Rome in the first and second centuries. Are weapons an ornament, as some cultures regarded them, and thus an item of clothing, or are they negative testimony to the existence of armed conflict, and thus a burden? At stake is how the Sages saw the war against the Romans, and something deeper: how they viewed the very culture of military valor. The Mishna (Shabbat 6:4) records the following disagreement:

> A man must not go out with a sword, bow, shield, lance, or spear, and if he does go out, he incurs a sin offering. R. Eliezer, however, said: They are ornaments for him. But the Sages maintain that they are merely shameful, for it is said, "They shall beat their swords into plowshares, their spears into pruning hooks. Nation shall not raise sword against nation" (Is. 2:4).

For R. Eliezer, weapons are "ornaments." There is honor in fighting for your freedom and resisting an imperial power. We can hear this sentiment in the victory songs recorded in our *parasha*. The Sages – the majority – disagree. Their proof text is the famous verse from Isaiah in which the prophet envisions a world without war. Military confrontation may sometimes be necessary in self-defense but it is not, in Judaism, a positive value. In the Messianic age there

made his sons fugitives, his daughters fugitives, to Siḥon
30 the Amorite king. Yet we – we threw them wholly down,
from Ḥeshbon to Divon, laid waste as far as Nofaḥ, as far
31 as Meideva." So Israel settled in the land of the Amorites.
32 And Moshe sent spies to Yazer. And Israel captured its
surrounding settlements and dispossessed the Amorites
33 who were there. Then they turned and journeyed along
the road toward Bashan. Og, king of Bashan, with all his
34 people came out to Edrei to engage them in battle. But MAFTIR
the LORD said to Moshe: "Do not be afraid of him, for
I have given him into your hand, with all his people and
his land. Do to him what you did to Siḥon, king of the
35 Amorites, who lived in Ḥeshbon." So they struck him
down, together with his sons and all his people until
there were no survivors, and they took possession of his
22 1 land. The Israelites moved on and encamped in the plains
of Moav across the Jordan from Yeriḥo.

The haftara for Parashat Ḥukat is on page 1572.
When Ḥukat and Balak are read together, read the haftara on page 1578.
On Rosh Ḥodesh Tamuz read the haftara on page 1640.

ל סִיחֽוֹן׃ וַנִּירָ֛ם אָבַ֥ד חֶשְׁבּ֖וֹן עַד־דִּיבֹ֑ן וַנַּשִּׁ֣ים עַד־נֹ֔פַח אֲשֶׁ֖ר
לא לב עַד־מֵֽידְבָֽא׃ וַיֵּ֙שֶׁב֙ יִשְׂרָאֵ֔ל בְּאֶ֖רֶץ הָאֱמֹרִֽי׃ וַיִּשְׁלַ֤ח מֹשֶׁה֙
לְרַגֵּ֣ל אֶת־יַעְזֵ֔ר וַֽיִּלְכְּד֖וּ בְּנֹתֶ֑יהָ ויירש אֶת־הָאֱמֹרִ֥י אֲשֶׁר־ וַיּ֖וֹרֶשׁ
לג שָֽׁם׃ וַיִּפְנוּ֙ וַֽיַּעֲל֔וּ דֶּ֖רֶךְ הַבָּשָׁ֑ן וַיֵּצֵ֣א ע֣וֹג מֶֽלֶךְ־הַ֠בָּשָׁן לִקְרָאתָ֜ם
לד ה֧וּא וְכָל־עַמּ֛וֹ לַמִּלְחָמָ֖ה אֶדְרֶֽעִי׃ וַיֹּ֨אמֶר יהוה אֶל־מֹשֶׁה֙ מפטיר
אַל־תִּירָ֣א אֹת֔וֹ כִּ֣י בְיָדְךָ֞ נָתַ֧תִּי אֹת֛וֹ וְאֶת־כָּל־עַמּ֖וֹ וְאֶת־
אַרְצ֑וֹ וְעָשִׂ֣יתָ לּ֔וֹ כַּאֲשֶׁ֣ר עָשִׂ֗יתָ לְסִיחֹן֙ מֶ֣לֶךְ הָֽאֱמֹרִ֔י אֲשֶׁ֥ר
לה יוֹשֵׁ֖ב בְּחֶשְׁבּֽוֹן׃ וַיַּכּ֨וּ אֹת֤וֹ וְאֶת־בָּנָיו֙ וְאֶת־כָּל־עַמּ֔וֹ עַד־בִּלְתִּ֥י
כב א הִשְׁאִֽיר־ל֖וֹ שָׂרִ֑יד וַיִּֽירְשׁ֖וּ אֶת־אַרְצֽוֹ׃ וַיִּסְע֖וּ בְּנֵ֣י יִשְׂרָאֵ֑ל וַֽיַּחֲנוּ֙
בְּעַֽרְב֣וֹת מוֹאָ֔ב מֵעֵ֖בֶר לְיַרְדֵּ֥ן יְרֵחֽוֹ׃

The הפטרה *for* פרשת חקת *is on page 1573.*
When חקת *and* בלק *are read together, read the* הפטרה *on page 1579.*
On ראש חודש תמוז *read the* הפטרה *on page 1641.*

Parashat Balak

22 2 And Balak son of Tzipor had seen all that the Israelites
3 had done to the Amorites. The Moabites were in deep
dread of the people because they were so numerous.
4 Fearful of the Israelites, the Moabites said to the elders of
Midyan, "This horde will now lick up everything around
us, as an ox licks up grass in the field." Balak son of Tzipor
5 was king of Moav at that time. He sent messengers to
summon Bilam son of Beor who was at Petor near the
River in his native land: "A people has come out of Egypt,

---

a man whom the Sages compared with Moshe himself – yet at the same time a figure of flawed character that eventually led to his downfall and to his reputation as an evildoer – one of those mentioned by the Mishna as having been denied a share in the World to Come.

What is his flaw? There are many speculations, but one suggestion given in the Talmud infers the answer from his name. What is the meaning of Bilam? Answers the Talmud (Sanhedrin 105a): it means "a man without a people" (*belo am*). This is a fine insight. Bilam is a prophet for hire, a man without loyalties. He has supernatural powers. He can bless someone and that person will succeed. He can curse and that person will be blighted by misfortune. But there is no hint in any of the reports, biblical or otherwise, that Bilam is a prophet in the moral sense: that he is concerned with justice, desert, the rights and wrongs of those whose lives he affects. Bilam has skills, and he uses them with devastating effect. But he has no commitments, no loyalties, no rootedness in humanity. He is the man *belo am*, without a people. Moshe is the opposite. God Himself says of him, "He is trusted [literally, 'loyal'] in all My House" (Num. 12:7). The Hebrew word *emuna* is usually translated as "faith," and that is what it came to mean in the Middle Ages. But in Biblical Hebrew it is better translated as faithfulness, reliability, loyalty. It means not walking away from the other party when times are tough. It is a key covenantal virtue. There are people with great gifts, intellectual and sometimes even spiritual, who nonetheless fail to achieve what they might have done. They lack the basic moral qualities of integrity, honesty, humility, and above all, loyalty. What they do, they do brilliantly. But often they do the wrong things. Conscious of their unusual endowments, they give way to pride, arrogance, and a belief that they can somehow get away with great crimes. Bilam is the classic example.

פרשת בלק

כב ב וַיַּרְא בָּלָק בֶּן־צִפּוֹר אֵת כׇּל־אֲשֶׁר־עָשָׂה יִשְׂרָאֵל לָאֱמֹרִי׃ יט
ג וַיָּגׇר מוֹאָב מִפְּנֵי הָעָם מְאֹד כִּי רַב־הוּא וַיָּקׇץ מוֹאָב מִפְּנֵי
ד בְּנֵי יִשְׂרָאֵל׃ וַיֹּאמֶר מוֹאָב אֶל־זִקְנֵי מִדְיָן עַתָּה יְלַחֲכוּ הַקָּהָל
אֶת־כׇּל־סְבִיבֹתֵינוּ כִּלְחֹךְ הַשּׁוֹר אֵת יֶרֶק הַשָּׂדֶה וּבָלָק בֶּן־
ה צִפּוֹר מֶלֶךְ לְמוֹאָב בָּעֵת הַהִוא׃ וַיִּשְׁלַח מַלְאָכִים אֶל־בִּלְעָם
בֶּן־בְּעוֹר פְּתוֹרָה אֲשֶׁר עַל־הַנָּהָר אֶרֶץ בְּנֵי־עַמּוֹ לִקְרֹא־לוֹ

BALAK

The Israelites are approaching the end of their forty years in the wilderness. Already they have fought and won wars against Siḥon, king of the Amorites, and Og, king of Bashan. They have arrived at the plains of Moav – today, southern Jordan at the point where it touches the Dead Sea. Balak, king of Moav is concerned, and he shares his distress with the elders of Midyan. The strategy Balak adopts is to seek the help of the seer and diviner Bilam.

Three times at different places they prepare altars and sacrifices, but each time, Bilam utters blessings instead of curses. Balak leaves in anger and frustration. Having been spared Bilam's curses, however, the Israelites bring disaster on themselves through adultery and idolatry, seduced by the local women. Twenty-four thousand people die in a plague that strikes the camp until Pinḥas, in an act of zealotry, rises up against one of the wrongdoers.

The character of Bilam remains ambiguous, both in the Torah and subsequent Jewish tradition. Is he a diviner (reading omens and signs) or a sorcerer (practicing occult arts)? Is he a genuine prophet or a fraud? Does he assent to the divine blessings placed in his mouth, or does he wish to curse Israel? The causal link between the blessings of Bilam and the catastrophic story at the end of the *parasha* will be fully explained only in Parashat Mattot.

BILAM THE PROPHET

We are introduced to Bilam as a religious virtuoso in his society, a sought-after shaman, magus, spellbinder, and miracle worker. On the phrase "there has never arisen a prophet in Israel like Moshe, whom the LORD knew face-to-face" (Deut. 34:10), the Sages went so far as to say: "In Israel there was no other prophet as great as Moshe, but among the nations there was. Who was he? Bilam" (Sifrei, Devarim 357). Yet the ultimate verdict on Bilam is negative. The picture that emerges from the Jewish sources is of a man with great gifts, a genuine prophet,

and now they cover the face of the land – and they have
6 settled down alongside me. Please, come now and curse
this people for me, for they are stronger than I. Perhaps
then I will be able to defeat them and drive them from the
land, for I know that whomsoever you bless is blessed and
7 whomsoever you curse is cursed." So the elders of Moav
and Midyan went, carrying with them payment for
divination. They came to Bilam and repeated Balak's
8 words to him. "Spend the night here," he said, "and I will
give you your reply that the LORD speaks to me." So the
9 princes of Moav stayed the night with Bilam. God came
10 to Bilam and said, "Who are these men with you?" And
Bilam replied to God, "Balak son of Tzipor, king of Moav,
11 has sent me a message: 'A people has come out of Egypt
and covers the face of the land. Now come and curse
them for me. Perhaps I will be able to fight against them
12 and drive them away.'" "Do not go with them," said God
to Bilam. "Do not curse this people, for they are blessed."
13 Then Bilam arose in the morning and said to Balak's SHENI /ḤAMISHI/
princes, "Go back to your land, because the LORD has
14 refused to let me go with you." The princes of Moav rose
and went to Balak and said, "Bilam refuses to go with us."
15 Balak then sent other princes, yet more numerous and
16 eminent than the first. They came to Bilam and said to
him, "This is what Balak son of Tzipor says: 'Do not let
17 anything prevent you from coming to me, for I will do
you great honor, and whatever else you ask of me.
18 Please – come and curse this people for me.'" Bilam
replied to Balak's servants, "Even if Balak were to give me
his palace full of silver and gold, I could not do anything,
small or great, to transgress the word of the LORD my
19 God. But now, you too remain here tonight so that I may

book of Exodus: "'The Israelite people are *many* (*rav*) and more *powerful* (*atzum*) than we.'… And the Egyptians *came to dread* (*vayakutzu*) the Israelites" (Ex. 1:9, 12). Again we are given an insight into the perspective of other nations on Israel, which may differ from Israel's experience of themselves.

לֵאמֹר הִנֵּה עַם יָצָא מִמִּצְרַיִם הִנֵּה כִסָּה אֶת־עֵין הָאָרֶץ
ו וְהוּא יֹשֵׁב מִמֻּלִי: וְעַתָּה לְכָה־נָּא אָרָה־לִּי אֶת־הָעָם הַזֶּה
כִּי־עָצוּם הוּא מִמֶּנִּי אוּלַי אוּכַל נַכֶּה־בּוֹ וַאֲגָרְשֶׁנּוּ מִן־הָאָרֶץ
ז כִּי יָדַעְתִּי אֵת אֲשֶׁר־תְּבָרֵךְ מְבֹרָךְ וַאֲשֶׁר תָּאֹר יוּאָר: וַיֵּלְכוּ
זִקְנֵי מוֹאָב וְזִקְנֵי מִדְיָן וּקְסָמִים בְּיָדָם וַיָּבֹאוּ אֶל־בִּלְעָם
ח וַיְדַבְּרוּ אֵלָיו דִּבְרֵי בָלָק: וַיֹּאמֶר אֲלֵיהֶם לִינוּ פֹה הַלַּיְלָה
וַהֲשִׁבֹתִי אֶתְכֶם דָּבָר כַּאֲשֶׁר יְדַבֵּר יהוה אֵלָי וַיֵּשְׁבוּ שָׂרֵי־
ט מוֹאָב עִם־בִּלְעָם: וַיָּבֹא אֱלֹהִים אֶל־בִּלְעָם וַיֹּאמֶר מִי
י הָאֲנָשִׁים הָאֵלֶּה עִמָּךְ: וַיֹּאמֶר בִּלְעָם אֶל־הָאֱלֹהִים בָּלָק
יא בֶּן־צִפֹּר מֶלֶךְ מוֹאָב שָׁלַח אֵלָי: הִנֵּה הָעָם הַיֹּצֵא מִמִּצְרַיִם
וַיְכַס אֶת־עֵין הָאָרֶץ עַתָּה לְכָה קָבָה־לִּי אֹתוֹ אוּלַי אוּכַל
יב לְהִלָּחֶם בּוֹ וְגֵרַשְׁתִּיו: וַיֹּאמֶר אֱלֹהִים אֶל־בִּלְעָם לֹא תֵלֵךְ
יג עִמָּהֶם לֹא תָאֹר אֶת־הָעָם כִּי בָרוּךְ הוּא: וַיָּקָם בִּלְעָם בַּבֹּקֶר שני
וַיֹּאמֶר אֶל־שָׂרֵי בָלָק לְכוּ אֶל־אַרְצְכֶם כִּי מֵאֵן יהוה לְתִתִּי /חמישי/
יד לַהֲלֹךְ עִמָּכֶם: וַיָּקוּמוּ שָׂרֵי מוֹאָב וַיָּבֹאוּ אֶל־בָּלָק וַיֹּאמְרוּ
טו מֵאֵן בִּלְעָם הֲלֹךְ עִמָּנוּ: וַיֹּסֶף עוֹד בָּלָק שְׁלֹחַ שָׂרִים רַבִּים
טז וְנִכְבָּדִים מֵאֵלֶּה: וַיָּבֹאוּ אֶל־בִּלְעָם וַיֹּאמְרוּ לוֹ כֹּה אָמַר
יז בָּלָק בֶּן־צִפּוֹר אַל־נָא תִמָּנַע מֵהֲלֹךְ אֵלָי: כִּי־כַבֵּד אֲכַבֶּדְךָ
מְאֹד וְכֹל אֲשֶׁר־תֹּאמַר אֵלַי אֶעֱשֶׂה וּלְכָה־נָּא קָבָה־לִּי אֵת
יח הָעָם הַזֶּה: וַיַּעַן בִּלְעָם וַיֹּאמֶר אֶל־עַבְדֵי בָלָק אִם־יִתֶּן־לִי
בָלָק מְלֹא בֵיתוֹ כֶּסֶף וְזָהָב לֹא אוּכַל לַעֲבֹר אֶת־פִּי יהוה
יט אֱלֹהָי לַעֲשׂוֹת קְטַנָּה אוֹ גְדוֹלָה: וְעַתָּה שְׁבוּ נָא בָזֶה גַּם־

Prophecy is a form of leadership – but leadership without loyalty is not leadership. Skills alone cannot substitute for the moral qualities that make people follow those who demonstrate them. We follow those we trust, because they have acted so as to earn our trust. That was what made Moshe the great leader Bilam might have been but never was.

22:6 עָצוּם הוּא מִמֶּנִּי *Stronger than I* – The language the Torah uses here and in verse 3 is reminiscent of the reaction of the Egyptians at the beginning of the

20 know what else the LORD may tell me." God came to
Bilam that night and said to him, "If the men have come
to summon you, you may get up and go with them; but
21 do only what I tell you to do." So Bilam rose in the SHELISHI
morning, saddled his donkey, and went along with the
22 princes of Moav. God was furious at his going, and an
angel of the LORD stood in the road to oppose him as he
23 was riding on his donkey, his two servants with him. The
donkey saw the angel of the LORD standing in the road,
drawn sword in hand, and she swerved from the road into
a field. And Bilam beat the donkey to urge her back onto
24 the road. Then the angel of the LORD was standing in a
narrow path between vineyards with a wall on either side.
25 When the donkey saw the angel of the LORD, she pressed
against the wall, crushing Bilam's foot against it. He beat
26 her once again. And the angel of the LORD went ahead
and stood in a narrow place where there was no room at
27 all to turn right or left. When the donkey saw the angel of
the LORD, she lay down under Bilam. Bilam was furious
28 and beat the donkey with his stick. Then the LORD opened
the donkey's mouth and – "What have I done to you," she

---

their purpose or intention. God is angry when Bilam goes, because he identifies with their mission.

There is another possible answer. The hardest word to hear in any language is the word "no." Bilam asked God once. God said no. That should have sufficed. Yet now Bilam asks a second time. God does not change His mind. Therefore Bilam's delay says something not about God but about himself. He has not accepted the divine refusal. He wants to hear the answer "yes" – and that is indeed what he hears. Not because God wants him to go, but because God speaks once, and if we refuse to accept what He says, God does not force His will upon us. As the Sages of the Talmud put it: "Man is led down the path he chooses to tread" (Makkot 10b).

The true meaning of God's second reply, "Go with them," is: "If you insist, then I cannot stop you going – but I am angry that you should have asked a second time."

If God speaks and we do not listen, He does not intervene to save us from our choices. But God is not prepared to let Bilam proceed as if he has divine consent. This is to be Bilam's lesson, and what we, too, must discover if we are to be open to the voice of God.

כ אַתֶּם הַלָּיְלָה וְאֵדְעָה מַה־יֹּסֵף יְהוָה דַּבֵּר עִמִּי: וַיָּבֹא
אֱלֹהִים ׀ אֶל־בִּלְעָם לַיְלָה וַיֹּאמֶר לוֹ אִם־לִקְרֹא לְךָ בָּאוּ
הָאֲנָשִׁים קוּם לֵךְ אִתָּם וְאַךְ אֶת־הַדָּבָר אֲשֶׁר־אֲדַבֵּר אֵלֶיךָ
כא אֹתוֹ תַעֲשֶׂה: וַיָּקָם בִּלְעָם בַּבֹּקֶר וַיַּחֲבֹשׁ אֶת־אֲתֹנוֹ וַיֵּלֶךְ שלישי
כב עִם־שָׂרֵי מוֹאָב: וַיִּחַר־אַף אֱלֹהִים כִּי־הוֹלֵךְ הוּא וַיִּתְיַצֵּב
מַלְאַךְ יְהוָה בַּדֶּרֶךְ לְשָׂטָן לוֹ וְהוּא רֹכֵב עַל־אֲתֹנוֹ וּשְׁנֵי
כג נְעָרָיו עִמּוֹ: וַתֵּרֶא הָאָתוֹן אֶת־מַלְאַךְ יְהוָה נִצָּב בַּדֶּרֶךְ
וְחַרְבּוֹ שְׁלוּפָה בְּיָדוֹ וַתֵּט הָאָתוֹן מִן־הַדֶּרֶךְ וַתֵּלֶךְ בַּשָּׂדֶה
כד וַיַּךְ בִּלְעָם אֶת־הָאָתוֹן לְהַטֹּתָהּ הַדָּרֶךְ: וַיַּעֲמֹד מַלְאַךְ יְהוָה
כה בְּמִשְׁעוֹל הַכְּרָמִים גָּדֵר מִזֶּה וְגָדֵר מִזֶּה: וַתֵּרֶא הָאָתוֹן אֶת־
מַלְאַךְ יְהוָה וַתִּלָּחֵץ אֶל־הַקִּיר וַתִּלְחַץ אֶת־רֶגֶל בִּלְעָם
כו אֶל־הַקִּיר וַיֹּסֶף לְהַכֹּתָהּ: וַיּוֹסֶף מַלְאַךְ־יְהוָה עֲבוֹר וַיַּעֲמֹד
כז בְּמָקוֹם צָר אֲשֶׁר אֵין־דֶּרֶךְ לִנְטוֹת יָמִין וּשְׂמֹאול: וַתֵּרֶא
הָאָתוֹן אֶת־מַלְאַךְ יְהוָה וַתִּרְבַּץ תַּחַת בִּלְעָם וַיִּחַר־אַף
כח בִּלְעָם וַיַּךְ אֶת־הָאָתוֹן בַּמַּקֵּל: וַיִּפְתַּח יְהוָה אֶת־פִּי הָאָתוֹן

22:20 קוּם לֵךְ אִתָּם *You may… go with them* – At first God said, "Do not go." Now He says, "Go." Then immediately, "God was furious at his going" (v. 22). Does God change His mind – not once but twice in the course of a single narrative?

The commentators offer various ways of resolving the apparent contradictions. According to Ramban (on Num. 22:20), God's first statement, "Don't go with them" meant "Don't curse the Israelites." His second – "Go with them" – meant "Go but make it clear that you will only say the words I put in your mouth, even if they are words of blessing." God was angry with Bilam, not because he went but because he did not tell them of the proviso.

In the nineteenth century, Malbim and Rabbi Tzvi Hirsch Mecklenberg suggested another, ingenious answer (Malbim on Num. 22:21; *HaKetav VeHaKabbala* on Num. 22:12). The Torah uses two different words for "with them" in the first and second divine replies. When God says, "Don't go with them," the Hebrew is *imahem*. When He later says, "Go with them," the corresponding word is *itam*. The two prepositions have subtly different meanings. *Imahem* means "with them mentally as well as physically," going along with their plans. *Itam* means "with them physically but not mentally"; in other words, Bilam could accompany them but not share

said to Bilam, "that you have struck me these three times?"
29 "You are playing games with me," said Bilam to the donkey.
"If only I had a sword in my hand, I would kill you here
30 and now." But the donkey said to Bilam, "Am I not your
donkey on whom you have always ridden to this day?
Have I been in the habit of doing this to you?" "No,"
31 he replied. Then the LORD uncovered Bilam's eyes, and
he saw the angel of the LORD standing in the road,
drawn sword in hand. He bowed and prostrated himself
32 facedown. The angel of the LORD said to him, "Why have
you beaten your donkey these three times? It was I who
came out here to oppose you, because your way is
33 perverse to me. The donkey saw me and turned away
from me these three times. If she had not turned away
from me, I would certainly have killed you by now and let
34 her live." Bilam said to the angel of the LORD, "I have
sinned, for I did not know that you were standing against
me in the road. Now, if you consider it wrong, I will go
35 back." The angel of the LORD said to Bilam, "Go with the
men, but say nothing except what I tell you." So Bilam
36 continued on with Balak's princes. When Balak heard
that Bilam was coming, he went out to meet him at the
city of Moav, at the Arnon border on the edge of his
37 territory. Balak said to Bilam, "Did I not send to summon
you? Why did you not come to me? Am I really not able
38 to offer you any honor?" Bilam replied to Balak, "Well, I
have come to you now. But can I speak any words I
choose? I can only say the word God puts into my mouth."
39 Then Bilam went with Balak and they came to Kiryat REVI'I /SHISHI/

successes to God and their failures to themselves. Far from making them weak, this made them strong. So it is with us as individuals. Pagan prophets like Bilam had not yet learned the lesson we must all one day learn: that what matters is not that God does what we want, but that we do what He wants. God laughs at those who think they have godlike powers. The smaller we see ourselves, the greater we become.

וַתֹּאמֶר לְבִלְעָם מֶה־עָשִׂיתִי לְךָ כִּי הִכִּיתַנִי זֶה שָׁלֹשׁ רְגָלִים׃
כט וַיֹּאמֶר בִּלְעָם לָאָתוֹן כִּי הִתְעַלַּלְתְּ בִּי לוּ יֶשׁ־חֶרֶב בְּיָדִי כִּי
ל עַתָּה הֲרַגְתִּיךְ׃ וַתֹּאמֶר הָאָתוֹן אֶל־בִּלְעָם הֲלוֹא אָנֹכִי אֲתֹנְךָ
אֲשֶׁר־רָכַבְתָּ עָלַי מֵעוֹדְךָ עַד־הַיּוֹם הַזֶּה הַהַסְכֵּן הִסְכַּנְתִּי
לא לַעֲשׂוֹת לְךָ כֹּה וַיֹּאמֶר לֹא׃ וַיְגַל יהוה אֶת־עֵינֵי בִלְעָם וַיַּרְא
אֶת־מַלְאַךְ יהוה נִצָּב בַּדֶּרֶךְ וְחַרְבּוֹ שְׁלֻפָה בְּיָדוֹ וַיִּקֹּד
לב וַיִּשְׁתַּחוּ לְאַפָּיו׃ וַיֹּאמֶר אֵלָיו מַלְאַךְ יהוה עַל־מָה הִכִּיתָ
אֶת־אֲתֹנְךָ זֶה שָׁלוֹשׁ רְגָלִים הִנֵּה אָנֹכִי יָצָאתִי לְשָׂטָן כִּי־יָרַט
לג הַדֶּרֶךְ לְנֶגְדִּי׃ וַתִּרְאַנִי הָאָתוֹן וַתֵּט לְפָנַי זֶה שָׁלֹשׁ רְגָלִים
אוּלַי נָטְתָה מִפָּנַי כִּי עַתָּה גַּם־אֹתְכָה הָרַגְתִּי וְאוֹתָהּ הֶחֱיֵיתִי׃
לד וַיֹּאמֶר בִּלְעָם אֶל־מַלְאַךְ יהוה חָטָאתִי כִּי לֹא יָדַעְתִּי כִּי
אַתָּה נִצָּב לִקְרָאתִי בַּדָּרֶךְ וְעַתָּה אִם־רַע בְּעֵינֶיךָ אָשׁוּבָה
לה לִּי׃ וַיֹּאמֶר מַלְאַךְ יהוה אֶל־בִּלְעָם לֵךְ עִם־הָאֲנָשִׁים וְאֶפֶס
אֶת־הַדָּבָר אֲשֶׁר־אֲדַבֵּר אֵלֶיךָ אֹתוֹ תְדַבֵּר וַיֵּלֶךְ בִּלְעָם
לו עִם־שָׂרֵי בָלָק׃ וַיִּשְׁמַע בָּלָק כִּי־בָא בִלְעָם וַיֵּצֵא לִקְרָאתוֹ
אֶל־עִיר מוֹאָב אֲשֶׁר עַל־גְּבוּל אַרְנֹן אֲשֶׁר בִּקְצֵה הַגְּבוּל׃
לז וַיֹּאמֶר בָּלָק אֶל־בִּלְעָם הֲלֹא שָׁלֹחַ שָׁלַחְתִּי אֵלֶיךָ לִקְרֹא־לָךְ
לח לָמָּה לֹא־הָלַכְתָּ אֵלָי הַאֻמְנָם לֹא אוּכַל כַּבְּדֶךָ׃ וַיֹּאמֶר
בִּלְעָם אֶל־בָּלָק הִנֵּה־בָאתִי אֵלֶיךָ עַתָּה הֲיָכֹל אוּכַל דַּבֵּר
לט מְאוּמָה הַדָּבָר אֲשֶׁר יָשִׂים אֱלֹהִים בְּפִי אֹתוֹ אֲדַבֵּר׃ וַיֵּלֶךְ

רביעי
/ששי/

22:33 וַתִּרְאַנִי הָאָתוֹן *The donkey saw me* – One thing provokes divine laughter in the Tanakh, namely human pretension. It can be heard between the lines of the story of the Tower of Bavel, in the defeat of Egypt's hubris, and in our *parasha*. There is deliberate humor in the episode of the talking donkey. Bilam is known as the man who held the secrets of blessing and curse. His fame has spread to Moav and Midyan. Yet God now proceeds to show Bilam that when He so chooses, even a donkey is a greater prophet than he. God humbles the self-important, just as He grants importance to the humble.

Hubris always eventually becomes nemesis. In a world in which rulers engaged in endless projects of self-aggrandizement, Israel produced a literature in which they attributed their

40 Ḥutzot. Balak sacrificed oxen and sheep and sent them to
41 Bilam and the princes who were with him. In the morning
Balak took Bilam up to Bamot Baal, where he could see
23 1 part of the people. Bilam said to Balak, "Build me seven
altars here and prepare for me seven bulls and seven
2 rams." Balak did as Bilam said, and Balak and Bilam
3 offered a bull and a ram on each altar. Then Bilam said to
Balak, "Stand by your offerings and I will go; perhaps the
Lord will come to meet me. Whatever He shows me, I
4 will tell you." And he went off alone. God met Bilam, who
said to Him, "I have prepared seven altars; on each altar I
5 have offered a bull and a ram." And the Lord put a word
6 in Bilam's mouth, "Go back to Balak and say this." He
went back to him, and found him standing by his offering
7 together with all the princes of Moav. And Bilam took up
his oracle and said: "Balak brought me from Aram, the
king of Moav from the eastern hills. 'Go: curse Yaakov for
8 me; go: denounce Israel.' How can I curse whom God has
not cursed? How can I denounce whom the Lord has

---

end of our *parasha*, He sends a plague against them. A generation has passed in the desert. This is the new generation in which all the hopes of the future are invested. Yet they too stumble at the first fence, fall in the first trial. Malakhi, last of the prophets, speaks aptly:

> From one end of the earth to the other, My name is great among the nations. Incense is offered in My name, a pure offering everywhere, for My name is great among the nations, says the Lord of Hosts. Yet you desecrate it. (Mal. 1:11–12)

Why then choose Israel? Moshe is to answer explicitly: "The Lord your God chose not to listen to Bilam; the Lord your God turned the curse into a blessing for you – *because the Lord your God loves you*" (Deut. 23:6).

God is often exasperated by Israel's conduct, but He cannot relinquish that love for them. Where in the Torah does God express this love? In the blessings of Bilam. That is where He gives voice to His feelings for this people. "Who can number the dust of Yaakov, count even a fourth of Israel?" (Num. 23:10). "A people – see – rises like a lioness, lifts itself up like a lion" (23:24). "How good are your tents, Yaakov, your homes, O Israel!" (24:5). These famous words are not Bilam's. They are God's – the most eloquent expression of His love for this small, otherwise undistinguished

מ בִלְעָם עִם־בָּלָק וַיָּבֹאוּ קִרְיַת חֻצוֹת: וַיִּזְבַּח בָּלָק בָּקָר וָצֹאן
מא וַיְשַׁלַּח לְבִלְעָם וְלַשָּׂרִים אֲשֶׁר אִתּוֹ: וַיְהִי בַבֹּקֶר וַיִּקַּח בָּלָק
אֶת־בִּלְעָם וַיַּעֲלֵהוּ בָּמוֹת בָּעַל וַיַּרְא מִשָּׁם קְצֵה הָעָם:
כג א וַיֹּאמֶר בִּלְעָם אֶל־בָּלָק בְּנֵה־לִי בָזֶה שִׁבְעָה מִזְבְּחֹת וְהָכֵן
ב לִי בָּזֶה שִׁבְעָה פָרִים וְשִׁבְעָה אֵילִים: וַיַּעַשׂ בָּלָק כַּאֲשֶׁר
ג דִּבֶּר בִּלְעָם וַיַּעַל בָּלָק וּבִלְעָם פַּר וָאַיִל בַּמִּזְבֵּחַ: וַיֹּאמֶר
בִּלְעָם לְבָלָק הִתְיַצֵּב עַל־עֹלָתֶךָ וְאֵלְכָה אוּלַי יִקָּרֶה יהוה
ד לִקְרָאתִי וּדְבַר מַה־יַּרְאֵנִי וְהִגַּדְתִּי לָךְ וַיֵּלֶךְ שֶׁפִי: וַיִּקָּר
אֱלֹהִים אֶל־בִּלְעָם וַיֹּאמֶר אֵלָיו אֶת־שִׁבְעַת הַמִּזְבְּחֹת
ה עָרַכְתִּי וָאַעַל פַּר וָאַיִל בַּמִּזְבֵּחַ: וַיָּשֶׂם יהוה דָּבָר בְּפִי בִלְעָם
ו וַיֹּאמֶר שׁוּב אֶל־בָּלָק וְכֹה תְדַבֵּר: וַיָּשָׁב אֵלָיו וְהִנֵּה נִצָּב
ז עַל־עֹלָתוֹ הוּא וְכָל־שָׂרֵי מוֹאָב: וַיִּשָּׂא מְשָׁלוֹ וַיֹּאמַר מִן־
אֲרָם יַנְחֵנִי בָלָק מֶלֶךְ־מוֹאָב מֵהַרְרֵי־קֶדֶם לְכָה אָרָה־לִּי
ח יַעֲקֹב וּלְכָה זֹעֲמָה יִשְׂרָאֵל: מָה אֶקֹּב לֹא קַבֹּה אֵל וּמָה

BILAM'S BLESSINGS

God puts into Bilam's mouth the extraordinary poetry that makes this among the most lyrical passages in the Torah. Why? All He really needs Bilam to say – and Bilam does eventually say it (Num. 24:9) – is the promise He gave to Avraham: "I will bless those who bless you, and those who curse you I will curse" (Gen. 12:3). In Bilam's blessings, the Israelites are rescued from a danger they know nothing about by a deliverance they know nothing about. Even Moshe would not know what had happened, were God not to tell him. Yet the story leaves a deep impression. Moshe will remind the people of it in Deuteronomy 23:4–5. Yehoshua, at Gilgal, giving an abridged summary of Jewish history, is to single out this event for attention (Josh. 24:9–10). At the culmination of the reforms instituted by Ezra and Neḥemya after the Babylonian exile, Neḥemya reminds the people that an Amonite or Moabite may not enter "the congregation of God" because they "hired Bilam to curse them" (Neh. 13:2). Why the resonance of an event that seemingly had no impact on any of the parties involved (see Num. 25:1 and note there) and made no difference to what happened thereafter?

The answer may lie in the very misdemeanors that precede and follow the story. God has threatened twice to destroy the people, after the golden calf and the episode of the spies. Toward the

9 not denounced? From the tops of crags I see him; from
the hills I gaze down: a people that dwells alone; not
10 reckoning itself among nations. Who can number the
dust of Yaakov, count even a fourth of Israel? Let me die
11 the death of the upright, and let my end be like his." And
Balak said to Bilam, "What have you done to me? I
brought you to curse my enemies, and you have blessed

23:9 וּבַגּוֹיִם לֹא יִתְחַשָּׁב *Not reckoning itself among nations* – Ibn Ezra interprets this verse as meaning that unlike all other nations, Jews, even when they are a minority in a non-Jewish culture, will not assimilate. Ramban says that their culture and creed will remain pure, not a cosmopolitan mix of multiple traditions and nationalities. The Netziv gives the sharp interpretation, clearly directed against the Jews of his time, that "if Jews live distinctive and apart from others they will dwell safely, but if they seek to emulate 'the nations' they 'will not be reckoned' as anything special at all." Rabbi Samson Raphael Hirsch offered a fine insight by focusing on the nuance between "people" (*am*) and "nation" (*goy*) – or as we might say nowadays, "society" and "state" (commentary on Num. 23:9). Israel uniquely became a society before it was a state. It had laws before it had a land. It was a people – a group bound together by a common code and culture – before it was a nation, that is, a political entity.

Jews, certainly from the Babylonian exile onward, had none of the conventional attributes of a nation. They did not live in the same land. Some lived in Israel, others in Babylon, yet others in Egypt. Later they would be scattered throughout the world. They did not share a language of everyday speech. There were many Jewish vernaculars. They did not live under the same political dispensation. They did not share the same cultural environment. Nor did they experience the same fate. Despite all their many differences though, they always saw themselves and were seen by others as one nation: the world's first, and for long the world's only, global people.

What makes Jews "a people that dwells alone, not reckoning itself among nations" is that their nationhood is not a matter of geography, politics, or ethnicity. It is a matter of religious vocation as God's covenant partners, summoned to be a living example of a nation among the nations made distinctive by its faith and way of life. Israel's strength lies not in nationalism but in building a society based on justice and human dignity.

This verse, then, expresses the uniqueness of the Jewish people – its isolation on the one hand, its defiance and resilience on the other. Though it has faced opposition and persecution from some of the greatest superpowers the world has ever known, it has so far outlived them all.

ט אֶזְעֹם לֹא זָעַם יְהוָה׃ כִּי־מֵרֹאשׁ צֻרִים אֶרְאֶנּוּ וּמִגְּבָעוֹת
י אֲשׁוּרֶנּוּ הֶן־עָם לְבָדָד יִשְׁכֹּן וּבַגּוֹיִם לֹא יִתְחַשָּׁב׃ מִי מָנָה כ
עֲפַר יַעֲקֹב וּמִסְפָּר אֶת־רֹבַע יִשְׂרָאֵל תָּמֹת נַפְשִׁי מוֹת
יא יְשָׁרִים וּתְהִי אַחֲרִיתִי כָּמֹהוּ׃ וַיֹּאמֶר בָּלָק אֶל־בִּלְעָם מֶה

---

people. Bilam, the pagan prophet, is the most unlikely vehicle for God's blessings. But that is God's way. He chose an aged, infertile couple to be the grandparents of the Jewish people. He chose a man who couldn't speak to be the mouthpiece of His word. He chose Bilam, an indifferent man in the service of a hateful one, to express His love.

That is what the story is about: not Balak, or Bilam, or Moav, or Midyan, or what happened next. It is about God's love for a people, their strength, resilience, their willingness to be different, their family life (tents, homes), and their ability to outlive empires. Bilam's poetry bears a message rarely so clearly conveyed in prose. *Love can turn curses into blessings. Love heals the wounds of the world.*

23:9 עָם לְבָדָד יִשְׁכֹּן *A people that dwells alone* – This is a very ambiguous blessing. Being alone, from a Torah perspective, is not a good thing. The first time the words "not good" appear in the Torah is in the verse "It is not good for man to be alone" (Gen. 2:18). The second time is when Moshe's father-in-law Yitro sees him leading alone and says, "What you are doing is not good" (Ex. 18:17). We cannot live and thrive alone. Isolation is not a blessing – quite the opposite.

The word *badad* appears in two other profoundly negative contexts. First is the case of the leper: "He shall live apart; outside the camp shall be his dwelling" (Lev. 13:46). The second is the opening line of the book of Lamentations, "How the city that overflowed with people sits alone" (Lam. 1:1). The only context in which *badad* has a positive sense is when it is applied to God (Deut. 32:12), for obvious theological reasons. In the Rabbis' view, "a people that dwells alone" eventually became not a blessing but a curse.

What is more, "a people that dwells alone" risks turning from an ambiguous prophecy to a self-fulfilling one. Why bother to make friends and allies if you know in advance that you will fail? Those who take refuge in solitude compound their problems rather than solving them.

Nowhere in Tanakh are we told that it will be the fate of Israel, or Jews, to be hated. To the contrary, the prophets foresaw that there would come a time when the nations would turn to Israel for inspiration. Isolation may at times be the Jewish condition, but it is not the Jewish vocation. We must treat this pronouncement with caution. It is Bilam's curse, not God's blessing.

12 them." He answered, "Am I not obliged to speak strictly
13 the words the LORD puts in my mouth?" Then Balak said ḤAMISHI
to him, "Come with me to another place where you will
see them. You will see only part of them; you will not see
14 them all. Curse them for me from there." He took him to
the field of Tzofim, to the top of Pisga. He built seven
15 altars and on each altar offered a bull and a ram. Then
Bilam said to Balak, "Stand here beside your offering,
16 while I seek a meeting there." The LORD met Bilam and
put a word in his mouth. "Go back to Balak," He said,
17 "and tell him this." He came to him and found him
standing by his offering together with the princes of
18 Moav. Balak asked him, "What did the LORD say?" So he
took up his oracle and said: "Stand up, Balak, listen; pay
19 attention, son of Tzipor. Not man is God, to lie; no
mortal, to change His mind. Would He speak and not
20 fulfill, would He promise and not keep? I received an
21 order to bless. He has blessed; I cannot revoke it. He has
glimpsed no wrong in Yaakov, He has seen no sin in Israel.
The LORD their God is with them, in them the King's
22 horn blasts sounds. God, who freed them from Egypt, is
23 like the oryx's proud horn for them. There is no divination
over Yaakov, no spell against Israel can hold. It will now
24 be said of Yaakov, of Israel, 'See what God has done.' A

Friends praise and bless. Enemies criticize and curse. To make an impression, to be credible, the order had to be reversed.

Might this be the explanation for the remarkable fact that more than any other national literature, the Hebrew Bible records Israel's failings, its shortcomings, its sins, its faults? It is a literature of unparalleled self-criticism. Yet somehow, somewhere, the people must be assured that they are loved not just for their ancestors but for themselves.

Bilam is God's messenger delivering a love letter to His people in such a way as to leave no doubt that the message has come directly from God – since there is nothing in Bilam's character and conduct that would explain it in any other way. Bilam is, if one can say such a thing, God's way of fulfilling Proverbs's principle: "Let another person praise you, not your own mouth; a stranger, not your own lips" (Prov. 27:2).

Bilam is the most unlikely messenger but the one who delivers the most beautiful of messages.

יב עָשִׂיתָ לִי לָקֹב אֹיְבַי לְקַחְתִּיךָ וְהִנֵּה בֵּרַכְתָּ בָרֵךְ: וַיַּעַן וַיֹּאמַר
יג הֲלֹא אֵת אֲשֶׁר יָשִׂים יהוה בְּפִי אֹתוֹ אֶשְׁמֹר לְדַבֵּר: וַיֹּאמֶר חמישי
אֵלָיו בָּלָק לְךָ־נָּא אִתִּי אֶל־מָקוֹם אַחֵר אֲשֶׁר תִּרְאֶנּוּ מִשָּׁם
יד אֶפֶס קָצֵהוּ תִרְאֶה וְכֻלּוֹ לֹא תִרְאֶה וְקָבְנוֹ־לִי מִשָּׁם: וַיִּקָּחֵהוּ
שְׂדֵה צֹפִים אֶל־רֹאשׁ הַפִּסְגָּה וַיִּבֶן שִׁבְעָה מִזְבְּחֹת וַיַּעַל פַּר
טו וָאַיִל בַּמִּזְבֵּחַ: וַיֹּאמֶר אֶל־בָּלָק הִתְיַצֵּב כֹּה עַל־עֹלָתֶךָ וְאָנֹכִי
טז אִקָּרֶה כֹּה: וַיִּקָּר יהוה אֶל־בִּלְעָם וַיָּשֶׂם דָּבָר בְּפִיו וַיֹּאמֶר
יז שׁוּב אֶל־בָּלָק וְכֹה תְדַבֵּר: וַיָּבֹא אֵלָיו וְהִנּוֹ נִצָּב עַל־עֹלָתוֹ
יח וְשָׂרֵי מוֹאָב אִתּוֹ וַיֹּאמֶר לוֹ בָּלָק מַה־דִּבֶּר יהוה: וַיִּשָּׂא
יט מְשָׁלוֹ וַיֹּאמַר קוּם בָּלָק וּשְׁמָע הַאֲזִינָה עָדַי בְּנוֹ צִפֹּר: לֹא
אִישׁ אֵל וִיכַזֵּב וּבֶן־אָדָם וְיִתְנֶחָם הַהוּא אָמַר וְלֹא יַעֲשֶׂה
כ וְדִבֶּר וְלֹא יְקִימֶנָּה: הִנֵּה בָרֵךְ לָקָחְתִּי וּבֵרֵךְ וְלֹא אֲשִׁיבֶנָּה:
כא לֹא־הִבִּיט אָוֶן בְּיַעֲקֹב וְלֹא־רָאָה עָמָל בְּיִשְׂרָאֵל יהוה אֱלֹהָיו
כב עִמּוֹ וּתְרוּעַת מֶלֶךְ בּוֹ: אֵל מוֹצִיאָם מִמִּצְרָיִם כְּתוֹעֲפֹת רְאֵם
כג לוֹ: כִּי לֹא־נַחַשׁ בְּיַעֲקֹב וְלֹא־קֶסֶם בְּיִשְׂרָאֵל כָּעֵת יֵאָמֵר
כד לְיַעֲקֹב וּלְיִשְׂרָאֵל מַה־פָּעַל אֵל: הֶן־עָם כְּלָבִיא יָקוּם וְכַאֲרִי

23:21 לֹא־רָאָה עָמָל בְּיִשְׂרָאֵל *He has seen no sin in Israel* – From the beginning of Exodus to the end of Numbers, not a word is spoken in praise of the Israelites – *except by Bilam*. Nor are these faint praises. This verse is a prime example, suggesting that the people are almost flawless. Who said these words? Ostensibly Bilam. But we know he is only speaking the words God put in his mouth. A comment in Midrash Rabba adds:

> It would have been appropriate for the reprimands [delivered to Israel] to be delivered by Bilam and the blessings by Moshe. However, if Bilam had spoken the reprimands, the Israelites would have said, "Our enemy is reprimanding us." And had Moshe delivered the blessings, the nations of the world would have said, "One who loves them is blessing them." Therefore, said the Holy One, blessed be He, "Let Moshe who loves them reprimand them, and let Bilam who hates them bless them, so that both the reprimands and the blessings make a clear impression on Israel." (Devarim Rabba 1:4)

When people say what they are expected to say, their words tend to be discounted.

▶

people – see – rises like a lioness, lifts itself up like a lion.
It will not lie down until it eats its meat and drinks the
25 blood of the slain." Balak said to Bilam, "Do not curse or
26 bless them." But Bilam answered, "Did I not tell you, 'I
27 must do whatever the LORD says'?" Then Balak said to SHISHI /SHEVI'I/
Bilam, "Come now and I will take you to another place.
Perhaps God will deem it right to let you curse them for
28 me there." So Balak took Bilam to the top of Peor,
29 overlooking the wasteland. Bilam said to Balak, "Build
me seven altars here and prepare for me seven bulls and
30 seven rams." Balak did as Bilam had said, and offered a
24 1 bull and a ram on each altar. When Bilam saw that it
pleased the LORD to bless the Israelites, he did not go as
at other times to seek omens. Instead, he turned toward
2 the wilderness. And Bilam raised his eyes and saw Israel
encamped there tribe by tribe, and God's spirit came
3 upon him. He took up his oracle and said: "The word of
Bilam, son of Beor; the word of the man whose eye is
4 opened. The word of one who hears God's speech, who
sees a vision of Shaddai, who falls, but with eyes unveiled.
5 How good are your tents, Yaakov, your homes, O Israel.
6 Like palm groves stretching forth, like gardens by the

things" (Wordsworth, *Lines Composed a Few Miles Above Tintern Abbey*).

This is what Bilam experiences against his will. Far from the uproar of the camp, viewing it from above, he is "a man whose eye is opened." He sees Israel momentarily from the perspective of God, and cannot do otherwise than bless them.

24:5 מִשְׁכְּנֹתֶיךָ יִשְׂרָאֵל *Your homes, O Israel* – This blessing, as understood by the Rabbis, was prophetic. "How good are your tents, Yaakov, your homes, O Israel." The home, *mishkan,* meant the synagogue, home of both the community and the Divine Presence. The Rabbis added to this interpretation a further note. They said: All of Bilam's blessings eventually turned into curses, except this. Israel lost all its earthly glory, but it never lost its synagogues. Because of this, it survived. No other people maintained its identity through two thousand years of dispersion, but Jews did, because though they had lost their geographic home they preserved their spiritual home, and though they were no longer a sovereign nation they were still a constituted people, the "congregation of Israel."

יִתְנַשָּׂא לֹא יִשְׁכַּב עַד־יֹאכַל טֶרֶף וְדַם־חֲלָלִים יִשְׁתֶּה׃
כה וַיֹּאמֶר בָּלָק אֶל־בִּלְעָם גַּם־קֹב לֹא תִקֳּבֶנּוּ גַּם־בָּרֵךְ לֹא
כו תְבָרְכֶנּוּ׃ וַיַּעַן בִּלְעָם וַיֹּאמֶר אֶל־בָּלָק הֲלֹא דִּבַּרְתִּי אֵלֶיךָ
כז לֵאמֹר כֹּל אֲשֶׁר־יְדַבֵּר יהוה אֹתוֹ אֶעֱשֶׂה׃ וַיֹּאמֶר בָּלָק אֶל־ ששי /שביעי/
בִּלְעָם לְכָה־נָּא אֶקָּחֲךָ אֶל־מָקוֹם אַחֵר אוּלַי יִישַׁר בְּעֵינֵי
כח הָאֱלֹהִים וְקַבֹּתוֹ לִי מִשָּׁם׃ וַיִּקַּח בָּלָק אֶת־בִּלְעָם רֹאשׁ
כט הַפְּעוֹר הַנִּשְׁקָף עַל־פְּנֵי הַיְשִׁימֹן׃ וַיֹּאמֶר בִּלְעָם אֶל־בָּלָק
בְּנֵה־לִי בָזֶה שִׁבְעָה מִזְבְּחֹת וְהָכֵן לִי בָּזֶה שִׁבְעָה פָרִים
ל וְשִׁבְעָה אֵילִם׃ וַיַּעַשׂ בָּלָק כַּאֲשֶׁר אָמַר בִּלְעָם וַיַּעַל פַּר
כד א וָאַיִל בַּמִּזְבֵּחַ׃ וַיַּרְא בִּלְעָם כִּי טוֹב בְּעֵינֵי יהוה לְבָרֵךְ אֶת־
יִשְׂרָאֵל וְלֹא־הָלַךְ כְּפַעַם־בְּפַעַם לִקְרַאת נְחָשִׁים וַיָּשֶׁת
ב אֶל־הַמִּדְבָּר פָּנָיו׃ וַיִּשָּׂא בִלְעָם אֶת־עֵינָיו וַיַּרְא אֶת־יִשְׂרָאֵל
ג שֹׁכֵן לִשְׁבָטָיו וַתְּהִי עָלָיו רוּחַ אֱלֹהִים׃ וַיִּשָּׂא מְשָׁלוֹ וַיֹּאמַר
ד נְאֻם בִּלְעָם בְּנוֹ בְעֹר וּנְאֻם הַגֶּבֶר שְׁתֻם הָעָיִן׃ נְאֻם שֹׁמֵעַ
ה אִמְרֵי־אֵל אֲשֶׁר מַחֲזֵה שַׁדַּי יֶחֱזֶה נֹפֵל וּגְלוּי עֵינָיִם׃ מַה־טֹּבוּ
ו אֹהָלֶיךָ יַעֲקֹב מִשְׁכְּנֹתֶיךָ יִשְׂרָאֵל׃ כִּנְחָלִים נִטָּיוּ כְּגַנֹּת עֲלֵי

24:2 וַיִּשָּׂא בִלְעָם אֶת־עֵינָיו וַיַּרְא *Bilam raised his eyes and saw* – Blessing, prayer, is a way of seeing, not unlike the account Iris Murdoch gives of the aesthetic sense:

> I am looking out of my window in an anxious and resentful frame of mind, oblivious of my surroundings, brooding perhaps on some damage done to my prestige. Then suddenly I observe a hovering kestrel. In a moment, everything is altered. The brooding self with its hurt vanity has disappeared. There is nothing now but kestrel. And when I return to the thinking of the other matter it seems less important. (*The Sovereignty of Good*)

She calls this "unselfing," and sees it as essential to the moral life. This is what happens, or ought to happen, when we pray. The relentless first-person singular falls silent and we become aware that we are not the center of the universe. There is a reality outside. That is a moment of transformation. For a moment we still the clamor of desire and experience instead "that serene and blessed mood, / in which…with an eye made quiet by the power / of harmony, and the deep power of joy, / we see into the life of

river, like aloes the LORD planted, like cedars by the
7 waters. Water will drip from his branches; his seed has
abundant water; his king will be higher than Agag, his
8 kingdom exalted. God, who freed him from Egypt, is the
oryx's proud horn to him. He will devour enemy nations,
9 break their bones, pierce them with arrows. Like a lion he
crouches, lies down, like a lioness; who dares to rouse
him? Blessing on all who bless you, on those who curse
10 you, curse." Balak was furious with Bilam. He struck his
hands together. Balak said to Bilam, "I summoned you to
curse my enemies. Instead you have blessed them these
11 three times over. Now get away from here and go home. I
said that I would honor you, but the LORD has denied
12 you all honor." Bilam replied to Balak, "Did I not tell the
13 messengers whom you sent to me, 'Even if Balak were to
give me his palace full of silver and gold, I could not do
anything to transgress the word of the LORD, doing either
good or bad of my own accord. What the LORD says is
14 what I must say.' So now that I am going back to my SHEVI'I
people, let me advise you what this people will do to your
15 people in days to come." He took up his oracle, saying:
"The word of Bilam son of Beor, the word of a man whose
16 eye is opened. The word of one who hears God's speech,
and has knowledge from the Most High, who sees a
17 vision of Shaddai, who falls, but with eyes unveiled. I see
him, but not now; I gaze upon him, though not near: A
star will shoot forth from Yaakov; a scepter will arise from
Israel, and smash the brow of Moav, and devastate all
18 children of Shet. Edom will become a possession, Se'ir
the possession of its foes. But Israel will act valiantly.
19 From Yaakov will come forth a ruler and empty the city
20 of survivors." He looked at Amalek; he took up his oracle
and said: "Amalek is first among nations, but its end will
21 be death forever." He looked at the Kenites; he took up
his oracle and said: "Invincible your dwelling, your nest
22 set in the rock. Yet Kayin is destined for burning, when
23 Assyria seizes you captive." And he took up his oracle and

ז נָהָר כַּאֲהָלִים נָטַע יְהוָה כַּאֲרָזִים עֲלֵי־מָיִם׃ יִזַּל־מַיִם מִדָּלְיָו
ח וְזַרְעוֹ בְּמַיִם רַבִּים וְיָרֹם מֵאֲגַג מַלְכּוֹ וְתִנַּשֵּׂא מַלְכֻתוֹ׃ אֵל
מוֹצִיאוֹ מִמִּצְרַיִם כְּתוֹעֲפֹת רְאֵם לוֹ יֹאכַל גּוֹיִם צָרָיו
ט וְעַצְמֹתֵיהֶם יְגָרֵם וְחִצָּיו יִמְחָץ׃ כָּרַע שָׁכַב כַּאֲרִי וּכְלָבִיא מִי
י יְקִימֶנּוּ מְבָרְכֶיךָ בָרוּךְ וְאֹרְרֶיךָ אָרוּר׃ וַיִּחַר־אַף בָּלָק אֶל־
בִּלְעָם וַיִּסְפֹּק אֶת־כַּפָּיו וַיֹּאמֶר בָּלָק אֶל־בִּלְעָם לָקֹב אֹיְבַי
יא קְרָאתִיךָ וְהִנֵּה בֵּרַכְתָּ בָרֵךְ זֶה שָׁלֹשׁ פְּעָמִים׃ וְעַתָּה בְּרַח־
לְךָ אֶל־מְקוֹמֶךָ אָמַרְתִּי כַּבֵּד אֲכַבֶּדְךָ וְהִנֵּה מְנָעֲךָ יְהוָה
יב מִכָּבוֹד׃ וַיֹּאמֶר בִּלְעָם אֶל־בָּלָק הֲלֹא גַּם אֶל־מַלְאָכֶיךָ
יג אֲשֶׁר־שָׁלַחְתָּ אֵלַי דִּבַּרְתִּי לֵאמֹר׃ אִם־יִתֶּן־לִי בָלָק מְלֹא
בֵיתוֹ כֶּסֶף וְזָהָב לֹא אוּכַל לַעֲבֹר אֶת־פִּי יְהוָה לַעֲשׂוֹת טוֹבָה
יד אוֹ רָעָה מִלִּבִּי אֲשֶׁר־יְדַבֵּר יְהוָה אֹתוֹ אֲדַבֵּר׃ וְעַתָּה הִנְנִי שביעי
הוֹלֵךְ לְעַמִּי לְכָה אִיעָצְךָ אֲשֶׁר יַעֲשֶׂה הָעָם הַזֶּה לְעַמְּךָ
טו בְּאַחֲרִית הַיָּמִים׃ וַיִּשָּׂא מְשָׁלוֹ וַיֹּאמַר נְאֻם בִּלְעָם בְּנוֹ בְעֹר
טז וּנְאֻם הַגֶּבֶר שְׁתֻם הָעָיִן׃ נְאֻם שֹׁמֵעַ אִמְרֵי־אֵל וְיֹדֵעַ דַּעַת
יז עֶלְיוֹן מַחֲזֵה שַׁדַּי יֶחֱזֶה נֹפֵל וּגְלוּי עֵינָיִם׃ אֶרְאֶנּוּ וְלֹא עַתָּה
אֲשׁוּרֶנּוּ וְלֹא קָרוֹב דָּרַךְ כּוֹכָב מִיַּעֲקֹב וְקָם שֵׁבֶט מִיִּשְׂרָאֵל
יח וּמָחַץ פַּאֲתֵי מוֹאָב וְקַרְקַר כָּל־בְּנֵי־שֵׁת׃ וְהָיָה אֱדוֹם יְרֵשָׁה
יט וְהָיָה יְרֵשָׁה שֵׂעִיר אֹיְבָיו וְיִשְׂרָאֵל עֹשֶׂה חָיִל׃ וְיֵרְדְּ מִיַּעֲקֹב
כ וְהֶאֱבִיד שָׂרִיד מֵעִיר׃ וַיַּרְא אֶת־עֲמָלֵק וַיִּשָּׂא מְשָׁלוֹ וַיֹּאמַר
כא רֵאשִׁית גּוֹיִם עֲמָלֵק וְאַחֲרִיתוֹ עֲדֵי אֹבֵד׃ וַיַּרְא אֶת־הַקֵּינִי
כב וַיִּשָּׂא מְשָׁלוֹ וַיֹּאמַר אֵיתָן מוֹשָׁבֶךָ וְשִׂים בַּסֶּלַע קִנֶּךָ׃ כִּי
כג אִם־יִהְיֶה לְבָעֵר קָיִן עַד־מָה אַשּׁוּר תִּשְׁבֶּךָּ׃ וַיִּשָּׂא מְשָׁלוֹ

24 said, "Alas! Who will live when God does this? Ships from
the coast of Kitim will afflict Assyria, afflict Ever; they too
25 will perish for all time." Then Bilam rose and returned
home, and Balak also set off upon his way.
25 1 Israel was dwelling at Shitim. And the men began to
2 consort with Moabite women, who invited the people
to join the sacrifices to their god; the men ate, and then
3 they worshipped the women's god. Israel allied itself
with Baal Peor, and the LORD was filled with fury against
4 Israel. "Take all the people's leaders," said the LORD to
Moshe, "and have them impaled before the LORD in
broad daylight, so that the LORD's fury with Israel may
5 be allayed." Moshe said to Israel's judges, "Each of you
kill those of your men who have allied themselves with
6 Baal Peor." At that moment, an Israelite man brought a
Midianite woman to his friends before the eyes of Moshe
and the entire Israelite community, who were weeping at
7 the entrance to the Tent of Meeting. When Pinḥas son of MAFTIR
Elazar son of Aharon the priest saw this, he rose from the
8 midst of the community, took a spear in his hand, went

suggest that Moshe's own background renders him powerless in this situation, for he is himself married to a Midianite woman, the daughter of one of their priests (Sanhedrin 82a). Any attempt on Moshe's part to do what Pinḥas does would expose him to the charge of hypocrisy, and make the situation worse, not better. Pinḥas, then, acts on his own initiative.

Not by accident did tradition fix the *parasha* break between Parashat Balak and Parashat Pinḥas at the most counterintuitive point, between Pinḥas's act (Num. 25:6–9) and the divine verdict on the act (25:10–15). The result is that we are forced to wait a week before hearing whether he did right or wrong. It is as if the Sages wanted us to live with that ambiguity so that we would not too readily conclude that Pinḥas is a hero. His act is fraught with moral hazard.

THE END OF THE BAAL PEOR AFFAIR

This may be the first time the Israelites have committed the cardinal sin of idolatry. Most of the commentators do not regard the golden calf as an idol. It was intended as a substitute Moshe – a vehicle for receiving divine messages – rather than an object of worship in its own right. But the idolatry at Shitim is real.

כד וַיֹּאמַר אוֹי מִי יִחְיֶה מִשֻּׂמוֹ אֵל: וְצִים מִיַּד כִּתִּים וְעִנּוּ אַשּׁוּר
כה וְעִנּוּ־עֵבֶר וְגַם־הוּא עֲדֵי אֹבֵד: וַיָּקָם בִּלְעָם וַיֵּלֶךְ וַיָּשָׁב
לִמְקֹמוֹ וְגַם־בָּלָק הָלַךְ לְדַרְכּוֹ:
כה א וַיֵּשֶׁב יִשְׂרָאֵל בַּשִּׁטִּים וַיָּחֶל הָעָם לִזְנוֹת אֶל־בְּנוֹת מוֹאָב: כא
ב וַתִּקְרֶאןָ לָעָם לְזִבְחֵי אֱלֹהֵיהֶן וַיֹּאכַל הָעָם וַיִּשְׁתַּחֲווּ
ג לֵאלֹהֵיהֶן: וַיִּצָּמֶד יִשְׂרָאֵל לְבַעַל פְּעוֹר וַיִּחַר־אַף יְהֹוָה
ד בְּיִשְׂרָאֵל: וַיֹּאמֶר יְהֹוָה אֶל־מֹשֶׁה קַח אֶת־כָּל־רָאשֵׁי הָעָם
וְהוֹקַע אוֹתָם לַיהֹוָה נֶגֶד הַשָּׁמֶשׁ וְיָשֹׁב חֲרוֹן אַף־יְהֹוָה
ה מִיִּשְׂרָאֵל: וַיֹּאמֶר מֹשֶׁה אֶל־שֹׁפְטֵי יִשְׂרָאֵל הִרְגוּ אִישׁ
ו אֲנָשָׁיו הַנִּצְמָדִים לְבַעַל פְּעוֹר: וְהִנֵּה אִישׁ מִבְּנֵי יִשְׂרָאֵל בָּא
וַיַּקְרֵב אֶל־אֶחָיו אֶת־הַמִּדְיָנִית לְעֵינֵי מֹשֶׁה וּלְעֵינֵי כָּל־עֲדַת
ז בְּנֵי־יִשְׂרָאֵל וְהֵמָּה בֹכִים פֶּתַח אֹהֶל מוֹעֵד: וַיַּרְא פִּינְחָס מפטיר
בֶּן־אֶלְעָזָר בֶּן־אַהֲרֹן הַכֹּהֵן וַיָּקָם מִתּוֹךְ הָעֵדָה וַיִּקַּח רֹמַח
ח בְּיָדוֹ: וַיָּבֹא אַחַר אִישׁ־יִשְׂרָאֵל אֶל־הַקֻּבָּה וַיִּדְקֹר אֶת־

25:1 לִזְנוֹת אֶל־בְּנוֹת מוֹאָב *To consort with Moabite women* – Bilam's failure to curse Israel does not, in the end, affect the Moabites. They proceed to enlist their women to successfully entice the Israelite men. A plague then strikes the Israelites, taking twenty-four thousand lives.

It does not affect the Midianites, whose hostility to Israel will later cause God to instruct Moshe to take military vengeance against them (Num. 31).

It does not affect Bilam himself; we will find this out in chapter 31. We see immediately here that it has not changed the Israelites either. Had the Israelites known the danger they were in, and how they were saved from it, it would have given them pause for thought before engaging in immorality and idol worship with the Moabite women. They would have known that the Moabites were not their friends.

In the story of Bilam, fearing that the Israelites derive strength from a supernatural force, the Moabites tried to counter it with another supernatural force. The plan failed and "Bilam rose and returned home, and Balak also set off upon his way" (24:25). It quickly becomes clear, however, that no supernatural means were needed. The Israelites bring their own downfall upon themselves.

25:7 וַיָּקָם מִתּוֹךְ הָעֵדָה *He rose from the midst of the community* – The Rabbis

after the Israelite man into the tent, and stabbed both
of them, the Israelite man and the woman, through the
stomach – and the plague among the Israelites ended.
9 Those who had died by the plague numbered twenty-four
thousand.

The haftara for Parashat Balak is on page 1578 (even when Ḥukat and Balak are read together).

view of the people, as brazen an offense as we have seen since Datan and Aviram joined the Koraḥ rebellion. Only the human zealousness of Pinḥas – killing them both as they are cavorting – saves the day.

It is a shocking awakening. God saves Israel from its enemies but even God cannot save Israel from itself. To be defended by the Holy One, Israel must be holy, and that includes – as Leviticus insists in chapters 18 and 20 – a strict sexual ethic. Lose that and the nation will lose everything. If the Israelites act like the Canaanites, they will suffer the fate of the Canaanites. If, on the other hand, it honors and sanctifies fidelity between husband and wife and tender care between parents and children, then Israel will eventually be blessed even by its enemies. If unworthy, it can expect no special indulgence from God. Loyalty begins in our most intimate relationships and extends outward to the nation and upward to God. Disloyalty, as the Israelites showed in Shitim, can only end in disaster.

The book of Numbers has been a counterpoint between order and chaos, law and narrative, God's faith and the people's faithlessness, the blessings God brings forth from the mouth of an enemy and the curses the people bring upon themselves. It is a story of innocence lost and responsibility to be gained – less a chronicle of what happened in the course of forty years than a tutorial in what it is to find or lose direction in the wilderness of time. The enduring lesson remains. God may save us from our enemies, but only we can save us from ourselves.

שְׁנֵיהֶ֔ם אֵ֚ת אִ֣ישׁ יִשְׂרָאֵ֔ל וְאֶת־הָאִשָּׁ֖ה אֶל־קֳבָתָ֑הּ וַתֵּֽעָצַר֙
ט הַמַּגֵּפָ֔ה מֵעַ֖ל בְּנֵ֥י יִשְׂרָאֵֽל׃ וַיִּהְי֕וּ הַמֵּתִ֖ים בַּמַּגֵּפָ֑ה אַרְבָּעָ֥ה
וְעֶשְׂרִ֖ים אָֽלֶף׃

The הפטרה *for* פרשת בלק *is on page 1579 (even when* חקת *and* בלק *are read together).*

For the first time we see the Israelites bowing down to Baal, the Canaanite god. It is a betrayal of everything they should stand for.

What is more, this is the first time the Israelites have sinned gratuitously. Previously they have been driven by fear or hunger or thirst or disappointment. None of these is operative in the case of the Moabite women. This is sheer sexual self-indulgence, yielding to temptation unthinkingly. Even the idolatrous act is undertaken not in any spirit of rebelliousness, but almost as an afterthought: they "began to *consort* with Moabite women… *ate,* and then they *worshipped* the women's god" (vv. 1–2). If the first, why not the second and the third?

Idolatry and adultery are closely related. Idolatry is worship of power – and in human terms the worship of power translates into the untrammeled pursuit of sexual desire. To paraphrase Thucydides, the strong do what they wish and the weak suffer as they must. For Israel to slip into the same sin at the first opportunity bodes ill for the future. It also makes a nonsense of Bilam's blessing, "How good are your tents, Yaakov, your homes, O Israel" (Num. 24:5), if, as the rabbis thought, this refers to the modesty of Israel's family life (Rashi on Num. 24:5). That they could fall so quickly is a frightening sign of how little they have learned about the nature of their mission as an exemplary people.

God issues a sharp and painful punishment. But it fails to restore order to the camp. One of the tribal leaders, Zimri from the tribe of Shimon, brings a Midianite woman into the center of the camp and cohabits with her in full

Parashat Pinḥas

25 10 11 The Lord spoke to Moshe: "Pinḥas son of Elazar son
of Aharon the priest has allayed My rage against the
Israelites. Because he was passionate on My behalf among
you, I did not destroy the Israelites in My own passion.
12 Therefore, say this: I grant him My covenant of peace.
13 For him and for his descendants, it shall be a covenant of

---

by giving him "My covenant of peace" (Num. 25:12), intimating that God will ensure that he never again acts the part of a zealot. Indeed, some years later, in the days of Yehoshua, he is to play a vital role as a diplomatic man of peace by averting a civil war between the rest of the Israelites and the two and a half tribes – Reuven, Gad, and half of Menashe – who have settled to the east of the Jordan (Josh. 22).

As for Eliyahu, he is implicitly rebuked by God in one of the great scenes of the Bible. Standing at Ḥorev, God shows him a whirlwind, an earthquake, and a fire, but God is not in any of these. Then He comes to Eliyahu in a "faint sound of silence" (I Kings 19:11–12). He asks Eliyahu, for the second time, "Why are you here?" and Eliyahu replies with exactly the same words he had used before: "I acted out of fervor, out of passion for the Lord, God of Hosts" (19:13–14). He has not understood that God has been trying to tell him that He is not to be found in violent confrontation, but in gentleness. God then tells him to appoint Elisha as his successor.

What is great about the zealot is also what is dangerous. *The zealot acts the part of God.* Rashi, commenting on the phrase "Pinḥas… has allayed My rage against the Israelites, because he was passionate on My behalf" (Num. 25:11), interprets this to mean that God was saying that Pinḥas had "executed My vengeance and showed the anger that was for Me to show." He had done what normally only God would do. The zealot, on his own initiative, acts on behalf of God. But human beings are not God. They do not know what God knows.

Pinḥas and Eliyahu are heroes of the spiritual life. Yet both are implicitly reprimanded by God. God does not say that they are wrong to do what they do. To the contrary, God praises Pinḥas and answers Eliyahu's prayer. But He also makes it clear that once is enough. Pinḥas is now to take on the role of priesthood and the way of peace. Eliyahu is to appoint his successor. There are forms of justice that, in essence, are God's domain, not ours.

25:12 בְּרִיתִי שָׁלוֹם *My covenant of peace* – To any onlooker, Pinḥas might have seemed simply a man of violence. On the one hand, he saved countless lives;

פרשת פינחס

כה יא וַיְדַבֵּר יְהוָה אֶל־מֹשֶׁה לֵּאמֹר: פִּינְחָס בֶּן־אֶלְעָזָר בֶּן־אַהֲרֹן כב
הַכֹּהֵן הֵשִׁיב אֶת־חֲמָתִי מֵעַל בְּנֵי־יִשְׂרָאֵל בְּקַנְאוֹ אֶת־
יב קִנְאָתִי בְּתוֹכָם וְלֹא־כִלִּיתִי אֶת־בְּנֵי־יִשְׂרָאֵל בְּקִנְאָתִי: לָכֵן
יג אֱמֹר הִנְנִי נֹתֵן לוֹ אֶת־בְּרִיתִי שָׁלוֹם: וְהָיְתָה לּוֹ וּלְזַרְעוֹ אַחֲרָיו
בְּרִית כְּהֻנַּת עוֹלָם תַּחַת אֲשֶׁר קִנֵּא לֵאלֹהָיו וַיְכַפֵּר עַל־בְּנֵי

PINḤAS

Parashat Pinḥas begins by completing the episode that began in Parashat Balak: Pinḥas ends the plague, which was the result of the Israelites' seduction into idolatry by the Moabite and Midianite women. Pinḥas's reward for his zealotry is a "covenant of peace" (Num. 25:12) and "everlasting priesthood" (25:13).

The *parasha* then moves on to the second census in the book, this time of the new generation, the one to enter the land. There then follow two narratives, one about the daughters of Tzelofḥad and God's positive reply to their request for a share in the land, and the second about Moshe's request that God appoint a successor. The narrative in which Yehoshua is chosen as Moshe's successor raises questions about the fact that Moshe is unable to hand on his leadership role to his children. The *parasha* ends with two chapters about the sacrifices to be brought at different times, daily, weekly, monthly, and on festivals. Not for the first time in the Torah, stories of chaos and disruption give way to a detailed account of priestly order.

PINḤAS THE ZEALOT

With Pinḥas, a new type of character enters the world of Israel: the zealot (translated here as "passionate"). Through his passion for God, Pinḥas succeeds in allaying God's passion. He is to be followed, many centuries later, by the one other figure in Tanakh described as a zealot, the prophet Eliyahu. Asked by God on Mount Ḥorev, "Why are you here, Eliyahu?" Eliyahu replies, "I acted out of fervor, out of passion for the Lord, God of Hosts" (I Kings 19:9–10). In fact, tradition identifies these two men with each other: "Pinḥas *is* Eliyahu," say the Sages (*Yalkut Shimoni* I:771).

Pinḥas and Eliyahu are religious heroes. They step into the breach at a time when the nation is facing religious and moral crisis and palpable divine anger. They risk their lives by so doing. And God Himself is called "zealous" many times in the Torah. Zealousness must therefore be a virtue, or so it seems.

Yet the treatment of the two men in both the Written and Oral Torah is ambivalent. God rewards Pinḥas

everlasting priesthood, because he was passionate for his
God and made atonement on the part of the Israelites."
14 The name of the slain Israelite man who was killed with
the Midianite woman was Zimri son of Salu, leader of the
15 ancestral House of Shimon. The name of the Midianite
woman who was killed was Kozbi, daughter of Tzur the
tribal leader of a Midianite ancestral house.
16 17 And the LORD spoke to Moshe: "Attack the Midianites
18 and defeat them, for they attacked you by the deception
they practiced against you in the Peor affair, and in the
affair of their sister Kozbi, daughter of a Midianite leader,
who was killed on the day of the plague in the Peor affair."
26 1 After the plague –
the LORD said to Moshe and Elazar son of Aharon the
2 priest: "Take a census of the entire Israelite community,

PREFACE TO THE SECOND CENSUS

The Rabbis said: "Whenever you find the word *vayehi*, 'and it came to pass,' this is always a sign of suffering" (Megilla 10b). They could hear this in the very sound of the word – "*Vai, vayehi*" (Shemot Rabba 20:1), and nowhere is it better illustrated than in this preface to the second census in the book of Numbers.

The previous chapter described the terrible events at Shitim, where God saved the Israelites from their enemies, only to see them commit the ultimate betrayal. Twenty-four thousand people died in a plague. God tells Moshe to take revenge against the Midianites (Num. 25:17). Immediately after, we read: "*Vayehi* after the plague." At this point, there is a *piska be'emtza pasuk*, a paragraph break in the middle of a sentence. It is a moment of radical discontinuity, one of the rare occasions when the Torah signals a break in the sequence of words. In a Torah scroll, the rest of the line is left empty. The sentence continues on the next line. This creates a deliberate pause until we can begin to take in the enormity of the offense. There is an audible silence in which the absence of words speaks more powerfully than any words could. Seeing what His people had done, God might have destroyed them.

Yet now, after the silence, comes a new beginning. It may be that the space in the middle of a sentence is there not to break but to join. The Torah wants us to understand that it is not merely after the plague but also because of it that God orders a new census. There are acts that are unforgivable, but the story must continue somehow.

Crisis in Jewish history has always led to renewal, not to despair. "Whenever you find the word *vayehi*, 'and it

יד יִשְׂרָאֵל: וְשֵׁם אִישׁ יִשְׂרָאֵל הַמֻּכֶּה אֲשֶׁר הֻכָּה אֶת־הַמִּדְיָנִית
טו זִמְרִי בֶּן־סָלוּא נְשִׂיא בֵית־אָב לַשִּׁמְעֹנִי: וְשֵׁם הָאִשָּׁה
הַמֻּכָּה הַמִּדְיָנִית כָּזְבִּי בַת־צוּר רֹאשׁ אֻמּוֹת בֵּית־אָב בְּמִדְיָן
הוּא:
טז יז וַיְדַבֵּר יְהוָה אֶל־מֹשֶׁה לֵּאמֹר: צָרוֹר אֶת־הַמִּדְיָנִים
יח וְהִכִּיתֶם אוֹתָם: כִּי־צֹרְרִים הֵם לָכֶם בְּנִכְלֵיהֶם אֲשֶׁר־
נִכְּלוּ לָכֶם עַל־דְּבַר פְּעוֹר וְעַל־דְּבַר כָּזְבִּי בַת־נְשִׂיא מִדְיָן
כו א אֲחֹתָם הַמֻּכָּה בְיוֹם־הַמַּגֵּפָה עַל־דְּבַר פְּעוֹר: וַיְהִי אַחֲרֵי
הַמַּגֵּפָה
וַיֹּאמֶר יְהוָה אֶל־מֹשֶׁה וְאֶל אֶלְעָזָר בֶּן־אַהֲרֹן הַכֹּהֵן לֵאמֹר:
ב שְׂאוּ אֶת־רֹאשׁ | כָּל־עֲדַת בְּנֵי־יִשְׂרָאֵל מִבֶּן עֶשְׂרִים שָׁנָה

no more people died of the plague. On the other hand, he could not have known that in advance. Is he then a hero or a murderer? Parashat Balak ends with this ambiguity unresolved. Only in our *parasha* do we hear God's answer. Pinḥas, we are assured, is a hero. He has saved the Israelites from destruction, showed the zeal that counterbalanced the people's faithlessness, and as a reward, God makes a personal covenant with him.

Halakha, however, dramatically circumscribes his act in multiple ways. First, it rules that if Zimri had turned and killed Pinḥas in self-defense, he would be declared innocent in a court of law (Sanhedrin 82a). Second, it rules that if Pinḥas had killed Zimri and Kozbi just before or after they were engaged in cohabitation, he would have been guilty of murder (Sanhedrin 81b). Third, had Pinḥas consulted a *beit din* and asked whether he was permitted to do what he was proposing to do, the answer would have been no (Sanhedrin 82a).

This is one of the rare cases where we say: *Halakha ve'ein morin ken*, "It is the law, but it should not be taught." That is why it is hedged with qualifications. It only applied when the offense was committed in public, when the sentence was carried out while the sin or crime was being committed, and only when the person carrying it out was a "zealot."

An act like that of Pinḥas can only be justified in retrospect, when it does actually produce the consequences it was intended to achieve. What is more, it is essential that it never becomes the basis of a general rule. Rare indeed are the circumstances in which Pinḥas-like zealotry is justified, and if anyone asks whether he may do the same, the answer must always be: no.

from twenty years of age and upward, by their ancestral
houses: everyone in Israel capable of active service."
3 Moshe and Elazar the priest spoke to them in the plains
4 of Moav by the Jordan opposite Yeriḥo: "Take a census
of those twenty years of age and upward just as the
LORD commanded Moshe and the Israelites who came
5 out of Egypt." Reuven was Yisrael's firstborn. Reuven's SHENI
descendants: of Ḥanokh, the clan of Ḥanokh; of Palu,
6 the clan of Palu; of Ḥetzron, the clan of Ḥetzron; of
7 Karmi, the clan of Karmi. These are the Reubenite clans.
8 9 Their tally was 43,730. Palu's descendants: Eliav. Eliav's
descendants: Nemuel, Datan, and Aviram. These were
the same Datan and Aviram, elect of the community,
who rebelled against Moshe and Aharon in the company
10 of Koraḥ, when they rebelled against the LORD. The
earth opened its mouth and swallowed them, along with
Koraḥ, when the company died and fire consumed the
11 two hundred fifty men; and they became a sign. But the
12 sons of Koraḥ did not die. Shimon's descendants
by their clans: of Nemuel, the clan of Nemuel; of Yamin,
13 the clan of Yamin; of Yakhin, the clan of Yakhin; of Zeraḥ,
14 the clan of Zeraḥ; of Sha'ul, the clan of Sha'ul. These are
15 the Simeonite clans: 22,200. Gad's descendants
by their clans: of Tzefon, the clan of Tzefon; of Ḥagi, the
16 clan of Ḥagi; of Shuni, the clan of Shuni; of Ozni, the clan
17 of Ozni; of Eri, the clan of Eri; of Arod, the clan of Arod;
18 of Areli, the clan of Areli. These are the Gadite clans. Their
19 tally was 40,500. Among Yehuda's sons were
Er and Onan; Er and Onan died in the land of Canaan.
20 Yehuda's descendants by their clans: of Shela, the clan

---

we create the micro-universe that is our life. The past might give us cause for lamentation, but the future still holds its promise.

The first census in Numbers documented the people of Israel who had recently left Egypt. The census taken now, "after the plague," shows the population that, having survived all the hazards and hardships of the desert, will take possession of the Promised Land.

ג וּמַעְלָה לְבֵית אֲבֹתָם כָּל־יֹצֵא צָבָא בְּיִשְׂרָאֵל׃ וַיְדַבֵּר מֹשֶׁה
וְאֶלְעָזָר הַכֹּהֵן אֹתָם בְּעַרְבֹת מוֹאָב עַל־יַרְדֵּן יְרֵחוֹ לֵאמֹר׃
ד מִבֶּן עֶשְׂרִים שָׁנָה וָמָעְלָה כַּאֲשֶׁר צִוָּה יהוה אֶת־מֹשֶׁה וּבְנֵי
ה יִשְׂרָאֵל הַיֹּצְאִים מֵאֶרֶץ מִצְרָיִם׃ רְאוּבֵן בְּכוֹר יִשְׂרָאֵל בְּנֵי
רְאוּבֵן חֲנוֹךְ מִשְׁפַּחַת הַחֲנֹכִי לְפַלּוּא מִשְׁפַּחַת הַפַּלֻּאִי׃
ו ז לְחֶצְרֹן מִשְׁפַּחַת הַחֶצְרוֹנִי לְכַרְמִי מִשְׁפַּחַת הַכַּרְמִי׃ אֵלֶּה
מִשְׁפְּחֹת הָרֻאוּבֵנִי וַיִּהְיוּ פְקֻדֵיהֶם שְׁלֹשָׁה וְאַרְבָּעִים אֶלֶף
ח ט וּשְׁבַע מֵאוֹת וּשְׁלֹשִׁים׃ וּבְנֵי פַלּוּא אֱלִיאָב׃ וּבְנֵי אֱלִיאָב
נְמוּאֵל וְדָתָן וַאֲבִירָם הוּא־דָתָן וַאֲבִירָם קרואי הָעֵדָה אֲשֶׁר קְרִיאֵי
הִצּוּ עַל־מֹשֶׁה וְעַל־אַהֲרֹן בַּעֲדַת־קֹרַח בְּהַצֹּתָם עַל־יהוה׃
י וַתִּפְתַּח הָאָרֶץ אֶת־פִּיהָ וַתִּבְלַע אֹתָם וְאֶת־קֹרַח בְּמוֹת
הָעֵדָה בַּאֲכֹל הָאֵשׁ אֵת חֲמִשִּׁים וּמָאתַיִם אִישׁ וַיִּהְיוּ לְנֵס׃
יא יב וּבְנֵי־קֹרַח לֹא־מֵתוּ׃ בְּנֵי שִׁמְעוֹן לְמִשְׁפְּחֹתָם
לִנְמוּאֵל מִשְׁפַּחַת הַנְּמוּאֵלִי לְיָמִין מִשְׁפַּחַת הַיָּמִינִי לְיָכִין
יג מִשְׁפַּחַת הַיָּכִינִי׃ לְזֶרַח מִשְׁפַּחַת הַזַּרְחִי לְשָׁאוּל מִשְׁפַּחַת
יד הַשָּׁאוּלִי׃ אֵלֶּה מִשְׁפְּחֹת הַשִּׁמְעֹנִי שְׁנַיִם וְעֶשְׂרִים אֶלֶף
טו וּמָאתָיִם׃ בְּנֵי גָד לְמִשְׁפְּחֹתָם לִצְפוֹן מִשְׁפַּחַת
טז הַצְּפוֹנִי לְחַגִּי מִשְׁפַּחַת הַחַגִּי לְשׁוּנִי מִשְׁפַּחַת הַשּׁוּנִי׃ לְאָזְנִי
יז מִשְׁפַּחַת הָאָזְנִי לְעֵרִי מִשְׁפַּחַת הָעֵרִי׃ לַאֲרוֹד מִשְׁפַּחַת
יח הָאֲרוֹדִי לְאַרְאֵלִי מִשְׁפַּחַת הָאַרְאֵלִי׃ אֵלֶּה מִשְׁפְּחֹת בְּנֵי־גָד
יט לִפְקֻדֵיהֶם אַרְבָּעִים אֶלֶף וַחֲמֵשׁ מֵאוֹת׃ בְּנֵי
כ יְהוּדָה עֵר וְאוֹנָן וַיָּמָת עֵר וְאוֹנָן בְּאֶרֶץ כְּנָעַן׃ וַיִּהְיוּ בְנֵי־יְהוּדָה

came to pass,' this is always a sign of suffering"; conversely, "whenever you find the phrase *vehaya,* 'and it shall come to pass,' this is always a sign of joy" (Bemidbar Rabba 13:5). The Jewish way of telling a story, the Mishna instructs us, is *mathil bigenut umesayem beshevaḥ,* to "begin with the bad and end with the good" (Pesaḥim 10:4). This is also a mode of being in the world. Leaders don't wait for things to come to pass. They say not *vayehi* but *yehi,* "Let there be." That was the word with which God created the universe. It is also the word with which

of Shela; of Peretz, the clan of Peretz; of Zeraḥ, the clan
21 of Zeraḥ. Peretz's descendants: of Ḥetzron, the clan of
22 Ḥetzron; of Ḥamul, the clan of Ḥamul. These are the clans
23 of Yehuda. Their tally was 76,500. Yissakhar's
descendants by their clans: of Tola, the clan of Tola; of
24 Puva, the clan of Puva; of Yashuv, the clan of Yashuv;
25 of Shimron, the clan of Shimron. These are the clans of
26 Yissakhar. Their tally was 64,300. Zevulun's
descendants by their clans: of Sered, the clan of
Sered; of Elon, the clan of Elon; of Yaḥle'el, the clan of
27 Yaḥle'el. These are the Zebulunite clans. Their tally was
28 60,500. Yosef's descendants by their clans:
29 Menashe and Efrayim – Menashe's descendants: of Makhir,
the clan of Makhir. Makhir had a son Gilad. Of Gilad, the
30 clan of Gilad. These are Gilad's descendants: of I'ezer, the
31 clan of I'ezer; of Ḥelek, the clan of Ḥelek; of Asriel, the clan
32 of Asriel; of Shekhem, the clan of Shekhem; of Shemida,

individuals than childless widows. But Tamar and Ruth were in a far worse situation still. They came from groups traditionally despised by the Israelites: the Canaanites and the Moabites. They had no natural place in the society in which they found themselves. *It was these two women, Tamar and Ruth, whose loyalty and steadfastness were the key factors in giving birth eventually to King David,* the man who became king of Israel, united the nation, initiated the plans for building the Temple, and wrote some of the finest poetry in the religious history of humankind.

This is worthy of serious reflection. Otto Rank, in his classic *The Myth of the Birth of the Hero,* points out that there are common elements in the stories told about the heroes of myth. Though raised by lowly adoptive parents, they are of noble birth. They have royal blood or are descended from the gods. The story of David turns this convention on its head. David has the kind of family background most people would seek to hide. His unlikely rise to greatness is due, not to any hidden divinity, but to the unexpected courage of his foremothers' love.

It is interesting too that this reminder of Tamar and foreshadowing of Ruth appear in the same census as the daughters of Tzelofḥad (Num. 26:33). They too are courageous women who find their way to insist that the family line will not be broken despite the absence of sons. Their path is to be easier, however. They are able to challenge the law to secure their place in the land.

לְמִשְׁפְּחֹתָם֒ לְשֵׁלָ֗ה מִשְׁפַּ֙חַת֙ הַשֵּׁ֣לָנִ֔י לְפֶ֕רֶץ מִשְׁפַּ֖חַת הַפַּרְצִ֑י
כא לְזֶ֕רַח מִשְׁפַּ֖חַת הַזַּרְחִֽי׃ וַיִּהְי֣וּ בְנֵי־פֶ֔רֶץ לְחֶצְרֹ֕ן מִשְׁפַּ֖חַת
כב הַֽחֶצְרֹנִ֑י לְחָמ֕וּל מִשְׁפַּ֖חַת הֶחָמוּלִֽי׃ אֵ֛לֶּה מִשְׁפְּחֹ֥ת יְהוּדָ֖ה
כג לִפְקֻדֵיהֶ֑ם שִׁשָּׁ֧ה וְשִׁבְעִ֛ים אֶ֖לֶף וַחֲמֵ֥שׁ מֵאֽוֹת׃ בְּנֵ֤י
יִשָּׂשכָר֙ לְמִשְׁפְּחֹתָ֔ם תּוֹלָ֕ע מִשְׁפַּ֖חַת הַתּֽוֹלָעִ֑י לְפֻוָ֕ה מִשְׁפַּ֖חַת
כד הַפּוּנִֽי׃ לְיָשׁ֕וּב מִשְׁפַּ֖חַת הַיָּשֻׁבִ֑י לְשִׁמְרֹ֕ן מִשְׁפַּ֖חַת הַשִּׁמְרֹנִֽי׃
כה אֵ֛לֶּה מִשְׁפְּחֹ֥ת יִשָּׂשכָ֖ר לִפְקֻדֵיהֶ֑ם אַרְבָּעָ֧ה וְשִׁשִּׁ֛ים אֶ֖לֶף
כו וּשְׁלֹ֥שׁ מֵאֽוֹת׃ בְּנֵ֤י זְבוּלֻן֙ לְמִשְׁפְּחֹתָ֔ם לְסֶ֗רֶד
מִשְׁפַּ֙חַת֙ הַסַּרְדִּ֔י לְאֵל֕וֹן מִשְׁפַּ֖חַת הָאֵלֹנִ֑י לְיַ֨חְלְאֵ֔ל מִשְׁפַּ֖חַת
כז הַיַּחְלְאֵלִֽי׃ אֵ֛לֶּה מִשְׁפְּחֹ֥ת הַזְּבוּלֹנִ֖י לִפְקֻדֵיהֶ֑ם שִׁשִּׁ֥ים
כח אֶ֖לֶף וַחֲמֵ֥שׁ מֵאֽוֹת׃ בְּנֵ֥י יוֹסֵ֖ף לְמִשְׁפְּחֹתָ֑ם
כט מְנַשֶּׁ֖ה וְאֶפְרָֽיִם׃ בְּנֵ֣י מְנַשֶּׁ֗ה לְמָכִיר֙ מִשְׁפַּ֣חַת הַמָּֽכִירִ֔י
ל וּמָכִ֖יר הוֹלִ֣יד אֶת־גִּלְעָ֑ד לְגִלְעָ֕ד מִשְׁפַּ֖חַת הַגִּלְעָדִֽי׃ אֵ֚לֶּה
בְּנֵ֣י גִלְעָ֔ד אִיעֶ֕זֶר מִשְׁפַּ֖חַת הָֽאִיעֶזְרִ֑י לְחֵ֕לֶק מִשְׁפַּ֖חַת
לא הַֽחֶלְקִֽי׃ וְאַ֨שְׂרִיאֵ֔ל מִשְׁפַּ֖חַת הָֽאַשְׂרְאֵלִ֑י וְשֶׁ֕כֶם מִשְׁפַּ֖חַת
לב הַשִּׁכְמִֽי׃ וּשְׁמִידָ֕ע מִשְׁפַּ֖חַת הַשְּׁמִידָעִ֑י וְחֵ֕פֶר מִשְׁפַּ֖חַת

26:21 בְּנֵי־פֶרֶץ *Peretz's descendants* – The text has obliquely reminded us of the narrative that led to Peretz's birth – Tamar's courageous plot to form an unorthodox Levirate relationship with her father-in-law (see Gen. 38 and comments there). Later, Ruth's relationship with Peretz's descendent, Boaz, will in many ways reflect the heroism of Tamar.

The book of Ruth ends with a family tree listing ten generations from Peretz to the birth of David. A ten-generation genealogy is a highly charged phenomenon in the Bible. There are ten generations from Adam to Noaḥ, and ten from Noaḥ to Avraham. The ten generations from Peretz to David carry the same sense of preordained destiny. The beginning of such a family tree is significant. So too is the seventh, the number associated with holiness. *David's family tree begins with Peretz, the son born to Yehuda and Tamar. The seventh generation is Oved, the son born to Ruth and Boaz.* The key progenitors of Israel's great and future king are Tamar and Ruth. Theirs are in fact the only stories told in any detail about David's female forebears.

The heroes in David's background are two women who stand at the very edge of Israelite society. In the biblical era there were no more vulnerable

33 the clan of Shemida; and of Ḥefer, the clan of Ḥefer. But
Tzelofḥad son of Ḥefer had no sons, only daughters. The
names of Tzelofḥad's daughters were Maḥla, Noa, Ḥogla,
34 Milka, and Tirtza. These are the clans of Menashe. Their
35 tally was 52,700. These are Efrayim's descendants
by their clans: of Shutelaḥ, the clan of Shutelaḥ; of Bekher,
36 the clan of Bekher; of Taḥan, the clan of Taḥan. These are
37 Shutelaḥ's descendants: of Eran, the clan of Eran. These
are the clans of Efrayim. Their tally was 32,500. All these
38 are Yosef's descendants by their clans. Binyamin's
descendants by their clans: of Bela, the clan of Bela; of
Ashbel, the clan of Ashbel; of Aḥiram, the clan of Aḥiram;
39 of Shefufam, the clan of Shefufam; of Ḥufam, the clan of
40 Ḥufam. Bela's descendants were Ard and Naaman: the
41 clan of Ard; of Naaman, the clan of Naaman. These are the
42 clans of Binyamin. Their tally was 45,600. These
are Dan's descendants by their clans: of Shuḥam, the clan
43 of Shuḥam. These are the clans of Dan; all the Shuhamite
44 clans according to their tally were 64,400. Asher's
descendants by their clans: of Yimna, the clan of Yimna;
of Yishvi, the clan of Yishvi; of Beria, the clan of Beria.
45 Of Beria's descendants: of Ḥever, the clan of Ḥever; of
46 Malkiel, the clan of Malkiel. The name of Asher's daughter
47 was Seraḥ. These are the clans of Asher; their tally was
48 53,400. Naftali's descendants by their clans:
of Yaḥtze'el, the clan of Yaḥtze'el; of Guni, the clan of
49 Guni; of Yetzer, the clan of Yetzer; of Shilem, the clan
50 of Shilem. These are all the clans of Naftali. Their tally
51 was 45,400. The total number of those Israelite men was
601,730.

52 53 The LORD spoke to Moshe: "The land shall be apportioned SHELISHI

לג הַחֶפְרִי: וּצְלׇפְחָד בֶּן־חֵפֶר לֹא־הָיוּ לוֹ בָּנִים כִּי אִם־בָּנוֹת
וְשֵׁם בְּנוֹת צְלׇפְחָד מַחְלָה וְנֹעָה חׇגְלָה מִלְכָּה וְתִרְצָה:
לד אֵלֶּה מִשְׁפְּחֹת מְנַשֶּׁה וּפְקֻדֵיהֶם שְׁנַיִם וַחֲמִשִּׁים אֶלֶף וּשְׁבַע
לה מֵאוֹת: אֵלֶּה בְנֵי־אֶפְרַיִם לְמִשְׁפְּחֹתָם לְשׁוּתֶלַח
מִשְׁפַּחַת הַשֻּׁתַלְחִי לְבֶכֶר מִשְׁפַּחַת הַבַּכְרִי לְתַחַן מִשְׁפַּחַת
לו לז הַתַּחֲנִי: וְאֵלֶּה בְּנֵי שׁוּתָלַח לְעֵרָן מִשְׁפַּחַת הָעֵרָנִי: אֵלֶּה
מִשְׁפְּחֹת בְּנֵי־אֶפְרַיִם לִפְקֻדֵיהֶם שְׁנַיִם וּשְׁלֹשִׁים אֶלֶף וַחֲמֵשׁ
לח מֵאוֹת אֵלֶּה בְנֵי־יוֹסֵף לְמִשְׁפְּחֹתָם: בְּנֵי בִנְיָמִן
לְמִשְׁפְּחֹתָם לְבֶלַע מִשְׁפַּחַת הַבַּלְעִי לְאַשְׁבֵּל מִשְׁפַּחַת
לט הָאַשְׁבֵּלִי לַאֲחִירָם מִשְׁפַּחַת הָאֲחִירָמִי: לִשְׁפוּפָם מִשְׁפַּחַת
מ הַשּׁוּפָמִי לְחוּפָם מִשְׁפַּחַת הַחוּפָמִי: וַיִּהְיוּ בְנֵי־בֶלַע אַרְדְּ
מא וְנַעֲמָן מִשְׁפַּחַת הָאַרְדִּי לְנַעֲמָן מִשְׁפַּחַת הַנַּעֲמִי: אֵלֶּה
בְנֵי־בִנְיָמִן לְמִשְׁפְּחֹתָם וּפְקֻדֵיהֶם חֲמִשָּׁה וְאַרְבָּעִים אֶלֶף
מב וְשֵׁשׁ מֵאוֹת: אֵלֶּה בְנֵי־דָן לְמִשְׁפְּחֹתָם
לְשׁוּחָם מִשְׁפַּחַת הַשּׁוּחָמִי אֵלֶּה מִשְׁפְּחֹת דָּן לְמִשְׁפְּחֹתָם:
מג כׇּל־מִשְׁפְּחֹת הַשּׁוּחָמִי לִפְקֻדֵיהֶם אַרְבָּעָה וְשִׁשִּׁים אֶלֶף
מד וְאַרְבַּע מֵאוֹת: בְּנֵי אָשֵׁר לְמִשְׁפְּחֹתָם
לְיִמְנָה מִשְׁפַּחַת הַיִּמְנָה לְיִשְׁוִי מִשְׁפַּחַת הַיִּשְׁוִי לִבְרִיעָה
מה מִשְׁפַּחַת הַבְּרִיעִי: לִבְנֵי בְרִיעָה לְחֶבֶר מִשְׁפַּחַת הַחֶבְרִי
מו לְמַלְכִּיאֵל מִשְׁפַּחַת הַמַּלְכִּיאֵלִי: וְשֵׁם בַּת־אָשֵׁר שָׂרַח:
מז אֵלֶּה מִשְׁפְּחֹת בְּנֵי־אָשֵׁר לִפְקֻדֵיהֶם שְׁלֹשָׁה וַחֲמִשִּׁים אֶלֶף
מח וְאַרְבַּע מֵאוֹת: בְּנֵי נַפְתָּלִי לְמִשְׁפְּחֹתָם לְיַחְצְאֵל
מט מִשְׁפַּחַת הַיַּחְצְאֵלִי לְגוּנִי מִשְׁפַּחַת הַגּוּנִי: לְיֵצֶר מִשְׁפַּחַת
נ הַיִּצְרִי לְשִׁלֵּם מִשְׁפַּחַת הַשִּׁלֵּמִי: אֵלֶּה מִשְׁפְּחֹת נַפְתָּלִי
לְמִשְׁפְּחֹתָם וּפְקֻדֵיהֶם חֲמִשָּׁה וְאַרְבָּעִים אֶלֶף וְאַרְבַּע מֵאוֹת:
נא אֵלֶּה פְּקוּדֵי בְּנֵי יִשְׂרָאֵל שֵׁשׁ־מֵאוֹת אֶלֶף וָאָלֶף שְׁבַע מֵאוֹת
וּשְׁלֹשִׁים:
נב נג וַיְדַבֵּר יְהֹוָה אֶל־מֹשֶׁה לֵּאמֹר: לָאֵלֶּה תֵּחָלֵק הָאָרֶץ בְּנַחֲלָה כג שלישי

54 to them for inheritance by the tally of their names. To
those who are many, give a large inheritance; to those
who are few, a small inheritance. Let each be given its
55 inheritance in keeping with its number. The land must be
apportioned by lot. By the names of their ancestral tribes
56 they shall inherit. Whether large or small, each tribe
57 will inherit by means of the lot." These are the
numbers of the Levites by their clans: of Gershon, the clan
of Gershon; of Kehat, the clan of Kehat; of Merari, the clan
58 of Merari. These are the Levite clans: the clan of Livna,
the clan of Ḥevron, the clan of Maḥli, the clan of Mushi,
59 and the clan of Koraḥ. Kehat had a son Amram. The name
of Amram's wife was Yokheved daughter of Levi; she had
been born to Levi in Egypt. She bore to Amram Aharon,
60 Moshe, and their sister Miriam. To Aharon were born
61 Nadav, Avihu, Elazar, and Itamar. Nadav and Avihu died
when they offered unauthorized fire before the Lord.
62 Their number was 23,000, this including every male one
month of age and upward. They were not numbered
along with the Israelites because no land inheritance was
63 given to them in the Israelites' midst. This was the census
that Moshe and Elazar the priest took of the Israelites
64 on the plains of Moav by the Jordan opposite Yeriḥo. It
contained not one man who had been counted by Moshe
and Aharon the priest when they took the census of the
65 Israelites in the Sinai Desert. For the Lord had said of
those, "They shall die in the wilderness." Not one of
them was left now except for Kalev son of Yefuneh and
27 1 Yehoshua son of Nun. Then the daughters of
Tzelofḥad son of Ḥefer son of Gilad son of Makhir son
of Menashe, of the clans of Menashe son of Yosef, came

them" (Num. 27:7). And so it comes to pass.

The Sages spoke of Tzelofḥad's daughters in terms of highest praise. They were, they said, very wise and chose the right time to present their request. They knew how to interpret Scripture, and they were perfectly virtuous (Bava Batra 110b). Even more consequentially, their love of the land of Israel was in striking

נד בְּמִסְפַּר שֵׁמוֹת: לָרַב תַּרְבֶּה נַחֲלָתוֹ וְלַמְעַט תַּמְעִיט נַחֲלָתוֹ
נה אִישׁ לְפִי פְקֻדָיו יֻתַּן נַחֲלָתוֹ: אַךְ־בְּגוֹרָל יֵחָלֵק אֶת־הָאָרֶץ
נו לִשְׁמוֹת מַטּוֹת־אֲבֹתָם יִנְחָלוּ: עַל־פִּי הַגּוֹרָל תֵּחָלֵק נַחֲלָתוֹ
נז בֵּין רַב לִמְעָט: וְאֵלֶּה פְקוּדֵי הַלֵּוִי לְמִשְׁפְּחֹתָם
לְגֵרְשׁוֹן מִשְׁפַּחַת הַגֵּרְשֻׁנִּי לִקְהָת מִשְׁפַּחַת הַקְּהָתִי לִמְרָרִי
נח מִשְׁפַּחַת הַמְּרָרִי: אֵלֶּה ׀ מִשְׁפְּחֹת לֵוִי מִשְׁפַּחַת הַלִּבְנִי
מִשְׁפַּחַת הַחֶבְרֹנִי מִשְׁפַּחַת הַמַּחְלִי מִשְׁפַּחַת הַמּוּשִׁי
נט מִשְׁפַּחַת הַקָּרְחִי וּקְהָת הוֹלִד אֶת־עַמְרָם: וְשֵׁם ׀ אֵשֶׁת
עַמְרָם יוֹכֶבֶד בַּת־לֵוִי אֲשֶׁר יָלְדָה אֹתָהּ לְלֵוִי בְּמִצְרָיִם וַתֵּלֶד
ס לְעַמְרָם אֶת־אַהֲרֹן וְאֶת־מֹשֶׁה וְאֵת מִרְיָם אֲחֹתָם: וַיִּוָּלֵד
לְאַהֲרֹן אֶת־נָדָב וְאֶת־אֲבִיהוּא אֶת־אֶלְעָזָר וְאֶת־אִיתָמָר:
סא סב וַיָּמָת נָדָב וַאֲבִיהוּא בְּהַקְרִיבָם אֵשׁ־זָרָה לִפְנֵי יהוה: וַיִּהְיוּ
פְקֻדֵיהֶם שְׁלֹשָׁה וְעֶשְׂרִים אֶלֶף כָּל־זָכָר מִבֶּן־חֹדֶשׁ וָמָעְלָה
כִּי ׀ לֹא הָתְפָּקְדוּ בְּתוֹךְ בְּנֵי יִשְׂרָאֵל כִּי לֹא־נִתַּן לָהֶם נַחֲלָה
סג בְּתוֹךְ בְּנֵי יִשְׂרָאֵל: אֵלֶּה פְּקוּדֵי מֹשֶׁה וְאֶלְעָזָר הַכֹּהֵן אֲשֶׁר
סד פָּקְדוּ אֶת־בְּנֵי יִשְׂרָאֵל בְּעַרְבֹת מוֹאָב עַל יַרְדֵּן יְרֵחוֹ: וּבְאֵלֶּה
לֹא־הָיָה אִישׁ מִפְּקוּדֵי מֹשֶׁה וְאַהֲרֹן הַכֹּהֵן אֲשֶׁר פָּקְדוּ
סה אֶת־בְּנֵי יִשְׂרָאֵל בְּמִדְבַּר סִינָי: כִּי־אָמַר יהוה לָהֶם מוֹת
יָמֻתוּ בַּמִּדְבָּר וְלֹא־נוֹתַר מֵהֶם אִישׁ כִּי אִם־כָּלֵב בֶּן־יְפֻנֶּה
כז א וִיהוֹשֻׁעַ בִּן־נוּן: וַתִּקְרַבְנָה בְּנוֹת צְלָפְחָד בֶּן־חֵפֶר
בֶּן־גִּלְעָד בֶּן־מָכִיר בֶּן־מְנַשֶּׁה לְמִשְׁפְּחֹת מְנַשֶּׁה בֶן־יוֹסֵף
וְאֵלֶּה שְׁמוֹת בְּנֹתָיו מַחְלָה נֹעָה וְחָגְלָה וּמִלְכָּה וְתִרְצָה:

THE DAUGHTERS OF TZELOFḤAD

Tzelofḥad, of the tribe of Menashe, died in the wilderness before the allocation of the land, leaving five daughters. Now the daughters come before Moshe, arguing that it would be unjust for his family to be denied their share in the land simply because he had daughters but not sons. Moshe brings their case before God, who tells him: "What Tzelofḥad's daughters say is right. You must certainly give them a heritable portion of land along with their father's kin. Transfer their father's portion to

forward; the daughters' names were Maḥla, Noa, Ḥogla,
2 Milka, and Tirtza. And they stood before Moshe, Elazar
the priest, the princes, and all the community at the
3 entrance to the Tent of Meeting, and said, "Our father
died in the wilderness. He was not among the company
of those who gathered together against the Lord in the
company of Koraḥ; he died in his own sin, and had no
4 sons. Why should our father's name be lost to his family
only because he had no son? Give us a portion of land
5 along with our father's brothers." Moshe brought their
case before the Lord.
6 7 And the Lord said to Moshe: "What Tzelofḥad's REVI'I
daughters say is right. You must certainly give them a
heritable portion of land along with their father's kin.
8 Transfer their father's portion to them. Speak to the
Israelites; tell them: If a man dies and has no son, you shall
9 transfer his property to his daughters. If he does not have
10 a daughter, you shall give his property to his brothers. If he
has no brothers, you shall give his property to his father's
11 brothers. If his father had no brothers, give his property to
the closest relative in his clan, and that person shall inherit
it." This shall be a decree of law for the Israelites, as the
Lord commanded Moshe.
12 The Lord said to Moshe, "Ascend this mountain of
Avarim, and gaze upon the land that I have given to the

---

but renewal. I call this "homeostatic change." Homeostatic temperature control will be continually changing, switching the air-conditioning on or off to maintain an even temperature. An airliner on automatic pilot is making adjustments every microsecond to stay on course. Change takes place in Judaism, but its aim is to stay true to the essential principles.

When the five daughters of Tzelofḥad come to Moshe, he is able to ask God their question directly. Yet it is an early instance of what we now call the Oral Torah: Torah applied to a time or a circumstance that is different from the one where it was given. This is the ongoing process that gives Judaism its unbroken continuity while at the same time relating to the challenge of each age, in each age.

27:12 עֲלֵה אֶל־הַר הָעֲבָרִים הַזֶּה *Ascend this mountain* – God grants Moshe one last gift: not entry into the land, but a glimpse of it from afar, from a mountaintop on

ב וַתַּעֲמֹדְנָה לִפְנֵי מֹשֶׁה וְלִפְנֵי אֶלְעָזָר הַכֹּהֵן וְלִפְנֵי הַנְּשִׂיאִם
ג וְכָל־הָעֵדָה פֶּתַח אֹהֶל־מוֹעֵד לֵאמֹר: אָבִינוּ מֵת בַּמִּדְבָּר
וְהוּא לֹא־הָיָה בְּתוֹךְ הָעֵדָה הַנּוֹעָדִים עַל־יְהֹוָה בַּעֲדַת־קֹרַח
ד כִּי־בְחֶטְאוֹ מֵת וּבָנִים לֹא־הָיוּ לוֹ: לָמָּה יִגָּרַע שֵׁם־אָבִינוּ
מִתּוֹךְ מִשְׁפַּחְתּוֹ כִּי אֵין לוֹ בֵּן תְּנָה־לָּנוּ אֲחֻזָּה בְּתוֹךְ אֲחֵי
ה אָבִינוּ: וַיַּקְרֵב מֹשֶׁה אֶת־מִשְׁפָּטָן לִפְנֵי יְהֹוָה:
ו ז וַיֹּאמֶר יְהֹוָה אֶל־מֹשֶׁה לֵּאמֹר: כֵּן בְּנוֹת צְלָפְחָד דֹּבְרֹת רביעי
נָתֹן תִּתֵּן לָהֶם אֲחֻזַּת נַחֲלָה בְּתוֹךְ אֲחֵי אֲבִיהֶם וְהַעֲבַרְתָּ
ח אֶת־נַחֲלַת אֲבִיהֶן לָהֶן: וְאֶל־בְּנֵי יִשְׂרָאֵל תְּדַבֵּר לֵאמֹר
אִישׁ כִּי־יָמוּת וּבֵן אֵין לוֹ וְהַעֲבַרְתֶּם אֶת־נַחֲלָתוֹ לְבִתּוֹ:
ט י וְאִם־אֵין לוֹ בַּת וּנְתַתֶּם אֶת־נַחֲלָתוֹ לְאֶחָיו: וְאִם־אֵין לוֹ
יא אַחִים וּנְתַתֶּם אֶת־נַחֲלָתוֹ לַאֲחֵי אָבִיו: וְאִם־אֵין אַחִים
לְאָבִיו וּנְתַתֶּם אֶת־נַחֲלָתוֹ לִשְׁאֵרוֹ הַקָּרֹב אֵלָיו מִמִּשְׁפַּחְתּוֹ
וְיָרַשׁ אֹתָהּ וְהָיְתָה לִבְנֵי יִשְׂרָאֵל לְחֻקַּת מִשְׁפָּט כַּאֲשֶׁר צִוָּה
יְהֹוָה אֶת־מֹשֶׁה:
יב וַיֹּאמֶר יְהֹוָה אֶל־מֹשֶׁה עֲלֵה אֶל־הַר הָעֲבָרִים הַזֶּה וּרְאֵה

---

contrast to that of the men. The spies had come back with a negative report about the land, and the people had said, "Let us appoint a [new] leader and go back to Egypt" (Num. 14:4). But Tzelofḥad's daughters wanted to have a share in the land, which they were duly granted. We have seen Rabbi Ephrayim Luntschitz's reading of this in his *Keli Yakar* (commentary on Num. 13:2). We can lose a priceless legacy simply because, not loving it, we do not come to appreciate its true value. What we love, we inherit.

The incident is also significant in the history of halakha. As Jews we believe that there is a *Torah Shebikhtav*, a Written Torah which never changes, and a *Torah Shebe'al Peh*, an Oral Torah which is, as it were, subject to ongoing interpretation. This is a highly sensitive process and it is entrusted to the great sages of each generation. Their task is to hear in the word of God for all time, the word of God for this time. In many cases the process begins, as with the daughters of Tzelofḥad, with a challenging question respectfully asked.

In halakha, as in other areas, there is a difference between change, or *shinui*, and *ḥiddush*. *Ḥiddush* means not change,

13 Israelites. After you have seen it, you too will be gathered
14 to your people, like Aharon your brother, because when
the community rebelled in the Wilderness of Tzin, you
disobeyed Me, failing to affirm My sanctity in their eyes
through the water." These were the waters of Merivat
15 Kadesh in the Wilderness of Tzin. Moshe
16 spoke to the LORD: "Let the LORD, God of the spirit of
17 all flesh, appoint a man over the community who will

---

territory of Efrayim and hired a Levite to officiate in the shrine. Some men from the tribe of Dan, moving north to find more suitable land for themselves, came upon Mikha's house and seized both the idolatrous artifacts and the Levite, whom they persuaded to become their priest, saying, "Come with us.... Would you rather be the priest of one man's household or the priest of a whole tribal clan in Israel?" (Judges 18:19).

Only at the end of the story (18:30) are we told the name of this priest: Yonatan son of Gershom son of Moshe. In our texts, the letter *nun* has been inserted into the last of these names, so that it can be read as Menashe rather than Moshe. However, the letter, unusually, is written above the line, as a superscription. The Talmud says that the *nun* was added to avoid besmirching the name of Moshe himself, by disclosing that his grandson had become an idolator.

How are we to explain Moshe's apparent failure to pass on his Torah? There are hints here and there that Moshe was so preoccupied with leading the people that he did not have time to attend to the spiritual needs of his family. The Sages, however, offered a quite different explanation. God did not want the "crown of Torah" to pass from parent to child in automatic succession. Kingship and priesthood did. But the crown of Torah, the Sages said, belongs to anyone who chooses to take hold of it. "Moshe charged us with the Law, heritage of Yaakov's assembly" (Deut. 33:4), meaning that it belongs to all of us. If the crown of Torah were hereditary, it might become the prerogative of the rich. Children of great scholars might take their inheritance for granted. It could lead to arrogance and contempt for others. Learning might become a mere intellectual pursuit rather than a spiritual exercise.

Moshe's tragedy, then, was Israel's consolation. The fact that his successor was not his son but his disciple meant that one form of leadership – historically and spiritually the most important one – could be aspired to by everyone.

27:16 אֱלֹהֵי הָרוּחֹת לְכָל־בָּשָׂר *God of the spirit of all flesh* – Why, asked the Sages, did Moshe add the phrase "God of the spirit of all flesh"? The answer, given by Rashi quoting a midrash, is that he was signaling what he saw as an essential quality of anyone leading the Jewish

יג אֶת־הָאָרֶץ אֲשֶׁר נָתַתִּי לִבְנֵי יִשְׂרָאֵל׃ וְרָאִיתָה אֹתָהּ וְנֶאֱסַפְתָּ
יד אֶל־עַמֶּיךָ גַּם־אָתָּה כַּאֲשֶׁר נֶאֱסַף אַהֲרֹן אָחִיךָ׃ כַּאֲשֶׁר
מְרִיתֶם פִּי בְּמִדְבַּר־צִן בִּמְרִיבַת הָעֵדָה לְהַקְדִּישֵׁנִי בַמַּיִם
טו לְעֵינֵיהֶם הֵם מֵי־מְרִיבַת קָדֵשׁ מִדְבַּר־צִן׃ וַיְדַבֵּר כד
טז מֹשֶׁה אֶל־יְהוָה לֵאמֹר׃ יִפְקֹד יְהוָה אֱלֹהֵי הָרוּחֹת לְכָל־
יז בָּשָׂר אִישׁ עַל־הָעֵדָה׃ אֲשֶׁר־יֵצֵא לִפְנֵיהֶם וַאֲשֶׁר יָבֹא

the other side of the river. Moshe's life has not been in vain. He has taken the people almost all the way, but it will be a new generation who will complete the journey.

Martin Luther King reminded his audience of the last day of Moshe's life on what turned out to be the last day of his.

> We've got some difficult times ahead. But it doesn't matter with me now. Because I've been to the mountaintop.… And I've looked over. And I've seen the Promised Land. I may not get there with you. But I want you to know tonight that we as a people will get to the Promised Land.

King knew what the Rabbis knew: "It is not for you to complete the task, but neither are you free to stand aside from it" (Avot 2:16). The Jewish story, in many ways, is the West's meta-narrative of hope.

MOSHE'S CONTINUITY

Seven chapters earlier, God told Moshe and Aharon that they would die without entering the land, and shortly thereafter we read of the death of Aharon. Why then is Moshe now told "You too will be gathered to your people, like Aharon your brother," and why does Moshe now pray for a successor?

The Sages sensed two clues. The first is that this story appears immediately after the episode in which the daughters of Tzelofḥad sought and were granted their father's share in the land. A midrash explains:

> Moshe reasoned: The time is right for me to make my own request. If daughters are allowed to inherit, it is surely right that my sons should inherit my glory. (Bemidbar Rabba 21:14)

The second clue lies in the words "like Aharon your brother" (Num. 27:13). The midrash says: "This teaches us that Moshe wanted to die the way Aharon did." *Ktav Sofer* explains: Aharon had the privilege of knowing that his children would follow in his footsteps. To this day, *kohanim* are direct descendants of Aharon. Moshe likewise longed to see one of his sons, Gershom or Eliezer, take his place as leader of the people. It was not to be. That is the story beneath the story.

It had an aftermath. In the book of Judges we read of a man named Mikha who established an idolatrous cult in the

go out before them and come in before them, who will
lead them out and bring them home. Let not the Lord's
18 community be like sheep without a shepherd." The Lord

---

was palpable in the case of Yehoshua. After the making of the golden calf, he was waiting for Moshe at the foot of the mountain so he could inform him about what had happened in his absence (Ex. 32:17). When Eldad and Meidad began prophesying, which Yehoshua saw as a potential threat to Moshe's leadership, his concern for Moshe was immediate and deeply felt (Num. 11:28). Yet when Moshe told him to assemble a military force and fight the Amalekites, he did so without demur, and won (Ex. 17:9–13).

27:17 אֲשֶׁר־יֵצֵא לִפְנֵיהֶם וַאֲשֶׁר יָבֹא לִפְנֵיהֶם *Who will lead them out and bring them home* – The first phrase in this verse, "who will go out before them and come in before them," is clear enough. It means one who will lead from the front, who will not send his people into battle while staying behind in safety himself. Rashi quotes a verse (I Sam. 18:16) in which the Torah says: "All of Israel and Yehuda loved David, *for he went out and came in before them.*"

It is the second phrase that is difficult: "who will lead them out and bring them home." Surely that follows from the first without saying anything new. Rashi offers two different explanations. One is that it means "who will lead them [to victory] *through his merits*" (Rashi, quoting Sifrei ad loc.). The other is that Moshe is protesting to God: "Do not do to my successor what You did to me, denying me the chance to lead the people into the land" (based on *Tanḥuma*, Buber, ad loc.). Moshe is saying: "Let Yehoshua, unlike me, reach his destination." This is striking, but not the plain sense of the verse.

There is another interpretation. A leader must indeed lead from the front. But he or she must also understand the pace at which people can go. Leadership is not effective if leaders are so far ahead of those they lead that when they turn their heads round, they discover that there is no one following. Leaders must go out in front and come back in front. But they must also "lead the people out and bring them home," meaning, they must take people with them.

A leader must have vision, but also realism. He or she must think the impossible but know the possible. People are slow to change. A leader of the people must go at the people's pace. He or she must educate them, prepare them for the challenges ahead, listen to their grievances, give them courage, lift their sights, and be prepared to slow down if they are unable to keep up. He or she must be impatient and patient all at once – a difficult balancing act. Leaders must not go on ahead so far and fast that, nearing their destination, they find themselves alone.

לִפְנֵיהֶם וַאֲשֶׁר יוֹצִיאֵם וַאֲשֶׁר יְבִיאֵם וְלֹא תִהְיֶה עֲדַת יהוה
יח כַּצֹּאן אֲשֶׁר אֵין־לָהֶם רֹעֶה: וַיֹּאמֶר יהוה אֶל־מֹשֶׁה קַח־

people: "Master of the Universe, the character of each person is revealed to You, and no two are alike. Appoint over them a leader *who will bear with each person according to his individual character*" (Rashi on Num. 27:16, based on *Tanḥuma,* Pinḥas 11). A true leader, even as he or she seeks to communicate a shared vision and common purpose, is nonetheless sensitive to the differences between people. One of the most striking facts about Judaism is its insistence on *the dignity of difference.* No two human beings are exactly alike. This, we believe, is not something to be lamented, but to be honored. It is the basis of one of the most striking sentences in the Mishna, that "a single soul is like a whole universe" (Sanhedrin 4:5), meaning that none of us is substitutable for any other. Leaders honor diversity. They recognize our distinctive gifts and help us realize them. They understand our role in the team. They help us make the contribution only we can make to the project we all share.

27:16 יִפְקֹד יהוה...אִישׁ *Appoint a man* – We might reasonably conclude that Moshe is talking about gender, meaning a man, not a woman. However, Jewish tradition did not read it this way. There were female prophets as well as male. There was a woman tribal and military leader, Devora, in the era of the judges. *Ish* in this context does not mean a man as opposed to a woman. What it does mean can be inferred from the two places in the Torah where we find the phrase *ha'ish Moshe,* "the man Moshe." One occurs in the story of the exodus: "The man Moshe, too, was held in high regard (*gadol meod,* literally, 'very great') in the land of Egypt, among both Pharaoh's officials and the people" (Ex. 11:3). The other appears in the episode in which his own sister and brother, Miriam and Aharon, criticize him: "Now the man Moshe was very humble (*anav meod*), more so than any other man on earth" (Num. 12:3).

These two characteristics – greatness and humility – often appear to be opposed. People whom the world considers great are rarely humble, and those who are humble rarely achieve greatness, at least in the public eye. But Moshe was both. The Torah goes out of its way to apply the same adverb, *meod,* "very," to both attributes. He was very great and at the same time very humble.

The word *ish* in the context of leadership does not mean "a man" but rather, "a mensch," one whose greatness is lightly worn, who cares about the people others often ignore, "the fatherless, the widow, and the stranger," who spends as much time with the people at the margins of society as with the elites, who is courteous to everyone equally and who receives respect because he or she gives respect.

Humility is one of the most important qualities of a leader. That humility

said to Moshe, "Take Yehoshua son of Nun, a man infused
19 with My spirit, and lay your hand upon him. Have him
stand before Elazar the priest and the entire community,
20 and in their sight, give him this charge. Give over to
him some of your majesty, so that the entire Israelite
21 community will obey him. Let him stand before Elazar
the priest, who shall seek the decision of the Urim before
the LORD on his behalf. By this word they will go out and
by this word they will return, he and all Israel, the entire
22 community." Moshe did as the LORD commanded him.
He took Yehoshua and had him stand before Elazar the
23 priest and the entire community. And he laid his hands
upon him and commissioned him, as the LORD had
spoken through Moshe.
28 1 2 The LORD spoke to Moshe: "Command the Israelites; say ḤAMISHI
to them: Take care to present My offering of foodstuffs –
fire offerings of pleasing aroma to Me – at its appointed

responsibilities of freedom. Hence their frequent false nostalgia about how things were in Egypt, and their regret that they ever left.

Moshe lived through this time and again. Perhaps this is why he was initially so reluctant to accept the role of leader. Being exposed to people's anger is the price leaders have to pay if they are to move a people from where they are to where they need to be. The highest form of leadership is the kind that changes people by a combination of vision, education, and giving people a sense of possibility and responsibility – helping them to achieve greatness. When the leader is good, people say, "The leader did it." When the leader is great, they say, "We did it ourselves."

This always carries a price because people often want the leader to do it for them. When they realize that the leader cannot relieve people of responsibility, there is anger. That is what the Sages meant when they said that God told Moshe to inform Yehoshua that the people "are troublesome and obstinate" and that being their leader came with the condition that "you accept this."

Learning to "take the heat" and live with people's anger is one of the hardest tasks of leadership, but it is essential. The leader has to hold steady, be respectful of people's pain, and defend the vision without becoming personally defensive. "Receiving anger" is, in Heifetz's words, "a sacred task."

THE SACRIFICIAL YEAR

As the rupture and disorder of the Baal Peor incident and its aftermath give way to the order and structure that

לְךָ אֶת־יְהוֹשֻׁעַ בִּן־נוּן אִישׁ אֲשֶׁר־רוּחַ בּוֹ וְסָמַכְתָּ אֶת־יָדְךָ
יט עָלָיו׃ וְהַעֲמַדְתָּ אֹתוֹ לִפְנֵי אֶלְעָזָר הַכֹּהֵן וְלִפְנֵי כָּל־הָעֵדָה
כ וְצִוִּיתָה אֹתוֹ לְעֵינֵיהֶם׃ וְנָתַתָּה מֵהוֹדְךָ עָלָיו לְמַעַן יִשְׁמְעוּ
כא כָּל־עֲדַת בְּנֵי יִשְׂרָאֵל׃ וְלִפְנֵי אֶלְעָזָר הַכֹּהֵן יַעֲמֹד וְשָׁאַל לוֹ
בְּמִשְׁפַּט הָאוּרִים לִפְנֵי יְהוָה עַל־פִּיו יֵצְאוּ וְעַל־פִּיו יָבֹאוּ הוּא
כב וְכָל־בְּנֵי־יִשְׂרָאֵל אִתּוֹ וְכָל־הָעֵדָה׃ וַיַּעַשׂ מֹשֶׁה כַּאֲשֶׁר צִוָּה
יְהוָה אֹתוֹ וַיִּקַּח אֶת־יְהוֹשֻׁעַ וַיַּעֲמִדֵהוּ לִפְנֵי אֶלְעָזָר הַכֹּהֵן
כג וְלִפְנֵי כָּל־הָעֵדָה׃ וַיִּסְמֹךְ אֶת־יָדָיו עָלָיו וַיְצַוֵּהוּ כַּאֲשֶׁר דִּבֶּר
יְהוָה בְּיַד־מֹשֶׁה׃
כח א ב וַיְדַבֵּר יְהוָה אֶל־מֹשֶׁה לֵּאמֹר׃ צַו אֶת־בְּנֵי יִשְׂרָאֵל וְאָמַרְתָּ חמישי
אֲלֵהֶם אֶת־קָרְבָּנִי לַחְמִי לְאִשַּׁי רֵיחַ נִיחֹחִי תִּשְׁמְרוּ לְהַקְרִיב

27:18 קַח־לְךָ אֶת־יְהוֹשֻׁעַ בִּן־נוּן *Take Yehoshua son of Nun* – On this phrase, Rashi says, "Persuade him, saying, 'Happy are you to merit leading the children of God'" (Rashi, quoting Sifrei, Pinḥas 23). In the end, leadership is a privilege. It is one of the richest sources of meaning in life.

Walter Lippmann once wrote, "The final test of a leader is that he leaves behind him in other men the conviction and the will to carry on." The measure of Moshe's greatness is that he not only inspired Yehoshua to continue the task he had begun, but did so to an unending flow of prophets, sages, and people of spirit who, lifted by his vision, carried it forward in generation after generation. In his lifetime he knew the bitterness of failure, but few if any have inspired so many for so long.

27:19 וְצִוִּיתָה אֹתוֹ *Give him this charge* – Rashi here makes a startling comment: "You shall command him about the Israelites, saying, 'Be aware that they are troublesome and obstinate. [You may be their leader only] on condition that you accept this'" (based on Shemot Rabba 7:3 and Sifrei, Behaalotekha 91).

This comment is a rabbinic anticipation of Ronald Heifetz's theory of adaptive leadership. Adaptive leadership is needed when, to meet a new challenge, the people have to change. This cannot be done by the leader alone. He or she has to educate the people and hand the challenge back to them.

People resist change, especially when it means giving up long-standing habits that have become deeply embedded in their character. They can go through all the emotions associated with loss: denial, anger, bargaining, and depression. That is one of the bass notes of Numbers: the people's anger at Moshe for forcing them to face the

3 times. Say to them: This is the fire offering you must
present to the LORD: two yearling lambs without blemish
4 as a regular burnt offering each day. Offer one lamb in the
5 morning and the second in the afternoon, with a tenth
of an ephah of fine flour as a grain offering mixed with
6 a quarter of a hin of beaten oil. This is the regular burnt
offering instituted at Mount Sinai, as a pleasing aroma,
7 a fire offering to the LORD. Its libation shall be a quarter
of a hin for each lamb, to be poured out in the Sanctuary
8 as a libation of fermented drink to the LORD. Offer the
other lamb in the afternoon together with a grain offering
and libation as in the morning; a fire offering, a pleasing
aroma to the LORD.

9 On the Sabbath day: two yearling lambs without blemish
and two-tenths of a measure of fine flour as a grain
10 offering, mixed with oil, and its libation. This is the burnt
offering for every Sabbath, to be brought in addition to
the regular daily burnt offering and its libation.

11 On your New Moons you shall present a burnt offering to
the LORD: two young bulls, one ram, and seven yearling
12 lambs, all without blemish. There shall be a grain offering

(Berakhot 51b). When a festival falls on the Sabbath, for instance, the Sabbath takes priority, and its additions to the prayers are said before those of the festival. This is in itself an expression of Jewish values. In many faiths, a sense of holiness and spirituality belongs to moments that are rare, unusual, exceptional. In Judaism what is holy is the texture of everyday life itself. It is the religious drama of daily deeds, words, and relationships. God is not distant but in the here and now – if we create space in our hearts for His presence. We encounter Him, as the journey through the desert nears its end, not in the thunder and lightning of Sinai but every morning and evening in ritual and routine. That is what life is and what faith transfigures.

28:11 וּבְרָאשֵׁי חָדְשֵׁיכֶם *On your New Moons* – Rosh Ḥodesh (the New Moon), like the new year, is understood in Judaism as a time of renewal and rededication, in which we pray for forgiveness and atonement and seek to begin again. As with the festivals, the Musaf prayer now commemorates the special offerings that were brought for the occasion in the Tabernacle and Temple. The central blessings of Musaf begin with a brief statement of the nature of the day and a prayer for the restoration of the Temple and its sacrifices. Our *parasha* is

ג לִי בְּמוֹעֲדוֹ: וְאָמַרְתָּ לָהֶם זֶה הָאִשֶּׁה אֲשֶׁר תַּקְרִיבוּ לַיהוָה
ד כְּבָשִׂים בְּנֵי־שָׁנָה תְמִימִם שְׁנַיִם לַיּוֹם עֹלָה תָמִיד: אֶת־
הַכֶּבֶשׂ אֶחָד תַּעֲשֶׂה בַבֹּקֶר וְאֵת הַכֶּבֶשׂ הַשֵּׁנִי תַּעֲשֶׂה בֵּין
ה הָעַרְבָּיִם: וַעֲשִׂירִית הָאֵיפָה סֹלֶת לְמִנְחָה בְּלוּלָה בְּשֶׁמֶן
ו כָּתִית רְבִיעִת הַהִין: עֹלַת תָּמִיד הָעֲשֻׂיָה בְּהַר סִינַי לְרֵיחַ
ז נִיחֹחַ אִשֶּׁה לַיהוָה: וְנִסְכּוֹ רְבִיעִת הַהִין לַכֶּבֶשׂ הָאֶחָד
ח בַּקֹּדֶשׁ הַסֵּךְ נֶסֶךְ שֵׁכָר לַיהוָה: וְאֵת הַכֶּבֶשׂ הַשֵּׁנִי תַּעֲשֶׂה
בֵּין הָעַרְבָּיִם כְּמִנְחַת הַבֹּקֶר וּכְנִסְכּוֹ תַּעֲשֶׂה אִשֵּׁה רֵיחַ
נִיחֹחַ לַיהוָה:
ט וּבְיוֹם הַשַּׁבָּת שְׁנֵי־כְבָשִׂים בְּנֵי־שָׁנָה תְּמִימִם וּשְׁנֵי עֶשְׂרֹנִים
י סֹלֶת מִנְחָה בְּלוּלָה בַשֶּׁמֶן וְנִסְכּוֹ: עֹלַת שַׁבַּת בְּשַׁבַּתּוֹ עַל־
עֹלַת הַתָּמִיד וְנִסְכָּהּ:
יא וּבְרָאשֵׁי חָדְשֵׁיכֶם תַּקְרִיבוּ עֹלָה לַיהוָה פָּרִים בְּנֵי־בָקָר
יב שְׁנַיִם וְאַיִל אֶחָד כְּבָשִׂים בְּנֵי־שָׁנָה שִׁבְעָה תְּמִימִם: וּשְׁלֹשָׁה

characterize the rest of the book of Numbers, Moshe recaps the Jewish calendar, viewed entirely through the prism of the sacrificial rituals of each day.

We have already encountered the astonishing midrashic passage (quoted in the preface to *Ein Yaakov*, 6b; see Ex. 29, "The Regular Burnt Offering") in which the Sages discuss the question: what is the one sentence that summarizes Judaism?

Ben Zoma holds that it is "Listen, Israel…" (Deut. 6:4) – faith in the One God. Ben Nannas chooses, "Love your neighbor as your own self" (Lev. 19:18) – Judaism's ethic of love. But Ben Pazi says, "There is a more embracing verse still: 'Offer one lamb in the morning and the second in the afternoon'" (Num. 28:4) – the routine of daily service. The midrash concludes: "A certain rabbi stood up and declared: 'The law is in accordance with Ben Pazi.'"

Judaism, suggests Ben Pazi, is not just poetry but also prose, not just the fire of romantic love but the daily kindnesses of a successful marriage, not just an exalted faith in the transcendent God but the way it takes faith and translates it into everyday life.

This account of the yearly calendar of sacrifices begins with ordinary days, then the Sabbath, then the New Moon, and finally the annual cycle of festivals. The order is reflected in the general rule in Judaism that "when a frequent obligation coincides with a rare one, the more frequent one takes precedence"

▶

of three-tenths of a measure of fine flour mixed with oil
for each bull, a grain offering of two-tenths of fine flour
13 mixed with oil for each ram, and a grain offering of one-
tenth of fine flour mixed with oil for each lamb. This shall
be a burnt offering of pleasing aroma, a fire offering to
14 the LORD. Their libations shall be half a hin of wine for a
bull, a third of a hin of wine for a ram, and a quarter of a
hin of wine for a lamb. This is the monthly burnt offering
15 for each New Moon of the year. One male goat shall be
brought as a purification offering to the LORD, in addition
16 to the regular burnt offering and its libation. On SHISHI
the fourteenth day of the first month, a Passover sacrifice
17 shall be brought to the LORD. And the fifteenth day of this
month will be a festival. For seven days unleavened bread
18 shall be eaten. The first day shall be a sacred assembly;
19 you shall perform no laborious work. You shall offer a
burnt fire offering to the LORD: two young bulls, one ram,
20 and seven yearling lambs, all unblemished. Their grain
offering shall be fine flour mixed with oil: three-tenths of
21 a measure for each bull, two-tenths for the ram, and one-
22 tenth for each of the seven lambs, together with one male
goat as a purification offering to make your atonement.
23 These you shall offer in addition to the morning burnt
24 offering, the regular daily offering. In the same way you
shall offer daily for seven days the foodstuffs of a fire
offering, a pleasing aroma to the LORD. It shall be offered
in addition to the regular burnt offering and its libation.
25 The seventh day shall be for you a sacred assembly; you
26 shall perform no laborious work. The day of
first produce, when you bring an offering of new grain
to the LORD on your Festival of Weeks, shall be a sacred
assembly for you. On it you shall perform no laborious

But each also has a historical dimension. Passover recalls the exodus from Egypt. Sukkot is a reminder of the forty years in the desert when the Israelites lived in temporary dwellings. What, then, is the historical dimension of Shavuot in the Torah? Shavuot, I would speculate, was the day, commanded in the desert, that was to celebrate the Promised Land.

There is evidence to support this.

עֶשְׂרֹנִים סֹלֶת מִנְחָה בְּלוּלָה בַשֶּׁמֶן לַפָּר הָאֶחָד וּשְׁנֵי
יג עֶשְׂרֹנִים סֹלֶת מִנְחָה בְּלוּלָה בַשֶּׁמֶן לָאַיִל הָאֶחָד: וְעִשָּׂרֹן
עִשָּׂרוֹן סֹלֶת מִנְחָה בְּלוּלָה בַשֶּׁמֶן לַכֶּבֶשׂ הָאֶחָד עֹלָה רֵיחַ
יד נִיחֹחַ אִשֶּׁה לַיהוָה: וְנִסְכֵּיהֶם חֲצִי הַהִין יִהְיֶה לַפָּר וּשְׁלִישִׁת
הַהִין לָאַיִל וּרְבִיעִת הַהִין לַכֶּבֶשׂ יָיִן זֹאת עֹלַת חֹדֶשׁ בְּחָדְשׁוֹ
טו לְחָדְשֵׁי הַשָּׁנָה: וּשְׂעִיר עִזִּים אֶחָד לְחַטָּאת לַיהוָה עַל־
טז עֹלַת הַתָּמִיד יֵעָשֶׂה וְנִסְכּוֹ: וּבַחֹדֶשׁ הָרִאשׁוֹן ששי
יז בְּאַרְבָּעָה עָשָׂר יוֹם לַחֹדֶשׁ פֶּסַח לַיהוָה: וּבַחֲמִשָּׁה עָשָׂר יוֹם
יח לַחֹדֶשׁ הַזֶּה חָג שִׁבְעַת יָמִים מַצּוֹת יֵאָכֵל: בַּיּוֹם הָרִאשׁוֹן
יט מִקְרָא־קֹדֶשׁ כָּל־מְלֶאכֶת עֲבֹדָה לֹא תַעֲשׂוּ: וְהִקְרַבְתֶּם
אִשֶּׁה עֹלָה לַיהוָה פָּרִים בְּנֵי־בָקָר שְׁנַיִם וְאַיִל אֶחָד וְשִׁבְעָה
כ כְבָשִׂים בְּנֵי שָׁנָה תְּמִימִם יִהְיוּ לָכֶם: וּמִנְחָתָם סֹלֶת בְּלוּלָה
בַשָּׁמֶן שְׁלֹשָׁה עֶשְׂרֹנִים לַפָּר וּשְׁנֵי עֶשְׂרֹנִים לָאַיִל תַּעֲשׂוּ:
כא עִשָּׂרוֹן עִשָּׂרוֹן תַּעֲשֶׂה לַכֶּבֶשׂ הָאֶחָד לְשִׁבְעַת הַכְּבָשִׂים:
כב כג וּשְׂעִיר חַטָּאת אֶחָד לְכַפֵּר עֲלֵיכֶם: מִלְּבַד עֹלַת הַבֹּקֶר אֲשֶׁר
כד לְעֹלַת הַתָּמִיד תַּעֲשׂוּ אֶת־אֵלֶּה: כָּאֵלֶּה תַּעֲשׂוּ לַיּוֹם שִׁבְעַת
יָמִים לֶחֶם אִשֵּׁה רֵיחַ־נִיחֹחַ לַיהוָה עַל־עוֹלַת הַתָּמִיד יֵעָשֶׂה
כה וְנִסְכּוֹ: וּבַיּוֹם הַשְּׁבִיעִי מִקְרָא־קֹדֶשׁ יִהְיֶה לָכֶם כָּל־מְלֶאכֶת
כו עֲבֹדָה לֹא תַעֲשׂוּ: וּבְיוֹם הַבִּכּוּרִים בְּהַקְרִיבְכֶם כה
מִנְחָה חֲדָשָׁה לַיהוָה בְּשָׁבֻעֹתֵיכֶם מִקְרָא־קֹדֶשׁ יִהְיֶה לָכֶם

cited, describing the offering of the day. On Rosh Ḥodesh, we pray that the new month be blessed for good.

A midrashic tradition associates Rosh Ḥodesh with Jewish women, as a tribute to their faithfulness and to their generosity in providing gifts for the construction of the Tabernacle. From the first month of the second year after the exodus, the day the Tabernacle was dedicated, it became a women's festival (Rashi, Megilla 22b; *Shulkhan Arukh, Oraḥ Ḥayim* 417:1).

28:26 וּבְיוֹם הַבִּכּוּרִים *The day of the first produce* – Nowhere does the Torah link Shavuot to a specific historical event. Passover and Sukkot both, like Shavuot, are agricultural and seasonal. Passover is the festival of spring. Sukkot is the festival of ingathering, the autumn harvest.

27 work. You shall present a burnt offering as a pleasing
aroma to the LORD: two young bulls, one ram, and seven
28 yearling lambs. Their grain offering shall be fine flour
mixed with oil: three-tenths of a measure for each bull,
29 two-tenths for the one ram, and one-tenth for each of the
30 31 seven lambs. Offer one male goat to atone for you. These
you shall offer in addition to the regular burnt offering,
its grain offering and libations. They shall be without
blemish.
29 1 The first day of the seventh month shall be a sacred
assembly for you; you shall perform no laborious work
on it. It shall be for you a day of the horn's sounding.

---

law did Jews fully realize that this – a deeper source of identity even than the land – is what Shavuot had been about from the very beginning.

29:1 יוֹם תְּרוּעָה *A day of the horn's sounding* – The Torah does not use the phrase *Rosh HaShana*, the beginning or "head" of the year, and the only time that expression appears in Tanakh (Ezek. 40:1), it refers to Yom Kippur. In fact, the Torah seems to make it clear that Rosh HaShana is *not* the beginning of the year. The first month is not Tishrei, but Nisan. The biblical names for the festival, *Yom Terua* and *Zikhron Terua*, literally "the day of *terua*" and "a commemoration or remembrance of *terua*" (Lev. 23:24), are the only hints we are given of what the day represents. Nor does the Torah specify what instrument is to be used for the "sounding." It might be a horn. But equally it might refer to the silver trumpets the Israelites were commanded to make to summon the people. Sometimes the word refers to a shout or cry on the part of a crowd. Furthermore, we do not know what the sound of *terua* symbolizes. Is it the sound of celebration, of warning, of fear or tears? We are not told.

The Sages ultimately identified *terua* with the shofar for a simple reason. Rosh HaShana is not the only time that a *terua* was sounded in the seventh month. It was also sounded on Yom Kippur of the Jubilee year, when slaves went free and ancestral land returned to its original owners. There (25:9) the instrument is specified: "Then you shall sound the ram's horn (*shofar terua*)." It became a simple inference to conclude that this applied to the *terua* of the first day of the seventh month as well.

What was special about the shofar? In several places in Tanakh it is the sound of battle (see, for example, Josh. 6; I Sam. 4; Jer. 4:19, 49:2). It could also be the sound of celebration (see II Sam. 6:15). But in a number of places, especially the historical books, the shofar was

כז כׇּל־מְלֶ֥אכֶת עֲבֹדָ֖ה לֹ֥א תַעֲשֽׂוּ׃ וְהִקְרַבְתֶּ֨ם עוֹלָ֜ה לְרֵ֤יחַ נִיחֹ֙חַ֙
לַֽיהֹוָ֔ה פָּרִ֧ים בְּנֵי־בָקָ֛ר שְׁנַ֖יִם אַ֣יִל אֶחָ֑ד שִׁבְעָ֥ה כְבָשִׂ֖ים בְּנֵ֥י
כח שָׁנָֽה׃ וּמִ֨נְחָתָ֔ם סֹ֖לֶת בְּלוּלָ֣ה בַשָּׁ֑מֶן שְׁלֹשָׁ֤ה עֶשְׂרֹנִים֙ לַפָּ֣ר
כט הָאֶחָ֔ד שְׁנֵי֙ עֶשְׂרֹנִ֔ים לָאַ֖יִל הָאֶחָֽד׃ עִשָּׂרוֹן֙ עִשָּׂר֔וֹן לַכֶּ֖בֶשׂ
ל הָאֶחָ֑ד לְשִׁבְעַ֖ת הַכְּבָשִֽׂים׃ שְׂעִ֥יר עִזִּ֖ים אֶחָ֑ד לְכַפֵּ֖ר עֲלֵיכֶֽם׃
לא מִלְּבַ֞ד עֹלַ֧ת הַתָּמִ֛יד וּמִנְחָת֖וֹ תַּעֲשׂ֑וּ תְּמִימִ֥ם יִהְיוּ־לָכֶ֖ם
וְנִסְכֵּיהֶֽם׃

כט א וּבַחֹ֨דֶשׁ הַשְּׁבִיעִ֜י בְּאֶחָ֣ד לַחֹ֗דֶשׁ מִֽקְרָא־קֹ֙דֶשׁ֙ יִהְיֶ֣ה לָכֶ֔ם
כׇּל־מְלֶ֥אכֶת עֲבֹדָ֖ה לֹ֣א תַעֲשׂ֑וּ י֥וֹם תְּרוּעָ֖ה יִהְיֶ֥ה לָכֶֽם׃

Passover is about the start of the journey from Egypt. Sukkot recalls the forty years of the journey itself. What is missing is a festival of celebrating the journey's end, the arrival at the destination. Logic would suggest that this was Shavuot. Were it not so, there would have been no annual celebration of the single most important fact about Israel's existence as a nation, namely, that it lived in the land given by God in fulfillment of the promise He had made to their ancestors at the dawn of their history. Shavuot completes the cycle of the three pilgrimage festivals by being the festival of homecoming. That was its historical dimension, made explicit in the *vidui bikkurim* (Deut. 26:1–11), the declaration accompanying the first fruits, and symbolized in the two loaves of wheat (Lev. 23:17) that were the special offering of Shavuot.

It would also follow that the three pilgrimage festivals correspond to three different kinds of bread. Passover is about "the bread of affliction" (Deut. 16:3) that our ancestors ate in Egypt. Sukkot is about the manna, the "bread from heaven" (Ex. 16:4) that they ate for forty years in the wilderness, the sukka itself symbolizing the clouds of glory that appeared just before the manna fell for the first time (13:21, 16:10). Shavuot, "the day of first produce," is about the bread of freedom made with the grain of the land itself.

In the Talmud, Shavuot became known as *zeman matan Torateinu,* "the time of the giving of our Torah," the anniversary of the revelation at Mount Sinai (see, for example, Pesaḥim 68b, among others). At Mount Sinai, a mere seven weeks after leaving Egypt, the Israelites underwent a unique experience that transformed their identity. They made a covenant with God. They pledged themselves to live by His laws. This was their foundational moment as a body politic – uniquely in the history of nations, first came the law, and only then the land.

It seems to me that only when they lost the land but knew they still had the

2 You shall present a burnt offering as a pleasing aroma to
the LORD: one young bull, one ram, and seven yearling
3 lambs, all without blemish. Their grain offering shall be
fine flour mixed with oil, three-tenths of a measure for
4 the bull, two-tenths for the ram, and one-tenth for each
5 of the seven lambs; and there shall be one male goat as
6 a purification offering to atone for you. This will be in
addition to the monthly burnt offering with its grain
offering, and the regular burnt offering with its grain
offering and libations as prescribed. It shall be a pleasing
7 aroma, a fire offering to the LORD. The tenth
day of this seventh month shall be a sacred assembly
for you; you shall afflict yourselves on it and perform
8 no work at all. You shall present a burnt offering to the
LORD for a pleasing aroma: one young bull, one ram, and
9 seven yearling lambs, all without blemish. Their grain
offering shall be fine flour mixed with oil, three-tenths
of a measure for the bull, two-tenths for the single ram,
10 11 and one-tenth for each of the seven sheep. There shall
be one male goat as a purification offering, in addition
to the special purification offering of atonement and
the regular burnt offering with its grain offering and
12 libations. The fifteenth day of the seventh month SHEVI'I
shall be a sacred assembly for you; you shall perform
no laborious work on it; you shall celebrate a festival to
13 the LORD for seven days. And you shall present a burnt
offering, a fire offering, for a pleasing aroma to the LORD:
thirteen young bulls, two rams, and fourteen yearling

---

celebrate God not just as creator of the world, but as its ruler also. Rabbi Joseph B. Soloveitchik told the story of his first Hebrew teacher, who made an indelible impression on him as a child by telling him that Rosh HaShana was God's coronation. "And who puts the crown on His head?" asked the teacher. "We do."

29:13 פָּרִים בְּנֵי־בָקָר שְׁלֹשָׁה עָשָׂר *Thirteen young bulls* – On the seven days of Sukkot, seventy young bulls were offered. Connecting this to Zekharya's prophecy that in the Messianic age all nations would celebrate Sukkot, the Sages concluded that the seventy sacrifices of Sukkot represented the seventy nations of the world as

ב וַעֲשִׂיתֶם עֹלָה לְרֵיחַ נִיחֹחַ לַיהוָה פַּר בֶּן־בָּקָר אֶחָד אַיִל
ג אֶחָד כְּבָשִׂים בְּנֵי־שָׁנָה שִׁבְעָה תְּמִימִם׃ וּמִנְחָתָם סֹלֶת
בְּלוּלָה בַשָּׁמֶן שְׁלֹשָׁה עֶשְׂרֹנִים לַפָּר שְׁנֵי עֶשְׂרֹנִים לָאָיִל׃
ד ה וְעִשָּׂרוֹן אֶחָד לַכֶּבֶשׂ הָאֶחָד לְשִׁבְעַת הַכְּבָשִׂים׃ וּשְׂעִיר־
ו עִזִּים אֶחָד חַטָּאת לְכַפֵּר עֲלֵיכֶם׃ מִלְּבַד עֹלַת הַחֹדֶשׁ
וּמִנְחָתָהּ וְעֹלַת הַתָּמִיד וּמִנְחָתָהּ וְנִסְכֵּיהֶם כְּמִשְׁפָּטָם לְרֵיחַ
ז נִיחֹחַ אִשֶּׁה לַיהוָה׃ וּבֶעָשׂוֹר לַחֹדֶשׁ הַשְּׁבִיעִי
הַזֶּה מִקְרָא־קֹדֶשׁ יִהְיֶה לָכֶם וְעִנִּיתֶם אֶת־נַפְשֹׁתֵיכֶם כָּל־
ח מְלָאכָה לֹא תַעֲשׂוּ׃ וְהִקְרַבְתֶּם עֹלָה לַיהוָה רֵיחַ נִיחֹחַ
פַּר בֶּן־בָּקָר אֶחָד אַיִל אֶחָד כְּבָשִׂים בְּנֵי־שָׁנָה שִׁבְעָה
ט תְּמִימִם יִהְיוּ לָכֶם׃ וּמִנְחָתָם סֹלֶת בְּלוּלָה בַשָּׁמֶן שְׁלֹשָׁה
י עֶשְׂרֹנִים לַפָּר שְׁנֵי עֶשְׂרֹנִים לָאַיִל הָאֶחָד׃ עִשָּׂרוֹן עִשָּׂרוֹן
יא לַכֶּבֶשׂ הָאֶחָד לְשִׁבְעַת הַכְּבָשִׂים׃ שְׂעִיר־עִזִּים אֶחָד
חַטָּאת מִלְּבַד חַטַּאת הַכִּפֻּרִים וְעֹלַת הַתָּמִיד וּמִנְחָתָהּ
יב וְנִסְכֵּיהֶם׃ וּבַחֲמִשָּׁה עָשָׂר יוֹם לַחֹדֶשׁ הַשְּׁבִיעִי שביעי
מִקְרָא־קֹדֶשׁ יִהְיֶה לָכֶם כָּל־מְלֶאכֶת עֲבֹדָה לֹא תַעֲשׂוּ
יג וְחַגֹּתֶם חַג לַיהוָה שִׁבְעַת יָמִים׃ וְהִקְרַבְתֶּם עֹלָה אִשֵּׁה
רֵיחַ נִיחֹחַ לַיהוָה פָּרִים בְּנֵי־בָקָר שְׁלֹשָׁה עָשָׂר אֵילִם שְׁנָיִם

sounded at the coronation of a king. So we find, for instance, at the proclamation of Shlomo as king. "Tzadok…anointed Shlomo. They sounded the ram's horn, and all the people cried, 'Long live King Shlomo!'" (I Kings 1:39).

The book of Psalms associates the shofar not with a human king but with the declaration of God as king. A key text is Psalm 47, said in many congregations before the shofar blowing on Rosh HaShana: "God ascends amid shouts of joy – the Lord – to the blast of the ram's horn…. For God is King over all the earth" (Ps. 47:6, 8).

Psalm 98 makes a clear connection between God's kingship and His judgment:

> With trumpets and the sound of the ram's horn, shout for joy before the Lord, the King…. For He is coming to judge the earth. He will judge the world with justice and the peoples with equity. (Ps. 98:6, 9)

Rosh HaShana, then, is the day we

14 lambs, all without blemish. Their grain offering shall be
fine flour mixed with oil: three-tenths of a measure for
each of the thirteen bulls, two-tenths for each of the
15 two rams, and one-tenth for each of the fourteen lambs.
16 There shall be one male goat as a purification offering,
in addition to the regular burnt offering with its grain
17 offering and libation. On the second day: twelve
young bulls, two rams, and fourteen yearling lambs, all
18 without blemish. The grain offering and libations for the
bulls, rams, and sheep shall be as prescribed for their
19 number. There shall be one male goat as a purification
offering, in addition to the regular burnt offering with
20 its grain offering and libations. On the third
day: eleven bulls, two rams, and fourteen yearling lambs,
21 all without blemish. The grain offering and libations for
the bulls, rams, and lambs shall be as prescribed for their
22 number. There shall be one male goat as a purification
offering, in addition to the regular burnt offering with
23 its grain offering and libation. On the fourth
day: ten bulls, two rams, and fourteen yearling lambs,
24 all without blemish. The grain offering and libations for
the bulls, rams, and sheep shall be as prescribed for their
25 number. And there shall be one male goat as a purification
offering, in addition to the regular burnt offering with its
26 grain offering and libation. On the fifth day: nine
bulls, two rams, and fourteen yearling lambs, all without
27 blemish. The grain offering and libations for the bulls,
rams, and lambs shall be as prescribed for their number.
28 And there shall be one male goat as a purification offering,
in addition to the regular burnt offering with its grain
29 offering and libation. On the sixth day: eight
bulls, two rams, and fourteen yearling lambs, all without

Sages said that on Sukkot, the world is judged for rain (Rosh HaShana 1:2). All peoples, especially in the Middle East, need rain. These facets make Sukkot the most universalistic of all festivals.

יד כְּבָשִׂים בְּנֵי־שָׁנָה אַרְבָּעָה עָשָׂר תְּמִימִם יִהְיוּ: וּמִנְחָתָם
סֹלֶת בְּלוּלָה בַשָּׁמֶן שְׁלֹשָׁה עֶשְׂרֹנִים לַפָּר הָאֶחָד לִשְׁלֹשָׁה
עָשָׂר פָּרִים שְׁנֵי עֶשְׂרֹנִים לָאַיִל הָאֶחָד לִשְׁנֵי הָאֵילִם:
טו וְעִשָּׂרוֹן עִשָּׂרוֹן לַכֶּבֶשׂ הָאֶחָד לְאַרְבָּעָה עָשָׂר כְּבָשִׂים:
טז וּשְׂעִיר־עִזִּים אֶחָד חַטָּאת מִלְּבַד עֹלַת הַתָּמִיד מִנְחָתָהּ
יז וְנִסְכָּהּ: וּבַיּוֹם הַשֵּׁנִי פָּרִים בְּנֵי־בָקָר שְׁנֵים
עָשָׂר אֵילִם שְׁנָיִם כְּבָשִׂים בְּנֵי־שָׁנָה אַרְבָּעָה עָשָׂר תְּמִימִם:
יח וּמִנְחָתָם וְנִסְכֵּיהֶם לַפָּרִים לָאֵילִם וְלַכְּבָשִׂים בְּמִסְפָּרָם
יט כַּמִּשְׁפָּט: וּשְׂעִיר־עִזִּים אֶחָד חַטָּאת מִלְּבַד עֹלַת הַתָּמִיד
כ וּמִנְחָתָהּ וְנִסְכֵּיהֶם: וּבַיּוֹם הַשְּׁלִישִׁי פָּרִים עַשְׁתֵּי־
עָשָׂר אֵילִם שְׁנָיִם כְּבָשִׂים בְּנֵי־שָׁנָה אַרְבָּעָה עָשָׂר תְּמִימִם:
כא וּמִנְחָתָם וְנִסְכֵּיהֶם לַפָּרִים לָאֵילִם וְלַכְּבָשִׂים בְּמִסְפָּרָם
כב כַּמִּשְׁפָּט: וּשְׂעִיר חַטָּאת אֶחָד מִלְּבַד עֹלַת הַתָּמִיד וּמִנְחָתָהּ
כג וְנִסְכָּהּ: וּבַיּוֹם הָרְבִיעִי פָּרִים עֲשָׂרָה אֵילִם
כד שְׁנָיִם כְּבָשִׂים בְּנֵי־שָׁנָה אַרְבָּעָה עָשָׂר תְּמִימִם: מִנְחָתָם
וְנִסְכֵּיהֶם לַפָּרִים לָאֵילִם וְלַכְּבָשִׂים בְּמִסְפָּרָם כַּמִּשְׁפָּט:
כה וּשְׂעִיר־עִזִּים אֶחָד חַטָּאת מִלְּבַד עֹלַת הַתָּמִיד מִנְחָתָהּ
כו וְנִסְכָּהּ: וּבַיּוֹם הַחֲמִישִׁי פָּרִים תִּשְׁעָה אֵילִם שְׁנָיִם
כז כְּבָשִׂים בְּנֵי־שָׁנָה אַרְבָּעָה עָשָׂר תְּמִימִם: וּמִנְחָתָם וְנִסְכֵּיהֶם
כח לַפָּרִים לָאֵילִם וְלַכְּבָשִׂים בְּמִסְפָּרָם כַּמִּשְׁפָּט: וּשְׂעִיר חַטָּאת
כט אֶחָד מִלְּבַד עֹלַת הַתָּמִיד וּמִנְחָתָהּ וְנִסְכָּהּ: וּבַיּוֹם
הַשִּׁשִּׁי פָּרִים שְׁמֹנָה אֵילִם שְׁנָיִם כְּבָשִׂים בְּנֵי־שָׁנָה אַרְבָּעָה

described in Genesis 10. Zekharya foresaw a day when

> all those remaining from all the nations who came up against Jerusalem will go up year after year to bow down to the King, Lord of Hosts, and to celebrate the Festival of Tabernacles. (Zech. 14:16)

Even though Zekharya's vision had not yet been realized, sacrifices were already to be made on behalf of the seventy nations of the world. Furthermore, the

30 blemish. The grain offering and libations for the bulls,
rams, and lambs shall be as prescribed for their number.
31 And there shall be one male goat as a purification offering,
in addition to the regular burnt offering with its grain
32 offering and libations. On the seventh day: seven
bulls, two rams, and fourteen yearling lambs, all without
33 blemish. The grain offering and libation for the bulls,
rams, and lambs shall be as prescribed for their number.
34 And there shall be one male goat as a purification offering,
in addition to the regular burnt offering with its grain
35 offering and libation. On the eighth day you MAFTIR
shall hold an assembly; you shall perform no laborious
36 work on it. You shall present a burnt offering, a fire
offering, for a pleasing aroma to the LORD: one bull, one
37 ram, and seven yearling lambs, all without blemish. The
grain offering and libations for the bull, ram, and lambs
38 shall be as prescribed for their number. And there shall be
one male goat as a purification offering, in addition to the
regular burnt offering with its grain offering and libation.

---

not a symphony. It is quiet time with God. We are reluctant to leave, and we dare to think that He is reluctant to see us go. There are some things we share because we are human. But there are other things, constitutive of our identity, that are uniquely ours – most importantly, our relationships to those who form our family. On Sukkot we are among strangers and friends. On Shemini Atzeret we are with family.

When the Temple stood, it was as if God had said to His people: "Stop. Pause. Stand in My courtyard, in Jerusalem the holy city, and feel My presence in the quiet of the day, the still blue sky, and the breeze gently rustling the trees." Even though the Temple has not been rebuilt, its sacrificial rituals are gone, Israel remains surrounded by enemies, and all we have of the Temple Mount is a wall, the most abstract of all religious symbols, still today in Jerusalem you can feel the Divine Presence as nowhere else on earth – a presence that does not have to be announced with clarions, robes, and rituals. We know that though God is God of all the world, to us He is also father, husband, neighbor, shepherd, king, and we are His children, and this is our private time together, breathing each other's being, blessed by the gift of being present to one another.

ל עָשָׂר תְּמִימִם׃ וּמִנְחָתָם וְנִסְכֵּיהֶם לַפָּרִים לָאֵילִם וְלַכְּבָשִׂים
לא בְּמִסְפָּרָם כַּמִּשְׁפָּט׃ וּשְׂעִיר חַטָּאת אֶחָד מִלְּבַד עֹלַת
לב הַתָּמִיד מִנְחָתָהּ וּנְסָכֶיהָ׃ וּבַיּוֹם הַשְּׁבִיעִי
פָּרִים שִׁבְעָה אֵילִם שְׁנָיִם כְּבָשִׂים בְּנֵי־שָׁנָה אַרְבָּעָה עָשָׂר
לג תְּמִימִם׃ וּמִנְחָתָם וְנִסְכֵּהֶם לַפָּרִים לָאֵילִם וְלַכְּבָשִׂים
לד בְּמִסְפָּרָם כְּמִשְׁפָּטָם׃ וּשְׂעִיר חַטָּאת אֶחָד מִלְּבַד עֹלַת
לה הַתָּמִיד מִנְחָתָהּ וְנִסְכָּהּ׃ בַּיּוֹם הַשְּׁמִינִי עֲצֶרֶת תִּהְיֶה מפטיר
לו לָכֶם כָּל־מְלֶאכֶת עֲבֹדָה לֹא תַעֲשׂוּ׃ וְהִקְרַבְתֶּם עֹלָה אִשֵּׁה
רֵיחַ נִיחֹחַ לַיהוה פַּר אֶחָד אַיִל אֶחָד כְּבָשִׂים בְּנֵי־שָׁנָה
לז שִׁבְעָה תְּמִימִם׃ מִנְחָתָם וְנִסְכֵּיהֶם לַפָּר לָאַיִל וְלַכְּבָשִׂים
לח בְּמִסְפָּרָם כַּמִּשְׁפָּט׃ וּשְׂעִיר חַטָּאת אֶחָד מִלְּבַד עֹלַת

29:35 עֲצֶרֶת תִּהְיֶה לָכֶם *You shall hold an assembly* – Shemini Atzeret is a strange, even unique day in the Jewish calendar. It is described as the eighth day, and thus part of Sukkot, but it is also designated by a name, Atzeret, of its own. Is it, or is it not, a separate festival in its own right? It seems to be both. How are we to understand this fact?

What guided the Sages was the detail that whereas on the seven days of Sukkot seventy young bulls were offered (see note on v. 13), on Atzeret, the eighth day, there was only one. It was as if all humanity were in some sense present in Jerusalem on Sukkot. On the eighth day, as they were leaving, it was as if God were inviting the Jewish people to a small private reception. The word *atzeret* itself was interpreted to mean, "Stop, stay a while." Shemini Atzeret was private time between God and His people. It was a day of particularity after the universality of the seven days of Sukkot.

In some versions of this narrative, the emphasis was on the length of time before the people would return to the Temple, virtually half a year until Passover. Others stressed the sudden shift from seventy sacrifices to one. The memorable phrase that shines through, though, is the one mentioned by Rashi (on Lev. 23:36), in which God says to Israel, "It is hard for Me to see you go." This is the language of intimacy.

So, when all the universality of Judaism has been expressed, there remains something that cannot be universalized: that sense of intimacy with and closeness to God that we feel on Shemini Atzeret, when all the other guests have left. Shemini Atzeret is chamber music,

39 These you shall offer to the Lord on your festivals, in
addition to your vows and freewill offerings: your burnt
offerings, grain offerings, libations, and peace offerings."
30 1 And Moshe told the Israelites all that the Lord had
commanded him.

The haftara for Parashat Pinḥas is on page 1582.
If the parasha falls before the Seventeenth of Tamuz, read this haftara. If it falls after, read the haftara on page 1586.

לט הַתָּמִ֔יד וּמִנְחָתָ֖הּ וְנִסְכָּֽהּ׃ אֵ֛לֶּה תַּעֲשׂ֥וּ לַיהוָ֖ה בְּמוֹעֲדֵיכֶ֑ם
לְ֠בַד מִנִּדְרֵיכֶ֨ם וְנִדְבֹתֵיכֶ֜ם לְעֹלֹתֵיכֶ֗ם וּלְמִנְחֹתֵיכֶ֛ם וּלְנִסְכֵּיכֶ֖ם
ל א וּלְשַׁלְמֵיכֶֽם׃ וַיֹּ֥אמֶר מֹשֶׁ֖ה אֶל־בְּנֵ֣י יִשְׂרָאֵ֑ל כְּכֹ֛ל אֲשֶׁר־צִוָּ֥ה
יְהוָ֖ה אֶת־מֹשֶֽׁה׃

The הפטרה *for* פרשת פינחס *is on page 1583.*
If the פרשה *falls before the Seventeenth of* תמוז*, read this* הפטרה*.*
If it falls after, read the הפטרה *on page 1587.*

Parashat Mattot

30 2 Moshe spoke to the tribal heads of the Israelites: "This
3 is what the LORD has commanded: When a man makes
a vow to the LORD or takes an oath binding himself to
an obligation, he must not break his word; whatever he

Israel, and the moral is still relevant today. A free society depends on trust, and trust depends on keeping your word. Only under very special and precisely formulated circumstances can you be released from your undertakings.

If you seek liberty, treat words as holy, vows and oaths as sacrosanct. When that happens, then, just as God used words to create the natural universe, so we use words to create a social universe. Words create moral obligations, and moral obligations, undertaken responsibly and honored faithfully, create the possibility of a free society.

This accounts for the appearance of the laws of vows and oaths prior to the episode of the tribes of Reuven and Gad. Just like the appearance of the laws of the red heifer (purification after contact with the dead) before the story of the deaths of Miriam and Aharon and the announcement of the death of Moshe, it is an instance of the rule that "God provides the cure before the disease" (Megilla 13b; see ch. 19, "The Red Heifer"). The law is stated before the narrative to which it applies.

30:3 אוֹ־הִשָּׁבַע שְׁבֻעָה *Or takes an oath* – Vows and oaths are obligations created by words. The difference between them is that a vow, *neder*, affects the status of an object (*ḥeftza*). It dedicates it in such a way as to render it inaccessible to me for my personal use. However, an oath, *shevua*, affects the person (*gavra*), not the object.

This distinction led Rabbi Joseph B. Soloveitchik into a fascinating reflection. The difference between *gavra* and *ḥeftza*, he suggests, is the difference between subject and object. "When I say that I am writing a letter, I am the *gavra*, the subject of the action, while the letter is the *ḥeftza*." A *gavra* acts; a *ḥeftza* is acted on. A judge passes sentence; a prisoner is sentenced. These are two different modes of being. Sometimes we are one, sometimes the other.

Rabbi Soloveitchik quotes the statement in the Gemara that an oath is administered to each of us before we are born, saying, "Be righteous and not wicked" (Nidda 30b). The fact that this is an oath requires us to be a *gavra*, not a *ḥeftza*, to be a free and responsible choosing subject, not the passive object of other people's acts. "If a human being is to act as an emissary of God, then they must be a *gavra*, constantly moving upward."

פרשת מטות

ל ב וַיְדַבֵּר מֹשֶׁה אֶל־רָאשֵׁי הַמַּטּוֹת לִבְנֵי יִשְׂרָאֵל לֵאמֹר זֶה כו
ג הַדָּבָר אֲשֶׁר צִוָּה יְהוָה׃ אִישׁ כִּי־יִדֹּר נֶדֶר לַיהוָה אוֹ־הִשָּׁבַע
שְׁבֻעָה לֶאְסֹר אִסָּר עַל־נַפְשׁוֹ לֹא יַחֵל דְּבָרוֹ כְּכָל־הַיֹּצֵא

MATTOT

Parashat Mattot opens with an account of Moshe instructing the leaders of the tribes on the laws of vows and oaths. The Israelites are then commanded to wage war against the Midianites because of their hostility. There is an account of what is to be done with the spoils of war. Two tribes, Reuven and Gad, together with half the tribe of Menashe, ask permission to stay east of the Jordan where the land is ideal pasture for their cattle. Moshe is initially angered but eventually agrees on condition that they first join and lead in the battles for the land west of the Jordan.

As Numbers draws toward its close, there is a new tone to the narrative. We no longer hear the querulous complaints that had been the bass note of so much of the wilderness years. That undertone was the sound of the generation born into slavery that had left Egypt. By now, the people of the generation born in freedom and toughened by conditions in the desert have a more purposeful feel about them. Battle-tried, they no longer doubt their ability, with God's help, to fight and win. The problems they face now are of a different kind, and they are newly equipped to deal with them.

VOWS AND OATHS

The laws of vows and oaths represent one of the most distinctive features of Judaism as a way of life, namely, its intense focus on the way we create or destroy worlds by words. With words, God created the world: "God said, 'Let there be…' and there was" (Gen. 2:19). One of the gifts God gave the first human was language: the ability to name the animals. When the Torah says that "the Lord God formed man from the dust of the land and breathed the breath of life into his nostrils, and the man became a living being" (2:7), the Targum translates the last phrase as "and the man became a speaking being." For Judaism, speaking is life itself.

If trust in others' words breaks down, social relationships break down. Society will then depend on law enforcement agencies or some other use of force. When force is widely used, society is no longer free. The only way free human beings can form collaborative and cooperative relationships without recourse to force is by the use of verbal undertakings honored by those who make them.

The insistence on honoring your word is axiomatic to the creation of the kind of society the Torah envisages in

4 speaks, that he must fulfill. When a woman makes a vow to
the LORD or takes an oath binding herself to an obligation
5 while still a girl in her father's house, and her father hears
of her vow or self-imposed obligation and remains silent,
then all her vows and self-imposed obligations stand.
6 But if her father restrains her on the day he hears her,
none of her vows or self-imposed obligations shall stand.

---

that Jews did not feel themselves bound by their word, a claim later repeated by antisemitic writers. In vain, Jews explained that the prayer had nothing to do with promises between man and man. It referred only to private commitments between man and God. All in all, it was and is a strange way to begin the holiest of days.

Yet the prayer survived all attempts to have it dislodged. One theory is that it had its origins in the forced conversion of Spanish Jews to Christianity under the Visigoths in the seventh century. These Jews, the first Marranos, publicly abandoned their faith rather than face torture and death, but they remained Jews in secret. On the Day of Atonement they made their way back to the synagogue and prayed to have their vow of conversion annulled. That, surely, is the significance of *Kol Nidrei* in the Jewish imagination. It is the moment when the doors of belonging are opened, and when those who have been estranged return. During the year – albeit less dramatically than their medieval predecessors – they may have been Marranos, hidden Jews. They have worn other masks, carried different identities. But tonight the music of *Kol Nidrei* has spoken to them and they have said: Here is where I belong. Among my people and its faith. I am a Jew.

30:6 וְאִם־הֵנִיא אָבִיהָ אֹתָהּ *If her father restrains her* – The text appears to give a father or husband power of veto over a woman's vows. This jars with our sense of women's autonomy. There is no hint, for instance, that Elkana was consulted over Ḥana's vow (1 Sam. 1:11). Indeed, the Sages expounded the law to limit men's power of veto to very specific circumstances. The passage highlights the fact, however, that commitments are not made in a vacuum but within a web of social connections. Our *parasha* is addressed, uniquely, not to "all Israel" but to "the tribal heads," hinting at the concentric circles of commitment which are the background of the specific commitments we undertake as individuals.

In stable families, nurtured by those who brought us into existence, we learn to give and receive love. There is no greater crucible of trust than the family bond. There we find, if we are lucky, that love given is not given in vain.

Communities are our closest approximation to the extended families of the Torah, where the concept of virtue was born and our ethical tradition has its origins. Communities are where we acquire a sense of place and belonging. They are usually small enough to allow

ד מִפִּיו יַעֲשֶׂה׃ וְאִשָּׁה כִּי־תִדֹּר נֶדֶר לַיהוָה וְאָסְרָה אִסָּר בְּבֵית
ה אָבִיהָ בִּנְעֻרֶיהָ׃ וְשָׁמַע אָבִיהָ אֶת־נִדְרָהּ וֶאֱסָרָהּ אֲשֶׁר אָסְרָה
עַל־נַפְשָׁהּ וְהֶחֱרִישׁ לָהּ אָבִיהָ וְקָמוּ כָּל־נְדָרֶיהָ וְכָל־אִסָּר
ו אֲשֶׁר־אָסְרָה עַל־נַפְשָׁהּ יָקוּם׃ וְאִם־הֵנִיא אָבִיהָ אֹתָהּ
בְּיוֹם שָׁמְעוֹ כָּל־נְדָרֶיהָ וֶאֱסָרֶיהָ אֲשֶׁר־אָסְרָה עַל־נַפְשָׁהּ

The difference between a vow and an oath thus becomes a metaphor for two different kinds of life, one defined by others and one self-created. One kind of person, Rabbi Soloveitchik says, is "receptive, passive… wholly under the influence of other people and their views." The other is "not passive but active.… He does not simply abandon himself to the rule of the species but blazes his own individual trail."

Things happen to us and they affect us, sometimes very deeply. To that extent, we are a *ḥeftza*. We are the object of events, and of other people's deeds, and we are shaped by them. But the challenge of faith is to become a *gavra*, to be our best self, undeflected and undefeated by what others do or say. It is not easy; it is never less than challenging. Faith is the call to be not an object but a subject, to influence more than to be influenced by our environment. We are called on to be more than others make us.

30:3 נדר... שבעה... לאסר אסר על־נפשו *Vow… oath… obligation* – This vocabulary is to be adopted and adapted as the annulment of vows that marks the start of the holiest day of the year, Yom Kippur. As the *ḥazan* sings *Kol Nidrei*, we hear in that ancient tune the deepest music of the Jewish soul, elegiac yet striving, pained but resolute, the music of our ancestors which stretches out to us from the past and enfolds us in its cadences, making us and them one. The music is pure poetry, but the words are prosaic prose.

Kol nidrei literally means "all vows." The passage itself is not a prayer at all, but a dry legal formula annulling in advance all vows, oaths, and promises between us and God in the coming year, or in some traditions, retroactively annulling those of the previous year. Nothing could be more incongruous, less apparently in keeping with the solemnity of the day. Indeed, for more than a thousand years there have been attempts to remove it from the liturgy. Why annul vows? Better not to make them in the first place if they could not be kept. Besides which, though Jewish law admits the possibility of annulment, it does so only after patient examination of individual cases. To do so globally for the whole community was difficult to justify. From the eighth century onward we read of *geonim*, rabbinic leaders, who condemned the prayer and sought to have it abolished. Five centuries later, a new note of concern was added. In the Christian-Jewish disputation in Paris in 1240, the Christian protagonist Nicholas Donin attacked *Kol Nidrei* as evidence

The Lord will forgo them for her, because her father
7 has restrained her. If she marries, having made vows or
8 verbally bound herself, and her husband hears of it and on
the day he does so keeps silent, then her vow or any pledge
9 by which she has bound herself shall stand. But if, on the
day her husband hears of it, he restrains her, he can annul
her vow or the pledge by which she has bound herself, and
10 the Lord will forgo them for her. The vow of a widow or a
11 divorcée – whatever she binds herself by – stands. If, while
in her husband's house, a woman makes a vow or takes an
12 oath binding herself to an obligation and her husband
hears and keeps silent, and does not restrain her, then all
her vows and the obligations by which she binds herself
13 shall stand. But if her husband annuls them on the day
when he hears them, then the words she spoke as a vow
or the obligation by which she bound herself will not
stand. Her husband has annulled them, and the Lord will
14 forgo them for her. Every vow or binding by oath may be
upheld by her husband or else annulled by her husband.
15 But if her husband keeps silent from that day to the next,
then he has upheld all her vows and the obligations by
which she has bound herself. He has upheld them by
16 remaining silent on the day when he heard them. If he
nullifies them some time after he has heard of them, he
17 shall bear her guilt." These are the decrees that the Lord
issued to Moshe, between a husband and his wife and
between a father and his daughter while she is a girl in her
father's home.

---

applies to both: say little, do much, and always do what you said you would. Vows can be annulled, but "better not to vow" (Eccl. 5:4) than to vow and then annul, for the latter causes an erosion of trust that devalues the sanctity of the commitment implicit in a vow.

There is such a thing as an ecology of hope – a web of circumstances that teaches us that it is worth working together for a better tomorrow. There are environments in which hope flourishes and others in which it dies. Hope is born with trust, and has its being in the context of family, community, and faith.

לֹא יָקוּם וַיהוה יִסְלַח־לָהּ כִּי־הֵנִיא אָבִיהָ אֹתָהּ: וְאִם־הָיוֹ ז
תִהְיֶה לְאִישׁ וּנְדָרֶיהָ עָלֶיהָ אוֹ מִבְטָא שְׂפָתֶיהָ אֲשֶׁר אָסְרָה
עַל־נַפְשָׁהּ: וְשָׁמַע אִישָׁהּ בְּיוֹם שָׁמְעוֹ וְהֶחֱרִישׁ לָהּ וְקָמוּ ח
נְדָרֶיהָ וֶאֱסָרֶהָ אֲשֶׁר־אָסְרָה עַל־נַפְשָׁהּ יָקֻמוּ: וְאִם בְּיוֹם ט
שְׁמֹעַ אִישָׁהּ יָנִיא אוֹתָהּ וְהֵפֵר אֶת־נִדְרָהּ אֲשֶׁר עָלֶיהָ וְאֵת
מִבְטָא שְׂפָתֶיהָ אֲשֶׁר אָסְרָה עַל־נַפְשָׁהּ וַיהוה יִסְלַח־לָהּ:
וְנֵדֶר אַלְמָנָה וּגְרוּשָׁה כֹּל אֲשֶׁר־אָסְרָה עַל־נַפְשָׁהּ יָקוּם י
עָלֶיהָ: וְאִם־בֵּית אִישָׁהּ נָדָרָה אוֹ־אָסְרָה אִסָּר עַל־נַפְשָׁהּ יא
בִּשְׁבֻעָה: וְשָׁמַע אִישָׁהּ וְהֶחֱרִשׁ לָהּ לֹא הֵנִיא אֹתָהּ וְקָמוּ יב
כָּל־נְדָרֶיהָ וְכָל־אִסָּר אֲשֶׁר־אָסְרָה עַל־נַפְשָׁהּ יָקוּם: וְאִם־ יג
הָפֵר יָפֵר אֹתָם ׀ אִישָׁהּ בְּיוֹם שָׁמְעוֹ כָּל־מוֹצָא שְׂפָתֶיהָ
לִנְדָרֶיהָ וּלְאִסַּר נַפְשָׁהּ לֹא יָקוּם אִישָׁהּ הֲפֵרָם וַיהוה יִסְלַח־
לָהּ: כָּל־נֵדֶר וְכָל־שְׁבֻעַת אִסָּר לְעַנֹּת נָפֶשׁ אִישָׁהּ יְקִימֶנּוּ יד
וְאִישָׁהּ יְפֵרֶנּוּ: וְאִם־הַחֲרֵשׁ יַחֲרִישׁ לָהּ אִישָׁהּ מִיּוֹם אֶל־יוֹם טו
וְהֵקִים אֶת־כָּל־נְדָרֶיהָ אוֹ אֶת־כָּל־אֱסָרֶיהָ אֲשֶׁר עָלֶיהָ הֵקִים
אֹתָם כִּי־הֶחֱרִשׁ לָהּ בְּיוֹם שָׁמְעוֹ: וְאִם־הָפֵר יָפֵר אֹתָם טז
אַחֲרֵי שָׁמְעוֹ וְנָשָׂא אֶת־עֲוֺנָהּ: אֵלֶּה הַחֻקִּים אֲשֶׁר צִוָּה יז
יהוה אֶת־מֹשֶׁה בֵּין אִישׁ לְאִשְׁתּוֹ בֵּין־אָב לְבִתּוֹ בִּנְעֻרֶיהָ
בֵּית אָבִיהָ:

us to recognize one another, to value the contribution of each to the welfare of all.

Families and communities are in turn undergirded by faith. Religious faith suggests that our commitments to fidelity and interdependence are not arbitrary. They mirror the deep structure of reality. The bonds between husband and wife, parent and child, and us and our neighbors partake of the covenantal bond between God and humanity. The moral rules and virtues which constrain and enlarge our aspirations are not mere subjective devices and desires. They are "out there" as well as "in here."

All this is the background and training ground for commitments undertaken, trust given and earned. In a passage on speech, Ecclesiastes moves from relationships between humans to those between us and God. The same rule

31 1 2 The Lord spoke to Moshe: "Take revenge for the SHENI
Israelites against the Midianites; after that you will be
3 gathered in to your people." Moshe spoke to the people:
"Equip men from among you for active service, to go
out against Midyan, to execute the Lord's vengeance
4 against Midyan. For this service, call up one thousand
5 from each of Israel's tribes." And so, of the thousands of
Israel, one thousand men were selected from each tribe,
6 twelve thousand in all, all armed for battle. Moshe sent
them, a thousand from each tribe, into service, together
with Pinḥas son of Elazar the priest, who was in charge
of the sacred utensils and the trumpets for sounding the
7 blast. And they did battle against Midyan as the Lord
8 had commanded Moshe, and killed every male. And,
among the slain, they killed the kings of Midyan: Evi,
Rekem, Tzur, Ḥur, and Reva – all five kings of Midyan. At

---

for all time, but the word of the Lord for *this* time. There are things – including a revenge attack such as this – that may be justified in an age of prophecy that are wholly unjustifiable at other times.

As a general rule, the application of every ancient text to another age involves an act of interpretation, and there is nothing inherently religious about this. It is a central problem in secular law and jurisprudence, deliberated over in every Supreme Court. How is a law enacted then to be understood now? It is a problem every theatrical director faces in deciding how, for example, to stage *The Merchant of Venice* for a contemporary audience. In each case, the issue is how to apply the-word-then to the-world-now, bridging the hermeneutical abyss of time and change. Religions develop rules of interpretation and structures of authority. Without these, any group can do almost anything in the name of religion, selecting texts, taking them out of context, reading them literally, and ignoring the rest. Without rules, principles, and authority, sacred texts provide the charisma of seemingly divine authority for purposes that are all too human. As Shakespeare said, "The devil can cite Scripture for his purpose."

Never say, then, "I hate, I kill, because my religion says so." Every text needs interpretation. Every interpretation needs wisdom. Every wisdom needs careful negotiation between the timeless and time. Fundamentalism reads texts as if God were as simple as we are. That is unlikely to be true. Hard texts need interpreting; without it, they lead to violence. God has given us both the mandate and the responsibility to do just that. We are guardians of His word for the sake of His world.

לא א ב וידבר יהוה אל־משה לאמר: נקם נקמת בני ישראל מאת כז שני
ג המדינים אחר תאסף אל־עמיך: וידבר משה אל־העם
לאמר החלצו מאתכם אנשים לצבא ויהיו על־מדין לתת
ד נקמת־יהוה במדין: אלף למטה אלף למטה לכל מטות
ה ישראל תשלחו לצבא: וימסרו מאלפי ישראל אלף למטה
ו שנים־עשר אלף חלוצי צבא: וישלח אתם משה אלף
למטה לצבא אתם ואת־פינחס בן־אלעזר הכהן לצבא
ז וכלי הקדש וחצצרות התרועה בידו: ויצבאו על־מדין
ח כאשר צוה יהוה את־משה ויהרגו כל־זכר: ואת־מלכי
מדין הרגו על־חלליהם את־אוי ואת־רקם ואת־צור ואת־
חור ואת־רבע חמשת מלכי מדין ואת בלעם בן־בעור הרגו

A WAR OF RETRIBUTION

Religions, especially religions of the Book, have hard texts: verses, commands, episodes, narratives that if understood literally and applied directly would not merely offend our moral sense. They would also go against our best understanding of the religion itself. The war of revenge against the Midianites is one. The war mandated against the seven nations in the land is another. They strike us as barbaric and out of key with an ethic of compassion and with the just-war doctrine that is to emerge in the Jewish tradition.

These texts – and there are notorious examples in the holy texts of most religions – require the most careful interpretation if they are not to do great harm. That is why every text-based religion develops its own traditions of interpretation. Rabbinic Judaism declared Biblicism – accepting the authority of the written word while rejecting the Oral Tradition, the position of the Sadducees and Karaites – as heresy. The Rabbis said: 'One who translates a verse literally is a liar' (Kiddushin 49a). The point is clear: no text without interpretation; no interpretation without tradition.

Why must it be so? One reason is that these ancient texts were originally directed to times and conditions quite unlike ours. The war commands of Deuteronomy and the book of Joshua, for example, belong to a time when warfare was systemic, endemic, and brutal. The massacre of populations, such as we read of here, was commonplace. Another reason is that we are dealing with sacred Scripture, texts invested with the ultimate authority of God Himself. How do you take the word of eternity and apply it to the here and now? That is never simple and self-understood. For much of the biblical era, ancient Israel had its prophets who delivered, not the word of the Lord

▶

9 the sword's edge they also killed Bilam son of Beor. The
Israelites took captive the Midianite women and children,
and took as booty all their cattle, flocks, and wealth.
10 They burned all the towns where they lived and their
11 encampments. They gathered all the spoil and plunder,
12 people and animals, and they brought the captives and
the plunder and spoil to Moshe, Elazar the priest, and the
Israelite community, at the camp on the plains of Moav
13 by the Jordan across from Yeriḥo. Moshe, Elazar SHELISHI /SHENI/
the priest, and all the community princes went to meet
14 them outside the camp. And Moshe grew furious with the
commanders of the forces, the officers of thousands and
15 of hundreds, now returned from the service of war. "Have
16 you left all the women alive?" Moshe demanded. "These
were the very ones who, on Bilam's advice, induced the
Israelites to betray the Lord during the Peor affair, so
17 that a plague struck down the Lord's community. Now,
therefore, kill every male child and kill every woman who
18 has had relations with a man. All the young girls who have
not had relations with any man – them you may spare
19 alive. You must stay outside the camp for seven days.
Every one among you or your captives who has killed a
person or touched a corpse must purify himself or herself
20 on the third and seventh days. You must also purify every
garment, as well as every article of leather, goats' hair, or
21 wood." Elazar the priest said to the soldiers
returning from war, "This is the Law's decree that the

---

fact that He had given him permission to do so. Evidently, God detected in Bilam's mind a persisting malevolence toward Israel, which eventually found expression in the plan to have the women seduce the Israelite men.

The real effect of concealing the information about Bilam, though, is to focus attention on the Israelites. It is they who sinned. Had Bilam's name been mentioned at the outset, we would have focused on him. It would have been his malice, his cunning, his defiance of God's purposes that would have been the story. The Torah is signaling to us that it was not the story. God saves Israel from its enemies but only we can save us from ourselves.

ט בחרב: וישבו בני־ישראל את־נשי מדין ואת־טפם ואת
י כל־בהמתם ואת־כל־מקנהם ואת־כל־חילם בזזו: ואת
יא כל־עריהם במושבתם ואת כל־טירתם שרפו באש: ויקחו
יב את־כל־השלל ואת כל־המלקוח באדם ובבהמה: ויבאו
אל־משה ואל־אלעזר הכהן ואל־עדת בני־ישראל את־
השבי ואת־המלקוח ואת־השלל אל־המחנה אל־ערבת
יג מואב אשר על־ירדן ירחו: ויצאו שלישי /שני/
משה ואלעזר הכהן וכל־נשיאי העדה לקראתם אל־
יד מחוץ למחנה: ויקצף משה על פקודי החיל שרי האלפים
טו ושרי המאות הבאים מצבא המלחמה: ויאמר אליהם
טז משה החייתם כל־נקבה: הן הנה היו לבני ישראל בדבר
בלעם למסר־מעל ביהוה על־דבר פעור ותהי המגפה
יז בעדת יהוה: ועתה הרגו כל־זכר בטף וכל־אשה ידעת
יח איש למשכב זכר הרגו: וכל הטף בנשים אשר לא־ידעו
יט משכב זכר החיו לכם: ואתם חנו מחוץ למחנה שבעת
ימים כל הרג נפש וכל | נגע בחלל תתחטאו ביום השלישי
כ וביום השביעי אתם ושביכם: וכל־בגד וכל־כלי־עור וכל־
כא מעשה עזים וכל־כלי־עץ תתחטאו: ויאמר
אלעזר הכהן אל־אנשי הצבא הבאים למלחמה זאת

31:16 בדבר בלעם *On Bilam's advice* – In chapter 25, we read of the sequel to the episode of Bilam's curses/blessings. The Israelites, having been saved by God from the would-be curses of Moav and Midyan, suffered a self-inflicted tragedy by allowing themselves to be enticed by the women of the land. God's anger burned against them. Here, several chapters later, it emerges that it was Bilam who devised this strategy. Having failed to curse the Israelites, Bilam eventually succeeds in doing them great harm.

When the Torah withholds a fact essential to understanding a passage and reveals it only later, it is forcing us to realize that events are not always what they first seem. In this case, certain puzzling aspects of the Bilam story become clear. We now understand why God was angry with Bilam for going along with the Moabites and Midianites despite the

▶

22 Lord commanded Moshe: Gold, silver, bronze, iron, tin,
23 and lead – anything that can withstand fire – you shall
pass through the fire and it will be purified, though it must
also be purified with the water of lustration. Anything
that cannot withstand fire, you must immerse in water.
24 You shall wash your clothes on the seventh day and you
25 will then be pure, and may enter the camp." The REVI'I
26 Lord said to Moshe: "Together with Elazar the priest
and the family heads of the community, you must make
an inventory of the plunder that was taken, people and
27 animals, giving half to the soldiers who went into battle
28 and half to the rest of the community. Levy a tribute to
the Lord. From the soldiers who took part in the battle,
take one part of every five hundred, be it of people, oxen,
29 donkeys, or flocks. Take this from their half and give it to
30 Elazar the priest as an upraised gift to the Lord. From
the Israelites' half, take one out of every fifty, be it of
people, cattle, donkeys, or flock – all the animals – and
give them to the Levites who carry out the duties of the
31 Lord's Tabernacle." Moshe and Elazar the priest did as

R. Yoḥanan responded, "I conferred on you the benefit of bringing you under the wings of the Divine Presence."

Scarred by this encounter, Reish Lakish became ill and eventually died and R. Yoḥanan grieved for him deeply. Reminding a penitent of his past is forbidden; once he has undergone a true repentance, he is no longer the same person he was.

Perhaps it was speaking from his own experience that Reish Lakish had said: Great is repentance, because *through it deliberate sins are accounted as though they were merits* (Yoma 86b). Any act we perform has multiple consequences, some good, some bad. When we intend evil, the bad consequences are attributed to us because they are what we sought to achieve. The good consequences are not; they are mere unintended outcomes. However, once one has undergone complete repentance, their original intent is canceled out. It is then possible to see the good, as well as the bad, consequences of the original act – and to be accredited with the former. There are two concepts of the past. The first is what happened. That is something we cannot change. The second is the *significance*, the *meaning*, of what happened. That is something we *can* change. Though we may need to pass through fire and water, we can reclaim our past through our choices for the future.

כב חֻקַּת הַתּוֹרָה אֲשֶׁר־צִוָּה יהוה אֶת־מֹשֶׁה: אַךְ אֶת־הַזָּהָב
וְאֶת־הַכָּסֶף אֶת־הַנְּחֹשֶׁת אֶת־הַבַּרְזֶל אֶת־הַבְּדִיל וְאֶת־
כג הָעֹפָרֶת: כָּל־דָּבָר אֲשֶׁר־יָבֹא בָאֵשׁ תַּעֲבִירוּ בָאֵשׁ וְטָהֵר אַךְ
בְּמֵי נִדָּה יִתְחַטָּא וְכֹל אֲשֶׁר לֹא־יָבֹא בָּאֵשׁ תַּעֲבִירוּ בַמָּיִם:
כד וְכִבַּסְתֶּם בִּגְדֵיכֶם בַּיּוֹם הַשְּׁבִיעִי וּטְהַרְתֶּם וְאַחַר תָּבֹאוּ
כה אֶל־הַמַּחֲנֶה: וַיֹּאמֶר יהוה אֶל־מֹשֶׁה לֵּאמֹר: כח רביעי
כו שָׂא אֵת רֹאשׁ מַלְקוֹחַ הַשְּׁבִי בָּאָדָם וּבַבְּהֵמָה אַתָּה וְאֶלְעָזָר
כז הַכֹּהֵן וְרָאשֵׁי אֲבוֹת הָעֵדָה: וְחָצִיתָ אֶת־הַמַּלְקוֹחַ בֵּין תֹּפְשֵׂי
כח הַמִּלְחָמָה הַיֹּצְאִים לַצָּבָא וּבֵין כָּל־הָעֵדָה: וַהֲרֵמֹתָ מֶכֶס
לַיהוה מֵאֵת אַנְשֵׁי הַמִּלְחָמָה הַיֹּצְאִים לַצָּבָא אֶחָד נֶפֶשׁ
מֵחֲמֵשׁ הַמֵּאוֹת מִן־הָאָדָם וּמִן־הַבָּקָר וּמִן־הַחֲמֹרִים וּמִן־
כט הַצֹּאן: מִמַּחֲצִיתָם תִּקָּחוּ וְנָתַתָּה לְאֶלְעָזָר הַכֹּהֵן תְּרוּמַת
ל יהוה: וּמִמַּחֲצִת בְּנֵי־יִשְׂרָאֵל תִּקַּח ׀ אֶחָד ׀ אָחֻז מִן־הַחֲמִשִּׁים
מִן־הָאָדָם מִן־הַבָּקָר מִן־הַחֲמֹרִים וּמִן־הַצֹּאן מִכָּל־הַבְּהֵמָה
לא וְנָתַתָּה אֹתָם לַלְוִיִּם שֹׁמְרֵי מִשְׁמֶרֶת מִשְׁכַּן יהוה: וַיַּעַשׂ

31:23 תַּעֲבִירוּ בָאֵשׁ וְטָהֵר *Pass through the fire and it will be purified* – The spoils of war, which had been used as vessels and tools of idolatry, must undergo a ritual of renewal, passing through fire and water, before they can be used by the people. The process is echoed in a poignant debate in the Talmud between R. Yoḥanan and his learning partner, Reish Lakish (Bava Metzia 84a). According to tradition, Reish Lakish was originally a robber or highwayman, who was persuaded by R. Yoḥanan, the leading Sage in the land of Israel at the time, to devote his life to talmudic study.

One day, in the house of study, the question arose as to when instruments like swords, spears, daggers, and knives are considered complete, and thus capable of becoming ritually unclean. R. Yoḥanan said they are complete when they have been tempered in a furnace. Reish Lakish said they are not complete until they have been quenched in water. In the heat of the argument, R. Yoḥanan said, "Trust a robber to be expert in his trade."

Reish Lakish, wounded by the jibe, turned on R. Yoḥanan and said, "What benefit have you conferred on me by persuading me to give up robbery and become a rabbi? There, among robbers, I was called master, and here in the house of study I am called a master."

32 the LORD commanded Moshe. The plunder, aside from
33 the spoil the troops had taken, was 675,000 sheep, 72,000
34, 35 oxen, 61,000 donkeys, and 32,000 women who had not
36 had relations with a man. The half share of those who had
37 served in battle was 337,500 sheep, of which the LORD's
38 tribute was 675. The cattle were 36,000, of which the
39 LORD's tribute was 72. The donkeys were 30,500, of which
40 the LORD's tribute was 61. There were 16,000 people, of
41 which the LORD's tribute was 32 persons. Moshe gave
the tribute, an upraised gift for the LORD, to Elazar the
42 priest, as the LORD had commanded Moshe. The half HAMISHI
share that Moshe took for the Israelites from those who
43 had served in battle as the community's half consisted of
44, 45, 46 337,500 sheep, 36,000 heads of cattle, 30,500 donkeys, and
47 16,000 people. Moshe took from the Israelites' half one
out of every 50 humans and animals. These he gave to the
Levites who keep the charge of the LORD's Tabernacle,
48 as the LORD had commanded Moshe. The commanders
over the thousands of the warriors – officers over
thousands and officers over hundreds – approached
49 Moshe and said to him, "Your servants have counted the
50 warriors in our charge; not one of us is missing. And so
we make an offering to the LORD of the gold articles each
man found – anklets, bracelets, signet rings, earrings, and
pendants – to make our atonement before the LORD."
51 Moshe and Elazar the priest took all the gold from them,
52 all the crafted objects. All the gold for the upraised gift
presented to the LORD by the officers of thousands and
53 the officers of hundreds was worth 16,750 shekel. Yet the

לב מֹשֶׁ֔ה וְאֶלְעָזָ֖ר הַכֹּהֵ֑ן כַּאֲשֶׁ֛ר צִוָּ֥ה יְהוָ֖ה אֶת־מֹשֶֽׁה׃ וַיְהִי֙
הַמַּלְק֔וֹחַ יֶ֣תֶר הַבָּ֔ז אֲשֶׁ֥ר בָּזְז֖וּ עַ֣ם הַצָּבָ֑א צֹ֗אן שֵׁשׁ־מֵא֥וֹת
לג אֶ֛לֶף וְשִׁבְעִ֥ים אֶ֖לֶף וַחֲמֵ֥שֶׁת אֲלָפִֽים׃ וּבָקָ֕ר שְׁנַ֥יִם וְשִׁבְעִ֖ים
לד לה אָֽלֶף׃ וַחֲמֹרִ֕ים אֶחָ֥ד וְשִׁשִּׁ֖ים אָֽלֶף׃ וְנֶ֣פֶשׁ אָדָ֔ם מִן־הַנָּשִׁ֕ים
אֲשֶׁ֥ר לֹא־יָדְע֖וּ מִשְׁכַּ֣ב זָכָ֑ר כָּל־נֶ֕פֶשׁ שְׁנַ֥יִם וּשְׁלֹשִׁ֖ים אָֽלֶף׃
לו וַתְּהִי֙ הַֽמֶּחֱצָ֔ה חֵ֕לֶק הַיֹּצְאִ֖ים בַּצָּבָ֑א מִסְפַּ֣ר הַצֹּ֗אן שְׁלֹשׁ־
מֵא֥וֹת אֶ֙לֶף֙ וּשְׁלֹשִׁ֣ים אֶ֔לֶף וְשִׁבְעַ֥ת אֲלָפִ֖ים וַחֲמֵ֥שׁ מֵאֽוֹת׃
לז וַיְהִ֛י הַמֶּ֥כֶס לַֽיהוָ֖ה מִן־הַצֹּ֑אן שֵׁ֥שׁ מֵא֖וֹת חָמֵ֥שׁ וְשִׁבְעִֽים׃
לח וְהַ֨בָּקָ֔ר שִׁשָּׁ֥ה וּשְׁלֹשִׁ֖ים אָ֑לֶף וּמִכְסָ֥ם לַֽיהוָ֖ה שְׁנַ֥יִם וְשִׁבְעִֽים׃
לט וַחֲמֹרִ֕ים שְׁלֹשִׁ֥ים אֶ֖לֶף וַחֲמֵ֣שׁ מֵא֑וֹת וּמִכְסָ֥ם לַֽיהוָ֖ה אֶחָ֥ד
מ וְשִׁשִּֽׁים׃ וְנֶ֣פֶשׁ אָדָ֔ם שִׁשָּׁ֥ה עָשָׂ֖ר אָ֑לֶף וּמִכְסָם֙ לַֽיהוָ֔ה שְׁנַ֥יִם
מא וּשְׁלֹשִׁ֖ים נָֽפֶשׁ׃ וַיִּתֵּ֣ן מֹשֶׁ֗ה אֶת־מֶ֙כֶס֙ תְּרוּמַ֣ת יְהוָ֔ה לְאֶלְעָזָ֖ר
מב הַכֹּהֵ֑ן כַּאֲשֶׁ֛ר צִוָּ֥ה יְהוָ֖ה אֶת־מֹשֶֽׁה׃ וּמִֽמַּחֲצִ֖ית בְּנֵ֣י יִשְׂרָאֵ֑ל חמישי
מג אֲשֶׁר֙ חָצָ֣ה מֹשֶׁ֔ה מִן־הָאֲנָשִׁ֖ים הַצֹּבְאִֽים׃ וַתְּהִ֛י מֶחֱצַ֥ת הָעֵדָ֖ה
מִן־הַצֹּ֑אן שְׁלֹשׁ־מֵא֥וֹת אֶ֙לֶף֙ וּשְׁלֹשִׁ֣ים אֶ֔לֶף שִׁבְעַ֥ת אֲלָפִ֖ים
מד מה וַחֲמֵ֥שׁ מֵאֽוֹת׃ וּבָקָ֕ר שִׁשָּׁ֥ה וּשְׁלֹשִׁ֖ים אָֽלֶף׃ וַחֲמֹרִ֕ים שְׁלֹשִׁ֥ים
מו מז אֶ֖לֶף וַחֲמֵ֥שׁ מֵאֽוֹת׃ וְנֶ֣פֶשׁ אָדָ֔ם שִׁשָּׁ֥ה עָשָׂ֖ר אָֽלֶף׃ וַיִּקַּ֨ח
מֹשֶׁ֜ה מִמַּחֲצִ֣ת בְּנֵֽי־יִשְׂרָאֵ֗ל אֶת־הָֽאָחֻז֙ אֶחָ֣ד מִן־הַחֲמִשִּׁ֔ים
מִן־הָאָדָ֖ם וּמִן־הַבְּהֵמָ֑ה וַיִּתֵּ֨ן אֹתָ֜ם לַלְוִיִּ֗ם שֹׁמְרֵי֙ מִשְׁמֶ֙רֶת֙
מח מִשְׁכַּ֣ן יְהוָ֔ה כַּאֲשֶׁ֛ר צִוָּ֥ה יְהוָ֖ה אֶת־מֹשֶֽׁה׃ וַיִּקְרְבוּ֙ אֶל־מֹשֶׁ֔ה
הַפְּקֻדִ֕ים אֲשֶׁ֖ר לְאַלְפֵ֣י הַצָּבָ֑א שָׂרֵ֥י הָאֲלָפִ֖ים וְשָׂרֵ֥י הַמֵּאֽוֹת׃
מט וַיֹּֽאמְרוּ֙ אֶל־מֹשֶׁ֔ה עֲבָדֶ֣יךָ נָֽשְׂא֔וּ אֶת־רֹ֛אשׁ אַנְשֵׁ֥י הַמִּלְחָמָ֖ה
נ אֲשֶׁ֣ר בְּיָדֵ֑נוּ וְלֹֽא־נִפְקַ֥ד מִמֶּ֖נּוּ אִֽישׁ׃ וַנַּקְרֵ֞ב אֶת־קָרְבַּ֣ן יְהוָ֗ה
אִישׁ֩ אֲשֶׁ֨ר מָצָ֤א כְלִי־זָהָב֙ אֶצְעָדָ֣ה וְצָמִ֔יד טַבַּ֖עַת עָגִ֣יל וְכוּמָ֑ז
נא לְכַפֵּ֥ר עַל־נַפְשֹׁתֵ֖ינוּ לִפְנֵ֥י יְהוָֽה׃ וַיִּקַּ֨ח מֹשֶׁ֜ה וְאֶלְעָזָ֧ר הַכֹּהֵ֛ן
נב אֶת־הַזָּהָ֖ב מֵאִתָּ֑ם כֹּ֖ל כְּלִ֥י מַעֲשֶֽׂה׃ וַיְהִ֣י ׀ כָּל־זְהַ֣ב הַתְּרוּמָ֗ה
אֲשֶׁ֤ר הֵרִ֙ימוּ֙ לַֽיהוָ֔ה שִׁשָּׁ֨ה עָשָׂ֥ר אֶ֛לֶף שְׁבַֽע־מֵא֖וֹת וַחֲמִשִּׁ֣ים
נג שָׁ֑קֶל מֵאֵת֙ שָׂרֵ֣י הָאֲלָפִ֔ים וּמֵאֵ֖ת שָׂרֵ֥י הַמֵּאֽוֹת׃ אַנְשֵׁי֙ הַצָּבָ֔א

54 men of the army each kept plunder for themselves. Moshe
and Elazar the priest took the gold from the officers of
thousands and of hundreds, and brought it to the Tent
of Meeting as a remembrance for the Israelites before the
Lord.

32 1 The people of Reuven and Gad had much cattle – in SHISHI /SHELISHI/
this they were very rich. And seeing the lands of Yazer
2 and Gilad they noticed that this was cattle country. So
the people of Gad and Reuven came to Moshe, Elazar
the priest, and the princes of the community and said:
3 "Atarot, Divon, Yazer, Nimra, Ḥeshbon, Elaleh, Sevam,
4 Nevo, and Beon, the land that the Lord struck down
before the community of Israel, is good cattle country,
5 and your servants keep cattle." They said, "If we
have found favor with you, let this land be given to your
servants as our possession. Do not make us cross the
6 Jordan." But Moshe asked the Gadites and Reubenites,
7 "Are your brothers to go to war while you stay here? Why

> once again leave them in the wilderness, and you will destroy this entire people. (Num. 32:14–15)

Moshe is blunt, honest, and confrontational.

One of the hardest tasks of any leader – from prime ministers to parents – is conflict resolution. Yet it is also the most vital. Where there is leadership, there is long-term cohesiveness within the group, whatever the short-term problems. Where there is a lack of leadership – where leaders lack authority, grace, generosity of spirit, and the ability to respect positions other than their own – then there is divisiveness, rancor, backbiting, resentment, internal politics, and a lack of trust. True leaders are the people who put the interests of the group above those of any subsection of the group. Moshe succeeds here, not because he is weak, not because he is willing to compromise on the integrity of the nation as a whole, not because he uses honeyed words and diplomatic evasions, but because he is honest, principled, and focused on the common good. We all face conflicts in our lives. This is how to resolve them.

32:6 הַאַחֵיכֶם יָבֹאוּ לַמִּלְחָמָה וְאַתֶּם תֵּשְׁבוּ פֹה *Are your brothers to go… while you stay here?* – The extent to which Moshe's concerns for the unity of the nation are justified will become apparent many years later. The Reubenites and Gadites do indeed fulfill their promise in the days of Yehoshua. The rest of the tribes conquer and settle the land of Israel while they

נד בָּזְזוּ אִישׁ לוֹ: וַיִּקַּח מֹשֶׁה וְאֶלְעָזָר הַכֹּהֵן אֶת־הַזָּהָב מֵאֵת
שָׂרֵי הָאֲלָפִים וְהַמֵּאוֹת וַיָּבִאוּ אֹתוֹ אֶל־אֹהֶל מוֹעֵד זִכָּרוֹן
לִבְנֵי־יִשְׂרָאֵל לִפְנֵי יְהוָה:

לב א וּמִקְנֶה ׀ רַב הָיָה לִבְנֵי רְאוּבֵן וְלִבְנֵי־גָד עָצוּם מְאֹד וַיִּרְאוּ כט ששי /שלישי/
אֶת־אֶרֶץ יַעְזֵר וְאֶת־אֶרֶץ גִּלְעָד וְהִנֵּה הַמָּקוֹם מְקוֹם מִקְנֶה:
ב וַיָּבֹאוּ בְנֵי־גָד וּבְנֵי רְאוּבֵן וַיֹּאמְרוּ אֶל־מֹשֶׁה וְאֶל־אֶלְעָזָר
ג הַכֹּהֵן וְאֶל־נְשִׂיאֵי הָעֵדָה לֵאמֹר: עֲטָרוֹת וְדִיבֹן וְיַעְזֵר
ד וְנִמְרָה וְחֶשְׁבּוֹן וְאֶלְעָלֵה וּשְׂבָם וּנְבוֹ וּבְעֹן: הָאָרֶץ אֲשֶׁר
הִכָּה יְהוָה לִפְנֵי עֲדַת יִשְׂרָאֵל אֶרֶץ מִקְנֶה הִוא וְלַעֲבָדֶיךָ
ה מִקְנֶה: וַיֹּאמְרוּ אִם־מָצָאנוּ חֵן בְּעֵינֶיךָ יֻתַּן אֶת־
הָאָרֶץ הַזֹּאת לַעֲבָדֶיךָ לַאֲחֻזָּה אַל־תַּעֲבִרֵנוּ אֶת־הַיַּרְדֵּן:
ו וַיֹּאמֶר מֹשֶׁה לִבְנֵי־גָד וְלִבְנֵי רְאוּבֵן הַאַחֵיכֶם יָבֹאוּ לַמִּלְחָמָה
ז וְאַתֶּם תֵּשְׁבוּ פֹה: וְלָמָּה תנואון אֶת־לֵב בְּנֵי יִשְׂרָאֵל מֵעֲבֹר תְּנִיאוּן

THE NEGOTIATION

At this stage in the journey, the people have their attention focused on the destination: the land west of the river Jordan, the place that even the spies confirmed to be "flowing with milk and with honey" (Num. 13:27). Yet it is at just this point that a problem arises, different in kind from those that came before.

The members of the tribes of Reuven and Gad begin to have different thoughts. Seeing that the land through which they are traveling is ideal for raising cattle, they decide that they would prefer to stay there, to the east of the Jordan, and they propose this to Moshe. Unsurprisingly, he is angry at the suggestion. The two tribes are putting their own interests above those of the nation as a whole. As Moshe put it to the tribes: "Are your brothers to go to war while you stay here? Why would you discourage the Israelites from crossing into the land the Lord has given them?" (32:6–7). The proposal is potentially disastrous.

Moshe reminds the men of Reuven and Gad what happened in the incident of the spies. The spies demoralized the people, ten of them saying that they could not conquer the land. The result of that one moment was to condemn an entire generation to die in the wilderness and to delay the eventual conquest by forty years.

> And here you are, a brood of sinners, taking your fathers' places and bringing yet more of the Lord's burning rage down upon Israel. If you turn back from following Him, He will

would you discourage the Israelites from crossing into the
8 land the LORD has given them? That is what your fathers
did when I sent them from Kadesh Barnea to see the land.
9 They went as far as the Eshkol Ravine and saw the land,
but they discouraged the Israelites from entering the land
10 the LORD had given them, and on that day the LORD's rage
11 burned, and He swore: None of the men twenty years of
age or above who left Egypt will see the land that I swore
to give Avraham, Yitzḥak, and Yaakov, because they did
12 not follow Me wholeheartedly – none except Kalev son of
Yefuneh the Kenizzite and Yehoshua son of Nun, because
13 they wholeheartedly followed the LORD. The LORD was
incensed at Israel, and He made them wander in the
wilderness for forty years until the whole generation that
14 had done evil in the LORD's sight was gone. And here you
are, a brood of sinners, taking your fathers' places and
bringing yet more of the LORD's burning rage down upon
15 Israel. If you turn back from following Him, He will once
again leave them in the wilderness, and you will destroy
16 this entire people." Then they set forward and
said to him, "Let us build sheep pens here for our livestock
17 and towns for our children. But we will arm ourselves and
go ahead of the Israelites until we have seen them safely
to their place. Meanwhile, our children will remain in
the fortified towns, protected from the inhabitants of the
18 land. We will not return to our homes until every one of

a symbol and a sign to future generations that they too are Israelites. Pinḥas and the rest of the delegation are satisfied with this answer, and once again civil war is averted.

32:16 וַיִּגְּשׁוּ אֵלָיו *Then they set forward* – The tribes do not argue with Moshe's claim. They accept its validity, but they point out that his concern is not incompatible with their own objectives. They are able to invent an option for mutual gain. If you allow us to make temporary provisions for our cattle and children, they say, we will not only fight in the army. We will be its advance guard. We will benefit, knowing that our request has been granted. The nation will benefit by our willingness to take on the most demanding military task.

ח אֶל־הָאָרֶץ אֲשֶׁר־נָתַן לָהֶם יהוה׃ כֹּה עָשׂוּ אֲבֹתֵיכֶם בְּשָׁלְחִי
ט אֹתָם מִקָּדֵשׁ בַּרְנֵעַ לִרְאוֹת אֶת־הָאָרֶץ׃ וַיַּעֲלוּ עַד־נַחַל
אֶשְׁכּוֹל וַיִּרְאוּ אֶת־הָאָרֶץ וַיָּנִיאוּ אֶת־לֵב בְּנֵי יִשְׂרָאֵל לְבִלְתִּי־
י בֹא אֶל־הָאָרֶץ אֲשֶׁר־נָתַן לָהֶם יהוה׃ וַיִּחַר־אַף יהוה בַּיּוֹם
יא הַהוּא וַיִּשָּׁבַע לֵאמֹר׃ אִם־יִרְאוּ הָאֲנָשִׁים הָעֹלִים מִמִּצְרַיִם
מִבֶּן עֶשְׂרִים שָׁנָה וָמַעְלָה אֵת הָאֲדָמָה אֲשֶׁר נִשְׁבַּעְתִּי
יב לְאַבְרָהָם לְיִצְחָק וּלְיַעֲקֹב כִּי לֹא־מִלְאוּ אַחֲרָי׃ בִּלְתִּי כָּלֵב
יג בֶּן־יְפֻנֶּה הַקְּנִזִּי וִיהוֹשֻׁעַ בִּן־נוּן כִּי מִלְאוּ אַחֲרֵי יהוה׃ וַיִּחַר־
אַף יהוה בְּיִשְׂרָאֵל וַיְנִעֵם בַּמִּדְבָּר אַרְבָּעִים שָׁנָה עַד־תֹּם
יד כָּל־הַדּוֹר הָעֹשֶׂה הָרַע בְּעֵינֵי יהוה׃ וְהִנֵּה קַמְתֶּם תַּחַת
אֲבֹתֵיכֶם תַּרְבּוּת אֲנָשִׁים חַטָּאִים לִסְפּוֹת עוֹד עַל חֲרוֹן
טו אַף־יהוה אֶל־יִשְׂרָאֵל׃ כִּי תְשׁוּבֻן מֵאַחֲרָיו וְיָסַף עוֹד לְהַנִּיחוֹ
טז בַּמִּדְבָּר וְשִׁחַתֶּם לְכָל־הָעָם הַזֶּה׃ וַיִּגְּשׁוּ אֵלָיו
יז וַיֹּאמְרוּ גִּדְרֹת צֹאן נִבְנֶה לְמִקְנֵנוּ פֹּה וְעָרִים לְטַפֵּנוּ׃ וַאֲנַחְנוּ
נֵחָלֵץ חֻשִׁים לִפְנֵי בְּנֵי יִשְׂרָאֵל עַד אֲשֶׁר אִם־הֲבִיאֹנֻם אֶל־
יח מְקוֹמָם וְיָשַׁב טַפֵּנוּ בְּעָרֵי הַמִּבְצָר מִפְּנֵי יֹשְׁבֵי הָאָרֶץ׃ לֹא
יט נָשׁוּב אֶל־בָּתֵּינוּ עַד הִתְנַחֵל בְּנֵי יִשְׂרָאֵל אִישׁ נַחֲלָתוֹ׃ כִּי

(together with half the tribe of Menashe) establish their presence in Transjordan. Despite this, within a brief space of time there is almost civil war.

Chapter 22 of the book of Joshua describes how, after returning to their families and settling their land, the Reubenites and Gadites build "an altar" (Josh. 22:10) on the east side of the Jordan. Seeing this as an act of secession, the rest of the Israelites prepare to do battle against them. Yehoshua, in a striking act of diplomacy, sends Pinḥas, the former zealot, now man of peace, to negotiate. He warns them of the terrible consequences of what they have done by, in effect, creating a religious center outside the land of Israel. It will split the nation in two.

The Reubenites and Gadites make it clear that this was not their intention at all. To the contrary, they themselves were worried that in the future, the rest of the Israelites would see them living across the Jordan and conclude that they no longer want to be part of the nation. That is why they have built the altar, not to offer sacrifices, not as a rival to the nation's Sanctuary, but merely as

19 the Israelites has taken possession of his inheritance. We,
however, will not take possession with them on the far
side of the Jordan, for our inheritance will be on the east
side of the Jordan."
20 Moshe replied to them, "If you do this – if you arm SHEVI'I /REVI'I/
21 yourselves for battle before the LORD, and each of your
armed men crosses the Jordan before the LORD until He
22 has driven out His enemies before Him, and the land has
been subdued before the LORD – then you may return
and be clear before the LORD and before Israel, and this
23 land will be yours as a possession before the LORD. But if

---

halakhic principles. The first is known as *ḥashad*, "suspicion," namely, that certain acts, permitted in themselves, are forbidden on the grounds that performing them may lead others to suspect one of doing something forbidden. A closely related halakhic principle is the idea known as *marit haayin*, "appearances." These twin principles of *ḥashad* and *marit haayin* mean that we should act in such a way as to be held as a role model and that, just as a book of instructions should be unambiguous, so should be our conduct. People should be able to observe the way we behave and learn from us how a Jew should live.

These rules apply to every Jew, not just to religious leaders. Each of us is bidden to become a role model. We are not allowed to say, when we have acted in a way conducive to suspicion, "I have done nothing wrong; to the contrary, the other person, by harboring doubts about me, is in the wrong." To be sure, he is. But that does not relieve us of the responsibility to conduct our lives in a way that is above suspicion. Each of us must play our part in constructing a society of mutual respect.

Suspicion is a pervasive feature of social life. Judaism – a central project of which is the construction of a gracious society built on responsibility and trust – confronts the problem from both directions. On the one hand, it commands us not to harbor suspicions but to judge people generously. On the other, it bids each of us to act in a way that is above suspicion, keeping (as the rabbis put it) "far from unseemly conduct, from whatever resembles it, and from what may merely appear to resemble it" (Bemidbar Rabba 10:8).

We will not always succeed. Despite our best endeavors, others may still accuse us (as they accused Moshe) of things of which we are genuinely innocent. Yet we must do our best, by being charitable in our judgment of others and scrupulous in the way we conduct ourselves.

לֹא נִנְחַל אִתָּם מֵעֵבֶר לַיַּרְדֵּן וָהָלְאָה כִּי בָאָה נַחֲלָתֵנוּ אֵלֵינוּ
מֵעֵבֶר הַיַּרְדֵּן מִזְרָחָה׃
כ וַיֹּאמֶר אֲלֵיהֶם מֹשֶׁה אִם־תַּעֲשׂוּן אֶת־הַדָּבָר הַזֶּה אִם־תֵּחָלְצוּ שביעי
כא לִפְנֵי יהוה לַמִּלְחָמָה׃ וְעָבַר לָכֶם כָּל־חָלוּץ אֶת־הַיַּרְדֵּן לִפְנֵי /רביעי/
כב יהוה עַד הוֹרִישׁוֹ אֶת־אֹיְבָיו מִפָּנָיו׃ וְנִכְבְּשָׁה הָאָרֶץ לִפְנֵי
יהוה וְאַחַר תָּשֻׁבוּ וִהְיִיתֶם נְקִיִּם מֵיהוה וּמִיִּשְׂרָאֵל וְהָיְתָה
כג הָאָרֶץ הַזֹּאת לָכֶם לַאֲחֻזָּה לִפְנֵי יהוה׃ וְאִם־לֹא תַעֲשׂוּן כֵּן
הִנֵּה חֲטָאתֶם לַיהוה וּדְעוּ חַטַּאתְכֶם אֲשֶׁר תִּמְצָא אֶתְכֶם׃

32:20 אִם־תַּעֲשׂוּן אֶת־הַדָּבָר הַזֶּה *If you do this* – Moshe recognizes the fact that the two and a half tribes have met his objections. He restates their position to make sure he and they have understood the proposal and they are ready to stand by it. He extracts from them agreement to a *tenai kaful*, a double condition, both positive and negative: if we do this, these will be the consequences, but if we fail to do this, those will be the consequences. They agree on objective criteria to assess the fulfillment of the conditions, and Moshe leaves them no escape from their commitment. The Reubenites and Gadites will not return to the east bank of the Jordan until all the other tribes are safely settled in their territories. And so it happens, as narrated in the book of Joshua:

> Then Yehoshua summoned the Reubenites, the Gadites, and half the tribe of Menashe and said to them, "You have performed everything that Moshe, the LORD's servant, commanded you, and you have obeyed me in all that I commanded you. You have not abandoned your brothers all this time – to this very day – and you have fulfilled the charge of the LORD your God's command. Now the LORD your God has granted rest to your brothers, as He promised them, so turn now and make your way home to the lands of your holding, which Moshe, the LORD's servant, assigned to you beyond the Jordan. (Josh. 22:1–4)

Conflict has been averted. The Reubenites and Gadites achieve what they want but the interests of the other tribes and of the nation as a whole are secured.

32:22 וִהְיִיתֶם נְקִיִּם מֵיהוה וּמִיִּשְׂרָאֵל *Be clear before the LORD and before Israel* – We learn from this that it is not enough to do what is right in the eyes of God. One must also act in such a way as to be seen to have done right in the eyes of one's fellow man. That is the rule of *viheyitem nekiyim*, "Be clear before the LORD and before Israel."

This concern became the basis of two

you do not do this, you will have sinned against the Lord,
24 and know that your sin will find you. Build towns for
your children and pens for your flocks, but do what you
25 have promised." The people of Gad and Reuven replied
to Moshe, "Your servants will do just as my lord charges
26 us. Our children, wives, livestock, and all our animals
27 will remain here in the towns of Gilad, but your servants,
all equipped for war, will cross over to do battle before
28 the Lord, as my lord has said." Moshe gave instructions
concerning them to Elazar the priest, Yehoshua son of
29 Nun, and the family heads of the Israelite tribes. Moshe
said to them, "If the men of Gad and Reuven cross the
Jordan with you, each equipped for battle before the
Lord, and the land is subdued before you, then you shall
30 give them the land of Gilad as a possession. But if they
do not cross with you, equipped for war, then they must
have their possession with you in the land of Canaan."
31 The Gadites and the Reubenites answered, "What the
32 Lord has spoken to your servants, we will do. We will
cross into the land of Canaan equipped for war before
the Lord, and we shall then have our hereditary land
33 across the Jordan." So Moshe gave to them – the people

Hence, infers the midrash, the men of Reuven and Gad put "wealth and honor" before faith and posterity. Moshe hints that their priorities are wrong. The midrash continues: "The Holy One, blessed be He, said to them: 'Seeing that you have shown greater love for your cattle than for human souls, by your life, there will be no blessing in it.'"

This will turn out to be not a minor incident in the wilderness long ago, but a consistent pattern throughout Jewish history. The fate of Jewish communities was determined by their decision to put children and their education first. The Rabbis ruled that "any town that lacks children at school is to be excommunicated" (Shabbat 119b). Already in the first century, the Jewish community in Israel had established a network of schools at which attendance was compulsory (Bava Batra 21a) – the first such system in history.

Moshe's implied rebuke to the tribes of Reuven and Gad is a fundamental statement of Jewish priorities. Property is secondary, children primary. Those who invest in the future have a future. It is not what we own that gives us a share in eternity, but those to whom we give birth and the effort we make to ensure that they carry our faith and way of life into the next generation.

כד בְּנוּ־לָכֶם עָרִים לְטַפְּכֶם וּגְדֵרֹת לְצֹנַאֲכֶם וְהַיֹּצֵא מִפִּיכֶם
כה תַּעֲשׂוּ׃ וַיֹּאמֶר בְּנֵי־גָד וּבְנֵי רְאוּבֵן אֶל־מֹשֶׁה לֵאמֹר עֲבָדֶיךָ
כו יַעֲשׂוּ כַּאֲשֶׁר אֲדֹנִי מְצַוֶּה׃ טַפֵּנוּ נָשֵׁינוּ מִקְנֵנוּ וְכָל־בְּהֶמְתֵּנוּ
כז יִהְיוּ־שָׁם בְּעָרֵי הַגִּלְעָד׃ וַעֲבָדֶיךָ יַעַבְרוּ כָּל־חֲלוּץ צָבָא
כח לִפְנֵי יהוה לַמִּלְחָמָה כַּאֲשֶׁר אֲדֹנִי דֹּבֵר׃ וַיְצַו לָהֶם מֹשֶׁה
אֵת אֶלְעָזָר הַכֹּהֵן וְאֵת יְהוֹשֻׁעַ בִּן־נוּן וְאֶת־רָאשֵׁי אֲבוֹת
כט הַמַּטּוֹת לִבְנֵי יִשְׂרָאֵל׃ וַיֹּאמֶר מֹשֶׁה אֲלֵהֶם אִם־יַעַבְרוּ
בְנֵי־גָד וּבְנֵי־רְאוּבֵן ׀ אִתְּכֶם אֶת־הַיַּרְדֵּן כָּל־חָלוּץ לַמִּלְחָמָה
לִפְנֵי יהוה וְנִכְבְּשָׁה הָאָרֶץ לִפְנֵיכֶם וּנְתַתֶּם לָהֶם אֶת־אֶרֶץ
ל הַגִּלְעָד לַאֲחֻזָּה׃ וְאִם־לֹא יַעַבְרוּ חֲלוּצִים אִתְּכֶם וְנֹאחֲזוּ
לא בְתֹכְכֶם בְּאֶרֶץ כְּנָעַן׃ וַיַּעֲנוּ בְנֵי־גָד וּבְנֵי רְאוּבֵן לֵאמֹר אֵת
לב אֲשֶׁר דִּבֶּר יהוה אֶל־עֲבָדֶיךָ כֵּן נַעֲשֶׂה׃ נַחְנוּ נַעֲבֹר חֲלוּצִים
לִפְנֵי יהוה אֶרֶץ כְּנָעַן וְאִתָּנוּ אֲחֻזַּת נַחֲלָתֵנוּ מֵעֵבֶר לַיַּרְדֵּן׃
לג וַיִּתֵּן לָהֶם ׀ מֹשֶׁה לִבְנֵי־גָד וְלִבְנֵי רְאוּבֵן וְלַחֲצִי ׀ שֵׁבֶט ׀ מְנַשֶּׁה

32:24 עָרִים לְטַפְּכֶם וּגְדֵרֹת לְצֹנַאֲכֶם *Towns for your children and pens for your flocks* – Let us listen carefully to what the Reubenites and Gadites said: "Then they set forward and said to him, 'Let us build sheep pens here for our livestock and towns for our children'" (Num. 32:16). Moshe replied: "Build towns for your children, and pens for your flocks, but do what you have promised" (32:24).

Note the ordering of the nouns here. The men of Reuven and Gad put property before people: they speak of their flocks first, their children second. Moshe reverses the order. As Rashi notes (on Num. 32:16):

> They paid more regard to their property than to their sons and daughters, because they mentioned their cattle before the children. Moshe said to them: "Not so. Make the main thing primary and the subordinate thing secondary. First build cities for your children, and only then, folds for your flocks."

A midrash (Bemidbar Rabba 22:9) makes the same point through an ingenious interpretation of a verse in Ecclesiastes: "A wise man's mind is to his right, as the mind of a fool is to his left" (Eccl. 10:2). The midrash identifies "right" with Torah and life: "At his right hand, darting fire" (Deut. 33:2). "Left," by contrast, refers to worldly goods: "Long life is in its right hand; in its left hand is wealth and honor" (Prov. 3:16).

of Gad and Reuven, and half the tribe of Menashe son
of Yosef – the kingdom of Siḥon, king of the Amorites,
and the kingdom of Og, king of Bashan, the land along
with its towns and the territory of the surrounding towns.
35 34 The Gadites rebuilt Divon, Atarot, Aroer, Atrot Shofan,
36 Yazer, Yogbeha, Beit Nimra, and Beit Haran, as fortified
37 towns and enclosures for flocks. The Reubenites built
38 Ḥeshbon, Elaleh, Kiryatayim, Nevo and Baal Meon – the
names of which were changed – and Sivma. They named
39 the cities that they built up. The descendants of Makhir
son of Menashe went to Gilad and captured it, driving
40 out the Amorites who were there. So Moshe gave Gilad MAFTIR
41 to Makhir son of Menashe, and he settled there. Yair son
of Menashe went and captured their villages, naming
42 them Hamlets of Yair. Novaḥ went and captured Kenat
and its surrounding villages, renaming it Novaḥ after
himself.

The haftara for Parashat Mattot is on page 1586.
Read this haftara on the first Shabbat after the Seventeenth of Tamuz.

בֶּן־יוֹסֵף אֶת־מַמְלֶכֶת סִיחֹן מֶלֶךְ הָאֱמֹרִי וְאֶת־מַמְלֶכֶת עוֹג
לד מֶלֶךְ הַבָּשָׁן הָאָרֶץ לְעָרֶיהָ בִּגְבֻלֹת עָרֵי הָאָרֶץ סָבִיב: וַיִּבְנוּ
לה בְנֵי־גָד אֶת־דִּיבֹן וְאֶת־עֲטָרֹת וְאֵת עֲרֹעֵר: וְאֶת־עַטְרֹת
לו שׁוֹפָן וְאֶת־יַעְזֵר וְיָגְבְּהָה: וְאֶת־בֵּית נִמְרָה וְאֶת־בֵּית הָרָן
לז עָרֵי מִבְצָר וְגִדְרֹת צֹאן: וּבְנֵי רְאוּבֵן בָּנוּ אֶת־חֶשְׁבּוֹן וְאֶת־
לח אֶלְעָלֵא וְאֵת קִרְיָתָיִם: וְאֶת־נְבוֹ וְאֶת־בַּעַל מְעוֹן מוּסַבֹּת
שֵׁם וְאֶת־שִׂבְמָה וַיִּקְרְאוּ בְשֵׁמֹת אֶת־שְׁמוֹת הֶעָרִים אֲשֶׁר
לט בָּנוּ: וַיֵּלְכוּ בְּנֵי מָכִיר בֶּן־מְנַשֶּׁה גִּלְעָדָה וַיִּלְכְּדֻהָ וַיּוֹרֶשׁ אֶת־
מ הָאֱמֹרִי אֲשֶׁר־בָּהּ: וַיִּתֵּן מֹשֶׁה אֶת־הַגִּלְעָד לְמָכִיר בֶּן־מְנַשֶּׁה מפטיר
מא וַיֵּשֶׁב בָּהּ: וְיָאִיר בֶּן־מְנַשֶּׁה הָלַךְ וַיִּלְכֹּד אֶת־חַוֺּתֵיהֶם וַיִּקְרָא
מב אֶתְהֶן חַוֺּת יָאִיר: וְנֹבַח הָלַךְ וַיִּלְכֹּד אֶת־קְנָת וְאֶת־בְּנֹתֶיהָ
וַיִּקְרָא לָה נֹבַח בִּשְׁמוֹ:

The הפטרה *for* פרשת מטות *is on page 1587.*
Read this הפטרה *on the first* שבת *after the Seventeenth of* תמוז.

PARASHAT MASEI

33 1 These were the journeys of the Israelites when they left
Egypt by their divisions under the leadership of Moshe
2 and Aharon. Moshe recorded the places of their setting
out on every journey at the LORD's command. These are
their journeys, by the places from which they set out.
3 They set out from Ramesses on the fifteenth day of the

"the long walk to freedom." The real journey to freedom is not a physical one. It is a mental, moral, and spiritual one. It is long, arduous, and demanding, and there are challenges and failures along the way. That is what the book of Numbers has been all about.

Rambam saw the journey through the desert not as a diversion, but as a necessary stage: a situation where, by sheer necessity, the people would acquire strength and endurance. He made this point in the course of his larger argument that it is impossible in human nature to go from one extreme to another, from the established way of doing things to a completely new one. If so, then the forty-two stopping points on the way may be a literary device to communicate just how many stages we must go through to get from here to there when the destination is liberty itself.

The road from slavery to freedom is as long or short as it takes for people to develop the habits of responsibility for their and their children's future. Freedom means making sacrifices in the present for the sake of peace and prosperity in the future. It means obeying laws for the sake of the common good. It requires virtue, courage, and discipline. Parashat Masei is about the many small journeys it took before the people were ready to enter the land and begin to construct a society of freedom under the sovereignty of God.

The journey is Judaism's first metaphor for a life worth living. Judaism is not a state of being; it is about walking, about the way, about following the call of God. For Avraham, it was following the call. For Moshe and the Israelites it was following that pillar of cloud by day, and fire by night, across the wilderness. It is this journey that has inspired men and women throughout human history to dedicate their lives to the uncertain proposition that by constant struggle we can reduce suffering and enhance dignity not for ourselves alone but for all those amongst whom we live; that our lives have a moral purpose, that redemption can be sought in this world with all its imperfections, and that by our efforts we can leave society better than we found it. None of this is the work of a moment – it is a journey, stage by stage and step by step.

33:2 לְמַסְעֵיהֶם עַל־פִּי יהוה *Every journey at the* LORD*'s command* – The Jewish

פרשת מסעי

לג א אֵ֣לֶּה מַסְעֵ֣י בְנֵֽי־יִשְׂרָאֵ֔ל אֲשֶׁ֥ר יָצְא֛וּ מֵאֶ֥רֶץ מִצְרַ֖יִם לְצִבְאֹתָ֑ם ל
ב בְּיַד־מֹשֶׁ֖ה וְאַהֲרֹֽן׃ וַיִּכְתֹּ֨ב מֹשֶׁ֜ה אֶת־מוֹצָאֵיהֶ֛ם לְמַסְעֵיהֶ֖ם
ג עַל־פִּ֣י יהוה וְאֵ֥לֶּה מַסְעֵיהֶ֖ם לְמוֹצָאֵיהֶֽם׃ וַיִּסְע֤וּ מֵֽרַעְמְסֵס֙

MASEI

Parashat Masei begins with an itinerary of the forty-two stopping points of the Israelites on their forty-year journey through the wilderness, culminating in their encampment on the plains of Moav, where they will stay until the death of Moshe. As we shall see, there is great significance to the lengthy descriptions of all their travels and sojourns. With their destination already close, the *parasha* sets out the boundaries of the Promised Land. It also specifies certain places that will become cities of refuge where people guilty of manslaughter are to be protected against possible vengeance on the part of a relative of the person who died. The *parasha,* and with it the book of Numbers, ends with a claim by the leaders of the tribe of Menashe that the ruling that the daughters of Tzelofḥad were entitled to inherit their late father's share in the land could mean that the land will be lost to the tribe if any of them marries members of another tribe. A divine decision resolves the conflict: the daughters have a right to inherit the land but must marry only within the tribe. This seemingly strange conclusion to the book of Numbers sheds important light on the theme of the book in its entirety.

THESE WERE THE JOURNEYS

"They set out from X and camped at Y. They set out from Y and camped at Z." The *parasha* begins with a recitation of the forty-two journeys the Israelites made during their years in the wilderness. It is for the most part a tedious recitation, deliberately so.

This is puzzling. The word "Torah," the name given to the five Mosaic books, means "instruction," "teaching," "guidance." It does not record events merely because they happened. Nowhere is this more manifest than in the book of Numbers, where almost thirty-eight of the forty wilderness years are passed over in silence, evidently because, although things happened in those years, they were mere events with no teaching to be drawn for the generations. Where then is the teaching in this list of place-names?

Look at a map and you will see that the distance between Egypt and the land of Israel is not far. In Genesis 12 we read of how Avraham traveled there after arriving in the land of Canaan because there was a famine and he needed to buy food. The physical journey is a matter of weeks, not years. The forty-year itinerary of Israel's travels, then, is a reminder for all time of what Nelson Mandela called

first month. On the day after the Passover the Israelites
4 went out defiantly, before all the Egyptians' eyes, while
the Egyptians were burying their firstborns, whom
the Lord had struck down, every one. The Lord had
5 executed judgments even against their gods. The Israelites
6 set out from Ramesses and camped at Sukkot. They set
out from Sukkot and camped at Etam on the edge of the

---

own strengths and contributions to our people and to humanity.

33:5 סֻכֹּת *Sukkot* – The first stop on the journey is apparently named for the structures the freed Israelites were to live in for the rest of their lives. There is no more potent symbol of Jewish history than the sukka, the temporary dwelling. For that, for the greater part of four thousand years, is where Jews have lived. Our story has been one of exiles and dispersions, as if wandering in the wilderness was not just the fate of Moshe's generation but a recurring theme of Jewish life. In the Middle Ages alone, Jews were expelled from England in 1290, Vienna in 1421, Cologne in 1424, Bavaria in 1442, Milan in 1489, and most traumatically from Spain in 1492. In the late nineteenth century, the wave of pogroms in Eastern Europe sent millions of Jews into flight to the West, and these great migrations continue even today. Jewish history reads like a vast continuation of the stages of the Israelites' journey in this chapter: "They set out… and camped.… They set out… and camped." More than most, Jews have known insecurity, whether in the land of Israel or elsewhere. Too often, home turned out to be no more than a temporary dwelling, a sukka.

Yet with its genius for the unexpected, Judaism declared the festival of Sukkot to be not a time of sadness but the "season of our rejoicing." For the sukka in all its vulnerability symbolizes faith: the faith of a people who set out long ago on a risk-laden journey across a desert of space and time with no more protection than the sheltering Divine Presence. Sitting in the sukka underneath its canopy of leaves, I often think of my ancestors and their wanderings across Europe in search of safety, and I begin to understand how faith was their only home. It was fragile, chillingly exposed to the storms of prejudice and hate. But it proved stronger. Faith survived. The Jewish people has outlived all its persecutors.

To know that life is full of risk and yet to affirm it, to sense the full insecurity of the human situation and yet to rejoice: this, for me, is the essence of faith. Judaism is no comforting illusion that all is well in this dark world. It is instead the courage to celebrate in the midst of uncertainty and to rejoice even in the transitory shelter of the sukka, the Jewish symbol of home.

בַּחֹדֶשׁ הָרִאשׁוֹן בַּחֲמִשָּׁה עָשָׂר יוֹם לַחֹדֶשׁ הָרִאשׁוֹן
מִמָּחֳרַת הַפֶּסַח יָצְאוּ בְנֵי־יִשְׂרָאֵל בְּיָד רָמָה לְעֵינֵי כָּל־
ד מִצְרָיִם׃ וּמִצְרַיִם מְקַבְּרִים אֵת אֲשֶׁר הִכָּה יְהוָה בָּהֶם כָּל־
ה בְּכוֹר וּבֵאלֹהֵיהֶם עָשָׂה יְהוָה שְׁפָטִים׃ וַיִּסְעוּ בְנֵי־יִשְׂרָאֵל
ו מֵרַעְמְסֵס וַיַּחֲנוּ בְּסֻכֹּת׃ וַיִּסְעוּ מִסֻּכֹּת וַיַּחֲנוּ בְאֵתָם אֲשֶׁר

story began when Avraham first heard the words *lekh lekha,* with their call to leave where he was and travel "to the land that I will show you" (Gen. 12:1). We are the people who travel. We are the people who do not stand still. We are the people for whom time itself is a journey through the wilderness in search of the Promised Land.

This is a familiar theme from the world of myth. In many cultures, stories are told about the journey of the hero. Joseph Campbell analyzed these tales in his book *The Hero with a Thousand Faces.* Nonetheless, the Jewish story is different in significant ways:

1. The journey, set out in the books of Exodus and Numbers, is undertaken by everyone – men, women, and children. It is as if, in Judaism, we are all heroes, or at least all summoned to a heroic challenge.
2. It takes longer than a single generation. Perhaps, had the spies not demoralized the nation with their report, it might have taken only a short while. But there is a deeper truth here. The Jewish journey began before we were born and it is our responsibility to hand it on to those who will continue it after us.
3. In myth, the hero usually encounters a major trial: an adversary, a dragon, a dark force. He (it is usually a he) may even die and be resurrected. As Campbell puts it:

   > A hero ventures forth from the world of common day into a region of supernatural wonder: fabulous forces are there encountered....The hero comes back from this mysterious adventure with the power to bestow boons on his fellow man.

   The Jewish story is different. The main adversary the Israelites encounter is themselves: their fears, their weaknesses, their constant urge to return and regress.

The Torah here is not myth but anti-myth. It focuses relentlessly on the human drama of courage versus fear and hope versus despair. It emphasizes the call, not to some larger-than-life hero but to all-of-us-together, given strength by our ties to our people's past and the bonds between us in the present. The Torah is not some fabled escape from reality but reality itself, seen as a journey we must all undertake, each with our

7 wilderness. They set out from Etam and turned back to
Pi HaḤirot, which faces Baal Tzefon, and camped before
8 Migdol. They set out from Pi HaḤirot and passed through
the sea into the wilderness – and they made a three-day
journey through the Wilderness of Etam and camped
9 at Mara. They set out from Mara and came to Eilim. At
Eilim there were twelve springs and seventy date palms,
10 and they encamped there. They set out from Eilim and
11 camped by the Sea of Reeds. They set out from the Sea of SHENI
12 Reeds and camped in the Wilderness of Sin. They set out
13 from the wilderness of Sin and camped at Dofka. They
14 set out from Dofka and camped at Alush. They set out
from Alush and camped at Refidim, where there was no
15 water for the people to drink. They set out from Refidim
16 and camped in the Sinai Desert. They set out from the
17 Sinai Desert and camped at Kivrot HaTaava. They set out
18 from Kivrot HaTaava and camped at Ḥatzerot. They set

mark the transition from one state to the next – from childhood to adulthood, for example, or from being single to being married – and they involve three stages. The first is *separation*, a symbolic break with the past. The last is *incorporation*, reentering society with a new identity. Between the two comes the crucial stage of *transition* when, having cast off one identity but not yet donned another, you are remade, reborn, refashioned.

Van Gennep used the term *liminal*, from the Latin word for "threshold," to describe this transitional state when you are in a kind of no-man's-land between the old and the new. That is what the wilderness signifies for Israel: liminal space between slavery and freedom, past and future, exile and return, Egypt and the Promised Land. The desert was the space that made transition and transformation possible. There, in no-man's-land, the Israelites, alone with God and with one another, could cast off one identity and assume another. There they could be reborn, no longer slaves to Pharaoh, instead servants of God, summoned to become "a kingdom of priests and a holy nation" (Ex. 19:6).

The desert thus became the birthplace of a wholly new relationship between God and humankind, a relationship built on covenant. Distant from the great centers of civilization, a people found themselves alone with God and there consummated a bond that neither exile nor tragedy could break. That is the moral truth at the beating heart of our faith: that it is not power or politics that link us to God, but love.

ז בִּקְצֵה הַמִּדְבָּר: וַיִּסְעוּ מֵאֵתָם וַיָּשָׁב עַל־פִּי הַחִירֹת אֲשֶׁר
ח עַל־פְּנֵי בַּעַל צְפוֹן וַיַּחֲנוּ לִפְנֵי מִגְדֹּל: וַיִּסְעוּ מִפְּנֵי הַחִירֹת
וַיַּעַבְרוּ בְתוֹךְ־הַיָּם הַמִּדְבָּרָה וַיֵּלְכוּ דֶּרֶךְ שְׁלֹשֶׁת יָמִים
ט בְּמִדְבַּר אֵתָם וַיַּחֲנוּ בְּמָרָה: וַיִּסְעוּ מִמָּרָה וַיָּבֹאוּ אֵילִמָה
י וּבְאֵילִם שְׁתֵּים עֶשְׂרֵה עֵינֹת מַיִם וְשִׁבְעִים תְּמָרִים וַיַּחֲנוּ־
יא שָׁם: וַיִּסְעוּ מֵאֵילִם וַיַּחֲנוּ עַל־יַם־סוּף: וַיִּסְעוּ מִיַּם־סוּף וַיַּחֲנוּ שני
יב יג בְּמִדְבַּר־סִין: וַיִּסְעוּ מִמִּדְבַּר־סִין וַיַּחֲנוּ בְּדָפְקָה: וַיִּסְעוּ
יד מִדָּפְקָה וַיַּחֲנוּ בְּאָלוּשׁ: וַיִּסְעוּ מֵאָלוּשׁ וַיַּחֲנוּ בִּרְפִידִם וְלֹא־
טו הָיָה שָׁם מַיִם לָעָם לִשְׁתּוֹת: וַיִּסְעוּ מֵרְפִידִם וַיַּחֲנוּ בְּמִדְבַּר
טז יז סִינָי: וַיִּסְעוּ מִמִּדְבַּר סִינָי וַיַּחֲנוּ בְּקִבְרֹת הַתַּאֲוָה: וַיִּסְעוּ
יח מִקִּבְרֹת הַתַּאֲוָה וַיַּחֲנוּ בַּחֲצֵרֹת: וַיִּסְעוּ מֵחֲצֵרֹת וַיַּחֲנוּ

33:16 קִבְרֹת הַתַּאֲוָה *Kivrot HaTaava* – Difficult memories hide behind this place-name (see ch. 11). Yet including it as merely one element in a list has removed the sting, as hindsight often does. In later generations, the prophets remembered the wilderness years as the formative time in which the Israelites, having left Egypt and not yet entered the land, were alone with God. Their prophecies speak of the desert period as a honeymoon in which God and the people, imagined as bridegroom and bride, were alone together, consummating their union in love. Hoshea, speaking in God's name regarding a future second honeymoon with the Israelites, says:

> I will lead her back to the open desert
> and I will speak to her heart....
> She will return to Me in song as in the first days of her youth,
> As on the day when she came up out of the land of Egypt. (Hos. 2:16–17)

Yirmeyahu says in God's name:

> I recall on your behalf the devotion of your youth, your bridal love, when you followed Me into the wilderness, a land unseeded. (Jer. 2:2)

To be sure, in the Torah itself we see the Israelites as a recalcitrant, obstinate people complaining and rebelling against God. Yet the prophets in retrospect saw things differently. The wilderness was a kind of *yiḥud*, an alone-togetherness, in which the people and God bonded in love.

We can sharpen our understanding of the Israelites' desert period with reference to the work of anthropologist Arnold van Gennep, who focused attention on the importance of *rites of passage*. Societies develop rituals to

19 out from Ḥatzerot and camped at Ritma. They set out
20 from Ritma and camped at Rimon Peretz. They set out
21 from Rimon Peretz and camped at Livna. They set out
22 from Livna and camped at Risa. They set out from Risa
23 and camped at Kehelata. They set out from Kehelata and
24 camped at Mount Shefer. They set out from Mount Shefer
25 and camped at Ḥarada. They set out from Ḥarada and
26 camped at Mak'helot. They set out from Mak'helot and
27 camped at Taḥat. They set out from Taḥat and camped
28 at Teraḥ. They set out from Teraḥ and camped at Mitka.
29 30 They set out from Mitka and camped at Ḥashmona. They
31 set out from Ḥashmona and camped at Moserot. They set
32 out from Moserot and camped at Benei Yaakan. They set
out from Benei Yaakan and camped at Ḥor HaGidgad.
33 They set out from Ḥor HaGidgad and camped at Yotvata.
34 35 They set out from Yotvata and camped at Avrona. They
36 set out from Avrona and camped at Etzyon Gever. They
set out from Etzyon Gever and camped in the Wilderness
37 of Tzin, that is, Kadesh. They set out from Kadesh and
camped at Mount Hor, at the edge of the land of Edom.
38 And Aharon the priest ascended Mount Hor at the
Lord's command, and he died there in the fortieth year,
on the first day of the fifth month after the Israelites left
39 Egypt. Aharon was one hundred and twenty-three years
40 old when he died on Mount Hor. And the
Canaanite king of Arad, who lived in the Negev in the
land of Canaan, heard that the Israelites were coming.
41 They set out from Mount Hor and camped at Tzalmona.
42 43 They set out from Tzalmona and camped at Punon. They
44 set out from Punon and camped at Ovot. They set out
from Ovot and camped at Iyei HaAvarim in the territory
45 of Moav. They set out from Iyim and camped at Divon
46 Gad. They set out from Divon Gad and camped at Almon
47 Divlatayma. They set out from Almon Divlatayma and
48 camped in the Mountains of Avarim, before Nevo. They
set out from the Mountains of Avarim and camped in
the plains of Moav by the Jordan across from Yeriḥo.

יט כ בְּרִתְמָה: וַיִּסְעוּ מֵרִתְמָה וַיַּחֲנוּ בְּרִמֹּן פָּרֶץ: וַיִּסְעוּ מֵרִמֹּן
כא כב פָּרֶץ וַיַּחֲנוּ בְּלִבְנָה: וַיִּסְעוּ מִלִּבְנָה וַיַּחֲנוּ בְּרִסָּה: וַיִּסְעוּ מֵרִסָּה
כג כד וַיַּחֲנוּ בִּקְהֵלָתָה: וַיִּסְעוּ מִקְּהֵלָתָה וַיַּחֲנוּ בְּהַר־שָׁפֶר: וַיִּסְעוּ
כה מֵהַר־שָׁפֶר וַיַּחֲנוּ בַּחֲרָדָה: וַיִּסְעוּ מֵחֲרָדָה וַיַּחֲנוּ בְּמַקְהֵלֹת:
כו כז וַיִּסְעוּ מִמַּקְהֵלֹת וַיַּחֲנוּ בְּתָחַת: וַיִּסְעוּ מִתָּחַת וַיַּחֲנוּ
כח כט בְּתָרַח: וַיִּסְעוּ מִתָּרַח וַיַּחֲנוּ בְּמִתְקָה: וַיִּסְעוּ מִמִּתְקָה וַיַּחֲנוּ
ל לא בְּחַשְׁמֹנָה: וַיִּסְעוּ מֵחַשְׁמֹנָה וַיַּחֲנוּ בְּמֹסֵרוֹת: וַיִּסְעוּ מִמֹּסֵרוֹת
לב וַיַּחֲנוּ בִּבְנֵי יַעֲקָן: וַיִּסְעוּ מִבְּנֵי יַעֲקָן וַיַּחֲנוּ בְּחֹר הַגִּדְגָּד:
לג לד וַיִּסְעוּ מֵחֹר הַגִּדְגָּד וַיַּחֲנוּ בְּיָטְבָתָה: וַיִּסְעוּ מִיָּטְבָתָה וַיַּחֲנוּ
לה לו בְּעַבְרֹנָה: וַיִּסְעוּ מֵעַבְרֹנָה וַיַּחֲנוּ בְּעֶצְיֹן גָּבֶר: וַיִּסְעוּ מֵעֶצְיֹן
לז גָּבֶר וַיַּחֲנוּ בְמִדְבַּר־צִן הִוא קָדֵשׁ: וַיִּסְעוּ מִקָּדֵשׁ וַיַּחֲנוּ
לח בְּהֹר הָהָר בִּקְצֵה אֶרֶץ אֱדוֹם: וַיַּעַל אַהֲרֹן הַכֹּהֵן אֶל־הֹר
הָהָר עַל־פִּי יְהוָה וַיָּמָת שָׁם בִּשְׁנַת הָאַרְבָּעִים לְצֵאת
בְּנֵי־יִשְׂרָאֵל מֵאֶרֶץ מִצְרַיִם בַּחֹדֶשׁ הַחֲמִישִׁי בְּאֶחָד
לט לַחֹדֶשׁ: וְאַהֲרֹן בֶּן־שָׁלֹשׁ וְעֶשְׂרִים וּמְאַת שָׁנָה בְּמֹתוֹ בְּהֹר
מ הָהָר: וַיִּשְׁמַע הַכְּנַעֲנִי מֶלֶךְ עֲרָד וְהוּא־
מא יֹשֵׁב בַּנֶּגֶב בְּאֶרֶץ כְּנָעַן בְּבֹא בְּנֵי יִשְׂרָאֵל: וַיִּסְעוּ מֵהֹר הָהָר
מב מג וַיַּחֲנוּ בְּצַלְמֹנָה: וַיִּסְעוּ מִצַּלְמֹנָה וַיַּחֲנוּ בְּפוּנֹן: וַיִּסְעוּ מִפּוּנֹן
מד וַיַּחֲנוּ בְּאֹבֹת: וַיִּסְעוּ מֵאֹבֹת וַיַּחֲנוּ בְּעִיֵּי הָעֲבָרִים בִּגְבוּל
מה מו מוֹאָב: וַיִּסְעוּ מֵעִיִּים וַיַּחֲנוּ בְּדִיבֹן גָּד: וַיִּסְעוּ מִדִּיבֹן גָּד וַיַּחֲנוּ
מז בְּעַלְמֹן דִּבְלָתָיְמָה: וַיִּסְעוּ מֵעַלְמֹן דִּבְלָתָיְמָה וַיַּחֲנוּ בְּהָרֵי
מח הָעֲבָרִים לִפְנֵי נְבוֹ: וַיִּסְעוּ מֵהָרֵי הָעֲבָרִים וַיַּחֲנוּ בְּעַרְבֹת

33:48 וַיִּסְעוּ... וַיַּחֲנוּ *They set out... and camped* – The dialectic between setting out and encamping, walking and standing still, is part of the rhythm of Jewish life. Rabbi Avraham HaKohen Kook spoke of the two symbols in Bilam's blessing, "How good are your tents, Yaakov, your homes, O Israel" (Num. 24:5). Tents are for people on a journey. Homes are for people who have found permanence.

In life, there are journeys and encampments. Without the encampments, we suffer burnout. Without the journey, we do not grow. Rabbi Aharon ▶

49 And they camped by the Jordan from Beit HaYeshimot
50 to Avel HaShitim in the plains of Moav. And SHELISHI /ḤAMISHI/
the LORD spoke to Moshe on the plains of Moav by the
51 Jordan across from Yeriḥo: "Speak to the Israelites. Say:
52 When you cross the Jordan into the land of Canaan, you
shall drive out all the inhabitants of the land before you.
You shall destroy all their carved images and all their
53 molten idols and demolish all their high shrines. You
shall take possession of the land and settle there, for I
54 have given you the land to possess. You shall divide up

The paradox of Jewish history is that although a specific territory, the Holy Land, is at its heart, Jews have spent more time longing for it than dwelling in it. On the one hand, monotheism must understand God as non-territorial. The God of *everywhere* can be found *anywhere*. On the other hand, it must be impossible to live fully as a Jew outside Israel, for if not, Jews would not have been commanded to go there initially, or to return subsequently. On this tension, the Jewish existence is built.

What then is special about Israel? In *The Kuzari*, Rabbi Yehuda HaLevi says that different environments have different ecologies. Just as there are some countries, climates, and soils particularly suited to growing vines, so there is a country, Israel, particularly suited to growing prophets – indeed a whole divinely inspired people (*Kuzari* II:9–12). Ramban (on Lev. 18:25) gives a different explanation:

> Though every land and nation is under the overarching sovereignty of God, only Israel is *directly* so. Others are ruled by intermediaries earthly and heavenly. Their fate is governed by other factors. Only in the land and people of Israel do we find a nation's fortunes and misfortunes directly attributable to their relationship with God.

HaLevi and Ramban both expound what we might call *mystical geography*. For both of them, religious experience is possible outside Israel, but it is a pale shadow of what it is in the land. There is a way of stating this non-mystically, in concepts and categories closer to ordinary experience.

The Torah is not merely a code of personal perfection. It is the framework for the construction of a society, a nation, a culture. Israel is the sole place on earth where Jews have had the sustained chance to create an entire society on Jewish lines. Only there are they able to construct a political system, an economy, and an environment on the template of Jewish values. There alone can Judaism be what it is meant to be – not just a code of conduct for individuals, but

מט מוֹאָב עַל יַרְדֵּן יְרֵחוֹ׃ וַיַּחֲנוּ עַל־הַיַּרְדֵּן מִבֵּית הַיְשִׁמֹת עַד
נ אָבֵל הַשִּׁטִּים בְּעַרְבֹת מוֹאָב׃ וַיְדַבֵּר יְהוָה אֶל־ שלישי /חמישי/
נא מֹשֶׁה בְּעַרְבֹת מוֹאָב עַל־יַרְדֵּן יְרֵחוֹ לֵאמֹר׃ דַּבֵּר אֶל־בְּנֵי
יִשְׂרָאֵל וְאָמַרְתָּ אֲלֵהֶם כִּי אַתֶּם עֹבְרִים אֶת־הַיַּרְדֵּן אֶל־אֶרֶץ
נב כְּנָעַן׃ וְהוֹרַשְׁתֶּם אֶת־כָּל־יֹשְׁבֵי הָאָרֶץ מִפְּנֵיכֶם וְאִבַּדְתֶּם
אֵת כָּל־מַשְׂכִּיֹּתָם וְאֵת כָּל־צַלְמֵי מַסֵּכֹתָם תְּאַבֵּדוּ וְאֵת
נג כָּל־בָּמוֹתָם תַּשְׁמִידוּ׃ וְהוֹרַשְׁתֶּם אֶת־הָאָרֶץ וִישַׁבְתֶּם־
נד בָהּ כִּי לָכֶם נָתַתִּי אֶת־הָאָרֶץ לָרֶשֶׁת אֹתָהּ׃ וְהִתְנַחַלְתֶּם

Lichtenstein illustrated this idea with a beautiful reading of Robert Frost's poem, "Stopping by Woods on a Snowy Evening":

> The woods are lovely, dark, and deep.
> But I have promises to keep,
> And miles to go before I sleep,
> And miles to go before I sleep.

Rabbi Lichtenstein analyzes the poem in terms of Kierkegaard's distinction between the aesthetic and ethical dimensions of life. The poet is enchanted by the aesthetic beauty of the scene, the soft silence of the falling snow, the dark dignity of the tall trees. He would love to stay here in this timeless moment, this eternity-in-an hour. But he knows that life has an ethical dimension also, and this demands action, not just contemplation. He has promises to keep; he has duties toward the world. So he must walk on despite his fatigue. He has miles to go before he sleeps: he has work to do while the breath of life is within him.

For us as Jews, as for Robert Frost the poet, ethics takes priority over aesthetics. Yes, there are moments when we should, indeed must, pause to see the beauty of the world, but then, like the Israelites in Parashat Masei, we must move on, for – to ourselves and to God – we have promises to keep.

THE LAND OF ISRAEL

The long journey is nearing its close. The Jordan is almost within sight. Finally we are reaching the end of the list of encampments, and God tells Moshe: "Take possession of the land and settle there" (Num. 33:53). This, according to Ramban on that verse, is the source of the command to dwell in the land of Israel.

The centrality of the land of Israel to Judaism cannot be doubted. Whatever the subplots and subsidiary themes of Tanakh, its overarching narrative is the promise of and journey to the land. Jewish history begins with Avraham and Sara's journey to it. Tanakh as a whole ends with Koresh, king of Persia, granting permission to Jews, exiled in Babylon, to return to their land (II Chr. 36:23).

the land by lot among your clans: to a large clan give a
large inheritance, and to a small one a small inheritance.
Whatever falls to them by lot will be theirs. According
55 to your ancestral tribes you shall inherit. But if you do
not drive the inhabitants out of the land before you, then
those you allow to remain will be barbs in your eyes and
thorns in your sides. They will harass you in the land
56 where you settle. Then, what I intended to do to them, I
will do instead to you."
34 1 2 The LORD said to Moshe: "Command the Israelites. Say
to them: As you enter the land of Canaan – this is the land
that will become your possession, the land of Canaan
3 with its borders: Your southern sector shall extend from
the Wilderness of Tzin alongside Edom; your southern
4 border to the east begins at the end of the Dead Sea. The
border shall then turn south of Scorpion Ascent and
cross toward Tzin. Its outer limit shall be south of Kadesh
Barnea, extending to Ḥatzar Adar and continuing toward
5 Atzmon. The border shall then turn from Atzmon to the
6 Ravine of Egypt and end at the sea. Your western border
will be the Great Sea and its coast; this shall be your
7 western border. This shall be your northern border: from
8 the Great Sea, mark a line to Mount Hor. From Mount
Hor mark a line to Levo Ḥamat. The outer limit of the
9 border shall be at Tzedad; the border shall then extend
to Zifron, and its outer limit shall be Ḥatzar Einan. This
10 shall be your northern border. Mark your eastern border
11 from Ḥatzar Einan to Shefam. The border will run down

---

sense of mission. Thus the prophets knew that without social justice and a sense of divine vocation, the nation would eventually fall and suffer exile again.

These are, as it were, the empirical foundations of the mysticism of HaLevi and Ramban. History tells us that the project of constructing a society under divine sovereignty in a vulnerable land is the highest of high-risk strategies. Yet the risk was worth taking. For only in Israel is God so close that you can feel Him in the sun and wind, sense Him just beyond the hills, hear Him in the inflections of everyday speech, breathe His presence in the early morning air and live, dangerously but confidently, under the shadow of His wings.

אֶת־הָאָרֶץ בְּגוֹרָל לְמִשְׁפְּחֹתֵיכֶם לָרַב תַּרְבּוּ אֶת־נַחֲלָתוֹ
וְלַמְעַט תַּמְעִיט אֶת־נַחֲלָתוֹ אֶל אֲשֶׁר־יֵצֵא לוֹ שָׁמָּה הַגּוֹרָל
נה לוֹ יִהְיֶה לְמַטּוֹת אֲבֹתֵיכֶם תִּתְנֶחָלוּ׃ וְאִם־לֹא תוֹרִישׁוּ
אֶת־יֹשְׁבֵי הָאָרֶץ מִפְּנֵיכֶם וְהָיָה אֲשֶׁר תּוֹתִירוּ מֵהֶם לְשִׂכִּים
בְּעֵינֵיכֶם וְלִצְנִינִם בְּצִדֵּיכֶם וְצָרְרוּ אֶתְכֶם עַל־הָאָרֶץ אֲשֶׁר
נו אַתֶּם יֹשְׁבִים בָּהּ׃ וְהָיָה כַּאֲשֶׁר דִּמִּיתִי לַעֲשׂוֹת לָהֶם אֶעֱשֶׂה
לָכֶם׃

לד א ב וַיְדַבֵּר יְהוָה אֶל־מֹשֶׁה לֵּאמֹר׃ צַו אֶת־בְּנֵי יִשְׂרָאֵל וְאָמַרְתָּ לא
אֲלֵהֶם כִּי־אַתֶּם בָּאִים אֶל־הָאָרֶץ כְּנָעַן זֹאת הָאָרֶץ אֲשֶׁר
ג תִּפֹּל לָכֶם בְּנַחֲלָה אֶרֶץ כְּנַעַן לִגְבֻלֹתֶיהָ׃ וְהָיָה לָכֶם פְאַת־
נֶגֶב מִמִּדְבַּר־צִן עַל־יְדֵי אֱדוֹם וְהָיָה לָכֶם גְּבוּל נֶגֶב מִקְצֵה
ד יָם־הַמֶּלַח קֵדְמָה׃ וְנָסַב לָכֶם הַגְּבוּל מִנֶּגֶב לְמַעֲלֵה עַקְרַבִּים
וְעָבַר צִנָה והיה תּוֹצְאֹתָיו מִנֶּגֶב לְקָדֵשׁ בַּרְנֵעַ וְיָצָא חֲצַר־ וְהָיוּ
ה אַדָּר וְעָבַר עַצְמֹנָה׃ וְנָסַב הַגְּבוּל מֵעַצְמוֹן נַחְלָה מִצְרָיִם
ו וְהָיוּ תוֹצְאֹתָיו הַיָּמָּה׃ וּגְבוּל יָם וְהָיָה לָכֶם הַיָּם הַגָּדוֹל
ז וּגְבוּל זֶה־יִהְיֶה לָכֶם גְּבוּל יָם׃ וְזֶה־יִהְיֶה לָכֶם גְּבוּל צָפוֹן
ח מִן־הַיָּם הַגָּדֹל תְּתָאוּ לָכֶם הֹר הָהָר׃ מֵהֹר הָהָר תְּתָאוּ לְבֹא
ט חֲמָת וְהָיוּ תּוֹצְאֹת הַגְּבֻל צְדָדָה׃ וְיָצָא הַגְּבֻל זִפְרֹנָה וְהָיוּ
י תוֹצְאֹתָיו חֲצַר עֵינָן זֶה־יִהְיֶה לָכֶם גְּבוּל צָפוֹן׃ וְהִתְאַוִּיתֶם
יא לָכֶם לִגְבוּל קֵדְמָה מֵחֲצַר עֵינָן שְׁפָמָה׃ וְיָרַד הַגְּבֻל מִשְּׁפָם

also and essentially the architectonics of a society.

But why Israel specifically? Because it has always been a key strategic location where three continents – Europe, Africa, and Asia – meet. Lacking the extended flat and fertile space of the Nile Delta or the Tigris-Euphrates valley, it could never be the base of an empire, but because of its location it was always sought after by empires. So it was politically vulnerable.

It was and is ecologically vulnerable, dependent on rains that are always unpredictable. Its existence could never be taken for granted. Small geographically and demographically, it would depend on outstanding achievement on the part of its people. This would depend, in turn, on their morale and

from Shefam to Rivla on the east side of Ayin. It will then
continue down to reach the eastern slope of the Sea of
12 Galilee. From there the border will run down along the
Jordan, ending at the Dead Sea. This is to be your land
13 with its borders on all sides." Moshe commanded the
Israelites: "This is the land of which you take possession
by lot, which the LORD has commanded to give to the
14 nine and a half tribes – for the tribe of Reuven by its
ancestral houses, and the tribe of Gad by its ancestral
houses, and half the tribe of Menashe have taken their
15 possession. The two and a half tribes have taken their
possession across the Jordan from Yeriḥo to the east as
the sun rises."

16 17 And the LORD spoke to Moshe: "These are the names of the REVI'I /SHISHI/
men who shall apportion the land to you for possession:
18 Elazar the priest and Yehoshua son of Nun. And you shall
also take one leader from each tribe to apportion the land.
19 These are the names of the men: for the tribe of Yehuda,
20 Kalev son of Yefuneh; for the tribe of the Simeonites,
21 Shmuel son of Amihud; for the tribe of Binyamin, Elidad
22 son of Kislon; for the tribe of the Danites, a leader, Buki
23 son of Yogli. For the descendants of Yosef: for the tribe of
24 the Manassites a leader, Ḥaniel son of Efod; for the tribe
25 of the Efraimites a leader, Kemuel son of Shiftan. For the
tribe of the Zebulunites a leader, Elitzafan son of Parnakh.
26 For the tribe of the Issakharites a leader, Paltiel son of
27 Azan. For the tribe of the Asherites a leader, Aḥihud son
28 of Shelomi. For the tribe of the Naftalites a leader, Pedahel
29 son of Amihud." These were the ones whom the LORD
commanded to apportion the possession for the Israelites
in the land of Canaan.

35 1 The LORD spoke to Moshe in the plains of Moav by the ḤAMISHI
2 Jordan across from Yeriḥo: "Command the Israelites to
grant the Levites towns to live in, among the inheritance
they will possess. Grant them also pasturelands around
3 the towns. The towns shall be theirs to live in, and the
pasturelands shall be for their cattle, all that they own,

הָרִבְלָה מִקֶּדֶם לָעָיִן וְיָרַד הַגְּבֻל וּמָחָה עַל־כֶּתֶף יָם־כִּנֶּרֶת
יב קֵדְמָה׃ וְיָרַד הַגְּבוּל הַיַּרְדֵּנָה וְהָיוּ תוֹצְאֹתָיו יָם הַמֶּלַח זֹאת
יג תִּהְיֶה לָכֶם הָאָרֶץ לִגְבֻלֹתֶיהָ סָבִיב׃ וַיְצַו מֹשֶׁה אֶת־בְּנֵי
יִשְׂרָאֵל לֵאמֹר זֹאת הָאָרֶץ אֲשֶׁר תִּתְנַחֲלוּ אֹתָהּ בְּגוֹרָל
אֲשֶׁר צִוָּה יְהוָה לָתֵת לְתִשְׁעַת הַמַּטּוֹת וַחֲצִי הַמַּטֶּה׃
יד כִּי לָקְחוּ מַטֵּה בְנֵי הָרְאוּבֵנִי לְבֵית אֲבֹתָם וּמַטֵּה בְנֵי־הַגָּדִי
טו לְבֵית אֲבֹתָם וַחֲצִי מַטֵּה מְנַשֶּׁה לָקְחוּ נַחֲלָתָם׃ שְׁנֵי הַמַּטּוֹת
וַחֲצִי הַמַּטֶּה לָקְחוּ נַחֲלָתָם מֵעֵבֶר לְיַרְדֵּן יְרֵחוֹ קֵדְמָה
מִזְרָחָה׃
טז יז וַיְדַבֵּר יְהוָה אֶל־מֹשֶׁה לֵּאמֹר׃ אֵלֶּה שְׁמוֹת הָאֲנָשִׁים רביעי /ששי/
אֲשֶׁר־יִנְחֲלוּ לָכֶם אֶת־הָאָרֶץ אֶלְעָזָר הַכֹּהֵן וִיהוֹשֻׁעַ בִּן־
יח נוּן׃ וְנָשִׂיא אֶחָד נָשִׂיא אֶחָד מִמַּטֶּה תִּקְחוּ לִנְחֹל אֶת־
יט הָאָרֶץ׃ וְאֵלֶּה שְׁמוֹת הָאֲנָשִׁים לְמַטֵּה יְהוּדָה כָּלֵב בֶּן־
כ כא יְפֻנֶּה׃ וּלְמַטֵּה בְּנֵי שִׁמְעוֹן שְׁמוּאֵל בֶּן־עַמִּיהוּד׃ לְמַטֵּה
כב בִנְיָמִן אֱלִידָד בֶּן־כִּסְלוֹן׃ וּלְמַטֵּה בְנֵי־דָן נָשִׂיא בֻּקִּי בֶּן־
כג יָגְלִי׃ לִבְנֵי יוֹסֵף לְמַטֵּה בְנֵי־מְנַשֶּׁה נָשִׂיא חַנִּיאֵל בֶּן־אֵפֹד׃
כד כה וּלְמַטֵּה בְנֵי־אֶפְרַיִם נָשִׂיא קְמוּאֵל בֶּן־שִׁפְטָן׃ וּלְמַטֵּה
כו בְנֵי־זְבוּלֻן נָשִׂיא אֱלִיצָפָן בֶּן־פַּרְנָךְ׃ וּלְמַטֵּה בְנֵי־יִשָּׂשכָר
כז נָשִׂיא פַּלְטִיאֵל בֶּן־עַזָּן׃ וּלְמַטֵּה בְנֵי־אָשֵׁר נָשִׂיא אֲחִיהוּד
כח בֶּן־שְׁלֹמִי׃ וּלְמַטֵּה בְנֵי־נַפְתָּלִי נָשִׂיא פְּדַהְאֵל בֶּן־עַמִּיהוּד׃
כט אֵלֶּה אֲשֶׁר צִוָּה יְהוָה לְנַחֵל אֶת־בְּנֵי־יִשְׂרָאֵל בְּאֶרֶץ
כְּנָעַן׃

לה א וַיְדַבֵּר יְהוָה אֶל־מֹשֶׁה בְּעַרְבֹת מוֹאָב עַל־יַרְדֵּן יְרֵחוֹ לֵאמֹר׃ חמישי
ב צַו אֶת־בְּנֵי יִשְׂרָאֵל וְנָתְנוּ לַלְוִיִּם מִנַּחֲלַת אֲחֻזָּתָם עָרִים
ג לָשָׁבֶת וּמִגְרָשׁ לֶעָרִים סְבִיבֹתֵיהֶם תִּתְּנוּ לַלְוִיִּם׃ וְהָיוּ הֶעָרִים
לָהֶם לָשָׁבֶת וּמִגְרְשֵׁיהֶם יִהְיוּ לִבְהֶמְתָּם וְלִרְכֻשָׁם וּלְכֹל

4 and all their animals. The pasturelands of the towns that
you shall give to the Levites shall extend from the town
5 wall outward for a thousand cubits in all directions; you
shall measure out from the town, two thousand cubits
on the east side, two thousand cubits on the south side,
two thousand cubits on the west side, and two thousand
cubits on the north side, with the town in the middle, and
this shall belong to them as pastureland for their towns.
6 Six of the towns that you give to the Levites shall be towns
of refuge, which you will designate as places to which a
manslayer may flee. In addition to these, you shall give
7 them forty-two more towns. Thus the total number of
towns you shall give to the Levites shall be forty-eight,
8 along with their pastureland. As for the towns that you
give from the possession of the Israelites, take more from
the larger tribes and fewer from the smaller so that each
grants towns to the Levites in proportion to its own
inheritance."
9 The LORD spoke to Moshe: "Speak to the Israelites. SHISHI
10 Tell them: When you cross the Jordan into the land of /SHEVI'I/

turns revenge into retribution, which makes all the difference.

People often find it difficult to distinguish between retribution and revenge, yet they are completely different concepts. Revenge is personal. You killed a member of my family so I will kill you. Retribution, by contrast, is *im*personal. Indeed, the best definition of the society the Torah seeks to create is *nomocracy*: the rule of laws, not men.

Retribution is the principled rejection of revenge. It says that we are not free to take the law into our own hands. Passion may not override the due process of the law, for that is a sure route to anarchy and bloodshed. Wrong must be punished, but only after it has been established by a fair trial, and only on behalf not just of the victim but of society as a whole. The cities of refuge were part of this process, by which vengeance was subordinated to, and replaced by, retributive justice.

The desire for revenge exists. But given free rein, it will reduce societies to violence and bloodshed without end. The alternative is to channel it through the operation of law, fair trial, and then either punishment or protection. That is what was introduced into civilization by the law of the cities of refuge, allowing retribution to take the place of revenge, and justice the place of retaliation.

ד חַיָּתָם׃ וּמִגְרְשֵׁי הֶעָרִים אֲשֶׁר תִּתְּנוּ לַלְוִיִּם מִקִּיר הָעִיר
ה וָחוּצָה אֶלֶף אַמָּה סָבִיב׃ וּמַדֹּתֶם מִחוּץ לָעִיר אֶת־פְּאַת־
קֵדְמָה אַלְפַּיִם בָּאַמָּה וְאֶת־פְּאַת־נֶגֶב אַלְפַּיִם בָּאַמָּה וְאֶת־
פְּאַת־יָם ׀ אַלְפַּיִם בָּאַמָּה וְאֵת פְּאַת צָפוֹן אַלְפַּיִם בָּאַמָּה
ו וְהָעִיר בַּתָּוֶךְ זֶה יִהְיֶה לָהֶם מִגְרְשֵׁי הֶעָרִים׃ וְאֵת הֶעָרִים
אֲשֶׁר תִּתְּנוּ לַלְוִיִּם אֵת שֵׁשׁ־עָרֵי הַמִּקְלָט אֲשֶׁר תִּתְּנוּ
לָנֻס שָׁמָּה הָרֹצֵחַ וַעֲלֵיהֶם תִּתְּנוּ אַרְבָּעִים וּשְׁתַּיִם עִיר׃
ז כָּל־הֶעָרִים אֲשֶׁר תִּתְּנוּ לַלְוִיִּם אַרְבָּעִים וּשְׁמֹנֶה עִיר אֶתְהֶן
ח וְאֶת־מִגְרְשֵׁיהֶן׃ וְהֶעָרִים אֲשֶׁר תִּתְּנוּ מֵאֲחֻזַּת בְּנֵי־יִשְׂרָאֵל
מֵאֵת הָרַב תַּרְבּוּ וּמֵאֵת הַמְעַט תַּמְעִיטוּ אִישׁ כְּפִי נַחֲלָתוֹ
אֲשֶׁר יִנְחָלוּ יִתֵּן מֵעָרָיו לַלְוִיִּם׃
ט וַיְדַבֵּר יְהוָה אֶל־מֹשֶׁה לֵּאמֹר׃ דַּבֵּר אֶל־בְּנֵי יִשְׂרָאֵל וְאָמַרְתָּ לב ששי /שביעי/

CITIES OF REFUGE

As the book of Numbers draws to a close, we encounter the law of the cities of refuge: three cities to the east of the Jordan and, later, three more within the land of Israel itself. There, people who commit homicide can flee and find protection until their case is heard by a court of law. If they are found guilty of murder (in biblical times), they are sentenced to death. If found innocent – if the death happened by accident or inadvertently, with neither deliberation nor malice – then they are to stay in a city of refuge "until the death of the High Priest" (Num. 35:25). By residing there, they are protected against revenge on the part of the *goel hadam*, the blood redeemer, usually the closest relative of the person who was killed.

Though the Torah rejects revenge except when commanded by God, something of the idea survives in the concept of the *goel hadam*. The desire for revenge is basic. It exists in all societies. The Torah recognizes the pain, the loss, and the moral indignation of the victim's family, understands that the desire for revenge is natural, and yet tames it. Torah legislates for people with all their passions, not for saints. It is a realistic code, not a utopian one.

Yet the Torah inserts one vital element *between* the killer and the victim's family: the principle of justice. There must be no direct act of revenge. The killer must be protected until his case has been heard in a court of law. If found guilty, he must pay the price. If he is found innocent of deliberate murder, though the vengeful instinct of the victim's family may be no less acute, he is given refuge from it. This due process

11 Canaan, select towns to be your refuge cities, to which
12 a person who kills another unintentionally may flee. The
cities shall be a refuge for you from avengers, so that no
person who has killed another may die without standing
13 trial before the community. The towns that you designate
14 shall be six cities of refuge for you; you shall designate
three towns across the Jordan and three in the land of
15 Canaan as cities of refuge. These six towns shall be a place
of refuge for Israelites, migrants, and temporary residents
alike, so that anyone who kills a person unintentionally
16 may flee there. If a person strikes another with an iron
object, however, and he dies, that person is a murderer;
17 the murderer must be put to death. If he strikes him with
a handheld stone that could cause death and he dies,
that person is a murderer; the murderer must be put to
18 death. Likewise, if he strikes him with a wooden tool that
could cause death and he dies, that person is a murderer;
19 the murderer must be put to death. The blood avenger
shall put the murderer to death; whenever he meets him,
20 he may put him to death. So too if one person pushes
another in hate, or throws something at him with prior
21 intent, he shall be put to death. If in enmity someone
strikes a person with his hand and he dies, the one who
struck the blow is a murderer and shall be put to death.
The blood avenger shall put the murderer to death
22 whenever they meet. If, however, one person pushes
another suddenly, without enmity, or throws an object at

---

helping us to see the world more clearly, think more deeply, argue more cogently, and decide more wisely.

34:12 וְהָיוּ תוֹצְאֹתָיו יָם הַמֶּלַח *Ending at the Dead Sea* – There are two seas in Israel: the Dead Sea and the Sea of Galilee. The latter is full of life: fish, birds, vegetation. The former, as its name suggests, contains no life at all. Yet they are both fed by the same river, the Jordan. The difference, says the Midrash, is that the Sea of Galilee receives water at one end and gives out water at the other. The Dead Sea receives but does not give. The Jordan ends there. To receive without reciprocating is a kind of death. To live is to give.

יא אֱלֵהֶם כִּי אַתֶּם עֹבְרִים אֶת־הַיַּרְדֵּן אַרְצָה כְּנָעַן: וְהִקְרִיתֶם
לָכֶם עָרִים עָרֵי מִקְלָט תִּהְיֶינָה לָכֶם וְנָס שָׁמָּה רֹצֵחַ מַכֵּה־
יב נֶפֶשׁ בִּשְׁגָגָה: וְהָיוּ לָכֶם הֶעָרִים לְמִקְלָט מִגֹּאֵל וְלֹא יָמוּת
יג הָרֹצֵחַ עַד־עָמְדוֹ לִפְנֵי הָעֵדָה לַמִּשְׁפָּט: וְהֶעָרִים אֲשֶׁר
יד תִּתֵּנוּ שֵׁשׁ־עָרֵי מִקְלָט תִּהְיֶינָה לָכֶם: אֵת ׀ שְׁלֹשׁ הֶעָרִים
תִּתְּנוּ מֵעֵבֶר לַיַּרְדֵּן וְאֵת שְׁלֹשׁ הֶעָרִים תִּתְּנוּ בְּאֶרֶץ כְּנָעַן
טו עָרֵי מִקְלָט תִּהְיֶינָה: לִבְנֵי יִשְׂרָאֵל וְלַגֵּר וְלַתּוֹשָׁב בְּתוֹכָם
תִּהְיֶינָה שֵׁשׁ־הֶעָרִים הָאֵלֶּה לְמִקְלָט לָנוּס שָׁמָּה כָּל־מַכֵּה־
טז נֶפֶשׁ בִּשְׁגָגָה: וְאִם־בִּכְלִי בַרְזֶל ׀ הִכָּהוּ וַיָּמֹת רֹצֵחַ הוּא מוֹת
יז יוּמַת הָרֹצֵחַ: וְאִם בְּאֶבֶן יָד אֲשֶׁר־יָמוּת בָּהּ הִכָּהוּ וַיָּמֹת
יח רֹצֵחַ הוּא מוֹת יוּמַת הָרֹצֵחַ: אוֹ בִּכְלִי עֵץ־יָד אֲשֶׁר־יָמוּת
יט בּוֹ הִכָּהוּ וַיָּמֹת רֹצֵחַ הוּא מוֹת יוּמַת הָרֹצֵחַ: גֹּאֵל הַדָּם
כ הוּא יָמִית אֶת־הָרֹצֵחַ בְּפִגְעוֹ־בוֹ הוּא יְמִתֶנּוּ: וְאִם־בְּשִׂנְאָה
כא יֶהְדָּפֶנּוּ אוֹ־הִשְׁלִיךְ עָלָיו בִּצְדִיָּה וַיָּמֹת: אוֹ בְאֵיבָה הִכָּהוּ
בְיָדוֹ וַיָּמֹת מוֹת־יוּמַת הַמַּכֶּה רֹצֵחַ הוּא גֹּאֵל הַדָּם יָמִית
כב אֶת־הָרֹצֵחַ בְּפִגְעוֹ־בוֹ: וְאִם־בְּפֶתַע בְּלֹא־אֵיבָה הֲדָפוֹ אוֹ־

34:11 עָרֵי מִקְלָט *Refuge cities* – The purpose of the cities of refuge was to make sure that someone judged innocent of murder was safe from being killed. This apparently simple concept was given a remarkable interpretation by the Talmud: "The Sages taught: If a student was exiled, his teacher was exiled with him, as it is said: 'That man may flee to one of these cities and live' (Deut. 19:5), meaning: do the things for him that will enable him to live" (Makkot 10a).

As Rambam explains: "Life without study is like death for scholars who seek wisdom" (*Hilkhot Rotze'aḥ UShmirat HaNefesh* 7:1). In Judaism, study is life itself, and study without a teacher is impossible. Teachers are like parents, only more so. Parents give us physical life; teachers give us spiritual life (*Hilkhot Talmud Torah* 5.1). Physical life is mortal, transient. Spiritual life is eternal. Therefore, we owe our teacher our life in its deepest sense.

Judaism made a wise decision when it made teachers its heroes and lifelong education its passion. We do not worship power or wealth. These things have their place, but not at the top of the hierarchy of values. Power forces us. Wealth induces us. But teachers develop us. They open us to the wisdom of the ages,

23 him unintentionally, or drops a fatal stone on him without
seeing him and he dies – they were not enemies, he
24 intended him no harm – then the community must judge
between the killer and the blood avenger in accordance
25 with these laws. And the community must protect the
manslayer from the avenger of blood and return him to
the refuge city to which he fled. There he shall live until
the death of the High Priest anointed with the sacred oil.
26 But if the manslayer ever goes outside the limits of the
27 city of refuge to which he fled and the blood avenger finds
him outside the limits of his city of refuge and kills him,
28 the avenger is not liable for murder; the manslayer must
stay in his city of refuge until the High Priest dies. After
the death of the High Priest the manslayer may return
29 to his own hereditary land. These shall be a decree of
law for you throughout your generations, wherever you
30 should live. If anyone kills a human being, the murderer
shall be put to death on the evidence of eyewitnesses.

---

to do with guilt or atonement, but simply with the fact that it causes great collective grief, in which people forget their own misfortunes in the face of larger national loss. That is when people let go of their individual sense of injustice and desire for revenge. It then becomes safe for the person found guilty of manslaughter to return home.

Rambam does not understand the law of the cities of refuge in terms of guilt or punishment. For him, the only relevant consideration is safety. The person guilty of manslaughter goes into exile, not because it is a form of atonement or expiation, but simply because it is safer for him to be a long way from those who might be seeking vengeance. He stays there until the death of the High Priest, because only after national tragedy can you assume that people have given up thoughts of taking revenge for their own lost family member.

This is a fundamentally different way to conceptualize the cities of refuge. The Talmud's explanation operates on the supernatural level; had the High Priest prayed hard and devotedly enough, there would have been no accidental deaths. Rambam's explanation is not supernatural. It is what we would call social psychology. There are events that evoke widespread and deep national grief, when our personal grievances seem simply too small to worry about. These collective sorrows bring the people together and move them beyond the resentments of the past.

כג הִשְׁלִיךְ עָלָיו כָּל־כְּלִי בְּלֹא צְדִיָּה׃ אוֹ בְכָל־אֶבֶן אֲשֶׁר־יָמוּת
בָּהּ בְּלֹא רְאוֹת וַיַּפֵּל עָלָיו וַיָּמֹת וְהוּא לֹא־אוֹיֵב לוֹ וְלֹא
כד מְבַקֵּשׁ רָעָתוֹ׃ וְשָׁפְטוּ הָעֵדָה בֵּין הַמַּכֶּה וּבֵין גֹּאֵל הַדָּם
כה עַל הַמִּשְׁפָּטִים הָאֵלֶּה׃ וְהִצִּילוּ הָעֵדָה אֶת־הָרֹצֵחַ מִיַּד גֹּאֵל
הַדָּם וְהֵשִׁיבוּ אֹתוֹ הָעֵדָה אֶל־עִיר מִקְלָטוֹ אֲשֶׁר־נָס שָׁמָּה
וְיָשַׁב בָּהּ עַד־מוֹת הַכֹּהֵן הַגָּדֹל אֲשֶׁר־מָשַׁח אֹתוֹ בְּשֶׁמֶן
כו הַקֹּדֶשׁ׃ וְאִם־יָצֹא יֵצֵא הָרֹצֵחַ אֶת־גְּבוּל עִיר מִקְלָטוֹ אֲשֶׁר
כז יָנוּס שָׁמָּה׃ וּמָצָא אֹתוֹ גֹּאֵל הַדָּם מִחוּץ לִגְבוּל עִיר מִקְלָטוֹ
כח וְרָצַח גֹּאֵל הַדָּם אֶת־הָרֹצֵחַ אֵין לוֹ דָּם׃ כִּי בְעִיר מִקְלָטוֹ יֵשֵׁב
עַד־מוֹת הַכֹּהֵן הַגָּדֹל וְאַחֲרֵי־מוֹת הַכֹּהֵן הַגָּדֹל יָשׁוּב הָרֹצֵחַ
כט אֶל־אֶרֶץ אֲחֻזָּתוֹ׃ וְהָיוּ אֵלֶּה לָכֶם לְחֻקַּת מִשְׁפָּט לְדֹרֹתֵיכֶם
ל בְּכֹל מוֹשְׁבֹתֵיכֶם׃ כָּל־מַכֵּה־נֶפֶשׁ לְפִי עֵדִים יִרְצַח אֶת־הָרֹצֵחַ

35:25 עַד־מוֹת הַכֹּהֵן הַגָּדֹל *Until the death of the High Priest* – There seems no connection between manslaughter, blood vengeance, and the High Priest, let alone his death. One explanation offered in the Talmud for the connection made in the law is that the death of the High Priest atoned for the lost life of the victim (Makkot 11b). To be sure, there was no malice aforethought. The killing was unintended. But it is precisely for unintended acts – sins committed *beshogeg*, unknowingly or unwittingly – that a purification offering had to be brought (Lev. 4). In the case of manslaughter, no purification offering is adequate. What has been lost is a life, and one life is like a universe. In the case of manslaughter, it seems as if it is the death of the High Priest that atones.

A second explanation – or it may be a variant on the first – is that in some way the High Priest shared in the responsibility for the death: "A venerable old scholar said: I heard an explanation at one of the sessional lectures of Rava that the High Priest should have implored divine grace for the generation, which he failed to do" (Makkot 11a).

According to this approach, the High Priest had a share, however small, in the guilt for the fact that someone died, albeit unintentionally. Manslaughter, because it is unintentional, is an event that might have been averted by the prayers of the High Priest. Therefore it is not fully atoned for until the High Priest dies. Only then can the manslaughterer go free.

Rambam offers a completely different kind of explanation in *Guide for the Perplexed* (III:40). According to him, the death of the High Priest has nothing

No one shall be put to death on the testimony of one
31 witness alone. You may not accept a ransom for the life
of a murderer found guilty of a capital crime; he must be
32 put to death. Nor may you accept a ransom for someone
who has fled to his city of refuge, to allow him to return
33 and live on his land before the priest dies. You shall not
pollute the land in which you live; blood pollutes the
land. And the land can have no atonement for the blood
that is shed in it – except through the blood of the one
34 who shed it. Do not defile the land in which you live, and
in the midst of which I dwell – for I the Lord dwell in the
midst of Israel."

36 1 The heads of the ancestral houses of the descendants of SHEVI'I
Gilad son of Makhir son of Menashe, one of the families
of Yosef's sons, came forward and spoke before Moshe
and the leaders, the heads of the ancestral houses of the
2 Israelites. "The Lord," they said, "commanded my lord to
give the land as an inheritance to the Israelites by lot. But
my lord was also commanded by the Lord to give the
3 inheritance of our brother Tzelofḥad to his daughters. If
they marry men from another Israelite tribe, their share
will be taken away from our ancestral inheritance and
given to the tribe into which they marry. It will be taken

Moshe with a request to be permitted to inherit their father's land based on the principles of justice. Now, at the end of the book, the Torah reports on another event arising from that case. Leaders of Tzelofḥad's tribe, Menashe, make the following complaint: If the land were to pass to Tzelofḥad's daughters and they married men from another tribe, the land would eventually pass to their husbands, and thus to their husbands' tribes. Thus, land that had initially been granted to the tribe of Menashe might be lost to it in perpetuity.

Again, Moshe takes the case to God, who offers a solution. The daughters of Tzelofḥad are entitled to the land, but so too is the tribe. If they wish to take possession of the land, they must marry men from within their own tribe. That way both claims can be honored. The daughters do not lose their right to the land but they do lose some freedom in choosing a marriage partner.

The two passages are intimately related. Why then are they separated in the text, and why does the book of Numbers end on this seemingly

לא וְעֵד אֶחָד לֹא־יַעֲנֶה בְנֶפֶשׁ לָמוּת: וְלֹא־תִקְחוּ כֹפֶר לְנֶפֶשׁ
לב רֹצֵחַ אֲשֶׁר־הוּא רָשָׁע לָמוּת כִּי־מוֹת יוּמָת: וְלֹא־תִקְחוּ כֹפֶר
לָנוּס אֶל־עִיר מִקְלָטוֹ לָשׁוּב לָשֶׁבֶת בָּאָרֶץ עַד־מוֹת הַכֹּהֵן:
לג וְלֹא־תַחֲנִיפוּ אֶת־הָאָרֶץ אֲשֶׁר אַתֶּם בָּהּ כִּי הַדָּם הוּא יַחֲנִיף
אֶת־הָאָרֶץ וְלָאָרֶץ לֹא־יְכֻפַּר לַדָּם אֲשֶׁר שֻׁפַּךְ־בָּהּ כִּי־אִם
לד בְּדַם שֹׁפְכוֹ: וְלֹא תְטַמֵּא אֶת־הָאָרֶץ אֲשֶׁר אַתֶּם יֹשְׁבִים
בָּהּ אֲשֶׁר אֲנִי שֹׁכֵן בְּתוֹכָהּ כִּי אֲנִי יהוה שֹׁכֵן בְּתוֹךְ בְּנֵי
יִשְׂרָאֵל:

לו א וַיִּקְרְבוּ רָאשֵׁי הָאָבוֹת לְמִשְׁפַּחַת בְּנֵי־גִלְעָד בֶּן־מָכִיר שביעי
בֶּן־מְנַשֶּׁה מִמִּשְׁפְּחֹת בְּנֵי יוֹסֵף וַיְדַבְּרוּ לִפְנֵי מֹשֶׁה וְלִפְנֵי
ב הַנְּשִׂאִים רָאשֵׁי אָבוֹת לִבְנֵי יִשְׂרָאֵל: וַיֹּאמְרוּ אֶת־אֲדֹנִי צִוָּה
יהוה לָתֵת אֶת־הָאָרֶץ בְּנַחֲלָה בְּגוֹרָל לִבְנֵי יִשְׂרָאֵל וַאדֹנִי
ג צֻוָּה בַיהוה לָתֵת אֶת־נַחֲלַת צְלָפְחָד אָחִינוּ לִבְנֹתָיו: וְהָיוּ
לְאֶחָד מִבְּנֵי שִׁבְטֵי בְנֵי־יִשְׂרָאֵל לְנָשִׁים וְנִגְרְעָה נַחֲלָתָן
מִנַּחֲלַת אֲבֹתֵינוּ וְנוֹסַף עַל נַחֲלַת הַמַּטֶּה אֲשֶׁר תִּהְיֶינָה

35:33 הַדָּם הוּא יַחֲנִיף אֶת־הָאָרֶץ *Blood pollutes the land* – The root *ḥ-n-f,* which appears twice in this verse and nowhere else in the Mosaic books, means "to pollute," "to soil," "to dirty," "to defile." There is something fundamentally blemished about a world in which murder goes unpunished. The book of Numbers draws to a close, then, with a statement of one of the fundamentals of Judaism: the sanctity of human life. As the people approach the land that will become holy, they are reminded: "You shall not pollute the land in which you live; blood pollutes the land" (Num. 35:33). With these words we are brought back almost to the beginning of the human story, to the scene in which the first child, Kayin, murders the second, Hevel, and is told by God, "The voice of your brother's blood cries out to Me from the land" (Gen. 4:10). Likewise we recall the central law of the covenant with Noaḥ: "One who sheds the blood of man, by man shall his blood be shed, for in God's image man was made" (9:6). Since the human person is the image of God, murder is not merely a crime; it is sacrilege. It defiles the land. It desecrates something holy, namely human life itself.

THE DAUGHTERS OF TZELOFḤAD – EPILOGUE

In Parashat Pinḥas we read of how the five daughters of Tzelofḥad came to

4 away from the allotted portion of our inheritance. When
the Israelites observe the Jubilee, their inheritance will
be added to that of the tribe into which they married;
their inheritance will be taken away from the inheritance
5 of our forefathers' tribe." Then Moshe, at the LORD's
word, commanded the Israelites: "What the tribe of
6 Yosef's descendants say is right. This is the word that the
LORD has commanded to Tzelofḥad's daughters: They
may marry whomever they wish as long as they marry
7 within a clan of their father's tribe, so that the Israelites'
inheritance does not pass from one tribe to another. Thus
the Israelites will each stay attached to the inheritance
8 of their ancestral tribes. Every daughter among the
Israelite tribes who inherits land must marry a member
of her father's tribe, so that the Israelites may possess
9 the inheritance of their ancestors. No inheritance may
pass from one tribe to another; each Israelite tribe shall
10 remain attached to its own inheritance." Tzelofḥad's
11 daughters did as the LORD commanded Moshe. Maḥla, MAFTIR
Tirtza, Ḥogla, Milka, and Noa, Tzelofḥad's daughters,
12 were each married to men who were their cousins. They
thus married into the families of Menashe son of Yosef,
and their inheritance remained within the tribe of their

develop our complex, vivid, face-to-face interactions and identities. This domain is known as civil society and a strong civil society is essential to liberty. We have rights as individuals; we have identities as members of communities. The existence of something like tribes is fundamental to a free society.

That is the Torah's point in dividing the story of the daughters of Tzelofḥad. The first part, in Pinḥas, is about individual rights, the rights of Tzelofḥad's daughters to a share in the land. The second, at the end of the book, is about group rights, the right of the tribe of Menashe to its territory.

A culture based solely on individual rights will undermine families, communities, traditions, loyalties, and shared codes of reverence and restraint. We should be free to live, worship, and identify as we choose. But despite its emphasis on the individual, Judaism also insists on the value of those institutions that preserve and protect our identities as members of groups. Honoring both is delicate, difficult, and necessary. Numbers ends by showing us how.

ד לָהֶם וּמִגּוֹרַל נַחֲלָתֵנוּ יִגָּרַע׃ וְאִם־יִהְיֶה הַיֹּבֵל לִבְנֵי יִשְׂרָאֵל
וְנוֹסְפָה נַחֲלָתָן עַל נַחֲלַת הַמַּטֶּה אֲשֶׁר תִּהְיֶינָה לָהֶם
ה וּמִנַּחֲלַת מַטֵּה אֲבֹתֵינוּ יִגָּרַע נַחֲלָתָן׃ וַיְצַו מֹשֶׁה אֶת־בְּנֵי
יִשְׂרָאֵל עַל־פִּי יְהוָה לֵאמֹר כֵּן מַטֵּה בְנֵי־יוֹסֵף דֹּבְרִים׃
ו זֶה הַדָּבָר אֲשֶׁר־צִוָּה יְהוָה לִבְנוֹת צְלָפְחָד לֵאמֹר לַטּוֹב
בְּעֵינֵיהֶם תִּהְיֶינָה לְנָשִׁים אַךְ לְמִשְׁפַּחַת מַטֵּה אֲבִיהֶם
ז תִּהְיֶינָה לְנָשִׁים׃ וְלֹא־תִסֹּב נַחֲלָה לִבְנֵי יִשְׂרָאֵל מִמַּטֶּה
אֶל־מַטֶּה כִּי אִישׁ בְּנַחֲלַת מַטֵּה אֲבֹתָיו יִדְבְּקוּ בְּנֵי
ח יִשְׂרָאֵל׃ וְכָל־בַּת יֹרֶשֶׁת נַחֲלָה מִמַּטּוֹת בְּנֵי יִשְׂרָאֵל
לְאֶחָד מִמִּשְׁפַּחַת מַטֵּה אָבִיהָ תִּהְיֶה לְאִשָּׁה לְמַעַן
ט יִירְשׁוּ בְּנֵי יִשְׂרָאֵל אִישׁ נַחֲלַת אֲבֹתָיו׃ וְלֹא־תִסֹּב נַחֲלָה
מִמַּטֶּה לְמַטֶּה אַחֵר כִּי־אִישׁ בְּנַחֲלָתוֹ יִדְבְּקוּ מַטּוֹת
י בְּנֵי יִשְׂרָאֵל׃ כַּאֲשֶׁר צִוָּה יְהוָה אֶת־מֹשֶׁה כֵּן עָשׂוּ בְּנוֹת
יא צְלָפְחָד׃ וַתִּהְיֶינָה מַחְלָה תִרְצָה וְחָגְלָה וּמִלְכָּה וְנֹעָה בְּנוֹת מפטיר
יב צְלָפְחָד לִבְנֵי דֹדֵיהֶן לְנָשִׁים׃ מִמִּשְׁפְּחֹת בְּנֵי־מְנַשֶּׁה בֶן־
יוֹסֵף הָיוּ לְנָשִׁים וַתְּהִי נַחֲלָתָן עַל־מַטֵּה מִשְׁפַּחַת אֲבִיהֶן׃

anticlimactic note? Numbers as a book is about individuals. It begins with a census, whose purpose is to "lift the heads" (in the literal Hebrew) of the Israelites. This is the unusual locution the Torah uses to convey that God orders a census to tell the people that they each count (see note on Num. 1:2). The book also focuses on the psychology of individuals. We read of Moshe's despair, of Aharon and Miriam's criticism of him, of the spies who lacked the courage to come back with a positive report, and of the malcontents, led by Koraḥ, who challenged Moshe's leadership. We read of Yehoshua and Kalev, Eldad and Meidad, Datan and Aviram, Zimri and Pinḥas, Balak and Bilam.

Against this backdrop we can understand the claim of Tzelofḥad's daughters. They were invoking their rights as individuals. Recognizing the justice of the women's cause, God affirmed their rights as individuals. But society is not built on individuals alone. We each have a series of identities, based partly on family background, partly on occupation, partly on locality and community. These "mediating structures," larger than the individual but smaller than the state, are where we

13 father's clan. All these are the commandments and laws
that the LORD gave through Moshe to the Israelites on the
plains of Moav, by the Jordan, across from Yeriḥo.

The haftara for Parashat Masei is on page 1588.
Read this haftara even when it is Rosh Ḥodesh Av.

---

command respect. Finally, after the story of Bilam comes the absolute nadir, when the Israelite men bring disaster on themselves by acts of immorality and idolatry. Complete chaos reigns in the camp, ended only by an act of violent zealotry on the part of Pinḥas.

After this stark contrast between order and chaos comes part 3, chapters 26–36, in which a new beginning is made, starting symbolically with a new census and a new generation. From here on, there are no rebellions. Order prevails. There are provisions for the sacrifices to be brought at their appointed times. The land is apportioned between the tribes. Levitical towns and cities of refuge are designated. Claims such as those of Tzelofḥad's daughters (ch. 27) and the heads of their tribe (ch. 36) are resolved peaceably, as is a potential conflict between the rest of the people and the Reubenites and Gadites. There is an orderly transition from Moshe's leadership to his successor Yehoshua. Battles are fought and won. The long journey is nearing its end, all its stages enumerated and recorded. For all the intervening chaos, order wins in the end.

The journey has not been only physical, a walk across the desert. It has been psychological, moral, and spiritual. It has taken as long as the time needed for human beings to change. Freedom, the Torah candidly acknowledges, is immensely demanding. It is *avoda*, hard work. It is striking that the Torah uses the same Hebrew word to describe slavery to Pharaoh and servitude to God. There is all the difference in the world between being enslaved to a human ruler and serving the Creator of the universe who made us all in His image, but the difference is not that the one is hard and the other is easy. They are both hard work, but one breaks the spirit, the other lifts and exalts it. A free society is a spiritual achievement. Maintaining liberty is as challenging today as it was in the days of Moshe. The book of Numbers remains one of its classic texts.

יג אֵלֶּה הַמִּצְוֺת וְהַמִּשְׁפָּטִים אֲשֶׁר צִוָּה יְהוָה בְּיַד־מֹשֶׁה אֶל־
בְּנֵי יִשְׂרָאֵל בְּעַרְבֹת מוֹאָב עַל יַרְדֵּן יְרֵחוֹ׃

The הפטרה *for* פרשת מסעי *is on page 1589.*
Read this הפטרה *even when it is* ראש חודש אב.

NUMBERS: THE NARRATIVE STRUCTURE

There have been times when the book of Numbers has resembled a bricolage of texts pasted together with no overarching structure or theme. Many of its laws read as if they more properly belong to Leviticus. Other passages read like repetitions of stories we encountered in the book of Exodus. Then there is the sheer overwhelming negativity of the narratives, culminating at Baal Peor in a complete breakdown of all that was supposed to characterize the Israelites as "a kingdom of priests and a holy nation" (Ex. 19:6). What is Numbers about? What hope is there to be rescued from this cumulative tale of failure and faithlessness? What is its overarching theme?

The central question of the Torah is how freedom and order, the essential elements in God's creation of the universe, can coexist in the universes human beings create (see Ex. 40, "Exodus: The Narrative Structure").

Understanding this, we notice that the book of Numbers is divided into three sections. The first, chapters 1–10, shows the Israelites preparing to begin the second half of their journey. The tribes are numbered. They are encamped, in precise formation, around the Sanctuary. There is a series of laws designed to maintain the purity of the camp and ward off potential threats to its peace. There is a lengthy account of the offerings brought by the tribes at the inauguration of the Sanctuary, each stated in the same words as if to avoid any favoritism. It is almost as if the Torah were describing the Israelites the way it describes the cosmos in the first chapter of Genesis, everything in its due proportion and proper place.

Then, in chapters 11–25, comes the chaos: dissension in the camp, complaints and criticism. The attempt to prepare the people for entry into the land by sending spies ends in disaster. The people panic and rebel. Kalev and Yehoshua attempt to calm them and fail. Next comes the story of the Koraḥ rebellion, a tale of the chaos that results when authority is challenged and ceases to

דברים
DEUTERONOMY

power or a land (though it longs for and is promised both) but on words – the words of God to Israel and the acceptance of those words by Israel. *So long as the word exists, Israel exists; and because God is eternal and never revokes His word, Israel will always exist.* Because Israel's very being as a nation is constituted by *devarim*, the "words" of God, there is always the possibility and promise of return. Israel, alone among the nations of the world, survives the loss of power and land because there is something it will never lose: God's word given and received in love. "Take words…" – the words of the covenant – "with you and return to the Lord" (Hos. 14:3). Israel survived because it never lost the words that bound it to God and God to it. That was the basis of its survival in exile. Those "words" were never rescinded. Hence Israel never lost the promise of return.

So the decision to call the fifth and final book of the Torah *Devarim* brought together in a single word the three main themes of the book: the uniqueness of Moshe as a prophet, the uniqueness of Israel as a nation, and the uniqueness of Jewish history as a narrative of exile and return. The book of *Devarim*, "words," is the supreme expression of the power of the word to link heaven and earth, God and a people, in an unbreakable bond of mutual loyalty.

THE BOOK OF DEUTERONOMY

The Hebrew names of the Mosaic books convey important insights into the nature of the book. The fifth book of the Torah is named in Hebrew *Devarim*, "words," taken from the opening verse. The whole of Torah is "words." What, then, is the connection between the title of this particular book and its contents?

The first connection is Moshe himself. He is a man transformed. Recall his words to God at the burning bush at the very outset of his mission: "Then Moshe said to the LORD, 'Please, my LORD, I am not a man of words (*ish devarim*).... I am slow of speech and tongue'" (Ex. 4:10). Of Moshe alone – "very humble, more so than any other man on earth" (Num. 12:3) – could it be said that his words, *devarim*, were the words of God. It was precisely because he said, "I am not a man of words" that he became the man of Devarim, the one whose words were not his own but those of the Divine Presence, the *Shekhina*, speaking through his lips – the most eloquent spokesman of God in all history.

The second significance of *devarim*, "words," is that it is the supreme expression of the politics of the word: a society founded on the basis of a covenant, a text, a set of mutual promises, by which God and His people pledge themselves in loyalty to one another.

The third significance is that Israel's existence as a nation is not based on

Parashat Devarim

1 1 These are the words that Moshe spoke to all Israel east of

---

century. It was then, under the twin influence of the Reformation and the spread of printing, that Europeans for the first time read the Hebrew Bible for themselves, in their homes and in their own language. Western freedom is biblical freedom.

Covenantal responsibility does not arise all at once. God makes one covenant with Noaḥ. He makes a further one with Avraham, and He makes a third with the Israelites at Sinai. The covenant with Noaḥ is entirely unilateral. God speaks, issuing certain rules, and nothing more is required from Noaḥ himself. The covenant with Avraham requires Avraham to perform an act – circumcision – for himself and the male members of his family. The covenant with the Israelites at Sinai is more demanding still in that God insists that Moshe indicate the nature of the agreement to the Israelites, and only when they agree, which they do three times (Ex. 19:8; 24:3, 7), does the covenant have force.

This is the key covenant of the Torah, and in principle should be its culmination. But it turned out not to be so. Despite the fact that the Jewish people agreed three times to accept the terms on which God was to become their sovereign, they were not yet ready for such responsibility. The story of the golden calf demonstrated that they were still in an age of magical thinking in which people do what the gods require and gods produce the outcome the people desire. It took the long journey through the desert to grow into an *ethic of responsibility*.

The covenants of Noaḥ, Avraham, and Sinai began with an act of divine initiative. The fourth, which comprises the whole of the book of Deuteronomy, is undertaken by human initiative. It is Moshe who rehearses and recites the whole content and context of the covenant. That is why Deuteronomy is the turning point in Jewish history. It marks the move from divine initiative to human responsibility.

Deuteronomy is the book of the covenant, the center point of Jewish theology. It aims at the construction of a society worthy of being a home for the Divine Presence – one that will moralize its members, inspire others, and serve as a role model of what might be achieved were humanity as a whole to worship the God who made us all in His image. "These are the words" of the covenant initiated by Moshe.

1:1 כָּל־יִשְׂרָאֵל *All Israel* – Rabbi Efrayim Luntschitz (1550–1619), in his commentary *Keli Yakar,* noted that the phrase *kol Yisrael,* which appears eleven times in Deuteronomy, exists nowhere else in the Mosaic books. Until now the Israelites

פרשת דברים

א א אֵלֶּה הַדְּבָרִים אֲשֶׁר דִּבֶּר מֹשֶׁה אֶל־כָּל־יִשְׂרָאֵל בְּעֵבֶר א

DEVARIM

The book of Deuteronomy as a whole is structured on the model of a covenant, and represents Moshe's renewal of the Sinai covenant with the next generation, who would enter the Promised Land and there create a covenant-based society. Accordingly, our *parasha* opens with the first two elements of a covenant document: a preamble identifying the speaker and context (Deut. 1:1–5) and a historical prologue recalling the events that led to the covenant and its renewal (beginning at 1:6).

The preamble identifies the time and place: the last weeks of Moshe's life, with the people encamped by the banks of the Jordan. Moshe recalls his appointments of leaders, the sending of the spies, and the people's failure of nerve that led to the forty-year stay in the wilderness. Moving to more recent episodes, he reminds the people of their victories over Moav and Ammon and the settlement of their land by the tribes of Reuven and Gad and part of Menashe. The *parasha* ends with Moshe's description of his appointment of, and encouragement to, Yehoshua as his successor. Moshe's role changes, in these last weeks of his life, as he becomes the great exemplar of the teacher as hero.

"THESE ARE THE WORDS"

The last book of the Ḥumash is the foundational text of covenantal politics, that is, a political order created out of words. Daniel Elazar, the political scientist who pioneered the study of covenantal politics, explains that there are three fundamental types of political structure, differentiated by the way they come into existence. The first is by conquest, the second is by organic development, and the third, born in ancient Israel, is covenant. "Covenantal foundings" suggests Elazar, "emphasize the deliberate coming together of humans as equals to establish bodies politic in such a way that all reaffirm their fundamental equality and retain their basic rights."

If conquest represents the politics of power, and organic development the politics of the elite, covenant is the politics of the word. It involves a document to which all sides agree to be bound. Deuteronomy defines Israel as a nation uniquely brought into being by a mutually binding pledge between a people and God in which God adopts the people as His own, and the people in turn agree to be bound to His authority and word.

Covenant is central to the emergence of free societies in the West. It is no accident that covenantal politics – movements rooted in the equality of dignity and shared responsibility of all citizens – emerged in the seventeenth

the Jordan, in the wilderness; in the Arava across from
Suf, between Paran and Tofel, Lavan, Ḥatzerot, and Di
2 Zahav. By way of Mount Se'ir, it takes eleven days to cross
3 from Ḥorev to Kadesh Barnea. In the fortieth year, on the
first day of the eleventh month, Moshe spoke to the
Israelites exactly as the Lord had commanded him
4 regarding them, after he had defeated Siḥon, king of the
Amorites, who lived in Ḥeshbon, and Og, king of Bashan,
5 who lived in Ashtarot and in Edre'i. On the east bank of
the Jordan, in the land of Moav, Moshe began to expound

Moshe, in this dramatic rereading, has been transformed into counsel for the defense. Yes, he says to God, the people committed a sin. But it was You who gave them the opportunity and the temptation. Without gold, they could not have made the calf. Who told them to ask their Egyptian neighbors for gold? It was You (Ex. 3:22, 11:2, 12:35). This was not something they did of their own accord. Therefore You must not blame them. Please, instead, forgive them.

We hear, in this aggadic passage, one of the most striking and humane motifs in rabbinic thought. It is called *limmud zekhut*, the act of judging favorably or arguing the case for the defense. It means placing a positive construction on events, pleading a cause, setting forth the case for mercy, or at least mitigation of sentence.

The Sages arranged for this *limmud zekhut* to occur specifically on *Shabbat Ḥazon*, the Sabbath before the Ninth of Av. They introduced into their reading of the first verse of *Devarim*, the *parasha* always read at this time of the year, a note of defense. It is true that Israel sinned, nowhere more so than when they made the golden calf, but do not blame them, says Moshe. They had gold only because You told them to take it. Moshe, often the Israelites' greatest critic, here becomes attorney for the defense. Thus the Sages brought a note of hope into what otherwise might have been the Sabbath of despair.

We are a self-critical people. The Tanakh is the most self-critical of all national literatures. We know our failings, and there is something admirable about this honesty. But it must never leave us bereft of hope. Jewish leadership, as the Sages understood it, is about giving expression to love, respect, and even awe for the Jewish people, who – though it has come through an unparalleled history of suffering – still survives, still flourishes, and still bears witness to the living God. We are not short of critics, internal and external. What we need by way of balance is the voice of those who are *melamed zekhut*, who see our faults but see our virtues also.

1:5 הוֹאִיל מֹשֶׁה בֵּאֵר אֶת־הַתּוֹרָה הַזֹּאת *Moshe began to expound this Law* – Over the last month of his life, Moshe, so to speak, changes career. He shifts his relationship

הַיַּרְדֵּן בַּמִּדְבָּר בָּעֲרָבָה מוֹל סוּף בֵּין־פָּארָן וּבֵין־תֹּפֶל וְלָבָן
ב וַחֲצֵרֹת וְדִי זָהָב׃ אַחַד עָשָׂר יוֹם מֵחֹרֵב דֶּרֶךְ הַר־שֵׂעִיר עַד
ג קָדֵשׁ בַּרְנֵעַ׃ וַיְהִי בְּאַרְבָּעִים שָׁנָה בְּעַשְׁתֵּי־עָשָׂר חֹדֶשׁ
בְּאֶחָד לַחֹדֶשׁ דִּבֶּר מֹשֶׁה אֶל־בְּנֵי יִשְׂרָאֵל כְּכֹל אֲשֶׁר צִוָּה
ד יְהוָה אֹתוֹ אֲלֵהֶם׃ אַחֲרֵי הַכֹּתוֹ אֵת סִיחֹן מֶלֶךְ הָאֱמֹרִי אֲשֶׁר
יוֹשֵׁב בְּחֶשְׁבּוֹן וְאֵת עוֹג מֶלֶךְ הַבָּשָׁן אֲשֶׁר־יוֹשֵׁב בְּעַשְׁתָּרֹת
ה בְּאֶדְרֶעִי׃ בְּעֵבֶר הַיַּרְדֵּן בְּאֶרֶץ מוֹאָב הוֹאִיל מֹשֶׁה בֵּאֵר

---

water, and gave them shelter. In the land of Israel, God will still be with them, but only rarely in the form of miracles. No longer will it be God serving the people, giving them all they need. It will be the people serving God. The nation will be defined by the covenant their parents made at Mount Sinai. It will be their constitution, their mission, their task, their destiny. They are about to change from a group of individuals with a common ancestry to a nation bound by collective responsibility. God does not choose, nor does He make a covenant with, individuals as individuals. He makes a covenant with an entire people, righteous and not-yet-righteous alike. This is the "all Israel" being addressed for the first time here.

1:1 דִי זָהָב *Di Zahav* – Di Zahav is the name of a place, but it has not been mentioned before. However, the name itself is suggestive. Di Zahav means "enough gold." Might there not be a subtle reference here to an episode which involved gold – namely, the golden calf, the worst sin of the previous generation? On this slender basis, the Sages (Berakhot 32a) built a daring interpretation.

have been described as *Bnei Yisrael*, literally "the children of Israel." Now for the first time they are no longer "the children of Israel" – they are simply "Israel." Until now, they have been linked by biological descent. They have a common ancestor: Yaakov, who was given the name Yisrael. They are part of the same family tree.

Now, Moshe is preparing the Israelites for a new mode of existence. They are no longer children, but are about to become moral adults. Their unity is no longer simply a matter of a common past; rather, they are to create a shared future. They are no longer to exist in a state of dependency – relying on Moshe and through him, God, to provide for their needs, welfare, and safety. Henceforth, they will have to take responsibility for one another.

Through this subtle linguistic shift, Moshe indicates that once the Israelites cross the Jordan they will become a nation, not just a family. They will have to fight wars, defend themselves, institute systems of justice and welfare, and learn the necessity for, as well as the limits of, politics.

None of that is necessary in the wilderness. God provided their needs, fought their battles, sent them food and

6 this Law: "The LORD our God spoke to us at Ḥorev; He
7 said: You have settled long enough at this mountain. Start
out and advance into the hill country of the Amorites and
all the neighboring regions – the Arava, the hill country,
the lowlands, the Negev, and the seacoast – the land of
the Canaanites and the Lebanon, as far as the Euphrates
8 River. See: I have set the land before you. Go in and take
possession of the land that the LORD swore He would
give to your ancestors – to Avraham, Yitzḥak, and
9 Yaakov – and to their descendants after them. At that
time I said to you, 'I cannot bear the burden of you alone.
10 The LORD your God has increased your numbers: today SHENI
11 you are as numerous as the stars of the heavens. May the
LORD, God of your ancestors, multiply you again a
12 thousandfold and bless you, as He has promised. But how
can I bear alone all your problems, your burdens, your
13 disputes? Choose for yourselves men who are wise,
discerning, and known to your tribes, and I will appoint
14 them as your leaders.' You answered me, 'The plan you
15 propose is a good one.' So I took the leaders of your tribes,
wise men and well known, and appointed them to be

---

always read on the Sabbath before the Ninth of Av. We can hear the verbal parallel between Moshe's exclamation, "How (*eikha*) can I bear" and the opening outcry of the Book of Lamentations: "How (*eikha*) the city that overflowed with people sits alone!" (Lam. 1:1). *Eikha* is not the only word these two verses have in common. They also share the word *levadi/badad*, meaning "lonely," "alone," "solitary." In both places, aloneness gives rise to a lament, for Judaism is a religion, not of isolated individuals, but of a people. Today's secular culture is highly individualistic, and contemporary forms of spirituality reflect that fact. Nowadays we often think that God is about me, not us. Nor is this new. Religion has often been thought of as a private engagement of the soul. Dean Inge defined it as "what a person does in his solitude." Walter Savage Landor called solitude the "audience chamber of God." Judaism holds the opposite. "It is not good for man to be alone."

Faith does not belong to the private recesses of the soul. It belongs to the life we live together. Where people meet is where God is to be found. As against the hyper-individualism of our late capitalist society, we find God in the "we," not the "I".

ו אֶת־הַתּוֹרָה הַזֹּאת לֵאמֹר׃ יְהוָה אֱלֹהֵינוּ דִּבֶּר אֵלֵינוּ בְּחֹרֵב
ז לֵאמֹר רַב־לָכֶם שֶׁבֶת בָּהָר הַזֶּה׃ פְּנוּ ׀ וּסְעוּ לָכֶם וּבֹאוּ הַר
הָאֱמֹרִי וְאֶל־כָּל־שְׁכֵנָיו בָּעֲרָבָה בָהָר וּבַשְּׁפֵלָה וּבַנֶּגֶב וּבְחוֹף
הַיָּם אֶרֶץ הַכְּנַעֲנִי וְהַלְּבָנוֹן עַד־הַנָּהָר הַגָּדֹל נְהַר־פְּרָת׃
ח רְאֵה נָתַתִּי לִפְנֵיכֶם אֶת־הָאָרֶץ בֹּאוּ וּרְשׁוּ אֶת־הָאָרֶץ אֲשֶׁר
נִשְׁבַּע יְהוָה לַאֲבֹתֵיכֶם לְאַבְרָהָם לְיִצְחָק וּלְיַעֲקֹב לָתֵת
ט לָהֶם וּלְזַרְעָם אַחֲרֵיהֶם׃ וָאֹמַר אֲלֵכֶם בָּעֵת הַהִוא לֵאמֹר
י לֹא־אוּכַל לְבַדִּי שְׂאֵת אֶתְכֶם׃ יְהוָה אֱלֹהֵיכֶם הִרְבָּה אֶתְכֶם
יא וְהִנְּכֶם הַיּוֹם כְּכוֹכְבֵי הַשָּׁמַיִם לָרֹב׃ יְהוָה אֱלֹהֵי אֲבוֹתֵכֶם שני
יֹסֵף עֲלֵיכֶם כָּכֶם אֶלֶף פְּעָמִים וִיבָרֵךְ אֶתְכֶם כַּאֲשֶׁר דִּבֶּר
יב יג לָכֶם׃ אֵיכָה אֶשָּׂא לְבַדִּי טָרְחֲכֶם וּמַשַּׂאֲכֶם וְרִיבְכֶם׃ הָבוּ
לָכֶם אֲנָשִׁים חֲכָמִים וּנְבֹנִים וִידֻעִים לְשִׁבְטֵיכֶם וַאֲשִׂימֵם
יד בְּרָאשֵׁיכֶם׃ וַתַּעֲנוּ אֹתִי וַתֹּאמְרוּ טוֹב־הַדָּבָר אֲשֶׁר־דִּבַּרְתָּ
טו לַעֲשׂוֹת׃ וָאֶקַּח אֶת־רָאשֵׁי שִׁבְטֵיכֶם אֲנָשִׁים חֲכָמִים וִידֻעִים
וָאֶתֵּן אֹתָם רָאשִׁים עֲלֵיכֶם שָׂרֵי אֲלָפִים וְשָׂרֵי מֵאוֹת וְשָׂרֵי

with the people. Moshe the liberator, the lawgiver, the worker of miracles, the intermediary between the Israelites and God, now becomes the figure known to Jewish memory: *Moshe Rabbeinu*, "Moshe, our teacher." That is how Deuteronomy begins – "Moshe began to expound this Law" (Deut. 1:5). Scripture uses a verb, *be'er*, that we have not encountered in this sense in the Torah and which appears only one more time, toward the end of the book: "On the boulders you shall write very clearly (*ba'er hetev*) all the words of this Law" (27:8). Moshe wants to explain, to make clear. He wants the people to understand that Judaism is not a religion of mysteries intelligible only to the few. It is a "heritage of Yaakov's [entire] assembly" (33:4). Moshe becomes, in the last month of his life, the master educator. At this defining moment of his life, Moshe understands that, though he will not be *physically* with the people when they enter the Promised Land, he can still be with them intellectually and emotionally if he gives them the teachings to take with them into the future. Moshe now becomes the pioneer of perhaps the single greatest contribution of Judaism to the concept of leadership: the idea of *the teacher as hero*.

1:12 אֵיכָה אֶשָּׂא לְבַדִּי *How can I bear alone* – As noted, the *parasha* of Devarim is

▶

leaders over you, chiefs of thousands, chiefs of hundreds,
chiefs of fifties, chiefs of tens, and officials, for your tribes.
16 I charged your judges at that time: 'Hear the disputes
among your people and judge fairly, between one person
17 and another, whether Israelite or migrant. Do not show
partiality in judgment: listen equally to the small and the
great. Do not be intimidated by any man, for judgment
belongs to God. Any case that is too difficult for you,
18 bring to me, and I will hear it.' I charged you at that time,
19 with all the things you are to do. Then we set out from
Ḥorev and journeyed through all that vast and fearful
wilderness that you have seen, toward the hill country of
the Amorites, as the Lord our God had commanded us,
20 until we reached Kadesh Barnea. I said to you, 'You have
reached the hill country of the Amorites, which the Lord
21 our God is giving us. See, the Lord your God has laid the
land out before you. Go up, take possession, as the Lord,
God of your ancestors, has promised. Do not fear and do

life. That needs law: law that represents justice, honoring all humans alike; law that judges impartially between rich and poor, powerful and powerless; law that links God, its giver, to us, its interpreters; law that alone allows freedom to coexist with order, so that my freedom is not bought at the cost of yours.

1:17 לֹא־תַכִּירוּ פָנִים בַּמִּשְׁפָּט *Do not show partiality in judgment* – The literal meaning of the phrase is "Do not recognize faces in judgment." That is to say, do not let kinship distort the course of justice. From the negative we can infer the positive, that when it comes not to justice but compassion, to "recognize a face" requires us to show the kind of care that family members should to one another.

1:17 הַמִּשְׁפָּט לֵאלֹהִים הוּא *Judgment belongs to God* – The Torah insists that justice is not a human artifact. Because judgment belongs to God, it must never be compromised – by fear, bribery, or favoritism. Judaism is a religion of love: you shall love the Lord your God; you shall love your neighbor as yourself; you shall love the stranger for you were once strangers. But it is also a religion of justice, for without justice, love corrupts (who would not bend the rules, if he could, to favor those he loves?). It is also a religion of compassion, for without compassion law itself can generate inequity. Justice plus compassion equals *tzedek*, the first precondition of a decent society.

טז חֲמִשִּׁים וְשָׂרֵי עֲשָׂרֹת וְשֹׁטְרִים לְשִׁבְטֵיכֶם: וָאֲצַוֶּה אֶת־
שֹׁפְטֵיכֶם בָּעֵת הַהִוא לֵאמֹר שָׁמֹעַ בֵּין־אֲחֵיכֶם וּשְׁפַטְתֶּם
יז צֶדֶק בֵּין־אִישׁ וּבֵין־אָחִיו וּבֵין גֵּרוֹ: לֹא־תַכִּירוּ פָנִים בַּמִּשְׁפָּט
כַּקָּטֹן כַּגָּדֹל תִּשְׁמָעוּן לֹא תָגוּרוּ מִפְּנֵי־אִישׁ כִּי הַמִּשְׁפָּט
לֵאלֹהִים הוּא וְהַדָּבָר אֲשֶׁר יִקְשֶׁה מִכֶּם תַּקְרִבוּן אֵלַי
יח וּשְׁמַעְתִּיו: וָאֲצַוֶּה אֶתְכֶם בָּעֵת הַהִוא אֵת כָּל־הַדְּבָרִים
יט אֲשֶׁר תַּעֲשׂוּן: וַנִּסַּע מֵחֹרֵב וַנֵּלֶךְ אֵת כָּל־הַמִּדְבָּר הַגָּדוֹל
וְהַנּוֹרָא הַהוּא אֲשֶׁר רְאִיתֶם דֶּרֶךְ הַר הָאֱמֹרִי כַּאֲשֶׁר צִוָּה
כ יְהוָה אֱלֹהֵינוּ אֹתָנוּ וַנָּבֹא עַד קָדֵשׁ בַּרְנֵעַ: וָאֹמַר אֲלֵכֶם
כא בָּאתֶם עַד־הַר הָאֱמֹרִי אֲשֶׁר־יְהוָה אֱלֹהֵינוּ נֹתֵן לָנוּ: רְאֵה
נָתַן יְהוָה אֱלֹהֶיךָ לְפָנֶיךָ אֶת־הָאָרֶץ עֲלֵה רֵשׁ כַּאֲשֶׁר דִּבֶּר

1:16 וּשְׁפַטְתֶּם צֶדֶק *Judge fairly* – Three features mark Judaism as a distinctive faith. First is the radical idea that when God reveals Himself to humans He does so in the form of law. In the ancient world, God was power. In Judaism, God is order, and order presupposes law. In the natural world of cause and effect, order takes the form of scientific law. But in the human world, where we have free will, order takes the form of moral law. Torah means "direction," "guidance," "teaching"; it also means "law." The most basic meaning of the most fundamental principle of Judaism, *Torah min haShamayim*, "Torah from Heaven," is that God, not humans, is the source of binding law.

Second, we are charged with being interpreters of the law. That is our responsibility as heirs and guardians of the *Torah Shebe'al Peh*, the Oral Tradition.

The Written Torah is *min haShamayim*, "from Heaven," but about the Oral Torah the Talmud insists: *Lo bashamayim hi*, "It is not in heaven" (Bava Metzia 59b). Judaism is a continuing conversation between the Giver of the law and the interpreters of the law. That is part of what the Talmud means when it says that "every judge who delivers a true judgment becomes a partner with the Holy One, blessed be He, in the work of creation" (Shabbat 10a).

Third, fundamental to Judaism is education, and fundamental to education is instruction in Torah, that is, the law. To be a Jewish child is to be, in the British phrase, "learned in the law." Why? Because Judaism is not just about spirituality. It is not simply a code for the salvation of the soul. It is a set of instructions for the creation of what Rabbi Aharon Lichtenstein called "societal beatitude." It is about bringing God into the shared spaces of our collective

22 not be dismayed.' Then all of you drew close to me and SHELISHI
said, 'Let us send men ahead of us to explore the land and
bring back a report to us about the route by which we
23 should go up and the towns we will come to.' The plan
seemed good to me, so I selected twelve of you, one man
24 from each tribe. They set out and went up into the hill
country. And, arriving at the Eshkol Ravine, they spied it
25 out. They took some of the fruit of the land, which they
brought down to us, and they brought us back a report:
26 'The land that the LORD our God is giving us is good.' But
you were unwilling to go up, and you rebelled against the
27 word of the LORD your God. You grumbled in your tents
and said, 'It is because the LORD hates us that He has

---

completely different activities, so why does the account in our *parasha* present what happened as a spying mission, while the account in Shelaḥ emphatically does not?

Addressing the discrepancy between the two accounts of the spies, Rabbi David Tzvi Hoffman argued that the account in Shelaḥ tells us what happened. The account in our *parasha,* on the other hand, was meant not to inform but to warn. They belong to different literary genres with different purposes. Parashat Shelaḥ is a historical narrative; our *parasha* is a sermon.

Rashi, however, explains that the two accounts, here and in Shelaḥ, are not two different versions of the same event. They are the same version of the same event split in two, half told there, half here. It was the people who requested spies (as stated here). Moshe took their request to God. God acceded to the request, but as a concession. "You may send," says God, not "You must send."

However, in granting permission, God made a provision. The people asked for spies. But God did not give Moshe permission to send spies. He specifically used the verb *latur,* meaning, He allowed the men to tour the land and testify that it is a good and fertile land, flowing with milk and honey.

The people did not need spies. As Moshe says, throughout the wilderness years God has been going "ahead of you on your journey, in fire by night and cloud by day, to seek out [*latur*] a place for you to camp and show you the way you should go" (1:33). They did, however, need eyewitness testimony of the beauty and fruitfulness of the land to which they had been traveling and for which they would have to fight. It is because they allowed the news that made them fearful to override that direct testimony to beauty that they were condemned never themselves to "see the good land" (1:35).

כב יהוה אֱלֹהֵי אֲבֹתֶיךָ לָךְ אַל־תִּירָא וְאַל־תֵּחָת׃ וַתִּקְרְבוּן שלישי
אֵלַי כֻּלְּכֶם וַתֹּאמְרוּ נִשְׁלְחָה אֲנָשִׁים לְפָנֵינוּ וְיַחְפְּרוּ־לָנוּ
אֶת־הָאָרֶץ וְיָשִׁבוּ אֹתָנוּ דָּבָר אֶת־הַדֶּרֶךְ אֲשֶׁר נַעֲלֶה־
כג בָּהּ וְאֵת הֶעָרִים אֲשֶׁר נָבֹא אֲלֵיהֶן׃ וַיִּיטַב בְּעֵינַי הַדָּבָר
כד וָאֶקַּח מִכֶּם שְׁנֵים עָשָׂר אֲנָשִׁים אִישׁ אֶחָד לַשָּׁבֶט׃ וַיִּפְנוּ
כה וַיַּעֲלוּ הָהָרָה וַיָּבֹאוּ עַד־נַחַל אֶשְׁכֹּל וַיְרַגְּלוּ אֹתָהּ׃ וַיִּקְחוּ
בְיָדָם מִפְּרִי הָאָרֶץ וַיּוֹרִדוּ אֵלֵינוּ וַיָּשִׁבוּ אֹתָנוּ דָבָר וַיֹּאמְרוּ
כו טוֹבָה הָאָרֶץ אֲשֶׁר־יהוה אֱלֹהֵינוּ נֹתֵן לָנוּ׃ וְלֹא אֲבִיתֶם
כז לַעֲלֹת וַתַּמְרוּ אֶת־פִּי יהוה אֱלֹהֵיכֶם׃ וַתֵּרָגְנוּ בְאָהֳלֵיכֶם

RETELLING THE STORY OF THE SPIES

Early in Moshe's final speech, he recalls the episode of the spies, the reason why the people's parents were denied the opportunity to enter the land, so that the next generation might learn the lessons of that event. But the story of the spies that he tells here is very different from the version in Parashat Shelaḥ (Num. 13–14), which described the events as they happened almost thirty-nine years earlier. The discrepancies between the two accounts are glaring and numerous. I want to focus only on two.

First, who proposed sending the spies? In Parashat Shelaḥ, it was God who told Moshe to do so: "Then the LORD spoke to Moshe: 'Send out men'" (Num. 13:1–2). In our *parasha*, it was the people who requested it: "Then all of you drew close to me and said, 'Let us send men'" (Deut. 1:22). The English does not convey the sense of menace in the original here. They came, says Rashi, "in a crowd," without respect, protocol, or order. They were a mob. This mirrors the people's behavior at the beginning of the story of the golden calf: "When the people saw that Moshe was long delayed in coming down the mountain, they *gathered around Aharon* and said to him…" (Ex. 32:1).

In Numbers (ch. 14, "The Spies' Report") we noted a second discrepancy: In our *parasha*, the people said, "Let us send men ahead of us to explore (*veyaḥperu*) the land" (Deut. 1:22). The twelve men "went up into the hill country. And, arriving at the Eshkol Ravine, they spied it out (*vayeraglu*)" (1:24). In other words, our *parasha* uses the two Hebrew verbs, *laḥpor* and *leragel*, that mean to spy.

But the account in Shelaḥ conspicuously does not mention spying. Instead, thirteen times, it uses the verb *latur*, which means to tour, explore, travel, inspect. According to Malbim, *latur* means to seek out what is good about a place. *Laḥpor* and *leragel* mean to seek out what is weak, vulnerable, exposed, defenseless. Touring and spying are

brought us out of the land of Egypt, to hand us over to the
28 Amorites to destroy us. Where can we go? Our brothers
have melted all the bravado from our hearts by telling us,
"The people are stronger and taller than we are. The cities
are large and walled to the sky; we even saw the Anakites
29 there."' And I said to you, 'Do not be terrified and have no
30 fear of them. The LORD your God, who is going before
you, He will fight for you, just as He did for you in Egypt
31 before your eyes, and in the wilderness, where you saw
the LORD your God carry you as a man carries his child,
all along the way you traveled until you reached this place.
32 And yet despite all this, you show no faith in the LORD
33 your God, who goes ahead of you on your journey – in
fire by night, and cloud by day – to seek out a place for
you to camp and show you the way you should go.'
34 Hearing your words, the LORD became furious and swore
35 an oath: 'Not one man of this evil generation shall see the
36 good land that I swore to give your ancestors, except for
Kalev son of Yefuneh. He will see it, and to him and his
descendants I will give the land on which he set foot,
37 because he followed the LORD wholeheartedly.' And
because of you, the LORD was enraged even with me, and
38 said, 'You also shall not enter it. Yehoshua son of Nun,

the land and come back and testify to its goodness. Moshe's error, if the analysis here is correct, was a subtle one, failing to make clear the difference between a spying mission and a morale-boosting eyewitness account of the land. In the face of a mob, a leader is not always in control of the situation. True leadership is impossible against the madness of crowds. Moshe implies that God was angry with him for not showing stronger leadership, but it was the people – or rather, their parents – who made that leadership impossible.

There is a famous saying of the Sages: "Make for yourself a teacher and acquire for yourself a friend" (Avot 1:6). You make a teacher by being willing to learn. You make a leader by being willing to follow. When people are unwilling to follow, even the greatest leader cannot lead. That is one reason why Yehoshua was chosen to be Moshe's successor. There were other distinguished candidates. But Yehoshua, serving Moshe throughout the wilderness years, is a role model of what it is to be a follower.

וַתֹּאמְרוּ בְּשִׂנְאַת יהוה אֹתָנוּ הוֹצִיאָנוּ מֵאֶרֶץ מִצְרָיִם לָתֵת
אֹתָנוּ בְּיַד הָאֱמֹרִי לְהַשְׁמִידֵנוּ׃ אָנָה ׀ אֲנַחְנוּ עֹלִים אַחֵינוּ כח
הֵמַסּוּ אֶת־לְבָבֵנוּ לֵאמֹר עַם גָּדוֹל וָרָם מִמֶּנּוּ עָרִים גְּדֹלֹת
וּבְצוּרֹת בַּשָּׁמָיִם וְגַם־בְּנֵי עֲנָקִים רָאִינוּ שָׁם׃ וָאֹמַר אֲלֵכֶם כט
לֹא־תַעַרְצוּן וְלֹא־תִירְאוּן מֵהֶם׃ יהוה אֱלֹהֵיכֶם הַהֹלֵךְ ל
לִפְנֵיכֶם הוּא יִלָּחֵם לָכֶם כְּכֹל אֲשֶׁר עָשָׂה אִתְּכֶם בְּמִצְרַיִם
לְעֵינֵיכֶם׃ וּבַמִּדְבָּר אֲשֶׁר רָאִיתָ אֲשֶׁר נְשָׂאֲךָ יהוה אֱלֹהֶיךָ לא
כַּאֲשֶׁר יִשָּׂא־אִישׁ אֶת־בְּנוֹ בְּכָל־הַדֶּרֶךְ אֲשֶׁר הֲלַכְתֶּם עַד־
בֹּאֲכֶם עַד־הַמָּקוֹם הַזֶּה׃ וּבַדָּבָר הַזֶּה אֵינְכֶם מַאֲמִינִם בַּיהוה לב
אֱלֹהֵיכֶם׃ הַהֹלֵךְ לִפְנֵיכֶם בַּדֶּרֶךְ לָתוּר לָכֶם מָקוֹם לַחֲנֹתְכֶם לג
בָּאֵשׁ ׀ לַיְלָה לַרְאֹתְכֶם בַּדֶּרֶךְ אֲשֶׁר תֵּלְכוּ־בָהּ וּבֶעָנָן יוֹמָם׃
וַיִּשְׁמַע יהוה אֶת־קוֹל דִּבְרֵיכֶם וַיִּקְצֹף וַיִּשָּׁבַע לֵאמֹר׃ אִם־ לד לה
יִרְאֶה אִישׁ בָּאֲנָשִׁים הָאֵלֶּה הַדּוֹר הָרָע הַזֶּה אֵת הָאָרֶץ
הַטּוֹבָה אֲשֶׁר נִשְׁבַּעְתִּי לָתֵת לַאֲבֹתֵיכֶם׃ זוּלָתִי כָּלֵב בֶּן־יְפֻנֶּה לו
הוּא יִרְאֶנָּה וְלוֹ־אֶתֵּן אֶת־הָאָרֶץ אֲשֶׁר דָּרַךְ־בָּהּ וּלְבָנָיו יַעַן
אֲשֶׁר מִלֵּא אַחֲרֵי יהוה׃ גַּם־בִּי הִתְאַנַּף יהוה בִּגְלַלְכֶם לֵאמֹר לז
גַּם־אַתָּה לֹא־תָבֹא שָׁם׃ יְהוֹשֻׁעַ בִּן־נוּן הָעֹמֵד לְפָנֶיךָ הוּא לח

1:37 גַּם־בִּי הִתְאַנַּף יהוה *The Lord was enraged even with me* – How could the episode of the spies have been Moshe's fault? It wasn't he who proposed sending them. Ramban suggests that Moshe was simply saying that, like the spies and the people, he too was condemned to die in the wilderness. Alternatively, he was hinting that no one should be able to say that Moshe avoided the fate of the generation he led.

However, Abrabanel offers a fascinating reading. Perhaps the reason Moshe and Aharon were not permitted to enter the land was not because of the episode of water and the rock at Kadesh. That is intended to distract attention from their real sins. Aharon's sin was the golden calf. Moshe's mistake was the episode of the spies. The hint to this is in Moshe's words here, "Because of you, the Lord was enraged even with me."

As we saw, different verbs are used here and in Shelaḥ (ch. 1, "Retelling the Story of the Spies," above). God did *not* give Moshe permission to send spies. He specifically used the verb *latur*, meaning, He allowed the men to tour

who stands before you – he shall enter there. Encourage
39 him, for he will give Israel their possession. As for your REVI'I
little ones, whom you thought would be taken captive,
and your children who do not yet know good from bad,
they shall enter, and I will give it to them, and they will
40 take possession of it. But you – turn around and set out
41 into the wilderness by way of the Sea of Reeds.' And you
answered me: 'We have sinned against the LORD! We will
go up and fight, as the LORD our God commanded us.' So
each of you strapped on your weapons thinking that it
42 would be easy to go up into the hill country. "The LORD
said to me, 'Tell them: Do not go up and do not fight, for
I will not be with you. Do not be struck down by your
43 enemies.' And I told you, but you would not listen. You
rebelled against the word of the LORD and willfully went
44 up into the hill country. The Amorites who lived in those
hills came out against you and chased you like a swarm of
45 bees. In Se'ir they struck you down, as far as Ḥorma. You
came back and wept before the LORD, but the LORD
46 would not listen to you, nor pay you any heed. And so
you remained at Kadesh for a long time – all that time
2 1 that you were there. Then we turned and journeyed back
into the wilderness, by way of the Sea of Reeds, as the
LORD had told me and, for a long time, made our way
2 around Mount Se'ir. Then the LORD said to me: ḤAMISHI
3 'You have circled about this hill country long enough
4 now. Turn to the north. And give the people these orders:
You are about to pass through the territory of your
kinsmen, the descendants of Esav, who live in Se'ir. They
5 will be afraid of you, but be very careful. Do not provoke
them, for I will not give you even a foot of their land; I
6 have given Mount Se'ir to Esav as his possession. You
shall pay them in silver for the food you eat, pay them
7 silver for the water that you buy from them and drink. For
the LORD your God has blessed you in all the work of
your hands. He has watched over your wanderings
through this vast wilderness. These forty years the LORD

לט יָבֹא שָׁמָּה אֹתוֹ חַזֵּק כִּי־הוּא יַנְחִלֶנָּה אֶת־יִשְׂרָאֵל׃ וְטַפְּכֶם רביעי
אֲשֶׁר אֲמַרְתֶּם לָבַז יִהְיֶה וּבְנֵיכֶם אֲשֶׁר לֹא־יָדְעוּ הַיּוֹם טוֹב
מ וָרָע הֵמָּה יָבֹאוּ שָׁמָּה וְלָהֶם אֶתְּנֶנָּה וְהֵם יִירָשׁוּהָ׃ וְאַתֶּם
מא פְּנוּ לָכֶם וּסְעוּ הַמִּדְבָּרָה דֶּרֶךְ יַם־סוּף׃ וַתַּעֲנוּ ׀ וַתֹּאמְרוּ
אֵלַי חָטָאנוּ לַיהוָה אֲנַחְנוּ נַעֲלֶה וְנִלְחַמְנוּ כְּכֹל אֲשֶׁר־צִוָּנוּ
יְהוָה אֱלֹהֵינוּ וַתַּחְגְּרוּ אִישׁ אֶת־כְּלֵי מִלְחַמְתּוֹ וַתָּהִינוּ לַעֲלֹת
מב הָהָרָה׃ וַיֹּאמֶר יְהוָה אֵלַי אֱמֹר לָהֶם לֹא תַעֲלוּ וְלֹא תִלָּחֲמוּ
מג כִּי אֵינֶנִּי בְּקִרְבְּכֶם וְלֹא תִּנָּגְפוּ לִפְנֵי אֹיְבֵיכֶם׃ וָאֲדַבֵּר אֲלֵיכֶם
וְלֹא שְׁמַעְתֶּם וַתַּמְרוּ אֶת־פִּי יְהוָה וַתָּזִדוּ וַתַּעֲלוּ הָהָרָה׃
מד וַיֵּצֵא הָאֱמֹרִי הַיֹּשֵׁב בָּהָר הַהוּא לִקְרַאתְכֶם וַיִּרְדְּפוּ אֶתְכֶם
כַּאֲשֶׁר תַּעֲשֶׂינָה הַדְּבֹרִים וַיַּכְּתוּ אֶתְכֶם בְּשֵׂעִיר עַד־חָרְמָה׃
מה וַתָּשֻׁבוּ וַתִּבְכּוּ לִפְנֵי יְהוָה וְלֹא־שָׁמַע יְהוָה בְּקֹלְכֶם וְלֹא
מו הֶאֱזִין אֲלֵיכֶם׃ וַתֵּשְׁבוּ בְקָדֵשׁ יָמִים רַבִּים כַּיָּמִים אֲשֶׁר
ב א יְשַׁבְתֶּם׃ וַנֵּפֶן וַנִּסַּע הַמִּדְבָּרָה דֶּרֶךְ יַם־סוּף כַּאֲשֶׁר דִּבֶּר
ב יְהוָה אֵלָי וַנָּסָב אֶת־הַר־שֵׂעִיר יָמִים רַבִּים׃ וַיֹּאמֶר ב חמישי
ג יְהוָה אֵלַי לֵאמֹר׃ רַב־לָכֶם סֹב אֶת־הָהָר הַזֶּה פְּנוּ לָכֶם
ד צָפֹנָה׃ וְאֶת־הָעָם צַו לֵאמֹר אַתֶּם עֹבְרִים בִּגְבוּל אֲחֵיכֶם
בְּנֵי־עֵשָׂו הַיֹּשְׁבִים בְּשֵׂעִיר וְיִירְאוּ מִכֶּם וְנִשְׁמַרְתֶּם מְאֹד׃
ה אַל־תִּתְגָּרוּ בָם כִּי לֹא־אֶתֵּן לָכֶם מֵאַרְצָם עַד מִדְרַךְ כַּף־רָגֶל
ו כִּי־יְרֻשָּׁה לְעֵשָׂו נָתַתִּי אֶת־הַר שֵׂעִיר׃ אֹכֶל תִּשְׁבְּרוּ מֵאִתָּם
ז בַּכֶּסֶף וַאֲכַלְתֶּם וְגַם־מַיִם תִּכְרוּ מֵאִתָּם בַּכֶּסֶף וּשְׁתִיתֶם׃ כִּי
יְהוָה אֱלֹהֶיךָ בֵּרַכְךָ בְּכֹל מַעֲשֵׂה יָדֶךָ יָדַע לֶכְתְּךָ אֶת־הַמִּדְבָּר

your God has been with you: you have lacked for nothing.'
8 So we passed by, away from our kinsmen, the descendants
of Esav who live in Se'ir. We turned from the route of the
Arava, away from Eilat and Etzyon Gever, and
journeyed in the direction of the Wilderness of Moav.
9 Then the LORD said to me: 'Do not mistreat the Moabites
or provoke them to war, for I will not give you any of their
land as a possession: I have given Ar to the descendants of
10 Lot for a possession.'" The Emim lived there originally – a
11 strong and numerous people, as tall as the Anakites. Like
the Anakites, they are considered Refaim, but the
12 Moabites call them Emim. Horites used to live in Se'ir, but
the descendants of Esav dispossessed them, destroying
them and settling in their place, as Israel did in the land
13 that the LORD gave them as a possession. "'Now, get up
and cross the Zered Stream.' So we crossed the Zered
14 Stream. From the time we left Kadesh Barnea to the time
we crossed the Zered Stream was thirty-eight years – until
the entire generation of warriors had perished from the
15 camp – as the LORD had sworn to them. And the LORD's
hand was against them to trouble them from the camp
16 until they had all perished. When all those warriors
17 among the people had died, the LORD spoke to
18 me: 'Today you are going to cross the border of Moav at
19 Ar. When you come to the Amonites, do not harass them
or provoke them to war, for I will not give you any of the

the disintegration of personality. As with individuals, so with a nation: it has a continuing identity to the extent that it can remember where it came from and who its ancestors were. We remember not what is objectively most remarkable but what shapes who we are. My predecessor as chief rabbi, Lord Jakobovits, pointed out that the word *yizkor*, the name given to the traditional Jewish prayer for the dead, is associated in the Torah with the future. "God remembered Noaḥ" (Gen. 8:1) and brought him out on dry land. He "remembered Avraham" (19:29) and rescued his nephew Lot from the destruction of the cities of the plain. "God remembered Raḥel" (30:23) and gave her a child. We remember for the sake of the future, and for life.

הַגָּדֹל הַזֶּה זֶה ׀ אַרְבָּעִים שָׁנָה יְהוָה אֱלֹהֶיךָ עִמָּךְ לֹא חָסַרְתָּ
ח דָּבָר: וַנַּעֲבֹר מֵאֵת אַחֵינוּ בְנֵי־עֵשָׂו הַיֹּשְׁבִים בְּשֵׂעִיר מִדֶּרֶךְ
הָעֲרָבָה מֵאֵילַת וּמֵעֶצְיֹן גָּבֶר   וַנֵּפֶן וַנַּעֲבֹר דֶּרֶךְ
ט מִדְבַּר מוֹאָב: וַיֹּאמֶר יְהוָה אֵלַי אַל־תָּצַר אֶת־מוֹאָב וְאַל־
תִּתְגָּר בָּם מִלְחָמָה כִּי לֹא־אֶתֵּן לְךָ מֵאַרְצוֹ יְרֻשָּׁה כִּי לִבְנֵי־
י לוֹט נָתַתִּי אֶת־עָר יְרֻשָּׁה: הָאֵמִים לְפָנִים יָשְׁבוּ בָהּ עַם גָּדוֹל
יא וְרַב וָרָם כָּעֲנָקִים: רְפָאִים יֵחָשְׁבוּ אַף־הֵם כָּעֲנָקִים וְהַמֹּאָבִים
יב יִקְרְאוּ לָהֶם אֵמִים: וּבְשֵׂעִיר יָשְׁבוּ הַחֹרִים לְפָנִים וּבְנֵי עֵשָׂו
יִירָשׁוּם וַיַּשְׁמִידוּם מִפְּנֵיהֶם וַיֵּשְׁבוּ תַּחְתָּם כַּאֲשֶׁר עָשָׂה
יג יִשְׂרָאֵל לְאֶרֶץ יְרֻשָּׁתוֹ אֲשֶׁר־נָתַן יְהוָה לָהֶם: עַתָּה קֻמוּ
יד וְעִבְרוּ לָכֶם אֶת־נַחַל זָרֶד וַנַּעֲבֹר אֶת־נַחַל זָרֶד: וְהַיָּמִים
אֲשֶׁר־הָלַכְנוּ ׀ מִקָּדֵשׁ בַּרְנֵעַ עַד אֲשֶׁר־עָבַרְנוּ אֶת־נַחַל זֶרֶד
שְׁלֹשִׁים וּשְׁמֹנֶה שָׁנָה עַד־תֹּם כָּל־הַדּוֹר אַנְשֵׁי הַמִּלְחָמָה
טו מִקֶּרֶב הַמַּחֲנֶה כַּאֲשֶׁר נִשְׁבַּע יְהוָה לָהֶם: וְגַם יַד־יְהוָה הָיְתָה
טז בָּם לְהֻמָּם מִקֶּרֶב הַמַּחֲנֶה עַד תֻּמָּם: וַיְהִי כַאֲשֶׁר־תַּמּוּ כָּל־
יז אַנְשֵׁי הַמִּלְחָמָה לָמוּת מִקֶּרֶב הָעָם: וַיְדַבֵּר יְהוָה
יח אֵלַי לֵאמֹר: אַתָּה עֹבֵר הַיּוֹם אֶת־גְּבוּל מוֹאָב אֶת־עָר:
יט וְקָרַבְתָּ מוּל בְּנֵי עַמּוֹן אַל־תְּצֻרֵם וְאַל־תִּתְגָּר בָּם כִּי לֹא־

2:10 וָרָם כָּעֲנָקִים *As tall as the Anakites* – The Anakites and Og, so vivid in the legends of the time, are no longer a helpful reference point to us. Moshe's story, however, repeated year after year, is as alive to us now as it ever was. The passing references to bygone peoples emphasize the profound difference between history and memory. History is *his* story – an event that happened sometime else to someone else. Memory is *my* story – something that happened to me and is part of who I am. History is information. Memory, by contrast, is part of identity. I can study the history of other peoples, cultures, and civilizations. They deepen my knowledge and broaden my horizons. But they do not make a claim on me. They are the past as past. Memory is the past as present, as it lives on in me. Without memory there can be no identity.

Alzheimer's disease, the progressive atrophying of memory function, is also

land of the Amonites as a possession: I have given it as a
20 possession to the descendants of Lot.'" This too was
considered a land of Refaim. Refaim lived there originally,
21 although the Amonites call them Zamzumim – a strong
and numerous people, as tall as the Anakites. The LORD
destroyed them so that the Amonites could dispossess
22 them and settle in their place, just as He did for the
descendants of Esav, who live in Se'ir, by destroying the
Horites before them so that they could dispossess them
and settle in their place to this day, where they still
23 remain; likewise the Avim, who had lived in villages as far
as Aza – the Caftorites, emerging from Caftor, destroyed
24 them and settled in their place. "'Set out and cross the
Arnon Stream. I have given over Siḥon, the Amorite king
of Ḥeshbon, with his land, into your hands. Begin to take
25 possession of it; enter into battle with him. This day I am
beginning to put the terror and fear of you upon the
peoples everywhere under the skies. When they hear
26 reports of you, they will tremble in dread of you.' So I sent
messengers from the Kedemot wilderness to Siḥon, king
27 of Ḥeshbon, with an offer of peace: 'Let us pass through
your land. We will stay on the main road, turning aside
28 neither to the right nor to the left. Provide us with food
and we will pay for it in silver and eat; give us water and
we will pay for it in silver and drink. Only let us pass
29 through on foot – just as the descendants of Esav living in

---

War, for Rambam, is never mandated except when the effort to make peace has been tried, and failed. Moshe's actions here express this fundamental principle.

2:29 כַּאֲשֶׁר עָשׂוּ־לִי בְּנֵי עֵשָׂו הַיֹּשְׁבִים בְּשֵׂעִיר *Just as the descendants of Esav living in Se'ir... did for us* – There is nothing in this passage to remind us of the eternal strife between the two nations predicted before their birth ("Two nations are inside your womb.... People will overpower people, and the greater shall the younger serve" [Gen. 25:23]). In recording the aid given by Esav's descendants to the Jewish people, the Torah teaches an important message: heroes have their faults and non-heroes their virtues, and these virtues are important to God. "The Holy One, blessed be He, does not withhold the reward of any creature," said the Sages (Pesaḥim 118a).

אֶתֵּן מֵאֶרֶץ בְּנֵי־עַמּוֹן לְךָ יְרֻשָּׁה כִּי לִבְנֵי־לוֹט נְתַתִּיהָ יְרֻשָּׁה׃
כ אֶרֶץ־רְפָאִים תֵּחָשֵׁב אַף־הִוא רְפָאִים יָשְׁבוּ־בָהּ לְפָנִים
כא וְהָעַמֹּנִים יִקְרְאוּ לָהֶם זַמְזֻמִּים׃ עַם גָּדוֹל וְרַב וָרָם כַּעֲנָקִים
כב וַיַּשְׁמִידֵם יהוה מִפְּנֵיהֶם וַיִּירָשֻׁם וַיֵּשְׁבוּ תַחְתָּם׃ כַּאֲשֶׁר
עָשָׂה לִבְנֵי עֵשָׂו הַיֹּשְׁבִים בְּשֵׂעִיר אֲשֶׁר הִשְׁמִיד אֶת־הַחֹרִי
כג מִפְּנֵיהֶם וַיִּירָשֻׁם וַיֵּשְׁבוּ תַחְתָּם עַד הַיּוֹם הַזֶּה׃ וְהָעַוִּים
הַיֹּשְׁבִים בַּחֲצֵרִים עַד־עַזָּה כַּפְתֹּרִים הַיֹּצְאִים מִכַּפְתֹּר
כד הִשְׁמִידֻם וַיֵּשְׁבוּ תַחְתָּם׃ קוּמוּ סְּעוּ וְעִבְרוּ אֶת־נַחַל אַרְנֹן
רְאֵה נָתַתִּי בְיָדְךָ אֶת־סִיחֹן מֶלֶךְ־חֶשְׁבּוֹן הָאֱמֹרִי וְאֶת־אַרְצוֹ
כה הָחֵל רָשׁ וְהִתְגָּר בּוֹ מִלְחָמָה׃ הַיּוֹם הַזֶּה אָחֵל תֵּת פַּחְדְּךָ
וְיִרְאָתְךָ עַל־פְּנֵי הָעַמִּים תַּחַת כָּל־הַשָּׁמָיִם אֲשֶׁר יִשְׁמְעוּן
כו שִׁמְעֲךָ וְרָגְזוּ וְחָלוּ מִפָּנֶיךָ׃ וָאֶשְׁלַח מַלְאָכִים מִמִּדְבַּר קְדֵמוֹת
כז אֶל־סִיחוֹן מֶלֶךְ חֶשְׁבּוֹן דִּבְרֵי שָׁלוֹם לֵאמֹר׃ אֶעְבְּרָה
כח בְאַרְצֶךָ בַּדֶּרֶךְ בַּדֶּרֶךְ אֵלֵךְ לֹא אָסוּר יָמִין וּשְׂמֹאול׃ אֹכֶל
בַּכֶּסֶף תַּשְׁבִּרֵנִי וְאָכַלְתִּי וּמַיִם בַּכֶּסֶף תִּתֶּן־לִי וְשָׁתִיתִי רַק
כט אֶעְבְּרָה בְרַגְלָי׃ כַּאֲשֶׁר עָשׂוּ־לִי בְּנֵי עֵשָׂו הַיֹּשְׁבִים בְּשֵׂעִיר

2:26 וָאֶשְׁלַח מַלְאָכִים... אֶל־סִיחוֹן מֶלֶךְ חֶשְׁבּוֹן דִּבְרֵי שָׁלוֹם *I sent messengers... to Siḥon, king of Ḥeshbon, with an offer of peace* – Rashi points out something remarkable here: that even though God does not tell Moshe to offer peace to Siḥon, Moshe takes it upon himself to do so. Despite the apparent militarism of the early texts of Judaism, their underlying value was always peace. Already in Leviticus we find the blessing "I will grant peace in the land... and through that land no sword shall pass" (26:6). The priestly benedictions end with a prayer for peace (Num. 6:26). Rambam summarized the laws about initiating a war as follows:

> No war, either permitted or obligatory [such as a war of self-defense] may be initiated without first offering terms of peace.... Joshua sent three messages before entering the land: the first, "Whoever wishes to flee, let him flee"; the second, "Whoever wishes to make peace, let him make peace"; the third, "Whoever wishes to make war, let him make war." (*Hilkhot Melakhim UMilḥemoteihem* 9:1)

Se'ir and the Moabites living in Ar did for us – until we
cross the Jordan into the land that the Lord our God is
30 giving us.' But Siḥon, king of Ḥeshbon, refused to let us
pass through, for the Lord your God had hardened his
spirit and made his heart defiant in order to give him over
31 into your hands, as He has now done. The Lord SHISHI
said to me, 'I have begun to give Siḥon and his land over to
32 you. Go: begin to conquer and possess his land.' Then
Siḥon and all his people came out to meet us in battle at
33 Yahatz. The Lord our God gave him over to us, and we
struck him down, together with his sons and all his people.
34 At that time we captured all his towns and completely
destroyed them, men, women, and children alike, leaving
35 not a single survivor. Only the livestock and the spoil of
the cities we captured did we keep as booty for ourselves.
36 From Aroer on the banks of the Arnon Stream, including
the town in the ravine, as far as Gilad, not one city was
unattainable to us. The Lord our God gave us all of them.
37 But you did not touch the land of the Amonites, not the
land around the Yabok Stream, nor the towns of the hill
country that the Lord our God commanded us to leave.
3 1 After this, we turned and journeyed along the road toward
Bashan. Og, king of Bashan, with all his people came out
2 to Edre'i to engage us in battle. But the Lord said to me,
'Do not be afraid of him, for I have given him into your
hand, with all his people and his land. Do to him what you
did to Siḥon, king of the Amorites, who lived in Ḥeshbon.'
3 So the Lord our God also gave over to us Og, king of
Bashan, and all his people. We struck him down until not
4 a single survivor remained. We captured all his towns at
that time; there was not a single town we did not take
from them – sixty towns, the entire region of Argov, Og's
5 kingdom in Bashan. And these were all fortress towns
with high walls, gates, and bars – there were a great many
6 unwalled towns besides. And we utterly destroyed them,
as we had done to Siḥon, king of Ḥeshbon, in each town
7 utterly destroying them: men, women, and children. All

וְהַמּוֹאָבִים הַיֹּשְׁבִים בְּעָר עַד אֲשֶׁר־אֶעֱבֹר אֶת־הַיַּרְדֵּן
ל אֶל־הָאָרֶץ אֲשֶׁר־יְהוָה אֱלֹהֵינוּ נֹתֵן לָנוּ׃ וְלֹא אָבָה סִיחֹן
מֶלֶךְ חֶשְׁבּוֹן הַעֲבִרֵנוּ בּוֹ כִּי־הִקְשָׁה יְהוָה אֱלֹהֶיךָ אֶת־רוּחוֹ
לא וְאִמֵּץ אֶת־לְבָבוֹ לְמַעַן תִּתּוֹ בְיָדְךָ כַּיּוֹם הַזֶּה׃ וַיֹּאמֶר ג ששי
יְהוָה אֵלַי רְאֵה הַחִלֹּתִי תֵּת לְפָנֶיךָ אֶת־סִיחֹן וְאֶת־אַרְצוֹ
לב הָחֵל רָשׁ לָרֶשֶׁת אֶת־אַרְצוֹ׃ וַיֵּצֵא סִיחֹן לִקְרָאתֵנוּ הוּא
לג וְכָל־עַמּוֹ לַמִּלְחָמָה יָהְצָה׃ וַיִּתְּנֵהוּ יְהוָה אֱלֹהֵינוּ לְפָנֵינוּ וַנַּךְ
לד אֹתוֹ וְאֶת־בָּנָו וְאֶת־כָּל־עַמּוֹ׃ וַנִּלְכֹּד אֶת־כָּל־עָרָיו בָּעֵת
הַהִוא וַנַּחֲרֵם אֶת־כָּל־עִיר מְתִם וְהַנָּשִׁים וְהַטָּף לֹא הִשְׁאַרְנוּ
לה שָׂרִיד׃ רַק הַבְּהֵמָה בָּזַזְנוּ לָנוּ וּשְׁלַל הֶעָרִים אֲשֶׁר לָכָדְנוּ׃
לו מֵעֲרֹעֵר אֲשֶׁר עַל־שְׂפַת־נַחַל אַרְנֹן וְהָעִיר אֲשֶׁר בַּנַּחַל
וְעַד־הַגִּלְעָד לֹא הָיְתָה קִרְיָה אֲשֶׁר שָׂגְבָה מִמֶּנּוּ אֶת־הַכֹּל
לז נָתַן יְהוָה אֱלֹהֵינוּ לְפָנֵינוּ׃ רַק אֶל־אֶרֶץ בְּנֵי־עַמּוֹן לֹא קָרָבְתָּ
כָּל־יַד נַחַל יַבֹּק וְעָרֵי הָהָר וְכֹל אֲשֶׁר־צִוָּה יְהוָה אֱלֹהֵינוּ׃
ג א וַנֵּפֶן וַנַּעַל דֶּרֶךְ הַבָּשָׁן וַיֵּצֵא עוֹג מֶלֶךְ־הַבָּשָׁן לִקְרָאתֵנוּ הוּא
ב וְכָל־עַמּוֹ לַמִּלְחָמָה אֶדְרֶעִי׃ וַיֹּאמֶר יְהוָה אֵלַי אַל־תִּירָא
אֹתוֹ כִּי בְיָדְךָ נָתַתִּי אֹתוֹ וְאֶת־כָּל־עַמּוֹ וְאֶת־אַרְצוֹ וְעָשִׂיתָ
לּוֹ כַּאֲשֶׁר עָשִׂיתָ לְסִיחֹן מֶלֶךְ הָאֱמֹרִי אֲשֶׁר יוֹשֵׁב בְּחֶשְׁבּוֹן׃
ג וַיִּתֵּן יְהוָה אֱלֹהֵינוּ בְּיָדֵנוּ גַּם אֶת־עוֹג מֶלֶךְ־הַבָּשָׁן וְאֶת־כָּל־
ד עַמּוֹ וַנַּכֵּהוּ עַד־בִּלְתִּי הִשְׁאִיר־לוֹ שָׂרִיד׃ וַנִּלְכֹּד אֶת־כָּל־עָרָיו
בָּעֵת הַהִוא לֹא הָיְתָה קִרְיָה אֲשֶׁר לֹא־לָקַחְנוּ מֵאִתָּם שִׁשִּׁים
ה עִיר כָּל־חֶבֶל אַרְגֹּב מַמְלֶכֶת עוֹג בַּבָּשָׁן׃ כָּל־אֵלֶּה עָרִים
בְּצֻרֹת חוֹמָה גְבֹהָה דְּלָתַיִם וּבְרִיחַ לְבַד מֵעָרֵי הַפְּרָזִי הַרְבֵּה
ו מְאֹד׃ וַנַּחֲרֵם אוֹתָם כַּאֲשֶׁר עָשִׂינוּ לְסִיחֹן מֶלֶךְ חֶשְׁבּוֹן
ז הַחֲרֵם כָּל־עִיר מְתִם הַנָּשִׁים וְהַטָּף׃ וְכָל־הַבְּהֵמָה וּשְׁלַל

the livestock and the spoil of the towns we kept as booty
8 for ourselves. At that time, then, we took from the two
kings of the Amorites the land beyond the Jordan, from
9 the Arnon Stream to Mount Ḥermon" – the Sidonians
10 call Ḥermon Siryon, and the Amorites call it Senir – "all
the towns of the plateau, the whole of Gilad, and the
whole of Bashan, as far as Salkha and Edre'i, towns of
11 Og's kingdom in Bashan." Only Og, king of Bashan, was
left then of the remaining Refaim. His bed, made of iron,
is still there, in Raba of the Amonites: it is nine cubits
long and four cubits wide, as measured by a man's
12 forearm. "Of the land that we took possession of at that
time, I gave to the Reubenites and Gadites the territory
from Aroer on the edge of the Arnon Stream, as well as
13 half the hill country of Gilad with its towns. To the half
tribe of Menashe I gave the rest of Gilad and all of Bashan,
Og's kingdom – the whole region of Argov: all that
portion of Bashan that used to be known as the land of
14 the Refaim." Yair of Menashe took the whole region of
Argov – that is, Bashan – as far as the border of the people
of Geshur and of Maakha – and named it after himself,
15 hamlets of Yair, as it is called to this day. "To Makhir I SHEVI'I
16 gave Gilad, and to the Reubenites and the Gadites I gave
the territory from Gilad as far as the Arnon Stream, with
the middle of the ravine as a border, and up to the Yabok
17 Stream and the Amonites' border. It included also the
Arava, with the Jordan and its banks, from the Sea of
Galilee down to the Arava Sea, the Dead Sea, with the
18 lower slopes of Pisga on the east. At that time, I charged
you: 'The LORD your God has given you this land to
possess, but all your troops must cross over armed before
19 your fellow Israelites. Only your wives, children, and
cattle – I know that you have much cattle – shall stay
20 behind in the towns I have given you, until the LORD MAFTIR

the group. They care for, and inspire others to care for, the common good. That is why this episode was of the highest consequence.

ח הֶעָרִים בַּזּוֹנוּ לָנוּ: וַנִּקַּח בָּעֵת הַהִוא אֶת־הָאָרֶץ מִיַּד שְׁנֵי
מַלְכֵי הָאֱמֹרִי אֲשֶׁר בְּעֵבֶר הַיַּרְדֵּן מִנַּחַל אַרְנֹן עַד־הַר
ט חֶרְמוֹן: צִידֹנִים יִקְרְאוּ לְחֶרְמוֹן שִׂרְיֹן וְהָאֱמֹרִי יִקְרְאוּ־לוֹ
י שְׂנִיר: כֹּל ׀ עָרֵי הַמִּישֹׁר וְכָל־הַגִּלְעָד וְכָל־הַבָּשָׁן עַד־סַלְכָה
יא וְאֶדְרֶעִי עָרֵי מַמְלֶכֶת עוֹג בַּבָּשָׁן: כִּי רַק־עוֹג מֶלֶךְ הַבָּשָׁן
נִשְׁאַר מִיֶּתֶר הָרְפָאִים הִנֵּה עַרְשׂוֹ עֶרֶשׂ בַּרְזֶל הֲלֹה הִוא
בְּרַבַּת בְּנֵי עַמּוֹן תֵּשַׁע אַמּוֹת אָרְכָּהּ וְאַרְבַּע אַמּוֹת רָחְבָּהּ
יב בְּאַמַּת־אִישׁ: וְאֶת־הָאָרֶץ הַזֹּאת יָרַשְׁנוּ בָּעֵת הַהִוא מֵעֲרֹעֵר
אֲשֶׁר־עַל־נַחַל אַרְנֹן וַחֲצִי הַר־הַגִּלְעָד וְעָרָיו נָתַתִּי לָראוּבֵנִי
יג וְלַגָּדִי: וְיֶתֶר הַגִּלְעָד וְכָל־הַבָּשָׁן מַמְלֶכֶת עוֹג נָתַתִּי לַחֲצִי
שֵׁבֶט הַמְנַשֶּׁה כֹּל חֶבֶל הָאַרְגֹּב לְכָל־הַבָּשָׁן הַהוּא יִקָּרֵא
יד אֶרֶץ רְפָאִים: יָאִיר בֶּן־מְנַשֶּׁה לָקַח אֶת־כָּל־חֶבֶל אַרְגֹּב
עַד־גְּבוּל הַגְּשׁוּרִי וְהַמַּעֲכָתִי וַיִּקְרָא אֹתָם עַל־שְׁמוֹ אֶת־
טו הַבָּשָׁן חַוֹּת יָאִיר עַד הַיּוֹם הַזֶּה: וּלְמָכִיר נָתַתִּי אֶת־הַגִּלְעָד: שביעי
טז וְלָראוּבֵנִי וְלַגָּדִי נָתַתִּי מִן־הַגִּלְעָד וְעַד־נַחַל אַרְנֹן תּוֹךְ הַנַּחַל
יז וּגְבֻל וְעַד יַבֹּק הַנַּחַל גְּבוּל בְּנֵי עַמּוֹן: וְהָעֲרָבָה וְהַיַּרְדֵּן וּגְבֻל
מִכִּנֶּרֶת וְעַד יָם הָעֲרָבָה יָם הַמֶּלַח תַּחַת אַשְׁדֹּת הַפִּסְגָּה
יח מִזְרָחָה: וָאֲצַו אֶתְכֶם בָּעֵת הַהִוא לֵאמֹר יְהוָה אֱלֹהֵיכֶם נָתַן
לָכֶם אֶת־הָאָרֶץ הַזֹּאת לְרִשְׁתָּהּ חֲלוּצִים תַּעַבְרוּ לִפְנֵי אֲחֵיכֶם
יט בְּנֵי־יִשְׂרָאֵל כָּל־בְּנֵי־חָיִל: רַק נְשֵׁיכֶם וְטַפְּכֶם וּמִקְנֵכֶם יָדַעְתִּי
כ כִּי־מִקְנֶה רַב לָכֶם יֵשְׁבוּ בְּעָרֵיכֶם אֲשֶׁר נָתַתִּי לָכֶם: עַד מפטיר

3:12 וְעָרָיו נָתַתִּי לָראוּבֵנִי וְלַגָּדִי *I gave to the the Reubenites and Gadites the territory* – Moshe here refers back to an immensely significant episode at the end of Parashat Mattot (Num. 32; see notes there). These words were the fruit of a model negotiation, and a sign of hope after the many destructive conflicts in the book of Numbers.

One of the hardest tasks of any leader – from prime ministers to parents – is conflict resolution. Yet it is also the most vital. Where there is leadership, there is long-term cohesiveness within the group, whatever the short-term problems. True leaders are the people who put the interests of the group above those of any subsection of

gives rest to your fellows as to you, and they too have
taken possession of the land that the LORD your God is
giving them beyond the Jordan. Then you may each
21 return to the land that I have given to you.' And I charged
Yehoshua also at that time: 'Your own eyes have seen all
that the LORD your God has done to these two kings; so
will the LORD do to all the kingdoms into which you are
22 about to cross. Do not fear them, for it is the LORD your
God who is fighting for you.'

The haftara for Parashat Devarim is on page 1594.

Moshe surely knows that some of his greatest achievements will not last forever. The people he has rescued will one day suffer exile and persecution again. The next time, though, they will not have a Moshe to do miracles. So he plants a vision in their minds, hope in their hearts, a discipline in their deeds, and a strength in their souls that will never fade. When leaders become educators they change lives. Judaism, with its acute concern for human dignity, favors leadership as education over leadership as power. And it began with Moshe, at the end of his life.

One of Moshe's final acts as a leader-educator is to appoint his successor, Yehoshua. It will be Yehoshua, whom Moshe has nurtured and educated as his successor, who will lead the people across the Jordan into the Promised Land. Good leaders create followers; great leaders create leaders. The paradigm case is Moshe.

אֲשֶׁר־יָנִיחַ יהוה ׀ לַאֲחֵיכֶם כָּכֶם וְיָרְשׁוּ גַם־הֵם אֶת־הָאָרֶץ
אֲשֶׁר יהוה אֱלֹהֵיכֶם נֹתֵן לָהֶם בְּעֵבֶר הַיַּרְדֵּן וְשַׁבְתֶּם אִישׁ
כא לִירֻשָּׁתוֹ אֲשֶׁר נָתַתִּי לָכֶם: וְאֶת־יְהוֹשׁוּעַ צִוֵּיתִי בָּעֵת הַהִוא
לֵאמֹר עֵינֶיךָ הָרֹאֹת אֵת כָּל־אֲשֶׁר עָשָׂה יהוה אֱלֹהֵיכֶם לִשְׁנֵי
הַמְּלָכִים הָאֵלֶּה כֵּן־יַעֲשֶׂה יהוה לְכָל־הַמַּמְלָכוֹת אֲשֶׁר אַתָּה
כב עֹבֵר שָׁמָּה: לֹא תִּירָאוּם כִּי יהוה אֱלֹהֵיכֶם הוּא הַנִּלְחָם
לָכֶם:

The הפטרה *for* פרשת דברים *is on page 1595.*

3:21 וְאֶת־יְהוֹשׁוּעַ צִוֵּיתִי *I charged Yehoshua* – By the end of the book of Numbers, Moshe's career as a leader appeared to have come to its end. Moshe seemed to have achieved everything he was destined to achieve. For him there would be no more battles to fight, no more miracles to perform, no more prayers to say on behalf of the people. It is what Moshe does next that bears the mark of greatness. For the final month of his life he stands before the assembled people, and delivers the series of addresses we know as the book of Deuteronomy or Devarim. In these addresses, he reviews the people's past and foresees their future. He gives them laws. Some he has given them before but in a different form. Others are new; he has delayed announcing them until the people are about to enter the land. Linking all these details of law and history into a single overarching vision, he teaches the people to see themselves as an *am kadosh*, a holy people, the only people whose sovereign and lawgiver is God Himself.

Parashat Vaetḥanan

3 23 At that time, I pleaded with the LORD: 'O Lord GOD,
24 You have begun to show Your servant Your greatness and
Your mighty hand; what force in heaven or earth can do
25 deeds and mighty acts like Yours! Please let me cross over
and see the good land beyond the Jordan, that good hill
26 country and the Lebanon.' But the LORD was enraged
with me because of you, and would not listen to me. 'It is
enough!' the LORD said to me. 'Never speak to Me about

Land, God did not grant him his request. He told him to stop praying. However hard or long Moshe prayed, it was not going to happen. This is the proof that prayer does not change God's mind in any simple sense. If it is good that something happens, God does not need my prayer to make it happen. If it is not good, then God will not bring it about, however hard I pray.

Prayer changes the world *because it changes us*. We pray not simply for God to fulfill our desires but in order to know what to desire. All animals act to satisfy their desires. Only human beings are capable of standing back and passing judgment on their desires. There are some desires we should not satisfy. Junk food is bad for us. So is smoking. So is wealth illicitly obtained. So is ambition achieved by betraying others. And so on. To be humanly mature is to know what to desire.

Prayer is the education of desire. The weekday *Amida*, as an example, teaches us to seek knowledge, wisdom, and understanding – not just material goods. It teaches us to want to return to God when, as happens so often, we drift in the winds of time, blown this way and that by the pressures of today. It teaches us to seek spiritual healing as well as physical health. It teaches us to seek the best not just for ourselves but also for our people and ultimately for all humanity.

Prayer opens our eyes to the wonders of the physical world. It trains us to give thanks for the sheer gift of being alive. Above all, prayer tells us we are not alone in the world.

Without a vessel to contain a blessing, there can be no blessing. If we have no receptacle to catch the rain, the rain may fall, but we will have none to drink. If we have no radio receiver, the sound waves will flow, but we will be unable to convert them into sound. God's blessings flow continuously, but unless we make ourselves into a vessel for them, they will flow elsewhere. Prayer is the act of turning ourselves into a vehicle for the Divine.

And so our *parasha* opens with a prayer that is not answered. "It is

פרשת ואתחנן

ג כג כד וָאֶתְחַנַּן אֶל־יהוה בָּעֵת הַהִוא לֵאמֹר: אֲדֹנָי יֱהֹוִה אַתָּה ד
הַחִלּוֹתָ לְהַרְאוֹת אֶת־עַבְדְּךָ אֶת־גָּדְלְךָ וְאֶת־יָדְךָ הַחֲזָקָה
אֲשֶׁר מִי־אֵל בַּשָּׁמַיִם וּבָאָרֶץ אֲשֶׁר־יַעֲשֶׂה כְמַעֲשֶׂיךָ
כה וְכִגְבוּרֹתֶךָ: אֶעְבְּרָה־נָּא וְאֶרְאֶה אֶת־הָאָרֶץ הַטּוֹבָה אֲשֶׁר
כו בְּעֵבֶר הַיַּרְדֵּן הָהָר הַטּוֹב הַזֶּה וְהַלְּבָנֹן: וַיִּתְעַבֵּר יהוה בִּי
לְמַעַנְכֶם וְלֹא שָׁמַע אֵלָי וַיֹּאמֶר יהוה אֵלַי רַב־לָךְ אַל־תּוֹסֶף

VAETḤANAN

Parashat Vaetḥanan contains some of the most sublime theological passages in the whole of Judaism. Moshe tells the people that their laws and history are unique, and will be seen as such by other nations. Their laws were given by God; their history was written by God – there is no other nation of which either can be said. Moshe then begins his second great speech. He reminds the people of the Ten Commandments and the revelation at Mount Sinai and commands them to set God at the center of their lives in the passage that became the first paragraph of the *Shema*, the supreme expression of the love of God. This love was to be more than an emotion. It was to be constantly spoken of to children, worn by men in the form of tefillin, and placed as mezuzot "on the doorposts of your houses" (Deut. 6:9).

There is much in Judaism about *what*: what is permitted, what is forbidden, what is sacred, what is secular. There is much, too, about *how*: how to learn, how to pray, how to grow in our relationship with God and with other people. In Parashat Vaetḥanan, Moshe says some of the most inspiring words ever uttered about the *why* of Jewish existence. Abrahamic monotheism believes there is an answer to the question *why*. Neither the universe nor human life is meaningless, an accident, a mere happenstance. Religious faith is faith in the meaningfulness of life.

Vaetḥanan tells us that we were called on to inspire the world. Our vocation is to be God's ambassadors to the world, giving testimony through the way we live that it is possible for a small people to survive and thrive under the most adverse conditions, to construct a society of law-governed liberty for which we all bear collective responsibility. Vaetḥanan is the mission statement of the Jewish people.

3:26 וְלֹא שָׁמַע אֵלָי *And would not listen to me* – When Moshe prayed for God to forgive the Israelites, God forgave them because God forgives. But when he prayed that he, Moshe, be allowed to cross the Jordan and enter the Promised

27 this again! Go up to the top of Pisga and gaze around you
to the west, to the north, to the south, and to the east. See
28 it with your eyes, for you will not cross this Jordan. But
charge Yehoshua, make him strong and determined, for
he will be the one to cross over at the head of this people
and who will secure their possession of the land that you
29 may only see.' And we came to rest in the valley beside
Beit Peor.
4 1 And now, Israel, listen to the decrees and laws that I am
teaching you to keep, so that you may live to enter and
take possession of the land that the LORD, God of your
2 ancestors, is giving to you. Do not add anything to that
which I command you, or subtract from it; keep the
commandments of the LORD your God with which I am
3 charging you. You saw with your own eyes what the LORD
did in the affair of Baal Peor – how the LORD your God
wiped out from among you everyone who followed Baal
4 Peor, while you, who held firmly to the LORD your God,
5 are all here living today. See: I have taught you decrees SHENI
and laws as the LORD my God commanded me, for you to
keep in the land that you are about to enter and possess.
6 Take care to keep them, for this will be your wisdom and
understanding in the eyes of the peoples: when they hear
all these decrees they will say, 'Surely this great nation is

---

Egyptians and the other peoples of his time. Moshe's contemporaries would have known far better than we do if this had been the case.…They would say that Israel is a foolish and inferior nation, because its laws were stolen from others." Moshe, suggests Luzzatto, knew that there was something different about the laws of Israel. This could not have been the case if Israel had simply adopted or adapted the practices of its time.

Whichever interpretation we take, the implication of Moshe's words is clear. The Torah would have an impact far beyond the boundaries, literal or metaphorical, of Israel. At no time in the biblical era could this be said to be true, but it did come true nonetheless. The Greeks, struck by the intensity with which Jews studied Torah, called them "a nation of philosophers." Then came Christianity and Islam, two faiths tracing their ancestry to Avraham and drawing much of their inspiration from the Hebrew Bible.

כז דַּבֵּר אֵלַי עוֹד בַּדָּבָר הַזֶּה׃ עֲלֵה ׀ רֹאשׁ הַפִּסְגָּה וְשָׂא עֵינֶיךָ
יָמָּה וְצָפֹנָה וְתֵימָנָה וּמִזְרָחָה וּרְאֵה בְעֵינֶיךָ כִּי־לֹא תַעֲבֹר
כח אֶת־הַיַּרְדֵּן הַזֶּה׃ וְצַו אֶת־יְהוֹשֻׁעַ וְחַזְּקֵהוּ וְאַמְּצֵהוּ כִּי־הוּא
יַעֲבֹר לִפְנֵי הָעָם הַזֶּה וְהוּא יַנְחִיל אוֹתָם אֶת־הָאָרֶץ אֲשֶׁר
כט תִּרְאֶה׃ וַנֵּשֶׁב בַּגָּיְא מוּל בֵּית פְּעוֹר׃
ד א וְעַתָּה יִשְׂרָאֵל שְׁמַע אֶל־הַחֻקִּים וְאֶל־הַמִּשְׁפָּטִים אֲשֶׁר
אָנֹכִי מְלַמֵּד אֶתְכֶם לַעֲשׂוֹת לְמַעַן תִּחְיוּ וּבָאתֶם וִירִשְׁתֶּם
ב אֶת־הָאָרֶץ אֲשֶׁר יְהוָה אֱלֹהֵי אֲבֹתֵיכֶם נֹתֵן לָכֶם׃ לֹא תֹסִפוּ
עַל־הַדָּבָר אֲשֶׁר אָנֹכִי מְצַוֶּה אֶתְכֶם וְלֹא תִגְרְעוּ מִמֶּנּוּ
לִשְׁמֹר אֶת־מִצְוֺת יְהוָה אֱלֹהֵיכֶם אֲשֶׁר אָנֹכִי מְצַוֶּה אֶתְכֶם׃
ג עֵינֵיכֶם הָרֹאוֹת אֵת אֲשֶׁר־עָשָׂה יְהוָה בְּבַעַל פְּעוֹר כִּי כָל־
הָאִישׁ אֲשֶׁר הָלַךְ אַחֲרֵי בַעַל־פְּעוֹר הִשְׁמִידוֹ יְהוָה אֱלֹהֶיךָ
ד מִקִּרְבֶּךָ׃ וְאַתֶּם הַדְּבֵקִים בַּיהוָה אֱלֹהֵיכֶם חַיִּים כֻּלְּכֶם הַיּוֹם׃
ה רְאֵה ׀ לִמַּדְתִּי אֶתְכֶם חֻקִּים וּמִשְׁפָּטִים כַּאֲשֶׁר צִוַּנִי יְהוָה שני
אֱלֹהָי לַעֲשׂוֹת כֵּן בְּקֶרֶב הָאָרֶץ אֲשֶׁר אַתֶּם בָּאִים שָׁמָּה
ו לְרִשְׁתָּהּ׃ וּשְׁמַרְתֶּם וַעֲשִׂיתֶם כִּי הִוא חָכְמַתְכֶם וּבִינַתְכֶם
לְעֵינֵי הָעַמִּים אֲשֶׁר יִשְׁמְעוּן אֵת כָּל־הַחֻקִּים הָאֵלֶּה וְאָמְרוּ

---

enough," says God. It is not time for Moshe to grasp after more life. It is time to climb the mountain, and survey what he has achieved.

IN THE EYES OF THE PEOPLES

According to Ramban, the meaning of the phrase "your wisdom and understanding in the eyes of the peoples" is that "the statutes and ordinances have the great benefit that they will bring honor from others to those who observe them. Even their enemies will praise them." Other nations will admire Israel's way of life.

Sforno interprets it differently: through the Torah "you will be able to refute a heretic by intellectual proofs." It is not so much that others will admire Israel as that they will acknowledge the divine source of its laws. The Jewish people will be living proof that God exists and has communicated with mankind.

Rabbi Shmuel David Luzzatto (1800–65), writing in a later age, sees the text from yet a different perspective. "This is a refutation," he writes, "of those who say that the statutes Moshe gave Israel were adopted from the

7 a wise and understanding people!' For what other great
nation has God so close to it as the Lord our God is to
8 us whenever we call out to Him? And what other great
nation has decrees and laws as just as this entire Torah
9 that I am setting before you today? But take care and be
very vigilant not to forget the things that your eyes have
seen, nor to let them fade from your mind, as long as you
live. Make known to your children and your children's
10 children, how you once stood before the Lord your God
at Ḥorev, when the Lord said to me, 'Assemble the people
for Me, and I will let them hear My words so that they
may learn to be in awe of Me as long as they live on earth,
11 and teach their children likewise.' And you came close
and stood at the foot of the mountain while the mountain
was ablaze to high heaven and shrouded in dark clouds.
12 Then the Lord spoke to you out of the fire. You heard the

---

when they hear all these decrees they will say, 'Surely this great nation is a wise and understanding people!'" (4:6).

4:6 עַם־חָכָם וְנָבוֹן *A wise and understanding people* – Judaism recognizes a dual epistemology, that there are two ways of knowing. One is called *ḥokhma*, "wisdom"; the other is Torah, "teaching," "instruction," "law," "guidance." The difference was stated clearly by the Sages: "If you are told that there is wisdom among the nations, believe it. If you are told there is Torah among the nations, do not believe it" (Eikha Rabba 2:13).

Wisdom is a biblical category. The word appears in the Tanakh some 341 times in various inflections. There are entire books dedicated to *ḥokhma*, known generically as the "wisdom literature." Wisdom is universal. We can also see this by examining where the concept of wisdom appears in the Mosaic books. In Genesis it appears solely in connection with Egypt. When Pharaoh dreams his dreams and wants to know what they mean, he summons his "sages" (Gen. 41:8). Yosef uses the word when speaking to Pharaoh, as does Pharaoh in describing Yosef ("There can be no one else as astute or as wise as you" – 41:39). It also appears in the description of Betzalel, the man who made the appurtenances of the Sanctuary. As Rambam notes in the last chapter of *Guide for the Perplexed*, one of the senses of *ḥokhma* is craftsmanship, a cultural universal. Here, when Moshe speaks of the universal significance of Torah itself – as opposed to its particular meaning to Israel – he says, "This will be your wisdom and understanding in the eyes of the peoples" (Deut. 4:6).

ז רַק עַם־חָכָם וְנָבוֹן הַגּוֹי הַגָּדוֹל הַזֶּה׃ כִּי מִי־גוֹי גָּדוֹל אֲשֶׁר־לוֹ
ח אֱלֹהִים קְרֹבִים אֵלָיו כַּיהוָה אֱלֹהֵינוּ בְּכׇל־קׇרְאֵנוּ אֵלָיו׃ וּמִי
גּוֹי גָּדוֹל אֲשֶׁר־לוֹ חֻקִּים וּמִשְׁפָּטִים צַדִּיקִם כְּכֹל הַתּוֹרָה
ט הַזֹּאת אֲשֶׁר אָנֹכִי נֹתֵן לִפְנֵיכֶם הַיּוֹם׃ רַק הִשָּׁמֶר לְךָ וּשְׁמֹר
נַפְשְׁךָ מְאֹד פֶּן־תִּשְׁכַּח אֶת־הַדְּבָרִים אֲשֶׁר־רָאוּ עֵינֶיךָ וּפֶן־
יָסוּרוּ מִלְּבָבְךָ כֹּל יְמֵי חַיֶּיךָ וְהוֹדַעְתָּם לְבָנֶיךָ וְלִבְנֵי בָנֶיךָ׃
י יוֹם אֲשֶׁר עָמַדְתָּ לִפְנֵי יהוה אֱלֹהֶיךָ בְּחֹרֵב בֶּאֱמֹר יהוה
אֵלַי הַקְהֶל־לִי אֶת־הָעָם וְאַשְׁמִעֵם אֶת־דְּבָרָי אֲשֶׁר יִלְמְדוּן
לְיִרְאָה אֹתִי כׇּל־הַיָּמִים אֲשֶׁר הֵם חַיִּים עַל־הָאֲדָמָה וְאֶת־
יא בְּנֵיהֶם יְלַמֵּדוּן׃ וַתִּקְרְבוּן וַתַּעַמְדוּן תַּחַת הָהָר וְהָהָר בֹּעֵר
יב בָּאֵשׁ עַד־לֵב הַשָּׁמַיִם חֹשֶׁךְ עָנָן וַעֲרָפֶל׃ וַיְדַבֵּר יהוה אֲלֵיכֶם
מִתּוֹךְ הָאֵשׁ קוֹל דְּבָרִים אַתֶּם שֹׁמְעִים וּתְמוּנָה אֵינְכֶם רֹאִים

Already in the twelfth century, Rambam could write (in a passage long censored and only recently restored):

> The whole world is already filled with the words of [the Christian] Messiah and the words of the commandments, and these words have spread to the farthest islands and among many unenlightened peoples, and they discuss these words and the commandments of the Torah. (*Hilkhot Melakhim UMilḥemoteihem* 11:4)

The effect of Christianity and Islam was to spread the Jewish message – albeit in ways with which Jews could not fully agree – throughout the world. At the time of this writing, these religions represent more than half of the people on the face of the earth. The "Judeo-Christian ethic" and the Abrahamic faiths have shaped much of the civilization of the West. The Torah really did become "your wisdom and understanding in the eyes of the peoples."

The people God chose to carry His message were not an obvious choice. They were not large: "It is not because you were more numerous than other peoples that the LORD desired you and chose you, for you are the smallest of all peoples" (Deut. 7:7). Nor were they especially pious: "Not for your righteousness or rectitude" (9:5). The impression we gain of the Israelites throughout is of a fractious, often wayward group, a "stiff-necked people."

Yet Moshe and the prophets were convinced that the message they carried was not for their people alone. It had a universal significance. Moshe said that the laws the Israelites had been commanded will show "your wisdom and understanding in the eyes of the peoples:

sound of words but saw no image; there was only a voice.
13 He announced to you His covenant, which He charged
you to keep – the Ten Commandments – and He wrote
14 them on two tablets of stone. And the Lord charged me
at that time to teach you decrees and laws for you to keep
in the land that you are about to cross into and possess.
15 You saw no image when the Lord spoke to you at Ḥorev
out of the fire, and so take great care for your own sake
16 not to act in self-destruction, making yourselves any idol,
17 an image of any shape, any form of man or of woman, or
in the form of any animal of the land, or any winged bird
18 that flies in the sky, or in the form of anything that crawls
on the ground, or of any fish in the waters below the
19 earth. And when you raise your eyes to the heavens and
see the sun, moon, and stars, all the heavenly array, do not
be led astray to bow down to them and worship them;
the Lord your God has allotted them to all the other
20 peoples beneath the sky. But you, the Lord took, and He
brought you out of the iron crucible that was Egypt, to
become the people of His heritage, as you are on this day.
21 The Lord was incensed with me because of your words,

---

emphatic in the Babylonian Talmud, as the Nazir, Rabbi David Cohen, pointed out in his book *Kol HaNevua*. When the Talmud brings a proof text, it says *Ta shema*, "Come and hear." When it draws an inference, it says *Shema mina*, "Hear from this." When it wants to signal agreement, it says *Shome'a ani*, "I hear." All of these are verbs of listening, attending with the ear. For the Greeks, truth is what we see. For Jews, it is what we hear (see note on Gen. 3:6).

Pagan cultures *saw* God, or rather, the gods. They were there in visible phenomena: the sun, the storm, the earth, the sea, the great forces that surround us and reduce us to a sense of insignificance. The polytheistic imagination views reality as the clash of powerful forces, each of which is indifferent to the fate of humankind. A tidal wave does not stop to think whom it will drown.

A world confined to the visible is an impersonal world, deaf to our prayers, blind to our hopes, a world without overarching meaning. Judaism, by contrast, is the supreme example of a person-centered civilization – and persons communicate by words. They speak and listen. Words bridge the metaphysical abyss between soul and soul.

יג זוּלָתִי קוֹל: וַיַּגֵּד לָכֶם אֶת־בְּרִיתוֹ אֲשֶׁר צִוָּה אֶתְכֶם לַעֲשׂוֹת
יד עֲשֶׂרֶת הַדְּבָרִים וַיִּכְתְּבֵם עַל־שְׁנֵי לֻחוֹת אֲבָנִים: וְאֹתִי צִוָּה
יְהוָה בָּעֵת הַהִוא לְלַמֵּד אֶתְכֶם חֻקִּים וּמִשְׁפָּטִים לַעֲשֹׂתְכֶם
טו אֹתָם בָּאָרֶץ אֲשֶׁר אַתֶּם עֹבְרִים שָׁמָּה לְרִשְׁתָּהּ: וְנִשְׁמַרְתֶּם
מְאֹד לְנַפְשֹׁתֵיכֶם כִּי לֹא רְאִיתֶם כָּל־תְּמוּנָה בְּיוֹם דִּבֶּר
טז יְהוָה אֲלֵיכֶם בְּחֹרֵב מִתּוֹךְ הָאֵשׁ: פֶּן־תַּשְׁחִתוּן וַעֲשִׂיתֶם
יז לָכֶם פֶּסֶל תְּמוּנַת כָּל־סָמֶל תַּבְנִית זָכָר אוֹ נְקֵבָה: תַּבְנִית
כָּל־בְּהֵמָה אֲשֶׁר בָּאָרֶץ תַּבְנִית כָּל־צִפּוֹר כָּנָף אֲשֶׁר תָּעוּף
יח בַּשָּׁמָיִם: תַּבְנִית כָּל־רֹמֵשׂ בָּאֲדָמָה תַּבְנִית כָּל־דָּגָה אֲשֶׁר־
יט בַּמַּיִם מִתַּחַת לָאָרֶץ: וּפֶן־תִּשָּׂא עֵינֶיךָ הַשָּׁמַיְמָה וְרָאִיתָ
אֶת־הַשֶּׁמֶשׁ וְאֶת־הַיָּרֵחַ וְאֶת־הַכּוֹכָבִים כֹּל צְבָא הַשָּׁמַיִם
וְנִדַּחְתָּ וְהִשְׁתַּחֲוִיתָ לָהֶם וַעֲבַדְתָּם אֲשֶׁר חָלַק יְהוָה אֱלֹהֶיךָ
כ אֹתָם לְכֹל הָעַמִּים תַּחַת כָּל־הַשָּׁמָיִם: וְאֶתְכֶם לָקַח יְהוָה
וַיּוֹצִא אֶתְכֶם מִכּוּר הַבַּרְזֶל מִמִּצְרָיִם לִהְיוֹת לוֹ לְעַם נַחֲלָה
כא כַּיּוֹם הַזֶּה: וַיהוָה הִתְאַנַּף־בִּי עַל־דִּבְרֵיכֶם וַיִּשָּׁבַע לְבִלְתִּי

4:12 זוּלָתִי קוֹל *There was only a voice* – Rabbi Yaakov Leiner (1814–78), leader of the hasidic community in Radzyn, Poland, made a profound point about the differences between the senses of sight and hearing:

> From a human perspective, it often seems as if seeing is a more precise form of knowledge than hearing. In fact, however, hearing has a greater power than seeing. Sight discloses the external aspect of things, but hearing reveals their inwardness. (*Beit Yaakov, Rosh Ḥodesh Menaḥem Av*)

God is not something we see, but a voice we hear. This has deep implications for the whole of Judaism. Its way of understanding the world and relating to it is fundamentally different from that of the Greeks and of the philosophical tradition of which they were the founders. A listening culture is not the same as a seeing culture.

To this day, the West, when it speaks of understanding, uses metaphors of sight. We talk of *insight*, *foresight*, and *hindsight*, of making an *observation*, of people of *vision*. When we understand something we say, "I *see*." These come to the West from ancient Greece.

In the Hebrew Bible, by contrast, instead of saying that someone thinks, the verse will say that he "said in his or her heart." Thought is not a form of sight but of speech. This becomes all the more

and He vowed that I would not cross the Jordan nor enter
the good land that the LORD your God is giving you as
22 a heritage. I will die in this land without crossing the
Jordan – but you will cross over and take possession of
23 that good land. Take care not to forget the covenant that
the LORD your God has forged with you. Do not make
yourselves an idol in any form: the LORD your God has
24 forbidden it. For the LORD your God is a consuming fire,
an impassioned God.
25 When you have had children and grandchildren, and
have lived long in the land, if you act destructively, forming
an idol in any image, wreaking evil in the sight of the LORD
26 your God and provoking Him to anger, I call heaven and
earth to witness against you today – to bear witness that
you will quickly perish from the land that you are crossing
the Jordan to take possession of. You will not live long
27 there; you will be utterly destroyed. The LORD will scatter
you among the peoples. Only a few of you will remain
among the nations that the LORD will drive you away
28 to. There you will worship man-made gods of wood and
of stone, ones that do not see, do not hear, do not eat or
29 smell. Yet there, if you seek the LORD your God, you will
find Him: if you search after Him with all your heart and
30 all your soul. In your distress, when all these things have
happened to you, in the days to come, you will finally
31 return to the LORD your God and heed His voice. For the
LORD your God is a merciful God. He will not forsake or
destroy you. He will not forget the covenant that He forged
32 on oath with your ancestors. For ask now about earliest
times, times long before your own, from the day God
created humans on the earth; ask from one end of heaven
to the other: Has anything as great as this ever happened

---

the momentous claim that history has meaning. It is not merely a sequence of disconnected events, but the long story of humanity's response to, or rebellion against, the voice of God as it echoes in the conscience of mankind.

עָבְרִי אֶת־הַיַּרְדֵּן וּלְבִלְתִּי־בֹא אֶל־הָאָרֶץ הַטּוֹבָה אֲשֶׁר
כב יהוה אֱלֹהֶיךָ נֹתֵן לְךָ נַחֲלָה׃ כִּי אָנֹכִי מֵת בָּאָרֶץ הַזֹּאת
אֵינֶנִּי עֹבֵר אֶת־הַיַּרְדֵּן וְאַתֶּם עֹבְרִים וִירִשְׁתֶּם אֶת־הָאָרֶץ
כג הַטּוֹבָה הַזֹּאת׃ הִשָּׁמְרוּ לָכֶם פֶּן־תִּשְׁכְּחוּ אֶת־בְּרִית יהוה
אֱלֹהֵיכֶם אֲשֶׁר כָּרַת עִמָּכֶם וַעֲשִׂיתֶם לָכֶם פֶּסֶל תְּמוּנַת כֹּל
כד אֲשֶׁר צִוְּךָ יהוה אֱלֹהֶיךָ׃ כִּי יהוה אֱלֹהֶיךָ אֵשׁ אֹכְלָה הוּא
אֵל קַנָּא׃
כה כִּי־תוֹלִיד בָּנִים וּבְנֵי בָנִים וְנוֹשַׁנְתֶּם בָּאָרֶץ וְהִשְׁחַתֶּם
וַעֲשִׂיתֶם פֶּסֶל תְּמוּנַת כֹּל וַעֲשִׂיתֶם הָרַע בְּעֵינֵי־יהוה אֱלֹהֶיךָ
כו לְהַכְעִיסוֹ׃ הַעִידֹתִי בָכֶם הַיּוֹם אֶת־הַשָּׁמַיִם וְאֶת־הָאָרֶץ
כִּי־אָבֹד תֹּאבֵדוּן מַהֵר מֵעַל הָאָרֶץ אֲשֶׁר אַתֶּם עֹבְרִים אֶת־
הַיַּרְדֵּן שָׁמָּה לְרִשְׁתָּהּ לֹא־תַאֲרִיכֻן יָמִים עָלֶיהָ כִּי הִשָּׁמֵד
כז תִּשָּׁמֵדוּן׃ וְהֵפִיץ יהוה אֶתְכֶם בָּעַמִּים וְנִשְׁאַרְתֶּם מְתֵי מִסְפָּר
כח בַּגּוֹיִם אֲשֶׁר יְנַהֵג יהוה אֶתְכֶם שָׁמָּה׃ וַעֲבַדְתֶּם־שָׁם אֱלֹהִים
מַעֲשֵׂה יְדֵי אָדָם עֵץ וָאֶבֶן אֲשֶׁר לֹא־יִרְאוּן וְלֹא יִשְׁמְעוּן
כט וְלֹא יֹאכְלוּן וְלֹא יְרִיחֻן׃ וּבִקַּשְׁתֶּם מִשָּׁם אֶת־יהוה אֱלֹהֶיךָ
ל וּמָצָאתָ כִּי תִדְרְשֶׁנּוּ בְּכָל־לְבָבְךָ וּבְכָל־נַפְשֶׁךָ׃ בַּצַּר לְךָ
וּמְצָאוּךָ כֹּל הַדְּבָרִים הָאֵלֶּה בְּאַחֲרִית הַיָּמִים וְשַׁבְתָּ עַד־
לא יהוה אֱלֹהֶיךָ וְשָׁמַעְתָּ בְּקֹלוֹ׃ כִּי אֵל רַחוּם יהוה אֱלֹהֶיךָ
לֹא יַרְפְּךָ וְלֹא יַשְׁחִיתֶךָ וְלֹא יִשְׁכַּח אֶת־בְּרִית אֲבֹתֶיךָ
לב אֲשֶׁר נִשְׁבַּע לָהֶם׃ כִּי שְׁאַל־נָא לְיָמִים רִאשֹׁנִים אֲשֶׁר־
הָיוּ לְפָנֶיךָ לְמִן־הַיּוֹם אֲשֶׁר בָּרָא אֱלֹהִים ׀ אָדָם עַל־הָאָרֶץ
וּלְמִקְצֵה הַשָּׁמַיִם וְעַד־קְצֵה הַשָּׁמָיִם הֲנִהְיָה כַּדָּבָר הַגָּדוֹל

4:32 הֲנִהְיָה כַּדָּבָר הַגָּדוֹל הַזֶּה *Has anything... happened before* – Israel knows God directly, through its own past. Where other faiths, ancient and modern, saw religion as the flight from history into a world without time, Judaism saw time itself as the arena where God and mankind met. Three-quarters of the Hebrew Bible is made up of historical narratives. Jews were the first to make

33 before? Has anyone heard of anything like this? Has any
people ever heard the voice of God speaking out of fire,
34 as you have, and lived? Has God ever taken one nation to
Himself, by miracles, from the midst of another, by trials,
signs, wonders, and war, with a mighty hand and an arm
stretched forth and terrifying displays of power, as the
LORD your God did for you in Egypt before your eyes?
35 To you this was shown – so that you may know that the
36 LORD is God; besides Him, there is no other. From heaven
He let you hear His voice to discipline you. On earth He
showed you His great fire, and from within the fire you
37 heard His words. And because He loved your ancestors
and chose their descendants after them He brought you
out of Egypt with His own presence and by His great
38 power, driving out from before you nations greater and
mightier than you, to bring you in and give you their land
39 as a possession, as it is on this day. Know today and take
to heart that the LORD is God in heaven above and on the
40 earth beneath; there is no other. Keep His decrees and
commandments, with which I am charging you today, so
that it may be well for you and your children after you,
and that you may live long in the land that the LORD your
God is giving you for all time."
41 Then Moshe designated three cities to the east side of the SHELISHI
42 Jordan to which a manslayer could flee, someone who
had killed a fellow human being without intent or prior
43 enmity. He could flee to one of these cities and live: Betzer
in the wilderness plateau for the people of Reuven, Ramot
in Gilad for the people of Gad, and Golan in Bashan for
44 the people of Menashe. This is the Law that Moshe set

Persians, Greeks, and Romans successively strode the stage of world dominion. Each empire played its part, and each in turn has gone. In our day, the two great powers which declared, as stated in the Merneptah Stele, "Israel is laid waste – its seed is no more" – the Third Reich and the Soviet Union – have been defeated, dismantled, and have disappeared. But the Jews survive. "Has anything as great as this ever happened before? Has anyone heard of anything like this?"

לג הֲזֶּה אוֹ הֲנִשְׁמַע כָּמֹהוּ: הֲשָׁמַע עָם קוֹל אֱלֹהִים מְדַבֵּר
לד מִתּוֹךְ־הָאֵשׁ כַּאֲשֶׁר־שָׁמַעְתָּ אַתָּה וַיֶּחִי: אוֹ ׀ הֲנִסָּה אֱלֹהִים
לָבוֹא לָקַחַת לוֹ גוֹי מִקֶּרֶב גּוֹי בְּמַסֹּת בְּאֹתֹת וּבְמוֹפְתִים
וּבְמִלְחָמָה וּבְיָד חֲזָקָה וּבִזְרוֹעַ נְטוּיָה וּבְמוֹרָאִים גְּדֹלִים
כְּכֹל אֲשֶׁר־עָשָׂה לָכֶם יהוה אֱלֹהֵיכֶם בְּמִצְרַיִם לְעֵינֶיךָ:
לה אַתָּה הָרְאֵתָ לָדַעַת כִּי יהוה הוּא הָאֱלֹהִים אֵין עוֹד מִלְּבַדּוֹ:
לו מִן־הַשָּׁמַיִם הִשְׁמִיעֲךָ אֶת־קֹלוֹ לְיַסְּרֶךָּ וְעַל־הָאָרֶץ הֶרְאֲךָ
לז אֶת־אִשּׁוֹ הַגְּדוֹלָה וּדְבָרָיו שָׁמַעְתָּ מִתּוֹךְ הָאֵשׁ: וְתַחַת כִּי
אָהַב אֶת־אֲבֹתֶיךָ וַיִּבְחַר בְּזַרְעוֹ אַחֲרָיו וַיּוֹצִאֲךָ בְּפָנָיו בְּכֹחוֹ
לח הַגָּדֹל מִמִּצְרָיִם: לְהוֹרִישׁ גּוֹיִם גְּדֹלִים וַעֲצֻמִים מִמְּךָ מִפָּנֶיךָ
לט לַהֲבִיאֲךָ לָתֶת־לְךָ אֶת־אַרְצָם נַחֲלָה כַּיּוֹם הַזֶּה: וְיָדַעְתָּ
הַיּוֹם וַהֲשֵׁבֹתָ אֶל־לְבָבֶךָ כִּי יהוה הוּא הָאֱלֹהִים בַּשָּׁמַיִם
מ מִמַּעַל וְעַל־הָאָרֶץ מִתָּחַת אֵין עוֹד: וְשָׁמַרְתָּ אֶת־חֻקָּיו
וְאֶת־מִצְוֺתָיו אֲשֶׁר אָנֹכִי מְצַוְּךָ הַיּוֹם אֲשֶׁר יִיטַב לְךָ וּלְבָנֶיךָ
אַחֲרֶיךָ וּלְמַעַן תַּאֲרִיךְ יָמִים עַל־הָאֲדָמָה אֲשֶׁר יהוה אֱלֹהֶיךָ
נֹתֵן לְךָ כָּל־הַיָּמִים:
מא אָז יַבְדִּיל מֹשֶׁה שָׁלֹשׁ עָרִים בְּעֵבֶר הַיַּרְדֵּן מִזְרְחָה שָׁמֶשׁ: ה שלישי
מב לָנֻס שָׁמָּה רוֹצֵחַ אֲשֶׁר יִרְצַח אֶת־רֵעֵהוּ בִּבְלִי־דַעַת וְהוּא
לֹא־שֹׂנֵא לוֹ מִתְּמֹל שִׁלְשֹׁם וְנָס אֶל־אַחַת מִן־הֶעָרִים
מג הָאֵל וָחָי: אֶת־בֶּצֶר בַּמִּדְבָּר בְּאֶרֶץ הַמִּישֹׁר לָראוּבֵנִי וְאֶת־
מד רָאמֹת בַּגִּלְעָד לַגָּדִי וְאֶת־גּוֹלָן בַּבָּשָׁן לַמְנַשִּׁי: וְזֹאת הַתּוֹרָה

4:32 הֲנִשְׁמַע כָּמֹהוּ *Has anyone heard of anything like this?* – At the very beginning of our national history Moshe recognizes that there will never be any other people quite like Israel. Turning to the new generation, he asks them this rhetorical question, one that still echoes, gathering force with each successive century. As we survey the breathtaking landscape of Jewish history, we know this: that those who sought to destroy the people of the covenant gather dust in the museums of mankind while *am Yisrael ḥai,* the people Israel lives. Ancient Egypt is no more. The Moabites have long since disappeared. The Assyrians, Babylonians,

45 before the people of Israel. These are the testimonies,
decrees, and laws that Moshe spoke to the Israelites when
46 they had come out of Egypt and were beyond the Jordan
in the valley opposite Beit Peor, in the land of Siḥon, king
of the Amorites, who reigned at Ḥeshbon, whom Moshe
and the Israelites defeated when they came out of Egypt.
47 They had taken possession of his land and the land of Og,
king of Bashan, the two Amorite kings east of the Jordan:
48 from Aroer on the edge of the Arnon Stream, as far as
49 Mount Siyon – that is, Ḥermon – together with all the
Arava on the east bank of the Jordan as far as the Arava
Sea, below the slopes of Pisga.

5 1 Moshe summoned all Israel, and said to them: "Listen, REVI'I
Israel, to the decrees and laws that I shall declare in your
hearing today; learn them and carefully observe them.
2 The LORD our God forged a covenant with us at Ḥorev.
3 Not with our ancestors did the LORD forge this covenant,
4 but with us who are here today, all of us, alive. Face-to-
face from amid the fire the LORD spoke to you at the
5 mountain. I was standing between the LORD and you at
that time to tell you the word of the LORD, because you
were afraid of the fire and did not go up the mountain.
6 He said: I am the LORD your God, who brought
you out of the land of Egypt, out of the house of slaves.

---

items of faith. Faith in the existence of God, or acceptance of the kingship of God, is not itself a command but a prelude to, and presupposition of, the commands. He quotes a passage from Mekhilta:

> "Have no other gods than me." Why is this said? Because it says, "I am the LORD your God." To explain this by way of a parable: A king of flesh and blood entered a province. His servants said to him, "Issue decrees for the people." He, however, told them, "No. When they accept my sovereignty, I will issue decrees. For if they do not accept my sovereignty, how will they carry out my decrees?"

According to Ramban, Halakhot Gedolot must have believed that the verse "I am the LORD your God, who brought you out of the land of Egypt, out of the house of slaves" is not itself a command, but a statement of why the Israelites should be bound by the will of God. He

מה אֲשֶׁר־שָׂם מֹשֶׁה לִפְנֵי בְּנֵי יִשְׂרָאֵל: אֵלֶּה הָעֵדֹת וְהַחֻקִּים
וְהַמִּשְׁפָּטִים אֲשֶׁר דִּבֶּר מֹשֶׁה אֶל־בְּנֵי יִשְׂרָאֵל בְּצֵאתָם
מו מִמִּצְרָיִם: בְּעֵבֶר הַיַּרְדֵּן בַּגַּיְא מוּל בֵּית פְּעוֹר בְּאֶרֶץ סִיחֹן
מֶלֶךְ הָאֱמֹרִי אֲשֶׁר יוֹשֵׁב בְּחֶשְׁבּוֹן אֲשֶׁר הִכָּה מֹשֶׁה וּבְנֵי
מז יִשְׂרָאֵל בְּצֵאתָם מִמִּצְרָיִם: וַיִּירְשׁוּ אֶת־אַרְצוֹ וְאֶת־אֶרֶץ ׀
עוֹג מֶלֶךְ־הַבָּשָׁן שְׁנֵי מַלְכֵי הָאֱמֹרִי אֲשֶׁר בְּעֵבֶר הַיַּרְדֵּן מִזְרַח
מח שָׁמֶשׁ: מֵעֲרֹעֵר אֲשֶׁר עַל־שְׂפַת־נַחַל אַרְנֹן וְעַד־הַר שִׂיאֹן
מט הוּא חֶרְמוֹן: וְכָל־הָעֲרָבָה עֵבֶר הַיַּרְדֵּן מִזְרָחָה וְעַד יָם
הָעֲרָבָה תַּחַת אַשְׁדֹּת הַפִּסְגָּה:

ה א וַיִּקְרָא מֹשֶׁה אֶל־כָּל־יִשְׂרָאֵל וַיֹּאמֶר אֲלֵהֶם שְׁמַע יִשְׂרָאֵל רביעי
אֶת־הַחֻקִּים וְאֶת־הַמִּשְׁפָּטִים אֲשֶׁר אָנֹכִי דֹּבֵר בְּאָזְנֵיכֶם
ב הַיּוֹם וּלְמַדְתֶּם אֹתָם וּשְׁמַרְתֶּם לַעֲשֹׂתָם: יְהוָה אֱלֹהֵינוּ כָּרַת
ג עִמָּנוּ בְּרִית בְּחֹרֵב: לֹא אֶת־אֲבֹתֵינוּ כָּרַת יְהוָה אֶת־הַבְּרִית
הַזֹּאת כִּי אִתָּנוּ אֲנַחְנוּ אֵלֶּה פֹה הַיּוֹם כֻּלָּנוּ חַיִּים: פָּנִים ׀
ה בְּפָנִים דִּבֶּר יְהוָה עִמָּכֶם בָּהָר מִתּוֹךְ הָאֵשׁ: אָנֹכִי עֹמֵד בֵּין־
יְהוָה וּבֵינֵיכֶם בָּעֵת הַהִוא לְהַגִּיד לָכֶם אֶת־דְּבַר יְהוָה כִּי
ו יְרֵאתֶם מִפְּנֵי הָאֵשׁ וְלֹא־עֲלִיתֶם בָּהָר לֵאמֹר: אָנֹכִי

THE TEN COMMANDMENTS

Though the Ten Commandments are a central text of Judaism, scholars have disagreed throughout the ages on how to count them. What was the first commandment? This was debated by, among others, Rambam (1138–1204) and the author of Halakhot Gedolot, probably Rabbi Shimon Kayyara (in the period of the *geonim* in the eighth century), who for the first time enumerated the 613 commands.

Rambam counts the opening line of the Ten Commandments, "I am the Lord your God, who brought you out of the land of Egypt, out of the house of slaves," as a positive command, to believe in God. Halakhot Gedolot does not count it as a command at all. Why not?

Ramban (1194–1270), in defense of Halakhot Gedolot, speculates that its author counted among the 613 commands only the specific laws enjoining us to do this or avoid doing that. The commands are rules of behavior, not

▶

7 8 Have no other gods than Me. Do not make for yourself
a carved image or likeness of any creature in the heavens
above or the earth beneath or the water beneath the
9 earth. Do not bow down to them or worship them, for I
the Lord your God demand absolute loyalty. For those
who hate Me, I hold the descendants to account for the
sins of the fathers to the third and fourth generation,

Yehuda HaLevi shifted the focus of this commandment. HaLevi was a great medieval Hebrew poet and also wrote one of Judaism's theological masterpieces, the Kuzari. In it, HaLevi draws a portrait diametrically opposed to Rambam's account. Judaism is not about abstract concepts but about concrete experiences: the taste of slavery, the feeling of liberation, the realization on the part of the people that God had heard their cry and set them free. The prophets were not philosophers. Philosophers found God in physics and metaphysics, but the prophets found God in history. This is how HaLevi explains his faith:

> I believe in the God of Avraham, Yitzḥak, and Yaakov, who led the children of Israel out of Egypt with signs and miracles, who fed them in the desert and gave them the land, after having brought them through the sea and the Jordan in a miraculous way. (Kuzari I:11)

He goes on to emphasize that God's opening words in the revelation at Mount Sinai were not, "I am the Lord your God, creator of heaven and earth" but "I am the Lord your God, who brought you out of the land of Egypt, out of the house of slaves" (Kuzari I:25). The covenant God made with the Israelites at Mount Sinai was not rooted in the ancient past of creation but in the recent past of the exodus.

What is at stake in this difference of opinion between Rambam and HaLevi? At the heart of Judaism is a twofold understanding of the nature of God and His relationship to the universe. On the one hand, God is creator of the universe and the maker of the human person "in His image." This aspect of God is universal. It is accessible to anyone, Jew or Gentile.

But there is a quite different aspect of God which predominates throughout most of Tanakh. This is God as He is involved in the fate of one family, one nation: the children of Israel. He intervened in their history. He made a highly specific covenant with them at Sinai, covering almost every aspect of life.

Rambam, the philosopher, emphasized the universal, metaphysical aspect of Judaism and the eternal, unchanging existence of God. Yehuda HaLevi, the poet, was more attuned to the particularistic and prophetic dimension of Judaism: the role of God in the historical drama of the Jewish people.

יהוה אֱלֹהֶיךָ אֲשֶׁר הוֹצֵאתִיךָ מֵאֶרֶץ מִצְרַיִם מִבֵּית עֲבָדִים:
ח לֹא־יִהְיֶה לְךָ אֱלֹהִים אֲחֵרִים עַל־פָּנָי: לֹא־תַעֲשֶׂה לְךָ פֶסֶל
כָּל־תְּמוּנָה אֲשֶׁר בַּשָּׁמַיִם מִמַּעַל וַאֲשֶׁר בָּאָרֶץ מִתָּחַת
ט וַאֲשֶׁר בַּמַּיִם מִתַּחַת לָאָרֶץ: לֹא־תִשְׁתַּחֲוֶה לָהֶם וְלֹא
תָעָבְדֵם כִּי אָנֹכִי יהוה אֱלֹהֶיךָ אֵל קַנָּא פֹּקֵד עֲוֺן אָבוֹת

---

had rescued them, liberated them, and brought them to safety. The first verse of the Decalogue is not a law but a statement of fact, a reason why the Israelites should accept God's sovereignty.

Thanks to recent archaeological discoveries, we now know that the biblical covenant has the same literary structure as ancient Near Eastern political treaties. These treaties usually follow a six-part pattern, of which the first three elements were: (1) the preamble, identifying the initiator of the treaty; (2) a historical review, summarizing the past relationship between the parties; and (3) the stipulations, namely, the terms and conditions of the covenant.

Fundamentally a covenant is a peace treaty. It can exist between states of roughly equivalent power (a parity treaty). But it can also exist between states of radically different power, in which case it is called a suzerainty treaty. Such is the covenant between Israel and God.

This was revolutionary. Covenants were common in the ancient Near East. But covenants between God and a people were unknown, indeed inconceivable. It was unimaginable that God would seek to constrain His own powers in the name of righteousness and justice, or that a supreme power would make a treaty with the supremely powerless.

Seen in this context, the first verse of the Ten Commandments is an abridged form of preamble ("I am the Lord your God") and historical review ("who brought you out of the land of Egypt, out of the house of slaves"). The verses that follow are the stipulations, or as we would call them, the commands. If so, then Halakhot Gedolot as understood by Ramban may well have been correct in seeing the verse as an introduction to the commands, not a command in its own right. From God's relationship with and redemption of Israel arises our commitment to all the commands that follow.

5:6 מִבֵּית עֲבָדִים *Out of the house of slaves* – For Rambam, as noted above, the first command is to believe in God, creator of heaven and earth:

> The basic principle of all basic principles and the pillar of all sciences is to realize that there is a First Being who brought every existing thing into being.... To acknowledge this truth is a positive command, as it is said: "I am the Lord your God" (Ex. 20:2; Deut. 5:6). (*Hilkhot Yesodei HaTorah* 1:1–5)

10 but to those who love Me and keep My commands – I
11 shall act with faithful love for thousands. Do not
speak the name of the Lord your God in vain, for the
Lord will not hold guiltless those who speak His name
12 in vain. Guard the Sabbath to keep it holy,
13 as the Lord your God has commanded you. Six days you
14 shall work and carry out all your labors, but the seventh
is a Sabbath to the Lord your God. On it, do no work
at all – neither you, nor your son or daughter, your male
or female servant, your ox, your donkey, nor any of your
livestock, or the migrant within your gates, so that your
15 male and female servants may rest as you do. Remember
that you were slaves in Egypt, and the Lord your God
brought you out of there with a mighty hand and an
arm stretched forth. That is why the Lord your God has
16 commanded you to keep the Sabbath day. Honor
your father and mother, as the Lord your God has
commanded you, so that you may live long and that it
may be well for you in the land that the Lord your God
17 is giving you. Do not murder. Do not commit
adultery. Do not steal. Do not bear false
18 witness against your neighbor. Do not crave
your neighbor's wife. Do not set your desire
on your neighbor's house, or field, or male or female
servant, his ox, his donkey, or anything else that is your
19 neighbor's. The Lord spoke these words with a HAMISHI
loud voice to your whole assembly at the mountain from

At many times in history, people have dreamed of an ideal world. The name given to such visions is "utopia," meaning "no place," because at no time or place have these dreams been realized on a society-wide basis. The Sabbath is the sole successful utopian experiment in history. It is based on the simple idea that utopia (in Judaism, the Messianic age) is not solely in the future. It is something we can experience in the midst of time, one day in seven. The Sabbath became the weekly rehearsal of an ideal world, one not yet reached but still lived as a goal, of a world at peace with itself, recognizing the createdness, and thus the integrity, of all people and all forms of life. If Egypt meant slavery, the Sabbath is collective freedom, a "foretaste of the World to Come."

י עַל־בָּנִים וְעַל־שִׁלֵּשִׁים וְעַל־רִבֵּעִים לְשֹׂנְאָי: וְעֹשֶׂה חֶסֶד
יא לַאֲלָפִים לְאֹהֲבַי וּלְשֹׁמְרֵי מצותו: לֹא תִשָּׂא אֶת־ מִצְוֹתָי
שֵׁם־יְהוָה אֱלֹהֶיךָ לַשָּׁוְא כִּי לֹא יְנַקֶּה יְהוָה אֵת אֲשֶׁר־יִשָּׂא
יב אֶת־שְׁמוֹ לַשָּׁוְא: שָׁמוֹר אֶת־יוֹם הַשַּׁבָּת לְקַדְּשׁוֹ
יג כַּאֲשֶׁר צִוְּךָ יְהוָה אֱלֹהֶיךָ: שֵׁשֶׁת יָמִים תַּעֲבֹד וְעָשִׂיתָ כָּל־
יד מְלַאכְתֶּךָ: וְיוֹם הַשְּׁבִיעִי שַׁבָּת לַיהוָה אֱלֹהֶיךָ לֹא־תַעֲשֶׂה
כָל־מְלָאכָה אַתָּה | וּבִנְךָ־וּבִתֶּךָ וְעַבְדְּךָ־וַאֲמָתֶךָ וְשׁוֹרְךָ
וַחֲמֹרְךָ וְכָל־בְּהֶמְתֶּךָ וְגֵרְךָ אֲשֶׁר בִּשְׁעָרֶיךָ לְמַעַן יָנוּחַ עַבְדְּךָ
טו וַאֲמָתְךָ כָּמוֹךָ: וְזָכַרְתָּ כִּי עֶבֶד הָיִיתָ בְּאֶרֶץ מִצְרַיִם וַיֹּצִאֲךָ
יְהוָה אֱלֹהֶיךָ מִשָּׁם בְּיָד חֲזָקָה וּבִזְרֹעַ נְטוּיָה עַל־כֵּן צִוְּךָ
טז יְהוָה אֱלֹהֶיךָ לַעֲשׂוֹת אֶת־יוֹם הַשַּׁבָּת: כַּבֵּד אֶת־
אָבִיךָ וְאֶת־אִמֶּךָ כַּאֲשֶׁר צִוְּךָ יְהוָה אֱלֹהֶיךָ לְמַעַן | יַאֲרִיכֻן
יָמֶיךָ וּלְמַעַן יִיטַב לָךְ עַל הָאֲדָמָה אֲשֶׁר־יְהוָה אֱלֹהֶיךָ נֹתֵן
יז לָךְ: לֹא תִרְצָח וְלֹא
תִנְאָף וְלֹא תִגְנֹב וְלֹא־
יח תַעֲנֶה בְרֵעֲךָ עֵד שָׁוְא: וְלֹא
תַחְמֹד אֵשֶׁת רֵעֶךָ וְלֹא
תִתְאַוֶּה בֵּית רֵעֶךָ שָׂדֵהוּ וְעַבְדּוֹ וַאֲמָתוֹ שׁוֹרוֹ וַחֲמֹרוֹ וְכֹל
יט אֲשֶׁר לְרֵעֶךָ: אֶת־הַדְּבָרִים הָאֵלֶּה דִּבֶּר יְהוָה חמישי
אֶל־כָּל־קְהַלְכֶם בָּהָר מִתּוֹךְ הָאֵשׁ הֶעָנָן וְהָעֲרָפֶל קוֹל

5:14 לֹא־תַעֲשֶׂה כָל־מְלָאכָה *Do no work at all* – Deuteronomy fuses theology, spirituality, morality, and law. The central emphasis is on society rather than the individual and his or her relationship with God. So in the first account of the Ten Commandments in the book of Exodus, the reason for keeping the Sabbath is because God created the universe in six days and rested on the seventh. In Deuteronomy, however, the Sabbath is given a quite different logic, namely the importance of freedom. The Sabbath is the ultimate expression of a free society, the antithesis of slavery in Egypt. On this day, all relationships of dominance and subordination are suspended. We may not work, or command others to work, "so that your male and female servants may rest as you do" (Deut. 5:14).

▶

amid the fire, cloud, and thick darkness, and He added
no more. And He wrote them on two stone tablets, and
20 gave them to me. When you heard the voice out of the
darkness, while the mountain was ablaze with fire, your
21 tribal leaders and elders came to me; they said, 'The LORD
our God has shown us His glory and greatness – we have
heard His voice from within the fire. Today we have seen
that God may speak to a person and that person still live.
22 But now, must we die? For this great fire will consume us.
If we hear the voice of the LORD our God for any longer,
23 we will die. For what mortal has heard the voice of the
Living God speaking from within the fire, as we have, and
24 yet lived? You go near and listen to all that the LORD our
God says. Then tell us all that the LORD our God tells
25 you, and we will heed and do it.' The LORD heard your
words when you spoke to me, and to me the LORD said:
'I have heard the words this people have spoken to you;
26 they did well to speak as they did. If only they would
have such a mind as this always, to hold Me in awe and
to keep all My commandments, so that it might be well
27 for them and for their children forever! Go, tell them to
28 go back to their tents. But you stay here by Me, and I will
tell you all the commandments, decrees, and laws that
you shall teach them, so that they may keep them in the
29 land that I am giving them to possess.' Take care to do as
the LORD your God has commanded you; do not turn
30 aside – neither to the right nor to the left. Follow only

---

here, Moshe cites the second tablets – the ones he engraved after breaking the first on seeing the golden calf. The second, carved out on the mountain by Moshe's hand, came together with *Torah Shebe'al Peh*, the Oral Law.

We can now grasp how the revelation can be a great voice that happened once and never again and a great voice that never stopped. The voice that was heard once was the Written Torah; the great voice that never ceased was the Oral Torah. The covenant laid out in Deuteronomy is based on a three-thousand-year-old conversation between Israel and God; not only a single revelation, but a voice that resonated forevermore.

גָּדוֹל וְלֹא יָסָף וַיִּכְתְּבֵם עַל־שְׁנֵי לֻחֹת אֲבָנִים וַיִּתְּנֵם אֵלָי׃
כ וַיְהִי כְּשָׁמְעֲכֶם אֶת־הַקּוֹל מִתּוֹךְ הַחֹשֶׁךְ וְהָהָר בֹּעֵר בָּאֵשׁ
כא וַתִּקְרְבוּן אֵלַי כָּל־רָאשֵׁי שִׁבְטֵיכֶם וְזִקְנֵיכֶם׃ וַתֹּאמְרוּ הֵן
הֶרְאָנוּ יהוה אֱלֹהֵינוּ אֶת־כְּבֹדוֹ וְאֶת־גָּדְלוֹ וְאֶת־קֹלוֹ שָׁמַעְנוּ
מִתּוֹךְ הָאֵשׁ הַיּוֹם הַזֶּה רָאִינוּ כִּי־יְדַבֵּר אֱלֹהִים אֶת־הָאָדָם
כב וָחָי׃ וְעַתָּה לָמָּה נָמוּת כִּי תֹאכְלֵנוּ הָאֵשׁ הַגְּדֹלָה הַזֹּאת
אִם־יֹסְפִים ׀ אֲנַחְנוּ לִשְׁמֹעַ אֶת־קוֹל יהוה אֱלֹהֵינוּ עוֹד
כג וָמָתְנוּ׃ כִּי מִי כָל־בָּשָׂר אֲשֶׁר שָׁמַע קוֹל אֱלֹהִים חַיִּים מְדַבֵּר
כד מִתּוֹךְ־הָאֵשׁ כָּמֹנוּ וַיֶּחִי׃ קְרַב אַתָּה וּשְׁמָע אֵת כָּל־אֲשֶׁר
יֹאמַר יהוה אֱלֹהֵינוּ וְאַתְּ ׀ תְּדַבֵּר אֵלֵינוּ אֵת כָּל־אֲשֶׁר יְדַבֵּר
כה יהוה אֱלֹהֵינוּ אֵלֶיךָ וְשָׁמַעְנוּ וְעָשִׂינוּ׃ וַיִּשְׁמַע יהוה אֶת־קוֹל
דִּבְרֵיכֶם בְּדַבֶּרְכֶם אֵלָי וַיֹּאמֶר יהוה אֵלַי שָׁמַעְתִּי אֶת־קוֹל
דִּבְרֵי הָעָם הַזֶּה אֲשֶׁר דִּבְּרוּ אֵלֶיךָ הֵיטִיבוּ כָּל־אֲשֶׁר דִּבֵּרוּ׃
כו מִי־יִתֵּן וְהָיָה לְבָבָם זֶה לָהֶם לְיִרְאָה אֹתִי וְלִשְׁמֹר אֶת־כָּל־
כז מִצְוֺתַי כָּל־הַיָּמִים לְמַעַן יִיטַב לָהֶם וְלִבְנֵיהֶם לְעֹלָם׃ לֵךְ
כח אֱמֹר לָהֶם שׁוּבוּ לָכֶם לְאָהֳלֵיכֶם׃ וְאַתָּה פֹּה עֲמֹד עִמָּדִי
וַאֲדַבְּרָה אֵלֶיךָ אֵת כָּל־הַמִּצְוָה וְהַחֻקִּים וְהַמִּשְׁפָּטִים
אֲשֶׁר תְּלַמְּדֵם וְעָשׂוּ בָאָרֶץ אֲשֶׁר אָנֹכִי נֹתֵן לָהֶם לְרִשְׁתָּהּ׃
כט וּשְׁמַרְתֶּם לַעֲשׂוֹת כַּאֲשֶׁר צִוָּה יהוה אֱלֹהֵיכֶם אֶתְכֶם לֹא
ל תָסֻרוּ יָמִין וּשְׂמֹאל׃ בְּכָל־הַדֶּרֶךְ אֲשֶׁר צִוָּה יהוה אֱלֹהֵיכֶם

5:19 וְלֹא יָסָף *And He added no more* – What was unique, transfiguring, and still hard to understand about this event was that the nation, as a nation, heard the voice of God. God spoke – not just to a prophet, not in a vision or a trance, not as a sound within the soul, but as an event in public space and time. It was a *kol gadol velo yasaf*, a phrase for which Rashi (ad loc.) offers two understandings: a great voice that was never heard again, and a great voice that was ever heard again – it happened once but it reverberated for all time.

How do we reconcile Rashi's two interpretations of this phrase? Note that the wording of the Ten Commandments in Exodus and Deuteronomy is not identical. The first represents the direct revelation at Sinai. In the second,

the path that the Lord your God has commanded you,
so that you may live and it may be well for you, and your
6 1 years may be long in the land you are to possess. This is
the command – the decrees and the laws – that the Lord
your God charged me to teach you to keep in the land
that you are about to cross over into and take possession
2 of, so that you and your children and grandchildren may
remain in awe of the Lord your God as long as you live,
keeping all His decrees and commandments that I am
commanding you and so that your years may be long.
3 Listen, Israel, and take care to keep them, so that it may
be well for you, and so that you may be abundantly fertile
in a land flowing with milk and with honey, as the Lord,
the God of your ancestors, promised you.
4 5 Listen, Israel: the Lord our God – the Lord is one. You SHISHI

It has yet other meanings in Rabbinic Hebrew, such as "to infer," "to accept," "to take into account as evidence," and "to receive as part of the Oral Tradition." No English word has this range of meanings. Perhaps the closest are "to hearken" and "to heed" – neither of them terms in common use today.

Shema Yisrael, then, does not mean "Hear, Israel." It means something like: "Listen. Concentrate. Give the word of God your most focused attention. Strive to understand. Engage all your faculties, intellectual and emotional. Make His will your own. For what He commands you to do is not irrational or arbitrary but for your welfare, the welfare of your people, and ultimately for the benefit of all humanity."

In Judaism, faith is a form of listening – to the song creation sings to its Creator, and to the message history delivers to those who strive to understand it. That is what Moshe says time and again in Deuteronomy: Stop looking; listen. Stop speaking; listen. Create a silence in the soul. Still the clamor of instinct, desire, fear, anger. Strive to listen to the still, small voice beneath the noise. Then you will know that the universe is the work of the One beyond the furthest star yet closer to you than you are to yourself – and then you will love your God with all your heart, all your soul, and all your might. In God's unity you will find unity, within yourself and between yourself and the world, and you will no longer fear the unknown.

6:4 יהוה אֶחָד *The Lord is one* – This sentence, the heart of Jewish faith, has two distinct meanings. As translated above, it is a theological statement of monotheism: there is but a single God. Equally, though, it can be translated as "Listen,

אֶתְכֶם תֵּלֵכוּ לְמַעַן תִּחְיוּן וְטוֹב לָכֶם וְהַאֲרַכְתֶּם יָמִים בָּאָרֶץ
ו א אֲשֶׁר תִּירָשׁוּן׃ וְזֹאת הַמִּצְוָה הַחֻקִּים וְהַמִּשְׁפָּטִים אֲשֶׁר צִוָּה
יְהוָה אֱלֹהֵיכֶם לְלַמֵּד אֶתְכֶם לַעֲשׂוֹת בָּאָרֶץ אֲשֶׁר אַתֶּם
ב עֹבְרִים שָׁמָּה לְרִשְׁתָּהּ׃ לְמַעַן תִּירָא אֶת־יְהוָה אֱלֹהֶיךָ
לִשְׁמֹר אֶת־כָּל־חֻקֹּתָיו וּמִצְוֺתָיו אֲשֶׁר אָנֹכִי מְצַוֶּךָ אַתָּה
ג וּבִנְךָ וּבֶן־בִּנְךָ כֹּל יְמֵי חַיֶּיךָ וּלְמַעַן יַאֲרִכֻן יָמֶיךָ׃ וְשָׁמַעְתָּ
יִשְׂרָאֵל וְשָׁמַרְתָּ לַעֲשׂוֹת אֲשֶׁר יִיטַב לְךָ וַאֲשֶׁר תִּרְבּוּן
מְאֹד כַּאֲשֶׁר דִּבֶּר יְהוָה אֱלֹהֵי אֲבֹתֶיךָ לָךְ אֶרֶץ זָבַת חָלָב
וּדְבָשׁ׃
ד ה שְׁמַע יִשְׂרָאֵל יְהוָה אֱלֹהֵינוּ יְהוָה ׀ אֶחָד׃ וְאָהַבְתָּ אֵת ו ששי

LISTEN

"Listen, Israel, the LORD our God – the LORD is one." These words are the supreme testimony of Jewish faith. The keyword of Judaism is *Shema*. God is not something we see, but a voice we hear (see above, 4:12 and note there) The patriarchs and prophets did not see God; they heard Him.

This has implications for the whole of Judaism. It is a way of understanding the world. Judaism, with its belief in the invisible God who transcends the universe, and its prohibition against visual representations of God, is supremely a civilization of the ear. To give dramatic force to the idea that God is heard, not seen, we cover our eyes with our hand as we say these words.

The verb *lishmoa* is a key term of the book of Deuteronomy, where it appears in one or other form some ninety-two times. It conveys a wide range of meanings, clustered around five primary senses:

1. To listen, to pay focused attention, as in "Be still and listen (*u'shema*), Israel" (Deut. 27:9)
2. To hear, as in "I heard (*shamati*) Your voice in the garden and I was afraid" (Gen. 3:10)
3. To understand, as in "Let us go down and confuse their language so that one will not understand (*yishme'u*) the speech of another" (11:7)
4. To internalize, register, take to heart, as in "As for Yishmael – I have heard you" (17:20), meaning, "I have taken into account what you have said; I will bear it in mind; it is a consideration that weighs with Me"
5. To respond in action, as in "Avram listened (*vayishma*) to Sarai" (16:2). This last sense is the closest *shema* comes to meaning "to obey."

shall love the LORD your God with all your heart, with all
6 your soul, and with all your might. Let these words that I
charge you with today remain impressed upon your heart.
7 Teach them to your children, speaking of them when you

---

and kindnesses, are sustained. Jewish law is the structure of behavior built around the love between God and His people, so that the love remains long after the first feelings of passion have grown old.

6:5 בְּכָל־לְבָבְךָ *With all your heart* – It is said that the Rebbe Menachem Mendel of Kotzk once asked his disciples, "Where does God live?" The disciples were perplexed. "What does the Rebbe mean, where does God live? Where does God not live? Surely we have been taught that no place is devoid of His presence? He fills the heavens and the earth." The Rebbe replied, "You have not understood. God lives *where we let Him in*."

On another occasion, he asked, "Why does it say in the *Shema*: 'Let these words…remain impressed upon your heart'? Why 'upon' and not 'in'?" He answered: "The heart is not always open. Therefore the Torah says: Lay these words *on* your heart, so that when your heart opens, they will be there, ready to fall in." In Judaism, spirituality means openness. To one who is open, God is closer than we are to ourselves. To one who is closed, He is farther away than the most distant galaxies. A question, asked with sincerity, is an opening in the soul. The task of education is to teach a child to be open – to the voice of God and the miracle of existence.

6:6 עַל־לְבָבֶךָ *Impressed upon your heart* – The ideal polity, so the Torah implies, is *nomocracy*: the rule not of men or women, but of law – not law carved in stone or written on scrolls but law engraved in the hearts of the people:

> "For this covenant, which I will make with the House of Israel after these days," declares the LORD, "I will deliver My teaching into their midst and inscribe it upon their hearts, and I will be their God, and they will be My people." (Jer. 31:32)

It was a utopian aspiration in Deuteronomy, and so it was to Yirmeyahu. It still is. This is why, in the book of Samuel, God says: If you want a king and are prepared to sacrifice some of the freedom I have given you, then appoint a king. But be aware that kings, courts, and governments carry a high price.

At the transition between the Israelites of the book of Judges and the birth of monarchy in the book of Samuel, a social contract formed the Israelite state. But the true foundational moment occurred here, centuries earlier, at Mount Sinai, when a social covenant created a society. God revealed Himself to the people and gave them the Ten Commandments. Unlike any other treaty in the ancient world, it is made not between two rulers but between

ו יְהוָה אֱלֹהֶיךָ בְּכָל־לְבָבְךָ וּבְכָל־נַפְשְׁךָ וּבְכָל־מְאֹדֶךָ: וְהָיוּ
ז הַדְּבָרִים הָאֵלֶּה אֲשֶׁר אָנֹכִי מְצַוְּךָ הַיּוֹם עַל־לְבָבֶךָ: וְשִׁנַּנְתָּם

Israel, the LORD is our God, the LORD alone," in which case it is the proclamation of God as the sole sovereign of the people Israel, what the Sages called *kabbalat ol malkhut Shamayim*, "acceptance of the yoke of the kingdom of Heaven," a theological-political statement of Israel as a nation under divine sovereignty. This is how the text is used in our daily prayers.

The words of the *Shema* are the first Hebrew words we learn as children, and the last words we say at the end of our life, the words Jewish martyrs said as they prepared to die for their faith. In these contexts they mean more than that God is One. You, God of the universe, are our God. We have no other. Our ancestors put their faith in You. We put our faith in You. You are the focus of our lives. You are the breath we breathe, the strength we feel, the voice we hear, the horizon of our hopes.

LOVE

Judaism is built around an act of mutual commitment, by God to a people and by the people to God. The commitment itself is an act of love. These famous words, "You shall love the LORD your God with all your heart, with all your soul, and with all your might" (Deut. 6:5), lie at its heart. The Torah is the foundational narrative of the fraught, sometimes tempestuous, marriage between God and an often obstinate people. It is a story of love.

How is this vision connected to the legal, halakhic content of much of Deuteronomy? On the one hand we have this passionate declaration of love by God for a people; on the other we have a detailed code of law covering most aspects of life for individuals and the nation as a whole once it enters the land. Law and love are not two things that go obviously together. What has the one to do with the other?

Commitment is falling in love with something and then building a structure of behavior around it to sustain that love over time. Law, the mitzvot, halakha, is that structure of behavior. Love is a passion, an emotion, a heightened state, a peak experience. But an emotional state cannot be guaranteed forever. We wed in poetry but we stay married in prose. Which is why we need laws, rituals, habits of deed. Rituals are the framework that keeps love alive. That is what the vast multiplicity of rituals in Judaism, many of them spelled out in the book of Deuteronomy, actually achieved. They sustained the love between God and a people. Could it have been done without the rituals, the 613 commands, that fill our days with reminders of God's presence? I think not. Without the rituals, eventually love dies. With them, the glowing embers remain and still have the power to burst into flame. Not every day in a long and happy marriage feels like a wedding, but even love grown old will still be strong, if the choreography of fond devotion, the ritual courtesies

sit at home and when you travel on the way, when you lie
8 down and when you rise. Bind them as a sign upon your
hand, and have them as an emblem between your eyes.
9 Write them on the doorposts of your houses and on your
10 gates. When the Lord your God brings you
into the land that He swore to your ancestors Avraham,
Yitzḥak, and Yaakov that He would give to you, a land
11 with great and goodly towns you did not build, houses
full of all good things that you did not provide, hewn
cisterns you did not hew, and vineyards and olive groves
that you did not plant – and you eat and are satisfied,
12 take care that you do not forget the Lord who brought
13 you out of Egypt, out of the house of slaves. It is the
Lord your God you must revere, Him you must serve,
14 and only by His name that you must swear. Do not walk
after other gods, after gods of the peoples around you,
15 for the Lord your God in your midst demands absolute
loyalty. The anger of the Lord your God would burn
against you and He would annihilate you from the face
16 of the earth. Do not test the Lord your God
17 as you tested Him at Masa. Be very vigilant to keep
the commandments of the Lord your God, and the

6:8 וּקְשַׁרְתָּם לְאוֹת *Bind them as a sign* – The word "tefillin" (here called *totafot*) means "emblem," "sign," "insignia," the visible symbol of an abstract idea. Tefillin are our reminder of the commandment "Love the Lord your God with all your heart, with all your soul, and with all your might" (Deut. 6:5). In verse 5, the words "*all your heart*" are understood to refer to the tefillin on the upper arm opposite the heart; "*all your soul*" to the head tefillin opposite the seat of consciousness, the soul; and "*all your might*" to the strap of the hand tefillin, symbolizing action, power, might. Tefillin thus symbolize the love for God in emotion (heart), thought (head), and deed (hand).

6:16 לֹא תְנַסּוּ אֶת־יהוה אֱלֹהֵיכֶם *Do not test the Lord your God* – This verse is the source of the prohibition against "relying on a miracle" – failing to take safety precautions on the basis that God will give supernatural protection.

The Talmud Bavli displays a fascinating attitude toward the miraculous. It tells the story of a man whose wife died giving birth. The man was so poor he was unable to pay for a wet nurse. A miracle happened, says the Talmud, and his

לְבָנֶ֔יךָ וְדִבַּרְתָּ֖ בָּ֑ם בְּשִׁבְתְּךָ֤ בְּבֵיתֶ֙ךָ֙ וּבְלֶכְתְּךָ֣ בַדֶּ֔רֶךְ וּֽבְשָׁכְבְּךָ֖
ח וּבְקוּמֶֽךָ׃ וּקְשַׁרְתָּ֥ם לְא֖וֹת עַל־יָדֶ֑ךָ וְהָי֥וּ לְטֹטָפֹ֖ת בֵּ֥ין עֵינֶֽיךָ׃
ט י וּכְתַבְתָּ֛ם עַל־מְזֻז֥וֹת בֵּיתֶ֖ךָ וּבִשְׁעָרֶֽיךָ׃ וְהָיָ֞ה כִּֽי־
יְבִֽיאֲךָ֣ ׀ יְהוָ֣ה אֱלֹהֶ֗יךָ אֶל־הָאָ֛רֶץ אֲשֶׁ֨ר נִשְׁבַּ֧ע לַאֲבֹתֶ֛יךָ
לְאַבְרָהָ֛ם לְיִצְחָ֥ק וּֽלְיַעֲקֹ֖ב לָ֣תֶת לָ֑ךְ עָרִ֛ים גְּדֹלֹ֥ת וְטֹבֹ֖ת
יא אֲשֶׁ֥ר לֹא־בָנִֽיתָ׃ וּבָ֨תִּ֜ים מְלֵאִ֣ים כָּל־טוּב֮ אֲשֶׁ֣ר לֹא־מִלֵּ֒אתָ֒
וּבֹרֹ֤ת חֲצוּבִים֙ אֲשֶׁ֣ר לֹא־חָצַ֔בְתָּ כְּרָמִ֥ים וְזֵיתִ֖ים אֲשֶׁ֣ר לֹא־
יב נָטָ֑עְתָּ וְאָכַלְתָּ֖ וְשָׂבָֽעְתָּ׃ הִשָּׁ֣מֶר לְךָ֔ פֶּן־תִּשְׁכַּ֖ח אֶת־יְהוָ֑ה
יג אֲשֶׁ֧ר הוֹצִֽיאֲךָ֛ מֵאֶ֥רֶץ מִצְרַ֖יִם מִבֵּ֥ית עֲבָדִֽים׃ אֶת־יְהוָ֧ה
יד אֱלֹהֶ֛יךָ תִּירָ֖א וְאֹת֣וֹ תַעֲבֹ֑ד וּבִשְׁמ֖וֹ תִּשָּׁבֵֽעַ׃ לֹ֣א תֵֽלְכ֔וּן אַחֲרֵ֖י
טו אֱלֹהִ֣ים אֲחֵרִ֑ים מֵֽאֱלֹהֵי֙ הָֽעַמִּ֔ים אֲשֶׁ֖ר סְבִיבוֹתֵיכֶֽם׃ כִּ֣י אֵ֤ל
קַנָּא֙ יְהוָ֣ה אֱלֹהֶ֔יךָ בְּקִרְבֶּ֑ךָ פֶּן־יֶ֩חֱרֶ֩ה אַף־יְהוָ֨ה אֱלֹהֶ֜יךָ בָּ֗ךְ
טז וְהִשְׁמִ֣ידְךָ֔ מֵעַ֖ל פְּנֵ֥י הָאֲדָמָֽה׃ לֹ֣א תְנַסּ֔וּ אֶת־
יז יְהוָ֖ה אֱלֹהֵיכֶ֑ם כַּאֲשֶׁ֥ר נִסִּיתֶ֖ם בַּמַּסָּֽה׃ שָׁמ֣וֹר תִּשְׁמְר֔וּן אֶת־

God and an entire people, the presence, knowledge, and consent of all of whom is essential. This is not democracy in the modern or even the Greek sense. But it is a corollary of the idea that the human person as such is in the image of God. In covenant as the Bible understands it, each individual has significance, dignity, moral worth, the right to be heard, a voice. The connection between the Law and every individual is not imposed by human authority but "impressed upon your heart."

6:7 וְשִׁנַּנְתָּם לְבָנֶיךָ *Teach them to your children* – Rashi translates this verb as "you shall sharpen" (compare Deut. 32:41). Education, in Judaism, is active, not passive. It is about honing the mind, sharpening the intellect, through question and answer, challenge and response. Four times the Torah refers to children asking questions (the "four sons" of the Haggada). Against cultures that see unquestioning obedience as the ideal behavior of a child, Jewish tradition regards the child "who does not know how to ask" as the lowest, not the highest, stage of development.

Judaism is God's perennial question mark against the condition of the world. That things are as they are is a fact, not a value. Should it be so? Why should it be so? Only one who asks whether the world should be as it is, is capable of changing what it is.

▶

testimonies and decrees with which He has charged you.
18 Do what is right and what is good in the LORD's eyes,
so that it may go well with you, and you may go in and
take possession of the good land that the LORD swore to
19 your ancestors to give you, driving out all your enemies
20 before you, as the LORD promised. And in the

> neighbors and friends, all his various transactions and the ordinances of all societies and countries. But since He mentioned many of them, such as "Do not go around as a gossipmonger" (Lev. 19:16), "Do not take revenge or bear a grudge" (19:18), "Do not stand by while your neighbor's life is in danger" (19:16), "Do not curse the deaf" (19:14), "Stand up in the presence of the white-haired" (19:32), and the like, He went on to state in a general way that in all matters one should do what is good and right, including even compromise and going beyond the strict requirement of the law.... Thus one should behave in every sphere of activity, such that one is worthy of being called "good and upright."

It seems as if Ramban is telling us that there are aspects of the moral life that are not caught by the concept of law at all. That is what he means by saying, "It is impossible to mention in the Torah all aspects of man's conduct with his neighbors and friends." Moral law is about universals, principles that apply in all places and times: Do not murder. Do not rob. Do not steal. Do not lie. Yet there are important features of the moral life that are not universal at all. They have to do with specific circumstances and the way we respond to them. What is it to be a good husband or wife, a good parent, a good teacher, a good friend? What is it to be a great leader, or follower, or member of a team? When is it right to praise, and when is it appropriate to say, "You could have done better"? There are aspects of the moral life that cannot be reduced to rules of conduct, because what matters is not only what we do, but the way in which we do it – with humility or gentleness or sensitivity or tact. Morality is not just a set of rules, even a code as elaborate as the 613 commandments and their rabbinic extensions. It is also about the way we respond to people as individuals.

This ultimately is the difference between the two great principles of Judaic ethics: justice and love. Justice is universal. It treats all people alike, rich and poor, powerful and powerless, making no distinctions on the basis of color or class. But love is particular. A parent loves his or her children for what makes them each unique. The moral life is a combination of both. That is why it cannot be reduced solely to universal laws. That is what the Torah means when it speaks of "what is right and what is good" over and above the commandments, statutes, and testimonies.

יח מִצְוֺת יהוה אֱלֹהֵיכֶם וְעֵדֹתָיו וְחֻקָּיו אֲשֶׁר צִוָּךְ׃ וְעָשִׂיתָ
הַיָּשָׁר וְהַטּוֹב בְּעֵינֵי יהוה לְמַעַן יִיטַב לָךְ וּבָאתָ וְיָרַשְׁתָּ
יט אֶת־הָאָרֶץ הַטֹּבָה אֲשֶׁר־נִשְׁבַּע יהוה לַאֲבֹתֶיךָ׃ לַהֲדֹף
כ אֶת־כָּל־אֹיְבֶיךָ מִפָּנֶיךָ כַּאֲשֶׁר דִּבֶּר יהוה׃ כִּי־

own breasts sprouted milk. What is fascinating is what the Talmud says next: "R. Yosef said: Come and see how great is this man that such a miracle was performed for him. Abaye said to him: To the contrary, come and see how lowly was this man, that he needed the natural order to be changed for him" (Shabbat 53b).

Abaye believed, with many of the Sages, that we should not need miracles, nor should we rely on them. Two prophets, Eliyahu and Elisha, both raise the dead to life (I Kings 17:17; II Kings 4:8–37). Yet neither the biblical text nor later Jewish tradition made any great fuss over this. The real miracle in both cases – as it is in the stories of the patriarchs and matriarchs in Genesis, and of Ḥana in the book of Samuel – is that infertile women were able to have children in the first place. In that sense, modern fertility treatments are our miracles. We should not need supernatural intervention to see children as the gift of God.

God is found in order, not in the miraculous suspension of that order; He is there in the law that tells us to provide for those in need, and in the human drive and ability to partner with Him in the work of creation and solve ever more of the problems we face. We are to "keep all these decrees, to revere the Lord our God… so that we might always prosper" (Deut. 6:24), but we are not to demand direct or miraculous connections between the two.

THE RIGHT AND THE GOOD

Verse 17 makes reference to commandments, testimonies, and decrees. This, on the face of it, is the whole of Judaism as far as conduct is concerned. What more then is meant, in the next verse, by the phrase "what is right and what is good"?

Rashi says that it refers to "compromise [that is, not strictly insisting on your rights] and action within or beyond the letter of the law (*lifnim mishurat hadin*)." The law, as it were, lays down a minimum threshold: this we must do. But the moral life aspires to more than simply doing what we must. The saints and heroes of the moral life go beyond. They do more than they are commanded. They go the extra mile. That, according to Rashi, is what the Torah means by "what is right and what is good."

Ramban, while citing Rashi and agreeing with him, goes on to say something different in his commentary on the same passage:

> Now this is a great principle, for it is impossible to mention in the Torah all aspects of man's conduct with his

future, when your child asks you, 'What is the meaning
of the testimonies, decrees, and laws that the Lord our
21 God has commanded you?' tell him, 'We were slaves to
Pharaoh in Egypt, but the Lord brought us out of Egypt
22 with a mighty hand. Before our eyes the Lord sent great
and awesome signs and wonders against Egypt and
23 Pharaoh and his whole household. And He freed us from
there, to bring us in and give us the land that He promised
24 on oath to our ancestors. The Lord commanded us to
keep all these decrees, to revere the Lord our God, so
that we might always prosper; to keep us alive, as we are
25 today. And if we carefully keep all this command before
the Lord our God, as He has charged us, this will be our
7 1 righteousness.' When the Lord your God brings SHEVI'I
you into the land that you are about to enter and possess,
when you drive out many nations before you – the Hittites,
Girgashites, Amorites, Canaanites, Perizzites, Hivites, and
2 Jebusites, seven nations larger and stronger than you – and
the Lord your God gives them over to you and you defeat
them, you must utterly destroy them. Make no covenant
3 with them and grant them no mercy. Do not intermarry
3 with them; do not give your daughters to their sons in
4 marriage or take their daughters for your sons. For they
will turn your children away from walking after Me, and
bring them to serve other gods. The Lord's anger will
5 burn against you, and He will quickly destroy you. Instead,
this is what you must do to them: tear down their altars,
smash their worship pillars, cut down their sacred trees,
6 and burn their idols with fire. For you are a holy people to
the Lord your God. The Lord your God has chosen you,
7 of all the peoples on earth, to be His treasured people. It is
not because you were more numerous than other peoples
that the Lord desired you and chose you, for you are the
8 smallest of all peoples. It was because of the love the Lord

a mere seventy when they went down to Egypt, "were fruitful and burgeoned, they multiplied and became exceptionally strong, until the land was filled with

יִשְׁאָלְךָ בִנְךָ מָחָר לֵאמֹר מָה הָעֵדֹת וְהַחֻקִּים וְהַמִּשְׁפָּטִים
כא אֲשֶׁר צִוָּה יְהוָה אֱלֹהֵינוּ אֶתְכֶם: וְאָמַרְתָּ לְבִנְךָ עֲבָדִים
הָיִינוּ לְפַרְעֹה בְּמִצְרָיִם וַיֹּצִיאֵנוּ יְהוָה מִמִּצְרַיִם בְּיָד חֲזָקָה:
כב וַיִּתֵּן יְהוָה אוֹתֹת וּמֹפְתִים גְּדֹלִים וְרָעִים ׀ בְּמִצְרַיִם בְּפַרְעֹה
כג וּבְכָל־בֵּיתוֹ לְעֵינֵינוּ: וְאוֹתָנוּ הוֹצִיא מִשָּׁם לְמַעַן הָבִיא אֹתָנוּ
כד לָתֶת לָנוּ אֶת־הָאָרֶץ אֲשֶׁר נִשְׁבַּע לַאֲבֹתֵינוּ: וַיְצַוֵּנוּ יְהוָה
לַעֲשׂוֹת אֶת־כָּל־הַחֻקִּים הָאֵלֶּה לְיִרְאָה אֶת־יְהוָה אֱלֹהֵינוּ
כה לְטוֹב לָנוּ כָּל־הַיָּמִים לְחַיֹּתֵנוּ כְּהַיּוֹם הַזֶּה: וּצְדָקָה תִּהְיֶה־
לָּנוּ כִּי־נִשְׁמֹר לַעֲשׂוֹת אֶת־כָּל־הַמִּצְוָה הַזֹּאת לִפְנֵי יְהוָה
ז א אֱלֹהֵינוּ כַּאֲשֶׁר צִוָּנוּ: כִּי יְבִיאֲךָ יְהוָה אֱלֹהֶיךָ שביעי
אֶל־הָאָרֶץ אֲשֶׁר־אַתָּה בָא־שָׁמָּה לְרִשְׁתָּהּ וְנָשַׁל גּוֹיִם־
רַבִּים ׀ מִפָּנֶיךָ הַחִתִּי וְהַגִּרְגָּשִׁי וְהָאֱמֹרִי וְהַכְּנַעֲנִי וְהַפְּרִזִּי
ב וְהַחִוִּי וְהַיְבוּסִי שִׁבְעָה גוֹיִם רַבִּים וַעֲצוּמִים מִמֶּךָּ: וּנְתָנָם
יְהוָה אֱלֹהֶיךָ לְפָנֶיךָ וְהִכִּיתָם הַחֲרֵם תַּחֲרִים אֹתָם לֹא־
ג תִכְרֹת לָהֶם בְּרִית וְלֹא תְחָנֵּם: וְלֹא תִתְחַתֵּן בָּם בִּתְּךָ לֹא־
ד תִתֵּן לִבְנוֹ וּבִתּוֹ לֹא־תִקַּח לִבְנֶךָ: כִּי־יָסִיר אֶת־בִּנְךָ מֵאַחֲרַי
וְעָבְדוּ אֱלֹהִים אֲחֵרִים וְחָרָה אַף־יְהוָה בָּכֶם וְהִשְׁמִידְךָ
ה מַהֵר: כִּי אִם־כֹּה תַעֲשׂוּ לָהֶם מִזְבְּחֹתֵיהֶם תִּתֹּצוּ וּמַצֵּבֹתָם
ו תְּשַׁבֵּרוּ וַאֲשֵׁירֵהֶם תְּגַדֵּעוּן וּפְסִילֵיהֶם תִּשְׂרְפוּן בָּאֵשׁ: כִּי
עַם קָדוֹשׁ אַתָּה לַיהוָה אֱלֹהֶיךָ בְּךָ בָּחַר ׀ יְהוָה אֱלֹהֶיךָ
לִהְיוֹת לוֹ לְעַם סְגֻלָּה מִכֹּל הָעַמִּים אֲשֶׁר עַל־פְּנֵי הָאֲדָמָה:
ז לֹא מֵרֻבְּכֶם מִכָּל־הָעַמִּים חָשַׁק יְהוָה בָּכֶם וַיִּבְחַר בָּכֶם
ח כִּי־אַתֶּם הַמְעַט מִכָּל־הָעַמִּים: כִּי מֵאַהֲבַת יְהוָה אֶתְכֶם

7:7 כִּי־אַתֶּם הַמְעַט מִכָּל־הָעַמִּים *You are the smallest of all peoples* – This remark gives a new complexion to the biblical image of the people Israel. It is not what we have heard thus far. In Genesis, God promised the patriarchs that their descendants would be like the stars of the heaven, the sand on the seashore, the dust of the earth, uncountable. Avraham will be the father, not just of one nation but of many. At the beginning of Exodus we read of how the covenantal family, numbering ▶

had for you, because of the oath He kept, that He swore
to your ancestors, that the LORD freed you with a mighty
hand, and redeemed you from the house of slaves, from the
9 grip of Pharaoh, king of Egypt. Know therefore that only MAFTIR
the LORD your God is God, the faithful God who keeps
His covenant and the love to a thousand generations of
10 those who love Him and keep His commandments, and
who instantly repays with destruction those who reject
11 Him, requiting them in a moment. Therefore, carefully
keep the command – the decrees and the laws – that I am
charging you with today.

The haftara for Parashat Vaethanan is on page 1598.

outlived all the world's great empires to deliver to humanity a message of hope: You need not be large to be great. What you need is to be open to a power greater than yourself.

7:9 שֹׁמֵר הַבְּרִית וְהַחֶסֶד *His covenant and the love* – The Hebrew phrase here, *shomer habrit vehaḥesed*, "the covenant and the loving-kindness," is a puzzling one. If you look, for instance, at the Jewish Publication Society translation, they translate only the word "covenant," because the *ḥesed* is included in the covenant. If you look at the New International version, *habrit vehaḥesed* is translated as "the covenant of love." But of course it doesn't mean that; it means "covenant and love." Everyone had a problem in understanding what else God does for the Jewish people at Mount Sinai, other than make a covenant with them. The answer, I believe, is that a covenant is what sociologists and anthropologists call reciprocal altruism. You do this for me. I will do this for you. "You serve Me," says God, "and I will protect you." Covenant is always reciprocal. But that makes one vulnerable, because what happens if we do not keep the covenant? The covenant is then rendered null and void.

Therefore, even covenant is not enough. God also has a relationship of *ḥesed* with us. An unconditional love, which is translated into deeds of kindness. The covenant is conditional, but *ḥesed* is unconditional. That is what Rambam meant when he said, in *Guide for the Perplexed* III:53, that *ḥesed* means doing something for somebody who has no claim on us.

We received a covenant at Mount Sinai, but we also received something still more long-lasting and profound, which is God's unconditional love.

וּמִשָּׁמְרוֹ אֶת־הַשְּׁבֻעָה אֲשֶׁר נִשְׁבַּע לַאֲבֹתֵיכֶם הוֹצִיא יְהוָה
אֶתְכֶם בְּיָד חֲזָקָה וַיִּפְדְּךָ מִבֵּית עֲבָדִים מִיַּד פַּרְעֹה מֶלֶךְ־
ט מִצְרָיִם: וְיָדַעְתָּ כִּי־יְהוָה אֱלֹהֶיךָ הוּא הָאֱלֹהִים הָאֵל הַנֶּאֱמָן מפטיר
שֹׁמֵר הַבְּרִית וְהַחֶסֶד לְאֹהֲבָיו וּלְשֹׁמְרֵי מִצְוֺתָו לְאֶלֶף דּוֹר:
י וּמְשַׁלֵּם לְשֹׂנְאָיו אֶל־פָּנָיו לְהַאֲבִידוֹ לֹא יְאַחֵר לְשֹׂנְאוֹ אֶל־
יא פָּנָיו יְשַׁלֶּם־לוֹ: וְשָׁמַרְתָּ אֶת־הַמִּצְוָה וְאֶת־הַחֻקִּים וְאֶת־
הַמִּשְׁפָּטִים אֲשֶׁר אָנֹכִי מְצַוְּךָ הַיּוֹם לַעֲשׂוֹתָם:

The הפטרה *for* פרשת ואתחנן *is on page 1599.*

them" (Ex. 1:7). In these texts and others it is the size, the numerical greatness, of the people that is emphasized. What then are we to make of Moshe's words that speak of its smallness? Targum Yonatan interprets it not to be about numbers at all but about self-image. He translates it not as "the fewest of all peoples" but as "the most lowly and humble of peoples." Rashi gives a similar reading, citing Avraham's words, "I am mere dust and ashes" (Gen. 18:27), and Moshe and Aharon's, "What are we?" (Ex. 16:7).

Whatever the explanation, there is something in this verse that resonates throughout Jewish history. Through the Jewish people, God is telling humankind that you do not need to be numerous to be great. Nations are judged not by their size but by their contribution. Of this the most compelling proof is that a nation as small as the Jews could produce an ever-renewed flow of prophets, priests, poets, philosophers, sages, and saints. It has also yielded some of the world's greatest writers, artists, musicians, filmmakers, intellectuals, doctors, lawyers, and technological innovators. Out of all proportion to their numbers, Jews could and can be found working as lawyers fighting injustice, economists fighting poverty, doctors fighting disease, teachers fighting ignorance, and therapists fighting depression and despair.

You do not need numbers to enlarge the spiritual and moral horizons of humankind. You need other things altogether: a sense of the worth and dignity of the individual, of the power of human possibility to transform the world, of the importance of giving everyone the best education they can have, of making each feel part of a collective responsibility to ameliorate the human condition. Judaism asks of us the willingness to take high ideals and enact them in the real world, unswayed by disappointments and defeats. This small people has

Parashat Ekev

7 12 If, indeed, you heed these laws, always vigilant to keep
them, the Lord your God will keep with you the
covenant and the love He forged on oath with your
13 ancestors. He will love you, bless you, and multiply you.
He will bless the fruit of your womb and the fruit of your
land, your grain and wine and oil, the calves of your herds
and the lambs of your flock, in the land that He swore
14 to your ancestors to give you. You shall be blessed above
all other peoples, and no male or female among you or
15 your livestock will be barren or childless. The Lord will
keep you free from all sickness. All the terrible diseases
of Egypt that you knew, He will not inflict upon you, but
16 He will lay them upon all those who hate you. You shall
devour all the peoples that the Lord your God is giving
over to you. Do not show them pity, and do not worship
17 their gods – for that would be a snare to you. You

This vision was unique in its time. In *Ethical Life: The Past and Present of Ethical Cultures*, philosopher Harry Redner distinguishes four basic visions of the ethical life in the history of civilizations. One he calls civic ethics, the ethics of ancient Greece and Rome. Second is the ethic of duty, which he identifies with Confucianism, Krishnaism, and late Stoicism. Third is the ethic of honor, a distinctive combination of courtly and military decorum to be found among Persians, Arabs, and Turks as well as in medieval Christianity and Islam. The fourth, which he calls simply morality, he traces to Leviticus and Deuteronomy. He defines it as "the ethic of love."

What is radical about this idea is that, first, the Torah insists, against virtually the whole of the ancient world, that the elements that constitute reality are neither hostile nor indifferent to humankind. We are here because Someone wanted us to be, One who cares about us, watches over us, and seeks our well-being. Second, the love with which God created the universe is not just divine. It is to serve as the model for us in our humanity. We are bidden to love the neighbor and the stranger, to engage in acts of kindness and compassion, and to build a society based on love (Deut. 10:18–19).

Having created the world in love and forgiveness, God asks us to love and forgive others.

פרשת עקב

ז יב וְהָיָה ׀ עֵקֶב תִּשְׁמְעוּן אֵת הַמִּשְׁפָּטִים הָאֵלֶּה וּשְׁמַרְתֶּם ז
וַעֲשִׂיתֶם אֹתָם וְשָׁמַר יהוה אֱלֹהֶיךָ לְךָ אֶת־הַבְּרִית וְאֶת־
יג הַחֶסֶד אֲשֶׁר נִשְׁבַּע לַאֲבֹתֶיךָ׃ וַאֲהֵבְךָ וּבֵרַכְךָ וְהִרְבֶּךָ וּבֵרַךְ
פְּרִי־בִטְנְךָ וּפְרִי־אַדְמָתֶךָ דְּגָנְךָ וְתִירֹשְׁךָ וְיִצְהָרֶךָ שְׁגַר־
אֲלָפֶיךָ וְעַשְׁתְּרֹת צֹאנֶךָ עַל הָאֲדָמָה אֲשֶׁר־נִשְׁבַּע לַאֲבֹתֶיךָ
יד לָתֶת לָךְ׃ בָּרוּךְ תִּהְיֶה מִכָּל־הָעַמִּים לֹא־יִהְיֶה בְךָ עָקָר
טו וַעֲקָרָה וּבִבְהֶמְתֶּךָ׃ וְהֵסִיר יהוה מִמְּךָ כָּל־חֹלִי וְכָל־מַדְוֵי
מִצְרַיִם הָרָעִים אֲשֶׁר יָדַעְתָּ לֹא יְשִׂימָם בָּךְ וּנְתָנָם בְּכָל־
טז שֹׂנְאֶיךָ׃ וְאָכַלְתָּ אֶת־כָּל־הָעַמִּים אֲשֶׁר יהוה אֱלֹהֶיךָ נֹתֵן
לָךְ לֹא־תָחוֹס עֵינְךָ עֲלֵיהֶם וְלֹא תַעֲבֹד אֶת־אֱלֹהֵיהֶם כִּי־
יז מוֹקֵשׁ הוּא לָךְ׃ כִּי תֹאמַר בִּלְבָבְךָ רַבִּים הַגּוֹיִם

EKEV

In Parashat Ekev, Moshe continues his second address, setting out in broad terms the principles of the covenant the Israelites made with God, and what it demands of them as a chosen nation in a promised land. If they are faithful to the covenant, they will be blessed materially as well as spiritually. But they should not attribute their success to themselves or their righteousness. Moshe reminds them of the people's sins during the wilderness years: the golden calf, the Koraḥ rebellion, and other such episodes. He reminds them, too, of God's forgiveness. Remembering their history, they are to love and revere God and teach their children to do likewise. This entire complex of beliefs is summarized in the passage that became the second paragraph of the *Shema* (Deut. 11:13–21). Israel's fate depends on Israel's faith.

GOD OF LOVE

Something implicit in the Torah from the very beginning becomes explicit in the book of Deuteronomy. God is the God of love. More than we love Him, He loves us.

The book of Deuteronomy is saturated with the language of love. The root *a-h-v* appears in Exodus twice, in Leviticus twice (both in Lev. 19), in Numbers not at all – and in Deuteronomy twenty-three times. Deuteronomy is a book about societal beatitude (see note on Deut. 1:16) and the transformative power of love.

▶

might say to yourself, 'These nations are more numerous
18 than I. How can I possibly dispossess them?' Do not be
afraid of them. Remember well what the LORD your God
19 did to Pharaoh and to all Egypt. Your own eyes saw the
great trials, the signs and wonders, the mighty hand and
the arm stretched forth, with which the LORD your God
brought you out. The LORD your God will do the same
20 to all the peoples you fear. The LORD your God will send
the hornet, too, against them until even the survivors
21 who hide from you are destroyed. Do not be terrified of
them, for the LORD your God, a great and awesome God,
22 is in your midst. The LORD your God will drive out these
nations before you, little by little. You may not put an end
to them at once, or the wild beasts would become too
23 numerous for you. But the LORD your God will give them
over to you, throwing them into great panic until they are
24 destroyed. He will give their kings over to your hands
and you shall wipe out their name from under heaven.
No one will be able to stand against you, until you have
25 destroyed them. You shall burn the images of their gods
with fire. Do not covet the silver or gold on them and take

---

view. The guardian of conscience is memory. Time and again the verb *zakhor*, "remember," resonates through Moshe's speeches in Deuteronomy:

> Remember that you were slaves in Egypt…that is why the LORD your God has commanded you to keep the Sabbath day. (5:15)
>
> Remember that the LORD your God has led you through all this journey of forty years in the wilderness. (8:2)
>
> Remember and never forget how you provoked the LORD your God to fury in the wilderness. (9:7)
>
> Remember what the LORD your God did to Miriam on your way when you left Egypt. (24:9)
>
> Remember what Amalek did to you on your way as you left Egypt. (25:17)
>
> Remember the days of old, consider the years of ages past. (32:7)

As Yosef Hayim Yerushalmi notes in his great treatise, *Zakhor*, "Only in Israel and nowhere else is the injunction to remember felt as a religious imperative to an entire people" (see also note on Ex. 16:33). Civilizations begin to die when they forget. Israel was commanded never to forget.

יח הָאֵלֶּה מִמֶּנִּי אֵיכָה אוּכַל לְהוֹרִישָׁם: לֹא תִירָא מֵהֶם זָכֹר
תִּזְכֹּר אֵת אֲשֶׁר־עָשָׂה יהוה אֱלֹהֶיךָ לְפַרְעֹה וּלְכָל־מִצְרָיִם:
יט הַמַּסֹּת הַגְּדֹלֹת אֲשֶׁר־רָאוּ עֵינֶיךָ וְהָאֹתֹת וְהַמֹּפְתִים וְהַיָּד
הַחֲזָקָה וְהַזְּרֹעַ הַנְּטוּיָה אֲשֶׁר הוֹצִאֲךָ יהוה אֱלֹהֶיךָ כֵּן־יַעֲשֶׂה
כ יהוה אֱלֹהֶיךָ לְכָל־הָעַמִּים אֲשֶׁר־אַתָּה יָרֵא מִפְּנֵיהֶם: וְגַם
אֶת־הַצִּרְעָה יְשַׁלַּח יהוה אֱלֹהֶיךָ בָּם עַד־אֲבֹד הַנִּשְׁאָרִים
כא וְהַנִּסְתָּרִים מִפָּנֶיךָ: לֹא תַעֲרֹץ מִפְּנֵיהֶם כִּי־יהוה אֱלֹהֶיךָ
כב בְּקִרְבֶּךָ אֵל גָּדוֹל וְנוֹרָא: וְנָשַׁל יהוה אֱלֹהֶיךָ אֶת־הַגּוֹיִם הָאֵל
מִפָּנֶיךָ מְעַט מְעָט לֹא תוּכַל כַּלֹּתָם מַהֵר פֶּן־תִּרְבֶּה עָלֶיךָ
כג חַיַּת הַשָּׂדֶה: וּנְתָנָם יהוה אֱלֹהֶיךָ לְפָנֶיךָ וְהָמָם מְהוּמָה
כד גְדֹלָה עַד הִשָּׁמְדָם: וְנָתַן מַלְכֵיהֶם בְּיָדֶךָ וְהַאֲבַדְתָּ אֶת־שְׁמָם
מִתַּחַת הַשָּׁמָיִם לֹא־יִתְיַצֵּב אִישׁ בְּפָנֶיךָ עַד הִשְׁמִדְךָ אֹתָם:
כה פְּסִילֵי אֱלֹהֵיהֶם תִּשְׂרְפוּן בָּאֵשׁ לֹא־תַחְמֹד כֶּסֶף וְזָהָב עֲלֵיהֶם

7:17 רַבִּים הַגּוֹיִם הָאֵלֶּה *These nations are more numerous* – Not only were the Israelites smaller than the great empires of the ancient world. They were smaller even than the other nations in the region. Compared to their origins, they had grown, but compared to their neighbors they remained tiny. But Moshe then tells them, "Do not be afraid of them; remember well what the LORD your God did to Pharaoh and to all Egypt" (Deut. 7:18). Israel will be the smallest of the nations for a reason that goes to the very heart of its existence as a nation. It will show the world that a people does not have to be large in order to defeat its enemies. Small groups can make a large difference. Israel's unique history will show that, in the words of the prophet Zekharya (Zech. 4:6), "'Not with valor and not with strength, but with My spirit,' says the LORD of Hosts."

7:18 זָכֹר תִּזְכֹּר *Remember well* – Throughout history there have been many attempts to ground ethics in universal attributes of humanity. Some, like Immanuel Kant, based it on reason. Others based it on duty. Bentham rooted it in consequences ("the greatest happiness for the greatest number"). David Hume attributed it to certain basic emotions: sympathy, empathy, compassion. Adam Smith predicated it on the capacity to stand back from situations and judge them with detachment ("the impartial spectator"). Each of these has its virtues, but none has proved fail-safe.

Judaism took and takes a different

it for yourself, because you would be ensnared by it, for
26 it is abhorrent to the LORD your God. Do not bring any
abhorrent thing into your house, or you, like it, will be set
apart for utter destruction. Detest and abhor it utterly, for
it is set apart for utter destruction.
8 1 Take care to keep every command that I am charging you
with on this day, so that you may survive and thrive, go in,
and take possession of the land that the LORD swore He
2 would give to your ancestors. Remember that the LORD
your God has led you through all this journey of forty
years in the wilderness, to humble you and to test you,
and to know what was in your heart: to know whether
you would keep His commandments or whether you
3 would fail to. He humbled you by leaving you hungry,
then feeding you manna, which neither you nor your
ancestors had ever known – to teach you that one does
not live by bread alone, but by all that comes forth from
4 the mouth of the LORD. Your clothes did not wear out,
5 nor did your feet swell these forty years. Know then in
your heart that just as a parent disciplines his child, so
6 the LORD your God disciplines you. And so keep the
commandments of the LORD your God, walking in
7 His ways and revering Him. For the LORD your God
is bringing you into a good land, a land of streams and
springs and deep waters gushing out to the valleys and
8 the hills, a land of wheat and barley, vines, fig trees and
9 pomegranates, a land of olive oil and honey, a land where
bread will not be scarce, where you will lack nothing, a
land where the rocks are iron and where you can hew
10 bronze from her hills. And when you eat and are satisfied,
you shall bless the LORD your God for the good land

beautiful tradition. It is a basic theme of Judaism. It is in the physical that we find the spiritual. God made the world; therefore it is in the world that we find God.

The commentators ask why Grace after Meals is a biblical command, whereas the blessing *before* meals is only a rabbinic injunction. Their answer is that to thank God when we are hungry is natural. To thank Him when we are

כו וְלָקַחְתָּ לָךְ פֶּן תִּוָּקֵשׁ בּוֹ כִּי תוֹעֲבַת יְהוָה אֱלֹהֶיךָ הוּא: וְלֹא־
תָבִיא תוֹעֵבָה אֶל־בֵּיתֶךָ וְהָיִיתָ חֵרֶם כָּמֹהוּ שַׁקֵּץ | תְּשַׁקְּצֶנּוּ
וְתַעֵב | תְּתַעֲבֶנּוּ כִּי־חֵרֶם הוּא:
ח א כָּל־הַמִּצְוָה אֲשֶׁר אָנֹכִי מְצַוְּךָ הַיּוֹם תִּשְׁמְרוּן לַעֲשׂוֹת לְמַעַן
תִּחְיוּן וּרְבִיתֶם וּבָאתֶם וִירִשְׁתֶּם אֶת־הָאָרֶץ אֲשֶׁר־נִשְׁבַּע
ב יְהוָה לַאֲבֹתֵיכֶם: וְזָכַרְתָּ אֶת־כָּל־הַדֶּרֶךְ אֲשֶׁר הוֹלִיכְךָ יְהוָה
אֱלֹהֶיךָ זֶה אַרְבָּעִים שָׁנָה בַּמִּדְבָּר לְמַעַן עַנֹּתְךָ לְנַסֹּתְךָ
ג לָדַעַת אֶת־אֲשֶׁר בִּלְבָבְךָ הֲתִשְׁמֹר מִצְוֹתָו אִם־לֹא: וַיְעַנְּךָ
וַיַּרְעִבֶךָ וַיַּאֲכִלְךָ אֶת־הַמָּן אֲשֶׁר לֹא־יָדַעְתָּ וְלֹא יָדְעוּן
אֲבֹתֶיךָ לְמַעַן הוֹדִיעֲךָ כִּי לֹא עַל־הַלֶּחֶם לְבַדּוֹ יִחְיֶה הָאָדָם
ד כִּי עַל־כָּל־מוֹצָא פִי־יְהוָה יִחְיֶה הָאָדָם: שִׂמְלָתְךָ לֹא
ה בָלְתָה מֵעָלֶיךָ וְרַגְלְךָ לֹא בָצֵקָה זֶה אַרְבָּעִים שָׁנָה: וְיָדַעְתָּ
עִם־לְבָבֶךָ כִּי כַּאֲשֶׁר יְיַסֵּר אִישׁ אֶת־בְּנוֹ יְהוָה אֱלֹהֶיךָ
ו מְיַסְּרֶךָּ: וְשָׁמַרְתָּ אֶת־מִצְוֹת יְהוָה אֱלֹהֶיךָ לָלֶכֶת בִּדְרָכָיו
ז וּלְיִרְאָה אֹתוֹ: כִּי יְהוָה אֱלֹהֶיךָ מְבִיאֲךָ אֶל־אֶרֶץ טוֹבָה אֶרֶץ
ח נַחֲלֵי מָיִם עֲיָנֹת וּתְהֹמֹת יֹצְאִים בַּבִּקְעָה וּבָהָר: אֶרֶץ חִטָּה
ט וּשְׂעֹרָה וְגֶפֶן וּתְאֵנָה וְרִמּוֹן אֶרֶץ־זֵית שֶׁמֶן וּדְבָשׁ: אֶרֶץ אֲשֶׁר
לֹא בְמִסְכֵּנֻת תֹּאכַל־בָּהּ לֶחֶם לֹא־תֶחְסַר כֹּל בָּהּ אֶרֶץ אֲשֶׁר
י אֲבָנֶיהָ בַרְזֶל וּמֵהֲרָרֶיהָ תַּחְצֹב נְחֹשֶׁת: וְאָכַלְתָּ וְשָׂבָעְתָּ
וּבֵרַכְתָּ אֶת־יְהוָה אֱלֹהֶיךָ עַל־הָאָרֶץ הַטֹּבָה אֲשֶׁר נָתַן־

8:10 וּבֵרַכְתָּ אֶת־יְהוָה אֱלֹהֶיךָ *You shall bless the LORD your God* – Grace after Meals is one of the elements of Jewish liturgy already specified in the Bible; it is commanded in this verse. Eating is a biological function. Judaism – with its emphasis on sanctifying the physical – is particularly concerned to turn the act of eating into a moment of spiritual affirmation.

It is said that Avraham and Sara drew people into the service of the One God by extending them hospitality. After their guests had eaten, they would turn to thank their hosts. Avraham would reply, "Thank not us but God, who provides food for all." "How shall we thank God?" "Say: Blessed is the LORD, who is blessed. Blessed be He who gives bread and food to all that lives" (*Tanḥuma*, Lekh Lekha 12). This is more than a

▶

11 that He has given you. Take care not to forget the LORD SHENI
your God, failing to keep His commandments, laws,
and decrees, with which I am charging you this day.
12 Otherwise, when you have eaten and been satisfied, and
13 have built fine houses and lived in them, when your herds
and flocks have grown abundant, and your silver and gold
is abundant, and all that you have has grown abundant,
14 your heart may become proud, forgetting the LORD your
God who brought you out of Egypt, the house of slaves,
15 who led you through the vast and terrifying wilderness,
an arid wasteland with venomous snakes and scorpions,
16 who brought forth water from flint rock for you, and fed
you manna in the wilderness, something your ancestors
did not know, to humble and to test you – so that in the
17 end it would be well for you. You might be tempted to
say to yourself, 'My power, the strength of my own hand,
18 have brought me this great wealth.' But remember the
LORD your God, for it is He who gives you the power to
do great things, upholding the covenant that He swore to
your ancestors, as He is doing on this day.

8:18 הוּא הַנֹּתֵן לְךָ כֹּחַ *It is He who gives you the power* – Everything will depend, Moshe teaches, on how the next generation responds to the good things that God promises them. *Either* you will eat and be satisfied and bless God, *remembering* that all things come from Him – *or* you will eat and be satisfied and *forget* to whom you owe all this. You will think it comes entirely from your own efforts: "My power, the strength of my own hand, have brought me this great wealth." Although this may seem a small difference, it will, says Moshe, make *all* the difference.

Moshe's argument is counterintuitive. You may think, he says, that the hard times are behind you. You have wandered for forty years without a home. There were times when you had no water, no food. You were attacked by enemies. You may think this was the test of your strength. It was not. *The real challenge is not poverty but affluence, not slavery but freedom, not homelessness but home.*

Many nations have been lifted to great heights when they faced difficulty and danger. They came through crises – droughts, plagues, recessions, defeats – and were toughened by them. When times are hard, people grow. There is a sense of community and solidarity, of neighbors and strangers pulling together. Many people who have lived

יא לָךְ׃ הִשָּׁמֶר לְךָ פֶּן־תִּשְׁכַּח אֶת־יְהוָה אֱלֹהֶיךָ לְבִלְתִּי שְׁמֹר שני
יב מִצְוֺתָיו וּמִשְׁפָּטָיו וְחֻקֹּתָיו אֲשֶׁר אָנֹכִי מְצַוְּךָ הַיּוֹם׃ פֶּן־
יג תֹּאכַל וְשָׂבָעְתָּ וּבָתִּים טֹבִים תִּבְנֶה וְיָשָׁבְתָּ׃ וּבְקָרְךָ וְצֹאנְךָ
יד יִרְבְּיֻן וְכֶסֶף וְזָהָב יִרְבֶּה־לָּךְ וְכֹל אֲשֶׁר־לְךָ יִרְבֶּה׃ וְרָם לְבָבֶךָ
וְשָׁכַחְתָּ אֶת־יְהוָה אֱלֹהֶיךָ הַמּוֹצִיאֲךָ מֵאֶרֶץ מִצְרַיִם מִבֵּית
טו עֲבָדִים׃ הַמּוֹלִיכְךָ בַּמִּדְבָּר ׀ הַגָּדֹל וְהַנּוֹרָא נָחָשׁ ׀ שָׂרָף
וְעַקְרָב וְצִמָּאוֹן אֲשֶׁר אֵין־מָיִם הַמּוֹצִיא לְךָ מַיִם מִצּוּר
טז הַחַלָּמִישׁ׃ הַמַּאֲכִלְךָ מָן בַּמִּדְבָּר אֲשֶׁר לֹא־יָדְעוּן אֲבֹתֶיךָ
יז לְמַעַן עַנֹּתְךָ וּלְמַעַן נַסֹּתֶךָ לְהֵיטִבְךָ בְּאַחֲרִיתֶךָ׃ וְאָמַרְתָּ
יח בִּלְבָבֶךָ כֹּחִי וְעֹצֶם יָדִי עָשָׂה לִי אֶת־הַחַיִל הַזֶּה׃ וְזָכַרְתָּ אֶת־
יְהוָה אֱלֹהֶיךָ כִּי הוּא הַנֹּתֵן לְךָ כֹּחַ לַעֲשׂוֹת חָיִל לְמַעַן הָקִים
אֶת־בְּרִיתוֹ אֲשֶׁר־נִשְׁבַּע לַאֲבֹתֶיךָ כַּיּוֹם הַזֶּה׃

---

sated is more difficult. It is precisely when we are most likely to forget that we need reminding – that what we have, we have from God, creator and sustainer of all.

8:17 כֹּחִי וְעֹצֶם יָדִי *My power, the strength of my own hand* – Gratitude – *hakarat hatov* – is at the heart of what Moshe has to say about the Israelites and their future in the Promised Land. Gratitude has not been their strong point in the desert. They have complained about the lack of food and water, about the manna and the lack of meat and vegetables, about the dangers they faced from the Egyptians as they were leaving, and about the inhabitants of the land they were about to enter. They lacked thankfulness during the difficult times. A greater danger still, says Moshe, would be a lack of gratitude during the good times.

Though you do not have to be religious to be grateful, there is something about belief in God as creator of the universe, shaper of history, and author of the laws of life that directs and facilitates our gratitude. It is hard to feel grateful to a universe that came into existence for no reason and is blind to us and our fate. It is our faith in a personal God that gives force and focus to our thanks.

The nation's history, Moshe asserts, should be engraved on people's souls and reenacted in the annual cycle of festivals; the nation, as a nation, should never attribute its achievements to itself – "my power, the strength of my own hand" – but should always ascribe its victories, indeed its very existence, to something higher than itself: God. This is a dominant theme of Deuteronomy, and it echoes throughout the book time and again.

19 If you do forget the LORD your God and follow other
gods, serving and worshipping them, I solemnly warn
20 you today that you will be altogether lost. Like the nations
that the LORD will cause to die before you, so shall you
be lost, because you would not listen to the voice of the
LORD your God.
9 1 Listen, Israel! You are now about to cross the Jordan, to
go in and dispossess nations larger and mightier than
2 you, with great cities, fortified to high heaven. The people
are strong and lofty – Anakites. You know of them; you
have heard it said of them, 'Who can stand up against
3 the descendants of Anak?' Know then today that it is
the LORD your God, who is crossing over before you
like a consuming fire: He will wipe them out, subduing
them before you, so that you may rapidly dispossess and
4 destroy them, as the LORD promised you. When the SHELISHI
LORD your God drives them out before you, do not say to
yourself, 'It is because of my righteousness that the LORD
has brought me in to take possession of this land.' The
LORD is dispossessing these nations before you because
5 of their own wickedness. Not for your righteousness

---

the history of other nations. He sends a prophet, Yona, to Israel's enemy, Assyria, to persuade them to repent and be saved from catastrophe. Yeshayahu even foresees a day when God will do for Israel's other great enemy, Egypt, what He did for the Israelites against Egypt itself – rescue them from oppression:

> On that day, in Egypt's heartlands, an altar to the LORD will stand; at her borders a pillar to the LORD. They will be sign and testament in the land of Egypt to the LORD of Hosts, for the people shall cry out to the LORD because of their oppressors; He will send them a rescuer, a fighter; he will save them. The LORD will be made known to Egypt, and Egypt will know the LORD on that day.... The LORD will plague Egypt – plague it and heal.... On that day a road will run from Egypt to Assyria. Assyria will come to Egypt. Egypt will come to Assyria, and Egypt with Assyria will worship. On that day, Israel will be one with Egypt and Assyria, a blessing on this earth. For the LORD of Hosts has blessed him, saying: Blessed are My people, Egypt, Assyria, work of My hands, and Israel, My own possession. (Is. 19:19–25)

יט וְהָיָה אִם־שָׁכֹחַ תִּשְׁכַּח אֶת־יְהוָה אֱלֹהֶיךָ וְהָלַכְתָּ אַחֲרֵי
אֱלֹהִים אֲחֵרִים וַעֲבַדְתָּם וְהִשְׁתַּחֲוִיתָ לָהֶם הַעִדֹתִי
כ בָכֶם הַיּוֹם כִּי אָבֹד תֹּאבֵדוּן׃ כַּגּוֹיִם אֲשֶׁר יְהוָה מַאֲבִיד
מִפְּנֵיכֶם כֵּן תֹּאבֵדוּן עֵקֶב לֹא תִשְׁמְעוּן בְּקוֹל יְהוָה
אֱלֹהֵיכֶם׃

ט א שְׁמַע יִשְׂרָאֵל אַתָּה עֹבֵר הַיּוֹם אֶת־הַיַּרְדֵּן לָבֹא לָרֶשֶׁת ח
גּוֹיִם גְּדֹלִים וַעֲצֻמִים מִמֶּךָּ עָרִים גְּדֹלֹת וּבְצֻרֹת בַּשָּׁמָיִם׃
ב עַם־גָּדוֹל וָרָם בְּנֵי עֲנָקִים אֲשֶׁר אַתָּה יָדַעְתָּ וְאַתָּה שָׁמַעְתָּ
ג מִי יִתְיַצֵּב לִפְנֵי בְּנֵי עֲנָק׃ וְיָדַעְתָּ הַיּוֹם כִּי יְהוָה אֱלֹהֶיךָ
הוּא־הָעֹבֵר לְפָנֶיךָ אֵשׁ אֹכְלָה הוּא יַשְׁמִידֵם וְהוּא יַכְנִיעֵם
לְפָנֶיךָ וְהוֹרַשְׁתָּם וְהַאֲבַדְתָּם מַהֵר כַּאֲשֶׁר דִּבֶּר יְהוָה לָךְ׃
ד אַל־תֹּאמַר בִּלְבָבְךָ בַּהֲדֹף יְהוָה אֱלֹהֶיךָ אֹתָם ׀ מִלְּפָנֶיךָ שלישי
לֵאמֹר בְּצִדְקָתִי הֱבִיאַנִי יְהוָה לָרֶשֶׁת אֶת־הָאָרֶץ הַזֹּאת
ה וּבְרִשְׁעַת הַגּוֹיִם הָאֵלֶּה יְהוָה מוֹרִישָׁם מִפָּנֶיךָ׃ לֹא בְצִדְקָתְךָ

through a war remember it as the most vivid time of their life.

The real test of a nation is not if it can survive a crisis but if it can survive the *lack* of a crisis. Can it stay strong during times of ease and plenty, power and prestige? That is the challenge that has defeated every civilization known to history. Let it not, says Moshe, defeat you.

The pages of history are littered with the relics of nations that seemed impregnable in their day, but which eventually declined and fell, always for the reason Moshe foresaw. *They forgot.* Memories fade. People lose sight of the values they once fought for – justice, equality, independence, freedom. The nation, its early battles over, becomes strong. Some of its members grow rich. They become lax, self-indulgent, over-sophisticated, decadent. They lose their sense of social solidarity. They begin to feel that such wealth and position as they have is theirs by right. The bonds of fraternity and collective responsibility begin to fray. That was the danger Moshe foresaw and about which he warned. The politics of free societies depends on the handing on of memory.

9:4 וּבְרִשְׁעַת הַגּוֹיִם הָאֵלֶּה *Because of their own wickedness* – There is no implication in the Tanakh that the Israelites' is the only story. To the contrary, as Amos 9:7 says: "Are you not to Me like the children of Kush, O children of Israel? Did I not bring up Israel from the land of Egypt as I brought the Philistines up from Kaftor, and Aram from Kir?" God is active in

or rectitude are you coming to take possession of their
land; it is for these nations' wickedness that the Lord
your God is driving them out before you and to fulfill the
promise that the Lord made on oath to your ancestors,
6 Avraham, Yitzḥak, and Yaakov. Know, then, that it is not
for your righteousness that the Lord your God is giving
you this good land to possess, for you are a stiff-necked
7 people. Remember and never forget how you provoked
the Lord your God to fury in the wilderness. From the
day you left Egypt until you arrived here, you have always
8 been rebellious against the Lord. At Ḥorev you provoked

The Sages lived through the disaster of the great rebellion against Rome, in which the Temple was destroyed, and in some ways the even greater disaster of the Bar Kokhba rebellion, the greatest human tragedy in Jewish history prior to the Holocaust. They knew they had been defeated because they were divided. How, then, could they continue? Should they encourage conformism and intellectual timidity? That was an option they rejected. What they did instead was to bring difference to the house of study, locate it within the protocols of "argument for the sake of Heaven," and thus create a culture in which strong individuals with strongly held beliefs could disagree without splitting apart. The contrariness identified by Moshe continued through the ages, but over time Judaism developed a culture of constructive dissent, in relation both to God and to other people.

9:7 מַמְרִים הֱיִיתֶם עִם־יהוה *You have always been rebellious against the Lord* – Criticism is easy to deliver but hard to bear. It is easy for people to close their ears, or even turn the criticism around ("He's blaming us, but he should be blaming himself. After all, he was in charge"). For criticism to be heeded, the people have to know, beyond any doubt, that the critic cares for them, wants the best for them, and is prepared to take personal risks for their sake. Moshe can be as critical as he is in the last month of his life because the people he is talking to know that he has defended them and their parents in his prayers for divine forgiveness, that he has risked challenging God, that he declined God's offer to abandon the Israelites and begin again with him – in short, that Moshe's whole life as a leader was dedicated to what was best for the people. When you know that about someone, you listen to their criticism. If you seek to change someone, make sure that you are willing to help them when they need your help, defend them when they need your defense, and see the good in them, not just the bad. Anyone can complain, but we have to earn the right to criticize.

וּבְיֹשֶׁר לְבָבְךָ אַתָּה בָא לָרֶשֶׁת אֶת־אַרְצָם כִּי בְּרִשְׁעַת ׀
הַגּוֹיִם הָאֵלֶּה יהוה אֱלֹהֶיךָ מוֹרִישָׁם מִפָּנֶיךָ וּלְמַעַן הָקִים
אֶת־הַדָּבָר אֲשֶׁר נִשְׁבַּע יהוה לַאֲבֹתֶיךָ לְאַבְרָהָם לְיִצְחָק
ו וּלְיַעֲקֹב: וְיָדַעְתָּ כִּי לֹא בְצִדְקָתְךָ יהוה אֱלֹהֶיךָ נֹתֵן לְךָ אֶת־
ז הָאָרֶץ הַטּוֹבָה הַזֹּאת לְרִשְׁתָּהּ כִּי עַם־קְשֵׁה־עֹרֶף אָתָּה: זְכֹר
אַל־תִּשְׁכַּח אֵת אֲשֶׁר־הִקְצַפְתָּ אֶת־יהוה אֱלֹהֶיךָ בַּמִּדְבָּר
לְמִן־הַיּוֹם אֲשֶׁר־יָצָאתָ ׀ מֵאֶרֶץ מִצְרַיִם עַד־בֹּאֲכֶם עַד־
ח הַמָּקוֹם הַזֶּה מַמְרִים הֱיִיתֶם עִם־יהוה: וּבְחֹרֵב הִקְצַפְתֶּם

Nor is there any intimation in the Bible that Avraham's family have a monopoly on virtue. One of the heroines of the exodus, without whom there would have been no Moshe, was Pharaoh's daughter. Raḥav, who shelters Yehoshua's spies, is a prostitute from Jericho (Josh. 2). Yael, the heroine who saves Israel from Sisera, is a Kenite (Judges 4). Uriya, whose faithfulness to David contrasts so sharply with David's faithlessness to him, is a Hittite (II Sam. 11). According to many of the Sages, Iyov, the Bible's most conspicuous example of a wholly righteous man, is not an Israelite; his book is also the Tanakh's most focused exploration of the question of individual providence. Just as we do not hold a monopoly on virtue, neither do we hold a monopoly on God's interest and concern.

9:5 לֹא בְצִדְקָתְךָ *Not for your righteousness* – Moshe criticizes the Israelites, telling them, "Not for your righteousness or rectitude are you coming to take possession of their land" (Deut. 9:5). This note is sustained to the end of the prophetic age. Malakhi, last of the prophets, says, "From one end of the earth to the other, My name is great among the nations… yet you desecrate it" (Mal. 1:11–12).

This is a point of immense consequence. A chosen people is the opposite of a master race, first, because it is not a race but a covenant; second, because it exists to serve God, not to master others. A master race worships itself; a chosen people worships something beyond itself. A master race produces monumental buildings, triumphal inscriptions, and a literature of self-congratulation. Israel, to a degree unique in history, produced a literature of almost uninterrupted self-criticism.

9:6 עַם־קְשֵׁה־עֹרֶף אָתָּה *You are a stiff-necked people* – Social cohesion requires a degree of submissiveness, but Jews are described across the Mosaic books as a "stiff-necked people." They submit (eventually) to God, but even then, to almost no one else. In this context can we understand why the Rabbis carefully constructed a culture of "argument for the sake of Heaven" (see Num. 16, "The Nature of the Argument").

the Lord to fury: so incensed was the Lord that He
9 was ready to destroy you. I had ascended the mountain
to receive the stone tablets, the tablets of the Covenant
the Lord made with you. I remained on the mountain
forty days and forty nights; I ate no bread and I drank
10 no water. The Lord gave me two stone tablets inscribed
by the finger of God. And upon them were all the words
that the Lord had spoken to you at the mountain out of
11 the fire, on the day of that assembly. And when the forty
days and forty nights were at an end, the Lord gave me
12 the two stone tablets, the tablets of the Covenant. And
then the Lord said to me, 'Get up; go down from here
immediately, because your people whom you brought
from Egypt have acted disastrously; how rapidly they
strayed from the path that I commanded them to
follow – they have made a molten image for themselves.'
13 The Lord said to me, 'I have seen this people, and they
14 are a stiff-necked people. Stand back from Me and I
will destroy them and erase their name from under the
heavens, and I will make of you a nation mightier and
15 more numerous than they.' I turned and went down from
the mountain while it was still ablaze with fire, and the
16 two tablets of the Covenant were in my two hands. When
I looked, I saw that you had indeed sinned against the
Lord your God. You had made for yourselves a molten
calf; you had strayed rapidly indeed from the path that
17 the Lord had commanded you to follow. So I took
hold of the two tablets and flung them from my hands,
18 smashing them to pieces before your eyes. Then I threw
myself down before the Lord as before, for forty days
and forty nights; I ate no bread and I drank no water,
because of the great sin you had committed, angering the
19 Lord by doing what was evil in His eyes. I was terrified
of the Lord's blazing fury and rage against you, ready
to destroy you. But the Lord listened to me that time
20 also. The Lord was so enraged with Aharon that He
was ready to destroy him, but I prayed for Aharon also

ט אֶת־יְהוָה וַיִּתְאַנַּף יְהוָה בָּכֶם לְהַשְׁמִיד אֶתְכֶם: בַּעֲלֹתִי
הָהָרָה לָקַחַת לוּחֹת הָאֲבָנִים לוּחֹת הַבְּרִית אֲשֶׁר־כָּרַת
יְהוָה עִמָּכֶם וָאֵשֵׁב בָּהָר אַרְבָּעִים יוֹם וְאַרְבָּעִים לַיְלָה לֶחֶם
י לֹא אָכַלְתִּי וּמַיִם לֹא שָׁתִיתִי: וַיִּתֵּן יְהוָה אֵלַי אֶת־שְׁנֵי לוּחֹת
הָאֲבָנִים כְּתֻבִים בְּאֶצְבַּע אֱלֹהִים וַעֲלֵיהֶם כְּכָל־הַדְּבָרִים
יא אֲשֶׁר דִּבֶּר יְהוָה עִמָּכֶם בָּהָר מִתּוֹךְ הָאֵשׁ בְּיוֹם הַקָּהָל: וַיְהִי
מִקֵּץ אַרְבָּעִים יוֹם וְאַרְבָּעִים לַיְלָה נָתַן יְהוָה אֵלַי אֶת־שְׁנֵי
יב לֻחֹת הָאֲבָנִים לֻחוֹת הַבְּרִית: וַיֹּאמֶר יְהוָה אֵלַי קוּם רֵד
מַהֵר מִזֶּה כִּי שִׁחֵת עַמְּךָ אֲשֶׁר הוֹצֵאתָ מִמִּצְרָיִם סָרוּ מַהֵר
יג מִן־הַדֶּרֶךְ אֲשֶׁר צִוִּיתִם עָשׂוּ לָהֶם מַסֵּכָה: וַיֹּאמֶר יְהוָה אֵלַי
לֵאמֹר רָאִיתִי אֶת־הָעָם הַזֶּה וְהִנֵּה עַם־קְשֵׁה־עֹרֶף הוּא:
יד הֶרֶף מִמֶּנִּי וְאַשְׁמִידֵם וְאֶמְחֶה אֶת־שְׁמָם מִתַּחַת הַשָּׁמָיִם
טו וְאֶעֱשֶׂה אוֹתְךָ לְגוֹי־עָצוּם וָרָב מִמֶּנּוּ: וָאֵפֶן וָאֵרֵד מִן־הָהָר
טז וְהָהָר בֹּעֵר בָּאֵשׁ וּשְׁנֵי לוּחֹת הַבְּרִית עַל שְׁתֵּי יָדָי: וָאֵרֶא
וְהִנֵּה חֲטָאתֶם לַיהוָה אֱלֹהֵיכֶם עֲשִׂיתֶם לָכֶם עֵגֶל מַסֵּכָה
יז סַרְתֶּם מַהֵר מִן־הַדֶּרֶךְ אֲשֶׁר־צִוָּה יְהוָה אֶתְכֶם: וָאֶתְפֹּשׂ
בִּשְׁנֵי הַלֻּחֹת וָאַשְׁלִכֵם מֵעַל שְׁתֵּי יָדָי וָאֲשַׁבְּרֵם לְעֵינֵיכֶם:
יח וָאֶתְנַפַּל לִפְנֵי יְהוָה כָּרִאשֹׁנָה אַרְבָּעִים יוֹם וְאַרְבָּעִים לַיְלָה
לֶחֶם לֹא אָכַלְתִּי וּמַיִם לֹא שָׁתִיתִי עַל כָּל־חַטַּאתְכֶם אֲשֶׁר
יט חֲטָאתֶם לַעֲשׂוֹת הָרַע בְּעֵינֵי יְהוָה לְהַכְעִיסוֹ: כִּי יָגֹרְתִּי
מִפְּנֵי הָאַף וְהַחֵמָה אֲשֶׁר קָצַף יְהוָה עֲלֵיכֶם לְהַשְׁמִיד אֶתְכֶם
כ וַיִּשְׁמַע יְהוָה אֵלַי גַּם בַּפַּעַם הַהִוא: וּבְאַהֲרֹן הִתְאַנַּף יְהוָה
מְאֹד לְהַשְׁמִידוֹ וָאֶתְפַּלֵּל גַּם־בְּעַד אַהֲרֹן בָּעֵת הַהִוא:

9:20 וָאֶתְפַּלֵּל גַּם־בְּעַד אַהֲרֹן בָּעֵת הַהִוא *I prayed for Aharon also at that time* – Only now, in the last month of Moshe's life, Moshe tells the people something that he has kept from them until this point: God, according to Moshe, was so angry with Aharon for the sin of the golden calf that He was about to kill him, and would have done so had it not been for Moshe's prayer.

21 at that time. Then I took that thing of sin you had made,
the calf, and burned it in fire. I crushed it and ground it
thoroughly, until it was as fine as dust, and I threw the
22 dust into a stream running down the mountain. At Tavera
also, and at Masa and Kivrot HaTaava, you provoked
23 the LORD. And when the LORD sent you from Kadesh
Barnea, saying, 'Go up and take possession of the land
that I have given you,' you rebelled against the command
of the LORD your God. You did not have faith in Him and
24 did not obey Him. You have rebelled against the LORD
25 as long as I have known you. I threw myself down before
the LORD, and as I lay prostrate those forty days and forty
26 nights, when the LORD had said He would destroy you, I
prayed to the LORD – 'Lord GOD,' I said, 'do not destroy
the people, Your heritage, those whom You redeemed in

---

this particular prayer, which are echoed twice weekly in the longer form of the *Taḥanun* prayer, and in some *Seliḥot*: "Remember Your servants Avraham, Yitzḥak, and Yaakov; do not attend to our stubbornness, wickedness, and sinfulness." *Taḥanun*, "plea," is a return to private prayer after the *ḥazan*'s repetition of the *Amida*. Knowing that our time in the direct presence of the supreme King of kings is drawing to an end, we approach Him directly, seeking, as it were, a private audience. Our voices drop; we whisper our deepest thoughts, we express our feelings of inadequacy and vulnerability. We know we are unworthy: we say nothing in our defense except that we have absolute faith in God.

What differentiates *Taḥanun* from other modes of prayer is the extent to which, echoing Moshe, "the humblest of men," we emphasize our failings and our lack of good deeds. We express our dependence on God's unconditional grace and mercy. *Taḥanun* is the chamber music rather than the symphony of the soul, and it has a unique intensity of tone.

The practice of following public prayer with private intercession was formalized in Temple times. After the daily sacrifice, "the Levites sang the psalm [of the day]. When they reached the end of each section [the psalm was divided into three parts], they blew the shofar and the people prostrated themselves" (Tamid 7:3). We preserve a trace of that gesture, and Moshe's here, by resting our heads on our arms and covering our faces as we say Psalm 6. The *ḥazan*'s repetition of the *Amida* stands in place of the daily sacrifice, which is why we subsequently "fall on our faces."

According to tradition, Moshe began his ascent of Mount Sinai to receive the second tablets on a Thursday and

כא וְֽאֶת־חַטַּאתְכֶ֞ם אֲשֶׁר־עֲשִׂיתֶ֣ם אֶת־הָעֵ֗גֶל לָקַ֘חְתִּי֮ וָאֶשְׂרֹ֣ף
אֹת֣וֹ ׀ בָּאֵ֗שׁ וָאֶכֹּ֨ת אֹת֤וֹ טָחוֹן֙ הֵיטֵ֔ב עַ֥ד אֲשֶׁר־דַּ֖ק לְעָפָ֑ר
כב וָֽאַשְׁלִךְ֙ אֶת־עֲפָר֔וֹ אֶל־הַנַּ֖חַל הַיֹּרֵ֥ד מִן־הָהָֽר׃ וּבְתַבְעֵרָה֙
וּבְמַסָּ֔ה וּבְקִבְרֹ֖ת הַֽתַּאֲוָ֑ה מַקְצִפִ֥ים הֱיִיתֶ֖ם אֶת־יְהוָֽה׃
כג וּבִשְׁלֹ֨חַ יהוה אֶתְכֶ֗ם מִקָּדֵ֤שׁ בַּרְנֵ֙עַ֙ לֵאמֹ֔ר עֲלוּ֙ וּרְשׁ֣וּ אֶת־
הָאָ֔רֶץ אֲשֶׁ֖ר נָתַ֣תִּי לָכֶ֑ם וַתַּמְר֗וּ אֶת־פִּ֤י יהוה֙ אֱלֹ֣הֵיכֶ֔ם וְלֹ֣א
כד הֶאֱמַנְתֶּם֙ ל֔וֹ וְלֹ֥א שְׁמַעְתֶּ֖ם בְּקֹלֽוֹ׃ מַמְרִ֥ים הֱיִיתֶ֖ם עִם־
כה יְהוָ֑ה מִיּ֖וֹם דַּעְתִּ֥י אֶתְכֶֽם׃ וָֽאֶתְנַפַּ֞ל לִפְנֵ֣י יהוה אֶת־אַרְבָּעִ֥ים
הַיּ֛וֹם וְאֶת־אַרְבָּעִ֥ים הַלַּ֖יְלָה אֲשֶׁ֣ר הִתְנַפָּ֑לְתִּי כִּֽי־אָמַ֥ר יהוה
כו לְהַשְׁמִ֥יד אֶתְכֶֽם׃ וָאֶתְפַּלֵּ֣ל אֶל־יהוה֮ וָאֹמַר֒ אֲדֹנָ֣י יֱהֹוִ֗ה אַל־
תַּשְׁחֵ֤ת עַמְּךָ֙ וְנַחֲלָתְךָ֔ אֲשֶׁ֥ר פָּדִ֖יתָ בְּגָדְלֶ֑ךָ אֲשֶׁר־הוֹצֵ֥אתָ

Faced with the sin of the calf, Aharon blamed the people. It was they who made the illegitimate request. He denied responsibility for making the calf. It just happened. "I threw it into the fire, and out came this calf!" (Ex. 32:24). In anyone such evasion is a moral failure; in a leader such as Aharon the High Priest, all the more so.

Yet Aharon was not immediately punished. According to the Torah he was condemned for another sin altogether when, years later, he and Moshe spoke angrily against the people complaining about the lack of water: "Aharon is to be gathered to his people. He shall not enter the land that I have given to the Israelites, because you disobeyed My command at the waters of Meriva" (Num. 20:24).

It is easy to be critical of people who fail the leadership test when, like Aharon, it involves blocking the path the majority are intent on taking. However, it is hard to oppose the mob. They can ignore you, remove you, even assassinate you. Even Moshe was helpless in the face of the people's demands during the later episode of the spies (14:5).

Tradition, therefore, dealt kindly with Aharon. He is portrayed as a man of peace. Perhaps that is why he was made High Priest. There is more than one kind of leadership, and priesthood does not involve swaying crowds. The fact that Aharon was not a leader in the same mold as Moshe does not mean that he was a failure. He failed when he was called on to be a Moshe, but he became a great leader in his own right in a different capacity. There are times when you need someone with the courage to stand against the crowd, others when you need a peacemaker.

MOSHE'S PRAYER

In Exodus we were not told the words of

Your greatness and brought out of Egypt with a mighty
27 hand. Remember Your servants Avraham, Yitzḥak, and
Yaakov; do not attend to the stubbornness of this people,
28 to their wickedness or sinfulness; otherwise the nation
from which You brought us will say, "It was because the
Lord was unable to bring them into the land that He
promised them, and because He hated them, that He
29 took them out to kill them in the wilderness." But they are
Your people, Your possession, whom You freed by Your
great power and Your arm stretched forth.'
10 1 And then the Lord said to me, 'Carve two tablets of REVI'I
stone like the first, and come up to Me on the mountain.
2 Make, as well, a wooden ark. I will inscribe upon these
tablets the words that were on the first, which you
3 smashed, and you shall place them in the ark.' So I made
an ark of acacia wood and carved two tablets of stone like
the first. I ascended the mountain with these two tablets
4 in my hand. And He inscribed on the tablets the same
words as before, the Ten Commandments that the Lord
had proclaimed to you on the mountain out of the fire
on the day of the assembly; and the Lord gave them to
5 me. I turned, came down from the mountain, and put the
tablets in the ark that I had made. And there they have
6 remained, as the Lord commanded me. And the Israelites
journeyed from Be'erot Benei Yaakan to Mosera. There
Aharon died and was buried. Elazar, his son, succeeded
7 him as priest. From there they journeyed to Gudgod, and

If we ever doubt the power of prayer to transform the human situation, here we find an answer. Despite being treated as a pariah people, Jews never allowed themselves to be defined by their enemies. They wept and gave voice to pain: "God, see how low our glory has sunk among the nations. They abhor us as if we were impure." Yet they remained the people of the covenant, children of the divine promise, unbroken and unbreakable. Prayer sustains hope, and hope defeats tragedy. In these profound and moving words, invoking Moshe's loving supplication to God on our behalf, Jews found the strength to survive.

כז מִמִּצְרַיִם בְּיָד חֲזָקָה׃ זְכֹר לַעֲבָדֶיךָ לְאַבְרָהָם לְיִצְחָק וּלְיַעֲקֹב
אַל־תֵּפֶן אֶל־קְשִׁי הָעָם הַזֶּה וְאֶל־רִשְׁעוֹ וְאֶל־חַטָּאתוֹ׃
כח פֶּן־יֹאמְרוּ הָאָרֶץ אֲשֶׁר הוֹצֵאתָנוּ מִשָּׁם מִבְּלִי יְכֹלֶת יהוה
לַהֲבִיאָם אֶל־הָאָרֶץ אֲשֶׁר־דִּבֶּר לָהֶם וּמִשִּׂנְאָתוֹ אוֹתָם
כט הוֹצִיאָם לַהֲמִתָם בַּמִּדְבָּר׃ וְהֵם עַמְּךָ וְנַחֲלָתֶךָ אֲשֶׁר הוֹצֵאתָ
בְּכֹחֲךָ הַגָּדֹל וּבִזְרֹעֲךָ הַנְּטוּיָה׃
י א בָּעֵת הַהִוא אָמַר יהוה אֵלַי פְּסָל־לְךָ שְׁנֵי־לוּחֹת אֲבָנִים ט רביעי
ב כָּרִאשֹׁנִים וַעֲלֵה אֵלַי הָהָרָה וְעָשִׂיתָ לְּךָ אֲרוֹן עֵץ׃ וְאֶכְתֹּב
עַל־הַלֻּחֹת אֶת־הַדְּבָרִים אֲשֶׁר הָיוּ עַל־הַלֻּחֹת הָרִאשֹׁנִים
ג אֲשֶׁר שִׁבַּרְתָּ וְשַׂמְתָּם בָּאָרוֹן׃ וָאַעַשׂ אֲרוֹן עֲצֵי שִׁטִּים
וָאֶפְסֹל שְׁנֵי־לֻחֹת אֲבָנִים כָּרִאשֹׁנִים וָאַעַל הָהָרָה וּשְׁנֵי
ד הַלֻּחֹת בְּיָדִי׃ וַיִּכְתֹּב עַל־הַלֻּחֹת כַּמִּכְתָּב הָרִאשׁוֹן אֵת
עֲשֶׂרֶת הַדְּבָרִים אֲשֶׁר דִּבֶּר יהוה אֲלֵיכֶם בָּהָר מִתּוֹךְ הָאֵשׁ
ה בְּיוֹם הַקָּהָל וַיִּתְּנֵם יהוה אֵלָי׃ וָאֵפֶן וָאֵרֵד מִן־הָהָר וָאָשִׂם
אֶת־הַלֻּחֹת בָּאָרוֹן אֲשֶׁר עָשִׂיתִי וַיִּהְיוּ שָׁם כַּאֲשֶׁר צִוַּנִי יהוה׃
ו וּבְנֵי יִשְׂרָאֵל נָסְעוּ מִבְּאֵרֹת בְּנֵי־יַעֲקָן מוֹסֵרָה שָׁם מֵת אַהֲרֹן
ז וַיִּקָּבֵר שָׁם וַיְכַהֵן אֶלְעָזָר בְּנוֹ תַּחְתָּיו׃ מִשָּׁם נָסְעוּ הַגֻּדְגֹּדָה

descended forty days later on a Monday (the tenth of Tishrei, Yom Kippur). The second tablets were a sign of God's forgiveness. Hence, these days were seen as "days of favor." They were also market days when people would come from villages to towns. Congregations were larger; the Torah was read; law courts were in session. The heightened atmosphere was the setting for more extended penitential prayer; therefore, on Mondays and Thursdays, *Taḥanun* is longer.

A tradition, found in the geonic literature, dates these prayers to the period of persecution under the Romans. Some passages may have been added in the wake of the Gothic and Frankish persecutions in the seventh century. Their mood bespeaks the tears of Jews throughout the centuries of exile who experienced persecution, expulsion, humiliation, and often bloodshed at the hand of those amongst whom they lived. Even in times of freedom, we continue to say these prayers, keeping faith with our ancestors and remembering their tears.

What is remarkable about the prayers is the absence of anger or despair.

8 from Gudgod to Yotvat, a region of flowing streams. At
that time the LORD set the tribe of Levi apart to carry the
Ark of the LORD's Covenant, to stand before the LORD
to minister to Him, and to give blessing in His name, as
9 they do to this day. This is why the Levites have no share
or inheritance among their fellow Israelites. The LORD is
their inheritance, as the LORD your God promised them.
10 I stayed on the mountain forty days and forty nights, as
I had the first time. And this time too, the LORD listened
11 to me; the LORD did not choose to destroy you. Then
the LORD said to me, 'Rise and resume your journey at
the head of the people, so that they may go in and take
possession of the land that I swore to their ancestors to
give to them.'
12 So now, Israel, what does the LORD your God ask of you? ḤAMISHI
Only this: to revere the LORD your God, to walk in all
His ways and love Him; to serve the LORD your God
13 with all your heart and all your soul, and to keep the
commandments and decrees of the LORD your God that
14 I am commanding you today, for your own good. Look:
the heavens, even the highest heavens, belong to the
15 LORD your God, with the earth and all it contains. Yet it
was on your ancestors alone that the LORD set His heart
in love, and it was you, their descendants after them, that

This is noted by philosopher Simon May, in his book *Love: A History*:

> [W]hat we must note here, for it is fundamental to the history of Western love, is the remarkable and radical justice that underlies the love commandment of Leviticus. Not a cold justice in which due deserts are mechanically handed out, but the justice that brings the other, as an individual with needs and interests, into a relationship of respect. All our neighbors are to be recognized as equal to ourselves before the law of love. Justice and love therefore become inseparable.

Love without justice leads to rivalry, and eventually to hate. Justice without love is devoid of the humanizing forces of compassion and mercy. We need both.

Israel is established as a nation and society held together by three loves: You shall love the LORD your God with all your heart, all your soul, and all your might. You shall love your neighbor as

ח וּמִן־הַגֻּדְגֹּדָה יָטְבָתָה אֶרֶץ נַחֲלֵי־מָיִם׃ בָּעֵת הַהִוא הִבְדִּיל
יְהוָה אֶת־שֵׁבֶט הַלֵּוִי לָשֵׂאת אֶת־אֲרוֹן בְּרִית־יְהוָה לַעֲמֹד
ט לִפְנֵי יְהוָה לְשָׁרְתוֹ וּלְבָרֵךְ בִּשְׁמוֹ עַד הַיּוֹם הַזֶּה׃ עַל־כֵּן לֹא־
הָיָה לְלֵוִי חֵלֶק וְנַחֲלָה עִם־אֶחָיו יְהוָה הוּא נַחֲלָתוֹ כַּאֲשֶׁר
י דִּבֶּר יְהוָה אֱלֹהֶיךָ לוֹ׃ וְאָנֹכִי עָמַדְתִּי בָהָר כַּיָּמִים הָרִאשֹׁנִים
אַרְבָּעִים יוֹם וְאַרְבָּעִים לָיְלָה וַיִּשְׁמַע יְהוָה אֵלַי גַּם בַּפַּעַם
יא הַהִוא לֹא־אָבָה יְהוָה הַשְׁחִיתֶךָ׃ וַיֹּאמֶר יְהוָה אֵלַי קוּם לֵךְ
לְמַסַּע לִפְנֵי הָעָם וְיָבֹאוּ וְיִירְשׁוּ אֶת־הָאָרֶץ אֲשֶׁר־נִשְׁבַּעְתִּי
לַאֲבֹתָם לָתֵת לָהֶם׃
יב וְעַתָּה יִשְׂרָאֵל מָה יְהוָה אֱלֹהֶיךָ שֹׁאֵל מֵעִמָּךְ כִּי אִם־לְיִרְאָה חמישי
אֶת־יְהוָה אֱלֹהֶיךָ לָלֶכֶת בְּכָל־דְּרָכָיו וּלְאַהֲבָה אֹתוֹ וְלַעֲבֹד
יג אֶת־יְהוָה אֱלֹהֶיךָ בְּכָל־לְבָבְךָ וּבְכָל־נַפְשֶׁךָ׃ לִשְׁמֹר אֶת־
מִצְוֹת יְהוָה וְאֶת־חֻקֹּתָיו אֲשֶׁר אָנֹכִי מְצַוְּךָ הַיּוֹם לְטוֹב לָךְ׃
יד הֵן לַיהוָה אֱלֹהֶיךָ הַשָּׁמַיִם וּשְׁמֵי הַשָּׁמָיִם הָאָרֶץ וְכָל־אֲשֶׁר־
טו בָּהּ׃ רַק בַּאֲבֹתֶיךָ חָשַׁק יְהוָה לְאַהֲבָה אוֹתָם וַיִּבְחַר בְּזַרְעָם

LOVE WITH JUSTICE

Why is it that love is so much stronger a theme in Deuteronomy than in the earlier books of Exodus, Leviticus (with the exception of Lev. 19), and Numbers? To answer this, first note that the book of Genesis contains many references to love. Avraham loves Yitzḥak. Yitzḥak loves Esav. Rivka loves Yaakov. Yaakov loves Raḥel. He also loves Yosef. There is plenty of interpersonal love. But almost all the loves of Genesis turn out to be divisive. They lead to tension between Yaakov and Esav, between Raḥel and Leah, and between Yosef and his brothers. Implicit in Genesis is a profound observation. Love by itself – real love, personal and passionate, the kind of love that suffuses much of the prophetic literature as well as Song of Songs, the greatest love song in the Tanakh, is not sufficient as a basis for society. It can divide as well as unite.

Hence it does not figure as a major motif until we reach the integrated social-moral-political vision of Deuteronomy which combines love and justice. *Tzedek*, justice, is to be another keyword of Deuteronomy, appearing eighteen times. It appears only four times in Exodus, not at all in Numbers, and in Leviticus only in chapter 19, the only chapter that also contains the word "love." In other words, in Judaism love and justice go hand in hand.

He chose among all the peoples, as He does to this day.
16 And so remove the hardness of your heart, and be stiff-
17 necked no longer. For the LORD your God is God of
gods and Lord of lords, the great, mighty, and awesome
18 God, who shows no partiality and accepts no bribe, who
executes justice for the orphan and the widow, and who
19 loves the stranger, giving him food and clothing. You too
must love the stranger, for you yourselves were strangers
20 in the land of Egypt. Revere the LORD your God and
21 worship Him. Hold fast to Him and swear by His name. He
is your praise; He is your God, who has done these great
and awesome things for you that your own eyes have seen.
22 When your ancestors went down to Egypt, they were but
seventy souls. Now the LORD your God has made you as

> Wherever you find the greatness of the Holy One, blessed be He, there you find His humility. This is written in the Torah, repeated in the Prophets, and stated a third time in the Writings. It is written in the Torah: "For the LORD your God is God of gods and LORD of lords, the great, mighty and awesome God, who shows no partiality and accepts no bribe" (Deut. 10:17). Immediately afterward it is written, "Who executes justice for the orphan and the widow, and who loves the stranger, giving him food and clothing" (10:18). It is repeated in the Prophets, as it says: "Thus says the high, the exalted One, abiding forever, whose name is holy: High and holy I abide, yet I am with the crushed and humbled, giving life to the humbled, giving life to crushed men's hearts" (Is. 57:15). It is stated a third time in the Writings: "Sing to God, sing praises to His name, laud Him who rides the clouds – the LORD is His name – and exult before Him" (Ps. 68:5). Immediately afterward it is written: "Father of orphans, judge of widows, God is in His holy abode" (68:6). (Megilla 31a)

This counterintuitive and life-changing idea is one of the great contributions of the Torah to Western civilization and it is first set out this *parasha*.

Physically, the taller you are the more you look down on others. Morally, the reverse is the case. The more we look up to others, the higher we stand. God's greatness lay not just in the fact that He was creator of the universe and shaper of history, but that He "executes justice for the orphan and the widow, and [He] loves the stranger, giving him food and clothing." Those who emulate Him and do this are the true men and women of God. For us, as for God, greatness is humility.

טז אַחֲרֵיהֶם בָּכֶם מִכָּל־הָעַמִּים כַּיּוֹם הַזֶּה: וּמַלְתֶּם אֵת עָרְלַת
יז לְבַבְכֶם וְעָרְפְּכֶם לֹא תַקְשׁוּ עוֹד: כִּי יהוה אֱלֹהֵיכֶם הוּא
אֱלֹהֵי הָאֱלֹהִים וַאֲדֹנֵי הָאֲדֹנִים הָאֵל הַגָּדֹל הַגִּבֹּר וְהַנּוֹרָא
יח אֲשֶׁר לֹא־יִשָּׂא פָנִים וְלֹא יִקַּח שֹׁחַד: עֹשֶׂה מִשְׁפַּט יָתוֹם
יט וְאַלְמָנָה וְאֹהֵב גֵּר לָתֶת לוֹ לֶחֶם וְשִׂמְלָה: וַאֲהַבְתֶּם אֶת־
כ הַגֵּר כִּי־גֵרִים הֱיִיתֶם בְּאֶרֶץ מִצְרָיִם: אֶת־יהוה אֱלֹהֶיךָ תִּירָא
כא אֹתוֹ תַעֲבֹד וּבוֹ תִדְבָּק וּבִשְׁמוֹ תִּשָּׁבֵעַ: הוּא תְהִלָּתְךָ וְהוּא
אֱלֹהֶיךָ אֲשֶׁר־עָשָׂה אִתְּךָ אֶת־הַגְּדֹלֹת וְאֶת־הַנּוֹרָאֹת הָאֵלֶּה
כב אֲשֶׁר רָאוּ עֵינֶיךָ: בְּשִׁבְעִים נֶפֶשׁ יָרְדוּ אֲבֹתֶיךָ מִצְרָיְמָה

---

yourself. And you shall love the stranger, for you were once strangers in the land of Egypt.

A society is thus formed on the basis of love of God, neighbor, and stranger. This is not merely abstract. It is translated into practical imperatives. Provide the poor with food from the corners of the field and the leavings of the harvest. Let them eat freely of the produce of the field in the seventh year and provide them with a tithe on the third and sixth. One year in seven, release debts and Hebrew slaves. Ensure that no one is left out of the festival celebrations, and no one denied access to dignity. Treat employees and debtors ethically and give slaves rest one day in seven. This is a unique vision that shaped the moral horizons of the West. The moral life as Judaism conceives it is a combination of love – *ḥesed* and *raḥamim* – and justice – *tzedek* and *mishpat*. Love is particular; justice is universal. Love is interpersonal; justice is impersonal. Love generates ethics: the duties we owe those to whom we are bound by kinship or consent. Justice generates morality: the duties we owe everyone because they are human.

This unique ethical vision – based ultimately on the love of God for humans and of humans for God, translated into an ethic of love toward both neighbor and stranger – is the foundation of Western civilization and its abiding glory.

10:19 וַאֲהַבְתֶּם אֶת־הַגֵּר *You too must love the stranger* – The juxtaposition of the two preceding verses – the first about God's supremacy, the second about His care for the low and lonely – could not be more striking. The Power of powers cares for the powerless. The Infinitely Great shows concern for the small. The Being at the heart of being listens to those at the margins: the orphan, the widow, the stranger, the poor, the outcast, the neglected.

On this idea, the third-century teacher R. Yoḥanan built the following homily:

▶

11 1 many as the stars of the heavens. And so – love the LORD
your God and keep His charge: His decrees, His laws,
2 and His commands through all your days. Know today
that it was not your children who knew or saw the LORD
your God's lesson – His greatness, His mighty hand, and
3 His arm stretched forth, the signs and the acts that He
performed in Egypt against Pharaoh, Egypt's king, and all
4 his land; what He did to the Egyptian fighting force, their
horses and their chariots, how He made the Reed Sea's
water flood over them as they pursued you, so that the
5 LORD destroyed them forever; what He did for you in the
6 wilderness until you came to this place; and what he did
to Datan and Aviram, sons of Eliav son of Reuven, in the
midst of all Israel, how the earth opened its mouth and
swallowed them, their families, tents, and every living
7 thing in their households: it is your own eyes that have
8 seen all these immense acts, all that the LORD did. And
so – keep all of this command with which I charge you
on this day, so that you may be empowered to go in and
take possession of the land that you are crossing over to

is unpredictable. We recall a whole series of earlier episodes in the book of Genesis in which we read the words "There was a famine in the land." This led first Avraham, then Yitzḥak, then Yaakov and his children into a series of journeys and exiles, a story echoed later in the Book of Ruth.

Life in Israel has never been stable and secure. Those who live there exist in a state of insecurity, never knowing whether the seeds they plant will grow. Israel is the land of promise, but it will always depend on He-who-promises.

The character of a country – its topography and climate – affects the society people build, and hence the culture and ethos that emerge. In Mesopotamia and Egypt, the most powerful reality was the regularity of nature, the succession of the seasons, which seemed to mirror the slow revolution of the stars. The cultures to which both places gave rise were cosmological and their sense of time cyclical. The universe seemed to be ruled by the heavenly bodies whose hierarchy and order were replicated in the hierarchy and order of life on earth. This is the mindset of the world of myth.

In Israel, by contrast, there was no guarantee that next year would be like this, or this year like last, no certainty that the rain would fall and the earth yield its crops or the trees their fruit. Thus in Israel a new sense of time was

יא א וְעַתָּה שָׂמְךָ יְהוָה אֱלֹהֶיךָ כְּכוֹכְבֵי הַשָּׁמַיִם לָרֹב: וְאָהַבְתָּ
אֵת יְהוָה אֱלֹהֶיךָ וְשָׁמַרְתָּ מִשְׁמַרְתּוֹ וְחֻקֹּתָיו וּמִשְׁפָּטָיו
ב וּמִצְוֹתָיו כָּל־הַיָּמִים: וִידַעְתֶּם הַיּוֹם כִּי ׀ לֹא אֶת־בְּנֵיכֶם
אֲשֶׁר לֹא־יָדְעוּ וַאֲשֶׁר לֹא־רָאוּ אֶת־מוּסַר יְהוָה אֱלֹהֵיכֶם
ג אֶת־גָּדְלוֹ אֶת־יָדוֹ הַחֲזָקָה וּזְרֹעוֹ הַנְּטוּיָה: וְאֶת־אֹתֹתָיו
וְאֶת־מַעֲשָׂיו אֲשֶׁר עָשָׂה בְּתוֹךְ מִצְרָיִם לְפַרְעֹה מֶלֶךְ־מִצְרַיִם
ד וּלְכָל־אַרְצוֹ: וַאֲשֶׁר עָשָׂה לְחֵיל מִצְרַיִם לְסוּסָיו וּלְרִכְבּוֹ
אֲשֶׁר הֵצִיף אֶת־מֵי יַם־סוּף עַל־פְּנֵיהֶם בְּרָדְפָם אַחֲרֵיכֶם
ה וַיְאַבְּדֵם יְהוָה עַד הַיּוֹם הַזֶּה: וַאֲשֶׁר עָשָׂה לָכֶם בַּמִּדְבָּר
ו עַד־בֹּאֲכֶם עַד־הַמָּקוֹם הַזֶּה: וַאֲשֶׁר עָשָׂה לְדָתָן וְלַאֲבִירָם
בְּנֵי אֱלִיאָב בֶּן־רְאוּבֵן אֲשֶׁר פָּצְתָה הָאָרֶץ אֶת־פִּיהָ וַתִּבְלָעֵם
וְאֶת־בָּתֵּיהֶם וְאֶת־אָהֳלֵיהֶם וְאֵת כָּל־הַיְקוּם אֲשֶׁר בְּרַגְלֵיהֶם
ז בְּקֶרֶב כָּל־יִשְׂרָאֵל: כִּי עֵינֵיכֶם הָרֹאֹת אֶת כָּל־מַעֲשֵׂה יְהוָה
ח הַגָּדֹל אֲשֶׁר עָשָׂה: וּשְׁמַרְתֶּם אֶת־כָּל־הַמִּצְוָה אֲשֶׁר אָנֹכִי
מְצַוְּךָ הַיּוֹם לְמַעַן תֶּחֶזְקוּ וּבָאתֶם וִירִשְׁתֶּם אֶת־הָאָרֶץ אֲשֶׁר

THE CONDITIONAL PROSPERITY OF THE LAND

Jewish destiny was to create a society that would honor the proposition that we are all created in the image and likeness of God. It would be a place in which the freedom of some would not lead to the enslavement of others, the opposite of Egypt, whose bread of affliction and bitter herbs of slavery they were to eat every year on the festival of Passover to remind them of what to avoid. Judaism is the code of a self-governing society. It is about the shared spaces of our collective lives, not just an interior drama of the soul. It formalizes the social virtues: righteousness (*tzedek/tzedaka*), justice (*mishpat*), loving-kindness (*ḥesed*), and compassion (*raḥamim*). These structure the template of biblical law, which covers all aspects of the life of society: its economy, its welfare systems, its education and family life. The broad principles driving this elaborate structure, traditionally enumerated as 613 commands, are clear. No one should be left in dire poverty. No one should lack access to justice and the courts. No family should be without its share of the land.

All this must be actualized in a territory. But the land of Israel, says Moshe, is not a fertile plain. It is a land of hills and valleys. It depends on rain – and rain in the Middle East, then and now,

9 possess, and so that your years may be long in the land
that the Lord swore to your ancestors to give to them
and their descendants, a land flowing with milk and with
10 honey. For the land that you are about to go into SHISHI
and take possession of is not like the land of Egypt you
left behind, where you could sow your seed and irrigate
11 by foot as in a vegetable garden. The land that you are
crossing over to possess is a land of hills and valleys; it is
12 watered by the sky's rains. It is a land the Lord your God
watches over; the eyes of the Lord your God are always
13 upon it, from the year's opening to its end. And
if you heed My commands, with which I charge you on

---

from yours. We may think, on the face of it, that this is a passage about obedience. Yet throughout Deuteronomy, Moshe tells us that God does not seek blind obedience. There is no word for "obedience" in Biblical Hebrew (Modern Hebrew had to borrow a verb, *letzayet*, from Aramaic). God wants us to listen, not just with our ears but with the deepest resources of our minds.

In making human beings free subjects "in His image," God created otherness. Listening to another human being, let alone God, is an act of opening ourselves up to a mind radically other than our own. This takes courage. To listen is to make myself vulnerable. My deepest certainties may be shaken by entering into the mind of one who thinks quite differently about the world. But it is essential to our humanity. It is the antidote to narcissism: the belief that we are the center of the universe. When we speak, we tell others who and what we are. But when we listen, we allow others to tell us who they are. This is the supremely revelatory moment.

In Judaism we believe that our relationship with God is an ongoing tutorial in our relationships with other people. If we can listen to other people, then we might possibly listen to God, whose otherness is not relative but absolute.

Listening is a profoundly spiritual act. It can also be painful. It is comfortable not to have to listen, not to be challenged, not to be moved outside our comfort zone. But it is the people not like us who make us grow. The bridge between self and other is conversation: speaking and listening. On superficial reading, this passage is a basic text of reward and punishment, obedience and disobedience. But it is addressed not only to our actions, but to the "heart and soul," to an inner act of listening and opening ourselves to influence.

Listening is the greatest gift we can give to another human being. To be listened to, to be heard, is to know that someone else

ט אַתֶּם עֹבְרִים שָׁמָּה לְרִשְׁתָּהּ: וּלְמַעַן תַּאֲרִיכוּ יָמִים עַל־
הָאֲדָמָה אֲשֶׁר נִשְׁבַּע יהוה לַאֲבֹתֵיכֶם לָתֵת לָהֶם וּלְזַרְעָם
י אֶרֶץ זָבַת חָלָב וּדְבָשׁ: כִּי הָאָרֶץ אֲשֶׁר אַתָּה ששי
בָא־שָׁמָּה לְרִשְׁתָּהּ לֹא כְאֶרֶץ מִצְרַיִם הִוא אֲשֶׁר יְצָאתֶם
מִשָּׁם אֲשֶׁר תִּזְרַע אֶת־זַרְעֲךָ וְהִשְׁקִיתָ בְרַגְלְךָ כְּגַן הַיָּרָק:
יא וְהָאָרֶץ אֲשֶׁר אַתֶּם עֹבְרִים שָׁמָּה לְרִשְׁתָּהּ אֶרֶץ הָרִים
יב וּבְקָעֹת לִמְטַר הַשָּׁמַיִם תִּשְׁתֶּה־מָּיִם: אֶרֶץ אֲשֶׁר־יהוה
אֱלֹהֶיךָ דֹּרֵשׁ אֹתָהּ תָּמִיד עֵינֵי יהוה אֱלֹהֶיךָ בָּהּ מֵרֵשִׁית
יג הַשָּׁנָה וְעַד אַחֲרִית שָׁנָה: וְהָיָה אִם־שָׁמֹעַ
תִּשְׁמְעוּ אֶל־מִצְוֺתַי אֲשֶׁר אָנֹכִי מְצַוֶּה אֶתְכֶם הַיּוֹם לְאַהֲבָה

born – the time we call historical. Those who lived, or live, in Israel exist in a state of radical contingency. They depend on something other than nature. To put it at its simplest: In Egypt, where the source of life was the Nile, you looked down. In Israel, where the source of life is rain, you had no choice but to look up.

When Moshe tells the Israelites about the land, he is telling them – whether or not they understand it at the time – that it is a place where not just wheat and barley but the human spirit also grew. It was the land where people were lifted beyond themselves because, time and again, they would have to believe in something beyond themselves. Not accidentally but essentially, by its climate, topography, and location, Israel is the Holy Land, the place where, merely to survive, the human eye must turn to Heaven and the human ear to Heaven's call.

11:13 אִם־שָׁמֹעַ תִּשְׁמְעוּ *If you heed* – There is urgency behind Moshe's double emphasis (*shamoa tishme'u* in the Hebrew) in the opening line of this passage, the second paragraph of the *Shema*. A more forceful translation might be: "If you listen – and I mean really listen."

One can almost imagine the Israelites saying to Moshe, "Enough; we hear you," and Moshe replying, "No you don't. You simply do not understand what is happening. The Creator of the entire universe is taking a personal interest in your welfare and destiny. Have you any idea of what that means?" Perhaps we still don't.

The root *sh-m-a* does not have a single direct translation in English (see ch. 6, "Listen"). When you encounter a word in any language that is untranslatable into your own, you are close to the beating pulse of that culture. To understand an untranslatable word, you have to move out of your comfort zone and enter a mindset that is significantly different

this day, to love the LORD your God and to serve Him
14 with all your heart and with all your soul, I will grant your
land's rain in its season, the early and the late rain; you
15 shall gather in your grain, your wine, your oil. I will grant
your fields grass for your cattle, and you will eat and be
16 satisfied. Be vigilant lest your heart be seduced and you
17 go astray and serve other gods and worship them. Then
the LORD's rage will blaze against you, and He will close
the skies; there will be no rain. The land will not yield its
crops, and you will swiftly perish from the good land that
18 the LORD is giving you. Therefore set these words of Mine
upon your heart and upon your soul. Bind them as a sign
upon your hand, and have them as an emblem between
19 your eyes. Teach them to your children, speaking of them
when you sit at home and when you travel on the way,
20 when you lie down and when you rise. Write them on the

---

the life of the mind. And it began, as this passage makes clear, in the context of the home. To be a parent, in Judaism, is to be a teacher. Education is the conversation between the generations.

There is a profound reason for this. The Torah envisages a society that will be more than just a reflection of the values that drive most human groups: the search for wealth and power. Instead, as a holy people in a holy land, Jews are to care about the poor and powerless. They are to become a nation driven by high ideals. They must seek to be an inspiration to others. They are charged with becoming a society that will bear testimony to something greater than themselves, namely, to God Himself.

But it is clear from the Torah's narrative thus far that the transformation of a people takes a long time. If any change in the human condition takes longer than a generation, education becomes fundamental. We need to hand on our memories, values, ideals, laws, and customs to our children, and they to theirs, if each generation is to continue the journey to a destination not yet reached.

This emphasis on education has given Judaism, from the very beginning, a future orientation that is unusual among the great religions of the world. Jews have always cared about children and placed them as their highest joy. Rather than look back exclusively to a vanished past, they have looked forward to a distant but promised future. A people that places children at the apex of its agenda does not grow old. It learns to see the world through the eyes of a child – with hope and wonder and aspiration unsullied by cynicism and despair.

אֶת־יְהוָה אֱלֹהֵיכֶם וּלְעָבְדוֹ בְּכָל־לְבַבְכֶם וּבְכָל־נַפְשְׁכֶם׃
יד וְנָתַתִּי מְטַר־אַרְצְכֶם בְּעִתּוֹ יוֹרֶה וּמַלְקוֹשׁ וְאָסַפְתָּ דְגָנֶךָ
טו וְתִירֹשְׁךָ וְיִצְהָרֶךָ׃ וְנָתַתִּי עֵשֶׂב בְּשָׂדְךָ לִבְהֶמְתֶּךָ וְאָכַלְתָּ
טז וְשָׂבָעְתָּ׃ הִשָּׁמְרוּ לָכֶם פֶּן־יִפְתֶּה לְבַבְכֶם וְסַרְתֶּם וַעֲבַדְתֶּם
יז אֱלֹהִים אֲחֵרִים וְהִשְׁתַּחֲוִיתֶם לָהֶם׃ וְחָרָה אַף־יְהוָה בָּכֶם
וְעָצַר אֶת־הַשָּׁמַיִם וְלֹא־יִהְיֶה מָטָר וְהָאֲדָמָה לֹא תִתֵּן אֶת־
יְבוּלָהּ וַאֲבַדְתֶּם מְהֵרָה מֵעַל הָאָרֶץ הַטֹּבָה אֲשֶׁר יְהוָה נֹתֵן
יח לָכֶם׃ וְשַׂמְתֶּם אֶת־דְּבָרַי אֵלֶּה עַל־לְבַבְכֶם וְעַל־נַפְשְׁכֶם
וּקְשַׁרְתֶּם אֹתָם לְאוֹת עַל־יֶדְכֶם וְהָיוּ לְטוֹטָפֹת בֵּין עֵינֵיכֶם׃
יט וְלִמַּדְתֶּם אֹתָם אֶת־בְּנֵיכֶם לְדַבֵּר בָּם בְּשִׁבְתְּךָ בְּבֵיתֶךָ
כ וּבְלֶכְתְּךָ בַדֶּרֶךְ וּבְשָׁכְבְּךָ וּבְקוּמֶךָ׃ וּכְתַבְתָּם עַל־מְזוּזוֹת

---

takes me seriously. That is a redemptive act. And it changes not only the one who is heard, but the listener as well.

11:19 וְלִמַּדְתֶּם אֹתָם *Teach them* – In Deuteronomy, a new word enters the biblical vocabulary: the verb based on the root *l-m-d*, meaning to learn or teach. The verb does not appear even once in Genesis, Exodus, Leviticus, or Numbers. In Deuteronomy it appears seventeen times.

When the Torah speaks about education it does so in a striking and unusual way. It speaks of parents and children and handing on the tradition from one generation to the next. Avraham is chosen – "so that he may direct his children and his household after him to keep the way of the Lord by doing what is right and just" (Gen. 18:19). The *Shema* commands us: "Teach them to your children, speaking of them when you sit at home and when you travel on the way, when you lie down and when you rise." The Seder service on Passover – Judaism's most intense and revolutionary educational experience – involves teaching a child to see himself or herself as part of a people and its memories, and it is achieved not by teachers in classrooms but by parents around the family table. Jewish education is not about the abstract contemplation of truth. It is about introducing the next generation to the covenant which they inherit from their parents and their parents' parents through a family line which stretches back to Sinai. Jewish education is about Jewish continuity.

11:19 אֶת־בְּנֵיכֶם *To your children* – Jews survived because they set as their highest priority handing on their heritage to the next generation. They placed education at the very heart of faith. Their heroes were teachers, their citadels were houses of study, and their passion learning and

21 doorposts of your house and on your gates, so that you
and your children may live long years in the land that the
Lord swore to your ancestors to give to them for as long
22 as the sky endures above the land. If you carefully SHEVI'I AND MAFTIR
keep all of this command with which I am charging you,
loving the Lord your God, walking in all His ways, and
23 holding fast to Him, then the Lord will drive all these
nations out before you, and you will dispossess nations
24 larger and mightier than you. Every place where you set

---

nothing exists except in Him – then one can preserve the state of communion and the not-self even when immersed in the world.

11:23 גְּדֹלִים וַעֲצֻמִים מִכֶּם *Larger and mightier than you* – These nations have their own story, which is not Moshe's concern here (see Deut. 9:4 and commentary there). To us as readers, these mighty nations symbolize the insecurity faced by Israel as it emerges into the arena of nations. There is no way of eliminating the objective conditions that create insecurity on many levels, now as then. We have, however, intellectual resources that enable us to cope with it. Of these the most important is a moral vision. We can travel at speed so long as we know where we are going. It is when we lose a sense of vision that we find ourselves, in effect, without a map or a destination. That is when people turn to populist leaders capable of manipulating public fear (see Num. 16, "The Koraḥ Rebellion") or to regressive identities and fundamentalisms that allow them to cope with fear by blaming some group or other for being the cause of the world's ills.

What morality restores to an increasingly uncertain world is the idea of *responsibility* – that what we do, severally and collectively, makes a difference, and that the future lies in our hands. Every era has produced its own philosophies or quasi-scientific systems to show that what happens could not have been otherwise, that the march of history is inevitable, that it is hubris to believe we can fight against fate. All we can do is to align ourselves to its flow, exploit it when we can, and render ourselves stoically indifferent to our fate when we cannot.

This way of thinking is a regression to a view of the universe that is very ancient indeed. It is the world of myth, in which mankind is alone in an environment dominated by irresistible forces blind to our presence, deaf to our prayers and hopes.

The great leap of the biblical imagination was to argue otherwise. There is a personal dimension to existence. Our hopes are not mere dreams, nor are our ideals illusions. Something at the core of being responds to us as persons, inviting us to exercise our freedom by shaping families, communities, and societies in

כא בֵּיתֶךָ וּבִשְׁעָרֶיךָ: לְמַעַן יִרְבּוּ יְמֵיכֶם וִימֵי בְנֵיכֶם עַל הָאֲדָמָה
אֲשֶׁר נִשְׁבַּע יְהוָה לַאֲבֹתֵיכֶם לָתֵת לָהֶם כִּימֵי הַשָּׁמַיִם עַל־
כב הָאָרֶץ: כִּי אִם־שָׁמֹר תִּשְׁמְרוּן אֶת־כָּל־ שביעי ומפטיר
הַמִּצְוָה הַזֹּאת אֲשֶׁר אָנֹכִי מְצַוֶּה אֶתְכֶם לַעֲשֹׂתָהּ לְאַהֲבָה
כג אֶת־יְהוָה אֱלֹהֵיכֶם לָלֶכֶת בְּכָל־דְּרָכָיו וּלְדָבְקָה־בוֹ: וְהוֹרִישׁ
יְהוָה אֶת־כָּל־הַגּוֹיִם הָאֵלֶּה מִלִּפְנֵיכֶם וִירִשְׁתֶּם גּוֹיִם גְּדֹלִים
כד וַעֲצֻמִים מִכֶּם: כָּל־הַמָּקוֹם אֲשֶׁר תִּדְרֹךְ כַּף־רַגְלְכֶם בּוֹ לָכֶם

11:22 וּלְדָבְקָה־בוֹ *Holding fast to Him* – There is a disagreement between Ramban and Ibn Ezra on the interpretation of this verse. Is it possible that man should hold fast to the Almighty, that he be in intimate relation with God at all times? Or must Majesty – the ultimate separateness of God – sometimes interfere with Covenant – the closeness of God?

Ibn Ezra comments, "Holding fast to Him – at the end, for it is a great mystery," implying perhaps that it is a communion reached only at death. Whereas Ramban says: "It is, in fact, the meaning of 'holding fast,' that one should remember God and His love at all times, and not be separated in thought from Him 'when you travel on the way, when you lie down, and when you rise' (Deut. 6:7, 11:19). At such a stage, one may be talking with other people but one's heart is not with (i.e., confined to) them, since one is in the presence of God." The suffusion of man's social existence with his covenantal intimacy with God is for Ramban a this-worldly possibility.

But for whom is it possible? Rambam held that by philosophy and meditation a man may reach the rank of prophecy, and this is the highest natural perfection. But he will still be a divided self. "When you have succeeded in properly performing these acts of divine service, and you have your thought during their performance entirely abstracted from worldly affairs, then take care that you be not disturbed by thinking of your wants or of superfluous things. In short, think of worldly matters when you eat, drink, bathe, talk with your wife and little children, or when you converse with other people" (*Guide for the Perplexed* III:51). *Devekut*, cleaving, is an act of seclusion, and prayer and meditation are its sanctuary. Emerging into everyday life, one relinquishes that union. Only at the highest level of prophecy, where Moshe and the patriarchs stand, does this partition dissolve.

We find Rambam's ideas mirrored in the kabbalistic tradition. He who makes *devekut* his aim must sever his contacts with the world and practice a meditative retreat. It is only in Hasidism that we find, as it were, a democratization of Rambam. Cleaving to God in all His ways is removed from Ibn Ezra's category of "mystery." Once one has perceived the implication of the unity of God – that

foot shall be yours. Your territory shall stretch from the
wilderness to the Lebanon, from the Euphrates River to
25 the Western Sea. No one will be able to stand against you.
The LORD your God will put the fear and dread of you
over all the land you set foot upon, just as He promised
you.

The haftara for Parashat Ekev is on page 1602.

imagination. It is this sense of responsibility – always opposed by determinisms ancient and modern – that Moshe seeks to impart to Israel in Deuteronomy.

יִהְיֶה מִן־הַמִּדְבָּר וְהַלְּבָנוֹן מִן־הַנָּהָר נְהַר־פְּרָת וְעַד הַיָּם
כה הָאַחֲרוֹן יִהְיֶה גְּבֻלְכֶם׃ לֹא־יִתְיַצֵּב אִישׁ בִּפְנֵיכֶם פַּחְדְּכֶם
וּמוֹרַאֲכֶם יִתֵּן ׀ יהוה אֱלֹהֵיכֶם עַל־פְּנֵי כׇל־הָאָרֶץ אֲשֶׁר
תִּדְרְכוּ־בָהּ כַּאֲשֶׁר דִּבֶּר לָכֶם׃

The הפטרה *for* פרשת עקב *is on page 1603.*

such a way as to honor the image of God that is mankind, investing each human life with ultimate dignity. This view sees choice, agency, and moral responsibility at the heart of the human project. We are not powerless in the face of fate. With every new power come choice, responsibility, and exercise of the moral

Parashat Re'eh

11 26 See this: I am setting before you on this day a blessing and
27 a curse: the blessing, if you obey the commandments of
the Lord your God that I am commanding you today;

---

reiteration of it. "See this: I am setting before you on this day a blessing and a curse."

What the Israelites are asked to see is words.

THE CHOICE

Having set out the broad principles of the covenant, Moshe now turns to the details, which extend over many chapters and several *parashot*. The long review of the laws that will govern Israel in its land begins and ends with Moshe posing a momentous choice.

Rambam (*Hilkhot Teshuva* 5:3) takes these passages as proof of our belief in free will, which indeed they are. But they are more than that. They are also a political statement. The connection between individual freedom (which Rambam is talking about) and collective choice (which Moshe is talking about) is this: if humans are free then they need a free society within which to exercise that freedom. The book of Deuteronomy represents the first attempt in history to create a free society.

Moshe insists on three interconnected things. First, we *are* free. Blessing or curse? Good or evil? Faithfulness or faithlessness? You decide, says Moshe. Never has freedom been so starkly defined, not just for an individual but for a nation as a whole. There is no defense, says Moshe, in protestations of powerlessness, in saying we could not help it, we were outnumbered, we were defeated, it was the fault of our leaders or our enemies. No, says Moshe. Your fate is in your hands. The sovereignty of God does not take away human responsibility. To the contrary, it places it center stage. If you are faithful to God, says Moshe, you will prevail over empires. If you are not, nothing else – neither military strength nor political alliances – will help you. The choice and responsibility are yours alone.

Second, we are collectively responsible. The phrase "All Israelites are responsible for one another" (Shevuot 39b) is rabbinic, but the idea is already present in the Torah. The fate of Israel depends on all Israel, from "the leaders among you, the tribes, the elders and officials" (Deut. 29:9) to your "woodcutters and water drawers" (Josh. 9:23). The people of the covenant did not believe their destiny was determined by a governing elite. It was determined by each of us as moral agents, jointly responsible for the common good.

Third, it is a God-centered politics. To borrow the American phrase, Israel

פרשת ראה

יא כו כז רְאֵה אָנֹכִי נֹתֵן לִפְנֵיכֶם הַיּוֹם בְּרָכָה וּקְלָלָה: אֶת־
הַבְּרָכָה אֲשֶׁר תִּשְׁמְעוּ אֶל־מִצְוֺת יהוה אֱלֹהֵיכֶם אֲשֶׁר

RE'EH

In Parashat Re'eh, Moshe turns from the general principles of the covenant to the specific details, prefacing them with a warning of the choice that lies before them: blessings if they are faithful to God's laws, curses if they are not. They are to proclaim these to the nation, on Mount Gerizim and Mount Eival, when they enter the land. They must destroy all traces of idolatry, and establish a central site that God will choose where they will worship, offer sacrifices, and eat consecrated food. Moshe then issues further warnings about idolatry, false prophets, clean and unclean animals, tithes, and the Sabbatical year, when debts are to be cancelled and Hebrew slaves set free. The *parasha* concludes with the laws of the three pilgrimage festivals, when the nation is to celebrate and the men "appear before the Lord" at the central place of worship. We learn that not only individually, but also collectively the nation must exercise its free will to choose the good and stay faithful to God. A free society must be a responsible society. And it is not enough to be free; we must also celebrate our freedom.

11:26 רְאֵה *See this – Re'eh,* the first word of the *parasha,* means "see." On the face of it, Moshe is making an appeal to the eye, not the ear. In fact, though, it is about listening to something heard, namely a blessing and a curse. The non sequitur is so marked that some English translations render the verb *re'eh* not as "see" but as "understand."

What are we to make of this apparent anomaly? The revolutionary doctrine known as *Torah min haShamayim,* "Torah from Heaven," maintains that God reveals Himself in speech. All religions have holy places, objects, and times. But in Judaism these are derivative, not primary. Things are holy only because God has said so. Judaism is the religion of holy words.

If you seek God, turn your attention to language. The hidden presence of God is everywhere. But the revealed presence of God is in the words He gave to humanity on the basis of which He made a series of covenants, first with Noaḥ, then with Avraham, then with the Israelites at Mount Sinai. The Mosaic books constitute the covenant binding Heaven and earth, God and mankind. Hence the philosophy of Israel. To meet God is to listen to God.

The apparent counterexample of *re'eh,* "see," turns out to be not a contradiction of this idea but a dramatic

28 and the curse, if you do not obey the commandments of
the LORD your God, and instead stray from the way I am
commanding you this day to follow, to walk after other
29 gods that you have not known. When the
LORD your God has brought you into the land that you
are entering to possess, you shall proclaim the blessing on
30 Mount Gerizim and the curse on Mount Eival. They are
across the Jordan, westward toward the setting sun, near
the Oaks of Moreh, in the territory of the Canaanites who
31 live in the Arava, near Gilgal. You are about to cross the
Jordan, to go into and take possession of the land that the
LORD your God is giving you. When you have possession
32 of it and live there, you must be vigilant to keep all the
decrees and laws that I am setting before you on this day.
12 1 These are the decrees and laws that you must take care to
keep in the land that the LORD, God of your ancestors,
has given you to possess for as long as you live on this
2 earth. Demolish completely all the shrines where the
nations you are about to dispossess served their gods: on
the high mountains, on the hills, and under every leafy

We have not the numbers, the wealth, nor the sophisticated weaponry of the great empires. As of now we do not even have a land. But we are different, and that difference defines who we are and why. God has chosen to make us His stake in history. He set us free from slavery and took us as His own covenantal partner.

Do not think, says Moshe, that we can survive as a nation among nations, worshipping what they worship and living as they live. If we do, we will be subject to the universal law that has governed the fate of nations from the dawn of civilization. Nations are born, they grow, they flourish; they become complacent, then corrupt, then divided, then defeated, then they die. In the case of Israel, small and intensely vulnerable, that fate would happen sooner rather than later. That is what Moshe calls "the curse."

The alternative is simple – even though it is demanding and detailed. It means taking God as our sovereign, framer of our laws, author of our liberty, defender of our destiny, object of our worship and our love. If we predicate our existence on something – some One – vastly greater than ourselves then we will be lifted higher than we could reach by ourselves.

כח אָנֹכִי מְצַוֶּה אֶתְכֶם הַיּוֹם׃ וְהַקְּלָלָה אִם־לֹא תִשְׁמְעוּ
אֶל־מִצְוֹת יְהוָה אֱלֹהֵיכֶם וְסַרְתֶּם מִן־הַדֶּרֶךְ אֲשֶׁר אָנֹכִי
מְצַוֶּה אֶתְכֶם הַיּוֹם לָלֶכֶת אַחֲרֵי אֱלֹהִים אֲחֵרִים אֲשֶׁר לֹא־
כט יְדַעְתֶּם׃ וְהָיָה כִּי יְבִיאֲךָ יְהוָה אֱלֹהֶיךָ אֶל־הָאָרֶץ
אֲשֶׁר־אַתָּה בָא־שָׁמָּה לְרִשְׁתָּהּ וְנָתַתָּה אֶת־הַבְּרָכָה עַל־הַר
ל גְּרִזִים וְאֶת־הַקְּלָלָה עַל־הַר עֵיבָל׃ הֲלֹא־הֵמָּה בְּעֵבֶר הַיַּרְדֵּן
אַחֲרֵי דֶּרֶךְ מְבוֹא הַשֶּׁמֶשׁ בְּאֶרֶץ הַכְּנַעֲנִי הַיֹּשֵׁב בָּעֲרָבָה מוּל
לא הַגִּלְגָּל אֵצֶל אֵלוֹנֵי מֹרֶה׃ כִּי אַתֶּם עֹבְרִים אֶת־הַיַּרְדֵּן לָבֹא
לָרֶשֶׁת אֶת־הָאָרֶץ אֲשֶׁר־יְהוָה אֱלֹהֵיכֶם נֹתֵן לָכֶם וִירִשְׁתֶּם
לב אֹתָהּ וִישַׁבְתֶּם־בָּהּ׃ וּשְׁמַרְתֶּם לַעֲשׂוֹת אֵת כָּל־הַחֻקִּים וְאֶת־
יב א הַמִּשְׁפָּטִים אֲשֶׁר אָנֹכִי נֹתֵן לִפְנֵיכֶם הַיּוֹם׃ אֵלֶּה הַחֻקִּים
וְהַמִּשְׁפָּטִים אֲשֶׁר תִּשְׁמְרוּן לַעֲשׂוֹת בָּאָרֶץ אֲשֶׁר נָתַן יְהוָה
אֱלֹהֵי אֲבֹתֶיךָ לְךָ לְרִשְׁתָּהּ כָּל־הַיָּמִים אֲשֶׁר־אַתֶּם חַיִּים
ב עַל־הָאֲדָמָה׃ אַבֵּד תְּאַבְּדוּן אֶת־כָּל־הַמְּקֹמוֹת אֲשֶׁר עָבְדוּ־
שָׁם הַגּוֹיִם אֲשֶׁר אַתֶּם יֹרְשִׁים אֹתָם אֶת־אֱלֹהֵיהֶם עַל־

11:32 וּשְׁמַרְתֶּם לַעֲשׂוֹת אֵת כָּל־הַחֻקִּים וְאֶת־הַמִּשְׁפָּטִים *To keep all the decrees and laws* – Moshe does not want the people to lose the big picture. Jewish law, with its 613 commands, is detailed. It aims at the sanctification of all aspects of life, from daily ritual to the structure of society and its institutions. Its aim is to shape a social world in which we turn even seemingly secular occasions into encounters with the Divine Presence. Despite the details, says Moshe, the choice I set before you is simple.

In effect, Moshe is here defining reality for the next generation and for all generations. We are unique, he tells the next generation. We are a small nation. was "one nation under God." It is a powerful, challenging idea. If God is our only sovereign, then all human power is delegated, limited, subject to moral constraints. Jews were the first to believe that an entire nation could govern itself in freedom and equal dignity. This has less to do with political structures (monarchy, oligarchy, democracy – Jews have tried them all), than with collective moral responsibility.

Moshe's words still challenge us today. God has given us freedom; it is for us to use it to create a just, generous, gracious society. God does not do it for us but He teaches us how it is done. As Moshe says: the choice is ours.

▶

3 tree. Tear down their altars, smash their worship pillars,
burn their sacred trees with fire, and cut down the statues
4 of their gods, obliterating their names from that place. Do
5 not make such things for the LORD your God; instead,
seek the place that the LORD your God will choose from
among all your tribes to set His name there, to be His
6 dwelling. Go there, bringing your burnt offerings and
peace offerings, your tithes and your offerings, your gifts
in fulfillment of vows and your freewill offerings, and the
7 firstborns of your herds and flocks. There you and your
families shall eat in the presence of the LORD your God,
rejoicing in all your endeavors in which the LORD your
8 God has granted blessing. Do not behave as we have
been behaving here, now, everyone doing what is right in
9 his own eyes. For you have not yet reached the resting

In Judaism joy is the supreme religious emotion. Here we are, in a world filled with beauty. Every breath we breathe is the spirit of God within us. Around us is the love that moves the sun and all the stars. We are here because someone wanted us to be. Robert Louis Stevenson rightly says: "Find out where joy resides and give it a voice far beyond singing. For to miss the joy is to miss all."

12:8 כָּל־הַיָּשָׁר בְּעֵינָיו *Right in his own eyes* – What liberal individualism takes as the highest virtue – each person doing that which is right in his own eyes – is for the Bible the absence or abdication of virtue, and indeed a way of describing the disintegration of society (see also Judges 17:6, 21:25).

At a certain point in the history of civilizations, a moral consensus breaks down and an attempt is made to solve the problem by conceiving law in minimalist terms. It is there to do no more than to prevent harm to others, to prevent us, in R. Ḥanina's words (Avot 3:2), from swallowing one another alive. The passage of time, however, invariably exposes the contradiction at the heart of this idea. Law is left to solve problems which it cannot solve alone. We then painfully rediscover the ancient truth of the Torah, that the rule of law is compatible with a sense of personal liberty only when supported by at least some collective moral code and by an educational system which allows successive generations to internalize it. Society cannot live by law alone. It needs our common commitment to the common good.

There is a deep connection between ethics and the human spirit, between *morality* and *morale*. If we lose the former, the latter begins to fail. It was Emile Durkheim in his classic study of suicide who coined the word *anomie* to describe

ג הֶהָרִים הָרָמִים וְעַל־הַגְּבָעוֹת וְתַחַת כָּל־עֵץ רַעֲנָן׃ וְנִתַּצְתֶּם
אֶת־מִזְבְּחֹתָם וְשִׁבַּרְתֶּם אֶת־מַצֵּבֹתָם וַאֲשֵׁרֵיהֶם תִּשְׂרְפוּן
בָּאֵשׁ וּפְסִילֵי אֱלֹהֵיהֶם תְּגַדֵּעוּן וְאִבַּדְתֶּם אֶת־שְׁמָם מִן־
ד ה הַמָּקוֹם הַהוּא׃ לֹא־תַעֲשׂוּן כֵּן לַיהוָה אֱלֹהֵיכֶם׃ כִּי אִם־אֶל־
הַמָּקוֹם אֲשֶׁר־יִבְחַר יהוה אֱלֹהֵיכֶם מִכָּל־שִׁבְטֵיכֶם לָשׂוּם
ו אֶת־שְׁמוֹ שָׁם לְשִׁכְנוֹ תִדְרְשׁוּ וּבָאתָ שָׁמָּה׃ וַהֲבֵאתֶם שָׁמָּה
עֹלֹתֵיכֶם וְזִבְחֵיכֶם וְאֵת מַעְשְׂרֹתֵיכֶם וְאֵת תְּרוּמַת יֶדְכֶם
ז וְנִדְרֵיכֶם וְנִדְבֹתֵיכֶם וּבְכֹרֹת בְּקַרְכֶם וְצֹאנְכֶם׃ וַאֲכַלְתֶּם־
שָׁם לִפְנֵי יהוה אֱלֹהֵיכֶם וּשְׂמַחְתֶּם בְּכֹל מִשְׁלַח יֶדְכֶם אַתֶּם
ח וּבָתֵּיכֶם אֲשֶׁר בֵּרַכְךָ יהוה אֱלֹהֶיךָ׃ לֹא תַעֲשׂוּן כְּכֹל אֲשֶׁר
ט אֲנַחְנוּ עֹשִׂים פֹּה הַיּוֹם אִישׁ כָּל־הַיָּשָׁר בְּעֵינָיו׃ כִּי לֹא־
בָאתֶם עַד־עָתָּה אֶל־הַמְּנוּחָה וְאֶל־הַנַּחֲלָה אֲשֶׁר־יהוה

12:7 וּשְׂמַחְתֶּם *Rejoicing* – The word "joy" (root *s-m-ḥ*) appears only once in Genesis, once in Exodus, once in Leviticus, once in Numbers, and twelve times in Deuteronomy. Moshe says again and again that joy is what we should feel in the land of Israel, the land given to us by God, the place to which the whole of Jewish life since the days of Avraham and Sara has been a journey. It will be there, said Moshe, that the narrative of Jewish history will become lucid, where a whole people will sing together, worship together, and celebrate the festivals together, knowing that history is not about empire or conquest, nor society about hierarchy and power; that commoner and king, Israelite and priest, are all equal in the sight of God, all voices in His holy choir, all dancers in the circle at whose center is the radiance of the Divine. This is what the covenant is about: the transformation of the human condition through what Wordsworth called "the deep power of joy."

Happiness is achieved over a lifetime, but joy lives in the moment. It is hard to feel happy in the midst of uncertainty. But you can still feel joy. King David in the book of Psalms spoke of danger, fear, dejection, sometimes even despair, but his songs usually end in the major key:

> For His wrath lasts but a moment,
> but His favor a lifetime;
> at night there may be weeping,
> but the morning brings joy....
> You have turned my mourning into dancing;
> You have untied my sackcloth and clothed me with joy,
> so that my soul may sing to You and not be silent.
> Lord my God, I will praise You forever. (Ps. 30:6–13)

place and inheritance that the LORD your God is giving
10 you. But you will cross the Jordan and live in the land
that the LORD your God is giving you as an inheritance.
When He gives you rest from all the enemies around
11 you so that you are living in safety, then you shall bring SHENI
everything that I command you to the place that the
LORD your God will choose as a dwelling for His name:
your burnt offerings and peace offerings, your tithes and
your offerings, and all the choice gifts that you commit by
12 vow to the LORD. And you shall rejoice before the LORD
your God, along with your sons and daughters, your male
and female servants, and the Levites living in your towns,
13 for they have no share or inheritance with you. Take care
not to offer your burnt offerings in any place you may
14 see. Only in the place that the LORD will choose of one
of your tribes – there you shall offer your burnt offerings

ancestral property to its original owners, restored essential elements of the economy to their default position of fairness. The first principle was: no one should be desperately poor.

The second element, which included *teruma* and *maaser rishon*, the priestly portion and the first tithe, went to support, respectively, the priests and the Levites. These were a religious elite within the nation in biblical times, whose role was to ensure that the service of God, especially in the Temple, continued at the heart of national life.

The third was more personal and spiritual. There were laws including bringing first fruits to Jerusalem, and the three agricultural pilgrimage festivals – Passover, Shavuot, and Sukkot – that imbued the lessons of gratitude and humility. They taught that the land belongs to God and we are merely His tenants and guests. The earth yields its produce, not through our power, but only because of God's blessing. Without such regular reminders, societies slowly but inexorably become materialistic and self-satisfied. Rulers and elites forget that their role is to serve the people, and instead they expect the people to serve them.

CENTRALIZED SACRIFICE, "SECULAR" SLAUGHTER

When the Israelites lived grouped around the Tabernacle, meat could be eaten only after sacrificial slaughter in the Sanctuary. There was no "secular" *sheḥita* to obtain kosher meat outside the Tabernacle. Now, our horizons broaden. When "God has enlarged your territory as He has promised" (Deut. 12:20), and established a centralized Temple, it will no longer be convenient to visit the altar whenever the people wish to eat meat. Israel is to build

י אֱלֹהֶיךָ נֹתֵן לָךְ: וַעֲבַרְתֶּם אֶת־הַיַּרְדֵּן וִישַׁבְתֶּם בָּאָרֶץ אֲשֶׁר־
יהוה אֱלֹהֵיכֶם מַנְחִיל אֶתְכֶם וְהֵנִיחַ לָכֶם מִכָּל־אֹיְבֵיכֶם
יא מִסָּבִיב וִישַׁבְתֶּם־בֶּטַח: וְהָיָה הַמָּקוֹם אֲשֶׁר־יִבְחַר יהוה שני
אֱלֹהֵיכֶם בּוֹ לְשַׁכֵּן שְׁמוֹ שָׁם שָׁמָּה תָבִיאוּ אֵת כָּל־אֲשֶׁר
אָנֹכִי מְצַוֶּה אֶתְכֶם עוֹלֹתֵיכֶם וְזִבְחֵיכֶם מַעְשְׂרֹתֵיכֶם וּתְרֻמַת
יב יֶדְכֶם וְכֹל מִבְחַר נִדְרֵיכֶם אֲשֶׁר תִּדְּרוּ לַיהוה: וּשְׂמַחְתֶּם לִפְנֵי
יהוה אֱלֹהֵיכֶם אַתֶּם וּבְנֵיכֶם וּבְנֹתֵיכֶם וְעַבְדֵיכֶם וְאַמְהֹתֵיכֶם
וְהַלֵּוִי אֲשֶׁר בְּשַׁעֲרֵיכֶם כִּי אֵין לוֹ חֵלֶק וְנַחֲלָה אִתְּכֶם:
יג יד הִשָּׁמֶר לְךָ פֶּן־תַּעֲלֶה עֹלֹתֶיךָ בְּכָל־מָקוֹם אֲשֶׁר תִּרְאֶה: כִּי
אִם־בַּמָּקוֹם אֲשֶׁר־יִבְחַר יהוה בְּאַחַד שְׁבָטֶיךָ שָׁם תַּעֲלֶה

---

a situation in which the individual loses his moorings in a shared moral order and becomes prone to a sense of meaninglessness and drift. A straight road leads from individualism to cynicism and despair. Individualism narrows the horizons of human happiness.

Moshe's first instruction for a covenant society is a decisive rejection of the idolatrous culture in which "they even offer their sons and daughters up in fire" (Deut. 12:31) to obtain favors from their gods. The God of Israel is to be found less in the "I" of individual devotion and self-interest than in the "we," in the relationships we make, the institutions we fashion, the duties we share, and the moral lives we lead.

12:11 וְכֹל מִבְחַר נִדְרֵיכֶם אֲשֶׁר תִּדְּרוּ לַיהוה *Choice gifts that you commit by vow to the* Lord – Biblical Israel was a predominantly agricultural society. Accordingly, it was through agriculture that the Torah pursued its religious and social program. This had three fundamental elements.

The first was the alleviation of poverty. The Torah accepts the basic principles of what we now call a market economy. But though the market is good at creating wealth, it is less good at distributing it equitably. Thus the Torah's social legislation aimed, in the words of Henry George, "to lay the foundations of a social state in which deep poverty and degrading want should be unknown." Hence institutions that left parts of the harvest for the poor: *leket, shikheha,* and *pe'a* – fallen ears of grain, the forgotten sheaf, and the corners of the field. On the third and sixth year of each septennial cycle, the second tithe, instead of being consumed by its owners in Jerusalem as in other years, is given locally to the poor and known as *maaser ani,* "poor person's tithe."

Shemitta, the seventh year, and *Yovel,* the Jubilee, with their release of debts, manumission of slaves, and return of

15 and there do all that I command you. Whenever you
desire, you may slaughter and eat meat in any of your
towns, according to the blessing that the LORD your God
gives you. People both impure and pure may eat of it, as
16 they would of gazelle or of deer. The blood, however, you
17 must not eat. Pour it out on the ground like water. You may
not eat the tithe of your grain, wine, and oil within your
towns, or the firstlings of your herds and flocks, or any of
the gifts that you commit by vow, your freewill offerings,
18 or your gifts. These you must eat in the presence of the
LORD your God at the place that the LORD your God will
choose, along with your sons and daughters, your male
and female servants, and the Levites living in your towns,

> Many dots scattered here and there certainly constitute a multiplicity, but the same number of dots ordered around a single point in the center form one circle. This is your duty in life, to place at the center of your life the "One," and then you need have no worry about dualities. Every new dot you acquire will then merely expand the circle, but its unity will remain.

It is all too easy to compartmentalize the religious life. There are sacred times and places: the Sabbath, the festivals, the synagogue, the home. And there are contexts – work, colleagues, the wider society – when we play our allotted roles and live by other rules. The result can be a divided personality and a sense of disconnection between inner and outer worlds. It does not have to be. What we take with us wherever we go is our character. To be gracious, thoughtful, sensitive, attentive; to have integrity, courage, and psychological strength; to be able to respond to different people in different ways, knowing what each needs to fulfill his or her part in the scheme of things – is to come as close as we can to living in the world as God lives in the world. If I were to sum up what faith asks us to be, I would say: a *healing presence*. Deuteronomy makes the concession of allowing "secular slaughter." It does, however, need to be performed "as I have commanded you" (Deut. 12:21) – referring, as the Rabbis understood, to humane slaughter. Meat need not emerge from the Sanctuary to be kosher, but it must be obtained with compassion.

12:18 וּבִנְךָ וּבִתֶּךָ וְעַבְדְּךָ וַאֲמָתֶךָ *Along with your sons and daughters, your male and female servants* – When you rejoice, Moshe says time and again, it must be "you and your sons and daughters, your male and female servants, the Levites, and the migrants, orphans, and widows living in your towns" (Deut. 16:14). A

טו עֹלֹתֶיךָ וְשָׁם תַּעֲשֶׂה כֹּל אֲשֶׁר אָנֹכִי מְצַוֶּךָּ׃ רַק בְּכָל־אַוַּת
נַפְשְׁךָ תִּזְבַּח ׀ וְאָכַלְתָּ בָשָׂר כְּבִרְכַּת יְהוָה אֱלֹהֶיךָ אֲשֶׁר
נָתַן־לְךָ בְּכָל־שְׁעָרֶיךָ הַטָּמֵא וְהַטָּהוֹר יֹאכְלֶנּוּ כַּצְּבִי וְכָאַיָּל׃
טז יז רַק הַדָּם לֹא תֹאכֵלוּ עַל־הָאָרֶץ תִּשְׁפְּכֶנּוּ כַּמָּיִם׃ לֹא־תוּכַל
לֶאֱכֹל בִּשְׁעָרֶיךָ מַעְשַׂר דְּגָנְךָ וְתִירֹשְׁךָ וְיִצְהָרֶךָ וּבְכֹרֹת
בְּקָרְךָ וְצֹאנֶךָ וְכָל־נְדָרֶיךָ אֲשֶׁר תִּדֹּר וְנִדְבֹתֶיךָ וּתְרוּמַת
יח יָדֶךָ׃ כִּי אִם־לִפְנֵי יְהוָה אֱלֹהֶיךָ תֹּאכְלֶנּוּ בַּמָּקוֹם אֲשֶׁר
יִבְחַר יְהוָה אֱלֹהֶיךָ בּוֹ אַתָּה וּבִנְךָ וּבִתֶּךָ וְעַבְדְּךָ וַאֲמָתֶךָ

and negotiate, for the first time in its life as a nation, a secular domain.

In 1954, Rabbi Yitzchak Hutner received a letter from a young man who was leaving a religious seminary to begin a secular career. The prospect was causing him distress. In the seminary he had found a sheltered environment within which he felt the intensity of a life devoted uninterruptedly to study. Pursuing a career seemed like a compromise that could only lead to a loss of single-mindedness. He was, he said, fearful of leading a "double life." Rabbi Hutner wrote him a powerful, dissenting reply:

> I would never agree to your leading a double life. One who rents a room in a house in which to live, and [at the same time] pays for a room in a hotel in which to be a guest is certainly leading a double life. But one who rents an apartment with two rooms is not leading a double life but a broad life.
>
> I remember once visiting the hospital in Jerusalem where [a certain Orthodox doctor worked] and I saw him approach a patient who was just about to undergo an operation. He asked him for the name of his mother so that he could say a prayer on his behalf for the success of the operation. When I mentioned this to one of the outstanding Torah sages in Jerusalem, he exclaimed, "How enviable to be such a Jew with so great an opportunity to serve as a vehicle for the glory of Heaven!" Tell me, beloved friend, is a doctor, about to perform an operation on a patient, who says a chapter of Psalms for the safe recovery of his patient, leading a double life?
>
> Beloved friend, God forbid that you should see yourself as leading a double life. [The Sages say that] "Whoever prolongs the word 'One' [in the first verse of the *Shema*, Deut. 6:4] prolongs his days and years" (Berakhot 13b). Therefore throughout your life you should be one of those who "prolongs the 'One'" – focusing on unity, not duality. It would grieve me very much if this point were not apparent to you.

rejoicing in all your endeavors in the presence of the
19 Lord your God. Take care not to neglect the Levite in all
20 your years living in your land. When the Lord
your God has enlarged your territory as He has promised,
and you say, 'I shall eat some meat,' because you have the
21 urge to eat it, you may eat meat whenever you desire it. If
the place where the Lord your God chooses to place His
name is too distant from you, you may slaughter animals
from the herds and flocks the Lord has given you, as I
have commanded you. These you may eat within your
22 towns whenever you wish. Eat them as you would eat
gazelle or a deer; the impure may eat together with the
23 pure. But make sure that you do not eat the blood, for
blood is life, and you must not eat the life with the meat.
24 25 Do not eat it; pour it out onto the ground like water; do
not eat it, so that all may be well for you and your children
after you, because you do what is right in the Lord's
26 eyes. But your sacred offerings and the gifts you commit
by vow you must bring to the place that the Lord will
27 choose. Present your burnt offerings – the meat and the
blood – on the altar of the Lord your God. Of your other
sacrifices, the blood shall be poured out on the altar of
28 the Lord your God, but you may eat the meat. Take
care to heed all these words that I command you today,
so that it may be well for you and for your children after
you forever, because you will be doing what is good and
29 right in the Lord your God's eyes. When the SHELISHI
Lord your God has cut down before you the nations that
you are about to come to and dispossess, after you have
30 dispossessed them and live in their land, beware being
tempted into their ways after they have been destroyed
before you. Do not inquire about their gods, saying, 'How
did these nations worship their gods? Let me do the same.'

---

moral. Not only was this a religious act of thanksgiving; it was also to be a form of social inclusion. No one was to be left out: not the stranger, the servant, the orphan, or the widow.

וְהַלֵּוִי אֲשֶׁר בִּשְׁעָרֶיךָ וְשָׂמַחְתָּ לִפְנֵי יְהוָה אֱלֹהֶיךָ בְּכֹל
יט מִשְׁלַח יָדֶךָ: הִשָּׁמֶר לְךָ פֶּן־תַּעֲזֹב אֶת־הַלֵּוִי כָּל־יָמֶיךָ עַל־
כ אַדְמָתֶךָ: כִּי־יַרְחִיב יְהוָה אֱלֹהֶיךָ אֶת־גְּבֻלְךָ יא
כַּאֲשֶׁר דִּבֶּר־לָךְ וְאָמַרְתָּ אֹכְלָה בָשָׂר כִּי־תְאַוֶּה נַפְשְׁךָ לֶאֱכֹל
כא בָּשָׂר בְּכָל־אַוַּת נַפְשְׁךָ תֹּאכַל בָּשָׂר: כִּי־יִרְחַק מִמְּךָ הַמָּקוֹם
אֲשֶׁר יִבְחַר יְהוָה אֱלֹהֶיךָ לָשׂוּם שְׁמוֹ שָׁם וְזָבַחְתָּ מִבְּקָרְךָ
וּמִצֹּאנְךָ אֲשֶׁר נָתַן יְהוָה לְךָ כַּאֲשֶׁר צִוִּיתִךָ וְאָכַלְתָּ בִּשְׁעָרֶיךָ
כב בְּכֹל אַוַּת נַפְשֶׁךָ: אַךְ כַּאֲשֶׁר יֵאָכֵל אֶת־הַצְּבִי וְאֶת־הָאַיָּל כֵּן
כג תֹּאכְלֶנּוּ הַטָּמֵא וְהַטָּהוֹר יַחְדָּו יֹאכְלֶנּוּ: רַק חֲזַק לְבִלְתִּי אֲכֹל
כד הַדָּם כִּי הַדָּם הוּא הַנָּפֶשׁ וְלֹא־תֹאכַל הַנֶּפֶשׁ עִם־הַבָּשָׂר: לֹא
כה תֹּאכְלֶנּוּ עַל־הָאָרֶץ תִּשְׁפְּכֶנּוּ כַּמָּיִם: לֹא תֹּאכְלֶנּוּ לְמַעַן יִיטַב
כו לְךָ וּלְבָנֶיךָ אַחֲרֶיךָ כִּי־תַעֲשֶׂה הַיָּשָׁר בְּעֵינֵי יְהוָה: רַק קָדָשֶׁיךָ
אֲשֶׁר־יִהְיוּ לְךָ וּנְדָרֶיךָ תִּשָּׂא וּבָאתָ אֶל־הַמָּקוֹם אֲשֶׁר־יִבְחַר
כז יְהוָה: וְעָשִׂיתָ עֹלֹתֶיךָ הַבָּשָׂר וְהַדָּם עַל־מִזְבַּח יְהוָה אֱלֹהֶיךָ
וְדַם־זְבָחֶיךָ יִשָּׁפֵךְ עַל־מִזְבַּח יְהוָה אֱלֹהֶיךָ וְהַבָּשָׂר תֹּאכֵל:
כח שְׁמֹר וְשָׁמַעְתָּ אֵת כָּל־הַדְּבָרִים הָאֵלֶּה אֲשֶׁר אָנֹכִי מְצַוֶּךָּ
לְמַעַן יִיטַב לְךָ וּלְבָנֶיךָ אַחֲרֶיךָ עַד־עוֹלָם כִּי תַעֲשֶׂה הַטּוֹב
כט וְהַיָּשָׁר בְּעֵינֵי יְהוָה אֱלֹהֶיךָ: כִּי־יַכְרִית יְהוָה שלישי
אֱלֹהֶיךָ אֶת־הַגּוֹיִם אֲשֶׁר אַתָּה בָא־שָׁמָּה לָרֶשֶׁת אוֹתָם
ל מִפָּנֶיךָ וְיָרַשְׁתָּ אֹתָם וְיָשַׁבְתָּ בְּאַרְצָם: הִשָּׁמֶר לְךָ פֶּן־תִּנָּקֵשׁ
אַחֲרֵיהֶם אַחֲרֵי הִשָּׁמְדָם מִפָּנֶיךָ וּפֶן־תִּדְרֹשׁ לֵאלֹהֵיהֶם
לֵאמֹר אֵיכָה יַעַבְדוּ הַגּוֹיִם הָאֵלֶּה אֶת־אֱלֹהֵיהֶם וְאֶעֱשֶׂה־

---

key theme of Parashat Re'eh is the idea of a central Sanctuary in "the place that the LORD your God will choose" (16:7). As we know from later Jewish history, during the reign of King David this was Jerusalem, where David's son Shlomo eventually built the Temple.

Moshe is articulating the idea of *simḥa* as communal, social, and national rejoicing. The nation was to be brought together not just by crisis, catastrophe, or impending war, but by collective celebration in the presence of God. The celebration itself was to be deeply

31 You must not worship the Lord your God in their way,
because they have done for their gods every abhorrent
thing that the Lord hates. They even offer their sons
13 1 and daughters up in fire to their gods. Take care: fulfill all
that I command you. Neither add to it nor subtract from
it.
2 If a prophet rises up among you, or one who divines
3 by dreams, and he tells you of some sign or omen, and
the sign or omen of which he spoke is realized – and
he had said, 'Let us walk after other gods and worship
4 them' – gods you have not known – do not listen to the
words of that prophet or dream diviner. The Lord your
God will be testing you, to know whether you really love
the Lord your God with all your heart and with all your
5 soul. Follow the Lord your God, revere Him, keep His
commandments, and listen to His voice. Worship Him;
6 stay close to Him. And that prophet or dream diviner – he
shall be put to death for inciting rebellion against the Lord
your God who brought you out of Egypt and redeemed
you from the house of slaves, seeking to make you stray
from the path the Lord your God commanded you to
7 walk. You must purge the evil from your midst. If
anyone, even your brother, your mother's son, or your
own son or daughter, the wife of your embrace, or the
friend who is like your own self to you, secretly tempts
you: 'Let us go and worship other gods' – whom neither
8 you nor your ancestors have known, gods of the peoples
9 around you, near or far, end to end of the earth – do not
acquiesce, do not listen to him, do not show him pity or
10 compassion, or cover up for him. You must put him to

---

temporary enactments for the sake of social order. Prophets were given the authority to command specific, time-bound acts. But no one could add to or subtract from the 613 commandments given by God through Moshe. Rather, the other prophets recalled the people to their mission. They reminded them of their duties. They spoke out against corruption and injustice within society. They were social critics, not innovators.

לא כֵּן גַּם־אָנִי: לֹא־תַעֲשֶׂה כֵן לַיהוָה אֱלֹהֶיךָ כִּי כָל־תּוֹעֲבַת
יְהוָה אֲשֶׁר שָׂנֵא עָשׂוּ לֵאלֹהֵיהֶם כִּי גַם אֶת־בְּנֵיהֶם וְאֶת־
יג א בְּנֹתֵיהֶם יִשְׂרְפוּ בָאֵשׁ לֵאלֹהֵיהֶם: אֵת כָּל־הַדָּבָר אֲשֶׁר
אָנֹכִי מְצַוֶּה אֶתְכֶם אֹתוֹ תִשְׁמְרוּ לַעֲשׂוֹת לֹא־תֹסֵף עָלָיו
וְלֹא תִגְרַע מִמֶּנּוּ:
ב כִּי־יָקוּם בְּקִרְבְּךָ נָבִיא אוֹ חֹלֵם חֲלוֹם וְנָתַן אֵלֶיךָ אוֹת
ג אוֹ מוֹפֵת: וּבָא הָאוֹת וְהַמּוֹפֵת אֲשֶׁר־דִּבֶּר אֵלֶיךָ לֵאמֹר
ד נֵלְכָה אַחֲרֵי אֱלֹהִים אֲחֵרִים אֲשֶׁר לֹא־יְדַעְתָּם וְנָעָבְדֵם: לֹא
תִשְׁמַע אֶל־דִּבְרֵי הַנָּבִיא הַהוּא אוֹ אֶל־חוֹלֵם הַחֲלוֹם הַהוּא
כִּי מְנַסֶּה יְהוָה אֱלֹהֵיכֶם אֶתְכֶם לָדַעַת הֲיִשְׁכֶם אֹהֲבִים
ה אֶת־יְהוָה אֱלֹהֵיכֶם בְּכָל־לְבַבְכֶם וּבְכָל־נַפְשְׁכֶם: אַחֲרֵי
יְהוָה אֱלֹהֵיכֶם תֵּלֵכוּ וְאֹתוֹ תִירָאוּ וְאֶת־מִצְוֹתָיו תִּשְׁמֹרוּ
ו וּבְקֹלוֹ תִשְׁמָעוּ וְאֹתוֹ תַעֲבֹדוּ וּבוֹ תִדְבָּקוּן: וְהַנָּבִיא הַהוּא אוֹ
חֹלֵם הַחֲלוֹם הַהוּא יוּמָת כִּי דִבֶּר־סָרָה עַל־יְהוָה אֱלֹהֵיכֶם
הַמּוֹצִיא אֶתְכֶם ׀ מֵאֶרֶץ מִצְרַיִם וְהַפֹּדְךָ מִבֵּית עֲבָדִים
לְהַדִּיחֲךָ מִן־הַדֶּרֶךְ אֲשֶׁר צִוְּךָ יְהוָה אֱלֹהֶיךָ לָלֶכֶת בָּהּ
ז וּבִעַרְתָּ הָרָע מִקִּרְבֶּךָ: כִּי יְסִיתְךָ אָחִיךָ בֶן־אִמֶּךָ
אוֹ־בִנְךָ אוֹ־בִתְּךָ אוֹ ׀ אֵשֶׁת חֵיקֶךָ אוֹ רֵעֲךָ אֲשֶׁר כְּנַפְשְׁךָ
בַּסֵּתֶר לֵאמֹר נֵלְכָה וְנַעַבְדָה אֱלֹהִים אֲחֵרִים אֲשֶׁר לֹא יָדַעְתָּ
ח אַתָּה וַאֲבֹתֶיךָ: מֵאֱלֹהֵי הָעַמִּים אֲשֶׁר סְבִיבֹתֵיכֶם הַקְּרֹבִים
אֵלֶיךָ אוֹ הָרְחֹקִים מִמֶּךָּ מִקְצֵה הָאָרֶץ וְעַד־קְצֵה הָאָרֶץ:
ט לֹא־תֹאבֶה לוֹ וְלֹא תִשְׁמַע אֵלָיו וְלֹא־תָחוֹס עֵינְךָ עָלָיו
י וְלֹא־תַחְמֹל וְלֹא־תְכַסֶּה עָלָיו: כִּי הָרֹג תַּהַרְגֶנּוּ יָדְךָ תִּהְיֶה־

13:4 לֹא תִשְׁמַע אֶל־דִּבְרֵי הַנָּבִיא הַהוּא *Do not listen to the words of that prophet* – In Judaism, what is primary is the covenant between Israel and God. A prophet who seeks to change the covenant or lead the people in a different direction must not be heeded. The classic prophets did not claim the authority to make changes in Judaism. Moshe was unique. Only he was authorized to proclaim Torah: he was Israel's sole legislator. The king and Sanhedrin both had powers to make

▶

death. Your own hand shall be first against him to kill
11 him, and after yours, the hand of all the people. Stone him
to death for seeking to make you abandon the LORD your
God who brought you out of Egypt, the house of slaves.
12 And all Israel shall hear, and fear, and never commit such
13 an evil again. If you hear it said about one of the
towns that the LORD your God is giving you to live in
14 that depraved men among you have gone out and led the
people of the town astray, saying, 'Let us go and worship
15 other gods' – gods you have not known – you shall seek
the truth, investigate, and inquire thoroughly abroad. If
it is true and is confirmed that this abhorrent thing has
16 been done among you, you shall put the inhabitants of
that town to the sword, destroying it and everything in it;
17 put even its animals to the sword. Gather all its spoil into
its public square, then burn with fire the town and all its
spoil, in its entirety, to the LORD your God. It shall be an

---

in truth. "Our faith in science is still based on a metaphysical faith. Even we know, as of today, we godless anti-metaphysicians, still date our fire from the blaze set alight by a faith thousands of years old... that God is truth. That truth is Divine."

In other words, says Nietzsche, our belief in truth and even science ultimately goes back to religious and philosophical foundations. There is nothing in nature that tends toward truth or truthfulness. Every animal that is the potential prey of a predator has to learn to conceal, to hide, to deceive. A free society, however, depends on trust. Trust depends on honesty in public life. And honesty in public life depends on truth as a norm.

13:17 וְהָיְתָה תֵּל עוֹלָם *It shall be an eternal ruin* – There are certain laws that the Rabbis found puzzling and morally problematic. This law of "the town led astray" is a classic example, alongside the law about a wayward and rebellious son who is to be put to death for what appears to us to be no worse than a serious case of juvenile delinquency (Deut. 21:18–21; see notes there). So incompatible did these laws seem with the principles of justice that the Talmud records the view that they were never put into effect and exist only for didactic purposes, not to be implemented in practice. In the case of the condemned city (see 13:13–19), R. Eliezer said that if it contained a single mezuza, the law was not enforced (Sanhedrin 71a).

Why did the Oral Tradition, or at least some of its exponents, narrow the scope of the law in some cases, and broaden it in others? The short answer is: we do not know. The rabbinic literature

יא בּוֹ בָרִאשֹׁנָה לַהֲמִיתוֹ וְיַד כָּל־הָעָם בָּאַחֲרֹנָה: וּסְקַלְתּוֹ
בָאֲבָנִים וָמֵת כִּי בִקֵּשׁ לְהַדִּיחֲךָ מֵעַל יהוה אֱלֹהֶיךָ הַמּוֹצִיאֲךָ
יב מֵאֶרֶץ מִצְרַיִם מִבֵּית עֲבָדִים: וְכָל־יִשְׂרָאֵל יִשְׁמְעוּ וְיִרָאוּן
יג וְלֹא־יוֹסִפוּ לַעֲשׂוֹת כַּדָּבָר הָרָע הַזֶּה בְּקִרְבֶּךָ: כִּי־
תִשְׁמַע בְּאַחַת עָרֶיךָ אֲשֶׁר יהוה אֱלֹהֶיךָ נֹתֵן לְךָ לָשֶׁבֶת
יד שָׁם לֵאמֹר: יָצְאוּ אֲנָשִׁים בְּנֵי־בְלִיַּעַל מִקִּרְבֶּךָ וַיַּדִּיחוּ
אֶת־יֹשְׁבֵי עִירָם לֵאמֹר נֵלְכָה וְנַעַבְדָה אֱלֹהִים אֲחֵרִים
טו אֲשֶׁר לֹא־יְדַעְתֶּם: וְדָרַשְׁתָּ וְחָקַרְתָּ וְשָׁאַלְתָּ הֵיטֵב
וְהִנֵּה אֱמֶת נָכוֹן הַדָּבָר נֶעֶשְׂתָה הַתּוֹעֵבָה הַזֹּאת בְּקִרְבֶּךָ:
טז הַכֵּה תַכֶּה אֶת־יֹשְׁבֵי הָעִיר הַהִוא לְפִי־חָרֶב הַחֲרֵם אֹתָהּ
יז וְאֶת־כָּל־אֲשֶׁר־בָּהּ וְאֶת־בְּהֶמְתָּהּ לְפִי־חָרֶב: וְאֶת־כָּל־
שְׁלָלָהּ תִּקְבֹּץ אֶל־תּוֹךְ רְחֹבָהּ וְשָׂרַפְתָּ בָאֵשׁ אֶת־הָעִיר
וְאֶת־כָּל־שְׁלָלָהּ כָּלִיל לַיהוה אֱלֹהֶיךָ וְהָיְתָה תֵּל עוֹלָם לֹא

13:15 וְדָרַשְׁתָּ וְחָקַרְתָּ וְשָׁאַלְתָּ הֵיטֵב *Seek the truth, investigate, and inquire thoroughly* – Essential to the justice system is the pursuit of the truth through careful investigation of evidence. This principle needs protection; the first reference to what could be referred to as a "post-truth society" is twenty-six centuries ago, in the sixth century BCE. This is Yirmeyahu (in chapter 9 of the book that bears his name):

> "They have drawn their tongue, their bow is falsehood. Not for faithfulness have they become powerful in the land.... Let each man be on guard against his fellow, and let no one trust his own brother, for every brother acts deceitfully, and every friend spreads slander. Each man defrauds his fellows and speaks untruth.... One speaks peaceably to another but secretly plans an ambush. Should I not hold them to account for these things?" demands the Lord. "For a nation such as this, should I not exact retribution?" (Jer. 9:2–8)

Yirmeyahu's faithful city, now the faithless city of Jerusalem, was indeed eventually conquered by the Babylonians and the people sent into exile. And although he was a moral extremist, Yirmeyahu was, at the same time, a political realist. He knew that in the absence of truth, no society can stand.

Nietzsche, in his book *On the Genealogy of Morality,* speaks about people who think of themselves as free spirits (in other words, atheists like him). He says that they are in fact very far from being free spirits because *they still believe*

18 eternal ruin, never to be rebuilt. Let nothing that has been
banned remain in your hands, so that the LORD may turn
away from His flaming rage, show you compassion, and
in His compassion increase your numbers, as He swore
19 to your ancestors, for you will have heeded the voice of
the LORD your God, keeping all His commandments
that I am giving you today and doing what is right in the
14 1 LORD your God's eyes. You are children of the REVI'I
LORD your God. Do not lacerate yourselves or make
2 bald patches in the middle of your heads for the dead. For

Rabbis is cruel (*akhzari*)" (*Hilkhot Evel* 13:12). At the same time, however, "one should not indulge in excessive grief over one's dead, for it is said, 'Weep not for the dead; do not bemoan him' (Jer. 22:10); that is to say, weep not too much, for [death] is the way of the world" (*Hilkhot Evel* 13:11).

Halakha, Jewish law, strives to create a balance between too much and too little grief. Hence the various stages of bereavement: *aninut* (the period between the death and burial), *shiva* (the week of mourning), *sheloshim* (thirty days in the case of other relatives) and *shana* (a year, in the case of parents). Judaism ordains a precisely calibrated sequence of grief, from the initial, numbing moment of loss itself, to the funeral and the return home, to the period of being comforted by friends and members of the community, to a more extended time during which one does not engage in activities associated with joy.

In this anti-traditional age, with its hostility to ritual and its preference for the public display of private emotion, the idea that grief has its laws and limits sounds strange. Yet many who have had the misfortune to be bereaved testify to the profound healing brought about by observance of the laws of *avelut* (mourning).

Torah and tradition knew how to honor both the dead and the living, sustaining the delicate balance between grief and consolation, the loss of life that gives us pain, and the re-affirmation of life that gives us hope.

14:1 בָּנִים אַתֶּם לַיהוה אֱלֹהֵיכֶם *You are children of the* LORD *your God* – We experience God in two ways: in awe and in love. In awe, for He is our sovereign, the supreme power of the universe. But also in love, for He brought us into being. He is a parent to us. Between a servant and a king there can be estrangement. A king can send a servant into exile. But between a father and a child there can be no permanent estrangement. However far removed they are from one another, the bond between parent and child still holds.

יח תִּבָּנֶה עוֹד׃ וְלֹא־יִדְבַּק בְּיָדְךָ מְאוּמָה מִן־הַחֵרֶם לְמַעַן יָשׁוּב
יְהוָה מֵחֲרוֹן אַפּוֹ וְנָתַן־לְךָ רַחֲמִים וְרִחַמְךָ וְהִרְבֶּךָ כַּאֲשֶׁר
יט נִשְׁבַּע לַאֲבֹתֶיךָ׃ כִּי תִשְׁמַע בְּקוֹל יְהוָה אֱלֹהֶיךָ לִשְׁמֹר אֶת־
כָּל־מִצְוֹתָיו אֲשֶׁר אָנֹכִי מְצַוְּךָ הַיּוֹם לַעֲשׂוֹת הַיָּשָׁר בְּעֵינֵי
יד א יְהוָה אֱלֹהֶיךָ׃ בָּנִים אַתֶּם לַיהוָה אֱלֹהֵיכֶם לֹא יב רביעי
ב תִתְגֹּדְדוּ וְלֹא־תָשִׂימוּ קָרְחָה בֵּין עֵינֵיכֶם לָמֵת׃ כִּי עַם קָדוֹשׁ

does not tell us. But we can speculate. A *posek*, seeking to interpret divine law in specific cases, will endeavor to do so in a way consistent with the total structure of biblical teaching. If a text seems to conflict with a basic principle of Jewish law, it will be understood restrictively, at least by some. If it exemplifies such a principle, it will be understood broadly.

The law of the condemned city, where all the inhabitants were sentenced to death, seems to conflict with the principle of individual justice. When Sedom was threatened with such a fate, Avraham argued that if there were only ten innocent people, the destruction of the entire population would be manifestly unfair: "Shall the judge of all the earth not do justice?" (Gen. 18:25). The Sages sought as far as possible to make their individual rulings consistent with the value structure of Jewish law as they understood it. On this view, the law of the condemned city exists to teach us that idolatry, once accepted in public, is contagious, as we see from the history of Israel's kings. Law exists not just to regulate but also to educate.

Living traditions constantly reinterpret their canonical texts. That is what makes fundamentalism – text *without* interpretation – an act of violence against tradition. In fact, fundamentalists and today's atheists share the same approach to texts. They read them directly and literally, ignoring the single most important fact about a sacred text, namely, that its meaning is not self-evident. It has a history and an authority of its own. Hard texts require not only covenantal commitment, but covenantal listening as well.

PROHIBITED MOURNING RITES

To lose a close member of one's family is a shattering experience. It is as if something of ourselves had died too. Yet we are commanded not to engage in excessive rituals of grief. Not to grieve is inhuman: Judaism does not command stoic indifference in the face of death. But to give way to wild expressions of sorrow – lacerating one's flesh, tearing out one's hair – is wrong. It is, the Torah suggests, not fitting to a holy people; it is the kind of behavior associated with idolatrous cults.

Here is how Rambam sets out the law: "Whoever does not mourn the dead in the manner enjoined by the

you are a people sacred to the Lord your God. The Lord
has chosen you of all the peoples on earth to be to Him
3 a treasured people. Do not eat any abhorrent
4 thing. These are the animals you may eat: the ox, the
5 sheep, the goat, the deer, the gazelle, the hartebeest, the
6 ibex, the oryx, the wild ox, and the giraffe. You may eat
any animal that has divided hoofs, fully split in two, and
7 chews the cud. Of those that chew the cud or that have
a cleft hoof, these you shall not eat: the camel, the hare,
and the hyrax, because they chew the cud but do not
8 have a divided hoof – they are impure for you; and the
pig, because it has a divided hoof but does not chew the
cud – it is impure for you. You may not eat their flesh or
9 touch their carcasses. These you may eat among
the creatures of the water: anything that has fins and
10 scales. Whatever does not have fins and scales you may
11 not eat; it is impure for you. You may eat any
12 pure species of bird. These you may not eat: the griffon
vulture, the bearded vulture, the lappet-faced vulture,

Particularly striking is the way these chapters deal with the animal kingdom. What Iyov sees are not domestic animals, but wild, untamable creatures, magnificent in their strength and beauty, living far from and utterly indifferent to humankind:

> Did you endow the horse with his valor? Did you clothe his neck with a mane?
>
> Do you make him rumble like locusts, neigh in majestic terror? …
>
> Is it by your wisdom the hawk flies, spreading his wings to head south?
>
> Does the vulture soar at your bidding? Is that why he builds his nest on high? (39:19–27)

This is the most radically non-anthropocentric passage in the Tanakh. It tells us that man is not the center of the universe, nor are we the measure of all things. Some of the most glorious aspects of nature have nothing to do with human needs. One of the few Jewish thinkers to state this clearly was Rambam:

> Consider how vast are the dimensions and how great the number of these corporeal beings. If the whole of the earth would not constitute even the smallest part of the sphere of the fixed stars, what is the relation of the human species to all these created things, and how can any of us imagine that they exist for his sake

אַתָּה לַיהוָה אֱלֹהֶיךָ וּבְךָ בָּחַר יְהוָה לִהְיוֹת לוֹ לְעַם סְגֻלָּה
ג מִכֹּל הָעַמִּים אֲשֶׁר עַל־פְּנֵי הָאֲדָמָה׃ לֹא תֹאכַל
ד כָּל־תּוֹעֵבָה׃ זֹאת הַבְּהֵמָה אֲשֶׁר תֹּאכֵלוּ שׁוֹר שֵׂה כְשָׂבִים
ה וְשֵׂה עִזִּים׃ אַיָּל וּצְבִי וְיַחְמוּר וְאַקּוֹ וְדִישֹׁן וּתְאוֹ וָזָמֶר׃
ו וְכָל־בְּהֵמָה מַפְרֶסֶת פַּרְסָה וְשֹׁסַעַת שֶׁסַע שְׁתֵּי פְרָסוֹת
ז מַעֲלַת גֵּרָה בַּבְּהֵמָה אֹתָהּ תֹּאכֵלוּ׃ אַךְ אֶת־זֶה לֹא תֹאכְלוּ
מִמַּעֲלֵי הַגֵּרָה וּמִמַּפְרִיסֵי הַפַּרְסָה הַשְּׁסוּעָה אֶת־הַגָּמָל
וְאֶת־הָאַרְנֶבֶת וְאֶת־הַשָּׁפָן כִּי־מַעֲלֵה גֵרָה הֵמָּה וּפַרְסָה לֹא
ח הִפְרִיסוּ טְמֵאִים הֵם לָכֶם׃ וְאֶת־הַחֲזִיר כִּי־מַפְרִיס פַּרְסָה
הוּא וְלֹא גֵרָה טָמֵא הוּא לָכֶם מִבְּשָׂרָם לֹא תֹאכֵלוּ וּבְנִבְלָתָם
ט לֹא תִגָּעוּ׃ אֶת־זֶה תֹּאכְלוּ מִכֹּל אֲשֶׁר בַּמָּיִם כֹּל
י אֲשֶׁר־לוֹ סְנַפִּיר וְקַשְׂקֶשֶׂת תֹּאכֵלוּ׃ וְכֹל אֲשֶׁר אֵין־לוֹ סְנַפִּיר
יא וְקַשְׂקֶשֶׂת לֹא תֹאכֵלוּ טָמֵא הוּא לָכֶם׃ כָּל־
יב צִפּוֹר טְהֹרָה תֹּאכֵלוּ׃ וְזֶה אֲשֶׁר לֹא־תֹאכְלוּ מֵהֶם הַנֶּשֶׁר

KOSHER AND NONKOSHER ANIMALS

Moshe returns here to the laws of *kashrut* first laid out in Parashat Shemini. The dietary laws, which seem to defy logical explanation, are as integral to the covenant as the laws of a just society. Why?

We may find some direction in the book of Job. Iyov is the paradigm of the righteous individual who suffers. He loses all he has, for no apparent reason. His companions tell him that he must have sinned. Only this can reconcile his fate with justice. Iyov maintains his innocence and demands a hearing in the heavenly tribunal. For some thirty-seven chapters the argument rages, then in chapter 38 God addresses Iyov "from the whirlwind" (Job 38:1). God offers no answers. Instead, for four chapters, He asks questions of His own, rhetorical questions that have no answer: "Where were you when I laid the earth's foundations?" (38:4); "Have you traveled as far as the sea's depths, walked through them, plumbing the abyss?" (38:16).

God shows Iyov the whole panoply of creation, but it is a very different view of the universe than that set out in Genesis 1–2. There the center of the narrative is the human person. Man and woman were created last, made in God's image, given dominion over all that lives. In Job we see not an anthropocentric, but a *theocentric,* universe. Iyov is the only person in Tanakh who sees the world, as it were, from God's point of view.

13 14 the glede, the buzzard, the kite of any kind, any kind of
15 raven, the ostrich, the swift, the gull, any kind of sparrow
16 17 hawk, the little owl, the short-eared owl, the barn owl, the
18 pelican, the Egyptian vulture, the cormorant, the stork,
19 any kind of heron, the hoopoe, and the bat. All swarming,
flying creatures are impure for you; they may not be eaten.
20 21 You may, however, eat any pure flying creature. Do not eat
any creature that has died of itself. Give it to the migrant
in your town to eat, or you may sell it to a foreigner. For
you are a people holy to the LORD your God. Do not boil
a kid in the milk of its mother.
22 Each year, set aside a tenth of the yield of all you have HAMISHI
23 sown in the field. You shall eat the tithe of your grain,
wine, and oil, as well as the firstborn of your herds and
flocks in the presence of the LORD your God in the place
that He will choose as a dwelling for His name, so that

Roger Scruton makes a fascinating observation in relation to the prohibition against "boiling a kid in the milk of its mother":

> The Jewish law which forbids us to seethe a young animal in its mother's milk may have little sense, when considered from the standpoint of a hard-nosed utilitarianism. But our disposition to hesitate before the mystery of nature, to renounce our presumption of mastery, and to respect the process by which life is made, must surely prompt us to sympathize with such an interdiction. And these very same feelings, had we allowed them to prevail, would have caused us to hesitate before feeding to cows, which live and thrive on pasture, the dead remains of their own and other species.

This practice, adopted to save money, ultimately caused the spread of deadly disease and led to untold damage.

All of the world's great faiths embody a sense of respect for nature, and thus constitute an important counterbalance to the indifference bordering on arrogance that has been one of the less lovely legacies of the Enlightenment. Civilizations at the height of their powers have found it hard to maintain a sense of limits. Each in turn has been captivated by the idea that it alone was immune to the laws of growth and decline, that it could consume resources indefinitely, pursuing present advantage without thought of future depletion. Never is this more likely than when we lose the sense of awe in the face of totality. The great faiths teach a different kind of wisdom: *reverence* in the face of creation, *responsibility* to future generations, and *restraint* in the knowledge

יג יד וְהַפֶּרֶס וְהָעׇזְנִיָּה: וְהָרָאָה וְאֶת־הָאַיָּה וְהַדַּיָּה לְמִינָהּ: וְאֵת
טו כׇּל־עֹרֵב לְמִינוֹ: וְאֵת בַּת הַיַּעֲנָה וְאֶת־הַתַּחְמָס וְאֶת־הַשָּׁחַף
טז וְאֶת־הַנֵּץ לְמִינֵהוּ: אֶת־הַכּוֹס וְאֶת־הַיַּנְשׁוּף וְהַתִּנְשָׁמֶת:
יז יח וְהַקָּאָת וְאֶת־הָרָחָמָה וְאֶת־הַשָּׁלָךְ: וְהַחֲסִידָה וְהָאֲנָפָה
יט לְמִינָהּ וְהַדּוּכִיפַת וְהָעֲטַלֵּף: וְכֹל שֶׁרֶץ הָעוֹף טָמֵא הוּא
כ כא לָכֶם לֹא יֵאָכֵלוּ: כׇּל־עוֹף טָהוֹר תֹּאכֵלוּ: לֹא־תֹאכְלוּ כׇל־
נְבֵלָה לַגֵּר אֲשֶׁר־בִּשְׁעָרֶיךָ תִּתְּנֶנָּה וַאֲכָלָהּ אוֹ מָכֹר לְנׇכְרִי
כִּי עַם קָדוֹשׁ אַתָּה לַיהֹוָה אֱלֹהֶיךָ לֹא־תְבַשֵּׁל גְּדִי בַּחֲלֵב
אִמּוֹ:

כב עַשֵּׂר תְּעַשֵּׂר אֵת כׇּל־תְּבוּאַת זַרְעֶךָ הַיֹּצֵא הַשָּׂדֶה שָׁנָה חמישי
כג שָׁנָה: וְאָכַלְתָּ לִפְנֵי ׀ יְהֹוָה אֱלֹהֶיךָ בַּמָּקוֹם אֲשֶׁר־יִבְחַר
לְשַׁכֵּן שְׁמוֹ שָׁם מַעְשַׂר דְּגָנְךָ תִּירֹשְׁךָ וְיִצְהָרֶךָ וּבְכֹרֹת בְּקָרְךָ
וְצֹאנֶךָ לְמַעַן תִּלְמַד לְיִרְאָה אֶת־יְהֹוָה אֱלֹהֶיךָ כׇּל־הַיָּמִים:

> and that they are instruments for his benefit? (*Guide for the Perplexed* III:14)

We now understand what is at stake in the prohibition of eating certain species of animals, birds, and fish, many of them predators like the creatures described in Job 38–41. They exist for their own sake, not for the sake of humankind. The vast universe, and earth itself with the myriad species it contains, has an integrity of its own. Yes, after the flood, God gave humans permission to eat meat, but this was a concession, as if to say: kill if you must, but let it be animals, not other humans, that you kill. The laws of *kashrut* limit our sense of possession over nature. We are placed in the world "to work it and safeguard it" (Gen. 2:15), but that does not give us license to take from it without exercising restraint.

14:21 בַּחֲלֵב אִמּוֹ *In the milk of its mother* – Religions are not philosophical systems. They are embodied truths, made real in the lives of communities. It is one thing to have an abstract conception of ecological responsibility, another to celebrate the Sabbath weekly – to renounce our mastery of nature one day in seven – and to make a blessing, as Jews do, over everything we eat or drink to remind ourselves of God's ownership of the world. Prayer, ritual, and narrative are ways we shape what Tocqueville called "habits of the heart." They form character, create behavioral dispositions, and educate us in patterns of self-restraint.

you may learn to hold the LORD your God in awe always.
24 But if the distance is too great for you to carry them,
because the place where the LORD your God chooses
to set His name is far from you and because the LORD
25 your God has blessed you, then you may exchange the
tithe for money. Wrap up the money in your hand, go
26 to the place that the LORD your God will choose, and
spend the money on whatever you choose: cattle, sheep,
wine, strong drink, or whatever else you like. There you
shall eat it in the presence of the LORD your God, and
27 rejoice together with your household. As for the Levites
living in your towns, do not neglect them, because they
28 have no share or inheritance as you do. At the
end of every third year, bring out the full tithe of your
29 produce for that year, and leave it within your towns, so
that the Levites, who have no share or inheritance as you
have, together with the migrants, orphans, and widows
in your towns, may come and eat and be satisfied, so
that the LORD your God will grant you blessing in all the
15 1 work of your hands. At the end of every seventh SHISHI
2 year, you shall grant a remission of debts. This is how the
remission is carried out: every creditor shall relinquish
any debt owed by his fellow. He shall not exact it from

---

would be a sense of shared citizenship, common belonging, and collective identity. The second tithe served to create social capital, bonds of trust and reciprocal altruism among the population, which came about through sharing food with strangers in the holy precincts of Jerusalem.

15:1 שְׁמִטָּה *A remission of debts* – The sequence here – the second and poor person's tithe, followed by the release of debts and slaves in the seventh year – are ways in which we serve God *bekhol meodekha* (Deut. 6:5), which some Sages understand to mean "with all your wealth" (Berakhot 9:5). We use our possessions to serve God when we ensure that those who have more than they need share their blessings with those who have less. In particular, we should ensure that no one in the nation God liberated from slavery is permanently enslaved, either by debt or poverty (the usual reason people sold themselves as slaves).

כד וְכִי־יִרְבֶּה מִמְּךָ הַדֶּרֶךְ כִּי לֹא תוּכַל שְׂאֵתוֹ כִּי־יִרְחַק מִמְּךָ
הַמָּקוֹם אֲשֶׁר יִבְחַר יְהוָה אֱלֹהֶיךָ לָשׂוּם שְׁמוֹ שָׁם כִּי יְבָרֶכְךָ
כה יְהוָה אֱלֹהֶיךָ׃ וְנָתַתָּה בַּכָּסֶף וְצַרְתָּ הַכֶּסֶף בְּיָדְךָ וְהָלַכְתָּ אֶל־
כו הַמָּקוֹם אֲשֶׁר יִבְחַר יְהוָה אֱלֹהֶיךָ בּוֹ׃ וְנָתַתָּה הַכֶּסֶף בְּכֹל
אֲשֶׁר־תְּאַוֶּה נַפְשְׁךָ בַּבָּקָר וּבַצֹּאן וּבַיַּיִן וּבַשֵּׁכָר וּבְכֹל אֲשֶׁר
תִּשְׁאָלְךָ נַפְשֶׁךָ וְאָכַלְתָּ שָּׁם לִפְנֵי יְהוָה אֱלֹהֶיךָ וְשָׂמַחְתָּ אַתָּה
כז וּבֵיתֶךָ׃ וְהַלֵּוִי אֲשֶׁר־בִּשְׁעָרֶיךָ לֹא תַעַזְבֶנּוּ כִּי אֵין לוֹ חֵלֶק
כח וְנַחֲלָה עִמָּךְ׃ מִקְצֵה ׀ שָׁלֹשׁ שָׁנִים תּוֹצִיא אֶת־
כט כָּל־מַעְשַׂר תְּבוּאָתְךָ בַּשָּׁנָה הַהִוא וְהִנַּחְתָּ בִּשְׁעָרֶיךָ׃ וּבָא
הַלֵּוִי כִּי אֵין־לוֹ חֵלֶק וְנַחֲלָה עִמָּךְ וְהַגֵּר וְהַיָּתוֹם וְהָאַלְמָנָה
אֲשֶׁר בִּשְׁעָרֶיךָ וְאָכְלוּ וְשָׂבֵעוּ לְמַעַן יְבָרֶכְךָ יְהוָה אֱלֹהֶיךָ
טו א בְּכָל־מַעֲשֵׂה יָדְךָ אֲשֶׁר תַּעֲשֶׂה׃ מִקֵּץ שֶׁבַע־ ששי
ב שָׁנִים תַּעֲשֶׂה שְׁמִטָּה׃ וְזֶה דְּבַר הַשְּׁמִטָּה שָׁמוֹט כָּל־בַּעַל

that not everything we can do, should we do.

14:23 לְמַעַן תִּלְמַד לְיִרְאָה אֶת־יְהוָה אֱלֹהֶיךָ כָּל־הַיָּמִים *You may learn to hold the Lord your God in awe always* – Unlike the other tithes, the "second tithe" described in this verse did not go to the poor, or to the priests and Levites. What then was its logic?

The Sages (Sifrei), focusing on the phrase "So that *you may learn* to hold the Lord your God in awe," said that it was to encourage people to study. Staying in Jerusalem while they consumed the tithe or the food bought with its monetary substitute, they would be influenced by the holy city, with its population engaged in divine service or sacred study.

Rambam gives a different explanation:

> The second tithe was commanded to be spent on food in Jerusalem; in this way the owner was compelled to give part of it away as charity. As he was not able to use it otherwise than by way of eating and drinking, he must have easily been induced to give it gradually away. This rule brought multitudes together in one place, and strengthened the bond of love and brotherhood among the children of men. (*Guide for the Perplexed* III:39)

For Rambam, the second tithe served a social purpose. It strengthened civil society, creating bonds of connectedness and friendship among the people. It encouraged visitors to share the blessings of the harvest with others. Strangers would meet and become friends. There

his brother, his fellow, because the LORD's remission
3 has been proclaimed. You may require payment from a
foreigner, but you must remit any debt owed to you by
4 a brother. There should be no poor among you, because
the LORD will bless you in the land that the LORD your
5 God is giving you to possess as your inheritance, if only
you obey the LORD your God, staying vigilant to keep all
6 the command with which I am charging you this day. For
the LORD your God will bless you as He has promised
you. You will lend to many nations, but will not borrow.
You will rule over many nations, and they will not rule
7 over you. If there be a poor person among your
kinsfolk in any of your towns in the land that the LORD
your God is giving you, do not harden your heart or close

What the Sabbath does for human beings and animals, the Sabbatical and Jubilee years do for the land. The earth too is entitled to its periodic rest. The Bible warns that if the Israelites do not respect this, they will suffer exile: "Then shall the land make appeasement for its Sabbaths (referring to Sabbatical years) for as long as it lies desolate and you are in your enemies' lands; then the land will rest and make appeasement for its Sabbaths" (Lev. 26:34). Behind this are two concerns. One is environmental. As Rambam points out (*Guide for the Perplexed* III:39), land which is overexploited is eventually eroded and loses its fertility. The Israelites were therefore commanded to conserve the soil by giving it periodic fallow years and not pursue short-term gain at the cost of long-term desolation. The second, no less significant, is theological: "The land," says God, "is Mine; you are merely migrants and visitors to Me" (Lev. 25:23). We are guests on earth. The same is true of material possessions; the Torah respects private property rights, but our claims over debtors are not absolute and must be relinquished if the poor are unable to pay by the seventh year.

LAWS OF TZEDAKA

The focus of the Torah from Exodus onward is the creation of a society in the land of Israel – the society that emerged from the days of Yehoshua to the close of the biblical era. Its economy was primarily agricultural. Therefore, the Torah sets out its program of distributive justice in terms of an agrarian order (see note on Deut. 12:11). But the Torah does not predicate its social vision on a single era or economic order. Alongside the specifics is a broad statement of timeless ideals, and this passage is to serve as the basis for extensive rabbinic legislation on tzedaka.

In postbiblical times, when Israel was no longer a nation in its own land,

מַשֵּׁה יָדוֹ אֲשֶׁר יַשֶּׁה בְּרֵעֵהוּ לֹא־יִגֹּשׂ אֶת־רֵעֵהוּ וְאֶת־אָחִיו
ג כִּי־קָרָא שְׁמִטָּה לַיהוָה׃ אֶת־הַנָּכְרִי תִּגֹּשׂ וַאֲשֶׁר יִהְיֶה
ד לְךָ אֶת־אָחִיךָ תַּשְׁמֵט יָדֶךָ׃ אֶפֶס כִּי לֹא יִהְיֶה־בְּךָ אֶבְיוֹן
כִּי־בָרֵךְ יְבָרֶכְךָ יהוה בָּאָרֶץ אֲשֶׁר יהוה אֱלֹהֶיךָ נֹתֵן־לְךָ
ה נַחֲלָה לְרִשְׁתָּהּ׃ רַק אִם־שָׁמוֹעַ תִּשְׁמַע בְּקוֹל יהוה אֱלֹהֶיךָ
לִשְׁמֹר לַעֲשׂוֹת אֶת־כָּל־הַמִּצְוָה הַזֹּאת אֲשֶׁר אָנֹכִי מְצַוְּךָ
ו הַיּוֹם׃ כִּי־יהוה אֱלֹהֶיךָ בֵּרַכְךָ כַּאֲשֶׁר דִּבֶּר־לָךְ וְהַעֲבַטְתָּ
גּוֹיִם רַבִּים וְאַתָּה לֹא תַעֲבֹט וּמָשַׁלְתָּ בְּגוֹיִם רַבִּים וּבְךָ
ז לֹא יִמְשֹׁלוּ׃ כִּי־יִהְיֶה בְךָ אֶבְיוֹן מֵאַחַד יג
אַחֶיךָ בְּאַחַד שְׁעָרֶיךָ בְּאַרְצְךָ אֲשֶׁר־יהוה אֱלֹהֶיךָ נֹתֵן
לָךְ לֹא תְאַמֵּץ אֶת־לְבָבְךָ וְלֹא תִקְפֹּץ אֶת־יָדְךָ מֵאָחִיךָ

History is full of ideal worlds, known as utopias. The word means "no place," because no utopias have ever happened. They never happen because they come without a realistic map of how to get from here to there. The Torah has a different approach to ideal worlds. We live them, periodically, in the here and now. The Sabbath is one example (see note on Deut. 5:14). Something similar is true of the *Shemitta*, the Sabbatical year, and *Yovel*, the Jubilee year. By cancelling debts, releasing slaves, leaving the produce of the land to be enjoyed by everyone equally, and restoring ancestral property to its original owners, we inhabit a world in which the inequities of the market economy have been redressed. For a year, sometimes two, we suspend the world of competition and live in a world of cooperation and the fellowship of equals.

15:4 בָּאָרֶץ אֲשֶׁר יהוה אֱלֹהֶיךָ נֹתֵן־לְךָ נַחֲלָה לְרִשְׁתָּהּ *The land that the Lord your God is giving you to possess* – Though we must exercise caution when reading twenty-first century concerns into ancient texts, there seems little doubt that much biblical legislation is concerned with what we would nowadays call "sustainability." This is particularly true of the three great commands ordaining periodic rest: the Sabbath, the Sabbatical year, and the Jubilee year. On the Sabbath all agricultural work is forbidden, "so that your ox and donkey may rest" (Ex. 23:12). It is a day that sets a limit to our intervention in nature and the pursuit of economic activity. We become conscious of being creations, not creators. The earth is not ours but God's. For six days it is handed over to us, but on the seventh day we symbolically abdicate that power. We may perform no "work," which is to say an act that alters the state of something for human purposes. The Sabbath is a weekly reminder of the integrity of nature and the boundaries of human striving.

8 your hand toward your brother in need. Open your hand
generously and freely lend him enough to answer all his
9 needs. Be vigilant: let your heart not whisper a depraved

---

know God is to act with justice and compassion, to recognize His image in other people, and to hear the silent cry of those in need.

15:8 דֵּי מַחְסֹרוֹ אֲשֶׁר יֶחְסַר לוֹ *To answer all his needs* – Judaism conceives poverty not only in material terms, that the poor lack the means of sustenance. It also sees it in psychological terms. Poverty humiliates. It robs people of dignity, makes them dependent on others, and deprives them of self-respect.

So tzedaka is addressed not only to people's physical needs but also to their psychological ones. The Rabbis (Ketubot 67b) based their approach on a finely nuanced understanding of this verse, which contains, in the Hebrew, a double phrasing. The first provision ("to answer all his needs") refers to an absolute subsistence level. In Jewish law this was taken to include food, housing, basic furniture, and, if necessary, funds to pay for a wedding. The second ("that which he lacks") means relative poverty – relative, however, not to others but to the individual's own previous standard of living.

Protecting dignity and avoiding humiliation was a systematic element of rabbinical law. So, for example, the Rabbis ruled that even the richest should be buried plainly so as not to shame the poor. The rabbis intervened to lower the prices of religious necessities so that no one would be excluded from communal celebrations. Work conditions had to be such that employees were treated with basic respect. Freedom presupposes self-respect, and a free society will therefore be one that robs no one of that basic human entitlement.

Rambam teaches that out of concern for recipients' dignity, Jewish law focuses not only on how much we must give but also on the manner in which we do so. Ideally, the donor should not know to whom he or she is giving, nor the recipient know from whom he or she is receiving. If a poor person does not want to accept tzedaka, we should practice a form of benign deception and give it to him under the guise of a loan (*Hilkhot Mattenot Aniyyim* 7:9).

Giving someone a job or making him your partner would not normally be considered charity at all. It costs you nothing. But this further serves to show that tzedaka does not mean charity. It means giving people the means to live a dignified life, and any form of employment is more dignified, within the Jewish value system, than dependence (see *Guide for the Perplexed* III:27).

Consider the law that "even a poor person who is dependent on tzedaka is obliged to give tzedaka" (*Hilkhot Mattenot Aniyyim* 7:5). The law seems absurd. Why give money to the poor so that they may give to the poor? It makes

ח הָאֶבְיוֹן: כִּי־פָתֹחַ תִּפְתַּח אֶת־יָדְךָ לוֹ וְהַעֲבֵט תַּעֲבִיטֶנּוּ דֵּי
ט מַחְסֹרוֹ אֲשֶׁר יֶחְסַר לוֹ: הִשָּׁמֶר לְךָ פֶּן־יִהְיֶה דָבָר עִם־לְבָבְךָ

and most of its people no longer worked on farms, tzedaka took on new forms. From earliest rabbinic times there were such institutions as the *tamḥui*, or mobile kitchen, which distributed food daily to whoever applied, and the *kuppa*, or community chest, which distributed money weekly to the poor of the city, together with specific funds for clothing, raising dowries for poor brides, and providing burial expenses for the poor. Thus the Torah established the first form of what came to be known as a welfare state – with one significant difference. It did not depend on a state. It was part of society, implemented not by power but by moral responsibility, not by governments but by individuals and local communities.

Tzedaka was to be constitutive of Jewish community life, the moral bond between people. It is foundational to the concept of covenantal society: society as an ethical enterprise is constructed on the basis of mutual responsibility.

Fundamental to the concept of tzedaka is, firstly, an absolute refusal on the part of the Sages to romanticize poverty. It is not, for them, a blessed state. It is an unmitigated evil. Many of the Sages were poor themselves. Hillel lacked the small sum needed to secure entrance to the house of study (Yoma 35b). Ḥanina b. Dosa is said to have survived on a *kav* of carobs from one week to the next (Berakhot 17b). They knew that poverty does not dignify, nor does it refine the soul. It deadens the sensibilities, turns a person in on himself, crushes the spirit, and humiliates the soul. "If there is no meal," said the Sages, "there can be no Torah" (Avot 3:17). On this the Rabbis would have agreed with Marx, that statements in praise of poverty are indefensible defenses of the status quo by those with privilege and power.

The whole tenor of the Torah is based on the idea that God is to be found in the physical world and its blessings. We are commanded to serve God in joy out of the abundance of good things, not through self-denial. Asceticism – always a temptation in the religious life – was never embraced by the Jewish mainstream. On the contrary, it was an implicit disavowal of this world which God created and pronounced good. Having regard for the poor did not mean in Judaism embracing poverty oneself. No poor person was ever helped by knowing that a saint had joined his ranks. He was helped by being given the chance not to be poor.

With its combination of charity and justice, tzedaka is a unique institution. It is deeply humanitarian, but it could not exist without the essentially religious concepts of divine ownership and social covenant. The prophet Yirmeyahu says of King Yoshiyahu, "'He took up the cause of the poor and the destitute with good results. That is the way to know Me,' declares the Lord" (Jer. 22:16). To

thought: 'The seventh year, the year of remission, is close,'
making you miserly toward your brother in need, giving
him nothing. He will cry out to the LORD about you, and
10 you will be held guilty. Give to him generously, and do
not let your heart begrudge it, for by merit of this the
LORD your God will grant you blessing in all your work
11 and all your hands' endeavors. There will never cease to
be poor people in the land. And so I command you: open
your hand generously to your kinsmen, your poor and
12 needy, who share your land. If a fellow Hebrew,
man or woman, is sold to you, he or she shall work for you
for six years; in the seventh year you shall send him or her
13 forth free. And when you send one forth free, do not send
14 him empty-handed. Provide for him liberally from your
flock, your threshing floor, and your winepress, giving
him a share in the things with which the LORD your God
15 has blessed you. Remember: you were a slave in Egypt
and the LORD your God redeemed you; and so I give you
16 this command today. But if he says to you, 'I do not want
to leave you' – because he loves you and your household
17 and he fares well with you, then take an awl and put it
through his ear into the door, and he will be your slave
18 for all time; you shall do the same with a female slave. Do

---

abrogated an established right of the less well-off. And Hillel was himself a man whose poverty was legendary.

With the transition from an agricultural to a more commercial economy, loans had become less a response to a disastrous harvest than a normal precondition of trading. A moral appeal to cancel debts was accordingly less likely to succeed and less plausible. The biblical law, whose original intent was explicitly to benefit the poor, was now working to their disfavor: they could not obtain loans in certain years. Clearly, forfeiting the redistribution in their favor would be more than compensated by the assistance they would receive in building up their own trade. Here was an instance, drawn from the Second Temple period, of redistribution of wealth yielding to economic growth – on the moral grounds agreed to be strong enough to justify inverting a biblical procedure. Hillel adapted the law dramatically to new circumstances and changing economic systems, still managing to preserve its original intent.

בְלִיַּעַל לֵאמֹר קָרְבָה שְׁנַת־הַשֶּׁבַע שְׁנַת הַשְּׁמִטָּה וְרָעָה
עֵינְךָ בְּאָחִיךָ הָאֶבְיוֹן וְלֹא תִתֵּן לוֹ וְקָרָא עָלֶיךָ אֶל־יהוה
י וְהָיָה בְךָ חֵטְא: נָתוֹן תִּתֵּן לוֹ וְלֹא־יֵרַע לְבָבְךָ בְּתִתְּךָ לוֹ
כִּי בִּגְלַל ׀ הַדָּבָר הַזֶּה יְבָרֶכְךָ יהוה אֱלֹהֶיךָ בְּכׇל־מַעֲשֶׂךָ
יא וּבְכֹל מִשְׁלַח יָדֶךָ: כִּי לֹא־יֶחְדַּל אֶבְיוֹן מִקֶּרֶב הָאָרֶץ עַל־
כֵּן אָנֹכִי מְצַוְּךָ לֵאמֹר פָּתֹחַ תִּפְתַּח אֶת־יָדְךָ לְאָחִיךָ לַעֲנִיֶּךָ
יב וּלְאֶבְיֹנְךָ בְּאַרְצֶךָ: כִּי־יִמָּכֵר לְךָ אָחִיךָ הָעִבְרִי
אוֹ הָעִבְרִיָּה וַעֲבָדְךָ שֵׁשׁ שָׁנִים וּבַשָּׁנָה הַשְּׁבִיעִת תְּשַׁלְּחֶנּוּ
יג חׇפְשִׁי מֵעִמָּךְ: וְכִי־תְשַׁלְּחֶנּוּ חׇפְשִׁי מֵעִמָּךְ לֹא תְשַׁלְּחֶנּוּ
יד רֵיקָם: הַעֲנֵיק תַּעֲנִיק לוֹ מִצֹּאנְךָ וּמִגׇּרְנְךָ וּמִיִּקְבֶךָ אֲשֶׁר
טו בֵּרַכְךָ יהוה אֱלֹהֶיךָ תִּתֶּן־לוֹ: וְזָכַרְתָּ כִּי עֶבֶד הָיִיתָ בְּאֶרֶץ
מִצְרַיִם וַיִּפְדְּךָ יהוה אֱלֹהֶיךָ עַל־כֵּן אָנֹכִי מְצַוְּךָ אֶת־הַדָּבָר
טז הַזֶּה הַיּוֹם: וְהָיָה כִּי־יֹאמַר אֵלֶיךָ לֹא אֵצֵא מֵעִמָּךְ כִּי אֲהֵבְךָ
יז וְאֶת־בֵּיתֶךָ כִּי־טוֹב לוֹ עִמָּךְ: וְלָקַחְתָּ אֶת־הַמַּרְצֵעַ וְנָתַתָּה
בְאׇזְנוֹ וּבַדֶּלֶת וְהָיָה לְךָ עֶבֶד עוֹלָם וְאַף לַאֲמָתְךָ תַּעֲשֶׂה־
יח כֵּן: לֹא־יִקְשֶׁה בְעֵינֶךָ בְּשַׁלֵּחֲךָ אֹתוֹ חׇפְשִׁי מֵעִמָּךְ כִּי מִשְׁנֶה

---

sense only on the assumption that giving is essential to human dignity and tzedaka is the obligation to ensure that everyone has that dignity.

15:9 וְהָיָה בְךָ חֵטְא *You will be held guilty* – There is a danger that the wealthy simply will not give loans prior to the seventh year; hence the invocation here of divine concern – always an accompaniment of a law which is difficult for humans to enforce. What happened to this law in a more complex economy? The Mishna records one of the most daring of all rabbinic innovations: "When he saw that the people refrained from giving loans to one another and thus transgressed the biblical warning... Hillel enacted the *pruzbul*" (Gittin 36a). The *pruzbul* was a technical device whereby a loan was transacted through the court, ceased to be an agreement between individuals, and so bypassed the terms of the year of release. Creditors no longer had to relinquish their claims in the seventh year. Hillel – perhaps the founding father of rabbinic Judaism – had set aside the law.

How he had the authority to do so is a technical question which need not concern us. But why he should wish to do so is another matter. In effect, he had

not consider it a hardship when you set him free, because
for six years he has given you twice the service of a hired
laborer; and the LORD your God will bless you in all your
work.
19 Every firstborn male among your herd and flock you shall SHEVI'I
consecrate to the LORD your God. Do not work your
20 firstborn ox or shear your firstborn sheep. You and your
household shall eat them year by year in the presence
of the LORD your God in the place that the LORD will
21 choose. If the animal has a blemish, a serious blemish such
as lameness or blindness, you shall not sacrifice it to the
22 LORD your God. The impure as well as the pure among
you shall eat it within your towns, as you would a gazelle
23 or a deer. Its blood, however, you must not eat. You must
pour it out onto the ground like water.
16 1 Observe the month of Aviv by offering a Passover sacrifice
to the LORD your God; for in the month of Aviv the LORD
2 your God brought you out of Egypt by night. You shall

---

sanctuary, or shrine. That is why, when it comes to the festivals, Moshe speaks only of Passover, Shavuot, and Sukkot, the three on which there is a duty of *aliya lar-egel*, pilgrimage to the Temple.

Moshe's presentation here has a strong emphasis on the seasons of the agricultural year: Passover is the festival of spring, the countdown to Shavuot begins "at the time when you first put sickle to standing grain" (Deut. 16:9), and Sukkot is celebrated at the time when "you have gathered the produce from your threshing floor and winepress" (16:13). These are dimensions of the festivals the people have not yet experienced as desert nomads, but they will once they enter and make their home in the land which God has blessed.

Equally significant is Deuteronomy's focus – not found elsewhere – on social inclusion: "You and your sons and daughters, your male and female slaves, and the Levites living in your towns, together with the migrants, orphans, and widows among you" (16:11). Deuteronomy is less about individual spirituality than about the kind of society that honors the presence of God by honoring our fellow humans, especially those at the margins of society. The idea that we can serve God while being indifferent to, or dismissive of, our fellow human beings is utterly alien to the vision of Deuteronomy. The festivals are times when people are to invite those at the margins of society. No one is to be left out.

שְׂכַר שָׂכִיר עֲבָדְךָ שֵׁשׁ שָׁנִים וּבֵרַכְךָ יְהוָה אֱלֹהֶיךָ בְּכֹל
אֲשֶׁר תַּעֲשֶׂה׃
יט כָּל־הַבְּכוֹר אֲשֶׁר יִוָּלֵד בִּבְקָרְךָ וּבְצֹאנְךָ הַזָּכָר תַּקְדִּישׁ לַיהוָה שביעי
כ אֱלֹהֶיךָ לֹא תַעֲבֹד בִּבְכֹר שׁוֹרֶךָ וְלֹא תָגֹז בְּכוֹר צֹאנֶךָ׃ לִפְנֵי
יְהוָה אֱלֹהֶיךָ תֹאכְלֶנּוּ שָׁנָה בְשָׁנָה בַּמָּקוֹם אֲשֶׁר־יִבְחַר
כא יְהוָה אַתָּה וּבֵיתֶךָ׃ וְכִי־יִהְיֶה בוֹ מוּם פִּסֵּחַ אוֹ עִוֵּר כֹּל מוּם
כב רָע לֹא תִזְבָּחֶנּוּ לַיהוָה אֱלֹהֶיךָ׃ בִּשְׁעָרֶיךָ תֹּאכְלֶנּוּ הַטָּמֵא
כג וְהַטָּהוֹר יַחְדָּו כַּצְּבִי וְכָאַיָּל׃ רַק אֶת־דָּמוֹ לֹא תֹאכֵל עַל־
הָאָרֶץ תִּשְׁפְּכֶנּוּ כַּמָּיִם׃
טז א שָׁמוֹר אֶת־חֹדֶשׁ הָאָבִיב וְעָשִׂיתָ פֶּסַח לַיהוָה אֱלֹהֶיךָ כִּי
בְּחֹדֶשׁ הָאָבִיב הוֹצִיאֲךָ יְהוָה אֱלֹהֶיךָ מִמִּצְרַיִם לָיְלָה׃
ב וְזָבַחְתָּ פֶּסַח לַיהוָה אֱלֹהֶיךָ צֹאן וּבָקָר בַּמָּקוֹם אֲשֶׁר יִבְחַר

THE THREE PILGRIMAGE FESTIVALS

There are five passages in the Torah dedicated to the festivals of the Jewish year. Two, both in the book of Exodus (23:14–17 and 34:18, 22–23), are very brief. They refer only to the three pilgrimage festivals, Passover, Shavuot, and Sukkot. They do not specify their dates, merely their rough position in the agricultural year. Nor do they mention the specific commands related to the festivals.

This leaves three other festival accounts, one in Leviticus 23, a second one in Numbers 28–29, and the third here. The three are very different. This is not, as critics maintain, because the Torah is a composite document, but rather because it comes at its subject matter from multiple perspectives – a characteristic of the Torah mindset as a whole.

The long section on the festivals in Numbers is wholly dedicated to the special additional sacrifices (the *musaf*) brought on holy days including the Sabbath and Rosh Ḥodesh. A memory of this is preserved in the Musaf prayers for these days. These are holy times from the perspective of the Tabernacle, the Temple, and later, the synagogue.

The account in Deuteronomy is about society. Moshe at the end of his life tells the next generation where they came from, where they are going to, and the kind of society they are to construct. It is to be the opposite of Egypt. It must strive for justice, freedom, and human dignity.

One of Deuteronomy's most important themes is its insistence that worship be centralized "in the place that the Lord will choose" (Deut. 12:14). The unity of God is to be mirrored in the unity of the nation, something that could not be achieved if every tribe had its own temple,

offer up the Passover sacrifice to the LORD your God,
from the flock and the herd, at the place that the LORD
3 will choose as a dwelling for His name. You must not eat
anything leavened with it. For seven days, eat unleavened
bread – the bread of affliction – because you left Egypt
in haste. This is for you to remember the day you left
4 Egypt all the days of your life. For seven days no leaven
shall be found with you in all your land. And do not let
any of the meat that you sacrificed on the evening of the
5 first day remain until morning. You may not slaughter the
Passover sacrifice in any of the towns that the LORD your
6 God is giving you. Only at the place that the LORD your
God chooses as a dwelling for His name, there shall you
slaughter the Passover sacrifice in the evening; at sunset,
7 at the time appointed to leave Egypt, you shall cook and
eat it at the place that the LORD your God will choose,
and on the following morning you may set out to your
8 tents. For six days you shall eat unleavened bread and,
on the seventh day, you shall hold an assembly for the
9 LORD your God and perform no work. You shall
count seven weeks. At the time when you first put sickle
10 to standing grain, begin your count of seven weeks. And
then celebrate the Festival of Weeks to the LORD your
God, bringing a freewill offering, tribute proportionate
to the blessing the LORD your God has granted you.
11 And rejoice before the LORD your God – you and your
sons and daughters, your male and female slaves, and the
Levites living in your towns, together with the migrants,
orphans, and widows among you – at the place that the
LORD your God will choose as a dwelling for His name.
12 Remember that you were a slave in Egypt, and so take
care to fulfill these decrees.

13 You shall keep the Festival of Tabernacles for seven days, MAFTIR
after you have gathered the produce from your threshing
14 floor and winepress. Rejoice in your festival, you and
your sons and daughters; your male and female servants;
the Levites; and the migrants, orphans, and widows living

ג יְהוָה לְשַׁכֵּן שְׁמוֹ שָׁם׃ לֹא־תֹאכַל עָלָיו חָמֵץ שִׁבְעַת יָמִים
תֹּאכַל־עָלָיו מַצּוֹת לֶחֶם עֹנִי כִּי בְחִפָּזוֹן יָצָאתָ מֵאֶרֶץ מִצְרַיִם
לְמַעַן תִּזְכֹּר אֶת־יוֹם צֵאתְךָ מֵאֶרֶץ מִצְרַיִם כֹּל יְמֵי חַיֶּיךָ׃
ד וְלֹא־יֵרָאֶה לְךָ שְׂאֹר בְּכָל־גְּבֻלְךָ שִׁבְעַת יָמִים וְלֹא־יָלִין
ה מִן־הַבָּשָׂר אֲשֶׁר תִּזְבַּח בָּעֶרֶב בַּיּוֹם הָרִאשׁוֹן לַבֹּקֶר׃ לֹא
תוּכַל לִזְבֹּחַ אֶת־הַפָּסַח בְּאַחַד שְׁעָרֶיךָ אֲשֶׁר־יְהוָה אֱלֹהֶיךָ
ו נֹתֵן לָךְ׃ כִּי אִם־אֶל־הַמָּקוֹם אֲשֶׁר־יִבְחַר יְהוָה אֱלֹהֶיךָ
לְשַׁכֵּן שְׁמוֹ שָׁם תִּזְבַּח אֶת־הַפֶּסַח בָּעָרֶב כְּבוֹא הַשֶּׁמֶשׁ
ז מוֹעֵד צֵאתְךָ מִמִּצְרָיִם׃ וּבִשַּׁלְתָּ וְאָכַלְתָּ בַּמָּקוֹם אֲשֶׁר יִבְחַר
ח יְהוָה אֱלֹהֶיךָ בּוֹ וּפָנִיתָ בַבֹּקֶר וְהָלַכְתָּ לְאֹהָלֶיךָ׃ שֵׁשֶׁת
יָמִים תֹּאכַל מַצּוֹת וּבַיּוֹם הַשְּׁבִיעִי עֲצֶרֶת לַיהוָה אֱלֹהֶיךָ
ט לֹא תַעֲשֶׂה מְלָאכָה׃ שִׁבְעָה שָׁבֻעֹת תִּסְפָּר־לָךְ
י מֵהָחֵל חֶרְמֵשׁ בַּקָּמָה תָּחֵל לִסְפֹּר שִׁבְעָה שָׁבֻעוֹת׃ וְעָשִׂיתָ
חַג שָׁבֻעוֹת לַיהוָה אֱלֹהֶיךָ מִסַּת נִדְבַת יָדְךָ אֲשֶׁר תִּתֵּן
יא כַּאֲשֶׁר יְבָרֶכְךָ יְהוָה אֱלֹהֶיךָ׃ וְשָׂמַחְתָּ לִפְנֵי ׀ יְהוָה אֱלֹהֶיךָ
אַתָּה וּבִנְךָ וּבִתֶּךָ וְעַבְדְּךָ וַאֲמָתֶךָ וְהַלֵּוִי אֲשֶׁר בִּשְׁעָרֶיךָ וְהַגֵּר
וְהַיָּתוֹם וְהָאַלְמָנָה אֲשֶׁר בְּקִרְבֶּךָ בַּמָּקוֹם אֲשֶׁר יִבְחַר יְהוָה
יב אֱלֹהֶיךָ לְשַׁכֵּן שְׁמוֹ שָׁם׃ וְזָכַרְתָּ כִּי־עֶבֶד הָיִיתָ בְּמִצְרָיִם
וְשָׁמַרְתָּ וְעָשִׂיתָ אֶת־הַחֻקִּים הָאֵלֶּה׃
יג חַג הַסֻּכֹּת תַּעֲשֶׂה לְךָ שִׁבְעַת יָמִים בְּאָסְפְּךָ מִגָּרְנְךָ וּמִיִּקְבֶךָ׃ מפטיר
יד וְשָׂמַחְתָּ בְּחַגֶּךָ אַתָּה וּבִנְךָ וּבִתֶּךָ וְעַבְדְּךָ וַאֲמָתֶךָ וְהַלֵּוִי וְהַגֵּר

15 in your towns. For seven days, celebrate before the LORD
your God at the place that the LORD will choose, for the
LORD your God will grant you blessing in all your harvest
and in all the work of your hands, and you shall be wholly
16 joyful. Three times a year, all the males among you shall
appear before the LORD your God in the place that He
will choose: on the Festival of Unleavened Bread, the
Festival of Weeks, and the Festival of Tabernacles. They
17 shall not appear before the LORD empty-handed; each
shall bring a gift, in keeping with the blessing that the
LORD your God has given you.

The haftara for Parashat Re'eh is on page 1606.
This haftara is read even on Erev Rosh Ḥodesh Elul.
On Rosh Ḥodesh Elul, Ashkenazim read the haftara on page 1640, while Sephardim read this haftara.

seven days in a hut with only leaves for a roof, exposed to the wind, cold, and rain, is the festival of insecurity. Nonetheless, it is, supremely, the "time of our joy."

There is something profoundly spiritual about our capacity to live in a state of total insecurity and yet feel the joy of simply being, under the shelter of the Divine Presence. Yes, there is danger, risk, uncertainty, vulnerability. But we are here, with a world to live in, family and friends to love and be loved by, and we are not alone, for with us is the Torah, God's unbreakable word, and though we walk through the valley of the shadow, we walk toward the redemptive light.

טו וְהַיָּת֥וֹם וְהָאַלְמָנָ֖ה אֲשֶׁ֥ר בִּשְׁעָרֶֽיךָ׃ שִׁבְעַ֣ת יָמִ֗ים תָּחֹג֙ לַיהוָ֣ה
אֱלֹהֶ֔יךָ בַּמָּק֖וֹם אֲשֶׁר־יִבְחַ֣ר יְהוָ֑ה כִּ֣י יְבָרֶכְךָ֞ יְהוָ֣ה אֱלֹהֶ֗יךָ
טז בְּכֹ֤ל תְּבוּאָֽתְךָ֙ וּבְכֹל֙ מַעֲשֵׂ֣ה יָדֶ֔יךָ וְהָיִ֖יתָ אַ֥ךְ שָׂמֵֽחַ׃ שָׁל֣וֹשׁ
פְּעָמִ֣ים ׀ בַּשָּׁנָ֡ה יֵרָאֶ֨ה כָל־זְכוּרְךָ֜ אֶת־פְּנֵ֣י ׀ יְהוָ֣ה אֱלֹהֶ֗יךָ
בַּמָּקוֹם֙ אֲשֶׁ֣ר יִבְחָ֔ר בְּחַ֧ג הַמַּצּ֛וֹת וּבְחַ֥ג הַשָּׁבֻע֖וֹת וּבְחַ֣ג
יז הַסֻּכּ֑וֹת וְלֹ֧א יֵרָאֶ֛ה אֶת־פְּנֵ֥י יְהוָ֖ה רֵיקָֽם׃ אִ֖ישׁ כְּמַתְּנַ֣ת יָד֑וֹ
כְּבִרְכַּ֛ת יְהוָ֥ה אֱלֹהֶ֖יךָ אֲשֶׁ֥ר נָתַן־לָֽךְ׃

The הפטרה *for* פרשת ראה *is on page 1607.*
This הפטרה *is read even on* ערב ראש חודש אלול.
On ראש חודש אלול, אשכנזים *read the* הפטרה *on page 1641,*
while ספרדים *read this* הפטרה.

16:15 וְהָיִיתָ אַךְ שָׂמֵחַ *You shall be wholly joyful* – The verb "to rejoice" appears three times in the *parasha* in connection with a festival: not at all in connection with Passover, once in relation to Shavuot, but twice in connection with Sukkot: "Rejoice in your festival … and you shall be wholly joyful" (Deut. 16:14–15). It is for this reason that Sukkot (and Shemini Atzeret) are called *zeman simḥatenu*, "the time of our joy."

This is counterintuitive. We could understand why Passover should be a festival of joy: it recalls our ancestors' liberation from slavery. Shavuot celebrates the giving of the Torah, God's great gift to us as a people. But why Sukkot?

It represents not a positive event, but forty years of wandering in the wilderness without a permanent home. A sukka is, by halakhic definition, a temporary dwelling. Sukkot, when we live for

Parashat Shofetim

16 18 Appoint judges and officials for your tribes in all the
towns that the Lord your God is giving you, to govern
19 the people with equitable justice. Do not pervert justice
or show partiality. Do not take bribes, for bribes blind the
20 eyes of the wise and subvert the cause of the just. Pursue
justice, only justice, so that you may live and possess the
21 land that the Lord your God is giving you. Do

---

expresses a principle of collective responsibility. The inhabitants of Shekhem, knowing that their prince had committed a crime and failing to bring him to court, were collectively guilty of injustice. We are responsible not only for our own conduct but for those around us, amongst whom we live. Or perhaps this flows not from the concept of society but simply from the nature of moral obligation. If X is wrong, then not only must I not do it. I must, if I can, stop others from doing it, and if I fail to do so, then I share in the guilt. We would call this nowadays the guilt of the bystander. Clearly, however, the issue is a complex one that needs nuance. There is a difference between a perpetrator and a bystander. It is one thing to commit a crime, another to witness someone committing a crime and fail to prevent it.

Ramban's position, and Yaakov's in Genesis, was that Shimon and Levi may have been right in thinking that the men of Shekhem were guilty of doing nothing when their prince abducted and assaulted Dina, but that does not mean that they were entitled to execute summary justice by killing all the males. Bystander guilt, though real, cannot be reduced to legal categories; this subject will be addressed at the end of the *parasha* (Deut. 21:1–9; see notes there). On the other hand, the responsibility of society to set up an effective and equitable justice system is so fundamental an ethical principle that it is incumbent not only on Israel, but on all the descendants of Noaḥ.

"PURSUE JUSTICE"

For Jews, and not only Jews, the religious voice is above all a moral voice. Avraham is chosen so that he will instruct his children "to do righteousness and justice." Yeshayahu begins his prophetic mission with the most powerful speech ever made against the idea that you can serve God in the house of prayer while ignoring Him in the marketplace. Mikha sums up the religious quest in three imperatives: "To do justice, love goodness, and walk modestly with your God" (Mic. 6:8). And here in the text of the covenant, Moshe tells the Israelites, "Pursue justice, only justice."

No idea in the Hebrew Bible has

פרשת שפטים

טז יח שֹׁפְטִים וְשֹׁטְרִים תִּתֶּן־לְךָ בְּכָל־שְׁעָרֶיךָ אֲשֶׁר יְהוָה אֱלֹהֶיךָ יד
יט נֹתֵן לְךָ לִשְׁבָטֶיךָ וְשָׁפְטוּ אֶת־הָעָם מִשְׁפַּט־צֶדֶק: לֹא־
תַטֶּה מִשְׁפָּט לֹא תַכִּיר פָּנִים וְלֹא־תִקַּח שֹׁחַד כִּי הַשֹּׁחַד
כ יְעַוֵּר עֵינֵי חֲכָמִים וִיסַלֵּף דִּבְרֵי צַדִּיקִם: צֶדֶק צֶדֶק תִּרְדֹּף
לְמַעַן תִּחְיֶה וְיָרַשְׁתָּ אֶת־הָאָרֶץ אֲשֶׁר־יְהוָה אֱלֹהֶיךָ נֹתֵן
כא לָךְ: לֹא־תִטַּע לְךָ אֲשֵׁרָה כָּל־עֵץ אֵצֶל מִזְבַּח

SHOFETIM

Having dealt with many of the aspects of worship in the Promised Land, Moshe now turns to the institutions of governance. He begins with the overarching imperative of justice: there must be courts, judges, and officers in every city. Justice must be accessible and impartial. Procedures must be followed for the prosecution of idolatry, and there is to be a supreme court to deal with hard cases.

There are to be three main types of leaders: a king, priests and Levites, and prophets. Warnings are issued against sorcery and witchcraft, and against false prophets. Cities of refuge are to be provided as sanctuaries for those who kill accidentally or unintentionally. Conspiring witnesses who testify falsely are to be punished.

Moshe then turns to the laws of warfare. The *parasha*, which has covered several aspects of the criminal law process, concludes with the atonement procedure to be followed in the case of an unsolved murder.

16:18 שֹׁפְטִים... תִּתֶּן־לְךָ *Appoint judges* – In his law code, the Mishneh Torah, Rambam explains that the establishment of justice and the rule of law is one of the seven Laws of Noaḥ, binding on all humanity:

> And how are the Gentiles commanded to establish law courts? They are required to establish judges and officers in every area of habitation to rule in accordance with the enforcement of the other six commands, to warn the citizenry concerning these laws and to punish any transgressor with death by the sword. And it is on this basis that all the people of Shekhem were liable to execution [at the hands of Shimon and Levi, sons of Yaakov]: because Shekhem [their prince] stole [and raped] Dina, which they saw and knew about, but did not bring him to justice. (*Hilkhot Melakhim UMilḥemoteihem* 9:14)

According to Rambam, the universal requirement to establish courts

not plant a sacred tree of any kind beside the altar that you
22 make for the LORD your God, and do not erect a worship
pillar, for these are things that the LORD your God
17 1 hates. Do not sacrifice an ox or a sheep that has
any blemish, any serious defect, to the LORD your God, for
2 that to the LORD your God would be abhorrent. If
a man or woman living among you in one of the towns the
LORD your God is giving you is found doing what is evil
3 in the LORD your God's eyes, breaking His covenant by
going off to serve or bow to other gods – the sun or moon
4 or any of the heavenly host, which I have forbidden – if you

---

and the justice it asks us to fight for is human justice.

Underlying all this is a proposition which even today has not lost its power to surprise and inspire. In the beginning God created the world as a home for humanity. Since then He has challenged humanity to create a world that will be a home for Him. God lives wherever we treat one another as beings in His image.

17:3 וַיֵּלֶךְ וַיַּעֲבֹד *By going off to serve* – "Evil" in the Torah is often framed not as an act of striking out alone, but as a form of obedience to the wrong gods, an irresistible temptation likely to foster a similar temptation in others. God's call, in contrast, is almost inaudible. But it is there, and if, from time to time throughout our lives, we create a silence in the soul, we will hear it.

Sin is rarely original, but a good deed sometimes is. Just as every life has a task, so every day brings an opportunity. If we are where we are because God wanted us to be, then there must be, in every situation, something He wants us to do, some act of redemption He wants us to perform. I found the best way of knowing what it is, is to turn the situation upside down. I used to hope that people would praise my work; then I realized that what I was here to do was to praise the work of others. There were times when, in crisis, I would await the reassuring word from a friend, until I suddenly saw that I should be the one giving reassurance. The discovery changed my life. That was when I knew that we experience pain to sensitize us to the pain of others. Turning our emotions outward, we can use them as the key to free someone else from the locked room of suffering or disappointment or grief.

God commands in generalities but calls in particulars. He knows our gifts and he knows the needs of the world. That is why we are here. There is an act only we can do, and only at this time, and that is our task. To miss God's quiet call amid the clamour of other temptations would be to overlook the meaning of our life, the purpose of our existence.

כב יְהוָה אֱלֹהֶיךָ אֲשֶׁר תַּעֲשֶׂה־לָּךְ׃ וְלֹא־תָקִים לְךָ מַצֵּבָה אֲשֶׁר
יז א שָׂנֵא יְהוָה אֱלֹהֶיךָ׃ לֹא־תִזְבַּח לַיהוָה
אֱלֹהֶיךָ שׁוֹר וָשֶׂה אֲשֶׁר יִהְיֶה בוֹ מוּם כֹּל דָּבָר רָע כִּי תוֹעֲבַת
ב יְהוָה אֱלֹהֶיךָ הוּא׃ כִּי־יִמָּצֵא בְקִרְבְּךָ בְּאַחַד
שְׁעָרֶיךָ אֲשֶׁר־יְהוָה אֱלֹהֶיךָ נֹתֵן לָךְ אִישׁ אוֹ־אִשָּׁה אֲשֶׁר
ג יַעֲשֶׂה אֶת־הָרַע בְּעֵינֵי יְהוָה־אֱלֹהֶיךָ לַעֲבֹר בְּרִיתוֹ׃ וַיֵּלֶךְ
וַיַּעֲבֹד אֱלֹהִים אֲחֵרִים וַיִּשְׁתַּחוּ לָהֶם וְלַשֶּׁמֶשׁ ׀ אוֹ לַיָּרֵחַ
ד אוֹ לְכָל־צְבָא הַשָּׁמַיִם אֲשֶׁר לֹא־צִוִּיתִי׃ וְהֻגַּד־לְךָ וְשָׁמַעְתָּ

been more influential than this, that society is founded on a moral covenant between its members, vested in an authority that transcends all earthly powers, and whose most famous symbol is the Ten Commandments engraved in stone. Law as envisaged by the Torah makes no distinction between rich and poor, powerful and powerless, home-born or stranger. Equality before the law is the translation into human terms of equality before God. Time and again the Torah insists that justice is not a human artifact: "Do not be intimidated by any man, for judgment belongs to God" (Deut. 1:17). Because it belongs to God, it must never be compromised – by intimidation, bribery, or favoritism. It is an inalienable right and also an inescapable duty – something that must be pursued actively.

One might suppose that the divinity of justice reduces our accountability for justice on earth. God exists, therefore the universe is just. We, however, are human, and God has empowered us to seek the justice that is human – not justice from the point of view of the universe and eternity but from the point of view of the fallible, frail, ephemeral, vulnerable beings that we are. We who live in space and time cannot but see injustice. We cannot know the rewards of a life beyond the grave. Our pain is not made less by the belief that it is necessary for the good of the whole. Still less is it made bearable that it is justified as punishment for sin. That – as Iyov's comforters belatedly discovered – is not a form of comfort but a double affliction. In the book of Job (42:7), the comforters who defend the justice of God are condemned by God Himself, because He asks of us *not* to take His part but to be human, defending one another, as Avraham defended Sedom, in the name of human solidarity.

God, in making humanity, conferred on us the right and duty to see things from a human point of view. If evil exists within our horizons, then it is real no matter how limited those horizons are. Making us human, not divine, God calls on us to judge and act within the terms of our humanity. "The Torah was not given to ministering angels," said the Sages (Berakhot 25b). It was given to human beings,

have been told of this or have heard about it, then you must
make thorough inquiry. If it is true and is confirmed that
5 this abhorrent deed has been done in Israel, then you shall
take the man or woman who has done this evil act out to
the town gates and stone that man or that woman to death.
6 The accused shall be put to death only on the testimony of
two or three witnesses; no one shall be put to death on the
7 evidence of one witness alone. The hand of the witnesses
shall be the first against him to kill him, and after theirs, the
hand of all the people. You must purge the evil from your
midst.
8 If a case is beyond your judgment, be it a conflict over
bloodshed, over civil claims or over injury – any dispute
in your town courts – then you shall go up to the place
9 that the LORD your God will choose. There you shall
approach the Levitical priests or the judge who is in
office at that time. Inquire of them and they will give you
10 the verdict. You must act in accordance with the ruling
they give you from the place that the LORD will choose,
11 taking care to do exactly as they instruct you. You shall
act in accord with the Law as they interpret it for you and

---

this second sense is, as it were, passing a sentence, outside a court of law, on what we or other people have done. It is backward-looking, after the event. We are reluctant, today, to be judgmental in this second sense. But so we were always taught to be. "Do not judge your fellow human being until you have been in his place," said the Rabbis (Avot 2:4).

There is a difference between righteousness and self-righteousness. The righteous are humble; the self-righteous are proud. The righteous understand doubt, the self-righteous only certainty. The righteous see the good in people, the self-righteous only the bad. The righteous leave you feeling enlarged; the self-righteous make you feel small.

King Shlomo, acceding to the throne, is said by the Bible to have been granted one wish. He asked not for wealth or long life or the defeat of his enemies but simply this: "Grant Your servant an understanding heart to judge Your people, to distinguish between good and evil" (I Kings 3:9). In the siddur, "knowledge, understanding, and discernment" are the things we pray for before all else. This is the "good judgment" we seek in our teachers and leaders, and even in our individualistic age it would be a mistake to dismiss it.

וְדָרַשְׁתָּ הֵיטֵב וְהִנֵּה אֱמֶת נָכוֹן הַדָּבָר נֶעֶשְׂתָה הַתּוֹעֵבָה
ה הַזֹּאת בְּיִשְׂרָאֵל׃ וְהוֹצֵאתָ אֶת־הָאִישׁ הַהוּא אוֹ אֶת־הָאִשָּׁה
הַהִוא אֲשֶׁר עָשׂוּ אֶת־הַדָּבָר הָרָע הַזֶּה אֶל־שְׁעָרֶיךָ אֶת־
ו הָאִישׁ אוֹ אֶת־הָאִשָּׁה וּסְקַלְתָּם בָּאֲבָנִים וָמֵתוּ׃ עַל־פִּי ׀
שְׁנַיִם עֵדִים אוֹ שְׁלֹשָׁה עֵדִים יוּמַת הַמֵּת לֹא יוּמַת עַל־פִּי
ז עֵד אֶחָד׃ יַד הָעֵדִים תִּהְיֶה־בּוֹ בָרִאשֹׁנָה לַהֲמִיתוֹ וְיַד כָּל־
הָעָם בָּאַחֲרֹנָה וּבִעַרְתָּ הָרָע מִקִּרְבֶּךָ׃
ח כִּי יִפָּלֵא מִמְּךָ דָבָר לַמִּשְׁפָּט בֵּין־דָּם ׀ לְדָם בֵּין־דִּין לְדִין וּבֵין
נֶגַע לָנֶגַע דִּבְרֵי רִיבֹת בִּשְׁעָרֶיךָ וְקַמְתָּ וְעָלִיתָ אֶל־הַמָּקוֹם
ט אֲשֶׁר יִבְחַר יְהוָה אֱלֹהֶיךָ בּוֹ׃ וּבָאתָ אֶל־הַכֹּהֲנִים הַלְוִיִּם
וְאֶל־הַשֹּׁפֵט אֲשֶׁר יִהְיֶה בַּיָּמִים הָהֵם וְדָרַשְׁתָּ וְהִגִּידוּ לְךָ אֵת
י דְּבַר הַמִּשְׁפָּט׃ וְעָשִׂיתָ עַל־פִּי הַדָּבָר אֲשֶׁר יַגִּידוּ לְךָ מִן־
הַמָּקוֹם הַהוּא אֲשֶׁר יִבְחַר יְהוָה וְשָׁמַרְתָּ לַעֲשׂוֹת כְּכֹל אֲשֶׁר
יא יוֹרוּךָ׃ עַל־פִּי הַתּוֹרָה אֲשֶׁר יוֹרוּךָ וְעַל־הַמִּשְׁפָּט אֲשֶׁר־

17:9 וְדָרַשְׁתָּ *Inquire of them* – The Levites were both judges and teachers. The idea of moral authority has become taboo in our society – largely because of a fallacy. The word "judgment" has two distinct, if related, meanings. The first is what we are looking for when we seek advice. Whether the counsel we wish for is moral or practical, we turn to those who have had long and successful encounters with the problem at hand. Whether we go to a tennis coach or a master craftsman or a lawyer, the very act of taking advice presupposes that there is excellence within an activity and that it is learned rather than immediately acquired. If this applies to specialized compartments of human behavior, how much more so does it apply to life itself taken as a whole. There may not be – indeed there is not – a single model of the good life. Even in a world as cohesive and structured as eighteenth-century East European Jewry, you went to Vilna for scholarship, to Mezerich for mysticism, and to Lubavitch for piety. But within each form of life there are exemplars and sages, and consensus tells us who they are. When we seek judgment in this sense, what we want is something forward-looking, the bringing to bear of considered experience on decisions we have to make.

We sometimes confuse this with judgment in a second sense, a metaphorical extension of what judges do, as here, in court. They pass a verdict. They acquit or condemn. Moral judgment in

the judgment as they tell you, not deviating from their
12 declaration to the right or to the left. Should anyone act
in wickedness, refusing to listen to the priest appointed
to minister there to the LORD your God, or the judge,
that person shall be put to death. You must purge the
13 evil from Israel. All the people will hear and fear and will
14 not act in such wickedness again. When you SHENI
enter the land that the LORD your God is giving you,
and have taken possession of it and settled in it, should
you say, 'I will set a king over me, like all the surrounding
15 nations,' set over you a king whom the LORD your God
chooses. The king you set over you must be one of your
own people. You may not set a foreigner over you, who
16 is not your brother. Further, he must not acquire many

---

was a permission, not an obligation. For Abrabanel it was a concession to human weakness. For Rabbeinu Baḥya, it was its own punishment. Why is the Torah so ambivalent about this central element of its political program?

The simplest answer was given by historian Lord Acton who saw the Hebrew Bible as the world's first tutorial in freedom. He wrote: "Thus the example of the Hebrew nation laid down the parallel lines on which all freedom has been won…the principle that all political authorities must be tested and reformed according to a code which was not made by man."

Judaism is not an argument for powerlessness. The briefest glance at two thousand years of Jewish history in the Diaspora tells us that there is nothing dignified in powerlessness. Instead, Judaism is an argument for the limitation, secularization, and transformation of power.

Limitation: Israel's kings were the only rulers in the ancient world without the power to legislate. For us, the laws that matter come from God, not from human beings. In Jewish law, kings may issue temporary regulations for the better ordering of society, but so may rabbis or courts.

Secularization: In Judaism, kings were not High Priests and High Priests were not kings. When some of the Hasmonean rulers sought to combine the two offices, the Talmud (Kiddushin 66a) records the objection of the Sages: "Let the royal crown be sufficient for you; leave the priestly crown to the descendants of Aharon."

Transformation: Fundamental to Judaism is the idea of servant leadership. The king must not "consider himself superior to his people, or stray from the commandments to the right or to the left" (Deut. 17:20). Humility is the essence of royalty, because to lead is to serve.

יֹאמְרוּ לְךָ תַּעֲשֶׂה לֹא תָסוּר מִן־הַדָּבָר אֲשֶׁר־יַגִּידוּ לְךָ יָמִין
יב וּשְׂמֹאל׃ וְהָאִישׁ אֲשֶׁר־יַעֲשֶׂה בְזָדוֹן לְבִלְתִּי שְׁמֹעַ אֶל־
הַכֹּהֵן הָעֹמֵד לְשָׁרֶת שָׁם אֶת־יְהוָה אֱלֹהֶיךָ אוֹ אֶל־הַשֹּׁפֵט
יג וּמֵת הָאִישׁ הַהוּא וּבִעַרְתָּ הָרָע מִיִּשְׂרָאֵל׃ וְכָל־הָעָם יִשְׁמְעוּ
יד וְיִרָאוּ וְלֹא יְזִידוּן עוֹד׃ כִּי־תָבֹא אֶל־הָאָרֶץ טו שני
אֲשֶׁר יְהוָה אֱלֹהֶיךָ נֹתֵן לָךְ וִירִשְׁתָּהּ וְיָשַׁבְתָּה בָּהּ וְאָמַרְתָּ
טו אָשִׂימָה עָלַי מֶלֶךְ כְּכָל־הַגּוֹיִם אֲשֶׁר סְבִיבֹתָי׃ שׂוֹם תָּשִׂים
עָלֶיךָ מֶלֶךְ אֲשֶׁר יִבְחַר יְהוָה אֱלֹהֶיךָ בּוֹ מִקֶּרֶב אַחֶיךָ תָּשִׂים
עָלֶיךָ מֶלֶךְ לֹא תוּכַל לָתֵת עָלֶיךָ אִישׁ נָכְרִי אֲשֶׁר לֹא־אָחִיךָ
טז הוּא׃ רַק לֹא־יַרְבֶּה־לּוֹ סוּסִים וְלֹא־יָשִׁיב אֶת־הָעָם מִצְרַיְמָה

SELECTING A MONARCH

In the eighth chapter of I Samuel, as this passage predicts, the people come to the prophet and demand a king. On the instruction of God, Shmuel tells them that if they appoint a king he will eventually seize their children, land, and a percentage of their harvests and cattle. Even constitutional monarchy, in other words, will involve a sacrifice of rights of property and person. "And on that day, you will cry out because of your own king, whom you yourselves chose, but the Lord will not answer you" (I Sam. 8:18).

Is having a king, then, a good thing or a bad thing, from a Jewish perspective? The question turns out to be almost unanswerable.

On the one hand, our *parasha* does say, "Set over you a king." Rambam counts it among the 613 commandments (*Mitzvat Aseh* 173). On the other hand, of no other command anywhere does it say that it is to be acted on when the people say that they want to be "like all the surrounding nations." The Torah doesn't tell us to be like everyone else. Jews are supposed to have the courage to be different.

The episode in the days of Shmuel makes matters no clearer. Shmuel is upset. He thinks the people are rejecting him. Not so, says God, the people are rejecting Me (I Sam. 8:7). Yet God does not command Shmuel to resist the request. He says, in effect: Tell them what monarchy will cost, what the people stand to lose. If they still want a king, give them a king.

If having a king is a good thing, why does God say that it means that the people are rejecting Him? If it is a bad thing, why does God tell Shmuel to give the people what they want even if it is not what God would wish them to want?

The great commentators run the entire spectrum on this issue. For Rambam, having a king was a good thing and a positive command. For Ibn Ezra it

horses for himself, he must not make the people return
to Egypt to acquire more horses, since the LORD has
17 told you: You must not go back that way again. He must
not accumulate wives and let his heart be led astray, nor
18 should he amass large amounts of silver and gold. As he
presides upon his royal throne, he must inscribe a copy
of this Law for himself upon a scroll in the presence of
19 the Levitical priests. It must always be with him, and he
shall read from it all the days of his life, so that he may
learn to revere the LORD his God, taking care to keep all
20 the words of this commandment and these decrees, not
considering himself superior to his people, or straying

---

elders, counselors, an inner court of sages and literati. In addition, biblical kings had prophets – Shmuel to Sha'ul, Natan to David, Yeshayahu to Ḥizkiyahu, and so on – to bring them the word of God. But those on whom the destiny of the nation turns may not delegate the task of thinking, reading, studying, and remembering. They are not entitled to say: I have affairs of state to worry about. I have no time for books. Leaders must be scholars, *benei Torah*, "children of the Book," if they are to direct and lead the people of the Book.

The two greatest kings of early Israel, David and Shlomo, were both authors, David of Psalms, Shlomo (according to tradition) of Song of Songs, Proverbs, and Ecclesiastes. What separate the statesman from the mere politician are reading and writing.

The key biblical word associated with kings is *ḥokhma*, "wisdom." We should note that *ḥokhma* means something slightly different from Torah, which is more commonly associated with priests and prophets than kings. *Ḥokhma* includes worldly wisdom, which is human and universal rather than a special heritage of Jews and Judaism. Broadly speaking, in contemporary terms *ḥokhma* refers to the sciences and humanities – to whatever allows us to see the universe as the work of God and the human person as the image of God. Torah is the specific moral and spiritual heritage of Israel.

Leaders take time to familiarize themselves with the world of ideas. Only thus do they gain the perspective to be able to see farther and clearer than others. To be a Jewish leader means spending time to study both Torah and *ḥokhma*: *ḥokhma* to understand the world as it is, Torah to understand the world as it ought to be.

17:20 לְבִלְתִּי רוּם־לְבָבוֹ מֵאֶחָיו *Not considering himself superior to his people* – Consistent with the fundamental Judaic idea that leadership is service, not dominion or power or status or superiority, the king is commanded to be humble: he

לְמַעַן הַרְבּוֹת סוּס וַיהוה אָמַר לָכֶם לֹא תֹסִפוּן לָשׁוּב בַּדֶּרֶךְ
יז הַזֶּה עוֹד: וְלֹא יַרְבֶּה־לּוֹ נָשִׁים וְלֹא יָסוּר לְבָבוֹ וְכֶסֶף וְזָהָב
יח לֹא יַרְבֶּה־לּוֹ מְאֹד: וְהָיָה כְשִׁבְתּוֹ עַל כִּסֵּא מַמְלַכְתּוֹ וְכָתַב
לוֹ אֶת־מִשְׁנֵה הַתּוֹרָה הַזֹּאת עַל־סֵפֶר מִלִּפְנֵי הַכֹּהֲנִים
יט הַלְוִיִּם: וְהָיְתָה עִמּוֹ וְקָרָא בוֹ כָּל־יְמֵי חַיָּיו לְמַעַן יִלְמַד
לְיִרְאָה אֶת־יהוה אֱלֹהָיו לִשְׁמֹר אֶת־כָּל־דִּבְרֵי הַתּוֹרָה
כ הַזֹּאת וְאֶת־הַחֻקִּים הָאֵלֶּה לַעֲשֹׂתָם: לְבִלְתִּי רוּם־לְבָבוֹ

17:17 וְכֶסֶף וְזָהָב לֹא יַרְבֶּה־לּוֹ מְאֹד *Nor should he amass large amounts of silver and gold* – Unique commands are given to the king. He must not accumulate horses so as not to establish trading links with Egypt. He should not have too many wives lest he "let his heart be led astray." He should not accumulate wealth. These were all standing temptations to a king. It was these three prohibitions that Shlomo, wisest of men, broke, marking the beginning of the long, slow slide into corruption that marked much of the history of the monarchy in ancient Israel. It led, after his death, to the division of the kingdom.

But these were symptoms, not the cause. The cause was the feeling on the part of the king that since he is above the people, he is above the law. As the Rabbis said (Sanhedrin 21b), Shlomo justified his breach of these prohibitions by saying:

> The only reason that a king may not accumulate wives is that they will lead his heart astray, so I will marry many wives and not let my heart be led astray. And since the only reason not to have many horses is not to establish links with Egypt, I will have many horses but not do business with Egypt. (Sanhedrin 21b)

In both cases he fell into the trap of which the Torah had warned. Shlomo's wives did lead his heart astray (1 Kings 11:3), and his horses were imported from Egypt (10:28–29). The arrogance of power is its downfall. Hence the Torah's insistence on humility, not as merely a good thing to have, but as essential to the role.

17:19 וְקָרָא בוֹ כָּל־יְמֵי חַיָּיו *He shall read from it all the days of his life* – We see that the king is commanded to study constantly. Later, in the book that bears his name, Yehoshua – Moshe's successor – is commanded in very similar terms:

> This book of Torah must never leave your lips; contemplate it day and night, so that you will faithfully uphold all that is written within it. For then your course will succeed; then you will triumph. (Josh. 1:8)

Leaders learn. True, they have advisers,

from the commandments to the right or to the left. Then
he and his descendants will reign long in the midst of
18 1 Israel. The Levitical priests, the whole tribe of SHELISHI
Levi, will have no share or inheritance with Israel. They
2 will eat the LORD's fire offerings as their inheritance, but
will have no inheritance among their kinsfolk. The LORD is
3 their inheritance, as He has promised them. This
shall be the priests' due from the people: those offering a
sacrifice – an ox or a sheep – shall give to the priest the
4 shoulder, the cheeks, and the stomach. You shall give
him the first yield of your grain, wine, and oil, and the
5 first wool from the shearing of your sheep. For the LORD
your God has chosen him out of all your tribes to stand
and minister in the name of the LORD – him and his sons
6 for all time. If a Levite leaves any of your towns REVI'I

The king recruited an army, levied taxes, and was responsible for civic order. It was his task to defend the nation from enemies outside and lawlessness within. He was immersed in the demands of statecraft, a civil rather than religious leader.

The priest mediated between the people and God. He served in the Temple, offered sacrifices on behalf of the people, and ensured that the holy was at the heart of national life. He was also a teacher and adjudicator of the law. He was the guardian of the holy, preserver of the boundaries between sacred and secular. Yet the priest was not the only kind of spiritual leader in biblical Israel. There was also the prophet. The prophet heard the word of God and conveyed it to the people.

Thus, we have in the Torah an intimation of the doctrine of the separation of powers that would emerge in the West in the eighteenth century, so as to avoid the concentration of power in a single individual or institution.

The Torah does not spell out explicitly why this separation was important, but we can guess. Power tends to corrupt, therefore no one should have absolute power. Parashat Shofetim signals a radical break from the pagan model of kingship. In Judaism, a king is not a High Priest, and a High Priest is not a king.

The result is a structure which limits the powers of king and priest alike, and which gives prominence to the prophet, who has no power but lasting influence. True power, in the Judaic view of things, belongs to God alone. All earthly power is merely delegated – Heaven's conditional gift to human beings. This means that any attempt by king, priest, or prophet to subvert or contravene the revealed will of God is automatically *ultra vires*, lacking in authority.

מאחיו ולבלתי סור מן־המצוה ימין ושמאול למען יאריך
יח א ימים על־ממלכתו הוא ובניו בקרב ישראל: שלישי לא־
יהיה לכהנים הלוים כל־שבט לוי חלק ונחלה עם־ישראל
ב אשי יהוה ונחלתו יאכלון: ונחלה לא־יהיה־לו בקרב אחיו
ג יהוה הוא נחלתו כאשר דבר־לו: וזה יהיה
משפט הכהנים מאת העם מאת זבחי הזבח אם־שור
ד אם־שה ונתן לכהן הזרע והלחיים והקבה: ראשית דגנך
ה תירשך ויצהרך וראשית גז צאנך תתן־לו: כי בו בחר
יהוה אלהיך מכל־שבטיך לעמד לשרת בשם־יהוה הוא
ו ובניו כל־הימים: וכי־יבא הלוי מאחד רביעי
שעריך מכל־ישראל אשר־הוא גר שם ובא בכל־אות

must constantly read the Torah "so that he may learn to revere the Lord his God... not considering himself superior to his people" (Deut. 17:19–20). It is not easy to be humble when everyone is bowing down before you and when you have the power of life and death over your subjects. If a king, whom all are bound to honor, is commanded to be humble – "not considering himself superior to his people" – how much more so the rest of us. Moshe, the greatest leader the Jewish people ever had, was "very humble, more so than any other man on earth" (Num. 12:3). Was it that he was great because he was humble, or humble because he was great? Either way, as R. Yoḥanan said of God Himself, "Wherever you find His greatness there you find His humility" (Megilla 31a). This is a clear example of how spirituality makes a difference to the way we act, feel, and think. *Believing that there is a God in whose presence we stand means that we are not the center of our world.* Humility means living by the light of that which is greater than me. When God is at the center of our lives, we open ourselves up to the glory of creation and the beauty of other people. The smaller the self, the wider the radius of our world.

17:20 למען יאריך ימים על־ממלכתו הוא ובניו *Then he and his descendants will reign long* – In the ancient world, the pharaohs of Egypt, like the kings of Mesopotamian city-states, combined temporal and ecclesiastical power. They were both head of state and head of the religion of the state. They claimed to be, and were seen as being, god made manifest or the child of the gods or the chief intercessor with the gods. The Torah's model of leadership is different. There was not to be one leader, but three, each of a very different kind: the king, the priest, and the prophet.

throughout Israel where he has been living, and comes
to the place that the LORD will choose – he may do so
7 whenever he wishes – then he may minister in the name
of the LORD his God, alongside any of his brother Levites
8 who serve there before the LORD. They shall have equal
portions to eat, regardless of income they may have from
9 the sale of family possessions. When you come
into the land that the LORD your God is giving you, do
not learn to partake in the abhorrent practices those
10 nations carry out. Let no one be found among you who
makes a son or daughter pass through fire, or who casts
11 spells, or is an augur or diviner or soothsayer, or who
practices sorcery, or consults ghosts or spirits, or seeks
12 oracles from the dead. For anyone who does these things
is abhorrent to the LORD; it is because of such abhorrent
acts that the LORD your God is driving them out before
13 you. You must be wholly loyal to the LORD your God.
14 The nations that you are driving out listen to augurs and HAMISHI
to those who cast spells. But as for you – the LORD your
15 God does not permit you these. The LORD your God
will raise up another prophet like me from among your
16 own people. To him you must listen. For this is what you
asked of the LORD your God at Ḥorev on the day of the
assembly when you said: 'If I hear the voice of the LORD
my God any more, or continue to see this great fire, I will
17 18 die.' The LORD said to me: They have spoken well. I will
raise up for them a prophet like you from among their
own people. I will put My words in the prophet's mouth
19 and he will tell them all that I command. Anyone who

But He is also in nature itself. Science does not displace God: it reveals, in ever more intricate and wondrous ways, the design within nature. Far from diminishing our religious sense, science (rightly understood) should enlarge it, teaching us to see "how many are Your works, LORD; You made them all in wisdom" (Ps. 104:24). Above all, however, God is to be found in the voice heard at Sinai, teaching us how to construct a society that will be the opposite of Egypt, in which the few do not enslave the many, nor are strangers mistreated.

ז נַפְשׁוֹ אֶל־הַמָּקוֹם אֲשֶׁר־יִבְחַר יְהוָה׃ וְשֵׁרֵת בְּשֵׁם יְהוָה
ח אֱלֹהָיו כְּכָל־אֶחָיו הַלְוִיִּם הָעֹמְדִים שָׁם לִפְנֵי יְהוָה׃ חֵלֶק
ט כְּחֵלֶק יֹאכֵלוּ לְבַד מִמְכָּרָיו עַל־הָאָבוֹת׃ כִּי
אַתָּה בָּא אֶל־הָאָרֶץ אֲשֶׁר־יְהוָה אֱלֹהֶיךָ נֹתֵן לָךְ לֹא־תִלְמַד
י לַעֲשׂוֹת כְּתוֹעֲבֹת הַגּוֹיִם הָהֵם׃ לֹא־יִמָּצֵא בְךָ מַעֲבִיר בְּנוֹ־
יא וּבִתּוֹ בָּאֵשׁ קֹסֵם קְסָמִים מְעוֹנֵן וּמְנַחֵשׁ וּמְכַשֵּׁף׃ וְחֹבֵר חָבֶר
יב וְשֹׁאֵל אוֹב וְיִדְּעֹנִי וְדֹרֵשׁ אֶל־הַמֵּתִים׃ כִּי־תוֹעֲבַת יְהוָה
כָּל־עֹשֵׂה אֵלֶּה וּבִגְלַל הַתּוֹעֵבֹת הָאֵלֶּה יְהוָה אֱלֹהֶיךָ מוֹרִישׁ
יג יד אוֹתָם מִפָּנֶיךָ׃ תָּמִים תִּהְיֶה עִם יְהוָה אֱלֹהֶיךָ׃ כִּי ׀ הַגּוֹיִם חמישי
הָאֵלֶּה אֲשֶׁר אַתָּה יוֹרֵשׁ אוֹתָם אֶל־מְעֹנְנִים וְאֶל־קֹסְמִים
טו יִשְׁמָעוּ וְאַתָּה לֹא כֵן נָתַן לְךָ יְהוָה אֱלֹהֶיךָ׃ נָבִיא מִקִּרְבְּךָ
טז מֵאַחֶיךָ כָּמֹנִי יָקִים לְךָ יְהוָה אֱלֹהֶיךָ אֵלָיו תִּשְׁמָעוּן׃ כְּכֹל
אֲשֶׁר־שָׁאַלְתָּ מֵעִם יְהוָה אֱלֹהֶיךָ בְּחֹרֵב בְּיוֹם הַקָּהָל לֵאמֹר
לֹא אֹסֵף לִשְׁמֹעַ אֶת־קוֹל יְהוָה אֱלֹהָי וְאֶת־הָאֵשׁ הַגְּדֹלָה
יז הַזֹּאת לֹא־אֶרְאֶה עוֹד וְלֹא אָמוּת׃ וַיֹּאמֶר יְהוָה אֵלָי הֵיטִיבוּ
יח אֲשֶׁר דִּבֵּרוּ׃ נָבִיא אָקִים לָהֶם מִקֶּרֶב אֲחֵיהֶם כָּמוֹךָ וְנָתַתִּי
יט דְבָרַי בְּפִיו וְדִבֶּר אֲלֵיהֶם אֵת כָּל־אֲשֶׁר אֲצַוֶּנּוּ׃ וְהָיָה הָאִישׁ

18:10 לֹא־יִמָּצֵא בְךָ... קֹסֵם קְסָמִים *Let no one be found among you…who casts spells* – Witchcraft and magic must be divorced from our reasons for religious belief. On this, Rambam is unequivocal:

> Israel did not believe in Moshe our teacher because of the signs he performed. When faith is predicated on signs, a lurking doubt always remains that these signs may have been performed with the aid of occult arts and witchcraft. All the signs Moshe performed in the wilderness, he did because they were necessary, not to authenticate his status as a prophet.… When we needed food, he brought down manna. When the people were thirsty, he cleaved the rock. When Korah's supporters denied his authority, the earth swallowed them up. So too with all the other signs. What then were our grounds for believing in him? The revelation at Sinai, in which we saw with our own eyes and heard with our own ears. (*Hilkhot Yesodei HaTorah* 8:1)

To be sure, God is in the events which, seeming to defy nature, we call miracles.

does not listen to My words that he speaks in My name,
20 I Myself will call him to account. But a prophet who acts
in wickedness, speaking anything I have not commanded
in My name, or speaking in the name of other gods – that
21 prophet shall die. You may say to yourself, 'How can we
22 recognize a message that the Lord has not spoken?' If
what a prophet proclaims in the name of the Lord does
not take place or come true, that is a message that the
Lord has not spoken. The prophet has proclaimed it in
19 1 wickedness. Do not be afraid of him. When the
Lord your God has cut down the nations whose land the
Lord your God is giving you, and you have driven them
2 out and are living in their towns and in their houses, you
shall set aside three cities in that land that the Lord your
3 God gives you to possess. Determine the distances and
divide the land that the Lord your God is giving you as
a heritage into three equal parts – so that any manslayer
4 will be able to flee to one of these cities. This is the rule
for a manslayer who may flee to one of these and live:
it is one who has killed another person unintentionally,

> character. We are not to say, "See, he spoke and his prediction has not come to pass." For God is long-suffering and abounding in kindness and repents of evil.... But if the prophet, in the name of God, assures good fortune, declaring that a particular event would come to pass, and the benefit promised has not been realized, he is unquestionably a false prophet, for no blessing decreed by the Almighty, even if promised conditionally, is ever revoked. (*Hilkhot Yesodei HaTorah* 10:4)

Precisely because Judaism believes in free will, the human future can never be unfailingly predicted. People change. God forgives: "Prayer, penitence, and charity avert the evil decree." There is no decree that cannot be revoked. A prophet does not foretell. He warns. If a prophecy of doom comes true, it has failed.

Calamity, catastrophe, disaster prove nothing. Anyone can foretell these things without risking his reputation or authority. It is only by the realization of a positive vision that prophecy is put to the test. A true prophet is an agent of hope.

אֲשֶׁר לֹא־יִשְׁמַע אֶל־דְּבָרַי אֲשֶׁר יְדַבֵּר בִּשְׁמִי אָנֹכִי אֶדְרֹשׁ
כ מֵעִמּוֹ: אַךְ הַנָּבִיא אֲשֶׁר יָזִיד לְדַבֵּר דָּבָר בִּשְׁמִי אֵת אֲשֶׁר
לֹא־צִוִּיתִיו לְדַבֵּר וַאֲשֶׁר יְדַבֵּר בְּשֵׁם אֱלֹהִים אֲחֵרִים וּמֵת
כא הַנָּבִיא הַהוּא: וְכִי תֹאמַר בִּלְבָבֶךָ אֵיכָה נֵדַע אֶת־הַדָּבָר
כב אֲשֶׁר לֹא־דִבְּרוֹ יהוה: אֲשֶׁר יְדַבֵּר הַנָּבִיא בְּשֵׁם יהוה וְלֹא־
יִהְיֶה הַדָּבָר וְלֹא יָבֹא הוּא הַדָּבָר אֲשֶׁר לֹא־דִבְּרוֹ יהוה בְּזָדוֹן
יט א דִּבְּרוֹ הַנָּבִיא לֹא תָגוּר מִמֶּנּוּ: כִּי־יַכְרִית יהוה
אֱלֹהֶיךָ אֶת־הַגּוֹיִם אֲשֶׁר יהוה אֱלֹהֶיךָ נֹתֵן לְךָ אֶת־אַרְצָם
ב וִירִשְׁתָּם וְיָשַׁבְתָּ בְעָרֵיהֶם וּבְבָתֵּיהֶם: שָׁלוֹשׁ עָרִים תַּבְדִּיל
ג לָךְ בְּתוֹךְ אַרְצְךָ אֲשֶׁר יהוה אֱלֹהֶיךָ נֹתֵן לְךָ לְרִשְׁתָּהּ: תָּכִין
לְךָ הַדֶּרֶךְ וְשִׁלַּשְׁתָּ אֶת־גְּבוּל אַרְצְךָ אֲשֶׁר יַנְחִילְךָ יהוה
ד אֱלֹהֶיךָ וְהָיָה לָנוּס שָׁמָּה כָּל־רֹצֵחַ: וְזֶה דְּבַר הָרֹצֵחַ אֲשֶׁר־
יָנוּס שָׁמָּה וָחָי אֲשֶׁר יַכֶּה אֶת־רֵעֵהוּ בִּבְלִי־דַעַת וְהוּא לֹא־

18:21 אֵיכָה נֵדַע אֶת־הַדָּבָר אֲשֶׁר לֹא־דִבְּרוֹ יהוה *How can we recognize a message that the Lord has not spoken?* – How does one tell a true prophet from a false one? On the face of it, if what the prophet predicts comes to pass, he is a true prophet; if not, not. Clearly, though, it is not that simple.

The prophet Yirmeyahu makes a fundamental distinction between prophesies of good news and bad.

> The prophets who were before me and before you long ago – they prophesied war, catastrophe, and pestilence to many lands and to great kingdoms. The prophet who shall prophesy peace, when his words come true, that prophet shall be acknowledged as one whom the Lord has truly sent. (Jer. 28:8–9)

It is easy to prophesy disaster. If the prophecy comes true, then you have spoken the truth. If it does not, then you can say: God relented and forgave. A negative prophecy cannot be refuted, but a positive one can. If the good foreseen comes to pass, then the prophecy is true. If it does not, then you cannot say, "God changed His mind," because God does not retract from a promise He has made of good, or peace, or return.

This is how Rambam puts it:

> As for calamities predicted by a prophet, if, for example, he foretells the death of a certain individual or declares that in a particular year there will be famine or war and so forth, the non-fulfillment of his forecast does not disprove his prophetic

5 without prior hatred. For instance, a man may go into the
forest with a neighbor to cut wood, and as he swings the
ax to cut down a tree, the ax-head may fly off the handle
and strike the neighbor and kill him; that man may flee
6 to one of these cities and live. Should the distance be too
great, the avenger of blood might pursue him in hot anger,
overtake, and kill him even though he did not deserve to
die, there having been no prior enmity between the two.
7 That is why I charge you thus: three cities must you set
8 aside. If the Lord your God enlarges your territory, as
He swore to your ancestors, and gives you all of that land
9 that He promised to give your ancestors, if you vigilantly
observe all of this commandment with which I charge you
today, loving the Lord your God and walking in all His
ways, then you shall add to these three, three cities more
10 so that innocent blood is not shed, bringing bloodguilt
upon you, in the land that the Lord your God is giving
you as a possession.

Man was created alone to teach you that whoever destroys a single soul is as if he destroyed an entire world, and whoever saves a single life is as if he had saved an entire world.... And also [he was created alone] to proclaim the greatness of the Holy One, blessed be He, for if a person makes many coins from one mold, they are all the same, but the supreme King of kings, the Holy One, blessed be He, made every person in the stamp of the first man, yet not one of them is identical to another. Therefore every single person is obliged to say: the world was created for my sake. (Sanhedrin 4:5)

The concept of God, singular and alone, gives rise to the concept of the human person, singular and alone. This is the birth of the individual in Western civilization.

It is also vital to Jewish survival in exile. Jews were always a minority, and the minority usually conforms to the majority. Had this been the case among Jews, there would be no Judaism today. Jews, however, have had a long history of valuing the individual over the group. Jews did not bend to the majority. Despite the vital importance of solidarity and communal responsibility, the one is not subsumed into the many.

ה שֹׂנֵא לוֹ מִתְּמֹל שִׁלְשֹׁם: וַאֲשֶׁר יָבֹא אֶת־רֵעֵהוּ בַיַּעַר לַחְטֹב
עֵצִים וְנִדְּחָה יָדוֹ בַגַּרְזֶן לִכְרֹת הָעֵץ וְנָשַׁל הַבַּרְזֶל מִן־הָעֵץ
וּמָצָא אֶת־רֵעֵהוּ וָמֵת הוּא יָנוּס אֶל־אַחַת הֶעָרִים־הָאֵלֶּה
ו וָחָי: פֶּן־יִרְדֹּף גֹּאֵל הַדָּם אַחֲרֵי הָרֹצֵחַ כִּי יֵחַם לְבָבוֹ וְהִשִּׂיגוֹ
כִּי־יִרְבֶּה הַדֶּרֶךְ וְהִכָּהוּ נָפֶשׁ וְלוֹ אֵין מִשְׁפַּט־מָוֶת כִּי לֹא־
ז שֹׂנֵא הוּא לוֹ מִתְּמוֹל שִׁלְשׁוֹם: עַל־כֵּן אָנֹכִי מְצַוְּךָ לֵאמֹר
ח שָׁלֹשׁ עָרִים תַּבְדִּיל לָךְ: וְאִם־יַרְחִיב יהוה אֱלֹהֶיךָ אֶת־גְּבֻלְךָ
כַּאֲשֶׁר נִשְׁבַּע לַאֲבֹתֶיךָ וְנָתַן לְךָ אֶת־כָּל־הָאָרֶץ אֲשֶׁר דִּבֶּר
ט לָתֵת לַאֲבֹתֶיךָ: כִּי־תִשְׁמֹר אֶת־כָּל־הַמִּצְוָה הַזֹּאת לַעֲשֹׂתָהּ
אֲשֶׁר אָנֹכִי מְצַוְּךָ הַיּוֹם לְאַהֲבָה אֶת־יהוה אֱלֹהֶיךָ וְלָלֶכֶת
בִּדְרָכָיו כָּל־הַיָּמִים וְיָסַפְתָּ לְךָ עוֹד שָׁלֹשׁ עָרִים עַל הַשָּׁלֹשׁ
י הָאֵלֶּה: וְלֹא יִשָּׁפֵךְ דָּם נָקִי בְּקֶרֶב אַרְצְךָ אֲשֶׁר יהוה אֱלֹהֶיךָ
נֹתֵן לְךָ נַחֲלָה וְהָיָה עָלֶיךָ דָּמִים:

19:5 הוּא יָנוּס אֶל־אַחַת הֶעָרִים־הָאֵלֶּה וָחָי *That man may flee to one of these cities and live* – The cities of refuge were havens, shelters, places of safety designed to protect manslaughterers from "blood vengeance" by a member of the family of the victim. Rambam, following the Talmud, includes the following unexpected detail in his legislation about the cities:

> One who has been exiled does not leave the city of refuge at all, even to perform a mitzva, or to give evidence in a monetary or capital case, or to save someone by his testimony, or to rescue someone from a non-Jew or a river or a fire or a collapsed building. Even if all Israel needs his help, like Yoav ben Tzeruya [King David's chief of staff], he never leaves the city of refuge until the death of the High Priest, and if he leaves, he makes himself vulnerable to death. (*Hilkhot Rotze'aḥ UShmirat HaNefesh* 7:8)

Only within the city of refuge was the manslaughterer safe. To leave the city of refuge was to put his life at risk. No one in Judaism is commanded to put his life at risk to save the life of another – even to save the entire Jewish people ("even if all Israel needs his help"). Despite the fact that Judaism is an intensely communal faith, nonetheless in Jewish law *the individual takes priority over the community.*

This illustrates the supreme importance of the individual in Judaism. This is how a famous Mishna puts it:

11 But if one person hates his fellow, lies in wait for him, and
attacks and kills him, and then flees to one of these cities,
12 the elders of his town shall have him brought back from
13 there and handed over to the avenger of blood to die. Show
him no pity. You must purge the guilt of innocent blood
14 from Israel, so that it may be well for you. Do not SHISHI
move back your neighbor's boundary marker, set up by
those long ago in the allotted land that the LORD your God
15 is giving you to possess. One witness alone is not
enough to convict a person of any crime or wrongdoing.
A case is to be established only on the evidence of two
16 or three witnesses. If a corrupt witness comes forward
17 to accuse someone of wrongdoing, both parties to the
dispute shall appear before the LORD, before the priests
18 and judges in office in that time. The judges shall make a
thorough investigation. If the man who testified proves to
be a false witness, having testified falsely against his fellow,
19 then inflict upon the false witness what the false witness
had intended to inflict upon his fellow; you must purge
20 the evil from your midst. Others will hear and fear, and

disqualification. A reputation for truth telling will be an essential test of character. A world of truth is a world of trust, and vice versa. Truth becomes the intellectual equivalent of a public space we can all inhabit, whatever our desires and predilections. Where there is honesty, truth, and truthfulness, there tends to be law, order, and prosperity. A respect for truth is essential for authority, collaborative endeavor, and human graciousness.

THE PROHIBITION ON DESTROYING FRUIT TREES

War is, the Torah implies, inevitably destructive. That is why Judaism's highest value is peace. Nonetheless, there is a difference between necessary and needless destruction. Trees are a source of wood for siege works. But some trees, those that bear fruit, are also a source of food. Therefore, do not destroy them. Do not needlessly deprive yourself and others of a productive resource, or engage in scorched earth tactics.

The sages saw in this command something more than a detail in the laws of war. They saw it as a *binyan av*, a specific example of a more general principle. They called this the rule of *bal tashḥit*, the prohibition against needless destruction of any kind. This is how Rambam summarizes it: "Not only does this apply to trees, but also whoever breaks vessels or tears garments,

יא וְכִֽי־יִהְיֶ֥ה אִישׁ֙ שֹׂנֵ֣א לְרֵעֵ֔הוּ וְאָ֤רַב לוֹ֙ וְקָ֣ם עָלָ֔יו וְהִכָּ֥הוּ
יב נֶ֖פֶשׁ וָמֵ֑ת וְנָ֕ס אֶל־אַחַ֖ת הֶעָרִ֥ים הָאֵֽל׃ וְשָֽׁלְחוּ֙ זִקְנֵ֣י
עִיר֔וֹ וְלָקְח֥וּ אֹת֖וֹ מִשָּׁ֑ם וְנָתְנ֣וּ אֹת֗וֹ בְּיַ֛ד גֹּאֵ֥ל הַדָּ֖ם וָמֵֽת׃
יג לֹא־תָח֥וֹס עֵינְךָ֖ עָלָ֑יו וּבִעַרְתָּ֧ דַם־הַנָּקִ֛י מִיִּשְׂרָאֵ֖ל וְט֥וֹב
יד לָֽךְ׃ לֹ֤א תַסִּיג֙ גְּב֣וּל רֵֽעֲךָ֔ אֲשֶׁ֥ר גָּבְל֖וּ רִאשֹׁנִ֑ים ששי
בְּנַחֲלָֽתְךָ֙ אֲשֶׁ֣ר תִּנְחַ֔ל בָּאָ֕רֶץ אֲשֶׁר֙ יְהוָ֣ה אֱלֹהֶ֔יךָ נֹתֵ֥ן לְךָ֖
טו לְרִשְׁתָּֽהּ׃ לֹֽא־יָק֨וּם עֵ֜ד אֶחָ֣ד בְּאִ֗ישׁ לְכָל־
עָוֺן֙ וּלְכָל־חַטָּ֔את בְּכָל־חֵ֖טְא אֲשֶׁ֣ר יֶחֱטָ֑א עַל־פִּ֣י ׀ שְׁנֵ֣י עֵדִ֗ים
טז א֛וֹ עַל־פִּ֥י שְׁלֹשָֽׁה־עֵדִ֖ים יָק֥וּם דָּבָֽר׃ כִּֽי־יָק֥וּם עֵד־חָמָ֖ס
יז בְּאִ֑ישׁ לַעֲנ֥וֹת בּ֖וֹ סָרָֽה׃ וְעָמְד֧וּ שְׁנֵֽי־הָאֲנָשִׁ֛ים אֲשֶׁר־לָהֶ֥ם
הָרִ֖יב לִפְנֵ֣י יְהוָ֑ה לִפְנֵ֤י הַכֹּֽהֲנִים֙ וְהַשֹּׁ֣פְטִ֔ים אֲשֶׁ֥ר יִהְי֖וּ בַּיָּמִ֥ים
יח הָהֵֽם׃ וְדָרְשׁ֥וּ הַשֹּׁפְטִ֖ים הֵיטֵ֑ב וְהִנֵּ֤ה עֵֽד־שֶׁ֙קֶר֙ הָעֵ֔ד שֶׁ֖קֶר
יט עָנָ֥ה בְאָחִֽיו׃ וַעֲשִׂ֣יתֶם ל֔וֹ כַּאֲשֶׁ֥ר זָמַ֖ם לַעֲשׂ֣וֹת לְאָחִ֑יו וּבִֽעַרְתָּ֥
כ הָרָ֖ע מִקִּרְבֶּֽךָ׃ וְהַנִּשְׁאָרִ֖ים יִשְׁמְע֣וּ וְיִרָ֑אוּ וְלֹֽא־יֹסִ֨פוּ לַעֲשׂ֜וֹת

19:11 וְכִי־יִהְיֶה אִישׁ שֹׂנֵא לְרֵעֵהוּ *If one person hates his fellow* – The protection of the city of refuge is given only to those who kill by accident, not to those who "hate" the victim, whose killing, even in the absence of witnesses, cannot be judged to be accidental. This poses an obvious problem for the court. How can human beings know whether the accused hated his victim or not? We cannot look into another person's heart. The law needs a behavioral criterion of hate. The sages ruled that it is deemed to be present if the killer was *not on speaking terms* with the victim ("He had not spoken with him for three days because of hatred," says Rambam, *Hilkhot Rotze'aḥ UShmirat HaNefesh* 6:10). We are told (Lev. 19:17): "Do not hate your brother in your heart. Admonish your fellow and do not bear guilt on his account." The second sentence, says Rambam, is the antidote to the first. If someone offends you, say so and do not be silent, for otherwise you will come to hate him in your heart. That has led, most obviously in the case of Avshalom and Amnon (II Sam. 13:22), to murder. Silence incubates hate; speech can heal it.

19:19 וּבִעַרְתָּ הָרָע מִקִּרְבֶּךָ *You must purge the evil from your midst* – The Torah well understands that a culture of truth telling is fundamental to a free society. Where there is a strong moral arena, then truth stands a chance of surviving intact against the assaults that will be made against it. Telling a lie will be a

such an evil will not be committed again in your midst.
21 Show no pity: life for life, eye for eye, tooth for tooth,
20 1 hand for hand, foot for foot. When you go out
to battle your enemies, and see horses and chariots, an
army greater than yours, do not be afraid of them; for
the LORD your God, who brought you out of Egypt, He
2 will be with you. Before you engage in battle, the priest
3 shall come forward and address the men. 'Listen, Israel,'
he shall say to them, 'this day you are going into battle
against your enemies. Do not lose heart or be afraid, do
4 not panic or dread them; for it is the LORD your God
who goes with you, to fight against your enemies for you,
5 to bring you victory.' Then the officers shall address the
men: 'Is there a man here who has built a new house but
not yet dedicated it? Let him go back home, or he may die
6 in battle and someone else will dedicate it. Is there a man
here who has planted a vineyard but not yet harvested it?
Let him go back home, or he may die in the battle and
7 someone else will harvest it. Is there a man here who has
betrothed a woman but not yet married her? Let him go
back home, or he may die in battle and someone else will
8 marry her.' And further, 'Is there a man here,' the officers
shall say to the men, 'who is afraid or fainthearted? Let
him go back home so that his comrades do not become

---

interfere with it is sacrilegious. The first allows technology to run rampant while the second turns its back on it altogether. Neither extreme, we believe, does justice to the challenge of human civilization.

God, said Yeshayahu (48:18), did not create the world to be desolate. He formed it to be inhabited. He gave man the intelligence to control nature. Therein lies his dignity. But He charged him with the duty of preserving nature. Therein lies his responsibility.

The rabbis put it simply. They said: When God made the first man, He took him to see all the trees of the Garden of Eden. He said to him: "See how beautiful are My works. All that I have created I have made for you. But be careful that you do not ruin My world, for if you do there is no one else to put right what you have destroyed" (Kohelet Rabba 7). That is as lucid a way as any of stating one of the great imperatives of our time.

כא עוֹד כַּדָּבָר הָרָע הַזֶּה בְּקִרְבֶּךָ: וְלֹא תָחוֹס עֵינֶךָ נֶפֶשׁ בְּנֶפֶשׁ
כ א עַיִן בְּעַיִן שֵׁן בְּשֵׁן יָד בְּיָד רֶגֶל בְּרָגֶל: כִּי־תֵצֵא
לַמִּלְחָמָה עַל־אֹיְבֶךָ וְרָאִיתָ סוּס וָרֶכֶב עַם רַב מִמְּךָ לֹא
תִירָא מֵהֶם כִּי־יהוה אֱלֹהֶיךָ עִמָּךְ הַמַּעַלְךָ מֵאֶרֶץ מִצְרָיִם:
ב וְהָיָה כְּקָרָבְכֶם אֶל־הַמִּלְחָמָה וְנִגַּשׁ הַכֹּהֵן וְדִבֶּר אֶל־הָעָם:
ג וְאָמַר אֲלֵהֶם שְׁמַע יִשְׂרָאֵל אַתֶּם קְרֵבִים הַיּוֹם לַמִּלְחָמָה
עַל־אֹיְבֵיכֶם אַל־יֵרַךְ לְבַבְכֶם אַל־תִּירְאוּ וְאַל־תַּחְפְּזוּ וְאַל־
ד תַּעַרְצוּ מִפְּנֵיהֶם: כִּי יהוה אֱלֹהֵיכֶם הַהֹלֵךְ עִמָּכֶם לְהִלָּחֵם
ה לָכֶם עִם־אֹיְבֵיכֶם לְהוֹשִׁיעַ אֶתְכֶם: וְדִבְּרוּ הַשֹּׁטְרִים אֶל־
הָעָם לֵאמֹר מִי־הָאִישׁ אֲשֶׁר בָּנָה בַיִת־חָדָשׁ וְלֹא חֲנָכוֹ יֵלֵךְ
ו וְיָשֹׁב לְבֵיתוֹ פֶּן־יָמוּת בַּמִּלְחָמָה וְאִישׁ אַחֵר יַחְנְכֶנּוּ: וּמִי־
הָאִישׁ אֲשֶׁר נָטַע כֶּרֶם וְלֹא חִלְּלוֹ יֵלֵךְ וְיָשֹׁב לְבֵיתוֹ פֶּן־יָמוּת
ז בַּמִּלְחָמָה וְאִישׁ אַחֵר יְחַלְּלֶנּוּ: וּמִי־הָאִישׁ אֲשֶׁר אֵרַשׂ אִשָּׁה
וְלֹא לְקָחָהּ יֵלֵךְ וְיָשֹׁב לְבֵיתוֹ פֶּן־יָמוּת בַּמִּלְחָמָה וְאִישׁ אַחֵר
ח יִקָּחֶנָּה: וְיָסְפוּ הַשֹּׁטְרִים לְדַבֵּר אֶל־הָעָם וְאָמְרוּ מִי־הָאִישׁ
הַיָּרֵא וְרַךְ הַלֵּבָב יֵלֵךְ וְיָשֹׁב לְבֵיתוֹ וְלֹא יִמַּס אֶת־לְבַב אֶחָיו

---

destroys a building, blocks a wellspring of water, or destructively wastes food transgresses the command of *bal tashḥit*" (*Hilkhot Melakhim UMilḥemoteihem* 6:10). This is the halakhic basis of an ethic of ecological responsibility.

The ruling represents a remarkable constraint on human ownership. Normally, to own something is to be able to dispose of it as one wishes. Jewish law denies absolute property in this sense. You may not break plates, tear clothes, or set fire to furniture in a spirit of vandalism even if they belong to you and no one else is harmed. Vandalism is a betrayal of the condition on which things are given over to the stewardship of man.

To be sure, conservation is not an absolute value in Jewish law. Halakha permits the destruction of natural resources in the course of constructive projects that will ultimately enhance human welfare. But the onus of proof is on the developer.

Judaism categorically rejects two attitudes to the environment. One, associated with the Stoic tradition, is that we have no moral duties toward nature. The other, drawn from some Eastern religions, is that nature is holy and to

9 fainthearted along with him.' When the officers have
finished addressing the men, they shall appoint the
10 commanders to lead them. When you approach SHEVI'I
11 a town to fight against it, first offer it peace. If it accepts
your terms of peace and lets you in, all the people found
12 there shall serve you a tribute of forced labor. If it rejects
your peace offer and wages war against you, you shall lay
13 siege. When the LORD your God gives it over into your
14 hands, you shall put all its males to the sword. You may,
however, take as your plunder the women, children,
livestock, and all else in the town, all its spoil; you may
use the spoil of your enemies, which the LORD your
15 God has given you. This is how you are to treat all the
towns that are distant from you and do not belong to the
16 nations nearby. However, in the towns of the nations that
the LORD your God is giving you as an inheritance, let
17 nothing that breathes remain alive. These, the Hittites
and Amorites, Canaanites and Perizzites, Hivites and
Jebusites, you must utterly destroy as the LORD your God
18 has commanded you, so that they cannot teach you to do
all the abhorrent things that they do for their gods, causing
19 you to sin against your God, the LORD. When
you lay siege to a town and wage war against it for a long
time to capture it, do not destroy its trees; do not wield
an ax against them. You may eat from them; you must not

---

the saints of early rabbinic times, Ḥoni the Circle-Drawer:

> One day Ḥoni was journeying on the road and saw a man plating a carob tree. He asked him, "How long does it take for a carob tree to bear fruit?" The man replied, "Seventy years." Ḥoni asked, "Are you certain that you will live another seventy years?" The man answered, "I found carob trees in the world. As my forefathers planted them for me, so I too plant these for my children." (Taanit 23a)

Trees are a symbol of the long-term nature of the human enterprise. In the book of Psalms, the wicked grow like grass, the righteous slowly like cedars. Our decisions – economic, political, and military – must be taken on the basis of calculation of distant consequences (the Israelites, for example, are warned against too rapid a conquest "lest the

ט כִּלְבָבוֹ: וְהָיָה כְּכַלֹּת הַשֹּׁטְרִים לְדַבֵּר אֶל־הָעָם וּפָקְדוּ שָׂרֵי
י צְבָאוֹת בְּרֹאשׁ הָעָם: כִּי־תִקְרַב אֶל־עִיר לְהִלָּחֵם טז שביעי
יא עָלֶיהָ וְקָרָאתָ אֵלֶיהָ לְשָׁלוֹם: וְהָיָה אִם־שָׁלוֹם תַּעַנְךָ וּפָתְחָה
לָךְ וְהָיָה כָּל־הָעָם הַנִּמְצָא־בָהּ יִהְיוּ לְךָ לָמַס וַעֲבָדוּךָ:
יב וְאִם־לֹא תַשְׁלִים עִמָּךְ וְעָשְׂתָה עִמְּךָ מִלְחָמָה וְצַרְתָּ עָלֶיהָ:
יג וּנְתָנָהּ יהוה אֱלֹהֶיךָ בְּיָדֶךָ וְהִכִּיתָ אֶת־כָּל־זְכוּרָהּ לְפִי־חָרֶב:
יד רַק הַנָּשִׁים וְהַטַּף וְהַבְּהֵמָה וְכֹל אֲשֶׁר יִהְיֶה בָעִיר כָּל־שְׁלָלָהּ
תָּבֹז לָךְ וְאָכַלְתָּ אֶת־שְׁלַל אֹיְבֶיךָ אֲשֶׁר נָתַן יהוה אֱלֹהֶיךָ
טו לָךְ: כֵּן תַּעֲשֶׂה לְכָל־הֶעָרִים הָרְחֹקֹת מִמְּךָ מְאֹד אֲשֶׁר לֹא־
טז מֵעָרֵי הַגּוֹיִם־הָאֵלֶּה הֵנָּה: רַק מֵעָרֵי הָעַמִּים הָאֵלֶּה אֲשֶׁר
יז יהוה אֱלֹהֶיךָ נֹתֵן לְךָ נַחֲלָה לֹא תְחַיֶּה כָּל־נְשָׁמָה: כִּי־הַחֲרֵם
תַּחֲרִימֵם הַחִתִּי וְהָאֱמֹרִי הַכְּנַעֲנִי וְהַפְּרִזִּי הַחִוִּי וְהַיְבוּסִי
יח כַּאֲשֶׁר צִוְּךָ יהוה אֱלֹהֶיךָ: לְמַעַן אֲשֶׁר לֹא־יְלַמְּדוּ אֶתְכֶם
לַעֲשׂוֹת כְּכֹל תּוֹעֲבֹתָם אֲשֶׁר עָשׂוּ לֵאלֹהֵיהֶם וַחֲטָאתֶם
יט לַיהוה אֱלֹהֵיכֶם: כִּי־תָצוּר אֶל־עִיר יָמִים רַבִּים
לְהִלָּחֵם עָלֶיהָ לְתָפְשָׂהּ לֹא־תַשְׁחִית אֶת־עֵצָהּ לִנְדֹּחַ עָלָיו
גַּרְזֶן כִּי מִמֶּנּוּ תֹאכֵל וְאֹתוֹ לֹא תִכְרֹת כִּי הָאָדָם עֵץ הַשָּׂדֶה

20:19 וְאֹתוֹ לֹא תִכְרֹת *You must not cut them down* – Václav Havel made a fundamental point in *The Art of the Impossible*: "I believe that we have little chance of averting an environmental catastrophe unless we recognize that we are not the masters of Being, but only a part of Being." That is why a religious vision is so important, reminding us that we are not owners of our resources. They belong not to us but to the Eternal and eternity. Hence we may not needlessly destroy. If that applies even in war, how much more so in times of peace. "The LORD owns the earth and all it contains" (Ps. 24:1). We are its guardians, on behalf of its Creator, for the sake of future generations.

20:19 כִּי הָאָדָם עֵץ הַשָּׂדֶה *Are trees of the field human beings* – There is a deep-seated reverence for trees in Judaism, expressed in modern times by the afforestation of Israel and the celebration of Tu BiShvat, the "New Year" for trees. No Jew should be indifferent to the destruction of rainforests.

The Talmud tells the story of one of

cut them down. Are trees of the field human beings that
20 you should besiege them too? Only trees that you know
do not produce food may you cut down for use building
siege works until the town that has made war against you
falls.
21 1 If a person is found lying slain in a field on the land that
the LORD your God is giving you to possess, and it is not
2 known who killed him, your elders and judges must go
out and measure the distances from the slain person to
3 each of the surrounding towns. The elders of the town
nearest the body shall take a female calf that has never
4 been worked or drawn a load with a yoke, and lead it to
a valley with a flowing stream that has not been plowed
or planted, and there in the valley the elders of that town
5 shall break the calf's neck. The priests, sons of Levi,
shall step forward, for it is them the LORD your God has
chosen to minister to Him, to give blessing in the LORD's
6 name, and to decide all cases of dispute and assault. Then
all the elders of the town nearest the slain person shall
wash their hands over the calf whose neck was broken in
7 the valley and declare: 'Our hands did not shed this blood MAFTIR

> Whoever can forbid his household [to commit a sin] but does not, he is seized for [the sins of] his household; [if he can forbid] his fellow citizens, he is seized for [the sins of] his fellow citizens; if the whole world, he is seized for [the sins of] the whole world. (Shabbat 54b)

The phrase "is seized" may mean that the bystander is morally guilty. He can be called to account. He may be punished by "the heavenly court" in this world or the next. It does not mean that he can be summoned to an earthly court and sentenced for criminal negligence. We might hold a bystander guilty, but not in the same degree as the perpetrator.

Nonetheless, we have to think long and hard before we can say, "Our hands did not shed this blood." Morality cannot be outsourced. It is about taking responsibility, not handing it away or sloughing it off. It needs for us to think about the "we" and not just the "I." When we assume responsibility for what happens around us, we start to change the moral climate in which we live, move, and have our being. Morality begins with us.

כ לָבֹא מִפָּנֶיךָ בַּמָּצוֹר׃ רַק עֵץ אֲשֶׁר־תֵּדַע כִּי־לֹא־עֵץ מַאֲכָל
הוּא אֹתוֹ תַשְׁחִית וְכָרָתָּ וּבָנִיתָ מָצוֹר עַל־הָעִיר אֲשֶׁר־הִוא
עֹשָׂה עִמְּךָ מִלְחָמָה עַד רִדְתָּהּ׃
כא א כִּי־יִמָּצֵא חָלָל בָּאֲדָמָה אֲשֶׁר יהוה אֱלֹהֶיךָ נֹתֵן לְךָ לְרִשְׁתָּהּ
ב נֹפֵל בַּשָּׂדֶה לֹא נוֹדַע מִי הִכָּהוּ׃ וְיָצְאוּ זְקֵנֶיךָ וְשֹׁפְטֶיךָ וּמָדְדוּ
ג אֶל־הֶעָרִים אֲשֶׁר סְבִיבֹת הֶחָלָל׃ וְהָיָה הָעִיר הַקְּרֹבָה
אֶל־הֶחָלָל וְלָקְחוּ זִקְנֵי הָעִיר הַהִוא עֶגְלַת בָּקָר אֲשֶׁר לֹא־
ד עֻבַּד בָּהּ אֲשֶׁר לֹא־מָשְׁכָה בְּעֹל׃ וְהוֹרִדוּ זִקְנֵי הָעִיר הַהִוא
אֶת־הָעֶגְלָה אֶל־נַחַל אֵיתָן אֲשֶׁר לֹא־יֵעָבֵד בּוֹ וְלֹא יִזָּרֵעַ
ה וְעָרְפוּ־שָׁם אֶת־הָעֶגְלָה בַּנָּחַל׃ וְנִגְּשׁוּ הַכֹּהֲנִים בְּנֵי לֵוִי כִּי בָם
בָּחַר יהוה אֱלֹהֶיךָ לְשָׁרְתוֹ וּלְבָרֵךְ בְּשֵׁם יהוה וְעַל־פִּיהֶם
ו יִהְיֶה כָּל־רִיב וְכָל־נָגַע׃ וְכֹל זִקְנֵי הָעִיר הַהִוא הַקְּרֹבִים
אֶל־הֶחָלָל יִרְחֲצוּ אֶת־יְדֵיהֶם עַל־הָעֶגְלָה הָעֲרוּפָה בַנָּחַל׃
ז וְעָנוּ וְאָמְרוּ יָדֵינוּ לֹא שפכה אֶת־הַדָּם הַזֶּה וְעֵינֵינוּ לֹא רָאוּ׃ שָׁפְכוּ מפטיר

---

land become desolate and the wild animals too numerous for you" [Ex. 23:29]). The world we inherit is due to the efforts of those who came before us. The world we leave our children is dependent on what we do. Conservation is part of what the philosopher Edmund Burke called the "partnership… between those who are living, those who are dead, and those who are to be born."

21:7 יָדֵינוּ לֹא שָׁפְכוּ אֶת־הַדָּם הַזֶּה *Our hands did not shed this blood* – If someone is found murdered outside a town, the elders of the nearest town have to undergo a penitential ritual and say a prayer for absolution that contains the words "Our hands did not shed this blood."

It is odd because no one was accusing them. The Talmud (Sota 46b) elaborates on the nature of the moral concern here. What the elders are really saying is: Did we create an environment in which such a crime could happen? Did we give the victim shelter? Did we protect them? Did we do all we could to make sure the roads were safe at night? We weren't legally responsible for their death, but were we in some larger sense morally responsible? Can we really say, "Our hands did not shed this blood"?

The Talmud discusses the accountability of those in the sphere of influence of a crime:

> Rav and R. Ḥanina, R. Yoḥanan and R. Ḥabiba taught [the following]:

8 and our eyes did not witness it. Absolve Your people
Israel, whom You redeemed, LORD, and do not leave the
guilt of innocent blood among Your people Israel.' So
9 shall atonement be made for the bloodshed, and so will
you purge the guilt of innocent blood from yourselves, by
doing what is right in the LORD's eyes.

The haftara for Parashat Shofetim is on page 1608.

ח כַּפֵּר֙ לְעַמְּךָ֤ יִשְׂרָאֵל֙ אֲשֶׁר־פָּדִ֔יתָ יְהֹוָ֔ה וְאַל־תִּתֵּן֙ דָּ֣ם נָקִ֔י
ט בְּקֶ֖רֶב עַמְּךָ֣ יִשְׂרָאֵ֑ל וְנִכַּפֵּ֥ר לָהֶ֖ם הַדָּֽם׃ וְאַתָּ֗ה תְּבַעֵ֛ר הַדָּ֥ם
הַנָּקִ֖י מִקִּרְבֶּ֑ךָ כִּֽי־תַעֲשֶׂ֥ה הַיָּשָׁ֖ר בְּעֵינֵ֥י יְהֹוָֽה׃

The הפטרה *for* פרשת שפטים *is on page 1609.*

Parashat Ki Tetzeh

21 10 When you wage war against your enemies, and the Lord
your God gives them into your hand and you take captives,
11 if you see a beautiful woman among the captives, and you
12 desire her and wish to marry her, bring her to your house.
13 Have her shave her head, pare her nails, and remove her
captive's garb. She shall sit in your house mourning for
her father and mother for a full month. Only after that
may you go in to her and be her husband, and she shall

There is a remarkable midrash about the creation of the world. It says that when God came to create man, the angel of peace objected because "man is full of strife." God ignored the angel and created mankind (Bereshit Rabba 8:5). The midrash raises the question that has hovered over human existence since the beginning of time: Why did God create a being capable of destroying all else He had made? Humanity has consistently disrupted the harmony of the world and engaged in violence and war. What answer did God give to the angel of peace? The answer implicit in the midrash is that God had faith that humanity would eventually learn that even a difficult peace is better than an easy war.

There are two words for "strength" in Hebrew: *koaḥ* and *gevura*. But they mean quite different things. *Koaḥ* means the strength to overcome your enemies. *Gevura* means the strength to overcome yourself. Defining *gevura*, the Rabbis said, "Who is strong? One who is capable of self-restraint" (Avot 4:1). *Koaḥ* is the strength to wage war. *Gevura* is the strength to make peace. Israel has needed both to survive.

21:11 בַּשִּׁבְיָה אֵשֶׁת יְפַת־תֹּאַר *A beautiful woman among the captives* – The *parasha*'s opening three laws – a captive woman taken in the course of war, the law about the rights of the firstborn, and the "wayward and rebellious son" (Deut. 21:18) – are all about dysfunction within the family. The Sages said that they were given in this order to hint that someone who takes a captive woman will suffer from strife at home, and the result will be a delinquent son (Sanhedrin 107a). In Judaism, marriage is seen as the foundation of society. Disorder there leads to disorder elsewhere. The Torah did not endorse the taking of the captive woman but rather "spoke only in response to the evil inclination" (Kiddushin 21b), warning by the juxtaposition to the rebellious son that no good would come of it.

פרשת כי תצא

כא י כִּי־תֵצֵא לַמִּלְחָמָה עַל־אֹיְבֶיךָ וּנְתָנוֹ יְהוָה אֱלֹהֶיךָ בְּיָדֶךָ
יא וְשָׁבִיתָ שִׁבְיוֹ׃ וְרָאִיתָ בַּשִּׁבְיָה אֵשֶׁת יְפַת־תֹּאַר וְחָשַׁקְתָּ
יב בָהּ וְלָקַחְתָּ לְךָ לְאִשָּׁה׃ וַהֲבֵאתָהּ אֶל־תּוֹךְ בֵּיתֶךָ וְגִלְּחָה
יג אֶת־רֹאשָׁהּ וְעָשְׂתָה אֶת־צִפָּרְנֶיהָ׃ וְהֵסִירָה אֶת־שִׂמְלַת
שִׁבְיָהּ מֵעָלֶיהָ וְיָשְׁבָה בְּבֵיתֶךָ וּבָכְתָה אֶת־אָבִיהָ וְאֶת־

KI TETZEH

Parashat Ki Tetzeh is about relationships: between men and women, parents and children, employers and employees, lenders and borrowers, and humans and animals. In this *parasha*, Moshe reaches the heart of the detailed provisions of the covenant. The *parasha* contains no fewer than seventy-four commands, more than any other in the Torah. Among them are laws about family dysfunction, moral and legal obligations toward neighbors and fellow citizens, sexual misdemeanors, moral behavior in relation to financial matters, and other rules of social responsibility. The *parasha* ends with the command to be eternally vigilant about Amalek, the Torah's paradigm case of hatred and cruelty.

21:10 כִּי־תֵצֵא לַמִּלְחָמָה *When you wage war* – Rambam summarized the Talmud's attitude to war in these words:

> No war, either permitted or obligatory [such as a war of self-defense] may be initiated without first offering terms of peace.… Yehoshua sent three messages before entering the land: the first, "Whoever wishes to flee, let him flee"; the second, "Whoever wishes to make peace, let him make peace"; the third, "Whoever wishes to make war, let him make war." (*Hilkhot Melakhim UMilḥemoteihem* 6:1, 5)

War, for Rambam, is *never* mandated except when the effort to make peace has been tried, and has failed. Even the command at the end of the *parasha* to "blot out the memory of Amalek" (Deut. 25:19), applied, according to Rambam, only if the Amalekites refused to make peace and accept the seven Noahide laws. Even here peace was preferable (*Hilkhot Melakhim UMilḥemoteihem* 6:4).

The Torah teaches a combination of idealism and realism in the political arena. We are neither pacifists nor militarists. We pray for peace, but we are prepared to go to war. We say, "How good and pleasant it is when brothers dwell together" (Ps. 133:1). But we also know, from the very beginning of Torah – from Kayin and Hevel – that brothers are capable of killing one another.

14 be your wife. But if you no longer desire her, you must
let her go free. You may not sell her for money or treat
15 her as a slave, since you have dishonored her. If
a man has two wives, and loves one but not the other,
and if both the loved and the unloved bear him sons, but

Torah takes the past as a guide to the future – often positively but sometimes negatively. Genesis tells us that Yaakov's favoritism toward Raḥel's firstborn, Yosef, over Leah's firstborn, Reuven, was a cause of lingering strife within the family. According to Ibn Ezra, the resentment felt by the descendants of Reuven endured for generations, which is why Datan and Aviram, both Reubenites, became key figures in the Koraḥ rebellion (Ibn Ezra on Num. 16:1).

Yaakov acted out of overwhelming love for Raḥel, and Yosef, her elder son. Love is central to Judaism – love between husband and wife, parent and child, love for God, neighbor, and stranger. But love is not enough. Love unites but it also divides. It leaves the less loved feeling neglected, "hated" (see note on Gen. 29:30). It can leave in its wake strife, envy, and a vortex of violence and revenge. There must also be justice, fairness, and the impartial application of the law.

That is what the Torah is telling us when it uses the verbal association *ahuva/senua*, "loved" and "unloved/hated," in precisely the way that it describes Raḥel and Leah – to link the law in this *parasha* with the story of Yaakov and his sons. It is teaching us that law is rooted in the experience of history. Law is itself a *tikkun*, a way of putting right what went wrong in the past. We must learn to love, but we must also know the limits of love, and the importance of justice-as-fairness in families as in society.

21:15 הָאַחַת אֲהוּבָה וְהָאַחַת שְׂנוּאָה *Loves one but not the other* – Although the Torah does not outlaw bigamy, it never presents it positively. Monogamy is seen as both the norm (Gen. 2:24) and the ideal (see, for instance, Prov. 31), and although the law protects the rights of the "unloved," marriage is meant to be characterized by love.

Rabbi Yosef Kolon (Maharik, 1420–80), discussing whether a child must obey his parents in his choice of marriage partner, refers to a responsum of Rabbeinu Asher in which the author rules that a son is not bound to obey his father if he tells him not to speak to X, with whom the father is in dispute. The command to love your neighbor overrides the command to obey your parents. Since the love of husband and wife is a supreme example of love-of-neighbor, it too takes priority over a parent's wishes (*Responsa Maharik* 166:3).

Rabbi Eliyahu Capsali (*Me'a She'arim, Shaar* 62) gave the following ruling in a case where a father forbade his son to marry the woman whom "his soul desired":

אִמָּהּ יֶרַח יָמִים וְאַחַר כֵּן תָּבוֹא אֵלֶיהָ וּבְעַלְתָּהּ וְהָיְתָה
יד לְךָ לְאִשָּׁה׃ וְהָיָה אִם־לֹא חָפַצְתָּ בָּהּ וְשִׁלַּחְתָּהּ לְנַפְשָׁהּ
וּמָכֹר לֹא־תִמְכְּרֶנָּה בַּכָּסֶף לֹא־תִתְעַמֵּר בָּהּ תַּחַת אֲשֶׁר
טו עִנִּיתָהּ׃ כִּי־תִהְיֶיןָ לְאִישׁ שְׁתֵּי נָשִׁים הָאַחַת
אֲהוּבָה וְהָאַחַת שְׂנוּאָה וְיָלְדוּ־לוֹ בָנִים הָאֲהוּבָה וְהַשְּׂנוּאָה

LAW AND LOVE

In biblical Israel the firstborn was entitled to a double share in his father's inheritance. This passage tells us that the father cannot choose to transfer this privilege from one son to another by favoring the son of the wife he loves most if the firstborn came from another wife. The law seems to be in sharp conflict with the story of Yaakov and his two wives, Leah and Raḥel. Yaakov *did* transfer the right of the firstborn from Reuven, his actual firstborn, son of the less-loved Leah, to Yosef, the firstborn of his beloved Raḥel. Indeed, the Torah itself makes the verbal linkage, using the same pair of opposites, *ahuva/senua*, "loved" and "unloved/hated" both in our verse, and also to describe Raḥel and Leah (Gen. 29:30–31). Yaakov's conduct was the opposite of what is legislated here. How are we to resolve this? Abrabanel's explanation (see his commentary on these verses in Deuteronomy) is that Yaakov transferred the double portion from Reuven to Yosef because God told him to do so. The law in our *parasha* is stated to show that the case of Yosef was an exception, not a precedent. Sforno (on Deut. 21:16) suggests that the prohibition in Deuteronomy applies only when the transfer of the firstborn's rights happens because the father favors one wife over another. It does not apply when the firstborn has been guilty of a sin that forfeits his legal privilege, which is what happened with Reuven. This is stated explicitly in the book of Chronicles, which says that "Reuven… was Yisrael's firstborn, but when he defiled his father's bed, his birthright was granted to the sons of Yosef" (I Chr. 5:1).

There may be a different explanation. The Torah is a book about both law and history. Law answers the question "What may we do or not do?" History is an answer to the question "What happened?" There is no obvious relationship between these two.

In Judaism they are often connected. Especially in *mishpat*, civil law, there is frequently a link between law and history. Much of biblical law, for example, emerges directly from the Israelites' experience of slavery in Egypt, as if to say: This is what our ancestors suffered in Egypt; therefore, do not do likewise. Do not oppress your workers. Do not turn an Israelite into a lifelong slave. And so on.

Such biblical laws represent *truth learned through experience*, justice as it takes shape through history. The

16 the firstborn is the son of the one unloved, then on the
day he bequeaths his possessions to his sons, he may not
give the rights of the firstborn to the son of the loved in
preference to the son of the unloved, the true firstborn.
17 He must acknowledge the son of his unloved wife as
the firstborn, giving him a double portion of all that he
has. He is the first fruit of his manhood; the right of the
18 firstborn belongs to him. If a man has a wayward
and rebellious son who does not listen to his father and
mother and, though they discipline him, still will not

---

logic? How was it to be applied? Was it, in fact, ever applied?

Because of the apparent harshness of the law, the whole tendency of rabbinic interpretation was so restrictive as to make it difficult if not impossible for such a case to arise (see the discussion on the "town led astray," Deut. 13:17). The child must be within three months of attaining maturity (younger than that, he was still a minor; older, he was not still a child). He must have stolen money from his parents, used it to buy a specific measure of meat and Italian wine, eaten and drunk it in one go, in a place other than his parents' house, and so on (Sanhedrin 68b–71a). Some Sages suggested conditions that in practice would never be fulfilled. For example, R. Yehuda held that "if his mother is not like his father in voice, appearance, and stature, he does not become a rebellious son" (Sanhedrin 71a). R. Shimon b. Yoḥai firmly declared: There never was and never will be a "wayward and rebellious son" (Sanhedrin 71a).

Nevertheless, there were those who held that the law was intended to be, and actually was, applied. What, according to them, was the logic of the law? R. Yosei HaGelili said: "The Torah foresaw the ultimate destiny of the wayward and rebellious son. Having dissipated his father's wealth, he would seek to satisfy his wants and be unable to do so. He would then go to a crossroad as a highwayman. Therefore the Torah ordained: Let him die innocent rather than die guilty – for the death of the wicked benefits both themselves and the world" (Sanhedrin 71b).

On this view, the law of the wayward and rebellious son is a form of preemptive punishment for what he is likely to do in the future. The equivalent nowadays would be preventive detention, that is to say, putting someone in prison because he or she is judged to be a danger to society.

One of the most significant post-Enlightenment arguments about the nature of ethics was between Kantians and Benthamites. For Kant, ethics was a matter of duty, and justice, of retribution. If a wrong had been done, it had to be set right by wrong being done to the

טז וְהָיָה הַבֵּן הַבְּכֹר לַשְּׂנִיאָה׃ וְהָיָה בְּיוֹם הַנְחִילוֹ אֶת־בָּנָיו אֵת
אֲשֶׁר־יִהְיֶה לוֹ לֹא יוּכַל לְבַכֵּר אֶת־בֶּן־הָאֲהוּבָה עַל־פְּנֵי
יז בֶן־הַשְּׂנוּאָה הַבְּכֹר׃ כִּי אֶת־הַבְּכֹר בֶּן־הַשְּׂנוּאָה יַכִּיר לָתֶת
לוֹ פִּי שְׁנַיִם בְּכֹל אֲשֶׁר־יִמָּצֵא לוֹ כִּי־הוּא רֵאשִׁית אֹנוֹ לוֹ
יח מִשְׁפַּט הַבְּכֹרָה׃ כִּי־יִהְיֶה לְאִישׁ בֵּן סוֹרֵר
וּמוֹרֶה אֵינֶנּוּ שֹׁמֵעַ בְּקוֹל אָבִיו וּבְקוֹל אִמּוֹ וְיִסְּרוּ אֹתוֹ וְלֹא

Though the command of filial honor and reverence is inexpressibly great… nonetheless it appears in my humble opinion that if the girl about whom you ask is a proper wife for the aforementioned Reuven…then the command of filial honor and reverence is irrelevant, and the son is not to abandon her so as to fulfill his father's command.

For it is nearly certain that this father virtually commands his son to violate the Torah…for we see in the Talmud that a man ought not to marry a woman who does not please him. So that when the father commands his son not to marry this woman, it is as though he commands him to violate the Torah; and it is well known that the son is not to obey his father in such cases.…

Now, if we were to decide that the son is obliged to obey his parents and marry, though his heart is not in the match, we would cause the growth of hatred and strife in the home, which is not the way of our holy Torah – most certainly in this case, where he loves another. Indeed, we can cite in this situation: "Great waters cannot quench love, nor torrents sweep it by" (Song. 8:7).

There is great wisdom in this approach. The Jewish family is based on mutual respect – the children's respect for those who have brought them into the world, and the parents' respect for the right of adult children to make their choices free of excessive parental interference. In this respect, as in so many others, Jewish law is a reflex of Jewish theology. For what we find in the Torah is a profound sense of empowerment of human beings by God. "Walk before Me," says God to Avraham (Gen. 17:1). The prophets, meanwhile, saw marriage as the single most compelling metaphor for the relationship between God and us – because it involves commitment, a mutual pledge of openness and trust, a promise that neither will walk away in difficult times, a covenant of loyalty and love.

THE WAYWARD AND REBELLIOUS SON

The law of the wayward and rebellious son is one that generated considerable debate among the Sages. What was its

19 listen, his father and his mother shall take hold of him and
20 bring him out to the elders at the town gate. They shall
say to the town elders, 'This son of ours is wayward and
rebellious. He does not listen to us. He is a glutton and a
21 drunkard.' Then all the men of the town shall stone him to
death. Thus you shall purge the evil from your midst, and
22 all Israel will hear, and be afraid. When someone SHENI
is convicted of a capital crime and is executed and you
23 hang him from a post, do not let his corpse remain all night
upon that post. You must bury him that same day, because
a man left hanging is a slur upon God, and you must not
defile the land that the LORD your God is giving you as
22 1 your possession. If you see your kinsman's ox or
sheep straying away, do not ignore it; you must return it to
2 its owner. If the owner does not live nearby or you do not
know who the owner is, you must bring it home with you
and keep it until the owner claims it; then you must return
3 it. You must do the same with his donkey, the same with
his garment, the same with anything your kinsman loses
4 and you find. You cannot ignore it. You shall not
see your kinsman's donkey or ox fallen on the road and
5 ignore it. Help him to lift it. Men's clothing shall

---

incidence of serious crimes. R. Shimon holds that it does not. One cannot preempt a crime in this way, even if lives will be lost in the future as a result. In other words, though the law of the "wayward and rebellious son" represents divine justice, it always encounters the existential reality of divine mercy. We are only judged, like the first wayward and rebellious son, Yishmael, "where we are" now (see Gen. 21:17 and commentary there). And on that basis R. Shimon b. Yoḥai rests his faith that the law never was or will be put into effect.

22:4 הָקֵם תָּקִים עִמּוֹ *Help him to lift it* – The Sages debated the logic of this command. Some held that it is motivated by concern for the welfare of the animal involved, the ox or the donkey, and that accordingly *tzaar baalei ḥayyim*, prevention of suffering to animals, is a biblical command (Bava Metzia 31a). Others, notably Rambam, held that it had to do with the welfare of the animal's owner, who might be so distressed that he came to stay with the animal at a risk to his own safety – the key word here being "on the road." (*Hilkhot Rotze'aḥ*

יט ישמע אליהם: ותפשו בו אביו ואמו והוציאו אתו אל־
כ זקני עירו ואל־שער מקמו: ואמרו אל־זקני עירו בננו
כא זה סורר ומרה איננו שמע בקלנו זולל וסבא: ורגמהו
כל־אנשי עירו באבנים ומת ובערת הרע מקרבך וכל־
כב ישראל ישמעו ויראו: וכי־יהיה באיש חטא שני
כג משפט־מות והומת ותלית אתו על־עץ: לא־תלין נבלתו
על־העץ כי־קבור תקברנו ביום ההוא כי־קללת אלהים
תלוי ולא תטמא את־אדמתך אשר יהוה אלהיך נתן לך
א נחלה: לא־תראה את־שור אחיך או את־שיו כב
ב נדחים והתעלמת מהם השב תשיבם לאחיך: ואם־לא
קרוב אחיך אליך ולא ידעתו ואספתו אל־תוך ביתך והיה
ג עמך עד דרש אחיך אתו והשבתו לו: וכן תעשה לחמרו
וכן תעשה לשמלתו וכן תעשה לכל־אבדת אחיך אשר־
ד תאבד ממנו ומצאתה לא תוכל להתעלם: לא־
תראה את־חמור אחיך או שורו נפלים בדרך והתעלמת
ה מהם הקם תקים עמו: לא־יהיה כלי־גבר

wrongdoer. Bentham, by contrast, developed the theory known as utilitarianism. An act is right if it produces the best consequences for society as a whole. On this view, justice looks less to the past than to the future. If it deters wrongdoing and leads to less crime, it is justified.

According to Bentham, a punishment might be justified even if it were out of proportion to the crime, so long as it deterred others (an "exemplary punishment"). A Kantian would disagree. If it is disproportionate to the crime it is unjust, and no utilitarian benefits can justify injustice. Conversely, Kant considered the hypothetical case of a man who had committed murder on a desert island where the remaining inhabitants were about to leave. Should they sentence him to death and carry out the punishment? There would be no one else on the island to murder. Nonetheless, said Kant, the sentence should be carried out, for if it were not, it would be a failure of justice.

Some such disagreement seems to lie between R. Shimon and R. Yosei. R. Yosei believed that the Torah sometimes prescribes punishment-as-prevention in order to protect society and reduce the

not be seen on a woman, nor shall a man wear women's
dress. Whoever does such things is abhorrent to the
Lord your God.
6 If you come across a bird's nest containing fledglings or
eggs by the roadside, in a tree, or on the ground, and the
mother is sitting on the fledglings or the eggs, do not take
7 the mother with the young. Let the mother go; only then
may you take the young, so that it may be well for you and

---

1. The law of the mother bird is a divine decree with no obvious reason. "If the reason for sending the mother bird away were divine compassion toward animals, then, in consistency, God should have forbidden killing animals for food. The law therefore should be understood as a decree without an obvious rationale (*gezerat hakatuv*)" (*Hilkhot Tefilla UVirkat Kohanim* 9:7).

2. It is intended to spare the mother bird emotional pain. "It is also prohibited to kill an animal with its young on the same day, in order that people should be restrained and prevented from killing the two together in such a manner that the young is killed in the sight of the mother, for the pain of the animals under such circumstances is very great.... The same reason applies to the law which enjoins that we should let the mother bird fly away when we take the young" (*Guide for the Perplexed* III:48).

3. It is intended to have an effect on us, not the animal. The reason we must not cause animals pain or distress is not because the Torah is concerned about animals but because it is concerned about humans; we should not be cruel (*Guide for the Perplexed* III:17).

We can harmonize these explanations by noting that they answer different questions. The first view explains why we have the laws we have. The Torah forbids certain acts that are cruel to animals but not others. Why these and not those? Because that is the law. Laws will always seem arbitrary. But we observe the law because it is the law, even though, under certain circumstances, we may reason that we know better, or that it does not apply. The second view explains the immediate logic of the law. It exists to prevent needless suffering to animals, because they too feel physical pain and sometimes emotional distress. The third view sets the law in a larger perspective. Cruelty to animals is wrong, not because animals have rights but because we have duties. The duty not to be cruel is intended to promote virtue, and the primary context of virtue is the relationship between human beings. But virtues are indivisible. Those who are cruel to animals often become cruel to people. Hence we have a duty not to cause needless pain to animals because of its effect on us.

This is a nuanced approach. Animals are part of God's creation. They

עַל־אִשָּׁה וְלֹא־יִלְבַּשׁ גֶּבֶר שִׂמְלַת אִשָּׁה כִּי תוֹעֲבַת יהוָה
אֱלֹהֶיךָ כׇּל־עֹשֵׂה אֵלֶּה׃
ו כִּי יִקָּרֵא קַן־צִפּוֹר ׀ לְפָנֶיךָ בַּדֶּרֶךְ בְּכׇל־עֵץ ׀ אוֹ עַל־הָאָרֶץ יז
אֶפְרֹחִים אוֹ בֵיצִים וְהָאֵם רֹבֶצֶת עַל־הָאֶפְרֹחִים אוֹ עַל־
ז הַבֵּיצִים לֹא־תִקַּח הָאֵם עַל־הַבָּנִים׃ שַׁלֵּחַ תְּשַׁלַּח אֶת־
הָאֵם וְאֶת־הַבָּנִים תִּקַּח־לָךְ לְמַעַן יִיטַב לָךְ וְהַאֲרַכְתָּ

UShmirat HaNefesh 13:2, 14). The roadside in ancient times was a place of danger.

The Sages also discussed the relationship between this command and the similar but different one in Exodus (23:5): "If you see the donkey of someone who hates you, fallen under its load, resist the impulse to leave it there. Help him to release it." They said that, all other things being equal, if there is a choice between helping an enemy and helping a friend, helping an enemy takes precedence, since it may "overcome the inclination" (Bava Metzia 32b), that is, it may help end the animosity and turn an enemy into a friend.

In general, Rambam states, one should do for someone you find in distress what you would do for yourself in a similar situation. Better still, one should put aside all considerations of honor and go "beyond the limit of the law." Even a prince, he says, should ideally help the lowliest commoner, even if the circumstances do not accord with the dignity of his office or his personal standing (*Hilkhot Rotze'aḥ UShmirat HaNefesh* 13:4).

All of this is part of what sociologists nowadays call social capital. This is the level of trust within a society – the knowledge that you are surrounded by people who have your welfare at heart. They will return your lost property (see the lines immediately prior to the fallen donkey, Deut. 22:1–3), raise the alarm if someone is breaking into your house or car, keep an eye on the safety of your children. High trust levels make society a place where people are good neighbors and are willing to help even a stranger in distress. Its citizens care about the welfare of others. When they see someone in need of help, they do not "see … and ignore"; they do not walk on by.

LAWS OF A BIRD'S NEST

As mentioned in the commentary at the beginning of the *parasha*, Parashat Ki Tetzeh is about relationships: within families, in the marketplace, between nations. Strikingly, though, it is also about relationships between humans and animals.

Among several pieces of animal legislation in this *parasha*, the law of "letting the mother go" is perhaps the most discussed. Rambam, in his various writings, seems to embrace three different reasons for the command:

8 you may live long. When you build a new house, SHELISHI
erect a parapet for your roof. Otherwise you may bring
9 bloodguilt on your house should anyone fall from it. Do
not sow your vineyard with a second kind of seed, or the
whole yield – both the crop you have sown and the yield
10 of the vineyard – will have to be forfeited. Do
11 not plow with an ox and a donkey yoked together. Do
not wear clothes made of wool and linen woven
12 together. Make tassels on the four corners of the
13 garment with which you cover yourself. If a man
takes a wife and, after sleeping with her, he dislikes her,
14 and he makes up charges against her, sullying her name,
saying, 'I married this woman, but when I lay with her, I
15 did not find her to be a virgin,' the girl's father and mother
shall produce the evidence of the girl's virginity before
16 the town elders at the gate. The girl's father shall say to the

---

continuity of species. Though the Torah permits us to use some (but not all) animals for food, we must not cull them to extinction. (Later authorities were particularly strong in their condemnation of hunting: killing animals *not* for the sake of food; see *Responsa Shemesh Tzedaka* 57. This was wanton and destructive cruelty and had no place in Jewish life.)

No one attached more far-reaching significance to biblical decrees about animals and nature than Rabbi Samson Raphael Hirsch. For him, *ḥukkim* were laws which embodied the principle that "the same regard which you show to man you must also demonstrate to every lower creature, to the earth which bears and sustains all, and to the world of plants and animals." The reason these commandments are difficult to understand is that we approach them from the perspective of man and his needs. If we could put ourselves in the place of animals and plant life, we would find it as easy to comprehend the "decrees" as to understand the Torah's laws of social justice. "They ask you to regard all living things as God's property. Destroy none; abuse none; waste nothing; employ all things wisely.... Look upon all creatures as servants in the household of creation."

Rabbi Hirsch was what today would be called a "deep" ecologist. He believed that there is such a thing as "justice" toward nature and that the world cannot be subordinated to the interests of man. It was an extreme view in Jewish thought, but one shared by the great mystic Rabbi Avraham Kook, who held that animals have rights and that one should not needlessly even pick a flower. "All of creation," he said, "sings a song."

ח יָמִים׃ כִּי תִבְנֶה בַּיִת חָדָשׁ וְעָשִׂיתָ מַעֲקֶה שלישי
ט לְגַגֶּךָ וְלֹא־תָשִׂים דָּמִים בְּבֵיתֶךָ כִּי־יִפֹּל הַנֹּפֵל מִמֶּנּוּ׃ לֹא־
תִזְרַע כַּרְמְךָ כִּלְאָיִם פֶּן־תִּקְדַּשׁ הַמְלֵאָה הַזֶּרַע אֲשֶׁר תִּזְרָע
י וּתְבוּאַת הַכָּרֶם׃ לֹא־תַחֲרֹשׁ
יא בְּשׁוֹר־וּבַחֲמֹר יַחְדָּו׃ לֹא תִלְבַּשׁ שַׁעַטְנֵז צֶמֶר וּפִשְׁתִּים
יב יַחְדָּו׃ גְּדִלִים תַּעֲשֶׂה־לָּךְ עַל־אַרְבַּע כַּנְפוֹת
יג כְּסוּתְךָ אֲשֶׁר תְּכַסֶּה־בָּהּ׃ כִּי־יִקַּח אִישׁ אִשָּׁה
יד וּבָא אֵלֶיהָ וּשְׂנֵאָהּ׃ וְשָׂם לָהּ עֲלִילֹת דְּבָרִים וְהוֹצִא עָלֶיהָ
שֵׁם רָע וְאָמַר אֶת־הָאִשָּׁה הַזֹּאת לָקַחְתִּי וָאֶקְרַב אֵלֶיהָ
טו וְלֹא־מָצָאתִי לָהּ בְּתוּלִים׃ וְלָקַח אֲבִי הַנַּעֲרָ וְאִמָּהּ וְהוֹצִיאוּ
טז אֶת־בְּתוּלֵי הַנַּעֲרָ אֶל־זִקְנֵי הָעִיר הַשָּׁעְרָה׃ וְאָמַר אֲבִי הַנַּעֲרָ

have their own integrity in the scheme of things. This would not have been news to the heroes of the Bible. Avraham, Moshe, and David were all shepherds who lived their formative years caring for animals. That was their first tutorial in leadership. David knew that this was one way of understanding God Himself ("The Lord is my shepherd" [Ps. 23:1]).

Genesis 1 gives us the mandate to "subdue" and "rule" creation, including animals, but Genesis 2 gives us the responsibility to "work" and "safeguard." Animals may not have rights but they have feelings, and we have duties toward them. We must respect them if we are to honor our role as God's partners in creation.

22:9 כִּלְאָיִם *A second kind of seed* – The Torah groups together three prohibitions: against crossbreeding livestock, planting a field with mixed seeds, and wearing a garment of mixed wool and linen. It calls these rules *ḥukkim* or "decrees." Ramban and later Rabbi Samson Raphael Hirsch gave this word a novel interpretation.

They understood *ḥukkim* to mean laws which respected the integrity of nature (see Num. 19, "The Decree of the Law"). To mix different species, argued Ramban (on Lev. 19:19), was an affront to the Creator and an assault on the creation. Each species has its own internal laws of development and reproduction, and these must not be tampered with. "One who combines two different species thereby changes and defies the work of creation, as if he believes that the Holy One, blessed be He, has not completely perfected the world and now he wishes to improve it by adding new kinds of creatures." Ramban saw the law against taking the mother bird with its fledglings (vv. 6–7) as motivated by the same concern. Acts like these threaten the

elders: 'I gave my daughter in marriage to this man but he
17 dislikes her. Now he has made up charges against her,
saying, "I did not find your daughter to be a virgin." But
here is the evidence of my daughter's virginity.' They shall
18 spread out the cloth before the town elders. And then the
19 town elders shall take the man and flog him. They shall
fine him one hundred shekel of silver, and give it to the
girl's father, because he has sullied the name of an Israelite
virgin. She shall remain his wife; he does not have the
20 choice to divorce her as long as he lives. If,
however, the charge is true, no evidence being found that
21 the girl was a virgin, then the girl shall be brought to the
entrance of her father's house and the men of her town
shall stone her to death, for she committed an outrage in
Israel by acting immorally while in her father's house. You
22 shall purge the evil from your midst. If a man is
caught lying with the wife of another, both shall die, the
man and the woman with whom he lay. You shall purge
23 the evil from Israel. If a virgin is betrothed to be
married, and a man encounters her within a town and lies
24 with her, you shall bring them both to the town gate and
stone them to death, the girl because she did not cry for
help in the town, and the man because he violated the
wife of his fellow. You shall purge the evil from your
25 midst. But if the man encounters the betrothed
woman in the open country, forces her and lies with her,
26 only the man who did this shall die. You shall do nothing
to the girl; she did not commit the capital offense. Just as
one man at times attacks and murders his fellow man, so
27 too here; he came upon her in open country. The
betrothed woman may have cried out for help, but no one
28 was there to rescue her. If a man encounters a
virgin who is not betrothed and rapes her, and they are
29 caught in the act, the man who lay with her shall pay the
girl's father fifty shekel of silver, and she shall become his
wife. Because he violated her he does not have the choice
23 1 to divorce her as long as he lives. A man cannot

אֶל־הַזְּקֵנִים אֶת־בִּתִּי נָתַתִּי לָאִישׁ הַזֶּה לְאִשָּׁה וַיִּשְׂנָאֶהָ׃
יז וְהִנֵּה־הוּא שָׂם עֲלִילֹת דְּבָרִים לֵאמֹר לֹא־מָצָאתִי לְבִתְּךָ
בְּתוּלִים וְאֵלֶּה בְּתוּלֵי בִתִּי וּפָרְשׂוּ הַשִּׂמְלָה לִפְנֵי זִקְנֵי הָעִיר׃
יח יט וְלָקְחוּ זִקְנֵי הָעִיר־הַהִוא אֶת־הָאִישׁ וְיִסְּרוּ אֹתוֹ׃ וְעָנְשׁוּ
אֹתוֹ מֵאָה כֶסֶף וְנָתְנוּ לַאֲבִי הַנַּעֲרָה כִּי הוֹצִיא שֵׁם רָע עַל
בְּתוּלַת יִשְׂרָאֵל וְלוֹ־תִהְיֶה לְאִשָּׁה לֹא־יוּכַל לְשַׁלְּחָהּ כָּל־
כ יָמָיו׃ וְאִם־אֱמֶת הָיָה הַדָּבָר
כא הַזֶּה לֹא־נִמְצְאוּ בְתוּלִים לַנַּעֲרָ׃ וְהוֹצִיאוּ אֶת־הַנַּעֲרָ אֶל־
פֶּתַח בֵּית־אָבִיהָ וּסְקָלוּהָ אַנְשֵׁי עִירָהּ בָּאֲבָנִים וָמֵתָה כִּי־
עָשְׂתָה נְבָלָה בְּיִשְׂרָאֵל לִזְנוֹת בֵּית אָבִיהָ וּבִעַרְתָּ הָרָע
כב מִקִּרְבֶּךָ׃ כִּי־יִמָּצֵא אִישׁ שֹׁכֵב ׀ עִם־אִשָּׁה בְעֻלַת־
בַּעַל וּמֵתוּ גַּם־שְׁנֵיהֶם הָאִישׁ הַשֹּׁכֵב עִם־הָאִשָּׁה וְהָאִשָּׁה
כג וּבִעַרְתָּ הָרָע מִיִּשְׂרָאֵל׃ כִּי יִהְיֶה נַעֲרָ בְתוּלָה
כד מְאֹרָשָׂה לְאִישׁ וּמְצָאָהּ אִישׁ בָּעִיר וְשָׁכַב עִמָּהּ׃ וְהוֹצֵאתֶם
אֶת־שְׁנֵיהֶם אֶל־שַׁעַר ׀ הָעִיר הַהִוא וּסְקַלְתֶּם אֹתָם בָּאֲבָנִים
וָמֵתוּ אֶת־הַנַּעֲרָ עַל־דְּבַר אֲשֶׁר לֹא־צָעֲקָה בָעִיר וְאֶת־
הָאִישׁ עַל־דְּבַר אֲשֶׁר־עִנָּה אֶת־אֵשֶׁת רֵעֵהוּ וּבִעַרְתָּ הָרָע
כה מִקִּרְבֶּךָ׃ וְאִם־בַּשָּׂדֶה יִמְצָא הָאִישׁ אֶת־הַנַּעֲרָ
הַמְאֹרָשָׂה וְהֶחֱזִיק־בָּהּ הָאִישׁ וְשָׁכַב עִמָּהּ וּמֵת הָאִישׁ
כו אֲשֶׁר־שָׁכַב עִמָּהּ לְבַדּוֹ׃ וְלַנַּעֲרָ לֹא־תַעֲשֶׂה דָבָר אֵין לַנַּעֲרָ
חֵטְא מָוֶת כִּי כַּאֲשֶׁר יָקוּם אִישׁ עַל־רֵעֵהוּ וּרְצָחוֹ נֶפֶשׁ כֵּן
כז הַדָּבָר הַזֶּה׃ כִּי בַשָּׂדֶה מְצָאָהּ צָעֲקָה הַנַּעֲרָ הַמְאֹרָשָׂה וְאֵין
כח מוֹשִׁיעַ לָהּ׃ כִּי־יִמְצָא אִישׁ נַעֲרָ בְתוּלָה
כט אֲשֶׁר לֹא־אֹרָשָׂה וּתְפָשָׂהּ וְשָׁכַב עִמָּהּ וְנִמְצָאוּ׃ וְנָתַן הָאִישׁ
הַשֹּׁכֵב עִמָּהּ לַאֲבִי הַנַּעֲרָ חֲמִשִּׁים כָּסֶף וְלוֹ־תִהְיֶה לְאִשָּׁה
כג א תַּחַת אֲשֶׁר עִנָּהּ לֹא־יוּכַל שַׁלְּחָהּ כָּל־יָמָיו׃ לֹא־

marry his father's wife; he must not dishonor his father's
2 bed. No one whose testicles have been crushed
or whose member is severed shall be admitted to the
3 congregation of the LORD. No one born of an
illicit union shall be admitted to the congregation of the
LORD; even to the tenth generation, no descendant of
such a union may be admitted to the congregation of the
4 LORD. No Amonite or Moabite shall be admitted
to the congregation of the LORD; even to the tenth
generation, none of their descendants shall be admitted
5 to the congregation of the LORD, for they would not greet
you with food and water on your way when you came out
of Egypt; and in hostility against you they hired Bilam
son of Beor from Petor of Aram Naharayim to curse you.
6 But the LORD your God chose not to listen to Bilam; the
LORD your God turned the curse into a blessing for you,
7 because the LORD your God loves you. Do not seek their
8 ease or welfare as long as you live. Do not REVI'I
despise an Edomite, for he is your kin. Do not despise an

---

assumed to part from the majority of the group [in this case, other nations of the empire]." ...They then permitted [Yehuda the Amonite] to enter the congregation. (Berakhot 28a)

At a stroke, the entire biblical legislation relating to Israel's neighbors and enemies was declared inoperative, on the grounds that after Sanḥeriv's conquests and population transfers (722–705 BCE), the "nations" could no longer be identified. As Rambam writes about the seven nations against which Israel was commanded to wage war, "Their memory has already perished" (*Hilkhot Melakhim UMilḥemoteihem* 5:4). We no longer know who is who. That chapter in Jewish history is closed.

23:8 לֹא־תְתַעֵב אֲדֹמִי *Do not despise an Edomite* – Edom was another name of Esav. There was a time when Esav hated Yaakov and vowed to kill him. Before the twins were born, Rivka received an oracle (Gen. 25:23) that seemed to imply an eternal conflict between the two brothers and their descendants.

Later, during the Second Temple period, the prophet Malakhi said: "'Is Esav not a brother to Yaakov?' So says the LORD: 'Yet I loved Yaakov and hated Esav'" (Mal. 1:2–3). Centuries later still, R. Shimon b. Yoḥai said, "It is a halakha [rule, law, inescapable truth] that Esav hates Yaakov" (Sifrei, Behaalotekha 69.) Given this generational hostility, why does Moshe tell us not to despise Esav's descendants?

ב יִקַּח אִישׁ אֶת־אֵשֶׁת אָבִיו וְלֹא יְגַלֶּה כְּנַף אָבִיו׃ לֹא־
ג יָבֹא פְצוּעַ־דַּכָּה וּכְרוּת שָׁפְכָה בִּקְהַל יהוה׃ לֹא־
יָבֹא מַמְזֵר בִּקְהַל יהוה גַּם דּוֹר עֲשִׂירִי לֹא־יָבֹא לוֹ בִּקְהַל
ד יהוה׃ לֹא־יָבֹא עַמּוֹנִי וּמוֹאָבִי בִּקְהַל יהוה גַּם
ה דּוֹר עֲשִׂירִי לֹא־יָבֹא לָהֶם בִּקְהַל יהוה עַד־עוֹלָם׃ עַל־דְּבַר
אֲשֶׁר לֹא־קִדְּמוּ אֶתְכֶם בַּלֶּחֶם וּבַמַּיִם בַּדֶּרֶךְ בְּצֵאתְכֶם
מִמִּצְרָיִם וַאֲשֶׁר שָׂכַר עָלֶיךָ אֶת־בִּלְעָם בֶּן־בְּעוֹר מִפְּתוֹר
ו אֲרַם נַהֲרַיִם לְקַלְלֶךָּ׃ וְלֹא־אָבָה יהוה אֱלֹהֶיךָ לִשְׁמֹעַ אֶל־
בִּלְעָם וַיַּהֲפֹךְ יהוה אֱלֹהֶיךָ לְּךָ אֶת־הַקְּלָלָה לִבְרָכָה כִּי
ז אֲהֵבְךָ יהוה אֱלֹהֶיךָ׃ לֹא־תִדְרֹשׁ שְׁלֹמָם וְטֹבָתָם כָּל־יָמֶיךָ
ח לְעוֹלָם׃ לֹא־תְתַעֵב אֲדֹמִי כִּי אָחִיךָ הוּא לֹא־ רביעי

23:4 גַּם דּוֹר עֲשִׂירִי *Even to the tenth generation* – The Torah explicitly excludes Moabites from the "congregation of the Lord even to the tenth generation." Yet, as we read in the Book of Ruth, Ruth herself was a Moabite who pledged herself as part of the Jewish nation. The Rabbis solved this problem simply and ingeniously. The Hebrew for Moabite, *Moavi*, is masculine, not feminine. So the prohibition applies to men, not women (Yevamot 76b–77a). This, they said, was one of the rulings given "in the days when the judges ruled" (Ruth 1:1).

This resolved an exegetical problem. In practice, the Rabbis went much further still, and we can identify the period at which they did so. It took place at the time – the late first or early second century CE – when Rabban Gamliel II was deposed as spiritual head of the Jewish community in Israel for his autocratic behavior toward one of his colleagues, and R. Elazar b. Azarya was appointed in his place. At that time many disputed issues were resolved. This is how the Talmud describes one of them:

> On that day, Yehuda, an Amonite proselyte, came before them in the house of study and asked: "Am I permitted to enter the assembly?" R. Yehoshua said, "You are permitted to enter the congregation." Rabban Gamliel said, "Is it not a law that '*no Amonite or Moabite shall be admitted to the congregation of the Lord*'?" R. Yehoshua replied, "Do Amon and Moav still live in their original homes? Long ago, Sanḥeriv, king of Assyria, came and mixed up all the nations, as it says, '*I… sweep away the borders of peoples and take their leaders for plunder; like a wild bull I pull down all who preside*' (Is. 10:13), and anything that parts [from a group] is

9 Egyptian, for you lived as a stranger in his land. Children
born to them may be admitted, in the third generation, to
10 the congregation of the LORD. When you

Egyptians, or at the very least to look back with a sense of grievance, resentment, animosity, and pain. Why does Moshe say the opposite?

Because to be free, you have to let go of hate. If the Israelites continued to hate their erstwhile enemies, Moshe would have succeeded in taking the Israelites out of Egypt, but he would have failed to take Egypt out of the Israelites. Mentally, they would still be there, slaves to the past, prisoners of their memories.

Freedom involves the abandonment of hate, because hate is the abdication of freedom. It is the projection of our conflicts onto an external force whom we can then blame, but only at the cost of denying responsibility. That is Moshe's message to those who are about to enter the Promised Land: that a free society can be built only by people who accept the responsibility of freedom, subjects who refuse to see themselves as objects, people who define themselves by love of God, not hatred of the other.

23:9 דּוֹר שְׁלִישִׁי *In the third generation* – Judaism is often portrayed as a religion of justice rather than mercy and forgiveness. That is not the case: Justice and forgiveness go hand in hand. Each is an answer to the problem of revenge, and neither is sufficient on its own. Justice takes the sense of wrong and transforms it from personal retaliation – revenge – to the impersonal processes of law – retribution. Forgiveness is the further acknowledgment that justice alone may not be enough to silence the feelings of the afflicted. Even when the evidence has been taken, the verdict passed, and sentence imposed, there is a residue of pain and grief which has to be discharged. Justice is the impersonal, forgiveness the personal, the restoration of the moral order. Justice rights wrongs; forgiveness rebuilds broken relationships. There is no other way.

It is impossible to understand the force of forgiveness without, at the same time, acknowledging the difficulty. It is hard precisely because it conflicts with our sense of keeping faith with the past. If wrong has been done to me, it is natural to feel that wrong must be done to the wrongdoer in return. When that wrong is historic – when its victims are no longer alive – we feel that more than mere justice is at stake. Only the offended party can forgive, and he or she is no longer alive to be able to forgive. We, the family or friends of the victim, feel the pull of loyalty to the unappeased cry of those who are no longer here. Forgiveness can then come to seem like a betrayal.

How then is it possible? It is possible because, once the impartial processes of law have taken their course, justice done, sentences served, amends made and

ט תְתַעֵב מִצְרִי כִּי־גֵר הָיִיתָ בְאַרְצוֹ: בָּנִים אֲשֶׁר־יִוָּלְדוּ לָהֶם
י דּוֹר שְׁלִישִׁי יָבֹא לָהֶם בִּקְהַל יהוה: כִּי־תֵצֵא יח

The answer is: Esav may hate Yaakov, but it does not follow that Yaakov should hate Esav. As Martin Luther King Jr. wrote, "Darkness cannot drive out darkness; only light can do that. Hate cannot drive out hate; only love can do that." Those who quote R. Shimon's aphorism do so selectively. In context it refers to the moment at which Yaakov and Esav meet after their long estrangement. Yaakov has feared that Esav will try to kill him. Then "Esav ran to meet him [Yaakov] and embraced him. He threw his arms around his neck and kissed him, and they [both] wept" (Gen. 33:4). Over the letters of the word "kissed," as it appears in a *sefer Torah*, there are dots, signaling some special meaning. It was in this context that R. Shimon b. Yoḥai said: "Even though it is well known that Esav hates Yaakov, at that moment he was overcome with compassion and kissed him with a full heart" (see Rashi ad loc.). In other words, it is precisely the text cited to show that antisemitism is inevitable that proves the opposite: At the crucial encounter, Esav did *not* feel hate toward Yaakov. They met, embraced, and went their separate ways without ill will. Hate, especially between brothers, is not eternal and inexorable. Always be ready, Moshe seems to imply in our verse, for reconciliation between enemies.

Moshe's commands against hate are testimony to his greatness as a leader. It is easy to become a leader by mobilizing hate. The language of hate can create enmity between people of different faiths and ethnicities who have lived peaceably together for centuries. It has been the most destructive force in history, and even knowledge of the Holocaust has not ended it. It is the unmistakable mark of toxic leadership.

Great leaders make people better, kinder, nobler than they would otherwise be. The paradigm case was Moshe, the man who had more lasting influence than any other leader in history. A true leader knows: Hate the sin but not the sinner. Do not forget the past but do not be held captive by it. Be willing to fight your enemies but never allow yourself to be defined by them.

23:8 לֹא־תְתַעֵב מִצְרִי כִּי־גֵר הָיִיתָ בְאַרְצוֹ *Do not despise an Egyptian, for you lived as a stranger in his land* – This is a counterintuitive command. Recall what had happened. The Egyptians enslaved the Israelites. They initiated a policy of slow genocide, killing every male Israelite at birth. Moshe begged Pharaoh repeatedly to let the people go and he refused.

Moshe knows that this entire chapter of Israelite history was not accidental or incidental. It is their matrix as a nation, their formative experience. They were commanded to remember it forever, enacting it once a year on Passover, eating the unleavened bread of affliction and the bitter herbs of slavery. All these, on the face of it, are reasons to hate the

are encamped against your enemies, guard against any
11 impropriety. If one of the men becomes impure because
of a nocturnal emission, he shall go outside the camp and
12 not reenter it. As evening approaches, he shall bathe in
13 water, and at sunset he may reenter the camp. You must
designate an area outside the camp where you may relieve
14 yourself. Among your gear you shall have a trowel. When
you relieve yourself outside, you shall dig a hole with it
15 and cover up your excrement. The LORD your God travels
with your camp, to protect you and to deliver your
enemies to you. Therefore your camp must be holy; He
must not find any indecent thing among you and turn
16 away from you. If a slave seeks refuge with you

---

needed long-term planning and the decision to exercise restraint in the present for the sake of the viability of the future. Even in the nomadic days of the wilderness, pollution is understood to threaten the holiness of the camp.

23:16 לֹא־תַסְגִּיר עֶבֶד *Do not hand him back* – Rashi stresses that the fugitive merits our assistance even if he or she is a non-Jewish slave fleeing a Jewish master. This verse provides the basis of an ethic of assisting refugees. It is also a striking example of the Torah's refusal to see inequalities in society as the will of God. On this, the Talmud (Bava Batra 10a) records a fascinating debate between R. Akiva and the Roman governor of Israel, Turnus Rufus:

> Turnus Rufus asked R. Akiva, "If your God loves the poor, why does He not provide for them?"
>
> R. Akiva replied, "So that we may be saved through them from the punishment of Gehinnom [i.e., charity atones]."
>
> Rufus said, "On the contrary, it is this that will condemn you to Gehinnom. I will make my point clear by a parable. A king of flesh and blood became angry with his slave, put him in prison, and ordered that he be given neither food nor drink. A certain man went [to the prison] and gave him food and drink. When the king hears what that man did, will he not be angry with him? And after all, you are no more than God's servants, as it is written, 'For it is to Me that the Israelites are servants'" (Lev. 25:55).
>
> R. Akiva replied, "I will prove my point with another parable. A king of flesh and blood became angry with his child, put him in prison, and ordered that he be given neither food nor drink. A certain man went [to the prison] and gave him food and drink. When the king hears what the man

יא מַחֲנֶה עַל־אֹיְבֶיךָ וְנִשְׁמַרְתָּ מִכֹּל דָּבָר רָע׃ כִּי־יִהְיֶה בְךָ אִישׁ
אֲשֶׁר לֹא־יִהְיֶה טָהוֹר מִקְּרֵה־לָיְלָה וְיָצָא אֶל־מִחוּץ לַמַּחֲנֶה
יב לֹא יָבֹא אֶל־תּוֹךְ הַמַּחֲנֶה׃ וְהָיָה לִפְנוֹת־עֶרֶב יִרְחַץ בַּמָּיִם
יג וּכְבֹא הַשֶּׁמֶשׁ יָבֹא אֶל־תּוֹךְ הַמַּחֲנֶה׃ וְיָד תִּהְיֶה לְךָ מִחוּץ
יד לַמַּחֲנֶה וְיָצָאתָ שָׁמָּה חוּץ׃ וְיָתֵד תִּהְיֶה לְךָ עַל־אֲזֵנֶךָ וְהָיָה
טו בְּשִׁבְתְּךָ חוּץ וְחָפַרְתָּה בָהּ וְשַׁבְתָּ וְכִסִּיתָ אֶת־צֵאָתֶךָ׃ כִּי
יְהוָה אֱלֹהֶיךָ מִתְהַלֵּךְ ׀ בְּקֶרֶב מַחֲנֶךָ לְהַצִּילְךָ וְלָתֵת אֹיְבֶיךָ
לְפָנֶיךָ וְהָיָה מַחֲנֶיךָ קָדוֹשׁ וְלֹא־יִרְאֶה בְךָ עֶרְוַת דָּבָר וְשָׁב
טז מֵאַחֲרֶיךָ׃ לֹא־תַסְגִּיר עֶבֶד אֶל־אֲדֹנָיו אֲשֶׁר־יִנָּצֵל

---

apologies expressed, a halt must be called to the otherwise endless voice of implacable grief. Forgiveness does not mean forgetting, nor does it mean abandoning the claims of justice. It does mean, however, an acknowledgment that the past is past and must not be allowed to cast its shadow over the future. Forgiveness heals moral wounds the way the body heals physical wounds. At its height it is a process of shared mourning between those who commit and those who suffer the consequences of wrong – the former for harm done, the latter for harm suffered – and like all acts of mourning it is the only bridge from the pain of loss to reintegration with the present and its tasks.

23:13 וְיָד תִּהְיֶה לְךָ מִחוּץ לַמַּחֲנֶה *Designate an area outside the camp* – The rabbis extended the Torah's rule that waste should be disposed of far from human habitation. They banned garbage disposal that interfered with crops or amenities, pollution of the water supply, and activities that would foul the air or create intolerable noise in residential areas. The provision for open space around the Levitical cities is one of the earliest examples of town planning (Num. 35:1–3).

These rulings and others set precedents of environmental legislation as well as commands that educate us in respect for and restraint toward nature as God's creation (see note on Deut. 20:19). Admittedly, environmental ethics has not yet received the same intense halakhic treatment as has medical ethics. Probably that is because medical decisions are taken by individuals while environmental decisions are taken by governments. An individual turns to Jewish law for guidance. Governments rarely do. But it is not because Judaism regards ecological issues lightly. Rambam repeatedly insists that we cannot pursue spiritual ideals without first ensuring our physical survival (for example, *Hilkhot Deot* 4:1). That has always

17 from his master, do not hand him back to his master. He
shall live with you in the place he chooses, in whichever
18 of your towns he likes. Do not ill-treat him. No
woman of Israel shall be a cult prostitute; no man of Israel
19 shall be a male cult prostitute. Do not bring wages of
prostitution or the payment for a dog into the house of
the Lord your God in fulfillment of any vow, for both are
20 abhorrent to the Lord your God. Do not charge
interest on loans to your kinsmen, whether on money or
21 food or anything that could earn interest. You may charge
interest on loans to a foreigner, but on loans to your
kinsmen do not charge, so that the Lord your God may
bless you in all your endeavors in the land you are entering

---

minuet of giving and taking is part of their identity and growth as individuals. In this microcosm of community and its everyday transactions, we see something significant taking place: the making and sustaining of the moral life. I call such relationships – using a keyword of the Torah – *covenantal*. Whereas contracts are about the self, covenants are about the larger groupings in and through which we develop our identity. They are about the "we" in which I discover the "I." Covenant is a bond, not of interest or advantage, but of belonging. Religious communities are bound by covenantal ties; in such a sensitive transaction as a loan to someone in need, a fellow Jew must be treated as a "kinsman." Yet this does not preclude the possibility of lending in a contractual manner, for mutual profit, in an open marketplace.

Covenantal relationships – where we develop the grammar and syntax of reciprocity, where we help others and they help us without calculations of relative advantage – are where trust is born. Contracts, social or economic, mediate relationships between strangers. But if we were always and only strangers to one another, we would have no reason to trust one another. Markets depend on virtues not produced by the market, just as states depend on virtues not created by the state. They depend on a surrounding matrix of virtue and on the institutions that sustain it: families, communities, beliefs, and traditions. They need rules of integrity and fair dealing, and a mindset that sees the market as a place not of exploitation, but of mutual gain. Without these, the workings of the market are too arbitrary and abrasive. With them, it is the best way we know of matching one person's talents to another's desires, of encouraging freedom, creativity, and dignity, and of enhancing the conditions of life for all.

יז אֵלֶיךָ מֵעִם אֲדֹנָיו: עִמְּךָ יֵשֵׁב בְּקִרְבְּךָ בַּמָּקוֹם אֲשֶׁר־יִבְחַר
יח בְּאַחַד שְׁעָרֶיךָ בַּטּוֹב לוֹ לֹא תּוֹנֶנּוּ: לֹא־תִהְיֶה
קְדֵשָׁה מִבְּנוֹת יִשְׂרָאֵל וְלֹא־יִהְיֶה קָדֵשׁ מִבְּנֵי יִשְׂרָאֵל:
יט לֹא־תָבִיא אֶתְנַן זוֹנָה וּמְחִיר כֶּלֶב בֵּית יְהוָה אֱלֹהֶיךָ לְכׇל־
כ נֶדֶר כִּי תוֹעֲבַת יְהוָה אֱלֹהֶיךָ גַּם־שְׁנֵיהֶם: לֹא־
תַשִּׁיךְ לְאָחִיךָ נֶשֶׁךְ כֶּסֶף נֶשֶׁךְ אֹכֶל נֶשֶׁךְ כׇּל־דָּבָר אֲשֶׁר
כא יִשָּׁךְ: לַנׇּכְרִי תַשִּׁיךְ וּלְאָחִיךָ לֹא תַשִּׁיךְ לְמַעַן יְבָרֶכְךָ יְהוָה
אֱלֹהֶיךָ בְּכֹל מִשְׁלַח יָדֶךָ עַל־הָאָרֶץ אֲשֶׁר־אַתָּה בָא־שָׁמָּה

---

did, will he not reward him? And after all, we are called [God's] children, as it is written, 'You are children of the Lord your God'" (Deut. 14:1).

There is nothing inevitable or divinely willed about social or economic inequality. Judaism rejects the almost universal belief in antiquity and throughout the Middle Ages that hierarchy and divisions of class are written into the structure of society. What human beings have created, human beings can rectify. It follows that everyone should be provided with the basic requirements of a safe and dignified life.

However complex the application of this principle in a globalized world, it remains one of the Torah's most powerful imperatives: a society is judged by what it contributes to the welfare of the least advantaged, such as the runaway slave, the widow, the orphan, the poor, and the stranger. If someone turns to us for help when fleeing violence, we do not ignore it.

23:20 לֹא־תַשִּׁיךְ לְאָחִיךָ נֶשֶׁךְ *Do not charge interest on loans to your kinsmen* – Lending to the poor on interest led to inescapable cycles of debt bondage in the ancient world. At the same time, loans and investments are a necessary part of a market economy and often a way for someone without wealth to become self-sustaining. One example of how the Rabbis managed this tension can be found in the commentary on Deut. 15:9. Here we see a distinction in policy between Jewish loan recipients ("kinsmen"), from whom one cannot charge interest, and others, to whom one can lend on interest as long as the usual laws of business integrity are observed. Two forms of relationships are being described.

Political and economic relationships are *contractual.* They presuppose the coming together of self-interested parties, both of whom benefit from the exchange. Contractual relationships, however, are not the only or even the most fundamental forms of association. Family members, for instance, develop an unconscious choreography of mutuality. They help one another; they depend on one another; and that

22 to possess. When you make a vow to the LORD
your God, do not delay in fulfilling it, for the LORD your
God will certainly require it of you; you will incur guilt.
23 But if you refrain from vowing you will not incur guilt.
24 Whatever your lips utter, take care to do, since you have
voluntarily vowed to the LORD your God, with your own
25 mouth. When you enter your neighbor's HAMISHI
vineyard, you may eat as many grapes as you wish; eat
26 your fill, but do not put any in a container. When
you enter your neighbor's field of standing grain, you may
pluck ears with your hand, but you may not put a sickle to
24 1 your neighbor's grain. If a man takes a wife and
becomes her husband, but begins to dislike her because
he finds something indecent in her; if he writes her a bill
of divorce, puts it in her hand, and sends her from his
2 house, she may leave his house and become another
3 man's wife. However, if the second husband rejects her,
writes her a bill of divorce, puts it in her hand, and sends
4 her from his house, or the second husband dies, her first
husband, who sent her away, is not permitted to take her
again to be his wife after she has been defiled, for that
would be abhorrent to the LORD, and you must not bring
sin into the land that the LORD your God is giving you for
5 your possession. When a man is newly married, SHISHI
he shall not go out with the army or have any related duty
laid on him. He shall be exempt for one year, to be with
his home and bring happiness to the woman he has
6 married. Do not take an upper or lower millstone as
security for a debt, for that would be taking a person's
7 livelihood as security. If someone is found to

---

we love and trust, who we know will never desert us, who lifts us when we fall and believes in us even when we fail.

God lives in the unadorned heart of the human situation, in the covenantal love between husband and wife on which the republic of faith is built. Building the foundation of a home on the shared joy of the first year of marriage overrides even the collective interests of a nation going to war.

כב לְרִשְׁתָּהּ: כִּי־תִדֹּר נֶדֶר לַיהוָה אֱלֹהֶיךָ לֹא תְאַחֵר יט
לְשַׁלְּמוֹ כִּי־דָרֹשׁ יִדְרְשֶׁנּוּ יהוָה אֱלֹהֶיךָ מֵעִמָּךְ וְהָיָה בְךָ
כג כד חֵטְא: וְכִי תֶחְדַּל לִנְדֹּר לֹא־יִהְיֶה בְךָ חֵטְא: מוֹצָא שְׂפָתֶיךָ
תִּשְׁמֹר וְעָשִׂיתָ כַּאֲשֶׁר נָדַרְתָּ לַיהוָה אֱלֹהֶיךָ נְדָבָה אֲשֶׁר
כה דִּבַּרְתָּ בְּפִיךָ: כִּי תָבֹא בְּכֶרֶם רֵעֶךָ וְאָכַלְתָּ עֲנָבִים חמישי
כו כְּנַפְשְׁךָ שָׂבְעֶךָ וְאֶל־כֶּלְיְךָ לֹא תִתֵּן: כִּי תָבֹא
בְּקָמַת רֵעֶךָ וְקָטַפְתָּ מְלִילֹת בְּיָדֶךָ וְחֶרְמֵשׁ לֹא תָנִיף עַל
כד א קָמַת רֵעֶךָ: כִּי־יִקַּח אִישׁ אִשָּׁה וּבְעָלָהּ
וְהָיָה אִם־לֹא תִמְצָא־חֵן בְּעֵינָיו כִּי־מָצָא בָהּ עֶרְוַת דָּבָר
ב וְכָתַב לָהּ סֵפֶר כְּרִיתֻת וְנָתַן בְּיָדָהּ וְשִׁלְּחָהּ מִבֵּיתוֹ: וְיָצְאָה
ג מִבֵּיתוֹ וְהָלְכָה וְהָיְתָה לְאִישׁ־אַחֵר: וּשְׂנֵאָהּ הָאִישׁ הָאַחֲרוֹן
וְכָתַב לָהּ סֵפֶר כְּרִיתֻת וְנָתַן בְּיָדָהּ וְשִׁלְּחָהּ מִבֵּיתוֹ אוֹ כִי
ד יָמוּת הָאִישׁ הָאַחֲרוֹן אֲשֶׁר־לְקָחָהּ לוֹ לְאִשָּׁה: לֹא־יוּכַל
בַּעְלָהּ הָרִאשׁוֹן אֲשֶׁר־שִׁלְּחָהּ לָשׁוּב לְקַחְתָּהּ לִהְיוֹת לוֹ
לְאִשָּׁה אַחֲרֵי אֲשֶׁר הֻטַּמָּאָה כִּי־תוֹעֵבָה הִוא לִפְנֵי יהוָה
וְלֹא תַחֲטִיא אֶת־הָאָרֶץ אֲשֶׁר יהוָה אֱלֹהֶיךָ נֹתֵן לְךָ
ה נַחֲלָה: כִּי־יִקַּח אִישׁ אִשָּׁה חֲדָשָׁה לֹא יֵצֵא ששי
בַּצָּבָא וְלֹא־יַעֲבֹר עָלָיו לְכָל־דָּבָר נָקִי יִהְיֶה לְבֵיתוֹ שָׁנָה
ו אֶחָת וְשִׂמַּח אֶת־אִשְׁתּוֹ אֲשֶׁר־לָקָח: לֹא־יַחֲבֹל רֵחַיִם וָרָכֶב
ז כִּי־נֶפֶשׁ הוּא חֹבֵל: כִּי־יִמָּצֵא אִישׁ גֹּנֵב נֶפֶשׁ

24:5 וְשִׂמַּח אֶת־אִשְׁתּוֹ אֲשֶׁר־לָקָח *Bring happiness to the woman he has married* – Not by chance is marriage called *kiddushin*, "sanctification." Like covenant itself, marriage is a pledge of loyalty between two parties, each recognizing the other's integrity, honoring their differences, even as they come together to bring new life into being. Marriage is to society what covenant is to religious faith: a decision to make love – not power, wealth, or *force majeure* – the generative principle of life.

Marriage is the most personal and intimate of all forms of human association, and the deepest matrix of faith. There is no redemption of solitude deeper than to share a life with someone

have kidnapped another Israelite, enslaving or selling
him, the kidnapper shall die. You must purge the evil from
8 your midst. Take great care in cases of impure
blight. Carefully do whatever the Levitical priests instruct
9 you, as I have commanded them. Remember what the
LORD your God did to Miriam on your way when you left
10 Egypt. When you make your neighbor a
loan of any kind, do not go into his house to take his
11 pledge. Wait outside while the person to whom you are
12 making the loan brings the pledge out to you. If the
person is poor, do not go to sleep with the pledge in your
13 possession. You must return his pledge by sunset, so that
he may sleep in his cloak and bless you. This will be
accounted to you as a righteous act before the LORD your
14 God. Do not take advantage of a poor
and destitute laborer, whether he is a kinsman or a SHEVI'I
15 migrant living in one of the towns in your land. Pay him
his wages on the same day, before sunset, because he is
poor and his livelihood depends on it. Otherwise he
will cry out to the LORD against you, and you will bear
16 your guilt. Parents shall not be put to death for
their children, nor shall children be put to death for their
parents. A person shall be put to death only for his own
17 sin. Do not deprive a migrant or an orphan

---

from sinning, but they failed to do so" (Sanhedrin 27b; *Yalkut Shimoni* I:290).

What, then, is the scope of responsibility we bear in our roles as parents, neighbors, townspeople, citizens, and children of the covenant? Judicially, only the criminal is responsible for his crime. But, implies the Torah, we are also our brother's keeper. We share collective responsibility for the moral and spiritual health of society. "All Israelites," said the Sages, "are responsible for one another" (Shevuot 39a). Legal responsibility is relatively easy to define. But moral responsibility is larger, and necessarily more vague. "Let a person not say, 'I have not sinned, and if someone else commits a sin, that is a matter between him and God.' This is contrary to the Torah," writes Rambam in *Sefer HaMitzvot* (*Mitzvat Aseh* 205).

This is particularly so when it comes to the relationship between parents and children. The duty of parents to teach

מֵאֶחָיו מִבְּנֵי יִשְׂרָאֵל וְהִתְעַמֶּר־בּוֹ וּמְכָרוֹ וּמֵת הַגַּנָּב הַהוּא
ח וּבִעַרְתָּ הָרָע מִקִּרְבֶּךָ׃ הִשָּׁמֶר בְּנֶגַע־הַצָּרַעַת
לִשְׁמֹר מְאֹד וְלַעֲשׂוֹת כְּכֹל אֲשֶׁר־יוֹרוּ אֶתְכֶם הַכֹּהֲנִים הַלְוִיִּם
ט כַּאֲשֶׁר צִוִּיתִם תִּשְׁמְרוּ לַעֲשׂוֹת׃ זָכוֹר אֵת אֲשֶׁר־עָשָׂה יְהוָה
י אֱלֹהֶיךָ לְמִרְיָם בַּדָּרֶךְ בְּצֵאתְכֶם מִמִּצְרָיִם׃ כִּי־
תַשֶּׁה בְרֵעֲךָ מַשַּׁאת מְאוּמָה לֹא־תָבֹא אֶל־בֵּיתוֹ לַעֲבֹט
יא עֲבֹטוֹ׃ בַּחוּץ תַּעֲמֹד וְהָאִישׁ אֲשֶׁר אַתָּה נֹשֶׁה בוֹ יוֹצִיא
יב אֵלֶיךָ אֶת־הַעֲבוֹט הַחוּצָה׃ וְאִם־אִישׁ עָנִי הוּא לֹא תִשְׁכַּב
יג בַּעֲבֹטוֹ׃ הָשֵׁב תָּשִׁיב לוֹ אֶת־הָעֲבוֹט כְּבוֹא הַשֶּׁמֶשׁ
וְשָׁכַב בְּשַׂלְמָתוֹ וּבֵרֲכֶךָּ וּלְךָ תִּהְיֶה צְדָקָה לִפְנֵי יְהוָה
יד אֱלֹהֶיךָ׃ לֹא־תַעֲשֹׁק שָׂכִיר עָנִי וְאֶבְיוֹן מֵאַחֶיךָ שביעי
טו אוֹ מִגֵּרְךָ אֲשֶׁר בְּאַרְצְךָ בִּשְׁעָרֶיךָ׃ בְּיוֹמוֹ תִתֵּן שְׂכָרוֹ וְלֹא־
תָבוֹא עָלָיו הַשֶּׁמֶשׁ כִּי עָנִי הוּא וְאֵלָיו הוּא נֹשֵׂא אֶת־נַפְשׁוֹ
טז וְלֹא־יִקְרָא עָלֶיךָ אֶל־יְהוָה וְהָיָה בְךָ חֵטְא׃ לֹא־
יוּמְתוּ אָבוֹת עַל־בָּנִים וּבָנִים לֹא־יוּמְתוּ עַל־אָבוֹת אִישׁ
יז בְּחֶטְאוֹ יוּמָתוּ׃ לֹא תַטֶּה מִשְׁפַּט גֵּר יָתוֹם

24:14 לֹא־תַעֲשֹׁק שָׂכִיר עָנִי וְאֶבְיוֹן *Poor and destitute laborer* – The architectonics of biblical liberty are immensely detailed, but they can be summarized under clear themes. One of these is a humane concern for the poor – an insistence that they never suffer hunger, or be humiliated by their economic circumstances: There is something extraordinarily humane about these ordinances, and although they speak to an agrarian order more than three thousand years ago, the principle they adumbrate remains true and compelling today. Freedom involves more than an absence of constraints. A society in which the few have wealth and many are on the verge of starvation is not free by the standards of the Torah.

24:16 אִישׁ בְּחֶטְאוֹ יוּמָתוּ *A person shall be put to death only for his own sin* – In general, the Sages rejected the idea that children could be punished, even at the hands of Heaven, for the sins of their parents. As a result, they reinterpreted every passage that gave the opposite impression, that children were indeed being punished for their parents' sins. They explained biblical episodes in which children were punished with their parents by saying that the children "had the power to protest/prevent their parents

▶

of justice. Do not take a widow's garment as a pledge.
18 Remember that you were a slave in Egypt and the LORD
your God redeemed you from there. And so I command
19 you in this. When you reap the harvest in your
field and forget a sheaf in the field, do not go back to get
it. Leave it for the migrant, the orphan, and the widow, so
that the LORD your God may grant you blessing in all the

---

in ritual, retold in sacred story, never to be forgotten. Indeed, says God through the prophets from Moshe to Yirmeyahu, if you ever forget it, you will be forced to relive it, through further exiles, other persecutions.

Egypt was, for the Israelites, the school of the soul. They knew what it was like to be on the receiving end of absolute power: Ramesses II, the greatest ruler of the longest-lived empire the world has ever known. They had been rescued by the Creator of heaven and earth, who had brought them from slavery to freedom and then made a covenant with them, not for His sake but for theirs, inviting them under His sovereignty to build a society that would use their God-given freedom to honor the liberty of others. Memory is the driving force of morality.

24:19 לַגֵּר לַיָּתוֹם וְלָאַלְמָנָה יִהְיֶה *Leave it for the migrant, the orphan, and the widow* – The language of tzedaka is often that of kinship. And yet a series of statements from the mishnaic period specifies:

> For the sake of peace, the poor of the heathens should not be prevented from gathering gleanings, forgotten sheaves, and corners of the field. (Gittin 5:8)
>
> Our masters taught: For the sake of peace, the poor of the heathens should be supported as we support the poor of Israel, the sick of the heathens should be visited as we visit the sick of Israel, and the dead of the heathens should be buried as we bury the dead of Israel. (Gittin 61a)

All of these provisions are ordained because of the principle of *darkhei shalom*, "the ways of peace." The prophets of ancient Israel were the first people in history to conceive of peace as an ideal. They did so in words that have resonated from that day to this, most famously those of Yeshayahu: "They shall beat their swords into plowshares, their spears into pruning hooks. Nation shall not raise sword against nation; no more will they learn to make war" (Is. 2:4). Yeshayahu's younger contemporary, Mikha, repeated these words and added some of his own: "Every man will sit beneath his grapevine, under his fig tree, with none to trouble him" (Mic. 4:4–5).

It is difficult at this distance to sense how revolutionary this was in an age

יח וְלֹא תַחֲבֹל בֶּגֶד אַלְמָנָה׃ וְזָכַרְתָּ כִּי עֶבֶד הָיִיתָ בְּמִצְרַיִם
וַיִּפְדְּךָ יְהוָה אֱלֹהֶיךָ מִשָּׁם עַל־כֵּן אָנֹכִי מְצַוְּךָ לַעֲשׂוֹת אֶת־
יט הַדָּבָר הַזֶּה׃ כִּי תִקְצֹר קְצִירְךָ בְשָׂדֶךָ וְשָׁכַחְתָּ כ
עֹמֶר בַּשָּׂדֶה לֹא תָשׁוּב לְקַחְתּוֹ לַגֵּר לַיָּתוֹם וְלָאַלְמָנָה יִהְיֶה

their children is fundamental to Judaism. It appears in both the first two paragraphs of the *Shema,* as well as passages cited in the Four Sons section of the Haggada. Rambam counts as one of the gravest sins "one who sees his son falling into bad ways and does not stop him." The reason, he says, is that "since his son is under his authority, had he stopped him the son would have desisted." Therefore it is accounted to the father as if he had actively caused his son to sin (*Hilkhot Teshuva* 4:1).

We are not legally responsible for the sins of either our parents or our children. But what we do and how we live do have an effect on the future to the third and fourth generation. If we fail to honor our responsibilities as parents, then – though no law will hold us responsible – our children will pay the price. They will suffer because of our sins.

24:18 וְזָכַרְתָּ כִּי עֶבֶד הָיִיתָ *Remember that you were a slave* – The exodus functions not simply as a fact of history, but also and primarily as the fundamental principle of jurisprudence, the logic and justification of the law. The Israelites were commanded to create a society that was opposite to Egypt. It would be a society in which even slaves rested every seventh day and breathed the wide air of freedom. It would be one in which no one became trapped endlessly in debt, or was forced irretrievably to sell ancestral property. Everyone would have access to justice.

This made sense because the Israelites had been on the receiving end of Egyptian mores. They knew what it felt like to be poor, to be deprived of justice, to be treated as less than human. They knew from the inside what powerlessness feels like. We can now see something singular about the Jewish experience. For as long as human beings have thought about morality, they have asked the question: Why be moral? Why act for the benefit of others if it is to your advantage to behave otherwise? We are self-seeking creatures, driven by desire. Why desist from something you want to do and can do merely because you ought not to? Plato, in *The Republic* (Book II, 359a–360d), uses a thought experiment. He recalls the legend of Gyges's ring, which had the power to make anyone who wore it invisible. One who had such a ring could commit any crime and get away with it. Why then would such a person be moral?

The Torah gives the most powerful grounding for a moral system. It provides not a veil of ignorance but a sustaining stream of knowledge – acquired through experience, nurtured by memory, enacted

20 work of your hands. When you beat the fruit
from your olive trees, do not go over them again. Leave
what remains for the migrant, the orphan, and the widow.
21 When you gather the grapes of your vineyard, do not go
over the vines again. Leave what remains for the migrant,
22 the orphan, and the widow. Remember that you were a
slave in the land of Egypt. And so I command you in
25 1 this. When two people have a dispute they shall
go to the court of justice and the judges shall decide
between them, acquitting the innocent and condemning
2 the guilty. If the guilty person is to be flogged, the judge
shall make him lie down and have him flogged there in his
3 presence with the requisite number of lashes. He may be
given as many as forty lashes but no more; if he is given
more lashes than this, an excessive flogging, your kinsman
4 will be degraded in your eyes. Do not muzzle an ox while
5 it is treading out the grain. When brothers live

---

divine rather than human punishment; the human punishment was to receive lashes. The principle that "once he has been beaten, he becomes [again] your kinsman" was taken to mean that the human punishment cancels the divine punishment. Once the offender has been beaten, there is no residual guilt (Makkot 3:15).

In addition, the Sages inferred the wider principle that when the guilty has received the punishment his offense deserved, he is restored to his earlier status. For example, he is permitted to be a witness, and his testimony is not invalidated by his having previously been found guilty of an offense. The stain on his character is temporary. Offenders are to be rehabilitated.

Not only were these teachings centuries ahead of their time; they also have much to teach us today. Retributive justice is compatible with a sense of human dignity and freedom. In fact, it is based on them. Jewish law is concerned not only with protecting the rights of those who have been wronged, but also helping wrongdoers rebuild their future. Guilt, in Judaism, is about acts, not persons. It is the act, not the person, that is condemned. Once the criminal has served his punishment and repented of his crime, he becomes, once more, "your kinsman."

25:4 לֹא־תַחְסֹם שׁוֹר בְּדִישׁוֹ *Do not muzzle an ox while it is treading out the grain* – This law parallels provisions for human beings as well: "When you enter [to work in] your neighbor's vineyard, you may eat as many grapes as you wish, eat your fill.... When you enter [to work in] your

לְמַעַן יְבָרֶכְךָ יְהוָה אֱלֹהֶיךָ בְּכֹל מַעֲשֵׂה יָדֶיךָ׃ כִּי כ
תַחְבֹּט זֵיתְךָ לֹא תְפַאֵר אַחֲרֶיךָ לַגֵּר לַיָּתוֹם וְלָאַלְמָנָה יִהְיֶה׃
כִּי תִבְצֹר כַּרְמְךָ לֹא תְעוֹלֵל אַחֲרֶיךָ לַגֵּר לַיָּתוֹם וְלָאַלְמָנָה כא
יִהְיֶה׃ וְזָכַרְתָּ כִּי־עֶבֶד הָיִיתָ בְּאֶרֶץ מִצְרָיִם עַל־כֵּן אָנֹכִי כב
מְצַוְּךָ לַעֲשׂוֹת אֶת־הַדָּבָר הַזֶּה׃ כִּי־יִהְיֶה א כה
רִיב בֵּין אֲנָשִׁים וְנִגְּשׁוּ אֶל־הַמִּשְׁפָּט וּשְׁפָטוּם וְהִצְדִּיקוּ אֶת־
הַצַּדִּיק וְהִרְשִׁיעוּ אֶת־הָרָשָׁע׃ וְהָיָה אִם־בִּן הַכּוֹת הָרָשָׁע ב
וְהִפִּילוֹ הַשֹּׁפֵט וְהִכָּהוּ לְפָנָיו כְּדֵי רִשְׁעָתוֹ בְּמִסְפָּר׃ אַרְבָּעִים ג
יַכֶּנּוּ לֹא יֹסִיף פֶּן־יֹסִיף לְהַכֹּתוֹ עַל־אֵלֶּה מַכָּה רַבָּה וְנִקְלָה
אָחִיךָ לְעֵינֶיךָ׃ לֹא־תַחְסֹם שׁוֹר בְּדִישׁוֹ׃ כִּי־ ד ה

that saw war as inevitable and noble, the arena of virtue and the testing ground of courage. Yet the Rabbis' "ways of peace" are not peace as Yeshayahu or Mikha envisaged it. They are a set of positive obligations promoting social harmony, alongside the negative duties that arise from the corollary principle of *eiva*, "[the avoidance of] animosity" – things we should not do because they endanger peaceful relations.

At first sight these rabbinic laws lack the grandeur of the prophets; they are small scale, local, even prosaic. They envisage no transformation of the universe or human sensibility. They seem to be no more than pragmatism, generously conceived. They are attempts to avoid the kind of civil strife from which Jews suffered so often during the long night of exile. For these reasons "the ways of peace" has not been seen for the innovation it is. I believe that is a mistake. The prophets articulated utopian peace; the Sages, a *non*-utopian program for peace in the here and now. "The ways of peace" are a program for a peace of small steps, for peace in an unredeemed world.

25:3 וְנִקְלָה אָחִיךָ לְעֵינֶיךָ *Your kinsman will be degraded in your eyes* – The Sages derived from this a fundamental principle, namely, *the rehabilitation of an offender* once he has served his punishment. In the earlier part of the passage the offender is called *harasha*, translated here as "the guilty" but which literally means "the wicked." At the end, however, he is called "your kinsman." From this, the Sages drew the conclusion that "once he has been beaten, he becomes [again] your kinsman" (Sifrei ad loc.).

This has both a specific and more general application. The specific rule applies to offenses that carried with them the severe punishment of *karet*, literally, "being cut off" from one's people. In many cases this was interpreted as a

together, and one of them dies without a son, his widow
shall not be married to a stranger outside the family. Her
husband's brother shall come to her and take her in
6 marriage, fulfilling the duty of a brother-in-law. The
firstborn son whom she bears will perpetuate the name of
the dead brother, so that his name is not erased from
7 Israel. But if the man does not wish to marry his brother's
widow, she shall go up to the elders at the gate and say,
'My husband's brother refuses to perpetuate his brother's
name in Israel. He does not care to perform the duty of a
8 brother-in-law for me.' The elders of the town shall
summon him and they must talk to him. If he persists in
9 saying, 'I have no desire to marry her,' then his brother's
widow shall go up to him in the presence of the elders,
pull the sandal from his foot, spit in his face, and say, 'This
is what is done to the man who will not build up his
10 brother's house.' Throughout Israel his family shall be
known as 'the house of the one whose sandal was pulled
11 off.' If two men fight, and the wife of one comes
to defend her husband from the one who does him harm
12 by reaching out and seizing the man's genitals, you shall
13 cut off her hand: show no pity. Do not have two
different weights in your bag, one large and the other
14 small. Do not have in your house two different measures,
15 one large and the other small. You must have a full and
honest weight and a full and honest measure, so that your
days may be long on the land that the Lord your God is
16 giving you. Whoever does such things, whoever acts
dishonestly, is abhorrent to the Lord your God.

THE LAST OF THE ETHICAL COMMANDMENTS

With this reiteration of the importance of honest weights (see Lev. 19:36 and note there), we close Moshe's lengthy summary of the laws *shebein adam lahavero*, the duties we owe one another. In Jewish law, most commands require a blessing. Its standard form is "Blessed are you, Lord our God... who has sanctified us with His commandments and has commanded us to...." However, there are exceptions. The medieval Jewish sages searched for a general rule to

יֵשְׁבוּ אַחִים יַחְדָּו וּמֵת אַחַד מֵהֶם וּבֵן אֵין־לוֹ לֹא־תִהְיֶה
אֵשֶׁת־הַמֵּת הַחוּצָה לְאִישׁ זָר יְבָמָהּ יָבֹא עָלֶיהָ וּלְקָחָהּ לוֹ
ו לְאִשָּׁה וְיִבְּמָהּ׃ וְהָיָה הַבְּכוֹר אֲשֶׁר תֵּלֵד יָקוּם עַל־שֵׁם אָחִיו
ז הַמֵּת וְלֹא־יִמָּחֶה שְׁמוֹ מִיִּשְׂרָאֵל׃ וְאִם־לֹא יַחְפֹּץ הָאִישׁ
לָקַחַת אֶת־יְבִמְתּוֹ וְעָלְתָה יְבִמְתּוֹ הַשַּׁעְרָה אֶל־הַזְּקֵנִים
וְאָמְרָה מֵאֵן יְבָמִי לְהָקִים לְאָחִיו שֵׁם בְּיִשְׂרָאֵל לֹא אָבָה
ח יַבְּמִי׃ וְקָרְאוּ־לוֹ זִקְנֵי־עִירוֹ וְדִבְּרוּ אֵלָיו וְעָמַד וְאָמַר לֹא
ט חָפַצְתִּי לְקַחְתָּהּ׃ וְנִגְּשָׁה יְבִמְתּוֹ אֵלָיו לְעֵינֵי הַזְּקֵנִים וְחָלְצָה
נַעֲלוֹ מֵעַל רַגְלוֹ וְיָרְקָה בְּפָנָיו וְעָנְתָה וְאָמְרָה כָּכָה יֵעָשֶׂה
י לָאִישׁ אֲשֶׁר לֹא־יִבְנֶה אֶת־בֵּית אָחִיו׃ וְנִקְרָא שְׁמוֹ בְּיִשְׂרָאֵל
יא בֵּית חֲלוּץ הַנָּעַל׃ כִּי־יִנָּצוּ אֲנָשִׁים יַחְדָּו אִישׁ
וְאָחִיו וְקָרְבָה אֵשֶׁת הָאֶחָד לְהַצִּיל אֶת־אִישָׁהּ מִיַּד מַכֵּהוּ
יב וְשָׁלְחָה יָדָהּ וְהֶחֱזִיקָה בִּמְבֻשָׁיו׃ וְקַצֹּתָה אֶת־כַּפָּהּ לֹא
יג תָחוֹס עֵינֶךָ׃ לֹא־יִהְיֶה לְךָ בְּכִיסְךָ אֶבֶן וָאָבֶן
יד גְּדוֹלָה וּקְטַנָּה׃ לֹא־יִהְיֶה לְךָ בְּבֵיתְךָ אֵיפָה וְאֵיפָה גְּדוֹלָה
טו וּקְטַנָּה׃ אֶבֶן שְׁלֵמָה וָצֶדֶק יִהְיֶה־לָּךְ אֵיפָה שְׁלֵמָה וָצֶדֶק
יִהְיֶה־לָּךְ לְמַעַן יַאֲרִיכוּ יָמֶיךָ עַל הָאֲדָמָה אֲשֶׁר־יְהוָה
טז אֱלֹהֶיךָ נֹתֵן לָךְ׃ כִּי תוֹעֲבַת יְהוָה אֱלֹהֶיךָ כָּל־עֹשֵׂה אֵלֶּה
כֹּל עֹשֵׂה עָוֶל׃

neighbor's field of standing grain, you may pluck ears with your hand" (Deut. 23:25–26). The principle is the same in both cases: it is cruel to prevent those working with food from eating some of it. The parallel is instructive. Descartes thought that animals lacked souls. Therefore you could do with them as you pleased. Judaism does not believe that animals lack souls – "The righteous man knows his beast's *nefesh*," says the book of Proverbs (12:10). To be sure, *nefesh* here probably means "life" rather than "soul" (*neshama* in Hebrew). But Tanakh does regard animals as sentient beings. They may not think or speak, but they are capable of distress. Therefore there is such a thing as animal distress, *tzaar baalei ḥayyim*, and as far as possible it should be avoided. Animals, not just humans, have feelings, and they must be respected.

▶

17 Remember what Amalek did to you on your way as you MAFTIR
18 left Egypt, how he attacked you on the way, when you
were tired and exhausted, striking down all the stragglers

---

do good, relieve suffering, bring comfort. They redeem human solitude and bring those who suffer back into "the land of the living."

These universal values are embedded into the particularities of the Jewish covenant. From here the Torah moves on to the commandments of Jewish historical memory, and to the sealing of the covenant anew.

AMALEK

The Israelites had two enemies in the days of Moshe: the Egyptians and the Amalekites. The Egyptians enslaved the Israelites. They turned them into a forced labor colony. Pharaoh commanded them to drown every male Israelite child, attempted genocide. Yet about them, as we saw, Moshe commands: "Do not despise an Egyptian, for you lived as a stranger in his land" (Deut. 23:8).

The Amalekites did no more than attack the Israelites once, an attack that was successfully repelled (Ex. 17:13). Yet Moshe commands: "Remember." "Do not forget." "Blot out the memory." In Exodus, the Torah says that "the LORD will be at war with Amalek throughout the ages" (17:16). Why the difference? Why did Moshe tell the Israelites, in effect, to forgive the Egyptians but not the Amalekites?

What is more, the commandment to destroy Amalek no longer has practical application. It is no longer possible to identify the ethnicity of any of the original peoples against whom the Israelites were commanded to fight (see note on Deut. 23:4). Rambam added in *Guide for the Perplexed* (III:50) that the command only applied to people of specific biological descent. It is not to be applied in general to enemies or haters of the Jewish people. So the command to wage war against the Amalekites no longer applies, yet the command to remember does. What is it about the memory of Amalek that makes it so different from the memory of Egypt?

The answer may be that when hate is rational, based on some fear or disapproval that – justified or not – has some logic to it, then it can be reasoned with. The Egyptians feared the Israelites because they were numerous. Historians tell us that this fear was not groundless. Egypt had already suffered from one invasion of outsiders, the Hyksos, an Asiatic people with Canaanite names and beliefs who took over the Nile Delta during the Second Intermediate Period of the Egypt of the pharaohs. Eventually they were expelled from Egypt and all traces of their occupation were erased. But the memory persisted. It was not irrational for the Egyptians to fear that the Hebrews were another such population. The fear of the Egyptians was certainly unjustified. The Israelites did

יז זָכ֕וֹר אֵ֛ת אֲשֶׁר־עָשָׂ֥ה לְךָ֖ עֲמָלֵ֑ק בַּדֶּ֖רֶךְ בְּצֵאתְכֶ֥ם מִמִּצְרָֽיִם׃ מפטיר
יח אֲשֶׁ֨ר קָֽרְךָ֜ בַּדֶּ֗רֶךְ וַיְזַנֵּ֤ב בְּךָ֙ כָּל־הַנֶּחֱשָׁלִ֣ים אַֽחֲרֶ֔יךָ וְאַתָּ֖ה

distinguish commandments that require a blessing from those that do not. Various suggestions were made; few were deemed satisfactory. Rabbi Shlomo Ibn Aderet (Rashba), among others, doubted whether there was a simple criterion (*Responsa Rashba* III:283). Rambam, however, formulated one of breathtaking simplicity: commands between us and God, *bein adam laMakom*, require a blessing; commands between us and our fellow human beings, *bein adam laḥavero*, do not (*Hilkhot Berakhot* 11:2; *Kesef Mishneh*).

Why should this be so? Some offered the suggestion that commands between us and our fellows are not wholly within our control. In the case of charity, for example, the rich man may wish to give but the poor may not wish to accept. It would be wrong to make a blessing over a command that is not wholly in our power. I believe, however, that a different issue is at stake.

In the case of commands between us and God, what matters is the act and the intention with which it was performed. There is a debate in Jewish law as to whether, in general, commands require specific intent (*kavana*). It is clear, however, that a command between us and God must be directed to God. That is what makes it a religious act as opposed to, say, a custom, an ethnic folkway, or a habit. Intention gives the act the characteristic essential to a religious deed in Judaism, namely, that it is a response to a command of God. In that minimalist sense, intent is necessary.

An act between us and another human being, however, has a different character. What matters is not the act but its result (in philosophical terms, not the *peula* but the *nifal*). Hence, the Talmud makes the radical remark that "one who gives a sum to charity in order to gain a share in the World to Come or save the life of his child is regarded as perfectly righteous" (Bava Batra 10b). The doer of the deed in this case has ulterior motives, *but the motives are irrelevant to acts the purpose of which is to bring aid to those who are in need*. The religious character of the moment lies not in the act, its intention, or the motive for which it was performed, but the comfort given, the help received, the loneliness lifted. In such cases Judaism does not require specific intent. Hence there is no need to make the intent explicit in the form of a benediction.

Our good deeds – deeds that make a difference to the lives of our fellow human beings – constitute, as it were, a universal language. Our human situation as embodied souls, physical beings, means that we share needs and vulnerabilities. When it comes to acts that address such needs, it is irrelevant who performs them, for whom they are performed, and with what motive or intention. What matters is that they

19 in your rear, with no fear of God. And so, when the Lord
your God gives you rest from all the enemies around you
in the land that the Lord your God is giving you as an
inheritance to possess, you shall blot out the memory of
Amalek from beneath the sky. Do not forget.

The haftara for Parashat Ki Tetzeh is on page 1612.
If the haftara for Re'eh was not read (because of Rosh Ḥodesh Elul), it is read at the end of this haftara (see page 1606).

of irrational hatred. In the Middle Ages, Jews were accused of poisoning wells, spreading the plague, and in one of the most absurd claims ever – the blood libel – they were suspected of killing Christian children to use their blood to make matzot for Passover. This was self-evidently impossible, but that did not stop people from believing it.

Amalek-like, irrational hatred does not die and cannot be reasoned with. But the Jewish people survives as well. Attacked so many times over the centuries, it still lives, and in doing so, gives testimony to the victory of the God of love over the myths and madness of hate.

יט עָיֵף וְיָגֵעַ וְלֹא יָרֵא אֱלֹהִים׃ וְהָיָה בְּהָנִיחַ יְהוָה אֱלֹהֶיךָ ׀ לְךָ
מִכָּל־אֹיְבֶיךָ מִסָּבִיב בָּאָרֶץ אֲשֶׁר־יְהוָה אֱלֹהֶיךָ נֹתֵן לְךָ
נַחֲלָה לְרִשְׁתָּהּ תִּמְחֶה אֶת־זֵכֶר עֲמָלֵק מִתַּחַת הַשָּׁמָיִם
לֹא תִּשְׁכָּח׃

The הפטרה *for* פרשת כי תצא *is on page 1613.*
If the הפטרה *for* ראה *was not read (because of* ראש חודש אלול*), it is read at the end of this* הפטרה *(see page 1607).*

not want to take over Egypt. To the contrary, they would have preferred to leave. Not every rational emotion is justified. Yet that rational but unjustified emotion can, in principle, be cured through reasoning.

Precisely the opposite was true of the Amalekites. They attacked the Israelites when they were "tired and exhausted," focused their assault on the "stragglers in your rear." Those who are weak and lagging behind pose no danger. This was irrational, groundless hate. Therefore it may never go away. The hatred symbolized by Amalek lasts "throughout the ages" (Ex. 17:16). All one can do is to remember and not forget, to be constantly vigilant, and to fight it whenever and wherever it appears.

Antisemitism is the paradigm case

PARASHAT KI TAVO

26 1 "When you have come into the land that the LORD
your God is giving you as a possession, and have taken
2 possession and settled in it, you shall take some of every
first fruit of the soil, which you harvest from the land that
the LORD your God is giving you. Put it in a basket and

---

the Temple: the well-known passage, beginning "My ancestor was a wandering Aramean" that is still expounded as part of the Haggada on Seder night.

Here for the first time *the retelling of the nation's past becomes an obligation for every citizen of the nation.* The passage, known as *vidui bikkurim*, "the confession made over first fruits," was simple and elemental. It is the entire history of the nation in summary form. Most importantly, it is written in the first person: "*My* ancestor.... The LORD brought *us* out of Egypt." History is transformed into memory. This is not a detached tale of some disembodied past. It is the story of where I came from and who I am, which led the Sages of the Mishna to say, "In each generation, every person should see himself as if he personally came out of Egypt" (Pesaḥim 10:5).

It is impossible to overestimate the impact this had on the Jewish people from then to now. Identity is not just a matter of who my parents were. It is also a matter of *what they remembered and handed on to me.* Identity is shaped by memory. Telling the story, regularly, as a religious duty, sustained Jewish identity across the centuries, even in the absence of all the normal accompaniments of nationhood – land, geographical proximity, independence, self-determination.

To know who we are is in large part to understand of which story or stories we are a part. That is what makes Jewish identity so rich and resonant. In an age in which computer memories have grown while human memories have become foreshortened, this remains an important message, not just to Jews but also to humanity. Maybe you can delegate history to computers, looking it up when you need it. But you cannot delegate memory. Memory is inherently, inescapably personal. It is what makes us who we are. If you seek to sustain identity, you have to renew memory regularly and teach it to the next generation. Those who tell the story of their past have already begun to build their children's future.

26:2 מֵרֵאשִׁית כׇּל־פְּרִי הָאֲדָמָה *Some of every first fruit of the soil* – There is a rabbinic aphorism that "God creates the remedy before the disease" (Megilla 13b). Prior to the *tokheḥa* (literally defined as "remonstration" or "rebuke") curses, Moshe outlined the law of bringing first

פרשת כי תבוא

כו א וְהָיָה֙ כִּֽי־תָב֣וֹא אֶל־הָאָ֔רֶץ אֲשֶׁר֙ יְהוָ֣ה אֱלֹהֶ֔יךָ נֹתֵ֥ן לְךָ֖ נַחֲלָ֑ה כא
ב וִֽירִשְׁתָּ֖הּ וְיָשַׁ֥בְתָּ בָּֽהּ׃ וְלָקַחְתָּ֞ מֵרֵאשִׁ֣ית ׀ כָּל־פְּרִ֣י הָאֲדָמָ֗ה
אֲשֶׁ֨ר תָּבִ֧יא מֵֽאַרְצְךָ֛ אֲשֶׁ֨ר יְהוָ֧ה אֱלֹהֶ֛יךָ נֹתֵ֥ן לָ֖ךְ וְשַׂמְתָּ֣
בַטֶּ֑נֶא וְהָֽלַכְתָּ֙ אֶל־הַמָּק֔וֹם אֲשֶׁ֤ר יִבְחַר֙ יְהוָ֣ה אֱלֹהֶ֔יךָ לְשַׁכֵּ֥ן

KI TAVO

In Parashat Ki Tavo, Moshe reaches the end of the detailed provisions of the covenant, with commands about bringing first fruits to the central Sanctuary, as well as allocating the various tithes. He closes this section with a reminder of what the covenant is: a mutual pledge between the people and God. The people are to give God their total loyalty. God, in turn, will hold the people in special regard.

The text then turns to a distinctive feature of ancient covenants: the blessings and curses that will attend faithfulness on the one hand, disloyalty on the other. Given that Israel's entire existence as a nation is predicated on the covenant, it means that their fate will be an ongoing commentary on their relationship with God and the ideals, both sacred and social, to which the people have dedicated themselves as "a holy people to the Lord your God" (Deut. 7:6).

The *parasha* ends with Moshe summoning the people, at the end of their forty-year journey and in sight of the Promised Land, to renew the covenant their parents made with God at Mount Sinai.

THE CEREMONY OF THE FIRST FRUITS

Parashat Ki Tavo begins with the ceremony of bringing the first fruits to the Temple. The Mishna gives a detailed account of what happened:

> Those who were near to Jerusalem brought fresh figs and grapes, and those who were far away brought dried figs and raisins. Before them went the ox, its horns overlaid with gold, and with a wreath of olive leaves on its head.
>
> The flute was played before them until they came near Jerusalem. When they were near to Jerusalem, they sent messengers before them and bedecked their first fruits. The rulers and the prefects and the treasurers of the Temple went forth to meet them.... All the craftsmen in Jerusalem used to rise up for them and greet them, saying, "Brothers, men of such and such a place, you are welcome." (Bikkurim 3:3)

It was a magnificent celebration. Its most significant aspect was the declaration each individual had to make in

go to the place that the Lord your God will choose as a
3 dwelling for His name. You shall go to the priest officiating
at that time and say to him, 'I declare today to the Lord
your God that I have come into the land that the Lord
4 swore to our ancestors to give us.' The priest shall take the
basket from your hand and set it down before the altar of
5 the Lord your God. You shall then make this declaration
before the Lord your God: 'My ancestor was a wandering
Aramean. He went down into Egypt and lived there as a
stranger, just a handful of souls, and there he became a
6 nation – large, mighty, and great. And the Egyptians dealt

The sun and the wind were once arguing as to which was stronger. The sun said, "I am stronger, because I give light and warmth to the whole world." The wind said, "I am stronger, because nothing can stand in my way." Just then a farmer began plowing his field. The sun said to the wind, "Let us settle the matter once and for all. Let us see which of us can remove the jacket from the man. That will prove which is the stronger." The wind accepted the challenge and began to blow. But the harder it blew, the more tightly the famer clung to his jacket, until the wind gave up, exhausted. Then the sun began to shine. As soon as the farmer felt its heat, he took his jacket off. Warmth is more powerful than wind.

So it was with Israel. Pharaoh and his people afflicted the Israelites, but "the more they were oppressed, the more they increased" (Ex. 1:12). Lavan, in this reading, did not afflict Yaakov. To the contrary, while he was with Lavan, Yaakov grew rich. The danger was that he would remain with Lavan and forget who he was. Throughout Jewish history, the more Jews suffered, the more they prayed, studied, and kept the commands. Paradoxically, the danger to Jewish continuity has been not slavery and suffering, but affluence and freedom.

So Moshe warned at the end of his life: "Take care not to forget the Lord your God.... Otherwise, when you have eaten and been satisfied, and have built fine houses and lived in them...your heart may become proud, forgetting the Lord your God who brought you out of Egypt, the house of slaves" (Deut. 8:11–14).

26:5 וַיְהִי־שָׁם לְגוֹי *There he became a nation* – The Vilna Gaon explains that the word *goy*, "nation," is related to the word *geviya*, "body." A group of individuals becomes a nation when it becomes like a single body. R. Shimon b. Yoḥai taught, "Israel is like one body with a single soul. When one is injured, all feel the pain" (Vayikra Rabba 4:6).

Rabbi Joseph B. Soloveitchik (1903–93), in his essay *Kol Dodi Dofek*, spoke of the two covenants that bind Jews to one

ג שְׁמוֹ שָׁם: וּבָאתָ אֶל־הַכֹּהֵן אֲשֶׁר יִהְיֶה בַּיָּמִים הָהֵם וְאָמַרְתָּ
אֵלָיו הִגַּדְתִּי הַיּוֹם לַיהוָה אֱלֹהֶיךָ כִּי־בָאתִי אֶל־הָאָרֶץ אֲשֶׁר
ד נִשְׁבַּע יְהוָה לַאֲבֹתֵינוּ לָתֶת לָנוּ: וְלָקַח הַכֹּהֵן הַטֶּנֶא מִיָּדֶךָ
ה וְהִנִּיחוֹ לִפְנֵי מִזְבַּח יְהוָה אֱלֹהֶיךָ: וְעָנִיתָ וְאָמַרְתָּ לִפְנֵי ׀ יְהוָה
אֱלֹהֶיךָ אֲרַמִּי אֹבֵד אָבִי וַיֵּרֶד מִצְרַיְמָה וַיָּגָר שָׁם בִּמְתֵי מְעָט
ו וַיְהִי־שָׁם לְגוֹי גָּדוֹל עָצוּם וָרָב: וַיָּרֵעוּ אֹתָנוּ הַמִּצְרִים וַיְעַנּוּנוּ

---

fruits, in celebration, to the Temple. The Torah concludes the passage with the following words: "Then you, with the Levites and the migrants who live among you, shall rejoice in all the good that the Lord your God has bestowed on you and on your household" (Deut. 26:11).

Judaism is a religion of rejoicing; of remembering where we came from, and not taking our blessings for granted; of recalling the source of the good, and therefore not forgetting the larger truth that it comes to us from the hand of God.

Jewish history sometimes seems to have been written in tears. More than most other nations, our collective story is told in terms of exiles and expulsions, persecutions and martyrdoms, inquisitions, pogroms, and holocausts. Yet Jews mourn on the Ninth of Av and the other specified fasts but have not allowed the rest of our days to be darkened by grief. We hold on to the affirmation that finds God in the midst of life and its blessings. Judaism's greatest challenge is to make a blessing over life, turning material satisfactions into spiritual affirmations.

26:5 **אֲרַמִּי אֹבֵד אָבִי** *My ancestor was a wandering Aramean* – The exposition of these four verses constitutes, according to the Mishna (Pesaḥim 10:4), the core of the Passover Haggada. Most scholars take the view that this text was chosen because, as part of the first-fruits ceremony, it would have been well known to most Jews in Temple times, before texts of the Haggada were freely available. Another reason is that the "confession" is preceded by the words "I declare (*higadeti*) today." The verb is from the same root as the word *haggada*, recited on the night of Passover, when we are commanded to "declare" to our children (*vehigadeta levinkha*).

Nonetheless, it is a strange choice. The plain sense of the words *Arami oved avi* is "My ancestor was a wandering Aramean" (meaning Avraham, according to Rashbam; or Yaakov, according to Ibn Ezra and Sforno). The interpretation of the Passover Haggada – "An Aramean sought my ancestor's death" – is not the plain sense. What is more, that interpretation seems to cut across the whole theme of the Haggada, which is about slavery in Egypt. It is strange to begin by saying that what Pharaoh did was bad, but Lavan was worse. Rabbi Z. H. Ferber offered the following explanation:

cruelly with us and oppressed us, subjecting us to harsh
7 labor. We cried out to the Lord, God of our ancestors.
And the Lord heard our voice and He saw our oppression,
8 our toil, and our enslavement. The Lord brought us out
of Egypt with a mighty hand and His arm stretched forth,
9 with terrifying power, with signs, and with wonders. He
brought us into this place and He gave us this land, a land
10 flowing with milk and with honey. And now I am bringing
the first fruit of the land that You, O Lord, have given me.'
Set the basket down before the Lord your God, and then
11 bow down low before the Lord your God. Then you,
with the Levites and the migrants who live among you,
shall rejoice in all the good that the Lord your God has
12 bestowed on you and on your household. When SHENI
you have finished setting aside a tenth of all your produce
in the third year, the year of the tithe, and have given it to
the Levites, the migrants, the orphans, and the widows, so
13 that they may eat in your towns and be satisfied, you shall
declare before the Lord your God: 'I have removed the
consecrated portion from my house, and I have given it to
the Levites and the migrants, the orphans, and the widows,
just as You commanded me. I have not transgressed or
14 forgotten any of Your commandments. I have not eaten
of it while in mourning. I have not removed any of it while

The word *simḥa* has in the Torah a nuance untranslatable into English. Joy, happiness, pleasure, and the like are all states of mind, emotions. They belong to the individual. We can feel them alone. *Simḥa*, by contrast, is not a private emotion. It means *happiness shared*. It is a social state, a predicate of "we," not "I." There is no such thing as feeling *simḥa* alone.

Freedom, affluence, and security too often turn a nation into a collection of individuals, each pursuing his or her own happiness, indifferent to the fate of those who have less, the lonely, the marginal, and the excluded. When that happens, societies start to disintegrate.

The only way to avoid it, says Moshe, is to share your happiness with others, and, in the midst of that collective, national celebration, serve God. Blessings are not measured by how much we own or earn or spend or possess but by how much we share. *Simḥa* is the mark of a sacred society. It is a place of collective joy.

ז וַיִּתְּנוּ עָלֵינוּ עֲבֹדָה קָשָׁה: וַנִּצְעַק אֶל־יהוה אֱלֹהֵי אֲבֹתֵינוּ
וַיִּשְׁמַע יהוה אֶת־קֹלֵנוּ וַיַּרְא אֶת־עָנְיֵנוּ וְאֶת־עֲמָלֵנוּ וְאֶת־
ח לַחֲצֵנוּ: וַיּוֹצִאֵנוּ יהוה מִמִּצְרַיִם בְּיָד חֲזָקָה וּבִזְרֹעַ נְטוּיָה
ט וּבְמֹרָא גָּדֹל וּבְאֹתוֹת וּבְמֹפְתִים: וַיְבִאֵנוּ אֶל־הַמָּקוֹם הַזֶּה
י וַיִּתֶּן־לָנוּ אֶת־הָאָרֶץ הַזֹּאת אֶרֶץ זָבַת חָלָב וּדְבָשׁ: וְעַתָּה
הִנֵּה הֵבֵאתִי אֶת־רֵאשִׁית פְּרִי הָאֲדָמָה אֲשֶׁר־נָתַתָּה לִּי
יהוה וְהִנַּחְתּוֹ לִפְנֵי יהוה אֱלֹהֶיךָ וְהִשְׁתַּחֲוִיתָ לִפְנֵי יהוה
יא אֱלֹהֶיךָ: וְשָׂמַחְתָּ בְכָל־הַטּוֹב אֲשֶׁר נָתַן־לְךָ יהוה אֱלֹהֶיךָ
יב וּלְבֵיתֶךָ אַתָּה וְהַלֵּוִי וְהַגֵּר אֲשֶׁר בְּקִרְבֶּךָ: כִּי שני
תְכַלֶּה לַעְשֵׂר אֶת־כָּל־מַעְשַׂר תְּבוּאָתְךָ בַּשָּׁנָה הַשְּׁלִישִׁת
שְׁנַת הַמַּעֲשֵׂר וְנָתַתָּה לַלֵּוִי לַגֵּר לַיָּתוֹם וְלָאַלְמָנָה וְאָכְלוּ
יג בִשְׁעָרֶיךָ וְשָׂבֵעוּ: וְאָמַרְתָּ לִפְנֵי יהוה אֱלֹהֶיךָ בִּעַרְתִּי הַקֹּדֶשׁ
מִן־הַבַּיִת וְגַם נְתַתִּיו לַלֵּוִי וְלַגֵּר לַיָּתוֹם וְלָאַלְמָנָה כְּכָל־
מִצְוָתְךָ אֲשֶׁר צִוִּיתָנִי לֹא־עָבַרְתִּי מִמִּצְוֺתֶיךָ וְלֹא שָׁכָחְתִּי:
יד לֹא־אָכַלְתִּי בְאֹנִי מִמֶּנּוּ וְלֹא־בִעַרְתִּי מִמֶּנּוּ בְּטָמֵא וְלֹא־

---

another: *brit goral*, the "covenant of fate," and *brit yeud*, the "covenant of destiny." The first arises out of shared suffering in the past, the second out of a collective vision of the future (see also notes on Ex. 12:3 and Num. 10, "Community and Camp"). In Egypt the Israelites entered into the covenant of fate. They were united by suffering. A midrash states: "In Egypt the Israelites gathered to dwell as a group, all of them becoming as one, and they covenanted to act with loving-kindness toward one another" (Tanna DeVei Eliyahu). That is how they first became a nation.

26:11 וְשָׂמַחְתָּ... אַתָּה וְהַלֵּוִי וְהַגֵּר *Then you, with the Levites and the migrants... shall rejoice* – According to Ibn Ezra this means that "you must bring them to rejoice in the fruit of your land." The description fits the festival tradition we practice to this day. Rambam puts it strongly:

> When one eats and drinks [on a festival], one must also feed the stranger, the orphan, the widow, and others who are distressed and poor. But one who locks the door of his courtyard, and eats and drinks with his children and wife but does not feed the poor and the bitter at heart – this is not joy of a mitzva, but the joy of his belly. (*Hilkhot Yom Tov* 6:18)

impure. I have not offered any of it to the dead. I have
obeyed the LORD my God, doing just as You commanded
15 me. Look down from Your holy habitation, from heaven,
and bless Your people Israel and the land that You have
given us, as You swore to our ancestors – a land flowing
16 with milk and with honey.' The LORD your God is SHELISHI
commanding you this day to keep these decrees and laws.
Take care to keep them with all your heart and with all
17 your soul. Today you have proclaimed the LORD to be your
God, and that you will walk in His ways, keep His decrees,
18 commandments, and laws, and listen to His voice. And
today the LORD has proclaimed you to be, as He promised
19 you, His treasured people who guard His commands; He
will set you high above all the nations He has made, in
praise, fame, and honor. You will be a people holy to the
LORD your God, just as He has promised."
27 1 Then Moshe and the elders of Israel charged the people: REVI'I
"Keep all of the command that I charge you with this day.
2 On the day that you cross the Jordan to the land that the
LORD your God is giving you, set up large boulders, and

there was." Language creates worlds.

That is divine – not human – speech. However, there is a human counterpart. There are things we create with words when we use them in a particular way. J. L. Austin called this use of speech *performative utterance*. So, for example, when a judge says, "This court is now in session," he is not *describing* something but *doing* something.

The most basic type of performative utterance is *making a promise*. This involves the use of language to *create an obligation*. Some promises are unilateral, but others are mutual. Some are specific; others are open-ended. The supreme example of an open-ended mutual pledge between human beings is marriage. The supreme example of an open-ended mutual pledge between human beings and God is a covenant. That is what our two verses state: that God and the people of Israel pledged themselves to one another by making a covenant, a relationship brought into existence by words and sustained by honoring those words.

Language used to create a mutually binding relationship links God and humankind. Our verse means: "Today, through speech, you have made God your God, and God has made you His people." Words, an act of saying, have created an eternally binding relationship.

נָתַתִּי מִמֶּנּוּ לְמֵת שָׁמַעְתִּי בְּקוֹל יהוה אֱלֹהָי עָשִׂיתִי כְּכֹל
טו אֲשֶׁר צִוִּיתָנִי׃ הַשְׁקִיפָה מִמְּעוֹן קָדְשְׁךָ מִן־הַשָּׁמַיִם וּבָרֵךְ
אֶת־עַמְּךָ אֶת־יִשְׂרָאֵל וְאֵת הָאֲדָמָה אֲשֶׁר נָתַתָּה לָנוּ כַּאֲשֶׁר
טז נִשְׁבַּעְתָּ לַאֲבֹתֵינוּ אֶרֶץ זָבַת חָלָב וּדְבָשׁ׃ הַיּוֹם שלישי
הַזֶּה יהוה אֱלֹהֶיךָ מְצַוְּךָ לַעֲשׂוֹת אֶת־הַחֻקִּים הָאֵלֶּה וְאֶת־
הַמִּשְׁפָּטִים וְשָׁמַרְתָּ וְעָשִׂיתָ אוֹתָם בְּכָל־לְבָבְךָ וּבְכָל־נַפְשֶׁךָ׃
יז אֶת־יהוה הֶאֱמַרְתָּ הַיּוֹם לִהְיוֹת לְךָ לֵאלֹהִים וְלָלֶכֶת בִּדְרָכָיו
יח וְלִשְׁמֹר חֻקָּיו וּמִצְוֹתָיו וּמִשְׁפָּטָיו וְלִשְׁמֹעַ בְּקֹלוֹ׃ וַיהוה
הֶאֱמִירְךָ הַיּוֹם לִהְיוֹת לוֹ לְעַם סְגֻלָּה כַּאֲשֶׁר דִּבֶּר־לָךְ
יט וְלִשְׁמֹר כָּל־מִצְוֹתָיו׃ וּלְתִתְּךָ עֶלְיוֹן עַל כָּל־הַגּוֹיִם אֲשֶׁר
עָשָׂה לִתְהִלָּה וּלְשֵׁם וּלְתִפְאָרֶת וְלִהְיֹתְךָ עַם־קָדֹשׁ לַיהוה
אֱלֹהֶיךָ כַּאֲשֶׁר דִּבֵּר׃
כז א וַיְצַו מֹשֶׁה וְזִקְנֵי יִשְׂרָאֵל אֶת־הָעָם לֵאמֹר שָׁמֹר אֶת־כָּל־ רביעי
ב הַמִּצְוָה אֲשֶׁר אָנֹכִי מְצַוֶּה אֶתְכֶם הַיּוֹם׃ וְהָיָה בַּיּוֹם אֲשֶׁר
תַּעַבְרוּ אֶת־הַיַּרְדֵּן אֶל־הָאָרֶץ אֲשֶׁר־יהוה אֱלֹהֶיךָ נֹתֵן לָךְ

26:17 הֶאֱמַרְתָּ *You have proclaimed* – Any translation tends to conceal the difficulty in this key verb, associated with Israel here, and God in the next verse: *lehaamir*. While it is a form of one of the most common of all biblical verbs, *lemor*, "to say," the specific form used here – the *hifil*, causative, form – is unique. It appears nowhere else in this form in the Tanakh. Its meaning is, therefore, obscure.

The JPS translation reads it as "affirmed." Rabbi Aryeh Kaplan, in *The Living Torah*, reads it as "declared allegiance to." Robert Alter, like us, renders it: "proclaimed." Other interpretations include "separated to yourself" (Rashi), "recognized" (Rabbi Saadia Gaon), "betrothed" (Malbim), "exchanged everything else for" (Ḥizkuni), "accepted the uniqueness of" (Rashi on Ḥagiga 3a), or "caused God to declare" (Rabbi Yehuda HaLevi, cited by Ibn Ezra).

In the Torah, the unique bond between humanity and God is formed by *language, speech, words*. Hence the importance here of the verb meaning "to say," "to declare," "to affirm." There is a radical statement of this at the very beginning of the Torah. God *spoke* and the world came into being. Unlike every ancient myth about the beginning of things, there was no struggle, no use of force. Instead, the key verb is *lemor*, "God *said* [*vayomer*], 'Let there be' and

▶

3 coat them with plaster, and write on them all the words of
this Law when you cross over, that you may enter the land
that the LORD your God is giving you, a land flowing with
milk and with honey, as the LORD, God of your ancestors,
4 promised you. When you cross the Jordan, set up these
stones, as I command you today, on Mount Eival, and
5 coat them with plaster. And there, build an altar to the
LORD your God, an altar of stones. Do not take any iron
6 tool to them: of uncut stones you shall build the altar of
the LORD your God. On it, offer burnt offerings to the
7 LORD your God. You shall also sacrifice peace offerings
and eat them there, rejoicing before the LORD your God.
8 On the boulders you shall write very clearly all the words
9 of this Law." Then Moshe and the Levitical

---

of being owned by newcomers as well as by those whose families have been here for many generations. Storytelling can bind without dividing. Narrative politics, telling the story, can be egalitarian without being confrontational.

At the border of the land of Israel is to stand, not a gatekeeper, but a set of boulders engraved with a summary of the law (Rabbi Saadia Gaon) or the full text of the Torah from "When God began creating" (Ramban). This will display to all comers that, though we are a disparate collection of tribes and individuals, this covenant, this shared code, accessible to all, makes us together who we are.

27:8 בַּאֵר הֵיטֵב *Very clearly* – According to one tradition, the words of the Law on the stones were written in seventy languages. In rabbinic tradition, the phrase *ba'er heitev* came to refer to the need for interpretation to elucidate a text that presents particular difficulty.

Fundamentalism refers to many things in different contexts, but one of them is the tendency to read texts literally and apply them directly: to go straight from revelation to application without interpretation. It is a kind of principled impatience with the interpretative process, emerging when people feel that the world has been allowed to defeat the word. They, by contrast, are determined to defeat the world by means of the word.

In many religions, including Judaism, this is heretical. Every text needs interpretation. Every interpretation needs wisdom. Every wisdom needs careful negotiation between the timeless and time. It needs great wisdom together with a deep grounding in tradition to know how to apply the word to the world. The word, given in love, invites its interpretation in love (see note on Deut. 13:17).

ג וַהֲקֵמֹתָ לְךָ אֲבָנִים גְּדֹלוֹת וְשַׂדְתָּ אֹתָם בַּשִּׂיד: וְכָתַבְתָּ
עֲלֵיהֶן אֶת־כָּל־דִּבְרֵי הַתּוֹרָה הַזֹּאת בְּעָבְרֶךָ לְמַעַן אֲשֶׁר
תָּבֹא אֶל־הָאָרֶץ אֲשֶׁר־יהוה אֱלֹהֶיךָ ׀ נֹתֵן לְךָ אֶרֶץ
זָבַת חָלָב וּדְבַשׁ כַּאֲשֶׁר דִּבֶּר יהוה אֱלֹהֵי־אֲבֹתֶיךָ לָךְ:
ד וְהָיָה בְּעָבְרְכֶם אֶת־הַיַּרְדֵּן תָּקִימוּ אֶת־הָאֲבָנִים הָאֵלֶּה
אֲשֶׁר אָנֹכִי מְצַוֶּה אֶתְכֶם הַיּוֹם בְּהַר עֵיבָל וְשַׂדְתָּ אוֹתָם
ה בַּשִּׂיד: וּבָנִיתָ שָּׁם מִזְבֵּחַ לַיהוה אֱלֹהֶיךָ מִזְבַּח אֲבָנִים
ו לֹא־תָנִיף עֲלֵיהֶם בַּרְזֶל: אֲבָנִים שְׁלֵמוֹת תִּבְנֶה אֶת־
מִזְבַּח יהוה אֱלֹהֶיךָ וְהַעֲלִיתָ עָלָיו עוֹלֹת לַיהוה אֱלֹהֶיךָ:
ז וְזָבַחְתָּ שְׁלָמִים וְאָכַלְתָּ שָּׁם וְשָׂמַחְתָּ לִפְנֵי יהוה אֱלֹהֶיךָ:
ח וְכָתַבְתָּ עַל־הָאֲבָנִים אֶת־כָּל־דִּבְרֵי הַתּוֹרָה הַזֹּאת בַּאֵר
ט הֵיטֵב: וַיְדַבֵּר מֹשֶׁה וְהַכֹּהֲנִים הַלְוִיִּם אֶל־כָּל־

27:3 וְכָתַבְתָּ עֲלֵיהֶן *And write on them* – Whenever I visit Washington, D.C., I make a point of going to see the presidential memorials, Jefferson's, Roosevelt's, and Lincoln's. Each carries inscriptions taken from their words: Jefferson's "We hold these truths to be self-evident," Roosevelt's "The only thing we have to fear is fear itself," and Lincoln's Gettysburg Address and his second inaugural, "With malice toward none; with charity for all." London has no equivalent that I know of. There are memorials and statues everywhere, each with a brief inscription saying who the statue represents, but no speeches, quotations, sound bites. Even the statue of Churchill, whose speeches rivaled Lincoln's in power, carries only one word: "Churchill."

This phenomenon is of a piece with the fact that the clubs and gathering places of Britain's governing elite have no signs or nameplates. You only know where they are if someone in the know shows you. It is as if, if you have to ask, you don't belong. Knowledge that in America is publicly displayed, is in Britain tacit and taken for granted. Those who need to know, know.

America tells national stories; Britain doesn't. The reason is that the two nations have different political cultures. America's is based on covenant, Britain's on hierarchy and tradition. "Telling the story" is at the heart of covenantal politics. It sustains identity and creates a sense of collective belonging. It binds the generations, reminding us of where the nation came from and is going to. It locates national identity in a set of historic events, speaking of the values for which those who came before us fought, and of which we are the guardians for the sake of the future. It must be an inclusive narrative, capable

priests spoke to all Israel: "Be still and listen, Israel.
Today you have become the people of the Lord your
10 God. Therefore listen to the Lord your God, keeping His
commandments and decrees, with which I charge you on
11 this day." On that day Moshe charged the people: ḤAMISHI
12 "When you have crossed the Jordan, these shall stand on
Mount Gerizim to bless the people: Shimon, Levi, Yehuda,
13 Yissakhar, Yosef, and Binyamin. And these shall stand on
Mount Eival for the curse: Reuven, Gad, Asher, Zevulun,
14 Dan, and Naftali. The Levites shall then recite to all the
15 Israelites in a loud voice: 'Cursed be one who
makes a graven or molten image, abhorrent to the Lord,
the work of a craftsman, and secretly sets it up.' And all the

---

the good, and more significantly, that He punishes the guilty. It is specifically the punitive dimension of religious belief that is for them the fundamental difference that religion makes to a society. Essentially, they agree with Voltaire, who once said that whatever his personal views on the matter, he wanted those around him to believe in God because then he would be cheated less.

For both researchers, the fundamental problem to be overcome by any society is that of the free rider. We all seek the benefits of cooperative endeavor, while being reluctant to pay the costs. Norenzayan's thesis is that "social surveillance keeps people in line." What moves people to act in prosocial ways is not the idea of God as an abstract creative force, but rather the belief that He sees what we do – and not simply the belief but an active reminder of it. Even being exposed to drawings of human eyes subtly influences our behavior. Religion makes a difference because, through rituals, prayers, and holy days, people are *reminded* that we are seen.

The power of religion, Norenzayan and Johnson argue, is precisely its negative aspect of divine punishment. Norenzayan assembles research evidence that shows, counter-intuitively, that those who believe in a punitive God are more law abiding and also more forgiving than those who believe in a forgiving God. His conclusion is that "belief in divine punishment diminishes the motivation for earthly forms of costly punishment." Johnson regards the fear of divine punishment as, historically, a remarkably effective means of deterring free riders and encouraging cooperation on a large scale.

This may be why the tribes, looking one another, as it were, in the eye, repeat the refrain that even if the victim of a crime is unknown, unknowing, or powerless to protest, the people collectively denounce the crime, and God sees and will respond.

יִשְׂרָאֵל לֵאמֹר הַסְכֵּת ׀ וּשְׁמַע יִשְׂרָאֵל הַיּוֹם הַזֶּה נִהְיֵיתָ לְעָם
י לַיהוָה אֱלֹהֶיךָ׃ וְשָׁמַעְתָּ בְּקוֹל יְהוָה אֱלֹהֶיךָ וְעָשִׂיתָ אֶת־
יא מִצְוֹתָו וְאֶת־חֻקָּיו אֲשֶׁר אָנֹכִי מְצַוְּךָ הַיּוֹם׃ וַיְצַו חמישי
יב מֹשֶׁה אֶת־הָעָם בַּיּוֹם הַהוּא לֵאמֹר׃ אֵלֶּה יַעַמְדוּ לְבָרֵךְ אֶת־
הָעָם עַל־הַר גְּרִזִּים בְּעָבְרְכֶם אֶת־הַיַּרְדֵּן שִׁמְעוֹן וְלֵוִי וִיהוּדָה
יג וְיִשָּׂשכָר וְיוֹסֵף וּבִנְיָמִן׃ וְאֵלֶּה יַעַמְדוּ עַל־הַקְּלָלָה בְּהַר עֵיבָל
יד רְאוּבֵן גָּד וְאָשֵׁר וּזְבוּלֻן דָּן וְנַפְתָּלִי׃ וְעָנוּ הַלְוִיִּם וְאָמְרוּ אֶל־
טו כָּל־אִישׁ יִשְׂרָאֵל קוֹל רָם׃ אָרוּר הָאִישׁ אֲשֶׁר
יַעֲשֶׂה פֶסֶל וּמַסֵּכָה תּוֹעֲבַת יְהוָה מַעֲשֵׂה יְדֵי חָרָשׁ וְשָׂם

27:9 הַסְכֵּת וּשְׁמַע *Be still and listen* – Throughout Deuteronomy, Moshe becomes an educator, explaining to the next generation that the laws God has given them are not just divine decrees. They make sense in human terms. They respect human dignity. They honor the integrity of nature. They give the land the chance to rest and recuperate, and protect Israel against the otherwise inexorable laws of the decline and fall of nations.

That is why Moshe, consistently throughout Deuteronomy, uses the verb *sh-m-a*. He wants the Israelites to obey God, but not blindly or through fear alone. God did not give the Torah to Israel for His sake but for theirs, as partners in the law (see also note on Gen. 3:6).

That is the meaning of Moshe's words in our verse: "Be still and listen." Keeping the commands involves an act of listening, not just submission and blind obedience – in all of listening's multiple senses of attending, meditating, and reflecting. It does not involve abdication of the intellect or silencing of the questioning mind. Israel set it as their highest task to understand why the law is as it is.

Shema, listening, is the Torah's call to moral growth.

CURSES AND BLESSINGS

Here we turn to the sanctions associated with the covenant, namely, the blessings that will follow if it is adhered to, and the curses that will occur if it is broken. Facing one another on two mountainsides, the people hear and denounce a list of clandestine crimes – sins such as incest and "white-collar" theft (pushing back a neighbor's boundary marker) – which cause great social harm but often go undetected.

The research of Ara Norenzayan in *Big Gods* and Dominic Johnson in *God Is Watching You* shed an interesting light on this passage. They focus on the moral impact of the idea that God sees what we do, even in private, that He rewards

16 people shall respond and say, 'Amen!' 'Cursed
be one who degrades his father or mother.' And all the
17 people shall say, 'Amen!' 'Cursed be one who
moves back his neighbor's boundary marker.' And all the
18 people shall say, 'Amen!' 'Cursed be one who
leads a blind person astray along his way.' And all the
19 people shall say, 'Amen!' 'Cursed be one who
deprives the migrant, orphan, or widow of justice.' And
20 all the people shall say, 'Amen!' 'Cursed be one who lies
with his father's wife, dishonoring his father's bed.' And
21 all the people shall say, 'Amen!' 'Cursed be one
who lies with any animal.' And all the people shall say,
22 'Amen!' 'Cursed be anyone who lies with his sister,
whether she is the daughter of his father or of his mother.'
23 And all the people shall say, 'Amen!' 'Cursed be
one who lies with his mother-in-law.' And all the people
24 shall say, 'Amen!' 'Cursed be one who strikes
down his fellow in secret.' And all the people shall say,
25 'Amen!' 'Cursed be one who accepts a bribe to
execute an innocent man.' And all the people shall say,
26 'Amen!' 'Cursed be one who does not uphold
the words of this Law by keeping them.' And all the
people shall say, 'Amen!'
28 1 If you listen faithfully to the LORD your God, taking care
to keep all His commandments, which I am commanding
you today, the LORD your God will set you above all the
2 nations of this earth. All these blessings will come upon
you – overtake you – if you listen to the voice of the LORD
3 your God: Blessed shall you be in the town, and blessed
4 shall you be in the field. Blessed shall be the fruit of your
womb, the fruit of your land, and the fruit of your cattle,
5 the calves of your herd, the lambs of your flock. Blessed
6 shall be your basket and your kneading pan. Blessed shall

---

poverty. Throughout history, Judaism resisted any attempt to romanticize, rationalize, or anesthetize the pain of hunger, starvation, or need. One of the recurring themes of the book of Deuteronomy is "Then you... shall rejoice in all the good

טז בַּסָּתֶר וְעָנוּ כָל־הָעָם וְאָמְרוּ אָמֵן׃ אָרוּר
יז מַקְלֶה אָבִיו וְאִמּוֹ וְאָמַר כָּל־הָעָם אָמֵן׃ אָרוּר
יח מַסִּיג גְּבוּל רֵעֵהוּ וְאָמַר כָּל־הָעָם אָמֵן׃ אָרוּר
יט מַשְׁגֶּה עִוֵּר בַּדָּרֶךְ וְאָמַר כָּל־הָעָם אָמֵן׃ אָרוּר
כ מַטֶּה מִשְׁפַּט גֵּר־יָתוֹם וְאַלְמָנָה וְאָמַר כָּל־הָעָם אָמֵן׃ אָרוּר
שֹׁכֵב עִם־אֵשֶׁת אָבִיו כִּי גִלָּה כְּנַף אָבִיו וְאָמַר כָּל־הָעָם
כא אָמֵן׃ אָרוּר שֹׁכֵב עִם־כָּל־בְּהֵמָה וְאָמַר כָּל־
כב הָעָם אָמֵן׃ אָרוּר שֹׁכֵב עִם־אֲחֹתוֹ בַּת־אָבִיו אוֹ
כג בַת־אִמּוֹ וְאָמַר כָּל־הָעָם אָמֵן׃ אָרוּר שֹׁכֵב עִם־
כד חֹתַנְתּוֹ וְאָמַר כָּל־הָעָם אָמֵן׃ אָרוּר מַכֵּה רֵעֵהוּ
כה בַּסָּתֶר וְאָמַר כָּל־הָעָם אָמֵן׃ אָרוּר לֹקֵחַ שֹׁחַד
כו לְהַכּוֹת נֶפֶשׁ דַּם נָקִי וְאָמַר כָּל־הָעָם אָמֵן׃ אָרוּר
אֲשֶׁר לֹא־יָקִים אֶת־דִּבְרֵי הַתּוֹרָה־הַזֹּאת לַעֲשׂוֹת אוֹתָם
וְאָמַר כָּל־הָעָם אָמֵן׃

כח א וְהָיָה אִם־שָׁמוֹעַ תִּשְׁמַע בְּקוֹל יְהוָה אֱלֹהֶיךָ לִשְׁמֹר לַעֲשׂוֹת כב
אֶת־כָּל־מִצְוֹתָיו אֲשֶׁר אָנֹכִי מְצַוְּךָ הַיּוֹם וּנְתָנְךָ יְהוָה אֱלֹהֶיךָ
ב עֶלְיוֹן עַל כָּל־גּוֹיֵי הָאָרֶץ׃ וּבָאוּ עָלֶיךָ כָּל־הַבְּרָכוֹת הָאֵלֶּה
ג וְהִשִּׂיגֻךָ כִּי תִשְׁמַע בְּקוֹל יְהוָה אֱלֹהֶיךָ׃ בָּרוּךְ אַתָּה בָּעִיר
ד וּבָרוּךְ אַתָּה בַּשָּׂדֶה׃ בָּרוּךְ פְּרִי־בִטְנְךָ וּפְרִי אַדְמָתְךָ וּפְרִי
ה בְהֶמְתֶּךָ שְׁגַר אֲלָפֶיךָ וְעַשְׁתְּרוֹת צֹאנֶךָ׃ בָּרוּךְ טַנְאֲךָ
ו וּמִשְׁאַרְתֶּךָ׃ בָּרוּךְ אַתָּה בְּבֹאֶךָ וּבָרוּךְ אַתָּה בְּצֵאתֶךָ׃

28:5 בָּרוּךְ טַנְאֲךָ וּמִשְׁאַרְתֶּךָ *Your basket and your kneading pan* – These blessings are, by and large, material ones: healthy children, plentiful harvest, safety. Judaism takes a candid view of wealth as God's blessing, to be enjoyed as such. The world is God's creation; therefore it is good, and prosperity is a sign of God's blessing. Asceticism and self-denial have little place in Jewish spirituality. Rav, the third-century Sage, went so far as to say: "In the World to Come we will face judgment for every legitimate pleasure we denied ourselves in this life" (Yerushalmi, Kiddushin 4:12).

Economic growth has *religious* significance first and foremost because of the degree to which it allows us to alleviate

you be when you enter, and blessed shall you be when
7 you leave. The LORD will cause your enemies who rise SHISHI
against you to be vanquished before you. They will come
8 at you from one direction, but flee from you in seven. The
LORD will send you blessing in your barns and in all your
endeavors. He will bless you in the land that the LORD your
9 God is giving you. The LORD will establish you as His holy
people, just as He has sworn to you, if you keep the LORD
10 your God's commandments and walk in His ways. All the
peoples of earth shall see that you are called by the LORD's
11 name, and they shall hold you in awe. The LORD will make
you abound in prosperity, in the fruit of your womb, the
fruit of your cattle, and the fruit of your soil in the land that
12 the LORD swore to your ancestors to give you. The LORD
will open for you His treasury of good, the heavens, to give
your land rain in its season, to bless all the work of your
hands. You will lend to many nations, and borrow from
13 none. The LORD will make you the head, never the tail. You
shall be always above, and never beneath – if you obey the
commandments of the LORD your God that I am charging
14 you with on this day, taking care to keep them, and if you
do not stray from any of the words that I am commanding
you today, either to the right or to the left, to follow other
gods and serve them.

15 But if you do not listen to the voice of the LORD your
God, taking care to keep all His commandments and
decrees that I am charging you with on this day, all these

---

significance which lie beyond the scope of precise legislation. They cannot be spelled out in terms of exact, exhaustive rules, because life cannot be reduced to an exhaustive list of rules. They have to do with self-restraint, moderation, gentleness, alertness to the suffering of others, and the many other forms of moral literacy which you cannot learn from a book of rules, but only from experience and example.

THE TOKHEḤA

Twice in the Torah – once in Parashat Beḥukotai, the second time here – Moshe voices a series of prophecies of the sufferings that will befall the Jewish people if they fail to honor their mission as the

ז יִתֵּן יְהוָה אֶת־אֹיְבֶיךָ הַקָּמִים עָלֶיךָ נִגָּפִים לְפָנֶיךָ בְּדֶרֶךְ ששי
ח אֶחָד יֵצְאוּ אֵלֶיךָ וּבְשִׁבְעָה דְרָכִים יָנוּסוּ לְפָנֶיךָ: יְצַו יְהוָה
אִתְּךָ אֶת־הַבְּרָכָה בַּאֲסָמֶיךָ וּבְכֹל מִשְׁלַח יָדֶךָ וּבֵרַכְךָ בָּאָרֶץ
ט אֲשֶׁר־יְהוָה אֱלֹהֶיךָ נֹתֵן לָךְ: יְקִימְךָ יְהוָה לוֹ לְעַם קָדוֹשׁ
כַּאֲשֶׁר נִשְׁבַּע־לָךְ כִּי תִשְׁמֹר אֶת־מִצְוֺת יְהוָה אֱלֹהֶיךָ וְהָלַכְתָּ
י בִּדְרָכָיו: וְרָאוּ כָּל־עַמֵּי הָאָרֶץ כִּי שֵׁם יְהוָה נִקְרָא עָלֶיךָ
יא וְיָרְאוּ מִמֶּךָּ: וְהוֹתִרְךָ יְהוָה לְטוֹבָה בִּפְרִי בִטְנְךָ וּבִפְרִי
בְהֶמְתְּךָ וּבִפְרִי אַדְמָתֶךָ עַל הָאֲדָמָה אֲשֶׁר נִשְׁבַּע יְהוָה
יב לַאֲבֹתֶיךָ לָתֶת לָךְ: יִפְתַּח יְהוָה ׀ לְךָ אֶת־אוֹצָרוֹ הַטּוֹב
אֶת־הַשָּׁמַיִם לָתֵת מְטַר־אַרְצְךָ בְּעִתּוֹ וּלְבָרֵךְ אֵת כָּל־
יג מַעֲשֵׂה יָדֶךָ וְהִלְוִיתָ גּוֹיִם רַבִּים וְאַתָּה לֹא תִלְוֶה: וּנְתָנְךָ
יְהוָה לְרֹאשׁ וְלֹא לְזָנָב וְהָיִיתָ רַק לְמַעְלָה וְלֹא תִהְיֶה לְמָטָּה
כִּי־תִשְׁמַע אֶל־מִצְוֺת ׀ יְהוָה אֱלֹהֶיךָ אֲשֶׁר אָנֹכִי מְצַוְּךָ הַיּוֹם
יד לִשְׁמֹר וְלַעֲשׂוֹת: וְלֹא תָסוּר מִכָּל־הַדְּבָרִים אֲשֶׁר אָנֹכִי
מְצַוֶּה אֶתְכֶם הַיּוֹם יָמִין וּשְׂמֹאול לָלֶכֶת אַחֲרֵי אֱלֹהִים
אֲחֵרִים לְעָבְדָם:
טו וְהָיָה אִם־לֹא תִשְׁמַע בְּקוֹל יְהוָה אֱלֹהֶיךָ לִשְׁמֹר לַעֲשׂוֹת
אֶת־כָּל־מִצְוֺתָיו וְחֻקֹּתָיו אֲשֶׁר אָנֹכִי מְצַוְּךָ הַיּוֹם וּבָאוּ עָלֶיךָ

---

that the Lord your God has bestowed on you and on your household" (Deut. 26:10). And joy (as we saw in the note on that verse), is always something we share.

28:9 וְהָלַכְתָּ בִּדְרָכָיו *Walk in His ways* – From this verse, Rambam (*Hilkhot Deot* 1:5), quoting the Talmud (Sota 14a) infers that we are commanded to develop certain traits of character – to be gracious, merciful, and holy, as God is gracious, merciful, and holy. He holds that in addition to prescribing or forbidding specific actions, Judaism requires us to develop certain virtues. The Torah is concerned not only with behavior but also with character, not just with *what we do* but also *the kind of person we become.* Ramban (on Leviticus 19:2) locates this idea in the command "Be holy," which, he says, requires us to go beyond the letter of what the law mandates.

Rambam and Ramban believed that there are matters of great religious

16 curses will come upon you and overtake you: Cursed
shall you be in the town, and cursed shall you be in the
17 field. Cursed shall be your basket and your kneading pan.
18 Cursed shall be the fruit of your womb, the fruit of your
land, the calves of your herd, the lambs of your flock.
19 Cursed shall you be when you enter, and cursed shall you
20 be when you leave. The LORD will send upon you curse,
panic, and thwarting in every endeavor you undertake,
until you are destroyed and come to sudden ruin because
21 of the evil you have done in forsaking Me. The LORD will
make disease cling to you until it consumes you entirely
22 in the land you are coming into to possess. The LORD
will afflict you with consumption, fever, inflammation,
scorching heat and drought, blight and mildew. They will
23 pursue you until you die. The sky over your head will be
24 like bronze, and the earth beneath you iron. The LORD

---

the control of the rulers in whose lands they live. Their fate will depend on the whim of a king or the shifting winds of popular opinion. In this sense *galut*, exile, is a metaphysical dislocation – a lack of freedom in every sense of the word. The Torah calls this the "hiding of the face" of God (31:18).

Major Jewish thinkers of the Middle Ages, such as Rabbi Yehuda HaLevi and Ramban, agreed on this: that divine providence governs the affairs of Israel only when they exist as a sovereign people in their own land. This means that *what happens to the Jewish people in exile is not the work of God but of human beings*. Exile is the loss of the protection of God and subjection, instead, to human powers.

There are many differences between the two *tokheḥot*. The first is the reported speech of God, the second the direct speech of Moshe. The first is directed to the Israelites as a whole; it uses the second-person plural. The second is addressed to individuals, speaking in the singular. The first ends on a note of consolation. Despite the bad things that will happen, God will not abandon the Jewish people. He will remember His covenant with their ancestors. The Jewish people will survive. The second ends bleakly with no consolation offered. The people will be forced back to Egypt, where they will try to sell themselves as slaves but no one will buy them. According to Ramban, the first *tokheḥa* refers to events surrounding the destruction of the First Temple while the second is about the Second Temple and the sufferings of Jews under the Romans. Hope only arises again in Parashat Nitzavim, if Israel "return, you and your children, to the LORD your God, obeying Him with all your heart and all your soul" (30:2).

טז כָּל־הַקְּלָלוֹת הָאֵלֶּה וְהִשִּׂיגוּךָ׃ אָרוּר אַתָּה בָּעִיר וְאָרוּר
יז יח אַתָּה בַּשָּׂדֶה׃ אָרוּר טַנְאֲךָ וּמִשְׁאַרְתֶּךָ׃ אָרוּר פְּרִי־בִטְנְךָ
יט וּפְרִי אַדְמָתֶךָ שְׁגַר אֲלָפֶיךָ וְעַשְׁתְּרֹת צֹאנֶךָ׃ אָרוּר אַתָּה
כ בְּבֹאֶךָ וְאָרוּר אַתָּה בְּצֵאתֶךָ׃ יְשַׁלַּח יְהוָה ׀ בְּךָ אֶת־הַמְּאֵרָה
אֶת־הַמְּהוּמָה וְאֶת־הַמִּגְעֶרֶת בְּכָל־מִשְׁלַח יָדְךָ אֲשֶׁר תַּעֲשֶׂה
עַד הִשָּׁמֶדְךָ וְעַד־אֲבָדְךָ מַהֵר מִפְּנֵי רֹעַ מַעֲלָלֶיךָ אֲשֶׁר
כא עֲזַבְתָּנִי׃ יַדְבֵּק יְהוָה בְּךָ אֶת־הַדָּבֶר עַד כַּלֹּתוֹ אֹתְךָ מֵעַל
כב הָאֲדָמָה אֲשֶׁר־אַתָּה בָא־שָׁמָּה לְרִשְׁתָּהּ׃ יַכְּכָה יְהוָה
בַּשַּׁחֶפֶת וּבַקַּדַּחַת וּבַדַּלֶּקֶת וּבַחַרְחֻר וּבַחֶרֶב וּבַשִּׁדָּפוֹן
כג וּבַיֵּרָקוֹן וּרְדָפוּךָ עַד אָבְדֶךָ׃ וְהָיוּ שָׁמֶיךָ אֲשֶׁר עַל־רֹאשְׁךָ
כד נְחֹשֶׁת וְהָאָרֶץ אֲשֶׁר־תַּחְתֶּיךָ בַּרְזֶל׃ יִתֵּן יְהוָה אֶת־מְטַר

people of God. They are terrifying passages. To this day we read them so quietly that they are hardly audible. Each is known as *tokheḥa*, literally, "remonstration," and that is how we should understand them. Moshe's prophecies take as given that Israel's history is predicated on a covenant with God. Its successes will seem to point to a force greater than itself. On the other hand, if the people break the covenant, the collapse will be dramatic. It will happen because the unity of God is no longer reflected in the unity of the people. The institutions of power will become corrupt. Strains will develop in the social fabric. Prophets will warn of this, but their words will not be heeded. The people of Israel have always been obstinate. This is both a strength and a weakness. It helped them stand out against the idols of their age. But it also at times made them ungrateful to God, unmindful of their vulnerability, indifferent to their vocation.

The result, Moshe warns, will be catastrophe. The nation that once seemed invincible will be defeated. Worse, it will sometimes seem (as it did to Josephus, witnessing the disastrous revolt against Rome) as if Jews were more intent on fighting other Jews than the enemy at the gates. The people who once seemed to be under the special protection of God will now seem to be abandoned by God. As Moshe puts it in the *tokheḥa*: "You will become an object of horror, a proverb and a byword among all the peoples into whose midst the Lord will lead you" (Deut. 28:37).

The significance of Israel's exile is not merely geographical, but political and spiritual as well. Jews will no longer be under the unmediated, direct sovereignty of God. They will be under

will turn the rain of your land into powder and dust. It will
descend upon you from the sky until you are destroyed.
25 The LORD will cause you to be vanquished before your
enemies. You will come at them from one direction but
flee before them in seven. You will be an object of horror
26 to all the kingdoms on earth. Your corpses will be food
for all the birds of the sky, for the beasts of the earth; there
27 will be no one to make them afraid. The LORD will afflict
you with the boils of Egypt, with hemorrhoids, rashes,
28 and scabs, from which you shall never recover. The LORD
will afflict you with insanity, blindness, confusion of
29 mind. You will grope at noon as a blind man gropes in
darkness. Your way will not prosper. Day after day, you
will be abused and looted, and no one will be there to
30 rescue you. You will betroth a woman and some other
man will lie with her. You will build a house, but will not
live there. You will plant a vineyard, but not harvest its
31 fruit. Your ox will be slaughtered before your eyes, but
you will not eat of it. Your donkey will be stolen in front
of you, and never return. Your sheep will be given to your
32 enemies, and no one will be there to rescue you. Your
sons and daughters will be given over to another people.
You will see it with your own eyes and pine for them all
33 through the day but have no power to act. A people that
you do not know will eat the fruit of your land and of
your labor. You will be incessantly abused and crushed.
34 35 The sights you see will drive you to insanity. The LORD
will strike your knees and thighs with incurable infection,
spreading from the sole of your foot to the crown of your
36 head. The LORD will bring you and the king you set over
you to a nation that neither you nor your ancestors have

who else will have mercy on him? And to whom can the poor of Israel look for help? To those nations who hate and persecute them? They can look for help only to their brethren. Jews were often robbed of sustenance and security, yet they retained the freedom to choose how to respond.

כה ארצך אבק ועפר מן־השמים ירד עליך עד השמדך: יתנך
יהוה ׀ נגף לפני איביך בדרך אחד תצא אליו ובשבעה
דרכים תנוס לפניו והיית לזעוה לכל ממלכות הארץ:
כו והיתה נבלתך למאכל לכל־עוף השמים ולבהמת הארץ
כז ואין מחריד: יככה יהוה בשחין מצרים ובעפלים ובגרב ובטחורים
כח ובחרס אשר לא־תוכל להרפא: יככה יהוה בשגעון
כט ובעורון ובתמהון לבב: והיית ממשש בצהרים כאשר
ימשש העור באפלה ולא תצליח את־דרכיך והיית אך
ל עשוק וגזול כל־הימים ואין מושיע: אשה תארש ואיש
אחר ישגלנה בית תבנה ולא־תשב בו כרם תטע ולא ישכבנה
לא תחללנו: שורך טבוח לעיניך ולא תאכל ממנו חמרך גזול
מלפניך ולא ישוב לך צאנך נתנות לאיביך ואין לך מושיע:
לב בניך ובנתיך נתנים לעם אחר ועיניך ראות וכלות אליהם
לג כל־היום ואין לאל ידך: פרי אדמתך וכל־יגיעך יאכל עם
לד אשר לא־ידעת והיית רק עשוק ורצוץ כל־הימים: והיית
לה משגע ממראה עיניך אשר תראה: יככה יהוה בשחין רע
על־הברכים ועל־השקים אשר לא־תוכל להרפא מכף
לו רגלך ועד קדקדך: יולך יהוה אתך ואת־מלכך אשר תקים

28:33 פרי אדמתך וכל־יגיעך יאכל עם *A people... will eat the fruit... of your labor* – Rambam, the austere twelfth century sage, was not a man to confuse law with narrative. Yet in his law code, the *Mishneh Torah*, he is moved to a note of wonder: "We have never seen nor heard of an Israelite community that does not have an alms fund" (*Hilkhot Mattenot Aniyyim* 9:3). Powerless, stateless, and often living under conditions of great poverty, Jews throughout the centuries of their dispersion created a communal equivalent of a welfare state. They did so voluntarily, because it was a mitzva, because it is what Jews do, and because they knew that no one else would do it for them. As Rambam notes in another aside (*Hilkhot Mattenot Aniyyim* 10:2):

> All Jews and those attached to them are like brothers, as it is said, "You are children of the Lord your God" (Deut. 14:1) – and if a brother will not show mercy to his brother, then

known. There you will worship other gods, of wood and
37 of stone. You will become an object of horror, a proverb,
and a byword among all the peoples into whose midst the
38 LORD will lead you. You will carry much seed into the
39 field but gather little, because locusts will eat it. You will
plant vineyards and cultivate them, but you will not drink
the wine or gather the grapes, because worms will devour
40 them. You will have olive trees throughout your country,
but you will have no oil for anointing, because the olives
41 will fall away. You will bear sons and daughters, but they
will not remain yours, for they will be taken into captivity.
42 Crickets will take over all your trees and the fruit of your
43 land. Strangers in your midst will rise ever higher above
44 you, while you descend ever further beneath. They will
lend to you but you will be unable to lend to them. They
45 will be the head and you will be the tail. All these curses
will come upon you; they will pursue and overtake you,
until you are destroyed – because you did not listen to the
voice of the LORD your God, keeping the commandments
46 and decrees with which He charged you. They will be a
sign and portent to you and your descendants forever.
47 Because you did not serve the LORD your God with joy
and with a heart content in the abundance of all things,
48 you shall serve the enemies whom the LORD will send
against you, in hunger and thirst, in nakedness and the

---

is to be negated, yet Judaism is not a religion of acceptance, nor have Jews tended to seek the risk-free life. We can survive the failures and defeats if we do not lose the capacity for joy. Moshe insists that the capacity for joy is a vital part of the resilience that gives the Jewish people the strength to endure. Without it, we become vulnerable to the multiple disasters set out in the curses in this *parasha*. Celebrating together binds us as a people. Joy connects us to others and to God. It is the ability to celebrate life as such, knowing that whatever tomorrow may bring, we are here today, under God's heaven, in the universe He made, to which He has invited us as His guests.

A people that can know insecurity and still feel joy is one that can never be fully defeated, for its spirit can never be broken nor its hope destroyed.

28:48 אֹיְבֶיךָ אֲשֶׁר יְשַׁלְּחֶנּוּ יהוה בָּךְ *The enemies whom the LORD will send against*

עָלֶיךָ אֶל־גּוֹי אֲשֶׁר לֹא־יָדַעְתָּ אַתָּה וַאֲבֹתֶיךָ וְעָבַדְתָּ שָּׁם
לז אֱלֹהִים אֲחֵרִים עֵץ וָאָבֶן: וְהָיִיתָ לְשַׁמָּה לְמָשָׁל וְלִשְׁנִינָה
לח בְּכֹל הָעַמִּים אֲשֶׁר־יְנַהֶגְךָ יְהוָה שָׁמָּה: זֶרַע רַב תּוֹצִיא
לט הַשָּׂדֶה וּמְעַט תֶּאֱסֹף כִּי יַחְסְלֶנּוּ הָאַרְבֶּה: כְּרָמִים תִּטַּע
וְעָבָדְתָּ וְיַיִן לֹא־תִשְׁתֶּה וְלֹא תֶאֱגֹר כִּי תֹאכְלֶנּוּ הַתֹּלָעַת:
מ זֵיתִים יִהְיוּ לְךָ בְּכָל־גְּבוּלֶךָ וְשֶׁמֶן לֹא תָסוּךְ כִּי יִשַּׁל זֵיתֶךָ:
מא מב בָּנִים וּבָנוֹת תּוֹלִיד וְלֹא־יִהְיוּ לָךְ כִּי יֵלְכוּ בַּשֶּׁבִי: כָּל־עֵצְךָ
מג וּפְרִי אַדְמָתֶךָ יְיָרֵשׁ הַצְּלָצַל: הַגֵּר אֲשֶׁר בְּקִרְבְּךָ יַעֲלֶה עָלֶיךָ
מד מַעְלָה מָּעְלָה וְאַתָּה תֵרֵד מַטָּה מָּטָּה: הוּא יַלְוְךָ וְאַתָּה
מה לֹא תַלְוֶנּוּ הוּא יִהְיֶה לְרֹאשׁ וְאַתָּה תִּהְיֶה לְזָנָב: וּבָאוּ עָלֶיךָ
כָּל־הַקְּלָלוֹת הָאֵלֶּה וּרְדָפוּךָ וְהִשִּׂיגוּךָ עַד הִשָּׁמְדָךְ כִּי־לֹא
שָׁמַעְתָּ בְּקוֹל יְהוָה אֱלֹהֶיךָ לִשְׁמֹר מִצְוֺתָיו וְחֻקֹּתָיו אֲשֶׁר
מו מז צִוָּךְ: וְהָיוּ בְךָ לְאוֹת וּלְמוֹפֵת וּבְזַרְעֲךָ עַד־עוֹלָם: תַּחַת אֲשֶׁר
לֹא־עָבַדְתָּ אֶת־יְהוָה אֱלֹהֶיךָ בְּשִׂמְחָה וּבְטוּב לֵבָב מֵרֹב
מח כֹּל: וְעָבַדְתָּ אֶת־אֹיְבֶיךָ אֲשֶׁר יְשַׁלְּחֶנּוּ יְהוָה בָּךְ בְּרָעָב
וּבְצָמָא וּבְעֵירֹם וּבְחֹסֶר כֹּל וְנָתַן עֹל בַּרְזֶל עַל־צַוָּארֶךָ עַד

28:47 תַּחַת אֲשֶׁר לֹא־עָבַדְתָּ אֶת־יהוה אֱלֹהֶיךָ בְּשִׂמְחָה *Because you did not serve the* L*ORD your God with joy* – In the *tokheḥa* of Parashat Beḥukotai, God spoke of a fundamental breach between Israel and its Redeemer. The language was harsh: "If you spurn My decrees and despise My laws" (Lev. 26:15); "If you still walk contrary to Me" (26:21). This is an active rebellion of the Israelites against God. In Parashat Ki Tavo, the language is different. It does not speak of a willful, petulant nation deliberately spurning God, but of something that hardly sounds like a sin at all. Why would Israel suffer? "Because you did not serve the LORD your God with joy and with a heart content in the abundance of all things."

Joylessness may not be the best way to live, but it is not a sin, let alone one that warrants a litany of curses. Yet the Torah attributes to it a national disaster. Why?

Though our history has been shot through with tragedy, Jews did not lose the ability to rejoice, to sing the LORD's song even in a strange land. There are Eastern faiths that promise peace of mind if we can train ourselves into habits of acceptance. Epicurus taught his disciples to avoid risks like marriage or a career in public life. Neither of these approaches

lack of all things. He will lay an iron yoke upon your neck
49 until He has destroyed you. The LORD will bring against
you a nation from afar, from the end of the earth, and it will
dart down on you like an eagle; a nation whose language
50 you do not understand, a fierce-faced nation with no
51 respect for the old, no mercy for the young. They will eat
the fruit of your cattle and the fruit of your land until you
are destroyed. They will leave you no grain, wine, or oil,
no calves of your herd or lambs of your flock, until they
52 have brought you to death. They will lay siege to you in all
the towns throughout your land until the high, fortified
walls in which you placed your trust have fallen. In all
your towns throughout the land the LORD your God has
53 given you, they will lay siege to you. And you will eat the
fruit of your womb. When your enemies besiege you,
so fiercely will they crush you that you will eat the flesh
of your own sons and daughters whom the LORD your
54 God has given you. Even the most gentle and sensitive of
men among you will begrudge food to his own brother,

28:54 תֵּרַע עֵינוֹ *Will begrudge food* – The nightmare vision of this passage returns as reportage in the book of Lamentations. The deepest horror of all, we come to understand, is not the suffering inflicted on the people, but what they will discover they have become (compare v. 57 with Lam. 4:10).

Primo Levi survived Auschwitz. In his book *If This Is a Man*, he describes his experiences there. According to Levi, the worst time of all was when the Nazis left in January 1945, fearing the Russian advance. All prisoners who could walk were taken on the brutal death marches. The only people left in the camp were those too ill to move. For ten days they were left alone with only scraps of food and fuel. Levi describes how he worked to light a fire and bring some warmth to his fellow prisoners, many of them dying. He then writes:

> When the broken window was repaired and the stove began to spread its heat, something seemed to relax in everyone, and at that moment Towarowski (a Franco-Pole of twenty-three, typhus) proposed to the others that each of them offer a slice of bread to us three who had been working. And so it was agreed.
>
> Only a day before a similar event would have been inconceivable. The law of the Lager [concentration camps] said: "Eat your own bread,

מט הִשְׁמִידוֹ אֹתָךְ: יִשָּׂא יהוה עָלֶיךָ גּוֹי מֵרָחֹק מִקְצֵה הָאָרֶץ
נ כַּאֲשֶׁר יִדְאֶה הַנָּשֶׁר גּוֹי אֲשֶׁר לֹא־תִשְׁמַע לְשֹׁנוֹ: גּוֹי עַז פָּנִים
נא אֲשֶׁר לֹא־יִשָּׂא פָנִים לְזָקֵן וְנַעַר לֹא יָחֹן: וְאָכַל פְּרִי בְהֶמְתְּךָ
וּפְרִי־אַדְמָתְךָ עַד הִשָּׁמְדָךְ אֲשֶׁר לֹא־יַשְׁאִיר לְךָ דָּגָן תִּירוֹשׁ
וְיִצְהָר שְׁגַר אֲלָפֶיךָ וְעַשְׁתְּרֹת צֹאנֶךָ עַד הַאֲבִידוֹ אֹתָךְ:
נב וְהֵצַר לְךָ בְּכָל־שְׁעָרֶיךָ עַד רֶדֶת חֹמֹתֶיךָ הַגְּבֹהֹת וְהַבְּצֻרוֹת
אֲשֶׁר אַתָּה בֹּטֵחַ בָּהֵן בְּכָל־אַרְצֶךָ וְהֵצַר לְךָ בְּכָל־שְׁעָרֶיךָ
נג בְּכָל־אַרְצְךָ אֲשֶׁר נָתַן יהוה אֱלֹהֶיךָ לָךְ: וְאָכַלְתָּ פְרִי־בִטְנְךָ
בְּשַׂר בָּנֶיךָ וּבְנֹתֶיךָ אֲשֶׁר נָתַן־לְךָ יהוה אֱלֹהֶיךָ בְּמָצוֹר
נד וּבְמָצוֹק אֲשֶׁר־יָצִיק לְךָ אֹיְבֶךָ: הָאִישׁ הָרַךְ בְּךָ וְהֶעָנֹג מְאֹד
תֵּרַע עֵינוֹ בְאָחִיו וּבְאֵשֶׁת חֵיקוֹ וּבְיֶתֶר בָּנָיו אֲשֶׁר יוֹתִיר:

---

you – It is one of the essential aspects of the Torah, as the Sages and Rambam noted, that it can be read at many levels. The blessings and curses of our *parasha* are both supernatural and natural. On the one hand, the vision of the Torah is that Israel's destiny depends on divine intervention in history. In that sense it is supernatural. On the other hand, there is a sense that there is something natural at work also. Not by chance are the children of Israel and the land of Israel exemplars of the relationship between humanity and God. The people of Israel will always be small: "You are the smallest of all peoples" (Deut. 7:7). The land of Israel will always be vulnerable, occupying as it does a strategic location between three continents – Europe, Africa, and Asia – and two ancient birthplaces of empire, the Nile and Tigris-Euphrates valleys. Israel is a place from which it is impossible to build an empire.

Lacking a constant, predictable water supply, its people will constantly find themselves looking up to the heavens for rain. They will know that (agricultural) prosperity is not entirely in their own hands. They will know also that there will be times of drought and famine during which the poor (small farmers) will be dependent on the generosity of others. The strength of the social bond – tzedaka, the charity which is also justice – will be constantly tested. Any age in which the rich fail in their responsibilities to those less well-off, or in which the sellers exploit the buyers, will be full of danger because the nation can only survive on the basis of a strong sense of collective responsibility. Only by almost superhuman achievements of national unity and moral purpose will Israel survive as a nation in its land. So it was in biblical times; so it is today.

55 his beloved wife, those of his children who survive, and
give none of them any of the flesh of his own children
when he eats them, because he has nothing else left, so
fiercely will the besieging enemy crush you in all your
56 towns. The most gentle and sensitive of women among
you, so sensitive and gentle that she would not venture
to set the sole of her foot on the ground, will begrudge
food to the husband she loves, and to her own son and
57 daughter, the afterbirth from her womb and the children
she bears – she will eat them in secret for lack of anything
else, so fiercely will the besieging enemy crush you in
58 your towns. If you do not take care to keep all the words
of this Law, written in this scroll, to revere this glorious,
59 awesome name, the LORD your God, then the LORD will
overwhelm you and your descendants with terrible and
relentless plagues, and malignant and chronic diseases.
60 He will bring back on you all the diseases of Egypt that
61 you dreaded, and they will cling to you. Every other
sickness and plague – even those not recorded in this
scroll of the Law – the LORD will inflict upon you until
62 you are destroyed. Though you were once as numerous as
the stars in the sky, you will be left but a handful of souls,
63 because you did not listen to the LORD your God. And as
the LORD once delighted in making you prosperous and
numerous, so will the LORD delight in bringing you to
ruin and destruction. You will be torn away from the land
64 that you are now coming into to possess. The LORD will
scatter you among all nations, from one end of the earth
to the other, and there you will serve other gods, of wood
and of stone, which neither you nor your ancestors have

---

fellowship and faith, the two things from which hope is born. That is why we begin the Passover Seder by inviting others to join us ("Let all who are hungry come in and eat"). Bread shared is no longer the bread of oppression. Reaching out to others, giving help to the needy and companionship to those who are alone, we bring freedom into the world, and with freedom, God.

נה מִתֵּת ׀ לְאַחַד מֵהֶם מִבְּשַׂר בָּנָיו אֲשֶׁר יֹאכֵל מִבְּלִי הִשְׁאִיר־
לוֹ כֹּל בְּמָצוֹר וּבְמָצוֹק אֲשֶׁר יָצִיק לְךָ אֹיִבְךָ בְּכָל־שְׁעָרֶיךָ׃
נו הָרַכָּה בְךָ וְהָעֲנֻגָּה אֲשֶׁר לֹא־נִסְּתָה כַף־רַגְלָהּ הַצֵּג עַל־
הָאָרֶץ מֵהִתְעַנֵּג וּמֵרֹךְ תֵּרַע עֵינָהּ בְּאִישׁ חֵיקָהּ וּבִבְנָהּ
נז וּבְבִתָּהּ׃ וּבְשִׁלְיָתָהּ הַיּוֹצֵת ׀ מִבֵּין רַגְלֶיהָ וּבְבָנֶיהָ אֲשֶׁר תֵּלֵד
כִּי־תֹאכְלֵם בְּחֹסֶר־כֹּל בַּסָּתֶר בְּמָצוֹר וּבְמָצוֹק אֲשֶׁר יָצִיק
נח לְךָ אֹיִבְךָ בִּשְׁעָרֶיךָ׃ אִם־לֹא תִשְׁמֹר לַעֲשׂוֹת אֶת־כָּל־דִּבְרֵי
הַתּוֹרָה הַזֹּאת הַכְּתֻבִים בַּסֵּפֶר הַזֶּה לְיִרְאָה אֶת־הַשֵּׁם
נט הַנִּכְבָּד וְהַנּוֹרָא הַזֶּה אֵת יהוה אֱלֹהֶיךָ׃ וְהִפְלָא יהוה אֶת־
מַכֹּתְךָ וְאֵת מַכּוֹת זַרְעֶךָ מַכּוֹת גְּדֹלֹת וְנֶאֱמָנוֹת וָחֳלָיִם רָעִים
ס וְנֶאֱמָנִים׃ וְהֵשִׁיב בְּךָ אֵת כָּל־מַדְוֵה מִצְרַיִם אֲשֶׁר יָגֹרְתָּ
סא מִפְּנֵיהֶם וְדָבְקוּ בָּךְ׃ גַּם כָּל־חֳלִי וְכָל־מַכָּה אֲשֶׁר לֹא כָתוּב
בְּסֵפֶר הַתּוֹרָה הַזֹּאת יַעְלֵם יהוה עָלֶיךָ עַד הִשָּׁמְדָךְ׃
סב וְנִשְׁאַרְתֶּם בִּמְתֵי מְעָט תַּחַת אֲשֶׁר הֱיִיתֶם כְּכוֹכְבֵי הַשָּׁמַיִם
סג לָרֹב כִּי־לֹא שָׁמַעְתָּ בְּקוֹל יהוה אֱלֹהֶיךָ׃ וְהָיָה כַּאֲשֶׁר־שָׂשׂ
יהוה עֲלֵיכֶם לְהֵיטִיב אֶתְכֶם וּלְהַרְבּוֹת אֶתְכֶם כֵּן יָשִׂישׂ
יהוה עֲלֵיכֶם לְהַאֲבִיד אֶתְכֶם וּלְהַשְׁמִיד אֶתְכֶם וְנִסַּחְתֶּם
סד מֵעַל הָאֲדָמָה אֲשֶׁר־אַתָּה בָא־שָׁמָּה לְרִשְׁתָּהּ׃ וֶהֱפִיצְךָ
יהוה בְּכָל־הָעַמִּים מִקְצֵה הָאָרֶץ וְעַד־קְצֵה הָאָרֶץ וְעָבַדְתָּ
שָּׁם אֱלֹהִים אֲחֵרִים אֲשֶׁר לֹא־יָדַעְתָּ אַתָּה וַאֲבֹתֶיךָ עֵץ

and if you can, that of your neighbor," and left no room for gratitude. It really meant that the law of the Lager was dead.

It was the first human gesture that occurred among us. I believe that that moment can be dated as the beginning of the change by which we who had not died slowly changed from *Haftlinge* [prisoners] to men again.

Sharing food is the first act through which slaves become free human beings. One who fears tomorrow does not offer his bread to others. But one who is willing to divide his food with a stranger has already shown himself capable of

65 known. Yet even among those nations you shall find no
ease, no resting place for the sole of your foot. There the
Lord will give you a trembling heart, pining eyes, and a
66 languishing spirit. Your life will hang suspended before
you; you will dread both night and day, never sure you
67 will survive. In the morning you will say, 'Would that it
were evening!' In the evening you will say, 'Would that
it were morning!' – because of the dread in your heart
that you will dread, the scenes in your eyes that you will
68 see. The Lord will send you back in ships to Egypt, by
a route that I told you that you would never see again.
You will offer yourselves to your enemies for sale as male
69 and female slaves, but none will buy you." These
are the words of the covenant that the Lord commanded
Moshe to make with the Israelites in the land of Moav,
alongside the covenant that He had made with them at
Ḥorev.

29 1 Moshe summoned all Israel and said to them: "You have SHEVI'I
seen all that the Lord did before your eyes in the land
of Egypt, to Pharaoh, all his officials, and all of his land.
2 Your own eyes saw the great trials, the signs, and the great
3 wonders. But to this day the Lord has not given you a
mind that understands, or eyes that see, or ears that hear.
4 For forty years I brought you through the wilderness. The

---

the start of an old-new era in the life of the people of the covenant. Once again, as in the days of Yehoshua, Jews are faced with the challenge and opportunity of constructing a society on the principles of the covenant: an arena of justice and compassion, liberty and the rule of law, respect for life and for human dignity. It was never easy. Now, as then, Jews face enemies outside and tensions within. Now, as then, there have been moments when the people must have come close to despair. The principle of "the blessing and the curse" of which Moshe spoke so eloquently has helped Jews emerge from tragedy with hope intact. When Jews have suffered, their first reaction is not to blame others but to examine themselves. That is why bad times – the times spoken of in the *tokheḥa* – have always led to national renewal, and the worse the times, the greater the renewal. A people capable of seeing suffering as a call from God to return to the covenant, choosing and sanctifying life, is one that cannot be defeated because it can never lose hope.

סה וָאָבֶן׃ וּבַגּוֹיִם הָהֵם לֹא תַרְגִּיעַ וְלֹא־יִהְיֶה מָנוֹחַ לְכַף־רַגְלֶךָ
סו וְנָתַן יהוה לְךָ שָׁם לֵב רַגָּז וְכִלְיוֹן עֵינַיִם וְדַאֲבוֹן נָפֶשׁ׃ וְהָיוּ
חַיֶּיךָ תְּלֻאִים לְךָ מִנֶּגֶד וּפָחַדְתָּ לַיְלָה וְיוֹמָם וְלֹא תַאֲמִין
סז בְּחַיֶּיךָ׃ בַּבֹּקֶר תֹּאמַר מִי־יִתֵּן עֶרֶב וּבָעֶרֶב תֹּאמַר מִי־יִתֵּן
בֹּקֶר מִפַּחַד לְבָבְךָ אֲשֶׁר תִּפְחָד וּמִמַּרְאֵה עֵינֶיךָ אֲשֶׁר
סח תִּרְאֶה׃ וֶהֱשִׁיבְךָ יהוה ׀ מִצְרַיִם בָּאֳנִיּוֹת בַּדֶּרֶךְ אֲשֶׁר אָמַרְתִּי
לְךָ לֹא־תֹסִיף עוֹד לִרְאֹתָהּ וְהִתְמַכַּרְתֶּם שָׁם לְאֹיְבֶיךָ
סט לַעֲבָדִים וְלִשְׁפָחוֹת וְאֵין קֹנֶה׃ אֵלֶּה דִבְרֵי הַבְּרִית
אֲשֶׁר־צִוָּה יהוה אֶת־מֹשֶׁה לִכְרֹת אֶת־בְּנֵי יִשְׂרָאֵל בְּאֶרֶץ
מוֹאָב מִלְּבַד הַבְּרִית אֲשֶׁר־כָּרַת אִתָּם בְּחֹרֵב׃

כט א וַיִּקְרָא מֹשֶׁה אֶל־כָּל־יִשְׂרָאֵל וַיֹּאמֶר אֲלֵהֶם אַתֶּם רְאִיתֶם שביעי
אֵת כָּל־אֲשֶׁר עָשָׂה יהוה לְעֵינֵיכֶם בְּאֶרֶץ מִצְרַיִם לְפַרְעֹה
ב וּלְכָל־עֲבָדָיו וּלְכָל־אַרְצוֹ׃ הַמַּסּוֹת הַגְּדֹלֹת אֲשֶׁר רָאוּ עֵינֶיךָ
ג הָאֹתֹת וְהַמֹּפְתִים הַגְּדֹלִים הָהֵם׃ וְלֹא־נָתַן יהוה לָכֶם לֵב
ד לָדַעַת וְעֵינַיִם לִרְאוֹת וְאָזְנַיִם לִשְׁמֹעַ עַד הַיּוֹם הַזֶּה׃ וָאוֹלֵךְ
אֶתְכֶם אַרְבָּעִים שָׁנָה בַּמִּדְבָּר לֹא־בָלוּ שַׂלְמֹתֵיכֶם מֵעֲלֵיכֶם

28:65 וְלֹא־יִהְיֶה מָנוֹחַ *No resting place* – "The righteous have no rest, neither in this world nor the next," says the Talmud (Berakhot 64a). I remain in awe at the challenge God has set us in this imperfect world: to be different, iconoclasts of the politically correct, to be God's question mark against the conventional wisdom of the age, to build, to change, to mend the world until it becomes a place worthy of the Divine Presence because we have learned to honor the image of God that is humankind.

28:69 הַבְּרִית אֲשֶׁר־כָּרַת אִתָּם *The covenant that He had made with them* – The story of the Jewish people is an interweaving of history and prophecy, of the choices of human beings and the overarching tutelage of God. The suffering of Jews in the Diaspora is not to be regarded as divine punishment but rather a consequence of exile itself – the loss of providence, the hiding of the face of God, and being "left to chance" (see note on Lev. 26:27). The idea that there is one answer to the problem of evil and the sufferings of the innocent, true at all times, is wrong. There are different historical eras, and these represent different relationships between Israel and God.

The return of Jews to Israel marks

clothes on your back did not wear out, nor the sandals
5 on your feet. You ate no bread and drank no wine or
strong drink, so that you might know that I am the Lord
6 your God. When you came to this place, Siḥon, king of MAFTIR
Heshbon, and Og, king of Bashan, came out to meet us
7 in warfare, but we defeated them. We took their land and
gave it as a heritage to the Reubenites, the Gadites, and
8 half the tribe of Menashe. Therefore take great care to
keep the words of this covenant, that you may succeed in
all you undertake.

The haftara for Parashat Ki Tavo is on page 1614.

וְנַֽעַלְךָ֥ לֹא־בָלְתָ֖ה מֵעַ֥ל רַגְלֶֽךָ׃ לֶ֚חֶם לֹ֣א אֲכַלְתֶּ֔ם וְיַ֥יִן וְשֵׁכָ֖ר ה
מפטיר לֹ֣א שְׁתִיתֶ֑ם לְמַ֙עַן֙ תֵּֽדְע֔וּ כִּ֛י אֲנִ֥י יְהוָ֖ה אֱלֹהֵיכֶֽם׃ וַתָּבֹ֖אוּ ו
אֶל־הַמָּק֣וֹם הַזֶּ֑ה וַיֵּצֵ֣א סִיחֹ֣ן מֶֽלֶךְ־חֶ֠שְׁבּ֠וֹן וְע֨וֹג מֶֽלֶךְ־הַבָּשָׁ֧ן
לִקְרָאתֵ֛נוּ לַמִּלְחָמָ֖ה וַנַּכֵּֽם׃ וַנִּקַּח֙ אֶת־אַרְצָ֔ם וַנִּתְּנָ֣הּ לְנַחֲלָ֔ה ז
לָרֽאוּבֵנִ֖י וְלַגָּדִ֑י וְלַחֲצִ֖י שֵׁ֥בֶט הַֽמְנַשִּֽׁי׃ וּשְׁמַרְתֶּ֗ם אֶת־דִּבְרֵי֙ ח
הַבְּרִ֣ית הַזֹּ֔את וַעֲשִׂיתֶ֖ם אֹתָ֑ם לְמַ֙עַן֙ תַּשְׂכִּ֔ילוּ אֵ֖ת כָּל־אֲשֶׁ֥ר
תַּעֲשֽׂוּן׃

The הפטרה *for* פרשת כי תבוא *is on page 1615.*

Parashat Nitzavim

29 9 All of you are standing today before the Lord your
God – the leaders among you, the tribes, the elders and
10 officials, all the men of Israel, the children, the women,
the strangers in your camp, from woodcutter to water
11 drawer – to enter into the covenant of the Lord your
God, and the oath the Lord your God is making with
12 you today, to establish you today as His people, that He SHENI
may be your God, as He promised you and swore to your
13 ancestors, Avraham, Yitzḥak, and Yaakov. Not with you
14 alone am I making this covenant and oath; with you who
are standing here with us today before the Lord our God
I make it, and with those, too, who are not with us here

We-and-Thou, the Jewish people standing collectively before God.

A CHOICE FOR THE GENERATIONS

The covenant is forged anew with all the people present, and also "those … who are not with us here today." The commentators point out that this cannot refer to Israelites alive at the time who happened to be somewhere else, as the entire nation was assembled. It can only mean generations not yet born. The covenant is to bind all Jews from that day to this. As the Talmud (Yoma 73b; Nedarim 8a) says, each of us is *mushba veomed meHar Sinai*, "foresworn from Sinai." But how can this be so? How can we be subject to a covenant on the basis of a decision taken long ago by our distant ancestors? The Sages answered the question mystically. They said (Shemot Rabba 28:6) that even the souls of Jews not yet born were present at Sinai and ratified the covenant. Every Jew, in other words, *did* give his or her consent in the days of Moshe even though he or she had not yet been born.

The fifteenth-century Spanish scholar Rabbi Yitzḥak Arama (*Akedat Yitzḥak*, Nitzavim), however, reopened the question. God's covenant is not with souls only, but with embodied human beings. We can understand that the soul, which desires closeness to God, would agree to the covenant. But the assent that counts is, surely, that of living, breathing human beings with bodies. We cannot assume that they would agree to the Torah with its many physical restrictions. Only when we understand what is being asked of us can we give our binding consent.

Why, then, be Jewish? When Jews

פרשת נצבים

כט ט אַתֶּם נִצָּבִים הַיּוֹם כֻּלְּכֶם לִפְנֵי יהוה אֱלֹהֵיכֶם רָאשֵׁיכֶם כג
י שִׁבְטֵיכֶם זִקְנֵיכֶם וְשֹׁטְרֵיכֶם כֹּל אִישׁ יִשְׂרָאֵל: טַפְּכֶם נְשֵׁיכֶם
וְגֵרְךָ אֲשֶׁר בְּקֶרֶב מַחֲנֶיךָ מֵחֹטֵב עֵצֶיךָ עַד שֹׁאֵב מֵימֶיךָ:
יא לְעָבְרְךָ בִּבְרִית יהוה אֱלֹהֶיךָ וּבְאָלָתוֹ אֲשֶׁר יהוה אֱלֹהֶיךָ
יב כֹּרֵת עִמְּךָ הַיּוֹם: לְמַעַן הָקִים־אֹתְךָ הַיּוֹם ׀ לוֹ לְעָם וְהוּא שני
יִהְיֶה־לְּךָ לֵאלֹהִים כַּאֲשֶׁר דִּבֶּר־לָךְ וְכַאֲשֶׁר נִשְׁבַּע לַאֲבֹתֶיךָ
יג לְאַבְרָהָם לְיִצְחָק וּלְיַעֲקֹב: וְלֹא אִתְּכֶם לְבַדְּכֶם אָנֹכִי כֹּרֵת
יד אֶת־הַבְּרִית הַזֹּאת וְאֶת־הָאָלָה הַזֹּאת: כִּי אֶת־אֲשֶׁר יֶשְׁנוֹ
פֹּה עִמָּנוּ עֹמֵד הַיּוֹם לִפְנֵי יהוה אֱלֹהֵינוּ וְאֵת אֲשֶׁר אֵינֶנּוּ

NITZAVIM

Moshe assembles all the people – leaders, elders, officials, children, women, men, and strangers in the camp, from woodcutter to water drawer – to renew the covenant prior to their entry into the land. He warns them solemnly that their future depends on their faithfulness to it. If they break it, they will suffer defeat, devastation, and exile. Yet even then, the covenant and its promise will remain. Even in the midst of dispersion and dislocation, if the people return to God He will return to them and cause them to return to their land. The choice will always be theirs.

29:9 אַתֶּם...כֻּלְּכֶם *All of you* – Judaism is of its essence a collective endeavor. The liturgy, other than occasional meditations, is written in the first-person plural, not the singular. When we pray for an individual we include him or her amongst "all others in Israel" who need healing or consolation. We confess our sins together. When a couple stands under the bridal canopy, the blessings said on the occasion, the *sheva berakhot*, speak of "Zion rejoicing in her children" as if the whole Jewish people past and present joined in the celebration. Jewish mourning customs draw the bereaved gently back into the ambit of community at the very time when they feel most alone. Even the Jewish home is not a closed institution. Jewish teachings emphasize the open house, the extended family, and welcoming the stranger. Hospitality is "greater than welcoming the Divine Presence" (Shabbat 127a). We discover God in our togetherness, not our isolation. Martin Buber misdescribed the faith of Judaism when he spoke of I-and-Thou. The primary relationship in Judaism is

15 today. You yourselves know what it was like when we SHELISHI
lived in Egypt, and when we passed through the nations
16 we encountered. You saw their detestable things, their
abominations of wood and stone, of silver and gold.
17 Let there be among you no man or woman, family or
tribe, whose heart turns away from the LORD our God
to serve the gods of those nations. Let there be among
18 you no root whose fruit is poison and wormwood. When
such a person hears the words of this oath, he may think
himself immune, saying, 'I will be safe even if I go my own
19 stubborn way, sweeping away the moist and dry alike,' but
the LORD will not be willing to pardon him. Instead, the
LORD's anger and passion will smolder against him; all
the curses written in this scroll will fall on him, and the
20 LORD will erase his name from under the sky. The LORD
will single him out for disaster – from all the tribes of
Israel – in line with all the curses of the covenant written

---

the gratification of instinct – what Freud took to be the mark of civilization? Judaism gives us 613 exercises in the power of will to shape our choices. Choosing life, choosing Judaism, is how we, with God, become coauthors of our lives.

29:17 פֶּן־יֵשׁ בָּכֶם שֹׁרֶשׁ *Let there be among you no root* – "All Israel are responsible for one another" (Shevuot 39a). The idea that an individual within Israel – and this applies to a subgroup as well – can "consider himself immune" and depart from the collective morality without consequences is nipped in the bud.

The first philosophers of civil society were the prophets. Unlike the priests, who spoke in terms of holy and profane, permitted and forbidden, pure and impure, the prophets spoke the language of the covenantal virtues: righteousness (*tzedek*), justice (*mishpat*), loving-kindness (*ḥesed*), and compassion (*raḥamim*). Insofar as one can summarize the message of Eliyahu and Elisha, Amos and Hoshea, Yeshayahu and Yirmeyahu, and translate it into secular terms, it would be this: Israel is a small nation surrounded by empires. To survive, it needs the strongest possible cohesion and morale. People must feel that they are fighting for something precious, a society whose manifest justice and graciousness are apparent to all. Thus motivated, they will defeat powers greater than themselves. If, however, Israel worships the idols of power or wealth, it will lose its corporate identity. The poor will resent the rich; the weak will feel exploited by the strong. The nation will be divided, and a house divided against itself cannot stand.

טו פֹּה עִמָּנוּ הַיּוֹם: כִּי־אַתֶּם יְדַעְתֶּם אֵת אֲשֶׁר־יָשַׁבְנוּ בְּאֶרֶץ שלישי
מִצְרָיִם וְאֵת אֲשֶׁר־עָבַרְנוּ בְּקֶרֶב הַגּוֹיִם אֲשֶׁר עֲבַרְתֶּם:
טז וַתִּרְאוּ אֶת־שִׁקּוּצֵיהֶם וְאֵת גִּלֻּלֵיהֶם עֵץ וָאֶבֶן כֶּסֶף וְזָהָב
יז אֲשֶׁר עִמָּהֶם: פֶּן־יֵשׁ בָּכֶם אִישׁ אוֹ־אִשָּׁה אוֹ מִשְׁפָּחָה אוֹ־
שֵׁבֶט אֲשֶׁר לְבָבוֹ פֹנֶה הַיּוֹם מֵעִם יהוה אֱלֹהֵינוּ לָלֶכֶת
לַעֲבֹד אֶת־אֱלֹהֵי הַגּוֹיִם הָהֵם פֶּן־יֵשׁ בָּכֶם שֹׁרֶשׁ פֹּרֶה רֹאשׁ
יח וְלַעֲנָה: וְהָיָה בְּשָׁמְעוֹ אֶת־דִּבְרֵי הָאָלָה הַזֹּאת וְהִתְבָּרֵךְ
בִּלְבָבוֹ לֵאמֹר שָׁלוֹם יִהְיֶה־לִּי כִּי בִּשְׁרִרוּת לִבִּי אֵלֵךְ לְמַעַן
יט סְפוֹת הָרָוָה אֶת־הַצְּמֵאָה: לֹא־יֹאבֶה יהוה סְלֹחַ לוֹ כִּי
אָז יֶעְשַׁן אַף־יהוה וְקִנְאָתוֹ בָּאִישׁ הַהוּא וְרָבְצָה בּוֹ כָּל־
הָאָלָה הַכְּתוּבָה בַּסֵּפֶר הַזֶּה וּמָחָה יהוה אֶת־שְׁמוֹ מִתַּחַת
כ הַשָּׁמָיִם: וְהִבְדִּילוֹ יהוה לְרָעָה מִכֹּל שִׁבְטֵי יִשְׂרָאֵל כְּכֹל

ask this question, we know that we are in the presence of a major crisis in Jewish life. At most times in history, Jewish identity was a fact of birth, a destiny. It was not something you chose, any more than you choose to be born. In Rabbi Arama's day, for the first time Jews converted to another faith in significant numbers. Those who did so seemed to prosper. Those who remained loyal to their faith suffered ever-increasing persecution. In times such as those, what answer could Rabbi Arama give to someone who asked, "Why should I remain a Jew?"

The following was his reply. After thousands of years, Jewish identity was as deeply engraved in the minds of Jews as the instinct of life is in all living creatures. It was no more possible for Jews collectively to desert the covenant than it was for a species to commit suicide. Within all that lives, there is a desire for life, an instinct for survival. And for Jews that instinct is for Jewish survival.

I would like to suggest another answer, which lies in what Moshe himself said at the end of his address: "I call heaven and earth as witnesses against you today. I have set before you life and death, the blessing and the curse. Choose life" (Deut. 30:19). The ancients – with their belief in fate, the influence of the stars, or the arbitrariness of nature – did not fully believe in human freedom. Nor do most scientific atheists believe in it today. We are determined, they say, by our genes. Choice is an illusion of the conscious mind.

Judaism says no. Choice is like a muscle: use it or lose it. Jewish law is an ongoing training regime in willpower. Can you eat this and not that? Can you exercise spiritually three times a day? Can you rest one day in seven? Can you defer

21 in this scroll of the Law. A future generation – your
descendants who rise after you, and foreigners from
distant lands – will see the land's devastation and the
22 sicknesses with which the LORD has afflicted it, all its
soil a burning waste of sulfur and salt, nothing planted,
nothing sprouting, no vegetation growing on it, like the
ruins of Sedom and Amora, Adma and Tzevoyim, which
23 the LORD overturned in His fierce rage. All the nations
will ask, 'Why did the LORD do this to the land? Why
24 this great, blazing anger?' They will say, 'It is because
they abandoned the covenant of the LORD, God of their
ancestors, which He made with them when He brought
25 them out of Egypt. They went and served other gods
and worshipped them, gods they did not know and
26 whom He had not allotted to them. So the LORD's anger
burned against that land, bringing on it every curse that
27 is written in this scroll. The LORD uprooted them from
their land in anger, rage, and great fury, and threw them
28 into another land, as we now see them.' Hidden things
belong to the LORD our God, but as for overt acts – it is
for us and our children to eternity to keep all the words
30 1 of this Law. When all these things have come REVI'I /SHENI/
upon you, the blessings and the curses I have set before
you, and you – amidst all the nations where the LORD
2 your God has driven you – take them to heart, and return,
you and your children, to the LORD your God, obeying
Him with all your heart and all your soul, just as I am

or disobey. He gives Kayin the freedom to control his negative impulses, and the freedom to capitulate to them. The story of the Tanakh is of God's gift of freedom to humankind. Thus the future is unknown – "hidden things belong to the LORD," and responsibility – for "overt acts" – is ours.

RETURN

This passage is a set of variations on the Hebrew verb *lashuv*, which is related to the noun *teshuva*. This is lost in English translation. All the phrases – "take to heart," "return," "bring your captives back," and "turn" – are, in the Hebrew, forms of this verb. The Torah often

כא אָלוֹת הַבְּרִית הַכְּתוּבָה בְּסֵפֶר הַתּוֹרָה הַזֶּה׃ וְאָמַר הַדּוֹר
הָאַחֲרוֹן בְּנֵיכֶם אֲשֶׁר יָקוּמוּ מֵאַחֲרֵיכֶם וְהַנׇּכְרִי אֲשֶׁר יָבֹא
מֵאֶרֶץ רְחוֹקָה וְרָאוּ אֶת־מַכּוֹת הָאָרֶץ הַהִוא וְאֶת־תַּחֲלֻאֶיהָ
כב אֲשֶׁר־חִלָּה יהוה בָּהּ׃ גׇּפְרִית וָמֶלַח שְׂרֵפָה כׇל־אַרְצָהּ לֹא
תִזָּרַע וְלֹא תַצְמִחַ וְלֹא־יַעֲלֶה בָהּ כׇּל־עֵשֶׂב כְּמַהְפֵּכַת סְדֹם
וַעֲמֹרָה אַדְמָה וצביים אֲשֶׁר הָפַךְ יהוה בְּאַפּוֹ וּבַחֲמָתוֹ׃ וּצְבוֹיִם
כג וְאָמְרוּ כׇּל־הַגּוֹיִם עַל־מֶה עָשָׂה יהוה כָּכָה לָאָרֶץ הַזֹּאת
כד מֶה חֳרִי הָאַף הַגָּדוֹל הַזֶּה׃ וְאָמְרוּ עַל אֲשֶׁר עָזְבוּ אֶת־
בְּרִית יהוה אֱלֹהֵי אֲבֹתָם אֲשֶׁר כָּרַת עִמָּם בְּהוֹצִיאוֹ אֹתָם
כה מֵאֶרֶץ מִצְרָיִם׃ וַיֵּלְכוּ וַיַּעַבְדוּ אֱלֹהִים אֲחֵרִים וַיִּשְׁתַּחֲווּ
כו לָהֶם אֱלֹהִים אֲשֶׁר לֹא־יְדָעוּם וְלֹא חָלַק לָהֶם׃ וַיִּחַר־אַף
יהוה בָּאָרֶץ הַהִוא לְהָבִיא עָלֶיהָ אֶת־כׇּל־הַקְּלָלָה הַכְּתוּבָה
כז בַּסֵּפֶר הַזֶּה׃ וַיִּתְּשֵׁם יהוה מֵעַל אַדְמָתָם בְּאַף וּבְחֵמָה וּבְקֶצֶף
כח גָּדוֹל וַיַּשְׁלִכֵם אֶל־אֶרֶץ אַחֶרֶת כַּיּוֹם הַזֶּה׃ הַנִּסְתָּרֹת לַיהוה
אֱלֹהֵינוּ וְהַנִּגְלֹת לָנוּ וּלְבָנֵינוּ עַד־עוֹלָם לַעֲשׂוֹת אֶת־כׇּל־
ל א דִּבְרֵי הַתּוֹרָה הַזֹּאת׃ וְהָיָה כִי־יָבֹאוּ עָלֶיךָ רביעי /שני/
כׇּל־הַדְּבָרִים הָאֵלֶּה הַבְּרָכָה וְהַקְּלָלָה אֲשֶׁר נָתַתִּי לְפָנֶיךָ
וַהֲשֵׁבֹתָ אֶל־לְבָבֶךָ בְּכׇל־הַגּוֹיִם אֲשֶׁר הִדִּיחֲךָ יהוה אֱלֹהֶיךָ
ב שָׁמָּה׃ וְשַׁבְתָּ עַד־יהוה אֱלֹהֶיךָ וְשָׁמַעְתָּ בְקֹלוֹ כְּכֹל אֲשֶׁר־

29:28 הַנִּסְתָּרֹת לַיהוה *Hidden things belong to the LORD* – If God is not within nature, but is Himself the author of nature, then He is subject to no laws except those by which He chooses to bind Himself. When God says to Moshe, "I will be what I will be" (Ex. 3:14), and later, "I…will show mercy to whom I decide to show mercy" (33:19), He is saying that "I, God, am free. What I do, how I appear, how I intervene – none of these things can be predicted or controlled. I am what I choose." God is unknowable and the future is unknowable, and both for the same reason: because of the nature of freedom.

If God is free and He bestows His image on us, then we too, within the limits set by our bodily existence, are free. That is the point of the Torah from the beginning. God gives Adam and Ḥava a command that they are free to obey

3 commanding you today, then the LORD your God will
bring your captives back and show you compassion. He
will bring you back together from all the nations among
4 whom the LORD your God has scattered you. If you
should be expelled to the furthest of horizons, even from
there the LORD your God will gather you, from there He
5 will take you back. The LORD your God will bring you
into the land that belonged to your ancestors, and you
will possess it. He will make you yet more prosperous
6 and numerous than your ancestors were. The LORD your
God will circumcise your heart and the hearts of your
descendants, so that you may love the LORD your God
with all your heart, with all your soul, that you may live.
7 The LORD your God will inflict all these curses on your
8 enemies and on those who hate and persecute you. Then
you shall turn and heed the LORD's voice, keeping all
His commandments with which I am charging you this
9 day, and the LORD your God will grant you abundant

ḤAMISHI /SHELISHI/

children. The words of the prophets have acquired a new salience in our time.

Unlike Rambam, who traces the imperative of repentance back to sacrificial rituals of atonement (*Hilkhot Teshuva* 1:1), for Ramban, sin and repentance are part of the broader sweep of Jewish history. They belong to the world not of the priest but of the prophet, the figure who heard the voice of God in history, warned the people that public wrongdoing would lead to defeat and exile, and who, when the exile eventually occurred, summoned the people back to their vocation as a prelude to their return to the land.

Every individual act of *teshuva* recapitulates, in some way, this larger pattern of return. *Teshuva* in this sense is less *atonement* than *homecoming* – a subtle difference, but a difference nonetheless. The primary feeling of sin in priestly consciousness is *guilt*; in prophetic consciousness it is a sense of *alienation*. For the priest, *teshuva* is integrally linked with sacrifice. For the prophet, it is associated with behavioral change (*teshuva* as "returning" to the right way) and leads to healing and restoration.

Parashat Nitzavim is always read on the Sabbath before Rosh HaShana, when our thoughts are directed toward *teshuva*. The rituals of atonement are encoded into the Yom Kippur service, but it is worth recalling that *teshuva* has less to do with the Temple, and everything to do with a sense of the divine call ("Where are you?") within the events that happen to us, whether individually as a personal fate or collectively as Jewish history.

ג אָנֹכִי מְצַוְּךָ הַיּוֹם אַתָּה וּבָנֶיךָ בְּכָל־לְבָבְךָ וּבְכָל־נַפְשֶׁךָ: וְשָׁב
יְהוָה אֱלֹהֶיךָ אֶת־שְׁבוּתְךָ וְרִחֲמֶךָ וְשָׁב וְקִבֶּצְךָ מִכָּל־הָעַמִּים
ד אֲשֶׁר הֱפִיצְךָ יְהוָה אֱלֹהֶיךָ שָׁמָּה: אִם־יִהְיֶה נִדַּחֲךָ בִּקְצֵה
ה הַשָּׁמָיִם מִשָּׁם יְקַבֶּצְךָ יְהוָה אֱלֹהֶיךָ וּמִשָּׁם יִקָּחֶךָ: וֶהֱבִיאֲךָ
יְהוָה אֱלֹהֶיךָ אֶל־הָאָרֶץ אֲשֶׁר־יָרְשׁוּ אֲבֹתֶיךָ וִירִשְׁתָּהּ
ו וְהֵיטִבְךָ וְהִרְבְּךָ מֵאֲבֹתֶיךָ: וּמָל יְהוָה אֱלֹהֶיךָ אֶת־לְבָבְךָ
וְאֶת־לְבַב זַרְעֶךָ לְאַהֲבָה אֶת־יְהוָה אֱלֹהֶיךָ בְּכָל־לְבָבְךָ
ז וּבְכָל־נַפְשְׁךָ לְמַעַן חַיֶּיךָ: וְנָתַן יְהוָה אֱלֹהֶיךָ אֵת כָּל־הָאָלוֹת חמישי /שלישי/
ח הָאֵלֶּה עַל־אֹיְבֶיךָ וְעַל־שֹׂנְאֶיךָ אֲשֶׁר רְדָפוּךָ: וְאַתָּה תָשׁוּב
וְשָׁמַעְתָּ בְּקוֹל יְהוָה וְעָשִׂיתָ אֶת־כָּל־מִצְוֹתָיו אֲשֶׁר אָנֹכִי
ט מְצַוְּךָ הַיּוֹם: וְהוֹתִירְךָ יְהוָה אֱלֹהֶיךָ בְּכֹל | מַעֲשֵׂה יָדֶךָ בִּפְרִי

---

repeats a word several times to emphasize its significance as a keyword: sometimes three or five times, but usually seven, as in the present instance (taking "bring your captives back," *veshav et shevutekha*, as one composite phrase).

The next passage (Deut. 30:11) continues, "For *this commandment* that I am giving you today is not unattainable to you, neither is it distant." Hence, Ramban identifies our passage as the source of the command of repentance, *teshuva*. In the Torah, sin is something more than a transaction in the soul, or even an act of wrongdoing narrowly conceived. It is *an act in the wrong place*. It disturbs the moral order of the world. The words for sin – *ḥet* and *avera* – both have this significance. *Ḥet* comes from the same verb as "to miss a target." *Avera*, like the English word "transgression," means to cross a boundary, to enter forbidden territory, to be in a place one should not be.

Because a sin is an act in the wrong place, its consequence is that the one who performs it finds himself in the wrong place – in exile, meaning, not at home. Sin *alienates*; it distances us from God, and so from where we ought to be, where we belong. We become aliens, strangers. We say in our prayers, "Because of our sins we were exiled from our land." Hence the double meaning of *teshuva*, most clearly expressed in this *parasha*, but found throughout the entire prophetic literature. It has both a physical and spiritual dimension, and the two are inseparable: it means both *the physical return to the land* and *the spiritual return to God. Teshuva* is a double homecoming. In the course of the twentieth century, Jews returned. The State of Israel was reborn. There has been a *physical* homecoming to the land, but not yet a full spiritual homecoming to the faith. That challenge rests with us and our

prosperity in all the work of your hands, in the fruit of
your womb, the fruit of your cattle, and the fruit of your
land. The LORD will again delight in your well-being as
10 He did in your ancestors', when you heed the LORD your
God, keeping His commandments and decrees that are
written in this book of the Law, and have returned to the
LORD your God with all your heart and with all your
11 soul. For this commandment that I am giving SHISHI
you today is not unattainable to you, neither is it distant.
12 It is not in heaven, that you should say, 'Who will go up
to heaven for us and bring it to us that we may hear it and

Religion is a sustained process of using the deep power of joy to see into the life of things.

"For you to keep it" – in the rituals we perform. A ritual is an *enactment of meaning*. That is what makes a house of worship not a theater, and a congregation something other than an audience. A congregation participates in a ritual, lives the reality it encodes; an audience merely suspends its disbelief while the play is going on, knowing that what it is seeing is a fiction.

Meanings are socially constructed. They belong to the shared life of communities. They involve a living connection to a past to which we feel ourselves to belong, and a future for which we hold ourselves responsible. They are always particular – to this group, that nation, this faith, that tradition. Science may be universal. Meaning never is. *Sacred* meanings are those we make when we covenant with God, listening to His voice, heeding His call.

We could not fully understand God's truth without being gods ourselves. God does not ask us to be anything other than what we are, finite beings whose knowledge is limited, whose lifespan is short, and whose horizons are circumscribed. For God, in creating us, gave our lives significance. Faith, Abrahamic faith, is about God and human beings making meaning in covenant together.

30:12 לֹא בַשָּׁמַיִם *Not in heaven* – Here God empowers His children. He gives them His greatest gift: His will as encoded in His word. The Torah is "not in heaven"; it is intelligible to all. Each member of the covenantal community has something to contribute to the totality of its meaning. As Maharsha (Rabbi Shmuel Eliezer Edels, 1555–1631) put it: There are six hundred thousand possible interpretations of the Torah, which is why the Torah was given to six hundred thousand Israelites, so that the revelation would include all possible interpretations (Maharsha, novellae on Berakhot 58a).

בִּטְנְךָ֜ וּבִפְרִ֧י בְהֶמְתְּךָ֛ וּבִפְרִ֥י אַדְמָתְךָ֖ לְטֹבָ֑ה כִּ֣י ׀ יָשׁ֣וּב יְהוָ֗ה
י לָשׂ֤וּשׂ עָלֶ֙יךָ֙ לְט֔וֹב כַּאֲשֶׁר־שָׂ֖שׂ עַל־אֲבֹתֶֽיךָ׃ כִּ֣י תִשְׁמַ֗ע
בְּקוֹל֙ יְהוָ֣ה אֱלֹהֶ֔יךָ לִשְׁמֹ֤ר מִצְוֺתָיו֙ וְחֻקֹּתָ֔יו הַכְּתוּבָ֕ה בְּסֵ֖פֶר
הַתּוֹרָ֣ה הַזֶּ֑ה כִּ֤י תָשׁוּב֙ אֶל־יְהוָ֣ה אֱלֹהֶ֔יךָ בְּכָל־לְבָבְךָ֖ וּבְכָל־
יא נַפְשֶֽׁךָ׃ כִּ֚י הַמִּצְוָ֣ה הַזֹּ֔את אֲשֶׁ֛ר אָנֹכִ֥י מְצַוְּךָ֖ כד ששי
יב הַיּ֑וֹם לֹֽא־נִפְלֵ֥את הִוא֙ מִמְּךָ֔ וְלֹ֥א רְחֹקָ֖ה הִֽוא׃ לֹ֥א בַשָּׁמַ֖יִם
הִ֑וא לֵאמֹ֗ר מִ֣י יַעֲלֶה־לָּ֤נוּ הַשָּׁמַ֙יְמָה֙ וְיִקָּחֶ֣הָ לָּ֔נוּ וְיַשְׁמִעֵ֥נוּ

NOT IN HEAVEN

The Torah "is not in heaven," says Moshe. There is plenary truth in heaven; on earth we live among its reflections and refractions. The Tanakh does not deny that there are ultimate meanings in the universe. There are. That human life is sacred is one of them. But we will always be blind to the truths we do not like, that circumscribe our power or stand in the way of the fulfillment of our desires.

So the Torah turns to covenants. Covenant is about *the meanings we make together* – the agreements God makes with Noaḥ, then Avraham, then the Israelites at Sinai. These are meanings that have ceased to be facts and become instead morally binding commitments. Do not murder, do not rob, do not commit adultery, do not bear false witness. These are part of a total system of meanings, that include the historical memory of liberation from slavery in Egypt, by which a people agreed to bind itself and its descendants, taking on themselves a collective vocation. It is not meaning *discovered* or meaning *invented*, but meaning collectively *made and renewed* in the conscious presence of God – that is to say, an authority beyond ourselves and our merely human devices and desires.

Religion is, for the most part, the constant making and remaking of meaning, by the stories we tell, the prayers we say, and the rituals we perform. Religion is an authentic response to a real presence, but it is also a way of making that presence real by constantly living in response to it. It is truth translated into deed.

It is "in your mouth" – in the stories we tell: When I take part in a Seder service on Passover, I do not "consume" the story of the exodus; I enact it, making it part of me. It defines me as part of that story. It changes me, for I now know what it feels and tastes like to be oppressed, and I can no longer walk by when others are oppressed.

It is "in your heart" – in the prayers we say. Praying, we hear the universe singing a song to its Creator. We join our ancestors as they sang psalms in the Temple, or as they passed through the divided waters of the Sea of Reeds.

13 keep it?' Nor is it beyond the sea, that you should say,
'Who will cross to the far side of the sea for us, and bring
14 it to us that we may hear it and keep it?' This word is very
close to you. It is in your mouth and in your heart for you
15 to keep it. See: I have set before you today life SHEVI'I AND MAFTIR /REVI'I/
16 and goodness, and death and evil. For I charge you on
this day to love the LORD your God, walk in His ways,
and keep His commandments, decrees, and laws. Then
you will survive and thrive and the LORD your God will
17 bless you in the land you are coming into to possess. But
if your heart turns away and you do not listen and are led
astray, and bow down to other gods and worship them,
18 then I declare to you today that you will certainly perish;
you will not live long in the land that you are crossing
19 the Jordan to enter and possess. I call heaven and earth
as witnesses against you today: I have set before you life

The deepest roots of spirituality come from within a culture, a tradition, a sensibility. They come from the syntax and semantics of the native language of the soul: "This word is very close to you; it is in your mouth and in your heart" (Deut. 30:14). The beauty of Jewish spirituality is precisely that in Judaism God is close. You do not need to climb a mountain or enter an ashram to find the Divine Presence. It is there around the table on the Sabbath, in the light of the candles and the simple holiness of the Kiddush wine, in the blessing of children, in the peace of mind that comes when you leave the world to look after itself for a day while you celebrate the good things that come not from working but resting, not from buying but enjoying – the gifts you have had all along but did not have time to appreciate.

30:16 וְחָיִיתָ וְרָבִיתָ *Survive and thrive* – Judaism is about creating spiritual energy, the energy that, if used for the benefit of others, changes lives and begins to change the world. God is our bridge across the abyss that separates me from you, one person from the next. If I learn Torah rightly, then I will want to teach it. If I pray for what I need, I will become aware of what other people need. If I thank God for what He has given me, I will know that He wants me to give part of it to others. Those are litmus paper tests for knowing whether we are on the right or wrong track. Jewish spirituality is not a private starburst of the soul. Jewish life is not the search for personal salvation. It is a restless desire to change the world into a place in which God can feel at home.

יג אַתָּה וְנַעֲשֶׂנָּה: וְלֹא־מֵעֵבֶר לַיָּם הִוא לֵאמֹר מִי יַעֲבָר־לָנוּ
יד אֶל־עֵבֶר הַיָּם וְיִקָּחֶהָ לָּנוּ וְיַשְׁמִעֵנוּ אֹתָהּ וְנַעֲשֶׂנָּה: כִּי־קָרוֹב
טו אֵלֶיךָ הַדָּבָר מְאֹד בְּפִיךָ וּבִלְבָבְךָ לַעֲשֹׂתוֹ: רְאֵה
שביעי ומפטיר /רביעי/
נָתַתִּי לְפָנֶיךָ הַיּוֹם אֶת־הַחַיִּים וְאֶת־הַטּוֹב וְאֶת־הַמָּוֶת וְאֶת־
טז הָרָע: אֲשֶׁר אָנֹכִי מְצַוְּךָ הַיּוֹם לְאַהֲבָה אֶת־יהוה אֱלֹהֶיךָ
לָלֶכֶת בִּדְרָכָיו וְלִשְׁמֹר מִצְוֹתָיו וְחֻקֹּתָיו וּמִשְׁפָּטָיו וְחָיִיתָ
וְרָבִיתָ וּבֵרַכְךָ יהוה אֱלֹהֶיךָ בָּאָרֶץ אֲשֶׁר־אַתָּה בָא־שָׁמָּה
יז לְרִשְׁתָּהּ: וְאִם־יִפְנֶה לְבָבְךָ וְלֹא תִשְׁמָע וְנִדַּחְתָּ וְהִשְׁתַּחֲוִיתָ
יח לֵאלֹהִים אֲחֵרִים וַעֲבַדְתָּם: הִגַּדְתִּי לָכֶם הַיּוֹם כִּי אָבֹד
תֹּאבֵדוּן לֹא־תַאֲרִיכֻן יָמִים עַל־הָאֲדָמָה אֲשֶׁר אַתָּה עֹבֵר
יט אֶת־הַיַּרְדֵּן לָבוֹא שָׁמָּה לְרִשְׁתָּהּ: הַעִידֹתִי בָכֶם הַיּוֹם אֶת־
הַשָּׁמַיִם וְאֶת־הָאָרֶץ הַחַיִּים וְהַמָּוֶת נָתַתִּי לְפָנֶיךָ הַבְּרָכָה

GOD IS CLOSE

Over the ages, there have always been Jews who sought inspiration elsewhere – in heaven, across the sea, anywhere but here. During the First Temple period, the people were tempted by the gods of the people around them. Later, they were attracted to Hellenism. It is a strange phenomenon: some Jews have had a tendency to fall in love with people who do not love them and pursue almost any spiritual path but their own. This is debilitating. When those in search of spirituality go elsewhere, Jewish spirituality suffers.

It tends to happen in the paradoxical way that Moshe describes several times in Deuteronomy. It occurs in ages of affluence, not poverty, in eras of freedom, not slavery. The surrounding culture in most of these cases was hostile to Jews and Judaism. Becoming Baal worshippers did not lead to Israelites being welcomed by the Canaanites. Becoming Hellenized did not endear Jews to either the Greeks or the Romans. Abandoning Judaism in the nineteenth century did not end antisemitism; it inflamed it. Yet Jews often preferred to adopt the culture that rejected them rather than embrace the one that was theirs by birth and inheritance, where they had the chance of feeling at home. Was it the failure of Europe to accept the Jewishness of Jews and Judaism? Was it Judaism's failure to confront the challenge? The phenomenon defies any simple explanation. But in the process, we have lost great intellects, spirits, and minds.

Hence the power of Moshe's insistence: to find truth, beauty, and spirituality, you do not have to go elsewhere.

▶

and death, the blessing and the curse. Choose life – so
20 that you and your children may live, loving the LORD
your God, heeding His voice and holding fast to Him,
for this is your life and the length of your days, living in
the land that the LORD swore to give to your ancestors, to
Avraham, Yitzḥak, and Yaakov."

The haftara for Parashat Nitzavim is on page 1616 (even when Nitzavim and Vayelekh are read together).

the wicked or reward the righteous? (*Hilkhot Teshuva* 5:1)

Without free will, Judaism would not make sense. If we lacked freedom, there would be no point in God commanding us, "Do this. Don't do that." Nor would there be any logic in reward and punishment, both of which presuppose human responsibility for our actions.

"Choose life," our *parasha* teaches. Nothing sounds easier yet nothing has proved more difficult over time. Instead, people choose substitutes for life. They pursue wealth, possessions, status, power, fame, and to these gods they make the supreme sacrifice, realizing too late that true wealth is not what you own but what you are thankful for, that the highest status is not to care about status, and that influence is more powerful than power. That is why, though few faiths are more demanding, Jews have stayed faithful to Judaism, living Jewish lives, building Jewish homes, and continuing the Jewish story.

כ וְהַקְּלָלָ֑ה וּבָֽחַרְתָּ֙ בַּֽחַיִּ֔ים לְמַ֥עַן תִּחְיֶ֖ה אַתָּ֥ה וְזַרְעֶֽךָ׃ לְאַהֲבָה֙
אֶת־יְהוָ֣ה אֱלֹהֶ֔יךָ לִשְׁמֹ֥עַ בְּקֹל֖וֹ וּלְדׇבְקָה־ב֑וֹ כִּ֣י ה֤וּא חַיֶּ֙יךָ֙
וְאֹ֣רֶךְ יָמֶ֔יךָ לָשֶׁ֖בֶת עַל־הָֽאֲדָמָ֗ה אֲשֶׁר֩ נִשְׁבַּ֨ע יְהוָ֧ה לַאֲבֹתֶ֛יךָ
לְאַבְרָהָ֛ם לְיִצְחָ֥ק וּֽלְיַעֲקֹ֖ב לָתֵ֥ת לָהֶֽם׃

The הפטרה *for* פרשת נצבים *is on page 1617*
(even when נצבים *and* וילך *are read together).*

30:19 **וּבָחַרְתָּ בַּחַיִּים** *Choose life* – Against all the many determinisms in the history of thought – astrological, philosophical, Spinozist, Marxist, Freudian, neo-Darwinian – Judaism insists that we are masters of our fate. We are neither programmed nor predestined. We can choose. Rambam leaves us in no doubt that free will is one of the fundamental principles of Judaism:

> Free will is bestowed on every human being. If one desires to turn toward the good way and be righteous, he has the power to do so. If one wishes to turn toward the evil way and be wicked, he is at liberty to do so.... This doctrine is an important principle, the pillar of the law and the commandment.... We have it in us to be as righteous as Moshe or as evil as Yorovam.
>
> If God had decreed that a person should either be righteous or wicked... what room could there be for the whole of the Torah? By what right or justice could God punish

Parashat Vayelekh

31 1 2 Moshe went and spoke these words to all Israel. He told
them, "I am a hundred and twenty years old now, and no
longer able to enter and to leave. And the Lord has told
3 me, 'You shall not cross this Jordan.' The Lord your God
Himself will cross ahead of you. He will destroy these
nations before you, and you shall take possession in their
place. It is Yehoshua who will lead you across, as the Lord
4 has spoken. The Lord will do to those nations as He did SHENI
to Siḥon and to Og, kings of the Amorites, and to their
5 land, when He destroyed them. The Lord will deliver
them to you and you shall deal with them just as I have
6 commanded you. Be strong and be determined. Do not
fear or dread them, for the Lord your God is going with
7 you. He will not fail you or forsake you." Then SHELISHI /ḤAMISHI/
Moshe summoned Yehoshua and said to him in the sight
of all Israel: "Be strong and be determined, for it is you

The difference in Hebrew is even slighter than it is in English. Moshe uses the verb *tavo*, "come with." God uses the verb *tavi*, "bring." It is the slightest of nuances, but Rashi tells us the words refer to two different styles of leadership. Here is Rashi's comment:

> Moshe said to Yehoshua, "Make sure that the elders of the generation are with you. Always act according to their opinion and advice." However, the Holy One, blessed be He, said to Yehoshua, "Because you shall bring the Israelites into the land that I promised them" – meaning, "Bring them even against their will. It all depends on you. If necessary, take a stick and beat them over the head. There is only one leader for a generation, not two." (Rashi on Deut. 31:7)

Moshe advises his successor to lead by consultation and consensus. God tells Yehoshua to lead firmly and with authority. Even if people do not agree with you, lead from the front. Be decisive. Be strong.

It is interesting that the person urging consensus is Moshe. This is the man who almost had to drag the people out of Egypt, through the sea, and across a howling desert, the man who did things of his own initiative without even asking God. It seems that at the end of his life, Moshe recognizes one great failure of his leadership. He has taken the Israelites out of Egypt, but he has not taken Egypt

פרשת וילך

לא א וַיֵּלֶךְ מֹשֶׁה וַיְדַבֵּר אֶת־הַדְּבָרִים הָאֵלֶּה אֶל־כָּל־יִשְׂרָאֵל׃
ב וַיֹּאמֶר אֲלֵהֶם בֶּן־מֵאָה וְעֶשְׂרִים שָׁנָה אָנֹכִי הַיּוֹם לֹא־אוּכַל
עוֹד לָצֵאת וְלָבוֹא וַיהוה אָמַר אֵלַי לֹא תַעֲבֹר אֶת־הַיַּרְדֵּן
ג הַזֶּה׃ יהוה אֱלֹהֶיךָ הוּא ׀ עֹבֵר לְפָנֶיךָ הוּא־יַשְׁמִיד אֶת־הַגּוֹיִם
הָאֵלֶּה מִלְּפָנֶיךָ וִירִשְׁתָּם יְהוֹשֻׁעַ הוּא עֹבֵר לְפָנֶיךָ כַּאֲשֶׁר דִּבֶּר
ד יהוה׃ וְעָשָׂה יהוה לָהֶם כַּאֲשֶׁר עָשָׂה לְסִיחוֹן וּלְעוֹג מַלְכֵי שני
ה הָאֱמֹרִי וּלְאַרְצָם אֲשֶׁר הִשְׁמִיד אֹתָם׃ וּנְתָנָם יהוה לִפְנֵיכֶם
ו וַעֲשִׂיתֶם לָהֶם כְּכָל־הַמִּצְוָה אֲשֶׁר צִוִּיתִי אֶתְכֶם׃ חִזְקוּ וְאִמְצוּ
אַל־תִּירְאוּ וְאַל־תַּעַרְצוּ מִפְּנֵיהֶם כִּי ׀ יהוה אֱלֹהֶיךָ הוּא
ז הַהֹלֵךְ עִמָּךְ לֹא יַרְפְּךָ וְלֹא יַעַזְבֶךָּ׃ וַיִּקְרָא שלישי
מֹשֶׁה לִיהוֹשֻׁעַ וַיֹּאמֶר אֵלָיו לְעֵינֵי כָל־יִשְׂרָאֵל חֲזַק וֶאֱמָץ /חמישי/

VAYELEKH

The shortest of all *parashot*, Vayelekh is a mere thirty verses long. Poignantly, Moshe tells the people, "I am a hundred and twenty years old now, and no longer able to enter and to leave" (Deut. 31:2). He will not lead them across the Jordan into the Promised Land. He summons his successor Yehoshua and, in the presence of the people, gives him words of encouragement. He instructs the people to gather every seven years to hear a public reading of the Torah. God appears to Moshe and Yehoshua, warning them that the Israelites may eventually stray from the covenant. He instructs them to write down the Torah and teach it to the people, as permanent testimony of the covenant itself. He then encourages Yehoshua, assuring him that He will be with him as he leads the people.

COMMAND AND CONSENSUS

The great transition is about to take place. Moshe's leadership is coming to an end. Yehoshua's is about to begin. Moshe blesses his successor. Then God does. But they give different blessings. These are Moshe's words:

> Be strong and be determined, for it is you who will come with this people into the land. (Deut. 31:7)

And these are God's:

> Be strong, be determined, because you shall bring the Israelites into the land." (31:23)

who will come with this people into the land that the
Lord has sworn to their ancestors to give them, and
8 you will allocate it to them for an inheritance. The Lord
Himself will go before you. He will be with you. He will
not fail you or forsake you. Do not fear and do not be
9 dismayed." Then Moshe wrote down this Law and gave it
to the priests, descendants of Levi, who carried the Ark of
the Covenant of the Lord, and to all the elders of Israel.
10 Moshe then commanded them: "At the end of every REVI'I
seventh year, the year of remission, during the Festival of
11 Tabernacles, when all Israel comes to appear before the
Lord your God at the place that He will choose, you shall
read out this Law in the presence of all Israel, for them to

---

entity exists under the sacred canopy of the divine word. We are a people, the king is implicitly saying, formed by covenant. If we keep it, we will flourish; if not, we will fail.

Tanakh gives us vivid descriptions of covenant renewal ceremonies, similar to this one, in the days of Yehoshua (Josh. 24), Yoshiyahu (II Kings 23), Asa (II Chr. 15), and Ezra and Neḥemya (Neh. 8–10). These were historic moments when the nation consciously rededicated itself after a long period of religious relapse. Because of *hak'hel* and covenant renewal, Israel was eternally capable of becoming young again, recovering what Yirmeyahu called "the devotion of your youth" (Jer. 2:2).

What happened to *hak'hel* during the almost two thousand years in which Israel had no king, no country, no Temple? Some scholars have made the intriguing suggestion that the *minhag Eretz Yisrael*, the custom of Jews in and from the land of Israel, which lasted until about the thirteenth century, of reading the Torah not once every year but every three or three and a half years, was intended to create a seven-year cycle, so that the second reading would end at the same time as *hak'hel*, namely on the Sukkot following a Sabbatical year.

Indeed, the institution of the reading of the Torah on Sabbath morning, which goes back to antiquity, acquired new significance at times of exile. It incorporates customs that remind us of *hak'hel*: The Torah is read, as it was by the king at *hak'hel* and Ezra at his assembly, standing on a *bima*, a raised wooden platform. The Torah reader never stands alone; there are usually three people on the *bima*: the *segan* (*gabbai*), the reader, and the person called to the Torah, representing respectively God, Moshe, and the Israelites (see Levush's commentary on *Shulḥan Arukh, Orakh Ḥayyim* 141:4). According to most halakhists, the reading of the Torah is *ḥovat tzibbur*, an obligation of the community, as opposed to the study of Torah, which is *ḥovat*

כִּי אַתָּה תָּבוֹא אֶת־הָעָם הַזֶּה אֶל־הָאָרֶץ אֲשֶׁר נִשְׁבַּע
ח יהוה לַאֲבֹתָם לָתֵת לָהֶם וְאַתָּה תַּנְחִילֶנָּה אוֹתָם׃ וַיהוה
הוּא ׀ הַהֹלֵךְ לְפָנֶיךָ הוּא יִהְיֶה עִמָּךְ לֹא יַרְפְּךָ וְלֹא יַעַזְבֶךָּ
ט לֹא תִירָא וְלֹא תֵחָת׃ וַיִּכְתֹּב מֹשֶׁה אֶת־הַתּוֹרָה הַזֹּאת
וַיִּתְּנָהּ אֶל־הַכֹּהֲנִים בְּנֵי לֵוִי הַנֹּשְׂאִים אֶת־אֲרוֹן בְּרִית יהוה
י וְאֶל־כָּל־זִקְנֵי יִשְׂרָאֵל׃ וַיְצַו מֹשֶׁה אוֹתָם לֵאמֹר מִקֵּץ ׀ שֶׁבַע רביעי
יא שָׁנִים בְּמֹעֵד שְׁנַת הַשְּׁמִטָּה בְּחַג הַסֻּכּוֹת׃ בְּבוֹא כָל־יִשְׂרָאֵל
לֵרָאוֹת אֶת־פְּנֵי יהוה אֱלֹהֶיךָ בַּמָּקוֹם אֲשֶׁר יִבְחָר תִּקְרָא

out of the Israelites. He now realizes that for them to experience a change of character, there would have to be a different kind of leadership, one that handed back responsibility to the people as a whole, and to the elders in particular.

God, on the other hand, forged the covenant only after Moshe explained to the people what was being proposed (Ex. 19:4–6), and the people – "*as one*" (19:8) – assented to it "*with one voice*" (24:3). It seems that both God and Moshe want Yehoshua to know that true leadership cannot be a one-sided affair, be it the pursuit of consensus or command-and-control. It must be a deft balance of both. They want Yehoshua to hear this in the most striking way, so each says what they are least expected to say.

Leadership is not simple. You have to listen, and you have to lead. You have to strive for consensus, but ultimately, if there is none, you must take the risk of deciding. There is a time to discuss and a time to act, a time to seek agreement and a time to move ahead without waiting for agreement. That is what both God and Moshe are telling Yehoshua in their different ways.

THE *HAK'HEL* CEREMONY

Once every seven years, on the second day of Sukkot in the year after the Sabbatical year, the people are to gather together in the Temple courtyard and hear a public reading of the Torah – specifically, selections from Deuteronomy itself (the details are set out by Rambam in *Hilkhot Ḥagiga* 3).

The Torah does not specify who is to perform the reading, but tradition ascribed the role to the king. To be sure, the Torah tends to separate religion and politics. The king is not High Priest, and the High Priest is not king. But the king is bound by the Torah. He is commanded to have a special Torah scroll written for him; he is to keep it with him when he sits on the throne and to read it "all the days of his life" (see Deut. 17:14–20 and notes there).

Here too, by reading the Torah to the assembled people every seven years, he is to show that the nation as a political

12 hear. Assemble the people – men, women, and children,
including the migrants living in your towns – so that
they may listen and learn to fear the LORD your God and
13 carefully keep all the words of this Law, and so that their
children, who do not know it, may listen and learn to be in

at Sinai – "as on the day the Torah was given," "as though he had heard it from the mouth of God." The comparison almost certainly arises from Moshe's description of the giving of the Torah in Parashat Vaetḥanan:

> Make known…how you once stood before the LORD your God at Ḥorev, when the LORD said to me, "*Assemble* the people for Me, and I will let them *hear My words so that they may learn to be in awe of Me* as long as they live on earth, and *teach their children likewise*." (Deut. 4:9–10)

The italicized words are all echoed here, especially the word *hak'hel* itself, which only appears in one other place in the Torah. Sinai, then, is to be recreated in the Temple in Jerusalem every seven years, renewing the nation, men, women, children, and migrants, in its commitment to its founding principles.

31:12 הָאֲנָשִׁים וְהַנָּשִׁים וְהַטַּף וְגֵרְךָ *Men, women, and children…migrants* – Judaism sees universal access to knowledge as fundamental to human dignity and equality. Every other form of equality has been based on either equality of power or of wealth. But there is an inherent problem with these aspirations. Power and wealth are both what I call material goods. The trouble with material goods is the more you share, the less you have. If you have total power but you decide to share it with nine other people, the result is you only have a tenth as much power that you began with. If you have a thousand dollars and share it with nine other people, you're left with only a tenth of the money that you began with. If you have a certain amount of knowledge, however, and you share that with nine others, you do not have less. Maybe you have more. The more we teach our knowledge to others, the more we learn.

Because wealth and power, at least in the short term, are zero-sum games – the more I share, the less I have – wealth and power, the economy and the state, economics and politics, are always arenas of conflict. Knowledge is not, because the more I give away, the more I have.

That is why the Jewish version of an egalitarian society, a society in which everyone reaches his or her own full dignity by having access to education and to knowledge, is the only form of egalitarianism that really has worked. *Hak'hel* establishes a culture that enables and encourages learning, not just for an elite, but for everyone.

31:13 וּבְנֵיהֶם אֲשֶׁר לֹא־יָדְעוּ *Their children, who do not know it* – National narratives

יב אֶת־הַתּוֹרָה הַזֹּאת נֶגֶד כָּל־יִשְׂרָאֵל בְּאׇזְנֵיהֶם׃ הַקְהֵל אֶת־
הָעָם הָאֲנָשִׁים וְהַנָּשִׁים וְהַטַּף וְגֵרְךָ אֲשֶׁר בִּשְׁעָרֶיךָ לְמַעַן
יִשְׁמְעוּ וּלְמַעַן יִלְמְדוּ וְיָרְאוּ אֶת־יהוה אֱלֹהֵיכֶם וְשָׁמְרוּ
יג לַעֲשׂוֹת אֶת־כָּל־דִּבְרֵי הַתּוֹרָה הַזֹּאת׃ וּבְנֵיהֶם אֲשֶׁר לֹא־
יָדְעוּ יִשְׁמְעוּ וְלָמְדוּ לְיִרְאָה אֶת־יהוה אֱלֹהֵיכֶם כָּל־הַיָּמִים

---

yaḥid, an obligation of the individual. So, I believe, *keriat haTorah* should be translated not as "the *reading* of the Torah" but as "the *proclaiming* of Torah." It is our equivalent of *hak'hel*, transposed from the seventh year to the seventh day.

It is hard for individuals, let alone nations, to stay perennially young. We drift, lose our way, become distracted, lose our sense of purpose and with it our energy and drive. The best way to stay young is never to forget "the devotion of our youth," the defining experiences that made us who we are, the dreams we had long ago of how we might change the world to make it a better, fairer, more spiritually beautiful place. *Hak'hel* was Moshe's parting gift to us, showing us how this might be done.

31:12 הַקְהֵל אֶת־הָעָם *Assemble the people* – This is how Rambam describes the ceremony:

> Trumpets were blown throughout Jerusalem to assemble the people; and a high platform, made of wood, was brought and set up in the center of the court of women. The king went up and sat there so that his reading might be heard....
>
> The *ḥazan* of the synagogue would take a *sefer Torah* and hand it to the head of the synagogue, and the head of the synagogue would hand it to the deputy High Priest, and the deputy High Priest to the High Priest, and the High Priest to the king, to honor him by the service of many persons....
>
> The king would read the sections we have mentioned until he would come to the end. Then he would roll up the *sefer Torah* and recite a blessing after the reading, the way it is recited in the synagogue....
>
> Proselytes who did not know Hebrew were required to direct their hearts and listen with utmost awe and reverence, as on the day the Torah was given at Sinai. Even great scholars who knew the entire Torah were required to listen with utmost attention....
>
> Each had to regard himself as if he had been charged with the Torah now for the first time, and as though he had heard it from the mouth of God, for the king was an ambassador proclaiming the words of God. (*Hilkhot Ḥagiga* 3:4–6)

Apart from giving us a sense of the grandeur of the occasion, Rambam is making a radical suggestion: that *hak'hel* is a reenactment of the giving of the Torah

awe of the LORD your God, as long as you live in the land
that you are crossing the Jordan to possess."
14 The LORD said to Moshe, "Your time to die draws ḤAMISHI /SHISHI/
near. Call Yehoshua and come and stand in the Tent of
Meeting, so that I may give him his charge." So Moshe
and Yehoshua went and stood in the Tent of Meeting.
15 The LORD appeared in the Tent in a pillar of cloud; and
the pillar of cloud stood at the entrance to the Tent.
16 Then the LORD said to Moshe, "Soon, you are going to
rest with your ancestors. And this people will begin to
stray after the foreign gods of the land into which they
are going. They will forsake Me and break the covenant
17 I have made with them. My rage will flare against them
at that time. I will abandon them and hide My face from
them. They will become easy prey, and many evils and
troubles will come upon them. On that day they will ask,
'Have not these troubles come upon us because our God
18 is not in our midst?' And I – I will hide My face at that

story – recalling the nation's history, giving thanks to God, and rededicating ourselves to the terms of our vocation – ensures that this story belongs to latecomers as much as to elders.

THE HIDING OF GOD'S FACE

Defeat, exile, suffering, persecution, are full of pain. But perhaps the greatest pain is to seek God and not be able to find Him. "The LORD is my light and my salvation," said David in the book of Psalms, "whom need I fear?" (Ps. 27:1). "Though I walk through the valley of the shadow of death, I fear no evil, for You are with me" (23:4). But if You are *not* with me – what then? If God's light shines but we cannot see it, if God is close but we cannot feel it, if God speaks and we cannot hear, what then?

Once, in the Garden of Eden, God called out to man and asked, "*Ayeka* – Where are you?" But for nearly two thousand years we have called out to God, "*Ayeka*?" When the Temple was destroyed, where were You? When Your sages and saints were put to death as martyrs, where were You? When Your people were dispersed and forced to wander homeless across the earth, where were You? When they were tortured and murdered for their faith, where were You? Almighty God, when Your people cried out to You from Auschwitz and Bergen-Belsen and Sobibor and Majdanek, where were You? When one million Jewish

אֲשֶׁר אַתֶּם חַיִּים עַל־הָאֲדָמָה אֲשֶׁר אַתֶּם עֹבְרִים אֶת־
הַיַּרְדֵּן שָׁמָּה לְרִשְׁתָּהּ׃
יד וַיֹּאמֶר יהוה אֶל־מֹשֶׁה הֵן קָרְבוּ יָמֶיךָ לָמוּת קְרָא אֶת־ כה חמישי /ששי/
יְהוֹשֻׁעַ וְהִתְיַצְּבוּ בְּאֹהֶל מוֹעֵד וַאֲצַוֶּנּוּ וַיֵּלֶךְ מֹשֶׁה וִיהוֹשֻׁעַ
טו וַיִּתְיַצְּבוּ בְּאֹהֶל מוֹעֵד׃ וַיֵּרָא יהוה בָּאֹהֶל בְּעַמּוּד עָנָן
טז וַיַּעֲמֹד עַמּוּד הֶעָנָן עַל־פֶּתַח הָאֹהֶל׃ וַיֹּאמֶר יהוה אֶל־
מֹשֶׁה הִנְּךָ שֹׁכֵב עִם־אֲבֹתֶיךָ וְקָם הָעָם הַזֶּה וְזָנָה ׀ אַחֲרֵי ׀
אֱלֹהֵי נֵכַר־הָאָרֶץ אֲשֶׁר הוּא בָא־שָׁמָּה בְּקִרְבּוֹ וַעֲזָבַנִי וְהֵפֵר
יז אֶת־בְּרִיתִי אֲשֶׁר כָּרַתִּי אִתּוֹ׃ וְחָרָה אַפִּי בוֹ בַיּוֹם־הַהוּא
וַעֲזַבְתִּים וְהִסְתַּרְתִּי פָנַי מֵהֶם וְהָיָה לֶאֱכֹל וּמְצָאֻהוּ רָעוֹת
רַבּוֹת וְצָרוֹת וְאָמַר בַּיּוֹם הַהוּא הֲלֹא עַל כִּי־אֵין אֱלֹהַי
יח בְּקִרְבִּי מְצָאוּנִי הָרָעוֹת הָאֵלֶּה׃ וְאָנֹכִי הַסְתֵּר אַסְתִּיר פָּנַי

can be, indeed must be, inclusive of those of all ages. The book of Deuteronomy as a whole is a restatement of the covenant for a new generation. A similar event is described in the last chapter of the book of Joshua once Yehoshua had fulfilled his mandate as Moshe's successor, bringing the people across the Jordan, leading them in their battles, and settling the land.

Another occurred many centuries later, in very different circumstances, in the reign of King Yoshiyahu. His grandfather Menashe, who reigned for fifty-five years, was one of the worst of Yehuda's kings, introducing idolatry, including child sacrifice. Yoshiyahu sought to return the nation to its faith, ordering the cleansing and repair of the Temple. In the course of this restoration, a copy of the Torah was discovered, sealed in a hiding place, to prevent it being destroyed during the many decades in which the Torah was almost forgotten. The king, deeply affected by this discovery, "summoned all the elders of Yehuda and Jerusalem.... He read out to them all the words of the scroll of the covenant that had been found in the House of the Lord.... And all the people pledged themselves to the covenant" (II Kings 23:1–3).

The most famous *hak'hel*-type ceremony was the national gathering convened by Ezra and Neḥemya after the second wave of returnees from Babylon (Neh. 8–10). Standing on a platform by one of the gates to the Temple, Ezra read the Torah to the assembly. The ceremony began on Rosh HaShana and culminated after Sukkot with the people collectively "binding themselves by an oath, under the penalty of a curse, to follow in the way of God's teaching as given into the hand of God's servant Moshe" (10:30).

Periodically retelling our national

time because of all the evil they have done by turning to
19 other gods. So now write down this song and teach it to
the Israelites. Place it in their mouths, so that this song
20 may be My witness against them. When I have brought SHISHI /SHEVI'I/
them into the land that flows with milk and with honey,

"WRITE THIS SONG"

The final mitzva is to "write down this song and teach it to the Israelites. Place it in their mouths, so that this song may be My witness" (Deut. 31:19).

According to the plain sense of the verse, God is speaking to Moshe and Yehoshua and is referring to the song in the following chapter. However, Oral Tradition gave the verse a wider interpretation, understanding it as a command for every Jew to write, or at least take some part in writing, a *sefer Torah*:

> Said Rabba: Even though our ancestors have left us a scroll of the Torah, it is our religious duty to write one for ourselves, as it is said: "So now, write down [literally, 'for yourselves'] this song and teach it to the Israelites. Place it in their mouths, so that this song may be My witness against them." (Sanhedrin 21b)

The logic of this reading seems to be that the phrase "write down for yourselves" could be construed as referring to every Israelite (Ibn Ezra), not just Moshe and Yehoshua. The Talmud offers a further reason. The verse goes on to say: "So that this song may be My witness against them" – implying the Torah as a whole, not just the song in chapter 32 (Nedarim 38a). Thus understood, Moshe's final message to the Israelites is: "It is not enough that you have received the Torah from me. You must make it new again in every generation." The covenant is not to grow old. It has to be periodically renewed.

If we take the command to refer to the whole Torah and not just one chapter, then what is the significance of the word "song" (*shira*) which appears five times in this passage? It is clearly a keyword. On this, two nineteenth-century scholars offered striking explanations.

The Netziv (Rabbi Naftali Tzvi Yehuda Berlin, 1816–93, one of the great yeshiva heads of the nineteenth century) interprets it to mean that the whole Torah should be read as poetry, not prose; the word *shira* in Hebrew means both a song and a poem. To be sure, most of the Torah is written in prose, but the Netziv argued that it has characteristics of poetry. It is allusive rather than explicit. It leaves unsaid more than is said. Like poetry, it hints at deeper reservoirs of meaning, sometimes by the use of an unusual word or sentence construction. Descriptive prose carries its meaning on the surface. The Torah, like poetry, does not (preface to *Haamek Davar*, 3).

A different aspect is alluded to by Rabbi Yechiel Michel Epstein, author of the halakhic code *Arukh HaShulḥan*.

בַּיּוֹם הַהוּא עַל כׇּל־הָרָעָה אֲשֶׁר עָשָׂה כִּי פָנָה אֶל־אֱלֹהִים
יט אֲחֵרִים׃ וְעַתָּה כִּתְבוּ לָכֶם אֶת־הַשִּׁירָה הַזֹּאת וְלַמְּדָהּ
אֶת־בְּנֵי־יִשְׂרָאֵל שִׂימָהּ בְּפִיהֶם לְמַעַן תִּהְיֶה־לִּי הַשִּׁירָה
כ הַזֹּאת לְעֵד בִּבְנֵי יִשְׂרָאֵל׃ כִּי־אֲבִיאֶנּוּ אֶל־הָאֲדָמָה ׀ אֲשֶׁר־ ששי
/שביעי/

children were gassed, burned, or buried alive, where were You?

The rabbinic literature contains an extraordinary statement, which by a slight textual emendation turned the phrase "Who is like You, Lord, among the mighty (*ba'elim*)?" (Ex. 15:11) into "Who is like You *ba'ilmim* – among the silent?" "A day will come [says God] when I will hide My face." It came. But it was not a day. It was two thousand years.

Then something began to happen. In the midst of darkness, we began to see what looked like the first faint signs of light. One after another, prayers that Jews had said for hundreds of years, more in hope than expectation, began to come true.

"Sound the great shofar for our freedom." The ram's horn sounded and in one country after another Jews left the ghetto and were free.

"Raise the banner to gather our exiles." The banner of Zion was lifted and from across the globe Jews began to return to the land of our ancestors.

"Restore our judges as at first." The State of Israel was born. For the first time in almost two thousand years, Jews could rule over themselves instead of being ruled over by others. They could defend themselves instead of depending on others.

"Return in mercy to Your city, Jerusalem." In 1967, Jerusalem was reunited. Jews could pray again at the Temple wall.

And they streamed into the land. From Yemen, Iraq, and Iran, from Russia and Ethiopia, Jews who had been cut off from their people for decades, for centuries, came home. "If you should be expelled to the furthest of horizons, even from there the Lord your God will gather you, from there He will take you back" (Deut. 30:4).

Rabbi Joseph B. Soloveitchik once said that with the birth of the State of Israel there ended the "hiding of the face" of God. It was the beginning of the end of exile. God had reentered history.

31:18 בַּיּוֹם הַהוּא *At that time* – The Torah speaks of the "hiding of the face" of God in a particular context, namely the exile of Jews from their land. From the opening chapters of Genesis to the closing speeches of Deuteronomy, human transgression is seen in terms of dislocation, moral and physical. The divine withdrawal from history is described not as a timeless feature of human freedom but as a specific phase in the history of the covenant. If the children of Israel sin, exile will further deepen the alienation between man and God, until man experiences God in His absence, not His presence.

which I promised on oath to their ancestors, they will eat
their fill and grow fat, and they will turn to other gods and
worship them, rejecting Me and breaking My covenant.
21 And when they are beset by many evils and troubles, this
song will testify as a witness against them, for it will not
be forgotten by their descendants. For I know what they
are inclined to do even now, before I have brought them
22 into the land that I promised them on oath." So, that day,
Moshe wrote down this song and taught it to the Israelites.
23 And He charged Yehoshua son of Nun: "Be strong, be
determined, because you shall bring the Israelites into
the land that I promised them – and I will be with you."
24 Moshe finished writing down in a scroll the words of
25 this Law to the very end; and then Moshe instructed the SHEVI'I
Levites who carried the Ark of the Covenant of the LORD:
26 "Take this scroll of the Law and place it beside the Ark of
the Covenant of the LORD your God. Let it remain there
27 as a witness to you. For I know how rebellious and stiff-
necked you are. Even now, while I am still living among
you, you have been rebellious toward the LORD; how
28 much more so will you be after my death! Gather to me MAFTIR
all the elders of your tribes and your officials, so that I
may proclaim these words in their hearing and call heaven
29 and earth to witness against them. For I know that after
my death you will act in self-destruction, turning away
from the path that I have commanded you. In the days to
come evil will befall you, because you will do evil in the
sight of the LORD, angering Him with the work of your
30 hands." Then Moshe proclaimed the words of this song
in the hearing of the entire assembly of Israel, to the very
end.

The haftara for Parashat Vayelekh is on page 1620, Shabbat Shuva, the Shabbat between Rosh Hashana and Yom Kippur.

---

unity of the Divine, which transcends the oppositions of lower worlds. The Torah is God's song, and we collectively are its singers. It is with a poetic sense of closure, then, that Moshe's life ends with the command to begin again in every generation, writing our own scroll, adding our own commentaries, the people of the book endlessly reinterpreting the book of the people, and singing its song.

נשבעתי לאבתיו זבת חלב ודבש ואכל ושבע ודשן ופנה
אל־אלהים אחרים ועבדום ונאצוני והפר את־בריתי:
כא והיה כי־תמצאן אתו רעות רבות וצרות וענתה השירה
הזאת לפניו לעד כי לא תשכח מפי זרעו כי ידעתי את־
יצרו אשר הוא עשה היום בטרם אביאנו אל־הארץ
כב אשר נשבעתי: ויכתב משה את־השירה הזאת ביום
כג ההוא וילמדה את־בני ישראל: ויצו את־יהושע בן־נון
ויאמר חזק ואמץ כי אתה תביא את־בני ישראל אל־
כד הארץ אשר־נשבעתי להם ואנכי אהיה עמך: ויהי | ככלות
משה לכתב את־דברי התורה־הזאת על־ספר עד תמם:
כה ויצו משה את־הלוים נשאי ארון ברית־יהוה לאמר: שביעי
כו לקח את ספר התורה הזה ושמתם אתו מצד ארון
כז ברית־יהוה אלהיכם והיה־שם בך לעד: כי אנכי ידעתי
את־מריך ואת־ערפך הקשה הן בעודני חי עמכם היום
כח ממרים היתם עם־יהוה ואף כי־אחרי מותי: הקהילו אלי מפטיר
את־כל־זקני שבטיכם ושטריכם ואדברה באזניהם את
כט הדברים האלה ואעידה בם את־השמים ואת־הארץ: כי
ידעתי אחרי מותי כי־השחת תשחתון וסרתם מן־הדרך
אשר צויתי אתכם וקראת אתכם הרעה באחרית הימים
כי־תעשו את־הרע בעיני יהוה להכעיסו במעשה ידיכם:
ל וידבר משה באזני כל־קהל ישראל את־דברי השירה
הזאת עד תמם:

The הפטרה *for* פרשת וילך *is on page 1621,* שבת שובה*,*
the שבת *between* ראש השנה *and* יום כפור*.*

He points out that the rabbinic literature is full of arguments, about which the Sages said: "These and those are the words of the living God" (*Ḥoshen Mishpat*, introduction). This, he says, is one of the reasons the Torah is called a "song" – because a song becomes more beautiful when scored for many voices interwoven in complex harmonies.

When Jews speak they often argue, but when they sing, they sing in harmony, as the Israelites did at the Sea of Reeds, because music is the language of the soul, and at the level of the soul we enter the

Parashat Haazinu

32 1 "Listen, heavens, I will speak; / let the earth

6. Lastly there was a statement of the *witnesses* to the agreement – usually the gods of the nations involved – in Deuteronomy: "heaven and earth": 30:19–32:1.

The entire book until now is, in fact, structured as a covenant on a monumental scale.

We now see the extraordinary nature of the book. It has taken an ancient political formula and used it for an entirely new purpose. It follows precisely the structure of an ancient suzerainty treaty between a strong power, God, and a weak one, the Israelites. Politically, such treaties were well known in the ancient world, but religiously this is unique. For it means that God has taken an entire nation to be His "partners in the work of creation" by showing all humanity what it is to construct a society that honors each individual as the image of God.

We now understand the meaning of the traditional name for Deuteronomy, *Mishneh Torah*. It means that this book is a "copy" of the covenant between God and the people, made at Sinai, renewed on the banks of the Jordan, and renewed again at significant moments of Jewish history (see note on Deut. 31:13). It is the written record of the agreement, just as a *ketuba* is a written record of the obligations undertaken by a husband toward his wife.

We now also understand the place of Deuteronomy in Tanakh as a whole. Had the generation that left Egypt had the faith and courage to enter the Promised Land, all Jewish history would turn on the revelation at Sinai. In fact, though, the episode of the spies showed that that generation lacked the spirit to do so. Therefore the critical moment came for the next generation, when Moshe at the end of his life renewed the covenant with them as the condition of their inheritance of the land. The four previous books of the Torah lead up to this moment, and all the other books of Tanakh are a commentary on it – an account of how it worked out in the course of time. Deuteronomy is the book of the covenant, the center point of Jewish theology.

MOSHE'S SONG

For a month, Moshe has taught the people. He has told them their history and destiny, and the laws that will make theirs a unique society of people bound in covenant with one another and with God. He has renewed the covenant and then handed the leadership on to his successor and disciple Yehoshua. His final act will be blessing the people, tribe by tribe. But before that, there is one more thing he must do. He must sum up his

פרשת האזינו

לב א הַאֲזִינוּ הַשָּׁמַיִם וַאֲדַבֵּרָה וְתִשְׁמַע הָאָרֶץ אִמְרֵי־פִי׃ כו

HAAZINU

Parashat Haazinu consists of the song sung by Moshe as his last lesson to the Israelites before blessing them and ascending Mount Nevo to die. It expresses in poetic form the relationship between the God of righteousness and His often recalcitrant people. The idea behind the song belongs to the logic of covenant, in which one of the parties can bring a case against the other for non-fulfillment of duties agreed to in the covenant itself. This kind of lawsuit (known in Biblical Hebrew as a *riv*) is referred to often by the later prophets, usually an accusation by God against the Israelites but occasionally the opposite.

THE END OF THE COVENANT DOCUMENT

More perhaps than any other book in the Torah, Deuteronomy is a highly structured work, blending together genres in a meticulous composite form. A number of archaeological discoveries have thrown new light on this form. They are the engraved records of ancient treaties between neighboring powers. Among them are the Stele of the Vultures commemorating the victory of Eannatum, ruler of Lagash in southern Mesopotamia, over the people of Umma, and the Stele of Naram-Sin, king of Kish and Akkad, a treaty with the ruler of Elam. Both date from the third millennium BCE, before the time of Avraham.

What the treaties show is the precise form of ancient covenants – closely reflected in the book of Deuteronomy thus far. They had six parts:

1. They began with a *preamble,* establishing the identity of the person or power initiating the covenant – in Deuteronomy: 1:1–1:5.
2. This was followed by a *historical prologue,* reviewing the history of the relationship between the two parties to the covenant: 1:6–4:49.
3. Then came the provisions of the covenant itself, the *stipulations,* which were often stated in two forms: (a) general principles: 5:1–11:32; and (b) detailed provisions: 12:1–26:19.
4. There then followed a provision for the covenant to be *deposited* in a sacred place and *read on a regular basis*: 27:1–26, 31:1–30.
5. Next came the *sanctions* associated with the covenant: the blessings that would follow if it was adhered to, and the curses that would occur if it was broken: 28:1–69.

2 hear the words of my mouth. / May my teaching pour
down like rain, / let my speech fall like the
dew; / like gentle rain on tender plants, / like
3 showers upon the grasses. / As I call out the name of
the Lord – / come, praise the greatness of our

32:2 יַעֲרֹף כַּמָּטָר לִקְחִי *May my teaching pour down like rain* – We are invited to think of the Torah as being like the rain that waters the ground so that it brings forth produce. Sifrei puts it thus:

> "May my teaching pour down like rain": Just as the rain is one thing, yet it falls on trees, enabling each to produce tasty fruit according to the kind of tree it is – the vine in its way, the olive tree in its way, and the date palm in its way – so the Torah is one, yet its words yield Scripture, Mishna, laws, and lore.
>
> "Like showers upon the grasses": Just as showers fall upon plants and make them grow, some green, some red, some black, some white, so the words of Torah produce teachers, worthy individuals, sages, the righteous, and the pious." (Haazinu 306)

There is only one Torah, yet it has multiple effects. It gives rise to different kinds of teaching, different sorts of virtue. Torah is sometimes seen by its critics as overly prescriptive, as if it sought to make everyone the same. The Midrash argues otherwise. The Torah is compared to rain precisely to emphasize that its most important effect is to make each of us grow into what we could become. As the Mishna puts it: "When a human being makes many coins from the same mint, they are all the same. God makes everyone in the same image – His image – yet none is the same as another" (Yerushalmi, Sanhedrin 4:5). There is no single role model of the religious hero or heroine in Tanakh. The patriarchs and matriarchs each had their own unmistakable character. Kings, priests, and prophets had different roles to play. Even among the prophets, "no two prophesy in the same style," said the Sages (Sanhedrin 89a). Eliyahu was zealous, Elisha gentle. Hoshea speaks of love; Amos speaks of justice. Yeshayahu's visions are less opaque than those of Yeḥezkel.

The same applies to the revelation at Sinai itself. Each individual heard, in the same words, a different inflection:

> "The Lord's voice rings with power" (Ps. 29:4): that is, according to the power of each individual, young, old, the very small ones, each according to their power [of understanding]. Yet God said to Israel, "Do not believe that there are many gods in heaven because you heard many voices. Know that I alone am the Lord your God" (Shemot Rabba 29:1).

Judaism, in short, says: "Out of the One, many." The miracle of creation is

ב יַעֲרֹף כַּמָּטָר לִקְחִי תִּזַּל כַּטַּל אִמְרָתִי
כִּשְׂעִירִם עֲלֵי־דֶשֶׁא וְכִרְבִיבִים עֲלֵי־עֵשֶׂב׃
ג כִּי שֵׁם יְהוָה אֶקְרָא הָבוּ גֹדֶל לֵאלֹהֵינוּ׃

prophetic message in a way the people will always remember and be inspired by. He knows that the best way of doing so is in music. So the last thing Moshe does before giving the people his deathbed blessing is to teach them a song.

Jewish history is not so much read as sung. Every day, in Judaism, we preface our morning prayers with *Pesukei DeZimra*, the "Verses of Song," with their magnificent crescendo, Psalm 150, in which instruments and the human voice combine to sing God's praises. Mystics go further and speak of the song of the universe, what Pythagoras called "the music of the spheres." This is what Psalm 19 means when it says, "The heavens tell of God's glory…. There is no speech; there are no words; their voice is not heard, yet their music carries across the land, their words to the end of the earth" (Ps. 19:2–5). Beneath the silence, audible only to the inner ear, creation sings to its Creator.

Who hears this song? The priest thinks in terms of universal rules that are eternally valid. The prophet is attuned to the particularities of a given situation and the relationships between those involved. *The prophet has emotional intelligence.* He or she hears the silent cry of the oppressed, and the incipient anger of Heaven. The vehicle of biblical prophecy is not prose, but poetry – language that engages the senses and the unconscious memory through its music. This is what Rabbi Joseph B. Soloveitchik described as "the Torah of his mother." From his mother, he said:

> I learned that Judaism expresses itself not only in formal compliance with the law but also in a living experience. She taught me that there is a flavor, a scent and warmth to mitzvot. I learned from her the most important thing in life – to feel the presence of the Almighty and the gentle pressure of His hand resting upon my frail shoulders. Without her teachings, which quite often were transmitted to me in silence, I would have grown up a soulless being, dry and insensitive. ("A Tribute to the Rebbetzin of Talne")

At the very end of his life, the greatest of all the prophets turns to emotional intelligence, to the spirituality of song, knowing that unless he does so, his teachings might enter the minds of the Israelites but not their hearts, their passions, their emotive DNA. It is feelings that move us to act, give us the energy to aspire, and fuel our ability to hand on our commitments to those who come after us. As Robert Frost said, "Poetry is what is lost in translation." And faith is poetry, not prose.

4 God. / The Rock, His work is whole, / and
all His ways are justice. / A God of faith who does no
5 wrong, / just is He and upright. / Did He act
ruinously? No, with His children lies the fault, / a
6 warped and twisted generation. / Is this how you repay
the LORD, / you foolish, unwise people? / Is

---

are, He does not relinquish the faith that we will change. However lost, He does not cease to believe that one day we will find our way back to Him. *More than we search for God, God searches for us*, asking us, as He did to Adam, "Where are you?" Sifrei's comment is profound. Creation, even God's creation, when it involves endowing a creature with the capacity to act in freedom, involves risk and therefore faith. "God of faith" means "He who had *faith in the universe* and created it." I know of no lovelier account of the (often unlovely) human condition.

32:5 לֹא בָּנָיו מוּמָם *No, with His children lies the fault* – In this verse, we sense the closing of a drama that began in the beginning with Adam and Ḥava in the Garden of Eden. When they sinned, Adam blamed the woman, the woman blamed the serpent. So it was in the beginning and so it still is in the twenty-first century. The story of humanity has been, for the most part, a flight from responsibility. The culprits change. Only the sense of victimhood remains. It wasn't us. It was the politicians. Or the media, or our parents, or the system – be it capitalism, communism, or anything in between. Most of all, it is the fault of the others, the ones not like us, infidels, sons of Satan, children of darkness, the unredeemed. The perpetrators of the greatest crime against humanity in all of history were convinced it wasn't them. They were "only obeying orders." When all else fails, blame God. And if you do not believe in God, blame the people who do. To be human is to seek to escape from responsibility. The first humans lost paradise when they sought to hide from responsibility. We will only ever regain it if we accept responsibility.

32:6 עַם נָבָל וְלֹא חָכָם *Foolish, unwise people* – The Netziv (1816–93) cites the Targum, which paraphrases the words *am naval* not as "a foolish people" but as "the people who received the Torah." The Netziv explains that the word *naval* comes from the same root as *novelet*, which means "unripe fruit" or "the incomplete or lesser substitute for something else." Therefore, the phrase in this verse could be read as "the people who, though they received the Torah, remained unwise." This, says the Netziv, foreshadowed the situation during the last days of the Second Temple. We have no problem in understanding why the people of the First Temple suffered defeat. They were far removed from the Torah, guilty of cardinal sins. However, the men of the

ד הַצּוּר֙ תָּמִ֣ים פָּעֳל֔וֹ כִּ֥י כָל־דְּרָכָ֖יו מִשְׁפָּ֑ט
אֵ֤ל אֱמוּנָה֙ וְאֵ֣ין עָ֔וֶל צַדִּ֥יק וְיָשָׁ֖ר הֽוּא׃
ה שִׁחֵ֥ת ל֛וֹ לֹּ֖א בָּנָ֣יו מוּמָ֑ם דּ֥וֹר עִקֵּ֖שׁ וּפְתַלְתֹּֽל׃
ו הַ לְיהוה֙ תִּגְמְלוּ־זֹ֔את עַ֥ם נָבָ֖ל וְלֹ֣א חָכָ֑ם

that unity in heaven produces diversity on earth. Torah is the rain that feeds this diversity, allowing each of us to become what only we can be.

GOD OF FAITH

The Rabbis of the first centuries of the Common Era communicated profound truths in a deceptively simple way. Commenting on the phrase "a God of faith" (simply understood to mean that He is faithful to His promises), they said, "This means the God who had *faith in the world He was about to create*" (Sifrei 307). In that sentence lies an extraordinary suggestion of the risk God took when He made mankind.

Biblical faith, with its emphasis on free will and responsibility, constantly holds before us the paradox of human history. There are times when we scale the heights of goodness. But there are others when we descend to the depths of evil. Modern thought has focused on the wrong question. It has asked how God could have created nature. The Rabbis posed a question altogether more profound. How could God have created man? It is one thing to believe that God in His goodness made the universe. It is another to believe that God in His goodness made a form of life, *Homo sapiens*, capable of inflicting untold cruelty and suffering on its own members. The Torah says that before the flood, contemplating the violence that filled the world, God "regretted that He had made man on earth and His heart was touched with sorrow" (Gen. 6:6). After Auschwitz, that verse echoes with almost unbearable pathos.

The Rabbis gave a remarkable answer. Creation testifies not merely to God's power but also, as it were, to His belief in mankind. At the heart of religion is not just the faith we have in God. No less significant is *the faith God has in us*. That faith is surely often tested. It is tested when we turn our back on God. It is tested no less when we commit evil in His name. Yet He does not lose faith that one day we will learn this: that God, "lover of peoples" (Deut. 33:3), has given us many universes of faith but only one world in which to live together.

The grant of freedom to humanity was an immense act of self-limitation on the part of God – what the exponents of Lurianic Kabbala called *tzimtzum*. God has faith in man. That faith is often abused, not to say betrayed. Yet God has infinite patience – "in your white-haired years I shall still bear you" (Is. 46:4). Though human beings inflict suffering on one another, God does not give up on His creation. However corrupt we

not He your Father, your Maker, / who formed
7 you and set you on your feet? / Remember the days of SHENI
old, / consider the years of ages past; / ask your
father, and he will tell you; / your elders, and
8 they will speak. / When the Highest gave nations their
heritage, / when He divided humankind, /
He fixed the boundaries of peoples / by the
9 number of Israel's sons. / The LORD's own share is His
people, / Yaakov His allotted place. /
10 He found him in a desert land, / in a barren,
howling waste; / He encircled him, watched over
him, / guarded him close like the apple of
11 His eye. / As an eagle stirs up its nest, / and
hovers over its young; / as it spreads its plumes and
takes them, / bearing them aloft on its wings, /
12 just so, the LORD alone led him – / no strange
13 god at His side – / He set him astride the heights of the SHELISHI
earth, / and fed him the bounty of meadows; /
He nursed him with honey from the crag, / and
14 oil from flinty rock; / with curds from the herd, milk from
the flock, / and the fat of lambs and goats, /
choice rams of Bashan, / and the fattest
buds of wheat – / you drank fine wine from blood-red
15 grapes. / Yeshurun grew fat, and kicked; /
you grew fat, grew gross, grew coarse. / They

first sense what is necessary, then consider what is useful, next attend to comfort, later delight in pleasures, soon grow dissolute in luxury, and finally go mad squandering their estates." The only antidote to this, he argued, was religion, which motivates people to act with virtue and concern for the common good. Spiritual systems have the capacity to defeat the law of entropy that governs the life of nations.

Here, the first use of the name Yeshurun in the Torah – from the root *y-sh-r*, "upright" – seems deliberately ironic. Israel once knew what it was to be upright, but it will be led astray by a combination of affluence, security, and assimilation to the ways of its neighbors. It will betray the terms of the covenant, and when that happens the people will find that God is no longer with them. Separated from the source of their strength, they will be overpowered by enemies. All that the nation once enjoyed will be lost.

הֲלוֹא־הוּא֙ אָבִ֣יךָ קָּנֶ֔ךָ ה֥וּא עָֽשְׂךָ֖ וַֽיְכֹנְנֶֽךָ׃
ז זְכֹר֙ יְמ֣וֹת עוֹלָ֔ם בִּ֖ינוּ שְׁנ֣וֹת דֹּר־וָדֹ֑ר שני
שְׁאַ֤ל אָבִ֙יךָ֙ וְיַגֵּ֔דְךָ זְקֵנֶ֖יךָ וְיֹ֥אמְרוּ לָֽךְ׃
ח בְּהַנְחֵ֤ל עֶלְיוֹן֙ גּוֹיִ֔ם בְּהַפְרִיד֖וֹ בְּנֵ֣י אָדָ֑ם
יַצֵּב֙ גְּבֻלֹ֣ת עַמִּ֔ים לְמִסְפַּ֖ר בְּנֵ֥י יִשְׂרָאֵֽל׃
ט כִּ֛י חֵ֥לֶק יְהוָ֖ה עַמּ֑וֹ יַעֲקֹ֖ב חֶ֥בֶל נַחֲלָתֽוֹ׃
י יִמְצָאֵ֙הוּ֙ בְּאֶ֣רֶץ מִדְבָּ֔ר וּבְתֹ֖הוּ יְלֵ֣ל יְשִׁמֹ֑ן
יְסֹבְבֶ֙נְהוּ֙ יְב֣וֹנְנֵ֔הוּ יִצְּרֶ֖נְהוּ כְּאִישׁ֥וֹן עֵינֽוֹ׃
יא כְּנֶ֙שֶׁר֙ יָעִ֣יר קִנּ֔וֹ עַל־גּוֹזָלָ֖יו יְרַחֵ֑ף
יִפְרֹ֤שׂ כְּנָפָיו֙ יִקָּחֵ֔הוּ יִשָּׂאֵ֖הוּ עַל־אֶבְרָתֽוֹ׃
יב יְהוָ֖ה בָּדָ֣ד יַנְחֶ֑נּוּ וְאֵ֥ין עִמּ֖וֹ אֵ֥ל נֵכָֽר׃
יג יַרְכִּבֵ֙הוּ֙ עַל־בָּ֣מותי אָ֔רֶץ וַיֹּאכַ֖ל תְּנוּבֹ֣ת שָׂדָ֑י בָּ֥מֳתֵי שלישי
וַיֵּנִקֵ֤הוּ דְבַשׁ֙ מִסֶּ֔לַע וְשֶׁ֖מֶן מֵחַלְמִ֥ישׁ צֽוּר׃
יד חֶמְאַ֨ת בָּקָ֜ר וַחֲלֵ֣ב צֹ֗אן עִם־חֵ֨לֶב כָּרִ֜ים
וְאֵילִ֤ים בְּנֵֽי־בָשָׁן֙ וְעַתּוּדִ֔ים עִם־חֵ֖לֶב כִּלְי֣וֹת חִטָּ֑ה
טו וְדַם־עֵנָ֖ב תִּשְׁתֶּה־חָֽמֶר׃ וַיִּשְׁמַ֤ן יְשֻׁרוּן֙ וַיִּבְעָ֔ט

late Second Temple "studied and labored in the Torah, which prepares us to be righteous and upright." Yet they "remained unwise and were not careful to avoid bad conduct." The tragedy of the Second Temple period is that "some of the worst behavior came from those who were outstanding Torah scholars (*ba hakilkul al yedei gedolei Torah*)." The patriarchs of Genesis were generous in their behavior even to idolaters. The Torah scholars of the Second Temple – at least some of them – were vicious in their conduct even toward other religious Jews if they acted in any way differently from them, treating them as if they were heretics or sectarians.

That, suggests the Netziv, is why we must return time and again to Tanakh, especially to Genesis, for though it contains narrative rather than law, it teaches something that cannot be taught by law alone, namely, how to behave uprightly in one's dealings with others.

32:15 וַיִּשְׁמַן יְשֻׁרוּן וַיִּבְעָט *Yeshurun grew fat, and kicked* – One of the first historians to give a cyclical account of history, Giambattista Vico, argued that all civilizations were subject to a law of rise and decline. They are born in austerity. They rise to affluence and power. Then they become decadent and eventually decline: "People

abandoned God who made them, / rejected the Rock of
16 their rescue. / They provoked Him with strange
17 gods, / and angered Him with abominations. / They
sacrificed to demons, no-gods, / to deities they never
knew, / new ones, lately arisen, / whom your
18 forebears never feared. / You deserted the Rock that bore
19 you; / you forgot the God who gave you birth. / The REVI'I
LORD saw this and He in turn rejected / the sons and
20 daughters who angered Him so. / He said: I
will hide My face from them, / and see what their end
will be; / for they are a perverse generation, /
21 children with no faithfulness. / They
incensed Me with a no-god, / they angered Me with their
vanities; / I will incense them with a no-people, /
22 enrage them with a fool nation. / For a fire My
anger has kindled, / it burns to the depths of Sheol, / will
devour the land and its harvests, / and set fire to the hills'
23 foundations. / I will heap evils upon them, /
24 exhaust My arrows on them: / consuming
famine, flaming fever, bitter plague, / and
fanged beasts will I send against them, / and venomous
25 vipers crawling in the dust. / Sword outside and
terror within / will claim young men and women, /
26 nursing infants, and the gray-haired old. / I
thought I would scatter them, / erasing their memory from
27 man, / were it not for fear of the enemy's taunts, /
lest their adversaries misunderstand / and
say, 'Our hand has triumphed; / it was not the LORD who
28 did all this.' / They are a nation devoid of
29 sense; / they have no understanding. / If they ḤAMISHI
were wise, they would contemplate this, / and know

---

was this that led Jews, time and again, to emerge from tragedy, shaken, scarred, limping like Yaakov after his encounter with the angel, yet resolved to begin again, to rededicate themselves to their mission and faith.

שָׁמַנְתָּ עָבִיתָ כָּשִׂיתָ   וַיִּטֹּשׁ אֱלוֹהַ עָשָׂהוּ
טז וַיְנַבֵּל צוּר יְשֻׁעָתוֹ:   יַקְנִאֻהוּ בְּזָרִים
יז בְּתוֹעֵבֹת יַכְעִיסֻהוּ:   יִזְבְּחוּ לַשֵּׁדִים לֹא אֱלֹהַ
אֱלֹהִים לֹא יְדָעוּם   חֲדָשִׁים מִקָּרֹב בָּאוּ
יח לֹא שְׂעָרוּם אֲבֹתֵיכֶם: צוּר יְלָדְךָ תֶּשִׁי
יט וַתִּשְׁכַּח אֵל מְחֹלְלֶךָ:   וַיַּרְא יהוה וַיִּנְאָץ   רביעי
כ מִכַּעַס בָּנָיו וּבְנֹתָיו: וַיֹּאמֶר אַסְתִּירָה פָנַי מֵהֶם
אֶרְאֶה מָה אַחֲרִיתָם   כִּי דוֹר תַּהְפֻּכֹת הֵמָּה
כא בָּנִים לֹא־אֵמֻן בָּם: הֵם קִנְאוּנִי בְלֹא־אֵל
כִּעֲסוּנִי בְּהַבְלֵיהֶם   וַאֲנִי אַקְנִיאֵם בְּלֹא־עָם
כב בְּגוֹי נָבָל אַכְעִיסֵם: כִּי־אֵשׁ קָדְחָה בְאַפִּי
וַתִּיקַד עַד־שְׁאוֹל תַּחְתִּית   וַתֹּאכַל אֶרֶץ וִיבֻלָהּ
כג וַתְּלַהֵט מוֹסְדֵי הָרִים: אַסְפֶּה עָלֵימוֹ רָעוֹת
כד חִצַּי אֲכַלֶּה־בָּם: מְזֵי רָעָב וּלְחֻמֵי רֶשֶׁף
וְקֶטֶב מְרִירִי   וְשֶׁן־בְּהֵמֹת אֲשַׁלַּח־בָּם
כה עִם־חֲמַת זֹחֲלֵי עָפָר: מִחוּץ תְּשַׁכֶּל־חֶרֶב
וּמֵחֲדָרִים אֵימָה   גַּם־בָּחוּר גַּם־בְּתוּלָה
כו יוֹנֵק עִם־אִישׁ שֵׂיבָה: אָמַרְתִּי אַפְאֵיהֶם
כז אַשְׁבִּיתָה מֵאֱנוֹשׁ זִכְרָם: לוּלֵי כַּעַס אוֹיֵב אָגוּר
פֶּן־יְנַכְּרוּ צָרֵימוֹ   פֶּן־יֹאמְרוּ יָדֵנוּ רָמָה
כח וְלֹא יהוה פָּעַל כָּל־זֹאת: כִּי־גוֹי אֹבַד עֵצוֹת הֵמָּה
כט וְאֵין בָּהֶם תְּבוּנָה: לוּ חָכְמוּ יַשְׂכִּילוּ זֹאת   חמישי

It is a stark and terrifying message. Yet it contains a kernel of hope. Moshe insists that when trouble and tragedy appear, we should search for the cause within ourselves. God is upright and just. The defect is in us, His children. It is a difficult belief, this commitment to seeing justice in history under the sovereignty of God. Yet, throughout history it has led us to say: if bad things have happened, let us blame no one but ourselves, and let us labor to make them better. It

30 what their end would be. / How could one
man pursue a thousand, / and two put ten thousand
to flight, / unless their Rock had sold them, /
31 the LORD had handed them over? / For
their rock is not like our Rock; / even in our enemies'
32 judgment. / Their vine is from Sedom, / from
the vineyards of Amora; / their grapes are
33 grapes of poison, / their clusters bitter; / their
wine is serpents' venom, / cruel poison of the
34 viper. / Is this not kept in My reserve, / sealed
35 away in My treasury? / Vengeance is Mine; I
will repay: / in time, their foot will slip; / their
day of disaster is near, / their destiny hastens to meet
36 them. / For the LORD will vindicate His people, /
bring solace to His servants, / when He sees
their strength has slipped away, / no one remains, no bond
37 nor free. / He will say: Where are these gods of
38 theirs, / the rock they went to for refuge, / that

(or tacitly sanctioning its use by others). They deem the talk of God's judgment irreverent, but think nothing of entrusting judgment into human hands.... And so violence thrives, secretly nourished by belief in a God who refuses to wield the sword."

I think of the Jews of the Middle Ages, who saw their fellow Jews accused of killing Christian children to drink their blood, of poisoning wells, of desecrating the host and spreading the plague, and then murdered en masse in the name of the God of love. We can still hear their responses: they are recorded for us in many of the lamentations, *kinot*, we say on the Ninth of Av. Yes, they appeal to God's vengeance, which is to say, to God's justice. But Jews did not seek to take vengeance. That is something you leave to God. There is a justice we will not see this side of the end of days. In the meantime, it is sufficient to live, and affirm life, and seek no more than the right to be true to your faith without fear – no more than the right to live and defend that selfsame right for your children. Yes, we seek justice and we fight for justice, but the search for *perfect* justice is not for us, here, now. It is – as Moshe taught the Israelites in the great song he sang at the end of his life – something that faith demands we leave to God, who alone knows the human heart, who alone knows what is just in a world of conflicting claims, and who will establish perfect justice at a time, and in a way, of His choosing, not ours.

ל יָבִינוּ לְאַחֲרִיתָם׃ אֵיכָה יִרְדֹּף אֶחָד אֶלֶף
וּשְׁנַיִם יָנִיסוּ רְבָבָה אִם־לֹא כִּי־צוּרָם מְכָרָם
לא וַיהוָה הִסְגִּירָם׃ כִּי לֹא כְצוּרֵנוּ צוּרָם
לב וְאֹיְבֵינוּ פְּלִילִים׃ כִּי־מִגֶּפֶן סְדֹם גַּפְנָם
וּמִשַּׁדְמֹת עֲמֹרָה עֲנָבֵמוֹ עִנְּבֵי־רוֹשׁ
לג אַשְׁכְּלֹת מְרֹרֹת לָמוֹ׃ חֲמַת תַּנִּינִם יֵינָם
לד וְרֹאשׁ פְּתָנִים אַכְזָר׃ הֲלֹא־הוּא כָּמֻס עִמָּדִי
לה חָתוּם בְּאוֹצְרֹתָי׃ לִי נָקָם וְשִׁלֵּם
לְעֵת תָּמוּט רַגְלָם כִּי קָרוֹב יוֹם אֵידָם
לו וְחָשׁ עֲתִדֹת לָמוֹ׃ כִּי־יָדִין יהוה עַמּוֹ
וְעַל־עֲבָדָיו יִתְנֶחָם כִּי יִרְאֶה כִּי־אָזְלַת יָד
לז וְאֶפֶס עָצוּר וְעָזוּב׃ וְאָמַר אֵי אֱלֹהֵימוֹ
לח צוּר חָסָיוּ בוֹ׃ אֲשֶׁר חֵלֶב זְבָחֵימוֹ יֹאכֵלוּ

GOD'S VENGEANCE

God forbids revenge (Lev. 19:18). He commands forgiveness, as Yosef forgave his brothers – and as we, on Judaism's holiest day, ask Him to forgive us. To quote Rambam, "As long as one nurses a grievance and keeps it in mind, one may come to take revenge. The Torah therefore emphatically warns us not to bear a grudge, so that the impression of the wrong shall be wholly obliterated and no longer remembered. This is the right principle. It alone makes society and human interaction possible" (*Hilkhot Deot* 7:8). Note that Rambam means this as a general rule for humanity, not limited to Jews.

Yet this *parasha* contains lines such as "He will avenge His servants' blood," which are difficult to reconcile with an ethic of non-revenge. Three thinkers, Jan Assmann, Henri Atlan, and Miroslav Volf, help us to understand this tension. Assmann points out that in the Hebrew Bible anger is "theologized" and thus "transferred … from earth to heaven." Atlan argues likewise that "the best way to rid the world of the violent sacred is to project it onto a transcendence." The "transcendence of violence" results in "its being expelled from the normal horizon of things." In other words, vengeance is removed from human calculation. It is God, not man, who is entitled to exercise it. Volf agrees, adding that "in a world of violence we are faced with an inescapable alternative: either God's violence or human violence." He adds: "Most people who insist on God's 'nonviolence' cannot resist using violence themselves

ate their sacrificial fat / and drank their wine of
libation? / Let those rise up and help you
39 now, / let them be your protection! / See
now that I, I alone, am He; / there is no god apart from
Me. / I deal death and I bring life; / I
wounded but will heal; / and there is no
40 rescue from My hand. / For I lift My hand skyward and SHISHI
41 swear: / as sure as I live forever, / when I
whet My flashing sword, / and My
hand grasps justice; / I will wreak vengeance on My
42 foes, / and repay those who hate Me. / I will
make My arrows drunk with blood, / while
My sword devours flesh, / the blood of the slain and
the captives, / leaders of the long-haired foe. /
43 O nations, sing out of His people, / for He will
avenge His servants' blood, / take vengeance upon His
foes, / and cleanse His land and His people."

44 Moshe came and proclaimed all the words of this song SHEVI'I
in the hearing of the people, he and Hoshea son of Nun.
45 When Moshe had finished speaking all these words to
46 all Israel, he said to them: "Take to heart all the words I
testify to you today, and charge your children with them,
so that they may take care to keep all the words of this
47 Law. For these are not idle words for you; they are your

---

that sustained us through twenty centuries of exile. We dreamed of inspiring the world by the simplicity and grace of Judaism as a way of life. We dreamed of creating in the Holy Land a society of justice and compassion, where the dignity of the individual and the sanctity of human life would be maintained, where love of God would translate into love of the neighbor and the stranger, and religion itself would be the prime driver of social justice and inclusion. It was a utopian vision, but the mere act of aspiring to it lifted our ancestors to spiritual, intellectual, and moral heights. Bounded in a nutshell, they counted themselves kings of infinite space.

That is the future that beckons us now. Yes, there is antisemitism, and yes, we have enemies. But we survived them all in the past and we will do so again in the future. We need the courage to be

יִשְׁתּוּ יֵין נְסִיכָם   יָקוּמוּ וְיַעְזְרֻכֶם
לט יְהִי עֲלֵיכֶם סִתְרָה: רְאוּ ׀ עַתָּה כִּי אֲנִי אֲנִי הוּא
וְאֵין אֱלֹהִים עִמָּדִי   אֲנִי אָמִית וַאֲחַיֶּה
מָחַצְתִּי וַאֲנִי אֶרְפָּא   וְאֵין מִיָּדִי מַצִּיל:
מ כִּי־אֶשָּׂא אֶל־שָׁמַיִם יָדִי   וְאָמַרְתִּי חַי אָנֹכִי לְעֹלָם: ששי
מא אִם־שַׁנּוֹתִי בְּרַק חַרְבִּי   וְתֹאחֵז בְּמִשְׁפָּט יָדִי
אָשִׁיב נָקָם לְצָרָי   וְלִמְשַׂנְאַי אֲשַׁלֵּם:
מב אַשְׁכִּיר חִצַּי מִדָּם   וְחַרְבִּי תֹּאכַל בָּשָׂר
מִדַּם חָלָל וְשִׁבְיָה   מֵרֹאשׁ פַּרְעוֹת אוֹיֵב:
מג הַרְנִינוּ גוֹיִם עַמּוֹ   כִּי דַם־עֲבָדָיו יִקּוֹם
וְנָקָם יָשִׁיב לְצָרָיו   וְכִפֶּר אַדְמָתוֹ עַמּוֹ:

מד וַיָּבֹא מֹשֶׁה וַיְדַבֵּר אֶת־כָּל־דִּבְרֵי הַשִּׁירָה־הַזֹּאת בְּאָזְנֵי הָעָם שביעי
מה הוּא וְהוֹשֵׁעַ בִּן־נוּן: וַיְכַל מֹשֶׁה לְדַבֵּר אֶת־כָּל־הַדְּבָרִים
מו הָאֵלֶּה אֶל־כָּל־יִשְׂרָאֵל: וַיֹּאמֶר אֲלֵהֶם שִׂימוּ לְבַבְכֶם לְכָל־
הַדְּבָרִים אֲשֶׁר אָנֹכִי מֵעִיד בָּכֶם הַיּוֹם אֲשֶׁר תְּצַוֻּם אֶת־
מז בְּנֵיכֶם לִשְׁמֹר לַעֲשׂוֹת אֶת־כָּל־דִּבְרֵי הַתּוֹרָה הַזֹּאת: כִּי
לֹא־דָבָר רֵק הוּא מִכֶּם כִּי־הוּא חַיֵּיכֶם וּבַדָּבָר הַזֶּה תַּאֲרִיכוּ

32:47 **כִּי־הוּא חַיֵּיכֶם** *They are your very life* – The holiest object in Judaism is a *sefer Torah,* a scroll of the law. Still written today as it was thousands of years ago, by hand with a quill on parchment, it symbolizes some of Judaism's deepest beliefs: that God is to be found in words, that these words are to be found in the Torah, and that they form the basis of the covenant – the bond of love – between God and the Jewish people.

I wonder if any people has ever loved a book as we love the Torah. We stand when it passes as if it were a king. We dance with it as if it were a bride. If it is desecrated or destroyed, we bury it as if it were a relative or friend. We study it endlessly as if in it were hidden all the secrets of our being. Heinrich Heine once called the Torah the "portable homeland" of the Jewish people. When we lacked a land, we found our home in words.

"These words" contain the dream

▶

very life. By this word you may live long in the land that
you are crossing over the Jordan to possess."
48 49 On that very day the LORD spoke to Moshe: "Ascend this MAFTIR
mountain of Avarim, Mount Nevo, in the land of Moav,
facing Yeriḥo, and gaze upon the land of Canaan, which
50 I am giving to the Israelites as a holding. There, on the
mountain that you ascend, you will die and be gathered
to your people, as your brother Aharon died on Mount
51 Hor and was gathered to his people; because both of
you broke faith with Me in the midst of the Israelites at
the waters of Merivat Kadesh in the Wilderness of Tzin,
52 failing to affirm My holiness among the Israelites. You will
see the land from afar, but you shall not enter it – the land
that I am giving to the people of Israel."

The haftara for Parashat Haazinu on page 1624.
On the Shabbat between Rosh Hashana and Yom Kippur, read the haftara for Shabbat Shuva on page 1620.

silence. Why not, then, pass over this too in silence, sparing Moshe's good name? What other religious literature has ever been so candid about the failings of even the greatest of its heroes?

Because that is what it is to be human. Even the greatest human beings make mistakes, fail as often as they succeed, and have moments of black despair. What makes them great is not that they are perfect but that they keep going. They learn from every error, refuse to give up hope, and eventually acquire the great gift that only failure can grant, namely humility. They understand that life is about falling a hundred times and getting up again. It is about never losing your ideals even when you know how hard it is to change the world. It is about getting up every morning and walking one more day toward the Promised Land even though you know you may never get there, but knowing also that you helped others get there.

Rambam writes that every human being can become "as righteous as Moshe or as evil as Yorovam" (*Hilkhot Teshuva* 5:2). That is an astonishing sentence. There only ever was one Moshe. The Torah says so. Yet what Rambam is saying is clear. Prophetically, there was only one Moshe. But morally, the choice lies before us every time we make a decision that will affect the lives of others. That Moshe was mortal, that the greatest leader who ever lived did not see his mission completed, that even he was capable of making a mistake, is the most profound gift God could give each of us.

יָמִים עַל־הָאֲדָמָה אֲשֶׁר אַתֶּם עֹבְרִים אֶת־הַיַּרְדֵּן שָׁמָּה
לְרִשְׁתָּהּ׃
מח מט וַיְדַבֵּר יהוה אֶל־מֹשֶׁה בְּעֶצֶם הַיּוֹם הַזֶּה לֵאמֹר׃ עֲלֵה אֶל־ מפטיר
הַר הָעֲבָרִים הַזֶּה הַר־נְבוֹ אֲשֶׁר בְּאֶרֶץ מוֹאָב אֲשֶׁר עַל־פְּנֵי
יְרֵחוֹ וּרְאֵה אֶת־אֶרֶץ כְּנַעַן אֲשֶׁר אֲנִי נֹתֵן לִבְנֵי יִשְׂרָאֵל
נ לַאֲחֻזָּה׃ וּמֻת בָּהָר אֲשֶׁר אַתָּה עֹלֶה שָׁמָּה וְהֵאָסֵף אֶל־
עַמֶּיךָ כַּאֲשֶׁר־מֵת אַהֲרֹן אָחִיךָ בְּהֹר הָהָר וַיֵּאָסֶף אֶל־עַמָּיו׃
נא עַל אֲשֶׁר מְעַלְתֶּם בִּי בְּתוֹךְ בְּנֵי יִשְׂרָאֵל בְּמֵי־מְרִיבַת קָדֵשׁ
מִדְבַּר־צִן עַל אֲשֶׁר לֹא־קִדַּשְׁתֶּם אוֹתִי בְּתוֹךְ בְּנֵי יִשְׂרָאֵל׃
נב כִּי מִנֶּגֶד תִּרְאֶה אֶת־הָאָרֶץ וְשָׁמָּה לֹא תָבוֹא אֶל־הָאָרֶץ
אֲשֶׁר־אֲנִי נֹתֵן לִבְנֵי יִשְׂרָאֵל׃

The הפטרה *for* פרשת האזינו *on page 1625.*
On the שבת *between* ראש השנה *and* יום כיפור,
read the הפטרה *for* שבת שובה *on page 1621.*

unashamedly ourselves, to educate our children in Judaic literacy, and to create in Israel a society of such moral force and spiritual generosity that it speaks to all those whose minds are open. The time has come to honor the trust our ancestors had in us, that when we had the chance we would light the dark places of the world with the radiance of the faith for which they risked life itself. "For these are not idle words for you; they are your very life."

MOSHE'S FAILING

Humanity at its highest is still human. We are mortal. We are creatures of flesh and blood. We are born, we grow, we learn, we make our way in the world. If we are lucky we find love. If we are blessed, we have children. But we also age. The body grows old even if the spirit stays young. We know that this gift of life does not last forever because in this physical universe, nothing lasts forever, not even planets or stars. We each have a destination we will not reach.

And so Moshe's death on the far side of the Jordan is a consolation for all of us. None of us should feel guilty or frustrated or angry or defeated that there are things we hoped to achieve but did not. That is what it is to be human.

Nor should we be haunted by our mistakes. That, I believe, is why the Torah tells us, and now reminds us, that Moshe sinned. Did it really have to include the episode of the water, the stick, the rock, and Moshe's anger (Num. 20)? It passes over thirty-eight of the forty years in the wilderness in

Parashat Vezot HaBerakha

33 1 This is the blessing with which Moshe, man of God, blessed
2 the Israelites before he died. Moshe said: "The Lord
came from Sinai, He shone upon them from Se'ir, He
appeared over the crest of Paran and came among myriads
3 of holy ones: at His right hand, darting fire. He is a lover
of peoples, all His holy ones are in Your hand; they place
4 themselves at Your feet, upholding Your words. Moshe
5 charged us with the Law, heritage of Yaakov's assembly. He
became king in Yeshurun, when the heads of the people

33:3 אַף חֹבֵב עַמִּים *He is a lover of peoples* – Many commentators understand "peoples" to refer to the tribes of Israel – a natural reading, given that the chapter is about Moshe blessing each of the tribes. Rashbam, however, suggests that it refers to Gentiles who join Israel and become proselytes. Before turning to the tribes, Moshe specifically includes converts – signaling that the children of Israel are not a race or ethnicity but a religious community defined by their covenant with God. Whoever wishes to join and undertake the responsibilities of that covenant may do so. Rashbam is here echoing the sentiment of Rambam's famous letter to Ovadya the Proselyte, written at about the same time, in which he explains that converts are the spiritual children of Avraham, and should not think of themselves as any less so than his biological children.

33:4 תּוֹרָה צִוָּה־לָנוּ מֹשֶׁה מוֹרָשָׁה קְהִלַּת יַעֲקֹב *Moshe charged us with the Law, heritage of Yaakov's assembly* – On the one hand, the Torah describes itself as an inheritance: "Moshe charged us with the Law, heritage (*morasha*) of Yaakov's assembly." On the other, the Sages were insistent that Torah is *not* an inheritance: "R. Yosei said: Prepare yourself to learn Torah, for it is not given to you as an inheritance (*yerusha*)" (Avot 2:12; see also Num. 27, "Moshe's Continuity").

The resolution of the contradiction is that there are two kinds of inheritance. Biblical Hebrew contains two different words for what we receive as a legacy: *yerusha/morasha* and *naḥala*. *Naḥala* is related to the word *naḥal*, "river." It signifies something passed down automatically across the generations, as river water flows downstream. *Yerusha* comes from the root *y-r-sh*, meaning "to *take* possession." It refers to something to which you have legitimate title, but which you need positive action to acquire. The Sages themselves put it more beautifully: "'Moshe charged us with the Law,

פרשת וזאת הברכה

לג א וְזֹאת הַבְּרָכָה אֲשֶׁר בֵּרַךְ מֹשֶׁה אִישׁ הָאֱלֹהִים אֶת־בְּנֵי כז
ב יִשְׂרָאֵל לִפְנֵי מוֹתוֹ: וַיֹּאמַר יהוה מִסִּינַי בָּא וְזָרַח מִשֵּׂעִיר
לָמוֹ הוֹפִיעַ מֵהַר פָּארָן וְאָתָה מֵרִבְבֹת קֹדֶשׁ מִימִינוֹ אשדת אֵשׁ דָּת
ג לָמוֹ: אַף חֹבֵב עַמִּים כָּל־קְדֹשָׁיו בְּיָדֶךָ וְהֵם תֻּכּוּ לְרַגְלֶךָ יִשָּׂא
ד מִדַּבְּרֹתֶיךָ: תּוֹרָה צִוָּה־לָנוּ מֹשֶׁה מוֹרָשָׁה קְהִלַּת יַעֲקֹב:
ה וַיְהִי בִישֻׁרוּן מֶלֶךְ בְּהִתְאַסֵּף רָאשֵׁי עָם יַחַד שִׁבְטֵי יִשְׂרָאֵל:

VEZOT HABERAKHA

The final *parasha* of the Torah consists of Moshe's blessing, delivered in the last day of his life, to the Israelites, tribe by tribe. It concludes poignantly with Moshe's death and his burial, seemingly by the hand of God, in the land of Moav, so that "to this day no one knows his burial place" (Deut. 34:6). The closing verses of the Torah are a tribute to the greatest leader and prophet the Israelites ever had, yet the ultimate accolade the Torah gives him is touching in its simplicity. He was "the man Moshe" (Num. 12:3), "the LORD's own servant" (Deut. 34:5). The Moshe we encounter in the Torah is simply a human being made great by the task he was set and by the humility that made him supremely one through whom the word and power of God flowed. The *parasha*, read not as an ordinary Sabbath portion, but on the festival of Simḥat Torah, is a profound commentary on mortality and the human condition. In one of the most intense convergences in Jewish time, this *parasha* brings together the last day in the life of Israel's greatest leader and the completion of the Torah.

33:1 בֵּרַךְ מֹשֶׁה אִישׁ הָאֱלֹהִים אֶת־בְּנֵי יִשְׂרָאֵל *Moshe, man of God, blessed the Israelites* – The book of Deuteronomy evokes the old Jewish custom that parents write their children *tzavaot*, ethical wills. The custom is based on the idea that the most important legacy we can give our children is not money or possessions, but spiritual ideals. Yaakov blessed his children at the end of his life, and likewise Moshe at the end of his blesses the next generation. Just as he handed on his role to his successor, Yehoshua, with a full heart, so here Moshe blesses them with a full heart, giving each tribe the words that would encourage them to fulfill their destiny. There is a beautiful midrash: "Moshe was not called 'the man of God' until he blessed the Israelites" (Pesikta DeRav Kahana, Vezot Haberakha). You do not need to be godly to criticize. Anyone can do that. Godliness lies with those who praise, defend, and bless.

6 gathered – the tribes of Israel together. May Reuven live,
7 and not die, even though his men are few." And
this he said of Yehuda: "Listen, LORD, to Yehuda's voice,
and bring him home to his people; strengthen his hands,
be his support against his foes."
8 And of Levi he said: "Let Your Tumim and Urim be with SHENI
Your faithful, the one You tested at Masa, and challenged
9 at the Meriva waters; who said of his father and mother,
'I do not regard them,' ignored his brothers, and did not
acknowledge his children – instead keeping Your word,
10 and guarding close Your covenant. They shall teach Your
laws to Yaakov, and Your instruction to Israel; they shall
place incense before You, and whole offerings on Your
11 altar. Bless, O LORD, his vigor, and accept the work of his
hands; crush the loins of his foes; let his enemies rise no
12 more." Of Binyamin he said: "Beloved of the LORD,
may he dwell in safety with Him – He protects him all day

---

of the LORD by doing what is right and just" (Gen. 18:19). Moshe has already told the people, as parents: "Teach them to your children" (Deut. 6:7). The Levites are now charged with being the first in a tradition of public teachers.

The Rabbis were therefore drawing on a long tradition when they organized perhaps the first genuinely universal system of education in history. Its evolution in the late Second Temple period is described in the Talmud: "At first, if a child had a father, his father taught him; if he had not a father, he did not learn at all.... Then they introduced an ordinance that teachers of children be appointed in Jerusalem.... Even so, if a child had a father, the father would take him to Jerusalem and have him learn there; but if he had no father, he would not go up there to learn. They therefore ordained that teachers be appointed in each district and that boys enter school at the age of sixteen or seventeen. But because a boy who was punished by his teacher would rebel and leave school, Yehoshua b. Gamla introduced a regulation that teachers of young children be appointed in each district and town, and that children begin their schooling at the age of six or seven" (Bava Batra 21a). This structure was in place by the time of the destruction of the Temple. A rabbinic dictum of the third century states that a town which lacks a school is to be excommunicated, on the grounds that "the world only exists in virtue of the breath of children at school" (Shabbat 119b). Here, Moshe "our teacher" accords to the Levites the blessing, and honor, of teaching others.

ו ז יְחִי רְאוּבֵן וְאַל־יָמֹת וִיהִי מְתָיו מִסְפָּר: וְזֹאת
לִיהוּדָה וַיֹּאמַר שְׁמַע יהוה קוֹל יְהוּדָה וְאֶל־עַמּוֹ תְּבִיאֶנּוּ
יָדָיו רָב לוֹ וְעֵזֶר מִצָּרָיו תִּהְיֶה:
ח וּלְלֵוִי אָמַר תֻּמֶּיךָ וְאוּרֶיךָ לְאִישׁ חֲסִידֶךָ אֲשֶׁר נִסִּיתוֹ שני
ט בְּמַסָּה תְּרִיבֵהוּ עַל־מֵי מְרִיבָה: הָאֹמֵר לְאָבִיו וּלְאִמּוֹ לֹא
רְאִיתִיו וְאֶת־אֶחָיו לֹא הִכִּיר וְאֶת־בָּנָו לֹא יָדָע כִּי שָׁמְרוּ
י אִמְרָתֶךָ וּבְרִיתְךָ יִנְצֹרוּ: יוֹרוּ מִשְׁפָּטֶיךָ לְיַעֲקֹב וְתוֹרָתְךָ
לְיִשְׂרָאֵל יָשִׂימוּ קְטוֹרָה בְּאַפֶּךָ וְכָלִיל עַל־מִזְבְּחֶךָ:
יא בָּרֵךְ יהוה חֵילוֹ וּפֹעַל יָדָיו תִּרְצֶה מְחַץ מָתְנַיִם קָמָיו
יב וּמְשַׂנְאָיו מִן־יְקוּמוּן: לְבִנְיָמִן אָמַר יְדִיד
יהוה יִשְׁכֹּן לָבֶטַח עָלָיו חֹפֵף עָלָיו כָּל־הַיּוֹם וּבֵין כְּתֵפָיו

heritage (*morasha*) of Yaakov's assembly' – read not 'inheritance (*morasha*)' but 'betrothed (*meorasa*)'" (Berakhot 57a). By a simple change in pronunciation – turning a *shin* ("sh") into a *sin* ("s"), "inheritance" into "betrothal" – the Rabbis signaled that, yes, there is an inheritance relationship between Torah and the Jew, but nonetheless, the former has to be loved if it is to be earned.

33:6 יְחִי רְאוּבֵן וְאַל־יָמֹת *May Reuven live, and not die* – The tribe of Reuven has chosen to live east of the Jordan, and will thus be highly exposed to enemy attacks – hence, the need for this blessing. Note the absence of Shimon from these blessings. Yaakov, in his deathbed speech, already predicted that the tribes of Shimon and Levi would be scattered among the other tribes (Gen. 49:7). According to Joshua 19:1–9, Shimon's townships all lay within the territory of Yehuda. Thus their blessing is included in that of the tribe of Yehuda.

33:10 יוֹרוּ מִשְׁפָּטֶיךָ לְיַעֲקֹב *They shall teach Your laws to Yaakov* – The priests and Levites had a special role as educators to the people (see Neh. 8:7–8). The prophet Malakhi says of the ideal priest: "True teaching was in his mouth, no sin from his lips; he walked with Me in peace and uprightness and returned many from iniquity. For a priest's lips should safeguard knowledge, and the people should seek teaching from his mouth, for he is a messenger of the Lord of Hosts" (Mal. 2:6–7).

The Jewish concern with education has its roots in the ancient history of Israel. In the book of Genesis, for example, the sole explanation for the covenant with Avraham is: "For I have chosen him so that he may direct his children and his household after him to keep the way

13 long as he rests between His shoulders." And of SHELISHI
Yosef he said: "Blessed by the LORD be his land, with the
bounty of heaven, with dew, and the deep waters that lie
14 below; with the bounty brought forth by the sun, and the
15 bounteous yield of the moon; with the best from the age-
old mountains, and the bounty of the everlasting hills;
16 with the bounty of earth and its fullness, and the will of
Him who dwelt in the bush. May these rest on Yosef's
17 head, on the brow of the prince among brothers. His
glory is that of a firstborn bull, his horns the grand horns
of the wild ox; with them he gores the peoples, all, to the
ends of the earth. These are the myriads of Efrayim, these
18 the thousands of Menashe." And of Zevulun he REVI'I
said: "Rejoice, Zevulun, as you set out; and Yissakhar,
19 in your tents. They summon peoples to the mountain;
there they offer righteous sacrifice; they will feast on
the plenty of oceans and the hidden, buried riches of
20 the sands." And of Gad he said: "Blessed be He ḤAMISHI
who enlarges Gad! He lives like a lion, he tears at arm
21 and scalp. He chose the first portion for himself, for there
the lawgiver's portion is reserved, where the heads of the
people come. He executed the LORD's justice, and His
22 ordinances for Israel." And of Dan he said: "Dan
23 is a lion's whelp springing forth from Bashan." And of
Naftali he said: "Naftali, sated with favor, filled with the
24 LORD's blessing, west and south possess." And
of Asher he said: "Most blessed of sons is Asher; may
25 he win his brothers' favor, and bathe his feet in oil. Your
bars are iron and bronze; may your strength be equal to

---

are a priest, more so if you are the High Priest – the less you can be in contact with or under the same roof as a dead person. God is not in death but in life.

We believe that the greatest mistake is to worship human beings as if they were gods. We admire human beings; we do not worship them. Moshe's hidden tomb is an honor to Gad, but not a pilgrimage site. "We do not make monuments for the dead; their words are their memorial" (Yerushalmi, Shekalim 2:5).

יג שָׁכֵן׃ וּלְיוֹסֵף אָמַר מְבֹרֶכֶת יְהֹוָה אַרְצוֹ שלישי
יד מִמֶּגֶד שָׁמַיִם מִטָּל וּמִתְּהוֹם רֹבֶצֶת תָּחַת׃ וּמִמֶּגֶד תְּבוּאֹת
טו שָׁמֶשׁ וּמִמֶּגֶד גֶּרֶשׁ יְרָחִים׃ וּמֵרֹאשׁ הַרְרֵי־קֶדֶם וּמִמֶּגֶד
טז גִּבְעוֹת עוֹלָם׃ וּמִמֶּגֶד אֶרֶץ וּמְלֹאָהּ וּרְצוֹן שֹׁכְנִי סְנֶה
יז תָּבוֹאתָה לְרֹאשׁ יוֹסֵף וּלְקָדְקֹד נְזִיר אֶחָיו׃ בְּכוֹר שׁוֹרוֹ
הָדָר לוֹ וְקַרְנֵי רְאֵם קַרְנָיו בָּהֶם עַמִּים יְנַגַּח יַחְדָּו אַפְסֵי־אָרֶץ
יח וְהֵם רִבְבוֹת אֶפְרַיִם וְהֵם אַלְפֵי מְנַשֶּׁה׃ וְלִזְבוּלֻן רביעי
יט אָמַר שְׂמַח זְבוּלֻן בְּצֵאתֶךָ וְיִשָּׂשכָר בְּאֹהָלֶיךָ׃ עַמִּים הַר־
יִקְרָאוּ שָׁם יִזְבְּחוּ זִבְחֵי־צֶדֶק כִּי שֶׁפַע יַמִּים יִינָקוּ וּשְׂפֻנֵי
כ טְמוּנֵי חוֹל׃ וּלְגָד אָמַר בָּרוּךְ מַרְחִיב גָּד כְּלָבִיא
כא שָׁכֵן וְטָרַף זְרוֹעַ אַף־קָדְקֹד׃ וַיַּרְא רֵאשִׁית לוֹ כִּי־שָׁם חֶלְקַת
מְחֹקֵק סָפוּן וַיֵּתֵא רָאשֵׁי עָם צִדְקַת יְהֹוָה עָשָׂה וּמִשְׁפָּטָיו
כב עִם־יִשְׂרָאֵל׃ וּלְדָן אָמַר דָּן גּוּר אַרְיֵה יְזַנֵּק מִן־ חמישי
כג הַבָּשָׁן׃ וּלְנַפְתָּלִי אָמַר נַפְתָּלִי שְׂבַע רָצוֹן וּמָלֵא בִּרְכַּת יְהֹוָה
כד יָם וְדָרוֹם יְרָשָׁה׃ וּלְאָשֵׁר אָמַר בָּרוּךְ מִבָּנִים
כה אָשֵׁר יְהִי רְצוּי אֶחָיו וְטֹבֵל בַּשֶּׁמֶן רַגְלוֹ׃ בַּרְזֶל וּנְחֹשֶׁת

33:21 חֶלְקַת מְחֹקֵק סָפוּן *The lawgiver's portion is reserved* – This "reserved (literally, 'hidden') portion" may refer to Moshe's gravesite in the territory of Gad. The Torah insists (Deut. 34:6) that no one knows exactly where Moshe is buried. His tomb must never become a place of pilgrimage and worship. What a contrast between Moshe and the heroes of other civilizations, whose burial places become monuments, shrines, places of pilgrimage.

An obsession with death ultimately devalues life. Fear of our own mortality led the ancient world to enslave the masses, turning them into giant labor forces to build monumental buildings that would stand as long as time itself. Why fight against the evils and injustices of the world if this life is only a preparation for the World to Come?

That is why in place of a pyramid or a temple such as Ramesses II built at Abu Simbel, all the Israelites had for almost five centuries until the days of Solomon was the *Mishkan*, a portable sanctuary, more like a tent than a temple. That is why, in Judaism, death defiles and why the rite of the red heifer was necessary to purify people from contact with it. That is why the holier you are – if you

26 your days. There is none like the God of Yeshurun, riding
27 the skies to help you, the heavens, in His grandeur. Your
refuge the God of time immemorial, you rest in eternal
arms. Dispelling every enemy before you, He spoke:
28 'Destroy!' So Israel dwells in safety; Yaakov takes refuge
alone in a land of grain and wine, where the skies drop
29 their dew. Happy are you, Israel. Who is like you, a
people rescued by the LORD? He is your shield of help,
your sword of triumph. Your enemies will cower before
34 1 you, and you shall tread their high places." Then
Moshe went up from the plains of Moav to Mount Nevo,
to the summit of Pisga, facing Yeriḥo. The LORD showed
2 him all the land: from Gilad to Dan, all of Naftali, the land
of Efrayim and Menashe, all the land of Yehuda as far as
3 the Westward Sea, the Negev, and the plain – the Valley of
4 Yeriḥo, city of palm trees – as far as Tzoar. The LORD said
to him, "This is the land I promised Avraham, Yitzḥak,
and Yaakov, saying, 'I will give this to your descendants';
I have let you see it with your eyes, but to that place you
5 will not cross over." Then Moshe, the LORD's own servant,

ḤATAN HATORAH

who loves us: "a people rescued by the LORD."

34:4 לֹא תַעֲבֹר *You will not cross over* – Franz Kafka gave voice to a compelling truth. Moshe

> is on the track of Canaan all his life; it is incredible that he should see the land only when on the verge of death. This dying vision of it can only be intended to illustrate how incomplete a moment is human life; incomplete because a life like this could last forever and still be nothing but a moment. Moses fails to enter Canaan not because his life was too short but because it is a human life. (Franz Kafka, *Diaries 1914–1923*)

Moshe at the end of his life becomes a symbol both of the possibilities of a human life and of its limits. "It is not for you to complete the task," said R. Tarfon, "but neither are you free to stand aside from it" (Avot 2:21). If we lived forever, life itself would have no shape, no edge, no urgency, no compelling purpose. We would not act. For anything we wished to do, there would always be time in the future. If we lived forever, we would not know love, for the very power of love is tied to the knowledge that its moment is all too brief and that soon it too will

כו מִנְעָלֶךָ וּכְיָמֶיךָ דָּבְאֶךָ׃ אֵין כָּאֵל יְשֻׁרוּן רֹכֵב שָׁמַיִם בְּעֶזְרֶךָ
כז וּבְגַאֲוָתוֹ שְׁחָקִים׃ מְעֹנָה אֱלֹהֵי קֶדֶם וּמִתַּחַת זְרֹעֹת עוֹלָם חתן התורה
כח וַיְגָרֶשׁ מִפָּנֶיךָ אוֹיֵב וַיֹּאמֶר הַשְׁמֵד׃ וַיִּשְׁכֹּן יִשְׂרָאֵל בֶּטַח
בָּדָד עֵין יַעֲקֹב אֶל־אֶרֶץ דָּגָן וְתִירוֹשׁ אַף־שָׁמָיו יַעַרְפוּ־
כט טָל׃ אַשְׁרֶיךָ יִשְׂרָאֵל מִי כָמוֹךָ עַם נוֹשַׁע בַּיהוה מָגֵן עֶזְרֶךָ
וַאֲשֶׁר־חֶרֶב גַּאֲוָתֶךָ וְיִכָּחֲשׁוּ אֹיְבֶיךָ לָךְ וְאַתָּה עַל־בָּמוֹתֵימוֹ
לד א תִדְרֹךְ׃ וַיַּעַל מֹשֶׁה מֵעַרְבֹת מוֹאָב אֶל־הַר
נְבוֹ רֹאשׁ הַפִּסְגָּה אֲשֶׁר עַל־פְּנֵי יְרֵחוֹ וַיַּרְאֵהוּ יהוה אֶת־
ב כָּל־הָאָרֶץ אֶת־הַגִּלְעָד עַד־דָּן׃ וְאֵת כָּל־נַפְתָּלִי וְאֶת־אֶרֶץ
אֶפְרַיִם וּמְנַשֶּׁה וְאֵת כָּל־אֶרֶץ יְהוּדָה עַד הַיָּם הָאַחֲרוֹן׃
ג וְאֶת־הַנֶּגֶב וְאֶת־הַכִּכָּר בִּקְעַת יְרֵחוֹ עִיר הַתְּמָרִים עַד־צֹעַר׃
ד וַיֹּאמֶר יהוה אֵלָיו זֹאת הָאָרֶץ אֲשֶׁר נִשְׁבַּעְתִּי לְאַבְרָהָם
לְיִצְחָק וּלְיַעֲקֹב לֵאמֹר לְזַרְעֲךָ אֶתְּנֶנָּה הֶרְאִיתִיךָ בְעֵינֶיךָ
ה וְשָׁמָּה לֹא תַעֲבֹר׃ וַיָּמָת שָׁם מֹשֶׁה עֶבֶד־יהוה בְּאֶרֶץ מוֹאָב

33:29 מִי כָמוֹךָ עַם נוֹשַׁע בַּיהוה *Who is like you, a people rescued by the LORD* – This verse contains Moshe's last words to the people he has led from slavery to freedom, through the wilderness, to the brink of the Promised Land. His message is moving and clear: If the people stay faithful to God, they will be safe from their enemies, and need have no fear. The real challenge will not be military but spiritual.

I find it moving that in all the centuries when they were considered pariahs by others, Jews were spared from the worst excesses of self-hatred. On the festivals they remembered the past and hoped for the future. On the Sabbath, however poor they were, they sat at the Sabbath table like free men and women, and sang. Though they could be racked by poverty, still they built houses of study and sat learning Talmud and cultivated the life of the mind. And though they were poor they knew there were others poorer than themselves, and they gave them aid, and invited them to their festive meals, and considered themselves bound by a covenant of mutual responsibility.

We are not defined by those who do not like us. This is how we have come through the Holocaust and still believe in life, lived through what Israel has lived through and still strive for peace, experienced the degree of hate poured out against us by some of Europe's greatest minds and remain undefiled. We still hear, every year, Moshe's loving words to us, his children: "Who is like you?" To be a Jew is to be defined by the One

6 died there in the land of Moav, at the Lord's word. He
buried him in Moav, in a valley opposite Beit Peor, and
7 to this day no one knows his burial place. Moshe was a
hundred and twenty years old when he died; his eyes had
8 not grown dim, nor his vitality fled. The Israelites wept for
Moshe in the plains of Moav for thirty days, until the time
9 of weeping and mourning for him was over. Yehoshua son
of Nun was filled with the spirit of wisdom, for Moshe
had laid his hands upon him, and the Israelites listened
to him, and did as the Lord had commanded Moshe.

---

that the first was an explanation of the second. Why had his vitality not fled? Because his eyes had not grown dim. He never lost the vision and high ideals of his youth. Despite the many setbacks he experienced, he did not allow himself to become disillusioned, or to give way to despair. He did not become embittered or sad, though he had sufficient reason to be. His undimmed faith in the God he served, the people he led, and the mission to which he dedicated his life was his energy source. His commitment to justice, compassion, liberty, and responsibility was unyielding. He was as passionate at the end as he was at the beginning. He knew there were things he would not live to achieve, so he taught the next generation how to achieve them. He was never afraid to learn something new. The result was that his vitality did not flee. His body was old, but his mind and soul stayed young.

Without passion you cannot be a transformative leader. Unless you yourself are inspired you cannot inspire others. Moshe never lost the vision of his first encounter with God at the bush that burned but was not consumed. That is how I see Moshe: as the man who burned but was not consumed. So long as that vision stayed with him, as it did until the end of his life, he remained full of energy. You feel that in the sustained power of the book of Deuteronomy, the greatest sequence of speeches in Tanakh. If you want to stay young, never give up on your ideals.

34:8 וַיִּבְכּוּ בְנֵי יִשְׂרָאֵל אֶת־מֹשֶׁה בְּעַרְבֹת מוֹאָב שְׁלֹשִׁים יוֹם *The Israelites wept for Moshe in the plains of Moav for thirty days* – Rashi notes that the mourning for Aharon was more widespread than for Moshe. Of Aharon it says, "The whole House of Israel wept" (Num. 20:29); in the case of Moshe the word "whole" is missing. Perhaps the reason is that Aharon was a man of peace; Moshe was a man of truth. People of truth have enemies as well as friends. Moshe was aflame with a passion for justice, and, unlike Aharon his brother, preferred principle to compromise. Even Moshe, the greatest of men, needed the peace-making skills of Aharon to maintain the balance of his leadership.

ו עַל־פִּי יהוה: וַיִּקְבֹּר אֹתוֹ בַגַּי בְּאֶרֶץ מוֹאָב מוּל בֵּית פְּעוֹר
ז וְלֹא־יָדַע אִישׁ אֶת־קְבֻרָתוֹ עַד הַיּוֹם הַזֶּה: וּמֹשֶׁה בֶּן־מֵאָה
ח וְעֶשְׂרִים שָׁנָה בְּמֹתוֹ לֹא־כָהֲתָה עֵינוֹ וְלֹא־נָס לֵחֹה: וַיִּבְכּוּ
בְנֵי יִשְׂרָאֵל אֶת־מֹשֶׁה בְּעַרְבֹת מוֹאָב שְׁלֹשִׁים יוֹם וַיִּתְּמוּ יְמֵי
ט בְכִי אֵבֶל מֹשֶׁה: וִיהוֹשֻׁעַ בִּן־נוּן מָלֵא רוּחַ חָכְמָה כִּי־סָמַךְ
מֹשֶׁה אֶת־יָדָיו עָלָיו וַיִּשְׁמְעוּ אֵלָיו בְּנֵי־יִשְׂרָאֵל וַיַּעֲשׂוּ כַּאֲשֶׁר

perish. Love lives in its vulnerability. It is our deepest longing for timelessness in the midst of time.

If we lived forever, we would not create – for the deepest source of the creative urge is the desire to make something that will live on after us, that will have the immortality we lack. Therefore we choose and plan and act. We become creators of the most consequential work of art we will ever execute – our life itself. We are the co-author and central character of our story – and because it is finite, life is capable of having a storylike structure. A novel that never ends is not a story. The ending itself – happy, tragic, serene, unfulfilled – gives the whole its color and tone.

We are mortal. But we have immortal longings. We live on because the story of which we are a part is itself immortal. The world did not begin with us, nor will it end with our departure. We belong to a larger narrative. From Moshe we learn: We are mortal; therefore make every day count. We are fallible; therefore learn to grow from each mistake. We will not complete the journey; therefore inspire others to continue what we began.

34:6 וַיִּקְבֹּר אֹתוֹ בַגַּי בְּאֶרֶץ מוֹאָב *He buried him in Moav* – The Torah ends as it began, with an act of loving-kindness on the part of God (Sota 14a). Just as at the beginning, He had breathed the breath of life into the first man, so now at the close of the Mosaic books He buries the greatest of men as the breath of life departs from him.

34:7 לֹא־כָהֲתָה עֵינוֹ וְלֹא־נָס לֵחֹה *His eyes had not grown dim, nor his vitality fled* – Moshe did not fade. Somehow, he defied the law of entropy that states that all systems lose energy over time. The law also applies to people, especially leaders. The kind of leadership Moshe undertook, getting people to change, persuading them to cease to think and feel like slaves and instead embrace the responsibilities of freedom – is stressful and exhausting. There were times when Moshe came close to burnout and despair. What then was the secret of the undiminished energy of his last years?

The Torah suggests the answer in the very words in which it describes the phenomenon. I used to think that "his eyes had not grown dim" and "his vitality [had not] fled" were simply two descriptions, until it dawned on me

10 There has never arisen a prophet in Israel like Moshe,
11 whom the Lord knew face-to-face, in all the signs and
wonders the Lord sent him to perform in Egypt, against
12 Pharaoh, all his officials, and all of his land, and in all the
acts of a mighty hand and of terrifying power that Moshe
performed before the eyes of all Israel.

The haftara for Parashat Vezot Haberakha is on page 1634.

past, but by looking forward to a time not yet reached. Ketuvim (the Writings), the third and final section, ends with King Koresh of Persia granting permission to the Jewish exiles in Babylon to return to their land and rebuild the Temple.

None of these is an ending in the conventional sense. Each leaves us with a sense of a promise not yet fulfilled, a task not yet completed, a future seen from afar but not yet reached. For each of us, likewise, there is a river we will not cross, a promised land we will not enter. Even the greatest life is an unfinished symphony.

Wallace Stevens, in his poem "Thirteen Ways of Looking at a Blackbird," wrote:

I do not know which to prefer,
The beauty of inflections
Or the beauty of innuendos,
The blackbird whistling
Or just after.

After the inflections, the innuendos remain, the hints, the intimations, Eliyahu's "faint sound of silence" (I Kings 19:12), Wordsworth's "sense of something far more deeply interfused." When all the data are in, the great questions still remain. Even when we close the book, the story continues.

Torah is God's book of humanity, and each of us is a chapter in its unfinished story. Every age has added its commentaries, and so must ours. Moshe is buried, but we wind the scroll back to Genesis and begin again. The words form our covenant with Heaven. And as we listen and respond, we add our voice to the unbroken conversation between the Jewish people and its destiny.

י צִוָּה יְהוָה אֶת־מֹשֶׁה: וְלֹא־קָם נָבִיא עוֹד בְּיִשְׂרָאֵל כְּמֹשֶׁה
יא אֲשֶׁר יְדָעוֹ יְהוָה פָּנִים אֶל־פָּנִים: לְכָל־הָאֹתֹת וְהַמּוֹפְתִים
אֲשֶׁר שְׁלָחוֹ יְהוָה לַעֲשׂוֹת בְּאֶרֶץ מִצְרָיִם לְפַרְעֹה וּלְכָל־
יב עֲבָדָיו וּלְכָל־אַרְצוֹ: וּלְכֹל הַיָּד הַחֲזָקָה וּלְכֹל הַמּוֹרָא הַגָּדוֹל
אֲשֶׁר עָשָׂה מֹשֶׁה לְעֵינֵי כָּל־יִשְׂרָאֵל:

The הפטרה *for* פרשת וזאת הברכה *is on page 1635.*

34:10 וְלֹא־קָם נָבִיא עוֹד בְּיִשְׂרָאֵל כְּמֹשֶׁה *There has never arisen a prophet in Israel like Moshe* – Moshe's greatness was his humility (Num. 12:3). It was his absence of self that allowed God's spirit to work through him, and his inability to speak (Ex. 4:10) that enabled God to place His words in his mouth. In a manuscript discovered after his death in 1778, Jean-Jacques Rousseau wrote:

> The Jews provide us with an astonishing spectacle: the laws of Numa, Lycurgus, Solon are dead; the very much older laws of Moses are still alive. Athens, Sparta, Rome have perished and no longer have children left on earth; Zion, destroyed, has not lost its children.

There never was another Moshe. There were other prophets but no other lawgiver, no other voice-of-God-for-eternity.

THE END OF THE TORAH

The Jewish story began with a repeated promise to Avraham that he would inherit the land of Canaan. Yet by the time we reach the end of the Torah, the Israelites have still not crossed the Jordan. Nevi'im (the Prophets), the second part of Tanakh, ends with Malakhi foreseeing the distant future, understood by tradition to mean the Messianic age:

> Behold, I will send you Eliya the prophet before the great and terrible day of the Lord. And he will return the hearts of parents back to their children, and the hearts of children back to their parents. (Mal. 3:23–24)

Nevi'im, which includes the great historical as well as prophetic books, thus concludes neither in the present nor the

הפטרות
HAFTAROT

Haftarat Bereshit

On Erev Rosh Ḥodesh Marḥeshvan, read the haftara on page 1644.

42 1 My servant, I uphold him, the one I chose, I wanted. I have ISAIAH *Yemenites begin here*
2 placed My spirit over him to draw justice out to nations; he will
not shout nor raise his voice; in the street he will not be heard;
3 not one crushed reed will break beneath him, no dimming wick
4 be quelled; he will open out judgment to truth, never himself
dimmed or crushed until he has brought the world justice, and all
5 the distant coastlands quake before his teaching. *So *Ashkenazim and Sepharadim begin here*
says God, the Lord, who created the skies, who stretched them
across and set down the land and all her children, and gave hu-
6 manity upon her breath, and spirit to those who walk her. I, the
Lord, call you forth in victory, and I will hold your hand; I shall
form you and make you a covenant people, make you a light unto
7 nations, to open blinded eyes, to bring prisoners out of captivity,
8 and those who dwell in darkness from their jail. I am the Lord;
this is My name, and I share not My glory with others, My praise
9 with idols. What I said at the beginning: see, it has come, and
I tell you now what will be afresh before it pushes through the
10 earth; you will hear it first from Me. Sing out to the
Lord a new song, His praise from the ends of the earth, You
who go to sea, and all that fill it, distant coastlands and you who
11 live there. Desert and its towns, raise your voices, Kedarites in
their scattered camps; those who dwell in the rocks must sing
12 out joy from the mountaintops, shout and give the Lord His
13 glory; His praise will be spoken in the distant coastlands. The
Lord sets out like a hero, rousing His passion like a man of
war; He gives the war cry, bellows the war cry, overthrows His
14 enemies. Always I held still and was silent, held back;
I will bellow out like one giving birth, breathing out, breathing
15 in all together, will vanquish hills and mountains and will dry up
all the green; I shall turn the rivers into coastlands and desiccate
16 the lakes, and lead the blind along a way they know not, on paths

---

theme common to these three contrasts is the emphasis on what is true and enduring as opposed to what is worthless and passing. This insight – that what endures will triumph over what is transient – is the basis for the path the prophet traces from the creation of the world to his vision of the end of days.

הפטרת בראשית

On ערב ראש חודש מרחשוון *some read the* הפטרה *on page 1645.*

ישעיה

Yemenites begin here

מב א הֵן עַבְדִּי אֶתְמָךְ־בּוֹ בְּחִירִי רָצְתָה נַפְשִׁי נָתַתִּי רוּחִי עָלָיו
ב מִשְׁפָּט לַגּוֹיִם יוֹצִיא: לֹא יִצְעַק וְלֹא יִשָּׂא וְלֹא־יַשְׁמִיעַ
ג בַּחוּץ קוֹלוֹ: קָנֶה רָצוּץ לֹא יִשְׁבּוֹר וּפִשְׁתָּה כֵהָה לֹא יְכַבֶּנָּה
ד לֶאֱמֶת יוֹצִיא מִשְׁפָּט: לֹא יִכְהֶה וְלֹא יָרוּץ עַד־יָשִׂים בָּאָרֶץ
ה מִשְׁפָּט וּלְתוֹרָתוֹ אִיִּים יְיַחֵלוּ: ★ כֹּה־אָמַר הָאֵל ׀

Ashkenazim and Sephardim begin here

יהוה בּוֹרֵא הַשָּׁמַיִם וְנוֹטֵיהֶם רֹקַע הָאָרֶץ וְצֶאֱצָאֶיהָ נֹתֵן
ו נְשָׁמָה לָעָם עָלֶיהָ וְרוּחַ לַהֹלְכִים בָּהּ: אֲנִי יהוה קְרָאתִיךָ
בְצֶדֶק וְאַחְזֵק בְּיָדֶךָ וְאֶצׇּרְךָ וְאֶתֶּנְךָ לִבְרִית עָם לְאוֹר גּוֹיִם:
ז לִפְקֹחַ עֵינַיִם עִוְרוֹת לְהוֹצִיא מִמַּסְגֵּר אַסִּיר מִבֵּית כֶּלֶא
ח יֹשְׁבֵי חֹשֶׁךְ: אֲנִי יהוה הוּא שְׁמִי וּכְבוֹדִי לְאַחֵר לֹא־אֶתֵּן
ט וּתְהִלָּתִי לַפְּסִילִים: הָרִאשֹׁנוֹת הִנֵּה־בָאוּ וַחֲדָשׁוֹת אֲנִי מַגִּיד
י בְּטֶרֶם תִּצְמַחְנָה אַשְׁמִיעַ אֶתְכֶם: שִׁירוּ לַיהוה
שִׁיר חָדָשׁ תְּהִלָּתוֹ מִקְצֵה הָאָרֶץ יוֹרְדֵי הַיָּם וּמְלֹאוֹ אִיִּים
יא וְיֹשְׁבֵיהֶם: יִשְׂאוּ מִדְבָּר וְעָרָיו חֲצֵרִים תֵּשֵׁב קֵדָר יָרֹנּוּ יֹשְׁבֵי
יב סֶלַע מֵרֹאשׁ הָרִים יִצְוָחוּ: יָשִׂימוּ לַיהוה כָּבוֹד וּתְהִלָּתוֹ
יג בָּאִיִּים יַגִּידוּ: יהוה כַּגִּבּוֹר יֵצֵא כְּאִישׁ מִלְחָמוֹת יָעִיר קִנְאָה
יד יָרִיעַ אַף־יַצְרִיחַ עַל־אֹיְבָיו יִתְגַּבָּר: הֶחֱשֵׁיתִי
מֵעוֹלָם אַחֲרִישׁ אֶתְאַפָּק כַּיּוֹלֵדָה אֶפְעֶה אֶשֹּׁם וְאֶשְׁאַף יָחַד:
טו אַחֲרִיב הָרִים וּגְבָעוֹת וְכׇל־עֶשְׂבָּם אוֹבִישׁ וְשַׂמְתִּי נְהָרוֹת
טז לָאִיִּים וַאֲגַמִּים אוֹבִישׁ: וְהוֹלַכְתִּי עִוְרִים בְּדֶרֶךְ לֹא יָדָעוּ

BERESHIT

During his life, the prophet Yeshayahu had to confront idolatrous worldviews that threatened faith in God, and fight for the place of the nation of Israel in the world. In this prophecy, he contrasts three opposed pairs: (1) God, the creator and ruler of the universe, versus the worthless idols of the nations; (2) Israel, God's eternal people, versus the wicked nations who will be punished; and (3) redemption and a perfected world versus the situation of sin and evil that he saw would bring ruin upon Israel. The

unknown shall guide them; I shall turn darkness to light before
them, the treacherous road to open highway; these things I will
17 perform, and will not fail.* Those who trust in idols will step
back ashamed, those who say to molded statuary, "You – you are
18 our gods." All you deaf ones – listen, and you who are
19 blind – now see. Who is blind if not My servant, who deaf like
the messenger I send? Who could be blind like him – who is de-
20 voted, blind like this, the LORD's servant? Many things seen, but
21 you remember not, with open ears, hear nothing. Yet the LORD
has desired them, that His righteousness be known, to raise aloft
22 His teachings, to confer majesty.** He is with this plundered, this
torn-apart people, who are trapped away in pits, hidden in prison,
plunder with none to save them, given over to looters with none
23 to cry, "Give back!" Who among you will listen to this, will hear
24 it and heed for the future? Who was it who gave Yaakov up for
looting, Israel for plunder – was it not the LORD? Him against
whom we sinned; whose ways they cared not to follow, whose
25 Law they did not heed. He poured out the fire of His rage against
them, His terrible warfare, and flames raged all around them,
yet they did not know; they burned but still they took it not
43 1 to heart. And now, Yaakov, so says the LORD, your
Creator, the One who formed you, Israel: Do not fear: I redeem
2 you; I name you: you are Mine. Though you pass through waters – I am with you; through rivers – they will not wash you
away. Though you walk right through the fire, you will not be
3 burned, and no flame will take hold of you, for I am the LORD
your God, the Holy One of Israel, your rescuer. I have paid Egypt
4 as your ransom, Kush and Seva in your place. Because you are
valued in My eyes, you are honored. I love you enough to give up
5 other men for you, whole nations in your place. Do not fear, for I
am with you. I will bring your children from the east, will gather
6 you back from the west. To the north I will say, "Give over"; to
the south, "Imprison no more." Bring My sons from far away, My
7 daughters back from the ends of the earth, all the people I called
by My name, created for My glory; I formed them, I made them.
8 He brought out a people – blind though they have eyes, deaf
9 though they have ears. Were all the nations to gather, the peoples
to come into session, who of them could tell of this? Who could
speak of this before? Let them bring their witnesses to vindicate
10 them, so that hearers may say, "This is truth." No – you are My

Yemenites end here

Sepharadim and Chabad end here

בִּנְתִיבוֹת לֹא־יָדְעוּ אַדְרִיכֵם אָשִׂים מַחְשָׁךְ לִפְנֵיהֶם לָאוֹר
וּמַעֲקַשִּׁים לְמִישׁוֹר אֵלֶּה הַדְּבָרִים עֲשִׂיתִם וְלֹא עֲזַבְתִּים:* *Yemenites end here*
יז נָסֹגוּ אָחוֹר יֵבֹשׁוּ בֹשֶׁת הַבֹּטְחִים בַּפָּסֶל הָאֹמְרִים לְמַסֵּכָה
יח אַתֶּם אֱלֹהֵינוּ: הַחֵרְשִׁים שְׁמָעוּ וְהַעִוְרִים הַבִּיטוּ
יט לִרְאוֹת: מִי עִוֵּר כִּי אִם־עַבְדִּי וְחֵרֵשׁ כְּמַלְאָכִי אֶשְׁלָח מִי
כ עִוֵּר כִּמְשֻׁלָּם וְעִוֵּר כְּעֶבֶד יהוה: רָאִית רַבּוֹת וְלֹא תִשְׁמֹר רָאוֹת
כא פָּקוֹחַ אָזְנַיִם וְלֹא יִשְׁמָע: יהוה חָפֵץ לְמַעַן צִדְקוֹ יַגְדִּיל
כב תּוֹרָה וְיַאְדִּיר:* וְהוּא עַם־בָּזוּז וְשָׁסוּי הָפֵחַ בַּחוּרִים כֻּלָּם *Sepharadim and Chabad end here*
וּבְבָתֵּי כְלָאִים הָחְבָּאוּ הָיוּ לָבַז וְאֵין מַצִּיל מְשִׁסָּה וְאֵין־
כג אֹמֵר הָשַׁב: מִי בָכֶם יַאֲזִין זֹאת יַקְשִׁב וְיִשְׁמַע לְאָחוֹר:
כד מִי־נָתַן למשוסה יַעֲקֹב וְיִשְׂרָאֵל לְבֹזְזִים הֲלוֹא יהוה זוּ לִמְשִׁסָּה
חָטָאנוּ לוֹ וְלֹא־אָבוּ בִדְרָכָיו הָלוֹךְ וְלֹא שָׁמְעוּ בְּתוֹרָתוֹ:
כה וַיִּשְׁפֹּךְ עָלָיו חֵמָה אַפּוֹ וֶעֱזוּז מִלְחָמָה וַתְּלַהֲטֵהוּ מִסָּבִיב
מג א וְלֹא יָדָע וַתִּבְעַר־בּוֹ וְלֹא־יָשִׂים עַל־לֵב: וְעַתָּה
כֹּה־אָמַר יהוה בֹּרַאֲךָ יַעֲקֹב וְיֹצֶרְךָ יִשְׂרָאֵל אַל־תִּירָא כִּי
ב גְאַלְתִּיךָ קָרָאתִי בְשִׁמְךָ לִי־אָתָּה: כִּי־תַעֲבֹר בַּמַּיִם אִתְּךָ אָנִי
וּבַנְּהָרוֹת לֹא יִשְׁטְפוּךָ כִּי־תֵלֵךְ בְּמוֹ־אֵשׁ לֹא תִכָּוֶה וְלֶהָבָה
ג לֹא תִבְעַר־בָּךְ: כִּי אֲנִי יהוה אֱלֹהֶיךָ קְדוֹשׁ יִשְׂרָאֵל מוֹשִׁיעֶךָ
ד נָתַתִּי כָפְרְךָ מִצְרַיִם כּוּשׁ וּסְבָא תַּחְתֶּיךָ: מֵאֲשֶׁר יָקַרְתָּ
בְעֵינַי נִכְבַּדְתָּ וַאֲנִי אֲהַבְתִּיךָ וְאֶתֵּן אָדָם תַּחְתֶּיךָ וּלְאֻמִּים
ה תַּחַת נַפְשֶׁךָ: אַל־תִּירָא כִּי אִתְּךָ־אָנִי מִמִּזְרָח אָבִיא זַרְעֶךָ
ו וּמִמַּעֲרָב אֲקַבְּצֶךָּ: אֹמַר לַצָּפוֹן תֵּנִי וּלְתֵימָן אַל־תִּכְלָאִי
ז הָבִיאִי בָנַי מֵרָחוֹק וּבְנוֹתַי מִקְצֵה הָאָרֶץ: כֹּל הַנִּקְרָא בִשְׁמִי
ח וְלִכְבוֹדִי בְּרָאתִיו יְצַרְתִּיו אַף־עֲשִׂיתִיו: הוֹצִיא עַם־עִוֵּר
ט וְעֵינַיִם יֵשׁ וְחֵרְשִׁים וְאָזְנַיִם לָמוֹ: כָּל־הַגּוֹיִם נִקְבְּצוּ יַחְדָּו
וְיֵאָסְפוּ לְאֻמִּים מִי בָהֶם יַגִּיד זֹאת וְרִאשֹׁנוֹת יַשְׁמִיעֻנוּ יִתְּנוּ
י עֵדֵיהֶם וְיִצְדָּקוּ וְיִשְׁמְעוּ וְיֹאמְרוּ אֱמֶת: אַתֶּם עֵדַי נְאֻם־יהוה

witnesses, so says the Lord, My servants whom I chose, so that
you should know, and trust in Me and understand that I am He;
before Me, no god was made, and after Me – no other.

Haftarat Noaḥ

On Rosh Ḥodesh Marḥeshvan, read the maftir from Numbers 28:9–15, and the haftara on page 1640.

54 1 Barren woman, never a mother, rejoice; break out in joyful song ISAIAH
though you have not given birth, for the children of the forsak-
en woman will outnumber those of the wife, so says the Lord.
2 Broaden the site of your tent; stretch out your canvas home; do
not hold back; lengthen your tent cords, and strengthen its pegs:
3 you shall overflow rightward and left, your children possessing
4 nations, and filling forsaken towns with life. Do not fear – you
will not be shamed; fear not, for none can disgrace you. You will
forget your youthful abjection; the debasement of your widow-
5 hood you will call no more to mind, for your husband, He who
made you – the Lord of Hosts is His name, and your redeemer,
6 Israel's Holy One – will be named God of all the world, for as a
woman abandoned, of sorrowful spirit, the Lord has called to
7 you: Can the young bride ever be rejected? says your God; for
one small moment I left you; with infinite care shall I gather you
8 back; in the flash of My fury I hid My face from you for just a moment, and in everlasting love will I care for you now. So speaks
9 the Lord, your redeemer. For these are the waters of
Noaḥ to Me, and I swore that the waters of Noaḥ would never
sweep again over the earth. And so did I swear no more to be
10 furious with you, no more to rebuke you. For mountains may
move, hills may crumble away; but My love for you will not be
moved, nor My pact of peace crumble. So speaks the Lord,

These words of the prophet Yeshayahu were spoken against the background of the exile of the kingdom of Israel, which occurred during his lifetime. For the first time since the people of Israel had arrived in the land, a great number of them were banished from it and a sizable portion of the territory laid waste. These words of encouragement and advice were appropriate for their time, and they remain trenchant today. Jews throughout the exile have taken heart reading this *haftara* every year.

וַעַבְדִּי אֲשֶׁר בָּחָרְתִּי לְמַעַן תֵּדְעוּ וְתַאֲמִינוּ לִי וְתָבִינוּ כִּי־אֲנִי
הוּא לְפָנַי לֹא־נוֹצַר אֵל וְאַחֲרַי לֹא יִהְיֶה׃

הפטרת נח

On ראש חודש מרחשוון *read the* מפטיר *from* במדבר כח, ט–טו*, and the* הפטרה *on page 1641.*

נד א רָנִּי עֲקָרָה לֹא יָלָדָה פִּצְחִי רִנָּה וְצַהֲלִי לֹא־חָלָה כִּי־רַבִּים ישעיה
ב בְּנֵי־שׁוֹמֵמָה מִבְּנֵי בְעוּלָה אָמַר יְהוָה׃ הַרְחִיבִי ׀ מְקוֹם
אָהֳלֵךְ וִירִיעוֹת מִשְׁכְּנוֹתַיִךְ יַטּוּ אַל־תַּחְשֹׂכִי הַאֲרִיכִי
ג מֵיתָרַיִךְ וִיתֵדֹתַיִךְ חַזֵּקִי׃ כִּי־יָמִין וּשְׂמֹאול תִּפְרֹצִי וְזַרְעֵךְ
ד גּוֹיִם יִירָשׁ וְעָרִים נְשַׁמּוֹת יוֹשִׁיבוּ׃ אַל־תִּירְאִי כִּי־לֹא
תֵבוֹשִׁי וְאַל־תִּכָּלְמִי כִּי לֹא תַחְפִּירִי כִּי בֹשֶׁת עֲלוּמַיִךְ
ה תִּשְׁכָּחִי וְחֶרְפַּת אַלְמְנוּתַיִךְ לֹא תִזְכְּרִי־עוֹד׃ כִּי בֹעֲלַיִךְ
עֹשַׂיִךְ יְהוָה צְבָאוֹת שְׁמוֹ וְגֹאֲלֵךְ קְדוֹשׁ יִשְׂרָאֵל אֱלֹהֵי כָל־
ו הָאָרֶץ יִקָּרֵא׃ כִּי־כְאִשָּׁה עֲזוּבָה וַעֲצוּבַת רוּחַ קְרָאָךְ יְהוָה
ז וְאֵשֶׁת נְעוּרִים כִּי תִמָּאֵס אָמַר אֱלֹהָיִךְ׃ בְּרֶגַע קָטֹן עֲזַבְתִּיךְ
ח וּבְרַחֲמִים גְּדֹלִים אֲקַבְּצֵךְ׃ בְּשֶׁצֶף קֶצֶף הִסְתַּרְתִּי פָנַי רֶגַע
ט מִמֵּךְ וּבְחֶסֶד עוֹלָם רִחַמְתִּיךְ אָמַר גֹּאֲלֵךְ יְהוָה׃ כִּי־
מֵי נֹחַ זֹאת לִי אֲשֶׁר נִשְׁבַּעְתִּי מֵעֲבֹר מֵי־נֹחַ עוֹד עַל־הָאָרֶץ
י כֵּן נִשְׁבַּעְתִּי מִקְּצֹף עָלַיִךְ וּמִגְּעָר־בָּךְ׃ כִּי הֶהָרִים יָמוּשׁוּ
וְהַגְּבָעוֹת תְּמוּטֶינָה וְחַסְדִּי מֵאִתֵּךְ לֹא־יָמוּשׁ וּבְרִית שְׁלוֹמִי

NOAḤ

The flood, which threw the world back into a state of chaos, came as a punishment for wickedness and oppression. The prophet draws a parallel between it and the destruction and exile of the Israelite kingdoms centuries later, which also came as a result of disobedience to God. He insists that crisis and suffering are not the natural way of things, even if they can seem never-ending. The covenant with God must be founded on the basis of justice and mercy – if we do this, we are promised blessing and light that will banish these difficult times. Then, in place of helplessness and sadness, we will find great mercy and eternal charity, for one good act leads to another.

11 who cares for you. * Oppressed and storm swept, never
comforted; behold: I am paving your ground with garnet, la-
12 pis lazuli your foundations. I am fitting your windows with
rubies, your gates with glowing granite, marking your borders
13 with stones men covet. All your children will be students of the
14 LORD, and great will be your children's peace. On righteousness
will you be founded; stay far from oppression; you will not fear,
15 and terror will never come near you. No strife can arise without My assent; who among you fears one who could come upon
16 you? For I create the craftsman who blows the charcoal fire and
brings forth the tools of his trade; I create also the destroyer to
17 do harm. No weapon made to harm you can prevail; any tongue
that calls you into judgment, you will prove its fault. This is the
birthright of the LORD's servants, for their innocence is Mine; so
55 1 says the LORD. You who are thirsty, all, come to water;
you who have no silver, come, take food and eat; come and take
2 food without silver, wine and milk without cost, for why should
you weigh out your silver for no bread, your labor bringing you
no fullness? Listen – listen to Me: let goodness nourish you, and
3 let your souls delight in plenty. Turn your ear to Me and come;
listen, that your souls may live; let Me forge an everlasting cov-
4 enant with you, like David's faithful promises,* for I make him a
5 witness to nations, a leader, a ruler of nations; for you shall call
out, call, to a people you know not, and a people who know you
not will come running out to you for the sake of the LORD your
God, the Holy One of Israel, your glory.

Sepharadim and Chabad end here

Yemenites end here

HAFTARAT LEKH LEKHA

ISAIAH

Yemenites begin here

40 25 Whom can you compare Me to – so speaks the Holy One – and
26 find them equal? Raise your eyes skyward and see: Who created

over and over the refrain "do not fear." This assurance creates a special sense of closeness between God and "the children of Avraham who loved Me," and it gives us strength to overcome our doubts and continue in our battle against the darkness of the world's idols with confidence. This prophecy was not directed at a specific time or context, and it is relevant throughout the long night of our people's struggle against foreign powers and their political and cultural influence.

יא לא תמוט אמר מרחמך יהוה:* עניה סערה לא *Sepharadim and Chabad end here*
נחמה הנה אנכי מרביץ בפוך אבניך ויסדתיך בספירים:
יב ושמתי כדכד שמשתיך ושעריך לאבני אקדח וכל־גבולך
יג יד לאבני־חפץ: וכל־בניך למודי יהוה ורב שלום בניך: בצדקה
תכונני רחקי מעשק כי־לא תיראי וממחתה כי לא־תקרב
טו טז אליך: הן גור יגור אפס מאותי מי־גר אתך עליך יפול: הן הנה
אנכי בראתי חרש נפח באש פחם ומוציא כלי למעשהו
יז ואנכי בראתי משחית לחבל: כל־כלי יוצר עליך לא
יצלח וכל־לשון תקום־אתך למשפט תרשיעי זאת נחלת
נה א עבדי יהוה וצדקתם מאתי נאם־יהוה: הוי כל־
צמא לכו למים ואשר אין־לו כסף לכו שברו ואכלו ולכו
ב שברו בלוא־כסף ובלוא מחיר יין וחלב: למה תשקלו־
כסף בלוא־לחם ויגיעכם בלוא לשבעה שמעו שמוע
ג אלי ואכלו־טוב ותתענג בדשן נפשכם: הטו אזנכם ולכו
אלי שמעו ותחי נפשכם ואכרתה לכם ברית עולם חסדי
ד דוד הנאמנים:* הן עד לאומים נתתיו נגיד ומצוה לאמים: *Yemenites end here*
ה הן גוי לא־תדע תקרא וגוי לא־ידעוך אליך ירוצו למען
יהוה אלהיך ולקדוש ישראל כי פארך:

הפטרת לך לך

מ כה כו ואל־מי תדמיוני ואשוה יאמר קדוש: שאו־מרום עיניכם ישעיה *Yemenites begin here*
וראו מי־ברא אלה המוציא במספר צבאם לכלם בשם

LEKH LEKHA

God's choice of Avraham – the first iconoclast – and his descendants put the Jewish people at the forefront of the war against the moral distortions that are the hallmark of idolatry. This bitter struggle throughout human history has often left the "worm of Yaakov" weak and pained, anxious to understand why God appears absent from our world. Against this backdrop, the strong words of consolation from the prophet Yeshayahu repeat

all these? Who summons their legions by number and calls each
man by name? In His great might, His adamantine strength, not
27 one of them is lost. *Why do you say, Yaakov; Israel,
why declare, "My way is hidden from the LORD; my God over-
28 looks my claim"? Do you not know this; have you not heard? The
LORD is God eternal, Creator of all horizons; He does not weary,
29 does not tire; no one can plumb His understanding. He gives the
30 weary strength, the helpless, power: more and more. Youths will
31 tire, grow weary; young men will falter and fall, but those who
wait for the LORD, their strength will be renewed; they will rise
on their wings like eagles, will run and never grow weary, will
41 1 walk on and never grow tired. Hush before Me, coastlands and nations; renew your strength, and then come forward,
2 speak, draw close; let us come into judgment. Who roused the
one from the east and called victory to his feet? Who herded nations before him, laid their kings low, and made his swords nu-
3 merous as dust, his bowshots like chaff in the wind? He pursued
them and came through in peace on paths that his feet never
4 walked. Who was it who acted and did this, who called forth generations long before? I, the LORD, am the first, and I shall be, I,
5 with the last who will be. Coastlands witness this and fear, earth's
6 horizons witness, tremble, draw near, come. *Each man helps his*
7 *fellow and tells his brother, "Be strong." "Strong," says the wright to*
the goldsmith, the hammerman to him who beats. He says of the glue,
8 *"This is good," and firms it up with nails, never to fall.* And
you, Israel, My servant, Yaakov whom I chose, children of Avra-
9 ham who loved Me, whom I lifted and brought from the ends of
the earth, calling you forth from its furthest corners, telling you:
You are My servant; You have I chosen, and I will not reject you;
10 do not fear, for I am with you; do not be afraid: I am your God;
I strengthen you and help you, uphold you with My right hand
11 of righteousness. All who rage against you will be shamed, de-
12 based; become like nothing, lost, all those who fight you. Look
for them then – you will not find them – the men with whom
you are wrestling, adversaries in war, like nothing, like no more.
13 For I am the LORD your God, holding your right hand, telling
14 you: Do not fear, for I am here: I help you. Yaakov:
worm, men of Israel, do not fear; I will help you, so speaks the
15 LORD, the Holy One of Israel, your redeemer. You shall see: I
have made you a slotted threshing board, new and razor edged;

Ashkenazim and Sepharadim begin here

Ashkenazim and Sephardim begin here

כו יקרא מרב אונים ואמיץ כח איש לא נעדר: *למה
תאמר יעקב ותדבר ישראל נסתרה דרכי מיהוה
כח ומאלהי משפטי יעבור: הלוא ידעת אם־לא שמעת
אלהי עולם ׀ יהוה בורא קצות הארץ לא ייעף ולא ייגע
כט אין חקר לתבונתו: נתן ליעף כח ולאין אונים עצמה
ל לא ירבה: ויעפו נערים ויגעו ובחורים כשול יכשלו: וקוי יהוה
יחליפו כח יעלו אבר כנשרים ירוצו ולא ייגעו ילכו ולא
מא א ייעפו: החרישו אלי איים ולאמים יחליפו כח
ב יגשו אז ידברו יחדו למשפט נקרבה: מי העיר ממזרח
צדק יקראהו לרגלו יתן לפניו גוים ומלכים ירד יתן כעפר
ג חרבו כקש נדף קשתו: ירדפם יעבור שלום ארח ברגליו
ד לא יבוא: מי־פעל ועשה קרא הדרות מראש אני יהוה
ה ראשון ואת־אחרנים אני־הוא: ראו איים וייראו קצות
ו הארץ יחרדו קרבו ויאתיון: איש את־רעהו יעזרו ולאחיו
ז יאמר חזק: ויחזק חרש את־צרף מחליק פטיש את־
הולם פעם אמר לדבק טוב הוא ויחזקהו במסמרים
ח לא ימוט: ואתה ישראל עבדי יעקב אשר
ט בחרתיך זרע אברהם אהבי: אשר החזקתיך מקצות
הארץ ומאציליה קראתיך ואמר לך עבדי־אתה בחרתיך
י ולא מאסתיך: אל־תירא כי עמך־אני אל־תשתע כי־אני
אלהיך אמצתיך אף־עזרתיך אף־תמכתיך בימין צדקי:
יא הן יבשו ויכלמו כל הנחרים בך יהיו כאין ויאבדו אנשי
יב ריבך: תבקשם ולא תמצאם אנשי מצתך יהיו כאין וכאפס
יג אנשי מלחמתך: כי אני יהוה אלהיך מחזיק ימינך האמר
יד לך אל־תירא אני עזרתיך: אל־תיראי
תולעת יעקב מתי ישראל אני עזרתיך נאם־יהוה וגאלך
טו קדוש ישראל: הנה שמתיך למורג חרוץ חדש בעל פיפיות

you will thresh mountains, turn them to powder, and hills into
16 chaff. As you winnow, the wind will lift them, and the storm will
spread them far; you will rejoice in the LORD and will, through
17 the Holy One of Israel, be praised. The oppressed,
impoverished, beg for water – there is none; their tongues are
seared with thirst. I am the LORD; I will answer them; Israel's
God, I will not leave them.

Ashkenazim and Sepharadim end here

HAFTARAT VAYERA

II KINGS

4 1 A woman – the wife of one of the brotherhood of the prophets – cried out to Elisha, "Your servant, my husband, is dead! You
know that your servant always feared the LORD. Now a creditor
2 has come to take my two children away to be his slaves." "What
can I do for you?" said Elisha. "Tell me, what do you have in the
house?" "Your servant has nothing at all at home," she said, "ex-
3 cept for a jar of oil." "Go out and borrow vessels from all your
neighbors," he said to her, "empty vessels – as many as you can.
4 When you come back in, close the door behind you and your
sons. Then pour away into all those vessels, setting them aside
5 when they are full." And so she left him. When she closed the
door behind her and her sons, they kept bringing vessels to her
6 while she kept pouring. When the vessels were full, she said to
her son, "Bring me another vessel," and he said to her, "There are
7 no more vessels" – and the oil stopped flowing. She came and
told the man of God, and he said, "Go, sell the oil and pay off your
8 debt, and you and your sons can live on the rest." One
day, Elisha was passing through Shunem, and a wealthy woman there urged him to have something to eat. So whenever he
9 passed through, he would stop there for some food. She said to
her husband, "Look, I am sure that the man who passes through

---

days of the dynasty of Yehu, Elisha the prophet battled against idol worship. He comforted and supported those loyal to God and emphasized the rewards God gives those who stand by Him. This was his way of inspiring the people to give over Baal worship in favor of devotion to the Almighty. At the same time, he promoted the idea that the connection between God and His people is strong and innate, like the experience of motherhood and a mother's connection to her children.

טז תָּדוּשׁ הָרִים וְתָדֹק וּגְבָעוֹת כַּמֹּץ תָּשִׂים׃ תִּזְרֵם וְרוּחַ תִּשָּׂאֵם
וּסְעָרָה תָּפִיץ אוֹתָם וְאַתָּה תָּגִיל בַּיהוָה בִּקְדוֹשׁ יִשְׂרָאֵל
יז תִּתְהַלָּל׃ הָעֲנִיִּים וְהָאֶבְיוֹנִים מְבַקְשִׁים מַיִם *Ashkenazim and Sepharadim end here*
וָאַיִן לְשׁוֹנָם בַּצָּמָא נָשָׁתָּה אֲנִי יְהוָה אֶעֱנֵם אֱלֹהֵי יִשְׂרָאֵל
לֹא אֶעֶזְבֵם׃

הפטרת וירא

ד א וְאִשָּׁה אַחַת מִנְּשֵׁי בְנֵי־הַנְּבִיאִים צָעֲקָה אֶל־אֱלִישָׁע מלכים ב׳
לֵאמֹר עַבְדְּךָ אִישִׁי מֵת וְאַתָּה יָדַעְתָּ כִּי עַבְדְּךָ הָיָה יָרֵא
אֶת־יְהוָה וְהַנֹּשֶׁה בָּא לָקַחַת אֶת־שְׁנֵי יְלָדַי לוֹ לַעֲבָדִים׃
ב וַיֹּאמֶר אֵלֶיהָ אֱלִישָׁע מָה אֶעֱשֶׂה־לָּךְ הַגִּידִי לִי מַה־יֶּשׁ־
לכי בַּבָּיִת וַתֹּאמֶר אֵין לְשִׁפְחָתְךָ כֹל בַּבַּיִת כִּי אִם־אָסוּךְ לָךְ
ג שָׁמֶן׃ וַיֹּאמֶר לְכִי שַׁאֲלִי־לָךְ כֵּלִים מִן־הַחוּץ מֵאֵת כָּל־
ד שכניכי כֵּלִים רֵקִים אַל־תַּמְעִיטִי׃ וּבָאת וְסָגַרְתְּ הַדֶּלֶת שְׁכֵנָיִךְ
בַּעֲדֵךְ וּבְעַד־בָּנַיִךְ וְיָצַקְתְּ עַל כָּל־הַכֵּלִים הָאֵלֶּה וְהַמָּלֵא
ה תַּסִּיעִי׃ וַתֵּלֶךְ מֵאִתּוֹ וַתִּסְגֹּר הַדֶּלֶת בַּעֲדָהּ וּבְעַד בָּנֶיהָ
ו הֵם מַגִּשִׁים אֵלֶיהָ וְהִיא מיצקת׃ וַיְהִי ׀ כִּמְלֹאת הַכֵּלִים מוּצָקֶת
וַתֹּאמֶר אֶל־בְּנָהּ הַגִּישָׁה אֵלַי עוֹד כֶּלִי וַיֹּאמֶר אֵלֶיהָ אֵין
ז עוֹד כֶּלִי וַיַּעֲמֹד הַשָּׁמֶן׃ וַתָּבֹא וַתַּגֵּד לְאִישׁ הָאֱלֹהִים וַיֹּאמֶר
לְכִי מִכְרִי אֶת־הַשֶּׁמֶן וְשַׁלְּמִי אֶת־נשיכי וְאַתְּ בניכי תִּחְיִי נִשְׁיֵךְ | וּבָנַיִךְ
ח בַּנּוֹתָר׃ וַיְהִי הַיּוֹם וַיַּעֲבֹר אֱלִישָׁע אֶל־שׁוּנֵם וְשָׁם
אִשָּׁה גְדוֹלָה וַתַּחֲזֶק־בּוֹ לֶאֱכָל־לָחֶם וַיְהִי מִדֵּי עָבְרוֹ יָסֻר
ט שָׁמָּה לֶאֱכָל־לָחֶם׃ וַתֹּאמֶר אֶל־אִישָׁהּ הִנֵּה־נָא יָדַעְתִּי

VAYERA

In this *haftara*, we find two instances of a mother's concern for her children. In both, the mother is aided by miracles worked by the prophet Elisha. The desire to have and raise children brings both of these mothers to the point of great sacrifice and commitment to a goal until it is accomplished. At the end of the reign of Aḥav and in the early

▶

10 here regularly is a holy man of God. Let us make him a small
enclosed upper chamber and provide him with a bed, table, chair,
and lamp there, so that whenever he comes to us, he can turn in
11 there." One day, he came by; he turned in to the upper chamber
12 and lay down there. He said to Geḥazi, his servant, "Call the Shu-
13 namite woman." He called her, and she stood before him. He said
to him, "Please say to her, 'You have shown us so much concern.
What can we do for you? Shall I speak to the king on your behalf, or to the army commander?'" "I live among my own people,"
14 she said. "Then what can be done for her?" he said. "Well, she is
15 childless," said Geḥazi, "and her husband is old." "Call her," he
16 said, and he called her, and she stood in the entrance. "At this
time next year," he said, "you will be embracing a son." "No, my
17 lord, man of God," she said. "Do not delude your servant." But
the woman did conceive, and she bore a son at that time dur-
18 ing the following year, just as Elisha had promised her. The child
grew up. One day, he went out to his father, who was with the
19 reapers. "My head! My head!" he said to his father, who said to
20 the servant, "Carry him to his mother." He carried him over and
brought him to his mother; he sat on her lap until noon, and
21 then he died. She went up and laid him on the man of God's bed,
22 closed the door behind him, and went out. Then she called to
her husband. "Send me one of the servants and one of the donkeys at once," she said. "I must rush over to the man of God and
23 come right back." "Why are you going to him today?" he said. "It
is not the New Moon, nor the Sabbath." "All is well," she said.* *Sepharadim end here*
24 She saddled the donkey and said to her servant, "Drive! Be off!
25 Do not stop riding on my account unless I tell you." She set out
and reached the man of God at Mount Carmel. When the man
of God saw her in the distance, he said to Geḥazi, his servant,
26 "Look, there is that Shunamite woman. Run to meet her straight-
away and say to her, 'Are you well? Is your husband well? Is your
27 child well?'" "All is well," she said. But she came up to the man of
God at the mountain and grasped his feet. Geḥazi came forward
to push her away, but the man of God said, "Leave her be, for she
is bitter of spirit, and the LORD has hidden this from me and did

י כִּי אִישׁ אֱלֹהִים קָדוֹשׁ הוּא עֹבֵר עָלֵינוּ תָּמִיד׃ נַעֲשֶׂה־נָּא
עֲלִיַּת־קִיר קְטַנָּה וְנָשִׂים לוֹ שָׁם מִטָּה וְשֻׁלְחָן וְכִסֵּא וּמְנוֹרָה
יא וְהָיָה בְּבֹאוֹ אֵלֵינוּ יָסוּר שָׁמָּה׃ וַיְהִי הַיּוֹם וַיָּבֹא שָׁמָּה וַיָּסַר
יב אֶל־הָעֲלִיָּה וַיִּשְׁכַּב־שָׁמָּה׃ וַיֹּאמֶר אֶל־גֵּיחֲזִי נַעֲרוֹ קְרָא
יג לַשּׁוּנַמִּית הַזֹּאת וַיִּקְרָא־לָהּ וַתַּעֲמֹד לְפָנָיו׃ וַיֹּאמֶר לוֹ אֱמָר־
נָא אֵלֶיהָ הִנֵּה חָרַדְתְּ | אֵלֵינוּ אֶת־כָּל־הַחֲרָדָה הַזֹּאת מֶה
לַעֲשׂוֹת לָךְ הֲיֵשׁ לְדַבֶּר־לָךְ אֶל־הַמֶּלֶךְ אוֹ אֶל־שַׂר הַצָּבָא
יד וַתֹּאמֶר בְּתוֹךְ עַמִּי אָנֹכִי יֹשָׁבֶת׃ וַיֹּאמֶר וּמֶה לַעֲשׂוֹת לָהּ
טו וַיֹּאמֶר גֵּיחֲזִי אֲבָל בֵּן אֵין־לָהּ וְאִישָׁהּ זָקֵן׃ וַיֹּאמֶר קְרָא־לָהּ
טז וַיִּקְרָא־לָהּ וַתַּעֲמֹד בַּפָּתַח׃ וַיֹּאמֶר לַמּוֹעֵד הַזֶּה כָּעֵת חַיָּה
אתי חֹבֶקֶת בֵּן וַתֹּאמֶר אַל־אֲדֹנִי אִישׁ הָאֱלֹהִים אַל־תְּכַזֵּב אַתְּ
יז בְּשִׁפְחָתֶךָ׃ וַתַּהַר הָאִשָּׁה וַתֵּלֶד בֵּן לַמּוֹעֵד הַזֶּה כָּעֵת חַיָּה
יח אֲשֶׁר־דִּבֶּר אֵלֶיהָ אֱלִישָׁע׃ וַיִּגְדַּל הַיָּלֶד וַיְהִי הַיּוֹם וַיֵּצֵא אֶל־
יט אָבִיו אֶל־הַקֹּצְרִים׃ וַיֹּאמֶר אֶל־אָבִיו רֹאשִׁי | רֹאשִׁי וַיֹּאמֶר
כ אֶל־הַנַּעַר שָׂאֵהוּ אֶל־אִמּוֹ׃ וַיִּשָּׂאֵהוּ וַיְבִיאֵהוּ אֶל־אִמּוֹ וַיֵּשֶׁב
כא עַל־בִּרְכֶּיהָ עַד־הַצָּהֳרַיִם וַיָּמֹת׃ וַתַּעַל וַתַּשְׁכִּבֵהוּ עַל־מִטַּת
כב אִישׁ הָאֱלֹהִים וַתִּסְגֹּר בַּעֲדוֹ וַתֵּצֵא׃ וַתִּקְרָא אֶל־אִישָׁהּ
וַתֹּאמֶר שִׁלְחָה נָא לִי אֶחָד מִן־הַנְּעָרִים וְאַחַת הָאֲתֹנוֹת
כג וְאָרוּצָה עַד־אִישׁ הָאֱלֹהִים וְאָשׁוּבָה׃ וַיֹּאמֶר מַדּוּעַ אתי אַתְּ
הלכתי אֵלָיו הַיּוֹם לֹא־חֹדֶשׁ וְלֹא שַׁבָּת וַתֹּאמֶר שָׁלוֹם׃* הֹלֶכֶת *Sepharadim end here*
כד וַתַּחֲבֹשׁ הָאָתוֹן וַתֹּאמֶר אֶל־נַעֲרָהּ נְהַג וָלֵךְ אַל־תַּעֲצָר־לִי
כה לִרְכֹּב כִּי אִם־אָמַרְתִּי לָךְ׃ וַתֵּלֶךְ וַתָּבוֹא אֶל־אִישׁ הָאֱלֹהִים
אֶל־הַר הַכַּרְמֶל וַיְהִי כִּרְאוֹת אִישׁ־הָאֱלֹהִים אֹתָהּ מִנֶּגֶד
כו וַיֹּאמֶר אֶל־גֵּיחֲזִי נַעֲרוֹ הִנֵּה הַשּׁוּנַמִּית הַלָּז׃ עַתָּה רוּץ־נָא
לִקְרָאתָהּ וֶאֱמָר־לָהּ הֲשָׁלוֹם לָךְ הֲשָׁלוֹם לְאִישֵׁךְ הֲשָׁלוֹם
כז לַיָּלֶד וַתֹּאמֶר שָׁלוֹם׃ וַתָּבֹא אֶל־אִישׁ הָאֱלֹהִים אֶל־הָהָר
וַתַּחֲזֵק בְּרַגְלָיו וַיִּגַּשׁ גֵּיחֲזִי לְהָדְפָהּ וַיֹּאמֶר אִישׁ הָאֱלֹהִים
הַרְפֵּה־לָהּ כִּי־נַפְשָׁהּ מָרָה־לָהּ וַיהוָה הֶעְלִים מִמֶּנִּי וְלֹא

28 not tell me." "Did I ask my lord for a son?" she said. "Did I not
29 say, 'Do not lead me on?'" "Hitch up your tunic," Elisha said to
Geḥazi. "Take my staff in your hand, and set out. If you meet anyone, do not greet them, and if anyone greets you, do not answer
30 them. Place my staff on the boy's face." "As the LORD lives, and
by your own life," said the boy's mother, "I will not leave you." So
31 he followed straight behind her. Geḥazi went on ahead of them
and placed the staff on the boy's face, but there was no sound
and no response. He went back to meet him and told him, "The
32 boy did not wake." Elisha entered the house, and there was the
33 boy laid out on his bed – dead. He entered and closed the door
34 behind the two of them, and he prayed to the LORD. Then he
mounted the bed and lay on top of the boy; he placed his mouth
on his mouth and his eyes on his eyes and his palms on his palms,
and he bent down over him, and the child's body became warm.
35 He went back down and paced about the house, back and forth,
then he climbed up and crouched down over him. And the boy
36 sneezed – seven times – and the boy opened his eyes. He called
to Geḥazi and said to him, "Call the Shunamite woman." He
37 called her, and she came to him. "Pick up your son," he said. And
she came and fell at his feet and bowed to the ground. Then she
picked up her son and went out.

HAFTARAT ḤAYEI SARA

1 1 King David was old, advanced in years, and though they covered I KINGS
2 him with bedclothes, he never felt warm. His servants said to
him, "Let a young virgin be sought out for our lord the king, to
wait upon the king and become his companion; when she lies in
3 your embrace, our lord the king will feel warm." They searched

on Adoniya as the next king. Natan the prophet, together with Shlomo's mother, Batsheva, informs David about the coup. David commands the two of them to quickly crown Shlomo, exposing Adoniya and his followers and rebels. This action succeeds in preventing a civil war during this fraught time of transition of power – a conflict which might have destroyed the united kingdom that it had taken David decades to build.

כח הִגִּיד לִי: וַתֹּאמֶר הֲשָׁאַלְתִּי בֵן מֵאֵת אֲדֹנִי הֲלֹא אָמַרְתִּי
כט לֹא תַשְׁלֶה אֹתִי: וַיֹּאמֶר לְגֵיחֲזִי חֲגֹר מׇתְנֶיךָ וְקַח מִשְׁעַנְתִּי
בְיָדְךָ וָלֵךְ כִּי־תִמְצָא אִישׁ לֹא תְבָרְכֶנּוּ וְכִי־יְבָרֶכְךָ אִישׁ לֹא
ל תַעֲנֶנּוּ וְשַׂמְתָּ מִשְׁעַנְתִּי עַל־פְּנֵי הַנָּעַר: וַתֹּאמֶר אֵם הַנַּעַר
לא חַי־יהוה וְחֵי־נַפְשְׁךָ אִם־אֶעֶזְבֶךָּ וַיָּקׇם וַיֵּלֶךְ אַחֲרֶיהָ: וְגֵחֲזִי
עָבַר לִפְנֵיהֶם וַיָּשֶׂם אֶת־הַמִּשְׁעֶנֶת עַל־פְּנֵי הַנַּעַר וְאֵין קוֹל
וְאֵין קָשֶׁב וַיָּשׇׁב לִקְרָאתוֹ וַיַּגֶּד־לוֹ לֵאמֹר לֹא הֵקִיץ הַנָּעַר:
לב וַיָּבֹא אֱלִישָׁע הַבָּיְתָה וְהִנֵּה הַנַּעַר מֵת מֻשְׁכָּב עַל־מִטָּתוֹ:
לג לד וַיָּבֹא וַיִּסְגֹּר הַדֶּלֶת בְּעַד שְׁנֵיהֶם וַיִּתְפַּלֵּל אֶל־יהוה: וַיַּעַל
וַיִּשְׁכַּב עַל־הַיֶּלֶד וַיָּשֶׂם פִּיו עַל־פִּיו וְעֵינָיו עַל־עֵינָיו וְכַפָּיו
לה עַל־כַּפָּו וַיִּגְהַר עָלָיו וַיָּחׇם בְּשַׂר הַיָּלֶד: וַיָּשׇׁב וַיֵּלֶךְ בַּבַּיִת
אַחַת הֵנָּה וְאַחַת הֵנָּה וַיַּעַל וַיִּגְהַר עָלָיו וַיְזוֹרֵר הַנַּעַר עַד־
לו שֶׁבַע פְּעָמִים וַיִּפְקַח הַנַּעַר אֶת־עֵינָיו: וַיִּקְרָא אֶל־גֵּיחֲזִי
וַיֹּאמֶר קְרָא אֶל־הַשֻּׁנַמִּית הַזֹּאת וַיִּקְרָאֶהָ וַתָּבֹא אֵלָיו
לז וַיֹּאמֶר שְׂאִי בְנֵךְ: וַתָּבֹא וַתִּפֹּל עַל־רַגְלָיו וַתִּשְׁתַּחוּ אָרְצָה
וַתִּשָּׂא אֶת־בְּנָהּ וַתֵּצֵא:

הפטרת חיי שרה

א א וְהַמֶּלֶךְ דָּוִד זָקֵן בָּא בַּיָּמִים וַיְכַסֻּהוּ בַּבְּגָדִים וְלֹא יִחַם לוֹ: מלכים א׳
ב וַיֹּאמְרוּ לוֹ עֲבָדָיו יְבַקְשׁוּ לַאדֹנִי הַמֶּלֶךְ נַעֲרָה בְתוּלָה
וְעָמְדָה לִפְנֵי הַמֶּלֶךְ וּתְהִי־לוֹ סֹכֶנֶת וְשָׁכְבָה בְחֵיקֶךָ וְחַם
ג לַאדֹנִי הַמֶּלֶךְ: וַיְבַקְשׁוּ נַעֲרָה יָפָה בְּכֹל גְּבוּל יִשְׂרָאֵל

ḤAYEI SARA

This *haftara* recounts an attempted coup by one of David's sons toward the end of the king's reign. Shlomo, David's intended successor, was still young, and Adoniya, his older brother, ought to have been the next king by right of being the eldest. Adoniya gathers a group of conspirators opposed to Shlomo and tries to seize the throne by putting on a show-coronation meant to imply that David has changed his mind and settled instead

▶

throughout Israel's borders for a beautiful girl, found Avishag the
4 Shunamite, and brought her to the king. The girl was most beautiful, and she became the king's companion and served him, but
5 the king was not intimate with her. Meanwhile, Adoniya son of
Ḥagit promoted himself, declaring, "I will become king," and he
procured a chariot and riders and fifty men to run before him.
6 Now his father had never disciplined him, saying, "Why have
you acted like that?" He was born after Avshalom, and he too
7 was devastatingly handsome. He conspired with Yoav son of
Tzeruya and Evyatar the priest, and they lent their support to
8 Adoniya. But Tzadok the priest, Benayahu son of Yehoyada, Natan the prophet, Shimi and Rei, and David's warriors were not on
9 Adoniyahu's side. Adoniyahu sacrificed sheep, oxen, and fatlings
by the Zoḥelet Stone near the Rogel Spring, and he invited all
his brothers – the king's sons – and all the men of Yehuda, the
10 king's subjects. But he did not invite the prophet Natan or Bena-
11 yahu or the warriors, or his brother Shlomo. And Natan said to
Batsheva, Shlomo's mother, "Have you heard? Adoniyahu the
son of Ḥagit has become king without our lord David's knowl-
12 edge. Come now, let me give you advice – to save your own life
13 and the life of your son Shlomo. Go to King David at once and
say to him, 'My lord the king, did you not swear to your handmaid, "Your son Shlomo will rule after me, and he will sit on my
14 throne"? Why, then, has Adoniyahu become king?' And while
you are still speaking there with the king, I will come in after
15 you and confirm your words." So Batsheva went to the king in
the inner chamber – the king had aged severely, and Avishag the
16 Shunamite was tending to him – and Batsheva bowed down low
17 in homage to the king. "What is the matter?" asked the king. "My
lord," she said to him, "you swore by the Lord your God to your
handmaid, 'Your son Shlomo will rule after me, and he will sit
18 on my throne.' But now, look – Adoniya has become king – and
19 you, my lord the king, did not even know! He has sacrificed a
wealth of oxen and fatlings and sheep and invited all the king's
sons, the priest Evyatar, and the army commander Yoav, but he
20 did not invite your servant Shlomo. But all the eyes of Israel look

ד וַיִּמְצְאוּ אֶת־אֲבִישַׁג הַשּׁוּנַמִּית וַיָּבִאוּ אֹתָהּ לַמֶּלֶךְ׃ וְהַנַּעֲרָה
יָפָה עַד־מְאֹד וַתְּהִי לַמֶּלֶךְ סֹכֶנֶת וַתְּשָׁרְתֵהוּ וְהַמֶּלֶךְ לֹא
ה יְדָעָהּ׃ וַאֲדֹנִיָּה בֶן־חַגִּית מִתְנַשֵּׂא לֵאמֹר אֲנִי אֶמְלֹךְ וַיַּעַשׂ
ו לוֹ רֶכֶב וּפָרָשִׁים וַחֲמִשִּׁים אִישׁ רָצִים לְפָנָיו׃ וְלֹא־עֲצָבוֹ
אָבִיו מִיָּמָיו לֵאמֹר מַדּוּעַ כָּכָה עָשִׂיתָ וְגַם־הוּא טוֹב־
ז תֹּאַר מְאֹד וְאֹתוֹ יָלְדָה אַחֲרֵי אַבְשָׁלוֹם׃ וַיִּהְיוּ דְבָרָיו עִם
יוֹאָב בֶּן־צְרוּיָה וְעִם אֶבְיָתָר הַכֹּהֵן וַיַּעְזְרוּ אַחֲרֵי אֲדֹנִיָּה׃
ח וְצָדוֹק הַכֹּהֵן וּבְנָיָהוּ בֶן־יְהוֹיָדָע וְנָתָן הַנָּבִיא וְשִׁמְעִי
ט וְרֵעִי וְהַגִּבּוֹרִים אֲשֶׁר לְדָוִד לֹא הָיוּ עִם־אֲדֹנִיָּהוּ׃ וַיִּזְבַּח
אֲדֹנִיָּהוּ צֹאן וּבָקָר וּמְרִיא עִם אֶבֶן הַזֹּחֶלֶת אֲשֶׁר־אֵצֶל עֵין
רֹגֵל וַיִּקְרָא אֶת־כָּל־אֶחָיו בְּנֵי הַמֶּלֶךְ וּלְכָל־אַנְשֵׁי יְהוּדָה
י עַבְדֵי הַמֶּלֶךְ׃ וְאֶת־נָתָן הַנָּבִיא וּבְנָיָהוּ וְאֶת־הַגִּבּוֹרִים
יא וְאֶת־שְׁלֹמֹה אָחִיו לֹא קָרָא׃ וַיֹּאמֶר נָתָן אֶל־בַּת־שֶׁבַע
אֵם־שְׁלֹמֹה לֵאמֹר הֲלוֹא שָׁמַעַתְּ כִּי מָלַךְ אֲדֹנִיָּהוּ בֶן־
יב חַגִּית וַאֲדֹנֵינוּ דָוִד לֹא יָדָע׃ וְעַתָּה לְכִי אִיעָצֵךְ נָא עֵצָה
יג וּמַלְּטִי אֶת־נַפְשֵׁךְ וְאֶת־נֶפֶשׁ בְּנֵךְ שְׁלֹמֹה׃ לְכִי וּבֹאִי ׀
אֶל־הַמֶּלֶךְ דָּוִד וְאָמַרְתְּ אֵלָיו הֲלֹא־אַתָּה אֲדֹנִי הַמֶּלֶךְ
נִשְׁבַּעְתָּ לַאֲמָתְךָ לֵאמֹר כִּי־שְׁלֹמֹה בְנֵךְ יִמְלֹךְ אַחֲרַי וְהוּא
יד יֵשֵׁב עַל־כִּסְאִי וּמַדּוּעַ מָלַךְ אֲדֹנִיָּהוּ׃ הִנֵּה עוֹדָךְ מְדַבֶּרֶת
שָׁם עִם־הַמֶּלֶךְ וַאֲנִי אָבוֹא אַחֲרַיִךְ וּמִלֵּאתִי אֶת־דְּבָרָיִךְ׃
טו וַתָּבֹא בַת־שֶׁבַע אֶל־הַמֶּלֶךְ הַחַדְרָה וְהַמֶּלֶךְ זָקֵן מְאֹד
טז וַאֲבִישַׁג הַשּׁוּנַמִּית מְשָׁרַת אֶת־הַמֶּלֶךְ׃ וַתִּקֹּד בַּת־שֶׁבַע
יז וַתִּשְׁתַּחוּ לַמֶּלֶךְ וַיֹּאמֶר הַמֶּלֶךְ מַה־לָּךְ׃ וַתֹּאמֶר לוֹ אֲדֹנִי
אַתָּה נִשְׁבַּעְתָּ בַּיהוָה אֱלֹהֶיךָ לַאֲמָתֶךָ כִּי־שְׁלֹמֹה בְנֵךְ
יח יִמְלֹךְ אַחֲרָי וְהוּא יֵשֵׁב עַל־כִּסְאִי׃ וְעַתָּה הִנֵּה אֲדֹנִיָּה מָלָךְ
יט וְעַתָּה אֲדֹנִי הַמֶּלֶךְ לֹא יָדָעְתָּ׃ וַיִּזְבַּח שׁוֹר וּמְרִיא־וְצֹאן לָרֹב
וַיִּקְרָא לְכָל־בְּנֵי הַמֶּלֶךְ וּלְאֶבְיָתָר הַכֹּהֵן וּלְיֹאָב שַׂר הַצָּבָא
כ וְלִשְׁלֹמֹה עַבְדְּךָ לֹא קָרָא׃ וְאַתָּה אֲדֹנִי הַמֶּלֶךְ עֵינֵי כָל־

to you, my lord the king, to tell them who will succeed my lord
21 the king on his throne. Otherwise, when my lord the king lies
with his ancestors, my son Shlomo and I will be considered of-
22 fenders." And as she was still speaking with the king, Natan the
23 prophet arrived. "Here is Natan the prophet," they announced
to the king, and he came before the king and bowed to him with
24 his face to the ground. "My lord the king," said Natan, "did you
yourself say, 'Adoniyahu will be king after me, and he will sit on
25 my throne'? For he went down today and sacrificed a wealth of
oxen, fatlings, and sheep and invited all the king's sons, the army
officers, and Evyatar the priest. And now they are feasting before
him and toasting him and declaring, 'Long live King Adoniyahu!'
26 But he did not invite me, your servant, or the priest Tzadok, or
27 Benayahu son of Yehoyada, or your servant Shlomo. Could it be
that my lord the king has decided this without informing your
28 servant who will succeed my lord the king on his throne?" "Summon Batsheva to me," King David said in response, and she came
29 before the king and stood in the king's presence. And the king
swore an oath. "As the LORD lives," he said, "who has rescued
30 me from every danger, what I swore to you by the LORD, God of
Israel – that Shlomo your son will rule after me, and that he will
31 sit on my throne in my place – I shall fulfill this very day." And
Batsheva bowed her face to the ground in royal homage and said,
"May my lord, King David, live forever!"

HAFTARAT TOLEDOT

On Erev Rosh Ḥodesh Kislev, read the haftara on page 1644.

1 1 An oracle: the word of the LORD to Israel through Malakhi. The MALACHI
2 LORD says, "I have loved you." But you say, "How have You loved
us?" Is Esav not a brother to Yaakov? So says the LORD: Yet I

Jews to Zion was not progressing as it should have. There was a great feeling of impotence, and the Jews had largely forsaken their spiritual lives. The behavior

יִשְׂרָאֵל עָלֶיךָ לְהַגִּיד לָהֶם מִי יֵשֵׁב עַל־כִּסֵּא אֲדֹנִי־הַמֶּלֶךְ
כא אַחֲרָיו׃ וְהָיָה כִּשְׁכַב אֲדֹנִי־הַמֶּלֶךְ עִם־אֲבֹתָיו וְהָיִיתִי אֲנִי
כב וּבְנִי שְׁלֹמֹה חַטָּאִים׃ וְהִנֵּה עוֹדֶנָּה מְדַבֶּרֶת עִם־הַמֶּלֶךְ וְנָתָן
כג הַנָּבִיא בָּא׃ וַיַּגִּידוּ לַמֶּלֶךְ לֵאמֹר הִנֵּה נָתָן הַנָּבִיא וַיָּבֹא
כד לִפְנֵי הַמֶּלֶךְ וַיִּשְׁתַּחוּ לַמֶּלֶךְ עַל־אַפָּיו אָרְצָה׃ וַיֹּאמֶר נָתָן
אֲדֹנִי הַמֶּלֶךְ אַתָּה אָמַרְתָּ אֲדֹנִיָּהוּ יִמְלֹךְ אַחֲרָי וְהוּא יֵשֵׁב
כה עַל־כִּסְאִי׃ כִּי ׀ יָרַד הַיּוֹם וַיִּזְבַּח שׁוֹר וּמְרִיא־וְצֹאן לָרֹב
וַיִּקְרָא לְכָל־בְּנֵי הַמֶּלֶךְ וּלְשָׂרֵי הַצָּבָא וּלְאֶבְיָתָר הַכֹּהֵן
וְהִנָּם אֹכְלִים וְשֹׁתִים לְפָנָיו וַיֹּאמְרוּ יְחִי הַמֶּלֶךְ אֲדֹנִיָּהוּ׃
כו וְלִי אֲנִי־עַבְדֶּךָ וּלְצָדֹק הַכֹּהֵן וְלִבְנָיָהוּ בֶן־יְהוֹיָדָע וְלִשְׁלֹמֹה
כז עַבְדְּךָ לֹא קָרָא׃ אִם מֵאֵת אֲדֹנִי הַמֶּלֶךְ נִהְיָה הַדָּבָר הַזֶּה
וְלֹא הוֹדַעְתָּ אֶת־עבדיך מִי יֵשֵׁב עַל־כִּסֵּא אֲדֹנִי־הַמֶּלֶךְ עַבְדְּךָ
כח אַחֲרָיו׃ וַיַּעַן הַמֶּלֶךְ דָּוִד וַיֹּאמֶר קִרְאוּ־לִי לְבַת־שָׁבַע וַתָּבֹא
כט לִפְנֵי הַמֶּלֶךְ וַתַּעֲמֹד לִפְנֵי הַמֶּלֶךְ׃ וַיִּשָּׁבַע הַמֶּלֶךְ וַיֹּאמַר
ל חַי־יְהוָה אֲשֶׁר־פָּדָה אֶת־נַפְשִׁי מִכָּל־צָרָה׃ כִּי כַּאֲשֶׁר
נִשְׁבַּעְתִּי לָךְ בַּיהוָה אֱלֹהֵי יִשְׂרָאֵל לֵאמֹר כִּי־שְׁלֹמֹה בְנֵךְ
יִמְלֹךְ אַחֲרַי וְהוּא יֵשֵׁב עַל־כִּסְאִי תַּחְתָּי כִּי כֵּן אֶעֱשֶׂה הַיּוֹם
לא הַזֶּה׃ וַתִּקֹּד בַּת־שֶׁבַע אַפַּיִם אֶרֶץ וַתִּשְׁתַּחוּ לַמֶּלֶךְ וַתֹּאמֶר
יְחִי אֲדֹנִי הַמֶּלֶךְ דָּוִד לְעֹלָם׃

הפטרת תולדת

On ערב ראש חודש כסלו *read the* הפטרה *on page 1645.*

א א ב מַשָּׂא דְבַר־יְהוָה אֶל־יִשְׂרָאֵל בְּיַד מַלְאָכִי׃ אָהַבְתִּי אֶתְכֶם מלאכי
אָמַר יְהוָה וַאֲמַרְתֶּם בַּמָּה אֲהַבְתָּנוּ הֲלוֹא־אָח עֵשָׂו לְיַעֲקֹב

TOLEDOT

Malakhi, the last of the prophets, lived during the beginning of the Second Temple Period. His time was a difficult one in the Persian province of Judea. The Temple was built, but the return of the ▶

3 loved Yaakov and hated Esav, so I made his mountains desolate
4 and gave his inheritance over to desert jackals. Even should Edom
say, "We have been destroyed, but we will return and rebuild the
ruins," says the LORD of Hosts, they will build; I will destroy, and
they will be called the territory of evil and the nation that suffers
5 the LORD's wrath forever. Your eyes will see this, and you will say,
6 "The LORD is great beyond the territory of Israel." A son honors
his father, and a slave his master; if I am a Father, where is My
honor, and if I am the Master, where is My reverence? So says
the LORD of Hosts to you, the priests who scorn My name. Yet
7 you say, "How have we scorned Your name?" You offer defiled
bread on My altar. Yet you say, "How have we defiled You?" In
8 saying the LORD's table is repugnant. When you offer a blind
animal to be sacrificed, is this no evil? And when you offer the
lame and the sick, is this no evil? Offer it if you will to your governor. Would he then accept you – let you lift your face to him?
9 So says the LORD of Hosts. Now, please, beseech God, and let
Him be gracious to us. This was in your hands – would He turn
10 His face for any one of you? So says the LORD of Hosts: O, who
is there among you who would close the doors so that you might
not light My altar for naught? I have no desire for you, says the
11 LORD of Hosts. I will accept no offering from your hands. For
from one end of the earth to the other, My name is great among
the nations. Incense is offered in My name, a pure offering everywhere, for My name is great among the nations, says the LORD
12 of Hosts. Yet you desecrate it by saying that the Lord's table is
13 defiled and its fruit too repugnant to be consumed. You say, "O,
how wearisome," and you snort at it, says the LORD of Hosts.
You bring what is stolen, the LORD says, what is lame, what is
ill; you bring this offering. Am I to accept it from your hands?
14 Cursed is the knave who has a ram in his flock but pledges and
sacrifices a damaged animal to the Lord. For I am a great King,
says the LORD of Hosts, and My name is revered among the na-
2 1 2 tions. Now, this is your command, priests: If you do not listen, if

---

The key to change lies in the hands of the priests, Malakhi proclaims. If they serve as a model of integrity for the people, they will draw the rest of the people after them toward truthfulness and godliness. This is also the key to advancing the process of the return to Zion and attaining the redemption it holds in store.

ג נְאֻם־יְהוָה וָאֹהַב אֶת־יַעֲקֹב: וְאֶת־עֵשָׂו שָׂנֵאתִי וָאָשִׂים
ד אֶת־הָרָיו שְׁמָמָה וְאֶת־נַחֲלָתוֹ לְתַנּוֹת מִדְבָּר: כִּי־תֹאמַר
אֱדוֹם רֻשַּׁשְׁנוּ וְנָשׁוּב וְנִבְנֶה חֳרָבוֹת כֹּה אָמַר יְהוָה צְבָאוֹת
הֵמָּה יִבְנוּ וַאֲנִי אֶהֱרוֹס וְקָרְאוּ לָהֶם גְּבוּל רִשְׁעָה וְהָעָם
ה אֲשֶׁר־זָעַם יְהוָה עַד־עוֹלָם: וְעֵינֵיכֶם תִּרְאֶינָה וְאַתֶּם תֹּאמְרוּ
ו יִגְדַּל יְהוָה מֵעַל לִגְבוּל יִשְׂרָאֵל: בֵּן יְכַבֵּד אָב וְעֶבֶד אֲדֹנָיו
וְאִם־אָב אָנִי אַיֵּה כְבוֹדִי וְאִם־אֲדוֹנִים אָנִי אַיֵּה מוֹרָאִי אָמַר ׀
יְהוָה צְבָאוֹת לָכֶם הַכֹּהֲנִים בּוֹזֵי שְׁמִי וַאֲמַרְתֶּם בַּמֶּה בָזִינוּ
ז אֶת־שְׁמֶךָ: מַגִּישִׁים עַל־מִזְבְּחִי לֶחֶם מְגֹאָל וַאֲמַרְתֶּם בַּמֶּה
ח גֵאַלְנוּךָ בֶּאֱמָרְכֶם שֻׁלְחַן יְהוָה נִבְזֶה הוּא: וְכִי־תַגִּשׁוּן עִוֵּר
לִזְבֹּחַ אֵין רָע וְכִי תַגִּישׁוּ פִּסֵּחַ וְחֹלֶה אֵין רָע הַקְרִיבֵהוּ נָא
ט לְפֶחָתֶךָ הֲיִרְצְךָ אוֹ הֲיִשָּׂא פָנֶיךָ אָמַר יְהוָה צְבָאוֹת: וְעַתָּה
חַלּוּ־נָא פְנֵי־אֵל וִיחָנֵנוּ מִיֶּדְכֶם הָיְתָה זֹּאת הֲיִשָּׂא מִכֶּם פָּנִים
י אָמַר יְהוָה צְבָאוֹת: מִי גַם־בָּכֶם וְיִסְגֹּר דְּלָתַיִם וְלֹא־תָאִירוּ
מִזְבְּחִי חִנָּם אֵין־לִי חֵפֶץ בָּכֶם אָמַר יְהוָה צְבָאוֹת וּמִנְחָה
יא לֹא־אֶרְצֶה מִיֶּדְכֶם: כִּי מִמִּזְרַח־שֶׁמֶשׁ וְעַד־מְבוֹאוֹ גָּדוֹל
שְׁמִי בַּגּוֹיִם וּבְכָל־מָקוֹם מֻקְטָר מֻגָּשׁ לִשְׁמִי וּמִנְחָה טְהוֹרָה
יב כִּי־גָדוֹל שְׁמִי בַּגּוֹיִם אָמַר יְהוָה צְבָאוֹת: וְאַתֶּם מְחַלְּלִים
אוֹתוֹ בֶּאֱמָרְכֶם שֻׁלְחַן אֲדֹנָי מְגֹאָל הוּא וְנִיבוֹ נִבְזֶה אָכְלוֹ:
יג וַאֲמַרְתֶּם הִנֵּה מַתְּלָאָה וְהִפַּחְתֶּם אוֹתוֹ אָמַר יְהוָה צְבָאוֹת
וַהֲבֵאתֶם גָּזוּל וְאֶת־הַפִּסֵּחַ וְאֶת־הַחוֹלֶה וַהֲבֵאתֶם אֶת־
יד הַמִּנְחָה הַאֶרְצֶה אוֹתָהּ מִיֶּדְכֶם אָמַר יְהוָה: וְאָרוּר נוֹכֵל
וְיֵשׁ בְּעֶדְרוֹ זָכָר וְנֹדֵר וְזֹבֵחַ מָשְׁחָת לַאדֹנָי כִּי מֶלֶךְ גָּדוֹל
ב א אָנִי אָמַר יְהוָה צְבָאוֹת וּשְׁמִי נוֹרָא בַגּוֹיִם: וְעַתָּה אֲלֵיכֶם
ב הַמִּצְוָה הַזֹּאת הַכֹּהֲנִים: אִם־לֹא תִשְׁמְעוּ וְאִם־לֹא תָשִׂימוּ

---

of the people and the priests in the Temple was so disgraceful that the prophet declares: "I have no desire for you.... I will accept no offering from your hands."

you do not take it to heart to honor My name, says the Lord of
Hosts, then I will set a curse on you, and I will curse your blessings – indeed, I have cursed your blessing, for you do not take it
3 to heart. I will drive away the crops because of you, and I will scatter filth in your face, the filth of your holiday sacrifices, and you
4 will be carried away after it. And you will know that I sent you
this command so that My covenant may endure with Levi, says
5 the Lord of Hosts. My covenant endures in him – life and peace.
I gave them to him so as to be revered. He revered Me and was in
6 awe of My name. True teaching was in his mouth, no sin from his
lips; he walked with Me in peace and uprightness and returned
7 many from iniquity. For a priest's lips should safeguard knowledge, and the people should seek teaching from his mouth, for
8 he is a messenger of the Lord of Hosts.* But you have strayed *Ashkenazim and Sepharadim end here*
from the path and caused many to stumble by your teaching. You
9 have destroyed the covenant of Levi, says the Lord of Hosts. So
indeed I will make you scorned and degraded before the whole
nation because you do not safeguard My ways, and you distort
10 the face of the Torah. Do we not all have one Father? Were we
not all created by one God? Why should a man be faithless to his
11 brother, desecrating the covenant of our fathers? For Yehuda has
been faithless, and an abomination has been perpetrated in Israel
and Jerusalem. For Yehuda, whom He loves, has desecrated that
which is holy to the Lord and married the daughter of a foreign
12 god. Let the man who does this be cut off by the Lord – kith
and kin – from the tents of Yaakov – even one who brings offer-
13 ings to the Lord of Hosts. And this you also do: flood
the Lord's altar with tears – weeping and sighing because He
no longer turns toward the offerings nor accepts favor from your
14 hands. And you say, "Why?" For the Lord is witness between
you and the wife of your youth, to whom you have been faithless,
15 though she is your companion and your covenantal wife. Did He
not make them one being? All remaining spirit accords with that.
And what does the One seek? Children of God. So take care of
your spirits, and let none of you be faithless to the wife of your
16 youth. If anyone hates and sends her away, says the Lord, God
of Israel, corruption covers his wedding clothes, says the Lord
of Hosts, and so, take care with your spirit and be not faith-
17 less. You have wearied the Lord with your talk. But

עַל־לֵ֗ב לָתֵ֤ת כָּבוֹד֙ לִשְׁמִ֔י אָמַר֙ יְהוָ֣ה צְבָא֔וֹת וְשִׁלַּחְתִּ֤י בָכֶם֙
אֶת־הַמְּאֵרָ֔ה וְאָרוֹתִ֖י אֶת־בִּרְכוֹתֵיכֶ֑ם וְגַם֙ אָר֣וֹתִיהָ֔ כִּ֥י אֵינְכֶ֖ם
ג שָׂמִ֥ים עַל־לֵֽב׃ הִנְנִ֨י גֹעֵ֤ר לָכֶם֙ אֶת־הַזֶּ֔רַע וְזֵרִ֤יתִי פֶ֙רֶשׁ֙ עַל־
ד פְּנֵיכֶ֔ם פֶּ֖רֶשׁ חַגֵּיכֶ֑ם וְנָשָׂ֥א אֶתְכֶ֖ם אֵלָֽיו׃ וִֽידַעְתֶּ֕ם כִּ֚י שִׁלַּ֣חְתִּי
אֲלֵיכֶ֔ם אֵ֖ת הַמִּצְוָ֣ה הַזֹּ֑את לִהְי֤וֹת בְּרִיתִי֙ אֶת־לֵוִ֔י אָמַ֖ר יְהוָ֥ה
ה צְבָאֽוֹת׃ בְּרִיתִ֣י ׀ הָיְתָ֣ה אִתּ֗וֹ הַֽחַיִּים֙ וְהַשָּׁל֔וֹם וָאֶתְּנֵֽם־ל֥וֹ
ו מוֹרָ֖א וַיִּֽירָאֵ֑נִי וּמִפְּנֵ֥י שְׁמִ֖י נִחַ֥ת הֽוּא׃ תּוֹרַ֤ת אֱמֶת֙ הָיְתָ֣ה
בְּפִ֔יהוּ וְעַוְלָ֖ה לֹא־נִמְצָ֣א בִשְׂפָתָ֑יו בְּשָׁל֤וֹם וּבְמִישׁוֹר֙ הָלַ֣ךְ
ז אִתִּ֔י וְרַבִּ֖ים הֵשִׁ֥יב מֵעָוֺֽן׃ כִּֽי־שִׂפְתֵ֤י כֹהֵן֙ יִשְׁמְרוּ־דַ֔עַת וְתוֹרָ֖ה
ח יְבַקְשׁ֣וּ מִפִּ֑יהוּ כִּ֛י מַלְאַ֥ךְ יְהוָֽה־צְבָא֖וֹת הֽוּא׃ * וְאַתֶּם֙ סַרְתֶּ֣ם

Ashkenazim and Sepharadim end here

מִן־הַדֶּ֔רֶךְ הִכְשַׁלְתֶּ֥ם רַבִּ֖ים בַּתּוֹרָ֑ה שִֽׁחַתֶּם֙ בְּרִ֣ית הַלֵּוִ֔י
ט אָמַ֖ר יְהוָ֥ה צְבָאֽוֹת׃ וְגַם־אֲנִ֗י נָתַ֧תִּי אֶתְכֶ֛ם נִבְזִ֥ים וּשְׁפָלִ֖ים
לְכָל־הָעָ֑ם כְּפִ֗י אֲשֶׁ֤ר אֵֽינְכֶם֙ שֹׁמְרִ֣ים אֶת־דְּרָכַ֔י וְנֹשְׂאִ֥ים
י פָּנִ֖ים בַּתּוֹרָֽה׃ הֲל֨וֹא אָ֤ב אֶחָד֙ לְכֻלָּ֔נוּ הֲל֛וֹא אֵ֥ל אֶחָ֖ד בְּרָאָ֑נוּ
יא מַדּ֗וּעַ נִבְגַּד֙ אִ֣ישׁ בְּאָחִ֔יו לְחַלֵּ֖ל בְּרִ֥ית אֲבֹתֵֽינוּ׃ בָּגְדָה֙ יְהוּדָ֔ה
וְתוֹעֵבָ֛ה נֶעֶשְׂתָ֥ה בְיִשְׂרָאֵ֖ל וּבִירוּשָׁלִָ֑ם כִּ֣י ׀ חִלֵּ֣ל יְהוּדָ֗ה קֹ֤דֶשׁ
יב יְהוָה֙ אֲשֶׁ֣ר אָהֵ֔ב וּבָעַ֖ל בַּת־אֵ֥ל נֵכָֽר׃ יַכְרֵ֨ת יְהוָ֜ה לָאִ֨ישׁ
אֲשֶׁ֤ר יַעֲשֶׂ֙נָּה֙ עֵ֣ר וְעֹנֶ֔ה מֵאָהֳלֵ֖י יַעֲקֹ֑ב וּמַגִּ֣ישׁ מִנְחָ֔ה לַיהוָ֖ה
יג צְבָאֽוֹת׃ וְזֹאת֙ שֵׁנִ֣ית תַּעֲשׂ֔וּ כַּסּ֤וֹת דִּמְעָה֙ אֶת־
מִזְבַּ֣ח יְהוָ֔ה בְּכִ֖י וַאֲנָקָ֑ה מֵאֵ֣ין ע֗וֹד פְּנוֹת֙ אֶל־הַמִּנְחָ֔ה וְלָקַ֥חַת
יד רָצ֖וֹן מִיֶּדְכֶֽם׃ וַאֲמַרְתֶּ֖ם עַל־מָ֑ה עַ֗ל כִּֽי־יְהוָ֞ה הֵעִ֣יד בֵּינְךָ֗
וּבֵ֣ין ׀ אֵ֣שֶׁת נְעוּרֶ֗יךָ אֲשֶׁ֤ר אַתָּה֙ בָּגַ֣דְתָּה בָּ֔הּ וְהִ֥יא חֲבֶרְתְּךָ֖
טו וְאֵ֥שֶׁת בְּרִיתֶֽךָ׃ וְלֹא־אֶחָ֣ד עָשָׂ֗ה וּשְׁאָ֥ר ר֙וּחַ֙ ל֔וֹ וּמָה֙ הָֽאֶחָ֔ד
מְבַקֵּ֖שׁ זֶ֣רַע אֱלֹהִ֑ים וְנִשְׁמַרְתֶּם֙ בְּר֣וּחֲכֶ֔ם וּבְאֵ֥שֶׁת נְעוּרֶ֖יךָ
טז אַל־יִבְגֹּֽד׃ כִּֽי־שָׂנֵ֣א שַׁלַּ֗ח אָמַ֤ר יְהוָה֙ אֱלֹהֵ֣י יִשְׂרָאֵ֔ל וְכִסָּ֤ה
חָמָס֙ עַל־לְבוּשׁ֔וֹ אָמַ֖ר יְהוָ֣ה צְבָא֑וֹת וְנִשְׁמַרְתֶּ֥ם בְּרוּחֲכֶ֖ם
יז וְלֹ֥א תִבְגֹּֽדוּ׃ הוֹגַעְתֶּ֤ם יְהוָה֙ בְּדִבְרֵיכֶ֔ם וַאֲמַרְתֶּ֖ם

you say, "How have we wearied Him?" By saying every evildoer
is good in the eyes of the LORD and it is them whom He desires;
3 1 or, "Where is the God of justice?" Behold: I am sending My messenger, and he will clear a path before Me. Suddenly, the Lord
whom you seek will arrive at His Temple. The angel of the covenant whom you desire – behold, he is coming, says the LORD
2 of Hosts. Who can survive the day of His coming, and who can
remain standing when He appears? For He is like the smelter's
3 fire and the washers' lye. And He will sit smelting and purifying
silver, and He will purify the sons of Levi and refine them like
gold and silver, and they will be the LORD's – bringing offerings
4 in righteousness. Then the offering of Yehuda and Jerusalem will
be pleasing to the LORD as in days of old and years past.

Haftarat Vayetze

HOSEA
Sepharadim, Chabad and Yemenites begin here

11 7 My people waver – whether to turn back to Me, although Israel
8 is summoned upward, they will not praise Him together. How
can I relinquish you, Efrayim; hand you over, Israel? How can I
make you like Adma and treat you like Tzevoyim? My heart has
9 turned upon Me; My compassion has been kindled. No, I will
not unleash My burning wrath, I will not turn again to destroy
Efrayim – for I am God, I am not a man; within you, My holiness
10 dwells; I will not enter the city with hatred. They will follow after
the LORD; He will roar like a lion. When He roars, His children
11 will rush forth from the west. They will be like a frightened bird
coming out of Egypt, like a dove leaving the land of Assyria. I
will bring them to settle safely in their homes. So declares the
12 1 LORD. Efrayim besieges Me with lies, the House of Israel with deception, but Yehuda still walks with God and remains

Israelites' betrayal of God and adherence to the idolatrous customs of the Assyrians represent ingratitude in the face of God's beneficence. Such ingratitude is distorted and unsustainable. The prophet paints a picture of the fate awaiting those who do not repent: "They will dissolve like morning mist, like dew at daybreak that swiftly fades." Like such fleeting visions that dissipate quickly, so too will the desire for Assyrian culture, at that time so intense and widespread, prove itself a mirage that will evaporate along with its adherents.

בַּמָּה הוֹגָעְנוּ בֶּאֱמָרְכֶם כָּל־עֹשֵׂה רָע טוֹב ׀ בְּעֵינֵי יהוה וּבָהֶם
ג א הוּא חָפֵץ אוֹ אַיֵּה אֱלֹהֵי הַמִּשְׁפָּט: הִנְנִי שֹׁלֵחַ מַלְאָכִי וּפִנָּה־
דֶרֶךְ לְפָנָי וּפִתְאֹם יָבוֹא אֶל־הֵיכָלוֹ הָאָדוֹן ׀ אֲשֶׁר־אַתֶּם
מְבַקְשִׁים וּמַלְאַךְ הַבְּרִית אֲשֶׁר אַתֶּם חֲפֵצִים הִנֵּה־בָא
ב אָמַר יהוה צְבָאוֹת: וּמִי מְכַלְכֵּל אֶת־יוֹם בּוֹאוֹ וּמִי הָעֹמֵד
ג בְּהֵרָאוֹתוֹ כִּי־הוּא כְּאֵשׁ מְצָרֵף וּכְבֹרִית מְכַבְּסִים: וְיָשַׁב
מְצָרֵף וּמְטַהֵר כֶּסֶף וְטִהַר אֶת־בְּנֵי־לֵוִי וְזִקַּק אֹתָם כַּזָּהָב
ד וְכַכָּסֶף וְהָיוּ לַיהוה מַגִּישֵׁי מִנְחָה בִּצְדָקָה: וְעָרְבָה לַיהוה
מִנְחַת יְהוּדָה וִירוּשָׁלִָם כִּימֵי עוֹלָם וּכְשָׁנִים קַדְמֹנִיּוֹת:

הפטרת ויצא

הושע

Sepharadim, Chabad and Yemenites begin here

יא ז וְעַמִּי תְלוּאִים לִמְשׁוּבָתִי וְאֶל־עַל יִקְרָאֻהוּ יַחַד לֹא יְרוֹמֵם:
ח אֵיךְ אֶתֶּנְךָ אֶפְרַיִם אֲמַגֶּנְךָ יִשְׂרָאֵל אֵיךְ אֶתֶּנְךָ כְאַדְמָה
ט אֲשִׂימְךָ כִּצְבֹאיִם נֶהְפַּךְ עָלַי לִבִּי יַחַד נִכְמְרוּ נִחוּמָי: לֹא
אֶעֱשֶׂה חֲרוֹן אַפִּי לֹא אָשׁוּב לְשַׁחֵת אֶפְרָיִם כִּי אֵל אָנֹכִי
י וְלֹא־אִישׁ בְּקִרְבְּךָ קָדוֹשׁ וְלֹא אָבוֹא בְּעִיר: אַחֲרֵי יהוה
יא יֵלְכוּ כְּאַרְיֵה יִשְׁאָג כִּי־הוּא יִשְׁאַג וְיֶחֶרְדוּ בָנִים מִיָּם: יֶחֶרְדוּ
כְצִפּוֹר מִמִּצְרַיִם וּכְיוֹנָה מֵאֶרֶץ אַשּׁוּר וְהוֹשַׁבְתִּים עַל־בָּתֵּיהֶם
יב א נְאֻם־יהוה: סְבָבֻנִי בְכַחַשׁ אֶפְרַיִם וּבְמִרְמָה בֵּית

VAYETZE

The prophet Hoshea accompanied the kings of Israel at the height of their power, from the reign of Yorovam son of Yoash (the greatest of the kings of the dynasty of Yehu) until the destruction during the reign of Hoshea son of Ela. At that time, the Assyrian Empire conquered the entire Levant. The prophet Hoshea (and others such as Yeshayahu, Amos, and Mikha) tried to prevent the fall of the kingdom of Israel. He called upon the Israelites to abandon their idolatrous ways and return to worship God. The verses of this *haftara* hint at events in Yaakov's life. The thread tying them together is God's providential guardianship over Yaakov in his struggles against Esav and Lavan. This providence was the secret to Yaakov's success in his lifetime, and it extends to all of his descendants even after his death. Because of this, the

2 faithful to the Holy One. Efrayim shepherds the wind; he chases
the east winds. Day and night he increases lies and ruin; he makes
3 pacts with Assyria and to Egypt bears oil. But also with Yehuda
the LORD has a dispute: He will visit upon Yaakov as he deserves,
4 as befits his deeds – He will repay him. In the womb he grasped
his brother by the heel, and with all his strength he struggled
5 with God. He struggled with an angel and prevailed; he cried
and pleaded with him; in Beit El He found him, and there He
6 spoke to us. But the LORD, God of Hosts, the LORD is His name.
7 Now you, too, return to your God, uphold compassion and
8 justice, and long for your God forever more. Still the merchant
9 possesses false scales; he loves to exploit. Efrayim exclaims, "I
have become wealthy; I have found fortune from my own labors;
in all the fruits of my toil they will find neither sin nor iniquity."
10 I am the LORD your God from the time you were in the land
of Egypt; once more I will settle you safely in tents as in days
11 of old. I have spoken by way of the prophets; I endowed them
with many visions, and through images I communicated with
12 the prophets. As Gilad is rampant with iniquity, so too they are
empty and vain; in Gilgal they sacrifice oxen, and their altars too
13 will become like rocks piled high in furrows of the fields. *Yaakov *Some end here*
fled to the lands of Aram, and Yisrael labored to acquire a bride;
14 for a bride he kept sheep. *With a prophet the LORD brought *Ashkenazim begin here*
Israel up out of Egypt, and with a prophet He kept watch over us.*
15 Efrayim has provoked bitter anger; the guilt from the blood he *Yemenites and Chabad end here*
shed will remain, and the Lord will turn his scorn back upon him.
13 1 So it was: when Efrayim spoke, they trembled in fear; he was
esteemed in Israel, but when found guilty of worshipping Baal,
2 he was as dead. Now their sinning goes on and on; they cast
graven images from their silver, mold idols as they understood,
each entirely the craft of men; of them they say, "Men who of-
3 fer sacrifices must kiss calves." So they will dissolve like morning mist, like dew at daybreak that swiftly fades. They will scatter
like chaff from the threshing floor, like smoke from the window.
4 I am the LORD your God from the land of Egypt; you know no
5 God other than Me; no one can save you except for Me. I knew
6 you, cared for you in the desert, in the parched, bereft land.* But *Sepharadim end here*
when they grazed, they became sated and satisfied; their hearts
7 became haughty – then they forgot Me. Therefore l will be as
8 a lion to them; as a leopard I will watch, lurking on the path. I

ב יִשְׂרָאֵל וִיהוּדָה עֹד רָד עִם־אֵל וְעִם־קְדוֹשִׁים נֶאֱמָן: אֶפְרַיִם
רֹעֶה רוּחַ וְרֹדֵף קָדִים כָּל־הַיּוֹם כָּזָב וָשֹׁד יַרְבֶּה וּבְרִית עִם־
ג אַשּׁוּר יִכְרֹתוּ וְשֶׁמֶן לְמִצְרַיִם יוּבָל: וְרִיב לַיהוָה עִם־יְהוּדָה
ד וְלִפְקֹד עַל־יַעֲקֹב כִּדְרָכָיו כְּמַעֲלָלָיו יָשִׁיב לוֹ: בַּבֶּטֶן עָקַב
ה אֶת־אָחִיו וּבְאוֹנוֹ שָׂרָה אֶת־אֱלֹהִים: וַיָּשַׂר אֶל־מַלְאָךְ וַיֻּכָל
ו בָּכָה וַיִּתְחַנֶּן־לוֹ בֵּית־אֵל יִמְצָאֶנּוּ וְשָׁם יְדַבֵּר עִמָּנוּ: וַיהוָה
ז אֱלֹהֵי הַצְּבָאוֹת יְהוָה זִכְרוֹ: וְאַתָּה בֵּאלֹהֶיךָ תָשׁוּב חֶסֶד
ח וּמִשְׁפָּט שְׁמֹר וְקַוֵּה אֶל־אֱלֹהֶיךָ תָּמִיד: כְּנַעַן בְּיָדוֹ מֹאזְנֵי
ט מִרְמָה לַעֲשֹׁק אָהֵב: וַיֹּאמֶר אֶפְרַיִם אַךְ עָשַׁרְתִּי מָצָאתִי
י אוֹן לִי כָּל־יְגִיעַי לֹא יִמְצְאוּ־לִי עָוֺן אֲשֶׁר־חֵטְא: וְאָנֹכִי יְהוָה
אֱלֹהֶיךָ מֵאֶרֶץ מִצְרָיִם עֹד אוֹשִׁיבְךָ בָאֳהָלִים כִּימֵי מוֹעֵד:
יא וְדִבַּרְתִּי עַל־הַנְּבִיאִים וְאָנֹכִי חָזוֹן הִרְבֵּיתִי וּבְיַד הַנְּבִיאִים
יב אֲדַמֶּה: אִם־גִּלְעָד אָוֶן אַךְ־שָׁוְא הָיוּ בַּגִּלְגָּל שְׁוָרִים זִבֵּחוּ
Some end here
Ashkenazim begin here
יג גַּם מִזְבְּחוֹתָם כְּגַלִּים עַל תַּלְמֵי שָׂדָי: * וַיִּבְרַח יַעֲקֹב שְׂדֵה
יד אֲרָם וַיַּעֲבֹד יִשְׂרָאֵל בְּאִשָּׁה וּבְאִשָּׁה שָׁמָר: וּבְנָבִיא הֶעֱלָה
Yemenites and Chabad end here
טו יְהוָה אֶת־יִשְׂרָאֵל מִמִּצְרָיִם וּבְנָבִיא נִשְׁמָר: * הִכְעִיס אֶפְרַיִם
יג א תַּמְרוּרִים וְדָמָיו עָלָיו יִטּוֹשׁ וְחֶרְפָּתוֹ יָשִׁיב לוֹ אֲדֹנָיו: כְּדַבֵּר
ב אֶפְרַיִם רְתֵת נָשָׂא הוּא בְּיִשְׂרָאֵל וַיֶּאְשַׁם בַּבַּעַל וַיָּמֹת: וְעַתָּה
יוֹסִפוּ לַחֲטֹא וַיַּעֲשׂוּ לָהֶם מַסֵּכָה מִכַּסְפָּם כִּתְבוּנָם עֲצַבִּים
מַעֲשֵׂה חָרָשִׁים כֻּלֹּה לָהֶם הֵם אֹמְרִים זֹבְחֵי אָדָם עֲגָלִים
ג יִשָּׁקוּן: לָכֵן יִהְיוּ כַּעֲנַן־בֹּקֶר וְכַטַּל מַשְׁכִּים הֹלֵךְ כְּמֹץ יְסֹעֵר
ד מִגֹּרֶן וּכְעָשָׁן מֵאֲרֻבָּה: וְאָנֹכִי יְהוָה אֱלֹהֶיךָ מֵאֶרֶץ מִצְרָיִם
ה וֵאלֹהִים זוּלָתִי לֹא תֵדָע וּמוֹשִׁיעַ אַיִן בִּלְתִּי: אֲנִי יְדַעְתִּיךָ
Sepharadim end here
ו בַּמִּדְבָּר בְּאֶרֶץ תַּלְאֻבוֹת: * כְּמַרְעִיתָם וַיִּשְׂבָּעוּ שָׂבְעוּ וַיָּרָם
ז לִבָּם עַל־כֵּן שְׁכֵחוּנִי: וָאֱהִי לָהֶם כְּמוֹ־שָׁחַל כְּנָמֵר עַל־

will fall upon them like a bear who mourns her whelps and tear
apart their sealed hearts; there I will consume them like a lion;
9 wild beasts will shred them to pieces. You have brought ruin
10 upon yourself, Israel, for your help is to be found in Me. I am
your King, then who will save you in all your cities, and what
of your judges of whom you said, "Appoint me a king and offi-
11 cers"? In My rage I gave you a king, and in My wrath I will take
12 him away. The sinfulness of Efrayim is tied together;
13 his sins are stored away. Pangs of birth will overcome him, but
he is not a wise son, for when the moment of birth comes, he
14 will break and not survive. I will rescue them from Sheol; I will
redeem them from the clutches of death. I shall be your plague,
O Death; I will be your destruction, O Sheol; any qualms will
15 be concealed from My eyes. For though he will flourish wildly
among the reeds, an east wind will come; a gust from the Lord
will rise from the wilderness. His fountain will dry up; his spring
14 1 will parch; his enemy will plunder all of his treasures. Shomron
will be held guilty, for she has rebelled against her God; she
will fall by the sword, her young smashed to pieces, her women
2 with child ripped apart. O Israel, return, go back to the
Lord your God, for you have stumbled in your own sinfulness.
3 Take words of remorse with you and return to the Lord; say
to Him, "Forgive all of our sins; accept our goodness – instead
4 of calves we offer You our words of prayer. Assyria will not save
us; no more will we ride upon horses; never again will we say,
'You are our god' to the work of our hands, for only in You will
5 the orphan find mercy." I will mend their rebellion with gracious
6 love, for I have turned My anger away from them. I will be as
dew to Israel; he will bloom like a lily and set down roots as
7 deep as the trees of Lebanon. His branches will spread wide; his
splendor will be as the olive tree, and his fragrance as the trees
8 of Lebanon. They who return will dwell beneath his shade; they
will revive once again as grain and flower like vines; their acclaim
9 will linger as the scent of the wine of Lebanon. Efrayim will say,
"What need do I have of these idols?" And I will answer him; I
will look after him. I will be as a cypress tree, lush and leafy; you
10 will find in Me your source of fruit. He who is wise will fathom
these words; the insightful will grasp them, for the ways of the
Lord are just, and the righteous will walk in them, but sinners
will stumble over them.

ח דֶּרֶךְ אַשּׁוּר׃ אֶפְגְּשֵׁם כְּדֹב שַׁכּוּל וְאֶקְרַע סְגוֹר לִבָּם וְאֹכְלֵם
ט שָׁם כְּלָבִיא חַיַּת הַשָּׂדֶה תְּבַקְּעֵם׃ שִׁחֶתְךָ יִשְׂרָאֵל כִּי־בִי
י בְעֶזְרֶךָ׃ אֱהִי מַלְכְּךָ אֵפוֹא וְיוֹשִׁיעֲךָ בְּכָל־עָרֶיךָ וְשֹׁפְטֶיךָ
יא אֲשֶׁר אָמַרְתָּ תְּנָה־לִּי מֶלֶךְ וְשָׂרִים׃ אֶתֶּן־לְךָ מֶלֶךְ בְּאַפִּי
יב וְאֶקַּח בְּעֶבְרָתִי׃ צָרוּר עֲוֺן אֶפְרָיִם צְפוּנָה
יג חַטָּאתוֹ׃ חֶבְלֵי יוֹלֵדָה יָבֹאוּ לוֹ הוּא־בֵן לֹא חָכָם כִּי־עֵת
יד לֹא־יַעֲמֹד בְּמִשְׁבַּר בָּנִים׃ מִיַּד שְׁאוֹל אֶפְדֵּם מִמָּוֶת אֶגְאָלֵם
אֱהִי דְבָרֶיךָ מָוֶת אֱהִי קָטָבְךָ שְׁאוֹל נֹחַם יִסָּתֵר מֵעֵינָי׃
טו כִּי הוּא בֵּין אַחִים יַפְרִיא יָבוֹא קָדִים רוּחַ יְהוָה מִמִּדְבָּר
עֹלֶה וְיֵבוֹשׁ מְקוֹרוֹ וְיֶחֱרַב מַעְיָנוֹ הוּא יִשְׁסֶה אוֹצַר כָּל־
יד א כְּלִי חֶמְדָּה׃ תֶּאְשַׁם שֹׁמְרוֹן כִּי מָרְתָה בֵּאלֹהֶיהָ בַּחֶרֶב
ב יִפֹּלוּ עֹלְלֵיהֶם יְרֻטָּשׁוּ וְהָרִיּוֹתָיו יְבֻקָּעוּ׃ שׁוּבָה
ג יִשְׂרָאֵל עַד יְהוָה אֱלֹהֶיךָ כִּי כָשַׁלְתָּ בַּעֲוֺנֶךָ׃ קְחוּ עִמָּכֶם
דְּבָרִים וְשׁוּבוּ אֶל־יְהוָה אִמְרוּ אֵלָיו כָּל־תִּשָּׂא עָוֺן וְקַח־טוֹב
ד וּנְשַׁלְּמָה פָרִים שְׂפָתֵינוּ׃ אַשּׁוּר ׀ לֹא יוֹשִׁיעֵנוּ עַל־סוּס לֹא
נִרְכָּב וְלֹא־נֹאמַר עוֹד אֱלֹהֵינוּ לְמַעֲשֵׂה יָדֵינוּ אֲשֶׁר־בְּךָ
ה יְרֻחַם יָתוֹם׃ אֶרְפָּא מְשׁוּבָתָם אֹהֲבֵם נְדָבָה כִּי שָׁב אַפִּי
ו מִמֶּנּוּ׃ אֶהְיֶה כַטַּל לְיִשְׂרָאֵל יִפְרַח כַּשּׁוֹשַׁנָּה וְיַךְ שָׁרָשָׁיו
ז כַּלְּבָנוֹן׃ יֵלְכוּ יֹנְקוֹתָיו וִיהִי כַזַּיִת הוֹדוֹ וְרֵיחַ לוֹ כַּלְּבָנוֹן׃
ח יָשֻׁבוּ יֹשְׁבֵי בְצִלּוֹ יְחַיּוּ דָגָן וְיִפְרְחוּ כַגָּפֶן זִכְרוֹ כְּיֵין לְבָנוֹן׃
ט אֶפְרַיִם מַה־לִּי עוֹד לָעֲצַבִּים אֲנִי עָנִיתִי וַאֲשׁוּרֶנּוּ אֲנִי כִּבְרוֹשׁ
י רַעֲנָן מִמֶּנִּי פֶּרְיְךָ נִמְצָא׃ מִי חָכָם וְיָבֵן אֵלֶּה נָבוֹן וְיֵדָעֵם
כִּי־יְשָׁרִים דַּרְכֵי יְהוָה וְצַדִּקִים יֵלְכוּ בָם וּפֹשְׁעִים יִכָּשְׁלוּ
בָם׃

2 26 You will eat, eat and be sated, and you will praise the name of
the LORD, your God, who has done wonders for you, for My na-
27 tion will never be ashamed. You will know that I am among Israel,
and I am the LORD, your God; there is no other. My nation will
never be ashamed.

YOEL
Some add

HAFTARAT VAYISHLAḤ

1 1 This is Ovadya's vision: So says the Lord GOD to Edom – we
have heard tidings from the LORD: and an envoy has been
sent among the nations, "Come, let us rise up in battle against
2 her." Look, I have made you small among nations; you are ut-
3 terly scorned. The arrogance of your heart deceived you, you
who dwell in the cliff's niches, your lofty abode, saying in
4 your heart, "Who could bring me down to earth?" But even if
you rise as high as an eagle, if you make your nest among the
5 stars, I shall bring you down from there, declares the LORD. If
thieves come upon you, bandits in the night, do they not take
only their fill? If grape gatherers come upon you, do they not
6 leave gleanings? Yet how has Esav been ransacked, his hidden
7 treasures laid bare. Your allies all have forced you to the borders; those with whom you had made peace all deceived you,
defeated you. Those with whom you broke your bread laid a
8 snare for you, bereft of awareness. Behold, on that day, says
the LORD, I will purge Edom of wise men, the mountains of
9 Esav of awareness. Your warriors will be frightened, Teiman,
10 for the mountains of Esav will be unmanned by slaughter. For
the violence you wrought against your brother Yaakov shame
11 will cover you, and you will be cut off forever. The day you
stood aside, the day strangers took captive his forces, and
foreigners entered his gates, casting lots for Jerusalem – you

OBADIAH
For Ashkenazim, Sepharadim, and Yemenites

---

a symbol of baseless hatred of Israel. The eradication of this hatred is part of the process of the world's redemption: "And saviors shall go up to Mount Zion to judge the mountains of Esav, and dominion shall be the LORD's." The exact time of Ovadya's life is unknown, but his words accurately reflect the atmosphere during the period of Jerusalem's destruction by the Babylonians.

יואל
Some add

ב כו וַאֲכַלְתֶּם אָכוֹל וְשָׂבוֹעַ וְהִלַּלְתֶּם אֶת־שֵׁם יהוה אֱלֹהֵיכֶם
אֲשֶׁר־עָשָׂה עִמָּכֶם לְהַפְלִיא וְלֹא־יֵבֹשׁוּ עַמִּי לְעוֹלָם׃
כז וִידַעְתֶּם כִּי בְקֶרֶב יִשְׂרָאֵל אָנִי וַאֲנִי יהוה אֱלֹהֵיכֶם וְאֵין
עוֹד וְלֹא־יֵבֹשׁוּ עַמִּי לְעוֹלָם׃

הפטרת וישלח

עובדיה
For Ashkenazim, Sephardim, and Yemenites

א א חֲזוֹן עֹבַדְיָה כֹּה־אָמַר אֲדֹנָי יֱהוִה לֶאֱדוֹם שְׁמוּעָה שָׁמַעְנוּ
מֵאֵת יהוה וְצִיר בַּגּוֹיִם שֻׁלָּח קוּמוּ וְנָקוּמָה עָלֶיהָ לַמִּלְחָמָה׃
ב ג הִנֵּה קָטֹן נְתַתִּיךָ בַּגּוֹיִם בָּזוּי אַתָּה מְאֹד׃ זְדוֹן לִבְּךָ הִשִּׁיאֶךָ
שֹׁכְנִי בְחַגְוֵי־סֶלַע מְרוֹם שִׁבְתּוֹ אֹמֵר בְּלִבּוֹ מִי יוֹרִדֵנִי אָרֶץ׃
ד אִם־תַּגְבִּיהַּ כַּנֶּשֶׁר וְאִם־בֵּין כּוֹכָבִים שִׂים קִנֶּךָ מִשָּׁם אוֹרִידְךָ
ה נְאֻם־יהוה׃ אִם־גַּנָּבִים בָּאוּ־לְךָ אִם־שׁוֹדְדֵי לַיְלָה אֵיךְ
נִדְמֵיתָה הֲלוֹא יִגְנְבוּ דַּיָּם אִם־בֹּצְרִים בָּאוּ לָךְ הֲלוֹא יַשְׁאִירוּ
ו ז עֹלֵלוֹת׃ אֵיךְ נֶחְפְּשׂוּ עֵשָׂו נִבְעוּ מַצְפֻּנָיו׃ עַד־הַגְּבוּל שִׁלְּחוּךָ
כֹּל אַנְשֵׁי בְרִיתֶךָ הִשִּׁיאוּךָ יָכְלוּ לְךָ אַנְשֵׁי שְׁלֹמֶךָ לַחְמְךָ
ח יָשִׂימוּ מָזוֹר תַּחְתֶּיךָ אֵין תְּבוּנָה בּוֹ׃ הֲלוֹא בַּיּוֹם הַהוּא נְאֻם־
ט יהוה וְהַאֲבַדְתִּי חֲכָמִים מֵאֱדוֹם וּתְבוּנָה מֵהַר עֵשָׂו׃ וְחַתּוּ
י גִבּוֹרֶיךָ תֵּימָן לְמַעַן יִכָּרֶת־אִישׁ מֵהַר עֵשָׂו מִקָּטֶל׃ מֵחֲמַס
יא אָחִיךָ יַעֲקֹב תְּכַסְּךָ בוּשָׁה וְנִכְרַתָּ לְעוֹלָם׃ בְּיוֹם עֲמָדְךָ מִנֶּגֶד
בְּיוֹם שְׁבוֹת זָרִים חֵילוֹ וְנָכְרִים בָּאוּ שְׁעָרָו וְעַל־יְרוּשָׁלַםִ יַדּוּ

VAYISHLAḤ

The relationship between Yaakov and Esav has become symbolic of the tension between Israel and the peoples of the world. In this *haftara*, the prophet Ovadya describes the cruelty of the nation Edom (Esav's descendants) to the neighboring people of Yehuda. Edom has allied itself with the enemy besieging Jerusalem, attacked refugees from Yehuda, and taken part in its plunder. This arrogant and willful behavior betrays the natural feelings of brotherhood that cousin peoples should feel for each other. It is no coincidence that Esav has become an enemy to Yaakov,

12 too were like one of them. Do not gloat over the day of your
brother's destruction, the day he becomes a stranger. Do not
rejoice over the children of Yehuda on the day of their destruc-
13 tion. Do not open your mouth on the day of trouble. Do not
enter My people's gate on the day of their ruin. Do not gloat
over its misfortune on the day of its ruin. Do not extend your
14 hands to take its wealth on the day of his ruin. Do not stand
at the crossroads to cut down his refugees. Do not surrender
15 his survivors on the day of trouble. For the day of the Lord
draws near for all the nations. What you have done shall be
done to you; what you have wrought will return upon your
16 head. What you drank on My holy mountain, all the nations
will always drink. They will drink and they will swallow, and
17 they will be as if they never were. There will be a remnant on
Mount Zion, and it will be holy, and the House of Yaakov will
18 possess their inheritance. The House of Yaakov will be fire,
the House of Yosef, flame; the House of Esav, straw. They will
blaze among them and consume them, and there will be no
19 survivors of the House of Esav, for the Lord has spoken. They
will take possession of the Negev, along with the mountains of
Esav, and the Shefela, from the Philistines. And they will take
possession of the land of Efrayim and the land of Shomron;
20 and Binyamin, along with the Gilad – they, the exiled force of
the children of Israel who are among the Canaanites as far as
Tzarfat and the exiled of Jerusalem who are in Sepharad will
21 take possession of the cities of the Negev. And saviors shall go
up to Mount Zion to judge the mountains of Esav, and dominion shall be the Lord's.

HOSEA
For Minhag Anglia

11 7 My people waver – whether to turn back to Me, although Israel
8 is summoned upward, they will not praise Him together. How
can I relinquish you, Efrayim; hand you over, Israel? How can I
make you like Adma and treat you like Tzevoyim? My heart has
9 turned upon Me; My compassion has been kindled. No, I will
not unleash My burning wrath, I will not turn again to destroy
Efrayim – for I am God, I am not a man; within you, My holiness
10 dwells; I will not enter the city with hatred. They will follow after
the Lord; He will roar like a lion. When He roars, His children
11 will rush forth from the west. They will be like a frightened bird

יב גּוֹרָל גַּם־אַתָּה כְּאַחַד מֵהֶם׃ וְאַל־תֵּרֶא בְיוֹם־אָחִיךָ בְּיוֹם
נָכְרוֹ וְאַל־תִּשְׂמַח לִבְנֵי־יְהוּדָה בְּיוֹם אָבְדָם וְאַל־תַּגְדֵּל
יג פִּיךָ בְּיוֹם צָרָה׃ אַל־תָּבוֹא בְשַׁעַר־עַמִּי בְּיוֹם אֵידָם אַל־
תֵּרֶא גַם־אַתָּה בְּרָעָתוֹ בְּיוֹם אֵידוֹ וְאַל־תִּשְׁלַחְנָה בְחֵילוֹ
יד בְּיוֹם אֵידוֹ׃ וְאַל־תַּעֲמֹד עַל־הַפֶּרֶק לְהַכְרִית אֶת־פְּלִיטָיו
טו וְאַל־תַּסְגֵּר שְׂרִידָיו בְּיוֹם צָרָה׃ כִּי־קָרוֹב יוֹם־יְהוָה עַל־
כָּל־הַגּוֹיִם כַּאֲשֶׁר עָשִׂיתָ יֵעָשֶׂה לָּךְ גְּמֻלְךָ יָשׁוּב בְּרֹאשֶׁךָ׃
טז כִּי כַּאֲשֶׁר שְׁתִיתֶם עַל־הַר קָדְשִׁי יִשְׁתּוּ כָל־הַגּוֹיִם תָּמִיד
יז וְשָׁתוּ וְלָעוּ וְהָיוּ כְּלוֹא הָיוּ׃ וּבְהַר צִיּוֹן תִּהְיֶה פְלֵיטָה וְהָיָה
יח קֹדֶשׁ וְיָרְשׁוּ בֵּית יַעֲקֹב אֵת מוֹרָשֵׁיהֶם׃ וְהָיָה בֵית־יַעֲקֹב
אֵשׁ וּבֵית יוֹסֵף לֶהָבָה וּבֵית עֵשָׂו לְקַשׁ וְדָלְקוּ בָהֶם וַאֲכָלוּם
יט וְלֹא־יִהְיֶה שָׂרִיד לְבֵית עֵשָׂו כִּי יְהוָה דִּבֵּר׃ וְיָרְשׁוּ הַנֶּגֶב
אֶת־הַר עֵשָׂו וְהַשְּׁפֵלָה אֶת־פְּלִשְׁתִּים וְיָרְשׁוּ אֶת־שְׂדֵה
כ אֶפְרַיִם וְאֵת שְׂדֵה שֹׁמְרוֹן וּבִנְיָמִן אֶת־הַגִּלְעָד׃ וְגָלֻת הַחֵל־
הַזֶּה לִבְנֵי יִשְׂרָאֵל אֲשֶׁר־כְּנַעֲנִים עַד־צָרְפַת וְגָלֻת יְרוּשָׁלִַם
כא אֲשֶׁר בִּסְפָרַד יִרְשׁוּ אֵת עָרֵי הַנֶּגֶב׃ וְעָלוּ מוֹשִׁעִים בְּהַר צִיּוֹן
לִשְׁפֹּט אֶת־הַר עֵשָׂו וְהָיְתָה לַיהוָה הַמְּלוּכָה׃

הושע

For Minhag Anglia

יא ז וְעַמִּי תְלוּאִים לִמְשׁוּבָתִי וְאֶל־עַל יִקְרָאֻהוּ יַחַד לֹא יְרוֹמֵם׃
ח אֵיךְ אֶתֶּנְךָ אֶפְרַיִם אֲמַגֶּנְךָ יִשְׂרָאֵל אֵיךְ אֶתֶּנְךָ כְאַדְמָה
ט אֲשִׂימְךָ כִּצְבֹאיִם נֶהְפַּךְ עָלַי לִבִּי יַחַד נִכְמְרוּ נִחוּמָי׃ לֹא
אֶעֱשֶׂה חֲרוֹן אַפִּי לֹא אָשׁוּב לְשַׁחֵת אֶפְרָיִם כִּי אֵל אָנֹכִי
י וְלֹא־אִישׁ בְּקִרְבְּךָ קָדוֹשׁ וְלֹא אָבוֹא בְּעִיר׃ אַחֲרֵי יְהוָה
יא יֵלְכוּ כְּאַרְיֵה יִשְׁאָג כִּי־הוּא יִשְׁאַג וְיֶחֶרְדוּ בָנִים מִיָּם׃ יֶחֶרְדוּ

coming out of Egypt, like a dove leaving the land of Assyria. I
will bring them to settle safely in their homes. So declares the
12 1 Lord. Efrayim besieges Me with lies, the House of
Israel with deception, but Yehuda still walks with God and re-
2 mains faithful to the Holy One. Efrayim shepherds the wind; he
chases the east winds. Day and night he increases lies and ruin;
3 he makes pacts with Assyria and to Egypt bears oil. But also with
Yehuda the Lord has a dispute: He will visit upon Yaakov as he
4 deserves, as befits his deeds – He will repay him. In the womb
he grasped his brother by the heel, and with all his strength he
5 struggled with God. He struggled with an angel and prevailed;
he cried and pleaded with him; in Beit El He found him, and
6 there He spoke to us. But the Lord, God of Hosts, the Lord
7 is His name. Now you, too, return to your God, uphold com-
8 passion and justice, and long for your God forever more. Still
9 the merchant possesses false scales; he loves to exploit. Efrayim
exclaims, "I have become wealthy; I have found fortune from
my own labors; in all the fruits of my toil they will find neither
10 sin nor iniquity." I am the Lord your God from the time you
were in the land of Egypt; once more I will settle you safely in
11 tents as in days of old. I have spoken by way of the prophets; I
endowed them with many visions, and through images I com-
12 municated with the prophets. As Gilad is rampant with iniquity,
so too they are empty and vain; in Gilgal they sacrifice oxen, and
their altars too will become like rocks piled high in furrows of
the fields.

Haftarat Vayeshev

On Ḥanukka, read the maftir from Numbers chapter 7 (Sepharadim and Yemenites begin at 6:22), and the haftara on *page 1648.*

2 6 So says the Lord: On account of Israel's three crimes and on AMOS
account of the fourth, I will not forgive them. They sold the righ-
7 teous for silver and the poor for the price of shoes. They are those
who trample the dust of the earth atop the heads of the poor; they

---

ben Yoash king of Israel. Both monarchs ruled for decades. Due to this stability, their commonwealths were strong and wealthy. Amos sounded his call in

כְצִפּוֹר מִמִּצְרַיִם וּכְיוֹנָה מֵאֶרֶץ אַשּׁוּר וְהוֹשַׁבְתִּים עַל־בָּתֵּיהֶם

יב א נְאֻם־יְהוָה׃ סְבָבֻנִי בְכַחַשׁ אֶפְרַיִם וּבְמִרְמָה

בֵּית יִשְׂרָאֵל וִיהוּדָה עֹד רָד עִם־אֵל וְעִם־קְדוֹשִׁים נֶאֱמָן׃

ב אֶפְרַיִם רֹעֶה רוּחַ וְרֹדֵף קָדִים כָּל־הַיּוֹם כָּזָב וָשֹׁד יַרְבֶּה

ג וּבְרִית עִם־אַשּׁוּר יִכְרֹתוּ וְשֶׁמֶן לְמִצְרַיִם יוּבָל׃ וְרִיב לַיהוָה

עִם־יְהוּדָה וְלִפְקֹד עַל־יַעֲקֹב כִּדְרָכָיו כְּמַעֲלָלָיו יָשִׁיב לוֹ׃

ד ה בַּבֶּטֶן עָקַב אֶת־אָחִיו וּבְאוֹנוֹ שָׂרָה אֶת־אֱלֹהִים׃ וַיָּשַׂר אֶל־

מַלְאָךְ וַיֻּכָל בָּכָה וַיִּתְחַנֶּן־לוֹ בֵּית־אֵל יִמְצָאֶנּוּ וְשָׁם יְדַבֵּר

ו ז עִמָּנוּ׃ וַיהוָה אֱלֹהֵי הַצְּבָאוֹת יְהוָה זִכְרוֹ׃ וְאַתָּה בֵּאלֹהֶיךָ

ח תָשׁוּב חֶסֶד וּמִשְׁפָּט שְׁמֹר וְקַוֵּה אֶל־אֱלֹהֶיךָ תָּמִיד׃ כְּנַעַן

ט בְּיָדוֹ מֹאזְנֵי מִרְמָה לַעֲשֹׁק אָהֵב׃ וַיֹּאמֶר אֶפְרַיִם אַךְ עָשַׁרְתִּי

מָצָאתִי אוֹן לִי כָּל־יְגִיעַי לֹא יִמְצְאוּ־לִי עָוֺן אֲשֶׁר־חֵטְא׃

י וְאָנֹכִי יְהוָה אֱלֹהֶיךָ מֵאֶרֶץ מִצְרָיִם עֹד אוֹשִׁיבְךָ בָאֳהָלִים

יא כִּימֵי מוֹעֵד׃ וְדִבַּרְתִּי עַל־הַנְּבִיאִים וְאָנֹכִי חָזוֹן הִרְבֵּיתִי וּבְיַד

יב הַנְּבִיאִים אֲדַמֶּה׃ אִם־גִּלְעָד אָוֶן אַךְ־שָׁוְא הָיוּ בַּגִּלְגָּל שְׁוָרִים

זִבֵּחוּ גַּם מִזְבְּחוֹתָם כְּגַלִּים עַל תַּלְמֵי שָׂדָי׃

הפטרת וישב

On חנוכה *read the* מפטיר *from* במדבר ז *(Sepharadim and Yemenites begin at* ו, כב*), and the* הפטרה *on page 1649.*

עמוס

ב ו כֹּה אָמַר יְהוָה עַל־שְׁלֹשָׁה פִּשְׁעֵי יִשְׂרָאֵל וְעַל־אַרְבָּעָה

לֹא אֲשִׁיבֶנּוּ עַל־מִכְרָם בַּכֶּסֶף צַדִּיק וְאֶבְיוֹן בַּעֲבוּר נַעֲלָיִם׃

ז הַשֹּׁאֲפִים עַל־עֲפַר־אֶרֶץ בְּרֹאשׁ דַּלִּים וְדֶרֶךְ עֲנָוִים יַטּוּ

VAYESHEV

Amos prophesied at the height of the Israelite kingdoms' power – the reigns of Uziyahu king of Yehuda and Yorovam

▶

turn the humble away from the path. A man and his father visit
8 the same girl to desecrate My holy name. They spread confiscat-
ed clothing beside every altar and drink wine bought with fines
9 in the house of their gods. But I had destroyed before them the
Amorite, whose height was as tall as cedars and whose strength
was like that of oaks. Yet I obliterated their fruit above and their
10 roots below. I brought you up from the land of Egypt and led
11 you in the desert for forty years to inherit Amorite lands. I raised
up into prophets some of your sons and into nazirites some of
your young men. Is this not so, children of Israel? said the LORD.
12 But you made the nazirites drink wine and ordered the prophets
13 not to prophesy. Behold, I will hold you back in your place, as a
14 wagon loaded with sheaves is held back. The swift will lose the
ability to flee; the strong will not gather their strength; the war-
15 rior will not escape with his life. The bowman will not stand; the
fleet of foot will not escape; the horse rider will not escape with
16 his life. He who considers himself strongest among warriors will
3 1 flee naked on that day, says the LORD. Hear this word,
which the LORD has spoken about you, children of Israel: About
2 the whole family I brought up from the land of Egypt, it is only
you that I have known from among all the families on earth, so I
3 will visit all your sins upon you. Would two walk together if they
4 had not met? Would a lion roar in the forest if it had not caught
prey? Would a young lion raise its voice from its den if it had not
5 seized prey? Would a bird plunge into a trap on the ground if it
were not baited? Would the trap spring up from the earth if it
6 had not trapped quarry? Would a warning horn blow in the city
and the people not be afraid? Would disaster come upon the city
7 were it not an act of the LORD? The Lord GOD does not do anything without revealing His secret to His servants, the prophets.
8 A lion roars; who would not fear?

---

coming to terms with our failures and accepting responsibility for correcting them. Ignoring the distorted and corrupt reality, denying our failures, only perpetuates them and ultimately leads to ruin. The *haftara* ends with a series of seven rhetorical questions. Each of them presents a necessary connection between a cause and an outcome. Anyone who cannot understand the causal connection between the state of society and the way it is run will come to destruction. "A lion roars; who would not fear?"

ואיש ואביו ילכו אל־הנערה למען חלל את־שם קדשי:
ח ועל־בגדים חבלים יטו אצל כל־מזבח ויין ענושים ישתו
ט בית אלהיהם: ואנכי השמדתי את־האמרי מפניהם אשר
כגבה ארזים גבהו וחסן הוא כאלונים ואשמיד פריו ממעל
י ושרשיו מתחת: ואנכי העליתי אתכם מארץ מצרים
ואולך אתכם במדבר ארבעים שנה לרשת את־ארץ
יא האמרי: ואקים מבניכם לנביאים ומבחוריכם לנזרים
יב האף אין־זאת בני ישראל נאם־יהוה: ותשקו את־הנזרים
יג יין ועל־הנביאים צויתם לאמר לא תנבאו: הנה אנכי
מעיק תחתיכם כאשר תעיק העגלה המלאה לה עמיר:
יד ואבד מנוס מקל וחזק לא־יאמץ כחו וגבור לא־ימלט
טו נפשו: ותפש הקשת לא יעמד וקל ברגליו לא ימלט
טז ורכב הסוס לא ימלט נפשו: ואמיץ לבו בגבורים ערום
ג א ינוס ביום־ההוא נאם־יהוה: שמעו את־הדבר
הזה אשר דבר יהוה עליכם בני ישראל על כל־המשפחה
ב אשר העליתי מארץ מצרים לאמר: רק אתכם ידעתי מכל
משפחות האדמה על־כן אפקד עליכם את כל־עונתיכם:
ג ד הילכו שנים יחדו בלתי אם־נועדו: הישאג אריה ביער
וטרף אין לו היתן כפיר קולו ממענתו בלתי אם־לכד:
ה התפל צפור על־פח הארץ ומוקש אין לה היעלה־פח מן־
ו האדמה ולכוד לא ילכוד: אם־יתקע שופר בעיר ועם לא
ז יחרדו אם־תהיה רעה בעיר ויהוה לא עשה: כי לא יעשה
אדני יהוה דבר כי אם־גלה סודו אל־עבדיו הנביאים:
ח אריה שאג מי לא יירא אדני יהוה דבר מי לא ינבא:

---

the kingdom of Israel, warning of the excesses of a lavish society, which lead to social and economic inequality and oppression. Such a society cannot endure.

At times, the reality in which we live can become corrupt. Despite the difficulties, it is possible to overcome this corruption, and there are fundamental conditions for accomplishing this: We must be courageously introspective,

HAFTARAT MIKETZ

On Ḥanukka, read the maftir from Numbers chapter 7, and the haftara on page 1652.

I KINGS

3 15 Then Shlomo awoke – it had all been a dream! When he came to
Jerusalem, he stood before the Ark of the Lord's Covenant and
offered up burnt offerings and presented peace offerings, and he
16 held a feast for all his servants. Then two harlot women
17 came before the king and stood before him. "If you please, my
lord," said the first woman, "this woman and I live in one house,
18 and I gave birth while she was in the house. On the third day
after I gave birth, this woman also gave birth. The two of us live
together – there was no one else in the house besides us, just the
19 two of us in the house. The son of this woman died in the night,
20 for she lay on him. But she got up during the night and took my
own son from me while your handmaid was sleeping and lay
down with him in her embrace, and laid her own dead son in my
21 embrace. I woke up in the morning to nurse my son to find that
he was dead! But when I looked at him closely in the morning,
22 why – it wasn't my own son, the one I had borne!" "No!" said
the other woman. "My son is the one who is alive, and your son
is the one who died!" "No," she said, "your son is dead, and my
23 son is alive!" and they continued arguing before the king. "This
one says, 'This is my son, who is alive, and your son is dead,'" said
the king, "and this one says, 'No, your son is dead, and my son is
24 alive.'" And the king said, "Fetch me a sword," and they
25 brought a sword before the king. "Cut the living child into two,"
26 the king declared, "and give half to one and half to the other." But
the woman whose son was alive spoke up, for she burned with
compassion for her son. "Please, my lord," she said, "give her the
living child; do anything but kill him!" while the other one said,

---

women of this low station would come to him for judgment; they knew that they would be given a serious and fair hearing by the king. Secondly, the legal challenge confronting Shlomo: Courts can only decide cases based on evidence. But here, there was no one to testify who was the true mother of the child. A king, however, has the right to issue rulings based on circumstantial evidence, such as a mother's instinctive psychological reactions. This story teaches us about the wondrous blessing inherent in worthy and wise leadership.

הפטרת מקץ

On חנוכה *read the* מפטיר *from* במדבר ז, *and the* הפטרה *on page 1653.*

ג טו וַיִּקַץ שְׁלֹמֹה וְהִנֵּה חֲלוֹם וַיָּבוֹא יְרוּשָׁלַ͏ִם וַיַּעֲמֹד ׀ לִפְנֵי | מלכים א׳
אֲרוֹן בְּרִית־אֲדֹנָי וַיַּעַל עֹלוֹת וַיַּעַשׂ שְׁלָמִים וַיַּעַשׂ מִשְׁתֶּה
טז לְכָל־עֲבָדָיו׃ אָז תָּבֹאנָה שְׁתַּיִם נָשִׁים זֹנוֹת
יז אֶל־הַמֶּלֶךְ וַתַּעֲמֹדְנָה לְפָנָיו׃ וַתֹּאמֶר הָאִשָּׁה הָאַחַת בִּי
אֲדֹנִי אֲנִי וְהָאִשָּׁה הַזֹּאת יֹשְׁבֹת בְּבַיִת אֶחָד וָאֵלֵד עִמָּהּ
יח בַּבָּיִת׃ וַיְהִי בַּיּוֹם הַשְּׁלִישִׁי לְלִדְתִּי וַתֵּלֶד גַּם־הָאִשָּׁה
הַזֹּאת וַאֲנַחְנוּ יַחְדָּו אֵין־זָר אִתָּנוּ בַּבַּיִת זוּלָתִי שְׁתַּיִם־
יט אֲנַחְנוּ בַּבָּיִת׃ וַיָּמָת בֶּן־הָאִשָּׁה הַזֹּאת לָיְלָה אֲשֶׁר שָׁכְבָה
כ עָלָיו׃ וַתָּקָם בְּתוֹךְ הַלַּיְלָה וַתִּקַּח אֶת־בְּנִי מֵאֶצְלִי וַאֲמָתְךָ
יְשֵׁנָה וַתַּשְׁכִּיבֵהוּ בְּחֵיקָהּ וְאֶת־בְּנָהּ הַמֵּת הִשְׁכִּיבָה בְחֵיקִי׃
כא וָאָקֻם בַּבֹּקֶר לְהֵינִיק אֶת־בְּנִי וְהִנֵּה־מֵת וָאֶתְבּוֹנֵן אֵלָיו
כב בַּבֹּקֶר וְהִנֵּה לֹא־הָיָה בְנִי אֲשֶׁר יָלָדְתִּי׃ וַתֹּאמֶר הָאִשָּׁה
הָאַחֶרֶת לֹא כִי בְּנִי הַחַי וּבְנֵךְ הַמֵּת וְזֹאת אֹמֶרֶת לֹא כִי
כג בְּנֵךְ הַמֵּת וּבְנִי הֶחָי וַתְּדַבֵּרְנָה לִפְנֵי הַמֶּלֶךְ׃ וַיֹּאמֶר הַמֶּלֶךְ
זֹאת אֹמֶרֶת זֶה־בְּנִי הַחַי וּבְנֵךְ הַמֵּת וְזֹאת אֹמֶרֶת לֹא כִי בְּנֵךְ
כד הַמֵּת וּבְנִי הֶחָי׃ וַיֹּאמֶר הַמֶּלֶךְ קְחוּ לִי־חָרֶב
כה וַיָּבִאוּ הַחֶרֶב לִפְנֵי הַמֶּלֶךְ׃ וַיֹּאמֶר הַמֶּלֶךְ גִּזְרוּ אֶת־הַיֶּלֶד
הַחַי לִשְׁנָיִם וּתְנוּ אֶת־הַחֲצִי לְאַחַת וְאֶת־הַחֲצִי לְאֶחָת׃
כו וַתֹּאמֶר הָאִשָּׁה אֲשֶׁר־בְּנָהּ הַחַי אֶל־הַמֶּלֶךְ כִּי־נִכְמְרוּ
רַחֲמֶיהָ עַל־בְּנָהּ וַתֹּאמֶר ׀ בִּי אֲדֹנִי תְּנוּ־לָהּ אֶת־הַיָּלוּד הַחַי
וְהָמֵת אַל־תְּמִיתֻהוּ וְזֹאת אֹמֶרֶת גַּם־לִי גַם־לָךְ לֹא יִהְיֶה

MIKETZ

The *haftara* describes a famous event from the beginning of the reign of King Shlomo. Two harlots come to the king, asking him to decide which of them is the true mother of a live child and which of a dead child. Two issues unique to this event emphasize the practical wisdom given to Shlomo by God, as he requested in his dream. Firstly, even

▶

27 "Neither of us will have him – cut him up." And the king spoke
up. "Give her the living child," he said, "and make no move to kill
28 him. She is his mother." When all of Israel heard about the case
that the king had judged, they held the king in awe, for they saw
4 1 that divine wisdom was within him to do justice. King Shlomo
was king of all Israel.

Haftarat Vayigash

37 15 16 The word of the Lord came to me, saying: "And you, Man, take EZEKIEL
a branch and write on it, 'For Yehuda and the children of Israel
associated with him.' Then take one branch and write on it, 'For
Yosef – the branch of Efrayim – and all of the House of Israel
17 associated with him.' Bring them together to make one branch,
18 so that they are one in your hand. When your people say to you,
19 'Tell us, what do these mean to you?' say to them: So says the
Lord God: See, I am going to take the branch of Yosef, which is
in the hand of Efrayim, and the tribes of Israel who are associated
with him, and join them with him, with the branch of Yehuda;
I will make them into one branch, and they will be one in My
20 hand. Let these branches that you write upon be in your hand
21 before their eyes. Speak to them: So says the Lord God: See that
I am taking the children of Israel from among the nations that
they went to; I will gather them from all around, and I will bring
22 them to their land. I will make them into one nation in the land,
in the mountains of Israel; one king will be king for all of them,
and they will no longer be two nations; they will no longer be

symbolic act from the field of agriculture: the grafting of a tree. When grafting, one joins the trunk of a strong, rooted tree with a branch of another tree that bears high-quality fruit, thus creating a hybrid better and stronger than both of the originals. This is the secret of "together," and it is the basis for many other aspects of the future redemption. These words, preached to those banished from their homes in Yehuda on the first occasion of destruction that affected the entire Jewish people (the Temple, the House of David, Jerusalem), breathed hope into the hearts of the people, and gave them the strength to carry on through their time of bitter crisis.

כז גְּזֹרוּ: וַיַּעַן הַמֶּלֶךְ וַיֹּאמֶר תְּנוּ־לָהּ אֶת־הַיָּלוּד הַחַי וְהָמֵת
כח לֹא תְמִיתֻהוּ הִיא אִמּוֹ: וַיִּשְׁמְעוּ כָל־יִשְׂרָאֵל אֶת־הַמִּשְׁפָּט
אֲשֶׁר שָׁפַט הַמֶּלֶךְ וַיִּרְאוּ מִפְּנֵי הַמֶּלֶךְ כִּי רָאוּ כִּי־חָכְמַת
ד א אֱלֹהִים בְּקִרְבּוֹ לַעֲשׂוֹת מִשְׁפָּט: וַיְהִי הַמֶּלֶךְ שְׁלֹמֹה מֶלֶךְ
עַל־כָּל־יִשְׂרָאֵל:

הפטרת ויגש

לז טו טז וַיְהִי דְבַר־יְהוָה אֵלַי לֵאמֹר: וְאַתָּה בֶן־אָדָם קַח־לְךָ עֵץ יחזקאל
אֶחָד וּכְתֹב עָלָיו לִיהוּדָה וְלִבְנֵי יִשְׂרָאֵל חֲבֵרָו וּלְקַח עֵץ
אֶחָד וּכְתוֹב עָלָיו לְיוֹסֵף עֵץ אֶפְרַיִם וְכָל־בֵּית יִשְׂרָאֵל חֲבֵרָו:
יז וְקָרַב אֹתָם אֶחָד אֶל־אֶחָד לְךָ לְעֵץ אֶחָד וְהָיוּ לַאֲחָדִים
יח בְּיָדֶךָ: וְכַאֲשֶׁר יֹאמְרוּ אֵלֶיךָ בְּנֵי עַמְּךָ לֵאמֹר הֲלוֹא־תַגִּיד
יט לָנוּ מָה־אֵלֶּה לָּךְ: דַּבֵּר אֲלֵהֶם כֹּה־אָמַר אֲדֹנָי יֱהֹוִה הִנֵּה
אֲנִי לֹקֵחַ אֶת־עֵץ יוֹסֵף אֲשֶׁר בְּיַד־אֶפְרַיִם וְשִׁבְטֵי יִשְׂרָאֵל
חֲבֵרָו וְנָתַתִּי אוֹתָם עָלָיו אֶת־עֵץ יְהוּדָה וַעֲשִׂיתִם לְעֵץ
כ אֶחָד וְהָיוּ אֶחָד בְּיָדִי: וְהָיוּ הָעֵצִים אֲשֶׁר־תִּכְתֹּב עֲלֵיהֶם
כא בְּיָדְךָ לְעֵינֵיהֶם: וְדַבֵּר אֲלֵיהֶם כֹּה־אָמַר אֲדֹנָי יֱהֹוִה הִנֵּה אֲנִי
לֹקֵחַ אֶת־בְּנֵי יִשְׂרָאֵל מִבֵּין הַגּוֹיִם אֲשֶׁר הָלְכוּ־שָׁם וְקִבַּצְתִּי
כב אֹתָם מִסָּבִיב וְהֵבֵאתִי אוֹתָם אֶל־אַדְמָתָם: וְעָשִׂיתִי אֹתָם
לְגוֹי אֶחָד בָּאָרֶץ בְּהָרֵי יִשְׂרָאֵל וּמֶלֶךְ אֶחָד יִהְיֶה לְכֻלָּם
לְמֶלֶךְ וְלֹא יהיה־עוֹד לִשְׁנֵי גוֹיִם וְלֹא יֵחָצוּ עוֹד לִשְׁתֵּי יִהְיוּ־

VAYIGASH

In his prophecies of comfort and encouragement, the prophet Yeḥezkel, who accompanied the Jewish exiles to Babylon, paints a picture of the future kingdom in the land of Israel when they return to their land, and describes its characteristics: the ingathering of exiles, the reestablishment of the dynasty of David, spiritual purity and adherence to the Torah and its commandments, and peace. He takes pains to discuss the unity of the nation. Unity, a central pillar of the future order, is described by the

▶

23 split into two kingdoms. They will no longer be defiled by their
idols or by their detestable things and all their transgressions; I
will deliver them from all the dwelling places where they have
sinned; I will purify them, and they will be My people, and I will
24 be their God. My servant David will be king over them; there
shall be one shepherd for all, and they will follow My laws, and
25 they will keep My statutes and perform them. They will live on
the land that I gave to My servant Yaakov, where your ancestors
lived. They will live upon it, they and their children and their
children's children, for eternity, and David My servant will be
26 their prince for eternity. I will make a covenant of peace with
them; it will be an everlasting covenant with them. I will place
them securely there, I will make them ever more numerous; I
27 will place My Sanctuary among them for eternity. My presence
will be upon them; I will be their God, and they will be My peo-
28 ple. And the nations will know that I the LORD make Israel holy
when My Sanctuary is among them for all eternity."

Haftarat Vayeḥi

2 1 The time of David's death was drawing near, and he gave instruc- I KINGS
2 tions to his son Shlomo. "I am going the way of all the earth," he
3 said. "You must be strong and prove yourself a man. You must
keep the charge of the LORD your God, following His ways and
keeping His laws and commandments, His rulings and decrees,
as written in the teaching of Moshe. For then you will succeed
4 in whatever you do, wherever you turn. For then, the LORD will
fulfill the promise He made to me, saying: If your sons keep to
their path and walk before Me truly, with all their heart and all
their soul, then no one of your lineage will be cut off from the

---

could pose a threat to the safety of the kingdom. In fateful and dangerous times such as this, Shlomo must work quickly and determinedly to forestall irrevocable damage to all his father had worked so hard to build. The Davidic kingdom was at that point a strong and united empire with wealth and standing. David understood this, and he saw it as an outcome of the principled adherence to the faith and values outlined at the beginning of his speech to Shlomo.

כג מַמְלָכוֹת עוֹד: וְלֹא יִטַּמְּאוּ עוֹד בְּגִלּוּלֵיהֶם וּבְשִׁקּוּצֵיהֶם
וּבְכֹל פִּשְׁעֵיהֶם וְהוֹשַׁעְתִּי אֹתָם מִכֹּל מוֹשְׁבֹתֵיהֶם אֲשֶׁר
חָטְאוּ בָהֶם וְטִהַרְתִּי אוֹתָם וְהָיוּ־לִי לְעָם וַאֲנִי אֶהְיֶה לָהֶם
כד לֵאלֹהִים: וְעַבְדִּי דָוִד מֶלֶךְ עֲלֵיהֶם וְרוֹעֶה אֶחָד יִהְיֶה לְכֻלָּם
כה וּבְמִשְׁפָּטַי יֵלֵכוּ וְחֻקּוֹתַי יִשְׁמְרוּ וְעָשׂוּ אוֹתָם: וְיָשְׁבוּ עַל־
הָאָרֶץ אֲשֶׁר נָתַתִּי לְעַבְדִּי לְיַעֲקֹב אֲשֶׁר יָשְׁבוּ־בָהּ אֲבוֹתֵיכֶם
וְיָשְׁבוּ עָלֶיהָ הֵמָּה וּבְנֵיהֶם וּבְנֵי בְנֵיהֶם עַד־עוֹלָם וְדָוִד עַבְדִּי
כו נָשִׂיא לָהֶם לְעוֹלָם: וְכָרַתִּי לָהֶם בְּרִית שָׁלוֹם בְּרִית עוֹלָם
יִהְיֶה אוֹתָם וּנְתַתִּים וְהִרְבֵּיתִי אוֹתָם וְנָתַתִּי אֶת־מִקְדָּשִׁי
כז בְּתוֹכָם לְעוֹלָם: וְהָיָה מִשְׁכָּנִי עֲלֵיהֶם וְהָיִיתִי לָהֶם לֵאלֹהִים
כח וְהֵמָּה יִהְיוּ־לִי לְעָם: וְיָדְעוּ הַגּוֹיִם כִּי אֲנִי יְהוָה מְקַדֵּשׁ אֶת־
יִשְׂרָאֵל בִּהְיוֹת מִקְדָּשִׁי בְּתוֹכָם לְעוֹלָם:

הפטרת ויחי

מלכים א׳

ב א ב וַיִּקְרְבוּ יְמֵי־דָוִד לָמוּת וַיְצַו אֶת־שְׁלֹמֹה בְנוֹ לֵאמֹר: אָנֹכִי
ג הֹלֵךְ בְּדֶרֶךְ כָּל־הָאָרֶץ וְחָזַקְתָּ וְהָיִיתָ לְאִישׁ: וְשָׁמַרְתָּ אֶת־
מִשְׁמֶרֶת ׀ יְהוָה אֱלֹהֶיךָ לָלֶכֶת בִּדְרָכָיו לִשְׁמֹר חֻקֹּתָיו מִצְוֹתָיו
וּמִשְׁפָּטָיו וְעֵדְוֹתָיו כַּכָּתוּב בְּתוֹרַת מֹשֶׁה לְמַעַן תַּשְׂכִּיל אֵת
ד כָּל־אֲשֶׁר תַּעֲשֶׂה וְאֵת כָּל־אֲשֶׁר תִּפְנֶה שָׁם: לְמַעַן יָקִים
יְהוָה אֶת־דְּבָרוֹ אֲשֶׁר דִּבֶּר עָלַי לֵאמֹר אִם־יִשְׁמְרוּ בָנֶיךָ אֶת־
דַּרְכָּם לָלֶכֶת לְפָנַי בֶּאֱמֶת בְּכָל־לְבָבָם וּבְכָל־נַפְשָׁם לֵאמֹר

VAYEḤI

King David conveys his last will and testament to his son Shlomo. In the first part, he emphasizes the importance of adhering to the Torah and its commandments as a condition for success in life and as a ruler. In the second, he prepares his son for the sensitive task of succession to power. Some personalities in the royal court are liable to take advantage of the period of instability to try to seize power. Such a struggle, against the best efforts of the old king to ensure stability by publicly designating Shlomo as his successor,

5 throne of Israel. Now you know what Yoav son of Tzeruya did
to me – how he dealt with the two commanders of Israel's forces,
Avner son of Ner and Amasa son of Yeter. By killing them, he
shed the blood of war in peacetime and tainted the belt around
6 his waist and the shoes upon his feet with the blood of war. Use
your wisdom – do not let his gray-haired head go down to Sheol
7 in peace. As for the sons of Barzilai the Gileadite, show
them loyalty and let them dine at your table, for they befriend-
8 ed me when I was fleeing from Avshalom your brother. Now,
look – though Shimi son of Gera the Benjaminite from Baḥurim
is with you, he cursed me with a vehement curse on the day I left
Maḥanayim. When he came down to meet me by the Jordan, I
swore to him by the Lord that I would not put him to death by
9 sword – but now, do not let him go free. You are a wise man, and
you will know how to deal with him – bring his gray-haired head
10 down in blood to Sheol." And David slept with his ancestors and
11 was buried in the City of David. The length of time
that David had reigned over Israel was forty years; he reigned in
Ḥevron for seven years, and he reigned in Jerusalem for thirty-
12 three years. Now Shlomo sat on his father David's throne, and his
kingdom was firmly established.

Haftarat Shemot

ISAIAH
For Ashkenazim and Chabad

27 6 In days to come, Yaakov will take root, Israel will put out buds
and flower, and all the land on all the earth will be covered with
7 the fruits. Was he beaten as are beaten those who beat
8 him? Was his slaying like the slaying of their slain? With a faithful
measure, driving them out You fight them; He blew them away
9 with His blasting spirit on the day of the gale. This, then, is how

redemption. Instead of hearing the call of the herald: "A great ram's horn will sound, and they will come, all those lost in the land of Assyria … and bow low to the Lord on the holy mount in Jerusalem," we will bemoan the "trampling underfoot the garland pride of Efrayim's drunkards."

ה לֹא־יִכָּרֵת לְךָ אִישׁ מֵעַל כִּסֵּא יִשְׂרָאֵל: וְגַם אַתָּה יָדַעְתָּ
אֵת אֲשֶׁר־עָשָׂה לִי יוֹאָב בֶּן־צְרוּיָה אֲשֶׁר עָשָׂה לִשְׁנֵי־שָׂרֵי
צִבְאוֹת יִשְׂרָאֵל לְאַבְנֵר בֶּן־נֵר וְלַעֲמָשָׂא בֶן־יֶתֶר וַיַּהַרְגֵם
וַיָּשֶׂם דְּמֵי־מִלְחָמָה בְּשָׁלֹם וַיִּתֵּן דְּמֵי מִלְחָמָה בַּחֲגֹרָתוֹ
ו אֲשֶׁר בְּמָתְנָיו וּבְנַעֲלוֹ אֲשֶׁר בְּרַגְלָיו: וְעָשִׂיתָ כְּחָכְמָתֶךָ
ז וְלֹא־תוֹרֵד שֵׂיבָתוֹ בְּשָׁלֹם שְׁאֹל: וְלִבְנֵי בַרְזִלַּי
הַגִּלְעָדִי תַּעֲשֶׂה־חֶסֶד וְהָיוּ בְּאֹכְלֵי שֻׁלְחָנֶךָ כִּי־כֵן קָרְבוּ
ח אֵלַי בְּבָרְחִי מִפְּנֵי אַבְשָׁלוֹם אָחִיךָ: וְהִנֵּה עִמְּךָ שִׁמְעִי
בֶן־גֵּרָא בֶן־הַיְמִינִי מִבַּחֻרִים וְהוּא קִלְלַנִי קְלָלָה נִמְרֶצֶת
בְּיוֹם לֶכְתִּי מַחֲנָיִם וְהוּא־יָרַד לִקְרָאתִי הַיַּרְדֵּן וָאֶשָּׁבַע לוֹ
ט בַיהוה לֵאמֹר אִם־אֲמִיתְךָ בֶּחָרֶב: וְעַתָּה אַל־תְּנַקֵּהוּ כִּי
אִישׁ חָכָם אָתָּה וְיָדַעְתָּ אֵת אֲשֶׁר תַּעֲשֶׂה־לּוֹ וְהוֹרַדְתָּ אֶת־
י שֵׂיבָתוֹ בְּדָם שְׁאוֹל: וַיִּשְׁכַּב דָּוִד עִם־אֲבֹתָיו וַיִּקָּבֵר בְּעִיר
יא דָּוִד: וְהַיָּמִים אֲשֶׁר מָלַךְ דָּוִד עַל־יִשְׂרָאֵל
אַרְבָּעִים שָׁנָה בְּחֶבְרוֹן מָלַךְ שֶׁבַע שָׁנִים וּבִירוּשָׁלַםִ מָלַךְ
יב שְׁלֹשִׁים וְשָׁלֹשׁ שָׁנִים: וּשְׁלֹמֹה יָשַׁב עַל־כִּסֵּא דָּוִד אָבִיו
וַתִּכֹּן מַלְכֻתוֹ מְאֹד:

הפטרת שמות

ישעיה
For Ashkenazim and Chabad

כז ו הַבָּאִים יַשְׁרֵשׁ יַעֲקֹב יָצִיץ וּפָרַח יִשְׂרָאֵל וּמָלְאוּ פְנֵי־תֵבֵל
ז תְּנוּבָה: הַכְּמַכַּת מַכֵּהוּ הִכָּהוּ אִם־כְּהֶרֶג הֲרֻגָיו
ח הֹרָג: בְּסַאסְּאָה בְּשַׁלְחָהּ תְּרִיבֶנָּה הָגָה בְּרוּחוֹ הַקָּשָׁה
ט בְּיוֹם קָדִים: לָכֵן בְּזֹאת יְכֻפַּר עֲוֹן־יַעֲקֹב וְזֶה כָּל־פְּרִי הָסִר

SHEMOT

Ashkenazim

The distance from success to excess is short. It is easy to be carried away by earthly achievements, and difficult to maintain a mindset of humility having made them. The drunkenness of society's successes causes us to become "wine benumbed." Such a society will fritter away its ability to achieve full

the iniquity of Israel may be atoned – and that, all the fruit of
removing his sin – by rendering all his altar stones smashed lime-
10 stone, no sacred trees or incense shrines rising again. The fortress
city will sit alone, a shelter left behind, lonely as desert. Calves
will graze there, there will they lie, and eat up all their branches.
11 When their yield dries up they will be broken down. Women
will come and use them as firewood, for this is not a wise people; and so its Maker will have no compassion, its Creator will
12 grant it no grace. On that day, the Lord will beat the
branches from the Euphrates's surge to the River of Egypt and
13 gather you up one by one, you children of Israel. It will
be, on that day: a great ram's horn will sound, and they will come,
all those lost in the land of Assyria, and those who are exiled to
the land of Egypt, and bow low to the Lord on the holy mount
28 1 in Jerusalem. Woe to the proud garland of Efrayim's
drunkards, for the withered lotus flower that was the glorious
2 supremacy crowning the oiled valley of the wine benumbed. See
what comes – something strong and determined of the Lord,
like pelting hail, like a cataclysmic storm, like a river of great
waters, flooding waters, heavy-handed, casting people down
3 to earth, trampling underfoot the garland pride of Efrayim's
4 drunkards. Like a withered lotus flower it shall be, its glorious
supremacy that crowned the fat valley like the first fig before
harvest; the one that all who saw would swallow up sooner than
5 hold it. On that day the Lord of Hosts will be a garland of splendor, the crown of supremacy, to the remnant of His
6 people, He will be the spirit of justice in those who preside over
justice, and of might in those who drive war back from the gate.
7 For these men too have gone astray with wine, they have lost
themselves in ale – priest and prophet – gone astray with their
ale, been swallowed up in wine, got lost by their ale, gone astray
8 in their vision, fallen over in judgment; the tables are soaked, all,
9 in vomit and filth, until there is no space left. Whom
would he teach knowledge, whom bring to comprehend his
words? Those barely weaned of milk, those just taken from the
10 breast? *Law after law, law after law, line after line, line after line, a*
11 *little bit here, a little bit there* – in a babble of words, in a different
12 tongue he speaks to this people. He told them, "This is rest: leave
13 the weary be; this is calm." They would not hear. So the word of
the Lord is to them law after law, law after law, line after line,

חַטָּאתוֹ בְּשׂוּמוֹ ׀ כׇּל־אַבְנֵי מִזְבֵּחַ כְּאַבְנֵי־גִר מְנֻפָּצוֹת לֹא־
י יָקֻמוּ אֲשֵׁרִים וְחַמָּנִים׃ כִּי עִיר בְּצוּרָה בָּדָד נָוֶה מְשֻׁלָּח
וְנֶעֱזָב כַּמִּדְבָּר שָׁם יִרְעֶה עֵגֶל וְשָׁם יִרְבָּץ וְכִלָּה סְעִפֶיהָ׃
יא בִּיבֹשׁ קְצִירָהּ תִּשָּׁבַרְנָה נָשִׁים בָּאוֹת מְאִירוֹת אוֹתָהּ כִּי
לֹא עַם־בִּינוֹת הוּא עַל־כֵּן לֹא־יְרַחֲמֶנּוּ עֹשֵׂהוּ וְיֹצְרוֹ לֹא
יב יְחֻנֶּנּוּ׃ וְהָיָה בַּיּוֹם הַהוּא יַחְבֹּט יְהֹוָה מִשִּׁבֹּלֶת
הַנָּהָר עַד־נַחַל מִצְרָיִם וְאַתֶּם תְּלֻקְּטוּ לְאַחַד אֶחָד בְּנֵי
יג יִשְׂרָאֵל׃ וְהָיָה ׀ בַּיּוֹם הַהוּא יִתָּקַע בְּשׁוֹפָר
גָּדוֹל וּבָאוּ הָאֹבְדִים בְּאֶרֶץ אַשּׁוּר וְהַנִּדָּחִים בְּאֶרֶץ מִצְרָיִם
כח א וְהִשְׁתַּחֲווּ לַיהֹוָה בְּהַר הַקֹּדֶשׁ בִּירוּשָׁלָ‍ִם׃ הוֹי
עֲטֶרֶת גֵּאוּת שִׁכֹּרֵי אֶפְרַיִם וְצִיץ נֹבֵל צְבִי תִפְאַרְתּוֹ אֲשֶׁר
ב עַל־רֹאשׁ גֵּיא־שְׁמָנִים הֲלוּמֵי יָיִן׃ הִנֵּה חָזָק וְאַמִּץ לַאדֹנָי
כְּזֶרֶם בָּרָד שַׂעַר קָטֶב כְּזֶרֶם מַיִם כַּבִּירִים שֹׁטְפִים הִנִּיחַ
ג לָאָרֶץ בְּיָד׃ בְּרַגְלַיִם תֵּרָמַסְנָה עֲטֶרֶת גֵּאוּת שִׁכּוֹרֵי אֶפְרָיִם׃
ד וְהָיְתָה צִיצַת נֹבֵל צְבִי תִפְאַרְתּוֹ אֲשֶׁר עַל־רֹאשׁ גֵּיא שְׁמָנִים
כְּבִכּוּרָהּ בְּטֶרֶם קַיִץ אֲשֶׁר יִרְאֶה הָרֹאֶה אוֹתָהּ בְּעוֹדָהּ בְּכַפּוֹ
ה יִבְלָעֶנָּה׃ בַּיּוֹם הַהוּא יִהְיֶה יְהֹוָה צְבָאוֹת לַעֲטֶרֶת
ו צְבִי וְלִצְפִירַת תִּפְאָרָה לִשְׁאָר עַמּוֹ׃ וּלְרוּחַ מִשְׁפָּט לַיּוֹשֵׁב
ז עַל־הַמִּשְׁפָּט וְלִגְבוּרָה מְשִׁיבֵי מִלְחָמָה שָׁעְרָה׃ וְגַם־אֵלֶּה
בַּיַּיִן שָׁגוּ וּבַשֵּׁכָר תָּעוּ כֹּהֵן וְנָבִיא שָׁגוּ בַשֵּׁכָר נִבְלְעוּ מִן־הַיַּיִן
ח תָּעוּ מִן־הַשֵּׁכָר שָׁגוּ בָּרֹאֶה פָּקוּ פְּלִילִיָּה׃ כִּי כׇּל־שֻׁלְחָנוֹת
ט מָלְאוּ קִיא צֹאָה בְּלִי מָקוֹם׃ אֶת־מִי יוֹרֶה דֵעָה
י וְאֶת־מִי יָבִין שְׁמוּעָה גְּמוּלֵי מֵחָלָב עַתִּיקֵי מִשָּׁדָיִם׃ כִּי צַו
יא לָצָו צַו לָצָו קַו לָקָו קַו לָקָו זְעֵיר שָׁם זְעֵיר שָׁם׃ כִּי בְּלַעֲגֵי
יב שָׂפָה וּבְלָשׁוֹן אַחֶרֶת יְדַבֵּר אֶל־הָעָם הַזֶּה׃ אֲשֶׁר ׀ אָמַר
אֲלֵיהֶם זֹאת הַמְּנוּחָה הָנִיחוּ לֶעָיֵף וְזֹאת הַמַּרְגֵּעָה וְלֹא אָבוּא
יג שְׁמוֹעַ׃ וְהָיָה לָהֶם דְּבַר־יְהֹוָה צַו לָצָו צַו לָצָו קַו לָקָו קַו לָקָו

line after line, a little bit here, a little bit there, for them to walk
and stumble on backward, be broken, be beaten, be caught.
29 22 And so, this is what the LORD has said – Avraham's redeemer –
to the House of Yaakov: No more will Yaakov be ashamed, his
23 face no more grow pale, for when he sees his children, the work
of My hands, in his midst, sanctifying My name, it is Yaakov's
Holy One they sanctify; it is Israel's God they worship.

JEREMIAH
For Sepharadim

1 1 The words of Yirmeyahu, son of Ḥilkiyahu, one of the priests
2 who were in Anatot in the land of Binyamin, to whom the word
of the LORD came in the days of Yoshiyahu son of Amon, king
3 of Yehuda, in the thirteenth year of his reign, and continued
during the days of Yehoyakim son of Yoshiyahu, king of Yehuda,
until the end of the eleventh year of Tzidkiyahu son of Yoshiyahu, king of Yehuda – until the exile of Jerusalem in the fifth
4 5 month: The word of the LORD came to me: "Before
I formed you in the womb I knew you. Before you were born
6 I consecrated you. I placed you as a prophet to the nations." I
said, "Please, Lord GOD, I am not capable of speaking, for I am
7 still only a boy." The LORD replied to me, "Do not say, 'I am a boy,'
for you shall go to all to whom I send you, and you shall speak as
8 I instruct you. Do not fear them, for I am with you to rescue you,
9 declares the LORD." The LORD extended His hand and touched
10 my mouth and the LORD said to me, "Look, I have placed My
words in your mouth. I have appointed you this day against the
kingdoms and against the nations to uproot and tear down, to
11 destroy and demolish, to build and to plant." The word
of the LORD came to me: "What do you see, Yirmeyahu?" I

the one hand he was a divine messenger, commanded to deliver a message of impending doom to the nation. On the other, he was one of the people and loved them. In this context God's words of encouragement to him take on special meaning: "Stand up and speak to them as I will instruct you. Do not break down because of them.... I have made you today a fortress city, an iron column, and walls of bronze.... They will wage battle against you, but they will not prevail." Yirmeyahu's attempts to avoid this terrible role, like Moshe's centuries earlier, testify to this difficulty as well.

זְעֵיר שָׁם זְעֵיר שָׁם לְמַעַן יֵלְכוּ וְכָשְׁלוּ אָחוֹר וְנִשְׁבָּרוּ וְנוֹקְשׁוּ
וְנִלְכָּדוּ׃
כט כב לָכֵן כֹּה־אָמַר יהוה אֶל־בֵּית יַעֲקֹב אֲשֶׁר פָּדָה אֶת־אַבְרָהָם
כג לֹא־עַתָּה יֵבוֹשׁ יַעֲקֹב וְלֹא עַתָּה פָּנָיו יֶחֱוָרוּ׃ כִּי בִרְאוֹתוֹ
יְלָדָיו מַעֲשֵׂה יָדַי בְּקִרְבּוֹ יַקְדִּישׁוּ שְׁמִי וְהִקְדִּישׁוּ אֶת־קְדוֹשׁ
יַעֲקֹב וְאֶת־אֱלֹהֵי יִשְׂרָאֵל יַעֲרִיצוּ׃

ירמיה
For Sepharadim

א א דִּבְרֵי יִרְמְיָהוּ בֶּן־חִלְקִיָּהוּ מִן־הַכֹּהֲנִים אֲשֶׁר בַּעֲנָתוֹת
ב בְּאֶרֶץ בִּנְיָמִן׃ אֲשֶׁר הָיָה דְבַר־יהוה אֵלָיו בִּימֵי יֹאשִׁיָּהוּ
ג בֶן־אָמוֹן מֶלֶךְ יְהוּדָה בִּשְׁלֹשׁ־עֶשְׂרֵה שָׁנָה לְמָלְכוֹ׃ וַיְהִי
בִּימֵי יְהוֹיָקִים בֶּן־יֹאשִׁיָּהוּ מֶלֶךְ יְהוּדָה עַד־תֹּם עַשְׁתֵּי־
עֶשְׂרֵה שָׁנָה לְצִדְקִיָּהוּ בֶן־יֹאשִׁיָּהוּ מֶלֶךְ יְהוּדָה עַד־גְּלוֹת
ד יְרוּשָׁלַםִ בַּחֹדֶשׁ הַחֲמִישִׁי׃ וַיְהִי דְבַר־יְהוָה אֵלַי
ה לֵאמֹר׃ בְּטֶרֶם אצורך בַבֶּטֶן יְדַעְתִּיךָ וּבְטֶרֶם תֵּצֵא מֵרֶחֶם אֶצָּרְךָ
ו הִקְדַּשְׁתִּיךָ נָבִיא לַגּוֹיִם נְתַתִּיךָ׃ וָאֹמַר אֲהָהּ אֲדֹנָי יֱהוִה
ז הִנֵּה לֹא־יָדַעְתִּי דַּבֵּר כִּי־נַעַר אָנֹכִי׃ וַיֹּאמֶר יהוה אֵלַי אַל־
תֹּאמַר נַעַר אָנֹכִי כִּי עַל־כָּל־אֲשֶׁר אֶשְׁלָחֲךָ תֵּלֵךְ וְאֵת
ח כָּל־אֲשֶׁר אֲצַוְּךָ תְּדַבֵּר׃ אַל־תִּירָא מִפְּנֵיהֶם כִּי־אִתְּךָ אֲנִי
ט לְהַצִּלֶךָ נְאֻם־יהוה׃ וַיִּשְׁלַח יהוה אֶת־יָדוֹ וַיַּגַּע עַל־פִּי וַיֹּאמֶר
י יהוה אֵלַי הִנֵּה נָתַתִּי דְבָרַי בְּפִיךָ׃ רְאֵה הִפְקַדְתִּיךָ ׀ הַיּוֹם
הַזֶּה עַל־הַגּוֹיִם וְעַל־הַמַּמְלָכוֹת לִנְתוֹשׁ וְלִנְתוֹץ וּלְהַאֲבִיד
יא וְלַהֲרוֹס לִבְנוֹת וְלִנְטוֹעַ׃ וַיְהִי דְבַר־יהוה אֵלַי
לֵאמֹר מָה־אַתָּה רֹאֶה יִרְמְיָהוּ וָאֹמַר מַקֵּל שָׁקֵד אֲנִי רֹאֶה׃

Sepharadim

Yirmeyahu prophesied during the reigns of the final kings of Yehuda up till the destruction of Jerusalem and afterward. His call to prophecy emphasizes the harsh daily reality of the prophet. Yirmeyahu's career was especially fraught. He was the first and only prophet that foretold the destruction as it occurred. His challenge stemmed from his complex nature: On

12 replied, "I see the branch of an almond tree." And the LORD
said to me: "You have seen well, for I am watchful about keeping
13 My word." The word of the LORD came to me a second time: "What do you see?" I answered, "I see a boiling caul-
14 dron facing the north." And the LORD said to me: "From the
north disaster shall burst forth upon all the inhabitants of the
15 land, for I am about to summon all the tribes of the kingdoms
of the north," declares the LORD. "They shall come; each shall
set up a throne at the entrance of the gates of Jerusalem against
her ramparts roundabout and against all the cities of Yehuda.
16 Thus will I pronounce My judgment upon them on account of
their wickedness: they abandoned Me, sacrificed to other gods,
17 and worshipped the works of their own hands. As for you, be
courageous; stand up and speak to them as I will instruct you. Do
not break down because of them lest I break you down before
18 them. I have made you today a fortress city, an iron column, and
walls of bronze against the entire land – against the kings of Ye-
19 huda, its princes, its priests, and the people of the land. They will
wage battle against you, but they will not prevail, for I am with
2 1 you," declares the LORD, "to rescue you." The
2 word of the LORD came to me: "Go and proclaim to the people
of Jerusalem: 'This is what the LORD has said: I recall on your
behalf the devotion of your youth, your bridal love, when you
3 followed Me into the wilderness, a land unseeded. Israel is a
treasure to the LORD, His choice harvest. All who eat of it will be
held to account. Evil will befall them, declares the LORD.'"

EZEKIEL
For Yemenites

16 1 2 The word of the LORD came to me, saying, "Man, make known
3 to Jerusalem her abominations and say: So says the Lord GOD to
Jerusalem: Your ancestry and your birth were in the land of the
4 Canaanites. Your father was Amorite, your mother Hittite and
as for your birth, on the day you were born your cord was not

---

strong woman, and then marries her. This story highlights the special providence of God for Israel from the nadir of the yoke of Egypt until the covenant at Sinai. Verses from this prophecy are woven into the Passover Haggada.

The continuation of the prophecy, after the conclusion of the *haftara*, describes the people's betrayal of God, despite all the good He did for them.

יב וַיֹּאמֶר יְהוָה אֵלַי הֵיטַבְתָּ לִרְאוֹת כִּי־שֹׁקֵד אֲנִי עַל־דְּבָרִי
יג לַעֲשֹׂתוֹ׃ וַיְהִי דְבַר־יְהוָה ׀ אֵלַי שֵׁנִית לֵאמֹר מָה
אַתָּה רֹאֶה וָאֹמַר סִיר נָפוּחַ אֲנִי רֹאֶה וּפָנָיו מִפְּנֵי צָפוֹנָה׃
יד וַיֹּאמֶר יְהוָה אֵלָי מִצָּפוֹן תִּפָּתַח הָרָעָה עַל כָּל־יֹשְׁבֵי הָאָרֶץ׃
טו כִּי ׀ הִנְנִי קֹרֵא לְכָל־מִשְׁפְּחוֹת מַמְלְכוֹת צָפוֹנָה נְאֻם־יְהוָה
וּבָאוּ וְנָתְנוּ אִישׁ כִּסְאוֹ פֶּתַח ׀ שַׁעֲרֵי יְרוּשָׁלִַם וְעַל כָּל־
טז חוֹמֹתֶיהָ סָבִיב וְעַל כָּל־עָרֵי יְהוּדָה׃ וְדִבַּרְתִּי מִשְׁפָּטַי
אוֹתָם עַל כָּל־רָעָתָם אֲשֶׁר עֲזָבוּנִי וַיְקַטְּרוּ לֵאלֹהִים אֲחֵרִים
יז וַיִּשְׁתַּחֲווּ לְמַעֲשֵׂי יְדֵיהֶם׃ וְאַתָּה תֶּאְזֹר מָתְנֶיךָ וְקַמְתָּ וְדִבַּרְתָּ
אֲלֵיהֶם אֵת כָּל־אֲשֶׁר אָנֹכִי אֲצַוֶּךָּ אַל־תֵּחַת מִפְּנֵיהֶם פֶּן־
יח אֲחִתְּךָ לִפְנֵיהֶם׃ וַאֲנִי הִנֵּה נְתַתִּיךָ הַיּוֹם לְעִיר מִבְצָר וּלְעַמּוּד
בַּרְזֶל וּלְחֹמוֹת נְחֹשֶׁת עַל־כָּל־הָאָרֶץ לְמַלְכֵי יְהוּדָה לְשָׂרֶיהָ
יט לְכֹהֲנֶיהָ וּלְעַם הָאָרֶץ׃ וְנִלְחֲמוּ אֵלֶיךָ וְלֹא־יוּכְלוּ לָךְ כִּי־
ב א אִתְּךָ אֲנִי נְאֻם־יְהוָה לְהַצִּילֶךָ׃ וַיְהִי דְבַר־יְהוָה
ב אֵלַי לֵאמֹר׃ הָלֹךְ וְקָרָאתָ בְאָזְנֵי יְרוּשָׁלִַם לֵאמֹר כֹּה אָמַר
יְהוָה זָכַרְתִּי לָךְ חֶסֶד נְעוּרַיִךְ אַהֲבַת כְּלוּלֹתָיִךְ לֶכְתֵּךְ אַחֲרַי
ג בַּמִּדְבָּר בְּאֶרֶץ לֹא זְרוּעָה׃ קֹדֶשׁ יִשְׂרָאֵל לַיהוָה רֵאשִׁית
תְּבוּאָתֹה כָּל־אֹכְלָיו יֶאְשָׁמוּ רָעָה תָּבֹא אֲלֵיהֶם נְאֻם־יְהוָה׃

יחזקאל

For Yemenites

טז א ב וַיְהִי דְבַר־יְהוָה אֵלַי לֵאמֹר׃ בֶּן־אָדָם הוֹדַע אֶת־יְרוּשָׁלִַם
ג אֶת־תּוֹעֲבֹתֶיהָ׃ וְאָמַרְתָּ כֹּה־אָמַר אֲדֹנָי יֱהֹוִה לִירוּשָׁלִַם
מְכֹרֹתַיִךְ וּמֹלְדֹתַיִךְ מֵאֶרֶץ הַכְּנַעֲנִי אָבִיךְ הָאֱמֹרִי וְאִמֵּךְ
ד חִתִּית׃ וּמוֹלְדוֹתַיִךְ בְּיוֹם הוּלֶּדֶת אֹתָךְ לֹא־כָרַּת שָׁרֵּךְ

Yemenites

Speaking to fellow exiles from Jerusalem, the prophet Yeḥezkel describes the reasons for the impending final destruction of the city. He surveys the relationship between God and Israel from the days of slavery in Egypt onward, using the metaphor of a man who takes in an abandoned child, a baby girl, thrown out into the street on the day she is born. The man, passing by the child, takes pity on her and takes her in, raising her into a mature, beautiful, and

cut, you were not washed clean with water, you were not rubbed
5 with salt, and you were not swaddled. No eye took enough pity
on you to do any of these things out of compassion for you. You
were thrown out into the open field, loathed, on the day you were
6 born. And when I passed by you, I saw you floundering in your
own blood, and I said to you, 'There in your blood, live'; I said to
7 you, 'In your blood, live!' I made you flourish like the shoots of
the field. You grew up, matured, were beautifully adorned – your
breasts were firm, your hair grew long – but you were naked and
8 bare. Then I passed by you and saw that you had reached the age
of love, so I spread My cloak out over you and covered your nakedness. I made My vow to you, entered into a covenant with
9 you, declares the Lord God, and you became Mine. I washed
you with water, I rinsed your blood off you, and I anointed you
10 with oil. I clothed you in embroidered cloth, I placed on you
leather shoes, I wound about your head fine linen, and I covered
11 you with silk. I adorned you with jewelry; I put bracelets upon
12 your arms and a necklace round your neck. I put a nose ring in
your nose, earrings in your ears, and a glorious crown upon your
13 head. You were adorned with gold and silver; your clothing was
fine linen, silk, and embroidered cloth; you ate fine flour, honey,
and oil; and you were exceptionally beautiful, fit to be a queen.
14 You became known among the nations for your beauty for, with
the splendor I placed upon you, it was perfect, declares the Lord
God."

Haftarat Vaera

On Rosh Ḥodesh Shevat read the maftir from Bemidbar 28:9–15, and the haftara on page 1640.

EZEKIEL

Yemenites begin here

Ashkenazim and Sepharadim begin here

28 24 The House of Israel will no longer suffer stabbing briars, scratch-
ing thorns, from those in their surroundings who scorn them,
25 and they will know that I am the Lord God. *So says
the Lord God: When I gather the House of Israel in from the
peoples where they have been scattered and I am sanctified

progressing. One of the questions being asked at that time was: Why has God given these nations the power to destroy His own Temple, the house of David, and the kingdom of Yehuda? In these chapters of prophecy for the surrounding nations, God clarifies that He will hold each of them accountable for the evil

וּבְמַיִם לֹא־רֻחַצְתְּ לְמִשְׁעִי וְהָמְלֵחַ לֹא הֻמְלַחַתְּ וְהָחְתֵּל
ה לֹא חֻתָּלְתְּ׃ לֹא־חָסָה עָלַיִךְ עַיִן לַעֲשׂוֹת לָךְ אַחַת מֵאֵלֶּה
לְחֻמְלָה עָלָיִךְ וַתֻּשְׁלְכִי אֶל־פְּנֵי הַשָּׂדֶה בְּגֹעַל נַפְשֵׁךְ בְּיוֹם
ו הֻלֶּדֶת אֹתָךְ׃ וָאֶעֱבֹר עָלַיִךְ וָאֶרְאֵךְ מִתְבּוֹסֶסֶת בְּדָמָיִךְ
ז וָאֹמַר לָךְ בְּדָמַיִךְ חֲיִי וָאֹמַר לָךְ בְּדָמַיִךְ חֲיִי׃ רְבָבָה כְּצֶמַח
הַשָּׂדֶה נְתַתִּיךְ וַתִּרְבִּי וַתִּגְדְּלִי וַתָּבֹאִי בַּעֲדִי עֲדָיִים שָׁדַיִם
ח נָכֹנוּ וּשְׂעָרֵךְ צִמֵּחַ וְאַתְּ עֵרֹם וְעֶרְיָה׃ וָאֶעֱבֹר עָלַיִךְ וָאֶרְאֵךְ
וְהִנֵּה עִתֵּךְ עֵת דֹּדִים וָאֶפְרֹשׂ כְּנָפִי עָלַיִךְ וָאֲכַסֶּה עֶרְוָתֵךְ
וָאֶשָּׁבַע לָךְ וָאָבוֹא בִבְרִית אֹתָךְ נְאֻם אֲדֹנָי יֱהֹוִה וַתִּהְיִי־
ט לִי׃ וָאֶרְחָצֵךְ בַּמַּיִם וָאֶשְׁטֹף דָּמַיִךְ מֵעָלָיִךְ וָאֲסֻכֵךְ בַּשָּׁמֶן׃
י וָאַלְבִּישֵׁךְ רִקְמָה וָאֶנְעֲלֵךְ תָּחַשׁ וָאֶחְבְּשֵׁךְ בַּשֵּׁשׁ וַאֲכַסֵּךְ
יא מֶשִׁי׃ וָאֶעְדֵּךְ עֶדִי וָאֶתְּנָה צְמִידִים עַל־יָדַיִךְ וְרָבִיד עַל־
יב גְּרוֹנֵךְ׃ וָאֶתֵּן נֶזֶם עַל־אַפֵּךְ וַעֲגִילִים עַל־אָזְנָיִךְ וַעֲטֶרֶת
יג תִּפְאֶרֶת בְּרֹאשֵׁךְ׃ וַתַּעְדִּי זָהָב וָכֶסֶף וּמַלְבּוּשֵׁךְ ששי וָמֶשִׁי שֵׁשׁ
וְרִקְמָה סֹלֶת וּדְבַשׁ וָשֶׁמֶן אכלתי וַתִּיפִי בִּמְאֹד מְאֹד וַתִּצְלְחִי אָכָלְתְּ
יד לִמְלוּכָה׃ וַיֵּצֵא לָךְ שֵׁם בַּגּוֹיִם בְּיָפְיֵךְ כִּי | כָּלִיל הוּא בַּהֲדָרִי
אֲשֶׁר־שַׂמְתִּי עָלַיִךְ נְאֻם אֲדֹנָי יֱהֹוִה׃

הפטרת וארא

On ראש חודש שבט *read the* מפטיר *from* במדבר כח, ט–טו*, and the* הפטרה *on page 1641.*

כח כד וְלֹא־יִהְיֶה עוֹד לְבֵית יִשְׂרָאֵל סִלּוֹן מַמְאִיר וְקוֹץ מַכְאִב יחזקאל *Yemenites begin here*
מִכֹּל סְבִיבֹתָם הַשָּׁאטִים אוֹתָם וְיָדְעוּ כִּי אֲנִי אֲדֹנָי
כה יֱהֹוִה׃ *כֹּה־אָמַר אֲדֹנָי יֱהֹוִה בְּקַבְּצִי | אֶת־בֵּית *Ashkenazim and Sepharadim begin here*
יִשְׂרָאֵל מִן־הָעַמִּים אֲשֶׁר נָפֹצוּ בָם וְנִקְדַּשְׁתִּי בָם לְעֵינֵי

VA'ERA

The middle portion of the book of Ezekiel contains prophecies concerning the nations surrounding Israel. Yeḥezkel pronounced these messages in Babylon to those Jews who had come with him into exile, around the same time as the final Babylonian siege on Jerusalem was

through them in the eyes of the nations, when they live on
26 their land that I gave to My servant Yaakov – they will live on
it in safety; they will build houses, plant vineyards, live safely;
when I execute judgments over all those from their surroundings who scorn them, they will know that I am the LORD, their
29 1 God." In the tenth year in the tenth month on the
2 twelfth of the month, the word of the LORD came to me: "Man,
set your face against Pharaoh, king of Egypt; prophesy against
3 him and against all of Egypt. Speak and say: So says the Lord
GOD: Behold, I am upon you, Pharaoh, king of Egypt, great
crocodile crouching in his Nile streams who says, 'It is mine, this
4 Nile; I made it for myself.' I will fix hooks into your jaw; I will
make the fish from your streams stick to your scales; I will drag
you up out of your streams, and all the fish from your streams
5 will stick to your scales; I will abandon you in the desert, you
and all the fish of your streams. You will fall in the open field
and be neither collected nor gathered up; to the animals of the
6 land and the birds of the skies I will give you over as food. All the
inhabitants of Egypt will know that I am the LORD – for they
7 were a reed staff to the House of Israel: when they grasped hold
of you, you crumbled, tearing their shoulders; when they leaned
8 upon you, you broke, buckling their loins. So the Lord
GOD says this: I will bring the sword down upon you, cut off
9 man and beast from you. The land of Egypt will be desolate, ruined, and they will know that I am the LORD. Because he said,
10 'The Nile is mine; I made it,' for this, I am coming down upon
you and your Nile streams. I will turn the land of Egypt into a
waste of desolate ruins from Migdol to Sevene and to the border
11 with Kush. The foot of no man will pass through her; the foot
of no animal will pass through her; she will not be inhabited for
12 forty years. For forty years I will make the land of Egypt desolate among desolate lands, and her cities will lie desolate among
ruined cities. I will strew Egypt among the nations, scatter them
13 over the lands. Yet, so says the Lord GOD, at the end of

---

that will be judged we see Egypt. After the plagues that God will inflict upon the Egyptians, "they will know that I am the LORD." Both Egypt and Israel will understand God's role as the orchestrator of history, for they will eventually see the return of Israel to its homeland.

הַגּוֹיִם וְיָשְׁבוּ עַל־אַדְמָתָם אֲשֶׁר נָתַתִּי לְעַבְדִּי לְיַעֲקֹב׃
כו וְיָשְׁבוּ עָלֶיהָ לָבֶטַח וּבָנוּ בָתִּים וְנָטְעוּ כְרָמִים וְיָשְׁבוּ לָבֶטַח
בַּעֲשׂוֹתִי שְׁפָטִים בְּכֹל הַשָּׁאטִים אֹתָם מִסְּבִיבוֹתָם וְיָדְעוּ
כט א כִּי אֲנִי יְהוָה אֱלֹהֵיהֶם׃ בַּשָּׁנָה הָעֲשִׂרִית בָּעֲשִׂרִי
ב בִּשְׁנֵים עָשָׂר לַחֹדֶשׁ הָיָה דְבַר־יְהוָה אֵלַי לֵאמֹר׃ בֶּן־אָדָם
שִׂים פָּנֶיךָ עַל־פַּרְעֹה מֶלֶךְ מִצְרָיִם וְהִנָּבֵא עָלָיו וְעַל־מִצְרַיִם
ג כֻּלָּהּ׃ דַּבֵּר וְאָמַרְתָּ כֹּה־אָמַר ׀ אֲדֹנָי יְהוִה הִנְנִי עָלֶיךָ פַּרְעֹה
מֶלֶךְ־מִצְרַיִם הַתַּנִּים הַגָּדוֹל הָרֹבֵץ בְּתוֹךְ יְאֹרָיו אֲשֶׁר אָמַר
ד לִי יְאֹרִי וַאֲנִי עֲשִׂיתִנִי׃ וְנָתַתִּי חחיים בִּלְחָיֶיךָ וְהִדְבַּקְתִּי חַחִים
דְגַת־יְאֹרֶיךָ בְּקַשְׂקְשֹׂתֶיךָ וְהַעֲלִיתִיךָ מִתּוֹךְ יְאֹרֶיךָ וְאֵת
ה כָּל־דְּגַת יְאֹרֶיךָ בְּקַשְׂקְשֹׂתֶיךָ תִּדְבָּק׃ וּנְטַשְׁתִּיךָ הַמִּדְבָּרָה
אוֹתְךָ וְאֵת כָּל־דְּגַת יְאֹרֶיךָ עַל־פְּנֵי הַשָּׂדֶה תִּפּוֹל לֹא
תֵאָסֵף וְלֹא תִקָּבֵץ לְחַיַּת הָאָרֶץ וּלְעוֹף הַשָּׁמַיִם נְתַתִּיךָ
ו לְאָכְלָה׃ וְיָדְעוּ כָּל־יֹשְׁבֵי מִצְרַיִם כִּי אֲנִי יְהוָה יַעַן הֱיוֹתָם
ז מִשְׁעֶנֶת קָנֶה לְבֵית יִשְׂרָאֵל׃ בְּתָפְשָׂם בְּךָ בככף תֵּרוֹץ בַכַּף
וּבָקַעְתָּ לָהֶם כָּל־כָּתֵף וּבְהִשָּׁעֲנָם עָלֶיךָ תִּשָּׁבֵר וְהַעֲמַדְתָּ
ח לָהֶם כָּל־מָתְנָיִם׃ לָכֵן כֹּה אָמַר אֲדֹנָי יְהוִה הִנְנִי
ט מֵבִיא עָלַיִךְ חָרֶב וְהִכְרַתִּי מִמֵּךְ אָדָם וּבְהֵמָה׃ וְהָיְתָה אֶרֶץ־
מִצְרַיִם לִשְׁמָמָה וְחָרְבָּה וְיָדְעוּ כִּי־אֲנִי יְהוָה יַעַן אָמַר יְאֹר לִי
י וַאֲנִי עָשִׂיתִי׃ לָכֵן הִנְנִי אֵלֶיךָ וְאֶל־יְאֹרֶיךָ וְנָתַתִּי אֶת־אֶרֶץ
מִצְרַיִם לְחָרְבוֹת חֹרֶב שְׁמָמָה מִמִּגְדֹּל סְוֵנֵה וְעַד־גְּבוּל
יא כּוּשׁ׃ לֹא תַעֲבָר־בָּהּ רֶגֶל אָדָם וְרֶגֶל בְּהֵמָה לֹא תַעֲבָר־בָּהּ
יב וְלֹא תֵשֵׁב אַרְבָּעִים שָׁנָה׃ וְנָתַתִּי אֶת־אֶרֶץ מִצְרַיִם שְׁמָמָה
בְּתוֹךְ ׀ אֲרָצוֹת נְשַׁמּוֹת וְעָרֶיהָ בְּתוֹךְ עָרִים מָחֳרָבוֹת תִּהְיֶיןָ
שְׁמָמָה אַרְבָּעִים שָׁנָה וַהֲפִצֹתִי אֶת־מִצְרַיִם בַּגּוֹיִם וְזֵרִיתִים
יג בָּאֲרָצוֹת׃ כִּי כֹּה אָמַר אֲדֹנָי יְהוִה מִקֵּץ אַרְבָּעִים

---

they have committed in lending a hand to the war against His people. There is a Judge, and there will be a reckoning even at the darkest hour. On the list of nations

forty years I will gather Egypt in from the people among whom
14 they were scattered. I will restore the fortunes of Egypt; I will
restore them to the land of Patros, the land of their origin, and
15 there they will be a lowly kingdom. She will be the lowest of the
kingdoms and will never again elevate herself above the nations;
I will reduce them to a state where they cannot dominate among
16 the nations. They will no longer be a source of trust for the
House of Israel but merely a reminder of Israel's sin in turning to
17 them, and they will know that I am the Lord God." It
was in the twenty-seventh year in the first month on the first
18 day of the month that the word of the Lord came to me: "Man:
Nevukhadretzar, king of Babylon, exerted his army to labor hard
against Tyre. Every head was rubbed raw, every shoulder worn
down bare, but from Tyre neither he nor his army received pay
19 for the hard work with which they toiled against her. So
the Lord God says this: See that to Nevukhadretzar, king of Babylon, I will give the land of Egypt. He will carry off her wealth,
ransack her spoils, and seize her loot; she will be the pay for his
20 army. I shall give him the land of Egypt as his payment, for which
he has labored, which he has done for Me, declares the Lord
21 God. On that day I will make a horn of strength grow for the
House of Israel, and you – I will let your voice be heard among
them, and they will know that I am the Lord."

Haftarat Bo

JEREMIAH

For Ashkenazim and Sephardim

46 13 The word that the Lord spoke to Yirmeyahu the prophet –
how Nevukhadretzar, king of Babylon, would come to attack
14 the land of Egypt: Tell it in Egypt, let it be heard in Migdol, and
let it be heard in Nof and in Taḥpanḥes! Say, "Stand firm and
prepare yourself, for the sword has devoured your surround-
15 ings." Why have your warriors been swept away? They did not

to Yehuda. In the prophet's eyes, all peoples are transient, and can cease to exist and be replaced once they have served their role in history. As such, they can be punished with utter destruction for their cruel and wicked acts in the context of world events. It is God who directs the course of world history, and it is He who will hold wicked states to account. It is He too who will always leave Israel standing on the world stage, even after punishing it for its sins.

שָׁנָה אֲקַבֵּץ אֶת־מִצְרַיִם מִן־הָעַמִּים אֲשֶׁר־נָפֹצוּ שָׁמָּה׃
יד וְשַׁבְתִּי אֶת־שְׁבוּת מִצְרַיִם וַהֲשִׁבֹתִי אֹתָם אֶרֶץ פַּתְרוֹס
טו עַל־אֶרֶץ מְכוּרָתָם וְהָיוּ שָׁם מַמְלָכָה שְׁפָלָה׃ מִן־הַמַּמְלָכוֹת
תִּהְיֶה שְׁפָלָה וְלֹא־תִתְנַשֵּׂא עוֹד עַל־הַגּוֹיִם וְהִמְעַטְתִּים
טז לְבִלְתִּי רְדוֹת בַּגּוֹיִם׃ וְלֹא יִהְיֶה־עוֹד לְבֵית יִשְׂרָאֵל
לְמִבְטָח מַזְכִּיר עָוֺן בִּפְנוֹתָם אַחֲרֵיהֶם וְיָדְעוּ כִּי אֲנִי אֲדֹנָי
יז יֱהֹוִה׃ וַיְהִי בְּעֶשְׂרִים וָשֶׁבַע שָׁנָה בָּרִאשׁוֹן בְּאֶחָד
יח לַחֹדֶשׁ הָיָה דְבַר־יְהֹוָה אֵלַי לֵאמֹר׃ בֶּן־אָדָם נְבוּכַדְרֶאצַּר
מֶלֶךְ־בָּבֶל הֶעֱבִיד אֶת־חֵילוֹ עֲבֹדָה גְדוֹלָה אֶל־צֹר כָּל־רֹאשׁ
מֻקְרָח וְכָל־כָּתֵף מְרוּטָה וְשָׂכָר לֹא־הָיָה לוֹ וּלְחֵילוֹ מִצֹּר עַל־
יט הָעֲבֹדָה אֲשֶׁר־עָבַד עָלֶיהָ׃ לָכֵן כֹּה אָמַר אֲדֹנָי
יֱהֹוִה הִנְנִי נֹתֵן לִנְבוּכַדְרֶאצַּר מֶלֶךְ־בָּבֶל אֶת־אֶרֶץ מִצְרָיִם
וְנָשָׂא הֲמֹנָהּ וְשָׁלַל שְׁלָלָהּ וּבָזַז בִּזָּהּ וְהָיְתָה שָׂכָר לְחֵילוֹ׃
כ פְּעֻלָּתוֹ אֲשֶׁר־עָבַד בָּהּ נָתַתִּי לוֹ אֶת־אֶרֶץ מִצְרָיִם אֲשֶׁר
כא עָשׂוּ לִי נְאֻם אֲדֹנָי יֱהֹוִה׃ בַּיּוֹם הַהוּא אַצְמִיחַ קֶרֶן לְבֵית
יִשְׂרָאֵל וּלְךָ אֶתֵּן פִּתְחוֹן־פֶּה בְּתוֹכָם וְיָדְעוּ כִּי־אֲנִי יְהֹוָה׃

הפטרת בא

ירמיה
For Ashkenazim and Sepharadim

מו יג הַדָּבָר אֲשֶׁר דִּבֶּר יְהֹוָה אֶל־יִרְמְיָהוּ הַנָּבִיא לָבוֹא
יד נְבוּכַדְרֶאצַּר מֶלֶךְ בָּבֶל לְהַכּוֹת אֶת־אֶרֶץ מִצְרָיִם׃ הַגִּידוּ
בְמִצְרַיִם וְהַשְׁמִיעוּ בְמִגְדּוֹל וְהַשְׁמִיעוּ בְנֹף וּבְתַחְפַּנְחֵס
טו אִמְרוּ הִתְיַצֵּב וְהָכֵן לָךְ כִּי־אָכְלָה חֶרֶב סְבִיבֶיךָ׃ מַדּוּעַ נִסְחַף

BO

For Ashkenazim and Sepharadim

The prophecies that close the book of Jeremiah address the nations of the Levant. They are harbingers of the doom that awaits those peoples who participated in the destruction of Yehuda and Jerusalem. In one, the prophet describes the expedition of Nevukhadnetzar to conquer Egypt, after he has laid waste

16 stand because the LORD pushed them down. He made many
falter. Each man fell upon his comrade and said, "Get up and let
us return to our people and to the land of our birth, away from
17 the sword of the oppressor." There they will taunt: "Pharaoh,
king of Egypt, king over a multitude, allowed the appointed
18 time to go by." As I live – declares the King, LORD of Hosts is
His name – just as Tabor is among the mountains, and Carmel
19 is by the sea, so will he come. Make for yourselves baggage for
exile, you who dwell securely, daughter Egypt, for Nof will be-
20 come a desolation, laid waste, with no inhabitant. A
very beautiful calf was Egypt, but a murderous enemy attacks
21 her from the north. Even her hired soldiers within her army
are like fattened calves. They too shall turn away, flee together,
and not stand firm. Their day of doom has arrived, when they
22 will meet their fate. Her voice will go forth like a snake's, for
they will attack her with force and come upon her with axes
23 like woodcutters. They shall cut down her forest, declares the
LORD, although it cannot be fathomed. There are more of
24 them than locusts; they are innumerable. Shamed is daughter
25 Egypt, given over into the hands of the northern people. Said
the LORD of Hosts, the God of Israel, I will inflict punishment
upon Amon of No, and upon Pharaoh, and upon Egypt, upon
her gods and upon her kings, upon Pharaoh and all who trust
26 in him. I will give them over into the hands of those who seek
their lives and into the hands of Nevukhadretzar, king of Babylon, and into the hands of his servants. Afterward, she shall be
27 inhabited as in days of old, declares the LORD. As for
you, My servant Yaakov, do not fear, and Israel, do not be terrified, for I will deliver you from a distant land and your descendants from their land of captivity. For Yaakov it will again
28 be quiet and tranquil, with none to frighten him. And you, My
servant Yaakov, do not fear, declares the LORD, for I am with
you. For I will make an end of all the nations among whom I
have scattered you, but of you I will not make an end. I will
discipline you justly, but I will surely not annihilate you.

טז אַבִּירֶיךָ לֹא עָמַד כִּי יְהוָה הֲדָפוֹ׃ הִרְבָּה כּוֹשֵׁל גַּם־נָפַל
אִישׁ אֶל־רֵעֵהוּ וַיֹּאמְרוּ קוּמָה ׀ וְנָשֻׁבָה אֶל־עַמֵּנוּ וְאֶל־אֶרֶץ
יז מוֹלַדְתֵּנוּ מִפְּנֵי חֶרֶב הַיּוֹנָה׃ קָרְאוּ שָׁם פַּרְעֹה מֶלֶךְ־מִצְרַיִם
יח שָׁאוֹן הֶעֱבִיר הַמּוֹעֵד׃ חַי־אָנִי נְאֻם־הַמֶּלֶךְ יְהוָה צְבָאוֹת
יט שְׁמוֹ כִּי כְּתָבוֹר בֶּהָרִים וּכְכַרְמֶל בַּיָּם יָבוֹא׃ כְּלֵי גוֹלָה עֲשִׂי
לָךְ יוֹשֶׁבֶת בַּת־מִצְרָיִם כִּי־נֹף לְשַׁמָּה תִהְיֶה וְנִצְּתָה מֵאֵין
כ יוֹשֵׁב׃ עֶגְלָה יְפֵה־פִיָּה מִצְרָיִם קֶרֶץ מִצָּפוֹן בָּא
כא בָא׃ גַּם־שְׂכִרֶיהָ בְקִרְבָּהּ כְּעֶגְלֵי מַרְבֵּק כִּי־גַם־הֵמָּה הִפְנוּ
נָסוּ יַחְדָּיו לֹא עָמָדוּ כִּי יוֹם אֵידָם בָּא עֲלֵיהֶם עֵת פְּקֻדָּתָם׃
כב קוֹלָהּ כַּנָּחָשׁ יֵלֵךְ כִּי־בְחַיִל יֵלֵכוּ וּבְקַרְדֻּמּוֹת בָּאוּ לָהּ כְּחֹטְבֵי
כג עֵצִים׃ כָּרְתוּ יַעְרָהּ נְאֻם־יְהוָה כִּי לֹא יֵחָקֵר כִּי רַבּוּ מֵאַרְבֶּה
כד וְאֵין לָהֶם מִסְפָּר׃ הֹבִישָׁה בַּת־מִצְרָיִם נִתְּנָה בְּיַד עַם־צָפוֹן׃
כה אָמַר יְהוָה צְבָאוֹת אֱלֹהֵי יִשְׂרָאֵל הִנְנִי פוֹקֵד אֶל־אָמוֹן מִנֹּא
וְעַל־פַּרְעֹה וְעַל־מִצְרַיִם וְעַל־אֱלֹהֶיהָ וְעַל־מְלָכֶיהָ וְעַל־
כו פַּרְעֹה וְעַל הַבֹּטְחִים בּוֹ׃ וּנְתַתִּים בְּיַד מְבַקְשֵׁי נַפְשָׁם וּבְיַד
נְבוּכַדְרֶאצַּר מֶלֶךְ־בָּבֶל וּבְיַד עֲבָדָיו וְאַחֲרֵי־כֵן תִּשְׁכֹּן כִּימֵי־
כז קֶדֶם נְאֻם־יְהוָה׃ וְאַתָּה אַל־תִּירָא עַבְדִּי יַעֲקֹב
וְאַל־תֵּחַת יִשְׂרָאֵל כִּי הִנְנִי מוֹשִׁעֲךָ מֵרָחוֹק וְאֶת־זַרְעֲךָ
כח מֵאֶרֶץ שִׁבְיָם וְשָׁב יַעֲקוֹב וְשָׁקַט וְשַׁאֲנַן וְאֵין מַחֲרִיד׃ אַתָּה
אַל־תִּירָא עַבְדִּי יַעֲקֹב נְאֻם־יְהוָה כִּי אִתְּךָ אָנִי כִּי אֶעֱשֶׂה
כָלָה בְּכָל־הַגּוֹיִם ׀ אֲשֶׁר הִדַּחְתִּיךָ שָׁמָּה וְאֹתְךָ לֹא־אֶעֱשֶׂה
כָלָה וְיִסַּרְתִּיךָ לַמִּשְׁפָּט וְנַקֵּה לֹא אֲנַקֶּךָּ׃

ISAIAH
For Yemenites

19 1 The burden of Egypt: Behold the LORD, riding upon swift cloud
and coming to Egypt. The gods of Egypt all sway before Him;
2 the heart of Egypt will dissolve. I shall make Egypt wrestle with
Egypt; brother will fight against brother, friend against friend,
3 city against city, realm against realm. Egypt will empty its spirit
from within, and I shall confound all its plans. The people will
seek after their false gods and mutterers, necromancers, medi-
4 ums. I shall dam Egypt through a hard-handed master; a mighty
king will tyrannize them, so says the Master, LORD of Hosts.
5 The sea will be emptied of water; the river will be scorched dry.
6 Rivers will be forsaken; Egypt's canals will dwindle and dry, and
7 rush and reed wither. Naked land on the Nile bed, naked the
bank of the Nile, and all that seeds and grows in the Nile will dry
8 up, disperse, be gone. The fishermen will lament; all who throw
hooks to the river will mourn, all who spread nets over water left
9 waste. The many who work combed flax will be shamed with all
10 those who weave fine cotton; Egypt's foundations – crushed, its
11 dam builders mired spirits. The princes of Tzoan are fools; the
wisest of Pharaoh's advisors give idiots' counsel. How can you
say to Pharaoh, "I am a son of wise men, heir to the ancient
12 kings?" Where, then – where are these wise men of yours? Surely they would tell you, surely they must know what the LORD
13 of Hosts has planned for Egypt. The princes of Tzoan are fools;
the princes of Nof, deceived. They have lead Egypt astray, the
14 very mainstay of its tribes. The LORD has poured into her a spirit
of madness, and they have led Egypt awry in all it does, like a
15 drunk man lurching through his vomit. Nothing in Egypt will
be done that is done by head or by tail, by palm or by bulrush
16 of them. On that day, Egypt will be like women who
quake and fear the LORD of Hosts' raised hand brandished over
17 them; the land of Judah will be the terror of Egypt. Whoever

---

recognition will lead to a change of perspective in Egypt and in Assyria as well, who will ultimately join Israel in worshipping God alone.

Scholars and commentators debate what events or period of time is referred to in this prophecy. Some identify the tyrannical foreign ruler as a king of Ethiopia, and some hold him to be the emperor of Assyria or even Persia. In its second section, the prophecy clearly describes the end of days, the conditions for which have not yet been fulfilled.

ישעיה
For Yemenites

יט א מַשָּׂא מִצְרָיִם הִנֵּה יְהוָה רֹכֵב עַל־עָב קַל וּבָא מִצְרַיִם וְנָעוּ
ב אֱלִילֵי מִצְרַיִם מִפָּנָיו וּלְבַב מִצְרַיִם יִמַּס בְּקִרְבּוֹ׃ וְסִכְסַכְתִּי
מִצְרַיִם בְּמִצְרַיִם וְנִלְחֲמוּ אִישׁ בְּאָחִיו וְאִישׁ בְּרֵעֵהוּ עִיר
ג בְּעִיר מַמְלָכָה בְּמַמְלָכָה׃ וְנָבְקָה רוּחַ־מִצְרַיִם בְּקִרְבּוֹ וַעֲצָתוֹ
אֲבַלֵּעַ וְדָרְשׁוּ אֶל־הָאֱלִילִים וְאֶל־הָאִטִּים וְאֶל־הָאֹבוֹת
ד וְאֶל־הַיִּדְּעֹנִים׃ וְסִכַּרְתִּי אֶת־מִצְרַיִם בְּיַד אֲדֹנִים קָשֶׁה וּמֶלֶךְ
ה עַז יִמְשָׁל־בָּם נְאֻם הָאָדוֹן יְהוָה צְבָאוֹת׃ וְנִשְּׁתוּ־מַיִם מֵהַיָּם
ו וְנָהָר יֶחֱרַב וְיָבֵשׁ׃ וְהֶאֶזְנִיחוּ נְהָרוֹת דָּלְלוּ וְחָרְבוּ יְאֹרֵי מָצוֹר
ז קָנֶה וָסוּף קָמֵלוּ׃ עָרוֹת עַל־יְאוֹר עַל־פִּי יְאוֹר וְכֹל מִזְרַע
ח יְאוֹר יִיבַשׁ נִדַּף וְאֵינֶנּוּ׃ וְאָנוּ הַדַּיָּגִים וְאָבְלוּ כָּל־מַשְׁלִיכֵי
ט בַיְאוֹר חַכָּה וּפֹרְשֵׂי מִכְמֹרֶת עַל־פְּנֵי־מַיִם אֻמְלָלוּ׃ וּבֹשׁוּ
י עֹבְדֵי פִשְׁתִּים שְׂרִיקוֹת וְאֹרְגִים חוֹרָי׃ וְהָיוּ שָׁתֹתֶיהָ מְדֻכָּאִים
יא כָּל־עֹשֵׂי שֶׂכֶר אַגְמֵי־נָפֶשׁ׃ אַךְ־אֱוִלִים שָׂרֵי צֹעַן חַכְמֵי יֹעֲצֵי
פַרְעֹה עֵצָה נִבְעָרָה אֵיךְ תֹּאמְרוּ אֶל־פַּרְעֹה בֶּן־חֲכָמִים אֲנִי
יב בֶּן־מַלְכֵי־קֶדֶם׃ אַיָּם אֵפוֹא חֲכָמֶיךָ וְיַגִּידוּ נָא לָךְ וְיֵדְעוּ מַה־
יג יָּעַץ יְהוָה צְבָאוֹת עַל־מִצְרָיִם׃ נוֹאֲלוּ שָׂרֵי צֹעַן נִשְּׁאוּ שָׂרֵי
יד נֹף הִתְעוּ אֶת־מִצְרַיִם פִּנַּת שְׁבָטֶיהָ׃ יְהוָה מָסַךְ בְּקִרְבָּהּ
רוּחַ עִוְעִים וְהִתְעוּ אֶת־מִצְרַיִם בְּכָל־מַעֲשֵׂהוּ כְּהִתָּעוֹת
טו שִׁכּוֹר בְּקִיאוֹ׃ וְלֹא־יִהְיֶה לְמִצְרַיִם מַעֲשֶׂה אֲשֶׁר יַעֲשֶׂה
טז רֹאשׁ וְזָנָב כִּפָּה וְאַגְמוֹן׃ בַּיּוֹם הַהוּא יִהְיֶה
מִצְרַיִם כַּנָּשִׁים וְחָרַד ׀ וּפָחַד מִפְּנֵי תְּנוּפַת יַד־יְהוָה צְבָאוֹת
יז אֲשֶׁר־הוּא מֵנִיף עָלָיו׃ וְהָיְתָה אַדְמַת יְהוּדָה לְמִצְרַיִם לְחָגָּא

For Yemenites

In the prophecy of Yeshayahu, as part of a collection of prophecies directed at various nations, we find one singling out Egypt and describing its future in two stages. At the first stage, there will be internal strife within the Egyptian state that will lead to its conquest by a tyrannical foreign ruler who will dominate it. All strata of Egyptian society will be humiliated, and the economy of Egypt will be greatly damaged. All this will lead the Egyptians to recognize the sovereignty of God, who directs all these events. This

▶

may mention its name will strike them with fear of the LORD
18 of Hosts' plan – of what He has destined for them. On
that day, five cities of Egypt shall speak the language of Canaan
and swear their oaths by the LORD of Hosts. City of Calamity,
19 one shall be named. On that day, in Egypt's heartlands,
an altar to the LORD will stand; at her borders a pillar to the
20 LORD. They will be sign and testament in the land of Egypt to
the LORD of Hosts, for the people shall cry out to the LORD because of their oppressors; He will send them a rescuer, a fighter;
21 he will save them. The LORD will be made known to Egypt, and
Egypt will know the LORD on that day. And they will serve by
sacrifice and offering; they will make the LORD vows and honor
22 them. The LORD will plague Egypt – plague it and heal. They
will come back to the LORD, and He will receive their appeal
23 and heal. On that day a road will run from Egypt to
Assyria. Assyria will come to Egypt. Egypt will come to Assyria,
24 and Egypt with Assyria will worship. On that day, Israel will be one with Egypt and Assyria, a blessing on this earth.
25 For the LORD of Hosts has blessed him, saying: Blessed are My
people, Egypt, Assyria, work of My hands, and Israel, My own
possession.

HAFTARAT BESHALAḤ

JUDGES

Ashkenazim and Chabad begin here

4 4 Devora was a prophetess, the wife of Lapidot; she was judging
5 Israel at that time. She sat beneath Devora's palm between Rama
and Beit El in the Efrayim hills; the Israelites would go up to her

created a division between the northern and central tribes. Following God's commandment to the prophetess Devora, an army of volunteers came onto the field under the leadership of Barak son of Avinoam to fight the Canaanite armies. Following the Israelites' surprising and dramatic victory over the Canaanites and their chariots, Devora and Barak sang this song of praise to God, just as generations earlier, the nation redeemed from Egypt had sung the Song at the Sea after their miraculous rescue from the Egyptian cavalry.

כֹּל אֲשֶׁר יַזְכִּיר אֹתָהּ אֵלָיו יִפְחָד מִפְּנֵי עֲצַת יְהוָה צְבָאוֹת
יח אֲשֶׁר־הוּא יוֹעֵץ עָלָיו׃ בַּיּוֹם הַהוּא יִהְיוּ
חָמֵשׁ עָרִים בְּאֶרֶץ מִצְרַיִם מְדַבְּרוֹת שְׂפַת כְּנַעַן וְנִשְׁבָּעוֹת
יט לַיהוָה צְבָאוֹת עִיר הַהֶרֶס יֵאָמֵר לְאֶחָת׃ בַּיּוֹם
הַהוּא יִהְיֶה מִזְבֵּחַ לַיהוָה בְּתוֹךְ אֶרֶץ מִצְרָיִם וּמַצֵּבָה אֵצֶל־
כ גְּבוּלָהּ לַיהוָה׃ וְהָיָה לְאוֹת וּלְעֵד לַיהוָה צְבָאוֹת בְּאֶרֶץ
מִצְרָיִם כִּי־יִצְעֲקוּ אֶל־יְהוָה מִפְּנֵי לֹחֲצִים וְיִשְׁלַח לָהֶם
כא מוֹשִׁיעַ וָרָב וְהִצִּילָם׃ וְנוֹדַע יְהוָה לְמִצְרַיִם וְיָדְעוּ מִצְרַיִם
אֶת־יְהוָה בַּיּוֹם הַהוּא וְעָבְדוּ זֶבַח וּמִנְחָה וְנָדְרוּ־נֵדֶר לַיהוָה
כב וְשִׁלֵּמוּ׃ וְנָגַף יְהוָה אֶת־מִצְרַיִם נָגֹף וְרָפוֹא וְשָׁבוּ עַד־יְהוָה
כג וְנֶעְתַּר לָהֶם וּרְפָאָם׃ בַּיּוֹם הַהוּא תִּהְיֶה מְסִלָּה
מִמִּצְרַיִם אַשּׁוּרָה וּבָא־אַשּׁוּר בְּמִצְרַיִם וּמִצְרַיִם בְּאַשּׁוּר
כד וְעָבְדוּ מִצְרַיִם אֶת־אַשּׁוּר׃ בַּיּוֹם הַהוּא יִהְיֶה
יִשְׂרָאֵל שְׁלִישִׁיָּה לְמִצְרַיִם וּלְאַשּׁוּר בְּרָכָה בְּקֶרֶב הָאָרֶץ׃
כה אֲשֶׁר בֵּרְכוֹ יְהוָה צְבָאוֹת לֵאמֹר בָּרוּךְ עַמִּי מִצְרַיִם וּמַעֲשֵׂה
יָדַי אַשּׁוּר וְנַחֲלָתִי יִשְׂרָאֵל׃

הפטרת בשלח

שופטים
Ashkenazim and Chabad begin here

ד ד וּדְבוֹרָה אִשָּׁה נְבִיאָה אֵשֶׁת לַפִּידוֹת הִיא שֹׁפְטָה אֶת־
ה יִשְׂרָאֵל בָּעֵת הַהִיא׃ וְהִיא יוֹשֶׁבֶת תַּחַת־תֹּמֶר דְּבוֹרָה בֵּין
הָרָמָה וּבֵין בֵּית־אֵל בְּהַר אֶפְרָיִם וַיַּעֲלוּ אֵלֶיהָ בְּנֵי יִשְׂרָאֵל

BESHALAḤ

The period of the Judges was characterized by a vacuum of centralized power. This reality projected an appearance of weakness within Israelite society and without, causing the tribes to become ready prey for their aggressive neighbors. Such was the case in the generation of Devora and Barak. The Canaanites relied on iron chariotry for military power, and they disrupted the everyday life of the Israelite tribes that lived next to them in the valley of Yizre'el. The danger of Canaanite raids on the main roads

6 for judgment. One day, she summoned Barak son of Avinoam
from Kedesh Naftali and said to him, "The LORD, God of Israel,
has commanded: Go, take ten thousand men of the people of
7 Naftali and Zevulun and lead them to Mount Tavor. And at the
Kishon Stream I shall lead to you to Sisera, Yavin's general, along
with his chariots and his hordes, and deliver him into your hands."
8 Barak said to her, "If you go with me, I will go; if not, I will not."
9 "Then I shall go with you," she said, "but you will find no glory
on the path you are taking, for the LORD will deliver Sisera into
the hands of a woman." So Devora arose and accompanied Barak
10 to Kedesh. Barak mustered Zevulun and Naftali at Kedesh and
advanced with ten thousand men behind him, and Devora went
11 up with him. Ḥever the Kenite had parted ways from the Kenites,
who were descended from Ḥovav, Moshe's father-in-law. He had
pitched his tent at Elon BeTzaananim, which was by Kedesh.
12 Sisera was informed that Barak son of Avinoam had advanced
13 to Mount Tavor. And Sisera mustered all his chariots – nine hundred iron chariots – and all his warriors from Ḥaroshet HaGoyim
14 to Kishon Stream. "Rise up!" Devora said to Barak. "For on this
day, the LORD will deliver Sisera into your hands – the LORD
marches before you!" Barak charged down Mount Tavor with
15 ten thousand men behind him. And the LORD threw Sisera, all
his chariots, and his entire force into panic before Barak's swords.
16 Sisera dismounted from his chariot and fled on foot. Barak
chased the chariots and warriors to Ḥaroshet HaGoyim, and
all of Sisera's army fell by the sword; not a single man survived.
17 Now Sisera had fled on foot to the tent of Yael, the wife of Ḥever
the Kenite, for there was peace between Yavin, king of Ḥatzor,
18 and Ḥever's family. Yael went out to meet Sisera. "Turn aside, my
lord," she said to him, "turn aside to me – do not fear." He turned
19 aside into her tent, and she covered him with a blanket. "Give
me a little water, please," he asked her, "for I am thirsty." She
opened a skin of milk, gave him some to drink, and covered him
20 once again. "Stand at the entrance to the tent," he told her, "and

ו לְמִשְׁפָּט: וַתִּשְׁלַח וַתִּקְרָא לְבָרָק בֶּן־אֲבִינֹעַם מִקֶּדֶשׁ נַפְתָּלִי
וַתֹּאמֶר אֵלָיו הֲלֹא־צִוָּה ׀ יְהוָה אֱלֹהֵי־יִשְׂרָאֵל לֵךְ וּמָשַׁכְתָּ
בְּהַר תָּבוֹר וְלָקַחְתָּ עִמְּךָ עֲשֶׂרֶת אֲלָפִים אִישׁ מִבְּנֵי נַפְתָּלִי
ז וּמִבְּנֵי זְבֻלוּן: וּמָשַׁכְתִּי אֵלֶיךָ אֶל־נַחַל קִישׁוֹן אֶת־סִיסְרָא
שַׂר־צְבָא יָבִין וְאֶת־רִכְבּוֹ וְאֶת־הֲמוֹנוֹ וּנְתַתִּיהוּ בְּיָדֶךָ:
ח וַיֹּאמֶר אֵלֶיהָ בָּרָק אִם־תֵּלְכִי עִמִּי וְהָלָכְתִּי וְאִם־לֹא תֵלְכִי
ט עִמִּי לֹא אֵלֵךְ: וַתֹּאמֶר הָלֹךְ אֵלֵךְ עִמָּךְ אֶפֶס כִּי לֹא תִהְיֶה
תִּפְאַרְתְּךָ עַל־הַדֶּרֶךְ אֲשֶׁר אַתָּה הוֹלֵךְ כִּי בְיַד־אִשָּׁה יִמְכֹּר
יְהוָה אֶת־סִיסְרָא וַתָּקָם דְּבוֹרָה וַתֵּלֶךְ עִם־בָּרָק קֶדְשָׁה:
י וַיַּזְעֵק בָּרָק אֶת־זְבוּלֻן וְאֶת־נַפְתָּלִי קֶדְשָׁה וַיַּעַל בְּרַגְלָיו
יא עֲשֶׂרֶת אַלְפֵי אִישׁ וַתַּעַל עִמּוֹ דְּבוֹרָה: וְחֶבֶר הַקֵּינִי נִפְרָד
מִקַּיִן מִבְּנֵי חֹבָב חֹתֵן מֹשֶׁה וַיֵּט אָהֳלוֹ עַד־אֵלוֹן בצענים בְּצַעֲנַנִּים
יב אֲשֶׁר אֶת־קֶדֶשׁ: וַיַּגִּדוּ לְסִיסְרָא כִּי עָלָה בָּרָק בֶּן־אֲבִינֹעַם
יג הַר־תָּבוֹר: וַיַּזְעֵק סִיסְרָא אֶת־כָּל־רִכְבּוֹ תְּשַׁע מֵאוֹת רֶכֶב
בַּרְזֶל וְאֶת־כָּל־הָעָם אֲשֶׁר אִתּוֹ מֵחֲרֹשֶׁת הַגּוֹיִם אֶל־נַחַל
יד קִישׁוֹן: וַתֹּאמֶר דְּבֹרָה אֶל־בָּרָק קוּם כִּי זֶה הַיּוֹם אֲשֶׁר
נָתַן יְהוָה אֶת־סִיסְרָא בְּיָדֶךָ הֲלֹא יְהוָה יָצָא לְפָנֶיךָ וַיֵּרֶד
טו בָּרָק מֵהַר תָּבוֹר וַעֲשֶׂרֶת אֲלָפִים אִישׁ אַחֲרָיו: וַיָּהָם יְהוָה
אֶת־סִיסְרָא וְאֶת־כָּל־הָרֶכֶב וְאֶת־כָּל־הַמַּחֲנֶה לְפִי־חֶרֶב
טז לִפְנֵי בָרָק וַיֵּרֶד סִיסְרָא מֵעַל הַמֶּרְכָּבָה וַיָּנָס בְּרַגְלָיו: וּבָרָק
רָדַף אַחֲרֵי הָרֶכֶב וְאַחֲרֵי הַמַּחֲנֶה עַד חֲרֹשֶׁת הַגּוֹיִם וַיִּפֹּל
יז כָּל־מַחֲנֵה סִיסְרָא לְפִי־חֶרֶב לֹא נִשְׁאַר עַד־אֶחָד: וְסִיסְרָא
נָס בְּרַגְלָיו אֶל־אֹהֶל יָעֵל אֵשֶׁת חֶבֶר הַקֵּינִי כִּי שָׁלוֹם בֵּין
יח יָבִין מֶלֶךְ־חָצוֹר וּבֵין בֵּית חֶבֶר הַקֵּינִי: וַתֵּצֵא יָעֵל לִקְרַאת
סִיסְרָא וַתֹּאמֶר אֵלָיו סוּרָה אֲדֹנִי סוּרָה אֵלַי אַל־תִּירָא וַיָּסַר
יט אֵלֶיהָ הָאֹהֱלָה וַתְּכַסֵּהוּ בַּשְּׂמִיכָה: וַיֹּאמֶר אֵלֶיהָ הַשְׁקִינִי־
נָא מְעַט־מַיִם כִּי צָמֵאתִי וַתִּפְתַּח אֶת־נֹאוד הֶחָלָב וַתַּשְׁקֵהוּ
כ וַתְּכַסֵּהוּ: וַיֹּאמֶר אֵלֶיהָ עֲמֹד פֶּתַח הָאֹהֶל וְהָיָה אִם־אִישׁ

21 if anyone comes and asks you if someone is here, say, 'No.'" Then
Yael, wife of Ḥever, picked up a tent peg, grasped a mallet, crept
up to him – he had fallen asleep, exhausted – and hammered the
tent peg through his temple until it sunk into the ground and he
22 died. Now Barak was chasing Sisera, and Yael went out to meet
him. "Come," she said to him, "I will show you the man you seek."
He came to her, and there was Sisera, sprawled out dead, with
23 the tent peg through his temple. *On that day, God subdued *Yemenites begin here*
24 Yavin, king of Canaan, before the Israelites. And the hand of the
Israelites grew harsher and harsher against Yavin, king of Canaan,
until they had destroyed him.

5 1 *And Devora sang – and Barak son of Avinoam with her – on *Sepharadim begin here*
2 that day: / When chaos was loosed in Israel, / when people of-
3 fered themselves willingly – / bless the LORD! / Hear, O kings, /
give ear, O rulers, / I – to the LORD I will sing, / I will chant
4 to the LORD, God of Israel. / O LORD, when You left Se'ir, /
when You marched from the fields of Edom, / the earth shook, /
5 the heavens poured – / rain poured from the clouds, / the
mountains melted before the LORD, / Sinai itself before the
6 LORD, God of Israel! / In the days of Shamgar son of Anat, / in
the days of Yael, / there were no caravans; / wayfarers walked
7 roundabout paths. / There were no unwalled cities in Israel, /
none – / until you arose, Devora, / until you arose, a mother
8 in Israel! / When they chose new gods, / there was war at the
gates – / but no shield or spear was seen / amid forty thousand
9 of Israel! / My heart is with Israel's leaders, / the people who
10 offer themselves willingly – / bless the LORD! / O riders of
white she-donkeys, / mounted on fine saddles, / O wayfarers: /

כא יָבֹא וּשְׁאֵלֵךְ וְאָמַר הֲיֵשׁ־פֹּה אִישׁ וְאָמַרְתְּ אָיִן׃ וַתִּקַּח יָעֵל
אֵשֶׁת־חֶבֶר אֶת־יְתַד הָאֹהֶל וַתָּשֶׂם אֶת־הַמַּקֶּבֶת בְּיָדָהּ
וַתָּבוֹא אֵלָיו בַּלָּאט וַתִּתְקַע אֶת־הַיָּתֵד בְּרַקָּתוֹ וַתִּצְנַח
כב בָּאָרֶץ וְהוּא־נִרְדָּם וַיָּעַף וַיָּמֹת׃ וְהִנֵּה בָרָק רֹדֵף אֶת־סִיסְרָא
וַתֵּצֵא יָעֵל לִקְרָאתוֹ וַתֹּאמֶר לוֹ לֵךְ וְאַרְאֶךָּ אֶת־הָאִישׁ
אֲשֶׁר־אַתָּה מְבַקֵּשׁ וַיָּבֹא אֵלֶיהָ וְהִנֵּה סִיסְרָא נֹפֵל מֵת
Yemenites begin here
כג וְהַיָּתֵד בְּרַקָּתוֹ׃ *וַיַּכְנַע אֱלֹהִים בַּיּוֹם הַהוּא אֵת יָבִין מֶלֶךְ־
כד כְּנָעַן לִפְנֵי בְּנֵי יִשְׂרָאֵל׃ וַתֵּלֶךְ יַד בְּנֵי־יִשְׂרָאֵל הָלוֹךְ וְקָשָׁה
עַל יָבִין מֶלֶךְ־כְּנָעַן עַד אֲשֶׁר הִכְרִיתוּ אֵת יָבִין מֶלֶךְ־כְּנָעַן׃

Sepharadim begin here
ה א *וַתָּשַׁר דְּבוֹרָה וּבָרָק בֶּן־אֲבִינֹעַם בַּיּוֹם הַהוּא
ב לֵאמֹר׃ בִּפְרֹעַ פְּרָעוֹת בְּיִשְׂרָאֵל בְּהִתְנַדֵּב
ג עָם בָּרְכוּ יהוה׃ שִׁמְעוּ מְלָכִים הַאֲזִינוּ
רֹזְנִים אָנֹכִי לַיהוה אָנֹכִי אָשִׁירָה אֲזַמֵּר
ד לַיהוה אֱלֹהֵי יִשְׂרָאֵל׃ יהוה בְּצֵאתְךָ
מִשֵּׂעִיר בְּצַעְדְּךָ מִשְּׂדֵה אֱדוֹם אֶרֶץ
רָעָשָׁה גַּם־שָׁמַיִם נָטָפוּ גַּם־עָבִים נָטְפוּ
ה מָיִם׃ הָרִים נָזְלוּ מִפְּנֵי יהוה זֶה
ו סִינַי מִפְּנֵי יהוה אֱלֹהֵי יִשְׂרָאֵל׃ בִּימֵי שַׁמְגַּר בֶּן־
עֲנָת בִּימֵי יָעֵל חָדְלוּ אֳרָחוֹת וְהֹלְכֵי
ז נְתִיבוֹת יֵלְכוּ אֳרָחוֹת עֲקַלְקַלּוֹת׃ חָדְלוּ פְרָזוֹן בְּיִשְׂרָאֵל
חָדֵלּוּ עַד שַׁקַּמְתִּי דְּבוֹרָה שַׁקַּמְתִּי
ח אֵם בְּיִשְׂרָאֵל׃ יִבְחַר אֱלֹהִים
חֲדָשִׁים אָז לָחֶם שְׁעָרִים מָגֵן
אִם־יֵרָאֶה וָרֹמַח בְּאַרְבָּעִים אֶלֶף
ט בְּיִשְׂרָאֵל׃ לִבִּי לְחוֹקְקֵי יִשְׂרָאֵל הַמִּתְנַדְּבִים
י בָּעָם בָּרְכוּ יהוה׃ רֹכְבֵי אֲתֹנוֹת
צְחֹרוֹת יֹשְׁבֵי עַל־מִדִּין וְהֹלְכֵי

11 speak out – / louder than the sound of archers / by the watering places; / there they shall recount the LORD's graces, / how
He graced the unwalled cities in Israel; / then, down to the
12 gates / marched the people of the LORD! / Awake, awake, Devora – / awake, awake, burst into song! / Arise, Barak – / seize
13 your captives, son of Avinoam; / then the remnant ruled over
the mighty people, / the LORD ruled over the warriors for me! /
14 From Efrayim, rooted in Amalek: / "After you, Binyamin, with
your people!" / From Makhir marched down leaders, / from
15 Zevulun, wielders of the scribal staff. / Yissakhar's chiefs were
with Devora, / Yissakhar, like Barak, charged into the valley, /
while amongst the clans of Reuven / was great soul-search-
16 ing. / Why did you linger among the sheepfolds / to hear the
whistling for the flocks? / Amongst the clans of Reuven / was
17 great soul-searching. / Gilad stayed put across the Jordan, /
and why did Dan stay by the ships? / Asher lingered by the
18 seashore, / staying put by its harbors. / Zevulun, a people who
risked their lives for death / with Naftali on the open heights; /
19 then came the kings to do battle, / then Canaan's kings did
battle / at Tanakh, by the waters of Megiddo – / but they took
20 no spoil of silver! / From the heavens they fought; / the stars
21 from their courses fought against Sisera! / Kishon Stream swept
them away, / the ancient stream, the Kishon Stream – / march
22 on, my soul, with might! / The hooves of horses hammered /
23 with the gallop, the gallop of the steeds! / "Curse Meroz," said
the LORD's angel, / "curse its people harshly, / for they did not
come to the aid of the LORD, / to the aid of the LORD amidst

יא עַל־דֶּ֖רֶךְ שִֽׂיחוּ׃ מִקּ֣וֹל מְחַֽצְצִ֗ים בֵּ֚ין
מַשְׁאַבִּ֔ים שָׁ֚ם יְתַנּוּ֙ צִדְק֣וֹת יְהוָ֔ה צִדְקֹ֥ת
פִּרְזֹנ֖וֹ בְּיִשְׂרָאֵ֑ל אָ֛ז יָרְד֥וּ לַשְּׁעָרִ֖ים עַם־
יב יְהוָֽה׃ ע֤וּרִי ע֙וּרִי֙ דְּב֣וֹרָ֔ה ע֥וּרִי
ע֖וּרִי דַּבְּרִי־שִׁ֑יר ק֥וּם בָּרָ֛ק וּֽשֲׁבֵ֥ה שֶׁבְיְךָ֖ בֶּן־
יג אֲבִינֹֽעַם׃ אָ֚ז יְרַ֣ד שָׂרִ֔יד לְאַדִּירִ֖ים עָ֑ם יְהוָ֕ה
יד יְרַד־לִ֖י בַּגִּבּוֹרִֽים׃ מִנִּ֣י אֶפְרַ֗יִם שָׁרְשָׁם֙
בַּעֲמָלֵ֔ק אַחֲרֶ֥יךָ בִנְיָמִ֖ין בַּעֲמָמֶ֑יךָ מִנִּ֣י
מָכִ֗יר יָֽרְדוּ֙ מְחֹ֣קְקִ֔ים וּמִ֨זְּבוּלֻ֔ן מֹשְׁכִ֖ים בְּשֵׁ֥בֶט
טו סֹפֵֽר׃ וְשָׂרַ֤י בְּיִשָּׂשכָר֙ עִם־דְּבֹרָ֔ה וְיִשָּׂשכָר֙
כֵּ֣ן בָּרָ֔ק בָּעֵ֖מֶק שֻׁלַּ֣ח
בְּרַגְלָ֑יו בִּפְלַגּ֣וֹת רְאוּבֵ֔ן גְּדֹלִ֖ים
טז חִקְקֵי־לֵֽב׃ לָ֣מָּה יָשַׁ֗בְתָּ בֵּ֚ין
הַמִּשְׁפְּתַ֔יִם לִשְׁמֹ֖עַ שְׁרִק֣וֹת עֲדָרִ֑ים לִפְלַגּ֣וֹת
יז רְאוּבֵ֔ן גְּדוֹלִ֖ים חִקְרֵי־לֵֽב׃ גִּלְעָ֞ד בְּעֵ֤בֶר הַיַּרְדֵּן֙
שָׁכֵ֔ן וְדָ֕ן לָ֥מָּה יָג֖וּר אֳנִיּ֑וֹת אָשֵׁ֗ר
יָשַׁב֙ לְח֣וֹף יַמִּ֔ים וְעַ֥ל מִפְרָצָ֖יו
יח יִשְׁכּֽוֹן׃ זְבֻל֗וּן עַ֣ם חֵרֵ֥ף נַפְשׁ֛וֹ לָמ֖וּת וְנַפְתָּלִ֑י
יט עַ֖ל מְר֥וֹמֵי שָׂדֶֽה׃ בָּ֤אוּ מְלָכִים֙
נִלְחָ֔מוּ אָ֚ז נִלְחֲמוּ֙ מַלְכֵ֣י כְנַ֔עַן בְּתַעְנַ֖ךְ
עַל מֵ֣י מְגִדּ֑וֹ בֶּ֥צַע כֶּ֖סֶף לֹ֥א
כ לָקָֽחוּ׃ מִן־שָׁמַ֖יִם נִלְחָ֑מוּ הַכּֽוֹכָבִים֙
כא מִֽמְּסִלּוֹתָ֔ם נִלְחֲמ֖וּ עִם־סִֽיסְרָא׃ נַ֤חַל קִישׁוֹן֙
גְּרָפָ֔ם נַ֥חַל קְדוּמִ֖ים נַ֣חַל קִישׁ֑וֹן תִּדְרְכִ֥י
כב נַפְשִׁ֖י עֹֽז׃ אָ֛ז הָלְמ֥וּ עִקְּבֵי־
כג ס֖וּס מִֽדַּהֲר֖וֹת דַּהֲר֥וֹת אַבִּירָֽיו׃ א֣וֹרוּ
מֵר֗וֹז אָמַר֙ מַלְאַ֣ךְ יְהוָ֔ה אֹ֥רוּ אָר֖וֹר
יֹשְׁבֶ֑יהָ כִּ֣י לֹא־בָ֙אוּ֙ לְעֶזְרַ֣ת יְהוָ֔ה לְעֶזְרַ֥ת

24 the warriors." / Blessed beyond women be Yael, / wife of Ḥever
25 the Kenite, / blessed beyond women in tents! / Water he asked
26 for, milk she gave; / in a princely bowl she offered cream. / Her
hand shot out for the tent peg, / her right hand for the work-
man's hammer, / and hammered Sisera / and crushed his head /
27 and smashed and pierced his temple! / Between her legs he lay
slumped, sprawled, / between her legs he slumped, sprawled, /
28 where he slumped, there he sprawled, slain! / Through the window she peered, / Sisera's mother wailed through the lattice, /
"Why does his chariot tarry so? / Why so late, the clank of his
29 chariots?" / The wisest of her ladies reply – / she even answers
30 herself – / "Why, they are dividing up the spoil they found, /
a womb or two for every man, / a haul of colors for Sisera, /
a haul of colors of embroidery, / colored embroidery, two apiece,
31 for the spoilers' throats." / Thus may all Your enemies perish, O
Lord, / and may His friends be like the risen sun! / And the
land was quiet for forty years.

Haftarat Yitro

6 1 In the year in which King Uziyahu died I saw the Lord sitting on ISAIAH
a high, raised throne, the hem of His clothing filling the Sanc-
2 tuary. There were seraphim standing above Him, each with six
wings – with two they covered their faces, with two they covered

the year in which King Uziyahu died," the prophet volunteers for his calling – an unusual phenomenon. He is tasked with confronting the people of Israel and warning them of the coming destruction if they continue in their evil ways. In the vision, God is seen sitting on a great throne in the Temple hall, surrounded

כד יהוה בַּגִּבּוֹרִֽים׃ תְּבֹרַךְ֙ מִנָּשִׁ֔ים
יָעֵ֕ל אֵ֖שֶׁת חֶ֣בֶר הַקֵּינִ֑י מִנָּשִׁ֥ים
כה בָּאֹ֖הֶל תְּבֹרָֽךְ׃ מַ֥יִם שָׁאַ֖ל חָלָ֣ב
כו נָתָ֑נָה בְּסֵ֥פֶל אַדִּירִ֖ים הִקְרִ֥יבָה חֶמְאָֽה׃ יָדָהּ֙
לַיָּתֵ֣ד תִּשְׁלַ֔חְנָה וִימִינָ֖הּ לְהַלְמ֣וּת
עֲמֵלִ֑ים וְהָלְמָ֤ה סִֽיסְרָא֙ מָחֲקָ֣ה רֹאשׁ֔וֹ וּמָחֲצָ֥ה
כז וְחָלְפָ֖ה רַקָּתֽוֹ׃ בֵּ֣ין רַגְלֶ֔יהָ כָּרַ֥ע נָפַ֖ל
שָׁכָ֑ב בֵּ֤ין רַגְלֶ֙יהָ֙ כָּרַ֣ע נָפָ֔ל בַּאֲשֶׁ֣ר
כח כָּרַ֔ע שָׁ֖ם נָפַ֥ל שָׁדֽוּד׃ בְּעַ֨ד הַחַלּ֜וֹן נִשְׁקְפָ֨ה
וַתְּיַבֵּ֜ב אֵ֤ם סִֽיסְרָא֙ בְּעַ֣ד הָֽאֶשְׁנָ֔ב מַדּ֗וּעַ
בֹּשֵׁ֤שׁ רִכְבּוֹ֙ לָב֔וֹא מַדּ֣וּעַ אֶֽחֱר֔וּ פַּעֲמֵ֖י
כט מַרְכְּבוֹתָֽיו׃ חַכְמ֥וֹת שָׂרוֹתֶ֖יהָ תַּעֲנֶ֑ינָּה אַף־
ל הִ֕יא תָּשִׁ֥יב אֲמָרֶ֖יהָ לָֽהּ׃ הֲלֹ֨א יִמְצְא֜וּ יְחַלְּק֣וּ
שָׁלָ֗ל רַ֤חַם רַחֲמָתַ֙יִם֙ לְרֹ֣אשׁ גֶּ֔בֶר שְׁלַ֤ל
צְבָעִים֙ לְסִֽיסְרָ֔א שְׁלַ֥ל צְבָעִ֖ים
לא רִקְמָ֑ה צֶ֥בַע רִקְמָתַ֖יִם לְצַוְּארֵ֥י שָׁלָֽל׃ כֵּ֠ן
יֹאבְד֤וּ כָל־אוֹיְבֶ֙יךָ֙ יהוה וְאֹ֣הֲבָ֔יו כְּצֵ֥את הַשֶּׁ֖מֶשׁ
בִּגְבֻרָת֑וֹ וַתִּשְׁקֹ֥ט הָאָ֖רֶץ אַרְבָּעִ֥ים שָׁנָֽה׃

הפטרת יתרו

ו א בִּשְׁנַת־מוֹת֙ הַמֶּ֣לֶךְ עֻזִּיָּ֔הוּ וָאֶרְאֶ֧ה אֶת־אֲדֹנָ֛י יֹשֵׁ֥ב עַל־כִּסֵּ֖א ישעיה
ב רָ֣ם וְנִשָּׂ֑א וְשׁוּלָ֖יו מְלֵאִ֥ים אֶת־הַהֵיכָֽל׃ שְׂרָפִ֨ים עֹמְדִ֜ים ׀

YITRO

The first part of this *haftara* is read by all different Jewish communities; it describes God's revelation to Yeshayahu. This revelation, like other prophetic revelations described in the Tanakh, comprises two aspects: a verbal component – God's words to the prophet – and a visual component – what the prophet sees. These two parts of the revelation complement one another. In this prophecy, which was revealed to Yeshayahu "in

3 their feet, and with two they were flying. And they called out
one to another, "Holy, holy, holy – the LORD of Hosts – all
4 the world's fullness His glory." The door pillars shook with the
5 voice of him who called – and smoke filled the House. And I
said, "This ache – I am condemned, for my mouth has been defiled, one man among a people with their mouths defiled, and
6 my eyes see the King, the LORD of Hosts." One of the seraphim
flew to me, and in his hand was a coal, taken with tongs from the
7 altar top. With this he touched my lips and said, "When this has
touched your lips, your iniquity is gone, and all your sin forgiven."
8 I heard the voice of the Lord saying, "Whom shall I send, and
9 who will go for us?" And I said, "I am here. Send me." He said,
"Go – tell this people: Hear, you shall hear but understand it not,
10 see it all but know it not. Fatten the heart of this people; make
their ears heavy; coat their eyes with plaster, lest they see with
their eyes and hear with their ears, and their hearts understand
11 and they return – and are healed." I said, "My Lord, how long?"
And He said, "Until the towns are stripped of all who live in them,
12 houses left without people, the land stripped bare, and the LORD
13 dispatches man far hence, and swaths of land will be forsaken; if
a tenth there will survive, it will return and will be burnt like the
terebinth and oak tree that drop their leaves, and yet the trunk re-
7 1 mains – and the trunk is holy seed."* In the days of Aḥaz
son of Yotam son of Uziyahu, king of Yehuda, Retzin, king of
Aram, and Pekaḥ son of Remalyahu, king of Israel, launched an
2 attack on Jerusalem, but they could not conquer it. The House
of David was told, "Aram is allied with Efrayim." And his heart
swayed, and the hearts of his people, as trees of the forest will
3 sway with the wind. And the LORD said to Yeshayahu:
Go out now to meet Aḥaz, you and She'ar Yashuv your son, to
the end of the Upper Pool's conduit, by the road to the Fuller's

Sepharadim and Chabad end here; Yemenites continue with 9:5

instability mirror the state of the kingdom at the close of Uziyahu's reign, and they are meant to jar the listener to repentance before it is too late.

מִמַּעַל לוֹ שֵׁשׁ כְּנָפַיִם שֵׁשׁ כְּנָפַיִם לְאֶחָד בִּשְׁתַּיִם ׀ יְכַסֶּה
ג פָנָיו וּבִשְׁתַּיִם יְכַסֶּה רַגְלָיו וּבִשְׁתַּיִם יְעוֹפֵף׃ וְקָרָא זֶה אֶל־זֶה
וְאָמַר קָדוֹשׁ ׀ קָדוֹשׁ קָדוֹשׁ יהוה צְבָאוֹת מְלֹא כָל־הָאָרֶץ
ד כְּבוֹדוֹ׃ וַיָּנֻעוּ אַמּוֹת הַסִּפִּים מִקּוֹל הַקּוֹרֵא וְהַבַּיִת יִמָּלֵא
ה עָשָׁן׃ וָאֹמַר אוֹי־לִי כִי־נִדְמֵיתִי כִּי אִישׁ טְמֵא־שְׂפָתַיִם אָנֹכִי
וּבְתוֹךְ עַם־טְמֵא שְׂפָתַיִם אָנֹכִי יוֹשֵׁב כִּי אֶת־הַמֶּלֶךְ יהוה
ו צְבָאוֹת רָאוּ עֵינָי׃ וַיָּעָף אֵלַי אֶחָד מִן־הַשְּׂרָפִים וּבְיָדוֹ רִצְפָּה
ז בְּמֶלְקַחַיִם לָקַח מֵעַל הַמִּזְבֵּחַ׃ וַיַּגַּע עַל־פִּי וַיֹּאמֶר הִנֵּה
ח נָגַע זֶה עַל־שְׂפָתֶיךָ וְסָר עֲוֺנֶךָ וְחַטָּאתְךָ תְּכֻפָּר׃ וָאֶשְׁמַע
אֶת־קוֹל אֲדֹנָי אֹמֵר אֶת־מִי אֶשְׁלַח וּמִי יֵלֶךְ־לָנוּ וָאֹמַר
ט הִנְנִי שְׁלָחֵנִי׃ וַיֹּאמֶר לֵךְ וְאָמַרְתָּ לָעָם הַזֶּה שִׁמְעוּ שָׁמוֹעַ
י וְאַל־תָּבִינוּ וּרְאוּ רָאוֹ וְאַל־תֵּדָעוּ׃ הַשְׁמֵן לֵב־הָעָם הַזֶּה
וְאָזְנָיו הַכְבֵּד וְעֵינָיו הָשַׁע פֶּן־יִרְאֶה בְעֵינָיו וּבְאָזְנָיו יִשְׁמָע
יא וּלְבָבוֹ יָבִין וָשָׁב וְרָפָא לוֹ׃ וָאֹמַר עַד־מָתַי אֲדֹנָי וַיֹּאמֶר
עַד אֲשֶׁר אִם־שָׁאוּ עָרִים מֵאֵין יוֹשֵׁב וּבָתִּים מֵאֵין אָדָם
יב וְהָאֲדָמָה תִּשָּׁאֶה שְׁמָמָה׃ וְרִחַק יהוה אֶת־הָאָדָם וְרַבָּה
יג הָעֲזוּבָה בְּקֶרֶב הָאָרֶץ׃ וְעוֹד בָּהּ עֲשִׂרִיָּה וְשָׁבָה וְהָיְתָה
לְבָעֵר כָּאֵלָה וְכָאַלּוֹן אֲשֶׁר בְּשַׁלֶּכֶת מַצֶּבֶת בָּם זֶרַע קֹדֶשׁ
ז א מַצַּבְתָּהּ׃* וַיְהִי בִּימֵי אָחָז בֶּן־יוֹתָם בֶּן־עֻזִּיָּהוּ
מֶלֶךְ יְהוּדָה עָלָה רְצִין מֶלֶךְ־אֲרָם וּפֶקַח בֶּן־רְמַלְיָהוּ מֶלֶךְ־
יִשְׂרָאֵל יְרוּשָׁלַם לַמִּלְחָמָה עָלֶיהָ וְלֹא יָכֹל לְהִלָּחֵם עָלֶיהָ׃
ב וַיֻּגַּד לְבֵית דָּוִד לֵאמֹר נָחָה אֲרָם עַל־אֶפְרָיִם וַיָּנַע לְבָבוֹ
ג וּלְבַב עַמּוֹ כְּנוֹעַ עֲצֵי־יַעַר מִפְּנֵי־רוּחַ׃ וַיֹּאמֶר
יהוה אֶל־יְשַׁעְיָהוּ צֵא־נָא לִקְרַאת אָחָז אַתָּה וּשְׁאָר יָשׁוּב
בְּנֶךָ אֶל־קְצֵה תְּעָלַת הַבְּרֵכָה הָעֶלְיוֹנָה אֶל־מְסִלַּת שְׂדֵה

Sepharadim and Chabad end here; Yemenites continue with 9:5

by His heavenly retinue, but the door pillars are shaking and the Temple is filled with smoke, signs of an earthquake or volcanic eruption. These impressions of

4 Field. And say to him: Be guarded, stay still, do not fear, and let
your heart not soften before these smoking tails of firebrands,
before the rage of Retzin and Aram and the son of Remalyahu.
5 For Aram has conspired to harm you, along with Efrayim and
6 Remalyahu's son: "We shall go up to Jerusalem, bring about her
end; we shall break her walls open for ourselves and set a new
king over her: the son of Taval."

9 5 For a child is born to us, a son is given us; leadership rests on
his shoulders, and he shall be called Mighty God Is Planning
6 Wonders, Eternal Father, Prince of Peace. To instill great leadership, peace without end, on the throne of David, and over his
kingdom, founding and supporting it with justice and with righteousness now and forever; the passion of the Lord of Hosts
will bring all this to be.

Haftarat Mishpatim

On Rosh Ḥodesh Adar Rishon, read the maftir from Numbers 28:9–15, and the haftara on page 1640. On Erev Rosh Ḥodesh Adar Rishon, read the haftara on page 1644. On Shabbat Shekalim (even if it coincides with Rosh Ḥodesh or Erev Rosh Ḥodesh) read the maftir from Exodus 30:11–16 and the haftara on page 1654.

34 8 The word that came to Yirmeyahu from the Lord after King JEREMIAH
Tzidkiyahu had made a covenant with all the people of Jerusalem,
9 proclaiming their freedom: Everyone was to set free his Hebrew
manservant and his Hebrew maidservant. No one was to en-
10 slave his fellow man of Yehuda. All the officials and all the people who had entered into the covenant obeyed in that each person set free his manservant and his maidservant, Hebrew males
and females, never to enslave them again. They obeyed and
11 set them free. After a time, they regressed. They recovered the

freed their slaves subjugated them again. God's reaction to this affront was swift; Yirmeyahu prophesies here renewed and worse destruction.

Between the lines, we read about the special ceremony customary at that time for establishing a covenant. A covenant is an agreement, a joining, but it is undertaken through an act of severing. In the ceremony, a calf is killed and cut in two. The parties to the covenant pass between the pieces of the calf to symbolize the dependence of the agreement on the two sides: if each side keeps to its own promises, the covenant will endure.

ד כּוֹבֵֽס׃ וְאָמַרְתָּ֨ אֵלָ֜יו הִשָּׁמֵ֣ר וְהַשְׁקֵ֗ט אַל־תִּירָא֙ וּלְבָבְךָ֙ אַל־
יֵרַ֔ךְ מִשְּׁנֵ֨י זַנְב֧וֹת הָאוּדִ֛ים הָעֲשֵׁנִ֖ים הָאֵ֑לֶּה בָּחֳרִי־אַ֛ף רְצִ֥ין
ה וַאֲרָ֖ם וּבֶן־רְמַלְיָֽהוּ׃ יַ֚עַן כִּֽי־יָעַ֥ץ עָלֶ֛יךָ אֲרָ֖ם רָעָ֑ה אֶפְרַ֥יִם
ו וּבֶן־רְמַלְיָ֖הוּ לֵאמֹֽר׃ נַעֲלֶ֤ה בִֽיהוּדָה֙ וּנְקִיצֶ֔נָּה וְנַבְקִעֶ֖נָּה
אֵלֵ֑ינוּ וְנַמְלִ֥יךְ מֶ֙לֶךְ֙ בְּתוֹכָ֔הּ אֵ֖ת בֶּן־טָֽבְאַֽל׃

ט ה כִּי־יֶ֣לֶד יֻלַּד־לָ֗נוּ בֵּ֚ן נִתַּן־לָ֔נוּ וַתְּהִ֥י הַמִּשְׂרָ֖ה עַל־שִׁכְמ֑וֹ וַיִּקְרָ֨א
ו שְׁמ֜וֹ פֶּ֠לֶא יוֹעֵץ֙ אֵ֣ל גִּבּ֔וֹר אֲבִי־עַ֖ד שַׂר־שָׁלֽוֹם׃ לסרבּ֨ה לְמַרְבֵּ֨ה
הַמִּשְׂרָ֜ה וּלְשָׁל֣וֹם אֵֽין־קֵ֗ץ עַל־כִּסֵּ֤א דָוִד֙ וְעַל־מַמְלַכְתּ֔וֹ
לְהָכִ֤ין אֹתָהּ֙ וּֽלְסַעֲדָ֔הּ בְּמִשְׁפָּ֖ט וּבִצְדָקָ֑ה מֵעַתָּה֙ וְעַד־עוֹלָ֔ם
קִנְאַ֛ת יהוָ֥ה צְבָא֖וֹת תַּעֲשֶׂה־זֹּֽאת׃

הפטרת משפטים

On ראש חודש אדר א׳ *read the maftir from* במדבר כח, ט–טו*, and the* הפטרה *on page 1641. On* ערב ראש חודש אדר א׳ *read the* הפטרה *on page 1645. On* שבת שקלים *(even if it coincides with* ראש חודש *or* ערב ראש חודש*) read the* מפטיר *from* שמות ל, יא–טו*, and the* הפטרה *on page 1655.*

לד ח הַדָּבָ֛ר אֲשֶׁר־הָיָ֥ה אֶֽל־יִרְמְיָ֖הוּ מֵאֵ֣ת יהוָ֑ה אַחֲרֵ֡י כְּרֹת֩ ירמיה
הַמֶּ֨לֶךְ צִדְקִיָּ֜הוּ בְּרִ֗ית אֶת־כָּל־הָעָם֙ אֲשֶׁ֣ר בִּירֽוּשָׁלִַ֔ם
ט לִקְרֹ֥א לָהֶ֖ם דְּרֽוֹר׃ לְשַׁלַּ֞ח אִ֧ישׁ אֶת־עַבְדּ֛וֹ וְאִ֧ישׁ אֶת־
שִׁפְחָת֛וֹ הָעִבְרִ֥י וְהָעִבְרִיָּ֖ה חָפְשִׁ֑ים לְבִלְתִּ֧י עֲבָד־בָּ֛ם
י בִּיהוּדִ֥י אָחִ֖יהוּ אִֽישׁ׃ וַֽיִּשְׁמְעוּ֩ כָל־הַשָּׂרִ֨ים וְכָל־הָעָ֜ם אֲשֶׁר־
בָּ֣אוּ בַבְּרִ֗ית לְשַׁלַּ֞ח אִ֣ישׁ אֶת־עַבְדּ֗וֹ וְאִ֤ישׁ אֶת־שִׁפְחָתוֹ֙
יא חָפְשִׁ֔ים לְבִלְתִּ֥י עֲבָד־בָּ֖ם ע֑וֹד וַֽיִּשְׁמְע֖וּ וַיְשַׁלֵּֽחוּ׃ וַיָּשׁ֣וּבוּ

MISHPATIM

During the reign of Tzidkiyahu, at the time of the Babylonian siege on Jerusalem, the people staged a ceremony of mass emancipation of slaves. The need for such a dramatic move testifies to the social-economic crisis that gripped the people of Jerusalem in that time. The ceremony was inspired by the words of the prophet Yirmeyahu, spoken to the people as the siege worsened. Afterward, the military situation improved somewhat, and the siege lightened a bit. In response, many of those who had

manservants and maidservants that they had set free and forced
12 them to be manservants and maidservants. Then the
13 word of the LORD came to Yirmeyahu from the LORD. This is
what the LORD, God of Israel, said: "I made a covenant with
your ancestors at the time I took them out of the land of Egypt,
14 the house of bondage, saying, 'At the beginning of the seventh
year each of you should set free your brother Hebrew who
had been sold to you and who served you for six years – send
him forth from you free.' But your ancestors did not heed Me
15 and did not even bend their ears. You repented today and did
what was proper in My eyes, proclaiming freedom, every person
for his fellow, and you made a covenant in My presence in the
16 house which is called by My name. But you regressed and profaned My name. Each of you recovered his manservant and his
maidservant, whom you had set free to do as they desire, and
you forced them to remain manservants and maidservants for
17 yourselves." Therefore, this is what the LORD said: "Because you did not heed Me to proclaim freedom, everyone for
his brother and everyone for his fellow, so will I set free against
you," declares the LORD, "the sword, the pestilence, and the famine, and render you an object of shuddering for all the kingdoms
18 of the earth. And I will deliver to all the people who violated My
covenant and did not uphold the words of the covenant that they
made in My presence, the calf that they cut in two, the sections
19 of which they passed between – the officials of Yehuda and the
officials of Jerusalem, the courtiers and the priests, and all the
20 folk of the land who passed between the sections of the calf – I
will deliver them into the hands of their enemies, the hands of
those that seek their lives, and their corpses shall become fodder
21 for the birds of the skies and the beasts of the earth. I will deliver
Tzidkiyahu, king of Yehuda, and his officials into the hands of
their enemies and into the hands of those who seek their lives
and into the army of the king of Babylon, which is withdrawing
22 from you. I shall now utter a command," declares the LORD, "and
I shall bring them back to this city. They will attack it, capture it,
and burn it down by fire. The cities of Yehuda I shall render desolate, without an inhabitant."*

Yemenites continue with chapter 35

33 25 This is what the LORD said: Only if I had no covenant with day
and night, and if I had not established the laws of heaven and

אַחֲרֵי־כֵן וַיָּשֻׁבוּ אֶת־הָעֲבָדִים וְאֶת־הַשְּׁפָחוֹת אֲשֶׁר שִׁלְּחוּ
יב חָפְשִׁים ויכבישום לַעֲבָדִים וְלִשְׁפָחוֹת׃ וַיְהִי — וַיִּכְבְּשׁוּם
יג דְבַר־יְהוָה אֶל־יִרְמְיָהוּ מֵאֵת יְהוָה לֵאמֹר׃ כֹּה־אָמַר
יְהוָה אֱלֹהֵי יִשְׂרָאֵל אָנֹכִי כָּרַתִּי בְרִית אֶת־אֲבוֹתֵיכֶם
בְּיוֹם הוֹצִאִי אוֹתָם מֵאֶרֶץ מִצְרַיִם מִבֵּית עֲבָדִים לֵאמֹר׃
יד מִקֵּץ שֶׁבַע שָׁנִים תְּשַׁלְּחוּ אִישׁ אֶת־אָחִיו הָעִבְרִי אֲשֶׁר־
יִמָּכֵר לְךָ וַעֲבָדְךָ שֵׁשׁ שָׁנִים וְשִׁלַּחְתּוֹ חָפְשִׁי מֵעִמָּךְ וְלֹא־
טו שָׁמְעוּ אֲבוֹתֵיכֶם אֵלַי וְלֹא הִטּוּ אֶת־אָזְנָם׃ וַתָּשֻׁבוּ אַתֶּם
הַיּוֹם וַתַּעֲשׂוּ אֶת־הַיָּשָׁר בְּעֵינַי לִקְרֹא דְרוֹר אִישׁ לְרֵעֵהוּ
טז וַתִּכְרְתוּ בְרִית לְפָנַי בַּבַּיִת אֲשֶׁר־נִקְרָא שְׁמִי עָלָיו׃ וַתָּשֻׁבוּ
וַתְּחַלְּלוּ אֶת־שְׁמִי וַתָּשִׁבוּ אִישׁ אֶת־עַבְדּוֹ וְאִישׁ אֶת־שִׁפְחָתוֹ
אֲשֶׁר־שִׁלַּחְתֶּם חָפְשִׁים לְנַפְשָׁם וַתִּכְבְּשׁוּ אֹתָם לִהְיוֹת לָכֶם
יז לַעֲבָדִים וְלִשְׁפָחוֹת׃ לָכֵן כֹּה־אָמַר יְהוָה אַתֶּם
לֹא־שְׁמַעְתֶּם אֵלַי לִקְרֹא דְרוֹר אִישׁ לְאָחִיו וְאִישׁ לְרֵעֵהוּ
הִנְנִי קֹרֵא לָכֶם דְּרוֹר נְאֻם־יְהוָה אֶל־הַחֶרֶב אֶל־הַדֶּבֶר
וְאֶל־הָרָעָב וְנָתַתִּי אֶתְכֶם לזועה לְכֹל מַמְלְכוֹת הָאָרֶץ׃ — לְזַעֲוָה
יח וְנָתַתִּי אֶת־הָאֲנָשִׁים הָעֹבְרִים אֶת־בְּרִתִי אֲשֶׁר לֹא־הֵקִימוּ
אֶת־דִּבְרֵי הַבְּרִית אֲשֶׁר כָּרְתוּ לְפָנָי הָעֵגֶל אֲשֶׁר כָּרְתוּ
יט לִשְׁנַיִם וַיַּעַבְרוּ בֵּין בְּתָרָיו׃ שָׂרֵי יְהוּדָה וְשָׂרֵי יְרוּשָׁלַם
הַסָּרִסִים וְהַכֹּהֲנִים וְכֹל עַם הָאָרֶץ הָעֹבְרִים בֵּין בִּתְרֵי
כ הָעֵגֶל׃ וְנָתַתִּי אוֹתָם בְּיַד אֹיְבֵיהֶם וּבְיַד מְבַקְשֵׁי נַפְשָׁם
וְהָיְתָה נִבְלָתָם לְמַאֲכָל לְעוֹף הַשָּׁמַיִם וּלְבֶהֱמַת הָאָרֶץ׃
כא וְאֶת־צִדְקִיָּהוּ מֶלֶךְ־יְהוּדָה וְאֶת־שָׂרָיו אֶתֵּן בְּיַד אֹיְבֵיהֶם
וּבְיַד מְבַקְשֵׁי נַפְשָׁם וּבְיַד חֵיל מֶלֶךְ בָּבֶל הָעֹלִים מֵעֲלֵיכֶם׃
כב הִנְנִי מְצַוֶּה נְאֻם־יְהוָה וַהֲשִׁבֹתִים אֶל־הָעִיר הַזֹּאת וְנִלְחֲמוּ
עָלֶיהָ וּלְכָדוּהָ וּשְׂרָפֻהָ בָאֵשׁ וְאֶת־עָרֵי יְהוּדָה אֶתֵּן שְׁמָמָה
מֵאֵין יֹשֵׁב׃*

Yemenites continue with chapter 35

לג כה כֹּה אָמַר יְהוָה אִם־לֹא בְרִיתִי יוֹמָם וָלָיְלָה חֻקּוֹת שָׁמַיִם

26 earth, would I reject the offspring of Yaakov and of David My
servant, and not select any of his offspring as rulers over the offspring of Avraham, Yisḥak, and Yaakov – for I will bring them
back from their captivity and have compassion for them.* *Ashkenazim and Sepharadim end here*

35 1 The word that came to Yirmeyahu from the LORD in the days of
2 Yehoyakim, son of Yoshiyahu, king of Yehuda: "Go to the house
of the descendants of Rekhav and speak to them. Bring them
to the House of the LORD, to one of the chambers, and give
3 them wine to drink." I took Yaazanya son of Yirmeyahu son of
Ḥavatzinya, his brothers and all his children and the entire house
4 of the descendants of Rekhav, and I brought them to the House
of the LORD, to the chamber of the sons of Ḥanan son of Yigda-
lyahu, the man of God, that was adjacent to the chamber of the officials and above the chamber of Maaseyahu son of Shalum, the
5 gatekeeper. I placed goblets full of wine and cups before the sons
6 of the house of Rekhav and said to them, "Drink wine." They said,
"We will not drink wine because Yonadav son of Rekhav, our ancestor, commanded us: 'Do not drink wine, neither you nor your
7 children, forever! You are not to build houses, nor sow seed, nor
plant vineyards, nor even possess them for yourselves. Instead,
you are to live in tents all your lives so that you will thrive for
8 many days upon the land where you will reside.' We heeded the
voice of Yehonadav son of Rekhav our forefather in all that he
commanded us, never to drink wine, neither ourselves nor our
9 wives, nor our sons and daughters, and not to build houses in
10 which to live, and not to have vineyard, field, or seed. Rather,
we live in tents. We heeded Yonadav our ancestor, and we have
11 done all that he commanded us. However, when Nevukhadretzar, king of Babylon, rose up against the land, we said, 'Come
and let us go up to Jerusalem because of the army of the Chaldeans and because of the army of Aram.' And so we live in Jeru-
12 salem." Then the word of the LORD came to Yirmeyahu.
13 This is what the LORD of Hosts, God of Israel, said: "Go and say
to the men of Yehuda and to those that dwell in Jerusalem: It
would befit you to take instruction to heed My words, declares
14 the LORD. Fulfilled are the words of Yehonadav son of Rekhav,
who commanded his descendants not to drink wine. They have
not drunk wine to this very day, for they heeded the command
of their ancestor. But I spoke to you persistently, and yet you did

כו וָאָ֖רֶץ לֹא־שָֽׂמְתִּי׃ גַּם־זֶ֣רַע יַעֲק֞וֹב וְדָוִ֣ד עַבְדִּ֗י אֶמְאַס֙ מִקַּ֤חַת
מִזַּרְעוֹ֙ מֹֽשְׁלִ֔ים אֶל־זֶ֥רַע אַבְרָהָ֖ם יִשְׂחָ֣ק וְיַעֲקֹ֑ב כִּֽי־אָשׁ֥וב אָשִׁ֥יב
אֶת־שְׁבוּתָ֖ם וְרִחַמְתִּֽים׃ *

Ashkenazim and Sepharadim end here

לה א הַדָּבָ֞ר אֲשֶׁר־הָיָ֣ה אֶֽל־יִרְמְיָ֗הוּ מֵאֵ֤ת יהוה֙ בִּימֵ֨י יְהוֹיָקִ֧ים
ב בֶּן־יֹאשִׁיָּ֛הוּ מֶ֥לֶךְ יְהוּדָ֖ה לֵאמֹֽר׃ הָל֞וֹךְ אֶל־בֵּ֣ית הָרֵֽכָבִ֗ים
וְדִבַּרְתָּ֙ אוֹתָ֔ם וַהֲבֵאוֹתָם֙ בֵּ֣ית יהוה אֶל־אַחַ֖ת הַלְּשָׁכ֑וֹת
ג וְהִשְׁקִיתָ֥ אוֹתָ֖ם יָֽיִן׃ וָאֶקַּ֞ח אֶת־יַאֲזַנְיָ֣ה בֶן־יִרְמְיָ֗הוּ בֶּן־
חֲבַצִּנְיָ֔ה וְאֶת־אֶחָ֖יו וְאֶת־כָּל־בָּנָ֑יו וְאֵ֖ת כָּל־בֵּ֥ית הָרֵכָבִֽים׃
ד וָאָבִ֤א אֹתָם֙ בֵּ֣ית יהוה אֶל־לִשְׁכַּ֗ת בְּנֵי֙ חָנָ֣ן בֶּן־יִגְדַּלְיָ֔הוּ אִ֖ישׁ
הָאֱלֹהִ֑ים אֲשֶׁר־אֵ֙צֶל֙ לִשְׁכַּ֣ת הַשָּׂרִ֔ים אֲשֶׁ֣ר מִמַּ֗עַל לְלִשְׁכַּ֛ת
ה מַעֲשֵׂיָ֥הוּ בֶן־שַׁלֻּ֖ם שֹׁמֵ֥ר הַסַּֽף׃ וָאֶתֵּ֞ן לִפְנֵ֣י ׀ בְּנֵ֣י בֵית־הָרֵכָבִ֗ים
ו גְּבִעִ֛ים מְלֵאִ֥ים יַ֖יִן וְכֹס֑וֹת וָאֹמַ֥ר אֲלֵיהֶ֖ם שְׁתוּ־יָֽיִן׃ וַיֹּאמְר֖וּ
לֹ֣א נִשְׁתֶּה־יָּ֑יִן כִּי֩ יוֹנָדָ֨ב בֶּן־רֵכָ֜ב אָבִ֗ינוּ צִוָּ֤ה עָלֵ֙ינוּ֙ לֵאמֹ֔ר
ז לֹ֧א תִשְׁתּוּ־יַ֛יִן אַתֶּ֥ם וּבְנֵיכֶ֖ם עַד־עוֹלָֽם׃ וּבַ֣יִת לֹֽא־תִבְנ֗וּ וְזֶ֤רַע
לֹֽא־תִזְרָ֙עוּ֙ וְכֶ֥רֶם לֹֽא־תִטָּ֖עוּ וְלֹ֣א יִהְיֶ֣ה לָכֶ֑ם כִּ֣י בָּאֳהָלִ֗ים
תֵּשְׁבוּ֙ כָּל־יְמֵיכֶ֔ם לְמַ֨עַן תִּחְי֜וּ יָמִ֣ים רַבִּ֗ים עַל־פְּנֵ֣י הָאֲדָמָ֔ה
ח אֲשֶׁ֥ר אַתֶּ֖ם גָּרִ֥ים שָֽׁם׃ וַנִּשְׁמַ֗ע בְּק֨וֹל יְהוֹנָדָ֤ב בֶּן־רֵכָב֙ אָבִ֔ינוּ
לְכֹ֖ל אֲשֶׁ֣ר צִוָּ֑נוּ לְבִלְתִּ֨י שְׁתֽוֹת־יַ֜יִן כָּל־יָמֵ֗ינוּ אֲנַ֙חְנוּ֙ נָשֵׁ֔ינוּ
ט בָּנֵ֖ינוּ וּבְנֹתֵֽינוּ׃ וּלְבִלְתִּ֛י בְּנ֥וֹת בָּתִּ֖ים לְשִׁבְתֵּ֑נוּ וְכֶ֧רֶם וְשָׂדֶ֛ה
י וָזֶ֖רַע לֹ֥א יִֽהְיֶה־לָּֽנוּ׃ וַנֵּ֖שֶׁב בָּאֳהָלִ֑ים וַנִּשְׁמַ֣ע וַנַּ֔עַשׂ כְּכֹ֥ל אֲשֶׁר־
יא צִוָּ֖נוּ יוֹנָדָ֥ב אָבִֽינוּ׃ וַיְהִ֗י בַּעֲל֞וֹת נְבוּכַדְרֶאצַּ֣ר מֶֽלֶךְ־בָּבֶל֮
אֶל־הָאָרֶץ֒ וַנֹּ֗אמֶר בֹּ֚אוּ וְנָב֣וֹא יְרוּשָׁלִַ֔ם מִפְּנֵי֙ חֵ֣יל הַכַּשְׂדִּ֔ים
יב וּמִפְּנֵ֖י חֵ֣יל אֲרָ֑ם וַנֵּ֖שֶׁב בִּירוּשָׁלִָֽם׃ וַיְהִ֥י דְבַר־יהוה
יג אֶל־יִרְמְיָ֥הוּ לֵאמֹֽר׃ כֹּה־אָמַ֞ר יהוה צְבָאוֹת֙ אֱלֹהֵ֣י יִשְׂרָאֵ֔ל
הָלֹךְ֙ וְאָמַרְתָּ֙ לְאִ֣ישׁ יְהוּדָ֔ה וּלְיוֹשְׁבֵ֖י יְרוּשָׁלִָ֑ם הֲל֨וֹא תִקְח֥וּ
יד מוּסָ֛ר לִשְׁמֹ֥עַ אֶל־דְּבָרַ֖י נְאֻם־יהוה׃ הוּקַ֡ם אֶת־דִּבְרֵ֣י יְהוֹנָדָ֣ב
בֶּן־רֵ֠כָב אֲשֶׁר־צִוָּ֨ה אֶת־בָּנָ֜יו לְבִלְתִּ֣י שְׁתֽוֹת־יַ֗יִן וְלֹ֤א שָׁתוּ֙
עַד־הַיּ֣וֹם הַזֶּ֔ה כִּ֣י שָֽׁמְע֔וּ אֵ֖ת מִצְוַ֣ת אֲבִיהֶ֑ם וְאָנֹכִ֡י דִּבַּ֣רְתִּי

15 not heed Me. I sent to you My servants, the prophets, again and
again, to tell every one of you to turn away from his evil path,
to correct his actions, and not to follow other gods to worship
them. Then you would live upon the land which I gave you and
your ancestors. But you did not bend your ears. You did not lis-
16 ten to Me. For the children of Yehonadav son of Rekhav obeyed
their ancestor's command just as he had commanded them, but
17 this people have not obeyed Me. Therefore, this is what
the LORD, God of Hosts, God of Israel, said: Now I will bring
upon Yehuda, and upon all who dwell in Jerusalem, every disaster which I have decreed upon them, for I spoke to them and
they did not listen; I called to them and they did not respond."
18 Yirmeyahu said to the house of the Rekhabites, "This is what the
LORD of Hosts, God of Israel, said: Because you listened to the
command of Yehonadav your ancestor, and kept all his precepts,
19 and did exactly as he commanded you, this is what the LORD of
Hosts, God of Israel, therefore said: There will never cease to be
a descendant of Yonadav son of Rekhav who will stand before
Me, for all time."

Haftarat Teruma

On Rosh Ḥodesh Adar Rishon, read the maftir from Numbers 28:9–15, and the haftara on page 1640. On Shabbat Shekalim (even if it coincides with Rosh Ḥodesh or Erev Rosh Ḥodesh) read the maftir from Exodus 30:11–16, and the haftara on page 1654. On Shabbat Zakhor read the maftir from Deuteronomy 25:17–19, and the haftara on page 1658.

5 26 The LORD had endowed Shlomo with wisdom, as He had prom- I KINGS
ised him. There was peace between Ḥiram and Shlomo, and
27 the two of them formed an alliance. King Shlomo began to levy
forced labor upon all of Israel; the levy was thirty thousand men.

that Your hands established (Ex. 15:17). This Sanctuary was modest in its size, but splendid in its construction. No iron tool was used in building the Temple or the altar that stood within it. The *haftara* ends during the main phase of construction, with God's message to Shlomo: The observance of the Torah and the commandments is the true test for whether this structure and the Divine Presence within it will weather the storms of history.

טו אליכם השכם ודבר ולא שמעתם אלי: ואשלח אליכם
את־כל־עבדי הנבאים | השכם ושלח | לאמר שבו־נא
איש מדרכו הרעה והיטיבו מעלליכם ואל־תלכו אחרי
אלהים אחרים לעבדם ושבו אל־האדמה אשר־נתתי לכם
טז ולאבתיכם ולא הטיתם את־אזנכם ולא שמעתם אלי: כי
הקימו בני יהונדב בן־רכב את־מצות אביהם אשר צום
יז והעם הזה לא שמעו אלי: לכן כה־אמר יהוה
אלהי צבאות אלהי ישראל הנני מביא אל־יהודה ואל
כל־יושבי ירושלם את כל־הרעה אשר דברתי עליהם יען
יח דברתי אליהם ולא שמעו ואקרא להם ולא ענו: ולבית
הרכבים אמר ירמיהו כה־אמר יהוה צבאות אלהי ישראל
יען אשר שמעתם על־מצות יהונדב אביכם ותשמרו
יט את־כל־מצותיו ותעשו ככל אשר־צוה אתכם: לכן כה
אמר יהוה צבאות אלהי ישראל לא־יכרת איש ליונדב
בן־רכב עמד לפני כל־הימים:

הפטרת תרומה

On ראש חודש אדר א׳*, read the* מפטיר *from* במדבר כח, ט–טו *and the* הפטרה *on page 1641. On* שבת שקלים *(even if it coincides with* ראש חודש *or* ערב ראש חודש*) read the* מפטיר *from* שמות ל, יא–טז*, and the* הפטרה *on page 1655. On* שבת זכור *read the* מפטיר *from* דברים יז, יט–כה*, and the* הפטרה *on page 1659.*

מלכים א׳

ה כו ויהוה נתן חכמה לשלמה כאשר דבר־לו ויהי שלם בין
כז חירם ובין שלמה ויכרתו ברית שניהם: ויעל המלך שלמה

TERUMA

This *haftara* describes the building of the Temple during the reign of King Shlomo and the preparations for its opening. This project began during the fourth year of Shlomo's reign, 480 years after the exodus from Egypt. The exodus was the time Israel began to rise from its historical nadir of servitude in Egypt. And now, with the inauguration of the Temple, came the pinnacle of its spiritual existence, as we read in the Song at the Sea, "You will bring them, You will plant them on the mountain … the Sanctuary, Lord,

28 He had ten thousand men sent to Lebanon every month, in
shifts; they would spend a month in Lebanon and two months at
29 home. Adoniram was in charge of the forced labor. And
Shlomo had seventy thousand porters and eight thousand quar-
30 riers in the mountains, besides Shlomo's three thousand and
three hundred prefect officers in charge of the labor, who super-
31 vised the people who performed the labor. At the king's command, they quarried enormous blocks of prime stone so that the
32 foundations of the House would be laid with hewn stone. And
Shlomo's builders, together with Ḥiram's builders and the Ge-
valites, carved the wood and the stone in preparation for the con-
6 1 struction of the House. In the four hundred and eightieth year after the Israelites left Egypt, in the month of Ziv – the
second month – of the fourth year of Shlomo's reign over Israel,
2 he began to build the House for the LORD. The House that King
Shlomo built for the LORD was sixty cubits long, twenty cubits
3 wide, and thirty cubits high. The Hall leading up to the Sanctuary of the House was twenty cubits long along the width of the
4 House, and ten cubits wide leading up to the House. He made
5 recessed, paned windows for the House. Around the outer wall
of the House – the outer walls around the Sanctuary and Inner
Sanctuary – he built a tiered structure and made side chambers
6 all around. The lowest tier was five cubits wide, the middle tier
was six cubits wide, and the third tier was seven cubits wide, as
he had designed recesses around the outside of the House to
7 avoid making grooves in the walls of the House. The House was
entirely built of finished stones that had been cut at the quarry;
no hammer, ax, or iron tool was heard in the House during its
8 construction. There was an entrance through the central alcove
on the southern side of the House; a winding staircase led to the
9 middle tier and from the middle tier to the third one. When he
finished building the House, he paneled the House with beams
10 and planks of cedar. He built the tiered structure against the
whole house, each story five cubits high, so that the House was
11 encased with cedarwood. And the word of the LORD
12 came to Shlomo: "Concerning this House that you are building:
if you follow My laws and uphold My rulings and keep all My

כח מס מכל־ישראל ויהי המס שלשים אלף איש: וישלחם
לבנונה עשרת אלפים בחדש חליפות חדש יהיו בלבנון
כט שנים חדשים בביתו ואדנירם על־המס: ויהי
לשלמה שבעים אלף נשא סבל ושמנים אלף חצב בהר:
ל לבד משרי הנצבים לשלמה אשר על־המלאכה שלשת
לא אלפים ושלש מאות הרדים בעם העשים במלאכה: ויצו
המלך ויסעו אבנים גדלות אבנים יקרות ליסד הבית
לב אבני גזית: ויפסלו בני שלמה ובני חירום והגבלים ויכינו
ו א העצים והאבנים לבנות הבית: ויהי בשמונים
שנה וארבע מאות שנה לצאת בני־ישראל מארץ־מצרים
בשנה הרביעית בחדש זו הוא החדש השני למלך שלמה
ב על־ישראל ויבן הבית ליהוה: והבית אשר בנה המלך
שלמה ליהוה ששים־אמה ארכו ועשרים רחבו ושלשים
ג אמה קומתו: והאולם על־פני היכל הבית עשרים אמה
ארכו על־פני רחב הבית עשר באמה רחבו על־פני
ד ה הבית: ויעש לבית חלוני שקפים אטמים: ויבן על־קיר
הבית יצוע סביב את־קירות הבית סביב להיכל ולדביר יציע
ו ויעש צלעות סביב: היצוע התחתנה חמש באמה רחבה היציע
והתיכנה שש באמה רחבה והשלישית שבע באמה רחבה
כי מגרעות נתן לבית סביב חוצה לבלתי אחז בקירות
ז הבית: והבית בהבנתו אבן־שלמה מסע נבנה ומקבות
ח והגרזן כל־כלי ברזל לא־נשמע בבית בהבנתו: פתח
הצלע התיכנה אל־כתף הבית הימנית ובלולים יעלו
ט על־התיכנה ומן־התיכנה אל־השלשים: ויבן את־הבית
י ויכלהו ויספן את־הבית גבים ושדרת בארזים: ויבן את־
היצוע על־כל־הבית חמש אמות קומתו ויאחז את־הבית היציע
יא בעצי ארזים: ויהי דבר־יהוה אל־שלמה לאמר:
יב הבית הזה אשר־אתה בנה אם־תלך בחקתי ואת־משפטי

commandments by following them, then I will fulfill My prom-
13 ise through you, the promise that I made to your father David. I
will dwell in the midst of the Israelites, and I will never abandon
My people Israel."

Haftarat Tetzaveh

On Shabbat Zakhor, read the maftir from Deuteronomy 25:17–19, and the haftara on page 1658. On Purim Meshulash in Jerusalem, read from Exodus 17:8–16, and the haftara on page 1658.

EZEKIEL

43 10 You, Man, describe this House to the House of Israel so that
they feel ashamed of their sins, and let them take measure of the
11 plan. And if they do feel shame about all they have done, then
make known to them the design of the House and its architectural plan: its exits and entrances, all of its structures and all of
its rules, all its decorative shapes and all the instructions about
it. And write it down in front of them so that they can preserve
everything about its design and its rules so that they can carry
12 them out. This is the teaching of the House: the top of the mountain, all its boundary roundabout, is holy of holies. Behold – this
13 is the teaching of the House: These are the dimensions of the
altar in cubits, each cubit being a five-handbreadth cubit plus a
handbreadth. But the base is a smaller cubit, as is the cubit of its
width, and the border at its edge all around is one half-cubit, the
14 same as for the top level of the altar. Now from the base on the
ground up to the lower ledge there are two cubits, and its excess
width is one cubit, and from the smaller ledge up to the top of
the large ledge there are four cubits, with an excess width of one
15 cubit. Now the Harel hearth is four cubits, and from this Ariel
16 upward, there rise four horns. And the Ariel is twelve cubits long
17 by twelve cubits wide, square on its four sides. And the ledge
is fourteen in length by fourteen in width on its four sides, and
the border surrounding it is half a small cubit. A cubit of its base

---

everything that that had been destroyed. Nothing is irreversible. This powerful message, conveyed at the very hour of Israel's darkest nightmare, prevented the Jews from reaching the depths of despair. This *haftara* deals with the construction of the Temple, the altar, and the reconstitution of the priestly service.

תַּעֲשֶׂה וְשָׁמַרְתָּ אֶת־כָּל־מִצְוֺתַי לָלֶכֶת בָּהֶם וַהֲקִמֹתִי אֶת־
יג דְּבָרִי אִתָּךְ אֲשֶׁר דִּבַּרְתִּי אֶל־דָּוִד אָבִיךָ׃ וְשָׁכַנְתִּי בְּתוֹךְ בְּנֵי
יִשְׂרָאֵל וְלֹא אֶעֱזֹב אֶת־עַמִּי יִשְׂרָאֵל׃

הפטרת תצוה

On שבת זכור*, read the* מפטיר *from* דברים כה, יז–יט*, and the* הפטרה *on page 1659. On* פורים משולש *in Jerusalem, read the* שמות יז, ח–טז מפטיר *from*, *and the* הפטרה *on page 1659.*

מג י אַתָּה בֶן־אָדָם הַגֵּד אֶת־בֵּית־יִשְׂרָאֵל אֶת־הַבַּיִת וְיִכָּלְמוּ יחזקאל
יא מֵעֲוֺנוֹתֵיהֶם וּמָדְדוּ אֶת־תָּכְנִית׃ וְאִם־נִכְלְמוּ מִכֹּל אֲשֶׁר־
עָשׂוּ צוּרַת הַבַּיִת וּתְכוּנָתוֹ וּמוֹצָאָיו וּמוֹבָאָיו וְכָל־צוּרֹתָו
וְאֵת כָּל־חֻקֹּתָיו וְכָל־צוּרֹתָו וְכָל־תּוֹרֹתָו הוֹדַע אוֹתָם וּכְתֹב
לְעֵינֵיהֶם וְיִשְׁמְרוּ אֶת־כָּל־צוּרָתוֹ וְאֶת־כָּל־חֻקֹּתָיו וְעָשׂוּ
יב אוֹתָם׃ זֹאת תּוֹרַת הַבָּיִת עַל־רֹאשׁ הָהָר כָּל־גְּבֻלוֹ סָבִיב ׀
יג סָבִיב קֹדֶשׁ קָדָשִׁים הִנֵּה־זֹאת תּוֹרַת הַבָּיִת׃ וְאֵלֶּה מִדּוֹת
הַמִּזְבֵּחַ בָּאַמּוֹת אַמָּה אַמָּה וָטֹפַח וְחֵיק הָאַמָּה וְאַמָּה־רֹחַב
וּגְבוּלָהּ אֶל־שְׂפָתָהּ סָבִיב זֶרֶת הָאֶחָד וְזֶה גַּב הַמִּזְבֵּחַ׃
יד וּמֵחֵיק הָאָרֶץ עַד־הָעֲזָרָה הַתַּחְתּוֹנָה שְׁתַּיִם אַמּוֹת וְרֹחַב
אַמָּה אֶחָת וּמֵהָעֲזָרָה הַקְּטַנָּה עַד־הָעֲזָרָה הַגְּדוֹלָה אַרְבַּע
טו אַמּוֹת וְרֹחַב הָאַמָּה׃ וְהַהַרְאֵל אַרְבַּע אַמּוֹת וּמֵהָאֲרִאֵיל
טז וּלְמַעְלָה הַקְּרָנוֹת אַרְבַּע׃ וְהָאֲרִאֵיל שְׁתֵּים עֶשְׂרֵה אֹרֶךְ
יז בִּשְׁתֵּים עֶשְׂרֵה רֹחַב רָבוּעַ אֶל אַרְבַּעַת רְבָעָיו׃ וְהָעֲזָרָה
אַרְבַּע עֶשְׂרֵה אֹרֶךְ בְּאַרְבַּע עֶשְׂרֵה רֹחַב אֶל אַרְבַּעַת רְבָעֶיהָ

TETZAVEH

The final vision recounted in the book of Ezekiel offers a lengthy and detailed description of the future structure of Jerusalem and the Temple within it. This prophecy was relayed to the exiles in Babylon after the destruction of the First Temple, Jerusalem, and the dynasty of the House of David. The series of prophecies of comfort at the end of the book foretells the story of the return of the people of Israel to their land and the rebuilding of

extends all around, and its ramp is off-center, shifted eastward."
18 Then He said to me: "Man, thus says the Lord God: These are
the statutes pertaining to the altar on the day that it is fashioned,
to enable you to bring burnt offerings upon it and to sprinkle
19 blood upon it. You will pass on to the priests, the Levites who are
of the seed of Tzadok who approach Me to serve Me, the word
of the Lord God: a young bull from the cattle herd shall be a pu-
20 rification offering. Take from its blood and put some on the four
altar horns and four corners of the ledge and upon the border
all around: you shall purify it so that it can provide atonement.
21 Then take the bull of the purification offering and burn it in its
designated place in the bounds of the House, outside the Sanctu-
22 ary. And from the second day onward, you shall sacrifice a flawless male goat for a purification offering. They shall purify the
23 altar as they purified it before, by sacrificing the bull. When you
have finished the purification process, sacrifice a flawless young
bull from among the cattle and a flawless ram from among the
24 sheep. You shall bring them near the Lord, and the priests shall
throw salt upon them and offer them up as a burnt offering to
25 the Lord. For seven days you shall bring the goat of a purification offering daily, as well as a young bull from the cattle and a
26 ram from the sheep; they are all to be flawless. For seven days
27 they shall cleanse the altar and purify it and consecrate it. When
these days are over, from the eighth day onward, the priests may
prepare your burnt offerings and your peace offerings on the
altar, and I shall respond favorably to you. So spoke the Lord
God.

Haftarat Ki Tisa

On Purim Meshulash in Jerusalem read the maftir from Exodus 17:8–16, and the haftara on page 1658. On Shabbat Para read the maftir from Numbers 19:1–22, and the haftara on page 1662.

I KINGS

Ashkenazim and Yemenites begin here

18 1 A long time passed. In the third year, the word of the Lord came
to Eliyahu: "Go, present yourself to Aḥav, and I will send down

years. Eliyahu had battled the idolatrous influence of Queen Izevel and decreed a devastating drought to prove that only God, and not Baal, has the power to give rain. King Aḥav went along with Eliyahu and allowed him to organize a contest after which the drought would break. This contest mirrors in some ways the

וְהַגְּבוּל סָבִיב אוֹתָהּ חֲצִי הָאַמָּה וְהַחֵיק־לָהּ אַמָּה סָבִיב
יח וּמַעֲלֹתֵהוּ פְּנוֹת קָדִים׃ וַיֹּאמֶר אֵלַי בֶּן־אָדָם כֹּה אָמַר אֲדֹנָי
יֱהֹוִה אֵלֶּה חֻקּוֹת הַמִּזְבֵּחַ בְּיוֹם הֵעָשׂוֹתוֹ לְהַעֲלוֹת עָלָיו
יט עוֹלָה וְלִזְרֹק עָלָיו דָּם׃ וְנָתַתָּה אֶל־הַכֹּהֲנִים הַלְוִיִּם אֲשֶׁר
הֵם מִזֶּרַע צָדוֹק הַקְּרֹבִים אֵלַי נְאֻם אֲדֹנָי יֱהֹוִה לְשָׁרְתֵנִי פַּר
כ בֶּן־בָּקָר לְחַטָּאת׃ וְלָקַחְתָּ מִדָּמוֹ וְנָתַתָּה עַל־אַרְבַּע קַרְנֹתָיו
וְאֶל־אַרְבַּע פִּנּוֹת הָעֲזָרָה וְאֶל־הַגְּבוּל סָבִיב וְחִטֵּאתָ אוֹתוֹ
כא וְכִפַּרְתָּהוּ׃ וְלָקַחְתָּ אֵת הַפָּר הַחַטָּאת וּשְׂרָפוֹ בְּמִפְקַד הַבַּיִת
כב מִחוּץ לַמִּקְדָּשׁ׃ וּבַיּוֹם הַשֵּׁנִי תַּקְרִיב שְׂעִיר־עִזִּים תָּמִים
כג לְחַטָּאת וְחִטְּאוּ אֶת־הַמִּזְבֵּחַ כַּאֲשֶׁר חִטְּאוּ בַּפָּר׃ בְּכַלּוֹתְךָ
מֵחַטֵּא תַּקְרִיב פַּר בֶּן־בָּקָר תָּמִים וְאַיִל מִן־הַצֹּאן תָּמִים׃
כד וְהִקְרַבְתָּם לִפְנֵי יְהוָה וְהִשְׁלִיכוּ הַכֹּהֲנִים עֲלֵיהֶם מֶלַח וְהֶעֱלוּ
כה אוֹתָם עֹלָה לַיהוָה׃ שִׁבְעַת יָמִים תַּעֲשֶׂה שְׂעִיר־חַטָּאת
כו לַיּוֹם וּפַר בֶּן־בָּקָר וְאַיִל מִן־הַצֹּאן תְּמִימִים יַעֲשׂוּ׃ שִׁבְעַת
כז יָמִים יְכַפְּרוּ אֶת־הַמִּזְבֵּחַ וְטִהֲרוּ אֹתוֹ וּמִלְאוּ יָדוֹ׃ וִיכַלּוּ
אֶת־הַיָּמִים וְהָיָה בַיּוֹם הַשְּׁמִינִי וָהָלְאָה יַעֲשׂוּ הַכֹּהֲנִים עַל־
הַמִּזְבֵּחַ אֶת־עוֹלוֹתֵיכֶם וְאֶת־שַׁלְמֵיכֶם וְרָצֵאתִי אֶתְכֶם נְאֻם
אֲדֹנָי יֱהֹוִה׃

הפטרת כי תשא

On פורים משולש *in Jerusalem read the* מפטיר *from* שמות יז, ח–טז*, and the* הפטרה *on page 1659. On* שבת פרה *read the* מפטיר *from* במדבר יט, א–כב*, and the* הפטרה *on page 1663.*

מלכים א׳
Ashkenazim and Yemenites begin here

יח א וַיְהִי יָמִים רַבִּים וּדְבַר־יְהוָה הָיָה אֶל־אֵלִיָּהוּ בַּשָּׁנָה
הַשְּׁלִישִׁית לֵאמֹר לֵךְ הֵרָאֵה אֶל־אַחְאָב וְאֶתְּנָה מָטָר

KI TISA

The dramatic confrontation between the prophet Eliyahu and the priests of Baal on Mount Carmel, witnessed by all Israel, was the culmination of a titanic struggle that had lasted three

2 rain on the face of the earth." So Eliyahu set out to present himself to Aḥav. By then, famine was raging fiercely in Shomron.
3 Aḥav summoned Ovadyahu, who was in charge of the palace –
4 Ovadyahu had deep reverence for the LORD; when Izevel was
annihilating the prophets of the LORD, Ovadyahu had taken
one hundred prophets and hidden them, fifty men to a cave, and
5 provided them with food and water. "Go about the land to every
spring and every wadi," Aḥav said to Ovadyahu. "Perhaps we will
find some grass to keep the horses and mules alive so that our
6 animals will not be annihilated." They divided up the land between them for exploration; Aḥav set out alone in one direction,
7 while Ovadyahu set out alone in another. As Ovadyahu was on
the road, he was suddenly met by Eliyahu. He recognized him
at once and fell on his face. "Is that you, my lord Eliyahu?" he
8 said. "It is I," he said to him. "Go and tell your lord: Eliyahu is
9 here." "How have I offended you, that you hand your servant
10 over to Aḥav to be killed?" he said. "As the LORD your God lives –
is there a single nation or kingdom where my lord has not sent
and looked for you? And when they said, 'He is not here,' he had
every kingdom and every nation swear that you were nowhere
11 to be found. Now you say, 'Go, tell your lord that Eliyahu is here,'
12 but as soon as I leave you, the spirit of the LORD will carry you
off – to where, I know not – and when I go to tell Aḥav and he
does not find you, he will kill me, though I, your servant, have
13 revered the LORD from my youth. Has my lord not been told
what I did when Izevel was killing the LORD's prophets, how I
hid one hundred of the LORD's prophets, fifty men to a cave, and
14 provided them with food and water? Now you say, 'Go, tell your
15 lord that Eliyahu is here' – but he will kill me." "As the LORD of
Hosts lives, whom I serve," said Eliyahu, "today I will present my-
16 self to him." So Ovadyahu set out toward Aḥav and told him, and
17 Aḥav went to meet Eliyahu. When Aḥav saw Eliyahu, Aḥav said
18 to him, "Is that you, O scourge of Israel?" "I have not brought a
scourge upon Israel," he said, "but you and your father's house

---

the Carmel and Sinai, much of the people sat on the fence, waiting to see which side would emerge victorious. And in each of these contexts, the prophet resorts both to prayer before God and words of reproof to the nation.

ב עַל־פְּנֵי הָאֲדָמָה׃ וַיֵּלֶךְ אֵלִיָּהוּ לְהֵרָאוֹת אֶל־אַחְאָב וְהָרָעָב
ג חָזָק בְּשֹׁמְרוֹן׃ וַיִּקְרָא אַחְאָב אֶל־עֹבַדְיָהוּ אֲשֶׁר עַל־הַבָּיִת
ד וְעֹבַדְיָהוּ הָיָה יָרֵא אֶת־יְהוָה מְאֹד׃ וַיְהִי בְּהַכְרִית אִיזֶבֶל אֵת
נְבִיאֵי יְהוָה וַיִּקַּח עֹבַדְיָהוּ מֵאָה נְבִיאִים וַיַּחְבִּיאֵם חֲמִשִּׁים
ה אִישׁ בַּמְּעָרָה וְכִלְכְּלָם לֶחֶם וָמָיִם׃ וַיֹּאמֶר אַחְאָב אֶל־
עֹבַדְיָהוּ לֵךְ בָּאָרֶץ אֶל־כָּל־מַעְיְנֵי הַמַּיִם וְאֶל כָּל־הַנְּחָלִים
אוּלַי ׀ נִמְצָא חָצִיר וּנְחַיֶּה סוּס וָפֶרֶד וְלוֹא נַכְרִית מֵהַבְּהֵמָה׃
ו וַיְחַלְּקוּ לָהֶם אֶת־הָאָרֶץ לַעֲבָר־בָּהּ אַחְאָב הָלַךְ בְּדֶרֶךְ
ז אֶחָד לְבַדּוֹ וְעֹבַדְיָהוּ הָלַךְ בְּדֶרֶךְ־אֶחָד לְבַדּוֹ׃ וַיְהִי עֹבַדְיָהוּ
בַּדֶּרֶךְ וְהִנֵּה אֵלִיָּהוּ לִקְרָאתוֹ וַיַּכִּרֵהוּ וַיִּפֹּל עַל־פָּנָיו וַיֹּאמֶר
ח הַאַתָּה זֶה אֲדֹנִי אֵלִיָּהוּ׃ וַיֹּאמֶר לוֹ אָנִי לֵךְ אֱמֹר לַאדֹנֶיךָ הִנֵּה
ט אֵלִיָּהוּ׃ וַיֹּאמֶר מֶה חָטָאתִי כִּי־אַתָּה נֹתֵן אֶת־עַבְדְּךָ בְּיַד־
י אַחְאָב לַהֲמִיתֵנִי׃ חַי ׀ יְהוָה אֱלֹהֶיךָ אִם־יֶשׁ־גּוֹי וּמַמְלָכָה
אֲשֶׁר לֹא־שָׁלַח אֲדֹנִי שָׁם לְבַקֶּשְׁךָ וְאָמְרוּ אָיִן וְהִשְׁבִּיעַ
יא אֶת־הַמַּמְלָכָה וְאֶת־הַגּוֹי כִּי לֹא יִמְצָאֶכָּה׃ וְעַתָּה אַתָּה אֹמֵר
יב לֵךְ אֱמֹר לַאדֹנֶיךָ הִנֵּה אֵלִיָּהוּ׃ וְהָיָה אֲנִי ׀ אֵלֵךְ מֵאִתָּךְ וְרוּחַ
יְהוָה ׀ יִשָּׂאֲךָ עַל אֲשֶׁר לֹא־אֵדָע וּבָאתִי לְהַגִּיד לְאַחְאָב וְלֹא
יג יִמְצָאֲךָ וַהֲרָגָנִי וְעַבְדְּךָ יָרֵא אֶת־יְהוָה מִנְּעֻרָי׃ הֲלֹא־הֻגַּד
לַאדֹנִי אֵת אֲשֶׁר־עָשִׂיתִי בַּהֲרֹג אִיזֶבֶל אֵת נְבִיאֵי יְהוָה
וָאַחְבִּא מִנְּבִיאֵי יְהוָה מֵאָה אִישׁ חֲמִשִּׁים חֲמִשִּׁים אִישׁ
יד בַּמְּעָרָה וָאֲכַלְכְּלֵם לֶחֶם וָמָיִם׃ וְעַתָּה אַתָּה אֹמֵר לֵךְ אֱמֹר
טו לַאדֹנֶיךָ הִנֵּה אֵלִיָּהוּ וַהֲרָגָנִי׃ וַיֹּאמֶר אֵלִיָּהוּ חַי יְהוָה צְבָאוֹת
טז אֲשֶׁר עָמַדְתִּי לְפָנָיו כִּי הַיּוֹם אֵרָאֶה אֵלָיו׃ וַיֵּלֶךְ עֹבַדְיָהוּ
יז לִקְרַאת אַחְאָב וַיַּגֶּד־לוֹ וַיֵּלֶךְ אַחְאָב לִקְרַאת אֵלִיָּהוּ׃ וַיְהִי
כִּרְאוֹת אַחְאָב אֶת־אֵלִיָּהוּ וַיֹּאמֶר אַחְאָב אֵלָיו הַאַתָּה זֶה
יח עֹכֵר יִשְׂרָאֵל׃ וַיֹּאמֶר לֹא עָכַרְתִּי אֶת־יִשְׂרָאֵל כִּי אִם־אַתָּה

events that had occurred centuries earlier at Mount Sinai: The war against Baal is reminiscent of Moshe's fight against the worshippers of the golden calf. At both

have by abandoning the Lord's commandments and by fol-
19 lowing the Be'alim. Now summon all of Israel to gather to me at
Mount Carmel, together with the four hundred fifty prophets of
Baal and the four hundred prophets of Ashera, those who dine
20 at Izevel's table." *Aḥav summoned all the Israelites and gathered
21 the prophets to Mount Carmel. And Eliyahu drew close to all
the people and said, "How long will you sway from one side to
another? If the Lord is God, then follow Him, and if Baal, fol-
22 low him!" But the people had no reply. "I am the only prophet
left to the Lord," Eliyahu said to the people, "while the prophets
23 of Baal are four hundred fifty men. Let two bulls be given to us;
let them choose one bull for themselves, cut it up, and position
it on the wood without setting it alight, while I prepare the other
24 bull and place it on the wood without setting it alight. You will
invoke your god by name, while I will invoke the Lord by name,
and the God who answers with fire – He is God." And all the
25 people answered, "We accept." "Choose one bull for yourselves,
and go first," Eliyahu said to the prophets of Baal, "for you are
the majority. Do not set it alight yourselves; invoke your god by
26 name." They took the bull that was given to them and prepared
it, then invoked Baal by name from morning to noon, crying, "O
Baal, answer us," but there was no sound and no reply, and they
27 swayed around the altar that had been prepared. At noon, Eliyahu began to mock them: "Shout louder," he said, "for he is a
god – he may be in conversation, or busy, or out traveling; he
28 may be asleep – he might wake!" And they shouted louder and
gashed themselves with swords and spears, as was their custom,
29 until blood streamed down them. Noon passed by, and they
raved until the time of the grain offering, but there was no sound
30 and no answer and no response. Then Eliyahu said to all the
people, "Draw close to me." All the people drew close, and he be-
31 gan to repair the Lord's ruined altar. Eliyahu took twelve stones,
corresponding to the number of the tribes of the sons of Yaakov,
who received the word of the Lord: "Yisrael shall be your name."
32 With the stones he built an altar for the name of the Lord and

Sepharadim and Chabad begin here

וּבֵית אָבִיךָ בַּעֲזָבְכֶם אֶת־מִצְוֺת יהוה וַתֵּלֶךְ אַחֲרֵי הַבְּעָלִים׃
יט וְעַתָּה שְׁלַח קְבֹץ אֵלַי אֶת־כָּל־יִשְׂרָאֵל אֶל־הַר הַכַּרְמֶל
וְאֶת־נְבִיאֵי הַבַּעַל אַרְבַּע מֵאוֹת וַחֲמִשִּׁים וּנְבִיאֵי הָאֲשֵׁרָה
כ אַרְבַּע מֵאוֹת אֹכְלֵי שֻׁלְחַן אִיזָבֶל׃ *וַיִּשְׁלַח אַחְאָב בְּכָל־

Sepharadim and Chabad begin here

כא בְּנֵי יִשְׂרָאֵל וַיִּקְבֹּץ אֶת־הַנְּבִיאִים אֶל־הַר הַכַּרְמֶל׃ וַיִּגַּשׁ
אֵלִיָּהוּ אֶל־כָּל־הָעָם וַיֹּאמֶר עַד־מָתַי אַתֶּם פֹּסְחִים עַל־שְׁתֵּי
הַסְּעִפִּים אִם־יהוה הָאֱלֹהִים לְכוּ אַחֲרָיו וְאִם־הַבַּעַל לְכוּ
כב אַחֲרָיו וְלֹא־עָנוּ הָעָם אֹתוֹ דָּבָר׃ וַיֹּאמֶר אֵלִיָּהוּ אֶל־הָעָם
אֲנִי נוֹתַרְתִּי נָבִיא לַיהוה לְבַדִּי וּנְבִיאֵי הַבַּעַל אַרְבַּע־מֵאוֹת
כג וַחֲמִשִּׁים אִישׁ׃ וְיִתְּנוּ־לָנוּ שְׁנַיִם פָּרִים וְיִבְחֲרוּ לָהֶם הַפָּר
הָאֶחָד וִינַתְּחֻהוּ וְיָשִׂימוּ עַל־הָעֵצִים וְאֵשׁ לֹא יָשִׂימוּ וַאֲנִי
אֶעֱשֶׂה ׀ אֶת־הַפָּר הָאֶחָד וְנָתַתִּי עַל־הָעֵצִים וְאֵשׁ לֹא אָשִׂים׃
כד וּקְרָאתֶם בְּשֵׁם אֱלֹהֵיכֶם וַאֲנִי אֶקְרָא בְשֵׁם־יהוה וְהָיָה
הָאֱלֹהִים אֲשֶׁר־יַעֲנֶה בָאֵשׁ הוּא הָאֱלֹהִים וַיַּעַן כָּל־הָעָם
כה וַיֹּאמְרוּ טוֹב הַדָּבָר׃ וַיֹּאמֶר אֵלִיָּהוּ לִנְבִיאֵי הַבַּעַל בַּחֲרוּ
לָכֶם הַפָּר הָאֶחָד וַעֲשׂוּ רִאשֹׁנָה כִּי אַתֶּם הָרַבִּים וְקִרְאוּ
כו בְּשֵׁם אֱלֹהֵיכֶם וְאֵשׁ לֹא תָשִׂימוּ׃ וַיִּקְחוּ אֶת־הַפָּר אֲשֶׁר־נָתַן
לָהֶם וַיַּעֲשׂוּ וַיִּקְרְאוּ בְשֵׁם־הַבַּעַל מֵהַבֹּקֶר וְעַד־הַצָּהֳרַיִם
לֵאמֹר הַבַּעַל עֲנֵנוּ וְאֵין קוֹל וְאֵין עֹנֶה וַיְפַסְּחוּ עַל־הַמִּזְבֵּחַ
כז אֲשֶׁר עָשָׂה׃ וַיְהִי בַצָּהֳרַיִם וַיְהַתֵּל בָּהֶם אֵלִיָּהוּ וַיֹּאמֶר
קִרְאוּ בְקוֹל־גָּדוֹל כִּי־אֱלֹהִים הוּא כִּי־שִׂיחַ וְכִי־שִׂיג לוֹ וְכִי־
כח דֶרֶךְ לוֹ אוּלַי יָשֵׁן הוּא וְיִקָץ׃ וַיִּקְרְאוּ בְּקוֹל גָּדוֹל וַיִּתְגֹּדְדוּ
כט כְּמִשְׁפָּטָם בַּחֲרָבוֹת וּבָרְמָחִים עַד־שְׁפָךְ־דָּם עֲלֵיהֶם׃ וַיְהִי
כַּעֲבֹר הַצָּהֳרַיִם וַיִּתְנַבְּאוּ עַד לַעֲלוֹת הַמִּנְחָה וְאֵין־קוֹל
ל וְאֵין־עֹנֶה וְאֵין קָשֶׁב׃ וַיֹּאמֶר אֵלִיָּהוּ לְכָל־הָעָם גְּשׁוּ אֵלָי
לא וַיִּגְּשׁוּ כָל־הָעָם אֵלָיו וַיְרַפֵּא אֶת־מִזְבַּח יהוה הֶהָרוּס׃ וַיִּקַּח
אֵלִיָּהוּ שְׁתֵּים עֶשְׂרֵה אֲבָנִים כְּמִסְפַּר שִׁבְטֵי בְנֵי־יַעֲקֹב אֲשֶׁר
לב הָיָה דְבַר־יהוה אֵלָיו לֵאמֹר יִשְׂרָאֵל יִהְיֶה שְׁמֶךָ׃ וַיִּבְנֶה

made a trench large enough for two *se'a* of seed all around the
33 altar. He arranged the wood, cut up the bull, and placed it on the
34 wood. "Fill four jugs with water," he said, "and pour it over the offering and the wood. Now do it a second time," he said, and they
did it a second time. "Do it a third time," he said, and they did it a
35 third time. The water flowed around the altar; he even filled the
36 trench with water. At the time of the grain offering, the prophet
Eliyahu drew close and said, "O Lord, God of Avraham, Yitzḥak,
and Yisrael, let it be known today that You are the God in Israel
and that I am Your servant, and it was by Your word that I have
37 done all these things. Answer me, Lord, answer me, so that this
people will know that You, O Lord, are God; it was You who
38 turned their hearts backward." And fire from the Lord flared
down and consumed the offering, the wood, the stones, and the
39 dirt, and licked up the water in the trench. And all the people saw,
and they fell on their faces and cried, "The Lord – He is God!
40 The Lord – He is God!" *"Seize the prophets of Baal!" Eliyahu
said to them. "Let none of them escape!" They seized them, then
Eliyahu led them down to the Kishon Stream and slaughtered
41 them there. "Go up to eat and drink," Eliyahu then said to Aḥav,
42 "for here comes the sound of roaring rain." And Aḥav went up to
eat and drink while Eliyahu went up to the top of Mount Carmel.
He crouched down on the ground and pressed his face between
43 his knees. "Go up now," he said to his boy, "and look out to sea."
He went up and looked out. "Nothing is there," he said. Seven
44 times he said, "Go back." The seventh time, he said, "A tiny cloud,
the size of a man's hand, is rising up from the sea." "Go up," he
said, "and say to Aḥav, 'Harness up and make your way down
45 so that the rain will not hold you back.'" And all the while, the
skies grew dark with clouds and wind, and heavy rain began to
fall. Aḥav mounted his chariot and rode out to Yizre'el.

Ashkenazim and Sepharadim end here

אֶת־הָאֲבָנִים מִזְבֵּחַ בְּשֵׁם יְהוָה וַיַּעַשׂ תְּעָלָה כְּבֵית סָאתַיִם
לג זֶרַע סָבִיב לַמִּזְבֵּחַ: וַיַּעֲרֹךְ אֶת־הָעֵצִים וַיְנַתַּח אֶת־הַפָּר
לד וַיָּשֶׂם עַל־הָעֵצִים: וַיֹּאמֶר מִלְאוּ אַרְבָּעָה כַדִּים מַיִם וְיִצְקוּ
עַל־הָעֹלָה וְעַל־הָעֵצִים וַיֹּאמֶר שְׁנוּ וַיִּשְׁנוּ וַיֹּאמֶר שַׁלֵּשׁוּ
לה וַיְשַׁלֵּשׁוּ: וַיֵּלְכוּ הַמַּיִם סָבִיב לַמִּזְבֵּחַ וְגַם אֶת־הַתְּעָלָה מִלֵּא־
לו מָיִם: וַיְהִי ׀ בַּעֲלוֹת הַמִּנְחָה וַיִּגַּשׁ אֵלִיָּהוּ הַנָּבִיא וַיֹּאמַר
יְהוָה אֱלֹהֵי אַבְרָהָם יִצְחָק וְיִשְׂרָאֵל הַיּוֹם יִוָּדַע כִּי־אַתָּה
אֱלֹהִים בְּיִשְׂרָאֵל וַאֲנִי עַבְדֶּךָ ובדבריך עָשִׂיתִי אֵת כָּל־ וּבִדְבָרְךָ
לז הַדְּבָרִים הָאֵלֶּה: עֲנֵנִי יְהוָה עֲנֵנִי וְיֵדְעוּ הָעָם הַזֶּה כִּי־אַתָּה
לח יְהוָה הָאֱלֹהִים וְאַתָּה הֲסִבֹּתָ אֶת־לִבָּם אֲחֹרַנִּית: וַתִּפֹּל
אֵשׁ־יְהוָה וַתֹּאכַל אֶת־הָעֹלָה וְאֶת־הָעֵצִים וְאֶת־הָאֲבָנִים
לט וְאֶת־הֶעָפָר וְאֶת־הַמַּיִם אֲשֶׁר־בַּתְּעָלָה לִחֵכָה: וַיַּרְא כָּל־
הָעָם וַיִּפְּלוּ עַל־פְּנֵיהֶם וַיֹּאמְרוּ יְהוָה הוּא הָאֱלֹהִים יְהוָה
מ הוּא הָאֱלֹהִים:* וַיֹּאמֶר אֵלִיָּהוּ לָהֶם תִּפְשׂוּ ׀ אֶת־נְבִיאֵי *Ashkenazim and Sepharadim end here*
הַבַּעַל אִישׁ אַל־יִמָּלֵט מֵהֶם וַיִּתְפְּשׂוּם וַיּוֹרִדֵם אֵלִיָּהוּ אֶל־
מא נַחַל קִישׁוֹן וַיִּשְׁחָטֵם שָׁם: וַיֹּאמֶר אֵלִיָּהוּ לְאַחְאָב עֲלֵה אֱכֹל
מב וּשְׁתֵה כִּי־קוֹל הֲמוֹן הַגָּשֶׁם: וַיַּעֲלֶה אַחְאָב לֶאֱכֹל וְלִשְׁתּוֹת
וְאֵלִיָּהוּ עָלָה אֶל־רֹאשׁ הַכַּרְמֶל וַיִּגְהַר אַרְצָה וַיָּשֶׂם פָּנָיו בֵּין
מג בִּרְכָּו: וַיֹּאמֶר אֶל־נַעֲרוֹ עֲלֵה־נָא הַבֵּט דֶּרֶךְ־יָם וַיַּעַל וַיַּבֵּט
מד וַיֹּאמֶר אֵין מְאוּמָה וַיֹּאמֶר שֻׁב שֶׁבַע פְּעָמִים: וַיְהִי בַּשְּׁבִעִית
וַיֹּאמֶר הִנֵּה־עָב קְטַנָּה כְּכַף־אִישׁ עֹלָה מִיָּם וַיֹּאמֶר עֲלֵה
מה אֱמֹר אֶל־אַחְאָב אֱסֹר וָרֵד וְלֹא יַעַצָרְכָה הַגָּשֶׁם: וַיְהִי ׀
עַד־כֹּה וְעַד־כֹּה וְהַשָּׁמַיִם הִתְקַדְּרוּ עָבִים וְרוּחַ וַיְהִי גֶּשֶׁם
גָּדוֹל וַיִּרְכַּב אַחְאָב וַיֵּלֶךְ יִזְרְעֶאלָה:

Haftarat Vayak'hel

On Shabbat Shekalim, read the maftir from Exodus 30:11–16, and the haftara on page 1654. On Shabbat Para, read the maftir from Numbers 19:1–22, and the haftara on page 1662. On Shabbat HaḤodesh, read the maftir from Exodus 12:1–20, and the haftara on page 1666. When Vayak'hel and Pekudei are read together, read the haftara for Pekudei on page 1506.

I KINGS

For Sepharadim, Chabad and Yemenites

7 13 14 King Shlomo sent and had Ḥiram fetched from Tyre. He was the
son of a widow from the tribe of Naftali, and his father had been
a Tyrian coppersmith. He was brimming with the talent, expertise, and skill to craft any work in bronze; he came to King Shlo-
15 mo and crafted all his work. He formed the two pillars of bronze;
each pillar was eighteen cubits high, and the circumference of
16 both pillars was twelve cubits. He crafted two capitals, cast in
bronze, to place atop the pillars – the height of each capital was
17 five cubits – as well as fronds of meshwork and garlands of chain-
work for the capitals atop the pillars, seven for each of the two
18 capitals. He crafted the pillars with two rows around one mesh
to cover the capitals that were above the pomegranates, and he
19 did the same with the second capital. The capitals atop the pillars
20 in the Hall were crafted in the form of a lily four cubits high; the
capitals atop both pillars bulged out through the meshwork over
the rows of two hundred pomegranates encircling both capitals.
21 He erected the pillars by the Hall of the Sanctuary; he set up the
right pillar and named it Yakhin, and he set up the left pillar and
22 named it Boaz. Atop each pillar was the form of a lily; thus the
23 work of the pillars was complete. *He made the Mol-
ten Sea, ten cubits across from rim to rim and perfectly round. *Yemenites end here*
24 It was five cubits high and thirty cubits in circumference. There
were bulb-shaped knobs beneath its rim, encircling it all around,

---

VAYAK'HEL

The First Temple, built in the reign of King Shlomo, was constructed from the finest materials and using the most advanced methods in existence. The richness of the structure was a testament to God's glory. This *haftara* describes the work of Ḥiram, the architect charged with constructing the Temple, just as Betzalel had built the Tabernacle in an earlier generation. It details the beauty of the structure and its accoutrements, including the wonderful golden candelabra that gave light to the luxurious Temple. The work of building the Sanctuary was complex and arduous, but after seven years it was completed, and the Temple was dedicated with pomp and festivity.

הפטרת ויקהל

On שבת שקלים*, read the* מפטיר *from* שמות ל, יא–טז*, and the* הפטרה *on page 1655. On* שבת פרה*, read the* מפטיר *from* במדבר יט, א–כב*, and the* הפטרה *on page 1663. On* שבת החודש*, read the* מפטיר *from* שמות יב, א–כ*, and the* הפטרה *on page 1667. When* ויקהל *and* פקודי *are read together, read the* הפטרה *for* פקודי *on page 1507.*

מלכים א׳
For Sepharadim, Chabad and Yemenites

ז יג יד וישלח המלך שלמה ויקח את־חירם מצר: בן־אשה
אלמנה הוא ממטה נפתלי ואביו איש־צרי חרש נחשת
וימלא את־החכמה ואת־התבונה ואת־הדעת לעשות
כל־מלאכה בנחשת ויבוא אל־המלך שלמה ויעש את־
טו כל־מלאכתו: ויצר את־שני העמודים נחשת שמנה עשרה
אמה קומת העמוד האחד וחוט שתים־עשרה אמה יסב
טז את־העמוד השני: ושתי כתרת עשה לתת על־ראשי
העמודים מצק נחשת חמש אמות קומת הכתרת האחת
יז וחמש אמות קומת הכתרת השנית: שבכים מעשה שבכה
גדלים מעשה שרשרות לכתרת אשר על־ראש העמודים
יח שבעה לכתרת האחת ושבעה לכתרת השנית: ויעש את־
העמודים ושני טורים סביב על־השבכה האחת לכסות
את־הכתרת אשר על־ראש הרמנים וכן עשה לכתרת
יט השנית: וכתרת אשר על־ראש העמודים מעשה שושן
כ באולם ארבע אמות: וכתרת על־שני העמודים גם־ממעל
מלעמת הבטן אשר לעבר שבכה והרמונים מאתים טרים (השבכה)
כא סביב על הכתרת השנית: ויקם את־העמדים לאלם ההיכל
ויקם את־העמוד הימני ויקרא את־שמו יכין ויקם את־
כב העמוד השמאלי ויקרא את־שמו בעז: ועל ראש העמודים
כג מעשה שושן ותתם מלאכת העמודים:* ויעש
Yemenites end here
את־הים מוצק עשר באמה משפתו עד־שפתו עגל | סביב
וחמש באמה קומתו וקוה שלשים באמה יסב אתו סביב: (וקו)
כד ופקעים מתחת לשפתו | סביב סבבים אתו עשר באמה
מקפים את־הים סביב שני טורים הפקעים יצקים ביצקתו:

clustered around the Sea ten to a cubit; the two rows of bulbs
25 were cast together with it. It stood upon twelve oxen, three facing north, three facing west, three facing south, and three facing
east; the Sea was on top of them, and their haunches were all
26 turned inward. It was a handbreadth thick, and its rim was like
the rim of a cup, like the petals of a lily; its capacity was two thousand *bat*.

I KINGS
For Ashkenazim

7 40 Ḥiram crafted the lavers and the shovels and the basins. And
so Ḥiram completed all the work for the House of the Lord
41 as commissioned by King Shlomo: two pillars and two globe-
shaped capitals for the pillar tops; two pieces of meshwork to
42 cover the two globe-shaped capitals for the pillar tops; four hundred pomegranates for the two pieces of meshwork – two rows
of pomegranates for each piece of meshwork, which covered the
43 two globe-shaped capitals on top of the pillars; ten stands and
44 ten lavers for the stands; one Sea with twelve oxen beneath the
45 Sea; pots, shovels, and basins. All these vessels, which Ḥiram
crafted for King Shlomo, for the House of the Lord, were of
46 burnished bronze. The king had them cast in clay molds on the
47 Jordan plain between Sukkot and Tzartan. Due to their sheer
abundance, Shlomo left all the vessels out of account; the weight
48 of the bronze was not determined. Shlomo made all the vessels for the House of the Lord: the altar was of gold, and the
49 table for the showbread was of gold. The candelabra – five on
the right and five on the left, in front of the Inner Sanctuary –
were of solid gold; the flowers, the lamps, and the tongs were all
50 of gold. The bowls, shears, basins, spoons, and firepans were of
solid gold. The hinges of the doors to the inner House, to the
Holy of Holies, and of the doors of the House to the Sanctuary,
were of gold.

כה עֹמֵד עַל־שְׁנֵי עָשָׂר בָּקָר שְׁלֹשָׁה פֹנִים ׀ צָפוֹנָה וּשְׁלֹשָׁה
פֹּנִים ׀ יָמָּה וּשְׁלֹשָׁה ׀ פֹּנִים נֶגְבָּה וּשְׁלֹשָׁה פֹּנִים מִזְרָחָה וְהַיָּם
כו עֲלֵיהֶם מִלְמָעְלָה וְכָל־אֲחֹרֵיהֶם בָּיְתָה: וְעָבְיוֹ טֶפַח וּשְׂפָתוֹ
כְּמַעֲשֵׂה שְׂפַת־כּוֹס פֶּרַח שׁוֹשָׁן אַלְפַּיִם בַּת יָכִיל:

מלכים א׳

For Ashkenazim

ז מ וַיַּעַשׂ חִירוֹם אֶת־הַכִּיֹּרוֹת וְאֶת־הַיָּעִים וְאֶת־הַמִּזְרָקוֹת וַיְכַל
חִירָם לַעֲשׂוֹת אֶת־כָּל־הַמְּלָאכָה אֲשֶׁר עָשָׂה לַמֶּלֶךְ שְׁלֹמֹה
מא בֵּית יְהוָה: עַמֻּדִים שְׁנַיִם וְגֻלֹּת הַכֹּתָרֹת אֲשֶׁר־עַל־רֹאשׁ
הָעַמֻּדִים שְׁתָּיִם וְהַשְּׂבָכוֹת שְׁתַּיִם לְכַסּוֹת אֶת־שְׁתֵּי גֻּלֹּת
מב הַכֹּתָרֹת אֲשֶׁר עַל־רֹאשׁ הָעַמּוּדִים: וְאֶת־הָרִמֹּנִים אַרְבַּע
מֵאוֹת לִשְׁתֵּי הַשְּׂבָכוֹת שְׁנֵי־טוּרִים רִמֹּנִים לַשְּׂבָכָה הָאֶחָת
לְכַסּוֹת אֶת־שְׁתֵּי גֻּלֹּת הַכֹּתָרֹת אֲשֶׁר עַל־פְּנֵי הָעַמּוּדִים:
מג וְאֶת־הַמְּכֹנוֹת עֶשֶׂר וְאֶת־הַכִּיֹּרֹת עֲשָׂרָה עַל־הַמְּכֹנוֹת:
מד וְאֶת־הַיָּם הָאֶחָד וְאֶת־הַבָּקָר שְׁנֵים־עָשָׂר תַּחַת הַיָּם:
מה וְאֶת־הַסִּירוֹת וְאֶת־הַיָּעִים וְאֶת־הַמִּזְרָקוֹת וְאֵת כָּל־הַכֵּלִים
האהל אֲשֶׁר עָשָׂה חִירָם לַמֶּלֶךְ שְׁלֹמֹה בֵּית יְהוָה נְחֹשֶׁת הָאֵלֶּה
מו מְמֹרָט: בְּכִכַּר הַיַּרְדֵּן יְצָקָם הַמֶּלֶךְ בְּמַעֲבֵה הָאֲדָמָה בֵּין
מז סֻכּוֹת וּבֵין צָרְתָן: וַיַּנַּח שְׁלֹמֹה אֶת־כָּל־הַכֵּלִים מֵרֹב מְאֹד
מח מְאֹד לֹא נֶחְקַר מִשְׁקַל הַנְּחֹשֶׁת: וַיַּעַשׂ שְׁלֹמֹה אֵת כָּל־
הַכֵּלִים אֲשֶׁר בֵּית יְהוָה אֵת מִזְבַּח הַזָּהָב וְאֶת־הַשֻּׁלְחָן אֲשֶׁר
מט עָלָיו לֶחֶם הַפָּנִים זָהָב: וְאֶת־הַמְּנֹרוֹת חָמֵשׁ מִיָּמִין וְחָמֵשׁ
מִשְּׂמֹאול לִפְנֵי הַדְּבִיר זָהָב סָגוּר וְהַפֶּרַח וְהַנֵּרֹת וְהַמֶּלְקַחַיִם
נ זָהָב: וְהַסִּפּוֹת וְהַמְזַמְּרוֹת וְהַמִּזְרָקוֹת וְהַכַּפּוֹת וְהַמַּחְתּוֹת
זָהָב סָגוּר וְהַפֹּתוֹת לְדַלְתוֹת הַבַּיִת הַפְּנִימִי לְקֹדֶשׁ הַקֳּדָשִׁים
לְדַלְתֵי הַבַּיִת לְהֵיכָל זָהָב:

Haftarat Pekudei

When Vayak'hel and Pekudei are read together, read this haftara. On Shabbat Shekalim read the maftir from Exodus 30:11–16, and the haftara on page 1654. On Shabbat Para, read the maftir from Numbers 19:1–22, and the haftara on page 1662. On Shabbat HaḤodesh, read the maftir from Exodus 12:1–20, and the haftara on page 1666.

I KINGS

Sepharadim and Yemenites begin here

7 40 Ḥiram crafted the lavers and the shovels and the basins. And
so Ḥiram completed all the work for the House of the Lord
41 as commissioned by King Shlomo: two pillars and two globe-
shaped capitals for the pillar tops; two pieces of meshwork to
42 cover the two globe-shaped capitals for the pillar tops; four hundred pomegranates for the two pieces of meshwork – two rows
of pomegranates for each piece of meshwork, which covered the
43 two globe-shaped capitals on top of the pillars; ten stands and
44 ten lavers for the stands; one Sea with twelve oxen beneath the
45 Sea; pots, shovels, and basins. All these vessels, which Ḥiram
crafted for King Shlomo, for the House of the Lord, were of
46 burnished bronze. The king had them cast in clay molds on the
47 Jordan plain between Sukkot and Tzartan. Due to their sheer
abundance, Shlomo left all the vessels out of account; the weight
48 of the bronze was not determined. Shlomo made all the vessels for the House of the Lord: the altar was of gold, and the
49 table for the showbread was of gold. The candelabra – five on
the right and five on the left, in front of the Inner Sanctuary –
were of solid gold; the flowers, the lamps, and the tongs were all
50 of gold. The bowls, shears, basins, spoons, and firepans were of
solid gold. The hinges of the doors to the inner House, to the
Holy of Holies, and of the doors of the House to the Sanctuary,
51 were of gold. *When all the work that King Shlomo
did for the House of the Lord was finished, Shlomo brought
what David his father had dedicated – the silver, the gold, and

Sepharadim and Yemenites end here

Ashkenazim and Chabad begin here

---

celebrating for fourteen days during the month of Tishrei, until Shemini Atzeret. At the center of this celebration were two main events, described here in detail. First was the moving of the Ark built in Moshe's time, which contained the tablets of the covenant, from the City of David to the new Temple. From then on, its home would be the Holy of Holies in the structures' Sanctuary building. Second was Shlomo's long prayer of thanksgiving, designating the Temple as a house of prayer for the people of Israel and all humanity.

הפטרת פקודי

When ויקהל *and* פקודי *are read together, read this* הפטרה*. On* שבת שקלים*, read the* מפטיר *from* שמות ל, יא–טז*, and the* הפטרה *on page 1655. On* שבת פרה*, read the* מפטיר *from* במדבר יט, א–כב*, and the* הפטרה *on page 1663. On* שבת החודש*, read the* מפטיר *from* שמות יב, א–כ*, and the* הפטרה *on page 1667.*

מלכים א׳

Sepharadim and Yemenites begin here

ז מ וַיַּעַשׂ חִירוֹם אֶת־הַכִּיֹּרוֹת וְאֶת־הַיָּעִים וְאֶת־הַמִּזְרָקוֹת וַיְכַל
חִירָם לַעֲשׂוֹת אֶת־כָּל־הַמְּלָאכָה אֲשֶׁר עָשָׂה לַמֶּלֶךְ שְׁלֹמֹה
מא בֵּית יהוה: עַמֻּדִים שְׁנַיִם וְגֻלֹּת הַכֹּתָרֹת אֲשֶׁר־עַל־רֹאשׁ
הָעַמֻּדִים שְׁתָּיִם וְהַשְּׂבָכוֹת שְׁתַּיִם לְכַסּוֹת אֶת־שְׁתֵּי גֻּלּוֹת
מב הַכֹּתָרֹת אֲשֶׁר עַל־רֹאשׁ הָעַמּוּדִים: וְאֶת־הָרִמֹּנִים אַרְבַּע
מֵאוֹת לִשְׁתֵּי הַשְּׂבָכוֹת שְׁנֵי־טוּרִים רִמֹּנִים לַשְּׂבָכָה הָאֶחָת
לְכַסּוֹת אֶת־שְׁתֵּי גֻּלֹּת הַכֹּתָרֹת אֲשֶׁר עַל־פְּנֵי הָעַמּוּדִים:
מג וְאֶת־הַמְּכֹנוֹת עָשֶׂר וְאֶת־הַכִּיֹּרֹת עֲשָׂרָה עַל־הַמְּכֹנוֹת:
מד וְאֶת־הַיָּם הָאֶחָד וְאֶת־הַבָּקָר שְׁנֵים־עָשָׂר תַּחַת הַיָּם:
מה וְאֶת־הַסִּירוֹת וְאֶת־הַיָּעִים וְאֶת־הַמִּזְרָקוֹת וְאֵת כָּל־הַכֵּלִים
האהל אֲשֶׁר עָשָׂה חִירָם לַמֶּלֶךְ שְׁלֹמֹה בֵּית יהוה נְחֹשֶׁת הָאֵלֶּה
מו מְמֹרָט: בְּכִכַּר הַיַּרְדֵּן יְצָקָם הַמֶּלֶךְ בְּמַעֲבֵה הָאֲדָמָה בֵּין
מז סֻכּוֹת וּבֵין צָרְתָן: וַיַּנַּח שְׁלֹמֹה אֶת־כָּל־הַכֵּלִים מֵרֹב מְאֹד
מח מְאֹד לֹא נֶחְקַר מִשְׁקַל הַנְּחֹשֶׁת: וַיַּעַשׂ שְׁלֹמֹה אֵת כָּל־
הַכֵּלִים אֲשֶׁר בֵּית יהוה אֵת מִזְבַּח הַזָּהָב וְאֶת־הַשֻּׁלְחָן אֲשֶׁר
מט עָלָיו לֶחֶם הַפָּנִים זָהָב: וְאֶת־הַמְּנֹרוֹת חָמֵשׁ מִיָּמִין וְחָמֵשׁ
מִשְּׂמֹאול לִפְנֵי הַדְּבִיר זָהָב סָגוּר וְהַפֶּרַח וְהַנֵּרֹת וְהַמֶּלְקָחַיִם
נ זָהָב: וְהַסִּפּוֹת וְהַמְזַמְּרוֹת וְהַמִּזְרָקוֹת וְהַכַּפּוֹת וְהַמַּחְתּוֹת
זָהָב סָגוּר וְהַפֹּתוֹת לְדַלְתוֹת הַבַּיִת הַפְּנִימִי לְקֹדֶשׁ
נא הַקֳּדָשִׁים לְדַלְתֵי הַבַּיִת לַהֵיכָל זָהָב:* *וַתִּשְׁלַם
כָּל־הַמְּלָאכָה אֲשֶׁר עָשָׂה הַמֶּלֶךְ שְׁלֹמֹה בֵּית יהוה וַיָּבֵא

Sepharadim and Yemenites end here

Ashkenazi and Chabad begin here

PEKUDEI

With the conclusion of the construction of the Temple during the reign of King Shlomo, the people prepare for the dedication ceremony for the new Sanctuary. All Israel arrived for the festivities,

the vessels – and placed them in the treasury of the House of the
8 1 Lord. Then Shlomo assembled the elders of Israel – all
the heads of the tribes, the ancestral leaders of the Israelites – before King Shlomo in Jerusalem, to bring up the Ark of the Lord's
2 Covenant from the City of David, Zion. All the men of Israel
assembled before King Shlomo in the month of Etanim, the
3 seventh month, at the festival. When all the elders of Israel had
4 arrived, the priests lifted up the Ark and brought up the Ark of
the Lord, the Tent of Meeting, and all the sacred vessels in the
5 Tent. While the priests and the Levites brought them up, King
Shlomo and the whole community of Israel, who had met him
before the Ark, sacrificed sheep and oxen – far too many to num-
6 ber or count. The priests brought the Ark of the Lord's Covenant
to its place – to the House's Inner Sanctuary, the Holy of Holies,
7 to under the shade of the wings of the cherubim. For the wings
of the cherubim were spread over the place of the Ark so that
8 the cherubim sheltered the Ark and its poles from above. The
poles extended so that the ends of the poles were visible from
the Holy Place in front of the Inner Sanctuary, but they could
9 not be seen from the outside, and they are there to this day. The
Ark contained nothing but the two stone tablets Moshe placed
there at Ḥorev when the Lord made a covenant with the Isra-
10 elites as they left the land of Egypt. And as the priests left the
11 Holy Place, a cloud filled the House of the Lord; the priests
could not stand and serve because of the cloud, for the glory
12 of the Lord had filled the House of the Lord. Then
Shlomo declared: "The Lord promised that He would dwell in
13 deep mist; I have now built You an exalted House, a permanent
14 place for Your abode." And the king turned his face and blessed
the whole assembly of Israel, while the whole assembly of Israel
15 stood. "Blessed is the Lord, God of Israel," he said, "who made
a promise to my father David with His own mouth and has now
16 fulfilled it with His own hand, saying: From the day I brought My
people, Israel, out of Egypt, I never chose a city from among all
the tribes of Israel, to build a House where My name would be;
17 but I chose David to be over My people Israel. My father David
had his heart set on building a House for the name of the Lord,

שְׁלֹמֹה אֶת־קׇדְשֵׁי ׀ דָּוִד אָבִיו אֶת־הַכֶּסֶף וְאֶת־הַזָּהָב וְאֶת־
ח א הַכֵּלִים נָתַן בְּאֹצְרוֹת בֵּית יהוה׃ אָז יַקְהֵל שְׁלֹמֹה
אֶת־זִקְנֵי יִשְׂרָאֵל אֶת־כׇּל־רָאשֵׁי הַמַּטּוֹת נְשִׂיאֵי הָאָבוֹת
לִבְנֵי יִשְׂרָאֵל אֶל־הַמֶּלֶךְ שְׁלֹמֹה יְרוּשָׁלָ͏ִם לְהַעֲלוֹת אֶת־
ב אֲרוֹן בְּרִית־יהוה מֵעִיר דָּוִד הִיא צִיּוֹן׃ וַיִּקָּהֲלוּ אֶל־הַמֶּלֶךְ
שְׁלֹמֹה כׇּל־אִישׁ יִשְׂרָאֵל בְּיֶרַח הָאֵתָנִים בֶּחָג הוּא הַחֹדֶשׁ
ג הַשְּׁבִיעִי׃ וַיָּבֹאוּ כֹּל זִקְנֵי יִשְׂרָאֵל וַיִּשְׂאוּ הַכֹּהֲנִים אֶת־הָאָרוֹן׃
ד וַיַּעֲלוּ אֶת־אֲרוֹן יהוה וְאֶת־אֹהֶל מוֹעֵד וְאֶת־כׇּל־כְּלֵי הַקֹּדֶשׁ
ה אֲשֶׁר בָּאֹהֶל וַיַּעֲלוּ אֹתָם הַכֹּהֲנִים וְהַלְוִיִּם׃ וְהַמֶּלֶךְ שְׁלֹמֹה
וְכׇל־עֲדַת יִשְׂרָאֵל הַנּוֹעָדִים עָלָיו אִתּוֹ לִפְנֵי הָאָרוֹן מְזַבְּחִים
ו צֹאן וּבָקָר אֲשֶׁר לֹא־יִסָּפְרוּ וְלֹא יִמָּנוּ מֵרֹב׃ וַיָּבִאוּ הַכֹּהֲנִים
אֶת־אֲרוֹן בְּרִית־יהוה אֶל־מְקוֹמוֹ אֶל־דְּבִיר הַבַּיִת אֶל־
ז קֹדֶשׁ הַקֳּדָשִׁים אֶל־תַּחַת כַּנְפֵי הַכְּרוּבִים׃ כִּי הַכְּרוּבִים
פֹּרְשִׂים כְּנָפַיִם אֶל־מְקוֹם הָאָרוֹן וַיָּסֹכּוּ הַכְּרֻבִים עַל־הָאָרוֹן
ח וְעַל־בַּדָּיו מִלְמָעְלָה׃ וַיַּאֲרִכוּ הַבַּדִּים וַיֵּרָאוּ רָאשֵׁי הַבַּדִּים
מִן־הַקֹּדֶשׁ עַל־פְּנֵי הַדְּבִיר וְלֹא יֵרָאוּ הַחוּצָה וַיִּהְיוּ שָׁם עַד
ט הַיּוֹם הַזֶּה׃ אֵין בָּאָרוֹן רַק שְׁנֵי לֻחוֹת הָאֲבָנִים אֲשֶׁר הִנִּחַ
שָׁם מֹשֶׁה בְּחֹרֵב אֲשֶׁר כָּרַת יהוה עִם־בְּנֵי יִשְׂרָאֵל בְּצֵאתָם
י מֵאֶרֶץ מִצְרָיִם׃ וַיְהִי בְּצֵאת הַכֹּהֲנִים מִן־הַקֹּדֶשׁ וְהֶעָנָן מָלֵא
יא אֶת־בֵּית יהוה׃ וְלֹא־יָכְלוּ הַכֹּהֲנִים לַעֲמֹד לְשָׁרֵת מִפְּנֵי הֶעָנָן
יב כִּי־מָלֵא כְבוֹד־יהוה אֶת־בֵּית יהוה׃ אָז אָמַר
יג שְׁלֹמֹה יהוה אָמַר לִשְׁכֹּן בָּעֲרָפֶל׃ בָּנֹה בָנִיתִי בֵּית זְבֻל לָךְ
יד מָכוֹן לְשִׁבְתְּךָ עוֹלָמִים׃ וַיַּסֵּב הַמֶּלֶךְ אֶת־פָּנָיו וַיְבָרֶךְ אֵת
טו כׇּל־קְהַל יִשְׂרָאֵל וְכׇל־קְהַל יִשְׂרָאֵל עֹמֵד׃ וַיֹּאמֶר בָּרוּךְ
יהוה אֱלֹהֵי יִשְׂרָאֵל אֲשֶׁר דִּבֶּר בְּפִיו אֵת דָּוִד אָבִי וּבְיָדוֹ
טז מִלֵּא לֵאמֹר׃ מִן־הַיּוֹם אֲשֶׁר הוֹצֵאתִי אֶת־עַמִּי אֶת־יִשְׂרָאֵל
מִמִּצְרַיִם לֹא־בָחַרְתִּי בְעִיר מִכֹּל שִׁבְטֵי יִשְׂרָאֵל לִבְנוֹת בַּיִת
יז לִהְיוֹת שְׁמִי שָׁם וָאֶבְחַר בְּדָוִד לִהְיוֹת עַל־עַמִּי יִשְׂרָאֵל׃ וַיְהִי

18 God of Israel. But the LORD said to my father David: Though
you have set your heart on building a House for My name, and
19 though you have set your heart well, you will not be the one to
build the House. But your son, the issue of your own loins – he
20 will be the one to build the House for My name. The LORD has
fulfilled the promise He made; I have risen in my father's stead,
and I sit upon Israel's throne, as the LORD promised. I have built
21 the House for the name of the LORD, God of Israel. And there I
have set a place for the Ark, which contains the covenant that the
LORD made with our ancestors when He brought them out of
the land of Egypt."

HAFTARAT VAYIKRA

On Shabbat Zakhor, read the maftir from Deuteronomy 25:17–19, and the haftara on page 1658. On Shabbat HaḤodesh, read the maftir from Exodus 12:1–20, and the haftara on page 1666.

43 21 22 The people I have formed for Me, who are to tell My praises. It ISAIAH
23 is not Me you call for, Yaakov; Israel, you wearied of Me. You
did not bring Me the lamb of your offering; it was not Me your
sacrifice honored; I did not enslave you to My gifts or weary you
24 with frankincense. You did not pay silver for calamus for Me or
slake My thirst with fat of the sacrifice, yet you enslaved Me to
25 your iniquity and wearied Me with your sins. I am I, who ex-
punge your offenses for My own sake and will not keep your sins
26 in mind. Recall Me now; let us argue this out; tell Me so that
27 you may be vindicated. Your first father sinned, and those who
28 spoke for you rebelled against Me, so I desecrated your Sanctuary's ministers and marked you for destruction, Yaakov; Israel,

of Israel. To save Yehuda from Assyria was therefore a religious imperative as well as a political one. Israel, as God's people, must respond to the prophet's call in His name: "I am the first and I the last; beside Me is no God." If they internalize this, they will have no need to fear the threat from gods of wood and stone. The prophet mocks these idols, while stressing that in Israel's own religion, the sacrificial service is not an end in itself but a means, and that true closeness to God comes through the perfection of our character.

עִם־לְבַב דָּוִד אָבִי לִבְנוֹת בַּיִת לְשֵׁם יְהוָה אֱלֹהֵי יִשְׂרָאֵל׃
יח וַיֹּאמֶר יְהוָה אֶל־דָּוִד אָבִי יַעַן אֲשֶׁר הָיָה עִם־לְבָבְךָ לִבְנוֹת
יט בַּיִת לִשְׁמִי הֱטִיבֹתָ כִּי הָיָה עִם־לְבָבֶךָ׃ רַק אַתָּה לֹא תִבְנֶה
הַבָּיִת כִּי אִם־בִּנְךָ הַיֹּצֵא מֵחֲלָצֶיךָ הוּא־יִבְנֶה הַבַּיִת לִשְׁמִי׃
כ וַיָּקֶם יְהוָה אֶת־דְּבָרוֹ אֲשֶׁר דִּבֵּר וָאָקֻם תַּחַת דָּוִד אָבִי
וָאֵשֵׁב ׀ עַל־כִּסֵּא יִשְׂרָאֵל כַּאֲשֶׁר דִּבֶּר יְהוָה וָאֶבְנֶה הַבַּיִת
כא לְשֵׁם יְהוָה אֱלֹהֵי יִשְׂרָאֵל׃ וָאָשִׂם שָׁם מָקוֹם לָאָרוֹן אֲשֶׁר־
שָׁם בְּרִית יְהוָה אֲשֶׁר כָּרַת עִם־אֲבֹתֵינוּ בְּהוֹצִיאוֹ אֹתָם
מֵאֶרֶץ מִצְרָיִם׃

הפטרת ויקרא

On שבת זכור*, read the* מפטיר *from* דברים כה, יז–יט*,*
and the הפטרה *on page 1659. On* שבת החודש*, read the* מפטיר
from שמות יב, א–כ*, and the* הפטרה *on page 1667.*

ישעיה מג כא כב עַם־זוּ יָצַרְתִּי לִי תְּהִלָּתִי יְסַפֵּרוּ׃ וְלֹא־אֹתִי קָרָאתָ יַעֲקֹב
כג כִּי־יָגַעְתָּ בִּי יִשְׂרָאֵל׃ לֹא־הֵבֵיאתָ לִּי שֵׂה עֹלֹתֶיךָ וּזְבָחֶיךָ
לֹא כִבַּדְתָּנִי לֹא הֶעֱבַדְתִּיךָ בְּמִנְחָה וְלֹא הוֹגַעְתִּיךָ בִּלְבוֹנָה׃
כד לֹא־קָנִיתָ לִּי בַכֶּסֶף קָנֶה וְחֵלֶב זְבָחֶיךָ לֹא הִרְוִיתָנִי אַךְ
כה הֶעֱבַדְתַּנִי בְּחַטֹּאותֶיךָ הוֹגַעְתַּנִי בַּעֲוֺנֹתֶיךָ׃ אָנֹכִי אָנֹכִי הוּא
כו מֹחֶה פְשָׁעֶיךָ לְמַעֲנִי וְחַטֹּאתֶיךָ לֹא אֶזְכֹּר׃ הַזְכִּירֵנִי נִשָּׁפְטָה
כז יָחַד סַפֵּר אַתָּה לְמַעַן תִּצְדָּק׃ אָבִיךָ הָרִאשׁוֹן חָטָא וּמְלִיצֶיךָ
כח פָּשְׁעוּ בִי׃ וַאֲחַלֵּל שָׂרֵי קֹדֶשׁ וְאֶתְּנָה לַחֵרֶם יַעֲקֹב וְיִשְׂרָאֵל

VAYIKRA

The military conflicts that plagued Israel from their entry into the land until the time of Yeshayahu were on a small scale, and never came close to the destruction and exile that would be the people's fate later. In Yeshayahu's lifetime, however, during the reign of Ḥizkiyahu, the Assyrian superpower destroyed the kingdom of Israel utterly and exiled its people. Yehuda was in acute danger of suffering a similar fate. The confrontation with Assyria was presented by its emissaries as a struggle between deities. Victory for Assyria would be taken as a victory of Assyria's gods over the God

▶

44 1 to be denounced. And now listen, Yaakov My servant,
2 Israel whom I chose; so says the LORD who made you, the One
who made you in the womb, who helps you: Do not fear, My ser-
3 vant Yaakov, Yeshurun whom I chose. As I pour water on thirsty
earth, water upon parched land, I shall pour forth My spirit upon
4 your children, upon your offspring My blessing. They will sprout
5 among the grasses, like willows on streams of water, and a man
will say, "I am the LORD's," while another invokes the name of
Yaakov, and a third one will inscribe on his hand, "The LORD's,"
6 to name himself Israel. So says the LORD, King of Israel,
its rescue, the LORD of Hosts: I am the first and I the last; beside
7 Me is no God. Who like Me calls the future forth and tells it? Let *Yemenites end here*
them lay their claim before Me. I have formed an eternal people,
8 so let them bring out signs and tell what is to come. Do not fear,
do not lose faith; have I not let you hear this from the start? I told
it, and you are My witnesses: Is there any God but Me? There is
9 no rock I do not know. All those makers of images – all emptiness, their gorgeous objects useless, and all their witnesses see
10 nothing and know not and are shamed. Who has made a god
11 and molded an idol to bring him no good? All his company
will be shamed; craftsmen – they are human; let them come to-
12 gether, all, and stand and fear and feel their shame together, for
the craftsman in iron makes a chisel, works it over the coals and
forms it with hammers, works it with his arms' strength, grows
hungry and has no strength, fails to drink water until he grows
13 faint. The carpenter stretches out his line and marks it with a
thread; he forms it with his planes and marks it with a compass.
He is making it into the form of a man, a supreme human frame,
14 to sit in a house. He cuts down cedars for his work or chooses a
cypress or oak and sees it grow strong in the forest, plants a bay
15 laurel and lets rain nourish it to grow. These become firewood
for a man; he takes them and warms himself, kindles them and
bakes bread, and works the rest into a god, and worships a statue
16 and prostrates himself before it. Half of it he burns in the fire;
thanks to that half he eats meat, roasts the roast, feels fullness,
warms himself, says, "Ah – I am warmed; I have seen the flames."
17 And with what is left over, he makes a god, a statue to prostrate
himself in front of and to worship, pray to, say, "Save me, please:
18 you are my god." They know not; they do not comprehend, for
their eyes are smeared over, not to see, not to let understanding

מד א לִגְדוּפִים׃ וְעַתָּה שְׁמַע יַעֲקֹב עַבְדִּי וְיִשְׂרָאֵל
ב בָּחַרְתִּי בוֹ׃ כֹּה־אָמַר יהוה עֹשֶׂךָ וְיֹצֶרְךָ מִבֶּטֶן יַעְזְרֶךָּ
ג אַל־תִּירָא עַבְדִּי יַעֲקֹב וִישֻׁרוּן בָּחַרְתִּי בוֹ׃ כִּי אֶצָּק־מַיִם
עַל־צָמֵא וְנֹזְלִים עַל־יַבָּשָׁה אֶצֹּק רוּחִי עַל־זַרְעֶךָ וּבִרְכָתִי
ד עַל־צֶאֱצָאֶיךָ׃ וְצָמְחוּ בְּבֵין חָצִיר כַּעֲרָבִים עַל־יִבְלֵי־מָיִם׃
ה זֶה יֹאמַר לַיהוה אָנִי וְזֶה יִקְרָא בְשֵׁם־יַעֲקֹב וְזֶה יִכְתֹּב
ו יָדוֹ לַיהוה וּבְשֵׁם יִשְׂרָאֵל יְכַנֶּה׃ כֹּה־אָמַר יהוה
מֶלֶךְ־יִשְׂרָאֵל וְגֹאֲלוֹ יהוה צְבָאוֹת אֲנִי רִאשׁוֹן וַאֲנִי אַחֲרוֹן
ז וּמִבַּלְעָדַי אֵין אֱלֹהִים׃ וּמִי־כָמוֹנִי יִקְרָא וְיַגִּידֶהָ וְיַעְרְכֶהָ לִי *Yemenites end here*
ח מִשּׂוּמִי עַם־עוֹלָם וְאֹתִיּוֹת וַאֲשֶׁר תָּבֹאנָה יַגִּידוּ לָמוֹ׃ אַל־
תִּפְחֲדוּ וְאַל־תִּרְהוּ הֲלֹא מֵאָז הִשְׁמַעְתִּיךָ וְהִגַּדְתִּי וְאַתֶּם
ט עֵדָי הֲיֵשׁ אֱלוֹהַּ מִבַּלְעָדַי וְאֵין צוּר בַּל־יָדָעְתִּי׃ יֹצְרֵי־פֶסֶל
כֻּלָּם תֹּהוּ וַחֲמוּדֵיהֶם בַּל־יוֹעִילוּ וְעֵדֵיהֶם הֵמָּה בַּל־יִרְאוּ
י וּבַל־יֵדְעוּ לְמַעַן יֵבֹשׁוּ׃ מִי־יָצַר אֵל וּפֶסֶל נָסָךְ לְבִלְתִּי הוֹעִיל׃
יא הֵן כָּל־חֲבֵרָיו יֵבֹשׁוּ וְחָרָשִׁים הֵמָּה מֵאָדָם יִתְקַבְּצוּ כֻלָּם
יב יַעֲמֹדוּ יִפְחֲדוּ יֵבֹשׁוּ יָחַד׃ חָרַשׁ בַּרְזֶל מַעֲצָד וּפָעַל בַּפֶּחָם
וּבַמַּקָּבוֹת יִצְּרֵהוּ וַיִּפְעָלֵהוּ בִּזְרוֹעַ כֹּחוֹ גַּם־רָעֵב וְאֵין כֹּחַ
יג לֹא־שָׁתָה מַיִם וַיִּיעָף׃ חָרַשׁ עֵצִים נָטָה קָו יְתָאֲרֵהוּ בַשֶּׂרֶד
יַעֲשֵׂהוּ בַּמַּקְצֻעוֹת וּבַמְּחוּגָה יְתָאֳרֵהוּ וַיַּעֲשֵׂהוּ כְּתַבְנִית אִישׁ
יד כְּתִפְאֶרֶת אָדָם לָשֶׁבֶת בָּיִת׃ לִכְרָת־לוֹ אֲרָזִים וַיִּקַּח תִּרְזָה
טו וְאַלּוֹן וַיְאַמֶּץ־לוֹ בַּעֲצֵי־יָעַר נָטַע אֹרֶן וְגֶשֶׁם יְגַדֵּל׃ וְהָיָה
לְאָדָם לְבָעֵר וַיִּקַּח מֵהֶם וַיָּחָם אַף־יַשִּׂיק וְאָפָה לָחֶם אַף־
טז יִפְעַל־אֵל וַיִּשְׁתָּחוּ עָשָׂהוּ פֶסֶל וַיִּסְגָּד־לָמוֹ׃ חֶצְיוֹ שָׂרַף בְּמוֹ־
אֵשׁ עַל־חֶצְיוֹ בָּשָׂר יֹאכֵל יִצְלֶה צָלִי וְיִשְׂבָּע אַף־יָחֹם וְיֹאמַר
יז הֶאָח חַמּוֹתִי רָאִיתִי אוּר׃ וּשְׁאֵרִיתוֹ לְאֵל עָשָׂה לְפִסְלוֹ
יסגוד־לוֹ וְיִשְׁתַּחוּ וְיִתְפַּלֵּל אֵלָיו וְיֹאמַר הַצִּילֵנִי כִּי אֵלִי יִסְגָּד־
יח אָתָּה׃ לֹא יָדְעוּ וְלֹא יָבִינוּ כִּי טַח מֵרְאוֹת עֵינֵיהֶם מֵהַשְׂכִּיל

19 into their hearts, so they do not take it to heart, nor find mind
or wisdom to say, "I burned half in the fire; I baked bread on the
coals; I roasted meat and ate it; with the rest should I make this
20 disgusting thing, this slab of wood, and bow down?" He courts
ashes; his deceived heart has misled him; he cannot save himself;
21 he cannot say, "This in my right hand – it is a lie." Hold
these things in mind, Yaakov, Israel, for you are My servant. I
22 made you – you are My servant; do not forget Me, Israel. I dis-
pelled your offenses like mist, like a cloud all your sins – come
23 back to Me, for I have redeemed you. Sing out, heavens, for the
LORD has acted. Sound the trumpets, lowest depths of earth;
hills, break out in song, and forests, all their trees, for the LORD
has redeemed Yaakov; in Israel is He glorified.

HAFTARAT TZAV

On Shabbat Zakhor read the maftir from Deuteronomy 25:17–19, and the haftara on page 1658. On Purim Meshulash in Jerusalem read the maftir from Exodus 17:8–16, and the haftara on page 1658. On Shabbat Para read the maftir from Numbers 19:1–22, and the haftara on page 1662. On Shabbat HaGadol read the haftara on page 1672.

7 21 This is what the LORD of Hosts, the God of Israel, said: Heap JEREMIAH
your burnt offerings upon your other sacrifices and eat the
22 meat. For when I brought your forefathers out of Egypt, I did
not speak to them, nor did I command them about matters of
23 burnt offerings and sacrifices. Rather, this is what I commanded them: Heed My voice so that I will be your God and you
will be My people. Walk in all the ways as I will command you
24 so that it will be good for you. But they did not listen, nor even
bend an ear. They followed their own counsel, their stubborn,
25 wicked hearts. They went backward, not forward. From the day
your forefathers left the land of Egypt until this very day, I sent

the people that the institution of the sacrifices is meant to arouse worshippers to correct their ways, to repent, and draw closer to God. The important thing is a person's behavior, not the sacrifices he or she brings. Those who act in a perverse way and come to bring sacrifices in the Temple to atone are carrying out a pointless exercise, only exacerbating God's displeasure. Just as God does charity, kindness, and justice on earth, He commands that we humans act likewise.

יט לִבֹּתָם׃ וְלֹא־יָשִׁיב אֶל־לִבּוֹ וְלֹא דַעַת וְלֹא־תְבוּנָה לֵאמֹר
חֶצְיוֹ שָׂרַפְתִּי בְמוֹ־אֵשׁ וְאַף אָפִיתִי עַל־גֶּחָלָיו לֶחֶם אֶצְלֶה
כ בָשָׂר וְאֹכֵל וְיִתְרוֹ לְתוֹעֵבָה אֶעֱשֶׂה לְבוּל עֵץ אֶסְגּוֹד׃ רֹעֶה
אֵפֶר לֵב הוּתַל הִטָּהוּ וְלֹא־יַצִּיל אֶת־נַפְשׁוֹ וְלֹא יֹאמַר הֲלוֹא
כא שֶׁקֶר בִּימִינִי׃ זְכָר־אֵלֶּה יַעֲקֹב וְיִשְׂרָאֵל כִּי עַבְדִּי־
כב אָתָּה יְצַרְתִּיךָ עֶבֶד־לִי אַתָּה יִשְׂרָאֵל לֹא תִנָּשֵׁנִי׃ מָחִיתִי
כג כָעָב פְּשָׁעֶיךָ וְכֶעָנָן חַטֹּאותֶיךָ שׁוּבָה אֵלַי כִּי גְאַלְתִּיךָ׃ רָנּוּ
שָׁמַיִם כִּי־עָשָׂה יהוה הָרִיעוּ תַּחְתִּיּוֹת אָרֶץ פִּצְחוּ הָרִים
רִנָּה יַעַר וְכָל־עֵץ בּוֹ כִּי־גָאַל יהוה יַעֲקֹב וּבְיִשְׂרָאֵל יִתְפָּאָר׃

הפטרת צו

On שבת זכור *read the* מפטיר *from* דברים כה, יז–יט*, and the* הפטרה *on page 1659. On* פורים משולש *in Jerusalem read the* מפטיר *from* שמות יז, ח–טז*, and the* הפטרה *on page 1659. On* שבת פרה *read the* מפטיר *from* במדבר יט, א–כב*, and the* הפטרה *on page 1663. On* שבת הגדול *read the* הפטרה *on page 1673.*

ז כא כֹּה אָמַר יהוה צְבָאוֹת אֱלֹהֵי יִשְׂרָאֵל עֹלוֹתֵיכֶם סְפוּ עַל־ ירמיה
כב זִבְחֵיכֶם וְאִכְלוּ בָשָׂר׃ כִּי לֹא־דִבַּרְתִּי אֶת־אֲבוֹתֵיכֶם וְלֹא
צִוִּיתִים בְּיוֹם הוֹצִיא אוֹתָם מֵאֶרֶץ מִצְרָיִם עַל־דִּבְרֵי עוֹלָה
כג וָזָבַח׃ כִּי אִם־אֶת־הַדָּבָר הַזֶּה צִוִּיתִי אוֹתָם לֵאמֹר שִׁמְעוּ
בְקוֹלִי וְהָיִיתִי לָכֶם לֵאלֹהִים וְאַתֶּם תִּהְיוּ־לִי לְעָם וַהֲלַכְתֶּם
כד בְּכָל־הַדֶּרֶךְ אֲשֶׁר אֲצַוֶּה אֶתְכֶם לְמַעַן יִיטַב לָכֶם׃ וְלֹא שָׁמְעוּ
וְלֹא־הִטּוּ אֶת־אָזְנָם וַיֵּלְכוּ בְּמֹעֵצוֹת בִּשְׁרִרוּת לִבָּם הָרָע
כה וַיִּהְיוּ לְאָחוֹר וְלֹא לְפָנִים׃ לְמִן־הַיּוֹם אֲשֶׁר יָצְאוּ אֲבוֹתֵיכֶם
מֵאֶרֶץ מִצְרַיִם עַד הַיּוֹם הַזֶּה וָאֶשְׁלַח אֲלֵיכֶם אֶת־כָּל־עֲבָדַי

TZAV

During the reign of King Yehoyakim the fate of Jerusalem's destruction was sealed. The cruelty of this ruler, his cultivation of idolatry (including human sacrifice), and his persecution of God's prophets tipped the scales. Yirmeyahu prophesied the bitter decree, which put him in serious danger as well.

In this *haftara*, Yirmeyahu reminds

▶

to them all of My servants, the prophets – early every day, and
26 persistently. But they did not listen to Me, nor even bend an ear.
They stiffened their necks. They did worse than their fathers.
27 You will speak all these words to them, but they will not hear
28 you. You will call to them, but they will not answer you. You
shall say to them: "This is the nation that did not obey the voice
of the LORD its God and that did not accept correction. Gone
29 is faithfulness, severed from their mouths."* Shear
your hair and throw it away. Raise a lament upon the high places, for the LORD has despised and has abandoned the genera-
30 tion that enraged Him. For the children of Yehuda have done
evil in My eyes, declares the LORD. They have placed their vile
objects in the House which is called by My name, thereby de-
31 filing it. They have built the altars of Tofet, which are in the
Valley of Ben Hinom, to burn their sons and daughters in fire,
something that I did not command and that never entered My
32 mind. Therefore, days are fast approaching, declares
the LORD, when men will no longer speak of "Tofet" and "Valley of Ben Hinom" but rather of "Valley of Slaughter." They will
33 bury in Tofet for lack of space elsewhere. The carcasses of this
people will become food for the birds of the heavens and the
34 beasts of the earth, and none will frighten them away. I will
silence from the cities of Yehuda and the streets of Jerusalem
the sound of joy and the sound of happiness, the voice of the
groom and the voice of the bride, for the land shall come to
8 1 ruin. At that time, declares the LORD, they will remove the
bones of the kings of Yehuda and the bones of its princes, the
bones of the priests, and the bones of the prophets, and the
2 bones of the inhabitants of Jerusalem from their graves. They
will spread them beneath the sun, the moon, and all the host of
heaven that they loved, and that they served, after which they
followed, and which they sought, and to which they bowed.
They will neither be collected nor reburied but shall remain
3 as dung upon the face of the earth. Death will be preferable
to life for all the surviving remnant of this evil clan in all the
other places to which I have expelled them, declares the LORD
of Hosts.

Yemenites and Chabad continue in chapter 9

9 22 Thus said the LORD: Let not the wise man boast of his wisdom.
Let not the mighty man boast of his might. Let not the wealthy
23 boast of his wealth. Someone may boast only of his conscious

כו הַנְּבִיאִים יוֹם הַשְׁכֵּם וְשָׁלֹחַ: וְלוֹא שָׁמְעוּ אֵלַי וְלֹא הִטּוּ אֶת־
כז אָזְנָם וַיַּקְשׁוּ אֶת־עָרְפָּם הֵרֵעוּ מֵאֲבוֹתָם: וְדִבַּרְתָּ אֲלֵיהֶם
אֶת־כָּל־הַדְּבָרִים הָאֵלֶּה וְלֹא יִשְׁמְעוּ אֵלֶיךָ וְקָרָאתָ אֲלֵיהֶם
כח וְלֹא יַעֲנוּכָה: וְאָמַרְתָּ אֲלֵיהֶם זֶה הַגּוֹי אֲשֶׁר לוֹא־שָׁמְעוּ
בְּקוֹל יְהוָה אֱלֹהָיו וְלֹא לָקְחוּ מוּסָר אָבְדָה הָאֱמוּנָה וְנִכְרְתָה
כט מִפִּיהֶם:* גָּזִּי נִזְרֵךְ וְהַשְׁלִיכִי וּשְׂאִי עַל־שְׁפָיִם קִינָה
ל כִּי מָאַס יְהוָה וַיִּטֹּשׁ אֶת־דּוֹר עֶבְרָתוֹ: כִּי־עָשׂוּ בְנֵי־יְהוּדָה
הָרַע בְּעֵינַי נְאֻם־יְהוָה שָׂמוּ שִׁקּוּצֵיהֶם בַּבַּיִת אֲשֶׁר־נִקְרָא־
לא שְׁמִי עָלָיו לְטַמְּאוֹ: וּבָנוּ בָּמוֹת הַתֹּפֶת אֲשֶׁר בְּגֵיא בֶן־הִנֹּם
לִשְׂרֹף אֶת־בְּנֵיהֶם וְאֶת־בְּנֹתֵיהֶם בָּאֵשׁ אֲשֶׁר לֹא צִוִּיתִי וְלֹא
לב עָלְתָה עַל־לִבִּי: לָכֵן הִנֵּה יָמִים בָּאִים נְאֻם־יְהוָה
וְלֹא־יֵאָמֵר עוֹד הַתֹּפֶת וְגֵיא בֶן־הִנֹּם כִּי אִם־גֵּיא הַהֲרֵגָה
לג וְקָבְרוּ בְתֹפֶת מֵאֵין מָקוֹם: וְהָיְתָה נִבְלַת הָעָם הַזֶּה לְמַאֲכָל
לד לְעוֹף הַשָּׁמַיִם וּלְבֶהֱמַת הָאָרֶץ וְאֵין מַחֲרִיד: וְהִשְׁבַּתִּי ׀
מֵעָרֵי יְהוּדָה וּמֵחֻצוֹת יְרוּשָׁלִַם קוֹל שָׂשׂוֹן וְקוֹל שִׂמְחָה
ח א קוֹל חָתָן וְקוֹל כַּלָּה כִּי לְחָרְבָּה תִּהְיֶה הָאָרֶץ: בָּעֵת הַהִיא
נְאֻם־יְהוָה ויוציאו אֶת־עַצְמוֹת מַלְכֵי־יְהוּדָה וְאֶת־עַצְמוֹת יוֹצִיאוּ
שָׂרָיו וְאֶת־עַצְמוֹת הַכֹּהֲנִים וְאֵת ׀ עַצְמוֹת הַנְּבִיאִים וְאֵת
ב עַצְמוֹת יוֹשְׁבֵי־יְרוּשָׁלִָם מִקִּבְרֵיהֶם: וּשְׁטָחוּם לַשֶּׁמֶשׁ וְלַיָּרֵחַ
וּלְכֹל ׀ צְבָא הַשָּׁמַיִם אֲשֶׁר אֲהֵבוּם וַאֲשֶׁר עֲבָדוּם וַאֲשֶׁר הָלְכוּ
אַחֲרֵיהֶם וַאֲשֶׁר דְּרָשׁוּם וַאֲשֶׁר הִשְׁתַּחֲווּ לָהֶם לֹא יֵאָסְפוּ
ג וְלֹא יִקָּבֵרוּ לְדֹמֶן עַל־פְּנֵי הָאֲדָמָה יִהְיוּ: וְנִבְחַר מָוֶת מֵחַיִּים
לְכֹל הַשְּׁאֵרִית הַנִּשְׁאָרִים מִן־הַמִּשְׁפָּחָה הָרָעָה הַזֹּאת
בְּכָל־הַמְּקֹמוֹת הַנִּשְׁאָרִים אֲשֶׁר הִדַּחְתִּים שָׁם נְאֻם יְהוָה
צְבָאוֹת:

Yemenites and Chabad continue in chapter 9

ט כב כֹּה ׀ אָמַר יְהוָה אַל־יִתְהַלֵּל חָכָם בְּחָכְמָתוֹ וְאַל־יִתְהַלֵּל
כג הַגִּבּוֹר בִּגְבוּרָתוֹ אַל־יִתְהַלֵּל עָשִׁיר בְּעָשְׁרוֹ: כִּי אִם־בְּזֹאת

devotion to Me, for I the LORD act with loving-kindness, justice, and righteousness in the world. For it is these things that I desire, declares the LORD.

HAFTARAT SHEMINI

On Shabbat Para read the maftir from Numbers 19:1–22, and the haftara on page 1662. On Shabbat HaḤodesh, read the maftir from Exodus 12:1–20, and the haftara on page 1666.

6 1 David mustered all of Israel's elite once more, thirty thousand. II SAMUEL
Then David, along with all the troops with him, set out from
2 Baalim of Yehuda. From there they brought up the Ark of God,
which is called by a name: The Name of the LORD of Hosts En-
3 throned upon the Cherubim is upon it. They mounted the Ark
of God upon a new cart and conveyed it from the house of Avinadav in Giva, with Uza and Aḥyo, the sons of Avinadav, driving
4 the new cart. They conveyed it from the house of Avinadav in
5 Giva – the Ark of God, Aḥyo walking before the Ark, and David and all the House of Israel reveling before the LORD with
all kinds of instruments of cypress wood, lyres, harps, timbrels,
6 sistra, and cymbals. When they reached the threshing floor of
Nakhon, Uza reached out toward the Ark of God and grasped
7 hold of it, for the oxen had stumbled. And the LORD's rage
flared up against Uza, and God struck him down on the spot
8 for his impudence; he died there with the Ark of God. David
was enraged that the LORD had burst out against Uza, and that
9 place has been called Peretz Uza to this day. David feared the
LORD on that day, and he said, "How will the Ark of the LORD
10 come to me?" And David was not willing to have the Ark of
the LORD removed to him in the City of David; David had it
11 redirected to the house of Oved Edom, the Gittite. The Ark of

symbolic move of reclaiming the Ark and bringing it to be near his palace shows David's devotion to the Almighty and intention of having God's Torah be a source of power and inspiration for his rule. This idea characterizes David's interactions with his wife Michal, daughter of Sha'ul, and the prophet Natan. Standing before the Ark, David feels no different from or superior to any of his subjects, but this does nothing to truly compromise his standing. The honor of a ruler of Israel only grows the more he humbles himself before God.

יִתְהַלֵּל הַמִּתְהַלֵּל הַשְׂכֵּל וְיָדֹעַ אוֹתִי כִּי אֲנִי יהוה עֹשֶׂה
חֶסֶד מִשְׁפָּט וּצְדָקָה בָּאָרֶץ כִּי־בְאֵלֶּה חָפַצְתִּי נְאֻם־יהוה:

הפטרת שמיני

On שבת פרה read the מפטיר from במדבר יט, א–כב, and the הפטרה on page 1663. On שבת החודש, read the מפטיר from שמות יב, א–כ, and the הפטרה on page 1667.

ו א ב וַיֹּסֶף עוֹד דָּוִד אֶת־כָּל־בָּחוּר בְּיִשְׂרָאֵל שְׁלֹשִׁים אָלֶף: וַיָּקָם ׀ שמואל ב׳
וַיֵּלֶךְ דָּוִד וְכָל־הָעָם אֲשֶׁר אִתּוֹ מִבַּעֲלֵי יְהוּדָה לְהַעֲלוֹת
מִשָּׁם אֵת אֲרוֹן הָאֱלֹהִים אֲשֶׁר־נִקְרָא שֵׁם שֵׁם יהוה צְבָאוֹת
ג יֹשֵׁב הַכְּרֻבִים עָלָיו: וַיַּרְכִּבוּ אֶת־אֲרוֹן הָאֱלֹהִים אֶל־עֲגָלָה
חֲדָשָׁה וַיִּשָּׂאֻהוּ מִבֵּית אֲבִינָדָב אֲשֶׁר בַּגִּבְעָה וְעֻזָּא וְאַחְיוֹ
ד בְּנֵי אֲבִינָדָב נֹהֲגִים אֶת־הָעֲגָלָה חֲדָשָׁה: וַיִּשָּׂאֻהוּ מִבֵּית
אֲבִינָדָב אֲשֶׁר בַּגִּבְעָה עִם אֲרוֹן הָאֱלֹהִים וְאַחְיוֹ הֹלֵךְ לִפְנֵי
ה הָאָרוֹן: וְדָוִד ׀ וְכָל־בֵּית יִשְׂרָאֵל מְשַׂחֲקִים לִפְנֵי יהוה בְּכֹל
עֲצֵי בְרוֹשִׁים וּבְכִנֹּרוֹת וּבִנְבָלִים וּבְתֻפִּים וּבִמְנַעַנְעִים
ו וּבְצֶלְצֶלִים: וַיָּבֹאוּ עַד־גֹּרֶן נָכוֹן וַיִּשְׁלַח עֻזָּה אֶל־אֲרוֹן
ז הָאֱלֹהִים וַיֹּאחֶז בּוֹ כִּי שָׁמְטוּ הַבָּקָר: וַיִּחַר־אַף יהוה בְּעֻזָּה
וַיַּכֵּהוּ שָׁם הָאֱלֹהִים עַל־הַשַּׁל וַיָּמָת שָׁם עִם אֲרוֹן הָאֱלֹהִים:
ח וַיִּחַר לְדָוִד עַל אֲשֶׁר פָּרַץ יהוה פֶּרֶץ בְּעֻזָּה וַיִּקְרָא לַמָּקוֹם
ט הַהוּא פֶּרֶץ עֻזָּה עַד הַיּוֹם הַזֶּה: וַיִּרָא דָוִד אֶת־יהוה בַּיּוֹם
י הַהוּא וַיֹּאמֶר אֵיךְ יָבוֹא אֵלַי אֲרוֹן יהוה: וְלֹא־אָבָה דָוִד
לְהָסִיר אֵלָיו אֶת־אֲרוֹן יהוה עַל־עִיר דָּוִד וַיַּטֵּהוּ דָוִד בֵּית
יא עֹבֵד־אֱדֹם הַגִּתִּי: וַיֵּשֶׁב אֲרוֹן יהוה בֵּית עֹבֵד אֱדֹם הַגִּתִּי

SHEMINI

This *haftara* is one of a set of chapters in II Samuel that recounts the piety of King David's thirty-three-year rule in Jerusalem. Here, we are told of the journey of the Ark to David's new capital. The Ark had previously been taken captive from the Tabernacle by the Philistines and returned, but it had been kept since then at various temporary locations. The

the LORD remained at the house of Oved Edom, the Gittite,
for three months, and the LORD blessed Oved Edom and his
12 whole household. When it was reported to King David that the
LORD had blessed Oved Edom's household and all that was his
because of the Ark of God, David went and brought up the Ark
of God from the house of Oved Edom to the City of David, with
13 joy. When the bearers of the Ark of the LORD had advanced six
14 paces, he sacrificed an ox and a fatling. And David danced with
all his might before the LORD; David was clad in a linen ephod.
15 So David and all the House of Israel led the Ark of the LORD
16 up with joyous shouting and the sound of the ram's horn. As
the Ark of the LORD entered the City of David, Mikhal, Sha'ul's
daughter, was watching through the window; when she saw David – the king! – leaping and dancing before the LORD, she felt
17 a rush of contempt for him. They brought the Ark of the LORD
and set it in its place within the tent David had pitched for it,
and David offered burnt offerings and peace offerings before
18 the LORD. When David had finished offering the burnt offering
and the peace offerings, he blessed the people in the name of
19 the LORD of Hosts. He then distributed a ring of bread, a share
of meat, and a cake of raisins to all the people – to all the multitudes of Israel, every single man and woman. Then all the people,
20 every one, made their way home.* When David returned to *Sepharadim and Chabad end here*
bless his own household, Mikhal, Sha'ul's daughter, came out
to meet him. "How dignified the king of Israel was today," she
said, "exposing himself before all the eyes of his servants' slave
21 girls just as one of the rabble might expose himself!" "It was before the LORD, who chose me instead of your father and all his
household and appointed me as ruler over the LORD's people,
22 Israel," David said to Mikhal. "I danced before the LORD. And I
would have lowered myself even further and been humiliated in
my own eyes – but to the slave girls you speak of, I would still be
23 dignified." And Mikhal, Sha'ul's daughter, never had a child – to
7 1 her dying day. Once the king had settled in his palace,
and the LORD had granted him repose from all his surrounding
2 enemies, the king said to the prophet Natan, "Look now – I am
dwelling in a cedarwood palace while the Ark of God is dwell-
3 ing in a tent." "Go – do whatever you have in mind," Natan said
4 to the king, "for the LORD is with you."* But that same *Yemenites end here*

שְׁלֹשָׁה חֳדָשִׁים וַיְבָרֶךְ יהוה אֶת־עֹבֵד אֱדֹם וְאֶת־כָּל־בֵּיתוֹ׃
יב וַיֻּגַּד לַמֶּלֶךְ דָּוִד לֵאמֹר בֵּרַךְ יהוה אֶת־בֵּית עֹבֵד אֱדֹם
וְאֶת־כָּל־אֲשֶׁר־לוֹ בַּעֲבוּר אֲרוֹן הָאֱלֹהִים וַיֵּלֶךְ דָּוִד וַיַּעַל
אֶת־אֲרוֹן הָאֱלֹהִים מִבֵּית עֹבֵד אֱדֹם עִיר דָּוִד בְּשִׂמְחָה׃
יג וַיְהִי כִּי צָעֲדוּ נֹשְׂאֵי אֲרוֹן־יהוה שִׁשָּׁה צְעָדִים וַיִּזְבַּח שׁוֹר
יד וּמְרִיא׃ וְדָוִד מְכַרְכֵּר בְּכָל־עֹז לִפְנֵי יהוה וְדָוִד חָגוּר אֵפוֹד
טו בָּד׃ וְדָוִד וְכָל־בֵּית יִשְׂרָאֵל מַעֲלִים אֶת־אֲרוֹן יהוה בִּתְרוּעָה
טז וּבְקוֹל שׁוֹפָר׃ וְהָיָה אֲרוֹן יהוה בָּא עִיר דָּוִד וּמִיכַל בַּת־
שָׁאוּל נִשְׁקְפָה ׀ בְּעַד הַחַלּוֹן וַתֵּרֶא אֶת־הַמֶּלֶךְ דָּוִד מְפַזֵּז
יז וּמְכַרְכֵּר לִפְנֵי יהוה וַתִּבֶז לוֹ בְּלִבָּהּ׃ וַיָּבִאוּ אֶת־אֲרוֹן יהוה
וַיַּצִּגוּ אֹתוֹ בִּמְקוֹמוֹ בְּתוֹךְ הָאֹהֶל אֲשֶׁר נָטָה־לוֹ דָּוִד וַיַּעַל
יח דָּוִד עֹלוֹת לִפְנֵי יהוה וּשְׁלָמִים׃ וַיְכַל דָּוִד מֵהַעֲלוֹת הָעוֹלָה
יט וְהַשְּׁלָמִים וַיְבָרֶךְ אֶת־הָעָם בְּשֵׁם יהוה צְבָאוֹת׃ וַיְחַלֵּק
לְכָל־הָעָם לְכָל־הֲמוֹן יִשְׂרָאֵל לְמֵאִישׁ וְעַד־אִשָּׁה לְאִישׁ
חַלַּת לֶחֶם אַחַת וְאֶשְׁפָּר אֶחָד וַאֲשִׁישָׁה אֶחָת וַיֵּלֶךְ כָּל־
Sepharadim and Chabad end here
כ הָעָם אִישׁ לְבֵיתוֹ׃* וַיָּשָׁב דָּוִד לְבָרֵךְ אֶת־בֵּיתוֹ וַתֵּצֵא מִיכַל
בַּת־שָׁאוּל לִקְרַאת דָּוִד וַתֹּאמֶר מַה־נִּכְבַּד הַיּוֹם מֶלֶךְ
יִשְׂרָאֵל אֲשֶׁר נִגְלָה הַיּוֹם לְעֵינֵי אַמְהוֹת עֲבָדָיו כְּהִגָּלוֹת
כא נִגְלוֹת אַחַד הָרֵקִים׃ וַיֹּאמֶר דָּוִד אֶל־מִיכַל לִפְנֵי יהוה
אֲשֶׁר בָּחַר־בִּי מֵאָבִיךְ וּמִכָּל־בֵּיתוֹ לְצַוֹּת אֹתִי נָגִיד עַל־
כב עַם יהוה עַל־יִשְׂרָאֵל וְשִׂחַקְתִּי לִפְנֵי יהוה׃ וּנְקַלֹּתִי עוֹד
מִזֹּאת וְהָיִיתִי שָׁפָל בְּעֵינָי וְעִם־הָאֲמָהוֹת אֲשֶׁר אָמַרְתְּ
כג עִמָּם אִכָּבֵדָה׃ וּלְמִיכַל בַּת־שָׁאוּל לֹא־הָיָה לָהּ יָלֶד עַד יוֹם
ז א מוֹתָהּ׃ וַיְהִי כִּי־יָשַׁב הַמֶּלֶךְ בְּבֵיתוֹ וַיהוה הֵנִיחַ־
ב לוֹ מִסָּבִיב מִכָּל־אֹיְבָיו׃ וַיֹּאמֶר הַמֶּלֶךְ אֶל־נָתָן הַנָּבִיא רְאֵה
נָא אָנֹכִי יוֹשֵׁב בְּבֵית אֲרָזִים וַאֲרוֹן הָאֱלֹהִים יֹשֵׁב בְּתוֹךְ
ג הַיְרִיעָה׃ וַיֹּאמֶר נָתָן אֶל־הַמֶּלֶךְ כֹּל אֲשֶׁר בִּלְבָבְךָ לֵךְ עֲשֵׂה
Yemenites end here
ד כִּי יהוה עִמָּךְ׃* וַיְהִי בַּלַּיְלָה הַהוּא וַיְהִי

5 night, the word of the Lord came to Natan. "Go, and
say to My servant David: Thus says the Lord: Shall you be the
6 one to build a house for Me, for My abode? For I have not dwelt
in a house from the day I brought the Israelites out of Egypt to
7 this day; I have roamed in tent and tabernacle. But wherever I
roamed, among all the Israelites, have I ever spoken a word to
any of the tribes of Israel whom I charged to shepherd My people
Israel, saying, 'Why have you not built Me a cedarwood palace?'
8 Now you shall say so to My servant David: Thus says the Lord
of Hosts: I took you out of the pastures, from following the sheep,
9 to be ruler over My people Israel. I have been with you wherever you went, and I have cut down all your enemies before you.
I will make your name great – one of the greatest names on earth.
10 I will set aside a place for My people Israel and let them take root
and settle down within it, and they will be disturbed no longer;
11 violent men will no longer oppress them as they once did in the
days when I appointed judges over My people Israel. To you I
will grant repose from all your enemies; moreover, the Lord
12 declares that the Lord will establish a house for you. For when
your days are done and you lie with your ancestors, I will raise
up your own seed after you – the issue of your own loins – and
13 I will establish his kingdom. He will build a house in My name,
14 and I will firmly establish his royal throne forever. I will be a father to him, and he will be a son to Me; and should he do wrong,
I will berate him with the rod of mortals and with human afflic-
15 tions. But My loyalties shall not move from him, as I removed
16 them from Sha'ul, whom I removed before you. And your house
and your kingdom will be ever steadfast before you, and your
17 throne will be secure forever." Natan related all these words and
all this vision to David.

ה דְּבַר־יְהוָה אֶל־נָתָן לֵאמֹר: לֵךְ וְאָמַרְתָּ אֶל־עַבְדִּי אֶל־
דָּוִד כֹּה אָמַר יְהוָה הַאַתָּה תִּבְנֶה־לִּי בַיִת לְשִׁבְתִּי:
ו כִּי לֹא יָשַׁבְתִּי בְּבַיִת לְמִיּוֹם הַעֲלֹתִי אֶת־בְּנֵי יִשְׂרָאֵל מִמִּצְרַיִם
ז וְעַד הַיּוֹם הַזֶּה וָאֶהְיֶה מִתְהַלֵּךְ בְּאֹהֶל וּבְמִשְׁכָּן: בְּכֹל אֲשֶׁר־
הִתְהַלַּכְתִּי בְּכָל־בְּנֵי יִשְׂרָאֵל הֲדָבָר דִּבַּרְתִּי אֶת־אַחַד שִׁבְטֵי
יִשְׂרָאֵל אֲשֶׁר צִוִּיתִי לִרְעוֹת אֶת־עַמִּי אֶת־יִשְׂרָאֵל לֵאמֹר
ח לָמָּה לֹא־בְנִיתֶם לִי בֵּית אֲרָזִים: וְעַתָּה כֹּה־תֹאמַר לְעַבְדִּי
לְדָוִד כֹּה אָמַר יְהוָה צְבָאוֹת אֲנִי לְקַחְתִּיךָ מִן־הַנָּוֶה מֵאַחַר
ט הַצֹּאן לִהְיוֹת נָגִיד עַל־עַמִּי עַל־יִשְׂרָאֵל: וָאֶהְיֶה עִמְּךָ בְּכֹל
אֲשֶׁר הָלַכְתָּ וָאַכְרִתָה אֶת־כָּל־אֹיְבֶיךָ מִפָּנֶיךָ וְעָשִׂתִי לְךָ
י שֵׁם גָּדוֹל כְּשֵׁם הַגְּדֹלִים אֲשֶׁר בָּאָרֶץ: וְשַׂמְתִּי מָקוֹם לְעַמִּי
לְיִשְׂרָאֵל וּנְטַעְתִּיו וְשָׁכַן תַּחְתָּיו וְלֹא יִרְגַּז עוֹד וְלֹא־יֹסִיפוּ
יא בְנֵי־עַוְלָה לְעַנּוֹתוֹ כַּאֲשֶׁר בָּרִאשׁוֹנָה: וּלְמִן־הַיּוֹם אֲשֶׁר
צִוִּיתִי שֹׁפְטִים עַל־עַמִּי יִשְׂרָאֵל וַהֲנִיחֹתִי לְךָ מִכָּל־אֹיְבֶיךָ
יב וְהִגִּיד לְךָ יְהוָה כִּי־בַיִת יַעֲשֶׂה־לְּךָ יְהוָה: כִּי ׀ יִמְלְאוּ יָמֶיךָ
וְשָׁכַבְתָּ אֶת־אֲבֹתֶיךָ וַהֲקִימֹתִי אֶת־זַרְעֲךָ אַחֲרֶיךָ אֲשֶׁר
יג יֵצֵא מִמֵּעֶיךָ וַהֲכִינֹתִי אֶת־מַמְלַכְתּוֹ: הוּא יִבְנֶה־בַּיִת לִשְׁמִי
יד וְכֹנַנְתִּי אֶת־כִּסֵּא מַמְלַכְתּוֹ עַד־עוֹלָם: אֲנִי אֶהְיֶה־לּוֹ לְאָב
וְהוּא יִהְיֶה־לִּי לְבֵן אֲשֶׁר בְּהַעֲוֺתוֹ וְהֹכַחְתִּיו בְּשֵׁבֶט אֲנָשִׁים
טו וּבְנִגְעֵי בְּנֵי אָדָם: וְחַסְדִּי לֹא־יָסוּר מִמֶּנּוּ כַּאֲשֶׁר הֲסִרֹתִי
טז מֵעִם שָׁאוּל אֲשֶׁר הֲסִרֹתִי מִלְּפָנֶיךָ: וְנֶאְמַן בֵּיתְךָ וּמַמְלַכְתְּךָ
יז עַד־עוֹלָם לְפָנֶיךָ כִּסְאֲךָ יִהְיֶה נָכוֹן עַד־עוֹלָם: כְּכֹל הַדְּבָרִים
הָאֵלֶּה וּכְכֹל הַחִזָּיוֹן הַזֶּה כֵּן דִּבֶּר נָתָן אֶל־דָּוִד:

Haftarat Tazria

On Shabbat HaḤodesh read the maftir from Exodus 12:1–20, and the haftara on page 1666. When Tazria and Metzora are read together, read the haftara for Metzora on page 1528.

4 42 A man came from Baal Shalisha and brought the man of God II KINGS
bread made of the first grain: twenty loaves of barley bread
and some fresh grain in his sack. "Give it to the people and let
43 them eat," he said. "How can I set this before a hundred people?" asked his attendant. "Give it to the people and let them
eat," he said, "for thus says the Lord: They will eat and leave
44 some over." So he set it before them and they ate, and there
5 1 was some left over, fulfilling the word of the Lord. Naaman, the commander of the king of Aram's army, was highly
esteemed by his master and held in favor, for the Lord had
granted victory to Aram through him. But this powerful man suf-
2 fered from an impure blight. Once, when the Arameans were
out raiding, they captured a young girl from the land of Israel,
3 and she became a servant of Naaman's wife. She said to her mistress, "If only my master would present himself to the prophet in
4 Shomron, he would cure him of his blight." Naaman then went
and told his own master about what the girl from the land of Is-
5 rael had said. "Prepare to set out," said the king of Aram, "and
I will send along a letter to the king of Israel." He set out, taking ten talents of silver, six thousand pieces of gold, and ten sets
6 of clothing with him. And he brought the letter to the king of
Israel, which read: "Now, as this letter reaches you, I have sent
my servant Naaman to you, that you may cure him of his blight."
7 When the king of Israel read the letter, he rent his clothes. "Am
I God, dealing death and granting life, that this one sends me a

---

instructions, and is instantly healed. Shaken, he returns to thank the prophet and declare his faith in the God of Israel. He offers Elisha a rich reward, but the prophet refuses adamantly.

Elisha's behavior toward Naaman carries a message: It is God who heals; the prophet does nothing by himself – this is why he refuses to accept Naaman's reward. Naaman understands this, and thus learns the difference between a prophet and a magician.

Aram had been the bitter enemy of Israel for two centuries. Naaman, the enemy warlord, converted to worship God, and this had a profound impact on both Aram and Israel. This was another aim of Elisha.

הפטרת תזריע

On שבת החודש read the מפטיר from שמות יב, א–כ, and the הפטרה on page 1667. When תזריע and מצרע are read together, read the הפטרה for מצרע on page 1529.

מלכים ב׳

ד מב וְאִישׁ בָּא מִבַּעַל שָׁלִשָׁה וַיָּבֵא לְאִישׁ הָאֱלֹהִים לֶחֶם
בִּכּוּרִים עֶשְׂרִים־לֶחֶם שְׂעֹרִים וְכַרְמֶל בְּצִקְלֹנוֹ וַיֹּאמֶר תֵּן
מג לָעָם וְיֹאכֵלוּ: וַיֹּאמֶר מְשָׁרְתוֹ מָה אֶתֵּן זֶה לִפְנֵי מֵאָה אִישׁ
מד וַיֹּאמֶר תֵּן לָעָם וְיֹאכֵלוּ כִּי כֹה אָמַר יְהוָה אָכֹל וְהוֹתֵר: וַיִּתֵּן
ה א לִפְנֵיהֶם וַיֹּאכְלוּ וַיּוֹתִרוּ כִּדְבַר יְהוָה: וְנַעֲמָן
שַׂר־צְבָא מֶלֶךְ־אֲרָם הָיָה אִישׁ גָּדוֹל לִפְנֵי אֲדֹנָיו וּנְשֻׂא
פָנִים כִּי־בוֹ נָתַן־יְהוָה תְּשׁוּעָה לַאֲרָם וְהָאִישׁ הָיָה גִּבּוֹר
ב חַיִל מְצֹרָע: וַאֲרָם יָצְאוּ גְדוּדִים וַיִּשְׁבּוּ מֵאֶרֶץ יִשְׂרָאֵל
ג נַעֲרָה קְטַנָּה וַתְּהִי לִפְנֵי אֵשֶׁת נַעֲמָן: וַתֹּאמֶר אֶל־גְּבִרְתָּהּ
אַחֲלֵי אֲדֹנִי לִפְנֵי הַנָּבִיא אֲשֶׁר בְּשֹׁמְרוֹן אָז יֶאֱסֹף אֹתוֹ
ד מִצָּרַעְתּוֹ: וַיָּבֹא וַיַּגֵּד לַאדֹנָיו לֵאמֹר כָּזֹאת וְכָזֹאת דִּבְּרָה
ה הַנַּעֲרָה אֲשֶׁר מֵאֶרֶץ יִשְׂרָאֵל: וַיֹּאמֶר מֶלֶךְ־אֲרָם לֶךְ־בֹּא
וְאֶשְׁלְחָה סֵפֶר אֶל־מֶלֶךְ יִשְׂרָאֵל וַיֵּלֶךְ וַיִּקַּח בְּיָדוֹ עֶשֶׂר
כִּכְּרֵי־כֶסֶף וְשֵׁשֶׁת אֲלָפִים זָהָב וְעֶשֶׂר חֲלִיפוֹת בְּגָדִים:
ו וַיָּבֵא הַסֵּפֶר אֶל־מֶלֶךְ יִשְׂרָאֵל לֵאמֹר וְעַתָּה כְּבוֹא הַסֵּפֶר
הַזֶּה אֵלֶיךָ הִנֵּה שָׁלַחְתִּי אֵלֶיךָ אֶת־נַעֲמָן עַבְדִּי וַאֲסַפְתּוֹ
ז מִצָּרַעְתּוֹ: וַיְהִי כִּקְרֹא מֶלֶךְ־יִשְׂרָאֵל אֶת־הַסֵּפֶר וַיִּקְרַע
בְּגָדָיו וַיֹּאמֶר הַאֱלֹהִים אָנִי לְהָמִית וּלְהַחֲיוֹת כִּי־זֶה

TAZRIA

This *haftara* describes the miraculous healing of the leprosy of general Naaman, head of the armies of Aram. This miracle is one of several worked by the prophet Elisha as described in the book of Kings. Naaman appears at Elisha's home in Shomron, accompanied by his retinue. He expects the prophet to come out to him and work his magic in order to heal him. Elisha, however, ignores him and instead sends him some simple instructions that will heal him. Naaman becomes angry with Elisha and goes on his way, but when he comes to the Jordan River he carries out Elisha's

man to cure his blight?" he said, "Be aware now, look – he must
8 be provoking a quarrel with me." When Elisha, the man of God,
heard that the king of Israel had rent his clothes, he sent to the
king, saying, "Why have you rent your clothes? Let him come
9 to me now, and he will know that there is a prophet in Israel." So
Naaman came with his horses and chariots and halted at the en-
10 trance of Elisha's house. And Elisha sent a messenger to him, saying, "Go and bathe in the Jordan seven times; your skin will be
11 restored to you, and you will be cleansed." Naaman was furious
and walked away. "I was certain he would come out to me," he
said, "and stand and invoke the name of the Lord, his God, and
12 wave his hand toward the affected area and cure my blight. Why,
Amana and Parpar, the rivers of Damascus, are better than all the
waters of Israel – if I bathe in them, will I not be cleansed?" And
13 he turned and stormed off in a rage. But his servants approached
him and spoke to him. "Father," they said, "had the prophet
given you more difficult instructions, would you not carry them
out? All the more so when he has only said to you, 'Bathe and be
14 cleansed.'" So he went down and immersed in the Jordan seven
times, fulfilling the instruction of the man of God, and his skin
15 became like the skin of a young boy, and he was cleansed. He
went back to the man of God along with all his company, and he
came and stood before him. "Now I know that there is no God in
all the world except in Israel," he said. "Now, please accept your
16 servant's gift." "As the Lord lives, whom I serve," he said, "I will
17 not accept it." He urged him to accept, but he refused. "If not,"
said Naaman, "may your servant be given two mule loads' worth
of soil, for your servant will no longer offer burnt offering or sac-
18 rifice to other gods, but only to the Lord. But may the Lord
forgive your servant this: when my master comes to the temple
of Rimon to bow down there, he leans on my hand so that I must
bow down in the temple of Rimon. So when I bow down in the
temple of Rimon, may the Lord forgive your servant for this."
19 "Go in peace," he said to him. When he had traveled some distance away from him.

שֹׁלֵחַ אֵלַי לֶאֱסֹף אִישׁ מִצָּרַעְתּוֹ כִּי אַךְ־דְּעוּ־נָא וּרְאוּ כִּי־
ח מִתְאַנֶּה הוּא לִי׃ וַיְהִי כִּשְׁמֹעַ ׀ אֱלִישָׁע אִישׁ־הָאֱלֹהִים
כִּי־קָרַע מֶלֶךְ־יִשְׂרָאֵל אֶת־בְּגָדָיו וַיִּשְׁלַח אֶל־הַמֶּלֶךְ
לֵאמֹר לָמָּה קָרַעְתָּ בְּגָדֶיךָ יָבֹא־נָא אֵלַי וְיֵדַע כִּי יֵשׁ נָבִיא
ט בְּיִשְׂרָאֵל׃ וַיָּבֹא נַעֲמָן בְּסוּסָו וּבְרִכְבּוֹ וַיַּעֲמֹד פֶּתַח־הַבַּיִת
י לֶאֱלִישָׁע׃ וַיִּשְׁלַח אֵלָיו אֱלִישָׁע מַלְאָךְ לֵאמֹר הָלוֹךְ
וְרָחַצְתָּ שֶׁבַע־פְּעָמִים בַּיַּרְדֵּן וְיָשֹׁב בְּשָׂרְךָ לְךָ וּטְהָר׃
יא וַיִּקְצֹף נַעֲמָן וַיֵּלַךְ וַיֹּאמֶר הִנֵּה אָמַרְתִּי אֵלַי ׀ יֵצֵא יָצוֹא
וְעָמַד וְקָרָא בְּשֵׁם־יְהוָה אֱלֹהָיו וְהֵנִיף יָדוֹ אֶל־הַמָּקוֹם וְאָסַף
יב הַמְּצֹרָע׃ הֲלֹא טוֹב אבנה וּפַרְפַּר נַהֲרוֹת דַּמֶּשֶׂק מִכֹּל מֵימֵי אֲמָנָה
יג יִשְׂרָאֵל הֲלֹא־אֶרְחַץ בָּהֶם וְטָהָרְתִּי וַיִּפֶן וַיֵּלֶךְ בְּחֵמָה׃ וַיִּגְּשׁוּ
עֲבָדָיו וַיְדַבְּרוּ אֵלָיו וַיֹּאמְרוּ אָבִי דָּבָר גָּדוֹל הַנָּבִיא דִּבֶּר
יד אֵלֶיךָ הֲלוֹא תַעֲשֶׂה וְאַף כִּי־אָמַר אֵלֶיךָ רְחַץ וּטְהָר׃ וַיֵּרֶד
וַיִּטְבֹּל בַּיַּרְדֵּן שֶׁבַע פְּעָמִים כִּדְבַר אִישׁ הָאֱלֹהִים וַיָּשָׁב בְּשָׂרוֹ
טו כִּבְשַׂר נַעַר קָטֹן וַיִּטְהָר׃ וַיָּשָׁב אֶל־אִישׁ הָאֱלֹהִים הוּא וְכָל־
מַחֲנֵהוּ וַיָּבֹא וַיַּעֲמֹד לְפָנָיו וַיֹּאמֶר הִנֵּה־נָא יָדַעְתִּי כִּי אֵין
אֱלֹהִים בְּכָל־הָאָרֶץ כִּי אִם־בְּיִשְׂרָאֵל וְעַתָּה קַח־נָא בְרָכָה
טז מֵאֵת עַבְדֶּךָ׃ וַיֹּאמֶר חַי־יְהוָה אֲשֶׁר־עָמַדְתִּי לְפָנָיו אִם־אֶקָּח
יז וַיִּפְצַר־בּוֹ לָקַחַת וַיְמָאֵן׃ וַיֹּאמֶר נַעֲמָן וָלֹא יֻתַּן־נָא לְעַבְדְּךָ
מַשָּׂא צֶמֶד־פְּרָדִים אֲדָמָה כִּי לוֹא־יַעֲשֶׂה עוֹד עַבְדְּךָ עֹלָה
יח וָזֶבַח לֵאלֹהִים אֲחֵרִים כִּי אִם־לַיהוָה׃ לַדָּבָר הַזֶּה יִסְלַח
יְהוָה לְעַבְדֶּךָ בְּבוֹא אֲדֹנִי בֵית־רִמּוֹן לְהִשְׁתַּחֲוֺת שָׁמָּה
וְהוּא ׀ נִשְׁעָן עַל־יָדִי וְהִשְׁתַּחֲוֵיתִי בֵּית רִמֹּן בְּהִשְׁתַּחֲוָיָתִי
יט בֵּית רִמֹּן יִסְלַח־נא־יְהוָה לְעַבְדְּךָ בַּדָּבָר הַזֶּה׃ וַיֹּאמֶר לוֹ נא כתיב ולא קרי
לֵךְ לְשָׁלוֹם וַיֵּלֶךְ מֵאִתּוֹ כִּבְרַת אָרֶץ׃

Haftarat Metzora

When Tazria and Metzora are read together, read this haftara.
On Shabbat HaGadol read the haftara on page 1672.
On Rosh Ḥodesh Iyar, read the maftir from Numbers 28:9–15, and the haftara on page 1640. On Erev Rosh Ḥodesh Iyar read the haftara on page 1644.

7 1 And Elisha said, "Hear the word of the Lord. Thus says the II KINGS
Lord: By this time tomorrow, a *se'a* of fine flour will sell for a *Yemenites*
shekel, and two *se'a* of barley will sell for a shekel at the gate *begin here*
2 of Shomron." The adjutant upon whose arm the king leaned
spoke up and said to the man of God, "Even if the Lord were to
make floodgates in the heavens, how could this possibly come
to pass?" "You will see it with your own eyes," he said, "but you
3 will not eat of it." *There were four men, who were *Ashkenazim and*
lepers, at the entrance to the gate, and they said to one another, *Sephardim begin here*
4 "Why should we sit here until we die? If we decide to enter the
city when there is famine in the city, we will die there; and if
we stay here, we will die. So let us now defect to the Aramean
camp; if they let us live, we will live, and if they kill us, we will
5 die." They set out at dusk to reach the Aramean camp, but when
they reached the edge of the Aramean camp, there was no one
6 there. For the Lord had caused the Aramean camp to hear
the sound of chariots, the sound of horses, the sound of a vast
army – and the men had said to one another, "Look, the king of
Israel must have hired the Hittite kings and the kings of Egypt
7 against us, to attack us!" They rose and fled at dusk, leaving their
tents, their horses and their donkeys, and the camp as it was,
8 and they ran for their lives. When those lepers reached the edge
of the camp, they entered one tent and ate and drank. Then they
carried off silver and gold and garments from there and went
and hid them. When they came back, they went into another
9 tent, carried off what was in it, and went and hid it. But then
one man said to another, "We are not doing what is right. This
is a day of good news, yet we are silent. If we wait until the light

---

the besieging Aramean army. As they approach the camp, they are shocked to discover that it has been abandoned; the whole army has fled in the middle of the night, leaving large amounts of food and property. The hungry lepers set upon their spoils and eat until they satisfy their hunger. Then they return to the city and inform the inhabitants of what they have seen. After checking the

הפטרת מצרע

When תזריע *and* מצרע *are read together, read this* הפטרה.
On שבת הגדול *read the* הפטרה *on page 1673. On* ראש חודש אייר *read the* מפטיר *from* במדבר כח, ט–טו *and the* הפטרה *on page 1641.*
On ערב ראש חודש אייר *read the* הפטרה *on page 1645.*

ז א וַיֹּאמֶר אֱלִישָׁע שִׁמְעוּ דְּבַר־יְהוָה כֹּה ׀ אָמַר יְהוָה כָּעֵת ׀ — מלכים ב׳
מָחָר סְאָה־סֹלֶת בְּשֶׁקֶל וְסָאתַיִם שְׂעֹרִים בְּשֶׁקֶל בְּשַׁעַר — *Yemenites begin here*
ב שֹׁמְרוֹן: וַיַּעַן הַשָּׁלִישׁ אֲשֶׁר לַמֶּלֶךְ נִשְׁעָן עַל־יָדוֹ אֶת־
אִישׁ הָאֱלֹהִים וַיֹּאמַר הִנֵּה יְהוָה עֹשֶׂה אֲרֻבּוֹת בַּשָּׁמַיִם
הֲיִהְיֶה הַדָּבָר הַזֶּה וַיֹּאמֶר הִנְּכָה רֹאֶה בְּעֵינֶיךָ וּמִשָּׁם לֹא
ג תֹּאכֵל: *וְאַרְבָּעָה אֲנָשִׁים הָיוּ מְצֹרָעִים פֶּתַח — *Ashkenazim and Sephardim begin here*
הַשָּׁעַר וַיֹּאמְרוּ אִישׁ אֶל־רֵעֵהוּ מָה אֲנַחְנוּ יֹשְׁבִים פֹּה עַד־
ד מָתְנוּ: אִם־אָמַרְנוּ נָבוֹא הָעִיר וְהָרָעָב בָּעִיר וָמַתְנוּ שָׁם
וְאִם־יָשַׁבְנוּ פֹה וָמָתְנוּ וְעַתָּה לְכוּ וְנִפְּלָה אֶל־מַחֲנֵה אֲרָם
ה אִם־יְחַיֻּנוּ נִחְיֶה וְאִם־יְמִיתֻנוּ וָמָתְנוּ: וַיָּקֻמוּ בַנֶּשֶׁף לָבוֹא
אֶל־מַחֲנֵה אֲרָם וַיָּבֹאוּ עַד־קְצֵה מַחֲנֵה אֲרָם וְהִנֵּה אֵין־
ו שָׁם אִישׁ: וַאדֹנָי הִשְׁמִיעַ ׀ אֶת־מַחֲנֵה אֲרָם קוֹל רֶכֶב קוֹל
סוּס קוֹל חַיִל גָּדוֹל וַיֹּאמְרוּ אִישׁ אֶל־אָחִיו הִנֵּה שָׂכַר־
עָלֵינוּ מֶלֶךְ יִשְׂרָאֵל אֶת־מַלְכֵי הַחִתִּים וְאֶת־מַלְכֵי מִצְרַיִם
ז לָבוֹא עָלֵינוּ: וַיָּקוּמוּ וַיָּנוּסוּ בַנֶּשֶׁף וַיַּעַזְבוּ אֶת־אָהֳלֵיהֶם
וְאֶת־סוּסֵיהֶם וְאֶת־חֲמֹרֵיהֶם הַמַּחֲנֶה כַּאֲשֶׁר הִיא וַיָּנֻסוּ
ח אֶל־נַפְשָׁם: וַיָּבֹאוּ הַמְצֹרָעִים הָאֵלֶּה עַד־קְצֵה הַמַּחֲנֶה
וַיָּבֹאוּ אֶל־אֹהֶל אֶחָד וַיֹּאכְלוּ וַיִּשְׁתּוּ וַיִּשְׂאוּ מִשָּׁם כֶּסֶף וְזָהָב
וּבְגָדִים וַיֵּלְכוּ וַיַּטְמִנוּ וַיָּשֻׁבוּ וַיָּבֹאוּ אֶל־אֹהֶל אַחֵר וַיִּשְׂאוּ
ט מִשָּׁם וַיֵּלְכוּ וַיַּטְמִנוּ: וַיֹּאמְרוּ אִישׁ אֶל־רֵעֵהוּ לֹא־כֵן ׀ אֲנַחְנוּ
עֹשִׂים הַיּוֹם הַזֶּה יוֹם־בְּשֹׂרָה הוּא וַאֲנַחְנוּ מַחְשִׁים וְחִכִּינוּ

METZORA

The Aramean siege on Shomron in the time of the prophet Elisha cut off the Israelite capital from the surrounding country. Outside the city stood four lepers. The harsh famine afflicting the city affected them as well, and they decide to try their luck looking for food with

of morning, we will be found guilty. We must go and report to
10 the royal palace right now." When they arrived, they called out
to the city gatekeepers and reported to them, "We came to the
Aramean camp, but there was not a man or a human voice there,
with the horses still tied up and the donkeys still tied up and
11 the tents just as they were." The gatekeepers called out, and it
12 was reported inside the royal palace. The king rose in the night
and said to his servants, "Let me tell you what the Arameans
are doing to us. They know we are starving, so they have left the
camp to hide in the field, planning, 'When they leave the city,
13 we will catch them alive and enter the city.'" One of his servants
spoke up. "Let them take five of the remaining horses that are
still here," he said. "Look, either they will be like all the masses
of Israelites who remain or like all the masses of Israelites who
14 have perished. Let us send and find out." So they took two chariots with horses, and the king sent them after the Aramean camp,
15 ordering them, "Go and find out." They followed them as far as
the Jordan to find that the whole road was full of garments and
vessels that Aram had cast aside in their haste, and the messen-
16 gers went back and reported to the king. Then the people went
out and ransacked the Aramean camp, so that a *se'a* of fine flour
fetched a shekel, and two *se'a* of barley fetched a shekel, fulfilling
17 the word of the Lord. Meanwhile, the king had stationed the
adjutant on whose arm he leaned by the gate, and the people
trampled him to death by the gate – just as the man of God had
18 pronounced when the king came down to him. For when the
man of God had told the king, "Two *se'a* of barley will fetch a
shekel, and a *se'a* of fine flour will fetch a shekel by this time
19 tomorrow at the gate of Shomron," the adjutant had retorted to
the man of God, "Even if the Lord were to make floodgates in
the heavens, how could this possibly come to pass?" "You will
see it with your own eyes," he had said, "but you will not eat
20 of it." And that is exactly what happened to him – the people
trampled him to death by the gate.

---

story, it is specifically lepers who discover that the siege has lifted. In returning to the city, they are the bearers of good news, rather than hurtful stories, and thus serve to correct their ways and bring blessing on their fellows in the city and themselves.

עַד־אוֹר הַבֹּקֶר וּמְצָאָנוּ עָווֹן וְעַתָּה לְכוּ וְנָבֹאָה וְנַגִּידָה בֵּית
י הַמֶּלֶךְ: וַיָּבֹאוּ וַיִּקְרְאוּ אֶל־שֹׁעֵר הָעִיר וַיַּגִּידוּ לָהֶם לֵאמֹר
בָּאנוּ אֶל־מַחֲנֵה אֲרָם וְהִנֵּה אֵין־שָׁם אִישׁ וְקוֹל אָדָם כִּי
אִם־הַסּוּס אָסוּר וְהַחֲמוֹר אָסוּר וְאֹהָלִים כַּאֲשֶׁר הֵמָּה:
יא יב וַיִּקְרָא הַשֹּׁעֲרִים וַיַּגִּידוּ בֵּית הַמֶּלֶךְ פְּנִימָה: וַיָּקָם הַמֶּלֶךְ
לַיְלָה וַיֹּאמֶר אֶל־עֲבָדָיו אַגִּידָה־נָּא לָכֶם אֵת אֲשֶׁר־עָשׂוּ
לָנוּ אֲרָם יָדְעוּ כִּי־רְעֵבִים אֲנַחְנוּ וַיֵּצְאוּ מִן־הַמַּחֲנֶה לְהֵחָבֵה
בהשדה לֵאמֹר כִּי־יֵצְאוּ מִן־הָעִיר וְנִתְפְּשֵׂם חַיִּים וְאֶל־ בַּשָּׂדֶה
יג הָעִיר נָבֹא: וַיַּעַן אֶחָד מֵעֲבָדָיו וַיֹּאמֶר וְיִקְחוּ־נָא חֲמִשָּׁה
מִן־הַסּוּסִים הַנִּשְׁאָרִים אֲשֶׁר נִשְׁאֲרוּ־בָהּ הִנָּם כְּכָל־ההמון הֶהָמוֹן
יִשְׂרָאֵל אֲשֶׁר נִשְׁאֲרוּ־בָהּ הִנָּם כְּכָל־הֲמוֹן יִשְׂרָאֵל אֲשֶׁר־
יד תָּמּוּ וְנִשְׁלְחָה וְנִרְאֶה: וַיִּקְחוּ שְׁנֵי רֶכֶב סוּסִים וַיִּשְׁלַח הַמֶּלֶךְ
טו אַחֲרֵי מַחֲנֵה־אֲרָם לֵאמֹר לְכוּ וּרְאוּ: וַיֵּלְכוּ אַחֲרֵיהֶם עַד־
הַיַּרְדֵּן וְהִנֵּה כָל־הַדֶּרֶךְ מְלֵאָה בְגָדִים וְכֵלִים אֲשֶׁר־הִשְׁלִיכוּ
טז אֲרָם בהחפזם וַיָּשֻׁבוּ הַמַּלְאָכִים וַיַּגִּדוּ לַמֶּלֶךְ: וַיֵּצֵא הָעָם בְּחָפְזָם
וַיָּבֹזּוּ אֵת מַחֲנֵה אֲרָם וַיְהִי סְאָה־סֹלֶת בְּשֶׁקֶל וְסָאתַיִם
יז שְׂעֹרִים בְּשֶׁקֶל כִּדְבַר יהוה: וְהַמֶּלֶךְ הִפְקִיד אֶת־הַשָּׁלִישׁ
אֲשֶׁר־נִשְׁעָן עַל־יָדוֹ עַל־הַשַּׁעַר וַיִּרְמְסֻהוּ הָעָם בַּשַּׁעַר וַיָּמֹת
כַּאֲשֶׁר דִּבֶּר אִישׁ הָאֱלֹהִים אֲשֶׁר דִּבֶּר בְּרֶדֶת הַמֶּלֶךְ אֵלָיו:
יח וַיְהִי כְּדַבֵּר אִישׁ הָאֱלֹהִים אֶל־הַמֶּלֶךְ לֵאמֹר סָאתַיִם שְׂעֹרִים
בְּשֶׁקֶל וּסְאָה־סֹלֶת בְּשֶׁקֶל יִהְיֶה כָּעֵת מָחָר בְּשַׁעַר שֹׁמְרוֹן:
יט וַיַּעַן הַשָּׁלִישׁ אֶת־אִישׁ הָאֱלֹהִים וַיֹּאמַר וְהִנֵּה יהוה עֹשֶׂה
אֲרֻבּוֹת בַּשָּׁמַיִם הֲיִהְיֶה כַּדָּבָר הַזֶּה וַיֹּאמֶר הִנְּךָ רֹאֶה בְּעֵינֶיךָ
כ וּמִשָּׁם לֹא תֹאכֵל: וַיְהִי־לוֹ כֵּן וַיִּרְמְסוּ אֹתוֹ הָעָם בַּשַּׁעַר
וַיָּמֹת:

---

truthfulness of their claims, the people of Shomron too are able to take part in the victory.

Leprosy is traditionally seen as a divine punishment for slander and gossip. It is interesting to note that in this

13 23 But the Lord was gracious and compassionate toward them; *Yemenites add*
He turned to them for the sake of His covenant with Avraham,
Yitzḥak, and Yaakov, and He was unwilling to destroy them or
cast them away from His presence – for now.

Haftarat Aḥarei Mot

When Aḥarei Mot and Kedoshim are read together, read the haftara for Kedoshim on page 1534. On Shabbat HaGadol read the haftara on page 1672.
Chabad: Aharei Mot, Aharei Mot-Kedoshim: Amos 9:7-15;
Kedoshim: Ezekiel 20:2-20 (See the haftara for Kedoshim on page 1534).

22 1 2 The word of the Lord came to me, saying, "And you, Man, will EZEKIEL
you accuse – will you accuse the bloody city? Make all her abomi-
3 nations known to her. Say: So says the Lord God: City that spills
blood in her own midst, hastening her time and making idols in
4 her to defile her, in spilling your own blood, you have become
guilty; in making your own idols, you have been defiled. You have
brought your days near; you have come to the end of your years,
so I give you over as a reproach to the nations, a mockery to all
5 the lands. Those near and far will mock you, you of impure name,
6 filled with panic. Here are the leaders of Israel: each used his
7 power to spill blood among you; they have dishonored mother
and father within you; they have oppressed the foreigner in your
8 midst; they have mistreated orphan and widow within you. You
9 despised My holy things; you desecrated My Sabbaths. Slander-
ers have been among you so as to spill blood; on the mountains
they have eaten among you; depravities they have performed in
10 your midst. Their father's nakedness they have uncovered within
you; the impure, menstrual woman they have forced within you.
11 One man committed abominations with another's wife; another
has defiled his daughter-in-law with depravity; another in you
12 has forced his sister, the daughter of his father – within you! They
have taken bribes within you so as to spill blood; you have taken

---

this question. He reviews the terrible mistakes that characterized the Israelites' behavior, both among themselves and toward God. This moral rot, which we brought upon ourselves, is the root of our suffering. Understanding the causes of the disaster mitigates the bitterness of defeat and allows for us to move on and mend our ways. This is the path to future redemption.

יג כג וַיָּחָן יְהוָה אֹתָם וַיְרַחֲמֵם וַיִּפֶן אֲלֵיהֶם לְמַעַן בְּרִיתוֹ אֶת־
אַבְרָהָם יִצְחָק וְיַעֲקֹב וְלֹא אָבָה הַשְׁחִיתָם וְלֹא־הִשְׁלִיכָם
מֵעַל־פָּנָיו עַד־עָתָּה׃

Yemenites add

הפטרת אחרי מות

When אחרי מות *and* קדשים *are read together, read the* הפטרה *for* קדשים *on page 1535. On* שבת הגדול *read the* הפטרה *on page 1673.*

Chabad: אחרי מות*,* קדשים*,* אחרי מות-קדשים*:* עמוס *9:7–15;* קדשים*:* יחזקאל *20:2–20 (see the* הפטרה *for* קדשים *on page 1535).*

יחזקאל

כב א ב וַיְהִי דְבַר־יְהוָה אֵלַי לֵאמֹר׃ וְאַתָּה בֶן־אָדָם הֲתִשְׁפֹּט
הֲתִשְׁפֹּט אֶת־עִיר הַדָּמִים וְהוֹדַעְתָּהּ אֵת כָּל־תּוֹעֲבוֹתֶיהָ׃
ג וְאָמַרְתָּ כֹּה אָמַר אֲדֹנָי יֱהוִה עִיר שֹׁפֶכֶת דָּם בְּתוֹכָהּ לָבוֹא
ד עִתָּהּ וְעָשְׂתָה גִלּוּלִים עָלֶיהָ לְטָמְאָה׃ בְּדָמֵךְ אֲשֶׁר־שָׁפַכְתְּ
אָשַׁמְתְּ וּבְגִלּוּלַיִךְ אֲשֶׁר־עָשִׂית טָמֵאת וַתַּקְרִיבִי יָמַיִךְ וַתָּבוֹא
עַד־שְׁנוֹתָיִךְ עַל־כֵּן נְתַתִּיךְ חֶרְפָּה לַגּוֹיִם וְקַלָּסָה לְכָל־
ה הָאֲרָצוֹת׃ הַקְּרֹבוֹת וְהָרְחֹקוֹת מִמֵּךְ יִתְקַלְּסוּ־בָךְ טְמֵאַת
ו הַשֵּׁם רַבַּת הַמְּהוּמָה׃ הִנֵּה נְשִׂיאֵי יִשְׂרָאֵל אִישׁ לִזְרֹעוֹ הָיוּ
ז בָךְ לְמַעַן שְׁפָךְ־דָּם׃ אָב וָאֵם הֵקַלּוּ בָךְ לַגֵּר עָשׂוּ בַעֹשֶׁק
ח בְּתוֹכֵךְ יָתוֹם וְאַלְמָנָה הוֹנוּ בָךְ׃ קָדָשַׁי בָּזִית וְאֶת־שַׁבְּתֹתַי
ט חִלָּלְתְּ׃ אַנְשֵׁי רָכִיל הָיוּ בָךְ לְמַעַן שְׁפָךְ־דָּם וְאֶל־הֶהָרִים
י אָכְלוּ בָךְ זִמָּה עָשׂוּ בְתוֹכֵךְ׃ עֶרְוַת־אָב גִּלָּה־בָךְ טְמֵאַת
יא הַנִּדָּה עִנּוּ־בָךְ׃ וְאִישׁ ׀ אֶת־אֵשֶׁת רֵעֵהוּ עָשָׂה תּוֹעֵבָה
וְאִישׁ אֶת־כַּלָּתוֹ טִמֵּא בְזִמָּה וְאִישׁ אֶת־אֲחֹתוֹ בַת־אָבִיו
יב עִנָּה־בָךְ׃ שֹׁחַד לָקְחוּ־בָךְ לְמַעַן שְׁפָךְ־דָּם נֶשֶׁךְ וְתַרְבִּית

AḤAREI MOT

The terrible crisis in the twilight of the kingdom of Yehuda was when, for the first time in history, all the physical symbols of Jewish peoplehood were destroyed. The Temple, Jerusalem, and the dynasty of David were no more, and the human suffering brought by the destruction and exile were so immense as to make everyone ask: "Why could such a thing have been brought upon us?" The prophet Yeḥezkel, who had been exiled a generation previously with King Yehoyakhin, prepares his fellow Jews to deal with

both advanced and accrued interest; you have taken advantage
of your friend with extortion; and Me you have forgotten, de-
13 clares the Lord God. See: I clap My hands over the dishonest
gain you have taken and over the bloodshed that were in your
14 midst. Will your heart stand firm, will your hands stay strong for
the days when I deal with you? I am the Lord; I have spoken
15 and will do it. I will strew you among the nations, scatter you
16 over the lands: I will purge your impurity from you. You will be
debased in yourself before the eyes of nations, and you will know
17 that I am the Lord." * And the word of the Lord came
18 to me, saying, "Man, to Me the House of Israel are dross; they
are bronze, tin, iron, and lead in a crucible; they are the dross of
19 silver. So the Lord God says this: Because you have all
become dross, I am gathering you in to Jerusalem.

Ashkenazim, Sepharadim, and Yemenites end here
Minhag Anglia continues

Haftarat Kedoshim

When Aḥarei Mot and Kedoshim are read together, read this haftara. On Rosh Ḥodesh Iyar, read the maftir from Numbers 28:9–15, and the haftara on page 1640.

AMOS
For Ashkenazim and Chabad

9 7 Are you not to Me like the children of Kush, O children of Israel?
Did I not bring up Israel from the land of Egypt as I brought the
8 Philistines up from Kaftor and Aram from Kir? Yes, the eyes of
the Lord God are upon the sinning kingdom; I will wipe it off
the face of the earth, but the House of Yaakov I will never de-
9 stroy, says the Lord. For I will but command, and I will shake
the House of Israel among all the nations as one shakes a sieve;
10 not one pebble will fall to the earth. All the sinners of My nation will be killed by the sword – those who say, "Disaster will

that also led to corruption and oppression among the Israelites. Amos warns against these moral ills that can accompany success and reminds the people that no one can guarantee the continuation of their privileged existence. Only moral behavior and observance of the commandments can preserve what they have gained. This *haftara*, the conclusion of the book of Amos, ends with a note of hope and promise for the future redemption.

לָקַחַתְּ וַתְּבַצְּעִי רֵעַיִךְ בַּעֹשֶׁק וְאֹתִי שָׁכַחַתְּ נְאֻם אֲדֹנָי
יג יֱהוִה׃ וְהִנֵּה הִכֵּיתִי כַפִּי אֶל־בִּצְעֵךְ אֲשֶׁר עָשִׂית וְעַל־דָּמֵךְ
יד אֲשֶׁר הָיוּ בְּתוֹכֵךְ׃ הֲיַעֲמֹד לִבֵּךְ אִם־תֶּחֱזַקְנָה יָדַיִךְ לַיָּמִים
טו אֲשֶׁר אֲנִי עֹשֶׂה אוֹתָךְ אֲנִי יְהוָה דִּבַּרְתִּי וְעָשִׂיתִי׃ וַהֲפִיצוֹתִי
אוֹתָךְ בַּגּוֹיִם וְזֵרִיתִיךְ בָּאֲרָצוֹת וַהֲתִמֹּתִי טֻמְאָתֵךְ מִמֵּךְ׃
טז יז וְנִחַלְתְּ בָּךְ לְעֵינֵי גוֹיִם וְיָדַעַתְּ כִּי־אֲנִי יְהוָה׃★ וַיְהִי

Ashkenazim, Sephardim, and Yemenites end here
Minhag Anglia continues

יח דְבַר־יְהוָה אֵלַי לֵאמֹר׃ בֶּן־אָדָם הָיוּ־לִי בֵית־יִשְׂרָאֵל לְסוּג לְסִיג
כֻּלָּם נְחֹשֶׁת וּבְדִיל וּבַרְזֶל וְעוֹפֶרֶת בְּתוֹךְ כּוּר סִגִים כֶּסֶף
יט הָיוּ׃ לָכֵן כֹּה אָמַר אֲדֹנָי יֱהוִה יַעַן הֱיוֹת כֻּלְּכֶם
לְסִגִים לָכֵן הִנְנִי קֹבֵץ אֶתְכֶם אֶל־תּוֹךְ יְרוּשָׁלִָם׃

הפטרת קדשים

When אחרי מות *and* קדשים *are read together, read this* הפטרה.
On ראש חודש אייר *read the* מפטיר *from* במדבר כח, ט–טו *and the* הפטרה *on page 1641.*

עמוס
For Ashkenazim and Chabad

ט ז הֲלוֹא כִבְנֵי כֻשִׁיִּים אַתֶּם לִי בְּנֵי יִשְׂרָאֵל נְאֻם־יְהוָה הֲלוֹא אֶת־
יִשְׂרָאֵל הֶעֱלֵיתִי מֵאֶרֶץ מִצְרַיִם וּפְלִשְׁתִּיִּים מִכַּפְתּוֹר וַאֲרָם
ח מִקִּיר׃ הִנֵּה עֵינֵי ׀ אֲדֹנָי יֱהוִה בַּמַּמְלָכָה הַחַטָּאָה וְהִשְׁמַדְתִּי
אֹתָהּ מֵעַל פְּנֵי הָאֲדָמָה אֶפֶס כִּי לֹא הַשְׁמֵיד אַשְׁמִיד אֶת־בֵּית
ט יַעֲקֹב נְאֻם־יְהוָה׃ כִּי־הִנֵּה אָנֹכִי מְצַוֶּה וַהֲנִעוֹתִי בְכָל־הַגּוֹיִם
אֶת־בֵּית יִשְׂרָאֵל כַּאֲשֶׁר יִנּוֹעַ בַּכְּבָרָה וְלֹא־יִפּוֹל צְרוֹר אָרֶץ׃
י בַּחֶרֶב יָמוּתוּ כֹּל חַטָּאֵי עַמִּי הָאֹמְרִים לֹא־תַגִּישׁ וְתַקְדִּים
יא בַּעֲדֵינוּ הָרָעָה׃ בַּיּוֹם הַהוּא אָקִים אֶת־סֻכַּת דָּוִיד הַנֹּפֶלֶת

KEDOSHIM

Ashkenazim

The prophet Amos was active throughout the kingdom of Israel during the era when it and the kingdom of Yehuda were at their strongest, under the reign of Uziyahu king of Yehuda and Yorovam son of Yoash king of Israel. Both monarchs reigned for decades, contributing unprecedented stability and wealth

▶

11 not reach, will not advance upon us." On that day, I will lift up
David's fallen tabernacle, repair its breaches, and lift up its ruins,
12 rebuild it as it was in days of yore. And so they will possess the
remnants of Edom and all the nations who are called in My name,
13 says the LORD who does this. Behold, days are coming.
The LORD has spoken. The plow man will meet the reaper, and
the grape crusher the seed sower; the mountains will drip with
14 sweet wine, and all the hills will dissolve. I will bring back the exiled of My nation, Israel. They will build ruined cities and settle.
They will plant vineyards and drink their wine. They will grow
15 gardens and eat their fruit. I will plant them on their land, and
never again will they be uprooted from the land which I gave to
them, says the LORD, your God.

EZEKIEL

Yemenites begin here

Sepharadim and Chabad begin here

20 1 And it was in the seventh year in the fifth month on the tenth
day of the month that men from the elders of Israel came and
2 sat before me to consult the LORD. *And the word of
3 the LORD came to me: "Man, speak to the elders of Israel; say
to them: So says the Lord GOD: Have you come to seek Me? As
4 I live, I will not be sought by you, declares the Lord GOD. Will
you accuse them, Man, will you accuse them? Make known to
5 them their fathers' abominations. Say to them: So says the Lord
GOD: On the day that I chose Israel, raising My hand in promise
to the descendants of the House of Yaakov and making Myself
known to them in the land of Egypt, I raised My hand in promise
6 to them, saying: 'I the LORD am your God.' On that day, I raised
My hand in promise to them to take them from the land of Egypt
to the land that flows with milk and honey, the most beautiful of
7 all lands, that I had sought out for them. I said to them: 'Throw

---

wickedness, times when they deserved to be destroyed, but God treated them with mercy out of concern for His own honor among the nations. At the end of this prophecy, Yeḥezkel formulates the historical logic that governs all Israel's special relationship with God. Whatever happens, nothing can break the bond between God and Israel. If Israel breaks the terms of their covenant with God, they will be punished – but they will never be wiped out, and they will never be able to constitute themselves in any other land and govern it. This is what makes the ultimate redemption inevitable, no matter how long it may take.

וגדרתי את־פרציהן והרסתיו אקים ובניתיה כימי עולם:
יב למען יירשו את־שארית אדום וכל־הגוים אשר־נקרא
יג שמי עליהם נאם־יהוה עשה זאת: הנה ימים
באים נאם־יהוה ונגש חורש בקצר ודרך ענבים במשך
הזרע והטיפו ההרים עסיס וכל־הגבעות תתמוגגנה:
יד ושבתי את־שבות עמי ישראל ובנו ערים נשמות וישבו
ונטעו כרמים ושתו את־יינם ועשו גנות ואכלו את־פריהם:
טו ונטעתים על־אדמתם ולא ינתשו עוד מעל אדמתם אשר
נתתי להם אמר יהוה אלהיך:

יחזקאל
Yemenites begin here

כ א ויהי | בשנה השביעית בחמשי בעשור לחדש
באו אנשים מזקני ישראל לדרש את־יהוה וישבו
ב ג לפני: *ויהי דבר־יהוה אלי לאמר: בן־אדם

Sepharadim and Chabad begin here

דבר את־זקני ישראל ואמרת אלהם כה אמר אדני
יהוה הלדרש אתי אתם באים חי־אני אם־אדרש לכם
ד נאם אדני יהוה: התשפט אתם התשפוט בן־אדם את־
ה תועבת אבותם הודיעם: ואמרת אליהם כה־אמר אדני
יהוה ביום בחרי בישראל ואשא ידי לזרע בית יעקב
ואודע להם בארץ מצרים ואשא ידי להם לאמר אני
ו יהוה אלהיכם: ביום ההוא נשאתי ידי להם להוציאם
מארץ מצרים אל־ארץ אשר־תרתי להם זבת חלב ודבש
ז צבי היא לכל־הארצות: ואמר אלהם איש שקוצי עיניו

Sepharadim and Yemenites

After the exile of Yehoyakhin and many residents of Jerusalem to Babylon, but still four years before the final destruction of the city and the Temple, the exiled Jewish elders gather in the home of the prophet Yeḥezkel to hear his explanation for the dramatic events they have witnessed. In addressing them, the prophet reviews the history of the relationship between God and Israel ever since the days of Egyptian servitude, and up until the coming destruction. Yeḥezkel cites historical examples of Israel's

off, each of you, the detestable things before your eyes; do not
defile yourselves with Egyptian idols: I the LORD am your God.'
8 But they defied Me; they were not prepared to listen to Me; none
threw off the detestable things before their eyes; they did not relinquish their Egyptian idols. And I thought of pouring out My
fury, exhausting My anger upon them in the midst of the land of
9 Egypt. But I acted for the sake of My name so that it would not
be desecrated in the eyes of the nations among whom they were –
and before whose eyes I had made Myself known in taking them
10 out from the land of Egypt. I took them out from the land of
11 Egypt and brought them into the wilderness. I gave them My
statutes, made My laws known to them, by which a person shall
12 live. I even gave them My Sabbaths as a sign between Myself and
them so that they should know that I, the LORD, make them holy.
13 But the House of Israel defied me in the wilderness. They did not
follow My statutes; they rejected My laws, by which each person
was to live; they wholly desecrated My Sabbaths. I thought of
pouring out My fury upon them in the wilderness and destroy-
14 ing them, but I acted for the sake of My name so that it would
not be desecrated in the eyes of the nations before whose eyes I
15 had taken them out. I even raised My hand in promise to them in
the desert not to bring them to the land that flows with milk and
honey, the most beautiful of all lands, which I had given them,* *Yemenites end here*
16 because they rejected My laws, did not follow My statutes, desecrated My Sabbaths – for their hearts followed after their idols.
17 But My eye pitied them, and I could not destroy them; I did not
18 bring them to their end in the wilderness. I said to their children
in the wilderness: 'Do not follow the statutes of your fathers, do
19 not keep their laws; do not be defiled by their idols. I the LORD
am your God: follow My statutes, keep My laws, perform them,
20 make My Sabbaths holy – it will be a sign between Me and you
to know that I the LORD am your God.'"

הַשְׁלִ֔יכוּ וּבְגִלּוּלֵ֥י מִצְרַ֖יִם אַל־תִּטַּמָּ֑אוּ אֲנִ֖י יְהוָ֥ה אֱלֹהֵיכֶֽם׃
ח וַיַּמְרוּ־בִ֗י וְלֹ֤א אָבוּ֙ לִשְׁמֹ֣עַ אֵלַ֔י אִ֣ישׁ אֶת־שִׁקּוּצֵ֤י עֵֽינֵיהֶם֙
לֹ֣א הִשְׁלִ֔יכוּ וְאֶת־גִּלּוּלֵ֥י מִצְרַ֖יִם לֹ֣א עָזָ֑בוּ וָאֹמַ֞ר לִשְׁפֹּ֧ךְ
ט חֲמָתִ֣י עֲלֵיהֶ֗ם לְכַלּ֤וֹת אַפִּי֙ בָּהֶ֔ם בְּת֖וֹךְ אֶ֥רֶץ מִצְרָֽיִם׃ וָאַ֙עַשׂ֙
לְמַ֣עַן שְׁמִ֔י לְבִלְתִּ֥י הֵחֵ֖ל לְעֵינֵ֣י הַגּוֹיִ֑ם אֲשֶׁר־הֵ֣מָּה בְתוֹכָ֔ם
אֲשֶׁ֨ר נוֹדַ֤עְתִּי אֲלֵיהֶם֙ לְעֵ֣ינֵיהֶ֔ם לְהוֹצִיאָ֖ם מֵאֶ֥רֶץ מִצְרָֽיִם׃
י יא וָאוֹצִיאֵ֖ם מֵאֶ֣רֶץ מִצְרָ֑יִם וָאֲבִאֵ֖ם אֶל־הַמִּדְבָּֽר׃ וָאֶתֵּ֤ן לָהֶם֙
אֶת־חֻקּוֹתַ֔י וְאֶת־מִשְׁפָּטַ֖י הוֹדַ֣עְתִּי אוֹתָ֑ם אֲשֶׁ֨ר יַעֲשֶׂ֥ה אוֹתָ֛ם
יב הָאָדָ֖ם וָחַ֥י בָּהֶֽם׃ וְגַ֤ם אֶת־שַׁבְּתוֹתַי֙ נָתַ֣תִּי לָהֶ֔ם לִהְי֥וֹת לְא֖וֹת
יג בֵּינִ֣י וּבֵינֵיהֶ֑ם לָדַ֕עַת כִּ֛י אֲנִ֥י יְהוָ֖ה מְקַדְּשָֽׁם׃ וַיַּמְרוּ־בִ֨י בֵֽית־
יִשְׂרָאֵ֜ל בַּמִּדְבָּ֗ר בְּחֻקּוֹתַ֤י לֹא־הָלָ֙כוּ֙ וְאֶת־מִשְׁפָּטַ֣י מָאָ֔סוּ
אֲשֶׁ֨ר יַעֲשֶׂ֤ה אֹתָם֙ הָֽאָדָם֙ וָחַ֣י בָּהֶ֔ם וְאֶת־שַׁבְּתֹתַ֖י חִלְּל֣וּ מְאֹ֑ד
יד וָאֹמַ֞ר לִשְׁפֹּ֨ךְ חֲמָתִ֧י עֲלֵיהֶ֛ם בַּמִּדְבָּ֖ר לְכַלּוֹתָֽם׃ וָאֶעֱשֶׂ֖ה לְמַ֣עַן
שְׁמִ֑י לְבִלְתִּ֤י הֵחֵל֙ לְעֵינֵ֣י הַגּוֹיִ֔ם אֲשֶׁ֥ר הוֹצֵאתִ֖ים לְעֵינֵיהֶֽם׃
טו וְגַם־אֲנִ֗י נָשָׂ֧אתִי יָדִ֛י לָהֶ֖ם בַּמִּדְבָּ֑ר לְבִלְתִּ֡י הָבִיא֩ אוֹתָ֨ם
אֶל־הָאָ֜רֶץ אֲשֶׁר־נָתַ֗תִּי זָבַ֤ת חָלָב֙ וּדְבַ֔שׁ צְבִ֥י הִ֖יא לְכָל־
טז הָאֲרָצֽוֹת׃* יַ֗עַן בְּמִשְׁפָּטַ֤י מָאָ֙סוּ֙ וְאֶת־חֻקּוֹתַי֙ לֹא־הָלְכ֣וּ בָהֶ֔ם

Yemenites end here

יז וְאֶת־שַׁבְּתוֹתַ֖י חִלֵּ֑לוּ כִּ֛י אַחֲרֵ֥י גִלּוּלֵיהֶ֖ם לִבָּ֥ם הֹלֵֽךְ׃ וַתָּ֧חָס
עֵינִ֛י עֲלֵיהֶ֖ם מִשַּׁחֲתָ֑ם וְלֹא־עָשִׂ֧יתִי אוֹתָ֛ם כָּלָ֖ה בַּמִּדְבָּֽר׃
יח וָאֹמַ֤ר אֶל־בְּנֵיהֶם֙ בַּמִּדְבָּ֔ר בְּחוּקֵּ֤י אֲבֽוֹתֵיכֶם֙ אַל־תֵּלֵ֔כוּ וְאֶת־
יט מִשְׁפְּטֵיהֶ֖ם אַל־תִּשְׁמֹ֑רוּ וּבְגִלּוּלֵיהֶ֖ם אַל־תִּטַּמָּֽאוּ׃ אֲנִי֙ יְהוָ֣ה
אֱלֹהֵיכֶ֔ם בְּחֻקּוֹתַ֖י לֵ֑כוּ וְאֶת־מִשְׁפָּטַ֥י שִׁמְר֖וּ וַעֲשׂ֥וּ אוֹתָֽם׃
כ וְאֶת־שַׁבְּתוֹתַ֖י קַדֵּ֑שׁוּ וְהָי֤וּ לְאוֹת֙ בֵּינִ֣י וּבֵֽינֵיכֶ֔ם לָדַ֕עַת כִּ֥י
אֲנִ֖י יְהוָ֥ה אֱלֹהֵיכֶֽם׃

Haftarat Emor

EZEKIEL

44 15 But the priests who are Levites descended from Tzadok, who
protected the preciousness of My Sanctuary when the children
of Israel strayed from Me, they are the ones who may draw near
Me in order to serve Me, and they shall stand before Me to offer
16 Me fat and blood: this is the word of the Lord God. They are the
ones who will enter My Sanctuary, and they shall approach My
table to serve Me; they shall dutifully protect My precious things.
17 This is how it shall be when they approach the gates of the inner
courtyard: they will wear linen garments, and no wool shall be
upon them when they serve at the gates of the inner courtyard
18 and within. There will be linen turbans on their heads and linen
trousers on their loins; they shall not gird themselves in a way
19 that causes perspiration. And when they leave to go to the outer
courtyard – to the outer courtyard to the people – they shall remove the garments in which they serve, leaving them in the holy
chambers, and put on other clothing, in order not to give the
impression, by mingling with them wearing their holy garments,
20 that the people are equal to them in sanctity. They shall not shave
their heads nor grow their hair long in disarray; they shall keep
21 their heads carefully trimmed. Nor shall any priest drink wine
22 when they enter the inner courtyard. And they shall not take as a
wife a widow or a divorcée. Rather, they shall take as wives only
virgins of the seed of the House of Israel, or a widow who is the
23 widow of a priest. And they shall teach My people the difference
between the sacred and the profane and make known to them
24 the difference between impure and pure. When there is controversy, they shall stand in judgment, adjudicating it according to
My laws. And they shall keep My teachings and My statutes at all
25 the times I have appointed, and sanctify My Sabbaths. The priest
shall not approach a human corpse and become impure because
of it, though for a father or a mother, for a son or a daughter, for

responsibility of sustaining the Levites, who have no land of their own. They do this through the institutions of the tithes and the priestly gifts. This system of support comes directly from the people; it is not collected or managed by the king or government. And in turn, the king has no right to influence the religious and moral content taught by the Levites to the people. "The priests who are Levites," i.e., the educational system, are thus in their own right a separate branch of governance, independent of the executive.

הפטרת אמר

יחזקאל

מד טו וְהַכֹּהֲנִים הַלְוִיִּם בְּנֵי צָדוֹק אֲשֶׁר שָׁמְרוּ אֶת־מִשְׁמֶרֶת מִקְדָּשִׁי
בִּתְעוֹת בְּנֵי־יִשְׂרָאֵל מֵעָלַי הֵמָּה יִקְרְבוּ אֵלַי לְשָׁרְתֵנִי וְעָמְדוּ
טז לְפָנַי לְהַקְרִיב לִי חֵלֶב וָדָם נְאֻם אֲדֹנָי יֱהֹוִה׃ הֵמָּה יָבֹאוּ
אֶל־מִקְדָּשִׁי וְהֵמָּה יִקְרְבוּ אֶל־שֻׁלְחָנִי לְשָׁרְתֵנִי וְשָׁמְרוּ
יז אֶת־מִשְׁמַרְתִּי׃ וְהָיָה בְּבוֹאָם אֶל־שַׁעֲרֵי הֶחָצֵר הַפְּנִימִית
בִּגְדֵי פִשְׁתִּים יִלְבָּשׁוּ וְלֹא־יַעֲלֶה עֲלֵיהֶם צֶמֶר בְּשָׁרְתָם
יח בְּשַׁעֲרֵי הֶחָצֵר הַפְּנִימִית וָבָיְתָה׃ פַּאֲרֵי פִשְׁתִּים יִהְיוּ עַל־
רֹאשָׁם וּמִכְנְסֵי פִשְׁתִּים יִהְיוּ עַל־מָתְנֵיהֶם לֹא יַחְגְּרוּ בַּיָּזַע׃
יט וּבְצֵאתָם אֶל־הֶחָצֵר הַחִיצוֹנָה אֶל־הֶחָצֵר הַחִיצוֹנָה אֶל־
הָעָם יִפְשְׁטוּ אֶת־בִּגְדֵיהֶם אֲשֶׁר־הֵמָּה מְשָׁרְתִם בָּם וְהִנִּיחוּ
אוֹתָם בְּלִשְׁכֹת הַקֹּדֶשׁ וְלָבְשׁוּ בְּגָדִים אֲחֵרִים וְלֹא־יְקַדְּשׁוּ
כ אֶת־הָעָם בְּבִגְדֵיהֶם׃ וְרֹאשָׁם לֹא יְגַלֵּחוּ וּפֶרַע לֹא יְשַׁלֵּחוּ
כא כָּסוֹם יִכְסְמוּ אֶת־רָאשֵׁיהֶם׃ וְיַיִן לֹא־יִשְׁתּוּ כָּל־כֹּהֵן בְּבוֹאָם
כב אֶל־הֶחָצֵר הַפְּנִימִית׃ וְאַלְמָנָה וּגְרוּשָׁה לֹא־יִקְחוּ לָהֶם
לְנָשִׁים כִּי אִם־בְּתוּלֹת מִזֶּרַע בֵּית יִשְׂרָאֵל וְהָאַלְמָנָה אֲשֶׁר־
כג תִּהְיֶה אַלְמָנָה מִכֹּהֵן יִקָּחוּ׃ וְאֶת־עַמִּי יוֹרוּ בֵּין קֹדֶשׁ לְחֹל
כד וּבֵין־טָמֵא לְטָהוֹר יוֹדִעֻם׃ וְעַל־רִיב הֵמָּה יַעַמְדוּ לשפט לְמִשְׁפָּט
בְּמִשְׁפָּטַי ושפטהו וְאֶת־תּוֹרֹתַי וְאֶת־חֻקֹּתַי בְּכָל־מוֹעֲדַי יִשְׁפְּטֻהוּ
כה יִשְׁמֹרוּ וְאֶת־שַׁבְּתוֹתַי יְקַדֵּשׁוּ׃ וְאֶל־מֵת אָדָם לֹא יָבוֹא
לְטָמְאָה כִּי אִם־לְאָב וּלְאֵם וּלְבֵן וּלְבַת לְאָח וּלְאָחוֹת אֲשֶׁר־

EMOR

In Yeḥezkel's prophetic virtual tour of the future reconstructed Temple, communicated twenty-four years after the destruction, the prophet reassures the exiles that the redemption will come one day. The *haftara* opens with the words "the priests who are Levites," evoking the role of the priests as educators and religious guides, mentioned in Moshe's final blessings in the book of Deuteronomy (33:10): "They shall teach Your laws to Yaakov, and Your instruction to Israel."

The people of Israel, whom the tribe of Levi represents before God and on whose behalf they work, bears the

a brother or for a sister who is unmarried, they may become im-
26 pure. After a priest's purification process begins, seven days are
27 counted for him. And on the day he comes to the Sanctuary, into
the inner courtyard to minister in the Sanctuary, he is to bring
28 his purification offering – this is the word of the Lord God. And
this shall be the priests' inheritance: I am their inheritance. Give
them no territory to possess in the land of Israel; I am their pos-
29 session. They shall eat the grain offering and the purification offering and the guilt offering, and everything consecrated by vow
30 in Israel shall be theirs. The choicest of all first fruits of every kind
and every gift offering out of all your various donations belongs
to the priests. And your first kneading you shall give to the priest
31 so that a blessing settles upon your home. Whether it be bird or
beast, the priests may not eat any creature that died on its own or
was torn to pieces as prey.

Haftarat Behar

When Behar and Beḥukotai are read together, read the haftara for Beḥukotai on page 1548.

JEREMIAH

For Ashkenazim and Sepharadim

32 6 And Yirmeyahu said: The word of the Lord came to me:
7 Ḥanamel, son of your uncle Shalum, shall come to you and
say, "Purchase for yourself my field that is in Anatot, for yours
8 is the right of redemption by purchase." Ḥanamel, my uncle's
son, came to me – just as the Lord had said – to the prison
courtyard, and said to me, "Please purchase my field in Anatot,
in the territory of Binyamin, for yours is the right of inheritance, and it is your right to redeem it. Purchase it for your-
9 self." Then I knew that this was the word of the Lord. And so
I purchased the field that was in Anatot from my uncle's son
Ḥanamel. I weighed out the silver to him: seven shekel and ten

siege makes no logical sense, Yirmeyahu follows God's command. The purchasing ceremony is carried out following all the customary and legal forms. Afterward, Yirmeyahu turns to God and requests an explanation for the strange mission. God's answer clarifies that the punishment of destruction is not irreversible. The symbolic act of purchasing a field right before the kingdom's demise concretizes this idea. The purchase and sale of land evokes the normality of day-to-day life, which will one day return to the hills and cities of Yehuda.

כו לֹא־הָיְתָה לְאִישׁ יִטַּמָּאוּ: וְאַחֲרֵי טָהֳרָתוֹ שִׁבְעַת יָמִים
כז יִסְפְּרוּ־לוֹ: וּבְיוֹם בֹּאוֹ אֶל־הַקֹּדֶשׁ אֶל־הֶחָצֵר הַפְּנִימִית
כח לְשָׁרֵת בַּקֹּדֶשׁ יַקְרִיב חַטָּאתוֹ נְאֻם אֲדֹנָי יֱהֹוִה: וְהָיְתָה
לָהֶם לְנַחֲלָה אֲנִי נַחֲלָתָם וַאֲחֻזָּה לֹא־תִתְּנוּ לָהֶם בְּיִשְׂרָאֵל
כט אֲנִי אֲחֻזָּתָם: הַמִּנְחָה וְהַחַטָּאת וְהָאָשָׁם הֵמָּה יֹאכְלוּם
ל וְכָל־חֵרֶם בְּיִשְׂרָאֵל לָהֶם יִהְיֶה: וְרֵאשִׁית כָּל־בִּכּוּרֵי כֹל
וְכָל־תְּרוּמַת כֹּל מִכֹּל תְּרוּמוֹתֵיכֶם לַכֹּהֲנִים יִהְיֶה וְרֵאשִׁית
עֲרִיסוֹתֵיכֶם תִּתְּנוּ לַכֹּהֵן לְהָנִיחַ בְּרָכָה אֶל־בֵּיתֶךָ:
לא כָּל־נְבֵלָה וּטְרֵפָה מִן־הָעוֹף וּמִן־הַבְּהֵמָה לֹא יֹאכְלוּ
הַכֹּהֲנִים:

הפטרת בהר

When בהר and בחקתי are read together, read the הפטרה for בחקתי on page 1549.

ירמיה
For Ashkenazim and Sepharadim

לב ו ז וַיֹּאמֶר יִרְמְיָהוּ הָיָה דְּבַר־יְהוָה אֵלַי לֵאמֹר: הִנֵּה חֲנַמְאֵל
בֶּן־שַׁלֻּם דֹּדְךָ בָּא אֵלֶיךָ לֵאמֹר קְנֵה לְךָ אֶת־שָׂדִי אֲשֶׁר
ח בַּעֲנָתוֹת כִּי לְךָ מִשְׁפַּט הַגְּאֻלָּה לִקְנוֹת: וַיָּבֹא אֵלַי חֲנַמְאֵל
בֶּן־דֹּדִי כִּדְבַר יְהוָה אֶל־חֲצַר הַמַּטָּרָה וַיֹּאמֶר אֵלַי קְנֵה
נָא אֶת־שָׂדִי אֲשֶׁר־בַּעֲנָתוֹת אֲשֶׁר ׀ בְּאֶרֶץ בִּנְיָמִין כִּי לְךָ
מִשְׁפַּט הַיְרֻשָּׁה וּלְךָ הַגְּאֻלָּה קְנֵה־לָךְ וָאֵדַע כִּי דְבַר־יְהוָה
ט הוּא: וָאֶקְנֶה אֶת־הַשָּׂדֶה מֵאֵת חֲנַמְאֵל בֶּן־דֹּדִי אֲשֶׁר
בַּעֲנָתוֹת וָאֶשְׁקֲלָה־לּוֹ אֶת־הַכֶּסֶף שִׁבְעָה שְׁקָלִים וַעֲשָׂרָה

BEHAR

Ashkenazim and Sepharadim

A few months before the destruction of the Temple, at the darkest hour of the Babylonian siege, Yirmeyahu is imprisoned by King Tzidkiyahu, who fears Yirmeyahu's prophecies of destruction. In his dungeon, Yirmeyahu receives a prophetic command to buy a field from a cousin, who arrives at the prison to visit him. Even though the financial investment in such a purchase by a prisoner during a

10 silver coins. I wrote it upon a scroll and sealed it, and I had
11 it witnessed; and I weighed out the silver on a scale. I took
the deed of purchase, sealed as prescribed by law and custom,
12 along with the unsealed document. And I gave the deed of
purchase to Barukh son of Neriya son of Maḥseya in the presence of Ḥanamel my uncle, in the presence of the witnesses
who were listed in the deed of purchase, and in the presence
of all the men of Yehuda who were sitting in the prison court-
13 14 yard. In their presence I instructed Barukh, saying, "This is
what the Lord of Hosts, God of Israel, said: Take these scrolls,
this deed of purchase, the sealed section and the unsealed section, and place it in a clay vessel, so that it might be preserved
15 for many days." For this is what the Lord of Hosts,
God of Israel, has said: Houses, fields, and vineyards shall once
16 again be purchased in this land. After I gave this deed
of purchase to Barukh son of Neriya, I prayed to the Lord, say-
17 ing, "O Lord God! You made the heavens and the earth with
Your great strength and with Your arm stretched forth. Noth-
18 ing is too wonderful for You. You perform loving-kindness to
thousands but repay the sins of fathers unto the bosoms of
their children after them. The great and mighty God, Lord of
19 Hosts is His name. Great in counsel, mighty in deed, Your eyes
are open to all of the ways of humans, to give each one according to his ways, to each according to the fruits of his actions.
20 You set signs and wonders in the land of Egypt to this day for
Israel and for humankind, and You made a name for Yourself
21 as on this day. You brought out Your people Israel from the
land of Egypt with signs and wonders, a mighty hand and an
22 arm stretched forth, and with terrifying power. You gave them
this land that You swore to their fathers that You would give
23 them, a land flowing with milk and honey. They came and pos- *Chabad end here*
sessed it, but they neither heeded Your voice nor followed Your
teaching. All that You had commanded them to do they did
not do, and so You caused all this disaster to come upon them.
24 The siege ramps have come near the city in order to capture
it, and the city is about to be delivered, because of the sword
and the famine and the pestilence, into the hands of the Chaldeans who are attacking it. That which you spoke about has
25 happened, and You see it for Yourself. And yet You say to me,
Lord God, 'Purchase this field for yourself for silver and have

י הַכֶּסֶף׃ וָאֶכְתֹּב בַּסֵּפֶר וָאֶחְתֹּם וָאָעֵד עֵדִים וָאֶשְׁקֹל הַכֶּסֶף
יא בְּמֹאזְנָיִם׃ וָאֶקַּח אֶת־סֵפֶר הַמִּקְנָה אֶת־הֶחָתוּם הַמִּצְוָה
יב וְהַחֻקִּים וְאֶת־הַגָּלוּי׃ וָאֶתֵּן אֶת־הַסֵּפֶר הַמִּקְנָה אֶל־בָּרוּךְ
בֶּן־נֵרִיָּה בֶּן־מַחְסֵיָה לְעֵינֵי חֲנַמְאֵל דֹּדִי וּלְעֵינֵי הָעֵדִים
הַכֹּתְבִים בְּסֵפֶר הַמִּקְנָה לְעֵינֵי כָּל־הַיְּהוּדִים הַיֹּשְׁבִים בַּחֲצַר
יג יד הַמַּטָּרָה׃ וָאֲצַוֶּה אֶת־בָּרוּךְ לְעֵינֵיהֶם לֵאמֹר׃ כֹּה־אָמַר יְהוָה
צְבָאוֹת אֱלֹהֵי יִשְׂרָאֵל לָקוֹחַ אֶת־הַסְּפָרִים הָאֵלֶּה אֵת סֵפֶר
הַמִּקְנָה הַזֶּה וְאֵת הֶחָתוּם וְאֵת סֵפֶר הַגָּלוּי הַזֶּה וּנְתַתָּם
טו בִּכְלִי־חָרֶשׂ לְמַעַן יַעַמְדוּ יָמִים רַבִּים׃ כִּי כֹה
אָמַר יְהוָה צְבָאוֹת אֱלֹהֵי יִשְׂרָאֵל עוֹד יִקָּנוּ בָתִּים וְשָׂדוֹת
טז וּכְרָמִים בָּאָרֶץ הַזֹּאת׃ וָאֶתְפַּלֵּל אֶל־יְהוָה אַחֲרֵי
יז תִתִּי אֶת־סֵפֶר הַמִּקְנָה אֶל־בָּרוּךְ בֶּן־נֵרִיָּה לֵאמֹר׃ אֲהָהּ
אֲדֹנָי יֱהוִה הִנֵּה ׀ אַתָּה עָשִׂיתָ אֶת־הַשָּׁמַיִם וְאֶת־הָאָרֶץ
בְּכֹחֲךָ הַגָּדוֹל וּבִזְרֹעֲךָ הַנְּטוּיָה לֹא־יִפָּלֵא מִמְּךָ כָּל־דָּבָר׃
יח עֹשֶׂה חֶסֶד לַאֲלָפִים וּמְשַׁלֵּם עֲוֺן אָבוֹת אֶל־חֵיק בְּנֵיהֶם
יט אַחֲרֵיהֶם הָאֵל הַגָּדוֹל הַגִּבּוֹר יְהוָה צְבָאוֹת שְׁמוֹ׃ גְּדֹל
הָעֵצָה וְרַב הָעֲלִילִיָּה אֲשֶׁר־עֵינֶיךָ פְקֻחוֹת עַל־כָּל־דַּרְכֵי
כ בְּנֵי אָדָם לָתֵת לְאִישׁ כִּדְרָכָיו וְכִפְרִי מַעֲלָלָיו׃ אֲשֶׁר שַׂמְתָּ
אֹתוֹת וּמֹפְתִים בְּאֶרֶץ מִצְרַיִם עַד־הַיּוֹם הַזֶּה וּבְיִשְׂרָאֵל
כא וּבָאָדָם וַתַּעֲשֶׂה־לְּךָ שֵׁם כַּיּוֹם הַזֶּה׃ וַתֹּצֵא אֶת־עַמְּךָ אֶת־
יִשְׂרָאֵל מֵאֶרֶץ מִצְרָיִם בְּאֹתוֹת וּבְמוֹפְתִים וּבְיָד חֲזָקָה
כב וּבְאֶזְרוֹעַ נְטוּיָה וּבְמוֹרָא גָּדוֹל׃ וַתִּתֵּן לָהֶם אֶת־הָאָרֶץ
הַזֹּאת אֲשֶׁר־נִשְׁבַּעְתָּ לַאֲבוֹתָם לָתֵת לָהֶם אֶרֶץ זָבַת חָלָב
כג וּדְבָשׁ׃* וַיָּבֹאוּ וַיִּרְשׁוּ אֹתָהּ וְלֹא־שָׁמְעוּ בְקוֹלֶךָ ובתרותך
וּבְתוֹרָתְךָ
Chabad end here
לֹא־הָלָכוּ אֵת כָּל־אֲשֶׁר צִוִּיתָה לָהֶם לַעֲשׂוֹת לֹא עָשׂוּ וַתַּקְרֵא
כד אֹתָם אֵת כָּל־הָרָעָה הַזֹּאת׃ הִנֵּה הַסֹּלְלוֹת בָּאוּ הָעִיר
לְלָכְדָהּ וְהָעִיר נִתְּנָה בְּיַד הַכַּשְׂדִּים הַנִּלְחָמִים עָלֶיהָ מִפְּנֵי
כה הַחֶרֶב וְהָרָעָב וְהַדָּבֶר וַאֲשֶׁר דִּבַּרְתָּ הָיָה וְהִנְּךָ רֹאֶה׃ וְאַתָּה

it witnessed, when the city is about to be delivered into the
26 hands of the Chaldeans'?" And the word of the LORD
27 came to Yirmeyahu: "Look, I am the LORD, God of all flesh. Is
anything beyond My power?"

JEREMIAH
For Yemenites

16 19 The LORD is my strength and my might, my refuge in a day
of trouble. To You the nations will come from the ends of the
earth, and they will say: "Our ancestors inherited nothing but
20 falsehood, futility, and things of no use. Can a human make gods
21 for himself when they are not gods?" Therefore, I am about to
make them know; this time I will make them know of My power
and My strength, and they shall come to know that My name
17 1 is the LORD. Yehuda's sin is written with an iron pen
with a diamond point, engraved upon the tablets of their hearts
2 and upon the corners of your altars. As they yearn for their children, so do they for their altars and their sacred trees beside ver-
3 dant trees upon the high hills. Mountain dweller – because of
the sin of your high places in all your territories, I will turn your
4 wealth and all your treasures into booty upon the field. You will
forfeit, by your own fault, the heritage which I have given you. I
will make you a slave to your enemies in a land that you never
knew, for you kindled a fire in My nostrils which shall blaze
5 forever. This is what the LORD said: Cursed is he who
trusts in man, who makes flesh his strength and who turns his
6 heart away from the LORD. He will be like a shrub in the desert,
never witnessing prosperity. He will dwell scorched in the wil-
7 derness, a salty, uninhabited land. Blessed is the person
8 who trusts in the LORD. The LORD will be his protector. He will
be like a tree planted beside the water, its roots spreading along

---

who favored the status quo. His relationship with God gave him strength to overcome the hostility directed at him by the people.

The word "land" (*eretz*) appears in this *haftara* with four different senses. It means the whole earth, a specific country, the ground from which plants grow, and a low place that is trodden on. To summarize the *haftara*: The people of Israel are located in the "land" of Israel. All the peoples of the "land" (i.e., of the earth) are supposed to learn from us the proper and pious way to behave. If Israel does not set a proper example, the "land" will become barren, the people will go into exile, and its honor will be brought down to the "land" (i.e., to the ground).

אָמַרְתָּ אֵלַי אֲדֹנָי יֱהֹוִה קְנֵה־לְךָ הַשָּׂדֶה בַּכֶּסֶף וְהָעֵד עֵדִים
כו וְהָעִיר נִתְּנָה בְּיַד הַכַּשְׂדִּים: וַיְהִי דְּבַר־יְהוָה אֶל־
כז יִרְמְיָהוּ לֵאמֹר: הִנֵּה אֲנִי יְהוָה אֱלֹהֵי כָּל־בָּשָׂר הֲמִמֶּנִּי יִפָּלֵא
כָּל־דָּבָר:

ירמיה
For Yemenites

טז יט יְהוָה עֻזִּי וּמָעֻזִּי וּמְנוּסִי בְּיוֹם צָרָה אֵלֶיךָ גּוֹיִם יָבֹאוּ מֵאַפְסֵי־
אֶרֶץ וְיֹאמְרוּ אַךְ־שֶׁקֶר נָחֲלוּ אֲבוֹתֵינוּ הֶבֶל וְאֵין־בָּם מוֹעִיל:
כ כא הֲיַעֲשֶׂה־לּוֹ אָדָם אֱלֹהִים וְהֵמָּה לֹא אֱלֹהִים: לָכֵן הִנְנִי
מוֹדִיעָם בַּפַּעַם הַזֹּאת אוֹדִיעֵם אֶת־יָדִי וְאֶת־גְּבוּרָתִי וְיָדְעוּ
יז א כִּי־שְׁמִי יְהוָה: חַטַּאת יְהוּדָה כְּתוּבָה בְּעֵט בַּרְזֶל
בְּצִפֹּרֶן שָׁמִיר חֲרוּשָׁה עַל־לוּחַ לִבָּם וּלְקַרְנוֹת מִזְבְּחוֹתֵיכֶם:
ב כִּזְכֹּר בְּנֵיהֶם מִזְבְּחוֹתָם וַאֲשֵׁרֵיהֶם עַל־עֵץ רַעֲנָן עַל גְּבָעוֹת
ג הַגְּבֹהוֹת: הֲרָרִי בַּשָּׂדֶה חֵילְךָ כָל־אוֹצְרוֹתֶיךָ לָבַז אֶתֵּן בָּמֹתֶיךָ
ד בְּחַטָּאת בְּכָל־גְּבוּלֶיךָ: וְשָׁמַטְתָּה וּבְךָ מִנַּחֲלָתְךָ אֲשֶׁר נָתַתִּי
לָךְ וְהַעֲבַדְתִּיךָ אֶת־אֹיְבֶיךָ בָּאָרֶץ אֲשֶׁר לֹא־יָדָעְתָּ כִּי־אֵשׁ
ה קְדַחְתֶּם בְּאַפִּי עַד־עוֹלָם תּוּקָד: כֹּה | אָמַר יְהוָה
אָרוּר הַגֶּבֶר אֲשֶׁר יִבְטַח בָּאָדָם וְשָׂם בָּשָׂר זְרֹעוֹ וּמִן־יְהוָה
ו יָסוּר לִבּוֹ: וְהָיָה כְּעַרְעָר בָּעֲרָבָה וְלֹא יִרְאֶה כִּי־יָבוֹא טוֹב
ז וְשָׁכַן חֲרֵרִים בַּמִּדְבָּר אֶרֶץ מְלֵחָה וְלֹא תֵשֵׁב: בָּרוּךְ
ח הַגֶּבֶר אֲשֶׁר יִבְטַח בַּיהוָה וְהָיָה יְהוָה מִבְטַחוֹ: וְהָיָה כְּעֵץ |
שָׁתוּל עַל־מַיִם וְעַל־יוּבַל יְשַׁלַּח שָׁרָשָׁיו וְלֹא יִרְאֶ כִּי־יָבֹא

Yemenites

Yirmeyahu prophesied during the final forty years of the kingdom of Yehuda. It seems that the prophecy in this *haftara* was delivered during the reign of King Yoshiyahu. Yoshiyahu worked hard to correct the many evils that were present in the kingdom when he inherited it, and he was helped in this work by Yirmeyahu. The pair saw two options laid out before them: the nation could mend its ways, or idolatry could triumph, bringing destruction and exile on the people of Israel. Because Yirmeyahu aided Yoshiyahu in pressuring the people to repent, he met concerted resistance from those

the stream. It need not be concerned when heat comes, for its
leaves will remain verdant. It need not worry in a year of drought,
9 for it will never cease to produce fruit. More devious is the heart
10 than all else, and it is hopelessly sick. Who can know it? I, the
LORD, search out the heart and examine inner thoughts so as to
treat each person according to his ways, according to the fruits of
11 his actions. Like the bird that hatches what she did not
lay, so is he who accumulated his wealth unjustly. After half of his
days, his fortune will leave him, and in the end he will be proven
12 a fool. Like the throne of glory, elevated from the beginning, so
13 is the place of our Temple. The hope of Israel is the LORD. All
who forsake You will be humiliated. Those who stray from Me
will be written in the earth, for they have forsaken the source of
14 living waters, declares the LORD. Heal me, LORD, so
that I may be healed. Save me so that I may be saved, for it is You
whom I praise.

HAFTARAT BEḤUKOTAI

When Behar and Beḥukotai are read together, read this haftara.

JEREMIAH
For Ashkenazim and Sepharadim

16 19 The LORD is my strength and my might, my refuge in a day
of trouble. To You the nations will come from the ends of the
earth, and they will say: "Our ancestors inherited nothing but
20 falsehood, futility, and things of no use. Can a human make gods
21 for himself when they are not gods?" Therefore, I am about to
make them know; this time I will make them know of My power
and My strength, and they shall come to know that My name
17 1 is the LORD. Yehuda's sin is written with an iron pen
with a diamond point, engraved upon the tablets of their hearts
2 and upon the corners of your altars. As they yearn for their children, so do they for their altars and their sacred trees beside ver-
3 dant trees upon the high hills. Mountain dweller – because of
the sin of your high places in all your territories, I will turn your

idolatry could triumph, bringing destruction and exile on the people of Israel. Because Yirmeyahu aided Yoshiyahu in pressuring the people to repent, he met concerted resistance from those who favored the status quo. His relationship with God gave him strength to overcome the hostility directed at him by the people.

חֹם וְהָיָה עָלֵהוּ רַעֲנָן וּבִשְׁנַת בַּצֹּרֶת לֹא יִדְאָג וְלֹא יָמִישׁ
ט י מֵעֲשׂוֹת פֶּרִי: עָקֹב הַלֵּב מִכֹּל וְאָנֻשׁ הוּא מִי יֵדָעֶנּוּ: אֲנִי
יהוה חֹקֵר לֵב בֹּחֵן כְּלָיוֹת וְלָתֵת לְאִישׁ כִּדְרָכָו כִּפְרִי
יא מַעֲלָלָיו: קֹרֵא דָגַר וְלֹא יָלָד עֹשֶׂה עֹשֶׁר וְלֹא
יב בְמִשְׁפָּט בַּחֲצִי יָמָו יַעַזְבֶנּוּ וּבְאַחֲרִיתוֹ יִהְיֶה נָבָל: כִּסֵּא
יג כָבוֹד מָרוֹם מֵרִאשׁוֹן מְקוֹם מִקְדָּשֵׁנוּ: מִקְוֵה יִשְׂרָאֵל יהוה
כָּל־עֹזְבֶיךָ יֵבֹשׁוּ יסורי בָּאָרֶץ יִכָּתֵבוּ כִּי עָזְבוּ מְקוֹר מַיִם־ וְסוּרַי
יד חַיִּים אֶת־יהוה: רְפָאֵנִי יהוה וְאֵרָפֵא הוֹשִׁיעֵנִי
וְאִוָּשֵׁעָה כִּי תְהִלָּתִי אָתָּה:

הפטרת בחקתי

When בהר *and* בחקתי *are read together, read this* הפטרה.

ירמיה
For Ashkenazim and Sepharadim

טז יט יהוה עֻזִּי וּמָעֻזִּי וּמְנוּסִי בְּיוֹם צָרָה אֵלֶיךָ גּוֹיִם יָבֹאוּ מֵאַפְסֵי־
אֶרֶץ וְיֹאמְרוּ אַךְ־שֶׁקֶר נָחֲלוּ אֲבוֹתֵינוּ הֶבֶל וְאֵין־בָּם מוֹעִיל:
כ כא הֲיַעֲשֶׂה־לּוֹ אָדָם אֱלֹהִים וְהֵמָּה לֹא אֱלֹהִים: לָכֵן הִנְנִי
מוֹדִיעָם בַּפַּעַם הַזֹּאת אוֹדִיעֵם אֶת־יָדִי וְאֶת־גְּבוּרָתִי וְיָדְעוּ
יז א כִּי־שְׁמִי יהוה: חַטַּאת יְהוּדָה כְּתוּבָה
בְּעֵט בַּרְזֶל בְּצִפֹּרֶן שָׁמִיר חֲרוּשָׁה עַל־לוּחַ לִבָּם וּלְקַרְנוֹת
ב מִזְבְּחוֹתֵיכֶם: כִּזְכֹּר בְּנֵיהֶם מִזְבְּחוֹתָם וַאֲשֵׁרֵיהֶם עַל־עֵץ
ג רַעֲנָן עַל גְּבָעוֹת הַגְּבֹהוֹת: הֲרָרִי בַּשָּׂדֶה חֵילְךָ כָל־אוֹצְרוֹתֶיךָ

BEḤUKOTAI

Ashkenazim and Sepharadim

Yirmeyahu prophesied during the final forty years of the kingdom of Yehuda. It seems that the prophecy in this *haftara* was delivered during the reign of King Yoshiyahu. Yoshiyahu worked hard to correct the many evils that were present in the kingdom when he inherited it, and he was helped in this work by Yirmeyahu. The pair saw two options laid out before them: the nation could mend its ways, or

4 wealth and all your treasures into booty upon the field. You will
forfeit, by your own fault, the heritage which I have given you. I
will make you a slave to your enemies in a land that you never
knew, for you kindled a fire in My nostrils which shall blaze
5 forever. This is what the LORD said: Cursed is he who
trusts in man, who makes flesh his strength and who turns his
6 heart away from the LORD. He will be like a shrub in the desert,
never witnessing prosperity. He will dwell scorched in the wil-
7 derness, a salty, uninhabited land. Blessed is the person
8 who trusts in the LORD. The LORD will be his protector. He will
be like a tree planted beside the water, its roots spreading along
the stream. It need not be concerned when heat comes, for its
leaves will remain verdant. It need not worry in a year of drought,
9 for it will never cease to produce fruit. More devious is the heart
10 than all else, and it is hopelessly sick. Who can know it? I, the
LORD, search out the heart and examine inner thoughts so as to
treat each person according to his ways, according to the fruits of
11 his actions. Like the bird that hatches what she did not
lay, so is he who accumulated his wealth unjustly. After half of his
days, his fortune will leave him, and in the end he will be proven
12 a fool. Like the throne of glory, elevated from the beginning, so
13 is the place of our Temple. The hope of Israel is the LORD. All
who forsake You will be humiliated. Those who stray from Me
will be written in the earth, for they have forsaken the source of
14 living waters, declares the LORD. Heal me, LORD, so
that I may be healed. Save me so that I may be saved, for it is You
whom I praise.

EZEKIEL
For Yemenites

34 1 The word of the LORD came to me: "Man, prophesy against
2 the shepherds of Israel; prophesy and say to them, to the shepherds: So says the Lord GOD: Woe, shepherds of Israel who

Yemenites

After news of the destruction of Jerusalem and the Temple reaches the exiles in Babylon, in the twelfth year after the exile of Yehoyakhin, Yeḥezkel begins to issue prophecies of comfort and reassurance. The exiles present in Babylon are joined by more refugees fleeing the final destruction of the kingdom of Yehuda. Everyone begins to look toward the future – the return to Zion several decades in the future. To correct the Jews' situation means correcting the mistakes of the past. And one of the most

ד לְבַז אֶתֵּן בָּמֹתֶיךָ בְּחַטָּאת בְּכָל־גְּבוּלֶיךָ׃ וְשָׁמַטְתָּה
וּבְךָ מִנַּחֲלָתְךָ אֲשֶׁר נָתַתִּי לָךְ וְהַעֲבַדְתִּיךָ אֶת־אֹיְבֶיךָ
בָּאָרֶץ אֲשֶׁר לֹא־יָדָעְתָּ כִּי־אֵשׁ קְדַחְתֶּם בְּאַפִּי עַד־עוֹלָם
ה תּוּקָד׃ כֹּה ׀ אָמַר יהוה אָרוּר הַגֶּבֶר אֲשֶׁר יִבְטַח
ו בָּאָדָם וְשָׂם בָּשָׂר זְרֹעוֹ וּמִן־יהוה יָסוּר לִבּוֹ׃ וְהָיָה כְּעַרְעָר
בָּעֲרָבָה וְלֹא יִרְאֶה כִּי־יָבוֹא טוֹב וְשָׁכַן חֲרֵרִים בַּמִּדְבָּר
ז אֶרֶץ מְלֵחָה וְלֹא תֵשֵׁב׃ בָּרוּךְ הַגֶּבֶר אֲשֶׁר יִבְטַח
ח בַּיהוה וְהָיָה יהוה מִבְטַחוֹ׃ וְהָיָה כְּעֵץ ׀ שָׁתוּל עַל־מַיִם וְעַל־
יוּבַל יְשַׁלַּח שָׁרָשָׁיו וְלֹא ירא כִּי־יָבֹא חֹם וְהָיָה עָלֵהוּ רַעֲנָן
ט וּבִשְׁנַת בַּצֹּרֶת לֹא יִדְאָג וְלֹא יָמִישׁ מֵעֲשׂוֹת פֶּרִי׃ עָקֹב הַלֵּב
י מִכֹּל וְאָנֻשׁ הוּא מִי יֵדָעֶנּוּ׃ אֲנִי יהוה חֹקֵר לֵב בֹּחֵן כְּלָיוֹת
יא וְלָתֵת לְאִישׁ כדרכו כִּפְרִי מַעֲלָלָיו׃ קֹרֵא דָגַר וְלֹא
יָלָד עֹשֶׂה עֹשֶׁר וְלֹא בְמִשְׁפָּט בַּחֲצִי יָמָו יַעַזְבֶנּוּ וּבְאַחֲרִיתוֹ
יב יִהְיֶה נָבָל׃ כִּסֵּא כָבוֹד מָרוֹם מֵרִאשׁוֹן מְקוֹם מִקְדָּשֵׁנוּ׃
יג מִקְוֵה יִשְׂרָאֵל יהוה כָּל־עֹזְבֶיךָ יֵבֹשׁוּ יסורי בָּאָרֶץ יִכָּתֵבוּ וְסוּרַי
יד כִּי עָזְבוּ מְקוֹר מַיִם־חַיִּים אֶת־יהוה׃ רְפָאֵנִי יהוה
וְאֵרָפֵא הוֹשִׁיעֵנִי וְאִוָּשֵׁעָה כִּי תְהִלָּתִי אָתָּה׃

יחזקאל
For Yemenites

לד א ב וַיְהִי דְבַר־יהוה אֵלַי לֵאמֹר׃ בֶּן־אָדָם הִנָּבֵא עַל־רוֹעֵי
יִשְׂרָאֵל הִנָּבֵא וְאָמַרְתָּ אֲלֵיהֶם לָרֹעִים כֹּה־אָמַר ׀ אֲדֹנָי יֱהֹוִה

The word "land" (*eretz*) appears in this *haftara* with four different senses. It means the whole earth, a specific country, the ground from which plants grow, and a low place that is trodden on. To summarize the *haftara*: The people of Israel are located in the "land" of Israel. All the peoples of the "land" (i.e., of the earth) are supposed to learn from us the proper and pious way to behave. If Israel does not set a proper example, the "land" will become barren, the people will go into exile, and its honor will be brought down to the "land" (i.e., to the ground).

▶

have been tending themselves when surely it is the sheep the
3 shepherds should tend. You ate the fat, you wore the wool, and
4 you slaughtered the fattest, but you did not tend the sheep: you
did not strengthen the weak, you did not nurse the sick, you did
not bind the broken, you did not recover the stray, and you did
not search for the lost; you ruled over them with force and with
5 harshness. They scattered, for they had no shepherd; they be-
6 came food for every animal of the field and scattered. My sheep
are wandering upon all the mountains, all the high hills; My
sheep have scattered over the face of the earth; no one searches
7 for them; no one seeks them out. So, shepherds, listen to the
8 word of the LORD: Surely as I live, declares the Lord GOD, because My sheep were spoils, My sheep became the food of every animal of the field for want of a shepherd, and because My
shepherds did not search for My sheep but tended themselves
9 and did not tend My sheep, so, shepherds, listen to the word of
10 the LORD: So says the Lord GOD: Behold, I am coming down upon the shepherds; I will seek redress for My sheep
from their hands and put an end to their shepherding; no more
will the shepherds tend themselves; I will save My sheep from
11 their mouths; it will not be their food. For so says the
Lord GOD: Behold, it is I; I will search for My sheep and care
12 for them; just as a shepherd cares for his flock when he is among
his sheep who have dispersed, so will I care for My sheep. I will
save them from all the places they have been scattered on a day
13 of heavy cloud, thick fog. I will take them out from the nations;
I will gather them in from the lands and bring them to their soil.
I will tend them on the mountains of Israel, in the ravines, in all
14 the settled parts of the land. I will tend them on good grazing-
land; the high hills of Israel will be their pasture; there will they
lie down on lush pasture; they will graze on rich grazing-land in
15 the hills of Israel. I Myself will tend My sheep: I will lay them
16 down, declares the Lord GOD; I will seek the lost, I will recover
the stray, I will bind the broken, I will strengthen the sick, but the
robust, the strong, I will destroy; I will tend them with justice.

exploiting the resources and funds of the kingdom for their own personal gain. Here, the prophet describes two types of government: that of the past saw only itself and its own good as its goals; that of the future sees its aim as promoting the good of the people. Making this shift is the root of redemption.

הוֹי רֹעֵי יִשְׂרָאֵל אֲשֶׁר הָיוּ רֹעִים אוֹתָם הֲלוֹא הַצֹּאן יִרְעוּ
ג הָרֹעִים׃ אֶת־הַחֵלֶב תֹּאכֵלוּ וְאֶת־הַצֶּמֶר תִּלְבָּשׁוּ הַבְּרִיאָה
ד תִּזְבָּחוּ הַצֹּאן לֹא תִרְעוּ׃ אֶת־הַנַּחְלוֹת לֹא חִזַּקְתֶּם וְאֶת־
הַחוֹלָה לֹא־רִפֵּאתֶם וְלַנִּשְׁבֶּרֶת לֹא חֲבַשְׁתֶּם וְאֶת־הַנִּדַּחַת
לֹא הֲשֵׁבֹתֶם וְאֶת־הָאֹבֶדֶת לֹא בִקַּשְׁתֶּם וּבְחָזְקָה רְדִיתֶם
ה אֹתָם וּבְפָרֶךְ׃ וַתְּפוּצֶינָה מִבְּלִי רֹעֶה וַתִּהְיֶינָה לְאָכְלָה לְכָל־
ו חַיַּת הַשָּׂדֶה וַתְּפוּצֶינָה׃ יִשְׁגּוּ צֹאנִי בְּכָל־הֶהָרִים וְעַל כָּל־
גִּבְעָה רָמָה וְעַל כָּל־פְּנֵי הָאָרֶץ נָפֹצוּ צֹאנִי וְאֵין דּוֹרֵשׁ וְאֵין
ז ח מְבַקֵּשׁ׃ לָכֵן רֹעִים שִׁמְעוּ אֶת־דְּבַר יהוה׃ חַי־אָנִי נְאֻם | אֲדֹנָי
יֱהֹוִה אִם־לֹא יַעַן הֱיוֹת־צֹאנִי | לָבַז וַתִּהְיֶינָה צֹאנִי לְאָכְלָה
לְכָל־חַיַּת הַשָּׂדֶה מֵאֵין רֹעֶה וְלֹא־דָרְשׁוּ רֹעַי אֶת־צֹאנִי
ט וַיִּרְעוּ הָרֹעִים אוֹתָם וְאֶת־צֹאנִי לֹא רָעוּ׃ לָכֵן הָרֹעִים שִׁמְעוּ
י דְּבַר־יהוה׃ כֹּה־אָמַר אֲדֹנָי יֱהֹוִה הִנְנִי אֶל־הָרֹעִים
וְדָרַשְׁתִּי אֶת־צֹאנִי מִיָּדָם וְהִשְׁבַּתִּים מֵרְעוֹת צֹאן וְלֹא־
יִרְעוּ עוֹד הָרֹעִים אוֹתָם וְהִצַּלְתִּי צֹאנִי מִפִּיהֶם וְלֹא־תִהְיֶיןָ
יא לָהֶם לְאָכְלָה׃ כִּי כֹּה אָמַר אֲדֹנָי יֱהֹוִה הִנְנִי־אָנִי
יב וְדָרַשְׁתִּי אֶת־צֹאנִי וּבִקַּרְתִּים׃ כְּבַקָּרַת רֹעֶה עֶדְרוֹ בְּיוֹם־
הֱיוֹתוֹ בְתוֹךְ־צֹאנוֹ נִפְרָשׁוֹת כֵּן אֲבַקֵּר אֶת־צֹאנִי וְהִצַּלְתִּי
אֶתְהֶם מִכָּל־הַמְּקוֹמֹת אֲשֶׁר נָפֹצוּ שָׁם בְּיוֹם עָנָן וַעֲרָפֶל׃
יג וְהוֹצֵאתִים מִן־הָעַמִּים וְקִבַּצְתִּים מִן־הָאֲרָצוֹת וַהֲבִיאוֹתִים
אֶל־אַדְמָתָם וּרְעִיתִים אֶל־הָרֵי יִשְׂרָאֵל בָּאֲפִיקִים וּבְכֹל
יד מוֹשְׁבֵי הָאָרֶץ׃ בְּמִרְעֶה־טּוֹב אֶרְעֶה אֹתָם וּבְהָרֵי מְרוֹם־
יִשְׂרָאֵל יִהְיֶה נְוֵהֶם שָׁם תִּרְבַּצְנָה בְּנָוֶה טּוֹב וּמִרְעֶה שָׁמֵן
טו תִּרְעֶינָה אֶל־הָרֵי יִשְׂרָאֵל׃ אֲנִי אֶרְעֶה צֹאנִי וַאֲנִי אַרְבִּיצֵם
טז נְאֻם אֲדֹנָי יֱהֹוִה׃ אֶת־הָאֹבֶדֶת אֲבַקֵּשׁ וְאֶת־הַנִּדַּחַת אָשִׁיב
וְלַנִּשְׁבֶּרֶת אֲחַבֹּשׁ וְאֶת־הַחוֹלָה אֲחַזֵּק וְאֶת־הַשְּׁמֵנָה וְאֶת־

---

serious of the past problems that must be correct is corrupt leadership. The kings of Yehuda and Israel had oppressed the people rather than helping them,

17 As for you, My sheep, so says the Lord GOD: Behold that I will
18 judge between one sheep and another, rams and he-goats. Is it
not enough for you to graze on good grazing-land; must your
feet trample the rest of your grazing-land? And when you drink
19 clear waters, must you muddy the rest with your feet? My sheep
graze on what has been trampled by your feet and drink from
20 what has been muddied by your feet. So the Lord GOD
says this to them: Behold, it is I – I will judge between the fat
21 sheep and the thin sheep. Because you pushed with flank and
shoulder and rammed all the weak with your horns until you scat-
22 tered them, I will save My sheep; they will no longer be spoils;
23 I will judge between one sheep and another. I will establish
over them one single shepherd who will tend them; My servant,
24 David, he will tend them; he will be a shepherd to them; I, the
LORD, will be their God, and My servant David will be prince
25 among them; I, the LORD, have spoken. I will make a covenant
of peace with them, I will rid the land of wild animals, and even
26 in the wilderness they will live securely and sleep in the forests. I
will make them and all around My hill a blessing; I will make rain
27 fall at its right time – they will be blessed rains; the trees of the
field will bear their fruit, and the land will yield its produce. They
will be secure upon their soil, and they will know that I am the
LORD when I break the bars of their yoke and save them from
those who enslave them.

HAFTARAT BEMIDBAR

On Erev Rosh Ḥodesh Sivan read the haftara on page 1644.

2 1 Yet the children of Israel will number like the sands of the sea, not HOSEA
measurable or countable, and rather than being told, "You are
Not My People," they will be told, "You are the sons of the living

terms of the connection between a husband and wife. At first, the couple is in love, and they lead a charmed existence together. After a time, however, the wife betrays the husband – her adulterous affairs symbolize the Israelites' dalliance with foreign nations and gods. This betrayal leads ultimately to disaster, and

יז הַחֲזָקָה אַשְׁמִיד אֶרְעֶנָּה בְמִשְׁפָּט: וְאַתֵּנָה צֹאנִי כֹּה אָמַר
אֲדֹנָי יֱהֹוִה הִנְנִי שֹׁפֵט בֵּין־שֶׂה לָשֶׂה לָאֵילִים וְלָעַתּוּדִים:
יח הַמְעַט מִכֶּם הַמִּרְעֶה הַטּוֹב תִּרְעוּ וְיֶתֶר מִרְעֵיכֶם תִּרְמְסוּ
בְּרַגְלֵיכֶם וּמִשְׁקַע־מַיִם תִּשְׁתּוּ וְאֵת הַנּוֹתָרִים בְּרַגְלֵיכֶם
יט תִּרְפֹּשׂוּן: וְצֹאנִי מִרְמַס רַגְלֵיכֶם תִּרְעֶינָה וּמִרְפַּשׂ רַגְלֵיכֶם
כ תִּשְׁתֶּינָה: לָכֵן כֹּה אָמַר אֲדֹנָי יֱהֹוִה אֲלֵיהֶם הִנְנִי־
כא אָנִי וְשָׁפַטְתִּי בֵּין־שֶׂה בִרְיָה וּבֵין שֶׂה רָזָה: יַעַן בְּצַד וּבְכָתֵף
תֶּהְדֹּפוּ וּבְקַרְנֵיכֶם תְּנַגְּחוּ כָּל־הַנַּחְלוֹת עַד אֲשֶׁר הֲפִיצוֹתֶם
כב אוֹתָנָה אֶל־הַחוּצָה: וְהוֹשַׁעְתִּי לְצֹאנִי וְלֹא־תִהְיֶינָה עוֹד
כג לָבַז וְשָׁפַטְתִּי בֵּין שֶׂה לָשֶׂה: וַהֲקִמֹתִי עֲלֵיהֶם רֹעֶה אֶחָד
וְרָעָה אֶתְהֶן אֵת עַבְדִּי דָוִיד הוּא יִרְעֶה אֹתָם וְהוּא יִהְיֶה
כד לָהֶן לְרֹעֶה: וַאֲנִי יְהוָה אֶהְיֶה לָהֶם לֵאלֹהִים וְעַבְדִּי דָוִד
כה נָשִׂיא בְתוֹכָם אֲנִי יְהוָה דִּבַּרְתִּי: וְכָרַתִּי לָהֶם בְּרִית שָׁלוֹם
וְהִשְׁבַּתִּי חַיָּה־רָעָה מִן־הָאָרֶץ וְיָשְׁבוּ בַמִּדְבָּר לָבֶטַח וְיָשְׁנוּ
כו ביעורים: וְנָתַתִּי אוֹתָם וּסְבִיבוֹת גִּבְעָתִי בְּרָכָה וְהוֹרַדְתִּי בַּיְּעָרִים
כז הַגֶּשֶׁם בְּעִתּוֹ גִּשְׁמֵי בְרָכָה יִהְיוּ: וְנָתַן עֵץ הַשָּׂדֶה אֶת־פִּרְיוֹ
וְהָאָרֶץ תִּתֵּן יְבוּלָהּ וְהָיוּ עַל־אַדְמָתָם לָבֶטַח וְיָדְעוּ כִּי־
אֲנִי יְהוָה בְּשִׁבְרִי אֶת־מֹטוֹת עֻלָּם וְהִצַּלְתִּים מִיַּד הָעֹבְדִים
בָּהֶם:

הפטרת במדבר

On ערב ראש חודש סיוון *read the* הפטרה *on page 1645.*

ב א וְהָיָה מִסְפַּר בְּנֵי־יִשְׂרָאֵל כְּחוֹל הַיָּם אֲשֶׁר לֹא־יִמַּד וְלֹא יִסָּפֵר הושע
וְהָיָה בִּמְקוֹם אֲשֶׁר־יֵאָמֵר לָהֶם לֹא־עַמִּי אַתֶּם יֵאָמֵר לָהֶם

BEMIDBAR

The prophet Hoshea was active from the height of the reign of Yorovam son of Yoash king of Israel until the destruction of the northern kingdom during the reign of Hoshea son of Ela.

The relationship between God and Israel is described in this *haftara* in

2 God." Then the children of Yehuda and the children of Israel will
gather together; they will designate one leader and escape from
3 the land, for the day of Yizre'el will be a great one. Say then to
4 your brothers "People," and to your sisters "Loved." Berate your
mother, for she is not my wife, nor I her husband. Let her remove
her prostitute's rouge from her face, her adulterous acts from be-
5 tween her breasts, lest I strip her naked as the day she was born
and make her as a desert wilderness. I will make her into parched
6 wasteland and let her die from thirst. As for her sons, I will have
7 no mercy, for they are the sons of a harlot, for their mother has
whored; she has conceived them in shame. She said, "I will follow after my lovers; it is they who give me bread and water, keep
8 me in wools and linens, lotions and wines," so I will obstruct her
path with prickly shrubs; I will fence her in with walls; her way
9 will be lost to her. She will pursue her lovers but not catch them;
she will search them out but never find them. Then she will say,
"I will go and return to my first husband, for I fared better then
10 than now." But she did not care to know that it was I who fur-
nished her with grain, wine, and oil, I who lavished silver upon
11 her and gold which they used for Baal. Hence I will take back My
grain as it ripens in its season, My wine as it ages; I will seize My
12 wools and My linens meant to cover her nakedness. And now I
will expose her indecency for her lovers to see, and there will be
13 no one to rescue her from My hand. I will put an end to all her
joyous occasions – her holidays, her New Moons, her Sabbaths,
14 and all her festive seasons. I will ravage her vines and fig trees, of
which she once said, "These are my harlot's favors, given to me
by my lovers." I will make them into abandoned woodlands, and
15 wild animals will feed on them. I will revisit upon her the days of
the Be'alim, for whom she burned incense and adorned herself
with earrings and jewels, how she followed after her lovers and
16 forgot Me. So declares the Lord. Behold, now I will
coax her, I will lead her back to the open desert, and I will speak
17 to her heart. Then and there I will give her vineyards to her, and
the Valley of the Scourge will be a doorway to hope; she will return to Me in song as in the first days of her youth, as on the day

---

them in their moment of need. Despite all this, God allows His wife to return to Him, renews His covenant with her, and restores her fortunes as of old.

ב בְּנֵי אֵל־חָי: וְנִקְבְּצוּ בְּנֵי־יְהוּדָה וּבְנֵי־יִשְׂרָאֵל יַחְדָּו וְשָׂמוּ
לָהֶם רֹאשׁ אֶחָד וְעָלוּ מִן־הָאָרֶץ כִּי גָדוֹל יוֹם יִזְרְעֶאל:
ג ד אִמְרוּ לַאֲחֵיכֶם עַמִּי וְלַאֲחוֹתֵיכֶם רֻחָמָה: רִיבוּ בְאִמְּכֶם רִיבוּ
כִּי־הִיא לֹא אִשְׁתִּי וְאָנֹכִי לֹא אִישָׁהּ וְתָסֵר זְנוּנֶיהָ מִפָּנֶיהָ
ה וְנַאֲפוּפֶיהָ מִבֵּין שָׁדֶיהָ: פֶּן־אַפְשִׁיטֶנָּה עֲרֻמָּה וְהִצַּגְתִּיהָ כְּיוֹם
הִוָּלְדָהּ וְשַׂמְתִּיהָ כַמִּדְבָּר וְשַׁתִּהָ כְּאֶרֶץ צִיָּה וַהֲמִתִּיהָ בַּצָּמָא:
ו ז וְאֶת־בָּנֶיהָ לֹא אֲרַחֵם כִּי־בְנֵי זְנוּנִים הֵמָּה: כִּי זָנְתָה אִמָּם
הֹבִישָׁה הוֹרָתָם כִּי אָמְרָה אֵלְכָה אַחֲרֵי מְאַהֲבַי נֹתְנֵי
ח לַחְמִי וּמֵימַי צַמְרִי וּפִשְׁתִּי שַׁמְנִי וְשִׁקּוּיָי: לָכֵן הִנְנִי־שָׂךְ
אֶת־דַּרְכֵּךְ בַּסִּירִים וְגָדַרְתִּי אֶת־גְּדֵרָהּ וּנְתִיבוֹתֶיהָ לֹא
ט תִמְצָא: וְרִדְּפָה אֶת־מְאַהֲבֶיהָ וְלֹא־תַשִּׂיג אֹתָם וּבִקְשָׁתַם
וְלֹא תִמְצָא וְאָמְרָה אֵלְכָה וְאָשׁוּבָה אֶל־אִישִׁי הָרִאשׁוֹן
י כִּי טוֹב לִי אָז מֵעָתָּה: וְהִיא לֹא יָדְעָה כִּי אָנֹכִי נָתַתִּי לָהּ
הַדָּגָן וְהַתִּירוֹשׁ וְהַיִּצְהָר וְכֶסֶף הִרְבֵּיתִי לָהּ וְזָהָב עָשׂוּ
יא לַבָּעַל: לָכֵן אָשׁוּב וְלָקַחְתִּי דְגָנִי בְּעִתּוֹ וְתִירוֹשִׁי בְּמוֹעֲדוֹ
יב וְהִצַּלְתִּי צַמְרִי וּפִשְׁתִּי לְכַסּוֹת אֶת־עֶרְוָתָהּ: וְעַתָּה אֲגַלֶּה
אֶת־נַבְלֻתָהּ לְעֵינֵי מְאַהֲבֶיהָ וְאִישׁ לֹא־יַצִּילֶנָּה מִיָּדִי:
יג וְהִשְׁבַּתִּי כָּל־מְשׂוֹשָׂהּ חַגָּהּ חָדְשָׁהּ וְשַׁבַּתָּהּ וְכֹל מוֹעֲדָהּ:
יד וַהֲשִׁמֹּתִי גַּפְנָהּ וּתְאֵנָתָהּ אֲשֶׁר אָמְרָה אֶתְנָה הֵמָּה לִי אֲשֶׁר
נָתְנוּ־לִי מְאַהֲבָי וְשַׂמְתִּים לְיַעַר וַאֲכָלָתַם חַיַּת הַשָּׂדֶה:
טו וּפָקַדְתִּי עָלֶיהָ אֶת־יְמֵי הַבְּעָלִים אֲשֶׁר תַּקְטִיר לָהֶם וַתַּעַד
נִזְמָהּ וְחֶלְיָתָהּ וַתֵּלֶךְ אַחֲרֵי מְאַהֲבֶיהָ וְאֹתִי שָׁכְחָה נְאֻם־
טז יְהוָה: לָכֵן הִנֵּה אָנֹכִי מְפַתֶּיהָ וְהֹלַכְתִּיהָ הַמִּדְבָּר
יז וְדִבַּרְתִּי עַל־לִבָּהּ: וְנָתַתִּי לָהּ אֶת־כְּרָמֶיהָ מִשָּׁם וְאֶת־עֵמֶק
עָכוֹר לְפֶתַח תִּקְוָה וְעָנְתָה שָּׁמָּה כִּימֵי נְעוּרֶיהָ וּכְיוֹם עֲלֹתָהּ

---

all the wife's erstwhile lovers are revealed in fact to hate her, not lifting a finger to help her in her time of trouble. This was the situation of the Israelites at the time of the destruction, when all the peoples they thought to be allies turned upon

18 when she came up out of the land of Egypt. It will be
on that day, says the LORD: you will call Me "my Husband"; no
19 longer will you call Me "my Master." I will eradicate the names
of the Be'alim from her mouth; no more will they be mentioned
20 by name. On that day I will make a covenant with them: with
the beasts of the fields, and the birds of heaven, and the crawling
creatures of the ground. I will break the bow and the sword; I
21 will crush conflict out from the land, and you will rest in safety. I
will betroth you to Me forever; I will betroth you to Me in righ-
22 teousness and justice, in kindness and compassion. I will betroth
you to Me in faithfulness, and you will know the LORD.

HAFTARAT NASO

13 2 There was a man of Tzora whose name was Manoaḥ, from the JUDGES
family of Dan. His wife was barren and had never given birth.
3 An angel of the LORD appeared to the woman and said to her:
"Look! Though you have been barren and have never given birth,
4 you shall conceive and bear a son. Take care: drink neither wine
5 nor strong drink, and eat nothing unclean. For indeed, you shall
be with child; you shall bear a son. Let no razor touch his head,
for the boy shall be a nazirite to God from the womb. He will
6 begin to save Israel from the hands of the Philistines." The woman went and told her husband, "A man of God came to me; he
looked like an angel of God – dazzling, awe-inspiring. I did not
7 ask him where he was from, and he did not tell me his name. He
said to me, 'You shall be with child, and you shall bear a son;
drink neither wine nor strong drink and eat nothing unclean, for

caution and deliberation. Therefore, even before Shimshon was born, when he was in his mother's womb, she was commanded to take on the ascetic restrictions of a nazirite. Shimshon himself would grow up as a nazirite and would be subject to the restrictions of that status all his life, in order to constantly be reminded of the source and purpose of his great strength. When his long hair, the symbol of his dedication, is removed, his strength will also dissipate. A nazirite, therefore, is one who takes concrete steps to dedicate his or her powers to a higher purpose.

יח מֵאֶרֶץ־מִצְרָיִם: וְהָיָה בַיּוֹם־הַהוּא נְאֻם־יְהוָה
יט תִּקְרְאִי אִישִׁי וְלֹא־תִקְרְאִי־לִי עוֹד בַּעְלִי: וַהֲסִרֹתִי אֶת־
כ שְׁמוֹת הַבְּעָלִים מִפִּיהָ וְלֹא־יִזָּכְרוּ עוֹד בִּשְׁמָם: וְכָרַתִּי
לָהֶם בְּרִית בַּיּוֹם הַהוּא עִם־חַיַּת הַשָּׂדֶה וְעִם־עוֹף הַשָּׁמַיִם
וְרֶמֶשׂ הָאֲדָמָה וְקֶשֶׁת וְחֶרֶב וּמִלְחָמָה אֶשְׁבּוֹר מִן־הָאָרֶץ
כא וְהִשְׁכַּבְתִּים לָבֶטַח: וְאֵרַשְׂתִּיךְ לִי לְעוֹלָם וְאֵרַשְׂתִּיךְ לִי
כב בְּצֶדֶק וּבְמִשְׁפָּט וּבְחֶסֶד וּבְרַחֲמִים: וְאֵרַשְׂתִּיךְ לִי בֶּאֱמוּנָה
וְיָדַעַתְּ אֶת־יְהוָה:

הפטרת נשא

יג ב וַיְהִי אִישׁ אֶחָד מִצָּרְעָה מִמִּשְׁפַּחַת הַדָּנִי וּשְׁמוֹ מָנוֹחַ וְאִשְׁתּוֹ שופטים
ג עֲקָרָה וְלֹא יָלָדָה: וַיֵּרָא מַלְאַךְ־יְהוָה אֶל־הָאִשָּׁה וַיֹּאמֶר
אֵלֶיהָ הִנֵּה־נָא אַתְּ־עֲקָרָה וְלֹא יָלַדְתְּ וְהָרִית וְיָלַדְתְּ בֵּן:
ד וְעַתָּה הִשָּׁמְרִי נָא וְאַל־תִּשְׁתִּי יַיִן וְשֵׁכָר וְאַל־תֹּאכְלִי כָּל־
ה טָמֵא: כִּי הִנָּךְ הָרָה וְיֹלַדְתְּ בֵּן וּמוֹרָה לֹא־יַעֲלֶה עַל־רֹאשׁוֹ
כִּי־נְזִיר אֱלֹהִים יִהְיֶה הַנַּעַר מִן־הַבָּטֶן וְהוּא יָחֵל לְהוֹשִׁיעַ
ו אֶת־יִשְׂרָאֵל מִיַּד פְּלִשְׁתִּים: וַתָּבֹא הָאִשָּׁה וַתֹּאמֶר לְאִישָׁהּ
לֵאמֹר אִישׁ הָאֱלֹהִים בָּא אֵלַי וּמַרְאֵהוּ כְּמַרְאֵה מַלְאַךְ
הָאֱלֹהִים נוֹרָא מְאֹד וְלֹא שְׁאִלְתִּיהוּ אֵי־מִזֶּה הוּא וְאֶת־
ז שְׁמוֹ לֹא־הִגִּיד לִי: וַיֹּאמֶר לִי הִנָּךְ הָרָה וְיֹלַדְתְּ בֵּן וְעַתָּה

NASO

This *haftara* describes the events leading up to the birth of the judge Shimshon. Shimshon's mother was barren, and at that point in time the Israelites were dominated by the Philistines. Everything changes when one day an angel appears to Shimshon's parents, heralding to them the birth of a son who will in the future save Israel from their Philistine oppressors. Shimshon will be blessed with unnatural strength that will aid him in overcoming the enemy. But one given so much power must also act with supreme

the boy will be a nazirite to the Lord from the womb until his
dying day.'"
8 Then Manoaḥ appealed to the LORD. "Please, my Lord," he
said, "let the man of God whom You sent come to us again and
9 teach us what to do with the boy who will be born." God heard
Manoaḥ's voice, and God's angel came to the woman once more.
She was sitting in the field, her husband Manoaḥ not with her.
10 The woman rushed to tell her husband. "Look!" she said to him.
11 "The man who came to visit me that day has appeared!" Manoaḥ
rose and followed his wife. When he reached the man, he said
to him, "Are you the man who spoke to this woman?" "I am," he
12 said. "Now," said Manoaḥ, "may your words come to pass. How
13 should the boy be properly dealt with?" The LORD's angel replied to Manoaḥ, "The woman must be kept from all that I said
14 to her. She must eat nothing derived from the grapevine, drink
neither wine nor strong drink, and eat nothing unclean; she
15 must follow all my instructions." Manoaḥ said to the LORD's angel, "Please let us detain you, and we will prepare a young goat
16 for you." "Even if you detain me, I will not eat your food," the
LORD's angel said to Manoaḥ, "but if you prepare a burnt offering, offer it to the LORD." For Manoaḥ did not realize that he was
17 an angel of the LORD. "What is your name," Manoaḥ asked the
LORD's angel, "so that when your words come to pass, we may
18 honor you?" "Why should you ask my name?" the LORD's angel
19 replied to him. "For it is wondrous." Manoaḥ took the young goat
and the grain offering and offered them up on the rock to the
LORD. As Manoaḥ and his wife were watching, He performed
20 wonders: as the flames flared up from the altar to the heavens,
the LORD's angel ascended in the altar's flames while Manoaḥ
and his wife were watching. They threw themselves down with
21 their faces to the ground. When the LORD's angel did not appear
again to Manoaḥ and his wife, Manoaḥ realized that he had been
22 an angel of the LORD. "We will surely die," Manoaḥ said to his
23 wife, "for it was God we saw!" "Had the LORD wanted to kill us,"
his wife said to him, "He would not have accepted burnt offerings or grain offerings from us. And He would not have shown us

אַל־תִּשְׁתִּי ׀ יַיִן וְשֵׁכָר וְאַל־תֹּאכְלִי כָּל־טֻמְאָה כִּי־נְזִיר
אֱלֹהִים יִהְיֶה הַנַּעַר מִן־הַבֶּטֶן עַד־יוֹם מוֹתוֹ׃
ח וַיֶּעְתַּר מָנוֹחַ אֶל־יְהוָה וַיֹּאמַר בִּי אֲדוֹנָי אִישׁ הָאֱלֹהִים אֲשֶׁר
שָׁלַחְתָּ יָבוֹא־נָא עוֹד אֵלֵינוּ וְיוֹרֵנוּ מַה־נַּעֲשֶׂה לַנַּעַר הַיּוּלָּד׃
ט וַיִּשְׁמַע הָאֱלֹהִים בְּקוֹל מָנוֹחַ וַיָּבֹא מַלְאַךְ הָאֱלֹהִים עוֹד
אֶל־הָאִשָּׁה וְהִיא יוֹשֶׁבֶת בַּשָּׂדֶה וּמָנוֹחַ אִישָׁהּ אֵין עִמָּהּ׃
י וַתְּמַהֵר הָאִשָּׁה וַתָּרָץ וַתַּגֵּד לְאִישָׁהּ וַתֹּאמֶר אֵלָיו הִנֵּה
יא נִרְאָה אֵלַי הָאִישׁ אֲשֶׁר־בָּא בַיּוֹם אֵלָי׃ וַיָּקָם וַיֵּלֶךְ מָנוֹחַ
אַחֲרֵי אִשְׁתּוֹ וַיָּבֹא אֶל־הָאִישׁ וַיֹּאמֶר לוֹ הַאַתָּה הָאִישׁ
יב אֲשֶׁר־דִּבַּרְתָּ אֶל־הָאִשָּׁה וַיֹּאמֶר אָנִי׃ וַיֹּאמֶר מָנוֹחַ עַתָּה
יג יָבֹא דְבָרֶיךָ מַה־יִּהְיֶה מִשְׁפַּט־הַנַּעַר וּמַעֲשֵׂהוּ׃ וַיֹּאמֶר
מַלְאַךְ יְהוָה אֶל־מָנוֹחַ מִכֹּל אֲשֶׁר־אָמַרְתִּי אֶל־הָאִשָּׁה
יד תִּשָּׁמֵר׃ מִכֹּל אֲשֶׁר־יֵצֵא מִגֶּפֶן הַיַּיִן לֹא תֹאכַל וְיַיִן וְשֵׁכָר
אַל־תֵּשְׁתְּ וְכָל־טֻמְאָה אַל־תֹּאכַל כֹּל אֲשֶׁר־צִוִּיתִיהָ תִּשְׁמֹר׃
טו וַיֹּאמֶר מָנוֹחַ אֶל־מַלְאַךְ יְהוָה נַעְצְרָה־נָּא אוֹתָךְ וְנַעֲשֶׂה
טז לְפָנֶיךָ גְּדִי עִזִּים׃ וַיֹּאמֶר מַלְאַךְ יְהוָה אֶל־מָנוֹחַ אִם־תַּעְצְרֵנִי
לֹא־אֹכַל בְּלַחְמֶךָ וְאִם־תַּעֲשֶׂה עֹלָה לַיהוָה תַּעֲלֶנָּה כִּי
יז לֹא־יָדַע מָנוֹחַ כִּי־מַלְאַךְ יְהוָה הוּא׃ וַיֹּאמֶר מָנוֹחַ אֶל־
יח מַלְאַךְ יְהוָה מִי שְׁמֶךָ כִּי־יָבֹא דבריך וְכִבַּדְנוּךָ׃ וַיֹּאמֶר דְּבָרְךָ
יט לוֹ מַלְאַךְ יְהוָה לָמָּה זֶּה תִּשְׁאַל לִשְׁמִי וְהוּא־פֶלִאי׃ וַיִּקַּח
מָנוֹחַ אֶת־גְּדִי הָעִזִּים וְאֶת־הַמִּנְחָה וַיַּעַל עַל־הַצּוּר לַיהוָה
כ וּמַפְלִא לַעֲשׂוֹת וּמָנוֹחַ וְאִשְׁתּוֹ רֹאִים׃ וַיְהִי בַעֲלוֹת הַלַּהַב
מֵעַל הַמִּזְבֵּחַ הַשָּׁמַיְמָה וַיַּעַל מַלְאַךְ־יְהוָה בְּלַהַב הַמִּזְבֵּחַ
כא וּמָנוֹחַ וְאִשְׁתּוֹ רֹאִים וַיִּפְּלוּ עַל־פְּנֵיהֶם אָרְצָה׃ וְלֹא־יָסַף
עוֹד מַלְאַךְ יְהוָה לְהֵרָאֹה אֶל־מָנוֹחַ וְאֶל־אִשְׁתּוֹ אָז יָדַע
כב מָנוֹחַ כִּי־מַלְאַךְ יְהוָה הוּא׃ וַיֹּאמֶר מָנוֹחַ אֶל־אִשְׁתּוֹ מוֹת
כג נָמוּת כִּי אֱלֹהִים רָאִינוּ׃ וַתֹּאמֶר לוֹ אִשְׁתּוֹ לוּ חָפֵץ יְהוָה
לַהֲמִיתֵנוּ לֹא־לָקַח מִיָּדֵנוּ עֹלָה וּמִנְחָה וְלֹא הֶרְאָנוּ אֶת־כָּל־

24 all that we saw or made this announcement." The woman bore a
son and named him Shimshon. The boy grew up and the LORD
25 blessed him.* The spirit of the LORD first stirred him in the Dan *Yemenites end here*
encampment between Tzora and Eshtaol.

HAFTARAT BEHAALOTEKHA

2 14 Shout out and be joyful, daughter Zion, for I am coming, and I ZECHARIAH
15 will dwell in your midst – the LORD has spoken. Many nations
will join themselves to the LORD on that day, and they will be
My people. I will dwell in your midst, and you will know that the
16 LORD of Hosts sent me to you. The LORD will take possession
of Yehuda as His portion of holy ground, and He will choose
17 Jerusalem once again. Hush, all flesh, before the LORD, for He
3 1 has stirred from His holy abode. Then He showed me
Yehoshua the High Priest standing before an angel of the LORD
2 with the Adversary on his right to oppose him. The LORD said
to the Adversary: The LORD drives you away, Adversary. The
LORD, who has chosen Jerusalem, drives you away. Yes, this is
3 a firebrand saved from the fire. And Yehoshua, wearing filthy
4 clothing, was standing before the angel, who spoke and said to
those standing before him, "Take those filthy clothes off him."
Then the angel said to him, "See, I have removed your guilt from
5 you and dressed you in finery." I said, "Place a pure turban on his
head," and they placed a pure turban on his head. They dressed
him in clothing. The angel of the LORD remained standing.
6 7 Then that angel of the LORD testified regarding Yehoshua: "So
says the LORD of Hosts: If you walk in My ways, if you keep My
watch, if you judge My House, and guard My courtyards, then

enemy nations bordering the Jews in the province of Judea. Zekharya's tireless involvement, preaching God's message, put life into the long-stymied project. The prophet described to them the many obstacles on the path to redemption, and to this end he describes his famous vision of the candelabrum. The candelabrum – the source of light – has become a quintessential Jewish symbol, and it traces the path from the Tabernacle to Shlomo's Temple, to the new structure that was to be built.

כד אֵלֶּה וְכָעֵת לֹא הִשְׁמִיעָנוּ כָּזֹאת: וַתֵּלֶד הָאִשָּׁה בֵּן וַתִּקְרָא
כה אֶת־שְׁמוֹ שִׁמְשׁוֹן וַיִּגְדַּל הַנַּעַר וַיְבָרְכֵהוּ יהוה:* וַתָּחֶל רוּחַ *Yemenites end here*
יהוה לְפַעֲמוֹ בְּמַחֲנֵה־דָן בֵּין צָרְעָה וּבֵין אֶשְׁתָּאוֹל:

הפטרת בהעלתך

ב יד רָנִּי וְשִׂמְחִי בַּת־צִיּוֹן כִּי הִנְנִי־בָא וְשָׁכַנְתִּי בְתוֹכֵךְ נְאֻם־ זכריה
טו יהוה: וְנִלְווּ גוֹיִם רַבִּים אֶל־יהוה בַּיּוֹם הַהוּא וְהָיוּ לִי לְעָם
וְשָׁכַנְתִּי בְתוֹכֵךְ וְיָדַעַתְּ כִּי־יהוה צְבָאוֹת שְׁלָחַנִי אֵלָיִךְ:
טז וְנָחַל יהוה אֶת־יְהוּדָה חֶלְקוֹ עַל אַדְמַת הַקֹּדֶשׁ וּבָחַר
יז עוֹד בִּירוּשָׁלָםִ: הַס כָּל־בָּשָׂר מִפְּנֵי יהוה כִּי נֵעוֹר מִמְּעוֹן
ג א קָדְשׁוֹ: וַיַּרְאֵנִי אֶת־יְהוֹשֻׁעַ הַכֹּהֵן הַגָּדוֹל עֹמֵד
ב לִפְנֵי מַלְאַךְ יהוה וְהַשָּׂטָן עֹמֵד עַל־יְמִינוֹ לְשִׂטְנוֹ: וַיֹּאמֶר
יהוה אֶל־הַשָּׂטָן יִגְעַר יהוה בְּךָ הַשָּׂטָן וְיִגְעַר יהוה בְּךָ
ג הַבֹּחֵר בִּירוּשָׁלָםִ הֲלוֹא זֶה אוּד מֻצָּל מֵאֵשׁ: וִיהוֹשֻׁעַ הָיָה
ד לָבֻשׁ בְּגָדִים צוֹאִים וְעֹמֵד לִפְנֵי הַמַּלְאָךְ: וַיַּעַן וַיֹּאמֶר אֶל־
הָעֹמְדִים לְפָנָיו לֵאמֹר הָסִירוּ הַבְּגָדִים הַצֹּאִים מֵעָלָיו וַיֹּאמֶר
אֵלָיו רְאֵה הֶעֱבַרְתִּי מֵעָלֶיךָ עֲוֺנֶךָ וְהַלְבֵּשׁ אֹתְךָ מַחֲלָצוֹת:
ה וָאֹמַר יָשִׂימוּ צָנִיף טָהוֹר עַל־רֹאשׁוֹ וַיָּשִׂימוּ הַצָּנִיף הַטָּהוֹר
ו עַל־רֹאשׁוֹ וַיַּלְבִּשֻׁהוּ בְּגָדִים וּמַלְאַךְ יהוה עֹמֵד: וַיָּעַד
ז מַלְאַךְ יהוה בִּיהוֹשֻׁעַ לֵאמֹר: כֹּה־אָמַר יהוה צְבָאוֹת אִם־
בִּדְרָכַי תֵּלֵךְ וְאִם אֶת־מִשְׁמַרְתִּי תִשְׁמֹר וְגַם־אַתָּה תָּדִין
אֶת־בֵּיתִי וְגַם תִּשְׁמֹר אֶת־חֲצֵרָי וְנָתַתִּי לְךָ מַהְלְכִים בֵּין

BEHAALOTEKHA

The prophet Zekharya was active in Jerusalem in the second year of the reign of Daryavesh, king of Persia. He gave strength and encouragement to the returnees to Zion after the Babylonian exile, urging them to rebuild the Temple. The construction, which was expressly authorized by the decree of the emperor Koresh, was frozen by the Persian government soon after the cornerstone had been laid, due to lobbying by the

8 I will give you walkers among these who are standing. Listen,
Yehoshua the High Priest, you and your friends who sit before
you, for they are men of wonders: Behold, I am bringing My
9 servant Tzemaḥ. Upon the stone that I set before Yehoshua,
one stone with seven eyes, I will engrave its inscription, and I
10 will wipe away the guilt of this land in one day. On that day –
the LORD of Hosts has spoken – you will call one to another:
Come under the shade of the vine; come under the shade of the
4 1 fig." Then the angel with whom I had spoken returned
2 and roused me like a man stirring from his sleep. He said to me,
"What do you see?" I said, "I see a candelabrum of pure gold, its
bowl at the top. It has seven lamps – seven – and seven indenta-
3 tions for the lamps, which are at the top. Next to it are two olive
4 trees, one to the right of the bowl and one to its left." I spoke and
said to the angel with whom I spoke, "What are these, my lord?"
5 And the angel with whom I spoke replied and said, "You know
6 what these are." I said, "No, my lord." Then he spoke and said
to me, "This is the word of the LORD to Zerubavel: Not with
valor and not with strength, but with My spirit, says the LORD
7 of Hosts. Who are you, great mountain before Zerubavel? Surely
it will become a level plain. He will remove the re-foundation
8 stone with clamor: Favor, favor to her!" *Then the *Yemenites add*
9 word of the Lord came to me: "Zerubavel's hands founded
this House, and his hands will complete it.

HAFTARAT SHELAḤ

2 1 Yehoshua son of Nun had sent two men as spies from Shitim, in JOSHUA
secret: "Go forth and survey the land and the region of Yeriḥo."
So the men had set out, arriving at the house of a harlot named

point, the nation was occupying the plains of Moav, on the eastern side of the Jordan River, opposite Yeriḥo. God's instructions to Yehoshua to prepare for crossing into the land of Israel were followed on three planes: the nation as

ח הָעֹמְדִים הָאֵלֶּה׃ שְׁמַע־נָא יְהוֹשֻׁעַ ׀ הַכֹּהֵן הַגָּדוֹל אַתָּה
וְרֵעֶיךָ הַיֹּשְׁבִים לְפָנֶיךָ כִּי־אַנְשֵׁי מוֹפֵת הֵמָּה כִּי־הִנְנִי מֵבִיא
ט אֶת־עַבְדִּי צֶמַח׃ כִּי ׀ הִנֵּה הָאֶבֶן אֲשֶׁר נָתַתִּי לִפְנֵי יְהוֹשֻׁעַ
עַל־אֶבֶן אַחַת שִׁבְעָה עֵינָיִם הִנְנִי מְפַתֵּחַ פִּתֻּחָהּ נְאֻם יְהוָה
י צְבָאוֹת וּמַשְׁתִּי אֶת־עֲוֺן הָאָרֶץ־הַהִיא בְּיוֹם אֶחָד׃ בַּיּוֹם
הַהוּא נְאֻם יְהוָה צְבָאוֹת תִּקְרְאוּ אִישׁ לְרֵעֵהוּ אֶל־תַּחַת
ד א גֶּפֶן וְאֶל־תַּחַת תְּאֵנָה׃ וַיָּשָׁב הַמַּלְאָךְ הַדֹּבֵר בִּי
ב וַיְעִירֵנִי כְּאִישׁ אֲשֶׁר־יֵעוֹר מִשְּׁנָתוֹ׃ וַיֹּאמֶר אֵלַי מָה אַתָּה
רֹאֶה ויאמר רָאִיתִי וְהִנֵּה מְנוֹרַת זָהָב כֻּלָּהּ וְגֻלָּהּ עַל־רֹאשָׁהּ וָאֹמַר
וְשִׁבְעָה נֵרֹתֶיהָ עָלֶיהָ שִׁבְעָה וְשִׁבְעָה מוּצָקוֹת לַנֵּרוֹת אֲשֶׁר
ג עַל־רֹאשָׁהּ׃ וּשְׁנַיִם זֵיתִים עָלֶיהָ אֶחָד מִימִין הַגֻּלָּה וְאֶחָד
ד עַל־שְׂמֹאלָהּ׃ וָאַעַן וָאֹמַר אֶל־הַמַּלְאָךְ הַדֹּבֵר בִּי לֵאמֹר
ה מָה־אֵלֶּה אֲדֹנִי׃ וַיַּעַן הַמַּלְאָךְ הַדֹּבֵר בִּי וַיֹּאמֶר אֵלַי הֲלוֹא
ו יָדַעְתָּ מָה־הֵמָּה אֵלֶּה וָאֹמַר לֹא אֲדֹנִי׃ וַיַּעַן וַיֹּאמֶר אֵלַי
לֵאמֹר זֶה דְּבַר־יְהוָה אֶל־זְרֻבָּבֶל לֵאמֹר לֹא בְחַיִל וְלֹא בְכֹחַ
ז כִּי אִם־בְּרוּחִי אָמַר יְהוָה צְבָאוֹת׃ מִי־אַתָּה הַר־הַגָּדוֹל לִפְנֵי
זְרֻבָּבֶל לְמִישֹׁר וְהוֹצִיא אֶת־הָאֶבֶן הָרֹאשָׁה תְּשֻׁאוֹת חֵן ׀
ח ט חֵן לָהּ׃ *וַיְהִי דְבַר־יְהוָה אֵלַי לֵאמֹר׃ יְדֵי זְרֻבָּבֶל *Yemenites add*
יִסְּדוּ הַבַּיִת הַזֶּה וְיָדָיו תְּבַצַּעְנָה וְיָדַעְתָּ כִּי־יְהוָה צְבָאוֹת
שְׁלָחַנִי אֲלֵיכֶם׃

הפטרת שלח

ב א וַיִּשְׁלַח יְהוֹשֻׁעַ בִּן־נוּן מִן־הַשִּׁטִּים שְׁנַיִם אֲנָשִׁים מְרַגְּלִים יהושע
חֶרֶשׁ לֵאמֹר לְכוּ רְאוּ אֶת־הָאָרֶץ וְאֶת־יְרִיחוֹ וַיֵּלְכוּ וַיָּבֹאוּ

SHELAḤ

The events of this *haftara* took place between the seventh and the tenth of Nisan in the fortieth year after the exodus from Egypt, after the mourning period for Moshe had ended. At this

2 Raḥav, where they lay down for the night. And word reached the
king of Yeriḥo: "Listen, people have come here tonight – Israel-
3 ites – to probe the land." The king of Yeriḥo sent word to Raḥav:
"Bring out those men who came to you, who arrived at your
4 house, for they have come to probe the land." Now, the woman
had taken the two men and hidden them, and she replied, "Yes,
5 men came to me, but I did not know where they were from. Just
as the gate was being closed at nightfall, the men left, and I do
not know where they went. Go after them quickly, for you can
6 overtake them." She had taken the spies up to the roof and hidden them amongst the stalks of flax she had laid out on the roof.
7 The king's men ran after them toward the Jordan route, over
the river fords; and the moment the pursuers left, the gate was
8 closed behind them. They were not yet asleep when she went
9 up to them on the roof. "I know that the Lord has given you
the land," she said to the men, "and that dread of you has fallen
10 upon us; for all the inhabitants of the land quake before you. For
we have heard that the Lord dried up the waters of the Sea of
Reeds before you when you left Egypt, and we have heard what
you did to the two Amorite kings across the Jordan – how you
11 utterly destroyed Siḥon and Og. We heard it and our hearts dissolved; no one has the spirit to face you, for the Lord your God
12 is God of heaven above and earth below. Now, please swear to
me by the Lord – for I have shown you loyalty – that you, too,
13 will be loyal to my father's house. Give me a true sign that you
will spare my father and mother and my brothers and sisters and
14 all that is theirs. Please, save our souls from death!" The men replied to her, "We pledge to die in your place, if you speak no word
of this, and when the Lord gives us the land, we will show you

---

and Yehoshua sent two spies to study the environs of Yeriḥo. This third tactic is the subject of our *haftara*.

The collection of intelligence must follow specific guidelines. Only the political-military leader (Yehoshua) can be the one to send spies, and the information must go back to him alone. Competent intelligence gatherers must operate in absolute secrecy. Yehoshua's spies were well trained and mission focused, and so even after their expedition encountered difficulties they were able to complete it successfully.

ב בֵּית אִשָּׁה זוֹנָה וּשְׁמָהּ רָחָב וַיִּשְׁכְּבוּ־שָׁמָּה: וַיֵּאָמַר לְמֶלֶךְ
יְרִיחוֹ לֵאמֹר הִנֵּה אֲנָשִׁים בָּאוּ הֵנָּה הַלַּיְלָה מִבְּנֵי יִשְׂרָאֵל
ג לַחְפֹּר אֶת־הָאָרֶץ: וַיִּשְׁלַח מֶלֶךְ יְרִיחוֹ אֶל־רָחָב לֵאמֹר
הוֹצִיאִי הָאֲנָשִׁים הַבָּאִים אֵלַיִךְ אֲשֶׁר־בָּאוּ לְבֵיתֵךְ כִּי לַחְפֹּר
ד אֶת־כָּל־הָאָרֶץ בָּאוּ: וַתִּקַּח הָאִשָּׁה אֶת־שְׁנֵי הָאֲנָשִׁים
וַתִּצְפְּנוֹ וַתֹּאמֶר כֵּן בָּאוּ אֵלַי הָאֲנָשִׁים וְלֹא יָדַעְתִּי מֵאַיִן
ה הֵמָּה: וַיְהִי הַשַּׁעַר לִסְגּוֹר בַּחֹשֶׁךְ וְהָאֲנָשִׁים יָצָאוּ לֹא יָדַעְתִּי
ו אָנָה הָלְכוּ הָאֲנָשִׁים רִדְפוּ מַהֵר אַחֲרֵיהֶם כִּי תַשִּׂיגוּם: וְהִיא
הֶעֱלָתַם הַגָּגָה וַתִּטְמְנֵם בְּפִשְׁתֵּי הָעֵץ הָעֲרֻכוֹת לָהּ עַל־
ז הַגָּג: וְהָאֲנָשִׁים רָדְפוּ אַחֲרֵיהֶם דֶּרֶךְ הַיַּרְדֵּן עַל הַמַּעְבְּרוֹת
ח וְהַשַּׁעַר סָגָרוּ אַחֲרֵי כַּאֲשֶׁר יָצְאוּ הָרֹדְפִים אַחֲרֵיהֶם: וְהֵמָּה
ט טֶרֶם יִשְׁכָּבוּן וְהִיא עָלְתָה עֲלֵיהֶם עַל־הַגָּג: וַתֹּאמֶר אֶל־
הָאֲנָשִׁים יָדַעְתִּי כִּי־נָתַן יְהוָה לָכֶם אֶת־הָאָרֶץ וְכִי־נָפְלָה
י אֵימַתְכֶם עָלֵינוּ וְכִי נָמֹגוּ כָּל־יֹשְׁבֵי הָאָרֶץ מִפְּנֵיכֶם: כִּי
שָׁמַעְנוּ אֵת אֲשֶׁר־הוֹבִישׁ יְהוָה אֶת־מֵי יַם־סוּף מִפְּנֵיכֶם
בְּצֵאתְכֶם מִמִּצְרָיִם וַאֲשֶׁר עֲשִׂיתֶם לִשְׁנֵי מַלְכֵי הָאֱמֹרִי
אֲשֶׁר בְּעֵבֶר הַיַּרְדֵּן לְסִיחֹן וּלְעוֹג אֲשֶׁר הֶחֱרַמְתֶּם אוֹתָם:
יא וַנִּשְׁמַע וַיִּמַּס לְבָבֵנוּ וְלֹא־קָמָה עוֹד רוּחַ בְּאִישׁ מִפְּנֵיכֶם
כִּי יְהוָה אֱלֹהֵיכֶם הוּא אֱלֹהִים בַּשָּׁמַיִם מִמַּעַל וְעַל־הָאָרֶץ
יב מִתָּחַת: וְעַתָּה הִשָּׁבְעוּ־נָא לִי בַּיהוָה כִּי־עָשִׂיתִי עִמָּכֶם חָסֶד
וַעֲשִׂיתֶם גַּם־אַתֶּם עִם־בֵּית אָבִי חֶסֶד וּנְתַתֶּם לִי אוֹת אֱמֶת:
יג וְהַחֲיִתֶם אֶת־אָבִי וְאֶת־אִמִּי וְאֶת־אַחַי וְאֶת־אחותי וְאֵת אַחְיוֹתַי
יד כָּל־אֲשֶׁר לָהֶם וְהִצַּלְתֶּם אֶת־נַפְשֹׁתֵינוּ מִמָּוֶת: וַיֹּאמְרוּ לָהּ
הָאֲנָשִׁים נַפְשֵׁנוּ תַחְתֵּיכֶם לָמוּת אִם לֹא תַגִּידוּ אֶת־דְּבָרֵנוּ
זֶה וְהָיָה בְּתֵת־יְהוָה לָנוּ אֶת־הָאָרֶץ וְעָשִׂינוּ עִמָּךְ חֶסֶד

---

a whole prepared for the crossing; the vanguard troops from the tribes that would settle the east bank of the Jordan moved to the front of the battle lines,

15 true loyalty." She let them down by a rope through the window,
for her house was built into the city wall; she lived inside the
16 wall. "Flee toward the hills," she said to them, "lest the pursuers
run into you. Hide there for three days until the pursuers have
17 returned; only then be on your way." They said to her, "We will
18 be free of this oath you have sworn us to unless, when we come
back to the land, you tie this scarlet thread in the window you
let us down from. Bring your father, your mother, your siblings,
19 and all your father's household into your home. If anyone ventures outside the doors of your house, his blood will be upon
his own head – we will be free of blame – while if a hand is laid
on anyone who remains in the house with you, his blood shall
20 be upon ours. But if you speak a word of this, we shall be free of
21 the oath we swore to you." "As you say, so be it," she said, and she
sent them away. They left, and she tied the scarlet thread in the
22 window. They set out and arrived at the hills. They stayed there
for three days until the pursuers turned back, for the pursuers
23 had searched the entire route but failed to find them. The two
men then went back, descended the hills, and crossed over. They
came to Yehoshua son of Nun and reported all that had befallen
24 them. "The LORD has delivered the whole land into our hands,"
they said to Yehoshua, "and what is more, all the people of the
land quake before us."

HAFTARAT KORAḤ

On Rosh Ḥodesh Tamuz read the maftir from Numbers 28:9–15, and the haftara on page 1640.

I SAMUEL

11 14 And Shmuel said to the people, "Come, let us go to Gilgal, and
15 we will renew the kingship there." All the people went to Gilgal,
and they crowned Sha'ul king there at Gilgal before the LORD.

---

leaders of the people saw the benefits, but were unclear about the downsides, and it fell to Shmuel to explain these to them. This *haftara* is the conclusion of this discussion, wherein Shmuel passes the reins of political and military leadership to Sha'ul. Shmuel, in his summation of the events, talks about the institution

וֶאֱמֶת: וַתּוֹרִדֵם בַּחֶבֶל בְּעַד הַחַלּוֹן כִּי בֵיתָהּ בְּקִיר הַחוֹמָה טו
וּבַחוֹמָה הִיא יוֹשָׁבֶת: וַתֹּאמֶר לָהֶם הָהָרָה לֵּכוּ פֶּן־יִפְגְּעוּ טז
בָכֶם הָרֹדְפִים וְנַחְבֵּתֶם שָׁמָּה שְׁלֹשֶׁת יָמִים עַד שׁוֹב הָרֹדְפִים
וְאַחַר תֵּלְכוּ לְדַרְכְּכֶם: וַיֹּאמְרוּ אֵלֶיהָ הָאֲנָשִׁים נְקִיִּם אֲנַחְנוּ יז
מִשְּׁבֻעָתֵךְ הַזֶּה אֲשֶׁר הִשְׁבַּעְתָּנוּ: הִנֵּה אֲנַחְנוּ בָאִים בָּאָרֶץ יח
אֶת־תִּקְוַת חוּט הַשָּׁנִי הַזֶּה תִּקְשְׁרִי בַּחַלּוֹן אֲשֶׁר הוֹרַדְתֵּנוּ
בוֹ וְאֶת־אָבִיךְ וְאֶת־אִמֵּךְ וְאֶת־אַחַיִךְ וְאֵת כָּל־בֵּית אָבִיךְ
תַּאַסְפִי אֵלַיִךְ הַבָּיְתָה: וְהָיָה כֹּל אֲשֶׁר־יֵצֵא מִדַּלְתֵי בֵיתֵךְ ׀ יט
הַחוּצָה דָּמוֹ בְרֹאשׁוֹ וַאֲנַחְנוּ נְקִיִּם וְכֹל אֲשֶׁר יִהְיֶה אִתָּךְ
בַּבַּיִת דָּמוֹ בְרֹאשֵׁנוּ אִם־יָד תִּהְיֶה־בּוֹ: וְאִם־תַּגִּידִי אֶת־ כ
דְּבָרֵנוּ זֶה וְהָיִינוּ נְקִיִּם מִשְּׁבֻעָתֵךְ אֲשֶׁר הִשְׁבַּעְתָּנוּ: וַתֹּאמֶר כא
כְּדִבְרֵיכֶם כֶּן־הוּא וַתְּשַׁלְּחֵם וַיֵּלֵכוּ וַתִּקְשֹׁר אֶת־תִּקְוַת הַשָּׁנִי
בַּחַלּוֹן: וַיֵּלְכוּ וַיָּבֹאוּ הָהָרָה וַיֵּשְׁבוּ שָׁם שְׁלֹשֶׁת יָמִים עַד־שָׁבוּ כב
הָרֹדְפִים וַיְבַקְשׁוּ הָרֹדְפִים בְּכָל־הַדֶּרֶךְ וְלֹא מָצָאוּ: וַיָּשֻׁבוּ כג
שְׁנֵי הָאֲנָשִׁים וַיֵּרְדוּ מֵהָהָר וַיַּעַבְרוּ וַיָּבֹאוּ אֶל־יְהוֹשֻׁעַ בִּן־נוּן
וַיְסַפְּרוּ־לוֹ אֵת כָּל־הַמֹּצְאוֹת אוֹתָם: וַיֹּאמְרוּ אֶל־יְהוֹשֻׁעַ כד
כִּי־נָתַן יהוה בְּיָדֵנוּ אֶת־כָּל־הָאָרֶץ וְגַם־נָמֹגוּ כָּל־יֹשְׁבֵי
הָאָרֶץ מִפָּנֵינוּ:

הפטרת קרח

On ראש חודש תמוז *read the* מפטיר *from* במדבר
כח, ט–טו*, and the* הפטרה *on page 1641.*

שמואל א׳ וַיֹּאמֶר שְׁמוּאֵל אֶל־הָעָם לְכוּ וְנֵלְכָה הַגִּלְגָּל וּנְחַדֵּשׁ שָׁם יד יא
הַמְּלוּכָה: וַיֵּלְכוּ כָל־הָעָם הַגִּלְגָּל וַיַּמְלִכוּ שָׁם אֶת־שָׁאוּל לִפְנֵי טו

KORAḤ

The prophet Shmuel founded the Israelite monarchy after 350 years of leadership by judges. The prospect of choosing a king led to a heated discussion between Shmuel and the people.

The institution of a king brings with it both advantages and dangers. The

They sacrificed peace offerings before the LORD, and Sha'ul
12 1 rejoiced greatly along with all the men of Israel. Then
Shmuel addressed all of Israel. "Now, I have heeded your voices
2 in all you said to me, and I have crowned a king over you – and
now, here is the king, walking before you. I have grown old and
gray, but my sons are here with you; I have been walking before
3 you from my youth until this day. Here I am – testify against me
in front of the LORD and in front of His anointed – whose ox
have I seized, and whose donkey have I seized? Whom have I
cheated, and whom have I oppressed, and from whose hand
have I taken a bribe and averted my eyes from him? Let me repay
4 you." And they said, "You have not cheated us, nor oppressed
5 us, nor taken anything from anyone." "The LORD is witness
against you," he said to them, "and His anointed is witness on
this day, that you have found nothing in my possession." And it
6 was declared, "The witness is… the LORD," Shmuel
said to the people, "who appointed Moshe and Aharon and
7 brought your ancestors out of the land of Egypt. Now take your
stand, and I will plead my case with you before the LORD: all the
LORD's acts of loyalty that He has done for you and your ances-
8 tors. When Yaakov arrived in Egypt and your ancestors cried out
to the LORD, the LORD sent Moshe and Aharon to take them
9 out of Egypt, and they settled them in this place. But they forgot
the LORD their God, and He sold them into the hands of Sisera,
the general of Ḥatzor, and into the hands of the Philistines, and
10 into the hands of the king of Moav, who attacked them. Then
they cried out to the LORD. 'We have sinned,' they said, 'for
we left the LORD and served the Be'alim and the Ashterot – oh,
save us from the hands of our enemies, and we will serve You.'
11 So the LORD sent Yerubaal and Bedan and Yiftaḥ and Shmuel
and saved you from the hands of the enemies around you, and
12 you dwelled in safety. But when you saw that King Naḥash of
the Amonites came upon you, you told me, 'No, we must have
a king to reign over us,' though the LORD your God is your

---

seized? Whom have I cheated, and whom have I oppressed?" A leader must be able, when he retires, to stand before his subjects and say truthfully that he has not abused his position for personal gain. He must be able to say that everything he has done has been for the sake of Heaven and the community.

יְהוָה בַּגִּלְגָּל וַיִּזְבְּחוּ־שָׁם זְבָחִים שְׁלָמִים לִפְנֵי יְהוָה וַיִּשְׂמַח
יב א שָׁם שָׁאוּל וְכָל־אַנְשֵׁי יִשְׂרָאֵל עַד־מְאֹד׃ וַיֹּאמֶר
שְׁמוּאֵל אֶל־כָּל־יִשְׂרָאֵל הִנֵּה שָׁמַעְתִּי בְקֹלְכֶם לְכֹל אֲשֶׁר־
ב אֲמַרְתֶּם לִי וָאַמְלִיךְ עֲלֵיכֶם מֶלֶךְ׃ וְעַתָּה הִנֵּה הַמֶּלֶךְ ׀
מִתְהַלֵּךְ לִפְנֵיכֶם וַאֲנִי זָקַנְתִּי וָשַׂבְתִּי וּבָנַי הִנָּם אִתְּכֶם וַאֲנִי
ג הִתְהַלַּכְתִּי לִפְנֵיכֶם מִנְּעֻרַי עַד־הַיּוֹם הַזֶּה׃ הִנְנִי עֲנוּ בִי
נֶגֶד יְהוָה וְנֶגֶד מְשִׁיחוֹ אֶת־שׁוֹר ׀ מִי לָקַחְתִּי וַחֲמוֹר מִי
לָקַחְתִּי וְאֶת־מִי עָשַׁקְתִּי אֶת־מִי רַצּוֹתִי וּמִיַּד־מִי לָקַחְתִּי
ד כֹפֶר וְאַעְלִים עֵינַי בּוֹ וְאָשִׁיב לָכֶם׃ וַיֹּאמְרוּ לֹא עֲשַׁקְתָּנוּ
ה וְלֹא רַצּוֹתָנוּ וְלֹא־לָקַחְתָּ מִיַּד־אִישׁ מְאוּמָה׃ וַיֹּאמֶר אֲלֵיהֶם
עֵד יְהוָה בָּכֶם וְעֵד מְשִׁיחוֹ הַיּוֹם הַזֶּה כִּי לֹא מְצָאתֶם בְּיָדִי
ו מְאוּמָה וַיֹּאמֶר עֵד׃ וַיֹּאמֶר שְׁמוּאֵל אֶל־הָעָם
יְהוָה אֲשֶׁר עָשָׂה אֶת־מֹשֶׁה וְאֶת־אַהֲרֹן וַאֲשֶׁר הֶעֱלָה
ז אֶת־אֲבוֹתֵיכֶם מֵאֶרֶץ מִצְרָיִם׃ וְעַתָּה הִתְיַצְּבוּ וְאִשָּׁפְטָה
אִתְּכֶם לִפְנֵי יְהוָה אֵת כָּל־צִדְקוֹת יְהוָה אֲשֶׁר־עָשָׂה אִתְּכֶם
ח וְאֶת־אֲבֹתֵיכֶם׃ כַּאֲשֶׁר־בָּא יַעֲקֹב מִצְרָיִם וַיִּזְעֲקוּ אֲבֹתֵיכֶם
אֶל־יְהוָה וַיִּשְׁלַח יְהוָה אֶת־מֹשֶׁה וְאֶת־אַהֲרֹן וַיּוֹצִיאוּ אֶת־
ט אֲבוֹתֵיכֶם מִמִּצְרַיִם וַיֹּשִׁבוּם בַּמָּקוֹם הַזֶּה׃ וַיִּשְׁכְּחוּ אֶת־יְהוָה
אֱלֹהֵיהֶם וַיִּמְכֹּר אֹתָם בְּיַד סִיסְרָא שַׂר־צְבָא חָצוֹר וּבְיַד־
י פְּלִשְׁתִּים וּבְיַד מֶלֶךְ מוֹאָב וַיִּלָּחֲמוּ בָּם׃ וַיִּזְעֲקוּ אֶל־יְהוָה
וַיֹּאמֶר חָטָאנוּ כִּי עָזַבְנוּ אֶת־יְהוָה וַנַּעֲבֹד אֶת־הַבְּעָלִים
יא וְאֶת־הָעַשְׁתָּרוֹת וְעַתָּה הַצִּילֵנוּ מִיַּד אֹיְבֵינוּ וְנַעַבְדֶךָּ׃ וַיִּשְׁלַח
יְהוָה אֶת־יְרֻבַּעַל וְאֶת־בְּדָן וְאֶת־יִפְתָּח וְאֶת־שְׁמוּאֵל וַיַּצֵּל
יב אֶתְכֶם מִיַּד אֹיְבֵיכֶם מִסָּבִיב וַתֵּשְׁבוּ בֶּטַח׃ וַתִּרְאוּ כִּי נָחָשׁ
מֶלֶךְ בְּנֵי־עַמּוֹן בָּא עֲלֵיכֶם וַתֹּאמְרוּ לִי לֹא כִּי־מֶלֶךְ יִמְלֹךְ

---

of monarchy. A ruler who has amassed status and power can become intoxicated from it, endangering himself and the people in his charge. Shmuel stood before the people and asked: "Whose ox have I seized, and whose donkey have I

13 King. And now, here is the king that you yourselves have chosen – that you yourselves demanded – here, the LORD has set a
14 king over you! If you fear the LORD, then serve Him and heed
His voice, and do not spurn the word of GOD; both you and
the king who reigns over you must follow the LORD your God.
15 But if you do not heed the LORD's voice and rebel against the
LORD's word, then the LORD's hand shall bear down against
16 you and your ancestral houses. And now, stand by and see
what a tremendous feat the LORD is about to perform before
17 your very eyes: Is it not the wheat harvest today? I will call
out to the LORD, and He will unleash thunder and rain. Then
you will know, and then you will see, how great an evil you
have committed in the eyes of the LORD by asking for a king
18 for yourselves." Then Shmuel called out to the LORD,
and the LORD unleashed thunder and rain on that day. All the
people were struck with terror of the LORD, and of Shmuel as
19 well. And all the people said to Shmuel, "Pray on your servants'
behalf to the LORD your God so that we will not die; for we
have added yet another evil to all our offenses by asking for
20 a king for ourselves." "Do not fear, though you have
done all this evil," Shmuel said to the people, "so long as you
do not turn away from the LORD; serve the LORD with all your
21 heart. But do not turn away to follow futilities that neither help
22 nor save, for they are futile. For the LORD will not desert His
people for the sake of His great name, because the LORD has
undertaken to make you His people.

HAFTARAT ḤUKAT

On Rosh Ḥodesh Tamuz read the maftir from Numbers 28:9–15, and the haftara on page 1640.

When Ḥukat and Balak are read together, read the haftara on page 1578.

JUDGES

11 1 Yiftaḥ the Gileadite was a valiant warrior. He was the son of
2 a harlot; Gilad sired Yiftaḥ, but Gilad's wife bore him sons as

the aggression of the Amonites. With no central government, the tribes sought a leader with military experience that could lead them in defending themselves. Yiftaḥ had the necessary experience, and after negotiations with the

יג עָלֵינוּ וַיהוָה אֱלֹהֵיכֶם מַלְכְּכֶם: וְעַתָּה הִנֵּה הַמֶּלֶךְ אֲשֶׁר
יד בְּחַרְתֶּם אֲשֶׁר שְׁאֶלְתֶּם וְהִנֵּה נָתַן יהוה עֲלֵיכֶם מֶלֶךְ: אִם־
תִּירְאוּ אֶת־יהוה וַעֲבַדְתֶּם אֹתוֹ וּשְׁמַעְתֶּם בְּקֹלוֹ וְלֹא תַמְרוּ
אֶת־פִּי יהוה וִהְיִתֶם גַּם־אַתֶּם וְגַם־הַמֶּלֶךְ אֲשֶׁר מָלַךְ עֲלֵיכֶם
טו אַחַר יהוה אֱלֹהֵיכֶם: וְאִם־לֹא תִשְׁמְעוּ בְּקוֹל יהוה וּמְרִיתֶם
טז אֶת־פִּי יהוה וְהָיְתָה יַד־יהוה בָּכֶם וּבַאֲבֹתֵיכֶם: גַּם־עַתָּה
הִתְיַצְּבוּ וּרְאוּ אֶת־הַדָּבָר הַגָּדוֹל הַזֶּה אֲשֶׁר יהוה עֹשֶׂה
יז לְעֵינֵיכֶם: הֲלוֹא קְצִיר־חִטִּים הַיּוֹם אֶקְרָא אֶל־יהוה וְיִתֵּן
קֹלוֹת וּמָטָר וּדְעוּ וּרְאוּ כִּי־רָעַתְכֶם רַבָּה אֲשֶׁר עֲשִׂיתֶם
יח בְּעֵינֵי יהוה לִשְׁאוֹל לָכֶם מֶלֶךְ: וַיִּקְרָא שְׁמוּאֵל
אֶל־יהוה וַיִּתֵּן יהוה קֹלֹת וּמָטָר בַּיּוֹם הַהוּא וַיִּירָא כָל־הָעָם
יט מְאֹד אֶת־יהוה וְאֶת־שְׁמוּאֵל: וַיֹּאמְרוּ כָל־הָעָם אֶל־שְׁמוּאֵל
הִתְפַּלֵּל בְּעַד־עֲבָדֶיךָ אֶל־יהוה אֱלֹהֶיךָ וְאַל־נָמוּת כִּי־יָסַפְנוּ
כ עַל־כָּל־חַטֹּאתֵינוּ רָעָה לִשְׁאֹל לָנוּ מֶלֶךְ: וַיֹּאמֶר
שְׁמוּאֵל אֶל־הָעָם אַל־תִּירָאוּ אַתֶּם עֲשִׂיתֶם אֵת כָּל־הָרָעָה
הַזֹּאת אַךְ אַל־תָּסוּרוּ מֵאַחֲרֵי יהוה וַעֲבַדְתֶּם אֶת־יהוה
כא בְּכָל־לְבַבְכֶם: וְלֹא תָּסוּרוּ כִּי ׀ אַחֲרֵי הַתֹּהוּ אֲשֶׁר לֹא־יוֹעִילוּ
כב וְלֹא יַצִּילוּ כִּי־תֹהוּ הֵמָּה: כִּי לֹא־יִטֹּשׁ יהוה אֶת־עַמּוֹ בַּעֲבוּר
שְׁמוֹ הַגָּדוֹל כִּי הוֹאִיל יהוה לַעֲשׂוֹת אֶתְכֶם לוֹ לְעָם:

הפטרת חקת

On ראש חודש תמוז *read the* מפטיר *from* במדבר
כח, ט–טו, and the הפטרה *on page 1641.*
When חקת *and* בלק *are read together, read the* הפטרה *on page 1579.*

יא א וַיִּפְתָּח הַגִּלְעָדִי הָיָה גִּבּוֹר חַיִל וְהוּא בֶּן־אִשָּׁה זוֹנָה וַיּוֹלֶד שופטים
ב גִּלְעָד אֶת־יִפְתָּח: וַתֵּלֶד אֵשֶׁת־גִּלְעָד לוֹ בָּנִים וַיִּגְדְּלוּ בְנֵי־

ḤUKAT
During the later years of the period of the judges, the tribes of Gilad, on the eastern side of the Jordan, suffered from

well. When the wife's sons grew up, they drove Yiftaḥ away, telling him, "You shall have no share in our father's estate, for you
3 are the son of another woman." So Yiftaḥ fled from his brothers; he settled in the land of Tov. Worthless men were drawn
4 to him and went out raiding with him. Time passed,
5 and the Amonites waged war upon Israel. When the Amonites
attacked Israel, the elders of Gilad set out to bring Yiftaḥ back
6 from the land of Tov. "Come with us," they said to Yiftaḥ, "and
be our commander, so that we can fight against the Amonites."
7 "But you despised me," Yiftaḥ said to the elders of Gilad, "and
drove me away from my father's house. Why do you come to
8 me now, when you are in trouble?" "For that reason we ourselves have come back to you now," the elders of Gilad said to
Yiftaḥ. "You shall march out with us and fight the Amonites,
9 and you shall be the leader of all the people of Gilad." "If you
bring me back to fight against the Amonites," Yiftaḥ replied to
the elders of Gilad, "and the Lord delivers them to me, then
10 I shall be your leader." The elders of Gilad said to Yiftaḥ, "The
Lord shall bear witness between us if we do not comply with
11 your words." So Yiftaḥ went with the elders of Gilad, and the
people made him their head and commander. Yiftaḥ repeated
12 all his terms before the Lord at Mitzpa. Yiftaḥ sent
messengers to the king of the Amonites: "What do you have
13 against us, that you came to attack our land?" The king of the
Amonites replied to Yiftaḥ's messengers, "Israel seized my
lands when they came out of Egypt – from the Arnon to the
Yabok and up to the Jordan. Now hand them back peacefully."
14 Once again Yiftaḥ sent messengers to the king of the Amonites.
15 "Thus says Yiftaḥ," they said. "Israel did not seize the land of
16 Moav nor the land of the Amonites. For when they came out
of Egypt, Israel trekked through the wilderness to the Sea of
17 Reeds, then they arrived at Kadesh. And Israel sent messengers

---

we can see his thorough knowledge of the historical circumstances of the Israelites' arrival in Canaan generations earlier and their rights to the Gilad. He had this erudition despite having been banished from his home at a young age due to a family conflict. When all efforts to arrive at a peaceful accommodation have failed, Yiftaḥ leads the Gileadites in a preemptive strike that defeats the army of Amon.

הָאִשָּׁה וַיְגָרְשׁוּ אֶת־יִפְתָּח וַיֹּאמְרוּ לוֹ לֹא־תִנְחַל בְּבֵית־
ג אָבִינוּ כִּי בֶּן־אִשָּׁה אַחֶרֶת אָתָּה: וַיִּבְרַח יִפְתָּח מִפְּנֵי אֶחָיו
וַיֵּשֶׁב בְּאֶרֶץ טוֹב וַיִּתְלַקְּטוּ אֶל־יִפְתָּח אֲנָשִׁים רֵיקִים
ד וַיֵּצְאוּ עִמּוֹ: וַיְהִי מִיָּמִים וַיִּלָּחֲמוּ בְנֵי־עַמּוֹן
ה עִם־יִשְׂרָאֵל: וַיְהִי כַּאֲשֶׁר־נִלְחֲמוּ בְנֵי־עַמּוֹן עִם־יִשְׂרָאֵל
ו וַיֵּלְכוּ זִקְנֵי גִלְעָד לָקַחַת אֶת־יִפְתָּח מֵאֶרֶץ טוֹב: וַיֹּאמְרוּ
לְיִפְתָּח לְכָה וְהָיִיתָה לָּנוּ לְקָצִין וְנִלָּחֲמָה בִּבְנֵי עַמּוֹן:
ז וַיֹּאמֶר יִפְתָּח לְזִקְנֵי גִלְעָד הֲלֹא אַתֶּם שְׂנֵאתֶם אוֹתִי
וַתְּגָרְשׁוּנִי מִבֵּית אָבִי וּמַדּוּעַ בָּאתֶם אֵלַי עַתָּה כַּאֲשֶׁר צַר
ח לָכֶם: וַיֹּאמְרוּ זִקְנֵי גִלְעָד אֶל־יִפְתָּח לָכֵן עַתָּה שַׁבְנוּ אֵלֶיךָ
וְהָלַכְתָּ עִמָּנוּ וְנִלְחַמְתָּ בִּבְנֵי עַמּוֹן וְהָיִיתָ לָּנוּ לְרֹאשׁ לְכֹל
ט יֹשְׁבֵי גִלְעָד: וַיֹּאמֶר יִפְתָּח אֶל־זִקְנֵי גִלְעָד אִם־מְשִׁיבִים
אַתֶּם אוֹתִי לְהִלָּחֵם בִּבְנֵי עַמּוֹן וְנָתַן יהוה אוֹתָם לְפָנָי
י אָנֹכִי אֶהְיֶה לָכֶם לְרֹאשׁ: וַיֹּאמְרוּ זִקְנֵי־גִלְעָד אֶל־יִפְתָּח
יהוה יִהְיֶה שֹׁמֵעַ בֵּינוֹתֵינוּ אִם־לֹא כִדְבָרְךָ כֵּן נַעֲשֶׂה:
יא וַיֵּלֶךְ יִפְתָּח עִם־זִקְנֵי גִלְעָד וַיָּשִׂימוּ הָעָם אוֹתוֹ עֲלֵיהֶם
לְרֹאשׁ וּלְקָצִין וַיְדַבֵּר יִפְתָּח אֶת־כָּל־דְּבָרָיו לִפְנֵי יהוה
יב בַּמִּצְפָּה: וַיִּשְׁלַח יִפְתָּח מַלְאָכִים אֶל־מֶלֶךְ בְּנֵי־
עַמּוֹן לֵאמֹר מַה־לִּי וָלָךְ כִּי־בָאתָ אֵלַי לְהִלָּחֵם בְּאַרְצִי:
יג וַיֹּאמֶר מֶלֶךְ בְּנֵי־עַמּוֹן אֶל־מַלְאֲכֵי יִפְתָּח כִּי־לָקַח יִשְׂרָאֵל
אֶת־אַרְצִי בַּעֲלוֹתוֹ מִמִּצְרַיִם מֵאַרְנוֹן וְעַד־הַיַּבֹּק וְעַד־הַיַּרְדֵּן
יד וְעַתָּה הָשִׁיבָה אֶתְהֶן בְּשָׁלוֹם: וַיּוֹסֶף עוֹד יִפְתָּח וַיִּשְׁלַח
טו מַלְאָכִים אֶל־מֶלֶךְ בְּנֵי עַמּוֹן: וַיֹּאמֶר לוֹ כֹּה אָמַר יִפְתָּח
טז לֹא־לָקַח יִשְׂרָאֵל אֶת־אֶרֶץ מוֹאָב וְאֶת־אֶרֶץ בְּנֵי עַמּוֹן: כִּי
בַּעֲלוֹתָם מִמִּצְרָיִם וַיֵּלֶךְ יִשְׂרָאֵל בַּמִּדְבָּר עַד־יַם־סוּף וַיָּבֹא
יז קָדֵשָׁה: וַיִּשְׁלַח יִשְׂרָאֵל מַלְאָכִים ׀ אֶל־מֶלֶךְ אֱדוֹם לֵאמֹר

---

tribal elders he accepts the position. He begins a parley with the kingdom of Amon, to try to convince them to leave off without bloodshed. In his arguments,

to the king of Edom, saying, 'Please let us pass through your
land,' but the king of Edom would not listen; they also reached
out to the king of Moav, but he would not comply. So Israel
18 remained in Kadesh. They trekked through the wilderness,
making their way around the land of Edom and the land of
Moav until they reached the eastern side of the land of Moav,
where they encamped across the Arnon. They did not enter
19 Moabite territory, for the Arnon is the Moabite border. Then
Israel sent messengers to Siḥon, king of the Amorites, the king
of Ḥeshbon. Israel said to him, 'Please, let us pass through your
20 land to our own place.' But Siḥon did not trust Israel to pass
through his territory. And Siḥon assembled all his troops, en-
21 camped at Yahtza, and attacked Israel. The Lord, God of Israel,
delivered Siḥon and all of his people into Israel's hands; they
defeated them, and the Israelites took possession of the entire
22 land of the Amorites, who lived in that land. They took possession of all the Amorite territory from Arnon to the Yabok, and
23 from the wilderness to the Jordan. Now, the Lord, God of Israel, dispossessed the Amorites before His people, Israel – why
24 should you possess it? You take possession of what Kemosh,
your god, grants you, and we will take possession of everything
25 the Lord, our God, grants us. Now, are you any better than
Balak son of Tzipor, king of Moav? Did he pick a quarrel with
26 Israel? Did he wage war against them? Israel has been dwelling in Ḥeshbon and its boroughs, Aroer and its boroughs, and
in all the towns near Arnon, for three hundred years – why
27 have you not reclaimed them all this time? I have never offended you, yet you do me wrong by fighting against me. May
the Lord, who judges, judge between the Israelites and the
28 Amonites today." But the king of the Amonites did not listen
29 to the words Yiftaḥ delivered to him. The spirit of the
Lord settled upon Yiftaḥ, and he crossed through Gilad and
Menashe; he crossed Mitzpeh Gilad; and from Mitzpeh Gilad
30 he crossed over to the Amonites. Then Yiftaḥ swore a vow to
the Lord. He said, "If You deliver the Amonites into my hand,
31 then whatever comes out of the doors of my home to meet me
when I return safely from the Amonites shall be for the Lord,
and I shall offer it up as a burnt offering."

32 Yiftaḥ crossed over to the Amonites and attacked them, and the

אֶעְבְּרָה־נָּא בְאַרְצֶךָ וְלֹא שָׁמַע מֶלֶךְ אֱדוֹם וְגַם אֶל־מֶלֶךְ
יח מוֹאָב שָׁלַח וְלֹא אָבָה וַיֵּשֶׁב יִשְׂרָאֵל בְּקָדֵשׁ׃ וַיֵּלֶךְ בַּמִּדְבָּר
וַיָּסָב אֶת־אֶרֶץ אֱדוֹם וְאֶת־אֶרֶץ מוֹאָב וַיָּבֹא מִמִּזְרַח־שֶׁמֶשׁ
לְאֶרֶץ מוֹאָב וַיַּחֲנוּן בְּעֵבֶר אַרְנוֹן וְלֹא־בָאוּ בִּגְבוּל מוֹאָב
יט כִּי אַרְנוֹן גְּבוּל מוֹאָב׃ וַיִּשְׁלַח יִשְׂרָאֵל מַלְאָכִים אֶל־סִיחוֹן
מֶלֶךְ־הָאֱמֹרִי מֶלֶךְ חֶשְׁבּוֹן וַיֹּאמֶר לוֹ יִשְׂרָאֵל נַעְבְּרָה־נָּא
כ בְאַרְצְךָ עַד־מְקוֹמִי׃ וְלֹא־הֶאֱמִין סִיחוֹן אֶת־יִשְׂרָאֵל עֲבֹר
בִּגְבֻלוֹ וַיֶּאֱסֹף סִיחוֹן אֶת־כָּל־עַמּוֹ וַיַּחֲנוּ בְּיָהְצָה וַיִּלָּחֶם עִם־
כא יִשְׂרָאֵל׃ וַיִּתֵּן יהוה אֱלֹהֵי־יִשְׂרָאֵל אֶת־סִיחוֹן וְאֶת־כָּל־עַמּוֹ
בְּיַד יִשְׂרָאֵל וַיַּכּוּם וַיִּירַשׁ יִשְׂרָאֵל אֵת כָּל־אֶרֶץ הָאֱמֹרִי יוֹשֵׁב
כב הָאָרֶץ הַהִיא׃ וַיִּירְשׁוּ אֵת כָּל־גְּבוּל הָאֱמֹרִי מֵאַרְנוֹן וְעַד־
כג הַיַּבֹּק וּמִן־הַמִּדְבָּר וְעַד־הַיַּרְדֵּן׃ וְעַתָּה יהוה ׀ אֱלֹהֵי יִשְׂרָאֵל
כד הוֹרִישׁ אֶת־הָאֱמֹרִי מִפְּנֵי עַמּוֹ יִשְׂרָאֵל וְאַתָּה תִּירָשֶׁנּוּ׃ הֲלֹא
אֵת אֲשֶׁר יוֹרִישְׁךָ כְּמוֹשׁ אֱלֹהֶיךָ אוֹתוֹ תִירָשׁ וְאֵת כָּל־אֲשֶׁר
כה הוֹרִישׁ יהוה אֱלֹהֵינוּ מִפָּנֵינוּ אוֹתוֹ נִירָשׁ׃ וְעַתָּה הֲטוֹב טוֹב
אַתָּה מִבָּלָק בֶּן־צִפּוֹר מֶלֶךְ מוֹאָב הֲרוֹב רָב עִם־יִשְׂרָאֵל
כו אִם־נִלְחֹם נִלְחַם בָּם׃ בְּשֶׁבֶת יִשְׂרָאֵל בְּחֶשְׁבּוֹן וּבִבְנוֹתֶיהָ
וּבְעַרְעוֹר וּבִבְנוֹתֶיהָ וּבְכָל־הֶעָרִים אֲשֶׁר עַל־יְדֵי אַרְנוֹן שְׁלֹשׁ
כז מֵאוֹת שָׁנָה וּמַדּוּעַ לֹא־הִצַּלְתֶּם בָּעֵת הַהִיא׃ וְאָנֹכִי לֹא־
חָטָאתִי לָךְ וְאַתָּה עֹשֶׂה אִתִּי רָעָה לְהִלָּחֶם בִּי יִשְׁפֹּט יהוה
כח הַשֹּׁפֵט הַיּוֹם בֵּין בְּנֵי יִשְׂרָאֵל וּבֵין בְּנֵי עַמּוֹן׃ וְלֹא שָׁמַע מֶלֶךְ
כט בְּנֵי עַמּוֹן אֶל־דִּבְרֵי יִפְתָּח אֲשֶׁר שָׁלַח אֵלָיו׃ וַתְּהִי
עַל־יִפְתָּח רוּחַ יהוה וַיַּעֲבֹר אֶת־הַגִּלְעָד וְאֶת־מְנַשֶּׁה וַיַּעֲבֹר
ל אֶת־מִצְפֵּה גִלְעָד וּמִמִּצְפֵּה גִלְעָד עָבַר בְּנֵי עַמּוֹן׃ וַיִּדַּר יִפְתָּח
לא נֶדֶר לַיהוה וַיֹּאמַר אִם־נָתוֹן תִּתֵּן אֶת־בְּנֵי עַמּוֹן בְּיָדִי׃ וְהָיָה
הַיּוֹצֵא אֲשֶׁר יֵצֵא מִדַּלְתֵי בֵיתִי לִקְרָאתִי בְּשׁוּבִי בְשָׁלוֹם
מִבְּנֵי עַמּוֹן וְהָיָה לַיהוה וְהַעֲלִיתִהוּ עוֹלָה׃
לב וַיַּעֲבֹר יִפְתָּח אֶל־בְּנֵי עַמּוֹן לְהִלָּחֶם בָּם וַיִּתְּנֵם יהוה

33 Lord delivered them into his hand. He defeated them from
Aroer to Minit, twenty towns, all the way to Avel Keramim – a
crushing defeat – and the Amonites were conquered by the Is-
34 raelites. *Yiftaḥ arrived home in Mitzpa – and there *Yemenites add*
was his daughter, coming out to meet him, drumming and
dancing! She was his one and only – he had no son or daughter
35 besides her. When he saw her, he rent his clothes. "O, O, my
daughter," he said, "you have brought me down low – you have
become my scourge! I have gone and opened up my mouth
36 to the Lord, and I cannot go back." "O, Father," she said to
him, "If you opened your mouth up to the Lord, do to me
whatever it was that came out of your mouth – after what the
Lord has done for you, defeating your enemies the Amonites.
37 Only grant me this one thing," she said to her father. "Let me
go for two months so that I may roam the hills and weep for my
38 maidenhood, my friends and I." "Go," he said to her, and sent
her off for two months; she and her friends went and wept for
39 her maidenhood upon the hills. At the end of two months, she
returned to her father. He did to her what he had vowed to do.
40 She never knew a man. It became a custom in Israel: every year,
the daughters of Israel would go and lament the daughter of
Yiftaḥ the Gileadite for four days a year.

Haftarat Balak

When Ḥukat and Balak are read together, read this haftara.

5 6 And the remnant of Yaakov will be found amid countless peo- MICAH
ples as dew brought down from the Lord, as ample rains shower
upon grass; they will not look to any man, nor place their hopes
7 in humankind. The remnant of Yaakov will be among nations,
amid countless peoples, like a lion among wild beasts of the

brought into focus questions of Israel's special status as God's chosen people and of the proper way of worshipping God. The fact that Assyria could destroy the northern kingdom and exile its inhabitants while the southern kingdom of Yehuda survived was difficult for the people to understand.

לג בְּיָדוֹ: וַיַּכֵּם מֵעֲרוֹעֵר וְעַד־בּוֹאֲךָ מִנִּית עֶשְׂרִים עִיר וְעַד
אָבֵל כְּרָמִים מַכָּה גְּדוֹלָה מְאֹד וַיִּכָּנְעוּ בְּנֵי עַמּוֹן מִפְּנֵי בְּנֵי
לד יִשְׂרָאֵל: *וַיָּבֹא יִפְתָּח הַמִּצְפָּה אֶל־בֵּיתוֹ וְהִנֵּה *Yemenites add*
בִתּוֹ יֹצֵאת לִקְרָאתוֹ בְּתֻפִּים וּבִמְחֹלוֹת וְרַק הִיא יְחִידָה
לה אֵין־לוֹ מִמֶּנּוּ בֵּן אוֹ־בַת: וַיְהִי כִרְאוֹתוֹ אוֹתָהּ וַיִּקְרַע אֶת־
בְּגָדָיו וַיֹּאמֶר אֲהָהּ בִּתִּי הַכְרֵעַ הִכְרַעְתִּנִי וְאַתְּ הָיִית בְּעֹכְרָי
לו וְאָנֹכִי פָּצִיתִי פִי אֶל־יהוה וְלֹא אוּכַל לָשׁוּב: וַתֹּאמֶר אֵלָיו
אָבִי פָּצִיתָה אֶת־פִּיךָ אֶל־יהוה עֲשֵׂה לִי כַּאֲשֶׁר יָצָא מִפִּיךָ
אַחֲרֵי אֲשֶׁר עָשָׂה לְךָ יהוה נְקָמוֹת מֵאֹיְבֶיךָ מִבְּנֵי עַמּוֹן:
לז וַתֹּאמֶר אֶל־אָבִיהָ יֵעָשֶׂה לִּי הַדָּבָר הַזֶּה הַרְפֵּה מִמֶּנִּי שְׁנַיִם
חֳדָשִׁים וְאֵלְכָה וְיָרַדְתִּי עַל־הֶהָרִים וְאֶבְכֶּה עַל־בְּתוּלַי
לח אָנֹכִי ורעיתי: וַיֹּאמֶר לֵכִי וַיִּשְׁלַח אוֹתָהּ שְׁנֵי חֳדָשִׁים וַתֵּלֶךְ וְרֵעוֹתַי
לט הִיא וְרֵעוֹתֶיהָ וַתֵּבְךְּ עַל־בְּתוּלֶיהָ עַל־הֶהָרִים: וַיְהִי מִקֵּץ ׀
שְׁנַיִם חֳדָשִׁים וַתָּשָׁב אֶל־אָבִיהָ וַיַּעַשׂ לָהּ אֶת־נִדְרוֹ אֲשֶׁר
מ נָדָר וְהִיא לֹא־יָדְעָה אִישׁ וַתְּהִי־חֹק בְּיִשְׂרָאֵל: מִיָּמִים ׀
יָמִימָה תֵּלַכְנָה בְּנוֹת יִשְׂרָאֵל לְתַנּוֹת לְבַת־יִפְתָּח הַגִּלְעָדִי
אַרְבַּעַת יָמִים בַּשָּׁנָה:

הפטרת בלק

When חקת *and* בלק *are read together, read this* הפטרה.

ה ו וְהָיָה ׀ שְׁאֵרִית יַעֲקֹב בְּקֶרֶב עַמִּים רַבִּים כְּטַל מֵאֵת יהוה מיכה
כִּרְבִיבִים עֲלֵי־עֵשֶׂב אֲשֶׁר לֹא־יְקַוֶּה לְאִישׁ וְלֹא יְיַחֵל
ז לִבְנֵי אָדָם: וְהָיָה שְׁאֵרִית יַעֲקֹב בַּגּוֹיִם בְּקֶרֶב עַמִּים רַבִּים
כְּאַרְיֵה בְּבַהֲמוֹת יַעַר כִּכְפִיר בְּעֶדְרֵי־צֹאן אֲשֶׁר אִם עָבַר

BALAK

The prophet Mikha was active in the kingdom of Yehuda at the same time as his teacher, the prophet Yeshayahu. At this time, the Assyrian Empire was on the ascent, and the northern kingdom of Israel had now been destroyed. The confrontation with this formidable enemy

forest, like a young lion among flocks of sheep whom, as they
pass, he tramples and rips to pieces; there is no one to save them.
8 Your hand shall be raised over your foes; your enemies will be cut
9 down. On that day, so says the LORD: I will cut out the
10 horses from among you, I will destroy your chariots, and I will
cut down the fortified cities of your land and demolish all your
11 fortresses. I will cut out all practice of witchcraft, and there will
12 be no more fortune tellers among you. I will cut down your idols,
the worship pillars from your midst; no longer will you bow
13 down to the craft of your hands. I will rip out the Ashera from
14 your midst, and I will destroy your cities. I will lash out with My
anger and wrath in vengeance against nations who did not heed
6 1 My words. Hear now what the LORD says: Arise; argue
2 your case before the mountains; let the hills hear your plea. Hear,
O mountains, the LORD's dispute – you, earth's everlasting foundations. For the LORD has a dispute with His people; He will
3 contend with Israel: My people! How have I wronged you? How
4 have I worn you down? Bear witness against Me, for I brought
you up from the land of Egypt; I redeemed you from the house
5 of slavery; I sent Moshe, Aharon, and Miriam to lead you. My
people, remember now how Balak, king of Moav, schemed, and
how Bilam son of Beor responded; remember from Shitim to
Gilgal so that you may come to realize the righteous ways of the
6 LORD. What then can I offer the LORD when I bow low to the
God Most High? Should I come before Him with burnt offerings,
7 with year-old calves? Would the LORD want a thousand rams,
untold rivulets of oil? Should I offer my firstborn as payment for
8 my crimes, the fruit of my womb for the sins of my being? Man,
God has told you what is good and what the LORD seeks from
you: only to do justice, love goodness, and walk modestly with
your God.

---

our religious consciousness, while forgetting about the demands of charity and justice that the Torah places on us, turns a means into an end. When we do so, we are serving only ourselves and our own conceptions, rather than God.

ח וְרָמַס וְטָרַף וְאֵין מַצִּיל: תָּרֹם יָדְךָ עַל־צָרֶיךָ וְכָל־אֹיְבֶיךָ
ט יִכָּרֵתוּ: וְהָיָה בַיּוֹם־הַהוּא נְאֻם־יהוה וְהִכְרַתִּי
י סוּסֶיךָ מִקִּרְבֶּךָ וְהַאֲבַדְתִּי מַרְכְּבֹתֶיךָ: וְהִכְרַתִּי עָרֵי אַרְצֶךָ
יא וְהָרַסְתִּי כָּל־מִבְצָרֶיךָ: וְהִכְרַתִּי כְשָׁפִים מִיָּדֶךָ וּמְעוֹנְנִים
יב לֹא יִהְיוּ־לָךְ: וְהִכְרַתִּי פְסִילֶיךָ וּמַצֵּבוֹתֶיךָ מִקִּרְבֶּךָ וְלֹא־
יג תִשְׁתַּחֲוֶה עוֹד לְמַעֲשֵׂה יָדֶיךָ: וְנָתַשְׁתִּי אֲשֵׁירֶיךָ מִקִּרְבֶּךָ
יד וְהִשְׁמַדְתִּי עָרֶיךָ: וְעָשִׂיתִי בְּאַף וּבְחֵמָה נָקָם אֶת־הַגּוֹיִם
ו א אֲשֶׁר לֹא שָׁמֵעוּ: שִׁמְעוּ־נָא אֵת אֲשֶׁר־יהוה
אֹמֵר קוּם רִיב אֶת־הֶהָרִים וְתִשְׁמַעְנָה הַגְּבָעוֹת קוֹלֶךָ:
ב שִׁמְעוּ הָרִים אֶת־רִיב יהוה וְהָאֵתָנִים מֹסְדֵי אָרֶץ כִּי רִיב
ג לַיהוה עִם־עַמּוֹ וְעִם־יִשְׂרָאֵל יִתְוַכָּח: עַמִּי מֶה־עָשִׂיתִי לְךָ
ד וּמָה הֶלְאֵתִיךָ עֲנֵה בִי: כִּי הֶעֱלִתִיךָ מֵאֶרֶץ מִצְרַיִם וּמִבֵּית
ה עֲבָדִים פְּדִיתִיךָ וָאֶשְׁלַח לְפָנֶיךָ אֶת־מֹשֶׁה אַהֲרֹן וּמִרְיָם: עַמִּי
זְכָר־נָא מַה־יָּעַץ בָּלָק מֶלֶךְ מוֹאָב וּמֶה־עָנָה אֹתוֹ בִּלְעָם
בֶּן־בְּעוֹר מִן־הַשִּׁטִּים עַד־הַגִּלְגָּל לְמַעַן דַּעַת צִדְקוֹת יהוה:
ו בַּמָּה אֲקַדֵּם יהוה אִכַּף לֵאלֹהֵי מָרוֹם הַאֲקַדְּמֶנּוּ בְעוֹלוֹת
ז בַּעֲגָלִים בְּנֵי שָׁנָה: הֲיִרְצֶה יהוה בְּאַלְפֵי אֵילִים בְּרִבְבוֹת
נַחֲלֵי־שָׁמֶן הַאֶתֵּן בְּכוֹרִי פִּשְׁעִי פְּרִי בִטְנִי חַטַּאת נַפְשִׁי:
ח הִגִּיד לְךָ אָדָם מַה־טּוֹב וּמָה־יהוה דּוֹרֵשׁ מִמְּךָ כִּי אִם־עֲשׂוֹת
מִשְׁפָּט וְאַהֲבַת חֶסֶד וְהַצְנֵעַ לֶכֶת עִם־אֱלֹהֶיךָ:

In this *haftara*, the prophet preaches a message of reassurance to the people. At the same time, he points out the difference between means and ends in serving God. He points out Israel's central mission in the world: modeling the ideal way of serving the Almighty. To put the sacrificial service at the center of

Haftarat Pinḥas

Read this haftara if Shabbat Parashat Pinḥas falls before the Seventeenth of Tamuz. If it falls afterward, read the haftara on page 1586.

18 46 The hand of the LORD settled on Eliyahu, and he hitched up his I KINGS
19 1 tunic and ran before Aḥav until he reached Yizre'el. When Aḥav
told Izevel all that Eliyahu had done and how he had put all the
2 prophets to the sword, Izevel sent a messenger to Eliyahu: "So
may the gods do to me and more if by this time tomorrow, I have
3 not treated your life like one of theirs." Frightened, he understood and fled for his life at once, and he reached Be'er Sheva of
4 Yehuda and left his servant boy there. But he continued a day's
journey into the wilderness, then came and sat under a certain
broom tree and prayed that he might die. "Enough!" he said.
"O LORD, take my life now, for I am no better than my ancestors."
5 Then he lay down and fell asleep beneath that broom tree. Sud-
6 denly, an angel was touching him, urging him, "Get up; eat." He
looked up and there, at his head, was a stone-baked cake and a
7 flask of water. He ate and drank and lay back down. The angel
of the LORD came back a second time and touched him. "Get
up; eat," it said, "or the long journey will prove too much for
8 you." He got up and ate and drank, and by the strength of that
food, he walked forty days and forty nights to the mountain of
9 God, Ḥorev. There he reached a cave, and there he spent the
night. Suddenly, the word of the LORD came to him and said to
10 him, "Why are you here, Eliyahu?" "I acted out of fervor, out of
passion for the LORD, God of Hosts," he said, "for the Israelites
have abandoned Your covenant, destroyed Your altars, and put
Your prophets to the sword. I am the only one left, and they seek
11 to take my life." "Go out and stand on the mountain before the
LORD," He said, "for the LORD is about to pass by." And a great,

afflicting Israel has run its course, and it has not been enough to induce the people to mend their ways. Fire from heaven is impressive and has the power to shock people out of their torpor, but its effect is short. Only repentance that answers a "faint sound of silence" can withstand the passage of time.

Eliyahu, nevertheless, is not willing to change his methods, and his answers to God's repeated questions do not change. Ultimately, God commands him to appoint Elisha as prophet in his stead.

הפטרת פינחס

Read this הפטרה *if* שבת פרשת פינחס *falls before* שבעה עשר בתמוז*. If it falls afterward, read the* הפטרה *on page 1587.*

If it falls afterward, read the הפטרה *on page 1587.*

יח מו וְיַד־יהוה הָיְתָה אֶל־אֵלִיָּהוּ וַיְשַׁנֵּס מָתְנָיו וַיָּרָץ לִפְנֵי אַחְאָב מלכים א׳
יט א עַד־בֹּאֲכָה יִזְרְעֶאלָה: וַיַּגֵּד אַחְאָב לְאִיזֶבֶל אֵת כָּל־אֲשֶׁר
עָשָׂה אֵלִיָּהוּ וְאֵת כָּל־אֲשֶׁר הָרַג אֶת־כָּל־הַנְּבִיאִים בֶּחָרֶב:
ב וַתִּשְׁלַח אִיזֶבֶל מַלְאָךְ אֶל־אֵלִיָּהוּ לֵאמֹר כֹּה־יַעֲשׂוּן אֱלֹהִים
וְכֹה יוֹסִפוּן כִּי־כָעֵת מָחָר אָשִׂים אֶת־נַפְשְׁךָ כְּנֶפֶשׁ אַחַד
ג מֵהֶם: וַיַּרְא וַיָּקָם וַיֵּלֶךְ אֶל־נַפְשׁוֹ וַיָּבֹא בְּאֵר שֶׁבַע אֲשֶׁר
ד לִיהוּדָה וַיַּנַּח אֶת־נַעֲרוֹ שָׁם: וְהוּא־הָלַךְ בַּמִּדְבָּר דֶּרֶךְ
יוֹם וַיָּבֹא וַיֵּשֶׁב תַּחַת רֹתֶם אחת וַיִּשְׁאַל אֶת־נַפְשׁוֹ לָמוּת אֶחָד
וַיֹּאמֶר ׀ רַב עַתָּה יהוה קַח נַפְשִׁי כִּי לֹא־טוֹב אָנֹכִי מֵאֲבֹתָי:
ה וַיִּשְׁכַּב וַיִּישַׁן תַּחַת רֹתֶם אֶחָד וְהִנֵּה־זֶה מַלְאָךְ נֹגֵעַ בּוֹ וַיֹּאמֶר
ו לוֹ קוּם אֱכוֹל: וַיַּבֵּט וְהִנֵּה מְרַאֲשֹׁתָיו עֻגַת רְצָפִים וְצַפַּחַת
ז מָיִם וַיֹּאכַל וַיֵּשְׁתְּ וַיָּשָׁב וַיִּשְׁכָּב: וַיָּשָׁב מַלְאַךְ יהוה ׀ שֵׁנִית
ח וַיִּגַּע־בּוֹ וַיֹּאמֶר קוּם אֱכֹל כִּי רַב מִמְּךָ הַדָּרֶךְ: וַיָּקָם וַיֹּאכַל
וַיִּשְׁתֶּה וַיֵּלֶךְ בְּכֹחַ ׀ הָאֲכִילָה הַהִיא אַרְבָּעִים יוֹם וְאַרְבָּעִים
ט לַיְלָה עַד הַר הָאֱלֹהִים חֹרֵב: וַיָּבֹא־שָׁם אֶל־הַמְּעָרָה וַיָּלֶן
שָׁם וְהִנֵּה דְבַר־יהוה אֵלָיו וַיֹּאמֶר לוֹ מַה־לְּךָ פֹה אֵלִיָּהוּ:
י וַיֹּאמֶר קַנֹּא קִנֵּאתִי לַיהוה ׀ אֱלֹהֵי צְבָאוֹת כִּי־עָזְבוּ בְרִיתְךָ
בְּנֵי יִשְׂרָאֵל אֶת־מִזְבְּחֹתֶיךָ הָרָסוּ וְאֶת־נְבִיאֶיךָ הָרְגוּ בֶחָרֶב
יא וָאִוָּתֵר אֲנִי לְבַדִּי וַיְבַקְשׁוּ אֶת־נַפְשִׁי לְקַחְתָּהּ: וַיֹּאמֶר צֵא
וְעָמַדְתָּ בָהָר לִפְנֵי יהוה וְהִנֵּה יהוה עֹבֵר וְרוּחַ גְּדוֹלָה וְחָזָק

PINḤAS

When the wicked Queen Izevel hears of Eliyahu's victory over the priests of Baal in the contest on Mount Carmel, she declares war on Eliyahu. Eliyahu realizes that despite the outcome of the contest, he remains alone in the battle against Izevel. Disappointed and desperate, he flees to Mount Sinai and there has an encounter with God. Speaking to God, Eliyahu requests to end his mission as a prophet. God understands that the terrible drought

powerful wind split mountains and shattered rocks before the
Lord – but the Lord was not in the wind. And after the wind,
12 an earthquake – but the Lord was not in the earthquake. And
after the earthquake, fire – but the Lord was not in the fire.
13 And after the fire – a faint sound of silence. And when Eliyahu
heard, he wrapped his face in his cloak and went out and stood
by the entrance of the cave. And suddenly a voice came to him
14 and said, "Why are you here, Eliyahu?" "I acted out of fervor,
out of passion for the Lord, God of Hosts," he said, "for the
Israelites have abandoned Your covenant, destroyed Your altars,
and put Your prophets to the sword. I am the only one left, and
15 they seek to take my life." And the Lord answered
him, "Set back out on your way to the Wilderness of Damas-
16 cus. When you arrive, anoint Ḥazael as king over Aram. As for
Yehu son of Nimshi, anoint him as king over Israel; and as for
Elisha son of Shafat of Avel Meḥola, anoint him as a prophet
17 in your place. Whoever escapes the sword of Ḥazael will be
killed by Yehu, and whoever escapes the sword of Yehu will be
18 killed by Elisha. I will leave but seven thousand of Israel: every
knee that has not bowed to Baal and every mouth that has not
19 kissed him." He set out from there and found Elisha son of Shafat. He was plowing with twelve pairs of oxen before him, and
he was with the twelfth. When Eliyahu reached him, he tossed
20 his cloak over him. He left the oxen and went running after Eliyahu. "Let me just kiss my father and mother," he said, "and I
will follow you." "Go back, then," he said to him. "What have
21 I done to you?" He turned back from him and took the pair of
oxen; he slaughtered them, and, using the oxen gear, he boiled
their meat and gave it out to the people to eat. Then he set out
and followed Eliyahu and became his attendant.

מְפָרֵק הָרִים וּמְשַׁבֵּר סְלָעִים לִפְנֵי יְהוָה לֹא בָרוּחַ יְהוָה
יב וְאַחַר הָרוּחַ רַעַשׁ לֹא בָרַעַשׁ יְהוָה: וְאַחַר הָרַעַשׁ אֵשׁ לֹא
יג בָאֵשׁ יְהוָה וְאַחַר הָאֵשׁ קוֹל דְּמָמָה דַקָּה: וַיְהִי | כִּשְׁמֹעַ
אֵלִיָּהוּ וַיָּלֶט פָּנָיו בְּאַדַּרְתּוֹ וַיֵּצֵא וַיַּעֲמֹד פֶּתַח הַמְּעָרָה
יד וְהִנֵּה אֵלָיו קוֹל וַיֹּאמֶר מַה־לְּךָ פֹה אֵלִיָּהוּ: וַיֹּאמֶר קַנֹּא
קִנֵּאתִי לַיהוָה | אֱלֹהֵי צְבָאוֹת כִּי־עָזְבוּ בְרִיתְךָ בְּנֵי יִשְׂרָאֵל
אֶת־מִזְבְּחֹתֶיךָ הָרָסוּ וְאֶת־נְבִיאֶיךָ הָרְגוּ בֶחָרֶב וָאִוָּתֵר אֲנִי
טו לְבַדִּי וַיְבַקְשׁוּ אֶת־נַפְשִׁי לְקַחְתָּהּ: וַיֹּאמֶר יְהוָה
אֵלָיו לֵךְ שׁוּב לְדַרְכְּךָ מִדְבַּרָה דַמָּשֶׂק וּבָאתָ וּמָשַׁחְתָּ אֶת־
טז חֲזָאֵל לְמֶלֶךְ עַל־אֲרָם: וְאֵת יֵהוּא בֶן־נִמְשִׁי תִּמְשַׁח לְמֶלֶךְ
עַל־יִשְׂרָאֵל וְאֶת־אֱלִישָׁע בֶּן־שָׁפָט מֵאָבֵל מְחוֹלָה תִּמְשַׁח
יז לְנָבִיא תַּחְתֶּיךָ: וְהָיָה הַנִּמְלָט מֵחֶרֶב חֲזָאֵל יָמִית יֵהוּא
יח וְהַנִּמְלָט מֵחֶרֶב יֵהוּא יָמִית אֱלִישָׁע: וְהִשְׁאַרְתִּי בְיִשְׂרָאֵל
שִׁבְעַת אֲלָפִים כָּל־הַבִּרְכַּיִם אֲשֶׁר לֹא־כָרְעוּ לַבַּעַל וְכָל־הַפֶּה
יט אֲשֶׁר לֹא־נָשַׁק לוֹ: וַיֵּלֶךְ מִשָּׁם וַיִּמְצָא אֶת־אֱלִישָׁע בֶּן־שָׁפָט
וְהוּא חֹרֵשׁ שְׁנֵים־עָשָׂר צְמָדִים לְפָנָיו וְהוּא בִּשְׁנֵים הֶעָשָׂר
כ וַיַּעֲבֹר אֵלִיָּהוּ אֵלָיו וַיַּשְׁלֵךְ אַדַּרְתּוֹ אֵלָיו: וַיַּעֲזֹב אֶת־הַבָּקָר
וַיָּרָץ אַחֲרֵי אֵלִיָּהוּ וַיֹּאמֶר אֶשְּׁקָה־נָּא לְאָבִי וּלְאִמִּי וְאֵלְכָה
כא אַחֲרֶיךָ וַיֹּאמֶר לוֹ לֵךְ שׁוּב כִּי מֶה־עָשִׂיתִי לָךְ: וַיָּשָׁב מֵאַחֲרָיו
וַיִּקַּח אֶת־צֶמֶד הַבָּקָר וַיִּזְבָּחֵהוּ וּבִכְלִי הַבָּקָר בִּשְּׁלָם הַבָּשָׂר
וַיִּתֵּן לָעָם וַיֹּאכֵלוּ וַיָּקָם וַיֵּלֶךְ אַחֲרֵי אֵלִיָּהוּ וַיְשָׁרְתֵהוּ:

Haftarat Pinḥas or Matot

Read this haftara on the Shabbat following the Seventeenth of Tamuz.

1 1 The words of Yirmeyahu, son of Ḥilkiyahu, one of the priests JEREMIAH
2 who were in Anatot in the land of Binyamin, to whom the word
of the LORD came in the days of Yoshiyahu son of Amon, king
3 of Yehuda, in the thirteenth year of his reign, and continued
during the days of Yehoyakim son of Yoshiyahu, king of Yehuda,
until the end of the eleventh year of Tzidkiyahu son of Yoshiyahu, king of Yehuda – until the exile of Jerusalem in the fifth
4 5 month: The word of the LORD came to me: "Before I
formed you in the womb I knew you. Before you were born I
6 consecrated you. I placed you as a prophet to the nations." I said,
"Please, Lord GOD, I am not capable of speaking, for I am still
7 only a boy." The LORD replied to me, "Do not say, 'I am a boy,'
for you shall go to all to whom I send you, and you shall speak as
8 I instruct you. Do not fear them, for I am with you to rescue you,
9 declares the LORD." The LORD extended His hand and touched
10 my mouth and the LORD said to me, "Look, I have placed My
words in your mouth. I have appointed you this day against the
kingdoms and against the nations to uproot and tear down, to
11 destroy and demolish, to build and to plant." The word
of the LORD came to me: "What do you see, Yirmeyahu?" I re-
12 plied, "I see the branch of an almond tree." And the LORD said
to me: "You have seen well, for I am watchful about keeping My
13 word." The word of the LORD came to me a second
time: "What do you see?" I answered, "I see a boiling cauldron
14 facing the north." And the LORD said to me: "From the north
disaster shall burst forth upon all the inhabitants of the land,
15 for I am about to summon all the tribes of the kingdoms of the
north," declares the LORD. "They shall come; each shall set up

---

of impending doom to the nation. On the other, he was one of the people and loved them. In this context God's words of encouragement to him take on special meaning: "Stand up and speak to them as I will instruct you. Do not break down because of them…. I have made you today a fortress city, an iron column, and walls of bronze…. They will wage battle against you, but they will not prevail." Yirmeyahu's attempts to avoid this terrible role, like Moshe's centuries earlier, testify to this difficulty as well.

הפטרת פינחס או מטות

Read this הפטרה *on the* שבת *following* שבעה עשר בתמוז.

א א דִּבְרֵי יִרְמְיָהוּ בֶּן־חִלְקִיָּהוּ מִן־הַכֹּהֲנִים אֲשֶׁר בַּעֲנָתוֹת ירמיה
ב בְּאֶרֶץ בִּנְיָמִן׃ אֲשֶׁר הָיָה דְבַר־יהוה אֵלָיו בִּימֵי יֹאשִׁיָּהוּ
ג בֶן־אָמוֹן מֶלֶךְ יְהוּדָה בִּשְׁלֹשׁ־עֶשְׂרֵה שָׁנָה לְמָלְכוֹ׃ וַיְהִי
בִּימֵי יְהוֹיָקִים בֶּן־יֹאשִׁיָּהוּ מֶלֶךְ יְהוּדָה עַד־תֹּם עַשְׁתֵּי־
עֶשְׂרֵה שָׁנָה לְצִדְקִיָּהוּ בֶן־יֹאשִׁיָּהוּ מֶלֶךְ יְהוּדָה עַד־גְּלוֹת
ד יְרוּשָׁלִַם בַּחֹדֶשׁ הַחֲמִישִׁי׃ וַיְהִי דְבַר־יְהוָה אֵלַי
ה לֵאמֹר׃ בְּטֶרֶם אצורך בַבֶּטֶן יְדַעְתִּיךָ וּבְטֶרֶם תֵּצֵא מֵרֶחֶם אֶצָּרְךָ
ו הִקְדַּשְׁתִּיךָ נָבִיא לַגּוֹיִם נְתַתִּיךָ׃ וָאֹמַר אֲהָהּ אֲדֹנָי יֱהוִה
ז הִנֵּה לֹא־יָדַעְתִּי דַּבֵּר כִּי־נַעַר אָנֹכִי׃ וַיֹּאמֶר יהוה אֵלַי אַל־
תֹּאמַר נַעַר אָנֹכִי כִּי עַל־כָּל־אֲשֶׁר אֶשְׁלָחֲךָ תֵּלֵךְ וְאֵת
ח כָּל־אֲשֶׁר אֲצַוְּךָ תְּדַבֵּר׃ אַל־תִּירָא מִפְּנֵיהֶם כִּי־אִתְּךָ אֲנִי
ט לְהַצִּלֶךָ נְאֻם־יְהוָה׃ וַיִּשְׁלַח יהוה אֶת־יָדוֹ וַיַּגַּע עַל־פִּי וַיֹּאמֶר
י יהוה אֵלַי הִנֵּה נָתַתִּי דְבָרַי בְּפִיךָ׃ רְאֵה הִפְקַדְתִּיךָ ׀ הַיּוֹם
הַזֶּה עַל־הַגּוֹיִם וְעַל־הַמַּמְלָכוֹת לִנְתוֹשׁ וְלִנְתוֹץ וּלְהַאֲבִיד
יא וְלַהֲרוֹס לִבְנוֹת וְלִנְטוֹעַ׃ וַיְהִי דְבַר־יהוה אֵלַי
לֵאמֹר מָה־אַתָּה רֹאֶה יִרְמְיָהוּ וָאֹמַר מַקֵּל שָׁקֵד אֲנִי רֹאֶה׃
יב וַיֹּאמֶר יְהוָה אֵלַי הֵיטַבְתָּ לִרְאוֹת כִּי־שֹׁקֵד אֲנִי עַל־דְּבָרִי
יג לַעֲשֹׂתוֹ׃ וַיְהִי דְבַר־יְהוָה ׀ אֵלַי שֵׁנִית לֵאמֹר מָה
אַתָּה רֹאֶה וָאֹמַר סִיר נָפוּחַ אֲנִי רֹאֶה וּפָנָיו מִפְּנֵי צָפוֹנָה׃
יד וַיֹּאמֶר יְהוָה אֵלָי מִצָּפוֹן תִּפָּתַח הָרָעָה עַל כָּל־יֹשְׁבֵי הָאָרֶץ׃
טו כִּי ׀ הִנְנִי קֹרֵא לְכָל־מִשְׁפְּחוֹת מַמְלְכוֹת צָפוֹנָה נְאֻם־יְהוָה

MATOT

Yirmeyahu prophesied during the reigns of the final kings of Yehuda up till the destruction of Jerusalem and afterward. His call to prophecy emphasizes the harsh daily reality of the prophet. Yirmeyahu's career was especially fraught. He was the first and only prophet who foretold the destruction as it occurred. His challenge stemmed from his complex nature: On the one hand he was a divine messenger, commanded to deliver a message

a throne at the entrance of the gates of Jerusalem against her
16 ramparts roundabout and against all the cities of Yehuda. Thus
will I pronounce My judgment upon them on account of their
wickedness: they abandoned Me, sacrificed to other gods, and
17 worshipped the works of their own hands. As for you, be courageous; stand up and speak to them as I will instruct you. Do not
break down because of them lest I break you down before them.
18 I have made you today a fortress city, an iron column, and walls
of bronze against the entire land – against the kings of Yehuda,
19 its princes, its priests, and the people of the land. They will wage
battle against you, but they will not prevail, for I am with you,"
2 1 declares the Lord, "to rescue you." The word of the
2 Lord came to me: "Go and proclaim to the people of Jerusalem:
'This is what the Lord has said: I recall on your behalf the devotion of your youth, your bridal love, when you followed Me into
3 the wilderness, a land unseeded. Israel is a treasure to the Lord,
His choice harvest. All who eat of it will be held to account. Evil
will befall them, declares the Lord.'"

Haftarat Masei

When Matot and Masei are read together, read this haftara, even on Rosh Ḥodesh Av.

JEREMIAH
For Ashkenazim and Sepharadim

2 4 Listen to the word of the Lord, House of Yaakov and all the
5 tribes of the House of Israel. This is what the Lord said: What
fault did your forefathers find with Me that they distanced themselves from Me? They followed nothingness and became noth-
6 ing. They did not say, "Where is the Lord who lifted us up from
the land of Egypt, who guided us in the wilderness, a land of deserts and pits, an arid land, deathly dark, a land never traversed by

One who has access to such a source of water would be foolish to give it up in exchange for other, inferior sources. If he does so, he loses the important benefits he has received and endangers himself. He will either find himself without water after making himself dependent on cracked cisterns that do not hold water (a metaphor for the empty idolatrous religions), or he will be swept away when he tries to drink from the raging river (symbolizing the strong but unreliable river-valley empires of Assyria and Egypt). If Israel gives up on its political and religious independence, it will become empty and worthless, a dead limb appended to the world.

וּבָאוּ וְנָתְנוּ אִישׁ כִּסְאוֹ פֶּתַח ׀ שַׁעֲרֵי יְרוּשָׁלַםִ וְעַל כָּל־
טז חוֹמֹתֶיהָ סָבִיב וְעַל כָּל־עָרֵי יְהוּדָה: וְדִבַּרְתִּי מִשְׁפָּטַי
אוֹתָם עַל כָּל־רָעָתָם אֲשֶׁר עֲזָבוּנִי וַיְקַטְּרוּ לֵאלֹהִים אֲחֵרִים
יז וַיִּשְׁתַּחֲווּ לְמַעֲשֵׂי יְדֵיהֶם: וְאַתָּה תֶּאְזֹר מָתְנֶיךָ וְקַמְתָּ וְדִבַּרְתָּ
אֲלֵיהֶם אֵת כָּל־אֲשֶׁר אָנֹכִי אֲצַוֶּךָּ אַל־תֵּחַת מִפְּנֵיהֶם פֶּן־
יח אֲחִתְּךָ לִפְנֵיהֶם: וַאֲנִי הִנֵּה נְתַתִּיךָ הַיּוֹם לְעִיר מִבְצָר וּלְעַמּוּד
בַּרְזֶל וּלְחֹמוֹת נְחֹשֶׁת עַל־כָּל־הָאָרֶץ לְמַלְכֵי יְהוּדָה לְשָׂרֶיהָ
יט לְכֹהֲנֶיהָ וּלְעַם הָאָרֶץ: וְנִלְחֲמוּ אֵלֶיךָ וְלֹא־יוּכְלוּ לָךְ כִּי־
ב א אִתְּךָ אֲנִי נְאֻם־יהוה לְהַצִּילֶךָ: וַיְהִי דְבַר־יהוה
ב אֵלַי לֵאמֹר: הָלֹךְ וְקָרָאתָ בְאָזְנֵי יְרוּשָׁלַםִ לֵאמֹר כֹּה אָמַר
יהוה זָכַרְתִּי לָךְ חֶסֶד נְעוּרַיִךְ אַהֲבַת כְּלוּלֹתָיִךְ לֶכְתֵּךְ אַחֲרַי
ג בַּמִּדְבָּר בְּאֶרֶץ לֹא זְרוּעָה: קֹדֶשׁ יִשְׂרָאֵל לַיהוה רֵאשִׁית
תְּבוּאָתֹה כָּל־אֹכְלָיו יֶאְשָׁמוּ רָעָה תָּבֹא אֲלֵיהֶם נְאֻם־יהוה:

הפטרת מסעי

When מטות *and* מסעי *are read together, read this* הפטרה*, even on* ראש חודש אב*.*

ירמיה
For Ashkenazim and Sepharadim

ב ד שִׁמְעוּ דְבַר־יהוה בֵּית יַעֲקֹב וְכָל־מִשְׁפְּחוֹת בֵּית יִשְׂרָאֵל:
ה כֹּה ׀ אָמַר יהוה מַה־מָּצְאוּ אֲבוֹתֵיכֶם בִּי עָוֶל כִּי רָחֲקוּ מֵעָלָי
ו וַיֵּלְכוּ אַחֲרֵי הַהֶבֶל וַיֶּהְבָּלוּ: וְלֹא אָמְרוּ אַיֵּה יהוה הַמַּעֲלֶה
אֹתָנוּ מֵאֶרֶץ מִצְרָיִם הַמּוֹלִיךְ אֹתָנוּ בַּמִּדְבָּר בְּאֶרֶץ עֲרָבָה
וְשׁוּחָה בְּאֶרֶץ צִיָּה וְצַלְמָוֶת בְּאֶרֶץ לֹא־עָבַר בָּהּ אִישׁ וְלֹא־

MASEI

Ashkenazim and Sepharadim

The first prophecy of Yirmeyahu, pronounced during the reign of Yoshiyahu, deals with two topics: (1) abandoning idolatry and returning to God, and (2) retreating from overinvolvement in international politics, since alliances with powerful foreign nations invariably lead to negative foreign influences. To concretize these ideas, the prophet uses metaphors having to do with water. "Flowing water," i.e., clean water found in springs, is cold, and its movement gives it the appearance of life – this symbolizes God's life-giving words and commands.

7 man, where no one ever dwelt?" I brought you to a fertile land,
to eat its fruits and bounty, but you came and defiled My land,
8 and made My heritage an abomination. The priests did not say,
"Where is the LORD?" The teachers of the Torah did not know
Me. The shepherds betrayed Me. The prophets prophesied in
9 the name of Baal. They pursued that which was useless. Therefore, I will continue to contend with them, declares the LORD.
10 I will contend with their children's children. Cross over to the
islands of the Kittites and observe. Send emissaries to Kedar and
11 ponder well. See if anything like this ever happened before. Has
a people ever exchanged its gods, and they are non-gods? Yet my
12 nation exchanged its glory for something useless. Heavens, be
astounded by this. Storm and become utterly desolate, declares
13 the LORD. For My nation has performed two wrongs: they have
forsaken Me, the source of living waters, to dig wells, broken
14 wells that cannot hold water. Is Israel a slave? Is he born to a
15 maidservant? Why has he become an object of plunder? Young
lions roar at him. They voiced their cries. They laid waste to his
16 land. His cities have been set afire, with no inhabitants. Even
17 the men of Nof and Taḥpanḥes crush your skull. This has been
done to you because you deserted the LORD your God during
18 the time He guided you upon the journey. Now of what use is
it to you to approach Egypt to drink the waters of Shiḥor? Of
what use is it to you to approach Assyria to drink the waters of
19 the river? Your own evil will discipline you; your own wayward-
ness will rebuke you. Know and see that your abandonment of
the LORD your God has been bad and bitter. There is no fear of
20 Me in you, says the Almighty, LORD of Hosts. I broke your yoke
long ago. I tore your restraints asunder. You said, "I will never
again transgress!" Yet on every high hilltop and under every leafy
21 tree you recline like a harlot. I planted you as a choice grape: perfect and genuine seed. How did you change on Me into a weed?
22 Rotten grapes of a strange vine! Although you scrub yourself
with natron and heap soap on yourselves, your guilt is stained
23 before Me, declares the Lord GOD. How can you say that you
were never defiled? That you never followed the Be'alim? Look
back upon your path in the valley. Recognize what you did, like
24 a young she-camel clinging to her wild ways. Like a wild ass accustomed to the wilderness; inhaling wind as she pleases, her
wailing cannot be silenced. Yet those who seek her need not
25 be weary. In her month they will find her. Spare your foot from

ז יֹשֵׁב אָדָם שָׁם׃ וָאָבִיא אֶתְכֶם אֶל־אֶרֶץ הַכַּרְמֶל לֶאֱכֹל
פִּרְיָהּ וְטוּבָהּ וַתָּבֹאוּ וַתְּטַמְּאוּ אֶת־אַרְצִי וְנַחֲלָתִי שַׂמְתֶּם
ח לְתוֹעֵבָה׃ הַכֹּהֲנִים לֹא אָמְרוּ אַיֵּה יְהוָה וְתֹפְשֵׂי הַתּוֹרָה לֹא
יְדָעוּנִי וְהָרֹעִים פָּשְׁעוּ בִי וְהַנְּבִאִים נִבְּאוּ בַבַּעַל וְאַחֲרֵי לֹא־
ט יוֹעִלוּ הָלָכוּ׃ לָכֵן עֹד אָרִיב אִתְּכֶם נְאֻם־יְהוָה וְאֶת־בְּנֵי בְנֵיכֶם
י אָרִיב׃ כִּי עִבְרוּ אִיֵּי כִתִּיִּים וּרְאוּ וְקֵדָר שִׁלְחוּ וְהִתְבּוֹנְנוּ
יא מְאֹד וּרְאוּ הֵן הָיְתָה כָּזֹאת׃ הַהֵימִיר גּוֹי אֱלֹהִים וְהֵמָּה לֹא
יב אֱלֹהִים וְעַמִּי הֵמִיר כְּבוֹדוֹ בְּלוֹא יוֹעִיל׃ שֹׁמּוּ שָׁמַיִם עַל־זֹאת
יג וְשַׂעֲרוּ חָרְבוּ מְאֹד נְאֻם־יְהוָה׃ כִּי־שְׁתַּיִם רָעוֹת עָשָׂה עַמִּי
אֹתִי עָזְבוּ מְקוֹר ׀ מַיִם חַיִּים לַחְצֹב לָהֶם בֹּארוֹת בֹּארֹת
יד נִשְׁבָּרִים אֲשֶׁר לֹא־יָכִלוּ הַמָּיִם׃ הַעֶבֶד יִשְׂרָאֵל אִם־יְלִיד
טו בַּיִת הוּא מַדּוּעַ הָיָה לָבַז׃ עָלָיו יִשְׁאֲגוּ כְפִרִים נָתְנוּ קוֹלָם
טז וַיָּשִׁיתוּ אַרְצוֹ לְשַׁמָּה עָרָיו נצתה מִבְּלִי יֹשֵׁב׃ גַּם־בְּנֵי־נֹף נִצְּתוּ
יז ותחפנס יִרְעוּךְ קָדְקֹד׃ הֲלוֹא־זֹאת תַּעֲשֶׂה־לָּךְ עָזְבֵךְ אֶת־ וְתַחְפַּנְחֵס
יח יְהוָה אֱלֹהַיִךְ בְּעֵת מוֹלִכֵךְ בַּדָּרֶךְ׃ וְעַתָּה מַה־לָּךְ לְדֶרֶךְ
מִצְרַיִם לִשְׁתּוֹת מֵי שִׁחוֹר וּמַה־לָּךְ לְדֶרֶךְ אַשּׁוּר לִשְׁתּוֹת מֵי
יט נָהָר׃ תְּיַסְּרֵךְ רָעָתֵךְ וּמְשֻׁבוֹתַיִךְ תּוֹכִחֻךְ וּדְעִי וּרְאִי כִּי־רַע
וָמָר עָזְבֵךְ אֶת־יְהוָה אֱלֹהָיִךְ וְלֹא פַחְדָּתִי אֵלַיִךְ נְאֻם־אֲדֹנָי
כ יֱהוִה צְבָאוֹת׃ כִּי מֵעוֹלָם שָׁבַרְתִּי עֻלֵּךְ נִתַּקְתִּי מוֹסְרוֹתַיִךְ
וַתֹּאמְרִי לֹא אעבוד כִּי עַל־כָּל־גִּבְעָה גְּבֹהָה וְתַחַת כָּל־עֵץ אֶעֱבוֹר
כא רַעֲנָן אַתְּ צֹעָה זֹנָה׃ וְאָנֹכִי נְטַעְתִּיךְ שׂוֹרֵק כֻּלֹּה זֶרַע אֱמֶת
כב וְאֵיךְ נֶהְפַּכְתְּ לִי סוּרֵי הַגֶּפֶן נָכְרִיָּה׃ כִּי אִם־תְּכַבְּסִי בַּנֶּתֶר
כג וְתַרְבִּי־לָךְ בֹּרִית נִכְתָּם עֲוֹנֵךְ לְפָנַי נְאֻם אֲדֹנָי יֱהוִה׃ אֵיךְ
תֹּאמְרִי לֹא נִטְמֵאתִי אַחֲרֵי הַבְּעָלִים לֹא הָלַכְתִּי רְאִי דַרְכֵּךְ
כד בַגַּיְא דְּעִי מֶה עָשִׂית בִּכְרָה קַלָּה מְשָׂרֶכֶת דְּרָכֶיהָ׃ פֶּרֶה ׀
לִמֻּד מִדְבָּר בְּאַוַּת נפשו שָׁאֲפָה רוּחַ תַּאֲנָתָהּ מִי יְשִׁיבֶנָּה נַפְשָׁהּ
כה כָּל־מְבַקְשֶׁיהָ לֹא יִיעָפוּ בְּחָדְשָׁהּ יִמְצָאוּנְהָ׃ מִנְעִי רַגְלֵךְ

becoming bare and your throat from suffering thirst! But you
said, "Never mind. No. I have loved strangers; it is them whom
26 I will follow." Like the shame of a thief when he is found out, so
will the House of Israel be shamed: They, their kings, their noble-
27 men, their priests, and their prophets. They say to the tree, "You
are my father!" And to the stone, "You gave birth to me!" They
have turned their backs to Me, not their faces but in their time
28 of trouble they say, "Arise and save us!" Where are the gods that
you have crafted for yourself? Let them rise if they can save you
in your time of trouble. For your gods, Yehuda, are as numerous
as your cities.

Ashkenazim and Minhag Anglia add

3 4 By now, you should have called Me: "Father! You were my childhood companion!"

Sepharadim, Chabad and Minhag Anglia add

4 1 If you, Israel, return to Me, declares the LORD, I will welcome
your return. If you remove your abominations from My presence,
2 you shall not suffer exile. You will utter oaths – exclaiming "as
the LORD lives" truthfully, justly, and righteously – so that other
nations will bless themselves by Him and come to take pride in
Him.

ISAIAH

For Yemenites

1 1 The vision of Yeshayahu son of Amotz, which he saw regarding Yehuda and Jerusalem in the days of Uziyahu, Yotam, Aḥaz,
2 and Ḥizkiyahu, kings of Yehuda: Listen, heavens, hear, O earth:
the LORD has spoken: I brought up children, raised them;
3 they rebelled against Me. Even an ox knows its owner, an ass
its master's trough. Israel does not know; My people does not
4 try to understand. Woe to the sinning nation, a people weighed
down with iniquity, seed of the wicked, vicious children, they
forsook the LORD, defamed the Holy One of Israel, fell away.
5 Why should you suffer more beatings? Yet you spawn more
6 defiance, your head sickened, all, your whole heart ailing. From
sole to crown – nothing is sound; laceration, bruise, and open
wound never squeezed or bandaged; never eased with oil:

wicked life. The destruction of many parts of the land of Israel by enemies should have given the Israelites pause to consider the error of their ways, but even these misfortunes could not convince them to repent. The prophet calls on the people to mend their behavior before the final hammer falls.

מִיָּחֵף וגורנך מִצִּמְאָה וַתֹּאמְרִי נוֹאָשׁ לוֹא כִּי־אָהַבְתִּי זָרִים | וּגְרוֹנֵךְ
כו וְאַחֲרֵיהֶם אֵלֵךְ: כְּבֹשֶׁת גַּנָּב כִּי יִמָּצֵא כֵּן הֹבִישׁוּ בֵּית יִשְׂרָאֵל
כז הֵמָּה מַלְכֵיהֶם שָׂרֵיהֶם וְכֹהֲנֵיהֶם וּנְבִיאֵיהֶם: אֹמְרִים לָעֵץ
אָבִי אַתָּה וְלָאֶבֶן אַתְּ ילדתני כִּי־פָנוּ אֵלַי עֹרֶף וְלֹא פָנִים | יְלִדְתָּנוּ
כח וּבְעֵת רָעָתָם יֹאמְרוּ קוּמָה וְהוֹשִׁיעֵנוּ: וְאַיֵּה אֱלֹהֶיךָ אֲשֶׁר
עָשִׂיתָ לָּךְ יָקוּמוּ אִם־יוֹשִׁיעוּךָ בְּעֵת רָעָתֶךָ כִּי מִסְפַּר עָרֶיךָ
הָיוּ אֱלֹהֶיךָ יְהוּדָה:
ג ד *הֲלוֹא מֵעַתָּה קראתי לִי אָבִי אַלּוּף נְעֻרַי אָתָּה: | קָרָאת
ד א ▪אִם־תָּשׁוּב יִשְׂרָאֵל | נְאֻם־יְהוָה אֵלַי תָּשׁוּב וְאִם־תָּסִיר
ב שִׁקּוּצֶיךָ מִפָּנַי וְלֹא תָנוּד: וְנִשְׁבַּעְתָּ חַי־יְהוָה בֶּאֱמֶת בְּמִשְׁפָּט
וּבִצְדָקָה וְהִתְבָּרְכוּ בוֹ גּוֹיִם וּבוֹ יִתְהַלָּלוּ:

**Ashkenazim and Minhag Anglia add*
▪Sepharadim, Chabad and Minhag Anglia add

ישעיה
For Yemenites

א א חֲזוֹן יְשַׁעְיָהוּ בֶן־אָמוֹץ אֲשֶׁר חָזָה עַל־יְהוּדָה וִירוּשָׁלָ͏ִם
ב בִּימֵי עֻזִּיָּהוּ יוֹתָם אָחָז יְחִזְקִיָּהוּ מַלְכֵי יְהוּדָה: שִׁמְעוּ שָׁמַיִם
וְהַאֲזִינִי אֶרֶץ כִּי יְהוָה דִּבֵּר בָּנִים גִּדַּלְתִּי וְרוֹמַמְתִּי וְהֵם
ג פָּשְׁעוּ בִי: יָדַע שׁוֹר קֹנֵהוּ וַחֲמוֹר אֵבוּס בְּעָלָיו יִשְׂרָאֵל
ד לֹא יָדַע עַמִּי לֹא הִתְבּוֹנָן: הוֹי | גּוֹי חֹטֵא עַם כֶּבֶד עָוֺן
זֶרַע מְרֵעִים בָּנִים מַשְׁחִיתִים עָזְבוּ אֶת־יְהוָה נִאֲצוּ אֶת־
ה קְדוֹשׁ יִשְׂרָאֵל נָזֹרוּ אָחוֹר: עַל מֶה תֻכּוּ עוֹד תּוֹסִיפוּ סָרָה
ו כָּל־רֹאשׁ לָחֳלִי וְכָל־לֵבָב דַּוָּי: מִכַּף־רֶגֶל וְעַד־רֹאשׁ אֵין־
בּוֹ מְתֹם פֶּצַע וְחַבּוּרָה וּמַכָּה טְרִיָּה לֹא־זֹרוּ וְלֹא חֻבָּשׁוּ

Yemenites

When we look at the words of reproach with which the prophet Yeshayahu berated the people, two lines of thought in particular stand out. First, God is disappointed with the people's disloyal behavior after all He has done for them. Second, God cares nothing about the sacrificial service in the Temple if the worshipper at the same time leads a

▶

7 your land is laid waste, your towns burned up in fire; your own
land – before your eyes strangers consume it – laid waste: a vi-
8 sion of strangers' overturning. Only daughter Zion stands like
the watchman's shack in a vineyard, like the hut in a cucumber
9 field – a town besieged. *Were it not for the Lord of Hosts, who left*
of us a bare remnant, we would have been like Sedom, like Amora –
10 *gone.* Listen to the Lord's word, you officers of Sedom;
11 hear the teaching of our God, you townsmen of Amora. Why,
says the Lord, would I want all these offerings? I am sated with
burnt offerings, with rams and fleshy creatures' fat, the blood of
12 bulls and sheep and goats – I do not want them. You come, appear before Me. Who asked all this of you, who asked you for all
13 this: trampling My courtyards? Bring no more your empty gifts –
they are foul incense to Me; New Moon and Sabbath, the feast
days you proclaim – I cannot endure these sins and assemblies.
14 Your New Moons and festivals, how I hate them; they have be-
15 come a burden to Me; I am weary, I cannot bear them. When you
spread your hands out skyward, I must turn My eyes away; when
you pray with such verbosity, I am not listening. Your hands, they
16 are covered in blood. Wash them, be clean now, remove your ter-
17 rible deeds from My sight; stop bringing about such evils. Learn
to do good. Seek justice. Correct what is cruel. Rule justice for
18 orphans. Fight the widows' cause. Come, let us argue
this out; so says the Lord. Though your sins may be like scarlet, they will grow whiter than snow. Though they redden you
19 more than dye worms, they will be clean wool again. If you will
20 it and listen, the best of this earth is yours to eat, but if you refuse
and rebel against Me, the sword will devour you; the Lord has
spoken.

Haftarat Devarim

1 1 The vision of Yeshayahu son of Amotz, which he saw regarding Yehuda and Jerusalem in the days of Uziyahu, Yotam, Aḥaz,
2 and Ḥizkiyahu, kings of Yehuda: Listen, heavens, hear, O earth:

ISAIAH

Ashkenazim and Sepharadim begin here

political-military, and social turmoil. In this *haftara*, Yeshayahu mentions the city of Sedom twice, both for the terrible punishment meted out on it and for the extreme wickedness with which it was saturated. Leaders have a crucial role

ז וְלֹא רֻכְּכָה בַּשָּׁמֶן׃ אַרְצְכֶם שְׁמָמָה עָרֵיכֶם שְׂרֻפוֹת אֵשׁ
אַדְמַתְכֶם לְנֶגְדְּכֶם זָרִים אֹכְלִים אֹתָהּ וּשְׁמָמָה כְּמַהְפֵּכַת
ח זָרִים׃ וְנוֹתְרָה בַת־צִיּוֹן כְּסֻכָּה בְכָרֶם כִּמְלוּנָה בְמִקְשָׁה
ט כְּעִיר נְצוּרָה׃ לוּלֵי יְהוָה צְבָאוֹת הוֹתִיר לָנוּ שָׂרִיד כִּמְעָט
י כִּסְדֹם הָיִינוּ לַעֲמֹרָה דָּמִינוּ׃ שִׁמְעוּ דְבַר־יְהוָה
יא קְצִינֵי סְדֹם הַאֲזִינוּ תּוֹרַת אֱלֹהֵינוּ עַם עֲמֹרָה׃ לָמָּה לִּי
רֹב־זִבְחֵיכֶם יֹאמַר יְהוָה שָׂבַעְתִּי עֹלוֹת אֵילִים וְחֵלֶב מְרִיאִים
יב וְדַם פָּרִים וּכְבָשִׂים וְעַתּוּדִים לֹא חָפָצְתִּי׃ כִּי תָבֹאוּ לֵרָאוֹת
יג פָּנָי מִי־בִקֵּשׁ זֹאת מִיֶּדְכֶם רְמֹס חֲצֵרָי׃ לֹא תוֹסִיפוּ הָבִיא
מִנְחַת־שָׁוְא קְטֹרֶת תּוֹעֵבָה הִיא לִי חֹדֶשׁ וְשַׁבָּת קְרֹא
יד מִקְרָא לֹא־אוּכַל אָוֶן וַעֲצָרָה׃ חָדְשֵׁיכֶם וּמוֹעֲדֵיכֶם שָׂנְאָה
טו נַפְשִׁי הָיוּ עָלַי לָטֹרַח נִלְאֵיתִי נְשֹׂא׃ וּבְפָרִשְׂכֶם כַּפֵּיכֶם
אַעְלִים עֵינַי מִכֶּם גַּם כִּי־תַרְבּוּ תְפִלָּה אֵינֶנִּי שֹׁמֵעַ יְדֵיכֶם
טז דָּמִים מָלֵאוּ׃ רַחֲצוּ הִזַּכּוּ הָסִירוּ רֹעַ מַעַלְלֵיכֶם מִנֶּגֶד עֵינָי
יז חִדְלוּ הָרֵעַ׃ לִמְדוּ הֵיטֵב דִּרְשׁוּ מִשְׁפָּט אַשְּׁרוּ חָמוֹץ שִׁפְטוּ
יח יָתוֹם רִיבוּ אַלְמָנָה׃ לְכוּ־נָא וְנִוָּכְחָה יֹאמַר יְהוָה
אִם־יִהְיוּ חֲטָאֵיכֶם כַּשָּׁנִים כַּשֶּׁלֶג יַלְבִּינוּ אִם־יַאְדִּימוּ כַתּוֹלָע
יט כ כַּצֶּמֶר יִהְיוּ׃ אִם־תֹּאבוּ וּשְׁמַעְתֶּם טוּב הָאָרֶץ תֹּאכֵלוּ׃ וְאִם־
תְּמָאֲנוּ וּמְרִיתֶם חֶרֶב תְּאֻכְּלוּ כִּי פִּי יְהוָה דִּבֵּר׃

הפטרת דברים

ישעיה
Ashkenazim and Sepharadim begin here

א א חֲזוֹן יְשַׁעְיָהוּ בֶן־אָמוֹץ אֲשֶׁר חָזָה עַל־יְהוּדָה וִירוּשָׁלָםִ
ב בִּימֵי עֻזִּיָּהוּ יוֹתָם אָחָז יְחִזְקִיָּהוּ מַלְכֵי יְהוּדָה׃ שִׁמְעוּ שָׁמַיִם

DEVARIM

Yeshayahu prophesied in the kingdom of Yehuda and Jerusalem for decades, during the reigns of Uziyahu, Yotam, Aḥaz, and Ḥizkiyahu. During this period, Yehuda went through spiritual,

the LORD has spoken: I brought up children, raised them;
3 they rebelled against Me. Even an ox knows its owner, an ass
its master's trough. Israel does not know; My people does not
4 try to understand. Woe to the sinning nation, a people weighed
down with iniquity, seed of the wicked, vicious children, they
forsook the LORD, defamed the Holy One of Israel, fell away.
5 Why should you suffer more beatings? Yet you spawn more
6 defiance, your head sickened, all, your whole heart ailing. From
sole to crown – nothing is sound; laceration, bruise, and open
wound never squeezed or bandaged; never eased with oil:
7 your land is laid waste, your towns burned up in fire; your own
land – before your eyes strangers consume it – laid waste: a vi-
8 sion of strangers' overturning. Only daughter Zion stands like
the watchman's shack in a vineyard, like the hut in a cucumber
9 field – a town besieged. *Were it not for the LORD of Hosts, who left*
of us a bare remnant, we would have been like Sedom, like Amora –
10 *gone.* Listen to the LORD's word, you officers of Sedom;
11 hear the teaching of our God, you townsmen of Amora. Why,
says the LORD, would I want all these offerings? I am sated with
burnt offerings, with rams and fleshy creatures' fat, the blood of
12 bulls and sheep and goats – I do not want them. You come, appear before Me. Who asked all this of you, who asked you for all
13 this: trampling My courtyards? Bring no more your empty gifts –
they are foul incense to Me; New Moon and Sabbath, the feast
days you proclaim – I cannot endure these sins and assemblies.
14 Your New Moons and festivals, how I hate them; they have be-
15 come a burden to Me; I am weary, I cannot bear them. When you
spread your hands out skyward, I must turn My eyes away; when
you pray with such verbosity, I am not listening. Your hands,
16 they are covered in blood. Wash them, be clean now, remove
your terrible deeds from My sight; stop bringing about such
17 evils. Learn to do good. Seek justice. Correct what is cruel. Rule
18 justice for orphans. Fight the widows' cause. Come,
let us argue this out; so says the LORD. Though your sins may
be like scarlet, they will grow whiter than snow. Though they

---

filled with murderers. Israel can only succeed in correcting these evils if the corrupt leadership is replaced. This is a vision (*ḥazon*) that we must all take to heart on the Shabbat before the Ninth of Av, Shabbat Ḥazon.

וְהַאֲזִינִי אֶרֶץ כִּי יְהוָה דִּבֵּר בָּנִים גִּדַּלְתִּי וְרוֹמַמְתִּי וְהֵם
ג פָּשְׁעוּ בִי׃ יָדַע שׁוֹר קֹנֵהוּ וַחֲמוֹר אֵבוּס בְּעָלָיו יִשְׂרָאֵל
ד לֹא יָדַע עַמִּי לֹא הִתְבּוֹנָן׃ הוֹי ׀ גּוֹי חֹטֵא עַם כֶּבֶד עָוֺן
זֶרַע מְרֵעִים בָּנִים מַשְׁחִיתִים עָזְבוּ אֶת־יְהוָה נִאֲצוּ אֶת־
ה קְדוֹשׁ יִשְׂרָאֵל נָזֹרוּ אָחוֹר׃ עַל מֶה תֻכּוּ עוֹד תּוֹסִיפוּ סָרָה
ו כָּל־רֹאשׁ לָחֳלִי וְכָל־לֵבָב דַּוָּי׃ מִכַּף־רֶגֶל וְעַד־רֹאשׁ אֵין־
בּוֹ מְתֹם פֶּצַע וְחַבּוּרָה וּמַכָּה טְרִיָּה לֹא־זֹרוּ וְלֹא חֻבָּשׁוּ
ז וְלֹא רֻכְּכָה בַּשָּׁמֶן׃ אַרְצְכֶם שְׁמָמָה עָרֵיכֶם שְׂרֻפוֹת אֵשׁ
אַדְמַתְכֶם לְנֶגְדְּכֶם זָרִים אֹכְלִים אֹתָהּ וּשְׁמָמָה כְּמַהְפֵּכַת
ח זָרִים׃ וְנוֹתְרָה בַת־צִיּוֹן כְּסֻכָּה בְכָרֶם כִּמְלוּנָה בְמִקְשָׁה
ט כְּעִיר נְצוּרָה׃ לוּלֵי יְהוָה צְבָאוֹת הוֹתִיר לָנוּ שָׂרִיד כִּמְעָט
י כִּסְדֹם הָיִינוּ לַעֲמֹרָה דָּמִינוּ׃ שִׁמְעוּ דְבַר־
יא יְהוָה קְצִינֵי סְדֹם הַאֲזִינוּ תּוֹרַת אֱלֹהֵינוּ עַם עֲמֹרָה׃ לָמָּה
לִּי רֹב־זִבְחֵיכֶם יֹאמַר יְהוָה שָׂבַעְתִּי עֹלוֹת אֵילִים וְחֵלֶב
יב מְרִיאִים וְדַם פָּרִים וּכְבָשִׂים וְעַתּוּדִים לֹא חָפָצְתִּי׃ כִּי תָבֹאוּ
יג לֵרָאוֹת פָּנָי מִי־בִקֵּשׁ זֹאת מִיֶּדְכֶם רְמֹס חֲצֵרָי׃ לֹא תוֹסִיפוּ
הָבִיא מִנְחַת־שָׁוְא קְטֹרֶת תּוֹעֵבָה הִיא לִי חֹדֶשׁ וְשַׁבָּת
יד קְרֹא מִקְרָא לֹא־אוּכַל אָוֶן וַעֲצָרָה׃ חָדְשֵׁיכֶם וּמוֹעֲדֵיכֶם
טו שָׂנְאָה נַפְשִׁי הָיוּ עָלַי לָטֹרַח נִלְאֵיתִי נְשֹׂא׃ וּבְפָרִשְׂכֶם
כַּפֵּיכֶם אַעְלִים עֵינַי מִכֶּם גַּם כִּי־תַרְבּוּ תְפִלָּה אֵינֶנִּי שֹׁמֵעַ
טז יְדֵיכֶם דָּמִים מָלֵאוּ׃ רַחֲצוּ הִזַּכּוּ הָסִירוּ רֹעַ מַעַלְלֵיכֶם מִנֶּגֶד
יז עֵינָי חִדְלוּ הָרֵעַ׃ לִמְדוּ הֵיטֵב דִּרְשׁוּ מִשְׁפָּט אַשְּׁרוּ חָמוֹץ
יח שִׁפְטוּ יָתוֹם רִיבוּ אַלְמָנָה׃ לְכוּ־נָא וְנִוָּכְחָה
יֹאמַר יְהוָה אִם־יִהְיוּ חֲטָאֵיכֶם כַּשָּׁנִים כַּשֶּׁלֶג יַלְבִּינוּ אִם־

to play in shaping the communal atmosphere of a place, for good and for bad. The prophet describes a corrupt leadership, which takes advantage of its power for its own purposes and oppresses the weakest members of society, and whose dishonesty filters down into the streets and shops of ordinary citizens. Fake goods are marketed as authentic, and what had once been a city of justice is

redden you more than dye worms, they will be clean wool
19 again. If you will it and listen, the best of this earth is yours to
20 eat, but if you refuse and rebel against Me, the sword will devour
21 you; the LORD has spoken. *How like a whore is she *Yemenites begin here*
now, the faithful metropolis. How full she was of justice once;
22 righteousness lodged with her, now murderers. Your silver has
23 turned into dross, your wine is watered down, your ministers
are wayward, friends to thieves, loving corruption, all of them,
chasing bribes. They do not judge an orphan's case; a widow's
24 claim does not even come before them. And so, says
the Master, the LORD of Hosts, the Mighty One of Israel: This
woe! – I shall seek consolation, crush My foes, wreak vengeance
25 on My enemies. I shall set My hand against you again, as if smelt-
26 ing, refining away your dross; all your lead will I remove. I shall
set up your judges again as first they were, your counselors as
long ago. And then you shall be called Righteous City, Faithful
27 Metropolis. Zion will be redeemed by justice, by righteousness –
28 those who return to her;* rebels and sinners will all be broken, *Ashkenazim and Sepharadim end here*
29 those who forsook the LORD all gone. How ashamed you will be
of the oaks that you longed for, how mortified over the gardens
30 you chose. For you will be like an oak with withered leaves, like
31 a garden that sees no water. That mighty oak will become flax
fibers and the one who once carved them the spark; the two will
burn together, and no one will be there to quench the fire. *Yemenites end here*

HAFTARAT VAETḤANAN

40 1 Comfort, comfort, My people – these are your God's words – ISAIAH
2 speak to Jerusalem's heart and call out to her that her term is
served, her guilt appeased, that she has received at the LORD's
3 hand twice over for all her sins. A voice calls out:

---

true, and the redemption is inevitable. This first prophecy of reassurance after the destruction was perhaps issued by Yeshayahu after the destruction of the northern kingdom of Israel by Assyria in the sixth year of the reign of Ḥizkiyahu king of Yehuda. Still, the themes here remain relevant to all subsequent exiles, and they echo in our synagogues every year on the first Shabbat after the Ninth of Av.

יט יאדימו כתולע כצמר יהיו: אם־תאבו ושמעתם טוב
כ הארץ תאכלו: ואם־תמאנו ומריתם חרב תאכלו כי פי
כא יהוה דבר: *איכה היתה לזונה קריה נאמנה *Yemenites begin here*
כב מלאתי משפט צדק ילין בה ועתה מרצחים: כספך היה
כג לסיגים סבאך מהול במים: שריך סוררים וחברי גנבים
כלו אהב שחד ורדף שלמנים יתום לא ישפטו וריב אלמנה
כד לא־יבוא אליהם: לכן נאם האדון יהוה צבאות
כה אביר ישראל הוי אנחם מצרי ואנקמה מאויבי: ואשיבה
כו ידי עליך ואצרף כבר סיגיך ואסירה כל־בדיליך: ואשיבה
שפטיך כבראשנה ויעציך כבתחלה אחרי־כן יקרא לך
כז עיר הצדק קריה נאמנה: ציון במשפט תפדה ושביה
כח בצדקה:* ושבר פשעים וחטאים יחדו ועזבי יהוה יכלו: *Ashkenazim and Sepharadim end here*
כט כי יבשו מאילים אשר חמדתם ותחפרו מהגנות אשר
ל בחרתם: כי תהיו כאלה נבלת עלה וכגנה אשר־מים אין
לא לה: והיה החסן לנערת ופעלו לניצוץ ובערו שניהם יחדו
ואין מכבה: *Yemenites end here*

הפטרת ואתחנן

מ א ב נחמו נחמו עמי יאמר אלהיכם: דברו על־לב ירושלם ישעיה
וקראו אליה כי מלאה צבאה כי נרצה עונה כי לקחה
ג מיד יהוה כפלים בכל־חטאתיה: קול קורא

VAETḤANAN

The central idea of this *haftara* is the smallness of human beings when compared to the eternal God. The attempts by the nations of the world to erect idolatrous alternatives to the true God are futile. Human beings and their creations are transient. God, who created and controls the world through His providence, determines the course of history. The nation of Israel is in exile not because of the victory of foreign gods but because of the abandonment of its own.

God's call to comfort His people is

"Clear the Lord's way in the desert: smooth across the arid
4 plain a road for our God." Every valley will be raised, each hill
and mountain leveled; the twisted road will be made straight;
5 the mountain ranges, open land, to let the Lord's glory be
revealed, and all flesh see as one – the voice of the Lord has
6 spoken. A voice speaks: "Call out!" I say, "What shall
I call?" All life is nothing more than grass, and all its love, green
7 shoots upon the land. And grass dries up; shoots wither, when
the Lord's breath blows over them and yes – this people is
8 but grass. Grass dries up, and shoots will wither, but the word
9 of our God stands firm; always. O lady, ascend the
high mountain, you who bear tidings to Zion; raise your voice in
strength, with tidings to Jerusalem. Raise it – do not fear – call
10 out loud to the cities of Yehuda: "Behold: your God." Behold:
the Lord your God coming in all His strength, His mighty
arm ruling. Behold: with Him, His prize; His reward walks be-
11 fore Him; like a shepherd He pastures His flock, gathering the
lambs into His arms, bearing them in His embrace, guiding His
12 young. Who was it who measured out the waters in His
palm and gauged the skies by His handspan? Who measured in
His fingers all the dust of earth; who weighed out the hills on
13 His balance and the mountains upon a hand scale? Who could
survey the wind? The Lord. Who is the confidant He would
14 tell? To gain His insight, with whom did He hold counsel; who
taught Him the path of justice? Who ever taught Him awareness;
15 who showed Him the way of insight? Whole nations are like the
drop left in His bucket, as inconsequential as dust on the balance.
16 He sweeps up the distant isles like powder. All Lebanon has not
17 wood enough, or animals, for the burnt offering. All
the nations are as nothing before Him, less than absence, than
18 emptiness, to Him. And what will you liken to God; what im-
19 age will you draw of Him? A smith molds a statue; the jeweler
20 plates it with gold and fashions chains of silver for it. Mulberry
wood his offering, he chooses a tree that will not rot; he chooses
21 a skilled craftsman to build a statue that cannot fall. Do you not
know it, have you not heard, was it not told to you long before?
22 Have you paid no attention to the world's foundations? He sits
over the dome of the sky, its dwellers like grasshoppers below;
He spreads out the skies like a canvas and pulls them taut like
23 a tent to dwell in. He turns great rulers to nothing, the judges

בַּמִּדְבָּר פַּנּוּ דֶּרֶךְ יְהוָה יַשְּׁרוּ בָּעֲרָבָה מְסִלָּה לֵאלֹהֵינוּ׃
ד כָּל־גֶּיא יִנָּשֵׂא וְכָל־הַר וְגִבְעָה יִשְׁפָּלוּ וְהָיָה הֶעָקֹב לְמִישׁוֹר
ה וְהָרְכָסִים לְבִקְעָה׃ וְנִגְלָה כְּבוֹד יְהוָה וְרָאוּ כָל־בָּשָׂר יַחְדָּו כִּי
ו פִּי יְהוָה דִּבֵּר׃ קוֹל אֹמֵר קְרָא וְאָמַר מָה אֶקְרָא
ז כָּל־הַבָּשָׂר חָצִיר וְכָל־חַסְדּוֹ כְּצִיץ הַשָּׂדֶה׃ יָבֵשׁ חָצִיר נָבֵל
ח צִיץ כִּי רוּחַ יְהוָה נָשְׁבָה בּוֹ אָכֵן חָצִיר הָעָם׃ יָבֵשׁ חָצִיר נָבֵל
ט צִיץ וּדְבַר אֱלֹהֵינוּ יָקוּם לְעוֹלָם׃ עַל הַר־גָּבֹהַּ
עֲלִי־לָךְ מְבַשֶּׂרֶת צִיּוֹן הָרִימִי בַכֹּחַ קוֹלֵךְ מְבַשֶּׂרֶת יְרוּשָׁלָםִ
י הָרִימִי אַל־תִּירָאִי אִמְרִי לְעָרֵי יְהוּדָה הִנֵּה אֱלֹהֵיכֶם׃ הִנֵּה
אֲדֹנָי יֱהוִה בְּחָזָק יָבוֹא וּזְרֹעוֹ מֹשְׁלָה לוֹ הִנֵּה שְׂכָרוֹ אִתּוֹ
יא וּפְעֻלָּתוֹ לְפָנָיו׃ כְּרֹעֶה עֶדְרוֹ יִרְעֶה בִּזְרֹעוֹ יְקַבֵּץ טְלָאִים
יב וּבְחֵיקוֹ יִשָּׂא עָלוֹת יְנַהֵל׃ מִי־מָדַד בְּשָׁעֳלוֹ מַיִם
וְשָׁמַיִם בַּזֶּרֶת תִּכֵּן וְכָל בַּשָּׁלִשׁ עֲפַר הָאָרֶץ וְשָׁקַל בַּפֶּלֶס
יג הָרִים וּגְבָעוֹת בְּמֹאזְנָיִם׃ מִי־תִכֵּן אֶת־רוּחַ יְהוָה וְאִישׁ עֲצָתוֹ
יד יוֹדִיעֶנּוּ׃ אֶת־מִי נוֹעָץ וַיְבִינֵהוּ וַיְלַמְּדֵהוּ בְּאֹרַח מִשְׁפָּט
טו וַיְלַמְּדֵהוּ דַעַת וְדֶרֶךְ תְּבוּנוֹת יוֹדִיעֶנּוּ׃ הֵן גּוֹיִם כְּמַר מִדְּלִי
טז וּכְשַׁחַק מֹאזְנַיִם נֶחְשָׁבוּ הֵן אִיִּים כַּדַּק יִטּוֹל׃ וּלְבָנוֹן אֵין
יז דֵּי בָּעֵר וְחַיָּתוֹ אֵין דֵּי עוֹלָה׃ כָּל־הַגּוֹיִם כְּאַיִן
יח נֶגְדּוֹ מֵאֶפֶס וָתֹהוּ נֶחְשְׁבוּ־לוֹ׃ וְאֶל־מִי תְּדַמְּיוּן אֵל וּמַה־
יט דְּמוּת תַּעַרְכוּ־לוֹ׃ הַפֶּסֶל נָסַךְ חָרָשׁ וְצֹרֵף בַּזָּהָב יְרַקְּעֶנּוּ
כ וּרְתֻקוֹת כֶּסֶף צוֹרֵף׃ הַמְסֻכָּן תְּרוּמָה עֵץ לֹא־יִרְקַב יִבְחָר
כא חָרָשׁ חָכָם יְבַקֶּשׁ־לוֹ לְהָכִין פֶּסֶל לֹא יִמּוֹט׃ הֲלוֹא תֵדְעוּ
הֲלוֹא תִשְׁמָעוּ הֲלוֹא הֻגַּד מֵרֹאשׁ לָכֶם הֲלוֹא הֲבִינֹתֶם
כב מוֹסְדוֹת הָאָרֶץ׃ הַיֹּשֵׁב עַל־חוּג הָאָרֶץ וְיֹשְׁבֶיהָ כַּחֲגָבִים
כג הַנּוֹטֶה כַדֹּק שָׁמַיִם וַיִּמְתָּחֵם כָּאֹהֶל לָשָׁבֶת׃ הַנּוֹתֵן רוֹזְנִים

24 of this earth to emptiness, as if they were not planted, were not
sown, as if their stem had no root within the earth. He breathes
on them and they dry up to nothing; the storm will sweep them
25 all away like straw. Whom can you compare Me to –
26 so speaks the Holy One – and find them equal? Raise your eyes
skyward and see: Who created all these? Who summons their legions by number and calls each man by name? In His great might,
His adamantine strength, not one of them is lost.* Why *Ashkenazim and Sepharadim end here*
do you say, Yaakov; Israel, why declare, "My way is hidden from
the LORD; my God overlooks my claim"?

41 17 The oppressed, impoverished, beg for water – there is none;
their tongues are seared with thirst. I am the LORD; I will answer
them; Israel's God, I will not leave them.

HAFTARAT EKEV

49 14 Zion speaks: "The LORD has forsaken me; my Lord, He has for- ISAIAH
15 gotten me." Can a mother forget her own baby; can she fail to
care for the child of her womb? These too may yet forget, but I
16 will not forget you. I have etched you on My palms; your walls
17 are before My eyes always. Your children will run to you; your
18 destroyers, your demolishers, will all be gone from you. Raise
your eyes; look around and see: the children all gathered and
coming back to you. As I live, so says the LORD, you will wear
19 them all as jewels, which you will bind on like a bride. For your
ruins, for your wastelands, for the land of your destruction, for
you will be too narrow for your dwellers, while those who would
20 destroy you will be far away from you. You will yet hear the children say, of whom you were bereaved, "The place is too tight for
21 me; make space for me to sit," while you say in your heart, "Who
bore these children, mine, to me, bereft and left alone, exiled

---

illustrate this connection Yeshayahu uses two metaphors: that of a woman and her child, and that of a husband and wife. These human connections are natural, powerful, and deep. But the prophet pledges in God's name that the link between Him and the people of Israel is even deeper and more powerful than these. It is this link that will bring about the ingathering of the exiles and the reconstitution of the people of Israel in their land, belying the exile and destruction that Yeshayahu's listeners saw before their eyes.

כד לְאַיִן שֹׁפְטֵי אֶרֶץ כַּתֹּהוּ עָשָׂה: אַף בַּל־נִטָּעוּ אַף בַּל־זֹרָעוּ
אַף בַּל־שֹׁרֵשׁ בָּאֶרֶץ גִּזְעָם וְגַם־נָשַׁף בָּהֶם וַיִּבָשׁוּ וּסְעָרָה כַּקַּשׁ
כה תִּשָּׂאֵם: וְאֶל־מִי תְדַמְּיוּנִי וְאֶשְׁוֶה יֹאמַר קָדוֹשׁ:
כו שְׂאוּ־מָרוֹם עֵינֵיכֶם וּרְאוּ מִי־בָרָא אֵלֶּה הַמּוֹצִיא בְמִסְפָּר
צְבָאָם לְכֻלָּם בְּשֵׁם יִקְרָא מֵרֹב אוֹנִים וְאַמִּיץ כֹּחַ אִישׁ לֹא
כז נֶעְדָּר:* לָמָּה תֹאמַר יַעֲקֹב וּתְדַבֵּר יִשְׂרָאֵל נִסְתְּרָה
דַרְכִּי מֵיהוה וּמֵאֱלֹהַי מִשְׁפָּטִי יַעֲבוֹר:

Ashkenazim and Sepharadim end here

מא יז הָעֲנִיִּים וְהָאֶבְיוֹנִים מְבַקְשִׁים מַיִם וָאַיִן לְשׁוֹנָם בַּצָּמָא נָשָׁתָּה
אֲנִי יהוה אֶעֱנֵם אֱלֹהֵי יִשְׂרָאֵל לֹא אֶעֶזְבֵם:

הפטרת עקב

ישעיה

מט יד טו וַתֹּאמֶר צִיּוֹן עֲזָבַנִי יהוה וַאדֹנָי שְׁכֵחָנִי: הֲתִשְׁכַּח אִשָּׁה עוּלָהּ
מֵרַחֵם בֶּן־בִּטְנָהּ גַּם־אֵלֶּה תִשְׁכַּחְנָה וְאָנֹכִי לֹא אֶשְׁכָּחֵךְ:
טז יז הֵן עַל־כַּפַּיִם חַקֹּתִיךְ חוֹמֹתַיִךְ נֶגְדִּי תָּמִיד: מִהֲרוּ בָּנָיִךְ
יח מְהָרְסַיִךְ וּמַחֲרִבַיִךְ מִמֵּךְ יֵצֵאוּ: שְׂאִי־סָבִיב עֵינַיִךְ וּרְאִי
כֻּלָּם נִקְבְּצוּ בָאוּ־לָךְ חַי־אָנִי נְאֻם־יהוה כִּי כֻלָּם כַּעֲדִי
יט תִלְבָּשִׁי וּתְקַשְּׁרִים כַּכַּלָּה: כִּי חָרְבֹתַיִךְ וְשֹׁמְמֹתַיִךְ וְאֶרֶץ
כ הֲרִסֻתֵךְ כִּי עַתָּה תֵּצְרִי מִיּוֹשֵׁב וְרָחֲקוּ מְבַלְּעָיִךְ: עוֹד יֹאמְרוּ
כא בְאָזְנַיִךְ בְּנֵי שִׁכֻּלָיִךְ צַר־לִי הַמָּקוֹם גְּשָׁה־לִּי וְאֵשֵׁבָה: וְאָמַרְתְּ
בִּלְבָבֵךְ מִי יָלַד־לִי אֶת־אֵלֶּה וַאֲנִי שְׁכוּלָה וְגַלְמוּדָה גֹּלָה ׀

EKEV

Two central topics feature in this *haftara*: the ingathering of the exiles and the rebuilding of the land of Israel. Without the return of the Israelites to their land, and without the building of the infrastructure there by them, redemption of the people of Israel cannot occur and none of its other aspects can come to fruition. In the lifetime of Yeshayahu, ten of the tribes of Israel were forced from the northern kingdom into exile, and Shomron, the capital of Israel, was laid waste, and this gave Yeshayahu's prophecies of redemption an air of relevance. At the heart of the process of redemption lies the unbreakable connection between God and His people, and to

▶

and expelled; these children – who has raised them? I was left all
22 alone, and these – who can they be?" So says the Lord
God: Behold: I shall raise My hands to nations, lift My banner
toward peoples; they will bring your sons back in the folds of
23 their robes, bearing your daughters upon their shoulders; kings
will be your caregivers, their princesses your nursemaids. They
will bow to the ground before you and kiss the dust you tread
upon, and you will know: I am the Lord, and those who wait
24 for Me will not be shamed. Can a mighty warrior be
25 plundered; can a victor's captives flee? For so says the Lord:
The mighty man's captives may yet be taken, the tyrant's plunder
flee, but I shall fight against those who fight you, I will save your
26 children. To those who wrong you, I will feed their own flesh;
their blood will intoxicate them like wine, and all flesh will know
then that I am the Lord, your rescue, your redeemer, Mighty
50 1 One of Yaakov. So says the Lord: Where is your mother's bill of divorce with which I banished her? Which one of My
creditors have I, then, sold you to? No, it was for your sins that
you were sold; for your faithlessness your mother was sent hence.
2 Why is it that I came, and no man was here; I cried out, and no
one answered? Does My arm fall short to redeem you; have I not
strength to rescue? No – at My rebuke I dry the sea; I turn whole
rivers to desert land. Their fish will stink for lack of water, dead
3 of thirst. I will dress the skies in darkness and make mourning
4 sack their covering. The Lord my God made me a
learning tongue to sustain the weary with words; morning, early
morning, He wakens my ears, He wakes them, like students, to
5 hear. The Lord my God opened my ears, and I did not reject
6 Him; I never shrank back; I gave up my back to beating, my
cheeks to those who scratched them. I never hid my face from
7 humiliations, spittle, but the Lord my God will help me, and
so no humiliation; I set my face as flint and know I will not be
8 ashamed. He is near who shows me righteous. Who, then, will
contend with me? Let us stand up opposing one another. Who
9 has a claim against me? Let him come to me, for the Lord God,
He will help me; who then can condemn me? They will wear out
10 like an old cloak; moths will eat them. Who of you re-
veres the Lord, and listens to His servant's voice? Let one who
walked in darkness, nothing shining for him, trust in the Lord's
11 name, and lean on his God. You – you light your fire and gird

וְסֹרָה וְאֵלֶּה מִי גִדֵּל הֵן אֲנִי נִשְׁאַרְתִּי לְבַדִּי אֵלֶּה אֵיפֹה
כב הֵם: כֹּה־אָמַר אֲדֹנָי יֱהֹוִה הִנֵּה אֶשָּׂא אֶל־גּוֹיִם
יָדִי וְאֶל־עַמִּים אָרִים נִסִּי וְהֵבִיאוּ בָנַיִךְ בְּחֹצֶן וּבְנֹתַיִךְ עַל־
כג כָּתֵף תִּנָּשֶׂאנָה: וְהָיוּ מְלָכִים אֹמְנַיִךְ וְשָׂרוֹתֵיהֶם מֵינִיקֹתַיִךְ
אַפַּיִם אֶרֶץ יִשְׁתַּחֲווּ־לָךְ וַעֲפַר רַגְלַיִךְ יְלַחֵכוּ וְיָדַעַתְּ כִּי־אֲנִי
כד יְהֹוָה אֲשֶׁר לֹא־יֵבֹשׁוּ קֹוָי: הֲיֻקַּח מִגִּבּוֹר מַלְקוֹחַ
כה וְאִם־שְׁבִי צַדִּיק יִמָּלֵט: כִּי־כֹה ׀ אָמַר יְהֹוָה גַּם־שְׁבִי גִבּוֹר
יֻקָּח וּמַלְקוֹחַ עָרִיץ יִמָּלֵט וְאֶת־יְרִיבֵךְ אָנֹכִי אָרִיב וְאֶת־בָּנַיִךְ
כו אָנֹכִי אוֹשִׁיעַ: וְהַאֲכַלְתִּי אֶת־מוֹנַיִךְ אֶת־בְּשָׂרָם וְכֶעָסִיס
דָּמָם יִשְׁכָּרוּן וְיָדְעוּ כָל־בָּשָׂר כִּי אֲנִי יְהֹוָה מוֹשִׁיעֵךְ וְגֹאֲלֵךְ
נ א אֲבִיר יַעֲקֹב: כֹּה ׀ אָמַר יְהֹוָה אֵי זֶה סֵפֶר כְּרִיתוּת
אִמְּכֶם אֲשֶׁר שִׁלַּחְתִּיהָ אוֹ מִי מִנּוֹשַׁי אֲשֶׁר־מָכַרְתִּי אֶתְכֶם
לוֹ הֵן בַּעֲוֺנֹתֵיכֶם נִמְכַּרְתֶּם וּבְפִשְׁעֵיכֶם שֻׁלְּחָה אִמְּכֶם:
ב מַדּוּעַ בָּאתִי וְאֵין אִישׁ קָרָאתִי וְאֵין עוֹנֶה הֲקָצוֹר קָצְרָה
יָדִי מִפְּדוּת וְאִם־אֵין־בִּי כֹחַ לְהַצִּיל הֵן בְּגַעֲרָתִי אַחֲרִיב יָם
אָשִׂים נְהָרוֹת מִדְבָּר תִּבְאַשׁ דְּגָתָם מֵאֵין מַיִם וְתָמֹת בַּצָּמָא:
ג ד אַלְבִּישׁ שָׁמַיִם קַדְרוּת וְשַׂק אָשִׂים כְּסוּתָם: אֲדֹנָי
יֱהֹוִה נָתַן לִי לְשׁוֹן לִמּוּדִים לָדַעַת לָעוּת אֶת־יָעֵף דָּבָר
ה יָעִיר ׀ בַּבֹּקֶר בַּבֹּקֶר יָעִיר לִי אֹזֶן לִשְׁמֹעַ כַּלִּמּוּדִים: אֲדֹנָי
ו יֱהֹוִה פָּתַח־לִי אֹזֶן וְאָנֹכִי לֹא מָרִיתִי אָחוֹר לֹא נְסוּגֹתִי: גֵּוִי
נָתַתִּי לְמַכִּים וּלְחָיַי לְמֹרְטִים פָּנַי לֹא הִסְתַּרְתִּי מִכְּלִמּוֹת
ז וָרֹק: וַאדֹנָי יֱהֹוִה יַעֲזָר־לִי עַל־כֵּן לֹא נִכְלָמְתִּי עַל־כֵּן שַׂמְתִּי
ח פָנַי כַּחַלָּמִישׁ וָאֵדַע כִּי־לֹא אֵבוֹשׁ: קָרוֹב מַצְדִּיקִי מִי־יָרִיב
ט אִתִּי נַעַמְדָה יָּחַד מִי־בַעַל מִשְׁפָּטִי יִגַּשׁ אֵלָי: הֵן אֲדֹנָי
יֱהֹוִה יַעֲזָר־לִי מִי־הוּא יַרְשִׁיעֵנִי הֵן כֻּלָּם כַּבֶּגֶד יִבְלוּ עָשׁ
י יֹאכְלֵם: מִי בָכֶם יְרֵא יְהֹוָה שֹׁמֵעַ בְּקוֹל עַבְדּוֹ
אֲשֶׁר ׀ הָלַךְ חֲשֵׁכִים וְאֵין נֹגַהּ לוֹ יִבְטַח בְּשֵׁם יְהֹוָה וְיִשָּׁעֵן
יא בֵּאלֹהָיו: הֵן כֻּלְּכֶם קֹדְחֵי אֵשׁ מְאַזְּרֵי זִיקוֹת לְכוּ ׀ בְּאוּר

yourselves with torchlight. Walk by the light of your own fire,
by torches that you burn. From My hand, all this came to you;
51 1 you will lie down in pain. You who chase righteous-
2 ness, listen to Me, you who seek the LORD: Look to the rock
you are hewed from, the quarry from which you were carved;
look to your father, Avraham, to Sara who gave you birth, for I
3 called him, one alone, and blessed him, made him many. And
the LORD has comforted Zion, brought comfort to all her ruins;
He has made her desert like Eden, her arid land like the LORD's
garden; celebration, joy are found in her, and thanks, and sounds
of song.

HAFTARAT RE'EH

On Rosh Ḥodesh Elul, read the maftir from Numbers 28:9–15. Sepharadim read this haftara even if Shabbat coincides with Erev Rosh Ḥodesh or Rosh Ḥodesh. They conclude the haftara by reading the first and last verses of the haftarot for those days. Ashkenazim read this haftara even if Shabbat coincides with Erev Rosh Ḥodesh; however, on Rosh Ḥodesh Elul, they read the haftara on page 1640. Yemenites read the haftara for Rosh Ḥodesh on page 1640. On Erev Rosh Ḥodesh, some read this haftara, while others read the haftara on page 1644.

54 11 Oppressed and storm swept, never comforted; behold: I am pav- ISAIAH
12 ing your ground with garnet, lapis lazuli your foundations. I am
fitting your windows with carnelians, your gates with glowing
13 granite, marking your borders with stones men covet. All your
children will be students of the LORD, and great will be your chil-
14 dren's peace. On righteousness will you be founded; stay far from
oppression; you will not fear, and terror will never come near
15 you. No strife can arise without My assent; who among you fears
16 one who could come upon you? For I create the craftsman who
blows the charcoal fire and brings forth the tools of his trade; I
17 create also the destroyer to do harm. No weapon made to harm
you can prevail; any tongue that calls you into judgment, you
will prove its fault. This is the birthright of the LORD's servants,

---

as a model of morality and justice for the peoples of the world, God promises that we will not be harmed in this spiritual struggle against foreign influences. The success of Israel in its mission to perfect the world and reveal God's sovereignty in it is a main stage in the process of redemption.

אֶשְׁכֶם וּבְזִיקוֹת בִּעַרְתֶּם מִיָּדִי הָיְתָה־זֹּאת לָכֶם לְמַעֲצֵבָה
נא א תִּשְׁכָּבוּן׃ שִׁמְעוּ אֵלַי רֹדְפֵי צֶדֶק מְבַקְשֵׁי יְהוָה
ב הַבִּיטוּ אֶל־צוּר חֻצַּבְתֶּם וְאֶל־מַקֶּבֶת בּוֹר נֻקַּרְתֶּם׃ הַבִּיטוּ
אֶל־אַבְרָהָם אֲבִיכֶם וְאֶל־שָׂרָה תְּחוֹלֶלְכֶם כִּי־אֶחָד קְרָאתִיו
ג וַאֲבָרְכֵהוּ וְאַרְבֵּהוּ׃ כִּי־נִחַם יְהוָה צִיּוֹן נִחַם כׇּל־חׇרְבֹתֶיהָ
וַיָּשֶׂם מִדְבָּרָהּ כְּעֵדֶן וְעַרְבָתָהּ כְּגַן־יְהוָה שָׂשׂוֹן וְשִׂמְחָה
יִמָּצֵא בָהּ תּוֹדָה וְקוֹל זִמְרָה׃

הפטרת ראה

On ראש חודש אלול*, read the* מפטיר *from* במדבר ט, טו–כח*. Sephardim read this* הפטרה *even if* שבת *coincides with* ערב ראש חודש *or* ראש חודש*. They conclude the* הפטרה *by reading the first and last verses of the* הפטרות *for those days. Ashkenazim read this* הפטרה *even if* שבת *coincides with* ערב ראש חודש*; however, on* ראש חודש אלול*, they read the* הפטרה *on page 1641. Yemenites read the* הפטרה *for* ראש חודש *on page page 1641. On* ערב ראש חודש*, some read this* הפטרה*, while others read the* הפטרה *on page 1645.*

נד יא עֲנִיָּה סֹעֲרָה לֹא נֻחָמָה הִנֵּה אָנֹכִי מַרְבִּיץ בַּפּוּךְ אֲבָנַיִךְ ישעיה
יב וִיסַדְתִּיךְ בַּסַּפִּירִים׃ וְשַׂמְתִּי כַּדְכֹד שִׁמְשֹׁתַיִךְ וּשְׁעָרַיִךְ לְאַבְנֵי
יג אֶקְדָּח וְכׇל־גְּבוּלֵךְ לְאַבְנֵי־חֵפֶץ׃ וְכׇל־בָּנַיִךְ לִמּוּדֵי יְהוָה
יד וְרַב שְׁלוֹם בָּנָיִךְ׃ בִּצְדָקָה תִּכּוֹנָנִי רַחֲקִי מֵעֹשֶׁק כִּי־לֹא
טו תִירָאִי וּמִמְּחִתָּה כִּי לֹא־תִקְרַב אֵלָיִךְ׃ הֵן גּוֹר יָגוּר אֶפֶס
טז מֵאוֹתִי מִי־גָר אִתָּךְ עָלַיִךְ יִפּוֹל׃ הן אָנֹכִי בָּרָאתִי חָרָשׁ נֹפֵחַ הִנֵּה
בְּאֵשׁ פֶּחָם וּמוֹצִיא כְלִי לְמַעֲשֵׂהוּ וְאָנֹכִי בָּרָאתִי מַשְׁחִית
יז לְחַבֵּל׃ כׇּל־כְּלִי יוּצַר עָלַיִךְ לֹא יִצְלָח וְכׇל־לָשׁוֹן תָּקוּם־
אִתָּךְ לַמִּשְׁפָּט תַּרְשִׁיעִי זֹאת נַחֲלַת עַבְדֵי יְהוָה וְצִדְקָתָם

RE'EH

The connection between God and Israel is a central theme throughout the Tanakh and history. The mission of the Jewish people is to bring God's word to humanity. But this mission brings us into conflict with other cultures. If Israel remains loyal to God's Torah and serves

▶

55 1 for their innocence is Mine; so says the LORD. You
who are thirsty, all, come to water; you who have no silver, come,
take food and eat; come and take food without silver, wine and
2 milk without cost, for why should you weigh out your silver for
no bread, your labor bringing you no fullness? Listen – listen to
Me: let goodness nourish you, and let your souls delight in plen-
3 ty. Turn your ear to Me and come; listen, that your souls may
live; let Me forge an everlasting covenant with you, like David's
4 faithful promises, for I make him a witness to nations, a leader, a
5 ruler of nations; for you shall call out, call, to a people you know
not, and a people who know you not will come running out to
you for the sake of the LORD your God, the Holy One of Israel,
your glory.

HAFTARAT SHOFETIM

51 12 It is I, I who comfort you. Who are you to fear mortal man, hu- ISAIAH
13 manity, that ends like grass, forgetting the LORD who made you,
who stretches out the skies, lays down the earth? All day you fear
the oppressor's rage as he makes his schemes of violence, yet
14 where is the oppressor's rage? The man bent under his burden –
how fast will he be freed; he will not die into the pit, nor will his
15 bread be lacking. I am the LORD your God. I trouble the ocean;
16 its waves roar; the LORD of Hosts is My name. I have placed My
words in your mouth and covered you in My hand's shade, planting the skies, laying down the earth, and saying to Zion: "You are
17 My people." Rouse, rouse yourself and rise, Jerusalem,
you who have drunk from the LORD's hand His full cup of rage,
18 the poisoned goblet, drunk and drained it. No one will guide her
back, of all the children she has borne; of all the sons she raised
19 there is none to hold her hand. Two things came to you, but who
is moved for you? Massacre and breaking, hunger and the sword;

The destruction and exile will create a tremendous rupture in the people's spirit. To help overcome this crisis, God pledges His own active involvement: "It is I, I who comfort you." God the omnipotent calls to us to return from exile; the feeling of powerlessness dissipates and is replaced by the joy of redemption.

נה א מֵאִתִּי נְאֻם־יהוה׃ הוֹי כָּל־צָמֵא לְכוּ לַמַּיִם וַאֲשֶׁר
אֵין־לוֹ כָּסֶף לְכוּ שִׁבְרוּ וֶאֱכֹלוּ וּלְכוּ שִׁבְרוּ בְּלוֹא־כֶסֶף וּבְלוֹא
ב מְחִיר יַיִן וְחָלָב׃ לָמָּה תִשְׁקְלוּ־כֶסֶף בְּלוֹא־לֶחֶם וִיגִיעֲכֶם
בְּלוֹא לְשָׂבְעָה שִׁמְעוּ שָׁמוֹעַ אֵלַי וְאִכְלוּ־טוֹב וְתִתְעַנַּג
ג בַּדֶּשֶׁן נַפְשְׁכֶם׃ הַטּוּ אָזְנְכֶם וּלְכוּ אֵלַי שִׁמְעוּ וּתְחִי נַפְשְׁכֶם
ד וְאֶכְרְתָה לָכֶם בְּרִית עוֹלָם חַסְדֵי דָוִד הַנֶּאֱמָנִים׃ הֵן עֵד
ה לְאוּמִּים נְתַתִּיו נָגִיד וּמְצַוֵּה לְאֻמִּים׃ הֵן גּוֹי לֹא־תֵדַע תִּקְרָא
וְגוֹי לֹא־יְדָעוּךָ אֵלֶיךָ יָרוּצוּ לְמַעַן יהוה אֱלֹהֶיךָ וְלִקְדוֹשׁ
יִשְׂרָאֵל כִּי פֵאֲרָךְ׃

הפטרת שפטים

נא יב אָנֹכִי אָנֹכִי הוּא מְנַחֶמְכֶם מִי־אַתְּ וַתִּירְאִי מֵאֱנוֹשׁ יָמוּת ישעיה
יג וּמִבֶּן־אָדָם חָצִיר יִנָּתֵן׃ וַתִּשְׁכַּח יהוה עֹשֶׂךָ נוֹטֶה שָׁמַיִם
וְיֹסֵד אָרֶץ וַתְּפַחֵד תָּמִיד כָּל־הַיּוֹם מִפְּנֵי חֲמַת הַמֵּצִיק
יד כַּאֲשֶׁר כּוֹנֵן לְהַשְׁחִית וְאַיֵּה חֲמַת הַמֵּצִיק׃ מִהַר צֹעֶה
טו לְהִפָּתֵחַ וְלֹא־יָמוּת לַשַּׁחַת וְלֹא יֶחְסַר לַחְמוֹ׃ וְאָנֹכִי יהוה
טז אֱלֹהֶיךָ רֹגַע הַיָּם וַיֶּהֱמוּ גַּלָּיו יהוה צְבָאוֹת שְׁמוֹ׃ וָאָשִׂם
דְּבָרַי בְּפִיךָ וּבְצֵל יָדִי כִּסִּיתִיךָ לִנְטֹעַ שָׁמַיִם וְלִיסֹד אָרֶץ
יז וְלֵאמֹר לְצִיּוֹן עַמִּי־אָתָּה׃ הִתְעוֹרְרִי הִתְעוֹרְרִי
קוּמִי יְרוּשָׁלִַם אֲשֶׁר שָׁתִית מִיַּד יהוה אֶת־כּוֹס חֲמָתוֹ אֶת־
יח קֻבַּעַת כּוֹס הַתַּרְעֵלָה שָׁתִית מָצִית׃ אֵין־מְנַהֵל לָהּ מִכָּל־
יט בָּנִים יָלָדָה וְאֵין מַחֲזִיק בְּיָדָהּ מִכָּל־בָּנִים גִּדֵּלָה׃ שְׁתַּיִם
הֵנָּה קֹרְאֹתַיִךְ מִי יָנוּד לָךְ הַשֹּׁד וְהַשֶּׁבֶר וְהָרָעָב וְהַחֶרֶב מִי

SHOFETIM

The prophecy in this *haftara* features four sets of doubled words: *anokhi anokhi* ("I, I"), *hitoreri hitoreri* ("rouse, rouse"), *uri uri* ("rise, rise"), and *suru suru* ("turn, turn aside"). These phrases emphasize the active role of the people, the prophet's listeners, in the process of redemption.

▶

20 through whom may I comfort you? Your children fainted, fallen
at every street corner, like netted wild oxen, full of the LORD's
21 rage, your God's rebuke. So listen, woman oppressed and drunk
22 but not with wine. So says the LORD, your Lord; so
your God fights His people's cause: Behold: I have taken the
poisoned cup from your hand, the goblet of My rage; you will
23 drink from it no more. I shall place it in the hands of those who
torment you, who have said to your face, "Bow down to let us
pass." You made your back like earth, like the road to be walked
52 1 over. Rise, rise, Zion, and don your dress of might; wear
your garb of glory, Jerusalem, holy town, for no more will uncir-
2 cumcised, impure ones enter you. Shake yourself free of the dust;
rise up to take your place, Jerusalem. Break free of the chains
3 around your neck, captive daughter Jerusalem. For
so says the LORD: You were sold away for nothing, and it is not
4 for silver that you will be redeemed. For so says the
Lord GOD: My people went down long ago to Egypt, to live
5 there for a time; for nothing, Assyria oppressed them, and now,
what is there here for Me? So says the LORD: For nothing My
people is taken captive, its rulers baying. So says the LORD: Un-
6 ceasingly, all day, My name is defamed, and so – My people will
know My name, and so – on that day – they will know that it is I
7 who spoke, that I am here. How lovely upon the mountains: the steps of the bringer of tidings, resounding with peace,
tidings of good, resounding of rescue, saying to Zion: "Your God
8 has ascended the throne." The voice of your watchmen, their
voices rise as one, singing, for they will see with their own eyes
9 the LORD's return to Zion. Break out in song; sing out together,
ruins of Jerusalem, for the LORD has comforted His people, re-
10 deemed His Jerusalem. The LORD has uncovered His holy arm
before the eyes of all nations, and all ends of this earth will see
11 rescue from our God. Turn, turn aside – leave that
place without touching the defiled. Go out from there; cleanse
12 yourselves, you who bear the LORD's vessels; this time you will
not leave in haste, you will not leave in flight. The LORD will go
before you, the God of Israel your rear guard behind.

כ אֲנַחֲמֵךְ׃ בָּנַיִךְ עֻלְּפוּ שָׁכְבוּ בְּרֹאשׁ כָּל־חוּצוֹת כְּתוֹא מִכְמָר
כא הַמְלֵאִים חֲמַת־יְהוָה גַּעֲרַת אֱלֹהָיִךְ׃ לָכֵן שִׁמְעִי־נָא זֹאת
כב עֲנִיָּה וּשְׁכֻרַת וְלֹא מִיָּיִן׃ כֹּה־אָמַר אֲדֹנַיִךְ יְהוָה
וֵאלֹהַיִךְ יָרִיב עַמּוֹ הִנֵּה לָקַחְתִּי מִיָּדֵךְ אֶת־כּוֹס הַתַּרְעֵלָה
כג אֶת־קֻבַּעַת כּוֹס חֲמָתִי לֹא־תוֹסִיפִי לִשְׁתּוֹתָהּ עוֹד׃ וְשַׂמְתִּיהָ
בְּיַד־מוֹגַיִךְ אֲשֶׁר־אָמְרוּ לְנַפְשֵׁךְ שְׁחִי וְנַעֲבֹרָה וַתָּשִׂימִי
נב א כָאָרֶץ גֵּוֵךְ וְכַחוּץ לַעֹבְרִים׃ עוּרִי עוּרִי לִבְשִׁי
עֻזֵּךְ צִיּוֹן לִבְשִׁי ׀ בִּגְדֵי תִפְאַרְתֵּךְ יְרוּשָׁלַםִ עִיר הַקֹּדֶשׁ
ב כִּי לֹא יוֹסִיף יָבֹא־בָךְ עוֹד עָרֵל וְטָמֵא׃ הִתְנַעֲרִי מֵעָפָר
קוּמִי שְּׁבִי יְרוּשָׁלָםִ התפתחו מוֹסְרֵי צַוָּארֵךְ שְׁבִיָּה בַּת־ הִתְפַּתְּחִי
ג צִיּוֹן׃ כִּי־כֹה אָמַר יְהוָה חִנָּם נִמְכַּרְתֶּם וְלֹא בְכֶסֶף
ד תִּגָּאֵלוּ׃ כִּי כֹה אָמַר אֲדֹנָי יֱהוִה מִצְרַיִם יָרַד־עַמִּי
ה בָרִאשֹׁנָה לָגוּר שָׁם וְאַשּׁוּר בְּאֶפֶס עֲשָׁקוֹ׃ וְעַתָּה מַה־לִּי־פֹה
נְאֻם־יְהוָה כִּי־לֻקַּח עַמִּי חִנָּם מֹשְׁלָו יְהֵילִילוּ נְאֻם־יְהוָה
ו וְתָמִיד כָּל־הַיּוֹם שְׁמִי מִנֹּאָץ׃ לָכֵן יֵדַע עַמִּי שְׁמִי לָכֵן בַּיּוֹם
ז הַהוּא כִּי־אֲנִי־הוּא הַמְדַבֵּר הִנֵּנִי׃ מַה־נָּאווּ עַל־
הֶהָרִים רַגְלֵי מְבַשֵּׂר מַשְׁמִיעַ שָׁלוֹם מְבַשֵּׂר טוֹב מַשְׁמִיעַ
ח יְשׁוּעָה אֹמֵר לְצִיּוֹן מָלַךְ אֱלֹהָיִךְ׃ קוֹל צֹפַיִךְ נָשְׂאוּ קוֹל יַחְדָּו
ט יְרַנֵּנוּ כִּי עַיִן בְּעַיִן יִרְאוּ בְּשׁוּב יְהוָה צִיּוֹן׃ פִּצְחוּ רַנְּנוּ יַחְדָּו
י חָרְבוֹת יְרוּשָׁלָםִ כִּי־נִחַם יְהוָה עַמּוֹ גָּאַל יְרוּשָׁלָםִ׃ חָשַׂף
יְהוָה אֶת־זְרוֹעַ קָדְשׁוֹ לְעֵינֵי כָּל־הַגּוֹיִם וְרָאוּ כָּל־אַפְסֵי־
יא אָרֶץ אֵת יְשׁוּעַת אֱלֹהֵינוּ׃ סוּרוּ סוּרוּ צְאוּ מִשָּׁם
יב טָמֵא אַל־תִּגָּעוּ צְאוּ מִתּוֹכָהּ הִבָּרוּ נֹשְׂאֵי כְּלֵי יְהוָה׃ כִּי לֹא
בְחִפָּזוֹן תֵּצֵאוּ וּבִמְנוּסָה לֹא תֵלֵכוּן כִּי־הֹלֵךְ לִפְנֵיכֶם יְהוָה
וּמְאַסִּפְכֶם אֱלֹהֵי יִשְׂרָאֵל׃

Haftarat Ki Tetzeh

The custom of the Ashkenazim is that if the haftara for Parashat Re'eh was not read due to it coinciding with Rosh Ḥodesh Elul, that haftara is read after this haftara.

54 1 Barren woman, never a mother, rejoice; break out in joyful song ISAIAH
though you have not given birth, for the children of the forsak-
en woman will outnumber those of the wife, so says the Lord.
2 Broaden the site of your tent; stretch out your canvas home; do
not hold back; lengthen your tent cords, and strengthen its pegs:
3 you shall overflow rightward and left, your children possessing
4 nations, and filling forsaken towns with life. Do not fear – you
will not be shamed; fear not, for none can disgrace you. You will
forget your youthful abjection; the debasement of your widow-
5 hood you will call no more to mind, for your husband, He who
made you – the Lord of Hosts is His name, and your redeemer,
6 Israel's Holy One – will be named God of all the world, for as a
woman abandoned, of sorrowful spirit, the Lord has called to
7 you: Can the young bride ever be rejected? says your God; for
one small moment I left you; with infinite care shall I gather you
8 back; in the flash of My fury I hid My face from you for just a moment, and in everlasting love will I care for you now. So speaks
9 the Lord, your redeemer. For these are the waters of
Noaḥ to Me, and I swore that the waters of Noaḥ would never
sweep again over the earth. And so did I swear no more to be
10 furious with you, no more to rebuke you. For mountains may
move, hills may crumble away; but My love for you will not be
moved, nor My pact of peace crumble. So speaks the Lord, who
cares for you.

if they can seem never-ending. The covenant with God must be founded on the basis of justice and mercy – if we do this, we are promised blessing and light that will banish these difficult times. Then, in place of helplessness and sadness, we will find great mercy and eternal charity, for one good act leads to another.

הפטרת כי תצא

The custom of the Ashkenazim is that if the הפטרה *for* פרשת ראה *was not read due to it coinciding with* ראש חודש אלול*, that* הפטרה *is read after this* הפטרה*.*

נד א רָנִּי עֲקָרָה לֹא יָלָדָה פִּצְחִי רִנָּה וְצַהֲלִי לֹא־חָלָה כִּי־רַבִּים ישעיה
ב בְנֵי־שׁוֹמֵמָה מִבְּנֵי בְעוּלָה אָמַר יהוה: הַרְחִיבִי ׀ מְקוֹם אׇהֳלֵךְ
וִירִיעוֹת מִשְׁכְּנוֹתַיִךְ יַטּוּ אַל־תַּחְשֹׂכִי הַאֲרִיכִי מֵיתָרַיִךְ
ג וִיתֵדֹתַיִךְ חַזֵּקִי: כִּי־יָמִין וּשְׂמֹאול תִּפְרֹצִי וְזַרְעֵךְ גּוֹיִם יִירָשׁ
ד וְעָרִים נְשַׁמּוֹת יוֹשִׁיבוּ: אַל־תִּירְאִי כִּי־לֹא תֵבוֹשִׁי וְאַל־
תִּכָּלְמִי כִּי לֹא תַחְפִּירִי כִּי בֹשֶׁת עֲלוּמַיִךְ תִּשְׁכָּחִי וְחֶרְפַּת
ה אַלְמְנוּתַיִךְ לֹא תִזְכְּרִי־עוֹד: כִּי בֹעֲלַיִךְ עֹשַׂיִךְ יהוה צְבָאוֹת
ו שְׁמוֹ וְגֹאֲלֵךְ קְדוֹשׁ יִשְׂרָאֵל אֱלֹהֵי כׇל־הָאָרֶץ יִקָּרֵא: כִּי־
כְאִשָּׁה עֲזוּבָה וַעֲצוּבַת רוּחַ קְרָאָךְ יהוה וְאֵשֶׁת נְעוּרִים כִּי
ז תִמָּאֵס אָמַר אֱלֹהָיִךְ: בְּרֶגַע קָטֹן עֲזַבְתִּיךְ וּבְרַחֲמִים גְּדֹלִים
ח אֲקַבְּצֵךְ: בְּשֶׁצֶף קֶצֶף הִסְתַּרְתִּי פָנַי רֶגַע מִמֵּךְ וּבְחֶסֶד עוֹלָם
ט רִחַמְתִּיךְ אָמַר גֹּאֲלֵךְ יהוה: כִּי־מֵי נֹחַ זֹאת לִי
אֲשֶׁר נִשְׁבַּעְתִּי מֵעֲבֹר מֵי־נֹחַ עוֹד עַל־הָאָרֶץ כֵּן נִשְׁבַּעְתִּי
י מִקְּצֹף עָלַיִךְ וּמִגְּעׇר־בָּךְ: כִּי הֶהָרִים יָמוּשׁוּ וְהַגְּבָעוֹת
תְּמוּטֶינָה וְחַסְדִּי מֵאִתֵּךְ לֹא־יָמוּשׁ וּבְרִית שְׁלוֹמִי לֹא תָמוּט
אָמַר מְרַחֲמֵךְ יהוה:

KI TETZEH

The flood, which threw the world back into a state of chaos, came as a punishment for wickedness and oppression. The prophet draws a parallel between it and the destruction and exile of the Israelite kingdoms centuries later, which also came as a result of disobedience to God. He insists that crisis and suffering are not the natural way of things, even

Haftarat Ki Tavo

60 1 Rise, give light, for your light has come: the glory of the Lord ISAIAH
2 shines over you, for darkness may cover the earth, and clouds
shroud nations, but over you, the Lord will be shining, His
3 glory manifest over you; nations will walk toward your light,
4 and kings into the brilliance you shine forth. Raise your eyes;
look around and see: all of them gathered in, and come to
you; your sons have come from far away, your daughters as
5 if clinging to nursemaids' hips. Then you will see and shine;
your heart will fill with awe and open wide, for the ocean's
abundance will turn to you; the wealth of nations will come to
6 you; herds of camels will cover your land, young camels from
Midyan and Eifa, all having come to you from Sheba, carrying
7 gold and frankincense and tidings of the Lord's praise. All the
flocks of Kedar will be gathered in to you; the rams of Nevayot
will be in your service. Offered on My altar, they will be de-
8 sired; I shall glorify the House of My glory. Who are these sail-
9 ing like clouds, like doves come back to their roosting cote? It
is Me the distant islands wait for; ships of Tarshish come the
first, to bring your children from far away, their silver and gold
with them, for the name of the Lord your God, the Holy One
10 of Israel: He has glorified you. The children of strangers will
build your walls; their kings will be in your service, for in My
11 fury I beat you, but, desiring you now, I show you mercy, and
your gates will be always open, day and night, never closed, as
the wealth of nations is brought in to you, their kings led to you,
12 for the nations and kingdoms that do not serve you will be
13 lost, nations desolate, destroyed. Lebanon's glory will come to
you: junipers, cypress trees, and pencil pines together, to lend
the place of My Sanctuary splendor; I shall glorify the place
14 of My footstool. The children of those who once oppressed
you will come before you prostrate, bowing themselves to the
soles of your feet; all who once denounced you, they will call

---

the nations, we must place emphasis on the idea that justice must be done. The nations will ultimately recognize the injustices they have committed against Israel and will make amends. Having repented, the peoples of the world will recognize God's sovereignty and Israel's chosenness, and they will become full partners in the redeemed world.

הפטרת כי תבוא

ס א ב קוּמִי אוֹרִי כִּי בָא אוֹרֵךְ וּכְבוֹד יְהוָה עָלַיִךְ זָרָח׃ כִּי־הִנֵּה ישעיה
הַחֹשֶׁךְ יְכַסֶּה־אֶרֶץ וַעֲרָפֶל לְאֻמִּים וְעָלַיִךְ יִזְרַח יְהוָה וּכְבוֹדוֹ
ג ד עָלַיִךְ יֵרָאֶה׃ וְהָלְכוּ גוֹיִם לְאוֹרֵךְ וּמְלָכִים לְנֹגַהּ זַרְחֵךְ׃ שְׂאִי־
סָבִיב עֵינַיִךְ וּרְאִי כֻּלָּם נִקְבְּצוּ בָאוּ־לָךְ בָּנַיִךְ מֵרָחוֹק יָבֹאוּ
ה וּבְנֹתַיִךְ עַל־צַד תֵּאָמַנָה׃ אָז תִּרְאִי וְנָהַרְתְּ וּפָחַד וְרָחַב
ו לְבָבֵךְ כִּי־יֵהָפֵךְ עָלַיִךְ הֲמוֹן יָם חֵיל גּוֹיִם יָבֹאוּ לָךְ׃ שִׁפְעַת
גְּמַלִּים תְּכַסֵּךְ בִּכְרֵי מִדְיָן וְעֵיפָה כֻּלָּם מִשְּׁבָא יָבֹאוּ זָהָב
ז וּלְבוֹנָה יִשָּׂאוּ וּתְהִלֹּת יְהוָה יְבַשֵּׂרוּ׃ כָּל־צֹאן קֵדָר יִקָּבְצוּ לָךְ
אֵילֵי נְבָיוֹת יְשָׁרְתוּנֶךְ יַעֲלוּ עַל־רָצוֹן מִזְבְּחִי וּבֵית תִּפְאַרְתִּי
ח אֲפָאֵר׃ מִי־אֵלֶּה כָּעָב תְּעוּפֶינָה וְכַיּוֹנִים אֶל־אֲרֻבֹּתֵיהֶם׃
ט כִּי־לִי ׀ אִיִּים יְקַוּוּ וָאֳנִיּוֹת תַּרְשִׁישׁ בָּרִאשֹׁנָה לְהָבִיא בָנַיִךְ
מֵרָחוֹק כַּסְפָּם וּזְהָבָם אִתָּם לְשֵׁם יְהוָה אֱלֹהַיִךְ וְלִקְדוֹשׁ
י יִשְׂרָאֵל כִּי פֵאֲרָךְ׃ וּבָנוּ בְנֵי־נֵכָר חֹמֹתַיִךְ וּמַלְכֵיהֶם יְשָׁרְתוּנֶךְ
יא כִּי בְקִצְפִּי הִכִּיתִיךְ וּבִרְצוֹנִי רִחַמְתִּיךְ׃ וּפִתְּחוּ שְׁעָרַיִךְ תָּמִיד
יוֹמָם וָלַיְלָה לֹא יִסָּגֵרוּ לְהָבִיא אֵלַיִךְ חֵיל גּוֹיִם וּמַלְכֵיהֶם
יב נְהוּגִים׃ כִּי־הַגּוֹי וְהַמַּמְלָכָה אֲשֶׁר לֹא־יַעַבְדוּךְ יֹאבֵדוּ
יג וְהַגּוֹיִם חָרֹב יֶחֱרָבוּ׃ כְּבוֹד הַלְּבָנוֹן אֵלַיִךְ יָבוֹא בְּרוֹשׁ תִּדְהָר
וּתְאַשּׁוּר יַחְדָּו לְפָאֵר מְקוֹם מִקְדָּשִׁי וּמְקוֹם רַגְלַי אֲכַבֵּד׃
יד וְהָלְכוּ אֵלַיִךְ שְׁחוֹחַ בְּנֵי מְעַנַּיִךְ וְהִשְׁתַּחֲווּ עַל־כַּפּוֹת רַגְלַיִךְ

KI TAVO

The phrase that concludes this *haftara*, "When the time is right, in a flash I will bring it to be," expresses two dynamics of redemption. On the one hand, God will hasten the process so that it will seem to happen in an instant. On the other hand, redemption must wait its turn, coming about at the pace of the natural order of things. How will these two opposed dynamics express themselves? Will the divine light shine through us to illuminate the world for all the nations in a flash? Or will we be unable to project such influence, in which case the perfection of the world will drag on for numerous generations? When we think of the relationship between Israel and

15 you The LORD's City, Zion of Israel's Holy One. Where once
you were forsaken, hated, never even passed through, I have
16 made you everlasting majesty, the joy of generations. You shall
suckle the milk of nations, suckle at kings' breasts, and know
that I am the LORD, your rescue, your redeemer, the Mighty
17 One of Yaakov. Where once there was bronze, I shall bring
gold, and where there was iron, silver. Where once there was
wood, I shall bring bronze, and where there was stone, now
iron. I shall make peace your commander, your ruling class:
18 righteousness. No more will violence be heard of in your land,
nor plunder or destruction in your borders. You shall name
19 your walls Rescue, and your gates, Praise. No more, by day,
will the sun be your light, nor the moon's radiance shine for
you, for the LORD will be your light forever; your God will
20 be your glory. Your sun will set no longer, nor your moon be
gathered in, for the LORD is your light forever; the days of
21 your mourning are done. Your people, all of them righteous,
will inherit the land forever, the shoots of My planting, works
22 of My hands, spreading branches in glory. The little son will
become a thousand strong, the youngest child a mighty nation; I am the LORD: when the time is right, in a flash I will
bring it all to be.

HAFTARAT NITZAVIM

When Nitzavim and Vayelekh are read together, read this haftara.

ISAIAH

Yemenites begin here

Ashkenazim and Sephardim begin here

61 9 Their children will be known among the nations, their offspring
among peoples, for all those who see them will know who they
10 are: children of the LORD's own blessing. * I shall rejoice, rejoice in the LORD; my soul exults in my God; He has
wrapped me in garb of rescue, on my shoulders the mantle of
righteousness, as a bridegroom attends in splendor, and a bride
11 puts on her jewels; just as the land brings forth green life, having
all that is planted in her flower like a garden, so will the Lord

as the heart beats, the body can live. But with the silencing of Jerusalem, the heart of the Jewish people, the exile began in earnest. The rebuilding of Jerusalem thus signals the end of the exile, for Jerusalem is no ordinary city; it is the seat of God on earth.

טו כָּל־מְנַאֲצָיִךְ וְקָרְאוּ לָךְ עִיר יְהוָה צִיּוֹן קְדוֹשׁ יִשְׂרָאֵל׃ תַּחַת
הֱיוֹתֵךְ עֲזוּבָה וּשְׂנוּאָה וְאֵין עוֹבֵר וְשַׂמְתִּיךְ לִגְאוֹן עוֹלָם
טז מְשׂוֹשׂ דּוֹר וָדוֹר׃ וְיָנַקְתְּ חֲלֵב גּוֹיִם וְשֹׁד מְלָכִים תִּינָקִי וְיָדַעַתְּ
יז כִּי אֲנִי יְהוָה מוֹשִׁיעֵךְ וְגֹאֲלֵךְ אֲבִיר יַעֲקֹב׃ תַּחַת הַנְּחֹשֶׁת
אָבִיא זָהָב וְתַחַת הַבַּרְזֶל אָבִיא כֶסֶף וְתַחַת הָעֵצִים נְחֹשֶׁת
וְתַחַת הָאֲבָנִים בַּרְזֶל וְשַׂמְתִּי פְקֻדָּתֵךְ שָׁלוֹם וְנֹגְשַׂיִךְ צְדָקָה׃
יח לֹא־יִשָּׁמַע עוֹד חָמָס בְּאַרְצֵךְ שֹׁד וָשֶׁבֶר בִּגְבוּלָיִךְ וְקָרָאת
יט יְשׁוּעָה חוֹמֹתַיִךְ וּשְׁעָרַיִךְ תְּהִלָּה׃ לֹא־יִהְיֶה־לָּךְ עוֹד הַשֶּׁמֶשׁ
לְאוֹר יוֹמָם וּלְנֹגַהּ הַיָּרֵחַ לֹא־יָאִיר לָךְ וְהָיָה־לָךְ יְהוָה לְאוֹר
כ עוֹלָם וֵאלֹהַיִךְ לְתִפְאַרְתֵּךְ׃ לֹא־יָבוֹא עוֹד שִׁמְשֵׁךְ וִירֵחֵךְ
לֹא יֵאָסֵף כִּי יְהוָה יִהְיֶה־לָּךְ לְאוֹר עוֹלָם וְשָׁלְמוּ יְמֵי אֶבְלֵךְ׃
כא וְעַמֵּךְ כֻּלָּם צַדִּיקִים לְעוֹלָם יִירְשׁוּ אָרֶץ נֵצֶר מטעו מַעֲשֵׂה מַטָּעַי
כב יָדַי לְהִתְפָּאֵר׃ הַקָּטֹן יִהְיֶה לָאֶלֶף וְהַצָּעִיר לְגוֹי עָצוּם אֲנִי
יְהוָה בְּעִתָּהּ אֲחִישֶׁנָּה׃

הפטרת נצבים

When נצבים *and* וילך *are read together, read this* הפטרה.

ישעיה / *Yemenites begin here*

סא ט וְנוֹדַע בַּגּוֹיִם זַרְעָם וְצֶאֱצָאֵיהֶם בְּתוֹךְ הָעַמִּים כָּל־רֹאֵיהֶם
י יַכִּירוּם כִּי הֵם זֶרַע בֵּרַךְ יְהוָה׃ *שׂוֹשׂ אָשִׂישׂ

Ashkenazim and Sepharadim begin here

בַּיהוָה תָּגֵל נַפְשִׁי בֵּאלֹהַי כִּי הִלְבִּישַׁנִי בִּגְדֵי־יֶשַׁע מְעִיל
יא צְדָקָה יְעָטָנִי כֶּחָתָן יְכַהֵן פְּאֵר וְכַכַּלָּה תַּעְדֶּה כֵלֶיהָ׃ כִּי
כָאָרֶץ תּוֹצִיא צִמְחָהּ וּכְגַנָּה זֵרוּעֶיהָ תַצְמִיחַ כֵּן ׀ אֲדֹנָי יֱהוִה

NITZAVIM

From the time Jerusalem became the capital of the kingdom of Israel in the time of King David, it has been the heart of the Jewish people and the place to which all nations turn in prayer. It has also turned into a site of conflict as different nations battle for control of the holy city. The consciousness of the exile begins with the destruction of Jerusalem. As long

▶

God bring forth righteousness and glory before all the nations.
62 1 For Zion's sake I cannot be silent, for Jerusalem's I cannot be still
until righteousness bursts forth shining, and rescue burns like a
2 brand, and all nations see your righteousness, all the kings your
glory. They will call you by a new name spoken from the Lord's
3 own mouth. You will be a crown of glory in the Lord's hand, a
4 kingly diadem in your God's palms. No more will they say of you,
"Abandoned," "Desolate" of your land, for you shall be called "My
Desire," your land renamed "Embraced," for it is you the Lord
5 desires, and your land shall be embraced; as a young man embraces a maid, so will your children embrace you, while the joy
of a bridegroom over his bride is the joy your God will take in
6 you. Over your walls, Jerusalem, I have appointed watchmen, all
day, all night long, always, and they will not keep silence; you
7 who call the Lord by name, none of you be quiet, and do not
give Him quiet until He has established, until He has raised Jeru-
8 salem to be the glory of this earth. The Lord has sworn by His
right hand and by His mighty arm: never again to give away your
grain as your foes' food, never to let strangers drink the wine that
9 you have labored for. No – the ones who harvest it will eat and
sing out the Lord's praise, and those He has gathered in will
10 drink within My sacred courtyards. Pass, pass through
the gates, and make way for the people. Mark, mark a road here;
11 clear the stones; raise a banner above all peoples. Behold: the
Lord resounding to the earth's ends; tell daughter Zion, your
rescue is come, and with Him, His prize: His work walking be-
12 fore Him. They will call them a holy people, redeemed ones of
the Lord. And you – you shall be called the One Sought After,
63 1 the City That Will Never Be Abandoned. "Who is this,
coming from Edom, from Botzra, in reddened clothes? Who,
His clothing glorious, striding forth in might?" It is I who speak
2 with rectitude, powerful to rescue. "And why is Your clothing red,
3 your garments, as if You trod the winepress?" I have trodden the
vat alone; no man of any nation was there with Me; I trod them
in My fury, trampling them in rage, until their lifeblood steeped
4 My clothes, befouling all My garments, for today in My heart is
5 a day of vengeance; My year of redemption is come. I look, and
no one is there to help; with dismay I see – no aid; so My arm
6 will bear My rescue; My rage is My support. My fury will tread
peoples low; in My rage I shall make them drunk and pour down

סב א יַצְמִיחַ צְדָקָה וּתְהִלָּה נֶגֶד כָּל־הַגּוֹיִם: לְמַעַן צִיּוֹן לֹא אֶחֱשֶׁה
וּלְמַעַן יְרוּשָׁלַםִ לֹא אֶשְׁקוֹט עַד־יֵצֵא כַנֹּגַהּ צִדְקָהּ וִישׁוּעָתָהּ
ב כְּלַפִּיד יִבְעָר: וְרָאוּ גוֹיִם צִדְקֵךְ וְכָל־מְלָכִים כְּבוֹדֵךְ וְקֹרָא
ג לָךְ שֵׁם חָדָשׁ אֲשֶׁר פִּי יְהוָה יִקֳּבֶנּוּ: וְהָיִית עֲטֶרֶת תִּפְאֶרֶת
ד בְּיַד־יְהוָה וצנוף מְלוּכָה בְּכַף־אֱלֹהָיִךְ: לֹא־יֵאָמֵר לָךְ עוֹד וּצְנִיף
עֲזוּבָה וּלְאַרְצֵךְ לֹא־יֵאָמֵר עוֹד שְׁמָמָה כִּי לָךְ יִקָּרֵא חֶפְצִי־
ה בָהּ וּלְאַרְצֵךְ בְּעוּלָה כִּי־חָפֵץ יְהוָה בָּךְ וְאַרְצֵךְ תִּבָּעֵל: כִּי־
יִבְעַל בָּחוּר בְּתוּלָה יִבְעָלוּךְ בָּנָיִךְ וּמְשׂוֹשׂ חָתָן עַל־כַּלָּה
ו יָשִׂישׂ עָלַיִךְ אֱלֹהָיִךְ: עַל־חוֹמֹתַיִךְ יְרוּשָׁלַםִ הִפְקַדְתִּי שֹׁמְרִים
כָּל־הַיּוֹם וְכָל־הַלַּיְלָה תָּמִיד לֹא יֶחֱשׁוּ הַמַּזְכִּרִים אֶת־יְהוָה
ז אַל־דֳּמִי לָכֶם: וְאַל־תִּתְּנוּ דֳמִי לוֹ עַד־יְכוֹנֵן וְעַד־יָשִׂים אֶת־
ח יְרוּשָׁלַםִ תְּהִלָּה בָּאָרֶץ: נִשְׁבַּע יְהוָה בִּימִינוֹ וּבִזְרוֹעַ עֻזּוֹ
אִם־אֶתֵּן אֶת־דְּגָנֵךְ עוֹד מַאֲכָל לְאֹיְבַיִךְ וְאִם־יִשְׁתּוּ בְנֵי־נֵכָר
ט תִּירוֹשֵׁךְ אֲשֶׁר יָגַעַתְּ בּוֹ: כִּי מְאַסְפָיו יֹאכְלֻהוּ וְהִלְלוּ אֶת־
י יְהוָה וּמְקַבְּצָיו יִשְׁתֻּהוּ בְּחַצְרוֹת קָדְשִׁי: עִבְרוּ
עִבְרוּ בַּשְּׁעָרִים פַּנּוּ דֶּרֶךְ הָעָם סֹלּוּ סֹלּוּ הַמְסִלָּה סַקְּלוּ מֵאֶבֶן
יא הָרִימוּ נֵס עַל־הָעַמִּים: הִנֵּה יְהוָה הִשְׁמִיעַ אֶל־קְצֵה הָאָרֶץ
אִמְרוּ לְבַת־צִיּוֹן הִנֵּה יִשְׁעֵךְ בָּא הִנֵּה שְׂכָרוֹ אִתּוֹ וּפְעֻלָּתוֹ
יב לְפָנָיו: וְקָרְאוּ לָהֶם עַם־הַקֹּדֶשׁ גְּאוּלֵי יְהוָה וְלָךְ יִקָּרֵא
סג א דְרוּשָׁה עִיר לֹא נֶעֱזָבָה: מִי־זֶה ׀ בָּא מֵאֱדוֹם
חֲמוּץ בְּגָדִים מִבָּצְרָה זֶה הָדוּר בִּלְבוּשׁוֹ צֹעֶה בְּרֹב כֹּחוֹ אֲנִי
ב מְדַבֵּר בִּצְדָקָה רַב לְהוֹשִׁיעַ: מַדּוּעַ אָדֹם לִלְבוּשֶׁךָ וּבְגָדֶיךָ
ג כְּדֹרֵךְ בְּגַת: פּוּרָה ׀ דָּרַכְתִּי לְבַדִּי וּמֵעַמִּים אֵין־אִישׁ אִתִּי
וְאֶדְרְכֵם בְּאַפִּי וְאֶרְמְסֵם בַּחֲמָתִי וְיֵז נִצְחָם עַל־בְּגָדַי וְכָל־
ד מַלְבּוּשַׁי אֶגְאָלְתִּי: כִּי יוֹם נָקָם בְּלִבִּי וּשְׁנַת גְּאוּלַי בָּאָה:
ה וְאַבִּיט וְאֵין עֹזֵר וְאֶשְׁתּוֹמֵם וְאֵין סוֹמֵךְ וַתּוֹשַׁע לִי זְרֹעִי
ו וַחֲמָתִי הִיא סְמָכָתְנִי: וְאָבוּס עַמִּים בְּאַפִּי וַאֲשַׁכְּרֵם בַּחֲמָתִי

7 their lifeblood to earth. Let me speak the Lord's acts
of kindness, praises of the Lord for all the Lord has done for
us, for His great goodness to Israel, performed in all compassion,
8 in all His loving-kindness. He said: They, they are My people,
My children who would not lie to Me – and He was their rescue.
9 Wherever they suffered, He too suffered, and His presence, its
emissary rescued them; in His love, in His mercy He redeemed
them and took them up and bore them through all those long-
past days.

Haftara for Shabbat Shuva

This haftara is read on the Shabbat between Rosh HaShana and Yom Kippur, no matter which parasha is read (Vayelekh or Haazinu). Minhag Anglia reads in this order: Hosea, Micah, Joel.

HOSEA

14 2 O Israel, return, go back to the Lord your God, for you have
3 stumbled in your own sinfulness. Take words of remorse with
you and return to the Lord; say to Him, "Forgive all of our
sins; accept our goodness – instead of calves we offer You our
4 words of prayer. Assyria will not save us; no more will we ride
upon horses; never again will we say, 'You are our god' to the
work of our hands, for only in You will the orphan find mercy."
5 I will mend their rebellion with gracious love, for I have turned
6 My anger away from them. I will be as dew to Israel; he will
bloom like a lily and set down roots as deep as the trees of Leb-
7 anon. His branches will spread wide; his splendor will be as the
8 olive tree, and his fragrance as the trees of Lebanon. They who
return will dwell beneath his shade; they will revive once again
as grain and flower like vines; their acclaim will linger as the
9 scent of the wine of Lebanon. Efrayim will say, "What need do
I have of these idols?" And I will answer him; I will look after
him. I will be as a cypress tree, lush and leafy; you will find
10 in Me your source of fruit. He who is wise will fathom these
words; the insightful will grasp them, for the ways of the Lord

---

fetishizing military power, is sure to result in the corruption of the divine image in us. The prophet urges his listeners to return to God; repentance will bring the people to a better, more worthy state of existence.

ז וְאוֹרִיד לָאָרֶץ נִצְחָם׃ חַסְדֵי יְהוָה ׀ אַזְכִּיר תְּהִלֹּת
יְהוָה כְּעַל כֹּל אֲשֶׁר־גְּמָלָנוּ יְהוָה וְרַב־טוּב לְבֵית יִשְׂרָאֵל
ח אֲשֶׁר־גְּמָלָם כְּרַחֲמָיו וּכְרֹב חֲסָדָיו׃ וַיֹּאמֶר אַךְ־עַמִּי הֵמָּה
ט בָּנִים לֹא יְשַׁקֵּרוּ וַיְהִי לָהֶם לְמוֹשִׁיעַ׃ בְּכָל־צָרָתָם ׀ לֹא לוֹ
צָר וּמַלְאַךְ פָּנָיו הוֹשִׁיעָם בְּאַהֲבָתוֹ וּבְחֶמְלָתוֹ הוּא גְאָלָם
וַיְנַטְּלֵם וַיְנַשְּׂאֵם כָּל־יְמֵי עוֹלָם׃

הפטרה לשבת שובה

This הפטרה *is read on the* שבת *between* ראש השנה *and* יום כיפור*, no matter which* פרשה *is read* (האזינו *or* וילך).
Minhag Anglia reads in this order: הושע, מיכה, יואל.

יד ב ג שׁוּבָה יִשְׂרָאֵל עַד יְהוָה אֱלֹהֶיךָ כִּי כָשַׁלְתָּ בַּעֲוֺנֶךָ׃ קְחוּ הושע
עִמָּכֶם דְּבָרִים וְשׁוּבוּ אֶל־יְהוָה אִמְרוּ אֵלָיו כָּל־תִּשָּׂא עָוֺן
ד וְקַח־טוֹב וּנְשַׁלְּמָה פָרִים שְׂפָתֵינוּ׃ אַשּׁוּר ׀ לֹא יוֹשִׁיעֵנוּ
עַל־סוּס לֹא נִרְכָּב וְלֹא־נֹאמַר עוֹד אֱלֹהֵינוּ לְמַעֲשֵׂה יָדֵינוּ
ה אֲשֶׁר־בְּךָ יְרֻחַם יָתוֹם׃ אֶרְפָּא מְשׁוּבָתָם אֹהֲבֵם נְדָבָה כִּי שָׁב
ו אַפִּי מִמֶּנּוּ׃ אֶהְיֶה כַטַּל לְיִשְׂרָאֵל יִפְרַח כַּשּׁוֹשַׁנָּה וְיַךְ שָׁרָשָׁיו
ז כַּלְּבָנוֹן׃ יֵלְכוּ יֹנְקוֹתָיו וִיהִי כַזַּיִת הוֹדוֹ וְרֵיחַ לוֹ כַּלְּבָנוֹן׃
ח יָשֻׁבוּ יֹשְׁבֵי בְצִלּוֹ יְחַיּוּ דָגָן וְיִפְרְחוּ כַגָּפֶן זִכְרוֹ כְּיֵין לְבָנוֹן׃
ט אֶפְרַיִם מַה־לִּי עוֹד לָעֲצַבִּים אֲנִי עָנִיתִי וַאֲשׁוּרֶנּוּ אֲנִי כִּבְרוֹשׁ
י רַעֲנָן מִמֶּנִּי פֶּרְיְךָ נִמְצָא׃ מִי חָכָם וְיָבֵן אֵלֶּה נָבוֹן וְיֵדָעֵם

HAFTARA FOR SHABBAT SHUVA

In Tanakh, the horse represents military power. The Assyrians, who possessed a large force of chariots (drawn by horses) and mounted cavalry, were considered the most powerful empire of the age. The prophet Hoshea calls on Israel not to pin their hopes on Assyria. The key to a good life is the understanding of the place of human beings in comparison to God. If one fails to comprehend this, they begin to attribute God-like characteristics to human beings, and this is the root of idolatry and the basis of moral degeneration. Centering human beings and their desires, while at the same time

are just, and the righteous will walk in them, but sinners will
stumble over them.*

Yemenites end here

JOEL

Some Ashkenazim continue from here

2 11 Then the LORD raises His voice before His troops – for His
camp is vast, and mighty are the ones who carry out His words.
For great and terrifying is the day of the LORD – who could
12 withstand it? Even now, so says the LORD, return to Me whole-
13 heartedly, with fasting, weeping, and grief. Rend your hearts,
not your clothing, and come back to the LORD your God. For
He is gracious and compassionate, slow to anger and abound-
14 ing in kindness; He may well relent and forswear the evil. Who
knows? Maybe He will reconsider and relent and leave behind
blessings; offer grain offerings and libations to the LORD, your
15 God. *Blow a ram's horn in Zion, sanctify a fast day,
16 convene an assembly, gather the people, sanctify the masses,
convene the old, and gather the children and infants. Let the
groom come from his room and the bride from her wedding
17 chamber. Let the priests, attendants of the LORD, weep between
the hallway and the altar. Let them say: "Have compassion, O
LORD, upon Your people, and do not allow Your possession to
become a reproach – ruled by nations." Why should it be said
18 among the peoples, "Where is their God?" Then the LORD will
be fiercely zealous toward His land, and He will have mercy
19 upon His nation. He will reply and say to His nation: So I will
send to you grain, and sweet wine, and young oil. You will be
sated with it. I will no longer allow you to become a reproach
20 among the nations. I will drive the northerner away from you – I
will banish them to a dry and desolate land; their vanguard to
the east sea, their rearguard to the west sea. Their foul smell will
ascend, their stench will rise, for they have done terrible things.
21 Fear not, earth. Rejoice! Be glad! For the LORD has done great
22 things. Fear not, animals of My fields, for the desert pasture is
green with grass; the tree has borne fruit: the fig and vine have
23 blossomed. Rejoice and be glad in the LORD, your God, children of Zion. For He has given you the first rain out of generosity.
He will rain down for you the first and last rain as it was in the
24 beginning. The granaries will fill with grain, and the press will
25 overflow with sweet wine and young oil. I will repay you for all

Most Ashkenazim continue from here

כִּי־יְשָׁרִים דַּרְכֵי יְהוָה וְצַדִּקִים יֵלְכוּ בָם וּפֹשְׁעִים יִכָּשְׁלוּ
בָם:★

Yemenites end here

ב יא וַיהוָה נָתַן קוֹלוֹ לִפְנֵי חֵילוֹ כִּי רַב מְאֹד מַחֲנֵהוּ כִּי עָצוּם עֹשֵׂה יואל

Some Ashkenazim continue from here

יב דְבָרוֹ כִּי־גָדוֹל יוֹם־יְהוָה וְנוֹרָא מְאֹד וּמִי יְכִילֶנּוּ: וְגַם־עַתָּה
נְאֻם־יְהוָה שֻׁבוּ עָדַי בְּכָל־לְבַבְכֶם וּבְצוֹם וּבִבְכִי וּבְמִסְפֵּד:
יג וְקִרְעוּ לְבַבְכֶם וְאַל־בִּגְדֵיכֶם וְשׁוּבוּ אֶל־יְהוָה אֱלֹהֵיכֶם כִּי־
יד חַנּוּן וְרַחוּם הוּא אֶרֶךְ אַפַּיִם וְרַב־חֶסֶד וְנִחָם עַל־הָרָעָה: מִי
יוֹדֵעַ יָשׁוּב וְנִחָם וְהִשְׁאִיר אַחֲרָיו בְּרָכָה מִנְחָה וָנֶסֶךְ לַיהוָה

Most Ashkenazim continue from here

טו אֱלֹהֵיכֶם: ★תִּקְעוּ שׁוֹפָר בְּצִיּוֹן קַדְּשׁוּ־צוֹם קִרְאוּ
טז עֲצָרָה: אִסְפוּ־עָם קַדְּשׁוּ קָהָל קִבְצוּ זְקֵנִים אִסְפוּ עוֹלָלִים
יז וְיֹנְקֵי שָׁדָיִם יֵצֵא חָתָן מֵחֶדְרוֹ וְכַלָּה מֵחֻפָּתָהּ: בֵּין הָאוּלָם
וְלַמִּזְבֵּחַ יִבְכּוּ הַכֹּהֲנִים מְשָׁרְתֵי יְהוָה וְיֹאמְרוּ חוּסָה יְהוָה
עַל־עַמֶּךָ וְאַל־תִּתֵּן נַחֲלָתְךָ לְחֶרְפָּה לִמְשָׁל־בָּם גּוֹיִם לָמָּה
יח יֹאמְרוּ בָעַמִּים אַיֵּה אֱלֹהֵיהֶם: וַיְקַנֵּא יְהוָה לְאַרְצוֹ וַיַּחְמֹל
יט עַל־עַמּוֹ: וַיַּעַן יְהוָה וַיֹּאמֶר לְעַמּוֹ הִנְנִי שֹׁלֵחַ לָכֶם אֶת־
הַדָּגָן וְהַתִּירוֹשׁ וְהַיִּצְהָר וּשְׂבַעְתֶּם אֹתוֹ וְלֹא־אֶתֵּן אֶתְכֶם
כ עוֹד חֶרְפָּה בַּגּוֹיִם: וְאֶת־הַצְּפוֹנִי אַרְחִיק מֵעֲלֵיכֶם וְהִדַּחְתִּיו
אֶל־אֶרֶץ צִיָּה וּשְׁמָמָה אֶת־פָּנָיו אֶל־הַיָּם הַקַּדְמֹנִי וְסֹפוֹ
אֶל־הַיָּם הָאַחֲרוֹן וְעָלָה בָאְשׁוֹ וְתַעַל צַחֲנָתוֹ כִּי הִגְדִּיל
כא לַעֲשׂוֹת: אַל־תִּירְאִי אֲדָמָה גִּילִי וּשְׂמָחִי כִּי־הִגְדִּיל יְהוָה
כב לַעֲשׂוֹת: אַל־תִּירְאוּ בַּהֲמוֹת שָׂדַי כִּי דָשְׁאוּ נְאוֹת מִדְבָּר
כג כִּי־עֵץ נָשָׂא פִרְיוֹ תְּאֵנָה וָגֶפֶן נָתְנוּ חֵילָם: וּבְנֵי צִיּוֹן גִּילוּ
וְשִׂמְחוּ בַּיהוָה אֱלֹהֵיכֶם כִּי־נָתַן לָכֶם אֶת־הַמּוֹרֶה לִצְדָקָה
כד וַיּוֹרֶד לָכֶם גֶּשֶׁם מוֹרֶה וּמַלְקוֹשׁ בָּרִאשׁוֹן: וּמָלְאוּ הַגֳּרָנוֹת בָּר
כה וְהֵשִׁיקוּ הַיְקָבִים תִּירוֹשׁ וְיִצְהָר: וְשִׁלַּמְתִּי לָכֶם אֶת־הַשָּׁנִים

the seasons consumed by the locusts, the springing-locusts, the
finisher-locusts, and the chewer-locusts – My great army, which
26 I sent among you. You will eat, eat and be sated, and you will
praise the name of the LORD, your God, who has done wonders
27 for you, for My nation will never be ashamed. You will know that
I am among Israel, and I am the LORD, your God; there is no
other. My nation will never be ashamed.

MICAH
Sepharadim and some Ashkenazim add

7 18 Is there any God like You who forgives iniquities, who looks beyond the sins of the remnant of His own people, who does not
19 hold onto His wrath forever because He desires kindness? He
will again have compassion for us; He will subdue our iniquities
20 and hurl all of our sins into the deepest of seas. You will show
truth to Yaakov, kindness to Avraham, as You swore to our fathers in the earliest days.

Haftarat Haazinu

This haftara is read on the Shabbat between Yom Kippur and Sukkot. If Shabbat Parashat Haazinu falls between Rosh HaShana and Yom Kippur, read the haftara on page 1620.

II SAMUEL
For Ashkenazim and Sepharadim

22 1 David uttered these words of song to the LORD on the day that
the LORD saved him from the hands of all his enemies and
2 from the hand of Sha'ul. He said: The LORD is my Rock and my
3 fortress, my own rescuer; // my God is the Rock of my refuge /
my shield, the horn of my salvation, my haven, / my refuge, my
4 savior who delivers me from violence. // Praise! When I call on
5 the LORD, / I am saved from my enemies. // For when waves
6 of death assailed me, / deadly torrents engulfed me, the cords
of Sheol entangled me, / snares of death confronted me, //
7 in my distress I called on the LORD; / I called out to my God; /
He heard my voice from His Temple, / and my cry rang in His

numerous and prolonged wars and built the kingdom of Israel into a regional empire. Throughout, he always understood that the source of his strength, wisdom, and dedication was God. This song is a song of praise to the Almighty for his achievements. Reading it, we are reminded to always act with the knowledge that our successes are not solely our own.

אֲשֶׁר֙ אָכַ֣ל הָֽאַרְבֶּ֔ה הַיֶּ֖לֶק וְהֶחָסִ֣יל וְהַגָּזָ֑ם חֵילִי֙ הַגָּד֔וֹל אֲשֶׁ֥ר
כו שִׁלַּ֖חְתִּי בָּכֶֽם׃ וַאֲכַלְתֶּ֤ם אָכוֹל֙ וְשָׂב֔וֹעַ וְהִֽלַּלְתֶּ֗ם אֶת־שֵׁ֤ם
יְהוָה֙ אֱלֹ֣הֵיכֶ֔ם אֲשֶׁר־עָשָׂ֥ה עִמָּכֶ֖ם לְהַפְלִ֑יא וְלֹא־יֵבֹ֥שׁוּ עַמִּ֖י
כז לְעוֹלָֽם׃ וִֽידַעְתֶּ֗ם כִּ֣י בְקֶ֤רֶב יִשְׂרָאֵל֙ אָ֔נִי וַאֲנִ֛י יְהוָ֥ה אֱלֹהֵיכֶ֖ם
וְאֵ֣ין ע֑וֹד וְלֹא־יֵבֹ֥שׁוּ עַמִּ֖י לְעוֹלָֽם׃

מיכה
Sepharadim and some Ashkenazim add

ז יח מִי־אֵ֣ל כָּמ֗וֹךָ נֹשֵׂ֤א עָוֺן֙ וְעֹבֵ֣ר עַל־פֶּ֔שַׁע לִשְׁאֵרִ֖ית נַחֲלָת֑וֹ
יט לֹא־הֶחֱזִ֤יק לָעַד֙ אַפּ֔וֹ כִּֽי־חָפֵ֥ץ חֶ֖סֶד הֽוּא׃ יָשׁ֣וּב יְרַחֲמֵ֔נוּ
כ יִכְבֹּ֖שׁ עֲוֺנֹתֵ֑ינוּ וְתַשְׁלִ֛יךְ בִּמְצֻל֥וֹת יָ֖ם כָּל־חַטֹּאתָֽם׃ תִּתֵּ֤ן
אֱמֶת֙ לְיַעֲקֹ֔ב חֶ֖סֶד לְאַבְרָהָ֑ם אֲשֶׁר־נִשְׁבַּ֥עְתָּ לַאֲבֹתֵ֖ינוּ מִ֥ימֵי
קֶֽדֶם׃

הפטרת האזינו

This הפטרה *is read on the* שבת *between* יום כיפור *and* סוכות*.*
If שבת פרשת האזינו *falls between* ראש השנה *and* יום כיפור*, read the* הפטרה *on page 1621.*

שמואל ב׳
For Ashkenazim and Sepharadim

כב א וַיְדַבֵּ֤ר דָּוִד֙ לַֽיהוָ֔ה אֶת־דִּבְרֵ֖י הַשִּׁירָ֣ה הַזֹּ֑את בְּיוֹם֩
הִצִּ֨יל יְהוָ֥ה אֹת֛וֹ מִכַּ֥ף כָּל־אֹיְבָ֖יו וּמִכַּ֥ף שָׁאֽוּל׃
ב ג וַיֹּאמַ֑ר   יְהוָ֥ה סַלְעִ֛י וּמְצֻדָתִ֖י וּמְפַלְטִי־לִֽי׃   אֱלֹהֵ֥י
צוּרִ֖י אֶֽחֱסֶה־בּ֑וֹ   מָֽגִנִּי֙ וְקֶ֣רֶן יִשְׁעִ֔י מִשְׂגַּבִּ֖י
ד וּמְנוּסִ֑י   מֹשִׁעִ֕י מֵחָמָ֖ס תֹּשִׁעֵֽנִי׃   מְהֻלָּ֖ל
ה אֶקְרָ֣א יְהוָ֑ה וּמֵאֹיְבַ֖י אִוָּשֵֽׁעַ׃   כִּ֥י אֲפָפֻ֖נִי מִשְׁבְּרֵי־
ו מָ֑וֶת   נַחֲלֵ֥י בְלִיַּ֖עַל יְבַעֲתֻֽנִי׃   חֶבְלֵ֥י
שְׁא֖וֹל סַבֻּ֑נִי   קִדְּמֻ֖נִי מֹ֥קְשֵׁי־
ז מָֽוֶת׃   בַּצַּר־לִי֙ אֶקְרָ֣א יְהוָ֔ה   וְאֶל־
אֱלֹהַ֖י אֶקְרָ֑א   וַיִּשְׁמַ֤ע מֵֽהֵיכָלוֹ֙

HAAZINU

Ashkenazim and Sepharadim

This *haftara* is from the closing chapters of the book of Samuel, which summarize the reign of King David. David was an unparalleled military leader. He survived

8 ears. // Then the earth shook and shuddered; / the foundations of heaven trembled; / they shuddered from His wrath. //
9 Smoke issued from His nostrils; / devouring flames flared from
10 His mouth; / from Him gleaming coals blazed forth. // He
bent the heavens and descended, / dense cloud beneath His
11 feet; / He mounted a cherub and flew, / appearing on wings of
12 wind. // He surrounded Himself with a shelter of darkness, /
13 of heavy storm clouds dense with rain. // From the brilliant
14 glow of His presence / blazed fiery coals. // The LORD thundered from the heavens; / the Most High raised His voice; /
15 He shot arrows to scatter them, / lightning bolts to rout them. //
16 The ocean bed was exposed, / the foundations of the world
laid bare / by the onslaught of the LORD, / by the blast of His
17 breath. // From on high He reached down and took me; / He
18 drew me out of the mighty waters. // He saved me from my
19 fierce enemy, / from foes too strong for me. // They confront-
20 ed me on my direst day, / but the LORD was my support. //
He brought me out to freedom; / He rescued me because He de-
21 lighted in me. // The LORD rewarded me as I deserved; / as my
22 hands were clean, He repaid me, / for I kept the ways of the LORD /
23 and did not betray my God, / for all His laws are before me; /
24 I will not turn away from His statutes. / I am blameless to Him /
25 and keep myself from sin. / So the LORD repaid me as I de-
26 served / as I was pure in His sight. // You deal loyally with
those who are loyal, / to the blameless warrior You show Your-
27 self blameless; / You are pure with those who are pure, / but
28 with the crooked, You are shrewd. / You bring salvation to a
humble people; / You cast Your eyes down on the haughty. //

ח קוֹלִי וְשַׁוְעָתִי בְּאָזְנָיו׃ ותגעש וַיִּתְגָּעַשׁ
וַתִּרְעַשׁ הָאָרֶץ מוֹסְדוֹת הַשָּׁמַיִם
ט יִרְגָּזוּ וַיִּתְגָּעֲשׁוּ כִּי־חָרָה לוֹ׃ עָלָה
עָשָׁן בְּאַפּוֹ וְאֵשׁ מִפִּיו
י תֹּאכֵל גֶּחָלִים בָּעֲרוּ מִמֶּנּוּ׃ וַיֵּט
שָׁמַיִם וַיֵּרַד וַעֲרָפֶל תַּחַת
יא רַגְלָיו׃ וַיִּרְכַּב עַל־כְּרוּב וַיָּעֹף וַיֵּרָא
יב עַל־כַּנְפֵי־רוּחַ׃ וַיָּשֶׁת חֹשֶׁךְ סְבִיבֹתָיו
יג סֻכּוֹת חַשְׁרַת־מַיִם עָבֵי שְׁחָקִים׃ מִנֹּגַהּ
יד נֶגְדּוֹ בָּעֲרוּ גַּחֲלֵי־אֵשׁ׃ יַרְעֵם מִן־שָׁמַיִם
טו יְהוָה וְעֶלְיוֹן יִתֵּן קוֹלוֹ׃ וַיִּשְׁלַח
טז חִצִּים וַיְפִיצֵם בָּרָק ויהמם׃ וַיֵּרָאוּ אֲפִקֵי וַיָּהֹם
יָם יִגָּלוּ מֹסְדוֹת תֵּבֵל בְּגַעֲרַת
יז יְהוָה מִנִּשְׁמַת רוּחַ אַפּוֹ׃ יִשְׁלַח מִמָּרוֹם
יח יִקָּחֵנִי יַמְשֵׁנִי מִמַּיִם רַבִּים׃ יַצִּילֵנִי
מֵאֹיְבִי עָז מִשֹּׂנְאַי כִּי אָמְצוּ
יט מִמֶּנִּי׃ יְקַדְּמֻנִי בְּיוֹם אֵידִי וַיְהִי
כ יְהוָה מִשְׁעָן לִי׃ וַיֹּצֵא לַמֶּרְחָב
כא אֹתִי יְחַלְּצֵנִי כִּי־חָפֵץ בִּי׃ יִגְמְלֵנִי
יְהוָה כְּצִדְקָתִי כְּבֹר יָדַי יָשִׁיב
כב לִי׃ כִּי שָׁמַרְתִּי דַּרְכֵי יְהוָה וְלֹא
כג רָשַׁעְתִּי מֵאֱלֹהָי׃ כִּי כָל־מִשְׁפָּטָו
כד לְנֶגְדִּי וְחֻקֹּתָיו לֹא־אָסוּר מִמֶּנָּה׃ וָאֶהְיֶה
כה תָמִים לוֹ וָאֶשְׁתַּמְּרָה מֵעֲוֺנִי׃ וַיָּשֶׁב יְהוָה לִי
כו כְּצִדְקָתִי כְּבֹרִי לְנֶגֶד עֵינָיו׃ עִם־
חָסִיד תִּתְחַסָּד עִם־גִּבּוֹר תָּמִים
כז תִּתַּמָּם׃ עִם־נָבָר תִּתָּבָר וְעִם־
כח עִקֵּשׁ תִּתַּפָּל׃ וְאֶת־עַם עָנִי

29 For You are my lamp, LORD; / the LORD lights up my dark-
30 ness. / With You I can rush a ridge; / with my God I can leap
31 over a wall. // God's ways are blameless; / the LORD's words
32 are pure; / He is a shield to all who take refuge in Him. // For
who is a god besides the LORD; / who is a Rock besides our
33 God? / God is my powerful stronghold; / He frees my way so
34 it is sound. / He makes my legs like a deer's / and stands me
35 on the heights. / He trains my hands for battle / so that my
36 arms can bend a bow of bronze. // You gave me the shield of
37 Your victory; / Your battle cry stirred me with power. / You
38 made my steps broad and firm; / my feet never faltered. / I
pursued my enemy to destroy them, / never turning back until
39 they perished. / I cut them down and crushed them, and they
40 did not rise; / they fell beneath my feet. / You girded me with
power for battle / and sunk my adversaries far beneath me; /
41 You made my enemies turn tail before me; / my foes, too, I de-
42 stroyed. / They looked wildly about, but there was no savior – /
43 called out to the LORD, but He did not answer them – // while
I ground them up like dust of the earth; / I crushed and pound-
44 ed them like street-mud. // You rescued me from civil strife; /
You kept me as the head of nations; / peoples I never knew
45 of serve me. / Foreign peoples come cringing before me; /
46 they merely hear me and obey; / foreign peoples lose heart /
47 and come trembling out of their forts. // The LORD lives! /
Blessed is my Rock; / exalted is God, Rock of my rescue! /
48 God who grants vengeance to me, / who subjugates people un-
49 der me, / my redeemer from my enemies, / You raise me above
those who rise against me; / You save me from violent men. //

כט תּוֹשִׁ֑יעַ וְעֵינֶ֖יךָ עַל־רָמִ֥ים תַּשְׁפִּֽיל׃ כִּֽי־
אַתָּ֥ה נֵירִ֖י יְהוָ֑ה וַיהוָ֖ה יַגִּ֥יהַּ
ל חָשְׁכִּֽי׃ כִּ֥י בְכָ֖ה אָר֣וּץ גְּד֑וּד בֵּאלֹהַ֖י
לא אֲדַלֶּג־שֽׁוּר׃ הָאֵ֖ל תָּמִ֣ים
דַּרְכּ֑וֹ אִמְרַ֤ת יְהוָה֙ צְרוּפָ֔ה מָגֵ֣ן
לב ה֔וּא לְכֹ֖ל הַחֹסִ֥ים בּֽוֹ׃ כִּ֥י מִי־אֵ֖ל מִבַּלְעֲדֵ֣י
לג יְהוָ֑ה וּמִ֥י צ֖וּר מִבַּלְעֲדֵ֥י אֱלֹהֵֽינוּ׃ הָאֵ֖ל
מָֽעוּזִּ֣י חָ֑יִל וַיַּתֵּ֥ר תָּמִ֖ים
לד דרכו׃ מְשַׁוֶּ֥ה רגליו כָּאַיָּל֑וֹת וְעַל־ דַּרְכִּ֑י | רַגְלַ֖י
לה בָּמוֹתַ֖י יַעֲמִדֵֽנִי׃ מְלַמֵּ֥ד יָדַ֖י
לו לַמִּלְחָמָ֑ה וְנִחַ֥ת קֶֽשֶׁת־נְחוּשָׁ֖ה זְרֹעֹתָֽי׃ וַתִּתֶּן־
לז לִ֖י מָגֵ֣ן יִשְׁעֶ֑ךָ וַעֲנֹתְךָ֖ תַּרְבֵּֽנִי׃ תַּרְחִ֥יב צַעֲדִ֖י
לח תַּחְתֵּ֑נִי וְלֹ֥א מָעֲד֖וּ קַרְסֻלָּֽי׃ אֶרְדְּפָ֥ה
אֹיְבַ֖י וָאַשְׁמִידֵ֑ם וְלֹ֥א אָשׁ֖וּב עַד־
לט כַּלּוֹתָֽם׃ וָאֲכַלֵּ֥ם וָאֶמְחָצֵ֖ם וְלֹ֣א יְקוּמ֑וּן וַיִּפְּל֖וּ
מ תַּ֥חַת רַגְלָֽי׃ וַתַּזְרֵ֥נִי חַ֖יִל
מא לַמִּלְחָמָ֑ה תַּכְרִ֥יעַ קָמַ֖י תַּחְתֵּֽנִי׃ וְאֹ֣יְבַ֔י
מב תַּ֥תָּה לִּ֖י עֹ֑רֶף מְשַׂנְאַ֖י וָאַצְמִיתֵֽם׃ יִשְׁע֖וּ וְאֵ֣ין
מג מֹשִׁ֑יעַ אֶל־יְהוָ֖ה וְלֹ֥א עָנָֽם׃ וְאֶשְׁחָקֵ֖ם
כַּעֲפַר־אָ֑רֶץ כְּטִיט־חוּצ֥וֹת אֲדִקֵּ֖ם
מד אֶרְקָעֵֽם׃ וַתְּפַלְּטֵ֔נִי מֵרִיבֵ֖י עַמִּ֑י תִּשְׁמְרֵ֙נִי֙
לְרֹ֣אשׁ גּוֹיִ֔ם עַ֥ם לֹא־יָדַ֖עְתִּי
מה יַֽעַבְדֻֽנִי׃ בְּנֵ֥י נֵכָ֖ר יִתְכַּחֲשׁוּ־לִ֑י לִשְׁמ֥וֹעַ
מו אֹ֖זֶן יִשָּׁ֥מְעוּ לִֽי׃ בְּנֵ֥י נֵכָ֖ר יִבֹּ֑לוּ וְיַחְגְּר֖וּ
מז מִמִּסְגְּרוֹתָֽם׃ חַי־יְהוָ֖ה וּבָר֣וּךְ צוּרִ֑י וְיָרֻ֕ם
מח אֱלֹהֵ֖י צ֥וּר יִשְׁעִֽי׃ הָאֵ֕ל הַנֹּתֵ֥ן נְקָמֹ֖ת
מט לִ֑י וּמוֹרִ֥יד עַמִּ֖ים תַּחְתֵּֽנִי׃ וּמֽוֹצִיאִ֖י
מֵאֹֽיְבָ֑י וּמִקָּמַי֙ תְּר֣וֹמְמֵ֔נִי מֵאִ֥ישׁ חֲמָסִ֖ים

50 So I praise You, LORD, among the nations, / and sing to Your
51 name. // He is a tower of victory for His king / and shows loyalty to His anointed, / to David and his seed forever.

EZEKIEL
For Yemenites

17 22 "So says the Lord GOD: I will take from the soaring crown of the
cedar and place it, I will pluck from the topmost, tender stalks,
23 and I will plant it upon a high and lofty mountain; in the moun-
tainous height of Israel I will plant it. It will bear branches, grow
fruit; it will become a majestic cedar, and every bird of every type
24 will settle beneath it; in the shade of its arms they will dwell. And
all the trees of the field will know that I, the LORD, have brought
down the high tree and raised the lowly tree; I have withered the
green tree and made the withered tree bloom; I, the LORD, have
18 1 spoken and will do it." And the word of the LORD came
2 to me, saying: "What are you doing, using this proverb on the
soil of Israel: 'Fathers eat sour grapes, but the teeth of the chil-
3 dren are set on edge'? As I live, declares the Lord GOD, you will
4 no longer use this proverb in Israel. Behold: all lives are Mine;
the life of father and son alike are Mine; that person who sins
5 will die. The person who is righteous, who acts in a way
6 that is just and right – he does not eat on the mountains or look
up to the idols of the House of Israel, he does not defile another's
7 wife or approach a menstruating woman, he mistreats no one, he
returns his debtor's pledge to him, he commits no robbery, he
gives his bread to the hungry, he covers the naked with clothes,
8 he does not lend with advanced interest or take accrued interest,

futility, as a matter both of principle and of practice. First of all, God's justice in the world works on an individual level: "That person who sins will die; the son will not bear the iniquity of the father." No one is forced to bear the punishment for their forebears' sins, since we always have the chance to repent. And so, while the fate of destruction for Jerusalem is final, the people have the opportunity to repair the damage done by the willful behavior that the prophets had identified as its cause. The people of Israel can make themselves a foundation for building a better future. The destruction can be undone, but despair will only exacerbate it. Yeḥezkel, at God's behest, was fighting against despair.

נ תַּצִּילֵנִי: עַל־כֵּן אוֹדְךָ יְהוָה בַּגּוֹיִם וּלְשִׁמְךָ
נא אֲזַמֵּר: מגדיל יְשׁוּעוֹת מִגְדּוֹל
מַלְכּוֹ וְעֹשֶׂה־חֶסֶד לִמְשִׁיחוֹ
לְדָוִד וּלְזַרְעוֹ עַד־עוֹלָם:

יחזקאל

For Yemenites

יז כב כֹּה אָמַר אֲדֹנָי יֱהוִה וְלָקַחְתִּי אָנִי מִצַּמֶּרֶת הָאֶרֶז הָרָמָה וְנָתָתִּי
מֵרֹאשׁ יֹנְקוֹתָיו רַךְ אֶקְטֹף וְשָׁתַלְתִּי אָנִי עַל הַר־גָּבֹהַּ וְתָלוּל:
כג בְּהַר מְרוֹם יִשְׂרָאֵל אֶשְׁתֳּלֶנּוּ וְנָשָׂא עָנָף וְעָשָׂה פֶרִי וְהָיָה
לְאֶרֶז אַדִּיר וְשָׁכְנוּ תַחְתָּיו כֹּל צִפּוֹר כָּל־כָּנָף בְּצֵל דָּלִיּוֹתָיו
כד תִּשְׁכֹּנָּה: וְיָדְעוּ כָּל־עֲצֵי הַשָּׂדֶה כִּי אֲנִי יְהוָה הִשְׁפַּלְתִּי ׀ עֵץ
גָּבֹהַּ הִגְבַּהְתִּי עֵץ שָׁפָל הוֹבַשְׁתִּי עֵץ לָח וְהִפְרַחְתִּי עֵץ יָבֵשׁ
יח א אֲנִי יְהוָה דִּבַּרְתִּי וְעָשִׂיתִי: וַיְהִי דְבַר־יְהוָה אֵלַי
ב לֵאמֹר: מַה־לָּכֶם אַתֶּם מֹשְׁלִים אֶת־הַמָּשָׁל הַזֶּה עַל־אַדְמַת
ג יִשְׂרָאֵל לֵאמֹר אָבוֹת יֹאכְלוּ בֹסֶר וְשִׁנֵּי הַבָּנִים תִּקְהֶינָה: חַי־
אָנִי נְאֻם אֲדֹנָי יֱהוִה אִם־יִהְיֶה לָכֶם עוֹד מְשֹׁל הַמָּשָׁל הַזֶּה
ד בְּיִשְׂרָאֵל: הֵן כָּל־הַנְּפָשׁוֹת לִי הֵנָּה כְּנֶפֶשׁ הָאָב וּכְנֶפֶשׁ הַבֵּן
ה לִי־הֵנָּה הַנֶּפֶשׁ הַחֹטֵאת הִיא תָמוּת: וְאִישׁ
ו כִּי־יִהְיֶה צַדִּיק וְעָשָׂה מִשְׁפָּט וּצְדָקָה: אֶל־הֶהָרִים לֹא
אָכָל וְעֵינָיו לֹא נָשָׂא אֶל־גִּלּוּלֵי בֵּית יִשְׂרָאֵל וְאֶת־אֵשֶׁת
ז רֵעֵהוּ לֹא טִמֵּא וְאֶל־אִשָּׁה נִדָּה לֹא יִקְרָב: וְאִישׁ לֹא יוֹנֶה
חֲבֹלָתוֹ חוֹב יָשִׁיב גְּזֵלָה לֹא יִגְזֹל לַחְמוֹ לְרָעֵב יִתֵּן וְעֵירֹם
ח יְכַסֶּה־בָּגֶד: בַּנֶּשֶׁךְ לֹא־יִתֵּן וְתַרְבִּית לֹא יִקָּח מֵעָוֶל יָשִׁיב

Yemenites

The prophet Yeḥezkel faces those exiled with him to Babylonia during the reign of Yehoyakhin. "Fathers eat sour grapes, but the teeth of the children are set on edge" – this was the mistaken lesson that the exiles took away from their harrowing experience – our ancestors sinned, and we are bearing their punishments. Such thinking brought about despair among the people, and contributed to an air of passivity and resignation. Yeḥezkel imparts God's word to the people, taking issue with their dejected attitude of

▶

he resists doing wrong, he judges between man and man with
9 true justice, he follows My statutes, keeps My laws, acts with
10 truth – he is righteous; he will live, declares the Lord GOD. If
he bears a violent son, a bloodshedder, who commits any one of
11 these – although he himself committed none of these – who eats
12 on the mountains, who defiles another's wife, who mistreats the
poor and needy, commits robbery, does not return his debtor's
pledge, who looks up to the idols, who commits abominable
13 things, who lends with advanced interest and takes accrued interest, will he live? He will not live; he has committed all these
14 abominable acts; he will die – his blood is on his own head. And
if he bears a son, who sees all the sins that his father has commit-
15 ted, who considers them but does not act similarly – he does
not eat on the mountains, he does not look up to the idols of the
16 House of Israel, he does not defile another's wife, he mistreats no
one, he does not retain his debtor's pledge, he does not commit
robbery, he gives his bread to the hungry, he covers the naked
17 with clothes, he refrains from harming the poor, he takes neither
advanced nor accrued interest, he keeps My laws, follows My
statutes – he will not die for the iniquity of his father; he will live.
18 Because his father practiced extortion, robbed his own brother,
acted in a way that was no good among his people, behold: he
19 will die in his iniquity. And you say: Why does the son not bear
the iniquity of the father? The son has acted in a way that is just
and right, has kept all My statutes, has performed them – he will
20 live. That person who sins will die; the son will not bear the iniquity of the father, and the father will not bear the iniquity of the
son; the righteous one's righteousness will be on him, and the
21 wicked one's wickedness will be on him. The wicked
one who turns back from all the sins he committed and keeps
all My statutes and acts in a way that is just and right – he will
22 live; he will not die. All the transgressions he committed will not
be remembered against him; through the righteousness he has
23 performed he will live. Do I desire the death of the wicked, declares the Lord GOD, not that he should turn from his ways and
24 live? And the righteous one who turns from his
righteousness and does wrong similar to all the abominable acts
the wicked one committed, shall he live? None of the righteous
deeds he has done will be remembered; his betrayal and the sins
25 that he has sinned – because of these he will die. You say, 'The

ט יָדוֹ מִשְׁפַּט אֱמֶת יַעֲשֶׂה בֵּין אִישׁ לְאִישׁ: בְּחֻקּוֹתַי יְהַלֵּךְ
וּמִשְׁפָּטַי שָׁמַר לַעֲשׂוֹת אֱמֶת צַדִּיק הוּא חָיֹה יִחְיֶה נְאֻם
י אֲדֹנָי יֱהֹוִה: וְהוֹלִיד בֵּן־פָּרִיץ שֹׁפֵךְ דָּם וְעָשָׂה אָח מֵאַחַד
יא מֵאֵלֶּה: וְהוּא אֶת־כׇּל־אֵלֶּה לֹא עָשָׂה כִּי גַם אֶל־הֶהָרִים
יב אָכַל וְאֶת־אֵשֶׁת רֵעֵהוּ טִמֵּא: עָנִי וְאֶבְיוֹן הוֹנָה גְּזֵלוֹת גָּזָל
חֲבֹל לֹא יָשִׁיב וְאֶל־הַגִּלּוּלִים נָשָׂא עֵינָיו תּוֹעֵבָה עָשָׂה:
יג בַּנֶּשֶׁךְ נָתַן וְתַרְבִּית לָקַח וָחָי לֹא יִחְיֶה אֵת כׇּל־הַתּוֹעֵבוֹת
יד הָאֵלֶּה עָשָׂה מוֹת יוּמָת דָּמָיו בּוֹ יִהְיֶה: וְהִנֵּה הוֹלִיד בֵּן
וַיַּרְא אֶת־כׇּל־חַטֹּאת אָבִיו אֲשֶׁר עָשָׂה וַיִּרְאֶה וְלֹא יַעֲשֶׂה
טו כָּהֵן: עַל־הֶהָרִים לֹא אָכָל וְעֵינָיו לֹא נָשָׂא אֶל־גִּלּוּלֵי בֵּית
טז יִשְׂרָאֵל אֶת־אֵשֶׁת רֵעֵהוּ לֹא טִמֵּא: וְאִישׁ לֹא הוֹנָה חֲבֹל
לֹא חָבָל וּגְזֵלָה לֹא גָזָל לַחְמוֹ לְרָעֵב נָתָן וְעֵרוֹם כִּסָּה־בָגֶד:
יז מֵעָנִי הֵשִׁיב יָדוֹ נֶשֶׁךְ וְתַרְבִּית לֹא לָקָח מִשְׁפָּטַי עָשָׂה
יח בְּחֻקּוֹתַי הָלָךְ הוּא לֹא יָמוּת בַּעֲוֺן אָבִיו חָיֹה יִחְיֶה: אָבִיו
כִּי־עָשַׁק עֹשֶׁק גָּזַל גֵּזֶל אָח וַאֲשֶׁר לֹא־טוֹב עָשָׂה בְּתוֹךְ עַמָּיו
יט וְהִנֵּה־מֵת בַּעֲוֺנוֹ: וַאֲמַרְתֶּם מַדֻּעַ לֹא־נָשָׂא הַבֵּן בַּעֲוֺן הָאָב
וְהַבֵּן מִשְׁפָּט וּצְדָקָה עָשָׂה אֵת כׇּל־חֻקּוֹתַי שָׁמַר וַיַּעֲשֶׂה
כ אֹתָם חָיֹה יִחְיֶה: הַנֶּפֶשׁ הַחֹטֵאת הִיא תָמוּת בֵּן לֹא־יִשָּׂא ׀
בַּעֲוֺן הָאָב וְאָב לֹא יִשָּׂא בַּעֲוֺן הַבֵּן צִדְקַת הַצַּדִּיק עָלָיו
כא תִּהְיֶה וְרִשְׁעַת רשע עָלָיו תִּהְיֶה: וְהָרָשָׁע הָרָשָׁע
כִּי יָשׁוּב מִכׇּל־חַטֹּאתָו אֲשֶׁר עָשָׂה וְשָׁמַר אֶת־כׇּל־חֻקּוֹתַי
כב וְעָשָׂה מִשְׁפָּט וּצְדָקָה חָיֹה יִחְיֶה לֹא יָמוּת: כׇּל־פְּשָׁעָיו
כג אֲשֶׁר עָשָׂה לֹא יִזָּכְרוּ לוֹ בְּצִדְקָתוֹ אֲשֶׁר־עָשָׂה יִחְיֶה: הֶחָפֹץ
אֶחְפֹּץ מוֹת רָשָׁע נְאֻם אֲדֹנָי יֱהֹוִה הֲלוֹא בְּשׁוּבוֹ מִדְּרָכָיו
כד וְחָיָה: וּבְשׁוּב צַדִּיק מִצִּדְקָתוֹ וְעָשָׂה עָוֶל
כְּכֹל הַתּוֹעֵבוֹת אֲשֶׁר־עָשָׂה הָרָשָׁע יַעֲשֶׂה וָחָי כׇּל־צִדְקֹתָו
אֲשֶׁר־עָשָׂה לֹא תִזָּכַרְנָה בְּמַעֲלוֹ אֲשֶׁר־מָעַל וּבְחַטָּאתוֹ
כה אֲשֶׁר־חָטָא בָּם יָמוּת: וַאֲמַרְתֶּם לֹא יִתָּכֵן דֶּרֶךְ אֲדֹנָי שִׁמְעוּ־

way of the Lord is not fair.' Listen, House of Israel: Is My way not
26 fair? Surely, your ways are not fair. When the righteous one turns
from his righteousness and does wrong and dies for it, he dies for
27 that which he has done wrong. And when the wicked
one turns from the wickedness that he has done and acts in a way
28 that is just and right, he preserves his life. When he considers
them and turns from all the transgressions he has committed, he
29 will live; he will not die. And the House of Israel says, 'The way
of the Lord is not fair.' Are My ways not fair, House of Israel? It
is your ways that are not fair. So I will judge you, House of Israel,
each man according to his ways, declares the Lord GOD; return –
turn back from all your transgressions so that they will not be the
31 obstacle that is sin for you. Throw off all the transgressions you
have committed; make yourselves a new heart, a new spirit. Why
32 should you die, House of Israel? For I do not desire the death of
those who die, declares the Lord GOD; turn back and live!

HAFTARAT VEZOT HABERAKHA

1 1 After the death of Moshe, the LORD's servant, the LORD said to JOSHUA
2 Moshe's disciple, Yehoshua son of Nun: "Moshe, My servant, is
dead; now arise, cross the Jordan here – you and all this people –
3 to the land that I am giving to the Israelites. I have given you ev-
4 ery place your foot will tread, just as I promised Moshe. Your territory shall stretch from the wilderness and Lebanon here to the
Great River, the Euphrates River, and all the land of the Hittites,
5 to the Great Sea where the sun sets. No one will be able to stand
against you for as long as you live; just as I was with Moshe, I will

against the peoples of Canaan were formidable. In his first prophecy, Yehoshua receives threefold encouragement from God in advance of the objectives he must set out to attain. Three times God says to him: "Be strong and brave." In answer to his call to the tribes of the eastern side of the Jordan to fulfill their pledge and take the lead in the invasion, Yehoshua receives additional support and affirmation of his leadership. These votes of confidence from God and the people were crucial in this sensitive time.

נָא בֵּית יִשְׂרָאֵל הֲדַרְכִּי לֹא יִתָּכֵן הֲלֹא דַרְכֵיכֶם לֹא יִתָּכֵנוּ׃
כו בְּשׁוּב־צַדִּיק מִצִּדְקָתוֹ וְעָשָׂה עָוֶל וּמֵת עֲלֵיהֶם בְּעַוְלוֹ אֲשֶׁר־
כז עָשָׂה יָמוּת׃ וּבְשׁוּב רָשָׁע מֵרִשְׁעָתוֹ אֲשֶׁר
כח עָשָׂה וַיַּעַשׂ מִשְׁפָּט וּצְדָקָה הוּא אֶת־נַפְשׁוֹ יְחַיֶּה׃ וַיִּרְאֶה
כט וישוב מִכָּל־פְּשָׁעָיו אֲשֶׁר עָשָׂה חָיוֹ יִחְיֶה לֹא יָמוּת׃ וְאָמְרוּ וַיָּשָׁב
בֵּית יִשְׂרָאֵל לֹא יִתָּכֵן דֶּרֶךְ אֲדֹנָי הַדְּרָכַי לֹא יִתָּכְנוּ בֵּית
ל יִשְׂרָאֵל הֲלֹא דַרְכֵיכֶם לֹא יִתָּכֵן׃ לָכֵן אִישׁ כִּדְרָכָיו אֶשְׁפֹּט
אֶתְכֶם בֵּית יִשְׂרָאֵל נְאֻם אֲדֹנָי יֱהֹוִה שׁוּבוּ וְהָשִׁיבוּ מִכָּל־
לא פִּשְׁעֵיכֶם וְלֹא־יִהְיֶה לָכֶם לְמִכְשׁוֹל עָוֹן׃ הַשְׁלִיכוּ מֵעֲלֵיכֶם
אֶת־כָּל־פִּשְׁעֵיכֶם אֲשֶׁר פְּשַׁעְתֶּם בָּם וַעֲשׂוּ לָכֶם לֵב חָדָשׁ
לב וְרוּחַ חֲדָשָׁה וְלָמָּה תָמֻתוּ בֵּית יִשְׂרָאֵל׃ כִּי לֹא אֶחְפֹּץ בְּמוֹת
הַמֵּת נְאֻם אֲדֹנָי יֱהֹוִה וְהָשִׁיבוּ וִחְיוּ׃

הפטרת וזאת הברכה

א א וַיְהִי אַחֲרֵי מוֹת מֹשֶׁה עֶבֶד יְהוָה וַיֹּאמֶר יְהוָה אֶל־יְהוֹשֻׁעַ יהושע
ב בִּן־נוּן מְשָׁרֵת מֹשֶׁה לֵאמֹר׃ מֹשֶׁה עַבְדִּי מֵת וְעַתָּה קוּם
עֲבֹר אֶת־הַיַּרְדֵּן הַזֶּה אַתָּה וְכָל־הָעָם הַזֶּה אֶל־הָאָרֶץ אֲשֶׁר
ג אָנֹכִי נֹתֵן לָהֶם לִבְנֵי יִשְׂרָאֵל׃ כָּל־מָקוֹם אֲשֶׁר תִּדְרֹךְ כַּף־
ד רַגְלְכֶם בּוֹ לָכֶם נְתַתִּיו כַּאֲשֶׁר דִּבַּרְתִּי אֶל־מֹשֶׁה׃ מֵהַמִּדְבָּר
וְהַלְּבָנוֹן הַזֶּה וְעַד־הַנָּהָר הַגָּדוֹל נְהַר־פְּרָת כֹּל אֶרֶץ הַחִתִּים
ה וְעַד־הַיָּם הַגָּדוֹל מְבוֹא הַשָּׁמֶשׁ יִהְיֶה גְּבוּלְכֶם׃ לֹא־יִתְיַצֵּב
אִישׁ לְפָנֶיךָ כֹּל יְמֵי חַיֶּיךָ כַּאֲשֶׁר הָיִיתִי עִם־מֹשֶׁה אֶהְיֶה

VEZOT HABERAKHA

This *haftara* is the direct continuation of the end of the events described in the book of Deuteronomy. Moshe's death, and the assumption of the mantle of responsibility by the prophet Yehoshua, were events that created challenges for all the people set to enter the land of Israel, especially Yehoshua. Moshe, who had led the people for forty years, left enormous shoes to fill. The difficulties posed in crossing the Jordan and waging war

▶

6 be with you. I will never let you go, and I will never leave you. Be
strong and brave, for you will bring this people into possession
7 of the land I swore to their ancestors to give them. But you must
be strong and brave indeed to uphold faithfully all the Torah that
Moshe My servant commanded you; do not stray from it – neither right nor left – so that you may triumph wherever you go.
8 This book of Torah must never leave your lips; contemplate it
day and night, so that you will faithfully uphold all that is written within it. For then your course will succeed; then you will
9 triumph. Hear now – I have charged you to be strong and brave.
Do not be frightened or dismayed, for the LORD your God is
10 with you wherever you go."* Yehoshua commanded
11 the officers of the people: "Cross through the camp and instruct
the people: 'Prepare provisions for yourselves, for in three days'
time you are to cross the Jordan here, to come and take possession of the land that the LORD your God is giving you as your
12 own.'" Yehoshua then told the Reubenites, the Gadites,
13 and half the tribe of Menashe: "Remember what Moshe, the
LORD's servant, commanded you: The LORD your God has
14 granted you rest and given you this land. Your wives and little
ones and your cattle shall dwell in the land that Moshe gave you
across the Jordan, but all your warriors shall cross over armed to
15 join your brothers and assist them, until the LORD grants rest
like yours to your brothers and they too take possession of the
land that the LORD your God is giving them. Then you shall return to your own land, which Moshe, the LORD's servant, gave
you on the eastern side of the Jordan – and you shall take pos-
16 17 session of it." They answered Yehoshua, "As we obeyed Moshe,
so we will obey you as long as the LORD your God is with you,
18 as He was with Moshe. Whoever rebels against your word or
disobeys anything you command shall be put to death; only be
strong and brave."

Sepharadim end here
Yemenites skip to Joshua 6:27

Ashkenazim end here

6 27 The LORD was with Yehoshua, and his fame rang out across the
land.

ו עִמְּךָ לֹא אַרְפְּךָ וְלֹא אֶעֶזְבֶךָּ׃ חֲזַק וֶאֱמָץ כִּי אַתָּה תַּנְחִיל
אֶת־הָעָם הַזֶּה אֶת־הָאָרֶץ אֲשֶׁר־נִשְׁבַּעְתִּי לַאֲבוֹתָם לָתֵת
ז לָהֶם׃ רַק חֲזַק וֶאֱמַץ מְאֹד לִשְׁמֹר לַעֲשׂוֹת כְּכָל־הַתּוֹרָה
אֲשֶׁר צִוְּךָ מֹשֶׁה עַבְדִּי אַל־תָּסוּר מִמֶּנּוּ יָמִין וּשְׂמֹאול לְמַעַן
ח תַּשְׂכִּיל בְּכֹל אֲשֶׁר תֵּלֵךְ׃ לֹא־יָמוּשׁ סֵפֶר הַתּוֹרָה הַזֶּה מִפִּיךָ
וְהָגִיתָ בּוֹ יוֹמָם וָלַיְלָה לְמַעַן תִּשְׁמֹר לַעֲשׂוֹת כְּכָל־הַכָּתוּב
ט בּוֹ כִּי־אָז תַּצְלִיחַ אֶת־דְּרָכֶךָ וְאָז תַּשְׂכִּיל׃ הֲלוֹא צִוִּיתִיךָ
חֲזַק וֶאֱמָץ אַל־תַּעֲרֹץ וְאַל־תֵּחָת כִּי עִמְּךָ יְהוָה אֱלֹהֶיךָ

Sepharadim end here
Yemenites skip to Joshua 6:27

י בְּכֹל אֲשֶׁר תֵּלֵךְ׃* וַיְצַו יְהוֹשֻׁעַ אֶת־שֹׁטְרֵי הָעָם
יא לֵאמֹר׃ עִבְרוּ ׀ בְּקֶרֶב הַמַּחֲנֶה וְצַוּוּ אֶת־הָעָם לֵאמֹר הָכִינוּ
לָכֶם צֵידָה כִּי בְּעוֹד ׀ שְׁלֹשֶׁת יָמִים אַתֶּם עֹבְרִים אֶת־הַיַּרְדֵּן
הַזֶּה לָבוֹא לָרֶשֶׁת אֶת־הָאָרֶץ אֲשֶׁר יְהוָה אֱלֹהֵיכֶם נֹתֵן
יב לָכֶם לְרִשְׁתָּהּ׃ וְלָראוּבֵנִי וְלַגָּדִי וְלַחֲצִי שֵׁבֶט
יג הַמְנַשֶּׁה אָמַר יְהוֹשֻׁעַ לֵאמֹר׃ זָכוֹר אֶת־הַדָּבָר אֲשֶׁר צִוָּה
אֶתְכֶם מֹשֶׁה עֶבֶד־יְהוָה לֵאמֹר יְהוָה אֱלֹהֵיכֶם מֵנִיחַ לָכֶם
יד וְנָתַן לָכֶם אֶת־הָאָרֶץ הַזֹּאת׃ נְשֵׁיכֶם טַפְּכֶם וּמִקְנֵיכֶם יֵשְׁבוּ
בָּאָרֶץ אֲשֶׁר נָתַן לָכֶם מֹשֶׁה בְּעֵבֶר הַיַּרְדֵּן וְאַתֶּם תַּעַבְרוּ
טו חֲמֻשִׁים לִפְנֵי אֲחֵיכֶם כֹּל גִּבּוֹרֵי הַחַיִל וַעֲזַרְתֶּם אוֹתָם׃ עַד
אֲשֶׁר־יָנִיחַ יְהוָה ׀ לַאֲחֵיכֶם כָּכֶם וְיָרְשׁוּ גַם־הֵמָּה אֶת־הָאָרֶץ
אֲשֶׁר־יְהוָה אֱלֹהֵיכֶם נֹתֵן לָהֶם וְשַׁבְתֶּם לְאֶרֶץ יְרֻשַּׁתְכֶם
וִירִשְׁתֶּם אוֹתָהּ אֲשֶׁר ׀ נָתַן לָכֶם מֹשֶׁה עֶבֶד יְהוָה בְּעֵבֶר
טז הַיַּרְדֵּן מִזְרַח הַשָּׁמֶשׁ׃ וַיַּעֲנוּ אֶת־יְהוֹשֻׁעַ לֵאמֹר כֹּל אֲשֶׁר־
יז צִוִּיתָנוּ נַעֲשֶׂה וְאֶל־כָּל־אֲשֶׁר תִּשְׁלָחֵנוּ נֵלֵךְ׃ כְּכֹל אֲשֶׁר־
שָׁמַעְנוּ אֶל־מֹשֶׁה כֵּן נִשְׁמַע אֵלֶיךָ רַק יִהְיֶה יְהוָה אֱלֹהֶיךָ
יח עִמָּךְ כַּאֲשֶׁר הָיָה עִם־מֹשֶׁה׃ כָּל־אִישׁ אֲשֶׁר־יַמְרֶה אֶת־פִּיךָ
וְלֹא־יִשְׁמַע אֶת־דְּבָרֶיךָ לְכֹל אֲשֶׁר־תְּצַוֶּנּוּ יוּמָת רַק חֲזַק

Ashkenazim end here

וֶאֱמָץ׃*

ו כז וַיְהִי יְהוָה אֶת־יְהוֹשֻׁעַ וַיְהִי שָׁמְעוֹ בְּכָל־הָאָרֶץ׃

עשרת הדיברות שבפרשת יתרו
בטעם העליון

אָנֹכִי יְהוָה אֱלֹהֶיךָ אֲשֶׁר הוֹצֵאתִיךָ
מֵאֶרֶץ מִצְרַיִם מִבֵּית עֲבָדִים לֹא יִהְיֶה לְךָ אֱלֹהִים
אֲחֵרִים עַל־פָּנַי לֹא תַעֲשֶׂה־לְךָ פֶסֶל ׀ וְכָל־תְּמוּנָה אֲשֶׁר
בַּשָּׁמַיִם ׀ מִמַּעַל וַאֲשֶׁר בָּאָרֶץ מִתַּחַת וַאֲשֶׁר בַּמַּיִם ׀
מִתַּחַת לָאָרֶץ לֹא־תִשְׁתַּחְוֶה לָהֶם וְלֹא תָעָבְדֵם כִּי אָנֹכִי
יְהוָה אֱלֹהֶיךָ אֵל קַנָּא פֹּקֵד עֲוֺן אָבֹת עַל־בָּנִים עַל־שִׁלֵּשִׁים
וְעַל־רִבֵּעִים לְשֹׂנְאָי וְעֹשֶׂה חֶסֶד לַאֲלָפִים לְאֹהֲבַי וּלְשֹׁמְרֵי
מִצְוֺתָי׃ לֹא תִשָּׂא אֶת־שֵׁם־יְהוָה אֱלֹהֶיךָ לַשָּׁוְא
כִּי לֹא יְנַקֶּה יְהוָה אֵת אֲשֶׁר־יִשָּׂא אֶת־שְׁמוֹ לַשָּׁוְא׃
זָכוֹר אֶת־יוֹם הַשַּׁבָּת לְקַדְּשׁוֹ שֵׁשֶׁת יָמִים תַּעֲבֹד וְעָשִׂיתָ
כָל־מְלַאכְתֶּךָ וְיוֹם הַשְּׁבִיעִי שַׁבָּת ׀ לַיהוָה אֱלֹהֶיךָ לֹא
תַעֲשֶׂה כָל־מְלָאכָה אַתָּה וּבִנְךָ וּבִתֶּךָ עַבְדְּךָ וַאֲמָתְךָ
וּבְהֶמְתֶּךָ וְגֵרְךָ אֲשֶׁר בִּשְׁעָרֶיךָ כִּי שֵׁשֶׁת־יָמִים עָשָׂה יְהוָה
אֶת־הַשָּׁמַיִם וְאֶת־הָאָרֶץ אֶת־הַיָּם וְאֶת־כָּל־אֲשֶׁר־בָּם

This superimposition led to much confusion and disagreement, particularly with regard to the first verse. The *taam elyon* presented here is according to the position of Rabbi Yaakov Emden (Germany, 1696–1776). However, according to Rabbi Wolf Heidenheim (Germany, 1757–1832), the first commandment (until the words מבית עבדים) ought to be read the same in *taam elyon* and *taam taḥton.*

Rabbi Ḥizkiya ben Manoaḥ, author of the commentary *Ḥizkuni,* writes that on the holiday of Shavuot, the Ten Commandments should be read in the synagogue using *taam elyon,* while when read as part of the weekly *parasha, taam taḥton* should be used. This is the custom of most Ashkenazic congregations. However, Rabbi Menaḥem de Lonzano (Middle East, sixteenth century) in his book *Or Torah* writes that *taam elyon* should always be used when reading publicly in the synagogue, and only individuals reading to themselves should use *taam taḥton.* This is the custom of Sephardic congregations. In the communities of Yemen, only *taam elyon* was extant, since the Yemenite customs largely mirror the traditions of the Babylonian Jews.

עשרת הדיברות שבפרשת ואתחנן
בטעם העליון

אָנֹכִי יְהוָה אֱלֹהֶיךָ
אֲשֶׁר הוֹצֵאתִיךָ מֵאֶרֶץ מִצְרַיִם מִבֵּית עֲבָדִים לֹא־יִהְיֶה
לְךָ אֱלֹהִים אֲחֵרִים עַל־פָּנַי לֹא תַעֲשֶׂה־לְךָ פֶסֶל ׀ כָּל־
תְּמוּנָה אֲשֶׁר בַּשָּׁמַיִם ׀ מִמַּעַל וַאֲשֶׁר בָּאָרֶץ מִתַּחַת וַאֲשֶׁר
בַּמַּיִם ׀ מִתַּחַת לָאָרֶץ לֹא־תִשְׁתַּחֲוֶה לָהֶם וְלֹא תָעָבְדֵם
כִּי אָנֹכִי יְהוָה אֱלֹהֶיךָ אֵל קַנָּא פֹּקֵד עֲוֺן אָבוֹת עַל־בָּנִים
וְעַל־שִׁלֵּשִׁים וְעַל־רִבֵּעִים לְשֹׂנְאָי וְעֹשֶׂה חֶסֶד לַאֲלָפִים
לְאֹהֲבַי וּלְשֹׁמְרֵי מצותו: לֹא תִשָּׂא אֶת־שֵׁם־יְהוָה מִצְוֺתָי
אֱלֹהֶיךָ לַשָּׁוְא כִּי לֹא יְנַקֶּה יְהוָה אֵת אֲשֶׁר־יִשָּׂא אֶת־שְׁמוֹ
לַשָּׁוְא: שָׁמוֹר אֶת־יוֹם הַשַּׁבָּת לְקַדְּשׁוֹ כַּאֲשֶׁר צִוְּךָ
׀ יְהוָה אֱלֹהֶיךָ שֵׁשֶׁת יָמִים תַּעֲבֹד וְעָשִׂיתָ כָּל־מְלַאכְתֶּךָ וְיוֹם
הַשְּׁבִיעִי שַׁבָּת ׀ לַיהוָה אֱלֹהֶיךָ לֹא־תַעֲשֶׂה כָל־מְלָאכָה
אַתָּה וּבִנְךָ־וּבִתֶּךָ וְעַבְדְּךָ־וַאֲמָתֶךָ וְשׁוֹרְךָ וַחֲמֹרְךָ וְכָל־
בְּהֶמְתֶּךָ וְגֵרְךָ אֲשֶׁר בִּשְׁעָרֶיךָ לְמַעַן יָנוּחַ עַבְדְּךָ וַאֲמָתְךָ
כָּמוֹךָ וְזָכַרְתָּ כִּי־עֶבֶד הָיִיתָ ׀ בְּאֶרֶץ מִצְרַיִם וַיֹּצִאֲךָ יְהוָה

THE TEN COMMANDMENTS IN TAAM ELYON

There are two traditional sets of *taamim* (cantillation marks) for the Ten Commandments. One is called *taam elyon,* and the other *taam taḥton*. In *taam elyon,* each commandment (except for perhaps the first; see below) comprises one and only one verse. This results in some verses that are very long, with a wealth of elaborate *taamim* such as *pazer* and *telisha*. This gives the reading a dignified and festive air. The difference between *taam elyon* and *taam taḥton* can also result in slight differences in the vocalization of the words – *nikkud*.

It seems that the original division of the verses customary in the land of Israel was *taam taḥton,* while the *taam elyon* has roots in the Babylonian Jewish tradition. Nevertheless, even the oldest extant manuscripts include both systems, though the most ancient ones superimposed them on the same quoted text.

▶

וַיָּנַח בַּיּוֹם הַשְּׁבִיעִי עַל־כֵּן בֵּרַךְ יְהוָה אֶת־יוֹם הַשַּׁבָּת
וַיְקַדְּשֵׁהוּ׃ כַּבֵּד אֶת־אָבִיךָ וְאֶת־
אִמֶּךָ לְמַעַן יַאֲרִכוּן יָמֶיךָ עַל הָאֲדָמָה אֲשֶׁר־יְהוָה אֱלֹהֶיךָ
נֹתֵן לָךְ׃ לֹא תִרְצָח׃ לֹא
תִנְאָף׃ לֹא תִגְנֹב׃ לֹא־
תַעֲנֶה בְרֵעֲךָ עֵד שָׁקֶר׃ לֹא
תַחְמֹד בֵּית רֵעֶךָ לֹא־
תַחְמֹד אֵשֶׁת רֵעֶךָ וְעַבְדּוֹ וַאֲמָתוֹ וְשׁוֹרוֹ וַחֲמֹרוֹ וְכֹל אֲשֶׁר
לְרֵעֶךָ׃

HAFTARA FOR SHABBAT ROSH ḤODESH

The maftir for Shabbat Rosh Ḥodesh is read from Numbers 28:9–15. If Rosh Ḥodesh is on Shabbat and Sunday, Sepharadim and Chabad conclude this haftara by reading the first and last verses of the haftara for Erev Rosh Ḥodesh, on page 1644.

ISAIAH

66 1 Thus speaks the LORD: The heavens are My throne; the world,
My footstool. What house, then, would You build for Me, where
2 could I rest? All this – My own hands made, all these are Mine,
so says the LORD. And these are the ones I look toward: the
3 poor, of humbled spirit, who tremble at My words. While he,
killing his ox is like a murderer of men, the one who offers up a
lamb might so well behead a dog; the offering brought may just
as well be pigs' blood; and his remembrance incense is a blessing of iniquity. These men, they choose their paths, their souls
4 desire their disgusting things, and so I too will choose – will
choose their torments, and bring to them what they most fear.
I called out – no one answered; I spoke, but none was listening.

(Sanhedrin 94a) teaches: "The Holy One, blessed be He, sought to make Ḥizkiyahu king of Yehuda the Messiah." This chance was never realized because Ḥizkiyahu neglected to write a song of praise for God as his ancestor David had done, and hence expressed insufficient gratitude for his salvation from the Assyrians. In the future redemption, however, all the peoples of the world will give praise to God for His providence, and the song will thus be completed.

אֱלֹהֶיךָ מִשָּׁם בְּיָד חֲזָקָה וּבִזְרֹעַ נְטוּיָה עַל־כֵּן צִוְּךָ יְהוָה
אֱלֹהֶיךָ לַעֲשׂוֹת אֶת־יוֹם הַשַּׁבָּת׃ כַּבֵּד אֶת־
אָבִיךָ וְאֶת־אִמֶּךָ כַּאֲשֶׁר צִוְּךָ יְהוָה אֱלֹהֶיךָ לְמַעַן ׀ יַאֲרִיכֻן
יָמֶיךָ וּלְמַעַן יִיטַב לָךְ עַל הָאֲדָמָה אֲשֶׁר־יְהוָה אֱלֹהֶיךָ נֹתֵן
לָךְ׃ לֹא תִּרְצָח׃ וְלֹא
תִּנְאָף׃ וְלֹא תִּגְנֹב׃ וְלֹא
תַעֲנֶה בְרֵעֲךָ עֵד שָׁוְא׃ וְלֹא
תַחְמֹד אֵשֶׁת רֵעֶךָ וְלֹא
תִתְאַוֶּה בֵּית רֵעֶךָ שָׂדֵהוּ וְעַבְדּוֹ וַאֲמָתוֹ שׁוֹרוֹ וַחֲמֹרוֹ וְכֹל
אֲשֶׁר לְרֵעֶךָ׃

הפטרת שבת ראש חודש

The מפטיר *for* שבת ראש חודש *is read from* במדבר כח, ט–טו*.*
If ראש חודש *is on* שבת *and Sunday, Sepharadim and Chabad conclude this* הפטרה *by reading the first and last verses of the* הפטרה *for* ערב ראש חודש*, on page 1645.*

סו א כֹּה אָמַר יְהוָה הַשָּׁמַיִם כִּסְאִי וְהָאָרֶץ הֲדֹם רַגְלָי אֵי־זֶה בַיִת ישעיה
ב אֲשֶׁר תִּבְנוּ־לִי וְאֵי־זֶה מָקוֹם מְנוּחָתִי׃ וְאֶת־כָּל־אֵלֶּה יָדִי
עָשָׂתָה וַיִּהְיוּ כָל־אֵלֶּה נְאֻם־יְהוָה וְאֶל־זֶה אַבִּיט אֶל־עָנִי
ג וּנְכֵה־רוּחַ וְחָרֵד עַל־דְּבָרִי׃ שׁוֹחֵט הַשּׁוֹר מַכֵּה־אִישׁ זוֹבֵחַ
הַשֶּׂה עֹרֵף כֶּלֶב מַעֲלֵה מִנְחָה דַּם־חֲזִיר מַזְכִּיר לְבֹנָה מְבָרֵךְ
אָוֶן גַּם־הֵמָּה בָּחֲרוּ בְּדַרְכֵיהֶם וּבְשִׁקּוּצֵיהֶם נַפְשָׁם חָפֵצָה׃

HAFTARA FOR SHABBAT ROSH ḤODESH

The conclusion of this *haftara*, which is also the close of the book of Isaiah, describes a vision of the future in which all humanity will come to the Temple to offer homage to God. In it, we see emphasis on the tension between the fallen present and the redeemed future. The transition from reality to vision is a central theme in all the book of Isaiah. The prophet Yeshayahu preached during the first exile – that of the northern kingdom of Israel – while at the same time, in the southern kingdom, there was an opportunity for full redemption, as the Talmud

They did what was evil in My sight, and chose what I never de-
5 sired. You who tremble to hear His word, listen to the
LORD's word: Your brothers said, the ones who hated you, who
cast you out, "Because of my name, the LORD is honored." We
6 will see your joy, and they will be shamefaced. A voice roaring
out from the city, a voice, out of the Sanctuary, a voice – it is the
7 LORD's, as He repays His enemies. Before she had writhed in labor she gave birth; before the agonies took her she was delivered
8 of a boy. Who ever heard of anything like this? Who ever saw
such happenings as these? Can the land give birth in a day? Can
a nation be born at a single step? Yet Zion has labored, and has
9 birthed her children. Would I bring on the labor and not deliver?
So the LORD speaks: Would I who fathered close the womb? So
10 your God speaks. Bring Jerusalem joy, exult in her, all
of you who love her; celebrate her joy with her, all of you who
11 mourned her. That you may suck your fill from the bosom of
her comforting; may suckle, take delight in the brilliance of her
12 glory. For thus says the LORD: See Me make peace flow
to her like a river, and the substance of nations – like a rushing
brook – and you shall suckle. You will be borne upon hips, play-
13 ing upon loving laps; as a man is consoled by his mother, just so
14 shall I comfort you, and in Jerusalem, you shall be consoled. You
shall look on, your heart rejoicing, while your bones grow vigor-
ous, like grass, and the hand of the LORD becomes known to His
15 servants, and His rage known to all His foes. For see: the LORD
is coming in fire, His chariots a storm wind, to slake His fury in
16 rage, His rebuke in flames of fire. For in fire, the LORD comes
to judgment, and by the sword, to all flesh, and many are those
17 the LORD will execute. Those in the gardens, sanctifying and
cleansing themselves, one after the other in the midst of it, while
eating the flesh of pigs and pests and mice, they will all be gath-
18 ered in together: so the LORD has spoken. For I – I know their
works, their thoughts; and time will come, to gather all nations
19 and tongues, and they will come, and look upon My glory. I shall
place a sign among them, send out survivors from them to all nations, to Tarshish, Pul, and Lud, to the great archers, Tuval, Yavan,
to the distant coastlands where none ever heard tell of Me or saw
20 My glory, and they will tell of My glory to the nations. And they
will bring back all your brothers from among all other nations,
an offering to the LORD, on horseback and on chariot, on camels,

ד גַּם־אֲנִי אֶבְחַר בְּתַעֲלֻלֵיהֶם וּמְגוּרֹתָם אָבִיא לָהֶם יַעַן קָרָאתִי
וְאֵין עוֹנֶה דִּבַּרְתִּי וְלֹא שָׁמֵעוּ וַיַּעֲשׂוּ הָרַע בְּעֵינַי וּבַאֲשֶׁר לֹא־
ה חָפַצְתִּי בָּחָרוּ׃ שִׁמְעוּ דְּבַר־יְהוָה הַחֲרֵדִים אֶל־
דְּבָרוֹ אָמְרוּ אֲחֵיכֶם שֹׂנְאֵיכֶם מְנַדֵּיכֶם לְמַעַן שְׁמִי יִכְבַּד יְהוָה
ו וְנִרְאֶה בְשִׂמְחַתְכֶם וְהֵם יֵבֹשׁוּ׃ קוֹל שָׁאוֹן מֵעִיר קוֹל מֵהֵיכָל
ז קוֹל יְהוָה מְשַׁלֵּם גְּמוּל לְאֹיְבָיו׃ בְּטֶרֶם תָּחִיל יָלָדָה בְּטֶרֶם
ח יָבוֹא חֵבֶל לָהּ וְהִמְלִיטָה זָכָר׃ מִי־שָׁמַע כָּזֹאת מִי רָאָה כָּאֵלֶּה
הֲיוּחַל אֶרֶץ בְּיוֹם אֶחָד אִם־יִוָּלֵד גּוֹי פַּעַם אֶחָת כִּי־חָלָה גַּם־
ט יָלְדָה צִיּוֹן אֶת־בָּנֶיהָ׃ הַאֲנִי אַשְׁבִּיר וְלֹא אוֹלִיד יֹאמַר יְהוָה
י אִם־אֲנִי הַמּוֹלִיד וְעָצַרְתִּי אָמַר אֱלֹהָיִךְ׃ שִׂמְחוּ
אֶת־יְרוּשָׁלִַם וְגִילוּ בָהּ כָּל־אֹהֲבֶיהָ שִׂישׂוּ אִתָּהּ מָשׂוֹשׂ כָּל־
יא הַמִּתְאַבְּלִים עָלֶיהָ׃ לְמַעַן תִּינְקוּ וּשְׂבַעְתֶּם מִשֹּׁד תַּנְחֻמֶיהָ
יב לְמַעַן תָּמֹצּוּ וְהִתְעַנַּגְתֶּם מִזִּיז כְּבוֹדָהּ׃ כִּי־כֹה ׀
אָמַר יְהוָה הִנְנִי נֹטֶה־אֵלֶיהָ כְּנָהָר שָׁלוֹם וּכְנַחַל שׁוֹטֵף כְּבוֹד
יג גּוֹיִם וִינַקְתֶּם עַל־צַד תִּנָּשֵׂאוּ וְעַל־בִּרְכַּיִם תְּשָׁעֳשָׁעוּ׃ כְּאִישׁ
אֲשֶׁר אִמּוֹ תְּנַחֲמֶנּוּ כֵּן אָנֹכִי אֲנַחֶמְכֶם וּבִירוּשָׁלִַם תְּנֻחָמוּ׃
יד וּרְאִיתֶם וְשָׂשׂ לִבְּכֶם וְעַצְמוֹתֵיכֶם כַּדֶּשֶׁא תִפְרַחְנָה וְנוֹדְעָה
טו יַד־יְהוָה אֶת־עֲבָדָיו וְזָעַם אֶת־אֹיְבָיו׃ כִּי־הִנֵּה יְהוָה בָּאֵשׁ
יָבוֹא וְכַסּוּפָה מַרְכְּבֹתָיו לְהָשִׁיב בְּחֵמָה אַפּוֹ וְגַעֲרָתוֹ בְּלַהֲבֵי־
טז אֵשׁ׃ כִּי בָאֵשׁ יְהוָה נִשְׁפָּט וּבְחַרְבּוֹ אֶת־כָּל־בָּשָׂר וְרַבּוּ חַלְלֵי
יז יְהוָה׃ הַמִּתְקַדְּשִׁים וְהַמִּטַּהֲרִים אֶל־הַגַּנּוֹת אַחַר אחד בַּתָּוֶךְ אַחַת
אֹכְלֵי בְּשַׂר הַחֲזִיר וְהַשֶּׁקֶץ וְהָעַכְבָּר יַחְדָּו יָסֻפוּ נְאֻם־יְהוָה׃
יח וְאָנֹכִי מַעֲשֵׂיהֶם וּמַחְשְׁבֹתֵיהֶם בָּאָה לְקַבֵּץ אֶת־כָּל־הַגּוֹיִם
יט וְהַלְּשֹׁנוֹת וּבָאוּ וְרָאוּ אֶת־כְּבוֹדִי׃ וְשַׂמְתִּי בָהֶם אוֹת וְשִׁלַּחְתִּי
מֵהֶם ׀ פְּלֵיטִים אֶל־הַגּוֹיִם תַּרְשִׁישׁ פּוּל וְלוּד מֹשְׁכֵי קֶשֶׁת
תֻּבַל וְיָוָן הָאִיִּים הָרְחֹקִים אֲשֶׁר לֹא־שָׁמְעוּ אֶת־שִׁמְעִי
כ וְלֹא־רָאוּ אֶת־כְּבוֹדִי וְהִגִּידוּ אֶת־כְּבוֹדִי בַּגּוֹיִם׃ וְהֵבִיאוּ אֶת־
כָּל־אֲחֵיכֶם ׀ מִכָּל־הַגּוֹיִם ׀ מִנְחָה ׀ לַיהוָה בַּסּוּסִים וּבָרֶכֶב

mules, dromedaries, to My holy mount, Jerusalem – so says the
Lord – just as the children of Israel would bring up their offer-
21 ings in pure vessels, to the Lord's House, and from among them
22 also I shall take priests and Levites, so says the Lord. For just as
the new heavens, the new earth that I am now forming, will stand
forever before Me, so says the Lord, so will stand your children,
23 your name. And it will be – every New Moon, every Sabbath –
24 all flesh will come to worship Me, so says the Lord. Going out,
they will see bodies of those people who sinned against Me, for
the worms will not die nor the fire be quenched, and they will be
repugnant to all flesh.

And it will be – every New Moon, every Sabbath –
all flesh will come to worship Me, so says the Lord.

Haftara for Shabbat Erev Rosh Ḥodesh

20 18 Yehonatan then said to David, "Tomorrow is the New Month, I SAMUEL
19 and you shall be missed, for your seat will be empty. Now
wait three days, then on the day people go back to work, make
your way swiftly down to your hiding place, and stay close to
20 the Ezel Stone. As for me – I will shoot three arrows to its side,
21 as though aiming at a target. Now, when I send the boy off to
find the arrows, if I say to him, 'Look, the arrows are just past
you, come take them,' then come, for all is well with you, and
22 there is nothing wrong – as the Lord lives. But if I say to the
boy, 'Look, the arrows are far past you,' then go, for the Lord
23 has sent you away. As for the matter we spoke of, you and I –
24 the Lord is between me and you forever." David hid
out in the field. The New Month came around, and the king
25 sat down at the feast to eat. When the king sat in his usual

realizes that he must flee from Sha'ul, but first he wants to check if all other recourses are exhausted. He designs a test together with his friend, Sha'ul's son Yonatan, to see how Sha'ul will respond to his absence from the customary Rosh Ḥodesh festivities in the palace. Sha'ul's reaction is extreme, and Yonatan confirms to David in his hiding place that they must separate. The two hold a touching final meeting.

וּבַצַּבִּים וּבַפְּרָדִים וּבַכִּרְכָּרוֹת עַל הַר קָדְשִׁי יְרוּשָׁלִַם אָמַר
יְהוָה כַּאֲשֶׁר יָבִיאוּ בְנֵי יִשְׂרָאֵל אֶת־הַמִּנְחָה בִּכְלִי טָהוֹר בֵּית
כא כב יְהוָה: וְגַם־מֵהֶם אֶקַּח לַכֹּהֲנִים לַלְוִיִּם אָמַר יְהוָה: כִּי כַאֲשֶׁר
הַשָּׁמַיִם הַחֲדָשִׁים וְהָאָרֶץ הַחֲדָשָׁה אֲשֶׁר אֲנִי עֹשֶׂה עֹמְדִים
כג לְפָנַי נְאֻם־יְהוָה כֵּן יַעֲמֹד זַרְעֲכֶם וְשִׁמְכֶם: וְהָיָה מִדֵּי־חֹדֶשׁ
בְּחָדְשׁוֹ וּמִדֵּי שַׁבָּת בְּשַׁבַּתּוֹ יָבוֹא כָל־בָּשָׂר לְהִשְׁתַּחֲוֹת לְפָנַי
כד אָמַר יְהוָה: וְיָצְאוּ וְרָאוּ בְּפִגְרֵי הָאֲנָשִׁים הַפֹּשְׁעִים בִּי כִּי
תוֹלַעְתָּם לֹא תָמוּת וְאִשָּׁם לֹא תִכְבֶּה וְהָיוּ דֵרָאוֹן לְכָל־בָּשָׂר:

והיה מדי חדש בחדשו ומדי שבת בשבתו
יבוא כל בשר להשתחות לפני אמר יהוה

הפטרת שבת
ערב ראש חודש

שמואל א׳

כ יח וַיֹּאמֶר־לוֹ יְהוֹנָתָן מָחָר חֹדֶשׁ וְנִפְקַדְתָּ כִּי יִפָּקֵד מוֹשָׁבֶךָ:
יט וְשִׁלַּשְׁתָּ תֵּרֵד מְאֹד וּבָאתָ אֶל־הַמָּקוֹם אֲשֶׁר־נִסְתַּרְתָּ שָּׁם
כ בְּיוֹם הַמַּעֲשֶׂה וְיָשַׁבְתָּ אֵצֶל הָאֶבֶן הָאָזֶל: וַאֲנִי שְׁלֹשֶׁת
כא הַחִצִּים צִדָּה אוֹרֶה לְשַׁלַּח־לִי לְמַטָּרָה: וְהִנֵּה אֶשְׁלַח אֶת־
הַנַּעַר לֵךְ מְצָא אֶת־הַחִצִּים אִם־אָמֹר אֹמַר לַנַּעַר הִנֵּה
הַחִצִּים ׀ מִמְּךָ וָהֵנָּה קָחֶנּוּ וָבֹאָה כִּי־שָׁלוֹם לְךָ וְאֵין דָּבָר
כב חַי־יְהוָה: וְאִם־כֹּה אֹמַר לָעֶלֶם הִנֵּה הַחִצִּים מִמְּךָ וָהָלְאָה
כג לֵךְ כִּי שִׁלַּחֲךָ יְהוָה: וְהַדָּבָר אֲשֶׁר דִּבַּרְנוּ אֲנִי וָאָתָּה הִנֵּה
כד יְהוָה בֵּינִי וּבֵינְךָ עַד־עוֹלָם: וַיִּסָּתֵר דָּוִד בַּשָּׂדֶה

HAFTARA FOR SHABBAT EREV ROSH ḤODESH

The events described in this *haftara* occur over the space of four days, from the day before Rosh Ḥodesh until the day after the second day of Rosh Ḥodesh. During this period, the tension between King Sha'ul and David reaches its peak. Sha'ul understands that David will be the next ruler, and he makes the decision to kill him. Once Sha'ul has twice threatened to skewer David with his spear, David

seat by the wall, Yehonatan rose, and Avner sat by Sha'ul's
26 side while David's seat remained empty. Sha'ul did not mention anything that day. "It must be by chance that he is not
27 clean," he thought; "he must be unclean." But the
next day, on the second day of the New Month, David's seat
was still empty, and Sha'ul asked Yehonatan, his son, "Why
did the son of Yishai fail to come to the feast – both yester-
28 day and today?" "David urgently asked me for leave to Beit
29 Leḥem," Yehonatan answered Sha'ul. "He said, 'Please let me
go, for we have a family feast in the city, and my brother has
bid me – so now, if I have gained your favor, please let me
get away to see my brothers.' That is why he has not come
30 to the king's table." Sha'ul burst into a rage at Yehonatan. "Son of a perverse, wayward woman!" he said. "Oh, I
knew you would side with the son of Yishai – to your own
31 disgrace and the disgrace of your mother's nakedness! But
as long as the son of Yishai lives on this earth, you and your
kingship will not endure – so bring him to me now, for he
32 is a dead man!" But Yehonatan answered Sha'ul, his
father. "Why should he be killed?" he said to him. "What has
33 he done?" And Sha'ul hurled the spear toward him to strike
him down, and Yehonatan realized that his father was de-
34 termined to kill David. Furious, Yehonatan rose up
from the table; he ate no food on the second day of the New
Month out of anguish for David, for his father had humili-
35 ated him. In the morning, Yehonatan went out to the
field for the rendezvous with David, a young boy with him.
36 He said to his boy, "Now, run and find the arrows I am about
to shoot." The boy ran off, and he shot the arrows past him.
37 When the boy reached the place where Yehonatan's arrows
had fallen, Yehonatan called out after the boy, "Oh – the arrows are far past you." Then Yehonatan called out after the
38 boy, "Quick – hurry, do not linger." When Yehonatan's boy
39 gathered up the arrows and came back to his master – the
boy knew nothing; only Yehonatan and David knew about
40 the arrangement – Yehonatan gave his gear to his boy and
41 said to him, "Go – bring these back to town." When the boy
had left, David emerged from the southern side of the stone,
flung his face to the ground, and bowed three times. And they
kissed each other and wept with each other until David's sobs

כה וַיְהִי הַחֹדֶשׁ וַיֵּשֶׁב הַמֶּלֶךְ עַל־הַלֶּחֶם לֶאֱכוֹל׃ וַיֵּשֶׁב הַמֶּלֶךְ (אֶל־)
עַל־מוֹשָׁבוֹ כְּפַעַם ׀ בְּפַעַם אֶל־מוֹשַׁב הַקִּיר וַיָּקָם יְהוֹנָתָן
כו וַיֵּשֶׁב אַבְנֵר מִצַּד שָׁאוּל וַיִּפָּקֵד מְקוֹם דָּוִד׃ וְלֹא־דִבֶּר שָׁאוּל
מְאוּמָה בַּיּוֹם הַהוּא כִּי אָמַר מִקְרֶה הוּא בִּלְתִּי טָהוֹר הוּא
כז כִּי־לֹא טָהוֹר׃ וַיְהִי מִמָּחֳרַת הַחֹדֶשׁ הַשֵּׁנִי וַיִּפָּקֵד
מְקוֹם דָּוִד וַיֹּאמֶר שָׁאוּל אֶל־יְהוֹנָתָן בְּנוֹ מַדּוּעַ לֹא־בָא בֶן־
כח יִשַׁי גַּם־תְּמוֹל גַּם־הַיּוֹם אֶל־הַלָּחֶם׃ וַיַּעַן יְהוֹנָתָן אֶת־שָׁאוּל
כט נִשְׁאֹל נִשְׁאַל דָּוִד מֵעִמָּדִי עַד־בֵּית לָחֶם׃ וַיֹּאמֶר שַׁלְּחֵנִי
נָא כִּי זֶבַח מִשְׁפָּחָה לָנוּ בָּעִיר וְהוּא צִוָּה־לִי אָחִי וְעַתָּה
אִם־מָצָאתִי חֵן בְּעֵינֶיךָ אִמָּלְטָה נָּא וְאֶרְאֶה אֶת־אֶחָי עַל־
ל כֵּן לֹא־בָא אֶל־שֻׁלְחַן הַמֶּלֶךְ׃ וַיִּחַר־אַף שָׁאוּל
בִּיהוֹנָתָן וַיֹּאמֶר לוֹ בֶּן־נַעֲוַת הַמַּרְדּוּת הֲלוֹא יָדַעְתִּי כִּי־בֹחֵר
לא אַתָּה לְבֶן־יִשַׁי לְבָשְׁתְּךָ וּלְבֹשֶׁת עֶרְוַת אִמֶּךָ׃ כִּי כָל־הַיָּמִים
אֲשֶׁר בֶּן־יִשַׁי חַי עַל־הָאֲדָמָה לֹא תִכּוֹן אַתָּה וּמַלְכוּתֶךָ
לב וְעַתָּה שְׁלַח וְקַח אֹתוֹ אֵלַי כִּי בֶן־מָוֶת הוּא׃ וַיַּעַן
יְהוֹנָתָן אֶת־שָׁאוּל אָבִיו וַיֹּאמֶר אֵלָיו לָמָּה יוּמַת מֶה עָשָׂה׃
לג וַיָּטֶל שָׁאוּל אֶת־הַחֲנִית עָלָיו לְהַכֹּתוֹ וַיֵּדַע יְהוֹנָתָן כִּי־כָלָה
לד הִיא מֵעִם אָבִיו לְהָמִית אֶת־דָּוִד׃ וַיָּקָם יְהוֹנָתָן
מֵעִם הַשֻּׁלְחָן בָּחֳרִי־אָף וְלֹא־אָכַל בְּיוֹם־הַחֹדֶשׁ הַשֵּׁנִי לֶחֶם
לה כִּי נֶעְצַב אֶל־דָּוִד כִּי הִכְלִמוֹ אָבִיו׃ וַיְהִי בַבֹּקֶר
לו וַיֵּצֵא יְהוֹנָתָן הַשָּׂדֶה לְמוֹעֵד דָּוִד וְנַעַר קָטֹן עִמּוֹ׃ וַיֹּאמֶר
לְנַעֲרוֹ רֻץ מְצָא־נָא אֶת־הַחִצִּים אֲשֶׁר אָנֹכִי מוֹרֶה הַנַּעַר
לז רָץ וְהוּא־יָרָה הַחֵצִי לְהַעֲבִרוֹ׃ וַיָּבֹא הַנַּעַר עַד־מְקוֹם הַחֵצִי
אֲשֶׁר יָרָה יְהוֹנָתָן וַיִּקְרָא יְהוֹנָתָן אַחֲרֵי הַנַּעַר וַיֹּאמֶר הֲלוֹא
לח הַחֵצִי מִמְּךָ וָהָלְאָה׃ וַיִּקְרָא יְהוֹנָתָן אַחֲרֵי הַנַּעַר מְהֵרָה
חוּשָׁה אַל־תַּעֲמֹד וַיְלַקֵּט נַעַר יְהוֹנָתָן אֶת־הַחִצִּי וַיָּבֹא אֶל־ (הַחִצִּים)
לט אֲדֹנָיו׃ וְהַנַּעַר לֹא־יָדַע מְאוּמָה אַךְ יְהוֹנָתָן וְדָוִד יָדְעוּ אֶת־
מ הַדָּבָר׃ וַיִּתֵּן יְהוֹנָתָן אֶת־כֵּלָיו אֶל־הַנַּעַר אֲשֶׁר־לוֹ וַיֹּאמֶר

42 reached a crescendo. "Go in peace," Yehonatan said to David,
"for the two of us have sworn in the name of the LORD, 'May
the Lord be between me and you, and between my seed and
your seed, forever.'"

HAFTARA FOR THE FIRST SHABBAT OF ḤANUKKA

On the first day of Ḥanukka, Sepharadim and Yemenites read the maftir from Numbers 6:22–7:17. Ashkenazim begin the maftir at Numbers 7:1.

On subsequent days of Ḥanukka, read the maftir for the appropriate day from Numbers chapter 7.

When the Shabbat of Ḥanukka coincides with Rosh Ḥodesh, three Torah scrolls are removed from the ark. The first six aliyot are read from Parashat Miketz. The seventh consists of the addition for Rosh Ḥodesh, Numbers 28:9–15. Afterward, half-Kaddish is recited, and the maftir is read for the sixth day of Ḥanukka.

2 14 Shout out and be joyful, daughter Zion, for I am coming, and I ZECHARIAH
15 will dwell in your midst – the LORD has spoken. Many nations
will join themselves to the LORD on that day, and they will be
My people. I will dwell in your midst, and you will know that the
16 LORD of Hosts sent me to you. The LORD will take possession
of Yehuda as His portion of holy ground, and He will choose
17 Jerusalem once again. Hush, all flesh, before the LORD, for He
3 1 has stirred from His holy abode. Then He showed me
Yehoshua the High Priest standing before an angel of the LORD
2 with the Adversary on his right to oppose him. The LORD said
to the Adversary: The LORD drives you away, Adversary. The
LORD, who has chosen Jerusalem, drives you away. Yes, this is a
3 firebrand saved from the fire. And Yehoshua, wearing filthy cloth-
4 ing, was standing before the angel, who spoke and said to those

Zekharya's tireless involvement, preaching God's message, put life into the long-stymied project. The prophet described to them the many obstacles on the path to redemption, and to this end he describes his famous vision of the candelabrum. The candelabrum – the source of light – has become a quintessential Jewish symbol, and it traces the path from the Tabernacle to Shlomo's Temple, the new structure that was to be built.

מא לוֹ לֵךְ הָבֵיא הָעִיר׃ הַנַּעַר בָּא וְדָוִד קָם מֵאֵצֶל הַנֶּגֶב וַיִּפֹּל
לְאַפָּיו אַרְצָה וַיִּשְׁתַּחוּ שָׁלֹשׁ פְּעָמִים וַיִּשְּׁקוּ ׀ אִישׁ אֶת־רֵעֵהוּ
מב וַיִּבְכּוּ אִישׁ אֶת־רֵעֵהוּ עַד־דָּוִד הִגְדִּיל׃ וַיֹּאמֶר יְהוֹנָתָן לְדָוִד
לֵךְ לְשָׁלוֹם אֲשֶׁר נִשְׁבַּעְנוּ שְׁנֵינוּ אֲנַחְנוּ בְּשֵׁם יהוה לֵאמֹר
יהוה יִהְיֶה ׀ בֵּינִי וּבֵינֶךָ וּבֵין זַרְעִי וּבֵין זַרְעֲךָ עַד־עוֹלָם׃

הפטרה לשבת ראשונה של חנוכה

On the first day of חנוכה*, Sepharadim and Yemenites read the* מפטיר *from* במדבר ז, א *at* במדבר ו, כב – ז, יז*. Ashkenazim begin the* מפטיר *at* במדבר ז, א*.*

On subsequent days of חנוכה*, read the* מפטיר *for the appropriate day from* במדבר ז*.*

When the שבת *of* חנוכה *coincides with* ראש חודש*, three Torah scrolls are removed from the ark. The first six* עליות *are read from* פרשת מקץ*. The seventh consists of the addition for* ראש חודש*,* במדבר כח, ט–טו*. Afterward,* חצי קדיש *is recited, and the* מפטיר *is read for the sixth day of* חנוכה*.*

ב יד רָנִּי וְשִׂמְחִי בַּת־צִיּוֹן כִּי הִנְנִי־בָא וְשָׁכַנְתִּי בְתוֹכֵךְ נְאֻם־ זכריה
טו יהוה׃ וְנִלְווּ גוֹיִם רַבִּים אֶל־יהוה בַּיּוֹם הַהוּא וְהָיוּ לִי לְעָם
וְשָׁכַנְתִּי בְתוֹכֵךְ וְיָדַעַתְּ כִּי־יהוה צְבָאוֹת שְׁלָחַנִי אֵלָיִךְ׃
טז וְנָחַל יהוה אֶת־יְהוּדָה חֶלְקוֹ עַל אַדְמַת הַקֹּדֶשׁ וּבָחַר
יז עוֹד בִּירוּשָׁלִָם׃ הַס כָּל־בָּשָׂר מִפְּנֵי יהוה כִּי נֵעוֹר מִמְּעוֹן
ג א קָדְשׁוֹ׃ וַיַּרְאֵנִי אֶת־יְהוֹשֻׁעַ הַכֹּהֵן הַגָּדוֹל עֹמֵד
ב לִפְנֵי מַלְאַךְ יהוה וְהַשָּׂטָן עֹמֵד עַל־יְמִינוֹ לְשִׂטְנוֹ׃ וַיֹּאמֶר
יהוה אֶל־הַשָּׂטָן יִגְעַר יהוה בְּךָ הַשָּׂטָן וְיִגְעַר יהוה בְּךָ
ג הַבֹּחֵר בִּירוּשָׁלִָם הֲלוֹא זֶה אוּד מֻצָּל מֵאֵשׁ׃ וִיהוֹשֻׁעַ הָיָה

HAFTARA FOR THE FIRST SHABBAT OF ḤANUKKA

The prophet Zekharya was active in Jerusalem in the second year of the reign of Daryavesh, king of Persia. He gave strength and encouragement to the returnees to Zion after the Babylonian exile, urging them to rebuild the Temple. The construction, which was expressly authorized by the decree of the emperor Koresh, was frozen by the Persian government soon after the cornerstone had been laid, due to lobbying by the enemy nations bordering the Jews in the province of Judea.

standing before him, "Take those filthy clothes off him." Then
the angel said to him, "See, I have removed your guilt from you
5 and dressed you in finery." I said, "Place a pure turban on his
head," and they placed a pure turban on his head. They dressed
him in clothing. The angel of the LORD remained standing.
6 Then that angel of the LORD testified regarding Yehoshua: "So
says the LORD of Hosts: If you walk in My ways, if you keep My
watch, if you judge My House, and guard My courtyards, then
8 I will give you walkers among these who are standing. Listen,
Yehoshua the High Priest, you and your friends who sit before
you, for they are men of wonders: Behold, I am bringing My
9 servant Tzemaḥ. Upon the stone that I set before Yehoshua,
one stone with seven eyes, I will engrave its inscription, and
10 I will wipe away the guilt of this land in one day. On that day –
the LORD of Hosts has spoken – you will call one to another:
Come under the shade of the vine; come under the shade of
4 1 the fig." Then the angel with whom I had spoken re-
2 turned and roused me like a man stirring from his sleep. He
said to me, "What do you see?" I said, "I see a candelabrum of
pure gold, its bowl at the top. It has seven lamps – seven – and
3 seven indentations for the lamps, which are at the top. Next
to it are two olive trees, one to the right of the bowl and one
4 to its left." I spoke and said to the angel with whom I spoke,
5 "What are these, my lord?" And the angel with whom I spoke
replied and said, "You know what these are." I said, "No, my
6 lord." Then he spoke and said to me, "This is the word of the
LORD to Zerubavel: Not with valor and not with strength, but
7 with My spirit, says the LORD of Hosts. Who are you, great
mountain before Zerubavel? Surely it will become a level plain.
He will remove the re-foundation stone with clamor: Favor,
8 favor to her!"* Then the word of the LORD came to
9 me: "Zerubavel's hands founded this House, and his hands will
complete it. You will know that the LORD of Hosts sent me to
you."

Ashkenazim and Sepharadim end here

ד לבש בגדים צואים ועמד לפני המלאך: ויען ויאמר אל־
העמדים לפניו לאמר הסירו הבגדים הצאים מעליו ויאמר
אליו ראה העברתי מעליך עונך והלבש אתך מחלצות:
ה ואמר ישימו צניף טהור על־ראשו וישימו הצניף הטהור
ו על־ראשו וילבשהו בגדים ומלאך יהוה עמד: ויעד
ז מלאך יהוה ביהושע לאמר: כה־אמר יהוה צבאות אם־
בדרכי תלך ואם את־משמרתי תשמר וגם־אתה תדין
את־ביתי וגם תשמר את־חצרי ונתתי לך מהלכים בין
ח העמדים האלה: שמע־נא יהושע | הכהן הגדול אתה
ורעיך הישבים לפניך כי־אנשי מופת המה כי־הנני מביא
ט את־עבדי צמח: כי | הנה האבן אשר נתתי לפני יהושע
על־אבן אחת שבעה עינים הנני מפתח פתחה נאם יהוה
י צבאות ומשתי את־עון הארץ־ההיא ביום אחד: ביום
ההוא נאם יהוה צבאות תקראו איש לרעהו אל־תחת
ד א גפן ואל־תחת תאנה: וישב המלאך הדבר בי
ב ויעירני כאיש אשר־יעור משנתו: ויאמר אלי מה אתה
ראה ויאמר ראיתי והנה מנורת זהב כלה וגלה על־ראשה ואמר
ושבעה נרתיה עליה שבעה ושבעה מוצקות לנרות אשר
ג על־ראשה: ושנים זיתים עליה אחד מימין הגלה ואחד
ד על־שמאלה: ואען ואמר אל־המלאך הדבר בי לאמר
ה מה־אלה אדני: ויען המלאך הדבר בי ויאמר אלי הלוא
ו ידעת מה־המה אלה ואמר לא אדני: ויען ויאמר אלי
לאמר זה דבר־יהוה אל־זרבבל לאמר לא בחיל ולא בכח
ז כי אם־ברוחי אמר יהוה צבאות: מי־אתה הר־הגדול לפני
זרבבל למישר והוציא את־האבן הראשה תשאות חן | חן
ח ט לה:* ויהי דבר־יהוה אלי לאמר: ידי זרבבל
יסדו הבית הזה וידיו תבצענה וידעת כי־יהוה צבאות
שלחני אליכם:

Ashkenazim and Sepharadim end here

Haftara for the Second Shabbat of Ḥanukka

The maftir for the second Shabbat of Ḥanukka is read from Numbers 7:54–8:4.

7 40 Ḥiram crafted the lavers and the shovels and the basins. And I KINGS
so Ḥiram completed all the work for the House of the Lord
41 as commissioned by King Shlomo: two pillars and two globe-
shaped capitals for the pillar tops; two pieces of meshwork to
42 cover the two globe-shaped capitals for the pillar tops; four hundred pomegranates for the two pieces of meshwork – two rows
of pomegranates for each piece of meshwork, which covered the
43 two globe-shaped capitals on top of the pillars; ten stands and
44 ten lavers for the stands; one Sea with twelve oxen beneath the
45 Sea; pots, shovels, and basins. All these vessels, which Ḥiram
crafted for King Shlomo, for the House of the Lord, were of
46 burnished bronze. The king had them cast in clay molds on the
47 Jordan plain between Sukkot and Tzartan. Due to their sheer
abundance, Shlomo left all the vessels out of account; the weight
48 of the bronze was not determined. Shlomo made all the vessels for the House of the Lord: the altar was of gold, and the
49 table for the showbread was of gold. The candelabra – five on
the right and five on the left, in front of the Inner Sanctuary –
were of solid gold; the flowers, the lamps, and the tongs were all
50 of gold. The bowls, shears, basins, spoons, and firepans were of
solid gold. The hinges of the doors to the inner House, to the
Holy of Holies, and of the doors of the House to the Sanctuary,
were of gold.

Ḥiram, the architect charged with constructing the Temple just as Betzalel had built the Tabernacle in an earlier generation. It details the beauty of the structure and its accoutrements, including the wonderful golden candelabra that gave light to the luxurious Temple. The work of building the Sanctuary was complex and arduous, but after seven years it was completed, and the Temple was dedicated with pomp and festivity.

הפטרה לשבת
שנייה של חנוכה

The מפטיר *for the second* שבת *of* חנוכה
is read from במדבר ז, נד – ח, ד.

ז מ וַיַּעַשׂ חִירוֹם אֶת־הַכִּיֹּרוֹת וְאֶת־הַיָּעִים וְאֶת־הַמִּזְרָקוֹת מלכים א׳
וַיְכַל חִירָם לַעֲשׂוֹת אֶת־כָּל־הַמְּלָאכָה אֲשֶׁר עָשָׂה לַמֶּלֶךְ
מא שְׁלֹמֹה בֵּית יְהוָה׃ עַמֻּדִים שְׁנַיִם וְגֻלֹּת הַכֹּתָרֹת אֲשֶׁר־
עַל־רֹאשׁ הָעַמֻּדִים שְׁתָּיִם וְהַשְּׂבָכוֹת שְׁתַּיִם לְכַסּוֹת
מב אֶת־שְׁתֵּי גֻּלּוֹת הַכֹּתָרֹת אֲשֶׁר עַל־רֹאשׁ הָעַמּוּדִים׃ וְאֶת־
הָרִמֹּנִים אַרְבַּע מֵאוֹת לִשְׁתֵּי הַשְּׂבָכוֹת שְׁנֵי־טוּרִים רִמֹּנִים
לַשְּׂבָכָה הָאֶחָת לְכַסּוֹת אֶת־שְׁתֵּי גֻּלּוֹת הַכֹּתָרֹת אֲשֶׁר
מג עַל־פְּנֵי הָעַמּוּדִים׃ וְאֶת־הַמְּכֹנוֹת עֶשֶׂר וְאֶת־הַכִּיֹּרֹת עֲשָׂרָה
מד עַל־הַמְּכֹנוֹת׃ וְאֶת־הַיָּם הָאֶחָד וְאֶת־הַבָּקָר שְׁנֵים־עָשָׂר
מה תַּחַת הַיָּם׃ וְאֶת־הַסִּירוֹת וְאֶת־הַיָּעִים וְאֶת־הַמִּזְרָקוֹת וְאֵת
כָּל־הַכֵּלִים הָאֹהֶל אֲשֶׁר עָשָׂה חִירָם לַמֶּלֶךְ שְׁלֹמֹה בֵּית הָאֵלֶּה
מו יְהוָה נְחֹשֶׁת מְמֹרָט׃ בְּכִכַּר הַיַּרְדֵּן יְצָקָם הַמֶּלֶךְ בְּמַעֲבֵה
מז הָאֲדָמָה בֵּין סֻכּוֹת וּבֵין צָרְתָן׃ וַיַּנַּח שְׁלֹמֹה אֶת־כָּל־הַכֵּלִים
מח מֵרֹב מְאֹד מְאֹד לֹא נֶחְקַר מִשְׁקַל הַנְּחֹשֶׁת׃ וַיַּעַשׂ שְׁלֹמֹה
אֵת כָּל־הַכֵּלִים אֲשֶׁר בֵּית יְהוָה אֵת מִזְבַּח הַזָּהָב וְאֶת־
מט הַשֻּׁלְחָן אֲשֶׁר עָלָיו לֶחֶם הַפָּנִים זָהָב׃ וְאֶת־הַמְּנֹרוֹת חָמֵשׁ
מִיָּמִין וְחָמֵשׁ מִשְּׂמֹאול לִפְנֵי הַדְּבִיר זָהָב סָגוּר וְהַפֶּרַח
נ וְהַנֵּרֹת וְהַמֶּלְקַחַיִם זָהָב׃ וְהַסִּפּוֹת וְהַמְזַמְּרוֹת וְהַמִּזְרָקוֹת
וְהַכַּפּוֹת וְהַמַּחְתּוֹת זָהָב סָגוּר וְהַפֹּתוֹת לְדַלְתוֹת הַבַּיִת
הַפְּנִימִי לְקֹדֶשׁ הַקֳּדָשִׁים לְדַלְתֵי הַבַּיִת לַהֵיכָל זָהָב׃

HAFTARA FOR THE SECOND SHABBAT OF ḤANUKKA

The First Temple, built in the reign of King Shlomo, was constructed from the finest materials and most advanced methods in existence. The richness of the structure was a testament to God's glory. This *haftara* describes the work of

▶

Haftarat Parashat Shekalim

The maftir of Parashat Shekalim is read from Exodus 30:11–16. When Shabbat Shekalim coincides with Rosh Ḥodesh Adar, three Torah scrolls are removed from the ark. The first six aliyot are read from the weekly parasha. The seventh consists of the addition for Rosh Ḥodesh, Numbers 28:9–15. Afterward, half-Kaddish is recited, and the maftir is read from Parashat Shekalim.

II KINGS

Sepharadim, Chabad and Minhag Anglia begin here

11 17 Then Yehoyada reinstated the covenant between the Lord, the
king, and the people, to be the Lord's people; and between
18 the king and the people. All the people of the land came to the
temple of Baal and tore it down and shattered its altars and
images through and through, and killed Matan, the priest of
Baal, in front of the altars. The priest set watchmen over the
19 House of the Lord, and he had the officers of the hundreds,
the Keretites, the sentry, and all the people of the land escort
the king down from the House of the Lord. They came in
through the sentry gate of the royal palace, and he took his
20 seat upon the royal throne. All the people of the land rejoiced,
and calm settled over the city. As for Atalya, they had put her
12 1 to death by sword in the royal palace. *Yehoash was
2 seven years old when he became king; Yehoash became king
in the seventh year of Yehu, and for forty years, he reigned in
3 Jerusalem. His mother's name was Tzivya, of Be'er Sheva. Yehoash did what was right in the eyes of the Lord all his days, as
4 the priest Yehoyada had taught him. Yet the high shrines were
not removed; the people still offered sacrifices and incense at
5 the high shrines. Yehoash said to the priests, "All the dedicated
money brought to the House of the Lord – the money from
the census, the money equivalent to a person's worth, or any
money that a person is moved to bring to the House of the
6 Lord – let the priests accept it, each from his donor, and they

Ashkenazim and Yemenites begin here

Yoash's father, was killed, the regime of Atalya, the introduction of idolatry into the Temple, and waning political and military power, a process that began at the end of the rule of Aḥav king of Israel and Yehoshafat king of Yehuda. The state required many reforms to correct its principal ills, and Yehoyada, who acted as regent until Yoash came of age, knew that he must turn over a new leaf in his kingdom's history. He worked hard to collect the money necessary to renovate the Temple, and to that purpose he made use of the annual collection of silver shekels mentioned in the Torah.

הפטרת פרשת שקלים

The מפטיר *of* פרשת שקלים *is read from* שמות ל, יא–טז.
When שבת שקלים *coincides with* ראש חודש אדר, *three Torah scrolls are removed from the ark. The first six* עליות *are read from the weekly* פרשה. *The seventh consists of the addition for* ראש חודש, במדבר כח, ט–טו. *Afterward,* חצי קדיש *is recited, and the* מפטיר *is read from* פרשת שקלים.

מלכים ב׳

Sepharadim, Chabad and Minhag Anglia begin here

יא יז ויכרת יהוידע את־הברית בין יהוה ובין המלך ובין העם
יח להיות לעם ליהוה ובין המלך ובין העם: ויבאו כל־עם
הארץ בית־הבעל ויתצהו את־מזבחתו ואת־צלמיו שברו
היטב ואת מתן כהן הבעל הרגו לפני המזבחות וישם
יט הכהן פקדת על־בית יהוה: ויקח את־שרי המאות ואת־
הכרי ואת־הרצים ואת | כל־עם הארץ וירידו את־המלך
מבית יהוה ויבואו דרך־שער הרצים בית המלך וישב על־
כ כסא המלכים: וישמח כל־עם־הארץ והעיר שקטה ואת־
יב א עתליהו המיתו בחרב בית מלך: ★בן־שבע המלך:

Ashkenazim and Yemenites begin here

ב שנים יהואש במלכו: בשנת־שבע ליהוא מלך יהואש
וארבעים שנה מלך בירושלם ושם אמו צביה מבאר
ג שבע: ויעש יהואש הישר בעיני יהוה כל־ימיו אשר הורהו
ד יהוידע הכהן: רק הבמות לא־סרו עוד העם מזבחים
ה ומקטרים בבמות: ויאמר יהואש אל־הכהנים כל כסף
הקדשים אשר יובא בית־יהוה כסף עובר איש כסף נפשות
ערכו כל־כסף אשר יעלה על לב־איש להביא בית יהוה:
ו יקחו להם הכהנים איש מאת מכרו והם יחזקו את־בדק

HAFTARAT PARASHAT SHEKALIM

The events of this *haftara* transpire during the reign of Yoash king of Yehuda and Yehoyada the High Priest, his uncle. Before Yoash was crowned, the kingdom had been ruled for six years by the wicked Queen Atalya from the family of King Aḥav of Israel. Atalya had despised and neglected the Temple in Jerusalem, and her tyrannical rule was ended by a revolution in which she was killed.

Spiritual and political crises plagued the kingdom of Yehuda: the revolt of Yehu to the north, in which Aḥazya,

will see to the repair of the House wherever damage may be
7 found." But by the twenty-third year of King Yehoash,
8 the priests had not seen to the repair of the House, and King
Yehoash summoned the priest Yehoyada and the priests. "Why
have you not kept the House in repair?" he said to them. "From
now on, do not take any money from your donors; rather, you
9 must donate it toward the repair of the House." The priests
agreed that they would neither take money from the people
10 nor see to the House's repair. So the priest Yehoyada took a
chest, made a hole in its lid, and placed it to the right of the
altar, where people entered the House of the Lord. There, the
priestly guardians of the threshold placed all the money that
11 was brought to the House of the Lord. Whenever they saw
that there was a considerable amount of money in the chest,
the royal scribe and the High Priest would come up, tie it into
a bundle, and count the money found in the House of the
12 Lord. They then gave the weighed-out money to the foremen
in charge of the House of the Lord, who would use it to pay
the carpenters and the builders who worked in the House of
13 the Lord, and the masons and stonecutters, and to purchase
timber and quarry stones to keep the House of the Lord in repair, and for any other expenses for maintenance of the House.
14 However, no silver bowls, shears, basins, or trumpets – or any
golden or silver vessels – were made from the money that
15 was brought to the House of the Lord, as it was given to the
overseers, who used it to keep the House of the Lord in re-
16 pair. They did not need to keep track of the men who received
the money to pay out to the workers, for they dealt honestly.
17 Money from guilt offerings and money from purification offerings was not brought to the House of the Lord; it belonged to
the priests.

ז הַבַּ֔יִת לְכֹ֛ל אֲשֶׁר־יִמָּצֵ֥א שָׁ֖ם בָּֽדֶק׃ וַיְהִ֗י בִּשְׁנַ֨ת
עֶשְׂרִ֧ים וְשָׁלֹ֛שׁ שָׁנָ֖ה לַמֶּ֣לֶךְ יְהוֹאָ֑שׁ לֹֽא־חִזְּק֥וּ הַכֹּהֲנִ֖ים אֶת־
ח בֶּ֥דֶק הַבָּֽיִת׃ וַיִּקְרָא֩ הַמֶּ֨לֶךְ יְהוֹאָ֜שׁ לִיהוֹיָדָ֣ע הַכֹּהֵ֗ן וְלַכֹּֽהֲנִים֙
וַיֹּ֣אמֶר אֲלֵהֶ֔ם מַדּ֛וּעַ אֵינְכֶ֥ם מְחַזְּקִ֖ים אֶת־בֶּ֣דֶק הַבָּ֑יִת וְעַתָּ֗ה
אַל־תִּקְחוּ־כֶ֙סֶף֙ מֵאֵ֣ת מַכָּרֵיכֶ֔ם כִּֽי־לְבֶ֥דֶק הַבַּ֖יִת תִּתְּנֻֽהוּ׃
ט וַיֵּאֹ֖תוּ הַכֹּֽהֲנִ֑ים לְבִלְתִּ֤י קְחַת־כֶּ֙סֶף֙ מֵאֵ֣ת הָעָ֔ם וּלְבִלְתִּ֥י חַזֵּ֖ק
י אֶת־בֶּ֥דֶק הַבָּֽיִת׃ וַיִּקַּ֞ח יְהוֹיָדָ֤ע הַכֹּהֵן֙ אֲר֣וֹן אֶחָ֔ד וַיִּקֹּ֥ב חֹ֖ר
בְּדַלְתּ֑וֹ וַיִּתֵּ֣ן אֹת֡וֹ אֵ֣צֶל הַמִּזְבֵּ֡חַ בימין בְּבוֹא־אִ֣ישׁ בֵּ֣ית יְהוָ֔ה מִיָּמִ֔ין
וְנָֽתְנוּ־שָׁ֙מָּה֙ הַכֹּהֲנִים֙ שֹׁמְרֵ֣י הַסַּ֔ף אֶֽת־כָּל־הַכֶּ֖סֶף הַמּוּבָ֥א
יא בֵּית־יְהוָֽה׃ וַיְהִי֙ כִּרְאוֹתָ֔ם כִּי־רַ֥ב הַכֶּ֖סֶף בָּאָר֑וֹן וַיַּ֨עַל סֹפֵ֤ר
הַמֶּ֙לֶךְ֙ וְהַכֹּהֵ֣ן הַגָּד֔וֹל וַיָּצֻ֙רוּ֙ וַיִּמְנ֔וּ אֶת־הַכֶּ֖סֶף הַנִּמְצָ֥א בֵית־
יב יְהוָֽה׃ וְנָֽתְנוּ֙ אֶת־הַכֶּ֣סֶף הַֽמְתֻכָּ֔ן עַל־יַ֛ד עֹשֵׂ֥י הַמְּלָאכָ֖ה
הפקדים בֵּ֣ית יְהוָ֑ה וַיּוֹצִיאֻ֜הוּ לְחָרָשֵׁ֤י הָעֵץ֙ וְלַבֹּנִ֔ים הָעֹשִׂ֖ים הַמֻּפְקָדִ֖ים
יג בֵּ֥ית יְהוָֽה׃ וְלַגֹּֽדְרִים֙ וּלְחֹצְבֵ֣י הָאֶ֔בֶן וְלִקְנ֤וֹת עֵצִים֙ וְאַבְנֵ֣י
מַחְצֵ֔ב לְחַזֵּ֖ק אֶת־בֶּ֣דֶק בֵּית־יְהוָ֑ה וּלְכֹ֛ל אֲשֶׁר־יֵצֵ֥א עַל־
יד הַבַּ֖יִת לְחָזְקָֽה׃ אַךְ֩ לֹ֨א יֵעָשֶׂ֜ה בֵּ֣ית יְהוָ֗ה סִפּ֥וֹת כֶּ֙סֶף֙ מְזַמְּר֤וֹת
מִזְרָק֙וֹת חֲצֹ֣צְר֔וֹת כָּל־כְּלִ֥י זָהָ֖ב וּכְלִי־כָ֑סֶף מִן־הַכֶּ֖סֶף הַמּוּבָ֥א
טו בֵית־יְהוָֽה׃ כִּֽי־לְעֹשֵׂ֥י הַמְּלָאכָ֖ה יִתְּנֻ֑הוּ וְחִזְּקוּ־ב֖וֹ אֶת־בֵּ֥ית
טז יְהוָֽה׃ וְלֹ֧א יְחַשְּׁב֣וּ אֶת־הָאֲנָשִׁ֗ים אֲשֶׁ֨ר יִתְּנ֤וּ אֶת־הַכֶּ֙סֶף֙ עַל־
יז יָדָ֔ם לָתֵ֖ת לְעֹשֵׂ֣י הַמְּלָאכָ֑ה כִּ֥י בֶאֱמֻנָ֖ה הֵ֥ם עֹשִֽׂים׃ כֶּ֤סֶף אָשָׁם֙
וְכֶ֣סֶף חַטָּא֔וֹת לֹ֥א יוּבָ֖א בֵּ֣ית יְהוָ֑ה לַכֹּהֲנִ֖ים יִהְיֽוּ׃

Haftarat Parashat Zakhor

The maftir of Parashat Zakhor is read from Deuteronomy 25:17–19.
The maftir of Purim Meshulash is read from Exodus 17:8–16.

14 52 There was fierce war against the Philistines all the days of I SAMUEL *Yemenites begin here*
Sha'ul, and whenever Sha'ul saw any strong man or valiant
15 1 warrior, he would recruit him. *Shmuel *Sepharadim and*
said to Sha'ul, "It was I whom the Lord sent to anoint you as *Minhag Anglia begin here*
king over His people, over Israel; now, heed the words of the
2 Lord. *Thus says the Lord of Hosts: I have taken *Ashkenazim and Chabad begin here*
note of what Amalek did to Israel; how they set upon them on
3 the way as they came out of Egypt. Now, go and strike down
Amalek; you must utterly destroy all that is theirs – spare nothing. You must slay man and woman; child and infant; ox and
4 sheep; camel and donkey." Sha'ul summoned the men
and mustered them at Telaim; two hundred thousand infantry-
5 men and ten thousand men from Yehuda. Sha'ul reached the
6 city of Amalek and lay in wait in the wadi. And Sha'ul said to
the Kenites, "Leave; turn and withdraw from among the Amalekites lest I destroy you together with them; you dealt loyally
with all the Israelites when they left Egypt," and the Kenites
7 departed from Amalek. Then Sha'ul struck down Amalek from
8 Ḥavila up to Shur, which is east of Egypt. He captured King Agag
of Amalek alive and utterly destroyed the entire people by the
9 sword. But Sha'ul and the men spared Agag and the best of the
sheep, cattle, fat calves, and lambs – the very best of everything;
they were not willing to destroy them. As for all the spurned,

---

by great wickedness and cruelty, like that which that same nation had brought to bear against the Israelites when they left Egypt centuries earlier. So it was late in Sha'ul's reign: the Amalekites would attack their neighbors, Israelites, Philistines, or Egyptians, unprovoked, for the sake of plunder and human trafficking, including of women and children. Just like the ancient city of Sedom, the symbol of a society of organized and systematic evil, Amalek had turned into an incarnation of pure wickedness, which had to be pulled out from the root. In Sha'ul's time, circumstances came about that allowed for a protracted military campaign against this ancient and ruthless foe. And only one who could mount a relentless fight to the death against this evil could be considered worthy to rule Israel.

When we read Parashat Zakhor, the Jewish people raise the standard of good against evil in the world, in all its forms.

הפטרת פרשת זכור

The מפטיר *of* פרשת זכור *is read from* דברים כה, יז–יט.
The מפטיר *of* פורים משולש *is read from* שמות יז, ח–טז.

שמואל א׳
Yemenites begin here

יד נב וַתְּהִי הַמִּלְחָמָה חֲזָקָה עַל־פְּלִשְׁתִּים כֹּל יְמֵי שָׁאוּל
וְרָאָה שָׁאוּל כָּל־אִישׁ גִּבּוֹר וְכָל־בֶּן־חַיִל וַיַּאַסְפֵהוּ

Sepharadim and Minhag Anglia begin here

טו א אֵלָיו׃ *וַיֹּאמֶר שְׁמוּאֵל אֶל־שָׁאוּל אֹתִי
שָׁלַח יהוה לִמְשָׁחֲךָ לְמֶלֶךְ עַל־עַמּוֹ עַל־יִשְׂרָאֵל וְעַתָּה

Ashkenazim and Chabad begin here

ב שְׁמַע לְקוֹל דִּבְרֵי יהוה׃ *כֹּה אָמַר
יהוה צְבָאוֹת פָּקַדְתִּי אֵת אֲשֶׁר־עָשָׂה עֲמָלֵק לְיִשְׂרָאֵל
ג אֲשֶׁר־שָׂם לוֹ בַּדֶּרֶךְ בַּעֲלֹתוֹ מִמִּצְרָיִם׃ עַתָּה לֵךְ וְהִכִּיתָה
אֶת־עֲמָלֵק וְהַחֲרַמְתֶּם אֶת־כָּל־אֲשֶׁר־לוֹ וְלֹא תַחְמֹל
עָלָיו וְהֵמַתָּה מֵאִישׁ עַד־אִשָּׁה מֵעֹלֵל וְעַד־יוֹנֵק מִשּׁוֹר
ד וְעַד־שֶׂה מִגָּמָל וְעַד־חֲמוֹר׃ וַיְשַׁמַּע שָׁאוּל
אֶת־הָעָם וַיִּפְקְדֵם בַּטְּלָאִים מָאתַיִם אֶלֶף רַגְלִי וַעֲשֶׂרֶת
ה אֲלָפִים אֶת־אִישׁ יְהוּדָה׃ וַיָּבֹא שָׁאוּל עַד־עִיר עֲמָלֵק
ו וַיָּרֶב בַּנָּחַל׃ וַיֹּאמֶר שָׁאוּל אֶל־הַקֵּינִי לְכוּ סֻּרוּ רְדוּ
מִתּוֹךְ עֲמָלֵקִי פֶּן־אֹסִפְךָ עִמּוֹ וְאַתָּה עָשִׂיתָה חֶסֶד עִם־
כָּל־בְּנֵי יִשְׂרָאֵל בַּעֲלוֹתָם מִמִּצְרָיִם וַיָּסַר קֵינִי מִתּוֹךְ
ז עֲמָלֵק׃ וַיַּךְ שָׁאוּל אֶת־עֲמָלֵק מֵחֲוִילָה בּוֹאֲךָ שׁוּר אֲשֶׁר
ח עַל־פְּנֵי מִצְרָיִם׃ וַיִּתְפֹּשׂ אֶת־אֲגַג מֶלֶךְ־עֲמָלֵק חָי וְאֶת־
ט כָּל־הָעָם הֶחֱרִים לְפִי־חָרֶב׃ וַיַּחְמֹל שָׁאוּל וְהָעָם עַל־אֲגָג
וְעַל־מֵיטַב הַצֹּאן וְהַבָּקָר וְהַמִּשְׁנִים וְעַל־הַכָּרִים וְעַל־כָּל־
הַטּוֹב וְלֹא אָבוּ הַחֲרִימָם וְכָל־הַמְּלָאכָה נְמִבְזָה וְנָמֵס אֹתָהּ

HAFTARAT PARASHAT ZAKHOR

Sha'ul was the first king in Israel after 350 years of decentralized leadership by the judges. The enemies of Israel during this time had sensed their weakness and attacked them again and again. The judges were charged with warding off the marauding neighboring armies, and then they would return to their normal daily lives. One of the enemies long involved in hostilities with Israel was Amalek. These attacks were characterized

10 worthless property – that, they utterly destroyed. Then
11 the word of the Lord reached Shmuel: "I regret that I crowned
Sha'ul as king, for he has turned away from following Me and
he has failed to fulfill My words." This enraged Shmuel, and he
12 cried out to the Lord all night long. And Shmuel set out early
in the morning toward Sha'ul, and Shmuel was told, "Sha'ul has
gone to Carmel, where he set up a monument for himself; then
13 he turned off and made his way down to Gilgal." When Shmuel
reached Sha'ul, Sha'ul said to him, "Blessed are you to the Lord!
14 I have fulfilled the Lord's word." "Then what is this bleating of
sheep in my ears," said Shmuel, "and the lowing of cattle that I
15 hear?" "They brought them from the Amalekites," said Sha'ul,
"for the men spared the best of the sheep and cattle for sacrificing to the Lord, your God – but we utterly destroyed the
16 rest." "Stop," said Shmuel, "and let me tell you what the
17 Lord told me last night." "Speak," he said to him. And
Shmuel said, "Though you may seem small in your own eyes,
you are the head of the tribes of Israel, and the Lord anointed
18 you as king over Israel. The Lord sent you on a mission, bid-
ding, 'Go and utterly destroy the offenders – Amalek – and fight
19 them until you have destroyed them.' But why did you fail to
heed the voice of the Lord, pouncing on the spoil and doing
20 evil in the eyes of the Lord?" "But I did heed the voice
of the Lord," Sha'ul said to Shmuel. "I set out on the mission
the Lord assigned me, and I brought Agag, king of Amalek, and
21 utterly destroyed Amalek. And the men took of the spoil – the
choicest sheep and cattle from what was banned – to sacrifice
22 to the Lord, your God, at Gilgal." And Shmuel said,
"Does the Lord delight in burnt offerings and sacrifices as
much as obedience to the Lord's voice? Behold – obedience
23 is better than sacrifice, and compliance than the fat of rams. For
rebellion is as bad as the sin of divination, and presumption as
corruption and idolatry. Because you rejected the word of the
24 Lord, He has rejected you as king." "I have sinned,"
Sha'ul said to Shmuel, "for I violated the Lord's command and
your word, because I feared the people and heeded their voice.
25 But now, please forgive my sin and return with me, so I may wor-
26 ship before the Lord." "I will not return with you," Shmuel said
to Sha'ul, "for you have rejected the word of the Lord – and the

י הֶחֱרִימוּ׃ וַיְהִי דְּבַר יְהוָה אֶל־שְׁמוּאֵל לֵאמֹר׃
יא נִחַמְתִּי כִּי־הִמְלַכְתִּי אֶת־שָׁאוּל לְמֶלֶךְ כִּי־שָׁב מֵאַחֲרַי
וְאֶת־דְּבָרַי לֹא הֵקִים וַיִּחַר לִשְׁמוּאֵל וַיִּזְעַק אֶל־יְהוָה
יב כָּל־הַלָּיְלָה׃ וַיַּשְׁכֵּם שְׁמוּאֵל לִקְרַאת שָׁאוּל בַּבֹּקֶר וַיֻּגַּד
לִשְׁמוּאֵל לֵאמֹר בָּא־שָׁאוּל הַכַּרְמֶלָה וְהִנֵּה מַצִּיב לוֹ יָד
יג וַיִּסֹּב וַיַּעֲבֹר וַיֵּרֶד הַגִּלְגָּל׃ וַיָּבֹא שְׁמוּאֵל אֶל־שָׁאוּל וַיֹּאמֶר
יד לוֹ שָׁאוּל בָּרוּךְ אַתָּה לַיהוָה הֲקִימֹתִי אֶת־דְּבַר יְהוָה׃ וַיֹּאמֶר
שְׁמוּאֵל וּמֶה קוֹל־הַצֹּאן הַזֶּה בְּאָזְנָי וְקוֹל הַבָּקָר אֲשֶׁר אָנֹכִי
טו שֹׁמֵעַ׃ וַיֹּאמֶר שָׁאוּל מֵעֲמָלֵקִי הֱבִיאוּם אֲשֶׁר חָמַל הָעָם
עַל־מֵיטַב הַצֹּאן וְהַבָּקָר לְמַעַן זְבֹחַ לַיהוָה אֱלֹהֶיךָ וְאֶת־
טז הַיּוֹתֵר הֶחֱרַמְנוּ׃ וַיֹּאמֶר שְׁמוּאֵל אֶל־שָׁאוּל
הֶרֶף וְאַגִּידָה לְּךָ אֵת אֲשֶׁר דִּבֶּר יְהוָה אֵלַי הַלָּיְלָה ויאמרו וַיֹּאמֶר
יז לוֹ דַּבֵּר׃ וַיֹּאמֶר שְׁמוּאֵל הֲלוֹא אִם־קָטֹן אַתָּה
בְּעֵינֶיךָ רֹאשׁ שִׁבְטֵי יִשְׂרָאֵל אָתָּה וַיִּמְשָׁחֲךָ יְהוָה לְמֶלֶךְ
יח עַל־יִשְׂרָאֵל׃ וַיִּשְׁלָחֲךָ יְהוָה בְּדָרֶךְ וַיֹּאמֶר לֵךְ וְהַחֲרַמְתָּה
אֶת־הַחַטָּאִים אֶת־עֲמָלֵק וְנִלְחַמְתָּ בוֹ עַד־כַּלּוֹתָם אֹתָם׃
יט וְלָמָּה לֹא־שָׁמַעְתָּ בְּקוֹל יְהוָה וַתַּעַט אֶל־הַשָּׁלָל וַתַּעַשׂ הָרַע
כ בְּעֵינֵי יְהוָה׃ וַיֹּאמֶר שָׁאוּל אֶל־שְׁמוּאֵל אֲשֶׁר
שָׁמַעְתִּי בְּקוֹל יְהוָה וָאֵלֵךְ בַּדֶּרֶךְ אֲשֶׁר־שְׁלָחַנִי יְהוָה וָאָבִיא
כא אֶת־אֲגַג מֶלֶךְ עֲמָלֵק וְאֶת־עֲמָלֵק הֶחֱרַמְתִּי׃ וַיִּקַּח הָעָם
מֵהַשָּׁלָל צֹאן וּבָקָר רֵאשִׁית הַחֵרֶם לִזְבֹּחַ לַיהוָה אֱלֹהֶיךָ
כב בַּגִּלְגָּל׃ וַיֹּאמֶר שְׁמוּאֵל הַחֵפֶץ לַיהוָה בְּעֹלוֹת
וּזְבָחִים כִּשְׁמֹעַ בְּקוֹל יְהוָה הִנֵּה שְׁמֹעַ מִזֶּבַח טוֹב לְהַקְשִׁיב
כג מֵחֵלֶב אֵילִים׃ כִּי חַטַּאת־קֶסֶם מֶרִי וְאָוֶן וּתְרָפִים הַפְצַר יַעַן
כד מָאַסְתָּ אֶת־דְּבַר יְהוָה וַיִּמְאָסְךָ מִמֶּלֶךְ׃ וַיֹּאמֶר
שָׁאוּל אֶל־שְׁמוּאֵל חָטָאתִי כִּי־עָבַרְתִּי אֶת־פִּי־יְהוָה וְאֶת־
כה דְּבָרֶיךָ כִּי יָרֵאתִי אֶת־הָעָם וָאֶשְׁמַע בְּקוֹלָם׃ וְעַתָּה שָׂא נָא
כו אֶת־חַטָּאתִי וְשׁוּב עִמִּי וְאֶשְׁתַּחֲוֶה לַיהוָה׃ וַיֹּאמֶר שְׁמוּאֵל

27 LORD has rejected you from being king over Israel." And Shmuel turned to go, but Sha'ul grabbed the corner of his robe, and
28 it tore. "The LORD has torn the kingship of Israel away from
you today," Shmuel said to him, "and has granted it to your peer,
29 who is better than you. What is more, Israel's Eternal will not
30 betray or waver, for He is not a mere wavering human." "I have
sinned," he said. "Now please honor me in front of the elders of
my people and in front of Israel; return with me and I will wor-
31 ship the LORD your God." So Shmuel followed Sha'ul back, and
32 Sha'ul worshipped the LORD. Shmuel then gave the
order, "Bring Agag, king of Amalek, to me." Agag walked up to
him with stately steps. "So," said Agag, "the bitterness of death
33 is upon me." And Shmuel said, "As your sword has made wom-
en childless, so your mother shall be childless among women!"
And Shmuel hacked Agag to pieces before the LORD at Gil-
34 gal.* Then Shmuel went to Rama while Sha'ul made his *Yemenites end here*
way up to his home in Givat Sha'ul.

HAFTARAT PARASHAT PARA

The maftir of Parashat Para is read from Numbers 19:1–22.

36 16 17 The word of the LORD came to me: "Man, the House of Israel EZEKIEL
dwelled upon their soil and defiled it with their ways and their
deeds – their ways were like the impurity of the menstrual wom-
18 an before Me. I poured out My fury upon them for the blood
they spilled upon the land and the idols they defiled her with.
19 I scattered them among the nations – they were strewn across

in exile is a desecration of God's name, and their return to their land will be a sanctification of God's name. The ingathering of exiles is a crucial stage of the process of redemption. When the people return to their land, they must purge themselves of their impurity in order to raise themselves to a state of piety and observance. A lyrical description of the softening of the people's "stone heart" and its replacement by a "heart of flesh" expresses this idea.

Earthly expressions of redemption will be material abundance and thriving, flourishing settlements. What had been a wasteland will become a paradise.

אֶל־שָׁאוּל לֹא אָשׁוּב עִמָּךְ כִּי מָאַסְתָּה אֶת־דְּבַר יהוה
כז וַיִּמְאָסְךָ יהוה מִהְיוֹת מֶלֶךְ עַל־יִשְׂרָאֵל: וַיִּסֹּב שְׁמוּאֵל
כח לָלֶכֶת וַיַּחֲזֵק בִּכְנַף־מְעִילוֹ וַיִּקָּרַע: וַיֹּאמֶר אֵלָיו שְׁמוּאֵל
קָרַע יהוה אֶת־מַמְלְכוּת יִשְׂרָאֵל מֵעָלֶיךָ הַיּוֹם וּנְתָנָהּ
כט לְרֵעֲךָ הַטּוֹב מִמֶּךָּ: וְגַם נֵצַח יִשְׂרָאֵל לֹא יְשַׁקֵּר וְלֹא יִנָּחֵם
ל כִּי לֹא אָדָם הוּא לְהִנָּחֵם: וַיֹּאמֶר חָטָאתִי עַתָּה כַּבְּדֵנִי
נָא נֶגֶד זִקְנֵי־עַמִּי וְנֶגֶד יִשְׂרָאֵל וְשׁוּב עִמִּי וְהִשְׁתַּחֲוֵיתִי
לא לַיהוה אֱלֹהֶיךָ: וַיָּשָׁב שְׁמוּאֵל אַחֲרֵי שָׁאוּל וַיִּשְׁתַּחוּ שָׁאוּל
לב לַיהוה: וַיֹּאמֶר שְׁמוּאֵל הַגִּישׁוּ אֵלַי אֶת־אֲגַג
מֶלֶךְ עֲמָלֵק וַיֵּלֶךְ אֵלָיו אֲגַג מַעֲדַנֹּת וַיֹּאמֶר אֲגָג אָכֵן סָר
לג מַר־הַמָּוֶת: וַיֹּאמֶר שְׁמוּאֵל כַּאֲשֶׁר שִׁכְּלָה נָשִׁים חַרְבֶּךָ כֵּן־
תִּשְׁכַּל מִנָּשִׁים אִמֶּךָ וַיְשַׁסֵּף שְׁמוּאֵל אֶת־אֲגָג לִפְנֵי יהוה
לד בַּגִּלְגָּל:* וַיֵּלֶךְ שְׁמוּאֵל הָרָמָתָה וְשָׁאוּל עָלָה *Yemenites end here*
אֶל־בֵּיתוֹ גִּבְעַת שָׁאוּל:

הפטרת פרשת פרה

The מפטיר *of* פרשת פרה *is read from* במדבר יט, א–כב.

לו טז יז וַיְהִי דְבַר־יהוה אֵלַי לֵאמֹר: בֶּן־אָדָם בֵּית יִשְׂרָאֵל יֹשְׁבִים יחזקאל
עַל־אַדְמָתָם וַיְטַמְּאוּ אוֹתָהּ בְּדַרְכָּם וּבַעֲלִילוֹתָם כְּטֻמְאַת
יח הַנִּדָּה הָיְתָה דַרְכָּם לְפָנָי: וָאֶשְׁפֹּךְ חֲמָתִי עֲלֵיהֶם עַל־הַדָּם
יט אֲשֶׁר־שָׁפְכוּ עַל־הָאָרֶץ וּבְגִלּוּלֵיהֶם טִמְּאוּהָ: וָאָפִיץ אֹתָם

HAFTARAT PARASHAT PARA

The prophet Yeḥezkel accompanied the people into exile in Babylon during the reign of Yehoyakhin king of Yehuda, eleven years before the destruction of Jerusalem, the Temple, and the House of David. He prepared them mentally and spiritually for the coming blow. When the news of the destruction arrived, the prophet shifted to messages of comfort and reassurance, and prepared them for the coming redemption. This *haftara* is one of these prophecies.

It is natural for a people to be settled in their own land. It is their sins which cause them to be exiled. For Israel to be

the countries – and I punished them according to their ways
20 and their deeds. There, in whichever nations they came to, they
desecrated My holy name because it was said of them, 'These
21 are the LORD's people, and they have left His land.' And I am
concerned for My holy name, which the House of Israel has des-
22 ecrated among the nations to which they have come. So,
say to the House of Israel: So says the Lord GOD: It is not for
your sake that I do this, House of Israel, but for My holy name
23 that you desecrated among the nations to which you came. I will
sanctify My great name that has been desecrated among the nations – that you desecrated among them. The nations will know
that I am the LORD, declares the Lord GOD, when I am sancti-
24 fied through you before their eyes. I will take you from the nations; I will gather you from all the countries and bring you to
25 your land. I will sprinkle over you purifying waters, and you will
be cleansed; I will cleanse you of all your impurities and all your
26 idols. I will give you a new heart and put a new spirit into you;
I will remove the heart of stone from your flesh and give you a
27 heart of flesh; I will put My spirit into you; make sure that you
follow My decrees and that you keep My laws and fulfill them.
28 You will live in the land that I gave to your fathers; you will be
29 My people, and I will be your God. I will deliver you from all
your impurities; I will summon the grain, make it plentiful; I will
30 not bring famine upon you. I will make the fruit of the trees and
the produce of the fields plentiful so that you will no longer have
31 to endure the reproach of famine among the nations. You will
remember your evil ways and your actions that were no good;
you will loathe yourselves for your iniquities and your abomi-
32 nations. Not for your sake do I act, declares the Lord GOD; let
that be known to you; be ashamed, disgraced by your own ways,
House of Israel.

33 So says the Lord GOD: On the day when I cleanse you of all
your iniquities, I will reinhabit the cities; the ruins will be
34 rebuilt. The desolate land will be tilled there, where she was
35 desolate in the sight of every passerby. They will say, 'This land
that was desolate has become like the garden of Eden; its towns
that were ruined, devastated, and destroyed have been fortified

כ בַּגּוֹיִם וַיִּזָּרוּ בָּאֲרָצוֹת כְּדַרְכָּם וְכַעֲלִילוֹתָם שְׁפַטְתִּים׃ וַיָּבוֹא
אֶל־הַגּוֹיִם אֲשֶׁר־בָּאוּ שָׁם וַיְחַלְּלוּ אֶת־שֵׁם קָדְשִׁי בֶּאֱמֹר לָהֶם
כא עַם־יְהוָה אֵלֶּה וּמֵאַרְצוֹ יָצָאוּ׃ וָאֶחְמֹל עַל־שֵׁם קָדְשִׁי אֲשֶׁר
כב חִלְּלֻהוּ בֵּית יִשְׂרָאֵל בַּגּוֹיִם אֲשֶׁר־בָּאוּ שָׁמָּה׃ לָכֵן
אֱמֹר לְבֵית־יִשְׂרָאֵל כֹּה אָמַר אֲדֹנָי יֱהוִה לֹא לְמַעַנְכֶם
אֲנִי עֹשֶׂה בֵּית יִשְׂרָאֵל כִּי אִם־לְשֵׁם־קָדְשִׁי אֲשֶׁר חִלַּלְתֶּם
כג בַּגּוֹיִם אֲשֶׁר־בָּאתֶם שָׁם׃ וְקִדַּשְׁתִּי אֶת־שְׁמִי הַגָּדוֹל הַמְחֻלָּל
בַּגּוֹיִם אֲשֶׁר חִלַּלְתֶּם בְּתוֹכָם וְיָדְעוּ הַגּוֹיִם כִּי־אֲנִי יְהוָה
כד נְאֻם אֲדֹנָי יֱהוִה בְּהִקָּדְשִׁי בָכֶם לְעֵינֵיהֶם׃ וְלָקַחְתִּי אֶתְכֶם
מִן־הַגּוֹיִם וְקִבַּצְתִּי אֶתְכֶם מִכָּל־הָאֲרָצוֹת וְהֵבֵאתִי אֶתְכֶם
כה אֶל־אַדְמַתְכֶם׃ וְזָרַקְתִּי עֲלֵיכֶם מַיִם טְהוֹרִים וּטְהַרְתֶּם
כו מִכֹּל טֻמְאוֹתֵיכֶם וּמִכָּל־גִּלּוּלֵיכֶם אֲטַהֵר אֶתְכֶם׃ וְנָתַתִּי
לָכֶם לֵב חָדָשׁ וְרוּחַ חֲדָשָׁה אֶתֵּן בְּקִרְבְּכֶם וַהֲסִרֹתִי אֶת־
כז לֵב הָאֶבֶן מִבְּשַׂרְכֶם וְנָתַתִּי לָכֶם לֵב בָּשָׂר׃ וְאֶת־רוּחִי אֶתֵּן
בְּקִרְבְּכֶם וְעָשִׂיתִי אֵת אֲשֶׁר־בְּחֻקַּי תֵּלֵכוּ וּמִשְׁפָּטַי תִּשְׁמְרוּ
כח וַעֲשִׂיתֶם׃ וִישַׁבְתֶּם בָּאָרֶץ אֲשֶׁר נָתַתִּי לַאֲבֹתֵיכֶם וִהְיִיתֶם
כט לִי לְעָם וְאָנֹכִי אֶהְיֶה לָכֶם לֵאלֹהִים׃ וְהוֹשַׁעְתִּי אֶתְכֶם
מִכֹּל טֻמְאוֹתֵיכֶם וְקָרָאתִי אֶל־הַדָּגָן וְהִרְבֵּיתִי אֹתוֹ וְלֹא־
ל אֶתֵּן עֲלֵיכֶם רָעָב׃ וְהִרְבֵּיתִי אֶת־פְּרִי הָעֵץ וּתְנוּבַת הַשָּׂדֶה
לא לְמַעַן אֲשֶׁר לֹא תִקְחוּ עוֹד חֶרְפַּת רָעָב בַּגּוֹיִם׃ וּזְכַרְתֶּם
אֶת־דַּרְכֵיכֶם הָרָעִים וּמַעַלְלֵיכֶם אֲשֶׁר לֹא־טוֹבִים וּנְקֹטֹתֶם
לב בִּפְנֵיכֶם עַל עֲוֺנֹתֵיכֶם וְעַל תּוֹעֲבוֹתֵיכֶם׃ לֹא לְמַעַנְכֶם אֲנִי־
עֹשֶׂה נְאֻם אֲדֹנָי יֱהוִה יִוָּדַע לָכֶם בּוֹשׁוּ וְהִכָּלְמוּ מִדַּרְכֵיכֶם
בֵּית יִשְׂרָאֵל׃

לג כֹּה אָמַר אֲדֹנָי יֱהוִה בְּיוֹם טַהֲרִי אֶתְכֶם מִכֹּל עֲוֺנוֹתֵיכֶם
לד וְהוֹשַׁבְתִּי אֶת־הֶעָרִים וְנִבְנוּ הֶחֳרָבוֹת׃ וְהָאָרֶץ הַנְּשַׁמָּה
לה תֵּעָבֵד תַּחַת אֲשֶׁר הָיְתָה שְׁמָמָה לְעֵינֵי כָּל־עוֹבֵר׃ וְאָמְרוּ
הָאָרֶץ הַלֵּזוּ הַנְּשַׁמָּה הָיְתָה כְּגַן־עֵדֶן וְהֶעָרִים הֶחֳרֵבוֹת

36 and inhabited.' And the nations that remain around you will
know that I, the LORD, have rebuilt what was destroyed, have
sown what was desolated; I the LORD have spoken and will do
37 it.* So says the Lord GOD: This, too – I will respond
to the House of Israel's request to do this for them: I will multi-
38 ply their people like a flock of sheep, like the flocks for sacred offerings, like the flocks of Jerusalem during her holy times; this
is how the ruined cities will be, filled with flocks of people, and
they will know that I am the LORD."

Sepharadim, Chabad and Yemenites end here

HAFTARAT PARASHAT HAḤODESH

The maftir of Parashat HaḤodesh is read from Exodus 12:1–20. When Shabbat HaḤodesh coincides with Rosh Ḥodesh Nisan, three Torah scrolls are removed from the ark. The first six aliyot are read from the weekly parasha. The seventh consists of the addition for Rosh Ḥodesh, Numbers 28:9–15. Afterward, half-Kaddish is recited, and the maftir is read from Parashat HaḤodesh.

EZEKIEL

Yemenites begin here

45 9 "Thus says the Lord GOD: You have gone far enough, O princes
of Israel! Stop your violence and robbery, do what is just and
right! Remove from My people your exacting taxes that evict
10 them from their land, says the Lord GOD. You shall have honest
11 scales and honest measures of the ephah and the *bat*. The ephah
and the *bat* contain the same amount, so the *bat* contains one-
tenth of a homer, and one-tenth of a homer is also an ephah: their
12 measure is relative to the homer. Now the shekel is twenty gerah.
Twenty shekel, twenty-five shekel, fifteen shekel together shall be
13 your maneh. This is the contribution that you shall offer up: one-
sixth of an ephah per homer of wheat and one-sixth of an ephah

However, this lofty status is not for their own sake. The prince receives his power from the people in order to improve their condition, just like a cloud, sent up over the fields, is charged with watering them and helping them grow. When a cloud is emptied of its life-giving waters, it dissipates and is gone.

In a redeemed world, all the classes of people will be present in the Temple, from the king to the lowest commoner. The service of the king in the Temple will be "for all the people," i.e., on behalf of a nation that stands before God. "When they enter, he enters, and when they leave, they leave together."

לו וְהַנְּשַׁמּוֹת וְהַנֶּהֱרָסוֹת בְּצוּרוֹת יָשָׁבוּ: וְיָדְעוּ הַגּוֹיִם אֲשֶׁר
יִשָּׁאֲרוּ סְבִיבוֹתֵיכֶם כִּי ׀ אֲנִי יהוה בָּנִיתִי הַנֶּהֱרָסוֹת נָטַעְתִּי
לז הַנְּשַׁמָּה אֲנִי יהוה דִּבַּרְתִּי וְעָשִׂיתִי:* כֹּה אָמַר אֲדֹנָי
יֱהֹוִה עוֹד זֹאת אִדָּרֵשׁ לְבֵית־יִשְׂרָאֵל לַעֲשׂוֹת לָהֶם אַרְבֶּה
לח אֹתָם כַּצֹּאן אָדָם: כְּצֹאן קָדָשִׁים כְּצֹאן יְרוּשָׁלַםִ בְּמוֹעֲדֶיהָ
כֵּן תִּהְיֶינָה הֶעָרִים הֶחֳרֵבוֹת מְלֵאוֹת צֹאן אָדָם וְיָדְעוּ כִּי־
אֲנִי יהוה:

Sepharadim, Chabad and Yemenites end here

הפטרת פרשת החודש

The מפטיר *of* פרשת החודש *is read from* שמות יב, א–כ.
When שבת החודש *coincides with* ראש חודש ניסן,
three Torah scrolls are removed from the ark. The first six עליות
are read from the weekly פרשה. *The seventh consists of the*
addition for ראש חודש, במדבר כח, ט–טו. *Afterward,* חצי קדיש
is recited, and the מפטיר *is read from* פרשת החודש.

יחזקאל

Yemenites begin here

מה ט כֹּה־אָמַר אֲדֹנָי יֱהֹוִה רַב־לָכֶם נְשִׂיאֵי יִשְׂרָאֵל חָמָס וָשֹׁד
הָסִירוּ וּמִשְׁפָּט וּצְדָקָה עֲשׂוּ הָרִימוּ גְרֻשֹׁתֵיכֶם מֵעַל עַמִּי
י נְאֻם אֲדֹנָי יֱהֹוִה: מֹאזְנֵי־צֶדֶק וְאֵיפַת־צֶדֶק וּבַת־צֶדֶק
יא יְהִי לָכֶם: הָאֵיפָה וְהַבַּת תֹּכֶן אֶחָד יִהְיֶה לָשֵׂאת מַעְשַׂר
הַחֹמֶר הַבָּת וַעֲשִׂירִת הַחֹמֶר הָאֵיפָה אֶל־הַחֹמֶר יִהְיֶה
יב מַתְכֻּנְתּוֹ: וְהַשֶּׁקֶל עֶשְׂרִים גֵּרָה עֶשְׂרִים שְׁקָלִים חֲמִשָּׁה
וְעֶשְׂרִים שְׁקָלִים עֲשָׂרָה וַחֲמִשָּׁה שֶׁקֶל הַמָּנֶה יִהְיֶה לָכֶם:
יג זֹאת הַתְּרוּמָה אֲשֶׁר תָּרִימוּ שִׁשִּׁית הָאֵיפָה מֵחֹמֶר הַחִטִּים

HAFTARAT PARASHAT HAḤODESH

The prophecy that appears in this week's *haftara* was communicated by Yeḥezkel to the exiles in Babylon fourteen years after the destruction of Jerusalem. In a prophetic virtual tour of the future rebuilt Jerusalem, we are informed about the daily rituals in the Temple, including the Passover sacrifice. The "prince" (*nasi*), i.e., the king, is the representative of the people in the Temple and works alongside the priests. A *nasi* in Hebrew can be a prince, but the word also means "cloud." Both stand above others: a leader of the people is held up over his charges, while a cloud hovers above the ground.

14 per homer of barley. The rule regarding oil: the *bat* is the measure
of oil; you shall offer one-tenth of a *bat* out of the *kor*, which is a
15 homer of ten *bat*, for ten *bat* make up a homer. And you shall offer
one lamb out of two hundred from your flock in the well-watered
pastureland of Israel. These shall serve as the grain offering and
as the burnt offering and as the peace offering to atone for them,
16 says the Lord GOD. *All the people of the land *Ashkenazim begin here*
17 shall give this contribution to the prince of Israel. And it shall be
the prince's duty to provide burnt offerings and grain offerings
and libations on festivals, New Moons, and Sabbaths; at all the
times appointed for the House of Israel, he shall prepare the purification offering and the grain offering and the burnt offering
and the peace offering to provide atonement for the House of
18 Israel. Thus says the Lord GOD: In the first month, on *Sepharadim and Chabad begin here*
the first day of the month, you shall take a young bull with no
19 blemish to purify the Sanctuary. And the priest shall take from
the blood of this purification offering and put it on the doorposts of the House, on the four corners of the ledge of the altar,
20 and on the doorpost of the gate of the inner courtyard. And so
shall you do on the seventh day of the month for anyone who
has sinned by mistake or due to ignorance: thus you shall pro-
21 vide atonement for the House. In the first month, on the fourteenth day of the month, you shall bring the Passover sacrifice,
22 for a festival of seven days, unleavened bread shall be eaten. On
that day the prince shall prepare a bull as a purification offering
23 for himself and for all the people of the land. And on every one
of the seven days of the festival he shall prepare a burnt offering
to the LORD: seven bulls and seven rams with no blemish every
day for seven days, and a daily purification offering consisting of
24 one male goat. And he shall prepare a grain offering consisting
of one ephah for each bull and one ephah for each ram and a
25 hin of oil for each ephah. In the seventh month, on the fifteenth
day of the month, during the festival, he shall prepare offerings
just like those on the seven days: a similar purification offering,
a similar burnt offering, and a similar grain offering, and a like
46 1 amount of oil. Thus says the Lord GOD: The gate of the
inner courtyard that faces eastward shall be closed during the six
days of labor, but on the Sabbath it shall be opened, and on the
2 day of the New Moon it shall be opened. The prince shall enter
from outside by way of the entrance hall of the gate and shall

יד וְשִׁשִּׁיתֶם הָאֵיפָה מֵחֹמֶר הַשְּׂעֹרִים׃ וְחֹק הַשֶּׁמֶן הַבַּת הַשֶּׁמֶן
מַעְשַׂר הַבַּת מִן־הַכֹּר עֲשֶׂרֶת הַבַּתִּים חֹמֶר כִּי־עֲשֶׂרֶת
טו הַבַּתִּים חֹמֶר׃ וְשֶׂה־אַחַת מִן־הַצֹּאן מִן־הַמָּאתַיִם מִמַּשְׁקֵה
יִשְׂרָאֵל לְמִנְחָה וּלְעוֹלָה וְלִשְׁלָמִים לְכַפֵּר עֲלֵיהֶם נְאֻם אֲדֹנָי
טז יֱהֹוִה׃ *כֹּל הָעָם הָאָרֶץ יִהְיוּ אֶל־הַתְּרוּמָה הַזֹּאת

Ashkenazim begin here

יז לַנָּשִׂיא בְּיִשְׂרָאֵל׃ וְעַל־הַנָּשִׂיא יִהְיֶה הָעוֹלוֹת וְהַמִּנְחָה
וְהַנֶּסֶךְ בַּחַגִּים וּבֶחֳדָשִׁים וּבַשַּׁבָּתוֹת בְּכָל־מוֹעֲדֵי בֵּית יִשְׂרָאֵל
הוּא־יַעֲשֶׂה אֶת־הַחַטָּאת וְאֶת־הַמִּנְחָה וְאֶת־הָעוֹלָה וְאֶת־
יח הַשְּׁלָמִים לְכַפֵּר בְּעַד בֵּית־יִשְׂרָאֵל׃ *כֹּה־אָמַר

Sepharadim and Chabad begin here

אֲדֹנָי יֱהֹוִה בָּרִאשׁוֹן בְּאֶחָד לַחֹדֶשׁ תִּקַּח פַּר־בֶּן־בָּקָר
יט תָּמִים וְחִטֵּאתָ אֶת־הַמִּקְדָּשׁ׃ וְלָקַח הַכֹּהֵן מִדַּם הַחַטָּאת
וְנָתַן אֶל־מְזוּזַת הַבַּיִת וְאֶל־אַרְבַּע פִּנּוֹת הָעֲזָרָה לַמִּזְבֵּחַ
כ וְעַל־מְזוּזַת שַׁעַר הֶחָצֵר הַפְּנִימִית׃ וְכֵן תַּעֲשֶׂה בְּשִׁבְעָה
כא בַחֹדֶשׁ מֵאִישׁ שֹׁגֶה וּמִפֶּתִי וְכִפַּרְתֶּם אֶת־הַבָּיִת׃ בָּרִאשׁוֹן
בְּאַרְבָּעָה עָשָׂר יוֹם לַחֹדֶשׁ יִהְיֶה לָכֶם הַפָּסַח חָג שְׁבֻעוֹת
כב יָמִים מַצּוֹת יֵאָכֵל׃ וְעָשָׂה הַנָּשִׂיא בַּיּוֹם הַהוּא בַּעֲדוֹ וּבְעַד
כג כָּל־עַם הָאָרֶץ פַּר חַטָּאת׃ וְשִׁבְעַת יְמֵי־הֶחָג יַעֲשֶׂה עוֹלָה
לַיהוָה שִׁבְעַת פָּרִים וְשִׁבְעַת אֵילִים תְּמִימִם לַיּוֹם שִׁבְעַת
כד הַיָּמִים וְחַטָּאת שְׂעִיר עִזִּים לַיּוֹם׃ וּמִנְחָה אֵיפָה לַפָּר וְאֵיפָה
כה לָאַיִל יַעֲשֶׂה וְשֶׁמֶן הִין לָאֵיפָה׃ בַּשְּׁבִיעִי בַּחֲמִשָּׁה עָשָׂר
יוֹם לַחֹדֶשׁ בֶּחָג יַעֲשֶׂה כָאֵלֶּה שִׁבְעַת הַיָּמִים כַּחַטָּאת
מו א כָּעֹלָה וְכַמִּנְחָה וְכַשָּׁמֶן׃ כֹּה־אָמַר אֲדֹנָי יֱהֹוִה
שַׁעַר הֶחָצֵר הַפְּנִימִית הַפֹּנֶה קָדִים יִהְיֶה סָגוּר שֵׁשֶׁת יְמֵי
ב הַמַּעֲשֶׂה וּבְיוֹם הַשַּׁבָּת יִפָּתֵחַ וּבְיוֹם הַחֹדֶשׁ יִפָּתֵחַ׃ וּבָא
הַנָּשִׂיא דֶּרֶךְ אוּלָם הַשַּׁעַר מִחוּץ וְעָמַד עַל־מְזוּזַת הַשַּׁעַר

stand by the doorpost of the gate. The priests shall prepare his
burnt offering and his peace offering, and he shall bow down at
the threshold of the gate and then leave, but the gate shall not be
3 closed until the evening so that the ordinary people can also bow
down before the LORD at the threshold of that gate on Sabbaths
4 and New Moons. The burnt offering that the prince shall offer
to the LORD on every Sabbath day consists of six lambs with
5 no blemish and a ram with no blemish. And his accompanying
grain offering shall be one ephah for the ram; as for the lambs,
his grain offering shall be whatever he chooses to give as well as
6 a hin of oil for each ephah of grain. And on the day of the New
Moon his offering shall consist of a young bull with no blemish
7 as well as six lambs and a ram, all without blemish. He shall prepare a grain offering of one ephah for the bull and one ephah for
the ram; as for the lambs, his grain offering shall be whatever he
8 chooses to give as well as a hin of oil for each ephah of grain. And
when the prince comes, he shall enter by way of the entrance hall
9 of the gate – and by way of it shall he exit. But when the people
come before the LORD on festivals, a person who enters by way
of the northern gate in order to bow down shall exit by the southern gate, and a person who enters by way of the southern gate
shall exit by way of the northern gate. He shall not return by way
of the gate through which he entered but shall exit through the
10 one across from it. And the prince shall be among the people on
those days: when they enter, he enters, and when they leave, they
11 leave together. And on the festivals and at the appointed times
the grain offering shall be an ephah for the bull, an ephah for the
ram, and as for the lambs, whatever he chooses to give as well as
12 a hin of oil for each ephah of grain.* Now, should the *Yemenites end here*
prince make a voluntary offering, a burnt offering or peace offering, voluntarily offered to the LORD on a weekday, the gate facing eastward shall be open for him, and he shall prepare his burnt
offering or peace offering just as he would do on the Sabbath, but
13 when he leaves, the gate will be closed after his exit. And you
shall prepare a daily burnt offering to the LORD consisting of
a lamb in its first year without blemish; you shall prepare it ev-
14 ery morning. And you shall prepare a grain offering for it every
morning: one-sixth of an ephah and one-third of a hin of oil to
moisten the finely ground flour as a grain offering to the LORD:
15 a perpetual, everlasting decree. Thus shall they prepare the lamb

וְעָשׂ֨וּ הַכֹּהֲנִ֜ים אֶת־עוֹלָתוֹ֙ וְאֶת־שְׁלָמָ֔יו וְהִֽשְׁתַּחֲוָ֛ה עַל־
ג מִפְתַּ֥ן הַשַּׁ֖עַר וְיָצָ֑א וְהַשַּׁ֥עַר לֹא־יִסָּגֵ֖ר עַד־הָעָֽרֶב׃ וְהִשְׁתַּחֲו֣וּ
עַם־הָאָ֗רֶץ פֶּ֚תַח הַשַּׁ֣עַר הַה֔וּא בַּשַּׁבָּת֖וֹת וּבֶחֳדָשִׁ֑ים לִפְנֵ֖י
ד יְהוָֽה׃ וְהָ֣עֹלָ֔ה אֲשֶׁר־יַקְרִ֥ב הַנָּשִׂ֖יא לַיהוָ֑ה בְּי֣וֹם הַשַּׁבָּ֗ת
ה שִׁשָּׁ֧ה כְבָשִׂ֛ים תְּמִימִ֖ם וְאַ֥יִל תָּמִֽים׃ וּמִנְחָה֙ אֵיפָ֣ה לָאַ֔יִל
ו וְלַכְּבָשִׂ֥ים מִנְחָ֖ה מַתַּ֣ת יָד֑וֹ וְשֶׁ֖מֶן הִ֥ין לָאֵיפָֽה׃ וּבְי֣וֹם הַחֹ֔דֶשׁ
פַּ֥ר בֶּן־בָּקָ֖ר תְּמִימִ֑ם וְשֵׁ֧שֶׁת כְּבָשִׂ֛ם וָאַ֖יִל תְּמִימִ֥ם יִהְיֽוּ׃
ז וְאֵיפָ֨ה לַפָּ֜ר וְאֵיפָ֤ה לָאַ֙יִל֙ יַעֲשֶׂ֣ה מִנְחָ֔ה וְלַכְּבָשִׂ֕ים כַּאֲשֶׁ֥ר
ח תַּשִּׂ֖יג יָד֑וֹ וְשֶׁ֖מֶן הִ֥ין לָאֵיפָֽה׃ וּבְב֖וֹא הַנָּשִׂ֑יא דֶּ֣רֶךְ אוּלָ֤ם
ט הַשַּׁ֙עַר֙ יָב֔וֹא וּבְדַרְכּ֖וֹ יֵצֵֽא׃ וּבְב֨וֹא עַם־הָאָ֜רֶץ לִפְנֵ֤י יְהוָה֙
בַּמּֽוֹעֲדִ֔ים הַבָּ֡א דֶּרֶךְ֩ שַׁ֨עַר צָפ֜וֹן לְהִֽשְׁתַּחֲוֺ֗ת יֵצֵא֙ דֶּרֶךְ־
שַׁ֣עַר נֶ֔גֶב וְהַבָּא֙ דֶּרֶךְ־שַׁ֣עַר נֶ֔גֶב יֵצֵ֖א דֶּרֶךְ־שַׁ֣עַר צָפ֑וֹנָה
י לֹ֣א יָשׁ֗וּב דֶּ֤רֶךְ הַשַּׁ֙עַר֙ אֲשֶׁר־בָּ֣א ב֔וֹ כִּ֥י נִכְח֖וֹ יצאו׃ וְהַנָּשִׂ֕יא יֵצֵֽא
יא בְּתוֹכָ֖ם בְּבוֹאָ֣ם יָב֔וֹא וּבְצֵאתָ֖ם יֵצֵֽאוּ׃ וּבַחַגִּ֣ים וּבַמּֽוֹעֲדִ֗ים
תִּהְיֶ֤ה הַמִּנְחָה֙ אֵיפָ֤ה לַפָּר֙ וְאֵיפָ֣ה לָאַ֔יִל וְלַכְּבָשִׂ֖ים מַתַּ֣ת
יב יָד֑וֹ וְשֶׁ֖מֶן הִ֥ין לָאֵיפָֽה׃* וְכִֽי־יַעֲשֶׂ֨ה הַנָּשִׂ֜יא נְדָבָ֗ה *Yemenites end here*
עוֹלָ֣ה אֽוֹ־שְׁלָמִים֮ נְדָבָ֣ה לַיהוָה֒ וּפָ֣תַח ל֗וֹ אֶת־הַשַּׁ֙עַר֙ הַפֹּנֶ֣ה
קָדִ֔ים וְעָשָׂ֤ה אֶת־עֹֽלָתוֹ֙ וְאֶת־שְׁלָמָ֔יו כַּאֲשֶׁ֥ר יַעֲשֶׂ֖ה בְּי֣וֹם
יג הַשַּׁבָּ֑ת וְיָצָ֕א וְסָגַ֥ר אֶת־הַשַּׁ֖עַר אַחֲרֵ֥י צֵאתֽוֹ׃ וְכֶ֨בֶשׂ בֶּן־
שְׁנָת֜וֹ תָּמִ֗ים תַּעֲשֶׂ֥ה עוֹלָ֛ה לַיּ֖וֹם לַיהוָ֑ה בַּבֹּ֥קֶר בַּבֹּ֖קֶר תַּעֲשֶׂ֥ה
יד אֹתֽוֹ׃ וּמִנְחָה֩ תַעֲשֶׂ֨ה עָלָ֜יו בַּבֹּ֣קֶר בַּבֹּ֗קֶר שִׁשִּׁ֤ית הָֽאֵיפָה֙
וְשֶׁ֛מֶן שְׁלִישִׁ֥ית הַהִ֖ין לָרֹ֣ס אֶת־הַסֹּ֑לֶת מִנְחָה֙ לַֽיהוָ֔ה חֻקּ֥וֹת
טו עוֹלָ֖ם תָּמִֽיד׃ ועשו אֶת־הַכֶּ֧בֶשׂ וְאֶת־הַמִּנְחָ֛ה וְאֶת־הַשֶּׁ֖מֶן יַעֲשׂ֥וּ

and the grain offering with the oil every morning as a regular
16 burnt offering.* Thus says the Lord GOD: Should the prince give a gift to one of his sons, it is his estate that will belong *Sepharadim and Chabad end here*
17 to his sons; it is their possession by inheritance. But should he
give a gift from his estate to one of his servants, the servant owns
it until the year of freedom, when it returns to the prince, for his
18 heritors are his sons: it belongs to them. This is so that the prince
does not take anything from the people's inheritance, throwing
them wrongfully out of their landholding. He shall pass his own
landholding onto his sons so that My people will not be scattered, each ousted from his landholding."

Haftarat Shabbat HaGadol

3 4 Then the offering of Yehuda and Jerusalem will be pleasing to the MALACHI
5 LORD as in days of old and years past. I will draw close to you
in judgment, and I will be a swift witness against the sorcerers
and adulterers and those who falsely swear; against those who
withhold payment from the worker or the widow or the orphan;
against those who turn away the stranger. They do not fear Me,
6 says the LORD of Hosts. For I am the LORD. I have not changed.
7 And you, children of Yaakov, you have not perished. Ever since
the days of your forefathers you have strayed from My statutes,
and you did not keep them. Come back to Me, and I will come
back to you, says the LORD of Hosts. But you say, "How shall we
8 come back?" Can a person steal from God? Yet you steal from
Me. But you say, "What have we stolen from You?" The tithes
9 and donations. You are being cursed with the curse because you
10 steal from Me – the whole nation. Bring the entire tithe to the
treasury, and it will be food for My House, and put Me to the
test, please, in this, says the LORD of Hosts. See if I do not open

"Return the hearts of parents back to their children and the hearts of children back to their parents." The process of return is reciprocal. The people (the children) must return to God (their Father), and vice versa. The past (symbolized by the parents) must make its peace with the future (the children), and vice versa. On the night of the Seder, all the family sits together. The parents speak to the children about the exodus from Egypt, and these founding values are the basis for the Jewish people's future, which continues to climb higher and higher.

טז בַּבֹּקֶר בַּבֹּקֶר עוֹלַת תָּמִיד:* כֹּה־אָמַר אֲדֹנָי
יֱהֹוִה כִּי־יִתֵּן הַנָּשִׂיא מַתָּנָה לְאִישׁ מִבָּנָיו נַחֲלָתוֹ הִיא לְבָנָיו
יז תִּהְיֶה אֲחֻזָּתָם הִיא בְּנַחֲלָה: וְכִי־יִתֵּן מַתָּנָה מִנַּחֲלָתוֹ לְאַחַד
מֵעֲבָדָיו וְהָיְתָה לּוֹ עַד־שְׁנַת הַדְּרוֹר וְשָׁבַת לַנָּשִׂיא אַךְ נַחֲלָתוֹ
יח בָּנָיו לָהֶם תִּהְיֶה: וְלֹא־יִקַּח הַנָּשִׂיא מִנַּחֲלַת הָעָם לְהוֹנֹתָם
מֵאֲחֻזָּתָם מֵאֲחֻזָּתוֹ יַנְחִל אֶת־בָּנָיו לְמַעַן אֲשֶׁר לֹא־יָפֻצוּ עַמִּי
אִישׁ מֵאֲחֻזָּתוֹ:

Sepharadim and Chabad end here

הפטרת שבת הגדול

מלאכי ג ד וְעָרְבָה לַיהֹוָה מִנְחַת יְהוּדָה וִירוּשָׁלָ͏ִם כִּימֵי עוֹלָם וּכְשָׁנִים
ה קַדְמֹנִיּוֹת: וְקָרַבְתִּי אֲלֵיכֶם לַמִּשְׁפָּט וְהָיִיתִי ׀ עֵד מְמַהֵר
בַּמְכַשְּׁפִים וּבַמְנָאֲפִים וּבַנִּשְׁבָּעִים לַשָּׁקֶר וּבְעֹשְׁקֵי שְׂכַר־
שָׂכִיר אַלְמָנָה וְיָתוֹם וּמַטֵּי־גֵר וְלֹא יְרֵאוּנִי אָמַר יְהֹוָה
ו צְבָאוֹת: כִּי אֲנִי יְהֹוָה לֹא שָׁנִיתִי וְאַתֶּם בְּנֵי־יַעֲקֹב לֹא
ז כְלִיתֶם: לְמִימֵי אֲבֹתֵיכֶם סַרְתֶּם מֵחֻקַּי וְלֹא שְׁמַרְתֶּם שׁוּבוּ
אֵלַי וְאָשׁוּבָה אֲלֵיכֶם אָמַר יְהֹוָה צְבָאוֹת וַאֲמַרְתֶּם בַּמֶּה
ח נָשׁוּב: הֲיִקְבַּע אָדָם אֱלֹהִים כִּי אַתֶּם קֹבְעִים אֹתִי וַאֲמַרְתֶּם
ט בַּמֶּה קְבַעֲנוּךָ הַמַּעֲשֵׂר וְהַתְּרוּמָה: בַּמְּאֵרָה אַתֶּם נֵאָרִים
י וְאֹתִי אַתֶּם קֹבְעִים הַגּוֹי כֻּלּוֹ: הָבִיאוּ אֶת־כָּל־הַמַּעֲשֵׂר אֶל־
בֵּית הָאוֹצָר וִיהִי טֶרֶף בְּבֵיתִי וּבְחָנוּנִי נָא בָּזֹאת אָמַר יְהֹוָה

HAFTARAT SHABBAT HAGADOL

Malakhi was the last of the prophets, living around the time of Neḥemya. At that time, the Jews newly returned to the land of Israel were in distress. An economic crisis and complicated social and spiritual situation sowed confusion and despair among the populace. To break out of such a situation required a communal conversation about the values on which their new reality would be founded. The discourse between the prophet and the people was meant to start such a conversation.

The prophet declares: "Come back to Me, and I will come back to you," and

up the floodgates of heaven for you and pour out blessings upon
11 you endlessly. I will drive away for you that which devours. Your
produce will not be destroyed, and your vines in the field will
12 not be barren, says the Lord of Hosts. All the nations will call
you happy, for you, yours will be a desired land, says the Lord
13 of Hosts. The Lord says, "You have spoken harshly
14 against Me." Yet you say, "What have we said of You?" You say,
"It is useless to serve God, and what do we gain in keeping His
watch, or by walking in dark sorrow before the Lord of Hosts?
15 Now we call the arrogant happy; evildoers have built themselves
16 up; they have tested God and escaped." Then those who fear
the Lord spoke one to another, and the Lord listened and
He heard, and it was written – a book of remembrance before
Him for those who fear the Lord and keep His name in mind.
17 And they shall be Mine, says the Lord of Hosts, on the day on
which I choose My cherished possession, and I will take pity
18 on them as a man takes pity on his son who serves him. And
you will once again distinguish between the righteous and the
wicked, between one who serves God and one who does not
19 serve Him. For behold, the day is coming, burning like
an oven; the arrogant and the evildoers will be straw, and the
coming day will consume them, says the Lord of Hosts, so that
20 neither root nor branch will remain of them. But for you, fear-
ers of My name, a sun of righteousness will shine with healing
under its wings, and you will go out and frolic like stall-fatted
21 calves. You will trample evildoers – for they will be ashes under
the soles of your feet on the day on which I act, says the Lord of
22 Hosts. Remember the Teaching of Moshe My servant,
which I commanded to him at Ḥorev, statutes and laws for all of
23 Israel. Behold, I will send you Eliya the prophet before the great
24 and terrible day of the Lord. And he will return the hearts of
parents back to their children and the hearts of children back to
their parents, lest I come and lay the earth waste.

Behold, I will send you Eliya the prophet
before the great and terrible day of the Lord.

צְבָא֑וֹת אִם־לֹ֧א אֶפְתַּ֣ח לָכֶ֗ם אֵ֚ת אֲרֻבּ֣וֹת הַשָּׁמַ֔יִם וַהֲרִיקֹתִ֥י
יא לָכֶ֛ם בְּרָכָ֖ה עַד־בְּלִי־דָֽי׃ וְגָעַרְתִּ֤י לָכֶם֙ בָּֽאֹכֵ֔ל וְלֹֽא־יַשְׁחִ֥ת
לָכֶ֖ם אֶת־פְּרִ֣י הָאֲדָמָ֑ה וְלֹא־תְשַׁכֵּ֨ל לָכֶ֤ם הַגֶּ֙פֶן֙ בַּשָּׂדֶ֔ה אָמַ֖ר
יב יְהוָ֥ה צְבָאֽוֹת׃ וְאִשְּׁר֥וּ אֶתְכֶ֖ם כָּל־הַגּוֹיִ֑ם כִּֽי־תִהְי֤וּ אַתֶּם֙ אֶ֣רֶץ
יג חֵ֔פֶץ אָמַ֖ר יְהוָ֥ה צְבָאֽוֹת׃ חָזְק֥וּ עָלַ֛י דִּבְרֵיכֶ֖ם
יד אָמַ֣ר יְהוָ֑ה וַאֲמַרְתֶּ֕ם מַה־נִּדְבַּ֖רְנוּ עָלֶֽיךָ׃ אֲמַרְתֶּ֕ם שָׁ֖וְא עֲבֹ֣ד
אֱלֹהִ֑ים וּמַה־בֶּ֗צַע כִּ֤י שָׁמַ֙רְנוּ֙ מִשְׁמַרְתּ֔וֹ וְכִ֤י הָלַ֙כְנוּ֙ קְדֹ֣רַנִּ֔ית
טו מִפְּנֵ֖י יְהוָ֥ה צְבָאֽוֹת׃ וְעַתָּ֕ה אֲנַ֖חְנוּ מְאַשְּׁרִ֣ים זֵדִ֑ים גַּם־נִבְנוּ֙
טז עֹשֵׂ֣י רִשְׁעָ֔ה גַּ֧ם בָּחֲנ֛וּ אֱלֹהִ֖ים וַיִּמָּלֵֽטוּ׃ אָ֧ז נִדְבְּר֛וּ יִרְאֵ֥י יְהוָ֖ה
אִ֣ישׁ אֶל־רֵעֵ֑הוּ וַיַּקְשֵׁ֤ב יְהוָה֙ וַיִּשְׁמָ֔ע וַ֠יִּכָּתֵב סֵ֣פֶר זִכָּר֤וֹן לְפָנָיו֙
יז לְיִרְאֵ֣י יְהוָ֔ה וּלְחֹשְׁבֵ֖י שְׁמֽוֹ׃ וְהָ֣יוּ לִ֗י אָמַר֙ יְהוָ֣ה צְבָא֔וֹת לַיּ֕וֹם
אֲשֶׁ֥ר אֲנִ֖י עֹשֶׂ֣ה סְגֻלָּ֑ה וְחָמַלְתִּ֣י עֲלֵיהֶ֔ם כַּאֲשֶׁר֙ יַחְמֹ֣ל אִ֔ישׁ
יח עַל־בְּנ֖וֹ הָעֹבֵ֥ד אֹתֽוֹ׃ וְשַׁבְתֶּם֙ וּרְאִיתֶ֔ם בֵּ֥ין צַדִּ֖יק לְרָשָׁ֑ע בֵּ֚ין
יט עֹבֵ֣ד אֱלֹהִ֔ים לַאֲשֶׁ֖ר לֹ֥א עֲבָדֽוֹ׃ כִּֽי־הִנֵּ֤ה הַיּוֹם֙ בָּ֔א
בֹּעֵ֖ר כַּתַּנּ֑וּר וְהָי֨וּ כָל־זֵדִ֜ים וְכָל־עֹשֵׂ֤ה רִשְׁעָה֙ קַ֔שׁ וְלִהַ֨ט
אֹתָ֜ם הַיּ֣וֹם הַבָּ֗א אָמַר֙ יְהוָ֣ה צְבָא֔וֹת אֲשֶׁ֛ר לֹא־יַעֲזֹ֥ב לָהֶ֖ם
כ שֹׁ֥רֶשׁ וְעָנָֽף׃ וְזָרְחָ֨ה לָכֶ֜ם יִרְאֵ֤י שְׁמִי֙ שֶׁ֣מֶשׁ צְדָקָ֔ה וּמַרְפֵּ֖א
כא בִּכְנָפֶ֑יהָ וִיצָאתֶ֥ם וּפִשְׁתֶּ֖ם כְּעֶגְלֵ֥י מַרְבֵּֽק׃ וְעַסּוֹתֶ֣ם רְשָׁעִ֔ים
כִּֽי־יִהְי֣וּ אֵ֔פֶר תַּ֖חַת כַּפּ֣וֹת רַגְלֵיכֶ֑ם בַּיּוֹם֙ אֲשֶׁ֣ר אֲנִ֣י עֹשֶׂ֔ה
כב אָמַ֖ר יְהוָ֥ה צְבָאֽוֹת׃ זִכְר֕וּ תּוֹרַ֖ת מֹשֶׁ֣ה עַבְדִּ֑י
אֲשֶׁ֩ר צִוִּ֨יתִי אוֹת֤וֹ בְחֹרֵב֙ עַל־כָּל־יִשְׂרָאֵ֔ל חֻקִּ֖ים וּמִשְׁפָּטִֽים׃
כג הִנֵּ֤ה אָֽנֹכִי֙ שֹׁלֵ֣חַ לָכֶ֔ם אֵ֖ת אֵלִיָּ֣ה הַנָּבִ֑יא לִפְנֵ֗י בּ֚וֹא י֣וֹם יְהוָ֔ה
כד הַגָּד֖וֹל וְהַנּוֹרָֽא׃ וְהֵשִׁ֤יב לֵב־אָבוֹת֙ עַל־בָּנִ֔ים וְלֵ֥ב בָּנִ֖ים עַל־
אֲבוֹתָ֑ם פֶּן־אָב֕וֹא וְהִכֵּיתִ֥י אֶת־הָאָ֖רֶץ חֵֽרֶם׃

הנה אנכי שלח לכם את אליה הנביא
לפני בוא יום יהוה הגדול והנורא

Haftara for the First Day of Pesaḥ

The maftir of the first day of Pesaḥ is read from Numbers 28:16–25.

JOSHUA

Ashkenazim begin here

3 5 And Yehoshua told the people, "Sanctify yourselves, for tomor-
6 row the Lord will perform wonders in your midst." "Raise up
the Ark of the Covenant," said Yehoshua to the priests, "and cross
before the people." So they raised up the Ark of the Covenant
7 and advanced to the front of the people. And the Lord
said to Yehoshua, "Today I shall begin to exalt you in the eyes of
all Israel so that they may know that I shall be with you as I was
with Moshe.

Sepharadim and Yemenites begin here

5 2 At that time, the Lord said to Yehoshua, "Make yourselves
3 knives of flint and circumcise the Israelites a second time." So Yehoshua made knives of flint and circumcised the Israelites at the
4 Hill of Foreskins. This is why Yehoshua circumcised them: all the
men who left Egypt – all the males fit for battle – had died in the
wilderness during the journey, as they came away from Egypt.
5 And while all the men who left there had been circumcised, all
those who were born in the wilderness during the journey away
6 from Egypt had not been circumcised. For forty years the Israelites had wandered in the wilderness until those among the
nation who had left Egypt fit for battle had perished. They disobeyed the voice of the Lord, and the Lord swore not to show
them the land He had sworn to our ancestors that He would give
7 us – a land flowing with milk and honey. Yehoshua circumcised
those children that He raised in their stead, for they still had
their foreskins, not having been circumcised during the journey.
8 When the whole nation's circumcision was over, they remained
9 in place in the camp until they recovered. The Lord
said to Yehoshua, "Today, I have rolled the shame of Egypt away

---

God's commandment (Ex. 12:48): "No uncircumcised man may eat of it." The leader then assures the people that by doing so, they have rid themselves of the "shame of Egypt," and can celebrate the festival as free men and women, confident that God's promise to give them the land of Israel as an inheritance will soon be realized. This promise is emphasized by the discontinuance of the manna, signaling that the era of the exodus has ended and the time to settle the land has arrived. The *haftara* ends with Yehoshua encountering the angelic general of God's army, presaging the miraculous conquest of Canaan that will soon follow.

הפטרת יום ראשון של פסח

The מפטיר *of* יום ראשון של פסח *is read from* במדבר כח, טז–כה.

יהושע *Ashkenazim begin here*

ג ה וַיֹּאמֶר יְהוֹשֻׁעַ אֶל־הָעָם הִתְקַדָּשׁוּ כִּי מָחָר יַעֲשֶׂה יְהוָה
ו בְּקִרְבְּכֶם נִפְלָאוֹת׃ וַיֹּאמֶר יְהוֹשֻׁעַ אֶל־הַכֹּהֲנִים לֵאמֹר שְׂאוּ
אֶת־אֲרוֹן הַבְּרִית וְעִבְרוּ לִפְנֵי הָעָם וַיִּשְׂאוּ אֶת־אֲרוֹן הַבְּרִית
ז וַיֵּלְכוּ לִפְנֵי הָעָם׃ וַיֹּאמֶר יְהוָה אֶל־יְהוֹשֻׁעַ הַיּוֹם
הַזֶּה אָחֵל גַּדֶּלְךָ בְּעֵינֵי כָּל־יִשְׂרָאֵל אֲשֶׁר יֵדְעוּן כִּי כַּאֲשֶׁר
הָיִיתִי עִם־מֹשֶׁה אֶהְיֶה עִמָּךְ׃

Sepharadim and Yemenites begin here

ה ב *בָּעֵת הַהִיא אָמַר יְהוָה אֶל־יְהוֹשֻׁעַ עֲשֵׂה לְךָ חַרְבוֹת צֻרִים
ג וְשׁוּב מֹל אֶת־בְּנֵי־יִשְׂרָאֵל שֵׁנִית׃ וַיַּעַשׂ־לוֹ יְהוֹשֻׁעַ חַרְבוֹת
ד צֻרִים וַיָּמָל אֶת־בְּנֵי יִשְׂרָאֵל אֶל־גִּבְעַת הָעֲרָלוֹת׃ וְזֶה הַדָּבָר
אֲשֶׁר־מָל יְהוֹשֻׁעַ כָּל־הָעָם הַיֹּצֵא מִמִּצְרַיִם הַזְּכָרִים כֹּל ׀
אַנְשֵׁי הַמִּלְחָמָה מֵתוּ בַמִּדְבָּר בַּדֶּרֶךְ בְּצֵאתָם מִמִּצְרָיִם׃
ה כִּי־מֻלִים הָיוּ כָּל־הָעָם הַיֹּצְאִים וְכָל־הָעָם הַיִּלֹּדִים בַּמִּדְבָּר
ו בַּדֶּרֶךְ בְּצֵאתָם מִמִּצְרַיִם לֹא־מָלוּ׃ כִּי ׀ אַרְבָּעִים שָׁנָה הָלְכוּ
בְנֵי־יִשְׂרָאֵל בַּמִּדְבָּר עַד־תֹּם כָּל־הַגּוֹי אַנְשֵׁי הַמִּלְחָמָה
הַיֹּצְאִים מִמִּצְרַיִם אֲשֶׁר לֹא־שָׁמְעוּ בְּקוֹל יְהוָה אֲשֶׁר נִשְׁבַּע
יְהוָה לָהֶם לְבִלְתִּי הַרְאוֹתָם אֶת־הָאָרֶץ אֲשֶׁר נִשְׁבַּע יְהוָה
ז לַאֲבוֹתָם לָתֶת לָנוּ אֶרֶץ זָבַת חָלָב וּדְבָשׁ׃ וְאֶת־בְּנֵיהֶם הֵקִים
תַּחְתָּם אֹתָם מָל יְהוֹשֻׁעַ כִּי־עֲרֵלִים הָיוּ כִּי לֹא־מָלוּ אוֹתָם
ח בַדָּרֶךְ׃ וַיְהִי כַּאֲשֶׁר־תַּמּוּ כָל־הַגּוֹי לְהִמּוֹל וַיֵּשְׁבוּ תַחְתָּם
ט בַּמַּחֲנֶה עַד חֲיוֹתָם׃ וַיֹּאמֶר יְהוָה אֶל־יְהוֹשֻׁעַ
הַיּוֹם גַּלּוֹתִי אֶת־חֶרְפַּת מִצְרַיִם מֵעֲלֵיכֶם וַיִּקְרָא שֵׁם הַמָּקוֹם

FIRST DAY OF PESAḤ

The Torah reading for the first day of Pesaḥ describes the first Paschal sacrifice offered by the people of Israel, in the land of Egypt. The *haftara*, read from the book of Joshua, describes the first paschal sacrifice offered in the land of Israel. Having just crossed the Jordan river, Yehoshua orders the people first to circumcise themselves, in keeping with

from you." He has named that place Gilgal, as it is known to this
10 day. The Israelites encamped at Gilgal and performed the Passover sacrifice on the fourteenth day of the month at dusk on the
11 plains of Yeriḥo. On the day after the Passover sacrifice, they ate
of the yield of the land – unleavened bread and roasted grain –
12 that very day. The manna stopped falling the day after they had
eaten from the yield of the land. The Israelites never had manna
again; from that year on they ate from the crops of the land of
13 Canaan. When Yehoshua was near Yeriḥo, he looked
up and suddenly saw a man standing opposite him, drawn sword
in hand. Yehoshua approached him and asked, "Are you for us or
14 for our enemies?" He said, "No, for I am the commander of the
Lord's hosts. Now I have come!" Yehoshua flung his face to the
ground and prostrated himself, asking him, "What does my lord
15 bid his servant?" The commander of the Lord's hosts said to Yehoshua, "Remove the shoes from your feet, for the place where
6 1 you stand is holy." And Yehoshua did so. Yeriḥo was barred and
bolted against the Israelites; no one came out, and no one went
in.

Haftara for the Second Day of Pesaḥ in the Diaspora

The maftir of the second day of Pesaḥ in the Diaspora is read from Numbers 28:16–25.

II KINGS
Yemenites begin here

22 1 Yoshiyahu was eight years old when he became king, and for thir-
ty-one years he reigned in Jerusalem. His mother's name was Ye-
2 dida daughter of Adaya, from Botzkat. He did what was right in
the eyes of the Lord and followed in all the ways of his ancestor

rediscovered a copy of the Torah, which had been forgotten under the reigns of his father and grandfather. Inspired by its words, Yoshiyahu calls a gathering of all the leaders of the people to renew the covenant with God and forswear idolatry in all its forms. Yoshiyahu's enactments culminate in the grand and festive celebration of the Paschal offering. "No such Passover sacrifice had been made since the days of the judges who ruled Israel, nor throughout all the time of the kings of Israel or the kings of Yehuda."

י הַהוּא גִּלְגָּל עַד הַיּוֹם הַזֶּה: וַיַּחֲנוּ בְנֵי־יִשְׂרָאֵל בַּגִּלְגָּל וַיַּעֲשׂוּ
אֶת־הַפֶּסַח בְּאַרְבָּעָה עָשָׂר יוֹם לַחֹדֶשׁ בָּעֶרֶב בְּעַרְבוֹת
יא יְרִיחוֹ: וַיֹּאכְלוּ מֵעֲבוּר הָאָרֶץ מִמָּחֳרַת הַפֶּסַח מַצּוֹת וְקָלוּי
יב בְּעֶצֶם הַיּוֹם הַזֶּה: וַיִּשְׁבֹּת הַמָּן מִמָּחֳרָת בְּאָכְלָם מֵעֲבוּר
הָאָרֶץ וְלֹא־הָיָה עוֹד לִבְנֵי יִשְׂרָאֵל מָן וַיֹּאכְלוּ מִתְּבוּאַת
יג אֶרֶץ כְּנַעַן בַּשָּׁנָה הַהִיא: וַיְהִי בִּהְיוֹת יְהוֹשֻׁעַ
בִּירִיחוֹ וַיִּשָּׂא עֵינָיו וַיַּרְא וְהִנֵּה־אִישׁ עֹמֵד לְנֶגְדּוֹ וְחַרְבּוֹ
שְׁלוּפָה בְּיָדוֹ וַיֵּלֶךְ יְהוֹשֻׁעַ אֵלָיו וַיֹּאמֶר לוֹ הֲלָנוּ אַתָּה אִם־
יד לְצָרֵינוּ: וַיֹּאמֶר ׀ לֹא כִּי אֲנִי שַׂר־צְבָא־יְהוָה עַתָּה בָאתִי
וַיִּפֹּל יְהוֹשֻׁעַ אֶל־פָּנָיו אַרְצָה וַיִּשְׁתָּחוּ וַיֹּאמֶר לוֹ מָה אֲדֹנִי
טו מְדַבֵּר אֶל־עַבְדּוֹ: וַיֹּאמֶר שַׂר־צְבָא יְהוָה אֶל־יְהוֹשֻׁעַ שַׁל־
נַעַלְךָ מֵעַל רַגְלֶךָ כִּי הַמָּקוֹם אֲשֶׁר אַתָּה עֹמֵד עָלָיו קֹדֶשׁ
ו א הוּא וַיַּעַשׂ יְהוֹשֻׁעַ כֵּן: וִירִיחוֹ סֹגֶרֶת וּמְסֻגֶּרֶת מִפְּנֵי בְּנֵי
יִשְׂרָאֵל אֵין יוֹצֵא וְאֵין בָּא:

הפטרת יום שני של פסח בחוץ לארץ

The מפטיר *of* יום שני של פסח בחוץ לארץ *is read from* במדבר כח, טו–כה.

מלכים ב׳
Yemenites begin here

כב א בֶּן־שְׁמֹנֶה שָׁנָה יֹאשִׁיָּהוּ בְמָלְכוֹ וּשְׁלֹשִׁים וְאַחַת שָׁנָה מָלַךְ
ב בִּירוּשָׁלִָם וְשֵׁם אִמּוֹ יְדִידָה בַת־עֲדָיָה מִבָּצְקַת: וַיַּעַשׂ הַיָּשָׁר
בְּעֵינֵי יְהוָה וַיֵּלֶךְ בְּכָל־דֶּרֶךְ דָּוִד אָבִיו וְלֹא־סָר יָמִין וּשְׂמֹאול:

SECOND DAY OF PESAḤ IN THE DIASPORA

In this *haftara* we read of the far-reaching reforms of King Yoshiyahu of Yehuda. The rule of his grandfather, Menashe, had been catastrophic, normalizing idolatry throughout the kingdom and converting the Temple of Jerusalem into a house of worship for Ashera. After the short rule and violent death of his father, Amon, Yoshiyahu sought to make amends, in consultation with the High Priest Ḥilkiyahu. He renovated the Temple, removing the idols there, and

3 David, straying neither right nor left. In the eighteenth year of
King Yoshiyahu, the king sent the scribe Shafan son of Atzalyahu
son of Meshulam to the House of the LORD with this message:
4 "Go up to Ḥilkiyahu the High Priest and have him calculate the
silver that has been brought to the House of the LORD, which the
5 guardians of the threshold have collected from the people. Have
them give it to the foremen in charge of the House of the LORD,
and they will pay it out to the workers in the House of the LORD
6 to keep the House in repair – to the carpenters, builders, and
masons – and to purchase wood and quarry stones to repair the
7 House. But there is no need to keep track of the silver entrusted
to them, for they deal honestly."
23 1 The king summoned all the elders of Yehuda and Jerusalem,
2 who gathered to him. And the king went up to the House of the
LORD, along with all the men of Yehuda and all the inhabitants
of Jerusalem, the priests and the prophets and all the people,
from the smallest to the greatest. And he read out to them all
the words of the scroll of the covenant that had been found in
3 the House of the LORD. The king stood on the platform and reinstated the covenant before the LORD: to follow the LORD and
to keep His commandments, decrees, and laws with all their
heart and all their soul; to fulfill the words of this covenant as
written in this book. And all the people pledged themselves to
4 the covenant. The king then commanded Ḥilkiyahu, the High
Priest, the deputy priests, and the guardians of the threshold to
remove from the LORD's Sanctuary all the vessels that had been
made for Baal, Ashera, and all the heavenly hosts. He burned
them outside of Jerusalem in the fields of Kidron and removed
5 their ashes to Beit El. He shut down the idolatrous priests whom
the kings of Yehuda had appointed to offer sacrifices at the high
shrines in the towns of Yehuda and the area around Jerusalem as
well as those who offered sacrifices to Baal, to the sun and moon
6 and stars, and to all the heavenly hosts. He brought out the Ashera from the House of the LORD to the Kidron Valley outside
of Jerusalem, and he burned it in the Kidron Valley and ground
it to dust, then he scattered the dust over the common burial
7 ground. He tore down the booths of the male ritual prostitutes
in the House of the LORD, where the women would weave cov-
8 erings for Ashera. He brought in all the priests from the towns
of Yehuda and defiled the high shrines where the priests had

Ashkenazim and Sepharadim begin here
Yemenites skip this

ג וַיְהִי בִּשְׁמֹנֶה עֶשְׂרֵה שָׁנָה לַמֶּלֶךְ יֹאשִׁיָּהוּ שָׁלַח הַמֶּלֶךְ אֶת־
ד שָׁפָן בֶּן־אֲצַלְיָהוּ בֶן־מְשֻׁלָּם הַסֹּפֵר בֵּית יְהוָה לֵאמֹר׃ עֲלֵה
אֶל־חִלְקִיָּהוּ הַכֹּהֵן הַגָּדוֹל וְיַתֵּם אֶת־הַכֶּסֶף הַמּוּבָא בֵּית
ה יְהוָה אֲשֶׁר אָסְפוּ שֹׁמְרֵי הַסַּף מֵאֵת הָעָם׃ וְיִתְּנֻה עַל־יַד עֹשֵׂי
הַמְּלָאכָה הַמֻּפְקָדִים בבית יְהוָה וְיִתְּנוּ אֹתוֹ לְעֹשֵׂי הַמְּלָאכָה בֵּית
ו אֲשֶׁר בְּבֵית יְהוָה לְחַזֵּק בֶּדֶק הַבָּיִת׃ לֶחָרָשִׁים וְלַבֹּנִים
וְלַגֹּדְרִים וְלִקְנוֹת עֵצִים וְאַבְנֵי מַחְצֵב לְחַזֵּק אֶת־הַבָּיִת׃
ז אַךְ לֹא־יֵחָשֵׁב אִתָּם הַכֶּסֶף הַנִּתָּן עַל־יָדָם כִּי בֶאֱמוּנָה הֵם
עֹשִׂים׃

Ashkenazim and Sephardim begin here Yemenites skip this

כג א וַיִּשְׁלַח הַמֶּלֶךְ וַיַּאַסְפוּ אֵלָיו כָּל־זִקְנֵי יְהוּדָה וִירוּשָׁלִָם׃ ב וַיַּעַל
הַמֶּלֶךְ בֵּית־יְהוָה וְכָל־אִישׁ יְהוּדָה וְכָל־יֹשְׁבֵי יְרוּשָׁלִַם אִתּוֹ
וְהַכֹּהֲנִים וְהַנְּבִיאִים וְכָל־הָעָם לְמִקָּטֹן וְעַד־גָּדוֹל וַיִּקְרָא
בְאָזְנֵיהֶם אֶת־כָּל־דִּבְרֵי סֵפֶר הַבְּרִית הַנִּמְצָא בְּבֵית יְהוָה׃
ג וַיַּעֲמֹד הַמֶּלֶךְ עַל־הָעַמּוּד וַיִּכְרֹת אֶת־הַבְּרִית ׀ לִפְנֵי יְהוָה
לָלֶכֶת אַחַר יְהוָה וְלִשְׁמֹר מִצְוֺתָיו וְאֶת־עֵדְוֺתָיו וְאֶת־חֻקֹּתָיו
בְּכָל־לֵב וּבְכָל־נֶפֶשׁ לְהָקִים אֶת־דִּבְרֵי הַבְּרִית הַזֹּאת
ד הַכְּתֻבִים עַל־הַסֵּפֶר הַזֶּה וַיַּעֲמֹד כָּל־הָעָם בַּבְּרִית׃ וַיְצַו
הַמֶּלֶךְ אֶת־חִלְקִיָּהוּ הַכֹּהֵן הַגָּדוֹל וְאֶת־כֹּהֲנֵי הַמִּשְׁנֶה וְאֶת־
שֹׁמְרֵי הַסַּף לְהוֹצִיא מֵהֵיכַל יְהוָה אֵת כָּל־הַכֵּלִים הָעֲשׂוּיִם
לַבַּעַל וְלָאֲשֵׁרָה וּלְכֹל צְבָא הַשָּׁמָיִם וַיִּשְׂרְפֵם מִחוּץ לִירוּשָׁלִַם
ה בְּשַׁדְמוֹת קִדְרוֹן וְנָשָׂא אֶת־עֲפָרָם בֵּית־אֵל׃ וְהִשְׁבִּית אֶת־
הַכְּמָרִים אֲשֶׁר נָתְנוּ מַלְכֵי יְהוּדָה וַיְקַטֵּר בַּבָּמוֹת בְּעָרֵי
יְהוּדָה וּמְסִבֵּי יְרוּשָׁלִָם וְאֶת־הַמְקַטְּרִים לַבַּעַל לַשֶּׁמֶשׁ וְלַיָּרֵחַ
ו וְלַמַּזָּלוֹת וּלְכֹל צְבָא הַשָּׁמָיִם׃ וַיֹּצֵא אֶת־הָאֲשֵׁרָה מִבֵּית
יְהוָה מִחוּץ לִירוּשָׁלִַם אֶל־נַחַל קִדְרוֹן וַיִּשְׂרֹף אֹתָהּ בְּנַחַל
קִדְרוֹן וַיָּדֶק לְעָפָר וַיַּשְׁלֵךְ אֶת־עֲפָרָהּ עַל־קֶבֶר בְּנֵי הָעָם׃
ז וַיִּתֹּץ אֶת־בָּתֵּי הַקְּדֵשִׁים אֲשֶׁר בְּבֵית יְהוָה אֲשֶׁר הַנָּשִׁים
ח אֹרְגוֹת שָׁם בָּתִּים לָאֲשֵׁרָה׃ וַיָּבֵא אֶת־כָּל־הַכֹּהֲנִים מֵעָרֵי

offered sacrifices from Geva to Be'er Sheva. And he tore down
the high shrines by the gates, those by the entrance to the gate
of Joshua, the city governor; they were on a person's left at the
9 city gate. Though the shrine priests could not go up to the Altar
of the LORD in Jerusalem, they did eat of the unleavened bread
along with their kin.
21 The king then commanded all the people: "Make the Passover *Yemenites continue here*
sacrifice to the LORD your God, as it is written in this book of
22 the covenant." Now no such Passover sacrifice had been made
since the days of the judges who ruled Israel, nor throughout all
23 the time of the kings of Israel or the kings of Yehuda. But in the
eighteenth year of King Yoshiyahu, such a Passover sacrifice was
24 made to the LORD in Jerusalem. As for the necromancers, me-
diums, household gods, idols, and all the detestable things that
had appeared in the land of Yehuda and Jerusalem, Yoshiyahu
stamped them out in order to uphold the words of the teaching
written in the book that Ḥilkiyahu the priest had found in the
25 House of the LORD. There was none like him before him – a king
who returned to the LORD with all his heart, all his soul, and all
his might, following all the teaching of Moshe, and none like him
ever arose after him.

HAFTARAT SHABBAT ḤOL HAMOED PESAḤ

The maftir of Shabbat Ḥol HaMoed Pesaḥ is read from Numbers 28:19–25.

36 37 So says the Lord GOD: This, too – I will respond to the House EZEKIEL *Yemenites begin here*
of Israel's request to do this for them: I will multiply their people
38 like a flock of sheep, like the flocks for sacred offerings, like the

graves of the people of Israel, resurrecting them, clothing them in flesh and sinew, and breathing the spirit of life back into them echoes the themes of hope and redemption that are the primary focus of the holiday of Pesaḥ. The culmination

יְהוּדָה וַיְטַמֵּא אֶת־הַבָּמוֹת אֲשֶׁר קִטְּרוּ־שָׁמָּה הַכֹּהֲנִים
מִגֶּבַע עַד־בְּאֵר שָׁבַע וְנָתַץ אֶת־בָּמוֹת הַשְּׁעָרִים אֲשֶׁר־פֶּתַח
שַׁעַר יְהוֹשֻׁעַ שַׂר־הָעִיר אֲשֶׁר־עַל־שְׂמֹאול אִישׁ בְּשַׁעַר
ט הָעִיר: אַךְ לֹא יַעֲלוּ כֹּהֲנֵי הַבָּמוֹת אֶל־מִזְבַּח יהוה בִּירוּשָׁלָם
כִּי אִם־אָכְלוּ מַצּוֹת בְּתוֹךְ אֲחֵיהֶם:
Yemenites continue here
כא וַיְצַו הַמֶּלֶךְ אֶת־כָּל־הָעָם לֵאמֹר עֲשׂוּ פֶסַח לַיהוה אֱלֹהֵיכֶם
כב כַּכָּתוּב עַל סֵפֶר הַבְּרִית הַזֶּה: כִּי לֹא נַעֲשָׂה כַּפֶּסַח הַזֶּה מִימֵי
הַשֹּׁפְטִים אֲשֶׁר שָׁפְטוּ אֶת־יִשְׂרָאֵל וְכֹל יְמֵי מַלְכֵי יִשְׂרָאֵל
כג וּמַלְכֵי יְהוּדָה: כִּי אִם־בִּשְׁמֹנֶה עֶשְׂרֵה שָׁנָה לַמֶּלֶךְ יֹאשִׁיָּהוּ
כד נַעֲשָׂה הַפֶּסַח הַזֶּה לַיהוה בִּירוּשָׁלָם: וְגַם אֶת־הָאֹבוֹת וְאֶת־
הַיִּדְּעֹנִים וְאֶת־הַתְּרָפִים וְאֶת־הַגִּלֻּלִים וְאֵת כָּל־הַשִּׁקֻּצִים
אֲשֶׁר נִרְאוּ בְּאֶרֶץ יְהוּדָה וּבִירוּשָׁלַם בִּעֵר יֹאשִׁיָּהוּ לְמַעַן
הָקִים אֶת־דִּבְרֵי הַתּוֹרָה הַכְּתֻבִים עַל־הַסֵּפֶר אֲשֶׁר מָצָא
כה חִלְקִיָּהוּ הַכֹּהֵן בֵּית יהוה: וְכָמֹהוּ לֹא־הָיָה לְפָנָיו מֶלֶךְ
אֲשֶׁר־שָׁב אֶל־יהוה בְּכָל־לְבָבוֹ וּבְכָל־נַפְשׁוֹ וּבְכָל־מְאֹדוֹ
כְּכֹל תּוֹרַת מֹשֶׁה וְאַחֲרָיו לֹא־קָם כָּמֹהוּ:

הפטרת שבת
חול המועד פסח

The מפטיר *of* שבת חול המועד פסח *is read from* במדבר כח, יט–כה.

יחזקאל
Yemenites begin here

לו לז כֹּה אָמַר אֲדֹנָי יֱהוִה עוֹד זֹאת אִדָּרֵשׁ לְבֵית־יִשְׂרָאֵל לַעֲשׂוֹת
לח לָהֶם אַרְבֶּה אֹתָם כַּצֹּאן אָדָם: כְּצֹאן קָדָשִׁים כְּצֹאן יְרוּשָׁלַם

SHABBAT ḤOL HAMOED PESAḤ
The famous vision of the dry bones, shown by God to Yeḥezkel in the aftermath of the destruction of Jerusalem, has earned a place of prominence in the popular consciousness as a powerfully moving allegory for salvation and deliverance. The image of God opening up the

▶

flocks of Jerusalem during her holy times; this is how the ruined
cities will be, filled with flocks of people, and they will know that
I am the LORD."

Ashkenazim and Sephardim begin here

37 1 And the hand of the LORD came upon me. He brought me out
by the spirit of the LORD and set me down in the valley. It was
2 full of bones. He led me around through them all; there were so
very many of them out upon the valley, and they were utterly dry.
3 And He said to me, "Man, can they come to life, these bones?"
4 And I said, "My Lord GOD, You know." He said to me: "Prophesy
to these bones; say to them: Dry bones – hear the word of the
5 LORD! So says the Lord GOD to these bones: See – I will bring
6 breath into you, and you will come to life. I will give you sinews,
I will make flesh grow on you, I will spread skin over you, I will
put breath into you, you will come to life, and you will know that
7 I am the LORD." I prophesied as I had been commanded. There
was a noise as I was prophesying, and then a rattling, and the
8 bones moved together, each bone to its bone. And I saw there
on them sinews, flesh forming, and skin spreading a cover over
9 them – but there was no breath in them. And He said to me:
"Prophesy to the breath; Man, prophesy and say to the breath: So
says the Lord GOD: From the four winds, come; breath, breathe
10 into these slain so that they come to life." I prophesied as He had
commanded me, and the breath entered them, and they came to
11 life; they stood upon their feet, a vast army. And He said to me:
"Man, these bones are the whole House of Israel. See, they say,
'Our bones are dried out, our hope is lost, and we are completely
12 cut off.' So, prophesy; say to them: So says the Lord GOD: See, I
am opening up your graves; I will lift you out of your graves, My
13 people, and I will bring you to the soil of Israel. You will know
that I am the LORD when I open up your graves, when I lift you
14 out of your graves, My people. I will put My breath into you, and
you will come to life; I will set you upon your soil, and you will
know that I am the LORD; I have spoken, and I will do it, declares the LORD."

---

exile and complete restoration, just as the Israelites were saved from Egypt and brought to the promised land so many years ago.

בְּמוֹעֲדֶיהָ כֵּן תִּהְיֶינָה הֶעָרִים הֶחֳרֵבוֹת מְלֵאוֹת צֹאן אָדָם
וְיָדְעוּ כִּי־אֲנִי יְהוָה׃

Ashkenazim and Sepharadim begin here

לז א הָיְתָה עָלַי יַד־יְהוָה וַיּוֹצִאֵנִי בְרוּחַ יְהוָה וַיְנִיחֵנִי בְּתוֹךְ
ב הַבִּקְעָה וְהִיא מְלֵאָה עֲצָמוֹת׃ וְהֶעֱבִירַנִי עֲלֵיהֶם סָבִיב ׀
סָבִיב וְהִנֵּה רַבּוֹת מְאֹד עַל־פְּנֵי הַבִּקְעָה וְהִנֵּה יְבֵשׁוֹת מְאֹד׃
ג וַיֹּאמֶר אֵלַי בֶּן־אָדָם הֲתִחְיֶינָה הָעֲצָמוֹת הָאֵלֶּה וָאֹמַר אֲדֹנָי
ד יֱהוִה אַתָּה יָדָעְתָּ׃ וַיֹּאמֶר אֵלַי הִנָּבֵא עַל־הָעֲצָמוֹת הָאֵלֶּה
ה וְאָמַרְתָּ אֲלֵיהֶם הָעֲצָמוֹת הַיְבֵשׁוֹת שִׁמְעוּ דְּבַר־יְהוָה׃ כֹּה
אָמַר אֲדֹנָי יֱהוִה לָעֲצָמוֹת הָאֵלֶּה הִנֵּה אֲנִי מֵבִיא בָכֶם רוּחַ
ו וִחְיִיתֶם׃ וְנָתַתִּי עֲלֵיכֶם גִּידִים וְהַעֲלֵתִי עֲלֵיכֶם בָּשָׂר וְקָרַמְתִּי
עֲלֵיכֶם עוֹר וְנָתַתִּי בָכֶם רוּחַ וִחְיִיתֶם וִידַעְתֶּם כִּי־אֲנִי יְהוָה׃
ז וְנִבֵּאתִי כַּאֲשֶׁר צֻוֵּיתִי וַיְהִי־קוֹל כְּהִנָּבְאִי וְהִנֵּה־רַעַשׁ
ח וַתִּקְרְבוּ עֲצָמוֹת עֶצֶם אֶל־עַצְמוֹ׃ וְרָאִיתִי וְהִנֵּה־עֲלֵיהֶם גִּדִים
וּבָשָׂר עָלָה וַיִּקְרַם עֲלֵיהֶם עוֹר מִלְמָעְלָה וְרוּחַ אֵין בָּהֶם׃
ט וַיֹּאמֶר אֵלַי הִנָּבֵא אֶל־הָרוּחַ הִנָּבֵא בֶן־אָדָם וְאָמַרְתָּ אֶל־
הָרוּחַ כֹּה־אָמַר ׀ אֲדֹנָי יֱהוִה מֵאַרְבַּע רוּחוֹת בֹּאִי הָרוּחַ
י וּפְחִי בַּהֲרוּגִים הָאֵלֶּה וְיִחְיוּ׃ וְהִנַּבֵּאתִי כַּאֲשֶׁר צִוָּנִי וַתָּבוֹא
בָהֶם הָרוּחַ וַיִּחְיוּ וַיַּעַמְדוּ עַל־רַגְלֵיהֶם חַיִל גָּדוֹל מְאֹד מְאֹד׃
יא וַיֹּאמֶר אֵלַי בֶּן־אָדָם הָעֲצָמוֹת הָאֵלֶּה כָּל־בֵּית יִשְׂרָאֵל הֵמָּה
הִנֵּה אֹמְרִים יָבְשׁוּ עַצְמוֹתֵינוּ וְאָבְדָה תִקְוָתֵנוּ נִגְזַרְנוּ לָנוּ׃
יב לָכֵן הִנָּבֵא וְאָמַרְתָּ אֲלֵיהֶם כֹּה־אָמַר אֲדֹנָי יֱהוִה הִנֵּה אֲנִי
פֹתֵחַ אֶת־קִבְרוֹתֵיכֶם וְהַעֲלֵיתִי אֶתְכֶם מִקִּבְרוֹתֵיכֶם עַמִּי
יג וְהֵבֵאתִי אֶתְכֶם אֶל־אַדְמַת יִשְׂרָאֵל׃ וִידַעְתֶּם כִּי־אֲנִי יְהוָה
בְּפִתְחִי אֶת־קִבְרוֹתֵיכֶם וּבְהַעֲלוֹתִי אֶתְכֶם מִקִּבְרוֹתֵיכֶם
יד עַמִּי׃ וְנָתַתִּי רוּחִי בָכֶם וִחְיִיתֶם וְהִנַּחְתִּי אֶתְכֶם עַל־
אַדְמַתְכֶם וִידַעְתֶּם כִּי אֲנִי יְהוָה דִּבַּרְתִּי וְעָשִׂיתִי נְאֻם־יְהוָה׃

of the vision – a divine promise to bring the great, resurrected host and replant them on the soil of Israel – inspires us today with hope for a future end to the

Haftara for the Seventh Day of Pesaḥ

The maftir of the seventh day of Pesaḥ is read from Numbers 28:19–25.

22 1 David uttered these words of song to the Lord on the day that II SAMUEL
the Lord saved him from the hands of all his enemies and
2 from the hand of Sha'ul. He said: The Lord is my Rock and
3 my fortress, my own rescuer; // my God is the Rock of my
refuge / my shield, the horn of my salvation, my haven, / my
4 refuge, my savior who delivers me from violence. // Praise!
When I call on the Lord, / I am saved from my enemies. //
5 For when waves of death assailed me, / deadly torrents en-
6 gulfed me, the cords of Sheol entangled me, / snares of death
7 confronted me, // in my distress I called on the Lord; /
I called out to my God; / He heard my voice from His
8 temple, / and my cry rang in His ears. // Then the earth
shook and shuddered; / the foundations of heaven trembled; /
9 they shuddered from His wrath. //Smoke issued from His
nostrils; / devouring flames flared from His mouth; / from
10 Him gleaming coals blazed forth. // He bent the heavens and
11 descended, / dense cloud beneath His feet; / He mounted
12 a cherub and flew, / appearing on wings of wind. // He surrounded Himself with a shelter of darkness, / of heavy storm
13 clouds dense with rain. // From the brilliant glow of His pres-
14 ence / blazed fiery coals. // The Lord thundered from the
15 heavens; / the Most High raised His voice; / He shot arrows
16 to scatter them, / lightning bolts to rout them. // The ocean

subdued, oppressed, and persecuted, like the Israelites in Egypt generations before. Overshadowed at first by his brothers, his rise to prominence was frustrated by the jealousy of King Sha'ul, and he was forced to spend years in hiding. Even after Sha'ul's death, the early days of David's reign were fraught with dangers from Sha'ul's loyalists and foreign kings and warlords bent on quashing his kingdom before it could grow. David's constant loyalty to God, however, was repaid in full by a series of miraculous and improbable victories over all who sought to stymie him. At every stage, David recognized that triumph and salvation comes not through our own strength or talents, but by God's favor. Now, finally victorious over all his enemies, David offers a paean of thanks to the Almighty for his deliverance, no less stirring than that of his ancient ancestors.

הפטרת יום שביעי
של פסח

The מפטיר *of* יום שביעי של פסח *is read from* במדבר כח, יט–כה.

כב א וַיְדַבֵּר דָּוִד לַיהוָה אֶת־דִּבְרֵי הַשִּׁירָה הַזֹּאת בְּיוֹם שמואל ב׳
הִצִּיל יְהוָה אֹתוֹ מִכַּף כָּל־אֹיְבָיו וּמִכַּף שָׁאוּל:
ב וַיֹּאמַר יְהוָה סַלְעִי וּמְצֻדָתִי וּמְפַלְטִי־לִי: ג אֱלֹהֵי
צוּרִי אֶחֱסֶה־בּוֹ מָגִנִּי וְקֶרֶן יִשְׁעִי מִשְׂגַּבִּי
ד וּמְנוּסִי מֹשִׁעִי מֵחָמָס תֹּשִׁעֵנִי: מְהֻלָּל
ה אֶקְרָא יְהוָה וּמֵאֹיְבַי אִוָּשֵׁעַ: כִּי אֲפָפֻנִי מִשְׁבְּרֵי־
ו מָוֶת נַחֲלֵי בְלִיַּעַל יְבַעֲתֻנִי: חֶבְלֵי
שְׁאוֹל סַבֻּנִי קִדְּמֻנִי מֹקְשֵׁי־
ז מָוֶת: בַּצַּר־לִי אֶקְרָא יְהוָה וְאֶל־
אֱלֹהַי אֶקְרָא וַיִּשְׁמַע מֵהֵיכָלוֹ
ח קוֹלִי וְשַׁוְעָתִי בְּאָזְנָיו: ותגעש וַיִּתְגָּעַשׁ
וַתִּרְעַשׁ הָאָרֶץ מוֹסְדוֹת הַשָּׁמַיִם
ט יִרְגָּזוּ וַיִּתְגָּעֲשׁוּ כִּי־חָרָה לוֹ: עָלָה
עָשָׁן בְּאַפּוֹ וְאֵשׁ מִפִּיו
י תֹּאכֵל גֶּחָלִים בָּעֲרוּ מִמֶּנּוּ: וַיֵּט
שָׁמַיִם וַיֵּרַד וַעֲרָפֶל תַּחַת
יא רַגְלָיו: וַיִּרְכַּב עַל־כְּרוּב וַיָּעֹף וַיֵּרָא
יב עַל־כַּנְפֵי־רוּחַ: וַיָּשֶׁת חֹשֶׁךְ סְבִיבֹתָיו
יג סֻכּוֹת חַשְׁרַת־מַיִם עָבֵי שְׁחָקִים: מִנֹּגַהּ
יד נֶגְדּוֹ בָּעֲרוּ גַּחֲלֵי־אֵשׁ: יַרְעֵם מִן־שָׁמַיִם
טו יְהוָה וְעֶלְיוֹן יִתֵּן קוֹלוֹ: וַיִּשְׁלַח
טז חִצִּים וַיְפִיצֵם בָּרָק ויהמם: וַיֵּרָאוּ אֲפִקֵי וַיָּהֹם

SEVENTH DAY OF PESAḤ

Having just read the triumphant Song of the Sea in the wake of God's rescue of Israel from Pharaoh's armies, we now turn to a parallel song in the words of the prophets. King David began his life

bed was exposed, / the foundations of the world laid bare /
by the onslaught of the LORD, / by the blast of His breath. //
17 From on high He reached down and took me; / He drew me out
18 of the mighty waters. // He saved me from my fierce enemy, /
19 from foes too strong for me. // They confronted me on my dir-
20 est day, / but the LORD was my support. // He brought me out
to freedom; / He rescued me because He delighted in me. //
21 The LORD rewarded me as I deserved; / as my hands were
22 clean, He repaid me, / for I kept the ways of the LORD / and
23 did not betray my God, / for all His laws are before me; / I will
24 not turn away from His statutes. / I am blameless to Him / and
25 keep myself from sin. / So the LORD repaid me as I deserved /
26 as I was pure in His sight. // You deal loyally with those who are
loyal, / to the blameless warrior You show Yourself blameless;
27 / You are pure with those who are pure, / but with the crooked,
28 You are shrewd. / You bring salvation to a humble people; / You
29 cast Your eyes down on the haughty. // For You are my lamp,
30 LORD; / the LORD lights up my darkness. / With You I can rush
31 a ridge; / with my God I can leap over a wall. // God's ways are
blameless; / the LORD's words are pure; / He is a shield to all who
32 take refuge in Him. // For who is a god besides the LORD; / who
33 is a Rock besides our God? / God is my powerful stronghold; /
34 He frees my way so it is sound. / He makes my legs like a deer's
35 / and stands me on the heights. / He trains my hands for battle
36 / so that my arms can bend a bow of bronze. // You gave me the
shield of Your victory; / Your battle cry stirred me with power. /
37 You made my steps broad and firm; / my feet never faltered. / I

יָ֔ם יִגָּל֖וּ מֹסְד֣וֹת תֵּבֵ֑ל בְּגַעֲרַ֣ת
יז יְהוָ֔ה מִנִּשְׁמַ֖ת ר֥וּחַ אַפּֽוֹ׃ יִשְׁלַ֥ח מִמָּר֖וֹם
יח יִקָּחֵ֑נִי יַמְשֵׁ֖נִי מִמַּ֥יִם רַבִּֽים׃ יַצִּילֵ֕נִי
מֵאֹיְבִ֖י עָ֑ז מִשֹּׂנְאַ֕י כִּ֥י אָמְצ֖וּ
יט מִמֶּֽנִּי׃ יְקַדְּמֻ֖נִי בְּי֣וֹם אֵידִ֑י וַיְהִ֧י
כ יְהוָ֛ה מִשְׁעָ֖ן לִֽי׃ וַיֹּצֵ֥א לַמֶּרְחָ֖ב
כא אֹתִ֑י יְחַלְּצֵ֖נִי כִּי־חָ֥פֵֽץ בִּֽי׃ יִגְמְלֵ֥נִי
יְהוָ֖ה כְּצִדְקָתִ֑י כְּבֹ֥ר יָדַ֖י יָשִׁ֥יב
כב לִֽי׃ כִּ֥י שָׁמַ֖רְתִּי דַּרְכֵ֣י יְהוָ֑ה וְלֹ֥א
כג רָשַׁ֖עְתִּי מֵאֱלֹהָֽי׃ כִּ֥י כָל־מִשְׁפָּטָ֖ו
כד לְנֶגְדִּ֑י וְחֻקֹּתָ֖יו לֹא־אָס֥וּר מִמֶּֽנָּה׃ וָאֶהְיֶ֥ה
כה תָמִ֖ים ל֑וֹ וָאֶשְׁתַּמְּרָ֖ה מֵעֲוֺנִֽי׃ וַיָּ֧שֶׁב יְהוָ֛ה לִ֖י
כו כְּצִדְקָתִ֑י כְּבֹרִ֖י לְנֶ֥גֶד עֵינָֽיו׃ עִם־
חָסִ֖יד תִּתְחַסָּ֑ד עִם־גִּבּ֥וֹר תָּמִ֖ים
כז תִּתַּמָּֽם׃ עִם־נָבָ֖ר תִּתָּבָ֑ר וְעִם־
כח עִקֵּ֖שׁ תִּתַּפָּֽל׃ וְאֶת־עַ֥ם עָנִ֖י
כט תּוֹשִׁ֑יעַ וְעֵינֶ֖יךָ עַל־רָמִ֥ים תַּשְׁפִּֽיל׃ כִּֽי־
אַתָּ֥ה נֵירִ֖י יְהוָ֑ה וַיהוָ֖ה יַגִּ֥יהַּ
ל חָשְׁכִּֽי׃ כִּ֥י בְכָ֖ה אָר֣וּץ גְּד֑וּד בֵּאלֹהַ֖י
לא אֲדַלֶּג־שֽׁוּר׃ הָאֵ֖ל תָּמִ֣ים
דַּרְכּ֑וֹ אִמְרַ֤ת יְהוָה֙ צְרוּפָ֔ה מָגֵ֣ן
לב ה֔וּא לְכֹ֖ל הַחֹסִ֥ים בּֽוֹ׃ כִּ֥י מִי־אֵ֖ל מִבַּלְעֲדֵ֣י
לג יְהוָ֑ה וּמִ֥י צ֖וּר מִבַּלְעֲדֵ֥י אֱלֹהֵֽינוּ׃ הָאֵ֖ל
מָעוּזִּ֣י חָ֑יִל וַיַּתֵּ֥ר תָּמִ֖ים
לד דרכו׃ מְשַׁוֶּ֥ה רגליו כָּֽאַיָּל֑וֹת וְעַל־ דַּרְכִּ֖י | רַגְלַ֑י
לה בָּמֹתַ֖י יַֽעֲמִדֵֽנִי׃ מְלַמֵּ֥ד יָדַ֖י
לו לַמִּלְחָמָ֑ה וְנִחַ֥ת קֶֽשֶׁת־נְחוּשָׁ֖ה זְרֹעֹתָֽי׃ וַתִּתֶּן־
לז לִ֖י מָגֵ֣ן יִשְׁעֶ֑ךָ וַעֲנֹתְךָ֖ תַּרְבֵּֽנִי׃ תַּרְחִ֥יב צַעֲדִ֖י

pursued my enemy to destroy them, / never turning back until
39 they perished. / I cut them down and crushed them, and they
40 did not rise; / they fell beneath my feet. / You girded me with
41 power for battle / and sunk my adversaries far beneath me; / You
made my enemies turn tail before me; / my foes, too, I destroyed.
42 / They looked wildly about, but there was no savior – / called out
43 to the LORD, but He did not answer them – // while I ground
them up like dust of the earth; / I crushed and pounded them
44 like street-mud. // You rescued me from civil strife; / you kept
me as the head of nations; / peoples I never knew of serve me. /
45 Foreign peoples come cringing before me; / they merely hear me
46 and obey; / foreign peoples lose heart / and come trembling out
47 of their forts. // The LORD lives! / Blessed is my Rock; / exalted
48 is God, Rock of my rescue! / God who grants vengeance to me, /
49 who subjugates people under me, / my redeemer from my enemies, / You raise me above those who rise against me; / You
50 save me from violent men. // So I praise You, LORD, among the
51 nations, / and sing to Your name. // He is a tower of victory for
His king / and shows loyalty to His anointed, / to David and his
seed forever.

לח תַּחְתֵּנִי וְלֹא מָעֲדוּ קַרְסֻלָּי׃ אֶרְדְּפָה
אֹיְבַי וָאַשְׁמִידֵם וְלֹא אָשׁוּב עַד־
לט כַּלּוֹתָם׃ וָאֲכַלֵּם וָאֶמְחָצֵם וְלֹא יְקוּמוּן וַיִּפְּלוּ
מ תַּחַת רַגְלָי׃ וַתַּזְרֵנִי חַיִל
מא לַמִּלְחָמָה תַּכְרִיעַ קָמַי תַּחְתֵּנִי׃ וְאֹיְבַי
מב תַּתָּה לִּי עֹרֶף מְשַׂנְאַי וָאַצְמִיתֵם׃ יִשְׁעוּ וְאֵין
מג מֹשִׁיעַ אֶל־יְהוָה וְלֹא עָנָם׃ וְאֶשְׁחָקֵם
כַּעֲפַר־אָרֶץ כְּטִיט־חוּצוֹת אֲדִקֵּם
מד אֶרְקָעֵם׃ וַתְּפַלְּטֵנִי מֵרִיבֵי עַמִּי תִּשְׁמְרֵנִי
לְרֹאשׁ גּוֹיִם עַם לֹא־יָדַעְתִּי
מה יַעַבְדֻנִי׃ בְּנֵי נֵכָר יִתְכַּחֲשׁוּ־לִי לִשְׁמוֹעַ
מו אֹזֶן יִשָּׁמְעוּ לִי׃ בְּנֵי נֵכָר יִבֹּלוּ וְיַחְגְּרוּ
מז מִמִּסְגְּרוֹתָם׃ חַי־יְהוָה וּבָרוּךְ צוּרִי וְיָרֻם
מח אֱלֹהֵי צוּר יִשְׁעִי׃ הָאֵל הַנֹּתֵן נְקָמֹת
מט לִי וּמוֹרִיד עַמִּים תַּחְתֵּנִי׃ וּמוֹצִיאִי
מֵאֹיְבָי וּמִקָּמַי תְּרוֹמְמֵנִי מֵאִישׁ חֲמָסִים
נ תַּצִּילֵנִי׃ עַל־כֵּן אוֹדְךָ יְהוָה בַּגּוֹיִם וּלְשִׁמְךָ
נא אֲזַמֵּר׃ מגדיל יְשׁוּעוֹת מִגְדּוֹל
מַלְכּוֹ וְעֹשֶׂה־חֶסֶד לִמְשִׁיחוֹ
לְדָוִד וּלְזַרְעוֹ עַד־עוֹלָם׃

Haftara for the Eighth Day of Pesaḥ in the Diaspora

The maftir for the eighth day of Pesaḥ in the Diaspora is read from Numbers 28:19–25.

10 32 This very day, he stands at Nov, waving his hand toward the ISAIAH
33 mount of daughter Zion, Jerusalem's hill. Behold the
Master, the Lord of Hosts, stirring dread, shearing off branches.
Those who held their heads high are brought down; the exalted
34 will be laid low. He fells the forest groves with iron, Lebanon falls
11 1 to the blows of majesty. A new shoot will grow from
2 the stem of Yishai; from his roots a branch will bud. And the
spirit of the Lord will rest upon him – a spirit of wisdom, of
knowing, a spirit of guidance and might, a spirit of insight and
3 awe of the Lord. With awe of the Lord infusing his senses,
he will not judge by his eyes' perception, nor rule by what his
4 ears can grasp; he will judge poor people justly, render judgment rightly for oppressed ones in the land; he will strike the
land with the staff of his speech, and the spirit that crosses his
5 lips will execute those who do evil. He will gird his loins with
6 righteousness: his battle dress is truth. Wolf will lie down beside lamb, the leopard will lie beside the young goat; calf, lion
7 cub, fatted lamb together – a little child will tend them. The cow
and the bear will graze with their young lying down together,
8 and lion, like ox, will feed upon straw. A baby will play at the
cobra's hole, and an infant's hand will explore the viper's nest.
9 There will be no wrong or violence on all My holy mountain,
for knowledge of the Lord will fill the earth as waters cover the
10 ocean. On that day, that offshoot of Yishai that stands
as a banner to all the peoples, nations will come to seek him, and
11 his resting place will be glorious. On that day this will
be: The Lord will stretch forth His hand again to take back the

held captive for so long. This includes an oblique allusion to the splitting of the Sea of Reeds, commemorated on the last day of Pesaḥ: "The Lord will destroy the Egyptian Sea gulf and wave His hand over the River through His fearsome wind; He will beat it into seven separate streams that people may cross in their shoes. A path will be there for the remnant of His people, those who remain, from Assyria, as there was for the people of Israel on the day they came up from the land of Egypt."

הפטרת יום שמיני של פסח בחוץ לארץ

The מפטיר *of* יום שביעי של פסח *is read from* במדבר כח, יט–כה.

י לב עוֹד הַיּוֹם בְּנֹב לַעֲמֹד יְנֹפֵף יָדוֹ הַר בית־צִיּוֹן גִּבְעַת ישעיה בַּת־
לג יְרוּשָׁלִָם׃ הִנֵּה הָאָדוֹן יְהוָה צְבָאוֹת מְסָעֵף
לד פֻּארָה בְּמַעֲרָצָה וְרָמֵי הַקּוֹמָה גְּדֻעִים וְהַגְּבֹהִים יִשְׁפָּלוּ׃ וְנִקַּף
יא א סִבְכֵי הַיַּעַר בַּבַּרְזֶל וְהַלְּבָנוֹן בְּאַדִּיר יִפּוֹל׃ וְיָצָא
ב חֹטֶר מִגֵּזַע יִשָׁי וְנֵצֶר מִשָּׁרָשָׁיו יִפְרֶה׃ וְנָחָה עָלָיו רוּחַ יְהוָה
רוּחַ חָכְמָה וּבִינָה רוּחַ עֵצָה וּגְבוּרָה רוּחַ דַּעַת וְיִרְאַת
ג יְהוָה׃ וַהֲרִיחוֹ בְּיִרְאַת יְהוָה וְלֹא־לְמַרְאֵה עֵינָיו יִשְׁפּוֹט
ד וְלֹא־לְמִשְׁמַע אָזְנָיו יוֹכִיחַ׃ וְשָׁפַט בְּצֶדֶק דַּלִּים וְהוֹכִיחַ
בְּמִישׁוֹר לְעַנְוֵי־אָרֶץ וְהִכָּה־אֶרֶץ בְּשֵׁבֶט פִּיו וּבְרוּחַ שְׂפָתָיו
ה יָמִית רָשָׁע׃ וְהָיָה צֶדֶק אֵזוֹר מָתְנָיו וְהָאֱמוּנָה אֵזוֹר חֲלָצָיו׃
ו וְגָר זְאֵב עִם־כֶּבֶשׂ וְנָמֵר עִם־גְּדִי יִרְבָּץ וְעֵגֶל וּכְפִיר וּמְרִיא
ז יַחְדָּו וְנַעַר קָטֹן נֹהֵג בָּם׃ וּפָרָה וָדֹב תִּרְעֶינָה יַחְדָּו יִרְבְּצוּ
ח יַלְדֵיהֶן וְאַרְיֵה כַּבָּקָר יֹאכַל־תֶּבֶן׃ וְשִׁעֲשַׁע יוֹנֵק עַל־חֻר
ט פָּתֶן וְעַל מְאוּרַת צִפְעוֹנִי גָּמוּל יָדוֹ הָדָה׃ לֹא־יָרֵעוּ וְלֹא־
יַשְׁחִיתוּ בְּכָל־הַר קָדְשִׁי כִּי־מָלְאָה הָאָרֶץ דֵּעָה אֶת־יְהוָה
י כַּמַּיִם לַיָּם מְכַסִּים׃ וְהָיָה בַּיּוֹם הַהוּא שֹׁרֶשׁ
יִשַׁי אֲשֶׁר עֹמֵד לְנֵס עַמִּים אֵלָיו גּוֹיִם יִדְרֹשׁוּ וְהָיְתָה מְנֻחָתוֹ
יא כָּבוֹד׃ וְהָיָה ׀ בַּיּוֹם הַהוּא יוֹסִיף אֲדֹנָי ׀ שֵׁנִית
יָדוֹ לִקְנוֹת אֶת־שְׁאָר עַמּוֹ אֲשֶׁר יִשָּׁאֵר מֵאַשּׁוּר וּמִמִּצְרַיִם

EIGHTH DAY OF PESAḤ IN THE DIASPORA

Having read throughout the holiday of Pesaḥ of God's numerous deliverances of the Jewish people over history, we now, on the last day, turn to Isaiah's famous vision of the future redemption. This account includes some of the most well-known descriptions of that future time, an account of the Messiah and his personality, the image of the "lion lying down with the lamb," and the ingathering of the exiles from all the lands – including Egypt – where they will have been

remnant of His people, those who remain, from Assyria and
Egypt, from Patros and from Kush, from Eilam and from Shinar,
12 Ḥamat and the islands of the sea. He will lift up a banner to nations and gather in the banished ones of Israel; He will gather
in the scattered ones of Israel from all four edges of the world.
13 Efrayim's jealousy will fall away, the enemies in Yehuda will be
cut down, Efrayim will no more be jealous of Yehuda; Yehuda
14 will bear toward Efrayim no more enmity. They will fly west to
the Philistines, shoulder to shoulder; together they will sack the
people of the East; they will thrust their hand against Edom and
15 Moav, and the people of Amon will obey them. The LORD will
destroy the Egyptian Sea gulf and wave His hand over the River
through His fearsome wind; He will beat it into seven separate
16 streams that people may cross in their shoes. A path will be there
for the remnant of His people, those who remain, from Assyria,
as there was for the people of Israel on the day they came up
12 1 from the land of Egypt. And you will say on that day: *I thank You,*
LORD for You raged against me, but You turned back Your rage, and
2 *now You console me. Behold the God of my salvation; I trust and will*
not fear, for God, the LORD, is my strength and song, and now my sal-
3 *vation.* With joy you will draw water from the flowing springs of
4 rescue. And you will say upon that day: *Give thanks to the LORD;*
call on His name; proclaim His acts among the peoples; recount:
5 *His name is transcendent. Sing out to the LORD: He has performed*
6 *grandeur; all across the world this thing is known. Cry out, sing out*
joy, all you who dwell in Zion; for great in your midst is the Holy
One of Israel.

Haftara for the First Day of Shavuot

The maftir of the first day of Shavuot is read from Numbers 28:26–31.

1 1 It was in the thirtieth year in the fourth month on the fifth day EZEKIEL
of the month. I was in the exile, by the Kevar River; the heavens

God's majesty to the prophet Yeḥezkel, in exile in Babylon. The symbolism of the strange vision of God's chariot and the creatures bearing it has long been the subject of intense debate, and the Sages taught that speculation about it

וּמִפַּתְרוֹס וּמִכּוּשׁ וּמֵעֵילָם וּמִשִּׁנְעָר וּמֵחֲמָת וּמֵאִיֵּי הַיָּם׃
יב וְנָשָׂא נֵס לַגּוֹיִם וְאָסַף נִדְחֵי יִשְׂרָאֵל וּנְפֻצוֹת יְהוּדָה יְקַבֵּץ
יג מֵאַרְבַּע כַּנְפוֹת הָאָרֶץ׃ וְסָרָה קִנְאַת אֶפְרַיִם וְצֹרְרֵי יְהוּדָה
יִכָּרֵתוּ אֶפְרַיִם לֹא־יְקַנֵּא אֶת־יְהוּדָה וִיהוּדָה לֹא־יָצֹר אֶת־
יד אֶפְרָיִם׃ וְעָפוּ בְכָתֵף פְּלִשְׁתִּים יָמָּה יַחְדָּו יָבֹזּוּ אֶת־בְּנֵי־קֶדֶם
טו אֱדוֹם וּמוֹאָב מִשְׁלוֹחַ יָדָם וּבְנֵי עַמּוֹן מִשְׁמַעְתָּם׃ וְהֶחֱרִים
יהוה אֵת לְשׁוֹן יָם־מִצְרַיִם וְהֵנִיף יָדוֹ עַל־הַנָּהָר בַּעְיָם רוּחוֹ
טז וְהִכָּהוּ לְשִׁבְעָה נְחָלִים וְהִדְרִיךְ בַּנְּעָלִים׃ וְהָיְתָה מְסִלָּה
לִשְׁאָר עַמּוֹ אֲשֶׁר יִשָּׁאֵר מֵאַשּׁוּר כַּאֲשֶׁר הָיְתָה לְיִשְׂרָאֵל
יב א בְּיוֹם עֲלֹתוֹ מֵאֶרֶץ מִצְרָיִם׃ וְאָמַרְתָּ בַּיּוֹם הַהוּא אוֹדְךָ
ב יהוה כִּי אָנַפְתָּ בִּי יָשֹׁב אַפְּךָ וּתְנַחֲמֵנִי׃ הִנֵּה אֵל יְשׁוּעָתִי
אֶבְטַח וְלֹא אֶפְחָד כִּי־עָזִּי וְזִמְרָת יָהּ יהוה וַיְהִי־לִי לִישׁוּעָה׃
ג ד וּשְׁאַבְתֶּם־מַיִם בְּשָׂשׂוֹן מִמַּעַיְנֵי הַיְשׁוּעָה׃ וַאֲמַרְתֶּם בַּיּוֹם
הַהוּא הוֹדוּ לַיהוה קִרְאוּ בִשְׁמוֹ הוֹדִיעוּ בָעַמִּים עֲלִילֹתָיו
ה הַזְכִּירוּ כִּי נִשְׂגָּב שְׁמוֹ׃ זַמְּרוּ יהוה כִּי גֵאוּת עָשָׂה מידעת מוּדַעַת
ו זֹאת בְּכָל־הָאָרֶץ׃ צַהֲלִי וָרֹנִּי יוֹשֶׁבֶת צִיּוֹן כִּי־גָדוֹל בְּקִרְבֵּךְ
קְדוֹשׁ יִשְׂרָאֵל׃

הפטרת יום ראשון של שבועות

The מפטיר *of* יום ראשון של שבועות *is read from* במדבר כח, כו–לא.

א א וַיְהִי ׀ בִּשְׁלֹשִׁים שָׁנָה בָּרְבִיעִי בַּחֲמִשָּׁה לַחֹדֶשׁ וַאֲנִי בְתוֹךְ־ יחזקאל
הַגּוֹלָה עַל־נְהַר־כְּבָר נִפְתְּחוּ הַשָּׁמַיִם וָאֶרְאֶה מַרְאוֹת

FIRST DAY OF SHAVUOT

The holiday of Shavuot celebrates God's miraculous and awe-inspiring revelation at Mount Sinai. This *haftara* offers a fitting continuation of this theme by describing the incredible revelation of

2 opened up, and I saw Godly visions. On the fifth day of the
3 month, the fifth year of the exile of King Yoyakhin, so it was: the
word of the LORD came to Yeḥezkel son of Buzi the priest, in the
land of the Chaldeans by the Kevar River; there the hand of the
4 LORD was upon him. And I looked: Behold, a storm wind came
from the north, a great cloud and a flaring fire with a radiance
around it, and inside it, within the fire, the look of something lu-
5 minous, and within that was the form of four living beings. This
6 was their appearance: they had the form of a man; each one had
7 four faces, and each one of them had four wings; their legs were
straight-standing, and their feet were like a calf's hoof, gleaming
8 with a look of burnished bronze; they had man's hands beneath
their wings on their four sides, and the four of them had faces
9 and wings. Their wings were joined to each other; they did not
turn when they moved but moved in the direction of one of the
10 faces. Their faces were in the form of the face of a man with the
face of a lion on the right of the four, the face of an ox on the left
11 of the four, and the face of an eagle on all four of them. Their
faces and their wings were separated above: each one had two
12 joining it to the others and two covering its body; each moved
in the direction of one of the faces – wherever the spirit would
13 move, they moved – they did not turn when they moved. The
form of the living beings, their appearance, was like coals burning, like the appearance of torch flames; it passed among the
living beings; the fire had a radiance, lightning flashed out from
14 the fire, and the living beings ran forward and back with the
15 appearance of darting flames. I looked at the living beings, and
there, a wheel was on the ground beside each of the living be-
16 ings with the four faces. The appearance of the wheels and their
design had the look of an aquamarine gem, all four of them with
the same form; their appearance and their design were as though
17 one wheel were inside the other. When they moved, they moved
18 on any of their four sides; they did not turn as they moved. Their
rims, towering, inspired fear; and the rims of all four of them were
19 covered, all around, with eyes. When the living beings moved,
the wheels moved beside them, and when the living beings
20 rose above the ground, the wheels also rose; wherever the spirit

along with its reminder that even through the mist of God's incomprehensibility and strangeness, we can discern how we were created in His image.

ב אֱלֹהִים: בַּחֲמִשָּׁה לַחֹדֶשׁ הִיא הַשָּׁנָה הַחֲמִישִׁית לְגָלוּת
ג הַמֶּלֶךְ יוֹיָכִין: הָיֹה הָיָה דְבַר־יְהוָה אֶל־יְחֶזְקֵאל בֶּן־בּוּזִי
הַכֹּהֵן בְּאֶרֶץ כַּשְׂדִּים עַל־נְהַר־כְּבָר וַתְּהִי עָלָיו שָׁם יַד־
ד יְהוָה: וָאֵרֶא וְהִנֵּה רוּחַ סְעָרָה בָּאָה מִן־הַצָּפוֹן עָנָן גָּדוֹל
וְאֵשׁ מִתְלַקַּחַת וְנֹגַהּ לוֹ סָבִיב וּמִתּוֹכָהּ כְּעֵין הַחַשְׁמַל
ה מִתּוֹךְ הָאֵשׁ: וּמִתּוֹכָהּ דְּמוּת אַרְבַּע חַיּוֹת וְזֶה מַרְאֵיהֶן
ו דְּמוּת אָדָם לָהֵנָּה: וְאַרְבָּעָה פָנִים לְאֶחָת וְאַרְבַּע כְּנָפַיִם
ז לְאַחַת לָהֶם: וְרַגְלֵיהֶם רֶגֶל יְשָׁרָה וְכַף רַגְלֵיהֶם כְּכַף רֶגֶל
ח עֵגֶל וְנֹצְצִים כְּעֵין נְחֹשֶׁת קָלָל: וידו אָדָם מִתַּחַת כַּנְפֵיהֶם וִידֵי
ט עַל אַרְבַּעַת רִבְעֵיהֶם וּפְנֵיהֶם וְכַנְפֵיהֶם לְאַרְבַּעְתָּם: חֹבְרֹת
אִשָּׁה אֶל־אֲחוֹתָהּ כַּנְפֵיהֶם לֹא־יִסַּבּוּ בְלֶכְתָּן אִישׁ אֶל־עֵבֶר
י פָּנָיו יֵלֵכוּ: וּדְמוּת פְּנֵיהֶם פְּנֵי אָדָם וּפְנֵי אַרְיֵה אֶל־הַיָּמִין
לְאַרְבַּעְתָּם וּפְנֵי־שׁוֹר מֵהַשְּׂמֹאול לְאַרְבַּעְתָּן וּפְנֵי־נֶשֶׁר
יא לְאַרְבַּעְתָּן: וּפְנֵיהֶם וְכַנְפֵיהֶם פְּרֻדוֹת מִלְמָעְלָה לְאִישׁ שְׁתַּיִם
יב חֹבְרוֹת אִישׁ וּשְׁתַּיִם מְכַסּוֹת אֵת גְּוִיֹּתֵיהֶנָה: וְאִישׁ אֶל־
עֵבֶר פָּנָיו יֵלֵכוּ אֶל אֲשֶׁר יִהְיֶה־שָׁמָּה הָרוּחַ לָלֶכֶת יֵלֵכוּ לֹא
יג יִסַּבּוּ בְּלֶכְתָּן: וּדְמוּת הַחַיּוֹת מַרְאֵיהֶם כְּגַחֲלֵי־אֵשׁ בֹּעֲרוֹת
כְּמַרְאֵה הַלַּפִּדִים הִיא מִתְהַלֶּכֶת בֵּין הַחַיּוֹת וְנֹגַהּ לָאֵשׁ
יד וּמִן־הָאֵשׁ יוֹצֵא בָרָק: וְהַחַיּוֹת רָצוֹא וָשׁוֹב כְּמַרְאֵה הַבָּזָק:
טו וָאֵרֶא הַחַיּוֹת וְהִנֵּה אוֹפַן אֶחָד בָּאָרֶץ אֵצֶל הַחַיּוֹת לְאַרְבַּעַת
טז פָּנָיו: מַרְאֵה הָאוֹפַנִּים וּמַעֲשֵׂיהֶם כְּעֵין תַּרְשִׁישׁ וּדְמוּת אֶחָד
לְאַרְבַּעְתָּן וּמַרְאֵיהֶם וּמַעֲשֵׂיהֶם כַּאֲשֶׁר יִהְיֶה הָאוֹפַן בְּתוֹךְ
יז הָאוֹפָן: עַל־אַרְבַּעַת רִבְעֵיהֶן בְּלֶכְתָּם יֵלֵכוּ לֹא יִסַּבּוּ בְּלֶכְתָּן:
יח וְגַבֵּיהֶן וְגֹבַהּ לָהֶם וְיִרְאָה לָהֶם וְגַבֹּתָם מְלֵאֹת עֵינַיִם סָבִיב
יט לְאַרְבַּעְתָּן: וּבְלֶכֶת הַחַיּוֹת יֵלְכוּ הָאוֹפַנִּים אֶצְלָם וּבְהִנָּשֵׂא
כ הַחַיּוֹת מֵעַל הָאָרֶץ יִנָּשְׂאוּ הָאוֹפַנִּים: עַל אֲשֶׁר יִהְיֶה־שָּׁם

should be reserved for only those with advanced wisdom and knowledge. But the wonder and amazement it inspires is nonetheless fitting for the sacred day,

would move, they moved; there where the spirit moved, the
wheels rose with them, for the spirit of the living being was also
21 in the wheels: when they moved, they too moved, and when
they stood still, they too stood still, and when they rose from
the ground, the wheels too rose with them because the spirit of
22 the living being was in the wheels. Above the head of the living
being was the form of an expanse with a look of ice, its overaw-
23 ing glare, suspended over their heads from above, and beneath
the expanse, their wings reached out toward each other. Each
had a pair covering them; each had a pair covering their bod-
24 ies. I heard the sound of their wings when they moved; it was
like the sound of great rushing waters, like the voice of Shaddai, a clamor like the noise of a gathered army. Standing ;still,
25 they lowered their wings; a voice came from upon the expanse
which was over their heads – standing still, they lowered their
26 wings. Above the film which was over their heads, with the appearance of a sapphire, was the form of a throne; and upon the
form of the throne – upon it, above – was a form with the ap-
27 pearance of a man. And I saw: something that looked luminous,
the appearance of fire encasing it from what appeared to be his
waist and above; and from what appeared to be his waist and
below, I saw an appearance like fire with a radiance around it;
28 it was like the appearance of a rainbow in the clouds on a rainy
day; the radiance around it had that appearance. This was the
appearance of the form of the glory of the Lord. I saw it and I
2 1 fell upon my face, and I heard a voice speak. He said
2 to me: "Man, stand on your feet, and I will speak to you." As He
spoke to me, a spirit came into me and set me on my feet, and I
heard him speaking to me.

Ashkenazim and Sepharadim skip these verses

3 12 A spirit then lifted me up, and I heard a great, thunderous noise
behind me: "Blessed is the Lord's glory from its place!"

Ashkenazim and Sepharadim continue here

הָרוּחַ לָלֶכֶת יֵלֵכוּ שָׁמָּה הָרוּחַ לָלֶכֶת וְהָאוֹפַנִּים יִנָּשְׂאוּ
כא לְעֻמָּתָם כִּי רוּחַ הַחַיָּה בָּאוֹפַנִּים׃ בְּלֶכְתָּם יֵלֵכוּ וּבְעָמְדָם
יַעֲמֹדוּ וּבְהִנָּשְׂאָם מֵעַל הָאָרֶץ יִנָּשְׂאוּ הָאוֹפַנִּים לְעֻמָּתָם
כב כִּי רוּחַ הַחַיָּה בָּאוֹפַנִּים׃ וּדְמוּת עַל־רָאשֵׁי הַחַיָּה רָקִיעַ
כג כְּעֵין הַקֶּרַח הַנּוֹרָא נָטוּי עַל־רָאשֵׁיהֶם מִלְמָעְלָה׃ וְתַחַת
הָרָקִיעַ כַּנְפֵיהֶם יְשָׁרוֹת אִשָּׁה אֶל־אֲחוֹתָהּ לְאִישׁ שְׁתַּיִם
מְכַסּוֹת לָהֵנָּה וּלְאִישׁ שְׁתַּיִם מְכַסּוֹת לָהֵנָּה אֵת גְּוִיֹּתֵיהֶם׃
כד וָאֶשְׁמַע אֶת־קוֹל כַּנְפֵיהֶם כְּקוֹל מַיִם רַבִּים כְּקוֹל־שַׁדַּי
בְּלֶכְתָּם קוֹל הֲמֻלָּה כְּקוֹל מַחֲנֶה בְּעָמְדָם תְּרַפֶּינָה כַנְפֵיהֶן׃
כה וַיְהִי־קוֹל מֵעַל לָרָקִיעַ אֲשֶׁר עַל־רֹאשָׁם בְּעָמְדָם תְּרַפֶּינָה
כו כַנְפֵיהֶן׃ וּמִמַּעַל לָרָקִיעַ אֲשֶׁר עַל־רֹאשָׁם כְּמַרְאֵה אֶבֶן־
סַפִּיר דְּמוּת כִּסֵּא וְעַל דְּמוּת הַכִּסֵּא דְּמוּת כְּמַרְאֵה אָדָם
כז עָלָיו מִלְמָעְלָה׃ וָאֵרֶא ׀ כְּעֵין חַשְׁמַל כְּמַרְאֵה־אֵשׁ בֵּית־לָהּ
סָבִיב מִמַּרְאֵה מָתְנָיו וּלְמָעְלָה וּמִמַּרְאֵה מָתְנָיו וּלְמַטָּה
כח רָאִיתִי כְּמַרְאֵה־אֵשׁ וְנֹגַהּ לוֹ סָבִיב׃ כְּמַרְאֵה הַקֶּשֶׁת אֲשֶׁר
יִהְיֶה בֶעָנָן בְּיוֹם הַגֶּשֶׁם כֵּן מַרְאֵה הַנֹּגַהּ סָבִיב הוּא מַרְאֵה
דְּמוּת כְּבוֹד־יהוה וָאֶרְאֶה וָאֶפֹּל עַל־פָּנַי וָאֶשְׁמַע קוֹל

Ashkenazim and Sephardim skip these verses

ב א מְדַבֵּר׃ וַיֹּאמֶר אֵלָי בֶּן־אָדָם עֲמֹד עַל־רַגְלֶיךָ
ב וַאֲדַבֵּר אֹתָךְ׃ וַתָּבֹא בִי רוּחַ כַּאֲשֶׁר דִּבֶּר אֵלַי וַתַּעֲמִדֵנִי
עַל־רַגְלָי וָאֶשְׁמַע אֵת מִדַּבֵּר אֵלָי׃

Ashkenazim and Sephardim continue here

ג יב וַתִּשָּׂאֵנִי רוּחַ וָאֶשְׁמַע אַחֲרַי קוֹל רַעַשׁ גָּדוֹל בָּרוּךְ כְּבוֹד־
יהוה מִמְּקוֹמוֹ׃

Haftara for the Second Day of Shavuot in the Diaspora

The maftir of the second day of Shavuot in the Diaspora is read from Numbers 28:26–31.

HABAKKUK

2 20 But the LORD is in His heavenly dwelling. All the earth, be si-
3 1 lent before Him. A prayer Ḥavakuk the prophet sung
2 with *shiggayon*: LORD, I have heard accounts of You and am
afraid. O LORD, in the coming years renew Your deeds; in the
coming years, make Yourself known; in wrath, remember mercy.
3 God appears from Teiman, the Holy One from Mount Paran.
Selah His splendor covers the heavens; the earth is filled with
4 His glory. His radiance illuminates like light; rays emanate from
5 His every side; therein lies His hidden strength. Before Him will
6 come plague, fiery blight at His feet. He stands and the earth
shakes; He looks and nations tremble; age-old mountains shat-
7 ter; everlasting hills bow low; all the world's ways are His. I saw
Kushan's tents afflicted for sinning, the curtains in the land of
8 Midyan quiver. Is the LORD angry at the rivers; is it
against the rivers that You rage? Is Your fury against the ocean so
that You ride upon Your horses of war, Your chariots of deliver-
9 ance? Your bow is unsheathed; You keep Your word, Your oath to
10 the tribes, Selah, and split the earth open with rivers. When the
mountains see You they shiver; streams of water flow through;
11 the deep sounds with thunder, lifting its hands up high. The sun,
the moon stand still in their spheres; by the light of Your bolts
12 the world will march, by the glow of Your flashing spear. In rage,
13 You tread the earth; in wrath, You trample nations. You emerge
to liberate Your people, to liberate Your king. You crush the head
of the house of evil, stripping it from the core up to its neck, Se-
14 lah. You pierce heads of cities with their own spears,
they who come in a storm to shatter me, rejoicing as though
15 secretly devouring the needy. You trample the ocean floor with
16 Your steeds, stirring mighty seas. I hear this, and my gut churns;
my lips tremble at the sound. Rot eats at my bones; I shudder
in my place. Could I rest on the day of terror, the day God rises

oceans. The natural world melds to His will as He performs wonders mirroring the thunder and fire of the revelation at Sinai.

הפטרת יום שני של שבועות בחוץ לארץ

The מפטיר *of* יום שני של שבועות בחוץ לארץ *is read from* במדבר כח, כו–לא.

ב כ וַיהוָה בְּהֵיכַל קׇדְשׁוֹ הַס מִפָּנָיו כׇּל־הָאָרֶץ: ג א תְּפִלָּה חבקוק
ב לַחֲבַקּוּק הַנָּבִיא עַל שִׁגְיֹנוֹת: יְהוָה שָׁמַעְתִּי שִׁמְעֲךָ יָרֵאתִי
יְהוָה פׇּעׇלְךָ בְּקֶרֶב שָׁנִים חַיֵּיהוּ בְּקֶרֶב שָׁנִים תּוֹדִיעַ בְּרֹגֶז
ג רַחֵם תִּזְכּוֹר: אֱלוֹהַּ מִתֵּימָן יָבוֹא וְקָדוֹשׁ מֵהַר־פָּארָן סֶלָה
ד כִּסָּה שָׁמַיִם הוֹדוֹ וּתְהִלָּתוֹ מָלְאָה הָאָרֶץ: וְנֹגַהּ כָּאוֹר תִּהְיֶה
ה קַרְנַיִם מִיָּדוֹ לוֹ וְשָׁם חֶבְיוֹן עֻזֹּה: לְפָנָיו יֵלֶךְ דָּבֶר וְיֵצֵא רֶשֶׁף
ו לְרַגְלָיו: עָמַד ׀ וַיְמֹדֶד אֶרֶץ רָאָה וַיַּתֵּר גּוֹיִם וַיִּתְפֹּצְצוּ הַרְרֵי־
ז עַד שַׁחוּ גִּבְעוֹת עוֹלָם הֲלִיכוֹת עוֹלָם לוֹ: תַּחַת אָוֶן רָאִיתִי
ח אׇהֳלֵי כוּשָׁן יִרְגְּזוּן יְרִיעוֹת אֶרֶץ מִדְיָן: הֲבִנְהָרִים
חָרָה יְהוָה אִם בַּנְּהָרִים אַפֶּךָ אִם־בַּיָּם עֶבְרָתֶךָ כִּי תִרְכַּב
ט עַל־סוּסֶיךָ מַרְכְּבֹתֶיךָ יְשׁוּעָה: עֶרְיָה תֵעוֹר קַשְׁתֶּךָ שְׁבֻעוֹת
י מַטּוֹת אֹמֶר סֶלָה נְהָרוֹת תְּבַקַּע־אָרֶץ: רָאוּךָ יָחִילוּ הָרִים
יא זֶרֶם מַיִם עָבָר נָתַן תְּהוֹם קוֹלוֹ רוֹם יָדֵיהוּ נָשָׂא: שֶׁמֶשׁ
יָרֵחַ עָמַד זְבֻלָה לְאוֹר חִצֶּיךָ יְהַלֵּכוּ לְנֹגַהּ בְּרַק חֲנִיתֶךָ:
יב יג בְּזַעַם תִּצְעַד־אָרֶץ בְּאַף תָּדוּשׁ גּוֹיִם: יָצָאתָ לְיֵשַׁע עַמֶּךָ
לְיֵשַׁע אֶת־מְשִׁיחֶךָ מָחַצְתָּ רֹּאשׁ מִבֵּית רָשָׁע עָרוֹת יְסוֹד
יד עַד־צַוָּאר סֶלָה: נָקַבְתָּ בְמַטָּיו רֹאשׁ פְּרָזָו
טו יִסְעֲרוּ לַהֲפִיצֵנִי עֲלִיצֻתָם כְּמוֹ־לֶאֱכֹל עָנִי בַּמִּסְתָּר: דָּרַכְתָּ
טז בַיָּם סוּסֶיךָ חֹמֶר מַיִם רַבִּים: שָׁמַעְתִּי ׀ וַתִּרְגַּז בִּטְנִי לְקוֹל
צָלְלוּ שְׂפָתַי יָבוֹא רָקָב בַּעֲצָמַי וְתַחְתַּי אֶרְגָּז אֲשֶׁר אָנוּחַ

SECOND DAY OF SHAVUOT IN THE DIASPORA

Like the *haftara* of the first day of Shavuot, that of the second day provides an image of God's majestic figure as revealed to the prophet, this time in His "heavenly dwelling" [*heikhal kodsho*] – which can also be seen as a reference to the holy Temple on earth. The prophet describes God's tremendous might, moving mountains and

17 up for His nation? Though the fig tree will not flower, nor will
fruit fill the vines, olives will grow gaunt and grain fields yield
no produce, sheep will be removed from their pens, and cattle
18 will not be found in the sheds, yet I will delight in the LORD;
19 I will rejoice in the God who will save me. GOD, my Lord, my
strength, He makes my legs like a deer's and guides me to stride
to the heights. This song is for the conductor; to Him I offer my
melodies.

HAFTARA FOR THE FIRST DAY OF SUKKOT

13

The maftir of the first day of Sukkot is read from Numbers 29:12–16.

9 I will pass that third through fire and refine them as one refines ZECHARIAH
silver, and test them as one tests gold. He will call in My name, *Yemenites begin here*
and I will answer him. I will say, "He is My nation," and he will
14 1 say, "The LORD is my God." *Behold, a day of the LORD *Ashkenazim and*
2 is coming; your spoil will be divided up in your midst. I will gath- *Sepharadim begin here*
er all the nations to Jerusalem in war: the city will be taken, the
houses will be plundered, and the women will be raped; half of
the city will go into exile, but the remainder of the people will
3 not be cut off from the city. The LORD will go out, and He will
4 fight against these nations as He has fought on days of battle. On
that day His feet will stand upon the Mount of Olives which
faces Jerusalem on the east, and the Mount of Olives will split
through its middle – into a great valley – from east to west. Half
5 the mountain will shift northward and half southward. And you
will flee from this Valley of the Mountains, for the Valley of the
Mountains will reach as far as Atzal; you will flee as you fled from
the earthquake in the days of Uziya, the king of Yehuda, and the
LORD will come – my God, and all the holy ones with You.

---

conquest of Jerusalem by foreign armies, it will seem that all is lost. But God Himself will appear to fight on behalf of Israel, punishing those nations that oppressed her with fire and plague. Afterward, all people will know that God alone rules the earth, and they will show their newfound loyalty by appearing in Jerusalem every year for the Sukkot festival.

יז לְיוֹם צָרָה לַעֲלוֹת לְעַם יְגוּדֶנּוּ: כִּי־תְאֵנָה לֹא־תִפְרָח וְאֵין
יְבוּל בַּגְּפָנִים כִּחֵשׁ מַעֲשֵׂה־זַיִת וּשְׁדֵמוֹת לֹא־עָשָׂה אֹכֶל
יח גָּזַר מִמִּכְלָה צֹאן וְאֵין בָּקָר בָּרְפָתִים: וַאֲנִי בַּיהוָה אֶעְלוֹזָה
יט אָגִילָה בֵּאלֹהֵי יִשְׁעִי: יְהוִה אֲדֹנָי חֵילִי וַיָּשֶׂם רַגְלַי כָּאַיָּלוֹת
וְעַל־בָּמוֹתַי יַדְרִכֵנִי לַמְנַצֵּחַ בִּנְגִינוֹתָי:

הפטרת יום ראשון של סוכות

The מפטיר *of* יום ראשון של סוכות *is read from* במדבר כט, יב–טז.

זכריה
Yemenites begin here

יג ט וְהֵבֵאתִי אֶת־הַשְּׁלִשִׁית בָּאֵשׁ וּצְרַפְתִּים כִּצְרֹף אֶת־
הַכֶּסֶף וּבְחַנְתִּים כִּבְחֹן אֶת־הַזָּהָב הוּא ׀ יִקְרָא בִשְׁמִי
וַאֲנִי אֶעֱנֶה אֹתוֹ אָמַרְתִּי עַמִּי הוּא וְהוּא יֹאמַר יְהוָה
יד א אֱלֹהָי: *הִנֵּה יוֹם־בָּא לַיהוָה וְחֻלַּק שְׁלָלֵךְ
ב בְּקִרְבֵּךְ: וְאָסַפְתִּי אֶת־כָּל־הַגּוֹיִם ׀ אֶל־יְרוּשָׁלִַם לַמִּלְחָמָה
וְנִלְכְּדָה הָעִיר וְנָשַׁסּוּ הַבָּתִּים וְהַנָּשִׁים תשגלנה וְיָצָא חֲצִי
ג הָעִיר בַּגּוֹלָה וְיֶתֶר הָעָם לֹא יִכָּרֵת מִן־הָעִיר: וְיָצָא יְהוָה
ד וְנִלְחַם בַּגּוֹיִם הָהֵם כְּיוֹם הִלָּחֲמוֹ בְּיוֹם קְרָב: וְעָמְדוּ רַגְלָיו
בַּיּוֹם־הַהוּא עַל־הַר הַזֵּיתִים אֲשֶׁר עַל־פְּנֵי יְרוּשָׁלִַם מִקֶּדֶם
וְנִבְקַע הַר הַזֵּיתִים מֵחֶצְיוֹ מִזְרָחָה וָיָמָּה גֵּיא גְּדוֹלָה מְאֹד
ה וּמָשׁ חֲצִי הָהָר צָפוֹנָה וְחֶצְיוֹ נֶגְבָּה: וְנַסְתֶּם גֵּיא־הָרַי כִּי־יַגִּיעַ
גֵּי־הָרִים אֶל־אָצַל וְנַסְתֶּם כַּאֲשֶׁר נַסְתֶּם מִפְּנֵי הָרַעַשׁ בִּימֵי

Ashkenazim and Sepharadim begin here

תִּשָּׁכַבְנָה

FIRST DAY OF SUKKOT

According to the Sages, Sukkot is a holiday of judgment for the entire world. The seventy sacrificial bulls brought in the Temple signified the seventy nations of the earth, teaching that on these days that God decides the fate of all peoples – for war or peace, plenty or hunger, rain or drought. As an expression of this idea, we read as today's *haftara* Zekharya's chilling account of God's future judgment of the nations. After a violent and ruthless

6 This is what will be: on that day there will be neither bright
7 light nor thick darkness. This is what will be: there will be a day
known to the LORD; it will be neither day nor night, but at eve-
8 ning time there will be light. This is what will be: on that day
living waters will flow out from Jerusalem, half to the eastern
sea and half to the western sea; in summer and winter it will
9 be so. Then the LORD shall be King over all the earth; on that
10 day the LORD shall be One and His name One. Then the land
will be smoothed out like a plain from Geva to Rimon, until
the area south of Jerusalem, and Jerusalem will be lifted up in
her place. From the Gate of Binyamin to the site of the First
Gate and to the Corner Gate, from the Tower of Ḥananel to
11 the king's winery, they will inhabit her. There will be no more
12 devastation, and Jerusalem will live in safety. This will
be the plague that the LORD will bring upon all the peoples
who fought against Jerusalem: their flesh will rot away as they
stand on their feet, their eyes will rot in their sockets, and their
13 tongues will rot in their mouths. This is what will be: on that
day the turmoil the LORD brings on them will be great, and
each man will seize another by the arm and raise his fist against
14 his neighbor's fist. And Yehuda too will fight in Jerusalem, and
the wealth of all the surrounding nations, great quantities of
15 gold, silver, and clothing, will be gathered in. There will be a
plague just like this plague on the horses, the mules, the camels,
16 and the donkeys, and on every animal in those camps. This is
what will be: all those remaining from all the nations who came
up against Jerusalem will go up year after year to bow down to
the King, LORD of Hosts, and to celebrate the Festival of Tab-
17 ernacles. This is what will be: the families of the land who do
not go up to Jerusalem and bow down to the King, LORD of
18 Hosts, rain shall not fall for them. If the family of Egypt does
not go up, does not come, it shall not be upon them. This will
be the plague that the LORD will bring upon the nations who
19 do not go up to celebrate the Festival of Tabernacles. Such will
be the punishment of Egypt and the punishment of all the nations who do not come up to celebrate the Festival of Taberna-
20 cles. On that day even the bells of the horses will be inscribed
"sacred to the LORD," and the pots in the House of the LORD

ו עֻזִּיָּה מֶלֶךְ־יְהוּדָה וּבָא יְהוָה אֱלֹהַי כָּל־קְדֹשִׁים עִמָּךְ: וְהָיָה
ז בַּיּוֹם הַהוּא לֹא־יִהְיֶה אוֹר יְקָרוֹת יקפאון: וְהָיָה יוֹם־אֶחָד וְקִפָּאוֹן
הוּא יִוָּדַע לַיהוָה לֹא־יוֹם וְלֹא־לָיְלָה וְהָיָה לְעֵת־עֶרֶב יִהְיֶה־
ח אוֹר: וְהָיָה ׀ בַּיּוֹם הַהוּא יֵצְאוּ מַיִם־חַיִּים מִירוּשָׁלִַם חֶצְיָם
אֶל־הַיָּם הַקַּדְמוֹנִי וְחֶצְיָם אֶל־הַיָּם הָאַחֲרוֹן בַּקַּיִץ וּבָחֹרֶף
ט יִהְיֶה: וְהָיָה יְהוָה לְמֶלֶךְ עַל־כָּל־הָאָרֶץ בַּיּוֹם הַהוּא יִהְיֶה
י יְהוָה אֶחָד וּשְׁמוֹ אֶחָד: יִסּוֹב כָּל־הָאָרֶץ כָּעֲרָבָה מִגֶּבַע
לְרִמּוֹן נֶגֶב יְרוּשָׁלִָם וְרָאֲמָה וְיָשְׁבָה תַחְתֶּיהָ לְמִשַּׁעַר בִּנְיָמִן
עַד־מְקוֹם שַׁעַר הָרִאשׁוֹן עַד־שַׁעַר הַפִּנִּים וּמִגְדַּל חֲנַנְאֵל
יא עַד יִקְבֵי הַמֶּלֶךְ: וְיָשְׁבוּ בָהּ וְחֵרֶם לֹא יִהְיֶה־עוֹד וְיָשְׁבָה
יב יְרוּשָׁלִַם לָבֶטַח: וְזֹאת ׀ תִּהְיֶה הַמַּגֵּפָה אֲשֶׁר
יִגֹּף יְהוָה אֶת־כָּל־הָעַמִּים אֲשֶׁר צָבְאוּ עַל־יְרוּשָׁלִָם הָמֵק ׀
בְּשָׂרוֹ וְהוּא עֹמֵד עַל־רַגְלָיו וְעֵינָיו תִּמַּקְנָה בְחֹרֵיהֶן וּלְשׁוֹנוֹ
יג תִּמַּק בְּפִיהֶם: וְהָיָה בַּיּוֹם הַהוּא תִּהְיֶה מְהוּמַת־יְהוָה רַבָּה
בָּהֶם וְהֶחֱזִיקוּ אִישׁ יַד רֵעֵהוּ וְעָלְתָה יָדוֹ עַל־יַד רֵעֵהוּ:
יד וְגַם־יְהוּדָה תִּלָּחֵם בִּירוּשָׁלִָם וְאֻסַּף חֵיל כָּל־הַגּוֹיִם סָבִיב
טו זָהָב וָכֶסֶף וּבְגָדִים לָרֹב מְאֹד: וְכֵן תִּהְיֶה מַגֵּפַת הַסּוּס הַפֶּרֶד
הַגָּמָל וְהַחֲמוֹר וְכָל־הַבְּהֵמָה אֲשֶׁר יִהְיֶה בַּמַּחֲנוֹת הָהֵמָּה
טז כַּמַּגֵּפָה הַזֹּאת: וְהָיָה כָּל־הַנּוֹתָר מִכָּל־הַגּוֹיִם הַבָּאִים עַל־
יְרוּשָׁלִָם וְעָלוּ מִדֵּי שָׁנָה בְשָׁנָה לְהִשְׁתַּחֲוֹת לְמֶלֶךְ יְהוָה
יז צְבָאוֹת וְלָחֹג אֶת־חַג הַסֻּכּוֹת: וְהָיָה אֲשֶׁר לֹא־יַעֲלֶה מֵאֵת
מִשְׁפְּחוֹת הָאָרֶץ אֶל־יְרוּשָׁלִַם לְהִשְׁתַּחֲוֹת לְמֶלֶךְ יְהוָה
יח צְבָאוֹת וְלֹא עֲלֵיהֶם יִהְיֶה הַגָּשֶׁם: וְאִם־מִשְׁפַּחַת מִצְרַיִם
לֹא־תַעֲלֶה וְלֹא בָאָה וְלֹא עֲלֵיהֶם תִּהְיֶה הַמַּגֵּפָה אֲשֶׁר יִגֹּף
יט יְהוָה אֶת־הַגּוֹיִם אֲשֶׁר לֹא יַעֲלוּ לָחֹג אֶת־חַג הַסֻּכּוֹת: זֹאת
תִּהְיֶה חַטַּאת מִצְרָיִם וְחַטַּאת כָּל־הַגּוֹיִם אֲשֶׁר לֹא יַעֲלוּ
כ לָחֹג אֶת־חַג הַסֻּכּוֹת: בַּיּוֹם הַהוּא יִהְיֶה עַל־מְצִלּוֹת הַסּוּס
קֹדֶשׁ לַיהוָה וְהָיָה הַסִּירוֹת בְּבֵית יְהוָה כַּמִּזְרָקִים לִפְנֵי

21 will be like basins before the Altar. This is what will be: every
pot in Jerusalem and in Yehuda will be sacred to the LORD of
Hosts, and all those who come to sacrifice will take them and
will cook in them. On that day, there will be no more need for
traders in the House of the LORD of Hosts.

Haftara for the Second Day of Sukkot in the Diaspora

The maftir of the second day of Sukkot in the Diaspora is read from Numbers 29:12–16.

I KINGS

Yemenites begin here

7 51 When all the work that King Shlomo did for the House of the
LORD was finished, Shlomo brought what David his father had
dedicated – the silver, the gold, and the vessels – and placed
8 1 them in the treasury of the House of the LORD. Then
Shlomo assembled the elders of Israel – all the heads of the tribes,
the ancestral leaders of the Israelites – before King Shlomo in
Jerusalem, to bring up the Ark of the Lord's Covenant from the
2 City of David, Zion. *All the men of Israel assembled before
King Shlomo in the month of Etanim, the seventh month, at the
3 festival. When all the elders of Israel had arrived, the priests lift-
4 ed up the Ark and brought up the Ark of the LORD, the Tent of
Meeting, and all the sacred vessels in the Tent. While the priests
5 and the Levites brought them up, King Shlomo and the whole
community of Israel, who had met him before the Ark, sacri-
6 ficed sheep and oxen – far too many to number or count. The
priests brought the Ark of the Lord's Covenant to its place – to
the House's Inner Sanctuary, the Holy of Holies, to under the
7 shade of the wings of the cherubim. For the wings of the cherubim were spread over the place of the Ark so that the cherubim

Ashkenazim and Sepharadim begin here

ceremony with a long address, the conclusion of which will be read as the *haftara* of Shemini Atzeret, calling on God to answer the prayers of His people. The role of the Temple as an address of prayer and supplication echoes the themes of prayers for rain and deliverance that characterize Sukkot's special *hoshanot* petitions. During these *hoshanot*, we march around the synagogue *bima*, in remembrance of those prayers that took place on that holiday in that ancient Temple, around its enormous altar.

כא הַמִּזְבֵּחַ׃ וְהָיָה כָּל־סִיר בִּירוּשָׁלִַם וּבִיהוּדָה קֹדֶשׁ לַיהוָה
צְבָאוֹת וּבָאוּ כָּל־הַזֹּבְחִים וְלָקְחוּ מֵהֶם וּבִשְּׁלוּ בָהֶם וְלֹא־
יִהְיֶה כְנַעֲנִי עוֹד בְּבֵית־יְהוָה צְבָאוֹת בַּיּוֹם הַהוּא׃

הפטרת יום שני של סוכות בחוץ לארץ

The מפטיר *of* יום שני של סוכות בחוץ לארץ *is read from* במדבר כט, יב–טז.

מלכים א׳
Yemenites begin here

ז נא וַתִּשְׁלַם כָּל־הַמְּלָאכָה אֲשֶׁר עָשָׂה הַמֶּלֶךְ שְׁלֹמֹה בֵּית
יהוה וַיָּבֵא שְׁלֹמֹה אֶת־קָדְשֵׁי ׀ דָּוִד אָבִיו אֶת־הַכֶּסֶף וְאֶת־
ח א הַזָּהָב וְאֶת־הַכֵּלִים נָתַן בְּאֹצְרוֹת בֵּית יהוה׃ אָז
יַקְהֵל שְׁלֹמֹה אֶת־זִקְנֵי יִשְׂרָאֵל אֶת־כָּל־רָאשֵׁי הַמַּטּוֹת
נְשִׂיאֵי הָאָבוֹת לִבְנֵי יִשְׂרָאֵל אֶל־הַמֶּלֶךְ שְׁלֹמֹה יְרוּשָׁלִָם
לְהַעֲלוֹת אֶת־אֲרוֹן בְּרִית־יהוה מֵעִיר דָּוִד הִיא צִיּוֹן׃

Ashkenazim and Sepharadim begin here

ב *וַיִּקָּהֲלוּ אֶל־הַמֶּלֶךְ שְׁלֹמֹה כָּל־אִישׁ יִשְׂרָאֵל בְּיֶרַח הָאֵתָנִים
ג בֶּחָג הוּא הַחֹדֶשׁ הַשְּׁבִיעִי׃ וַיָּבֹאוּ כֹּל זִקְנֵי יִשְׂרָאֵל וַיִּשְׂאוּ
ד הַכֹּהֲנִים אֶת־הָאָרוֹן׃ וַיַּעֲלוּ אֶת־אֲרוֹן יהוה וְאֶת־אֹהֶל מוֹעֵד
וְאֶת־כָּל־כְּלֵי הַקֹּדֶשׁ אֲשֶׁר בָּאֹהֶל וַיַּעֲלוּ אֹתָם הַכֹּהֲנִים
ה וְהַלְוִיִּם׃ וְהַמֶּלֶךְ שְׁלֹמֹה וְכָל־עֲדַת יִשְׂרָאֵל הַנּוֹעָדִים עָלָיו
אִתּוֹ לִפְנֵי הָאָרוֹן מְזַבְּחִים צֹאן וּבָקָר אֲשֶׁר לֹא־יִסָּפְרוּ
ו וְלֹא יִמָּנוּ מֵרֹב׃ וַיָּבִאוּ הַכֹּהֲנִים אֶת־אֲרוֹן בְּרִית־יהוה אֶל־
מְקוֹמוֹ אֶל־דְּבִיר הַבַּיִת אֶל־קֹדֶשׁ הַקֳּדָשִׁים אֶל־תַּחַת כַּנְפֵי
ז הַכְּרוּבִים׃ כִּי הַכְּרוּבִים פֹּרְשִׂים כְּנָפַיִם אֶל־מְקוֹם הָאָרוֹן

SECOND DAY OF SUKKOT IN THE DIASPORA

The *haftara* recounts the most important event of Jewish history to have occurred on Sukkot: the inauguration of King Shlomo's Temple. With pomp and fanfare, all the people of Israel convene in Jerusalem, and the priests bring the holy Ark into the new Sanctuary to begin its service. King Shlomo opens the

▶

8 sheltered the Ark and its poles from above. The poles extended
so that the ends of the poles were visible from the Holy Place in
front of the Inner Sanctuary, but they could not be seen from
9 the outside, and they are there to this day. The Ark contained
nothing but the two stone tablets Moshe placed there at Ḥorev
when the LORD made a covenant with the Israelites as they left
10 the land of Egypt. And as the priests left the Holy Place, a cloud
11 filled the House of the LORD; the priests could not stand and
serve because of the cloud, for the glory of the LORD had filled
12 the House of the LORD. Then Shlomo declared: "The
13 LORD promised that He would dwell in deep mist; I have now
built You an exalted House, a permanent place for Your abode."
14 And the king turned his face and blessed the whole assembly of
15 Israel, while the whole assembly of Israel stood. "Blessed is the
LORD, God of Israel," he said, "who made a promise to my father
David with His own mouth and has now fulfilled it with His own
16 hand, saying: From the day I brought My people, Israel, out of
Egypt, I never chose a city from among all the tribes of Israel, to
build a House where My name would be; but I chose David to
17 be over My people Israel. My father David had his heart set on
18 building a House for the name of the LORD, God of Israel. But
the LORD said to my father David: Though you have set your
heart on building a House for My name, and though you have
19 set your heart well, you will not be the one to build the House.
But your son, the issue of your own loins – he will be the one to
20 build the House for My name. The LORD has fulfilled the promise He made; I have risen in my father's stead, and I sit upon Israel's throne, as the LORD promised. I have built the House for
21 the name of the LORD, God of Israel. And there I have set a place
for the Ark, which contains the covenant that the LORD made
with our ancestors when He brought them out of the land of
Egypt."

ח וַיָּסֹכּוּ הַכְּרֻבִים עַל־הָאָרוֹן וְעַל־בַּדָּיו מִלְמָעְלָה: וַיַּאֲרִכוּ
הַבַּדִּים וַיֵּרָאוּ רָאשֵׁי הַבַּדִּים מִן־הַקֹּדֶשׁ עַל־פְּנֵי הַדְּבִיר
ט וְלֹא יֵרָאוּ הַחוּצָה וַיִּהְיוּ שָׁם עַד הַיּוֹם הַזֶּה: אֵין בָּאָרוֹן רַק
שְׁנֵי לֻחוֹת הָאֲבָנִים אֲשֶׁר הִנִּחַ שָׁם מֹשֶׁה בְּחֹרֵב אֲשֶׁר כָּרַת
י יְהוָה עִם־בְּנֵי יִשְׂרָאֵל בְּצֵאתָם מֵאֶרֶץ מִצְרָיִם: וַיְהִי בְּצֵאת
יא הַכֹּהֲנִים מִן־הַקֹּדֶשׁ וְהֶעָנָן מָלֵא אֶת־בֵּית יְהוָה: וְלֹא־יָכְלוּ
הַכֹּהֲנִים לַעֲמֹד לְשָׁרֵת מִפְּנֵי הֶעָנָן כִּי־מָלֵא כְבוֹד־יְהוָה
יב אֶת־בֵּית יְהוָה: אָז אָמַר שְׁלֹמֹה יְהוָה אָמַר
יג לִשְׁכֹּן בָּעֲרָפֶל: בָּנֹה בָנִיתִי בֵּית זְבֻל לָךְ מָכוֹן לְשִׁבְתְּךָ
יד עוֹלָמִים: וַיַּסֵּב הַמֶּלֶךְ אֶת־פָּנָיו וַיְבָרֶךְ אֵת כָּל־קְהַל יִשְׂרָאֵל
טו וְכָל־קְהַל יִשְׂרָאֵל עֹמֵד: וַיֹּאמֶר בָּרוּךְ יְהוָה אֱלֹהֵי יִשְׂרָאֵל
טז אֲשֶׁר דִּבֶּר בְּפִיו אֵת דָּוִד אָבִי וּבְיָדוֹ מִלֵּא לֵאמֹר: מִן־הַיּוֹם
אֲשֶׁר הוֹצֵאתִי אֶת־עַמִּי אֶת־יִשְׂרָאֵל מִמִּצְרַיִם לֹא־בָחַרְתִּי
בְעִיר מִכֹּל שִׁבְטֵי יִשְׂרָאֵל לִבְנוֹת בַּיִת לִהְיוֹת שְׁמִי שָׁם
יז וָאֶבְחַר בְּדָוִד לִהְיוֹת עַל־עַמִּי יִשְׂרָאֵל: וַיְהִי עִם־לְבַב דָּוִד
יח אָבִי לִבְנוֹת בַּיִת לְשֵׁם יְהוָה אֱלֹהֵי יִשְׂרָאֵל: וַיֹּאמֶר יְהוָה
אֶל־דָּוִד אָבִי יַעַן אֲשֶׁר הָיָה עִם־לְבָבְךָ לִבְנוֹת בַּיִת לִשְׁמִי
יט הֱטִיבֹתָ כִּי הָיָה עִם־לְבָבֶךָ: רַק אַתָּה לֹא תִבְנֶה הַבָּיִת כִּי
כ אִם־בִּנְךָ הַיֹּצֵא מֵחֲלָצֶיךָ הוּא־יִבְנֶה הַבַּיִת לִשְׁמִי: וַיָּקֶם
יְהוָה אֶת־דְּבָרוֹ אֲשֶׁר דִּבֵּר וָאָקֻם תַּחַת דָּוִד אָבִי וָאֵשֵׁב
עַל־כִּסֵּא יִשְׂרָאֵל כַּאֲשֶׁר דִּבֶּר יְהוָה וָאֶבְנֶה הַבַּיִת לְשֵׁם יְהוָה
כא אֱלֹהֵי יִשְׂרָאֵל: וָאָשִׂם שָׁם מָקוֹם לָאָרוֹן אֲשֶׁר־שָׁם בְּרִית
יְהוָה אֲשֶׁר כָּרַת עִם־אֲבֹתֵינוּ בְּהוֹצִיאוֹ אֹתָם מֵאֶרֶץ מִצְרָיִם:

Haftarat Shabbat Ḥol HaMoed Sukkot

The maftir of Shabbat Ḥol HaMoed Sukkot is read the offering for the respective day (in the Diaspora adding the offering for the previous day).

38 1 2 The word of the Lord came to me: "Man, set your face toward EZEKIEL
Gog of the land of Magog, the chief prince of Meshekh and Tu- *Yemenites begin here*
3 val. Prophesy against him; say: So says the Lord God: Behold –
4 I am against you, Gog, chief prince of Meshekh and Tuval. I
will turn you around, fix hooks into your jaw, and bring you out
with all your troops, horses, and cavalry in complete regalia, a
5 great horde with shields and bucklers, all wielding swords. And
with them Persia, Kush, and Put, all with shields and helmets;
6 Gomer and all her forces; Beit Togarma from the far edges of
7 the north and all her forces – many peoples with you. Prepare,
ready yourself, you and all of the hordes assembled around
8 you; you are their guarding commander. After many days you
will be summoned; at the end of years, you will come against
the land which has been restored after the sword, which has
been gathered back from many nations upon the mountains of
Israel that long lay in ruins – she who will have been brought
9 out from the nations, a people who all now live securely. You
will advance, you will come like a devastating storm, and you
will be like a cloud covering the land – you, all your forces, and
10 the many peoples with you. So says the Lord
God: On that day, certain thoughts will occur to you; you will
11 devise an evil scheme. You will say, 'I will advance against the
land of open villages; I will come upon those who are tranquil,
living securely, all of whom live in unwalled towns and with-
12 out bars or gates,' to ransack spoils and seize loot, to turn your
hand against reinhabited ruins and a people gathered in from
the nations who have built up livestock and possessions, who
13 live at the center of the land. Sheba, Dedan, and the merchants

---

the besieging nations and devastating them with supernatural wonders and plagues. As a result, God promises, "I will be magnified, I will be sanctified, and I will make Myself known in the eyes of many nations – and they will know that I am the Lord." This recognition by all peoples that God alone is sovereign in the world is the universalist vision of the holiday of Sukkot.

הפטרת שבת
חול המועד סוכות

The מפטיר *of* שבת חול המועד סוכות *is read from the offering for the respective day (in the Diaspora adding the offering for the previous day).*

יחזקאל

Yemenites begin here

לח א ב וַיְהִי דְבַר־יְהוָה אֵלַי לֵאמֹר: בֶּן־אָדָם שִׂים פָּנֶיךָ אֶל־גּוֹג
ג אֶרֶץ הַמָּגוֹג נְשִׂיא רֹאשׁ מֶשֶׁךְ וְתֻבָל וְהִנָּבֵא עָלָיו: וְאָמַרְתָּ
כֹּה אָמַר אֲדֹנָי יֱהוִה הִנְנִי אֵלֶיךָ גּוֹג נְשִׂיא רֹאשׁ מֶשֶׁךְ וְתֻבָל:
ד וְשׁוֹבַבְתִּיךָ וְנָתַתִּי חַחִים בִּלְחָיֶיךָ וְהוֹצֵאתִי אוֹתְךָ וְאֶת־
כָּל־חֵילֶךָ סוּסִים וּפָרָשִׁים לְבֻשֵׁי מִכְלוֹל כֻּלָּם קָהָל רָב
ה צִנָּה וּמָגֵן תֹּפְשֵׂי חֲרָבוֹת כֻּלָּם: פָּרַס כּוּשׁ וּפוּט אִתָּם כֻּלָּם
ו מָגֵן וְכוֹבָע: גֹּמֶר וְכָל־אֲגַפֶּיהָ בֵּית תּוֹגַרְמָה יַרְכְּתֵי צָפוֹן
ז וְאֶת־כָּל־אֲגַפָּיו עַמִּים רַבִּים אִתָּךְ: הִכֹּן וְהָכֵן לְךָ אַתָּה
ח וְכָל־קְהָלֶךָ הַנִּקְהָלִים עָלֶיךָ וְהָיִיתָ לָהֶם לְמִשְׁמָר: מִיָּמִים
רַבִּים תִּפָּקֵד בְּאַחֲרִית הַשָּׁנִים תָּבוֹא ׀ אֶל־אֶרֶץ ׀ מְשׁוֹבֶבֶת
מֵחֶרֶב מְקֻבֶּצֶת מֵעַמִּים רַבִּים עַל הָרֵי יִשְׂרָאֵל אֲשֶׁר־הָיוּ
לְחָרְבָּה תָּמִיד וְהִיא מֵעַמִּים הוּצָאָה וְיָשְׁבוּ לָבֶטַח כֻּלָּם:
ט וְעָלִיתָ כַּשֹּׁאָה תָבוֹא כֶּעָנָן לְכַסּוֹת הָאָרֶץ תִּהְיֶה אַתָּה
י וְכָל־אֲגַפֶּיךָ וְעַמִּים רַבִּים אוֹתָךְ: כֹּה אָמַר
אֲדֹנָי יֱהוִה וְהָיָה ׀ בַּיּוֹם הַהוּא יַעֲלוּ דְבָרִים עַל־לְבָבֶךָ
יא וְחָשַׁבְתָּ מַחֲשֶׁבֶת רָעָה: וְאָמַרְתָּ אֶעֱלֶה עַל־אֶרֶץ פְּרָזוֹת
אָבוֹא הַשֹּׁקְטִים יֹשְׁבֵי לָבֶטַח כֻּלָּם יֹשְׁבִים בְּאֵין חוֹמָה
יב וּבְרִיחַ וּדְלָתַיִם אֵין לָהֶם: לִשְׁלֹל שָׁלָל וְלָבֹז בַּז לְהָשִׁיב יָדְךָ
עַל־חֳרָבוֹת נוֹשָׁבֹת וְאֶל־עַם מְאֻסָּף מִגּוֹיִם עֹשֶׂה מִקְנֶה
יג וְקִנְיָן יֹשְׁבֵי עַל־טַבּוּר הָאָרֶץ: שְׁבָא וּדְדָן וְסֹחֲרֵי תַרְשִׁישׁ

SHABBAT ḤOL HAMOED SUKKOT

The fitting counterpart to Zekharya's apocalyptic prophecy, read on the first day of Sukkot, is Yeḥezkel's premonition of the war of Gog and Magog, read on Shabbat of Ḥol HaMoed. Here too we witness a titanic assault against Israel by the surrounding nations in the end of days. And here too, it is God who will save Israel, fighting by Himself against

of Tarshish and all her young warriors will say to you, 'Have
you come to ransack spoils? Have you assembled your hordes
to seize loot – to carry off silver and gold, to take livestock and
14 possessions, to ransack great spoils?' So, prophesy,
Man; say to Gog: So says the Lord God: Surely, on the day that
15 My people Israel lives securely, you will know it, and you will
come from your place, from the far edges of the north, you and
many peoples with you, all of them on horseback, with a great
16 horde and a mighty army. You will advance against My people
Israel like a cloud covering the land. This is what will be in the
end of days, and I will bring you to My land so that the nations
will know Me when I am sanctified through you before their
17 eyes, Gog. So says the Lord God: It is you whom I
spoke of in former days through My servants the prophets of
Israel, who in those days, for years, prophesied that I would
18 bring you against them. *And it shall be, on that day, *Ashkenazim and Sepharadim begin here*
on the day that Gog comes onto the soil of Israel, says the Lord
19 God: My fury will blaze; in My passionate anger, in the fire of
My rage I have spoken: Surely on that day there will be a great
20 quaking upon the soil of Israel; they will quake before Me: the
fish of the seas and the birds of the sky, the animals of the field,
every creeping thing that crawls upon the earth, and every man
on the face of the earth; the mountains will be demolished, the
terraces will collapse, and every wall shall fall to the ground.
21 I will call the sword down against him across My mountains,
says the Lord God; each man's sword will be turned against his
22 brother. I will execute judgment on him with pestilence and
blood; I will pour down torrential rain and crystal hailstone,
fire and sulfur over him and his troops, and over the many peo-
23 ples who are with him. I will be magnified, I will be sanctified,
and I will make Myself known in the eyes of many nations – and
39 1 they will know that I am the Lord.* And you, *Yemenites end here*
Man, prophesy against Gog and say: So says the Lord God:
Behold – I am against you, Gog, chief prince of Meshekh and
2 Tuval. I will turn you around; I will drive you forward; I will
make you advance from the far edges of the north and bring
3 you to the mountains of Israel. I will strike your bow from your
4 left hand; I will make the arrows fall from your right; upon the
mountains of Israel you will fall – you, all your troops, and the
peoples who are with you. I will give you up to birds of prey

וְכָל־כְּפִרֶיהָ יֹאמְרוּ לְךָ הֲלִשְׁלֹל שָׁלָל אַתָּה בָא הֲלָבֹז בַּז
הִקְהַלְתָּ קְהָלֶךָ לָשֵׂאת ׀ כֶּסֶף וְזָהָב לָקַחַת מִקְנֶה וְקִנְיָן
יד לִשְׁלֹל שָׁלָל גָּדוֹל׃ לָכֵן הִנָּבֵא בֶן־אָדָם
וְאָמַרְתָּ לְגוֹג כֹּה אָמַר אֲדֹנָי יֱהֹוִה הֲלוֹא ׀ בַּיּוֹם הַהוּא בְּשֶׁבֶת
טו עַמִּי יִשְׂרָאֵל לָבֶטַח תֵּדָע׃ וּבָאתָ מִמְּקוֹמְךָ מִיַּרְכְּתֵי צָפוֹן
אַתָּה וְעַמִּים רַבִּים אִתָּךְ רֹכְבֵי סוּסִים כֻּלָּם קָהָל גָּדוֹל וְחַיִל
טז רָב׃ וְעָלִיתָ עַל־עַמִּי יִשְׂרָאֵל כֶּעָנָן לְכַסּוֹת הָאָרֶץ בְּאַחֲרִית
הַיָּמִים תִּהְיֶה וַהֲבִאוֹתִיךָ עַל־אַרְצִי לְמַעַן דַּעַת הַגּוֹיִם
יז אֹתִי בְּהִקָּדְשִׁי בְךָ לְעֵינֵיהֶם גּוֹג׃ כֹּה־אָמַר אֲדֹנָי
יֱהֹוִה הַאַתָּה־הוּא אֲשֶׁר־דִּבַּרְתִּי בְּיָמִים קַדְמוֹנִים בְּיַד עֲבָדַי
נְבִיאֵי יִשְׂרָאֵל הַנִּבְּאִים בַּיָּמִים הָהֵם שָׁנִים לְהָבִיא אֹתְךָ
Ashkenazim and Sepharadim begin here
יח עֲלֵיהֶם׃ *וְהָיָה ׀ בַּיּוֹם הַהוּא בְּיוֹם בּוֹא גוֹג
עַל־אַדְמַת יִשְׂרָאֵל נְאֻם אֲדֹנָי יֱהֹוִה תַּעֲלֶה חֲמָתִי בְּאַפִּי׃
יט וּבְקִנְאָתִי בְאֵשׁ־עֶבְרָתִי דִּבַּרְתִּי אִם־לֹא ׀ בַּיּוֹם הַהוּא יִהְיֶה
כ רַעַשׁ גָּדוֹל עַל אַדְמַת יִשְׂרָאֵל׃ וְרָעֲשׁוּ מִפָּנַי דְּגֵי הַיָּם וְעוֹף
הַשָּׁמַיִם וְחַיַּת הַשָּׂדֶה וְכָל־הָרֶמֶשׂ הָרֹמֵשׂ עַל־הָאֲדָמָה
וְכֹל הָאָדָם אֲשֶׁר עַל־פְּנֵי הָאֲדָמָה וְנֶהֶרְסוּ הֶהָרִים וְנָפְלוּ
כא הַמַּדְרֵגוֹת וְכָל־חוֹמָה לָאָרֶץ תִּפּוֹל׃ וְקָרָאתִי עָלָיו לְכָל־הָרַי
כב חֶרֶב נְאֻם אֲדֹנָי יֱהֹוִה חֶרֶב אִישׁ בְּאָחִיו תִּהְיֶה׃ וְנִשְׁפַּטְתִּי
אִתּוֹ בְּדֶבֶר וּבְדָם וְגֶשֶׁם שׁוֹטֵף וְאַבְנֵי אֶלְגָּבִישׁ אֵשׁ וְגָפְרִית
אַמְטִיר עָלָיו וְעַל־אֲגַפָּיו וְעַל־עַמִּים רַבִּים אֲשֶׁר אִתּוֹ׃
כג וְהִתְגַּדִּלְתִּי וְהִתְקַדִּשְׁתִּי וְנוֹדַעְתִּי לְעֵינֵי גּוֹיִם רַבִּים וְיָדְעוּ
Yemenites end here
לט א כִּי־אֲנִי יְהוָה׃* וְאַתָּה בֶן־אָדָם הִנָּבֵא עַל־גּוֹג
וְאָמַרְתָּ כֹּה אָמַר אֲדֹנָי יֱהֹוִה הִנְנִי אֵלֶיךָ גּוֹג נְשִׂיא רֹאשׁ
ב מֶשֶׁךְ וְתֻבָל׃ וְשֹׁבַבְתִּיךָ וְשִׁשֵּׁאתִיךָ וְהַעֲלִיתִיךָ מִיַּרְכְּתֵי
ג צָפוֹן וַהֲבִאוֹתִךָ עַל־הָרֵי יִשְׂרָאֵל׃ וְהִכֵּיתִי קַשְׁתְּךָ מִיַּד
ד שְׂמֹאולְךָ וְחִצֶּיךָ מִיַּד יְמִינְךָ אַפִּיל׃ עַל־הָרֵי יִשְׂרָאֵל תִּפּוֹל
אַתָּה וְכָל־אֲגַפֶּיךָ וְעַמִּים אֲשֶׁר אִתָּךְ לְעֵיט צִפּוֹר כָּל־כָּנָף

5 of every kind and to the animals of the field as food; upon the
open field you will fall, for I have spoken, says the Lord God.
6 I will set loose fire on Magog and on those living securely in
7 the coastlands, and they will know that I am the Lord. I will
make My holy name known among My people Israel; I will no
longer allow My holy name to be desecrated, and the nations
8 will know that I am the Lord, holy in Israel. Behold: it is coming, it will be, says the Lord God: This is the day I have spoken
9 of. The inhabitants of the cities of Israel will come out, and they
will kindle and burn the weapons, the shields and bucklers, the
bows and arrows, and the clubs and spears; they will burn
10 them as fuel for fire for seven years. They will not take wood
from the fields or chop down trees from the forests, for they
will fuel their fires with weapons. They will ransack those who
despoiled them and loot those who looted them, says the Lord
11 God. And it will happen on that day: I will grant Gog
a burial place there in Israel, the Valley of the Travelers, east of
the sea, and it will block the travelers. Here they will bury Gog
and his horde; they will call it the Valley of the Horde of Gog.
12 For seven months the House of Israel will bury them to purify
13 the land. All the people in the land shall bury them, and it will
make them renowned on the day of My glory, says the Lord
14 God. They shall select men to cross the land constantly, burying the invaders' remains that lie upon the ground – to purify it.
15 They will search for a period of seven months. Whenever these
men assigned to cross the land see a human bone, they shall
place a sign next to it until the buriers have buried it in the Val-
16 ley of the Horde of Gog. There will also be a city named Horde.
Thus they shall purify the land.

ה וְחַיַּת הַשָּׂדֶה נְתַתִּיךָ לְאָכְלָה׃ עַל־פְּנֵי הַשָּׂדֶה תִּפּוֹל כִּי
ו אֲנִי דִבַּרְתִּי נְאֻם אֲדֹנָי יֱהֹוִה׃ וְשִׁלַּחְתִּי־אֵשׁ בְּמָגוֹג וּבְיֹשְׁבֵי
ז הָאִיִּים לָבֶטַח וְיָדְעוּ כִּי־אֲנִי יְהוָה׃ וְאֶת־שֵׁם קָדְשִׁי אוֹדִיעַ
בְּתוֹךְ עַמִּי יִשְׂרָאֵל וְלֹא־אַחֵל אֶת־שֵׁם־קָדְשִׁי עוֹד וְיָדְעוּ
ח הַגּוֹיִם כִּי־אֲנִי יְהוָה קָדוֹשׁ בְּיִשְׂרָאֵל׃ הִנֵּה בָאָה וְנִהְיָתָה
ט נְאֻם אֲדֹנָי יֱהֹוִה הוּא הַיּוֹם אֲשֶׁר דִּבַּרְתִּי׃ וְיָצְאוּ יֹשְׁבֵי ׀ עָרֵי
יִשְׂרָאֵל וּבִעֲרוּ וְהִשִּׂיקוּ בְּנֶשֶׁק וּמָגֵן וְצִנָּה בְּקֶשֶׁת וּבְחִצִּים
י וּבְמַקֵּל יָד וּבְרֹמַח וּבִעֲרוּ בָהֶם אֵשׁ שֶׁבַע שָׁנִים׃ וְלֹא־יִשְׂאוּ
עֵצִים מִן־הַשָּׂדֶה וְלֹא יַחְטְבוּ מִן־הַיְּעָרִים כִּי בַנֶּשֶׁק יְבַעֲרוּ־
אֵשׁ וְשָׁלְלוּ אֶת־שֹׁלְלֵיהֶם וּבָזְזוּ אֶת־בֹּזְזֵיהֶם נְאֻם אֲדֹנָי
יא יֱהֹוִה׃ וְהָיָה בַיּוֹם הַהוּא אֶתֵּן לְגוֹג ׀ מְקוֹם־
שָׁם קֶבֶר בְּיִשְׂרָאֵל גֵּי הָעֹבְרִים קִדְמַת הַיָּם וְחֹסֶמֶת הִיא
אֶת־הָעֹבְרִים וְקָבְרוּ שָׁם אֶת־גּוֹג וְאֶת־כָּל־הֲמוֹנֹה וְקָרְאוּ
יב גֵּיא הֲמוֹן גּוֹג׃ וּקְבָרוּם בֵּית יִשְׂרָאֵל לְמַעַן טַהֵר אֶת־הָאָרֶץ
יג שִׁבְעָה חֳדָשִׁים׃ וְקָבְרוּ כָּל־עַם הָאָרֶץ וְהָיָה לָהֶם לְשֵׁם
יד יוֹם הִכָּבְדִי נְאֻם אֲדֹנָי יֱהֹוִה׃ וְאַנְשֵׁי תָמִיד יַבְדִּילוּ עֹבְרִים
בָּאָרֶץ מְקַבְּרִים אֶת־הָעֹבְרִים אֶת־הַנּוֹתָרִים עַל־פְּנֵי הָאָרֶץ
טו לְטַהֲרָהּ מִקְצֵה שִׁבְעָה־חֳדָשִׁים יַחְקֹרוּ׃ וְעָבְרוּ הָעֹבְרִים
בָּאָרֶץ וְרָאָה עֶצֶם אָדָם וּבָנָה אֶצְלוֹ צִיּוּן עַד קָבְרוּ אֹתוֹ
טז הַמְקַבְּרִים אֶל־גֵּיא הֲמוֹן גּוֹג׃ וְגַם שֶׁם־עִיר הֲמוֹנָה וְטִהֲרוּ
הָאָרֶץ׃

Haftarat Shemini Atzeret in the Diaspora

The maftir of Shemini Atzeret in the Diaspora is read from Numbers 29:35–30:1.

8 54 When Shlomo had finished offering the whole of this prayer
and plea to the Lord, he rose from before the Altar of the Lord,
where he had been kneeling on his knees with his palms raised
55 heavenward. And he stood and blessed the whole assembly of
56 Israel in a loud voice: "Blessed is the Lord, who has granted rest
to His people Israel, fulfilling all His promises," he said. "Not one
thing is unfulfilled from all the good promises He made through
57 Moshe, His servant. May the Lord our God be with us as He
was with our ancestors; may He never leave us or abandon us.
58 May He sway our hearts toward Him so that we follow in all His
ways and keep His commandments, laws and rulings that He
59 commanded our ancestors. May these words of mine, which I
have pleaded before the Lord, stay close to the Lord our God
day and night, to uphold the cause of His servant and the cause
60 of His people Israel as each day's needs arise – so that all the
peoples of the land will know that the Lord is God, and there is
61 no other. May your hearts be fully with the Lord our God, fol-
62 lowing His laws and keeping His commandments, as today." And
the king, together with all of Israel, offered sacrifices before the
63 Lord; Shlomo sacrificed the peace sacrifices he offered to the
Lord – twenty-two thousand cattle and one hundred twenty
thousand sheep – and thus the king and all of Israel dedicated
64 the House of the Lord. On that day, the king consecrated the
center of the courtyard in front of the House of the Lord, for
it was there that he prepared the burnt offering, the grain offering, and the fats of the peace offerings. The bronze altar before

---

all the peoples of the land will know that the Lord is God, and there is no other." The desire to see God recognized and worshipped by "all peoples of the land" is a central theme of Sukkot, expressed in the other *haftarot* read on the days leading up to Shemini Atzeret. His prayer and blessing ended, Shlomo turns to the service of the Sukkot holiday, which they celebrate for seven days. On the eighth day, Shemini Atzeret, he releases the people to their homes, but the Sages teach that they chose to remain to feast and rejoice for this last day of Shemini Atzeret, and returned home only afterward.

הפטרת שמיני עצרת
בחוץ לארץ

The מפטיר *of* שמיני עצרת בחוץ לארץ *is read from* במדבר כט, לה – ל, א.

מלכים א׳

ח נד וַיְהִי ׀ כְּכַלּוֹת שְׁלֹמֹה לְהִתְפַּלֵּל אֶל־יהוה אֵת כָּל־הַתְּפִלָּה
וְהַתְּחִנָּה הַזֹּאת קָם מִלִּפְנֵי מִזְבַּח יהוה מִכְּרֹעַ עַל־בִּרְכָּיו
נה וְכַפָּיו פְּרֻשׂוֹת הַשָּׁמָיִם: וַיַּעֲמֹד וַיְבָרֶךְ אֵת כָּל־קְהַל יִשְׂרָאֵל
נו קוֹל גָּדוֹל לֵאמֹר: בָּרוּךְ יהוה אֲשֶׁר נָתַן מְנוּחָה לְעַמּוֹ
יִשְׂרָאֵל כְּכֹל אֲשֶׁר דִּבֵּר לֹא־נָפַל דָּבָר אֶחָד מִכֹּל דְּבָרוֹ הַטּוֹב
נז אֲשֶׁר דִּבֶּר בְּיַד מֹשֶׁה עַבְדּוֹ: יְהִי יהוה אֱלֹהֵינוּ עִמָּנוּ כַּאֲשֶׁר
נח הָיָה עִם־אֲבֹתֵינוּ אַל־יַעַזְבֵנוּ וְאַל־יִטְּשֵׁנוּ: לְהַטּוֹת לְבָבֵנוּ
אֵלָיו לָלֶכֶת בְּכָל־דְּרָכָיו וְלִשְׁמֹר מִצְוֺתָיו וְחֻקָּיו וּמִשְׁפָּטָיו
נט אֲשֶׁר צִוָּה אֶת־אֲבֹתֵינוּ: וְיִהְיוּ דְבָרַי אֵלֶּה אֲשֶׁר הִתְחַנַּנְתִּי
לִפְנֵי יהוה קְרֹבִים אֶל־יהוה אֱלֹהֵינוּ יוֹמָם וָלָיְלָה לַעֲשׂוֹת ׀
ס מִשְׁפַּט עַבְדּוֹ וּמִשְׁפַּט עַמּוֹ יִשְׂרָאֵל דְּבַר־יוֹם בְּיוֹמוֹ: לְמַעַן
דַּעַת כָּל־עַמֵּי הָאָרֶץ כִּי יהוה הוּא הָאֱלֹהִים אֵין עוֹד:
סא וְהָיָה לְבַבְכֶם שָׁלֵם עִם יהוה אֱלֹהֵינוּ לָלֶכֶת בְּחֻקָּיו וְלִשְׁמֹר
סב מִצְוֺתָיו כַּיּוֹם הַזֶּה: וְהַמֶּלֶךְ וְכָל־יִשְׂרָאֵל עִמּוֹ זֹבְחִים זֶבַח
סג לִפְנֵי יהוה: וַיִּזְבַּח שְׁלֹמֹה אֵת זֶבַח הַשְּׁלָמִים אֲשֶׁר זָבַח
לַיהוה בָּקָר עֶשְׂרִים וּשְׁנַיִם אֶלֶף וְצֹאן מֵאָה וְעֶשְׂרִים אָלֶף
סד וַיַּחְנְכוּ אֶת־בֵּית יהוה הַמֶּלֶךְ וְכָל־בְּנֵי יִשְׂרָאֵל: בַּיּוֹם הַהוּא
קִדַּשׁ הַמֶּלֶךְ אֶת־תּוֹךְ הֶחָצֵר אֲשֶׁר לִפְנֵי בֵית־יהוה כִּי־
עָשָׂה שָׁם אֶת־הָעֹלָה וְאֶת־הַמִּנְחָה וְאֵת חֶלְבֵי הַשְּׁלָמִים

SHEMINI ATZERET IN THE DIASPORA

This *haftara* concludes the great prayer of King Shlomo at the inauguration of the Temple, the beginning of which was read as the *haftara* for the second day of Sukkot. The petition ends with the memorable plea, recited at the end of each of the Sukkot *hoshana* prayers, that "these words of mine, which I have pleaded before the Lord, stay close to the Lord our God day and night, to uphold the cause of His servant and the cause of His people Israel as each day's needs arise – so that

the Lord was too small to contain the burnt offering, the grain
65 offering, and the fats of the peace offerings. At that same time,
Shlomo celebrated the festival together with all of Israel; they
were a great assembly, from Levo Ḥamat to the Wadi of Egypt,
before the Lord our God for seven days and seven days more –
66 fourteen days in all. On the eighth day he sent the people off, and
they blessed the king; they went back to their homes joyful and
glad at heart for all the goodness the Lord had shown to David,
9 1 His servant, and Israel, His people. * When Shlomo
had finished building the House of the Lord and the king's own
house, and fulfilled every desire he wished to fulfill.

Sepahardim, Yemenites, Chabad, and Minhag Anglia end here

Haftarat Simḥat Torah

The maftir of Simḥat Torah is read from Numbers 29:35–30:01.

1 1 After the death of Moshe, the Lord's servant, the Lord said to
2 Moshe's disciple, Yehoshua son of Nun: "Moshe, My servant, is
dead; now arise, cross the Jordan here – you and all this people –
3 to the land that I am giving to the Israelites. I have given you ev-
4 ery place your foot will tread, just as I promised Moshe. Your territory shall stretch from the wilderness and Lebanon here to the
Great River, the Euphrates River, and all the land of the Hittites,
5 to the Great Sea where the sun sets. No one will be able to stand
against you for as long as you live; just as I was with Moshe, I will
6 be with you. I will never let you go, and I will never leave you. Be
strong and brave, for you will bring this people into possession

us that the story of the Jewish people and its relationship to God did not end with the death of Moshe. Rather, it continued on through his successor Yehoshua, who would work to actualize Moshe's vision of settling the land of Israel and establishing there an Israelite society committed to the covenant with God. By implication, this same story, and that same work, continues with us today. We must therefore take to our own hearts God's repeated word of encouragement to Yehoshua, also shouted as a refrain upon the completion of every book of the Torah: *Ḥazak* – "Be strong!"

כִּֽי־מִזְבַּח הַנְּחֹשֶׁת אֲשֶׁר לִפְנֵי יהוה קָטֹן מֵהָכִיל אֶת־הָעֹלָה
סה וְאֶת־הַמִּנְחָה וְאֵת חֶלְבֵי הַשְּׁלָמִים: וַיַּעַשׂ שְׁלֹמֹה בָעֵת־
הַהִיא ׀ אֶת־הֶחָג וְכָל־יִשְׂרָאֵל עִמּוֹ קָהָל גָּדוֹל מִלְּבוֹא
חֲמָת ׀ עַד־נַחַל מִצְרַיִם לִפְנֵי יהוה אֱלֹהֵינוּ שִׁבְעַת יָמִים
סו וְשִׁבְעַת יָמִים אַרְבָּעָה עָשָׂר יוֹם: בַּיּוֹם הַשְּׁמִינִי שִׁלַּח אֶת־
הָעָם וַיְבָרֲכוּ אֶת־הַמֶּלֶךְ וַיֵּלְכוּ לְאָהֳלֵיהֶם שְׂמֵחִים וְטוֹבֵי
לֵב עַל כָּל־הַטּוֹבָה אֲשֶׁר עָשָׂה יהוה לְדָוִד עַבְדּוֹ וּלְיִשְׂרָאֵל
ט א עַמּוֹ:* וַיְהִי כְּכַלּוֹת שְׁלֹמֹה לִבְנוֹת אֶת־בֵּית־
יהוה וְאֶת־בֵּית הַמֶּלֶךְ וְאֵת כָּל־חֵשֶׁק שְׁלֹמֹה אֲשֶׁר חָפֵץ
לַעֲשׂוֹת:

Sepahardim, Yemenites, Chabad, and Minhag Anglia end here

הפטרת שמחת תורה

The מפטיר *of* שמחת תורה *is read from* במדבר כט, לה – ל, א.

א א וַיְהִי אַחֲרֵי מוֹת מֹשֶׁה עֶבֶד יהוה וַיֹּאמֶר יהוה אֶל־יְהוֹשֻׁעַ יהושע
ב בִּן־נוּן מְשָׁרֵת מֹשֶׁה לֵאמֹר: מֹשֶׁה עַבְדִּי מֵת וְעַתָּה קוּם
עֲבֹר אֶת־הַיַּרְדֵּן הַזֶּה אַתָּה וְכָל־הָעָם הַזֶּה אֶל־הָאָרֶץ אֲשֶׁר
ג אָנֹכִי נֹתֵן לָהֶם לִבְנֵי יִשְׂרָאֵל: כָּל־מָקוֹם אֲשֶׁר תִּדְרֹךְ כַּף־
ד רַגְלְכֶם בּוֹ לָכֶם נְתַתִּיו כַּאֲשֶׁר דִּבַּרְתִּי אֶל־מֹשֶׁה: מֵהַמִּדְבָּר
וְהַלְּבָנוֹן הַזֶּה וְעַד־הַנָּהָר הַגָּדוֹל נְהַר־פְּרָת כֹּל אֶרֶץ הַחִתִּים
ה וְעַד־הַיָּם הַגָּדוֹל מְבוֹא הַשָּׁמֶשׁ יִהְיֶה גְּבוּלְכֶם: לֹא־יִתְיַצֵּב
אִישׁ לְפָנֶיךָ כֹּל יְמֵי חַיֶּיךָ כַּאֲשֶׁר הָיִיתִי עִם־מֹשֶׁה אֶהְיֶה
ו עִמָּךְ לֹא אַרְפְּךָ וְלֹא אֶעֶזְבֶךָּ: חֲזַק וֶאֱמָץ כִּי אַתָּה תַּנְחִיל
אֶת־הָעָם הַזֶּה אֶת־הָאָרֶץ אֲשֶׁר־נִשְׁבַּעְתִּי לַאֲבוֹתָם לָתֵת

SIMḤAT TORAH

Simḥat Torah marks the close, and the opening, of the yearly cycle of Torah reading. No sooner do we read the Torah's final story, Moshe's death, than we begin again with the creation of the world, showing with our actions that there can be no beginning or ending to the Torah's wisdom or to our devotion to studying. The *haftara* continues this idea, reminding

possession of the land I swore to their ancestors to give them.
7 But you must be strong and brave indeed to uphold faithfully
all the Torah that Moshe My servant commanded you; do not
stray from it – neither right nor left – so that you may triumph
8 wherever you go. This book of Torah must never leave your lips;
contemplate it day and night, so that you will faithfully uphold
all that is written within it. For then your course will succeed;
9 then you will triumph. Hear now – I have charged you to be
strong and brave. Do not be frightened or dismayed, for the
10 Lord your God is with you wherever you go."* Ye- *Sepharadim end here*
11 hoshua commanded the officers of the people: "Cross through *Yemenites skip ahead*
the camp and instruct the people: 'Prepare provisions for yourselves,
for in three days' time you are to cross the Jordan here,
to come and take possession of the land that the Lord your
12 God is giving you as your own.'" Yehoshua then told
the Reubenites, the Gadites, and half the tribe of Menashe:
13 "Remember what Moshe, the Lord's servant, commanded
you: The Lord your God has granted you rest and given you
14 this land. Your wives and little ones and your cattle shall dwell
in the land that Moshe gave you across the Jordan, but all your
warriors shall cross over armed to join your brothers and assist
15 them, until the Lord grants rest like yours to your brothers and
they too take possession of the land that the Lord your God
is giving them. Then you shall return to your own land, which
Moshe, the Lord's servant, gave you on the eastern side of the
16 Jordan – and you shall take possession of it." They answered Yehoshua, saying, "Whatever you have commanded us we shall do;
17 wherever you send us we shall go. As we obeyed Moshe, so we
will obey you as long as the Lord your God is with you, as He
18 was with Moshe. Whoever rebels against your word or disobeys
anything you command shall be put to death; only be strong and
brave."

6 27 The Lord was with Yehoshua, and his fame rang out across the *Yemenites add*
land.

ז לָהֶם: רַק חֲזַק וֶאֱמַץ מְאֹד לִשְׁמֹר לַעֲשׂוֹת כְּכָל־הַתּוֹרָה
אֲשֶׁר צִוְּךָ מֹשֶׁה עַבְדִּי אַל־תָּסוּר מִמֶּנּוּ יָמִין וּשְׂמֹאול לְמַעַן
ח תַּשְׂכִּיל בְּכֹל אֲשֶׁר תֵּלֵךְ: לֹא־יָמוּשׁ סֵפֶר הַתּוֹרָה הַזֶּה מִפִּיךָ
וְהָגִיתָ בּוֹ יוֹמָם וָלַיְלָה לְמַעַן תִּשְׁמֹר לַעֲשׂוֹת כְּכָל־הַכָּתוּב
ט בּוֹ כִּי־אָז תַּצְלִיחַ אֶת־דְּרָכֶךָ וְאָז תַּשְׂכִּיל: הֲלוֹא צִוִּיתִיךָ
חֲזַק וֶאֱמָץ אַל־תַּעֲרֹץ וְאַל־תֵּחָת כִּי עִמְּךָ יְהוָה אֱלֹהֶיךָ
Sepharadim end here
י בְּכֹל אֲשֶׁר תֵּלֵךְ:* וַיְצַו יְהוֹשֻׁעַ אֶת־שֹׁטְרֵי הָעָם
Yemenites skip ahead
יא לֵאמֹר: עִבְרוּ | בְּקֶרֶב הַמַּחֲנֶה וְצַוּוּ אֶת־הָעָם לֵאמֹר הָכִינוּ
לָכֶם צֵידָה כִּי בְּעוֹד | שְׁלֹשֶׁת יָמִים אַתֶּם עֹבְרִים אֶת־הַיַּרְדֵּן
הַזֶּה לָבוֹא לָרֶשֶׁת אֶת־הָאָרֶץ אֲשֶׁר יְהוָה אֱלֹהֵיכֶם נֹתֵן
יב לָכֶם לְרִשְׁתָּהּ: וְלָראוּבֵנִי וְלַגָּדִי וְלַחֲצִי שֵׁבֶט
יג הַמְנַשֶּׁה אָמַר יְהוֹשֻׁעַ לֵאמֹר: זָכוֹר אֶת־הַדָּבָר אֲשֶׁר צִוָּה
אֶתְכֶם מֹשֶׁה עֶבֶד־יְהוָה לֵאמֹר יְהוָה אֱלֹהֵיכֶם מֵנִיחַ לָכֶם
יד וְנָתַן לָכֶם אֶת־הָאָרֶץ הַזֹּאת: נְשֵׁיכֶם טַפְּכֶם וּמִקְנֵיכֶם יֵשְׁבוּ
בָּאָרֶץ אֲשֶׁר נָתַן לָכֶם מֹשֶׁה בְּעֵבֶר הַיַּרְדֵּן וְאַתֶּם תַּעַבְרוּ
טו חֲמֻשִׁים לִפְנֵי אֲחֵיכֶם כֹּל גִּבּוֹרֵי הַחַיִל וַעֲזַרְתֶּם אוֹתָם: עַד
אֲשֶׁר־יָנִיחַ יְהוָה | לַאֲחֵיכֶם כָּכֶם וְיָרְשׁוּ גַם־הֵמָּה אֶת־הָאָרֶץ
אֲשֶׁר־יְהוָה אֱלֹהֵיכֶם נֹתֵן לָהֶם וְשַׁבְתֶּם לְאֶרֶץ יְרֻשַּׁתְכֶם
וִירִשְׁתֶּם אוֹתָהּ אֲשֶׁר | נָתַן לָכֶם מֹשֶׁה עֶבֶד יְהוָה בְּעֵבֶר
טז הַיַּרְדֵּן מִזְרַח הַשָּׁמֶשׁ: וַיַּעֲנוּ אֶת־יְהוֹשֻׁעַ לֵאמֹר כֹּל אֲשֶׁר־
יז צִוִּיתָנוּ נַעֲשֶׂה וְאֶל־כָּל־אֲשֶׁר תִּשְׁלָחֵנוּ נֵלֵךְ: כְּכֹל אֲשֶׁר־
שָׁמַעְנוּ אֶל־מֹשֶׁה כֵּן נִשְׁמַע אֵלֶיךָ רַק יִהְיֶה יְהוָה אֱלֹהֶיךָ
יח עִמָּךְ כַּאֲשֶׁר הָיָה עִם־מֹשֶׁה: כָּל־אִישׁ אֲשֶׁר־יַמְרֶה אֶת־פִּיךָ
וְלֹא־יִשְׁמַע אֶת־דְּבָרֶיךָ לְכֹל אֲשֶׁר־תְּצַוֶּנּוּ יוּמָת רַק חֲזַק
וֶאֱמָץ:

Yemenites add
ו כז וַיְהִי יְהוָה אֶת־יְהוֹשֻׁעַ וַיְהִי שָׁמְעוֹ בְּכָל־הָאָרֶץ:

FOR FURTHER READING

SEFER BERESHIT

The Ḥumash commentary was compiled with great care from Rabbi Sacks' vast array of books, articles, commentaries, and lectures. The following section is not intended as a comprehensive bibliography for each comment in the commentary; rather, it points the reader toward Rabbi Sacks' works containing similar ideas for further reading and insights.

Due to the various editions of Rabbi Sacks' books in print, we have noted chapter numbers rather than specific page numbers, for relevance across all editions.

For liturgical sources, we used the Ashkenaz editions of *siddurim* and *maḥzorim* (the most widely used editions at the time of printing).

Abbreviations for *Covenant & Conversation* (C&C) volumes:

LL – Lessons in Leadership

SS – Studies in Spirituality

EE – Essays on Ethics

JLCI – Judaism's Life-Changing Ideas

Bereshit

THE BOOK OF GENESIS: Genesis: An Introduction (C&C Genesis).

BERESHIT: Introduction to Bereshit (C&C Genesis).

1:1 When God began: Bereshit: The Book of Teaching (C&C Genesis).

1:1 Heaven and earth: Rabbi Sacks Torah and *Ḥokhma* lecture; Bereshit: The Book of Teaching (C&C Genesis); *The Great Partnership*, ch. 3; *Radical Then, Radical Now*, ch. 7; *Faith in the Future*, ch. 12.

LET THERE BE . . . : Bereshit: Three Stages of Creation (C&C Genesis).

1:4 It was good: Bereshit: The Genesis of Justice (C&C EE).

1:4 God separated the light from the darkness: Rabbi Sacks Lecture at Kings: "Confronting Violence in the Name of God"; Haazinu: The Arc of the Moral Universe (C&C EE).

1:6 Let it separate: Kedoshim: The Priestly Moral Imagination (C&C Leviticus).

1:12 Each of its kind: Humanitas Lecture 1; Leviticus: The Democratization of Holiness (C&C Leviticus).

1:14 To serve for signs and seasons: *The Great Partnership*, ch. 3.

1:21 The great sea serpents: *The Great Partnership*, ch. 3; *Radical Then, Radical Now*, ch. 6; Video: "Rabbi Sacks on *The Great Partnership*."

1:21 All the kinds of crawling, living things: *The Great Partnership*, ch. 11.

1:22 God blessed them: *Faith in the Future*, ch. 29.

MAN IN GOD'S IMAGE: Bereshit: The Genesis of Justice (C&C EE); *Faith in the Future*, ch. 29.

1:26 Let us make humankind: *Faith in the Future*, ch. 29.

1:28 Be fertile and multiply: *Tradition in an Untraditional Age*, ch. 1.

1:28 Fill the earth and subdue it: *Faith in the Future*, ch. 30.

1:31 Very good: Kedoshim: The Priestly Moral Imagination (C&C Leviticus).

THE SEVENTH DAY: *Faith in the Future*, ch. 20.

2:3 That God had created and done: *The Great Partnership*, ch. 11.

THE SECOND STORY OF CREATION: *Radical Then, Radical Now*, ch. 7; Shofetim: The Ecological Imperative (C&C Deuteronomy).

2:7 The man became a living being: Bereshit: Three Stages of Creation (C&C Genesis).

2:15 To work it and safeguard it: Video: "The Stewardship Paradigm – A Thought for Tu BiShvat."

THE TREE OF KNOWLEDGE OF GOOD AND EVIL: Bereshit: The Art of Listening (C&C SS); *Morality*, ch. 15.

2:17 You may not eat: Shemini: The Eighth Day (C&C Leviticus).

2:18 It is not good: *Radical Then, Radical Now*, ch. 7.

2:18 For man to be alone: Bereshit: The Genesis of Love (C&C Rabbi Sacks Website).

2:19 To see what he would call them: Article: "It's Good to Talk – Perhaps Even Holy Too," *The Times*, June 2011; *Morality*, ch. 20.

2:23 For from man was this one taken: *Radical Then, Radical Now*, ch. 7; *Future Tense*, ch. 9.

2:24 And cleaves to his wife: *Morality*, ch. 4.

3:6 Enticing to the eyes… insight: Bereshit: Taking Responsibility (C&C LL).

3:9 Where are you? Bereshit: Taking Responsibility (C&C LL).

3:12 *The woman You put here:* Bereshit: Taking Responsibility (C&C LL); *Celebrating Life*, ch. 30.

3:15 *Between your children and hers:* *The Great Partnership*, ch. 11.

3:16 *You will long…but he will rule over you:* *The Koren Sacks Pesaḥ Maḥzor*, pp. 964–65.

3:19 *By the sweat of your brow:* *Faith in the Future*, ch. 28.

3:19 *You are dust, and you will return to dust:* Bereshit: Garments of Light (C&C Genesis).

3:21 *God made garments of skins for Adam and his wife and clothed them:* Bereshit: Garments of Light (C&C Genesis).

3:22 *He must not be allowed to…live forever:* Ḥukat: The Consolations of Mortality (C&C Rabbi Sacks Website).

3:23 *To work the land:* Shemini: The Eighth Day (C&C Leviticus).

4:1 *The man knew:* *The Great Partnership*, ch. 3; Video: "Rabbi Sacks in Conversation with Professor Fania Oz-Salzberger, Hosted by Makom."

4:1 *With the Lord's help I have made a man:* Bereshit: Garments of Light (C&C Genesis); Bereshit: The Genesis of Love (C&C Rabbi Sacks Website); *The Great Partnership*, ch. 3.

4:2 *Hevel:* Article: "Happiness Is to Be Found in Being, Not in Having," *The Times*, October 2008.

4:5 *Kayin became very angry:* Bereshit: Violence in the Name of God (C&C Genesis).

4:7 *But you must rule over it:* *The Great Partnership*, ch. 6; Beḥukkotai: The Politics of Responsibility (C&C EE).

4:8 *Kayin said to his brother Hevel:* *Future Tense*, ch. 9.

THE FIRST MURDER: *The Home We Build Together*, ch. 5; *Not in God's Name*, ch. 1.

4:19 *Lemekh:* *The Great Partnership*, ch. 11.

4:24 *Lemekh, seventy-seven:* *Not in God's Name*, ch. 4.

5:3 *In his own likeness and image:* Bereshit: The Essence of Man (C&C Genesis); *The Koren Sacks Yom Kippur Maḥzor*, introduction.

5:29 *This one will bring us comfort:* *To Heal a Fractured World*, ch. 10.

6:6 *The Lord regretted:* *Not in God's Name*, ch. 1.

Noaḥ

NOAḤ: Noaḥ: Drama in Four Acts (C&C Genesis).

THE FLOOD AND THE TOWER: Noaḥ: Individual and Collective Responsibility (C&C Rabbi Sacks Website).

6:9 Righteous… in his generation: *To Heal a Fractured World*, ch. 10.

6:9 Noaḥ walked with God: Noaḥ: Righteousness Is Not Leadership (C&C LL); Noaḥ: Beyond Obedience (C&C Genesis).

6:11 Corrupt…full of violence: Noaḥ: Individual and Collective Responsibility (C&C Rabbi Sacks Website).

6:14 Make yourself an ark of cypress wood: *To Heal a Fractured World*, ch. 10.

6:16 Make a window: Noaḥ: The Light in the Ark (C&C Rabbi Sacks Website); *Future Tense*, ch. 10.

7:1 I have seen you alone to be righteous: Noaḥ: Righteousness Is Not Leadership (C&C LL).

7:5 Noaḥ did all that the LORD commanded him: *A Judaism Engaged with the World*, p. 18; Noaḥ: Righteousness Is Not Leadership (C&C LL).

8:16 Leave the ark: Noaḥ: Hero or Zero? (C&C Rabbi Sacks Website).

THE NOAHIDE COVENANT: Noaḥ: Trace of God (C&C JLCI); Humanitas Lecture 3; *To Heal a Fractured World*, ch. 5.

8:21 The devisings of the human heart: Noaḥ: Beyond Nature (C&C EE).

8:21 Evil from its youth: *Not in God's Name*, ch. 9.

8:22 As long as earth and time endure: Bereshit: The Faith of God (C&C JLCI).

THE NOAHIDE COVENANT: "OBJECTIVE" MORALITY: Lecture: "Markets, Governments and Virtues – The Mais Lectures"; Noaḥ: The Objectivity of Morality (C&C Genesis).

9:3 I allow them all to you: Tzav: Violence and the Sacred (C&C EE).

9:6 By man shall his blood be shed: *Koren Shalem Siddur*, pp. xxxix–xxx.

9:6 In God's image: *Not in God's Name*, ch. 11.

9:10 Every living creature on earth: *To Heal a Fractured World*, ch. 9.

9:13 The sign of the covenant: Lecture: "Faith and Fate: The Lambeth Conference Address"; *Future Tense*, ch. 4.

9:17 The covenant that I have established: Noaḥ: The Trace of God (C&C JLCI).

9:23 The nakedness of their father: Noaḥ: Beyond Obedience (C&C Genesis).

THE TOWER OF BAVEL: *To Heal a Fractured World*, ch. 10.

11:1 The whole world spoke... the same words: *Not in God's Name,* ch. 11; Humanitas Lecture 1; *Future Tense,* ch. 4.

11:3 Let us bake them thoroughly: *The Dignity of Difference,* ch. 3.

11:4 A city and a tower: Noaḥ: Babel: A Story of Heaven and Earth (C&C Genesis).

11:4 Otherwise we will be scattered: Humanitas Lecture 1; Noaḥ: A Tale of Four Cities (Rabbi Sacks Website); Naso: What Counts? (C&C Numbers).

11:4 Across the face of the earth: Humanitas Lecture 1.

11:5 The Lord came down: Noaḥ: Babel: A Story of Heaven and Earth (C&C Genesis).

11:7 Confuse their language: Humanitas Lecture 1; Noaḥ: Babel: A Story of Heaven and Earth (C&C Genesis).

11:9 From there the Lord scattered them: *Not in God's Name,* ch. 11.

11:31 Teraḥ took his son Avram: Lekh Lekha: Fathers and Sons (C&C Genesis).

Lekh Lekha

LEKH LEKHA: Introduction to Lekh Lekha (C&C Genesis); *To Heal a Fractured World,* ch. 10; Lekh Lekha: The Long Walk to Freedom (C&C Genesis).

AVRAHAM'S CALL: *Radical Then, Radical Now,* ch. 5.

12:1 Go: Lekh Lekha: The Heroism of Ordinary Life (C&C Rabbi Sacks Website).

12:1 Go – from your land: Lekh Lekha: The Heroism of Ordinary Life (C&C Rabbi Sacks Website).

12:1 From your land, your birthplace, and your father's house: *To Heal a Fractured World,* ch. 10.

12:1 To the land that I will show you: Lekh Lekha: Four Dimensions of the Journey (C&C Genesis).

12:2 You will become a blessing: Lekh Lekha: A New Kind of Hero (C&C Genesis).

12:3 All the families of the earth will be blessed: *Faith in the Future,* ch. 27.

12:4 As the Lord had told him: Lekh Lekha: The Long Walk to Freedom (C&C Genesis).

12:10 Avram went down to Egypt: Lekh Lekha: How Perfect Were the Patriarchs and Matriarchs? (C&C EE).

13:10 Lot raised his eyes: Lekh Lekha: Promise and Fulfillment (C&C Genesis).

14:14 He marshaled: Lekh Lekha: The Courage Not to Conform (C&C LL).

14:14 He…went in pursuit: *Not in God's Name,* ch. 11; Vayeshev: What is the Theme of the Stories of Genesis? (C&C Rabbi Sacks Website).

14:18 Malki Tzedek, king of Shalem: *Future Tense,* ch. 4.

15:1 Do not be afraid, Avram: Video: "In the Room with Jonathan Sacks."

THE PROMISE OF CHILDREN: *The Koren Sacks Rosh Hashana Maḥzor,* pp. 736–41.

15:2 Eliezer of Damascus: Lekh Lekha: Promise and Fulfillment (C&C Genesis).

15:6 Avram put his trust in the LORD: *Community of Faith,* ch. 9.

15:14 Afterward they will go free: *Faith in the Future,* introduction.

15:14 Afterward…with great wealth: *The Jonathan Sacks Haggada,* pp. 59–61.

HAGAR: *Not in God's Name,* ch. 6.

16:6 Sarai treated her harshly: *Not in God's Name,* ch. 6.

16:12 A wild donkey of a man: Lekh Lekha: How Perfect Were the Patriarchs and Matriarchs? (C&C EE).

17:7 An eternal covenant: *Will We Have Jewish Grandchildren?,* ch. 1.

17:10 Every male among you shall be circumcised: *Radical Then, Radical Now,* ch. 7.

17:20 Twelve princes: *Not in God's Name,* ch. 6.

17:21 I will establish My covenant with Yitzḥak: Lekh Lekha: Promise and Fulfillment (C&C Genesis).

VAYERA

VAYERA: Lekh Lekha: The Long Walk to Freedom (C&C Genesis); Introduction to Vayera (C&C Genesis).

THE THREE VISITORS: Vayera: God and Strangers (C&C Genesis).

18:1 The LORD appeared to him…in the heat of the day: Vayera: God and Strangers (C&C Genesis).

18:4 Rest under the tree: *The Koren Sacks Sukkot Maḥzor,* pp. 180–83.

18:8 Standing by them: Vayera: God and Strangers (C&C Genesis).

AVRAHAM INTERCEDES FOR SEDOM: Vayera: Challenging God (C&C Genesis).

18:19 By doing what is right and just: *The Great Partnership*, epilogue; *Will We Have Jewish Grandchildren?*, ch. 1.

18:24 Righteous people in the city: *Will We Have Jewish Grandchildren?*, ch. 7.

18:25 Shall the judge of all the earth not do justice? *Faith in the Future*, ch. 7.

LOT IN SEDOM: Vayera: The Ambivalent Jew (C&C Genesis).

19:3 Unleavened bread: *The Jonathan Sacks Haggada*: "The First Pesaḥ," p. 159.

19:16 He hesitated: Vayera: The Music of Ambivalence (C&C Rabbi Sacks Website).

19:26 Lot's wife looked back: Article: "Thoughts for Elul: The Future of the Past," September 2014.

19:29 The overthrow that overturned the cities: *The Home We Build Together*, ch. 11.

20:11 They will kill me because of my wife: Vayeshev: What Is the Theme of the Stories of Genesis? (C&C Rabbi Sacks Website).

21:3 Yitzḥak: *The Koren Sacks Rosh Hashana Maḥzor*, pp. 466–67.

21:9 Mocking: *Not in God's Name*, ch. 6.

21:13 Because he is your child: *Not in God's Name*, ch. 6.

THE BANISHMENT OF YISHMAEL: *Not in God's Name*, ch. 6.

21:17 God has heard the boy's cry: *Tradition in an Untraditional Age*, ch. 11.

21:17 There, where he is: *Tradition in an Untraditional Age*, ch. 11.

AKEDAT YITZḤAK: Vayera: The Binding of Isaac: A New Interpretation (C&C EE).

22:2 Go: Vayera: The Space Between Us (C&C JLCI).

22:8 God will see to… my son: Vayera: Negative Capability (C&C Rabbi Sacks Website).

22:23 Rivka: Toledot: Isaac and Esau (C&C Rabbi Sacks Website).

Ḥayei Sara

ḤAYEI SARA: Introduction to Ḥayei Sara (C&C Genesis); Ḥayei Sara: Land and Children (C&C Genesis).

THE YEARS OF SARA'S LIFE: Ḥayei Sara: To Have a Why (C&C Rabbi Sacks Website).

23:3 Then Avraham rose: Ḥayei Sara: A Call from the Future (C&C Rabbi Sacks Website).

23:4 A migrant and a visitor: *Not in God's Name*, ch. 10.

23:4 Sell me a burial site: Ḥayei Sara: Land and Children (C&C Genesis).

23:6 You are a prince of God in our midst: *A Judaism Engaged with the World*, pp.18–19.

THE SERVANT'S TEST: Ḥayei Sara: The Kindness of Strangers (C&C EE).

24:12 He said: Vayera: The Music of Ambivalence (C&C Rabbi Sacks Website).

24:19 I will draw water for your camels, too: *To Heal a Fractured World*, ch. 1.

24:20 And ran back: Video: "On Leadership"; *Morality*, ch. 17; Article: "Marriage Is a Song for Two Voices in Harmony," *The Times*, June 2000.

24:34 I am Avraham's servant: Ḥayei Sara: Parental Authority and the Choice of a Marriage Partner (C&C Genesis).

24:55 Let the young woman stay… or ten months: Ḥayei Sara: Hopes and Fears (C&C Rabbi Sacks Website).

24:58 I will: *Celebrating Life*, ch. 26.

24:60 They blessed Rivka: *The Koren Shalem Siddur*, p. 1035.

24:63 Toward evening: Ḥayei Sara: Prayer and Conversation (C&C Genesis).

24:63 To meditate: Ḥayei Sara: Prayer and Conversation (C&C Genesis).

24:64 Rivka too looked up – and saw Yitzḥak: Ḥayei Sara: Isaac and Prayer (C&C Rabbi Sacks Website).

25:1 Ketura: Ḥayei Sara: On Judaism and Islam (C&C Genesis).

AVRAHAM'S DEATH: Ḥayei Sara: A Journey of a Thousand Miles (C&C Rabbi Sacks Website).

25:9 His sons, Yitzḥak and Yishmael: Ḥayei Sara: On Judaism and Islam (C&C Genesis).

Toledot

TOLEDOT: Introduction to Toledot (C&C Genesis); *Not in God's Name*, ch. 5.

YAAKOV AND ESAV: *Not in God's Name*, chs. 5, 7.

25:19 Avraham was Yitzḥak's father: Toledot: On Clones and Identity (C&C Genesis).

25:22 *So she went to inquire of the* L*ORD*: Toledot: The Price of Silence (C&C LL).

25:23 *Two nations are inside your womb:* Toledot: The Future of the Past (C&C Genesis); *Not in God's Name*, ch. 7.

25:23 *The greater will the younger serve:* Toledot: The Future of the Past (C&C Genesis).

25:28 *Yitzḥak loved Esav:* Toledot: A Father's Love (C&C SS).

25:34 *Esav disdained his birthright:* *Not in God's Name*, ch. 7.

26:6 *So Yitzḥak now settled in Gerar:* Toledot: The Courage of Persistence (C&C Genesis).

STOPPING UP THE WELLS: Toledot: The Courage of Persistence (C&C Genesis).

26:18 *The same names his father had given them:* Toledot: The Courage of Persistence (C&C Genesis).

26:22 *Reḥovot:* Toledot: The Courage of Persistence (C&C Genesis).

27:4 *Prepared in the way that I love:* Toledot: A Father's Love (C&C SS).

27:10 *So that he may give you his blessing:* Toledot: Was Jacob Right to Take Esau's Blessing? (C&C EE).

27:22 *But the hands are the hands of Esav:* *Not in God's Name*, ch. 7.

27:38 *Have you only one blessing, father?* Toledot: The Other Face of Esau (C&C Genesis).

"BLESS ME TOO": Toledot: Isaac and Esau (C&C Rabbi Sacks Website).

27:39 *Of the cream of the land:* *Not in God's Name*, ch. 7.

27:40 *But when you break loose:* Toledot: The Future of the Past (C&C Genesis).

27:44 *Stay with him a while:* Article: "The Family Is Where We Find Passion, Affection and Companionship," *The Times*, May 2004.

28:4 *Avraham's blessing:* Toledot: Was Jacob Right to Take Esau's Blessing? (C&C EE).

28:4 *The land where…you live as a stranger:* *Faith in the Future*, ch. 27.

28:8 *Esav realized:* Toledot: The Price of Silence (C&C LL).

Vayetze

VAYETZE: Introduction to Vayetze (C&C Genesis); Vayetze: Out of the Depths (C&C JLCI).

THE VISION OF THE LADDER: Vayetze: The Ladder of Prayer (C&C Genesis).

28:11 He chanced upon a certain place: Vayetze: How the Light Gets In (C&C SS); Vayetze: Encountering God (C&C Genesis).

28:12 And he dreamed: Vayetze: Encountering God (C&C Genesis).

28:14 Like the dust of the earth.... all the families of the earth will be blessed: *Faith in the Future*, ch. 27.

28:16 And I did not know it: Vayetze: How the Light Gets In (C&C SS); Vayetze: Encountering God (C&C Genesis).

28:17 This the gate of the heavens: Vayetze: The Ladder of Prayer (C&C Genesis); Vayetze: When the "I" Is Silent (C&C Genesis).

28:22 I will dedicate a tenth: *To Heal a Fractured World*, ch. 3.

29:10 When Yaakov saw Raḥel: Vayetze: On Love and Justice (C&C Genesis).

29:13 Embraced and kissed him: Vayetze: The Birth of the World's Oldest Hate (C&C Rabbi Sacks Website).

29:17 Leah had sensitive eyes: *Not in God's Name*, ch. 9.

29:20 Seemed to him but a few days: Vayetze: On Love and Justice (C&C Genesis).

29:25 And it was Leah: Vayetze: The Birth of the World's Oldest Hate (C&C Rabbi Sacks Website); Vayetze: On Love and Justice (C&C Genesis); Vayetze: Love Is Not Enough (C&C EE).

29:25 Why did you deceive me? Vayetze: On Love and Justice (C&C Genesis).

THE RIVALRY OF LEAH AND RAḤEL: Vayetze: Hearing the Torah (C&C Genesis); Vayetze: On Love and Justice (C&C Genesis); Vayetze: Love Is Not Enough (C&C EE).

29:32 She named him: Vayetze: Hearing the Torah (C&C Genesis).

29:32 The LORD has seen: Vayeshev: How Praise Can Empower (C&C Rabbi Sacks Website).

29:35 This time I will praise the LORD: *Celebrating Life*, ch. 4.

30:2 Am I in place of God... : Bereshit: The Art of Listening (C&C SS).

30:14 He brought them to his mother Leah: Vayeshev: Reuben: The Might-Have-Been (C&C Rabbi Sacks Website).

AN ARAMEAN SOUGHT MY FATHER'S DEATH: Vayetze: Laban the Aramean (C&C Rabbi Sacks Website).

30:31 Do not give me anything: Vayetze: The Birth of the World's Oldest Hate (C&C Rabbi Sacks Website).

30:37 Yaakov took fresh shoots…: Vayetze: The Character of Jacob (C&C Rabbi Sacks Website).

31:2 Not what it had been: Vayetze: The Birth of the World's Oldest Hate (C&C Rabbi Sacks Website).

31:19 Raḥel had stolen: Vayigash: Does My Father Love Me? (C&C Genesis).

31:42 Had the God of my father… not been with me: Vayetze: How the Light Gets In (C&C SS).

31:43 All that you see is mine: Vayetze: The Birth of the World's Oldest Hate (C&C Rabbi Sacks Website).

31:50 God is the witness: *Faith in the Future*, ch. 10.

31:55 And blessed them: Vayetze: The Birth of the World's Oldest Hate (C&C Rabbi Sacks Website).

32:2 He named the place Maḥanayim: Vayetze: Out of the Depths (C&C JLCI).

Vayishlaḥ

VAYISHLAḤ: Introduction to Vayishlaḥ (C&C Genesis); Vayishlaḥ: The Parable of the Tribes (C&C EE).

YAAKOV FACES ESAV: Vayishlaḥ: Be Thyself (C&C LL).

32:7 Yaakov was acutely afraid and distressed: Vayishlaḥ: Physical Fear, Moral Distress (C&C Genesis).

32:24 And Yaakov was left alone: Vayishlaḥ: Surviving Crisis (C&C Genesis).

32:24 And a man wrestled with him: Vayishlaḥ: Surviving Crisis (C&C Genesis).

32:26 I will not let you go unless you bless me: Vayishlaḥ: Surviving Crisis (C&C Genesis).

32:30 For I have seen God: Vayishlaḥ: Wrestling Face to Face (C&C Genesis).

32:31 Limping on his thigh: Vayishlaḥ: Surviving Crisis (C&C Genesis).

32:32 To this day: *Crisis & Covenant*, ch. 9.

33:4 Esav ran… and embraced him: Vayishlaḥ: Jacob Wrestling (C&C Rabbi Sacks Website).

33:10 Like seeing the face of God: *Not in God's Name*, ch. 7.

33:11 Please accept my blessing: Vayishlaḥ: Jacob Wrestling (C&C Rabbi Sacks Website).

Vayeshev

37:26 What do we gain by killing our brother? *Ceremony & Celebration*, Shavuot: The Greatest Gift.

37:28 And they sold him: Miketz: Man proposes, God disposes (C&C Genesis).

37:35 He refused to be comforted: *The Great Partnership*, ch. 12.

TAMAR: Vayeshev: A Tale of Two Women (C&C Genesis).

38:25 To whom this seal and cord and staff belong: Vayeshev: The Heroism of Tamar (C&C EE).

38:26 She is more righteous than I: Vayeshev: The Heroism of Tamar (C&C EE).

39:8 But he refused: Vayera: The Ambivalent Jew (C&C Genesis).

40:8 Tell me your dreams: Vayeshev: How to Change the World (C&C SS).

40:23 He forgot him: Vayeshev: Improbable Endings and the Defeat of Despair (C&C JLCI).

Miketz

MIKETZ: Introduction to Miketz (C&C Genesis).

"TWO YEARS PASSED": Miketz: To Wait Without Despair (C&C SS).

41:16 Not I: Miketz: The Author of Our Lives (C&C Rabbi Sacks Website).

41:27 Seven years of famine: Miketz: The Power of Dreams (C&C LL).

41:32 He is soon to bring it about: Miketz: Between Freedom and Providence (C&C Genesis); Miketz: Man Proposes, God Disposes (C&C Genesis).

41:37 The plan seemed good: Miketz: The Power of Dreams (C&C LL).

PHARAOH, YOSEF, AND *ELOKIM*: Miketz: Faith, Universal and Particular (C&C Rabbi Sacks Website).

41:49 It was beyond measure: Miketz: Jews and Economics (C&C JLCI).

41:52 Fruitful in the land of my affliction: "On Creative Minorities," Erasmus Lecture, October 2013.

YOSEF AND HIS BROTHERS MEET AGAIN: *Not in God's Name*, ch. 8.

42:7 Yosef recognized: *Not in God's Name*, ch. 8.

42:8 They did not recognize him: Miketz: Appearance and Reality (C&C EE).

42:20 So that your words can be verified: *Not in God's Name*, ch. 8.

42:21 We are guilty: *Faith in the Future*, ch. 30.

42:38 In grief to Sheol: *The Koren Pesaḥ Maḥzor,* p. 966.
43:9 I myself am the guarantee: *To Heal a Fractured World,* ch. 7.
43:30 And there he wept: Vayeḥi: The Last Tears (C&C Rabbi Sacks Website).
44:10 The one… shall be my slave: *Not in God's Name,* ch. 8.
44:16 We are now my LORD's slaves: *Not in God's Name,* ch. 8.

Vayigash

VAYIGASH: Introduction to Vayigash (C&C Genesis); Vayigash: Forgiveness (C&C Genesis).
44:18 Yehuda stepped forward to him: Vayigash: The Space Between (C&C Rabbi Sacks Website).
YEHUDA'S TEST: Vayigash: Penitential Man (C&C Genesis).
44:28 "He must have been torn to pieces": Vayigash: Does My Father Love Me? (C&C Genesis).
YOSEF FORGIVES HIS BROTHERS: Article: "Thoughts for Yom Kippur – The Day Forgiveness was Born."
45:3 I am Yosef: Vayigash: In Search of Repentance (C&C Genesis).
45:8 It was not you who sent me here, but God: Vayigash: Forgiveness (C&C Genesis).
45:15 Only after that: Vayigash: Reframing (C&C SS).
46:17 Their sister was Seraḥ: Haazinu: The Spirituality of Song (C&C Deuteronomy).
46:30 You are still alive: Vayeshev: Refusing Comfort, Keeping Hope (C&C Genesis).
46:34 The Egyptians abominate all who keep sheep: *The Koren Sacks Pesaḥ Maḥzor,* introduction; Noah: A Tale of Four Cities (C&C Rabbi Sacks Website).
THE EGYPTIANS BECOME SLAVES: Miketz: Joseph and the Risks of Power (C&C Rabbi Sacks Website).
47:27 Settled in the land of Egypt: Vayigash: Forgiveness (C&C Genesis).

Vayeḥi

VAYEḤI: Introduction to Vayeḥi (C&C Genesis).
48:2 Yisrael summoned his strength and sat up: Behaalotekha: From Despair to Hope (C&C SS).

48:11 And now God has shown me your children as well: Vayeḥi: Grandparents (C&C Rabbi Sacks Website).

EFRAYIM AND MENASHE – THE FIRST CHILDREN OF EXILE: Vayeḥi: Forgetfulness and Fruitfulness (C&C Genesis).

48:20 Like Efrayim and Menashe: Vayeḥi: Family, Faith and Freedom (C&C Rabbi Sacks Website); Vayeḥi: Grandparents (C&C Rabbi Sacks Website).

Yaakov's Deathbed Speech: Vayeḥi: On Not Predicting the Future (C&C SS).

49:2 Assemble and listen: Vayeḥi: Family, Faith and Freedom (C&C Rabbi Sacks Website).

49:3-4 Excelling in power. Unstable as water: Vayeshev: Reuben the Might-Have-Been (C&C Rabbi Sacks Website).

49:5 Weapons of violence their wares: Vayishlaḥ: The Parable of the Tribes (C&C EE).

49:12 His eyes are darker than wine, and his teeth whiter than milk: Vayigash: The Unexpected Leader (C&C LL).

49:28 Giving each his particular blessing: Metzora: How to Praise (C&C LL).

50:16 Your father gave these instructions: Vayeḥi: When Can We Lie? (C&C Rabbi Sacks Website); Vayeḥi: The White Lie (C&C Genesis).

50:17 Yosef wept: Vayeḥi: The Last Tears (C&C Rabbi Sacks Website).

50:19 Am I in place of God?: Vayeḥi: The Future of the Past (C&C Genesis).

50:20 God intended it for good: *Not in God's Name*, ch. 9.

50:21 And he comforted them: *Not in God's Name*, ch. 8.

50:25 Carry my bones up from this place: *The Jonathan Sacks Haggada*, pp. 48–51.

THE ENDING THAT IS NOT AN ENDING: Vayeḥi: Jewish Time (C&C Genesis).

SEFER SHEMOT

A number of the comments in the *parashot* that follow are taken directly from Rabbi Sacks' own commentary drafts. These have not been referenced for further reading because they are unpublished works, but many of the ideas they contain are reflected in his other writings on the book of Exodus.

Shemot

THE BOOK OF EXODUS: Exodus: The Birth of a Nation (C&C Exodus); Lecture: "A New Concept of Freedom," a *shiur* at UCL for Passover, March 2018.

SHEMOT: Introduction to Shemot (C&C Exodus).

1:1 And these: *Future Tense*, ch. 11.

1:1 The names: Rabbi Sacks draft commentary.

THE PEOPLE OF ISRAEL: Exodus: The Birth of a Nation (C&C Exodus).

1:8 A new king: Ki Tetzeh: Two Types of Hate (C&C Rabbi Sacks Website).

1:8 Who had not known Yosef: Shemot: Turning Curses into Blessings (C&C SS).

1:9 The Israelite people: *Will We Have Jewish Grandchildren?*, introduction.

1:9 More powerful than we: Vayetzeh: The Birth of the World's Oldest Hate (C&C Rabbi Sacks Website).

1:10 Deal wisely with them: *The Jonathan Sacks Haggada*, pp. 54–57.

1:10 They may join our enemies: *The Jonathan Sacks Haggada*, pp. 14–15.

1:11 Pitom and Ramesses: Rabbi Sacks draft commentary.

1:14 Embittering their lives: *The Jonathan Sacks Haggada*, p. 57.

MIDWIVES TO THE HEBREWS : *The Jonathan Sacks Haggada*, pp. 123–124; Shemot: Civil Disobedience (C&C Exodus).

1:21 He granted them households: Shemot: Civil Disobedience (C&C Exodus).

1:22 Then Pharaoh commanded his entire people: Shemot: Civil Disobedience (C&C Exodus).

2:1 A man of the house of Levi went and married a daughter of Levi: *Crisis and Covenant*, ch. 2.

2:2 She saw what a fine child he was: Rabbi Sacks draft commentary.

2:2 She kept him hidden: Numbers: Then and Now (C&C Numbers).

2:3 Placed it among the reeds by the bank of the Nile: *The Jonathan Sacks Haggada*, pp. 117–18.

PHARAOH'S DAUGHTER: Shemot: The Light at the Heart of Darkness (C&C Exodus).

2:6 The boy was crying: *The Jonathan Sacks Haggada*, p. 59.

2:7 Then his sister asked Pharaoh's daughter: Shemot: The Light at the Heart of Darkness (C&C Exodus).

2:10 She named him Moshe: *The Koren Sacks Pesaḥ Maḥzor,* pp. xxxiv–xxxv.

2:11 Went out to his people: Rabbi Sacks draft commentary.

2:17 Moshe stood up to defend them: Article: "Seven Principles of Jewish Leadership," *Jewish Chronicle,* June 2021.

2:22 I have been a stranger in an alien land: Massei: Miles to Go Before I Sleep (C&C JLCI).

2:24 And God heard: *The Jonathan Sacks Haggada,* pp. 58–59.

2:25 And God knew: *The Jonathan Sacks Haggada,* pp. 60–61.

THE BURNING BUSH: *Faith in the Future,* ch. 6.

3:2 From the midst of a bush: Rabbi Sacks draft commentary.

3:4 Here I am: *The Koren Sacks Yom Kippur Maḥzor,* pp. 770–71.

3:5 Remove the shoes from your feet: Rabbi Sacks draft commentary.

3:11 Who am I: Vayishlaḥ: Feeling the Fear (C&C SS).

I WILL BE WHAT I WILL BE: Shemot: Faith in the Future (C&C Rabbi Sacks Website); *The Great Partnership,* ch. 3.

3:15 The LORD God of your fathers: Ki Tavo: We Are What We Remember (C&C Deuteronomy).

4:1 They will not believe me: Shemot: The Belief of a Leader (C&C Exodus).

4:6 White as snow: Shemot: Leadership and the People (C&C Rabbi Sacks Website).

4:10 I am not a man of words: Shemini: When Weakness Becomes Strength (C&C JLCI).

4:13 Send someone else: Article: "Strength from Faith Is God's Faith in Us," *The Times,* October 2012.

4:14 His heart will rejoice: Tetzaveh: Brothers: A Drama in Five Acts (C&C Exodus); *Not in God's Name,* ch. 9.

THE ENCOUNTER ON THE WAY TO EGYPT: Vayishlaḥ: Feeling the Fear (C&C SS).

4:20 Moshe took his wife and sons: Rabbi Sacks draft commentary.

4:22 Israel is My son, My firstborn: *The Jonathan Sacks Haggada,* p. 125.

4:25 Tzipora took a flint knife: Exodus: The Birth of a Nation (C&C Exodus).

5:1 Send My people forth: Rabbi Sacks draft commentary.

5:2 *I do not know the Lord:* Video: "The Home of the Book for the People of the Book."

5:21 *May the Lord look on you and judge:* Vaera: Overcoming Setbacks (C&C LL).

5:22 *Why, Lord, have You brought harm to this people?*: *The Koren Sacks Rosh Hashana Maḥzor*, pp. 580–82.

Vaera

VAERA: Introduction to Vaera (C&C Exodus).

I AM THE LORD: Vaera: The God Who Acts in History (C&C Exodus).

6:2 *I am the Lord*: Rabbi Sacks draft commentary.

6:3 *But by My name the Lord I did not make Myself known:* Rabbi Sacks draft commentary.

6:6 *I will free you from the forced labor of the Egyptians:* Vaera: The God Who Acts in History (C&C Exodus).

6:8 *I will bring you:* Vaera: The Cup of Hope (C&C Exodus).

6:9 *They did not listen to him:* Vaera: Spirits in a Material World (C&C SS).

6:12 *How then will Pharaoh listen?:* Rabbi Sacks draft commentary.

6:12 *Uncircumcised lips:* Rabbi Sacks draft commentary.

6:14 *These were the heads:* Rabbi Sacks draft commentary.

6:20 *Amram married Yokheved, his father's sister:* Rabbi Sacks draft commentary.

6:26 *Aharon and Moshe:* Rabbi Sacks draft commentary.

7:1 *Like a god to Pharaoh:* Rabbi Sacks draft commentary.

THE HARDENING OF PHARAOH'S HEART: Rabbi Sacks draft commentary.

7:9 *A serpent:* Rabbi Sacks draft commentary.

THE PLAGUES: Bo: Heart of Darkness (C&C Exodus).

7:17 *It will become blood:* Rabbi Sacks draft commentary.

7:22 *But the Egyptian magicians did the same thing by their sorcery:* Rabbi Sacks draft commentary.

7:27 *I will scourge your land with frogs:* Rabbi Sacks draft commentary.

8:4 *Pray to the Lord:* Rabbi Sacks draft commentary.

8:4 *And I will send your people forth:* Rabbi Sacks draft commentary.

8:5 *Gloat over me:* Rabbi Sacks draft commentary.

8:6 *Then you will know:* Rabbi Sacks draft commentary.

8:10 They gathered them up: Rabbi Sacks draft commentary.
8:10 The stench filled the whole land: Rabbi Sacks draft commentary.
THE FINGER OF GOD: Vaera: A Handful of Dust (C&C Exodus).
8:16 Send My people forth, so that they may serve Me: Rabbi Sacks draft commentary.
8:17 Swarms of insects: Rabbi Sacks draft commentary.
8:18 That I am the LORD, here on earth: Rabbi Sacks draft commentary.
8:19 I will mark out a separation: Rabbi Sacks draft commentary.
8:21 Pharaoh called for Moshe and Aharon: Rabbi Sacks draft commentary.
8:22 An abomination to the Egyptian: Rabbi Sacks draft commentary.
MOSHE'S REQUEST: Vaera: Freedom and Truth (C&C Rabbi Sacks Website).
9:3 The LORD's hand: Rabbi Sacks draft commentary.
9:3 A deadly epidemic: Rabbi Sacks draft commentary.
9:7 Pharaoh investigated the matter: Rabbi Sacks draft commentary.
9:8 A handful of soot: Rabbi Sacks draft commentary.
9:12 But the LORD strengthened Pharaoh's heart: Rabbi Sacks draft commentary.
9:14 I will set the full force of My plagues upon you: Rabbi Sacks draft commentary.
9:16 My name known throughout the land: Exodus: The Birth of a Nation (C&C Exodus).
9:22 Reach your hand out: Rabbi Sacks draft commentary.
9:24 The hail, with fire blazing inside it: Rabbi Sacks draft commentary.
9:27 This time I have sinned: Rabbi Sacks draft commentary.
9:29 As I leave the city: *The Great Partnership*, chs. 3, 7, 14.

Bo

BO: Bo: The Story We Tell (C&C JLCI).
10:1 His heart and his officials': Rabbi Sacks draft commentary.
10:3 How much longer will you refuse to submit to Me?: Rabbi Sacks draft commentary.
10:2 And so that you may tell your children and grandchildren: Rabbi Sacks draft commentary.
10:4 Locusts: Rabbi Sacks draft commentary.
10:6 Your parents and grandparents: Rabbi Sacks draft commentary.

10:6 Then Moshe turned: Vaera: The Hardened Heart (C&C Exodus).
10:9 With our youths and our elderly folk: Rabbi Sacks draft commentary.
10:10 Evil is staring you in the face: Rabbi Sacks draft commentary.
10:13 The Lord caused an east wind: Rabbi Sacks draft commentary.
10:17 Forgive my sin: Rabbi Sacks draft commentary.
THE PLAGUE OF DARKNESS: Bo: Heart of Darkness (C&C Exodus).
10:21 Darkness so deep it can be felt: Bo: Heart of Darkness (C&C Exodus).
11:3 The Lord granted the people favor in the eyes of the Egyptians: Rabbi Sacks draft commentary.
11:3 The man Moshe: Rabbi Sacks draft commentary.
11:8 Blazing with anger: Article: "Seven Principles of Jewish Leadership," *Jewish Chronicle* and *Jerusalem Post*, June 2012.
"THIS MONTH SHALL BE TO YOU…": Article: "To Master Time Is to Be Truly Free," *The Times*, April 2012; *The Jonathan Sacks Haggada*, p. 15.
12:2 To you: Emor: The Duality of Jewish Time (C&C Rabbi Sacks Website).
12:2 The beginning of months: Rabbi Sacks draft commentary.
12:3 Community of Israel: *Future Tense*, ch. 2.
12:4 Let him and a close neighbor take a lamb together: *The Jonathan Sacks Haggada*, pp. 21–23.
12:7 Two sides and top of the doorframes: Rabbi Sacks draft commentary.
12:8 Unleavened bread: *The Jonathan Sacks Haggada*, p. 23.
12:8 Bitter herbs: Video: "Inspiration for Shabbat HaGadol and Pesach 2020."
12:11 Passover: *The Jonathan Sacks Haggada*, "Matza," p. 87.
12:14 This day… a memorial for you: *Future Tense*, ch. 11.
12:15 You shall have removed leaven from your houses: *The Koren Sacks Pesaḥ Maḥzor*, pp. 2–3.
EDUCATION: Bo: The Spiritual Child (C&C SS).
12:32 But bless me too: *The Koren Sacks Pesaḥ Maḥzor*, pp. 456–547.
12:35 Items of silver and gold: Ki Tetzeh: Letting Go of Hate (C&C Rabbi Sacks Website).
12:38 A great variety of other people: *The Home We Build Together*, ch. 8; Humanitas Lecture 1.
12:39 They… could not delay: *The Koren Sacks Pesaḥ Maḥzor*, p. 548.

12:49 The stranger who lives among you: *The Koren Sacks Pesaḥ Maḥzor,* pp. 550–51.
13:2 Consecrate every firstborn: *The Koren Shalem Siddur,* pp. 1026–27.
13:8 You must tell your child: Rabbi Sacks draft commentary.
13:9 It shall be a sign: *Community of Faith,* ch. 10.
13:14 What is this?: Bo: The Spiritual Child (C&C SS).
13:14 You shall answer: Bo: Schools of Freedom (C&C Exodus).

Beshalaḥ

BESHALAḤ: Beshalaḥ: The Turning Point (C&C Exodus).
THE JOURNEY BEGINS: Beshalaḥ: Time and Social Transformation (C&C Exodus).
13:19 The remains of Yosef: *The Koren Sacks Pesaḥ Maḥzor,* pp. 562–65.
13:21 A column of cloud to guide them: Video: "Rabbi Sacks Speaks on a Life Worth Living"; Video: "J Insider: Rabbi Sacks on Doubt"; Beshalaḥ: The Longer, Shorter Road (C&C JLCI).
14:13 Fear not: Beshalaḥ: The Turning Point (C&C Exodus).
14:20 Keeping the two apart all night: *The Koren Sacks Pesaḥ Maḥzor,* p. 512; *The Jonathan Sacks Haggada,* pp. 70, 73.
THE SPLITTING OF THE SEA: Beshalaḥ: The Divided Sea: Natural or Supernatural? (C&C Exodus).
14:22 To their right and left: Behar: Eminent Domain (C&C Leviticus); Beshalaḥ: The Turning Point (C&C Exodus).
14:25 Clogging their chariot wheels: *The Koren Sacks Pesaḥ Maḥzor,* p. 568; Beshalaḥ: The Turning Point (C&C Exodus); Beshalaḥ: The Power of Ruaḥ (C&C Rabbi Sacks Website).
14:28 Not one of them remained: *The Koren Sacks Pesaḥ Maḥzor,* p. 571.
14:31 They believed in Him and in Moshe His servant: Beshalaḥ: Four Models of Leadership (C&C Exodus); *The Koren Sacks Pesaḥ Maḥzor,* p. 570.
THE SONG OF THE SEA: *The Koren Sacks Sukkot Maḥzor,* pp. 346–49; *The Koren Sacks Pesaḥ Maḥzor,* pp. 444–47; Beshalaḥ: Music, Language of the Soul (C&C Rabbi Sacks Website).
15:2 The LORD is my strength and song: *The Koren Sacks Pesaḥ Maḥzor,* p. 573; Beshalaḥ: Music, Language of the Soul (C&C Rabbi Sacks Website); Video: "The Soul's Language."

15:2 My father's God, I will exalt Him: Video: "J Insider: Rabbi Sacks on Parenting."

15:11 Awesome in glory: Video: "Understanding Prayer #3, 'Praise.'"

15:13 In Your love, You guided.... In Your strength, You led: *The Koren Sacks Pesaḥ Maḥzor*, pp. 572–75.

15:17 The Sanctuary... that Your hands established: *The Jonathan Sacks Haggada*, p. 80.

15:18 The LORD will reign for ever: *The Koren Sacks Pesaḥ Maḥzor*, p. 574.

15:19 The Israelites had walked on dry land through the sea: Beshalaḥ: The Divided Sea: Natural or Supernatural? (C&C Exodus).

15:22 Three days: *Crisis & Covenant*, ch. 8.

15:25 The LORD showed him a piece of wood, which he threw into the water: *To Heal a Fractured World*, ch. 15.

16:1 The fifteenth day of the second month: Video: "*Shiur* on Sefirat Haomer"; *The Great Partnership*, ch. 4.

THE SABBATH: Beshalaḥ: Renewable Energy (C&C SS).

16:33 For future generations: Video: "Faith in the Future: A Templeton Conversation"; Studies in Renewal 1; *Future Tense*, ch. 8.

17:3 They railed against Moshe: Vaera: Overcoming Setbacks (C&C Rabbi Sacks Website); *The Koren Sacks Pesaḥ Maḥzor*, p. 567.

AMALEK: Beshalaḥ: Looking Up (C&C LL).

17:9 Do battle against Amalek: Beshalaḥ: Crossing the Sea (C&C Rabbi Sacks Website).

17:16 Throughout the ages: Beshalaḥ: The Turning Point (C&C Exodus).

Yitro

YITRO: Yitro: A Nation of Leaders (C&C LL).

18:10 Blessed be the LORD: Miketz: The Universal and the Particular (C&C Genesis); *Future Tense*, ch. 4.

YITRO ADVISES MOSHE: Yitro: A Nation of Leaders (C&C LL); *Faith in the Future*, ch. 17.

18:17 Not good: Yitro: Justice or Peace (C&C Exodus).

18:21 Seek out... capable men: Miketz: Three Approaches to Dreams (C&C Genesis).

18:21 Leaders of thousands, hundreds, fifties, and tens: Yitro: Justice or Peace (C&C Exodus).

19:2 There Israel camped: *Community of Faith*, ch. 5.

19:3 The House of Yaakov: Yitro: Mount Sinai and the Birth of Freedom (C&C Exodus); Video: "The Torah of Kindness and Truth."

19:4 You yourselves have seen: *The Koren Sacks Shavuot Maḥzor,* p. 404.

19:5 My treasure among all the peoples: *The Koren Sacks Shavuot Maḥzor,* p. 404; Video: "10 Questions with Rabbi Sacks"; *Not in God's Name,* ch. 11.

A KINGDOM OF PRIESTS AND A HOLY NATION: Yitro: A Nation of Leaders (C&C LL).

19:6 A holy nation: Yitro: A Holy Nation (C&C Exodus).

19:8 And the people answered as one: *The Koren Sacks Shavuot Maḥzor,* pp. 406–7; *Future Tense,* ch. 8.

19:20 And the Lord descended: *The Koren Sacks Shavuot Maḥzor,* p. 96.

THE TEN COMMANDMENTS: Yitro: The Structure of the Good Society (C&C EE).

20:2 I am the Lord your God: *Celebrating Life,* ch. 23; Ten Paths to God: Faith Study Guide.

20:5 To the third and fourth generation: *The Koren Sacks Shavuot Maḥzor,* p. 410; *Will We Have Jewish Grandchildren?,* ch. 3.

20:7 Do not speak the name... in vain: *The Persistence of Faith,* Lecture 5; *Morality,* introduction; *Not in God's Name,* ch. 1.

20:10 You, nor your son or daughter...servant...livestock... migrant: *The Koren Sacks Shavuot Maḥzor,* pp. 412–13; *Faith in the Future,* ch. 19.

20:10 Made it holy: Leviticus: The Democratisation of Holiness (C&C Leviticus); Yitro: A Holy Nation (C&C Exodus); Lecture: "Markets and Morals – The 1998 Hayek Lecture."

20:12 Honor your father and mother: *The Koren Sacks Shavuot Maḥzor,* p. 412; Yitro: The Structure of the Good Society (C&C EE).

20:13 Do not commit adultery: *The Politics of Hope,* ch. 16.

20:13 Do not steal: Yitro: The Structure of the Good Society (C&C EE); *The Dignity of Difference,* ch. 5.

20:13 Do not bear false witness: Yitro: The Structure of the Good Society (C&C EE).

20:14 Do not crave: Yitro: To Thank Before We Think (C&C SS).

20:22 In wielding a sword upon it, you profane it: *Not in God's Name,* ch. 12.

Mishpatim

MISHPATIM: (C&C Exodus); Mishpatim: God Is in the Details (C&C Exodus).

21:1 And these are the laws: Mishpatim: God Is in the Details (C&C Exodus).

SLAVERY: Mishpatim: The Slow End of Slavery (C&C Rabbi Sacks Website).

21:6 Pierce his ear with an awl: Yitro: Justice or Peace? (C&C Exodus); Mishpatim: God's Nudge (C&C Rabbi Sacks Website).

21:7 If a man sells his daughter as a maidservant: *Faith in the Future,* ch. 28.

TEXT AND INTERPRETATION: THE CASE OF ACCIDENTAL MISCARRIAGE: Mishpatim: Text and Interpretation: The Case of Abortion (C&C Exodus).

21:29 Its owner was warned: *The Dignity of Difference,* ch. 6.

22:1 If a burglar is caught tunneling in: Vayishlaḥ: Physical Fear, Moral Distress (C&C Genesis).

22:20 For you yourselves were strangers in the land of Egypt: Mishpatim: Loving the Stranger (C&C Exodus).

22:24 If you lend money to one of My people who is poor: *The Koren Sacks Pesaḥ Maḥzor,* p. 814; *Morality,* introduction.

22:26 I will be listening: Va'etḥanan; Listening Is an Art (C&C Deuteronomy); Video: "Rabbi Sacks on Connecting to God" (J Insider).

22:26 I am gracious: Mishpatim: God Is in the Details (C&C Exodus).

23:2 Do not pervert justice: Mishpatim: God Is in the Details (C&C Exodus).

23:2 Siding with the crowd: *The Koren Sacks Pesaḥ Maḥzor,* p. 816.

23:3 Do not show favoritism even to a poor man: Mishpatim; God Is in the Details (C&C Exodus); *The Koren Sacks Pesaḥ Maḥzor,* p. 816.

23:4 Your enemy's ox: Mishpatim: Helping an Enemy (C&C Exodus).

23:7 The innocent and righteous: *The Koren Sacks Pesaḥ Maḥzor,* p. 819.

23:9 For you yourselves were strangers in the land of Egypt: Mishpatim: Loving the Stranger (C&C Exodus); *Not in God's Name,* ch. 10; *To Heal a Fractured World,* ch. 8.

SHEMITTA AND THE SABBATH: Shofetim: Environmental Responsibility (C&C EE); Behar: Eminent Domain (C&C Leviticus).

23:18 Do not boil a kid in the milk of its mother: *The Koren Sacks Pesaḥ Maḥzor,* p. 821; Shemini: Food for Thought (C&C Rabbi Sacks Website).

23:20 I am sending a messenger: *The Jonathan Sacks Haggada,,* pp. 62–65.

24:7 We shall do: Mishpatim: Doing and Hearing (C&C SS); Mishpatim: We Will Do and We Will Hear (C&C Rabbi Sacks Website).

WE SHALL DO AND WE SHALL HEED: Mishpatim: Doing and Hearing (C&C SS).

24:8 Regarding all these words: Mishpatim: Vision and Detail (C&C LL).

24:10 They saw a vision: *To Heal a Fractured World,* ch. 10.

Teruma

TERUMA: Introduction to Teruma (C&C Exodus); *Community of Faith,* ch. 2.

CALLING FOR CONTRIBUTIONS: *The Home We Build Together,* ch. 12.

25:2 All whose heart moves them to give: Teruma: Voluntary Contribution (C&C Exodus).

25:3 The offerings you shall receive from them: Teruma: The Gift of Giving (C&C SS).

25:8 In their midst: Teruma: A Portable Home (C&C Exodus).

THE DETAILS OF THE TABERNACLE: Teruma: The Architecture of Holiness (C&C Rabbi Sacks Website); *The Home We Build Together,* ch. 12.

25:10 Make an Ark of acacia wood: Teruma: The Making of an Ark (C&C Exodus).

25:20 They should face one another: *The Koren Sacks Rosh Hashana Maḥzor,* pp. 634–37; *To Heal a Fractured World,* ch. 4.

25:22 There, from above the cover: *To Heal a Fractured World,* ch. 5; Pekudei: Making Space (C&C JLCI).

25:31 A candelabrum of pure gold: Vayak'hel: God's Shadow (C&C Rabbi Sacks Website); Vayak'hel: The Beauty of Holiness or the Holiness of Beauty (C&C Family Edition); Article: "The Festival of Lights Signifies an Inextinguishable Faith," *The Times,* December 2012.

A TENT: *The Home We Build Together,* ch. 12.

27:1 Make the altar: Tzav: Understanding Sacrifice (C&C SS).

Tetzaveh

TETZAVEH: Introduction to Tetzaveh (C&C Exodus); Tetzaveh: The Ethic of Holiness (C&C EE).

27:20 To kindle the lamp, every night: Tetzaveh: Crushed for the Light (C&C JLCI).

27:21 Aharon and his sons: Tetzaveh: Priests and Prophets (C&C Exodus).
28:1 To serve Me as priests: Tetzaveh: Priests and Prophets (C&C Exodus).
PRIESTLY VESTMENTS: Tetzaveh: Dressing to Impress (C&C Rabbi Sacks Website).
28:3 Speak: Tetzaveh: Leadership Means Making Space (C&C Rabbi Sacks Website).
THE AESTHETIC IN JUDAISM: Tetzaveh: The Aesthetic in Judaism (C&C Rabbi Sacks Website).
28:15 Make a breast piece: *The Koren Sacks Yom Kippur Maḥzor*, p. 404; Tetzaveh: The Aesthetic in Judaism (C&C Rabbi Sacks Website).
28:21 Yisrael's sons.... the twelve tribes: Vayeshev: A Tale of Two Women (C&C Genesis); *The Dignity of Difference*, ch. 6.
PROPHETIC AND PRIESTLY PRAYER: Tetzaveh: Whose Footsteps Do We Follow When We Pray? (C&C Exodus); Ki Tisa: Between Truth and Peace (C&C Rabbi Sacks Website); Ḥayei Sara: Prayer and Conversation (C&C Genesis).
28:35 So that he will not die: Tetzaveh: The Ethic of Holiness (C&C EE).
28:43 A law for Aharon and his descendants for all time: Tetzaveh: Who Is Honored? (C&C Rabbi Sacks Website).
29:24 A wave offering before the Lord: *The Great Partnership*, introduction; *Celebrating Life*, ch. 50.
29:33 Through which atonement will be made: *Radical Then, Radical Now*, ch. 11.
THE REGULAR BURNT OFFERING: Tetzaveh: Inspiration and Perspiration (C&C SS).

Ki Tisa

KI TISA: Introduction to Ki Tisa (C&C Exodus); Ki Tisa: A Stiff-Necked People (C&C Exodus).
THE CENSUS: *From Renewal to Responsibility*; Ki Tisa: Counting Jews (C&C Exodus).
30:13 Half a shekel: *To Heal a Fractured World*, ch. 20.
31:2 Betzalel: *Faith in the Future*, ch. 20.
31:17 And on the seventh day He ceased and was revived: *Faith in the Future*, ch. 20.
THE GOLDEN CALF: Leviticus: The Democratisation of Holiness (C&C Leviticus).

32:2 Bring them to me: Ki Tisa: Between Truth and Peace (C&C Rabbi Sacks Website).

32:3 Brought them to Aharon: *Will We Have Jewish Grandchildren?*, ch. 5.

32:11 Moshe implored: Ki Tisa: Moses Annuls a Vow (C&C Rabbi Sacks Website).

32:16 Engraved on the tablets: Ki Tisa: The Birth of a New Freedom (C&C Rabbi Sacks Website).

32:24 They gave it to me: Ki Tisa: How Leaders Fail (C&C LL).

32:32 The book You have written: *The Koren Sacks Rosh Hashana Maḥzor* p. 68.

33:8 When Moshe went out: Ki Tisa: The Closeness of God (C&C SS).

33:13 Please show me Your ways: Ki Tisa: The Closeness of God (C&C SS).

33:18 Show me, please, Your glory: Ki Tisa: The Closeness of God (C&C SS).

33:19 Will show mercy to whom I decide to show mercy: Ki Tisa: The Closeness of God (C&C SS).

34:1 Carve two tablets of stone like the first: Ki Tisa: Awakening from Above, Awakening from Below (C&C Exodus).

THE THIRTEEN ATTRIBUTES OF MERCY: *The Koren Sacks Yom Kippur Maḥzor*, pp. 134–36; Ki Tisa: Can There Be Compassion Without Justice? (C&C EE).

34:7 Who does not acquit the guilty: Ki Tisa: Can There Be Compassion Without Justice? (C&C EE).

34:9 Though this is a stiff-necked people: Ki Tisa: A Stiff-Necked People (C&C Exodus).

34:21 On the seventh day you shall rest: Ki Tisa: Shabbat and the Golden Calf: Reflections on the Great Crash of 2008 (C&C Exodus).

34:26 Do not cook a kid in the milk of its mother: *The Koren Sacks Sukkot Maḥzor*, p. 868.

34:29 The skin of his face shone with light: Ki Tisa: Two Types of Religious Encounter (C&C Rabbi Sacks Website).

Vayak'hel

VAYAK'HEL: Introduction to Vayak'hel (C&C Exodus).

THE SABBATH AND THE SANCTUARY: Video: "Vayak'hel-Pekudei in the Time of the Coronavirus Pandemic."

35:3 ***On the Sabbath day:*** Vayak'hel: The Sabbath: First Day or the Last? (C&C Exodus).

35:29 ***All the men and women whose hearts moved them to bring anything… as a freewill offering to the LORD:*** Vayak'hel: Three Kinds of Community (C&C Exodus).

35:33 ***Working in every other craft:*** Vayak'hel: The Beauty of Holiness or the Holiness of Beauty (C&C Exodus).

36:35 ***With a design of cherubim worked into it:*** Vayak'hel: God's Shadow (C&C Exodus); *The Dignity of Difference*, ch. 5; *Future Tense*, ch. 10.

37:29 ***With the skill of a perfumer… the fragrant incense:*** Video: "Understanding Prayer – Framing Beliefs."

WOMEN AND THE MAKING OF THE TABERNACLE: Vayak'hel: Mirrors of Love (C&C Rabbi Sacks Website).

THE COMPLETION OF THE BUILDING WORK: Vayak'hel: Three Kinds of Community (C&C Exodus); Teruma: The Home We Build Together (C&C LL); *The Home We Build Together*, ch. 20; Vayak'hel: Nation-Building: Ancient Answer, Contemporary Problem (C&C Exodus).

Pekudei

PEKUDEI: Introduction to Pekudei (C&C Exodus); Pekudei: Encampments and Journeys (C&C Exodus).

THE ACCOUNTS OF THE TABERNACLE: Pekudei: Integrity in Public Life (C&C EE).

39:1 ***As the LORD commanded Moshe:*** Pekudei: God at the Center (C&C Exodus).

39:32 ***Thus all the work on the tabernacle, the Tent of Meeting, was completed:*** Pekudei: God at the Center (C&C Exodus).

39:35 ***The ARK… its carrying staves:*** Pekudei: Encampments and Journeys (C&C Exodus).

39:43 ***And Moshe blessed them:*** Pekudei: Celebrate (C&C LL).

THE COMPLETION AND CONSTRUCTION OF THE TABERNACLE: *The Home We Build Together*, ch. 12; *Radical Then, Radical Now*, ch. 11; Exodus: The Narrative Structure (C&C Exodus).

40:34 ***The glory of the LORD filled the Tabernacle:*** Ki Tisa: Awakening from Above, Awakening from Below (C&C Exodus).

EXODUS: THE NARRATIVE STRUCTURE: Exodus: The Narrative Structure (C&C Exodus).

40:34 Through all their journeys: Pekudei: Encampments and Journeys (C&C Exodus).

SEFER VAYIKRA

Vayikra

THE BOOK OF VAYIKRA: The Democratisation of Holiness (C&C Leviticus); Introduction to Vayikra (C&C Leviticus).

VAYIKRA: Introduction to Vayikra (C&C Leviticus); Vayikra: Between Destiny and Chance (C&C Leviticus).

THE LORD CALLED: Vayikra: Between Destiny and Chance (C&C Leviticus).

1:2 An animal offering: Vayikra: What Do We Sacrifice? (C&C Leviticus).

1:2 From the herd or from the flock: Vayikra: What Do We Sacrifice? (C&C Leviticus).

1:9 A pleasing aroma to the Lord: *Koren Shalem Siddur*, pages xliii–xliv.

2:1 Fine flour: Leviticus: The Democratisation of Holiness (C&C Leviticus).

PEACE OFFERING: Vayikra: The Prophetic View of Sacrifice (C&C Rabbi Sacks Website).

4:2 If a person sins unintentionally: Vayikra: Dimensions of Sin (C&C Leviticus).

THE SINS OF LEADERS: Vayikra: The Sins of a Leader (C&C Leviticus).

5:5 He shall confess: Article: "The Challenge of Jewish Repentance," *Wall Street Journal*, September 2017.

5:7 Offering: *The Koren Sacks Yom Kippur Maḥzor*, pp. 870–71.

5:21 A trespass against the Lord: Community of Faith, ch. 9.

5:26 This guilt: *Morality*, ch. 15; Article: "Doing Guilt Obliges Us to Accept Responsibility for Our Sins," *The Times*, August 2010.

Tzav

TZAV: Introduction to Tzav (C&C Leviticus); Tzav: Jeremiah on Sacrifices (C&C Leviticus).

6:2 Instruct Aharon and his sons: This is the law of the burnt offering: Tzav: Left- and Right-Brain Judaism (C&C Rabbi Sacks Website).

6:6 Every morning the priest shall add wood ... it shall not go out: *Will We Have Jewish Grandchildren?*, chs. 6, 7.

6:7 The law of the grain offering: *The Koren Sacks Yom Kippur Maḥzor*, pp. 870–71.

6:13 On the day when he is anointed: Leviticus: The Democratisation of Holiness (C&C Leviticus).

THANKSGIVING: Tzav: Giving Thanks (C&C Leviticus).

7:13 Peace sacrifice of thanksgiving: Tzav: Giving Thanks (C&C JLCI).

7:19 Flesh that touches any impure thing: Leviticus: The Democratisation of Holiness (C&C Leviticus).

THE PROHIBITION AGAINST EATING BLOOD: Tzav: Blood, Idolatry, and War (C&C Leviticus).

7:37 This, then, is the law for the burnt offering: Leviticus: The Democratisation of Holiness (C&C Leviticus).

8:3 Assemble the whole community: *The Great Partnership*, ch. 13; *Faith in the Future*, ch. 17.

8:23 It was slaughtered: Tzav: On Not Trying to Be What You Are Not (C&C LL).

JUSTICE AND OBEDIENCE: Vayikra: The Prophetic View of Sacrifice (C&C Rabbi Sacks Website).

Shemini

SHEMINI: Shemini: Fire: Holy and Unholy (C&C Leviticus); Shemini: Spontaneity: Good or Bad? (C&C Leviticus); Shemini: The Integrity of Nature (C&C Leviticus).

THE EIGHTH DAY: Shemini: The Eighth Day (C&C Leviticus).

9:7 Approach the altar: Shemini: Reticence vs. Impetuosity (C&C LL).

NADAV AND AVIHU: Shemini: Fire: Holy and Unholy (C&C Leviticus).

10:2 And fire came forth: Shemini: Fire: Holy and Unholy (C&C Leviticus).

10:2 They died before the Lord: *The Koren Sacks Yom Kippur Maḥzor*, introduction; Shemini: Spontaneity: Good or Bad? (C&C Leviticus).

10:3 Aharon was silent: Shemini: Between Hope and Humanity (C&C Leviticus).

10:9 Wine or strong drink: Shemini: Reticence vs. Impetuosity (C&C LL); Shemini: The Dangers of Enthusiasm (C&C SS).

10:10 Between impure and pure: Metzora: The Laws of Purity (C&C Leviticus); Shemini: The Eighth Day (C&C Leviticus).

10:20 Moshe listened; and it was right in his eyes: Shemini: Between Hope and Humanity (C&C Leviticus).

THE DIETARY LAWS: Shemini: The Integrity of Nature (C&C Leviticus); Shemini: The Eighth Day (C&C Leviticus).

11:19 The stork: *Faith in the Future*, ch. 12.

11:44 Be holy, for I am holy: Shemini: The Integrity of Nature (C&C Leviticus).

11:46 This is the law concerning… all creatures: *Future Tense*, ch. 10.

Tazria

TAZRIA: Introduction to Tazria (C&C Leviticus).

CIRCUMCISION: Tazria: Circumcision, Sex, and Violence (C&C Leviticus); Tazria: The Sign of the Covenant (Rabbi Sacks C&C Website); Tazria: The Circumcision of Desire (C&C Leviticus).

12:3 The child's foreskin shall be circumcised: Tazria: Circumcision, Sex, and Violence (C&C Leviticus); Tazria: The Sign of the Covenant (C&C Rabbi Sacks Website); Tazria: The Circumcision of Desire (C&C Leviticus).

OFFERINGS AFTER CHILDBIRTH: Tazria: The Sacrifices of Childbirth (C&C Leviticus); Leviticus: The Democratisation of Holiness (C&C Leviticus).

12:6 When the days of her purification are complete: Tazria: Holiness and Childbirth (C&C Leviticus).

12:7 The law for a woman who bears a child: Tetzaveh: The Ethic of Holiness (C&C EE); Tazria: Holiness and Childbirth (C&C Leviticus); *The Koren Shalem Siddur*, p. 1031.

12:8 One for the burnt offering: Tazria: The Sacrifices of Childbirth (C&C Leviticus).

TZARAAT: THE IMPURE BLIGHT : Tazria: Of Skin Disease, Mildew, and Evil Speech (C&C Leviticus); Leviticus: The Democratisation of Holiness (C&C Leviticus).

13:10 The priest shall look: Tazria: Of Skin Disease, Mildew, and Evil Speech (C&C Leviticus); *To Heal a Fractured World*, ch. 20.

13:21 Shall quarantine the patient for seven days: Tazria: The Power of Bad (C&C JLIC); The Price of Free Speech (C&C LL); The Plague of Evil

Speech (C&C Rabbi Sacks Website); Metzora: The Power of Praise (C&C JLIC).

ILLNESS AND OSTRACIZATION: Metzora: The Power of Shame (C&C EE); *Faith in the Future*, ch. 30.

Metzora

METZORA: Introduction to Metzora (C&C Leviticus).

REINTEGRATION: Tazria: The Power of Bad (C&C JLCI); Metzora: The Power of Speech (C&C Leviticus); The Power of Praise (C&C JLCI); How to Praise (C&C LL).

14:20 Thus shall the priest make his atonement, and he shall be purified: Vayikra: Why Do We Sacrifice? (C&C Rabbi Sacks Website).

14:22 Such as he can afford: *Tradition in an Untraditional Age*, ch. 10.

14:34 And I afflict a house: Tazria: Othello, WikiLeaks, and Mildewed Walls (C&C Rabbi Sacks Website); Metzora: Language and Relationship (C&C Leviticus); Leviticus: The Democratisation of Holiness (C&C Leviticus).

15:2 A genital discharge: Leviticus: The Democratisation of Holiness (C&C Leviticus).

15:18 Remain impure until evening: Leviticus: The Democratisation of Holiness (C&C Leviticus); Metzora: The Laws of Purity (C&C Leviticus).

15:31 Making My Tabernacle impure: Metzora: The Laws of Purity (C&C Leviticus).

Aḥarei Mot

AḤAREI MOT: Introduction to Aḥarei Mot (C&C Leviticus).

YOM KIPPUR: *Faith in the Future*, ch. 25.

16:4 Sacred linen tunic: *The Koren Sacks Yom Kippur Maḥzor*, p. 729.

THE RITUAL OF THE TWO GOATS: Aḥarei Mot: The Scapegoat: Shame and Guilt (C&C Leviticus); Aḥarei Mot: Thinking Fast and Slow (C&C Leviticus).

16:6 His purification: *The Koren Sacks Yom Kippur Maḥzor*, pp. 309, 729, 886–87.

16:8 For Azazel: Aḥarei Mot: The Scapegoat: Shame and Guilt (C&C

Leviticus); *The Koren Sacks Yom Kippur Maḥzor*, p. 728; Aḥarei Mot: The Scapegoat: Perversion of an Idea (C&C Leviticus).

16:21 All of their sins: Aḥarei Mot: The Scapegoat: Shame and Guilt (C&C Leviticus).

16:29 An Everlasting Statute: Aḥarei Mot: The Courage to Admit Mistakes (C&C SS).

16:29 You must afflict yourselves: *The Koren Sacks Yom Kippur Maḥzor*, p. 733.

16:30 You shall be purified before the Lord: *The Koren Sacks Yom Kippur Maḥzor*, pp. 732–33.

16:34 An everlasting statute for you: Aḥarei Mot: Surviving Catastrophe (C&C Leviticus).

17:4 Severed from his people: *Faith in the Future*, ch. 25.

FORBIDDEN RELATIONSHIPS: *The Koren Sacks Yom Kippur Maḥzor*, pp. 992–97.

THE LAW AND THE LAND: Aḥarei Mot: Why Judaism Needs a Land (C&C Leviticus).

Kedoshim

KEDOSHIM: Kedoshim: From Priest to People (C&C Leviticus).

19:2 Speak to all: Kedoshim: From Priest to People (C&C Leviticus).

BE HOLY: Kedoshim: Being Holy (C&C Leviticus); In Search of Jewish Identity (C&C SS); *The Koren Sacks Sukkot Maḥzor*, p. 490.

19:14 Do not curse the deaf or put a stumbling-block before the blind: *Faith in the Future*, ch. 30.

19:15 Do not show partiality to the poor: *Tradition in an Untraditional Age*, ch. 1.

19:16 Do not stand by: *The Jonathan Sacks Haggada*, pp. 118–19.

LAWS OF SOCIAL RELATIONS: Kedoshim: The Logic of Love (C&C Leviticus).

19:17 Do not hate your brother in your heart: *The Dignity of Difference*, ch. 10.

19:17 Admonish: Kedoshim: Followership (C&C LL).

19:18 Do not take revenge: Kedoshim: Do Not Take Revenge (C&C Leviticus).

19:18 Or bear a grudge: Kedoshim: Do Not Take Revenge (C&C Leviticus).

"LOVE YOUR NEIGHBOR AS YOUR OWN SELF": Article: "The Practical Implications of Infinity" (Rabbi Sacks Website, February 2005).

19:32 Show respect to the elderly: Article: "Honouring the Elderly Adds Life to Their Years" (BBC Radio 4's *Thought for the Day,* May 2013).

19:34 Love him as your own self: Mishpatim: Loving the Stranger (C&C Exodus).

19:36 Honest scales: *Faith in the Future,* ch. 28; Lecture: "Markets and Morals – The 1998 Hayek Lecture," June 1998.

20:18 He has laid her hidden source bare: *The Politics of Hope,* ch. 16; Video: "A Life Worth Living."

20:26 I have set you apart: Kedoshim: Made with Love (C&C Rabbi Sacks Website).

Emor

EMOR: Introduction to Emor (C&C Leviticus).

21:1 No one of you shall render himself impure: Emor: Eternity and Mortality (C&C Rabbi Sacks Website).

A PRIEST WITH A PHYSICAL BLEMISH: Emor: Eternity and Mortality (C&C Rabbi Sacks Website); *Faith in the Future,* ch. 18.

21:11 But if a priest acquires a slave: *The Home We Build Together,* ch. 11; Behar: Evolution or Revolution? (C&C Leviticus); Article: "Giving and Belonging: The Lesson Jews Can Offer New Immigrants," *The Times,* October 2005.

21:32 Do not profane My holy name: Emor: On Not Being Afraid of Greatness (C&C LL).

21:32 In the midst of the Israelites: *Community of Faith,* ch. 10.

21:32 I am the Lord, who makes you holy: *To Heal a Fractured World,* ch. 5.

THE JEWISH CALENDAR: Emor: Holy Times (C&C SS).

23:3 Sabbath of complete rest: Emor: Three Versions of Shabbat (C&C Leviticus).

23:5 Passover: *The Jonathan Sacks Haggada,* p. 87.

COUNTING THE OMER: Emor: Counting Time (C&C Rabbi Sacks Website).

23:34 Festival of Tabernacles: Emor: Sukkot: The Dual Festival (C&C Leviticus).

23:43 I brought them out of the land of Egypt: Article: "In Memory of Yoni Jesner," *Jewish Telegraph,* September 2002.

23:44 The LORD's appointed times to the Israelites: Emor: In the Diary (C&C JLCI).

THE EXECUTION OF THE BLASPHEMER: Emor: The Blasphemer (C&C Leviticus).

24:20 An eye for an eye: Emor: The Blasphemer (C&C Leviticus); Ekev: The Morality of Love (C&C Deuteronomy).

24:22 There shall be one law: Emor: The Blasphemer (C&C Leviticus); Video: "Just Punishment and the Holocaust."

BEHAR

BEHAR: Introduction to Behar (C&C Leviticus).

25:1 On Mount Sinai: Leviticus: The Democratisation of Holiness (C&C Leviticus).

25:4 To the land a Sabbath: *The Koren Sacks Shalem Siddur,* introduction; Behar: The Chronological Imagination (C&C Leviticus); *The Jonathan Sacks Haggada,* pp. 32–33.

***25:8 And you shall count*:** Behar: Think Long (C&C LL).

THE JUBILEE YEAR: Emor: Real Responsibilities (C&C Rabbi Sacks Website); Lecture: "Markets and Morals – The 1998 Hayek Lecture," June 1998.

25:14 [His] Brother: Behar: Family Feeling (C&C SS).

25:14 Brother must not cheat brother: *Faith in the Future,* ch. 28.

25:23 The land is Mine: Behar: Eminent Domain (C&C Leviticus).

REDEMPTION: Behar: The Concept of Redemption (C&C Leviticus).

25:29 The period of redemption: Emor: New Light on an Old Controversy (C&C Leviticus); *The Dignity of Difference,* ch. 5.

THE RIGHTS OF STRANGERS: Behar: Minority Rights (C&C Leviticus).

25:35 That he may live among you: *To Heal a Fractured World,* ch. 3; *Tradition in an Untraditional Age,* ch. 10.

25:44 Acquire a male or female slave: Behar: Evolution or Revolution? (C&C Leviticus).

25:55 For it is to Me that the Israelites are servants: *Celebrating Life,* ch. 13.

BEḤUKOTAI

BEḤUKOTAI: Introduction to Beḥukotai (C&C Leviticus); Beḥukotai: Birth of Hope (C&C Leviticus).

26:3 If you follow My decrees: Leviticus: The Democratisation of Holiness (C&C Leviticus).

COVENANTAL POLITICS: Beḥukotai: The Politics of Responsibility (C&C EE).

26:6 I will grant peace: The Dignity of Difference, ch. 5.

THE CURSES: Beḥukotai: The Power of a Curse (C&C Rabbi Sacks Website); Beḥukotai: When Curses Are a Blessing (C&C Leviticus); Beḥukotai: The Eternal People (C&C Rabbi Sacks Website); Beḥukotai: The Politics of Responsibility (C&C EE).

26:18 And if, in spite of all this, you still will not listen to Me: Beḥukotai: The Politics of Responsibility (C&C EE).

26:21 Walk contrary: Beḥukotai: In Search of the Why (C&C JLCI).

COLLECTIVE RESPONSIBILITY: Beḥukotai: "We the People"(C&C LL); Beḥukotai: All Israel Are Responsible for One Another (C&C Leviticus); *Future Tense,* ch. 2.

THE BIRTH OF HOPE: Beḥukotai: The Birth of Hope (C&C Leviticus).

26:44 For I am the LORD their God: Beḥukotai: The Rejection of Rejection (C&C Leviticus).

26:45 I am the LORD: Beḥukotai: The Eternal People (Rabbi Sacks Website C&C).

LAWS OF CONSECRATION: Vayikra: The Pursuit of Meaning (C&C SS); *Morality,* ch. 18.

SEFER BEMIDBAR

Bemidbar

THE BOOK OF NUMBERS: Numbers: Then and Now (C&C Numbers).

BEMIDBAR: Introduction to Bemidbar (C&C Numbers).

1:1 The Sinai Desert: Numbers: Wilderness and Word (C&C Numbers); Numbers: Wilderness and Revelation (C&C Rabbi Sacks Website).

1:2 Take a census: Elul WhatsApp, Day 2.

PRINCES OF THE TRIBES: Tetzaveh: The Counterpoint of Leadership (C&C LL).

TO BE COUNTED: *Radical Then, Radical Now,* ch. 4.

1:46 603,550: Bemidbar: Leading a Nation of Individuals (C&C LL).

1:53 Encamp around the Tabernacle of the Testimony: Bemidbar: The

Human Story: Act 4 (C&C Deuteronomy); Ki Tisa: The Closeness of God (C&C SS).

2:2 Positioned around the Tent of Meeting at a distance: Bemidbar: The Space Between (C&C Numbers).

2:9 They shall be the first to set out: Noaḥ: The Courage to Live with Uncertainty (C&C SS).

2:34 They camped by their banners: Bemidbar: The Ever-Repeated Story (C&C Rabbi Sacks Website).

3:1 Descendants of Aharon and Moshe: Devarim: The Teacher as Hero (C&C Deuteronomy).

3:14 Then the Lord spoke to Moshe in the Sinai Desert: Bemidbar: The Sound of Silence (C&C SS).

3:41 In place of all the firstborn of the Israelites: Kedoshim: From Priest to People (C&C Leviticus).

THE JOURNEY ONWARD: Bemidbar: The Two Journeys (C&C JLCI).

Naso

NASO: Numbers: Then and Now (C&C Numbers); Naso: Pursuing Peace (C&C Numbers).

THE CENSUS: Naso: What Counts? (C&C Numbers).

4:46 All the Levites: Naso: The Politics of Envy (C&C LL).

THE RITUAL OF THE ACCUSED WIFE: Naso: Pursuing Peace (C&C Numbers); *The Dignity of Difference*, ch. 3; *To Heal a Fractured World*, ch. 8.

5:23 Wash them off into the bitter water: Naso: Pursuing Peace (C&C Numbers); *To Heal a Fractured World*, ch. 8.

THE NAZIRITE: Naso: Sages and Saints (C&C Numbers).

6:4 Anything that comes from the grapevine: Naso: Sages and Saints (C&C Numbers).

THE PRIESTLY BLESSING: Naso: The Blessing of Love (C&C SS); Naso: The Priestly Blessings (C&C Numbers).

6:24 May the Lord bless you and watch over you: Naso: The Priestly Blessings (C&C Numbers).

6:25 May the Lord make His face shine upon you and be gracious to you: Naso: The Priestly Blessings (C&C Numbers).

6:26 May the Lord raise His face toward you and grant you peace: Naso: The Priestly Blessings (C&C Numbers).

6:27 I will bless them: Naso: The Priestly Blessings (C&C Numbers).

THE OFFERINGS OF THE PRINCES: Naso: Tribes (C&C Numbers).
7:18 ***On the second day:*** Naso: Pursuing Peace (C&C Numbers).
A LITANY OF GIFTS: Video: "On Living a Responsible Life," *J Insider* (March 2010); *Celebrating Life*, ch. 14; Video: "On Love as Deed" *J Insider* (March 2010).
7:89 ***When Moshe entered:*** Naso: The Politics of Envy (C&C LL); Naso: Pursuing Peace (C&C Numbers).

Behaalotekha

BEHAALOTEKHA: Numbers: Then and Now (C&C Numbers); Introduction to Behaalotekha (C&C Numbers).
LIGHTING THE CANDELABRUM: Video: "The Light of Judaism" (Rabbi Sacks Website).
8:3 ***Aharon did so:*** Behaalotekha: The Book Between the Books (C&C Numbers).
9:1 ***The first month of the second year:*** Video: "An Unforgiving Age" (Midnight Selichot 5779).
CONGREGATION AND CAMP: Behaalotekha: Camp and Congregation (C&C Numbers).
10:30 ***I will not come:*** Behaalotekha: Seventy Elders (C&C Numbers).
A BOOK BETWEEN THE BOOKS: Behaalotekha: The Book Between the Books (C&C Numbers).
10:35 ***When the Ark set out:*** Behaalotekha: The Book Between the Books (C&C Numbers).
11:1 ***The people began to rail bitterly:*** Behaalotekha: Miriam's Error (C&C Numbers).
11:6 ***Nothing at all but this manna:*** Behaalotekha: From Despair to Hope (C&C SS); *The Jonathan Sacks Haggada*, pp. 76–77.
11:12 ***As a nursemaid carries a baby:*** Behaalotekha: Is a Leader a Nursing Father? (C&C Numbers).
THE SEVENTY ELDERS: Behaalotekha: The Seventy Elders (C&C Numbers).
11:17 ***You will not have to bear it alone:*** Behaalotekha: Faith and Friendship (C&C JLCI).
11:29 ***The LORD would put His spirit upon them all:*** Behaalotekha: Power or Influence? (C&C LL).

11:30 Together with the elders of Israel: Behaalotekha: From Despair to Hope (C&C SS).

MIRIAM AND AHARON SPEAK ABOUT MOSHE: Behaalotekha: The Book Between the Books (C&C Numbers).

12:1 Because of his Kushite wife: Ki Tetzeh: Against Hate (C&C LL).

12:3 Now the man Moshe was very humble: Behaalotekha: From Pain to Humility (C&C EE).

12:7 Not so with Moshe: *Tradition in an Untraditional Age*, ch. 15.

12:13 Heal her now: Behaalotekha: Miriam's Error (C&C Numbers); *To Heal a Fractured World*, ch. 4.

Shelaḥ

SHELAḤ: Introduction to Shelaḥ (C&C Numbers).

THE SENDING OF THE SPIES: Shelaḥ: Confidence (C&C LL); *Tradition in an Untraditional Age*, ch. 12; *Future Tense*, ch. 10.

13:2 Men: Pinḥas: The Lost Masterpiece (C&C JLCI).

13:16 And Moshe named Hoshea…Yehoshua: Shelaḥ: What Made Yehoshua and Kalev Different? (C&C Numbers); Shelaḥ: Confidence (C&C LL).

13:28 The cities are fortified: Shelaḥ: Without Walls (C&C Numbers).

13:33 And so we were in theirs: Shelaḥ: Law and Narrative: Believing and Seeing (C&C Numbers); Shelaḥ: Confidence (C&C LL).

THE SPIES' REPORT: Shelaḥ: What Is Going On? (C&C Rabbi Sacks Website).

14:17 The LORD is slow to anger: *The Koren Sacks Yom Kippur Maḥzor*, pp. 122–123.

14:35 In this wilderness they shall come to their end: Shelaḥ: Time as a Factor in Politics (C&C Numbers).

14:41 It will not work: Shelaḥ: Freedom Needs Patience (C&C Rabbi Sacks Website).

15:15 You and the migrant shall be the same before the LORD: *The Jonathan Sacks Haggada*, p. 32.

15:26 Because all the people acted in error: *The Koren Sacks Yom Kippur Maḥzor*, pp. 74–75.

15:32 A man gathering wood on the Sabbath: *Tradition in an Untraditional Age*, ch. 10; Shelaḥ: Assembling Reminders (C&C EE).

TZITZIT: Shelaḥ: Law and Narrative: Believing and Seeing (C&C Numbers); *The Koren Sacks Rosh Hashana Maḥzor,* pp. 58–63.

15:38 Throughout the generations: Shelaḥ: Fringe Phenomena (C&C Numbers).

15:39 You shall remember: Shelaḥ: Assembling Reminders (C&C EE).

15:39 Your heart or of your eyes: Shelaḥ: Seeing What Isn't There (C&C JLCI).

Koraḥ

KORAḤ: Introduction to Koraḥ (C&C Numbers).

THE KORAḤ REBELLION: Koraḥ: Argument for the Sake of Heaven (C&C Numbers); Koraḥ: The First Populist (C&C JLCI); *Morality* , ch. 13; *Future Tense,* ch. 9.

16:1 Son of Kehat son of Levi: Koraḥ: Servant Leadership (C&C Numbers).

16:1 Descendants of Reuven: Koraḥ: Servant Leadership (C&C Numbers); Koraḥ: A Lesson in Conflict Resolution (C&C Rabbi Sacks Website).

16:1 Took: Koraḥ: A Cloak Entirely Blue (C&C Numbers).

16:3 All the community is holy, every one of them: Koraḥ: The Egalitarian Impulse in Judaism (C&C Numbers).

16:4 He fell upon his face: Koraḥ: Not Taking It Personally (C&C Numbers).

16:5 In the morning: Koraḥ: Not Taking It Personally (C&C Numbers).

16:10 Yet you seek the priesthood also: Koraḥ: Not Taking It Personally (C&C Numbers).

16:13 Out of a land flowing with milk and with honey: *Morality,* ch. 13.

16:15 Pay no attention to their offering: Koraḥ: Not Taking It Personally (C&C Numbers).

16:15 I have not taken a single donkey from them: Koraḥ: Not Taking It Personally (C&C Numbers).

THE NATURE OF THE ARGUMENT: Koraḥ: Argument for the Sake of Heaven (C&C Numbers); *Morality,* ch. 13; Koraḥ: The First Populist (C&C JLCI).

16:32 The earth opened its mouth: *The Koren Shalem Siddur,* pp. 668–71.

17:6 You have killed the LORD's people: Koraḥ: Argument for the Sake of Heaven (C&C Numbers).

17:11 Go quickly.... the plague has begun: *Faith in the Future*, ch. 31; *The Koren Shalem Siddur*, p. 153.

THE SIGN OF THE STAFFS: Koraḥ: A Lesson in Conflict Resolution (C&C Rabbi Sacks Website).

17:23 Bearing almonds: Koraḥ: Argument for the Sake of Heaven (C&C Numbers); Koraḥ: Not Taking It Personally (C&C Numbers).

18:6 I have singled out your brothers: Koraḥ: The Egalitarian Impulse in Judaism (C&C Numbers).

18:20 I am your share, your inheritance: *To Heal a Fractured World*, ch. 19.

Ḥukat

ḤUKAT: Introduction to Ḥukat (C&C Numbers).

THE DECREE OF THE LAW: Ḥukat: Kohelet, Tolstoy, and the Red Heifer (C&C JLCI).

THE RED HEIFER: Ḥukat: Kohelet, Tolstoy, and the Red Heifer (C&C JLCI); Ḥukat: The Consolations of Mortality (C&C Rabbi Sacks Website).

19:11 Seven Days: Ḥukat: Kohelet, Tolstoy, and the Red Heifer (C&C JLCI).

19:17 Living water: Ḥukat: Law and Narrative (C&C Rabbi Sacks Website).

MOSHE AND MIRIAM: Ḥukat: Miriam, Moshe's Friend (C&C LL); Healing the Trauma of Loss (C&C SS).

20:10 Listen now, rebels: Ḥukat: Anger Management (C&C EE).

MOSHE'S PUNISHMENT: Ḥukat: Why was Moses Not Destined to Enter the Land (C&C Rabbi Sacks Website); *Future Tense*, introduction.

20:29 The whole House of Israel wept for Aharon for thirty days: Ḥukat: Statute and Story (C&C Numbers).

THE BOOK OF THE WARS OF THE LORD: Ḥukat: Love in the End (C&C Numbers).

21:17 Then the Israelites sang this song: Haazinu, The Spirituality of Song (C&C Deuteronomy); Vayikra: Why do we sacrifice? (C&C Rabbi Sacks Website).

THE FIRST CONQUEST OF LAND: *Not in God's Name*, ch. 12.

Balak

Pinḥas

Numbers); Pinḥas: Moral vs. Political Decisions (C&C Rabbi Sacks Website).

PREFACE TO THE SECOND CENSUS: *Will We Have Jewish Grandchildren?*, ch. 2; The Torah You Learn from Life: Introduction to Leadership (C&C Rabbi Sacks Website); Pinḥas: When Words Fail (C&C Numbers).

26:21 Peretz's descendants: *The Koren Sacks Shavuot Maḥzor*, introduction.

THE DAUGHTERS OF TZELOFḤAD: Pinḥas: The Lost Masterpiece (C&C JLCI); Video: "Questions Answered, Part 2"; Video: "Bridging the Divides: A Conversation with Yair Lapid."

27:12 Ascend this mountain: *Future Tense*, ch. 1.

MOSHE'S CONTINUITY: Pinḥas: Moshe's Disappointment (C&C SS); Pinḥas: The Crown All Can Wear (C&C Numbers).

27:16 God of the spirit of all flesh: Pinḥas: Lessons of a Leader (C&C LL).

27:16 Appoint a man: Pinḥas: Lessons of a Leader (C&C LL).

27:17 Who will lead them out and bring them home: Pinḥas: Leadership and the Art of Pacing (C&C Numbers).

27:18 Take Yehoshua son of Nun: Pinḥas: Lessons of a Leader (C&C LL).

27:19 Give him this charge: Pinḥas: Lessons of a Leader (C&C LL).

THE SACRIFICIAL YEAR: Leviticus: The Democratisation of Holiness (C&C Leviticus); *The Jonathan Sacks Haggada*, p. 17.

28:11 On your New Moons: *The Koren Shalem Siddur*, pp. 744–47.

28:26 The day of the first produce: *The Koren Sacks Shavuot Maḥzor*, introduction.

29:1 A day of the horn's sounding: *The Koren Sacks Rosh Hashana Maḥzor*, introduction

29:13 Thirteen young bulls: Emor: Sukkot, the Dual Festival (C&C Leviticus); *The Koren Sacks Sukkot Maḥzor*, introduction.

29:35 You shall hold an assembly: *The Koren Sacks Sukkot Maḥzor*, introduction.

MATOT

MATOT: Matot: Priorities (C&C Numbers).

VOWS AND OATHS: Matot: The World We Make with Words (C&C Numbers).

30:3 Or takes an oath: Matot: Subject/Object (C&C JLCI).

30:3 Vow... oath... obligation: Matot: Oaths and Vows (C&C Rabbi Sacks Website); *Faith in the Future*, ch. 25.

30:6 If her father restrains her: *Faith in the Future*, introduction; *The Koren Sacks Sukkot Maḥzor*, pp. 826–27.

A WAR OF RETRIBUTION: *Not in God's Name*, ch. 1.

31:16 On Bilam's advice: Bereshit: Taking Responsibility (C&C LL); Balak: Tragic Irony (C&C Numbers).

31:23 Pass through the fire and it will be purified: *Future Tense*, ch. 9; Vayehi: Transforming the Story (C&C Rabbi Sacks Website).

THE NEGOTIATION: Matot: Priorities (C&C Numbers); Matot: Conflict Resolution (C&C LL).

32:6 Are your brothers to go... while you stay here?: Matot: Conflict Resolution (C&C LL).

32:16 Then they set forward: Matot: Priorities (C&C Numbers); Matot: Conflict Resolution (C&C LL)

32:20 If you do this: Matot: Conflict Resolution (C&C LL).

32:22 Be clear before the LORD and before Israel: Matot: Above Suspicion (C&C Numbers).

32:24 Towns for your children and pens for your flocks: Matot: Priorities (C&C Numbers).

Masei

MASEI: Introduction to Masei (C&C Numbers).

THESE WERE THE JOURNEYS: Masei: The Long Walk to Freedom (C&C Numbers); Numbers: Then and Now (C&C Numbers); *Faith in the Future*, introduction.

33:2 Every journey at the LORD's command: Masei: Miles to Go Before I Sleep (C&C JLCI).

33:5 Sukkot: *Faith in the Future*, ch. 23.

33:16 Kivrot HaTaava: Bemidbar: Law as Love (C&C EE).

33:48 They set out.... And camped: Masei: Miles to Go Before I Sleep (C&C JLCI).

THE LAND OF ISRAEL: Masei: The Religious Significance of Israel (C&C Numbers).

CITIES OF REFUGE: Masei: Retribution and Revenge (C&C EE).

34:11 Refuge cities: Mattot: My Teacher: In Memoriam (C&C Rabbi Sacks Website).

34:12 Ending at the Dead Sea: *To Heal a Fractured World,* ch. 3.
35:25 Until the death of the High Priest: Masei: The Death of the High Priest (C&C Numbers).
35:33 Blood pollutes the land: Masei: Individual and Community (C&C Numbers).
THE DAUGHTERS OF TZELOFḤAD – EPILOGUE: Masei: The Complexity of Human Rights (C&C Numbers).
NUMBERS: THE NARRATIVE STRUCTURE: Numbers: Then and Now (C&C Numbers); Bemidbar: The Ever-Repeated Story (C&C Rabbi Sacks Website).

SEFER DEVARIM

Devarim

THE BOOK OF DEUTERONOMY: Devarim: Words (C&C Rabbi Sacks Website).
DEVARIM: Devarim: The World We Make with Words (C&C Deuteronomy).
"THESE ARE THE WORDS": Devarim: Words (C&C Rabbi Sacks Website); Vaetḥanan: The First Commandment (C&C Rabbi Sacks Website).
1:1 All Israel: Devarim: The Birth of a Nation (C&C Rabbi Sacks Website).
1:1 Di Zahav: Devarim: Counsel for the Defence (C&C Deuteronomy).
1:5 Moshe began to expound this Law: Devarim: The Teacher as Hero (C&C Deuteronomy).
1:12 How can I bear alone: The Birth of a Nation (C&C Rabbi Sacks Website).
1:16 Judge fairly: Devarim: Why Are There So Many Jewish Lawyers? (C&C EE).
1:17 Do not show partiality in judgment: *The Koren Sacks Shavuot Maḥzor,* p. ixx; *Ceremony & Celebration,* p. 315.
1:17 Judgment belongs to God: Devarim: *Tzedek*: Justice Tempered by Compassion (C&C Deuteronomy).
RETELLING THE STORY OF THE SPIES: Devarim: The First Follower (C&C Rabbi Sacks Website).
1:37 The Lord was enraged even with me: Devarim: The First Follower (C&C Rabbi Sacks Website).

2:10 As tall as the Anakites: *The Jonathan Sacks Haggada,* pp. 38–39.

2:26 I sent messengers… to Siḥon, king of Ḥeshbon, with an offer of peace: *Not in God's Name,* ch. 12.

2:29 Just as the descendants of Esav living in Se'ir… did for us: Toledot: The Other Face of Esau (C&C Rabbi Sacks Website).

3:12 I gave to the Reubenites and Gadites the territory: Mattot: Conflict Resolution (C&C LL).

3:21 I charged Yehoshua: Devarim: The Leader as Teacher (C&C LL).

Vaetḥanan

VAETḤANAN: Introduction to Vaetḥanan (C&C Deuteronomy); Vaetḥanan: The Power of Why (C&C SS).

3:26 And would not listen to me: *Letters to the Next Generation,* Letter 12.

IN THE EYES OF THE PEOPLES: *Future Tense,* ch. 4; Vaetḥanan: In the Eyes of the Nations (C&C Deuteronomy).

4:6 A wise and understanding people: *Future Tense,* ch. 10.

4:12 There was only a voice: Vaetḥanan: Listening Is an Art (C&C Deuteronomy).

4:32 Has anything… happened before: *The Jonathan Sacks Haggada,* pp. 36–37.

4:32 Has anyone heard of anything like this?: *Will We Have Jewish Grandchildren?,* ch. 1.

THE TEN COMMANDMENTS: Vaetḥanan: Philosophy or Prophecy? (C&C Rabbi Sacks Website).

5:6 Out of the house of slaves: Vaetḥanan: Philosophy or Prophecy? (C&C Rabbi Sacks Website).

5:14 Do no work at all: Deuteronomy: Covenant Society (C&C Deuteronomy).

5:19 And He added no more: *The Koren Sacks Shavuot Maḥzor,* p. xxxix; *Ceremony & Celebration,* p. 283; Video: "Conversation with Daniel Taub – Not in God's Name: Confronting Religious Violence."

LISTEN: Vaetḥanan: The Meanings of *Shema* (C&C Deuteronomy); *The Koren Shalem Siddur,* pp. 470–71.

6:4 The LORD is one: *The Koren Sacks Yom Kippur Maḥzor,* p. 1196.

LOVE: Vaetḥanan: Making Love Last (C&C JLCI).

6:5 With all your heart: *The Jonathan Sacks Haggada,* p. 40.

6:6 Impressed upon your heart: *The Home We Build Together,* ch. 9.

6:7 Teach them to your children: Devarim: The Teacher as Hero (C&C Deuteronomy); *Will We Have Jewish Grandchildren?*, ch. 9.

6:8 Bind them as a sign: *The Koren Shalem Siddur*, pp. 14–15.

6:16 Do not test the Lord your God: *The Great Partnership*, ch. 4.

THE RIGHT AND THE GOOD: Vaetḥanan: The Right and the Good (C&C EE).

7:7 You are the smallest of all peoples: Vaetḥanan: Why Is the Jewish People So Small? (C&C Deuteronomy).

7:9 Keeps His covenant and the love: Video: "A Life of Vertical and Horizontal Responsibility: Shavuot During the Coronavirus Pandemic," May 2020.

Ekev

EKEV: Introduction to Ekev (C&C Deuteronomy)

GOD OF LOVE: Ekev: The Morality of Love (C&C Deuteronomy).

7:17 These nations are more numerous: Vaetḥanan: The Fewest of All Peoples (C&C LIL); *Letters to the Next Generation*, Letter 2.

7:18 Remember well: Ekev: The Politics of Memory (C&C Deuteronomy).

8:10 You shall bless the Lord your God: *The Jonathan Sacks Haggada*, pp. 102–5.

8:17 My power, the strength of my own hand: Ekev: The Power of Gratitude (C&C EE).

8:18 It is He who gives you the power: Ekev: The Politics of Memory (C&C Deuteronomy).

9:4 Because of their own wickedness: *Not in God's Name*, ch. 11.

9:5 Not for your righteousness: *Not in God's Name*, ch. 11.

9:6 You are a stiff-necked people: *Future Tense*, ch. 9.

9:7 You have always been rebellious against the Lord: Devarim: The Effective Critic (C&C JLCI).

9:20 I prayed for Aharon also at that time: Ki Tisa: How Leaders Fail (C&C LIL).

MOSHE'S PRAYER: *The Koren Sacks Shalem Siddur*, pp. 142–45.

LOVE WITH JUSTICE: Ekev: The Morality of Love (C&C Deuteronomy).

10:19 You too must love the stranger: Ekev: Greatness and Humility (C&C Deuteronomy).

THE CONDITIONAL PROSPERITY OF THE LAND: *Future Tense*, ch. 7.

11:13 If you heed: Ekev: Listen, Really Listen (C&C JLCI).

11:19 Teach them: *To Heal a Fractured World*, ch. 2.
11:19 To your children: Ekev: A Nation of Educators (C&C Deuteronomy).
11:22 Holding fast to Him: *Tradition in an Untraditional Age*, ch. 11.
11:23 Larger and mightier than you: *The Dignity of Difference*, ch. 4.

Re'eh

RE'EH: Introduction to Re'eh (C&C Deuteronomy).
11:26 See this: Re'eh: Seeing and Hearing (C&C Rabbi Sacks Website).
THE CHOICE: Re'eh: The Politics of Freedom (C&C Deuteronomy).
11:32 To keep all the decrees and laws: Re'eh: Defining Reality (C&C LIL).
12:7 Rejoicing: Re'eh: The Deep Power of Joy (C&C SIS); Re'eh: Defining Reality (C&C LIL).
12:8 Right in his own eyes: *Faith in the Future*, chs.2, 7.
12:11 Choice gifts that you commit by vow to the Lord: Re'eh: The Second Tithe and the Making of a Strong Society (C&C EE); *The Koren Sacks Sukkot Maḥzor*, p. 1092.
CENTRALIZED SACRIFICE, "SECULAR" SLAUGHTER: *To Heal a Fractured World*, ch. 18.
12:18 Along with your sons and daughters, your male and female servants: Re'eh: Collective Joy (C&C Deuteronomy).
13:4 Do not listen to the words of that prophet: Nitzavim: Not in Heaven (C&C Deuteronomy); Shofetim: The Sage Is Greater than the Prophet (C&C Rabbi Sacks Website).
13:15 Seek the truth, investigate, and inquire thoroughly: Video: "Post-Truth and the Erosion of Trust," June 2017.
13:17 It shall be an eternal ruin: *Not in God's Name*, ch. 12; Shofetim: Environmental Responsibility (C&C EE).
PROHIBITED MOURNING RITES: Re'eh: The Limits of Grief (C&C Rabbi Sacks Website).
14:1 You are children of the Lord your God: *The Koren Sacks Rosh Hashana Maḥzor*, pp. 718–19.
KOSHER AND NON-KOSHER ANIMALS: Shemini: The Integrity of Nature (C&C Leviticus).
14:21 In the milk of its mother: *The Dignity of Difference*, ch. 9.
14:23 You may learn to hold the Lord your God in awe always: Re'eh: The Second Tithe and the Making of a Strong Society (C&C EE).

15:1 A remission of debts: *The Koren Sacks Sukkot Maḥzor*, pp. 1094–95; Behar: The Chronological Imagination (C&C Leviticus).

15:4 The land that the Lord your God is giving you to possess: *The Dignity of Difference*, ch. 9.

LAWS OF *TZEDAKA*: Re'eh: The Untranslatable Virtue (C&C Deuteronomy); *To Heal a Fractured World*, ch. 3.

15:8 To answer all his needs: Re'eh: The Psychology of Dignity (C&C Deuteronomy); Re'eh: The Untranslatable Virtue (C&C Deuteronomy).

15:9 You will be held guilty: *Wealth and Poverty*, pp. 6–7.

THE THREE PILGRIMAGE FESTIVALS: Emor: Holy Times (C&C SIS); *The Koren Sacks Sukkot Maḥzor*, pp. 1092–93.

16:15 You shall be wholly joyful: Re'eh: Insecurity and Joy (C&C Deuteronomy).

Shofetim

SHOFETIM: Introduction to Shofetim (C&C Deuteronomy).

16:18 Appoint judges: Vayishlaḥ: Collective Responsibility (C&C Rabbi Sacks Website).

"PURSUE JUSTICE": *Faith in the Future*, ch. 1; Devarim: *Tzedek*: Justice and Compassion (C&C Rabbi Sacks Website); *To Heal a Fractured World*, ch. 2.

17:3 By going off to serve: *To Heal a Fractured World*, ch. 19.

17:9 Inquire of them: *Faith in the Future*, ch. 6; *The Great Partnership*, epilogue.

SELECTING A MONARCH: *The Dignity of Difference*, ch. 5; Shofetim: To Lead Is to Serve (C&C JLCI)

17:17 Nor should he amass large amounts of silver and gold: Shofetim: Greatness Is Humility (C&C Rabbi Sacks Website).

17:19 He shall read from it all the days of his life: Shofetim: Learning and Leadership (C&C LIL).

17:20 Not considering himself superior to his people: Shofetim: The Greatness of Humility (C&C SIS).

17:20 Then he and his descendants will reign long: *The Dignity of Difference*, ch. 10; Shofetim: The Three Crowns (C&C Deuteronomy).

18:10 Let no one be found among you… who casts spells: Vaera: Of Lice and Men (C&C Rabbi Sacks Website).

18:21 How can we recognize a message that the Lord has not spoken? Shofetim: True and False Prophets (C&C Deuteronomy).

19:5 That man may flee to one of these cities and live: Masei: Individual and Community (C&C Numbers).

19:11 If one person hates his fellow: *Future Tense*, ch. 9.

19:19 You must purge the evil from your midst: *Morality*, ch. 11.

THE PROHIBITION OF DESTROYING FRUIT TREES: Shofetim: The Ecological Imperative (C&C Deuteronomy); *Faith in the Future*, ch. 29.

20:19 You must not cut them down: Shofetim: The Ecological Imperative (C&C Deuteronomy).

20:19 Are trees of the field human beings: *Faith in the Future*, ch. 29.

21:7 Our hands did not shed this blood: "We Have to Ask the Wider Question of Moral Responsibility" (BBC Radio 4's *Thought for the Day*, August 2015); Vayishlaḥ: Collective Responsibility (C&C Rabbi Sacks Website).

Ki Tetzeh

KI TETZEH: Ki Tetzeh: Animal Welfare (C&C Deuteronomy).

21:10 When you wage war: *Not in God's Name*, ch. 12; *Faith in the Future*, ch. 14.

21:11 A beautiful woman among the captives: Ki Tetzeh: Love Is Not Enough (C&C Deuteronomy).

LAW AND LOVE: Ki Tetzeh: Love Is Not Enough (C&C Deuteronomy).

21:15 Loves one but not the other: Ḥayei Sara: Parental Authority and the Choice of a Marriage Partner (C&C Genesis); "Marriage as a Metaphor for our Relationship with God," *The Times*, April 2003.

THE WAYWARD AND REBELLIOUS SON: Ki Tetzeh: Stubborn and Rebellious Sons (C&C Deuteronomy); *Tradition in an Untraditional Age*, ch. 10.

22:4 Help him to lift it: Ki Tetzeh: Social Capital and Fallen Donkeys (C&C JLCI).

LAWS OF A BIRD'S NEST: Ki Tetzeh: Animal Welfare (C&C Deuteronomy).

22:9 A second kind of seed: *Faith in the Future*, ch. 29.

23:4 Even to the tenth generation: *The Koren Sacks Shavuot Maḥzor*. p. lxvi; *Ceremony and Celebration*, p. 310; *Not in God's Name*, ch. 12.

23:8 Do not despise an Edomite: Ki Tetzeh: Against Hate (C&C LIL).

23:8 Do not despise an Egyptian, for you lived as a stranger in his land: *Not in God's Name*, ch. 14; Ki Tetzeh: Letting Go (C&C Deuteronomy).

23:9 In the third generation: *The Dignity of Difference*, ch. 10.

23:13 Designate an area outside the camp: *Faith in the Future*, ch. 29.

23:16 Do not hand him back: *To Heal a Fractured World*, ch. 3.

23:20 Do not charge interest on loans to your kinsmen: *The Dignity of Difference*, ch. 8; *Faith in the Future*, ch. 28.

24:5 Bring happiness to the woman he has married: Tazria: The Circumcision of Desire (C&C EE); *The Home We Build Together*, ch. 18; *Radical Then, Radical Now*, ch. 7.

24:14 Poor and destitute laborer: *The Jonathan Sacks Haggada*, pp. 31–32.

24:16 A person shall be put to death only for his own sin: Ki Tetzeh: To the Third and Fourth Generations (C&C EE).

24:18 Remember that you were a slave: *The Koren Sacks Pesaḥ Maḥzor*, pp. xxii–xxvi; *Faith in the Future*, ch. 13.

24:19 Leave it for the migrant, the orphan, and the widow: *To Heal a Fractured World*, ch. 8; Video: "The Challenge to Faith in the Twenty-First Century," lecture at the University of Dallas, 2014.

25:3 Your kinsman will be degraded in your eyes: Ki Tetzeh: Rehabilitation of Offenders (C&C Deuteronomy).

25:4 Do not muzzle an ox while it is treading out the grain: Ki Tetzeh: Animal Welfare (C&C Deuteronomy).

THE LAST OF THE ETHICAL COMMANDMENTS: *To Heal a Fractured World*, ch. 8.

AMALEK: Ki Tetzeh: Hate: Curable and Incurable (C&C Deuteronomy).

Ki Tavo

KI TAVO: Introduction to Ki Tavo (C&C Deuteronomy).

THE CEREMONY OF THE FIRST FRUITS: Ki Tavo: History and Memory (C&C Deuteronomy).

26:2 Some of every first fruit of the soil: Ki Tavo: The Greatest Challenge (C&C Deuteronomy); Ki Tavo: A Sense of History (C&C Rabbi Sacks Website).

26:5 My ancestor was a wandering Aramean: *The Jonathan Sacks Haggada*, pp. 46–49.

26:5 There he became a nation: *The Jonathan Sacks Haggada*, pp. 50–53.

26:11 Then you, with the Levites and the migrants… shall rejoice: Re'eh: Collective Joy (C&C Deuteronomy).

26:17 You have proclaimed: Ki Tavo: Covenant and Conversation (C&C Deuteronomy).

27:3 And write on them: *The Home We Build Together*, ch. 14; Ki Tavo: A Nation of Storytellers (C&C LIL).

27:8 Very clearly: *Not in God's Name*, ch. 12.

27:9 Be still and listen: Ki Tavo: Listening and Moral Growth (C&C Deuteronomy).

CURSES AND BLESSINGS: Deuteronomy: Covenant Society (C&C introduction), p. 12; *Morality*, ch. 21.

28:5 Your basket and your kneading pan: *The Dignity of Difference*, ch. 5; Ki Tavo: The Pursuit of Joy (C&C EE).

28:9 Walk in His ways: Kedoshim: Being Holy (C&C Leviticus); *To Heal a Fractured World*, ch. 2.

THE *TOKHEḤA*: Ki Tavo: Judaism's Greatest Challenge (C&C Rabbi Sacks Website); Ki Tavo: The Blessing and the Curse (C&C Deuteronomy).

28:33 A people… will eat the fruit… of your labor: *To Heal a Fractured World*, chs. 3, 16.

28:47 Because you did not serve the LORD your God with joy: Ki Tavo: The Pursuit of Joy (C&C EE); Ki Tavo: Judaism's Greatest Challenge (C&C Rabbi Sacks Website).

28:48 The enemies whom the LORD will send against you: Ki Tavo: The Blessing and the Curse (C&C Deuteronomy).

28:54 Will begrudge food: *The Jonathan Sacks Haggada*, pp. 24–25.

28:65 No resting place: *To Heal a Fractured World*, ch. 2.

28:69 The covenant that He had made with them: Ki Tavo: The Blessing and the Curse (C&C Deuteronomy).

NITZAVIM

NITZAVIM: Introduction to Nitzavim (C&C Deuteronomy).

29:9 All of you: Community of Faith, ch. 9.

A CHOICE FOR THE GENERATIONS: Nitzavim: Why Judaism? (C&C EE); *Radical Then, Radical Now*, ch. 1.

29:17 Let there be among you no root: *Future Tense*, ch. 8.

29:28 Hidden things belong to the LORD: *Future Tense*, ch. 11.

RETURN: Nitzavim: Two Concepts of *Teshuva* (C&C Deuteronomy).

NOT IN HEAVEN: *To Heal a Fractured World,* ch. 2; *The Great Partnership,* ch. 10.

30:12 Not in heaven: Nitzavim: Not in Heaven (C&C Deuteronomy).

GOD IS CLOSE: Nitzavim: Not Beyond the Sea (C&C Deuteronomy).

30:16 Survive and thrive: *From Renewal to Responsibility,* "An Open Letter to British Jewry."

30:19 Choose life: Nitzavim: The Fourteenth Principle of Faith (C&C Deuteronomy); Nitzavim: Why Judaism? (C&C EE).

Vayelekh

VAYELEKH: Introduction to Vayelekh (C&C Deuteronomy).

COMMAND AND CONSENSUS: Vayelekh: Leadership: Consensus or Command? (C&C Deuteronomy).

THE *HAK'HEL* CEREMONY: Vayelekh: How to Renew a Nation (C&C Rabbi Sacks Website); Vayelekh: Covenantal Politics (C&C Rabbi Sacks Website).

31:12 Assemble the people: Vayelekh: How to Renew a Nation (C&C Rabbi Sacks Website).

31:12 Men, women, and children… migrants: Video: "The Home of the Book for the People of the Book," May 2014.

31:13 Their children, who do not know it: *Future Tense,* ch. 8; Vayelekh: To Renew Our Days (C&C Deuteronomy); Vayelekh: Covenantal Politics (C&C Rabbi Sacks Website).

THE HIDING OF GOD'S FACE: *Faith in the Future,* chs. 14, 33.

31:18 At that time: *Crisis and Covenant,* ch. 2.

"WRITE THIS SONG": Vayelekh: The Singers and the Song (C&C Rabbi Sacks Website); Vayelekh: The Torah as God's Song (C&C Deuteronomy).

Haazinu

HAAZINU: Introduction to Haazinu (C&C Deuteronomy).

THE END OF THE COVENANT DOCUMENT: Deuteronomy: Covenant Society (C&C Deuteronomy).

MOSHE'S SONG: Haazinu: The Spirituality of Song (C&C Deuteronomy); Haazinu: Emotional Intelligence (C&C JLCI); Humanitas Lecture 2 (2012).

32:2 *May My teaching pour down like rain:* Haazinu: Let my Teaching Drop as Rain (C&C Deuteronomy).

GOD OF FAITH: Haazinu: The Faith of God (C&C Deuteronomy); *Faith in the Future*, ch. 11.

32:5 *No, with His children lies the fault:* Haazinu: A Leader's Call to Responsibility (C&C LL).

32:6 *Foolish, unwise people:* Haazinu: A Warped and Twisted Generation (C&C Deuteronomy).

32:15 *Yeshurun grew fat, and kicked:* *The Great Partnership*, ch. 14; Haazinu: The Arc of the Moral Universe (C&C SS).

GOD'S VENGEANCE: Haazinu: Vengeance (C&C Deuteronomy).

32:47 *They are your very life:* *Radical Then, Radical Now*, ch. 4; Lecture: "What Will Be the Condition of the Jewish Community 50 Years from Now?" *Commentary Magazine*, October 2015.

MOSHE'S FAILING: Vezot Haberakha: The Unfinished Symphony (C&C JLCI).

Vezot Haberakha

VEZOT HABERAKHA: Introduction to Vezot Haberakha (C&C Deuteronomy).

33:1 *Moshe, man of God, blessed the Israelites:* *Letters to the Next Generation*, Letter 1; Vezot Haberakha: The Love of Nations (C&C Deuteronomy).

33:3 *He is a lover of peoples:* Vezot Haberakha: The Love of Nations (C&C Deuteronomy).

33:4 *Moshe charged us with the Law, heritage of Yaakov's assembly:* Pinḥas: The Crown All Can Wear (C&C Numbers).

33:6 *May Reuven live, and not die:* *The Koren Sacks Sukkot Maḥzor*, p. 1232.

33:10 *They shall teach Your laws to Yaakov:* *The Koren Sacks Sukkot Maḥzor*, p. 1235; *The Politics of Hope*, ch. 13.

33:21 *The lawgiver's portion is reserved:* Vezot Haberakha: Moses' Death, Moses' Life (C&C EE); Nitzavim: Defeating Death (C&C LL); *The Koren Sacks Pesaḥ Maḥzor*, pp. xxxiii–xxxiv.

33:29 *Who is like you, a people rescued by the Lord:* *The Koren Sacks Sukkot Maḥzor*, pp. 1240–43; *Future Tense*, ch. 11; Nitzavim: Two Concepts of *Teshuva* (C&C Deuteronomy).

34:4 *You will not cross over:* Vezot Haberakha: Moses the Man (C&C

Deuteronomy); Vezot Haberakha: The Unfinished Symphony (C&C JLCI).

34:6 He buried him in Moav: Vezot Haberakha: Moses the Man (C&C Deuteronomy).

34:7 His eyes had not grown dim, nor his vitality fled: Vezot Haberakha: Staying Young (C&C LL).

34:8 The Israelites wept for Moshe in the plains of Moav for thirty days: Moses the Man (C&C Deuteronomy).

34:10 There has never arisen a prophet in Israel like Moshe: *The Koren Sacks Sukkot Maḥzor*, p. 1245.

THE END OF THE TORAH: Vayeḥi: Jewish Time (C&C Genesis); *The Great Partnership*, ch. 14; Vezot Haberakha: The Unfinished Symphony (C&C JLCI); Genesis: An Introduction (C&C Genesis).

KOREN JERUSALEM